CW00384939

☆ INSIDE THE ROPES ☆
WRESTLING ALMANAC

INSIDE
THE
ROPES
WRESTLING MAGAZINE

www.insidetheropesmagazine.com

Copyright © Dante Richardson, 2023

Published by Titan Insider Press
contact@titaninsiderpress.com

All rights reserved. No part of this publication may be reproduced, stored in a retrieval system, or transmitted in any form by any process — electronic, mechanical, photocopying, recording, or otherwise — without the prior written permission of the copyright holders and Titan Insider Press. The scanning, uploading, and distribution of this book via the Internet or via any other means without the permission of the publisher is illegal and punishable by law. Please purchase only authorized electronic editions, and do not participate in or encourage electronic piracy of copyrighted materials.
Your support of the authors' rights is appreciated.

Designed and typeset by STK Design
Cover design by STK Design
Cover images: George Tahinos and George Napolitano

Printed and bound in the United Kingdom

www.insidetheropesmagazine.com

CONTENTS

5   **A NOTE FROM THE EDITOR**
An introduction to the INSIDE THE ROPES WRESTLING ALMANAC

7   **THE BIGGEST STORIES OF 2022**
The most important happenings of the year

17   **2022 SUPERCARDS AND TV SPECIALS**
Results and review from 2022's major supercards around the world

41   **2022 TELEVISION RESULTS**
All of the results from this year's wrestling on television

42	WWE Monday Night RAW	46	WWE SmackDown
49	WWE Kickoff	49	WWE Main Event
51	WWE 205 Live	51	WWE NXT 2.0
54	WWE NXT	55	WWE NXT Level Up
57	WWE NXT Kickoff	57	WWE NXT UK
58	AEW Dynamite	62	AEW Rampage
65	AEW Buy-In	65	AEW Dark
70	AEW Dark Elevation	75	Impact Wrestling
79	Impact Before The Impact	80	MLW Fusion
81	NWA Power	84	NJPW Strong

87   **TELEVISION RATINGS**
Nielsen TV viewership for all of the major cable and network shows

93   **2022 WRESTLER TELEVISION RECORDS**
TV results and match times for wrestlers in all of the major promotions

261   **WRESTLER CAREER HISTORIES**
Stats and career info for all of the notable wrestlers of the year

295   **TITLE HISTORIES**
The lineage of wrestling's active championships

343   **TOURNAMENT RECORDS**
Winners and results from notable wrestling tournaments, current and historic

383   **HISTORICAL PS50 & ITR50 RANKINGS**
Annual wrestler rankings lists from Power Slam Magazine and Inside The Ropes Magazine

393   **END OF YEAR AWARDS**
Annual awards from major publications down the years

415   **WRESTLING HALLS OF FAME**
Year-by-year inductions from all of wrestling's major Halls Of Fame

423   **WRESTLING OBSERVER FIVE-STAR MATCHES**
Every match rated five-star (or above) by the Wrestling Observer Newsletter

429   **EVENTS DIRECTORY**
A comprehensive chronological list of major events with PPV buy rates and show ratings

453   **HISTORIC EVENT RESULTS**
Results, match times and ratings from every major supercard and television special

595   **IN MEMORIUM**
Remembering those that left us for the great ring in the sky in 2022

A NOTE FROM THE EDITOR . . .

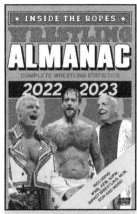

One of the things I look forward each year is the arrival on my doorstep of English football's annual Utilita Football Yearbook (formerly known and most fondly remembered as the "Rothmans"). This famous blue tome has become a footballing institution since it was launched in the 1970s, thanks to its 1,000 incredible pages chronicling every result, statistic and record that you could hope to consume. It is my dream that our annual INSIDE THE ROPES WRESTLING ALMANAC will one day be considered with the same level of reverence in wrestling circles as the Football Yearbook is amongst football fans and writers. Thanks to the sheer scope and size of the 2022-23 edition, I feel we are one step closer to that.

The addition of several hundred more pages and a new easier to consume format should certainly help matters. This year, thanks to the incredible efforts of our new recruit Danny Schmitz, who's passion for this project has been an inspiration for its growth, we have added features that we think will significantly improve the experience for the user.

The most notable of these is significant expansion of the extensive Supercards Directory at the back of the book, which now features the results and match times of over 1,600 pay-per-views, television specials, televised house shows, cards released on VHS, closed circuit broadcasts and more. In fact, it's got more than double the shows it had in last year's edition. We have also given every card a rating on a one-to-five scale - inspired by the annual Christmas TV guide magazines that do the same - which should serve as a handy guide for fans.

And for the first time, we have also reviewed every single match in this section (some 10,000 matches) using a combination of personal objective opinions, consensus fan opinion and critics' opinions. As ever, we consider both one star and five star ratings to be exceedingly rare and much consideration is taken before one is awarded. As noted in previous editions, our star ratings for shows and matches are likely quite different to what you may be familiar with already. Our system has no negative stars, no "DUDs", no fractions of stars and nothing beyond five stars. As alluded to, we intend for our ratings to be more in line with what you would see for movie reviews than your typical wrestling ratings. A key to what our star ratings mean can be found in the appropriate sections where they appear throughout this publication.

With our first retro Almanac, the 1989-90 edition that was released in 2022, we introduced several new features, including wrestler TV records and year-by-year career data for hundreds of grapplers. These have been introduced to the modern Almanac for the first time, which was a painstaking task but one that should serve as a handy guide to a given wrestler's output for the year. These features shall be retained going forwards.

As with last year, there are a few notes that remain relevant: Our title histories may differ slightly from a promotion's official records, sometimes intentionally (such as in the case of Antonio Inoki's WWF Title reign, which we do recognise and WWE does not) and sometimes because the promotion in question has got its own history wrong (usually with slightly incorrect dates). We also recognise title reigns as beginning and ending on the day they aired on television or PPV (unless the switch took place at an untelevised event and was recognised as such) and count the day a wrestler lost the title as the final day of their reign and the next day as the first of the new champion's reign.

Thirdly, our pay-per-view buy rate information (which is restricted to North American buys only) has been gleamed from a number of reliable sources and in some cases will differ from the early predicted buys widely reported by some websites and newsletters. We are confident that we have assembled numbers that are as accurate as they can be.

As ever, putting the Almanac together was a difficult task and a team effort, but we feel the results have made it worthwhile. The 2022-23 edition is the most complete and accurate guide to wrestling in 2022 that you will find anywhere, be it online or in print, we are confident of that.

Thank you, once again, for your support in our quest to preserve the history of wrestling and to keep the vital medium of wrestling print media alive and kicking.

Dante Richardson
Editor

PUBLISHER
Titan Insider Press

EDITOR
Dante Richardson

ASSISTANT EDITOR
Danny Schmitz

CONTRIBUTING WRITERS AND RESEARCH ASSISTANTS
Benjamin Richardson
Findlay Martin
Justin Henry
Kenny McIntosh
Liam Wyatt
Richard Land
Tom Fordy

PHOTOGRAPHERS
Brad McFarlin
George Napolitano
George Tahinos
Howard Baum
John Barrett
Mike Lano
Ryan Brenna

WITH THANKS TO
All Elite Wrestling
Cagematch
New Japan Pro Wrestling
OSW Review
Ring Of Honor
The History Of WWE
Wrestlenomics
Wrestlingdata
Wrestling Observer
WWE

DESIGN
STK Design

THE BIGGEST STORIES OF 2022

VINCE MCMAHON ANNOUNCES RETIREMENT

In what is likely the most unbelievable and surreal wrestling-related development in generations, WWE owner Vince McMahon, the most omnipresent figure in all of professional wrestling, abruptly announced his retirement on July 22.

McMahon simply tweeted, "At 77, time for me to retire. Thank you, WWE Universe. Then. Now. Forever. Together #WWE #thankful"

More than five weeks earlier, on June 15, The Wall Street Journal reported that McMahon had been under internal investigation since March for a $3 million payout he'd given to a former employee that he'd allegedly had an affair with. The woman was reportedly a company paralegal that later became an assistant to talent relations head John Laurinaitis.

These accusations came from an anonymous friend of the woman, who e-mailed WWE's Board of Directors with the story. Among the details, the writer claimed that McMahon "gave (the friend) like a toy" to Laurinaitis. The e-mail also claimed, "My friend was so scared so she quit after Vince McMahon and lawyer Jerry (McDevitt) paid her millions of dollars to shut up."

Two days following the revelation, McMahon stepped down from his position as CEO of WWE, ceding the role to daughter Stephanie. Vince, however, would hold onto his standing as showrunner for the time being.

On the same date he gave up his CEO position, McMahon appeared in a bizarre cameo on WWE's SmackDown broadcast, during which he made no mention of the stories, but instead recited the company's, "Then. Now. Forever." slogan, adding "Together" at the end.

Over the weeks ahead, McMahon continued to make random, mostly disconnected appearances on WWE television, for reasons that are unclear.

Then on July 8, The Wall Street Journal published a follow-up report that levied even more troubling accusations against McMahon. The new report claimed that an additional $12 million had been paid out to four different women in exchange for their silence on matters of alleged sexual impropriety and infidelity. Of that $12 million, $7.5 million was paid out to one woman (an unnamed former on-screen talent) whom McMahon allegedly coerced into sexual favors. The report contends that this individual's contract later went unrenewed after she refused later requests. McMahon's short television cameos ceased after the running of this story.

Two weeks later, McMahon tweeted out his apparent professional farewell. At the time of his tweet, the Securities and Exchange Commission, as well as federal prosecutors, were launching inquiries into the approximately $15 million in secret payouts.

On August 8, stories surfaced that Laurinaitis was officially gone from WWE. McMahon son-in-law Paul Levesque took over Laurinaitis' talent relations role, while also assuming McMahon's chair in creative. WWE President Nick Khan became co-CEO with Stephanie McMahon.

After working for his father's WWWF (later WWF) throughout the 1970s and early-1980s, Vince McMahon bought the territory in 1982, and quickly expanded it into a national powerhouse. Through many changes and permutations, McMahon was the primary overseer of WWE from the time of his purchase to his July 2022 retirement. Despite the changes, McMahon does remain WWE's primary owner, and, at press time, still holds the majority of voting power.

TONY KHAN BUYS RING OF HONOR

A little more than 20 years after Ring of Honor held its first event in Philadelphia, AEW President Tony Khan announced his purchase of the ailing organisation on March 2.

Khan's purchase of ROH from the Sinclair Broadcasting Group included assets, intellectual properties, and a video library that spans 20 years. Days later, following AEW's Revolution pay-per-view, Khan stated that he intended to run ROH separately from All Elite Wrestling (with himself as the booker), while also noting that ROH could be used as a development brand of sorts for AEW. As of late-2022, no television deal for a separate ROH had been secured, though Khan was hopeful to have a TV outlet in 2023.

Since starting up in 2002, ROH had been home to ascending stars and underutilised castaways. Its list of World Champions includes Samoa Joe, Bryan Danielson, CM Punk, Tyler Black (Seth Rollins), Kevin Steen (Owens), Cody Rhodes, and dozens more. ROH featured some of the finest in-ring wrestlers on the planet, oftentimes in realistic, gritty rivalries that strongly emphasised the competition aspect of wrestling.

By 2021, ROH had whittled down to a shell of its former glory. Losing Rhodes, Adam Page, and The Young Bucks to upstart AEW in late 2018 kicked off ROH's swift drop to America's number three promotion, at best. Attendance and general popularity fell, and the 2020 pandemic made matters worse, as ROH had next to no new output or presence for many months.

Though ROH allowed crowds again by the summer of 2021, the promotion was limping along with diminished fan interest. That October, it was announced that Ring of Honor would go on hiatus after December's Final Battle pay-per-view, and that all personnel would be released from their contracts.

Final Battle took place that December 11, and concluded with Jonathan Gresham defeating Jay Lethal to win the vacated ROH World championship.

The reborn ROH held three pay-per-views in 2022— one in the midst of Khan's purchase, and two after it was finalised. Without a television time slot, Khan has allotted time on AEW broadcasts for Ring of Honor matters to play out, such as Chris Jericho becoming the group's World Champion (to which he dubbed himself "The Ocho", as it marked his eighth World Title win). While the pay-per-views have been critically praised, the integration of ROH into AEW programs has been criticised for detracting from the overall AEW product, with some feeling there are too many belts and characters.

AEW AND NJPW COME TOGETHER FOR FORBIDDEN DOOR

Though the road to the event was riddled with frequent changes due to injuries and other developments, AEW and NJPW's joint Forbidden Door pay-per-view on June 26 was nonetheless hailed by fans and critics alike.

On April 20, Tony Khan and NJPW President Takami Ohbari (with an assist from Adam Cole) formally announced the event for Chicago's United Center. Before any matches were announced, 11,000 pre-sale tickets sold out in under 40 minutes on May 5.

When the time came to start promoting matches, however, misfortune continually reared itself. New AEW World Champion CM Punk was scheduled to wrestle Hiroshi Tanahashi in a first-time encounter, but was forced to pull out due to requiring foot surgery. Plans were then made to crown an interim AEW Champion, with Tanahashi facing Jon Moxley to fill the void.

A match between mat-wrestling virtuosos Bryan Danielson and Zack Sabre Jr had to be modified, due to Danielson being out with a concussion. Tomohiro Ishii's

participation in a four way match to crown the first ever AEW All-Atlantic Champion was scrapped for medical reasons. Both Kyle O'Reilly and Hiromu Takahashi had to be pulled from the show as well.

While Forbidden Door looked like a jinxed card, more than 16,000 fans on hand were nonetheless treated to one of the most critically-acclaimed pay-per-views of 2022, while an estimated 140,000 households witnessed the event as well.

Pre-show included, 13 matches took place at Forbidden Door, culminating with Moxley defeating Tanahashi to claim the interim AEW World Title.

Elsewhere on the card, Claudio Castagnoli made his AEW debut, filling in for Danielson against Sabre in the expected showcase of scientific brilliance. Castagnoli won his debut outing with AEW, and continued onward as the newest member of the Blackpool Combat Club.

Jay White retained the IWGP World Heavyweight belt over Kazuchika Okada, Adam Page, and Adam Cole. Unfortunately, Cole was knocked out late in the match, suffering a concussion that kept him sidelined for the rest of 2022.

Pac became the first ever AEW All-Atlantic Champion by defeating Malakai Black, Miro, and Clark Connors in a four way bout. ROH and AAA Tag Team Champions FTR added more gold to their collection by defeating United Empire and Roppongi Vice in a three-way match to win IWGP's tag straps.

In a surprise appearance, Katsuyori Shibata attacked IWGP United States Champion Will Ospreay, after Ospreay retained his title over Orange Cassidy in a frenetic contest.

CM PUNK SENSATIONALLY DEPARTS AEW FOLLOWING POST-ALL OUT PIPEBOMB AND BRAWL WITH THE ELITE

CM Punk's World Title win, and MJF's grand return, should have been the lasting memories of AEW All Out on September 4. Instead, events that transpired both on and off screen after the show's conclusion swiftly took focus over all else.

When all was said and done, following a physical altercation, Punk, Kenny Omega, Matt and Nick Jackson, backstage official Ace Steel (a friend and mentor to Punk), and other witnesses in the vicinity of the incident were all suspended from AEW.

All Out in Punk's native Chicago concluded with him defeating Jon Moxley to regain the AEW World Title he'd lost 11 nights earlier on an episode of Dynamite. Punk's celebration, however, was cut short by the return of MJF, who had (under a mask) won a top contenders' ladder match earlier in the night, and had chosen this moment to show his face. MJF had been absent since early June, and this ending set the stage for the next big angle.

Instead, an irritated Punk made all sorts of inflammatory

remarks at the post-event media scrum, while seated next to AEW President Tony Khan. Punk first mentioned the issue concerning former friend, AEW performer Colt Cabana, addressing rumours that Punk tried to get Cabana fired. Punk shot down those rumours, and claimed that they were spread by "irresponsible people who call themselves EVPs" (referring to Omega and both Jacksons), while questioning their management skills.

Punk also sharply criticised "Hangman" Adam Page, for comments Page made on-screen while the two were working a main event angle in May over the AEW World Title. Punk had initially retaliated by making his own off-script remarks about Page during an August episode of Dynamite, which created a stir at the time.

While details remain murky, it's alleged that Matt and Nick Jackson (along with company legal counsel Megha Parekh) went to Punk's locker room afterward to speak with him. That scene quickly became violent, reportedly with Nick Jackson being hit with a chair, punches being thrown, and Steel biting Omega when Omega tried to remove Punk's dog from the room.

All primary and secondary parties at the site were suspended, pending an investigation. Punk vacated his World Title, while Omega and The Young Bucks relinquished the Trios Titles they'd just won that night. Steel was fired from AEW in mid-October following the investigation, while Punk was reportedly in the midst of negotiating a contractual buyout. Omega and the Bucks returned in November at Full Gear.

TRIPLE H ANNOUNCES IN-RING RETIREMENT

Nearly three years after wrestling his most recent match, WWE executive Paul Levesque announced his retirement from in-ring activity in an ESPN interview on March 25.

Levesque revealed that shortly after the 2021 SummerSlam, he began to feel sick, and was diagnosed with viral pneumonia. After he began coughing up blood, doctors found that Levesque had fluid in his lungs and around his heart.

Levesque then experienced heart failure, with 100 percent blockage in his left anterior descending artery. At its worst, Levesque's heart was only at 12 percent functionality. Levesque ended up undergoing a reported 15 hours of surgery, and was fitted with an implantable cardioverter defibrillator.

With the defibrillator installed in his chest, Levesque ended his days inside the ring. To signify the end of his career, Levesque appeared at WrestleMania XXXVIII in Dallas a week following the announcement, and symbolically left his boots inside the ring.

As Triple H, Levesque had not wrestled since June of 2019, when he teamed with Shinsuke Nakamura on a WWE house show in Tokyo, against Robert Roode and Samoa Joe. He hadn't wrestled a regular schedule since the turn of the 2010s, when he assumed more of a backstage role, while restricting his wrestling to a part-time schedule.

In 2022, Levesque assumed a greater backstage role, following the retirement of father-in-law Vince McMahon. Levesque now heads up both of WWE's creative and talent relations departments (the latter after the exit of John Laurinaitis, shortly after McMahon confirmed his retirement).

Beginning his wrestling career in 1992, Levesque's first big break came in WCW in 1994. The following year, he jumped to the WWF, where he became Hunter Hearst Helmsley, a snobbish aristocrat. Over time, Levesque went through radical changes on screen, before settling upon the winningest version of 'Triple H'—a musclebound, cunning villain that dominated WWE's main event scene throughout most of the 2000s, amassing 14 reigns as World Champion. Levesque was also a founding member of D-Generation X, alongside Shawn Michaels.

As a semi-active performer, Triple H cultivated WWE's NXT development brand, growing it into a popular alternative to WWE's main roster.

CODY RHODES LEAVES AEW, RETURNS TO WWE

Cody Rhodes, one of the ground-floor members of the All Elite Wrestling locker room, announced on February 15 that he was leaving the organisation.

Rhodes and wife Brandi's contracts with AEW expired on December 31, and both were in ongoing negotiations for new deals. However, terms could not be reached, and Rhodes tweeted out his thank yous and goodbyes to the AEW faculty and fans in February.

With Cody leaving, immediate speculation was that he would return to WWE, where he last worked in 2016. On March 18, it was announced by multiple outlets that Rhodes had re-signed with his previous employer.

Rhodes ultimately made his return as a (not so) mystery opponent to Seth Rollins on the first night of WrestleMania XXXVIII. Notably, Rhodes entered to the 'Kingdom' entrance theme he began using in his post-WWE career.

Rhodes went on to defeat Rollins at WrestleMania, and again five weeks later at WrestleMania Backlash. The two met once again at Hell In A Cell on June 5, which Rhodes worked with a torn right pectoral. Rhodes won the match, but would be sidelined for months after the fact.

Across his two and a half years wrestling for AEW, Rhodes feuded with the likes of Chris Jericho, MJF, Mr. Brodie Lee, Malakai Black, and others. His match with brother Dustin at the 2019 Double Or Nothing (AEW's inaugural event) was heralded as an instant classic. As part of his entrance that night, Rhodes used a sledgehammer to destroy a Triple H-esque throne.

Both Cody and Brandi Rhodes had executive positions in AEW, with Cody working as an Executive Vice President, and Brandi as the Chief Branding Officer. The two were also stars of the TNT reality series Rhodes To

The Top.

Rhodes was the inaugural AEW TNT Champion, after defeating Lance Archer in a tournament final in 2020, and went on to hold the title on two more occasions. His last match with AEW took place on January 26, as he lost the TNT Championship to Sammy Guevara in a ladder match. Coincidentally, Rhodes and Guevara faced each other in the first match in AEW Dynamite history in October 2019.

STEVE AUSTIN RETURNS TO THE RING AT WRESTLEMANIA

Nineteen years after his presumed career finale, 57-year-old Stone Cold Steve Austin had "one more round" at WrestleMania XXXVIII on April 2 in Dallas, taking on Kevin Owens at the end of the event's first night.

The match had been speculated about for weeks, but was not formally advertised for the card, and was instead facilitated by an in-show confrontation with Owens.

Owens hosted Austin in his Kevin Owens Show talk segment, and ran down the state of Texas, before telling Austin that he wanted to fight him in a no holds barred match. Austin accepted the challenge, saying his first ever match was in Dallas, and his last match would be as well.

The match played out like a greatest hits of Stone Cold, mixing classic Austin spots with intense brawling in an expansive stadium environment. At one juncture, Owens went to steal Austin's ATV to try and get out of dodge, but Austin prevented his escape.

Late in the brawl, Owens swung a chair at Austin, who moved away, causing the chair to bounce off the ropes and ricochet back, hitting Owens in the face. Austin followed up with a Stunner to win the 14-minute skirmish. True to form, post-match, Austin drank beer and doled out more Stunners, including one to announcer Byron Saxton.

Austin also got physically involved on the second night of WrestleMania, showing up after Vince McMahon defeated Pat McAfee in another impromptu match. There, Austin dispensed more Stunners, including a particularly sad-looking one to 76-year old McMahon that soon went viral across social media.

Due to compounding spinal injuries, Austin had retired from the ring in 2003 at age 38, following a 13 and a half year career. Before WrestleMania, he last wrestled against The Rock in Seattle at WrestleMania XIX, putting his rival over after three Rock Bottoms.

NXT UK SHUTS DOWN

After four and a half years of existence, NXT UK shut down as of September 4, and its championships were unified with their American NXT counterparts.

WWE made the announcement on August 18 that the NXT UK brand would take a "brief hiatus", before returning in 2023 under the name NXT Europe. On the date of the announcement, numerous NXT UK personalities confirmed that they had been released from WWE, including Flash Morgan Webster, Mark Andrews, Millie McKenzie, Xia Brookside, Trent Seven, Dave Mastiff, and many others.

The final NXT UK card was a joint production with the American NXT called Worlds Collide, which took place at WWE's Performance Center in Orlando on September 4.

Three unification matches were held at Worlds Collide. Pretty Deadly won a four way match to capture both the NXT and NXT UK tag belts, defeating The Creed

Brothers, Brooks Jensen and Josh Briggs, and Gallus. NXT Women's Champion Mandy Rose defeated UK titleholder Meiko Satomura and Blair Davenport to combine those belts.

In the main event, NXT Champion Bron Breakker defeated UK champ Tyler Bate to unify the titles.

In January 2017, WWE held a tournament to crown the first ever United Kingdom Champion, which Bate won after defeating Pete Dunne in the finals. A year and a half later, NXT UK officially started up as a wrestling brand, largely as a counter to the revival of World Of Sport on ITV in the United Kingdom (which was officially cancelled in late 2019).

NXT UK ran three events under the TakeOver banner: Blackpool in January 2019, Cardiff that August, and Blackpool in January 2020. The brand was shut down for about six months during the early stages of the pandemic, and it never really recovered, puttering along until the August 2022 announcement.

WWE DRAWS STADIUM CROWD FOR CLASH AT THE CASTLE IN THE UK

WWE ran its first United Kingdom stadium show in three decades on September 3, bringing Clash At The Castle to Principality Stadium in the city of Cardiff.

The location was officially announced in mid-April. Weeks later, Drew McIntyre revealed the Clash At The Castle name at a WWE house show at London's O2 Arena. Anticipation was such that in the 24 hours after Clash was first announced, a reported 59,000 individuals had pre-registered for tickets, setting a new company record. It would be the first time WWE staged a stadium card in the United Kingdom since August 29, 1992, when that year's SummerSlam was held at London's old Wembley Stadium, and broadcast on tape delay in the United States two days later.

In all, a reported crowd of 62,296 witnessed what many rank among the greatest WWE events of the year.

In the main event, Roman Reigns continued his now two-year-plus reign as Universal Champion, successfully defending the unified belts over Drew McIntyre, after interference from debuting Bloodline member Solo Sikoa. After the match, heavyweight boxing champion Tyson Fury shared a faceoff with Reigns, before initiating a singalong inside the ring with McIntyre (in a bit that apparently wasn't supposed to air).

Elsewhere on the card, Gunther retained his Intercontinental Title over Sheamus in a hard-hitting, critically-acclaimed battle. After the match, Sheamus received a standing ovation from the stadium crowd.

Dominik Mysterio turned heel on the card, turning on father Rey and his tag team partner Edge after they defeated Judgment Day members Finn Balor and Damian Priest. Dominik formally joined the heel stable on the following Monday's RAW.

There were no title changes at Clash At The Castle. In the SmackDown Women's Title match, Liv Morgan retained her belt over Shayna Baszler.

SASHA BANKS AND NAOMI QUIT WWE

Reigning WWE Women's Tag Team Champions Sasha Banks and Naomi walked out of a Monday Night RAW taping on May 16, amid apparent creative differences.

Banks and Naomi were booked to take part in a six-way match on that night's RAW that would help set up the singles title challengers for the June 5 Hell In A Cell pay-per-view. Sources have it that Naomi was supposed

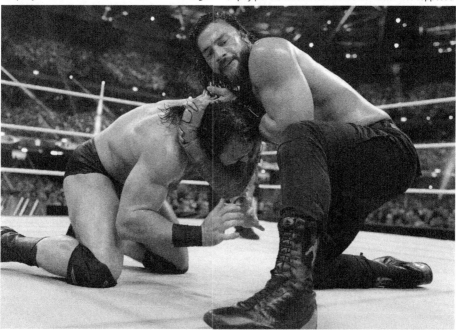

to pin Banks in the match in order to earn a title match with RAW Women's champion Bianca Belair, while a later angle would lead to Banks challenging Ronda Rousey for the SmackDown belt at the same event. Both Naomi and Banks were intended to lose those matches, before resuming life as the women's tag champs.

Banks and Naomi reportedly requested a tag title defense instead at Hell In A Cell, which Vince McMahon shot down. Banks and Naomi then left their belts with John Laurinaitis, and departed the arena.

Announcer Corey Graves later made an in-show reference to the walkout, and called the exit "unprofessional". Four nights later on SmackDown, Michael Cole informed the home audience that both Banks and Naomi had been suspended indefinitely, and that a tournament would be held to crown new tag team champions. Among Cole's obviously prepared remarks, he said that Banks and Naomi, "...let us all down."

The vacated belts were won in a tournament final by Raquel Rodriguez and Aliyah on August 29. The two only reigned as champions for two weeks before dropping the belts to Dakota Kai and Iyo Sky on September 12.

MJF CREATES A STIR AROUND DOUBLE OR NOTHING

Maxwell Jacob Friedman was the subject of much drama, confusion, and speculation during AEW Double Or Nothing weekend, beginning Saturday, May 28.

MJF was booked to face former bodyguard Wardlow on the pay-per-view, to blow off their long simmering feud. However, more than 24 hours before the event, stories emerged that MJF had no-showed his appearance at the weekend's fan fest. Follow-up stories claimed that AEW was considering conducting a welfare check on MJF, while other stories said that MJF had been spotted at one of the casinos in Las Vegas, when he was supposed to be at the meet and greet.

Late that Saturday night, the newest development was that MJF had reportedly booked a flight out of Las Vegas, leaving fans to speculate whether or not MJF would even make it to the pay-per-view.

Videos advertising the MJF-Wardlow match were pulled from, then reposted to, AEW's media sites several times on Sunday, giving the impression that the situation was still in flux.

However, MJF did appear at Double Or Nothing, losing to Wardlow in the opener via ten riveting powerbombs, which necessitated a stretcher job. Before the match, MJF made a mocking "airplane" gesture to play off the headlines.

At Wednesday's Dynamite in Los Angeles, MJF cut a blistering worked/shoot promo where he lambasted Tony Khan for paying ex-WWE wrestlers more than him, called Khan a mark that shouldn't be running a company, dared Khan to fire him from AEW, and teased a jump to WWE. During the obscenity-filled rant (during which one F-bomb was bleeped), MJF's mic was suddenly cut, and the segment hastily faded into commercial.

That marked MJF's last appearance for AEW until September 4, when he returned at All Out in Chicago. He went on to become AEW World Champion on November 19, defeating Jon Moxley at Full Gear.

LOGAN PAUL SIGNS WITH WWE

Popular YouTube star Logan Paul signed a multi-event contract with WWE on June 30. The deal calls for Paul to appear on select TV shows and pay-per-views in 2022 and 2023.

Paul had already taken part in the previous couple of WrestleManias. At WrestleMania XXXVII, Paul sat ringside for a match between Kevin Owens and Sami Zayn. He had been incorporated into the angle as an acquaintance of Zayn, who had screened his "conspiracy" documentary for Paul.

After Owens defeated Zayn, Paul celebrated with Owens, but ended up receiving a post-match Stunner for his troubles.

At WrestleMania XXXVIII, Paul wrestled in his first ever match, teaming with The Miz to defeat Rey and Dominik Mysterio. After the match, Miz turned on Paul.

After Paul signed with WWE, the wheels were set in motion for Paul to face Miz at SummerSlam on July 30. Paul won the match, pinning Miz with his own Skull Crushing Finale. Paul earned strong praise for his work, especially for somebody wrestling only their second match.

In September, WWE announced that Paul would challenge undisputed Universal Champion Roman Reigns at Crown Jewel in Riyadh. Paul ended up losing the match, but earned even more praise for his performance, in which he looked like a polished, main event-caliber wrestler. On a down note, however, it came out after the match that Paul suffered a sprained meniscus and PCL.

In addition to wrestling, Paul has shown his athletic side in boxing matches with English YouTuber KSI, as well as an exhibition fight with former World champion Floyd Mayweather, Jr.

RIC FLAIR HAS ONE MORE "LAST MATCH"

At age 73, Ric Flair took to the ring for his apparent final match on July 31 in Nashville, with many fans and critics hoping he sticks to his word.

Flair announced in May that he would take to the ring one last time for an event held under the banner of the revived Jim Crockett Promotions, co-promoted by David Crockett and Conrad Thompson.

The Nature Boy nominally retired at WrestleMania XXIV in 2008, after losing to Shawn Michaels in a featured bout. Both immediately after the match and the next night on RAW, Flair was given a sizable sendoff by WWE. However, Flair broke his retirement vow the following year, taking part in a tour of Australia where he headlined several events with Hulk Hogan. Flair then wrestled several bouts for TNA, the last of which came against Sting in 2011.

For this match, Flair teamed with son-in-law Andrade el Idolo to face Jay Lethal and Jeff Jarrett at the Nashville Municipal Auditorium, before a crowd of 6,800 fans.

What those fans got in the main event of an 11 match supercard was an uncomfortable spectacle in which Flair (wrestling in a t-shirt and noticeably limping due to a foot issue) quickly ran out of gas, struggled to perform basic moves, and spent long periods in a near motionless state on the canvas. Despite his jarring struggles, a blood-stained Flair managed to perform the finish, which was trapping Jarrett in the figure four and scoring a pinfall victory off of the hold.

SHANE MCMAHON FIRED FROM WWE

Among all the WWE firings and releases over the last few years, few were as surprising on the surface as the termination of Shane McMahon on February 2.

McMahon's firing was confirmed days after the 2022 Royal Rumble pay-per-view, in which McMahon both wrestled in and helped assemble the 30-man gauntlet. His involvement on both ends was subject of much criticism and derision.

Stories indicated that McMahon attempted to book the latter stages of the men's Rumble match around himself, and acted unprofessionally to those involved in the booking process when his ideas and suggestions were shot down. McMahon was said to be especially crude toward fellow organiser Jamie Noble, and talked down to others as well. McMahon also reportedly clashed with Brock Lesnar over the proposed match layout.

One source cited in The Wrestling Observer Newsletter said that because of McMahon's actions toward numerous individuals, father Vince had, "...no options but to fire him."

McMahon entered the match from the number 28 position and managed to eliminate former rival Kevin Owens. He was part of the final four, where he was soon thrown out by eventual winner Lesnar. The 2022 Royal Rumble was largely panned, with most criticism levied toward the 30-man match.

Before his firing, McMahon was scheduled to take part in the Elimination Chamber match the following month, and later a singles match with Seth Rollins at WrestleMania XXXVIII. McMahon's most recent match prior to the Rumble was at WrestleMania XXXVII in 2021, where he lost to Braun Strowman in a steel cage match.

BIG E SUFFERS BROKEN NECK

Former WWE Champion Big E suffered a broken neck during a tag team match on the March 11 episode of SmackDown.

Big E was teaming with New Day partner Kofi Kingston against Sheamus and Ridge Holland in Birmingham, AL, when, whilst outside the ring, Holland performed an overhead belly to belly suplex on Big E. Unfortunately, Big E came down on the top of his head, and needed to be stretchered out of ringside.

It was later revealed that the New Day member suffered fractures to his C1 and C6 vertebrae, though he managed to avoid spinal damage, and wouldn't require any surgery.

Big E later had a reunion with Kingston and Xavier Woods on the May 20 episode of SmackDown, but a return to the ring remains uncertain. Kingston indicated in an October interview that his recovering friend and partner was still taking things slowly.

While inactive from the ring, Big E has been a part of WWE's recruitment efforts, in the role of evaluator. He was on hand at WWE's tryouts in Nashville during SummerSlam weekend, as well as tryouts at Tampa's IMG Academy later in the year. An alumnus of the University of Iowa, Big E was a featured guest at the school's October football game against Michigan.

Big E actually entered the year as WWE Champion, having won the title from Bobby Lashley in September 2021 via a Money In The Bank cash-in. He dropped the gold to Brock Lesnar in a five-way match at WWE Day 1 on New Year's Day 2022.

2022 SUPERCARDS AND TV SPECIALS

THE NEW YEAR '22
01-01-22, Tokyo, Japan **NOAH**

Junta Miyawaki and **Kinya Okada** defeated **Kai Fujimura** and **Yasutaka Yano** in 8:39; **Akitoshi Saito, King Tany** and **Mohammed Yone** defeated **Manabu Soya, Nio** and **Tadasuke** in 8:45; **Aleja** and **Hao** defeated **Seiki Yoshioka** and **Yuya Susumu** in 11:44; **Hajime Ohara, Atsushi Kotoge, Daisuke Harada** and **Ultimo Dragon** defeated **Eita, Kotaro Suzuki, Nosawa Rongai** and **Yo-Hey** in 13:51; **Kazuyuki Fujita** and **Kendo Kashin** defeated **Ikuto Hidaka** and **Masakatsu Funaki** in 12:17; **Hayata** defeated **Yoshinari Ogawa** in 20:54; **Keiji Muto** and **Naomichi Marufuji** defeated **Masaaki Mochizuki** and **Masato Tanaka** in 20:50; **Kenta, Kazushi Sakuraba** and **Takashi Sugiura** defeated **Daiki Inaba, Masa Kitamiya** and **Yoshiki Inamura** in 25:46; **Kenoh** defeated **Kaito Kiyomiya** in 24:42; **Katsuhiko Nakajima** defeated **Go Shiozaki** in 30:10.

Was It Any Good? This was a very good card overall, with a killer stretch of three matches to close the show that were each of very high quality indeed. The undercard was largely solid, save a relatively static tag match between Kazuyuki Fujita and Kendo Kashin, and Ikuto Hidaka and Masakatsu Funaki. Things heated up later in the evening with the NOAH return of KENTA, who had been absent from his home promotion since 2018. This match sizzled in large part due to the tensions surrounding KENTA's absence and decision to join New Japan following his stint with WWE, and laid the groundwork for some mouth-watering clashes down the road. In the co-main, blood rivals Kenoh and Kaito Kiyomiya clashed once again, this time for the former's GHC National Championship. The story between these two is so richly developed that it would be impossible to do it justice here, but certainly this match, in which Kenoh retained his title, was another worthy addition to what will likely be a career-long rivalry. The main event clash between former partners turned bitter enemies, Katsuhiko Nakajima and Go Shiozaki, was every bit as compelling as one might expect given the quality of the combatants. Shiozaki plays NOAH's shining hero perfectly and with the devilish Nakajima, he had found a perfect foil. Nakajima won the battle, and retained the GHC Heavyweight Championship, capping off a strong start to the year from The Ark.

DAY 1
01-01-22, Atlanta, Georgia **WWE**

The Usos (**Jey Uso** and **Jimmy Uso**) defeated **The New Day** (**Kofi Kingston** and **Xavier Woods**) in 18:05; **Drew McIntyre** defeated **Madcap Moss** in 9:45; **RK-Bro** (**Randy Orton** and **Riddle**) defeated **The Street Profits** (**Angelo Dawkins** and **Montez Ford**) in 11:15; **Edge** defeated **The Miz** in 20:00; **Becky Lynch** defeated **Liv Morgan** in 17:00; **Brock Lesnar** defeated **Big E, Seth Rollins, Kevin Owens** and **Bobby Lashley** in a Fatal Five-Way Match to win the WWE Title in 8:19.

Was It Any Good? Not particularly. Day 1 was the brainchild of WWE President Nick Khan, who wanted the New Year's Day show to become not only an annual tradition, but a major event on the calendar to rival the likes of WrestleMania and SummerSlam. WWE's creative team evidently did not get the memo, as Day 1 was booked to look and feel like every other B-show, with the exception of the planned main event between Roman Reigns and Brock Lesnar. However, just hours before the event, Reigns was pulled from the show due to COVID-19, causing a last minute scramble that saw Lesnar added to the already-scheduled four-way bout for Big E's WWE Title. The expectation was that WWE would go all guns blazing for the headliner given the schedule change, but that did not happen, with the bout only lasting a deeply unsatisfying eight minutes. The rest of the card was fairly humdrum, with only the Usos' win over eternal rivals New Day in the opener and an entertaining clash between Edge and The Miz getting out of second gear.

WRESTLE KINGDOM 16 NIGHT #1
04-01-22, Tokyo, Japan **NJPW**

Yoh defeated **Sho** in 12:32; **Kenta, Taiji Ishimori** and **El Phantasmo** defeated **Hiroshi Tanahashi, Ryusuke Taguchi** and **Rocky Romero** by DQ in 8:40; **Will Ospreay, Great-O-Khan** and **Jeff Cobb** defeated **Tetsuya Naito, Sanada** and **Bushi** in 9:27; **Katsuyori Shibata** defeated **Ren Narita** in 11:46; **Evil** defeated **Tomohiro Ishii** to win the NEVER Openweight Title in 12:10; **Hirooki Goto** and **Yoshi-Hashi** defeated **Taichi** and **Zack Sabre Jr.** to win the IWGP Tag Team Title in 15:27; **El Desperado** defeated **Hiromu Takahashi** in 16:18; **Kazuchika Okada** defeated **Shingo Takagi** to win the IWGP World Heavyweight Title in 35:44.

Was It Any Good? It's difficult to say. New Japan has built such an incredible reputation around its Wrestle Kingdom shows, but since the beginning of the pandemic, and the subsequent closure of borders, the show quality has understandably taken a hit. Then factor in the decision to split the event over two nights (night three is a different beast) and one can appreciate how the shows may struggle to live up to their pre-pandemic predecessors. So, was it any good? Yes, it was, but nowhere near the level of Kingdoms gone by and the natural comparisons of which hung heavy over both nights. Like many of the company's premier pairings, Kazuchika Okada and Shingo Takagi must be pushing towards the outer limits of what they can achieve together now, having produced several superlative contests in recent years. This one was certainly a worthy addition to their catalogue, with Okada claiming the IWGP World Heavyweight Title. Another rivalry revisited on the show was between Hiromu Takahashi and El Desperado who, like in the main event, fought bitterly to outdo some of their previous tussles. They didn't quite achieve it, but this was an enjoyable battle, nonetheless. Two notable moments from the undercard included Katsuyori Shibata's impromptu return to action and Tomoshiro Ishii's interminable clash with EVIL. Of the former, Shibata had reportedly been scheduled for a 'safety first' grappling exchange but instead called an audible, on the mic no less, forcing student Ren Narita into a full contact match. The live crowd loved it and Shibata himself looked fantastic, scoring the win with his trademark PK. The Ishii encounter was noteworthy purely for the fact that it was not very good. For anyone who has followed the 'Stone Pitbull' for any stretch of time, the notion that he had been involved in a poorly received contest will be as big a shock as anything else on the card!

WRESTLE KINGDOM 16 NIGHT #2
05-01-22, Tokyo, Japan **NJPW**

Robbie Eagles and **Tiger Mask** defeated **Ryusuke Taguchi** and **Rocky Romero,** and **El Phantasmo** in a Three Way Match in 12:07; **Tam Nakano** and **Saya Kamitani** defeated **Mayu Iwatani** and **Starlight Kid** in 9:14; **Minoru Suzuki** defeated **Chase Owens, Cima** and **Toru Yano** in a Four Way Match to win the Provisional KOPW 2022 Trophy in 6:08; **Evil, Yujiro Takahashi** and **Sho** defeated **Hirooki Goto, Yoshi-Hashi** and **Yoh** in 9:37; **Sanada** defeated **Great-O-Khan** in 13:21; **Tetsuya Naito** defeated **Jeff Cobb** in 15:34; **Hiroshi Tanahashi** defeated **Kenta** in a No DQ Match to win the IWGP United States Heavyweight Title in 22:40; **Kazuchika Okada** defeated **Will Ospreay** in 32:52.

Was It Any Good? Night two arguably ended with

more headlines than night one and certainly did more to generate intrigue into the coming year. Will Ospreay and Kazuchika Okada provided the event with some much-needed quality in a phenomenal closing bout in which 'The Rainmaker' reigned supreme. Both men should be given credit for delivering a bout of such quality within the constraints of New Japan's mandated 'clap crowds' Hiroshi Tanahashi and KENTA at the very least tried to do something different with their no disqualification bout for the US Title. This one definitely fell flat with the live crowd though, who were not used to seeing such stylings in a Tokyo Dome setting. One of the more unique moments of the show came when the Pro Wrestling NOAH roster marched to the ring en masse, ahead of the forthcoming inter-promotional showdown between the two companies. This was a rare moment of spectacle, and the likes of Kenoh, Kaito Kiyomiya and Keiji Muto standing proudly within the New Japan ring was comfortably the most noteworthy moment of the first two nights of Wrestle Kingdom 16.

WRESTLE KINGDOM 16 NIGHT #3
08-01-22, Yokohama, Japan *NJPW/NOAH*
Tomohiro Ishii, Hirooki Goto, Yoshi-Hashi, Master Wato and **Ryusuke Taguchi** defeated **Daisuke Harada, Hajime Ohara, Daiki Inaba, Yoshiki Inamura** and **Kinya Okada** in 11:42; **Sho** defeated **Atsushi Kotoge** in 8:20; **Hayata** and **Seiki Yoshioka** defeated **Taiji Ishimori** and **Gedo** in 5:59; **El Desperado** and **Douki** defeated **Yo-Hey** and **Nosawa Rongai** in 9:09; **Takashi Sugiura, Kazushi Sakuraba** and **Toru Yano** defeated **Taichi, Minoru Suzuki** and **Taka Michinoku** in 9:37; **Go Shiozaki** and **Masa Kitamiya** defeated **Evil** and **Dick Togo** in 9:53; **Naomichi Marufuji** and **Yoshinari Ogawa** defeated **Zack Sabre Jr.** and **Yoshinobu Kanemaru** in 15:20; **Tetsuya Naito, Shingo Takagi, Sanada, Bushi** and **Hiromu Takahashi** defeated **Katsuhiko Nakajima, Kenoh, Manabu Soya, Tadasuke** and **Aleja** in 26:33; **Kazuchika Okada** and **Hiroshi Tanahashi** defeated **Keiji Mutoh** and **Kaito Kiyomiya** in 24:34.
Was It Any Good? It was a step in the right direction. The top three matches were pretty notable and beyond that, this event was a fun, if tentative, experiment between two companies eager to do something different but not entirely sure of how to do it. There were some big seeds planted here, particularly with regards to Kaito Kiyomiya's ongoing quest to face Kazuchika Okada and the ideological clash between Tetsuya Naito's Los Ingobernables de Japón troop and Kenoh's Kongoh stable. In fact, the five-on five-clash between the two groups was arguably the match of the night, with the two highly characterised leaders generating a wonderful, organic rivalry in a relatively short space of time. New Japan ended up winning the inter-promotional war with six wins to NOAH's four, but both companies were big winners here, with the card boasting a freshness not seen in either promotion in quite some time.

BATTLE OF THE BELTS I
08-01-22, Charlotte, North Carolina *AEW*
Sammy Guevara defeated **Dustin Rhodes** in 16:15; **Ricky Starks** defeated **Matt Sydal** in 9:00; **Dr. Britt Baker D.M.D.** defeated **Riho** in 12:47.
Was It Any Good? It was an easy-to-watch hour of professional wrestling, but nothing special. Sammy Guevara's interim TNT Title victory over Dustin Rhodes was the highlight, with the pair engaging in a fun opener. Guevara looked like a star here and the veteran Rhodes continued to wind back the clock and more than kept up with his high flying opponent. Elsewhere, Ricky Starks defended the unrecognised FTW Title against Matt Sydal in a decent match bereft of stakes (both in the

championship itself and in the likelihood of it changing hands). In the main event, Britt Baker retained the AEW Women's Championship against arguably her strongest opponent in Riho. These two have decent chemistry and typically deliver when paired against one another. This bout was no exception, with Baker ultimately sealing the win with the Lockjaw submission.

HARD TO KILL '22
08-01-22, Dallas, Texas *Impact*
Tasha Steelz defeated **Alisha Edwards, Chelsea Green, Jordynne Grace, Lady Frost** and **Rosemary** in an Ultimate X Match in 9:00; **Trey Miguel** defeated **Steve Maclin** in 12:50; **Jonathan Gresham** defeated **Chris Sabin** in 12:40; **Josh Alexander** defeated **Jonah** in 17:05; **Eddie Edwards, Rich Swann, Willie Mack, Heath** and **Rhyno** defeated **The Good Brothers (Luke Gallows** and **Karl Anderson)** and **Violent By Design (Eric Young, Deaner** and **Joe Doering)** in a Hardcore War in 23:25; **Moose** defeated **Matt Cardona** and **W. Morrissey** in a Three Way Match in 16:00; **Mickie James** defeated **Deonna Purrazzo** in a Texas Deathmatch in 19:40.
Was It Any Good? It was a very good night of wrestling overall. Despite arriving just eight days into the year, Hard To Kill was arguably IMPACT's 2022 peak in terms of a card delivering from top to bottom. Of particular note were rising star Josh Alexander's big man clash with the gargantuan JONAH, Jonathan Gresham's ROH World Title victory over Chris Sabin (fought under ROH Pure Rules) and Trey Miguel's X-Division Title triumph over Steve Maclin, which was bumped onto the main card at short notice. The IMPACT World Title match between Moose, W. Morrisey and Matt Cardona was much better than it had any right to be, while history was made in the show opener as Tasha Steelz emerged victorious in the first ever women's Ultimate X match. Mickie James and Deonna Purrazzo closed the show in a Texas Death Match for the former's IMPACT Knockouts Title. This was well received and indeed well wrestled, albeit slightly below par from what had come before it.

NAGOYA SUPREME FIGHT
29-01-22, Nagoya, Japan *Stardom*
Hanan defeated **Lady C** in 5:56; **Momo Watanabe** and **Starlight Kid** defeated **AZM** and **Utami Hayashishita** in 9:43; **Thekla** defeated **Mina Shirakawa** to win the vacant SWA Undisputed World Women's Title in 9:58; **Hazuki** and **Koguma** defeated **Himeka** and **Maika** in 13:27; **Saya Kamitani** defeated **Unagi Sayaka** in 18:47; **Giulia** vs. **Mayu Iwatani** ended in a draw in 30:00; **Syuri** defeated **Mirai** in 26:47.
Was It Any Good? It was fine if unspectacular save for the main event and one killer angle. This was Stardom's first pay per view of the year and it in many ways served as a reset show following the conclusion of 2021's storylines and several of its title reigns. And as with any first episode, this had a much slower feel than the promotion's meatier shows, as the building blocks were positioned for the year ahead. That said, the main event between World of Stardom Champion Syuri and recent Tokyo Joshi Pro defector Mirai was very good, and worthy of your time. Mirai was a huge pick-up for Stardom and is packed with potential. Here, she was made to look a star by the company's top dog, which is perhaps indicative of her longer-term prospects. The other big story from the show was the arrival of Prominence, a breakaway group from fellow *joshi* promotion Ice Ribbon, whose membership specialised in the deathmatch style. Principle members Suzu Suzuki and Risa Sera each had history with several of Stardom's top talents, particularly Giulia, whose Donna del Mundo stable appeared in the firing line here. This was a big story, not least for the potential

matches it could create but for Stardom's willingness to engage with outside talent and promotions, something that would become a key theme throughout 2022.

ROYAL RUMBLE '22
29-01-22, St. Louis, Missouri **WWE**

Seth Rollins defeated **Roman Reigns** by DQ in 14:25; **Ronda Rousey** won the 30-Woman Royal Rumble Match in 59:40; **Becky Lynch** defeated **Doudrop** in 13:00; **Bobby Lashley** defeated **Brock Lesnar** to win the WWE Title in 10:15; **Edge** and **Beth Phoenix** defeated **The Miz** and **Maryse** in 12:30; **Brock Lesnar** won the 30-Man Royal Rumble Match in 51:10.

Was It Any Good? No. From start to finish, Royal Rumble '22 was a bit of a disaster. The opener between former Shield teammates Roman Reigns and Seth Rollins was developing into a fine bout until the unsatisfying DQ finish, which may have served the story but it left viewers feeling short-changed. The returning Ronda Rousey's ring rust was evident as she sleepwalked through the motions to win the women's Royal Rumble bout. Her uninterested performance was unfortunately a precursor to the rest of her output in 2022. Becky Lynch's RAW Women's Title defence against Doudrop was as routine as they come—nobody bought Doudrop as a realistic challenger to Lynch, as they had not been given any reason to. There were more storyline shenanigans in the WWE Title bout between Bobby Lashley and Brock Lesnar, another anticipated bout that suffered from layout issues (namely the short run time) and overbooking, when Paul Heyman turned on Brock at the climax to cost him the title and firmly establish himself in the camp of Roman Reigns and The Bloodline. Edge and Beth Phoenix's win over The Miz and Maryse was typical sports entertainment fare, albeit not executed with much panache and ruined by the silly rules that forbid the men and women from interacting, essentially reducing it to two disconnected singles bouts. It was down to the men's Rumble to save the show, and it failed on all fronts. The surprises were groan-inducing (celebs Johnny Knoxville and Bad Bunny and the returning Shane McMahon—who incredibly made it to the final four), the participants were mostly midcard fodder who had no hope of winning, and the bout was rushed at just over 50 minutes. Rather than using the Rumble to set the stage for WrestleMania with stories and character development, WWE rushed through the bout and achieved nothing other than confirming that Brock Lesnar would meet Reigns at the show of shows, which everyone already knew going into the card. Widely panned, this was one of the most pointless Rumble matches ever.

ELIMINATION CHAMBER '22
19-02-22, Jeddah, Saudi Arabia **WWE**

Roman Reigns defeated **Goldberg** in 6:00; **Bianca Belair** defeated **Alexa Bliss**, **Doudrop**, **Liv Morgan**, **Nikki A.S.H.** and **Rhea Ripley** in an Elimination Chamber Match in 15:45; **Naomi** and **Ronda Rousey** defeated **Charlotte Flair** and **Sonya Deville** in 9:14; **Drew McIntyre** defeated **Madcap Moss** in a Falls Count Anywhere Match in 9:00; **Becky Lynch** defeated **Lita** in 12:10; **Brock Lesnar** defeated **Bobby Lashley**, **AJ Styles**, **Austin Theory**, **Riddle** and **Seth Rollins** in an Elimination Chamber Match to win the WWE Title in 14:55.

Was It Any Good? Nope. WWE took its now-traditional last stop before WrestleMania to the Kingdom of Saudi Arabia for the first time, and the show managed to live down to the low standards set by previous events in the nation. Goldberg's performance in his quick-fire loss to Roman Reigns in the opener was closer to his catastrophic display opposite The Undertaker in Saudi three years prior than his bamburner there with Lashley in 2021. The women's Elimination Chamber match

was unremarkable, but at least had the right winner. Ronda Rousey was forced to wrestle with one arm tied behind her back when she teamed with Naomi in a throwaway tag bout opposite Sonya Deville and WrestleMania opponent Charlotte Flair, a stipulation which did little to improve Ronda's ropey—no pun intended —performances since her WWE return. Drew McIntyre did his best to get something watchable out of Madcap Moss, who just about kept up with the former WWE Champion. Match of the night honours went to Becky Lynch and the returning Lita, who gave one of the finest in-ring performances of her career and received a deserved standing ovation for her efforts. The main event men's Chamber was one of the stipulation's weakest ever. Brock Lesnar annihilated the field in short order—but not WWE Champion Bobby Lashley, who was removed from the match due to "injury" after Seth Rollins powerbombed Austin Theory through his pod, causing Lashley to fall over. Apparently that was enough to take The Allmighty out of the match, leaving Lesnar a clear path to crush everyone else and regain the strap, rendering his Royal Rumble title loss a total waste of time.

REY DE REYES '22
19-02-22, Veracruz, Mexico **AAA**

Taya Valkyrie defeated **Flammer**, **Keyra**, **Lady Shani** and **Maravilla** in a Five Way Match in 12:20; **Abismo Negro Jr.**, **Latigo** and **Psicosis** defeated **Mr. Iguana**, **Myzteziz Jr.** and **Nino Hamburguesa** in 10:58; **Arez** and **Chik Tormenta** defeated **La Hiedra** and **Villano III Jr.**, and **Octagon Jr.** and **Sexy Star** in a Three Way Lumberjack Match in 11:31; **El Hijo de LA Park**, **LA Park** and **LA Park Jr.** vs. **DMT Azul**, **Puma King** and **Sam Adonis** vs. **El Cuatrero**, **Forastero** and **Sanson** ended in a no contest in a Three Way Match in 13:05; **Psycho Clown** defeated **Heavy Metal**, **Bandido**, **Cibernetico** and **Laredo Kid** in a Five Way Elimination Match in 10:17; **Pentagon Jr.** defeated **Dralistico** in 13:19; **El Hijo del Vikingo** defeated **Johnny Superstar** in 13:07.

Was It Any Good? No, not really. While a reasonable card on paper, Rey de Reyes was full to the brim with run ins, screwy finishes and baffling booking. Right up until the co-main event, any gains made by the in-ring action were hastily cancelled out by unintelligible interference that, at best, hampered the contest and at worst, outright ruined it. As has been the case for many a Triple A show in recent years, the responsibility fell to El Hijo del Vikingo to deliver a show-saving performance and the superhuman luchador certainly did his best, in the main event against John Superstar (formerly WWE's John Morrison). The bout was comfortably match of the night, and while not the best Vikingo of the year, it absolutely had its moments, including Vikingo's stunning ropewalk poisonrana. Unfortunately, the main event alone could do little to offset the rest of the show, which was a challenging watch.

50TH ANNIVERSARY SHOW
01-03-22, Tokyo, Japan **NJPW**

Evil, **Yujiro Takahashi** and **Sho** defeated **Tiger Mask**, **Yoh** and **Ryohei Oiwa** in 6:35; **Bad Luck Fale**, **Taiji Ishimori** and **El Phantasmo** defeated **Taichi**, **Taka Michinoku** and **Minoru Tanaka** in 9:50; **Cima**, **T-Hawk** and **El Lindaman** defeated **El Desperado**, **Yoshinobu Kanemaru** and **Douki** in 9:22; **Great-O-Khan**, **Will Ospreay**, **Jeff Cobb** and **Aaron Henare** defeated **Satoshi Kojima**, **Yuji Nagata**, **Kosei Fujita** and **Yuto Nakashima** in 9:20; **Sanada**, **Tetsuya Naito**, **Shingo Takagi**, **Bushi** and **Hiromu Takahashi** defeated **Togi Makabe**, **Tomoaki Honma**, **Tomohiro Ishii**, **Toru Yano** and **Shiro Koshinaka** in 12:38; **Hirooki Goto** and **Yoshi-Hashi** defeated **Ryusuke Taguchi** and **Master Wato** in 15:04; **Kazuchika**

Okada, **Hiroshi Tanahashi** and **Tatsumi Fujinami** defeated **Zack Sabre Jr., Minoru Suzuki** and **Yoshiaki Fujiwara** in 18:12.

Was It Any Good? Yes, but not in the conventional sense of being a New Japan card filled with strong style star-fests. Indeed, there was little to write home about from an in-ring perspective, instead, this was a more nostalgia-driven affair that played to the long-time fan and paid homage to the company's rich history. The tag team encounter between Bishamon and Six or Nine was fun, as was the main event offering which saw Kazuchika Okada, Hiroshi Tanahashi and Tatsumi Fujinami defeat Minoru Suzuki, Zack Sabre Jr. and Yoshiaki Fujiwara. Arguably the best bout of the night came much earlier in proceedings, when the STRONGHEARTS stable of CIMA, T-Hawk and El Lindaman made their presence felt against the Suzuki-gun trio of DOUKI, El Desperado and Yoshinobu Kanemaru. The group, now residing in lesser known promotion GLEAT, picked up the win over the New Japan trio and brought a unique sense of freshness along with them. In general, this was an enjoyable stroll of a show that featured plenty of good wrestling alongside a neat shot of nostalgia.

REVOLUTION '22
06-03-22, Orlando, Florida **AEW**

Eddie Kingston defeated **Chris Jericho** in 13:40; **Jurassic Express (Jungle Boy** and **Luchasaurus)** defeated **reDRagon (Bobby Fish** and **Kyle O'Reilly)** and **The Young Bucks (Matt Jackson** and **Nick Jackson)** in a Three Way Match in 18:55; **Wardlow** defeated **Christian Cage, Keith Lee, Orange Cassidy, Powerhouse Hobbs** and **Ricky Starks** in a Face Of The Revolution Ladder Match in 17:20; **Jade Cargill** defeated **Tay Conti** in 6:40; **CM Punk** defeated **MJF** in a Dog Collar Match in 26:45; **Dr. Britt Baker D.M.D.** defeated **Thunder Rosa** in 17:25; **Jon Moxley** defeated **Bryan Danielson** in 21:05; **Darby Allin, Sammy Guevara** and **Sting** defeated **The Andrade-Hardy Family Office (Andrade El Idolo, Matt Hardy** and **Isiah Kassidy)** in a Tornado Tag Team Match in 13:20; **Hangman Page** defeated **Adam Cole** in 25:45.

Was It Any Good? It was indeed. Revolution was one of AEW's strongest pay per view offerings of the year, with several high-quality match ups of varying stipulations. Chief among these was the Dog Collar match between CM Punk and MJF, which not only served as a feud-ending bloodbath between the pair but also facilitated Wardlow's face turn, which had been building for months. The 'War Dog' swerved his former employer who was begging for his trusty Dynamite Diamond Ring to finish the match. While Wardlow was searching his pockets, Punk took advantage and nailed the brash New Yorker with a Go to Sleep. It was at this point that 'Mr Mayhem' conveniently managed to locate Friedman's weapon of choice, leaving it on the apron for Punk to collect and eventually gain the victory with. This was brilliantly executed. Jon Moxley's hard hitting victory over Bryan Danielson prompted the shocking debut of William Regal, in an excellent post-match segment. With the two combatants engaged in a pull apart brawl, Regal hit the ring, slapping both men in the face in a bid to restore order—and incredibly, it worked! Mox and Bryan shook hands and thus, the Blackpool Combat Club was born. Swerve Strickland also made his debut at the show in a brief segment with Tony Schiavone. Other notable moments included Eddie Kingston's shock submission victory over Chris Jericho in the opener, Hangman Page's sterling AEW World Title defence versus Adam Cole and Sting once again going full New Jack in a chaotic six-man tag match. The 60-year-old has clearly been hanging around with Darby Allin for too long. The strength of Revolution was in its variety, there was

something for everyone a show that captured the original spirit of the company perfectly.

GRAND PRINCESS '22
19-03-22, Tokyo, Japan **TJPW**

Arisu Endo and **Suzume** defeated **Juria Nagano** and **Moka Miyamoto** in 9:44; **Harukaze, Moeka Haruhi, Yuna Manase** and **Yuuri** defeated **Haruna Neko, Kaya Toribami, Mahiro Kiryu** and **Nao Kakuta** in 12:20; **Hyper Misao** defeated **Sanshiro Takagi** in a Falls Count Anywhere Match in 12:01; **Asuka** defeated **Yuki Kamifuku** in 9:38; **Yuki Aino** defeated **Nodoka Tenma** in 9:24; **Martha, Mei Saint-Michel, Sakisama** and **Yukio Saint Laurent** defeated **Marika Kobashi, Pom Harajuku, Raku** and **Ram Kaicho** in 10:52; **Hikaru Shida** defeated **Hikari Noa** in 8:33; **Maki Ito** defeated **Yuki Arai** in 16:18; **Mizuki** and **Yuka Sakazaki** defeated **Miu Watanabe** and **Rika Tatsumi** in 17:05; **Shoko Nakajima** defeated **Miyu Yamashita** to win the Princess Of Princess Title in 19:06.

Was It Any Good? It was a very enjoyable event, as Tokyo Joshi Pro turned up the pomp and pageantry for one of its biggest shows of the year. The match card had several high stakes title matches, alongside some more personal rivalries and meaningful exhibitions. Chief among them was the Princess of Princess Championship match between two of the promotion's top contenders, Miyu Yamashita and Shoko Nakajima. This was a very well-constructed contest, with Yamashita playing her role of unstoppable killer with aplomb, only for the underdog Nakajima to come from behind and score the victory. Of equal note was Miu Watanabe's standout performance in the Princess Tag Title match alongside Rika Tatsumi against champions Yuka Sakazaki and Mizuki, otherwise known as the Magical Sugar Rabbits. Watanabe is a real prospect, with charisma, athleticism and surprising power. Her double big swing was a spectacular moment in what was otherwise a very good contest. Also of note was Maki Itoh's successful International Princess Title defence over fellow idol-turned-wrestler Yuki Arai. The ever-improving Arai looked good here, and already has a keen grasp of selling and garnering sympathy from her audience. This rivalry has echoes of Itoh's previous conflicts with Mizuki and Yamashita, only this time, she is in the role of senpai and it is Akai who is having to overcome. This made for a compelling instalment in what should be a lengthy feud between the pair. Elsewhere on the card, AEW's Hikaru Shida made a flying visit to best the promising Hikari Noa while Nodoka Tenma bowed out of the industry in a fun bout against tag team partner Yuki Aino. A stellar show top-to-bottom.

CROCKETT CUP '22 NIGHT #1
19-03-22, Nashville, Tennessee **NWA**

Hawx Aerie (Luke Hawx and **PJ Hawx)** defeated **The End (Odinson** and **Parrow)** in 9:20; **The Cardonas (Mike Knox** and **VSK)** defeated **Da Pope** and **Mims** in 9:59; **The Dirty Sexy Boys (Dirty Dango** and **JTG)** defeated **Aron Stevens** and **The Blue Meanie** in 6:40; **Gold Rushhh (Jordan Clearwater** and **Marshe Rockett)** defeated **Strictly Business (Chris Adonis** and **Thom Latimer)** in 4:18; **The Commonwealth Connection (Doug Williams** and **Harry Smith)** defeated **The Ill Begotten (Alex Taylor** and **Rush Freeman)** in 6:38; **La Rebelion (Bestia 666** and **Mecha Wolf)** defeated **The Bad News Boyz (Brandon Tate** and **Brent Tate)** in 8:59; **The Cardonas (Mike Knox** and **VSK)** defeated **The Fixers (Jay Bradley** and **Wrecking Ball Legursky)** in 7:03; **The Briscoe Brothers (Jay Briscoe** and **Mark Briscoe)** defeated **The Dirty Sexy Boys (Dirty Dango** and **JTG)** in 8:13; **La Rebelion (Bestia 666** and **Mecha Wolf)** defeated **PJ Hawx** in a Handicap Match in 7:25; **The**

Commonwealth Connection (**Doug Williams** and **Harry Smith**) defeated **Gold Rushhh** (**Jordan Clearwater** and **Marshe Rockett**) in 12:50.

Was It Any Good? It was pretty good, with plenty of well wrestled tag team action on display. The big winners of the night were arguably The Commonwealth Connection (Doug Williams and Harry Smith), who cruised to the quarter finals where they had a very good match with Gold Rushhh (Jordan Clearwater and Marshe Rockett). The Briscoes were on typically good form throughout, as were Hawx Aerie and La Rebelión—two of the company's more established tandems. With no contest breaking the 10-minute mark, this was a fairly comfortable watch with some enjoyable bouts throughout.

JUDGMENT '22: DDT 25TH ANNIVERSARY
20-03-22, Tokyo, Japan **DDT**

Mikami, **Thanomsak Toba**, **Gentaro**, **Poison Sawada Julie** and **Takashi Sasaki** defeated **Kazuki Hirata**, **Toru Owashi**, **Antonio Honda** and **Yoshihiko** in a Handicap Match to win the KO-D 10-Man Tag Team Title in 8:49; **Saki Akai** defeated **Maya Yukihi** in 10:40; **Sanshiro Takagi** defeated **Michael Nakazawa** in an "I'm Sorry" Match in 10:20; **Shunma Katsumata** and **Yuki Ueno** defeated **Isami Kodaka** and **Yukio Sakaguchi** in 11:02; **Danshoku Dino**, **Yuki Ino** and **Yumehito Imanari** defeated **Akito**, **LiLiCo** and **Ryohei Odai** in 16:52; **Jun Akiyama** and **Takao Omori** defeated **Hideki Okatani** and **Kazusada Higuchi** in 12:36; **Mao** defeated **Daisuke Sasaki** and **Jun Kasai** in a Three Way Hardcore Match to win the DDT Univeral Title in 19:56; **Chris Brookes** and **Masahiro Takanashi** defeated **Harashima** and **Naomi Yoshimura** to win the KO-D Tag Team Title in 18:56; **Tetsuya Endo** defeated **Konosuke Takeshita** to win the KO-D Openweight Title in 46:30.

Was It Any Good? Definitely. This event, marking DDT-Pro's 25th anniversary, contained all the hallmarks of the promotion, namely, variety, wacky Japanese comedy, and excellent pro wrestling. Too often pigeonholed as a comedy promotion, DDT has built its name developing homegrown talent such as Konosuke Takeshita, Tetsuya Endo and Yuki Ueno, none of whom would look out of place on any top card in Japan or America (as evidenced by Takeshita's recent run in AEW). Very much on his way out of the promotion, Takeshita looked at the lights for perennial foe Endo in the show's main event, dropping the KO-D Openweight Championship in the process. This was an excellent encounter between two of Japan's best. Also worth seeking out was the KO-D Tag Title match between the Calamari Drunken Kings (Chris Brookes and Masahiro Takanashi) and outgoing champions HARASHIMA and Naomi Yoshimura of the DISASTER BOX stable, as well the DDT Universal Title Hardcore Match in which MAO emerged victorious over Daisuke Sasaki and Jun Kasai. Earlier in the card, Saki Akai bested freelance star Maya Yukihi in a decent ten-minute bout which was arguably the best singles encounter of Akai's career. The comedy spots throughout the show will divide opinion among western viewers, as it is certainly geared towards the Japanese palate, however there was plenty to enjoy here, while celebrating one of the most unique companies in Japan.

CROCKETT CUP '22 NIGHT #2
20-03-22, Nashville, Tennessee **NWA**

The Briscoe Brothers (**Jay Briscoe** and **Mark Briscoe**) defeated **The Cardonas** (**Mike Knox** and **VSK**) in 7:45; **The Commonwealth Connection** (**Doug Williams** and **Harry Smith**) defeated **La Rebelion** (**Bestia 666** and **Mecha Wolf**) in 8:58; **Anthony Mayweather** defeated **Jax Dane** in 10:11; **Jax Dane** defeated **Anthony Mayweather** to win the NWA National Title in :31;

The Hex (**Allysin Kay** and **Marti Belle**) defeated **Pretty Empowered** (**Ella Envy** and **Kenzie Paige**) in 7:09; **Homicide** defeated **Austin Aries**, **Colby Corino** and **Darius Lockhart** in a Four Way Match to win the vacant NWA World Junior Heavyweight Title in 9:39; **Kamille** defeated **Chelsea Green** and **Kylie Rae** in a Three Way Match in 12:02; **Tyrus** defeated **Rodney Mack** in 8:14; **The Briscoe Brothers** (**Jay Briscoe** and **Mark Briscoe**) defeated **The Commonwealth Connection** (**Doug Williams** and **Harry Smith**) to win the Crockett Cup in 13:55; **Matt Cardona** defeated **Nick Aldis** by DQ in 21:11.

Was It Any Good? With just the semi-finals and finals remaining in the tournament, there was plenty of room for some of the NWA's other storylines to breathe on night two, with all other belts on-the-line over the course of the event. Sticking with the tournament, The Briscoes were the eventual winners after seeing off Mike Knox and VSK in the semis and the Commonwealth Connection in a stellar final. In the singles ranks, Matt Cardona's burgeoning NWA World Title reign survived Nick Aldis' challenge, thanks in part to some shenanigans, while Kamille bested Chelsea Green and Kylie Rae in a fun three-way outing. In the battle of former WWE talents no one expected to be talking about in 2022, Tyrus successfully defended his NWA TV Title against Rodney Mack, while Homicide claimed the revived Junior Heavyweight strap in a four-way with Austin Aries, Colby Corino and Darius Lockheart. Good stuff overall, if a little stuffy in places.

MULTIVERSE OF MATCHES
01-04-22, Dallas, Texas **Impact**

Trey Miguel defeated **Chris Bey**, **Jordynne Grace**, **Rich Swann**, **Vincent** and **Willie Mack** in an Ultimate X Match in 7:27; **Mickie James** and **Nick Aldis** defeated **Chelsea Green** and **Matt Cardona** in 7:04; **Mike Bailey** defeated **Alex Shelley** in 15:03; **The Influence** (**Madison Rayne** and **Tenille Dashwood**) defeated **Tasha Steelz** and **Savannah Evans**, **Gisele Shaw** and **Lady Frost**, and **Decay** (**Havok** and **Rosemary**) in a Four Way Match in 9:02; **Tomohiro Ishii** defeated **Eddie Edwards** in 14:09; **Josh Alexander** and **Jonah** defeated **Moose** and **PCO** in 12:47; **Deonna Purrazzo** defeated **Faby Apache** in 8:52; **Chris Sabin** defeated **Jay White** in 16:00; **The Good Brothers** (**Luke Gallows** and **Karl Anderson**) defeated **The Briscoe Brothers** (**Jay Briscoe** and **Mark Briscoe**) in 9:46.

Was It Any Good? Largely, although some of the action flattered to deceive. Multiverse Of Matches was a clever concept for IMPACT's WrestleMania weekend offering, and featured talent from neighbouring promotions such as the NWA, AAA and New Japan. Many of the storylines on hand had been built across the various promotions' respective outlets, giving the card a unique build and feel. There were several noteworthy moments on the show itself, including Nick Aldis' return to IMPACT in which the former NWA World Champion teamed with wife Mickie James to upend another real-life couple, Matt Cardona and Chelsea Green. Taya Valkyrie also made her return to the promotion following Deonna Purrazzo's victory over AAA star Faby Apache, and challenged The Virtuosa for a match at Rebellion. From a bell-to-bell perspective, Mike Bailey's victory over Alex Shelley was the match of the night, while Chris Sabin's shock victory over Jay White and Tomohiro Ishii's triumph over Eddie Edwards each had quality. The main event contest between The Briscoes and The Good Brothers sagged a little but fortunately did not outstay its welcome and capped off what was a decent outing for IMPACT Wrestling and its new concept show.

LONESTAR SHOOTOUT
01-04-22, Dallas, Texas **NJPW**

Ren Narita defeated **Rocky Romero** in 7:42; **Clark Connors**, **Karl Fredericks**, **Mascara Dorada** and **Yuya Uemura** defeated **FinJuice** (**David Finlay** and **Juice Robinson**), **Daniel Garcia** and **Kevin Knight** in 10:45; **Minoru Suzuki** defeated **Killer Kross** in 9:48; **Jay White** defeated **Mike Bailey** in 14:10; **Tomohiro Ishii** defeated **Chris Dickinson** in 16:11.

Was It Any Good? It was fine, albeit extremely brief. At a shade over ninety minutes, the running time for Lonestar Shootout may have caught some off guard, but there was good work squeezed into the session. Match of the night honours went to Jay White and Mike Bailey, who put forth an exhilarating effort in the show's co-main event. So much so that the actual main event between Tomohiro Ishii and Chris Dickinson could not surpass it, leaving the show finale feeling flatter than usual. Killer Kross was given a rare New Japan run out, but did little to enhance his stature within the company after submitting a relatively tame display against an agitated Minoru Suzuki. A shame, as Kross has the look and feel of someone who should excel in this type of environment but for whatever reason, it was not to be on the night.

SUPERCARD OF HONOR XV
01-04-22, Garland, Texas **ROH**

Swerve Strickland defeated **Alex Zayne** in 11:40; **Brian Cage** defeated **Ninja Mack** in 2:50; **Jay Lethal** defeated **Lee Moriarty** in 14:50; **Mercedes Martinez** defeated **Willow Nightingale** to win the interim ROH Women's World Title in 12:45; **FTR** (**Dax Harwood** and **Cash Wheeler**) defeated **The Briscoe Brothers** (**Jay Briscoe** and **Mark Briscoe**) to win the ROH World Tag Team Title in 27:25; **Minoru Suzuki** defeated **Rhett Titus** to win the ROH World Television Title in 6:00; **Wheeler Yuta** defeated **Josh Woods** in a Pure Wrestling Rules Match to win the ROH Pure Title in 12:55; **Jonathan Gresham** defeated **Bandido** in 24:55.

Was It Any Good? Yes. Tony Khan's first outing with Ring Of Honor felt bigger and better than the company's previous efforts, with higher production values providing a fresh coat of paint for a product that had grown stale. Supercard Of Honor afforded Khan the opportunity to clear the decks and install several new champions in what was essentially a reboot for the ROH brand. Of the five belts that were on the line, only one champion held firm on the night. ROH World Champion Jonathan Gresham saw off Bandido in the match that was supposed to headline ROH's final show, End Of An Era, prior to Khan's acquisition. This was a decent styles clash, with Bandido's unusual blend of strength and agility shining through prior to his eventual defeat. Post-match, Samoa Joe made his return to the promotion with which he was synonymous for so many years, assisting Gresham in fending off Jay Lethal and Sonjay Dutt. Earlier in the evening, FTR and The Briscoe Brothers launched one of the year's best rivalries, as the Top Guys lifted the ROH Tag Team Titles in an excellent encounter. Wheeler Yuta's stock continued to rise as he was handed the ROH Pure Title following a fun bout with Josh Woods. In one of the more surprising moments of the night, Minoru Suzuki ran through Rhett Titus to claim the ROH World TV Championship. To qualify, absolutely no one viewed Titus as on Suzuki's level, but it was still a shock nonetheless to see the New Japan star lift his first championship on US soil. The interim ROH Women's World Title was also on the line, as lineal champion Deonna Purrazzo was unable to make the event. Veteran performer Mercedes Martinez took the belt following a physical tussle with highly rated prospect Willow Nightingale.

STAND & DELIVER '22
02-04-22, Dallas, Texas **NXT**

Cameron Grimes defeated **Carmelo Hayes**, **Santos Escobar**, **Solo Sikoa** and **Grayson Waller** in a Five Way Ladder Match to win the NXT North American Title in 21:01; **Tony D'Angelo** defeated **Tommaso Ciampa** in 13:11; **MSK** (**Nash Carter** and **Wes Lee**) defeated **Imperium** (**Fabian Aichner** and **Marcel Barthel**) and **The Creed Brothers** (**Brutus Creed** and **Julius Creed**) in a Three Way Match to win the NXT Tag Team Title in 11:22; **Mandy Rose** defeated **Cora Jade**, **Kay Lee Ray** and **Io Shirai** in a Fatal Four-Way Match in 13:28; **Gunther** defeated **LA Knight** in 10:24; **Dolph Ziggler** defeated **Bron Breakker** in 16:13.

Was It Any Good? Fairly. The show-opening ladder match was the usual high spot filled stunt-fest, and while it did not reinvent the wheel, it did enough to hold viewer's attention for its duration. Tommaso Ciampa's NXT swansong putting over Tony D'Angelo was an underwhelming way for the former NXT champ to depart the brand. MSK's tag title win in a three-way over Imperium and The Creed Brothers was entertaining enough, but rendered pointless mere days later when MSK's Nash Carter was fired stemming from domestic assault allegations made by his ex-wife and a leaked picture of him performing a Nazi salute. Mandy Rose again proved herself a worthy holder of the NXT Women's Title by outlasting the competition in a spirited four-way, before unlikely NXT Champion Dolph Ziggler surprisingly retained the belt against NXT standout Bron Breakker in a so-so headliner. The decision was made to save Breakker's return to the NXT summit for the post-WrestleMania RAW in order for it to be seen by more eyes. A reasonable tactic, but one which left Stand & Deliver ending with a whimper rather than a bang, and meant Breakker was forced to eat another aura-hurting defeat.

WRESTLEMANIA XXXVIII NIGHT #1
02-04-22, Dallas, Texas **WWE**

The Usos (**Jey Uso** and **Jimmy Uso**) defeated **Shinsuke Nakamura** and **Rick Boogs** in 6:55; **Drew McIntyre** defeated **Happy Corbin** in 8:35; **The Miz** and **Logan Paul** defeated **The Mysterios** (**Rey Mysterio** and **Dominik Mysterio**) in 11:15; **Bianca Belair** defeated **Becky Lynch** to win the WWE RAW Women's Title in 19:10; **Cody Rhodes** defeated **Seth Rollins** in 21:40; **Charlotte Flair** defeated **Ronda Rousey** in 18:30; **Steve Austin** defeated **Kevin Owens** in a No Holds Barred Match in 13:55.

Was It Any Good? It was tremendous—everything WrestleMania should be. The first two matches were damp squibs, but debutant Logan Paul—of all people—upped the ante with a superb performance in the annual WrestleMania celebrity bout, oozing charisma and natural ability as he and The Miz downed the Mysterios. The post-match angle where the despised Paul was drilled with a Skull Crushing Finale by his tag partner failed to hit the mark, however; fans wildly cheered The Miz's betrayal, which was supposed to be Paul's face turn. Bianca Belair and Becky Lynch had arguably the match of the night, with Belair putting her damaging SummerSlam '21 squash defeat behind her in emphatic fashion as she regained the RAW Women's Title. Seth Rollins' opponent was a mystery going into the show, although most fans were well aware that his opponent would be the returning prodigal son Cody Rhodes, who became the first major name to jump from AEW to WWE. Rhodes received a hero's welcome and delivered a main event calibre performance en route to defeating Rollins, in what was another high quality match-up. Charlotte Flair and Ronda Rousey were unable to hit the heights of their previous supercard meeting at Survivor Series '18, with

Rousey again looking unconvincing. The advertised main event was a talk show segment with Stone Cold Steve Austin appearing on The Kevin Owens Show, which—as had been rumoured—turned into a match, Austin's first since WrestleMania XIX in 2003, which delivered everything one could reasonably expect from Austin. The bout was essentially Stone Cold's greatest hits, which is exactly what the fans in attendance wanted to see, and Owens more than played his part in helping the 57-year-old look as good as possible. The sight of WrestleMania ending with Austin hitting Stone Cold Stunners and drinking beers was a nostalgic feel-good moment that will live long in the memory and was a perfect end to a scintillating first night of a WrestleMania card that flew by.

WRESTLEMANIA XXXVIII NIGHT #2
03-04-22, Dallas, Texas **WWE**

RK-Bro (Randy Orton and **Riddle)** defeated **The Street Profits (Angelo Dawkins** and **Montez Ford)** and **Alpha Academy (Chad Gable** and **Otis)** in a Three Way Match in 11:30; **Bobby Lashley** defeated **Omos** in 6:35; **Johnny Knoxville** defeated **Sami Zayn** in an Anything Goes Match in 14:25; **Sasha Banks** and **Naomi** defeated **Carmella** and **Queen Zelina, Liv Morgan** and **Rhea Ripley,** and **Natalya** and **Shayna Baszler** in a Four Way Match to win the WWE Women's Tag Team Title in 10:50; **Edge** defeated **AJ Styles** in 24:05; **Sheamus** and **Ridge Holland** defeated **The New Day (Kofi Kingston** and **Xavier Woods)** in 1:40; **Pat McAfee** defeated **Austin Theory** in 9:40; **Vince McMahon** defeated **Pat McAfee** in 3:45; **Roman Reigns** defeated **Brock Lesnar** to win the WWE Title in 12:15.

Was It Any Good? It was nowhere near as strong as the first night, but it certainly had its moments. The opening three-way for the RAW tag straps was an energetic outing that could have been a classic had it been afforded an extra five minutes. Lashley's win over the lumbering Omos was thankfully brief. Night 2's celebrity bout pitting Jackass star Johnny Knoxville against Sami Zayn was a laugh-out-loud romp that ticked all of the boxes for celebrity involvement in wrestling, and featured enough memorable—albeit wacky—moments to deliver what it promised. The women's tag title bout was the usual thrown-together affair that it is at every 'Mania, although at least it was afforded more time than The Brawling Brutes and New Day, who had less than two minutes to strut their stuff. Kofi Kingston's WrestleMania record since his memorable WWE Title win at WrestleMania XXXV has been underwhelming to say the least. Conversely, the heavily-hyped clash between Edge and AJ Styles would have benefited from a shorter run time, as the 24:05 contest dragged in places. Pat McAfee gave another decent in-ring account of himself against Austin Theory, who was seconded by Vince McMahon. Post-match, McMahon then challenged McAfee to a match, which ranks amongst the worst in 'Mania history, in purely sporting terms. It was not entirely devoid of merit though, particularly when Stone Cold Steve Austin broke up the post-match party and drilled McMahon with a Stunner that was so badly executed Austin could not hold back his laughter. The main event between Roman Reigns and Brock Lesnar was the third meeting between the two rivals at WrestleMania, putting them in a very exclusive club with Steve Austin and The Rock. Their match could not hold a candle to the classics between those two greats, but it provided enough thrills and spills to feel like a worthy headliner to the biggest show of the year.

HYPER BATTLE '22
09-04-22, Tokyo, Japan **NJPW**

Hiroshi Tanahashi, Tama Tonga, Tanga Loa and **Jado** defeated **Bad Luck Fale, Chase Owens, Yujiro Takahashi** and **Gedo** in 10:28; **Tetsuya Naito** and **Shingo Takagi** defeated **Will Ospreay** and **Aaron Henare** in 9:23; **Ryusuke Taguchi** and **Master Wato** defeated **Taiji Ishimori** and **El Phantasmo** in 15:13; **Taichi** defeated **Toru Yano** in a No Rope Ring Out Match to win the Provisional KOPW 2022 Trophy in 4:18; **Evil** defeated **Hiromu Takahashi** in 15:47; **Great-O-Khan** and **Jeff Cobb** defeated **Hirooki Goto** and **Yoshi-Hashi** to win the IWGP Tag Team Title in 16:05; **El Desperado** defeated **Sho** in 20:33; **Kazuchika Okada** defeated **Zack Sabre Jr.** in 28:25.

Was It Any Good? It was a little uninspiring, despite several eye-catching performances throughout the show. The issue appeared more to do with booking and product momentum rather than any lack of effort on the part of the wrestlers. For example, the ice cold House of Torture stable were present in two of the event's title matches and while they were both reasonable in-ring affairs, there was little desire from the crowd to see them. Likewise, the main event clash between company kingpin Kazuchika Okada and Zack Sabre Jr. was of superior quality bell-to-bell but suffered from its predictability, in that nobody through that the Brit might win. It's a challenging position for the New Japan matchmakers, particularly when booking a champion as strong as Okada, but more has to be done to plant doubt in the minds of fans who can otherwise see the writing on the wall. So, while there was nothing wrong with Hyper Battle per se, the ring work was overshadowed by a more overarching issue of roster stagnation and repetitive booking.

WINDY CITY RIOT
16-04-22, Villa Park, Illinois **NJPW**

QT Marshall, Aaron Solo and **Nick Comoroto** defeated **Karl Fredericks, Clark Connors** and **Yuya Uemura** in 11:56; **Fred Rosser, Josh Alexander, Alex Coughlin, Ren Narita** and **Chris Dickinson** defeated **Royce Isaacs, Jorel Nelson, JR Kratos, Black Tiger** and **Danny Limelight** in 13:50; **Tom Lawlor** defeated **Yuji Nagata** in 13:57; **Aaron Henare, Great-O-Khan, Jeff Cobb, TJP, Mark Davis** and **Kyle Fletcher** defeated **Hikuleo, Chris Bey, El Phantasmo, Karl Anderson, Luke Gallows** and **Scott Norton** in 11:58; **David Finlay, Juice Robinson** and **Brody King** defeated **Jonah, Shane Haste** and **Bad Dude Tito** in a Chicago Street Fight in 24:11; **Jay White** defeated **Shota Umino** in 15:45; **Tomohiro Ishii** defeated **Minoru Suzuki** in 18:46; **Jon Moxley** defeated **Will Ospreay** in 21:24.

Was It Any Good? It was fun, if a little overcrowded in the earlier portions of the event. The key matches delivered though, particularly Jon Moxley and Will Ospreay which was a perfect example of how "styles make fights". This was Moxley at his brutish best, with the more technically gifted Ospreay lifting the violence level in a bid to meet his opponent halfway. The finish was a touch cluttered, with Ospreay seemingly kicking out on three, leaving Moxley to apply a choke in the post-match while his music was playing. This appeared to be planned but left the live crowd unclear about who or what they should be cheering. Nonetheless, it was a great effort by two of the year's best performers. The other notable contest was between veterans Tomohiro Ishii and Minoru Suzuki, who did exactly what fans expected them to do in a hard-hitting war which captured the live crowd. It was nice to see the Stone Pitbull grab a meaningful victory here, as he put Suzuki away with his trademark brainbuster. The undercard did little to offend but equally scarcely offered an opportunity to commit anything to memory.

BATTLE OF THE BELTS II
16-04-22, Garland, Texas **AEW**

Sammy Guevara defeated **Scorpio Sky** in 12:45; **Jonathan Gresham** defeated **Dalton Castle** in 10:35; **Thunder Rosa** defeated **Nyla Rose** in 14:10.
Was It Any Good? It certainly wasn't bad, but like its predecessor, suffered from lacking any real intrigue or stakes. The one match that felt genuinely in the balance was the TNT Championship bout between two of the belt's more frequent fliers, Sammy Guevara and Scorpio Sky. Clearly, with two competitors of that calibre, the in-ring aspect of the contest was always going to deliver, however the bout was hampered throughout from the negative crowd reaction towards supposed babyface Guevara. The Spanish God got the headlines but in truth, both men were miscast, with the likeable Sky a more natural babyface. Still, this was a fun contest ending with Sammy G embarking on his third reign as champion. Also on the card was the maiden voyage of ROH World Champion Jonathan Gresham, who competed in an AEW ring for the first time against fellow debutant Dalton Castle. Given that neither man had been afforded any prior exposure on AEW programming, this was a success, as the crowd got bought into the charismatic Castle. Gresham scored the win with the Octopus Stretch and was subject to a post-match brawl involving Jay Lethal's crew and ROH TV Champion Samoa Joe. In theory, the idea was to get a closing shot of Ring Of Honor's two lead titlists together, but a cynic might suggest that AEW really just wanted footage of its shortest roster member (Gresham stands at 5'4) stood across from its tallest (the 7'2 Satnam Singh). This image did Gresham no favours whatsoever. Thunder Rosa was also on the card, defending the AEW Women's belt against Nyla Rose in a match that felt like a foregone conclusion but included some decent action nonetheless.

REBELLION '22
23-04-22, Poughkeepsie, New York **Impact**

Steve Maclin defeated **Chris Sabin** and **Jay White** in a Three Way Match in 12:07; **Taya Valkyrie** defeated **Deonna Purrazzo** to win the AAA Reina de Reinas Title in 9:03; **Ace Austin** defeated **Trey Miguel** and **Mike Bailey** in a Three Way Match to win the Impact X Division Title in 10:25; **Tomohiro Ishii** defeated **Jonah** in 14:34; **Violent By Design (Eric Young** and **Joe Doering)** won an Eight-Team Elimination Challenge Match in 33:02); **Tasha Steelz** defeated **Rosemary** in 11:45; **Josh Alexander** defeated **Moose** to win the Impact World Title in 23:56.
Was It Any Good? I'd say. Rebellion was a very strong show indeed, featuring two high profile title changes and a bevy of fun match-ups across the card. Most important, of course, was Josh Alexander's IMPACT World Title victory over Moose in the show's main event. The talented Canadian had long been the company's standard bearer and as such, his coronation as World Champion felt like a seminal moment, not just for Alexander but for the company itself. Also of note was Taya Valkyrie's spirited win over Deonna Purrazzo for the AAA Reina de Reinas belt. This had implications for further shows down the line and played a key part in the annual trajectories of both women. A special mention as well for Tomohiro Ishii's cracking dust-up with JONAH, which felt more like a G1 semifinal than a midcard pay-per-view match. Overall, this was a decent, well-booked event with several noteworthy moments that ultimately helped reposition the company for the months ahead.

TRIPLEMANIA XXX: MONTERREY
30-04-22, Monterrey, Mexico **AAA**

Ultimo Dragon defeated **Pentagon Jr.** in 9:19; **Sammy Guevara** and **Tay Conti** defeated **Komander** and **Sexy Star**, **Latigo** and **Maravilla**, and **Los Vipers (Arez** and **Chik Tormenta)** in a Four Way Match to win the AAA World Mixed Tag Team Title in 12:35; **LA Park** defeated **Villano IV** in 18:01; **Johnny Caballero** defeated **Hermanos Lee (Dragon Lee** and **Dralistico)**, and **Jack Cartwheel** and **Laredo Kid** in a Three Way Match in 13:29; **El Rayo de Jalisco Jr.** defeated **Blue Demon Jr.** in 14:18; **Bandido**, **Pagano** and **Taya Valkyrie** defeated **Andrade El Idolo**, **Cibernetico** and **Deonna Purrazzo** by DQ in 18:53; **El Canek** defeated **Psycho Clown** in 13:08; **The Young Bucks (Matt Jackson** and **Nick Jackson)** defeated **El Hijo del Vikingo** and **Rey Fenix** in 15:58.
Was It Any Good? It wasn't bad and featured a great match event between The Young Bucks and the dream pairing of Rey Fenix and El Hijo del Vikingo. This was certainly the bout to watch going in and it delivered on its promise with the expected levels of athleticism and creativity. Perhaps the only let down was the slightly botched final pinfall in which the official appeared reluctant to count to three, but beyond that, this was an excellent showcase for all four performers and provided Fenix and Vikingo with some needle headed into their anticipated showdown later in the year. Elsewhere, the Ruleta de la Muerte matches varied in quality, in large part due to the advanced years of some of the combatants. Certainly Pentagon Jr. and Ultimo Dragon were on the more positive end of that spectrum, in a fun match that stayed short and sweet at around eight minutes, while the bout between veterans Rayo de Jalisco Jr. and Blue Demon Jr. represented the nadir of the card. There was an AEW influence running throughout the show, with Tay Conti and Sammy Guevara on hand to collect the AAA World Mixed Tag Team Championships and Andrade El Idolo in trios action.

WRESTLING DONTAKU '22
01-05-22, Fukuoka, Japan **NJPW**

Taichi, **Zack Sabre Jr.** and **Taka Michinoku** defeated **Shingo Takagi**, **Bushi** and **Shiro Koshinaka** in 10:15; **Hiromu Takahashi** defeated **Yoh** in 9:59; **Tanga Loa** defeated **Yujiro Takahashi** in 11:33; **Ryusuke Taguchi** and **Master Wato** defeated **Yoshinobu Kanemaru** and **Douki** in 9:10; **Bad Luck Fale** and **Chase Owens** defeated **Great-O-Khan** and **Jeff Cobb**, and **Hirooki Goto** and **Yoshi-Hashi** in a Three Way Match to win the IWGP Tag Team Title in 9:43; **Tama Tonga** defeated **Evil** to win the NEVER Openweight Title in 13:25; **Taiji Ishimori** defeated **El Desperado** to win the IWGP Junior Heavyweight Title in 14:40; **Hiroshi Tanahashi** defeated **Tomohiro Ishii** to win the vacant IWGP United States Title in 23:20; **Kazuchika Okada** defeated **Tetsuya Naito** in 34:12.
Was It Any Good? Yes, this was arguably one of the strongest large-scale cards from New Japan's domestic offerings. Wrestling Dontaku featured a murderer's row of title matches leading up to a stellar main event. Following a moderate undercard that gradually grew in stature, Taiji Ishimori's IWGP Junior Heavyweight Title win over El Desperado was the launch point for this card. The two divisional stars had an excellent bout here, with a surprising finish, as most had expected the masked man to retain. Next was the blistering IWGP US Title match between two of the company's greatest servants, Hiroshi Tanahashi and Tomohiro Ishii. This was top drawer stuff from two of the best to ever do it, with The Ace narrowly escaping with the win. In the post-match, Juice Robinson, who had been rumoured to be leaving the company,

was revealed as the latest member of the Bullet Club and had Tanahashi's title within his sights. Finally, in the main event, frequent opponents Kazuchika Okada and Tetsuya Naito did battle once more, in a typically brilliant affair for the company's top honours. Yes, we've been here before, but there's no denying the chemistry between the pair. Post-match, another of Okada's regular rivals reappeared in the form of Jay White, who laid out The Rainmaker and staked his claim for the title. Good fun all round.

WRESTLEMANIA BACKLASH '22
08-05-22, Providence, Rhode Island **WWE**

Cody Rhodes defeated **Seth Rollins** in 20:45; **Omos** defeated **Bobby Lashley** in 8:50; **Edge** defeated **AJ Styles** in 16:25; **Ronda Rousey** defeated **Charlotte Flair** in an "I Quit" Match to win the WWE SmackDown Women's Title in 16:35; **Madcap Moss** defeated **Happy Corbin** in 8:40; **The Bloodline (Roman Reigns, Jey Uso** and **Jimmy Uso)** defeated **Drew McIntyre** and **RK-Bro (Randy Orton** and **Riddle)** in 22:20.

Was It Any Good? For the most part, yes, although the sheer amount of WrestleMania rematches was jarring. In the opener, Cody Rhodes again exhibited a superstar aura in his second consecutive PLE win over Seth Rollins, which cemented his status as a major player in WWE. Omos evened the score with Lashley in a useless bout, before Edge again put down AJ Styles, in a match that was briefer and thus better than their WrestleMania collision. Ronda Rousey's SmackDown Women's Title victory over Charlotte Flair was also a vast improvement on their WM outing, and easily Rousey's finest display since her return. Unfortunately, it would also be her peak. The main event elevated WrestleMania Backlash from middling to worth seeing, with all six participants in the six-man tag putting in a shift. If there was a negative it's that the show did very little to advance anything, feeling more like a post-'Mania European show from the 90s than a major happening. Still, the in-ring action was just about good enough to carry it through.

CAPITAL COLLISION
14-05-22, Washington, D.C. **NJPW**

Karl Fredericks defeated **Ren Narita** in 10:32; **Tom Lawlor, Jorel Nelson, Royce Isaacs, JR Kratos** and **Danny Limelight** defeated **The DKC, Yuya Uemura, David Finlay, Tanga Loa** and **Fred Rosser** in 14:48; **Chase Owens** defeated **Great-O-Khan** in 8:46; **Mikey Nicholls, Shane Haste, Jonah** and **Bad Dude Tito** defeated **Aaron Henare, Kyle Fletcher, Mark Davis** and **Jeff Cobb** in 12:09; **Brody King** defeated **Minoru Suzuki** in 9:05; **Tomohiro Ishii** defeated **Eddie Kingston** in 16:07; **Jay White** and **Hikuleo** defeated **Kazuchika Okada** and **Rocky Romero** in 15:59; **Juice Robinson** defeated **Hiroshi Tanahashi, Will Ospreay** and **Jon Moxley** in a Four Way Match to win the IWGP United States Title in 15:45.

Was It Any Good? It was another fun outing for New Japan's US arm, featuring a decent main event and one particularly good undercard bout in Eddie Kingston versus Tomohiro Ishii. The two battle-tested warriors let their hands fly in this super-stiff slugfest, which saw the New Japan man come out on top. Brody King picked up a useful W over veteran star Minoru Suzuki in tidy match-up. The show's co-main event of Hikuleo and Jay White against Kazuchika Okada and Rocky Romero was great fun, and added fuel to the existing fire between White and The Rainmaker. Uniquely for New Japan, the main event clash for the US strap was a four-way match, featuring the eclectic mix of Juice Robinson, Jon Moxley, Will Ospreay and defending champion, Hiroshi Tanahashi. This was a pacy battle, with some clever

near falls and interesting exchanges, and had a surprise winner in the unfancied Robinson. While not packed with the sort of substance that New Japan main events have become famed for, this was a sugary finale to another eminently easy watch from NJPW USA.

HANA KIMURA MEMORIAL SHOW 2
23-05-22, Tokyo, Japan **N/A**

Kenoh defeated **Menso-re Oyaji** in 7:06; **Chihiro Hashimoto** and **Mika Iwata** won an 11-Team Battle Royal in 27:16; **Jungle Kyona** defeated **Kyoko Kimura** in 11:23; **Sakura Hirota** defeated **Kaori Yoneyama** and **Saori Anou** in a Handicap Match in 6:25; **Aja Kong** defeated **Sakura Hirota** in :15; **Aja Kong** defeated **Sakura Hirota** in 4:52; **Rina** defeated **Sakura Hirota** in 7:32; **Syuri** defeated **Asuka** in 19:09.

Was It Any Good? It feels somewhat trite to qualify this card as "good" or otherwise, but certainly, it was an enjoyable celebration of a life lost too soon. The second annual show for the late Hana Kimura featured talent from across Japan alongside several emotional tributes to the Tokyo Cyber Squad leader, not least from Kairi, who helped open the show. There was not a dry eye in the house for the exhibition bout between Kimura's mother, the legendary Kyoko Kimura and her TCS stablemate Jungle Kyona. This brief but engaging contest felt like a much-needed catharsis for the pair, who expressed their love in the best way they knew how. A special mention should also be given to NOAH's Kenoh and Okinawa PW's Menso-re Oyaji who put on a fine opener filled with humour, and provided some much needed levity for the audience. Kenoh is a wonderful example of the power of character work, and having long established his uber-serious demeanour, is able to manipulate it perfectly for comedic purposes when the moment presents. Fun, touching, and crucially, a fitting tribute to Hana Kimura.

DOUBLE OR NOTHING '22
29-05-22, Paradise, Nevada **AEW**

Wardlow defeated **MJF** in 7:30; **The Hardys (Matt Hardy** and **Jeff Hardy)** defeated **The Young Bucks (Matt Jackson** and **Nick Jackson)** in 19:15; **Jade Cargill** defeated **Anna Jay** in 7:25; **The House Of Black (Malakai Black, Buddy Matthews** and **Brody King)** defeated **Death Triangle (Pac, Penta Oscuro** and **Rey Fenix)** in 15:35; **Adam Cole** defeated **Samoa Joe** to win the Men's Owen Hart Foundation Tournament in 12:30; **Dr. Britt Baker D.M.D.** defeated **Ruby Soho** to win the Women's Owen Hart Foundation Tournament in 13:20; **American Top Team (Ethan Page, Scorpio Sky** and **Paige VanZant)** defeated **Frankie Kazarian, Sammy Guevara** and **Tay Conti** in 12:30; **Kyle O'Reilly** defeated **Darby Allin** in 9:50; **Thunder Rosa** defeated **Serena Deeb** in 16:55; **The Jericho Appreciation Society (Chris Jericho, Daniel Garcia, Jake Hager, Angelo Parker** and **Matt Menard)** defeated **The Blackpool Combat Club (Bryan Danielson** and **Jon Moxley), Eddie Kingston, Santana** and **Ortiz** in an Anarchy In Arena Match in 22:45; **Jurassic Express (Jungle Boy** and **Luchasaurus)** defeated **Swerve In Our Glory (Keith Lee** and **Swerve Strickland)** and **Team Taz (Powerhouse Hobbs** and **Ricky Starks)** in a Three Way Match in 17:15; **CM Punk** defeated **Hangman Page** to win the AEW World Title in 25:40.

Was It Any Good? It had its moments and was packed with well-worked matches, but it was too long. With a running time in excess of four hours for the main card alone, Double Or Nothing had a lot of fat on it that perhaps could have found a home on a Dynamite or a forthcoming special. However, putting that to one side, there were several noteworthy matches on display here, including the incredible Anarchy In The Arena match pitting The Jericho Appreciation Society against the

Blackpool Combat Club, Eddie Kingston, Santana and Ortiz. This was a wild contest and comfortably the match of the night. In the main event, CM Punk completed his comeback story by relieving Hangman Page of the AEW World Title. Despite the reported issues between the pair, this was a well-worked match that went just shy of the 30-minute mark and while some may have felt it too soon to dislodge the cowboy, the title change went down well with those inside Las Vegas' T-Mobile Arena. The other bit of lingering heat heading into the event was surrounding MJF, who had failed to appear at a scheduled autograph signing and had reportedly considered no-showing the pay-per-view. Friedman did eventually appear, and was soundly beaten by former charge Wardlow, although the furore around his antics certainly distracted from what should have been a seminal moment for the big man. In other notable moments, both Athena and Stokely Hathaway made their respective debuts on the card. Former UFC fighter Paige VanZant made her in-ring debut and looked very green while toppling Sammy Guevara, Tay Conti and Frankie Kazarian alongside the Men of the Year. Real-life couple Britt Baker and Adam Cole each won their respective Owen Hart Tournament final, after which Martha Hart gave a rousing speech.

IN YOUR HOUSE '22
04-06-22, Orlando, Florida **NXT**

The D'Angelo Family (Tony D'Angelo, Channing Lorenzo and **Troy Donovan)** defeated **Legado del Fantasma (Santos Escobar, Cruz Del Toro** and **Joaquin Wilde)** in 12:45; **Toxic Attraction (Gigi Dolin** and **Jacy Jayne)** defeated **Katana Chance** and **Kayden Carter** in 9:01; **Carmelo Hayes** defeated **Cameron Grimes** to win the NXT North American Title in 15:30; **Mandy Rose** defeated **Wendy Choo** in 11:08; **The Creed Brothers (Brutus Creed** and **Julius Creed)** defeated **Pretty Deadly (Elton Prince** and **Kit Wilson)** to win the NXT Tag Team Title in 15:19; **Bron Breakker** defeated **Joe Gacy** in 15:50.
Was It Any Good? Not really. NXT's second special of the year featured too much filler and nothing that stood out, highlighting how far WWE's third brand had fallen since the peak TakeOver years, when every event was a must-see show featuring some of the finest talent and matches on the planet. The opening six-man tag and the North American Title bout were both highly watchable, but NXT Women's Title match was a mess and the main event was far below the standards one expects from an NXT special.

HELL IN A CELL '22
05-06-22, Rosemont, Illinois **WWE**

Bianca Belair defeated **Asuka** and **Becky Lynch** in a Three Way Match in 18:55; **Bobby Lashley** defeated **Omos** and **MVP** in a Handicap Match in 8:25; **Kevin Owens** defeated **Ezekiel** in 9:20; **The Judgment Day (Edge, Damian Priest** and **Rhea Ripley)** defeated **AJ Styles, Finn Balor** and **Liv Morgan** in 16:00; **Madcap Moss** defeated **Happy Corbin** in a No Holds Barred Match in 12:05; **Theory** defeated **Mustafa Ali** in 10:25; **Cody Rhodes** defeated **Seth Rollins** in a Hell In A Cell Match in 24:20.
Was It Any Good? Yes. Thanks to a cracking opener and an all-time classic headliner, Hell In A Cell was a fine supercard. Bianca Belair firmly established herself as the new face of the women's division in the opening three-way, which was a high-energy, all-action affair for the majority of its near 20-minute run time. Judgment Day six-person aside—which felt like a good TV bout at best—the midcard matches that followed were useless, with Ezekiel's inept performance against Kevin Owens

particularly weak. And indeed, what a fall from grace it was for Owens to be reduced to messing around in a nothing comedy feud with Ezekiel two months after headlining WM with Steve Austin. Similarly, Mustafa Ali must have been wondering why he had allowed himself to be talked out of quitting WWE, given the burial he had received since his return. But none of that mattered after the main event—a third consecutive PLE meeting between Cody Rhodes and Seth Rollins. Taking place inside Hell In A Cell, this was by far the best match of their series and, indeed, the best WWE bout of the entire year. Rhodes came into the contest sporting a massive unsightly bruise across his pec and bicep, the result of a training injury that would keep him out for the remainder of the year. Most wrestlers would have pulled out of the match but Rhodes was determined to see his commitment through. The crowd audibly gasped when the extent of Rhodes' very real injury was revealed, and thus the two grapplers had the audience with them from the start of their HIAC thrill-ride. Reminiscent of Shawn Michaels' comeback match against Triple H at SummerSlam '02, fans winced and reacted to every blow the clearly pained Rhodes endured, then cheered him on as he rallied to an heroic victory, firmly establishing himself as a bona fide WWE main event superstar for the first time in his career. A career-defining performance from The American Nightmare.

ALWAYZ READY '22
11-06-22, Knoxville, Tennessee **NWA**

Trevor Murdoch defeated **Aron Stevens** in 4:38; **Pretty Empowered (Ella Envy** and **Kenzie Paige)** defeated **The Hex (Allysin Kay** and **Marti Belle)** to win the NWA World Women's Tag Team Title in 8:35; **Homicide** defeated **PJ Hawx** in 10:50; **Homicide** defeated **Colby Corino** in 9:06; **Natalia Markova** defeated **Taya Valkyrie** in 8:43; **Jax Dane** defeated **Chris Adonis** in 10:19; **Thom Latimer** defeated **Cyon** in 12:30; **Tyrus** defeated **Mims** in 8:37; **The Commonwealth Connection (Doug Williams** and **Harry Smith)** defeated **La Rebelion (Bestia 666** and **Mecha Wolf)** to win the NWA World Tag Team Title in 13:54; **Kamille** defeated **KiLynn King** in 17:25; **Trevor Murdoch** defeated **Nick Aldis, Thom Latimer** and **Sam Shaw** in a Four Way Match to win the vacant NWA Worlds Heavyweight Title in 18:10.
Was It Any Good? It was a good event top-to-bottom. One could argue that the promo segments between Matt Cardona, Bully Ray and Thom Latimer outstayed their welcome, but the story was executed well enough with injured NWA Worlds Heavyweight Champion Cardona vacating the belt and a four way featuring Latimer, Nick Aldis, Trevor Murdoch and Sam Shaw hastily arranged. The match itself was fine, if a little soggy in parts, with Murdoch ultimately reinstalled at company top dog. NWA Women's Champion Kamille enjoyed another solid outing, this time against the increasingly popular KiLynn King. That wasn't all for women's action on the card, as Natalia Markova bested the returning Taya Valkyrie in a decent undercard affair. UK legend Doug Williams was able to turn back the clock once more, as he alongside Harry Smith claimed NWA tag team gold at the expense of La Rebelión. There were a few dips along the way but by and large, this was a varied and enjoyable event from the National Wrestling Alliance.

DOMINION '22
12-06-22, Osaka, Japan **NJPW**

Aaron Henare, TJP and **Francesco Akira** defeated **Ryusuke Taguchi, Master Wato** and **Hiroyoshi Tenzan** in 10:31; **Taiji Ishimori, El Phantasmo** and **Ace Austin** defeated **Tetsuya Naito, Bushi** and **Hiromu Takahashi** in 8:04; **Toru Yano** defeated **Luke Gallows** in 4:05; **Evil,**

Sho and **Yujiro Takahashi** defeated **Zack Sabre Jr.**, **El Desperado** and **Yoshinobu Kanemaru** in 9:26; **Jeff Cobb** and **Great-O-Khan** defeated **Bad Luck Fale** and **Chase Owens** to win the IWGP Tag Team Title in 11:52; **Hiroshi Tanahashi** defeated **Hirooki Goto** in 12:40; **Shingo Takagi** defeated **Taichi** 11-10 in a 10 Minute Unlimited Pinfall Scramble Match in 10:00; **Karl Anderson** defeated **Tama Tonga** to win the NEVER Openweight Title in 16:27; **Will Ospreay** defeated **Sanada** to win the vacant IWGP United States Heavyweight Title in 12:48; **Jay White** defeated **Kazuchika Okada** to win the IWGP World Heavyweight Title in 36:04.

Was It Any Good? This was one of the weaker Dominion shows of recent years. The bell-to-bell output ranged from great-to-bad, but the booking felt uninspired throughout, and the show struggled to break through as a consequence. Case in point was the main event clash between Kazuchika Okada and Jay White for the IWGP World Heavyweight Championship. This was the latest in a long line of high quality contests between the pair and therein lies the headache facing the New Japan brass—it was good, really good even, but we've seen it all before. Still, viewed in a vacuum, this was another decent encounter with the New Zealander upsetting Okada to reclaim the gold. The remainder of the card was somewhat disappointing. Will Ospreay had a decent outing against SANADA which only suffered from its predictability—the Brit was red hot and his opponent the exact opposite. Shingo Takagi's KOPW trophy defence against Taichi surprised to the upside, although the former Suzuki Gun man really does deserve more credit at this point. While unconventional, this match certainly felt different, which was a massive positive amidst the overall malaise. Outside of those, there was nothing particularly noteworthy on the undercard which was a surprise given the quality of previous iterations of the event.

CYBERFIGHT FESTIVAL '22
12-06-22, Saitama, Japan **DDT/NOAH/TJPW**

Kai Fujimura and **Kinya Okada** defeated **Toi Kojima** and **Yuya Koroku** in 11:45; **Maki Ito**, **Miyu Yamashita** and **Juria Nagano** defeated **Hikari Noa**, **Suzume** and **Yuki Arai** in 10:54; **Akito Nishigaki**, **Danshoku Dino**, **Yuki Ino** and **Yumehito Imanari** defeated **Kendo Kashin**, **Sanshiro Takagi**, **Shinya Aoki** and **Yumiko Hotta** in 13:21; **Rika Tatsumi** defeated **Miu Watanabe**, **Mizuki** and **Yuki Kamifuku** in a Four Way Match in 9:37; **El Hijo del Dr. Wagner Jr.**, **Michael Elgin**, **Rene Dupree**, **Simon Gotch** and **Timothy Thatcher** defeated **Daiki Inaba**, **Kazuyuki Fujita**, **Masa Kitamiya**, **Shuhei Taniguchi** and **Takashi Sugiura** in 14:01; **Chris Brookes**, **Masahiro Takanashi**, **Harashima** and **Naomi Yoshimura** defeated **Mao**, **Shunma Katsumata**, **Yuki Ueno** and **Asuka** in 14:29; **Hayata**, **Yoshinari Ogawa** and **Rob Van Dam** defeated **Daisuke Harada**, **Kaito Kiyomiya** and **Yo-Hey** in 12:03; **Atsushi Kotoge**, **Katsuhiko Nakajima** and **Yoshiki Inamura** defeated **Jun Akiyama**, **Tetsuya Endo** and **Kazusada Higuchi** in 6:20; **Kenoh** defeated **Daisuke Sasaki** in a Hardcore Match in 21:28; **Shoko Nakajima** defeated **Yuka Sakazaki** in 14:57; **Satoshi Kojima** defeated **Go Shiozaki** to win the GHC Heavyweight Title in 21:11.

Was It Any Good? It was, particularly from a production standpoint. The look and feel of the CyberFight stable's annual get-together was deeply impressive, with several entrances afforded a significant portion of the production budget and the overall vibe of the show feeling bigger and more special. The wrestling on the card was in large part good, if lacking in stakes. The top end of the card naturally had more riding on it, as was the case with Satoshi Kojima's shock GHC Heavyweight Title victory

over Go Shoizaki. With NOAH having only recently returned Shiozaki to the top table, this felt like a curious piece of booking, but certainly one that generated headlines. NOAH straight man Kenoh once again flexed his comedic muscles in a fun inter-promotional match with DDT-Pro hellraiser Daisuke Sasaki. Fought under No DQ rules, this was fun and again highlighted the NOAH man's versatility. Rob Van Dam was a surprising inclusion on the card but certainly a fun one, teaming with Yoshinari Ogawa and HAYATA to defeat Kaito Kiyomiya, Daisuke Harada and YO-HEY. Also worth mentioning was the TJPW Princess of Princess title match between Shoko Nakajima and Yuka Sakazaki in which the champion successfully retained in a good match that fell slightly below the pair's lofty standards. The unfortunate injury to DDT's Tetsuya Endo midway through the card certainly slowed its momentum but overall, this gets a thumbs in the middle for the action but two thumbs up for the stunning production values.

TRIPLEMANIA XXX: TIJUANA
18-06-22, Tijuana, Mexico **AAA**

Nino Hamburguesa won a 13 Man Copa TripleMania XXX Match in 21:57; **Rey Fenix** defeated **Bandido**, **El Hijo del Vikingo**, **Laredo Kid** and **Taurus** in a Five Way Match to win the AAA Cruiserweight Title and Latin American Title in 20:37; **Blue Demon Jr.** defeated **Pentagon Jr.** in 11:52; **Flammer** defeated **Chik Tormenta** in a Mask vs. Mask Match in 12:58; **Psycho Clown** defeated **Villano IV** in 17:19; **Hermanos Lee (Dragon Lee** and **Dralistico)** defeated **Johnny Hardy** and **Matt Hardy** in 13:35.

Was It Any Good? This was perhaps the most well balanced of the three TripleMania shows of 2022, with decent action peppered throughout the card. One could certainly pick holes with the event's running order, specifically the early placement of the AAA World Cruiserweight / Latin America unification five-way match, which was by far and away the best thing on the card. This was high level lucha libre with five of the best modern exhibitors of the style (Vikingo, Fenix, Taurus, Bandido and Laredo Kid) going hell for leather for 20 minutes. AEW's Rey Fenix ultimately walked away with the amalgamated gold, in what was the show's in-ring apex. That's not to say the remainder was bad, just not at the same level. Both Ruleta De La Muerte semi-finals were stellar, particularly Psycho Clown's victory over Villano IV. The main event between Hermanos Lee (Dragon Lee and Dralistico) and Matt Hardy and late-replacement partner Johnny Hardy (John Morrison) was a reasonable contest, although not in the same universe as the aforementioned five-way, which should really have topped the bill. Still, overall a decent outing for the Mexican powerhouse promotion.

SLAMMIVERSARY XX
19-06-22, Nashville, Tennessee **Impact**

Mike Bailey defeated **Ace Austin**, **Alex Zayne**, **Andrew Everett**, **Kenny King** and **Trey Miguel** in an Ultimate X Match to win the Impact X Divison Title in 9:50; **Rosemary** and **Taya Valkyrie** defeated **The Influence (Madison Rayne** and **Tenille Dashwood)** to win the Impact Knockouts World Tag Team Title in 7:20; **Sami Callihan** defeated **Moose** in a Monster's Ball Match in 16:00; **The Good Brothers (Luke Gallows** and **Karl Anderson)** defeated **The Briscoe Brothers (Jay Briscoe** and **Mark Briscoe)** to win the Impact World Tag Team Title in 10:00; **Impact Originals (Alex Shelley**, **Chris Sabin**, **Davey Richards**, **Frankie Kazarian** and **Magnus)** defeated **Honor No More (Eddie Edwards**, **Matt Taven**, **Mike Bennett**, **PCO** and **Vincent)** in 18:45; **Jordynne Grace** defeated **Tasha Steelz**, **Chelsea Green**, **Deonna Purrazzo** and **Mia Yim** in a Queen Of The Mountain

Match to win the Impact Knockouts World Title in 18:15; **Josh Alexander** defeated **Eric Young** in 18:50.

Was It Any Good? This was a solid show with big ideas that coasted along nicely until its final three matches, at which point business picked up significantly. IMPACT rightly leant into its sizeable history at points throughout Slammiversary, with acts from yesteryear such as America's Most Wanted (James Storm and Chris Harris) making an appearance following The Goodbrothers' victory over The Briscoes. But the brand's legacy was felt most keenly in the 10-man tag team match between the insurgent Ring Of Honor stable, Honor No More, and the IMPACT originals team of Nick Aldis, Frankie Kazarian, The Motor City Machine Guns and mystery partner, Davey Richards. Too often IMPACT is ridiculed for its mistakes, particularly from its Hogan/Bischoff period, but it was right to remind fans of its role in the development of talent such as Shelley, Sabin and co. here, in what was a fun, nostalgia-fuelled contest. Another slice of history for Knockouts division was also on tap, as Mia Yim, Deonna Purrazzo, Chelsea Green, Tasha Steelz and Jordynne Grace competed in the first ever Queen of the Mountain match. Grace, who had long felt like the division's champion-elect, was finally installed as Knockouts Champion following a very fun match. Josh Alexander's IMPACT World Title defence against Eric Young was another minor dip into the nostalgia pool for the promotion, given Young's rich history with the company. And while not necessarily a fashionable main event on paper, the two Canadians delivered in spades here, with Alexander rightly coming out on top.

FORBIDDEN DOOR

26-06-22, Chicago, Illinois **AEW/NJPW**

Minoru Suzuki and **Le Sex Gods (Chris Jericho** and **Sammy Guevara)** defeated **Eddie Kingston, Shota Umino** and **Wheeler Yuta** in 18:58; **FTR (Cash Wheeler** and **Dax Harwood)** defeated **United Empire (Great-O-Khan** and **Jeff Cobb)** and **Roppongi Vice (Rocky Romero** and **Trent Beretta)** in a Three Way Match to win the IWGP Tag Team Title in 16:19; **Pac** defeated **Clark Connors, Miro** and **Malakai Black** in a Four Way Match to win the inaugural AEW All-Atlantic Title in 15:10; **Dudes With Attitudes (Darby Allin, Sting** and **Shingo Takagi)** defeated **Bullet Club (El Phantasmo, Matt Jackson** and **Nick Jackson)** in 13:01; **Thunder Rosa** defeated **Toni Storm** in 10:42; **Will Ospreay** defeated **Orange Cassidy** in 16:43; **Claudio Castagnoli** defeated **Zack Sabre Jr.** in 18:26; **Jay White** defeated **Hangman Page, Kazuchika Okada** and **Adam Cole** in a Four Way Match in 21:05; **Jon Moxley** defeated **Hiroshi Tanahashi** to win the interim AEW World Title in 18:14.

Was It Any Good? Purely from an in-ring perspective, it was one of the best shows of the year top-to-bottom. Having endured a build-up to forget, this co-promotion between AEW and New Japan shrugged off weeks of disjointed television to present an excellent wrestling show. The main event was amongst the highlights, with Jon Moxley clashing with Hiroshi Tanahashi for the vacant AEW Interim World Title. The bout contained a masterful babyface performance from The Ace, who gradually turned the pro-Moxley crowd to his favour and caught one of the best near falls of the year by landing a last ditch High Fly Flow at the match's apex for a long two count. Mox eventually won with the Paradigm Shift ahead of a show-closing brawl between The Jericho Appreciation Society and Moxley's troop of the BBC, Eddie Kingston, Santana and Ortiz. Earlier in the evening, strange bedfellows Will Ospreay and Orange Cassidy gelled brilliantly to put on the sleeper match of the card. The Brit retained his IWGP United States Heavyweight Championship, after which his United Empire teammates

descended on 'Freshly Squeezed' only to be run off by Katsuyori Shibata. That was a shocker. Clark Connors was the beneficiary of the underdog role in the four way match to crown the inaugural All Atlantic champion. The 'Wild Rhino' was the least known contestant in the match and was afforded plenty by Pac, Miro and Malakai Black, who appeared happy to put the New Japan man over (figuratively speaking). Pac eventually won, picking up his first piece of silverware in AEW. Claudio Castagnoli made his debut on the show as Zack Sabre Jr's mystery opponent. The pair had a fun 15-minute tussle. Adam Cole's injury in the IWGP World Heavyweight four-way alongside an oddly positioned AEW Women's Title match were the only dips in an otherwise enthralling event.

MONEY IN THE BANK '22

02-07-22, Paradise, Nevada **WWE**

Liv Morgan defeated **Alexa Bliss, Asuka, Becky Lynch, Lacey Evans, Raquel Rodriguez** and **Shotzi** in a Money In The Bank Ladder Match in 16:35; **Bobby Lashley** defeated **Theory** to win the WWE United States Title in 11:05; **Bianca Belair** defeated **Carmella** in 7:10; **The Usos (Jey Uso** and **Jimmy Uso)** defeated **The Street Profits (Angelo Dawkins** and **Montez Ford)** in 23:00; **Ronda Rousey** defeated **Natalya** in 12:30; **Liv Morgan** defeated **Ronda Rousey** to win the WWE SmackDown Women's Title in :35; **Theory** defeated **Drew McIntyre, Madcap Moss, Omos, Riddle, Sami Zayn, Seth Rollins** and **Sheamus** in a Money In The Bank Ladder Match in 25:25.

Was It Any Good? It was hit and miss. The final supercard of the Vince McMahon era featured many of the traits that had left fans feeling so frustrated with WWE over the years, from counterproductive booking (Lashley hammering rising star Austin Theory), to unwarranted pushes (Carmella again getting elevated to the women's title picture), to groan-inducing surprises that nobody except McMahon wanted to see (Theory miraculously recovering from his beating to outlast the entire field in the men's Money In The Bank Ladder Match to snare the briefcase). The opener featured a truly shambolic performance from Shotzi, who managed to botch every spot she was involved in and was a danger to herself and others. There were some positives though. Liv Morgan's women's MITB win and subsequent cash-in over Ronda Rousey were warmly received and the Usos vs. Street Profits clash was a near-fall laden banger that ranks amongst the best WWE tag matches of the year. MITB was the third consecutive WWE supercard that did not feature a title defence from undisputed WWE Univeral Champion Roman Reigns, begging the question why WWE bothered unifying the belts in the first place. As a result, Money In The Bank felt largely missable. Perhaps it is no surprise, then, that the show was supposed to take place in a stadium setting but was moved to a much smaller arena because of a lack of interest.

SUMMER SUN PRINCESS '22

09-07-22, Toyko, Japan **TJPW**

Moka Miyamoto defeated **Juria Nagano** in 4:58; **Aja Kong, Pom Harajuku, Raku** and **Yuki Aino** defeated **Haruna Neko, Hyper Misao, Kaya Toribami** and **Nao Kakuta** in 12:28; **Ryo Mizunami** defeated **Miu Watanabe** in 11:53; **Hikari Noa** and **Hikaru Shida** defeated **Mahiro Kiryu** and **Yuki Kamifuku** in 13:32; **Mei Suruga** and **Suzume** defeated **Arisu Endo** and **Riho** in 14:21; **Alex Windsor** defeated **Maki Ito** to win the International Princess Title in 13:22; **Miyu Yamashita** defeated **Thunder Rosa** in 13:39; **Saki Akai** and **Yuki Arai** defeated **Mizuki** and **Yuka Sakazaki** to win the Princess Tag Team Title in 24:28; **Shoko Nakajima** defeated **Rika Tatsumi** in 19:23.

Was It Any Good? Definitely. This was an incredibly easy watch with only two matches stretching beyond the 15-minute mark and featured great action throughout. The show also featured a roster seemingly buoyed by the return of international stars following a lengthy period of closed borders due to Covid-19. Principally, the Ota City General Gymnasium played host to the return of AEW Women's World Champion Thunder Rosa, who had previously wrestled for the company prior to the pandemic. Rosa was matched against company ace Miyu Yamashita in what was a very good, and hard-hitting affair. To the surprise of many, The Pink Striker picked up with the win and thus booked a return bout on US television. The other notable import was rising UK star Alex Windsor, who claimed the International Princess Title in a decent encounter with Maki Itoh. In other prominent bouts, Shoko Nakajima retained her Princess of Princess Championship over former titlist Rika Tatsumi in a good match, while Saki Akai and Yuki Arai upset the Magical Sugar Rabbits to claim the Princess Tag Titles in a match that played to the likeable Arai's strengths in the selling department. AEW grapplers Hikaru Shida and Riho were both present, wrestling in separate tag matches, as was All Elite alumni Ryo Mizunami, who gave the upstart Miu Watanabe her greatest challenge to date in a very good one-on-one encounter.

DESTINATION '22
16-07-22, Toyko, Japan NOAH

Hajime Ohara, Hi69, Shuji Kondo and Tadasuke defeated Atsushi Kotoge, Daisuke Harada, Xtreme Tiger and Yo-Hey in 11:17; Anthony Greene, El Hijo del Dr. Wagner Jr., Rene Dupree, Simon Gotch and Stallion Rogers defeated Daiki Inaba, Kazushi Sakuraba, Kinya Okada, Masaaki Mochizuki and Shuhei Taniguchi in 13:29; Eita and Kotaro Suzuki defeated Yoshinari Ogawa and Yuya Susumu in 5:38; Ninja Mack defeated Dante Leon in 14:24; Masato Tanaka and Rob Van Dam defeated Nosawa Rongai and Super Crazy in a Hardcore Match in 10:46; Go Shiozaki, Kazuyuki Fujita and Takashi Sugiura defeated Katsuhiko Nakajima, Manabu Soya and Masakatsu Funaki in 12:59; Kaito Kiyomiya defeated Keiji Mutoh in 26:28; Hideki Suzuki and Timothy Thatcher defeated Masa Kitamiya and Yoshiki Inamura to win the vacant GHC Tag Team Title in 20:38; Hayata defeated Seiki Yoshioka in 20:45; Kenoh defeated Satoshi Kojima to win the GHC Heavyweight Title in 28:17.
Was It Any Good? It was a show of two halves. The undercard, while inoffensive, was a bit of a hotchpotch of names and felt slightly inconsequential as a result, while the show's bigger matches delivered with aplomb. Chief among these were two torch-passing match-ups between the older generation and NOAH's new guard. In the main event, Kenoh (although not exactly a spring chicken at 37) relieved New Japan veteran Satoshi Kojima of the GHC Heavyweight Title that he had won in such surprising fashion one month prior. This was a good match with the correct result, as there are few better suited to NOAH's main event scene than the character-driven Kenoh. Equally beneficial was Kaito Kiyomiya's revenge over Keiji Muto who had previously embarrassed him in singles competition. The youthful Kiyomiya carried the 59-year-old to a compelling contest. Also of note was the punchy GHC Tag Team Title match between the team of Hideki Suzuki and Timothy Thatcher and NOAH hosses Masa Kitamiya and Yoshiki Inamura. This was big, burly, bruising puro at its finest.

DEATH BEFORE DISHONOR XIX
23-07-22, Lowell, Massachusetts ROH

Claudio Castagnoli defeated Jonathan Gresham to win the ROH World Title in 11:30; Dalton Castle and The Boys (Brandon Tate and Brent Tate) defeated The Righteous (Vincent, Bateman and Dutch) to win the ROH World Six-Man Tag Team Title in 9:40; Wheeler Yuta defeated Daniel Garcia in a Pure Wrestling Rules Match in 15:55; Rush defeated Dragon Lee in 15:50; Mercedes Martinez defeated Serena Deeb in 17:20; Samoa Joe defeated Jay Lethal in 12:20; FTR (Cash Wheeler and Dax Harwood) defeated The Briscoe Brothers (Jay Briscoe and Mark Briscoe) 2-1 in a Best Two Out Of Three Falls Match in 43:25.
Was It Any Good? Absolutely. Death Before Dishonor was another very strong outing for the revamped ROH product. Like many AEW-related shows of the period, it wasn't without its share of backstage controversy, as then-ROH World Champion Jonathan Gresham reportedly clashed with Tony Khan backstage and subsequently left the promotion. Gresham's mood was clear as he made his way to the ring in what was, surprisingly, the pay-per-view's opening contest. Sans his usual entrance outfit and flag, the stony-faced Gresham marched solemnly to the ring seemingly in a hurry to get the whole ordeal over with. And he wasn't made to wait long, with Claudio Castagnoli lifting the title after just over 11 minutes of action. The live crowd cared not one jot and revelled in the Swiss Superman's victory, but it was a shame to see the man who had carried the belt throughout so much uncertainty reduced to such a undistinguished finale. The other big story of the show was the second clash between FTR and The Briscoes, this time in a two-out-of-three falls match. This was another spectacular battle between two of the planet's premier partnerships, with the Top Guys cinching another victory over their newfound rivals. Samoa Joe wrestled in an ROH ring for the first time since 2015, besting former protégé Jay Lethal to retain the ROH TV title. Wheeler Yuta and Mercedes Martinez each kept hold of their titles, with wins over Daniel Garcia and Serena Deeb, respectively. The ROH Six-Man Tag Titles returned to the fray, with The Righteous conceding the gold to Dalton Castle and The Boys. Away from the belts, Rush and Dragon Lee had one of the best matches of the night in a hard-fought lucha brawl, with Rush ultimately picking up the victory.

MUSIC CITY MAYHEM
30-07-22, Nashville, Tennessee NJPW

Fred Yehi, Shota Umino and Yuya Uemura defeated Kevin Knight, Ren Narita and The DKC in 13:12; Davey Richards defeated Rocky Romero in 11:29; Fred Rosser defeated Big Damo in 13:01; Hiromu Takahashi defeated Blake Christian in 13:59; Aussie Open (Kyle Fletcher, Mark Davis) and TJP defeated Alex Zayne and FTR (Cash Wheeler and Dax Harwood) in 14:30; Alex Shelley vs. Kushida ended in a draw in 20:00; Jon Moxley defeated El Desperado in a No DQ Match in 17:20.
Was It Any Good? Like many of New Japan's Stateside events, Music City Mayhem was a watchable if entirely unremarkable event, with a handful of top-drawer offerings to help punctuate proceedings. Chief among these was the main event clash between Jon Moxley and junior heavyweight sensation El Desperado. Fought under no disqualification rules, this contest neatly summarised why Desperado needs a more permanent move away for the Junior Heavyweights. Here, the masked man was at home against Moxley, wrestling the hardcore style and lapping up both the theatrics and the physicality. Moxley walked away with win, but it was another noteworthy performance from the form Junior kingpin. Of equal

quality, albeit for entirely different reasons, was Blake Christian's battle with Hiromu Takahashi. 'All Heart' has shown his class in spurts, but this was exactly the type of contest needed to help pull the best out of him. Outside of these two matches, the remainder of the card coasted along nicely, with Fred Rosser's STRONG Openweight Title defence against Big Damo and Alex Shelley's exhibition with Kushida among the other notable contests.

SUMMERSLAM '22
30-07-22, Nashville, Tennessee **WWE**

Bianca Belair defeated **Becky Lynch** in 15:10; **Logan Paul** defeated **The Miz** in 14:15; **Bobby Lashley** defeated **Theory** in 4:45; **The Mysterios (Rey Mysterio** and **Dominik Mysterio)** defeated **The Judgment Day (Finn Balor** and **Damian Priest)** in 11:05; **Pat McAfee** defeated **Happy Corbin** in 10:40; **The Usos (Jey Uso** and **Jimmy Uso)** defeated **The Street Profits (Angelo Dawkins** and **Montez Ford)** in 13:25; **Liv Morgan** defeated **Ronda Rousey** in 4:35; **Roman Reigns** defeated **Brock Lesnar** in a Last Man Standing Match in 23:00.

Was It Any Good? Yes it was. The Triple H era got off to a strong start, thanks to the stadium setting, a quality card of action, unexpected returns and some memorable moments. Bianca Belair and Becky Lynch had another gripping encounter, following which Lynch turned babyface—which fans had been waiting for since her return the year prior—and a new faction was established in the post-match when Bayley returned and brought Iyo Sky (Io Shirai) and the returning Dakota Kai with her. Logan Paul again over-delivered, looking every bit the multi-year veteran in a slick effort against The Miz, who deserves credit for carrying his end of the bargain and making Paul look like a million bucks. The card trailed off somewhat after that, as WWE supercards tend to do, but the Last Man Standing main event between eternal rivals Roman Reigns and Brock Lesnar helped take SummerSlam up another notch with their chaotic, rip-roaring brawl, punctuated by an all-time classic visual when Lesnar lifted the ring high into the air with his tractor. Featuring matches that people wanted to see and plenty of talking points, this was SummerSlam done right.

RIC FLAIR'S LAST MATCH
31-07-22, Nashville, Tennessee **JCP**

The Motor City Machine Guns (Alex Shelley and **Chris Sabin)** defeated **The Wolves (Davey Richards** and **Eddie Edwards)** in 11:06; **Killer Kross** defeated **Davey Boy Smith Jr.** in 5:22; **Jonathan Gresham** defeated **Alan Angels, Konosuke Takeshita** and **Nick Wayne** in a Four Way Match in 5:40; **The Four Horsemen (Brian Pillman Jr.** and **Brock Anderson)** defeated **The Rock 'N' Roll Express (Ricky Morton** and **Kerry Morton)** in 7:21; **Rey Fenix** defeated **Bandido, Laredo Kid** and **Black Taurus** in a Four Way Match in 11:45; **Josh Alexander** vs. **Jacob Fatu** ended in a no contest in 10:14; **The Briscoe Brothers (Jay Briscoe** and **Mark Briscoe)** defeated **The Von Erichs (Marshall Von Erich** and **Ross Von Erich)** in 7:43; **Jordynne Grace** defeated **Deonna Purrazzo** and **Rachael Ellering** in a Three Way Match in 9:17; **Ric Flair** and **Andrade El Idolo** defeated **Jay Lethal** and **Jeff Jarrett** in 26:40.

Was It Any Good? As an overall event, it was okay. With the spirit of cooperation thick in the air and good will flowing throughout, the show featured contributions from several of the world's premier wrestling promotions, affording the event a unique "festival of wrestling" feel and offering a huge sense of variety. In fact, the only really bad thing about Ric Flair's Last Match was, well, Ric Flair's last match. North of 70 and having not wrestled in a decade, The Nature Boy looked every inch of a man who should not have been stood in a wrestling ring, much less taking bumps and blading. Throughout the bout, a discombobulated Flair appeared to frequently lose consciousness and despite the good work of the seasoned professionals around him (Jeff Jarrett, Jay Lethal and Andrade El Idolo), the match felt on the precipice of tragedy throughout. Thankfully, everyone involved lived to tell the tale, but regardless, this did nothing to enhance Flair's reputation and even less to threaten WrestleMania XXIV as the Hall of Famer's true retirement match in the eyes of many. Most notable of the undercard bouts was the lucha libre four-way match between Rey Fenix, Bandido, Laredo Kid and Taurus, which was spectacular.

BATTLE OF THE BELTS III
06-08-22, Grand Rapids, Michigan **AEW**

Wardlow defeated **Jay Lethal** in 7:21; **Thunder Rosa** defeated **Jamie Hayter** in 11:31; **Claudio Castagnoli** defeated **Konosuke Takeshita** in 19:59.

Was It Any Good? While none of the Battle Of The Belts specials were afforded much in the way of hype or build, this was comfortably the concept's best in-ring presentation of the year. Claudio Castagnoli vs. Konosuke Takeshita topped the bill, with the former defending his ROH World Championship for the first time. Unsurprisingly, the pair had an excellent back-and-forth encounter which the live audience in Grand Rapids, Michigan lapped up. Castagnoli picked up the win after 20 minutes of frenetic action, pinning the DDT-Pro star following a Ricola Bomb. This was very much a win-win affair, with both men growing in stature; Castagnoli as a fighting champion and Takeshita as one to watch. Earlier in the card, Thunder Rosa's bested Jamie Hayter to retain the AEW Women's Title in one of the finest outings of her reign. The contest was hard-hitting, to say the least, with Hayter ending the night with broken nose—reportedly the source of some backstage heat between the two. The show opener between Wardlow and Jay Lethal for the TNT strap was a perfectly acceptable affair.

WRESTLE PETER PAN '22
20-08-22, Tokyo, Japan **DDT**

Yusuke Okada, Yuya Koroku and **Illusion** defeated **Toui Kojima, Yuki Ishida** and **Takeshi Masada** in 9:11; **Yuki Iino, Danshoku Dino** and **Koju Takeda** defeated **Yuji Hino, Yukio Naya** and **Super Sasadango Machine,** and **Toru Owashi, Kazuki Hirata** and **Antonio Honda** in a Three Way Match in 12:18; **Harashima, Yukio Sakaguchi** and **Hideki Okatani** defeated **Naomi Yoshimura, Kota Umeda** and **Keisuke Okuda** in 12:44; **Osamu Nishimura, Makoto Oishi** and **Akito** defeated **Shinichiro Kawamatsu, Sanshiro Takagi** and **Soma Takao** in 14:47; **Jun Akiyama** and **Saki Akai** defeated **Chris Brookes** and **Asuka** in 15:21; **Joey Janela** defeated **Shunma Katsumata** in a Hardcore Match in 18:56; **Yuki Ueno** defeated **Masahiro Takahashi** to win the DDT Universal Title in 14:26; **Konosuke Takeshita, Mao** and **Yasu Urano** defeated **Dick Togo, Daisuke Sasaki** and **Kanon** in 20:41; **Kazusada Higuchi** defeated **Tetsuya Endo** in 25:24.

Was It Any Good? In places, but it was arguably a leg down from some of the promotion's other big events. The main event pitting KO-D Openweight Champion Kazusada Higuchi opposite former champion Tetsuya Endo absolutely delivered. Endo, who had vacated the belt following his injury at CyberFight Festival, came into the bout with plenty to prove but ran into a surging Higuchi at just the wrong time. The back-and-forth affair was one of DDT's best matches of the year and proved a significant feather in the cap for the relatively new champion, Higuhci. Other highlights included Yuki Ueno's DDT Universal Title win over Masa Takanashi. Ueno has been on the cusp for some time now, and excelled here against the unorthodox Takanashi. The DDT Extreme Title match between Joey Janela and Shunma Katsumata had its moments but arguably overstayed its welcome. Overall, a decent event from Japan's most diverse promotion, but with nothing blow away barring the main event.

74TH ANNIVERSARY SHOW NIGHT #1
27-08-22, St. Louis, Missouri **NWA**

EC3 defeated **Mims** in 4:52; **The Miserable Faithful (Judais, Sal The Pal** and **Gaagz The Gymp)** defeated **The Ill Begotten (Alex Taylor, Jeremiah Plunkett** and **Danny Dealz)** in a Beelzebub's Bedlam Match in 9:41; **Chris Adonis** defeated **Odinson** by DQ in 7:26; **Homicide** defeated **Kerry Morton** in 12:38; **Rolando Freeman** defeated **Matt Cardona** in 5:41; **Max The Impaler** won a Burke Invitational Gauntlet in 17:24; **Cyon** defeated **Jax Dane** in 7:26; **Bully Ray** defeated **Mike Knox** in a Tables Match in 8:38; **La Rebelion (Bestia 666** and **Mecha Wolf)** defeated **Hawx Aerie (Luke Hawx** and **PJ Hawx)** to win the vacant NWA World Tag Team Title in 13:10; **Kamille** defeated **Taya Valkyrie** in 18:57.
Was It Any Good? It wasn't bad, although at 13 matches, one of which being a 10-person gauntlet, the card felt fatty and subsequently certain matches were a little squashed. That said, there was plenty to like, particularly from the company's expanding women's division. The Mildred Burke Invitational Gauntlet featured several decent performances from the likes of KiLynn King, Madi Wrenkowski and Jennacyde and eventual winner Max the Impaler has an excellent look and plenty of potential. In the show's main event, reigning NWA Women's Champion Kamille took on her stiffest test yet in the form of decorated women's wrestler Taya Valkyrie. This was decent, with both performers working hard. Elsewhere, La Rebelión continued their winning ways with a successful tag title defence over Luke and PJ Hawx, while Bully Ray's clunky Tables Match with Mike Knox at the very least had the right result (ie. Knox going through a table).

74TH ANNIVERSARY SHOW NIGHT #2
28-08-22, St. Louis, Missouri **NWA**

Colby Corino defeated **Caprice Coleman** 2-1 in a Best Two Out Of Three Falls Match in 9:57; **The Fixers (Jay Bradley** and **Wrecking Ball Legursky)** won a Tag Team Battle Royal to win the vacant NWA United States Tag Team Title in 14:07; **Magic Jake Dumas** defeated **Mercurio** in 7:15; **Davey Richards** defeated **Thrillbilly Silas** in 10:24; **Cyon** defeated **Anthony Mayweather** in 8:18; **Pretty Empowered (Ella Envy** and **Kenzie Paige)** defeated **The Hex (Allysin Kay** and **Marti Belle)** in a Kingshighway Street Fight in 10:02; **Homicide** defeated **Ricky Morton** in 6:12; **Nick Aldis** defeated **Flip Gordon** in 8:43; **JR Kratos** and **Da Pope** defeated **Aron Stevens** and **Rodney Mack** in a Missouri Tornado Match in 9:40; **Thom Latimer** vs. **EC3** ended in a no contest in 6:42; **Kamille** defeated **Max The Impaler** in 11:07; **Trevor Murdoch** defeated **Tyrus** in 13:44.
Was It Any Good? Bearing in mind the main critique for the night one was the number of matches, night two boasted an excessive 16 separate contests (including the pre-show)—which way too many. And while the quantity was heavy here, the quality was a little lighter, with far fewer noteworthy matches and moments than the prior night. Kamille's title retention over Max the Impaler was fun, as was Homicides NWA World Junior Heavyweight victory over Kerry Morton. Trevor Murdoch bested Tyrus in a sluggish main event that did little for either man while company stalwart Nick Aldis was confined to a midcard victory over Flip Gordon (remember him?). Not terrible, but certainly not as strong as night one.

CLASH AT THE CASTLE
03-09-22, Cardiff, Wales **WWE**

Damage CTRL (Bayley, Dakota Kai and Iyo Sky) defeated **Bianca Belair, Alexa Bliss** and **Asuka** in 18:44; **Gunther** defeated **Sheamus** in 19:33; **Liv Morgan** defeated **Shayna Baszler** in 11:02; **Edge** and **Rey Mysterio** defeated **The Judgment Day (Finn Balor** and **Damian Priest)** in 12:35; **Seth Rollins** defeated **Matt Riddle** in 17:22; **Roman Reigns** defeated **Drew McIntyre** in 30:47.
Was It Any Good? It certainly was. A strong card from top to bottom, WWE's first UK stadium show in 30 years was a triumph. From a purely in-ring perspective, few WWE supercards have come close to matching it. Match of the night honours belonged to Gunther and Sheamus, who's collision for the IC title was up their with SummerSlam '92's legendary IC title scrap between Bret Hart and The British Bulldog. Beating seven bells out of each other for almost 20 gruelling minutes, fans were spellbound by the action on offer, and were moved to give Sheamus a much-deserved standing ovation following the bout's conclusion. Nothing else could top it, but Seth Rollins and Matt Riddle's thrill-a-minute scrap and the rollercoaster ride of a main event that saw Drew McIntyre come perilously close to unseating the invincible Roman Reigns came very close.

WORLDS COLLIDE '22
04-09-22, Orlando, Florida **NXT**

Carmelo Hayes defeated **Ricochet** in 15:57; **Pretty Deadly (Elton Prince** and **Kit Wilson)** defeated **The Creed Brothers (Brutus Creed** and **Julius Creed), Brooks Jensen** and **Josh Briggs,** and **Gallus (Mark Coffey** and **Wolfgang)** in a Four Way Elimination Match to unify the NXT Tag Team Title and NXT UK Tag Team Title in 15:34; **Mandy Rose** defeated **Meiko Satomura** and **Blair Davenport** in a Three Way Match to unify the NXT Women's Title and NXT UK Women's Title in 13:17; **Katana Chance** and **Kayden Carter** defeated **Doudrop** and **Nikki A.S.H.** in 10:19; **Bron Breakker** defeated **Tyler Bate** to unify the NXT Title and NXT United Kingdom Title in 17:11.
Was It Any Good? Mostly. The death of NXT UK meant the unification of all of its titles with their American NXT counterparts, which made for an interesting concept show on paper but also led to a lot of predictable outcomes. With the main roster shackles off, Ricochet looked great in his explosive opener with rising star Carmelo Hayes. Pretty Deadly were the surprise winners of a four-way to unify the tag straps, but the match was nothing to write home about. Mandy Rose's victory over Meiko Satomura and the shoehorned-in Blair Davenport—who was there to eat the fall—was fairly routine. Main roster loanees Doudrop and Nikki A.S.H. were on the card to put over women's tag champs Katana Chance and Kayden Carter, but the basic match did little to elevate the new generation. Fortunately the main event was a belter, with NXT UK standout Tyler Bate once again proving he has an immensely bright future in WWE, taking Bron Breakker to the limit in a cracking scrap that would not have been out of place on a TakeOver show of old.

ALL OUT '22
04-09-22, Hoffman Estates, Illinois **AEW**

MJF defeated **Claudio Castagnoli, Wheeler Yuta, Penta El Zero M, Rey Fenix, Rush, Andrade El Idolo** and **Dante Martin** in a Casino Ladder Match in 14:15; **The Elite (Kenny Omega, Matt Jackson** and **Nick Jackson)** defeated **The Dark Order (Hangman Page, Alex Reynolds** and **John Silver)** to win the inaugural AEW World Trios Title in 19:50; **Jade Cargill** defeated

Athena in 4:20; **Wardlow** and **FTR (Cash Wheeler** and **Dax Harwood)** defeated **Jay Lethal** and **The Motor City Machine Guns (Chris Sabin** and **Alex Shelley)** in 16:30; **Powerhouse Hobbs** defeated **Ricky Starks** in 5:05; **Swerve In Our Glory (Keith Lee** and **Swerve Strickland)** defeated **The Acclaimed (Anthony Bowens** and **Max Caster)** in 22:30; **Toni Storm** defeated **Dr. Britt Baker D.M.D., Jamie Hayter** and **Hikaru Shida** in a Four Way Match to win the vacant interim AEW Women's World Title in 14:20; **Christian Cage** defeated **Jungle Boy** in :20; **Chris Jericho** defeated **Bryan Danielson** in 23:40; **Darby Allin, Sting** and **Miro** defeated **The House Of Black (Malakai Black, Brody King** and **Buddy Matthews)** in 12:10; **CM Punk** defeated **Jon Moxley** to win the AEW World Title in 19:55.

Was It Any Good? Not that anyone remembers the show itself, due to events in the immediate aftermath, but All Out was a decent, if somewhat disjointed, affair built around MJF's shocking return. Before the pay-per-view itself began, the pre-show encounter between New Japan's Tomohiro Ishii and Eddie Kingston had threatened to overshadow proceedings, as the two engaged in a brutal chop-fest for the ages. The PPV launched with the Casino Ladder Match, affording the winner a shot at the AEW World Championship. The match itself was okay but the unique finish was where things got interesting. First, Stokely Hathaway's new group, The Firm, cleared the ring while Hathaway himself retrieved the chip. Then the match's masked final entrant, announced as The Joker, sauntered to the ring to The Rolling Stones' hit 'Sympathy For The Devil', was handed the chip by Hathaway and subsequently won the match. It was both a unique and perplexing finish, to say the least. The pay off came later in the night, after CM Punk had regained his World Title from Jon Moxley in the main event. The Joker appeared once more, revealed himself to be Friedman and signalled his intention of taking Punk's freshly won silverware. The juice was worth the squeeze. Elsewhere, despite Anthony Bowens' previous assertions, All Out was the night The Acclaimed officially arrived. The duo's tag team title challenge against Swerve In Our Glory had few talking beforehand, but the Chicago crowd had decided that tonight was the night, and went crazy for Bowens, Caster and of course, Daddy Ass. What unfolded was an incredible spectacle, as The Acclaimed and SIOG manoeuvred on the fly to play into the live crowd's reaction. The Acclaimed didn't win the match that night, but they did become one of the company's hottest properties seemingly overnight.

89. ANIVERSARIO
16-09-22, Mexico City, Mexico **CMLL**

Dulce Gardenia, Espiritu Negro and **Rey Cometa** defeated **Arkalis, Guerrero Maya Jr.** and **Stigma** in 15:15; **Euforia, Hechicero** and **Mephisto** defeated **Negro Casas, Star Jr.** and **Titan** 2-1 in a Best Two Out Of Three Falls Match in 19:19; **Angel de Oro** defeated **Mistico** and **Volador Jr.** in a Three Way Match in 19:20; **Atlantis Jr.** and **Dragon Rojo Jr.** defeated **Averno** and **Fuerza Guerrera** in a Four Way Elimination Match in 3:03; **Averno** and **Ultimo Guerrero** defeated **Atlantis** and **Fuerza Guerrera** in 8:21; **Atlantis Jr.** and **Stuka Jr.** defeated **Dragon Rojo Jr.** and **Soberano Jr.** in 9:49; **Atlantis Jr.** and **Stuka Jr.** defeated **Averno** and **Ultimo Guerrero** in 2:36; **La Jarochita** defeated **Reyna Isis** in a Best Two Out Of Three Falls Mask vs. Match Match in 18:23; **Atlantis Jr.** defeated **Stuka Jr.** in a Best Two Out Of Three Falls Mask vs. Match Match in 16:17.

Was It Any Good? It was. CMLL has made a habit of delivering on their big shows and that was certainly the case here. Most notable were the two Mask vs. Mask matches, where the bell-to-bell action was excellent and

delivered on the huge stakes in both encounters. The first of these matches was the women's contest between La Jarochita and Reyna Isis, which gradually evolved into one of the country's finest bouts of the year. Jarochita eventually took the win, unmasking her foe in the ritual humiliation of lucha libre. The show's main event also had a mask up for grabs, as the highly touted Atlantis Jr submitted Stuka Jr. with his La Atlantida finisher to claim the scalp. Elsewhere on the card, there was some decent tag and trios action to be found, most notably in the form of the Mexican National Trios Title match pitting Los Dulce Atrapsuenos against Fuerza Poblana. A fun watch overall which is certainly worth revisiting, particularly for the Mask matches.

50TH ANNIVERSARY SHOW
18-09-22, Tokyo, Japan **AJPW**

Rising Hayato and **Ryo Inoue** defeated **Oji Shiiba** and **Yusuke Kodama** in 4:18; **ATM, Mitsuya Nagai, Tajiri** and **Yoshitatsu** defeated **Andy Wu, Black Menso-re, Izanagi** and **Sushi** in 6:04; **Cyrus, Jun Saito** and **Rei Saito** defeated **Kohei Sato, Shuji Ishikawa** and **Yukio Naya** in 7:38; **Dan Tamura** and **Hikaru Sato** defeated **Minoru** and **Toshizo** to win the AJPW All Asia Tag Team Title in 14:22; **Minoru Suzuki** defeated **Hokuto Omori** in 12:04; **Yuji Nagata** defeated **Yuma Anzai** in 9:09; **Yuma Aoyagi** defeated **Christopher Daniels** in 11:31; **Atsushi Onita, Masanobu Fuchi** and **Shiro Koshinaka** defeated **Great Kojika, Masao Inoue** and **Yoshiaki Yatsu** in 11:55; **Ryuki Honda** and **Shotaro Ashino** defeated **Manabu Soya** and **Takao Omori** in 16:22; **Atsuki Aoyagi** defeated **Tiger Mask IV** to win the AJPW World Junior Heavyweight Title in 13:23; **Naoya Nomura** defeated **Jake Lee** in :43; **Kento Miyahara** defeated **Suwama** to win the Triple Crown Title in 16:35.

Was It Any Good? It was solid. All Japan's 50th anniversary show continued the company's long march back to prominence following years on the periphery of the puro scene. The event drew a live gate just shy of 5,000, making it the company's most well-attended event since 2017. There was plenty to like here, with company ace Kento Miyahara claiming the Triple Crown Championship in a good main event versus AJPW stalwart Suwama. It was also pleasing to see the legendary Stan Hansen and Kenta Kobashi at ringside for this one, adding grandeur to a fitting main event. AEW's Christopher Daniels continued his role as company ambassador, this time in putting over one of the company's brightest prospects, Yuma Aoyagi. Given that All Elite have working relationships with practically every other company in Japan, there's no reason why AJPW shouldn't be pushing for some exposure stateside going forward and Aoyagi would certainly be a prime candidate for that role. The collaborative nature of the event did not end there, with the likes of New Japan's Yuji Nagata and Minoru Suzuki featured elsewhere on a card that delivered good quality without ever threatening to shoot the lights out.

BURNING SPIRIT '22
25-09-22, Kobe, Japan **NJPW**

Bushi, Hiromu Takahashi and **Shingo Takagi** defeated **El Phantasmo, Hikuleo** and **Kenta** in 8:43; **Luke Gallows** vs. **Toru Yano** ended in a double count out in 3:45; **Great-O-Khan** and **Jeff Cobb** defeated **Bad Luck Fale** and **Chase Owens** in 7:57; **Taichi** and **Zack Sabre Jr.** defeated **Sanada** and **Tetsuya Naito** in 9:32; **Bad Dude Tito, Jonah** and **Shane Haste** defeated **Togi Makabe, Tomoaki Honma** and **Kazuchika Okada** in 12:09; **Jay White** and **Taiji Ishimori** defeated **Jado** and **Tama Tonga** in 10:39; **Francesco Akira** and **TJP** defeated **Ryusuke Taguchi** and **Master Wato** in 12:43; **Karl**

Anderson defeated **Hiroshi Tanahashi** in 13:37; **Will Ospreay** defeated **David Finlay** in 28:22.

Was It Any Good? It was somewhere in the middle for a bigger NJPW show this year, with a decent main event and several enjoyable, if somewhat uneventful, undercard match-ups. Will Ospreay's IWGP US Heavyweight Championship clash with David Finlay was a worthy main event, with both men working hard throughout. Having met several times in recent years, there was palpable needle between the two from the open, which resulted in an aggressive start from the fiery Brit. At just shy of 30 minutes, this could have benefited from a modest trim, but beyond that, it was a decent effort from both competitors. In a curious contest, Karl Anderson continued to underwhelm in his latest New Japan stint, this time against Hiroshi Tanahashi, in what would have been an unthinkable prospect in years gone by. The match was really the backdrop for a bigger story, however, as the fraying Bullet Club continued to rip apart at the seams. This time, the towering Hikuleo decided he'd had enough of Jay White and co., turning on his stablemates to the benefit of Tama Tonga, whom was the recipient of a BC beat down up until that point. There weren't masses of talking points beyond those, in what was a fine, if somewhat pedestrian affair from the Cerulean Blue.

ROYAL QUEST II NIGHT #1
01-10-22, London, England **NJPW**

Gabriel Kidd defeated **Dan Moloney** in 9:19; **Michael Oku** and **Ricky Knight Jr.** defeated **Great-O-Khan** and **Gideon Grey** in 12:17; **Ava White** and **Alex Windsor** defeated **Jazzy Gabert** and **Kanji** in 6:18; **Tetsuya Naito, Sanada** and **Hiromu Takahashi** defeated **Zack Sabre Jr., El Desperado** and **Douki** in 14:29; **Kazuchika Okada** and **Tomohiro Ishii** defeated **Bad Dude Tito** and **Zak Knight** in 12:47; **Hiroshi Tanahashi, Tama Tonga, Hikuleo** and **Jado** defeated **Jay White, Karl Anderson, Luke Gallows** and **Gedo** in 12:15; **Will Ospreay** defeated **Shota Umino** in 15:30; **FTR (Cash Wheeler** and **Dax Harwood)** defeated **Aussie Open (Kyle Fletcher** and **Mark Davis)** in 31:59.

Was It Any Good? It was a bit of a one-match card in truth, but it was a particularly good match! Aussie Open and FTR were comfortably two of the top five tag teams on the planet and were set to collide for the first time in London, England. The meeting did not disappoint and generated significant hype for the event which in turn took an eternity to arrive on the promotion's streaming service, New Japan World. In other notes, Will Ospreay took out Shota Umino in a decent encounter while several Brits were afforded opportunities to impress, including Dan Moloney, Michael Oku, Ricky Knight Jr and Alex Windsor.

ROYAL QUEST II NIGHT #2
02-10-22, London, England **NJPW**

El Desperado and **Douki** defeated **Michael Oku** and **Robbie X** in 9:33; **Sanada** and **Hiromu Takahashi** defeated **North West Strong (Ethan Allen** and **Luke Jacob)** in 14:04; **Jazzy Gabert** defeated **Ava White** in 10:34; **Will Ospreay, Great-O-Khan, Mark Davis, Kyle Fletcher** and **Gideon Grey** defeated **FTR (Cash Wheeler** and **Dax Harwood), Shota Umino, Gabriel Kidd** and **Ricky Knight Jr.** in 16:57; **Hiroshi Tanahashi, Tama Tonga** and **Hikuleo** defeated **Jay White, Luke Gallows** and **Karl Anderson** in 10:54; **Kazuchika Okada** defeated **Bad Dude Tito** in 8:13; **Tomohiro Ishii** defeated **Yota Tsuji** in 17:36; **Tetsuya Naito** defeated **Zack Sabre Jr.** in 21:05.

Was It Any Good? Night two was perhaps a more balanced affair, with several interesting matches on the bill. Top of the card was UK export Zack Sabre Jr. who fell to Tetsuya Naito in a match that was good but fell short of the pair's previous efforts. More impressive was Tomohiro Ishii's clash with recent young lion graduate Yota Tsuji, who had been plying his trade in the UK while on excursion. This was a very good match indeed and did much to enhance Tsuji's stature ahead of an eventual return to New Japan proper. The remainder of the card passed without incident but was in large part forgettable.

BOUND FOR GLORY '22
07-10-22, Albany, New York **Impact**

Frankie Kazarian defeated **Mike Bailey** to win the Impact X Division Title in 12:30; **Mickie James** defeated **Mia Yim** in a Last Rodeo Match in 10:56; **The Death Dollz (Jessicka** and **Taya Valkyrie)** defeated **VXT (Chelsea Green** and **Deonna Purrazzo)** to win the Impact Knockouts World Tag Team Title in 7:24; **The Kingdom (Matt Taven** and **Mike Bennett)** defeated **The Motor City Machine Guns (Alex Shelley** and **Chris Sabin)** in 16:35; **Bully Ray** won a 20-Person Call Your Shot Gauntlet Match in 29:18; **Jordynne Grace** defeated **Masha Slamovich** in 16:00; **Josh Alexander** defeated **Eddie Edwards** in 28:02.

Was It Any Good? It was, bar a few questionable booking decisions. Certainly from an in-ring perspective, BFG largely brought the goods, with several top tier bouts on display. Chief among these was Josh Alexander's title retention over former champion Eddie Edwards. Both men are hard workers and this was a notably crunching affair, with Alexander put under real duress while having to fight from underneath. Also of note was Jordynne Grace's Knockouts Title victory over the rampaging Masha Slamovich. This was arguably the best Knockouts match of the year, which is significant praise when you consider the depth of the IMPACT women's locker room. While there was no knocking the content of Frankie Kazarian's X-Division Title win over Mike Bailey, the result was something of a head-scratcher given Bailey's trajectory until that point. Similarly, the decision to have veteran performer Bully Ray win the Call Your Shot Gauntlet Match at the expense of younger talent such as Steve Maclin, whom fans appeared ready to get behind, left some cold and appeared a step backwards.

BATTLE OF THE BELTS IV
07-10-22, Washington, D.C. **AEW**

Pac defeated **Trent Beretta** in 14:25; **Jade Cargill** defeated **Willow Nightingale** in 7:30; **FTR (Cash Wheeler** and **Dax Harwood)** defeated **Gates Of Agony (Toa Liona** and **Kaun)** in 13:26.

Was It Any Good? It wasn't exactly noteworthy. There were no title changes on the show, but the All-Atlantic Championship match between Pac and Trent Beretta is worth seeking out. The pair had an engaging encounter that finished just prior to the 15-mintue mark and contained plenty of impressive action. Also on the card, Jade Cargill extended her AEW record to 39-0 with a win over the spirited Willow Nightingale. A far cry from the match prior, this was another step up for the TBS Champion, who looked better against the more complete Nightingale. The main event saw FTR defend their ROH World Tag Team Titles against the Gates Of Agony, Bishop Kaun and Toa Liona. The match was good, if unexceptional, and featured a funny cameo from The Gunns who continued to get under the champions' skin. As an hour's worth of pro wrestling, it was an easy watch.

EXTREME RULES '22
08-10-22, Philadelphia, Pennsylvania **WWE**

The Brawling Brutes (Sheamus, Butch and **Ridge Holland)** defeated **Imperium (Gunther, Ludwig Kaiser** and **Giovanni Vinci)** in a Good Old Fashioned Donnybrook Match in 17:50; **Ronda Rousey** defeated **Liv Morgan** in an Extreme Rules Match to win the WWE SmackDown Women's Title in 12:05; **Karrion Kross** defeated **Drew McIntyre** in a Strap Match in 10:20; **Bianca Belair** defeated **Bayley** in a Ladder Match in 16:40; **Finn Balor** defeated **Edge** in an "I Quit" Match in 29:55; **Matt Riddle** defeated **Seth Rollins** in a Fight Pit Match in 16:35.

Was It Any Good? It was okay. Sheamus and Gunther again carried the load between the ropes, this time with their Imperium and Brawling Brutes buddies on hand for a wild brawl that set things off with a bang. Unfortunately, Extreme Rules came crashing down to earth with Ronda Rousey's SmackDown Women's Title victory over Liv Morgan, a sloppy encounter with a result that pleased nobody. The recently-returned Karrion Kross looked a pale imitation of the top-level superstar he was being pushed as in his strap match over Drew McIntyre. Kross's act seems impressive on first glance, but falls apart as soon as the bell rings. Bianca Belair and Bayley gave plenty of effort in their Ladder Match, but there were some sloppy moments that dragged it down. Finn Balor and Edge dragged out their "I Quit" Match for half an hour—the first half of which was just punch-kick brawling around the arena. The second half, though, was WWE sports entertainment at its finest, featuring high drama with Edge handcuffed to the ropes, Rey Mysterio getting involved and Edge's wife Beth Phoenix getting wiped out with a conchairto. The Fight Pit main event between Seth Rollins and Matt Riddle—refereed by UFC veteran Daniel Cormier—was a better idea on paper than in execution. The nature of the cage meant the bout was almost impossible to film and thus difficult to watch, and Cormier did nothing of note to warrant his inclusion. WWE's strict "no blood" policy also hurts stipulation bouts like these. The real main event came afterwards when Bray Wyatt made his long-awaited WWE return to a huge response, sans his Fiend gimmick. Doing very little other than making a brief appearance in the aisle, Wyatt and WWE left fans both pleased and wanting more, the hallmarks of a job well done.

DECLARATION OF POWER
10-10-22, Tokyo, Japan **NJPW**

David Finlay, Robbie Eagles and **Ren Narita** defeated **El Desperado, Yoshinobu Kanemaru** and **Douki** in 7:28; **Taichi** and **Zack Sabre Jr.** defeated **Shane Haste** and **Bad Dude Tito** in 9:58; **Hiroshi Tanahashi, Hikuelo** and **Ryusuke Taguchi** defeated **Evil, Yujiro Takahashi** and **Sho** in 7:14; **Great-O-Khan** and **Jeff Cobb** defeated **Hirooki Goto** and **Yoshi-Hashi** in 10:09; **Tetsuya Naito, Sanada, Bushi** and **Hiromu Takahashi** defeated **Will Ospreay, Aaron Henare, TJP** and **Francesco Akira** in 8:07; **Master Wato** defeated **Taiji Ishimori** in 14:40; **Shingo Takagi** defeated **El Phantasmo** in a Who's Your Daddy Match in 16:01; **Kazuchika Okada** defeated **Jonah** in 19:53; **Jay White** defeated **Tama Tonga** in 31:07.

Was It Any Good? This was another decent show from New Japan that moved a few things forward without ever threatening to become a must-see event. Pleasingly, there were some different pairings on tap throughout the card, which was welcomed following a series of repetitive booking choices. This was highlighted in the main event, when freshly babyface Tama Tonga fell to IWGP World Heavyweight Champion Jay White in a solid effort. Of similar quality was the return match between Kazuchika Okada and JONAH, following the Australian's shock victory during the G1 Climax. However, unlike the G1 clash, the stakes were null and void here, as Okada had already stamped his ticket to Wrestle Kingdom and appeared in little danger of losing a second time. Elsewhere on the card, Master Wato continued making strides in a decent encounter with veteran junior ace Taiji Ishimori, while El Phantasmo's transition into the heavyweight ranks continued to gather steam, despite eating the loss here to Shingo Takagi. Overall, this was a relatively light-hearted affair which featured some fresh match-ups but within minimal stakes.

TRIPLEMANIA XXX: MEXICO CITY
15-10-22, Mexico City, Mexico **AAA**

Hermanos Lee (Dragon Lee and **Dralistico)** defeated **Los Vipers (Latigo** and **Toxin), Arez** and **Willie Mack,** and **Komander** and **Myzteziz Jr.** in a Four Way Match in 9:00; **Taya Valkyrie** defeated **Kamille** in 15:18; **Brian Cage, Johnny Caballero** and **Sam Adonis** defeated **El Cuatrero, Forastero** and **Sanson,** and **Bandido, Laredo Kid** and **Psycho Clown** in a Three Way Match in 12:44; **Pagano** defeated **Cibernetico** in a Lucha de Apuestas Hair vs. Hair Match in 21:43; **El Hijo del Vikingo** defeated **Rey Fenix** in 19:27; **Pentagon Jr.** defeated **Villano IV** in the Ruleta De La Muerte Final Mask vs. Mask Match in 25:30.

Was It Any Good? The top two matches were outstanding, but a patchy undercard dragged down the overall quality of the show. Starting with the positives, the highly anticipated clash between Rey Fenix and El Hijo del Vikingo somehow managed to meet, if not exceed, expectations, with Vikingo eventually retaining his AAA Mega Championship. This was state-of-the-art lucha libre, packed with finely tuned storytelling and breathtaking moves—a must watch for fans of the genre. Sticking with the impactful storytelling was the main event, and finale of the Ruleta de la Muerte tournament, between Pentagon Jr. and veteran Villano IV. In contrast to the Mega Championship bout, this was a violent, blood-soaked brawl in which the AEW man was back in his element, looking every inch the star as he terrorised the tenured luchador. Sealing the victory with his brutal arm breaker, Pentagon was awarded his opponent's coveted mask as the curtain fell on Villano's historic career. Earlier in the card, the Hair vs Hair match between Pagano and Cibernetico was a bit of a mess, while the AAA Trios Title bout was fine but nothing more. Taya Valkyrie upended the nigh-on-unbeatable NWA Women's champion Kamille in a AAA Reina de Reinas Championship match (Kamille's belt was not on the line) which had its moments. Certainly worth seeking out for the two big matches, as well as the fun opening sprint for the AAA Tag Title number one contendership.

HALLOWEEN HAVOC '22
22-10-22, Orlando, Florida **NXT**

Wes Lee defeated **Carmelo Hayes, Oro Mensa, Von Wagner** and **Nathan Frazer** in a Ladder Match to win the vacant NXT North American Title in 22:25; **Apollo Crews** defeated **Grayson Waller** in a Casket Match in 14:27; **Roxanne Perez** defeated **Cora Jade** in a Weapons Wild Match in 12:25; **Julius Creed** defeated **Damon Kemp** in an Ambulance Match in 14:09; **Mandy Rose** defeated **Alba Fyre** in 7:07; **Bron Breakker** defeated **Ilja Dragunov** and **JD McDonagh** in a Three Way Match in 23:47.

Was It Any Good? The main event was, but the rest of the card suffered from forced stipulations that were more miss than hit. By loading the show with gimmick matches, Halloween Havoc felt more like a low rent Extreme Rules tribute show than a standalone special.

There were enjoyable moments in the opening ladder match but it was nothing that has not already been done a thousand times before, and was largely just a collection of unrelated spots. The three-way headliner carried the show, but it was former NXT UK stars JD McDonagh and Ilja Dragunov who shined brightest in the bout rather than its victor Bron Breakker.

RUMBLE ON 44TH STREET
28-10-22, New York City, New York **NJPW**

Yujiro Takahashi and Sho defeated **Rocky Romero** and **Yoh** in 7:42; **The Motor City Machine Guns (Alex Shelley** and **Chris Sabin)** defeated **Aussie Open (Kyle Fletcher** and **Mark Davis)**, and **Kevin Knight** and **The DKC** in a Three Way Match to win the Strong Openweight Tag Team Title in 13:42; **Fred Rosser** defeated **Jonathan Gresham** in 14:37; **Homicide, Wheeler Yuta** and **Shota Umino** defeated **Tom Lawlor, Royce Isaacs** and **Jorel Nelson** in 12:15; **Minoru Suzuki** defeated **Clark Connors** in 15:50; **Mayu Iwatani** defeated **KiLynn King** in 11:47; **Shingo Takagi** defeated **El Phantasmo** in a New York City Street Fight in 20:59; **Bullet Club (Jay White** and **Juice Robinson)** defeated **Kazuchika Okada** and **Eddie Kingston** in 20:15.

Was It Any Good? There was nothing spectacular here but that didn't take away from what was a fun and easy watch, peppered with unique pairings and the beginnings of New Japan's foray into women's wrestling. NJPW had gone to the trouble of bringing Stardom ace Mayu Iwatani to New York for this one, pairing her with rising US star KiLynn King in a SWA Title defence. This was a decent showing from both, with King staking a claim for future involvement in New Japan's burgeoning female division. Shingo Takagi and El Phantasmo arguably had the match of the night in a chaotic New York City Street Fight for the KOPW Title. After initial scepticism, KOPW has proven to be a welcome addition to New Japan shows, offering talent (and fans) something different to sink their teeth into. Also on the card was a fairly run of the mill tag match between Bullet Club's Jay White and Juice Robinson, and Kazuchika Okada and Eddie Kingston, a STRONG Openweight Title defence for Fred Rosser versus Jonathan Gresham, and a fun dust-up between Minoru Suzuki and Clark Connors, who was flanked by Ken Shamrock, no less. The STRONG Openweight Tag Titles changed hands on the night as well, in a good match between The Motor City Machine Guns and outgoing titlists Aussie Open which didn't quite hit the heights expected of two teams of that calibre. All in all, an eclectic mix and a step in the right direction for New Japan's US arm.

BATTLE AUTUMN '22
05-11-22, Osaka, Japan **NJPW**

TJP and Francesco Akira defeated **Bushi** and **Titan** in 11:36; **Aaron Henare, Gideon Grey, Kyle Fletcher** and **Mark Davis** defeated **Hiroshi Tanahashi, Toru Yano, David Finlay** and **Alex Zayne** in 9:50; **Hikuleo** defeated **Yujiro Takahashi** in :28; **Ren Narita** defeated **Sanada** in 14:31; **Zack Sabre Jr.** defeated **Evil** in 4:48; **Master Wato** and **El Desperado** defeated **Taiji Ishimori** and **Hiromu Takahashi** in 16:48; **Kazuchika Okada** and **Tama Tonga** defeated **Jay White** and **Kenta** in 17:34; **FTR (Cash Wheeler** and **Dax Harwood)** defeated **Great-O-Khan** and **Jeff Cobb** in 17:31; **Will Ospreay** defeated **Tetsuya Naito** in 30:07.

Was It Any Good? It had a lot going for it, that's for sure, and when reviewed alongside New Japan's other marquee events of the year, Battle Autumn compares favourably. Despite not being one of the bigger cards of the year, the event held a refreshing aura more akin to spring than autumn. That was in part due to the ongoing

Television Title tournament which condensed matches down to 15 minutes, prompting some much-needed urgency for a company whose title tilts tend to go long. Ren Narita and Zack Sabre Jr. both performed well in this environment. TJP and Francesco Akira continued their enjoyable reign atop the junior tag team division with a fun victory over Busgi and Titán. IWGP tag champs FTR finally got their Japanese bow on the card, having represented the company in both the US and UK previously. The pair's tussle with Great-O-Khan and Jeff Cobb was well-received and added another layer of star power to the middle of the card. Finally, at the top of the bill, Will Ospreay and Tetsuya Naito were afforded plenty of room to work in an enjoyable main event that benefited from what was a relatively fresh pairing relative to other NJPW finales. Generally speaking this was one of the company's more easy-to-watch events of the year, with very few dips and plenty of highs.

CROWN JEWEL '22
05-11-22, Riyadh, Saudi Arabia **WWE**

Brock Lesnar defeated **Bobby Lashley** in 6:00; **Damage CTRL (Dakota Kai** and **Iyo Sky)** defeated **Alexa Bliss** and **Asuka** to win the WWE Women's Tag Team Title in 12:50; **Drew McIntyre** defeated **Karrion Kross** in a Steel Cage Match in 13:00; **The Judgment Day (Finn Balor, Damian Priest** and **Dominik Mysterio)** defeated **The O.C. (AJ Styles, Luke Gallows** and **Karl Anderson)** in 14:00; **Braun Strowman** defeated **Omos** in 7:20; **The Usos (Jey Uso** and **Jimmy Uso)** defeated **The Brawling Brutes (Ridge Holland** and **Butch)** in 10:45; **Bianca Belair** defeated **Bayley** in a Last Woman Standing Match in 20:20; **Roman Reigns** defeated **Logan Paul** in 24:50.

Was It Any Good? It was solid, but mostly forgettable. Brock Lesnar and Bobby Lashley went at it hammer and tongs in the opener, in which Lashley surprisingly dominated before the banana skin finish The six minute run time left viewers feeling somewhat short-changed, however. Damage CTRL regained the Women's Tag Team Titles less than a week after dropping them to Alexa Bliss and Asuka and felt like an exercise in futility. Clearly WWE wanted to have a title change in Saudi Arabia on the record books, for whatever reason. Karrion Kross again failed to impress in his cage match defeat to Drew McIntyre, as his brief push came crashing to an end. Judgment Day vs. The O.C. had its moments but rarely ventured beyond the realms of a decent TV outing. The most positive thing one can say about the clash of the giants between Braun Strowman and Omos is that it was nowhere near as bad as it could have been. Bianca Belair and Bayley again worked hard in their Last Woman Standing Match, with their effort levels making up for the surprising lack of chemistry they have together. An ill-advised spot involving a golf cart should have been scrapped though, as it went wrong repeatedly and hurt the flow of the contest. The real standout from the show was the main event, in which Roman Reigns once again defended his titles in Saudi against an unlikely opponent. In this case, Logan Paul, who built on his impressive form in his previous two WWE bouts and took things to the next level, giving a main event calibre performance that elevated this to one of WWE's best matches of the year, setting a new high bar for all celebrity gimmick matches to live up to.

HARD TIMES 3
12-11-22, Chalmette, Louisiana **NWA**

Max The Impaler defeated **Natalia Markova** in a Voodoo Queen Casket Match in 8:14; **Davey Richards** defeated **Colby Corino** in 6:42; **The Question Mark II** defeated **The Question Mark** in a Mask vs. Mask Match in 6:00; **Kerry Morton** defeated **Homicide** to win the

NWA World Junior Heavyweight Title in 10:02; **Thrillbilly Silas** defeated **Odinson** in 4:43; **The Fixers (Jay Bradley** and **Wrecking Ball Legursky)** defeated **The Spectaculars (Brady Pierce** and **Rush Freeman)** in 9:15; **Cyon** defeated **Dak Draper** in 6:01; **Pretty Empowered (Ella Envy** and **Kenzie Paige)** defeated **Madi Wrenkowski** and **Missa Kate** in 8:12; **EC3** defeated **Thom Latimer** by DQ in 8:31; **La Rebelion (Bestia 666** and **Mecha Wolf)** defeated **Hawx Aerie (Luke Hawx** and **PJ Hawx)** in 10:48; **Kamille** defeated **Chelsea Green** and **KiLynn King** in a Three Way Match in 8:59; **Tyrus** defeated **Trevor Murdoch** and **Matt Cardona** in a Three Way Match to win the NWA Worlds Heavyweight Title in 10:03.

Was It Any Good? The show was in-line with the general NWA offering of relatively vanilla professional wrestling complemented by highly characterised promos and character work. The latter point was hit and miss here, particularly in the mid-match dialogue between EC3 and Thom Latimer, where the former NXT star alluded to Latimer's very real run-ins with the police and domestic abuse charges. This was beyond the pale, to say the least. In terms of match quality, there were a few contests that stepped outside of the prescribed formula, most notably the NWA Tag Title match between champions Mecha Wolf and Bestia 666, and Luke and PJ Hawx. The NWA Women's Title three-way was also decent, with KiLynn King again shining. Davey Richards' MLW National Openweight Title defence over Colby Corino was fun while it lasted, and Kerry Morton's NWA Junior Heavyweight Title triumph over Homicide was just fine. The main event saw the hulking Tyrus add his name to the 'Ten Pounds of Gold' when he bested Trevor Murdoch and Matt Cardona to become champion. There's a marketing edge here, given Tyrus' relative prominence as a contributor to FOX News, however this still felt like a dubious booking decision. Overall, Hard Times 3 was decent enough, but could have benefited from a thinner undercard and allowing more time for the title matches to unfold.

FULL GEAR '22
19-11-22, Newark, New Jersey **AEW**

Jungle Boy defeated **Luchasaurus** in a Steel Cage Match in 18:40; **Death Triangle (Pac, Penta El Zero Miedo** and **Rey Fenix)** defeated **The Elite (Kenny Omega, Matt Jackson** and **Nick Jackson)** in 18:40; **Jade Cargill** defeated **Nyla Rose** in 8:00; **Chris Jericho** defeated **Bryan Danielson, Claudio Castagnoli** and **Sammy Guevara** in a Four Way Match in 21:30; **Saraya** defeated **Dr. Britt Baker D.M.D.** in 12:30; **Samoa Joe** defeated **Wardlow** and **Powerhouse Hobbs** in a Three Way Match to win the AEW TNT Title in 9:55; **Sting** and **Darby Allin** defeated **Jeff Jarrett** and **Jay Lethal** in a No DQ Match in 11:00; **Jamie Hayter** defeated **Toni Storm** to win the interim AEW Women's Title in 15:00; **The Acclaimed (Anthony Bowens** and **Max Caster)** defeated **Swerve In Our Glory (Swerve Strickland** and **Keith Lee)** in 19:40; **MJF** defeated **Jon Moxley** to win the AEW World Title in 23:15.

Was It Any Good? Full Gear was a much-needed return to form following the fallout of All Out. With excellent matches throughout the card and the return of The Elite, the PPV had plenty to keep fans happy. However, more importantly, Full Gear installed several new, homegrown champions at the top of their respective divisions, providing a soft reset of sorts for the company amidst increasing angst surrounding ex-WWE talents. The big news, of course, was MJF's coronation as AEW World Champion. The brash New Yorker dislodged company workhorse Jon Moxley thanks to a double cross from William Regal to take his rightful place atop the AEW mountain. Likewise, Tony Khan capitalised on

the groundswell of support for Jamie Hayter, booking the Brit to knock off Toni Storm in a decent contest for the AEW Women's World Title. The Acclaimed crystallised their ascension with a series-winning victory over Swerve In Our Glory, whom they had lifted the tag straps from at September's Grand Slam while 'Jungle Boy' Jack Perry scored the biggest victory of his career in defeating former partner Luchasaurus in a very good cage match opener. There were a few curious results on the night, not least in Death Triangle's Trios Title retention over the returning Young Bucks and Kenny Omega—that one seemed to confuse the live crowd following what was a very compelling contest. Likewise, Samoa Joe's TNT Title win over Wardlow seemed ill-timed, with the 'War Dog' already struggling for momentum. Britt Baker did what she could with a rusty Saraya in what was a decent match on a card full of bangers. But overall, Full Gear was the perfect tonic for what had been a tumultuous few months for All Elite Wrestling.

HISTORIC X-OVER
20-11-22, Tokyo, Japan **NJPW/Stardom**

Lio Rush, Tomohiro Ishii, Yoh and **Yoshi-Hashi** defeated **Dick Togo, Evil, Sho** and **Yujiro Takahashi** in 7:05; **AZM, Lady C** and **Saya Kamitami** defeated **Himeka, Mai Sakurai** and **Thekla** in 9:20; **Giulia** and **Zack Sabre Jr.** defeated **Syuri** and **Tom Lawlor** in 10:20; **Tam Nakano, Natsupoi, Taichi** and **Yoshinobu Kanemaru** defeated **Momo Watanabe, Starlight Kid, El Desperado** and **Douki** in 12:01; **Hiroshi Tanahashi** and **Utami Hayashishita** defeated **Hirooki Goto** and **Maika** in 9:36; **Kyle Fletcher, Mark Davis, Francesco Akira, TJP** and **Gideon Grey** defeated **Bushi, Hiromu Takahashi, Sanada, Shingo Takagi** and **Tetsuya Naito** in 9:55; **Kazuchika Okada, Toru Yano** and **The Great Muta** defeated **Great-O-Khan, Jeff Cobb** and **Aaron Henare** in 9:48; **Will Ospreay** defeated **Shota Umino** in 23:30; **Kairi** defeated **Mayu Iwatani** to win the inaugural IWGP Women's Title in 25:28.

Was It Any Good? It was very good. The crossover between the New Japan and Stardom rosters breathed a hitherto unseen freshness into the New Japan ranks, and yielded some very good matches indeed. Chiefly though, this was enjoyable due to the differing dynamics between NJPW and Stardom performers and the unique interactions it presented. For example, the serially snide Zack Sabre Jr. cracked arguably his first genuine smile in a New Japan presser following his interactions with tag partner Giulia, while Syuri's relative bemusement over 'Filthy' Tom Lawlor's well publicised fandom was a joy to behold. One match that needed no crossover frivolity was the inaugural IWGP Women's Championship match between Kairi and Mayu Iwatani. This was an excellent showcase for both wrestlers, who put on a thrilling, hard-hitting bout which finished a shade over the 25 minute mark. Kairi's incredible elbow drop will seemingly never get old and that was again the case here, as the Pirate Princess unleashed her trademark dive to carve her name into the history books. All told, this event was a lot of fun and highlighted how beneficial the relationship between the two Bushiroad owned companies can potentially be.

SURVIVOR SERIES WARGAMES
26-11-22, Boston, Massachusetts **WWE**

Team Belair (Bianca Belair, Alexa Bliss, Asuka, Mia Yim and **Becky Lynch)** defeated **Team Bayley (Bayley, Dakota Kai, Iyo Sky, Nikki Cross** and **Rhea Ripley)** in a WarGames Match in 39:40; **AJ Styles** defeated **Finn Balor** in 18:25; **Ronda Rousey** defeated **Shotzi** in 7:15; **Austin Theory** defeated **Seth Rollins** and **Bobby Lashley** in a Three Way Match to win the WWE United States Title in 14:50; **The Bloodline (Roman Reigns, Sami Zayn, Solo**

Sikoa, Jey Uso and Jimmy Uso) defeated The Brawling Brutes (Sheamus, Butch and Ridge Holland), Drew McIntyre and Kevin Owens in a WarGames Match in 38:30.

Was It Any Good? In places it was. Dropping the RAW vs. SmackDown concept in favour of debuting WarGames on the main roster was a masterstroke from Triple H, but presenting two such bouts on the same card was overkill. The inherent issue is down to the rules of the bout, which essentially render the majority of it pointless until the "match beyond", which is the only time a finish can occur. If the bout features superior workers with an ongoing storyline thread and a reason to go at it, then it can work wonders, as it did so successfully for WCW from 1987-1989, and again in 1991 and 1992. Unfortunately, the women's WarGames match did not have that, and instead was just a parade of spots and moments that dragged on for 40 interminable minutes. It was not bad, per se, but it was a slog to endure. Shotzi again proved that she should be nowhere near the main roster with another error-laden display opposite the obviously uninterested Ronda Rousey; this match belonged nowhere near a WWE supercard. Fortunately, the rest of the show was very much worthwhile. Austin Theory's push was reignited when he snared the US Title in an invigorating three-way with Seth Rollins and Bobby Lashley, AJ Styles and Finn Balor had a competent and engaging wrestling match, and the main event WarGames clash was WWE's unique brand of sports entertainment at its finest. Although it suffered from the same issues as the women's bout, the ongoing thread surrounding Sami Zayn's loyalty to the Bloodline's cause and whether he would prove himself to the sceptics in the group by willingly fighting his best friend Kevin Owens was compelling viewing. Zayn duly proved himself, preventing Owens from pinning Roman Reigns and assisting Roman in putting KO down for the three count, thus cementing his status as a genuine Bloodline ally and finally receiving acceptance from the entire group. It was brilliant storytelling.

DEADLINE
10-12-22, Orlando, Florida **NXT**

Roxanne Perez (2) defeated Zoey Stark (1), Cora Jade (1), Indi Hartwell (1) and Kiana James (0) in an Iron Survivor Challenge in 25:00; Isla Dawn defeated Alba Fyre in 9:52; The New Day (Kofi Kingston and Xavier Woods) defeated Pretty Deadly (Elton Prince and Kit Wilson) to win the NXT Tag Team Title in 14:05; Grayson Waller (3) defeated Carmelo Hayes (2), Joe Gacy (2), Axiom (2) and JD McDonagh (0) in an Iron Survivor Challenge in 25:00; Bron Breakker defeated Apollo Crews in 14:34.

Was It Any Good? It was. The new Iron Survivor Challenge concept that debuted on the show was a triumph, providing WWE with a fresh gimmick match that could and should become firmly entrenched in WWE lore in the future. The women's bout set up the concept nicely in the opener, and with fans more familiar with the rules the men's bout was even better received. The action varied in quality elsewhere, as is typically the case on modern NXT shows, but there was a memorable moment with main roster loanees New Day capturing the NXT Tag Titles, before Bron Breakker later reasserted his dominance with a victory over Apollo Crews in a decent main event.

FINAL BATTLE '22
10-12-22, Arlington, Texas **ROH**

Blake Christian and AR Fox defeated La Faccion Ingobernable (Rush and Dralistico) in 10:35; Athena defeated Mercedes Martinez to win the ROH Women's

World Title in 13:10; Swerve In Our Glory (Keith Lee and Swerve Strickland) defeated Shane Taylor Promotions (Shane Taylor and JD Griffey) in 13:50; The Embassy (Brian Cage, Kaun and Toa Liona) defeated Dalton Castle and The Boys (Brandon Tate and Brent Tate) to win the ROH World Six-Man Tag Team Title in 10:05; Wheeler Yuta defeated Daniel Garcia in a Pure Rules Match to win the ROH Pure Title in 14:50; The Briscoe Brothers (Jay Briscoe and Mark Briscoe) defeated FTR (Cash Wheeler and Dax Harwood) in a Double Dog Collar Match to win the ROH World Tag Team Title in 22:20; Samoa Joe defeated Juice Robinson in 13:40; Claudio Castagnoli defeated Chris Jericho to win the ROH World Title in 17:15.

Was It Any Good? As an overall show, it was perhaps a step down from Death Before Dishonor, but was still a very strong outing nonetheless, and contained one of the year's best matches in the final meeting between The Briscoes and FTR in a dog collar match. Between this match and the CM Punk-MJF affair from AEW Revolution, 2022 did more to rejuvenate the dog collar stipulation than any year in the past two decades. This was a gruelling, blood-soaked affair, packed with emotion and world class action. The Briscoes eventually went over their rivals and were restored to their default as ROH's top tandem (a win made all the more poignant in hindsight). In the main event, Claudio Castagnoli ended Chris Jericho's fleeting run with the ROH World Title, with Jericho unexpectedly tapping out mid-big swing in one of the more unique finishes of the year. Wheeler Yuta also reclaimed his gold, relieving Daniel Garcia of the ROH Pure Title in a really good effort. Athena upended Mercedes Martinez to become the brand's women's champ after a fair outing. This was the right call as Martinez had struggled to catch on as champion, although her booking hadn't exactly helped. Brian Cage was clearly back in Tony Khan's good graces, as alongside The Gates of Agony, 'The Machine' ripped the company's trios straps from Dalton Castle and The Boys. Swerve In Our Glory got another run out on the show, dispatching Lee's old running buddy Shane Taylor and partner JD Griffey in a placeholder match to continue the duo's gradual dissension.

TRIBUTE TO THE TROOPS '22
17-12-22, Indianapolis, Indiana **WWE**

Braun Strowman defeated LA Knight in 2:12; Ronda Rousey and Shayna Baszler defeated Emma and Tamina in 7:34; Drew McIntyre, Ricochet and Sheamus defeated Imperium (Gunther, Giovanni Vinci and Ludwig Kaiser) in 16:34.

Was It Any Good? No. WWE's annual Tribute To The Troops used to feel like a special event back in the days when it took place on military bases in war zones and featured random cameos to please the servicemen in attendance, but the unique setting has long since been dropped in favour of a generic arena in the US. As a result, Tribute To The Troops has lost its appeal as an entertainment spectacle and feels like little more than a truncated version of RAW or SmackDown. While it is commendable that WWE continues to honour and support US soldiers, there's simply nothing worthwhile on the non-canon Tribute show in terms of in-ring action or storyline progression.

DREAM QUEENDOM '22
29-12-22, Tokyo, Japan **Stardom**

Hanan, Mayu Iwatani and Momo Kohgo defeated Hazuki, Koguma and Saya Iida in a Pre-Triangle Derby Match in 12:04; Mina Shirakawa and Unagi Sayaka defeated Mai Sakurai and Thekla in 10:13; Himeka and Maika defeated Ami Sourei and Mirai, and Natsuko

Tora and **Ruaka** in a Three Way Match in 10:06; **Kairi** vs. **Utami Hayashishita** ended in a draw in 15:00; **Hiragi Kurumi, Risa Sera** and **Suzu Suzuki** defeated **Momo Watanabe, Saki Kashima** and **Starlight Kid** in a Hardcore Match to win the Artist Of Stardom Title in 15:54; **Nanae Takahashi** and **Yuu** defeated **Natsupoi** and **Tam Nakano** to win the Goddesses Of Stardom Title in 15:57; **Saya Kamitani** defeated **Haruka Umesaki** in 16:33; **Giulia** defeated **Syuri** to win the World Of Stardom Title in 29:51.

Was It Any Good? 2022 was a strong year for Stardom on PPV and this was no exception. The crux of the show was the conclusion of a story that had been brewing gradually for years, that being the inevitable clash between former stablemates Giulia and World of Stardom Champion Syuri. The pair's slow-burn rivalry had been incredibly unique in that it was almost bereft of animosity but yet still had plenty of heat. Only in this instance, that was born out of emotion, rather than the typical grudge matches we see in pro wrestling. The match delivered tenfold, and was comfortably one of the best matches of the year, with Giulia taking the title with seconds left to spare (ahead of a time limit draw). Engaging stuff. Elsewhere, there was plenty of good action to get into, not least the High Speed Title opener between champion AZM and challenger Saya Iida. At the time of writing, Stardom's High Speed division feels like a well-kept secret from western audiences but one wonders how much longer they can contain it. Kairi notched another strong outing on her comeback trail, this time in a spirited 15-minute draw with former champion Utami Hayashishita, while the insurgent Prominence stable overturned Stardom mainstays Oedo Tai in a Hardcore Match to pick up the Artist of Stardom belts. Practically every match on this card delivered and credit must be given to booker Rossy Ogawa for its structure, with built carefully towards the impactful main event.

2022 TELEVISION RESULTS

WWE MONDAY NIGHT RAW

JANUARY 3 *Greenville, SC*

Alpha Academy (Chad Gable and Otis) defeated RK-Bro (Randy Orton and Riddle) in 2:40; Reggie and Dana Brooke defeated Tamina and Akira Tozawa in 1:10; Queen Zelina and Carmella defeated Super Brutality (Rhea Ripley and Nikki A.S.H.) in 2:40; The Street Profits (Angelo Dawkins and Montez Ford) defeated Apollo Crews and Commander Azeez in 2:15; Damian Priest defeated Dolph Ziggler in 9:00; Omos defeated AJ Styles in 3:45; Bobby Lashley defeated Big E, Seth Rollins and Kevin Owens in a Fatal Four Way Match in 18:40.

JANUARY 10 *Philadelphia, PA*

Alpha Academy (Chad Gable and Otis) defeated RK-Bro (Randy Orton and Riddle) to win the WWE RAW Tag Team Title in 8:57; The Dirty Dawgs (Dolph Ziggler and Robert Roode) and Apollo Crews defeated Damian Priest and The Street Profits (Angelo Dawkins and Montez Ford) in 8:30; Seth Rollins defeated Big E in 18:00; Omos defeated Nick Sanders in 1:35; AJ Styles defeated Austin Theory by DQ in 7:00; Doudrop defeated Liv Morgan and Bianca Belair in a Triple Threat Match in 14:45.

JANUARY 17 *Tulsa, OK*

Becky Lynch and Doudrop defeated Bianca Belair and Liv Morgan in 3:00; Kevin Owens defeated Damian Priest in 10:55; Austin Theory defeated Finn Balor in 6:06; Omos defeated Reggie in :28; The Mysterios (Rey Mysterio and Dominik Mysterio) and The Street Profits (Angelo Dawkins and Montez Ford) defeated Apollo Crews, Commander Azeez and The Dirty Dawgs (Dolph Ziggler and Robert Roode) in 8:00; Bobby Lashley defeated Seth Rollins by DQ in 13:17.

JANUARY 24 *Toledo, OH*

Bianca Belair defeated Queen Zelina in 3:45; Kevin Owens defeated Damian Priest by DQ in 9:35; Rhea Ripley, Dana Brooke and Liv Morgan defeated Carmella, Tamina and Nikki A.S.H. in 2:20; Randy Orton defeated Chad Gable in 13:55; AJ Styles defeated Austin Theory in 17:00; The Mysterios (Rey Mysterio and Dominik Mysterio) defeated The Street Profits (Angelo Dawkins and Montez Ford) in 8:00.

JANUARY 31 *Cincinnati, OH*

Rhea Ripley defeated Nikki A.S.H. in 8:10; The Miz defeated Dominik Mysterio in 2:10; Austin Theory defeated Kevin Owens in 11:25; Angelo Dawkins defeated Dolph Ziggler in 4:30; Riddle defeated Otis in 7:25; Bianca Belair defeated Carmella in 5:30; AJ Styles defeated Rey Mysterio in 11:35.

FEBRUARY 7 *Denver, CO*

Alpha Academy (Chad Gable and Otis) defeated The Street Profits (Angelo Dawkins and Montez Ford) in 5:37; AJ Styles defeated Damian Priest in 4:58; Dominik Mysterio defeated The Miz in 1:47; Bianca Belair defeated Nikki A.S.H. in 4:01; Kevin Owens defeated Austin Theory in 9:06; Doudrop defeated Liv Morgan in 7:59; Riddle defeated Seth Rollins by DQ in 7:39; Seth Rollins and Kevin Owens defeated RK-Bro (Randy Orton and Riddle) in 8:05.

FEBRUARY 14 *Indianapolis, IN*

The Street Profits (Angelo Dawkins and Montez Ford) defeated The Dirty Dawgs (Dolph Ziggler and Robert Roode) in 2:50; Damian Priest defeated AJ Styles in 4:30; Omos defeated The Hurt Business (Cedric Alexander and Shelton Benjamin) in a Handicap Match in 1:25; Bianca Belair defeated Rhea Ripley, Nikki A.S.H., Liv Morgan and Doudrop in a Gauntlet Match in 44:04; Alpha Academy (Chad Gable and Otis) defeated The Mysterios (Rey Mysterio and Dominik Mysterio) in 10:34; Seth Rollins defeated Randy Orton in 15:17.

FEBRUARY 21 *Columbia, SC*

Alpha Academy (Chad Gable and Otis) defeated The Street Profits (Angelo Dawkins and Montez Ford) in 9:05; Tommaso Ciampa and Finn Balor defeated The Dirty Dawgs (Dolph Ziggler and Robert Roode) in 9:15; Rhea Ripley defeated Nikki A.S.H. in 2:35; Damian Priest defeated Shelton Benjamin in 3:10; Dana Brooke defeated Reggie to win the WWE 24/7 Title in 3:10; Bianca Belair defeated Doudrop in 11:20; Seth Rollins and Kevin Owens defeated RK-Bro (Randy Orton and Riddle) in 12:40.

FEBRUARY 28 *Columbus, OH*

Seth Rollins and Kevin Owens defeated Alpha Academy (Chad Gable and Otis) in 12:50; Omos defeated T-Bar in :40; Rhea Ripley, Bianca Belair and Liv Morgan defeated Becky Lynch, Doudrop and Nikki A.S.H. in 12:20; Tommaso Ciampa defeated Robert Roode in 2:40; Dana Brooke and Reggie defeated Tamina and Akira Tozawa in 1:40; The Hurt Business (Cedric Alexander and Shelton Benjamin) defeated The Mysterios (Rey Mysterio and Dominik Mysterio) in 4:30; The Street Profits (Angelo Dawkins and Montez Ford) defeated RK-Bro (Randy Orton and Riddle) in 8:35; Finn Balor defeated Damian Priest to win the WWE United States Title in 11:00.

MARCH 7 *Cleveland, OH*

RK-Bro (Randy Orton and Riddle) defeated Alpha Academy (Chad Gable and Otis) and Seth Rollins and Kevin Owens in a Triple Threat No DQ Match to win the WWE RAW Tag Team Title in 27:05; Dana Brooke defeated Tamina in 1:45; Bron Breakker and Tommaso Ciampa defeated The Dirty Dawgs (Dolph Ziggler and Robert Roode) in 9:37; Omos defeated Apollo Crews in 2:40; Rhea Ripley and Liv Morgan defeated Carmella and Queen Zelina in 9:05; Finn Balor defeated Austin Theory by DQ in 8:40.

MARCH 14 *Jacksonville, FL*

Damian Priest defeated Finn Balor in 7:35; Omos defeated Commander Azeez in 2:00; Liv Morgan defeated Queen Zelina in 2:55; The Mysterios (Rey Mysterio and Dominik Mysterio) defeated The Hurt Business (Cedric Alexander and Shelton Benjamin) in 3:25; Bianca Belair defeated Doudrop in 7:00; Riddle vs. Montez Ford ended in a no contest in 9:40; Kevin Owens defeated Seth Rollins in 16:20.

MARCH 21 *Rosemary, IL*

The Mysterios (Rey Mysterio and Dominik Mysterio) defeated The Dirty Dawgs (Dolph Ziggler and Robert Roode) in 9:25; Omos defeated Commander Azeez and Apollo Crews in a Handicap Match in 2:45; Natalya and Shayna Baszler defeated Liv Morgan and Rhea Ripley in 3:55; Finn Balor defeated Austin Theory in 7:55; RK-Bro (Randy Orton and Riddle) defeated Alpha Academy (Chad Gable and Otis) in 7:45; Dana

Brooke and **Reggie** defeated **Akira Tozawa** and **Tamina** in 1:05; **AJ Styles** defeated **Seth Rollins** by DQ in 22:45.

MARCH 28 *Pittsburgh, PA*
Rey Mysterio defeated **The Miz** in 5:30; **Omos** defeated **The Viking Raiders (Erik** and **Ivar)** via count out in a Handicap Match in :50; **Naomi, Sasha Banks, Liv Morgan** and **Rhea Ripley** defeated **Queen Zelina, Carmella, Natalya** and **Shayna Baszler** in 8:20; **Austin Theory** defeated **Ricochet** in 1:45; **Drew McIntyre** defeated **Happy Corbin** and **Madcap Moss** in a Handicap Match in 1:55; **RK-Bro (Randy Orton** and **Riddle)** defeated **The Usos (Jimmy Uso** and **Jey Uso)** by DQ in 16:20.

APRIL 4 *Dallas, TX*
Sasha Banks and **Naomi** defeated **Liv Morgan** and **Rhea Ripley** in 9:00; **The Miz** defeated **Dominik Mysterio** in :30; **Bron Breakker** defeated **Dolph Ziggler** to win the NXT Title in 10:45; **Austin Theory** and **The Usos (Jimmy Uso** and **Jey Uso)** defeated **Finn Balor** and **RK-Bro (Randy Orton** and **Riddle)** in 8:25; **The Street Profits (Angelo Dawkins** and **Montez Ford)** defeated **Alpha Academy (Chad Gable** and **Otis)** in 8:25.

APRIL 11 *Detroit, MI*
Veer Mahaan defeated **Dominik Mysterio** in 2:00; **Damian Priest** vs. **AJ Styles** ended in a no contest in 13:05; **Cody Rhodes** defeated **The Miz** in 11:45; **Naomi** defeated **Liv Morgan** in 2:20; **Bianca Belair** defeated **Queen Zelina** in 2:10; **RK-Bro (Randy Orton** and **Riddle)** defeated **Alpha Academy (Chad Gable** and **Otis)** in 8:30; **The Usos (Jimmy Uso** and **Jey Uso)** defeated **The Street Profits (Angelo Dawkins** and **Montez Ford)** in 15:10.

APRIL 18 *Buffalo, NY*
Sasha Banks and **Naomi** defeated **Liv Morgan** and **Rhea Ripley** in 7:25; **Veer Mahaan** defeated **Jeff Brooks** in 1:10; **Ezekiel** defeated **Chad Gable** by DQ in 3:30; **The Street Profits (Angelo Dawkins** and **Montez Ford)** defeated **RK-Bro (Randy Orton** and **Riddle)** in 7:50; **Theory** defeated **Finn Balor** to win the WWE United States Title in 11:35; **Cody Rhodes** defeated **Kevin Owens** via count out in 17:20.

APRIL 25 *Knoxville, TN*
Bianca Belair defeated **Sonya Deville** in 8:55; **Veer Mahaan** defeated **Sam Smothers** in :38; **Akira Tozawa** and **Tamina** defeated **Dana Brooke** and **Reggie** in 1:30; **Damian Priest** defeated **Finn Balor** in 7:20; **Mustafa Ali** defeated **The Miz** in 6:40; **Cody Rhodes, Ezekiel** and **RK-Bro (Randy Orton** and **Riddle)** defeated **Seth Rollins, Kevin Owens** and **The Usos (Jimmy Uso** and **Jey Uso)** in 14:58.

MAY 2 *Greensboro, NC*
Kevin Owens and **Alpha Academy (Chad Gable** and **Otis)** defeated **Ezekiel** and **The Street Profits (Angelo Dawkins** and **Montez Ford)** in 9:45; **Veer Mahaan** defeated **Burt Hanson** in 1:30; **AJ Styles** defeated **Damian Priest** in 11:00; **The Miz** and **Theory** defeated **Mustafa Ali** in a Handicap Match in 2:50; **Dana Brooke** defeated **Nikki A.S.H.** to win the WWE 24/7 Title in 1:30; **Bobby Lashley** defeated **Cedric Alexander** in 2:35; **Asuka, Liv Morgan** and **Bianca Belair** defeated **Becky Lynch, Rhea Ripley** and **Sonya Deville** in 15:15.

MAY 9 *Hartford, CT*
RK-Bro (Randy Orton and **Riddle)** defeated **The Street Profits (Angelo Dawkins** and **Montez Ford)** in 9:58; **Rhea Ripley** defeated **Liv Morgan** in 5:40; **Finn Balor** defeated **Damian Priest** by DQ in 5:59; **Alexa Bliss** defeated **Sonya Deville** in :40; **Veer Mahaan** defeated **Frank Loman** in 1:25; **Cody Rhodes** defeated **Theory** by DQ in 13:10; **Sasha Banks** and **Naomi** defeated **Doudrop** and **Nikki A.S.H.** in 4:25; **Ciampa** defeated **Mustafa Ali** in 3:55; **Asuka** vs. **Bianca Belair** ended in no contest in 3:05.

MAY 16 *Norfolk, VA*
Bobby Lashley defeated **Omos** in a Steel Cage Match in 7:30; **Veer Mahaan** defeated **Mustafa Ali** in 2:50; **Riddle** defeated **Jimmy Uso** in 10:50; **Finn Balor** and **AJ Styles** defeated **Los Lotharios (Angel** and **Humberto)** in 8:30; **Alexa Bliss** defeated **Sonya Deville** in 4:00; **Ezekiel** defeated **Chad Gable** in 11:00; **Asuka** defeated **Becky Lynch** in 9:55.

MAY 23 *Evansville, IN*
Riddle and **The Street Profits (Angelo Dawkins** and **Montez Ford)** defeated **Sami Zayn** and **The Usos (Jimmy Uso** and **Jey Uso)** in 12:35; **The Judgment Day (Damian Priest** and **Rhea Ripley)** defeated **AJ Styles** and **Liv Morgan** in 11:35; **Alexa Bliss** defeated **Nikki A.S.H.** in 3:00; **Cody Rhodes** defeated **The Miz** by DQ in 9:00; **Ezekiel** defeated **Chad Gable** in 4:10; **MVP** defeated **Bobby Lashley** via count out in 3:05; **Becky Lynch** defeated **Asuka** in 11:25.

MAY 30 *Des Moines, IA*
Bianca Belair defeated **Asuka** in 12:58; **Ezekiel** and **The Mysterios (Rey Mysterio** and **Dominik Mysterio)** defeated **Kevin Owens** and **Alpha Academy (Chad Gable** and **Otis)** in 8:30; **Alexa Bliss** defeated **Doudrop** in 3:20; **Mustafa Ali** defeated **Ciampa** by DQ in 3:24; **Theory** defeated **Mustafa Ali** in 1:45; **Riddle** and **Shinsuke Nakamura** defeated **The Usos (Jimmy Uso** and **Jey Uso)** in 12:30; **Liv Morgan** defeated **Rhea Ripley** in 10:15.

JUNE 6 *Green Bay, WI*
Becky Lynch vs. **Dana Brooke** ended in a no contest in 1:00; **Dana Brooke** defeated **Becky Lynch** in 2:10; **Riddle** defeated **The Miz** in 2:13; **The Street Profits (Angelo Dawkins** and **Montez Ford)** defeated **The Usos (Jimmy Uso** and **Jey Uso)** via count out in 16:30; **Veer Mahaan** defeated **Dominik Mysterio** by DQ in 9:20; **Omos** defeated **Cedric Alexander** in :12; **Ezekiel** defeated **Otis** in 2:20; **Rhea Ripley** defeated **Alexa Bliss, Liv Morgan** and **Doudrop** in a Fatal Four Way Match in 14:35.

JUNE 13 *Wichita, KS*
Jimmy Uso defeated **Montez Ford** in 13:00; **Alexa Bliss** and **Liv Morgan** defeated **Nikki A.S.H.** and **Doudrop** in 4:25; **Ezekiel** defeated **Kevin Owens** via count out in 8:30; **MVP** defeated **Cedric Alexander** in 1:40; **Seth Rollins** defeated **AJ Styles** in 15:05; **Riddle** defeated **Ciampa** in 4:30; **Chad Gable** defeated **Mustafa Ali** in 3:15; **Veer Mahaan** defeated **Rey Mysterio** in 3:45.

JUNE 20 *Lincoln, NE*
Carmella defeated **Alexa Bliss, Asuka, Becky Lynch** and **Liv Morgan** in a Fatal Five Way Match in 12:30; **Omos** defeated **Riddle** in 3:55; **Angelo Dawkins** defeated **Jey Uso** in 7:20; **Bobby Lashley** defeated **Chad Gable, Otis** and **Theory** in a Gauntlet Match in 16:45; **AJ Styles** defeated **Ciampa** in 4:30; **Asuka** defeated **Becky Lynch** in 12:00.

JUNE 27 Laredo, TX
Riddle won a Battle Royal in 19:25; **Montez Ford** defeated **Jey Uso** in 9:50; **AJ Styles** defeated **The Miz** via count out in 12:30; **Liv Morgan** defeated **Alexa Bliss** in 3:20; **Bobby Lashley** defeated **Alpha Academy (Chad Gable** and **Otis)** in a Handicap Match in 8:15; **Becky Lynch** defeated **Doudrop, Nikki A.S.H., Xia Li, Shayna Baszler** and **Tamina** in a Six Way Elimination Match in 13:20.

JULY 4 San Diego, CA
The Mysterios (Rey Mysterio and **Dominik Mysterio)** defeated **The Judgment Day (Finn Balor** and **Damian Priest)** by DQ in 11:30; **AJ Styles** defeated **The Miz** in 6:25; **Bianca Belair** and **Liv Morgan** defeated **Natalya** and **Carmella** in 13:25; **Seth Rollins** defeated **Ezekiel** in 10:15; **Bobby Lashley** and **The Street Profits (Angelo Dawkins** and **Montez Ford)** defeated **Theory** and **Alpha Academy (Chad Gable** and **Otis)** in 10:05; **Gunther** defeated **R-Truth** in :55; **Becky Lynch** defeated **Asuka** in a No Holds Barred Match in 11:40.

JULY 11 San Antonio, TX
Finn Balor defeated **Rey Mysterio** in 10:15; **Carmella** defeated **Bianca Belair** via count out in 11:50; **AJ Styles** and **Ezekiel** defeated **The Miz** and **Ciampa** by DQ in 11:29; **Alexa Bliss** and **Asuka** defeated **Nikki A.S.H.** and **Doudrop** in 4:15; **Omos** and **The Usos (Jimmy Uso** and **Jey Uso)** defeated **R-Truth** and **The Street Profits (Angelo Dawkins** and **Montez Ford)** in 11:30; **Bobby Lashley** and **Riddle** defeated **Seth Rollins** and **Theory** in 13:50.

JULY 18 Tampa, FL
Bianca Belair defeated **Carmella** in 10:25; **Damian Priest** defeated **Rey Mysterio** in 4:59; **Seth Rollins** defeated **Ezekiel** in 11:55; **Angelo Dawkins** defeated **Omos** by DQ in 1:20; **The Street Profits (Angelo Dawkins** and **Montez Ford)** defeated **MVP** and **Omos** by DQ in 4:50; **AJ Styles** defeated **Theory** via count out in 11:25; **Alexa Bliss, Asuka** and **Dana Brooke** defeated **Doudrop, Nikki A.S.H.** and **Tamina** in 2:35.

JULY 25 New York, NY
Drew McIntyre defeated **Theory** by DQ in 9:45; **Drew McIntyre** and **Bobby Lashley** defeated **Theory** and **Sheamus** in 12:20; **The Mysterios (Rey Mysterio** and **Dominik Mysterio)** defeated **The Judgment Day (Finn Balor** and **Damian Priest)** in 11:29; **Alexa Bliss** defeated **Doudrop** in 4:20; **AJ Styles** and **Dolph Ziggler** defeated **Alpha Academy (Chad Gable** and **Otis)** in 6:30; **The Bloodline (Roman Reigns, Jimmy Uso** and **Jey Uso)** defeated **Riddle** and **The Street Profits (Angelo Dawkins** and **Montez Ford)** in 19:25.

AUGUST 1 Houston, TX
AJ Styles defeated **The Miz** and **Mustafa Ali** in a Triple Threat Match in 8:50; **Seth Rollins** defeated **Montez Ford** in 10:59; **Alexa Bliss** vs. **Asuka** ended in a no contest in 2:20; **Ciampa** defeated **Dolph Ziggler** and **Chad Gable** in a Triple Threat Match in 10:30; **Bianca Belair** vs. **Iyo Sky** ended in a no contest in 17:15; **Ciampa** defeated **AJ Styles** in 13:30; **The Usos (Jimmy Uso** and **Jey Uso)** defeated **The Mysterios (Rey Mysterio** and **Dominik Mysterio)** in 15:50.

AUGUST 8 Cleveland, OH
Seth Rollins defeated **Angelo Dawkins** in 8:50; **Kevin Owens** vs. **Ezekiel** ended in a no contest in :50; **Finn Balor** defeated **Rey Mysterio** in 14:00; **Iyo Sky** and **Dakota Kai** defeated **Dana Brooke** and **Tamina** in

10:00; **Bobby Lashley** defeated **Ciampa** in 13:30; **Omos** defeated **Andrea Guercio** and **Spencer Slade** in a Handicap Match in 1:40; **Dolph Ziggler** defeated **Chad Gable** in 6:35; **AJ Styles** defeated **The Miz** in a No Disqualification Match in 12:30.

AUGUST 15 Washington, D.C
Alexa Bliss and **Asuka** defeated **Nikki A.S.H.** and **Doudrop** in 9:00; **The Miz** and **Ciampa** defeated **Cedric Alexander** and **Mustafa Ali** in 9:30; **Drew McIntyre** defeated **Kevin Owens** by DQ in 15:58; **Veer Mahaan** defeated **Beaux Keller** in 1:50; **Bobby Lashley** defeated **AJ Styles** in 21:40; **Dakota Kai** defeated **Dana Brooke** in 1:50; **Theory** defeated **Dolph Ziggler** in 16:15.

AUGUST 22 Toronto, Canada
Damage CTRL (Dakota Kai and **Iyo Sky)** defeated **Alexa Bliss** and **Asuka** in 18:30; **Finn Balor** defeated **Dolph Ziggler** in 13:05; **Kevin Owens** defeated **Chad Gable** in 11:10; **Bayley** defeated **Aliyah** in 6:45; **Ciampa** and **The Miz** defeated **AJ Styles** and **Bobby Lashley** by DQ in 13:30; **Edge** defeated **Damian Priest** in 19:35.

AUGUST 29 Pittsburgh, PA
The Judgment Day (Finn Balor and **Damian Priest)** defeated **AJ Styles** and **Dolph Ziggler** in 8:34; **Alexa Bliss, Asuka** and **Bianca Belair** defeated **Katie Ark, Kay Sparks** and **Dani Mo** in 3:19; **The Street Profits (Angelo Dawkins** and **Montez Ford)** defeated **Alpha Academy (Chad Gable** and **Otis)** in 16:04; **Bobby Lashley** defeated **The Miz** in 10:49; **Kevin Owens** defeated **Jey Uso** in 12:26; **Raquel Rodriguez** and **Aliyah** defeated **Damage CTRL (Dakota Kai** and **Iyo Sky)** to win the vacant WWE Women's Tag Team Title in 11:17.

SEPTEMBER 5 Kansas City, MO
Alpha Academy (Chad Gable and **Otis)** vs. **Los Lotharios (Angel** and **Humberto)** vs. **The New Day (Xavier Woods** and **Kofi Kingston)** vs. **The Street Profits (Angelo Dawkins** and **Montez Ford)** ended in a no contest in 14:30; **Raquel Rodriguez** and **Aliyah** defeated **Nikki A.S.H.** and **Doudrop** in 3:45; **Kevin Owens** defeated **Austin Theory** in 15:40; **Damian Priest** defeated **Rey Mysterio** in 13:35; **Bobby Lashley** defeated **The Miz** in a Steel Cage Match in 14:15.

SEPTEMBER 12 Portland, OR
Finn Balor defeated **Matt Riddle** in 13:35; **Damage CTRL (Dakota Kai** and **Iyo Sky)** defeated **Raquel Rodriguez** and **Aliyah** to win the WWE Women's Tag Team Title in 12:30; **Johnny Gargano** defeated **Chad Gable** in 13:50; **Bianca Belair** defeated **Sonya Deville** in 12:00; **Omos** defeated **Khash Morazzi** and **Ryan Toombs** in a Handicap Match in :40; **Edge** defeated **Dominik Mysterio** by DQ in 15:10.

SEPTEMBER 19 San Jose, CA
Bobby Lashley defeated **Seth Rollins** in 20:15; **Kevin Owens** defeated **Austin Theory** in 13:15; **The Brawling Brutes (Ridge Holland** and **Butch)** defeated **The Street Profits (Angelo Dawkins** and **Montez Ford)** in 12:57; **The Judgment Day (Finn Balor** and **Damian Priest)** defeated **Matt Riddle** and **Rey Mysterio** in 17:40; **Bayley** defeated **Alexa Bliss** in 15:05.

SEPTEMBER 26 Edmonton, Canada
Bianca Belair defeated **Iyo Sky** in 18:08; **Seth Rollins** defeated **Rey Mysterio** in 17:57; **Kevin Owens** and **Johnny Gargano** defeated **Alpha Academy (Chad Gable** and **Otis)** in 13:09; **Omos** defeated **Joey Gibson** and **Greg Lester** in a Handicap Match in 1:42; **Candice**

LeRae defeated **Nikki A.S.H.** in 1:45; **Sami Zayn** defeated **AJ Styles** in 20:02; **Matt Riddle** defeated **Damian Priest** in 19:21.

OCTOBER 3 *Saint Paul, MN*
The Judgment Day (Finn Balor and Damian Priest) defeated **AJ Styles and Rey Mysterio** in 10:42; **Bobby Lashley** defeated **Mustafa Ali** in 11:26; **Dakota Kai** defeated **Candice LeRae** in 11:00; **Otis** defeated **Johnny Gargano** in 5:40; **Braun Strowman** defeated **Chad Gable** in 8:45; **Solo Sikoa** defeated **Angelo Dawkins** in 12:20; **Iyo Sky** defeated **Alexa Bliss** in 9:15.

OCTOBER 10 *New York, NY*
Johnny Gargano defeated **Austin Theory** in 8:50; **Rey Mysterio** defeated **Chad Gable** in 7:50; **Omos** defeated **Joseph Torres and Robert Adams** in a Handicap Match in 1:20; **Seth Rollins** defeated **Bobby Lashley** to win the WWE United States Title in 2:35; **Matt Riddle** defeated **Sami Zayn** in 16:15.

OCTOBER 17 *Oklahoma City, OK*
The O.C (Luke Gallows and Karl Anderson) defeated **Alpha Academy (Chad Gable and Otis)** in 8:20; **Damage CTRL (Dakota Kai and Iyo Sky)** defeated **Bianca Belair and Candice LeRae** in 12:10; **Baron Corbin** defeated **Dolph Ziggler** in 13:35; **Dominik Mysterio** defeated **AJ Styles** in 14:30; **Seth Rollins** defeated **Matt Riddle** in 14:50.

OCTOBER 24 *Charlotte, NC*
Finn Balor defeated **Karl Anderson** in 17:15; **R-Truth** defeated **The Miz** in 2:45; **Austin Theory** defeated **Mustafa Ali** in 9:58; **Omos** defeated **Chrisifix, Dennis Daniels, Michael Stevens and Sal Rinauro** in a Handicap Match in 1:40; **Elias** defeated **Chad Gable** in 9:30; **Baron Corbin** defeated **Johnny Gargano** in 14:10; **Bayley** defeated **Bianca Belair** in 22:57.

OCTOBER 31 *Dallas, TX*
Bianca Belair defeated **Nikki Cross** in 9:30; **Seth Rollins** defeated **Austin Theory** in 14:40; **Karl Anderson** defeated **Damian Priest** in 7:17; **Matt Riddle** defeated **Otis** in a Trick Or Street Fight in 7:39; **Mustafa Ali** defeated **The Miz** in 10:00; **Alexa Bliss and Asuka** defeated **Damage CTRL (Dakota Kai and Iyo Sky)** in 16:25.

NOVEMBER 7 *Wilkes-Barre, PA*
The Bloodline (Solo Sikoa, Jey Uso and Jimmy Uso) defeated **Matt Riddle and The New Day (Xavier Woods and Kofi Kingston)** in 20:55; **Baron Corbin** defeated **Cedric Alexander** in 2:20; **Otis** defeated **Elias** in 3:00; **Austin Theory** defeated **Shelton Benjamin** in 2:40; **The Miz** defeated **Johnny Gargano** in 17:00; **Nikki Cross** defeated **Dana Brooke** to win the WWE 24/7 Championship in 2:15; **Seth Rollins** defeated **Austin Theory** in 5:00.

NOVEMBER 14 *Louisville, KY*
Bobby Lashley defeated **Mustafa Ali** in 4:30; **Mia Yim** defeated **Tamina** in 2:00; **Chad Gable** defeated **Matt Riddle** in 10:10; **Dominik Mysterio** defeated **Shelton Benjamin** in 5:00; **Iyo Sky** defeated **Dana Brooke** in 3:15; **Dolph Ziggler** defeated **Austin Theory** by DQ in 15:00; **Baron Corbin** defeated **Akira Tozawa** in 3:35; **Seth Rollins** defeated **Finn Balor** in 21:10.

NOVEMBER 21 *Albany, NY*
The Brawling Brutes (Sheamus, Ridge Holland and Butch) defeated **The Judgment Day (Finn Balor,**

Damian Priest and Dominik Mysterio) in 14:50; **Omos** defeated **Johnny Gargano** in 3:10; **Austin Theory** defeated **Mustafa Ali** in 5:45; **Elias and Matt Riddle** defeated **Alpha Academy (Chad Gable and Otis)** in 16:05; **Drew McIntyre** defeated **Baron Corbin** in 17:50; **Rhea Ripley** defeated **Asuka** in 17:58.

NOVEMBER 28 *Norfolk, VA*
Rhea Ripley vs. Mia Yim ended in a no contest in 7:05; **The Judgment Day (Finn Balor, Damian Priest, Dominik Mysterio and Rhea Ripley)** defeated **The O.C. (AJ Styles, Luke Gallows, Karl Anderson and Mia Yim)** in 14:20; **The Street Profits (Angelo Dawkins and Montez Ford)** defeated **Alpha Academy (Chad Gable and Otis)** in 12:00; **Dexter Lumis** defeated **The Miz** in an Anything Goes Match in 9:30; **Candice LeRae** defeated **Dakota Kai** in 14:00; **Kevin Owens** defeated **Jey Uso** in 21:55.

DECEMBER 5 *Washington, D.C.*
The Usos (Jey Uso and Jimmy Uso) defeated **Matt Riddle and Kevin Owens** in 14:10; **Bayley** defeated **Asuka and Rhea Ripley** in a Three Way Match in 15:15; **Austin Theory** defeated **Mustafa Ali** by DQ in 8:05; **The O.C. (AJ Styles, Luke Gallows and Karl Anderson)** defeated **Baron Corbin and Alpha Academy (Chad Gable and Otis)** in 14:30; **Dominik Mysterio** defeated **Akira Tozawa** in 2:50; **Alexa Bliss** defeated **Nikki Cross and Becky Lynch** in a Three Way Match in 16:30.

DECEMBER 12 *Milwaukee, WI*
Alexa Bliss defeated **Bayley** in 13:25; **AJ Styles** defeated **Chad Gable** in 9:05; **The Judgment Day (Finn Balor, Damian Priest and Dominik Mysterio)** defeated **Akira Tozawa and The Street Profits (Angelo Dawkins and Montez Ford)** in 14:45; **Iyo Sky** defeated **Candice LeRae** in 10:20; **Solo Sikoa** defeated **Elias** in 8:15; **Rhea Ripley** defeated **Asuka** in 11:40; **Seth Rollins** defeated **Bobby Lashley** in 12:55.

DECEMBER 19 *Des Moines, IA*
The Street Profits (Angelo Dawkins and Montez Ford) defeated **The Judgment Day (Finn Balor and Damian Priest)** in 9:00; **Rhea Ripley** defeated **Akira Tozawa** in 4:55; **The O.C. (Karl Anderson and Luke Gallows)** defeated **Alpha Academy (Chad Gable and Otis)** in 9:05; **The Miz** defeated **Dexter Lumis** in a Ladder Match in 18:20; **Sami Zayn** defeated **AJ Styles** in 12:15; **Bayley** defeated **Becky Lynch** in 14:20; **Seth Rollins and Kevin Owens** defeated **The Usos (Jey Uso and Jimmy Uso)** in 10:50.

DECEMBER 26
Highlights show

WWE SMACKDOWN

JANUARY 7 *Uncasville, CT*
Rick Boogs defeated **Sami Zayn** in 6:30; **Charlotte Flair** defeated **Naomi** in 12:15; **Happy Corbin and Madcap Moss** defeated **The Viking Raiders (Erik and Ivar)** in 3:30; **The Usos (Jimmy Uso and Jey Uso)** defeated **The New Day (Xavier Woods and Kofi Kingston)** in 17:45.

JANUARY 14 *Omaha, NE*
The Viking Raiders (Erik and Ivar) defeated **Los Lotharios (Angel and Humberto)** and **Cesaro & Mansoor** and **Jinder Mahal & Shanky** in a Fatal Four Way Match in 13:21; **Aliyah** defeated **Natalya** in :03;

Sheamus defeated Ricochet in 9:53; Madcap Moss defeated Kofi Kingston in 9:53.

JANUARY 21 Nashville, TN
Kofi Kingston defeated Madcap Moss in 7:40; Aliyah defeated Natalya by DQ in 2:10; The Viking Raiders (Erik and Ivar) defeated Los Lotharios (Angel and Humberto) in 2:20; Charlotte Flair defeated Naomi in 2:25; Sheamus defeated Ricochet in 3:20; Kevin Owens and Seth Rollins defeated The Usos (Jimmy Uso and Jey Uso) in 15:00.

JANUARY 28 Kansas City, MO
Ridge Holland and Sheamus defeated Ricochet and Cesaro in 10:45; Naomi defeated Sonya Deville in 11:45; Shinsuke Nakamura and Rick Boogs defeated Jinder Mahal and Shanky in 3:05; The New Day (Big E and Kofi Kingston) defeated Happy Corbin and Madcap Moss in 7:10.

FEBRUARY 4 Oklahoma City, OK
Ricochet defeated Ridge Holland in 2:20; Ridge Holland and Sheamus defeated Ricochet and Cesaro in 5:34; Jimmy Uso defeated Erik in 2:10; Aliyah defeated Natalya via count out in 4:08; Shinsuke Nakamura defeated Jinder Mahal in 3:09; The New Day (Big E and Kofi Kingston) defeated Los Lotharios (Angel and Humberto) in 8:58.

FEBRUARY 11 New Orleans, LA
Los Lotharios (Angel and Humberto) defeated The New Day (Big E and Kofi Kingston) in 10:20; Natalya defeated Aliyah in a Hart Dungeon Style Match in 2:40; Happy Corbin defeated Cesaro in 3:55; Charlotte Flair defeated Naomi in 19:55.

FEBRUARY 18 New Orleans, LA
Ricochet defeated Sheamus in 10:55; Ivar defeated Jey Uso by DQ in 2:35; Sami Zayn defeated Shinsuke Nakamura to win the WWE Intercontinental Title in 18:15.

FEBRUARY 25 Hershey, PA
The New Day (Big E and Kofi Kingston) defeated Los Lotharios (Angel and Humberto) in 10:30; Xia Li defeated Natalya in 4:00; Sasha Banks defeated Shotzi in 2:10; Drew McIntyre defeated Madcap Moss in 7:20.

MARCH 4 Miami, FL
Ricochet defeated Sami Zayn to win the WWE Intercontinental Title in 8:20; Naomi defeated Carmella in 2:10; Drew McIntyre defeated Jinder Mahal in 2:05; The Usos (Jimmy Uso and Jey Uso) defeated The Viking Raiders (Erik and Ivar) in 8:25; Ronda Rousey defeated Sonya Deville in 3:15.

MARCH 11 Birmingham, AL
Sheamus and Ridge Holland defeated The New Day (Big E and Kofi Kingston) in 8:49; Sasha Banks and Naomi defeated Shayna Baszler and Natalya in 3:19; Rick Boogs defeated Jey Uso in 2:25; Ricochet defeated Sami Zayn in 12:59.

MARCH 18 Charlotte, NC
Shinsuke Nakamura and Rick Boogs defeated Los Lotharios (Angel and Humberto) in 4:55; Drew McIntyre and The Viking Raiders (Erik and Ivar) defeated Happy Corbin, Jinder Mahal and Shanky in 7:10; Sasha Banks and Naomi vs. Rhea Ripley and Liv Morgan ended in a no contest in 12:00; Ridge Holland defeated Kofi Kingston in 6:00.

MARCH 25 New York, NY
Shinsuke Nakamura defeated Jimmy Uso in 8:48; Xavier Woods defeated Ridge Holland in :46; Angel defeated Ricochet in 2:10; Humberto defeated Ricochet by count out in 7:18; Sasha Banks defeated Queen Zelina, Shayna Baszler and Rhea Ripley in a Fatal Four Way Match in 8:43.

APRIL 1 Dallas, TX
Madcap Moss won the Andre The Giant Memorial Battle Royal in 8:05; Ricochet defeated Angel and Humberto in a Triple Threat Match in 11:20; Sasha Banks and Naomi defeated Carmella and Queen Zelina in 3:13; Rick Boogs vs. Jimmy Uso ended in a no contest in 3:13; Austin Theory and The Usos (Jimmy Uso and Jey Uso) defeated Finn Balor, Shinsuke Nakamura and Rick Boogs in 11:27.

APRIL 8 Milwaukee, WI
Xavier Woods defeated Butch in 8:35; Gunther defeated Joe Alonzo in 2:05; Drew McIntyre defeated Sami Zayn via count out in 3:40; Liv Morgan defeated Sasha Banks in 7:08.

APRIL 15 Worcester, MA
Rhea Ripley defeated Naomi in 9:04; Madcap Moss defeated Humberto in 2:46; Drew McIntyre defeated Sami Zayn via count out in 2:39; Ricochet defeated Jinder Mahal in 3:37; Riddle defeated Jimmy Uso in 8:32.

APRIL 22 Albany, NY
Xavier Woods defeated Butch in 9:00; Gunther defeated Teddy Goodz in 2:10; Riddle defeated Jey Uso in 12:10; Madcap Moss defeated Angel in 2:25; Drew McIntyre vs. Sami Zayn went to a no contest in a Lumberjack Match in 9:00.

APRIL 29 Albany, NY
Drew McIntyre defeated Sami Zayn in a Steel Cage Match in 10:36; Ricochet defeated Shanky in 3:34; Raquel Rodriguez defeated Cat Cardoza in 2:36; Naomi defeated Shayna Baszler in 2:27; Xavier Woods defeated Ridge Holland in 8:47; Sheamus defeated Kofi Kingston in 2:57; Ronda Rousey defeated Shotzi in an "I Quit" Beat The Clock Challenge Match in 1:41; Aliyah vs. Charlotte Flair ended in a time limit draw in an "I Quit" Beat The Clock Challenge Match in 1:41.

MAY 6 Uniondale, NY
Shayna Baszler defeated Sasha Banks in 8:05; Gunther defeated Drew Gulak in 2:05; Sheamus and Ridge Holland defeated The New Day (Xavier Woods and Kofi Kingston) in a Tables Match in 12:30; Sami Zayn defeated Shinsuke Nakamura via count out in 9:15.

MAY 13 Wilkes-Barre, PA
Riddle defeated Sami Zayn in 10:50; Ronda Rousey defeated Raquel Rodriguez in 6:00; Sasha Banks and Naomi defeated Natalya and Shayna Baszler in 8:30; Butch defeated Kofi Kingston in 8:20.

MAY 20 Grand Rapids, MI
Shinsuke Nakamura defeated Sami Zayn in 10:28; Gunther defeated Drew Gulak in 1:04; Raquel Rodriguez defeated Shotzi in 2:46; Xavier Woods defeated Butch in 3:28; The Usos (Jimmy Uso and Jey Uso) defeated RK-Bro (Randy Orton and Riddle) to win the WWE RAW Tag Team Title in 13:13.

MAY 27 *North Little Rock, AR*
Ronda Rousey vs. Raquel Rodriguez ended in a no contest in :55; Ronda Rousey and Raquel Rodriguez defeated Shayna Baszler and Natalya in 7:35; Los Lotharios (Angel and Humberto) defeated Jinder Mahal and Shanky in 2:15; Gunther and Ludwig Kaiser defeated Ricochet and Drew Gulak in 6:45; Drew McIntyre and The New Day (Xavier Woods and Kofi Kingston) defeated The Brawling Brutes (Sheamus, Ridge Holland and Butch) in 11:30.

JUNE 3 *Columbus, OH*
The Brawling Brutes (Sheamus, Ridge Holland and Butch) defeated Drew McIntyre and The New Day (Xavier Woods and Kofi Kingston) in 10:30; Jinder Mahal defeated Humberto in 3:34; Natalya defeated Raquel Rodriguez, Shotzi, Aliyah, Shayna Baszler and Xia Li in a Six Pack Challenge in 5:54.

JUNE 10 *Baton Rouge, LA*
Drew McIntyre vs. Sheamus ended in a no contest in 11:50; Lacey Evans defeated Xia Li in 2:30; Ronda Rousey defeated Shotzi in 7:20; Gunther defeated Ricochet to win the WWE Intercontinental Title in 8:35; Riddle defeated Sami Zayn in 13:05.

JUNE 17 *Minneapolis, MN*
Madcap Moss defeated Happy Corbin in a Last Laugh Match in 9:22; The New Day (Xavier Woods and Kofi Kingston) defeated Jinder Mahal and Shanky in 3:02; Raquel Rodriguez defeated Shayna Baszler in 3:15; Roman Reigns defeated Riddle in 16:56.

JUNE 24 *Austin, TX*
Sami Zayn defeated Shinsuke Nakamura in 9:55; Lacey Evans and Raquel Rodriguez defeated Sonya Deville in a Handicap Match in 3:05; Gunther defeated Ricochet in 3:10; Shotzi defeated Tamina in 2:40; Drew McIntyre and Sheamus defeated The Usos (Jimmy Uso and Jey Uso) in 11:20.

JULY 1 *Phoenix, AZ*
Happy Corbin won a Battle Royal in 14:36; Alexa Bliss, Liv Morgan and Asuka defeated Raquel Rodriguez, Lacey Evans and Shotzi in 13:14; Madcap Moss defeated The Miz, Ezekiel and Happy Corbin in a Fatal Four Way Match in 10:33.

JULY 8 *Fort Worth, TX*
The Viking Raiders (Erik and Ivar) defeated Jinder Mahal and Shanky in 1:15; Shinsuke Nakamura defeated Ludwig Kaiser in 6:40; Ronda Rousey defeated Natalya in 2:15; The Usos (Jimmy Uso and Jey Uso) defeated Los Lotharios (Angel and Humberto) in 2:00; Drew McIntyre defeated Butch in 1:30.

JULY 15 *Orlando, FL*
Liv Morgan defeated Natalya in 9:04; Drew McIntyre defeated Ridge Holland in 3:25; Madcap Moss defeated Theory by DQ in 11:34; Angelo Dawkins defeated Jimmy Uso in 7:00.

JULY 22 *Boston, MA*
Ludwig Kaiser defeated Shinsuke Nakamura in 9:30; The Viking Raiders (Erik and Ivar) defeated Jinder Mahal and Shanky via count out in 1:30; Raquel Rodriguez defeated Sonya Deville in 3:40; Madcap Moss and The Street Profits (Angelo Dawkins and Montez Ford) defeated Theory and The Usos (Jimmy Uso and Jey Uso) by DQ in 17:00.

JULY 29 *Atlanta, GA*
Drew McIntyre defeated Sheamus in a Donnybrook Match in 25:30; Shotzi defeated Aliyah in 3:20; Ronda Rousey and Liv Morgan defeated Sonya Deville and Natalya in 11:30; The Viking Raiders (Erik and Ivar) defeated The New Day (Xavier Woods and Kofi Kingston) in 9:15.

AUGUST 5 *Greenville, SC*
Ricochet defeated Happy Corbin in 11:50; Shinsuke Nakamura defeated Ludwig Kaiser in 8:45; Shayna Baszler defeated Sonya Deville, Raquel Rodriguez, Aliyah, Shotzi, Xia Li and Natalya in a Gauntlet Match in 21:05; The Viking Raiders (Erik and Ivar) defeated Jim Mulkey and Tommy Gibson in 1:35; Kofi Kingston defeated Erik in 3:45.

AUGUST 12 *Raleigh, NC*
Raquel Rodriguez and Aliyah defeated Shotzi and Xia Li in 9:35; Hit Row (Ashante Adonis and Top Dolla) defeated Trevor Urban and Brandon Scott in 1:50; Drew McIntyre and Madcap Moss defeated The Usos (Jimmy Uso and Jey Uso) in 9:15; Gunther defeated Shinsuke Nakamura in 14:20.

AUGUST 19 *Montreal, Canada*
Toxic Attraction (Jacy Jayne and Gigi Dolin) defeated Natalya and Sonya Deville in 8:48; Sheamus defeated Happy Corbin, Madcap Moss, Ricochet and Sami Zayn in a Five Way Match in 22:33; Liv Morgan defeated Shotzi in 6:48.

AUGUST 26 *Detroit, MI*
Ricochet defeated Happy Corbin in 12:20; Natalya and Sonya Deville defeated Doudrop and Nikki A.S.H., Dana Brooke and Tamina, and Shotzi and Xia Li in a Four Way Match in 3:10; Raquel Rodriguez and Aliyah defeated Natalya and Sonya Deville in 8:00; Drew McIntyre defeated Sami Zayn in 10:20.

SEPTEMBER 2 *Detroit, MI*
The Viking Raiders (Erik and Ivar) defeated The New Day (Xavier Woods and Kofi Kingston) in a Viking Rules Match in 22:15; Karrion Kross defeated Drew Gulak in 1:15; Hit Row (Ashante Adonis and Top Dolla) defeated Maximum Male Models (Mace and Mansoor) in 3:05; Shinsuke Nakamura defeated Happy Corbin in 2:20; Butch defeated Ludwig Kaiser in 9:10.

SEPTEMBER 9 *Seattle, WA*
Imperium (Gunther, Ludwig Kaiser and Giovanni Vinci) defeated The Brawling Brutes (Sheamus, Ridge Holland and Butch) in 19:05; Raquel Rodriguez and Aliyah defeated Toxic Attraction (Jacy Jayne and Gigi Dolin) in 5:00; Ronda Rousey defeated Sonya Deville, Xia Li, Natalya and Lacey Evans in a Five Way Elimination Match in 4:40; The Street Profits (Angelo Dawkins and Montez Ford) and Hit Row (Ashante Adonis and Top Dolla) defeated Los Lotharios (Angel and Humberto) and Maximum Male Models (Mace and Mansoor) in 8:35; Drew McIntyre defeated Solo Sikoa by DQ in 10:35.

SEPTEMBER 16 *Anaheim, CA*
Ricochet defeated Sami Zayn in 13:02; Bayley defeated Raquel Rodriguez in 8:20; Solo Sikoa defeated Madcap Moss in 10:49; The Brawling Brutes (Ridge Holland and Butch) defeated Hit Row (Ashante Adonis and Top Dolla), Imperium (Ludwig Kaiser and Giovanni Vinci) and The New Day (Xavier Woods and Kofi Kingston) in a Four Way Match in 18:44.

SEPTEMBER 23 *Salt Lake City, UT*
Liv Morgan defeated Lacey Evans in 8:44; The New Day (Xavier Woods and Kofi Kingston) defeated Maximum Male Models (Mace and Mansoor) in 3:18; Braun Strowman defeated Otis in 5:45; Raquel Rodriguez defeated Dakota Kai in 2:01; The Usos (Jimmy Uso and Jey Uso) defeated The Brawling Brutes (Ridge Holland and Butch) in 14:10.

SEPTEMBER 30 *Winnipeg, Canada*
Sami Zayn and Solo Sikoa defeated Ricochet and Madcap Moss in 12:44; Drew McIntyre defeated Austin Theory by DQ in 3:12; Hit Row (Ashante Adonis and Top Dolla) defeated Los Lotharios (Angel and Humberto) in 3:21; Ronda Rousey defeated Natalya in 4:18; Bayley defeated Shotzi in 6:42; Drew McIntyre, Kevin Owens and Johnny Gargano defeated Austin Theory and Alpha Academy (Chad Gable and Otis) in 13:38.

OCTOBER 7 *Worcester, MA*
Solo Sikoa defeated Ricochet in 8:16; Shotzi and Raquel Rodriguez defeated Sonya Deville and Xia Li in 2:16; Braun Strowman and The New Day (Xavier Woods and Kofi Kingston) defeated The Bloodline (Sami Zayn, Jimmy Uso and Jey Uso) in 10:30; Gunther defeated Sheamus in 18:18.

OCTOBER 14 *New Orleans, LA*
Sami Zayn defeated Kofi Kingston in 14:50; Braun Strowman defeated Brian Thomas and James Maverick in a Handicap Match in 1:57; LA Knight defeated Mansoor in 2:52; Damage CTRL (Bayley, Dakota Kai and Iyo Sky) defeated Raquel Rodriguez, Shotzi and Roxanne Perez in 6:42; Legado Del Fantasma (Joaquin Wilde and Cruz Del Toro) defeated Hit Row (Ashante Adonis and Top Dolla) in 1:22; Rey Mysterio defeated Ricochet, Solo Sikoa and Sheamus in a Four Way Match in 16:19.

OCTOBER 21 *Toledo, OH*
Solo Sikoa defeated Sheamus in 13:05; Liv Morgan vs. Sonya Deville ended in a double count out in 8:50; Damage CTRL (Dakota Kai and Iyo Sky) defeated Shotzi and Raquel Rodriguez in 9:58; Rey Mysterio defeated Ludwig Kaiser in 11:25.

OCTOBER 28 *St. Louis, MO*
The Brawling Brutes (Ridge Holland and Butch) defeated The Bloodline (Sami Zayn and Solo Sikoa) in 11:50; The New Day (Xavier Woods and Kofi Kingston) defeated Maximum Male Models (Mace and Mansoor) in 3:45; Ronda Rousey defeated Emma in 6:50; Shinsuke Nakamura and Hit Row (Ashante Adonis and Top Dolla) defeated Legado Del Fantasma (Santos Escobar, Joaquin Wilde and Cruz Del Toro) in 4:19; Karrion Kross defeated Madcap Moss in 9:35.

NOVEMBER 4 *St. Louis, MO*
Liv Morgan defeated Sonya Deville in a No Disqualification Match in 13:48; LA Knight defeated Ricochet in 9:54; Shayna Baszler defeated Natalya in 4:11; Gunther defeated Rey Mysterio in 18:18.

NOVEMBER 11 *Indianapolis, IN*
The Usos (Jimmy Uso and Jey Uso) defeated The New Day (Xavier Woods and Kofi Kingston) in 23:50; Santos Escobar defeated Shinsuke Nakamura in 8:20; Shotzi defeated Raquel Rodriguez, Sonya Deville, Liv Morgan, Xia Li and Lacey Evans in a Six-Pack Challenge in 11:58; Braun Strowman defeated Jinder Mahal in 1:50.

NOVEMBER 18 *Hartford, CT*
Ricochet defeated Mustafa Ali in 10:45; Karrion Kross defeated Madcap Moss in 6:48; Shotzi defeated Shayna Baszler in 5:01; Braun Strowman and The New Day (Xavier Woods and Kofi Kingston) defeated Imperium (Gunther, Ludwig Kaiser and Giovanni Vinci) in 7:38; Butch defeated Sami Zayn in 7:30.

NOVEMBER 25 *Providence, RI*
Santos Escobar defeated Butch in 6:41; The Viking Raiders (Erik and Ivar) defeated Hit Row (Ashante Adonis and Top Dolla) in 2:46; Ricochet defeated Braun Strowman in 3:45; Ronda Rousey and Shayna Baszler defeated Raquel Rodriguez and Shotzi in 3:26; Drew McIntyre and Sheamus defeated The Usos (Jimmy Uso and Jey Uso) in 14:43.

DECEMBER 2 *Buffalo, NY*
Sami Zayn defeated Sheamus in 18:02; Shayna Baszler defeated Emma in 4:10; Gunther defeated Kofi Kingston in 11:37; Ricochet defeated Santos Escobar to win the SmackDown World Cup Tournament in 20:45.

DECEMBER 9 *Pittsburgh, PA*
The Usos (Jey Uso and Jimmy Uso) defeated The Brawling Brutes (Butch and Sheamus) in 19:20; The Viking Raiders (Erik and Ivar) vs. Legado Del Fantasma (Joaquin Wilde and Cruz Del Toro) ended in a no contest in 1:53; Ricochet and The New Day (Kofi Kingston and Xavier Woods) defeated Imperium (Gunther, Ludwig Kaiser and Giovanni Vinci) in 18:47; Liv Morgan and Tegan Nox defeated Ronda Rousey and Shayna Baszler in 4:07.

DECEMBER 16 *Rosemont, IL*
Damage CTRL (Dakota Kai and Iyo Sky) defeated Liv Morgan and Tegan Nox in 14:48; Gunther defeated Ricochet in 21:37; Hit Row (Top Dolla and Ashante Adonis) defeated The Viking Raiders (Erik and Ivar) and Legado Del Fantasma (Joaquin Wilde and Cruz Del Toro) in a Three Way Match in 9:20.

DECEMBER 23 *Rosemont, IL*
The Usos (Jey Uso and Jimmy Uso) defeated Hit Row (Top Dolla and Ashante Adonis) in 9:43; Raquel Rodriguez defeated Xia Li, Emma, Liv Morgan, Sonya Deville, Tegan Nox and Shayna Baszler in a Gauntlet Match in 23:58; Rey Mysterio defeated Angel Garza in 4:18; Braun Strowman and Ricochet defeated Imperium (Ludwig Kaiser and Giovanni Vinci) in a Miracle On 34th Street Fight in 11:59.

DECEMBER 30 *Tampa, FL*
Solo Sikoa defeated Sheamus in 11:10; Ronda Rousey defeated Raquel Rodriguez in 16:43; Charlotte Flair defeated Ronda Rousey to win the WWE SmackDown Women's Title in :40; John Cena and Kevin Owens defeated Roman Reigns and Sami Zayn in 10:57.

WWE KICKOFF

JANUARY 1 - DAY 1 *Atlanta, GA*
Sheamus and Ridge Holland defeated Cesaro and Ricochet in 9:45.

FEBRUARY 19 - ELIMINATION CHAMBER *Saudi Arabia*
Rey Mysterio defeated The Miz in 8:20.

SEPTEMBER 3 - CLASH AT THE CASTLE *Cardiff, Wales*
Madcap Moss and The Street Profits (Angelo Dawkins and Montez Ford) defeated Austin Theory and Alpha Academy (Chad Gable and Otis) in 6:29.

WWE MAIN EVENT

JANUARY 6 *Greenville, SC*
T-Bar defeated Dennis Daniels in 1:59; The Mysterios (Dominik Mysterio and Rey Mysterio) defeated The Hurt Business (Cedric Alexander and Shelton Benjamin) in 5:41.

JANUARY 13 *Philadelphia, PA*
Tommaso Ciampa defeated T-Bar in 5:28; Pete Dunne defeated Akira Tozawa in 7:11.

JANUARY 20 *Tulsa, OK*
Tommaso Ciampa defeated Akira Tozawa in 5:33; Pete Dunne defeated T-Bar in 6:44.

JANUARY 27 *Toledo, OH*
LA Knight defeated Cedric Alexander in 5:02; T-Bar defeated Roderick Strong in 5:21.

FEBRUARY 3 *Cincinnati, OH*
Veer Mahaan defeated Akira Tozawa in 2:14; Liv Morgan defeated Doudrop in 7:21.

FEBRUARY 10 *Denver, CO*
Veer Mahaan defeated T-Bar in 5:36; The Hurt Business (Cedric Alexander and Shelton Benjamin) defeated The Dirty Dawgs (Dolph Ziggler and Robert Roode) in 7:01.

FEBRUARY 17 *Indianapolis, IN*
Tommaso Ciampa defeated T-Bar in 8:29; Veer Mahaan defeated Apollo Crews in 5:04.

FEBRUARY 24 *Columbia, SC*
Veer Mahaan defeated Apollo Crews in 4:59; Liv Morgan defeated Queen Zelina in 6:53.

MARCH 3 *Columbus, OH*
Veer Mahaan defeated Storm Grayson in 3:36.

MARCH 10 *Cleveland, OH*
Veer Mahaan defeated Savion Truitt in 4:50; The Street Profits (Angelo Dawkins and Montez Ford) defeated The Hurt Business (Cedric Alexander and Shelton Benjamin) in 9:23.

MARCH 17 *Jacksonville, FL*
Veer Mahaan defeated Gary Heck in 3:28; Tommaso Ciampa defeated T-Bar in 5:58.

MARCH 24 *Rosemont, IL*
Veer Mahaan defeated Joe Alonzo in 4:10; Cedric Alexander defeated T-Bar in 10:24.

MARCH 31 *Pittsburgh, PA*
Veer Mahaan defeated Cedric Alexander in 5:19; Finn Balor defeated Apollo Crews in 5:31.

APRIL 7 *Dallas, TX*
Apollo Crews defeated Greg Leslie in 3:49; Shelton Benjamin defeated T-Bar in 8:36.

APRIL 14 *Detroit, MI*
Tommaso Ciampa defeated T-Bar in 6:26; Apollo Crews and Commander Azeez defeated The Hurt Business (Cedric Alexander and Shelton Benjamin) in 6:59.

APRIL 21 *Buffalo, NY*
Apollo Crews defeated T-Bar in 5:06; Tommaso Ciampa defeated Cedric Alexander in 7:42.

APRIL 28 *Knoxville, TN*
Liv Morgan defeated Nikki A.S.H. in 5:03; The Street Profits (Angelo Dawkins and Montez Ford) defeated The Hurt Business (Cedric Alexander and Shelton Benjamin) in 9:31.

MAY 5 *Greensboro, NC*
Commander Azeez defeated T-Bar in 6:02; Ciampa defeated Apollo Crews in 7:29.

MAY 12 *Hartford, CT*
T-Bar defeated Reggie in 2:50; Apollo Crews defeated Akira Tozawa in 6:08.

MAY 19 *Norfolk, VA*
Ciampa defeated Reggie in 5:37; The Street Profits (Angelo Dawkins and Montez Ford) defeated Apollo Crews and Commander Azeez in 4:23.

MAY 26 *Evansville, IN*
Commander Azeez defeated Akira Tozawa in 4:22; Apollo Crews defeated T-Bar in 8:43.

JUNE 2 *Des Moines, IA*
R-Truth defeated T-Bar in 6:02; Apollo Crews defeated Akira Tozawa in 6:08.

JUNE 9 *Green Bay, WI*
Ciampa defeated Reggie in 5:29; Mustafa Ali defeated T-Bar in 7:13.

JUNE 16 *Wichita, KS*
Shelton Benjamin defeated Akira Tozawa in 6:16; T-Bar defeated Reggie in 6:29.

JUNE 23 *Lincoln, NE*
Doudrop defeated Dana Brooke to win the WWE 24/7 Title in 2:21; The Mysterios (Dominik Mysterio and Rey Mysterio) defeated The Judgment Day (Damian Priest and Finn Balor) by DQ in 7:31.

JUNE 30 *Laredo, TX*
Mustafa Ali defeated T-Bar in 4:57; Ciampa defeated Akira Tozawa in 8:39.

JULY 7 *San Diego, CA*
Cedric Alexander defeated T-Bar in 5:01; Veer Mahaan defeated Mustafa Ali in 7:09.

JULY 14 *San Antonio, TX*
Tamina defeated Jazmin Allure in 5:22; Mustafa Ali defeated Akira Tozawa in 8:28.

JULY 21 *Tampa, FL*
Akira Tozawa defeated Reggie in 6:12; Alpha Academy (Chad Gable and Otis) defeated Cedric Alexander and Mustafa Ali in 8:49.

JULY 28 *New York, NY*
Cedric Alexander and Mustafa Ali defeated Akira Tozawa and T-Bar in 4:38; Asuka and Dana Brooke defeated Carmella and Tamina in 7:09.

AUGUST 4 *Houston, TX*
Omos defeated Ezekiel in 4:06; T-Bar defeated Shelton Benjamin in 9:23.

AUGUST 11 *Cleveland, OH*
Cedric Alexander defeated Shelton Benjamin in 4:51; Mustafa Ali defeated T-Bar in 8:01.

AUGUST 18 *Washington, D.C.*
Shelton Benjamin defeated Akira Tozawa in 5:22; The Street Profits (Angelo Dawkins and Montez Ford) defeated Alpha Academy (Chad Gable and Otis) in 6:49.

AUGUST 25 *Toronto, Canada*
Doudrop and Nikki A.S.H. defeated Dana Brooke and Tamina in 5:14; Cedric Alexander and Mustafa Ali defeated Shelton Benjamin and T-Bar in 8:30.

SEPTEMBER 1 *Pittsburgh, PA*
Shelton Benjamin defeated R-Truth in 4:42; Cedric Alexander defeated T-Bar in 8:00.

SEPTEMBER 8 *Kansas City, MO*
Shelton Benjamin defeated Reggie in 6:09; T-Bar defeated Cedric Alexander in 6:46.

SEPTEMBER 15 *Portland, OR*
R-Truth defeated Akira Tozawa in 4:42; Shelton Benjamin defeated Cedric Alexander in 8:00.

SEPTEMBER 22 *San Jose, CA*
Dana Brooke defeated Tamina in 5:00; Alpha Academy (Chad Gable and Otis) defeated Mustafa Ali and Shelton Benjamin in 9:52.

SEPTEMBER 29 *Edmonton, Canada*
Mustafa Ali defeated T-Bar in 5:21; R-Truth defeated Shelton Benjamin in 8:57.

OCTOBER 6 *Saint Paul, MN*
Dana Brooke defeated Fallon Henley in 4:39; Brooks Jensen and Josh Briggs defeated R-Truth and Shelton Benjamin in 6:48.

OCTOBER 13 *New York, NY*
Carmelo Hayes defeated Cedric Alexander in 8:19; R-Truth defeated Von Wagner by DQ in 3:34.

OCTOBER 20 *Oklahoma City, OK*
Cameron Grimes defeated Akira Tozawa in 4:46; Cedric Alexander defeated Duke Hudson in 8:50.

OCTOBER 27 *Charlotte, NC*
Cedric Alexander defeated Von Wagner by DQ in 8:50; Dana Brooke defeated Kiana James in 4:56.

NOVEMBER 3 *Dallas, TX*
Kiana James defeated Dana Brooke in 4:19; R-Truth and Shelton Benjamin defeated Duke Hudson and Von Wagner in 6:31.

NOVEMBER 10 *Wilkes-Barre, PA*
Wendy Choo defeated Tamina in 5:25; Xyon Quinn defeated Akira Tozawa in 8:34.

NOVEMBER 17 *Louisville, KY*
Asuka defeated Kiana James in 4:15; Cedric Alexander defeated JD McDonagh in 10:00.

NOVEMBER 24 *Albany, NY*
Alba Fyre defeated Tamina in 5:21; Akira Tozawa defeated Grayson Waller in 7:02.

DECEMBER 1 *Norfolk, VA*
Zoey Stark defeated Dana Brooke in 5:42; Cedric Alexander defeated Joe Gacy in 8:02.

DECEMBER 8 *Washington, D.C.*
Katana Chance defeated Tamina in 1:47; Cedric Alexander defeated Trick Williams in 7:56.

DECEMBER 15 *Milwaukee, WI*
Dana Brooke defeated Briana Ray in 6:12; Cedric Alexander and Mustafa Ali defeated Edris Enofe and Malik Blade in 6:17.

DECEMBER 22 *Des Moines, IA*
Cedric Alexander defeated Andre Chase in 5:10; Mustafa Ali defeated Axiom in 7:19.

DECEMBER 29
Highlights show

WWE 205 LIVE

JANUARY 7 *Orlando, FL*
Malik Blade defeated Draco Anthony in 6:05; Nikkita Lyons defeated Erica Yan in 5:24; Ikemen Jiro defeated Ru Feng in 6:39.

JANUARY 14 *Orlando, FL*
Bodhi Hayward defeated Guru Raaj in 3:44; Ivy Nile defeated Valentina Feroz in 4:39.

JANUARY 21 *Orlando, FL*
Lash Legend defeated Fallon Henley in 4:25; Draco Anthony defeated Javier Bernal in 4:53; James Drake defeated Bodhi Hayward in 4:36.

JANUARY 28 *Orlando, FL*
Josh Briggs defeated Damon Kemp in 5:04; Valentina Feroz and Yulisa Leon defeated Amari Miller and Lash Legend in 6:29; Joe Gacy defeated Draco Anthony in 5:10.

FEBRUARY 4 *Orlando, FL*
Brooks Jensen defeated Bodhi Hayward in 6:06; Kacy Katanzaro and Kayden Carter defeated Fallon Henley and Lash Legend in 6:15; Kushida defeated Damon Kemp in 3:50.

FEBRUARY 11 *Orlando, FL*
Trick Williams defeated Ikemen Jiro in 5:09; Lash Legend defeated Erica Yan in 4:22; Joe Gacy defeated Xyon Quinn in 5:39.

WWE NXT 2.0

JANUARY 4 - NEW YEAR'S EVIL '22 *Orlando, FL*
Carmelo Hayes defeated Roderick Strong to win the Unified NXT North American and NXT Cruiserweight Title in 15:30; Riddle and MSK (Nash Carter and Wes Lee) defeated Imperium (Walter, Marcel Barthel and

Fabian Aichner) in 13:52; **Mandy Rose** defeated **Raquel Gonzalez** and **Cora Jade** in 12:32; **Bron Breakker** defeated **Tommaso Ciampa** to win the NXT Title in 15:28.

JANUARY 11 *Orlando, FL*
Santos Escobar defeated **Xyon Quinn** in 10:38; **Cameron Grimes** defeated **Damon Kemp** in 2:20; **Malik Blade** and **Edris Enofe** defeated **Joe Gacy** and **Harland** by DQ in 3:14; **Tony D'Angelo** defeated **Pete Dunne** in a Crowbar On A Pole Match in 13:17; **Wendy Choo**, **Indi Hartwell** and **Persia Pirotta** defeated **Kacy Catanzaro**, **Kayden Carter** and **Amari Miller** in 3:40; **Solo Sikoa** vs. **Boa** ended in a double count out in 3:47; **AJ Styles** defeated **Grayson Waller** in 14:15.

JANUARY 18 *Orlando, FL*
Grayson Waller defeated **Dexter Lumis** in 10:01; **The Creed Brothers (Julius Creed** and **Brutus Creed)** defeated **Josh Briggs** and **Brooks Jensen** in 5:33; **Dante Chen** vs. **Guru Raaj** ended in a no contest in :58; **Ivy Nile** defeated **Kay Lee Ray** in 4:25; **Malik Blade** and **Edris Enofe** defeated **Legado Del Fantasma (Joaquin Wilde** and **Raul Mendoza)** in 3:17; **Dakota Kai** defeated **Yulisa Leon** in 4:05; **Walter** defeated **Roderick Strong** in 12:15.

JANUARY 25 *Orlando, FL*
MSK (Nash Carter and **Wes Lee)** defeated **Jacket Time (Kushida** and **Ikemen Jiro)** in 11:32; **Solo Sikoa** defeated **Boa** in a Falls Count Anywhere No Disqualification Match in 8:08; **Duke Hudson** defeated **Guru Raaj** in 1:08; **Kay Lee Ray**, **Indi Hartwell** and **Persia Pirotta** defeated **Toxic Attraction (Mandy Rose, Gigi Dolin** and **Jacy Jayne)** in 10:25; **Grizzled Young Veterans (Zack Gibson** and **James Drake)** defeated **Andre Chase** and **Bodhi Hayward** in 5:11; **Io Shirai** defeated **Tiffany Stratton** in 4:18; **Cameron Grimes** defeated **Tony D'Angelo** in 11:41.

FEBRUARY 1 *Orlando, FL*
Imperium (Walter, Marcel Barthel and **Fabian Aichner)** defeated **The Diamond Mine (Roderick Strong, Julius Creed** and **Brutus Creed)** in 12:01; **Raquel Gonzalez** defeated **Cora Jade** in 6:02; **Sarray** defeated **Kayla Inlay** in 3:29; **Joe Gacy** defeated **LA Knight** in 4:18; **Wendy Choo** defeated **Amari Miller** in 3:26; **Andre Chase** defeated **Draco Anthony** in 4:36; **Bron Breakker** and **Tommaso Ciampa** defeated **Legado Del Fantasma (Joaquin Wilde** and **Raul Mendoza)** in 11:28.

FEBRUARY 8 *Orlando, FL*
The Creed Brothers (Julius Creed and **Brutus Creed)** defeated **Grizzled Young Veterans (Zack Gibson** and **James Drake)** in 12:03; **Tiffany Stratton** defeated **Wendy Choo** in 3:07; **Pete Dunne** defeated **Draco Anthony** in 6:53; **LA Knight** defeated **Sanga** in 3:12; **Sarray** defeated **Dakota Kai** in 6:20; **MSK (Nash Carter** and **Wes Lee)** defeated **Malik Blade** and **Edris Enofe** in 9:29; **Mandy Rose** defeated **Kay Lee Ray** in 7:59.

FEBRUARY 15 - VENGEANCE DAY '22 *Orlando, FL*
Pete Dunne defeated **Tony D'Angelo** in a Weaponized Steel Cage Match in 9:52; **Toxic Attraction (Gigi Dolin** and **Jacy Jayne)** defeated **Indi Hartwell** and **Persia Pirotta** in 7:54; **Carmelo Hayes** defeated **Cameron Grimes** in 15:57; **The Creed Brothers (Julius Creed** and **Brutus Creed)** defeated **MSK (Nash Carter** and **Wes Lee)** to win the Dusty Rhodes Tag Team Classic in 9:36; **Bron Breakker** defeated **Santos Escobar** in 12:05.

FEBRUARY 22 *Orlando, FL*
Grayson Waller defeated **LA Knight** in 9:58; **Io Shirai** and **Kay Lee Ray** defeated **Amari Miller** and **Lash Legend** in 2:44; **Duke Hudson** defeated **Dante Chen** in 2:20; **Cameron Grimes** defeated **Trick Williams** in 6:06; **Nikkita Lyons** defeated **Kayla Inlay** in 4:03; **Kayden Carter** and **Kacy Catanzaro** defeated **Ivy Nile** and **Tatum Paxley** in 3:26; **Dolph Ziggler** defeated **Tommaso Ciampa** in 15:37.

MARCH 1 *Orlando, FL*
Bron Breakker and **Tommaso Ciampa** defeated **The Dirty Dawgs (Dolph Ziggler** and **Robert Roode)** in 13:05; **Wendy Choo** and **Dakota Kai** defeated **Indi Hartwell** and **Persia Pirotta** in 5:21; **Lash Legend** defeated **Amari Miller** in 2:57; **Gunther** defeated **Solo Sikoa** in 7:37; **Harland** defeated **Draco Anthony** in 2:25; **Raquel Gonzalez** and **Cora Jade** defeated **Yulisa Leon** and **Valentina Feroz** in 4:47; **Von Wagner** defeated **Andre Chase** in 4:10; **Carmelo Hayes** defeated **Pete Dunne** in 12:31.

MARCH 8 - ROADBLOCK '22 *Orlando, FL*
Wendy Choo and **Dakota Kai** defeated **Raquel Gonzalez** and **Cora Jade** in 10:42; **Fallon Henley** defeated **Tiffany Stratton** in 2:48; **Grayson Waller** defeated **LA Knight** in a Last Man Standing Match in 16:01; **Io Shirai** and **Kay Lee Ray** defeated **Kayden Carter** and **Kacy Catanzaro** in 7:59; **Imperium (Marcel Barthel** and **Fabian Aichner)** vs. **MSK (Nash Carter** and **Wes Lee)** ended in a no contest in 5:33; **Dolph Ziggler** defeated **Bron Breakker** and **Tommaso Ciampa** in a Triple Threat Match to win the NXT Title in 12:24.

MARCH 15 *Orlando, FL*
Santos Escobar defeated **Cameron Grimes** in a Ladder Match in 11:30; **A-Kid** defeated **Kushida** in 4:58; **Tiffany Stratton** defeated **Sarray** in :54; **Indi Hartwell** defeated **Persia Pirotta** in 2:24; **Dominik Mysterio** defeated **Raul Mendoza** in 3:05; **Dolph Ziggler** defeated **LA Knight** in 11:48.

MARCH 22 *Orlando, FL*
Solo Sikoa defeated **Roderick Strong** in a Ladder Match in 9:18; **Tony D'Angelo** defeated **Dexter Lumis** in 7:15; **Elektra Lopez** defeated **Fallon Henley** in 3:33; **Bron Breakker** defeated **Robert Roode** in 15:14; **Grayson Waller** defeated **A-Kid** in a Ladder Match in 2:51; **The Creed Brothers (Julius Creed** and **Brutus Creed)** defeated **Grizzled Young Veterans (Zack Gibson** and **James Drake)** in 4:14; **Gunther** defeated **Duke Hudson** in 3:52; **Io Shirai** and **Kay Lee Ray** defeated **Wendy Choo** and **Dakota Kai** to win the Dusty Rhodes Tag Team Classic in 10:22.

MARCH 29 *Orlando, FL*
Imperium (Gunther, Marcel Barthel and **Fabian Aichner)** defeated **LA Knight** and **MSK (Nash Carter** and **Wes Lee)** in 12:11; **Ivy Nile** defeated **Tiffany Stratton** in 3:32; **Brooks Jensen** and **Josh Briggs** defeated **Legado Del Fantasma (Joaquin Wilde** and **Raul Mendoza)** in 5:36; **Von Wagner** defeated **Bodhi Hayward** in 3:42; **Joe Gacy** defeated **Draco Anthony** in 3:57; **Nikkita Lyons** defeated **Sloane Jacobs** in 1:47; **Cameron Grimes** defeated **A-Kid** and **Roderick Strong** in a Ladder Match in 10:55.

APRIL 5 *Orlando, FL*
The Creed Brothers (Julius Creed and **Brutus Creed)** defeated **Imperium (Marcel Barthel** and **Fabian Aichner)** in 11:24; **Dexter Lumis** vs. **Duke Hudson**

ended in a double count out in 4:55; **Toxic Attraction** (Gigi Dolin and Jacy Jayne) defeated **Dakota Kai** and **Raquel Gonzalez** in 8:31; **Nikkita Lyons** defeated **Lash Legend** in 4:39; **Bron Breakker** defeated **Gunther** in 13:08.

APRIL 12 *Orlando, FL*
Cameron Grimes defeated **Solo Sikoa** in 13:11; **Von Wagner** defeated **Ikemen Jiro** in 2:55; **Mandy Rose** defeated **Dakota Kai** in 10:48; **Xyon Quinn** defeated **Draco Anthony** in 2:58; **Pretty Deadly** (Elton Prince and Kit Wilson) defeated **Grayson Waller** and **Sanga**, **Legado Del Fantasma** (Joaquin Wilde and Raul Mendoza) and **The Creed Brothers** (Julius Creed and Brutus Creed) and **Brooks Jensen** and **Josh Briggs** in a Gauntlet Match to win the NXT Tag Team Title in 27:08.

APRIL 19 *Orlando, FL*
Tiffany Stratton defeated **Sarray** in 4:31; **Grayson Waller** defeated **Sanga** in 3:28; **Legado Del Fantasma** (Joaquin Wilde and Raul Mendoza) defeated **Grizzled Young Veterans** (Zack Gibson and James Drake) in 3:57; **Carmelo Hayes** defeated **Santos Escobar** in 13:54; **Natalya** defeated **Tatum Paxley** in 4:52; **Xyon Quinn** defeated **Wes Lee** in 3:29; **Roxanne Perez** defeated **Jacy Jayne** in 2:17; **Pretty Deadly** (Elton Prince and Kit Wilson) defeated **Dexter Lumis** and **Duke Hudson** in 11:47.

APRIL 26 *Orlando, FL*
Nikkita Lyons defeated **Lash Legend** in 5:09; **Von Wagner** defeated **Tony D'Angelo** in 10:44; **Katana Chance** and **Kayden Carter** defeated **Yulisa Leon** and **Valentina Feroz** in 6:01; **Legado Del Fantasma** (Joaquin Wilde, Cruz del Toro and Elektra Lopez) defeated **Fallon Henley** and **Josh Briggs** in a Handicap Match in 4:45; **Solo Sikoa** defeated **Trick Williams** in 5:08; **The Viking Raiders** (Erik and Ivar) defeated **Edris Enofe** and **Malik Blade** in 4:45; **Mandy Rose** defeated **Roxanne Perez** in 9:58.

MAY 3 - SPRING BREAKIN' *Orlando, FL*
Cameron Grimes defeated **Carmelo Hayes** and **Solo Sikoa** in a Triple Threat Match in 14:06; **Nathan Frazer** defeated **Grayson Waller** in 12:45; **Cora Jade** and **Nikkita Lyons** defeated **Natalya** and **Lash Legend** in 13:28; **The Creed Brothers** (Julius Creed and Brutus Creed) defeated **The Viking Raiders** (Erik and Ivar) in 12:58; **Bron Breakker** defeated **Joe Gacy** in 11:03.

MAY 10 *Orlando, FL*
Toxic Attraction (Gigi Dolin and Jacy Jayne) defeated **Roxanne Perez** and **Wendy Choo** in 10:01; **Fallon Henley** defeated **Sloane Jacobs** in 4:28; **Alba Fyre** defeated **Amari Miller** in 3:40; **Sarray** and **Andre Chase** defeated **Tiffany Stratton** and **Grayson Waller** in 7:00; **Nikkita Lyons** defeated **Arianna Grace** in 3:09; **Natalya** defeated **Cora Jade** in 14:08.

MAY 17 *Orlando, FL*
Cameron Grimes and **Solo Sikoa** defeated **Carmelo Hayes** and **Trick Williams** in 9:57; **Lash Legend** defeated **Tatum Paxley** in 3:50; **The Viking Raiders** (Erik and Ivar) defeated **The Creed Brothers** (Julius Creed and Brutus Creed) in 9:30; **Grayson Waller** defeated **Andre Chase** in 4:12; **Roxanne Perez** defeated **Kiana James** in 5:15; **Nathan Frazer** vs. **Wes Lee** ended in a no contest in 4:21; **Santos Escobar** defeated **Tony D'Angelo** in 12:49.

MAY 24 *Orlando, FL*
Channing Lorenzo and **Troy Donavan** defeated **Edris Enofe** and **Malik Blade** in 6:10; **Sanga** defeated **Wes Lee** in 3:51; **Alba Fyre** defeated **Elektra Lopez** in 2:53; **Roxanne Perez** defeated **Lash Legend** in 3:19; **Mandy Rose** defeated **Indi Hartwell** in 9:18; **Tiffany Stratton** defeated **Fallon Henley** in 5:02; **Von Wagner** defeated **Ikemen Jiro** in 4:13; **Duke Hudson** defeated **Bron Breakker** by DQ in 11:02.

MAY 31 *Orlando, FL*
Pretty Deadly (Elton Prince and Kit Wilson) defeated **Diamond Mine** (Roderick Strong and Damon Kemp) in 13:17; **Cora Jade** defeated **Elektra Lopez** in 5:06; **Wes Lee** defeated **Xyon Quinn** in 3:41; **Solo Sikoa** defeated **Duke Hudson** in 4:44; **Grayson Waller** defeated **Josh Briggs** in 3:33; **Ivy Nile** defeated **Kiana James** in 3:36; **Cameron Grimes** defeated **Nathan Frazer** in 10:09.

JUNE 7 *Orlando, FL*
Josh Briggs defeated **Von Wagner** in 3:04; **Nathan Frazer** defeated **Santos Escobar** in 11:54; **Roxanne Perez** defeated **Tiffany Stratton** to win the NXT Women's Breakout Tournament in 8:48; **Pretty Deadly** (Elton Prince and Kit Wilson) defeated **Andre Chase** in a Handicap Match in 3:16; **Alba Fyre** defeated **Tatum Paxley** in 2:38; **Solo Sikoa** and **Apollo Crews** defeated **Grayson Waller** and **Carmelo Hayes** in 13:45.

JUNE 14 *Orlando, FL*
The Creed Brothers (Julius Creed and Brutus Creed) defeated **Edris Enofe** and **Malik Blade** in 13:57; **Fallon Henley** defeated **Tiffany Stratton** in 3:10; **Wes Lee** defeated **Xyon Quinn** 2:50; **The Dyad** (Rip Fowler and Jagger Reid) defeated **Dante Chen** and **Javier Bernal** in 3:56; **Bron Breakker** defeated **Duke Hudson** in :46; **Giovanni Vinci** defeated **Guru Raaj** in 2:55; **Carmelo Hayes** and **Trick Williams** defeated **Troy Donavan** and **Channing Lorenzo** in 4:22; **Roxanne Perez, Cora Jade** and **Indi Hartwell** defeated **Toxic Attraction** (Mandy Rose, Gigi Dolin and Jacy Jayne) in 13:51.

JUNE 21 *Orlando, FL*
Grayson Waller defeated **Solo Sikoa** in 12:18; **Katana Chance** and **Kayden Carter** defeated **Valentina Feroz** and **Yulisa Leon** in 5:15; **Diamond Mine** (Roderick Strong and Damon Kemp) defeated **Cruz Del Toro** and **Joaquin Wilde** in 4:57; **Cameron Grimes** defeated **Edris Enofe** in 5:37; **Von Wagner** defeated **Brooks Jensen** in 4:45; **Alba Fyre** defeated **Lash Legend** by DQ in 3:31; **Carmelo Hayes** defeated **Tony D'Angelo** in 10:38.

JUNE 28 *Orlando, FL*
Cora Jade and **Roxanne Perez** defeated **Katana Chance** and **Kayden Carter** in 13:46; **Giovanni Vinci** defeated **Ikemen Jiro** in 2:59; **Kiana James** defeated **Indi Hartwell** in 3:51; **Joe Gacy** and **The Dyad** (Rip Fowler and Jagger Reid) defeated **Diamond Mine** (Roderick Strong, Julius Creed and Brutus Creed) in 13:56; **Sanga** defeated **Xyon Quinn** in 5:08; **Nikkita Lyons** defeated **Mandy Rose** by DQ in 5:29.

JULY 5 - GREAT AMERICAN BASH '22 *Orlando, FL*
Cora Jade and **Roxanne Perez** defeated **Toxic Attraction** (Gigi Dolin and Jacy Jayne) to win the NXT Women's Tag Team Title in 10:29; **Trick Williams** defeated **Wes Lee** in 3:46; **Tiffany Stratton** defeated **Wendy Choo** in 5:05; **Carmelo Hayes** defeated **Grayson Waller** in 11:43; **The Creed Brothers** (Julius Creed and Brutus Creed) defeated **Roderick Strong**

and **Damon Kemp** in 12:13; **Bron Breakker** defeated **Cameron Grimes** in 12:33.

JULY 12 *Orlando, FL*
Giovanni Vinci defeated **Apollo Crews** in 12:09; **Tatum Paxley** defeated **Kayden Carter** in 3:31; **Sanga** defeated **Duke Hudson** in 3:01; **Von Wagner** vs. **Solo Sikoa** ended in a double count out in 6:50; **Indi Hartwell** defeated **Lash Legend** in 3:45; **Tony D'Angelo** and **Channing Lorenzo** defeated **Edris Enofe** and **Malik Blade** in 5:23; **Mandy Rose** defeated **Roxanne Perez** in 9:17.

JULY 19 *Orlando, FL*
JD McDonagh defeated **Cameron Grimes** in 13:25; **Roderick Strong** defeated **Damon Kemp** in 5:55; **Josh Briggs** and **Brooks Jensen** defeated **Pretty Deadly** (**Elton Prince** and **Kit Wilson**) in 8:15; **Axiom** defeated **Dante Chen** in 3:00; **Zoey Stark** won a Battle Royal in 13:13.

JULY 26 *Orlando, FL*
Grayson Waller defeated **Wes Lee** in 10:59; **Apollo Crews** defeated **Xyon Quinn** in 5:40; **Zoey Stark** defeated **Gigi Dolin** in 2:48; **Giovanni Vinci** defeated **Andre Chase** in 9:10; **Indi Hartwell** defeated **Arianna Grace** in 3:59; **The D'Angelo Family** (**Tony D'Angelo, Channing Lorenzo, Joaquin Wilde** and **Cruz Del Toro**) defeated **Diamond Mine** (**Roderick Strong, Damon Kemp, Julius Creed** and **Brutus Creed**) in 11:39.

AUGUST 2 *Orlando, FL*
Kayden Carter and **Katana Chance** defeated **Valentina Feroz** and **Yulisa Leon, Ivy Nile** and **Tatum Paxley,** and **Toxic Attraction** (**Gigi Dolin** and **Jacy Jayne**) in a Four Way Elimination Match to win the vacant NXT Women's Tag Team Title in 12:09; **Carmelo Hayes** defeated **Nathan Frazer** in 5:41; **Mandy Rose** defeated **Sarray** in 5:44; **Axiom** defeated **Duke Hudson** in 2:10; **The Creed Brothers** (**Julius Creed** and **Brutus Creed**) defeated **Tony D'Angelo** and **Channing Lorenzo** in 10:46; **Joe Gacy** defeated **Brooks Jensen** in 3:00; **Alba Fyre** defeated **Lash Legend** in 5:31; **Solo Sikoa** defeated **Von Wagner** in a Falls Count Anywhere Match in 12:25.

AUGUST 9 *Orlando, FL*
Nikkita Lyons defeated **Kiana James** in 4:10; **Wes Lee** defeated **Trick Williams** 2-1 in a Rounds Match in 10:56; **Arianna Grace** defeated **Thea Hail** in 3:49; **Apollo Crews** defeated **Roderick Strong** in 11:55; **Pretty Deadly** (**Elton Prince** and **Kit Wilson**) defeated **Edris Enofe** and **Malik Blade** in 4:37; **Zoey Stark** defeated **Cora Jade** in 11:05.

AUGUST 16 - HEATWAVE *Orlando, FL*
Carmelo Hayes defeated **Giovanni Vinci** in 11:56; **Cora Jade** defeated **Roxanne Perez** in 11:41; **Tony D'Angelo** defeated **Santos Escobar** in a Street Fight in 12:44; **Mandy Rose** defeated **Zoey Stark** in 11:26; **Bron Breakker** defeated **JD McDonagh** in 13:17.

AUGUST 23 *Orlando, FL*
Gallus (**Mark Coffey** and **Wolfgang**) defeated **Josh Briggs** and **Brooks Jensen** via count out in 8:46; **Cameron Grimes** defeated **Javier Bernal** in 2:35; **Blair Davenport** defeated **Indi Hartwell** in 3:49; **The Dyad** (**Jagger Reid** and **Rip Fowler**) defeated **Joaquin Wilde** and **Cruz Del Toro** in 5:02; **Tyler Bate** defeated **Von Wagner** in 6:14; **Wendy Choo** defeated **Tiffany Stratton** in a Lights Out Match in 13:09.

AUGUST 30 *Orlando, FL*
Grayson Waller defeated **Apollo Crews** in 11:11; **Katana Chance** and **Kayden Carter** defeated **Ivy Nile** and **Tatum Paxley** in 4:17; **Lash Legend** and **Pretty Deadly** (**Elton Prince** and **Kit Wilson**) defeated **Fallon Henley, Josh Briggs** and **Brooks Jensen** in 11:31; **Andre Chase** defeated **Charlie Dempsey** in 5:17; **Zoey Stark** defeated **Kiana James** in 4:23; **Gallus** (**Joe Coffey, Mark Coffey** and **Wolfgang**) defeated **Diamond Mine** (**Damon Kemp, Julius Creed** and **Brutus Creed**) in 10:59.

SEPTEMBER 6 *Orlando, FL*
Nikki A.S.H. and **Doudrop** defeated **Toxic Attraction** (**Gigi Dolin** and **Jacy Jayne**) in 10:50; **JD McDonagh** defeated **Wes Lee** in 9:37; **Meiko Satomura** defeated **Roxanne Perez** in 11:19; **Ricochet** defeated **Trick Williams** in 5:13; **Axiom** defeated **Nathan Frazer** in 11:46; **Tyler Bate** and **Bron Breakker** defeated **Gallus** (**Mark Coffey** and **Joe Coffey**) in 10:51.

SEPTEMBER 13 *Orlando, FL*
Pretty Deadly (**Elton Prince** and **Kit Wilson**) defeated **The Creed Brothers** (**Julius Creed** and **Brutus Creed**) in a Steel Cage Match in 14:58; **Fallon Henley** defeated **Lash Legend** in 2:17; **Quincy Elliott** defeated **Sean Gallagher** in 1:21; **Cameron Grimes** and **Joe Gacy** defeated **Channing Lorenzo** and **Tony D'Angelo** in 5:36; **Nikkita Lyons** and **Zoey Stark** defeated **Kiana James** and **Arianna Grace** in 9:04; **Hank Walker** defeated **Javier Bernal** in 3:24; **Solo Sikoa** defeated **Carmelo Hayes** to win the NXT North American Title in 10:02.

WWE NXT

SEPTEMBER 20 *Orlando, FL*
Nathan Frazer defeated **Axiom** 13:14; **Toxic Attraction** (**Gigi Dolin** and **Jacy Jayne**) defeated **Ivy Nile** and **Tatum Paxley** in 3:58; **The Dyad** (**Jagger Reid** and **Rip Fowler**) defeated **Malik Blade** and **Edris Enofe** in 9:17; **Cora Jade** defeated **Wendy Choo** in 4:14; **Andre Chase** and **Bodhi Hayward** defeated **Carmelo Hayes** and **Trick Williams** in 4:15; **Von Wagner** defeated **Sanga** in 2:52; **Oro Mensah** defeated **Grayson Waller** in 5:23; **JD McDonagh** defeated **Tyler Bate** in 12:54.

SEPTEMBER 27 *Orlando, FL*
Mandy Rose defeated **Fallon Henley** in 5:40; **Wes Lee** defeated **Tony D'Angelo** in 8:45; **Sol Ruca** defeated **Amari Miller** in 4:48; **Joe Gacy** defeated **Cameron Grimes** in 3:17; **Nikkita Lyons** defeated **Kayden Carter** in 4:54; **Ilja Dragunov** defeated **Xyon Quinn** in 4:55; **Brutus Creed** defeated **Damon Kemp** by DQ in 3:05; **Brooks Jensen** and **Josh Briggs** defeated **Gallus** (**Mark Coffey** and **Wolfgang**) in a Pub Rules Match in 11:35.

OCTOBER 4 *Orlando, FL*
Carmelo Hayes defeated **Oro Mensah** in 5:35; **Von Wagner** defeated **Andre Chase** in 3:36; **Wendy Choo** defeated **Lash Legend** in 3:50; **Nikkita Lyons** and **Zoey Stark** defeated **Toxic Attraction** (**Gigi Dolin** and **Jacy Jayne**) in 10:28; **Julius Creed** defeated **Duke Hudson** in :52; **Xyon Quinn** defeated **Hank Walker** in 2:15; **Pretty Deadly** (**Elton Prince** and **Kit Wilson**) defeated **The Brawling Brutes** (**Ridge Holland** and **Butch**) in 12:27.

OCTOBER 11 *Orlando, FL*
Bron Breakker defeated Javier Bernal in 3:20; Nathan Frazer defeated Axiom in a Ladder Match in 12:53; Indi Hartwell defeated Valentina Feroz in 3:33; Edris Enofe and Malik Blade defeated The Dyad (Jagger Reid and Rip Fowler), and Brooks Jensen and Josh Briggs in a Three Way Match in 9:10; Alba Fyre defeated Jacy Jayne in 3:34; Wes Lee defeated Channing Lorenzo in 3:57; Kiana James defeated Thea Hail in 1:18; Ilja Dragunov defeated Grayson Waller in 11:07.

OCTOBER 18 *Orlando, FL*
Rhea Ripley defeated Roxanne Perez in a Pick Your Poison Match in 12:46; Shinsuke Nakamura defeated Channing Lorenzo in 5:22; Alba Fyre defeated Sonya Deville in 2:09; Carmelo Hayes and Trick Williams defeated Wes Lee and Oro Mensah in 2:43; Cameron Grimes and The O.C. (Luke Gallows and Karl Anderson) defeated Joe Gacy and The Dyad (Jagger Reid and Rip Fowler) in 11:56; Quincy Elliott defeated Xyon Quinn in 2:49; Cora Jade defeated Raquel Rodriguez by DQ in a Pick Your Poison Match in 2:42.

OCTOBER 25 *Orlando, FL*
Katana Chance and Kayden Carter defeated Zoey Stark and Nikkita Lyons in 12:52; Shotzi defeated Lash Legend in 3:42; Pretty Deadly (Elton Prince and Kit Wilson) defeated Malik Blade and Edris Enofe in 12:29; Indi Hartwell defeated Sol Ruca in 1:19; JD McDonagh defeated Ilja Dragunov in 9:58.

NOVEMBER 1 *Orlando, FL*
Grayson Waller defeated R-Truth in 7:13; Kiana James defeated Thea Hail in 4:20; Odyssey Jones defeated Javier Bernal in 3:20; Indi Hartwell defeated Zoey Stark in 6:30; Cora Jade defeated Valentina Feroz in 3:37; Pretty Deadly (Elton Prince and Kit Wilson) defeated Bron Breakker and Wes Lee in 11:57.

NOVEMBER 8 *Orlando, FL*
Joe Gacy defeated Cameron Grimes in 10:44; Elektra Lopez defeated Sol Ruca in 3:02; Charlie Dempsey defeated Andre Chase in 2:59; Channing Lorenzo defeated Hank Walker in 3:28; JD McDonagh defeated Axiom in 10:40; Damon Kemp defeated Brutus Creed by DQ in a Five Minute Challenge in 2:47; Katana Chance and Kayden Carter defeated Zoey Stark and Nikkita Lyons in 11:02.

NOVEMBER 15 *Orlando, FL*
Bron Breakker defeated Von Wagner in 12:42; Indus Sher (Veer and Sanga) defeated Ariel Dominguez and George Cannon in 3:26; Apollo Crews defeated JD McDonagh in 13:55; The Dyad (Jagger Reid and Rip Fowler) defeated Josh Briggs and Brooks Jensen in 4:10; Indi Hartwell defeated Tatum Paxley in 4:00; Mandy Rose defeated Alba Fyre in a Last Woman Standing Match in 11:56.

NOVEMBER 22 *Orlando, FL*
Cora Jade defeated Wendy Choo in 9:08; Ivy Nile defeated Kiana James in 4:43; Scrypts defeated Guru Raaj in 1:22; Zoey Stark defeated Sol Ruca in 4:17; Pretty Deadly (Elton Prince and Kit Wilson) defeated Chase U (Andre Chase and Duke Hudson) in 8:17; Wes Lee defeated Carmelo Hayes in 13:01.

NOVEMBER 29 *Orlando, FL*
Roxanne Perez defeated Indi Hartwell in 9:07; Dijak defeated Dante Chen in 3:48; Grayson Waller defeated Duke Hudson in 5:20; Kiana James defeated

Fallon Henley in 9:40; Axiom defeated Javier Bernal in 9:03; Julius Creed defeated JD McDonagh by DQ in 10:33; Von Wagner defeated Malik Blade in 2:43; Toxic Attraction (Mandy Rose, Gigi Dolin and Jacy Jayne) defeated Katana Chance, Kayden Carter and Nikkita Lyons in 8:54.

DECEMBER 6 *Orlando, FL*
Axiom defeated Von Wagner and Andre Chase in a Three Way Match in 11:54; Tony D'Angelo defeated Xyon Quinn in 1:55; Charlie Dempsey defeated Hank Walker in 4:06; Isla Dawn defeated Thea Hail in 2:51; Brooks Jensen and Josh Briggs defeated Malik Blade and Edris Enofe in 3:24; Indi Hartwell defeated Fallon Henley and Wendy Choo in a Three Way Match in 10:15.

DECEMBER 13 *Orlando, FL*
Wes Lee defeated Channing Lorenzo in 9:52; Toxic Attraction (Gigi Dolin and Jacy Jayne) defeated Ivy Nile and Tatum Paxley by DQ in 2:26; Odyssey Jones defeated Von Wagner in 2:54; Ikemen Jiro defeated Javier Bernal in 3:16; JD McDonagh defeated Brutus Creed in 4:18; Lyra Valkyria defeated Amari Miller in 3:03; Duke Hudson defeated Damon Kemp in 3:53; Roxanne Perez defeated Mandy Rose to win the NXT Women's Championship in 9:37.

DECEMBER 20 *Orlando, FL*
Carmelo Hayes defeated Axiom in 12:35; Zoey Stark defeated Nikkita Lyons in 5:23; Kayden Carter and Katana Chance defeated Toxic Attraction (Gigi Dolin and Jacy Jayne) and Ivy Nile and Tatum Paxley in a Three Way Match in 6:35; Elektra Lopez defeated Indi Hartwell in 3:35; The New Day (Kofi Kingston and Xavier Woods) defeated Brooks Jensen and Josh Briggs in 11:10.

DECEMBER 27 *Orlando, FL*
Julius Creed defeated JD McDonagh in 9:51; Wendy Choo defeated Cora Jade in 6:10; Scrypts defeated Ikemen Jiro in 4:14; Lyra Valkyria defeated Lash Legend in 3:32; The Schism (Jagger Reid, Rip Fowler and Joe Gacy) defeated Edris Enofe, Malik Blade and Odyssey Jones in 11:15; Fallon Henley defeated Kiana James in 5:13; Wes Lee defeated Tony D'Angelo in 14:48.

WWE NXT LEVEL UP

FEBRUARY 18 *Orlando, FL*
Harland defeated Javier Bernal in 1:55; Ivy Nile and Tatum Paxley defeated Fallon Henley and Kayla Inlay in 4:18; Edris Enofe defeated Kushida in 7:07.

FEBRUARY 25 *Orlando, FL*
James Drake defeated Xyon Quinn in 4:53; Elektra Lopez defeated Sarray in 3:43; Harland and Joe Gacy defeated Jacket Time (Ikemen Jiro and Kushida) in 6:55.

MARCH 4 *Orlando, FL*
Dante Chen defeated Javier Bernal in 3:59; Tiffany Stratton defeated Erica Yan in 3:51; Legado del Fantasma (Joaquin Wilde and Raul Mendoza) defeated Edris Enofe and Malik Blade in 8:45.

MARCH 11 *Orlando, FL*
Trick Williams defeated Guru Raaj in 4:08; Ivy Nile defeated Brooklyn Barlow in 3:50; Grizzled Young Veterans (Zack Gibson and James Drake) defeated Brooks Jensen and Josh Briggs in 5:58.

MARCH 18 *Orlando, FL*
Xyon Quinn defeated Damon Kemp in 5:24; Lash Legend defeated Valentina Feroz in 4:53; Dante Chen defeated Bodhi Hayward in 5:57.

MARCH 25 *Orlando, FL*
Joe Gacy defeated Quincy Elliott in 4:15; Ivy Nile defeated Kiana James in 4:15; Edris Enofe and Malik Blade defeated Jacket Time (Ikemen Jiro and Kushida) in 7:33.

APRIL 1 *Orlando, FL*
Xyon Quinn defeated Dante Chen in 4:48; Kayden Carter defeated Tatum Paxley in 6:01; Damon Kemp defeated James Drake in 6:22.

APRIL 8 *Orlando, FL*
Javier Bernal defeated Guru Raaj in 4:27; Ivy Nile defeated Thea Hail in 4:08; Andre Chase and Bodhi Hayward defeated Channing Lauren and Troy Donavan in 6:47.

APRIL 15 *Orlando, FL*
Roxanne Perez defeated Sloane Jacobs in 4:18; Damon Kemp defeated Troy Donavan in 6:00; Tatum Paxley defeated Kiana James in 3:58.

APRIL 22 *Orlando, FL*
Edris Enofe and Malik Blade defeated Damaris Griffin and Quincy Elliott in 6:36; Fallon Henley defeated Thea Hail in 4:21; Bodhi Hayward defeated Dante Chen in 5:50.

APRIL 29 *Orlando, FL*
Damon Kemp defeated Dante Chen in 5:17; Arianna Grace defeated Amari Miller in 5:15; Andre Chase defeated Quincy Elliott in 6:19.

MAY 6 *Orlando, FL*
Ivy Nile and Tatum Paxley defeated Erica Yan and Sarray in 5:32; Sloane Jacobs defeated Thea Hail in 5:07; Channing Lorenzo and Troy Donavan defeated Dante Chen and Javier Bernal in 6:04.

MAY 13 *Orlando, FL*
Sanga defeated Dante Chen in 5:08; Elektra Lopez defeated Thea Hail in 5:08; Trick Williams defeated Javier Bernal in 6:20.

MAY 20 *Orlando, FL*
Javier Bernal defeated Bryson Montana in 4:13; Ivy Nile defeated Yulisa Leon in 5:16; Josh Briggs defeated Quincy Elliott in 7:16.

MAY 27 *Orlando, FL*
Andre Chase and Bodhi Hayward defeated Bryson Montana and Damaris Griffin in 3:53; Amari Miller defeated Arianna Grace in 5:14; Trick Williams defeated Dante Chen in 6:05.

JUNE 3 *Orlando, FL*
Fallon Henley defeated Brooklyn Barlow in 4:19; Tatum Paxley defeated Sloane Jacobs in 5:48; Edris Enofe and Malik Blade defeated Dante Chen and Javier Bernal in 7:05.

JUNE 10 *Orlando, FL*
Valentina Feroz defeated Arianna Grace in 4:16; Sloane Jacobs defeated Sierra St. Pierre in 4:51; Ikemen Jiro defeated Dante Chen in 7:01.

JUNE 17 *Orlando, FL*
Thea Hail defeated Arianna Grace in 5:28; Guru Raaj defeated Myles Borne in 4:55; Ivy Nile defeated Elektra Lopez in 5:51.

JUNE 24 *Orlando, FL*
Quincy Elliott defeated Bryson Montana in 5:07; Kiana James defeated Brooklyn Barlow in 5:15; Ikemen Jiro defeated Ru Feng in 5:27.

JULY 1 *Orlando, FL*
Channing Lorenzo defeated Hank Walker in 4:13; Amari Miller defeated Sloane Jacobs in 5:54; Duke Hudson defeated Javier Bernal in 6:53.

JULY 8 *Orlando, FL*
Dante Chen defeated Myles Borne in 4:38; Yulisa Leon defeated Arianna Grace in 6:21; Edris Enofe and Malik Blade defeated Bryson Montana and Damaris Griffin in 5:29.

JULY 15 *Orlando, FL*
Ikemen Jiro defeated Quincy Elliott in 5:05; Kiana James defeated Sol Ruca in 4:20; Andre Chase and Bodhi Hayward defeated Javier Bernal and Myles Borne in 5:47.

JULY 22 *Orlando, FL*
Thea Hail defeated Brooklyn Barlow in 5:26; Bryson Montana defeated Ru Feng in 4:40; Duke Hudson defeated Hank Walker in 6:05.

JULY 29 *Orlando, FL*
Javier Bernal defeated Myles Borne in 4:04; Fallon Henley defeated Sol Ruca in 5:14; Edris Enofe and Malik Blade defeated Ikemen Jiro and Quincy Elliott in 6:01.

AUGUST 5 *Orlando, FL*
Dante Chen and Guru Raaj defeated Bryson Montana and Damaris Griffin in 5:20; Arianna Grace defeated Thea Hail in 5:03; Quincy Elliott defeated Xyon Quinn in 4:50.

AUGUST 12 *Orlando, FL*
Ikemen Jiro defeated Myles Borne in 5:12; Elektra Lopez defeated Sol Ruca in 3:56; Chase U (Andre Chase and Bodhi Hayward) defeated Bronco Nima and Lucien Price in 6:16.

AUGUST 19 *Orlando, FL*
Dante Chen defeated Javier Bernal in 4:31; Ivy Nile defeated Arianna Grace in 4:24; Axiom defeated Xyon Quinn in 6:10.

AUGUST 26 *Orlando, FL*
Edris Enofe and Malik Blade defeated Bronco Nima and Lucien Price in 5:50; Kiana James defeated Amari Miller in 4:59; Nathan Frazer defeated Ikemen Jiro in 6:29.

SEPTEMBER 2 *Orlando, FL*
Duke Hudson defeated Myles Borne in 5:42; Arianna Grace defeated Erica Yan in 4:43; Xyon Quinn defeated Dante Chen in 5:53.

SEPTEMBER 9 *Orlando, FL*
Charlie Dempsey defeated Bodhi Hayward in 7:49; Valentina Feroz defeated Sol Ruca in 5:52; Channing Lorenzo defeated Ikemen Jiro in 5:16.

SEPTEMBER 16 *Orlando, FL*
Ivy Nile and Tatum Paxley defeated Erica Yan and Sloane Jacobs in 5:21; Duke Hudson defeated Bronco Nima in 5:40; Indi Hartwell defeated Amari Miller in 5:10.

SEPTEMBER 23 *Orlando, FL*
Dante Chen defeated Bryson Montana in 5:47; Indi Hartwell defeated Valentina Feroz in 4:37; Andre Chase defeated Myles Borne in 5:34.

SEPTEMBER 30 *Orlando, FL*
Javier Bernal defeated Ru Feng in 5:20; Thea Hail defeated Valentina Feroz in 4:38; Edris Enofe and Malik Blade defeated Guru Raaj and Ikemen Jiro in 6:50.

OCTOBER 7 *Orlando, FL*
Indi Hartwell defeated Sloane Jacobs in 3:20; Myles Borne defeated Guru Raaj in 5:36; Fallon Henley and Sol Ruca defeated Arianna Grace and Kiana James in 5:06.

OCTOBER 14 *Orlando, FL*
Ikemen Jiro and Tank Ledger defeated Bryson Montana and Duke Hudson in 6:18; Myles Borne defeated Dante Chen in 5:14; Ivy Nile defeated Lash Legend in 6:16.

OCTOBER 21 *Orlando, FL*
Myles Borne defeated Ikemen Jiro in 5:18; Duke Hudson defeated Bryson Montana in 3:55; Andre Chase defeated Javier Bernal in 6:48.

OCTOBER 28 *Orlando, FL*
Channing Lorenzo defeated Tank Ledger in 5:42; Thea Hail defeaed Jakara Jackson in 4:25; Brooks Jensen defeated Trick Williams in 6:11.

NOVEMBER 4 *Orlando, FL*
Ivy Nile defeated Sol Ruca in 4:51; Hank Walker defeated Myles Borne in 4:15; Oro Mensah defeated Xyon Quinn in 6:08.

NOVEMBER 11 *Orlando, FL*
Ivy Nile and Tatum Paxley defeated Jakara Jackson and Lash Legend in 4:42; Javier Bernal defeated Ikemen Jiro in 5:07; Edris Enofe, Malik Blade and Odyssey Jones defeated Bronco Nima, Lucien Price and Xyon Quinn in 6:41.

NOVEMBER 18 *Orlando, FL*
Thea Hail defeated Dani Palmer in 4:41; Dante Chen defeated Oba Femi in 5:42; Channing Lorenzo defeated Oro Mensah in 5:41.

NOVEMBER 25 *Orlando, FL*
Xyon Quinn defeated Tank Ledger in 4:57; Elektra Lopez defeated Amari Miller in 4:30; Damon Kemp defeated Dante Chen in 6:13.

DECEMBER 2 *Orlando, FL*
Oro Mensah defeated Myles Borne in 6:11; Channing Lorenzo defeated Tavion Heights in 4:19; Thea Hail defeated Sol Ruca in 6:18.

DECEMBER 9 *Orlando, FL*
Odyssey Jones defeated Damon Kemp in 5:10; Sol Ruca defeated Valentina Feroz in 4:30; Trick Williams defeated Ikemen Jiro in 5:50.

DECEMBER 16 *Orlando, FL*
The Dyad (Jagger Reid and Rip Fowler) defeated Bronco Nima and Lucien Price in 5:39; Ivy Nile defeated Lash Legend in 5:03; Chase U (Andre Chase and Duke Hudson) defeated Javier Bernal and Xyon Quinn in 7:16.

DECEMBER 23 *Orlando, FL*
Charlie Dempsey defeated Myles Borne in 8:13; Sol Ruca defeated Dani Palmer in 3:01; Trick Williams defeated Hank Walker in 6:13.

DECEMBER 30 *Orlando, FL*
Thea Hail defeated Amari Miller in 5:53; Bronco Nima and Lucien Price defeated Bryson Montana and Oba Femi in 4:38; Oro Mensah defeated Javier Bernal in 6:18.

WWE NXT KICKOFF

APRIL 2 - STAND & DELIVER *Dallas, TX*
Raquel Gonzalez and Dakota Kai defeated Toxic Attraction (Gigi Dolin and Jacy Jayne) to win the NXT Women's Tag Team Title in 7:53.

WWE NXT UK

JANUARY 6 *London, England*
Ashton Smith and Oliver Carter defeated Symbiosis (Primate and T-Bone) in 9:37; Xia Brookside defeated Myla Grace in 3:51; Meiko Satomura defeated Blair Davenport in 12:58.

JANUARY 13 *London, England*
Dave Mastiff and Jack Starz defeated Die Familie (Rohan Raja and Teoman) in 9:24; Amale defeated Stevie Turner in 3:59; Walter defeated Nathan Frazer in 14:02.

JANUARY 20 *London, England*
Pretty Deadly (Lewis Howley and Sam Stoker) defeated Sam Gradwell and Saxon Huxley in 9:22; Isla Dawn defeated Emilia McKenzie in 5:30; Noam Dar vs. A-Kid ended in a draw in a Heritage Cup Rules Match in 18:00.

JANUARY 27 *London, England*
Die Familie (Charlie Dempsey, Rohan Raja and Teoman) defeated Gallus (Joe Coffey, Mark Coffey and Wolfgang) in 11:18; Jinny defeated Amale in 6:31; Ilja Dragunov defeated Jordan Devlin in an Empty Arena Match in 21:43.

FEBRUARY 3 *London, England*
Ashton Smith and Oliver Carter defeated Dave Mastiff and Jack Starz in 12:31; Isla Dawn defeated Myla Grace in 2:59; Meiko Satomura defeated Blair Davenport in a Japanese Street Fight in 9:16.

FEBRUARY 10 *London, England*
Amale defeated **Nina Samuels** in 5:17; **A-Kid** defeated **Saxon Huxley** in 7:03; **Nathan Frazer** defeated **Teoman** in 13:15.

FEBRUARY 17 *London, England*
Sam Gradwell defeated **Kenny Williams** in 3:54; **Emilia McKenzie** defeated **Angel Hayze** in 4:57; **Stevie Turner** defeated **Myla Grace** in 4:34; **Jordan Devlin** defeated **Wolfgang** in 13:40.

FEBRUARY 24 *London, England*
Amale defeated **Xia Brookside** in 6:14; **Rohan Raja** defeated **Danny Jones** in 5:00; **Moustache Mountain (Trent Seven** and **Tyler Bate)** defeated **Ashton Smith** and **Oliver Carter** in 13:02.

MARCH 3 *London, England*
Mark Coffey defeated **Sha Samuels** in 7:41; **Dave Mastiff** and **Jack Starz** defeated **Pretty Deadly (Lewis Howley** and **Sam Stoker)** in 10:34; **Ilja Dragunov** defeated **Nathan Frazer** in 14:42.

MARCH 10 *London, England*
Charlie Dempsey defeated **A-Kid** in 12:30; **Symbiosis (Primate** and **T-Bone)** defeated **Danny Jones** and **Josh Morrell** in 6:05; **Noam Dar** defeated **Joe Coffey** in a Heritage Cup Rules Match in 17:43.

MARCH 17 *London, England*
Oliver Carter defeated **Tyler Bate** in 10:07; **Emilia McKenzie** defeated **Nina Samuels** in 8:44; **Aleah James** defeated **Stevie Turner** in 4:10; **Roderick Strong** defeated **Wolfgang** in 9:51.

MARCH 24 *London, England*
Die Familie **(Charlie Dempsey** and **Rohan Raja)** defeated **A-Kid** and **Saxon Huxley** in 8:24; **Wild Boar** defeated **T-Bone** in 4:37; **Jordan Devlin** defeated **Danny Jones** in 4:44; **Meiko Satomura** defeated **Isla Dawn** in 8:04.

MARCH 31 *London, England*
Xia Brookside defeated **Amale** in 5:51; **Trent Seven** defeated **Ashton Smith** in 8:50; **Tate Mayfairs** defeated **Kenny Williams** via count out in 5:53; **Noam Dar** defeated **Mark Coffey** in 16:46.

APRIL 7 *London, England*
Primate defeated **Wild Boar** in 3:37; **Charlie Dempsey** defeated **Wolfgang** in 7:20; **Ilja Dragunov** defeated **Roderick Strong** in 14:40.

APRIL 14 *London, England*
Dave Mastiff and **Jack Starz** defeated **Gallus (Joe Coffey** and **Mark Coffey)** in 8:30; **Eliza Alexander** defeated **Angel Hayze** in 4:12; **Teoman** defeated **A-Kid** in 11:23.

APRIL 21 *London, England*
Sam Gradwell defeated **Kenny Williams** in a Back Alley Brawl Match in 9:42; **Emilia McKenzie** defeated **Stevie Turner** in 4:42; **Moustache Mountain (Trent Seven** and **Tyler Bate)** defeated **Ashton Smith** and **Oliver Carter** 2-1 in a Best Two Out Of Three Falls Match in 21:38.

APRIL 28 *London, England*
Mark Andrews and **Wild Boar** defeated **Symbiosis (Primate** and **T-Bone)** in 7:26; **Xia Brookside** defeated **Angel Hayze** in 5:05; **Von Wagner** defeated **Saxon Huxley** in 4:04.

MAY 5 *London, England*
Tiger Turan defeated **Tate Mayfairs** in 4:03; **Damon Kemp** defeated **Danny Jones** in 4:15; **Meiko Satomura** defeated **Isla Dawn** in a World Of Darkness Match in 12:48.

MAY 12 *London, England*
Ashton Smith and **Oliver Carter** defeated **Gallus (Joe Coffey** and **Mark Coffey)** in 10:24; **Ivy Nile** defeated **Nina Samuels** in 4:41; **Ilja Dragunov** defeated **Jordan Devlin** in a Loser Leaves NXT UK Match in 14:53.

MAY 19 *London, England*
Eliza Alexander and **Xia Brookside** defeated **Amale** and **Angel Hayze** in 5:54; **Die Familie (Charlie Dempsey** and **Rohan Raja)** defeated **Dave Mastiff** and **Jack Starz** in 8:01; **Kenny Williams** defeated **Josh Morrell** in 5:30; **Wild Boar** defeated **Eddie Dennis** in a Dog Collar Match in 10:17.

MAY 26 *London, England*
Mark Coffey defeated **Saxon Huxley** in 4:13; **Lash Legend** defeated **Emilia McKenzie** in 6:06; **Sha Samuels** defeated **Damon Kemp** in 5:42; **Charlie Dempsey** defeated **A-Kid** in a Heritage Cup Rules Match in 16:24.

JUNE 2 *London, England*
Von Wagner defeated **Sam Gradwell** in 6:47; **Stevie Turner** defeated **Angel Hayze** in 4:04; **Ashton Smith** and **Oliver Carter** defeated **Moustache Mountain (Trent Seven** and **Tyler Bate)** and **Die Familie (Charlie Dempsey** and **Rohan Raja)** in a Triple Threat Match to win the NXT UK Tag Team Championship in 14:17.

JUNE 9 *London, England*
Mark Andrews defeated **Kenny Williams** in 9:46; **Symbiosis (Primate** and **T-Bone)** defeated **Oli Blake** and **Tate Mayfairs** in 4:32; **Eliza Alexander** defeated **Amale** in 6:51; **Meiko Satomura** defeated **Ivy Nile** in 10:26.

JUNE 16 *London, England*
Tiger Turan defeated **Josh Morrell** in 3:03; **Lash Legend** defeated **Myla Grace** in 4:34; **Damon Kemp** and **Wolfgang** defeated **Noam Dar** and **Sha Samuels** in 12:41.

JUNE 23 *London, England*
Isla Dawn defeated **Myla Grace** in 5:03; **Sarray** defeated **Nina Samuels** in 5:34; **Brooks Jensen** and **Josh Briggs** defeated **Dave Mastiff** and **Jack Starz**, **Die Familie (Charlie Dempsey** and **Rohan Raja)**, and **Mark Andrews** and **Wild Boar** in a Four Way Elimination Match to win the vacant NXT UK Tag Team Championship in 18:15.

JUNE 30 *London, England*
Blair Davenport defeated **Angel Hayze** in 5:32; **Fallon Henley** defeated **Emilia McKenzie** in 8:31; **Wolfgang** defeated **Sha Samuels** in 10:18.

JULY 7 *London, England*
Tiger Turan defeated **Kenny Williams** in 6:33; **Josh Morrell** defeated **Primate** in 4:05; **Trent Seven** defeated **Tate Mayfairs** in 4:05; **Meiko Satomura** and **Sarray** defeated **Eliza Alexander** and **Xia Brookside** in 9:27.

JULY 14 *London, England*
Ashton Smith defeated **Teoman** in 7:24; **Amale** defeated **Stevie Turner** in 4:15; **Mark Coffey** defeated **Noam Dar** to win the NXT UK Heritage Cup Championship in 17:49.

JULY 21 *London, England*
Isla Dawn defeated **Fallon Henley** in 5:12; **Dave Mastiff** defeated **Josh Morrell** in 6:58; **Emilia McKenzie** defeated **Nina Samuels** in 4:58; **Trent Seven** defeated **Sam Gradwell** in 11:01.

JULY 28 *London, England*
Brooks Jensen and **Josh Briggs** defeated **Mark Andrews** and **Wild Boar** in 9:03; **Blair Davenport** defeated **Amale** in 5:46; **Ilja Dragunov** defeated **Wolfgang** in 15:55.

AUGUST 4 *London, England*
Oliver Carter defeated **Rohan Raja** in 5:25; **Sha Samuels** defeated **Bodhi Hayward** in 4:43; **Blair Davenport** vs. **Isla Dawn** ended in a no contest in 7:15.

AUGUST 11 *London, England*
Oliver Carter defeated **Charlie Dempsey** in 9:08; **Eliza Alexander** defeated **Thea Hail** in 4:12; **Sam Gradwell** defeated **Teoman** in 5:54; **Trent Seven** defeated **Wolfgang** in 9:03.

AUGUST 18 *London, England*
Joe Coffey defeated **Mark Andrews** in 7:40; **Amale** defeated **Nina Samuels** in 6:31; **Andre Chase** and **Bodhi Hayward** defeated **Eddie Dennis** and **Saxon Huxley** in 6:49.

AUGUST 25 *London, England*
Trent Seven defeated **Oliver Carter** in 9:15; **Tyler Bate** defeated **Joe Coffey** in 12:00; **Noam Dar** defeated **Mark Coffey** to win the NXT UK Heritage Cup Championship in 14:38.

SEPTEMBER 1 *London, England*
Blair Davenport defeated **Amale**, **Eliza Alexander** and **Isla Dawn** in a Four Way Elimination Match in 15:07; **Saxon Huxley** defeated **Kenny Williams** in 5:44; **Tyler Bate** defeated **Trent Seven** to win the vacant NXT United Kingdom Championship in 20:31.

AEW DYNAMITE

JANUARY 5 *Newark, NJ*
Hangman Page defeated **Bryan Danielson** in 29:06; **Shawn Dean** defeated **MJF** by DQ in :47; **Wardlow** defeated **Antonio Zambrano** in 1:23; **Jade Cargill** defeated **Ruby Soho** to win the inaugural AEW TBS Title in 11:13; **Malakai Black** defeated **Brian Pillman Jr.** in 6:02; **Jurassic Express** (**Jungle Boy** and **Luchasaurus**) defeated **The Lucha Brothers** (**Rey Fenix** and **Penta El Zero M**) to win the AEW World Tag Team Title in 14:03.

JANUARY 12 *Raleigh, NC*
CM Punk defeated **Wardlow** in 14:06; **Dante Martin** defeated **Powerhouse Hobbs** in 10:07; **Serena Deeb** defeated **Hikaru Shida** in 1:59; **Penta El Zero M** defeated **Matt Hardy** in 8:51; **The Acclaimed** (**Anthony Bowens** and **Max Caster**) defeated **Bear Country** (**Bear Bronson** and **Bear Boulder**) in 6:18; **Sammy Guevara** defeated **Daniel Garcia** in 12:34.

JANUARY 19 *Washington, D.C.*
Adam Cole and **Dr. Britt Baker D.M.D.** defeated **Orange Cassidy** and **Kris Statlander** in 14:25; **CM Punk** defeated **Shawn Spears** in :12; **Malakai Black** and

Brody King defeated **The Varsity Blondes** (**Brian Pillman Jr.** and **Griff Garrison**) in 1:53; **Lance Archer** defeated **Frankie Kazarian** in 10:02; **Serena Deeb** defeated **Skye Blue** in 2:51; **Sting** and **Darby Allin** defeated **The Acclaimed** (**Anthony Bowens** and **Max Caster**) in 9:22.

JANUARY 26 - BEACH BREAK *Cleveland, OH*
Sammy Guevara defeated **Cody Rhodes** in a Ladder Match to win the AEW TNT Title in 22:59; **Wardlow** defeated **James Alexander** and **Elijah Dean** in a Handicap Match in 1:23; **The Inner Circle** (**Chris Jericho**, **Santana** and **Ortiz**) defeated **Daniel Garcia** and **2.0** (**Matt Lee** and **Jeff Parker**) in 8:52; **Leyla Hirsch** defeated **Red Velvet** in 8:08; **Orange Cassidy** defeated **Adam Cole** in a Lights Out Match in 16:56.

FEBRUARY 2 *Chicago, IL*
Jon Moxley defeated **Wheeler Yuta** in 7:29; **House Of Black** (**Malakai Black** and **Brody King**) defeated **Death Triangle** (**Pac** and **Penta El Zero M**) in 10:23; **Nyla Rose** defeated **Ruby Soho** in 10:48; **MJF** defeated **CM Punk** in 38:09.

FEBRUARY 9 *Atlantic City, NJ*
Wardlow defeated **The Blade** in 6:15; **Keith Lee** defeated **Isiah Kassidy** in 4:29; **CM Punk** and **Jon Moxley** defeated **FTR** (**Dax Harwood** and **Cash Wheeler**) in 18:34; **Jade Cargill** defeated **AQA** in 7:44; **Serena Deeb** defeated **Katie Arquette** in 1:02; **Hangman Page** defeated **Lance Archer** in a Texas Death Match in 15:29.

FEBRUARY 16 *Nashville, TN*
Bryan Danielson defeated **Lee Moriarty** in 12:14; **Wardlow** defeated **Max Caster** in 5:18; **The Inner Circle** (**Santana** and **Ortiz**) defeated **The Inner Circle** (**Chris Jericho** and **Jake Hager**) in 10:43; **Thunder Rosa** defeated **Mercedes Martinez** in a No Disqualification Match in 9:31; **Sammy Guevara** defeated **Darby Allin** in 14:51.

FEBRUARY 23 *Bridgeport, CT*
ReDRagon (**Bobby Fish** and **Kyle O'Reilly**) won a Tag Team Battle Royal in 18:25; **Death Triangle** (**Pac** and **Penta Oscuro**) defeated **House Of Black** (**Malakai Black** and **Brody King**) in 7:31; **Ricky Starks** defeated **Ten** in 5:56; **Jade Cargill** defeated **The Bunny** in 6:50; **Bryan Danielson** defeated **Daniel Garcia** in 10:22.

MARCH 2 *Jacksonville, FL*
Bryan Danielson defeated **Christopher Daniels** in 11:17; **The Young Bucks** (**Matt Jackson** and **Nick Jackson**) won a Casino Tag Team Battle Royale in 27:01; **Thunder Rosa** and **Mercedes Martinez** defeated **Dr. Britt Baker D.M.D.** and **Jamie Hayter** in 8:32; **Wardlow** defeated **Cezar Bononi** in :50; **Adam Cole** and **ReDRagon** (**Bobby Fish** and **Kyle O'Reilly**) defeated **Hangman Page** and **The Dark Order** (**John Silver** and **Alex Reynolds**) in 12:43.

MARCH 9 *Fort Myters, FL*
Hangman Page defeated **Dante Martin** in 7:27; **Bryan Danielson** and **Jon Moxley** defeated **The Work Horsemen** (**JD Drake** and **Anthony Henry**) in 4:00; **Pac** defeated **Wheeler Yuta** in 5:40; **Jurassic Express** (**Jungle Boy** and **Luchasaurus**) defeated **The Acclaimed** (**Anthony Bowens** and **Max Caster**) in 9:26; **Thunder Rosa** defeated **Leyla Hirsch** in 8:51; **Scorpio Sky** defeated **Sammy Guevara** to win the AEW TNT Title in 11:50.

MARCH 16 - ST. PATRICK'S DAY SLAM *San Antonio*

Adam Cole and ReDRagon (Bobby Fish and Kyle O'Reilly) defeated Hangman Page and Jurassic Express (Jungle Boy and Luchasaurus) in 13:58; Blackpool Combat Club (Bryan Danielson and Jon Moxley) defeated Chuck Taylor and Wheeler Yuta in 11:45; Scorpio Sky defeated Wardlow in 9:20; The Hardys (Matt Hardy and Jeff Hardy) defeated Private Party (Isiah Kassidy and Marq Quen) in 12:22; Thunder Rosa defeated Dr. Britt Baker D.M.D. in a Steel Cage Match to win the AEW Women's World Title in 17:33.

MARCH 23 *Cedar Park, TX*

CM Punk defeated Dax Harwood in 12:51; Sting, Darby Allin and The Hardys (Matt Hardy and Jeff Hardy) defeated Private Party (Isiah Kassidy and Marq Quen) and The Butcher and The Blade in a Tornado Match in 9:27; Blackpool Combat Club (Bryan Danielson and Jon Moxley) defeated The Varsity Blonds (Brian Pillman Jr. and Griff Garrison) in 6:04; Adam Cole defeated Jay Lethal in 10:04; Leyla Hirsch defeated Red Velvet in 6:30; Chris Jericho and Daniel Garcia defeated The Dark Order (John Silver and Alex Reynolds) in 10:02.

MARCH 30 *Columbia, SC*

CM Punk defeated Max Caster in 7:09; Jon Moxley defeated Jay Lethal in 11:03; FTR (Dax Harwood and Cash Wheeler) defeated The Gunn Club (Austin Gunn and Colten Gunn) in 11:27; Bryan Danielson defeated Wheeler Yuta in 10:10; Toni Storm defeated The Bunny in 8:41; Andrade El Idolo defeated Darby Allin in 10:32.

APRIL 6 *Boston, MA*

Adam Cole defeated Christian Cage in 14:56; Samoa Joe defeated Max Caster in 2:52; Shawn Dean defeated Shawn Spears in 3:50; The Hardys (Matt Hardy and Jeff Hardy) defeated The Butcher and The Blade in a Tables Match in 11:54; Hikaru Shida defeated Julia Hart in 7:45; FTR (Dax Harwood and Cash Wheeler) defeated The Young Bucks (Matt Jackson and Nick Jackson) in 20:07.

APRIL 13 *New Orleans, LA*

CM Punk defeated Penta Oscuro in 13:38; Jurassic Express (Jungle Boy and Luchasaurus) defeated ReDRagon (Bobby Fish and Kyle O'Reilly) in 13:45; Shawn Dean defeated MJF via count out in 4:07; The Jericho Appreciation Society (Chris Jericho, Jake Hager and Daniel Garcia) defeated Eddie Kingston, Santana and Ortiz in 11:46; Marina Shafir defeated Skye Blue in 2:24; Ricky Starks and Powerhouse Hobbs defeated Keith Lee and Swerve Strickland in 12:32; Samoa Joe defeated Minoru Suzuki to win the ROH World Television Title in 11:37.

APRIL 20 *Pittsburgh, PA*

CM Punk defeated Dustin Rhodes in 17:26; Blackpool Combat Club (Bryan Danielson, Jon Moxley and Wheeler Yuta) defeated Lee Moriarty, Dante Martin and Brock Anderson in 8:08; Wardlow defeated The Butcher in 4:20; Kyle O'Reilly defeated Jungle Boy in 13:02; Hook defeated Anthony Henry in 1:23; Dr. Britt Baker D.M.D. defeated Danielle Kamela in 6:16; Darby Allin defeated Andrade El Idolo in a Coffin Match in 12:25.

APRIL 27 *Philadelphia, PA*

Dax Harwood defeated Cash Wheeler in 15:05; Blackpool Combat Club (Bryan Danielson, Jon Moxley and Wheeler Yuta) defeated The Factory (QT Marshall, Aaron Solo and Nick Comoroto) in 8:49;

Wardlow defeated Lance Archer in 5:29; Hikaru Shida defeated Serena Deeb in a Philly Street Fight in 11:40; Adam Cole, The Young Bucks (Matt Jackson and Nick Jackson) and ReDRagon (Bobby Fish and Kyle O'Reilly) defeated Dante Martin, Lee Johnson, Brock Anderson and The Varsity Blonds (Brian Pillman Jr. and Griff Garrison) in 6:28; Scorpio Sky defeated Sammy Guevara in a Ladder Match to win the AEW TNT Title in 14:06.

MAY 4 *Baltimore, MD*

Jeff Hardy defeated Bobby Fish in 10:20; Blackpool Combat Club (Bryan Danielson, Jon Moxley and Wheeler Yuta) defeated Andrade Family Office (Angelico, The Butcher and The Blade) in 7:27; Wardlow defeated W. Morrissey in 5:32; Chris Jericho defeated Santana in 9:05; Rey Fenix defeated Dante Martin in 9:38; Mercedes Martinez defeated Deonna Purrazzo to win the ROH Women's World Title in 10:35.

MAY 11 *Long Island, NY*

Adam Cole defeated Dax Harwood in 15:34; CM Punk defeated John Silver in 8:06; Tony Nese defeated Danhausen in :32; Ricky Starks defeated Jungle Boy in 10:01; Toni Storm defeated Jamie Hayter in 8:32; Jeff Hardy defeated Darby Allin in 10:16.

MAY 18 - WILD CARD WEDNESDAY *Houston, TX*

Samoa Joe defeated Johnny Elite in 10:25; Hangman Page defeated Konosuke Takeshita in 12:14; Keith Lee and Swerve Strickland defeated The Work Horsemen (JD Drake and Anthony Henry) in 2:24; Kyle O'Reilly defeated Rey Fenix in 12:00; Dr. Britt Baker D.M.D. defeated Maki Itoh in 6:44; Adam Cole defeated Jeff Hardy in 7:10.

MAY 25 - 3 YEAR ANNIVERSARY *Las Vegas, NV*

Wardlow defeated Shawn Spears in a Steel Cage Match in 6:56; Jon Moxley and Eddie Kingston defeated Private Party (Isiah Kassidy and Marq Quen) in 7:20; FTR (Dax Harwood and Cash Wheeler) vs. Roppongi Vice (Trent Baretta and Rocky Romero) ended in a no contest in 10:12; Swerve Strickland defeated Ricky Starks and Jungle Boy in a Three Way Match in 9:36; Dr. Britt Baker D.M.D. defeated Toni Storm in 9:02; Samoa Joe defeated Kyle O'Reilly in 12:38.

JUNE 1 *Los Angeles, CA*

CM Punk and FTR (Dax Harwood and Cash Wheeler) defeated Max Caster and The Gunn Club (Austin Gunn and Colten Gunn) in 11:50; Miro defeated Johnny Elite in 6:07; The Young Bucks (Matt Jackson and Nick Jackson), ReDRagon (Bobby Fish and Kyle O'Reilly) and Hikuleo defeated Christian Cage, Matt Hardy, Darby Allin and Jurassic Express (Jungle Boy and Luchasaurus) in 12:00; Wardlow defeated JD Drake in 1:11; Toni Storm and Ruby Soho defeated Jamie Hayter and Dr. Britt Baker D.M.D. in 9:48; Jon Moxley defeated Daniel Garcia in 11:32.

JUNE 8 *Independence, MO*

Kyle O'Reilly won a Casino Battle Royale in 24:59; Pac defeated Buddy Matthews in 10:46; Hangman Page defeated David Finlay in 10:22; Thunder Rosa defeated Marina Shafir in 8:26; Jon Moxley defeated Kyle O'Reilly in 14:15.

JUNE 15 - ROAD RAGER *St. Louis, MO*

Chris Jericho defeated Ortiz in a Hair vs. Hair Match in 11:06; Wardlow defeated 20 Plaintiffs in a Twenty-On-

One Handicap Match in 4:09; **Will Ospreay** defeated **Dax Harwood** in 13:43; **Miro** defeated **Ethan Page** in 9:31; **Toni Storm** defeated **Dr. Britt Baker D.M.D.** in 7:34; **The Young Bucks (Matt Jackson** and **Nick Jackson)** defeated **Jurassic Express (Jungle Boy** and **Luchasaurus)** in a Ladder Match to win the AEW World Tag Team Title in 14:53.

JUNE 22 *Milwaukee, WI*
Orange Cassidy and **Roppongi Vice (Trent Beretta** and **Rocky Romero)** defeated **United Empire (Will Ospreay, Kyle Fletcher** and **Mark Davis)** in 11:37; **Malakai Black** defeated **Penta Oscuro** in 9:56; **Hangman Page** defeated **Silas Young** in 8:44; **Toni Storm** defeated **Marina Shafir** in 7:22; **Jon Moxley** and **Hiroshi Tanahashi** defeated **Chris Jericho** and **Lance Archer** in 12:12.

JUNE 29 - BLOOD & GUTS *Detroit, MI*
Orange Cassidy defeated **Ethan Page** in 10:57; **Luchasaurus** defeated **Serpentico** in :49; **Danhausen** and **FTR (Dax Harwood** and **Cash Wheeler)** defeated **Max Caster** and **The Gunn Club (Austin Gunn** and **Colten Gunn)** in 9:31; **Jade Cargill** defeated **Leila Grey** in 1:55; **Blackpool Combat Club (Jon Moxley, Claudio Castagnoli** and **Wheeler Yuta), Eddie Kingston, Santana** and **Ortiz** defeated **The Jericho Appreciation Society (Chris Jericho, Daniel Garcia, Jake Hager, Matt Menard, Angelo Parker** and **Sammy Guevara)** in a Blood And Guts Match in 46:45.

JULY 6 *Rochester, NY*
Wardlow defeated **Scorpio Sky** in a Street Fight to win the AEW TNT Title in 8:29; **Swerve In Our Glory (Keith Lee** and **Swerve Strickland)** defeated **The Butcher** and **The Blade** in 9:38; **Rush** defeated **Penta Oscuro** in 11:04; **The Acclaimed (Anthony Bowens** and **Max Caster)** and **The Gunn Club (Austin Gunn** and **Colten Gunn)** defeated **Fuego Del Sol, Leon Ruffin** and **Bear Country (Bear Bronson** and **Bear Boulder)** in 2:14; **Thunder Rosa** and **Toni Storm** defeated **Marina Shafir** and **Nyla Rose** in 9:07; **Jon Moxley** defeated **Brody King** in 11:14.

JULY 13 - FYTER FEST *Savannah, GA*
Wardlow defeated **Orange Cassidy** in 11:36; **Jon Moxley** defeated **Konosuke Takeshita** in 13:22; **Luchasaurus** defeated **Griff Garrison** in 1:28; **Claudio Castagnoli** defeated **Jake Hager** in 11:32; **Serena Deeb** defeated **Anna Jay** in 8:22; **Swerve In Our Glory (Keith Lee** and **Swerve Strickland)** defeated **The Young Bucks (Matt Jackson** and **Nick Jackson)** and **Team Taz (Ricky Starks** and **Powerhouse Hobbs)** in a Three Way Match to win the AEW World Tag Team Title in 18:14.

JULY 20 - FYTER FEST *Duluth, GA*
Brody King defeated **Darby Allin** in 12:35; **Blackpool Combat Club (Jon Moxley** and **Wheeler Yuta)** defeated **Best Friends (Chuck Taylor** and **Trent Beretta)** in 11:53; **Christian Cage** and **Luchasaurus** defeated **The Varsity Blonds (Brian Pillman Jr.** and **Griff Garrison)** in 2:08; **Ricky Starks** defeated **Cole Karter** in 6:09; **Jade Cargill** and **Kiera Hogan** defeated **Athena** and **Willow Nightingale** in 8:25; **Chris Jericho** defeated **Eddie Kingston** in a Barbed Wire Death Match in 13:13.

JULY 27 - FIGHT FOR THE FALLEN *Worcester, MA*
Jon Moxley defeated **Rush** in 13:27; **Ricky Starks** defeated **Danhausen** in 1:31; **Hook** defeated **Ricky Starks** to win the FTW World Heavyweight Title in 1:32; **Sammy Guevara** defeated **Dante Martin** in 8:48;

Swerve Strickland defeated **Mark Sterling** and **Tony Nese** in a Handicap Match in 6:44; **Thunder Rosa** defeated **Miyu Yamashita** in 10:02; **Daniel Garcia** defeated **Bryan Danielson** in 17:12.

AUGUST 3 *Columbus, OH*
Jay Lethal defeated **Orange Cassidy** in 12:18; **Dr. Britt Baker D.M.D.** and **Jamie Hayter** defeated **Thunderstorm (Thunder Rosa** and **Toni Storm)** in 12:02; **Powerhouse Hobbs** defeated **Ren Jones** in :53; **Christian Cage** defeated **Matt Hardy** in 11:06; **The Acclaimed (Anthony Bowens** and **Max Caster)** defeated **The Gunn Club (Austin Gunn** and **Colten Gunn)** in 8:20; **Chris Jericho** defeated **Wheeler Yuta** in 12:33.

AUGUST 10 - QUAKE BY THE LAKE *Minneapolis, MN*
Darby Allin defeated **Brody King** in a Coffin Match in 13:28; **Andrade El Idolo** and **Rush** defeated **The Lucha Brothers (Penta El Zero M** and **Rey Fenix)** in a Tornado Tag Team Match in 13:45; **Luchasaurus** defeated **Anthony Henry** in :43; **Ricky Starks** defeated **Aaron Solo** in 2:13; **Jade Cargill** defeated **Madison Rayne** in 7:48; **Jon Moxley** defeated **Chris Jericho** in 22:38.

AUGUST 17 *Charleston, WV*
Bryan Danielson defeated **Daniel Garcia** 2-1 in a Best Two Out Of Three Falls Match in 26:16; **The Gunn Club (Austin Gunn** and **Colten Gunn)** defeated **The Varsity Blonds (Brian Pillman Jr.** and **Griff Garrison)** in :31; **Toni Storm** defeated **KiLynn King** in 6:49; **The Elite (Kenny Omega, Matt Jackson** and **Nick Jackson)** defeated **La Faccion Ingobernable (Andrade El Idolo, Rush** and **Dragon Lee)** in 20:54.

AUGUST 24 *Cleveland, OH*
Jay Lethal defeated **Dax Harwood** in 12:47; **Colten Gunn** defeated **Billy Gunn** in 6:16; **Dr. Britt Baker D.M.D.** defeated **KiLynn King** in 3:55; **Jon Moxley** defeated **CM Punk** to win the AEW World Heavyweight Title in 2:59; **United Empire (Will Ospreay, Kyle Fletcher** and **Mark Davis)** defeated **Death Triangle (Pac, Penta El Zero M** and **Rey Fenix)** in 25:18.

AUGUST 31 *Hoffman Estates, IL*
Bryan Danielson defeated **Jake Hager** in 10:46; **Toni Storm** and **Hikaru Shida** defeated **Dr. Britt Baker D.M.D.** and **Jamie Hayter** in 7:40; **Wardlow** and **FTR (Dax Harwood** and **Cash Wheeler)** defeated **Ren Jones, Vic Capri** and **Silas Young** in 2:02; **Wheeler Yuta** defeated **Dante Martin, Rush** and **Rey Fenix** in a Four Way Match in 8:06; **The Elite (Kenny Omega, Matt Jackson** and **Nick Jackson)** defeated **United Empire (Will Ospreay, Kyle Fletcher** and **Mark Davis)** in 18:54.

SEPTEMBER 7 *Buffalo, NY*
Death Triangle (Pac, Penta El Zero M and **Rey Fenix)** defeated **Orange Cassidy** and **Best Friends (Chuck Taylor** and **Trent Beretta)** to win the AEW World Trios Title in 12:58; **Toni Storm** defeated **Penelope Ford** in 5:50; **Wardlow** defeated **Tony Nese** in 1:24; **Bryan Danielson** defeated **Hangman Page** in 22:52; **Daniel Garcia** defeated **Wheeler Yuta** to win the ROH Pure Title in 16:04.

SEPTEMBER 14 *Albany, NY*
Jon Moxley defeated **Sammy Guevara** in 13:27; **Jungle Boy** defeated **Jay Lethal** in 10:38; **Powerhouse Hobbs** defeated **Matt DiMartino** in :29; **Swerve In Our Glory (Swerve Strickland** and **Keith Lee)** defeated **The Lucha Brothers (Penta El Zero M** and **Rey Fenix)** in 8:15;

Serena Deeb and Dr. Britt Baker D.M.D. defeated Toni Storm and Athena in 8:34; Bryan Danielson defeated Chris Jericho in 19:44.

SEPTEMBER 21 - GRAND SLAM *Queens, NY*
Chris Jericho defeated Claudio Castagnoli to win the ROH World Title in 14:49; The Acclaimed (Anthony Bowens and Max Caster) defeated Swerve In Our Glory (Swerve Strickland and Keith Lee) to win the AEW World Tag Team Title in 13:44; Pac defeated Orange Cassidy in 12:34; Toni Storm defeated Athena, Dr. Britt Baker D.M.D. and Serena Deeb in a Four Way Match in 9:50; Jon Moxley defeated Bryan Danielson to win the vacant AEW World Heavyweight Title in 19:31.

SEPTEMBER 28 *Philadelphia, PA*
Bryan Danielson defeated Matt Menard in 8:36; Jon Moxley defeated Juice Robinson in 11:18; Toni Storm defeated Serena Deeb in a Lumberjack Match in 11:09; Ricky Starks defeated Eli Isom in :51; Chris Jericho defeated Bandido in 18:24.

OCTOBER 5 - ANNIVERSARY *Washington, D.C.*
MJF defeated Wheeler Yuta in 15:06; Darby Allin defeated Jay Lethal in 10:15; Wardlow defeated Brian Cage in 10:04; Toni Storm, Athena and Willow Nightingale defeated Jamie Hayter, Serena Deeb and Penelope Ford in 9:29; Hangman Page defeated Rush in 9:05; Luchasaurus defeated Fuego Del Sol in :23; The Jericho Appreciation Society (Chris Jericho and Sammy Guevara) defeated Bryan Danielson and Daniel Garcia in 14:23.

OCTOBER 12 *Toronto, Canada*
Luchasaurus defeated Jungle Boy in 14:05; WarJoe (Samoa Joe and Wardlow) defeated The Factory (QT Marshall and Nick Comoroto) in 2:29; Swerve Strickland defeated Billy Gunn in 8:48; Chris Jericho defeated Bryan Danielson in 14:09; Toni Storm and Hikaru Shida defeated Dr. Britt Baker D.M.D. and Jamie Hayter in 8:18; Orange Cassidy defeated Pac to win the AEW All-Atlantic Title in 11:18.

OCTOBER 18 - TITLE TUESDAY *Cincinnati, OH*
Death Triangle (Pac, Penta El Zero M and Rey Fenix) defeated Orange Cassidy and Best Friends (Chuck Taylor and Trent Beretta) in 11:45; Toni Storm defeated Hikaru Shida in 8:44; Chris Jericho defeated Dalton Castle in 12:28; Jon Moxley defeated Hangman Page in 15:32.

OCTOBER 26 *Norfolk, VA*
Blackpool Combat Club (Claudio Castagnoli and Wheeler Yuta) defeated The Jericho Appreciation Society (Chris Jericho and Daniel Garcia) in 11:40; Swerve In Our Glory (Swerve Strickland and Keith Lee) defeated FTR (Dax Harwood and Cash Wheeler) in 15:06; Bryan Danielson defeated Sammy Guevara in 14:58; Jamie Hayter defeated Riho in 10:52; Jon Moxley defeated Penta El Zero M in 12:21.

NOVEMBER 2 *Baltimore, MD*
Jay Lethal defeated Darby Allin in 9:08; Jon Moxley defeated Lee Moriarty in 10:07; Chris Jericho defeated Colt Cabana in 9:12; Orange Cassidy defeated Luchasaurus and Rey Fenix in a Three Way Match in 9:59; Jade Cargill defeated Marina Shafir in 2:20; Samoa Joe defeated Brian Cage in 11:23.

NOVEMBER 9 *Boston, MA*
The Acclaimed (Anthony Bowens and Max Caster) and FTR (Dax Harwood and Cash Wheeler) defeated Swerve In Our Glory (Swerve Strickland and Keith Lee) and The Gunn Club (Austin Gunn and Colten Gunn) in 12:22; Ethan Page defeated Eddie Kingston in 9:18; Wardlow defeated Ari Daivari in 1:48; Jay Lethal defeated Trent Beretta in 7:17; Jamie Hayter defeated Skye Blue in 6:48; Bryan Danielson defeated Sammy Guevara 2-1 in a Best Two Out Of Three Falls Match in 20:33.

NOVEMBER 16 *Bridgeport, CT*
Blackpool Combat Club (Claudio Castagnoli and Bryan Danielson) defeated The Jericho Appreciation Society (Chris Jericho and Sammy Guevara) in 18:02; Swerve Strickland defeated Anthony Bowens in 9:36; Death Triangle (Pac, Penta El Zero M and Rey Fenix) defeated AR Fox and Top Flight (Dante Martin and Darius Martin) in 11:33; Ethan Page defeated Bandido in 9:08; Toni Storm defeated Anna Jay in 7:09.

NOVEMBER 23 - THANKSGIVING EVE *Chicago, IL*
Orange Cassidy defeated Jake Hager in 8:38; Ricky Starks defeated Ethan Page in 12:58; Death Triangle (Pac, Penta El Zero M and Rey Fenix) defeated The Elite (Kenny Omega, Matt Jackson and Nick Jackson) in 14:49; Dr. Britt Baker D.M.D. and Jamie Hayter defeated The Jericho Appreciation Society (Anna Jay and Tay Melo) and Willow Nightingale and Skye Blue in a Three Way Match in 8:05; Chris Jericho defeated Tomohiro Ishii in 15:29.

NOVEMBER 30 *Indianapolis, IN*
Bryan Danielson defeated Dax Harwood in 14:49; Samoa Joe defeated AR Fox in 6:36; Ricky Starks defeated Ari Daivari in :24; Willow Nightingale defeated Anna Jay in 7:29; The Elite (Kenny Omega, Matt Jackson and Nick Jackson) defeated Death Triangle (Pac, Penta El Zero M and Rey Fenix) in 17:20.

DECEMBER 7 *Cedar Park, TX*
Ricky Starks won the Dynamite Diamond Battle Royale in 13:10; Samoa Joe defeated Darby Allin in 10:29; Blackpool Combat Club (Claudio Castagnoli and Wheeler Yuta) defeated The Jericho Appreciation Society (Jake Hager and Daniel Garcia) in 12:42; Jade Cargill, Leila Grey and Red Velvet defeated Kiera Hogan, Skye Blue and Madison Rayne in 8:13; The Acclaimed (Anthony Bowens and Max Caster) defeated FTR (Dax Harwood and Cash Wheeler) in 16:46.

DECEMBER 14 - WINTER IS COMING *Garland, TX*
Death Triangle (Pac, Penta El Zero M and Rey Fenix) defeated The Elite (Kenny Omega, Matt Jackson and Nick Jackson) in 14:59; Jungle Boy defeated Brian Cage in 8:16; House Of Black (Malakai Black, Brody King and Buddy Matthews) defeated The Factory (QT Marshall, Aaron Solo and Cole Karter) in :23; Action Andretti defeated Chris Jericho in 9:35; Ruby Soho defeated Tay Melo in 7:22; MJF defeated Ricky Starks in 15:46.

DECEMBER 21 - HOLIDAY BASH *San Antonio, TX*
The Elite (Kenny Omega, Matt Jackson and Nick Jackson) defeated Death Triangle (Pac, Penta El Zero M and Rey Fenix) in a No DQ Match in 13:41; Hook defeated Exodus Prime in 1:04; Jon Moxley defeated Darius Martin in 8:49; The Gunn Club (Austin Gunn and Colten Gunn) defeated FTR (Dax Harwood and

Cash Wheeler) in 9:12; **Jamie Hayter** defeated **Hikaru Shida** in 16:16.

DECEMBER 28 *Broomfield, CO*
Bryan Danielson defeated **Ethan Page** in 16:25; **Blackpool Combat Club (Jon Moxley** and **Claudio Castagnoli)** defeated **Top Flight (Dante Martin** and **Darius Martin)** in 14:02; **Hook** defeated **Baylum Lynx** in :57; **The Elite (Kenny Omega, Matt Jackson** and **Nick Jackson)** defeated **Death Triangle (Pac, Penta El Zero M** and **Rey Fenix)** in a Falls Count Anywhere Match in 17:16; **The Jericho Appreciation Society (Tay Melo** and **Anna Jay)** defeated **Ruby Soho** and **Willow Nightingale** in 11:58; **Samoa Joe** defeated **Wardlow** in 12:12.

AEW RAMPAGE

JANUARY 7 *Newark, NJ*
Adam Cole defeated **Jake Atlas** in 9:39; **Hook** defeated **Aaron Solo** in 3:19; **Riho** and **Ruby Soho** defeated **Dr. Britt Baker D.M.D.** and **Jamie Hayter** in 8:10; **Eddie Kingston, Santana** and **Ortiz** defeated **Daniel Garcia** and **2point0 (Jeff Parker** and **Matt Lee)** in a No DQ No Holds Barred Match in 13:50.

JANUARY 14 *Raleigh, NC*
Adam Cole defeated **Trent Beretta** in 11:34; **Shawn Spears** defeated **Andrew Everett** in :57; **Penelope Ford, The Bunny** and **Nyla Rose** defeated **Red Velvet, Leyla Hirsch** and **Kris Statlander** in 8:12; **Jurassic Express (Jungle Boy** and **Luchasaurus)** defeated **The Dark Order (John Silver** and **Alex Reynolds)** in 12:37.

JANUARY 21 *Washington, D.C.*
Jon Moxley defeated **Ethan Page** in 10:15; **Trent Beretta** defeated **Nick Jackson** in 13:00; **Hook** defeated **Serpentico** in 1:10; **Jade Cargill** defeated **Anna Jay** in 8:45.

JANUARY 28 - BEACH BREAK *Cleveland, OH*
Jon Moxley defeated **Anthony Bowens** in 12:02; **FTR (Dax Harwood** and **Cash Wheeler)** defeated **Lee Johnson** and **Brock Anderson** in 9:10; **Jade Cargill** defeated **Julia Hart** in 2:28; **Jurassic Express (Jungle Boy** and **Luchasaurus)** defeated **Private Party (Marq Quen** and **Isiah Kassidy)** in 10:45.

FEBRUARY 4 *Chicago, IL*
Adam Cole defeated **Evil Uno** in 2:28; **Sammy Guevara** defeated **Isiah Kassidy** in 9:14; **Thunder Rosa** defeated **Mercedes Martinez** by DQ in 7:41; **Ricky Starks** defeated **Jay Lethal** in 12:51.

FEBRUARY 11 *Atlantic City, NJ*
The Young Bucks (Matt Jackson and Nick Jackson) defeated **Roppongi Vice (Trent Beretta** and **Rocky Romero)** in 13:23; **Dr. Britt Baker D.M.D.** defeated **Robyn Renegade** in 6:28; **Hook** defeated **Blake Li** in 2:51; **Jurassic Express (Jungle Boy** and **Luchasaurus)** defeated **The Gunn Club (Austin Gunn** and **Colten Gunn)** in 12:29.

FEBRUARY 18 - SLAM DUNK *Nashville, TN*
Adam Cole defeated **Ten** in 9:52; **Powerhouse Hobbs** defeated **Dante Martin** in 9:29; **Serena Deeb** defeated **Angelica Risk** in 2:04; **Jay White** defeated **Trent Beretta** in 15:11.

FEBRUARY 25 *Bridgeport, CT*
Sammy Guevara defeated **Andrade El Idolo** in 12:23; **Wardlow** defeated **Nick Comoroto** in 6:25; **Serena Deeb** defeated **Kayla Sparks** in 2:29; **Orange Cassidy** defeated **Anthony Bowens** in 10:15.

MARCH 4 *Orlando, FL*
Sammy Guevara defeated **Darby Allin** and **Andrade El Idolo** in a Three Way Match in 13:12; **Keith Lee** defeated **JD Drake** in 5:50; **Serena Deeb** defeated **Leila Gray** in :58; **Christian Cage** defeated **Ethan Page** in 8:57.

MARCH 11 *Fort Myers, FL*
Darby Allin defeated **Marq Quen** in 11:55; **Jamie Hayter** defeated **Mercedes Martinez** in 8:42; **Keith Lee** defeated **QT Marshall** in 4:05; **Swerve Strickland** defeated **Tony Nese** in 12:58.

MARCH 18 *San Antonio, TX*
Darby Allin defeated **The Butcher** via count out in 10:41; **Red Velvet** defeated **Leyla Hirsch** in 8:00; **House Of Black (Malakai Black, Brody King** and **Buddy Matthews)** defeated **Fuego Del Sol** and **Bear Country (Bear Bronson** and **Bear Boulder)** in 3:22; **Keith Lee** defeated **Max Caster** in 9:46.

MARCH 25 *Cedar Park, TX*
Dustin Rhodes defeated **Lance Archer** in 9:32; **ReDragon (Kyle O'Reilly** and **Bobby Fish)** defeated **The Dark Order (Alan Angels** and **Ten)** in 7:00; **Nyla Rose** defeated **Madi Wrenkowski** in :38; **Ricky Starks** defeated **Swerve Strickland** in 11:27.

APRIL 1 *Columbia, SC*
The Young Bucks (Matt Jackson and Nick Jackson) defeated **Top Flight (Dante Martin** and **Darius Martin)** in 10:48; **House Of Black (Malakai Black, Brody King** and **Buddy Matthews)** defeated **Fuego Del Sol** and **The Dark Order (Evil Uno** and **Stu Grayson)** in 7:15; **Jamie Hayter** defeated **Skye Blue** in 5:36; **Keith Lee** defeated **Powerhouse Hobbs** in 10:53.

APRIL 8 *Boston, MA*
Bryan Danielson defeated **Trent Beretta** in 13:39; **Swerve Strickland** defeated **QT Marshall** in 6:08; **Red Velvet** defeated **Willow Nightingale** in 5:16; **Jon Moxley** defeated **Wheeler Yuta** in 12:40.

APRIL 15 *Garland, TX*
Blackpool Combat Club (Bryan Danielson, Jon Moxley and Wheeler Yuta) defeated **The Gunn Club (Billy Gunn, Austin Gunn** and **Colten Gunn)** in 9:06; **The Butcher** defeated **Barrett Brown** in :55; **Ruby Soho** defeated **Robyn Renegade** in 8:22; **Hangman Page** defeated **Adam Cole** in a Texas Death Match in 20:06.

APRIL 22 *Pittsburgh, PA*
Adam Cole defeated **Tomohiro Ishii** in 11:14; **Lance Archer** defeated **Serpentico** in :33; **Eddie Kingston** defeated **Daniel Garcia** in 11:22; **Jade Cargill** defeated **Marina Shafir** in 11:41.

APRIL 29 *Philadelphia, PA*
Darby Allin defeated **Swerve Strickland** in 10:23; **Jade Cargill, Red Velvet** and **Kiera Hogan** defeated **Skye Blue, Willow Nightingale** and **Trish Adora** in 2:46; **Keith Lee** defeated **Colten Gunn** in 5:57; **Samoa Joe** defeated **Trent Beretta** in 9:57.

MAY 6 *Baltimore, MD*
Toni Storm and Ruby Soho defeated Dr. Britt Baker D.M.D. and Jamie Hayter in 8:38; Hook defeated JD Drake in 1:25; Riho defeated Yuka Sakazaki in 9:18; Jay Lethal defeated Konosuke Takeshita in 9:38.

MAY 13 *Long Island, NY*
Death Triangle (Pac, Penta El Zero M and Rey Fenix) defeated The Andrade Family Office (Marq Quen, The Butcher and The Blade) in 10:22; Shawn Spears defeated Bear Boulder in 2:03; Ruby Soho defeated Riho in 9:07; Scorpio Sky defeated Frankie Kazarian in 11:37.

MAY 20 *Houston, TX*
House Of Black (Malakai Black, Brody King and Buddy Matthews) defeated Fuego Del Sol and The Dark Order (Evil Uno and Ten) in 9:25; Shawn Spears defeated Big Damo in 1:40; Kris Statlander defeated Red Velvet in 7:50; Blackpool Combat Club (Bryan Danielson and Jon Moxley) defeated Dante Martin and Matt Sydal in 12:00.

MAY 27 *Las Vegas, NV*
Bryan Danielson defeated Matt Sydal in 11:09; The Young Bucks (Matt Jackson and Nick Jackson) defeated Jon Cruz and Taylor Rust in 2:34; Dante Martin defeated Max Caster in 6:12; Ruby Soho defeated Kris Statlander in 10:06.

JUNE 3 *Ontario, CA*
The Young Bucks (Matt Jackson and Nick Jackson) defeated The Lucha Brothers (Penta El Zero M and Rey Fenix) in 14:53; Team Taz (Ricky Starks and Powerhouse Hobbs) defeated Jordan Cruz and Ju Dizz in :47; Athena defeated Kiera Hogan in 8:21; Scorpio Sky defeated Dante Martin in 8:10.

JUNE 10 *Independence, MO*
Eddie Kingston defeated Jake Hager in 11:24; Jay Lethal and Satnam Singh defeated Mat Fitchett and Davey Vega in 1:37; Kris Statlander defeated Red Velvet in 8:55; Trent Beretta and FTR (Dax Harwood and Cash Wheeler) defeated United Empire (Will Ospreay, Kyle Fletcher and Mark Davis) in 13:59.

JUNE 17 - ROAD RAGER *St. Louis, MO*
Jon Moxley defeated Dante Martin in 11:58; Max Caster and The Gunn Club (Austin Gunn and Colten Gunn) defeated Leon Ruffin and Bear Country (Bear Bronson and Bear Boulder) in 1:15; Jade Cargill defeated Willow Nightingale in 4:58; Darby Allin defeated Bobby Fish in 11:45.

JUNE 24 *Milwaukee, WI*
Andrade El Idolo defeated Rex Fenix in 16:29; Mercedes Martinez and Serena Deeb defeated Laynie Luck and Sierra in 3:25; Hook defeated The DKC in 1:40; Jeff Cobb defeated Cash Wheeler in 10:55.

JULY 1 *Detroit, MI*
Brody King won a Royal Rampage Match in 22:41; The Young Bucks (Matt Jackson and Nick Jackson) defeated CHAOS (Hirooki Goto and Yoshi-Hashi) in 9:31; Toni Storm defeated Nyla Rose in 9:42.

JULY 8 *Rochester, NY*
Eddie Kingston defeated Konosuke Takeshita in 11:56; The Gates Of Agony (Kaun and Toa Liona) defeated Jonathan Gresham and Lee Moriarty in 7:27; Mercedes Martinez and Serena Deeb defeated

Christina Marie and Kayla Sparks in 2:23; Orange Cassidy defeated Tony Nese in 15:01.

JULY 15 *Savannah, GA*
House Of Black (Malakai Black and Brody King) defeated The Dark Order (Alex Reynolds and John Silver) in 8:18; Jonathan Gresham defeated Lee Moriarty in 9:01; Athena and Kris Statlander defeated The Renegades (Charlette Renegade and Robyn Renegade) in :25; The Lucha Brothers (Penta El Zero M and Rey Fenix) defeated Private Party (Marq Quen and Isiah Kassidy) in 11:16.

JULY 22 - FYTER FEST *Duluth, GA*
Hangman Page and John Silver defeated The Butcher and The Blade in 9:55; Lee Moriarty defeated Dante Martin in 9:00; Dr. Britt Baker D.M.D. and Jamie Hayter defeated Ashley D'Amboise and Skye Blue in 5:00; Jay Lethal defeated Christopher Daniels in 11:00.

JULY 29 *Worcester, MA*
Orange Cassidy and Best Friends (Chuck Taylor and Trent Beretta) defeated Jay Lethal, Satnam Singh and Sonjay Dutt in 7:29; Ethan Page defeated Leon Ruffin in 1:31; Lee Moriarty defeated Matt Sydal in 6:57; Anna Jay defeated Ruby Soho in 9:48.

AUGUST 5 *Grand Rapids, MI*
Jon Moxley defeated Mance Warner in 11:40; Konosuke Takeshita defeated Ryan Nemeth in 1:36; Madison Rayne defeated Leila Grey in 8:25; Swerve In Our Glory (Keith Lee and Swerve Strickland) defeated The Varsity Athletes (Tony Nese and Josh Woods) in a Friday Night Street Fight in 12:53.

AUGUST 12 - QUAKE BY THE LAKE *Minneapolis, MN*
Sammy Guevara and Tay Conti defeated Dante Martin and Skye Blue in 8:00; Parker Boudreaux defeated Sonny Kiss in 1:10; The Gunn Club (Austin Gunn and Colten Gunn) defeated Danhausen and Erick Redbeard in 4:33; Orange Cassidy defeated Ari Daivari in 10:00.

AUGUST 19 *Charleston, WV*
Swerve In Our Glory (Keith Lee and Swerve Strickland) defeated Private Party (Marq Quen and Isiah Kassidy) in 7:15; Hook defeated Zack Clayton in :30; Buddy Matthews defeated Serpentico in 1:33; Athena defeated Penelope Ford in 4:00; Orange Cassidy and Best Friends (Trent Beretta and Chuck Taylor) defeated The Trustbusters (Ari Daivari, Parker Boudreaux and Slim J) in 11:00.

AUGUST 26 *Cleveland, OH*
The Dark Order (Ten, John Silver and Alex Reynolds) defeated House Of Black (Malakai Black, Brody King and Buddy Matthews) in 9:03; Wardlow defeated Ryan Nemeth in 1:31; Powerhouse Hobbs defeated Ashton Day in 1:02 The Jericho Appreciation Society (Sammy Guevara and Tay Melo) defeated Ortiz and Ruby Soho in 8:35; Claudio Castagnoli defeated Dustin Rhodes in 12:27.

SEPTEMBER 2 *Hoffman Estates, IL*
Hangman Page and The Dark Order (John Silver and Alex Reynolds) defeated Orange Cassidy and Best Friends (Chuck Taylor and Trent Beretta) in 11:12; Rey Fenix defeated Blake Christian in 2:20; Ortiz and Ruby Soho defeated Sammy Guevara and Tay Melo in 7:40; Ricky Starks defeated QT Marshall in 7:10.

SEPTEMBER 9 *Buffalo, NY*
Sammy Guevara defeated Darby Allin in 11:06; Serena Deeb defeated Madison Rayne in 3:56; Claudio Castagnoli defeated Dax Harwood in 20:13.

SEPTEMBER 16 *Albany, NY*
Darby Allin defeated Matt Hardy in 9:59; Penelope Ford defeated Willow Nightingale in 7:28; Ethan Page defeated Danhausen in 1:25; Samoa Joe defeated Josh Woods in 10:10.

SEPTEMBER 23 - GRAND SLAM *Queens, NY*
Sting and Darby Allin defeated House Of Black (Buddy Matthews and Brody King) in a No DQ Match in 12:57; Action Bronson and Hook defeated The Jericho Appreciation Society (Angelo Parker and Matt Menard) in 5:10; WarJoe (Samoa Joe and Wardlow) defeated The Varsity Athletes (Tony Nese and Josh Woods) in 2:26; Jungle Boy defeated Rey Fenix in 16:40; Sammy Guevara defeated Eddie Kingston by DQ in 8:11; Jade Cargill defeated Diamante in 2:36; Hangman Page won a Golden Ticket Battle Royale in 12:16; Ricky Starks defeated Powerhouse Hobbs in a Lights Out Match in 11:52.

SEPTEMBER 30 *Philadelphia, PA*
The Acclaimed (Anthony Bowens and Max Caster) defeated Private Party (Marq Quen and Isiah Kassidy) and The Butcher and The Blade in a Three Way Match in 10:00; Jamie Hayter defeated Willow Nightingale in 7:12; Lee Moriarty defeated Fuego Del Sol in 1:56; Rush defeated John Silver in 10:58.

OCTOBER 7 *Washington, D.C.*
Blackpool Combat Club (Claudio Castagnoli, Jon Moxley and Wheeler Yuta) defeated Private Party (Marq Quen and Isiah Kassidy) and Rush in 10:16; The Varsity Athletes (Tony Nese and Josh Woods) defeated The Varsity Blonds (Brian Pillman Jr. and Griff Garrison) in 1:45; Anna Jay and Tay Melo defeated Madison Rayne and Skye Blue in 7:42; Death Triangle (Pac, Penta El Zero M and Rey Fenix) defeated The Dark Order (Alex Reynolds, John Silver and Ten) in 21:01.

OCTOBER 14 *Toronto, Canada*
Blackpool Combat Club (Jon Moxley and Claudio Castagnoli) defeated The Butcher and The Blade in 8:40; Nyla Rose defeated Anna Jay in 5:25; Ethan Page defeated Isiah Kassidy in 2:10; Shawn Spears and FTR (Dax Harwood and Cash Wheeler) defeated The Embassy (Brian Cage, Kaun and Toa Liona) in 10:29.

OCTOBER 21 *Jacksonville, FL*
The Acclaimed (Anthony Bowens and Max Caster) defeated The Varsity Athletes (Tony Nese and Josh Woods) in 8:06; Hook defeated Ari Daivari in 2:47; Willow Nightingale defeated Leila Grey in 7:51; Orange Cassidy defeated Rush and Ten in a Three Way Match in 11:53.

OCTOBER 28 *Uncasville, CT*
Jon Moxley defeated Matt Menard in 8:05; Keith Lee defeated Serpentico in :14; Tay Melo defeated Madison Rayne in 9:23; Wardlow defeated Matt Taven in 8:59.

NOVEMBER 4 *Atlantic City, NJ*
Orange Cassidy defeated Katsuyori Shibata in 14:00; Dr. Britt Baker D.M.D. and Jamie Hayter defeated Madison Rayne and Skye Blue in 7:18; WarJoe (Samoa Joe and Wardlow) defeated The Gates Of Agony (Kaun and Toa Liona) in 9:10.

NOVEMBER 11 *Boston, MA*
Brian Cage defeated Dante Martin in 7:15; Bandido defeated Rush in 8:45; Nyla Rose defeated Kayla Sparks in :45; Orange Cassidy defeated Lee Johnson in 9:12.

NOVEMBER 18 *Newark, NJ*
Ricky Starks defeated Lance Archer in 5:23; Hook defeated Lee Moriarty in 8:39; Athena defeated Madison Rayne in 2:50; Jun Akiyama and Konosuke Takeshita defeated Eddie Kingston and Ortiz in 12:17.

NOVEMBER 25 - BLACK FRIDAY *Chicago, IL*
FTR (Dax Harwood and Cash Wheeler) defeated Top Flight (Dante Martin and Darius Martin) in 11:12; Darby Allin defeated Anthony Henry in 8:09; Hikaru Shida defeated Queen Aminata in 1:18; Rush, The Butcher and The Blade defeated The Dark Order (John Silver, Alex Reynolds and Ten) in 7:24.

DECEMBER 2 *Indianapolis, IN*
Darby Allin defeated Cole Karter in 7:40; Jay Lethal and Jeff Jarrett defeated Private Party (Marq Quen and Isiah Kassidy) in 7:04; Athena defeated Dani Mo in 1:27; Orange Cassidy defeated QT Marshall in a Lumberjack Match in 9:31.

DECEMBER 9 *Cedar Park, TX*
Jon Moxley defeated Konosuke Takeshita in 14:30; Hikaru Shida defeated The Bunny in 7:26; The Firm (Big Bill and Lee Moriarty) defeated Clayton Bloodstone and Izzy James in 2:01; Orange Cassidy defeated Trent Seven in 11:55.

DECEMBER 16 *Garland, TX*
Jon Moxley defeated Sammy Guevara in 15:34; Dr. Britt Baker D.M.D. defeated Skye Blue in 6:15; Wardlow defeated Exodus Prime in 2:06; Orange Cassidy, Dustin Rhodes and Best Friends (Chuck Taylor and Trent Beretta) defeated Trent Seven, Kip Sabian, The Butcher and The Blade in 10:42.

DECEMBER 23 *San Antonio, TX*
AR Fox and Top Flight (Dante Martin and Darius Martin) won a $300,000 Three Kings Christmas Casino Trios Royale in 22:01; Jade Cargill defeated Vertvixen in 4:57; Jeff Jarrett and Jay Lethal defeated Anthony Bowens and Billy Gunn in 11:46.

DECEMBER 30 *Broomfield, CO*
Orange Cassidy defeated Trent Beretta in 14:36; Kip Sabian defeated Atiba in 1:12; Jade Cargill defeated Kiera Hogan in 6:26; Swerve Strickland defeated Wheeler Yuta in 13:58.

AEW BUY-IN

MARCH 6 - REVOLUTION BUY-IN *Orlando, FL*
Leyla Hirsch defeated Kris Statlander in 9:50; Hook defeated QT Marshall in 5:00; House Of Black (Malakai Black, Brody King and Buddy Matthews) defeated Pac, Penta Oscuro and Erick Redbeard in 17:20.

MAY 29 - DOUBLE OR NOTHING BUY-IN *Paradise, NV*
Hookhausen (Hook and Danhausen) defeated Tony Nese and Mark Sterling in 5:20.

JUNE 26 - FORBIDDEN DOOR BUY-IN *Chicago, IL*
Bishamon (Hirooki Goto and Yoshi-Hashi) defeated The Factory (Aaron Solo and QT Marshall) in 8:53; Lance Archer defeated Nick Comoroto in 6:08; Swerve In Our Glory (Keith Lee and Swerve Strickland) defeated Suzuki-gun (El Desperado and Yoshinobu Kanemaru) in 12:08; Max Caster and The Gunn Club (Billy Gunn, Austin Gunn and Colten Gunn) defeated Yuya Uemura, Alex Coughlin, The DKC and Kevin Knight in 5:35.

SEPTEMBER 4 - ALL OUT BUY-IN *Hoffman Estates, IL*
The Jericho Appreciation Society (Sammy Guevara and Tay Melo) defeated Ortiz and Ruby Soho in 6:00; Hook defeated Angelo Parker in 3:55; Pac defeated Kip Sabian in 10:00; Eddie Kingston defeated Tomohiro Ishii in 13:25.

NOVEMBER 19 - FULL GEAR BUY-IN *Newark, NJ*
Orange Cassidy, Chuck Taylor, Trent Beretta, Rocky Romero and Danhausen defeated The Factory (QT Marshall, Aaron Solo, Lee Johnson, Nick Comoroto and Cole Karter) in 11:55; Ricky Starks defeated Brian Cage in 10:00; Eddie Kingston defeated Jun Akiyama in 10:30.

AEW DARK

JANUARY 4 *Orlando, FL*
Tony Nese defeated Alan Angels in 6:46; Anna Jay defeated Dream Girl Ellie in 1:32; The Gunn Club (Billy Gunn, Austin Gunn and Colten Gunn) defeated Rolando Perez, Austin Green and Donnie Primetime in 3:06; Marina Shafir defeated Valentina Rossi 1:38; Bobby Fish defeated Ryzin in 2:08; Leyla Hirsch, Red Velvet and Kris Statlander defeated Renee Michelle, Sofia Castillo and Marina Tucker in 2:43; The Acclaimed (Anthony Bowens and Max Caster) defeated Blanco Loco and Axton Ray in 3:02; Jamie Hayter defeated Madi Wrenkowski in 3:36; Dante Martin defeated Chandler Hopkins in 2:59; Sammy Guevara defeated Ho Ho Lun in 4:11; Powerhouse Hobbs defeated Colt Cabana in 4:46; Brian Pillman Jr. defeated JD Drake in 6:06.

JANUARY 11 *Orlando, FL*
Shawn Dean defeated Liam Cross in 2:23; Anthony Ogogo defeated Baron Black in 4:24; Red Velvet defeated Shalonce Royal in 1:20; The Gunn Club (Billy Gunn, Austin Gunn and Colten Gunn) defeated Patrick Scott, Marcus Kross and T.I.M in :41; TayJay (Tay Conti and Anna Jay) defeated The Renegades (Charlette Renegade and Robyn Renegade) in 3:48; Orange Cassidy defeated JD Drake in 2:47; Dante Martin defeated Aaron Solo in 3:16; Eddie Kingston defeated Joey Janela in 8:33; Thunder Rosa defeated Kasey Fox in 2:00; Powerhouse Hobbs defeated Alexander Moss in :24; Daniel Garcia defeated Fuego Del Sol in 3:44; Jade Cargill defeated Skye Blue in 1:59; Jurassic Express (Jungle Boy and Luchasaurus) defeated Nick Comoroto and QT Marshall in 8:21; Hangman Page and The Dark Order (Alan Angels and Ten) defeated Matt Hardy, Serpentico and Isiah Kassidy in 14:27.

JANUARY 18 *Orlando, FL*
Adam Cole defeated Kaun in 7:53; The Gunn Club (Austin Gunn and Colten Gunn) defeated Bison XL and Larintiz XL in 2:20; Leyla Hirsch defeated Katalina Perez in 3:11; Lance Archer defeated Liam Cross in 1:57; The Varsity Blonds (Brian Pillman Jr. and Griff Garrison) defeated Adrian Alanis and Liam Gray in 2:03; Red Velvet defeated Vipress in 2:56; Skye Blue defeated Robyn Renegade in 2:51; Anna Jay defeated Tiffany Nieves in 1:57; Daniel Garcia defeated Anthony Greene in 7:36; Bear Country (Bear Boulder and Bear Bronson) defeated Brandon Bullock and Jameson Ryan in 2:06; Orange Cassidy and Wheeler Yuta defeated Peter Avalon and JD Drake in 7:32.

JANUARY 25 *Washington, D.C.*
The Bunny defeated Erica Leigh in 2:13; 2point0 (Jeff Parker and Matt Lee) defeated Daniel Garcia and Kekoa, Pat Brink and Rayo in 1:01; Lance Archer defeated Joe Keys in 4:11; Leyla Hirsch defeated Janai Kai in :43; The Acclaimed (Anthony Bowens and Max Caster) and The Gunn Club (Austin Gunn and Colten Gunn) defeated The Dark Order (Alan Angels, Alex Reynolds, Evil Uno and Ten) in 6:15; Penta El Zero M defeated Wheeler Yuta in 9:43; Jungle Boy defeated Nick Comoroto in 6:48.

FEBRUARY 1 *Orlando, FL*
Anthony Ogogo defeated Marcus Kross in 2:28; Penelope Ford defeated Angelica Risk in 4:02; QT Marshall defeated Toa Liona in 4:43; 2point0 (Jeff Parker and Matt Lee) defeated Kidd Bandit and Ish in 2:42; Lance Archer defeated Jordan Costa in 1:48; Marina Shafir defeated Reka Tehaka in 3:29; The Factory (Nick Comoroto and Aaron Solo) defeated Cam Stewart and Dante Casanova in 3:44; Tony Nese defeated Zack Clayton in 5:17; Kiera Hogan defeated Mazzerati in 3:36; The Dark Order (Alan Angels and Ten) defeated Ari Daivari and Invictus Khash in 7:44; Dante Martin and Matt Sydal defeated Bear Country (Bear Boulder and Bear Bronson) in 9:43; Lee Moriarty defeated Joey Janela in 11:44.

FEBRUARY 8 *Orlando, FL*
Julia Hart defeated Kelsey Heather in 2:23; Powerhouse Hobbs defeated Gus De La Vega in 2:01; The Gunn Club (Austin Gunn and Colten Gunn) defeated Adrian Alanis and Liam Gray in 2:07; Mercedes Martinez defeated Queen Aminata in 3:04; Anthony Ogogo defeated Tony Vincita in 3:38; Lee Moriarty defeated Anthony Henry in 6:01; Anna Jay defeated Kaci Lennox in 1:44; Fuego Del Sol defeated Serpentino in 5:42; Wheeler Yuta defeated Aaron Solo in 7:00.

FEBRUARY 10 *Washington, D.C.*
Aaron Solo defeated Sonny Kiss in 6:53; Abadon defeated Gia Scott in 1:51; Powerhouse Hobbs defeated Lee Johnson in 7:08; Dante Martin, Lee Moriarty and Matt Sydal defeated Andrade Hardy Family Office (Isiah Kassidy, Marq Quen and The Blade) in 9:05.

FEBRUARY 15 *Orlando, FL*
The Dark Order (John Silver and Alex Reynolds) defeated Ari Daivari and Invictus Khash in 5:40; QT Marshall defeated Pat Brink in 5:15; Max Caster defeated Cameron Stewart in 3:30; Tony Nese defeated Carlie Bravo in 3:51; Emi Sakura defeated Angelica Risk in 3:14; 2point0 (Jeff Parker and Matt Lee) defeated The Metro Brothers (Chris Metro and JC

Metro) in 1:57; **MT Nakazawa** defeated **Joey Sweets** in 3:48; **Frankie Kazarian** defeated **Luke Sampson** in 2:27; **Jora Johl** defeated **Axel Rico** in 2:43; **The Dark Order** (Alan Angels and Ten) defeated **Chaos Project** (Luther and Serpentico) in 8:16; **Anthony Bowens** defeated **Fuego Del Sol** in 4:30.

FEBRUARY 22 *Orlando, FL*
The Varsity Blonds (Brian Pillman Jr. and Griff Garrison) defeated **Guillermo Rosas** and **Marcus Kross** in 5:52; **The Wingmen** (Cezar Bononi, JD Drake, Peter Avalon and Ryan Nemeth) defeated **Caleb Teninity**, **Karam**, **Rohit Raju** and **Sotheara Chhun** in 2:29; **Skye Blue** defeated **Ruthie Jay** in 2:49; **Nick Comoroto** defeated **Lamar Diggs** in 3:54; **Ten** defeated **Ben Bishop** in 2:49; **Fuego Del Sol** defeated **David Ali** in 3:49; **Matt Sydal** defeated **Serpentico** in 6:27.

MARCH 1 *Orlando, FL*
Lee Johnson defeated **Darian Bengston** in 3:51; **Sonny Kiss** defeated **Ashton Starr** in 2:29; **The Acclaimed** (Anthony Bowens and Max Caster) defeated **B. Jack** and **Donovan Izzolena** in 2:46; **Marina Shafir** defeated **Danielle Kamela** in 3:24; **Dante Martin** defeated **Jack Evans** in 7:47; **Abadon** defeated **Sahara Seven** in 2:23; **Diamante** defeated **Vipress** in 1:53; **Kiera Hogan** defeated **Kelsey Raegan** in 2:41; **Daniel Garcia** defeated **Josh Woods** in 6:42; **Shawn Dean** defeated **Will Austin** in 2:50; **Orange Cassidy** and **Wheeler Yuta** defeated **The Factory** (Aaron Solo and Nick Comoroto) in 14:17.

MARCH 8 *Orlando, FL*
Anna Jay defeated **Marina Tucker** in 1:21; **Scorpio Sky** defeated **Sonny Kiss** in 5:42; **Red Velvet** defeated **Kiera Hogan** in 2:16; **Top Flight** (Dante Martin and Darius Martin) defeated **The Wingmen** (Peter Avalon and Ryan Nemeth) in 6:25; **Kris Statlander** defeated **Kelsey Raegan** in 1:52; **AQA** and **Ruby Soho** defeated **Diamante** and **Emi Sakura** in 5:02; **The Butcher** and **The Blade** defeated **The Dark Order** (Alan Angels and Colt Cabana) in 5:31; **Nyla Rose** defeated **Skye Blue** in 2:38; **Jay Lethal** defeated **Serpentico** in 5:12; **Private Party** (Isiah Kassidy and Marq Quen) defeated **Brock Anderson** and **Lee Johnson** in 5:05.

MARCH 15 *Orlando, FL*
Brandon Cutler and **The Young Bucks** (Matt Jackson and Nick Jackson) defeated **The Dark Order** (Alan Angels, Colt Cabana and Evil Uno) in 8:40; **Ruby Soho** defeated **Ashley D'Amboise** in 2:53; **Josh Woods** defeated **AC Adams** in 1:05; **Ricky Starks** defeated **Darian Bengston** in 3:22; **The Dark Order** (John Silver and Alex Reynolds) defeated **Chaos Project** (Luther and Serpentico) in 4:26; **Leyla Hirsch** defeated **Marina Tucker** in 2:06; **Top Flight** (Dante Martin and Darius Martin) defeated **Ari Daivari** and **Invictus Khash** in 7:30; **Ten** defeated **Aaron Solo** in 5:41; **Emi Sakura** defeated **Shalonce Royal** in 2:46; **Lance Archer** defeated **Sage Scott** in 2:10; **2point0** (Jeff Parker and Matt Lee) and **Daniel Garcia** defeated **Luke Sampson**, **Mike Reed** and **Shayne Stetson** in 2:19; **Frankie Kazarian** defeated **Jora Johl** in 4:33.

MARCH 22 *Orlando, FL*
Jay Lethal defeated **JD Drake** in 5:44; **The Butcher** and **The Blade** defeated **Carlie Bravo** and **Shawn Dean** in 2:41; **Anthony Ogogo** defeated **Ray Jaz** in 2:23; **Nyla Rose** defeated **Kaci Lennox** in 1:19; **Blake Christian** defeated **Rohit Raju** in 3:29; **The Acclaimed** (Anthony Bowens and Max Caster) defeated **Adrian Alanis** and

Liam Gray in 2:13; **AQA** defeated **Valentina Rossi** in 2:04; **Tony Nese** defeated **Karam** in 2:39; **Abadon** defeated **Angelica Risk** in 1:06; **The Gunn Club** (Austin Gunn and Colten Gunn) defeated **The Brick City Boyz** (JCruz and Victor Chase) in :29; **Mercedes Martinez** defeated **Gemma Jewels** in 1:33; **The Varsity Blonds** (Brian Pillman Jr. and Griff Garrison) defeated **Sotheara Chhun** and **Tony Vincita** in 3:36; **Marina Shafir** defeated **Leila Grey** in 1:20; **Powerhouse Hobbs** defeated **Fuego Del Sol** in 4:08.

MARCH 29 *Jacksonville, FL*
The Factory (Aaron Solo, Nick Comoroto and QT Marshall) defeated **Adam Priest**, **Gus De La Vega** and **Invictus Khash** in 4:30; **Emi Sakura** defeated **Leila Grey** in 2:55; **Diamante** defeated **Kelsey Heather** in 1:59; **The Dark Order** (Alan Angels, Evil Uno and Stu Grayson) defeated **Alexander Zane**, **Jay Marte** and **Richard King** in 3:09; **Frankie Kazarian** defeated **Kaun** in 3:20; **Tay Conti** defeated **Shalonce Royal** in 2:53; **The Dark Order** (John Silver, Alex Reynolds and Ten) defeated **Brandon Bullock**, **Foxx Vinyer** and **Jameson Ryan** in 3:20; **Nyla Rose** defeated **Kiera Hogan** in 3:01.

APRIL 5 *Orlando, FL*
Ryan Nemeth defeated **Chandler Hopkins** in 3:57; **Sonny Kiss** defeated **JP Harlow** in 1:56; **Abadon** defeated **Hyena Hera** in 1:35; **Cezar Bononi** and **Tiger Ruas** defeated **Guillermo Rosas** and **Luke Sampson** in 2:34; **Lance Archer** defeated **Dean Alexander** in 1:36; **The Dark Order** (Alan Angels and Ten) defeated **The Factory** (Aaron Solo and Nick Comoroto) in 8:08.

APRIL 12 *Orlando, FL*
Powerhouse Hobbs defeated **Axton Ray** in 1:17; **Max Caster** defeated **Mike Reed** in 4:10; **Diamante** defeated **Mylo** in 1:30; **Jora Johl** defeated **Teddy Goodz** in 2:30; **Emi Sakura** defeated **Charlette Renegade** in 2:15; **Shawn Dean** defeated **Rohit Raju** in 5:44.

APRIL 19 *Garland, TX*
Toni Storm defeated **Gigi Rey** in 3:10; **Danielle Kamela** defeated **Rache Chanel** in 2:10; **Team Taz** (Powerhouse Hobbs and Ricky Starks) defeated **The Dark Order** (Evil Uno and Stu Grayson) in 8:48; **Tony Nese** defeated **JD Griffey** in 1:54; **Marina Shafir** defeated **Alejandra Lion** in 2:00; **Keith Lee** and **Swerve Strickland** defeated **The Factory** (Aaron Solo and Nick Comoroto) in 8:40.

APRIL 26 *Garland, TX*
Red Velvet defeated **Dulce Tormenta** in 2:35; **Lee Moriarty** defeated **Serpentico** in 3:50; **Anna Jay** and **Skye Blue** defeated **Raychell Rose** and **The Bunny** in 5:07; **Penta Oscuro** defeated **QT Marshall** in 7:15; **Abadon** defeated **Charlette Renegade** in 1:09; **Frankie Kazarian**, **The Hardys** (Jeff Hardy and Matt Hardy) and **Top Flight** (Dante Martin and Darius Martin) defeated **Max Caster** and **Andrade Family Office** (Angelico, Isiah Kassidy, Marq Quen and The Blade) in 12:40.

MAY 3 *Orlando, FL*
John Silver defeated **Ryan Nemeth** in 6:43; **The Varsity Blonds** (Brian Pillman Jr. and Griff Garrison) defeated **The WorkHorsemen** (Anthony Henry and JD Drake) in 6:33; **Shawn Spears** defeated **Lord Crewe** in 3:50; **Team Taz** (Powerhouse Hobbs and Ricky Starks) defeated **Jay Lucas** and **Terry Yaki** in 3:55; **Julia Hart** defeated **Jaycie Love** in 1:55; **Tony Nese** defeated **Leon Ruffin** in 4:11; **Angelico** defeated **Yuya Uemura** in 8:55; **Dante Martin** defeated **Invictus Khash** in 6:00; **Toni Storm** defeated **Diamante** in 8:38.

MAY 10 *Orlando, FL*
Jay Lethal defeated **Jake Something** in 4:30; **Alex Reynolds** defeated **Jake Manning** in 4:00; **The Gunn Club (Austin Gunn** and **Colten Gunn)** defeated **Fly Def (Warren J** and **Zack Zilla)** in 3:30; **Shawn Dean** defeated **Serpentico** in 7:30; **Brock Anderson** and **Lee Johnson** defeated **The Brick City Boyz (JCruz** and **Victor Chase)** in 3:30; **Abadon** defeated **Vicky Dreamboat** in 2:00; **Jora Johl** defeated **Trip Jordy** in 3:30; **Kiera Hogan** defeated **Skye Blue** in 4:00; **The Factory (Aaron Solo** and **Nick Comoroto)** defeated **The DKC** and **Kevin Knight** in 8:30; **Rohit Raju** defeated **Adam Priest** in 3:00; **The Dark Order (Evil Uno** and **Ten)** defeated **Cezar Bononi** and **Tiger Ruas** in 8:30.

MAY 17 *Orlando, FL*
Max Caster defeated **Tyler Uriah** in 3:00; **Marina Shafir** defeated **Layna Lennox** in 3:00; **Bear Country (Bear Boulder** and **Bear Bronson)** defeated **The WorkHorsemen (Anthony Henry** and **JD Drake)** in 8:30; **Emi Sakura** defeated **Devlyn Macabre** in 3:30; **Andrade Family Office (Angelico** and **Jora Johl)** defeated **Anthony Catena** and **Baron Black** in 4:30; **Trent Beretta** defeated **Ryan Nemeth** in 3:30; **Skye Blue** defeated **Amber Nova** in 3:30; **Alex Coughlin, Clark Connors, Karl Fredericks, Kevin Knight** and **Yuya Uemura** defeated **The Factory (Aaron Solo, Blake Li, Brick Aldridge, Nick Comoroto** and **QT Marshall)** in 10:30; **Wheeler Yuta** defeated **Josh Woods** in 12:30; **Swerve In Our Glory (Keith Lee** and **Swerve Strickland)** defeated **Chaos Project (Luther** and **Serpentico)** in 6:00.

MAY 24 *Orlando, FL*
Kris Statlander defeated **Avery Breaux** in 2:59; **The Jericho Appreciation Society (Angelo Parker** and **Matt Menard)** defeated **Eli Isom** and **T.U.G. Cooper** in 1:42; **AQA** defeated **Brittany Jade** in 4:19; **Lee Moriarty** defeated **Alan Angels** in 9:44; **Sonny Kiss** defeated **Carlie Bravo** in 4:29; **Robyn Renegade** defeated **Vicky Dreamboat** in 3:31; **Anthony Ogogo** defeated **Trenton Storm** in 3:40; **Leva Bates** defeated **Kiah Dream** in 2:00; **Roppongi Vice (Rocky Romero** and **Trent Beretta)** defeated **The Wingmen (Peter Avalon** and **Ryan Nemeth)** in 7:02.

MAY 28 *Las Vegas, NV*
Darby Allin defeated **Brandon Cutler** in :59; **Anna Jay** defeated **Sandra Moone** in 2:42; **House Of Black (Malakai Black, Brody King** and **Buddy Matthews)** defeated **Adriel Noctis, Greg Sharpe** and **Matt Brannigan** in 3:50; **Riho, Skye Blue** and **Yuka Sakazaki** defeated **Diamante, Emi Sakura** and **Nyla Rose** in 6:11; **Death Triangle (Pac, Penta El Zero M** and **Rey Fenix)** defeated **The Factory (Aaron Solo, Nick Comoroto** and **QT Marshall)** in 10:32; **Johnny Elite** defeated **Marq Quen** in 6:00.

MAY 31 *Las Vegas, NV*
Mercedes Martinez defeated **Viva Van** in 2:40; **The Butcher** and **The Blade** defeated **Hunter Grey** and **Paul Titan** in 3:52; **Anthony Ogogo** defeated **Carlie Bravo** in 3:34; **Jamie Hayter** defeated **Danika Della Rouge** in 1:20; **The Dark Order (John Silver, Evil Uno** and **Ten)** defeated **Serpentico** and **The Wingmen (Peter Avalon** and **Ryan Nemeth)** in 5:37.

JUNE 7 *Ontario, CA*
Lance Archer defeated **Aaron Solo** in 2:46; **Christopher Daniels** defeated **Steve Andrews** in 3:04; **Marina Shafir** defeated **Skye Blue** in 3:32; **Ortiz** defeated **Serpentico** in 4:07; **Toni Storm** defeated **Zeda Zhang** in 3:37; **Max Caster** and **The Gunn Club (Austin Gunn** and **Colten Gunn)** defeated **The Dark Order (John Silver, Alex Reynolds** and **Ten)** in 5:26.

JUNE 14 *Ontario, CA*
QT Marshall defeated **Alan Angels** in 3:42; **Bobby Fish** defeated **Brock Anderson** in 5:57; **The Jericho Appreciation Society (Angelo Parker, Matt Menard** and **Daniel Garcia)** defeated **Jack Banning, Ray Rosas** and **Sinn Bodhi** in 2:38; **Anna Jay, Kris Statlander** and **Ruby Soho** defeated **Diamante, Emi Sakura** and **Nyla Rose** in 7:54; **Anthony Ogogo** defeated **Nick Ruiz** in 2:02; **Konosuke Takeshita** defeated **Nick Comoroto** in 6:42; **Matt Sydal** defeated **Taylor Rust** in 3:19; **Ethan Page** defeated **Frankie Kazarian** in 8:06.

JUNE 21 *Orlando, FL*
Max Caster defeated **Trever Aeon** in 3:19; **Serpentico** defeated **Vary Morales** in 3:16; **Kris Statlander** defeated **Ava Everett** in 1:42; **The Dark Order (John Silver** and **Alex Reynolds)** defeated **The Wingmen (Cezar Bononi** and **Peter Avalon)** in 5:01; **Brock Anderson** and **The Varsity Blonds (Brian Pillman Jr.** and **Griff Garrison)** defeated **Jay Lucas, Larry Lazard** and **Terry Yaki** in 3:00; **Diamante** defeated **Devlyn Macabre** in 3:06; **Tony Nese** defeated **JDX** in a Pure Rules Match in 3:08; **Mercedes Martinez** and **Serena Deeb** defeated **Anna Diaz** and **Yaide** in 2:21; **Jay Lethal** defeated **Blake Christian** in 9:54.

JUNE 28 *Orlando, FL*
Willow Nightingale defeated **Ashley D'Amboise** in 3:41; **The Factory (Aaron Solo** and **Nick Comoroto)** defeated **Knull** and **Matt Vandagriff** in 3:43; **Matt Sydal** defeated **Jake Something** in 5:53; **Athena** defeated **Amber Nova** in 3:03; **Dante Martin** defeated **Lucky Ali** in 4:49; **Julia Hart** defeated **Valentina Rossi** in 2:38; **Fuego Del Sol** defeated **Marcus Kross** in 4:05; **The Dark Order (Evil Uno** and **Ten)** defeated **The Wingmen (JD Drake** and **Ryan Nemeth)** in 8:16; **Ari Daivari** defeated **Caleb Konley** in 6:25; **Wheeler Yuta** defeated **Tony Nese** in 10:16.

JULY 5 *Orlando, FL*
Lee Moriarty defeated **Leon Ruffin** in 8:21; **Bear Country (Bear Boulder** and **Bear Bronson)** defeated **Adrian Alanis** and **Liam Gray** in 5:25; **AQA** defeated **Avery Breaux** in 3:42; **Josh Woods** defeated **Barrett Brown** in 2:35; **Sonny Kiss** defeated **Lamar Diggs** in 2:26; **Fuego Del Sol** defeated **Aaron Solo** in 5:27; **Jay Lethal** and **Satnam Singh** defeated **Darian Bengston** and **Gus De La Vega** in 4:11; **The Dark Order (John Silver, Alex Reynolds, Evil Uno** and **Ten)** defeated **The Wingmen (Cezar Bononi, JD Drake, Peter Avalon** and **Ryan Nemeth)** in 7:22.

JULY 12 *Orlando, FL*
Miyu Yamashita defeated **Thunder Rosa** in 13:39; **Private Party (Isiah Kassidy** and **Marq Quen)** defeated **Bear Country (Bear Boulder** and **Bear Bronson)** in 10:45; **Shawn Dean** defeated **Conan Lycan** in 4:48; **The Jericho Appreciation Society (Angelo Parker** and **Matt Menard)** defeated **Jake St. Patrick** and **Sage Scott** in :43; **Willow Nightingale** defeated **Mila Moore** in 3:02; **Rohit Raju** defeated **Baron Black** in 4:12; **Angelico** defeated **Logan Laroux** in 3:52; **Dante Martin** defeated **Nick Comoroto** in 7:53; **Pac** defeated **Shota Umino** in 18:43.

JULY 19 *Orlando, FL*

Jora Johl defeated Luke Sampson in 3:58; Lee Moriarty defeated Ren Jones in 5:10; Serena Deeb defeated Viva Van in 3:56; Marina Shafir defeated Amber Nova in 2:13; Konosuke Takeshita defeated Anthony Henry in 7:48; Jonathan Gresham defeated Jordan Oasis in 3:13; Wheeler Yuta defeated Bryce Donovan in 4:24; Danhausen defeated Jake Something in 3:55; The Renegades (Charlette Renegade and Robyn Renegade) defeated Avery Breaux and Valentina Rossi in 4:09; Mercedes Martinez defeated J-Rod in 4:45; The Varsity Blonds (Brian Pillman Jr. and Griff Garrison) defeated The Hughes Bros. (Terrell Hughes and Terrence Hughes) in 3:16; QT Marshall defeated Fuego Del Sol in 10:48; Jay Lethal defeated Logan Cruz in 2:20; Daniel Garcia defeated Alan Angels in 9:42.

JULY 26 *Orlando, FL*

Kiera Hogan defeated Allie Recks in 1:33; Alex Reynolds defeated Ryan Nemeth in 5:56; Marina Shafir defeated Tracy Nyxx in 2:12; Slim J defeated Blake Li in 2:53; Julia Hart defeated Renee Michelle in 2:51; Cole Karter defeated Mike Orlando in 2:29; Angelo Parker defeated Cameron Stewart in 1:39; Ari Daivari defeated Blake Christian in 4:59; Dante Martin defeated Peter Avalon in 5:08; Pac defeated LJ Cleary in 15:15.

AUGUST 2 *Orlando, FL*

The Trustbusters (Ari Daivari and Slim J) defeated Logan Cruz and Tyshon Price in 3:02; Willow Nightingale defeated Harley Cameron in 4:15; Diamante defeated Rocky Radley in 3:32; The Factory (Aaron Solo and Nick Comoroto) defeated Caleb Teninty and KC Rocker in 3:18; Shawn Dean defeated Jonathan Hudson in 2:22; Parker Boudreaux defeated Serpentico in 1:47; The Acclaimed (Anthony Bowens and Max Caster) defeated The Wingmen (Peter Avalon and Ryan Nemeth) in 5:00; Pac defeated Connor Mills in 18:16.

AUGUST 9 *Grand Rapids, MI*

The Butcher and The Blade and Private Party (Isiah Kassidy and Marq Quen) defeated Braden Lee, Isaiah Broner, James Alexander and Sam Moore in 2:22; Anna Jay defeated Megan Meyers in 1:20; Best Friends (Chuck Taylor and Trent Beretta) defeated Ren Jones and Rohit Raju in 3:28; The Dark Order (Evil Uno and Ten) defeated The Wingmen (JD Drake and Peter Avalon) in 4:15; Marina Shafir and Nyla Rose defeated Heather Reckless and Joseline Navarro in :46; Kris Statlander defeated Sierra in 2:16; The Trustbusters (Ari Daivari, Parker Boudreaux and Slim J) defeated Sonny Kiss, Xavier Walker and Zack Clayton in 3:10; Athena, Hikaru Shida and Ruby Soho defeated Emi Sakura, Leva Bates and Serena Deeb in 8:08; Orange Cassidy defeated Anthony Henry in 6:04.

AUGUST 16 *Orlando, FL*

Ari Daivari defeated Fuego Del Sol in 10:57; Willow Nightingale defeated Robyn Renegade in 4:01; Brock Anderson defeated Serpentico in 6:38; Abadon defeated Mafioso Rossi in 2:32; Angelico defeated Baliyan Akki in 3:04; Emi Sakura defeated Renee Michelle in 3:37; Josh Woods defeated Cobra in 2:50; Rohit Raju defeated Invictus Khash in 2:43; Skye Blue defeated Charlette Renegade in 4:44; Bear Country (Bear Boulder and Bear Bronson) defeated Axel Rico and Victor Iniestra in 3:59; Kayla Rossi defeated Avery Breaux in 2:29; Cezar Bononi defeated Marcus Kross in 2:43; Powerhouse Hobbs defeated Blake Christian in 4:45.

AUGUST 23 *Orlando, FL*

The Renegades (Charlette Renegade and Robyn Renegade) defeated Allie Recks and Rocky Radley in 3:24; Anthony Ogogo defeated Meto in 3:24; The Wingmen (Peter Avalon and Ryan Nemeth) defeated Adrian Alanis and Liam Gray in 2:40; Blake Christian defeated Lucky Ali in 4:38; Jora Johl defeated Vary Morales in 2:59; Max Caster defeated Justin Cotto in 2:37; Dante Martin and Matt Sydal defeated The Factory (Aaron Solo and Nick Comoroto) in 8:11; Daniel Garcia defeated Westin Blake in 5:52; The Trustbusters (Ari Daivari, Parker Boudreaux and Slim J) defeated Cash Flo, Omar Amir and Ryan Howe in 2:30; The Dark Order (John Silver, Alex Reynolds and Ten) defeated DK Vandu, Joey Sweets and Tyshaun Perez in 3:38; The Varsity Athletes (Tony Nese and Josh Woods) defeated GKM and Oliver Sawyer in 1:25; The Iron Savages (Boulder and Bronson) defeated Manny Lo and Sean Maluta in 1:59; The Work Horsemen (Anthony Henry and JD Drake) defeated Dean Alexander and Rosario Grillo in 3:41; KiLynn King defeated Mafiosa in 2:34.

AUGUST 30 *Orlando, FL*

John Silver defeated Serpentico in 4:10; Diamante defeated Charlette Renegade in 3:05; Angelo Parker defeated Gus De La Vega in :15; Kiera Hogan defeated Mylo in 2:19; The Trustbusters (Ari Daivari, Parker Boudreaux and Slim J) defeated Hermano, Logan Cruz and Tyshaun Perez in 3:35; Julia Hart defeated Vickie Dreamboat in 3:08; Kayla Rossi defeated Vipress in 1:47; The Varsity Blonds (Brian Pillman Jr. and Griff Garrison) defeated Dean Alexander and Rosario Grillo in 2:25; Dante Martin defeated AR Fox in 4:36; Brock Anderson defeated Tyson Maddux in 1:31; The Work Horsemen (Anthony Henry and JD Drake) defeated Manny Lo and Oliver Sawyer in 2:32; Leila Grey defeated Renee Michelle in 3:07; Rush defeated Blake Christian in 5:47.

SEPTEMBER 6 *Hoffman Estates, IL*

The Varsity Athletes (Tony Nese and Josh Woods) defeated Brandon Gore and Storm Grayson in 2:10; Marina Shafir defeated Laynie Luck in 3:19; Zack Clayton defeated Serpentico in 4:37; Julia Hart defeated Missa Kate in 2:36; Serena Deeb defeated Sierra in 4:48; Private Party (Isiah Kassidy and Marq Quen) defeated GPA and Robert Anthony in 5:16; Claudio Castagnoli defeated Ari Daivari in 9:19.

SEPTEMBER 13 *Hoffman Estates, IL*

Penelope Ford defeated Alice Crowley in 3:20; Dante Martin and Matt Sydal defeated The Wingmen (Cezar Bononi and Ryan Nemeth) in 6:19; Queen Aminata and Skye Blue defeated Diamante and Emi Sakura in 4:01; Danhausen defeated Peter Avalon in 2:15; Matt Hardy defeated Angelico in 6:32.

SEPTEMBER 20 *Orlando, FL*

The Dark Order (John Silver and Alex Reynolds) defeated Alexander Moss and Zuka in 4:50; Emi Sakura defeated Avery Breaux in 3:15; The Trustbusters (Ari Daivari, Parker Boudreaux and Slim J) defeated GKM, Marcus Kross and Mike Magnum in 4:08; Anthony Ogogo defeated Luke Kurtis in :43; Zack Clayton defeated Vary Morales in 3:04; Marina Shafir defeated La Rosa Negra in 3:01; Madison Rayne defeated Viva Van in 4:21; KiLynn King defeated Sahara Seven in 1:04; The Varsity Athletes (Tony Nese and Josh Woods) defeated Baliyan Akki and Ryan Matthews in 4:02; Sonny Kiss defeated Joe Ocasio in 1:30; Matt Sydal defeated JD Drake in 9:30.

SEPTEMBER 27 *Orlando, FL*

Fuego Del Sol defeated Jay Malachi in 4:57; Leila Grey defeated Tiara James in 2:45; Jeeves Kay defeated Gus De La Vega in 1:55; Jora Johl defeated Blake Li in 2:29; Anna Jay defeated Kelly Madan in 1:27; Ryan Nemeth defeated Arjun Singh in 2:37; Leon Ruffin defeated Bshp King in 1:43; Angelico defeated Caleb Konley in 3:42; The Renegades (Charlette Renegade and Robyn Renegade) defeated Mila Moore and Mylo in :21; Nick Comoroto defeated Shaheem Ali in 2:43; Dante Martin defeated Anthony Henry in 9:24.

OCTOBER 4 *Orlando, FL*

Marina Shafir defeated Sio Nieves in 2:37; Ari Daivari defeated AR Fox in 6:35; The Varsity Athletes (Tony Nese and Josh Woods) defeated Invictus Khash and Rohit Raju in 2:34; Abadon defeated Freya States in 2:06; Slim J defeated Blake Christian in 6:16; The Wingmen (Cezar Bononi and Ryan Nemeth) defeated Chris Pharoah and Eli Isom in 1:58; Parker Boudreaux defeated Terry Kid in :42; Skye Blue defeated Robyn Renegade in 3:19; The Iron Savages (Boulder and Bronson) defeated Levis Valenzuela and Vary Morales in 2:42; Dante Martin and Matt Sydal defeated The WorkHorsemen (Anthony Henry and JD Drake) in 9:34.

OCTOBER 11 *Washington, DC*

Lance Archer defeated Alec Odin in 3:53; Jamie Hayter, Penelope Ford and Serena Deeb defeated Brittany Blake, Jordan Blade and Trish Adora in 4:32; Hikaru Shida defeated Marina Shafir in 6:56; Brian Cage defeated Papadon in 4:29; Athena defeated Gia Scott in 4:39; QT Marshall defeated Action Andretti in 7:01; Dalton Castle and The Boys (Brandon Tate and Brent Tate) defeated BK Klein, Joe Keys and Josh Fuller in 3:35; Kip Sabian defeated Brandon Cutler in 6:01; Toni Storm defeated Emi Sakura in 8:53; Dante Martin and Matt Sydal defeated The Factory (Aaron Solo and Cole Karter) in 9:31.

OCTOBER 18 *Toronto, Canada*

Hikaru Shida defeated Vanessa Kraven in 4:25; The Dark Order (John Silver, Alex Reynolds, Evil Uno and Ten) defeated Jordano, Shayne Hawke, Tyler Tirva and Zak Patterson in 6:52; Eddie Kingston and Ortiz defeated Jake O'Reilly and Mo Jabari in 3:56; Orange Cassidy and Best Friends (Chuck Taylor and Trent Beretta) defeated Jessie V, Kobe Durst and Steven Mainz in 2:44; Ari Daivari defeated Brandon Cutler in 4:59; Willow Nightingale defeated Seleziya Sparx in 5:25; Dante Martin defeated QT Marshall in 9:19.

OCTOBER 25 *Toronto, Canada*

Lance Archer defeated Iseah Bronson in 3:39; Zack Clayton defeated Shane Saber in 3:57; Athena defeated Alexia Nicole in 2:51; Danhausen defeated James Stone in 2:18; Aaron Solo defeated Serpentico in 5:13; Riho defeated Jungle Kyona in 5:20; The Lucha Brothers (Penta El Zero M and Rey Fenix) defeated The WorkHorsemen (Anthony Henry and JD Drake) in 2:55; Emi Sakura and Serena Deeb defeated KC Spinelli and Taylor Rising in 4:34; Ricky Starks defeated Nick Comoroto in 8:47.

NOVEMBER 1 *Uncasville, CT*

Danhausen defeated Jon Cruz in 4:47; The Embassy (Brian Cage, Kaun and Toa Liona) defeated Fuego Del Sol and Waves And Curls (Jaylen Brandyn and Traevon Jordan) in 4:01; Nyla Rose defeated Leva Bates in 1:00; Dante Martin defeated Encore in 2:49; Toni Storm defeated Diamante in 6:43; Orange Cassidy and Best

Friends (Chuck Taylor and Trent Beretta) defeated Tony Deppen and The Trustbusters (Ari Daivari and Sonny Kiss) in 6:04; Kip Sabian defeated Dean Alexander in 2:31; Marina Shafir defeated Kennedi Copeland in :26; Rey Fenix defeated AR Fox in 4:52.

NOVEMBER 8 *Jacksonville, FL*

Zack Clayton defeated Blake Li in 1:41; Kayla Rossi defeated Ashley D'Amboise in 2:13; The Gunn Club (Austin Gunn and Colten Gunn) defeated BK Klein and Jarett Diaz in 3:05; Peter Avalon defeated Brandon Cutler in 6:37; The Factory (Cole Karter and QT Marshall) defeated The Varsity Blonds (Brian Pillman Jr. and Griff Garrison) in 4:13; Anna Jay defeated Sio Nieves in 2:06; Kip Sabian defeated Marcus Kross in 2:58; Athena defeated Diamante in 4:22; Powerhouse Hobbs defeated Rico Gonzalez in :54; The Dark Order (John Silver, Alex Reynolds and Evil Uno) defeated Ativalu, Fulton and Troy Hollywood in 2:22; Eddie Kingston and Ortiz defeated AR Fox and Caleb Konley in 1:49; Hikaru Shida and Toni Storm defeated Emi Sakura and Mei Suruga in 7:51; Blackpool Combat Club (Claudio Castagnoli and Wheeler Yuta) defeated The Wingmen (Cezar Bononi and Ryan Nemeth) in 4:40.

NOVEMBER 15 *Uncasville, CT*

Skye Blue defeated Paris Van Dale in 2:25; The Iron Savages (Boulder and Bronson) defeated Brando Lee and Lucas Chase in 2:40; Kiera Hogan defeated Kennedi Copeland in 2:41; Frankie Kazarian defeated Zack Clayton in 3:39; The Factory (Cole Karter, Lee Johnson and QT Marshall) defeated Channing Thomas, Man Scout and Teddy Goodz in 4:11; Athena defeated LMK in 3:42; The Dark Order (John Silver, Alex Reynolds and Evil Uno) defeated Arjun Singh, Brett Gosselin and Mike Magnum in 4:43; Daniel Garcia defeated Brock Anderson in 7:49.

NOVEMBER 22 *Newark, NJ*

The Varsity Athletes (Josh Woods and Tony Nese) defeated Dean Alexander and Rosario Grillo in 3:32; Willow Nightingale defeated Marina Shafir in 5:00; Wheeler Yuta defeated KM in 3:21; Jake Hager defeated Bryce Donavan in 2:41; Tay Melo defeated Skye Blue in 5:54; Rush defeated Leon Ruffin in 1:04; The Dark Order (John Silver, Alex Reynolds and Evil Uno) defeated The Trustbusters (Ari Daivari, Jeeves Kay and Sonny Kiss) in 5:26.

NOVEMBER 29 *Newark, NJ*

The Factory (Cole Karter, Lee Johnson and QT Marshall) defeated Justin Corino, Ryan Mooney and Steven Josifi in 3:40; Zack Clayton defeated Chris Wylde in 2:40; Hikaru Shida defeated Leyla Luciano in 2:37; The Jericho Appreciation Society (Angelo Parker, Daniel Garcia and Matt Menard) defeated Jack Tomlinson, LSG and Tracy Williams in 4:09; Brian Cage defeated Tony Deppen in 3:07; Angelico defeated Hagane Shinno in 4:25; Emi Sakura defeated Tiara James in 2:17; Matt Hardy and Private Party (Isiah Kassidy and Marq Quen) defeated The Wingmen (Cezar Bononi, Peter Avalon and Ryan Nemeth) in 7:16.

DECEMBER 6 *Atlantic City, NJ*

Dalton Castle and The Boys (Brandon Tate and Brent Tate) defeated Jaden Valo, Justin Corino and Sonny Defarge in 2:30; Abadon defeated Leva Bates in 2:39; Brian Cage defeated Leon Ruffin in 5:35; Jay Lethal and Satnam Singh defeated The Brick City Boyz (JCruz and Victor Chase) in 1:54; Athena defeated B3CCA in 3:11; Trent Beretta defeated Anthony Henry in 10:49.

DECEMBER 13 *Atlantic City, NJ*
Tay Melo defeated Miranda Vionette in 1:07; The Factory (Cole Karter, Lee Johnson and QT Marshall) defeated Chris Steeler, Joe Keys and LSG in 3:29; Zack Clayton defeated Steve Pena in 2:15; Kip Sabian defeated Tony Deppen in 5:27; Eddie Kingston and Ortiz defeated The Trustbusters (Jeeves Kay and Slim J) in 6:59

DECEMBER 20 *Orlando, FL*
Kenny Omega defeated Hagane Shinno in 11:16; Action Andretti defeated Invictus Khash in 3:57; Marina Shafir defeated Angelica Risk in :55; Parker Boudreaux defeated Gus De La Vega in 1:21; Angelico and Chaos Project (Luther and Serpentico) defeated Jarett Diaz, Jay Marti and Richard Adonis in 4:07; Julia Hart defeated Sahara Se7en in 1:07; Jeff Jarrett and Satnam Singh defeated Dean Alexander and Rosario Grillo in 2:32; The Wingmen (Peter Avalon and Ryan Nemeth) defeated Jake St. Patrick and Sage Scott in 3:27; Kip Sabian defeated Caleb Konley in 2:49; Jade Cargill defeated Dream Girl Ellie in 1:20; Ricky Starks defeated Cezar Bononi in 1:28.

DECEMBER 27 *Orlando, FL*
Angelico defeated Dante Casanova in 2:37; The WorkHorsemen (Anthony Henry and JD Drake) defeated The Hughes Bros. (Terrell Hughes and Terrence Hughes) in 5:38; Fuego Del Sol defeated Lucky Ali in 2:28; Matt Menard defeated Brock Anderson in 4:44; Evil Uno defeated Blake Li in 2:10; Red Velvet defeated Billie Starkz in 1:54; The Iron Savages (Boulder and Bronson) defeated Brandon Bullock and James Ryan in 2:13; Diamante defeated Mafiosa in 1:48; AR Fox defeated Slim J in 8:54.

AEW DARK ELEVATION

JANUARY 3 *Jacksonville, FL*
Riho defeated Valentina Rossi in 3:33; Andrade El Idolo defeated JP Harlow in 2:58; Megan Bayne defeated Leila Grey in 2:42; Scorpio Sky defeated Ray Jaz in 2:41; The Dark Order (John Silver and Alex Reynolds) defeated Mike Orlando and Shayne Stetson in 3:48; Jake Atlas defeated Serpentico in 2:19; Skye Blue defeated Angelica Risk in 2:56; Jay Lethal defeated Troy Hollywood in 3:58.

JANUARY 10 *Jacksonville, FL*
Jay Lethal and Sonny Kiss defeated Chris Steeler and Jaden Valo in 2:32; Emi Sakura and Nyla Rose defeated Skye Blue and Tina San Antonio in 2:44; FTR (Cash Wheeler and Dax Harwood) defeated Pat Brink and Myles Hawkins in 3:08; Leyla Hirsch and Red Velvet defeated B3CCA and Notorious Mimi in 1:50; Powerhouse Hobbs defeated Ryan Clancy in 1:23; QT Marshall defeated Zack Clayton in 2:53; Andrade El Idolo defeated Avery Good in 2:30; The Acclaimed (Anthony Bowens and Max Caster) defeated Joey Ace and Kevin Matthews in 3:29; Dante Martin defeated Action Andretti in 1:31; The Dark Order (John Silver, Alex Reynolds and Ten) defeated The Hardy Family Office (Isiah Kassidy, Marq Quen and The Blade) in 4:01.

JANUARY 17 *Raleigh, NC*
Lee Moriarty and Matt Sydal defeated JR Miller and Marcus Kross in 3:20; Tay Conti defeated Ameera in 1:57; The Gunn Club (Austin Gunn and Colten Gunn) defeated JB Cole and TIM in 2:55; Frankie Kazarian defeated LaBron Kozone in 3:15; Ruby Soho defeated Kenzie Paige in 3:07; Private Party (Isiah Kassidy and Marq Quen) defeated Chase Emory and Patrick Scott in 3:10; Jay Lethal defeated Alexander Moss in 4:40.

JANUARY 24 *Washington, D.C.*
Leyla Hirsch defeated Brittany Blake in 2:25; Private Party (Isiah Kassidy and Marq Quen) defeated Action Andretti and Myles Hawkins in 3:20; Brandi Rhodes defeated Willow Nightingale in 2:27; Men Of The Year (Ethan Page and Scorpio Sky) defeated Logan LaRoux and Mike Fowler in 3:00; Red Velvet defeated Janai Kai in 3:36; The Inner Circle (Santana and Ortiz) defeated Breaux Keller and Goldy in 3:10; Ruby Soho and Thunder Rosa defeated Jordan Blake and Leva Bates in 2:52; Team Taz (Powerhouse Hobbs and Ricky Starks) defeated Lee Moriarty and Matt Sydal in 5:21.

JANUARY 31 *Cleveland, OH*
Lance Archer defeated Chase Oliver in 1:12; Brandi Rhodes defeated KiLynn King in 4:00; Jay Lethal defeated Casey Carrington in 3:10; Anna Jay defeated Nikki Victory in 1:20; Dante Martin, Lee Moriarty and Matt Sydal defeated The Factory (Aaron Solo, Nick Comoroto and QT Marshall) in 7:46; Ruby Soho and Thunder Rosa defeated Joseline Navarro and Megan Meyers in 2:46; Penta El Zero M defeated Serpentico in 5:30.

FEBRUARY 7 *Chicago, IL*
Bobby Fish defeated Robert Anthony in 5:15; Diamante, Emi Sakura and The Bunny defeated Heather Reckless, Queen Aminata and Skye Blue in 4:02; Scorpio Sky defeated Stephen Wolf in 3:40; Julia Hart defeated Arie Alexander in 2:06; Dante Martin defeated Aaron Solo in 5:01; The Acclaimed (Anthony Bowens and Max Caster) and The Gunn Club (Austin Gunn and Colten Gunn) defeated Lee Moriarty, Matt Sydal and The Nightmare Family (Brock Anderson and Lee Johnson) in 7:11; Best Friends (Chuck Taylor and Trent Beretta) defeated Chaos Project (Luther and Serpentico) in 6:42.

FEBRUARY 14 *Atlantic City, NJ*
Dante Martin defeated Kevin Matthews in 3:34; Thunder Rosa defeated Riley Shepard in 2:24; Zack Clayton defeated Serpentico in 3:46; Powerhouse Hobbs defeated Matt Sydal in 5:19; Men Of The Year (Ethan Page and Scorpio Sky) defeated Jaden Valo and Steve Pena in 3:12; 2point0 (Jeff Parker and Matt Lee), Daniel Garcia and The Acclaimed (Anthony Bowens and Max Caster) defeated The Dark Order (John Silver, Alex Reynolds, Evil Uno, Alan Angels and Stu Grayson) in 5:56; Ruby Soho and TayJay (Anna Jay and Tay Conti) defeated Emi Sakura, Nyla Rose and The Bunny in 3:43.

FEBRUARY 21 *Nashville, TN*
Red Velvet and TayJay (Anna Jay and Tay Conti) defeated Angelica Risk, Arie Alexander and Freya States in 3:42; 2point0 (Jeff Parker and Matt Lee), Daniel Garcia and The Gunn Club (Austin Gunn and Colten Gunn) defeated Ariel Levy, Chico Adams, Dean Alexander, Dominic Garrini and Kevin Ku in 2:55; The Bunny defeated Kaitland Alexis in 2:05; AHFO (Andrade El Idolo, Isiah Kassidy, Marq Quen, The Butcher and The Blade) defeated Baron Black, Carlie Bravo, Chandler Hopkins, Jameson Ryan and Shawn Dean in 4:20; Ruby Soho defeated Haley J in

2:00; **Lance Archer** defeated **Joey O'Riley** in :23; **Emi Sakura**, **Leyla Hirsch** and **Nyla Rose** defeated **AQA**, **Kiera Hogan** and **Skye Blue** in 4:48; **Brock Anderson**, **Frankie Kazarian**, **Jay Lethal**, **Lee Johnson** and **Matt Sydal** defeated **Chaos Project** (**Luther** and **Serpentico**) and **The Wingmen** (**Cezar Bononi**, **JD Drake** and **Peter Avalon**) in 6:06.

FEBRUARY 28 *Bridgeport, CT*
Jay Lethal defeated **Jora Johl** in 3:27; **Red Velvet** defeated **Skye Blue** in 2:24; **Frankie Kazarian** defeated **Alan Angels** in 6:05; **Diamante**, **Emi Sakura** and **Nyla Rose** defeated **Kayla Sparks**, **LMK** and **Paris Van Dale** in 2:27; **Lance Archer** defeated **Fuego Del Sol** in 3:10; **Leyla Hirsch** defeated **Willow Nightingale** in 2:16; **The Dark Order** (**Evil Uno** and **Stu Grayson**) defeated **Chaos Project** (**Luther** and **Serpentico**) in 4:53.

MARCH 7 *Jacksonville, FL*
Lance Archer defeated **Cameron Stewart** in 1:50; **Ruby Soho** defeated **Session Moth Martina** in 3:50; **Daniel Garcia** defeated **Ray Jaz** in 1:06; **Scorpio Sky** defeated **Shawn Dean** in 5:11; **Kris Statlander** defeated **Emi Sakura** in 4:19; **Wheeler Yuta** defeated **Aaron Solo** in 7:07.

MARCH 14 *Fort Myers, FL*
Nyla Rose defeated **Katalina Perez** in 1:20; **Frankie Kazarian** defeated **Tiger Ruas** in 5:47; **Emi Sakura** and **The Bunny** defeated **KiLynn King** and **Skye Blue** in 6:00; **Jay Lethal** defeated **Merrik Donovan** in 2:23; **Ruby Soho** defeated **Amber Nova** in 3:34; **The Dark Order** (**John Silver** and **Alex Reynolds**) defeated **Chaos Project** (**Luther** and **Serpentico**) in 4:40.

MARCH 21 *San Antonio, TX*
Nyla Rose defeated **Robyn Renegade** in 1:24; **Julia Hart** defeated **Skye Blue** in 4:00; **The Gunn Club** (**Austin Gunn** and **Colten Gunn**) defeated **Aaron Mercer** and **Masada** in 3:42; **Top Flight** (**Dante Martin** and **Darius Martin**) defeated **Chaos Project** (**Luther** and **Serpentico**) in 4:54; **Anna Jay** and **Ruby Soho** defeated **Emi Sakura** and **The Bunny** in 4:20; **The Dark Order** (**John Silver**, **Evil Uno** and **Stu Grayson**) defeated **The Factory** (**Aaron Solo**, **Nick Comoroto** and **QT Marshall**) in 7:27.

MARCH 28 *Cedar Park, TX*
Lee Moriarty defeated **Serpentico** in 3:59; **Abadon** defeated **Danni Bee** in 1:23; **Penta Oscuro** defeated **JPH** in 1:55; **Frankie Kazarian** defeated **Brandon Cutler** in 3:46; **Jamie Hayter** defeated **Rache Chanel** in 1:44; **Max Caster** defeated **Sonny Kiss** in 4:17; **Hikaru Shida** defeated **Madi Wrenkowski** in 1:39; **Anna Jay** and **Ruby Soho** defeated **The Renegades** (**Charlette Renegade** and **Robyn Renegade**) in 2:17; **Roppongi Vice** (**Rocky Romero** and **Trent Beretta**) defeated **The Factory** (**Aaron Solo** and **QT Marshall**) in 5:23.

APRIL 4 *Columbia, SC*
Leyla Hirsch defeated **Ella Envy** in 1:35; **Brock Anderson** and **Lee Johnson** defeated **The Factory** (**Aaron Solo** and **QT Marshall**) in 6:59; **Serena Deeb** defeated **Dani Mo** in 2:15; **Frankie Kazarian** defeated **Lucky Ali** in 3:40; **Red Velvet** defeated **Brittany Jade** in 2:20; **Best Friends** (**Chuck Taylor** and **Trent Beretta**) defeated **The WorkHorsemen** (**Anthony Henry** and **JD Drake**) in 8:00; **Anna Jay** and **Ruby Soho** defeated **Ashley D'Amboise** and **Diamante** in 4:50; **Paul Wight** defeated **Austin Green** in 2:04.

APRIL 11 *Boston, MA*
Frankie Kazarian defeated **Teddy Goodz** in 3:18; **Diamante** defeated **Ashley D'Amboise** in 2:43; **The Dark Order** (**John Silver**, **Alex Reynolds**, **Alan Angels**, **Stu Grayson** and **Ten**) defeated **Chaos Project** (**Luther** and **Serpentico**) and **The Gunn Club** (**Austin Gunn**, **Billy Gunn** and **Colten Gunn**) in 5:20; **Anna Jay**, **Ruby Soho** and **Skye Blue** defeated **Emi Sakura**, **LuFisto** and **The Bunny** in 3:21; **Penta Oscuro** defeated **Jora Johl** in 3:50; **Top Flight** (**Dante Martin** and **Darius Martin**) defeated **The Factory** (**Aaron Solo** and **Nick Comoroto**) in 5:52.

APRIL 18 *New Orleans, LA*
Kris Statlander defeated **Ashley D'Amboise** in 1:30; **Andrade El Idolo** defeated **Alan Angels** in 4:24; **Tony Nese** defeated **J. Spade** in 2:35; **The Dark Order** (**John Silver**, **Alex Reynolds**, **Evil Uno** and **Stu Grayson**) defeated **Allen Russell**, **Dale Springs**, **Izaiah Zane** and **Kameron Russell** in 2:17; **Roppongi Vice** (**Rocky Romero** and **Trent Beretta**) defeated **The Factory** (**Aaron Solo** and **Nick Comoroto**) in 7:25; **Anna Jay**, **Hikaru Shida** and **Ruby Soho** defeated **Emi Sakura**, **Raychell Rose** and **The Bunny** in 3:20; **The Hardys** (**Jeff Hardy** and **Matt Hardy**) and **Top Flight** (**Dante Martin** and **Darius Martin**) defeated **Private Party** (**Isiah Kassidy** and **Marq Quen**) and **The Hybrid2** (**Angelico** and **Jack Evans**) in 9:45.

APRIL 25 *Pittsburgh, PA*
The Dark Order (**Evil Uno**, **Alex Reynolds**, **Alan Angels**, **Stu Grayson** and **Ten**) defeated **Bulk Nasty**, **Jake Omen**, **Luther**, **RC Dupree** and **Tito Ortic** in 3:09; **Kris Statlander** defeated **Julia Hart** in 6:19; **Konosuke Takeshita** defeated **Brandon Cutler** in 4:57; **Tony Nese** defeated **The Steel City Brawler** in 2:51; **Minoru Suzuki** defeated **QT Marshall** in 4:12; **John Silver** defeated **Vince Valor** in 1:29; **Anna Jay**, **Ruby Soho** and **Skye Blue** defeated **Emi Sakura**, **Nyla Rose** and **The Bunny** in 6:35; **Penta Oscuro** defeated **Max Caster** in 4:45.

MAY 2 *Philadelphia, PA*
Julia Hart defeated **Abby Jane** in 2:20; **Anthony Ogogo** defeated **Goldy** in 2:33; **Konosuke Takeshita** defeated **Rhett Titus** in 4:40; **Tony Nese** defeated **Cheeseburger** in 4:13; **Willow Nightingale** defeated **Gia Scott** in 1:24; **Max Caster** defeated **Zack Clayton** in 1:24; **Anna Jay** and **Kris Statlander** defeated **Emi Sakura** and **Nyla Rose** in 6:10; **The Dark Order** (**John Silver**, **Alex Reynolds**, **Alan Angels**, **Evil Uno**, **Colt Cabana** and **Ten**) defeated **Anthony Bennett**, **Bret Waters**, **Cory Bishop**, **Eli Isom**, **Jaden Valo** and **Mike Law** in 1:44.

MAY 9 *Baltimore, MD*
The Dark Order (**Alex Reynolds**, **Alan Angels**, **Evil Uno** and **Ten**) defeated **Brandon Scott**, **Diego**, **Josh Fuller** and **Ryan Mooney** in 4:27; **Abadon** defeated **Emi Sakura** in 4:29; **Sonny Kiss** defeated **Peter Avalon** in 4:12; **John Silver** defeated **Tony Deppen** in 2:34; **Keith Lee** and **Swerve Strickland** defeated **The Factory** (**Nick Comoroto** and **QT Marshall**) in 6:47.

MAY 16 *Elmont, NY*
Bear Bronson defeated **Brandon Cutler** in 2:20; **Brody King** defeated **Alex Reynolds** in 1:46; **Anna Jay** and **Yuka Sakazaki** defeated **Emi Sakura** and **Nyla Rose** in 3:32; **The Acclaimed** (**Anthony Bowens** and **Max Caster**) and **The Gunn Club** (**Austin Gunn** and **Colten Gunn**) defeated **Bryce Donovan**, **GKM**, **Lucas Chase** and **Zack Clayton** in 1:22; **The Dark Order** (**Evil**

Uno and Ten) defeated Eric James and VSK in 2:30; Mercedes Martinez defeated Trish Adora in 5:32.

MAY 23 Houston, TX
Ethan Page defeated JD Griffey in 2:07; Mercedes Martinez defeated Hyan in 5:01; The Butcher and The Blade defeated The Varsity Blonds (Brian Pillman Jr. and Griff Garrison) in 5:55; Lee Moriarty defeated Alex Reynolds in 4:04; Emi Sakura and Nyla Rose defeated Skye Blue and Yuka Sakazaki in 6:17; Anthony Ogogo defeated Mysterious Q in 4:10.

MAY 30 Las Vegas, NV
Konosuke Takeshita defeated Ryan Nemeth in 5:31; Mercedes Martinez defeated Mazzerati in 7:17.

JUNE 6 Los Angeles, CA
The Factory (Aaron Solo, Anthony Ogogo, Nick Comoroto and QT Marshall) defeated The Dark Order (Alan Angels, Evil Uno, John Silver and Ten) in 6:28; Frankie Kazarian defeated Serpentico in 5:00; Nyla Rose and Serena Deeb defeated Miyu Yamashita and Skye Blue in 7:40; Death Triangle (Pac, Penta Oscuro and Rey Fenix) defeated The Wingmen (Cezar Bononi, Peter Avalon and Ryan Nemeth) in 5:04.

JUNE 13 Independence, MO
Nyla Rose defeated Max The Impaler in 1:55; Private Party (Isiah Kassidy and Marq Quen) defeated Pharell Jackson and SK Bishop in 3:00; Ortiz defeated Anaya in 1:14; Mercedes Martinez and Serena Deeb defeated Miranda Gordy and Tootie Lynn in 4:15; The Jericho Appreciation Society (Angelo Parker and Matt Menard) defeated Danny Adams and Warhorse in 2:45; Ruby Soho defeated Heidi Howitzer in 3:17; The Dark Order (Evil Uno and Ten) defeated The Factory (Aaron Solo and QT Marshall) in 8:13.

JUNE 20 St. Louis, MO
Mercedes Martinez and Serena Deeb defeated Heather Reckless and Tootie Lynn in 4:29; Andrade El Idolo defeated Frankie Kazarian in 8:43; Marina Shafir and Nyla Rose defeated Heidi Howitzer and Max The Impaler in 3:25; Keith Lee and Swerve Strickland defeated Davey Vega and Mat Fitchett in 3:10; Anna Jay defeated Rebel in :56; Tony Nese defeated Warhorse in 2:53; Ruby Soho defeated Miranda Gordy in 2:05; Matt Sydal defeated QT Marshall in 7:28.

JUNE 27 Milwaukee, WI
Anna Jay defeated Heather Reckless in 1:52; Team Taz (Powerhouse Hobbs and Ricky Starks) defeated Joey Jett and Jordan Chaos in 3:28; Ruby Soho defeated Missa Kate in 2:39; Swerve In Our Glory (Keith Lee and Swerve Strickland) defeated GPA and Vic Capri in 4:07; Ethan Page defeated Serpentico in 1:37; John Silver defeated Kevin Matthews in 2:27; House Of Black (Brody King and Buddy Matthews) defeated Brubaker and CJ Esparza in 2:36; The Gunn Club (Austin Gunn and Colten Gunn) and Max Caster defeated The Dark Order (Alex Reynolds, Evil Uno and Ten) in 4:08.

JULY 4 Detroit, MI
Anna Jay defeated Megan Myers in 2:21; Best Friends (Chuck Taylor and Trent Beretta) defeated GPA and Isaiah Broner in 3:52; Jay Lethal and Satnam Singh defeated Cage Alexander and Ryan Jones in 2:30; Anthony Ogogo defeated Pat Monix in 2:38; Hikaru Shida and Yuka Sakazaki defeated Heather Reckless and Laynie Luck in 2:53; The Dark Order (Alex Reynolds, Evil Uno and Ten) defeated The Factory (Aaron Solo, Nick Comoroto and QT Marshall) in 7:56.

JULY 11 Rochester, NY
Emi Sakura defeated Paris Van Dale in 3:03; Dante Martin defeated JD Drake in 7:13; Julia Hart defeated JC in 2:02; Ethan Page defeated Colin Delaney in 5:10; Anna Jay defeated Shawna Reed in 1:50; Best Friends (Chuck Taylor and Trent Beretta) defeated The Factory (Aaron Solo and QT Marshall) in 9:40.

JULY 18 Savannah, GA
Bobby Fish defeated Blake Li in 2:59; Marina Shafir and Nyla Rose defeated Brittany Jade and Skye Blue in 4:30; Julia Hart defeated Amber Nova in 1:33; Ethan Page defeated Leon Ruffin in 5:38; The Dark Order (Evil Uno and Ten) defeated The Hughes Bros. (Terrell Hughes and Terrence Hughes) in 4:44; Angelico, The Butcher and The Blade defeated Brandon Bullock, Bryce Cannon and Jameson Ryan in 1:40; Tony Nese defeated John Walters in 2:34.

JULY 25 Duluth, GA
Private Party (Isiah Kassidy and Marq Quen) and Angelico defeated Adrian Alanis, AR Fox and Liam Gray in 3:59; Marina Shafir and Nyla Rose defeated Angelica Risk and Shalonce Royal in 2:17; Toni Storm defeated Emi Sakura in 7:33; Kris Statlander defeated Brittany Jade in 1:54; Hikaru Shida defeated Robyn Renegade in 5:33; The Dark Order (Evil Uno and Ten) defeated The Factory (Aaron Solo and Nick Comoroto) in 6:35; Baron Black defeated Brandon Cutler in 3:12; Konosuke Takeshita defeated JD Drake in 3:40.

AUGUST 1 Worcester, MA
Julia Hart defeated MLK in 2:35; Leila Grey defeated JC in 2:23; Private Party (Isiah Kassidy and Marq Quen), Angelico, The Butcher and The Blade defeated JCruz, Joey Ace, Victor Chase and Waves and Curls (Jaylen Brandyn and Treavon Jordan) in 2:12; The Factory (Aaron Solo, Anthony Ogogo, Nick Comoroto and QT Marshall) defeated Bobby Orlando, BRG, Bryce Donovan and TUG Cooper in 3:33; Cole Karter defeated Serpentico in 4:02; Athena defeated Christina Marie in 2:48; Hikaru Shida, Toni Storm and Willow Nightingale defeated Emi Sakura, Marina Shafir and Nyla Rose in 8:05.

AUGUST 4 Columbus, OH
Hikaru Shida defeated Emi Sakura in 5:40; Mance Warner defeated Serpentico in 3:57; The Varsity Athletes (Tony Nese and Josh Woods) defeated Damian Chambers and Dean Alexander in 2:52.

AUGUST 8 Columbus, OH
Ruby Soho and Skye Blue defeated Megan Myers and Nikki Victory in 3:11; Parker Boudreaux defeated Casey Carrington in 1:37; Athena defeated Queen Aminata in 2:59; Kiera Hogan and Leila Grey defeated Alice Crowley and Freya States in 2:00; The Dark Order (John Silver and Alex Reynolds) defeated Lord Crewe and TUG Cooper in 2:13; The Lucha Brothers (Penta El Zero M and Rey Fenix) defeated The Wingmen (Peter Avalon and Ryan Nemeth) in 4:50.

AUGUST 15 Minneapolis, MN
The Varsity Athletes (Tony Nese and Josh Woods) defeated Arik Cannon and Travis Titan in 2:40; The Dark Order (John Silver, Alex Reynolds, Evil Uno and Ten) defeated Adam Grace, Drew System, Rylie Jackson and TUG Cooper in 2:25; Serena Deeb defeated Sierra in 2:58; Konosuke Takeshita defeated Cezar Bononi in 2:37; Julia Hart defeated Free-Range Kara in 2:41; Private Party (Isiah Kassidy and Marq

Quen) defeated **Jah-C** and **JDX** in 1:49; **Penelope Ford** defeated **Heather Reckless** in 2:46; **The Acclaimed** (**Anthony Bowens** and **Max Caster**) defeated **JT Energy** and **Justin Fowler** in 1:47; **Hikaru Shida** and **ThunderStorm** (**Thunder Rosa** and **Toni Storm**) defeated **Emi Sakura, Marina Shafir** and **Nyla Rose** in 2:42.

AUGUST 22 *Charleston, WV*
Anna Jay defeated **Nikki Victory** in 1:02; **Ortiz** and **Ruby Soho** defeated **Mickey Midas** and **Queen Aminata** in 1:50; **Dante Martin** defeated **Jackson Drake** in 2:47; **Serena Deeb** defeated **Megan Meyers** in 2:57; **The Dark Order** (**John Silver, Alex Reynolds** and **Ten**) defeated **Alexander Apollo, D'Mone Solavino** and **RC Dupree** in 3:22; **Julia Hart** defeated **Hayley Shadows** in 2:08; **The Varsity Athletes** (**Tony Nese** and **Josh Woods**) defeated **Andrea Guercio** and **Logan James** in 2:16; **Death Triangle** (**Pac, Penta Oscuro** and **Rey Fenix**) defeated **Dean Alexander, Jake Manning** and **Rosario Grillo** in 2:36; **Emi Sakura** and **Maki Itoh** defeated **Hikaru Shida** and **Skye Blue** in 7:15.

AUGUST 29 *Cleveland, OH*
Dante Martin defeated **Wes Barkley** in 2:00; **Julia Hart** defeated **Arie Alexander** in 1:56; **Marina Shafir** and **Nyla Rose** defeated **Queen Aminata** and **Skye Blue** in 3:40; **Matt Hardy** defeated **RSP** in 3:16; **Serena Deeb** defeated **Katie Arquette** in 2:03; **Frankie Kazarian** defeated **Andrea Guercio** in 2:50; **Rush, The Butcher** and **The Blade** defeated **Chase Oliver, Elijah Dean** and **Zach Nystrom** in 3:20; **Hikaru Shida** defeated **Emi Sakura** in 6:30.

SEPTEMBER 3 *Hoffman Estates, IL*
The Jericho Appreciation Society (**Sammy Guevara** and **Tay Melo**) defeated **GPA** and **Laynie Luck** in 4:27; **Swerve In Our Glory** (**Keith Lee** and **Swerve Strickland**) defeated **Jah-C** and **Storm Grayson** in 3:54; **Hangman Page** and **The Dark Order** (**John Silver** and **Alex Reynolds**) defeated **The Factory** (**Aaron Solo, Cole Karter** and **Nick Comoroto**) in 6:00; **The Acclaimed** (**Anthony Bowens** and **Max Caster**) defeated **Invictus Khash** and **JPH** in 1:55; **Ortiz** and **Ruby Soho** defeated **Baliyan Akki** and **Emi Sakura** in 2:20; **Best Friends** (**Chuck Taylor** and **Trent Beretta**) and **Orange Cassidy** defeated **Angelico, The Butcher** and **The Blade** in 8:13.

SEPTEMBER 5 *Hoffman Estates, IL*
Julia Hart defeated **Alice Crowley** in 2:27; **The Varsity Athletes** (**Tony Nese** and **Josh Woods**) defeated **Jordan Kross** and **Renny D** in 2:27; **Serena Deeb** defeated **Nikki Victory** in 3:50; **Private Party** (**Isiah Kassidy** and **Marq Quen**) defeated **Brandon Gore** and **JDX** in 2:07; **Skye Blue** defeated **Diamante** in 4:37; **Marina Shafir** and **Nyla Rose** defeated **Madison Rayne** and **Queen Aminata** in 4:42.

SEPTEMBER 12 *Buffalo, NY*
Marina Shafir and **Nyla Rose** defeated **JC Storm** and **Joelle Clift** in 1:40; **Julia Hart** defeated **Tiara James** in 1:33; **Dante Martin** and **Matt Sydal** defeated **Serpentico** and **Zack Clayton** in :57; **Athena** defeated **Emi Sakura** in 4:43; **The House Of Black** (**Brody King** and **Buddy Matthews**) defeated **Isaiah Prince** and **Kubes** in 2:34; **Hikaru Shida** defeated **Christina Marie** in 2:11; **John Silver** defeated **Ryan Nemeth** in 3:33; **The Butcher** and **The Blade** defeated **The Factory** (**Aaron Solo** and **Nick Comoroto**) in 4:37.

SEPTEMBER 19 *Albany, NY*
Zack Clayton defeated **Conan Lycan** in 3:34; **Nyla Rose** defeated **B3CCA** in 1:04; **Private Party** (**Isiah Kassidy** and **Marq Quen**) defeated **Aggro** and **DangerKid** in 4:46; **Skye Blue** defeated **Chica Carreras** in 2:17; **Dalton Castle** and **The Boys** (**Brandon Tate** and **Brent Tate**) defeated **Boujii, Omar** and **Rick Recon** in 3:25; **Frankie Kazarian** defeated **Jora Johl** in 3:52; **Mascara Dorada** defeated **Serpentico** in 2:46; **The Butcher** and **The Blade** defeated **Liam Davis** and **Mike Anthony** in 2:48.

SEPTEMBER 26 *New York, NY*
Kip Sabian and **Penelope Ford** defeated **Shawn Dean** and **Skye Blue** in 5:16; **Ortiz** defeated **Serpentico** in 3:22.

OCTOBER 3 *Philadelphia, PA*
Skye Blue defeated **Trish Adora** in 2:30; **Brian Cage** defeated **Tracy Williams** in 5:18; **Lance Archer** defeated **Cheeseburger** in 3:00; **Abadon** defeated **Abby Jane** in 1:00; **Dalton Castle** and **The Boys** (**Brandon Tate** and **Brent Tate**) defeated **Primal Fear** (**Adrien Soriano, Gabriel Hodder** and **Matthew Omen**) in 4:07; **Kip Sabian** and **Penelope Ford** defeated **Gia Scott** and **LSG** in 3:20; **The Lucha Brothers** (**Penta El Zero M** and **Rey Fenix**) defeated **Dante Martin** and **Tony Deppen** in 6:20; **Best Friends** (**Chuck Taylor** and **Trent Beretta**), **Danhausen** and **Rocky Romero** defeated **The Factory** (**Aaron Solo, Cole Karter, Nick Comoroto** and **QT Marshall**) in 7:54.

OCTOBER 10 *Washington, D.C.*
Hikaru Shida defeated **Erica Leigh** in 2:40; **Lance Archer** defeated **Papadon** in 3:10; **Emi Sakura** defeated **Trish Adora** in 3:10; **The Varsity Athletes** (**Tony Nese** and **Josh Woods**) defeated **Action Andretti** and **Myles Hawkins** in 5:55; **Nyla Rose** defeated **Jordan Blade** in 2:15; **Dalton Castle** and **The Boys** (**Brandon Tate** and **Brent Tate**) defeated **Brett Waters, Goldy** and **Logan Laroux** in 4:00; **Brandon Cutler** defeated **Serpentico** in 5:45.

OCTOBER 17 *Toronto, Canada*
Kip Sabian and **Penelope Ford** defeated **Jeremy Prophet** and **Jessika Neri** in 3:58; **Frankie Kazarian** defeated **Matt Blackmon** in 2:23; **Athena** defeated **Jody Threat** in 4:57; **The Butcher** and **The Blade** defeated **Voros Twins** (**Chris Voros** and **Patrick Voros**) in 2:37; **Jay Lethal** and **Satnam Singh** defeated **Dylan Davis** and **Junior Benito** in 2:32; **Emi Sakura** and **Serena Deeb** defeated **Madison Rayne** and **Skye Blue** in 6:00; **The Gunn Club** (**Austin Gunn** and **Colten Gunn**) defeated **The Bollywood Boyz** (**Gurv Sihra** and **Harv Sihra**) in 4:16.

OCTOBER 24 *Cincinnati, OH*
Ten defeated **Baron Black** in :47; **Eddie Kingston** and **Ortiz** defeated **Russ Myers** and **T-Money** in 1:54; **Serena Deeb** defeated **Haley J** in 2:01; **The Varsity Blonds** (**Brian Pillman Jr.** and **Griff Garrison**) defeated **The WorkHorsemen** (**Anthony Henry** and **JD Drake**) in 5:47; **Emi Sakura** and **Mei Suruga** defeated **Jaylee** and **Nikki Victory** in 3:30; **Matt Hardy** defeated **Lord Crewe** in 1:44; **Claudio Castagnoli** defeated **QT Marshall** in 9:45.

OCTOBER 31 *Norfolk, VA*
Madison Rayne defeated **Diamante** in 3:12; **Frankie Kazarian** defeated **Rhett Titus** in 3:35; **Kiera Hogan** defeated **Skye Blue** in 2:05; **Dante Martin** defeated

Brandon Cutler in 2:05; **Athena** defeated **Janai Kai** in 2:30; **Orange Cassidy** and **Best Friends (Chuck Taylor and Trent Beretta)** defeated **Anthony Young, Patton** and **Victor Andrews** in 3:30; **Eddie Kingston** and **Ortiz** defeated **Breaux Keller** and **Myles Hawkins** in 1:30; **Jade Cargill** defeated **Trish Adora** in 1:50; **QT Marshall** defeated **Danhausen** in 9:00.

NOVEMBER 7 Baltimore, MD

Abadon defeated **Amy Rose** in 1:45; **Dalton Castle** and **The Boys (Brandon Tate** and **Brent Tate)** defeated **The Trustbusters (Ari Daivari, Jeeves Kay** and **Slim J)** in 5:25; **Athena** defeated **Abby Jane** in 3:00; **Tay Melo** defeated **Trish Adora** in 2:10; **Dante Martin** defeated **Eli Isom** in 6:35; **The Factory (Cole Karter, Lee Johnson** and **QT Marshall)** defeated **Cheeseburger, Logan Easton Laroux** and **Rhett Titus** in 6:45; **Eddie Kingston** and **Ortiz** defeated **Joe Keys** and **Myles Hawkins** in 3:25; **Kip Sabian** defeated **Alex Reynolds** in 8:15; **Rocky Romero** and **Best Friends (Chuck Taylor** and **Trent Beretta)** defeated **Angelico, The Butcher** and **The Blade** in 7:20.

NOVEMBER 14 Boston, MA

The Gates Of Agony (Kaun and **Toa Liona)** defeated **Big Cuzzo** and **Teddy Goodz** in 1:37; **Tay Melo** defeated **Paris Van Dale** in 1:33; **Matt Hardy** and **Private Party (Isiah Kassidy** and **Marq Quen)** defeated **Channing Thomas, Kyle Bradley** and **Smiley Fairchild** in 3:46; **Athena** defeated **Kayla Sparks** in 3:08; **The Butcher** and **The Blade** defeated **Waves and Curls (Jaylen Brandyn** and **Traevon Jordan)** in 1:15; **Daniel Garcia** defeated **Leon Ruffin** in 5:41; **Ten** defeated **Jora Johl** in 1:30; **AR Fox** defeated **Serpentico** in 3:07; **Riho** and **Willow Nightingale** defeated **Emi Sakura** and **Mei Suruga** in 6:14.

NOVEMBER 21 Bridgeport, CT

Rush, The Butcher and **The Blade** defeated **Brett Gosselin, Channing Thomas** and **Doug Love** in 2:20; **Hikaru Shida** and **Willow Nightingale** defeated **Emi Sakura** and **Leva Bates** in 4:28; **Brian Cage** defeated **Brandon Cutler** in 2:30; **The Jericho Appreciation Society (Angelo Parker, Daniel Garcia** and **Matt Menard)** defeated **Leon Ruffin, Tony Deppen** and **Tracy Williams** in 2:46; **Mercedes Martinez** defeated **JC** in 2:28; **Wheeler Yuta** defeated **Zack Clayton** in 1:55; **Matt Hardy** and **Private Party (Isiah Kassidy** and **Marq Quen)** defeated **Encore** and **The Trustbusters (Ari Daivari** and **Sonny Kiss)** in 3:15; **Alex Reynolds** defeated **Kip Sabian** in 1:56; **Orange Cassidy** and **Best Friends (Chuck Taylor** and **Trent Beretta)** defeated **The Factory (Aaron Solo, Cole Karter** and **Lee Johnson)** in 3:38.

NOVEMBER 28 Chicago, IL

The Bunny defeated **Blair Onyx** in 1:18; **Brandon Cutler** defeated **Man Scout** in 3:28; **Marina Shafir** and **Nyla Rose** defeated **Emi Sakura** and **Maki Itoh** in 4:17; **Konosuke Takeshita** defeated **Ari Daivari** in 4:45; **Lee Moriarty** defeated **Robert Anthony** in 4:08; **Jay Lethal** and **Satnam Singh** defeated **GPA** and **Joe Alonzo** in 1:44; **Rocky Romero** and **Best Friends (Chuck Taylor** and **Trent Beretta)** defeated **Davey Bang, Freedom Ramsey** and **Yabo** in 3:54; **Athena** defeated **Laynie Luck** in 2:05; **Matt Hardy** and **Private Party (Isiah Kassidy** and **Marq Quen)** defeated **Isaia Moore** and **Chaos Project (Luther** and **Serpentico)** in 4:50; **Eddie Kingston** and **Ortiz** defeated **The Factory (Aaron Solo** and **Nick Comoroto)** in 4:55.

DECEMBER 5 Indianapolis, IN

Hagane Shinno defeated **Nick Comoroto** in 3:15; **Marina Shafir** and **Nyla Rose** defeated **Alice Crowley** and **Kitty LaFleur** in 3:07; **Kiera Hogan** defeated **Nikki Victory** in 2:28; **Top Flight (Dante Martin** and **Darius Martin)** defeated **The Outrunners (Truth Magnum** and **Turbo Floyd)** in 4:03; **Emi Sakura** defeated **Madison Rayne** in 2:41; **Lee Moriarty** defeated **Serpentico** in 3:23; **The Embassy (Kaun, Brian Cage** and **Toa Liona)** defeated **Dan Adams, Facade** and **Star Rider** in 3:43; **Kip Sabian** defeated **Alex Reynolds** in 6:25; **Konosuke Takeshita** defeated **Aaron Solo** in 3:15.

DECEMBER 10 Cedar Park, TX

The Kingdom (Matt Taven and **Mike Bennett)** defeated **Ativalu** and **Sal Muscat** in 1:49; **Athena** defeated **Madi Wrenkowski** in 1:39; **Top Flight (Dante Martin** and **Darius Martin)** defeated **The Factory (Aaron Solo** and **Nick Comoroto)** in 3:35; **Juice Robinson** defeated **Hagane Shinno** in 4:30.

DECEMBER 12 Cedar Park, TX

Emi Sakura defeated **Danni Bee** in 1:40; **The Jericho Appreciation Society (Angelo Parker** and **Matt Menard)** defeated **Warren Johnson** and **Zack Mason** in :20; **Willow Nightingale** defeated **Vertvixen** in 2:10; **Best Friends (Chuck Taylor** and **Trent Beretta)** defeated **Zack Clayton** and **Zane Valero** in 3:00; **Ari Daivari** and **The Varsity Athletes (Josh Woods** and **Tony Nese)** defeated **Brandon Cutler** and **Chaos Project (Luther** and **Serpentico)** in 5:20.

DECEMBER 19 Garland, TX

Marina Shafir defeated **Jazmin Allure** in 1:30; **Emi Sakura** and **The Bunny** defeated **Gigi Rey** and **Lady Bird Monroe** in 2:45; **Ethan Page, Isiah Kassidy, Konosuke Takeshita, Matt Hardy** and **Top Flight (Dante Martin** and **Darius Martin)** defeated **The Trustbusters (Jeeves Kay, Slim J** and **Sonny Kiss)** and **The Wingmen (Cezar Bononi, Peter Avalon** and **Ryan Nemeth)** in 7:45; **Eddie Kingston** and **Ortiz** defeated **Hagane Shinno** and **Steven Andrews** in 3:50; **Athena** defeated **Vertvixen** in 2:45; **Blackpool Combat Club (Claudio Castagnoli** and **Wheeler Yuta)** defeated **The WorkHorsemen (Anthony Henry** and **JD Drake)** in 7:55.

DECEMBER 26 San Antonio, TX

Marina Shafir and **Nyla Rose** defeated **Karizma** and **Leva Bates** in 2:54; **Julia Hart** defeated **Promise Braxton** in 1:11; **The Bunny** defeated **Madison Rayne** in 3:00; **Konosuke Takeshita** defeated **Frankie Kazarian** in 5:01; **Ruby Soho** and **Willow Nightingale** defeated **Madi Wrenkowski** and **Vertvixen** in 4:47; **Athena** defeated **Kiera Hogan** in 5:59; **Dralistico** defeated **Blake Christian** in 3:59.

IMPACT WRESTLING

JANUARY 6 Las Vegas, NV

Tasha Steelz, Lady Frost and **Chelsea Green** defeated **Rosemary, Jordynne Grace** and **Rachael Ellering** in 7:19; **Jonah** defeated **Jake Something** in 8:22; **Masha Slamovich** defeated **Sandra Moone** in :45; **Deonna Purrazzo** defeated **Mercedes Martinez** in 13:00; **Ace Austin** and **Madman Fulton** defeated **Hernandez** and **Johnny Swinger** in 3:40; **Karl Anderson** defeated **Heath** in 11:02.

JANUARY 13 *Dallas, TX*
Laredo Kid defeated Chris Bey in 12:49; Mike Bailey defeated Jake Something in 4:17; Masha Slamovich defeated Vert Vixen in 1:05; Moose defeated Zicky Dice in :16; Jonah defeated Raj Singh in 1:24; Deonna Purrazzo defeated Rok-C in 14:24.

JANUARY 20 *Dallas, TX*
Tasha Steelz defeated Chelsea Green in 4:24; The Influence (Tenille Dashwood and Madison Rayne) defeated Decay (Rosemary and Havok) in 3:35; W. Morrissey defeated Zicky Dice and VSK in a Handicap Match in 1:08; Jonathan Gresham defeated Steve Maclin in 10:20; Luke Gallows and Joe Doering defeated Heath and Rhino in 8:39; Josh Alexander defeated Charlie Haas in 11:03.

JANUARY 27 *Pembroke Pines, FL*
Jake Something defeated Chris Bey in 9:22; The IInspiration (Cassie Lee and Jessie McKay) defeated Madison Rayne and Kaleb With A K in 10:57; W. Morrissey defeated VSK, Zicky Dice, D-Ray 3000, David Young, Elix Skipper, Mikey Batts, Lex Lovett, Jerrelle Clark and Shark Boy in a Handicap Match in 3:00; Jonah defeated Johnny Swinger in 1:11; PCO defeated Chris Sabin in 15:48.

FEBRUARY 3 *Pembroke Pines, FL*
Matt Cardona defeated Jordynne Grace to win the Impact Digitial Media Title in 8:49; Jonah defeated Crazzy Steve in 2:08; Steve Maclin defeated Jonathan Gresham by DQ in 11:52; Josh Alexander defeated Vincent in 10:28; Bhupinder Gujjar defeated John Skyler in 3:46; Masha Slamovich defeated Kaci Lennox in :45; Bullet Club (Chris Bey, Jay White, Tama Tonga and Tanga Loa) defeated Jake Something, Mike Bailey, Madman Fulton and Ace Austin in 16:49.

FEBRUARY 10 *Pembroke Pines, FL*
Josh Alexander defeated Big Kon in :38; Deonna Purrazzo defeated Santana Garrett in 9:00; Mickie James vs. Chelsea Green ended in a no contest in 3:58; Matt Taven and Mike Bennett defeated Rhino and Rich Swann in 8:42; W. Morrissey defeated Brian Myers in a No DQ Match in 14:22.

FEBRUARY 17 *Pembroke Pines, FL*
Masha Slamovich defeated Kiah Dream in :44; Ace Austin defeated Blake Christian and Laredo Kid in a Three Way Match in 11:57; Gisele Shaw defeated Lady Frost in 4:30; Chris Sabin defeated Kenny King in 8:37; Tasha Steelz and Savannah Evans defeated Chelsea Green and Mickie James in 12:26; Bullet Club (Jay White, Tama Tonga and Tanga Loa) defeated Violent By Design (Eric Young, Deaner and Joe Doering) in 13:19.

FEBRUARY 24 *Westwego, LA*
Matt Cardona defeated Jordynne Grace in a Dot Combat Match in 12:14; Bhupinder Gujjar defeated John Skyler in 3:34; Deonna Purrazzo defeated Lady Frost in 5:43; Jonah defeated Zicky Dice in 1:00; Honor No More (Kenny King, Matt Taven and Mike Bennett) defeated Chris Sabin, Rich Swann and Willie Mack) in 8:58.

MARCH 3 *Westwego, LA*
Steve Maclin defeated Eddie Edwards by DQ in 6:52; Heath defeated Vincent in 9:34; Masha Slamovich defeated Raychell Rose in 1:00; Cassie Lee defeated Madison Rayne in 4:13; Tasha Steelz defeated Chelsea

Green in 8:05; Jonah defeated Johnny Swinger in :49; Bullet Club (Chris Bey, Luke Gallows, Karl Anderson and Jay White) defeated Guerrillas Of Destiny (Tama Tonga and Tanga Loa) and Violent By Design (Deaner and Joe Doering) in 9:48.

MARCH 10 *Louisville, KY*
Willie Mack defeated Kenny King in 8:32; Ace Austin defeated Crazzy Steve and John Skyler in a Three Way Match in 10:45; The IInspiration (Cassie Lee and Jessie McKay), Chelsea Green and Mickie James defeated The Influence (Madison Rayne and Tenille Dashwood), Savannah Evans and Tasha Steelz in 6:00; Eddie Edwards defeated Rich Swann in 17:48.

MARCH 17 *Louisville, KY*
The Motor City Machine Guns (Alex Shelley and Chris Sabin) defeated Bullet Club (Chris Bey and Jay White) in 12:38; Steve Maclin defeated Rhino in 9:50; Bhupinder Gujjar defeated Larry D in 5:55; Deonna Purrazzo defeated Gisele Shaw and Lady Frost in a Three Way Match in 6:08; Jonah defeated Zicky Dice in :30; Masha Slamovich defeated Arie Alexander in 1:00; Josh Alexander defeated Matt Taven in 12:13.

MARCH 24 *Philadelphia, PA*
Mike Bailey defeated Laredo Kid and Willie Mack in a Three Way Match in 10:09; Steve Maclin defeated Heath in 4:50; Violent By Design (Eric Young and Joe Doering) defeated The Good Brothers (Karl Anderson and Luke Gallows) in a Lumberjack Match in 7:26; Eddie Edwards defeated Rocky Romero in 12:45; Tasha Steelz defeated Mickie James in a Street Fight in 16:00.

MARCH 31 *Philadelphia, PA*
Jonathan Gresham defeated Kenny King in 12:05; The Good Brothers (Luke Gallows and Karl Anderson) defeated Johnny Swinger and Zicky Dice in :50; Josh Alexander defeated Madman Fulton in 1:40; Rosemary won a Knockouts Battle Royal in 7:15; Bhupinder Gujjar defeated Aiden Prince in 4:36; Masha Slamovich defeated Abby Jane in :48; Bullet Club (Chris Bey and Jay White) defeated The Motor City Machine Guns (Alex Shelley and Chris Sabin) in 17:42.

APRIL 7 *Dallas, TX*
[All matches previously aired on Impact Wrestling Multiverse Of Matches]

APRIL 14 *Philadelphia, PA*
Deonna Purrazzo defeated Willow Nightingale in 9:32; Jonathan Gresham defeated Rocky Romero in 10:45; Alex Shelley defeated Steve Maclin in 10:00; Jonah defeated PCO in 14:00.

APRIL 21 *Philadelphia, PA*
Violent By Design (Eric Young and Deaner) defeated Decay (Black Taurus and Crazzy Steve) in 4:42; Matt Cardona defeated Little Guido in 4:59; Shera defeated Gabriel Rodriguez in :23; Bullet Club (Chris Bey, Luke Gallows, Jay White and Karl Anderson) defeated Honor No More (Kenny King, Matt Taven, Mike Bennett and Vincent) in 9:22; Laredo Kid and Trey Miguel defeated Ace Austin and Mike Bailey in 6:00.

APRIL 28 *Poughkeepsie, NY*
The Briscoe Brothers (Jay Briscoe and Mark Briscoe) defeated Heath and Rhino in 6:35; Bhupinder Gujjar defeated VSK in 4:31; Honor No More (Eddie Edwards, Matt Taven and Mike Bennett) defeated The Motor City Machine Guns (Alex Shelley and Chris Sabin) and

Mike Bailey in 7:35; **Decay** (**Havok** and **Rosemary**) defeated **Savannah Evans** and **Tasha Steelz** in 4:51; **Josh Alexander** defeated **Moose** in 12:40.

MAY 5 *Poughkeepsie, NY*
W. **Morrissey** defeated **Brian Myers** in a Tables Match in 10:42; **Ace Austin** defeated **Rocky Romero** in 11:39; **Masha Slamovich** defeated **Damarus** in :56; **Bullet Club** (**Chris Bey** and **Jay White**) defeated **Willie Mack** and **Rich Swann** in 6:28; **Tomohiro Ishii** defeated **Steve Maclin** in 13:58; **PCO** defeated **Jonah** in a Monster's Ball Match in 15:09.

MAY 12 *Newport, KY*
Kenny King defeated **Chris Bey** in 8:27; **The Influence** (**Madison Rayne** and **Tenille Dashwood**) defeated **Alisha Edwards** and **Gisele Shaw** in 12:00; **Josh Alexander** and **Tomohiro Ishii** defeated **Bullet Club** (**El Phantasmo** and **Jay White**) in 10:28; **Eric Young** won Gauntlet For The Gold in 39:00.

MAY 19 *Newport, KY*
Mike Bailey defeated **Laredo Kid** in 9:00; **Jordynne Grace**, **Mia Yim** and **Taya Valkyrie** defeated **Deonna Purrazzo**, **Savannah Evans** and **Tasha Steelz** in 12:00; **The Good Brothers** (**Luke Gallows** and **Karl Anderson**) defeated **Honor No More** (**Matt Taven** and **Mike Bennett**) in 10:00; **Masha Slamovich** defeated **Shawna Reed** in 1:00; **The Briscoe Brothers** (**Jay Briscoe** and **Mark Briscoe**) defeated **Violent By Design** (**Deaner** and **Joe Doering**) in 15:00.

MAY 26 *Kissimmee, FL*
Trey Miguel defeated **Alex Shelley** in 12:26; **Masha Slamovich** defeated **Havok** in 1:28; **Jordynne Grace** defeated **Chelsea Green** in 11:26; **Chris Sabin** vs. **Frankie Kazarian** ended in a no contest in 10:25; **Bhupinder Gujjar** and **W. Morrissey** defeated **Raj Singh** and **Shera** in 5:17; **Violent By Design** (**Deaner**, **Eric Young** and **Joe Doering**) defeated **Josh Alexander** and **The Briscoe Brothers** (**Jay Briscoe** and **Mark Briscoe**) in 17:09.

JUNE 2 *Kissimmee, FL*
Mia Yim defeated **Savannah Evans** in 7:51; **Kenny King** defeated **Blake Christian** in 9:30; **Rich Swann** defeated **Matthew Rehwoldt** in 5:13; **Honor No More** (**Matt Taven** and **Mike Bennett**) defeated **Heath** and **Rhino** in 6:15; **Moose** and **Steve Maclin** defeated **PCO** and **W. Morrissey** in 10:51.

JUNE 9 *Kissimmee, FL*
Rosemary defeated **Tenille Dashwood** in 6:10; **Steve Maclin** defeated **PCO** in 8:55; **Joe Doering** defeated **Josh Alexander** by DQ in 6:32; **Honor No More** (**Eddie Edwards**, **Matt Taven** and **Mike Bennett**) defeated **Frankie Kazarian** and **The Motor City Machine Guns** (**Alex Shelley** and **Chris Sabin**) in 16:47.

JUNE 16 *Kissimmee, FL*
Savannah Evans and **Tasha Steelz** defeated **Jordynne Grace** and **Mia Yim** in 6:49; **Trey Miguel** defeated **Mike Bailey** in 10:42; **Masha Slamovich** defeated **Alisha Edwards** in :58; **The Briscoe Brothers** (**Jay Briscoe** and **Mark Briscoe**) defeated **Bullet Club** (**Chris Bey** and **Jay White**) in 11:02; **Honor No More** (**Kenny King** and **Vincent**) defeated **Aces & Eights** (**Garrett Bischoff** and **Wes Brisco**) in 3:28.

JUNE 23 *Nashville, TN*
Mia Yim defeated **Chelsea Green** in 9:08; **Bhupinder Gujjar** and **Shark Boy** defeated **Johnny Swinger** and **Zicky Dice** in 3:50; **Josh Alexander** defeated **Deaner** in 5:23; **Sami Callihan** defeated **Jack Price** in 1:28; **Honor No More** (**Eddie Edwards**, **Matt Taven** and **Mike Bennett**) defeated **James Storm** and **The Briscoe Brothers** (**Jay Briscoe** and **Mark Briscoe**) in 12:12.

JUNE 30 *Nashville, TN*
Trey Miguel defeated **Chris Bey**, **Laredo Kid** and **Steve Maclin** in a Four Way Match in 6:12; **Gisele Shaw** defeated **Rosemary** in 5:51; **Jordynne Grace** defeated **Savannah Evans** in 3:47; **The Good Brothers** (**Luke Gallows** and **Karl Anderson**) defeated **Honor No More** (**PCO** and **Vincent**) in 5:19; **Ace Austin** defeated **Alex Zayne** in 6:57; **Chris Sabin** defeated **Frankie Kazarian** in 18:42.

JULY 7 *Atlanta, GA*
Mike Bailey defeated **Alan Angels** in 8:35; **Trey Miguel** defeated **Laredo Kid** in 7:41; **PCO** defeated **Black Taurus** in 6:04; **Rich Swann** defeated **Shera** in 3:49; **Mia Yim** defeated **Deonna Purrazzo** in 14:09.

JULY 14 *Atlanta, GA*
Josh Alexander and **The Motor City Machine Guns** (**Alex Shelley** and **Chris Sabin**) defeated **Violent By Design** (**Eric Young**, **Deaner** and **Joe Doering**) in 11:56; **Steve Maclin** defeated **James Storm** in 8:34; **Chelsea Green** defeated **Mickie James** in 12:41; **Masha Slamovich** defeated **Tenille Dashwood** in 1:16; **Honor No More** (**Eddie Edwards**, **Kenny King**, **Matt Taven** and **Mike Bennett**) defeated **Bullet Club** (**Ace Austin**, **Chris Bey**, **Luke Gallows** and **Karl Anderson**) in 12:34.

JULY 21 *Louisville, KY*
Chelsea Green and **Deonna Purrazzo** defeated **Jordynne Grace** and **Mia Yim** in 9:11; **Mike Bailey** defeated **Deaner** in 8:54; **Masha Slamovich** defeated **Madison Rayne** in 1:12; **Bullet Club** (**Ace Austin** and **Chris Bey**) defeated **Honor No More** (**Matt Taven** and **Mike Bennett**) in 10:32; **Alex Shelley** defeated **Chris Sabin** in 17:09.

JULY 28 *Louisville, KY*
Eddie Edwards defeated **Ace Austin** in 11:38; **Laredo Kid** and **Trey Miguel** defeated **Johnny Swinger** and **Zicky Dice** in 4:01; **Tiffany Nieves** defeated **Jada Stone** in 2:03; **Josh Alexander** defeated **Shera** in 3:12; **Kushida** defeated **Rich Swann** in 15:29.

AUGUST 4 *Louisville, KY*
Deonna Purrazzo defeated **Rosemary** in 7:11; **Brian Myers** defeated **Black Taurus** in 6:45; **Masha Slamovich** defeated **Gisele Shaw** in 2:42; **The Motor City Machine Guns** (**Alex Shelley** and **Chris Sabin**) defeated **Violent By Design** (**Deaner** and **Joe Doering**) in 6:23; **Sami Callihan** defeated **Raj Singh** in 1:56; **PCO** defeated **Luke Gallows** in a Derby City Street Fight in 11:59.

AUGUST 11 *Louisville, KY*
Karl Anderson defeated **Kenny King** in 7:53; **Kushida** defeated **Deaner** in 6:14; **Killer Kelly** defeated **Tiffany Nieves** in 1:14; **Mia Yim** defeated **Madison Rayne** in 9:18; **Mike Bailey** defeated **Rocky Romero** in 12:04.

AUGUST 18 *Cicero, IL*
Black Taurus defeated **Laredo Kid**, **Rey Horus** and **Trey Miguel** in a Four Way Match in 7:33; **Heath** defeated **Kenny King** in 3:28; **Killer Kelly** defeated **Savannah**

Evans in 3:30; **Mike Bailey** defeated **Chris Bey** in 8:25; **Eddie Edwards** defeated **Bandido, Moose, Rich Swann, Sami Callihan** and **Steve Maclin** in a Six Way Elimination Match in 18:25.

AUGUST 25 *Cicero, IL*
VXT (**Chelsea Green** and **Deonna Purrazzo**) defeated **Jordynne Grace** and **Mia Yim** in 7:24; **Karl Anderson** defeated **Mike Bennett** in 7:44; **Bhupinder Gujjar** defeated **Jason Hotch** in 2:17; **Josh Alexander** defeated **Vincent** in 4:05; **Jessicka** defeated **Alisha Edwards** in 1:56; **Kushida** and **The Motor City Machine Guns** (**Alex Shelley** and **Chris Sabin**) defeated **Violent By Design** (**Deaner, Eric Young** and **Joe Doering**) in 15:18.

SEPTEMBER 1 *Dallas, TX*
Honor No More (**Matt Taven** and **Mike Bennett**) defeated **The Good Brothers** (**Luke Gallows** and **Karl Anderson**) to win the Impact World Tag Team Title in 8:14; **Mike Bailey** defeated **Kenny King** in 7:38; **Mascara Dorada** defeated **Alex Zayne** in 8:08; **Masha Slamovich** defeated **Deonna Purrazzo** in 12:50.

SEPTEMBER 8 *Dallas, TX*
Aussie Open (**Kyle Fletcher** and **Mark Davis**) defeated **Bullet Club** (**Ace Austin** and **Chris Bey**) in 7:07; **Mickie James** defeated **Raychell Rose** in 3:17; **Yuya Uemura** defeated **Kenny King** in 9:02; **Chelsea Green** defeated **Taya Valkyrie** in 6:27; **Brian Myers** defeated **Bhupinder Gujjar** by DQ in 5:01; **Eddie Edwards** defeated **Heath** in 8:53.

SEPTEMBER 15 *Dallas, TX*
Mike Bailey defeated **Mascara Dorada** in 8:03; **Decay** (**Black Taurus** and **Crazzy Steve**) defeated **Moose** and **Steve Maclin** in 1:52; **Killer Kelly** defeated **Alisha Edwards** in 2:13; **Honor No More** (**Matt Taven** and **Mike Bennett**) defeated **Josh Alexander** and **Rich Swann** by DQ in 6:54; **Mickie James** defeated **Hyan** in 2:39; **The Motor City Machine Guns** (**Alex Shelley** and **Chris Sabin**) defeated **The Good Brothers** (**Luke Gallows** and **Karl Anderson**) in 14:39.

SEPTEMBER 22 *Dallas, TX*
Brian Myers defeated **Bhupinder Gujjar** in a Ladder Match in 12:11; **Jordynne Grace** defeated **Zicky Dice** in :43; **Black Taurus** defeated **Alex Zayne, Laredo Kid** and **Trey Miguel** in a Five Way Match in 11:58; **Heath** defeated **PCO** in a Street Fight in 9:12; **The Motor City Machine Guns** (**Alex Shelley** and **Chris Sabin**) defeated **Aussie Open** (**Kyle Fletcher** and **Mark Davis**) in 15:31.

SEPTEMBER 29 *Nashville, TN*
Bullet Club (**Ace Austin** and **Chris Bey**) defeated **Laredo Kid** and **Trey Miguel** in 8:16; **Brian Myers** defeated **Crazzy Steve** in 4:06; **Black Taurus** defeated **Delirious** in 5:03; **Heath** and **Rich Swann** defeated **Honor No More** (**PCO** and **Vincent**) in 4:32; **Masha Slamovich** defeated **Allie Katch** in a Monster's Ball Match in 15:12.

OCTOBER 6 *Nashville, TN*
Frankie Kazarian defeated **Kenny King** in 9:20; **Mia Yim** defeated **Gisele Shaw** in 7:15; **Steve Maclin** defeated **Moose** in 9:51; **Jessicka** and **Taya Valkyrie** defeated **Johnny Swinger's Swingerellas** (**Swingerella #1** and **Swingerella #2**) in 1:30; **Alex Shelley** defeated **Matt Taven** in 9:50.

OCTOBER 13 *Albany, NY*
Killer Kelly defeated **Tasha Steelz** in a No DQ Match in 6:52; **Trey Miguel** defeated **Alex Zayne, Black Taurus, Kenny King, Laredo Kid** and **Yuya Uemura** in a Six Way Match in 5:19; VXT (**Chelsea Green** and **Deonna Purrazzo**) and **Gisele Shaw** defeated **The Death Dollz** (**Jessicka, Rosemary** and **Taya Valkyrie**) in 5:40; **Matt Cardona** defeated **Bhupinder Gujjar** in 4:21; **Josh Alexander** defeated **Bobby Fish** in 12:55.

OCTOBER 20 *Albany, NY*
Bully Ray and **Tommy Dreamer** defeated **Bullet Club** (**Chris Bey** and **Juice Robinson**) in 6:23; **Taylor Wilde** defeated **Mia Yim** in 9:22; **Joe Hendry** defeated **Jason Hotch** in 1:54; **Rich Swann** defeated **Eric Young** in 3:14; **Heath** and **Rhino** defeated **Honor No More** (**Matt Taven** and **Mike Bennett**) to win the Impact World Tag Team Title in 10:02.

OCTOBER 27 *Las Vegas, NV*
Trey Miguel defeated **Alan Angels** in 8:17; **Rachelle Scheel** defeated **Tasha Steelz** by DQ in 1:57; **Chris Bey** defeated **Tommy Dreamer** in 6:50; **Matt Cardona** defeated **Alex Shelley** in 8:42; **Joe Hendry** defeated **Raj Singh** in 1:47; **Jordynne Grace, Mickie James** and **Taylor Wilde** defeated **Chelsea Green, Deonna Purrazzo** and **Gisele Shaw** in 13:46.

NOVEMBER 3 *Las Vegas, NV*
Mike Bailey defeated **Kenny King** in 8:44; **Savannah Evans** defeated **Jessicka** in 7:38; **Sami Callihan** defeated **Eric Young** by DQ in 6:11; **Ace Austin** defeated **Moose** in 7:42; **Frankie Kazarian** and **Josh Alexander** defeated **Aussie Open** (**Kyle Fletcher** and **Mark Davis**) in 15:56.

NOVEMBER 10 *Las Vegas, NV*
Joe Hendry defeated **Brian Myers** to win the Impact Digital Media Title in 5:58; **Trey Miguel** defeated **Mike Bailey** by DQ in 7:02; **Bhupinder Gujjar** defeated **G Sharpe** in 4:56; **Mickie James** defeated **Chelsea Green** in 10:37; **Bully Ray** defeated **Zicky Dice** in 1:10; **Jordynne Grace** defeated **Gisele Shaw** in 11:01.

NOVEMBER 17 *Las Vegas, NV*
Black Taurus defeated **PJ Black** in 6:18; **Bullet Club** (**Ace Austin** and **Chris Bey**) defeated **Aussie Open** (**Kyle Fletcher** and **Mark Davis**), **The Motor City Machine Guns** (**Alex Shelley** and **Chris Sabin**) and **Raj Singh** and **Shera** in a Four Way Match in 13:03; **Taya Valkyrie** defeated **Tasha Steelz** in 2:20; **Steve Maclin** defeated **Tommy Dreamer** in an Old School Rules Match in 8:10; **Rich Swann** defeated **Laredo Kid** in 3:40; **Sami Callihan** defeated **Eric Young** in a Death Machine's Double Jeopardy Match in 14:04.

NOVEMBER 24
Highlights show

DECEMBER 1 *Louisville, KY*
Rich Swann defeated **Bully Ray** by DQ in 5:53; **Moose** defeated **Bhupinder Gujjar** in 4:22; **Frankie Kazarian** defeated **Steve Maclin** by DQ in 7:26; **Mickie James** defeated **Deonna Purrazzo** in 16:01.

DECEMBER 8 *Louisville, KY*
Heath and **Rhino** vs. **The Motor City Machine Guns** (**Alex Shelley** and **Chris Sabin**) ended in a no contest in 8:34; **Savannah Evans** defeated **Taya Valkyrie** in 6:51; **Big Kon** defeated **Sami Callihan** in 5:46; **Josh Alexander** defeated **Mike Bailey** in 59:48.

DECEMBER 15 *Pembroke Pines, FL*
Eddie Edwards defeated **Delirious** in 6:36; **Bully Ray** defeated **John Skyler** in 1:06; **The Major Playerz** (**Matt Cardona** and **Brian Myers**) defeated **Decay** (**Black Taurus** and **Crazzy Steve**) in 4:24; **Sami Callihan** defeated **Alan Angels** in 6:53; **Bhupinder Gujjar** and **Joe Hendry** defeated **Johnny Swinger** and **Zicky Dice** in 3:17; **The Motor City Machine Guns** (**Alex Shelley** and **Chris Sabin**) defeated **Heath** and **Rhino** to win the Impact World Tag Team Title in 14:04.

DECEMBER 22 *Pembroke Pines, FL*
The Death Dollz (**Jessicka** and **Rosemary**) defeated **Deonna Purrazzo** and **Gisele Shaw** in 5:39; **Mike Bailey** defeated **Yuya Uemura** in 11:16; **Rich Swann** vs. **Steve Maclin** ended in a double count out in 6:27; **Jordynne Grace** and **Mickie James** defeated **Savannah Evans** and **Tasha Steelz** in 11:08.

DECEMBER 29
Highlights show

IMPACT WRESTLING BEFORE THE IMPACT

JANUARY 6 *Las Vegas, NV*
Juice Robinson defeated **Raj Singh** in 9:12.

JANUARY 13 *Dallas, TX*
Black Taurus defeated **Matthew Rehwoldt** in 7:17.

JANUARY 20 *Dallas, TX*
Jordynne Grace defeated **Lady Frost** in 8:18.

JANUARY 27 *Pembroke Pines, FL*
Laredo Kid defeated **Blake Christian** in 7:29.

FEBRUARY 3 *Pembroke Pines, FL*
Black Taurus defeated **Raj Singh** in 9:21.

FEBRUARY 10 *Pembroke Pines, FL*
Lady Frost defeated **Alisha Edwards** in 6:05.

FEBRUARY 17 *Pembroke Pines, FL*
Eddie Edwards defeated **Big Kon** in 8:23.

FEBRUARY 24 *Westwego, LA*
Ace Austin and **Mike Bailey** defeated **Trey Miguel** and **Jake Something** in 8:01.

MARCH 3 *Westwego, LA*
Brian Myers defeated **Crazzy Steve** in 8:05.

MARCH 10 *Louisville, KY*
Jordynne Grace defeated **Havok** in 8:20

MARCH 17 *Louisville, KY*
Karl Anderson defeated **Deaner** in 6:22.

MARCH 24 *Philadelphia, PA*
Shera defeated **Crazzy Steve** in 7:15.

MARCH 31 *Philadelphia, PA*
Black Taurus defeated **Deaner** in 8:21.

APRIL 7
Highlights show

APRIL 14 *Philadelphia, PA*
Madison Rayne defeated **Jessie McKay** in 6:34.

APRIL 21 *Philadelphia, PA*
Heath and **Rhino** defeated **Rich Swann** and **Willie Mack** in 7:56.

APRIL 28 *Poughkeepsie, NY*
Vincent defeated **Crazzy Steve** in 9:20.

MAY 5 *Poughkeepsie, NY*
Tenille Dashwood defeated **Gisele Shaw** in 7:58.

MAY 12 *Newport, KY*
Ace Austin defeated **Aiden Prince** in 8:02.

MAY 19 *Newport, KY*
Crazzy Steve defeated **Zicky Dice** in 9:13.

MAY 26 *Kissimmee, FL*
Laredo Kid defeated **Black Taurus** in 7:49.

JUNE 2 *Kissimmee, FL*
Alisha Edwards defeated **Renee Michelle** in 6:15.

JUNE 9 *Kissimmee, FL*
Decay (**Crazzy Steve** and **Black Taurus**) defeated **Johnny Swinger** and **Zicky Dice** in 8:18.

JUNE 16 *Kissimmee, FL*
Laredo Kid defeated **Blake Christian** in 8:47.

JUNE 23 *Nashville, TN*
Black Taurus defeated **Andrew Everett** in 8:13.

JUNE 30 *Nashville, TN*
Rich Swann defeated **Raj Singh** in 6:30.

JULY 7 *Atlanta, GA*
Gisele Shaw defeated **Alisha Edwards** in 8:21.

JULY 14 *Atlanta, GA*
Bhupinder Gujjar defeated **Johnny Swinger** in 8:37.

JULY 21 *Louisville, KY*
Laredo Kid defeated **Johnny Swinger** in 8:10.

JULY 28 *Louisville, KY*
Bhupinder Gujjar defeated **Vincent** in 6:12.

AUGUST 4 *Louisville, KY*
Savannah Evans defeated **Alisha Edwards** in 7:33.

AUGUST 11 *Louisville, KY*
Steve Maclin defeated **Crazzy Steve** in 7:37.

AUGUST 18 *Cicero, IL*
Gisele Shaw defeated **Rosemary** in 8:27.

AUGUST 25 *Cicero, IL*
Bullet Club (**Ace Austin** and **Hikuleo**) defeated **Johnny Swinger** and **Zicky Dice** in 7:46.

SEPTEMBER 1 *Dallas, TX*
Bullet Club (**Chris Bey** and **Ace Austin**) defeated **JD Griffey** and **Exodus Prime** in 8:03.

SEPTEMBER 8 *Dallas, TX*
Crazzy Steve defeated **Shane Taylor** in 8:17.

SEPTEMBER 15 *Dallas, TX*
Yuya Uemura defeated Raj Singh in 8:59.

SEPTEMBER 22 *Dallas, TX*
Gisele Shaw defeated Hyan in 6:20.

SEPTEMBER 29 *Nashville, TN*
Yuya Uemura defeated Jason Hotch in 8:30.

OCTOBER 6 *Nashville, TN*
Juice Robinson defeated Alex Zayne in 9:27.

OCTOBER 13 *Albany, NY*
The Motor City Machine Guns (Chris Sabin and Alex Shelley) defeated Raj Singh and Shera in 7:16.

OCTOBER 20 *Albany, NY*
Dirty Dango defeated Johnny Swinger in 8:23.

OCTOBER 27 *Las Vegas, NV*
Black Taurus defeated Laredo Kid in 8:05.

NOVEMBER 3 *Las Vegas, NV*
PJ Black defeated Yuya Uemura in 8:33.

NOVEMBER 10 *Las Vegas, NV*
Killer Kelly defeated Sandra Moone in 4:41.

NOVEMBER 17 *Las Vegas, NV*
Yuya Uemura defeated Andrew Everett in 8:00.

NOVEMBER 24 *Louisville, KY*
Raj Singh and Shera defeated Yuya Uemura and Delirious in 9:22.

DECEMBER 1 *Louisville, KY*
Ladybird Johnston (Jessicka) defeated Miss Bea Haven (Alisha Edwards) in 8:28.

DECEMBER 8 *Louisville, KY*
Trey Miguel defeated Jason Hotch in 8:27.

DECEMBER 15 *Pembroke Pines, FL*
Shera defeated Jack Price in 8:24.

DECEMBER 22 *Pembroke Pines, FL*
Taylor Wilde defeated KiLynn King in 7:20.

DECEMBER 29 *Pembroke Pines, FL*
Yuya Uemura and Delirious defeated The Good Hands (John Skyler and Jason Hotch) in 9:08.

MLW FUSION

FEBRUARY 10 *Dallas, TX*
King Muertes defeated Richard Holliday in 7:34; EJ Nduka defeated Ikuro Kwon in 2:23; Alexander Hammerstone defeated Pagano in a Falls Count Anywhere Match in 17:15.

FEBRUARY 17 *Dallas, TX*
Davey Richards defeated ACH in 8:58; The Saito Brothers (Jun Saito and Rei Saito) defeated Budd Heavy and Gnarls Garvin in 5:10; 5150 (Rivera and Slice Boogie) defeated El Hijo de LA Park and LA Park Jr. in a Ladder Match in 10:18.

FEBRUARY 24 *Dallas, TX*
Aramis, El Dragon and Micro Man defeated Arez, Gino Medina and Mini Abismo Negro in 15:46; Jacob Fatu defeated Mads Krugger in 4:54.

MARCH 3 *Dallas, TX*
Alex Kane defeated Calvin Tankman in 8:08; KC Navarro defeated Ho Ho Lun in 3:29; Myron Reed defeated Yoshihiro Tajiri, Bandido and Matt Cross in a Four Way Match to win the MLW World Middleweight Title in 8:48.

MARCH 10 *Charlotte, NC*
Alex Kane defeated ACH and Calvin Tankman in a Three Way Match in 8:00; nZo defeated KC Navarro in 2:48; Alexander Hammerstone defeated Davey Richards in 19:14.

MARCH 17 *Dallas, TX*
Miranda Gordy defeated Rok-C in 7:38; TJP defeated Buddy Matthews in 20:21.

MARCH 24 *Charlotte, NC*
Killer Kross defeated Budd Heavy in 2:23; Gangrel defeated Gnarls Garvin in 10:35; Mads Krugger defeated Jacob Fatu in a Stairway To Hell Match in 14:32.

MARCH 31 *Charlotte, NC*
Micro Man, Octagon Jr. and Puma King defeated Arez, Gino Medina and Mini Abismo Negro in 15:42; Ikuro Kwon defeated Ken Broadway in 2:26; Hustle And Power (Calvin Tankman and EJ Nduka) defeated 5150 (Rivera and Slice Boogie) to win the MLW World Tag Team Title in 8:08.

APRIL 7 *Charlotte, NC*
Myron Reed defeated TJP in 13:39; Richard Holliday defeated Matt Cross in 6:44; The Von Erichs (Marshall Von Erich and Ross Von Erich) defeated The Mortons (Kerry Morton and Ricky Morton) in 5:27.

APRIL 14 *Dallas, TX*
Matt Cross defeated TJP in 11:07; Holidead defeated Shazza McKenzie in 5:04; Alex Kane defeated ACH, Juicy Finau, Myron Reed and Puma King in a Five Way Scramble Match in 4:28.

APRIL 29 *Dallas, TX*
Gino Medina and Strange Sangre (Arez and Mini Abismo Negro) defeated Aramis, KC Navarro and Micro Man in 11:55; Alexander Hammerstone defeated Jacob Fatu and Mads Krugger in a Three Way Match in 13:34.

MAY 5 *Dallas, TX*
Richard Holliday defeated Davey Richards in 9:39; Hustle And Power (Calvin Tankman and EJ Nduka) defeated Budd Heavy and Red Pickins in 1:20; Myron Reed defeated Swerve Strickland in 7:54.

MAY 12 *Dallas, TX*
Holidead defeated Chik Tormenta in 4:07; Octagon Jr. defeated King Muertes, El Dragon and El Hijo de LA Park in a Four Way Match to win the MLW Caribbean Heavyweight Title in 9:26; Jacob Fatu defeated Bestia 666 in an Aztec Apocalypto Match in 9:41.

MAY 19 *Dallas, TX*
nZo defeated ACH in 6:21; Hustle And Power (Calvin Tankman and EJ Nduka) defeated The Bomaye Fight

Club (Alex Zayne and Mr. Thomas) in 7:26; The Von Erichs (Marshall Von Erich and Ross Von Erich) defeated 5150 (Hernandez and Rivera) in a Bunkhouse Brawl Match in 9:42.

MAY 26 *Dallas, TX*
Davey Richards defeated Danny Rivera in 8:29; Aero Star, El Dragon and Micro Man defeated Arez, Mini Abismo Negro and TJP in 10:36; Alexander Hammerstone defeated Cesar Duran by DQ in 1:40.

JUNE 2 *Dallas, TX*
Los Parks (LA Park and LA Park Jr.) defeated Gangrel and Pagano in a Mexican Death Match in 10:53; KC Navarro defeated nZo in 1:50; Bandido defeated Flamita in 12:13.

JUNE 9 *Dallas, TX*
Gino Medina defeated Aramis in a Mexican Strap Match in 5:37; Octagon Jr. defeated Matt Cross in 9:01; King Muertes, Mads Krugger and Richard Holliday defeated Alexander Hammerstone and The Von Erichs (Marshall Von Erich and Ross Von Erich) in 9:31.

JUNE 16 *Philadelphia, PA*
Gangrel defeated Budd Heavy in 1:30; Hustle And Power (Calvin Tankman and EJ Nduka) defeated 5150 (Rivera and Slice Boogie) and The Von Erichs (Marshall Von Erich and Ross Von Erich) in a Three Way Match in 9:12; Taya Valkyrie defeated Holidead to win the vacant MLW Women's Featherweight Title in 9:00.

JUNE 23 *Philadelphia, PA*
Myron Reed defeated Arez and KC Navarro in a Three Way Match in 6:09; Lox Maximos (Joel Maximo and Jose Maximo) defeated Jaden Valo and Kris Kage in 2:38; Jacob Fatu defeated Mads Krugger in a Weapons Of Mass Destruction Match in 16:27.

JUNE 30 *Philadelphia, PA*
Samoan Swat Team (Juicy Finau and Lance Anoa'i) defeated Aztecas (Cinco and Uno) in 2:24; Lince Dorado, Micro Man and Taya Valkyrie defeated Strange Sangre (Arez, Holidead and Mini Abismo Negro) in 6:32.

JULY 7 *Philadelphia, PA*
Real1 defeated Lince Dorado in 9:58; Alex Kane vs. Davey Richards ended in a draw in 20:00.

JULY 14 *Philadelphia, PA*
Brittany Blake defeated Zoey Skye in 2:37; Matt Cross defeated ACH in 6:17; Alexander Hammerstone defeated Richard Holliday in 9:53.

NOVEMBER 10 *New York, NY*
Myron Reed defeated Arez, La Estrella and Lince Dorado in a Four Way Match in 6:54; KC Navarro defeated Mini Abismo Negro in 4:04; Scarlett Bordeaux defeated Clara Carreras in 1:47; Jacob Fatu defeated Real1 by DQ in 2:01.

NOVEMBER 17 *New York, NY*
Samoan Swat Team (Juicy Finau and Lance Anoa'i) defeated Lox Maximos (Joel Maximo and Jose Maximo) in 3:14; Killer Kross defeated Matt Cross in 4:38; Davey Richards defeated Alex Kane to win the MLW National Openweight Title in 12:52.

NOVEMBER 24 *New York, NY*
Taya Valkyrie defeated Brittany Blake in 6:50; Alexander Hammerstone defeated Richard Holliday in a Falls Count Anywhere Match in 21:55.

DECEMBER 1 *Norcross, GA*
Lady Flammer defeated Lady Shani, La Hiedra and Reina Dorada in a Four Way Match in 8:04; Alexander Hammerstone defeated Bandido in 16:04.

DECEMBER 8 *Norcross, GA*
Samoan Swat Team (Juicy Finau and Lance Anoa'i) defeated La Anexion (Angel Fashion and Mark Davidson) in 4:23; EJ Nduka defeated Sultan del Aire in 2:54; Shun Skywalker defeated Myron Reed to win the MLW World Middleweight Title in 10:59.

DECEMBER 15 *Norcross, GA*
Star Roger defeated Cosmos in 10:45; Davey Richards defeated SB KENTo in 10:28.

DECEMBER 22 *Norcross, GA*
Mance Warner defeated Mads Krugger in a Tables Match in 7:38; Alex Kane defeated D3 in a Five Minute Challenge Match in 2:02; Taya Valkyrie defeated Lady Flammer in 8:48.

DECEMBER 29
Highlights show

NWA POWER

JANUARY 5 *Atlanta, GA*
Jamie Stanley defeated Alex Taylor, Jeremiah Plunkett and Miguel Robles in 5:31; Jordan Clearwater and Marshe Rockett defeated Cyon in a Handicap Match in 5:21; Kylie Rae and Tootie Lynn defeated Kamille and Missa Kate in 6:44; Matt Taven defeated Wrecking Ball Legursky in 6:29; Natalia Markova defeated Paola Blaze in 3:57; La Rebellion (Bestia 666 and Mecha Wolf) and Homicide defeated The Dane Event (Jax Dane, Odinson and Parrow) in 6:54.

JANUARY 11 *Atlanta, GA*
Kiera Hogan defeated Christi Jaynes, Jennacide and Kenzie Paige in 5:08; Anthony Mayweather defeated Mims via count out in 5:07; The Dirty Sexy Boys (Dirty Dango and JTG) defeated The Rude Dudes (Jamie Stanley and Sam Adonis) in 5:51; Tyrus defeated Jaden Roller in 2:54; Cyon defeated Judais by DQ in 2:53; Matt Cardona and Mike Knox defeated Strictly Business (Chris Adonis and Thom Latimer), and Tim Storm and Trevor Murdoch in a Three Way Match in 5:25.

JANUARY 18 *Atlanta, GA*
Kylie Rae defeated Allysin Kay in 5:43; Melina defeated Madi Wrenkowski in 4:42; The Fixers (Jay Bradley and Wrecking Ball Legursky) and Rush Freeman defeated The Dirty Sexy Boys (Dirty Dango and JTG) in a Handicap Match in 4:29; Hawx Aerie (Luke Hawx and PJ Hawx) defeated Church's Money Enterprises (Jordan Clearwater and Marshe Rockett) in 6:32.

FEBRUARY 1 *Atlanta, GA*
The Dirty Sexy Boys (Dirty Dango and JTG) defeated The Ill Begotten (Alex Taylor, Captain Yuma and Rush Freeman) in a Handicap Match in 4:09; Cyon defeated Sal Rinauro in a No DQ Match in 4:52; Trevor Murdoch defeated Matt Cardona in 5:02.

FEBRUARY 8 *Atlanta, GA*
Strictly Business (Chris Adonis and Thom Latimer) and El Rudo defeated The OGK (Matt Taven and Mike Bennett) and Victor Benjamin, La Rebellion (Bestia 666 and Mecha Wolf) and Homicide, and The Fixers (Jay Bradley and Wrecking Ball Legursky) and Colby Corino in a Team War Elimination Match in 11:09; Kamille defeated Kiera Hogan in 3:20; The End (Odinson and Parrow) and Rodney Mack defeated Idolmania Sports Entertainment (Jordan Clearwater, Marshe Rockett and Tyrus), The Ill Begotten (Alex Taylor, Jeremiah Plunkett and Rush Freeman), and Aron Stevens, JR Kratos and Judais in a Team War Elimination Match in 11:40.

FEBRUARY 15 *Atlanta, GA*
British Invasion (Doug Williams and Nick Aldis) defeated Fable Jake and Jaden Roller in 8:11; Tootie Lynn defeated Marti Belle in 4:36; Jennacide vs. Natalia Markova ended in a double count out in 5:32; Melina defeated Christi Jaynes in 6:14; Matt Cardona defeated Victor Benjamin in 6:06; Strictly Business (Chris Adonis and Thom Latimer) and El Rudo defeated The End (Odinson and Parrow) and Rodney Mack in a Team War Final Match in 11:35.

FEBRUARY 22 *Oak Grove, KY*
Jax Dane defeated Eric Jackson in 1:26; Chelsea Green defeated Kenzie Paige in 7:24; Colby Corino defeated Rhett Titus 2-1 in a Best Two Out Of Three Falls Match in 16:55; Kamille defeated Taryn Terrell in 7:48.

MARCH 1 *Oak Grove, KY*
The Fixers (Jay Bradley and Wrecking Ball Legursky) defeated The OGK (Matt Taven and Mike Bennett in 10:47; Mike Knox defeated Da Pope in 11:55; Anthony Mayweather defeated Chris Adonis to win the NWA National Heavyweight Title in 11:38.

MARCH 8 *Oak Grove, KY*
Idolmania Sports Entertainment (BLK Jeez, Jordan Clearwater, Marshe Rockett and Tyrus) defeated The Ill Begotten (Alex Taylor and Rush Freeman), Cyon and Mims in 6:59; Nick Aldis defeated Thom Latimer in an "I Quit" Match in 13:38; Matt Cardona defeated Trevor Murdoch to win the NWA World Heavyweight Title in 11:04.

MARCH 22 *Nashville, TN*
The Briscoe Brothers (Jay Briscoe and Mark Briscoe) defeated The OGK (Matt Taven and Mike Bennett) in 6:56; Trevor Murdoch defeated Brett Buffshay in 1:39; The Hex (Allysin Kay and Marti Belle) defeated Jennacide and Paola Blaze in 7:24; Homicide defeated Austin Aries in 8:04.

MARCH 29 *Nashville, TN*
Kamille defeated Madi Wrenkowski in 5:53; Jake Dumas defeated Rodney Mack in 4:08; The Cardonas (Mike Knox and VSK) defeated The Ill Begotten (Alex Taylor and Rush Freeman) in 4:18; Nick Aldis defeated Deonte Marshall in 1:10; La Rebellion (Bestia 666 and Mecha Wolf) defeated The End (Odinson and Parrow) in 7:17.

APRIL 5 *Nashville, TN*
Matt Cardona defeated Tim Storm in 5:21; Rhett Titus defeated Darius Lockhart by DQ in 7:24; Trevor Murdoch defeated Garrison Creed in :39; Cyon vs. Tyrus ended in a no contest in a Slam Challenge Match in 3:09.

APRIL 12 *Nashville, TN*
The Commonwealth Connection (Doug Williams and Harry Smith) defeated The Dirty Sexy Boys (Dirty Dango and JTG) in 6:52; KiLynn King defeated Natalia Markova in 6:02; The Miserably Faithful (Gaagz The Gymp, Judais and Sal The Pal) defeated The Fixers (Jay Bradley and Wrecking Ball Legursky) and Colby Corino in 6:27; Matt Cardona defeated Da Pope in 16:07.

APRIL 26 *Nashville, TN*
Nick Aldis defeated Jordan Clearwater in 6:54; Homicide defeated Rhett Titus in 7:53; Trevor Murdoch defeated Aron Stevens in 5:24; Angelina Love defeated Tootie Lynn in 5:14; La Rebellion (Bestia 666 and Mecha Wolf) defeated The Briscoe Brothers (Jay Briscoe and Mark Briscoe) in 9:56.

MAY 3 *Nashville, TN*
Nick Aldis defeated Mike Bennett in 7:01; The Fixers (Jay Bradley and Wrecking Ball Legursky) defeated The Rude Dudes (El Rudo and Jamie Stanley) in a no DQ Match in 8:33; Mims defeated Tyrus in a Slam Challenge Match in :47; Mickie James defeated Kenzie Paige in 7:55.

MAY 10 *Nashville, TN*
Kamille defeated Paola Blaze in 7:48; Matt Taven defeated Judais by DQ in 4:53; The Dirty Sexy Boys (Dirty Dango and JTG) defeated The Miserably Faithful (Gaagz The Gymp and Sal The Pal) in 6:37; KiLynn King defeated Chelsea Green and Jennacide in a Three Way Match in 6:36; Nick Aldis and The Commonwealth Connection (Doug Williams and Harry Smith) defeated Matt Cardona and The Cardonas (Mike Knox and VSK) in 8:15.

MAY 17 *Nashville, TN*
The Hex (Allysin Kay and Marti Belle) defeated Kenzie Paige and Madi Wrenkowski in 5:16; Colby Corino defeated AJ Cazana in 4:50; Jax Dane and The End (Odinson and Parrow) defeated Gold Rushhh (BLK Jeez, Jordan Clearwater and Marshe Rockett) and The Ill Begotten (Alex Taylor, Jeremiah Plunkett and Rush Freeman) in a Team War Match in 6:54; Mickie James defeated Natalia Markova in 6:44.

MAY 24 *Oak Grove, KY*
Max The Impaler defeated Ella Envy in 3:20; Cyon defeated Joe Alonzo in 16:32; Trevor Murdoch defeated Mike Knox in 7:58.

MAY 31 *Oak Grove, KY*
Matt Vine defeated Eric Jackson in 4:23; Thom Latimer defeated Rhett Titus in 9:25; Homicide defeated Colby Corino in 9:55.

JUNE 7 *Oak Grove, KY*
Nick Aldis defeated Brian Myers in 10:19; Tyrus defeated KC Roxx by DQ in 1:10; KiLynn King and Missa Kate defeated Kamille and Kenzie Paige in 9:07.

JUNE 14 *Knoxville, TN*
Taya Valkyrie defeated Taryn Terrell in 6:45; Strictly Business (Chris Adonis and Thom Latimer) defeated The Cardonas (Mike Knox and VSK) in 7:23.

JUNE 21 *Knoxville, TN*
Nick Aldis defeated Brett Buffshay in 3:28; Cyon and Tyrus defeated The Ill Begotten (Alex Taylor and Jeremiah Plunkett) in 7:40.

JUNE 28 *Knoxville, TN*
Chelsea Green and Max The Impaler defeated Jennacide and Missa Kate in 5:38; PJ Hawx defeated Gustavo Aguilar and Sal The Pal in a Three Way Match in 4:00; Rodney Mack defeated Anthony Andrews in 4:29; The Commonwealth Connection (Doug Williams and Harry Smith) defeated La Rebellion (Bestia 666 and Mecha Wolf) in a Lucha Rules Match in 5:08.

JULY 5 *Nashville, TN*
Odinson defeated Judais and AJ Cazana in a Three Way Match in 5:11; Trevor Murdoch defeated Thrillbilly Silas in 3:09; Kerry Morton defeated Jay Bradley in 5:16.

JULY 12 *Nashville, TN*
Thom Latimer defeated Chris Adonis in 6:48; Brian Myers defeated Da Pope in 6:56; KiLynn King defeated Allysin Kay in 6:47; Nick Aldis defeated Tim Storm by DQ in 8:30.

JULY 19 *Nashville, TN*
Max The Impaler defeated Ella Envy and Taya Valkyrie in a Three Way Match in 6:37; La Rebellion (Bestia 666 and Mecha Wolf) vs. The OGK (Matt Taven and Mike Bennett) ended in a no contest in 5:38; Jake Dumas defeated Eric Jackson in 1:45; Nick Aldis defeated Mike Knox, Brian Myers and Thom Latimer in a Four Way Match in 8:47.

JULY 26 *Nashville, TN*
Kenzie Paige defeated Kaci Lennox in 3:53; Taya Valkyrie defeated KiLynn King in 6:50; The Commonwealth Connection (Doug Williams and Harry Smith) defeated The Dirty Sexy Boys (Dirty Dango and JTG) in 6:13; Kamille defeated Chelsea Green in 9:37.

AUGUST 2 *Nashville, TN*
Cyon defeated Rodney Mack in 4:39; The Miserably Faithful (Gaagz The Gymp, Judais and Sal The Pal) defeated The Ill Begotten (Alex Taylor, Jeremiah Plunkett and Rush Freeman) in 8:08; Tyrus defeated Odinson in 4:04.

AUGUST 9 *Nashville, TN*
Mike Knox defeated De'Vin Graves in 4:16; Ricky Morton defeated Wrecking Ball Legursky in 3:42; Jordan Clearwater defeated Joe Alonzo in 5:48; Da Pope vs. Trevor Murdoch ended in a double count out in 7:30.

AUGUST 16 *Nashville, TN*
Angelina Love and Chelsea Green defeated Paola Blaze and Rylee Rockett in 4:00; Tim Storm defeated Larry D in 3:59; Kamille defeated Hayley Shadows in 3:04; Rodney Mack defeated BLK Jeez in 3:28.

AUGUST 23 *Nashville, TN*
Chris Adonis defeated Caprice Coleman in 6:12; Jennacide defeated Kayla Kassidy in 2:11; Hawx Aerie (Luke Hawx and PJ Hawx) defeated The Dirty Sexy

Boys (Dirty Dango and JTG) and Gustavo Aguilar and Rhett Titus in a Three Way Elimination Match in 5:56; Pretty Empowered (Ella Envy and Kenzie Paige) defeated Hayley Shadows and Jaylee in 2:24; The Commonwealth Connection (Doug Williams and Harry Smith) defeated The Spectaculars (Brady Pierce and Rush Freeman) in 4:48.

AUGUST 30 *Nashville, TN*
Matt Taven defeated Mecha Wolf in 9:56; The Question Mark II defeated De'Vin Graves in 1:43; Thom Latimer defeated Chris Sainz in 2:03; Rolando Freeman defeated Matt Cardona in a No DQ Match in 8:17.

SEPTEMBER 6 *Nashville, TN*
Taya Valkyrie defeated Chelsea Green, Jennacide and KiLynn King in a Four Way Match in 4:22; EC3 defeated Deonte Marshall in 3:49; Kamille vs. Allysin Kay ended in a draw in 10:00; Flip Gordon defeated Doug Williams in 9:30.

SEPTEMBER 13 *Nashville, TN*
JR Kratos and Da Pope defeated KC Roxx and The Question Mark II in 6:46; Cyon defeated Joe Alonzo in 7:09; Angelina Love, Max The Impaler and Natalia Markova defeated Pretty Empowered (Ella Envy and Kenzie Paige) and Roxy in 3:11; Angelina Love vs. Max The Impaler vs. Natalia Markova in a Three Way Match ended in a no contest in 3:48; Tyrus defeated Mims in 2:03.

SEPTEMBER 20 *Nashville, TN*
Dak Draper defeated Brian Myers in 6:34; Chris Adonis defeated Jake Dumas in 8:01; Marshe Rockett defeated Eric Jackson and Joe Ocasio in a Three Way Match in 2:49; Bully Ray and Thom Latimer defeated Mike Knox and VSK in 5:15.

OCTOBER 4 *Nashville, TN*
Odinson defeated Flip Gordon in 7:11; EC3 defeated Traxx in 3:52; Kamille defeated Jennacide in 7:20; The OGK (Matt Taven and Mike Bennett) and Rhett Titus defeated La Rebellion (Bestia 666 and Mecha Wolf) and Damian 666 in 8:16.

OCTOBER 11 *Nashville, TN*
The Hex (Allysin Kay and Marti Belle) defeated Natalia Markova and Taryn Terrell in 5:33; The Question Mark II defeated KC Roxx in 5:37; Dak Draper defeated Chris Adonis and Thrillbilly Silas in a Three Way Match in 5:15; KiLynn King defeated Taya Valkyrie in 8:57.

OCTOBER 18 *Nashville, TN*
Trevor Murdoch defeated Matt Taven in 5:39; The Question Mark II defeated JR Kratos in 5:37; Chelsea Green defeated Angelina Love in 8:02; Kerry Morton defeated Joe Alonzo in 5:46; EC3 defeated Mercurio in 5:20.

NOVEMBER 1 *Nashville, TN*
Colby Corino defeated Flip Gordon in 8:38; Hawx Aerie (Luke Hawx and PJ Hawx) defeated The Dirty Sexy Boys (Dirty Dango and JTG) in 6:22; Rolando Freeman and The Spectaculars (Brady Pierce and Rush Freeman) defeated The Cardona Family (Brian Myers, Mike Knox and VSK) in 6:54; Mims defeated Gustavo Aguilar and Judais in a Three Way Match in 6:45.

NOVEMBER 8 *Nashville, TN*
Kamille and KiLynn King defeated The Hex (Allysin Kay and Marti Belle) in 7:31; Odinson defeated Fodder in 5:16; Taya Valkyrie defeated Madi Wrenkowski in 6:22; Doug Williams, JR Kratos and Da Pope vs. Thom Latimer, Trevor Murdoch and Tyrus ended in a no contest in 6:49.

NOVEMBER 15 *Chalmette, LA*
Jordan Clearwater vs. Mims ended in a draw in 6:05; Odinson defeated Ryan Davidson in 6:21; JR Kratos defeated Aron Stevens by DQ in 1:35.

NOVEMBER 22 *Chalmette, LA*
Danny Flamingo and Thom Latimer defeated EC3 and Matt Lancie in 7:43; Chuck Devine defeated Nate Bradley in 5:49; Cyon defeated Thrillbilly Silas in 4:56; Kamille defeated Jazmin Allure in 7:50.

NOVEMBER 29 *Chalmette, LA*
Blunt Force Trauma (Carnage and Damage) defeated David Powers and Eddie Vero in 2:20; KiLynn King defeated Samantha Starr in 6:09; The Spectaculars (Brady Pierce and Rush Freeman) defeated The Cardonas (Matt Cardona and Mike Knox) by DQ in 11:19; Matt Cardona defeated Rolando Freeman in 7:40.

DECEMBER 6 *Nashville, TN*
Bully Ray vs. Odinson ended in a draw in 10:00; EC3 vs. Thom Latimer ended in a double DQ in 5:47; Rolando Freeman defeated Anthony Andrews, Jeremiah Plunkett and Sal The Pal in a Four Way Match in 5:36; Judais and PJ Hawx defeated Damage and Rush Freeman in 6:42; Thrillbilly Silas defeated JR Kratos in 8:08.

DECEMBER 13 *Nashville, TN*
Rhett Titus and Trevor Murdoch defeated Dak Draper and Mims in 9:14; Chris Adonis defeated Jax Dane by DQ in 7:17; Alex Taylor defeated Luke Hawx in 6:33; Colby Corino defeated AJ Cazana in 8:10.

DECEMBER 20 *Nashville, TN*
Jax Dane vs. Trevor Murdoch ended in a no contest in 8:47; Bully Ray, Judais and Thom Latimer defeated Chris Adonis, Dak Draper and Mims in 8:18; KiLynn King defeated Allysin Kay in 7:55; Alex Taylor defeated PJ Hawx in 7:11.

DECEMBER 27 *Nashville, TN*
Jordan Clearwater defeated Mercurio in 4:14; The Mortons (Kerry Morton and Ricky Morton) defeated The Fixers (Jay Bradley and Wrecking Ball Legursky) in 6:26; Jeremiah Plunkett defeated Garrison Creed and Traxx in a Three Way Match in 4:51; Damage defeated The Question Mark II in 4:11; Kamille defeated Kenzie Paige by DQ in 10:07; Idolmania Sports Management (Cyon, Jordan Clearwater and Tyrus) defeated Joe Alonzo and La Rebellion (Bestia 666 and Mecha Wolf) in 7:56.

NJPW STRONG

JANUARY 8 *Los Angeles, CA*
TJP defeated The DKC in 8:31; Bullet Club (Chris Bey and Hikuleo) defeated Jordan Clearwater and Keita Murray in 9:12; Eddie Kingston defeated Gabriel Kidd in 12:37.

JANUARY 15 *Los Angeles, CA*
Karl Fredericks and Kevin Knight defeated Stray Dog Army (Bateman and Misterioso) in 10:04; Brody King defeated Dave Dutra in 6:31; Jonah defeated David Finlay in 8:20.

JANUARY 22 *Los Angeles, CA*
Royce Isaacs defeated Lucas Riley in 7:24; Juice Robinson defeated Bad Dude Tito in 9:37; Fred Rosser, Rocky Romero and Taylor Rust defeated Team Filthy (Jorel Nelson and Tom Lawlor) and Black Tiger in 11:35.

JANUARY 29 *Los Angeles, CA*
Alex Zayne defeated Ari Daivari in 10:07; Alex Coughlin defeated JR Kratos in 9:22; Jay White defeated Christopher Daniels in 19:07.

FEBRUARY 5 *Seattle, WA*
Brody King defeated Yuya Uemura in 12:56; Lio Rush and Rocky Romero defeated West Coast Wrecking Crew (Jorel Nelson and Royce Isaacs) in 10:52; Clark Connors defeated TJP in 18:19.

FEBRUARY 12 *Seattle, WA*
Hikuleo defeated Cody Chhun in 7:34; Josh Barnett defeated Ren Narita in 10:15; FinJuice (David Finlay and Juice Robinson) defeated Bad Dude Tito and Jonah in 11:51.

FEBRUARY 19 *Seattle, WA*
Midnight Heat (Eddie Pearl and Ricky Gibson) defeated Kevin Knight and The DKC in 9:18; Fred Rosser defeated Gabriel Kidd in 14:52; Jay White defeated Jay Lethal in 20:07.

FEBRUARY 26 *Seattle, WA*
Karl Fredericks defeated Ethan HD in 11:51; El Phantasmo defeated Matt Rehwoldt in 9:45; Tom Lawlor defeated Taylor Rust in 19:11.

MARCH 5 *Los Angeles, CA*
TJP defeated Brogan Finlay in 9:06; Christopher Daniels defeated Karl Fredericks in 11:40; Bad Dude Tito and Jonah defeated FinJuice (David Finlay and Juice Robinson) in 8:16.

MARCH 12 *Los Angeles, CA*
Hikuleo defeated Kevin Knight in 8:13; Kevin Blackwood defeated Ari Daivari in 8:51; Jay White defeated Swerve Strickland in 17:15.

MARCH 19 *Los Angeles, CA*
Fred Yehi, Keita Murray and The DKC defeated Stray Dog Army (Barrett Brown, Bateman and Misterioso) in 10:05; Chris Bey defeated Blake Christian in 10:24; Buddy Matthews defeated Ren Narita in 15:32.

MARCH 26 *Los Angeles, CA*
Daniel Garcia defeated Yuya Uemura in 10:39; Black Tiger defeated Rocky Romero in 11:02; Team Filthy (Danny Limelight, Jorel Nelson, JR Kratos, Royce Isaacs and Tom Lawlor) defeated Adrian Quest, Clark Connors, Fred Rosser, Taylor Rust and The DKC in an Elimination Match in 16:29.

APRIL 2 *Tampa, FL*
Team Filthy (Black Tiger and JR Kratos) defeated Chaos (Rocky Romero and Wheeler Yuta) in 9:50; FinJuice (David Finlay and Juice Robinson) defeated TMDK (Jonah and Shane Haste) by DQ in 6:34; Tom Lawlor defeated Clark Connors in 13:58.

APRIL 9 *Tampa, FL*
Hikuleo defeated **Andy Brown** in 4:34; **Josh Alexander** defeated **Karl Fredericks** in 14:14; **Eddie Kingston** and **Fred Rosser** defeated **Daniel Garcia** and **Fred Yehi** in 9:27; **Jay White** defeated **Chris Sabin** in 18:12.

APRIL 23 *Tampa, FL*
Big Damo defeated **John Skyler** in 7:04; **Swerve Strickland** defeated **Blake Christian** in 11:27; **Buddy Matthews** defeated **Yuya Uemura** in 9:50.

APRIL 30 *Tampa, FL*
The DKC defeated **Kevin Knight** in 7:45; **Mascara Dorada** defeated **TJP** in 10:50; **Jay Lethal** defeated **Ren Narita** in 12:17.

MAY 7 *Dallas, TX*
Bullet Club (**Chris Bey** and **Hikuleo**) defeated **Stray Dog Army** (**Barrett Brown** and **Bateman**) in 12:16; **Jonah** defeated **Blake Christian** in 6:56; **Team Filthy** (**JR Kratos**, **Royce Isaacs** and **Tom Lawlor**) defeated **Alex Coughlin**, **Fred Rosser** and **The DKC** in 11:12.

MAY 13 *Los Angeles, CA*
Adrian Quest, **Alex Coughlin** and **Rocky Romero** defeated **Team Filthy** (**Black Tiger**, **Danny Limelight** and **JR Kratos**) in 8:33; **West Coast Wrecking Crew** (**Jorel Nelson** and **Royce Isaacs**) defeated **Fred Rosser** in a Handicap Match in 7:28; **Jay White** defeated **Hikuleo** in 18:33.

MAY 21 *Los Angeles, CA*
Chris Dickinson vs. **Ren Narita** ended in a draw in 15:00; **Clark Connors** and **Karl Fredericks** defeated **The Factory** (**Aaron Solo** and **Nick Comoroto**) in 8:21; **United Empire** (**Aaron Henare**, **Great-O-Khan** and **TJP**) defeated **Brody King**, **Mascara Dorada** and **Taylor Rust** in 14:04.

MAY 28 *Los Angeles, CA*
Stray Dog Army (**Barrett Brown**, **Bateman** and **Misterioso**) defeated **Fred Yehi**, **Kevin Knight** and **The DKC** in 10:06; **David Finlay** defeated **Blake Christian** in 10:07; **United Empire** (**Jeff Cobb**, **Kyle Fletcher** and **Mark Davis**) defeated **TMDK** (**Bad Dude Tito**, **Jonah** and **Shane Haste**) in 14:39.

JUNE 4 *Los Angeles, CA*
Keita Murray and **Yuya Uemura** defeated **Kevin Blackwood** and **Lucas Riley** in 8:33; **Bullet Club** (**Chris Bey** and **El Phantasmo**) defeated **Alex Zayne** and **Christopher Daniels** in 9:58; **Tomohiro Ishii** defeated **Big Damo** in 13:02.

JUNE 11 *Philadelphia, PA*
Killer Kross defeated **Yuya Uemura** in 7:50; **Karl Fredericks** defeated **QT Marshall** in 8:24; **Bullet Club** (**Luke Gallows**, **Hikuleo**, **Jay White**, **Juice Robinson** and **Karl Anderson**) defeated **Chaos** (**Chuck Taylor**, **Rocky Romero** and **Tomohiro Ishii**), **Mascara Dorada** and **Ren Narita** in 12:44.

JUNE 18 *Philadelphia, PA*
Jorel Nelson, **JR Kratos** and **Royce Isaacs** defeated **Alex Coughlin**, **Kevin Knight** and **The DKC** in 9:21; **Ari Daivari** defeated **Delirious** in 10:15; **Brody King** defeated **Jake Something** in 8:27; **Hiroshi Tanahashi** defeated **Chris Dickinson** in 13:15.

JUNE 25 *Philadelphia, PA*
David Finlay defeated **Danny Limelight** in 6:31; **Minoru Suzuki** defeated **Tony Deppen** in 10:32; **Fred Rosser** defeated **Tom Lawlor** to win the NJPW Strong Openweight Title in 24:19.

JULY 2 *Philadelphia, PA*
United Empire (**Aaron Henare**, **Great-O-Khan**, **Kyle Fletcher** and **Mark Davis**) defeated **TMDK** (**Bad Dude Tito**, **Jonah**, **Mikey Nicholls** and **Shane Haste**) in 11:35; **Jeff Cobb** defeated **Willie Mack** in 13:13; **Will Ospreay** defeated **Homicide** in 20:47.

JULY 9 *Los Angeles, CA*
Christopher Daniels and **Yuya Uemura** defeated **The Factory** (**Aaron Solo** and **Nick Comoroto**) in 9:17; **Jonah** defeated **Taylor Rust** in 12:50; **TMDK** (**Mikey Nicholls** and **Shane Haste**) defeated **West Coast Wrecking Crew** (**Jorel Nelson** and **Royce Isaacs**) in 10:21.

JULY 16 *Los Angeles, CA*
Stray Dog Army (**Barrett Brown** and **Misterioso**) defeated **Midnight Heat** (**Eddie Pearl** and **Ricky Gibson**) in 8:31; **Tom Lawlor** defeated **Bad Dude Tito** in 12:09; **Aussie Open** (**Kyle Fletcher** and **Mark Davis**) defeated **Dark Order** (**Alan Angels** and **Evil Uno**) in 12:47.

JULY 23 *Los Angeles, CA*
JR Kratos defeated **Jordan Cruz** in 4:11; **David Finlay**, **Mascara Dorada** and **Rocky Romero** defeated **Adrian Quest**, **Lucas Riley** and **Negro Casas** in 11:03; **Christopher Daniels** and **Yuya Uemura** defeated **TMDK** (**Mikey Nicholls** and **Shane Haste**) in 10:02.

JULY 30 *Los Angeles, CA*
Jeff Cobb defeated **Jordan Clearwater** in 4:27; **Fred Yehi** defeated **Bateman** in 7:30; **Aussie Open** (**Kyle Fletcher** and **Mark Davis**) defeated **Stray Dog Army** (**Barrett Brown** and **Misterioso**) in 7:27; **Bullet Club** (**Chase Owens**, **Hikuleo** and **Jay White**) defeated **Fred Rosser**, **Hiroshi Tanahashi** and **Kevin Knight** in 15:41.

AUGUST 13 *Charlotte, NC*
Jorel Nelson defeated **Shane Haste** in 8:16; **Hikuleo** defeated **Big Damo** in 6:18; **Aussie Open** (**Kyle Fletcher** and **Mark Davis**) defeated **Christopher Daniels** and **Yuya Uemura** to win the NJPW Strong Openweight Tag Team Title in 11:57.

AUGUST 20 *Charlotte, NC*
JR Kratos defeated **Drew Adler** in 4:43; **Dax Harwood** defeated **Rocky Romero** in 10:26; **El Desperado** defeated **Blake Christian** and **Hiromu Takahashi** in a Three Way Match in 19:19.

AUGUST 27 *Charlotte, NC*
Kevin Knight and **The DKC** defeated **The Heatseekers** (**Elliot Russell** and **Sigmon**) in 9:55; **QT Marshall** defeated **Parker Li** in 2:56; **TJP** defeated **Mascara Dorada** in 11:55; **Kushida** and **Ren Narita** defeated **The WorkHorsemen** (**Anthony Henry** and **JD Drake**) in 11:18.

SEPTEMBER 3 *Charlotte, NC*
John Skyler defeated **Lucky Ali** in 10:56; **Eddie Kingston** defeated **Jake Something** in 8:35; **Fred Rosser** defeated **Fred Yehi** in 8:20.

SEPTEMBER 10 *Los Angeles, CA*
Mascara Dorada defeated Misterioso in 9:41; Robbie Eagles defeated Kevin Blackwood in 11:32; Aussie Open (Kyle Fletcher and Mark Davis) defeated West Coast Wrecking Crew (Jorel Nelson and Royce Isaacs) in 11:38.

SEPTEMBER 17 *Los Angeles, CA*
Peter Avalon defeated Adrian Quest in 8:52; Team Filthy (JR Kratos and Tom Lawlor) defeated Cody Chhun and Jordan Cruz in 9:54; Bullet Club (Chase Owens, Hikuleo, Jay White and Juice Robinson) defeated Kushida, Taylor Rust and Roppongi Vice (Trent Beretta and Rocky Romero) in 14:46.

SEPTEMBER 24 *Los Angeles, CA*
QT Marshall defeated Keita Murray in 5:12; TMDK (Bad Dude Tito and Shane Haste) defeated Christopher Daniels and Yuya Uemura in 9:10; Ren Narita defeated Jakob Austin Young in 4:48; Taiji Ishimori defeated Alan Angels in 9:14.

OCTOBER 1 *Los Angeles, CA*
Kevin Knight and The DKC defeated Stray Dog Army (Barrett Brown and Bateman) in 8:16; Aaron Solo defeated Che Cabrera in 8:31; Fred Rosser defeated TJP in 17:20.

OCTOBER 8 *Las Vegas, NV*
Shota Umino defeated QT Marshall in 10:11; Ren Narita defeated Juice Robinson by DQ in 1:20; Ren Narita defeated Juice Robinson in a No DQ Match in 14:45; Bullet Club (Jay White and Karl Anderson) defeated Homicide and Wheeler Yuta in 14:37.

OCTOBER 15 *Las Vegas, NV*
Luke Gallows defeated Che Cabrera in 7:53; Aussie Open (Kyle Fletcher and Mark Davis) defeated Team Filthy (Danny Limelight and JR Kratos) in 10:08; Fred Rosser vs. Chris Dickinson ended in a double count out in 6:48.

OCTOBER 22 *Las Vegas, NV*
West Coast Wrecking Crew (Jorel Nelson and Royce Isaacs) defeated Greg Sharpe and Jakob Austin Young in 6:01; Yuya Uemura defeated Christopher Daniels in 9:48; Shingo Takagi defeated Rocky Romero in 15:51.

OCTOBER 29 *Las Vegas, NV*
Ari Daivari defeated Kevin Knight in 8:19; Alex Zayne and Mistico defeated Blake Christian and Mascara Dorada in 10:09; Tomohiro Ishii defeated Tom Lawlor in 15:31.

NOVEMBER 5 *Los Angeles, CA*
Christopher Daniels defeated Rocky Romero in 9:24; Stray Dog Army (Barrett Brown and Misterioso) defeated Kevin Knight and The DKC, TMDK (Bad Dude Tito and Shane Haste), and West Coast Wrecking Crew (Jorel Nelson and Royce Isaacs) in a Four Way Match in 12:36; Hiroshi Tanahashi defeated Gabriel Kidd in 11:30.

NOVEMBER 12 *Los Angeles, CA*
Kenny King defeated Che Cabrera in 8:06; Team Filthy (Danny Limelight and JR Kratos) defeated Adrian Quest and Jordan Cruz in 8:20; Minoru Suzuki defeated Fred Yehi in 16:27.

NOVEMBER 19 *Los Angeles, CA*
Peter Avalon defeated Keita Murray in 8:58; Bullet Club (Chris Bey and El Phantasmo) defeated Blake Christian and Mascara Dorada in 10:44; Homicide defeated Tom Lawlor in 13:44.

NOVEMBER 26 *Los Angeles, CA*
Aussie Open (Kyle Fletcher and Mark Davis) defeated Greg Sharpe and Jakob Austin Young in 5:51; Juice Robinson defeated Jake Something in 10:44; Jay White defeated Fred Rosser in 19:22.

DECEMBER 3 *Los Angeles, CA*
Adrian Quest and Rocky Romero defeated Atlantis Jr. and Virus in 10:33; Homicide defeated Danny Limelight in 11:14; Juice Robinson defeated Blake Christian in 9:33.

DECEMBER 10 *Los Angeles, CA*
Kenny King defeated Greg Sharpe in 9:43; Christopher Daniels defeated The DKC in 9:15; Alan Angels, David Finlay and Guerrilas Of Destiny (Hikuleo and Tama Tonga) defeated Bullet Club (El Phantasmo and Jay White) and West Coast Wrecking Crew (Jorel Nelson and Royce Isaacs) in 13:20.

DECEMBER 17 *Los Angeles, CA*
Bateman defeated Jakob Austin Young in 7:49; Kenta defeated Bad Dude Tito in 7:53; The Motor City Machine Guns (Alex Shelley and Chris Sabin) defeated Stray Dog Army (Barrett Brown and Misterioso) in 12:11.

DECEMBER 24 *Los Angeles, CA*
Lince Dorado and Mascara Dorada defeated C4 (Cody Chhun and Guillermo Rosas) in 10:35; Bobby Fish defeated Kevin Blackwood in 12:00; Fred Rosser defeated JR Kratos in 18:44.

DECEMBER 31
Highlights show

TELEVISION RATINGS

Listed below is the total number of viewers (in millions) who tuned in for the major cable and network wrestling shows in the United States, according to data provided by Nielsen. The number in parenthesis is the change in the number of viewers from the equivalent broadcast in 2021. For clarification, in 2022 WWE Monday Night RAW aired Mondays on the USA Network, NXT aired Tuesdays on the USA Network, AEW Dynamite aired Wednesdays on TBS, WWE SmackDown aired Fridays on Fox and AEW Rampage aired Fridays on TNT.

WEEK OF	RAW	NXT	DYNAMITE	SMACKDOWN	RAMPAGE
03/01/2022	1.717 (-0.411)	0.685 (+0.044)	1.010 (+0.348)	2.271 (+0.268)	0.588
10/01/2022	1.633 (-0.186)	0.647 (+0.096)	0.969 (+0.207)	2.174 (+0.021)	0.526
17/01/2022	1.613 (-0.241)	0.587 (-0.072)	1.032 (+0.178)	2.255 (-0.027)	0.594
24/01/2022	1.766 (-0.053)	0.593 (-0.127)	1.110 (+0.376)	2.217 (-0.011)	0.601
31/01/2022	1.865 (-0.027)	0.619 (+0.009)	0.954 (+0.110)	2.151 (-0.025)	0.54
07/02/2022	1.387 (-0.328)	0.400 (-0.158)	1.112 (+0.371)	2.231 (+0.347)	0.549
14/02/2022	1.602 (-0.208)	0.525 (-0.188)	0.869 (+0.122)	2.173 (+0.101)	0.471
21/02/2022	1.825 (-0.065)	0.621 (-0.113)	1.010 (+0.179)	2.114 (+0.063)	0.473
28/02/2022	1.753 (-0.131)	0.551 (-0.141)	0.966 (+0.032)	2.261 (+0.095)	0.545
07/03/2022	1.775 (-0.122)	0.613 (-0.078)	0.945 (+0.202)	2.226 (+0.216)	0.526
14/03/2022	1.700 (-0.143)	0.624 (+0.0027)	0.993 (+0.225)	2.147 (+0.201)	0.398
21/03/2022	1.769 (-0.047)	0.628 (-0.050)	1.046 (+0.289)	2.180 (+0.149)	0.425
28/03/2022	1.979 (+0.278)	0.626 (-0.028)	0.979 (+0.279)	2.359 (+0.323)	0.456
04/04/2022	2.101 (+0.400)	0.631 (-0.137)	0.989 (+0.301)	2.230 (+0.150)	0.6
11/04/2022	1.803 (-0.223)	0.610 (-0.195)	0.977 (-0.230)	2.142 (+0.145)	0.482
18/04/2022	1.647 (-0.260)	0.569 (-0.272)	0.930 (-0.174)	1.952 (-0.090)	0.518
25/04/2022	1.613 (-0.161)	0.577 (-0.167)	0.921 (+0.032)	1.953 (-0.065)	0.464
02/05/2022	1.581 (-0.291)	0.661 (-0.100)	0.833 (-0.257)	1.998 (-0.284)	0.292
09/05/2022	1.652 (-0.165)	0.533 (-0.164)	0.840 (-0.096)	1.893 (-0.024)	0.34
16/05/2022	1.736 (-0.087)	0.601 (-0.099)	0.922 (+0.101)	2.031 (+0.101)	0.41
23/05/2022	1.732 (+0.111)	0.551 (-0.147)	0.929 (+0.403)	1.878 (-0.050)	0.341
30/05/2022	1.497 (-0.054)	0.534 (-0.134)	0.969 (+0.507)	1.939 (+0.056)	0.475
06/06/2022	1.872 (+0.232)	0.675 (+0.006)	0.939 (+0.452)	2.031 (+0.087)	0.476
13/06/2022	1.695 (-0.047)	0.612 (-0.083)	0.761 (+0.210)	2.290 (+0.250)	0.369
20/06/2022	1.986 (+0.277)	0.673 (+0.008)	0.878 (+0.229)	2.231 (+0.260)	0.422
27/06/2022	1.951 (+0.381)	0.570 (-0.066)	1.023 (+0.140)	2.142 (+0.281)	0.486
04/07/2022	1.563 (+0.091)	0.593 (-0.061)	0.979 (+0.108)	2.129 (+0.143)	0.428
11/07/2022	1.735 (+0.126)	0.582 (-0.123)	0.942 (-0.083)	2.077 (-0.233)	0.435
18/07/2022	1.765 (-0.158)	0.588 (-0.121)	0.910 (-0.238)	2.256 (+0.119)	0.428
25/07/2022	1.901 (+0.087)	0.600 (+0.080)	0.976 (-0.132)	2.193 (+0.150)	0.375
01/08/2022	2.230 (+0.409)	0.649 (+0.129)	0.938 (-0.164)	2.093 (-0.076)	0.468
08/08/2022	1.956 (+0.166)	0.597 (-0.154)	0.972 (-0.007)	1.927 (-0.157)	0.528(-0.212)
15/08/2022	1.978 (+0.121)	0.723 (+0.069)	0.957 (-0.018)	2.084 (-0.018)	0.461(-0.668)
22/08/2022	2.005 (-0.062)	0.678 (-0.007)	1.049 (-0.123)	1.990 (-0.260)	0.431(-0.291)
29/08/2022	2.107 (+0.200)	0.676 (-0.041)	1.020 (-0.027)	2.077 (-0.143)	0.485(-0.211)
05/09/2022	2.054 (+0.205)	0.684 (+0.083)	1.035 (-0.284)	2.367 (-0.016)	0.429(-0.241)
12/09/2022	1.709 (+0.039)	0.728 (-0.042)	1.175 1.175 (=)	2.212 (-0.031)	0.470(-0.172)
19/09/2022	1.593 (-0.200)	0.688 (-0.058)	1.039 (-0.234)	2.535 (+0.400)	0.522(-0.205)
26/09/2022	1.674 (-0.037)	0.660 (+0.005)	0.990 (-0.162)	2.207 (-0.045)	0.472(-0.150)
03/10/2022	1.599 (-0.258)	0.625 (-0.007)	1.038 (-0.015)	2.243 (+0.096)	0.404(-0.098)
10/10/2022	1.824 (+0.242)	0.737 (+0.105)	0.983 (+0.256)	2.254 (+1.388)	0.458(-0.120)
17/10/2022	1.803 (+0.210)	0.676 (+0.070)	0.752 (+0.177)	2.231 (-0.018)	0.480(-0.053)
24/10/2022	1.641 (-0.018)	0.716 (-0.030)	0.997 (+0.056)	0.835 (-0.197)	0.378(-0.245)
31/10/2022	1.500 (-0.189)	0.670 (+0.039)	0.911 (+0.033)	2.138 (+0.045)	0.455(-0.144)
07/11/2022	1.593 (+0.044)	0.664 (+0.061)	0.930 (+0.017)	2.264 (+0.160)	0.456(-0.059)
14/11/2022	1.648 (+0.068)	0.663 (+0.089)	0.818 (-0.166)	2.232 (+0.158)	0.445(-0.111)
21/11/2022	1.646 (-0.054)	0.624 (-0.001)	0.880 (-0.018)	2.166 (+0.017)	0.411(-0.020)
28/11/2022	1.668 (-0.012)	0.644 (+0.007)	0.870 (+0.009)	0.902 (-1.130)	0.360(-0.139)
05/12/2022	1.536 (-0.064)	0.534 (-0.056)	0.840 (-0.032)	2.306 (+0.164)	0.457(-0.046)
12/12/2022	1.472 (-0.102)	0.666 (+0.105)	0.950 (+0.002)	2.151 (-0.152)	0.464(-0.107)
19/12/2022	1.705 (+0.153)	0.705 (+0.114)	0.957 (-0.063)	2.376 (-0.404)	0.556(-0.033)
26/12/2022	1.075 (-0.515)	0.588 (-0.074)	0.876 (-0.099)	2.629 (+2.251)	0.470(+0.017)

AEW BATTLE OF THE BELTS		WWE TRIBUTE TO THE TROOPS	
Jan-08	704,000	Dec-17	612,000
Apr-16	527,000		
Aug-06	437,000		
Oct-07	317,000		

Listed below is the rating share each show scored in the 18-49 demographic, which is now widely considered the most important ratings number, due to its value to advertisers. Historically, total viewers has typically been used to assess the performance of a show, but that has changed in recent years as advertising has become more focused towards targeted demos. The number in parenthesis is the change in the number of viewers from the equivalent broadcast in 2021.

WEEK OF	RAW	NXT	DYNAMITE	SMACKDOWN	RAMPAGE
03/01/2022	0.45 (-0.23)	0.16 0.16 (=)	0.43 (+0.18)	0.58 (+0.02)	0.24
10/01/2022	0.39 (-0.16)	0.14 0.14 (=)	0.39 (+0.09)	0.56 (-0.11)	0.20
17/01/2022	0.43 (-0.17)	0.11 (-0.04)	0.44 (+0.08)	0.64 (-0.01)	0.24
24/01/2022	0.46 (-0.06)	0.14 (-0.07)	0.41 (+0.12)	0.56 (-0.06)	0.25
31/01/2022	0.47 (-0.11)	0.13 (-0.02)	0.35 (+0.03)	0.51 (-0.14)	0.20
07/02/2022	0.36 (-0.13)	0.07 (-0.05)	0.41 (+0.12)	0.55 (-0.02)	0.19
14/02/2022	0.44 (-0.13)	0.11 (-0.05)	0.31 (=)	0.54 (-0.05)	0.20
21/02/2022	0.51 (-0.06)	0.12 (-0.06)	0.40 (+0.05)	0.57 (+0.03)	0.18
28/02/2022	0.47 (-0.11)	0.13 (-0.07)	0.36 (+0.03)	0.59 (-0.01)	0.22
07/03/2022	0.45 (-0.10)	0.13 (-0.05)	0.40 (+0.08)	0.57 (-0.04)	0.22
14/03/2022	0.48 (-0.08)	0.14 (+0.01)	0.38 (+0.10)	0.58 (+0.01)	0.13
21/03/2022	0.50 (-0.03)	0.14 (=)	0.41 (+0.11)	0.49 (-0.06)	0.14
28/03/2022	0.55 (-0.01)	0.14 (-0.07)	0.38 (+0.12)	0.61 (+0.04)	0.15
04/04/2022	0.63 (+0.11)	0.14 (-0.08)	0.38 (+0.10)	0.60 (-0.01)	0.25
11/04/2022	0.54 (-0.14)	0.12 (-0.10)	0.37 (-0.07)	0.48 (-0.08)	0.22
18/04/2022	0.57 (-0.14)	0.12 (-0.11)	0.37 (=)	0.47 (-0.07)	0.19
25/04/2022	0.44 (-0.05)	0.14 (-0.08)	0.33 (=)	0.38 (-0.11)	0.14
02/05/2022	0.38 (-0.15)	0.13 (-0.05)	0.32 (-0.10)	0.46 (-0.19)	0.11
09/05/2022	0.44 (-0.09)	0.10 (-0.07)	0.33 (+0.02)	0.40 (-0.04)	0.12
16/05/2022	0.45 (-0.03)	0.14 (-0.01)	0.33 (+0.05)	0.45 (-0.05)	0.15
23/05/2022	0.41 (-0.04)	0.13 (=)	0.35 (+0.15)	0.43 (-0.07)	0.14
30/05/2022	0.42 (+0.02)	0.12 (-0.07)	0.40 (+0.21)	0.47 (-0.03)	0.14
06/06/2022	0.52 (+0.04)	0.14 (-0.05)	0.34 (+0.15)	0.44 (-0.04)	0.16
13/06/2022	0.43 (-0.06)	0.12 (-0.07)	0.28 (+0.08)	0.57 (+0.03)	0.10
20/06/2022	0.54 (+0.05)	0.18 (+0.01)	0.31 (+0.10)	0.53 (-0.01)	0.12
27/06/2022	0.54 (+0.13)	0.11 (-0.02)	0.36 (+0.01)	0.49 (+0.03)	0.16
04/07/2022	0.37 (-0.04)	0.12 (-0.06)	0.36 (+0.03)	0.47 (-0.01)	0.15
11/07/2022	0.44 (+0.01)	0.14 (-0.05)	0.32 (-0.08)	0.47 (-0.19)	0.14
18/07/2022	0.46 (-0.11)	0.13 (-0.07)	0.32 (-0.12)	0.62 (+0.07)	0.17
25/07/2022	0.50 (+0.01)	0.13 (+0.01)	0.33 (-0.12)	0.52 (-0.05)	0.11
01/08/2022	0.61 (+0.10)	0.15 (+0.05)	0.32 (-0.14)	0.49 (-0.12)	0.15
08/08/2022	0.54 (+0.05)	0.13 (-0.06)	0.33 (-0.02)	0.44 (-0.14)	0.17 (-0.13)
15/08/2022	0.53 (-0.02)	0.18 (+0.03)	0.30 (-0.05)	0.47 (-0.10)	0.12 (-0.41)
22/08/2022	0.55 (-0.09)	0.14 (-0.02)	0.34 (-0.14)	0.48 (-0.11)	0.11 (-0.23)
29/08/2022	0.59 (+0.05)	0.15 (-0.02)	0.35 (-0.02)	0.49 (-0.13)	0.16 (-0.14)
05/09/2022	0.58 (+0.06)	0.16 (+0.02)	0.38 (-0.14)	0.57 (-0.08)	0.14 (-0.13)
12/09/2022	0.44 (+0.01)	0.15 (-0.06)	0.39 (-0.05)	0.50 (-0.08)	0.14 (-0.14)
19/09/2022	0.45 (-0.04)	0.15 (-0.05)	0.35 (-0.13)	0.63 (+0.08)	0.18 (-0.11)
26/09/2022	0.45 (-0.03)	0.16 (+0.02)	0.34 (-0.11)	0.54 (-0.08)	0.16 (-0.09)
03/10/2022	0.40 (-0.12)	0.13 (=)	0.33 (-0.04)	0.54 (+0.02)	0.13 (-0.04)
10/10/2022	0.55 (+0.13)	0.15 (=)	0.32 (+0.04)	0.54 (+0.30)	0.17 (-0.07)
17/10/2022	0.50 (+0.11)	0.18 (+0.04)	0.26 (+0.04)	0.52 (-0.06)	0.13 (-0.09)
24/10/2022	0.45 (-0.02)	0.15 (-0.03)	0.32 (-0.08)	0.23 (-0.06)	0.12 (-0.13)
31/10/2022	0.36 (-0.11)	0.13 (-0.02)	0.29 (-0.04)	0.48 (-0.09)	0.14 (-0.08)
07/11/2022	0.43 (+0.03)	0.15 (=)	0.32 (-0.03)	0.58 (+0.02)	0.11 (-0.09)
14/11/2022	0.44 (+0.02)	0.17 (+0.06)	0.28 (-0.09)	0.56 (+0.04)	0.14 (-0.08)
21/11/2022	0.41 (-0.08)	0.12 (-0.02)	0.32 (+0.01)	0.54 (-0.03)	0.11 (-0.07)
28/11/2022	0.40 (-0.05)	0.13 (-0.02)	0.26 (-0.05)	0.25 (-0.26)	0.08 (-0.10)
05/12/2022	0.41 (+0.06)	0.13 (+0.02)	0.29 (-0.04)	0.57 (+0.07)	0.11 (-0.07)
12/12/2022	0.37 (-0.02)	0.17 (+0.03)	0.33 (-0.05)	0.52 (=)	0.15 (-0.08)
19/12/2022	0.43 (+0.05)	0.14 (+0.03)	0.30 (-0.07)	0.55 (+0.07)	0.18 (-0.08)
26/12/2022	0.27 (-0.15)	0.12 (-0.04)	0.28 (-0.09)	0.64 (+0.56)	0.12 (-0.07)

AEW BATTLE OF THE BELTS		WWE TRIBUTE TO THE TROOPS	
Jan-08	0.27	Dec-17	0.17
Apr-16	0.18		
Aug-06	0.12		
Oct-07	0.1		

TELEVISION RECORDS AND HISTORICAL VIEWERSHIP AVERAGES

WWE PRIME TIME WRESTLING

1987	1,204,000
1988	1,285,000
1989	1,458,000
1990	1,580,000
1991	1,382,000
1992	1,241,000

WWE ALL AMERICAN WRESTLING

1987	1,181,000
1988	1,193,000
1989	1,207,000
1990	1,344,000
1991	1,303,000
1992	1,096,000
1993	1,280,000
1994	1,152,000

WWE MONDAY NIGHT RAW

1993	1,712,000
1994	1,856,000
1995	1,915,000
1996	1,735,000
1997	1,941,000
1998	3,146,000
1999	4,621,000
2000	5,134,000
2001	4,940,000
2002	4,195,000
2003	4,040,000
2004	4,355,000
2005	4,576,000
2006	4,950,000
2007	5,050,000
2008	4,810,000
2009	5,220,000
2010	4,800,000
2011	4,800,000
2012	4,330,000
2013	4,140,000
2014	4,150,000
2015	3,700,000
2016	3,200,000
2017	3,080,000
2018	2,820,000
2019	2,417,000
2020	1,879,000
2021	1,756,000
2022	1,735,000

Record High: 9,200,000
(May 10, 1999)
Record Low: 1,075,000
(Dec 26, 2022)

WWE MANIA

1993	705,000
1994	798,000
1995	842,000
1996	907,000

WWE ACTION ZONE

1994	1,149,000
1995	1,078,000
1996	1,098,000

WWE LIVEWIRE

1996	725,000
1997	936,000
1998	1,198,000
1999	1,371,000
2000	1,198,000

WWE SUPERSTARS

1996	1,220,000
1997	1,178,000
1998	1,298,000
1999	1,462,000
2000	1,287,000

WWE SUNDAY NIGHT HEAT

1998	2,707,000
1999	3,016,000
2000	2,077,000
2001	1,190,000
2002	1,169,000
2003	1,062,000
2004	1,027,000
2005	860,000

WWE SMACKDOWN

1999	4,405,000
2000	4,764,000
2001	4,208,000
2002	3,801,000
2003	3,573,000
2004	3,377,000
2005	4,547,000
2006	3,930,000
2007	4,410,000
2008	4,050,000
2009	3,290,000
2010	2,890,000
2011	2,870,000
2012	2,700,000
2013	2,660,000
2014	2,650,000
2015	2,360,000
2016	2,400,000
2017	2,550,000
2018	2,350,000
2019	2,160,000
2020	2,152,000
2021	2,046,000
2022	2,122,000

Record High: 5,470,000
(Jan 27, 2000)
Record Low: 835,000
(Oct 28, 2022)

WWE ECW

2006	2,138,000
2007	1,630,000
2008	1,622,000

WWE NXT

2019	826,000
2020	701,000
2021	666,000
2022	624,000

Record High: 1,179,000
(Sep 18, 2019)
Record Low: 400,000
(Feb 8, 2022)

WCW WORLD CHAMPIONSHIP WRESTLING/SATURDAY NIGHT

1987	1,239,000
1988	1,388,000
1989	1,147,000
1990	1,512,000
1991	1,480,000
1992	1,307,000
1993	1,601,000
1994	1,643,000
1995	1,601,000
1996	1,777,000
1997	1,619,000
1998	1,638,000
1999	1,393,000
2000	1,115,000

WCW MAIN EVENT

1987	1,000,000
1988	1,077,000
1989	1,175,000
1990	1,462,000
1991	1,407,000
1992	1,230,000
1993	1,351,000
1994	1,311,000
1995	1,232,000
1996	1,139,000
1997	895,000

WCW POWER HOUR

1989	925,000
1990	1,038,000
1991	941,000
1992	948,000
1993	963,000
1994	1,048,000

WCW PRO

1994	952,000
1995	1,002,000
1996	1,028,000
1997	1,029,000

WCW MONDAY NITRO

1995	1,672,000
1996	2,169,000
1997	2,654,000
1998	3,213,000
1999	2,829,000
2000	2,128,000
2001	1,791,000

WCW THUNDER

1998	2,706,000
1999	2,144,000
2000	1,807,000
2001	1,527,000

ECW ON TNN

1999	751,000
2000	735,000

AEW DYNAMITE
2019   903,000
2020   807,000
2021   892,000
2022   932,000

Record High: 1,409,000
(Oct 2, 2019)
Record Low: 462,000
(Jun 4, 2021)

AEW RAMPAGE
2021   614,000
2022   463,000

Record High: 1,129,000
(Aug 20, 2021)
Record Low: 292,000
(May 6, 2022)

AEW BATTLE OF THE BELTS
2022   496,000

Record High: 704,000
(Jan 8, 2022)
Record Low: 317,000
(Oct 7, 2022)

IMPACT WRESTLING
2005   927,000
2006   1,052,000
2007   1,222,000
2008   1,247,000
2009   1,580,000
2010   1,420,000
2011   1,620,000
2012   1,380,000
2013   1,263,000
2014   1,155,000
2015   340,000
2016   310,000
2017   282,000
2018   252,000
2019   N/A
2020   154,000
2021   119,000
2022   105,000

Record High: 2,200,000
(Jan 24, 2010)
Record Low: 48,000
(Nov 25, 2021)

TALES FROM THE TERRITORIES
S1   80,500

Record High: 113,000
(Oct 4, 2022)
Record Low: 34,000
(Nov 1, 2022)

RHODES TO THE TOP
S1   360,000

Record High: 422,000
(Sep 29, 2021)
Record Low: 309,000
(Oct 23, 2021)

DARK SIDE OF THE RING
S1   201,000
S2   258,000
S3   177,000

Record High: 349,000
(May 19, 2020)
Record Low: 109,000
(Oct 21, 2021)

MIZ & MRS
S1   1,064,000
S2   539,000
S3   551,000

Record High: 1,470,000
(Jul 24, 2018)
Record Low: 380,000
(Nov 26, 2020)

YOUNG ROCK
S1   3,036,000
S2   2,159,000

Record High: 5,320,000
(Feb 16, 2021)
Record Low: 1,870,000
(May 17, 2022)

TOTAL BELLAS
S1   630,000
S2   580,000
S3   630,000
S4   430,000
S5   504,000
S6   342,000

Record High: 750,000
(Oct 12, 2016)
Record Low: 220,000
(Dec 10, 2020)

TOTAL DIVAS
S1   1,320,000
S2   1,190,000
S3   1,110,000
S4   1,000,000
S5   720,000
S6   610,000
S7   570,000
S8   380,000
S9   253,000

Record High: 1,670,000
(Aug 11, 2013)
Record Low: 190,000
(Nov 5, 2019)

2022
WRESTLER
TELEVISION
RECORDS

AARON HENARE

Date	Opponents	Result	Event	Time
Mar 3	Satoshi Kojima, Yuji Nagata, Kosei Fujita & Yuto Nakashiam (w/Great-O-Khan, Will Ospreay & Jeff Cobb)	W	NJPW 50th Anniversary Show	9:20
Apr 9	Tetsuya Naito & Shingo Takagi (w/Will Ospreay)	L	NJPW Hyper Battle '22	9:23
Apr 16	Hikuleo, Chris Bey, El Phantasmo, Karl Anderson, Luke Gallows & Scott Norton (w/Great-O-Khan, Jeff Cobb, TJP, Mark Davis & Kyle Fletcher)	W	NJPW Windy City Riot	11:58
May 14	Mikey Nicholls, Shane Haste, Jonah & Bad Dude Tito (w/Kyle Fletcher, Mark Davis & Jeff Cobb)	L	NJPW Capital Collision	12:09
May 21	Brody King, Mascara Dorada & Taylor Rust (w/Great-O-Khan & TJP)	W	NJPW Strong	14:04
Jun 12	Ryusuke Taguchi, Master Wato & Hiroyoshi Tenzan (w/TJP & Francesco Akira)	W	NJPW Dominion '22	10:31
Jul 2	Bad Dude Tito, Jonah, Mikey Nicholls & Shane Haste (w/Great-O-Khan, Kyle Fletcher & Mark Davis)	W	NJPW Strong	11:35
Oct 10	Tetsuya Naito, Sanada, Bushi & Hiromu Takahashi (w/Will Ospreay, TJP & Francesco Akira)	L	NJPW Declaration Of Power	8:07
Nov 5	Hiroshi Tanahashi, Toru Yano, David Finlay & Alex Zayne (w/Gideon Grey, Kyle Fletcher & Mark Davis)	W	NJPW Battle Autumn '22	9:50
Nov 20	Kazuchika Okada, Toru Yano & The Great Muta (w/Great-O-Khan & Jeff Cobb)	L	NJPW x Stardom Historic X-Over	9:48

AARON SOLO

Date	Opponents	Result	Event	Time
Jan 7	Hook	L	AEW Rampage	3:19
Jan 11	Dante Martin	L	AEW Dark	3:16
Jan 31	Dante Martin, Lee Moriarty & Matt Sydal (w/Nick Comoroto & QT Marshall)	L	AEW Dark Elevation	7:46
Feb 1	Cam Stewart & Dante Casanova (w/Nick Comoroto)	W	AEW Dark	3:44
Feb 7	Dante Martin	L	AEW Dark Elevation	5:01
Feb 8	Wheeler Yuta	L	AEW Dark	7:00
Feb 10	Sonny Kiss	W	AEW Dark	6:53
Mar 1	Orange Cassidy & Wheeler Yuta (w/Nick Comoroto)	L	AEW Dark	14:17
Mar 7	Wheeler Yuta	L	AEW Dark Elevation	7:07
Mar 15	Ten	L	AEW Dark	5:41
Mar 21	John Silver, Evil Uno & Stu Grayson (w/Nick Comoroto & QT Marshall)	L	AEW Dark Elevation	7:27
Mar 28	Rocky Romero & Trent Beretta (w/QT Marshall)	L	AEW Dark Elevation	5:23
Mar 29	Adam Priest, Gus De La Vega & Invictus Khash (w/Nick Comoroto & QT Marshall)	W	AEW Dark	4:30
Apr 4	Brock Anderson & Lee Johnson (w/QT Marshall)	L	AEW Dark Elevation	6:59
Apr 5	Alan Angels & Ten (w/Nick Comoroto)	L	AEW Dark	8:08
Apr 11	Dante Martin & Darius Martin (w/Nick Comoroto)	L	AEW Dark Elevation	5:52
Apr 16	Karl Fredericks, Clark Connors & Yuya Uemura (w/QT Marshall & Nick Comoroto)	W	NJPW Windy City Riot	11:56
Apr 18	Rocky Romero & Trent Beretta (w/Nick Comoroto)	L	AEW Dark Elevation	7:25
Apr 19	Keith Lee & Swerve Strickland (w/Nick Comoroto)	L	AEW Dark	8:40
Apr 27	Bryan Danielson, Jon Moxley & Wheeler Yuta (w/Nick Comoroto & QT Marshall)	L	AEW Dynamite	8:49
May 10	The DKC & Kevin Knight (w/Nick Comoroto)	W	AEW Dark	8:30
May 17	Alex Coughlin, Clark Connors, Karl Fredericks, Kevin Knight & Yuya Uemura (w/Blake Li, Brick Aldridge, Nick Comoroto & QT Marshall)	L	AEW Dark	10:30
May 21	Clark Connors & Karl Fredericks (w/Nick Comoroto)	L	NJPW Strong	8:21
May 28	Pac, Penta El Zero M & Rey Fenix (w/Nick Comoroto & QT Marshall)	L	AEW Dark	10:32
Jun 6	Alan Angels, Evil Uno, John Silver & Ten (w/Anthony Ogogo, Nick Comoroto & QT Marshall)	W	AEW Dark Elevation	6:28
Jun 7	Lance Archer	L	AEW Dark	2:46
Jun 13	Evil Uno & Ten (w/QT Marshall)	L	AEW Dark Elevation	8:13
Jun 26	Hirooki Goto & Yoshi-Hashi (w/QT Marshall)	L	AEW x NJPW Forbidden Door Buy-In	8:53
Jun 28	Knull & Matt Vandagriff (w/Nick Comoroto)	W	AEW Dark	3:43
Jul 4	Alex Reynolds, Evil Uno & Ten (w/Nick Comoroto & QT Marshall)	L	AEW Dark Elevation	7:56
Jul 5	Fuego Del Sol	L	AEW Dark	5:27
Jul 9	Christopher Daniels & Yuya Uemura (w/Nick Comoroto)	L	NJPW Strong	9:17
Jul 11	Chuck Taylor & Trent Beretta (w/QT Marshall)	L	AEW Dark Elevation	9:40
Jul 25	Evil Uno & Ten (w/Nick Comoroto)	L	AEW Dark Elevation	6:35
Aug 1	Bobby Orlando, BRG, Bryce Donovan & TUG Cooper (w/Anthony Ogogo, Nick Comoroto & QT Marshall)	W	AEW Dark Elevation	3:33
Aug 2	Caleb Teninty & KC Rocker (w/Nick Comoroto)	W	AEW Dark	3:18
Aug 10	Ricky Starks	L	AEW Dynamite: Quake By The Lake	2:13
Aug 23	Dante Martin & Matt Sydal (w/Nick Comoroto)	W	AEW Dark	8:11
Sep 3	Hangman Page, John Silver & Alex Reynolds (w/Cole Karter & Nick Comoroto)	L	AEW Dark Elevation	6:00
Sep 12	The Butcher & The Blade (w/Nick Comoroto)	L	AEW Dark Elevation	4:37
Oct 1	Che Cabrera	W	NJPW Strong	8:31
Oct 3	Chuck Taylor, Trent Beretta, Danhausen & Rocky Romero (w/Cole Karter, Nick Comoroto & QT Marshall)	L	AEW Dark Elevation	7:54
Oct 11	Dante Martin & Matt Sydal (w/Cole Karter)	L	AEW Dark	9:31
Oct 25	Serpentico	L	AEW Dark	5:13
Nov 19	Orange Cassidy, Chuck Taylor, Trent Beretta, Rocky Romero & Danhausen (w/QT Marshall, Lee Johnson, Nick Comoroto & Cole Karter)	L	AEW Full Gear Buy-In	11:55
Nov 21	Orange Cassidy, Trent Beretta & Chuck Taylor (w/Cole Karter & Lee Johnson)	L	AEW Dark	3:38
Nov 28	Eddie Kingston & Ortiz (w/Nick Comoroto)	L	AEW Dark Elevation	4:55
Dec 5	Konosuke Takeshita	L	AEW Dark Elevation	3:15
Dec 10	Dante Martin & Darius Martin (w/Nick Comoroto)	L	AEW Dark Elevation	3:35

| Dec 14 | Malakai Black, Brody King & Buddy Matthews (w/QT Marshall & Cole Karter) | L | AEW Dynamite: Winter Is Coming | :23 |

ABADON

Feb 10	Gia Scott	W	AEW Dark	1:51
Mar 1	Sahara Seven	W	AEW Dark	2:23
Mar 22	Angelica Risk	W	AEW Dark	1:06
Mar 28	Danni Bee	W	AEW Dark Elevation	1:23
Apr 5	Hyena Hera	W	AEW Dark	1:35
Apr 26	Charlette Renegade	W	AEW Dark	1:09
May 9	Emi Sakura	W	AEW Dark Elevation	4:29
May 10	Vicky Dreamboat	W	AEW Dark	2:00
Aug 16	Mafioso Rossi	W	AEW Dark	2:32
Oct 3	Abby Jane	W	AEW Dark Elevation	1:00
Oct 4	Freya States	W	AEW Dark	2:06
Nov 7	Amy Rose	W	AEW Dark Elevation	1:45
Dec 6	Leva Bates	W	AEW Dark	2:39

ACE AUSTIN

Jan 6	Hernandez & Johnny Swinger (w/Madman Fulton)	W	IMPACT Wrestling	3:40
Feb 3	Chris Bey, Jay White, Tama Tonga & Tanga Loa (w/Jake Something, Mike Bailey & Madman Fulton)	L	IMPACT Wrestling	16:49
Feb 17	Blake Christian, Laredo Kid	W	IMPACT Wrestling	11:57
Feb 24	Trey Miguel & Jake Something (w/Mike Bailey)	W	IMPACT Before The Impact	8:01
Mar 10	Crazzy Steve, John Skyler	W	IMPACT Wrestling	10:45
Apr 21	Laredo Kid & Trey Miguel (w/Mike Bailey)	L	IMPACT Wrestling	6:00
Apr 23	Trey Miguel, Mike Bailey	W	IMPACT Rebellion '22	10:25
May 5	Rocky Romero	W	IMPACT Wrestling	11:39
May 12	Aiden Prince	W	IMPACT Before The Impact	8:02
Jun 12	Tetsuya Naito, Bushi & Hiromu Takahashi (w/Taiji Ishimori & El Phantasmo)	W	NJPW Dominion '22	8:04
Jun 19	Ultimate X Match: Mike Bailey, Alex Zayne, Andrew Everett, Kenny King, Trey Miguel	L	IMPACT Slammiversary XX	9:50
Jun 30	Alex Zayne	W	IMPACT Wrestling	6:57
Jul 14	Eddie Edwards, Kenny King, Matt Taven & Mike Bennett (w/Chris Bey, Luke Gallows & Karl Anderson)	L	IMPACT Wrestling	12:34
Jul 21	Matt Taven & Mike Bennett (w/Chris Bey)	W	IMPACT Wrestling	10:32
Jul 28	Eddie Edwards	L	IMPACT Wrestling	11:38
Aug 25	Johnny Swinger & Zicky Dice (w/Hikuleo)	W	IMPACT Before The Impact	7:46
Sep 1	JD Griffey & Exodus Prime (w/Chris Bey)	W	IMPACT Before The Impact	8:03
Sep 8	Kyle Fletcher & Mark Davis (w/Chris Bey)	L	IMPACT Wrestling	7:07
Sep 29	Laredo Kid & Trey Miguel (w/Chris Bey)	W	IMPACT Wrestling	8:16
Nov 3	Moose	W	IMPACT Wrestling	7:42
Nov 17	Kyle Fletcher & Mark Davis, Alex Shelley & Chris Sabin, Raj Singh & Shera (w/Chris Bey)	W	IMPACT Wrestling	13:03

ACH

Feb 17	Davey Richards	L	MLW Fusion	8:58
Mar 10	Alex Kane, Calvin Tankman	L	MLW Fusion	8:00
Apr 14	Alex Kane, Juicy Finau, Myron Reed, Puma King	L	MLW Fusion	4:28
May 19	nZo	L	MLW Fusion	6:21
Jul 14	Matt Cross	L	MLW Fusion	6:17

ACTION ANDRETTI

Jan 10	Dante Martin	L	AEW Dark Elevation	1:31
Jan 24	Isiah Kassidy & Marq Quen (w/Myles Hawkins)	L	AEW Dark Elevation	3:20
Oct 10	Josh Woods & Tony Nese (w/Myles Hawkins)	L	AEW Dark Elevation	5:55
Oct 11	QT Marshall	L	AEW Dark	7:01
Dec 14	Chris Jericho	W	AEW Dynamite: Winter Is Coming	9:35
Dec 20	Invictus Khash	W	AEW Dark	3:57

ADAM COLE

Jan 7	Jake Atlas	W	AEW Rampage	9:39
Jan 14	Trent Beretta	W	AEW Rampage	11:34
Jan 18	Kaun	W	AEW Dark	7:53
Jan 19	Orange Cassidy & Kris Statlander (w/Dr. Britt Baker D.M.D.)	W	AEW Dynamite	14:25
Jan 26	Lights Out Match: Orange Cassidy	L	AEW Dynamite: Beach Break	16:56
Feb 4	Evil Uno	W	AEW Rampage	2:28
Feb 18	Ten	W	AEW Rampage: Slam Dunk	9:52
Mar 2	Hangman Page, John Silver & Alex Reynolds (w/Bobby Fish & Kyle O'Reilly)	W	AEW Dynamite	12:43
Mar 6	Hangman Page	L	AEW Revolution '22	25:45
Mar 16	Hangman Page, Jungle Boy & Luchasaurua (w/Bobby Fish & Kyle O'Reilly)	W	AEW Dynamite: St. Patrick's Day Slam	13:58
Mar 23	Jay Lethal	W	AEW Dynamite	10:04
Apr 6	Christian Cage	W	AEW Dynamite	14:56
Apr 15	Texas Death Match: Hangman Page	L	AEW Rampage	20:06
Apr 22	Tomohiro Ishii	W	AEW Rampage	11:14
Apr 27	Dante Martin, Lee Johnson, Brock Anderson, Brian Pillman Jr. & Griff Garrison (w/Matt Jackson, Nick Jackson, Bobby Fish & Kyle O'Reilly)	W	AEW Dynamite	6:28
May 11	Dax Harwood	W	AEW Dynamite	15:34
May 18	Jeff Hardy	W	AEW Dynamite: Wild Card Wednesday	7:10
May 29	Samoa Joe	W	AEW Double Or Nothing '22	12:30
Jun 26	Hangman Page, Jay White, Kazuchika Okada	L	AEW x NJPW Forbidden Door	21:05

ADRIAN QUEST

Mar 26	Elimination Match: Danny Limelight, Jorel Nelson, JR Kratos, Tom Lawlor & Royce Isaacs (w/Clark Connors, Fred Rosser, Taylor Rust & The DKC)	L	NJPW Strong	16:29
May 13	Black Tiger, Danny Limelight & JR Kratos (w/Alex Coughlin & Rocky Romero)	W	NJPW Strong	8:33
Jul 23	David Finlay, Mascara Dorada & Rocky Romero (w/Lucas Riley & Negro Casas)	L	NJPW Strong	11:03
Sep 17	Peter Avalon	L	NJPW Strong	8:52
Nov 12	Danny Limelight & JR Kratos (w/Jordan Cruz)	L	NJPW Strong	8:20
Dec 3	Atlantis Jr. & Virus (w/Rocky Romero)	W	NJPW Strong	10:33

AJ CAZANA

May 17	Colby Corino	L	NWA Power	4:50
Jul 5	Odinson, Judais	L	NWA Power	5:11
Aug 28	Tag Team Battle Royal (w/Anthony Andrews)	L	NWA 74th Anniversary Show	14:07
Dec 13	Colby Corino	L	NWA Power	8:10

AJ STYLES

Jan 3	Omos	L	WWE Monday Night RAW	3:45
Jan 10	Austin Theory	W	WWE Monday Night RAW	7:00
Jan 11	Grayson Waller	W	NXT 2.0	14:15
Jan 24	Austin Theory	W	WWE Monday Night RAW	17:00
Jan 29	Royal Rumble Match	L	WWE Royal Rumble '22	29:06
Jan 31	Rey Mysterio	W	WWE Monday Night RAW	11:35
Feb 7	Damian Priest	W	WWE Monday Night RAW	4:58
Feb 14	Damian Priest	L	WWE Monday Night RAW	4:30
Feb 19	Elimination Chamber: Brock Lesnar, Austin Theory, Riddle, Seth Rollins	L	WWE Elimination Chamber '22	11:00
Mar 21	Seth Rollins	W	WWE Monday Night RAW	22:45
Apr 3	Edge	L	WWE WrestleMania XXXVIII	24:05
Apr 11	Damian Priest	D	WWE Monday Night RAW	13:05
May 2	Damian Priest	W	WWE Monday Night RAW	11:00
May 8	Edge	L	WWE WrestleMania Backlash '22	16:25
May 16	Angel & Humberto (w/Finn Balor)	W	WWE Monday Night RAW	8:30
May 23	Damian Priest & Rhea Ripley (w/Liv Morgan)	L	WWE Monday Night RAW	11:35
Jun 5	Edge, Damian Priest & Rhea Ripley (w/Liv Morgan & Finn Balor)	L	WWE Hell In A Cell '22	16:00
Jun 13	Seth Rollins	L	WWE Monday Night RAW	15:05
Jun 20	Ciampa	W	WWE Monday Night RAW	4:30
Jun 27	Battle Royal	L	WWE Monday Night RAW	19:25
Jun 27	The Miz	W	WWE Monday Night RAW	12:30
Jul 4	The Miz	W	WWE Monday Night RAW	6:25
Jul 11	The Miz & Ciampa (w/Ezekiel)	W	WWE Monday Night RAW	11:29
Jul 18	Theory	W	WWE Monday Night RAW	11:25
Jul 25	Chad Gable & Otis (w/Dolph Ziggler)	W	WWE Monday Night RAW	6:30
Aug 1	The Miz, Mustafa Ali	W	WWE Monday Night RAW	8:50
Aug 1	Ciampa	L	WWE Monday Night RAW	13:30
Aug 8	No DQ: The Miz	W	WWE Monday Night RAW	12:30
Aug 15	Bobby Lashley	L	WWE Monday Night RAW	21:40
Aug 22	The Miz & Ciampa (w/Bobby Lashley)	L	WWE Monday Night RAW	13:30
Aug 29	Finn Balor & Damian Priest (w/Dolph Ziggler)	L	WWE Monday Night RAW	8:34
Sep 26	Sami Zayn	L	WWE Monday Night RAW	20:02
Oct 3	Finn Balor & Damian Priest (w/Rey Mysterio)	L	WWE Monday Night RAW	10:42
Oct 17	Dominik Mysterio	L	WWE Monday Night RAW	14:30
Nov 5	Finn Balor, Damian Priest & Dominik Mysterio (w/Luke Gallows & Karl Anderson)	L	WWE Crown Jewel '22	14:00
Nov 26	Finn Balor	W	WWE Survivor Series WarGames	18:25
Nov 28	Finn Balor, Damian Priest, Dominik Mysterio & Rhea Ripley (w/Luke Gallows, Karl Anderson & Mia Yim)	L	WWE Monday Night RAW	14:20
Dec 5	Baron Corbin, Chad Gable & Otis (w/Luke Gallows & Karl Anderson)	W	WWE Monday Night RAW	14:30
Dec 12	Chad Gable	W	WWE Monday Night RAW	9:05
Dec 19	Sami Zayn	L	WWE Monday Night RAW	12:15

AKIRA TOZAWA

Jan 3	Dana Brooke & Reggie (w/Tamina)	L	WWE Monday Night RAW	1:10
Jan 13	Pete Dunne	L	WWE Main Event	7:11
Jan 20	Tommaso Ciampa	L	WWE Main Event	5:33
Feb 3	Veer Mahaan	L	WWE Main Event	2:14
Feb 28	Dana Brooke & Reggie (w/Tamina)	L	WWE Monday Night RAW	1:40
Mar 21	Dana Brooke & Reggie (w/Tamina)	L	WWE Monday Night RAW	1:05
Apr 1	Andre The Giant Memorial Battle Royal	L	WWE SmackDown	8:05
Apr 25	Dana Brooke & Reggie (w/Tamina)	W	WWE Monday Night RAW	1:30
May 12	Apollo Crews	L	WWE Main Event	6:08
May 26	Commander Azeez	L	WWE Main Event	4:22
Jun 2	Apollo Crews	L	WWE Main Event	6:08
Jun 16	Shelton Benjamin	L	WWE Main Event	6:16
Jun 27	Battle Royal	L	WWE Monday Night RAW	19:25
Jun 30	Ciampa	L	WWE Main Event	8:39
Jul 14	Mustafa Ali	L	WWE Main Event	8:28
Jul 21	Reggie	W	WWE Main Event	6:12
Jul 28	Cedric Alexander & Mustafa Ali (w/T-Bar)	L	WWE Main Event	4:38
Aug 18	Shelton Benjamin	L	WWE Main Event	5:22
Sep 15	R-Truth	L	WWE Main Event	4:42
Oct 20	Cameron Grimes	L	WWE Main Event	4:46

Nov 10	Xyon Quinn	L	WWE Main Event	8:34
Nov 14	Baron Corbin	L	WWE Monday Night RAW	3:35
Nov 24	Grayson Waller	W	WWE Main Event	7:02
Dec 5	Dominik Mysterio	L	WWE Monday Night RAW	2:50
Dec 12	Finn Balor, Damian Priest & Dominik Mysterio	L	WWE Monday Night RAW	14:45
	(w/Angelo Dawkins & Montez Ford)			
Dec 19	Rhea Ripley	L	WWE Monday Night RAW	4:55

ALAN ANGELS

Jan 4	Tony Nese	L	AEW Dark	6:46
Jan 11	Matt Hardy, Serpentico & Isiah Kassidy (w/Hangman Page & Ten)	W	AEW Dark	14:27
Jan 25	Anthony Bowens, Max Caster, Austin Gunn & Colten Gunn	L	AEW Dark	6:15
	(w/Alex Reynolds, Evil Uno & Ten)			
Feb 1	Ari Daivari & Ivictus Khash (w/Ten)	W	AEW Dark	7:44
Feb 14	Jeff Parker, Matt Lee, Daniel Garcia, Anthony Bowens & Max Caster	L	AEW Dark Elevation	5:56
	(w/John Silver, Alex Reynolds, Evil Uno & Stu Grayson)			
Feb 15	Luther & Serpentico (w/Ten)	W	AEW Dark	8:16
Feb 28	Frankie Kazarian	L	AEW Dark Elevation	6:05
Mar 2	Casino Battle Royale (w/Ten)	L	AEW Dynamite	5:07
Mar 8	The Butcher & The Blade (w/Colt Cabana)	L	AEW Dark	5:31
Mar 15	Brandon Cutler, Matt Jackson & Nick Jackson (w/Colt Cabana & Evil Uno)	L	AEW Dark	8:40
Mar 25	Kyle O'Reilly & Bobby Fish (w/Ten)	L	AEW Rampage	7:00
Mar 29	Alexander Zane, Jay Marte & Richard King (w/Evil Uno & Stu Grayson)	W	AEW Dark	3:09
Apr 5	Aaron Solo & Nick Comoroto (w/Ten)	W	AEW Dark	8:08
Apr 11	Luther, Serpentico, Austin Gunn, Colten Gunn & Billy Gunn	W	AEW Dark Elevation	5:20
	(w/John Silver, Alex Reynolds, Stu Grayson & Ten)			
Apr 18	Andrade El Idolo	L	AEW Dark Elevation	4:24
Apr 25	Bulk Nasty, Jake Omen, Luther, RC Dupress & Tito Ortic	W	AEW Dark Elevation	3:09
	(w/Evil Uno, Alex Reynolds, Stu Grayson & Ten)			
May 2	Anthony Bennett, Bret Waters, Cory Bishop, Eli Isom, Jaden Valo &	W	AEW Dark Elevation	1:44
	Mike Law (w/John Silver, Alex Reynolds, Evil Uno, Colt Cabana & Ten)			
May 9	Brandon Scott, Diego, Josh Fuller & Ryan Mooney	W	AEW Dark Elevation	4:27
	(w.Alex Reynolds, Evil Uno & Ten)			
May 24	Lee Moriarty	L	AEW Dark	9:44
Jun 6	Aaron Solo, Anthony Ogogo, Nick Comoroto & QT Marshall	L	AEW Dark Elevation	6:28
	(w/Evil Uno, John Silver & Ten)			
Jun 14	QT Marshall	L	AEW Dark	3:42
Jul 7	Mike Bailey	L	IMPACT Wrestling	8:35
Jul 16	Kyle Fletcher & Mark Davis (w/Evil Uno)	L	NJPW Strong	12:47
Jul 19	Daniel Garcia	L	AEW Dark	9:42
Jul 31	Jonathan Gresham, Konosuke Takeshita, Nick Wayne	L	JCP Ric Flair's Last Match	5:40
Sep 24	Taiji Ishimori	L	NJPW Strong	9:14
Oct 27	Trey Miguel	L	IMPACT Wrestling	8:17
Dec 10	El Phantasmo, Jay White, Jorel Nelson & Royce Isaacs	W	NJPW Strong	13:20
	(w/David Finlay, Hikuleo & Tama Tonga)			
Dec 15	Sami Callihan	L	IMPACT Wrestling	6:53

ALBA FYRE (AS KAY LEE RAY UNTIL MAY 10)

Jan 18	Ivy Nile	L	NXT 2.0	4:25
Jan 25	Mandy Rose, Gigi Dolin & Jacy Jayne (w/Indi Hartwell & Persia Pirotta)	W	NXT 2.0	10:25
Feb 8	Mandy Rose	L	NXT 2.0	7:59
Feb 22	Amari Miller & Lash Legend (w/Io Shirai)	W	NXT 2.0	2:44
Mar 8	Kacy Katanzaro & Kayden Carter (w/Io Shirai)	W	NXT 2.0	7:59
Mar 22	Wendy Choo & Dakota Kai (w/Io Shirai)	W	NXT 2.0	10:22
Apr 2	Mandy Rose, Cora Jade, Io Shirai	L	NXT Stand & Deliver '22	13:27
May 10	Amari Miller	W	NXT 2.0	3:40
May 24	Elektra Lopez	W	NXT 2.0	2:53
Jun 7	Tatum Paxley	W	NXT 2.0	2:38
Jun 21	Lash Legend	W	NXT 2.0	3:31
Jul 19	Battle Royal	L	NXT 2.0	13:13
Aug 2	Lash Legend	W	NXT 2.0	5:31
Oct 11	Jacy Jayne	W	NXT	3:34
Oct 18	Sonya Deville	W	NXT	2:09
Oct 22	Mandy Rose	L	NXT Halloween Havoc '22	7:07
Nov 15	Last Woman Standing: Mandy Rose	L	NXT	11:56
Nov 24	Tamina	W	WWE Main Event	5:21
Dec 10	Isla Dawn	L	NXT Deadline	9:52

ALEX COUGHLIN

Jan 29	JR Kratos	W	NJPW Strong	9:22
Apr 16	Royce Isaacsm Jorel Nelson, JR Kratos, Black Tiger & Danny Limelight	W	NJPW Windy City Riot	13:50
	(w/Fred Rosser, Josh Alexander, Ren Narita & Chris Dickinson)			
May 7	JR Kratos, Royce Isaacs & Tom Lawlor (w/Fred Rosser & The DKC)	L	NJPW Strong	11:12
May 13	JR Kratos, Black Tiger & Danny Limelight (w/Adrian Quest & Rocky Romero)	W	NJPW Strong	8:33
May 17	Aaron Solo, Blake Li, Brick Aldridge, Nick Comoroto & QT Marshall	W	AEW Dark	10:30
	(w/Clark Connors, Karl Fredericks, Kevin Knight & Yuya Uemura)			
Jun 18	JR Kratos, Jorel Nelson & Royce Isaacs (w/Kevin Knight & The DKC)	L	NJPW Strong	9:21
Jun 26	Max Caster, Billy Gunn, Austin Gunn & Colten Gunn	L	AEW x NJPW Forbidden Door Buy-In	5:35
	(w/The DKC, Kevin Knight & Yuya Uemura)			

ALEX KANE

Mar 3	Calvin Tankman	W	MLW Fusion	8:08
Mar 10	ACH, Calvin Tankman	W	MLW Fusion	8:00
Apr 14	ACH, Juicy Finau, Myron Reed, Puma King	W	MLW Fusion	4:28
Jul 7	Davey Richards	D	MLW Fusion	20:00
Nov 17	Davey Richards	L	MLW Fusion	12:52
Dec 22	Five Minute Challenge: D3	W	MLW Fusion	2:02

ALEX REYNOLDS

Jan 3	Mike Orlando & Shayne Stetson (w/John Silver)	W	AEW Dark Elevation	3:48
Jan 10	Isiah Kassidy, Marq Quen & The Blade (w/John Silver & Ten)	W	AEW Dark Elevation	4:01
Jan 14	Jungle Boy & Luchasaurus (w/John Silver)	L	AEW Rampage	12:37
Jan 25	Anthony Bowens, Max Caster, Austin Gunn & Colten Gunn (w/Alan Angels, Evil Uno & Ten)	L	AEW Dark	6:15
Feb 14	Jeff Parker, Matt Lee, Daniel Garcia, Anthony Bowens & Max Caster (w/John Silver, Evil Uno, Alan Angels & Stu Grayson)	L	AEW Dark Elevation	5:56
Feb 15	Ari Daivari & Invictus Khash (w/John Silver)	W	AEW Dark	5:40
Feb 23	Tag Team Battle Royal (w/John Silver)	L	AEW Dynamite	:51
Mar 2	Adam Cole, Bobby Fish & Kyle O'Reilly (w/Hangman Page & John Silver)	L	AEW Dynamite	12:43
Mar 14	Luther & Serpentico (w/John Silver)	W	AEW Dark Elevation	4:40
Mar 15	Luther & Serpentico (w/John Silver)	W	AEW Dark	4:26
Mar 23	Chris Jericho & Daniel Garcia (wJohn Silver)	L	AEW Dynamite	10:02
Mar 29	Brandon Bullock, Foxx Vinyer & Jameson Ryan (w/John Silver & Ten)	W	AEW Dark	3:20
Apr 11	Luther, Serpentico, Austin Gunn, Colten Gunn & Billy Gunn (w/John Silver, Alan Angels, Stu Grayson & Ten)	W	AEW Dark Elevation	5:20
Apr 18	Allen Russell, Dale Springs, Izaiah Zane & Kameron Russell (w/John Silver, Evil Uno & Stu Grayson)	W	AEW Dark Elevation	2:17
Apr 25	Bulk Nasty, Jake Omen, Luther, RC Dupree & Tito Ortic (w/Evil Uno, Alan Angels, Stu Grayson & Ten)	W	AEW Dark Elevation	3:09
May 2	Anthony Bennett, Bret Waters, Cory Bishop, Eli Isorn, Jaden Valo & Mike Law (w/John Silver, Alan Angels, Evil Uno, Colt Cabana & Ten)	W	AEW Dark Elevation	1:44
May 9	Brandon Scott, Diego, Josh Fuller & Ryan Mooney (w/Alan Angels, Evil Uno & Ten)	W	AEW Dark Elevation	4:27
May 10	Jake Manning	W	AEW Dark	4:00
May 16	Brody King	L	AEW Dark Elevation	1:46
May 23	Lee Moriarty	L	AEW Dark Elevation	4:04
Jun 7	Max Caster, Austin Gunn & Colten Gunn (w/John Silver & Ten)	L	AEW Dark	5:26
Jun 21	Cezar Bononi & Peter Avalon (w/John Silver)	W	AEW Dark	5:01
Jun 27	Max Caster, Austin Gunn & Colten Gunn (w/Evil Uno & Ten)	L	AEW Dark Elevation	4:08
Jul 4	Aaron Solo, Nick Comoroto & QT Marshall (w/Evil Uno & Ten)	W	AEW Dark Elevation	7:56
Jul 5	Cezar Bononi, JD Drake, Peter Avalon & Ryan Nemeth (w/John Silver, Evil Uno & Ten)	W	AEW Dark	7:22
Jul 15	Malakai Black & Brody King (w/John Silver)	L	AEW Rampage	8:18
Jul 26	Ryan Nemeth	W	AEW Dark	5:56
Aug 8	Lord Crew & TUG Cooper (w/John Silver)	W	AEW Dark Elevation	2:13
Aug 15	Adam Grace, Drew System, Rylie Jackson & TUG Cooper (w/John Silver, Evil Uno & Ten)	W	AEW Dark Elevation	2:25
Aug 22	Alexander Apollo, D'Mone Solavino & RC Dupree (w/John Silver & Ten)	W	AEW Dark Elevation	3:22
Aug 23	DK Vandu, Joey Sweets & Tyshaun Perez (w/John Silver & Ten)	W	AEW Dark	3:38
Aug 26	Malakai Black, Brody King & Buddy Matthews (w/Ten & John Silver)	W	AEW Rampage	9:03
Sep 2	Orange Cassidy, Chuck Taylor & Trent Beretta (w/Hangman Page & John Silver)	W	AEW Rampage	11:12
Sep 3	Aaron Solo, Cole Karter & Nick Comoroto (w/Hangman Page & John Silver)	W	AEW Dark Elevation	6:00
Sep 4	Kenny Omega, Matt Jackson & Nick Jackson (w/Hangman Page & John Silver)	L	AEW All Out '22	19:50
Sep 20	Alexander Moss & Zuka (w/John Silver)	W	AEW Dark	4:50
Oct 7	Pac, Penta El Zero M & Rey Fenix (w/Ten & John Silver)	L	AEW Rampage	21:01
Oct 18	Jordano, Shayne Hawke, Tyler Tirva & Zak Patterson (w/John Silver, Evil Uno & Ten)	W	AEW Dark	6:52
Nov 7	Kip Sabian	L	AEW Dark Elevation	8:15
Nov 8	Ativalu, Fulton & Troy Hollywood (w/John Silver & Evil Uno)	W	AEW Dark	2:22
Nov 15	Arjun Singh, Brett Gosselin & Mike Magnum (w/John Silver & Evil Uno)	W	AEW Dark	4:43
Nov 21	Kip Sabian	W	AEW Dark Elevation	1:56
Nov 22	Ari Daivari, Jeeves Jay & Sonny Kiss (w/John Silver & Evil Uno)	W	AEW Dark	5:26
Nov 25	Rush, The Butcher & The Blade (w/Ten & John Silver)	L	AEW Rampage: Black Friday	7:24
Dec 5	Kip Sabian	L	AEW Dark Elevation	6:25
Dec 23	$300,000 Three Kings Christmas Casino Trios Royale (w/Evil Uno & John Silver)	L	AEW Rampage	22:01

ALEX SHELLEY

Mar 17	Chris Bey & Jay White (w/Chris Sabin)	W	IMPACT Wrestling	12:38
Mar 31	Chris Bey & Jay White (w/Chris Sabin)	L	IMPACT Wrestling	17:42
Apr 1	Mike Bailey	L	IMPACT Multiverse Of Matches	15:03
Apr 14	Steve Maclin	W	IMPACT Wrestling	10:00
Apr 28	Eddie Edwards, Matt Taven & Mike Bennett (w/Chris Sabin & Mike Bailey)	L	IMPACT Wrestling	7:35
May 12	Gauntlet For The Gold	L	IMPACT Wrestling	39:00
May 26	Trey Miguel	L	IMPACT Wrestling	12:26
Jun 9	Eddie Edwards, Matt Taven & Mike Bennett (w/Chris Sabin & Frankie Kazarian)	L	IMPACT Wrestling	16:47
Jun 19	Eddie Edwards, Matt Taven, Mike Bennett, PCO & Vincent	W	IMPACT Slammiversary XX	18:45

	(w/Chris Sabin, Davey Richards, Frankie Kazarian & Magnus)			
Jul 14	Eric Young, Deaner & Joe Doering (w/Chris Sabin & Josh Alexander)	W	IMPACT Wrestling	11:56
Jul 21	Chris Sabin	W	IMPACT Wrestling	17:09
Jul 30	Kushida	D	NJPW Music City Mayhem	20:00
Jul 31	Davey Richards & Eddie Edwards (w/Chris Sabin)	W	JCP Ric Flair's Last Match	11:06
Aug 4	Deaner & Joe Doering (w/Chris Sabin)	W	IMPACT Wrestling	6:23
Aug 25	Deaner, Eric Young & Joe Doering (w/Chris Sabin & Kushida)	W	IMPACT Wrestling	15:18
Sep 4	Wardlow, Dax Harwood & Cash Wheeler (w/Jay Lethal & Chris Sabin)	L	AEW All Out '22	16:30
Sep 15	Luke Gallows & Karl Anderson (w/Chris Sabin)	W	IMPACT Wrestling	14:39
Sep 22	Kyle Fletcher & Mark Davis (w/Chris Sabin)	W	IMPACT Wrestling	15:31
Oct 6	Matt Taven	W	IMPACT Wrestling	9:50
Oct 7	Matt Taven & Mike Bennett (w/Chris Sabin)	L	IMPACT Bound For Glory '22	16:35
Oct 13	Raj Singh & Shera (w/Chris Sabin)	W	IMPACT Before The Impact	7:16
Oct 27	Matt Cardona	L	IMPACT Wrestling	8:42
Oct 28	Kyle Fletcher & Mark Davis, Kevin Knight & The DKC (w/Chris Sabin)	W	NJPW Rumble On 44th Street	13:42
Nov 17	Ace Austin & Chris Bey, Kyle Fletcher & Mark Davis, Raj Singh & Shera (w/Chris Sabin)	L	IMPACT Wrestling	13:03
Dec 8	Heath & Rhino (w/Chris Sabin)	D	IMPACT Wrestling	8:34
Dec 15	Heath & Rhino (w/Chris Sabin)	W	IMPACT Wrestling	14:04
Dec 17	Barrett Brown & Misterioso (w/Chris Sabin)	W	NJPW Strong	12:11

ALEX TAYLOR

Jan 5	Jamie Stanley, Jeremiah Plunkett, Miguel Robles	L	NWA Power	5:31
Feb 1	Handicap Match: Dirty Dango & JTG (w/Captain Yuma & Rush Freeman)	L	NWA Power	4:09
Feb 8	Team War: Odinson, Parrow & Rodney Mack, Jordan Clearwater, Tyrus & Marshe Rockett, Aron Stevens, JR Kratos & Judais (w/Rush Freeman & Jeremiah Plunkett)	L	NWA Power	11:40
Mar 8	BLK Jeez, Jordan Clearwater, Marshe Rockett & Tyrus (w/Rush Freeman, Cyon & Mims)	L	NWA Power	6:59
Mar 19	Doug Williams & Harry Smith (w/Rush Freeman)	L	NWA Crockett Cup '22	6:38
Mar 29	Mike Knox & VSK (w/Rush Freeman)	L	NWA Power	4:18
May 17	Team War: Jax Dane, Odinson & Parrow, BLK Jeez, Jordan Clearwater & Marshe Rockett (w/Jeremiah Plunkett & Rush Freeman)	L	NWA Power	6:54
Jun 21	Cyon & Tyrus (w/Jeremiah Plunkett)	L	NWA Power	7:40
Aug 2	Gaagz The Gymp, Judais & Sal The Pal (w/Jeremiah Plunkett & Rush Freeman)	L	NWA Power	8:08
Aug 27	Beelzebub's Bedlam Match: Judais, Sal The Pal & Gaagz The Gimp (w/Jeremiah Plunkett & Danny Dealz)	L	NWA 74th Anniversary Show	9:41
Aug 28	Tag Team Battle Royal (w/Jeremiah Plunkett)	L	NWA 74th Anniversary Show	14:07
Dec 13	Luke Hawx	W	NWA Power	6:33
Dec 20	PJ Hawx	W	NWA Power	7:11

ALEX ZAYNE

Jan 29	Ari Daivari	W	NJPW Strong	10:07
Apr 1	Swerve Strickland	L	ROH Supercard Of Honor XV	11:40
May 19	Calvin Tankman & EJ Nduka (w/Mr. Thomas)	L	MLW Fusion	7:26
Jun 4	Chris Bey & El Phantasmo (w/Christopher Daniels)	L	NJPW Strong	9:58
Jun 19	Ultimate X Match: Mike Bailey, Ace Austin, Andrew Everett, Kenny King, Trey Miguel	L	IMPACT Slammiversary XX	9:50
Jun 30	Ace Austin	L	IMPACT Wrestling	6:57
Jul 30	Kyle Fletcher, Mark Davis & TJP (w/Cash Wheeler & Dax Harwood)	L	NJPW Music City Mayhem	14:30
Sep 1	Mascara Dorada	L	IMPACT Wrestling	8:08
Sep 22	Black Taurus, Laredo Kid, Mia Yim, Trey Miguel	L	IMPACT Wrestling	11:58
Oct 6	Juice Robinson	L	IMPACT Before The Impact	9:27
Oct 13	Trey Miguel, Black Taurus, Kenny King, Laredo Kid, Yuya Uemura	L	IMPACT Wrestling	5:19
Oct 29	Blake Christian & Mascara Dorada (w/Mistico)	W	NJPW Strong	10:09
Nov 5	Aaron Henare, Gideon Grey, Kyle Fletcher & Mark Davis (w/Hiroshi Tanahashi, Toru Yano & David Finlay)	L	NJPW Battle Autumn '22	9:50

ALEXA BLISS

Feb 19	Elimination Chamber: Bianca Belair, Doudrop, Liv Morgan, Nikki A.S.H., Rhea Ripley	L	WWE Elimination Chamber '22	15:45
May 9	Sonya Deville	W	WWE Monday Night RAW	:40
May 16	Sonya Deville	W	WWE Monday Night RAW	4:00
May 23	Nikki A.S.H.	W	WWE Monday Night RAW	3:00
May 30	Doudrop	W	WWE Monday Night RAW	3:20
Jun 6	Rhea Ripley, Liv Morgan, Doudrop	L	WWE Monday Night RAW	14:35
Jun 13	Nikki A.S.H. & Doudrop (w/Liv Morgan)	W	WWE Monday Night RAW	4:25
Jun 20	Carmella, Asuka, Becky Lynch, Liv Morgan	L	WWE Monday Night RAW	12:30
Jun 27	Liv Morgan	L	WWE Monday Night RAW	3:20
Jul 1	Raquel Rodriguez, Lacey Evans & Shotzi (w/Liv Morgan & Asuka)	W	WWE SmackDown	13:14
Jul 2	Money In The Bank Ladder Match: Liv Morgan, Asuka, Becky Lynch Lacey Evans, Raquel Rodriguez, Shotzi	L	WWE Money In The Bank '22	16:35
Jul 11	Nikki A.S.H. & Doudrop (w/Asuka)	W	WWE Monday Night RAW	4:15
Jul 18	Nikki A.S.H., Doudrop & Tamina (w/Asuka & Dana Brooke)	W	WWE Monday Night RAW	2:35
Jul 25	Doudrop	W	WWE Monday Night RAW	4:20
Aug 1	Asuka	D	WWE Monday Night RAW	2:20
Aug 15	Nikki A.S.H. & Doudrop (w/Asuka)	W	WWE Monday Night RAW	9:00
Aug 22	Dakota Kai & Iyo Sky (w/Asuka)	L	WWE Monday Night RAW	18:30
Aug 27	Katie Ark, Kay Sparks & Dani Mo (w/Asuka & Bianca Belair)	W	WWE Monday Night RAW	3:19
Sep 3	Bayley, Dakota Kai & Iyo Sky (w/Asuka & Bianca Belair)	L	WWE Clash At The Castle	18:44
Sep 19	Bayley	L	WWE Monday Night RAW	15:05

Oct 3	Iyo Sky	L	WWE Monday Night RAW	9:15
Oct 31	Dakota Kai & Iyo Sky (w/Asuka)	W	WWE Monday Night RAW	16:25
Nov 5	Dakota Kai & Iyo Sky (w/Asuka)	L	WWE Crown Jewel '22	12:50
Nov 26	WarGames: Bayley, Dakota Kai, Iyo Sky, Nikki Cross, Rhea Ripley (w/Bianca Belair, Asuka, Mia Yim & Becky Lynch)	W	WWE Survivor Series WarGames	39:40
Dec 5	Nikki Cross, Becky Lynch	W	WWE Monday Night RAW	16:30
Dec 12	Bayley	W	WWE Monday Night RAW	13:25

ALEXANDER HAMMERSTONE

Feb 10	Falls Count Anywhere: Pagano	W	MLW Fusion	17:15
Mar 10	Davey Richards	W	MLW Fusion	19:14
Apr 29	Jacob Fatu, Mads Krugger	W	MLW Fusion	13:34
May 26	Cesar Duran	W	MLW Fusion	1:40
Jun 9	King Muertes, Mads Krugger & Richard Holliday (w/Marshall Von Erich & Ross Von Erich)	L	MLW Fusion	9:31
Jul 14	Richard Holliday	W	MLW Fusion	9:53
Nov 24	Falls Count Anywhere: Richard Holliday	W	MLW Fusion	21:55
Dec 1	Bandido	W	MLW Fusion	16:04

ALICIA FOX

Jan 29	Royal Rumble Match	L	WWE Royal Rumble '22	6:30

ALISHA EDWARDS

Jan 8	Ultimate X Match: Tasha Steelz, Chelsea Green, Jordynne Grace, Lady Frost, Rosemary	L	IMPACT Hard To Kill '22	9:00
Feb 10	Lady Frost	L	IMPACT Before The Impact	6:05
Mar 31	Battle Royal	L	IMPACT Wrestling	7:15
May 12	Madison Rayne & Tenille Dashwood (w/Gisele Shaw)	L	IMPACT Wrestling	12:00
Jun 2	Renee Michelle	W	IMPACT Before The Impact	6:15
Jun 16	Masha Slamovich	L	IMPACT Wrestling	:58
Jul 7	Gisele Shaw	L	IMPACT Before The Impact	8:21
Aug 4	Savannah Evans	L	IMPACT Before The Impact	7:33
Aug 25	Jessicka	L	IMPACT Wrestling	1:56
Sep 15	Killer Kelly	L	IMPACT Wrestling	2:13
Dec 1	Ladybird Johnson (Jessicka)	L	IMPACT Before The Impact	8:28

ALIYAH

Jan 14	Natalya	W	WWE SmackDown	:03
Jan 21	Natalya	W	WWE SmackDown	2:10
Jan 29	Royal Rumble Match	L	WWE Royal Rumble '22	22:50
Feb 4	Natalya	W	WWE SmackDown	4:08
Feb 11	Hart Dungeon Style Match: Natalya	L	WWE SmackDown	2:40
Apr 29	"I Quit" Beat The Clock Challenge: Charlotte Flair	D	WWE SmackDown	1:41
Jun 3	Natalya, Raquel Rodriguez, Shotzi, Shayna Baszler, Xia Li	L	WWE SmackDown	5:54
Jul 29	Shotzi	L	WWE SmackDown	3:20
Aug 5	Gauntlet Match: Shayna Baszler, Sonya Deville, Raquel Rodriguez, Shotzi, Xia Li, Natalya	L	WWE SmackDown	21:05
Aug 12	Shotzi & Xia Li (w/Raquel Rodriguez)	W	WWE SmackDown	9:35
Aug 22	Bayley	L	WWE Monday Night RAW	6:45
Aug 26	Natalya & Sonya Deville (w/Raquel Rodriguez)	W	WWE SmackDown	8:00
Aug 29	Dakota Kai & Iyo Sky (w/Raquel Rodriguez)	W	WWE Monday Night RAW	11:17
Sep 5	Nikki A.S.H. & Doudrop (w/Raquel Rodriguez)	W	WWE Monday Night RAW	3:45
Sep 9	Jacy Jayne & Gigi Dolin (w/Raquel Rodriguez)	W	WWE SmackDown	5:00
Sep 12	Dakota Kai & Iyo Sky (w/Raquel Rodriguez)	L	WWE Monday Night RAW	12:30

ALLYSIN KAY

Jan 18	Kylie Rae	L	NWA Power	5:43
Mar 20	Ella Envy & Kenzie Paige (w/Marti Belle)	W	NWA Crockett Cup '22	7:09
Mar 22	Jennacide & Paola Blaze (w/Marti Belle)	W	NWA Power	7:24
May 17	Kenzie Pge & Madi Wrenkowski (w/Martin Belle)	W	NWA Power	5:16
Jun 11	Ella Envy & Kenzie Paige (w/Marti Belle)	L	NWA Alwayz Ready '22	8:35
Jul 12	KiLynn King	L	NWA Power	6:47
Aug 28	Kingshighway Steet Fight: Ella Envy & Kenzie Paige (w/Marti Belle)	L	NWA 74th Anniversary Show	10:02
Sep 6	Kamille	D	NWA Power	10:00
Oct 11	Natalia Markova & Taryn Terrell (w/Marti Belle)	W	NWA Power	5:33
Nov 8	Kamille & KiLynn King (w/Marti Belle)	L	NWA Power	7:31
Dec 20	KiLynn King	L	NWA Power	7:55

AMALE

Jan 13	Stevie Turner	W	NXT UK	3:59
Jan 27	Jinny	L	NXT UK	6:31
Feb 10	Nina Samuels	W	NXT UK	5:17
Feb 24	Xia Brookside	W	NXT UK	6:14
Mar 31	Xia Brookside	L	NXT UK	5:51
May 19	Eliza Alexander & Xia Brookside (w/Angel Hayze)	L	NXT UK	5:54
Jun 9	Eliza Alexander	L	NXT UK	6:51
Jul 14	Stevie Turner	W	NXT UK	4:15
Jul 28	Blair Davenport	L	NXT UK	5:46
Aug 18	Nina Samuels	W	NXT UK	6:31
Sep 1	Elimination Match: Blair Davenport, Eliza Alexander, Isla Dawn	L	NXT UK	15:07

AMARI MILLER

Jan 11	Wendy Choo, Indi Hartwell & Persia Pirotta	L	NXT 2.0	3:40
	(w/Kacy Katanzara & Kayden Carter)			
Jan 28	Valentina Feroz & Yulisa Leon (w/Lash Legend)	L	WWE 205 Live	6:29
Feb 1	Wendy Choo	L	NXT 2.0	3:26
Feb 22	Io Shirai & Kay Lee Ray (w/Lash Legend)	L	NXT 2.0	2:44
Mar 1	Lash Legend	L	NXT 2.0	2:57
Apr 29	Arianna Grace	L	NXT 2.0	5:15
May 10	Alba Fyre	L	NXT 2.0	3:40
May 27	Arianna Grace	W	NXT Level Up	5:14
Jul 1	Sloane Jacobs	W	NXT Level Up	5:54
Jul 19	Battle Royal	L	NXT 2.0	13:13
Aug 26	Kiana James	L	NXT Level Up	4:59
Sep 16	Indi Hartwell	L	NXT Level Up	5:10
Sep 27	Sol Ruca	L	NXT	4:48
Nov 25	Elektra Lopez	L	NXT Level Up	4:30
Dec 13	Lyra Valkyria	L	NXT	3:03
Dec 30	Thea Hail	L	NXT Level Up	5:53

ANDRADE EL IDOLO

Jan 3	JP Harlow	W	AEW Dark Elevation	2:58
Jan 10	Avery Good	W	AEW Dark Elevation	2:30
Feb 21	Baron Black, Carlie Bravo, Chandler Hopkins, Jameson Ryan &	W	AEW Dark Elevation	4:20
	Shawn Dean (w/Isiah Kassidy, Marq Quen, The Butcher & The Blade)			
Feb 25	Sammy Guevara	L	AEW Rampage	12:23
Mar 4	Sammy Guevara, Darby Allin	L	AEW Rampage	13:12
Mar 6	Tornado Match: Darby Allin, Sammy Guevara & Sting	L	AEW Revolution '22	13:20
	(w/Matt Hardy & Isiah Kassidy)			
Mar 30	Darby Allin	W	AEW Dynamite	10:32
Apr 18	Alan Angels	W	AEW Dark Elevation	4:24
Apr 20	Coffin Match: Darby Allin	L	AEW Dynamite	12:25
Apr 30	Bandido, Pagano & Taya Valkyrie (w/Cibernetico & Deonna Purrazzo)	L	AAA TripleMania XXX: Monterrey	18:53
Jun 8	Casino Battle Royale	W	AEW Dynamite	24:59
Jun 20	Frankie Kazarian	W	AEW Dark Elevation	8:43
Jun 24	Rey Fenix	W	AEW Rampage	16:29
Jul 31	Jay Lethal & Jeff Jarrett (w/Ric Flair)	W	JCP Ric Flair's Last Match	26:40
Aug 10	Tornado Match: Penta El Zero M & Rey Fenix (w/Rush)	W	AEW Dynamite: Quake By The Lake	13:45
Aug 17	Kenny Omega, Matt Jackson & Nick Jackson (w/Rush & Dragon Lee)	L	AEW Dynamite	20:54
Sep 4	Casino Ladder Match: MJF, Claudio Castagnoli, Penta El Zero M,	L	AEW All Out '22	14:15
	Rey Fenix, Rush, Wheeler Yuta, Dante Martin			

ANDRE CHASE

Jan 25	Zack Gibson & James Drake (w/Bodhi Haward)	L	NXT 2.0	5:11
Feb 1	Draco Anthony	W	NXT 2.0	4:36
Mar 1	Von Wagner	L	NXT 2.0	4:10
Apr 8	Channing Lauren & Troy Donovan (w/Bodhi Hayward)	W	NXT Level Up	6:47
Apr 29	Quincy Elliott	W	NXT Level Up	6:18
May 10	Tiffany Stratton & Grayson Waller (w/Sarray)	W	NXT 2.0	7:00
May 17	Grayson Waller	L	NXT 2.0	4:12
May 27	Bryson Montana & Damaris Griffin (w/Bodhi Hayward)	W	NXT Level Up	3:53
Jun 7	Handicap Match: Elton Prince & Kit Wilson	L	NXT 2.0	3:16
Jul 15	Javier Bernal & Myles Borne (w/Bodhi Hayward)	W	NXT Level Up	5:47
Jul 26	Giovanni Vinci	L	NXT 2.0	9:10
Aug 12	Bronco Nima & Lucien Price	W	NXT Level Up	6:16
Aug 18	Eddie Dennis & Saxon Huxley (w/Bodhi Hayward)	W	NXT UK	6:49
Aug 30	Charlie Dempsey	W	NXT 2.0	5:17
Sep 20	Carmelo Hayes & Trick Williams (w/Bodhi Hayward)	W	NXT	4:15
Sep 23	Myles Borne	W	NXT Level Up	5:34
Oct 4	Von Wagner	L	NXT	3:36
Oct 21	Javier Bernal	W	NXT Level Up	6:48
Nov 8	Charlie Dempsey	L	NXT	2:59
Nov 22	Elton Prince & Kit Wilson (w/Duke Hudson)	L	NXT	8:17
Dec 6	Axiom, Von Wagner	L	NXT	11:54
Dec 16	Javier Bernal & Xyon Quinn (w/Duke Hudson)	W	NXT Level Up	7:16
Dec 22	Cedric Alexander	L	WWE Main Event	5:10

ANGEL

Jan 14	Erik & Ivar, Cesaro & Mansoor, Jinder Mahal & Shanky (w/Humberto)	L	WWE SmackDown	13:21
Jan 21	Erik & Ivar (w/Humberto)	L	WWE SmackDown	2:20
Feb 4	Big E & Kofi Kingston (w/Humberto)	L	WWE SmackDown	8:58
Feb 11	Big E & Kofi Kingston (w/Humberto)	W	WWE SmackDown	10:20
Feb 25	Big E & Kofi Kingston (w/Humberto)	L	WWE SmackDown	10:30
Mar 18	Shinsuke Nakamura & Rick Boogs (w/Humberto)	L	WWE SmackDown	4:55
Mar 25	Ricochet	W	WWE SmackDown	2:10
Apr 1	Ricochet, Humberto	L	WWE SmackDown	11:20
Apr 22	Madcap Moss	L	WWE SmackDown	2:25
May 16	Finn Balor & AJ Styles (w/Humberto)	L	WWE Monday Night RAW	8:30
May 27	Jinder Mahal & Shanky (w/Humberto)	W	WWE SmackDown	2:15
Jul 8	Jimmy Uso & Jey Uso (w/Humberto)	L	WWE SmackDown	2:00
Sep 5	Chad Gable & Otis, Kofi Kingston & Xavier Woods,	D	WWE Monday Night RAW	14:30
	Angelo Dawkins & Montez Ford (w/Humberto)			
Sep 9	Angelo Dawkins, Montez Ford, Ashante Adonis & Top Dolla	L	WWE SmackDown	8:35

	(w/Humberto, Mace & Mansoor)			
Sep 30	Ashante Adonis & Top Dolla (w/Humberto)	L	WWE SmackDown	3:21
Dec 23	Rey Mysterio	L	WWE SmackDown	4:18

ANGEL HAYZE

Feb 17	Emilia McKenzie	L	NXT UK	4:57
Apr 14	Eliza Alexander	L	NXT UK	4:12
Apr 28	Xia Brookside	L	NXT UK	5:05
May 19	Eliza Alexander & Xia Brookside (w/Amale)	L	NXT UK	5:54
Jun 2	Stevie Turner	L	NXT UK	4:04
Jun 30	Blair Davenport	L	NXT UK	5:32

ANGELICO

Apr 18	Jeff Hardy, Matt Hardy, Dante Martin & Darius Martin (w/Isiah Kassidy, Marq Quen & Jack Evans)	L	AEW Dark Elevation	9:45
Apr 26	Frankie Kazarian, Matt Hardy, Jeff Hardy, Dante Martin & Darius Martin (w/Max Caster, Isiah Kassidy, Marq Quen & The Blade)	L	AEW Dark	12:40
May 3	Yuya Uemura	W	AEW Dark	8:55
May 4	Bryan Danielson, Jon Moxley & Wheeler Yuta (w/The Butcher & The Blade)	L	AEW Dynamite	7:27
May 17	Anthony Catena & Baron Black (w/Jora Johl)	W	AEW Dark	4:30
Jul 12	Logan Laroux	W	AEW Dark	3:52
Jul 18	Brandon Bullock, Bryce Cannon & Jameson Ryan (w/The Butcher & The Blade)	W	AEW Dark Elevation	1:42
Jul 25	Adrian Alanis, AR Fox & Liam Gray (w/Isiah Kassidy & Marq Quen)	W	AEW Dark Elevation	3:59
Aug 1	JCruz, Joey Ace, Victory Chase, Jaylen Brandyn & Traevon Jordan (w/Isiah Kassidy, Marq Quen, The Butcher & The Blade)	W	AEW Dark Elevation	2:12
Aug 16	Baliyan Akki	W	AEW Dark	3:04
Sep 3	Orange Cassidy, Chuck Taylor & Trent Beretta (w/The Butcher & The Blade)	L	AEW Dark Elevation	8:13
Sep 13	Matt Hardy	L	AEW Dark	6:32
Sep 27	Caleb Konley	W	AEW Dark	3:42
Nov 7	Rocky Romero, Chuck Taylor & Trent Beretta (w/The Butcher & The Blade)	L	AEW Dark Elevation	7:20
Nov 29	Hagane Shinno	W	AEW Dark	4:25
Dec 20	Jarett Diaz, Jay Marti & Richard Adonis (w/Luther & Serpentico)	W	AEW Dark	4:07
Dec 23	$300,000 Three Kings Christmas Casino Trios Royale (w/Luther & Serpentico)	L	AEW Rampage	22:01
Dec 27	Dante Casanova	W	AEW Dark	2:37

ANGELINA LOVE

Apr 26	Tootie Lynn	W	NWA Power	5:14
Aug 16	Paola Blaze & Rylee Rockett (w/Chelsea Green)	W	NWA Power	4:00
Aug 27	Burke Invitational Gauntlet	L	NWA 74th Anniversary Show	17:24
Sep 13	Ella Envy, Kenzie Paige & Roxy (w/Max The Impaler & Natalia Markova)	W	NWA Power	3:11
Sep 13	Max The Impaler, Natalia Markova	D	NWA Power	3:48
Oct 18	Chelsea Green	L	NWA Power	8:02

ANGELO DAWKINS

Jan 1	Randy Orton & Riddle (w/Montez Ford)	L	WWE Day 1	11:15
Jan 3	Apollo Crews & Commander Azeez (w/Montez Ford)	W	WWE Monday Night RAW	2:15
Jan 10	Dolph Ziggler, Robert Roode & Apollo Crews (w/Montez Ford & Damian Priest)	L	WWE Monday Night RAW	8:30
Jan 17	Apollo Crews, Commander Azeez, Dolph Ziggler & Robert Roode (w/Rey Mysterio, Dominik Mysterio & Montez Ford)	W	WWE Monday Night RAW	8:00
Jan 24	Rey Mysterio & Dominik Mysterio (w/Montez Ford)	L	WWE Monday Night RAW	8:00
Jan 29	Royal Rumble Match	L	WWE Royal Rumble '22	2:15
Jan 31	Dolph Ziggler	W	WWE Monday Night RAW	4:30
Feb 7	Chad Gable & Otis (w/Montez Ford)	L	WWE Monday Night RAW	5:37
Feb 14	Dolph Ziggler & Robert Roode (w/Montez Ford)	W	WWE Monday Night RAW	2:50
Feb 21	Chad Gable & Otis (w/Montez Ford)	L	WWE Monday Night RAW	9:05
Feb 28	Randy Orton & Riddle (w/Montez Ford)	W	WWE Monday Night RAW	8:35
Mar 10	Cedric Alexander & Shelton Benjamin (w/Montez Ford)	W	WWE Main Event	9:23
Apr 3	Randy Orton & Riddle, Chad Gable & Otis (w/Montez Ford)	L	WWE WrestleMania XXXVIII	11:30
Apr 4	Chad Gable & Otis (w/Montez Ford)	W	WWE Monday Night RAW	8:25
Apr 11	Jimmy Uso & Jey Uso (w/Montez Ford)	L	WWE Monday Night RAW	15:10
Apr 18	Randy Orton & Riddle (w/Montez Ford)	W	WWE Monday Night RAW	7:50
Apr 28	Cedric Alexander & Shelton Benjamin (w/Montez Ford)	W	WWE Main Event	9:31
May 2	Kevin Owens, Chad Gable & Otis (w/Montez Ford & Ezekiel)	L	WWE Monday Night RAW	9:45
May 9	Randy Orton & Riddle (w/Montez Ford)	L	WWE Monday Night RAW	9:58
May 19	Apollo Crews & Commander Azeez (w/Montez Ford)	W	WWE Main Event	4:23
May 23	Sami Zayn, Jimmy Uso & Jey Uso (w/Riddle & Montez Ford)	W	WWE Monday Night RAW	12:35
Jun 6	Jimmy Uso & Jey Uso (w/Montez Ford)	W	WWE Monday Night RAW	16:30
Jun 20	Jey Uso	W	WWE Monday Night RAW	7:20
Jul 2	Jimmy Uso & Jey Uso (w/Montez Ford)	L	WWE Money In The Bank '22	23:00
Jul 4	Theory, Chad Gable & Otis (w/Bobby Lashley & Montez Ford)	W	WWE Monday Night RAW	10:05
Jul 11	Omos, Jimmy Uso & Jey Uso (w/R-Truth & Montez Ford)	L	WWE Monday Night RAW	11:30
Jul 15	Jimmy Uso	W	WWE SmackDown	7:00
Jul 18	Omos	W	WWE Monday Night RAW	1:20
Jul 18	MVP & Omos (w/Montez Ford)	W	WWE Monday Night RAW	4:50
Jul 22	Theory, Jimmy Uso & Jey Uso (w/Madcap Moss & Montez Ford)	W	WWE SmackDown	17:00
Jul 25	Roman Reigns, Jimmy Uso & Jey Uso (w/Riddle & Montez Ford)	L	WWE Monday Night RAW	19:25
Jul 30	Jimmy Uso & Jey Uso (w/Montez Ford)	L	WWE SummerSlam '22	13:25
Aug 8	Seth Rollins	L	WWE Monday Night RAW	8:50

Aug 18	Chad Gable & Otis (w/Montez Ford)	W	WWE Main Event	6:49
Aug 29	Chad Gable & Otis (w/Montez Ford)	W	WWE Monday Night RAW	16:04
Sep 3	Austin Theory, Chad Gable & Otis (w/Madcap Moss & Montez Ford)	W	WWE Clash At The Castle Kickoff	6:29
Sep 5	Chad Gable & Otis, Angel & Humberto, Xavier Woods & Kofi Kingston (w/Montez Ford)	D	WWE Monday Night RAW	14:30
Sep 9	Angel, Humberto, Mace & Mansoor (w/Montez Ford, Ashante Adonis & Top Dolla)	W	WWE SmackDown	8:35
Sep 19	Ridge Holland & Butch (w/Montez Ford)	L	WWE Monday Night RAW	12:57
Oct 3	Solo Sikoa	L	WWE Monday Night RAW	12:20
Nov 28	Chad Gable & Otis (w/Montez Ford)	W	WWE Monday Night RAW	12:00
Dec 12	Finn Balor, Damian Priest & Dominik Mysterio (w/Akira Tozawa & Montez Ford)	L	WWE Monday Night RAW	14:45
Dec 19	Finn Balor & Damian Priest (w/Montez Ford)	W	WWE Monday Night RAW	9:00

ANGELO PARKER

Jan 7	No DQ, No Holds Barred: Eddie Kingston, Santana & Ortiz (w/Daniel Garcia & Matt Lee)	L	AEW Rampage	13:50
Jan 25	Kekoa, Pat Brink & Rayo (w/Matt Lee & Daniel Garcia)	W	AEW Dark	1:01
Jan 26	Chris Jericho, Santana & Ortiz (w/Daniel Garcia & Matt Lee)	W	AEW Dynamite: Beach Break	8:52
Feb 1	Kidd Bandit & Ish (w/Matt Lee)	W	AEW Dark	2:42
Feb 14	John Silver, Alex Reynolds, Evil Uno, Alan Angels & Stu Grayson (w/Matt Lee, Daniel Garcia, Anthony Bowens & Max Caster)	W	AEW Dark Elevation	5:56
Feb 15	Chris Metro & JC Metro (w/Matt Lee)	W	AEW Dark	1:57
Feb 21	Ariel Levy, Chico Adams, Dean Alexander, Dominic Garrinin & Kevin Ku (w/Matt Lee, Daniel Garcia, Austin Gunn & Colten Gunn)	W	AEW Dark Elevation	2:55
Feb 23	Tag Team Battle Royal (w/Matt Lee)	L	AEW Dynamite	5:20
Mar 2	Casino Battle Royale (w/Matt Lee)	L	AEW Dynamite	22:14
Mar 15	Luke Sampson, Mike Reed & Shayne Stetson (w/Matt Lee & Daniel Garcia)	W	AEW Dark	2:19
May 24	Eli Isom & TUG Cooper (w/Matt Menard)	W	AEW Dark	1:42
May 29	Anarchy In The Arena: Bryan Danielson, Jon Moxley, Eddie Kingston, Santana & Ortiz (w/Daniel Garcia, Jake Hager, Chris Jericho & Matt Menard)	W	AEW Double Or Nothing '22	22:45
Jun 13	Danny Adams & Warhorse (w/Matt Menard)	W	AEW Dark Elevation	2:45
Jun 14	Jack Banning, Ray Rosas & Sinn Bodhi (w/Daniel Garcia & Matt Menard)	W	AEW Dark	2:38
Jun 29	Blood & Guts: Jon Moxley, Claudio Castagnoli, Wheeler Yuta, Eddie Kingston, Santana & Ortiz (w/Chris Jericho, Daniel Garcia, Jake Hager, Matt Menard & Sammy Guevara)	L	AEW Dynamite: Blood & Guts	46:45
Jul 12	Jake St. Patrick & Sage Scott (w/Matt Menard)	W	AEW Dark	:43
Jul 26	Cameron Stewart	W	AEW Dark	1:39
Aug 30	Gus De La Vega	W	AEW Dark	:15
Sep 4	Hook	L	AEW All Out Buy-In	3:55
Sep 23	Action Bronson & Hook (w/Matt Menard)	L	AEW Rampage: Grand Slam	5:10
Nov 21	Leon Ruffin, Tony Deppen & Tracy Williams (w/Matt Menard & Daniel Garcia)	W	AEW Dark Elevation	2:46
Nov 29	Jack Tomlinson, LSG & Tracy Williams (w/Matt Menard & Daniel Garcia)	W	AEW Dark	4:09
Dec 12	Warren Johnson & Zack Mason (w/Matt Menard)	W	AEW Dark Elevation	:20

ANNA JAY

Jan 4	Dream Girl Ellie	W	AEW Dark	1:32
Jan 11	Charlotte Renegade & Robyn Renegade (w/Tay Conti)	W	AEW Dark	3:48
Jan 18	Tiffany Nieves	W	AEW Dark	1:57
Jan 21	Jade Cargill	L	AEW Rampage	8:45
Jan 31	Nikki Victory	W	AEW Dark Elevation	1:20
Feb 8	Kaci Lennox	W	AEW Dark	1:44
Feb 14	Emi Sakura, Nyla Rose & The Bunny (w/Ruby Soho & Tay Conti)	W	AEW Dark Elevation	3:43
Feb 21	Angelica Risk, Arie Alexander & Freya States (w/Red Velvet & Tay Conti)	W	AEW Dark Elevation	3:42
Mar 8	Marina Tucker	W	AEW Dark	1:21
Mar 21	Emi Sakura & The Bunny (w/Ruby Soho)	W	AEW Dark Elevation	4:20
Mar 28	Charlotte Renegade & Ruby Renegade (w/Ruby Soho)	W	AEW Dark Elevation	2:17
Apr 4	Ashley D'Amboise & Diamante (w/Ruby Soho)	W	AEW Dark Elevation	4:50
Apr 11	Emi Sakura, LuFisto & The Bunny (w/Ruby Soho & Skye Blue)	W	AEW Dark Elevation	3:21
Apr 18	Emi Sakura, Raychell Rose & The Bunny (w/Hikaru Shida & Ruby Soho)	W	AEW Dark Elevation	3:20
Apr 25	Emi Sakura, Nyla Rose & The Bunny (w/Ruby Soho & Skye Blue)	W	AEW Dark Elevation	6:35
Apr 26	Raychell Rose & The Bunny (w/Skye Blue)	W	AEW Dark	5:07
May 2	Emi Sakura & Nyla Rose (w/Kris Statlander)	W	AEW Dark Elevation	6:10
May 16	Emi Sakura & Nyla Rose (w/Yuka Sakazaki)	W	AEW Dark Elevation	3:32
May 28	Sandra Moone	W	AEW Dark	2:42
May 29	Jade Cargill	L	AEW Double Or Nothing '22	7:25
Jun 14	Diamante, Emi Sakura & Nyla Rose (w/Kris Statlander & Ruby Soho)	W	AEW Dark	7:54
Jun 20	Rebel	W	AEW Dark Elevation	:56
Jun 27	Heather Reckless	W	AEW Dark Elevation	1:52
Jul 4	Megan Myers	W	AEW Dark Elevation	2:21
Jul 11	Shawna Reed	W	AEW Dark Elevation	1:50
Jul 13	Serena Deeb	L	AEW Dynamite: Fyter Fest	8:22
Jul 29	Ruby Soho	W	AEW Rampage	9:48
Aug 9	Megan Meyers	W	AEW Dark	1:20
Aug 22	Nikki Victory	W	AEW Dark Elevation	1:02
Sep 27	Kelly Madan	W	AEW Dark	1:27
Oct 7	Madison Rayne & Skye Blue (w/Tay Melo)	W	AEW Rampage	7:42
Oct 14	Nyla Rose	L	AEW Rampage	5:25
Nov 8	Sio Nieves	W	AEW Dark	2:06

Nov 16	Toni Storm	L	AEW Dynamite	7:09
Nov 23	Dr. Britt Baker D.M.D. & Jamie Hayter, Willow Nightingale & Skye Blue (w/Tay Melo)	L	AEW Dynamite: Thanksgiving Eve	8:05
Nov 30	Willow Nightingale	L	AEW Dynamite	7:29
Dec 28	Ruby Soho & Willow Nightingale (w/Tay Melo)	W	AEW Dynamite	11:58

ANTHONY ANDREWS

Jun 28	Rodney Mack	L	NWA Power	4:29
Aug 28	Tag Team Battle Royal (w/AJ Cazana)	L	NWA 74th Anniversary Show	14:07
Dec 6	Rolando Freeman, Jeremiah Plunkett, Sal The Pal	L	NWA Power	5:36

ANTHONY MAYWEATHER

Jan 11	Mims	W	NWA Power	5:07
Mar 1	Chris Adonis	W	NWA Power	11:38
Mar 20	Jax Dane	W	NWA Crockett Cup '22	10:11
Mar 20	Jax Dane	L	NWA Crockett Cup '22	:31
Aug 28	Cyon	L	NWA 74th Anniversary Show	8:18

ANTHONY BOWENS

Jan 4	Blanco Loco & Axton Ray (w/Max Caster)	W	AEW Dark	3:02
Jan 10	Joey Ace & Kevin Matthews (w/Max Caster)	W	AEW Dark Elevation	3:29
Jan 12	Bear Bronson & Bear Boulder (w/Max Caster)	W	AEW Dynamite	6:18
Jan 19	Sting & Darby Allin (w/Max Caster)	L	AEW Dynamite	9:22
Jan 25	Alan Angels, Alex Reynolds, Evil Uno & Ten (w/Max Caster, Austin Gunn & Colten Gunn)	W	AEW Dark	6:15
Jan 28	Jon Moxley	L	AEW Rampage: Beach Break	12:02
Feb 7	Lee Moriarty, Matt Sydal, Brock Anderson & Lee Johnson (w/Max Caster, Austin Gunn & Colten Gunn)	W	AEW Dark Elevation	7:11
Feb 14	John Silver, Alex Reynolds, Evil Uno, Alan Angels & Stu Grayson (w/Max Caster, Jeff Parker, Matt Lee & Daniel Garcia)	W	AEW Dark Elevation	5:56
Feb 15	Fuego Del Sol	W	AEW Dark	4:30
Feb 25	Orange Cassidy	L	AEW Rampage	10:15
Mar 1	B. Jack & Donovan Izzolena (w/Max Caster)	W	AEW Dark	2:46
Mar 2	Casino Battle Royale (w/Max Caster)	L	AEW Dynamite	20:33
Mar 9	Jungle Boy & Luchasaurus (w/Max Caster)	L	AEW Dynamite	9:26
Mar 22	Adrian Alanis & Liam Gray (w/Max Caster)	W	AEW Dark	2:13
May 16	Bryce Donovan, GKM, Lucas Chase & Zack Clayton (w/Max Caster, Austin Gunn & Colten Gunn)	W	AEW Dark Elevation	1:22
Jul 6	Fuego Del Sol, Leon Ruffin, Bear Bronson & Bear Boulder (w/Max Caster, Austin Gunn & Colten Gunn)	W	AEW Dynamite	2:14
Aug 2	Peter Avalon & Ryan Nemeth (w/Max Caster)	W	AEW Dark	5:00
Aug 3	Austin Gunn & Colten Gunn (w/Max Caster)	W	AEW Dynamite	8:20
Aug 15	JT Energy & Justin Fowler (w/Max Caster)	W	AEW Dark Elevation	1:47
Sep 3	Invictus Khash & JPH (w/Max Caster)	W	AEW Dark Elevation	1:55
Sep 4	Keith Lee & Swerve Strickland (w/Max Caster)	L	AEW All Out '22	22:30
Sep 21	Keith Lee & Swerve Strickland (w/Max Caster)	W	AEW Dynamite: Grand Slam	13:44
Sep 30	Marq Quen & Isiah Kassidy, The Butcher & The Blade (w/Max Caster)	W	AEW Rampage	10:00
Oct 21	Tony Nese & Josh Woods (w/Max Caster)	W	AEW Rampage	8:06
Nov 9	Keith Lee, Swerve Strickland, Austin Gunn & Colten Gunn (w/Max Caster, Dax Harwood & Cash Wheeler)	W	AEW Dynamite	12:22
Nov 16	Swerve Strickland	L	AEW Dynamite	9:36
Nov 19	Keith Lee & Swerve Strickland (w/Max Caster)	W	AEW Full Gear '22	19:40
Dec 7	Dax Harwood & Cash Wheeler (w/Max Caster)	W	AEW Dynamite	16:46
Dec 23	Jeff Jarrett & Jay Lethal (w/Billy Gunn)	L	AEW Rampage	11:46

ANTHONY HENRY

Feb 8	Lee Moriarty	L	AEW Dark	6:01
Mar 9	Bryan Danielson & Jon Moxley (w/JD Drake)	L	AEW Dynamite	4:00
Apr 4	Chuck Taylor & Trent Beretta (w/JD Drake)	L	AEW Dark Elevation	8:00
Apr 20	Hook	L	AEW Dynamite	1:23
May 3	Brian Pillman Jr. & Griff Garrison (w/JD Drake)	L	AEW Dark	6:33
May 17	Bear Boulder & Bear Bronson (w/JD Drake)	L	AEW Dark	8:30
May 18	Keith Lee & Swerve Strickland (w/JD Drake)	L	AEW Dynamite: Wild Card Wednesday	2:24
Jul 19	Konosuke Takeshita	L	AEW Dark	7:48
Aug 9	Orange Cassidy	L	AEW Dark	6:04
Aug 10	Luchasaurus	L	AEW Dynamite: Quake By The Lake	:43
Aug 23	Dean Alexander & Rosario Grillo (w/JD Drake)	W	AEW Dark	3:41
Aug 27	Kushida & Ren Narita (w/JD Drake)	L	NJPW Strong	11:18
Aug 30	Manny Lo & Oliver Sawyer (w/JD Drake)	W	AEW Dark	2:32
Sep 27	Dante Martin	L	AEW Dark	9:24
Oct 4	Dante Martin & Matt Sydal (w/JD Drake)	L	AEW Dark	9:34
Oct 24	Brian Pillman Jr. & Griff Garrison (w/JD Drake)	L	AEW Dark Elevation	5:47
Oct 25	Penta El Zero M & Rey Fenix (w/JD Drake)	L	AEW Dark	2:55
Nov 25	Darby Allin	L	AEW Rampage: Black Friday	8:09
Dec 6	Trent Beretta	L	AEW Dark	10:49
Dec 19	Claudio Castagnoli & Wheeler Yuta (w/JD Drake)	L	AEW Dark Elevation	7:55
Dec 27	Terrell Hughes & Terrence Hughes (w/JD Drake)	W	AEW Dark	5:38

ANTHONY OGOGO

Jan 11	Baron Black	W	AEW Dark	4:24
Feb 1	Marcus Kross	W	AEW Dark	2:28
Feb 8	Tony Vincita	W	AEW Dark	3:38

Mar 22	Ray Jaz	W	AEW Dark	2:23
May 2	Goldy	W	AEW Dark Elevation	2:33
May 23	Mysterious Q	W	AEW Dark Elevation	4:10
May 24	Trenton Storm	W	AEW Dark	3:40
May 31	Carlie Bravo	W	AEW Dark	3:34
Jun 6	Alan Angels, Evil Uno, John Silver & Ten	W	AEW Dark Elevation	6:28
	(w/Aaron Solo, Nick Comoroto & QT Marshall)			
Jun 14	Nick Ruiz	W	AEW Dark	2:02
Jul 4	Pat Monix	W	AEW Dark Elevation	2:38
Aug 1	Bobby Orlando, BRG, Bryce Donovan & TUG Cooper	W	AEW Dark Elevation	3:33
	(w/Aaron Solo, Nick Comoroto & QT Marshall)			
Aug 23	Meto	W	AEW Dark	3:24
Sep 20	Luke Kurtis	W	AEW Dark	:43

APOLLO CREWS

Jan 3	Angelo Dawkins & Montez Ford (w/Commander Azeez)	L	WWE Monday Night RAW	2:15
Jan 10	Damian Priest, Angelo Dawkins & Montez Ford	W	WWE Monday Night RAW	8:30
	(w/Dolph Ziggler & Robert Roode)			
Jan 17	Rey Mysterio, Dominik Mysterio, Angelo Dawkins & Montez Ford	L	WWE Monday Night RAW	8:00
	(w/Commander Azeez, Dolph Ziggler & Robert Roode)			
Feb 17	Veer Mahaan	L	WWE Main Event	5:04
Feb 24	Veer Mahaan	L	WWE Main Event	4:59
Mar 7	Omos	L	WWE Monday Night RAW	2:40
Mar 21	Handicap Match: Omos (w/Commander Azeez)	L	WWE Monday Night RAW	2:45
Mar 31	Finn Balor	L	WWE Main Event	5:31
Apr 1	Andre The Giant Memorial Battle Royal	L	WWE SmackDown	8:05
Apr 7	Greg Leslie	W	WWE Main Event	3:49
Apr 14	Cedric Alexander & Shelton Benjamin (w/Commander Azeez)	W	WWE Main Event	6:59
Apr 21	T-Bar	W	WWE Main Event	5:06
May 5	Ciampa	L	WWE Main Event	7:29
May 12	Akira Tozawa	W	WWE Main Event	6:08
May 19	Angelo Dawkins & Montez Ford (w/Commander Azeez)	L	WWE Main Event	4:23
May 26	T-Bar	W	WWE Main Event	8:43
Jun 2	Akira Tozawa	W	WWE Main Event	6:08
Jun 7	Grayson Waller & Carmelo Hayes (w/Solo Sikoa)	W	NXT 2.0	13:45
Jul 12	Giovanni Vinci	L	NXT 2.0	12:09
Jul 26	Xyon Quinn	W	NXT 2.0	5:40
Aug 9	Roderick Strong	W	NXT 2.0	11:55
Aug 30	Grayson Waller	L	NXT 2.0	11:11
Oct 22	Casket Match: Grayson Waller	W	NXT Halloween Havoc '22	14:27
Nov 15	JD McDonagh	W	NXT	13:55
Dec 10	Bron Breakker	L	NXT Deadline	14:34

AQA

Feb 9	Jade Cargill	L	AEW Dynamite	7:44
Feb 21	Emi Sakura, Leyla Hirsch & Nyla Rose (w/Kiera Hogan & Skye Blue)	L	AEW Dark Elevation	4:48
Mar 8	Diamante & Emi Sakura (w/Ruby Soho)	W	AEW Dark	5:02
Mar 22	Valentina Rossi	W	AEW Dark	2:04
May 24	Brittany Jade	W	AEW Dark	4:19
Jul 5	Avery Breaux	W	AEW Dark	3:42

AR FOX

Jul 25	Isiah Kassidy, Marq Quen & Angelico (w/Adrian Alanis & Liam Gray)	L	AEW Dark Elevation	3:59
Aug 30	Dante Martin	L	AEW Dark	4:36
Oct 4	Ari Daivari	L	AEW Dark	6:35
Nov 1	Rey Fenix	L	AEW Dark	4:52
Nov 8	Eddie Kingston & Ortiz (w/Caleb Konley)	L	AEW Dark	1:49
Nov 14	Serpentico	W	AEW Dark Elevation	3:07
Nov 16	Pac, Penta El Zero M & Rey Fenix (w/Dante Martin & Darius Martin)	L	AEW Dynamite	11:33
Nov 30	Samoa Joe	L	AEW Dynamite	6:36
Dec 10	Rush & Dralistico (w/Blake Christian)	W	ROH Final Battle '22	10:35
Dec 23	$300,000 Three Kings Christmas Casino Trios Royale	W	AEW Rampage	22:01

ARAMIS

Feb 24	Arez, Gino Medina & Mini Abismo Negro (w/El Dragon & Micro Man)	W	MLW Fusion	15:46
Apr 29	Gino Medina, Arez & Mini Abismo Negro (w/KC Navarro & Micro Man)	L	MLW Fusion	11:55
Jun 9	Mexican Strap Match: Gino Medina	L	MLW Fusion	5:37

AREZ

Feb 24	Aramis, El Dragon & Micro Man (w/Gino Medina & Mini Abismo Negro)	L	MLW Fusion	15:46
Mar 31	Micro Man, Octagon Jr. & Puma King	L	MLW Fusion	15:42
	(w/Gino Medina & Mini Abismo Negro)			
Apr 29	Aramis, KC Navarro & Micro Man (w/Gino Medina & Mini Abismo Negro)	W	MLW Fusion	11:55
May 26	Aero Star, El Dragon & Micro Man (w/Mini Abismo Negro & TJP)	L	MLW Fusion	10:36
Jun 23	Myron Reed, KC Navarro	L	MLW Fusion	6:09
Jun 30	Lince Dorado, Micro Man & Taya Valkyrie	L	MLW Fusion	6:32
	(w/Holidead & Mini Abismo Negro)			
Nov 10	Myron Reed, La Estrella, Lince Dorado	L	MLW Fusion	6:54

ARI DAIVARI

Jan 29	Alex Zayne	L	NJPW Strong	10:07
Feb 1	Alan Angels & Ten (w/Invictus Khash)	L	AEW Dark	7:44

Feb 15	John Silver & Alex Reynolds (w/Invictus Khash)	L	AEW Dark	5:40
Mar 12	Kevin Blackwood	L	NJPW Strong	8:51
Mar 15	Dante Martin & Darius Martin (w/Invictus Khash)	L	AEW Dark	7:30
Jun 18	Delirious	W	NJPW Strong	10:15
Jun 28	Caleb Konley	W	AEW Dark	6:25
Jul 26	Blake Christian	W	AEW Dark	4:59
Aug 2	Logan Cruz & Tyshon Price (w/Slim J)	W	AEW Dark	3:02
Aug 9	Sonny Kiss, Xavier Walker & Zack Clayton (w/Parker Boudreaux & Slim J)	W	AEW Dark	3:10
Aug 12	Orange Cassidy	L	AEW Rampage: Quake By The Lake	10:00
Aug 16	Fuego Del Sol	W	AEW Dark	10:57
Aug 19	Orange Cassidy, Trent Beretta & Chuck Taylor (w/Parker Boudreaux & Slim J)	L	AEW Rampage	11:00
Aug 23	Cash Flo, Omar Amir & Ryan Howe (w/Parker Boudreaux & Slim J)	W	AEW Dark	2:30
Aug 30	Hermano, Logan Cruz & Thshaun Perez (w/Parker Boudreaux & Slim J)	W	AEW Dark	3:35
Sep 6	Claudio Castagnoli	L	AEW Dark	9:19
Sep 20	GKM, Marcus Kross & Mike Magnum (w/Parker Boudreaux & Slim J)	W	AEW Dark	4:08
Sep 23	Golden Ticket Battle Royale	L	AEW Rampage: Grand Slam	12:16
Oct 4	AR Fox	W	AEW Dark	6:35
Oct 18	Brandon Cutler	W	AEW Dark	4:59
Oct 21	Hook	L	AEW Rampage	2:47
Oct 29	Kevin Knight	W	NJPW Strong	8:19
Nov 1	Orange Cassidy, Chuck Taylor & Trent Beretta (w/Sonny Kiss & Tony Depen)	L	AEW Dark	6:04
Nov 7	Dalton Castle, Brandon Tate & Brent Tate (w/Jeeves Kay & Slim J)	L	AEW Dark Elevation	5:25
Nov 9	Wardlow	L	AEW Dynamite	1:48
Nov 21	Matt Hardy, Isiah Kassidy & Marq Quen (w/Encore & Sonny Kiss)	L	AEW Dark Elevation	3:15
Nov 22	John Silver, Alex Reynolds & Evil Uno (w/Jeeves Kay & Sonny Kiss)	L	AEW Dark	5:26
Nov 28	Konosuke Takeshita	L	AEW Dark Elevation	4:45
Nov 30	Ricky Starks	L	AEW Dynamite	:24
Dec 12	Brandon Cutler, Luther & Serpentico (w/Josh Woods & Tony Nese)	W	AEW Dark Elevation	5:20
Dec 23	$300,000 Three Kings Christmas Casino Trios Royale (w/Josh Woods & Tony Nese)	L	AEW Rampage	22:01

ARIANNA GRACE

Apr 29	Amari Miller	W	NXT Level Up	5:15
May 10	Nikkita Lyons	L	NXT 2.0	3:09
May 27	Amari Miller	L	NXT Level Up	5:14
Jun 10	Valentina Feroz	L	NXT Level Up	4:16
Jun 17	Thea Hail	L	NXT Level Up	5:28
Jul 8	Yulisa Leon	L	NXT Level Up	6:21
Jul 19	Battle Royal	L	NXT 2.0	13:13
Jul 26	Indi Hartwell	L	NXT 2.0	3:59
Aug 5	Thea Hail	W	NXT Level Up	5:03
Aug 9	Thea Hail	W	NXT 2.0	3:49
Aug 19	Ivy Nile	L	NXT Level Up	4:24
Sep 2	Erica Yan	W	NXT Level Up	4:43
Sep 13	Nikkita Lyons & Zoey Stark (w/Kiana James)	L	NXT 2.0	9:04
Oct 7	Fallon Henley & Sol Ruca (w/Kiana James)	L	NXT Level Up	5:06

ARON STEVENS

Feb 8	Team War Elimination Match: Odinson, Parrow & Rodney Mack, Tyrus, Jordan Clearwater & Marshe Rockett, Alex Taylor, Jeremiah Plunkett & Rush Freeman (w/JR Kratos & Judais)	L	NWA Power	11:40
Mar 19	Dirty Dango & JTG (w/The Blue Meanie)	L	NWA Crockett Cup '22	6:40
Apr 26	Trevor Murdoch	L	NWA Power	5:24
Jun 11	Trevor Murdoch	L	NWA Alwayz Ready '22	4:38
Aug 28	Misssouri Tornado Match: JR Kratos & Da Pope (w/Rodney Mack)	L	NWA 74th Anniversary Show	9:40
Nov 15	JR Kratos	L	NWA Power	1:35

ASHANTE ADONIS

Aug 12	Trevor Urban & Brandon Scott (w/Top Dolla)	W	WWE SmackDown	1:50
Sep 2	Mace & Mansoor (w/Top Dolla)	W	WWE SmackDown	3:05
Sep 9	Angel, Humberto, Mace & Mansoor (w/Top Dolla, Angelo Dawkins & Montez Ford)	W	WWE SmackDown	8:35
Sep 16	Ridge Holland & Butch, Ludwig Kaiser & Giovanni Vinci, Xavier Woods & Kofi Kingston (w/Top Dolla)	L	WWE SmackDown	18:44
Sep 30	Angel & Humberto (w/Top Dolla)	W	WWE SmackDown	3:21
Oct 14	Joaquin Wilde & Cruz Del Toro (w/Top Dolla)	L	WWE SmackDown	1:22
Oct 28	Santos Escobar, Joaquin Wilde & Cruz Del Toro (w/Shinsuke Nakamura & Top Dolla)	W	WWE SmackDown	4:19
Nov 25	Erik & Ivar (w/Top Dolla)	L	WWE SmackDown	2:46
Dec 16	Erik & Ivar, Joaquin Wilde & Cruz Del Toro (w/Top Dolla)	W	WWE SmackDown	9:20
Dec 23	Jey Uso & Jimmy Uso (w/Top Dolla)	L	WWE SmackDown	9:43

ASHTON SMITH

Jan 6	Primate & T-Bone (w/Oliver Carter)	W	NXT UK	9:37
Feb 3	Dave Mastiff & Jack Starz (w/Oliver Carter)	W	NXT UK	12:31
Feb 24	Trent Seven & Tyler Bate (w/Oliver Carter)	L	NXT UK	13:02
Mar 31	Trent Seven	L	NXT UK	8:50
Apr 21	2/3 Falls: Trent Seven & Tyler Bate (w/Oliver Carter)	L	NXT UK	21:38
May 12	Joe Coffey & Mark Coffey (w/Oliver Carter)	W	NXT UK	10:24
Jun 2	Trent Seven & Tyler Bate, Charlie Dempsey & Rohan Raja (w/Oliver Carter)	W	NXT UK	14:17
Jul 14	Teoman	W	NXT UK	7:24

ASUKA

Date	Opponent(s)		Event	Time
May 2	Becky Lynch, Rhea Ripley & Sonya Deville (w/Liv Morgan & Bianca Belair)	W	WWE Monday Night RAW	15:15
May 9	Bianca Belair	D	WWE Monday Night RAW	3:05
May 16	Becky Lynch	W	WWE Monday Night RAW	9:55
May 23	Becky Lynch	L	WWE Monday Night RAW	11:25
May 30	Bianca Belair	L	WWE Monday Night RAW	12:58
Jun 5	Bianca Belair, Becky Lynch	L	WWE Hell In A Cell '22	18:55
Jun 20	Carmella, Alexa Bliss, Becky Lynch, Liv Morgan	L	WWE Monday Night RAW	12:30
Jun 20	Becky Lynch	W	WWE Monday Night RAW	12:00
Jul 1	Raquel Rodriguez, Lacey Evans & Shotzi (w/Liv Morgan & Alexa Bliss)	W	WWE SmackDown	13:14
Jul 2	Money In The Bank Ladder Match: Liv Morgan, Alexa Bliss, Becky Lynch Lacey Evans, Raquel Rodriguez, Shotzi	L	WWE Money In The Bank '22	16:35
Jul 4	No Holds Barred: Becky Lynch	L	WWE Monday Night RAW	11:40
Jul 11	Nikki A.S.H. & Doudrop (w/Alexa Bliss)	W	WWE Monday Night RAW	4:15
Jul 18	Doudrop, Nikki A.S.H. & Tamina (w/Alexa Bliss & Dana Brooke)	W	WWE Monday Night RAW	2:35
Jul 28	Carmella & Tamina (w/Dana Brooke)	W	WWE Main Event	7:09
Aug 1	Alexa Bliss	D	WWE Monday Night RAW	2:20
Aug 15	Nikki A.S.H. & Doudrop (w/Alexa Bliss)	W	WWE Monday Night RAW	9:00
Aug 22	Dakota Kai & Iyo Sky (w/Alexa Bliss)	L	WWE Monday Night RAW	18:30
Aug 29	Katie Ark, Kay Sparks & Dani Mo (w/Alexa Bliss & Bianca Belair)	W	WWE Monday Night RAW	3:19
Sep 3	Bayley, Dakota Kai & Iyo Sky (w/Alex Bliss & Bianca Belair)	L	WWE Clash At The Castle	18:44
Oct 31	Dakota Kai & Iyo Sky (w/Alexa Bliss)	W	WWE Monday Night RAW	16:25
Nov 5	Dakota Kai & Iyo Sky (w/Alexa Bliss)	L	WWE Crown Jewel '22	12:50
Nov 17	Kiana James	W	WWE Main Event	4:15
Nov 21	Rhea Ripley	L	WWE Monday Night RAW	17:58
Nov 26	WarGames: Bayley, Dakota Kai, Iyo Sky, Nikki Cross & Rhea Ripley (w/Bianca Belair, Alexa Bliss, Mia Yim & Becky Lynch)	W	WWE Survivor Series WarGames	39:40
Dec 5	Bayley, Rhea Ripley	L	WWE Monday Night RAW	15:15
Dec 12	Rhea Ripley	L	WWE Monday Night RAW	11:40

ATHENA

Date	Opponent(s)		Event	Time
Jun 3	Kiera Hogan	W	AEW Rampage	8:21
Jun 28	Amber Nova	W	AEW Dark	3:03
Jul 15	Charlette Renegade & Robyn Renegade (w/Kris Statlander)	W	AEW Rampage	:25
Jul 20	Jade Cargill & Kiera Hogan (w/Willow Nightingale)	L	AEW Dynamite: Fyter Fest	8:25
Aug 1	Christina Marie	W	AEW Dark Elevation	2:48
Aug 8	Queen Aminata	W	AEW Dark Elevation	2:59
Aug 9	Emi Sakura, Leva Bates & Serena Deeb (w/Hikaru Shida & Ruby Soho)	W	AEW Dark	8:08
Aug 19	Penelope Ford	W	AEW Rampage	4:00
Sep 4	Jade Cargill	L	AEW All Out '22	4:20
Sep 12	Emi Sakura	W	AEW Dark Elevation	4:43
Sep 14	Serena Deeb & Dr. Britt Baker D.M.D. (w/Toni Storm)	L	AEW Dynamite	8:34
Sep 21	Toni Storm, Serena Deeb, Dr. Britt Baker D.M.D.	L	AEW Dynamite: Grand Slam	9:50
Oct 5	Jamie Hayter, Serena Deeb & Penelope Ford (w/Toni Storm & Willow Nightingale)	W	AEW Dynamite: Anniversary	9:29
Oct 11	Gia Scott	W	AEW Dark	4:39
Oct 17	Jody Threat	W	AEW Dark Elevation	4:57
Oct 25	Alexia Nicole	W	AEW Dark	2:51
Oct 31	Janai Kai	W	AEW Dark Elevation	2:30
Nov 7	Abby Jane	W	AEW Dark Elevation	3:00
Nov 8	Diamante	W	AEW Dark	4:22
Nov 14	Kayla Sparks	W	AEW Dark Elevation	3:08
Nov 15	LMK	W	AEW Dark	3:42
Nov 18	Madison Rayne	W	AEW Rampage	2:50
Nov 28	Laynie Luck	W	AEW Dark Elevation	2:05
Dec 2	Dani Mo	W	AEW Rampage	1:27
Dec 6	B3CCA	W	AEW Dark	3:11
Dec 10	Madi Wrenkowski	W	AEW Dark Elevation	1:39
Dec 10	Mercedes Martinez	W	ROH Final Battle '22	13:10
Dec 19	Vertvixen	W	AEW Dark Elevation	2:45
Dec 26	Kiera Hogan	W	AEW Dark Elevation	5:59

AUSTIN ARIES

Date	Opponent(s)		Event	Time
Mar 20	Homicide, Colby Corino, Darius Lockhart	L	NWA Crockett Cup '22	9:39
Mar 22	Homicide	L	NWA Power	8:04

AUSTIN GUNN

Date	Opponent(s)		Event	Time
Jan 4	Rolando Perez, Austin Green & Donnie Primetime (w/Billy Gunn & Colten Gunn)	W	AEW Dark	3:06
Jan 11	Patrick Scott, Marcus Kross & T.I.M (w/Billy Gunn & Colten Gunn)	W	AEW Dark	:41
Jan 17	JB Cole & T.I.M (w/Colten Gunn)	W	AEW Dark Elevation	2:55
Jan 18	Bison XL & Larintiz XL (w/Colten Gunn)	W	AEW Dark	2:20
Jan 25	Alan Angels, Alex Reynolds, Evil Uno & Ten (w/Anthony Bowens, Max Caster & Colten Gunn)	W	AEW Dark	6:15
Feb 7	Lee Moriarty, Matt Sydal, Brock Anderson & Lee Johnson (w/Colten Gunn, Anthony Bowens & Max Caster)	W	AEW Dark Elevation	7:11
Feb 8	Adrian Alanis & Liam Gray (w/Colten Gunn)	W	AEW Dark	2:07
Feb 11	Jungle Boy & Luchasaurus (w/Colten Gunn)	L	AEW Rampage	12:29
Feb 21	Ariel Levy, Chico Adams, Dean Alexander, Dominic Garrini & Kevin Ku (w/Jeff Parker, Matt Lee, Daniel Garcia & Colten Gunn)	W	AEW Dark Elevation	2:55
Feb 23	Tag Team Battle Royal (w/Colten Gunn)	L	AEW Dynamite	1:40
Mar 2	Casino Battle Royale (w/Colten Gunn)	L	AEW Dynamite	17:07

Mar 21	Aaron Mercer & Masada (w/Colten Gunn)	W	AEW Dark Elevation	3:42
Mar 22	JCruz & Victor Chase (w/Colten Gunn)	W	AEW Dark	:29
Mar 30	Dax Harwood & Cash Wheeler (w/Colten Gunn)	L	AEW Dynamite	11:27
Apr 11	John Silver, Alex Reynolds, Alan Angels, Stu Grayson & Ten (w/Colten Gunn, Billy Gunn, Luther & Serpentico)	L	AEW Dark Elevation	5:20
Apr 15	Bryan Danielson, Jon Moxley & Wheeler Yuta (w/Billy Gunn & Colten Gunn)	L	AEW Rampage	9:06
May 10	Warren J & Zack Zilla (w/Colten Gunn)	W	AEW Dark	3:30
May 16	Bryce Donovan, GKM, Lucas Chase & Zack Clayton (w/Colten Gunn, Anthony Bowens & Max Caster)	W	AEW Dark Elevation	1:22
Jun 1	CM Punk, Dax Harwood & Cash Wheeler (w/Max Caster & Colten Gunn)	L	AEW Dynamite	11:50
Jun 7	John Silver, Alex Reynolds & Ten (w/Max Caster & Colten Gunn)	W	AEW Dark	5:26
Jun 8	Casino Battle Royale	L	AEW Dynamite	24:59
Jun 17	Leon Ruffin, Bear Bronson & Bear Boulder (w/Max Caster & Colten Gunn)	W	AEW Rampage: Road Rager	1:15
Jun 26	Yuya Uemura, Alex Coughlin, The DKC & Kevin Knight (w/Max Caster, Billy Gunn & Colten Gunn)	W	AEW x NJPW Forbidden Door Buy-In	5:35
Jun 27	Alex Reynolds, Evil Uno & Ten (w/Colten Gunn & Max Caster)	W	AEW Dark Elevation	4:08
Jun 29	Danhausen, Dax Harwood & Cash Wheeler (w/Max Caster & Colten Gunn)	L	AEW Dynamite: Blood & Guts	9:31
Jul 6	Fuego Del Sol, Leon Ruffin, Bear Bronson & Bear Boulder (w/Anthony Bowens, Max Caster & Colten Gunn)	W	AEW Dynamite	2:14
Aug 3	Anthony Bowens & Max Caster (w/Colten Gunn)	L	AEW Dynamite	8:20
Aug 12	Danhausen & Erick Redbeard (w/Colten Gunn)	W	AEW Rampage: Quake By The Lake	4:33
Aug 17	Brian Pillman Jr. & Griff Garrison (w/Colten Gunn)	W	AEW Dynamite	:31
Oct 17	Gurv Sihra & Harv Sihra (w/Colten Gunn)	W	AEW Dark Elevation	4:16
Nov 8	BK Klein & Jarett Diaz (w/Colten Gunn)	W	AEW Dark	3:05
Nov 9	Anthony Bowens, Max Caster, Dax Harwood & Cash Wheeler (w/Colten Gunn, Keith Lee & Swerve Strickland)	L	AEW Dynamite	12:22
Dec 21	Dax Harwood & Cash Wheeler (w/Colten Gunn)	W	AEW Dynamite: Holiday Bash	9:12

AUSTIN THEORY (AS THEORY UNTIL SEP 5)

Jan 10	AJ Styles	L	WWE Monday Night RAW	7:00
Jan 17	Finn Balor	W	WWE Monday Night RAW	6:06
Jan 24	AJ Styles	L	WWE Monday Night RAW	17:00
Jan 29	Royal Rumble Match	L	WWE Royal Rumble '22	22:06
Jan 31	Kevin Owens	W	WWE Monday Night RAW	11:25
Feb 7	Kevin Owens	L	WWE Monday Night RAW	9:06
Feb 19	Elimination Chamber: AJ Styles, Austin Theory, Riddle, Seth Rollins	L	WWE Elimination Chamber '22	14:55
Mar 7	Finn Balor	L	WWE Monday Night RAW	8:40
Mar 21	Finn Balor	L	WWE Monday Night RAW	7:55
Mar 28	Ricochet	W	WWE Monday Night RAW	1:45
Apr 1	Finn Balor, Shinsuke Nakamura & Rick Boogs (w/Jimmy Uso & Jey Uso)	W	WWE SmackDown	11:27
Apr 3	Pat McAfee	L	WWE WrestleMania XXXVIII	9:40
Apr 4	Finn Balor, Randy Orton & Riddle (w/Jimmy Uso & Jey Uso)	W	WWE Monday Night RAW	8:25
Apr 18	Finn Balor	W	WWE Monday Night RAW	11:35
May 2	Handicap Match: Mustafa Ali (w/The Miz)	W	WWE Monday Night RAW	2:50
May 9	Cody Rhodes	L	WWE Monday Night RAW	13:10
May 30	Mustafa Ali	W	WWE Monday Night RAW	1:45
Jun 5	Mustafa Ali	W	WWE Hell In A Cell '22	10:25
Jun 20	Gauntlet Match: Bobby Lashley, Chad Gable, Otis	L	WWE Monday Night RAW	16:45
Jul 2	Bobby Lashley	L	WWE Money In The Bank '22	11:05
Jul 2	Money In The Bank Ladder Match: Drew McIntyre, Madcap Moss, Omos, Riddle, Sami Zayn, Seth Rollins, Sheamus	W	WWE Money In The Bank '22	25:25
Jul 4	Bobby Lashley, Angelo Dawkins & Montez Ford (w/Chad Gable & Otis)	L	WWE Monday Night RAW	10:05
Jul 11	Bobby Lashley & Riddle (w/Seth Rollins)	L	WWE Monday Night RAW	13:50
Jul 15	Madcap Moss	L	WWE SmackDown	11:34
Jul 18	AJ Styles	L	WWE Monday Night RAW	11:25
Jul 22	Madcap Moss, Angelo Dawkins & Montez Ford (w/Jimmy Uso & Jey Uso)	L	WWE SmackDown	17:00
Jul 25	Drew McIntyre	L	WWE Monday Night RAW	9:45
Jul 25	Drew McIntyre & Bobby Lashley (w/Sheamus)	L	WWE Monday Night RAW	12:20
Jul 30	Bobby Lashley	L	WWE SummerSlam '22	4:45
Aug 15	Dolph Ziggler	W	WWE Monday Night RAW	16:15
Sep 3	Madcap Moss, Angelo Dawkins & Montez Ford (w/Chad Gable & Otis)	L	WWE Clash At The Castle Kickoff	6:29
Sep 5	Kevin Owens	L	WWE Monday Night RAW	15:40
Sep 19	Kevin Owens	L	WWE Monday Night RAW	13:15
Sep 30	Drew McIntyre	L	WWE SmackDown	3:12
Sep 30	Drew McIntyre, Kevin Owens & Johnny Gargano (w/Chad Gable & Otis)	L	WWE SmackDown	13:38
Oct 10	Johnny Gargano	L	WWE Monday Night RAW	8:50
Oct 24	Mustafa Ali	W	WWE Monday Night RAW	9:58
Oct 31	Seth Rollins	L	WWE Monday Night RAW	14:40
Nov 7	Shelton Benjamin	W	WWE Monday Night RAW	2:40
Nov 7	Seth Rollins	L	WWE Monday Night RAW	5:00
Nov 14	Dolph Ziggler	L	WWE Monday Night RAW	15:00
Nov 21	Mustafa Ali	W	WWE Monday Night RAW	5:45
Nov 26	Seth Rollins, Bobby Lashley	W	WWE Survivor Series WarGames	14:50
Dec 5	Mustafa Ali	W	WWE Monday Night RAW	8:05

AXIOM (AS A-KID UNTIL JUL 19)

Jan 20	Heritage Cup Rules: Noam Dar	D	NXT UK	18:00
Feb 10	Saxon Huxley	W	NXT UK	7:03
Mar 10	Charlie Dempsey	L	NXT UK	12:30
Mar 15	Kushida	W	NXT 2.0	4:58

Mar 22	Ladder Match: Grayson Waller	L	NXT 2.0	2:51
Mar 24	Charlie Dempsey & Rohan Raja (w/Saxon Huxley)	L	NXT UK	8:24
Mar 29	Ladder Match: Cameron Grimes, Roderick Strong	L	NXT 2.0	10:55
Apr 14	Teoman	L	NXT UK	11:23
May 26	Heritage Cup Rules: Charlie Dempsey	L	NXT UK	16:24
Jul 19	Dante Chen	W	NXT 2.0	3:00
Aug 2	Duke Hudson	W	NXT 2.0	2:10
Aug 19	Xyon Quinn	W	NXT Level Up	6:10
Sep 6	Nathan Frazer	W	NXT 2.0	11:46
Sep 20	Nathan Frazer	L	NXT	13:14
Oct 11	Ladder Match: Nathan Frazer	L	NXT	12:53
Nov 8	JD McDonagh	L	NXT	10:40
Nov 29	Javier Bernal	W	NXT	9:03
Dec 6	Von Wagner, Andre Chase	W	NXT	11:54
Dec 10	Iron Survivor Challenge: Grayson Waller, Carmelo Hayes, Joe Gacy, JD McDonagh	L	NXT Deadline	25:00
Dec 20	Carmelo Hayes	L	NXT	12:35
Dec 22	Mustafa Ali	L	WWE Main Event	7:19

BAD BUNNY

Jan 22	Juice Robinson	L	NJPW Strong	9:37
Feb 12	David Finlay & Juice Robinson (w/Jonah)	L	NJPW Strong	11:51
Mar 5	David Finlay & Juice Robinson (w/Jonah)	W	NJPW Strong	8:16
May 28	Jeff Cobb, Kyle Fletcher & Mark Davis (w/Jonah & Shane Haste)	L	NJPW Strong	14:39
Jul 2	Aaron Henare, Great-O-Khan, Kyle Fletcher & Mark Davis (w/Jonah, Mikey Nicholls & Shane Haste)	L	NJPW Strong	11:35
Jul 16	Tom Lawlor	L	NJPW Strong	12:09
Sep 24	Christopher Daniels & Yuya Uemura (w/Shane Haste)	W	NJPW Strong	9:10
Nov 5	Barrett Brown & Misterioso, Kevin Knight & The DKC, Jorel Nelson & Royce Isaacs (w/Shane Haste)	L	NJPW Strong	12:36
Dec 17	Kenta	L	NJPW Strong	7:53

BAD DUDE TITO

Jan 22	Juice Robinson	L	NJPW Strong	9:37
Feb 12	David Finlay & Juice Robinson (w/Jonah)	L	NJPW Strong	11:51
Mar 5	David Finlay & Juice Robinson (w/Jonah)	W	NJPW Strong	8:16
Apr 16	Chicago Street Fight: David Finlay, Juice Robinson & Brody King (w/Jonah & Shane Haste)	L	NJPW Windy City Riot	24:11
May 14	Aaron Henare, Kyle Fletcher, Mark Davis & Jeff Cobb (w/Mikey Nicholls, Shane Haste & Jonah)	W	NJPW Capital Collision	12:09
May 28	Jeff Cobb, Kyle Fletcher & Mark Davis (w/Jonah & Shane Haste)	L	NJPW Strong	14:39
Jul 2	Aaron Henare, Great-O-Khan, Kyle Fletcher & Mark Davis (w/Jonah, Mikey Nicholls & Shane Haste)	L	NJPW Strong	11:35
Jul 16	Tom Lawlor	L	NJPW Strong	12:09
Sep 24	Christopher Daniels & Yuya Uemura (w/Shane Haste)	W	NJPW Strong	9:10
Sep 25	Togi Makabe, Tomoaki Honma & Kazuchika Okada (w/Jonah & Shane Haste)	W	NJPW Burning Spirit '22	12:09
Oct 1	Kazuchika Okada & Tomohiro Ishii (w/Zak Knight)	L	NJPW Royal Quest II Night #1	12:47
Oct 2	Kazuchika Okada	L	NJPW Royal Quest II Night #2	8:13
Oct 10	Taichi & Zack Sabre Jr. (w/Shane Haste)	L	NJPW Declaration Of Power	9:58
Nov 5	Barrett Brown & Misterioso, Kevin Knight & The DKC, Jorel Nelson & Royce Isaacs (w/Shane Haste)	L	NJPW Strong	12:36
Dec 17	Kenta	L	NJPW Strong	7:53

BAD LUCK FALE

Mar 1	Taichi, Taka Michinoku & Minoru Tanaka (w/Taiji Ishimori & El Phantasmo)	W	NJPW 50th Anniversary Show	9:50
Apr 9	Hiroshi Tanahashi, Tama Tonga, Tanga Loa & Jado (w/Chase Owens, Yujiro Takahashi & Gedo)	L	NJPW Hyper Battle '22	10:28
May 1	Great-O-Khan & Jeff Cobb, Hirooki Goto & Yoshi-Hashi (w/Chase Owens)	W	NJPW Wrestling Dontaku '22	9:43
Jun 12	Great-O-Khan & Jeff Cobb (w/Chase Owens)	L	NJPW Dominion '22	11:52
Sep 25	Great-O-Khan & Jeff Cobb (w/Chase Owens)	L	NJPW Burning Spirit '22	7:57

BANDIDO

Feb 19	Elimination Match: Psycho Clown, Heavy Metal, Cibernetico, Laredo Kid	L	AAA Rey De Reyes '22	10:17
Mar 3	Myron Reed, Yoshihiro Tajiri, Matt Cross	L	MLW Fusion	8:48
Apr 1	Jonathan Gresham	L	ROH Supercard Of Honor XV	24:55
Apr 30	Andrade El Idolo, Cibernetico & Deonna Purrazzo (w/Pagano & Taya Valkyrie)	W	AAA TripleMania XXX: Monterrey	18:53
Jun 2	Flamita	W	MLW Fusion	12:13
Jun 18	Rey Fenix, El Hijo del Vikingo, Laredo Kid, Taurus	L	AAA TripleMania XXX: Tijuana	20:37
Jul 31	Rey Fenix, Laredo Kid, Black Taurus	L	JCP Ric Flair's Last Match	11:45
Aug 18	Eddie Edwards, Moose, Rich Swann, Sami Callihan, Steve Maclin	L	IMPACT Wrestling	18:25
Sep 28	Chris Jericho	L	AEW Dynamite	18:24
Oct 15	El Cuatrero, Forastero & Sanson, Brian Cage, Johnny Caballero & Sam Adonis (w/Laredo Kid & Psycho Clown)	L	AAA TripleMania XXX: Mexico City	12:44
Nov 11	Rush	W	AEW Rampage	8:45
Nov 16	Ethan Page	L	AEW Dynamite	9:08
Dec 1	Alexander Hammerstone	L	MLW Fusion	16:04

BARON CORBIN (AS HAPPY CORBIN UNTIL OCT 17)

Jan 7	Erik & Ivar (w/Madcap Moss)	W	WWE SmackDown	3:30
Jan 28	Big E & Kofi Kingston (w/Madcap Moss)	L	WWE SmackDown	7:10

Jan 29	Royal Rumble Match	L	WWE Royal Rumble '22	10:47
Feb 11	Cesaro	W	WWE SmackDown	3:55
Mar 18	Drew McIntyre, Erik & Ivar (w/Jinder Mahal & Shanky)	L	WWE SmackDown	7:10
Mar 28	Handicap Match: Drew McIntyre (w/Madcap Moss)	L	WWE Monday Night RAW	1:55
Apr 2	Drew McIntyre	L	WWE WrestleMania XXXVIII	8:35
May 8	Madcap Moss	L	WWE WrestleMania Backlash '22	8:40
Jun 5	No Holds Barred: Madcap Moss	L	WWE Hell In A Cell '22	12:05
Jun 17	Last Laugh Match: Madcap Moss	L	WWE SmackDown	9:22
Jul 1	Battle Royal	W	WWE SmackDown	14:36
Jul 1	Madcap Moss, The Miz, Ezekiel	L	WWE SmackDown	10:33
Jul 30	Pat McAfee	L	WWE SummerSlam '22	10:40
Aug 5	Ricochet	L	WWE SmackDown	11:50
Aug 19	Sheamus, Madcap Moss, Ricochet, Sami Zayn	L	WWE SmackDown	22:33
Aug 26	Ricochet	L	WWE SmackDown	12:20
Sep 2	Shinsuke Nakamura	L	WWE SmackDown	2:20
Oct 17	Dolph Ziggler	W	WWE Monday Night RAW	13:35
Oct 24	Johnny Gargano	W	WWE Monday Night RAW	14:10
Nov 7	Cedric Alexander	W	WWE Monday Night RAW	2:20
Nov 14	Akira Tozawa	W	WWE Monday Night RAW	3:35
Nov 21	Drew McIntyre	L	WWE Monday Night RAW	17:50
Dec 5	AJ Styles, Luke Gallows & Karl Anderson (w/Chad Gable & Otis)	L	WWE Monday Night RAW	14:30

BARRETT BROWN

Mar 19	Fred Yehi, Keita Murray & The DKC (w/Bateman & Misterioso)	W	NJPW Strong	10:05
May 7	Chris Bey & Hikuleo (w/Bateman)	L	NJPW Strong	12:16
May 28	Fred Yehi, Kevin Knight & The DKC (w/Bateman & Misterioso)	W	NJPW Strong	10:06
Jul 16	Eddie Pearl & Ricky Gibson (w/Misterioso)	W	NJPW Strong	8:31
Jul 30	Kyle Fletcher & Mark Davis (w/Misterioso)	L	NJPW Strong	7:27
Oct 1	Kevin Knight & The DKC (w/Bateman)	L	NJPW Strong	8:16
Nov 5	Kevin Knight & The DKC, Bad Dude Tito & Shane Haste, Jorel Nelson & Royce Isaacs (w/Misterioso)	W	NJPW Strong	12:36
Dec 17	Alex Shelley & Chris Sabin (w/Misterioso)	L	NJPW Strong	12:11

BATEMAN

Jan 15	Karl Fredericks & Kevin Knight (w/Misterioso)	L	NJPW Strong	10:04
Mar 19	Fred Yehi, Keita Murray & The DKC (w/Barrett Brown & Misterioso)	L	NJPW Strong	10:05
May 7	Chris Bey & Hikuleo (w/Barrett Brown)	L	NJPW Strong	12:16
May 28	Fred Yehi, Kevin Knight & The DKC (w/Barrett Brown & Misterioso)	W	NJPW Strong	10:06
Jul 23	Dalton Castle, Brandon Tate & Brent Tate (w/Vincent & Dutch)	L	ROH Death Before Dishonor XIX	9:40
Jul 30	Fred Yehi	L	NJPW Strong	7:30
Oct 1	Kevin Knight & The DKC (w/Barrett Brown)	L	NJPW Strong	8:16
Dec 17	Jakob Austin Young	W	NJPW Strong	7:49

BAYLEY

Aug 22	Aliyah	W	WWE Monday Night RAW	6:45
Sep 3	Bianca Belair, Alexa Bliss & Asuka (w/Dakota Kai & Iyo Sky)	W	WWE Clash At The Castle	18:44
Sep 16	Raquel Rodriguez	W	WWE SmackDown	8:20
Sep 19	Alexa Bliss	W	WWE Monday Night RAW	15:05
Sep 30	Shotzi	W	WWE Monday Night RAW	6:42
Oct 8	Ladder Match: Bianca Belair	L	WWE Extreme Rules '22	16:40
Oct 14	Raquel Rodriguez, Shotzi & Roxanne Perez (w/Dakota Kai & Iyo Sky)	W	WWE SmackDown	6:42
Oct 24	Bianca Belair	W	WWE Monday Night RAW	22:57
Nov 5	Last Woman Standing: Bianca Belair	L	WWE Crown Jewel '22	20:20
Nov 26	WarGames: Bianca Belair, Alexa Bliss, Asuka, Mia Yim & Becky Lynch (w/Dakota Kai, Iyo Sky, Nikki Cross & Rhea Ripley)	L	WWE Survivor Series WarGames	39:40
Dec 5	Asuka, Rhea Ripley	W	WWE Monday Night RAW	15:15
Dec 12	Alexa Bliss	L	WWE Monday Night RAW	13:25
Dec 19	Becky Lynch	W	WWE Monday Night RAW	14:20

BECKY LYNCH

Jan 1	Liv Morgan	W	WWE Day 1	17:00
Jan 17	Bianca Belair & Liv Morgan (w/Doudrop)	W	WWE Monday Night RAW	3:00
Jan 29	Doudrop	W	WWE Royal Rumble '22	13:00
Feb 19	Lita	W	WWE Elimination Chamber '22	12:10
Feb 28	Rhea Ripley, Bianca Belair & Liv Morgan (w/Doudrop & Nikki A.S.H.)	L	WWE Monday Night RAW	12:20
Apr 2	Bianca Belair	L	WWE WrestleMania XXXVIII	19:10
May 2	Asuka, Liv Morgan & Bianca Belair (w/Rhea Ripley & Sonya Deville)	L	WWE Monday Night RAW	15:15
May 16	Asuka	L	WWE Monday Night RAW	9:55
May 23	Asuka	W	WWE Monday Night RAW	11:25
Jun 5	Bianca Belair, Asuka	L	WWE Hell In A Cell '22	18:55
Jun 6	Dana Brooke	D	WWE Monday Night RAW	1:00
Jun 6	Dana Brooke	L	WWE Monday Night RAW	2:10
Jun 20	Carmella, Alexa Bliss, Asuka, Liv Morgan	L	WWE Monday Night RAW	12:30
Jun 20	Asuka	L	WWE Monday Night RAW	12:00
Jun 27	Doudrop, Nikki A.S.H., Xia Li, Shayna Baszler, Tamina	W	WWE Monday Night RAW	13:20
Jul 2	Money In The Bank Ladder Match: Liv Morgan, Alexa Bliss, Asuka, Lacey Evans, Raquel Rodriguez, Shotzi	L	WWE Money In The Bank '22	16:35
Jul 4	No Holds Barred: Asuka	W	WWE Monday Night RAW	11:40
Jul 30	Bianca Belair	L	WWE SummerSlam '22	15:10
Nov 26	WarGames: Bayley, Dakota Kai, Iyo Sky, Nikki Cross & Rhea Ripley (w/Bianca Belair, Alexa Bliss, Asuka & Mia Yim)	W	WWE Survivor Series '22	39:40
Dec 5	Alexa Bliss, Nikki Cross	L	WWE Monday Night RAW	16:30
Dec 19	Bayley	L	WWE Monday Night RAW	14:20

BESTIA 666

Jan 5	Jax Dane, Odinson & Parrow (w/Mecha Wolf & Homicide)	W	NWA Power	6:54
Feb 8	Team War Elimination Match: Chris Adonis, Thom Latimer & El Rudo, Matt Taven, Matt Bennett & Victor Benjamin, Jay Bradley, Wrecking Ball Legursky & Colby Corina (w/Mecha Wolf & Homicide)	L	NWA Power	11:09
Mar 19	Brandon Tate & Brent Tate (w/Mecha Wolf)	W	NWA Crockett Cup '22	8:59
Mar 19	Handicap Match: PJ Hawx (w/Mecha Wolf)	W	NWA Crockett Cup '22	7:25
Mar 20	Doug Williams & Harry Smith (w/Mecha Wolf)	L	NWA Crockett Cup '22	8:58
Mar 29	Odinson & Parrow (w/Mecha Wolf)	W	NWA Power	7:17
Apr 26	Jay Briscoe & Mark Briscoe (w/Mecha Wolf)	W	NWA Power	9:56
May 12	Aztec Apocalypo Match: Jacob Fatu	L	MLW Fusion	9:41
Jun 11	Doug Williams & Harry Smith (w/Mecha Wolf)	L	NWA Alwayz Ready '22	13:54
Jun 18	Copa TripleMania XXX Match	L	AAA TripleMania XXX: Tijuana	21:57
Jun 28	Lucha Rules: Doug Williams & Harry Smith (w/Mecha Wolf)	L	NWA Power	5:08
Jul 19	Matt Taven & Mike Bennett (w/Mecha Wolf)	D	NWA Power	5:38
Aug 27	Luke Hawx & PJ Hawx (w/Mecha Wolf)	W	NWA 74th Anniversary Show	13:10
Aug 28	Tag Team Battle Royal (w/Mecha Wolf)	L	NWA 74th Anniversary Show	14:07
Oct 4	Matt Taven, Mike Bennett & Rhett Titus (w/Mecha Wolf & Damian 666)	L	NWA Power	8:16
Nov 12	Luke Hawx & PJ Hawx (w/Mecha Wolf)	W	NWA Hard Times 3	10:48
Dec 27	Cyon, Jordan Clearwater & Tyrus (w/Mecha Wolf & Joe Alonzo)	L	NWA Power	7:56

BETH PHOENIX

Jan 29	The Miz & Maryse (w/Edge)	W	WWE Royal Rumble '22	12:30

BHUPINDER GUJJAR

Feb 3	John Skyler	W	IMPACT Wrestling	3:46
Feb 24	John Skyler	W	IMPACT Wrestling	3:34
Mar 17	Larry D	W	IMPACT Wrestling	5:55
Mar 31	Aiden Prince	W	IMPACT Wrestling	4:36
Apr 28	VSK	W	IMPACT Wrestling	4:31
May 12	Gauntlet For The Gold	L	IMPACT Wrestling	39:00
May 26	Raj Singh & Shera (w/W. Morrissey)	W	IMPACT Wrestling	5:17
Jun 23	Johnny Swinger & Zicky Dice (w/Shark Boy)	W	IMPACT Wrestling	3:50
Jul 14	Johnny Swinger	W	IMPACT Before The Impact	8:37
Jul 28	Vincent	W	IMPACT Before The Impact	6:12
Aug 25	Jason Hotch	W	IMPACT Wrestling	2:17
Sep 8	Brian Myers	L	IMPACT Wrestling	5:01
Sep 22	Ladder Match: Brian Myers	L	IMPACT Wrestling	12:11
Oct 7	Call Your Shot Gauntlet	L	IMPACT Bound For Glory '22	29:18
Oct 13	Matt Cardona	L	IMPACT Wrestling	4:21
Nov 10	G Sharpe	W	IMPACT Wrestling	4:56
Dec 1	Moose	L	IMPACT Wrestling	4:22
Dec 15	Johnny Swinger & Zicky Dice (w/Joe Hendry)	W	IMPACT Wrestling	3:17

BIANCA BELAIR

Jan 10	Doudrop, Liv Morgan	W	WWE Monday Night RAW	14:45
Jan 17	Becky Lynch & Doudrop (w/Liv Morgan)	L	WWE Monday Night RAW	3:00
Jan 24	Queen Zelina	W	WWE Monday Night RAW	3:45
Jan 29	Royal Rumble Match	L	WWE Royal Rumble '22	47:30
Jan 31	Carmella	W	WWE Monday Night RAW	5:30
Feb 7	Nikki A.S.H.	W	WWE Monday Night RAW	4:01
Feb 14	Gauntlet Match: Rhea Ripley, Nikki A.S.H., Liv Morgan, Doudrop	W	WWE Monday Night RAW	44:04
Feb 19	Elimination Chamber: Alexa Bliss, Doudrop, Liv Morgan, Nikki A.S.H. Rhea Ripley	W	WWE Elimination Chamber '22	15:45
Feb 21	Doudrop	W	WWE Monday Night RAW	11:20
Feb 28	Becky Lynch, Doudrop & Nikki A.S.H. (w/Rhea Ripley & Liv Morgan)	W	WWE Monday Night RAW	12:20
Mar 14	Doudrop	W	WWE Monday Night RAW	7:00
Apr 2	Becky Lynch	W	WWE WrestleMania XXXVIII	19:10
Apr 11	Queen Zelina	W	WWE Monday Night RAW	2:10
Apr 25	Sonya Deville	W	WWE Monday Night RAW	8:55
May 2	Becky Lynch, Rhea Ripley & Sonya Deville (w/Asuka & Liv Morgan)	W	WWE Monday Night RAW	15:15
May 9	Asuka	D	WWE Monday Night RAW	3:05
May 30	Asuka	W	WWE Monday Night RAW	12:58
Jun 5	Asuka, Becky Lynch	W	WWE Hell In A Cell '22	18:55
Jul 2	Carmella	W	WWE Money In The Bank '22	7:10
Jul 4	Natalya & Carmella (w/Liv Morgan)	W	WWE Monday Night RAW	13:25
Jul 11	Carmella	L	WWE Monday Night RAW	11:50
Jul 18	Carmella	W	WWE Monday Night RAW	10:25
Jul 30	Becky Lynch	W	WWE SummerSlam '22	15:10
Aug 1	Iyo Sky	D	WWE Monday Night RAW	17:15
Aug 29	Katie Ark, Kay Sparks & Dani Mo (w/Alexa Bliss & Asuka)	W	WWE Monday Night RAW	3:19
Sep 3	Bayley, Dakota Kai & Iyo Sky (w/Alexa Bliss & Asuka)	L	WWE Clash At The Castle	18:44
Sep 12	Sonya Deville	W	WWE Monday Night RAW	12:00
Sep 26	Iyo Sky	W	WWE Monday Night RAW	18:08
Oct 8	Ladder Match: Bayley	W	WWE Extreme Rules '22	16:40
Oct 17	Dakota Kai & Iyo Sky (w/Candice LeRae)	L	WWE Monday Night RAW	12:10
Oct 24	Bayley	L	WWE Monday Night RAW	22:57
Oct 31	Nikki Cross	W	WWE Monday Night RAW	9:30
Nov 5	Last Woman Standing: Bayley	W	WWE Crown Jewel '22	20:20
Nov 26	WarGames: Bayley, Dakota Kai, Iyo Sky, Nikki Cross & Rhea Ripley (w/Alexa Bliss, Asuka, Mia Yim & Becky Lynch)	W	WWE Survivor Series WarGames	39:40

BIG BILL (AS W. MORRISSEY UNTIL DECEMBER 9)

Jan 8	Moose, Matt Cardona	L	IMPACT Hard To Kill '22	16:00
Jan 20	Handicap Match: Zicky Dice & VSK	W	IMPACT Wrestling	1:08
Jan 27	Handicap Match: Zicky Dice, VSK, D-Ray 3000, David Young,	W	IMPACT Wrestling	3:00
	Elix Skipper, Mikey Batts, Lex Lovett, Jerrelle Clark & Shark Boy			
Feb 10	No DQ Match: Brian Myers	W	IMPACT Wrestling	14:22
Apr 23	Elimination Challenge Match (w/Jordynne Grace)	L	IMPACT Rebellion '22	33:02
May 4	Wardlow	L	AEW Dynamite	5:32
May 5	Tables Match: Brian Myers	W	IMPACT Wrestling	10:42
May 12	Gauntlet For The Gold	L	IMPACT Wrestling	39:00
May 26	Raj Singh & Shera (w/Bhupinder Gujjar)	W	IMPACT Wrestling	5:17
Jun 2	Moose & Steve Maclin (w/PCO)	L	IMPACT Wrestling	10:51
Dec 9	Clayton Bloodstone & Izzy James	W	AEW Rampage	2:01

BIG DAMO

Apr 23	John Skyler	W	NJPW Strong	7:04
May 20	Shawn Spears	L	AEW Rampage	1:40
Jun 4	Tomohiro Ishii	L	NJPW Strong	13:02
Jul 30	Fred Rosser	L	NJPW Music City Mayhem	13:01
Aug 13	Hikuleo	L	NJPW Strong	6:18

BIG E

Jan 1	Brock Lesnar, Seth Rollins, Kevin Owens, Bobby Lashley	L	WWE Day 1	8:19
Jan 3	Bobby Lashey, Seth Rollins, Kevin Owens	L	WWE Monday Night RAW	18:40
Jan 10	Seth Rollins	L	WWE Monday Night RAW	18:00
Jan 28	Happy Corbin & Madcap Moss (w/Kofi Kingston)	W	WWE SmackDown	7:10
Jan 29	Royal Rumble Match	L	WWE Royal Rumble '22	6:37
Feb 4	Angel & Humberto (w/Kofi Kingston)	W	WWE SmackDown	8:58
Feb 11	Angel & Humberto (w/Kofi Kingston)	L	WWE SmackDown	10:20
Feb 25	Angel & Humberto (w/Kofi Kingston)	W	WWE SmackDown	10:30
Mar 11	Sheamus & Ridge Holland (w/Kofi Kingston)	L	WWE SmackDown	8:49

BIG KON

Feb 10	Josh Alexander	L	IMPACT Wrestling	:38
Feb 17	Eddie Edwards	L	IMPACT Before The Impact	8:23
Dec 8	Sami Callihan	W	IMPACT Wrestling	5:46

BILLY GUNN

Jan 4	Rolando Perez, Austin Green & Donnie Primetime	W	AEW Dark	3:06
	(w/Austin Gunn & Colten Gunn)			
Jan 11	Patrick Scott, Marcus Kross & T.I.M. (w/Austin Gunn & Colten Gunn)	W	AEW Dark	:41
Apr 11	John Silver, Alex Reynolds, Alan Angels, Stu Grayson & Ten	L	AEW Dark Elevation	5:20
	(w/Austin Gunn, Colten Gunn, Luther & Serpentico)			
Apr 15	Bryan Danielson, Jon Moxley & Wheeler Yuta	L	AEW Rampage	9:06
	(w/Austin Gunn & Colten Gunn)			
Jun 26	Yuya Uemura, Alex Coughlin, The DKC & Kevin Knight	W	AEW Rampage	5:35
	(w/Max Caster, Austin Gunn & Colten Gunn)			
Aug 24	Colten Gunn	L	AEW Dynamite	6:16
Oct 12	Swerve Strickland	L	AEW Dynamite	8:48
Dec 23	Jeff Jarrett & Jay Lethal (w/Anthony Bowens)	L	AEW Rampage	11:46

BLACK TAURUS

Jan 13	Matthew Rehwoldt	W	IMPACT Before The Impact	7:17
Feb 3	Raj Singh	W	IMPACT Before The Impact	9:21
Mar 31	Deaner	W	IMPACT Before The Impact	8:21
Apr 21	Eric Young & Deaner (w/Crazzy Steve)	L	IMPACT Wrestling	4:42
Apr 30	Dragon Lee & Dralistico, Jack Cartwheel & Laredo Kid	W	AAA TripleMania XXX: Monterrey	13:29
	(w/Johnny Caballero)			
May 12	Gauntlet For The Gold	L	IMPACT Wrestling	39:00
May 26	Laredo Kid	L	IMPACT Before The Impact	7:49
Jun 9	Johnny Swinger & Zicky Dice (w/Crazzy Steve)	W	IMPACT Before The Impact	8:18
Jun 18	Rey Fenix, El Hijo del Vikingo, Laredo Kid, Bandido	L	AAA TripleMania XXX: Tijuana	20:37
Jun 23	Andrew Everett	W	IMPACT Before The Impact	8:13
Jul 7	PCO	L	IMPACT Wrestling	6:04
Jul 31	Rey Fenix, Laredo Kid, Bandido	L	JCP Ric Flair's Last Match	11:45
Aug 4	Brian Myers	W	IMPACT Wrestling	6:45
Aug 18	Laredo Kid, Rey Horus, Trey Miguel	W	IMPACT Wrestling	7:33
Sep 15	Moose & Steve Maclin (w/Crazzy Steve)	W	IMPACT Wrestling	1:52
Sep 22	Alex Zayne, Laredo Kid, Mia Yim, Trey Miguel	W	IMPACT Wrestling	11:58
Sep 29	Delirious	W	IMPACT Wrestling	5:03
Oct 13	Trey Miguel, Alex Zayne, Kenny King, Laredo Kid, Yuya Uemura	L	IMPACT Wrestling	5:19
Oct 27	Laredo Kid	W	IMPACT Before The Impact	8:05
Nov 17	PJ Black	W	IMPACT Wrestling	6:18
Dec 15	Matt Cardona & Brian Myers (w/Crazzy Steve)	L	IMPACT Wrestling	4:24

BLACK TIGER

Jan 22	Fred Rosser, Rocky Romero & Taylor Rust (w/Jorel Nelson & Tom Lawlor)	L	NJPW Strong	11:35
Mar 26	Rocky Romero	W	NJPW Strong	11:02
Apr 2	Rocky Romero & Wheeler Yuta (w/JR Kratos)	W	NJPW Strong	9:50
Apr 4	Fred Rosser, Josh Alexander, Alex Coughlin, Ren Narita & Chris Dickinson	L	NJPW Windy City Riot	13:50
	(w/Royce Isaacs, Jorel Nelson, JR Kratos & Danny Limelight)			
May 13	Adrian Quest, Alex Coughlin & Rocky Romero	L	NJPW Strong	8:33
	(w/Danny Limelight & JR Kratos)			

BLADE, THE

Jan 10	John Silver, Alex Reynolds & Ten (w/Isiah Kassidy & Marq Quen)	L	AEW Dark Elevation	4:01
Feb 9	Wardlow	L	AEW Dynamite	6:15
Feb 10	Dante Martin, lee Moriarty & Matt Sydal (w/Isiah Kassidy & Marq Quen)	L	AEW Dark	9:05
Feb 21	Baron Black, Carlie Bravo, Chandler Hopkins, James Ryan & Shawn Dean (w/Andrade El Idolo, Isiah Kassidy, Marq Quen & The Butcher)	W	AEW Dark Elevation	4:20
Feb 23	Tag Team Battle Royal (w/The Butcher)	L	AEW Dynamite	1:02
Mar 2	Casino Battle Royale (w/The Butcher)	L	AEW Dynamite	11:17
Mar 8	Alan Angels & Colt Cabana (w/The Butcher)	W	AEW Dark	5:31
Mar 22	Carlie Bravo & Shawn Dean (w/The Butcher)	W	AEW Dark	2:41
Mar 23	Tornado Match: Sting, Darby Allin, Matt Hardy & Jeff Hardy (w/Isiah Kassidy, Marq Quen & The Butcher)	L	AEW Dynamite	9:27
Apr 6	Tables Match: Matt Hardy & Jeff Hardy (w/The Butcher)	L	AEW Dynamite	11:54
Apr 26	Frankie Kazarian, Matt Hardy, Jeff Hardy, Dante Martin & Darius Martin (w/Max Caster, Angelico, Isiah Kassidy & Marq Quen)	L	AEW Dark	12:40
May 4	Bryan Danielson, Jon Moxley & Wheeler Yuta (w/Angelico & The Butcher)	L	AEW Dynamite	7:27
May 13	Pac, Penta El Zero M & Rey Fenix (w/Marq Quen & The Butcher)	L	AEW Rampage	10:22
May 23	Brian Pillman Jr. & Griff Garisson (w/The Butcher)	W	AEW Dark Elevation	5:55
May 31	Hunter Grey & Paul Titan (w/The Butcher)	W	AEW Dark	3:52
Jul 1	Royal Rampage Match	L	AEW Rampage	22:41
Jul 6	Keith Lee & Swerve Strickland (w/The Butcher)	L	AEW Dynamite	9:38
Jul 18	Brandon Bullock, Bryce Cannon & Jameson Ryan (w/Angelico & The Butcher)	W	AEW Dark Elevation	1:40
Jul 22	Hangman Page & John Silver (w/The Butcher)	L	AEW Rampage	9:55
Aug 1	JCruz, Joey Ace, Victor Chase, Jaylen Brandyn & Traevon Jordan (w/Isiah Kassidy, Marq Quen, Angelico & The Butcher)	W	AEW Dark Elevation	2:12
Aug 9	Braden Lee, Isaiah Broner, James Alexander & Sam Moore (w/The Butcher, Isiah Kassidy & Marq Quen)	W	AEW Dark	2:22
Aug 29	Chase Oliver, Elijah Dean & Zach Nystrom (w/Rush & The Butcher)	W	AEW Dark Elevation	3:20
Sep 3	Orange Cassidy, Chuck Taylor & Trent Beretta (w/Angelico & The Butcher)	W	AEW Dark Elevation	8:13
Sep 12	Aaron Solo & Nick Comoroto (w/The Butcher)	W	AEW Dark Elevation	4:37
Sep 19	Liam Davis & Mike Anthony (w/The Butcher)	W	AEW Dark Elevation	2:48
Sep 23	Golden Ticket Battle Royale	L	AEW Rampage: Grand Slam	12:16
Sep 30	Anthony Bowens & Max Caster, Marq Quen & Isiah Kassidy (w/The Butcher)	L	AEW Rampage	10:00
Oct 14	Jon Moxley & Claudio Castagnoli (w/The Butcher)	L	AEW Rampage	8:40
Oct 17	Chris Voros & Patrick Voros (w/The Butcher)	W	AEW Dark Elevation	2:37
Nov 7	Rocky Romero, Chuck Taylor & Trent Beretta (w/Angelico & The Butcher)	L	AEW Dark Elevation	7:20
Nov 14	Jaylen Brandyn & Traevon Jordan (w/The Butcher)			
Nov 21	Brett Gosselin, Channing Thomas & Doug Love (w/Rush & The Butcher)	W	AEW Dark Elevation	2:20
Nov 25	John Silver, Alex Reynolds & Ten (w/Rush & The Butcher)	W	AEW Rampage: Black Friday	7:24
Dec 16	Orange Cassidy, Dustin Rhodes, Chuck Taylor & Trent Beretta (w/Trent Seven, Kip Sabian & The Butcher)	L	AEW Rampage	10:42
Dec 23	$300,000 Three Kings Christmas Casino Trios Royale (w/The Butcher & Kip Sabian)	L	AEW Rampage	22:01

BLAIR DAVENPORT

Jan 6	Meiko Satomura	L	NXT UK	12:58
Feb 3	Japanese Street Fight: Meiko Satomura	L	NXT UK	9:16
Jun 30	Angel Hayze	W	NXT UK	5:32
Jul 28	Amale	W	NXT UK	5:46
Aug 4	Isla Dawn	D	NXT UK	7:15
Aug 23	Indi Hartwell	W	NXT 2.0	3:49
Sep 1	Elimination Match: Amale, Eliza Alexander, Isla Dawn	W	NXT UK	15:07
Sep 4	Mandy Rose, Meiko Satomura	L	NXT Worlds Collide '22	13:17

BLAKE CHRISTIAN

Jan 27	Laredo Kid	L	IMPACT Before The Impact	7:29
Feb 17	Ace Austin, Laredo Kid	L	IMPACT Wrestling	11:57
Mar 19	Chris Bey	L	NJPW Strong	10:24
Mar 22	Rohit Raju	W	AEW Dark	3:29
Apr 23	Swerve Strickland	L	NJPW Strong	11:27
May 7	Jonah	L	NJPW Strong	6:56
May 28	David Finlay	L	NJPW Strong	10:07
Jun 2	Kenny King	L	IMPACT Wrestling	9:30
Jun 16	Laredo Kid	L	IMPACT Before The Impact	8:47
Jun 21	Jay Lethal	L	AEW Dark	9:54
Jul 26	Ari Daivari	L	AEW Dark	4:59
Jul 30	Hiromu Takahashi	L	NJPW Music City Mayhem	13:59
Aug 16	Powerhouse Hobbs	L	AEW Dark	4:45
Aug 20	El Desperado, Hiromu Takahashi	L	NJPW Strong	19:19
Aug 23	Lucky Ali	W	AEW Dark	4:38
Aug 30	Rush	L	AEW Dark	5:47
Sep 2	Rey Fenix	L	AEW Rampage	2:20
Oct 4	Slim J	L	AEW Dark	6:16
Oct 29	Alex Zayne & Mistico (w/Mascara Dorada)	L	NJPW Strong	10:09
Nov 19	Chris Bey & El Phantasmo (w/Mascara Dorada)	L	NJPW Strong	10:44
Dec 3	Juice Robinson	L	NJPW Strong	9:33
Dec 10	Rush & Dralistico (w/AR Fox)	W	ROH Final Battle '22	10:35
Dec 26	Dralistico	L	AEW Dark	3:59

BLK JEEZ

Mar 8	Alex Taylor, Rush Freeman, Cyon & Mims (w/Jordan Clearwater, Marshe Rockett & Tyrus)	W	NWA Power	6:59
May 17	Team War: Jax Dane, Odinson & Parrow, Alex Taylor, Rush Freeman & Jeremiah Plunkett (w/Jordan Clearwater & Marshe Rockett)	L	NWA Power	6:54
Aug 16	Rodney Mack	L	NWA Power	3:28

BOA

Jan 11	Solo Sikoa	D	NXT 2.0	3:47
Jan 25	Falls Count Anywhere No DQ Match: Solo Sikoa	L	NXT 2.0	8:08

BOBBY FISH

Jan 4	Ryzin	W	AEW Dark	2:08
Feb 7	Robert Anthony	W	AEW Dark Elevation	5:15
Feb 23	Tag Team Battle Royal (w/Kyle O'Reilly)	W	AEW Dynamite	18:25
Mar 2	Hangman Page, John Silver & Alex Reynolds (w/Adam Cole & Kyle O'Reilly)	W	AEW Dynamite	12:43
Mar 6	Jungle Boy & Luchasaurus, Matt Jackson & Nick Jackson (w/Kyle O'Reilly)	L	AEW Revolution '22	18:55
Mar 16	Hangman Page, Jungle Boy & Luchasaurus (w/Adam Cole & Kyle O'Reilly)	W	AEW Dynamite: St. Patrick's Day Slam	13:58
Mar 25	Alan Angels & Ten (w/Kyle O'Reilly)	W	AEW Rampage	7:00
Apr 13	Jungle Boy & Luchasaurus (w/Kyle O'Reilly)	L	AEW Dynamite	13:45
Apr 27	Dante Martin, Lee Johnson, Brock Anderson, Brian Pillman Jr. & Griff Garrison (w/Matt Jackson, Nick Jackson, Adam Cole & Kyle O'Reilly)	W	AEW Dynamite	6:28
May 4	Jeff Hardy	L	AEW Dynamite	10:20
Jun 1	Christian Cage, Matt Hardy, Darby Allin, Jungle Boy & Luchasaurua (w/Matt Jackson, Nick Jackson, Kyle O'Reilly & Hikuleo)	W	AEW Dynamite	12:00
Jun 8	Casino Battle Royale	L	AEW Dynamite	24:59
Jun 14	Brock Anderson	W	AEW Dark	5:57
Jun 17	Darby Allin	L	AEW Rampage: Road Rager	11:45
Jul 18	Blake Li	W	AEW Dark Elevation	2:59
Oct 7	Call Your Shot Gauntlet	L	IMPACT Bound For Glory '22	29:18
Oct 13	Josh Alexander	L	IMPACT Wrestling	12:55
Dec 24	Kevin Blackwood	W	NJPW Strong	12:00

BOBBY LASHLEY

Jan 1	Brock Lesnar, Seth Rollins, Big E, Kevin Owens	L	WWE Day 1	8:19
Jan 3	Big E, Seth Rollins, Kevin Owens	W	WWE Monday Night RAW	18:40
Jan 17	Seth Rollins	W	WWE Monday Night RAW	13:17
Jan 29	Brock Lesnar	W	WWE Royal Rumble '22	10:15
Apr 3	Omos	W	WWE WrestleMania XXXVIII	6:35
May 2	Cedric Alexander	W	WWE Monday Night RAW	2:35
May 8	Omos	L	WWE WrestleMania Backlash '22	8:50
May 16	Steel Cage Match: Omos	W	WWE Monday Night RAW	7:30
May 23	MVP	L	WWE Monday Night RAW	3:05
Jun 5	Handicap Match: Omos & MVP	W	WWE Hell In A Cell '22	8:25
Jun 20	Gauntlet Match: Chad Gable, Otis, Theory	W	WWE Monday Night RAW	16:45
Jun 27	Handicap Match: Chad Gable & Otis	W	WWE Monday Night RAW	8:15
Jul 2	Theory	W	WWE Money In The Bank '22	11:05
Jul 4	Theory, Chad Gable & Otis (w/Angelo Dawkins & Montez Ford)	W	WWE Monday Night RAW	10:05
Jul 11	Seth Rollins & Theory (w/Riddle)	W	WWE Monday Night RAW	13:50
Jul 25	Theory & Sheamus (w/Drew McIntyre)	W	WWE Monday Night RAW	12:20
Jul 30	Theory	W	WWE SummerSlam '22	4:45
Aug 8	Ciampa	W	WWE Monday Night RAW	13:30
Aug 15	AJ Styles	W	WWE Monday Night RAW	21:40
Aug 22	Ciampa & The Miz (w/AJ Styles)	L	WWE Monday Night RAW	13:30
Aug 29	The Miz	W	WWE Monday Night RAW	10:49
Sep 5	Steel Cage Match: The Miz	W	WWE Monday Night RAW	14:15
Sep 19	Seth Rollins	W	WWE Monday Night RAW	20:15
Oct 3	Mustafa Ali	W	WWE Monday Night RAW	11:26
Oct 10	Seth Rollins	L	WWE Monday Night RAW	2:35
Nov 5	Brock Lesnar	L	WWE Crown Jewel '22	6:00
Nov 14	Mustafa Ali	W	WWE Monday Night RAW	4:30
Nov 26	Austin Theory, Seth Rollins	L	WWE Survivor Series WarGames	14:50
Dec 12	Seth Rollins	L	WWE Monday Night RAW	12:55

BODHI HAYWARD

Jan 14	Guru Raaj	W	WWE 205 Live	3:44
Jan 21	James Drake	L	WWE 205 Live	4:36
Jan 25	Zack Gibson & James Drake (w/Andre Chase)	L	NXT 2.0	5:11
Feb 4	Brooks Jensen	L	WWE 205 Live	6:06
Mar 18	Dante Chen	L	NXT Level Up	5:57
Mar 29	Von Wagner	L	NXT 2.0	3:42
Apr 8	Channing Lauren & Troy Donovan (w/Andre Chase)	W	NXT Level Up	6:47
Apr 22	Dante Chen	W	NXT Level Up	5:50
May 27	Bryson Montana & Damaris Griffin (w/Andre Chase)	W	NXT Level Up	3:53
Jul 15	Javier Bernal & Myles Borne (w/Andre Chase)	W	NXT Level Up	5:47
Aug 4	Sha Samuels	L	NXT UK	4:43
Aug 12	Bronco Nima & Lucien Price (w/Andre Chase)	W	NXT Level Up	6:16
Aug 18	Eddie Dennis & Saxon Huxley (w/Andre Chase)	W	NXT UK	6:49
Sep 9	Charlie Dempsey	L	NXT Level Up	7:49
Sep 20	Carmelo Hayes & Trick Williams (w/Andre Chase)	W	NXT	4:15

BOULDER

Jan 12	Anthony Bowens & Max Caster (w/Bear Bronson)	L	AEW Dynamite	6:18
Jan 18	Brandon Bullock & Jameson Ryan (w/Bear Bronson)	W	AEW Dark	2:06
Feb 1	Dante Martin & Matt Sydal (w/Bear Bronson)	L	AEW Dark	9:43
Mar 2	Casino Battle Royale (w/Bear Bronson)	L	AEW Dynamite	8:56
Mar 15	Malakai Black, Brody King & Buddy Matthews (w/Fuego Del Sol & Bear Bronson)	L	AEW Rampage	3:22
May 13	Shawn Spears	L	AEW Rampage	2:03
May 17	Anthony Henry & JD Drake (w/Bear Bronson)	W	AEW Dark	8:30
Jun 17	Max Caster, Austin Gunn & Colten Gunn (w/Leon Ruffin & Bear Bronson)	L	AEW Rampage	1:15
Jul 5	Adrian Alanis & Liam Gray (w/Bear Bronson)	W	AEW Dark	5:25
Jul 6	Anthony Bowens, Max Caster, Austin Gunn & Colten Gunn (w/Fuego Del Sol, Leon Ruffin & Bear Bronson)	L	AEW Dynamite	2:14
Jul 12	Isiah Kassidy & Marq Quen (w/Bear Bronson)	L	AEW Dark	10:45
Aug 16	Axel Rico & Victor Iniestra (w/Bear Bronson)	W	AEW Dark	3:59
Aug 23	Manny Lo & Sean Maluta (w/Bronson)	W	AEW Dark	1:59
Oct 4	Levis Valenzuela & Vary Morales (w/Bronson)	W	AEW Dark	2:42
Nov 15	Brando Lee & Lucas Chase (w/Bronson)	W	AEW Dark	2:40
Dec 27	Brandon Bullock & James Ryan (w/Bronson)	W	AEW Dark	2:13

BRADY PIERCE

Aug 23	Doug Williams & Harry Smith (w/Rush Freeman)	L	NWA Power	4:48
Aug 28	Tag Team Battle Royal (w/Rush Freeman)	L	NWA 74th Anniversary Show	14:07
Nov 1	Brian Myers, Mike Knox & VSK (w/Rush Freeman & Rolando Freeman)	W	NWA Power	6:54
Nov 12	Jay Bradley & Wrecking Ball Legursky (w/Rush Freeman)	L	NWA Hard Time 3	9:15
Nov 29	Matt Cardona & Mike Knox (w/Rush Freeman)	W	NWA Power	11:19

BRANDI RHODES

Jan 24	Willow Nightingale	W	AEW Dark Elevation	2:27
Jan 31	KiLynn King	W	AEW Dark Elevation	4:00

BRANDON CUTLER

Mar 15	Alan Angels, Colt Cabana & Evil Uno (w/Matt Jackson & Nick Jackson)	W	AEW Dark	8:40
Mar 28	Frankie Kazarian	L	AEW Dark Elevation	3:46
Apr 25	Konosuke Takeshita	L	AEW Dark Elevation	4:47
May 16	Bear Bronson	L	AEW Dark Elevation	2:20
May 28	Darby Allin	L	AEW Dark	:59
Jul 25	Baron Black	L	AEW Dark Elevation	3:12
Oct 10	Serpentico	W	AEW Dark Elevation	5:45
Oct 11	Kip Sabian	L	AEW Dark	6:01
Oct 18	Ari Daivari	L	AEW Dark	4:59
Oct 31	Dante Martin	L	AEW Dark Elevation	2:05
Nov 8	Peter Avalon	L	AEW Dark	6:37
Nov 21	Brian Cage	L	AEW Dark Elevation	2:30
Nov 28	Man Scout	W	AEW Dark Elevation	3:28
Dec 12	Ari Daivari, Josh Woods & Tony Nese (w/Luther & Serpentico)	L	AEW Dark Elevation	5:20

BRANDON TATE

Mar 19	Bestia 666 & Mecha Wolf (w/Brent Tate)	L	NWA Crockett Cup '22	8:59
Jul 23	Vincent, Bateman & Dutch (w/Dalton Castle & Brent Tate)	W	ROH Death Before Dishonor XIX	9:40
Sep 19	Boujii, Omar & Rick Recon (w/Dalton Castle & Brent Tate)	W	AEW Dark Elevation	3:25
Oct 3	Adrien Soriano, Gabriel Hodder & Matthew Omen (w/Dalton Castle & Brent Tate)	W	AEW Dark Elevation	4:07
Oct 10	Brett Waters, Goldy & Logan Laroux (w/Dalton Castle & Brent Tate)	W	AEW Dark Elevation	4:00
Oct 11	BK Klein, Joe Keys & Josh Fuller (w/Dalton Castle & Brent Tate)	W	AEW Dark	3:35
Nov 7	Ari Daivari, Jeeves Kay & Slim J (w/Dalton Castle & Brent Tate)	W	AEW Dark Elevation	5:25
Dec 6	Jaden Valo, Justin Corino & Sonny Defarge (w/Dalton Castle & Brent Tate)	W	AEW Dark	2:30
Dec 10	Brian Cage, Kaun & Toa Liona (w/Dalton Castle & Brent Tate)	L	ROH Final Battle '22	10:05

BRAUN STROWMAN

Sep 23	Otis	W	WWE SmackDown	5:45
Oct 3	Chad Gable	W	WWE Monday Night RAW	8:45
Oct 7	Sami Zayn, Jimmy Uso & Jey Uso (w/Xavier Woods & Kofi Kingston)	W	WWE SmackDown	10:30
Oct 14	Handicap Match: Brian Thomas & James Maverick	W	WWE SmackDown	1:57
Nov 5	Omos	W	WWE Crown Jewel '22	7:20
Nov 11	Jinder Mahal	W	WWE SmackDown	1:50
Nov 18	Gunther, Ludwig Kaiser & Giovanni Vinci (w/Kofi Kingston & Xavier Woods)	W	WWE SmackDown	7:38
Nov 25	Ricochet	L	WWE SmackDown	3:45
Dec 17	LA Knight	W	WWE Tribute To The Troops '22	2:12
Dec 23	Miracle On 34th Street Fight: Ludwig Kaiser & Giovanni Vinci (w/Ricochet)	W	WWE SmackDown	11:59

BRENT TATE

Mar 19	Bestia 666 & Mecha Wolf (w/Brandon Tate)	L	NWA Crockett Cup '22	8:59
Jul 23	Vincent, Bateman & Dutch (w/Dalton Castle & Brandon Tate)	W	ROH Death Before Dishonor XIX	9:40
Sep 19	Boujii, Omar & Rick Recon (w/Dalton Castle & Brandon Tate)	W	AEW Dark Elevation	3:25
Oct 3	Adrien Soriano, Gabriel Hodder & Matthew Omen (w/Dalton Castle & Brandon Tate)	W	AEW Dark Elevation	4:07
Oct 10	Brett Waters, Goldy & Logan Laroux (w/Dalton Castle & Brandon Tate)	W	AEW Dark Elevation	4:00
Oct 11	BK Klein, Joe Keys & Josh Fuller (w/Dalton Castle & Brandon Tate)	W	AEW Dark	3:35
Nov 7	Ari Daivari, Jeeves Kay & Slim J (w/Dalton Castle & Brandon Tate)	W	AEW Dark Elevation	5:25
Dec 6	Jaden Valo, Justin Corino & Sonny Defarge	W	AEW Dark	2:30

(w/Dalton Castle & Brandon Tate)

Dec 10	Brian Cage, Kaun & Toa Liona (w/Dalton Castle & Brandon Tate)	L	ROH Final Battle '22	10:05

BRIAN CAGE

Apr 1	Ninja Mack	W	ROH Supercard Of Honor XV	2:50
Sep 23	Golden Ticket Battle Royale	L	AEW Rampage: Grand Slam	12:16
Oct 3	Tracy Williams	W	AEW Dark Elevation	5:18
Oct 5	Wardlow	L	AEW Dynamite: Anniversary	10:04
Oct 11	Papadon	W	AEW Dark	4:29
Oct 14	Shawn Spears, Dax Harwood & Cash Wheeler (w/Kaun & Toa Liona)	L	AEW Rampage	10:29
Oct 15	El Cuatrero, Forastero & Sanson, Bandido, Laredo Kid & Psycho Clown (w/Johnny Caballero & Sam Adonis)	W	AAA TripleMania XXX: Mexico City	12:44
Nov 1	Fuego Del Sol, Jaylen Brandyn & Traevon Jordan (w/Kaun & Toa Liona)	W	AEW Dark	4:01
Nov 2	Samoa Joe	L	AEW Dynamite	11:23
Nov 11	Dante Martin	W	AEW Rampage	7:15
Nov 19	Ricky Starks	L	AEW Full Gear Buy-In	10:00
Nov 21	Brandon Cutler	W	AEW Dark Elevation	2:30
Nov 29	Tony Deppen	W	AEW Dark	3:07
Dec 5	Dan Adams, Facade & Star Rider (w/Kaun & Toa Liona)	W	AEW Dark Elevation	3:43
Dec 6	Leon Ruffin	W	AEW Dark	5:35
Dec 7	Dynamite Diamond Battle Royale	L	AEW Dynamite	13:10
Dec 10	Dalton Castle, Brandon Tate & Brent Tate (w/Kaun & Toa Liona)	W	ROH Final Battle '22	10:05
Dec 14	Jungle Boy	L	AEW Dynamite: Winter Is Coming	8:16

BRIAN MYERS

Feb 10	No DQ Match: W. Morrissey	L	IMPACT Wrestling	14:22
Mar 3	Crazzy Steve	W	IMPACT Before The Impact	8:05
Apr 23	Elimination Challenge Match (w/Matt Cardona)	L	IMPACT Rebellion '22	33:02
May 5	Tables Match: W. Morrissey	L	IMPACT Wrestling	10:42
Jun 7	Nick Aldis	L	NWA Power	10:19
Jul 12	Da Pope	W	NWA Power	6:56
Jul 19	Nick Aldis, Mike Knox, Thom Latimer	L	NWA Power	8:47
Aug 4	Black Taurus	W	IMPACT Wrestling	6:45
Sep 8	Bhupinder Gujjar	W	IMPACT Wrestling	5:01
Sep 20	Dak Draper	L	NWA Power	6:34
Sep 22	Ladder Match: Bhupinder Gujjar	W	IMPACT Wrestling	12:11
Sep 29	Crazzy Steve	W	IMPACT Wrestling	4:06
Nov 1	Brady Pierce, Rush Freeman & Rolando Freeman (w/Mike Knox & VSK)	L	NWA Power	6:54
Nov 10	Joe Hendry	L	IMPACT Wrestling	5:58
Dec 15	Black Taurus & Crazzy Steve (w/Matt Cardona)	W	IMPACT Wrestling	4:24

BRIAN PILLMAN JR.

Jan 4	JD Drake	W	AEW Dark	6:06
Jan 5	Malakai Black	L	AEW Dynamite	6:02
Jan 18	Adrian Alanis & Liam Gray (w/Griff Garrison)	W	AEW Dark	2:03
Jan 19	Malakai Black & Brody King (w/Griff Garrison)	L	AEW Dynamite	1:53
Feb 22	Guillermo Rosas & Marcus Kross (w/Griff Garrison)	W	AEW Dark	5:52
Mar 2	Casino Battle Royale (w/Griff Garrison)	L	AEW Dynamite	6:59
Mar 22	Sotheara Chhun & Tony Vincita (w/Griff Garrison)	W	AEW Dark	3:36
Mar 23	Bryan Danielson & Jon Moxley (w/Griff Garrison)	L	AEW Dynamite	6:04
Apr 27	Adam Cole, Matt Jackson, Nick Jackson, Bobby Fish, Kyle O'Reilly (w/Dante Martin, Lee Johnson, Brock Anderson & Griff Garrison)	L	AEW Dynamite	6:28
May 3	Anthony Henry & JD Drake (w/Griff Garrison)	W	AEW Dark	6:33
May 23	The Butcher & The Blade (w/Griff Garrison)	L	AEW Dark Elevation	5:55
Jun 21	Jay Lucas, Larry Lazard & Terry Yaki (w/Griff Garrison & Brock Anderson)	W	AEW Dark	3:00
Jul 19	Terrell Hughes & Terrence Hughes (w/Griff Garrison)	W	AEW Dark	3:16
Jul 20	Christian Cage & Luchasaurus (w/Griff Garrison)	L	AEW Dynamite: Fyter Fest	2:08
Jul 31	Ricky Morton & Kerry Morton (w/Brock Anderson)	W	JCP Ric Flair's Last Match	7:21
Aug 17	Austin Gunn & Colten Gunn (w/Griff Garrison)	L	AEW Dynamite	:31
Aug 30	Dean Alexander & Rosario Grillo (w/Griff Garrison)	W	AEW Dark	2:25
Oct 7	Josh Woods & Tony Nese (w/Griff Garrison)	L	AEW Rampage	1:45
Oct 24	Anthony Henry & JD Drake (w/Griff Garrison)	W	AEW Dark Elevation	5:47
Nov 8	Cole Karter & QT Marshall (w/Griff Garrison)	L	AEW Dark	4:13

BRIANA RAY (AS KYLIE RAE UNTIL DECEMBER 15)

Jan 5	Kamille & Missa Kate (w/Tootie Lynn)	W	NWA Power	6:44
Jan 18	Allysin Kay	W	NWA Power	5:43
Mar 20	Kamille, Chelsea Green	L	NWA Crockett Cup '22	12:02
Dec 15	Dana Brooke	L	WWE Main Event	6:12

BRIE BELLA

Jan 29	Royal Rumble Match	L	WWE Royal Rumble '22	19:21

BRITTANY BLAKE

Jan 24	Leyla Hirsch	L	AEW Dark Elevation	2:25
Jul 14	Zoey Stark	W	MLW Fusion	2:37
Oct 11	Jamie Hayter, Penelope Ford & Serena Deeb (w/Jordan Blade & Trish Adora)	L	AEW Dark	4:32
Nov 24	Taya Valkyrie	L	MLW Fusion	6:50

BROCK ANDERSON

Jan 28	Dax Harwood & Cash Wheeler (w/Lee Johnson)	L	AEW Rampage: Beach Break	9:10
Feb 7	Anthony Bowens, Max Caster, Austin Gunn & Colten Gunn (w/Lee Moriarty, Matt Sydal & Lee Johnson)	L	AEW Dark Elevation	7:11
Feb 21	Luther, Serpentico, Cezar Bononi, JD Drake & Peter Avalon (w/Frankie Kazarian, Jay Lethal, Lee Johnson & Matt Sydal)	W	AEW Dark Elevation	6:06
Mar 2	Casino Battle Royale (w/Lee Johnson)	L	AEW Dynamite	20:14
Mar 8	Isiah Kassidy & Marq Quen (w/Lee Johnson)	L	AEW Dark	5:05
Apr 4	Aaron Solo & QT Marshall (w/Lee Johnson)	W	AEW Dark Elevation	6:59
Apr 20	Bryan Danielson, Jon Moxley & Wheeler Yuta (w/Lee Moriarty & Dante Martin)	L	AEW Dynamite	8:08
Apr 27	Adam Cole, Matt Jackson, Nick Jackson, Bobby Fish & Kyle O'Reilly (w/Dante Martin, Lee Johnson, Brian Pillman Jr. & Griff Garrison)	L	AEW Dynamite	6:28
		W	AEW Dark	3:30
May 10	JCruz & Victor Chase (w/Lee Johnson)			
Jun 14	Bobby Fish	L	AEW Dark	5:57
Jun 21	Jay Lucas, Larry Lazard & Terry Yaki (w/Brian Pillman Jr. & Griff Garrison)	W	AEW Dark	3:00
Jul 31	Ricky Morton & Kerry Morton (w/Brian Pillman Jr.)	W	JCP Ric Flair's Last Match	7:21
Aug 16	Serpentico	W	AEW Dark	6:38
Aug 30	Tyson Maddux	W	AEW Dark	1:31
Nov 15	Daniel Garcia	L	AEW Dark	7:49
Dec 27	Matt Menard	L	AEW Dark	4:44

BROCK LESNAR

Jan 1	Big E, Seth Rollins, Kevin Owens, Bobby Lashley	W	WWE Day 1	8:19
Jan 29	Big E	L	WWE Royal Rumble '22	10:15
Jan 29	Royal Rumble Match	W	WWE Royal Rumble '22	2:32
Feb 19	Elimination Chamber: AJ Styles, Austin Theory, Riddle, Seth Rollins	W	WWE Elimination Chamber '22	14:55
Apr 3	Roman Reigns	L	WWE WrestleMania XXXVIII	12:15
Jul 30	Last Man Standing: Roman Reigns	L	WWE SummerSlam '22	23:00
Nov 5	Bobby Lashley	W	WWE Crown Jewel '22	6:00

BRODY KING

Jan 15	Dave Dutra	W	NJPW Strong	6:31
Jan 19	Brian Pillman Jr. & Griff Garrison (w/Malakai Black)	W	AEW Dynamite	1:53
Feb 2	Pac & Penta El Zero M (w/Malakai Black)	W	AEW Dynamite	10:23
Feb 5	Yuya Uemura	W	NJPW Strong	12:56
Feb 23	Pac & Penta Oscuro (w/Malakai Black)	L	AEW Dynamite	7:31
Mar 6	Pac, Penta Oscuro & Erick Redbeard (w/Malakai Black & Buddy Matthews)	W	AEW Revolution Buy-In	17:20
Mar 18	Fuego Del Sol, Bear Bronson & Bear Boulder (w/Malakai Black & Buddy Matthews)	W	AEW Rampage	3:22
Apr 1	Fuego Del Sol, Evil Uno & Stu Grayson (w/Malakai Black & Buddy Matthews)	W	AEW Rampage	7:15
Apr 16	Chicago Street Fight: Jonah, Shane Haste & Bad Dude Tito (w/David Finlay & Juice Robinson)	W	NJPW Windy City Riot	24:11
May 14	Minoru Suzuki	W	NJPW Capital Collision	9:05
May 16	Alex Reynolds	W	AEW Dark Elevation	1:46
May 20	Fuego Del Sol, Evil Uno & Ten (w/Malakai Black & Buddy Matthews)	W	AEW Rampage	9:25
May 21	Aaron Henare, Great-O-Khan & TJP (w/Mascara Dorada & Taylor Rust)	L	NJPW Strong	14:04
May 28	Adriel Noctis, Greg Sharpe & Matt Brannigan (w/Malakai Black & Buddy Matthews)	W	AEW Dark	3:50
May 29	Pac, Penta Oscuro & Rey Fenix (w/Buddy Matthews & Malakai Black)	W	AEW Double Or Nothing '22	15:35
Jun 18	Jake Something	W	NJPW Strong	8:27
Jun 27	Brubaker & CJ Esparza	W	AEW Dark Elevation	2:36
Jul 1	Royal Rampage Match	W	AEW Rampage	22:41
Jul 6	Jon Moxley	L	AEW Dynamite	11:14
Jul 15	Aley Reynolds & John Silver (w/Malakai Black)	W	AEW Rampage	8:18
Jul 20	Darby Allin	W	AEW Dynamite: Fyter Fest	12:35
Aug 10	Coffin Match: Darby Allin	L	AEW Dynamite: Quake By The Lake	13:28
Aug 26	Ten, John Silver & Alex Reynolds (w/Malakai Black & Buddy Matthews)	L	AEW Rampage	9:03
Sep 4	Darby Allin, Sting & Miro (w/Malakai Black & Buddy Matthews)	L	AEW All Out '22	12:10
Sep 12	Isaiah Prince & Kubes (w/Buddy Matthews)	W	AEW Dark Elevation	2:34
Sep 23	No DQ: Sting & Darby Allin (w/Buddy Matthews)	L	AEW Rampage: Grand Slam	12:57
Dec 14	QT Marshall, Aaron Solo & Cole Karter (w/Malakai Black & Buddy Matthews)	W	AEW Dynamite: Winter Is Coming	:23

BRON BREAKKER

Jan 4	Tommaso Ciampa	W	NXT 2.0: New Year's Evil '22	15:28
Feb 1	Joaquin Wilde & Raul Mendoza (w/Tommaso Ciampa)	W	NXT 2.0	11:28
Feb 15	Santos Escobar	W	NXT 2.0: Vengeance Day '22	12:05
Mar 1	Dolph Ziggler & Robert Roode (w/Tommaso Ciampa)	W	NXT 2.0	13:05
Mar 7	Dolph Ziggler & Robert Roode (w/Tommaso Ciampa)	W	WWE Monday Night RAW	9:37
Mar 8	Dolph Ziggler, Tommaso Ciampa	L	NXT 2.0: Roadblock '22	12:24
Mar 22	Robert Roode	W	NXT 2.0	15:14
Apr 2	Dolph Ziggler	L	NXT Stand & Deliver '22	16:13
Apr 4	Dolph Ziggler	W	WWE Monday Night RAW	10:45
Apr 5	Gunther	W	NXT 2.0	13:08
May 3	Joe Gacy	W	NXT 2.0: Spring Breakin'	11:03
May 24	Duke Hudson	L	NXT 2.0	11:02
Jun 4	Joe Gacy	W	NXT In Your House '22	15:50
Jun 13	Duke Hudson	W	NXT 2.0	:46
Jul 5	Cameron Grimes	W	NXT 2.0: Great American Bash	12:33
Aug 16	JD McDonagh	W	NXT 2.0: Heatwave	13:17

Sep 4	Tyler Bate	W	NXT Worlds Collide '22	17:11
Sep 6	Mark Coffey & Joe Coffey (w/Tyler Bate)	W	NXT 2.0	10:51
Oct 11	Javier Bernal	W	NXT	3:20
Oct 22	Ilja Dragunov, JD McDonagh	W	NXT Halloween Havoc '22	23:47
Nov 1	Elton Prince & Kit Wilson (w/Wes Lee)	L	NXT	11:57
Nov 15	Von Wagner	W	NXT	12:42
Dec 10	Apollo Crews	W	NXT Deadline	14:34

BRONCO NIMA

Aug 12	Andre Chase & Bodhi Hayward (w/Lucien Price)	L	NXT Level Up	6:16
Aug 26	Edris Enofe & Malik Blade (w/Lucien Price)	L	NXT Level Up	5:50
Sep 16	Duke Hudson	L	NXT Level Up	5:40
Nov 11	Edris Enofe, Malik Blade & Odyssey Jones (w/Lucien Price & Xyon Quinn)	L	NXT Level Up	6:41
Dec 16	Jagger Reid & Rip Fowler (w/Lucien Price)	L	NXT Level Up	5:39
Dec 30	Bryson Montana & Oba Femi (w/Lucien Price)	W	NXT Level Up	4:38

BRONSON

Jan 12	Anthony Bowens & Max Caster (w/Bear Boulder)	L	AEW Dynamite	6:18
Jan 18	Brandon Bullock & Jameson Ryan (w/Bear Boulder)	W	AEW Dark	2:06
Feb 1	Dante Martin & Matt Sydal (w/Bear Boulder)	L	AEW Dark	9:43
Mar 2	Casino Battle Royale (w/Matt Lee)	L	AEW Dynamite	8:50
Mar 18	Malakai Black, Brody King & Buddy Matthews (w/Fuego Del Sol & Bear Boulder)	L	AEW Rampage	3:22
May 16	Brandon Cutler	W	AEW Dark Elevation	2:20
May 17	Anthony Henry & JD Drake (w/Bear Boulder)	W	AEW Dark	8:30
Jun 17	Max Caster, Austin Gunn & Colten Gunn (w/Leon Ruffin & Bear Boulder)	L	AEW Rampage	1:15
Jul 5	Adrian Alanis & Liam Gray (w/Bear Boulder)	W	AEW Dark	5:25
Jul 6	Anthony Bowens, Max Caster, Austin Gunn & Colten Gunn (w/Fuego Del Sol, Leon Ruffin & Bear Boulder)	L	AEW Dynamite	2:14
Jul 12	Isiah Kassidy & Marq Quen (w/Bear Boulder)	L	AEW Dark	10:45
Aug 16	Axel Rico & Victor Iniestra (w/Bear Boulder)	W	AEW Dark	3:59
Aug 23	Manny Lo & Sean Maluta (w/Boulder)	W	AEW Dark	1:59
Oct 4	Levis Valenzuela & Vary Morales (w/Boulder)	W	AEW Dark	2:42
Nov 15	Brando Lee & Lucas Chase (w/Boulder)	W	AEW Dark	2:40
Dec 27	Brandon Bullock & James Ryan (w/Boulder)	W	AEW Dark	2:13

BROOKLYN BARLOW

Mar 11	Ivy Nile	L	NXT Level Up	3:50
Jun 3	Fallon Henley	L	NXT Level Up	4:19
Jun 24	Kiana James	L	NXT Level Up	5:15
Jul 22	Thea Hail	L	NXT Level Up	5:26

BROOKS JENSEN

Jan 18	Julius Creed & Brutus Creed (w/Josh Briggs)	L	NXT 2.0	5:33
Feb 4	Bodhi Hayward	W	WWE 205 Live	6:06
Mar 11	Zack Gibson & James Drake (w/Josh Briggs)	L	NXT Level Up	5:58
Mar 29	Joaquin Wilde & Raul Mendoza (w/Josh Briggs)	W	NXT 2.0	5:36
Apr 12	Gauntlet Match: Grayson Waller & Sanga, Kit Wilson & Elton Prince Joaquin Wilde & Raul Mendoza, Julius Creed & Brutus Creed (w/Josh Briggs)	L	NXT 2.0	27:08
Jun 21	Von Wagner	L	NXT 2.0	4:45
Jun 23	Elimination Match: Dave Mastiff & Jack Starz, Charlie Dempsey & Rohan Raja, Mark Andrews & Wild Boar (w/Josh Briggs)	W	NXT UK	18:15
Jul 19	Elton Prince & Kit Wilson (w/Josh Briggs)	W	NXT 2.0	8:15
Jul 28	Mark Andrews & Wild Boar (w/Josh Briggs)	W	NXT UK	9:03
Aug 2	Joe Gacy	L	NXT 2.0	3:00
Aug 23	Mark Coffey & Wolfgang (w/Josh Briggs)	L	NXT 2.0	8:46
Aug 30	Lash Legend, Elton Prince & Kit Wilson (w/Fallon Henley & Josh Briggs)	L	NXT 2.0	11:31
Sep 4	Elimination Match: Elton Prince & Kit Wilson, Brutus Creed & Julius Creed, Mark Coffey & Wolfgang (w/Josh Briggs)	L	NXT Worlds Collide '22	15:34
Sep 27	Pub Rules Match: Mark Coffey & Wolfsgang (w/Josh Briggs)	W	NXT	11:35
Oct 6	R-Truth & Shelton Benjamin (w/Josh Briggs)	W	WWE Main Event	6:48
Oct 11	Edris Enofe & Malik Blade, Jagger Reid & Rip Fowler (w/Josh Briggs)	L	NXT	9:10
Oct 28	Trick Williams	W	NXT Level Up	6:11
Nov 15	Jagger Reid & Rip Fowler (w/Josh Briggs)	L	NXT	4:10
Dec 6	Edris Enofe & Malik Blade (w/Josh Briggs)	W	NXT	3:24
Dec 20	Kofi Kingston & Xavier Woods (w/Josh Briggs)	L	NXT	11:10

BRUTUS CREED

Jan 18	Josh Briggs & Brooks Jensen (w/Julius Creed)	W	NXT 2.0	5:33
Feb 1	Walter, Marcel Barthel & Fabian Aichner (w/Julius Creed & Roderick Strong)	L	NXT 2.0	12:01
Feb 8	Zack Gibson & James Drake (w/Julius Creed)	W	NXT 2.0	12:03
Feb 15	Nash Carter & Wes Lee (w/Julius Creed)	W	NXT 2.0: Vengeance Day '22	9:36
Mar 22	Zack Gibson & James Drake (w/Julius Creed)	W	NXT 2.0	4:14
Apr 2	Wes Lee & Nash Carter, Marcel Barthel & Fabin Aichner (w/Julius Creed)	L	NXT Stand & Deliver '22	11:22
Apr 5	Marcel Barthel & Fabian Aichner (w/Julius Creed)	W	NXT 2.0	11:24
Apr 12	Gauntlet Match: Grayson Waller & Sanga, Kit Wilson & Elton Prince Joaquin Wilde & Raul Mendoza, Brooks Jensen & Josh Briggs (w/Julius Creed)	L	NXT 2.0	27:08
May 3	Erik & Ivar (w/Julius Creed)	W	NXT 2.0: Spring Breakin'	12:58
May 17	Erik & Ivar (w/Julius Creed)	L	NXT 2.0	9:30
Jun 4	Elton Prince & Kit Wilson (w/Julius Creed)	W	NXT In Your House '22	15:19
Jun 14	Edris Enofe & Malik Blade (w/Julius Creed)	W	NXT 2.0	13:57

Jun 28	Joe Gacy, Rip Fowler & Jagger Reid (w/Roderick Strong & Julius Creed)	L	NXT 2.0	13:56
Jul 5	Roderick Strong & Damon Kemp (w/Julius Creed)	W	NXT 2.0: Great American Bash	12:13
Jul 26	Tony D'Angelo, Channing Lorenzo, Joaquin Wilde & Cruz Del Toro (w/Roderick Strong, Damon Kemp & Julius Creed)	L	NXT 2.0	11:39
Aug 2	Tony D'Angelo & Channing Lorenzo (w/Julius Creed)	W	NXT 2.0	10:46
Aug 30	Joe Coffey, Mark Coffey & Wolfgang (w/Damon Kemp & Julius Creed)	L	NXT 2.0	10:59
Sep 4	Elimination Match: Elton Prince & Kit Wilson, Brooks Jensen & Josh Briggs, Mark Coffey & Wolfgang (w/Julius Creed)	L	NXT Worlds Collide '22	15:34
Sep 13	Steel Cage Match: Elton Prince & Kit Wilson (w/Julius Creed)	L	NXT 2.0	14:58
Sep 27	Damon Kemp	W	NXT	3:05
Nov 8	Five Minute Challenge: Damon Kemp	L	NXT	2:47
Dec 13	JD McDonagh	L	NXT	4:18

BRYAN DANIELSON

Jan 5	Hangman Page	L	AEW Dynamite	29:06
Feb 16	Lee Moriarty	W	AEW Dynamite	12:14
Feb 23	Daniel Garcia	W	AEW Dynamite	10:22
Mar 2	Christopher Daniels	W	AEW Dynamite	11:17
Mar 6	Jon Moxley	L	AEW Revolution '22	21:05
Mar 9	JD Drake & Anthony Henry (w/Jon Moxley)	W	AEW Dynamite	4:00
Mar 16	Chuck Taylor & Wheeler Yuta (w/Jon Moxley)	W	AEW Dynamite -St. Patrick's Day Slam	11:45
Mar 23	Brian Pillman Jr. & Griff Garrison (w/Jon Moxley)	W	AEW Dynamite	6:04
Mar 30	Wheeler Yuta	W	AEW Dynamite	10:10
Apr 8	Trent Beretta	W	AEW Rampage	13:39
Apr 15	Billy Gunn, Austin Gunn & Colten Gunn (w/Jon Moxley & Wheeler Yuta)	W	AEW Rampage	9:06
Apr 20	Lee Moriarty, Dante Martin & Brock Anderson (w/Jon Moxley & Wheeler Yuta)	W	AEW Dynamite	8:08
Apr 27	QT Marshall, Aaron Solo & Nick Comoroto (w/Jon Moxley & Wheeler Yuta)	W	AEW Dynamite	8:49
May 4	Angelico, The Butcher, The Blade (w/Jon Moxley & Wheeler Yuta)	W	AEW Dynamite	7:27
May 20	Dante Martin & Matt Sydal (w/Jon Moxley)	W	AEW Dynamite	12:00
May 27	Matt Sydal	W	AEW Rampage	11:09
May 29	Anarchy In The Arena: Chris Jericho, Daniel Garcia, Jake Hager, Angelo Parker & Matt Menard (w/Jon Moxley, Eddie Kingston, Santana & Ortiz)	L	AEW Double Or Nothing '22	22:45
Jul 27	Daniel Garcia	L	AEW Dynamite -Fight For The Fallen	17:12
Aug 17	2/3 Falls: Daniel Garcia	W	AEW Dynamite	26:16
Aug 31	Jake Hager	W	AEW Dynamite	10:46
Sep 4	Chris Jericho	L	AEW All Out '22	23:40
Sep 7	Hangman Page	W	AEW Dynamite	22:52
Sep 14	Chris Jericho	W	AEW Dynamite	19:44
Sep 21	Jon Moxley	L	AEW Dynamite	19:31
Sep 28	Matt Menard	W	AEW Dynamite	8:36
Oct 5	Chris Jericho & Sammu Guevara (w/Daniel Garcia)	L	AEW Dynamite -Anniversary	14:23
Oct 12	Chris Jericho	L	AEW Dynamite	14:09
Oct 26	Sammy Guevara	W	AEW Dynamite	14:58
Nov 9	2/3 Falls: Sammy Guevara	W	AEW Dynamite	20:33
Nov 16	Chris Jericho & Sammy Guevara (w/Claudio Castagnoli)	L	AEW Dynamite	18:02
Nov 19	Chris Jericho, Claudio Castagnoli, Sammy Guevara	L	AEW Full Gear '22	21:30
Nov 30	Dax Harwood	W	AEW Dynamite	14:49
Dec 28	Ethan Page	W	AEW Dynamite	16:25

BRYSON MONTANA

May 20	Javier Bernal	L	NXT Level Up	4:13
May 27	Andre Chase & Bodhi Hayward (w/Damaris Griffin)	L	NXT Level Up	3:53
Jun 24	Quincy Elliott	L	NXT Level Up	5:07
Jul 8	Edris Enofe & Malik Blade (w/Damaris Griffin)	L	NXT Level Up	5:29
Jul 22	Ru Feng	W	NXT Level Up	4:40
Aug 5	Dante Chen & Guru Raaj (w/Damaris Griffin)	L	NXT Level Up	5:20
Sep 23	Dante Chen	L	NXT Level Up	5:47
Oct 14	Ikemen Jiro & Tank Ledger (w/Duke Hudson)	L	NXT Level Up	6:18
Oct 21	Duke Hudson	L	NXT Level Up	3:55
Dec 30	Bronco Nima & Lucien Price (w/Oba Femi)	L	NXT Level Up	4:38

BUDDY MATTHEWS

Mar 6	Pac, Penta Oscuro & Erick Redbeard (w/Malakai Black & Brody King)	W	AEW Revolution Buy-In	17:20
Mar 17	TJP	L	MLW Fusion	20:21
Mar 18	Fuego Del Sol, Bear Bronson & Bear Boulder (w/Malakai Black & Brody King)	W	AEW Rampage	3:22
Mar 19	Ren Narita	W	NJPW Strong	15:32
Apr 1	Fuego Del Sol, Evil Uno & Stu Grayson (w/Malakai Black & Brody King)	W	AEW Rampage	7:15
Apr 23	Yuya Uemura	W	NJPW Strong	9:50
May 20	Fuego Del Sol, Evil Uno & Ten (w/Malakai Black & Brody King)	W	AEW Rampage	9:25
May 28	Adriel Noctis, Greg Sharpe & Matt Brannigan (w/Malakai Black & Brody King)	W	AEW Dark	3:50
May 29	Pac, Penta Oscuro & Rey Fenix (w/Malakai Black & Brody King)	W	AEW Double Or Nothing '22	15:35
Jun 8	Pac	L	AEW Dynamite	10:46
Jun 27	Brubaker & CJ Esparza (w/Brody King)	W	AEW Dark Elevation	2:36
Aug 19	Serpentico	W	AEW Rampage	1:33
Aug 26	Ten, John Silver & Alex Reynolds (w/Malakai Black & Brody King)	L	AEW Rampage	9:03
Sep 4	Darby Allin, Sting & Miro (w/Malakai Black & Brody King)	L	AEW All Out '22	12:10
Sep 12	Isaiah Prince & Kubes (w/Brody King)	W	AEW Dark Elevation	2:34

| Sep 23 | No DQ: Darby Allin & Sting (w/Brody King) | L | AEW Rampage: Grand Slam | 12:57 |
| Dec 14 | QT Marshall, Aaron Solo & Cole Karter (w/Malakai Black & Brody King) | W | AEW Dynamite: Winter Is Coming | :23 |

BULLY RAY

Aug 27	Tables Match: Mike Knox	W	NWA 74th Anniversary Show	8:38
Sep 20	Mike Knox & VSK (w/Thom Latimer)	W	NWA Power	5:15
Oct 7	Call Your Shot Gauntlet	W	IMPACT Bound For Glory '22	29:18
Oct 20	Chris Bey & Juice Robinson (w/Tommy Dreamer)	W	IMPACT Wrestling	6:23
Nov 10	Zicky Dice	W	IMPACT Wrestling	1:10
Dec 1	Rich Swann	L	IMPACT Wrestling	5:53
Dec 6	Odinson	D	NWA Power	10:00
Dec 15	John Skyler	W	IMPACT Wrestling	1:06
Dec 20	Chris Adonis, Dak Draper & Mims (w/Judais & Thom Latimer)	W	NWA Power	8:18

BUNNY, THE

Jan 14	Red Velvet, Leyla Hirsch & Kris Statlander (w/Penelope Ford & Nyla Rose)	W	AEW Rampage	8:12
Jan 25	Erica Leigh	W	AEW Dark	2:13
Feb 7	Heather Reckless, Queen Aminata & Skye Blue (w/Emi Sakura & Diamante)	W	AEW Dark Elevation	4:02
Feb 14	Ruby Soho, Anna Jay & Tay Conti (w/Emi Sakura & Nyla Rose)	L	AEW Dark Elevation	3:43
Feb 21	Kaitland Alexis	W	AEW Dark Elevation	2:05
Feb 23	Jade Cargill	L	AEW Dynamite	6:50
Mar 14	Kilynn King & Skye Blue (w/Emi Sakura)	W	AEW Dark Elevation	6:00
Mar 21	Anna Jay & Ruby Soho (w/Emi Sakura)	L	AEW Dark Elevation	4:20
Mar 30	Toni Storm	L	AEW Dynamite	8:41
Apr 11	Anna Jay, Ruby Soho & Skye Blue (w/Emi Sakura & LuFisto)	L	AEW Dark Elevation	3:21
Apr 18	Anna Jay, Hikaru Shida & Ruby Soho (w/Emi Sakura & Raychell Rose)	L	AEW Dark Elevation	3:20
Apr 25	Anna Jay, Ruby Soho & Skye Blue (w/Emi Sakura & Nyla Rose)	L	AEW Dark Elevation	6:35
Apr 26	Anna Jay & Skye Blue (w/Raychell Rose)	L	AEW Dark	5:07
Nov 28	Blair Onyx	W	AEW Dark Elevation	1:18
Dec 9	Hikaru Shida	L	AEW Rampage	7:26
Dec 19	Gigi Rey & Lady Bird Monroe (w/Emi Sakura)	W	AEW Dark Elevation	2:45
Dec 26	Madison Rayne	W	AEW Dark Elevation	3:00

BUSHI

Jan 4	Will Ospreay, Great-O-Khan & Jeff Cobb (w/Tetsuya Naito & Sanada)	L	NJPW Wrestle Kingdom 16 Night #1	9:27
Jan 8	Katsuhiko Nakajima, Kenoh, Manabu Soya, Tadasuke & Aleja (w/Tetsuya Naito, Shingo Takagi, Sanada & Hiromu Takahashi)	W	NJPW Wrestle Kingdom 16 Night #3	26:33
Mar 1	Togi Makabe, Tomoaki Honma, Tomohiro Ishii, Shiro Koshinaka & Toru Yano (w/Sanada, Tetsuya Naito, Shingo Takagi & Hiromu Takahashi)	W	NJPW 50th Anniversary Show	12:38
May 1	Taichi, Zack Sabre Jr. & Taka Michinoku (w/Shingo Takagi & Shiro Koshinaka)	L	NJPW Wrestling Dontaku '22	10:15
Jun 12	Taiji Ishimori, El Phantasmo & Ace Austin (w/Tetsuya Naito & Hiromu Takahashi)	L	NJPW Dominion '22	8:04
Sep 25	El Phantasmo, Hikuleo & Kenta (w/Hiromu Takahashi & Shingo Takagi)	W	NJPW Burning Spirit '22	8:43
Oct 10	Will Ospreay, Aaron Henare, TJP & Francesco Akira (w/Tetsuya Naito, Sanada & Hiromu Takahashi)	W	NJPW Declaration Of Power	8:07
Nov 5	TJP & Francesco Akira (w/Titan)	L	NJPW Battle Autumn '22	11:36
Nov 20	Kyle Fletcher, Mark David, Francesco Akira, TJP & Gideon Grey (w/Hiromu Takahashi, Sanada, Shingo Takagi & Tetsuya Naito)	L	NJPW x Stardom Historic X-Over	9:55

BUTCH (AS PETE DUNNE UNTIL APRIL 8)

Jan 11	Crowbar On A Pole Match: Tony D'Angelo	L	NXT 2.0	13:17
Jan 13	Akira Tozawa	W	WWE Main Event	7:11
Jan 20	T-Bar	W	WWE Main Event	6:44
Feb 8	Draco Anthony	W	NXT 2.0	6:53
Feb 15	Weaponized Steel Cage Match: Tony D'Angelo	W	NXT 2.0 Vengeance Day '22	9:52
Mar 1	Carmelo Hayes	L	NXT 2.0	12:31
Apr 8	Xavier Woods	L	WWE SmackDown	8:35
Apr 22	Xavier Woods	L	WWE SmackDown	9:00
May 13	Kofi Kingston	W	WWE SmackDown	8:20
May 20	Xavier Woods	L	WWE SmackDown	3:28
May 27	Drew McIntyre, Xavier Woods & Kofi Kingston (w/Sheamus & Ridge Holland)	L	WWE SmackDown	11:30
Jun 3	Drew McIntyre, Xavier Woods & Kofi Kingston (w/Sheamus & Ridge Holland)	W	WWE SmackDown	10:30
Jul 8	Drew McIntyre	L	WWE SmackDown	1:30
Sep 2	Ludwig Kaiser	W	WWE SmackDown	9:10
Sep 9	Gunther, Ludwig Kaiser & Giovanni Vinci (w/Sheamus & Ridge Holland)	L	WWE SmackDown	19:05
Sep 16	Ashante Adonis & Top Dolla, Ludwig Kaiser & Giovanni Vinci, Kofi Kingston & Xavier Woods (w/Ridge Holland)	W	WWE SmackDown	18:44
Sep 19	Angelo Dawkins & Montez Ford (w/Ridge Holland)	W	WWE Monday Night RAW	12:57
Sep 23	Jimmy Uso & Jey Uso (w/Ridge Holland)	L	WWE SmackDown	14:10
Oct 4	Elton Prince & Kit Wilson (w/Ridge Holland)	L	NXT	12:27
Oct 8	Good Old Fashioned Donnybrook Match: Gunther, Ludwig Kaiser & Giovanni Vinci (w/Sheamus & Ridge Holland)	W	WWE Extreme Rules '22	17:50
Oct 28	Sami Zayn & Solo Sikoa (w/Ridge Holland)	W	WWE SmackDown	11:50
Nov 5	Jey Uso & Jimmy Uso (w/Ridge Holland)	L	WWE Crown Jewel '22	10:45
Nov 18	Sami Zayn	W	WWE SmackDown	7:30
Nov 21	Finn Balor, Damian Priest & Dominik Mysterio (w/Ridge Holland & Sheamus)	W	WWE Monday Night RAW	14:50
Nov 25	Santos Escobar	L	WWE SmackDown	6:41

| Nov 26 | WarGames: Roman Reigns, Solo Sikoa, Sami Zayn, Jey Uso & Jimmy Uso (w/Sheamus, Ridge Holland, Drew McIntyre & Kevin Owens) | L | WWE Survivor Series WarGames | 38:30 |
| Dec 9 | Jey Uso & Jimmy Uso (w/Sheamus) | L | WWE SmackDown | 19:20 |

BUTCHER, THE

Feb 21	Baron Black, Carlie Bravo, Chandler Hopkins, James Ryan & Shawn Dean (w/Andrade El Idolo, Isiah Kassidy, Marq Quen & The Blade)	W	AEW Dark Elevation	4:20
Feb 23	Tag Team Battle Royal (w/The Blade)	L	AEW Dynamite	3:30
Mar 2	Casino Battle Royale (w/The Blade)	L	AEW Dynamite	11:52
Mar 8	Alan Angels & Colt Cabana (w/The Blade)	W	AEW Dark	5:31
Mar 18	Darby Allin	L	AEW Rampage	10:41
Mar 22	Carlie Bravo & Shawn Dean (w/The Blade)	W	AEW Dark	2:41
Mar 23	Tornado Match: Sting, Darby Allin, Matt Hardy & Jeff Hardy (w/Isiah Kassidy, Marq Quen & The Blade)	L	AEW Dynamite	9:27
Apr 6	Tables Match: Matt Hardy & Jeff Hardy (w/The Blade)	L	AEW Dynamite	11:54
Apr 15	Barrett Brown	W	AEW Rampage	:55
Apr 20	Wardlow	L	AEW Dynamite	4:20
May 4	Bryan Danielson, Jon Moxley & Wheeler Yuta (w/Angelo & The Blade)	L	AEW Dynamite	7:27
May 13	Pac, Penta El Zero M & Rey Fenix (w/Marq Quen & The Blade)	L	AEW Rampage	10:22
May 23	Brian Pillman Jr. & Griff Garisson (w/The Blade)	W	AEW Dark Elevation	5:55
May 31	Hunter Grey & Paul Titan (w/The Blade)	W	AEW Dark	3:52
Jul 1	Royal Rampage Match	L	AEW Rampage	22:41
Jul 6	Keith Lee & Swerve Strickland (w/The Blade)	L	AEW Dynamite	9:38
Jul 18	Brandon Bullock, Bryce Cannon & Jameson Ryan (w/Angelico & The Blade)	W	AEW Dark Elevation	1:40
Jul 22	Hangman Page & John Silver (w/The Blade)	L	AEW Rampage	9:55
Aug 1	JCruz, Joey Ace, Victor Chase, Jaylen Brandyn & Traevon Jordan (w/Isiah Kassidy, Marq Quen, Angelico & The Blade)	W	AEW Dark Elevation	2:12
Aug 9	Braden Lee, Isaiah Broner, James Alexander & Sam Moore (w/The Blade, Isiah Kassidy & Marq Quen)	W	AEW Dark	2:22
Aug 29	Chase Oliver, Elijah Dean & Zach Nystrom (w/Rush & The Blade)	W	AEW Dark Elevation	3:20
Sep 3	Orange Cassidy, Chuck Taylor & Trent Beretta (w/Angelico & The Blade)	W	AEW Dark Elevation	8:13
Sep 12	Aaron Solo & Nick Comoroto (w/The Blade)	W	AEW Dark Elevation	4:37
Sep 19	Liam Davis & Mike Anthony (w/The Blade)	W	AEW Dark Elevation	2:48
Sep 23	Golden Ticket Battle Royale	L	AEW Rampage: Grand Slam	12:16
Sep 30	Anthony Bowens & Max Caster, Marq Quen & Isiah Kassidy (w/The Blade)	L	AEW Rampage	10:00
Oct 14	Jon Moxley & Claudio Castagnoli (w/The Blade)	L	AEW Rampage	8:40
Oct 17	Chris Voros & Patrick Voros (w/The Blade)	W	AEW Dark Elevation	2:37
Nov 7	Rocky Romero, Chuck Taylor & Trent Beretta (w/Angelico & The Blade)	L	AEW Dark Elevation	7:20
Nov 14	Jaylen Brandyn & Traevon Jordan (w/The Blade)			
Nov 21	Brett Gosselin, Channing Thomas & Doug Love (w/Rush & The Blade)	W	AEW Dark Elevation	2:20
Nov 25	John Silver, Alex Reynolds & Ten (w/Rush & The Blade)	W	AEW Rampage: Black Friday	7:24
Dec 7	Dynamite Diamond Battle Royale	L	AEW Dynamite	13:10
Dec 16	Orange Cassidy, Dustin Rhodes, Chuck Taylor & Trent Beretta (w/Trent Seven, Kip Sabian & The Blade)	L	AEW Rampage	10:42
Dec 23	$300,000 Three Kings Christmas Casino Trios Royale (w/Kip Sabian & The Blade)	L	AEW Rampage	22:01

CALEB KONLEY

Jan 27	Cassie Lee & Jessie McKay (w/Madison Rayne)	L	IMPACT Wrestling	10:57
Jun 28	Ari Daivari	L	AEW Dark	6:25
Sep 27	Angelico	L	AEW Dark	3:42
Nov 8	Eddie Kingston & Ortiz (w/AR Fox)	L	AEW Dark	1:49
Dec 20	Kip Sabian	L	AEW Dark	2:49

CALVIN TANKMAN

Mar 3	Alex Kane	L	MLW Fusion	8:08
Mar 10	Alex Kane, ACH	L	MLW Fusion	8:00
Mar 31	Rivera & Slice Boogie (w/EJ Nduka)	W	MLW Fusion	8:08
May 5	Budd Heavy & Red Pickins (w/EJ Nduka)	W	MLW Fusion	1:20
May 19	Alex Zayne & Mr. Thomas (w/EJ Nduka)	W	MLW Fusion	7:26
Jun 16	Rivera & Slice Boogie, Marshall Von Erich & Ross Von Erich (w/EJ Nduka)	W	MLW Fusion	9:12

CAMERON

| Jan 29 | Royal Rumble Match | L | WWE Royal Rumble '22 | :51 |

CAMERON GRIMES

Jan 11	Damon Kemp	W	NXT 2.0	2:20
Jan 25	Tony D'Angelo	W	NXT 2.0	11:41
Feb 15	Carmelo Hayes	L	NXT 2.0: Vengeance Day '22	15:57
Feb 22	Trick Williams	W	NXT 2.0	6:06
Mar 15	Ladder Match: Santos Escobar	L	NXT 2.0	11:30
Mar 29	Ladder Match: A-Kid, Roderick Strong	W	NXT 2.0	10:55
Apr 2	Ladder Match: Carmelo Hayes, Santos Escobar, Solo Sikoa, Grayson Waller	W	NXT Stand & Deliver '22	21:01
Apr 12	Solo Sikoa	W	NXT 2.0	13:11
May 3	Carmelo Hayes, Solo Sikoa	W	NXT 2.0: Spring Breakin'	14:06
May 17	Carmelo Hayes & Trick Williams (w/Solo Sikoa)	W	NXT 2.0	9:57
May 31	Nathan Frazer	W	NXT 2.0	10:09
Jun 4	Carmelo Hayes	L	NXT In Your House '22	15:30
Jun 21	Edris Enofe	W	NXT 2.0	5:37
Jul 5	Bron Breakker	L	NXT 2.0: Great American Bash	12:33

Jul 19	JD McDonagh	L	NXT 2.0	13:25
Aug 23	Javier Bernal	W	NXT 2.0	2:35
Sep 13	Channing Lorenzo & Tony D'Angelo (w/Joe Gacy)	W	NXT 2.0	5:36
Sep 27	Joe Gacy	L	NXT	3:17
Oct 18	Joe Gacy, Jagger Reid & Rip Fowler (w/Luke Gallows & Karl Anderson)	W	NXT	11:56
Oct 20	Akira Tozawa	W	WWE Main Event	4:46
Nov 8	Joe Gacy	L	NXT	10:44

CANDICE LERAE

Sep 26	Nikki A.S.H.	W	WWE Monday Night RAW	1:45
Oct 3	Dakota Kai	L	WWE Monday Night RAW	11:00
Oct 17	Dakota Kai & Iyo Sky (w/Bianca Belair)	L	WWE Monday Night RAW	12:10
Nov 28	Dakota Kai	W	WWE Monday Night RAW	14:00
Dec 12	Iyo Sky	L	WWE Monday Night RAW	10:20

CARMELLA

Jan 3	Rhea Ripley & Nikki A.S.H. (w/Queen Zelina)	W	WWE Monday Night RAW	2:40
Jan 24	Rhea Ripley, Dana Brooke & Liv Morgan (w/Tamina & Nikki A.S.H.)	L	WWE Monday Night RAW	2:20
Jan 29	Royal Rumble Match	L	WWE Royal Rumble '22	:50
Jan 31	Bianca Belair	L	WWE Monday Night RAW	5:30
Mar 4	Naomi	L	WWE SmackDown	2:10
Mar 7	Rhea Ripley & Liv Morgan (w/Queen Zelina)	L	WWE Monday Night RAW	9:05
Mar 28	Naomi, Sasha Banks, Liv Morgan & Rhea Ripley (w/Queen Zelina, Natalya & Shayna Baszler)	L	WWE Monday Night RAW	8:20
Apr 1	Sasha Banks & Naomi (w/Queen Zelina)	L	WWE SmackDown	3:13
Apr 3	Sasha Banks & Naomi, Liv Morgan & Rhea Ripley, Natalya & Shayna Baszler (w/Queen Zelina)	L	WWE WrestleMania XXXVIII	10:50
Jun 20	Alexa Bliss, Asuka, Becky Lynch, Liv Morgan	W	WWE Monday Night RAW	12:30
Jul 2	Bianca Belair	L	WWE Money In The Bank '22	7:10
Jul 4	Bianca Belair & Liv Morgan (w/Natalya)	L	WWE Monday Night RAW	13:25
Jul 11	Bianca Belair	W	WWE Monday Night RAW	11:50
Jul 18	Bianca Belair	L	WWE Monday Night RAW	10:25
Jul 28	Asuka & Dana Brooke (w/Tamina)	L	WWE Main Event	7:09

CARMELO HAYES

Jan 4	Roderick Strong	W	NXT 2.0: New Year's Evil '22	15:30
Feb 15	Cameron Grimes	W	NXT 2.0: Vengeance Day '22	15:57
Mar 1	Pete Dunne	W	NXT 2.0	12:31
Apr 2	Ladder Match: Cameron Grimes, Santos Escobar, Solo Sikoa, Grayson Waller	W	NXT Stand & Deliver '22	21:01
Apr 19	Santos Escobar	W	NXT 2.0	13:54
May 3	Cameron Grimes, Solo Sikoa	L	NXT 2.0: Spring Breakin'	14:06
May 17	Cameron Grimes & Solo Sikoa (w/Trick Williams)	L	NXT 2.0	9:57
Jun 4	Cameron Grimes	W	NXT In Your House '22	15:30
Jun 7	Solo Sikoa & Apollo Crews (w/Grayson Waller)	L	NXT 2.0	13:45
Jun 14	Troy Donovan & Channing Lorenzo (w/Trick Williams)	W	NXT 2.0	4:22
Jun 21	Tony D'Angelo	W	NXT 2.0	10:38
Jul 5	Grayson Waller	W	NXT 2.0: Great American Bash	11:43
Aug 2	Nathan Frazer	W	NXT 2.0	5:41
Aug 16	Giovanni Vinci	W	NXT 2.0: Heatwave	11:56
Sep 4	Ricochet	W	NXT Worlds Collide '22	15:57
Sep 13	Solo Sikoa	L	NXT 2.0	10:02
Sep 20	Andre Chase & Bodhi Hayward (w/Trick Williams)	L	NXT	4:15
Oct 4	Oro Mensah	W	NXT	5:35
Oct 13	Cedric Alexander	W	WWE Main Event	8:19
Oct 18	Wes Lee & Oro Mensah (w/Trick Williams)	W	NXT	2:43
Oct 22	Ladder Match: Wes Lee, Oro Mensa, Von Wagner, Nathan Frazer	L	NXT Halloween Havoc '22	22:25
Nov 22	Wes Lee	L	NXT	13:01
Dec 10	Iron Survivor Challenge: Grayson Waller, Joe Gacy, Axiom, JD McDonagh	L	NXT Deadline	25:00
Dec 20	Axiom	W	NXT	12:35

CASH WHEELER

Jan 10	Pat Brink & Myles Hawkins (w/Dax Harwood)	W	AEW Dark Elevation	3:08
Jan 28	Lee Johnson & Brock Anderson (w/Dax Harwood)	W	AEW Rampage: Beach Break	9:10
Feb 9	CM Punk & Jon Moxley (w/Dax Harwood)	L	AEW Dynamite	18:34
Feb 23	Tag Team Battle Royal (w/Dax Harwood)	L	AEW Dynamite	12:05
Mar 2	Casino Battle Royale (w/Dax Harwood)	L	AEW Dynamite	23:44
Mar 30	Austin Gunn & Colten Gunn (w/Dax Harwood)	W	AEW Dynamite	11:27
Apr 1	Jay Briscoe & Mark Briscoe (w/Dax Harwood)	W	ROH Supercard Of Honor XV	27:25
Apr 6	Matt Jackson & Nick Jackson (w/Dax Harwood)	W	AEW Dynamite	20:07
Apr 27	Dax Harwood	L	AEW Dynamite	15:05
May 25	Trent Barretta & Rocky Romero (w/Dax Harwood)	D	AEW Dynamite: 3 Year Anniversary	10:12
Jun 1	Max Caster, Austin Gunn & Colten Gunn (w/CM Punk & Dax Harwood)	W	AEW Dynamite	11:50
Jun 10	Will Ospreay, Kyle Fletcher & Mark Davis (w/Trent Beretta & Dax Harwood)	W	AEW Rampage	13:59
Jun 24	Jeff Cobb	L	AEW Rampage	10:55
Jun 26	Great-O-Khan & Jeff Cobb, Rocky Romero & Trent Beretta (w/Dax Harwood)	W	AEW x NJPW Forbidden Door	16:19
Jun 29	Max Caster, Austin Gunn & Colten Gunn (w/Danhausen & Dax Harwood)	W	AEW Dynamite: Blood & Guts	9:31
Jul 23	2/3 Falls: Jay Briscoe & Mark Briscoe (w/Dax Harwood)	W	ROH Death Before Dishonor XIX	43:25
Jul 30	Kyle Fletcher, Mark Davis & TJP (w/Dax Harwood & Alex Zayne)	L	NJPW Music City Mayhem	14:30
Aug 31	Ren Jones, Vic Capri & Silas Young (w/Wardlow & Dax Harwood)	W	AEW Dynamite	2:02
Sep 4	Jay Lethal, Chris Sabin & Alex Shelley (w/Wardlow & Dax Harwood)	W	AEW All Out '22	16:30

Oct 1	Kyle Fletcher & Mark Davis (w/Dax Harwood)	W	NJPW Royal Quest II Night #1	31:59
Oct 2	Will Ospreay, Great-O-Khan, Mark Davis, Kyle Fletcher & Gideon Grey (w/Dax Harwood, Shota Umino, Gabriel Kidd & Ricky Knight Jr.)	L	NJPW Royal Quest II Night #2	16:57
Oct 7	Toa Liona & Kaun (w/Dax Harwood)	W	AEW Battle Of The Belts IV	13:26
Oct 14	Brian Cage, Kaun & Toa Liona (w/Shawn Spears & Dax Harwood)	L	AEW Rampage	10:29
Oct 26	Swerve Strickland & Keith Lee (w/Dax Harwood)	L	AEW Dynamite	15:06
Nov 5	Great-O-Khan & Jeff Cobb (w/Dax Harwood)	W	NJPW Battle Autumn '22	17:31
Nov 9	Swerve Strickland, Keith Lee, Austin Gunn & Colten Gunn (w/Anthony Bowens, Max Caster & Dax Harwood)	W	AEW Dynamite	12:22
Nov 25	Dante Martin & Darius Mart (w/Dax Harwood)	W	AEW Rampage: Black Friday	11:12
Dec 7	Anthony Bowens & Max Caster (w/Dax Harwood)	L	AEW Dynamite	16:46
Dec 10	Double Dog Collar Match: Jay Briscoe & Mark Briscoe (w/Dax Harwood)	W	ROH Final Battle '22	22:20
Dec 21	Austin Gunn & Colten Gunn (w/Dax Harwood)	L	AEW Dynamite: Holiday Bash	9:12

CASSIE LEE

Jan 27	Madison Rayne & Kaleb With A K (w/Jessie McKay)	W	IMPACT Wrestling	10:57
Mar 3	Madison Rayne	W	IMPACT Wrestling	4:13
Mar 10	Madison Rayne, Tenille Dashwood, Savannah Evans & Tasha Steelz (w/Jessie McKay, Chelsea Green & Mickie James)	W	IMPACT Wrestling	6:00

CEDRIC ALEXANDER

Jan 6	Rey Mysterio & Dominik Mysterio (w/Shelton Benjamin)	L	WWE Main Event	5:41
Jan 27	LA Knight	L	WWE Main Event	5:02
Feb 10	Dolph Ziggler & Robert Roode (w/Shelton Benjamin)	W	WWE Main Event	7:01
Feb 14	Handicap Match: Omos (w/Shelton Benjamin)	L	WWE Monday Night RAW	1:25
Feb 28	Rey Mysterio & Dominik Mysterio (w/Shelton Benjamin)	W	WWE Monday Night RAW	4:30
Mar 10	Angelo Dawkins & Montez Ford (w/Shelton Benjamin)	L	WWE Main Event	9:23
Mar 14	Rey Mysterio & Dominik Mysterio (w/Shelton Benjamin)	L	WWE Monday Night RAW	3:25
Mar 24	T-Bar	W	WWE Main Event	10:24
Mar 31	Veer Mahaan	L	WWE Main Event	5:19
Apr 1	Andre The Giant Memorial Battle Royal	L	WWE SmackDown	8:05
Apr 14	Apollo Crews & Commander Azeez (w/Shelton Benjamin)	L	WWE Main Event	6:59
Apr 21	Tommaso Ciampa	L	WWE Main Event	7:42
Apr 28	Angelo Dawkins & Montez Ford (w/Shelton Benjamin)	L	WWE Main Event	9:31
May 2	Bobby Lashley	L	WWE Monday Night RAW	2:35
Jun 6	Omos	L	WWE Monday Night RAW	:12
Jun 13	MVP	L	WWE Monday Night RAW	1:40
Jul 7	T-Bar	W	WWE Main Event	5:01
Jul 21	Chad Gable & Otis (w/Mustafa Ali)	L	WWE Main Event	8:49
Jul 28	Akira Tozawa & T-Bar (w/Mustafa Ali)	W	WWE Main Event	4:38
Aug 11	Shelton Benjamin	W	WWE Main Event	4:51
Aug 15	The Miz & Ciampa (w/Mustafa Ali)	L	WWE Monday Night RAW	9:30
Aug 25	Shelton Benjamin & T-Bar (w/Mustafa Ali)	W	WWE Main Event	8:30
Sep 1	T-Bar	W	WWE Main Event	8:00
Sep 8	T-Bar	L	WWE Main Event	6:46
Sep 15	Shelton Benjamin	L	WWE Main Event	8:00
Oct 13	Carmelo Hayes	L	WWE Main Event	8:19
Oct 20	Duke Hudson	W	WWE Main Event	8:50
Oct 27	Von Wagner	W	WWE Main Event	8:50
Nov 7	Baron Corbin	L	WWE Monday Night RAW	2:20
Nov 17	JD McDonagh	W	WWE Main Event	10:00
Dec 1	Joe Gacy	W	WWE Main Event	8:02
Dec 8	Trick Williams	W	WWE Main Event	7:56
Dec 15	Edris Enofe & Malik Blade (w/Mustafa Ali)	W	WWE Main Event	6:17
Dec 22	Andre Chase	W	WWE Main Event	5:10

CEZAR BONONI

Feb 21	Brock Anderson, Frankie Kazarian, Jay Lethal, Lee Johnson & Matt Sydal (w/Luther, Serpentico, JD Drake & Peter Avalon)	L	AEW Dark Elevation	6:06
Feb 22	Caleb Trinity, Karam, Rohit Raju & Sotheara Chhun (w/JD Drake, Peter Avalon & Ryan Nemeth)	W	AEW Dark	2:29
Mar 2	Wardlow	L	AEW Dynamite	:50
Apr 5	Guillermo Rosas & Luke Sampson (w/Tiger Ruas)	W	AEW Dark	2:34
May 10	Evil Uno & Ten (w/Tiger Ruas)	L	AEW Dark	8:30
Jun 6	Pac, Penta Oscuro & Rey Fenix (w/Peter Avalon & Ryan Nemeth)	L	AEW Dark Elevation	5:04
Jun 21	John Silver & Alex Reynolds (w/Peter Avalon)	L	AEW Dark	5:01
Jul 5	John Silver, Alex Reynolds, Evil Uno & Ten (w/JD Drake, Peter Avalon & Ryan Nemeth)	L	AEW Dark	7:22
Aug 15	Konosuke Takeshita	L	AEW Dark Elevation	2:37
Aug 16	Marcus Kross	W	AEW Dark	2:43
Sep 13	Dante Martin & Matt Sydal (w/Ryan Nemeth)	L	AEW Dark	6:19
Oct 4	Chris Pharaoh & Eli Isom (w/Ryan Nemeth)	W	AEW Dark	1:58
Nov 8	Claudio Castagnoli & Wheeler Yuta (w/Ryan Nemeth)	L	AEW Dark	4:40
Nov 29	Matt Hardy, Isiah Kassidy & Marq Quen (w/Peter Avalon & Ryan Nemeth)	L	AEW Dark	7:16
Dec 19	Ethan Page, Isiah Kassidy, Konosuke Takeshita, Matt Hardy, Dante Martin & Darius Martin (w/Jeeves Kay, Slim J, Sonny Kiss, Peter Avalon & Ryan Nemeth)	L	AEW Dark Elevation	7:45
Dec 20	Ricky Starks	L	AEW Dark	1:28

CHAD GABLE

Jan 3	Randy Orton & Riddle (w/Otis)	W	WWE Monday Night RAW	2:40
Jan 10	Randy Orton & Riddle (w/Otis)	W	WWE Monday Night RAW	8:57

Jan 24	Randy Orton	L	WWE Monday Night RAW	13:55
Jan 29	Royal Rumble Match	L	WWE Royal Rumble '22	8:18
Feb 7	Angelo Dawkins & Montez Ford (w/Otis)	W	WWE Monday Night RAW	5:37
Feb 14	Rey Mysterio & Dominik Mysterio (w/Otis)	W	WWE Monday Night RAW	10:34
Feb 21	Angelo Dawkins & Montez Ford (w/Otis)	W	WWE Monday Night RAW	9:05
Feb 28	Seth Rollins & Kevin Owens (w/Otis)	L	WWE Monday Night RAW	12:50
Mar 7	No DQ: Randy Orton & Riddle, Seth Rollins & Kevin Owens (w/Otis)	L	WWE Monday Night RAW	27:05
Mar 21	Randy Orton & Riddle (w/Otis)	L	WWE Monday Night RAW	7:45
Apr 3	Randy Orton & Riddle, Angelo Dawkins & Montez Ford (w/Otis)	L	WWE WrestleMania XXXVIII	11:30
Apr 4	Angelo Dawkins & Montez Ford (w/Otis)	L	WWE Monday Night RAW	8:25
Apr 11	Randy Orton & Riddle (w/Otis)	L	WWE Monday Night RAW	8:30
Apr 18	Ezekiel	L	WWE Monday Night RAW	3:30
May 2	Ezekiel, Angelo Dawkins & Montez Ford (w/Kevin Owens & Otis)	W	WWE Monday Night RAW	9:45
May 16	Ezekiel	L	WWE Monday Night RAW	11:00
May 23	Ezekiel	L	WWE Monday Night RAW	4:10
May 30	Ezekiel, Rey Mysterio & Dominik Mysterio (w/Kevin Owens & Otis)	L	WWE Monday Night RAW	8:30
Jun 13	Mustafa Ali	W	WWE Monday Night RAW	3:15
Jun 20	Gauntlet Match: Bobby Lashley, Otis, Theory	L	WWE Monday Night RAW	16:45
Jun 27	Handicap Match: Bobby Lashley (w/Otis)	L	WWE Monday Night RAW	8:15
Jul 4	Bobby Lashley, Angelo Dawkins & Montez Ford (w/Theory & Otis)	L	WWE Monday Night RAW	10:05
Jul 21	Cedric Alexander & Mustafa Ali (w/Otis)	W	WWE Main Event	8:49
Jul 25	AJ Styles & Dolph Ziggler (w/Otis)	L	WWE Monday Night RAW	6:30
Aug 1	Ciampa, Dolph Ziggler	L	WWE Monday Night RAW	10:30
Aug 8	Dolph Ziggler	L	WWE Monday Night RAW	6:35
Aug 18	Angelo Dawkins & Montez Ford (w/Otis)	L	WWE Main Event	6:49
Aug 22	Kevin Owens	L	WWE Monday Night RAW	11:10
Aug 29	Angelo Dawkins & Montez Ford (w/Otis)	L	WWE Monday Night RAW	16:04
Sep 3	Madcap Moss, Angelo Dawkins & Montez Ford (w/Austin Theory & Otis)	L	WWE Clash At The Castle Kickoff	6:29
Sep 5	Angel & Humberto, Xavier Woods & Kofi Kingston, Angelo Dawkins & Montez Ford (w/Otis)	D	WWE Monday Night RAW	14:30
Sep 12	Johnny Gargano	L	WWE Monday Night RAW	13:50
Sep 22	Mustafa Ali & Shelton Benjamin (w/Otis)	W	WWE Main Event	9:52
Sep 26	Kevin Owens & Johnny Gargano (w/Otis)	L	WWE Monday Night RAW	13:09
Sep 30	Drew McIntyre, Kevin Owens & Johnny Gargano (w/Austin Theory & Otis)	L	WWE SmackDown	13:38
Oct 3	Braun Strowman	L	WWE Monday Night RAW	8:45
Oct 10	Rey Mysterio	L	WWE Monday Night RAW	7:50
Oct 17	Luke Gallows & Karl Anderson (w/Otis)	L	WWE Monday Night RAW	8:20
Oct 24	Elias	L	WWE Monday Night RAW	9:30
Nov 14	Matt Riddle	W	WWE Monday Night RAW	10:10
Nov 21	Elias & Matt Riddle (w/Otis)	L	WWE Monday Night RAW	16:05
Nov 28	Angelo Dawkins & Montez Ford (w/Otis)	L	WWE Monday Night RAW	12:00
Dec 5	AJ Styles, Luke Gallows & Karl Anderson (w/Baron Corbin & Otis)	L	WWE Monday Night RAW	14:30
Dec 12	AJ Styles	L	WWE Monday Night RAW	9:05
Dec 19	Luke Gallows & Karl Anderson (w/Otis)	L	WWE Monday Night RAW	9:05

CHANNING LORENZO (AS CHANNING LAUREN UNTIL MAY 6)

Apr 8	Andre Chase & Bodhi Hayward (w/Troy Donovan)	W	NXT Level Up	6:47
May 6	Dante Chen & Javier Bernal (w/Troy Donovan)	W	NXT Level Up	6:04
May 24	Edris Enofe & Malik Blade (w/Troy Donovan)	W	NXT 2.0	6:10
Jun 14	Carmelo Hayes & Trick Williams (w/Troy Donovan)	L	NXT 2.0	4:22
Jul 1	Hank Walker	W	NXT Level Up	4:13
Jun 4	Santos Escobar, Cruz del Toro & Joaquin Wilde (w/Tony D'Angelo & Troy Donovan)	W	NXT In Your House '22	12:45
Jul 12	Edris Enofe & Malik Blade (w/Tony D'Angelo)	W	NXT 2.0	5:23
Jul 26	Roderick Strong, Damon Kemp, Julius Creed & Brutus Creed (w/Tony D'Angelo, Joaquin Wilde & Cruz Del Toro)	W	NXT 2.0	11:39
Aug 2	Julius Creed & Brutus Creed (w/Tony D'Angelo)	L	NXT 2.0	10:46
Sep 9	Ikemen Jiro	W	NXT Level Up	5:16
Sep 13	Cameron Grimes & Joe Gacy (w/Tony D'Angelo)	L	NXT 2.0	5:36
Oct 11	Wes Lee	L	NXT	3:57
Oct 18	Shinsuke Nakamura	L	NXT	5:22
Oct 28	Tank Ledger	W	NXT Level Up	5:42
Nov 8	Hank Walker	W	NXT	3:28
Nov 18	Oro Mensah	W	NXT Level Up	5:41
Dec 2	Tavion Heights	W	NXT Level Up	4:19
Dec 13	Wes Lee	L	NXT	9:52

CHARLETTE RENEGADE

Jan 11	Tay Conti & Anna Jay (w/Robyn Renegade)	L	AEW Dark	3:48
Mar 28	Anna Jay & Ruby Soho (w/Robyn Renegade)	L	AEW Dark Elevation	2:17
Apr 12	Emi Sakura	L	AEW Dark	2:15
Apr 26	Abadon	L	AEW Dark	1:09
Jul 15	Athena & Kris Statlander (w/Robyn Renegade)	L	AEW Rampage	:25
Jul 19	Avery Breaux & Valentina Rossi (w/Robyn Renegade)	W	AEW Dark	4:09
Aug 16	Skye Blue	L	AEW Dark	4:44
Aug 23	Allie Recks & Rocky Radley (w/Robyn Renegade)	W	AEW Dark	3:24
Aug 30	Diamante	L	AEW Dark	3:05
Sep 27	Mila Moore & Mylo (w/Robyn Renegade)	W	AEW Dark	:21

CHARLIE DEMPSEY

Jan 27	Joe Coffey, Mark Coffey & Wolfgang (w/Rohan Raja & Teoman)	W	NXT UK	11:18
Mar 10	A-Kid	W	NXT UK	12:30

Mar 24	A-Kid & Saxon Huxley (w/Rohan Raja)	W	NXT UK	8:24
Apr 7	Wolfgang	W	NXT UK	7:20
May 19	Dave Mastiff & Jack Starz (w/Rohan Raja)	W	NXT UK	8:01
May 26	Heritage Cup Rules: A-Kid	W	NXT UK	16:24
Jun 2	Ashton Smith & Oliver Carter, Trent Seven & Tyler Bate (w/Rohan Raja)	L	NXT UK	14:17
Jun 23	Elimination Match: Brooks Jensen & Josh Briggs, Dave Mastiff & Jack Starz, Mark Andrews & Wild Boar (w/Rohan Raja)	L	NXT UK	18:15
Aug 11	Oliver Carter	L	NXT UK	9:08
Aug 30	Andre Chase	L	NXT 2.0	5:17
Sep 9	Bodhi Hayward	W	NXT Level Up	7:49
Nov 8	Andre Chase	W	NXT	2:59
Dec 6	Hank Walker	W	NXT	4:06
Dec 23	Myles Borne	W	NXT Level Up	8:13

CHARLOTTE FLAIR

Jan 7	Naomi	W	WWE SmackDown	12:15
Jan 21	Naomi	W	WWE SmackDown	2:25
Jan 29	Royal Rumble Match	L	WWE Royal Rumble '22	31:23
Feb 11	Naomi	W	WWE SmackDown	19:55
Feb 19	Naomi & Ronda Rousey (w/Sonya Deville)	L	WWE Elimination Chamber '22	9:14
Apr 2	Ronda Rousey	W	WWE WrestleMania XXXVIII	18:30
Apr 29	"I Quit" Beat The Clock Challenge: Aliyah	D	WWE SmackDown	1:41
May 5	I Quit Match: Ronda Rousey	L	WWE WrestleMania Backlash '22	16:35
Dec 30	Ronda Rousey	W	WWE SmackDown	:40

CHASE OWENS

Jan 5	Minoru Suzuki, Cima, Toru Yano	L	NJPW Wrestle Kingdom 16 Night #2	6:08
Apr 9	Hiroshi Tanahashi, Tama Tonga, Tanga Loa & Jado (w/Bad Luck Fale, Yujiro Takahashi & Gedo)	L	NJPW Hyper Battle '22	10:28
May 1	Great-O-Khan & Jeff Cobb, Hirooki Goto & Yoshi-Hashi (w/Bad Luck Fale)	W	NJPW Wrestling Dontaku '22	9:43
May 14	Great-O-Khan	W	NJPW Capital Collision	8:46
Jun 12	Jeff Cobb & Great-O-Khan (w/Bad Luck Fale)	L	NJPW Dominion '22	11:52
Jul 30	Fred Rosser, Hiroshi Tanahashi & Kevin Knight (w/Hikuleo & Jay White)	W	NJPW Strong	15:41
Sep 17	Kushida, Taylor Rust, Trent Beretta & Rocky Romero (w/Hikuleo, Jay White & Juice Robinson)	W	NJPW Strong	14:46
Sep 25	Jeff Cobb & Great-O-Khan (w/Bad Luck Fale)	L	NJPW Burning Spirit '22	7:57

CHEESEBURGER

May 2	Tony Nese	L	AEW Dark Elevation	4:13
Oct 3	Lance Archer	L	AEW Dark Elevation	3:00
Nov 7	Cole Karter, Lee Johnson & QT Marshall (w/Logan Easton Laroux & Rhett Titus)	L	AEW Dark Elevation	6:45

CHELSEA GREEN

Jan 6	Rosemary, Jordynne Grace & Rachael Ellering (w/Tasha Steelz & Lady Frost)	W	IMPACT Wrestling	7:19
Jan 8	Ultimate X Match: Tasha Steelz, Alisha Edwards, Jordynne Grace, Lady Frost, Rosemary	L	IMPACT Hard To Kill '22	9:00
Jan 20	Tasha Steelz	L	IMPACT Wrestling	4:24
Feb 10	Mickie James	D	IMPACT Wrestling	3:58
Feb 17	Tasha Steelz & Savannah Evans (w/Mickie James)	L	IMPACT Wrestling	12:26
Feb 22	Kenzie Paige	W	NWA Power	7:24
Mar 3	Tasha Steelz	L	IMPACT Wrestling	8:05
Mar 10	Madison Rayne, Tenille Dashwood, Savannah Evans & Tasha Steelz (w/Mickie James, Cassie Lee & Jessie McKay)	W	IMPACT Wrestling	6:00
Mar 20	Kamille, Kylie Rae	L	NWA Crockett Cup '22	12:02
Apr 1	Mickie James & Nick Aldis (w/Matt Cardona)	L	IMPACT Multiverse Of Matches	7:04
May 10	KiLynn King, Jennacide	L	NWA Power	6:36
May 26	Jordynne Grace	L	IMPACT Wrestling	11:26
Jun 19	Queen Of The Mountain: Jordynne Grace, Tasha Steelz, Mia Yim, Deonna Purrazzo	L	IMPACT Slammiversary XX	18:15
Jun 23	Mia Yim	L	IMPACT Wrestling	9:08
Jun 28	Jennacide & Missa Kate (w/Max The Impaler)	W	NWA Power	5:38
Jul 14	Mickie James	W	IMPACT Wrestling	12:41
Jul 21	Jordynne Grace & Mia Yim (w/Deonna Purrazzo)	W	IMPACT Wrestling	9:11
Jul 26	Kamille	L	NWA Power	9:37
Aug 16	Paola Blaze & Rylee Rockett (w/Angelina Love)	W	NWA Power	4:00
Aug 25	Jordynne Grace & Mia Yim (w/Deonna Purrazzo)	W	IMPACT Wrestling	7:24
Sep 6	Taya Valkyrie, Jennacide, KiLynn King	L	NWA Power	4:22
Sep 8	Taya Valkyrie	W	IMPACT Wrestling	6:27
Oct 7	Jessicka & Taya Valkyrie (w/Deonna Purrazzo)	L	IMPACT Bound For Glory '22	7:24
Oct 13	Jessicka, Rosemary & Taya Valkyrie (w/Deonna Purrazzo & Gisele Shaw)	W	IMPACT Wrestling	5:40
Oct 18	Angelina Love	W	NWA Power	8:02
Oct 27	Jordynne Grace, Mickie James & Taylor Wilde (w/Deonna Purrazzo & Gisele Shaw)	L	IMPACT Wrestling	13:46
Nov 10	Mickie James	L	IMPACT Wrestling	10:37
Nov 12	Kamille, KiLynn King	L	NWA Hard Times 3	8:59

CHRIS ADONIS

Jan 11	Matt Cardona & Mike Knox, Tim Storm & Trevor Murdoch (w/Thom Latimer)	L	NWA Power	5:25
Feb 8	Team War Elimination Match: Matt Taven, Mike Bennett &	W	NWA Power	11:09

Victor Benjamin, Bestia 666, Mecha Wolf & Homicide, Jay Bradley,
Wrecking Ball Legursky & Colby Corino (w/Thom Latimer & El Rudo)

Feb 15	Odinson, Parrow & Rodney Mack (w/Thom Latimer & El Rudo)	W	NWA Power	11:35
Mar 1	Anthony Mayweather	L	NWA Power	11:38
Mar 19	Jordan Clearwater & Marshe Rockett (w/Thom Latimer)	L	NWA Crockett Cup '22	4:18
Jun 11	Jax Dane	L	NWA Alwayz Ready '22	10:19
Jun 14	Mike Knox & VSK (w/Thom Latimer)	W	NWA Power	7:23
Jul 12	Thom Latimer	L	NWA Power	6:48
Aug 23	Caprice Coleman	W	NWA Power	6:12
Aug 27	Odinson	W	NWA 74th Anniversary Show	7:26
Sep 20	Jake Dumas	W	NWA Power	8:01
Oct 11	Dak Draper, Thrillbilly Silas	L	NWA Power	5:15
Dec 13	Jax Dane	W	NWA Power	7:17
Dec 20	Bully Ray, Judais & Thom Latimer (w/Dak Draper & Mims)	L	NWA Power	8:18

CHRIS BEY

Jan 8	Jordan Clearwater & Keita Murray (w/Hikuleo)	W	NJPW Strong	9:12
Jan 13	Laredo Kid	L	IMPACT Wrestling	12:49
Jan 27	Jake Something	L	IMPACT Wrestling	9:22
Feb 3	Jake Something, Mike Bailey, Madman Fulton & Ace Austin (w/Jay White, Tama Tonga & Tanga Loa)	W	IMPACT Wrestling	16:49
Mar 3	Tama Tonga, Tanga Loa, Deaner & Joe Doering (w/Luke Gallows, Karl Anderson & Jay White)	W	IMPACT Wrestling	9:48
Mar 17	Alex Shelley & Chris Sabin (w/Jay White)	L	IMPACT Wrestling	12:38
Mar 19	Blake Christian	W	NJPW Strong	10:24
Mar 31	Alex Shelley & Chris Savin (w/Jay White)	W	IMPACT Wrestling	17:42
Apr 1	Ultimate X Match: Trey Miguel, Vincent, Jordynne Grace, Rich Swann, Willie Mack	L	IMPACT Multiverse Of Matches	7:27
Apr 16	Aaron Henare, Great-O-Khan, Jeff Cobb, TJP, Kyle Fletcher & Mark Davis (w/Hikuleo, El Phantasmo, Karl Anderson, Luke Gallows & Scott Norton)	L	NJPW Windy City Riot	11:58
Apr 21	Kenny King, Matt Taven, Mike Bennett & Vincent (w/Luke Gallows, Karl Anderson & Jay White)	W	IMPACT Wrestling	9:22
May 5	Willie Mack & Rich Swann (w/Jay White)	W	IMPACT Wrestling	6:28
May 7	Barrett Brown & Bateman (w/Hikuleo)	W	NJPW Strong	12:16
May 12	Kenny King	L	IMPACT Wrestling	8:27
Jun 4	Alex Zayne & Christopher Daniels (w/El Phantasmo)	W	NJPW Strong	9:58
Jun 16	Jay Briscoe & Mark Briscoe (w/Jay White)	L	IMPACT Wrestling	11:02
Jun 30	Trey Miguel, Laredo Kid, Steve Maclin	L	IMPACT Wrestling	6:12
Jul 14	Eddie Edwards, Kenny King, Matt Taven & Mike Bennett (w/Ace Austin, Luke Gallows & Karl Anderson)	W	IMPACT Wrestling	12:34
Jul 21	Matt Taven & Mike Bennett (w/Ace Austin)	W	IMPACT Wrestling	10:32
Aug 18	Mike Bailey	L	IMPACT Wrestling	8:25
Sep 1	JD Griffey & Exodus Prime (w/Ace Austin)	W	IMPACT Before The Impact	8:03
Sep 8	Kyle Fletcher & Mark Davis (w/Ace Austin)	L	IMPACT Wrestling	7:07
Sep 29	Laredo Kid & Trey Miguel (w/Ace Austin)	W	IMPACT Wrestling	8:16
Oct 20	Bully Ray & Tommy Dreamer (w/Juice Robinson)	L	IMPACT Wrestling	6:23
Oct 27	Tommy Dreamer	W	IMPACT Wrestling	6:50
Nov 17	Kyle Fletcher & Mark David, Alex Shelley & Chris Sabin, Raj Singh & Shera (w/Ace Austin)	W	IMPACT Wrestling	13:03
Nov 19	Blake Christian & Mascara Dorada (w/El Phantasmo)	W	NJPW Strong	10:44

CHRIS DICKINSON

Apr 1	Tomohiro Ishii	L	NJPW Lonestar Shootout	16:11
Apr 16	Royce Isaacs, Jorel Nelson, JR Kratos, Black Tiger & Danny Limelight (w/Fred Rosser, Josh Alexander, Alex Coughlin & Ren Narita)	W	NJPW Windy City Riot	13:50
May 21	Ren Narita	D	NJPW Strong	15:00
Jun 18	Hiroshi Tanahashi	L	NJPW Strong	13:15
Oct 15	Fred Rosser	D	NJPW Strong	6:48

CHRIS JERICHO

Jan 26	Daniel Garcia, Matt Lee & Jeff Parker (w/Santana & Ortiz)	W	AEW Dynamite: Beach Break	8:52
Feb 16	Santana & Ortiz (w/Jake Hager)	L	AEW Dynamite	10:43
Mar 6	Eddie Kingston	L	AEW Revolution '22	13:40
Mar 23	John Silver & Alex Reynolds (w/Daniel Garcia)	W	AEW Dynamite	10:02
Apr 13	Eddie Kingston, Santana & Ortiz (w/Daniel Garcia & Jake Hager)	W	AEW Dynamite	11:46
May 4	Santana	W	AEW Dynamite	9:05
May 29	Anarchy In The Arena: Bryan Danielson, Jon Moxley, Eddie Kingston, Santana & Ortiz (w/Daniel Garcia, Jake Hager, Angelo Parker & Matt Menard)	W	AEW Double Or Nothing '22	22:45
Jun 15	Hair vs. Hair: Santana	W	AEW Dynamite: Road Rager	11:06
Jun 22	Jon Moxley & Hiroshi Tanahashi (w/Lance Archer)	L	AEW Dynamite	12:12
Jun 26	Eddie Kingston, Shota Umino & Wheeler Yuta (w/Minoru Suzuki & Sammy Guevara)	W	AEW x NJPW Forbidden Door	18:58
Jun 29	Blood & Guts: Jon Moxley, Claudio Castagnoli, Wheeler Yuta, Eddie Kingston, Santana & Ortiz (w/Daniel Garcia, Jake Hager, Matt Menard, Angelo Parker & Sammy Guevara)	L	AEW Dynamite: Blood & Guts	46:45
Jul 20	Barbed Wire Death Match: Eddie Kingston	W	AEW Dynamite: Fyter Fest	13:13
Aug 3	Wheeler Yuta	W	AEW Dynamite	12:33
Aug 10	Jon Moxley	L	AEW Dynamite: Quake By The Lake	22:38
Sep 4	Bryan Danielson	W	AEW All Out '22	23:40
Sep 14	Bryan Danielson	L	AEW Dynamite	19:44
Sep 21	Claudio Castagnoli	W	AEW Dynamite: Grand Slam	14:49

Sep 28	Bandido	W	AEW Dynamite	18:24
Oct 5	Bryan Danielson & Daniel Garcia (w/Sammy Guevara)	W	AEW Dynamite: Anniversary	14:23
Oct 12	Bryan Danielson	W	AEW Dynamite	14:09
Oct 18	Dalton Castle	W	AEW Dynamite: Title Tuesday	12:28
Oct 26	Claudio Castagnoli & Wheeler Yuta (w/Daniel Garcia)	L	AEW Dynamite	11:40
Nov 2	Colt Cabana	W	AEW Dynamite	9:12
Nov 16	Claudio Castagnoli & Bryan Danielson (w/Sammy Guevara)	L	AEW Dynamite	18:02
Nov 19	Bryan Danielson, Claudio Castagnoli, Sammy Guevara	W	AEW Full Gear '22	21:30
Nov 23	Tomohiro Ishii	W	AEW Dynamite: Thanksgiving Eve	15:29
Dec 10	Claudio Castagnoli	L	ROH Final Battle '22	17:15
Dec 14	Action Andretti	L	AEW Dynamite: Winter Is Coming	9:35

CHRIS SABIN

Jan 8	Jonathan Gresham	L	IMPACT Hard To Kill '22	12:40
Jan 27	PCO	L	IMPACT Wrestling	15:48
Feb 17	Kenny King	W	IMPACT Wrestling	8:37
Feb 24	Kenny King, Matt Taven & Mike Bennett (w/Rich Swann & Willie Mack)	L	IMPACT Wrestling	8:58
Mar 17	Chris Bey & Jay White (w/Alex Shelley)	W	IMPACT Wrestling	12:38
Mar 31	Chris Bey & Jay White (w/Alex Shelley)	L	IMPACT Wrestling	17:42
Apr 1	Jay White	W	IMPACT Multiverse Of Matches	16:00
Apr 9	Jay White	L	NJPW Strong	18:12
Apr 23	Steve Maclin, Jay White	L	IMPACT Rebellion '22	12:07
Apr 28	Eddie Edwards, Matt Taven & Mike Bennett (w/Alex Shelley & Mike Bailey)	L	IMPACT Wrestling	7:35
May 12	Gauntlet For The Gold	L	IMPACT Wrestling	39:00
May 26	Frankie Kazarian	D	IMPACT Wrestling	10:25
Jun 9	Eddie Edwards, Matt Taven & Mike Bennett (w/Allex Shelley & Frankie Kazarian)	L	IMPACT Wrestling	16:47
Jun 19	Eddie Edwards, Matt Taven, Mike Bennett, PCO & Vincent (w/Alex Shelley, Davey Richards, Frankie Kazarian & Magnus)	W	IMPACT Slammiversary XX	18:45
Jun 30	Frankie Kazarian	W	IMPACT Wrestling	18:42
Jul 14	Eric Young, Deaner & Joe Doering (w/Alex Shelley & Josh Alexander)	W	IMPACT Wrestling	11:56
Jul 21	Alex Shelley	L	IMPACT Wrestling	17:09
Jul 31	Davey Richards & Eddie Edwards (w/Alex Shelley)	W	JCP Ric Flair's Last Match	11:06
Aug 4	Deaner & Joe Doering (w/Alex Shelley)	W	IMPACT Wrestling	6:23
Aug 25	Deaner, Eric Young & Joe Doering (w/Alex Shelley & Kushida)	W	IMPACT Wrestling	15:18
Sep 4	Wardlow, Dax Harwood & Cash Wheeler (w/Jay Lethal & Alex Shelley)	L	AEW All Out '22	16:30
Sep 15	Luke Gallows & Karl Anderson (w/Alex Shelley)	W	IMPACT Wrestling	14:39
Sep 22	Kyle Fletcher & Mark Davis (w/Alex Shelley)	W	IMPACT Wrestling	15:31
Oct 7	Matt Taven & Mike Bennett (w/Alex Shelley)	L	IMPACT Bound For Glory '22	16:35
Oct 13	Raj Singh & Shera (w/Alex Shelley)	W	IMPACT Before The Impact	7:16
Oct 28	Kyle Fletcher & Mark Davis, Kevin Knight & The DKC (w/Alex Shelley)	W	NJPW Rumble On 44th Street	13:42
Nov 17	Ace Austin & Chris Bey, Kyle Fletcher & Mark Davis, Raj Singh & Shera (w/Alex Shelley)	L	IMPACT Wrestling	13:03
Dec 8	Heath & Rhino (w/Alex Shelley)	D	IMPACT Wrestlling	8:34
Dec 15	Heath & Rhino (w/Alex Shelley)	W	IMPACT Wrestlling	14:04
Dec 17	Barrett Brown & Misterioso (w/Alex Shelley)	W	NJPW Strong	12:11

CHRISTIAN CAGE

Mar 4	Ethan Page	W	AEW Rampage	8:57
Mar 6	Ladder Match: Wardlow, Keith Lee, Orange Cassidy, Powerhouse Hobbs, Ricky Starks	L	AEW Revolution '22	17:20
Apr 6	Adam Cole	L	AEW Dynamite	14:56
Jun 1	Matt Jackson, Nick Jackson, Bobby Fish, Kyle O'Reilly & Hikuleo (w/Matt Hardy, Darby Allin, Jungle Boy & Luchasaurus)	L	AEW Dynamite	12:00
Jul 20	Brian Pillman Jr. & Griff Garrison (w/Luchasaurus)	W	AEW Dynamite: Fyter Fest	2:08
Aug 3	Matt Hardy	W	AEW Dynamite	11:06
Sep 4	Jungle Boy	W	AEW All Out '22	:20

CHRISTOPHER DANIELS

Jan 29	Jay White	L	NJPW Strong	19:07
Mar 2	Bryan Danielson	L	AEW Dynamite	11:17
Mar 5	Karl Fredericks	W	NJPW Strong	11:40
Jun 4	Chris Bey & El Phantasmo (w/Alex Zayne)	L	NJPW Strong	9:58
Jun 7	Steve Andrews	W	AEW Dark	3:04
Jul 9	Aaron Solo & Nick Comoroto (w/Yuya Uemura)	W	NJPW Strong	9:17
Jul 22	Jay Lethal	L	AEW Rampage	11:00
Jul 23	Mikey Nicholls & Shane Haste (w/Yuya Uemura)	W	NJPW Strong	10:02
Aug 13	Kyle Fletcher & Mark Davis (w/Yuya Uemura)	L	NJPW Strong	11:57
Sep 18	Yuma Aoyagi	L	AJPW 50th Anniversary Show	11:31
Sep 24	Bad Dude Tito & Shane Haste (w/Yuya Uemura)	L	NJPW Strong	9:10
Oct 22	Yuya Uemura	L	NJPW Strong	9:48
Nov 5	Rocky Romero	W	NJPW Strong	9:24
Dec 10	The DKC	W	NJPW Strong	9:15

CHUCK TAYLOR

Feb 7	Luther & Serpentico (w/Trent Beretta)	W	AEW Dark Elevation	6:42
Feb 23	Tag Team Battle Royal (w/Trent Beretta)	L	AEW Dynamite	4:14
Mar 2	Casino Battle Royale (w/Trent Beretta)	L	AEW Dynamite	18:34
Mar 16	Bryan Danielson & Jon Moxley (w/Wheeler Yuta)	L	AEW Dynamite: St. Patrick's Day Slam	11:45
Apr 4	Anthony Henry & JD Drake (w/Trent Beretta)	W	AEW Dark Elevation	8:00
Jun 11	Luke Gallows, Hikuleo, Jay White, Juice Robinson & Karl Anderson (w/Rocky Romero, Tomohiro Ishii, Mascara Dorada & Ren Narita)	L	NJPW Strong	12:44

Jul 4	GPA & Isaiah Broner (w/Trent Beretta)	W	AEW Dark Elevation	3:52
Jul 11	Aaron Solo & QT Marshall (w/Trent Beretta)	W	AEW Dark Elevation	9:40
Jul 20	Jon Moxley & Wheeler Yuta (w/Trent Beretta)	L	AEW Dynamite: Fyter Fest	11:53
Jul 29	Jay Lethal, Satnam Singh & Sonjay Dutt (w/Orange Cassidy & Trent Beretta)	W	AEW Rampage	7:29
Aug 9	Ren Jones & Rohit Raju (w/Trent Beretta)	W	AEW Dark	3:28
Aug 19	Ari Daivari, Parker Boudreaux & Slim J (w/Orange Cassidy & Trent Beretta)	W	AEW Rampage	11:00
Sep 2	Hangman Page, John Silver & Alex Reynolds (w/Orange Cassidy & Trent Beretta)	L	AEW Rampage	11:12
Sep 3	Angelico, The Butcher & The Blade (w/Orange Cassidy & Trent Beretta)	W	AEW Dark Elevation	8:13
Sep 7	Pac, Penta El Zero M & Rey Fenix (w/Orange Cassidy & Trent Beretta)	L	AEW Dynamite	12:58
Sep 23	Golden Ticket Battle Royale	L	AEW Rampage: Grand Slam	12:16
Oct 3	Aaron Solo, Cole Karter, Nick Comoroto & QT Marshall (w/Danhausen, Rocky Romero & Trent Beretta)	W	AEW Dark Elevation	7:54
Oct 18	Jessie V, Kobe Durst & Steven Mainz (w/Orange Cassidy & Trent Beretta)	W	AEW Dark	2:44
Oct 18	Pac, Penta El Zero M & Rey Fenix (w/Orange Cassidy & Trent Beretta)	L	AEW Dynamite: Title Tuesday	11:45
Oct 31	Anthony Young, Patton & Victor Andrews (w/Orange Cassidy & Trent Beretta)	W	AEW Dark Elevation	3:30
Nov 1	Tony Deppen, Ari Daivari & Sonny Kiss (w/Orange Cassidy & Trent Beretta)	W	AEW Dark	6:04
Nov 7	Angelico, The Butcher & The Blade (w/Rocky Romero & Trent Beretta)	W	AEW Dark Elevation	7:20
Nov 19	QT Marshall, Aaron Solo, Lee Johnson, Nick Comoroto & Cole Karter (w/Orange Cassidy, Trent Beretta, Rocky Romero & Danhausen)	W	AEW Full Gear Buy-In	11:55
Nov 21	Aaron Solo, Cole Karter & Lee Johnson (w/Orange Cassidy & Trent Beretta)	W	AEW Dark Elevation	3:38
Nov 28	Davey Bang, Freedom Ramsey & Yabo (w/Rocky Romero & Trent Beretta)	W	AEW Dark Elevation	3:54
Dec 12	Zack Clayton & Zane Valero (w/Trent Beretta)	W	AEW Dark Elevation	3:00
Dec 16	Trent Seven, Kip Sabian, The Butcher & The Blade (w/Orange Cassidy, Dustin Rhodes & Trent Beretta)	W	AEW Rampage	10:42
Dec 23	$300,000 Three Kings Christmas Casino Trios Royale (w/Orange Cassidy & Trent Beretta)	L	AEW Rampage	22:01

CLARK CONNORS

Feb 5	TJP	W	NJPW Strong	18:19
Mar 26	Elimination Match: Danny Limelight, Jorel Nelson, JR Kratos, Royce Isaacs & Tom Lawlor (w/Adrian Quest, Fred Rosser, Taylor Rust & The DKC)	L	NJPW Strong	16:29
Apr 1	David Finlay, Juice Robinson, Daniel Garcia & Kevin Knight (w/Karl Fredericks, Mascara Dorada & Yuya Uemura)	W	NJPW Lonestar Shootout	10:45
Apr 2	Tom Lawlor	L	NJPW Strong	13:58
Apr 16	QT Marshall, Aaron Solo & Nick Comoroto (w/Karl Fredericks & Yuya Uemura)	L	NJPW Windy City Riot	11:56
May 17	Aaron Solo, Blake Li, Brick Aldridge, Nick Comoroto & QT Marshall (w/Alex Coughlin, Karl Fredericks, Kevin Knight & Yuya Uemura)	W	AEW Dark	10:30
May 21	Aaron Solo & Nick Comoroto (w/Karl Fredericks)	W	NJPW Strong	8:21
Jun 26	Pac, Miro, Malakai Black	W	AEW x NJPW Forbidden Door	15:10
Oct 28	Minoru Suzuki	L	NJPW Rumble On 44th Street	15:50

CLAUDIO CASTAGNOLI

Jan 1	Ridge Holland & Sheamus (w/Ricochet)	L	WWE Day 1 Kickoff	9:45
Jan 14	Erik & Ivar, Angel & Humberto, Jinder Mahal & Shanky (w/Mansoor)	L	WWE SmackDown	13:21
Jan 28	Ridge Holland & Sheamus (w/Ricochet)	L	WWE SmackDown	10:45
Feb 4	Ridge Holland & Sheamus (w/Ricochet)	L	WWE SmackDown	5:34
Feb 11	Happy Corbin	L	WWE SmackDown	3:55
Jun 26	Zack Sabre Jr.	W	AEW x NJPW Forbidden Door	18:26
Jun 29	Blood & Guts: Chris Jericho, Daniel Garcia, Jake Hager, Angelo Parker, Matt Menard & Sammy Guevara (w/Jon Moxley, Wheeler Yuta, Eddie Kingston, Santana & Ortiz)	W	AEW Dynamite: Blood & Guts	46:45
Jul 13	Jake Hager	W	AEW Dynamite: Fyter Fest	11:32
Jul 23	Jonathan Gresham	W	ROH Death Before Dishonor XIX	11:30
Aug 6	Konosuke Takeshita	W	AEW Battle Of The Belts III	19:59
Aug 26	Dustin Rhodes	W	AEW Rampage	12:27
Sep 4	Casino Ladder Match: MJF, Wheeler Yuta, Penta El Zero M, Rey Fenix, Rush, Andrade El Idolo, Dante Martin	L	AEW All Out '22	14:15
Sep 6	Ari Daivari	W	AEW Dark	9:19
Sep 9	Dax Harwood	W	AEW Rampage	20:13
Sep 21	Chris Jericho	L	AEW Dynamite: Grand Slam	14:49
Oct 7	Rush, Marq Quen & Isiah Kassidy (w/Jox Moxley & Wheeler Yuta)	W	AEW Rampage	10:16
Oct 14	The Butcher & The Blade (w/Jon Moxley)	W	AEW Rampage	8:40
Oct 24	QT Marshall	W	AEW Dark Elevation	9:45
Oct 26	Chris Jericho & Daniel Garcia (w/Wheeler Yuta)	W	AEW Dynamite	11:40
Nov 8	Cezaro Bononi & Ryan Nemeth (w/Wheeler Yuta)	W	AEW Dark	4:40
Nov 16	Chris Jericho & Sammy Guevara (w/Bryan Danielson)	W	AEW Dynamite	18:02
Nov 19	Bryan Danielson, Chris Jericho, Sammy Guevara	L	AEW Full Gear '22	21:30
Dec 7	Jake Hager & Daniel Garcia (w/Wheeler Yuta)	W	AEW Dynamite	12:42
Dec 10	Chris Jericho	W	ROH Final Battle '22	17:15
Dec 19	Anthony Henry & JD Drake (w/Wheeler Yuta)	W	AEW Dark Elevation	7:55
Dec 23	$300,000 Three Kings Christmas Casino Trios Royale (w/Wheeler Yuta & Jon Moxley)	L	AEW Rampage	22:01
Dec 28	Dante Martin & Darius Martin (w/Jon Moxley)	W	AEW Dynamite	14:02

CM PUNK

Jan 12	Wardlow	W	AEW Dynamite	14:06
Jan 19	Shawn Spears	W	AEW Dynamite	:12

Feb 2	MJF	L	AEW Dynamite	38:09
Feb 9	Dax Harwood & Cash Wheeler (w/Jon Moxley)	W	AEW Dynamite	18:34
Mar 6	Dog Collar Match: MJF	W	AEW Revolution '22	26:45
Mar 23	Dax Harwood	W	AEW Dynamite	12:51
Mar 30	Max Caster	W	AEW Dynamite	7:09
Apr 13	Penta Oscuro	W	AEW Dynamite	13:38
Apr 20	Dustin Rhodes	W	AEW Dynamite	17:26
May 11	John Silver	W	AEW Dynamite	8:06
May 29	Hangman Page	W	AEW Double Or Nothing '22	25:40
Jun 1	Max Caster, Austin Gunn & Colten Gunn (w/Dax Harwood & Cash Wheeler)	W	AEW Dynamite	11:50
Aug 24	Jon Moxley	L	AEW Dynamite	2:59
Sep 4	Jon Moxley	W	AEW All Out '22	19:55

CODY CHHUN

Feb 12	Hikuleo	L	NJPW Strong	7:34
Feb 22	Cezar Bononi, JD Drake, Peter Avalon & Ryan Nemeth (w/Caleb Teninity, Karam & Rohit Raju)	L	AEW Dark	2:29
Mar 22	Brian Pillman Jr. & Griff Garrison (w/Tony Vincita)	L	AEW Dark	3:36
Sep 17	JR Kratos & Tom Lawlor (w/Jordan Cruz)	L	NJPW Strong	9:54
Dec 24	Lince Dorado & Mascara Dorada (w/Guillermo Rosas)	L	NJPW Strong	10:35

CODY RHODES

Jan 26	Ladder Match: Sammy Guevara	L	AEW Dynamite: Beach Break	22:59
Apr 2	Seth Rollins	W	WWE WrestleMania XXXVIII	21:40
Apr 11	The Miz	W	WWE Monday Night RAW	11:45
Apr 18	Kevin Owens	W	WWE Monday Night RAW	17:20
Apr 25	Seth Rollins, Kevin Owens, Jimmy Uso & Jey Uso (Ezekiel, Randy Orton & Riddle)	W	WWE Monday Night RAW	14:58
May 8	Seth Rollins	W	WWE WrestleMania Backlash '22	20:45
May 9	Theory	W	WWE Monday Night RAW	13:10
May 23	The Miz	W	WWE Monday Night RAW	9:00
Jun 5	Hell In A Cell: Seth Rollins	W	WWE Hell In A Cell '22	24:20

COLBY CORINO

Feb 8	Team War Elimination Match: Chris Adonis, Thom Latimer & El Rudo, Matt Taven, Mike Bennett & Victor Benjamin, Bestia 666, Mecha Wolf & Homicide (w/Jay Bradley & Wrecking Ball Legursky)	L	NWA Power	11:09
Feb 22	2/3 Falls: Rhett Titus	W	NWA Power	16:55
Mar 20	Homicide, Austin Aries, Darius Lockhart	L	NWA Crockett Cup '22	9:39
Apr 12	Gaagz The Gymp, Judais & Sal The Pal (w/Jay Bradley & Wrecking Ball Legursky)	L	NWA Power	6:27
May 17	AJ Cazana	W	NWA Power	4:50
May 31	Homicide	L	NWA Power	9:55
Jun 11	Homicide	L	NWA Alwayz Ready '22	9:06
Aug 28	2/3 Falls: Caprice Coleman	W	NWA 74th Anniversary Show	9:57
Nov 1	Flip Gordon	W	NWA Power	8:38
Nov 12	Davey Richards	L	NWA Hard Times 3	6:42
Dec 13	AJ Cazana	W	NWA Power	8:10

COLE KARTER (AS TROY DONOVAN UNTIL JULY 20)

Apr 8	Andre Chase & Bodhi Hayward (w/Channing Lorenzo)	W	NXT Level Up	6:47
Apr 15	Damon Kemp	L	NXT Level Up	6:00
May 6	Dante Chen & Javier Bernal (w/Channing Lorenzo)	W	NXT Level Up	6:04
May 24	Edris Enofe & Malik Blade (w/Channing Lorenzo)	W	NXT 2.0	6:10
Jun 4	Santos Escobar, Cruz del Toro & Joaquin Wilde (w/Channing Lorenzo & Tony D'Angelo)	W	NXT In Your House '22	12:45
Jun 14	Carmelo Hayes & Trick Williams (w/Channing Lorenzo)	L	NXT 2.0	4:22
Jul 20	Ricky Starks	L	AEW Dynamite: Fyter Fest	6:09
Jul 26	Mike Orlando	W	AEW Dark	2:29
Aug 1	Serpentico	W	AEW Dark Elevation	4:02
Sep 3	Hangman Page, John Silver & Alex Reynolds (w/Aaron Solo & Nick Comoroto)	L	AEW Dark Elevation	6:00
Sep 23	Golden Ticket Battle Royale	L	AEW Rampage: Grand Slam	12:16
Oct 3	Chuck Taylor, Trent Beretta, Danhausen & Rocky Romero (w/Aaron Solo, Nick Comoroto & QT Marshall)	L	AEW Dark Elevation	7:54
Oct 11	Dante Martin & Matt Sydal (w/Aaron Solo)	L	AEW Dark	9:31
Nov 7	Cheeseburger, Logan Easton Laroux & Rhett Titus (w/Lee Johnson & QT Marshall)	W	AEW Dark Elevation	6:45
Nov 8	Brian Pillman Jr. 7 Griff Garrison (w/QT Marshall)	W	AEW Dark	4:13
Nov 15	Channing Thomas, Man Scout & Teddy Goodz (w/Lee Johnson & QT Marshall)	W	AEW Dark	4:11
Nov 19	Orange Cassidy, Chuck Taylor, Trent Beretta, Rocky Romero & Danhausen (w/QT Marshall, Aaron Solo, Lee Johnson & Nick Comoroto)	L	AEW Full Gear Buy-In	11:55
Nov 21	Orange Cassidy, Chuck Taylor & Trent Beretta (w/Aaron Solo & Lee Johnson)	L	AEW Dark Elevation	3:38
Nov 29	Justin Corino, Ryan Mooney & Steven Josifi (w/Lee Johnson & QT Marshall)	W	AEW Dark	3:40
Dec 2	Darby Allin	L	AEW Rampage	7:40
Dec 13	Chris Steeler, Joe Keys & LSG (w/Lee Johnson & QT Marshall)	W	AEW Dark	3:29
Dec 14	Malakai Black, Brody King & Buddy Matthews (w/QT Marshall & Aaron Solo)	L	AEW Dynamite: Winter Is Coming	:23

COLT CABANA

Date	Opponent		Result	Promotion	Time
Jan 4	Powerhouse Hobbs		L	AEW Dark	4:46
Mar 8	The Butcher & The Blade (w/Alan Angels)		L	AEW Dark	5:31
Mar 15	Brandon Cutler, Matt Jackson & Matt Jackson (w/Alan Angels & Evil Uno)		L	AEW Dark	8:40
May 2	Anthony Bennett, Bret Waters, Cory Bishop, Eli Isom, Jaden Valo & Mike Law (w/John Silver, Alex Reynolds, Alan Angels, Evil Uno & Ten)		W	AEW Dark Elevation	1:44
Nov 2	Chris Jericho		L	AEW Dynamite	9:12

COLTEN GUNN

Date	Opponent		Result	Promotion	Time
Jan 4	Rolando Perez, Austin Green & Donnie Primetime (w/Billy Gunn & Austin Gunn)		W	AEW Dark	3:06
Jan 11	Patrick Scott, Marcus Kross & T.I.M (w/Billy Gunn & Austin Gunn)		W	AEW Dark	:41
Jan 17	JB Cole & T.I.M (w/Austin Gunn)		W	AEW Dark Elevation	2:55
Jan 18	Bison XL & Larintiz XL (w/Austin Gunn)		W	AEW Dark	2:20
Jan 25	Alan Angels, Alex Reynolds, Evil Uno & Ten (w/Anthony Bowens, Max Caster & Austin Gunn)		W	AEW Dark	6:15
Feb 7	Lee Moriarty, Matt Sydal, Brock Anderson & Lee Johnson (w/Austin Gunn, Anthony Bowens & Max Caster)		W	AEW Dark Elevation	7:11
Feb 8	Adrian Alanis & Liam Gray (w/Austin Gunn)		W	AEW Dark	2:07
Feb 11	Jungle Boy & Luchasaurus (w/Austin Gunn)		L	AEW Rampage	12:29
Feb 21	Ariel Levy, Chico Adams, Dean Alexander, Dominic Garrini & Kevin Ku (w/Jeff Parker, Matt Lee, Daniel Garcia & Austin Gunn)		W	AEW Dark Elevation	2:55
Feb 23	Tag Team Battle Royal (w/Austin Gunn)		L	AEW Dynamite	1:54
Mar 2	Casino Battle Royale (w/Austin Gunn)		L	AEW Dynamite	17:07
Mar 21	Aaron Mercer & Masada (w/Austin Gunn)		W	AEW Dark Elevation	3:42
Mar 22	JCruz & Victor Chase (w/Austin Gunn)		W	AEW Dark	:29
Mar 30	Dax Harwood & Cash Wheeler (w/Austin Gunn)		L	AEW Dynamite	11:27
Apr 11	John Silver, Alex Reynolds, Alan Angels, Stu Grayson & Ten (w/Austin Gunn, Billy Gunn, Luther & Serpentico)		L	AEW Dark Elevation	5:20
Apr 15	Bryan Danielson, Jon Moxley & Wheeler Yuta (w/Billy Gunn & Austin Gunn)		L	AEW Rampage	9:06
Apr 29	Keith Lee		L	AEW Rampage	5:57
May 10	Warren J & Zack Zilla (w/Austin Gunn)		W	AEW Dark	3:30
May 16	Bryce Donovan, GKM, Lucas Chase & Zack Clayton (w/Austin Gunn, Anthony Bowens & Max Caster)		W	AEW Dark Elevation	1:22
Jun 1	CM Punk, Dax Harwood & Cash Wheeler (w/Max Caster & Austin Gunn)		L	AEW Dynamite	11:50
Jun 7	John Silver, Alex Reynolds & Ten (w/Max Caster & Austin Gunn)		W	AEW Dark	5:26
Jun 8	Casino Battle Royale		L	AEW Dynamite	24:59
Jun 17	Leon Ruffin, Bear Bronson & Bear Boulder (w/Max Caster & Austin Gunn)		W	AEW Rampage: Road Rager	1:15
Jun 26	Yuya Uemura, Alex Coughlin, The DKC & Kevin Knight (w/Max Caster, Billy Gunn & Austin Gunn)		W	AEW x NJPW Forbidden Door Buy-In	5:35
Jun 27	Alex Reynolds, Evil Uno & Ten (w/Austin Gunn & Max Caster)		W	AEW Dark Elevation	4:08
Jun 29	Danhausen, Dax Harwood & Cash Wheeler (w/Max Caster & Austin Gunn)		L	AEW Dynamite: Blood & Guts	9:31
Jul 6	Fuego Del Sol, Leon Ruffin, Bear Bronson & Bear Boulder (w/Anthony Bowens, Max Caster & Austin Gunn)		W	AEW Dynamite	2:14
Aug 3	Anthony Bowens & Max Caster (w/Austin Gunn)		L	AEW Dynamite	8:20
Aug 12	Danhausen & Erick Redbeard (w/Austin Gunn)		W	AEW Rampage: Quake By The Lake	4:33
Aug 17	Brian Pillman Jr. & Griff Garrison (w/Austin Gunn)		W	AEW Dynamite	:31
Aug 24	Billy Gunn		W	AEW Dynamite	6:16
Oct 17	Gurv Sihra & Harv Sihra (w/Austin Gunn)		W	AEW Dark Elevation	4:16
Nov 8	BK Klein & Jarett Diaz (w/Austin Gunn)		W	AEW Dark	3:05
Nov 9	Anthony Bowens, Max Caster, Dax Harwood & Cash Wheeler (w/Austin Gunn, Keith Lee & Swerve Strickland)		L	AEW Dynamite	12:22
Dec 21	Dax Harwood & Cash Wheeler (w/Austin Gunn)		W	AEW Dynamite: Holiday Bash	9:12

COMMANDER AZEEZ

Date	Opponent		Result	Promotion	Time
Jan 3	Angelo Dawkins & Montez Ford (w/Apollo Crews)		L	WWE Monday Night RAW	2:15
Jan 17	Rey Mysterio, Dominik Mysterio, Angelo Dawkins & Montez Ford (w/Apollo Crews, Dolph Ziggler & Robert Roode)		L	WWE Monday Night RAW	8:00
Mar 14	Omos		L	WWE Monday Night RAW	2:00
Mar 21	Handicap Match: Omos (w/Apollo Crews)		L	WWE Monday Night RAW	2:45
Apr 1	Andre The Giant Memorial Battle Royal		L	WWE SmackDown	8:05
Apr 14	Cedric Alexander & Shelton Benjamin (w/Apollo Crews)		W	WWE Main Event	6:59
May 5	T-Bar		W	WWE Main Event	6:02
May 19	Angelo Dawkins & Montez Ford (w/Apollo Crews)		L	WWE Main Event	4:23
May 26	Akira Tozawa		W	WWE Main Event	4:22

CORA JADE

Date	Opponent		Result	Promotion	Time
Jan 4	Mandy Rose, Raquel Gonzalez		L	NXT 2.0: New Year's Evil '22	12:32
Feb 1	Raquel Gonzalez		L	NXT 2.0	6:02
Mar 1	Yulisa Leon & Valentina Feroz (w/Raquel Gonzalez)		W	NXT 2.0	4:47
Mar 8	Wendy Choo & Dakota Kai (w/Raquel Gonzalez)		L	NXT 2.0: Roadblock '22	10:42
Apr 2	Mandy Rose, Kay Lee Ray, Io Shirai		L	NXT Stand & Deliver '22	13:27
May 3	Natalya & Lash Legend (w/Nikkita Lyons)		W	NXT 2.0: Spring Breakin'	13:28
May 10	Natalya		L	NXT 2.0	14:08
May 31	Elektra Lopez		W	NXT 2.0	5:06
Jun 14	Mandy Rose, Gigi Dolin & Jacy Jayne (w/Roxanne Perez & Indi Hartwell)		W	NXT 2.0	13:51
Jun 28	Katana Chance & Kayden Carter (w/Roxanne Perez)		W	NXT 2.0	13:46
Jul 5	Gigi Dolin & Jacy Jayne (w/Roxanne Perez)		W	NXT 2.0: Great American Bash	10:29
Jul 19	Battle Royal		L	NXT 2.0	13:13
Aug 9	Zoey Stark		L	NXT 2.0	11:05

Aug 16	Roxanne Perez	W	NXT 2.0: Heatwave	11:41
Sep 20	Wendy Choo	W	NXT	4:14
Oct 18	Pick Your Poison Match: Raquel Rodriguez	W	NXT	2:42
Oct 22	Weapons Wild Match: Roxanne Perez	L	NXT Halloween Havoc '22	12:25
Nov 1	Valentina Feroz	W	NXT	3:37
Nov 22	Wendy Choo	W	NXT	9:08
Dec 10	Iron Survivor Challenge: Roxanne Perez, Zoey Stark, Indi Hartwell, Kiana James	L	NXT Deadline	25:00
Dec 27	Wendy Choo	L	NXT	6:10

CRAZZY STEVE

Feb 3	Jonah	L	IMPACT Wrestling	2:08
Mar 3	Brian Myers	L	IMPACT Before The Impact	8:05
Mar 10	Ace Austin, John Skyler	L	IMPACT Wrestling	10:45
Mar 24	Shera	L	IMPACT Before The Impact	7:15
Apr 21	Eric Young & Deaner (w/Black Taurus)	L	IMPACT Wrestling	4:42
Apr 28	Vincent	L	IMPACT Before The Impact	9:20
May 19	Zicky Dice	W	IMPACT Before The Impact	9:13
Jun 9	Johnny Swinger & Zicky Dice (w/Black Taurus)	W	IMPACT Before The Impact	8:18
Aug 11	Steve Maclin	L	IMPACT Before The Impact	7:37
Sep 8	Shane Taylor	W	IMPACT Before The Impact	8:17
Sep 15	Moose & Steve Maclin (w/Black Taurus)	W	IMPACT Wrestling	1:52
Sep 29	Brian Myers	L	IMPACT Wrestling	4:06
Dec 15	Matt Cardona & Brian Myers (w/Black Taurus)	L	IMPACT Wrestling	4:24

CRUZ DEL TORO (AS RAUL MENDOZA UNTIL APR 26)

Jan 18	Malik Blade & Edris Enofe (w/Joaquin Wilde)	L	NXT 2.0	3:17
Feb 1	Bron Breakker & Tommaso Ciampa (w/Joaquin Wilde)	L	NXT 2.0	11:28
Mar 4	Malik Blade & Edris Enofe (w/Joaquin Wilde)	W	NXT Level Up	8:45
Mar 15	Dominik Mysterio	L	NXT 2.0	3:05
Mar 29	Brooks Jensen & Josh Briggs (w/Joaquin Wilde)	L	NXT 2.0	5:36
Apr 12	Gauntlet Match: Brooks Jensen & Josh Briggs, Kit Wilson & Elton Prince Grayson Waller & Sanga, Julius Creed & Brutus Creed (w/Joaquin Wilde)	L	NXT 2.0	27:08
Apr 19	Zack Gibson & James Drake (w/Joaquin Wilde)	W	NXT 2.0	3:57
Apr 26	Handicap Match: Fallon Henley & Josh Briggs (w/Joaquin Wilde & Elektra Lopez)	W	NXT 2.0	4:45
Jun 4	Tony D'Angelo, Channing Lorenzo & Troy Donovan (w/Santos Escobar & Joaquin Wilde)	L	NXT In Your House '22	12:45
Jun 21	Roderick Strong & Damon Kemp (w/Joaquin Wilde)	L	NXT 2.0	4:57
Jul 26	Roderick Strong, Damon Kemp, Julius Creed & Brutus Creed (w/Tony D'Angelo, Channing Lorenzo & Joaquin Wilde)	W	NXT 2.0	11:39
Aug 23	Jagger Reid & Rip Fowler (w/Joaquin Wilde)	L	NXT 2.0	5:02
Oct 14	Ashante Adonis & Top Dolla (w/Joaquin Wilde)	W	WWE SmackDown	1:22
Oct 28	Ashante Adonis, Top Dolla & Shinsuke Nakamura (w/Santos Escobar & Joaquin Wilde)	L	WWE SmackDown	4:19
Dec 9	Erik & Ivar (w/Joaquin Wilde)	D	WWE SmackDown	1:53
Dec 16	Ashante Adonis & Top Dolla, Erik & Ivar (w/Joaquin Wilde)	L	WWE SmackDown	9:20

CYON

Jan 5	Handicap Match: Jordan Clearwater & Marshe Rockett	L	NWA Power	5:21
Jan 11	Judais	W	NWA Power	2:53
Feb 1	No DQ Match: Sal Rinauro	W	NWA Power	4:52
Mar 8	BLK Jeez, Jordan Clearwater, Marshe Rockett & Tyrus (w/Alex Taylor, Rush Freeman & Mims)	L	NWA Power	6:59
Apr 5	Slam Challenge Match: Tyrus	D	NWA Power	3:09
May 24	Joe Alonzo	W	NWA Power	16:32
Jun 11	Thom Latimer	L	NWA Alwayz Ready '22	12:30
Jun 21	Alex Taylor & Jeremiah Plunkett (w/Tyrus)	W	NWA Power	7:40
Aug 2	Rodney Mack	W	NWA Power	4:39
Aug 27	Jax Dane	W	NWA 74th Anniversary Show	7:26
Aug 28	Anthony Mayweather	W	NWA 74th Anniversary Show	8:18
Sep 13	Joe Alonzo	W	NWA Power	7:09
Nov 12	Dak Draper	W	NWA Hard Times 3	6:01
Nov 22	Thrillbilly Silas	W	NWA Power	4:56
Dec 27	Joe Alonzo, Bestia 666 & Mecha Wolf (w/Jordan Clearwater & Tyrus)	W	NWA Power	7:56

DA POPE

Mar 1	Mike Knox	L	NWA Power	11:55
Mar 19	Mike Knox & VSK (w/Mims)	L	NWA Crockett Cup '22	9:59
Apr 12	Matt Cardona	L	NWA Power	16:07
Jul 12	Brian Myers	L	NWA Power	6:56
Aug 9	Trevor Murdoch	D	NWA Power	7:30
Aug 28	Misouri Tornado Match: Aron Stevens & Rodney Mack (w/JR Kratos)	W	NWA 74th Anniversary Show	9:40
Sep 13	KC Roxx & The Question Mark II (w/JR Kratos)	W	NWA Power	6:46
Nov 8	Thom Latimer, Trevor Murdoch & Tyrus (w/Doug Williams & JR Kratos)	D	NWA Power	6:49

DAK DRAPER

Sep 20	Brian Myers	W	NWA Power	6:34
Oct 11	Chris Adonis, Thrillbilly Silas	W	NWA Power	5:15
Nov 12	Cyon	L	NWA Hard Times 3	6:01
Dec 13	Rhett Titus & Trevor Murdoch (w/Mims)	L	NWA Power	9:14
Dec 20	Bully Ray, Judais & Thomas Latimer (w/Chris Adonis & Mims)	L	NWA Power	8:18

DAKOTA KAI

Jan 18	Yulisa Leon	W	NXT 2.0	4:05
Feb 8	Sarray	L	NXT 2.0	6:20
Mar 1	Indi Hartwell & Persia Pirotta (w/Wendy Choo)	W	NXT 2.0	5:21
Mar 8	Raquel Gonzalez & Cora Jade (w/Wendy Choo)	W	NXT 2.0: Roadblock '22	10:42
Mar 22	Io Shirai & Kay Lee Ray (w/Wendy Choo)	L	NXT 2.0	10:22
Apr 2	Gigi Dolin & Jacy Jayne (w/Raquel Gonzalez)	W	NXT Stand & Deliver Kickoff	7:53
Apr 5	Gigi Dolin & Jacy Jayne (w/Raquel Gonzalez)	W	NXT 2.0	8:31
Apr 12	Mandy Rose	L	NXT 2.0	10:48
Aug 8	Dana Brooke & Tamina (w/Iyo Sky)	W	WWE Monday Night RAW	10:00
Aug 15	Dana Brooke	W	WWE Monday Night RAW	1:50
Aug 22	Alexa Bliss & Asuka (w/Iyo Sky)	W	WWE Monday Night RAW	18:30
Aug 29	Raquel Rodriguez & Aliyah (w/Iyo Sky)	L	WWE Monday Night RAW	11:17
Sep 3	Bianca Belair, Alexa Bliss & Asuka (w/Bayley & Iyo Sky)	W	WWE Clash At The Castle	18:44
Sep 12	Raquel Rodriguez & Aliyah (w/Iyo Sky)	W	WWE Monday Night RAW	12:30
Sep 23	Raquel Rodriguez	L	WWE SmackDown	2:01
Oct 3	Candice LeRae	W	WWE Monday Night RAW	11:00
Oct 14	Raquel Rodriguez, Shotzi & Roxanne Perez (w/Bayley & Iyo Sky)	W	WWE SmackDown	6:42
Oct 17	Bianca Belair & Candice LeRae (w/Iyo Sky)	W	WWE Monday Night RAW	12:10
Oct 21	Shotzi & Raquel Rodriguez (w/Iyo Sky)	W	WWE SmackDown	9:58
Oct 31	Alexa Bliss & Asuka (w/Iyo Sky)	L	WWE Monday Night RAW	16:25
Nov 5	Alexa Bliss & Asuka (w/Iyo Sky)	W	WWE Crown Jewel '22	12:50
Nov 26	WarGames: Bianca Belair, Alexa Bliss, Asuka, Mia Yim & Becky Lynch (w/Bayley, Iyo Sky, Nikki Cross & Rhea Ripley)	L	WWE Survivor Series WarGames	39:40
Nov 28	Candice LeRae	L	WWE Monday Night RAW	14:00
Dec 16	Liv Morgan & Tegan Nox (w/Iyo Sky)	W	WWE SmackDown	14:48

DALTON CASTLE

Apr 16	Jonathan Gresham	L	AEW Battle Of The Belts II	10:35
Jul 23	Vincent, Bateman & Dutch (w/Brandon Tate & Brent Tate)	W	ROH Death Before Dishonor XIX	9:40
Sep 19	Boujii, Omar & Rick Recon (w/Brandon Tate & Brent Tate)	W	AEW Dark Elevation	3:25
Sep 23	Golden Ticket Battle Royale	L	AEW Rampage: Grand Slam	12:16
Oct 3	Adrien Soriano, Gabriel Hodder & Matthew Omen (w/Brandon Tate & Brent Tate)	W	AEW Dark Elevation	4:07
Oct 10	Brett Waters, Goldy & Logan Laroux (w/Brandon Tate & Brent Tate)	W	AEW Dark Elevation	4:00
Oct 11	BK Klein, Joe Keys & Josh Fuller (w/Brandon Tate & Brent Tate)	W	AEW Dark	3:35
Oct 18	Chris Jericho	L	AEW Dynamite: Title Tuesday	12:28
Nov 7	Ari Daivari, Jeeves Kay & Slim J (w/Brandon Tate & Brent Tate)	W	AEW Dark Elevation	5:25
Dec 6	Jaden Valo, Justin Corino & Sonny Defarge (w/Brandon Tate & Brent Tate)	W	AEW Dark	2:30
Dec 7	Dynamite Diamond Battle Royale	L	AEW Dynamite	13:10
Dec 10	Brian Cage, Kaun & Toa Liona (w/Brandon Tate & Brent Tate)	L	ROH Final Battle '22	10:05

DAMAGE

Nov 29	David Powers & Eddie Vero (w/Carnage)	W	NWA Power	2:20
Dec 6	Judais & PJ Hawx (w/Rush Freeman)	L	NWA Power	6:42
Dec 27	The Question Mark II	W	NWA Power	4:11

DAMARIS GRIFFIN

Apr 22	Edris Enofe & Malik Blade (w/Quincy Elliott)	L	NXT Level Up	6:36
May 27	Andre Chase & Bodhi Hayward (w/Bryson Montana)	L	NXT Level Up	3:53
Jul 8	Edris Enofe & Malik Blade (w/Bryson Montana)	L	NXT Level Up	5:29
Aug 5	Dante Chen & Guru Raaj (w/Bryson Montana)	L	NXT Level Up	5:20

DAMIAN PRIEST

Jan 3	Dolph Ziggler	W	WWE Monday Night RAW	9:00
Jan 10	Dolph Ziggler, Robert Roode & Apollo Crews (w/Angelo Dawkins & Montez Ford)	L	WWE Monday Night RAW	8:30
Jan 17	Kevin Owens	L	WWE Monday Night RAW	10:55
Jan 24	Kevin Owens	L	WWE Monday Night RAW	9:35
Jan 29	Royal Rumble Match	L	WWE Royal Rumble '22	11:04
Feb 7	AJ Styles	L	WWE Monday Night RAW	4:58
Feb 14	AJ Styles	W	WWE Monday Night RAW	4:30
Feb 21	Shelton Benjamin	W	WWE Monday Night RAW	3:10
Feb 28	Finn Balor	L	WWE Monday Night RAW	11:00
Mar 14	Finn Balor	W	WWE Monday Night RAW	7:35
Apr 1	Andre The Giant Memorial Battle Royal	L	WWE SmackDown	8:05
Apr 11	AJ Styles	D	WWE Monday Night RAW	13:05
Apr 25	Finn Balor	W	WWE Monday Night RAW	7:20
May 2	AJ Styles	L	WWE Monday Night RAW	11:00
May 9	Finn Balor	L	WWE Monday Night RAW	5:59
May 23	AJ Styles & Liv Morgan (w/Rhea Ripley)	W	WWE Monday Night RAW	11:35
Jun 5	AJ Styles, Finn Balor & Liv Morgan (w/Edge & Rhea Ripley)	W	WWE Hell In A Cell '22	16:00
Jun 23	Rey Mysterio & Dominik Mysterio (w/Finn Balor)	L	WWE Main Event	7:31
Jul 4	Rey Mysterio & Dominik Mysterio (w/Finn Balor)	L	WWE Monday Night RAW	11:30
Jul 18	Rey Mysterio	W	WWE Monday Night RAW	4:59
Jul 25	Rey Mysterio & Dominik Mysterio (w/Finn Balor)	L	WWE Monday Night RAW	11:29
Jul 30	Rey Mysterio & Dominik Mysterio (w/Finn Balor)	L	WWE SummerSlam '22	11:05
Aug 22	Edge	L	WWE Monday Night RAW	19:35
Aug 29	AJ Styles & Dolph Ziggler (w/Finn Balor)	W	WWE Monday Night RAW	8:34
Sep 3	Rey Mysterio & Edge (w/Finn Balor)	L	WWE Clash At The Castle	12:35
Sep 5	Rey Mysterio	W	WWE Monday Night RAW	13:35
Sep 19	Matt Riddle & Rey Mysterio (w/Finn Balor)	W	WWE Monday Night RAW	17:40

Sep 26	Matt Riddle	L	WWE Monday Night RAW	19:21
Oct 3	AJ Styles & Rey Mysterio (w/Finn Balor)	W	WWE Monday Night RAW	10:42
Oct 31	Karl Anderson	L	WWE Monday Night RAW	7:17
Nov 5	AJ Styles, Luke Gallows & Karl Anderson (w/Finn Balor & Dominik Mysterio)	W	WWE Crown Jewel '22	14:00
Nov 21	Sheamus, Ridge Holland & Butch (w/Finn Balor & Dominik Mysterio)	L	WWE Monday Night RAW	14:50
Nov 28	AJ Styles, Luke Gallows, Karl Anderson & Mia Yim (w/Finn Balor, Dominik Mysterio & Rhea Ripley)	W	WWE Monday Night RAW	14:20
Dec 12	Akira Tozawa, Angelo Dawkins & Montez Ford (w/Finn Balor & Dominik Mysterio)	W	WWE Monday Night RAW	14:45
Dec 19	Angelo Dawkins & Montez Ford (w/Finn Balor)	L	WWE Monday Night RAW	9:00

DAMON KEMP

Jan 11	Cameron Grimes	L	NXT 2.0	2:20
Jan 28	Josh Briggs	L	WWE 205 Live	5:04
Feb 4	Kushida	L	WWE 205 Live	3:50
Mar 18	Xyon Quinn	L	NXT Level Up	5:24
Apr 1	James Drake	W	NXT Level Up	6:22
Apr 15	Troy Donovan	W	NXT Level Up	6:00
Apr 29	Dante Chen	W	NXT Level Up	5:17
May 5	Danny Jones	W	NXT UK	4:15
May 26	Sha Samuels	L	NXT UK	5:42
May 31	Elton Prince & Kit Wilson (w/Roderick Strong)	L	NXT 2.0	13:17
Jun 16	Noam Dar & Sha Samuels (w/Wolfgang)	W	NXT UK	12:41
Jun 21	Cruz Del Toro & Joaquin Wilde (w/Roderick Strong)	W	NXT 2.0	4:57
Jul 5	Julius Creed & Brutus Creed (w/Roderick Strong)	L	NXT 2.0: Great American Bash	12:13
Jul 19	Roderick Strong	L	NXT 2.0	5:55
Jul 26	Tony D'Angelo, Channing Lorenzo, Joaquin Wilde & Cruz Del Toro (w/Roderick Strong, Julius Creed & Brutus Creed)	L	NXT 2.0	11:39
Aug 30	Joe Coffey, Mark Coffey & Wolfgang (w/Julius Creed & Brutus Creed)	L	NXT 2.0	10:59
Sep 27	Brutus Creed	L	NXT	3:05
Oct 22	Ambulance Match: Julius Creed	L	NXT Halloween Havoc '22	14:09
Nov 8	Five Minute Challenge: Brutus Creed	W	NXT	2:47
Nov 25	Dante Chen	W	NXT Level Up	6:13
Dec 9	Odyssey Jones	L	NXT Level Up	5:10
Dec 13	Duke Hudson	L	NXT	3:53

DANA BROOKE

Jan 3	Tamina & Akira Tozawa (w/Reggie)	W	WWE Monday Night RAW	1:10
Jan 24	Tamina, Carmella & Nikki A.S.H. (w/Rhea Ripley & Liv Morgan)	W	WWE Monday Night RAW	2:20
Jan 29	Royal Rumble Match	L	WWE Royal Rumble '22	2:12
Feb 21	Reggie	W	WWE Monday Night RAW	3:10
Feb 28	Tamina & Akira Tozawa (w/Reggie)	W	WWE Monday Night RAW	1:40
Mar 7	Tamina	W	WWE Monday Night RAW	1:45
Mar 21	Tamina & Akira Tozawa (w/Reggie)	W	WWE Monday Night RAW	1:05
Apr 25	Tamina & Akira Tozawa (w/Reggie)	L	WWE Monday Night RAW	1:30
May 2	Nikki A.S.H.	W	WWE Monday Night RAW	1:30
Jun 6	Becky Lynch	D	WWE Monday Night RAW	1:00
Jun 6	Becky Lynch	W	WWE Monday Night RAW	2:10
Jun 23	Doudrop	L	WWE Main Event	2:21
Jul 18	Tamina, Doudrop & Nikki A.S.H.	W	WWE Monday Night RAW	2:35
Jul 28	Carmella & Tamina (w/Asuka)	W	WWE Main Event	7:09
Aug 8	Iyo Sky & Dakota Kai (w/Tamina)	L	WWE Monday Night RAW	10:00
Aug 15	Dakota Kai	L	WWE Monday Night RAW	1:50
Aug 25	Doudrop & Nikki A.S.H. (w/Tamina)	L	WWE Main Event	5:14
Aug 26	Natalya & Sonya Deville, Nikki A.S.H. & Doudrop, Shotzi & Xia Li (w/Tamina)	L	WWE SmackDown	3:10
Sep 22	Tamina	W	WWE Main Event	5:00
Oct 6	Fallon Henley	W	WWE Main Event	4:39
Oct 27	Kiana James	W	WWE Main Event	4:56
Nov 3	Kiana James	L	WWE Main Event	4:19
Nov 7	Nikki Cross	L	WWE Monday Night RAW	2:15
Nov 14	Iyo Sky	L	WWE Monday Night RAW	3:15
Dec 1	Zoey Stark	L	WWE Main Event	5:42
Dec 15	Briana Ray	W	WWE Main Event	6:12

DANI PALMER

Nov 18	Thea Hail	L	NXT Level Up	4:41
Dec 23	Sol Ruca	L	NXT Level Up	3:01

DANHAUSEN

May 11	Tony Nese	L	AEW Dynamite	:32
May 29	Tony Nese & Mark Sterling (w/Hook)	W	AEW Double Or Nothing Buy-In	5:20
Jun 29	Max Caster, Austin Gunn & Colten Gunn (w/Dax Harwood & Cash Wheeler)	W	AEW Dynamite: Blood & Guts	9:31
Jul 19	Jake Something	W	AEW Dark	3:55
Jul 27	Ricky Starks	L	AEW Dynamite: Fight For The Fallen	1:31
Aug 12	Austin Gunn & Colten Gunn (w/Erick Redbeard)	L	AEW Rampage: Quake By The Lake	4:33
Sep 13	Peter Avalon	W	AEW Dark	2:15
Sep 16	Ethan Page	L	AEW Rampage	1:25
Sep 23	Golden Ticket Battle Royale	L	AEW Rampage: Grand Slam	12:16
Oct 3	Aaron Solo, Cole Karter, Nick Comoroto & QT Marshall	W	AEW Dark Elevation	7:54

	(w/Chuck Taylor, Trent Beretta & Danhausen)			
Oct 25	James Stone	W	AEW Dark	2:18
Oct 31	QT Marshall	L	AEW Dark Elevation	9:00
Nov 1	Jon Cruz	W	AEW Dark	4:47
Nov 19	QT Marshall, Aaron Solo, Lee Johnson, Nick Comoroto & Cole Karter	W	AEW Full Gear Buy-In	11:55
	(w/Orange Cassidy, Chuck Taylor, Trent Beretta & Rocky Romero)			

DANIEL GARCIA

Jan 7	No DQ, No Holds Barred: Eddie Kingston, Santana & Ortiz	L	AEW Rampage	13:50
	(w/Jeff Parker & Matt Lee)			
Jan 11	Fuego Del Sol	W	AEW Dark	3:44
Jan 12	Sammy Guevara	L	AEW Dynamite	12:34
Jan 18	Anthony Greene	W	AEW Dark	7:36
Jan 25	Kekoa, Pat Brink & Rayo (w/Jeff Parker & Matt Lee)	W	AEW Dark	1:01
Jan 26	Chris Jericho, Santana & Ortiz (w/Matt Lee & Jeff Parker)	L	AEW Dynamite	8:52
Feb 14	John Silver, Alex Reynolds, Evil Uno, Alan Angels & Stu Grayson	W	AEW Dark Elevation	5:56
	(w/Jeff Parker, Matt Lee, Anthony Bowens & Max Caster)			
Feb 21	Ariel Levy, Chico Adams, Dean Alexander, Dominic Garrini & Kevin Ku	W	AEW Dark Elevation	2:55
	(w/Jeff Parker, Matt Lee, Austin Gunn & Colten Gunn)			
Feb 23	Bryan Danielson	L	AEW Dynamite	10:22
Mar 1	Josh Woods	W	AEW Dark	6:42
Mar 7	Ray Jaz	W	AEW Dark Elevation	1:06
Mar 15	Luke Sampson, Mike Reed & Shayne Stetson (w/Jeff Parker & Matt Lee)	W	AEW Dark	2:19
Mar 23	John Silver & Alex Reynolds (w/Chris Jericho)	W	AEW Dynamite	10:02
Mar 26	Yuya Uemura	W	NJPW Strong	10:39
Apr 1	Clark Connors, Karl Fredericks, Mascara Dorada & Yuya Uemura	L	NJPW Lonestar Shootout	10:45
	(w/Juice Robinson, David Finlay & Kevin Knight)			
Apr 9	Eddie Kingston & Fred Rosser (w/Fred Yehi)	L	NJPW Strong	9:27
Apr 13	Eddie Kingston, Santana & Ortiz (w/Chris Jericho & Jake Hager)	W	AEW Dynamite	11:46
Apr 22	Eddie Kingston	L	AEW Rampage	11:22
May 29	Anarchy In The Arena: Bryan Danielson, Jon Moxley, Eddie Kingston,	W	AEW Double Or Nothing '22	22:45
	Santana & Ortiz (w/Chris Jericho, Jake Hager, Angelo Parker &			
	Matt Menard)			
Jun 1	Jon Moxley	L	AEW Dynamite	11:32
Jun 8	Casino Battle Royale	L	AEW Dynamite	24:59
Jun 14	Jack Banning, Ray Rosas & Sinn Bodhi (w/Angelo Parker & Matt Menard)	W	AEW Dark	2:38
Jun 29	Blood & Guts: Jon Moxley, Claudio Castagnoli, Wheeler Yuta,	L	AEW Dynamite: Blood & Guts	46:45
	Eddie Kingston, Santana & Ortiz (w/Chris Jericho, Jake Hager,			
	Matt Menard, Angelo Parker & Sammy Guevara)			
Jul 19	Alan Angels	W	AEW Dark	9:42
Jul 23	Pure Wrestling Rules: Wheeler Yuta	L	ROH Death Before Dishonor XIX	15:55
Jul 27	Bryan Danielson	W	AEW Dynamite: Fight For The Fallen	17:12
Aug 17	2/3 Falls: Bryan Danielson	L	AEW Dynamite	26:16
Aug 23	Westin Blake	W	AEW Dark	5:52
Sep 7	Wheeler Yuta	W	AEW Dynamite	16:04
Sep 23	Golden Ticket Battle Royale	L	AEW Rampage: Grand Slam	12:16
Oct 5	Chris Jericho & Sammy Guevara (w/Bryan Danielson)	L	AEW Dynamite: Anniversary	14:23
Oct 26	Claudio Castagnoli & Wheeler Yuta (w/Chris Jericho)	L	AEW Dynamite	11:40
Nov 14	Leon Ruffin	W	AEW Dark Elevation	5:41
Nov 15	Brock Anderson	W	AEW Dark	7:49
Nov 21	Leon Ruffin, Tony Deppen & Tracy Williams	W	AEW Dark Elevation	2:46
	(w/Angelo Parker & Matt Menard)			
Nov 29	Jack Tomlinson, LSG & Tracy Williams (w/Angelo Parker & Matt Menard)	W	AEW Dark	4:09
Dec 7	Claudio Castagnoli & Wheeler Yuta (w/Jake Hager)	L	AEW Dynamite	12:42
Dec 10	Pure Wrestling Rules: Wheeler Yuta	L	ROH Final Battle '22	14:50

DANNY LIMELIGHT

Mar 26	Elimination Match: Adrian Quest, Clark Connors, Fred Rosser, The DKC	W	NJPW Strong	16:29
	& Taylor Rust (w/Jorel Nelson, JR Kratos, Royce Isaacs & Tom Lawlor)			
Apr 16	Fred Rosser, Josh Alexander, Alex Coughlin, Ren Narita & Chris Dickinson	L	NJPW Windy City Riot	13:50
	(w/Royce Isaacs, Jorel Nelson, JR Kratos & Black Tiger)			
May 13	Adrian Quest, Alex Coughlin & Rocky Romero (w/Black Tiger & JR Kratos)	L	NJPW Strong	8:33
May 14	The DKC, Yuya Uemura, David Finlay, Tanga Loa & Fred Rosser	W	NJPW Capital Collision	14:48
	(w/Tom Lawlor, Jorel Nelson, Royce Isaacs & JR Kratos)			
Jun 25	David Finlay	L	NJPW Strong	6:31
Oct 15	Kyle Fletcher & Mark Davis (w/JR Kratos)	L	NJPW Strong	10:08
Nov 12	Adrian Quest & Jordan Cruz (w/JR Kratos)	W	NJPW Strong	8:20
Dec 3	Homicide	L	NJPW Strong	11:14

DANTE CHEN

Jan 18	Guru Raaj	D	NXT 2.0	:58
Feb 22	Duke Hudson	L	NXT 2.0	2:20
Mar 4	Javier Bernal	W	NXT Level Up	3:59
Mar 18	Bodhi Hayward	W	NXT Level Up	5:57
Apr 1	Xyon Quin	L	NXT Level Up	4:48
Apr 22	Bodhi Hayward	L	NXT Level Up	5:50
Apr 29	Damon Kemp	L	NXT Level Up	5:17
May 6	Channing Lorenzo & Troy Donovan (w/Javier Bernal)	L	NXT Level Up	6:04
May 13	Sanga	L	NXT Level Up	5:08
May 27	Trick Williams	L	NXT Level Up	6:05
Jun 3	Edris Enofe & Malik Blade (w/Javier Bernal)	L	NXT Level Up	7:05
Jun 10	Ikemen Jiro	L	NXT Level Up	7:01

Jun 14	Rip Fowler & Jagger Reid (w/Javier Bernal)	L	NXT 2.0	3:56
Jul 8	Myles Borne	W	NXT Level Up	4:38
Jul 19	Axiom	L	NXT 2.0	3:00
Aug 5	Bryson Montana & Damaris Griffin (w/Guru Raaj)	W	NXT Level Up	5:20
Aug 19	Javier Bernal	W	NXT Level Up	4:31
Sep 2	Xyon Quinn	L	NXT Level Up	5:53
Sep 23	Bryson Montana	W	NXT Level Up	5:47
Oct 14	Myles Borne	L	NXT Level Up	5:14
Nov 18	Oba Femi	W	NXT Level Up	5:42
Nov 25	Damon Kemp	L	NXT Level Up	6:13
Nov 29	Dijak	L	NXT	3:48

DANTE MARTIN

Jan 4	Chandler Hopkins	W	AEW Dark	2:59
Jan 10	Action Andretti	W	AEW Dark Elevation	1:31
Jan 11	Aaron Solo	W	AEW Dark	3:16
Jan 12	Powerhouse Hobbs	W	AEW Dynamite	10:07
Jan 31	Aaron Solo, Nick Comoroto & QT Marshall (w/Lee Moriarty & Matt Sydal)	W	AEW Dark Elevation	7:46
Feb 1	Bear Boulder & Bear Bronson (w/Matt Sydal)	W	AEW Dark	9:43
Feb 7	Aaron Solo	W	AEW Dark Elevation	5:01
Feb 10	Isiah Kassidy, Marq Quen & The Blade (w/Lee Moriarty & Matt Sydal)	W	AEW Dark	9:05
Feb 14	Kevin Matthews	W	AEW Dark Elevation	3:34
Feb 18	Powerhouse Hobbs	L	AEW Rampage: Slam Dunk	9:29
Mar 1	Jack Evans	W	AEW Dark	7:47
Mar 2	Casino Battle Royale (w/Darius Martin)	L	AEW Dynamite	23:44
Mar 8	Peter Avalon & Ryan Nemeth (w/Darius Martin)	W	AEW Dark	6:25
Mar 9	Hangman Page	L	AEW Dynamite	7:27
Mar 15	Ari Daivari & Invictus Khash (w/Darius Martin)	W	AEW Dark	7:30
Mar 21	Luther & Serpentico (w/Darius Martin)	W	AEW Dark Elevation	4:54
Apr 1	Matt Jackson & Nick Jackson (w/Darius Martin)	L	AEW Rampage	10:48
Apr 11	Aaron Solo & Nick Comoroto (w/Darius Martin)	W	AEW Dark Elevation	5:52
Apr 18	Isiah Kassidy, Marq Quen, Angelico & Jack Evans (w/Jeff Hardy, Matt Hardy & Darius Martin)	W	AEW Dark Elevation	9:45
Apr 20	Bryan Danielson, Jon Moxley & Wheeler Yuta (w/Lee Moriarty & Brock Anderson)	L	AEW Dynamite	8:08
Apr 26	Max Caster, Angelico, Isiah Kassidy, Marq Quen & The Blade (w/Frankie Kazarian, Matt Hardy, Jeff Hardy & Darius Martin)	W	AEW Dark	12:40
Apr 27	Adam Cole, Matt Jackson, Nick Jackson, Bobby Fish & Kyle O'Reilly (w/Lee Johnson, Brock Anderson, Brian Pillman Jr. & Griff Garrison)	L	AEW Dynamite	6:28
May 3	Invictus Khash	W	AEW Dark	6:00
May 4	Rey Fenix	L	AEW Dynamite	9:38
May 20	Bryan Danielson & Jon Moxley (w/Matt Sydal)	L	AEW Rampage	12:00
May 27	Max Caster	W	AEW Rampage	6:12
Jun 3	Scorpio Sky	L	AEW Rampage	8:10
Jun 8	Casino Battle Royale	L	AEW Dynamite	24:59
Jun 17	Jon Moxley	L	AEW Rampage: Road Rager	11:58
Jun 28	Lucky Ali	W	AEW Dark	4:49
Jul 1	Royal Rampage Match	L	AEW Rampage	22:41
Jul 11	JD Drake	W	AEW Dark Elevation	7:13
Jul 12	Nick Comoroto	W	AEW Dark	7:53
Jul 22	Lee Moriarty	L	AEW Rampage: Fyter Fest	9:00
Jul 26	Peter Avalon	W	AEW Dark	5:08
Jul 27	Sammy Guevara	L	AEW Dynamite: Fight For The Fallen	8:48
Aug 12	Sammy Guevara & Tay Conti (w/Skye Blue)	L	AEW Rampage: Quake By The Lake	8:00
Aug 22	Jackson Drake	W	AEW Dark Elevation	2:47
Aug 23	Aaron Solo & Nick Comoroto (w/Matt Sydal)	W	AEW Dark	8:11
Aug 29	Wes Barkley	W	AEW Dark Elevation	2:00
Aug 30	AR Fox	W	AEW Dark	4:36
Aug 31	Wheeler Yuta, Rush, Rey Fenix	L	AEW Dynamite	8:06
Sep 4	Casino Ladder Match: MJF, Claudio Castagnoli, Penta El Zero M, Rey Fenix, Rush, Andrade El Idolo, Wheeler Yuta	L	AEW All Out '22	14:15
Sep 12	Serpentico & Zack Clayton (w/Matt Sydal)	W	AEW Dark	:57
Sep 13	Cezar Bononi & Ryan Nemeth (w/Matt Sydal)	W	AEW Dark	6:19
Sep 23	Golden Ticket Battle Royale	L	AEW Rampage: Grand Slam	12:16
Sep 27	Anthony Henry	W	AEW Dark	9:24
Oct 3	Penta El Zero M & Rey Fenix (w/Tony Deppen)	L	AEW Dark Elevation	6:20
Oct 4	Anthony Henry & JD Drake (w/Matt Sydal)	W	AEW Dark	9:34
Oct 11	Aaron Solo & Cole Karter (w/Matt Sydal)	W	AEW Dark	9:31
Oct 18	QT Marshall	W	AEW Dark	9:19
Oct 31	Brandon Cutler	W	AEW Dark Elevation	2:05
Nov 1	Encore	W	AEW Dark	2:49
Nov 7	Eli Isom	W	AEW Dark Elevation	6:35
Nov 11	Brian Cage	L	AEW Rampage	7:15
Nov 16	Pac, Penta El Zero M & Rey Fenix (w/AR Fox & Darius Martin)	L	AEW Dynamite	11:33
Nov 25	Dax Harwood & Cash Wheeler (w/Darius Martin)	L	AEW Rampage: Black Friday	11:12
Dec 5	Truth Magnum & Turbo Floyd (w/Darius Martin)	W	AEW Dark Elevation	4:03
Dec 10	Aaron Solo & Nick Comoroto (w/Darius Martin)	W	AEW Dark Elevation	3:35
Dec 19	Jeeves Kay, Slim J, Sonny Kiss, Cezar Bononi, Peter Avalon & Ryan Nemeth (w/Ethan Page, Isiah Kassidy, Konosuke Takeshita, Matt Hardy & Darius Martin)	W	AEW Dark Elevation	7:45
Dec 23	$300,000 Three Kings Christmas Casino Trios Royale (w/AR Fox & Darius Martin)	W	AEW Rampage	22:01
Dec 28	Jon Moxley & Claudio Castagnoli (w/Darius Martin)	L	AEW Dynamite	14:02

DANNY JONES

Feb 24	Rohan Raja	L	NXT UK	5:00
Mar 10	Primate & T-Bone (w/Josh Morrell)	L	NXT UK	6:05
Mar 24	Jordan Devlin	L	NXT UK	4:44
May 5	Damon Kemp	L	NXT UK	4:15

DARBY ALLIN

Jan 19	Anthony Bowens & Max Caster (w/Sting)	W	AEW Dynamite	9:22
Feb 16	Sammy Guevara	L	AEW Dynamite	14:51
Mar 4	Sammy Guevara, Andrade El Idolo	L	AEW Rampage	13:12
Mar 6	Tornado Match: Andrade El Idolo, Matt Hardy & Isiah Kassidy (w/Sammy Guevara & Sting)	W	AEW Revolution '22	13:20
Mar 11	Marq Quen	W	AEW Rampage	11:55
Mar 18	The Butcher	W	AEW Rampage	10:41
Mar 23	Tornado Match: Isiah Kassidy, Marq Quen, The Butcher & The Blade (w/Sting, Matt Hardy & Jeff Hardy)	W	AEW Dynamite	9:27
Mar 30	Andrade El Idolo	L	AEW Dynamite	10:32
Apr 20	Coffin Match: Andrade El Idolo	W	AEW Dynamite	12:25
Apr 29	Swerve Strickland	W	AEW Rampage	10:23
May 11	Jeff Hardy	L	AEW Dynamite	10:16
May 28	Brandon Cutler	W	AEW Dark	:59
May 29	Kyle O'Reilly	L	AEW Double Or Nothing '22	9:50
Jun 1	Matt Jackson, Nick Jackson, Bobby Fish, Kyle O'Reilly & Hikuleo (w/Christian Cage, Matt Hardy, Jungle Boy & Luchasaurus)	L	AEW Dynamite	12:00
Jun 8	Casino Battle Royale	L	AEW Dynamite	24:59
Jun 17	Bobby Fish	W	AEW Rampage: Road Rager	11:45
Jun 26	El Phantasmo, Matt Jackson & Nick Jackson (w/Sting & Shingo Takagi)	W	AEW x NJPW Forbidden Door	13:01
Jul 1	Royal Rampage Match	L	AEW Rampage	22:41
Jul 20	Brody King	L	AEW Dynamite: Fyter Fest	12:35
Aug 10	Coffin Match: Brody King	W	AEW Dynamite: Quake By The Lake	13:28
Sep 4	Malakai Black, Brody King & Buddy Matthews (w/Sting & Miro)	W	AEW All Out '22	12:10
Sep 9	Sammy Guevara	L	AEW Rampage	11:06
Sep 16	Matt Hardy	W	AEW Rampage	9:59
Sep 23	No DQ: Buddy Matthews & Brody King (w/Sting)	W	AEW Rampage: Grand Slam	12:57
Oct 5	Jay Lethal	W	AEW Dynamite: Anniversary	10:15
Nov 2	Jay Lethal	L	AEW Dynamite	9:08
Nov 19	No DQ: Jeff Jarrett & Jay Lethal (w/Sting)	W	AEW Full Gear '22	11:00
Nov 25	Anthony Henry	W	AEW Rampage: Black Friday	8:09
Dec 2	Cole Karter	W	AEW Rampage	7:40
Dec 7	Samoa Joe	L	AEW Dynamite	10:29

DARIUS MARTIN

Mar 2	Casino Battle Royale (w/Dante Martin)	L	AEW Dynamite	27:01
Mar 8	Peter Avalon & Ryan Nemeth (w/Dante Martin)	W	AEW Dark	6:25
Mar 15	Ari Daivari & Invictus Khash (w/Dante Martin)	W	AEW Dark	7:30
Mar 21	Luther & Serpentico (w/Dante Martin)	W	AEW Dark Elevation	4:54
Apr 1	Matt Jackson & Nick Jackson (w/Dante Martin)	L	AEW Rampage	10:48
Apr 11	Aaron Solo & Nick Comoroto (w/Dante Martin)	W	AEW Dark Elevation	5:52
Apr 18	Isiah Kassidy, Marq Quen, Angelico & Jack Evans (w/Jeff Hardy, Matt Hardy & Dante Martin)	W	AEW Dark Elevation	9:45
Apr 26	Max Caster, Angelico, Isiah Kassidy, Marq Quen & The Blade (w/Frankie Kazarian, Matt Hardy, Jeff Hardy & Dante Martin)	W	AEW Dark	12:40
Nov 16	Pac, Penta El Zero M & Rey Fenix (w/Dante Martin & AR Fox)	L	AEW Dynamite	11:33
Nov 25	Dax Harwood & Cash Wheeler (w/Dante Martin)	L	AEW Rampage: Black Friday	11:12
Dec 5	Truth Magnum & Turbo Floyd (w/Dante Martin)	W	AEW Dark Elevation	4:03
Dec 10	Aaron Solo & Nick Comoroto (w/Dante Martin)	W	AEW Dark Elevation	3:35
Dec 19	Jeeves Kay, Slim J, Sonny Kiss, Cezar Bononi, Peter Avalon & Ryan Nemeth (w/Ethan Page, Isiah Kassidy, Konosuke Takeshita, Matt Hardy & Dante Martin)	W	AEW Dark Elevation	7:45
Dec 21	Jon Moxley	L	AEW Dynamite: Holiday Bash	8:49
Dec 23	$300,000 Three Kings Christmas Casino Trios Royale (w/AR Fox & Dante Martin)	W	AEW Rampage	22:01
Dec 28	Jon Moxley & Claudio Castagnoli (w/Dante Martin)	L	AEW Dynamite	14:02

DAVE MASTIFF

Jan 13	Rohan Raja & Teoman (w/Jack Starz)	W	NXT UK	9:24
Feb 3	Ashton Smith & Oliver Carter (w/Jack Starz)	L	NXT UK	12:31
Mar 3	Lewis Howley & Sam Stoker (w/Jack Starz)	W	NXT UK	10:34
Apr 14	Joe Coffey & Mark Coffey (w/Jack Starz)	W	NXT UK	8:30
May 19	Charlie Dempsey & Rohan Raja (w/Jack Starz)	L	NXT UK	8:01
Jun 23	Elimination Match: Brooks Jensen & Josh Briggs, Charlie Dempsey & Rohan Raja, Mark Andrews & Wild Boar (w/Jack Starz)	L	NXT UK	18:15
Jul 21	Josh Morrell	W	NXT UK	6:58

DAVEY RICHARDS

Feb 17	ACH	W	MLW Fusion	8:58
Mar 10	Alexander Hammerstone	L	MLW Fusion	19:14
May 5	Richard Holliday	L	MLW Fusion	9:39
May 26	Danny Rivera	W	MLW Fusion	8:29
Jun 19	Eddie Edwards, Matt Taven, Mike Bennett, PCO & Vincent (w/Alex Shelley, Chris Sabin, Frankie Kazarian & Magnus)	W	IMPACT Slammiversary XX	18:45
Jul 7	Alex Kane	D	MLW Fusion	20:00

Jul 30	Rocky Romero	W	NJPW Music City Mayhem	11:29
Jul 31	Alex Shelley & Chris Sabin (w/Eddie Edwards)	L	JCP Ric Flair's Last Match	11:06
Aug 28	Thrillbilly Silas	W	NWA 74th Anniversary Show	10:24
Nov 12	Colby Corino	W	NWA Hard Times 3	6:42
Nov 17	Alex Kane	W	MLW Fusion	12:52
Dec 15	SB KENTo	W	MLW Fusion	10:28

DAVID FINLAY

Jan 15	Jonah	L	NJPW Strong	8:20
Feb 12	Bad Dude Tito & Jonah (w/Juice Robinson)	W	NJPW Strong	11:51
Mar 5	Bad Dude Tito & Jonah (w/Juice Robinson)	L	NJPW Strong	8:16
Apr 1	Clark Connors, Karl Fredericks, Mascara Dorada & Yuya Uemura (w/Juice Robinson, Daniel Garcia & Kevin Knight)	L	NJPW Lonestar Shootout	10:45
Apr 2	Jonah & Shane Haste (w/Juice Robinson)	W	NJPW Strong	6:34
Apr 16	Chicago Street Fight: Jonah, Shane Haste & Bad Dude Tito (w/Juice Robinson & Brody King)	W	NJPW Windy City Riot	24:11
May 14	Tom Lawlor, Jorel Nelson, Royce Isaacs, JR Kratos & Danny Limelight (w/The DKC, Yuya Uemura, Tanga Loa & Fred Rosser)	L	NJPW Capital Collision	14:48
May 28	Blake Christian	W	NJPW Strong	10:07
Jun 8	Hangman Page	L	AEW Dynamite	10:22
Jun 25	Danny Limelight	W	NJPW Strong	6:31
Jul 23	Adrian Quest, Lucas Riley & Negro Casas (w/Mascara Dorada & Rocky Romero)	W	NJPW Strong	11:03
Sep 25	Will Ospreay	L	NJPW Burning Spirit '22	28:22
Oct 10	El Desperado, Yoshinobu Kanemaru & Douki (w/Robbie Eagles & Ren Narita)	W	NJPW Declaration Of Power	7:28
Nov 5	Aaron Henare, Gideon Grey, Kyle Fletcher & Mark Davis (Hiroshi Tanahashi, Toru Yano, & Alex Zayne)	L	NJPW Battle Autumn '22	9:50
Dec 10	El Phantasmo, Jay White, Jorel Nelson & Royce Isaacs (w/Alan Angels, Hikuleo & Tama Tonga)	W	NJPW Strong	13:20

DAX HARWOOD

Jan 10	Pat Brink & Myles Hawkins (w/Cash Wheeler)	W	AEW Dark Elevation	3:08
Jan 28	Lee Johnson & Brock Anderson (w/Cash Wheeler)	W	AEW Rampage: Beach Break	9:10
Feb 9	CM Punk & Jon Moxley (w/Cash Wheeler)	L	AEW Dynamite	18:34
Feb 23	Tag Team Battle Royal (w/Cash Wheeler)	L	AEW Dynamite	16:51
Mar 2	Casino Battle Royale (w/Cash Wheeler)	L	AEW Dynamite	24:21
Mar 23	CM Punk	L	AEW Dynamite	12:51
Mar 30	Austin Gunn & Colten Gunn (w/Cash Wheeler)	W	AEW Dynamite	11:27
Apr 1	Jay Briscoe & Mark Briscoe (w/Cash Wheeler)	W	ROH Supercard Of Honor XV	27:25
Apr 6	Matt Jackson & Nick Jackson (w/Cash Wheeler)	W	AEW Dynamite	20:07
Apr 27	Cash Wheeler	W	AEW Dynamite	15:05
May 11	Adam Cole	L	AEW Dynamite	15:34
May 25	Trent Barretta & Rocky Romero (w/Cash Wheeler)	D	AEW Dynamite: 3 Year Anniversary	10:12
Jun 1	Max Caster, Austin Gunn & Colten Gunn (w/CM Punk & Cash Wheeler)	W	AEW Dynamite	11:50
Jun 10	Will Ospreay, Kyle Fletcher & Mark Davis (w/Trent Beretta & Cash Wheeler)	W	AEW Rampage	13:59
Jun 15	Will Ospreay	L	AEW Dynamite	13:43
Jun 26	Great-O-Khan & Jeff Cobb, Rocky Romero & Trent Beretta (w/Cash Wheeler)	W	AEW x NJPW Forbidden Door	16:19
Jun 29	Max Caster, Austin Gunn & Colten Gunn (w/Danhausen & Cash Wheeler)	W	AEW Dynamite: Blood & Guts	9:31
Jul 23	2/3 Falls: Jay Briscoe & Mark Briscoe (w/Cash Wheeler)	W	ROH Death Before Dishonor XIX	43:25
Jul 30	Kyle Fletcher, Mark Davis & TJP (w/Cash Wheeler & Alex Zayne)	L	NJPW Music City Mayhem	14:30
Aug 20	Rocky Romero	W	NJPW Strong	10:26
Aug 24	Jay Lethal	L	AEW Dynamite	12:47
Aug 31	Ren Jones, Vic Capri & Silas Young (w/Wardlow & Cash Wheeler)	W	AEW Dynamite	2:02
Sep 4	Jay Lethal, Chris Sabin & Alex Shelley (w/Cash Wheeler & Wardlow)	W	AEW All Out '22	16:30
Sep 9	Claudio Castagnoli	L	AEW Rampage	20:13
Oct 1	Kyle Fletcher & Mark Davis (w/Cash Wheeler)	W	NJPW Royal Quest II Night #1	31:59
Oct 2	Will Ospreay, Great-O-Khan, Mark Davis, Kyle Fletcher & Gideon Grey (w/Cash Wheeler, Shota Umino, Gabriel Kidd & Ricky Knight Jr.)	L	NJPW Royal Quest II Night #2	16:57
Oct 7	Toa Liona & Kaun (w/Cash Wheeler)	W	AEW Battle Of The Belts IV	13:26
Oct 14	Brian Cage, Kaun & Toa Liona (w/Shawn Spears & Cash Wheeler)	W	AEW Rampage	10:29
Oct 26	Swerve Strickland & Keith Lee (w/Cash Wheeler)	L	AEW Dynamite	15:06
Nov 5	Great-O-Khan & Jeff Cobb (w/Cash Wheeler)	W	NJPW Battle Autumn '22	17:31
Nov 9	Swerve Strickland, Keith Lee, Austin Gunn & Colten Gunn (w/Anthony Bowens, Max Caster & Cash Wheeler)	W	AEW Dynamite	12:22
Nov 25	Dante Martin & Darius Martin (w/Cash Wheeler)	W	AEW Rampage: Black Friday	11:12
Nov 30	Bryan Danielson	L	AEW Dynamite	14:49
Dec 7	Anthony Bowens & Max Caster (w/Cash Wheeler)	L	AEW Dynamite	16:46
Dec 10	Double Dog Collar Match: Jay Briscoe & Mark Briscoe (w/Cash Wheeler)	W	ROH Final Battle '22	22:20
Dec 21	Austin Gunn & Colten Gunn (w/Cash Wheeler)	L	AEW Dynamite: Holiday Bash	9:12

DEANER

Jan 8	Hardcore War: Eddie Edwards, Rich Swann, Willie Mack, Heath & Rhino (w/Luke Gallows, Karl Anderson, Eric Young & Joe Doering)	L	IMPACT Hard To Kill '22	23:25
Feb 17	Jay White, Tama Tonga & Tanga Loa (w/Deaner & Joe Doering)	L	IMPACT Wrestling	13:19
Mar 3	Chris Bey, Luke Gallows, Karl Anderson & Jay White (w/Tama Tonga, Tanga Loa & Joe Doering)	L	IMPACT Wrestling	9:48
Mar 17	Karl Anderson	L	IMPACT Before The Impact	6:22
Mar 31	Black Taurus	L	IMPACT Before The Impact	8:21
Apr 21	Black Taurus & Crazzy Steve (w/Eric Young)	W	IMPACT Wrestling	4:42
May 19	Jay Briscoe & Mark Briscoe (w/Joe Doering)	L	IMPACT Wrestling	15:00

May 26	Josh Alexander, Jay Briscoe & Mark Briscoe (w/Eric Young & Joe Doering)	W	IMPACT Wrestling	17:09
Jun 23	Josh Alexander	L	IMPACT Wrestling	5:23
Jul 14	Josh Alexander, Alex Shelley & Chris Sabin (w/Eric Young & Joe Doering)	L	IMPACT Wrestling	11:56
Jul 21	Mike Bailey	L	IMPACT Wrestling	8:54
Aug 4	Alex Shelley & Chris Sabin (w/Joe Doering)	L	IMPACT Wrestling	6:23
Aug 11	Kushida	L	IMPACT Wrestling	6:14
Aug 25	Kushida, Alex Shelley & Chris Sabin (w/Eric Young & Joe Doering)	L	IMPACT Wrestling	15:18

DELIRIOUS

Jun 18	Ari Daivari	L	NJPW Strong	10:15
Sep 29	Black Taurus	L	IMPACT Wrestling	5:03
Nov 24	Raj Singh & Shera (w/Yuya Uemura)	L	IMPACT Before The Impact	9:22
Dec 15	Eddie Edwards	L	IMPACT Wrestling	6:36
Dec 29	John Skyler & Jason Hotch (w/Yuya Uemura)	W	IMPACT Before The Impact	9:08

DEONNA PURRAZZO

Jan 6	Mercedes Martinez	W	IMPACT Wrestling	13:00
Jan 8	Texas Deathmatch: Mickie James	L	IMPACT Hard To Kill '22	19:40
Jan 13	Rok-C	W	IMPACT Wrestling	14:24
Feb 10	Santana Garrett	W	IMPACT Wrestling	9:00
Feb 24	Lady Frost	W	IMPACT Wrestling	5:43
Mar 17	Gisele Shaw, Lady Frost	W	IMPACT Wrestling	6:08
Apr 1	Faby Apache	W	IMPACT Multiverse Of Matches	8:52
Apr 14	Willow Nightingale	W	IMPACT Wrestling	9:32
Apr 23	Taya Valkyrie	L	IMPACT Rebellion '22	9:03
Apr 30	Bandido, Pagano & Taya Valkyrie (w/Cibernetico & Andrade El Idolo)	L	AAA TripleMania XXX: Monterrey	18:53
May 4	Mercedes Martinez	L	AEW Dynamite	10:35
May 19	Jordynne Grace, Mia Yim & Taya Valkyrie (w/Savannah Evans & Tasha Steelz)	L	IMPACT Wrestling	12:00
Jun 19	Queen Of The Mountain: Jordynne Grace, Tasha Steelz, Chelsea Green, Mia Yim	L	IMPACT Slammiversary XX	18:15
Jul 7	Mia Yim	L	IMPACT Wrestling	14:09
Jul 21	Jordynne Grace & Mia Yim (w/Chelsea Green)	W	IMPACT Wrestling	9:11
Jul 31	Jordynne Grace, Rachael Ellering	L	JCP Ric Flair's Last Match	9:17
Aug 4	Rosemary	W	IMPACT Wrestling	7:11
Aug 25	Jordynne Grace & Mia Yim (w/Chelsea Green)	W	IMPACT Wrestling	7:24
Sep 1	Masha Slamovich	L	IMPACT Wrestling	12:50
Oct 7	Jessicka & Taya Valkyrie (w/Chelsea Green)	L	IMPACT Bound For Glory '22	7:24
Oct 13	Jessicka, Rosemary & Taya Valkyrie (w/Chelsea Green & Gisele Shaw)	W	IMPACT Wrestling	5:40
Oct 27	Jordynne Grace, Mickie James & Taylor Wilde (w/Chelsea Green & Gisele Shaw)	L	IMPACT Wrestling	13:46
Dec 1	Mickie James	L	IMPACT Wrestling	16:01
Dec 22	Jessicka & Rosemary (w/Gisele Shaw)	L	IMPACT Wrestling	5:39

DEXTER LUMIS

Jan 18	Grayson Waller	L	NXT 2.0	10:01
Mar 22	Tony D'Angelo	L	NXT 2.0	7:15
Apr 5	Duke Hudson	D	NXT 2.0	4:55
Apr 19	Elton Prince & Kit Wilson (w/Duke Hudson)	L	NXT 2.0	11:47
Jun 11	Trevor Murdoch, Nick Aldis, Thom Latimer	L	NWA Alwayz Ready '22	18:10
Nov 28	Anything Goes Match: The Miz	W	WWE Monday Night RAW	9:30
Dec 19	Ladder Match: The Miz	L	WWE Monday Night RAW	18:20

DIAMANTE

Feb 7	Heather Reckless, Queen Aminata & Skye Blue (w/Emi Sakura & The Bunny)	W	AEW Dark Elevation	4:02
Feb 28	Kayla Sparks, LMK & Paris Van Dale (w/Emi Sakura & Nyla Rose)	W	AEW Dark Elevation	2:27
Mar 1	Vipress	W	AEW Dark	1:53
Mar 8	AQA & Ruby Soho (w/Emi Sakura)	L	AEW Dark	5:02
Mar 29	Kelsey Heather	W	AEW Dark	1:59
Apr 4	Anna Jay & Ruby Soho (w/Ashley D'Amboise)	L	AEW Dark Elevation	4:50
Apr 11	Ashley D'Amboise	W	AEW Dark Elevation	2:43
Apr 12	Mylo	W	AEW Dark	1:30
May 3	Toni Storm	L	AEW Dark	8:38
May 28	Riho, Skye Blue & Yuka Sakazaki (w/Emi Sakura & Nyla Rose)	L	AEW Dark	6:11
Jun 14	Anna Jay, Kris Statlander & Ruby Soho (w/Emi Sakura & Nyla Rose)	L	AEW Dark	7:54
Jun 21	Devlyn Macabre	W	AEW Dark	3:06
Aug 2	Rocky Radley	W	AEW Dark	3:32
Aug 30	Charlette Renegade	W	AEW Dark	3:05
Sep 5	Skye Blue	L	AEW Dark Elevation	4:37
Sep 13	Queen Aminata & Skye Blue (w/Emi Sakura)	L	AEW Dark	4:01
Sep 23	Jade Cargill	L	AEW Rampage: Grand Slam	2:36
Oct 31	Madison Rayne	L	AEW Dark Elevation	3:12
Nov 1	Toni Storm	L	AEW Dark	6:43
Nov 8	Athena	L	AEW Dark	4:22
Dec 27	Mafiosa	W	AEW Dark	1:48

DIJAK (AS T-BAR UNTIL NOVEMBER 29)

Jan 6	Dennis Daniels	W	WWE Main Event	1:59
Jan 13	Tommaso Ciampa	L	WWE Main Event	5:28
Jan 20	Pete Dunne	L	WWE Main Event	6:44
Jan 27	Roderick Strong	W	WWE Main Event	5:21

Feb 10	Veer Mahaan	L	WWE Main Event	5:36
Feb 17	Tommaso Ciampa	L	WWE Main Event	8:29
Feb 28	Omos	L	WWE Monday Night RAW	:40
Mar 17	Tommaso Ciampa	L	WWE Main Event	5:58
Mar 24	Cedric Alexander	L	WWE Main Event	10:24
Apr 7	Shelton Benjamin	L	WWE Main Event	8:36
Apr 14	Tommaso Ciampa	L	WWE Main Event	6:26
Apr 21	Apollo Crews	L	WWE Main Event	5:06
May 5	Commander Azeez	L	WWE Main Event	6:02
May 12	Reggie	W	WWE Main Event	2:50
May 26	Apollo Crews	L	WWE Main Event	8:43
Jun 2	R-Truth	L	WWE Main Event	6:02
Jun 9	Mustafa Ali	L	WWE Main Event	7:13
Jun 16	Reggie	W	WWE Main Event	6:29
Jun 27	Battle Royal	L	WWE Monday Night RAW	19:25
Jun 30	Mustafa Ali	L	WWE Main Event	4:57
Jul 7	Cedric Alexander	L	WWE Main Event	5:01
Jul 28	Cedric Alexander & Mustafa Ali (w/Akira Tozawa)	L	WWE Main Event	4:38
Aug 4	Shelton Benjamin	W	WWE Main Event	9:23
Aug 11	Mustafa Ali	L	WWE Main Event	8:01
Aug 25	Cedric Alexander & Mustafa Ali (w/Shelton Benjamin)	L	WWE Main Event	8:30
Sep 1	Cedric Alexander	L	WWE Main Event	8:00
Sep 8	Cedric Alexander	W	WWE Main Event	6:46
Sep 29	Mustafa Ali	L	WWE Main Event	5:21
Nov 29	Dante Chen	W	NXT	3:48

DIRTY DANGO

Jan 11	Jamie Stanley & Sam Adonis (w/JTG)	W	NWA Power	5:51
Jan 18	Handicap Match: Jay Bradley, Wrecking Ball Legursky & Rush Freeman (w/JTG)	L	NWA Power	4:29
Feb 1	Handicap Match: Alex Taylor, Captain Yuma & Rush Freeman (w/JTG)	W	NWA Power	4:09
Mar 19	Aron Stevens & The Blue Meanie (w/JTG)	W	NWA Crockett Cup '22	6:40
Mar 19	Jay Briscoe & Mark Briscoe (w/JTG)	L	NWA Crockett Cup '22	8:13
Apr 12	Doug Williams & Harry Smith (w/JTG)	L	NWA Power	6:52
May 10	Gaagz The Gymp & Sal The Pal (w/JTG)	W	NWA Power	6:37
Jul 26	Doug Williams & Harry Smith (w/JTG)	L	NWA Power	6:13
Aug 23	Luke Hawx & PJ Hawx, Gustavo Aguilar & Rhett Titus (w/JTG)	L	NWA Power	5:56
Oct 20	Johnny Swinger	W	IMPACT Before The Impact	8:22
Nov 1	Luke Hawx & PJ Hawx (w/JTG)	L	NWA Power	6:22

DKC, THE

Jan 8	TJP	L	NJPW Strong	8:31
Feb 19	Eddie Pearl & Ricky Gibson (w/Kevin Knight)	L	NJPW Strong	9:18
Mar 19	Barrett Brown, Bateman & Misterioso (w/Fred Yehi & Keita Murray)	W	NJPW Strong	10:05
Mar 26	Elimination Match: Danny Limelight, Jorel Nelson, JR Kratos, Royce Isaacs & Tom Lawlor (w/Adrian Quest, Clark Connors, Fred Rosser & Taylor Rust)	L	NJPW Strong	16:29
Apr 30	Kevin Knight	W	NJPW Strong	7:45
May 7	JR Kratos, Royce Isaacs & Tom Lawlor (w/Alex Coughlin & Fred Rosser)	L	NJPW Strong	11:12
May 10	Aaron Solo & Nick Comoroto (w/Kevin Knight)	L	AEW Dark	8:30
May 14	Tom Lawlor, Jorel Nelson, Royce Isaacs, JR Kratos & Danny Limelight (w/Yuya Uemura, David Finlay, Tanga Loa & Fred Rosser)	L	NJPW Capital Collision	14:48
May 28	Barrett Brown, Bateman & Misterioso (w/Fred Yehi & Kevin Knight)	L	NJPW Strong	10:06
Jun 18	Jorel Nelson, JR Kratos & Royce Isaacs (w/Alex Coughlin & Kevin Knight)	L	NJPW Strong	9:21
Jun 24	Hook	L	AEW Rampage	1:40
Jun 26	Max Caster, Billy Gunn, Austin Gunn & Colten Gunn (w/Yuya Uemura, Alex Coughlin & Kevin Knight)	L	AEW x NJPW Forbidden Door Buy-In	5:35
Jul 30	Fred Yehi, Shota Umino & Yuya Uemura (w/Kevin Knight & Ren Narita)	L	NJPW Music City Mayhem	13:12
Aug 27	Elliot Russell & Sigmon (w/Kevin Knight)	W	NJPW Strong	9:55
Oct 1	Barrett Brown & Bateman (w/Kevin Knight)	W	NJPW Strong	8:16
Oct 28	Alex Shelley & Chris Sabin, Kyle Fletcher & Mark Davis (w/Kevin Knight)	L	NJPW Rumble On 44th Street	13:42
Nov 5	Barrett Brown & Misterioso, Bad Dude Tito & Shane Haste, Jorel Nelson & Royce Isaacs (w/Kevin Knight)	L	NJPW Strong	12:36
Dec 10	Christopher Daniels	L	NJPW Strong	9:15

DOLPH ZIGGLER

Jan 3	Damian Priest	L	WWE Monday Night RAW	9:00
Jan 10	Damian Priest, Angelo Dawkins & Montez Ford (w/Robert Roode & Apollo Crews)	W	WWE Monday Night RAW	8:30
Jan 17	Rey Mysterio, Dominik Mysterio, Angelo Dawkins & Montez Ford (w/Robert Roode, Apollo Crews & Commander Azeez)	L	WWE Monday Night RAW	8:00
Jan 29	Royal Rumble Match	L	WWE Royal Rumble '22	20:46
Jan 31	Angelo Dawkins	L	WWE Monday Night RAW	4:30
Feb 10	Cedric Alexander & Shelton Benjamin (w/Robert Roode)	L	WWE Main Event	7:01
Feb 14	Angelo Dawkins & Montez Ford (w/Robert Roode)	L	WWE Monday Night RAW	2:50
Feb 21	Tommaso Ciampa & Finn Balor (w/Robert Roode)	L	WWE Monday Night RAW	9:15
Feb 22	Tommaso Ciampa	W	NXT 2.0	15:37
Mar 1	Bron Breakker & Tommaso Ciampa (w/Robert Roode)	L	NXT 2.0	13:05
Mar 7	Tommaso Ciampa & Bron Breakker (w/Robert Roode)	L	WWE Monday Night RAW	9:37
Mar 8	Bron Breakker, Tommaso Ciampa	W	NXT 2.0: Roadblock '22	12:24
Mar 15	LA Knight	W	NXT 2.0	11:48
Mar 21	Rey Mysterio & Dominik Mysterio (w/Robert Roode)	L	WWE Monday Night RAW	9:25
Apr 2	Bron Breakker	W	NXT Stand & Deliver '22	16:13

Apr 4	Bron Breakker	L	WWE Monday Night RAW	10:45
Jun 27	Battle Royal	L	WWE Monday Night RAW	19:25
Jul 25	Chad Gable & Otis (w/AJ Styles)	W	WWE Monday Night RAW	6:30
Aug 1	Ciampa, Chad Gable	L	WWE Monday Night RAW	10:30
Aug 8	Chad Gable	W	WWE Monday Night RAW	6:35
Aug 15	Theory	L	WWE Monday Night RAW	16:15
Aug 22	Finn Balor	L	WWE Monday Night RAW	13:05
Aug 29	Finn Balor & Damian Priest (w/AJ Styles)	L	WWE Monday Night RAW	8:34
Oct 17	Baron Corbin	L	WWE Monday Night RAW	13:35
Nov 14	Austin Theory	W	WWE Monday Night RAW	15:00

DOMINIK MYSTERIO

Jan 6	Cedric Alexander & Shelton Benjamin (w/Rey Mysterio)	W	WWE Main Event	5:41
Jan 17	Apollo Crews, Commander Azeez, Dolph Ziggler & Robert Roode (w/Rey Mysterio, Angelo Dawkins & Montez Ford)	W	WWE Monday Night RAW	8:00
Jan 24	Angelo Dawkins & Montez Ford (w/Rey Mysterio)	W	WWE Monday Night RAW	8:00
Jan 29	Royal Rumble Match	L	WWE Royal Rumble '22	3:44
Jan 31	The Miz	L	WWE Monday Night RAW	2:10
Feb 7	The Miz	W	WWE Monday Night RAW	1:47
Feb 14	Chad Gable & Otis (w/Rey Mysterio)	L	WWE Monday Night RAW	10:34
Feb 28	Cedric Alexander & Shelton Benjamin (w/Rey Mysterio)	L	WWE Monday Night RAW	4:30
Mar 14	Cedric Alexander & Shelton Benjamin (w/Rey Mysterio)	W	WWE Monday Night RAW	3:25
Mar 15	Raul Mendoza	W	NXT 2.0	3:05
Mar 21	Dolph Ziggler & Robert Roode (w/Rey Mysterio)	W	WWE Monday Night RAW	9:25
Apr 2	The Miz & Logan Paul (w/Rey Mysterio)	L	WWE WrestleMania XXXVIII	11:15
Apr 4	The Miz	L	WWE Monday Night RAW	:30
Apr 11	Veer Mahan	L	WWE Monday Night RAW	2:00
May 30	Kevin Owens, Chad Gable & Otis (w/Ezekiel & Rey Mysterio)	W	WWE Monday Night RAW	8:30
Jun 6	Veer Mahan	L	WWE Monday Night RAW	9:20
Jun 23	Finn Balor & Damian Priest (w/Rey Mysterio)	W	WWE Main Event	7:31
Jun 27	Battle Royal	L	WWE Monday Night RAW	19:25
Jul 4	Finn Balor & Damian Priest (w/Rey Mysterio)	W	WWE Monday Night RAW	11:30
Jul 25	Finn Balor & Damian Priest (w/Rey Mysterio)	W	WWE Monday Night RAW	11:29
Jul 30	Finn Balor & Damian Priest (w/Rey Mysterio)	W	WWE SummerSlam '22	11:05
Aug 1	Jimmy Uso & Jey Uso (w/Rey Mysterio)	L	WWE Monday Night RAW	15:50
Aug 12	Edge	L	WWE Monday Night RAW	15:10
Oct 17	AJ Styles	W	WWE Monday Night RAW	14:30
Nov 5	AJ Styles, Luke Gallows & Karl Anderson (w/Finn Balor & Damian Priest)	W	WWE Crowen Jewel '22	14:00
Nov 14	Shelton Benjamin	W	WWE Monday Night RAW	5:00
Nov 21	Sheamus, Ridge Holland & Butch (w/Finn Balor & Damian Priest)	L	WWE Monday Night RAW	14:50
Nov 28	AJ Styles, Luke Gallows, Karl Anderson & Mia Yim (w/Finn Balor, Damian Priest & Rhea Ripley)	W	WWE Monday Night RAW	14:20
Dec 5	Akira Tozawa	W	WWE Monday Night RAW	2:50
Dec 12	Akira Tozawa, Angelo Dawkins & Montez Ford (w/Finn Balor & Damian Priest)	W	WWE Monday Night RAW	14:45

DOUDROP

Jan 10	Liv Morgan, Bianca Belair	W	WWE Monday Night RAW	14:45
Jan 17	Liv Morgan & Bianca Belair (w/Becky Lynch)	W	WWE Monday Night RAW	3:00
Jan 29	Becky Lynch	L	WWE Royal Rumble '22	13:00
Feb 3	Liv Morgan	L	WWE Main Event	7:21
Feb 7	Liv Morgan	W	WWE Monday Night RAW	7:59
Feb 14	Gauntlet Match: Liv Morgan, Bianca Belair, Nikki A.S.H., Rhea Ripley	L	WWE Monday Night RAW	44:04
Feb 19	Elimination Chamber: Bianca Belair, Alexa Bliss, Liv Morgan, Nikki A.S..H., Rhea Ripley	L	WWE Elimination Chamber '22	8:50
Feb 21	Bianca Belair	L	WWE Monday Night RAW	11:20
Feb 28	Rhea Ripley, Bianca Belair & Liv Morgan (w/Becky Lynch & Nikki A.S.H.)	L	WWE Monday Night RAW	12:20
Mar 14	Bianca Belair	L	WWE Monday Night RAW	7:00
May 9	Sasha Banks & Naomi (w/Nikki A.S.H.)	L	WWE Monday Night RAW	4:25
May 30	Alexa Bliss	L	WWE Monday Night RAW	3:20
Jun 6	Liv Morgan, Alexa Bliss, Rhea Ripley	L	WWE Monday Night RAW	14:35
Jun 13	Liv Morgan & Alexa Bliss (w/Nikki A.S.H.)	L	WWE Monday Night RAW	4:25
Jun 23	Dana Brooke	W	WWE Main Event	2:21
Jun 27	Becky Lynch, Nikki A.S.H., Xia Lia, Shayna Baszler, Tamina	L	WWE Monday Night RAW	13:20
Jul 11	Alexa Bliss & Asuka (w/Nikki A.S.H.)	L	WWE Monday Night RAW	4:15
Jul 18	Alexa Bliss, Asuka & Dana Brooke (w/Nikki A.S.H. & Tamina)	L	WWE Monday Night RAW	2:35
Jul 25	Alexa Bliss	L	WWE Monday Night RAW	4:20
Aug 15	Alexa Bliss & Asuka (w/Nikki A.S.H.)	L	WWE Monday Night RAW	9:00
Aug 25	Dana Brooke & Tamina (w/Nikki A.S.H.)	W	WWE Main Event	5:14
Aug 26	Natalya & Sonya Deville, Dana Brooke & Tamina, Shotzi & Xia Li (w/Nikki A.S.H.)	L	WWE SmackDown	3:10
Sep 4	Katana Chance & Kayden Carter (w/Nikki A.S.H.)	L	NXT Worlds Collide '22	10:19
Sep 5	Raquel Rodriguez & Aliyah (w/Nikki A.S.H.)	L	WWE Monday Night RAW	3:45
Sep 6	Gigi Dolin & Jacy Jayne (w/Nikki A.S.H.)	W	NXT 2.0	10:50

DOUG WILLIAMS

Feb 15	Fable Jake & Jaden Roller (w/Nick Aldis)	W	NWA Power	8:11
Mar 19	Alex Taylor & Rush Freeman (w/Harry Smith)	W	NWA Crockett Cup '22	6:38
Mar 19	Jordan Clearwater & Marshe Rockett (w/Harry Smith)	W	NWA Crockett Cup '22	12:50
Mar 20	Bestia 666 & Mecha Wolf (w/Harry Smith)	W	NWA Crockett Cup '22	8:58
Mar 20	Jay Briscoe & Mark Briscoe (w/Harry Smith)	L	NWA Crockett Cup '22	13:55
Apr 12	Dirty Dango & JTR (w/Harry Smith)	W	NWA Power	6:52

May 10	Matt Cardona, Mike Knox & VSK (w/Harry Smith & Nick Aldis)	W	NWA Power	8:15
Jun 11	Bestia 666 & Mecha Wolf (w/Harry Smith)	W	NWA Alwayz Ready '22	13:54
Jun 28	Lucha Rules Match: Bestia 666 & Mecha Wolf (w/Harry Smith)	W	NWA Power	5:08
Jul 26	Dirty Dango & JTG (w/Harry Smith)	W	NWA Power	6:13
Aug 23	Brady Pierce & Rush Freeman (w/Harry Smith)	W	NWA Power	4:48
Sep 6	Flip Gordon	L	NWA Power	9:30
Nov 8	Thom Latimer, Trevor Murdoch & Tyrus (w/JR Kratos & Da Pope)	D	NWA Power	6:49

DOUKI

Jan 8	Yo-Hey & Nosawa Rongai (w/El Desperado)	W	NJPW Wrestle Kingdom 16 Night #1	9:09
Mar 1	Cima, T-Hawk & El Lindaman (w/El Desperado & Yoshinobu Kanemaru)	L	NJPW 50th Anniversary Show	9:22
May 1	Ryusuke Taguchi & Master Wato (w/Yoshinobu Kanemaru)	L	NJPW Wrestling Dontaku '22	9:10
Oct 1	Tetsuya Naito, Sanada & Hiromu Takahashi (w/Zack Sabre Jr. & El Desperado)	L	NJPW Royal Quest II Night #1	14:29
Oct 2	Michael Oku & Robbie X (w/El Desperado)	W	NJPW Royal Quest II Night #2	9:33
Oct 10	David Finlay, Robbie Eagles & Ren Narita (w/El Desperado & Yoshinobu Kanemaru)	L	NJPW Declaration Of Power	7:28
Nov 20	Tam Nakano, Natsupoi, Taichi & Yoshinobu Kanemaru (w/Momo Watanabe, Starlight Kid, El Desperado & Douki)	L	NJPW x Stardom Historic X-Over	12:01

DR. BRITT BAKER D.M.D.

Jan 7	Riho & Ruby Soho (w/Jamie Hayter)	L	AEW Rampage	8:10
Jan 8	Riho	W	AEW Battle Of The Belts I	12:47
Jan 19	Orange Cassidy & Kris Statlander (w/Adam Cole)	W	AEW Dynamite	14:25
Feb 11	Robyn Renegade	W	AEW Rampage	6:28
Mar 2	Thunder Rosa & Mercedes Martinez (w/Jamie Hayter)	L	AEW Dynamite	8:32
Mar 6	Thunder Rosa	W	AEW Revolution '22	17:25
Mar 16	Steel Cage Match: Thunder Rosa	L	AEW Dynamite: St. Patrick's Day Slam	17:33
Apr 20	Danielle Kamela	W	AEW Dynamite	6:16
May 6	Toni Storm & Ruby Soho (w/Jamie Hayter)	L	AEW Rampage	8:38
May 18	Maki Itoh	W	AEW Dynamite: Wild Card Wednesday	6:44
May 25	Toni Storm	W	AEW Dynamite: 3 Year Anniversary	9:02
May 29	Ruby Soho	W	AEW Double Or Nothing '22	13:20
Jun 1	Toni Storm & Ruby Soho (w/Jamie Hayter)	L	AEW Dynamite	9:48
Jun 15	Toni Storm	L	AEW Dynamite: Road Rager	7:34
Jul 22	Ashley D'Amboise & Skye Blue (w/Jamie Hayter)	W	AEW Rampage: Fyter Fest	5:00
Aug 3	Toni Storm & Thunder Rosa (w/Jamie Hayter)	W	AEW Dynamite	12:02
Aug 24	KiLynn King	W	AEW Dynamite	3:55
Aug 31	Toni Storm & Hikaru Shida (w/Jamie Hayter)	L	AEW Dynamite	7:40
Sep 4	Toni Storm, Jamie Hayter, Hikaru Shida	L	AEW All Out '22	14:20
Sep 14	Toni Storm & Athena (w/Serena Deeb)	W	AEW Dynamite	8:34
Sep 21	Toni Storm, Athena, Serena Deeb	L	AEW Dynamite: Grand Slam	9:50
Oct 12	Toni Storm & Hikaru Shida (w/Jamie Hayter)	L	AEW Dynamite	8:18
Nov 4	Madison Rayne & Skye Blue (w/Jamie Hayter)	W	AEW Rampage	7:18
Nov 19	Saraya	L	AEW Full Gear '22	12:30
Nov 23	Anna Jay & Tay Melo, Willor Nightingale & Skye Blue (w/Jamie Hayter)	W	AEW Dynamite: Thanksgiving Eve	8:05
Dec 16	Skye Blue	W	AEW Rampage	6:15

DRACO ANTHONY

Jan 7	Malik Blade	L	WWE 205 Live	6:05
Jan 21	Javer Bernal	W	WWE 205 Live	4:53
Jan 28	Joe Gacy	L	WWE 205 Live	5:10
Feb 1	Andre Chase	L	NXT 2.0	4:36
Feb 8	Pete Dunne	L	NXT 2.0	6:53
Mar 1	Harland	L	NXT 2.0	2:25
Mar 29	Joe Gacy	L	NXT 2.0	3:57
Apr 12	Xyon Quinn	L	NXT 2.0	2:58

DRAGON LEE

Apr 30	Johnny Caballero & Taurus, Jack Cartwheel & Laredo Kid (w/Dralistico)	L	AAA TripleMania XXX: Monterrey	13:29
Jun 18	Johnny Hardy & Matt Hardy (w/Dralistico)	W	AAA TripleMania XXX: Tijuana	13:35
Jul 23	Rush	L	ROH Death Before Dishonor XIX	15:50
Aug 17	Kenny Omega, Matt Jackson & Nick Jackson (w/Andrade El Idolo & Rush)	L	AEW Dynamite	20:54
Oct 15	Latigo & Toxin, Arez & Willie Mack, Komander & Myzteziz Jr. (w/Dralistico)	W	AAA TripleMania XXX: Mexico City	9:00

DRALISTICO

Feb 20	Pentagon Jr.	L	AAA Rey De Reyes '22	13:19
Apr 30	Johnny Caballero & Taurus, Jack Cartwheel & Laredo Kid (w/Dragon Lee)	L	AAA TripleMania XXX: Monterrey	13:29
Jun 18	Johnny Hardy & Matt Hardy (w/Dragon Lee)	W	AAA TripleMania XXX: Tijuana	13:35
Oct 15	Latigo & Toxin, Arez & Willie Mack, Komander & Myzteziz Jr. (w/Dragon Lee)	W	AAA TripleMania XXX: Mexico City	9:00
Dec 10	Blake Christian & AR Fox (w/Rush)	L	ROH Final Battle '22	10:35
Dec 23	$300,000 Three Kings Christmas Casino Trios Royale (w/Preston Vance & Rush)	L	AEW Rampage	22:01
Dec 26	Blake Christian	W	AEW Dark Elevation	3:59

DREW GULAK

Apr 1	Andre The Giant Memorial Battle Royal	L	WWE SmackDown	8:05
May 6	Gunther	L	WWE SmackDown	2:05
May 20	Gunther	L	WWE SmackDown	1:04
May 27	Gunther & Ludwig Kaiser (w/Ricochet)	L	WWE SmackDown	6:45
Sep 2	Karrion Kross	L	WWE SmackDown	1:15

DREW MCINTYRE

Jan 1	Madcap Moss	W	WWE Day 1	9:45
Jan 29	Royal Rumble Match	L	WWE Royal Rumble '22	19:18
Feb 19	Falls Count Anywhere: Madcap Moss	W	WWE Elimination Chamber '22	9:00
Feb 25	Madcap Moss	W	WWE SmackDown	7:20
Mar 4	Jinder Mahal	W	WWE SmackDown	2:05
Mar 18	Happy Corbin, Jinder Mahal & Shanky (w/Erik & Ivar)	W	WWE SmackDown	7:10
Mar 28	Handicap Match: Happy Corbin & Madcap Moss	W	WWE Monday Night RAW	1:55
Apr 2	Happy Corbin	W	WWE WrestleMania XXXVIII	8:35
Apr 8	Sami Zayn	W	WWE SmackDown	3:40
Apr 15	Sami Zayn	W	WWE SmackDown	2:39
Apr 22	Lumberjack Match: Sami Zayn	D	WWE SmackDown	9:00
Apr 29	Steel Cage Match: Sami Zayn	W	WWE SmackDown	10:36
May 8	Roman Reigns, Jey Uso & Jimmy Uso (w/Randy Orton & Riddle)	L	WWE WrestleMania Backlash '22	22:20
May 27	Sheamus, Ridge Holland & Butch (w/Xavier Woods & Kofi Kingston)	W	WWE SmackDown	11:30
Jun 3	Sheamus, Ridge Holland & Butch (w/Xavier Woods & Kofi Kingston)	L	WWE SmackDown	10:30
Jun 10	Sheamus	D	WWE SmackDown	11:50
Jun 24	Jimmy Uso & Jey Uso (w/Sheamus)	W	WWE SmackDown	11:20
Jul 1	Battle Royal	L	WWE SmackDown	14:36
Jul 2	Money In The Bank Ladder Match: Theory, Madcap Moss, Omos Riddle, Sami Zayn, Seth Rollins, Sheamus	L	WWE Money In The Bank '22	25:25
Jul 8	Butch	W	WWE SmackDown	1:30
Jul 15	Ridge Holland	W	WWE SmackDown	3:25
Jul 25	Theory	W	WWE Monday Night RAW	9:45
Jul 25	Theory & Sheamus (w/Bobby Lashley)	W	WWE Monday Night RAW	12:20
Jul 29	Donnybrook Match: Sheamus	W	WWE SmackDown	25:30
Aug 12	Jimmy Uso & Jey Uso (w/Madcap Moss)	W	WWE SmackDown	9:15
Aug 15	Kevin Owens	W	WWE Monday Night RAW	15:58
Aug 26	Sami Zayn	W	WWE SmackDown	10:20
Sep 3	Roman Reigns	L	WWE Clash At The Castle	30:47
Sep 9	Solo Sikoa	W	WWE SmackDown	10:35
Sep 30	Austin Theory	W	WWE SmackDown	3:12
Sep 30	Austin Theory, Chad Gable & Otis (w/Kevin Owens & Johnny Gargano)	W	WWE SmackDown	13:38
Oct 8	Strap Match: Karrion Kross	L	WWE Extreme Rules '22	10:20
Oct 20	Cedric Alexander	L	WWE Main Event	8:50
Nov 3	R-Truth & Shelton Benjamin (w/Von Wagner)	L	WWE Main Event	6:31
Nov 5	Steel Cage Match: Karrion Kross	W	WWE Crown Jewel '22	13:00
Nov 21	Baron Corbin	W	WWE Monday Night RAW	17:50
Nov 25	Jimmy Uso & Jey Uso (w/Sheamus)	W	WWE SmackDown	14:43
Nov 26	WarGames: Roman Reigns, Sami Zayn, Solo Sikoa, Jey Uso & Jimmy Uso (w/Sheamus, Butch, Ridge Holland & Kevin Owens)	L	WWE Survivor Series WarGames	38:30
Dec 17	Gunther, Giovanni Vinci & Ludwig Kaiser (w/Sheamus & Ricochet)	W	WWE Tribute To The Troops '22	16:34

DUKE HUDSON

Jan 25	Guru Raaj	W	NXT 2.0	1:08
Feb 22	Dante Chen	W	NXT 2.0	2:20
Mar 22	Gunther	L	NXT 2.0	3:52
Apr 5	Dexter Lumis	D	NXT 2.0	4:55
Apr 19	Elton Prince & Kit Wilson (w/Dexter Lumis)	L	NXT 2.0	11:47
May 24	Bron Breakker	W	NXT 2.0	11:02
May 31	Solo Sikoa	L	NXT 2.0	4:44
Jun 14	Bron Breakker	L	NXT 2.0	:46
Jul 1	Javier Bernal	W	NXT Level Up	6:53
Jul 12	Sanga	L	NXT 2.0	3:01
Jul 22	Hank Walker	W	NXT Level Up	6:05
Aug 2	Axiom	L	NXT 2.0	2:10
Sep 2	Myles Borne	W	NXT Level Up	5:42
Sep 16	Bronco Nima	W	NXT Level Up	5:40
Oct 4	Julius Creed	L	NXT	:52
Oct 14	Ikemen Jiro & Tank Ledger (w/Bryson Montana)	L	NXT Level Up	6:18
Oct 21	Bryson Montana	W	NXT Level Up	3:55
Nov 22	Elton Prince & Kit Wilson (w/Andre Chase)	L	NXT	8:17
Nov 29	Grayson Waller	L	NXT	5:20
Dec 13	Damon Kemp	W	NXT	3:53
Dec 16	Javier Bernal & Xyon Quin (w/Andre Chase)	W	NXT Level Up	7:16

DUSTIN RHODES

Jan 8	Sammy Guevara	L	AEW Battle Of The Belts I	16:15
Mar 25	Lance Archer	W	AEW Rampage	9:32
Apr 20	CM Punk	L	AEW Dynamite	17:26
Jul 1	Royal Rampage Match	L	AEW Rampage	22:41
Aug 26	Claudio Castagnoli	L	AEW Rampage	12:27
Dec 7	Dynamite Diamond Battle Royale	L	AEW Dynamite	13:10
Dec 16	Trent Seven, Kip Sabian, The Butcher & The Blade (w/Orange Cassidy, Chuck Taylor & Trent Beretta)	W	AEW Rampage	10:42

EC3

Aug 27	Mims	W	NWA 74th Anniversary Show	4:52
Aug 28	Thom Latimer	D	NWA 74th Anniversary Show	6:42
Sep 6	Deonte Marshall	W	NWA Power	3:49
Oct 4	Traxx	W	NWA Power	3:52
Oct 18	Mercurio	W	NWA Power	5:20

Nov 12	Thom Latimer	W	NWA Hard Times 3	8:31
Nov 22	Danny Flamingo & Thom Latimer (w/Matt Lancie)	L	NWA Power	7:43
Dec 6	Thom Latimer	D	NWA Power	5:47

EDDIE DENNIS

May 19	Dog Collar Match: Wild Boar	L	NXT UK	10:17
Aug 18	Andre Chase & Bodhi Hayward (w/Saxon Huxley)	L	NXT UK	6:49

EDDIE EDWARDS

Jan 8	Hardcore War: Luke Gallows, Karl Anderson, Eric Young, Joe Doering & Deaner (w/Rich Swann, Willie Mack, Heath & Rhino)	W	IMPACT Hard To Kill '22	23:25
Feb 17	Big Kon	W	IMPACT Before The Impact	8:23
Mar 3	Steve Maclin	L	IMPACT Wrestling	6:52
Mar 10	Rich Swann	W	IMPACT Wrestling	17:48
Mar 24	Rocky Romero	W	IMPACT Wrestling	12:45
Apr 1	Tomohiro Ishii	L	IMPACT Multiverse Of Matches	14:09
Apr 28	Alex Shelley, Chris Sabin & Mike Bailey (w/Matt Taven & Mike Bennett)	W	IMPACT Wrestling	7:35
May 12	Gauntlet For The Gold	L	IMPACT Wrestling	39:00
Jun 9	Frankie Kazarian, Alex Shelley & Chris Sabin (w/Matt Taven & Mike Bennett)	W	IMPACT Wrestling	16:47
Jun 19	Alex Shelley, Chris Sabin, Davey Richardson, Frankie Kazarian & Magnus (w/Matt Taven, Mike Bennett, PCO & Vincent)	L	IMPACT Slammiversary XX	18:45
Jun 23	James Storm, Jay Briscoe & Mark Briscoe (w/Matt Taven & Mike Bennett)	W	IMPACT Wrestling	12:12
Jul 14	Ace Austin, Chris Bey, Luke Gallows & Karl Anderson (w/Kenny King, Matt Taven & Mike Bennett)	W	IMPACT Wrestling	12:34
Jul 28	Ace Austin	W	IMPACT Wrestling	11:38
Jul 31	Alex Shelley & Chris Sabin (w/Davey Richards)	L	JCP Ric Flair's Last Match	11:06
Aug 18	Bandido, Moose, Rich Swann, Sami Callihan, Steve Maclin	W	IMPACT Wrestling	18:25
Sep 8	Heath	W	IMPACT Wrestling	8:53
Oct 7	Josh Alexander	L	IMPACT Bound For Glory '22	28:02
Dec 15	Delirious	W	IMPACT Wrestling	6:36

EDDIE KINGSTON

Jan 7	No DQ, No Holds Barred: Daniel Garcia, Jeff Parker & Matt Lee (w/Santana & Ortiz)	W	AEW Rampage	13:50
Jan 8	Gabriel Kidd	W	NJPW Strong	12:37
Jan 11	Joey Janela	W	AEW Dark	8:33
Mar 6	Chris Jericho	W	AEW Revolution '22	13:40
Apr 9	Daniel Garcia & Fred Yehi (w/Fred Rosser)	W	NJPW Strong	9:27
Apr 13	Chris Jericho, Jake Hager & Daniel Garcia (w/Santana & Ortiz)	L	AEW Dynamite	11:46
Apr 22	Daniel Garcia	W	AEW Rampage	11:22
May 14	Tomohiro Ishii	L	NJPW Capital Collision	16:07
May 25	Isiah Kassidy & Marq Quen (w/Jon Moxley)	W	AEW Dynamite: 3 Year Anniversary	7:20
May 29	Anarchy In The Arena: Chris Jericho, Daniel Garcia, Jake Hager, Angelo Parker & Matt Menard (w/Jon Moxley, Bryan Danielson, Santana & Ortiz)	L	AEW Double Or Nothing '22	22:45
Jun 8	Casino Battle Royale	L	AEW Dynamite	24:59
Jun 10	Jake Hager	W	AEW Rampage	11:24
Jun 26	Chris Jericho, Minoru Suzuki & Sammy Guevara (w/Shota Umino & Wheeler Yuta)	L	AEW x NJPW Forbidden Door	18:58
Jun 29	Blood & Guts: Chris Jericho, Daniel Garcia, Sammy Guevara, Jake Hager, Matt Menard & Angelo Parker (w/Jon Moxley, Santana, Ortiz, Claudio Castagnoli & Wheeler Yuta)	W	AEW Dynamite: Blood & Guts	46:45
Jul 8	Konosuke Takeshita	W	AEW Rampage	11:56
Jul 20	Barbed Wire Death Match: Chris Jericho	L	AEW Dynamite: Fyter Fest	13:13
Sep 3	Jake Something	W	NJPW Strong	8:35
Sep 4	Tomohiro Ishii	W	AEW All Out Buy-In	13:25
Sep 23	Sammy Guevara	L	AEW Rampage	8:11
Oct 18	Jake O'Reilly & Mo Jabari (w/Ortiz)	W	AEW Dark	3:56
Oct 24	Russ Myers & T-Money (w/Ortiz)	W	AEW Dark Elevation	1:54
Oct 28	Jay White & Juice Robinson (w/Kazuchika Okada)	L	NJPW Rumble On 44th Street	20:15
Oct 31	Breaux Keller & Myles Hawkins (w/Ortiz)	W	AEW Dark Elevation	1:30
Nov 7	Joe Keys & Myles Hawkins (w/Ortiz)	W	AEW Dark Elevation	3:25
Nov 8	AR Fox & Caleb Konley (w/Ortiz)	W	AEW Dark	1:49
Nov 9	Ethan Page	L	AEW Dynamite	9:18
Nov 18	Jun Akiyama & Konosuke Takeshita (w/Ortiz)	L	AEW Rampage	12:17
Nov 19	Jun Akiyama	W	AEW Full Gear Buy-In	10:30
Nov 28	Aaron Solo & Nick Comoroto (w/Ortiz)	W	AEW Dark Elevation	4:55
Dec 13	Jeeves Kay & Slim J (w/Ortiz)	W	AEW Dark	6:59
Dec 19	Hagane Shinno & Steven Andrews (w/Ortiz)	W	AEW Dark Elevation	3:50

EDGE

Jan 1	The Miz	W	WWE Day 1	20:00
Jan 29	The Miz & Marsye (w/Beth Phoenix)	W	WWE Royal Rumble '22	12:30
Apr 3	AJ Styles	W	WWE WrestleMania XXXVIII	24:05
May 8	AJ Styles	W	WWE WrestleMania Backlash '22	16:25
Jun 5	AJ Styles, Finn Balor & Liv Morgan (w/Damian Priest & Rhea Ripley)	W	WWE Hell In A Cell '22	16:00
Aug 22	Damian Priest	W	WWE Monday Night RAW	19:35
Sep 3	Finn Balor & Damian Priest (w/Rey Mysterio)	W	WWE Clash At The Castle	12:35
Sep 12	Dominik Mysterio	W	WWE Monday Night RAW	15:10
Oct 8	I Quit Match: Finn Balor	L	WWE Extreme Rules '22	29:55

EDRIS ENOFE

Jan 11	Joe Gacy & Harland (w/Malik Blade)	W	NXT 2.0	3:14
Jan 18	Joaquin Wilde & Raul Mendoza (w/Malik Blade)	W	NXT 2.0	3:17
Feb 8	Nash Carter & Wes Lee (w/Malik Blade)	L	NXT 2.0	9:29
Feb 18	Kushida	W	NXT Level Up	7:07
Mar 4	Joaquin Wilde & Raul Mendoza (w/Malik Blade)	L	NXT Level Up	8:45
Mar 25	Ikemen Jiro & Kushida (w/Malik Blade)	W	NXT Level Up	7:33
Apr 22	Damaris Griffin & Quincy Elliott (w/Malik Blade)	W	NXT Level Up	6:36
Apr 26	Erik & Ivar (w/Malik Blade)	L	NXT 2.0	4:45
May 24	Channing Lorenzo & Troy Donovan (w/Malik Blade)	L	NXT 2.0	6:10
Jun 3	Dante Chen & Javier Bernal (w/Malik Blade)	W	NXT Level Up	7:05
Jun 14	Julius Creed & Brutus Creed (w/Malik Blade)	L	NXT 2.0	13:57
Jun 21	Cameron Grimes	L	NXT 2/0	5:37
Jul 8	Bryson Montana & Damaris Griffin (w/Malik Blade)	W	NXT Level Up	5:29
Jul 12	Tony D'Angelo & Channing Lorenzo (w/Malik Blade)	L	NXT 2.0	5:23
Jul 29	Ikemen Jiro & Quincy Elliott (w/Malik Blade)	W	NXT Level Up	6:01
Aug 9	Elton Prince & Kit Wilson (w/Malik Blade)	L	NXT 2.0	4:37
Aug 26	Bronco Nima & Lucien Price (w/Malik Blade)	W	NXT Level Up	5:50
Sep 20	Jagger Reid & Rip Fowler (w/Malik Blade)	L	NXT	9:17
Sep 30	Guru Raaj & Ikemen Jiro (w/Malik Blade)	W	NXT Level Up	6:50
Oct 11	Jagger Reid & Rip Fowler, Brooks Jensen & Josh Briggs (w/Malik Blade)	W	NXT	9:10
Oct 25	Elton Prince & Kit Wilson (w/Malik Blade)	L	NXT	12:29
Nov 11	Bronco Nima, Lucien Price & Xyon Quinn (w/Malik Blade & Odyssey Jones)	W	NXT Level Up	6:41
Dec 6	Brooks Jensen & Josh Briggs (w/Malik Blade)	L	NXT	3:24
Dec 15	Cedric Alexander & Mustafa Ali (w/Malik Blade)	L	WWE Main Event	6:17
Dec 27	Jagger Reid, Rip Fowler & Joe Gacy (w/Malik Blade & Odyssey Jones)	L	NXT	11:15

EJ NDUKA

Feb 10	Ikuro Kwon	W	MLW Fusion	2:23
Mar 31	Rivera & Slice Boogie (w/Calvin Tankman)	W	MLW Fusion	8:08
May 5	Budd Heavy & Red Pickins (w/Calvin Tankman)	W	MLW Fusion	1:20
May 19	Alex Zayne & Mr. Thomas (w/Calvin Tankman)	W	MLW Fusion	7:26
Jun 16	Rivera & Slice Boogie, Marshall Von Erich & Ross Von Erich (w/Calvin Tankman)	W	MLW Fusion	9:12
Dec 8	Sultan del Aire	W	MLW Fusion	2:54

EL DESPERADO

Jan 4	Hiromu Takahashi	W	NJPW Wrestle Kingdom 16 Night #1	16:18
Jan 8	Yo-Hey & Nosawa Rongai (w/Douki)	W	NJPW Wrestle Kingdom 16 Night #3	9:09
Mar 1	Cima, T-Hawk & El Lindaman (w/Yoshinobu Kanemaru & Douki)	L	NJPW 50th Anniversary Show	9:22
Apr 9	Sho	W	NJPW Hyper Battle '22	20:33
May 1	Taiji Ishimori	L	NJPW Wrestling Dontaku '22	14:40
Jun 12	Evil, Sho & Yujiro Takahashi (w/Zack Sabre Jr. & Yoshinobu Kanemaru)	L	NJPW Dominion '22	9:26
Jun 26	Keith Lee & Swerve Strickland (w/Yoshinobu Kanemaru)	L	AEW x NJPW Forbidden Door Buy-In	12:08
Jul 30	No DQ: Jon Moxley	L	NJPW Music City Showdown	17:20
Aug 20	Blake Christian, Hiromu Takahashi	W	NJPW Strong	19:19
Oct 1	Tetsuya Naito, Sanada & Hiromu Takahashi (w/Zack Sabre Jr. & Douki)	L	NJPW Royal Quest II Night #1	14:29
Oct 2	Michael Oku & Robbie X (w/Douki)	W	NJPW Royal Quest II Night #2	9:33
Oct 10	David Finlay, Robbie Eagles & Ren Narita (w/Yoshinobu Kanemaru & Douki)	L	NJPW Declaration Of Power	7:28
Nov 5	Taiji Ishimori & Hiromu Takahashi (w/Master Wato)	W	NJPW Battle Autumn '22	16:48
Nov 20	Tam Nakano, Natsupoi, Taichi & Yoshinobu Kanemaru (w/Momo Watanabe, Starlight Kid & Douki)	L	NJPW x Stardom Historic X-Over	12:01

EL DRAGON

Feb 24	Arez, Gino Medina & Mini Abismo Negro (w/Aramis & Micro Man)	W	MLW Fusion	15:46
May 12	Octagon Jr., King Muertes, El Hijo de LA Park	L	MLW Fusion	9:26
May 26	Arez, Mini Abismo Negro & TJP (w/Aero Star & Micro Man)	W	MLW Fusion	10:36

EL HIJO DE LA PARK

Feb 17	Ladder Match: Rivera & Slice Boogie (w/LA Park Jr.)	L	MLW Fusion	10:18
Feb 19	DMT Azul, Puma King & Sam Adonis, El Cuatrero, Forastero & Sanson (w/LA Park & LA Park Jr.)	D	AAA Rey De Reyes '22	13:05
May 12	Octagon Jr., King Muertes, El Dragon	L	MLW Fusion	9:26

EL PHANTASMO

Jan 4	Hiroshi Tanahashi, Ryusuke Taguchi & Rocky Romero (w/Kenta & Taiji Ishimori)	W	NJPW Wrestle Kingdom 16 Night #1	8:40
Jan 5	Robbie Eagles & Tiger Mask, Ryusuke Taguchi & Rocky Romero (w/Taiji Ishimori)	L	NJPW Wrestle Kingdom 16 Night #2	12:07
Feb 26	Matt Rehwoldt	W	NJPW Strong	9:45
Mar 1	Taichi, Taka Michinoku & Minoru Tanaka (w/Bad Luck Fale & Taiji Ishimori)	W	NJPW 50th Anniversary Show	9:50
Apr 9	Ryusuke Taguchi & Master Wato (w/Taiji Ishimori)	L	NJPW Hyper Battle '22	15:13
Apr 16	Aaron Henare, Great-O-Khan, Jeff Cobb, TJP, Mark Davis & Kyle Fletcher (w/Hikuleo, Chris Bey, Karl Anderson, Luke Gallows & Scott Norton)	L	NJPW Windy City Riot	11:58
May 12	Josh Alexander & Tomohiro Ishii (w/Jay White)	L	IMPACT Wrestling	10:28
Jun 4	Alex Zayne & Christopher Daniels (w/Chris Bey)	W	NJPW Strong	9:58
Jun 12	Tetsuya Naito, Bushi & Hiromu Takahashi (w/Taiji Ishimori & Ace Austin)	W	NJPW Dominion '22	8:04
Jun 26	Darby Allin, Sting & Shingo Takagi (w/Matt Jackson & Nick Jackson)	L	AEW x NJPW Forbidden Door	13:01
Sep 25	Bushi, Hiromu Takahashi & Shingo Takagi (w/Hikuleo & Kenta)	L	NJPW Burning Spirit '22	8:43
Oct 10	Who's Your Daddy Match: Shingo Takagi	L	NJPW Declaration Of Power	16:01

Oct 28	New York City Street Fight: Shingo Takagi	L	NJPW Rumble On 44th Street	20:59
Nov 19	Blake Christian & Mascara Dorada (w/Chris Bey)	W	NJPW Strong	10:44
Dec 10	Alan Angels, David Finlay, Hikuleo & Tama Tonga (w/Jay White, Jorel Nelson & Royce Isaacs)	L	NJPW Strong	13:20

EL RUDO (*AS SAM ADONIS)

Jan 11	Dirty Dango & JTG (w/Jamie Stanley)	L	NWA Power	5:51*
Feb 8	Team War: Matt Taven, Mike Bennett & Victor Benjamin, Bestia 666, Mecha Wolf & Homicide, Jay Bradley, Wrecking Ball Legursky & Colby Corino (w/Chris Adonis & Thom Latimer)	W	NWA Power	11:09*
Feb 15	Team War: Odinson, Parrow & Rodney Mack (w/Chris Adonis & Thom Latimer)	W	NWA Power	11:35
Feb 19	El Hijo de LA Park, LA Park & LA Park Jr., El Cuatrero, Forastero & Sanson (w/DMT Azul & Puma King)	D	AAA Rey De Reyes '22	13:05
May 3	No DQ: Jay Bradley & Wrecking Ball Legursky (w/Jamie Stanley)	L	NWA Power	8:33
Oct 15	El Cuatrero, Forastero & Sanson, Bandido, Laredo Kid & Psycho Clown (w/Johnny Caballero & Brian Cage)	W	AAA TripleMania XXX: Mexico City	12:44*

ELEKTRA LOPEZ

Feb 25	Sarray	W	NXT Level Up	3:43
Mar 22	Fallon Henley	W	NXT 2.0	3:33
Apr 26	Handicap Match: Fallon Henley & Josh Briggs (w/Joaquin Wilde & Cruz del Toro)	W	NXT 2.0	4:45
May 13	Thea Hail	W	NXT Level Up	5:08
May 24	Alba Fyre	L	NXT 2.0	2:53
May 31	Cora Jade	L	NXT 2.0	5:06
Jun 17	Ivy Nile	L	NXT Level Up	5:51
Jul 19	Battle Royal	L	NXT 2.0	13:13
Aug 12	Sol Ruca	W	NXT Level Up	3:56
Nov 8	Sol Ruca	W	NXT	3:02
Nov 25	Amari Miller	W	NXT Level Up	4:30
Dec 20	Indi Hartwell	W	NXT	3:35

ELIAS (AS EZEKIEL UNTIL OCT 24)

Apr 18	Chad Gable	W	WWE Monday Night RAW	3:30
Apr 25	Seth Rollins, Kevin Owens, Jimmy Uso & Jey Uso (w/Cody Rhodes, Randy Orton & Riddle)	W	WWE Monday Night RAW	14:58
May 2	Kevin Owens, Chad Gable & Otis (w/Angelo Dawkins & Montez Ford)	L	WWE Monday Night RAW	9:45
May 16	Chad Gable	W	WWE Monday Night RAW	11:00
May 23	Chad Gable	W	WWE Monday Night RAW	4:10
May 30	Kevin Owens, Chad Gable & Otis (w/Rey Mysterio & Dominik Mysterio)	W	WWE Monday Night RAW	8:30
Jun 5	Kevin Owens	L	WWE Hell In A Cell '22	9:20
Jun 6	Otis	W	WWE Monday Night RAW	2:20
Jun 13	Kevin Owens	W	WWE Monday Night RAW	8:30
Jul 1	Battle Royal	L	WWE SmackDown	14:36
Jul 1	Madcap Moss, The Miz, Happy Corbin	L	WWE SmackDown	10:33
Jul 4	Seth Rollins	L	WWE Monday Night RAW	10:15
Jul 11	The Miz & Ciampa (w/AJ Styles)	W	WWE Monday Night RAW	11:29
Jul 18	Seth Rollins	L	WWE Monday Night RAW	11:55
Aug 4	Omos	L	WWE Main Event	4:06
Aug 8	Kevin Owens	D	WWE Monday Night RAW	:50
Oct 24	Chad Gable	W	WWE Monday Night RAW	9:30
Nov 7	Otis	L	WWE Monday Night RAW	3:00
Nov 21	Chad Gable & Otis (w/Matt Riddle)	W	WWE Monday Night RAW	16:05
Dec 12	Solo Sikoa	L	WWE Monday Night RAW	8:15

ELIZA ALEXANDER

Apr 14	Angel Hayze	W	NXT UK	4:12
May 19	Angel Hayze & Amale (w/Xia Brookside)	W	NXT UK	5:54
Jun 9	Amale	W	NXT UK	6:51
Jul 7	Meiko Satomura & Sarray (w/Xia Brookside)	L	NXT UK	9:27
Aug 11	Thea Hail	W	NXT UK	4:12
Sep 1	Blair Davenport, Amale, Isla Dawn	L	NXT UK	15:07

ELLA ENVY

Mar 20	Allysin Kay & Marti Belle (w/Kenzie Paige)	L	NWA Crockett Cup '22	7:09
May 24	Max The Impaler	L	NWA Power	3:20
Jun 11	Allysin Kay & Marti Belle (w/Kenzie Paige)	W	NWA Alwayz Ready '22	8:35
Jul 19	Max The Impaler, Taya Valkyrie	L	NWA Power	6:37
Aug 23	Hayley Shadows & Jaylee (w/Kenzie Paige)	W	NWA Power	2:24
Aug 28	Kingshighway Street Fight: Allysin Kay & Marti Belle (w/Kenzie Paige)	W	NWA 74th Anniversary Show	10:02
Sep 13	Angelina Love, Max The Impaler & Natalia Markova (w/Kenzie Paige & Roxy)	L	NWA Power	3:11
Nov 12	Madi Wrenkowski & Missa Kate (w/Kenzie Paige)	W	NWA Hard Times 3	8:12

ELTON PRINCE (AS LEWIS HOWLEY UNTIL APRIL 12)

Jan 20	Sam Gradwell & Saxon Huxley (w/Sam Stoker)	W	NXT UK	9:22
Mar 3	Dave Mastiff & Jack Starz (w/Sam Stoker)	L	NXT UK	10:34
Apr 12	Gauntlet Match: Julius Creed & Brutus Creed, Grayson Waller & Sanga, Joaquin Wilde & Raul Mendoza, Brooks Jensen & Josh Briggs (w/Kit Wilson)	W	NXT 2.0	27:08
Apr 19	Dexter Lumis & Duke Hudson (w/Kit Wilson)	W	NXT 2.0	11:47
May 31	Roderick Strong & Damon Kemp (w/Kit Wilson)	W	NXT 2.0	13:17

Jun 4	Julius Creed & Brutus Creed (w/Kit Wilson)	L	NXT In Your House '22	15:19
Jun 7	Handicap Match: Andre Chase (w/Kit Wilson)	W	NXT 2.0	3:16
Jul 19	Josh Briggs & Brooks Jensen (w/Kit Wilson)	L	NXT 2.0	8:15
Aug 9	Edris Enofe & Malik Blade (w/Kit Wilson)	W	NXT 2.0	4:37
Aug 30	Fallon Henley, Josh Briggs & Brooks Jensen (w/Lash Legend & Kit Wilson)	W	NXT 2.0	11:31
Sep 4	Elimination Match: Brutus Creed & Julius Creed, Mark Coffey & Wolfgang, Brooks Jensen & Josh Briggs (w/Kit Wilson)	W	NXT Worlds Collide '22	15:34
Sep 13	Steel Cage Match: Julius Creed & Brutus Creed (w/Kit Wilson)	W	NXT 2.0	14:58
Oct 4	Ridge Holland & Butch (w/Kit Wilson)	W	NXT	12:27
Oct 25	Malik Blade & Edris Enofe (w/Kit Wilson)	W	NXT	12:29
Nov 1	Bron Breakker & Wes Lee (w/Kit Wilson)	W	NXT	11:57
Nov 22	Andre Chase & Duke Hudson (w/Kit Wilson)	W	NXT	8:17
Dec 10	Kofi Kingston & Xavier Woods (w/Kit Wilson)	L	NXT Deadline	14:05

EMI SAKURA

Jan 10	Skye Blue & Tina San Antonio (w/Nyla Rose)	W	AEW Dark Elevation	2:44
Feb 7	Heather Reckless, Queen Aminata & Skye Blue (w/Diamante & The Bunny)	W	AEW Dark Elevation	4:02
Feb 14	Ruby Soho, Anna Jay & Tay Conti (w/Nyla Rose & The Bunny)	L	AEW Dark Elevation	3:43
Feb 15	Angelica Risk	W	AEW Dark	3:14
Feb 21	AQA, Kiera Hogan & Skye Blue (w/Leyla Hirsch & Nyla Rose)	W	AEW Dark Elevation	4:48
Feb 28	Kayla Sparks, LMK & Paris Van Dale (w/Diamante & Nyla Rose)	W	AEW Dark Elevation	2:27
Mar 7	Kris Statlander	L	AEW Dark	4:19
Mar 8	AQA & Ruby Soho (w/Diamante)	L	AEW Dark	5:02
Mar 14	KiLynn King & Skye Blue (w/The Bunny)	W	AEW Dark Elevation	6:00
Mar 15	Shalonce Royal	W	AEW Dark	2:46
Mar 21	Anna Jay & Ruby Soho (w/The Bunny)	L	AEW Dark Elevation	4:20
Mar 29	Leila Grey	W	AEW Dark	2:55
Apr 11	Anna Jay, Ruby Soho & Skye Blue (w/LuFisto & The Bunny)	L	AEW Dark Elevation	3:21
Apr 12	Charlette Renegade	W	AEW Dark	2:15
Apr 18	Anna Jay, Hikaru Shida & Ruby Soho (w/Raychell Rose & The Bunny)	L	AEW Dark Elevation	3:20
Apr 25	Anna Jay, Ruby Soho & Skye Blue (w/Nyla Rose & The Bunny)	L	AEW Dark Elevation	6:35
May 2	Anna Jay & Kris Statlander (w/Nyla Rose)	L	AEW Dark Elevation	6:10
May 9	Abadon	L	AEW Dark Elevation	4:29
May 16	Anna Jay & Yuka Sakazaki (w/Nyla Rose)	L	AEW Dark Elevation	3:32
May 17	Devlyn Macabre	W	AEW Dark	3:30
May 23	Skye Blue & Yuka Sakazaki (w/Nyla Rose)	L	AEW Dark Elevation	6:17
May 28	Riho, Sky Blue & Yuka Sakazaki (w/Diamante & Nyla Rose)	L	AEW Dark	6:11
Jun 14	Anna Jay, Kris Statlander & Ruby Soho (w/Diamante & Nyla Rose)	L	AEW Dark	7:54
Jul 11	Paris Van Dale	W	AEW Dark Elevation	3:03
Jul 25	Toni Storm	L	AEW Dark Elevation	7:33
Aug 1	Hikaru Shida, Toni Storm & Willow Nightingale (w/Marina Shafir & Nyla Rose)	L	AEW Dark Elevation	8:05
Aug 4	Hikaru Shida	L	AEW Dark Elevation	5:40
Aug 9	Athena, Hikaru Shida & Ruby Soho (w/Leva Bates & Serena Deeb)	L	AEW Dark	8:08
Aug 15	Hikaru Shida, Toni Storm & Thunder Rosa (w/Marina Shafir & Nyla Rose)	L	AEW Dark Elevation	2:42
Aug 16	Renee Michelle	W	AEW Dark	3:37
Aug 22	Hikaru Shida & Skye Blue (w/Maki Itoh)	W	AEW Dark Elevation	7:15
Aug 29	Hikaru Shida	L	AEW Dark Elevation	6:30
Sep 3	Ortiz & Ruby Soho (w/Baliyan Akki)	L	AEW Dark Elevation	2:20
Sep 12	Athena	L	AEW Dark Elevation	4:43
Sep 13	Queen Aminata & Skye Blue (w/Diamante)	L	AEW Dark	4:01
Sep 20	Avery Breaux	W	AEW Dark	3:15
Oct 10	Trish Adora	W	AEW Dark Elevation	3:10
Oct 11	Toni Storm	L	AEW Dark	8:53
Oct 17	Madison Rayne & Skye Blue (w/Serena Deeb)	W	AEW Dark Elevation	6:00
Oct 24	Jaylee & Nikki Victory (w/Mei Suruga)	W	AEW Dark Elevation	3:30
Oct 25	KC Spinelli & Taylor Rising (w/Serena Deeb)	W	AEW Dark	4:34
Nov 8	Toni Storm & Hikaru Shida (w/Mei Suruga)	W	AEW Dark	7:51
Nov 14	Riho & Willow Nightingale (w/Mei Suruga)	L	AEW Dark Elevation	6:14
Nov 21	Hikaru Shida & Willow Nightingale (w/Leva Bates)	L	AEW Dark Elevation	4:28
Nov 28	Marina Shafir & Nyla Rose (w/Maki Itoh)	L	AEW Dark Elevation	4:17
Nov 29	Tiara James	W	AEW Dark	2:17
Dec 5	Madison Rayne	W	AEW Dark Elevation	2:41
Dec 12	Danni Bee	W	AEW Dark Elevation	1:40
Dec 19	Gigi Rey & Lady Bird Monroe (w/Emi Sakura)	W	AEW Dark Elevation	2:45

EMILIA MCKENZIE

Jan 20	Isla Dawn	L	NXT UK	5:30
Feb 17	Angel Hayze	W	NXT UK	4:57
Mar 17	Nina Samuels	W	NXT UK	8:44
Apr 21	Stevie Turner	W	NXT UK	4:42
May 26	Lash Legend	L	NXT UK	6:06
Jun 30	Fallon Henley	L	NXT UK	8:31
Jul 21	Nina Samuels	W	NXT UK	4:58

EMMA (AS TENILLE DASHWOOD UNTIL OCTOBER 28)

Jan 20	Rosemary & Havok (w/Madison Rayne)	W	IMPACT Wrestling	3:35
Mar 10	Cassie Lee & Jessie McKay, Chelsea Green & Mickie James, Savannah Evans & Tasha Steelz (w/Madison Rayne)	L	IMPACT Wrestling	6:00
Mar 31	Battle Royal	L	IMPACT Wrestling	7:15
Apr 1	Tasha Steelz & Savannah Evans, Gisele Shaw & Lady Frost, Havok & Rosemark (w/Madison Rayne)	W	IMPACT Multiverse Of Matches	9:02

May 5	Gisele Shaw	W	IMPACT Before The Impact	7:58
May 12	Alisha Edwards & Gisele Shaw (w/Madison Rayne)	W	IMPACT Wrestling	12:00
Jun 9	Rosemary	L	IMPACT Wrestling	6:10
June 19	Rosemary & Taya Valkyrie (w/Madison Rayne)	L	IMPACT Slammiversary XX	7:20
Jul 14	Masha Slamovich	L	IMPACT Wrestling	1:16
Oct 28	Ronda Rousey	L	WWE SmackDown	6:50
Dec 2	Shayna Baszler	L	WWE SmackDown	4:10
Dec 17	Ronda Rousey & Shayna Baszler (w/Tamina)	L	WWE Tribute To The Troops '22	7:34
Dec 23	Gauntlet Match: Raquel Rodriguez, Xia Li, Liv Morgan, Sonya Deville, Tegan Nox, Shayna Baszler	L	WWE SmackDown	23:58

ERIC YOUNG

Jan 8	Hardcore War: Eddie Edwards, Rich Swann, Willie Mack, Heath & Rhino (w/Luke Gallows, Karl Anderson, Deaner & Joe Doering)	L	IMPACT Hard To Kill '22	23:25
Feb 17	Jay White, Tama Tonga & Tanga Loa (w/Deaner & Joe Doering)	L	IMPACT Wrestling	13:19
Mar 24	Lumberjack Match: Luke Gallows & Karl Anderson (w/Joe Doering)	W	IMPACT Wrestling	7:26
Apr 21	Black Taurus & Crazzy Steve (w/Deaner)	W	IMPACT Wrestling	4:42
Apr 23	Elimination Challenge Match (w/Joe Doering)	W	IMPACT Rebellion '22	33:02
May 12	Gauntlet For The Gold	W	IMPACT Wrestling	39:00
May 26	Josh Alexander, Jay Briscoe & Mark Briscoe (w/Deaner & Joe Doering)	W	IMPACT Wrestling	17:09
Jun 19	Josh Alexander	L	IMPACT Slammiversary XX	18:50
Jul 14	Josh Alexander, Alex Shelley & Chris Sabin (w/Deaner & Joe Doering)	L	IMPACT Wrestling	11:56
Aug 25	Kushida, Alex Shelley & Chris Sabin (w/Deaner & Joe Doering)	L	IMPACT Wrestling	15:18
Oct 7	Call Your Shot Gauntlet	L	IMPACT Bound For Glory '22	29:18
Oct 20	Rich Swann	L	IMPACT Wrestling	3:14
Nov 3	Sami Callihan	L	IMPACT Wrestling	6:11
Nov 17	Death Machine's Double Jeopardy Match: Sami Callihan	L	IMPACT Wrestling	14:04

ERICA YAN

Jan 7	Nikkita Lyons	L	WWE 205 Live	5:24
Feb 11	Lash Legend	L	WWE 205 Live	4:22
Mar 4	Tiffany Stratton	L	NXT Level Up	3:51
May 6	Ivy Nile & Tatum Paxley (w/Sarray)	L	NXT Level Up	5:32
Sep 2	Arianna Grace	L	NXT Level Up	4:43
Sep 16	Ivy Nile & Tatum Paxley (w/Sloane Jacobs)	L	NXT Level Up	5:21

ERICK REDBEARD

Mar 6	Malakai Black, Brody King & Buddy Matthews (w/Pac & Penta Oscuro)	L	AEW Revolution Buy-In	17:20
Aug 12	Austin Gunn & Colten Gunn (w/Danhausen)	L	AEW Rampage: Quake By The Lake	4:33

ERIK

Jan 7	Happy Corbin & Madcap Moss (w/Ivar)	L	WWE SmackDown	3:30
Jan 14	Angel & Humberto, Cesaro & Mansoon, Jinder Mahal & Shanky (w/Ivar)	W	WWE SmackDown	13:21
Jan 21	Angel & Humberto (w/Ivar)	W	WWE SmackDown	2:20
Feb 4	Jimmy Uso	L	WWE SmackDown	2:10
Mar 4	Jimmy Uso & Jey Uso (w/Ivar)	L	WWE SmackDown	8:25
Mar 18	Happy Corbin, Jinder Mahal & Shanky (w/Drew McIntyre & Ivar)	W	WWE SmackDown	7:10
Mar 28	Handicap Match: Omos (w/Ivar)	L	WWE Monday Night RAW	:50
Apr 1	Andre The Giant Memorial Battle Royal	L	WWE SmackDown	8:05
Apr 26	Edris Enofe & Malik Blade (w/Ivar)	W	NXT 2.0	4:45
May 3	Julius Creed & Brutus Creed (w/Ivar)	L	NXT 2.0: Spring Breakin'	12:58
May 17	Julius Creed & Brutus Creed (w/Ivar)	W	NXT 2.0	9:30
Jul 8	Jinder Mahal & Shanky (w/Ivar)	W	WWE SmackDown	1:15
Jul 22	Jinder Mahal & Shanky (w/Ivar)	W	WWE SmackDown	1:30
Jul 29	Xavier Woods & Kofi Kingston (w/Ivar)	W	WWE SmackDown	9:15
Aug 5	Jim Mulkey & Tommy Gibson (w/Ivar)	W	WWE SmackDown	1:35
Aug 5	Kofi Kingston	L	WWE SmackDown	3:45
Sep 2	Viking Rules Match: Kofi Kingston & Xavier Woods (w/Ivar)	W	WWE SmackDown	22:15
Nov 25	Ashante Adonis & Top Dolla (w/Ivar)	W	WWE SmackDown	2:46
Dec 9	Joaquin Wilde & Cruz Del Toro (w/Ivar)	D	WWE SmackDown	1:53
Dec 16	Ashante Adonis & Top Dolla, Joaquin Wilde & Cruz Del Toro (w/Ivar)	L	WWE SmackDown	9:20

ETHAN PAGE

Jan 21	Jon Moxley	L	AEW Rampage	10:15
Jan 24	Logan LaRoux & Mike Fowler (w/Scorpio Sky)	W	AEW Dark Elevation	3:00
Feb 14	Jaden Valo & Steve Pena (w/Scorpio Sky)	W	AEW Dark Elevation	3:12
Mar 4	Christian Cage	L	AEW Rampage	8:57
May 23	JD Griffey	W	AEW Dark Elevation	2:07
May 29	Frankie Kazarian, Sammy Guevara & Tay Conti (w/Scorpio Sky & Paige VanZant)	W	AEW Double Or Nothing '22	12:30
Jun 14	Frankie Kazarian	W	AEW Dark	8:06
Jun 15	Miro	L	AEW Dynamite: Road Rager	9:31
Jun 27	Serpentico	W	AEW Dark Elevation	1:37
Jun 29	Orange Cassidy	L	AEW Dynamite: Blood & Guts	10:57
Jul 11	Colin Delaney	W	AEW Dark Elevation	5:10
Jul 18	Leon Ruffin	W	AEW Dark Elevation	5:38
Jul 29	Leon Ruffin	W	AEW Rampage	1:31
Sep 16	Danhausen	W	AEW Rampage	1:25
Oct 14	Isiah Kassidy	W	AEW Rampage	2:10
Nov 9	Eddie Kingston	W	AEW Dynamite	9:18
Nov 16	Bandido	W	AEW Dynamite	9:08
Nov 23	Ricky Starks	L	AEW Dynamite: Thanksgiving Eve	12:58

Dec 7	Dynamite Diamond Battle Royale	L	AEW Dynamite	13:10
Dec 19	Jeeves Kay, Slim J, Sonny Kiss, Cezar Bononi, Peter Avalon & Ryan Nemeth (w/Isiah Kassidy, Konosuke Takeshita, Matt Hardy, Dante Martin & Darius Martin)	W	AEW Dark Elevation	7:45
Dec 28	Bryan Danielson	L	AEW Dynamite	16:25

EVIL

Jan 4	Tomohiro Ishii	W	NJPW Wrestle Kingdom 16 Night #1	12:10
Jan 5	Hirooki Goto, Yoshi-Hashi & Yoh (w/Yujiro Takahashi & Sho)	W	NJPW Wrestle Kingdom 16 Night #2	9:37
Jan 8	Go Shiozaki & Masa Kitamiya (w/Dick Togo)	L	NJPW Wrestle Kingdom 16 Night #3	9:53
Mar 1	Tiger Mask, Yoh & Ryusuke Taguchi (w/Yujiro Takahashi & Sho)	W	NJPW 50th Anniversary Show	6:35
Apr 9	Hiromu Takahashi	W	NJPW Hyper Battle '22	15:47
May 1	Tama Tonga	L	NJPW Wrestling Dontaku '22	13:25
Jun 12	Zack Sabre Jr., El Desperado & Yoshinobu Kanemaru (w/Sho & Yujiro Takahashi)	W	NJPW Dominion '22	9:26
Oct 10	Hiroshi Tanahashi, Hikuleo & Ryusuke Taguchi (w/Yujiro Takahashi & Sho)	L	NJPW Declaration Of Power	7:14
Nov 5	Zack Sabre Jr.	L	NJPW Battle Autumn '22	4:48
Nov 20	Lio Rush, Tomohiro Ishii, Yoh & Yoshi-Hashi (w/Dick Togo, Sho & Yujiro Takahashi)	L	NJPW x Stardom Historic X-Over	7:05

EVIL UNO

Jan 25	Anthony Bowens, Max Caster, Austin Gunn & Colten Gunn (w/Alan Angels, Alex Reynolds & Ten)	L	AEW Dark	6:15
Feb 4	Adam Cole	L	AEW Rampage	2:28
Feb 14	Jeff Parker, Matt Lee, Daniel Garcia, Anthony Bowens & Max Caster (w/John Silver, Alex Reynolds, Alan Angels & Stu Grayson)	L	AEW Dark Elevation	5:56
Feb 28	Luther & Serpentico (w/Stu Grayson)	W	AEW Dark Elevation	4:53
Mar 2	Casino Battle Royale (w/Stu Grayson)	L	AEW Dynamite	21:32
Mar 15	Brandon Cutler, Matt Jackson & Nick Jackson (w/Alan Angels & Colt Cabana)	L	AEW Dark	8:40
Mar 21	Aaron Solo, Nick Comoroto & QT Marshall (w/John Silver & Stu Grayson)	W	AEW Dark Elevation	7:27
Mar 29	Alexander Zane, Jay Marte & Richard King (w/Stu Grayson & Alan Angels)	W	AEW Dark	3:09
Apr 1	Malakai Black, Brody King & Buddy Matthews (w/Fuego Del Sol & Stu Grayson)	L	AEW Rampage	7:15
Apr 18	Allen Russell, Dale Springs, Izaiah Zane & Kameron Russell (w/John Silver, Alex Reynolds & Stu Grayson)	W	AEW Dark Elevation	2:17
Apr 19	Powerhouse Hobbs & Ricky Starks (w/Stu Grayson)	L	AEW Dark	8:48
Apr 25	Bulk Nasty, Jake Omen, Luther, RC Dupress & Tito Ortic (w/Alan Angels, Alex Reynolds, Stu Grayson & Ten)	W	AEW Dark Elevation	3:09
May 2	Anthony Bennett, Bret Waters, Cory Bishop, Eli Isom, Jaden Valo & Mike Law (w/John Silver, Alex Reynolds, Alan Angels, Colt Cabana & Ten)	W	AEW Dark Elevation	1:44
May 9	Brandon Scott, Diego, Josh Fuller & Ryan Mooney (w/Alex Reynolds, Alan Angels & Ten)	W	AEW Dark Elevation	4:27
May 10	Cezar Bononi & Tiger Ruas (w/Ten)	W	AEW Dark	8:30
May 16	Eric James & VSK (w/Ten)	W	AEW Dark Elevation	2:30
May 20	Malakai Black, Brody King & Buddy Matthews (w/Ten & Fuego Del Sol)	L	AEW Rampage	9:25
May 31	Serpentico, Peter Avalon & Ryan Nemeth (w/John Silver & Ten)	W	AEW Dark	5:37
Jun 6	Aaron Solo, Anthony Ogogo, Nick Comoroto & QT Marshall (w/Alan Angels, John Silver & Ten)	L	AEW Dark Elevation	6:28
Jun 13	Aaron Solo & QT Marshall (w/Ten)	W	AEW Dark Elevation	8:13
Jun 27	Max Caster, Austin Gunn & Colten Gunn (w/Alex Reynolds & Ten)	L	AEW Dark Elevation	4:08
Jun 28	JD Drake & Ryan Nemeth (w/Ten)	W	AEW Dark	8:16
Jul 4	Aaron Solo, Nick Comoroto & QT Marshall (w/Alex Reynolds & Ten)	W	AEW Dark Elevation	7:56
Jul 5	Cezar Bononi, JD Drake, Peter Avalon & Ryan Nemeth (w/John Silver, Alex Reynolds & Ten)	W	AEW Dark	7:22
Jul 16	Kyle Fletcher & Mark Davis (w/Alan Angels)	L	NJPW Strong	12:47
Jul 18	Terrell Hughes & Terrence Hughes (w/Ten)	W	AEW Dark Elevation	4:44
Jul 25	Aaron Solo & Nick Comoroto (w/Ten)	W	AEW Dark Elevation	6:35
Aug 9	JD Drake & Peter Avalon (w/Ten)	W	AEW Dark	4:15
Aug 15	Adam Grace, Drew System, Rylie Jackson & TUG Cooper (w/John Silver, Alex Reynolds & Ten)	W	AEW Dark Elevation	2:25
Sep 23	Golden Ticket Battle Royale	L	AEW Rampage: Grand Slam	12:16
Oct 18	Jordano, Shayne Hawke, Tyler Tirva & Zak Patterson (w/John Silver, Alex Reynolds & Ten)	W	AEW Dark	6:52
Nov 8	Ativalu, Fulton & Troy Hollywood (w/John Silver & Alex Reynolds)	W	AEW Dark	2:22
Nov 15	Arjun Singh, Brett Gosselin & Mike Magnum (w/John Silver & Alex Reynolds)	W	AEW Dark	4:43
Nov 22	Ari Daivari, Jeeves Kay & Sonny Kiss (w/John Silver & Alex Reynolds)	W	AEW Dark	5:26
Dec 23	$300,000 Three Kings Christmas Casino Trios Royale (w/Alex Reynolds & John Silver)	L	AEW Rampage	22:01
Dec 27	Blake Li	W	AEW Dark	2:10

FALLON HENLEY

Jan 21	Lash Legend	L	WWE 205 Live	4:25
Feb 4	Kacy Katanzaro & Kayden Carter (w/Lash Legend)	L	WWE 205 Live	6:15
Feb 18	Ivy Nile & Tatum Paxley (w/Kayla Inlay)	L	NXT Level Up	4:18
Mar 8	Tiffany Stratton	W	NXT 2.0: Roadblock '22	2:48
Mar 22	Elektra Lopez	L	NXT 2.0	3:33
Apr 22	Thea Hail	W	NXT Level Up	4:21
Apr 26	Handicap Match: Joaquin Wilde, Cruz del Toro & Elektra Lopez (w/Josh Briggs)	L	NXT 2.0	4:45
May 10	Sloane Jacobs	W	NXT 2.0	4:28

May 24	Tiffany Stratton	L	NXT 2.0	5:02
Jun 3	Brooklyn Barlow	W	NXT Level Up	4:19
Jun 14	Tiffany Stratton	W	NXT 2.0	3:10
Jun 30	Emilia McKenzie	W	NXT UK	8:31
Jul 19	Battle Royal	L	NXT 2.0	13:13
Jul 21	Isla Dawn	L	NXT UK	5:12
Jul 29	Sol Ruca	W	NXT Level Up	5:14
Aug 30	Lash Legend, Elton Prince & Kit Wilson (w/Josh Briggs & Brooks Jensen)	L	NXT 2.0	11:31
Sep 13	Lash Legend	W	NXT 2.0	2:17
Sep 27	Mandy Rose	L	NXT	5:40
Oct 6	Dana Brooke	L	WWE Main Event	4:39
Oct 7	Arianna Grace & Kiana James (w/Sol Ruca)	W	NXT Level Up	5:06
Nov 29	Kiana James	L	NXT	9:40
Dec 6	Indi Hartwell, Wendy Choo	L	NXT	10:15
Dec 27	Kiana James	W	NXT	5:13

FINN BALOR

Jan 17	Austin Theory	W	WWE Monday Night RAW	6:06
Feb 21	Dolph Ziggler & Robert Roode (w/Tommaso Ciampa)	W	WWE Monday Night RAW	9:15
Feb 28	Damian Priest	W	WWE Monday Night RAW	11:00
Mar 7	Austin Theory	W	WWE Monday Night RAW	8:40
Mar 14	Damian Priest	L	WWE Monday Night RAW	7:35
Mar 21	Austin Theory	W	WWE Monday Night RAW	7:55
Mar 31	Apollo Crews	W	WWE Main Event	5:31
Apr 1	Andre The Giant Memorial Battle Royal	W	WWE SmackDown	8:05
Apr 1	Austin Theory, Jimmy Uso & Jey Uso (w/Shinsuke Nakamura & Rick Boogs)	L	WWE SmackDown	11:27
Apr 4	Austin Theory, Jimmy Uso & Jey Uso (w/Randy Orton & Riddle)	L	WWE Monday Night RAW	8:25
Apr 18	Theory	L	WWE Monday Night RAW	11:35
Apr 25	Damian Priest	L	WWE Monday Night RAW	7:20
May 9	Damian Priest	W	WWE Monday Night RAW	5:59
May 16	Angel & Humberto (w/AJ Styles)	W	WWE Monday Night RAW	8:30
Jun 5	Edge, Damian Priest & Rhea Ripley (w/AJ Styles & Liv Morgan)	L	WWE Hell In A Cell '22	16:00
Jun 23	Rey Mysterio & Dominik Mysterio (w/Damian Priest)	L	WWE Main Event	7:31
Jul 4	Rey Mysterio & Dominik Mysterio (w/Damian Priest)	L	WWE Monday Night RAW	11:30
Jul 11	Rey Mysterio	W	WWE Monday Night RAW	10:15
Jul 25	Rey Mysterio & Dominik Mysterio (w/Damian Priest)	L	WWE Monday Night RAW	11:29
Jul 30	Rey Mysterio & Dominik Mysterio (w/Damian Priest)	L	WWE SummerSlam '22	11:05
Aug 8	Rey Mysterio	W	WWE Monday Night RAW	14:00
Aug 22	Dolph Ziggler	W	WWE Monday Night RAW	13:05
Aug 29	AJ Styles & Dolph Ziggler (w/Damian Priest)	W	WWE Monday Night RAW	8:34
Sep 3	Edge & Rey Mysterio (w/Damian Priest)	L	WWE Clash At The Castle	12:35
Sep 12	Matt Riddle	W	WWE Monday Night RAW	13:35
Sep 19	Matt Riddle & Rey Mysterio (w/Damian Priest)	W	WWE Monday Night RAW	17:40
Oct 3	AJ Styles & Rey Mysterio (w/Damian Priest)	W	WWE Monday Night RAW	10:42
Oct 8	I Quit Match: Edge	W	WWE Extreme Rules '22	29:55
Oct 24	Karl Anderson	W	WWE Monday Night RAW	17:15
Nov 5	AJ Styles, Luke Gallows & Karl Anderson (w/Damian Priest & Dominik Mysterio)	W	WWE Crown Jewel '22	14:00
Nov 14	Seth Rollins	L	WWE Monday Night RAW	21:10
Nov 21	Sheamus, Ridge Holland & Butch (w/Dominik Mytserio & Damian Priest)	L	WWE Monday Night RAW	14:50
Nov 26	AJ Styles	L	WWE Survivor Series WarGames	18:25
Nov 28	AJ Styles, Luke Gallows, Karl Anderson & Mia Yim (w/Damian Priest, Dominik Mysterio & Rhea Ripley)	W	WWE Monday Night RAW	14:20
Dec 12	Akira Tozawa, Luke Gallows & Karl Anderson (w/Damian Priest & Dominik Mysterio)	W	WWE Monday Night RAW	14:45
Dec 19	Angelo Dawkins & Montez Ford (w/Damian Priest)	L	WWE Monday Night RAW	9:00

FLIP GORDON

Aug 28	Nick Aldis	L	NWA 74th Anniversary Show	8:43
Sep 6	Doug Williams	W	NWA Power	9:30
Oct 4	Odinson	L	NWA Power	7:11
Nov 1	Colby Corino	L	NWA Power	8:38

FRANCESCO AKIRA

Jun 12	Ryusuke Taguchi, Master Wato & Hiroyoshi Tenzan (w/Aaron Henare & TJP)	W	NJPW Dominion '22	10:31
Sep 25	Ryusuke Taguchi & Master Wato (w/TJP)	W	NJPW Burning Spirit '22	12:43
Oct 10	Tetsuya Naito, Sanada, Bushi & Hiromu Takahashi (w/Will Ospreay, Aaron Henare & TJP)	L	NJPW Declaration Of Power	8:07
Nov 5	Bushi & Titan (w/TJP)	W	NJPW Battle Autumn '22	11:36
Nov 20	Bushi, Hiromu Takahashi, Sanada, Shingo Takagi & Tetsuya Naito (w/Kyle Fletcher, Mark Davis, TJP & Gideon Grey)	W	NJPW x Stardom Historic X-Over	9:55

FRANKIE KAZARIAN

Jan 17	LaBron Kozone	W	AEW Dark Elevation	3:15
Jan 19	Lance Archer	L	AEW Dynamite	10:02
Feb 15	Luke Sampson	W	AEW Dark	2:27
Feb 21	Luther, Serpentico, Cezar Bononi, JD Drake & Peter Avalon (w/Brock Anderson, Jay Lethal, Lee Johnson & Matt Sydal)	W	AEW Dark Elevation	6:06
Feb 28	Alan Angels	W	AEW Dark Elevation	6:05
Mar 14	Tiger Ruas	W	AEW Dark Elevation	5:47
Mar 15	Jora Johl	W	AEW Dark	4:33

Mar 28	Brandon Cutler	W	AEW Dark Elevation	3:46
Mar 29	Kaun	W	AEW Dark	3:20
Apr 4	Lucky Ali	W	AEW Dark Elevation	3:40
Apr 11	Teddy Goodz	W	AEW Dark Elevation	3:18
Apr 26	Max Caster, Angelico, Isiah Kassidy, Marq Quen & The Blade (w/Matt Hardy, Jeff Hardy, Dante Martin & Darius Martin)	W	AEW Dark	12:40
May 13	Scorpio Sky	L	AEW Rampage	11:37
May 26	Chris Sabin	D	IMPACT Wrestling	10:25
May 29	Ethan Page, Scorpio Sky & Paige VanZant (w/Sammy Guevara & Tay Conti)	L	AEW Double Or Nothing '22	12:30
Jun 6	Serpentico	W	AEW Dark Elevation	5:00
Jun 9	Eddie Edwards, Matt Taven & Mike Bennett (w/Alex Shelley & Chris Sabin)	L	IMPACT Wrestling	16:47
Jun 14	Ethan Page	L	AEW Dark	8:06
Jun 19	Eddie Edwards, Matt Taven, Mike Bennett, PCO & Vincent (w/Alex Shelley, Chris Sabin, Davey Richards & Magnus)	W	IMPACT Slammiversary XX	18:45
Jun 20	Andrade El Idolo	L	AEW Dark Elevation	8:43
Jun 30	Chris Sabin	L	IMPACT Wrestling	18:42
Jul 1	Royal Rampage Match	L	AEW Rampage	22:41
Aug 29	Andrea Guercio	W	AEW Dark Elevation	2:50
Sep 19	Jora Johl	W	AEW Dark Elevation	3:52
Oct 6	Kenny King	W	IMPACT Wrestling	9:20
Oct 7	Mike Bailey	W	IMPACT Bound For Glory '22	12:30
Oct 17	Matt Blackmon	W	AEW Dark Elevation	2:23
Oct 31	Rhett Titus	W	AEW Dark Elevation	3:35
Nov 13	Kyle Fletcher & Mark Davis (w/Josh Alexander)	W	IMPACT Wrestling	15:56
Nov 15	Zack Clayton	W	AEW Dark	3:39
Dec 1	Steve Maclin	W	IMPACT Wrestling	7:26
Dec 26	Konosuke Takeshita	L	AEW Dark Elevation	5:01

FRED ROSSER

Jan 22	Jorel Nelson, Tom Lawlor & Black Tiger (w/Rocky Romero & Taylor Rust)	W	NJPW Strong	11:35
Feb 19	Gabriel Kidd	W	NJPW Strong	14:52
Mar 26	Elimination Match: Danny Limelight, Jorel Nelson, JR Kratos, Royce Isaacs & Tom Lawlor (w/Adrian Quest, Clark Connors, Taylor Rust & The DKC)	L	NJPW Strong	16:29
Apr 9	Daniel Garcia & Fred Yehi (w/Eddie Kingston)	W	NJPW Strong	9:27
Apr 16	Royce Isaacs, Jorel Nelson, JR Kratos, Black Tiger & Danny Limelight (w/Josh Alexander, Alex Coughlin, Ren Narita & Chris Dickinson)	W	NJPW Windy City Riot	13:50
May 7	JR Kratos, Royce Isaacs & Tom Lawlor (w/Alex Coughlin & The DKC)	L	NJPW Strong	11:12
May 13	Handicap Match: Jorel Nelson & Rouce Isaacs	L	NJPW Strong	7:28
May 14	Tom Lawlor, Jorel Nelson, Royce Isaacs, JR Kratos & Danny Limelight (w/The DKC, Yuya Uemura, David Finlay & Tanga Loa)	L	NJPW Capital Collision	14:48
Jun 25	Tom Lawlor	W	NJPW Strong	24:19
Jul 30	Chase Owens, Hikuleo & Jay White (w/Hiroshi Tanahashi & Kevin Knight)	L	NJPW Strong	15:41
Jul 30	Big Damo	W	NJPW Music City Mayhem	13:01
Sep 3	Fred Yehi	W	NJPW Strong	8:20
Oct 1	TJP	W	NJPW Strong	17:20
Oct 15	Chris Dickinson	D	NJPW Strong	6:48
Oct 28	Jonathan Gresham	W	NJPW Rumble On 44th Street	14:37
Nov 26	Jay White	L	NJPW Strong	19:22
Dec 24	JR Kratos	W	NJPW Strong	18:44

FRED YEHI

Mar 19	Barrett Brown, Bateman & Misterioso (w/Keita Murray & The DKC)	W	NJPW Strong	10:05
Apr 9	Eddie Kingston & Fred Rosser (w/Daniel Garcia)	L	NJPW Strong	9:27
May 28	Barrett Brown, Bateman & Misterioso (w/Kevin Knight & The DKC)	L	NJPW Strong	10:06
Jul 30	Bateman	W	NJPW Strong	7:30
Jul 30	Kevin Knight, Ren Narita & The DKC (w/Shota Umino & Yuya Uemura)	W	NJPW Music City Mayhem	13:12
Sep 3	Fred Rosser	L	NJPW Strong	8:20
Nov 12	Minoru Suzuki	L	NJPW Strong	16:27

FUEGO DEL SOL

Jan 11	Daniel Garcia	L	AEW Dark	3:44
Feb 8	Serpentico	W	AEW Dark	5:42
Feb 15	Anthony Bowens	L	AEW Dark	4:30
Feb 22	David Ali	W	AEW Dark	3:49
Feb 28	Lance Archer	L	AEW Dark Elevation	3:10
Mar 18	Malakai Black, Brody King & Buddy Matthews (w/Bear Bronson & Bear Boulder)	L	AEW Rampage	3:22
Mar 22	Powerhouse Hobbs	L	AEW Dark	4:08
Apr 1	Malakai Black, Brody King & Buddy Matthews (w/Evil Uno & Stu Grayson)	L	AEW Rampage	7:15
May 20	Malakai Black, Brody King & Buddy Matthews (w/Evil Uno & Ten)	L	AEW Rampage	9:25
Jun 28	Marcus Kross	W	AEW Dark	4:05
Jul 5	Aaron Solo	W	AEW Dark	5:27
Jul 6	Anthony Bowens, Max Caster, Austin Gunn & Colten Gunn (w/Leon Ruffin, Bear Bronson & Bear Boulder)	L	AEW Dynamite	2:14
Jul 19	QT Marshall	L	AEW Dark	10:48
Aug 16	Ari Daivari	L	AEW Dark	10:57
Sep 27	Jay Malachi	W	AEW Dark	4:57
Sep 30	Lee Moriarty	L	AEW Rampage	1:56
Oct 5	Luchasaurus	L	AEW Dynamite: Anniversary	:23

| Nov 1 | Brian Cage, Kaun & Toa Liona (w/Jaylen Brandyn & Traevon Jordan) | L | AEW Dark | 4:01 |
| Dec 27 | Lucky Ali | W | AEW Dark | 2:28 |

GAAGZ THE GYMP (AS CAPTAIN YUMA UNTIL APRIL 12)

Feb 1	Handicap Match: Dirty Dango & JTG (w/Alex Taylor & Rush Freeman)	L	NWA Power	4:09
Apr 12	Jay Bradley, Wrecking Ball Legursky & Colby Corino (w/Judais & Sal The Pal)	W	NWA Power	6:27
May 10	Dirty Dango & JTG (w/Sal The Pal)	L	NWA Power	6:37
Aug 2	Alex Taylor, Jeremiah Plunkett & Rush Freeman (w/Judais & Sal The Pal)	W	NWA Power	8:08
Aug 27	Beelzebub's Bedlam Match: Danny Dealz, Alex Taylor & Jeremiah Plunkett (w/Sal The Pal & Judais)	W	NWA 74th Anniversary Show	9:41
Aug 28	Tag Team Battle Royal (w/Sal The Pal)	L	NWA 74th Anniversary Show	14:07

GABRIEL KIDD

Jan 8	Eddie Kingston	L	NJPW Strong	12:37
Feb 19	Fred Rosser	L	NJPW Strong	14:52
Oct 1	Dan Moloney	W	NJPW Royal Quest II Night #1	9:19
Oct 2	Will Ospreay, Great-O-Khan, Mark Davis, Kyle Fletcher & Gideon Grey (w/Cash Wheeler, Dax Harwood, Shota Umino & Ricky Knight Jr.)	L	NJPW Royal Quest II Night #2	16:57
Nov 15	Hiroshi Tanahashi	L	NJPW Strong	11:30

GANGREL

Mar 24	Gnarls Garvin	W	MLW Fusion	10:35
Jun 2	Mexican Death Match: LA Park & LA Park Jr. (w/Pagano)	L	MLW Fusion	10:53
Jun 16	Budd Heavy	W	MLW Fusion	1:30

GIGI DOLIN

Jan 25	Kay Lee Ray, Indi Hartwell & Persia Pirotta (w/Mandy Rose & Jacy Jayne)	L	NXT 2.0	10:25
Feb 15	Indi Hartwell & Persia Pirotta (w/Jacy Jayne)	W	NXT 2.0: Vengeance Day '22	7:54
Apr 2	Raquel Gonzalez & Dakota Kai (w/Jacy Jayne)	L	NXT Stand & Deliver Kickoff	7:53
Apr 5	Dakota Kai & Raquel Gonzalez (w/Jacy Jayne)	W	NXT 2.0	8:31
May 10	Roxanne Perez & Wendy Choo (w/Jacy Jayne)	W	NXT 2.0	10:01
Jun 4	Katana Chance & Kayden Carter (w/Jacy Jayne)	W	NXT In Your House '22	9:01
Jun 14	Roxanne Perez, Cora Jade & Indi Hartwell (w/Mandy Rose & Jacy Jayne)	L	NXT 2.0	13:51
Jul 5	Roxanne Perez & Cora Jade (w/Jacy Jayne)	L	NXT 2.0: Great American Bash	10:29
Jul 26	Zoey Stark	L	NXT 2.0	2:48
Aug 2	Elimination Match: Kayden Carter & Katana Chance, Valentina Feroz & Yulisa Leon, Ivy Nile & Tatum Paxley (w/Jacy Jayne)	L	NXT 2.0	12:09
Aug 19	Natalya & Sonya Deville (w/Jacy Jayne)	W	WWE SmackDown	8:48
Sep 6	Nikki A.S.H. & Doudrop (w/Jacy Jayne)	L	NXT 2.0	10:50
Sep 9	Raquel Rodriguez & Aliyah (w/Jacy Jayne)	L	WWE SmackDown	5:00
Sep 20	Ivy Nile & Tatum Paxley (w/Jacy Jayne)	W	NXT	3:58
Oct 4	Nikkita Lyons & Zoey Stark (w/Jacy Jayne)	L	NXT	10:28
Nov 29	Katana Chance, Kayden Carter & Nikkita Lyons (w/Jacy Jayne & Mandy Rose)	W	NXT	8:54
Dec 13	Ivy Nile & Tatum Paxley (w/Jacy Jayne)	W	NXT	2:26
Dec 20	Kayden Carter & Katana Chance, Ivy Nile & Tatum Paxley (w/Jacy Jayne)	L	NXT	6:35

GINO MEDINA

Feb 24	Aramis, El Dragon & Micro Man (w/Arez & Mini Abismo Negro)	L	MLW Fusion	15:46
Mar 31	Micro Man, Octagon Jr. & Puma King (w/Arez & Mini Abismo Negro)	L	MLW Fusion	15:42
Apr 29	Aramis, KC Navarro & Micro Man (w/Arez & Mini Abismo Negro)	W	MLW Fusion	11:55
Jun 9	Mexican Strap Match: Aramis	W	MLW Fusion	5:37

GIOVANNI VINCI (AS FABIAN AICHNER UNTIL JUNE 14)

Jan 4	Riddle, Nash Carter & Wes Lee (w/Walter & Marcel Barthel)	L	NXT 2.0: New Year's Evil '22	13:52
Feb 1	Roderick Strong, Julius Creed & Brutus Creed (w/Gunther & Marcel Barthel)	W	NXT 2.0	12:01
Mar 8	Nash Carter & Wes Lee (w/Marcel Barthel)	D	NXT 2.0: Roadblock '22	5:33
Mar 29	LA Knight, Nash Carter & Wes Lee (w/Gunther & Marcel Barthel)	W	NXT 2.0	12:11
Apr 2	Wes Lee & Nash Carter, Brutus Creed & Julius Creed (w/Marcel Barthel)	L	NXT Stand & Deliver '22	11:22
Apr 5	Julius Creed & Brutus Creed (w/Marcel Barthel)	L	NXT 2.0	11:24
Jun 14	Guru Raaj	W	NXT 2.0	2:55
Jun 28	Ikemen Jiro	W	NXT 2.0	2:59
Jul 12	Apollo Crews	W	NXT 2.0	12:09
Jul 26	Andre Chase	W	NXT 2.0	9:10
Aug 16	Carmelo Hayes	L	NXT 2.0	11:56
Sep 9	Sheamus, Ridge Holland & Butch (w/Gunther & Ludwig Kaiser)	W	WWE SmackDown	19:05
Sep 16	Ridge Holland & Butch, Ashante Adonis & Top Dolla, Kofi Kingston & Xavier Woods (w/Ludwig Kaiser)	L	WWE SmackDown	18:44
Oct 8	Good Old Fashioned Donnybrook Match: Sheamus, Ridge Holland & Butch (w/Gunther & Ludwig Kaiser)	L	WWE Extreme Rules '22	17:50
Nov 18	Braun Strowman, Kofi Kingston & Xaiver Woods (w/Ludwig Kaiser & Gunther)	L	WWE SmackDown	7:38
Dec 9	Ricochet, Kofi Kingston & Xavier Woods (w/Gunther & Ludwig Kaiser)	L	WWE SmackDown	18:47
Dec 17	Drew McIntyre, Sheamus & Ricochet (w/Gunther & Ludwig Kaiser)	L	WWE Tribute To The Troops '22	16:34
Dec 23	Miracle On 34th Street Fight: Braun Strowman & Ricochet (w/Ludwig Kaiser)	L	WWE SmackDown	11:59

GISELE SHAW

| Feb 14 | Lady Frost | W | IMPACT Wrestling | 4:30 |
| Mar 17 | Deonna Purrazzo, Lady Frost | L | IMPACT Wrestling | 6:08 |

Mar 31	Battle Royal	L	IMPACT Wrestling	7:15
Apr 1	Madison Rayne & Tenille Dashwood, Tasha Steelz & Savannah Evans, Havok & Rosemary (w/Lady Frost)	L	IMPACT Multiverse Of Matches	9:02
May 5	Tenille Dashwood	L	IMPACT Before The Impact	7:58
May 12	Madison Rayne & Tenille Dashwood (w/Alisha Edwards)	L	IMPACT Wrestling	12:00
Jun 30	Rosemary	W	IMPACT Wrestling	5:51
Jul 7	Alisha Edwards	W	IMPACT Before The Impact	8:21
Aug 4	Masha Slamovich	L	IMPACT Wrestling	2:42
Aug 18	Rosemary	W	IMPACT Before The Impact	8:27
Sep 22	Hyan	W	IMPACT Before The Impact	6:20
Oct 6	Mia Yim	L	IMPACT Wrestling	7:15
Oct 7	Call Your Shot Gauntlet	L	IMPACT Bound For Glory '22	29:18
Oct 13	Jessicka, Rosemary & Taya Valkyrie (w/Chelsea Green & Deonna Purrazzo)	W	IMPACT Wrestling	12:55
Oct 27	Jordynne Grace, Mickie James & Taylor Wilde (w/Chelsea Green & Deonna Purrazzo)	L	IMPACT Wrestling	13:46
Nov 10	Jordynne Grace	L	IMPACT Wrestling	11:01
Dec 22	Jessicka & Rosemary (w/Deonna Purrazzo)	L	IMPACT Wrestling	5:39

GOLDBERG

Feb 19	Roman Reigns	L	WWE Elimination Chamber '22	6:00

GRAYSON WALLER

Jan 11	AJ Styles	L	NXT 2.0	14:15
Jan 18	Dexter Lumis	W	NXT 2.0	10:01
Feb 22	LA Knight	W	NXT 2.0	9:58
Mar 8	Last Man Standing Match: LA Knight	W	NXT 2.0: Roadblock '22	16:01
Mar 22	Ladder Match: A-Kid	W	NXT 2.0	2:51
Apr 2	Ladder Match: Cameron Grimes, Carmelo Hayes, Solo Sikoa, Santos Escobar	L	NXT Stand & Deliver '22	21:01
Apr 12	Gauntlet Match: Julius Creed & Brutus Creed, Kit Wilson & Elton Prince Joaquin Wilde & Raul Mendoza, Brooks Jensen & Josh Briggs (w/Sanga)	L	NXT 2.0	27:08
Apr 19	Sanga	W	NXT 2.0	3:28
May 3	Nathan Frazer	L	NXT 2.0: Spring Breakin'	12:45
May 10	Sarray & Andre Chase (w/Tiffany Stratton)	L	NXT 2.0	7:00
May 17	Andre Chase	W	NXT 2.0	4:12
May 31	Josh Briggs	W	NXT 2.0	3:33
Jun 7	Solo Sikoa & Apollo Crews (w/Carmelo Hayes)	L	NXT 2.0	13:45
Jun 21	Solo Sikoa	W	NXT 2.0	12:18
Jul 5	Carmelo Hayes	L	NXT 2.0: Great American Bash	11:43
Jul 26	Wes Lee	W	NXT 2.0	10:59
Aug 30	Apollo Crews	W	NXT 2.0	11:11
Sep 20	Oro Mensah	L	NXT	5:23
Oct 11	Ilja Dragunov	L	NXT	11:07
Oct 22	Casket Match: Apollo Crews	L	NXT Halloween Havoc '22	14:27
Nov 1	R-Truth	W	NXT	7:13
Nov 24	Akira Tozawa	L	WWE Main Event	7:02
Nov 29	Duke Hudson	W	NXT	5:20
Dec 10	Iron Survivor Challenge: Carmelo Hayes, Joe Gacy, Axiom, JD McDonagh	W	NXT Deadline	25:00

GREAT-O-KHAN

Jan 4	Tetsuya Naito, Sanada & Bushi (w/Will Ospreay & Jeff Cobb)	W	NJPW Wrestle Kingdom 16 Night #1	9:27
Jan 5	Sanada	L	NJPW Wrestle Kingdom 16 Night #2	13:21
Mar 1	Satoshi Kojima, Yuji Nagata, Kosei Fujita & Yuto Nakashima (w/Will Ospreay, Jeff Cobb & Aaron Henare)	W	NJPW 50th Anniversary Show	9:20
Apr 9	Hirooki Goto & Yoshi-Hashi (w/Jeff Cobb)	W	NJPW Hyper Battle '22	16:05
Apr 16	Hikuleo, Chris Bey, El Phantasmo, Karl Anderson, Luke Gallows & Scott Norton (w/Aaron Henare, Jeff Cobb, TJP, Mark Davis & Kyle Fletcher)	W	NJPW Windy City Riot	11:58
May 1	Bad Luck Fale & Chase Owens, Hirooki Goto & Yoshi-Hashi (w/Jeff Cobb)	L	NJPW Wrestling Dontaku '22	9:43
May 14	Chase Owens	L	NJPW Capital Collision	8:46
May 21	Brody King, Mascara Dorada & Taylor Rush (w/Aaron Henare & TJP)	W	NJPW Strong	14:04
Jun 12	Bad Luck Fale & Chase Owens (w/Jeff Cobb)	W	NJPW Dominion '22	11:52
Jun 26	Dax Harwood & Cash Wheeler, Rocky Romero & Trent Beretta (w/Jeff Cobb)	L	AEW x NJPW Forbidden Door	16:19
Jul 2	Bad Dude Tito, Jonah, Mikey Nicholls & Shane Haste (w/Aaron Henare, Kyle Fletcher & Mark Davis)	W	NJPW Strong	11:35
Sep 25	Bad Luck Fale & Chase Owens (w/Jeff Cobb)	W	NJPW Burning Spirit '22	7:57
Oct 1	Michael Oku & Ricky Knight Jr. (w/Gideon Grey)	L	NJPW Royal Quest II Night #1	12:17
Oct 2	Cash Wheeler, Dax Harwood, Shota Umino, Gabriel Kidd & Ricky Knight Jr. (w/Will Ospreay, Kyle Fletcher, Mark Davis & Gideon Grey)	W	NJPW Royal Quest II Night #2	16:57
Oct 10	Hirooki Goto & Yoshi-Hashi (w/Jeff Cobb)	W	NJPW Declaration Of Power	10:09
Nov 5	Cash Wheeler & Dax Harwood (w/Jeff Cobb)	L	NJPW Battle Autumn '22	17:31
Nov 20	Kazuchika Okada, Toru Yano & The Great Muta (w/Jeff Cobb & Aaron Henare)	L	NJPW x Stardom Historic X-Over	9:48

GREG SHARPE

May 28	Malakai Black, Brody King & Buddy Matthews (w/Adriel Noctis & Matt Brannigan)	L	AEW Dark	3:50
Oct 22	Jorel Nelson & Royce Isaacs (w/Jakob Austin Young)	L	NJPW Strong	6:01
Nov 10	Bhupinder Gujjar	L	IMPACT Wrestling	4:56
Nov 26	Kyle Fletcher & Mark Davis (w/Jakob Austin Young)	L	NJPW Strong	5:51
Dec 10	Kenny King	L	NJPW Strong	9:43

GRIFF GARRISON

Jan 18	Adrian Alanis & Liam Gray (w/Brian Pillman Jr.)	W	AEW Dark	2:03
Jan 19	Malakai Black & Brody King (w/Brian Pillman Jr.)	L	AEW Dynamite	1:53
Feb 22	Guillermo Rosas & Marcus Kross (w/Brian Pillman Jr.)	W	AEW Dark	5:52
Mar 2	Casino Battle Royale (w/Brian Pillman Jr.)	L	AEW Dynamite	10:23
Mar 22	Sotheara Chhun & Tony Vincita (w/Brian Pillman Jr.)	W	AEW Dark	3:36
Mar 23	Bryan Danielson & Jon Moxley (w/Brian Pillman Jr.)	L	AEW Dynamite	6:04
Apr 27	Adam Cole, Matt Jackson, Nick Jackson, Bobby Fish, Kyle O'Reilly (w/Dante Martin, Lee Johnson, Brock Anderson & Brian Pillman Jr.)	L	AEW Dynamite	6:28
May 3	Anthony Henry & JD Drake (w/Brian Pillman Jr.)	W	AEW Dark	6:33
May 23	The Butcher & The Blade (w/Brian Pillman Jr.)	L	AEW Dark Elevation	5:55
Jun 21	Jay Lucas, Larry Lazard & Terry Yaki (w/Brian Pillman Jr. & Brock Anderson)	W	AEW Dark	3:00
Jul 13	Luchasaurus	L	AEW Dynamite: Fyter Fest	1:28
Jul 19	Terrell Hughes & Terrence Hughes (w/Brian Pillman Jr.)	W	AEW Dark	3:16
Jul 20	Christian Cage & Luchasaurus (w/Brian Pillman Jr.)	L	AEW Dynamite: Fyter Fest	2:08
Aug 17	Austin Gunn & Colten Gunn (w/Brian Pillman Jr.)	L	AEW Dynamite	:31
Aug 30	Dean Alexander & Rosario Grillo (w/Brian Pillman Jr.)	W	AEW Dark	2:25
Oct 7	Josh Woods & Tony Nese (w/Brian Pillman Jr.)	L	AEW Rampage	1:45
Oct 24	Anthony Henry & JD Drake (w/Brian Pillman Jr.)	W	AEW Dark Elevation	5:47
Nov 8	Cole Karter & QT Marshall (w/Brian Pillman Jr.)	L	AEW Dark	4:13

GUNTHER (AS WALTER UNTIL FEB 1)

Jan 4	Riddle, Nash Carter & Wes Lee (w/Marcel Barthel & Fabian Aichner)	L	NXT 2.0: New Year's Evil '22	13:52
Jan 13	Nathan Frazer	W	NXT UK	14:02
Jan 18	Roderick Strong	W	NXT 2.0	12:15
Feb 1	Roderick Strong, Julius Creed & Brutus Creed (w/Marcel Barthel & Fabian Aichner)	W	NXT 2.0	12:01
Mar 1	Solo Sikoa	W	NXT 2.0	7:37
Mar 22	Duke Hudson	W	NXT 2.0	3:52
Mar 29	LA Knight, Nash Carter & Wes Lee (w/Marcel Barthel & Fabian Aichner)	W	NXT 2.0	12:11
Apr 2	LA Knight	W	NXT Stand & Deliver '22	10:24
Apr 5	Bron Breakker	L	NXT 2.0	13:08
Apr 8	Joe Alonzo	W	WWE SmackDown	2:05
Apr 22	Teddy Goodz	W	WWE SmackDown	2:10
May 6	Drew Gulak	W	WWE SmackDown	2:05
May 20	Drew Gulak	W	WWE SmackDown	1:04
May 27	Ricochet & Drew Gulak (w/Ludwig Kaiser)	W	WWE SmackDown	6:45
Jun 10	Ricochet	W	WWE SmackDown	8:35
Jun 24	Ricochet	W	WWE SmackDown	3:10
Jul 4	R-Truth	W	WWE Monday Night RAW	:55
Aug 12	Shinsuke Nakamura	W	WWE SmackDown	14:20
Sep 3	Sheamus	W	WWE Clash At The Castle	19:33
Sep 9	Sheamus, Ridge Holland & Butch (w/Ludwig Kaiser & Giovanni Vinci)	W	WWE SmackDown	19:05
Oct 7	Sheamus	W	WWE SmackDown	18:18
Oct 8	Good Old Fashioned Donnybrook Match: Sheamus, Ridge Holland & Butch (w/Ludwig Kaiser & Giovanni Vinci)	L	WWE Extreme Rules '22	17:50
Nov 4	Rey Mysterio	W	WWE SmackDown	18:18
Nov 18	Braun Strowman, Kofi Kingston & Xaiver Woods (w/Ludwig Kaiser & Giovanni Vinci)	L	WWE SmackDown	7:38
Dec 2	Kofi Kingston	W	WWE SmackDown	11:37
Dec 9	Ricochet, Kofi Kingston & Xavier Woods (w/Ludwig Kaiser & Giovanni Vinci)	L	WWE SmackDown	18:47
Dec 16	Ricochet	W	WWE SmackDown	21:37
Dec 17	Drew McIntyre, Sheamus & Ricochet (w/Giovanni Vinci & Ludwig Kaiser)	L	WWE Tribute To The Troops '22	16:34

GURU RAAJ

Jan 14	Bodhi Hayward	L	WWE 205 Live	3:44
Jan 18	Dante Chen	D	NXT 2.0	:58
Jan 25	Duke Hudson	L	NXT 2.0	1:08
Mar 11	Trick Williams	L	NXT Level Up	4:08
Apr 8	Javier Bernal	L	NXT Level Up	4:27
Jun 14	Giovanni Vinci	L	NXT 2.0	2:55
Jun 17	Myles Borne	L	NXT Level Up	4:55
Aug 5	Bryson Montana & Damaris Griffin (w/Dante Chen)	W	NXT Level Up	5:20
Sep 30	Edris Enofe & Malik Blade (w/Ikemen Jiro)	L	NXT Level Up	6:50
Oct 7	Myles Borne	L	NXT Level Up	5:36
Nov 22	Scrypts	L	NXT	1:22

HANGMAN PAGE

Jan 5	Bryan Danielson	W	AEW Dynamite	29:06
Jan 11	Matt Hardy, Serpentico & Isiah Kassidy (w/Alan Angels & Ten)	W	AEW Dark	14:27
Feb 9	Texas Death Match: Lance Archer	W	AEW Dynamite	15:29
Mar 2	Adam Cole, Bobby Fish & Kyle O'Reilly (w/John Silver & Alex Reynolds)	L	AEW Dynamite	12:43
Mar 6	Adam Cole	W	AEW Revolution '22	25:45
Mar 9	Dante Martin	W	AEW Dynamite	7:27
Mar 16	Adam Cole, Bobby Fish & Kyle O'Reilly (w/Jungle Boy & Luchasaurus)	L	AEW Dynamite: St. Patrick's Day Slam	13:58
Apr 15	Texas Death Match: Adam Cole	W	AEW Rampage	20:06
May 18	Konosuke Takeshita	W	AEW Dynamite: Wild Card Wednesday	12:14
May 29	CM Punk	L	AEW Double Or Nothing '22	25:40
Jun 8	David Finlay	W	AEW Dynamite	10:22
Jun 22	Silas Young	W	AEW Dynamite	8:44
Jun 26	Jay White, Kazuchika Okada, Adam Cole	L	AEW x NJPW Forbidden Door	21:05

Jul 1	Royal Rampage Match	L	AEW Rampage	22:41
Jul 22	The Butcher & The Blade (w/John Silver)	W	AEW Rampage: Fyter Fest	9:55
Sep 2	Orange Cassidy, Chuck Taylor & Trent Beretta (w/John Silver & Alex Reynolds)	W	AEW Rampage	11:12
Sep 3	Aaron Solo, Cole Karter & Nick Comoroto (w/John Silver & Alex Reynolds)	W	AEW Dark Elevation	6:00
Sep 4	Kenny Omega, Matt Jackson & Nick Jackson (w/Alex Reynolds & John Silver)	L	AEW All Out '22	19:50
Sep 7	Bryan Danielson	L	AEW Dynamite	22:52
Sep 23	Golden Ticket Battle Royale	W	AEW Rampage: Grand Slam	12:16
Oct 5	Rush	W	AEW Dynamite: Anniversary	9:05
Oct 18	Jon Moxley	L	AEW Dynamite: Title Tuesday	15:32

HANK WALKER

Jul 1	Channing Lorenzo	W	NXT 2.0	4:13
Jul 22	Duke Hudson	L	NXT Level Up	6:05
Sep 13	Javier Bernal	W	NXT 2.0	3:24
Oct 4	Xyon Quinn	L	NXT	2:15
Nov 4	Myles Borne	W	NXT Level Up	4:15
Nov 8	Channing Lorenzo	L	NXT	3:28
Dec 6	Charlie Dempsey	L	NXT	4:06
Dec 23	Trick Williams	L	NXT Level Up	6:13

HARRY SMITH

Mar 19	Alex Taylor & Rush Freeman (w/Doug Williams)	W	NWA Crockett Cup '22	6:38
Mar 19	Jordan Clearwater & Marshe Rockett (w/Doug Williams)	W	NWA Crockett Cup '22	12:50
Mar 20	Bestia 666 & Mecha Wolf (w/Doug Williams)	W	NWA Crockett Cup '22	8:58
Mar 20	Jay Briscoe & Mark Briscoe (w/Doug Williams)	L	NWA Crockett Cup '22	13:55
Apr 12	Dirty Dango & JTG (w/Doug Williams)	W	NWA Power	6:52
May 10	Matt Cardona, Mike Knox & VSK (w/Doug Williams & Nick Aldis)	W	NWA Power	8:15
Jun 11	Bestia 666 & Mecha Wolf (w/Doug Williams)	W	NWA Alwayz Ready '22	13:54
Jun 28	Lucha Rules Match: Bestia 666 & Mecha Wolf (w/Doug Williams)	W	NWA Power	5:08
Jul 26	Dirty Dango & JTG (w/Doug Williams)	W	NWA Power	6:13
Jul 31	Killer Kross	L	JCP Ric Flair's Last Match	5:22
Aug 23	Brady Pierce & Rush Freeman (w/Doug Williams)	W	NWA Power	4:48

HEATH

Jan 6	Karl Anderson	L	IMPACT Wrestling	11:02
Jan 8	Hardcore War: Luke Gallows, Karl Anderson, Eric Young, Deaner & Joe Doering (w/Eddie Edwards, Rich Swann, Willie Mack & Rhino)	W	IMPACT Hard To Kill '22	23:25
Jan 20	Luke Gallows & Joe Doering (w/Rhino)	L	IMPACT Wrestling	8:39
Mar 3	Vincent	W	IMPACT Wrestling	9:34
Mar 24	Steve Maclin	L	IMPACT Wrestling	4:50
Apr 21	Rich Swann & Willie Mack (w/Rhino)	W	IMPACT Before The Impact	7:56
Apr 23	Elimination Challenge Match (w/Rhino)	L	IMPACT Rebellion '22	33:02
Apr 28	Jay Briscoe & Mark Briscoe (w/Rhino)	L	IMPACT Wrestling	6:35
May 12	Gauntlet For The Gold	L	IMPACT Wrestling	39:00
Jun 2	Matt Taven & Mike Bennett (w/Rhino)	L	IMPACT Wrestling	6:15
Aug 18	Kenny King	W	IMPACT Wrestling	3:28
Sep 8	Eddie Edwards	L	IMPACT Wrestling	8:53
Sep 22	Street Fight: PCO	W	IMPACT Wrestling	9:12
Sep 29	PCO & Vincent (w/Rich Swann)	W	IMPACT Wrestling	4:32
Oct 7	Call Your Shot Gauntlet	L	IMPACT Bound For Glory '22	29:18
Oct 20	Matt Taven & Mike Bennett (w/Rhino)	W	IMPACT Wrestling	10:02
Dec 8	Alex Shelley & Chris Sabin (w/Rhino)	D	IMPACT Wrestling	8:34
Dec 15	Alex Shelley & Chris Sabin (w/Rhino)	L	IMPACT Wrestling	14:04

HERNANDEZ

Jan 6	Ace Austin & Madman Fulton (w/Johnny Swinger)	L	IMPACT Wrestling	3:40
May 19	Bunkhouse Brawl: Marshall Von Erich & Ross Von Erich (w/Rivera)	L	MLW Fusion	9:42

HIKARU SHIDA

Jan 12	Serena Deeb	L	AEW Dynamite	1:59
Mar 19	Hikari Noa	W	TJPW Grand Princess '22	8:33
Mar 28	Madi Wrenkowski	W	AEW Dark Elevation	1:39
Apr 6	Julia Hart	W	AEW Dynamite	7:45
Apr 18	Emi Sakura, Raychell Rose & The Bunny (w/Anna Jay & Ruby Soho)	W	AEW Dark Elevation	3:20
Apr 27	Street Fight: Serena Deeb	W	AEW Dynamite	11:40
Jul 4	Heather Reckless & Laynie Luck (w/Yuka Sakazaki)	W	AEW Dark Elevation	2:53
Jul 9	Mahiro Kiryu & Yuki Kamifuku (w/Hikari Noa)	W	TJPW Summer Sun Princess '22	13:32
Jul 25	Robyn Renegade	W	AEW Dark Elevation	5:33
Aug 1	Emi Sakura, Marina Shafir & Nyla Rose (w/Toni Storm & Willow Nightingale)	W	AEW Dark Elevation	8:05
Aug 4	Emi Sakura	W	AEW Dark Elevation	5:40
Aug 9	Emi Sakura, Leva Bates & Serena Deeb (w/Athena & Ruby Soho)	W	AEW Dark	8:08
Aug 15	Emi Sakura, Marina Shafir & Nyla Rose (w/Toni Storm & Thunder Rosa)	W	AEW Dark Elevation	2:42
Aug 22	Emi Sakura & Maki Itoh (w/Skye Blue)	L	AEW Dark Elevation	7:15
Aug 29	Emi Sakura	W	AEW Dark Elevation	6:30
Aug 31	Dr. Britt Baker D.M.D. & Jamie Hayter (w/Toni Storm)	W	AEW Dynamite	7:40
Sep 4	Toni Storm, Jamie Hayter, Dr. Britt Baker D.M.D.	L	AEW All Out '22	14:20
Sep 12	Christina Marie	W	AEW Dark Elevation	2:11
Oct 10	Erica Leigh	W	AEW Dark Elevation	2:40
Oct 11	Marina Shafir	W	AEW Dark	6:56

Oct 12	Dr. Britt Baker D.M.D. & Jamie Hayter (w/Toni Storm)	W	AEW Dynamite	8:18
Oct 18	Vanessa Kraven	W	AEW Dark	4:25
Oct 18	Toni Storm	L	AEW Dynamite: Title Tuesday	8:44
Nov 8	Emi Sakura & Mei Suruga (w/Toni Storm)	W	AEW Dark	7:51
Nov 21	Emi Sakura & Leva Bates (w/Willow Nightingale)	W	AEW Dark Elevation	4:28
Nov 25	Queen Aminata	W	AEW Rampage: Black Friday	1:18
Nov 29	Leyla Luciano	W	AEW Dark	2:37
Dec 9	The Bunny	W	AEW Rampage	7:26
Dec 21	Jamie Hayter	L	AEW Dynamite: Holiday Bash	16:16

HIKULEO

Jan 8	Jordan Clearwater & Keita Murray (w/Chris Bey)	W	NJPW Strong	9:12
Feb 12	Cody Chhun	W	NJPW Strong	7:34
Mar 12	Kevin Knight	W	NJPW Strong	8:13
Apr 9	Andy Brown	W	NJPW Strong	4:34
Apr 16	Aaron Henare, Great-O-Khan, Jeff Cobb, TJP, Mark Davis & Kyle Fletcher (w/Chris Bey, El Phantasmo, Karl Anderson, Luke Gallows & Scott Norton)	L	NJPW Windy City Riot	11:58
May 7	Barrett Brown & Bateman (w/Chris Bey)	W	NJPW Strong	12:16
May 13	Jay White	L	NJPW Strong	18:33
May 14	Kazuchika Okada & Rocky Romero (w/Jay White)	W	NJPW Capital Collision	15:59
Jun 1	Christian Cage, Matt Hardy, Darby Allin, Jungle Boy & Luchasaurus (w/Matt Jackson, Nick Jackson, Bobby Fish & Kyle O'Reilly)	L	AEW Dynamite	12:00
Jun 11	Chuck Taylor, Rocky Romero, Tomohiro Ishii, Mascara Dorada & Ren Narita (w/Luke Gallows, Karl Anderson, Jay White & Juice Robinson)	W	NJPW Strong	12:44
Jul 30	Fred Rosser, Hiroshi Tanahashi & Kevin Knight (w/Chase Owens & Jay White)	W	NJPW Strong	15:41
Aug 13	Big Damo	W	NJPW Strong	6:18
Aug 25	Johnny Swinger & Zicky Dice (w/Ace Austin)	W	IMPACT Before The Impact	7:46
Sep 17	Kushida, Taylor Rust, Trent Beretta & Rocky Romero (w/Chase Owens, Jay White & Juice Robinson)	W	NJPW Strong	14:46
Sep 25	Bushi, Hiromu Takahashi & Shingo Takagi (w/El Phantasmo & Kenta)	L	NJPW Burning Spirit '22	8:43
Oct 1	Jay White, Karl Anderson, Luke Gallows & Gedo (w/Hiroshi Tanahashi, Tama Tonga & Jado)	W	NJPW Royal Quest II Night #1	12:15
Oct 2	Jay White, Luke Gallows & Karl Anderson (w/Hiroshi Tanahashi & Tama Tonga)	W	NJPW Royal Quest II Night #2	10:54
Oct 10	Evi, Yujiro Takahashi & Sho (w/Hiroshi Tanahashi & Ryusuke Taguchi)	W	NJPW Declaration Of Power	7:14
Nov 5	Yujiro Takahashi	W	NJPW Battle Autumn '22	:28
Dec 10	El Phantasmo, Jay White, Jorel Nelson & Royce Isaacs (w/Alan Angels, David Finlay & Tama Tonga)	W	NJPW Strong	13:20

HIROMU TAKAHASHI

Jan 4	El Desperado	L	NJPW Wrestle Kingdom 16 Night #1	16:18
Jan 8	Katsuhiko Nakajima, Kenoh, Manabu Soya, Tadasuke & Aljea (w/Tetsuya Naito, Shingo Takagi, Sanada & Bushi)	W	NJPW Wrestle Kingdom 16 Night #3	26:33
Mar 1	Togi Makabe, Tomoaki Honma, Tomohiro Ishii, Toru Yano & Shiro Koshinaka (w/Sanada, Tetsuya Naito, Shingo Takagi & Bushi)	W	NJPW 50th Anniversary Show	12:38
Apr 9	Evil	L	NJPW Hyper Battle '22	15:47
May 1	Yoh	W	NJPW Wrestling Dontaku '22	9:59
Jun 12	Taiji Ishimori, El Phantasmo & Ace Austin (w/Tetsuya Naito & Bushi)	L	NJPW Dominion '22	8:04
Jul 30	Blake Christian	W	NJPW Music City Mayhem	13:59
Aug 20	El Desperado, Blake Christian	L	NJPW Strong	19:19
Sep 25	El Phantasmo, Hikuleo & Kenta (w/Bushi & Shingo Takagi)	W	NJPW Burning Spirit '22	8:43
Oct 1	Zack Sabre Jr., El Desperado & Douki (w/Tetsuya Naito & Sanada)	W	NJPW Royal Quest II Night #1	14:29
Oct 2	Ethan Allen & Luke Jacob (w/Sanada)	W	NJPW Royal Quest II Night #2	14:04
Oct 10	Will Ospreay, Aaron Henare, TJP & Francesco Akira (w/Tetsuya Naito, Sanada & Bushi)	W	NJPW Declaration Of Power	8:07
Nov 5	Master Wato & El Desperado (w/Taiji Ishimori)	L	NJPW Battle Autumn '22	16:48
Nov 20	Kyle Fletcher, Mark David, Francesco Akira, TJP & Gideon Grey (w/Bushi, Sanada, Shingo Takagi & Tetsuya Naito)	L	NJPW x Stardom Historic X-Over	9:55

HIROOKI GOTO

Jan 4	Taichi & Zack Sabre Jr. (w/Yoshi-Hashi)	W	NJPW Wrestle Kingdom 16 Night #1	15:27
Jan 5	Evil, Yujiro Takahashi & Sho (w/Yoshi-Hashi & Yoh)	L	NJPW Wrestle Kingdom 16 Night #2	9:37
Jan 8	Daisuke Harada, Hajime Ohara, Daiki Inaba, Yoshiki Inamura & Kinya Okada (w/Tomohiro Ishii, Yoshi-Hashi, Master Wato & Ryusuke Taguchi)	W	NJPW Wrestle Kingdom 16 Night #3	11:42
Mar 1	Ryusuke Taguchi & Master Wato (w/Yoshi-Hashi)	W	NJPW 50th Anniversary Show	15:04
Apr 9	Great-O-Khan & Jeff Cobb (w/Yoshi-Hashi)	L	NJPW Hyper Battle '22	16:05
May 1	Bad Luck Fale & Chase Owens, Great-O-Khan & Jeff Cobb (w/Yoshi-Hashi)	L	NJPW Wrestling Dontaku '22	9:43
Jun 12	Hiroshi Tanahashi	L	NJPW Dominion '22	12:40
Jun 26	Aaron Solo & QT Marshall (w/Yoshi-Hashi)	W	AEW x NJPW Forbidden Door Buy-In	8:53
Jul 1	Matt Jackson & Nick Jackson (w/Yoshi-Hashi)	L	AEW Rampage	9:31
Oct 10	Great-O-Khan & Jeff Cobb (w/Yoshi-Hashi)	L	NJPW Declaration Of Power	10:09
Nov 20	Hiroshi Tanahashi & Utami Hayashishita (w/Maika)	L	NJPW x Stardom Historic X-Over	9:36

HIROSHI TANAHASHI

Jan 4	Kenta, Taiji Ishimori & El Phantasmo (w/Ryusuke Taguchi & Rocky Romero)	L	NJPW Wrestle Kingdom 16 Night #1	8:40
Jan 5	No DQ: Kenta	W	NJPW Wrestle Kingdom 16 Night #2	22:40
Jan 8	Keiji Mutoh & Kaito Kiyomiya (w/Kazuchika Okada)	W	NJPW Wrestle Kingdom 16 Night #3	24:34
Mar 1	Zack Sabre Jr., Minoru Suzuki & Yoshiaki Fujiwara (w/Kazuchika Okada & Tatsumi Fujinami)	W	NJPW 50th Anniversary Show	18:12
Apr 9	Bad Luck Fale, Chase Owens, Yujiro Takahashi & Gedo (w/Tama Tonga, Tanga Loa & Jado)	W	NJPW Hyper Battle '22	10:28

May 1	Tomohiro Ishii	W	NJPW Wrestling Dontaku '22	23:20
May 14	Juice Robinson, Will Ospreay, Jox Moxley	L	NJPW Capital Collision	15:45
Jun 12	Hirooki Goto	W	NJPW Dominion '22	12:40
Jun 18	Chris Dickinson	W	NJPW Strong	13:15
Jun 22	Chris Jericho & Lance Archer (w/Jon Moxley)	W	AEW Dynamite	12:12
Jun 26	Jon Moxley	L	AEW x NJPW Forbidden Door	18:14
Jul 30	Chase Owens, Hikuleo & Jay White (w/Fred Rosser & Kevin Knight)	L	NJPW Strong	15:41
Sep 25	Karl Anderson	L	NJPW Burning Spirit '22	13:37
Oct 1	Jay White, Karl Anderson, Luke Gallows & Gedo (w/Tama Tonga, Hikuleo & Jado)	W	NJPW Royal Quest II Night #1	12:15
Oct 2	Jay White, Luke Gallows, Karl Anderson (w/Tama Tonga & Hikuleo)	W	NJPW Royal Quest II Night #2	10:54
Oct 10	Evil, Yujiro Takahashi & Sho (w/Hikuleo & Ryusuke Taguchi)	W	NJPW Declaration Of Power	7:14
Nov 5	Gabriel Kidd	W	NJPW Strong	11:30
Nov 5	Aaron Henare, Gideon Grey, Kyle Fletcher & Mark Davis (w/Toru Yano, David Finlay & Alex Zayne)	L	NJPW Battle Autumn '22	9:50
Nov 20	Hirooki Goto & Maika (w/Utami Hayashishita)	W	NJPW x Stardom Historic X-Over	9:36

HOLIDEAD

Apr 14	Shazza McKenzie	L	MLW Fusion	5:04
May 12	Chik Tormenta	W	MLW Fusion	4:07
Jun 16	Taya Valkyrie	L	MLW Fusion	9:00
Jun 30	Lince Dorado, Micro Man & Taya Valkyrie (w/Arez & Mini Abismo Negro)	L	MLW Fusion	6:32

HOMICIDE

Jan 5	Jax Dane, Odinson & Parrow (w/Bestia 666 & Mecha Wolf)	W	NWA Power	6:54
Feb 8	Team War Elimination Match: Chris Adonis, Thom Latimer & El Rudo, Matt Taven, Mike Bennett & Victor Benjamin, Wrecking Ball Legusrky, Jay Bradley & Colby Corino (w/Bestia 666 & Mecha Wolf)	L	NWA Power	11:09
Mar 20	Austin Aries, Colby Corino, Darius Lockhart	W	NWA Crockett Cup '22	9:39
Mar 22	Austin Aries	W	NWA Power	8:04
Apr 26	Rhett Titus	W	NWA Power	7:53
May 31	Colby Corino	W	NWA Power	9:55
Jun 11	PJ Hawx	W	NWA Alwayz Ready '22	10:50
Jun 11	Colby Corino	W	NWA Alwayz Ready '22	9:06
Jul 2	Will Ospreay	L	NJPW Strong	20:47
Aug 27	Kerry Morton	W	NWA 74th Anniversary Show	12:38
Aug 28	Ricky Morton	W	NWA 74th Anniversary Show	6:12
Oct 8	Wheeler Yuta	W	NJPW Strong	14:37
Oct 28	Tom Lawlor, Royce Isaacs & Jorel Nelson (w/Wheeler Yuta & Shota Umino)	W	NJPW Rumble On 44th Street	12:15
Nov 12	Kerry Morton	L	NWA Hard Times 3	10:02
Nov 19	Tom Lawlor	W	NJPW Strong	13:44
Dec 3	Danny Limelight	W	NJPW Strong	11:14

HOOK

Jan 7	Aaron Solo	W	AEW Rampage	3:19
Jan 21	Serpentico	W	AEW Rampage	1:10
Feb 11	Blake Li	W	AEW Rampage	2:51
Mar 6	QT Marshall	W	AEW Revolution Buy-In	5:00
Apr 20	Anthony Henry	W	AEW Dynamite	1:23
May 6	JD Drake	W	AEW Rampage	1:25
May 29	Tony Nese & Mark Sterling (w/Danhausen)	W	AEW Double Or Nothing Buy-In	5:20
Jun 24	The DKC	W	AEW Rampage	1:40
Jul 27	Ricky Starks	W	AEW Dynamite: Fight For The Fallen	1:32
Aug 19	Zack Clayton	W	AEW Rampage	:30
Sep 4	Angelo Parker	W	AEW All Out Buy-In	3:55
Sep 23	Angelo Parker & Matt Menard (w/Action Bronson)	W	AEW Rampage: Grand Slam	5:10
Oct 21	Ari Daivari	W	AEW Rampage	2:47
Nov 18	Lee Moriarty	W	AEW Rampage	8:39
Dec 21	Exodus Prime	W	AEW Dynamite: Holiday Bash	1:04
Dec 28	Baylum Lynx	W	AEW Dynamite	:57

HUMBERTO

Jan 14	Erik & Ivar, Cesaro & Mansoor, Jinder Mahal & Shanky (w/Angel)	L	WWE SmackDown	13:21
Jan 21	Erik & Ivar (w/Angel)	L	WWE SmackDown	2:20
Feb 4	Big E & Kofi Kingston (w/Angel)	L	WWE SmackDown	8:58
Feb 11	Big E & Kofi Kingston (w/Angel)	W	WWE SmackDown	10:20
Feb 25	Big E & Kofi Kingston (w/Angel)	L	WWE SmackDown	10:30
Mar 18	Shinsuke Nakamura & Rick Boogs (w/Angel)	L	WWE SmackDown	4:55
Mar 25	Ricochet	W	WWE SmackDown	7:18
Apr 1	Ricochet, Angel	L	WWE SmackDown	11:20
Apr 15	Madcap Moss	L	WWE SmackDown	2:46
May 16	Finn Balor & AJ Styles (w/Angel)	L	WWE Monday Night RAW	8:30
May 27	Jinder Mahal & Shanky (w/Angel)	W	WWE SmackDown	2:15
Jun 3	Jinder Mahal	L	WWE SmackDown	3:34
Jul 8	Jimmy Uso & Jey Uso (w/Angel)	L	WWE SmackDown	2:00
Sep 5	Chad Gable & Otis, Kofi Kingston & Xavier Woods, Angelo Dawkins & Montez Ford (w/Angel)	D	WWE Monday Night RAW	14:30
Sep 9	Angelo Dawkins, Montez Ford, Ashante Adonis & Top Dolla (w/Angel, Mace & Mansoor)	L	WWE SmackDown	8:35
Sep 30	Ashante Adonis & Top Dolla (w/Angel)	L	WWE SmackDown	3:21

IKEMEN JIRO

Jan 7	Ru Feng	W	WWE 205 Live	6:39
Jan 25	Nash Carter & Wes Lee (w/Kushida)	L	NXT 2.0	11:32
Feb 11	Trick Williams	L	WWE 205 Live	5:09
Feb 25	Harland & Joe Gacy (w/Kushida)	L	NXT Level Up	6:55
Mar 25	Malik Blade & Edris Enofe (w/Kushida)	L	NXT Level Up	7:33
Apr 12	Von Wagner	L	NXT 2.0	2:55
May 24	Von Wagner	L	NXT 2.0	4:13
Jun 10	Dante Chen	W	NXT Level Up	7:01
Jun 24	Ru Feng	W	NXT Level Up	5:27
Jun 28	Giovanni Vinci	L	NXT 2.0	2:59
Jul 15	Quincy Elliott	W	NXT Level Up	5:05
Jul 29	Malik Blade & Edris Enofe (w/Quincy Elliott)	L	NXT Level Up	6:01
Aug 12	Myles Borne	W	NXT Level Up	5:12
Aug 26	Nathan Frazer	L	NXT Level Up	6:29
Sep 9	Channing Lorenzo	W	NXT Level Up	5:16
Sep 30	Edris Enofe & Malik Blade (w/Guru Raaj)	L	NXT Level Up	6:50
Oct 14	Bryson Montana & Duke Hudson (w/Tank Ledger)	W	NXT Level Up	6:18
Oct 21	Myles Borne	L	NXT Level Up	5:18
Nov 11	Javier Bernal	L	NXT Level Up	5:07
Dec 9	Trick Williams	L	NXT Level Up	5:50
Dec 13	Javier Bernal	W	NXT	3:16
Dec 27	Scypts	L	NXT	4:14

INDI HARTWELL

Jan 11	Kacy Katanzaro, Kayden Carter & Amari Miller (w/Wendy Choo & Persia Pirotta)	W	NXT 2.0	3:30
Jan 25	Mandy Rose, Gigi Dolin & Jacy Jayne (w/Kay Lee Ray & Persia Pirotta)	W	NXT 2.0	10:25
Feb 15	Gig Dolin & Jacy Jayne (w/Persia Pirotta)	L	NXT 2.0: Vengeance Day '22	7:54
Mar 1	Wendy Choo & Dakota Kai (w/Persia Pirotta)	L	NXT 2.0	5:21
Mar 15	Persia Pirotta	W	NXT 2.0	2:24
May 24	Mandy Rose	L	NXT 2.0	9:18
Jun 14	Mandy Rose, Gigi Dolin & Jacy Jayne (w/Roxanne Perez & Cora Jade)	W	NXT 2.0	13:51
Jun 28	Kiana James	L	NXT 2.0	3:51
Jul 12	Lash Legend	W	NXT 2.0	3:45
Jul 19	Battle Royal	L	NXT 2.0	13:13
Jul 26	Arianna Grace	W	NXT 2.0	3:59
Aug 23	Blair Davenport	L	NXT 2.0	3:49
Sep 16	Amari Miller	W	NXT Level Up	5:10
Sep 23	Valentina Feroz	W	NXT Level Up	4:37
Oct 7	Sloane Jacobs	W	NXT Level Up	3:20
Oct 11	Valentina Feroz	W	NXT	3:33
Oct 25	Sol Ruca	W	NXT	1:19
Nov 1	Zoey Stark	W	NXT	6:30
Nov 15	Tatum Paxley	W	NXT	4:00
Nov 29	Roxanne Perez	L	NXT	9:07
Dec 6	Fallon Henley, Wendy Choo	W	NXT	10:15
Dec 10	Iron Survivor Challenge: Roxanne Perez, Zoey Stark, Cora Jade, Kiana James	L	NXT Deadline	25:00
Dec 20	Elektra Lopez	L	NXT	3:35

ILJA DRAGUNOV

Jan 27	Empty Arena Match: Jordan Devlin	W	NXT UK	21:43
Mar 3	Nathan Frazer	W	NXT UK	14:42
Apr 7	Roderick Strong	W	NXT UK	14:40
May 12	Loser Leaves NXT UK: Jordan Devlin	W	NXT UK	14:53
Jul 28	Wolfgang	W	NXT UK	15:55
Sep 27	Xyon Quinn	W	NXT	4:55
Oct 11	Grayson Waller	W	NXT	11:07
Oct 22	Bron Breakker, JD McDonagh	L	NXT Halloween Havoc '22	23:47
Oct 25	JD McDonagh	L	NXT	9:58

ISIAH KASSIDY

Jan 10	John Silver, Alex Reynolds & Ten (w/Marq Quen & The Blade)	L	AEW Dark Elevation	4:01
Jan 11	Hangman Page, Alan Angels & Ten (w/Matt Hardy & Serpentico)	L	AEW Dark	14:27
Jan 17	Chase Emory & Patrick Scott (w/Marq Quen)	W	AEW Dark Elevation	3:10
Jan 24	Action Andretti & Myles Hawkins (w/Marq Quen)	W	AEW Dark Elevation	3:20
Jan 28	Jungle Boy & Luchasaurus (w/Marq Quen)	L	AEW Rampage: Beach Break	10:45
Feb 4	Sammy Guevara	L	AEW Rampage	9:14
Feb 9	Keith Lee	L	AEW Dynamite	4:29
Feb 10	Dante Martin, Lee Moriarty & Matt Sydal (w/Marq Quen & The Blade)	L	AEW Dark	9:05
Feb 21	Baron Black, Carlie Bravo, Chandler Hopkins, Jameson Ryan & Shawn Dean (w/Andrade El Idolo, Marq Quen, The Butcher & The Blade)	W	AEW Dark Elevation	4:20
Feb 23	Tag Team Battle Royal (w/Marq Quen)	L	AEW Dynamite	4:44
Mar 6	Tornado Match: Darby Allin, Sammy Guevara & Sting (w/Matt Hardy & Andrade El Idolo)	L	AEW Revolution '22	13:20
Mar 8	Brock Anderson & Lee Johnson (w/Marq Quen)	W	AEW Dark	5:05
Mar 16	Matt Hardy & Jeff Hardy (w/Marq Quen)	L	AEW Dynamite: St. Patrick's Day Slam	12:22
Mar 23	Tornado Match: Sting, Darby Allin, Matt Hardy & Jeff Hardy (w/Mark Quen, The Butcher & The Blade)	L	AEW Dynamite	9:27
Apr 18	Jeff Hardy, Matt Hardy, Dante Martin & Darius Martin (w/Marq Quen, Angelico & Jack Evans)	L	AEW Dark Elevation	9:45

Apr 26	Frankie Kazarian, Jeff Hardy, Matt Hardy, Dante Martin & Darius Martin (w/Max Caster, Angelico, Marq Quen & The Blade)	L	AEW Dark	12:40
May 25	Jon Moxley & Eddie Kingston (w/Marq Quen)	L	AEW Dynamite	7:20
Jun 13	Pharell Jackson & SK Bishop (w/Marq Quen)	W	AEW Dark Elevation	3:00
Jul 12	Bear Boulder & Bear Bronson (w/Marq Quen)	W	AEW Dark	10:45
Jul 15	Penta El Zero M & Rey Fenix (w/Marq Quen)	L	AEW Rampage	11:16
Jul 25	Adrian Alanis, AR Fox & Liam Gray (w/Marq Quen & Angelico)	W	AEW Dark Elevation	3:59
Aug 1	JCruz, Joey Ace, Victor Chase, Jaylen Brandyn & Traevon Jordan (w/Marq Quen, Angelico, The Butcher & The Blade)	W	AEW Dark Elevation	2:12
Aug 9	Braden Lee, Isaiah Broner, James Alexander & Sam Moore (w/The Butcher, The Blade & Marq Quen)	W	AEW Dark	2:22
Aug 15	Jah-C & JDX (w/Marq Quen)	W	AEW Dark Elevation	1:49
Aug 19	Keith Lee & Swerve Strickland (w/Marq Quen)	L	AEW Rampage	7:15
Sep 5	Brandon Gore & JDX (w/Marq Quen)	W	AEW Dark Elevation	2:07
Sep 6	GPA & Robert Anthony (w/Marq Quen)	W	AEW Dark	5:16
Sep 19	Aggro & DangerKid (w/Marq Quen)	W	AEW Dark Elevation	4:46
Sep 23	Golden Ticket Battle Royale	L	AEW Rampage: Grand Slam	12:16
Sep 30	Anthony Bowens & Max Caster, The Butcher & The Blade (w/Marq Quen)	L	AEW Rampage	10:00
Oct 7	Claudio Castagnoli, Jon Moxley & Wheeler Yuta (w/Rush & Marq Quen)	L	AEW Rampage	10:16
Oct 14	Ethan Page	L	AEW Rampage	2:10
Nov 14	Channing Thomas, Kyle Bradley & Smiley Fairchild (w/Matt Hardy & Marq Quen)	W	AEW Dark Elevation	3:46
Nov 21	Encore, Ari Daivari & Sonny Kiss (w/Matt Hardy & Marq Quen)	W	AEW Dark Elevation	3:15
Nov 28	Isaia Moore, Luther & Serpentico (w/Matt Hardy & Marq Quen)	W	AEW Dark Elevation	4:50
Nov 29	Cezar Bononi, Peter Avalon & Ryan Nemeth (w/Matt Hardy & Marq Quen)	W	AEW Dark	7:16
Dec 2	Jay Lethal & Jeff Jarrett (w/Marq Quen)	L	AEW Rampage	7:04
Dec 19	Jeeves Kay, Slim J, Sonny Kiss, Cezaro Bononi, Peter Avalon & Ryan Nemeth (w/Ethan Page, Konosuke Takeshita, Matt Hardy, Dante Martin & Darius Martin)	W	AEW Dark Elevation	7:45

ISLA DAWN

Jan 20	Emilia McKenzie	W	NXT UK	5:30
Feb 3	Myla Grace	W	NXT UK	2:59
Mar 24	Meiko Satomura	L	NXT UK	8:04
May 5	World Of Darkness Match: Meiko Satomura	L	NXT UK	12:48
Jun 23	Myla Grace	W	NXT UK	5:03
Jul 21	Fallon Henley	W	NXT UK	5:12
Aug 4	Blair Davenport	D	NXT UK	7:15
Sep 1	Elimination Match: Blair Davenport, Amale, Elize Alexander	L	NXT UK	15:07
Dec 6	Thea Hail	W	NXT	2:51
Dec 10	Alba Fyre	W	NXT Deadline	9:52

IVAR

Jan 7	Happy Corbin & Madcap Moss (w/Erik)	L	WWE SmackDown	3:30
Jan 14	Angel & Humberto, Cesaro & Mansoon, Jinder Mahal & Shanky (w/Erik)	W	WWE SmackDown	13:21
Jan 21	Angel & Humberto (w/Erik)	W	WWE SmackDown	2:20
Feb 18	Jey Uso	W	WWE SmackDown	2:35
Mar 4	Jimmy Uso & Jey Uso (w/Erik)	L	WWE SmackDown	8:25
Mar 18	Happy Corbin, Jinder Mahal & Shanky (w/Drew McIntyre & Erik)	W	WWE SmackDown	7:10
Mar 28	Handicap Match: Omos (w/Erik)	L	WWE Monday Night RAW	:50
Apr 1	Andre The Giant Memorial Battle Royal	L	WWE SmackDown	8:05
Apr 26	Edris Enofe & Malik Blade (w/Erik)	W	NXT 2.0	4:45
May 3	Julius Creed & Brutus Creed (w/Erik)	L	NXT 2.0: Spring Breakin'	12:58
May 17	Julius Creed & Brutus Creed (w/Erik)	W	NXT 2.0	9:30
Jul 8	Jinder Mahal & Shanky (w/Erik)	W	WWE SmackDown	1:15
Jul 22	Jinder Mahal & Shanky (w/Erik)	W	WWE SmackDown	1:30
Jul 29	Xavier Woods & Kofi Kingston (w/Erik)	W	WWE SmackDown	9:15
Aug 5	Jim Mulkey & Tommy Gibson (w/Erik)	W	WWE SmackDown	1:35
Sep 2	Viking Rules Match: Kofi Kingston & Xavier Woods (w/Erik)	W	WWE SmackDown	22:15
Nov 25	Ashante Adonis & Top Dolla (w/Erik)	W	WWE SmackDown	2:46
Dec 9	Joaquin Wilde & Cruz Del Toro (w/Erik)	D	WWE SmackDown	1:53
Dec 16	Ashante Adonis & Top Dolla, Joaquin Wilde & Cruz Del Toro (w/Erik)	L	WWE SmackDown	9:20

IVORY

Jan 29	Royal Rumble Match	L	WWE Royal Rumble '22	:25

IVY NILE

Jan 14	Valentina Feroz	W	WWE 205 Live	4:39
Jan 18	Kay Lee Ray	W	NXT 2.0	4:25
Feb 18	Fallon Henley & Kayla Inlay (w/Tatum Paxley)	W	NXT Level Up	4:18
Feb 22	Kayden Carter & Kacy Catanzaro (w/Tatum Paxley)	L	NXT 2.0	3:26
Mar 11	Brooklyn Barlow	W	NXT Level Up	3:50
Mar 25	Kiana James	W	NXT Level Up	4:15
Mar 29	Tiffany Stratton	W	NXT 2.0	3:32
Apr 8	Thea Hail	W	NXT Level Up	4:08
May 6	Erica Yan & Sarray (w/Tatum Paxley)	W	NXT Level Up	5:32
May 12	Nina Samuels	W	NXT UK	4:41
May 20	Yulisa Leon	W	NXT Level Up	5:16
May 31	Kiana James	W	NXT 2.0	3:36
Jun 9	Meiko Satomura	L	NXT UK	10:26
Jun 17	Elektra Lopez	W	NXT Level Up	5:51
Jul 19	Battle Royal	L	NXT 2.0	13:13

Aug 2	Elimination Match: Kayden Carter & Katana Chance, Valentina Feroz & Yulisa Leon, Gigi Dolin & Jacy Jayne (w/Tatum Paxley)	L	NXT 2.0	12:09
Aug 19	Arianna Grace	W	NXT Level Up	4:24
Aug 30	Kayden Carter & Katana Chance (w/Tatum Paxley)	L	NXT 2.0	4:17
Sep 16	Erica Yan & Sloane Jacobs (w/Tatum Paxley)	W	NXT Level Up	5:21
Sep 20	Gigi Dolin & Jacy Jayne (w/Tatum Paxley)	L	NXT	3:58
Oct 14	Lash Legend	W	NXT Level Up	6:16
Nov 4	Sol Ruca	W	NXT Level Up	4:51
Nov 11	Jakara Jackson & Lash Legend (w/Tatum Paxley)	W	NXT Level Up	4:42
Nov 22	Kiana James	W	NXT	4:43
Dec 13	Gigi Dolin & Jacy Jayne (w/Tatum Paxley)	L	NXT	2:26
Dec 16	Lash Legend	W	NXT Level Up	5:03
Dec 20	Kayden Carter & Katana Chance, Gigi Dolin & Jacy Jayne (w/Tatum Paxley)	L	NXT	6:35

IYO SKY (AS IO SHIRAI UNTIL AUGUST 1)

Jan 25	Tiffany Stratton	W	NXT 2.0	4:18
Feb 22	Amari Miller & Lash Legend (w/Kay Lee Ray)	W	NXT 2.0	2:44
Mar 8	Kacy Katanzara & Kayden Carter (w/Kay Lee Ray)	W	NXT 2.0: Roadblock '22	7:59
Mar 22	Wendy Choo & Dakota Kai (w/Kay Lee Ray)	W	NXT 2.0	10:22
Apr 2	Mandy Rose, Kay Lee Ray, Cora Jade	L	NXT Stand & Deliver '22	13:27
Aug 1	Bianca Belair	D	WWE Monday Night RAW	17:15
Aug 8	Dana Brooke & Tamina (w/Dakota Kai)	W	WWE Monday Night RAW	10:00
Aug 22	Alexa Bliss & Asuka (w/Dakota Kai)	W	WWE Monday Night RAW	18:30
Aug 29	Raquel Rodriguez & Aliyah (w/Dakota Kai)	L	WWE Monday Night RAW	11:17
Sep 3	Bianca Belair, Alexa Bliss & Asuka (w/Bayley & Dakota Kai)	W	WWE Clash At The Castle	18:44
Sep 12	Raquel Rodriguez & Aliyah (w/Dakota Kai)	W	WWE Monday Night RAW	12:30
Sep 26	Bianca Belair	L	WWE Monday Night RAW	18:08
Oct 3	Alexa Bliss	W	WWE Monday Night RAW	9:15
Oct 14	Raquel Rodriguez, Shotzi & Roxanne Perez (w/Bayley & Dakota Kai)	W	WWE SmackDown	6:42
Oct 17	Bianca Belair & Candice LeRae (w/Dakota Kai)	W	WWE Monday Night RAW	12:10
Oct 21	Shotzi & Raquel Rodriguez (w/Dakota Kai)	W	WWE SmackDown	9:58
Oct 31	Alexa Bliss & Asuka (w/Dakota Kai)	L	WWE Monday Night RAW	16:25
Nov 5	Alexa Bliss & Asuka (w/Dakota Kai)	W	WWE Crown Jewel '22	12:50
Nov 14	Dana Brooke	W	WWE Monday Night RAW	3:15
Nov 26	WarGames: Bianca Belair, Alexa Bliss, Asuka, Mia Yim & Becky Lynch (w/Bayley, Dakota Kai, Nikki Cross & Rhea Riplkey)	L	WWE Survivor Series WarGames	39:40
Dec 12	Candice LeRae	W	WWE Monday Night RAW	10:20
Dec 16	Liv Morgan & Tegan Nox (w/Dakota Kai)	W	WWE SmackDown	14:48

JACK EVANS

Mar 1	Dante Martin	L	AEW Dark	7:47
Apr 18	Jeff Hardy, Matt Hardy, Dante Martin & Darius Martin (w/Angelico, Isiah Kassidy & Marq Quen)	L	AEW Dark Elevation	9:45

JACK STARZ

Jan 13	Rohan Raja & Teoman (w/Dave Mastiff)	W	NXT UK	9:24
Feb 3	Ashton Smith & Oliver Carter (w/Dave Mastiff)	L	NXT UK	12:31
Mar 3	Lewis Howley & Sam Stoker (w/Dave Mastiff)	W	NXT UK	10:34
Apr 14	Joe Coffey & Mark Coffey (w/Dave Mastiff)	W	NXT UK	8:30
May 19	Charlie Dempsey & Rohan Raja (w/Dave Mastiff)	L	NXT UK	8:01
Jun 23	Elimination Match: Brooks Jensen & Josh Briggs, Charlie Dempsey & Rohan Raja, Mark Andrews & Wild Boar (w/Dave Mastiff)	L	NXT UK	18:15

JACOB FATU

Feb 24	Mads Krugger	W	MLW Fusion	4:54
Mar 24	Stairway To Hell Match: Mads Krugger	L	MLW Fusion	14:32
Apr 29	Alexander Hammerstone, Mds Krugger	L	MLW Fusion	13:34
May 12	Aztec Apocalypto Match: Bestia 666	W	MLW Fusion	9:41
Jun 23	Weapons Of Mass Destruction Match: Mads Krugger	W	MLW Fusion	16:27
Jul 31	Josh Alexander	D	JCP Ric Flair's Last Match	10:14
Nov 10	Real1	W	MLW Fusion	2:01

JACY JAYNE

Jan 25	Kay Lee Ray, Indi Hartwell & Persia Pirotta (w/Mandy Rose & Gigi Dolin)	L	NXT 2.0	10:25
Feb 15	Indi Hartwell & Persia Pirotta (w/Gigi Dolin)	W	NXT 2.0: Vengeance Day '22	7:54
Apr 2	Raquel Gonzalez & Dakota Kai (w/Gigi Dolin)	L	NXT Stand & Deliver Kickoff	7:53
Apr 5	Dakota Kai & Raquel Gonzalez (w/Gigi Dolin)	W	NXT 2.0	8:31
Apr 19	Roxanne Perez	L	NXT 2.0	2:17
May 10	Roxanne Perez & Wendy Choo (w/Gigi Dolin)	W	NXT 2.0	10:01
Jun 4	Katana Chance & Kayden Carter (w/Gigi Dolin)	W	NXT In Your House '22	9:01
Jun 14	Roxanne Perez, Cora Jade & Indi Hartwell (w/Mandy Rose & Gigi Dolin)	L	NXT 2.0	13:51
Jul 5	Roxanne Perez & Cora Jade (w/Gigi Dolin)	L	NXT 2.0: Great American Bash	10:29
Aug 2	Elimination Match: Kayden Carter & Katana Chance, Valentina Feroz & Yulisa Leon, Ivy Nile & Tatum Paxley (w/Gigi Dolin)	L	NXT 2.0	12:09
Aug 19	Natalya & Sonya Deville (w/Gigi Dolin)	W	WWE SmackDown	8:48
Sep 6	Nikki A.S.H. & Doudrop (w/Gigi Dolin)	L	NXT 2.0	10:50
Sep 9	Raquel Rodriguez & Aliyah (w/Gigi Dolin)	L	WWE SmackDown	5:00
Sep 20	Ivy Nile & Tatum Paxley (w/Gigi Dolin)	W	NXT	3:58
Oct 4	Nikkita Lyons & Zoey Stark (w/Gigi Dolin)	L	NXT	10:28
Oct 11	Alba Fyre	L	NXT	3:34
Nov 29	Katana Chance, Kayden Carter & Nikkita Lyons	W	NXT	8:54

	(w/Mandy Rose & Gigi Dolin)			
Dec 13	Ivy Nile & Tatum Paxley (w/Gigi Dolin)	W	NXT	2:26
Dec 20	Kayden Carter & Katana Chance, Ivy Nile & Tatum Paxley (w/Gigi Dolin)	L	NXT	6:35

JADE CARGILL

Jan 5	Ruby Soho	W	AEW Dynamite	11:13
Jan 11	Skye Blue	W	AEW Dark	1:59
Jan 21	Anna Jay	W	AEW Rampage	8:45
Jan 28	Julia Hart	W	AEW Rampage: Beach Break	2:28
Feb 9	AQA	W	AEW Dynamite	7:44
Feb 23	The Bunny	W	AEW Dynamite	6:50
Mar 6	Tay Conti	W	AEW Revolution '22	6:40
Apr 22	Marina Shafir	W	AEW Rampage	11:41
Apr 29	Skye Blue, Willow Nightingale, Trish Adora (w/Red Velvet & Kiera Hogan)	W	AEW Rampage	2:46
May 29	Anna Jay	W	AEW Double Or Nothing '22	7:25
Jun 17	Willow Nightingale	W	AEW Rampage: Road Rager	4:58
Jun 29	Leila Grey	W	AEW Dynamite -Blood & Guts	1:55
Jul 20	Athena & Willow Nightingale (w/Kiera Hogan)	W	AEW Dynamite	8:25
Aug 10	Madison Rayne	W	AEW Dynamite: Quake By The Lake	7:48
Sep 4	Athena	W	AEW All Out '22	4:20
Sep 23	Diamante	W	AEW Rampage: Grand Slam	2:36
Oct 7	Willow Nightingale	W	AEW Battle Of The Belts IV	7:30
Oct 31	Trish Adora	W	AEW Dark Elevation	1:50
Nov 2	Marina Shafir	W	AEW Dynamite	2:20
Nov 19	Nyla Rose	W	AEW Full Gear '22	8:00
Dec 7	Kiera Hogan, Skye Blue & Madison Rayne (w/Leila Grey & Red Velvet)	W	AEW Dynamite	8:13
Dec 20	Dream Girl Ellie	W	AEW Dark	1:20
Dec 23	Vertvixen	W	AEW Rampage	4:57
Dec 30	Kiera Hogan	W	AEW Rampage	6:26

JAGGER REID (AS JAMES DRAKE UNTIL JUNE 14)

Jan 21	Bodhi Hayward	W	WWE 205 Live	4:36
Jan 25	Andre Chase & Bodhi Hayward (w/Zack Gibson)	W	NXT 2.0	5:11
Feb 8	Julius Creed & Brutus Creed (w/Zack Gibson)	L	NXT 2.0	12:03
Feb 25	Xyon Quinn	W	NXT Level Up	4:53
Mar 11	Brooks Jensen & Josh Briggs (w/Zack Gibson)	W	NXT Level Up	5:58
Mar 22	Julius Creed & Brutus Creed (w/Zack Gibson)	L	NXT 2.0	4:14
Apr 1	Damon Kemp	L	NXT Level Up	6:22
Apr 19	Joaquin Wilde & Raul Mendoza (w/Zack Gibson)	L	NXT 2.0	3:57
Jun 14	Dante Chen & Javier Bernal (w/Rip Fowler)	W	NXT 2.0	3:56
Jun 28	Roderick Strong, Julius Creed & Brutus Creed (w/Joe Gacy & Rip Fowler)	W	NXT 2.0	13:56
Aug 23	Joaquin Wilde & Cruz Del Toro (w/Rip Fowler)	W	NXT 2.0	5:02
Sep 20	Malik Blade & Edris Enofe (w/Rip Fowler)	W	NXT	9:17
Oct 11	Malik Blade & Edris Enofe, Brooks Jensen & Josh Briggs (w/Rip Fowler)	L	NXT	9:10
Oct 18	Cameron Grimes, Luke Gallows & Karl Anderson (w/Rip Fowler & Joe Gacy)	L	NXT	11:56
Nov 15	Brooks Jensen & Josh Briggs (w/Rip Fowler)	W	NXT	4:10
Dec 16	Bronco Nima & Lucien Price (w/Rip Fowler)	W	NXT Level Up	5:39
Dec 27	Malik Blade, Edris Enofe & Odyssey Jones (w/Rip Fowler & Joe Gacy)	W	NXT	11:15

JAKARA JACKSON

Oct 28	Thea Hail	W	NXT Level Up	4:25
Nov 11	Ivy Nile & Tatum Paxley (w/Lash Legend)	L	NXT Level Up	4:42

JAKE ATLAS

Jan 3	Serpentico	W	AEW Dark Elevation	2:19
Jan 7	Adam Cole	L	AEW Rampage	9:39

JAKE HAGER

Feb 16	Santana & Ortiz (w/Chris Jericho)	L	AEW Dynamite	10:43
Apr 13	Eddie Kingston, Santana & Ortiz (w/Chris Jericho & Jake Hager)	W	AEW Dynamite	11:46
May 29	Anarchy In The Arena: Bryan Danielson, Jon Moxley, Eddie Kingston, Santana & Ortiz (w/Daniel Garcia, Chris Jericho, Angelo Parker & Matt Menard)	W	AEW Double Or Nothing '22	22:45
Jun 8	Casino Battle Royale	L	AEW Dynamite	24:59
Jun 10	Eddie Kingston	L	AEW Rampage	11:24
Jun 29	Blood & Guts: Jon Moxley, Claudio Castagnoli, Wheeler Yuta, Eddie Kingston, Santana & Ortiz (w/Daniel Garcia, Chris Jericho, Matt Menard, Angelo Parker & Sammy Guevara)	L	AEW Dynamite: Blood & Guts	46:45
Jul 13	Claudio Castagnoli	L	AEW Dynamite: Fyter Fest	11:32
Aug 31	Bryan Danielson	L	AEW Dynamite	10:46
Sep 23	Golden Ticket Battle Royale	L	AEW Rampage: Grand Slam	12:16
Nov 22	Bryce Donovan	W	AEW Dark	2:41
Nov 23	Orange Cassidy	L	AEW Dynamite: Thanksgiving Eve	8:38
Dec 7	Claudio Castagnoli & Wheeler Yuta (w/Daniel Garcia)	L	AEW Dynamite	12:42

JAKE SOMETHING

Jan 6	Jonah	L	IMPACT Wrestling	8:22
Jan 13	Mike Bailey	L	IMPACT Wrestling	4:17
Jan 27	Chris Bey	W	IMPACT Wrestling	9:22
Feb 3	Chris Bey, Jay White, Tama Tonga & Tanga Loa (w/Mike Bailey, Madman Fulton & Ace Austin)	L	IMPACT Wrestling	16:49

Feb 24	Ace Austin & Mike Bailey (w/Trey Miguel)	L	IMPACT Before The Impact	8:01
May 10	Jay Lethal	L	AEW Dark	4:30
Jun 18	Brody King	L	NJPW Strong	8:27
Jun 28	Matt Sydal	L	AEW Dark	5:53
Jul 19	Danhausen	L	AEW Dark	3:55
Sep 3	Eddie Kingston	L	NJPW Strong	8:35
Nov 26	Juice Robinson	L	NJPW Strong	10:44

JAMES STORM

Jun 23	Eddie Edwards, Matt Taven & Mike Bennett (w/Jay Briscoe & Mark Briscoe)	L	IMPACT Wrestling	12:12
Jul 14	Steve Maclin	L	IMPACT Wrestling	8:34

JAMIE HAYTER

Jan 4	Madi Wrenkowski	W	AEW Dark	3:36
Jan 7	Riho & Ruby Soho (w/Dr. Britt Baker D.M.D.)	L	AEW Rampage	8:10
Mar 2	Thunder Rosa & Mercedes Martinez (w/Dr. Britt Baker D.M.D.)	L	AEW Dynamite	8:32
Mar 11	Mercedes Martinez	W	AEW Rampage	8:42
Mar 28	Rache Chanel	W	AEW Dark Elevation	1:44
Apr 1	Skye Blue	W	AEW Rampage	5:36
May 6	Toni Storm & Ruby Soho (w/Dr. Britt Baker D.M.D.)	L	AEW Rampage	8:38
May 11	Toni Storm	L	AEW Dynamite	8:32
May 31	Danika Della Rouge	W	AEW Dark	1:20
Jun 1	Toni Storm & Ruby Soho (w/Dr. Britt Baker D.M.D.)	L	AEW Dynamite	9:48
Jul 22	Ashley D'Amboise & Skye Blue (w/Dr. Britt Baker D.M.D.)	W	AEW Rampage: Fyter Fest	5:00
Aug 3	Toni Storm & Thunder Rosa (w/Dr. Britt Baker D.M.D.)	W	AEW Dynamite	12:02
Aug 6	Thunder Rosa	L	AEW Battle Of The Belts III	11:31
Aug 31	Toni Storm & Hikaru Shida (w/Dr. Britt Baker D.M.D.)	L	AEW Dynamite	7:40
Sep 4	Toni Storm, Dr. Britt Baker D.M.D., Hikaru Shida	L	AEW All Out '22	14:20
Sep 30	Willow Nightingale	W	AEW Rampage	7:12
Oct 5	Toni Storm, Athena & Willow Nightingale (w/Serena Deeb & Penelope Ford)	L	AEW Dynamite: Anniversary	9:29
Oct 11	Brittany Blake, Jordan Blade & Trish Adora (w/Penelope Ford & Serena Deeb)	W	AEW Dark	4:32
Oct 12	Toni Storm & Hikaru Shida (w/Dr. Britt Baker D.M.D.)	L	AEW Dynamite	8:18
Oct 26	Riho	W	AEW Dynamite	10:52
Nov 4	Madison Rayne & Skye Blue (w/Dr. Britt Baker D.M.D.)	W	AEW Rampage	7:18
Nov 9	Skye Blue	W	AEW Dynamite	6:48
Nov 19	Toni Storm	W	AEW Full Gear '22	15:00
Nov 23	Anna Jay & Tay Melo, Willow Nightingale & Skye Blue (w/Dr. Britt Baker D.M.D.)	W	AEW Dynamite: Thanksgiving Eve	8:05
Dec 21	Hikaru Shida	W	AEW Dynamite: Holiday Bash	16:16

JASON HOTCH

Aug 25	Bhupinder Gujjar	L	IMPACT Wrestling	2:17
Sep 29	Yuya Uemura	L	IMPACT Before The Impact	8:30
Oct 20	Joe Hendry	L	IMPACT Wrestling	1:54
Dec 8	Trey Miguel	L	IMPACT Before The Impact	8:27
Dec 29	Yuya Uemura & Delirious (w/John Skyler)	L	IMPACT Before The Impact	9:08

JAVIER BERNAL

Jan 21	Draco Anthony	L	WWE 205 Live	4:53
Feb 18	Harland	L	NXT Level Up	1:55
Mar 4	Dante Chen	L	NXT Level Up	3:59
Apr 8	Guru Raaj	W	NXT Level Up	4:27
May 6	Channing Lorenzo & Troy Donovan (w/Dante Chen)	L	NXT Level Up	6:04
May 13	Trick Williams	L	NXT Level Up	6:20
May 20	Bryson Montana	W	NXT Level Up	4:13
Jun 3	Malik Blade & Edris Enofe (w/Dante Chen)	L	NXT Level Up	7:05
Jun 14	Rip Fowler & Jagger Reid (w/Dante Chen)	L	NXT 2.0	3:56
Jul 1	Duke Hudson	L	NXT Level Up	6:53
Jul 15	Andre Chase & Bodhi Hayward (w/Myles Borne)	L	NXT Level Up	5:47
Jul 29	Myles Borne	W	NXT Level Up	4:04
Aug 19	Dante Chen	L	NXT Level Up	4:31
Aug 23	Cameron Grimes	L	NXT 2.0	2:35
Sep 13	Hank Walker	L	NXT 2.0	3:24
Sep 30	Ru Feng	W	NXT Level Up	5:20
Oct 11	Bron Breakker	L	NXT	3:20
Oct 21	Andre Chase	L	NXT Level Up	6:48
Nov 1	Odyssey Jones	L	NXT	3:20
Nov 11	Ikemen Jiro	W	NXT Level Up	5:07
Nov 29	Axiom	L	NXT	9:03
Dec 13	Ikemen Jiro	L	NXT	3:16
Dec 16	Andre Chase & Duke Hudson (w/Xyon Quinn)	L	NXT Level Up	7:16
Dec 30	Oro Mensah	L	NXT Level Up	6:18

JAX DANE

Jan 5	Homicide, Bestia 666 & Mecha Wolf (w/Odinson & Parrow)	L	NWA Power	6:54
Feb 22	Eric Jackson	W	NWA Power	1:26
Mar 20	Anthony Mayweather	L	NWA Crockett Cup '22	10:11
Mar 20	Anthony Mayweather	W	NWA Crockett Cup '22	:31
May 17	Team War: BLK Jeez, Jordan Clearwater & Marshe Rockett, Alex Taylor,	W	NWA Power	6:54

Jeremiah Plunkett & Rush Freeman (w/Odinson & Parrow)

Jun 11	Chris Adonis	W	NWA Alwayz Ready '22	10:19
Aug 27	Cyon	L	NWA 74th Anniversary Show	7:26
Dec 13	Chris Adonis	L	NWA Power	7:17
Dec 20	Trevor Murdoch	D	NWA Power	8:47

JAY BRADLEY

Jan 18	Handicap Match: Dirty Dango & JTG	W	NWA Power	4:29
	(w/Wrecking Ball Legursky & Rush Freeman)			
Feb 8	Team War Elimination Match: Chris Adonis, Thom Latimer & El Rudo,	L	NWA Power	11:09
	Matt Taven, Mike Bennett & Victor Benjamin, Homicide, Bestia 666 &			
	Mecha Wolf (w/Wrecking Ball Legursky & Colby Corino)			
Mar 1	Matt Taven & Mike Bennett (w/Wrecking Ball Legursky)	W	NWA Power	10:47
Mar 19	Mike Knox & VSK (w/Wrecking Ball Legursky)	L	NWA Crockett Cup '22	7:03
Apr 12	Gaagz The Gymp, Judais & Sal The Pal	L	NWA Power	6:27
	(w/Wrecking Ball Legursky & Colby Corino)			
May 3	No DQ Match: El Rudo & Jamie Stanley (w/Wrecking Ball Legursky)	W	NWA Power	8:33
Jul 5	Kerry Morton	L	NWA Power	5:16
Aug 28	Tag Team Battle Royal (w/Wrecking Ball Legursky)	W	NWA 74th Anniversary Show	14:07
Nov 12	Brady Pierce & Rush Freeman (w/Wrecking Ball Legursky)	W	NWA Hard Times 3	9:15
Dec 27	Kerry Morton & Ricky Morton (w/Wrecking Ball Legursky)	L	NWA Power	6:26

JAY BRISCOE

Mar 19	Dirty Dango & JTG (w/Mark Briscoe)	W	NWA Crockett Cup '22	8:13
Mar 20	Mike Knox & VSK (w/Mark Briscoe)	W	NWA Crockett Cup '22	7:45
Mar 20	Doug Williams & Harry Smith (w/Mark Briscoe)	W	NWA Crockett Cup '22	13:55
Mar 22	Matt Taven & Mike Bennett (w/Mark Briscoe)	W	NWA Power	6:56
Apr 1	Luke Gallows & Karl Anderson (w/Mark Briscoe)	L	IMPACT Multiverse Of Matches	9:46
Apr 1	Dax Harwood & Cash Wheeler (w/Mark Briscoe)	L	ROH Supercard Of Honor XV	27:25
Apr 26	Bestia 666 & Mecha Wolf (w/Mark Briscoe)	L	NWA Power	9:56
Apr 28	Heath & Rhino (w/Mark Briscoe)	W	IMPACT Wrestling	6:35
May 19	Deaner & Joe Doering (w/Mark Briscoe)	W	IMPACT Wrestling	15:00
May 26	Deaner, Eric Young & Joe Doering (w/Mark Briscoe & Josh Alexander)	L	IMPACT Wrestling	17:09
Jun 16	Chris Bey & Jay White (w/Mark Briscoe)	W	IMPACT Wrestling	11:02
Jun 19	Luke Gallows & Karl Anderson (w/Mark Briscoe)	L	IMPACT Slammiversary XX	10:00
Jun 23	Eddie Edwards, Matt Taven & Mike Bennett	L	IMPACT Wrestling	12:12
	(w/Mark Briscoe & James Storm)			
Jul 23	2/3 Falls: Dax Harwood & Cash Wheeler (w/Mark Briscoe)	L	ROH Death Before Dishonor XIX	43:25
Jul 31	Marshall Von Erich & Ross Von Erich (w/Mark Briscoe)	W	JCP Ric Flair's Last Match	7:43
Dec 10	Double Dog Collar Match: Dax Harwood & Cash Wheeler	W	ROH Final Battle '22	22:20
	(w/Mark Briscoe)			

JAY LETHAL

Jan 3	Troy Hollywood	W	AEW Dark Elevation	3:58
Jan 10	Chris Steeler & Jaden Valo (w/Sonny Kiss)	W	AEW Dark Elevation	2:32
Jan 17	Alexander Moss	W	AEW Dark Elevation	4:40
Jan 31	Casey Carrington	W	AEW Dark Elevation	3:10
Feb 4	Ricky Starks	L	AEW Rampage	12:51
Feb 19	Jay White	L	NJPW Strong	20:07
Feb 21	Luther, Serpentico, Cezar Bononi, JD Drake & Peter Avalon	W	AEW Dark Elevation	6:06
	(w/Brock Anderson, Frankie Kazarian, Lee Johnson & Matt Sydal)			
Feb 28	Jora Johl	W	AEW Dark Elevation	3:27
Mar 8	Serpentico	W	AEW Dark	5:12
Mar 14	Merrik Donovan	W	AEW Dark Elevation	2:23
Mar 22	JD Drake	W	AEW Dark	5:44
Mar 23	Adam Cole	L	AEW Dynamite	10:04
Mar 30	Jon Moxley	L	AEW Dynamite	11:03
Apr 1	Lee Moriarty	W	ROH Supercard Of Honor XV	14:50
Apr 30	Ren Narita	W	NJPW Strong	12:17
May 6	Konosuke Takeshita	W	AEW Rampage	9:38
May 10	Jake Something	W	AEW Dark	4:30
Jun 10	Mat Fitchett & Davey Vega (w/Satnam Singh)	W	AEW Rampage	1:37
Jun 21	Blake Christian	W	AEW Dark	9:54
Jul 4	Cage Alexander & Ryan Jones (w/Satnam Singh)	W	AEW Dark Elevation	2:30
Jul 5	Darian Bengston & Gus De La Vega (w/Satnam Singh)	W	AEW Dark	4:11
Jul 19	Logan Cruz	W	AEW Dark	2:20
Jul 22	Christopher Daniels	W	AEW Rampage: Fyter Fest	11:00
Jul 23	Samoa Joe	L	ROH Death Before Dishonor XIX	12:20
Jul 29	Orange Cassidy, Chuck Taylor & Trent Beretta	L	AEW Rampage	7:29
	(w/Satnam Singh & Sonjay Dutt)			
Jul 31	Ric Flair & Andrade El Idolo (w/Jeff Jarrett)	L	JCP Ric Flair's Last Match	26:40
Aug 3	Orange Cassidy	W	AEW Dynamite	12:18
Aug 6	Wardlow	L	AEW Battle Of The Belts III	7:21
Aug 24	Dax Harwood	W	AEW Dynamite	12:47
Sep 4	Wardlow, Dax Harwood & Cash Wheeler (w/Chris Sabin & Alex Shelley)	L	AEW All Out '22	16:30
Sep 14	Jungle Boy	L	AEW Dynamite	10:38
Sep 23	Golden Ticket Battle Royale	L	AEW Rampage: Grand Slam	12:16
Oct 5	Darby Allin	L	AEW Dynamite: Anniversary	10:15
Oct 17	Dylan Davis & Junior Benito (w/Satnam Singh)	W	AEW Dark Elevation	2:32
Nov 2	Darby Allin	W	AEW Dynamite	9:08
Nov 9	Trent Beretta	W	AEW Dynamite	7:17
Nov 19	Darby Allin & Sting (w/Jeff Jarrett)	L	AEW Full Gear '22	11:00

Nov 28	GPA & Joe Alonzo (w/Satnam Singh)	W	AEW Dark Elevation	1:44
Dec 2	Marq Quen & Isiah Kassidy (w/Jeff Jarrett)	W	AEW Rampage	7:04
Dec 6	JCruz & Victor Chase (w/Satnam Singh)	W	AEW Dark	1:54
Dec 23	Anthony Bowens & Billy Gunn (w/Jeff Jarrett)	W	AEW Rampage	11:46

JAY WHITE

Jan 29	Christopher Daniels	W	NJPW Strong	19:07
Feb 3	Jake Something, Mike Bailey, Madman Fulton & Ace Austin (w/Chris Bey, Tama Tonga & Tanga Loa)	W	IMPACT Wrestling	16:49
Feb 17	Eric Young, Deaner & Joe Doering (w/Tama Tonga & Tanga Loa)	W	IMPACT Wrestling	13:19
Feb 18	Trent Beretta	W	AEW Rampage: Slam Dunk	15:11
Feb 19	Jay Lethal	W	NJPW Strong	20:07
Mar 3	Tama Tonga, Tanga Loa, Deaner & Joe Doering (w/Chris Bey, Luke Gallows & Karl Anderson)	W	IMPACT Wrestling	9:48
Mar 12	Swerve Strickland	W	NJPW Strong	17:15
Mar 17	Alex Shelley & Chris Sabin (w/Chris Bey)	L	IMPACT Wrestling	12:38
Mar 31	Alex Shelley & Chris Sabin (w/Chris Bey)	W	IMPACT Wrestling	17:42
Apr 1	Chris Sabin	L	IMPACT Multiverse Of Matches	16:00
Apr 1	Mike Bailey	W	NJPW Lonestar Shootout	14:10
Apr 9	Chris Sabin	W	NJPW Strong	18:12
Apr 16	Shota Umino	W	NJPW Windy City Riot	15:45
Apr 21	Kenny King, Matt Taven, Mike Bennett & Vincent (w/Chris Bey, Luke Gallows & Karl Anderson)	W	IMPACT Wrestling	9:22
Apr 23	Steve Maclin, Chris Sabin	L	IMPACT Rebellion '22	12:07
May 5	Willie Mack & Rich Swann (w/Chris Bey)	W	IMPACT Wrestling	6:28
May 12	Josh Alexander & Tomohiro Ishii (w/El Phantasmo)	L	IMPACT Wrestling	10:28
May 13	Hikuleo	W	NJPW Strong	18:33
May 14	Kazuchika Okada & Rocky Romero (w/Hikuleo)	W	NJPW Capital Collision	15:59
Jun 11	Chuck Taylor, Rocky Romero, Tomohiro Ishii, Mascara Dorada & Ren Narita (w/Luke Gallows, Karl Anderson, Juice Robinson & Hikuleo)	W	NJPW Strong	12:44
Jun 12	Kazuchika Okada	W	NJPW Dominion '22	36:04
Jun 16	Jay Briscoe & Mark Briscoe (w/Chris Bey)	L	IMPACT Wrestling	11:02
Jun 26	Hangman Page, Kazuchika Okada, Adam Cole	W	AEW x NJPW Forbidden Door	21:05
Jul 30	Fred Rosser, Hiroshi Tanahashi & Kevin Knight (w/Chase Owens & Hikuleo)	W	NJPW Strong	15:41
Sep 17	Kushida, Taylor Rust, Trent Beretta & Rocky Romero (w/Chase Owens, Hikuleo & Juice Robinson)	W	NJPW Strong	14:46
Sep 25	Jado & Tama Tonga (w/Taiji Ishimori)	W	NJPW Burning Spirit '22	10:39
Oct 1	Hiroshi Tanahashi, Tama Tonga, Hikuleo & Jado (w/Karl Anderson, Luke Gallows & Gedo)	L	NJPW Royal Quest II Night #1	12:15
Oct 2	Hiroshi Tanahashi, Tama Tonga & Hikuleo (w/Luke Gallows & Karl Anderson)	L	NJPW Royal Quest II Night #2	10:54
Oct 8	Homicide & Wheeler Yuta (w/Karl Anderson)	W	NJPW Strong	14:37
Oct 10	Tama Tonga	W	NJPW Declaration Of Power	31:07
Oct 28	Kazuchika Okada & Eddie Kingston (w/Juice Robinson)	W	NJPW Rumble On 44th Street	20:15
Nov 5	Kazuchika Okada & Tama Tonga (w/Kenta)	L	NJPW Battle Autumn '22	17:34
Nov 26	Fred Rosser	W	NJPW Strong	19:22
Dec 10	Jorel Nelson & Royce Isaacs (w/El Phantasmo)	W	NJPW Strong	13:20

JD DRAKE

Jan 4	Brian Pillman Jr.	L	AEW Dark	6:06
Jan 11	Orange Cassidy	L	AEW Dark	9:04
Jan 18	Orange Cassidy & Wheeler Yuta (w/Peter Avalon)	L	AEW Dark	7:32
Feb 21	Brock Anderson, Frankie Kazarian, Jay Lethal, Lee Johnson & Matt Sydal (w/Luther, Serpentico, Cezar Bononi & Peter Avalon)	L	AEW Dark Elevation	6:06
Feb 22	Caleb Teninity, Karam, Rohit Raju & Sotheara Chhun (w/Cezar Bononi, Peter Avalon & Ryan Nemeth)	W	AEW Dark	2:29
Mar 4	Keith Lee	L	AEW Rampage	5:50
Mar 9	Bryan Danielson & Jon Moxley (w/Anthony Henry)	L	AEW Dynamite	4:00
Mar 22	Jay Lethal	L	AEW Dark	5:44
Apr 4	Chuck Taylor & Trent Beretta (w/Anthony Henry)	L	AEW Dark Elevation	8:00
May 3	Brian Pillman Jr. & Griff Garrison (w/Anthony Henry)	L	AEW Dark	6:33
May 6	Hook	L	AEW Rampage	1:25
May 17	Bear Boulder & Bear Bronson (w/Anthony Henry)	L	AEW Dark	8:30
May 18	Keith Lee & Swerve Strickland (w/Anthony Henry)	L	AEW Dynamite: Wild Card Wednesday	2:24
Jun 1	Wardlow	L	AEW Dynamite	1:11
Jun 28	Evil Uno & Ten (w/Ryan Nemeth)	L	AEW Dark	8:16
Jul 5	John Silver, Alex Reynolds, Evil Uno & Ten (w/Cezar Bononi, Peter Avalon & Ryan Nemeth)	L	AEW Dark	7:22
Jul 11	Dante Martin	L	AEW Dark Elevation	7:13
Jul 25	Konosuke Takeshita	L	AEW Dark Elevation	3:40
Aug 9	Evil Uno & Ten (w/Peter Avalon)	L	AEW Dark	4:15
Aug 23	Dean Alexander & Rosario Grillo (w/Anthony Henry)	W	AEW Dark	3:41
Aug 27	Kushida & Ren Narita (w/Anthony Henry)	L	NJPW Strong	11:18
Aug 30	Manny Lo & Oliver Sawyer (w/Anthony Henry)	W	AEW Dark	2:32
Sep 20	Matt Sydal	L	AEW Dark	9:30
Oct 4	Dante Martin & Matt Sydal (w/Anthony Henry)	L	AEW Dark	9:34
Oct 24	Brian Pillman Jr. & Griff Garrison (w/Anthony Henry)	L	AEW Dark Elevation	5:47
Oct 25	Penta El Zero M & Rey Fenix (w/Anthony Henry)	L	AEW Dark	2:55
Dec 19	Claudio Castagnoli & Wheeler Yuta (w/Anthony Henry)	L	AEW Dark Elevation	7:55
Dec 27	Terrell Hughes & Terrence Hughes (w/Anthony Henry)	W	AEW Dark	5:38

JD MCDONAGH

Jan 27	Empty Arena Match: Ilja Dragunov	L	NXT UK	21:43
Feb 17	Wolfgang	W	NXT UK	13:40
Mar 24	Danny Jones	W	NXT UK	4:44
May 12	Loser Leaves NXT UK: Ilja Dragunov	L	NXT UK	14:53
Jul 19	Cameron Grimes	W	NXT 2.0	13:25
Aug 16	Bron Breakker	L	NXT 2.0: Heatwave	13:17
Sep 6	Wes Lee	W	NXT 2.0	9:37
Sep 20	Tyler Bate	W	NXT	12:54
Oct 22	Bron Breakker, Ilja Dragunov	L	NXT Halloween Havoc '22	23:47
Oct 25	Ilja Dragunov	W	NXT	9:58
Nov 8	Axiom	W	NXT	10:40
Nov 15	Apollo Crews	L	NXT	13:55
Nov 17	Cedric Alexander	L	WWE Main Event	10:00
Nov 29	Julius Creed	L	NXT	10:33
Dec 10	Iron Survivor Challenge: Grayson Waller, Carmelo Hayes, Joe Gacy, Axiom	L	NXT Deadline	25:00
Dec 13	Brutus Creed	W	NXT	4:18
Dec 27	Julius Creed	L	NXT	9:51

JEEVES KAY

Sep 27	Gus De La Vega	W	AEW Dark	1:55
Nov 7	Dalton Castle, Brandon Tate & Brent Tate (w/Ari Daivari & Slim J)	L	AEW Dark Elevation	5:25
Nov 22	John Silver, Alex Reynolds & Evil Uno (w/Ari Daivari & Sonny Kiss)	L	AEW Dark	5:26
Dec 13	Eddie Kingston & Ortiz (w/Slim J)	L	AEW Dark	6:59
Dec 19	Ethan Page, Isiah Kassidy, Konosuke Takeshita, Matt Hardy, Dante Martin & Darius Martin (w/Slim J, Sonny Kiss, Cezar Bononi, Peter Avalon & Ryan Nemeth)	L	AEW Dark Elevation	7:45

JEFF COBB

Jan 4	Tetsuya Naito, Sanada & Bushi (w/Will Ospreay & Great-O-Khan)	W	NJPW Wrestle Kingdom 16 Night #1	9:27
Jan 5	Tetsuya Naito	L	NJPW Wrestle Kingdom 16 Night #2	15:34
Mar 1	Satoshi Kojima, Yuji Nagata, Kosei Fujita & Yuto Nakashima (w/Great-O-Khan, Will Ospreay & Aaron Henare)	W	NJPW 50th Anniversary Show	9:20
Apr 9	Hirooki Goto & Yoshi-Hashi (w/Great-O-Khan)	W	NJPW Hyper Battle '22	16:05
Apr 16	Hikuleo, Chris Bey, El Phantasmo, Karl Anderson, Luke Gallows & Scott Norton (w/Aaron Henare, Great-O-Khan, TJP, Mark Davis & Kyle Fletcher)	W	NJPW Windy City Riot	11:58
May 1	Bad Luke Fale & Chase Owens, Hirooki Goto & Yoshi-Hashi (w/Great-O-Khan)	L	NJPW Wrestling Dontaku '22	9:43
May 14	Mikey Nicholls, Shane Haste, Jonah & Bad Dude Tito (w/Aaron Henare, Kyle Fletcher & Mark Davis)	L	NJPW Capital Collision	12:09
May 28	Bad Dude Tito, Jonah & Shane Haste (w/Kyle Fletcher & Mark Davis)	W	NJPW Strong	14:39
Jun 12	Bad Luck Fale & Chase Owens (w/Great-O-Khan)	W	NJPW Dominion '22	11:52
Jun 24	Cash Wheeler	W	AEW Rampage	10:55
Jun 26	Dax Harwood & Cash Wheeler, Rocky Romero & Trent Beretta (w/Great-O-Khan)	L	AEW x NJPW Forbidden Door	16:19
Jul 2	Willie Mack	W	NJPW Strong	13:13
Jul 30	Jordan Clearwater	W	NJPW Strong	4:27
Sep 25	Bad Luck Fale & Chase Owens (w/Great-O-Khan)	W	NJPW Burning Spirit '22	7:57
Oct 10	Hirooki Goto & Yoshi-Hashi (w/Great-O-Khan)	W	NJPW Declaration Of Power	10:09
Nov 5	Cash Wheeler & Dax Harwood (w/Great-O-Khan)	L	NJPW Battle Autumn '22	17:31
Nov 20	Kazuchika Okada, Toru Yano & The Great Muta (w/Great-O-Khan & Aaron Henare)	L	NJPW x Stardom Historic X-Over	9:48

JEFF HARDY

Mar 16	Isiah Kassidy & Marq Quen (w/Matt Hardy)	W	AEW Dynamite: St. Patrick's Day Slam	12:22
Mar 23	Tornado Match: Isiah Kassidy, Marq Quen, The Butcher & The Blade (w/Sting, Darby Allin & Matt Hardy)	W	AEW Dynamite	9:27
Apr 6	Tables Match: The Butcher & The Blade (w/Matt Hardy)	W	AEW Dynamite	11:54
Apr 18	Isiah Kassidy, Marq Quen, Angelico & Jack Evans (w/Matt Hardy, Dante Martin & Darius Martin)	W	AEW Dark Elevation	9:45
Apr 26	Max Caster, Angelico, Isiah Kassidy, Marq Quen & The Blade (w/Matt Hardy, Frankie Kazarian, Dante Martin & Darius Martin)	W	AEW Dark	12:40
May 4	Bobby Fish	W	AEW Dynamite	10:20
May 11	Darby Allin	W	AEW Dynamite	10:16
May 18	Adam Cole	L	AEW Dynamite: Wild Card Wednesday	7:10
May 29	Matt Jackson & Nick Jackson (w/Matt Hardy)	W	AEW Double Or Nothing '22	19:15

JEFF JARRETT

Jul 31	Ric Flair & Andrade El Idolo (w/Jay Lethal)	L	JCP Ric Flair's Last Match	26:40
Nov 19	Darby Allin & Sting (w/Jay Lethal)	L	AEW Full Gear '22	11:00
Dec 2	Marq Quen & Isiah Kassidy (w/Jay Lethal)	W	AEW Rampage	7:04
Dec 20	Dean Alexander & Rosario Grillo (w/Satnam Singh)	W	AEW Dark	2:32
Dec 23	Anthony Bowens & Billy Gunn (w/Jay Lethal)	W	AEW Rampage	11:46

JENNACIDE

Jan 11	Kiera Hogan, Christi Jaynes, Kenzie Paige	L	NWA Power	5:08
Feb 15	Natalia Markova	D	NWA Power	5:32
Mar 22	Allysin Kay & Martin Belle (w/Paola Blaze)	L	NWA Power	7:24
May 10	KiLynn King, Chelsea Green	L	NWA Power	6:36
Jun 28	Chelsea Green & Max The Impaler (w/Missa Kate)	L	NWA Power	5:38
Aug 23	Kayla Kassidy	W	NWA Power	2:11

Aug 27	Burke Invitational Gauntlet	L	NWA 74th Anniversary Show	17:24
Sep 6	Taya Valkyrie, Chelsea Green, KiLynn King	L	NWA Power	4:22
Oct 4	Kamille	L	NWA Power	7:20

JEREMIAH PLUNKETT

Jan 5	Jamie Stanley, Alex Taylor, Miguel Robles	L	NWA Power	5:31
Feb 8	Team War Match: Odinson, Parrow & Rodney Mack, Marshe Rockett, Tyrus & Jordan Clearwater, Aron Stevens, JR Kratos & Judais (w/Alex Taylor & Rush Freeman)	L	NWA Power	11:40
May 17	Team War Match: Jax Dane, Odinson & Parrow, Jordan Clearwater, BLK Jeez & Marshe Rockett (w/Alex Taylor & Rush Freeman)	L	NWA Power	6:54
Jun 21	Cyon & Tyrus (w/Alex Taylor)	L	NWA Power	7:40
Aug 2	Gaagz The Gymp, Judais & Sal The Pal (w/Alex Taylor & Rush Freeman)	L	NWA Power	8:08
Aug 27	Beelzebub's Bedlam Match: Judais, Sal The Pal & Gaagz The Gimp (w/Danny Dealz & Alex Taylor)	L	NWA 74th Anniversary Show	9:41
Aug 28	Tag Team Battle Royal (w/Alex Taylor)	L	NWA 74th Anniversary Show	14:07
Dec 6	Rolando Freeman, Anthony Andrews, Sal The Pal	L	NWA Power	5:36
Dec 27	Garrison Creed, Traxx	W	NWA Power	4:51

JESSICKA (AS HAVOK UNTIL AUGUST 25)

Jan 20	Tenille Dashwood & Madison Rayne (w/Rosemary)	L	IMPACT Wrestling	3:35
Mar 10	Jordynne Grace	L	IMPACT Before The Impact	8:20
Mar 31	Battle Royal	L	IMPACT Wrestling	7:15
Apr 1	Madison Rayne & Tenille Dashwood, Tasha Steelz & Savannah Evans, Gisele Shaw & Lady Frost (w/Rosemary)	L	IMPACT Multiverse Of Matches	9:02
Apr 28	Savannah Evans & Tasha Steelz (w/Rosemary)	W	IMPACT Wrestling	4:51
May 26	Masha Slamovich	L	IMPACT Wrestling	1:28
Aug 25	Alisha Edwards	W	IMPACT Wrestling	1:56
Oct 6	Swingerella #1 & Swingerella #2 (w/Taya Valkyrie)	W	IMPACT Wrestling	1:30
Oct 10	Chelsea Green & Deonna Purrazzo (w/Taya Valkyrie)	W	IMPACT Bound For Glory '22	7:24
Oct 13	Chelsea Green, Deonna Purrazzo & Gisele Shaw (w/Taya Valkyrie & Rosemary)	L	IMPACT Wrestling	5:40
Nov 3	Savannah Evans	L	IMPACT Wrestling	7:38
Dec 1	Miss Bea Haven (Alisha Edwards)	W	IMPACT Wrestling	8:28
Dec 22	Deonna Purrazzo & Gisele Shaw (w/Rosemary)	W	IMPACT Wrestling	5:39

JESSIE MCKAY

Jan 27	Madison Rayne & Kaleb With A K (w/Cassie Lee)	W	IMPACT Wrestling	10:57
Mar 10	Madison Rayne, Tenille Dashwood, Savannah Evans & Tasha Steelz (w/Cassie Lee, Chelsea Green & Mickie James)	W	IMPACT Wrestling	6:00
Mar 31	Battle Royal	L	IMPACT Wrestling	7:15
Apr 14	Madison Rayne	L	IMPACT Before The Impact	6:34

JEY USO

Jan 1	Kofi Kingston & Xavier Woods (w/Jimmy Uso)	W	WWE Day 1	18:05
Jan 7	Kofi Kingston & Xavier Woods (w/Jimmy Uso)	W	WWE SmackDown	17:45
Jan 21	Kevin Owens & Seth Rollins (w/Jimmy Uso)	L	WWE SmackDown	15:00
Feb 18	Ivar	L	WWE SmackDown	2:35
Mar 4	Erik & Ivar (w/Jimmy Uso)	W	WWE SmackDown	8:25
Mar 11	Rick Boogs	L	WWE SmackDown	2:25
Mar 28	Randy Orton & Riddle (w/Jimmy Uso)	L	WWE Monday Night RAW	16:20
Apr 1	Finn Balor, Shinsuke Nakamura & Rick Boogs (w/Austin Theory & Jimmy Uso)	W	WWE Monday Night RAW	11:27
Apr 2	Shinsuke Nakamura & Rick Boogs (w/Jimmy Uso)	W	WWE WrestleMania XXXVIII	6:55
Apr 4	Finn Balor, Randy Orton & Riddle (w/Austin Theory & Jimmy Uso)	W	WWE Monday Night RAW	8:25
Apr 11	Angelo Dawkins & Montez Ford (w/Jimmy Uso)	W	WWE Monday Night RAW	15:10
Apr 22	Riddle	L	WWE SmackDown	12:10
Apr 25	Cody Rhodes, Ezekiel, Randy Orton & Riddle (w/Seth Rollins, Kevin Owens & Jimmy Uso)	L	WWE Monday Night RAW	14:58
May 8	Drew McIntyre, Randy Orton & Riddle (w/Roman Reigns & Jimmy Uso)	W	WWE WrestleMania Backlash '22	22:20
May 20	Riddle & Randy Orton (w/Jimmy Uso)	W	WWE SmackDown	13:13
May 23	Riddle, Angelo Dawkins & Montez Ford (w/Sami Zayn & Jimmy Uso)	L	WWE Monday Night RAW	12:35
May 30	Riddle & Shinsuke Nakamura (w/Jimmy Uso)	L	WWE Monday Night RAW	12:30
Jun 6	Angelo Dawkins & Montez Ford (w/Jimmy Uso)	L	WWE Monday Night RAW	16:30
Jun 20	Angelo Dawkins	L	WWE Monday Night RAW	7:20
Jun 24	Drew McIntyre & Sheamus (w/Jimmy Uso)	L	WWE SmackDown	11:20
Jun 27	Montez Ford	L	WWE Monday Night RAW	9:50
Jul 2	Angelo Dawkins & Montez Ford (w/Jimmy Uso)	W	WWE Money In The Bank '22	23:00
Jul 8	Angel & Humberto (w/Jimmy Uso)	W	WWE SmackDown	2:00
Jul 11	R-Truth, Angelo Dawkins & Montez Ford (w/Omos & Jimmy Uso)	W	WWE Monday Night RAW	11:30
Jul 22	Madcap Moss, Angelo Dawkins & Montez Ford (w/Theory & Jimmy Uso)	L	WWE SmackDown	17:00
Jul 25	Riddle, Angelo Dawkins & Jey Uso (w/Roman Reigns & Jimmy Uso)	W	WWE Monday Night RAW	19:25
Jul 30	Angelo Dawkins & Montez Ford (w/Jimmy Uso)	W	WWE SummerSlam '22	13:25
Aug 1	Rey Mysterio & Dominik Mysterio (w/Jimmy Uso)	W	WWE Monday Night RAW	15:50
Aug 12	Drew McIntyre & Madcap Moss (w/Jimmy Uso)	L	WWE SmackDown	9:15
Aug 29	Kevin Owens	L	WWE Monday Night RAW	12:26
Sep 23	Ridge Holland & Butch (w/Jimmy Uso)	W	WWE SmackDown	14:10
Oct 7	Braun Strowman, Xavier Woods & Kofi Kingston (w/Jimmy Uso & Sami Zayn)	L	WWE SmackDown	10:30
Nov 5	Ridge Holland & Butch (w/Jimmy Uso)	W	WWE Crown Jewel '22	10:45
Nov 7	Matt Riddle, Xavier Woods & Kofi Kingston (w/Solo Sikoa & Jimmy Uso)	W	WWE Monday Night RAW	20:55
Nov 11	Xavier Woods & Kofi Kingston (w/Jimmy Uso)	W	WWE SmackDown	23:50

Nov 25	Drew McIntyre & Sheamus (w/Jimmy Uso)	L	WWE SmackDown	14:43
Nov 26	WarGames Match: Sheamus, Butch, Ridge Holland, Drew McIntyre & Kevin Owens (w/Roman Reigns, Solo Sikoa, Sami Zayn & Jimmy Uso)	W	WWE Survivor Series WarGames	38:30
Nov 28	Kevin Owens	L	WWE Monday Night RAW	21:55
Dec 5	Matt Riddle & Kevin Owens (w/Jimmy Uso)	W	WWE Monday Night RAW	14:10
Dec 9	Butch & Sheamus (w/Jimmy Uso)	W	WWE SmackDown	19:20
Dec 19	Seth Rollins & Kevin Owens (w/Jimmy Uso)	L	WWE Monday Night RAW	10:50
Dec 23	Ashante Adonis & Top Dolla (w/Jimmy Uso)	W	WWE SmackDown	9:43

JIMMY USO

Jan 1	Kofi Kingston & Xavier Woods (w/Jey Uso)	W	WWE Day 1	18:05
Jan 7	Kofi Kingston & Xavier Woods (w/Jey Uso)	W	WWE SmackDown	17:45
Jan 21	Kevin Owens & Seth Rollins (w/Jey Uso)	L	WWE SmackDown	15:00
Feb 4	Erik	W	WWE SmackDown	2:10
Mar 4	Erik & Ivar (w/Jey Uso)	W	WWE SmackDown	8:25
Mar 25	Shinsuke Nakamura	L	WWE SmackDown	8:48
Mar 28	Randy Orton & Riddle (w/Jey Uso)	L	WWE Monday Night RAW	16:20
Apr 1	Rick Boogs	D	WWE SmackDown	3:13
Apr 1	Finn Balor, Shinsuke Nakamura & Rick Boogs (w/Austin Theory & Jey Uso)	W	WWE SmackDown	11:27
Apr 2	Shinsuke Nakamura & Rick Boogs (w/Jey Uso)	W	WWE WrestleMania XXXVIII	6:55
Apr 4	Finn Balor, Randy Orton & Riddle (w/Austin Theory & Jey Uso)	W	WWE Monday Night RAW	8:25
Apr 11	Angelo Dawkins & Montez Ford (w/Jey Uso)	W	WWE Monday Night RAW	15:10
Apr 15	Riddle	L	WWE SmackDown	8:32
Apr 25	Cody Rhodes, Ezekiel, Randy Orton & Riddle (w/Seth Rollins, Kevin Owens & Jey Uso)	L	WWE Monday Night RAW	14:58
May 8	Drew McIntyre, Randy Orton & Riddle (w/Roman Reigns & Jey Uso)	W	WWE WrestleMania Backlash '22	22:20
May 16	Riddle	L	WWE Monday Night RAW	10:50
May 20	Riddle & Randy Orton (w/Jey Uso)	W	WWE SmackDown	13:13
May 23	Riddle, Angelo Dawkins & Montez Ford (w/Sami Zayn & Jey Uso)	L	WWE Monday Night RAW	12:35
May 30	Riddle & Shinsuke Nakamura (w/Jey Uso)	L	WWE Monday Night RAW	12:30
Jun 6	Angelo Dawkins & Montez Ford (w/Jey Uso)	L	WWE Monday Night RAW	16:30
Jun 13	Montez Ford	W	WWE Monday Night RAW	13:00
Jun 24	Drew McIntyre & Sheamus (w/Jey Uso)	L	WWE SmackDown	11:20
Jul 2	Angelo Dawkins & Montez Ford (w/Jey Uso)	W	WWE Money In The Bank '22	23:00
Jul 8	Angel & Humberto (w/Jey Uso)	W	WWE SmackDown	2:00
Jul 11	R-Truth, Angelo Dawkins & Montez Ford (w/Omos & Jey Uso)	W	WWE Monday Night RAW	11:30
Jul 15	Angelo Dawkins	L	WWE SmackDown	7:00
Jul 22	Madcap Moss, Angelo Dawkins & Montez Ford (w/Theory & Jey Uso)	L	WWE SmackDown	17:00
Jul 25	Riddle, Angelo Dawkins & Jey Uso (w/Roman Reigns & Jey Uso)	W	WWE Monday Night RAW	19:25
Jul 30	Angelo Dawkins & Montez Ford (w/Jey Uso)	W	WWE SummerSlam '22	13:25
Aug 1	Rey Mysterio & Dominik Mysterio (w/Jey Uso)	W	WWE Monday Night RAW	15:50
Aug 12	Drew McIntyre & Madcap Moss (w/Jey Uso)	L	WWE SmackDown	9:15
Sep 23	Ridge Holland & Butch (w/Jey Uso)	W	WWE SmackDown	14:10
Oct 7	Braun Strowman, Xavier Woods & Kofi Kingston (w/Jey Uso & Sami Zayn)	L	WWE SmackDown	10:30
Nov 5	Ridge Holland & Butch (w/Jey Uso)	W	WWE Crown Jewel '22	10:45
Nov 7	Matt Riddle, Xavier Woods & Kofi Kingston (w/Jey Uso & Solo Sikoa)	W	WWE Monday Night RAW	20:55
Nov 11	Xavier Woods & Kofi Kingston (w/Jey Uso)	W	WWE SmackDown	23:50
Nov 25	Drew McIntyre & Sheamus (w/Jey Uso)	L	WWE SmackDown	14:43
Nov 26	WarGames Match: Sheamus, Butch, Ridge Holland, Drew McIntyre & Kevin Owens (w/Roman Reigns, Solo Sikoa, Sami Zayn & Jey Uso)	W	WWE Survivor Series WarGames	38:30
Dec 5	Matt Riddle & Kevin Owens (w/Jey Uso)	W	WWE Monday Night RAW	14:10
Dec 9	Butch & Sheamus (w/Jey Uso)	W	WWE SmackDown	19:20
Dec 19	Seth Rollins & Kevin Owens (w/Jey Uso)	L	WWE Monday Night RAW	10:50
Dec 23	Ashante Adonis & Top Dolla (w/Jey Uso)	W	WWE SmackDown	9:43

JINDER MAHAL

Jan 14	Erik & Ivar, Angel & Humberto, Cesaro & Mansoor (w/Shanky)	L	WWE SmackDown	13:21
Jan 28	Shinsuke Nakamura & Rick Boogs (w/Shanky)	L	WWE SmackDown	3:05
Feb 4	Shinsuke Nakamura	L	WWE SmackDown	3:09
Mar 4	Drew McIntyre	L	WWE SmackDown	2:05
Mar 18	Drew McIntyre, Erik & Ivar (w/Happy Corbin & Shanky)	L	WWE SmackDown	7:10
Apr 1	Andre The Giant Memorial Battle Royal	L	WWE SmackDown	8:05
Apr 15	Ricochet	L	WWE SmackDown	3:37
May 27	Angel & Humberto (w/Shanky)	L	WWE SmackDown	2:15
Jun 3	Humberto	W	WWE SmackDown	3:34
Jun 17	Xavier Woods & Kofi Kingston (w/Shanky)	L	WWE SmackDown	3:02
Jun 27	Battle Royal	L	WWE Monday Night RAW	19:25
Jul 8	Erik & Ivar (w/Shanky)	L	WWE SmackDown	1:15
Jul 22	Erik & Ivar (w/Shanky)	L	WWE SmackDown	1:30
Nov 11	Braun Strowman	L	WWE SmackDown	1:50

JINNY

Jan 27	Amale	W	NXT UK	6:31

JOAQUIN WILDE

Jan 18	Malik Blade & Edris Enofe (w/Raul Mendoza)	L	NXT 2.0	3:17
Feb 1	Bron Breakker & Tommaso Ciampa (w/Raul Mendoza)	L	NXT 2.0	11:28
Mar 4	Malik Blade & Edris Enofe (w/Raul Mendoza)	W	NXT Level Up	8:45
Mar 29	Brooks Jensen & Josh Briggs (w/Raul Mendoza)	L	NXT 2.0	5:36
Apr 12	Gauntlet Match: Brooks Jensen & Josh Briggs, Kit Wilson & Elton Prince Grayson Waller & Sanga, Julius Creed & Brutus Creed (w/Raul Mendoza)	L	NXT 2.0	27:08
Apr 19	Zack Gibson & James Drake (w/Raul Mendoza)	W	NXT 2.0	3:57

Apr 26	Handicap Match: Fallon Henley & Josh Briggs (w/Cruz del Toro & Elektra Lopez)	W	NXT 2.0	4:45
Jun 4	Tony D'Angelo, Channing Lorenzo & Troy Donovan (w/Cruz del Toro & Santos Escobar)	L	NXT In Your House '22	12:45
Jun 21	Roderick Strong & Damon Kemp (w/Cruz del Toro)	L	NXT 2.0	4:57
Jul 26	Roderick Strong, Damon Kemp, Julius Creed & Brutus Creed (w/Tony D'Angelo, Channing Lorenzo & Cruz del Toro)	W	NXT 2.0	11:39
Aug 23	Jagger Reid & Rip Fowler (w/Cruz Del Toro)	L	NXT 2.0	5:02
Oct 14	Ashante Adonis & Top Dolla (w/Cruz del Toro)	W	WWE SmackDown	1:22
Oct 28	Ashante Adonis, Top Dolla & Shinsuke Nakamura (w/Santos Escobar & Cruz Del Toro)	L	WWE SmackDown	4:19
Dec 9	Erik & Ivar (w/Cruz Del Toro)	D	WWE SmackDown	1:53
Dec 16	Ashante Adonis & Top Dolla, Erik & Ivar (w/Cruz Del Toro)	L	WWE SmackDown	9:20

JOE ALONZO

May 24	Cyon	L	NWA Power	16:32
Aug 9	Jordan Clearwater	L	NWA Power	5:48
Sep 13	Cyon	L	NWA Power	7:09
Oct 18	Kerry Morton	L	NWA Power	5:46
Dec 27	Cyon, Jordan Clearwater & Tyrus (w/Bestia 666 & Mecha Wolf)	L	NWA Power	7:56

JOE COFFEY

Jan 27	Charlie Dempsey, Rohan Raja & Teoman (w/Mark Coffey & Wolfgang)	L	NXT UK	11:18
Mar 10	Heritage Cup Rules: Noam Dar	L	NXT UK	17:43
Apr 14	David Mastiff & Jack Starz (w/Mark Coffey)	L	NXT UK	8:30
May 12	Ashton Smith & Oliver Carter (w/Mark Coffey)	L	NXT UK	10:24
Aug 18	Mark Andrews	W	NXT UK	7:40
Aug 25	Tyler Bate	L	NXT UK	12:00
Aug 30	Damon Kemp, Julius Creed & Brutus Creed (w/Mark Coffey & Wolfgang)	W	NXT 2.0	10:59
Sep 6	Tyler Bate & Bron Breakker (w/Mark Coffey)	L	NXT 2.0	10:51

JOE DOERING

Jan 8	Hardcore War: Eddie Edwards, Rich Swann, Willie Mack, Heath & Rhino (w/Luke Gallows, Karl Anderson, Deaner & Eric Young)	L	IMPACT Hard To Kill '22	23:25
Jan 20	Heath & Rhino (w/Luke Gallows)	W	IMPACT Wrestling	8:39
Feb 17	Jay White, Tama Tonga & Tanga Loa (w/Eric Young & Deaner)	L	IMPACT Wrestling	13:19
Mar 3	Chris Bey, Luke Gallows, Karl Anderson & Jay White (w/Deaner, Tama Tonga & Tanga Loa)	L	IMPACT Wrestling	9:48
Mar 24	Lumberjack Match: Luke Gallows & Karl Anderson (w/Eric Young)	W	IMPACT Wrestling	7:26
Apr 23	Elimination Challenge Match (w/Eric Young)	W	IMPACT Rebellion '22	33:02
May 19	Jay Briscoe & Mark Briscoe (w/Deaner)	L	IMPACT Wrestling	15:00
May 26	Josh Alexander, Jay Briscoe & Mark Briscoe (w/Deaner & Eric Young)	W	IMPACT Wrestling	17:09
Jun 9	Josh Alexander	W	IMPACT Wrestling	6:32
Jul 14	Josh Alexander, Alex Shelley & Chris Sabin (w/Deaner & Eric Young)	L	IMPACT Wrestling	11:56
Aug 4	Alex Shelley & Chris Sabin (w/Deaner)	L	IMPACT Wrestling	6:23
Aug 25	Kushida, Alex Shelley & Chris Sabin (w/Deaner & Eric Young)	L	IMPACT Wrestling	15:18

JOE GACY

Jan 11	Malik Blade & Edris Enofe (w/Harland)	L	NXT 2.0	3:14
Jan 28	Draco Anthony	W	WWE 205 Live	5:10
Feb 1	LA Knight	W	NXT 2.0	4:18
Feb 11	Xyon Quinn	W	WWE 205 Live	5:39
Feb 25	Ikemen Jiro & Kushida (w/Harland)	W	NXT Level Up	6:55
Mar 25	Quincy Elliott	W	NXT Level Up	4:15
Mar 29	Draco Anthony	W	NXT 2.0	3:57
May 3	Bron Breakker	L	NXT 2.0: Spring Breakin'	11:03
Jun 4	Bron Breakker	L	NXT In Your House '22	15:50
Jun 28	Roderick Strong, Julius Creed & Brutus Creed (w/Rip Fowler & Jagger Reid)	W	NXT 2.0	13:56
Aug 2	Brooks Jensen	W	NXT 2.0	3:00
Sep 13	Channing Lorenzo & Tony D'Angelo (w/Cameron Grimes)	W	NXT 2.0	5:36
Sep 27	Cameron Grimes	W	NXT	3:17
Oct 18	Cameron Grimes, Luke Gallows & Karl Anderson (w/Jagger Reid & Rip Fowler)	L	NXT	11:56
Nov 8	Cameron Grimes	W	NXT	10:44
Dec 1	Cedric Alexander	L	WWE Main Event	8:02
Dec 10	Iron Survivor Challenge: Grayson Waller, Carmelo Hayes, Axiom, JD McDonagh	L	NXT Deadline	25:00
Dec 27	Edris Enofe, Malik Blade & Odyssey Jones (w/Jagger Reid & Rip Fowler)	W	NXT	11:15

JOE HENDRY

Oct 7	Call Your Shot Gauntlet	L	IMPACT Bound For Glory '22	29:18
Oct 20	Jason Hotch	W	IMPACT Wrestling	1:54
Oct 27	Raj Singh	W	IMPACT Wrestling	1:47
Nov 10	Brian Myers	W	IMPACT Wrestling	5:58
Dec 15	Johnny Swinger & Zicky Dice (w/Bhupinder Gujjar)	W	IMPACT Wrestling	3:17

JOEY JANELA

Jan 11	Eddie Kingston	L	AEW Dark	8:33
Feb 1	Lee Moriarty	L	AEW Dark	11:44
Aug 20	Hardcore Match: Shunma Katsumata	W	DDT Wrestle Peter Pan '22	18:56

JOHN CENA

Dec 30	Roman Reigns & Sami Zayn (w/Kevin Owens)	W	WWE SmackDown	10:57

JOHN SILVER

Jan 3	Mike Orlando & Shayne Stetson (w/Alex Reynolds)	W	AEW Dark Elevation	3:48
Jan 10	Isiah Kassidy, Marq Quen & The Blade (w/Alex Reynolds & Ten)	W	AEW Dark Elevation	4:01
Jan 14	Jungle Boy & Luchasaurus (w/Alex Reynolds)	L	AEW Rampage	12:37
Feb 14	Jeff Parker, Matt Lee, Daniel Garcia, Anthony Bowens & Max Caster (w/Alex Reynolds, Evil Uno, Alan Angels & Stu Grayson)	L	AEW Dark Elevation	5:56
Feb 15	Ari Daivari & Invictus Khash (w/Alex Reynolds)	W	AEW Dark	5:40
Feb 23	Tag Team Battle Royal (w/ Alex Reynolds)	L	AEW Dynamite	18:24
Mar 2	Adam Cole, Bobby Fish & Kyle O'Reilly (w/Hangman Page & Alex Reynolds)	L	AEW Dynamite	12:43
Mar 14	Luther & Serpentico (w/Alex Reynolds)	W	AEW Dark Elevation	4:40
Mar 15	Luther & Serpentico (w/Alex Reynolds)	W	AEW Dark	4:26
Mar 21	Aaron Solo, Nick Comoroto & QT Marshall (w/Evil Uno & Stu Grayson)	W	AEW Dark Elevation	7:27
Mar 23	Chris Jericho & Daniel Garcia (w/Alex Reynolds)	L	AEW Dynamite	10:02
Mar 29	Brandon Bullodkc, Foxx Vinyer & Jameson Ryan (w/Alex Reynolds & Ten)	W	AEW Dark	3:20
Apr 11	Luther, Serpentico, Austin Gunn, Colten Gunn & Billy Gunn (w/Alex Reynolds, Alan Angels, Stu Grayson & Ten)	W	AEW Dark Elevation	5:20
Apr 18	Allen Russell, Dale Springs, Izaiah Zane & Kameron Russell (w/Alex Reynolds, Evil Uno & Stu Grayson)	W	AEW Dark Elevation	2:17
Apr 25	Vince Valor	W	AEW Dark Elevation	1:29
May 2	Anthony Bennett, Bret Waters, Cory Bishop, Eli Isom, Jaden Valo & Mike Law (w/Alex Reynolds, Alan Angels, Evil Uno, Colt Cabana & Ten)	W	AEW Dark Elevation	1:44
May 3	Ryan Nemeth	W	AEW Dark	6:43
May 9	Tony Deppen	W	AEW Dark Elevation	2:34
May 11	CM Punk	L	AEW Dynamite	8:06
May 31	Serpentico, Peter Avalon & Ryan Nemeth (w/Evil Uno & Ten)	W	AEW Dark	5:37
Jun 6	Aaron Solo, Anthony Ogogo, Nick Comoroto & QT Marshall (w/Alan Angels, Evil Uno & Ten)	L	AEW Dark Elevation	6:28
Jun 7	Max Caster, Austin Gunn & Colten Gunn (w/Alex Reynolds & Ten)	W	AEW Dark	5:26
Jun 8	Casino Battle Royale	L	AEW Dynamite	24:59
Jun 21	Cezar Bononi & Peter Avalon (w/Alex Reynolds)	W	AEW Dark	5:01
Jun 27	Kevin Matthews	W	AEW Dark Elevation	2:27
Jul 1	Royal Rampage Match	L	AEW Rampage	22:41
Jul 5	Cezar Bononi, JD Drake, Peter Avalon & Ryan Nemeth (w/Alex Reynolds, Evil Uno & Ten)	W	AEW Dark	7:22
Jul 15	Malakai Black & Brody King (w/Alex Reynolds)	L	AEW Rampage	8:18
Jul 22	The Butcher & The Blade (w/Hangman Page)	W	AEW Rampage: Fyter Fest	9:55
Aug 8	Lord Crewe & TUG Cooper (w/Alex Reynolds)	W	AEW Dark Elevation	2:13
Aug 15	Adam Grace, Drew System, Rylie Jackson & TUG Cooper (w/Alex Reynolds, Evil Uno & Ten)	W	AEW Dark Elevation	2:25
Aug 22	Alexander Apollo, D'Mone Solavino & RC Dupree (w/Alex Reynolds & Ten)	W	AEW Dark Elevation	3:22
Aug 23	DK Vandu, Joey Sweets & Tyshaun Perez (w/Alex Reynolds & Ten)	W	AEW Dark	3:38
Aug 26	Malakai Black, Brody King & Buddy Matthews (w/Ten & Alex Reynolds)	W	AEW Rampage	9:03
Aug 30	Serpentico	W	AEW Dark	4:10
Sep 2	Orange Cassidy, Chuck Taylor & Trent Beretta (w/Hangman Page & Alex Reynolds)	W	AEW Rampage	11:12
Sep 3	Aaron Solo, Cole Karter & Nick Comoroto (w/Hangman Page & Alex Reynolds)	W	AEW Dark Elevation	6:00
Sep 4	Kenny Omega, Matt Jackson & Nick Jackson (w/Alex Reynolds & Hangman Page)	L	AEW All Out '22	19:50
Sep 12	Ryan Nemeth	W	AEW Dark Elevation	3:33
Sep 20	Alexander Moss & Zuka (w/Alex Reynolds)	W	AEW Dark	4:50
Sep 23	Golden Ticket Battle Royale	L	AEW Rampage: Grand Slam	12:16
Sep 30	Rush	L	AEW Rampage	10:58
Oct 7	Pac, Penta El Zero M & Rey Fenix (w/Ten & Alex Reynolds)	L	AEW Rampage	21:01
Oct 18	Jordano, Shayne Hawke, Tyler Tirva & Zak Patterson (w/Alex Reynolds, Evil Uno & Ten)	W	AEW Dark	6:52
Nov 8	Ativalu, Fulton & Troy Hollywood (w/Alex Reynolds & Evil Uno)	W	AEW Dark	2:22
Nov 15	Arjun Singh, Brett Gosselin & Mike Magnum (w/Alex Reynolds & Evil Uno)	W	AEW Dark	4:43
Nov 22	Ari Daivari, Jeeves Kay & Sonny Kiss (w/Alex Reynolds & Evil Uno)	W	AEW Dark	5:26
Nov 25	Rush, The Butcher & The Blade (w/Ten & Alex Reynolds)	L	AEW Rampage	7:24
Dec 23	$300,000 Three Kings Christmas Casino Trios Royale (w/Evil Uno & Alex Reynolds)	L	AEW Rampage	22:01

JOHN SKYLER

Feb 3	Bhupinder Gujjar	L	IMPACT Wrestling	3:46
Feb 24	Bhupinder Gujjar	L	IMPACT Wrestling	3:34
Mar 10	Ace Austin, Crazzy Steve	L	IMPACT Wrestling	10:45
Apr 23	Big Damo	L	NJPW Strong	7:04
Sep 3	Lucky Ali	W	NJPW Strong	10:56
Dec 15	Bully Ray	L	IMPACT Wrestling	1:06
Dec 29	Yuya Uemura & Delirious (w/Jason Hotch)	L	IMPACT Before The Impact	9:08

JOHNNY ELITE

Feb 19	El Hijo del Vikingo	L	AAA Rey De Reyes '22	13:07
Apr 30	Dragon Lee & Dralistico, Jack Cartwheel & Laredo Kid (w/Taurus)	W	AAA TripleMania XXX: Monterrey	13:29
May 18	Samoa Joe	L	AEW Dynamite: Wild Card Wednesday	10:25
May 28	Marq Quen	W	AEW Dark	6:00

Jun 1	Miro	L	AEW Dynamite	6:07
Jun 18	Dragon Lee & Dralistico (w/Matt Hardy)	L	AAA TripleMania XXX: Tijuana	13:35
Oct 15	El Cuatrero, Forastero & Sanson, Bandido, Laredo Kid & Psycho Clown (w/Brian Cage & Sam Adonis)	W	AAA TripleMania XXX: Mexico City	12:44

JOHNNY GARGANO

Sep 12	Chad Gable	W	WWE Monday Night RAW	13:50
Sep 26	Chad Gable & Otis (w/Kevin Owens)	W	WWE Monday Night RAW	13:09
Sep 30	Austin Theory, Chad Gable & Otis (w/Drew McIntyre & Kevin Owens)	W	WWE SmackDown	13:38
Oct 3	Otis	L	WWE Monday Night RAW	5:40
Oct 10	Austin Theory	W	WWE Monday Night RAW	8:50
Oct 24	Baron Corbin	L	WWE Monday Night RAW	14:10
Nov 7	The Miz	L	WWE Monday Night RAW	17:00
Nov 21	Omos	L	WWE Monday Night RAW	3:10

JOHNNY KNOXVILLE

| Jan 29 | Royal Rumble Match | L | WWE Royal Rumble '22 | 1:26 |
| Apr 3 | Anything Goes Match: Sami Zayn | W | WWE WrestleMania XXXVIII | 14:25 |

JOHNNY SWINGER

Jan 6	Ace Austin & Madman Fulton (w/Hernandez)	L	IMPACT Wrestling	3:40
Jan 27	Jonah	L	IMPACT Wrestling	1:11
Mar 3	Jonah	L	IMPACT Wrestling	:49
Mar 31	Luke Gallows & Karl Anderson (w/Zicky Dice)	L	IMPACT Wrestling	:50
Apr 23	Elimination Challenge Match (w/Zicky Dice)	L	IMPACT Rebellion '22	33:02
May 12	Gauntlet For The Gold	L	IMPACT Wrestling	39:00
Jun 9	Crazzy Steve & Black Taurus (w/Zicky Dice)	L	IMPACT Before The Impact	8:18
Jun 23	Bhupinder Gujjar & Shark Boy (w/Zicky Dice)	L	IMPACT Before The Impact	3:50
Jul 14	Bhupinder Gujjar	L	IMPACT Before The Impact	8:37
Jul 21	Laredo Kid	L	IMPACT Before The Impact	8:10
Jul 28	Laredo Kid & Trey Miguel (w/Zicky Dice)	L	IMPACT Wrestling	4:01
Aug 25	Ace Austin & Hikuleo (w/Zicky Dice)	L	IMPACT Before The Impact	7:46
Oct 7	Call Your Shot Gauntlet	L	IMPACT Bound For Glory '22	29:18
Oct 20	Dirty Dango	L	IMPACT Before The Impact	8:23
Dec 15	Bhupinder Gujjar & Joe Hendry (w/Zicky Dice)	L	IMPACT Wrestling	3:17

JON MOXLEY

Jan 21	Ethan Page	W	AEW Rampage	10:15
Jan 28	Anthony Bowens	W	AEW Rampage: Beach Break	12:02
Feb 2	Wheeler Yuta	W	AEW Dynamite	7:29
Feb 9	Dax Harwood & Cash Wheeler (w/CM Punk)	W	AEW Dynamite	18:34
Mar 6	Bryan Danielson	W	AEW Revolution '22	21:05
Mar 9	JD Drake & Anthony Henry (w/Bryan Danielson)	W	AEW Dynamite	4:00
Mar 16	Chuck Taylor & Wheeler Yuta (w/Bryan Danielson)	W	AEW Dynamite: St. Patrick's Day Slam	11:45
Mar 23	Brian Pillman Jr. & Griff Garrison (w/Bryan Danielson)	W	AEW Dynamite	6:04
Mar 30	Jay Lethal	W	AEW Dynamite	11:03
Apr 8	Wheeler Yuta	W	AEW Rampage	12:40
Apr 15	Billy Gunn, Austin Gunn & Colten Gunn (w/Bryan Danielson & Wheeler Yuta)	W	AEW Rampage	9:06
Apr 16	Will Ospreay	W	NJPW Windy City Riot	21:24
Apr 20	Lee Moriarty, Dante Martin & Brock Anderson (w/Bryan Danielson & Wheeler Yuta)	W	AEW Dynamite	8:08
Apr 27	QT Marshall, Aaron Solo & Nick Comoroto (w/Bryan Danielson & Wheeler Yuta)	W	AEW Dynamite	8:49
May 4	Angelico, The Butcher & The Blade (w/Bryan Danielson & Wheeler Yuta)	W	AEW Dynamite	7:27
May 14	Juice Robinson, Hiroshi Tanahashi, Will Ospreay	L	NJPW Capital Collision	15:45
May 20	Dante Martin & Matt Sydal (w/Bryan Danielson)	W	AEW Dynamite	12:00
May 25	Isiah Kassidy & Marq Quen (w/Eddie Kingston)	W	AEW Dynamite: 3 Year Anniversary	7:20
May 29	Anarchy In The Arena: Chris Jericho, Daniel Garcia, Jake Hager, Angelo Parker & Matt Menard (w/Bryan Danielson, Eddie Kingston, Santana & Ortiz)	L	AEW Double Or Nothing '22	22:45
Jun 1	Daniel Garcia	W	AEW Dynamite	11:32
Jun 8	Kyle O'Reilly	W	AEW Dynamite	14:15
Jun 17	Dante Martin	W	AEW Rampage: Road Rager	11:58
Jun 22	Chris Jericho & Lance Archer (w/Hiroshi Tanahashi)	W	AEW Dynamite	12:12
Jun 26	Hiroshi Tanahashi	W	AEW x NJPW Forbidden Door	18:14
Jun 29	Blood & Guts: Chris Jericho, Daniel Garcia, Jake Hager, Matt Menard, Angelo Parker & Sammy Guevara (w/Bryan Danielson, Wheeler Yuta, Eddie Kingston, Santana & Ortiz)	W	AEW Dynamite: Blood & Guts	46:45
Jul 6	Brody King	W	AEW Dynamite	11:14
Jul 13	Konosuke Takeshita	W	AEW Dynamite: Fyter Fest	13:22
Jul 20	Chuck Taylor & Trent Beretta (w/Wheeler Yuta)	W	AEW Dynamite: Fyter Fest	11:53
Jul 27	Rush	W	AEW Dynamite: Fight For The Fallen	13:27
Jul 30	No DQ: El Desperado	W	NJPW Music City Mayhem	17:20
Aug 5	Mance Warner	W	AEW Rampage	11:40
Aug 10	Chris Jericho	W	AEW Dynamite: Quake By The Lake	22:38
Aug 24	CM Punk	W	AEW Dynamite	2:59
Sep 4	CM Punk	L	AEW All Out '22	19:55
Sep 14	Sammy Guevara	W	AEW Dynamite	13:27
Sep 21	Bryan Danielson	W	AEW Dynamite: Grand Slam	19:31
Sep 28	Juice Robinson	W	AEW Dynamite	11:18
Oct 7	Rush, Marq Quen & Isiah Kassidy (w/Claudio Castagnoli & Wheeler Yuta)	W	AEW Rampage	10:16

Oct 14	The Butcher & The Blade (w/Claudio Castagnoli)	W	AEW Rampage	8:40
Oct 18	Hangman Page	W	AEW Dynamite: Title Tuesday	15:32
Oct 26	Penta El Zero M	W	AEW Dynamite	12:21
Oct 28	Matt Menard	W	AEW Rampage	8:05
Nov 2	Lee Moriarty	W	AEW Rampage	10:07
Nov 19	MJF	L	AEW Full Gear '22	23:15
Dec 9	Konosuke Takeshita	W	AEW Rampage	14:30
Dec 16	Sammy Guevara	W	AEW Rampage	15:34
Dec 21	Darius Martin	W	AEW Dynamite: Holiday Bash	8:49
Dec 23	$300,000 Three Kings Christmas Casino Trios Royale (w/Claudio Castagnoli & Wheeler Yuta)	L	AEW Rampage	22:01
Dec 28	Dante Martin & Darius Martin (w/Claudio Castagnoli)	W	AEW Dynamite	14:02

JONAH

Jan 6	Jake Something	W	IMPACT Wrestling	8:22
Jan 8	Josh Alexander	L	IMPACT Hard To Kill '22	17:05
Jan 13	Raj Singh	W	IMPACT Wrestling	1:24
Jan 15	David Finlay	W	NJPW Strong	8:20
Jan 27	Johnny Swinger	W	IMPACT Wrestling	1:11
Feb 3	Crazzy Steve	W	IMPACT Wrestling	2:08
Feb 12	David Finlay & Juice Robinson (w/Bad Dude Tito)	L	NJPW Strong	11:51
Feb 24	Zicky Dice	W	IMPACT Wrestling	1:00
Mar 3	Johnny Swinger	W	IMPACT Wrestling	:49
Mar 5	David Finlay & Juice Robinson (w/Bad Dude Tito)	W	NJPW Strong	8:16
Mar 17	Zicky Dice	W	IMPACT Wrestling	:30
Apr 1	Moose & PCO (w/Josh Alexander)	W	IMPACT Multiverse Of Matches	12:47
Apr 2	David Finlay & Juice Robinson (w/Shane Haste)	L	NJPW Strong	6:35
Apr 14	PCO	W	IMPACT Wrestling	14:00
Apr 16	Chicago Street Fight: David Finlay, Juice Robinson & Brody King (w/Shane Haste & Bad Dude Tito)	L	NJPW Windy City Riot	24:11
Apr 23	Tomohiro Ishii	L	IMPACT Rebellion '22	14:34
May 5	Monster's Ball Match: PCO	L	IMPACT Wrestling	15:09
May 7	Blake Christian	W	NJPW Strong	6:56
May 14	Aaron Henare, Kyle Fletcher, Mark Davis & Jeff Cobb (w/Mikey Nicholls, Shane Haste & Bad Dude Tito)	W	NJPW Capital Collision	12:09
May 28	Jeff Cobb, Kyle Fletcher & Mark Davis (w/Bad Dude Tito & Shane Haste)	L	NJPW Strong	14:39
Jul 2	Aaron Henare, Great-O-Khan, Kyle Fletcher & Mark Davis (w/Bad Dude Tito, Mikey Nicholls & Shane Haste)	L	NJPW Strong	11:35
Jul 9	Taylor Rust	W	NJPW Strong	12:50
Sep 25	Togi Makabe, Tomoaki Honma & Kazuchika Okada (w/Bad Dude Tito & Shane Haste)	W	NJPW Burning Spirit '22	12:09
Oct 10	Kazuchika Okada	L	NJPW Declaration Of Power	19:53

JONATHAN GRESHAM

Jan 8	Chris Sabin	W	IMPACT Hard To Kill '22	12:40
Jan 20	Steve Maclin	W	IMPACT Wrestling	10:20
Feb 3	Steve Maclin	L	IMPACT Wrestling	11:52
Mar 31	Kenny King	W	IMPACT Wrestling	12:05
Apr 1	Bandido	W	ROH Supercard Of Honor XV	24:55
Apr 14	Rocky Romero	W	IMPACT Wrestling	10:45
Apr 16	Dalton Castle	W	AEW Battle Of The Belts II	10:35
Jul 8	Kaun & Toa Liona (w/Lee Moriarty)	L	AEW Rampage	7:27
Jul 15	Lee Moriarty	W	AEW Rampage	9:01
Jul 19	Jordan Oasis	W	AEW Dark	3:13
Jul 23	Claudio Castagnoli	L	ROH Death Before Dishonor XIX	11:30
Jul 31	Alan Angels, Konosuke Takeshita, Nick Wayne	W	JCP Ric Flair's Last Match	5:40
Oct 28	Fred Rosser	L	NJPW Rumble On 44th Street	14:37

JORDAN CLEARWATER

Jan 5	Handicap Matvh: Cyon (w/Marshe Rockett)	W	NWA Power	5:21
Jan 8	Chris Bey & Hikuleo (w/Keita Murray)	L	NJPW Strong	9:12
Jan 18	Luke Hawx & PJ Hawx (w/Marshe Rockett)	W	NWA Power	6:32
Feb 8	Team War Match: Odinson, Parrow & Rodney Mack, Aron Stevens, JR Kratos & Judais, Jeremiah Plunkett, Alex Taylor & Rush Freeman (w/Marshe Rockett & Tyrus)	L	NWA Power	11:40
Mar 8	Alex Taylor, Rush Freeman, Cyon & Mims (w/BLK Jeez, Marshe Rockett & Tyrus)	W	NWA Power	6:59
Mar 19	Chris Adonis & Thom Latimer (w/Marshe Rockett)	W	NWA Crockett Cup '22	4:18
Mar 19	Doug Williams & Harry Smith (w/Marshe Rockett)	L	NWA Crockett Cup '22	12:50
Apr 26	Nick Aldis	L	NWA Power	6:54
May 17	Team War Match: Jax Dane, Odinson & Parrow, Alex Taylor, Jeremiah Plunkett & Rush Freeman (w/Marshe Rockett & BLK Jeez)	L	NWA Power	6:54
Jul 30	Jeff Cobb	L	NJPW Strong	4:27
Aug 9	Joe Alonzo	W	NWA Power	5:48
Aug 28	Tag Team Battle Royal (w/Marshe Rockett)	L	NWA 74th Anniversary Show	14:07
Nov 15	Mims	D	NWA Power	6:05
Dec 27	Mercurio	W	NWA Power	4:14
Dec 27	Joe Alonzo, Bestia 666 & Mecha Wolf (w/Cyon & Tyrus)	W	NWA Power	7:56

JORDAN CRUZ

Jun 3	Ricky Starks & Powerhouse Hobbs (w/Ju Dizz)	L	AEW Rampage	:47
Jul 23	JR Kratos	L	NJPW Strong	4:11

| Sep 17 | JR Kratos & Tom Lawlor (w/Cody Chhun) | L | NJPW Strong | 9:54 |
| Nov 12 | Danny Limelight & JR Kratos (w/Adrian Quest) | L | NJPW Strong | 8:20 |

JORDYNNE GRACE

Jan 6	Tasha Steelz, Lady Frost & Chelsea Green (w/Rosemary & Rachael Ellering)	L	IMPACT Wrestling	7:19
Jan 8	Ultimate X Match: Tasha Steelz, Alisha Edwards, Chelsea Green, Lady Frost, Rosemary	W	IMPACT Hard To Kill '22	9:00
Jan 20	Lady Frost	W	IMPACT Wrestling	8:18
Feb 3	Matt Cardona	L	IMPACT Wrestling	8:49
Feb 24	Dot Combat Match: Matt Cardona	L	IMPACT Wrestling	12:14
Mar 10	Havok	W	IMPACT Before The Impact	8:20
Mar 31	Battle Royal	L	IMPACT Wrestling	7:15
Apr 1	Ultimate X Match: Trey Miguel, Chris Bey, Rich Swann, Vincent, Willie Mack	L	IMPACT Multiverse Of Matches	7:27
Apr 23	Elimination Challenge Match (w/W. Morrissey)	L	IMPACT Rebellion '22	33:02
May 19	Deonna Purrazzo, Savannah Evans & Tasha Steelz (w/Mia Yim & Taya Valkyrie)	W	IMPACT Wrestling	12:00
May 26	Chelsea Green	W	IMPACT Wrestling	11:26
Jun 16	Savannah Evans & Tasha Steelz (w/Mia Yim)	L	IMPACT Wrestling	6:49
Jun 19	Queen Of The Mountain: Tasha Steelz, Chelsea Green, Mia Yim, Deonna Purrazzo	W	IMPACT Slammiversary XX	18:15
Jun 30	Savannah Evans	W	IMPACT Wrestling	3:47
Jul 21	Chelsea Green & Deonna Purrazzo (w/Mia Yim)	L	IMPACT Wrestling	9:11
Jul 31	Deonna Purrazzo, Rachael Ellering	W	JCP Ric Flair's Last Match	9:17
Aug 25	Chelsea Green & Deonna Purrazzo (w/Mia Yim)	L	IMPACT Wrestling	7:24
Sep 22	Zicky Dice	W	IMPACT Wrestling	:43
Oct 7	Masha Slamovich	W	IMPACT Bound For Glory '22	16:00
Oct 27	Chelsea Green, Deonna Purrazzo & Gisele Shaw (w/Mickie James & Taylor Wilde)	W	IMPACT Wrestling	13:46
Nov 10	Gisele Shaw	W	IMPACT Wrestling	11:01
Dec 22	Savannah Evans & Tasha Steelz (w/Mickie James)	W	IMPACT Wrestling	11:08

JOREL NELSON

Jan 22	Fred Rosser, Rocky Romero & Taylor Rust (w/Tom Lawlor & Black Tiger)	L	NJPW Strong	11:35
Feb 5	Lio Rush & Rocky Romero (w/Royce Isaacs)	L	NJPW Strong	10:52
Mar 26	Elimination Match: Adrian Quest, Clark Connors, Fred Rosser, The DKC & Taylor Rust (w/Danny Limelight, Royce Isaacs, JR Kratos & Tom Lawlor)	W	NJPW Strong	16:29
Apr 16	Fred Rosser, Josh Alexander, Alex Coughlin, Ren Narita & Chris Dickinson (w/Royce Isaacs, JR Kratos, Black Tiger & Danny Limelight)	L	NJPW Windy City Riot	13:50
May 13	Handicap Match: Fred Rosser (w/Royce Isaacs)	W	NJPW Strong	7:28
May 14	The DKC, Yuya Uemura, David Finlay, Tanga Loa & Fred Rosser (w/Tom Lawlor, Royce Isaacs, JR Kratos & Danny Limelight)	W	NJPW Capital Collision	14:48
Jun 18	Alex Coughlin, Kevin Knight & The DKC (w/Royce Isaacs & JR Kratos)	W	NJPW Strong	9:21
Jul 9	Mikey Nicholls & Shane Haste (w/Royce Isaacs)	L	NJPW Strong	10:21
Aug 13	Shane Haste	W	NJPW Strong	8:16
Sep 10	Kyle Fletcher & Mark Davis (w/Royce Isaacs)	L	NJPW Strong	11:38
Oct 22	Greg Sharpe & Jakob Austin Young (w/Royce Isaacs)	W	NJPW Strong	6:01
Oct 28	Homicide, Wheeler Yuta & Shota Umino (w/Tom Lawlor & Royce Isaacs)	L	NJPW Rumble On 44th Street	12:15
Nov 5	Barrett Brown & Misterioso, Kevin Knight & The DKC, Bad Dude Tito & Shane Haste (w/Royce Isaacs)	L	NJPW Strong	12:36
Dec 10	Alan Angels, David Finlay, Hikuleo & Tama Tonga (w/El Phantasmo, Jay White & Royce Isaacs)	L	NJPW Strong	13:20

JOSH ALEXANDER

Jan 8	Jonah	W	IMPACT Hard To Kill '22	17:05
Jan 20	Charlie Haas	W	IMPACT Wrestling	11:03
Feb 3	Vincent	W	IMPACT Wrestling	10:28
Feb 10	Big Kon	W	IMPACT Wrestling	:38
Mar 17	Matt Taven	W	IMPACT Wrestling	12:13
Mar 31	Madman Fulton	W	IMPACT Wrestling	1:40
Apr 1	Moose & PCO (w/Jonah)	W	IMPACT Multiverse Of Matches	12:47
Apr 9	Karl Fredericks	W	NJPW Wrestling	14:14
Apr 16	Royce Isaacs, Jorel Nelson, JR Kratos, Black Tiger & Danny Limelight (w/Fred Rosser, Alex Coughlin, Ren Narita & Chris Dickinson)	W	NJPW Windy City Riot	13:50
Apr 23	Moose	W	IMPACT Rebellion '22	23:56
Apr 28	Moose	W	IMPACT Wrestling	12:40
May 12	El Phantasmo & Jay White (w/Tomohiro Ishii)	W	IMPACT Wrestling	10:28
May 26	Deaner, Eric Young & Joe Doering (w/Jay Briscoe & Mark Briscoe)	L	IMPACT Wrestling	17:09
Jun 9	Joe Doering	L	IMPACT Wrestling	6:32
Jun 19	Eric Young	W	IMPACT Slammiversary XX	18:50
Jun 23	Deaner	W	IMPACT Wrestling	5:23
Jul 14	Eric Young, Deaner & Joe Doering (w/Alex Shelley & Chris Sabin)	W	IMPACT Wrestling	11:56
Jul 28	Shera	W	IMPACT Wrestling	3:12
Jul 31	Jacob Fatu	D	JCP Ric Flair's Last Match	10:14
Aug 25	Vincent	W	IMPACT Wrestling	4:05
Sep 15	Matt Taven & Mike Bennett (w/Rich Swann)	L	IMPACT Wrestling	6:54
Oct 7	Eddie Edwards	W	IMPACT Bound For Glory '22	28:02
Oct 13	Bobby Fish	W	IMPACT Wrestling	12:55
Nov 3	Kyle Fletcher & Mark Davis (w/Frankie Kazarian)	W	IMPACT Wrestling	15:56
Dec 8	Mike Bailey	W	IMPACT Wrestling	59:48

JOSH BARNETT

Feb 12	Ren Narita	W	NJPW Strong	10:15

JOSH BRIGGS

Jan 18	Julius Creed & Brutus Creed (w/Brooks Jensen)	W	NXT 2.0	5:33
Jan 28	Damon Kemp	W	WWE 205 Live	5:04
Mar 11	Zack Gibson & James Drake (w/Brooks Jensen)	L	NXT Level Up	5:58
Mar 29	Joaquin Wilde & Raul Mendoza (w/Brooks Jensen)	W	NXT 2.0	5:36
Apr 12	Gauntlet Match: Grayson Waller & Sanga, Kit Wilson & Elton Prince	L	NXT 2.0	27:08
	Joaquin Wilde & Raul Mendoza, Julius Creed & Brutus Creed (w/Brooks Jensen)			
Apr 26	Handicap Match: Joaquin Wilde, Cruz del Toro & Elektra Lopez	L	NXT 2.0	4:45
	(w/Fallon Henley)			
May 20	Quincy Elliott	W	NXT Level Up	7:16
May 31	Grayson Waller	L	NXT 2.0	3:33
Jun 7	Von Wagner	W	NXT 2.0	3:04
Jun 23	Elimination Match: Dave Mastiff & Jack Starz, Charlie Dempsey	W	NXT UK	18:15
	& Rohan Raja, Mark Andrews & Wilf Boar (w/Brooks Jensen)			
Jul 19	Elton Prince & Kit Wilson (w/Brooks Jensen)	W	NXT 2.0	8:15
Jul 28	Mark Andrews & Wild Boar (w/Brooks Jensen)	W	NXT UK	9:03
Aug 23	Mark Coffey & Wolfgang (w/Brooks Jensen)	L	NXT 2.0	8:46
Aug 30	Lash Legend, Elton Prince & Kit Wilson (w/Fallon Henley & Brooks Jensen)	K	NXT 2.0	11:31
Sep 4	Elimination Match: Elton Prince & Kit Wilson, Brutus Creed & Julius Creed,	L	NXT Worlds Collide '22	15:34
	Mark Coffey & Wolfgang (w/Brooks Jensen)			
Sep 27	Pub Rules Match: Mark Coffey & Wolfgang (w/Brooks Jensen)	W	NXT	11:35
Oct 6	R-Truth & Shelton Benjamin (w/Brooks Jensen)	W	WWE Main Event	6:48
Oct 11	Edris Enofe & Malik Blade, Jagger Reid & Rip Fowler (w/Brooks Jensen)	L	NXT	9:10
Nov 15	Jagger Reid & Rip Fowler (w/Brooks Jensen)	L	NXT	4:10
Dec 6	Edris Enofe & Malik Blade (w/Brooks Jensen)	W	NXT	3:24
Dec 20	Kofi Kingston & Xavier Woods (w/Brooks Jensen)	L	NXT	11:10

JOSH MORRELL

Mar 10	Primate & T-Bone (w/Danny Jones)	L	NXT UK	6:05
May 19	Kenny Williams	L	NXT UK	5:30
Jun 16	Tiger Turan	L	NXT UK	3:03
Jul 7	Primate	W	NXT UK	4:05
Jul 21	Dave Mastiff	L	NXT UK	6:58

JOSH WOODS

Mar 1	Daniel Garcia	L	AEW Dark	6:42
Mar 15	AC Adams	W	AEW Dark	1:05
Apr 1	Pure Wrestling Rules: Wheeler Yuta	L	ROH Supercard Of Honor XV	12:55
May 17	Wheeler Yuta	L	AEW Dark	12:30
Jul 5	Barrett Brown	W	AEW Dark	2:35
Aug 4	Damian Chambers & Dean Alexander (w/Tony Nese)	W	AEW Dark Elevation	2:52
Aug 5	Street Fight: Keith Lee & Swerve Strickland (w/Tony Nese)	L	AEW Rampage	12:53
Aug 15	Arik Cannon & Travis Titan (w/Tony Nese)	W	AEW Dark Elevation	2:40
Aug 16	Cobra	W	AEW Dark	2:50
Aug 22	Andrea Guercio & Logan James (w/Tony Nese)	W	AEW Dark Elevation	2:16
Aug 23	GKM & Oliver Sawyer (w/Tony Nese)	W	AEW Dark	1:25
Sep 5	Jordan Kross & Renny D (w/Tony Nese)	W	AEW Dark Elevation	2:27
Sep 6	Brandon Gore & Storm Grayson (w/Tony Nese)	W	AEW Dark	2:10
Sep 16	Samoa Joe	L	AEW Rampage	10:10
Sep 20	Baliyan Akki & Ryan Matthews (w/Tony Nese)	W	AEW Dark	4:02
Sep 23	Samoa Joe & Wardlow (w/Tony Nese)	L	AEW Rampage: Grand Slam	2:26
Oct 4	Invictus Khash & Rohit Raju (w/Tony Nese)	W	AEW Dark	2:34
Oct 7	Brian Pillman Jr. & Griff Garrison (w/Tony Nese)	W	AEW Rampage	1:45
Oct 10	Action Andretti & Myles Hawkins (w/Tony Nese)	W	AEW Dark Elevation	5:55
Oct 21	Anthony Bowens & Max Caster (w/Tony Nese)	L	AEW Rampage	8:06
Nov 22	Dean Alexander & Rosario Grillo (w/Tony Nese)	W	AEW Dark	3:32
Dec 12	Brandon Cutler, Luther & Serpentico (w/Tony Nese & Ari Daivari)	W	AEW Dark Elevation	5:20
Dec 23	$300,000 Three Kings Christmas Casino Trios Royale	L	AEW Rampage	22:01
	(w/Ari Daivari & Tony Nese)			

JR KRATOS

Jan 29	Alex Coughlin	L	NJPW Strong	9:22
Feb 8	Team War Match: Odinson, Parrow & Rodney Mack, Jordan Clearwater,	L	NWA Power	11:40
	Marshe Rockett & Tyrus, Alex Taylor, Jeremiah Plunkett & Rush Freeman			
	(w/Aron Stevens & Judais)			
Mar 26	Elimination Match: Adrian Quest, Clark Connors, Fred Rosser, Taylor Rust	W	NJPW Strong	16:29
	& The DKC (w/Danny Limelight, Jorel Nelson, Royce Isaacs & Tom Lawlor)			
Apr 2	Rocky Romero & Wheeler Yuta (w/Black Tiger)	W	NJPW Strong	9:50
Apr 16	Fred Rosser, Josh Alexander, Alex Coughlin, Ren Narita & Chris Dickinson	L	NJPW Windy City Riot	13:50
	(w/Royce Isaacs, Jorel Nelson, Black Tiger & Danny Limelight)			
May 7	Alex Coughlin, Fred Rosser & The DKC (w/Royce Isaacs & Tom Lawlor)	W	NJPW Strong	11:12
May 13	Adrian Quest, Alex Coughlin & Rocky Romero	L	NJPW Strong	8:33
	(w/Black Tiger & Danny Limelight)			
May 14	The DKC, Yuya Uemura, David Finlay, Tanga Loa & Fred Rosser	W	NJPW Capital Collision	14:48
	(w/Tom Lawlor, Jorel Nelson, Royce Isaacs & Danny Limelight)			
Jun 18	Alex Coughlin, Kevin Knight & The DKC (w/Jorel Nelson & Royce Isaacs)	W	NJPW Strong	9:21
Jul 23	Jordan Cruz	W	NJPW Strong	4:11
Aug 20	Drew Adler	W	NJPW Strong	4:43
Aug 28	Missouri Tornado Match: Aron Stevens & Rodney Mack (w/Da Pope)	W	NWA 74th Anniversary Show	9:40

Sep 13	KC Roxx & The Question Mark II (w/Da Pope)	W	NWA Power	6:46
Sep 17	Cody Chhun & Jordan Cruz (w/Tom Lawlor)	W	NJPW Strong	9:54
Oct 15	Kyle Fletcher & Mark Davis (w/Danny Limelight)	L	NJPW Strong	10:08
Oct 18	The Question Mark II	L	NWA Power	5:37
Nov 8	Thom Latimer, Trevor Murdoch & Tyrus (w/Doug Williams & Da Pope)	D	NWA Power	6:49
Nov 12	Adrian Quest & Jordan Cruz (w/Danny Limelight)	W	NJPW Strong	8:20
Nov 15	Aron Stevens	W	NWA Power	1:35
Dec 6	Thrillbilly Silas	L	NWA Power	8:08
Dec 24	Fred Rosser	L	NJPW Strong	18:44

JTG

Jan 11	Jamie Stanley & Sam Adonis (w/Dirty Dango)	W	NWA Power	5:51
Jan 18	Handicap Match: Jay Bradley, Wrecking Ball Legursky & Rush Freeman (w/Dirty Dango)	L	NWA Power	4:29
Feb 1	Handicap Match: Alex Taylor, Captain Yuma & Rush Freeman (w/Dirty Dango)	W	NWA Power	4:09
Mar 19	Aron Stevens & The Blue Meanie (w/Dirty Dango)	W	NWA Crockett Cup '22	6:40
Mar 19	Jay Briscoe & Mark Briscoe (w/Dirty Dango)	L	NWA Crockett Cup '22	8:13
Apr 12	Doug Williams & Harry Smith (w/Dirty Dango)	L	NWA Power	6:52
May 10	Gaagz The Gymp & Sal The Pal (w/Dirty Dango)	W	NWA Power	6:37
Jul 26	Doug Williams & Harry Smith (w/Dirty Dango)	L	NWA Power	6:13
Aug 23	Luke Hawx & PJ Hawx, Gustavo Aguilar & Rhett Titus (w/Dirty Dango)	L	NWA Power	5:56
Nov 1	Luke Hawx & PJ Hawx (w/Dirty Dango)	L	NWA Power	6:22

JUDAIS

Jan 11	Cyon	L	NWA Power	2:53
Feb 8	Team War Match: Odinson, Parrow & Rodney Mack, Jordan Clearwater, Marshe Rockett & Tyrus, Alex Taylor, Jeremiah Plunkett & Rush Freeman (w/Aron Stevens & JR Kratos)	L	NWA Power	11:40
Apr 12	Jay Bradley, Wrecking Ball Legursky & Colby Corino (w/Gaagz The Gymp & Sal The Pal)	W	NWA Power	6:27
May 10	Matt Taven	L	NWA Power	4:53
Jul 5	Odinson, AJ Cazana	L	NWA Power	5:11
Aug 2	Alex Taylor, Jeremiah Plunkett & Rush Freeman (w/Gaagz The Gymp & Sal The Pal)	W	NWA Power	8:08
Aug 27	Beelzebub's Bedlam Match: Danny Dealz, Alex Taylor & Jeremiah Plunkett (w/Sal The Pal & Gaagz The Gymp)	W	NWA 74th Anniversary Show	9:41
Nov 1	Mims, Gustavo Aguilar	L	NWA Power	6:45
Dec 6	Damage & Rush Freeman (w/PJ Hawx)	W	NWA Power	6:42
Dec 20	Chris Adonis, Dak Draper & Mims (w/Bully Ray & Thom Latimer)	W	NWA Power	8:18

JUICE ROBINSON

Jan 6	Raj Singh	W	IMPACT Before The Impact	9:12
Jan 22	Bad Dude Tito	W	NJPW Strong	9:37
Feb 12	Bad Dude Tito & Jonah (w/David Finlay)	W	NJPW Strong	11:51
Mar 5	Bad Dude Tito & Jonah (w/David Finlay)	L	NJPW Strong	8:16
Apr 1	Clark Connors, Karl Fredericks, Mascara Dorada & Yuya Uemura (w/David Finlay, Daniel Garcia & Kevin Knight)	L	NJPW Lonestar Shootout	10:45
Apr 2	Jonah & Shane Haste (w/David Finlay)	W	NJPW Strong	6:34
Apr 16	Chicago Street Fight: Jonah, Shane Haste & Bad Dude Tito (w/David Finlay & Brody King)	W	NJPW Windy City Riot	24:11
May 14	Hiroshi Tanahashi, Will Ospreay, Jon Moxley	W	NJPW Capital Collision	15:45
Jun 11	Chuck Taylor, Rocky Romero, Tomohiro Ishii, Mascara Dorada & Ren Narita (w/Luke Gallows, Karl Anderson, Hikuleo & Jay White)	W	NJPW Strong	12:44
Sep 17	Kushida, Taylor Rust, Trent Beretta & Rocky Romero (w/Chase Owens, Hikuleo & Jay White)	W	NJPW Strong	14:46
Sep 28	Jon Moxley	L	AEW Dynamite	11:18
Oct 6	Alex Zayne	W	IMPACT Before The Impact	9:27
Oct 8	Ren Narita	L	NJPW Strong	1:20
Oct 8	No DQ: Ren Narita	L	NJPW Strong	14:45
Oct 20	Bully Ray & Tommy Dreamer (w/Chris Bey)	L	IMPACT Wrestling	6:23
Oct 28	Kazuchika Okada & Eddie Kingston (w/Jay White)	W	NJPW Rumble On 44th Street	20:15
Nov 26	Jake Something	W	NJPW Strong	10:44
Dec 3	Blake Christian	W	NJPW Strong	9:33
Dec 10	Hagane Shinno	W	AEW Dark Elevation	4:30
Dec 10	Samoa Joe	L	ROH Final Battle '22	13:40

JUICY FINAU

Apr 14	Alex Kane, ACH, Myron Reed, Puma King	L	MLW Fusion	4:28
Jun 30	Cinco & Uno (w/Lance Anoa'i)	W	MLW Fusion	2:24
Nov 17	Joel Maximo & Jose Maximo (w/Lance Anoa'i)	W	MLW Fusion	3:14
Dec 8	Angel Fashion & Mark Davidson (w/Lance Anoa'i)	W	MLW Fusion	4:23

JULIA HART

Jan 28	Jade Cargill	L	AEW Rampage: Beach Break	2:28
Feb 7	Arie Alexander	W	AEW Dark Elevation	2:06
Feb 8	Kelsey Heather	W	AEW Dark	2:23
Mar 21	Skye Blue	W	AEW Dark Elevation	4:00
Apr 6	Hikaru Shida	L	AEW Dynamite	7:45
Apr 25	Kris Statlander	L	AEW Dark Elevation	6:19
May 2	Abby Jane	W	AEW Dark Elevation	2:20
May 3	Jaycie Love	W	AEW Dark	1:55

Jun 28	Valentina Rossi	W	AEW Dark	2:38
Jul 11	JC	W	AEW Dark Elevation	2:02
Jul 18	Amber Nova	W	AEW Dark Elevation	1:33
Jul 26	Renee Michelle	W	AEW Dark	2:51
Aug 1	MLK	W	AEW Dark Elevation	2:35
Aug 15	Free-Range Kara	W	AEW Dark Elevation	2:41
Aug 22	Hayley Shadows	W	AEW Dark Elevation	2:08
Aug 29	Arie Alexander	W	AEW Dark Elevation	1:56
Aug 30	Vickie Dreamboat	W	AEW Dark	3:08
Sep 5	Alice Crowley	W	AEW Dark Elevation	2:27
Sep 6	Missa Kate	W	AEW Dark	2:36
Sep 12	Tiara James	W	AEW Dark Elevation	1:33
Dec 20	Sahara Se7en	W	AEW Dark	1:07
Dec 26	Promise Braxton	W	AEW Dark Elevation	1:11

JULIUS CREED

Jan 18	Josh Briggs & Brooks Jensen (w/Brutus Creed)	W	NXT 2.0	5:33
Feb 1	Walter, Marcel Barthel & Fabian Aichner (w/Brutus Creed & Roderick Strong)	L	NXT 2.0	12:01
Feb 8	Zack Gibson & James Drake (w/Brutus Creed)	W	NXT 2.0	12:03
Feb 15	Nash Carter & Wes Lee (w/Brutus Creed)	W	NXT 2.0: Vengeance Day '22	9:36
Mar 22	Zack Gibson & James Drake (w/Brutus Creed)	W	NXT 2.0	4:14
Apr 2	Wes Lee & Nash Carter, Marcel Barthel & Fabin Aichner (w/Brutus Creed)	L	NXT Stand & Deliver '22	11:22
Apr 5	Marcel Barthel & Fabian Aichner (w/Brutus Creed)	W	NXT 2.0	11:24
Apr 12	Gauntlet Match: Grayson Waller & Sanga, Kit Wilson & Elton Prince Joaquin Wilde & Raul Mendoza, Brooks Jensen & Josh Briggs (w/Brutus Creed)	L	NXT 2.0	27:08
May 3	Erik & Ivar (w/Brutus Creed)	W	NXT 2.0: Spring Breakin'	12:58
May 17	Erik & Ivar (w/Brutus Creed)	L	NXT 2.0	9:30
Jun 4	Elton Prince & Kit Wilson (w/Brutus Creed)	W	NXT In Your House '22	15:19
Jun 14	Edris Enofe & Malik Blade (w/Brutus Creed)	W	NXT 2.0	13:57
Jun 28	Joe Gacy, Rip Fowler & Jagger Reid (w/Roderick Strong & Brutus Creed)	L	NXT 2.0	13:56
Jul 5	Roderick Strong & Damon Kemp (w/Brutus Creed)	W	NXT 2.0: Great American Bash	12:13
Jul 26	Tony D'Angelo, Channing Lorenzo, Joaquin Wilde & Cruz Del Toro (w/Roderick Strong, Damon Kemp & Brutus Creed)	L	NXT 2.0	11:39
Aug 2	Tony D'Angelo & Channing Lorenzo (w/Brutus Creed)	W	NXT 2.0	10:46
Aug 30	Joe Coffey, Mark Coffey & Wolfgang (w/Brutus Creed & Damon Kemp)	L	NXT 2.0	10:59
Sep 4	Elimination Match: Elton Prince & Kit Wilson, Brooks Jensen & Josh Briggs, Mark Coffey & Wolfgang (w/Brutus Creed)	L	NXT Worlds Collide '22	15:34
Sep 13	Steel Cage Match: Elton Prince & Kit Wilson (w/Brutus Creed)	L	NXT 2.0	14:58
Oct 4	Duke Hudson	W	NXT	:52
Oct 22	Ambulance Match: Damon Kemp	W	NXT Halloween Havoc '22	14:09
Nov 29	JD McDonagh	W	NXT	10:33
Dec 27	JD McDonagh	W	NXT	9:51

JUN AKIYAMA

Mar 20	Hideki Okatani & Kazusada Higuchi (w/Takao Omori)	W	DDT Judgment '22: 25th Anniversary	12:36
Jun 12	Atsushi Kotoge, Katsuhiko Nakajima & Yoshiaki Inamura (w/Tetsuya Endo & Kazusada Higuchi)	L	Cyberfight Festival '22	6:20
Nov 18	Eddie Kingston & Ortiz (w/Konosuke Takeshita)	W	AEW Rampage	12:17
Nov 19	Eddie Kingston	L	AEW Full Gear Buy-In	10:30

JUNGLE BOY

Jan 5	Rey Fenix & Penta El Zero M (w/Luchasaurus)	W	AEW Dynamite	14:03
Jan 11	Nick Comoroto & QT Marshall (w/Luchasaurus)	W	AEW Dark	8:21
Jan 14	John Silver & Alex Reynolds (w/Luchasaurus)	W	AEW Rampage	12:37
Jan 25	Nick Comoroto	W	AEW Dark	6:48
Jan 28	Marq Quen & Isiah Kassidy (w/Luchasaurus)	W	AEW Rampage: Beach Break	10:45
Feb 11	Austin Gunn & Colten Gunn (w/Luchasaurus)	W	AEW Rampage	12:29
Mar 6	Bobby Fish & Kyle O'Reilly, Matt Jackson & Nick Jackson (w/Luchasaurus)	W	AEW Revolution '22	18:55
Mar 9	Anthony Bowens & Max Caster (w/Luchasaurus)	W	AEW Dynamite	9:26
Mar 16	Adam Cole, Bobby Fish & Kyle O'Reilly (w/Hangman Page & Luchasaurus)	L	AEW Dynamite: St. Patrick's Day Slam	13:58
Apr 13	Bobby Fish & Kyle O'Reilly (w/Luchasaurus)	W	AEW Dynamite	13:45
Apr 20	Kyle O'Reilly	L	AEW Dynamite	13:02
May 11	Ricky Starks	L	AEW Dynamite	10:01
May 25	Swerve Strickland, Ricky Starks	L	AEW Dynamite: 3 Year Anniversary	9:36
May 29	Keith Lee & Swerve Strickland, Powerhouse Hobbs & Ricky Starks (w/Luchasaurus)	W	AEW Double Or Nothing '22	17:15
Jun 1	Matt Jackson, Nick Jackson, Bobby Fish, Kyle O'Reilly & Hikuleo (w/Christian Cage, Matt Hardy, Darby Allin & Luchasaurus)	L	AEW Dynamite	12:00
Jun 15	Ladder Match: Matt Jackson & Nick Jackson (w/Luchasaurus)	L	AEW Dynamite: Road Rager	14:53
Sep 4	Christian Cage	L	AEW All Out '22	:20
Sep 14	Jay Lethal	W	AEW Dynamite	10:38
Sep 23	Rey Fenix	W	AEW Rampage: Grand Slam	16:40
Oct 12	Luchasaurus	L	AEW Dynamite	14:05
Nov 19	Steel Cage Match: Luchasaurus	W	AEW Full Gear '22	18:40
Dec 7	Dynamite Diamond Battle Royale	L	AEW Dynamite	13:10
Dec 14	Brian Cage	W	AEW Dynamite: Winter Is Coming	8:16

KAMILLE

Jan 5	Kylie Rae & Tootie Lynn (w/Missa Kate)	L	NWA Power	6:44
Feb 8	Kiera Hogan	W	NWA Power	3:20
Feb 22	Taryn Terrell	W	NWA Power	7:48

Mar 20	Chelsea Green, Kylie Rae	W	NWA Crockett Cup '22	12:02
Mar 29	Madi Wrenkowski	W	NWA Power	5:53
May 10	Paola Blaze	W	NWA Power	7:48
Jun 7	KiLynn King & Missa Kate (w/Kenzie Paige)	L	NWA Power	9:07
Jun 11	KiLynn King	W	NWA Alwayz Ready '22	17:25
Jul 26	Chelsea Green	W	NWA Power	9:37
Aug 16	Hayley Shadows	W	NWA Power	3:04
Aug 27	Taya Valkyrie	W	NWA 74th Anniversary Show	18:57
Aug 28	Max The Impaler	W	NWA 74th Anniversary Show	11:07
Sep 6	Allysin Kay	D	NWA Power	10:00
Oct 4	Jennacide	W	NWA Power	7:20
Oct 15	Taya Valkyrie	L	AAA TripleMania XXX: Mexico City	15:18
Nov 8	Allysin Kay & Marti Belle (w/KiLynn King)	W	NWA Power	7:31
Nov 12	Chelsea Green, KiLynn King	W	NWA Hard Times 3	8:59
Nov 22	Jazmin Allure	W	NWA Power	7:50
Dec 27	Kenzie Paige	W	NWA Power	10:07

KARL ANDERSON

Jan 6	Heath	W	IMPACT Wrestling	11:02
Jan 8	Hardcore War: Eddie Edwards, Rich Swann, Willie Mack, Heath & Rhino (w/Luke Gallows, Eric Young, Deaner & Joe Doering)	L	IMPACT Hard To Kill '22	23:25
Mar 3	Tama Tonga, Tanga Loa, Deaner & Joe Doering (w/Chris Bey, Jay White & Luke Gallows)	W	IMPACT Wrestling	9:48
Mar 17	Deaner	W	IMPACT Before The Impact	6:22
Mar 24	Lumberjack Match: Eric Young & Joe Doering (w/Luke Gallows)	L	IMPACT Wrestling	7:26
Mar 31	Johnny Swinger & Zicky Dice (w/Luke Gallows)	W	IMPACT Wrestling	:50
Apr 1	Jay Briscoe & Mark Briscoe (w/Luke Gallows)	W	IMPACT Multiverse Of Matches	9:46
Apr 16	Aaron Henare, Great-O-Khan, Jeff Cobb, TJP, Mark Davis & Kyle Fletcher (w/Hikuleo, Chris Bey, El Phantasmo, Luke Gallows & Scott Norton)	L	NJPW Windy City Riot	11:58
Apr 21	Kenny King, Matt Taven, Mike Bennett & Vincent (w/Chris Bey, Jay White & Luke Gallows)	W	IMPACT Wrestling	9:22
Apr 23	Elimination Challenge Match (w/Luke Gallows)	L	IMPACT Rebellion '22	33:02
May 19	Matt Taven & Mike Bennett (w/Luke Gallows)	W	IMPACT Wrestling	10:00
Jun 11	Chuck Taylor, Rocky Romero, Tomohiro Ishii, Mascara Dorada & Ren Narita (w/Luke Gallows, Hikuleo, Jay White & Juice Robinson)	W	NJPW Strong	12:44
Jun 12	Tama Tonga	W	NJPW Dominion '22	16:27
Jun 19	Jay Briscoe & Mark Briscoe (w/Luke Gallows)	W	IMPACT Slammiversary XX	10:00
Jun 30	PCO & Vincent (w/Luke Gallows)	W	IMPACT Wrestling	5:19
Jul 14	Eddie Edwards, Kenny King, Matt Taven & Mike Bennett (w/Ace Austin, Chris Bey & Luke Gallows)	L	IMPACT Wrestling	12:34
Aug 11	Kenny King	W	IMPACT Wrestling	7:53
Aug 25	Mike Bennett	W	IMPACT Wrestling	7:44
Sep 1	Matt Taven & Mike Bennett (w/Luke Gallows)	L	IMPACT Wrestling	8:14
Sep 15	Alex Shelley & Chris Sabin (w/Luke Gallows)	L	IMPACT Wrestling	14:39
Sep 25	Hiroshi Tanahashi	W	NJPW Burning Spirit '22	13:37
Oct 1	Hiroshi Tanahashi, Tama Tonga, Hikuleo & Jado (w/Jay White, Luke Gallows & Gedo)	L	NJPW Royal Quest II Night #1	12:15
Oct 2	Hiroshi Tanahashi, Tama Tonga & Hikuleo (w/Jay White & Luke Gallows)	L	NJPW Royal Quest II Night #2	10:54
Oct 8	Homicide & Wheeler Yuta (w/Jay White)	W	NJPW Strong	14:37
Oct 17	Chad Gable & Otis (w/Luke Gallows)	W	WWE Monday Night RAW	8:20
Oct 18	Joe Gacy, Jagger Reid & Rip Fowler (w/Cameron Grimes & Luke Gallows)	W	NXT	11:56
Oct 24	Finn Balor	L	WWE Monday Night RAW	17:15
Oct 31	Damian Priest	W	WWE Monday Night RAW	7:17
Nov 5	Finn Balor, Damian Priest & Dominik Mysterio (w/Luke Gallows & AJ Styles)	L	WWE Crown Jewel '22	14:00
Nov 28	Finn Balor, Damian Priest, Dominik Mysterio & Rhea Ripley (w/AJ Styles, Luke Gallows & Mia Yim)	L	WWE Monday Night RAW	14:20
Dec 5	Baron Corbin, Chad Gable & Otis (w/AJ Styles & Luke Gallows)	W	WWE Monday Night RAW	14:30
Dec 19	Chad Gable & Otis (w/Luke Gallows)	W	WWE Monday Night RAW	9:05

KARL FREDERICKS

Jan 15	Bateman & Misterioso (w/Kevin Knight)	W	NJPW Strong	10:04
Feb 26	Ethan HD	W	NJPW Strong	11:51
Mar 5	Christopher Daniels	L	NJPW Strong	11:40
Apr 1	David Finlay, Juice Robinson, Daniel Garcia & Kevin Knight (w/Clark Connors, Mascara Dorada & Yuya Uemura)	W	NJPW Lonestar Shootout	10:45
Apr 9	Josh Alexander	L	NJPW Strong	14:14
Apr 16	QT Marshall, Aaron Solo & Nick Comoroto (w/Clark Connors & Yuya Uemura)	L	NJPW Windy City Riot	11:56
May 14	Ren Narita	W	NJPW Capital Collision	10:32
May 17	Aaron Solo, Blake Li, Brick Aldridge, Nick Comoroto & QT Marshall (w/Alex Coughlin, Clark Connors, Kevin Knight & Yuya Uemura)	W	AEW Dark	10:30
May 21	Aaron Solo & Nick Comoroto (w/Clark Connors)	W	NJPW Strong	8:21
Jun 11	QT Marshall	W	NJPW Strong	8:24

KARRION KROSS (AS KILLER KROSS UNTIL SEPTEMBER 2)

Mar 24	Budd Heavy	W	MLW Fusion	2:23
Apr 1	Minoru Suzuki	L	NJPW Lonestar Shootout	9:48
Jun 11	Yuya Uemura	W	NJPW Strong	7:50
Jul 31	Davey Boy Smith Jr.	W	JCP Ric Flair's Last Match	5:22
Sep 2	Drew Gulak	W	WWE SmackDown	1:15

Oct 8	Strap Match: Drew McIntyre	W	WWE Extreme Rules '22	10:20
Oct 28	Madcap Moss	W	WWE SmackDown	9:35
Nov 5	Steel Cage Match: Drew McIntyre	L	WWE Crown Jewel '22	13:00
Nov 17	Matt Cross	W	MLW Fusion	4:38
Nov 18	Madcap Moss	W	WWE SmackDown	6:48

KATANA CHANCE (AS KACY CATANZARO UNTIL APR 26)

Jan 11	Wendy Choo, Indi Hartwell & Persia Pirotta (w/Kayden Carter & Amari Miller)	L	NXT 2.0	3:40
Feb 4	Fallon Henley & Lash Legend (w/Kayden Carter)	W	WWE 205 Live	6:15
Feb 22	Ivy Nile & Tatum Paxley (w/Kayden Carter)	W	NXT 2.0	3:26
Mar 8	Io Shirai & Kay Lee Ray (w/Kayden Carter)	L	NXT 2.0: Roadblock '22	7:59
Apr 26	Yulisa Leon & Valentina Feroz (w/Kayden Carter)	W	NXT 2.0	6:01
Jun 4	Gigi Dolin & Jacy Jayne (w/Kayden Carter)	L	NXT In Your House '22	9:01
Jun 21	Yulisa Leon & Valentina Feroz (w/Kayden Carter)	W	NXT 2.0	5:15
Jun 28	Cora Jade & Roxanne Perez (w/Kayden Carter)	L	NXT 2.0	13:46
Jul 19	Battle Royal	L	NXT 2.0	13:13
Aug 2	Elimination Match: Valentina Feroz & Yulisa Leon, Ivy Nile & Tatum Paxley, Gigi Dolin & Jacy Jayne (w/Kayden Carter)	W	NXT 2.0	12:09
Aug 30	Ivy Nile & Tatum Paxley (w/Kayden Carter)	W	NXT 2.0	4:17
Sep 4	Doudrop & Nikki A.S.H. (w/Kayden Carter)	W	NXT Worlds Collide '22	10:19
Oct 25	Zoey Stark & Nikkita Lyons (w/Kayden Carter)	W	NXT	12:52
Nov 8	Zoey Stark & Nikkita Lyons (w/Kayden Carter)	W	NXT	11:02
Nov 29	Mandy Rose, Gigi Dolin & Jacy Jayne (w/Kayden Karter & Nikkita Lyons)	L	NXT	8:54
Dec 8	Tamina	W	WWE Main Event	1:47
Dec 20	Gigi Dolin & Jacy Jayne, Icy Nile & Tatum Paxley (w/Kayden Carter)	W	NXT	6:35

KATSUYORI SHIBATA

| Jan 4 | Ren Narita | W | NJPW Wrestle Kingdom 16 Night #1 | 11:46 |
| Nov 4 | Orange Cassidy | L | AEW Rampage | 14:00 |

KAUN

Jan 18	Adam Cole	L	AEW Dark	7:53
Mar 29	Frankie Kazarian	L	AEW Dark	3:20
Jul 8	Jonathan Gresham & Lee Moriarty (w/Toa Liona)	W	AEW Rampage	7:27
Oct 7	Dax Harwood & Cash Wheeler (w/Toa Liona)	L	AEW Battle Of The Belts IV	13:26
Oct 14	Shawn Spears, Dax Harwood & Cash Wheeler (w/Brian Cage & Toa Liona)	L	AEW Rampage	10:29
Nov 1	Fuego Del Sol, Jaylen Brandyn & Traevon Jordan (w/Brian Cage & Toa Liona)	W	AEW Dark	4:01
Nov 4	Wardlow & Samoa Joe (w/Toa Liona)	L	AEW Rampage	9:10
Nov 14	Big Cuzzo & Teddy Goodz (w/Toa Liona)	W	AEW Dark Elevation	1:37
Dec 5	Dan Adams, Facade & Star Rider (w/Brian Cage & Toa Liona)	W	AEW Dark Elevation	3:43
Dec 10	Dalton Castle, Brandon Tate & Brent Tate (w/Brian Cage & Toa Liona)	W	ROH Final Battle '22	10:05

KAYDEN CARTER

Jan 11	Wendy Choo, Indi Hartwell & Persia Pirotta (w/Kacy Catanzaro & Amari Miller)	L	NXT 2.0	3:40
Feb 4	Fallon Henley & Lash Legend (w/Kacy Catanzaro)	W	WWE 205 Live	6:15
Feb 22	Ivy Nile & Tatum Paxley (w/Kacy Catanzaro)	W	NXT 2.0	3:26
Mar 8	Io Shirai & Kay Lee Ray (w/Kacy Catanzaro)	L	NXT 2.0: Roadblock '22	7:59
Apr 1	Tatum Paxley	W	NXT Level Up	6:01
Apr 26	Yulisa Leon & Valentina Feroz (w/Katana Chance)	W	NXT 2.0	6:01
Jun 4	Gigi Dolin & Jacy Jayne (w/Katana Chance)	L	NXT In Your House '22	9:01
Jun 21	Yulisa Leon & Valentina Feroz (w/Katana Chance)	W	NXT 2.0	5:15
Jun 28	Cora Jade & Roxanne Perez (w/Katana Chance)	L	NXT 2.0	13:46
Jul 12	Tatum Paxley	L	NXT 2.0	3:31
Jul 19	Battle Royal	L	NXT 2.0	13:13
Aug 2	Elimination Match: Valentina Feroz & Yulisa Leon, Ivy Nile & Tatum Paxley, Gigi Dolin & Jacy Jayne (w/Katana Chance)	W	NXT 2.0	12:09
Aug 30	Ivy Nile & Tatum Paxley (w/Katana Chance)	W	NXT 2.0	4:17
Sep 4	Doudrop & Nikki A.S.H. (w/Katana Chance)	W	NXT Worlds Collide '22	10:19
Sep 27	Nikkita Lyons	L	NXT	4:54
Oct 25	Zoey Stark & Nikkita Lyons (w/Katana Chance)	W	NXT	12:52
Nov 8	Zoey Stark & Nikkita Lyons (w/Katana Chance)	W	NXT	11:02
Nov 29	Mandy Rose, Gigi Dolin & Jacy Jayne (w/Katana Chance & Nikkita Lyons)	L	NXT	8:54
Dec 20	Gigi Dolin & Jacy Jayne, Icy Nile & Tatum Paxley (w/Katana Chance)	W	NXT	6:35

KAZUCHIKA OKADA

Jan 4	Shingo Takagi	W	NJPW Wrestle Kingdom 16 Night #1	35:44
Jan 5	Will Ospreay	W	NJPW Wrestle Kingdom 16 Night #2	32:52
Jan 8	Keiji Mutoh & Kaito Kiyomiya (w/Hiroshi Tanahashi)	W	NJPW Wrestle Kingdom 16 Night #3	24:34
Mar 1	Zack Sabre Jr., Minoru Suzuki & Yoshiaki Fujiwara (w/Hiroshi Tanahashi & Tatsumi Fujinami)	W	NJPW 50th Anniversary Show	18:12
Apr 9	Zack Sabre Jr.	W	NJPW Hyper Battle '22	28:25
May 1	Tetsuya Naito	W	NJPW Wrestling Dontaku '22	34:12
May 14	Jay White & Hikuleo (w/Rocky Romero)	L	NJPW Capital Collision	15:59
Jun 12	Jay White	L	NJPW Dominion '22	36:04
Jun 26	Hangman Page, Jay White, Adam Cole	L	AEW x NJPW Forbidden Door	21:05
Sep 25	Bad Dude Tito, Jonah & Shane Haste (w/Togi Makabe & Tomoaki Honma)	L	NJPW Burning Spirit '22	12:09
Oct 1	Bad Dude Tito & Zak Knight (w/Tomohiro Ishii)	W	NJPW Royal Quest II Night #1	12:47

Oct 2	Bad Dude Tito	W	NJPW Royal Quest II Night #2	8:13
Oct 10	Jonah	W	NJPW Declaration Of Power	19:53
Oct 28	Jay White & Juice Robinson (w/Eddie Kingston)	L	NJPW Rumble On 44th Street	20:15
Nov 5	Jay White & Kenta (w/Tama Tonga)	W	NJPW Battle Autumn '22	17:34
Nov 20	Great-O-Khan, Jeff Cobb & Aaron Henare (w/Toru Yano & The Great Muta)	W	NJPW x Stardom Historic X-Over	9:48

KC NAVARRO

Mar 3	Ho Ho Lun	W	MLW Fusion	3:29
Mar 10	nZo	L	MLW Fusion	2:48
Apr 29	Gino Medina, Arez & Mini Abismo Negro (w/Aramis & Micro Man)	L	MLW Fusion	11:55
Jun 2	nZo	W	MLW Fusion	1:50
Jun 23	Myron Reed, Arez	W	MLW Fusion	6:09
Nov 10	Mini Abismo Negro	W	MLW Fusion	4:04

KEITA MURRAY

Jan 8	Chris Bey & Hikuleo (w/Jordan Clearwater)	L	NJPW Strong	9:12
Mar 19	Barrett Brown, Bateman & Misterioso (w/Fred Yehi & The DKC)	W	NJPW Strong	10:05
Jun 4	Kevin Blackwood & Lucas Riley (w/Yuya Uemura)	W	NJPW Strong	8:33
Sep 24	QT Marshall	L	NJPW Strong	5:12
Nov 19	Peter Avalon	L	NJPW Strong	8:58

KEITH LEE

Feb 9	Isiah Kassidy	W	AEW Dynamite	4:29
Mar 4	JD Drake	W	AEW Rampage	5:50
Mar 6	Ladder Match: Christian Cage, Wardlow, Orange Cassidy, Powerhouse Hobbs, Ricky Starks	L	AEW Revolution '22	17:20
Mar 11	QT Marshall	W	AEW Rampage	4:05
Mar 18	Max Caster	W	AEW Rampage	9:46
Apr 1	Powerhouse Hobbs	W	AEW Rampage	10:53
Apr 13	Ricky Starks & Powerhouse Hobbs (w/Swerve Strickland)	L	AEW Dynamite	12:32
Apr 19	Aaron Solo & Nick Comoroto (w/Swerve Strickland)	W	AEW Dark	8:40
Apr 29	Colten Gunn	W	AEW Rampage	5:57
May 9	Nick Comoroto & QT Marshall (w/Sweve Strickland)	W	AEW Dark Elevation	6:47
May 17	Luther & Serpentico (w/Swerve Strickland)	W	AEW Dark	6:00
May 18	JD Drake & Anthony Henry (w/Swerve Strickland)	W	AEW Dynamite: Wild Card Wednesday	2:24
May 29	Jungle Boy & Luchasaurus, Powerhouse Hobbs & Ricky Starks (w/Swerve Strickland)	L	AEW Double Or Nothing '22	17:15
Jun 8	Casino Battle Royale	L	AEW Dynamite	24:59
Jun 20	Davey Vega & Mat Fitchett (w/Swerve Strickland)	W	AEW Dark Elevation	3:10
Jun 26	El Desperado & Yoshinobu Kanemaru (w/Swerve Strickland)	W	AEW x NJPW Forbidden Door Buy-In	12:08
Jun 27	GPA & Vic Capri (w/Swerve Strickland)	W	AEW Dark Elevation	4:07
Jul 1	Royal Rampage Match	L	AEW Rampage	22:41
Jul 6	The Butcher & The Blade (w/Swerve Strickland)	W	AEW Dynamite	9:38
Jul 13	Matt Jackson & Nick Jackson, Ricky Starks & Powerhouse Hobbs (w/Swerve Strickland)	W	AEW Dynamite: Fyter Fest	18:14
Aug 5	Street Fight: Tony Nese & Josh Woods (w/Swerve Strickland)	W	AEW Rampage	12:53
Aug 19	Marq Quen & Isiah Kassidy (w/Swerve Strickland)	W	AEW Rampage	7:15
Sep 3	Jah-C & Storm Grayson (w/Swerve Strickland)	W	AEW Dark Elevation	3:54
Sep 4	Anthony Bowens & Max Caster (w/Swerve Strickland)	W	AEW All Out '22	22:30
Sep 14	Penta El Zero M & Rey Fenix (w/Swerve Strickland)	W	AEW Dynamite	8:15
Sep 21	Anthony Bowens & Max Caster (w/Swerve Strickland)	W	AEW Dynamite: Grand Slam	13:44
Oct 26	Dax Harwood & Cash Wheeler (w/Swerve Strickland)	W	AEW Dynamite	15:06
Oct 28	Serpentico	W	AEW Rampage	:14
Nov 9	Anthony Bowens, Max Caster, Dax Harwood & Cash Wheeler (w/Swerve Strickland, Austin Gunn & Colten Gunn)	L	AEW Dynamite	12:22
Nov 19	Anthony Bowens & Max Caster (w/Swerve Strickland)	L	AEW Full Gear '22	19:40
Dec 10	Shane Taylor & JD Griffey (w/Swerve Strickland)	W	ROH Final Battle '22	13:50

KELLY KELLY

| Jan 29 | Royal Rumble Match | L | WWE Royal Rumble '22 | 1:05 |

KENNY KING

Feb 17	Chris Sabin	L	IMPACT Wrestling	8:37
Feb 24	Chris Sabin, Rich Swann & Willie Mack (w/Matt Taven & Mike Bennett)	W	IMPACT Wrestling	8:58
Mar 10	Willie Mack	L	IMPACT Wrestling	8:32
Mar 31	Jonathan Gresham	L	IMPACT Wrestling	12:05
Apr 21	Chris Bey, Jay White, Luke Gallows & Karl Anderson (w/Matt Taven, Mike Bennett & Vincent)	L	IMPACT Wrestling	9:22
May 12	Chris Bey	W	IMPACT Wrestling	8:27
Jun 2	Blake Christian	W	IMPACT Wrestling	9:30
Jun 16	Garrett Bischoff & Wes Brisco (w/Vincent)	W	IMPACT Wrestling	3:28
Jun 19	Ultimate X Match: Mike Bailey, Ace Austin, Andrew Everett, Alex Zayne, Trey Miguel	L	IMPACT Slammiversary XX	9:50
Jul 14	Ace Austin, Chris Bey, Luke Gallows & Karl Anderson (w/Eddie Edwards, Matt Taven & Mike Bennett)	W	IMPACT Wrestling	12:34
Aug 11	Karl Anderson	L	IMPACT Wrestling	7:53
Aug 18	Heath	L	IMPACT Wrestling	3:28
Sep 1	Mike Bailey	L	IMPACT Wrestling	9:02
Sep 8	Yuya Uemura	L	IMPACT Wrestling	9:02
Oct 6	Frankie Kazarian	L	IMPACT Wrestling	9:20
Oct 13	Trey Miguel, Alex Zayne, Black Taurus, Laredo Kid, Yuya Uemura	L	IMPACT Wrestling	5:19

Nov 3	Mike Bailey		L	IMPACT Wrestling	8:44
Nov 12	Che Cabrera		W	NJPW Strong	8:06
Dec 10	Greg Sharpe		W	NJPW Strong	9:43

KENNY OMEGA

Aug 17	Andrade El Idolo, Rush & Dragon Lee (w/Nick Jackson & Matt Jackson)	W	AEW Dynamite	20:54
Aug 31	Will Ospreay, Kyle Fletcher & Mark Davis (w/Nick Jackson & Matt Jackson)	W	AEW Dynamite	18:54
Sep 4	Hangman Page, Alex Reynolds & John Silver (w/Matt Jackson & Nick Jackson)	W	AEW All Out '22	19:50
Nov 19	Pac, Penta El Zero M & Rey Fenix (w/Matt Jackson & Nick Jackson)	L	AEW Full Gear '22	18:40
Nov 23	Pac, Penta El Zero M & Rey Fenix (w/Nick Jackson & Matt Jackson)	L	AEW Dynamite: Thanksgiving Eve	14:49
Nov 30	Pac, Penta El Zero M & Rey Fenix (w/Nick Jackson & Matt Jackson)	W	AEW Dynamite	17:20
Dec 14	Pac, Penta El Zero M & Rey Fenix (w/Nick Jackson & Matt Jackson)	L	AEW Dynamite: Winter Is Coming	14:59
Dec 20	Hagane Shinno	W	AEW Dark	11:16
Dec 21	No DQ: Pac, Penta El Zero M & Rey Fenix (w/Nick Jackson & Matt Jackson)	W	AEW Dynamite: Holiday Bash	13:41
Dec 28	Falls Count Anywhere: Pac, Penta El Zero M & Rey Fenix (w/Nick Jackson & Matt Jackson)	W	AEW Dynamite	17:16

KENNY WILLIAMS

Feb 17	Sam Gradwell	L	NXT UK	3:54
Mar 31	Tate Mayfairs	L	NXT UK	5:53
Apr 21	Back Alley Brawl: Sam Gradwell	L	NXT UK	9:42
May 19	Josh Morrell	W	NXT UK	5:30
Jun 9	Mark Andrews	L	NXT UK	9:46
Jul 7	Tiger Turan	L	NXT UK	6:33
Sep 1	Saxon Huxley	L	NXT UK	5:44

KENTA

Jan 4	Hiroshi Tanahashi, Ryusuke Taguchi & Rocky Romero (w/Taiji Ishimori & El Phantasmo)	W	NJPW Wrestle Kingdom 16 Night #1	8:40
Jan 5	No DQ: Hiroshi Tanahashi	L	NJPW Wrestle Kingdom 16 Night #2	22:40
Sep 25	Bushi, Hiromu Takahashi & Shingo Takagi (w/El Phantasmo & Hikuleo)	L	NJPW Burning Spirit '22	8:43
Nov 5	Kazuchika Okada & Tama Tonga (w/Jay White)	L	NJPW Battle Autumn '22	17:34
Dec 17	Bad Dude Tito	W	NJPW Strong	7:53

KENZIE PAIGE

Jan 11	Kiera Hogan, Christi Jayne, Jennacide	L	NWA Power	5:08
Feb 22	Chelsea Green	L	NWA Power	7:24
Mar 20	Allysin Kay & Marti Belle (w/Ella Envy)	L	NWA Crockett Cup '22	7:09
May 3	Mickie James	L	NWA Power	7:55
May 17	Allysin Kay & Marti Belle (w/Madi Wrenkowski)	L	NWA Power	5:16
Jun 7	KiLynn King & Missa Kate (w/Kamille)	L	NWA Power	9:07
Jun 11	Allysin Kay & Marti Belle (w/Ella Envy)	W	NWA Alwayz Ready '22	8:35
Jul 26	Kaci Lennox	W	NWA Power	3:53
Aug 23	Hayley Shadows & Jaylee (w/Ella Envy)	W	NWA Power	2:24
Aug 28	Kingshighway Street Fight: Allysin Kay & Marti Belle (w/Ella Envy)	W	NWA 74th Anniversary Show	10:02
Sep 13	Angelina Love, Max The Impaler & Natalia Markova (w/Ella Envy & Roxy)	L	NWA Power	3:11
Nov 12	Madi Wrenkowski & Missa Kate (w/Ella Envy)	W	NWA Hard Times 3	8:12
Dec 27	Kamille	L	NWA Power	10:07

KERRY MORTON

Apr 7	Marshall Von Erich & Ross Von Erich (w/Ricky Morton)	L	MLW Fusion	5:27
Jul 5	Jay Bradley	W	NWA Power	5:16
Jul 31	Brock Anderson & Brian Pillman Jr. (w/Ricky Morton)	L	JCP Ric Flair's Last Match	7:21
Aug 27	Homicide	L	NWA 74th Anniversary Show	12:38
Oct 18	Joe Alonzo	W	NWA Power	5:46
Nov 12	Homicide	W	NWA Hard Times 3	10:02
Dec 27	Jay Bradley & Wrecking Ball Legursky (w/Ricky Morton)	W	NWA Power	6:26

KEVIN BLACKWOOD

Mar 12	Ari Daivari	W	NJPW Strong	8:51
Jun 4	Keita Murray & Yuya Uemura (w/Lucas Riley)	L	NJPW Strong	8:33
Sep 10	Robbie Eagles	L	NJPW Strong	11:32
Dec 24	Bobby Fish	L	NJPW Strong	12:00

KEVIN KNIGHT

Jan 15	Bateman & Misterioso (w/Karl Fredericks)	W	NJPW Strong	10:04
Feb 19	Eddie Pearl & Ricky Gibson (w/The DKC)	L	NJPW Strong	9:18
Mar 12	Hikuleo	L	NJPW Strong	8:13
Apr 1	Clark Connors, Karl Fredericks, Mascara Dorada & Yuya Uemura (w/Juice Robinson, Daniel Garcia & David Finlay)	L	NJPW Lonestar Shootout	10:45
Apr 30	The DKC	L	NJPW Strong	7:45
May 10	Aaron Solo & Nick Comoroto (w/The DKC)	L	AEW Dark	8:30
May 17	Aaron Solo, Blake Li, Brick Aldridge, Nick Comoroto & QT Marshall (w/Alex Coughlin, Clark Connors, Karl Fredericks & Yuya Uemura)	W	AEW Dark	10:30
May 28	Barrett Brown, Bateman & Misterioso (w/Fred Yehi & The DKC)	L	NJPW Strong	10:06
Jun 18	Jorel Nelson, JR Kratos & Royce Isaacs (w/Alex Coughlin & The DKC)	L	NJPW Strong	9:21
Jun 26	Max Caster, Billy Gunn, Austin Gunn & Colten Gunn (w/The DKC, Alex Coughlin & Yuya Uemura)	L	AEW x NJPW Forbidden Door Buy-In	5:35
Jul 30	Chase Owens, Hikuleo & Jay White (w/Fred Rosser & Hiroshi Tanahashi)	L	NJPW Strong	15:41

Jul 30	Fred Yehi, Shota Umino & Yuya Uemura (w/Ren Narita & The DKC)	L	NJPW Music City Mayhem	13:12
Aug 27	Elliot Russell & Sigmon (w/The DKC)	W	NJPW Strong	9:55
Oct 1	Barrett Brown & Bateman (w/The DKC)	W	NJPW Strong	8:16
Oct 28	Alex Shelley & Chris Sabin, Kyle Fletcher & Mark Davis (w/The DKC)	L	NJPW Rumble On 44th Street	13:42
Oct 29	Ari Daivari	L	NJPW Strong	8:19
Nov 5	Barrett Brown & Misterioso, Bad Dude Tito & Shane Haste, Jorel Nelson & Royce Isaacs (w/The DKC)	L	NJPW Strong	12:36

KEVIN OWENS

Jan 1	Brock Lesnar, Seth Rollins, Big E, Bobby Lashley	L	WWE Day 1	8:19
Jan 3	Bobby Lashley, Seth Rollins, Big E	L	WWE Monday Night RAW	18:40
Jan 17	Damian Priest	W	WWE Monday Night RAW	10:55
Jan 21	Jimmy Uso & Jey Uso (w/Seth Rollins)	W	WWE SmackDown	15:00
Jan 24	Damian Priest	W	WWE Monday Night RAW	9:35
Jan 29	Royal Rumble Match	L	WWE Royal Rumble '22	11:13
Jan 31	Austin Theory	L	WWE Monday Night RAW	11:25
Feb 7	Austin Theory	W	WWE Monday Night RAW	9:06
Feb 7	Randy Orton & Riddle (w/Seth Rollins)	W	WWE Monday Night RAW	8:05
Feb 21	Randy Orton & Riddle (w/Seth Rollins)	W	WWE Monday Night RAW	12:40
Feb 28	Chad Gable & Otis (w/Seth Rollins)	W	WWE Monday Night RAW	12:50
Mar 7	No DQ: Randy Orton & Riddle, Chad Gable & Otis (w/Seth Rollins)	L	WWE Monday Night RAW	27:05
Mar 14	Seth Rollins	W	WWE Monday Night RAW	16:20
Apr 2	No Holds Barred: Steve Austin	L	WWE WrestleMania XXXVIII	13:55
Apr 18	Cody Rhodes	L	WWE Monday Night RAW	17:20
Apr 25	Cody Rhodes, Ezekiel, Randy Orton & Riddle (w/Seth Rollins, Jimmy Uso & Jey Uso)	L	WWE Monday Night RAW	14:58
May 2	Ezekiel, Angelo Dawkins & Montez Ford (w/Chad Gable & Otis)	W	WWE Monday Night RAW	9:45
May 30	Ezekiel, Rey Mysterio & Dominik Mysterio (w/Chad Gable & Otis)	L	WWE Monday Night RAW	8:30
Jun 5	Ezekiel	W	WWE Hell In A Cell '22	9:20
Jun 13	Ezekiel	L	WWE Monday Night RAW	8:30
Aug 8	Ezekiel	D	WWE Monday Night RAW	:50
Aug 15	Drew McIntyre	L	WWE Monday Night RAW	15:58
Aug 22	Chad Gable	W	WWE Monday Night RAW	11:10
Aug 29	Jey Uso	W	WWE Monday Night RAW	12:26
Sep 5	Austin Theory	W	WWE Monday Night RAW	15:40
Sep 19	Austin Theory	W	WWE Monday Night RAW	13:15
Sep 26	Chad Gable & Otis (w/Johnny Gargano)	W	WWE Monday Night RAW	13:09
Sep 30	Austin Theory, Chad Gable & Otis (w/Drew McIntyre & Johnny Gargano)	W	WWE SmackDown	13:38
Nov 26	WarGames: Roman Reigns, Solo Sikoa, Sami Zayn, Jey Uso & Jimmy Uso (w/Sheamus, Butch, Ridge Holland & Drew McIntyre)	L	WWE Survivor Series WarGames	38:30
Nov 28	Jey Uso	W	WWE Monday Night RAW	21:55
Dec 5	Jey Uso & Jimmy Uso (w/Matt Riddle)	L	WWE Monday Night RAW	14:10
Dec 19	Jey Uso & Jimmy Uso (w/Seth Rollins)	W	WWE Monday Night RAW	10:50
Dec 30	Roman Reigns & Sami Zayn (w/John Cena)	W	WWE SmackDown	10:57

KIANA JAMES (AS KAYLA INLAY UNTIL MAY 17)

Feb 1	Sarray	L	NXT 2.0	3:29
Feb 18	Ivy Nile & Tatum Paxley (w/Fallon Henley)	L	NXT Level Up	4:18
Feb 22	Nikkita Lyon	L	NXT 2.0	4:03
Mar 25	Ivy Nile	L	NXT Level Up	4:15
Apr 15	Tatum Paxley	L	NXT Level Up	3:58
May 17	Roxanne Perez	L	NXT 2.0	5:15
May 31	Ivy Nile	L	NXT 2.0	3:36
Jun 24	Brooklyn Barlow	W	NXT Level Up	5:15
Jun 28	Indi Hartwell	W	NXT 2.0	3:51
Jul 15	Sol Ruca	W	NXT Level Up	4:20
Jul 19	Battle Royal	L	NXT 2.0	13:13
Aug 9	Nikkita Lyons	L	NXT 2.0	4:10
Aug 26	Amari Miller	W	NXT Level Up	4:59
Aug 30	Zoey Stark	L	NXT 2.0	4:23
Sep 13	Zoey Stark & Nikkita Lyons (w/Arianna Grace)	L	NXT 2.0	9:04
Oct 7	Fallon Henley & Sol Ruca (w/Arianna Grace)	L	NXT 2.0	5:06
Oct 11	Thea Hail	W	NXT 2.0	1:18
Oct 27	Dana Brooke	L	WWE Main Event	4:56
Nov 1	Thea Hail	W	NXT	4:20
Nov 3	Dana Brooke	W	WWE Main Event	4:19
Nov 17	Asuka	L	WWE Main Event	4:15
Nov 22	Ivy Nile	L	NXT	4:43
Nov 29	Fallon Henley	W	NXT	9:40
Dec 10	Iron Survivor Challenge: Roxanne Perez, Zoey Stark, Cora Jade, Indi Hartwell	L	NXT Deadline	25:00
Dec 27	Fallon Henley	L	NXT	5:13

KIERA HOGAN

Jan 11	Christi Jaynes, Jennacide, Kenzie Paige	W	NWA Power	5:08
Feb 1	Mazzerati	W	AEW Dark	3:36
Feb 8	Kamille	L	NWA Power	3:20
Feb 21	Emi Sakura, Leyla Hirsch & Nyla Rose (w/AQA & Skye Blue)	L	AEW Dark Elevation	4:48
Mar 1	Kelsey Raegan	W	AEW Dark	2:41
Mar 8	Red Velvet	L	AEW Dark	2:16
Mar 29	Nyla Rose	L	AEW Dark	3:01
Apr 29	Skye Blue, Willow Nightingale & Trish Adora (w/Jade Cargill & Red Velvet)	W	AEW Rampage	2:46

May 10	Skye Blue	W	AEW Dark	4:00
Jun 3	Athena	L	AEW Rampage	8:21
Jul 20	Athena & Willow Nightingale (w/Jade Cargill)	W	AEW Dynamite: Fyter Fest	8:25
Jul 26	Allie Recks	W	AEW Dark	1:33
Aug 8	Alice Crowley & Freya States (w/Leila Grey)	W	AEW Dark Elevation	2:00
Aug 30	Mylo	W	AEW Dark	2:19
Oct 31	Skye Blue	W	AEW Dark Elevation	2:05
Nov 15	Kennedi Copeland	W	AEW Dark	2:41
Dec 5	Nikki Victory	W	AEW Dark Elevation	2:28
Dec 7	Jade Cargill, Leila Grey & Red Velvet (w/Skye Blue & Madison Rayne)	L	AEW Dynamite	8:13
Dec 26	Athena	L	AEW Dark Elevation	5:59
Dec 30	Jade Cargill	L	AEW Rampage	6:26

KILLER KELLY

Aug 11	Tiffany Nieves	W	NWA Power	1:14
Aug 18	Savannah Evans	W	NWA Power	3:30
Sep 15	Alisha Edwards	W	NWA Power	2:13
Oct 7	Call Your Shot Gauntlet	L	IMPACT Bound For Glory '22	29:18
Oct 13	No DQ: Tasha Steelz	W	NWA Power	6:52
Nov 10	Sandra Moone	W	IMPACT Before The Impact	4:41

KILYNN KING

Jan 31	Brandi Rhodes	L	AEW Dark Elevation	4:00
Mar 14	Emi Sakura & The Bunny (w/Skye Blue)	L	AEW Dark Elevation	6:00
Apr 12	Natalia Markova	W	NWA Power	6:02
May 10	Chelsea Green, Jennacide	W	NWA Power	6:36
Jun 7	Kamille & Kenzie Paige (w/Missa Kate)	W	NWA Power	9:07
Jun 11	Kamille	L	NWA Alwayz Ready '22	17:25
Jul 12	Allysin Kay	W	NWA Power	6:47
Jul 26	Taya Valkyrie	L	NWA Power	6:50
Aug 17	Toni Storm	L	AEW Dynamite	6:49
Aug 23	Mafiosa	W	AEW Dark	2:34
Aug 24	Dr. Britt Baker D.M.D.	L	AEW Dynamite	3:55
Aug 27	Burke Invitational Gauntlet	L	NWA 74th Anniversary Show	17:24
Sep 6	Taya Valkyrie, Chelsea Green, Jennacide	L	NWA Power	4:22
Sep 20	Sahara Seven	W	AEW Dark	1:04
Oct 11	Taya Valkyrie	W	NWA Power	8:57
Oct 28	Mayu Iwatani	L	NJPW Rumble On 44th Street	11:47
Nov 8	Allysin Kay & Marti Belle (w/Kamille)	W	NWA Power	7:31
Nov 12	Kamille, Chelsea Green	L	NWA Hard Times 3	8:59
Nov 29	Samantha Starr	W	NWA Power	6:09
Dec 20	Allysin Kay	W	NWA Power	7:55
Dec 22	Taylor Wilde	L	IMPACT Before The Impact	7:20

KING MUERTES

Feb 10	Richard Holliday	W	MLW Fusion	7:34
May 12	Octagon Jr., El Dragon, El Hijo de LA Park	L	MLW Fusion	9:26
Jun 9	Alexander Hammerstone, Marshall Von Erich & Ross Von Erich (w/Mads Krugger & Richard Holliday)	W	MLW Fusion	9:31

KIP SABIAN

Sep 4	Pac	L	AEW All Out Buy-In	10:00
Sep 26	Shawn Dean & Skye Blue (w/Penelope Ford)	W	AEW Dark Elevation	5:16
Oct 3	Gia Scott & LSG (w/Penelope Ford)	W	AEW Dark Elevation	3:20
Oct 11	Brandon Cutler	W	AEW Dark	6:01
Oct 17	Jeremy Prophet & Jessika Neri (w/Penelope Ford)	W	AEW Dark Elevation	3:58
Nov 1	Dean Alexander	W	AEW Dark	2:31
Nov 7	Alex Reynolds	W	AEW Dark Elevation	8:15
Nov 8	Marcus Kross	W	AEW Dark	2:58
Nov 21	Alex Reynolds	L	AEW Dark Elevation	1:56
Dec 5	Alex Reynolds	W	AEW Dark Elevation	6:25
Dec 7	Dynamite Diamond Battle Royale	L	AEW Dynamite	13:10
Dec 13	Tony Deppen	W	AEW Dark	5:27
Dec 20	Caleb Konley	W	AEW Dark	2:49
Dec 16	Orange Cassidy, Dustin Rhodes, Chuck Taylor & Trent Beretta (w/Trent Seven, The Butcher & The Blade)	L	AEW Rampage	10:42
Dec 23	$300,000 Three Kings Christmas Casino Trios Royale (w/The Butcher & The Blade)	L	AEW Rampage	22:01
Dec 30	Atiba	W	AEW Rampage	1:12

KIT WILSON (AS SAM STOKER UNTIL APRIL 12)

Jan 20	Sam Gradewell & Saxon Huxley (w/Lewis Howley)	W	NXT UK	9:22
Mar 3	Dave Mastiff & Jack Starz (w/Lewis Howley)	L	NXT UK	10:34
Apr 12	Gauntlet Match: Julius Creed & Brutus Creed, Grayson Waller & Sanga Joaquin Wilde & Raul Mendoza, Brooks Jensen & Josh Briggs (w/Elton Prince)	W	NXT 2.0	27:08
Apr 19	Dexter Lumis & Duke Hudson (w/Elton Prince)	W	NXT 2.0	11:47
May 31	Roderick Strong & Damon Kemp (w/Elton Prince)	W	NXT 2.0	13:17
Jun 4	Julius Creed & Brutus Creed (w/Elton Prince)	L	NXT In Your House '22	15:19
Jun 7	Handicap Match: Andre Chase (w/Elton Prince)	W	NXT 2.0	3:16
Jul 19	Josh Briggs & Brooks Jensen (w/Elton Prince)	L	NXT 2.0	8:15
Aug 9	Edris Enofe & Malik Blade (w/Elton Prince)	W	NXT 2.0	4:37
Aug 30	Fallon Henley, Josh Briggs & Brooks Jensen (w/Elton Prince & Lash Legend)	W	NXT 2.0	11:31

Sep 4	Elimination Match: Brutus Creed & Julius Creed,	W	NXT Worlds Collide '22	15:34
	Mark Coffey & Wolfgang, Brooks Jensen & Josh Briggs (w/Elton Prince)			
Sep 13	Steel Cage Match: Julius Creed & Brutus Creed (w/Elton Prince)	W	NXT 2.0	14:48
Oct 4	Ridge Holland & Butch (w/Elton Prince)	W	NXT	12:27
Oct 25	Edris Enofe & Malik Blade (w/Elton Prince)	W	NXT	12:29
Nov 1	Bron Breakker & Wes Lee (w/Elton Prince)	W	NXT	11:57
Nov 22	Andre Chase & Duke Hudson (w/Elton Prince)	W	NXT	8:17
Dec 10	Kofi Kingston & Xavier Woods (w/Elton Prince)	L	NXT Deadline	14:05

KOFI KINGSTON

Jan 1	Jimmy Uso & Jey Uso (w/Xavier Woods)	L	WWE Day 1	18:05
Jan 7	Jimmy Uso & Jey Uso (w/Xavier Woods)	L	WWE SmackDown	17:45
Jan 14	Madcap Moss	L	WWE SmackDown	9:53
Jan 21	Madcap Moss	W	WWE SmackDown	7:40
Jan 28	Happy Corbin & Madcap Moss (w/Big E)	W	WWE SmackDown	7:10
Jan 29	Royal Rumble Match	L	WWE Royal Rumble '22	:21
Feb 4	Angel & Humberto (w/Big E)	W	WWE SmackDown	8:58
Feb 11	Angel & Humberto (w/Big E)	L	WWE SmackDown	10:20
Feb 25	Angel & Humberto (w/Big E)	W	WWE SmackDown	10:30
Mar 11	Sheamus & Ridge Holland (w/Big E)	L	WWE SmackDown	8:49
Mar 18	Ridge Holland	L	WWE SmackDown	6:00
Apr 3	Sheamus & Ridge Holland (w/Xavier Woods)	L	WWE WrestleMania XXXVIII	1:40
Apr 29	Sheamus	L	WWE SmackDown	2:57
May 6	Tables Match: Sheamus & Ridge Holland (w/Xavier Woods)	L	WWE SmackDown	12:30
May 13	Butch	L	WWE SmackDown	8:20
May 27	Sheamus, Ridge Holland & Butch (w/Drew McIntyre & Xavier Woods)	W	WWE SmackDown	11:30
Jun 3	Sheamus, Ridge Holland & Butch (w/Drew McIntyre & Xavier Woods)	L	WWE SmackDown	10:30
Jun 17	Jinder Mahal & Shanky (w/Xavier Woods)	W	WWE SmackDown	3:02
Jul 29	Erik & Ivar (w/Xavier Woods)	L	WWE SmackDown	9:15
Aug 5	Erik	W	WWE SmackDown	3:45
Sep 2	Viking Rules Match: Erik & Ivar (w/Xavier Woods)	L	WWE SmackDown	22:15
Sep 5	Chad Gable & Otis, Angel & Humberto, Angelo Dawkins & Montez Ford	D	WWE Monday Night RAW	14:30
	(w/Xavier Woods)			
Sep 16	Ridge Holland & Butch, Ludwig Kaiser & Giovanni Vinci,	L	WWE SmackDown	18:44
	Ashante Adonis & Top Dolla (w/Xavier Woods)			
Sep 23	Mace & Mansoor (w/Xavier Woods)	W	WWE SmackDown	3:18
Oct 7	Sami Zayn, Jimmy Uso & Jey Uso (w/Braun Strowman & Xavier Woods)	W	WWE SmackDown	10:30
Oct 14	Sami Zayn	L	WWE SmackDown	14:50
Oct 28	Mace & Mansoor (w/Xavier Woods)	W	WWE SmackDown	3:45
Nov 7	Jimmy Uso, Jey Uso & Solo Sikoa (w/Xavier Woods & Matt Riddle)	L	WWE Monday Night RAW	20:55
Nov 11	Jey Uso & Jimmy Uso (w/Xavier Woods)	L	WWE SmackDown	23:50
Nov 18	Gunther, Ludwig Kaiser & Giovanni Vinci	W	WWE SmackDown	7:38
	(w/Braun Strowman & Xavier Woods)			
Dec 2	Gunther	L	WWE SmackDown	11:37
Dec 9	Gunther, Ludwig Kaiser & Giovanni Vinci (w/Ricochet & Xavier Woods)	W	WWE SmackDown	18:47
Dec 10	Elton Prince & Kit Wilson (w/Xavier Woods)	W	NXT Deadline	14:05
Dec 20	Brooks Jensen & Josh Briggs (w/Xavier Woods)	W	NXT	11:10

KONOSUKE TAKESHITA

Mar 20	Tetsuya Endo	L	DDT Judgment '22: 25th Anniversary	46:30
Apr 25	Brandon Cutler	W	AEW Dark Elevation	4:57
May 2	Rhett Titus	W	AEW Dark Elevation	4:40
May 6	Jay Lethal	L	AEW Rampage	9:38
May 18	Hangman Page	L	AEW Dynamite: Wild Card Wednesday	12:24
May 30	Ryan Nemeth	W	AEW Dark Elevation	5:31
Jun 8	Casino Battle Royale	L	AEW Dynamite	24:59
Jun 14	Nick Comoroto	W	AEW Dark	6:42
Jul 1	Royal Rampage Match	L	AEW Rampage	22:41
Jul 8	Eddie Kingston	L	AEW Rampage	11:56
Jul 13	Jon Moxley	L	AEW Dynamite: Fyter Fest	13:22
Jul 19	Anthony Henry	W	AEW Dark	7:48
Jul 25	JD Drake	W	AEW Dark Elevation	3:40
Jul 31	Jonathan Gresham, Alan Angels, Nick Wayne	L	JCP Ric Flair's Last Match	5:40
Aug 5	Ryan Nemeth	W	AEW Rampage	1:36
Aug 6	Claudio Castagnoli	L	AEW Battle Of The Belts III	19:59
Aug 15	Cezar Bononi	W	AEW Dark Elevation	2:37
Aug 20	Dick Togo, Daisuke Sasaki & Kanon (w/Mao & Yasu Urano)	W	DDT Wrestle Peter Pan '22	20:41
Nov 18	Eddie Kingston & Ortiz (w/Jun Akiyama)	W	AEW Rampage	12:17
Nov 28	Ari Daivari	W	AEW Dark Elevation	4:45
Dec 5	Aaron Solo	W	AEW Dark Elevation	3:15
Dec 9	Jon Moxley	L	AEW Rampage	14:30
Dec 19	Jeeves Kay, Slim J, Sonny Kiss, Cezar Bononi, Peter Avalon & Ryan	W	AEW Dark Elevation	7:45
	Nemeth (w/Ethan Page, Isiah Kassidy, Matt Hardy, Dante Martin			
	& Darius Martin)			
Dec 26	Frankie Kazarian	W	AEW Dark Elevation	5:01

KRIS STATLANDER

Jan 4	Renee Michelle, Sofia Castillo & Marina Tucker	W	AEW Dark	2:43
	(w/Leyla Hirsch & Red Velvet)			
Jan 14	Penelope Ford, The Bunny & Nyla Rose (w/Red Velvet & Leyla Hirsch)	L	AEW Rampage	8:12
Jan 19	Adam Cole & Dr. Britt Baker D.M.D. (w/Orange Cassidy)	L	AEW Dynamite	14:25
Mar 6	Leyla Hirsch	L	AEW Revolution Buy-In	9:50

Mar 7	Emi Sakura	W	AEW Dark Elevation	4:19
Mar 8	Kelsey Raegan	W	AEW Dark	1:52
Apr 18	Ashley D'Amboise	W	AEW Dark Elevation	1:30
Apr 25	Julia Hart	W	AEW Dark Elevation	6:19
May 2	Emi Sakura & Nyla Rose (w/Anna Jay)	W	AEW Dark Elevation	6:10
May 20	Red Velvet	W	AEW Rampage	7:50
May 24	Avery Breaux	W	AEW Dark	2:59
May 27	Ruby Soho	L	AEW Rampage	10:06
Jun 10	Red Velvet	W	AEW Rampage	8:55
Jun 14	Diamante, Emi Sakura & Nyla Rose (w/Anna Jay & Ruby Soho)	W	AEW Dark	7:54
Jun 21	Ava Everett	W	AEW Dark	1:42
Jul 15	Charlette Renegade & Robyn Renegade (w/Athena)	W	AEW Rampage	:25
Jul 25	Brittany Jade	W	AEW Dark Elevation	1:54
Aug 9	Sierra	W	AEW Dark	2:16

KUSHIDA

Jan 25	Nash Carter & Wes Lee (w/Ikemen Jiro)	L	NXT 2.0	11:32
Feb 4	Damon Kemp	W	WWE 205 Live	3:50
Feb 18	Edris Enofe	L	NXT Level Up	7:07
Feb 25	Harland & Joe Gacy (w/Ikemen Jiro)	L	NXT Level Up	6:55
Mar 15	A-Kid	L	NXT 2.0	4:58
Mar 25	Edris Enofe & Malik Blade (w/Ikemen Jiro)	L	NXT Level Up	7:33
Jul 28	Rich Swann	W	IMPACT Wrestling	15:29
Jul 30	Alex Shelley	D	NJPW Music City Mayhem	20:00
Aug 11	Deaner	W	IMPACT Wrestling	6:14
Aug 25	Deaner, Eric Young & Joe Doering (w/Alex Shelley & Chris Sabin)	W	IMPACT Wrestling	15:18
Aug 27	Anthony Henry & JD Drake (w/Ren Narita)	W	NJPW Strong	11:18
Sep 17	Chase Owens, Hikuleo, Jay White & Juice Robinson (w/Taylor Rust, Trent Beretta & Rocky Romero)	L	NJPW Strong	14:46

KYLE FLETCHER

Apr 16	Hikuleo, Chris Bey, El Phantasmo, Karl Anderson, Luke Gallows & Scott Norton (w/Aaron Henarem Great-O-Khan, Jeff Cobb, TJP & Mark Davis)	W	NJPW Windy City Riot	11:58
May 14	Mikey Nicholls, Shane Haste, Jonah & Bad Dude Tito (w/Aaron Henare, Mark Davis & Jeff Cobb)	L	NJPW Capital Collision	12:09
May 28	Bad Dude Tito, Jonah & Shane Haste (w/Jeff Cobb & Mark Davis)	W	NJPW Strong	14:39
Jun 10	Trent Beretta, Dax Harwood & Cash Wheeler (w/Will Ospreay & Mark Davis)	L	AEW Rampage	13:59
Jun 22	Orange Cassidy, Trent Beretta & Rocky Romero (w/Mark Davis & Will Ospreay)	L	AEW Dynamite	11:37
Jul 2	Bad Dude Tito, Jonah, Mikey Nicholls & Shane Haste (w/Aaron Henare, Great-O-Khan & Mark Davis)	W	IMPACT Wrestling	11:35
Jul 16	Alan Angels & Evil Uno (w/Mark Davis)	W	NJPW Strong	12:47
Jul 30	Barrett Brown & Misterioso (w/Mark Davis)	W	NJPW Strong	7:27
Jul 30	Alex Zayne, Cash Wheeler & Dax Harwood (w/Mark Davis & TJP)	W	NJPW Music City Mayhem	14:30
Aug 13	Christopher Daniels & Yuya Uemura (w/Mark Davis)	W	NJPW Strong	11:57
Aug 24	Pac, Penta El Zero M & Rey Fenix (w/Mark Davis & Will Ospreay)	W	AEW Dynamite	25:18
Aug 31	Kenny Omega, Matt Jackson & Nick Jackson (w/Mark Davis & Will Ospreay)	L	AEW Dynamite	18:54
Sep 8	Ace Austin & Chris Bey (w/Mark Davis)	W	IMPACT Wrestling	7:07
Sep 10	Jorel Nelson & Royce Isaacs (w/Mark Davis)	W	NJPW Strong	11:38
Sep 22	Alex Shelley & Chris Sabin (w/Mark Davis)	L	IMPACT Wrestling	15:31
Oct 1	Cash Wheeler & Dax Harwood (w/Mark Davis)	L	NJPW Royal Quest II Night #1	31:59
Oct 2	Cash Wheeler, Dax Harwood, Shota Umino, Gabriel Kidd & Ricky Knight Jr. (w/Will Ospreay, Great-O-Khan, Mark Davis & Gideon Grey)	W	NJPW Royal Quest II Night #2	16:57
Oct 15	Danny Limelight & JR Kratos (w/Mark Davis)	W	NJPW Strong	10:08
Oct 28	Alex Shelley & Chris Sabin, Kevin Knight & The DKC (w/Mark Davis)	L	NJPW Rumble On 44th Street	13:42
Nov 3	Frankie Kazarian & Josh Alexander (w/Mark Davis)	L	IMPACT Wrestling	15:46
Nov 5	Hiroshi Tanahashi, Toru Yano, David Finlay & Alex Zayne (w/Aaron Henare, Gideon Grey & Mark Davis)	W	NJPW Battle Autumn '22	9:50
Nov 17	Ace Austin & Chris Bey, Alex Shelley & Chris Sabin, Raj Singh & Shera (w/Mark Davis)	L	IMPACT Wrestling	13:03
Nov 20	Bushi, Hiromu Takahashi, Sanada, Shingo Takagi & Tetsuya Naito (w/Mark Davis, Francesco Akira, TJP & Gideon Grey)	W	NJPW x Stardom Historic X-Over	9:55
Nov 26	Greg Sharpe & Jakob Austin Young (w/Mark Davis)	W	NJPW Strong	5:51

KYLE O'REILLY

Feb 23	Tag Team Battle Royal (w/Bobby Fish)	W	AEW Dynamite	18:25
Mar 2	Hangman Page, John Silver & Alex Reynolds (w/Adam Cole & Bobby Fish)	W	AEW Dynamite	12:43
Mar 6	Jungle Boy & Luchasaurus, Matt Jackson & Nick Jackson (w/Bobby Fish)	L	AEW Revolution '22	18:55
Mar 16	Hangman Page, Jungle Boy & Luchasaurus (w/Adam Cole & Bobby Fish)	W	AEW Dynamite: St. Patrick's Day Slam	13:58
Mar 25	Alan Angels & Ten (w/Bobby Fish)	W	AEW Rampage	7:00
Apr 13	Jungle Boy & Luchasaurus (w/Bobby Fish)	L	AEW Dynamite	13:45
Apr 20	Jungle Boy	W	AEW Dynamite	13:02
Apr 27	Dante Martin, Lee Johnson, Brock Anderson, Brian Pillman Jr. & Griff Garrison (w/Matt Jackson, Nick Jackson, Adam Cole & Bobby Fish)	W	AEW Dynamite	6:28
May 18	Rey Fenix	W	AEW Dynamite: Wild Card Wednesday	12:00
May 25	Samoa Joe	L	AEW Dynamite: 3 Year Anniversary	12:38
May 29	Darby Allin	W	AEW Double Or Nothing '22	9:50
Jun 1	Christian Cage, Matt Hardy, Darby Allin, Jungle Boy & Luchasaurua	W	AEW Dynamite	12:00

	(w/Matt Jackson, Nick Jackson, Bobby Fish & Hikuleo)			
Jun 8	Casino Battle Royale	W	AEW Dynamite	24:59
Jun 8	Jon Moxley	L	AEW Dynamite	14:15

LA KNIGHT

Feb 1	Joe Gacy	L	NXT 2.0	4:18
Feb 8	Sanga	W	NXT 2.0	3:12
Feb 22	Grayson Waller	L	NXT 2.0	9:58
Mar 8	Last Man Standing: Grayson Waller	L	NXT 2.0	16:01
Mar 15	Dolph Ziggler	L	NXT 2.0	11:48
Mar 29	Gunther, Marcel Barthel & Fabian Aichner (w/Nash Carter & Wes Lee)	L	NXT 2.0	12:11
Apr 2	Gunther	L	NXT Stand & Deliver '22	10:24
Oct 14	Mansoor	W	WWE SmackDown	2:52
Nov 4	Ricochet	W	WWE SmackDown	9:54
Dec 17	Braun Strowman	L	WWE Tribute To The Troops '22	2:12

LACEY EVANS

Jun 10	Xia Li	W	WWE SmackDown	2:30
Jun 24	Handicap Match: Sonya Deville (w/Raquel Rodriguez)	W	WWE SmackDown	3:05
Jul 1	Alexa Bliss, Liv Morgan & Asuka (w/Raquel Rodriguez & Shotzi)	L	WWE SmackDown	13:14
Jul 2	Money In The Bank Ladder Match: Alexa Bliss, Asuka, Becky Lynch Liv Morgan, Raquel Rodriguez, Shotzi	L	WWE Money In The Bank '22	16:35
Sep 9	Ronda Rousey, Sonya Deville, Xia Li, Natalya	L	WWE SmackDown	4:40
Sep 23	Liv Morgan	L	WWE SmackDown	8:44
Nov 11	Six-Pack Challenge: Shotzi, Raquel Rodriguez, Sonya Deville, Liv Morgan, Xia Li	L	WWE SmackDown	11:58

LADY FROST

Jan 6	Rosemary, Jordynne Grace & Rachael Ellering (w/Tasha Steelz & Chelsea Green)	W	IMPACT Wrestling	7:19
Jan 8	Ultimate X Match: Tasha Steelz, Alisha Edwards, Chelsea Green, Jordynne Grace, Rosemary	W	IMPACT Hard To Kill '22	9:00
Jan 20	Jordynne Grace	L	IMPACT Before The Impact	8:18
Feb 10	Alisha Edwards	W	IMPACT Before The Impact	6:05
Feb 17	Gisele Shaw	L	IMPACT Wrestling	4:30
Feb 24	Deonna Purrazzo	L	IMPACT Wrestling	5:43
Mar 17	Deonna Purrazzo, Gisele Shaw	L	IMPACT Wrestling	6:08
Mar 31	Battle Royal	L	IMPACT Wrestling	7:15
Apr 1	Madison Rayne & Tenille Dashwood, Tasha Steelz & Savannah Evans, Havok & Rosemary (w/Gisele Shaw)	L	IMPACT Multiverse Of Matches	9:02

LANCE ANOA'I

Jun 30	Cinco & Uno (w/Juice Finau)	W	MLW Fusion	2:24
Nov 17	Joel Maximo & Jose Maximo (w/Juice Finau)	W	MLW Fusion	3:14
Dec 8	Angel Fashion & Mark Davidson (w/Juice Finau)	W	MLW Fusion	4:23

LANCE ARCHER

Jan 18	Liam Cross	W	AEW Dark	1:57
Jan 19	Frankie Kazarian	W	AEW Dynamite	10:02
Jan 25	Joe Keys	W	AEW Dark	4:11
Jan 31	Chase Oliver	W	AEW Dark Elevation	1:12
Feb 1	Jordan Costa	W	AEW Dark	1:48
Feb 9	Texas Death Match: Hangman Page	L	AEW Dynamite	15:29
Feb 21	Joey O'Riley	W	AEW Dark Elevation	:23
Feb 28	Fuego Del Sol	W	AEW Dark Elevation	3:10
Mar 7	Cameron Stewart	W	AEW Dark Elevation	1:50
Mar 15	Sage Scott	W	AEW Dark	2:10
Mar 25	Dustin Rhodes	L	AEW Rampage	9:32
Apr 5	Dean Alexander	W	AEW Dark	1:36
Apr 22	Serpentico	W	AEW Rampage	:33
Apr 27	Wardlow	L	AEW Dynamite	5:29
Jun 7	Aaron Solo	W	AEW Dark	2:46
Jun 8	Casino Battle Royale	L	AEW Dynamite	24:59
Jun 22	Jon Moxley & Hiroshi Tanahashi (w/Chris Jericho)	L	AEW Dynamite	12:12
Jun 26	Nick Comoroto	W	AEW Forbidden Door Buy-In	6:08
Sep 23	Golden Ticket Battle Royale	L	AEW Rampage: Grand Slam	12:16
Oct 3	Cheeseburger	W	AEW Dark Elevation	3:00
Oct 10	Papadon	W	AEW Dark Elevation	3:10
Oct 11	Alex Odin	W	AEW Dark	3:53
Oct 25	Iseah Bronson	W	AEW Dark	3:39
Nov 18	Ricky Starks	L	AEW Rampage	5:23

LAREDO KID

Jan 13	Chris Bey	W	IMPACT Wrestling	12:49
Jan 27	Blake Christian	W	IMPACT Before The Impact	7:29
Feb 17	Ace Austin, Blake Christian	L	IMPACT Wrestling	11:57
Feb 19	Elimination Match: Psycho Clown, Heavy Metal, Bandido, Cibernetico	L	AAA Rey De Reyes '22	10:17
Mar 24	Mike Bailey, Willie Mack	L	IMPACT Wrestling	10:09
Apr 21	Ace Austin & Mike Bailey (w/Trey Miguel)	W	IMPACT Wrestling	6:00
Apr 30	Johnny Caballero & Taurus, Dragon Lee & Dralistico (w/Jack Cartwheel)	L	AAA TripleMania XXX: Monterrey	13:29
May 19	Mike Bailey	L	IMPACT Wrestling	9:00
May 26	Black Taurus	W	IMPACT Before The Impact	7:49

Jun 16	Blake Christian		W	IMPACT Before The Impact	8:47
Jun 18	Rey Fenix, El Hijo del Vikingo, Bandido, Taurus		L	AAA TripleMania XXX: Tijuana	20:37
Jun 30	Trey Miguel, Chris Bey, Steve Maclin		L	IMPACT Wrestling	6:12
Jul 7	Trey Miguel		L	IMPACT Wrestling	7:41
Jul 21	Johnny Swinger		W	IMPACT Before The Impact	8:10
Jul 28	Johnny Swinger & Zicky Dice (w/Trey Miguel)		W	IMPACT Wrestling	4:01
Jul 31	Rey Fenix, Black Taurus, Bandido		L	JCP Ric Flair's Last Match	11:45
Aug 18	Black Taurus, Rey Horus, Trey Miguel		L	IMPACT Wrestling	7:33
Sep 22	Black Taurus, Alex Zayne, Mia Yim, Trey Miguel		L	IMPACT Wrestling	11:58
Sep 29	Ace Austin & Chris Bey (w/Trey Miguel)		L	IMPACT Wrestling	8:16
Oct 13	Trey Miguel, Alex Zayne, Black Taurus, Kenny King, Yuya Uemura		L	IMPACT Wrestling	5:19
Oct 15	El Cuatrero, Forastero & Sanson, Brian Cage, Johnny Caballero & Sam Adonis (w/Bandido & Psycho Clown)		L	AAA TripleMania XXX: Mexico City	12:44
Oct 27	Black Taurus		L	IMPACT Before The Impact	8:05
Nov 17	Rich Swann		L	IMPACT Wrestling	3:40

LASH LEGEND

Jan 21	Fallon Henley		W	WWE 205 Live	4:25
Jan 28	Valentina Feroz & Yulisa Leon (w/Amari Miller)		L	WWE 205 Live	6:29
Feb 4	Kacy Katanzaro & Kayden Carter (w/Fallon Henley)		L	WWE 205 Live	6:15
Feb 11	Erica Yan		W	WWE 205 Live	4:22
Feb 22	Io Shirai & Kay Lee Ray (w/Amari Miller)		L	NXT 2.0	2:44
Mar 1	Amari Miller		W	NXT 2.0	2:57
Mar 18	Valentina Feroz		W	NXT Level Up	4:53
Apr 5	Nikkita Lyons		L	NXT 2.0	4:39
Apr 26	Nikkita Lyon		L	NXT 2.0	5:09
May 3	Cora Jade & Nikkita Lyons (w/Natalya)		L	NXT 2.0: Spring Breakin'	13:28
May 17	Tatum Paxley		W	NXT 2.0	3:50
May 24	Roxanne Perez		L	NXT 2.0	3:19
May 26	Emilia McKenzie		W	NXT UK	6:06
Jun 16	Myla Grace		W	NXT UK	4:34
Jun 21	Alba Fyre		L	NXT 2.0	3:31
Jul 12	Indi Hartwell		L	NXT 2.0	3:45
Jul 19	Battle Royal		L	NXT 2.0	13:13
Aug 2	Alba Fyre		L	NXT 2.0	5:31
Aug 30	Fallon Henley, Josh Briggs & Brooks Jensen (w/Kit Wilson & Elton Prince)		W	NXT 2.0	11:31
Sep 13	Fallon Henley		L	NXT 2.0	2:17
Oct 4	Wendy Choo		L	NXT	3:50
Oct 14	Ivy Nile		L	NXT Level Up	6:16
Oct 25	Shotzi		L	NXT	3:42
Nov 11	Ivy Nile & Tatum Paxley (w/Jakara Jackson)		L	NXT Level Up	4:42
Dec 16	Ivy Nile		L	NXT Level Up	5:03
Dec 27	Lyra Valkyria		L	NXT	3:32

LEE JOHNSON

Jan 28	Dax Harwood & Cash Wheeler (w/Brock Anderson)		L	AEW Rampage: Beach Break	9:10
Feb 7	Anthony Bowens, Max Caster, Austin Gunn & Colten Gunn (w/Lee Moriarty, Matt Sydal & Brock Anderson)		L	AEW Dark Elevation	7:11
Feb 10	Powerhouse Hobbs		L	AEW Dark	7:08
Feb 21	Luther, Serpentico, Cezar Bononi, JD Drake & Peter Avalon (w/Brock Anderson, Frankie Kazarian, Jay Lethal & Matt Sydal)		W	AEW Dark Elevation	6:06
Mar 1	Darian Bengston		W	AEW Dark	3:51
Mar 2	Casino Battle Royale (w/Brock Anderson)		L	AEW Dynamite	20:19
Mar 8	Isiah Kassidy & Marq Quen (w/Brock Anderson)		L	AEW Dark	5:05
Apr 4	Aaron Solo & QT Marshall (w/Brock Anderson)		W	AEW Dark Elevation	6:59
Apr 27	Adam Cole, Matt Jackson, Nick Jackson, Bobby Fish & Kyle O'Reilly (w/Dante Martin, Brock Anderson, Brian Pillman Jr. & Griff Garrison)		L	AEW Dynamite	6:28
May 10	JCruz & Victor Chase (w/Brock Anderson)		W	AEW Dark	3:30
Nov 7	Cheeseburger, Logan Easton Laroux & Rhett Titus (w/Cole Karter & QT Marshall)		W	AEW Dark Elevation	6:45
Nov 11	Orange Cassidy		L	AEW Rampage	9:12
Nov 15	Channing Thomas, Man Scout & Teddy Goodz (w/Cole Karter & QT Marshall)		W	AEW Dark	4:11
Nov 19	Orange Cassidy, Chuck Taylor, Trent Beretta, Rocky Romero & Danhausen (w/QT Marshall, Aaron Solo, Nick Comoroto & Cole Karter)		L	AEW Full Gear Buy-In	11:55
Nov 21	Orange Cassidy, Chuck Taylor & Trent Beretta (w/Aaron Solo & Cole Karter)		L	AEW Dark Elevation	3:38
Nov 29	Justin Corino, Ryan Mooney & Steven Josifi (w/Cole Karter & QT Marshall)		W	AEW Dark	3:40
Dec 13	Chris Steeler, Joe Keys & LSG (w/Cole Karter & QT Marshall)		W	AEW Dark	3:29

LEE MORIARTY

Jan 17	JR Miller & Marcus Kross (w/Matt Sydal)		W	AEW Dark Elevation	3:20
Jan 24	Powerhouse Hobbs & Ricky Starks (w/Matt Sydal)		L	AEW Dark Elevation	5:21
Jan 31	Aaron Solo, Nick Comoroto & QT Marshall (w/Dante Martin & Matt Sydal)		W	AEW Dark Elevation	7:46
Feb 1	Joey Janela		W	AEW Dark	11:44
Feb 7	Anthony Bowens, Max Caster, Austin Gunn & Colten Gunn (w/Matt Sydal, Brock Anderson & Lee Johnson)		L	AEW Dark Elevation	7:11
Feb 8	Anthony Henry		W	AEW Dark	6:01
Feb 10	Isiah Kassidy, Marq Quen & The Blade (w/Dante Martin & Matt Sydal)		W	AEW Dark	9:05
Feb 16	Bryan Danielson		L	AEW Dynamite	12:14
Mar 28	Serpentico		W	AEW Dark Elevation	3:59
Apr 1	Jay Lethal		L	ROH Supercard Of Honor XV	14:50

Date	Opponent	Result	Show	Time
Apr 20	Bryan Danielson, Jon Moxley & Wheeler Yuta (w/Dante Martin & Brock Anderson)	L	AEW Dynamite	8:08
Apr 26	Serpentico	W	AEW Dark	3:50
May 23	Alex Reynolds	W	AEW Dark Elevation	4:04
May 24	Alan Angels	W	AEW Dark	9:44
Jul 5	Leon Ruffin	W	AEW Dark	8:21
Jul 8	Kaun & Toa Liona (w/Jonathan Gresham)	L	AEW Rampage	7:27
Jul 15	Jonathan Gresham	L	AEW Rampage	9:01
Jul 19	Ren Jones	W	AEW Dark	5:10
Jul 22	Dante Martin	W	AEW Rampage: Fyter Fest	9:00
Jul 29	Matt Sydal	W	AEW Rampage	6:57
Sep 23	Golden Ticket Battle Royale	L	AEW Rampage: Grand Slam	12:16
Sep 30	Fuego Del Sol	W	AEW Rampage	1:56
Nov 2	Jon Moxley	L	AEW Dynamite	10:07
Nov 18	Hook	L	AEW Rampage	8:39
Nov 28	Robert Anthony	W	AEW Dark Elevation	4:08
Dec 5	Serpentico	W	AEW Dark Elevation	3:23
Dec 7	Dynamite Diamond Battle Royale	L	AEW Dynamite	13:10
Dec 9	Clayton Bloodstone & Izzy James (w/Big Bill)	W	AEW Rampage	2:01

LEILA GREY

Date	Opponent	Result	Show	Time
Jan 3	Megan Bayne	L	AEW Dark Elevation	2:42
Mar 4	Serena Deeb	L	AEW Rampage	:58
Mar 22	Marina Shafir	L	AEW Dark	1:20
Mar 29	Emi Sakura	L	AEW Dark	2:55
Apr 22	Raquel Rodriguez	L	WWE SmackDown	2:36
Jun 29	Jade Cargill	L	AEW Dynamite: Blood & Guts	1:55
Aug 1	JC	W	AEW Dark Elevation	2:23
Aug 5	Madison Rayne	L	AEW Rampage	8:25
Aug 8	Alice Crowley & Freya States (w/Kiera Hogan)	W	AEW Dark Elevation	2:00
Aug 30	Renee Michelle	W	AEW Dark	3:07
Sep 27	Tiara James	W.	AEW Dark	2:45
Oct 21	Willow Nightingale	W	AEW Rampage	7:51
Dec 7	Kiera Hogan, Skye Blue & Madison Rayne (w/Jade Cargill & Red Velvet)	W	AEW Dynamite	8:13

LEON RUFFIN

Date	Opponent	Result	Show	Time
May 3	Tony Nese	L	AEW Dark	4:11
Jun 17	Max Caster, Austin Gunn & Colten Gunn (w/Bear Bronson & Bear Boulder)	L	AEW Rampage: Road Rager	1:15
Jul 5	Lee Moriarty	L	AEW Dark	8:21
Jul 6	Anthony Bowens, Max Caster, Austin Gunn & Colten Gunn (w/Fuego Del Sol, Bear Bronson & Bear Boulder)	L	AEW Dynamite	2:14
Jul 18	Ethan Page	L	AEW Dark Elevation	5:38
Jul 29	Ethan Page	L	AEW Rampage	1:31
Sep 27	Bshp King	W	AEW Dark	1:43
Nov 14	Daniel Garcia	L	AEW Dark Elevation	5:41
Nov 21	Daniel Garcia, Angelo Parker & Matt Menard (w/Tony Deppen & Tracy Williams)	L	AEW Dark Elevation	2:46
Nov 22	Rush	L	AEW Dark	1:04
Dec 6	Brian Cage	L	AEW Dark	5:35

LEVA BATES

Date	Opponent	Result	Show	Time
Jan 24	Ruby Soho & Thunder Rosa (w/Jordan Blake)	L	AEW Dark Elevation	2:52
May 24	Kiah Dream	W	AEW Dark	2:00
Aug 9	Athena, Hikaru Shida & Ruby Soho (w/Emi Sakura & Serena Deeb)	L	AEW Dark	8:08
Nov 1	Nyla Rose	L	AEW Dark	1:00
Nov 21	Hikaru Shida & Willow Nightingale (w/Emi Sakura)	L	AEW Dark Elevation	4:28
Dec 6	Abadon	L	AEW Dark	2:39
Dec 26	Marina Shafir & Nyla Rose (w/Karizma)	L	AEW Dark Elevation	2:54

LEYLA HIRSCH

Date	Opponent	Result	Show	Time
Jan 4	Renee Michelle, Sofia Castillo & Marina Tucker (w/Red Velvet & Kris Statlander)	W	AEW Dark	2:43
Jan 10	B3CCA & Notorious Mimi (w/Red Velvet)	W	AEW Dark Elevation	1:50
Jan 14	Penelope Ford, The Bunny & Nyla Rose (w/Red Velvet & Kris Statlander)	L	AEW Rampage	8:12
Jan 18	Katalina Perez	W	AEW Dark	3:11
Jan 24	Brittany Blake	W	AEW Dark Elevation	2:25
Jan 25	Janai Kai	W	AEW Dark	:43
Jan 26	Red Velvet	W	AEW Dynamite: Beach Break	8:08
Feb 21	AQA, Kiera Hogan & Skye Blue (w/Emi Sakura & Nyla Rose)	W	AEW Dark Elevation	4:48
Feb 28	Willow Nightingale	W	AEW Dark Elevation	2:16
Mar 6	Kris Statlander	W	AEW Revolution Buy-In	9:50
Mar 9	Thunder Rosa	L	AEW Dynamite	8:51
Mar 15	Marina Tucker	W	AEW Dark	2:06
Mar 18	Red Velvet	L	AEW Rampage	8:00
Mar 23	Red Velvet	W	AEW Dynamite	6:30
Apr 4	Ella Envy	W	AEW Dark Elevation	1:35

LINCE DORADO

Date	Opponent	Result	Show	Time
Jun 30	Arez, Holidead & Mini Abismo Negro (w/Micro Man & Taya Valkyrie)	W	MLW Fusion	6:32
Jul 7	Real1	L	MLW Fusion	9:58
Nov 10	Myron Reed, Arez, La Estrella	L	MLW Fusion	6:54
Dec 24	Cody Chhun & Guillermo Rosas (w/Mascara Dorada)	W	NJPW Strong	10:35

LIO RUSH

| Feb 5 | Jorel Nelson & Royce Isaacs (w/Rocky Romero) | W | NJPW Strong | 10:52 |
| Nov 20 | Dick Togo, Evil, Sho & Yujiro Takahashi (w/Tomohiro Ishii, Yoh & Yoshi-Hashi) | W | NJPW x Stardom Historic X-Over | 7:05 |

LITA

| Jan 29 | Royal Rumble Match | L | WWE Royal Rumble '22 | 10:21 |
| Feb 19 | Becky Lynch | L | WWE Elimination Chamber '22 | 12:10 |

LIV MORGAN

Jan 1	Becky Lynch	L	WWE Day 1	17:00
Jan 10	Doudrop, Bianca Belair	L	WWE Monday Night RAW	14:45
Jan 17	Becky Lynch & Doudrop (w/Bianca Belair)	L	WWE Monday Night RAW	3:00
Jan 24	Carmella, Tamina & Nikki A.S.H. (w/Rhea Ripley & Dana Brooke)	W	WWE Monday Night RAW	2:20
Jan 29	Royal Rumble Match	L	WWE Royal Rumble '22	37:20
Feb 3	Doudrop	W	WWE Main Event	7:21
Feb 7	Doudrop	L	WWE Monday Night RAW	7:59
Feb 14	Gauntlet Match: Doudrop, Bianca Belair, Rhea Ripley, Nikki A.S.H.	L	WWE Monday Night RAW	44:04
Feb 19	Elimination Chamber: Bianca Belair, Alexa Bliss, Doudrop, Nikki A.S.H., Rhea Ripley	L	WWE Elimination Chamber '22	12:10
Feb 24	Queen Zelina	W	WWE Main Event	6:53
Feb 28	Becky Lynch, Doudrop & Nikki A.S.H. (w/Rhea Ripley & Bianca Belair)	W	WWE Monday Night RAW	12:20
Mar 7	Carmella & Queen Zelina (w/Rhea Ripley)	W	WWE Monday Night RAW	9:05
Mar 14	Queen Zelina	W	WWE Monday Night RAW	2:55
Mar 18	Sasha Banks & Naomi (w/Rhea Ripley)	D	WWE SmackDown	12:00
Mar 21	Natalya & Shayna Baszler (w/Rhea Ripley)	L	WWE Monday Night RAW	3:55
Mar 28	Queen Zelina, Carmella, Natalya & Shayna Baszler (w/Naomi, Sasha Banks & Rhea Ripley)	W	WWE Monday Night RAW	8:20
Apr 3	Sasha Banks & Naomi, Carmella & Queen Zelina, Natalya & Shayna Baszler (w/Rhea Ripley)	L	WWE WrestleMania XXXVIII	10:50
Apr 4	Sasha Banks & Naomi (w/Rhea Ripley)	L	WWE Monday Night RAW	9:00
Apr 8	Sasha Banks	W	WWE SmackDown	7:08
Apr 11	Naomi	L	WWE Monday Night RAW	2:20
Apr 18	Sasha Banks & Naomi (w/Rhea Ripley)	L	WWE Monday Night RAW	7:25
Apr 28	Nikki A.S.H.	W	WWE Main Event	5:03
May 2	Becky Lynch, Rhea Ripley & Sonya Deville (w/Asuka & Bianca Belair)	W	WWE Monday Night RAW	15:15
May 9	Rhea Ripley	L	WWE Monday Night RAW	5:40
May 23	Damian Priest & Rhea Ripley (w/AJ Styles)	L	WWE Monday Night RAW	11:35
May 30	Rhea Ripley	W	WWE Monday Night RAW	10:15
Jun 5	Edge, Damian Priest & Rhea Ripley (w/AJ Styles & Finn Balor)	L	WWE Hell In A Cell '22	16:00
Jun 6	Rhea Ripley, Alexa Bliss, Doudrop	L	WWE Monday Night RAW	14:35
Jun 13	Doudrop & Nikki A.S.H. (w/Alexa Bliss)	W	WWE Monday Night RAW	4:25
Jun 20	Carmella, Alexa Bliss, Asuka, Becky Lynch	L	WWE Monday Night RAW	12:30
Jun 27	Alexa Bliss	W	WWE Monday Night RAW	3:20
Jul 1	Raquel Rodriguez, Lacey Evans & Shotzi (w/Alexa Bliss & Asuka)	W	WWE SmackDown	13:14
Jul 2	Money In The Bank Ladder Match: Alexa Bliss, Asuka, Becky Lynch, Lacey Evans, Raquel Rodriguez, Shotzi	W	WWE Money In The Bank '22	16:35
Jul 2	Ronda Rousey	W	WWE Money In The Bank '22	:35
Jul 4	Natalya & Carmella (w/Bianca Belair)	W	WWE Monday Night RAW	13:25
Jul 15	Natalya	W	WWE SmackDown	9:04
Jul 29	Sonya Deville & Natalya (w/Ronda Rousey)	W	WWE SmackDown	11:30
Jul 30	Ronda Rousey	W	WWE SummerSlam '22	4:35
Aug 19	Shotzi	W	WWE SmackDown	6:48
Sep 3	Shayna Baszler	W	WWE Clash At The Castle	11:02
Sep 23	Lacey Evans	W	WWE SmackDown	8:44
Oct 8	Extreme Rules Match: Ronda Rousey	L	WWE Extreme Rules '22	12:05
Oct 21	Sonya Deville	D	WWE SmackDown	8:50
Nov 4	No DQ: Sonya Deville	W	WWE SmackDown	13:48
Nov 11	Six-Pack Challenge: Shotzi, Raquel Rodriguez, Sonya Deville, Xia Li, Lacey Evans	L	WWE SmackDown	11:58
Dec 9	Ronda Rousey & Shayna Baszler (w/Tegan Nox)	W	WWE SmackDown	4:07
Dec 16	Dakota Kai & Iyo Sky (w/Tegan Nox)	L	WWE SmackDown	14:48
Dec 23	Gauntlet Match: Raquel Rodriguez, Xia Li, Emma, Sonya Deville, Tegan Nox, Shayna Baszler	L	WWE SmackDown	23:58

LOGAN PAUL

Apr 2	Rey Mysterio & Dominik Mysterio (w/The Miz)	W	WWE WrestleMania XXXVIII	11:15
Jul 30	The Miz	W	WWE SummerSlam '22	14:15
Nov 5	Roman Reigns	L	WWE Crown Jewel '22	24:50

LUCHASAURUS

Jan 5	Rey Fenix & Penta El Zero M (w/Jungle Boy)	W	AEW Dynamite	14:03
Jan 11	Nick Comoroto & QT Marshall (w/Jungle Boy)	W	AEW Dark	8:21
Jan 14	John Silver & Alex Reynolds (w/Jungle Boy)	W	AEW Rampage	12:37
Jan 28	Marq Quen & Isiah Kassidy (w/Jungle Boy)	W	AEW Rampage: Beach Break	10:45
Feb 11	Austin Gunn & Colten Gunn (w/Jungle Boy)	W	AEW Rampage	12:29
Mar 6	Bobby Fish & Kyle O'Reilly, Matt Jackson & Nick Jackson (w/Jungle Boy)	W	AEW Revolution '22	18:55
Mar 9	Anthony Bowens & Max Caster (w/Jungle Boy)	W	AEW Dynamite	9:26
Mar 16	Adam Cole, Bobby Fish & Kyle O'Reilly (w/Hangman Page & Jungle Boy)	L	AEW Dynamite: St. Patrick's Day Slam	13:58
Apr 13	Bobby Fish & Kyle O'Reilly (w/Jungle Boy)	W	AEW Dynamite	13:45
May 29	Keith Lee & Swerve Strickland, Powerhouse Hobbs & Ricky Starks (w/Jungle Boy)	W	AEW Double Or Nothing '22	17:15
Jun 1	Matt Jackson, Nick Jackson, Bobby Fish, Kyle O'Reilly & Hikuleo	L	AEW Dynamite	12:00

(w/Christian Cage, Matt Hardy, Darby Allin & Jungle Boy)

Jun 15	Ladder Match: Matt Jackson & Nick Jackson (w/ Jungle Boy)	L	AEW Dynamite: Road Rager	14:53
Jun 29	Serpentico	W	AEW Dynamite: Blood & Guts	:49
Jul 13	Griff Garrison	W	AEW Dynamite: Fyter Fest	1:28
Jul 20	Brian Pillman Jr. & Griff Garrison (w/Christian Cage)	W	AEW Dynamite: Fyter Fest	2:08
Aug 10	Anthony Henry	W	AEW Dynamite: Quake By The Lake	:43
Oct 5	Fuego Del Sol	W	AEW Dynamite: Anniversary	:23
Oct 12	Jungle Boy	W	AEW Dynamite	14:05
Nov 2	Orange Cassidy, Rey Fenix	L	AEW Dynamite	9:59
Nov 19	Steel Cage Match: Jungle Boy	L	AEW Full Gear '22	18:40

LUCIEN PRICE

Aug 12	Andre Chase & Bodhi Hayward (w/Bronco Nima)	L	NXT Level Up	6:16
Aug 26	Edris Enofe & Malik Blade (w/Bronco Nima)	L	NXT Level Up	5:50
Nov 11	Edris Enofe, Malik Blade & Odyssey Jones (w/Bronco Nima & Xyon Quinn)	L	NXT Level Up	6:41
Dec 16	Jagger Reid & Rip Fowler (w/Bronco Nima)	L	NXT Level Up	5:39
Dec 30	Bryson Montana & Oba Femi (w/Bronco Nima)	W	NXT Level Up	4:38

LUDWIG KAISER (AS MARCEL BARTHEL UNTIL MAY 27)

Jan 4	Riddle, Nash Carter & Wes Lee (w/Walter & Fabian Aichner)	L	NXT 2.0: New Year's Evil '22	13:52
Feb 1	Roderick Strong, Julius Creed & Brutus Creed (w/Gunther & Fabian Aichner)	W	NXT 2.0	12:01
Mar 8	Nash Carter & Wes Lee (w/Fabian Aichner)	D	NXT 2.0: Roadblock '22	5:33
Mar 29	LA Knight, Nash Carter & Wes Lee (w/Gunther & Fabian Aichner)	W	NXT 2.0	12:11
Apr 2	Wes Lee & Nash Carter, Brutus Creed & Julius Creed (w/Fabian Aichner)	L	NXT Stand & Deliver '22	11:22
Apr 5	Julius Creed & Brutus Creed (w/Fabian Aichner)	L	NXT 2.0	11:24
May 27	Ricochet & Drew Gulak (w/Gunther)	W	WWE SmackDown	6:45
Jul 8	Shinsuke Nakamura	L	WWE SmackDown	6:40
Jul 22	Shinsuke Nakamura	W	WWE SmackDown	9:30
Aug 5	Shinsuke Nakamura	L	WWE SmackDown	8:45
Sep 2	Butch	L	WWE SmackDown	9:10
Sep 9	Sheamus, Ridge Holland & Butch (w/Gunther & Giovanni Vinci)	W	WWE SmackDown	19:05
Sep 16	Ridge Holland & Butch, Ashante Adonis & Top Dolla, Kofi Kingston & Xavier Woods (w/Giovanni Vinci)	L	WWE SmackDown	18:44
Oct 8	Good Old Fashioned Donnybrook Match: Sheamus, Ridge Holland & Butch (w/Gunther & Giovanni Vinci)	L	WWE Extreme Rules '22	17:50
Oct 21	Rey Mysterio	L	WWE SmackDown	11:25
Nov 18	Braun Strowman, Kofi Kingston & Xaiver Woods (w/Gunther & Giovanni Vinci)	L	WWE SmackDown	7:38
Dec 9	Ricochet, Kofi Kingston & Xavier Woods (w/Gunther & Giovanni Vinci)	L	WWE SmackDown	18:47
Dec 17	Drew McIntyre, Sheamus & Ricochet (w/Giovanni Vinci & Gunther)	L	WWE Tribute To The Troops '22	16:34
Dec 23	Miracle On 34th Street Fight: Braun Strowman & Ricochet (w/Giovanni Vinci)	L	WWE SmackDown	11:59

LUKE GALLOWS

Jan 8	Hardcore War: Eddie Edwards, Rich Swann, Willie Mack, Heath & Rhino (w/Karl Anderson, Eric Young, Deaner & Joe Doering)	L	IMPACT Hard To Kill '22	23:25
Jan 20	Heath & Rhino (w/Joe Doering)	W	IMPACT Wrestling	8:39
Mar 3	Tama Tonga, Tanga Loa, Deaner & Joe Doering (w/Karl Anderson, Chris Bey & Jay White)	W	IMPACT Wrestling	9:48
Mar 24	Lumberjack Match: Eric Young & Joe Doering (w/Karl Anderson)	L	IMPACT Wrestling	7:26
Mar 31	Johnny Swinger & Zicky Dice (w/Karl Anderson)	W	IMPACT Wrestling	:50
Apr 1	Jay Briscoe & Mark Briscoe (w/Karl Anderson)	W	IMPACT Multiverse Of Matches	9:46
Apr 16	Aaron Henare, Great-O-Khan, Jeff Cobb, TJP, Mark Davis & Kyle Fletcher (w/Hikuleo, Chris Bey, El Phantasmo, Karl Anderson & Scott Norton)	L	NJPW Windy City Riot	11:58
Apr 21	Kenny King, Matt Taven, Mike Bennett & Vincent (w/Karl Anderson, Jay White & Chris Bey)	W	IMPACT Wrestling	9:22
Apr 23	Elimination Challenge Match (w/Karl Anderson)	L	IMPACT Rebellion '22	33:02
May 19	Matt Taven & Mike Bennett (w/Karl Anderson)	W	IMPACT Wrestling	10:00
Jun 11	Chuck Taylor, Rocky Romero, Tomohiro Ishii, Mascara Dorada & Ren Narita (w/Karl Anderson, Hikuleo, Jay White & Juice Robinson)	W	NJPW Strong	12:44
Jun 12	Toru Yano	L	NJPW Dominion '22	4:05
Jun 19	Jay Briscoe & Mark Briscoe (w/Karl Anderson)	W	IMPACT Slammiversary XX	10:00
Jun 30	PCO & Vincent (w/Karl Anderson)	W	IMPACT Wrestling	5:19
Jul 14	Eddie Edwards, Kenny King, Matt Taven & Mike Bennett (w/Karl Anderson, Ace Austin & Chris Bey)	W	IMPACT Wrestling	12:34
Aug 4	Derby City Street Fight: PCO	L	IMPACT Wrestling	11:59
Sep 1	Matt Taven & Mike Bennett (w/Karl Anderson)	W	IMPACT Wrestling	8:14
Sep 15	Alex Shelley & Chris Sabin (w/Karl Anderson)	L	IMPACT Wrestling	14:39
Sep 25	Toru Yano	D	NJPW Burning Spirit '22	3:45
Oct 1	Hiroshi Tanahashi, Tama Tonga, Hikuleo & Jado (w/Jay White, Karl Anderson & Gedo)	L	NJPW Royal Quest II Night #1	12:15
Oct 2	Hiroshi Tanahashi, Tama Tonga & Hikuleo (w/Jay White & Karl Anderson)	L	NJPW Royal Quest II Night #2	10:54
Oct 15	Che Cabrera	W	NJPW Strong	7:53
Oct 17	Chad Gable & Otis (w/Karl Anderson)	W	WWE Monday Night RAW	8:20
Oct 18	Joe Gacy, Jagger Reid & Rip Fowler (w/Karl Anderson & Cameron Grimes)	W	NXT	11:56
Nov 5	Finn Balor, Damian Priest & Dominik Mysterio (w/AJ Styles & Karl Anderson)	L	WWE Crown Jewel '22	14:00
Nov 28	Finn Balor, Damian Priest, Dominik Mysterio & Rhea Ripley (w/AJ Styles, Karl Anderson & Mia Yim)	L	WWE Monday Night RAW	14:20
Dec 5	Baron Corbin, Chad Gable & Otis (w/AJ Styles & Karl Anderson)	W	WWE Monday Night RAW	14:30
Dec 19	Chad Gable & Otis (w/Karl Anderson)	W	WWE Monday Night RAW	9:05

LUKE HAWX

Jan 18	Jordan Clearwater & Marshe Rockett (w/PJ Hawx)	W	NWA Power	6:32
Mar 3	Odinson & Parrow (w/PJ Hawx)	W	NWA Crockett Cup '22	9:20
Aug 23	Dirty Dango & JTG, Gustavo Aguilar & Rhett Titus (w/PJ Hawx)	W	NWA Power	5:56
Aug 27	Bestia 666 & Mecha Wolf (w/PJ Hawx)	L	NWA 74th Anniversary Show	13:10
Aug 28	Tag Team Battle Royal (w/PJ Hawx)	L	NWA 74th Anniversary Show	14:07
Nov 1	Dirty Dango & JTG (w/PJ Hawx)	W	NWA Power	6:22
Nov 12	Bestia 666 & Mecha Wolf (w/PJ Hawx)	L	NWA Hard Times 3	10:48
Dec 13	Alex Taylor	L	NWA Power	6:33

LUTHER

Feb 7	Chuck Taylor & Trent Beretta (w/Serpentico)	L	AEW Dark Elevation	6:42
Feb 15	Alan Angels & Ten (w/Serpentico)	L	AEW Dark	8:16
Feb 21	Brock Anderson, Frankie Kazarian, Jay Lethal, Lee Johnson & Matt Sydal (w/Serpentico, Cezar Bononi, JD Drake & Peter Avalon)	L	AEW Dark Elevation	6:06
Feb 28	Evil Uno & Stu Grayson (w/Serpentico)	L	AEW Dark Elevation	4:53
Mar 14	John Silver & Alex Reynolds (w/Serpentico)	L	AEW Dark Elevation	4:40
Mar 15	John Silver & Alex Reynolds (w/Serpentico)	L	AEW Dark	4:26
Mar 21	Dante Martin & Darius Martin (w/Serpentico)	L	AEW Dark Elevation	4:54
Apr 11	John Silver, Alex Reynolds, Alan Angels, Stu Grayson & Ten (w/Serpentico, Austin Gunn, Colten Gunn & Billy Gunn)	L	AEW Dark Elevation	5:20
Apr 25	Evil Uno, Alex Reynolds, Alan Angels, Stu Grayson & Ten (w/Bulk Nasty, Jake Omen, RC Dupree & Tito Ortic)	L	AEW Dark Elevation	3:09
May 17	Keith Lee & Swerve Strickland (w/Serpentico)	L	AEW Dark	6:00
Nov 28	Matt Hardy, Isiah Kassidy & Marq Quen (w/Isaia Moore & Serpentico)	L	AEW Dark Elevation	4:50
Dec 12	Ari Daivari, Josh Woods & Tony Nese (w/Brandon Cutler & Serpentico)	L	AEW Dark Elevation	5:20
Dec 20	Jarett Diaz, Jay Marti & Richard Adonis (w/Angelico & Serpentico)	W	AEW Dark	4:07
Dec 23	$300,000 Three Kings Christmas Casino Trios Royale (w/Angelico & Serpentico)	L	AEW Rampage	22:01

LYRA VALKYRIA

Dec 13	Amari Miller	W	NXT	3:03
Dec 27	Lash Legend	W	NXT	3:32

MACE

Sep 2	Ashante Adonis & Top Dolla (w/Mansoor)	L	WWE SmackDown	3:05
Sep 9	Angelo Dawkins, Montez Ford, Ashante Adonis & Top Dolla (w/Mansoor, Angel & Humberto)	L	WWE SmackDown	8:35
Sep 23	Kofi Kingston & Xavier Woods (w/Mansoor)	L	WWE SmackDown	3:18
Oct 28	Kofi Kingston & Xavier Woods (w/Mansoor)	L	WWE SmackDown	3:45

MADCAP MOSS

Jan 1	Drew McIntyre	L	WWE Day 1	9:45
Jan 7	Erik & Ivar (w/Happy Corbin)	W	WWE SmackDown	3:30
Jan 14	Kofi Kingston	W	WWE SmackDown	9:53
Jan 21	Kofi Kingston	L	WWE SmackDown	7:40
Jan 28	Big E & Kofi Kingston (w/Happy Corbin)	L	WWE SmackDown	7:10
Jan 29	Royal Rumble Match	L	WWE Royal Rumble '22	4:24
Feb 19	Falls Count Anywhere: Drew McIntyre	L	WWE Elimination Chamber '22	9:00
Feb 25	Drew McIntyre	L	WWE SmackDown	7:20
Mar 28	Handicap Match: Drew McIntyre (w/Happy Corbin)	L	WWE Monday Night RAW	1:55
Apr 1	Andre The Giant Memorial Battle Royal	W	WWE SmackDown	8:05
Apr 15	Humberto	W	WWE SmackDown	2:46
Apr 22	Angel	W	WWE SmackDown	2:25
May 8	Happy Corbin	W	WWE WrestleMania Backlash '22	8:40
Jun 6	No Holds Barred: Happy Corbin	W	WWE Hell In A Cell '22	12:05
Jun 17	Last Laugh Match: Happy Corbin	W	WWE SmackDown	9:22
Jul 1	Battle Royal	L	WWE SmackDown	14:36
Jul 1	The Miz, Ezekiel, Happy Corbin	W	WWE SmackDown	10:33
Jul 2	Money In The Bank Ladder Match: Theory, Drew McIntyre, Omos, Riddle Sami Zayn, Seth Rollins, Sheamus	L	WWE Money In The Bank '22	25:25
Jul 15	Theory	W	WWE SmackDown	11:34
Jul 22	Theory, Jimmy Uso & Jey Uso (w/Angelo Dawkins & Montez Ford)	W	WWE SmackDown	17:00
Aug 12	Jimmy Uso & Jey Uso (w/Drew McIntyre)	W	WWE SmackDown	9:15
Aug 19	Sheamus, Happy Corbin, Ricochet, Sami Zayn	L	WWE SmackDown	22:33
Sep 3	Austin Theory, Chad Gable & Otis (w/Angelo Dawkins & Montez Ford)	W	WWE Clash At The Castle Kickoff	6:29
Sep 16	Solo Sikoa	L	WWE SmackDown	10:49
Sep 30	Sami Zayn & Solo Sikoa (w/Ricochet)	L	WWE SmackDown	12:44
Oct 28	Karrion Kross	L	WWE SmackDown	9:35
Nov 18	Karrion Kross	L	WWE SmackDown	6:48

MADI WRENKOWSKI

Jan 4	Jamie Hayter	L	AEW Dark	3:36
Jan 18	Melina	L	NWA Power	4:42
Mar 25	Nyla Rose	L	AEW Rampage	:38
Mar 28	Hikaru Shida	L	AEW Dark Elevation	1:39
Mar 29	Kamille	L	NWA Power	5:53
May 17	Allysin Kay & Marti Belle (w/Kenzie Paige)	L	NWA Power	5:16
Aug 27	Burke Invitational Gauntlet	L	NWA 74th Anniversary Show	17:24
Nov 8	Taya Valkyrie	L	NWA Power	6:22
Nov 12	Ella Envy & Kenzie Paige (w/Missa Kate)	L	NWA Hard Times 3	8:12
Dec 10	Athena	L	AEW Dark Elevation	1:39
Dec 26	Ruby Soho & Willow Nightingale (w/Vertvixen)	L	AEW Dark Elevation	4:47

MADISON RAYNE

Jan 20	Rosemary & Havok (w/Tenille Dashwood)	W	IMPACT Wrestling	3:35
Jan 27	Cassie Lee & Jessie McKay (w/Kaleb With A K)	L	IMPACT Wrestling	10:57
Mar 3	Cassie Lee	L	IMPACT Wrestling	4:13
Mar 10	Cassie Lee & Jessie McKay, Chelsea Green & Mickie James, Savannah Evans & Tasha Steelz (w/Tenille Dashwood)	L	IMPACT Wrestling	6:00
Mar 31	Battle Royal	L	IMPACT Wrestling	7:15
Apr 1	Tasha Steelz & Savannah Evans, Gisele Shaw & Lady Frost, Havok & Rosemary (w/Tenille Dashwood)	W	IMPACT Multiverse Of Matches	9:02
Apr 14	Jessie McKay	W	IMPACT Before The Impact	6:34
May 12	Alisha Edwards & Gisele Shaw (w/Tenille Dashwood)	W	IMPACT Wrestling	12:00
Jun 19	Rosemary & Taya Valkyrie (w/Tenille Dashwood)	L	IMPACT Slammiversary XX	7:20
Jul 21	Masha Slamovich	L	IMPACT Wrestling	1:12
Aug 5	Leila Grey	W	AEW Rampage	8:25
Aug 10	Jade Cargill	L	AEW Dynamite: Quake By The Lake	7:48
Aug 11	Mia Yim	L	IMPACT Wrestling	9:18
Sep 5	Marina Shafir & Nyla Rose (w/Queen Aminata)	L	AEW Dark Elevation	4:42
Sep 9	Serena Deeb	L	AEW Rampage	3:56
Sep 20	Viva Van	W	AEW Dark	4:21
Oct 7	Anna Jay & Tay Melo (w/Skye Blue)	L	AEW Rampage	7:42
Oct 17	Emi Sakura & Serena Deeb (w/Skye Blue)	L	AEW Dark Elevation	6:00
Oct 28	Tay Melo	L	AEW Rampage	9:23
Oct 31	Diamante	W	AEW Dark Elevation	3:12
Nov 4	Dr. Britt Baker D.M.D. & Jamie Hayter (w/Skye Blue)	L	AEW Rampage	7:18
Nov 18	Athena	L	AEW Rampage	2:50
Dec 5	Emi Sakura	L	AEW Dark Elevation	2:41
Dec 7	Jade Cargill, Leila Grey & Red Velvet (w/Kiera Hogan & Skye Blue)	L	AEW Dynamite	8:13
Dec 26	The Bunny	L	AEW Dark Elevation	3:00

MADMAN FULTON

Jan 6	Hernandez & Johnny Swinger (w/Ace Austin)	W	IMPACT Wrestling	3:40
Feb 3	Chris Bey, Jay White, Tama Tonga & Tanga Loa (w/Jake Something, Mike Bauley & Ace Austin)	L	IMPACT Wrestling	16:49
Mar 31	Josh Alexander	L	IMPACT Wrestling	1:40

MADS KRUGGER

Feb 24	Jacob Fatu	L	MLW Fusion	4:54
Mar 24	Stairway To Hell Match: Jacob Fatu	W	MLW Fusion	14:32
Apr 29	Alexander Hammerstone, Jacob Fatu	L	MLW Fusion	13:34
Jun 9	Alexander Hammerstone, Marshall Von Erich & Ross Von Erich (w/King Muertes & Richard Holliday)	W	MLW Fusion	9:31
Jun 23	Weapons Of Mass Destruction Match: Jacob Fatu	L	MLW Fusion	16:27
Dec 22	Tables Match: Mance Warner	L	MLW Fusion	7:38

MAGIC JAKE DUMAS

Mar 29	Rodney Mack	W	NWA Power	4:08
Jul 19	Eric Jackson	W	NWA Power	1:45
Aug 28	Mercurio	W	NWA 74th Anniversary Show	7:15
Sep 20	Chris Adonis	L	NWA Power	8:01

MAKI ITOH

Mar 19	Yuki Arai	W	TJPW Grand Princess '22	16:18
May 18	Dr. Britt Baker D.M.D.	L	AEW Dynamite: Wild Card Wednesday	6:44
Jun 12	Hikari Noa, Suzume & Yuki Arai (w/Miyu Yamashita & Juria Nagano)	W	Cyberfight Festival '22	11:54
Jul 9	Alex Windsor	L	TJPW Summer Sun Princess '22	13:22
Aug 22	Hikaru Shida & Skye Blue (w/Emi Sakura)	W	AEW Dark Elevation	7:15
Nov 28	Marina Shafir & Nyla Rose (w/Emi Sakura)	L	AEW Dark Elevation	4:17

MALAKAI BLACK

Jan 5	Brian Pillman Jr.	W	AEW Dynamite	6:02
Jan 19	Brian Pillman Jr. & Griff Garrison (w/Brody King)	W	AEW Dynamite	1:53
Feb 2	Pac & Penta El Zero M (w/Brody King)	W	AEW Dynamite	10:23
Feb 23	Pac & Penta Oscuro (w/Brody King)	L	AEW Dynamite	7:31
Mar 6	Pac, Penta Oscuro & Erick Redbeard (w/Brody King & Buddy Matthews)	W	AEW Revolution Buy-In	17:20
Mar 18	Fuego Del Sol, Bear Bronson & Bear Boulder (w/Brody King & Buddy Matthews)	W	AEW Rampage	3:22
Apr 1	Fuego Del Sol, Evil Uno & Stu Grayson (w/Brody King & Buddy Matthews)	W	AEW Rampage	7:15
May 20	Fuego Del Sol, Evil Uno & Ten (w/Brody King & Buddy Matthews)	W	AEW Rampage	9:25
May 28	Adriel Noctis, Greg Sharpe & Matt Brannigan (w/Brody King & Buddy Matthews)	W	AEW Dark	3:50
May 29	Pac, Penta Oscuro & Rey Fenix (w/Buddy Matthews & Brody King)	W	AEW Double Or Nothing '22	15:35
Jun 22	Penta Oscuro	W	AEW Dynamite	9:56
Jun 26	Clark Connors, Miro, Pac	W	AEW x NJPW Forbidden Door	15:10
Jul 15	Alex Reynolds & John Silver (w/Brody King)	W	AEW Rampage	8:18
Aug 26	Ten, John Silver & Alan Reynolds (w/Brody King & Buddy Matthews)	L	AEW Rampage	9:03
Sep 4	Darby Allin, Sting & Miro (w/Brody King & Buddy Matthews)	L	AEW All Out '22	12:10
Dec 14	QT Marshall, Aaron Solo & Cole Karter (w/Brody King & Buddy Matthews)	W	AEW Dynamite: Winter Is Coming	:23

MALIK BLADE

Jan 7	Draco Anthony	W	WWE 205 Live	6:05
Jan 11	Joe Gacy & Harland (w/Edris Enofe)	W	NXT 2.0	3:14

Jan 18	Joaquin Wilde & Raul Mendoza (w/Edris Enofe)	W	NXT 2.0	3:17
Feb 8	Nash Carter & Wes Lee (w/Edris Enofe)	L	NXT 2.0	9:29
Mar 4	Joaquin Wilde & Raul Mendoza (w/Edris Enofe)	L	NXT Level Up	8:45
Mar 25	Ikemen Jiro & Kushida (w/Edris Enofe)	W	NXT Level Up	7:33
Apr 22	Damaris Griffin & Quincy Elliott (w/Edris Enofe)	W	NXT Level Up	6:36
Apr 26	Erik & Ivar (w/Edris Enofe)	L	NXT 2.0	4:45
May 24	Channing Lorenzo & Troy Donovan (w/Edris Enofe)	L	NXT 2.0	6:10
Jun 3	Dante Chen & Javier Bernal (w/Edris Enofe)	W	NXT Level Up	7:05
Jun 14	Julius Creed & Brutus Creed (w/Edris Enofe)	L	NXT 2.0	13:57
Jul 8	Bryson Montana & Damaris Griffin (w/Edris Enofe)	W	NXT Level Up	5:29
Jul 12	Tony D'Angelo & Channing Lorenzo (w/Edris Enofe)	L	NXT 2.0	5:23
Jul 29	Ikemen Jiro & Quincy Elliott (w/Edris Enofe)	W	NXT Level Up	6:01
Aug 9	Elton Prince & Kit Wilson (w/Edris Enofe)	L	NXT 2.0	4:37
Aug 26	Bronco Nima & Lucien Price (w/Edris Enofe)	W	NXT Level Up	5:50
Sep 20	Jagger Reid & Rip Fowler (w/Edris Enofe)	L	NXT	9:17
Sep 30	Edris Enofe & Guru Raaj (w/Edris Enofe)	W	NXT Level Up	6:50
Oct 11	Jadder Reid & Rip Fowler, Brooks Jensen & Josh Briggs (w/Edris Enofe)	W	NXT	9:10
Oct 25	Elton Prince & Kit Wilson (w/Edris Enofe)	L	NXT	12:29
Nov 11	Bronco Nima, Lucien Price & Xyon Quinn (w/Edris Enofe & Odyssey Jones)	W	NXT Level Up	6:41
Nov 29	Von Wagner	L	NXT	2:43
Dec 6	Brooks Jensen & Josh Briggs (w/Edris Enofe)	L	NXT	3:24
Dec 15	Cedric Alexander & Mustafa Ali (w/Edris Enofe)	L	WWE Main Event	6:17
Dec 27	Joe Gacy, Jagger Reid & Rip Fowler (w/Edris Enofe & Odyssey Jones)	L	NXT	11:15

MANCE WARNER

Aug 4	Serpentico	W	AEW Dark Elevation	3:57
Aug 5	Jon Moxley	L	AEW Rampage	11:40
Dec 22	Tables Match: Mads Krugger	W	MLW Fusion	7:38

MANDY ROSE

Jan 4	Raquel Gonzalez, Cora Jade	W	NXT 2.0: New Year's Evil '22	12:32
Jan 25	Kay Lee Ray, Indi Hartwell & Persia Pirotta (w/Gigi Dolin & Jacy Jayne)	L	NXT 2.0	10:25
Feb 8	Kay Lee Ray	W	NXT 2.0	7:59
Apr 2	Cora Jade, Kay Lee Ray, Io Shirai	W	NXT Stand & Deliver '22	13:27
Apr 12	Dakota Kai	W	NXT 2.0	10:48
Apr 26	Roxanne Perez	W	NXT 2.0	9:58
May 24	Indi Hartwell	W	NXT 2.0	9:18
Jun 4	Wendy Choo	W	NXT In Your House '22	11:08
Jun 14	Roxanne Perez, Cora Jade & Indi Hartwell (w/Gigi Dolin & Jacy Jayne)	L	NXT 2.0	13:51
Jun 28	Nikkita Lyons	L	NXT 2.0	5:29
Jul 12	Roxanne Perez	W	NXT 2.0	9:17
Aug 2	Sarray	W	NXT 2.0	5:44
Aug 16	Zoey Stark	W	NXT 2.0: Heatwave	11:26
Sep 4	Meiko Satomura, Blair Davenport	W	NXT Worlds Collide '22	13:17
Sep 27	Fallon Henley	W	NXT	5:40
Oct 22	Alba Fyre	W	NXT Halloween Havoc '22	7:07
Nov 15	Last Woman Standing: Alba Fyre	W	NXT	11:56
Nov 29	Katana Chance, Kayden Carter & Nikkita Lyons (w/Gigi Dolin & Jacy Jayne)	W	NXT	8:54
Dec 13	Roxanne Perez	L	NXT	9:37

MANSOOR

Jan 14	Erik & Ivar, Angel & Humberto, Jinder Mahal & Shanky (w/Cesaro)	L	WWE SmackDown	13:21
Apr 1	Andre The Giant Memorial Battle Royal	L	WWE SmackDown	8:05
Sep 2	Ashante Adonis & Top Dolla (w/Mace)	L	WWE SmackDown	3:05
Sep 9	Angelo Dawkins, Montez Ford, Ashante Adonis & Top Dolla (w/Mace, Angel & Humberto)	L	WWE SmackDown	8:35
Sep 23	Kofi Kingston & Xavier Woods (w/Mace)	L	WWE SmackDown	3:18
Oct 14	LA Knight	L	WWE SmackDown	2:52
Oct 28	Kofi Kingston & Xavier Woods (w/Mace)	L	WWE SmackDown	3:45

MARINA SHAFIR

Jan 4	Valentina Rossi	W	AEW Dark	1:38
Feb 1	Reka Tehaka	W	AEW Dark	3:29
Mar 1	Danielle Kamela	W	AEW Dark	3:24
Mar 22	Leila Grey	W	AEW Dark	1:20
Apr 13	Skye Blue	W	AEW Dynamite	2:24
Apr 19	Alejandra Lion	W	AEW Dark	2:00
Apr 22	Jade Cargill	L	AEW Rampage	11:41
May 17	Layna Lennox	W	AEW Dark	3:00
Jun 7	Skye Blue	W	AEW Dark	3:32
Jun 8	Thunder Rosa	L	AEW Dynamite	8:26
Jun 20	Heidi Howitzer & Max The Impaler (w/Nyla Rose)	W	AEW Dark Elevation	3:25
Jun 22	Toni Storm	L	AEW Dynamite	7:22
Jul 6	Thunder Rosa & Toni Storm (w/Nyla Rose)	L	AEW Dynamite	9:07
Jul 18	Brittany Jade & Skye Blue (w/Nyla Rose)	W	AEW Dark Elevation	4:30
Jul 19	Amber Nova	W	AEW Dark	2:13
Jul 25	Angelica Risk & Shalonce Royal (w/Nyla Rose)	W	AEW Dark Elevation	2:17
Jul 26	Tracy Nyxx	W	AEW Dark	2:12
Aug 1	Hikaru Shida, Toni Storm & Willow Nightingale (w/Emi Sakura & Nyla Rose)	L	AEW Dark Elevation	8:05
Aug 9	Heather Reckless & Joseline Navarro (w/Nyla Rose)	W	AEW Dark	:46

Aug 15	Hikaru Shida, Thunder Rosa & Toni Storm (w/Emi Sakura & Nyla Rose)	L	AEW Dark Elevation	2:42
Aug 29	Queen Aminata & Skye Blue (w/Nyla Rose)	W	AEW Dark Elevation	3:40
Sep 5	Madison Rayne & Queen Aminata (w/Nyla Rose)	W	AEW Dark Elevation	4:42
Sep 6	Laynie Luck	W	AEW Dark	3:19
Sep 20	Le Rosa Negra	W	AEW Dark	3:01
Sep 22	JC Storm & Joelle Clift (w/Nyla Rose)	W	AEW Dark Elevation	1:40
Oct 4	Sio Nieves	W	AEW Dark	2:37
Oct 11	Hikaru Shida	L	AEW Dark	6:56
Nov 1	Kennedi Copeland	W	AEW Dark	:26
Nov 2	Jade Cargill	L	AEW Dynamite	2:20
Nov 22	Willow Nightingale	L	AEW Dark	5:00
Nov 28	Emi Sakura & Maki Itoh (w/Nyla Rose)	W	AEW Dark Elevation	4:17
Dec 5	Alice Crowley & Kitty LaFleur (w/Nyla Rose)	W	AEW Dark Elevation	3:07
Dec 19	Jazmin Allure	W	AEW Dark Elevation	1:30
Dec 20	Angelica Risk	W	AEW Dark	:55
Dec 26	Karizma & Leva Bates (w/Nyla Rosa)	W	AEW Dark Elevation	2:54

MARK ANDREWS

Apr 28	Primate & T-Bone (w/Wild Boar)	W	NXT UK	7:26
Jun 9	Kenny Williams	W	NXT UK	9:46
Jun 23	Elimination Match: Brooks Jensen & Josh Briggs, Dave Mastiff & Jack Starz, Charlie Dempsey & Rohan Raja (w/Wild Boar)	L	NXT UK	18:15
Jul 28	Brooks Jensen & Josh Briggs (w/Wild Boar)	L	NXT UK	9:03
Aug 18	Joe Coffey	L	NXT UK	7:40

MARK BRISCOE

Mar 19	Dirty Dango & JTG (w/Jay Briscoe)	W	NWA Crockett Cup '22	8:13
Mar 20	Mike Knox & VSK (w/Jay Briscoe)	W	NWA Crockett Cup '22	7:45
Mar 20	Doug Williams & Harry Smith (w/Jay Briscoe)	W	NWA Crockett Cup '22	13:55
Mar 22	Matt Taven & Mike Bennett (w/Jay Briscoe)	W	NWA Power	6:56
Apr 1	Luke Gallows & Karl Anderson (w/Jay Briscoe)	L	IMPACT Multiverse Of Matches	9:46
Apr 1	Dax Harwood & Cash Wheeler (w/Jay Briscoe)	L	ROH Supercard Of Honor XV	27:25
Apr 26	Bestia 666 & Mecha Wolf (w/Jay Briscoe)	L	NWA Power	9:56
Apr 28	Heath & Rhino (w/Jay Briscoe)	W	IMPACT Wrestling	6:35
May 19	Deaner & Joe Doering (w/Jay Briscoe)	W	IMPACT Wrestling	15:00
May 26	Deaner, Eric Young & Joe Doering (w/Jay Briscoe & Josh Alexander)	L	IMPACT Wrestling	17:09
Jun 16	Chris Bey & Jay White (w/Jay Briscoe)	W	IMPACT Wrestling	11:02
Jun 19	Luke Gallows & Karl Anderson (w/Jay Briscoe)	L	IMPACT Slammiversary XX	10:00
Jun 23	Eddie Edwards, Matt Taven & Mike Bennett (w/Jay Briscoe & James Storm)	L	IMPACT Wrestling	12:12
Jul 23	2/3 Falls: Dax Harwood & Cash Wheeler (w/Jay Briscoe)	L	ROH Death Before Dishonor XIX	43:25
Jul 31	Marshall Von Erich & Ross Von Erich (w/Jay Briscoe)	W	JCP Ric Flair's Last Match	7:43
Dec 10	Double Dog Collar Match: Dax Harwood & Cash Wheeler (w/Jay Briscoe)	W	ROH Final Battle '22	22:20

MARK COFFEY

Jan 27	Charlie Dempsey, Rohan Raja & Teoman (w/Wolfgang & Joe Coffey)	L	NXT UK	11:18
Mar 3	Sha Samuels	W	NXT UK	7:41
Mar 31	Noam Dar	L	NXT UK	16:46
Apr 14	Dave Mastiff & Jack Starz (w/Joe Coffey)	L	NXT UK	8:30
May 12	Ashton Smith & Oliver Carter (w/Joe Coffey)	L	NXT UK	10:24
May 26	Saxon Huxley	W	NXT UK	4:13
Jul 14	Noam Dar	W	NXT UK	17:49
Aug 23	Josh Briggs & Brooks Jensen (w/Wolfgang)	W	NXT 2.0	8:46
Aug 25	Noam Dar	L	NXT UK	14:38
Aug 30	Damon Kemp, Julius Creed & Brutus Creed (w/Joe Coffey & Wolfgang)	W	NXT 2.0	10:59
Sep 4	Elimination Match: Elton Prince & Kit Wilson, Brutus Creed & Julius Creed, Brooks Jensen & Josh Briggs (w/Wolfgang)	L	NXT Worlds Collide '22	15:34
Sep 6	Tyler Bate & Bron Breakker (w/Joe Coffey)	L	NXT 2.0	10:51
Sep 27	Pub Rules Match: Brooks Jensen & Josh Briggs (w/Wolfgang)	L	NXT	11:35

MARK DAVIS

Apr 16	Hikuleo, Chris Bey, El Phantasmo, Karl Anderson, Luke Gallows & Scott Norton (w/Aaron Henare, Great-O-Khan, Jeff Cobb, TJP & Kyle Fletcher)	W	NJPW Windy City Riot	11:58
May 14	Mikey Nicholls, Shane Haste, Jonah & Bad Dude Tito (w/Aaron Henare, Kyle Fletcher & Jeff Cobb)	L	NJPW Capital Collision	12:09
May 28	Bad Dude Tito, Jonah & Shane Haste (w/Jeff Cobb & Kyle Fletcher)	W	NJPW Strong	14:39
Jun 10	Trent Beretta, Dax Harwood & Cash Wheeler (w/Kyle Fletcher & Will Ospreay)	L	AEW Rampage	13:59
Jun 22	Orange Cassidy, Trent Beretta & Rocky Romero (w/Kyle Fletcher & Will Ospreay)	L	AEW Dynamite	11:37
Jul 2	Bad Dude Tito, Jonah, Mikey Nicholls & Shane Haste (w/Aaron Henare, Great-O-Khan & Kyle Fletcher)	W	NJPW Strong	11:35
Jul 16	Alan Angels & Evil Uno (w/Kyle Fletcher)	W	NJPW Strong	12:47
Jul 30	Barrett Brown & Misterioso (w/Kyle Fletcher)	W	NJPW Strong	7:27
Jul 30	Alex Zayne, Cash Wheeler & Dax Harwood (w/Kyle Fletcher & TJP)	W	NJPW Music City Mayhem	14:30
Aug 13	Christopher Daniels & Yuya Uemura (w/Kyle Fletcher)	W	NJPW Strong	11:57
Aug 24	Pac, Penta El Zero M & Rey Fenix (w/Kyle Fletcher & Will Ospreay)	W	AEW Dynamite	25:18
Aug 31	Kenny Omega, Matt Jackson & Nick Jackson (w/Kyle Fletcher & Will Ospreay)	L	AEW Dynamite	18:54
Sep 8	Ace Austin & Chris Bey (w/Kyle Fletcher)	W	IMPACT Wrestling	7:07
Sep 10	Jorel Nelson & Royce Isaacs (w/Kyle Fletcher)	W	NJPW Strong	11:38
Sep 22	Alex Shelley & Chris Sabin (w/Kyle Fletcher)	L	IMPACT Wrestling	15:31

Oct 1	Cash Wheeler & Dax Harwood (w/Kyle Fletcher)	L	NJPW Royal Quest II Night #1	31:59
Oct 2	Cash Wheeler, Dax Harwood, Shota Umino, Ricky Knight Jr. & Gabriel Kidd (w/Will Ospreay, Great-O-Khan, Kyle Fletcher & Gideon Grey)	W	NJPW Royal Quest II Night #2	16:57
Oct 15	Danny Limelight & JR Kratos (w/Kyle Fletcher)	W	NJPW Strong	10:08
Oct 28	Alex Shelley & Chris Sabin, Kevin Knight & The DKC (w/Kyle Fletcher)	L	NJPW Rumble On 44th Street	13:42
Nov 3	Frankie Kazarian & Josh Alexander (w/Kyle Fletcher)	L	IMPACT Wrestling	15:56
Nov 5	Hiroshi Tanahashi, Toru Yano, David Finlay & Alex Zayne (w/Kyle Fletcher, Aaron Henare & Gideon Grey)	W	NJPW Battle Autumn '22	9:50
Nov 17	Ace Austin & Chris Bey, Alex Shelley & Chris Sabin, Raj Singh & Shera (w/Kyle Fletcher)	L	IMPACT Wrestling	13:03
Nov 20	Bushi, Hiromu Takahashi, Sanada, Shingo Takagi & Tetsuya Naito (w/Kyle Fletcher, Francesco Akira, TJP & Gideon Grey)	W	NJPW x Stardom Historic X-Over	9:55
Nov 26	Greg Sharpe & Jakob Austin Young (w/Kyle Fletcher)	W	NJPW Strong	5:51

MARK STERLING

May 29	Hook & Danhausen (w/Tony Nese)	L	AEW Double Or Nothing Buy-In	5:20
Jul 27	Handicap Match: Swerve Strickland (w/Tony Nese)	L	AEW Dynamite	6:44

MARQ QUEN

Jan 10	John Silver, Alex Reynolds & Ten (w/Isiah Kassidy & The Blade)	L	AEW Dark Elevation	4:01
Jan 17	Chase Emory & Patrick Scott (w/Isiah Kassidy)	W	AEW Dark Elevation	3:10
Jan 24	Action Andretti & Myles Hawkins (w/Isiah Kassidy)	W	AEW Dark Elevation	3:20
Jan 28	Jungle Boy & Luchasaurus (w/Isiah Kassidy)	L	AEW Rampage: Beach Break	10:45
Feb 10	Dante Martin, Lee Moriarty & Matt Sydal (w/Isiah Kassidy & The Blade)	L	AEW Dark	9:05
Feb 21	Baron Black, Carlie Bravo, Chandler Hopkins, Jameson Ryan & Shawn Dean (w/Andrade El Idolo, Isiah Kassidy, The Butcher & The Blade)	W	AEW Dark Elevation	4:20
Feb 23	Tag Team Battle Royal (w/Isiah Kassidy)	L	AEW Dynamite	4:34
Mar 8	Brock Anderson & Lee Johnson (w/Isiah Kassidy)	W	AEW Dark	5:05
Mar 11	Darby Allin	L	AEW Rampage	11:55
Mar 16	Matt Hardy & Jeff Hardy (w/Isiah Kassidy)	L	AEW Dynamite: St. Patrick's Day Slam	12:22
Mar 23	Tornado Match: Sting, Darby Allin, Matt Hardy & Jeff Hardy (w/Isiah Kassidy, The Butcher & The Blade)	L	AEW Dynamite	9:27
Apr 18	Jeff Hardy, Matt Hardy, Dante Martin & Darius Martin (w/Isiah Kassidy, Angelico & Jack Evans)	L	AEW Dark Elevation	9:45
Apr 26	Frankie Kazarian, Jeff Hardy, Matt Hardy, Dante Martin & Darius Martin (w/Max Caster, Angelico, Isiah Kassidy & The Blade)	L	AEW Dark	12:40
May 13	Pac, Penta El Zero M & Rey Fenix (w/The Butcher & The Blade)	L	AEW Rampage	10:22
May 25	Jon Moxley & Eddie Kingston (w/Isiah Kassidy)	L	AEW Dynamite	7:20
May 28	Johnny Elite	L	AEW Dark	6:00
Jun 13	Pharell Jackson & SK Bishop (w/Isiah Kassidy)	W	AEW Dark Elevation	3:00
Jul 12	Bear Boulder & Bear Bronson (w/Isiah Kassidy)	W	AEW Dark	10:45
Jul 15	Penta El Zero M & Rey Fenix (w/Isiah Kassidy)	L	AEW Rampage	11:16
Jul 25	Adrian Alanis, AR Fox & Liam Gray (w/Isiah Kassidy & Angelico)	W	AEW Dark Elevation	3:59
Aug 1	JCruz, Joey Ace, Victor Chase, Jaylen Brandyn & Traevon Jordan (w/Isiah Kassidy, Angelico, The Butcher & The Blade)	W	AEW Dark Elevation	2:12
Aug 9	Braden Lee, Isaiah Broner, James Alexander & Sam Moore (w/The Butcher, The Blade & Isiah Kassidy)	W	AEW Dark	2:22
Aug 15	Jah-C & JDX (w/Isiah Kassidy)	W	AEW Dark Elevation	1:49
Aug 19	Keith Lee & Swerve Strickland (w/Isiah Kassidy)	L	AEW Rampage	7:15
Sep 5	Brandon Gore & JDX (w/Isiah Kassidy)	W	AEW Dark Elevation	2:07
Sep 6	GPA & Robert Anthony (w/Isiah Kassidy)	W	AEW Dark	5:16
Sep 19	Aggro & DangerKid (w/Isiah Kassidy)	W	AEW Dark Elevation	4:46
Sep 23	Golden Ticket Battle Royale	L	AEW Rampage: Grand Slam	12:16
Sep 30	Anthony Bowens & Max Caster, The Butcher & The Blade (w/Isiah Kassidy)	L	AEW Rampage	10:00
Oct 7	Claudio Castagnoli, Jon Moxley & Wheeler Yuta (w/Rush & Isiah Kassidy)	L	AEW Rampage	10:16
Nov 14	Channing Thomas, Kyle Bradley & Smiley Fairchild (w/Matt Hardy & Isiah Kassidy)	W	AEW Dark Elevation	3:46
Nov 21	Encore, Ari Daivari & Sonny Kiss (w/Matt Hardy & Isiah Kassidy)	W	AEW Dark Elevation	3:15
Nov 28	Isaia Moore, Luther & Serpentico (w/Matt Hardy & Isiah Kassidy)	W	AEW Dark Elevation	4:50
Nov 29	Cezar Bononi, Peter Avalon & Ryan Nemeth (w/Matt Hardy & Isiah Kassidy)	W	AEW Dark	7:16
Dec 2	Jay Lethal & Jeff Jarrett (w/Isiah Kassidy)	L	AEW Rampage	7:04

MARSHALL VON ERICH

Apr 7	Kerry Morton & Ricky Morton (w/Ross Von Erich)	W	MLW Fusion	5:27
May 19	Bunkhouse Match: Hernandez & Rivera (w/Ross Von Erich)	W	MLW Fusion	9:42
Jun 9	King Muertes, Mads Krugger & Richard Holliday (w/Alexander Hammerstone & Ross Von Erich)	L	MLW Fusion	9:31
Jun 16	Calvin Tankman & EJ Nduka, Rivera & Slice Boogie (w/Ross Von Erich)	L	MLW Fusion	9:12
Jul 31	Jay Briscoe & Mark Briscoe (w/Ross Von Erich)	L	JCP Ric Flair's Last Match	7:43

MARSHE ROCKETT

Jan 5	Handicap Match: Cyon (w/Jordan Clearwater)	W	NWA Power	5:21
Jan 18	Luke Hawx & PJ Hawx (w/Jordan Clearwater)	L	NWA Power	6:32
Feb 8	Team War: Odinson, Parrow & Rodney Mack, Alex Taylor, Rush Freeman & Jeremiah Plunkett, Aron Stevens, JR Kratos & Judais (w/Jordan Clearwater & Tyrus)	L	NWA Power	11:40
Mar 8	Alex Taylor, Rush Freeman, Cyon & Mims (w/BLK Jeez, Jordan Clearwater & Tyrus)	W	NWA Power	6:59
Mar 19	Chris Adonis & Thom Latimer (w/Jordan Clearwater)	W	NWA Crockett Cup '22	4:18
Mar 19	Doug Williams & Harry Smith (w/Jordan Clearwater)	L	NWA Crockett Cup '22	12:50

May 17	Team War: Jax Dane, Odinson & Parrow, Alex Taylor, Jeremiah Plunkett & Rush Freeman (w/BLK Jeez & Jordan Clearwater)	L	NWA Power	6:54
Aug 28	Tag Team Battle Royal (w/Jordan Clearwater)	L	NWA 74th Anniversary Show	14:07
Sep 20	Eric Jackson, Joe Ocasio	W	NWA Power	2:49

MARTI BELLE

Feb 15	Tootie Lynn	L	NWA Power	4:36
Mar 20	Ella Envy & Kenzie Paige (w/Allysin Kay)	W	NWA Crockett Cup '22	7:09
Mar 22	Jennacide & Paola Blaze (w/Allysin Kay)	W	NWA Power	7:24
May 17	Kenzie Paige & Madi Wrenkowski (w/Allysin Kay)	W	NWA Power	5:16
Jun 11	Ella Envy & Kenzie Paige (w/Allysin Kay)	L	NWA Alwayz Ready '22	8:35
Aug 28	Kingshighway Steet Fight: Ella Envy & Kenzie Paige (w/Allysin Kay)	L	NWA 74th Anniversary Show	10:02
Oct 11	Natalia Markova & Taryn Terrell (w/Allysin Kay)	W	NWA Power	5:33
Nov 8	Kamille & KiLynn King (w/Allysin Kay)	L	NWA Power	7:31

MARYSE

Jan 29	Edge & Beth Phoenix (w/The Miz)	L	WWE Royal Rumble '22	12:30

MASCARA DORADA

Apr 1	David Finlay, Juice Robinson, Daniel Garcia & Kevin Knight (w/Karl Fredericks, Clark Connors & Yuya Uemura)	W	NJPW Lonestar Shootout	10:45
Apr 30	TJP	W	NJPW Strong	10:50
May 21	Aaron Henare, Great-O-Khan & TJP (w/Brody King & Taylor Rust)	L	NJPW Strong	14:04
Jun 11	Luke Gallows, Karl Anderson, Hikuleo, Jay White & Juice Robinson (w/Chuck Taylor, Rocky Romero, Tomohiro Ishii & Ren Narita)	L	NJPW Strong	12:44
Jul 23	Adrian Quest, Lucas Riley & Negro Casas (w/David Finlay & Rocky Romero)	W	NJPW Strong	11:03
Aug 27	TJP	L	NJPW Strong	11:55
Sep 1	Alex Zayne	W	IMPACT Wrestling	8:08
Sep 10	Misterioso	W	NJPW Strong	9:41
Sep 15	Mike Bailey	L	IMPACT Wrestling	8:03
Sep 19	Serpentico	W	AEW Dark Elevation	2:46
Oct 29	Alex Zayne & Mistico (w/Blake Christian)	L	NJPW Strong	10:09
Nov 19	Chris Bey & El Phantasmo (w/Blake Christian)	L	NJPW Strong	10:44
Dec 24	Cody Chhun & Guillermo Rosas (w/Lince Dorado)	W	NJPW Strong	10:35

MASHA SLAMOVICH

Jan 6	Sandra Moone	W	IMPACT Wrestling	:45
Jan 13	Vert Vixen	W	IMPACT Wrestling	1:05
Feb 3	Kaci Lennox	W	IMPACT Wrestling	:45
Feb 17	Kiah Dream	W	IMPACT Wrestling	:44
Mar 3	Raychell Rose	W	IMPACT Wrestling	1:00
Mar 17	Arie Alexander	W	IMPACT Wrestling	1:00
Mar 31	Abby Jane	W	IMPACT Wrestling	:48
May 5	Damarus	W	IMPACT Wrestling	:56
May 19	Shawna Reed	W	IMPACT Wrestling	1:00
May 26	Havok	W	IMPACT Wrestling	1:28
Jun 16	Alisha Edwards	W	IMPACT Wrestling	:58
Jul 14	Tenille Dashwood	W	IMPACT Wrestling	1:16
Jul 21	Madison Rayne	W	IMPACT Wrestling	1:12
Aug 4	Gisele Shaw	W	IMPACT Wrestling	2:42
Sep 1	Deonna Purrazzo	W	IMPACT Wrestling	12:50
Sep 29	Monster's Ball Match: Allie Katch	W	IMPACT Wrestling	15:12
Oct 7	Jordynne Grace	L	IMPACT Bound For Glory '22	16:00

MASTER WATO

Jan 8	Daisuke Harada, Hajime Ohara, Daiki Inaba, Yoshiaki Inamura & Kinya Okada (w/Tomohiro Ishii, Hirooki Goto, Yoshi-Hashi & Ryusuke Taguchi)	W	NJPW Wrestle Kingdom 16 Night #3	11:42
Mar 1	Hirooki Goto & Yoshi-Hashi (w/Ryusuke Taguchi)	L	NJPW 50th Anniversary Show	15:04
Apr 9	Taiji Ishimori & El Phantasmo (wRysuke Taguchi)	W	NJPW Hyper Battle '22	15:13
May 1	Yoshinobu Kanemaru & Douki (w/Ryusuke Taguchi)	W	NJPW Wrestling Dontaku '22	9:10
Jun 12	Aaron Henare, TJP & Francesco Akira (w/Ryusuke Taguchi & Hiroyoshi Tenzan)	L	NJPW Dominion '22	10:31
Sep 25	Francesco Akira & TJP (w/Ryusuke Taguchi)	L	NJPW Burning Spirit '22	12:43
Oct 10	Taiji Ishimori	W	NJPW Declaration Of Power	14:40
Nov 5	Taiji Ishimori & Hiromu Takahashi (w/El Desperado)	W	NJPW Battle Autumn '22	16:48

MATT CARDONA

Jan 8	Moose, W. Morrissey	L	IMPACT Hard To Kill '22	16:00
Jan 11	Chris Adonis & Thom Latimer, Tim Storm & Trevor Murdoch (w/Mike Knox)	W	NWA Power	5:25
Feb 1	Trevor Murdoch	L	NWA Power	5:02
Feb 3	Jordynne Grace	W	IMPACT Wrestling	8:49
Feb 15	Victor Benjamin	W	NWA Power	6:06
Feb 24	Dot Combat Match: Jordynne Grace	W	IMPACT Wrestling	12:14
Mar 8	Trevor Murdoch	W	NWA Power	11:04
Mar 20	Nick Aldis	W	NWA Crockett Cup '22	21:11
Apr 1	Mickie James & Nick Aldis (w/Chelsea Green)	L	IMPACT Multiverse Of Matches	7:04
Apr 5	Tim Storm	W	NWA Power	5:21
Apr 12	Da Pope	W	NWA Power	16:07
Apr 21	Little Guido	W	IMPACT Wrestling	4:59
Apr 23	Elimination Challenge Match (w/Brian Myers)	L	IMPACT Rebellion '22	33:02
May 10	Nick Aldis, Doug Williams & Harry Smith (w/Mike Knox & VSK)	L	NWA Power	8:15

Aug 27	Rolando Freeman	L	NWA 74th Anniversary Show	5:41
Aug 30	No DQ Match: Rolando Freeman	L	NWA Power	8:17
Oct 7	Call Your Shot Gauntlet	L	IMPACT Bound For Glory '22	29:18
Oct 13	Bhupinder Gujjar	W	IMPACT Wrestling	4:21
Oct 27	Alex Shelley	W	IMPACT Wrestling	8:42
Nov 12	Tyrus, Trevor Murdoch	L	NWA Hard Times 3	10:03
Nov 29	Brady Pierce & Rush Freeman (w/Mike Knox)	L	NWA Power	11:19
Nov 29	Rolando Freeman	W	NWA Power	7:40
Dec 15	Black Taurus & Crazzy Steve (w/Brian Myers)	W	IMPACT Wrestling	4:24

MATT CROSS

Mar 3	Myron Reed, Yoshihiro Tajiri, Bandido	L	MLW Fusion	8:48
Apr 7	Richard Holliday	L	MLW Fusion	6:44
Apr 14	TJP	W	MLW Fusion	11:07
Jun 9	Octagon Jr.	L	MLW Fusion	9:01
Jul 14	ACH	W	MLW Fusion	6:17
Nov 17	Killer Kross	L	MLW Fusion	4:38

MATT HARDY

Jan 11	Hangman Page, Alan Angels & Ten (w/Serpentico & Isiah Kassidy)	L	AEW Dark	14:27
Jan 12	Penta El Zero M	L	AEW Dynamite	8:51
Mar 6	Tornado Match: Darby Allin, Sammy Guevara & Sting (w/Andrade El Idolo & Isiah Kassidy)	L	AEW Revolution '22	13:20
Mar 16	Isiah Kassidy & Marq Quen (w/Jeff Hardy)	W	AEW Dynamite: St. Patrick's Day Slam	12:22
Mar 23	Tornado Match: Isiah Kassidy, Marq Quen, The Butcher & The Blade (w/Sting, Darby Allin & Jeff Hardy)	W	AEW Dynamite	9:27
Apr 6	Tables Match: The Butcher & The Blade (w/Jeff Hardy)	W	AEW Dynamite	11:54
Apr 18	Isiah Kassidy, Marq Quen, Angelico & Jack Evans (w/Jeff Hardy, Dante Martin & Darius Martin)	W	AEW Dark Elevation	9:45
Apr 26	Max Caster, Angelico, Isiah Kassidy, Marq Quen & The Blade (w/Frankie Kazarian, Jeff Hardy, Dante Martin & Darius Martin)	W	AEW Dark	12:40
May 5	Matt Jackson & Nick Jackson (w/Jeff Hardy)	W	AEW Double Or Nothing '22	19:15
Jun 1	Matt Jackson, Nick Jackson, Bobby Fish, Kyle O'Reilly & Hikuleo (w/Christian Cage, Darby Allin, Jungle Boy & Luchasaurus)	L	AEW Dynamite	12:00
Jun 18	Dragon Lee & Dralistico (w/Johnny Hardy)	L	AAA TripleMania XXX: Tijuana	13:35
Jul 1	Royal Rampage Match	L	AEW Rampage	22:41
Aug 3	Christian Cage	L	AEW Dynamite	11:06
Aug 29	RSP	W	AEW Dark Elevation	3:16
Sep 13	Angelico	W	AEW Dark	6:32
Sep 16	Darby Allin	L	AEW Rampage	9:59
Sep 23	Golden Ticket Battle Royale	L	AEW Rampage: Grand Slam	12:16
Oct 24	Lord Crewe	W	AEW Dark Elevation	1:44
Nov 14	Channing Thomas, Kyle Bradley & Smiley Fairchild (w/Isiah Kassidy & Marq Quen)	W	AEW Dark Elevation	3:46
Nov 21	Encore, Ari Daivari & Sonny Kiss (w/Isiah Kassidy & Marq Quen)	W	AEW Dark Elevation	3:15
Nov 28	Isaia Moore, Luther & Serpentico (w/Isiah Kassidy & Marq Quen)	W	AEW Dark Elevation	4:50
Nov 29	Cezar Bononi, Peter Avalon & Ryan Nemeth (w/Isiah Kassidy & Marq Quen)	W	AEW Dark	7:16
Dec 7	Dynamite Diamond Battle Royale	L	AEW Dynamite	13:10
Dec 19	Jeeves Kay, Slim J, Sonny Kiss, Cezar Bononi, Peter Avalon & Ryan Nemeth (w/Ethan Page, Isiah Kassidy, Konosuke Takeshita, Dante Martin & Darius Martin)	W	AEW Dark Elevation	7:45

MATT JACKSON

Feb 11	Trent Beretta & Rocky Romero (w/Nick Jackson)	W	AEW Rampage	13:23
Feb 23	Tag Team Battle Royal (w/Nick Jackson)	L	AEW Dynamite	18:25
Mar 2	Casino Battle Royale (w/Nick Jackson)	W	AEW Dynamite	27:01
Mar 6	Jungle Boy & Luchasaurus, Bobby Fish & Kyle O'Reilly (w/Nick Jackson)	L	AEW Revolution '22	18:55
Mar 15	Alan Angels, Colt Cabana & Evil Uno (w/Brandon Cutler & Nick Jackson)	W	AEW Dark	8:40
Apr 1	Dante Martin & Darius Martin (w/Nick Jackson)	W	AEW Rampage	10:48
Apr 6	Dax Harwood & Cash Wheeler (w/Nick Jackson)	L	AEW Dynamite	20:07
Apr 27	Dante Martin, Lee Johnson, Brock Anderson, Brian Pillman Jr. & Griff Garrison (w/Adam Cole, Nick Jackson, Bobby Fish & Kyle O'Reilly)	W	AEW Dynamite	6:28
Apr 30	El Hijo del Vikingo & Rey Fenix (w/Nick Jackson)	W	AAA TripleMania XXX: Monterrey	15:58
May 5	Matt Hardy & Jeff Hardy (w/Nick Jackson)	L	AEW Double Or Nothing '22	19:15
May 27	Jon Cruz & Taylor Rust (w/Nick Jackson)	W	AEW Rampage	2:34
Jun 1	Christian Cage, Matt Hardy, Darby Allin, Jungle Boy & Luchasaurus (w/Nick Jackson, Bobby Fish, Kyle O'Reilly & Hikuleo)	W	AEW Dynamite	12:00
Jun 3	Penta El Zero M & Rey Fenix (w/Nick Jackson)	W	AEW Rampage	14:53
Jun 15	Ladder Match: Jungle Boy & Luchasaurus (w/Nick Jackson)	W	AEW Dynamite: Road Rager	14:53
Jun 26	Darby Allin, Sting & Shingo Takagi (w/El Phantasmo & Nick Jackson)	L	AEW x NJPW Forbidden Door	13:01
Jul 1	Hirooki Goto & Yoshi-Hashi (w/Nick Jackson)	W	AEW Rampage	9:31
Jul 13	Keith Lee & Swerve Strickland, Ricky Starks & Powerhouse Hobbs (w/Nick Jackson)	L	AEW Dynamite: Fyter Fest	18:14
Aug 17	Andrade El Idolo, Rush & Dragon Lee (w/Kenny Omega & Nick Jackson)	W	AEW Dynamite	20:54
Aug 31	Will Ospreay, Kyle Fletcher & Mark Davis (w/Kenny Omega & Nick Jackson)	W	AEW Dynamite	18:54
Sep 4	Hangman Page, Alex Reynolds & John Silver (w/Kenny Omega & Nick Jackson)	W	AEW All Out '22	19:50
Nov 19	Pac, Penta El Zero M & Rey Fenix (w/Kenny Omega & Nick Jackson)	L	AEW Full Gear '22	18:40
Nov 23	Pac, Penta El Zero M & Rey Fenix (w/Kenny Omega & Nick Jackson)	L	AEW Dynamite: Thanksgiving Eve	14:49
Nov 30	Pac, Penta El Zero M & Rey Fenix (w/Kenny Omega & Nick Jackson)	W	AEW Dynamite	17:20

Dec 14	Pac, Penta El Zero M & Rey Fenix (w/Kenny Omega & Nick Jackson)	L	AEW Dynamite: Winter Is Coming	14:59
Dec 21	No DQ: Pac, Penta El Zero M & Rey Fenix (w/Kenny Omega & Nick Jackson)	W	AEW Dynamite: Holiday Bash	13:41
Dec 28	Falls Count Anywhere: Pac, Penta El Zero M & Rey Fenix (w/Nick Jackson & Kenny Omega)	W	AEW Dynamite	17:16

MATT MENARD

Jan 7	No DQ, No Holds Barred: Eddie Kingston, Santana & Ortiz (w/Daniel Garcia & Jeff Parker)	L	AEW Rampage	13:50
Jan 25	Kekoa, Pat Brink & Rayo (w/Jeff Parker & Daniel Garcia)	W	AEW Dark	1:01
Jan 26	Chris Jericho, Santana & Ortiz (w/Daniel Garcia & Jeff Parker)	W	AEW Dynamite: Beach Break	8:52
Feb 1	Kidd Bandit & Ish (w/Jeff Parker)	W	AEW Dark	2:42
Feb 14	John Silver, Alex Reynolds, Evil Uno, Alan Angels & Stu Grayson (w/Jeff Parker, Daniel Garcia, Anthony Bowens & Max Caster)	W	AEW Dark Elevation	5:56
Feb 15	Chris Metro & JC Metro (w/Jeff Parker)	W	AEW Dark	1:57
Feb 21	Ariel Levy, Chico Adams, Dean Alexander, Dominic Garrinin & Kevin Ku (w/Jeff Parker, Daniel Garcia, Austin Gunn & Colten Gunn)	W	AEW Dark Elevation	2:55
Feb 23	Tag Team Battle Royal (w/Jeff Parker)	L	AEW Dynamite	5:21
Mar 2	Casino Battle Royale (w/Jeff Parker)	L	AEW Dynamite	22:19
Mar 15	Luke Sampson, Mike Reed & Shayne Stetson (w/Jeff Parker & Daniel Garcia)	W	AEW Dark	2:19
May 24	Eli Isom & TUG Cooper (w/Angelo Parker)	W	AEW Dark	1:42
May 29	Anarchy In The Arena: Bryan Danielson, Jon Moxley, Eddie Kingston, Santana & Ortiz (w/Daniel Garcia, Jake Hager, Angelo Parker & Chris Jericho)	W	AEW Double Or Nothing '22	22:45
Jun 13	Danny Adams & Warhorse (w/Angelo Parker)	W	AEW Dark Elevation	2:45
Jun 14	Jack Banning, Ray Rosas & Sinn Bodhi (w/Daniel Garcia & Angelo Parker)	W	AEW Dark	2:38
Jun 29	Blood & Guts: Jon Moxley, Claudio Castagnoli, Wheeler Yuta, Eddie Kingston, Santana & Ortiz (w/Chris Jericho, Daniel Garcia, Jake Hager, Angelo Parker & Sammy Guevara)	L	AEW Dynamite: Blood & Guts	46:45
Jul 12	Jake St. Patrick & Sage Scott (w/Angelo Parker)	W	AEW Dark	:43
Sep 23	Action Bronson & Hook (w/Angelo Parker)	L	AEW Rampage: Grand Slam	5:10
Sep 28	Bryan Danielson	L	AEW Dynamite	8:36
Oct 28	Jon Moxley	L	AEW Rampage	8:05
Nov 21	Leon Ruffin, Tony Deppen & Tracy Williams (w/Angelo Parker & Daniel Garcia)	W	AEW Dark Elevation	2:46
Nov 29	Jack Tomlinson, LSG & Tracy Williams (w/Angelo Parker & Daniel Garcia)	W	AEW Dark	4:09
Dec 12	Warren Johnson & Zack Mason (w/Angelo Parker)	W	AEW Dark Elevation	:20
Dec 27	Brock Anderson	W	AEW Dark	4:44

MATT RIDDLE (AS RIDDLE UNTIL SEPTEMBER 12)

Jan 1	Angelo Dawkins & Montez Ford (w/Randy Orton)	W	WWE Day 1	11:15
Jan 3	Chad Gable & Otis (w/Randy Orton)	L	WWE Monday Night RAW	2:40
Jan 4	Walter, Marcel Barthel & Fabian Aichner (w/Nash Carter & Wes Lee)	W	NXT 2.0: New Year's Evil '22	13:52
Jan 10	Chad Gable & Otis (w/Randy Orton)	L	WWE Monday Night RAW	8:57
Jan 29	Royal Rumble Match	L	WWE Royal Rumble '22	19:46
Jan 31	Otis	W	WWE Monday Night RAW	7:25
Feb 7	Seth Rollins	W	WWE Monday Night RAW	7:39
Feb 7	Seth Rollins & Kevin Owens (w/Randy Orton)	L	WWE Monday Night RAW	8:05
Feb 19	Elimination Chamber: AJ Styles, Austin Theory, Brock Lesnar, Seth Rollins	L	WWE Elimination Chamber '22	10:05
Feb 21	Seth Rollins & Kevin Owens (w/Randy Orton)	L	WWE Monday Night RAW	12:40
Feb 28	Angelo Dawkins & Montez Ford (w/Riddle)	L	WWE Monday Night RAW	8:35
Mar 7	No DQ: Chad Gable & Otis, Seth Rollins & Kevin Owens (w/Randy Orton)	W	WWE Monday Night RAW	27:05
Mar 14	Montez Ford	D	WWE Monday Night RAW	9:40
Mar 21	Chad Gable & Otis (w/Randy Orton)	W	WWE Monday Night RAW	7:45
Mar 28	Jimmy Uso & Jey Uso (w/Randy Orton)	W	WWE Monday Night RAW	16:20
Apr 3	Angelo Dawkins & Montez Ford, Chad Gable & Otis (w/Randy Orton)	W	WWE WrestleMania XXXVIII	11:30
Apr 4	Austin Theory, Jimmy Uso & Jey Uso (w/Randy Orton & Finn Balor)	L	WWE Monday Night RAW	8:25
Apr 11	Chad Gable & Otis (w/Randy Orton)	W	WWE Monday Night RAW	8:30
Apr 15	Jimmy Uso	W	WWE SmackDown	8:32
Apr 18	Angelo Dawkins & Montez Ford (w/Randy Orton)	L	WWE Monday Night RAW	7:50
Apr 22	Jey Uso	W	WWE SmackDown	12:10
Apr 25	Seth Rollins, Kevin Owens, Jimmy Uso & Jey Uso (w/Randy Orton, Cody Rhodes & Ezekiel)	W	WWE Monday Night RAW	14:58
May 8	Roman Reigns, Jey Uso & Jimmy Uso (w/Randy Orton & Drew McIntyre)	L	WWE WrestleMania Backlash '22	22:20
May 9	Angelo Dawkins & Montez Ford (w/Randy Orton)	W	WWE Monday Night RAW	9:58
May 13	Sami Zayn	W	WWE SmackDown	10:50
May 16	Jimmy Uso	W	WWE Monday Night RAW	10:50
May 20	Jimmy Uso & Jey Uso (w/Randy Orton)	L	WWE SmackDown	13:13
May 23	Sami Zayn, Jimmy Uso & Jey Uso (w/Angelo Dawkins & Montez Ford)	W	WWE Monday Night RAW	12:35
May 30	Jimmy Uso & Jey Uso (w/Shinsuke Nakamura)	W	WWE Monday Night RAW	12:30
Jun 6	The Miz	W	WWE Monday Night RAW	2:13
Jun 10	Sami Zayn	W	WWE SmackDown	13:05
Jun 13	Ciampa	W	WWE Monday Night RAW	4:30
Jun 17	Roman Reigns	L	WWE SmackDown	16:56
Jun 20	Omos	L	WWE Monday Night RAW	3:55
Jun 27	Battle Royal	W	WWE Monday Night RAW	19:25
Jul 1	Battle Royal	L	WWE SmackDown	14:36
Jul 2	Money In The Bank Ladder Match: Drew McIntyre, Madcap Moss, Theory, Omos, Sami Zayn, Seth Rollins, Sheamus	L	WWE Money In The Bank '22	25:25
Jul 11	Seth Rollins & Theory (w/Bobby Lashley)	W	WWE Monday Night RAW	13:50

Jul 25	Roman Reigns, Jimmy Uso & Jey Uso (w/Angelo Dawkins & Montez Ford)	L	WWE Monday Night RAW	19:25
Sep 3	Seth Rollins	L	WWE Clash At The Castle	17:22
Sep 12	Finn Balor	L	WWE Monday Night RAW	13:35
Sep 19	Finn Balor & Damian Priest (w/Rey Mysterio)	L	WWE Monday Night RAW	17:40
Sep 26	Damien Priest	W	WWE Monday Night RAW	19:21
Oct 8	Fight Pit Match: Seth Rollins	W	WWE Extreme Rules '22	16:35
Oct 10	Sami Zayn	W	WWE Monday Night RAW	16:15
Oct 17	Seth Rollins	L	WWE Monday Night RAW	14:50
Oct 31	Trick Or Street Fight: Otis	W	WWE Monday Night RAW	7:39
Nov 7	Jimmy Uso, Jey Uso & Solo Sikoa (w/Xavier Woods & Kofi Kingston)	L	WWE Monday Night RAW	20:55
Nov 14	Chad Gable	L	WWE Monday Night RAW	10:10
Nov 21	Chad Gable & Otis (w/Elias)	W	WWE Monday Night RAW	16:05
Dec 5	Jey Uso & Jimmy Uso (w/Kevin Owens)	L	WWE Monday Night RAW	14:10

MATT SYDAL

Jan 8	Ricky Starks	L	AEW Battle Of The Belts I	9:00
Jan 17	JR Miller & Marcus Kross (w/Lee Moriarty)	W	AEW Dark Elevation	3:20
Jan 24	Powerhouse Hobbs & Ricky Starks (w/Lee Moriarty)	L	AEW Dark Elevation	5:21
Jan 31	Aaron Solo, Nick Comoroto & QT Marshall (w/Dante Martin & Lee Moriarty)	W	AEW Dark Elevation	7:46
Feb 1	Bear Boulder & Bear Bronson (w/Dante Martin)	W	AEW Dark	9:43
Feb 7	Anthony Bowens, Max Caster, Austin Gunn & Colten Gunn (w/Lee Moriarty, Brock Anderson & Lee Johnson)	L	AEW Dark Elevation	7:11
Feb 10	Isiah Kassidy, Marq Quen & The Blade (w/Dante Martin & Lee Moriarty)	W	AEW Dark	9:05
Feb 14	Powerhouse Hobbs	L	AEW Dark Elevation	5:19
Feb 21	Luther, Serpentico, Cezar Bononi, JD Drake & Peter Avalon (w/Brock Anderson, Frankie Kazarian, Jay Lethal & Lee Johnson)	W	AEW Dark Elevation	6:06
Feb 22	Serpentico	W	AEW Dark	6:27
May 20	Bryan Danielson & Jon Moxley (w/Dante Martin)	L	AEW Rampage	12:00
May 27	Bryan Danielson	L	AEW Rampage	11:09
Jun 14	Taylor Rust	W	AEW Dark	3:19
Jun 20	QT Marshall	W	AEW Dark Elevation	7:28
Jun 28	Jake Something	W	AEW Dark	5:53
Jul 29	Lee Moriarty	L	AEW Rampage	6:57
Aug 23	Aaron Solo & Nick Comoroto (w/Dante Martin)	W	AEW Dark	8:11
Sep 12	Serpentico & Zack Clayton (w/Dante Martin)	W	AEW Dark Elevation	:57
Sep 13	Cezar Bononi & Ryan Nemth (w/Dante Martin)	W	AEW Dark	6:19
Sep 20	JD Drake	W	AEW Dark	9:30
Oct 4	Anthony Henry & JD Drake (w/Dante Martin)	W	AEW Dark	9:34
Oct 11	Aaron Solo & Cole Karter (w/Dante Martin)	W	AEW Dark	9:31

MATT TAVEN

Jan 5	Wrecking Ball Legursky	W	NWA Power	6:29
Feb 8	Team War: Chris Adonis, Thom Latimer & El Rudo, Bestia 666, Mecha Wolf & Homicide, Jay Bradley, Wrecking Ball Legursky & Colby Corino (w/Mike Bennett & Victor Benjamin)	L	NWA Power	11:09
Feb 10	Rhino & Rich Swann (w/Mike Bennett)	W	IMPACT Wrestling	8:42
Feb 24	Chris Sabin, Rich Swann & Willie Mack (w/Mike Bennett & Kenny King)	W	IMPACT Wrestling	8:58
Mar 1	Jay Bradley & Wrecking Ball Legursky (w/Mike Bennett)	L	NWA Power	10:47
Mar 17	Josh Alexander	L	IMPACT Wrestling	12:13
Mar 22	Jay Briscoe & Mark Briscoe (w/Mike Bennett)	L	NWA Power	6:56
Apr 21	Chris Bey, Luke Gallows, Karl Anderson & Jay White (w/Kenny King, Mike Bennett & Vincent)	L	IMPACT Wrestling	9:22
Apr 23	Elimination Challenge Match (w/Mike Bennett)	L	IMPACT Rebellion '22	33:02
Apr 28	Alex Shelley, Chris Sabin & Mike Bailey (w/Eddie Edwards & Mike Bennett)	W	IMPACT Wrestling	7:35
May 10	Judais	W	NWA Power	4:53
May 19	Luke Gallows & Karl Anderson (w/Mike Bennett)	L	IMPACT Wrestling	10:00
Jun 2	Heath & Rhino (w/Mike Bennett)	W	IMPACT Wrestling	6:15
Jun 9	Frankie Kazarian, Alex Shelley & Chris Sabin (w/Eddie Edwards & Mike Bennett)	W	IMPACT Wrestling	16:47
Jun 19	Alex Shelley, Chris Sabin, Davey Richards, Frankie Kazarian & Magnus (w/Eddie Edwards, Mike Bennett, PCO & Vincent)	L	IMPACT Slammiversary XX	18:45
Jun 23	James Storm, Jay Briscoe & Mark Briscoe (w/Eddie Edwards & Mike Bennett)	W	IMPACT Wrestling	12:12
Jul 14	Ace Austin, Chris Bey, Karl Anderson & Luke Gallows (w/Eddie Edwards, Kenny King & Mike Bennett)	W	IMPACT Wrestling	12:34
Jul 19	Bestia 666 & Mecha Wolf (w/Mike Bennett)	D	NWA Power	5:38
Jul 21	Ace Austin & Chris Bey (w/Mike Bennett)	L	IMPACT Wrestling	10:32
Aug 28	Tag Team Battle Royal (w/Mike Bennett)	L	NWA 74th Anniversary Show	14:07
Aug 30	Mecha Wolf	W	NWA Power	9:56
Sep 1	Luke Gallows & Karl Anderson (w/Mike Bennett)	W	IMPACT Wrestling	8:14
Sep 15	Josh Alexander & Rich Swann (w/Mike Bennett)	W	IMPACT Wrestling	6:54
Oct 4	Bestia 666, Mecha Wolf & Damian 666 (w/Mike Bennett & Rhett Titus)	W	NWA Power	8:16
Oct 6	Alex Shelley	L	IMPACT Wrestling	9:50
Oct 7	Alex Shelley & Chris Sabin (w/Mike Bennett)	W	IMPACT Bound For Glory '22	16:35
Oct 18	Trevor Murdoch	L	NWA Power	5:39
Oct 20	Heath & Rhino (w/Mike Bennett)	L	IMPACT Wrestling	10:02
Oct 28	Warlow	L	AEW Rampage	8:59
Dec 10	Ativalu & Sal Muscat (w/Mike Bennett)	W	AEW Dark Elevation	1:49

MATTHEW REHWOLDT

Jan 13	Black Taurus	L	IMPACT Before The Impact	7:17
Feb 26	El Phantasmo	L	NJPW Strong	9:45
May 12	Gauntlet For The Gold	L	IMPACT Wrestling	39:00
Jun 2	Rich Swann	L	IMPACT Wrestling	5:13

MAX CASTER

Jan 4	Blanco Loco & Axton Ray (w/Anthony Bowens)	W	AEW Dark	3:02
Jan 10	Joey Ace & Kevin Matthews (w/Anthony Bowens)	W	AEW Dark Elevation	3:29
Jan 12	Bear Bronson & Bear Boulder (w/Anthony Bowens)	W	AEW Dynamite	6:18
Jan 19	Sting & Darby Allin (w/Anthony Bowens)	L	AEW Dynamite	9:22
Jan 25	Alan Angels, Alex Reynolds, Evil Uno & Ten (w/Anthony Bowens, Austin Gunn & Colten Gunn)	W	AEW Dark	6:15
Feb 7	Lee Moriarty, Matt Sydal, Brock Anderson & Lee Johnson (w/Anthony Bowens, Austin Gunn & Colten Gunn)	W	AEW Dark Elevation	7:11
Feb 14	John Silver, Alex Reynolds, Evil Uno, Alan Angels & Stu Grayson (w/Anthony Bowens, Jeff Parker, Matt Lee & Daniel Garcia)	W	AEW Dark Elevation	5:56
Feb 15	Cameron Stewart	W	AEW Dark	3:30
Feb 16	Wardlow	L	AEW Dynamite	5:18
Mar 1	B. Jack & Donovan Izzolena (w/Anthony Bowens)	W	AEW Dark	2:46
Mar 2	Casino Battle Royale (wAnthony Bowens)	L	AEW Dynamite	9:13
Mar 9	Jungle Boy & Luchasaurus (w/Anthony Bowens)	L	AEW Dynamite	9:26
Mar 18	Keith Lee	L	AEW Rampage	9:46
Mar 22	Adrian Alanis & Liam Gray (w/Anthony Bowens)	W	AEW Dark	2:13
Mar 28	Sonny Kiss	W	AEW Dark Elevation	4:17
Mar 30	CM Punk	L	AEW Dynamite	7:09
Apr 6	Samoa Joe	L	AEW Dynamite	2:52
Apr 12	Mike Reed	W	AEW Dark	4:10
Apr 25	Penta Oscuro	L	AEW Dark Elevation	4:45
Apr 26	Frankie Kazarian, Jeff Hardy, Matt Hardy, Dante Martin & Darius Martin (w/Angelico, Isiah Kassidy, Marq Quen & The Blade)	L	AEW Dark	12:40
May 2	Zack Clayton	W	AEW Dark Elevation	1:24
May 16	Bryce Donovan, GKM, Lucas Chase & Zack Clayton (w/Anthony Bowens, Austin Gunn & Colten Gunn)	W	AEW Dark Elevation	1:22
May 17	Tyler Uriah	W	AEW Dark	3:00
May 27	Dante Martin	L	AEW Rampage	6:12
Jun 1	CM Punk, Dax Harwood & Cash Wheeler (w/Austin Gunn & Colten Gunn)	L	AEW Dynamite	11:50
Jun 7	John Silver, Alex Reynolds & Ten (w/Austin Gunn & Colten Gunn)	W	AEW Dark	5:26
Jun 8	Casino Battle Royale	L	AEW Dynamite	24:59
Jun 17	Leon Ruffin, Bear Bronson & Bear Boulder (w/Austin Gunn & Colten Gunn)	W	AEW Rampage: Road Rager	1:15
Jun 21	Trever Aeon	W	AEW Dark	3:19
Jun 26	Yuya Uemura, Alex Coughlin, The DKC & Kevin Knight (w/Billy Gunn, Austin Gunn & Colten Gunn)	W	AEW x NJPW Forbidden Door Buy-In	5:35
Jun 27	Alex Reynolds, Evil Uno & Ten (w/Austin Gunn & Colten Gunn)	W	AEW Dark Elevation	4:08
Jun 29	Danhausen, Dax Harwood & Cash Wheeler (w/Austin Gunn & Colten Gunn)	L	AEW Dynamite: Blood & Guts	9:31
Jul 1	Royal Rampage Match	L	AEW Rampage	22:41
Jul 6	Fuego Del Sol, Leon Ruffin, Bear Bronson & Bear Boulder (w/Anthony Bowens, Austin Gunn & Colten Gunn)	W	AEW Dynamite	2:14
Aug 2	Peter Avalon & Ryan Nemeth (w/Anthony Bowens)	W	AEW Dark	5:00
Aug 3	Austin Gunn & Colten Gunn (w/Anthony Bowens)	W	AEW Dynamite	8:20
Aug 15	JT Energy & Justin Fowler (w/Anthony Bowens)	W	AEW Dark Elevation	1:47
Aug 23	Justin Cotto	W	AEW Dark	2:37
Sep 3	Invictus Khash & JPH (w/Anthony Bowens)	W	AEW Dark Elevation	1:55
Sep 4	Keith Lee & Swerve Strickland (w/Anthony Bowens)	L	AEW All Out '22	22:30
Sep 21	Keith Lee & Swerve Strickland (w/Anthony Bowens)	W	AEW Dynamite: Grand Slam	13:44
Sep 30	Marq Quen & Isiah Kassidy, The Butcher & The Blade (w/Anthony Bowens)	W	AEW Rampage	10:00
Oct 21	Tony Nese & Josh Woods (w/Anthony Bowens)	W	AEW Rampage	8:06
Nov 9	Keith Lee, Swerve Strickland, Austin Gunn & Colten Gunn (w/Anthony Bowens, Dax Harwood & Cash Wheeler)	W	AEW Dynamite	12:22
Nov 19	Keith Lee & Swerve Strickland (w/Anthony Bowens)	W	AEW Full Gear '22	19:40
Dec 7	Dax Harwood & Cash Wheeler (w/Anthony Bowens)	W	AEW Dynamite	16:46

MAX THE IMPALER

May 24	Ella Envy	W	NWA Power	3:20
Jun 13	Nyla Rose	L	AEW Dark Elevation	1:55
Jun 20	Marina Shafir & Nyla Rose (w/Heidi Howitzer)	L	AEW Dark Elevation	3:25
Jun 28	Jennacide & Missa Kate (w/Chelsea Green)	W	NWA Power	5:38
Jul 19	Ella Envy, Taya Valkyrie	W	NWA Power	6:37
Aug 27	Burke Invitational Gauntlet	W	NWA 74th Anniversary Show	17:24
Aug 28	Kamille	L	NWA 74th Anniversary Show	11:07
Sep 13	Ella Envy, Kenzie Paige & Roxy (w/Natalia Markova & Angelina Love)	W	NWA Power	3:11
Sep 13	Angelina Love, Natalia Markova	D	NWA Power	3:48
Nov 12	Voodoo Queen Casket Match: Natalia Markova	W	NWA Hard Times 3	8:14

MECHA WOLF

Jan 5	Jax Dane, Odinson & Parrow (w/Bestia 666 & Homicide)	W	NWA Power	6:54
Feb 8	Team War: Chris Adonis, Thom Latimer & El Rudo, Matt Taven, Mike Bennett & Victor Benjamin, Jay Bradley, Wrecking Ball Legursky & Colby Corino (w/Bestia 666 & Homicide)	L	NWA Power	11:09
Mar 19	Brandon Tate & Brent Tate (w/Bestia 666)	W	NWA Crockett Cup '22	8:59

Mar 19	Handicap Match: PJ Hawx (w/Bestia 666)	W	NWA Crockett Cup '22	7:25
Mar 20	Doug Williams & Harry Smith (w/Bestia 666)	L	NWA Crockett Cup '22	8:58
Mar 29	Odinson & Parrow (w/Bestia 666)	W	NWA Power	7:17
Apr 26	Jay Briscoe & Mark Briscoe (w/Bestia 666)	W	NWA Power	9:56
Jun 11	Doug Williams & Harry Smith (w/Bestia 666)	L	NWA Alwayz Ready '22	13:54
Jun 18	Copa TripleMania XXX Match	L	AAA TripleMania XXX: Tijuana	21:57
Jun 28	Lucha Rules Match: Doug Williams & Harry Smith (w/Bestia 666)	L	NWA Power	5:08
Jul 19	Matt Taven & Mike Bennett (w/Bestia 666)	D	NWA Power	5:38
Aug 27	Luke Hawx & PJ Hawx (w/Bestia 666)	W	NWA 74th Anniversary Show	13:10
Aug 28	Tag Team Battle Royal (w/Bestia 666)	L	NWA 74th Anniversary Show	14:07
Aug 30	Matt Taven	L	NWA Power	9:56
Oct 4	Matt Taven, Mike Bennett & Rhett Titus (w/Bestia 666 & Damian 666)	L	NWA Power	8:16
Nov 12	Luke Hawx & PJ Hawx (w/Bestia 666)	W	NWA Hard Times 3	10:48
Dec 27	Cyon, Jordan Clearwater & Tyrus (w/Joe Alonzo & Bestia 666)	L	NWA Power	7:56

MEI SURUGA

Jul 9	Arisu Endo & Riho (w/Suzume)	W	TJPW Summer Sun Princess '22	14:21
Oct 24	Jaylee & Nikki Victory (w/Emi Sakura)	W	AEW Dark Elevation	3:30
Nov 8	Hikaru Shida & Toni Storm (w/Emi Sakura)	L	AEW Dark	7:51
Nov 14	Riho & Willow Nightingale (w/Emi Sakura)	L	AEW Dark Elevation	6:14

MEIKO SATOMURA

Jan 6	Blair Davenport	W	NXT UK	12:58
Feb 3	Japanese Street Fight: Blair Davenport	W	NXT UK	9:16
Mar 24	Isla Dawn	W	NXT UK	8:04
May 5	World Of Darkness Match: Isla Dawn	W	NXT UK	12:48
Jun 9	Ivy Nile	W	NXT UK	10:26
Jul 7	Eliza Alexander & Xia Brookside (w/Sarray)	W	NXT UK	9:27
Sep 4	Mandy Rose, Blair Davenport	L	NXT Worlds Collide '22	13:17
Sep 6	Roxanne Perez	W	NXT 2.0	11:19

MELINA

Jan 18	Madi Wrenkowski	W	NWA Power	4:42
Jan 29	Royal Rumble Match	L	WWE Royal Rumble '22	:53
Feb 15	Christi Jaynes	W	NWA Power	6:14

MERCEDES MARTINEZ

Jan 6	Deonna Purrazzo	L	IMPACT Wrestling	13:00
Feb 4	Thunder Rosa	L	AEW Rampage	7:41
Feb 8	Queen Aminata	W	AEW Dark	3:04
Feb 16	No DQ Match: Thunder Rosa	L	AEW Dynamite	9:31
Mar 2	Dr. Britt Baker D.M.D. & Jamie Hayter (w/Thunder Rosa)	W	AEW Dynamite	8:32
Mar 11	Jamie Hayter	L	AEW Rampage	8:42
Mar 22	Gemma Jewels	W	AEW Dark	1:33
Apr 1	Willow Nightingale	W	ROH Supercard Of Honor XV	12:45
May 4	Deonna Purrazzo	W	AEW Dynamite	10:35
May 16	Trish Adora	W	AEW Dark Elevation	5:32
May 23	Hyan	W	AEW Dark Elevation	5:01
May 30	Mazzerati	W	AEW Dark Elevation	7:17
May 31	Viva Van	W	AEW Dark	2:40
Jun 13	Miranda Gordy & Tootie Lynn (w/Serena Deeb)	W	AEW Dark Elevation	4:15
Jun 20	Heather Reckless & Tootie Lynn (w/Serena Deeb)	W	AEW Dark Elevation	4:29
Jun 21	Anna Diaz & Yaide (w/Serena Deeb)	W	AEW Dark	2:21
Jun 24	Laynie Luck & Sierra (w/Serena Deeb)	W	AEW Rampage	3:25
Jul 8	Christina Marie & Kayla Sparks (w/Serena Deeb)	W	AEW Rampage	2:23
Jul 19	J-Rod	W	AEW Dark	4:45
Jul 23	Serena Deeb	W	ROH Death Before Dishonor XIX	17:20
Nov 21	JC	W	AEW Dark Elevation	2:28
Dec 10	Athena	L	ROH Final Battle '22	13:10

MIA YIM

May 19	Deonnna Purrazzo, Savannah Evans & Tasha Steelz (w/Jordynne Grace & Taya Valkyrie)	W	IMPACT Wrestling	12:00
Jun 2	Savannah Evans	W	IMPACT Wrestling	7:51
Jun 16	Savannah Evans & Tasha Steelz (w/Jordynne Grace)	L	IMPACT Wrestling	6:49
Jun 19	Queen Of The Mountain: Jordynne Grace, Tasha Steelz, Chelsea Green, Deonna Purrazzo	L	IMPACT Slammiversary XX	18:15
Jun 23	Chelsea Green	W	IMPACT Wrestling	9:08
Jul 7	Deonna Purrazzo	W	IMPACT Wrestling	14:09
Jul 21	Chelsea Green & Deonna Purrazzo (w/Jordynne Grace)	L	IMPACT Wrestling	9:11
Aug 11	Madison Rayne	W	IMPACT Wrestling	9:18
Aug 25	Chelsea Green & Deonna Purrazzo (w/Jordynne Grace)	L	IMPACT Wrestling	7:24
Sep 22	Black Taurus, Alex Zayne, Laredo Kid, Trey Miguel	L	IMPACT Wrestling	11:58
Oct 6	Gisele Shaw	W	IMPACT Wrestling	7:15
Oct 7	Last Rodeo Match: Mickie James	L	IMPACT Bound For Glory '22	10:56
Oct 20	Taylor Wilde	L	IMPACT Wrestling	9:22
Nov 14	Tamina	W	WWE Monday Night RAW	2:00
Nov 26	WarGames: Bayley, Dakota Kai, Iyo Sky, Nikki Cross & Rhea Ripley (w/Bianca Belair, Alexa Bliss, Asuka & Becky Lynch)	W	WWE Survivor Series WarGames	39:40
Nov 28	Rhea Ripley	D	WWE Monday Night RAW	7:05
Nov 28	Finn Balor, Damian Priest, Dominik Mysterio & Rhea Ripley (w/AJ Styles, Luke Gallows & Karl Anderson)	L	WWE Monday Night RAW	14:20

MICHELLE MCCOOL

Jan 29	Royal Rumble Match	L	WWE Royal Rumble '22	20:50

MICKIE JAMES

Jan 8	Texas Deathmatch: Deonna Purrazzo	W	IMPACT Hard To Kill '22	19:40
Jan 29	Royal Rumble Match	L	WWE Royal Rumble '22	11:40
Feb 10	Chelsea Green	D	IMPACT Wrestling	3:58
Feb 17	Tasha Steelz & Savannah Evans (w/Chelsea Green)	L	IMPACT Wrestling	12:26
Mar 10	Cassie Lee & Jessie McKay, Madison Rayne & Tenille Dashwood, Savannah Evans & Tasha Steelz (w/Chelsea Green)	L	IMPACT Wrestling	6:00
Mar 24	Street Fight: Tasha Steelz	L	IMPACT Wrestling	16:00
Apr 1	Chelsea Green & Matt Cardona (w/Nick Aldis)	W	IMPACT Multiverse Of Matches	7:04
May 3	Kenzie Paige	W	NWA Power	7:55
May 17	Natalia Markova	W	NWA Power	6:44
Jul 14	Chelsea Green	L	IMPACT Wrestling	12:41
Sep 8	Raychell Rose	W	IMPACT Wrestling	3:17
Sep 15	Hyan	W	IMPACT Wrestling	2:39
Oct 7	Last Rodeo Match: Mia Yim	W	IMPACT Bound For Glory '22	10:56
Oct 27	Chelsea Green, Deonna Purrazzo & Gisele Shaw (w/Jordynne Grace & Taylor Wilde)	W	IMPACT Wrestling	13:46
Nov 10	Chelsea Green	W	IMPACT Wrestling	10:37
Dec 1	Deonna Purrazzo	W	IMPACT Wrestling	16:01
Dec 22	Savannah Evans, Tasha Steelz	W	IMPACT Wrestling	11:08

MICRO MAN

Feb 24	Arez, Gino Medina & Mini Abismo Negro (w/Aramis & El Dragon)	W	MLW Fusion	15:46
Mar 31	Arez, Gino Medina & Mini Abismo Negro (w/Octagon Jr. & Puma King)	W	MLW Fusion	15:42
Apr 29	Arez, Gino Medina & Mini Abusmo Negro (w/Aramis & KC Navarro)	L	MLW Fusion	11:55
May 26	Arez, Mini Abismo Negro & TJP (w/Aero Star & El Dragon)	W	MLW Fusion	10:36
Jun 30	Arez, Holidead & Mini Abismo Negro (w/Lince Dorado & Taya Valkyrie)	W	MLW Fusion	6:32

MIGHTY MOLLY

Jan 29	Royal Rumble Match	L	WWE Royal Rumble '22	:20

MIKE BAILEY

Jan 13	Jake Something	W	IMPACT Wrestling	4:17
Feb 3	Chris Bey, Jay White, Tama Tonga & Tanga Loa (w/Jake Something, Madman Fulton & Ace Austin)	L	IMPACT Wrestling	16:49
Feb 24	Trey Miguel & Jake Something (w/Ace Austin)	W	IMPACT Before The Impact	8:01
Mar 24	Laredo Kid, Willie Mack	W	IMPACT Wrestling	10:09
Apr 1	Alex Shelley	W	IMPACT Multiverse Of Matches	15:03
Apr 1	Jay White	L	NJPW Lonestar Shootout	14:10
Apr 21	Laredo Kid & Trey Miguel (w/Ace Austin)	L	IMPACT Wrestling	6:00
Apr 23	Ace Austin, Trey Miguel	L	IMPACT Rebellion '22	10:25
Apr 28	Eddie Edwards, Matt Taven & Mike Bennett (w/Alex Shelly & Chris Sabin)	L	IMPACT Wrestling	7:35
May 19	Laredo Kid	W	IMPACT Wrestling	9:00
Jun 16	Trey Miguel	L	IMPACT Wrestling	10:42
Jun 19	Ultimate X Match: Ace Austin, Alex Zayne, Andrew Everett, Kenny King & Trey Miguel	W	IMPACT Slammiversary XX	9:50
Jul 7	Alan Angels	W	IMPACT Wrestling	8:35
Jul 21	Deaner	W	IMPACT Wrestling	8:54
Aug 11	Rocky Romero	W	IMPACT Wrestling	12:04
Aug 18	Chris Bey	W	IMPACT Wrestling	8:25
Sep 1	Kenny King	W	IMPACT Wrestling	7:38
Sep 15	Mascara Dorada	W	IMPACT Wrestling	8:03
Oct 7	Frankie Kazarian	L	IMPACT Bound For Glory '22	12:30
Nov 3	Kenny King	W	IMPACT Wrestling	8:44
Nov 10	Trey Miguel	L	IMPACT Wrestling	7:02
Dec 8	Josh Alexander	L	IMPACT Wrestling	59:48
Dec 22	Yuya Uemura	W	IMPACT Wrestling	11:16

MIKE BENNETT

Feb 8	Team War: Chris Adonis, Thom Latimer & El Rudo, Bestia 666, Mecha Wolf & Homicide, Jay Bradley, Wrecking Ball Legursky & Colby Corino (w/Matt Taven & Victor Benjamin)	L	NWA Power	11:09
Feb 10	Rhino & Rich Swann (w/Matt Taven)	W	IMPACT Wrestling	8:42
Feb 24	Chris Sabin, Rich Swann & Willie Mack (w/Kenny King & Matt Taven)	W	IMPACT Wrestling	8:58
Mar 1	Jay Bradley & Wrecking Ball Legursky (w/Matt Taven)	L	NWA Power	10:47
Mar 22	Jay Briscoe & Mark Briscoe (w/Matt Taven)	L	NWA Power	6:56
Apr 21	Chris Bey, Jay White, Luke Gallows & Karl Anderson (w/Kenny King, Matt Taven & Vincent)	L	IMPACT Wrestling	9:22
Apr 23	Elimination Challenge Match (w/Matt Taven)	L	IMPACT Rebellion '22	33:02
Apr 28	Alex Shelley, Chris Sabin & Mike Bailey (w/Eddie Edwards & Matt Taven)	W	IMPACT Wrestling	7:35
May 3	Nick Aldis	L	NWA Power	7:01
May 19	Luke Gallows & Karl Anderson (w/Matt Taven)	L	IMPACT Wrestling	10:00
Jun 2	Heath & Rhino (w/Matt Taven)	W	IMPACT Wrestling	6:15
Jun 9	Frankie Kazarian, Alex Shelley & Chris Sabin (w/Eddie Edwards & Matt Taven)	W	IMPACT Wrestling	16:47
Jun 19	Alex Shelley, Chris Sabin, Davey Richards, Frankie Kazarian & Magnus (w/Eddie Edwards, Matt Taven, PCO & Vincent)	L	IMPACT Slammiversary XX	18:45
Jun 23	James Storm, Jay Briscoe & Mark Briscoe (w/Eddie Edwards & Matt Taven)	W	IMPACT Wrestling	12:12
Jul 14	Ace Austin, Chris Bey, Luke Gallows & Karl Anderson	W	IMPACT Wrestling	12:34

	(w/Eddie Edwards, Kenny King & Matt Taven)			
Jul 19	Bestia 666 & Mecha Wolf (w/Matt Taven)	D	NWA Power	5:38
Jul 21	Ace Austin & Chris Bey (w/Matt Taven)	L	IMPACT Wrestling	10:32
Aug 25	Karl Anderson	L	IMPACT Wrestling	7:44
Aug 28	Tag Team Battle Royal (w/Matt Taven)	L	NWA 74th Anniversary Show	14:07
Sep 1	Luke Gallows & Karl Anderson (w/Matt Taven)	W	IMPACT Wrestling	8:14
Sep 15	Josh Alexander & Rich Swann (w/Matt Taven)	W	IMPACT Wrestling	6:54
Oct 4	Bestia 666, Mecha Wolf & Damian 666 (w/Matt Taven & Rhett Titus)	W	NWA Power	8:16
Oct 7	Alex Shelley & Chris Sabin (w/Matt Taven)	W	IMPACT Bound For Glory '22	16:35
Oct 20	Heath & Rhino (w/Matt Taven)	L	IMPACT Wrestling	10:02
Dec 10	Ativalu & Sal Muscat (w/Matt Taven)	W	AEW Dark Elevation	1:49

MIKE KNOX

Jan 11	Chris Adonis & Thom Latimer, Tim Storm & Trevor Murdoch	W	NWA Power	5:25
	(w/Matt Cardona)			
Mar 1	Da Pope	W	NWA Power	11:55
Mar 19	Da Pope & Mims (w/VSK)	W	NWA Crockett Cup '22	9:59
Mar 19	Jay Bradley & Wrecking Ball Legursky (w/VSK)	W	NWA Crockett Cup '22	7:03
Mar 20	Jay Briscoe & Mark Briscoe (w/VSK)	L	NWA Crockett Cup '22	7:45
Mar 29	Alex Taylor & Rush Freeman (w/VSK)	W	NWA Power	4:18
May 10	Nick Aldis, Doug Williams & Harry Smith (w/Matt Cardona & VSK)	L	NWA Power	8:15
May 24	Trevor Murdoch	L	NWA Power	7:58
Jun 14	Chris Adonis & Thom Latimer (w/VSK)	L	NWA Power	7:23
Jul 19	Nick Aldis, Brian Myers, Thom Latimer	L	NWA Power	8:47
Aug 9	De'Vin Graves	W	NWA Power	4:16
Aug 27	Tables Match: Bully Ray	L	NWA 74th Anniversary Show	8:38
Sep 20	Bully Ray & Thom Latimer (w/VSK)	L	NWA Power	5:15
Nov 1	Rolando Freeman, Brady Pierce & Rush Freeman (w/Brian Myers & VSK)	L	NWA Power	6:54
Nov 29	Brady Pierce & Rush Freeman (w/Matt Cardona)	L	NWA Power	11:19

MIKEY NICHOLLS

May 14	Aaron Henare, Kyle Fletcher, Mark Davis & Jeff Cobb	W	NJPW Capital Collision	12:09
	(w/Shane Haste, Jonah & Bad Dude Tito)			
Jul 2	Aaron Henare, Great-O-Khan, Kyle Fletcher & Mark Davis	L	NJPW Strong	11:35
	(w/Bad Dude Tito, Jonah & Shane Haste)			
Jul 9	Jorel Nelson & Royce Isaacs (w/Shane Haste)	W	NJPW Strong	10:21
Jul 23	Christopher Daniels & Yuya Uemura (w/Shane Haste)	L	NJPW Strong	10:02

MIMS

Jan 11	Anthony Mayweather	L	NWA Power	5:07
Mar 8	BLK Jeez, Jordan Clearwater, Marshe Rockett & Tyrus	L	NWA Power	6:59
	(w/Alex Taylor, Rush Freeman & Cyon)			
Mar 19	Mike Knox & VSK (w/Da Pope)	L	NWA Crockett Cup '22	9:59
May 3	Slam Challenge: Tyrus	W	NWA Power	:47
Jun 11	Tyrus	L	NWA Alwayz Ready '22	8:37
Aug 27	EC3	L	NWA 74th Anniversary Show	4:52
Sep 13	Tyrus	L	NWA Power	2:03
Nov 1	Gustavo Aguilar, Judais	W	NWA Power	6:45
Nov 15	Jordan Clearwater	D	NWA Power	6:05
Dec 13	Rhett Titus & Trevor Murdoch (w/Dak Draper)	L	NWA Power	9:14
Dec 20	Bully Ray, Judais & Thom Latimer (w/Chris Adonis & Dak Draper)	L	NWA Power	8:18

MINI ABISMO NEGRO

Feb 24	Aramis, El Dragon & Micro Man (w/Arez & Gino Medina)	L	MLW Fusion	15:46
Mar 31	Micro Man, Octagon Jr. & Puma King (w/Arez & Gino Medina)	L	MLW Fusion	15:42
Apr 29	Aramis, KC Navarro & Micro Man (w/Gino Medina & Arez)	W	MLW Fusion	11:55
May 26	Aero Star, El Dragon & Micro Man (w/Arez & TJP)	L	MLW Fusion	10:36
Jun 30	Lince Dorado, Micro Man & Taya Valkyrie (w/Arez & Holidead)	L	MLW Fusion	6:32
Nov 10	KC Navarro	L	MLW Fusion	4:04

MINORU SUZUKI

Jan 5	Chase Owens, Cima, Toru Yano	W	NJPW Wrestle Kingdom 16 Night #1	6:08
Jan 6	Takashi Sugiura, Kazushi Sakuraba & Toru Yano	L	NJPW Wrestle Kingdom 16 Night #3	9:37
	(w/Taichi & Taka Michinoku)			
Mar 1	Kazuchika Okada, Hiroshi Tanahashi & Tatsumi Fujinami	L	NJPW 50th Anniversary Show	18:12
	(w/Zack Sabre Jr. & Yoshiaki Fujiwara)			
Apr 1	Killer Kross	W	NJPW Lonestar Shootout	9:48
Apr 1	Rhett Titus	W	ROH Supercard Of Honor XV	6:00
Apr 13	Samoa Joe	L	AEW Dynamite	11:37
Apr 16	Tomohiro Ishii	L	NJPW Windy City Riot	18:46
Apr 25	QT Marshall	W	AEW Dark Elevation	4:12
May 14	Brody King	L	NJPW Capital Collision	9:05
Jun 25	Tony Deppen	W	NJPW Strong	10:32
Jun 26	Eddie Kingston, Shota Umino & Wheeler Yuta	W	AEW x NJPW Forbidden Door	18:58
	(w/Chris Jericho & Sammy Guevara)			
Sep 18	Hokuto Omori	W	AJPW 50th Anniversary Show	12:04
Oct 28	Clark Connors	W	NJPW Rumble On 44th Street	15:50
Nov 12	Fred Yehi	W	NJPW Strong	16:27

MIRANDA GORDY

Mar 17	Rok-C	W	MLW Fusion	7:38
Jun 13	Mercedes Martinez & Serena Deeb (w/Tootie Lynn)	L	AEW Dark Elevation	4:15
Jun 20	Ruby Soho	L	AEW Dark Elevation	2:05

MIRO

Jun 1	Johnny Elite	W	AEW Dynamite	6:07
Jun 15	Ethan Page	W	AEW Dynamite: Road Rager	9:31
Jun 26	Clark Connors, Pac, Malakai Black	L	AEW x NJPW Forbidden Door	15:10
Sep 4	Malakai Black, Brody King & Buddy Matthews (w/Sting & Darby Allin)	W	AEW All Out '22	12:10

MISSA KATE

Jan 5	Kylie Rae & Tootie Lynn (w/Kamille)	L	NWA Power	6:44
Jun 7	Kamille & Kenzie Paige (w/KiLynn King)	W	NWA Power	9:07
Jun 28	Chelsea Green & Max The Impaler (w/Jennacide)	L	NWA Power	5:38
Aug 27	Burke Invitational Gauntlet	L	NWA 74th Anniversary Show	17:24
Nov 12	Ella Envy & Kenzie Paige (w/Madi Wrenkowski)	L	NWA Hard Times 3	8:12

MISTERIOSO

Jan 15	Karl Fredericks & Kevin Knight (w/Bateman)	L	NJPW Strong	10:04
Mar 19	Fred Yehi, Keita Murray & The DKC (w/Bateman & Barrett Brown)	W	NJPW Strong	10:05
May 28	Fred Yehi, Kevin Knight & The DKC (w/Barrett Brown)	W	NJPW Strong	10:06
Jul 16	Eddie Pearl & Ricky Gibson (w/Barrett Brown)	W	NJPW Strong	8:31
Jul 30	Kyle Fletcher & Mark Davis (w/Barrett Brown)	L	NJPW Strong	7:27
Sep 10	Mascara Dorada	L	NJPW Strong	9:41
Nov 5	Kevin Knight & The DKC, Bad Dude Tito & Shane Haste, Jorel Nelson & Royce Isaacs (w/Barrett Brown)	W	NJPW Strong	12:36
Dec 17	Alex Shelley & Chris Sabin (w/Barrett Brown)	L	NJPW Strong	12:11

MIYU YAMASHITA

Mar 19	Shoko Nakajima	L	TJPW Grand Princess '22	19:06
Jun 6	Nyla Rose & Serena Deeb (w/Skye Blue)	L	AEW Dark Elevation	7:40
Jun 12	Hikari Noa, Suzume & Yuki Arai (w/Maki Ito & Juria Nagano)	W	Cyberfight Festival '22	11:54
Jul 9	Thunder Rosa	W	TJPW Summer Sun Princess '22	13:39
Jul 27	Thunder Rosa	L	AEW Dynamite: Fight For The Fallen	10:02

MIZ, THE

Jan 1	Edge	L	WWE Day 1	20:00
Jan 29	Edge & Beth Phoenix (w/Maryse)	L	WWE Royal Rumble '22	12:30
Jan 31	Dominik Mysterio	W	WWE Monday Night RAW	2:10
Feb 7	Dominik Mysterio	L	WWE Monday Night RAW	1:47
Feb 19	Rey Mysterio	L	WWE Elimination Chamber Kickoff	8:20
Mar 28	Rey Mysterio	L	WWE Monday Night RAW	5:30
Apr 2	Rey Mysterio & Dominik Mysterio (w/Logan Paul)	W	WWE WrestleMania XXXVIII	11:15
Apr 4	Dominik Mysterio	W	WWE Monday Night RAW	:30
Apr 11	Cody Rhodes	L	WWE Monday Night RAW	11:45
Apr 25	Mustafa Ali	L	WWE Monday Night RAW	6:40
May 2	Handicap Match: Mustafa Ali (w/Theory)	W	WWE Monday Night RAW	2:50
May 23	Cody Rhodes	L	WWE Monday Night RAW	9:00
Jun 6	Riddle	L	WWE Monday Night RAW	2:13
Jun 27	Battle Royal	L	WWE Monday Night RAW	19:25
Jun 27	AJ Styles	L	WWE Monday Night RAW	12:30
Jul 1	Battle Royal	L	WWE SmackDown	14:36
Jul 1	Madcap Moss, Ezekiel, Happy Corbin	L	WWE SmackDown	10:33
Jul 4	AJ Styles	L	WWE Monday Night RAW	6:25
Jul 11	AJ Styles & Ezekiel (w/Ciampa)	L	WWE Monday Night RAW	11:29
Jul 30	Logan Paul	L	WWE SummerSlam '22	14:15
Aug 1	AJ Styles, Mustafa Ali	L	WWE Monday Night RAW	8:50
Aug 8	No DQ: AJ Styles	L	WWE Monday Night RAW	12:30
Aug 15	Cedric Alexander & Mustafa Ali (w/Ciampa)	W	WWE Monday Night RAW	9:30
Aug 22	AJ Styles & Bobby Lashley (w/Ciampa)	W	WWE Monday Night RAW	13:30
Aug 29	Bobby Lashley	L	WWE Monday Night RAW	10:49
Sep 5	Steel Cage Match: Bobby Lashley	L	WWE Monday Night RAW	14:15
Oct 24	R-Truth	L	WWE Monday Night RAW	2:45
Oct 31	Mustafa Ali	L	WWE Monday Night RAW	10:00
Nov 7	Johnny Gargano	W	WWE Monday Night RAW	17:00
Nov 28	Anything Goes Match: Dexter Lumis	L	WWE Monday Night RAW	9:30
Dec 19	Ladder Match: Dexter Lumis	W	WWE Monday Night RAW	18:20

MJF

Jan 5	Shawn Dean	L	AEW Dynamite	:47
Feb 2	CM Punk	W	AEW Dynamite	38:09
Mar 6	Dog Collar Match: CM Punk	L	AEW Revolution '22	26:45
Apr 13	Shawn Dean	L	AEW Dynamite	4:07
May 29	Wardlow	L	AEW Double Or Nothing '22	7:30
Sep 4	Casino Ladder Match: Claudio Castagnoli, Wheeler Yuta, Penta El Zero M, Rey Fenix, Rush, Andrade El Idolo, Dante Martin	W	AEW All Out '22	14:15
Oct 5	Wheeler Yuta	W	AEW Dynamite: Anniversary	15:06
Nov 19	Jon Moxley	W	AEW Full Gear '22	23:15
Dec 14	Ricky Starks	W	AEW Dynamite: Winter Is Coming	15:46

MONTEZ FORD

Jan 1	Randy Orton & Riddle (w/Angelo Dawkins)	L	WWE Day 1	11:15
Jan 3	Apollo Crews & Commander Azeez (w/Angelo Dawkins)	W	WWE Monday Night RAW	2:15
Jan 10	Dolph Ziggler, Robert Roode & Apollo Crews (w/Angelo Dawkins & Damian Priest)	L	WWE Monday Night RAW	8:30
Jan 17	Apollo Crews, Commander Azeez, Dolph Ziggler & Robert Roode	W	WWE Monday Night RAW	8:00

	(w/Rey Mysterio, Dominik Mysterio & Angelo Dawkins)			
Jan 24	Rey Mysterio & Dominik Mysterio (w/Angelo Dawkins)	L	WWE Monday Night RAW	8:00
Jan 29	Royal Rumble Match	L	WWE Royal Rumble '22	9:10
Feb 7	Chad Gable & Otis (w/Angelo Dawkins)	L	WWE Monday Night RAW	5:37
Feb 14	Dolph Ziggler & Robert Roode (w/Angelo Dawkins)	W	WWE Monday Night RAW	2:50
Feb 21	Chad Gable & Otis (w/Angelo Dawkins)	L	WWE Monday Night RAW	9:05
Feb 28	Randy Orton & Riddle (w/Angelo Dawkins)	W	WWE Monday Night RAW	8:35
Mar 10	Cedric Alexander & Shelton Benjamin (w/Angelo Dawkins)	W	WWE Main Event	9:23
Mar 14	Riddle	D	WWE Monday Night RAW	9:40
Apr 3	Randy Orton & Riddle, Chad Gable & Otis (w/Angelo Dawkins)	L	WWE WrestleMania XXXVIII	11:30
Apr 4	Chad Gable & Otis (w/Angelo Dawkins)	W	WWE Monday Night RAW	8:25
Apr 11	Jimmy Uso & Jey Uso (w/Angelo Dawkins)	L	WWE Monday Night RAW	15:10
Apr 18	Randy Orton & Riddle (w/Angelo Dawkins)	W	WWE Monday Night RAW	7:50
Apr 28	Cedric Alexander & Shelton Benjamin (w/Angelo Dawkins)	W	WWE Main Event	9:31
May 2	Kevin Owens, Chad Gable & Otis (w/Angelo Dawkins & Ezekiel)	L	WWE Monday Night RAW	9:45
May 9	Randy Orton & Riddle (w/Angelo Dawkins)	L	WWE Monday Night RAW	9:58
May 19	Apollo Crews & Commander Azeez (w/Angelo Dawkins)	W	WWE Main Event	4:23
May 23	Sami Zayn, Jimmy Uso & Jey Uso (w/Riddle & Angelo Dawkins)	W	WWE Monday Night RAW	12:35
Jun 6	Jimmy Uso & Jey Uso (w/Angelo Dawkins)	W	WWE Monday Night RAW	16:30
Jun 13	Jimmy Uso	L	WWE Monday Night RAW	13:30
Jun 27	Jey Uso	W	WWE Monday Night RAW	9:50
Jul 2	Jimmy Uso & Jey Uso (w/Angelo Dawkins)	L	WWE Money In The Bank '22	23:00
Jul 4	Theory, Chad Gable & Otis (w/Bobby Lashley & Angelo Dawkins)	W	WWE Monday Night RAW	10:05
Jul 11	Omos, Jimmy Uso & Jey Uso (w/R-Truth & Angelo Dawkins)	L	WWE Monday Night RAW	11:30
Jul 18	MVP & Omos (w/Angelo Dawkins)	W	WWE Monday Night RAW	4:50
Jul 22	Theory, Jimmy Uso & Jey Uso (w/Madcap Moss & Angelo Dawkins)	W	WWE SmackDown	17:00
Jul 25	Roman Reigns, Jimmy Uso & Jey Uso (w/Riddle & Angelo Dawkins)	L	WWE Monday Night RAW	19:25
Jul 30	Jimmy Uso & Jey Uso (w/Angelo Dawkins)	L	WWE SummerSlam '22	13:25
Aug 1	Seth Rollins	L	WWE Monday Night RAW	10:59
Aug 18	Chad Gable & Otis (w/Angelo Dawkins)	W	WWE Main Event	6:49
Aug 29	Chad Gable & Otis (w/Angelo Dawkins)	W	WWE Monday Night RAW	16:04
Sep 3	Austin Theory, Chad Gable & Otis (w/Madcap Moss & Angelo Dawkins)	W	WWE Clash At The Castle Kickoff	6:29
Sep 5	Chad Gable & Otis, Angel & Humberto, Xavier Woods & Kofi Kingston (w/Angelo Dawkins)	D	WWE Monday Night RAW	14:30
Sep 9	Angel, Humberto, Mace & Mansoor (w/Angelo Dawkins, Ashante Adonis & Top Dolla)	W	WWE SmackDown	8:35
Sep 19	Ridge Holland & Butch (w/Angelo Dawkins)	L	WWE Monday Night RAW	12:57
Nov 28	Chad Gable & Otis (w/Angelo Dawkins)	W	WWE Monday Night RAW	12:00
Dec 12	Finn Balor, Damian Priest & Dominik Mysterio (w/Akira Tozawa & Angelo Dawkins)	L	WWE Monday Night RAW	14:45
Dec 19	Finn Balor & Damian Priest (w/Angelo Dawkins)	W	WWE Monday Night RAW	9:00

MOOSE

Jan 8	Matt Cardona, W. Morrissey	W	IMPACT Hard To Kill '22	16:00
Jan 13	Zicky Dice	W	IMPACT Wrestling	:16
Apr 1	Josh Alexander & Jonah (w/PCO)	L	IMPACT Multiverse Of Matches	12:47
Apr 23	Josh Alexander	L	IMPACT Rebellion '22	23:56
Apr 28	Josh Alexander	L	IMPACT Wrestling	12:40
May 12	Gauntlet For The Gold	L	IMPACT Wrestling	39:00
Jun 2	PCO & W. Morrissey (w/Steve Maclin)	W	IMPACT Wrestling	10:51
Jun 16	Monster's Ball Match: Sami Callihan	L	IMPACT Slammiversary XX	16:00
Aug 18	Eddie Edwards, Bandido, Rich Swann, Sami Callihan, Steve Maclin	L	IMPACT Wrestling	18:25
Sep 15	Black Taurus & Crazzy Steve (w/Steve Maclin)	L	IMPACT Wrestling	1:52
Oct 6	Steve Maclin	L	IMPACT Wrestling	9:51
Oct 7	Call Your Shot Gauntlet	L	IMPACT Bound For Glory '22	29:18
Nov 3	Ace Austin	L	IMPACT Wrestling	7:42
Dec 1	Bhupinder Gujjar	W	IMPACT Wrestling	4:22

MUSTAFA ALI

Apr 25	The Miz	W	WWE Monday Night RAW	6:40
May 2	Handicap Match: The Miz & Theory	L	WWE Monday Night RAW	2:50
May 9	Ciampa	L	WWE Monday Night RAW	3:44
May 16	Veer Mahan	L	WWE Monday Night RAW	2:50
May 30	Ciampa	W	WWE Monday Night RAW	3:24
May 30	Theory	L	WWE Monday Night RAW	1:45
Jun 5	Theory	L	WWE Hell In A Cell '22	10:25
Jun 9	T-Bar	W	WWE Main Event	7:13
Jun 13	Chad Gable	L	WWE Monday Night RAW	3:15
Jun 27	Battle Royal	L	WWE Monday Night RAW	19:25
Jun 30	T-Bar	W	WWE Main Event	4:57
Jul 7	Veer Mahaan	L	WWE Main Event	7:09
Jul 14	Akira Tozawa	W	WWE Main Event	8:28
Jul 21	Chad Gable & Otis (w/Cedric Alexander)	L	WWE Main Event	8:49
Jul 28	Akira Tozawa & T-Bar (w/Cedric Alexander)	W	WWE Main Event	4:38
Aug 1	AJ Styles, The Miz	L	WWE Monday Night RAW	8:50
Aug 11	T-Bar	W	WWE Main Event	8:01
Aug 15	The Miz & Ciampa (w/Cedric Alexander)	L	WWE Monday Night RAW	9:30
Aug 25	Shelton Benjamin & T-Bar (w/Cedric Alexander)	W	WWE Main Event	8:30
Sep 22	Chad Gable & Otis (w/Shelton Benjamin)	L	WWE Main Event	9:52
Sep 29	T-Bar	W	WWE Main Event	5:21
Oct 3	Bobby Lashley	L	WWE Monday Night RAW	11:26
Oct 24	Austin Theory	L	WWE Monday Night RAW	9:58

Oct 31	The Miz	W	WWE Monday Night RAW	10:00
Nov 14	Bobby Lashley	L	WWE Monday Night RAW	4:30
Nov 18	Ricochet	L	WWE SmackDown	10:45
Nov 21	Austin Theory	L	WWE Monday Night RAW	5:45
Dec 5	Austin Theory	L	WWE Monday Night RAW	8:05
Dec 15	Edris Enofe & Malik Blade (w/Cedric Alexander)	W	WWE Main Event	6:17
Dec 22	Axiom	W	WWE Main Event	7:19

MVP

May 23	Bobby Lashley	W	WWE Monday Night RAW	3:05
Jun 5	Handicap Match: Bobby Lashley (w/Omos)	L	WWE Hell In A Cell '22	8:25
Jun 13	Cedric Alexander	W	WWE Monday Night RAW	1:40
Jul 18	Angelo Dawkins & Montez Ford (w/Omos)	L	WWE Monday Night RAW	4:50

MYLA GRACE

Jan 6	Xia Brookside	L	NXT UK	3:51
Feb 3	Isla Dawn	L	NXT UK	2:59
Feb 17	Stevie Turner	L	NXT UK	4:34
Jun 16	Lash Legend	L	NXT UK	4:34
Jun 23	Isla Dawn	L	NXT UK	5:03

MYLES BORNE

Jun 17	Guru Raaj	L	NXT Level Up	4:55
Jul 8	Dante Chen	L	NXT Level Up	4:38
Jul 15	Andre Chase & Bodhi Hayward (w/Javier Bernal)	L	NXT Level Up	5:47
Jul 29	Javier Bernal	L	NXT Level Up	4:04
Aug 12	Ikemen Jiro	L	NXT Level Up	5:12
Sep 2	Duke Hudson	L	NXT Level Up	5:42
Sep 23	Andre Chase	L	NXT Level Up	5:34
Oct 7	Guru Raaj	W	NXT Level Up	5:36
Oct 14	Dante Chen	W	NXT Level Up	5:14
Oct 21	Ikemen Jiro	W	NXT Level Up	5:18
Nov 4	Hank Walker	L	NXT Level Up	4:15
Dec 2	Oro Mensah	L	NXT Level Up	6:11
Dec 23	Charlie Dempsey	L	NXT Level Up	8:13

MYRON REED

Mar 3	Yoshihiro Tajiri, Bandido, Matt Cross	W	MLW Fusion	8:48
Apr 7	TJP	W	MLW Fusion	13:39
Apr 14	Alex Kane, ACH, Juicy Finau, Puma King	L	MLW Fusion	4:28
May 5	Swerve Strickland	W	MLW Fusion	7:54
Jun 23	Arez, KC Navarro	W	MLW Fusion	6:09
Nov 10	Arez, La Estrella, Lince Dorado	W	MLW Fusion	6:54
Dec 8	Shun Skywalker	L	MLW Fusion	10:59

NAOMI

Jan 7	Charlotte Flair	L	WWE SmackDown	12:15
Jan 21	Charlotte Flair	L	WWE SmackDown	2:25
Jan 28	Sonya Deville	W	WWE SmackDown	11:45
Jan 29	Royal Rumble Match	L	WWE Royal Rumble '22	7:18
Feb 11	Charlotte Flair	L	WWE SmackDown	19:55
Feb 19	Charlotte Flair & Sonya Deville (w/Ronda Rousey)	W	WWE Elimination Chamber '22	9:14
Mar 4	Carmella	W	WWE SmackDown	2:10
Mar 11	Natalya & Shayna Baszler (w/Sasha Banks)	W	WWE SmackDown	3:19
Mar 18	Rhea Ripley & Liv Morgan (w/Sasha Banks)	D	WWE SmackDown	12:00
Mar 28	Queen Zelina, Carmella, Natalya & Shayna Baszler (w/Sasha Banks, Liv Morgan & Rhea Ripley)	W	WWE Monday Night RAW	8:20
Apr 1	Carmella & Queen Zelina (w/Sasha Banks)	W	WWE SmackDown	3:13
Apr 3	Natalya & Shayna Baszler, Carmella & Queen Zelina, Rhea Ripley & Liv Morgan (w/Sasha Banks)	W	WWE WrestleMania XXXVIII	10:50
Apr 4	Liv Morgan & Rhea Ripley (w/Sasha Banks)	W	WWE Monday Night RAW	9:00
Apr 11	Liv Morgan	W	WWE Monday Night RAW	2:20
Apr 15	Rhea Ripley	L	WWE SmackDown	9:04
Apr 18	Liv Morgan & Rhea Ripley (w/Sasha Banks)	W	WWE Monday Night RAW	7:25
Apr 29	Shayna Baszler	W	WWE SmackDown	2:27
May 9	Doudrop & Nikki A.S.H. (w/Sasha Banks)	W	WWE Monday Night RAW	4:25
May 13	Natalya & Shayna Baszler (w/Sasha Banks)	W	WWE SmackDown	8:30

NASH CARTER

Jan 4	Walter, Marcel Barthel & Fabian Aichner (w/Riddle & Wes Lee)	W	NXT 2.0: New Year's Evil '22	13:52
Jan 25	Kushida & Ikemen Jiro (w/Wes Lee)	W	NXT 2.0	11:32
Feb 8	Malik Blade & Edris Enofe (w/Wes Lee)	W	NXT 2.0	9:29
Feb 15	Julius Creed & Brutus Creed (w/Wes Lee)	L	NXT 2.0: Vengeance Day '22	9:36
Mar 8	Marcel Barthel & Fabian Aichner (w/Wes Lee)	D	NXT 2.0: Roadblock '22	5:33
Mar 29	Gunther, Marcel Barthel & Fabian Aichner (w/LA Knight & Wes Lee)	L	NXT 2.0	12:11
Apr 2	Fabian Aichner & Marcel Barthel, Brutus Creed & Julius Creed (w/Wes Lee)	W	NXT Stand & Deliver '22	11:22

NATALIA MARKOVA

Jan 5	Paola Blaze	W	NWA Power	3:57
Feb 15	Jennacide	D	NWA Power	5:32
Apr 12	KiLynn King	L	NWA Power	6:02

May 17	Mickie James	L	NWA Power	6:44
Jun 11	Taya Valkyrie	W	NWA Alwayz Ready '22	8:43
Aug 27	Burke Invitational Gauntlet	L	NWA 74th Anniversary Show	17:24
Sep 13	Ella Envy, Kenzie Paige & Roxy (w/Angelina Love & Max The Impaler)	W	NWA Power	3:11
Sep 13	Angelina Love, Max The Impaler	D	NWA Power	3:48
Oct 11	Allysin Hex & Marti Belle (w/Taryn Terrell)	L	NWA Power	5:33
Nov 12	Voodoo Queen Casket Match: Max The Impaler	L	NWA Hard Times 3	8:14

NATALYA

Jan 14	Aliyah	L	WWE SmackDown	:03
Jan 21	Aliyah	L	WWE SmackDown	2:10
Jan 29	Royal Rumble Match	L	WWE Royal Rumble '22	36:17
Feb 4	Aliyah	L	WWE SmackDown	4:08
Feb 11	Hart Dungeon Style Match: Aliyah	W	WWE SmackDown	2:40
Feb 25	Xia Li	L	WWE SmackDown	4:00
Mar 11	Sasha Banks & Naomi (w/Shayna Baszler)	L	WWE SmackDown	3:19
Mar 21	Liv Morgan & Rhea Ripley (w/Shayna Baszler)	W	WWE Monday Night RAW	3:55
Mar 28	Naomi, Sasha Banks, Liv Morgan & Rhea Ripley (w/Queen Zelina, Carmella & Shayna Baszler)	L	WWE Monday Night RAW	8:20
Apr 3	Sasha Banks & Naomi, Carmella & Queen Zelina, Rhea Ripley & Liv Morgan (w/Shayna Baszler)	L	WWE WrestleMania XXXVIII	10:50
Apr 19	Tatum Paxley	W	NXT 2.0	4:52
May 3	Cora Jade & Nikkita Lyons (w/Lash Legend)	L	NXT 2.0: Spring Breakin'	13:28
May 10	Cora Jade	W	NXT 2.0	14:08
May 13	Sasha Banks & Naomi (w/Shayna Baszler)	L	WWE SmackDown	8:30
May 27	Ronda Rousey & Raquel Rodriguez (w/Shayna Baszler)	L	WWE SmackDown	7:35
Jun 3	Aliyah, Raquel Rodriguez, Shotzi, Shayna Baszler, Xia Li	W	WWE SmackDown	5:54
Jul 2	Ronda Rousey	L	WWE Money In The Bank '22	12:30
Jul 4	Bianca Belair & Liv Morgan (w/Carmella)	L	WWE Monday Night RAW	13:25
Jul 8	Ronda Rousey	L	WWE SmackDown	2:15
Jul 15	Liv Morgan	L	WWE SmackDown	9:04
Jul 29	Ronda Rousey & Liv Morgan (w/Sonya Deville)	L	WWE SmackDown	11:30
Aug 5	Gauntlet Match: Shayna Baszler, Sonya Deville, Raquel Rodriguez, Shotzi, Xia Li, Aliyah	L	WWE SmackDown	21:05
Aug 19	Jacy Jayne & Gigi Dolin (w/Sonya Deville)	L	WWE SmackDown	8:48
Aug 26	Nikki A.S.H. & Doudrop, Dana Brooke & Tamina, Shotzi & Xia Li (w/Sonya Deville)	W	WWE SmackDown	3:10
Aug 26	Raquel Rodriguez & Aliyah (w/Sonya Deville)	L	WWE SmackDown	8:00
Sep 9	Ronda Rousey, Sonya Deville, Xia Li, Lacey Evans	L	WWE SmackDown	4:40
Sep 30	Ronda Rousey	L	WWE SmackDown	4:18
Nov 4	Shayna Baszler	L	WWE SmackDown	4:11

NATHAN FRAZER

Jan 13	Walter	L	NXT UK	14:02
Feb 10	Teoman	W	NXT UK	13:15
Mar 3	Ilja Dragunov	L	NXT UK	14:42
May 3	Grayson Waller	W	NXT 2.0: Spring Breakin'	12:45
May 17	Wes Lee	D	NXT 2.0	4:21
May 31	Cameron Grimes	L	NXT 2.0	10:09
Jun 7	Santos Escobar	W	NXT 2.0	11:54
Aug 2	Carmelo Hayes	L	NXT 2.0	5:41
Aug 26	Ikemen Jiro	W	NXT Level Up	6:29
Sep 6	Axiom	L	NXT 2.0	11:46
Sep 20	Axiom	W	NXT	13:14
Oct 11	Ladder Match: Axiom	W	NXT	12:53
Oct 22	Ladder Match: Carmelo Hayes, Oro Mensa, Von Wagner, Wes Lee	L	NXT Halloween Havoc '22	22:25

NICK ALDIS

Feb 15	Fable Jake & Jaden Roller (w/Doug Williams)	W	NWA Power	8:11
Mar 8	"I Quit" Match: Thom Latimer	W	NWA Power	13:38
Mar 20	Matt Cardona	L	NWA Crockett Cup '22	21:11
Mar 29	Deonte Marshall	W	NWA Power	1:10
Apr 1	Matt Cardona & Chelsea Green (w/Mickie James)	W	IMPACT Multiverse Of Matches	7:04
Apr 26	Jordan Clearwater	W	NWA Power	6:54
May 3	Mike Bennett	W	NWA Power	7:01
May 10	Matt Cardona, Mike Knox & VSK (w/Doug Williams & Harry Smith)	W	NWA Power	8:15
Jun 7	Brian Myers	W	NWA Power	10:19
Jun 11	Trevor Murdoch, Thom Latimer, Sam Shaw	L	NWA Alwayz Ready '22	18:10
Jun 19	Eddie Edwards, Matt Taven, Mike Bennett, PCO & Vincent (w/Alex Shelley, Chris Sabin, Davey Richards & Frankie Kazarian)	W	IMPACT Slammiversary XX	18:45
Jun 21	Brett Buffshay	W	NWA Power	3:28
Jul 12	Tim Storm	W	NWA Power	8:30
Jul 19	Mike Knox, Brian Myers, Thom Latimer	W	NWA Power	8:47
Aug 28	Flip Gordon	W	NWA 74th Anniversary Show	8:43

NICK COMOROTO

Jan 11	Jungle Boy & Luchasaurus (w/QT Marshall)	L	AEW Dark	8:21
Jan 25	Jungle Boy	L	AEW Dark	6:48
Jan 31	Dante Martin, Lee Moriarty & Matt Sydal (w/Aaron Solo & QT Marshall)	L	AEW Dark Elevation	7:46
Feb 1	Cam Stewart & Dante Casanova (w/Aaron Solo)	W	AEW Dark	3:44
Feb 22	Lamar Diggs	W	AEW Dark	3:54
Feb 25	Wardlow	L	AEW Rampage	6:25

Mar 1	Orange Cassidy & Wheeler Yuta (w/Aaron Solo)	L	AEW Dark	14:17
Mar 21	John Silver, Evil Uno & Stu Grayson (w/Aaron Solo & QT Marshall)	L	AEW Dark Elevation	7:27
Mar 29	Adam Priest, Gus De La Vega & Invictus Khash (w/Aaron Solo & QT Marshall)	W	AEW Dark	4:30
Apr 5	Alan Angels & Ten (w/Aaron Solo)	L	AEW Dark	8:08
Apr 11	Dante Martin & Darius Martin (w/Aaron Solo)	L	AEW Dark Elevation	5:52
Apr 16	Karl Fredericks, Clark Connors & Yuya Uemura (w/QT Marshall & Aaron Solo)	W	NJPW Windy City Riot	11:56
Apr 18	Rocky Romero & Trent Beretta (w/Aaron Solo)	L	AEW Dark	7:25
Apr 19	Keith Lee & Swerve Strickland (w/Aaron Solo)	L	AEW Dark	8:40
Apr 27	Bryan Danielson, Jon Moxley & Wheeler Yuta (w/QT Marshall & Aaron Solo)	L	AEW Dynamite	8:49
May 9	Keith Lee & Swerve Strickland (w/QT Marshall)	L	AEW Dark Elevation	6:47
May 10	The DKC & Kevin Knight (w/Aaron Solo)	W	AEW Dark	8:30
May 17	Alex Coughlin, Clark Connors, Karl Fredericks, Kevin Knight & Yuya Uemura (w/Blake Li, Brick Aldridge, Aaron Solo & QT Marshall)	L	AEW Dark	10:30
May 21	Clark Connors & Karl Fredericks (w/Aaron Solo)	L	NJPW Strong	8:21
May 28	Pac, Penta El Zero M & Rey Fenix (w/Aaron Solo & QT Marshall)	L	AEW Dark	10:32
Jun 6	Alan Angels, Evil Uno, John Silver & Ten (w/Anthony Ogogo, Aaron Solo & QT Marshall)	W	AEW Dark Elevation	6:28
Jun 14	Konosuke Takeshita	L	AEW Dark	6:42
Jun 26	Lance Archer	L	AEW x NJPW Forbidden Door Buy-In	6:08
Jun 28	Knull & Matt Vandagriff (w/Aaron Solo)	W	AEW Dark	3:43
Jul 4	Alex Reynolds, Evil Uno & Ten (w/Aaron Solo & QT Marshall)	L	AEW Dark Elevation	7:56
Jul 9	Christopher Daniels & Yuya Uemura (w/Aaron Solo)	L	NJPW Strong	9:17
Jul 12	Dante Martin	L	AEW Dark	7:53
Jul 25	Evil Uno & Ten (w/Aaron Solo)	L	AEW Dark Elevation	6:35
Aug 1	Bobby Orlando, BRG, Bryce Donovan & TUG Cooper (w/Anthony Ogogo, Aaron Solo & QT Marshall)	W	AEW Dark Elevation	3:33
Aug 2	Caleb Teninty & KC Rocker (w/Aaron Solo)	W	AEW Dark	3:18
Aug 23	Dante Martin & Matt Sydal (w/Aaron Solo)	W	AEW Dark	8:11
Sep 3	Hangman Page, John Silver & Alex Reynolds (w/Cole Karter & Aaron Solo)	L	AEW Dark Elevation	6:00
Sep 12	The Butcher & The Blade (w/Aaron Solo)	L	AEW Dark Elevation	4:37
Sep 27	Shaheem Ali	W	AEW Dark	2:43
Oct 3	Chuck Taylor, Trent Beretta, Danhausen & Rocky Romero (w/Cole Karter, Aaron Solo & QT Marshall)	L	AEW Dark Elevation	7:54
Oct 12	Samoa Joe & Wardlow (w/QT Marshall)	L	AEW Dynamite	2:29
Oct 25	Ricky Starks	L	AEW Dark	8:47
Nov 19	Orange Cassidy, Chuck Taylor, Trent Beretta, Rocky Romero & Danhausen (w/QT Marshall, Aaron Solo, Lee Johnson & Cole Karter)	L	AEW Full Gear Buy-In	11:55
Nov 28	Eddie Kingston & Ortiz (w/Aaron Solo)	L	AEW Dark Elevation	4:55
Dec 5	Hagane Shinno	L	AEW Dark Elevation	3:15
Dec 10	Dante Martin & Darius Martin (w/Aaron Solo)	L	AEW Dark Elevation	3:35

NICK JACKSON

Jan 21	Trent Beretta	L	AEW Rampage	13:00
Feb 11	Trent Beretta & Rocky Romero (w/Matt Jackson)	W	AEW Rampage	13:23
Feb 23	Tag Team Battle Royal (w/Matt Jackson)	L	AEW Dynamite	7:41
Mar 2	Casino Battle Royale (w/Matt Jackson)	W	AEW Dynamite	25:54
Mar 6	Jungle Boy & Luchasaurus, Bobby Fish & Kyle O'Reilly (w/Matt Jackson)	L	AEW Revolution '22	18:55
Mar 15	Alan Angels, Colt Cabana & Evil Uno (w/Brandon Cutler & Matt Jackson)	W	AEW Dark	8:40
Apr 1	Dante Martin & Darius Martin (w/Matt Jackson)	W	AEW Rampage	10:48
Apr 6	Dax Harwood & Cash Wheeler (w/Matt Jackson)	L	AEW Dynamite	20:07
Apr 27	Dante Martin, Lee Johnson, Brock Anderson, Brian Pillman Jr. & Griff Garrison (w/Adam Cole, Matt Jackson, Bobby Fish & Kyle O'Reilly)	W	AEW Dynamite	6:28
Apr 30	El Hijo del Vikingo & Rey Fenix (w/Matt Jackson)	W	AAA TripleMania XXX: Monterrey	15:58
May 5	Matt Hardy & Jeff Hardy (w/Matt Jackson)	W	AEW Double Or Nothing '22	19:15
May 27	Jon Cruz & Taylor Rust (w/Matt Jackson)	W	AEW Rampage	2:34
Jun 1	Christian Cage, Matt Hardy, Darby Allin, Jungle Boy & Luchasaurus (w/Matt Jackson, Bobby Fish, Kyle O'Reilly & Hikuleo)	W	AEW Dynamite	12:00
Jun 3	Penta El Zero M & Rey Fenix (w/Matt Jackson)	W	AEW Rampage	14:53
Jun 15	Ladder Match: Jungle Boy & Luchasaurus (w/Matt Jackson)	W	AEW Dynamite: Road Rager	14:53
Jun 26	Darby Allin, Sting & Shingo Takagi (w/Matt Jackson & El Phantasmo)	L	AEW x NJPW Forbidden Door	13:01
Jul 1	Hirooki Goto & Yoshi-Hashi (w/Matt Jackson)	W	AEW Rampage	9:31
Jul 13	Keith Lee & Swerve Strickland, Ricky Starks & Powerhouse Hobbs (w/Matt Jackson)	L	AEW Dynamite: Fyter Fest	18:14
Aug 17	Andrade El Idolo, Rush & Dragon Lee (w/Kenny Omega & Matt Jackson)	W	AEW Dynamite	20:54
Aug 31	Will Ospreay, Kyle Fletcher & Mark Davis (w/Kenny Omega & Matt Jackson)	W	AEW Dynamite	18:54
Sep 4	Hangman Page, Alex Reynolds & John Silver (w/Matt Jackson & Kenny Omega)	W	AEW All Out '22	19:50
Nov 19	Pac, Penta El Zero M & Rey Fenix (w/Kenny Omega & Matt Jackson)	L	AEW Full Gear '22	18:40
Nov 23	Pac, Penta El Zero M & Rey Fenix (w/Kenny Omega & Matt Jackson)	L	AEW Dynamite: Thanksgiving Eve	14:49
Nov 30	Pac, Penta El Zero M & Rey Fenix (w/Kenny Omega & Matt Jackson)	W	AEW Dynamite	17:20
Dec 14	Pac, Penta El Zero M & Rey Fenix (w/Kenny Omega & Matt Jackson)	L	AEW Dynamite: Winter Is Coming	14:59
Dec 21	No DQ: Pac, Penta El Zero M & Rey Fenix (w/Kenny Omega & Matt Jackson)	W	AEW Dynamite: Holiday Bash	13:41
Dec 28	Falls Count Anywhere: Pac, Penta El Zero M & Rey Fenix (w/Matt Jackson & Kenny Omega)	W	AEW Dynamite	17:16

NIKKI CROSS (AS NIKKI A.S.H. UNTIL OCT 31)

Jan 3	Queen Zelina & Carmella (w/Rhea Ripley)	L	WWE Monday Night RAW	2:40
Jan 24	Rhea Ripley, Dana Brooke & Liv Morgan (w/Carmella & Tamina)	L	WWE Monday Night RAW	2:20
Jan 29	Royal Rumble Match	L	WWE Royal Rumble '22	12:13
Jan 31	Rhea Ripley	L	WWE Monday Night RAW	8:10
Feb 7	Bianca Belair	L	WWE Monday Night RAW	4:01
Feb 14	Gauntlet Match: Bianca Belair, Rhea Ripley, Liv Morgan, Doudrop	L	WWE Monday Night RAW	44:04
Feb 19	Elimination Chamber: Bianca Belair, Alexa Bliss, Doudrop, Liv Morgan, Rhea Ripley	L	WWE Elimination Chamber '22	6:20
Feb 21	Rhea Ripley	L	WWE Monday Night RAW	2:35
Feb 28	Rhea Ripley, Bianca Belair & Liv Morgan (w/Becky Lynch & Doudrop)	L	WWE Monday Night RAW	12:20
Apr 28	Liv Morgan	L	WWE Main Event	5:03
May 2	Dana Brooke	L	WWE Monday Night RAW	1:30
May 9	Sasha Banks & Naomi (w/Doudrop)	L	WWE Monday Night RAW	4:25
May 23	Alexa Bliss	L	WWE Monday Night RAW	3:00
Jun 13	Alexa Bliss & Liv Morgan (w/Doudrop)	L	WWE Monday Night RAW	4:25
Jun 27	Becky Lynch, Doudrop, Xia Li, Shayna Baszler, Tamina	L	WWE Monday Night RAW	13:20
Jul 11	Alexa Bliss & Asuka (w/Doudrop)	L	WWE Monday Night RAW	4:15
Jul 18	Alexa Bliss, Asuka & Dana Brooke (w/Doudrop & Tamina)	L	WWE Monday Night RAW	2:35
Aug 15	Alexa Bliss & Asuka (w/Doudrop)	L	WWE Monday Night RAW	9:00
Aug 25	Dana Brooke & Tamina (w/Doudrop)	W	WWE Main Event	5:14
Aug 26	Natalya & Sonya Deville, Dana Brooke & Tamina, Shotzi & Xia Li (w/Doudrop)	L	WWE SmackDown	3:10
Sep 4	Katana Chance & Kayden Carter (w/Doudrop)	L	NXT Worlds Collide '22	10:19
Sep 5	Raquel Rodriguez & Aliyah (w/Doudrop)	L	WWE Monday Night RAW	3:45
Sep 6	Gigi Dolin & Jacy Jayne (w/Doudrop)	W	NXT 2.0	10:50
Sep 26	Candice LeRae	L	WWE Monday Night RAW	1:45
Oct 31	Bianca Belair	L	WWE Monday Night RAW	9:30
Nov 7	Dana Brooke	W	WWE Monday Night RAW	2:15
Nov 26	WarGames: Bianca Belair, Alexa Bliss, Asuka, Mia Yim & Becky Lynch (w/Bayley, Dakota Kai, Iyo Sky & Rhea Ripley)	L	WWE Survivor Series WarGames	39:40
Dec 5	Alexa Bliss, Becky Lynch	L	WWE Monday Night RAW	16:30

NIKKI BELLA

Jan 29	Royal Rumble Match	L	WWE Royal Rumble '22	8:40

NIKKITA LYONS

Jan 7	Erica Yan	W	WWE 205 Live	5:24
Feb 22	Kayla Inlay	W	NXT 2.0	4:03
Mar 29	Sloane Jacobs	W	NXT 2.0	1:47
Apr 5	Lash Legend	W	NXT 2.0	4:39
Apr 26	Lash Legend	W	NXT 2.0	5:09
May 3	Natalya & Lash Legend (w/Cora Jade)	W	NXT 2.0: Spring Breakin'	13:28
May 10	Arianna Grace	W	NXT 2.0	3:09
Jun 28	Mandy Rose	W	NXT 2.0	5:29
Jul 19	Battle Royal	L	NXT 2.0	13:13
Aug 9	Kiana James	W	NXT 2.0	4:10
Sep 13	Kiana James & Arianna Grace (w/Zoey Stark)	W	NXT 2.0	9:04
Sep 27	Kayden Carter	W	NXT	4:54
Oct 4	Gigi Dolin & Jacy Jayne (w/Zoey Stark)	W	NXT	10:28
Oct 25	Katana Chance & Kayden Carter (w/Zoey Stark)	L	NXT	12:52
Nov 8	Katana Chance & Kayden Carter (w/Zoey Stark)	L	NXT	11:02
Nov 29	Mandy Rose, Gigi Dolin & Jacy Jayne (w/Katana Chance & Kayden Carter)	L	NXT	8:54
Dec 20	Zoey Stark	L	NXT	5:23

NINA SAMUELS

Feb 10	Amale	L	NXT UK	5:17
Mar 17	Emilia McKenzie	L	NXT UK	8:44
May 12	Ivy Nile	L	NXT UK	4:41
Jun 23	Sarray	L	NXT UK	5:34
Jul 21	Emilia McKenzie	L	NXT UK	4:58
Aug 18	Amale	L	NXT UK	6:31

NOAM DAR

Jan 20	Heritage Cup Rules: A-Kid	D	NXT UK	18:00
Mar 10	Heritage Cup Rules: Joe Coffey	W	NXT UK	17:43
Mar 31	Mark Coffey	W	NXT UK	16:46
Jun 16	Damon Kemp & Wolfgang (w/Sha Samuels)	L	NXT UK	12:41
Jul 14	Mark Coffey	L	NXT UK	17:49
Aug 25	Mark Coffey	W	NXT UK	14:38

NYLA ROSE

Jan 10	Skye Blue & Tina San Antonio (w/Emi Sakura)	W	AEW Dark Elevation	2:44
Jan 14	Red Velvet, Leyla Hirsch & Kris Statlander (w/Penelope Ford & The Bunny)	W	AEW Rampage	8:12
Feb 2	Ruby Soho	W	AEW Dynamite	10:58
Feb 14	Ruby Soho, Anna Jay & Tay Conti (w/Emi Sakura & The Bunny)	L	AEW Dark Elevation	3:43
Feb 21	AQA, Kiera Hogan & Skye Blue (w/Emi Sakura & Leyla Hirsch)	W	AEW Dark Elevation	4:48
Feb 28	Kayla Sparks, LMK & Paris Van Dale (w/Emi Sakura & Diamante)	W	AEW Dark Elevation	2:27
Mar 8	Skye Blue	W	AEW Dark	2:38
Mar 14	Katalina Perez	W	AEW Dark Elevation	1:20
Mar 21	Robyn Renegade	W	AEW Dark Elevation	1:24

Mar 22	Kaci Lennox	W	AEW Dark	1:19
Mar 25	Madi Wrenkowski	W	AEW Rampage	:38
Mar 29	Kiera Hogan	W	AEW Dark	3:01
Apr 16	Thunder Rosa	L	AEW Battle Of The Belts II	14:10
Apr 25	Anna Jay, Ruby Soho & Skye Blue (w/Emi Sakura & The Bunny)	L	AEW Dark Elevation	6:35
May 2	Anna Jay & Kris Statlander (w/Emi Sakura)	L	AEW Dark Elevation	6:10
May 16	Anna Jay & Yuka Sakazaki (w/Emi Sakura)	L	AEW Dark Elevation	3:32
May 23	Skye Blue & Yuka Sakazaki (w/Emi Sakura)	W	AEW Dark Elevation	6:17
May 28	Riho, Skye Blue & Yuka Sakazaki (w/Diamante & Emi Sakura)	L	AEW Dark	6:11
Jun 6	Miyu Yamashita & Skye Blue (w/Serena Deeb)	W	AEW Dark Elevation	7:40
Jun 13	Max The Impaler	W	AEW Dark Elevation	1:55
Jun 14	Anna Jay, Kris Statlander & Ruby Soho (w/Diamante & Emi Sakura)	L	AEW Dark	7:54
Jun 20	Heidi Howitzer & Max The Impaler (w/Marina Shafir)	W	AEW Dark Elevation	3:25
Jul 1	Toni Storm	L	AEW Rampage	9:42
Jul 6	Thunder Rosa & Toni Storm (w/Marina Shafir)	L	AEW Dynamite	9:07
Jul 18	Brittany Jade & Skye Blue (w/Marina Shafir)	W	AEW Dark Elevation	4:30
Jul 25	Angelica Risk & Shalonce Royal (w/Marina Shafir)	W	AEW Dark Elevation	2:17
Aug 1	Hikaru Shida, Toni Storm & Willow Nightingale (w/Emi Sakura & Marina Shafir)	L	AEW Dark Elevation	8:05
Aug 9	Heather Reckless & Joseline Navarro (w/Marina Shafir)	W	AEW Dark	:46
Aug 15	Hikaru Shida, Thunder Rosa & Toni Storm (w/Emi Sakura & Marina Shafir)	L	AEW Dark Elevation	2:42
Aug 29	Queen Aminata & Skye Blue (w/Marina Shafir)	W	AEW Dark Elevation	3:40
Sep 5	Madison Rayne & Queen Aminata (w/Marina Shafir)	W	AEW Dark Elevation	4:42
Sep 12	JC Storm & Joelle Clift (w/Marina Shafir)	W	AEW Dark Elevation	1:40
Sep 19	B3CCA	W	AEW Dark Elevation	1:04
Oct 10	Jordan Blade	W	AEW Dark Elevation	2:15
Oct 14	Anna Jay	W	AEW Rampage	5:25
Nov 1	Leva Bates	W	AEW Dark	1:00
Nov 11	Kayla Sparks	W	AEW Rampage	:45
Nov 19	Jade Cargill	L	AEW Full Gear '22	8:00
Nov 28	Emi Sakura & Maki Itoh (w/Marina Shafir)	W	AEW Dark Elevation	4:17
Dec 5	Alice Crowley & Kitty LaFleur (w/Marina Shafir)	W	AEW Dark Elevation	3:07
Dec 26	Karizma & Leva Bates (w/Marina Shafir)	W	AEW Dark Elevation	2:54

OBA FEMI

Nov 18	Dante Chen	L	NXT Level Up	5:42
Dec 30	Bronco Nima & Lucien Price (w/Bryson Montana)	L	NXT Level Up	4:38

OCTAGON JR.

Mar 31	Arez, Gino Medina & Mino Abismo Negro (w/Micro Man & Puma King)	W	MLW Fusion	15:42
May 12	King Muertes, El Dragon, El Hijo de LA Park	W	MLW Fusion	9:26
Jun 9	Matt Cross	W	MLW Fusion	9:01

ODINSON

Jan 5	Bestia 666, Mecha Wolf & Homicide (w/Jax Dane & Parrow)	L	NWA Power	6:54
Feb 8	Team War: Jordan Clearwater, Marshe Rockett & Tyrus, Alex Taylor, Jeremiah Plunkett & Rush Freeman, Aron Stevens, JR Kratos & Judais (w/Parrow & Rodney Mack)	W	NWA Power	11:40
Feb 15	Team War: Chris Adonis, Thom Latimer & El Rudo (w/Parrow & Rodney Mack)	L	NWA Power	11:35
Mar 19	Luke Hawx & PJ Hawx (w/Parrow)	L	NWA Crockett Cup '22	9:20
Mar 29	Bestia 666 & Mecha Wolf (w/Parrow)	L	NWA Power	7:17
May 17	Team WarL BLK Jeez, Jordan Clearwater & Marshe Rockett, Alex Taylor, Jeremiah Plunkett & Rush Freeman (w/Parrow & Jax Dane)	W	NWA Power	6:54
Jul 5	Judais, AJ Cazana	W	NWA Power	5:11
Aug 2	Tyrus	L	NWA Power	4:04
Aug 27	Chris Adonis	L	NWA 74th Anniversary Show	7:26
Oct 4	Flip Gordon	W	NWA Power	7:11
Nov 8	Fodder	W	NWA Power	5:16
Nov 12	Thrillbilly Silas	L	NWA Hard Times 3	4:43
Nov 15	Ryan Davidson	W	NWA Power	6:21
Dec 6	Bully Ray	D	NWA Power	10:00

ODYSSEY JONES

Nov 1	Javier Bernal	W	NXT	3:20
Nov 11	Bronco Nima, Lucien Price & Xyon Quinn (w/Edris Enofe & Malik Blade)	W	NXT Level Up	6:41
Dec 9	Damon Kemp	W	NXT Level Up	5:10
Dec 13	Von Wagner	W	NXT	2:54
Dec 27	Jagger Reid, Rip Fowler & Joe Gacy (w/Edris Enofe & Malik Blake)	L	NXT	11:15

OMOS

Jan 3	AJ Styles	W	WWE Monday Night RAW	3:45
Jan 10	Nick Sanders	W	WWE Monday Night RAW	1:35
Jan 17	Reggie	W	WWE Monday Night RAW	:28
Jan 29	Royal Rumble Match	L	WWE Royal Rumble '22	4:24
Feb 14	Handicap Match: Cedric Alexander & Shelton Benjamin	W	WWE Monday Night RAW	1:25
Feb 28	T-Bar	W	WWE Monday Night RAW	:40
Mar 7	Apollo Crews	W	WWE Monday Night RAW	2:40
Mar 14	Commander Azeez	W	WWE Monday Night RAW	2:00
Mar 21	Handicap Match: Apollo Crews & Commander Azeez	W	WWE Monday Night RAW	2:45
Mar 28	Handicap Match: Erik & Ivar	W	WWE Monday Night RAW	:50
Apr 3	Bobby Lashley	L	WWE WrestleMania XXXVIII	6:35

May 8	Bobby Lashley	W	WWE WrestleMania Backlash '22	8:50
May 16	Steel Cage Match: Bobby Lashley	L	WWE Monday Night RAW	7:30
Jun 5	Handicap Match: Bobby Lashley (w/MVP)	L	WWE Hell In A Cell '22	8:25
Jun 6	Cedric Alexander	W	WWE Monday Night RAW	:12
Jun 20	Riddle	W	WWE Monday Night RAW	3:55
Jul 1	Battle Royal	L	WWE SmackDown	14:36
Jul 2	Money In The Bank Ladder Match: Drew McIntyre, Madcap Moss, Theory, Riddle, Sami Zayn, Seth Rollins, Sheamus	L	WWE Money In The Bank '22	25:25
Jul 11	R-Truth, Angelo Dawkins & Montez Ford (w/Jimmy Uso & Jey Uso)	W	WWE Monday Night RAW	11:30
Jul 18	Angelo Dawkins	L	WWE Monday Night RAW	1:20
Jul 18	Angelo Dawkins & Montez Ford (w/MVP)	L	WWE Monday Night RAW	4:50
Aug 4	Ezekiel	W	WWE Main Event	4:06
Aug 8	Handicap Match: Andrea Guercio & Spencer Slade	W	WWE Monday Night RAW	1:40
Sep 12	Handicap Match: Khash Morazzi & Ryan Tombs	W	WWE Monday Night RAW	:40
Sep 26	Handicap Match: Joey Gibson & Greg Lester	W	WWE Monday Night RAW	1:42
Oct 10	Handicap Match: Joseph Torres & Robert Adams	W	WWE Monday Night RAW	1:20
Oct 24	Handicap Match: Chrisifix, Dennis Daniels, Michael Stevens & Sal Rinauro	W	WWE Monday Night RAW	1:40
Nov 5	Braun Strowman	L	WWE Crown Jewel '22	7:20
Nov 21	Johnny Gargano	W	WWE Monday Night RAW	3:10

ORANGE CASSIDY

Jan 11	JD Drake	W	AEW Dark	9:04
Jan 18	Peter Avalon & JD Drake (w/Wheeler Yuta)	W	AEW Dark	7:32
Jan 19	Adam Cole & Dr. Britt Baker D.M.D. (w/Kris Statlander)	L	AEW Dynamite	14:25
Jan 26	Lights Out Match: Adam Cole	W	AEW Dynamite: Beach Break	16:56
Feb 25	Anthony Bowens	W	AEW Rampage	10:15
Mar 1	Aaron Solo & Nick Comoroto (w/Wheeler Yuta)	W	AEW Dark	14:17
Mar 6	Ladder Match: Christian Cage, Keith Lee, Wardlow, Powerhouse Hobbs, Ricky Starks	W	AEW Revolution '22	17:20
Jun 22	Will Ospreay, Kyle Fletcher & Mark Davis (w/Trent Beretta & Rocky Romero)	W	AEW Dynamite	11:37
Jun 26	Will Ospreay	L	AEW x NJPW Forbidden Door	16:43
Jun 29	Ethan Page	W	AEW Dynamite: Blood & Guts	10:57
Jul 1	Royal Rampage Match	L	AEW Rampage	22:41
Jul 8	Tony Nese	W	AEW Rampage	15:01
Jul 13	Warlow	L	AEW Dynamite: Fyter Fest	11:36
Jul 29	Jay Lethal, Satnam Singh & Sonjay Dutt (w/Chuck Taylor & Trent Beretta)	W	AEW Rampage	7:29
Aug 3	Jay Lethal	L	AEW Dynamite	12:18
Aug 9	Anthony Henry	W	AEW Dark	6:04
Aug 12	Ari Daivari	W	AEW Rampage: Quake By The Lake	10:00
Aug 19	Ari Daivari, Parker Boudreaux & Slim J (w/Trent Beretta & Chuck Taylor)	W	AEW Rampage	11:00
Sep 2	Hangman Page, John Silver & Alex Reynolds (w/Trent Beretta & Chuck Taylor)	L	AEW Rampage	11:12
Sep 3	Angelico, The Butcher & The Blade (w/Trent Beretta & Chuck Taylor)	W	AEW Dark Elevation	8:13
Sep 7	Pac, Penta El Zero M & Rey Fenix (w/Trent Beretta & Chuck Taylor)	L	AEW Dynamite	12:58
Sep 21	Pac	L	AEW Dynamite: Grand Slam	12:34
Oct 12	Pac	W	AEW Dynamite	11:18
Oct 18	Jessie V, Kobe Durst & Steven Mainz (w/Trent Beretta & Chuck Taylor)	W	AEW Dark	2:44
Oct 18	Pac, Penta El Zero M & Rey Fenix (w/Trent Beretta & Chuck Taylor)	L	AEW Dynamite: Title Tuesday	11:45
Oct 21	Rush, Ten	W	AEW Rampage	11:53
Oct 31	Anthony Young, Patton & Victor Andrews (w/Trent Beretta & Chuck Taylor)	W	AEW Dark Elevation	3:30
Nov 1	Tony Deppen, Ari Daivari & Sonny Kiss (w/Trent Beretta & Chuck Taylor)	W	AEW Dark	6:04
Nov 2	Luchasaurus, Rey Fenix	W	AEW Dynamite	9:59
Nov 4	Katsuyori Shibata	W	AEW Rampage	14:00
Nov 11	Lee Johnson	W	AEW Rampage	9:12
Nov 19	QT Marshall, Aaron Solo, Lee Johnson, Nick Comoroto & Cole Karter (w/Chuck Taylor, Trent Beretta, Rocky Romero & Danhausen)	W	AEW Full Gear Buy-In	11:55
Nov 21	Aaron Solo, Cole Karter & Lee Johnson (w/Trent Beretta & Chuck Taylor)	W	AEW Dark Elevation	3:38
Nov 23	Jake Hager	W	AEW Dynamite: Thanksgiving Eve	8:38
Dec 2	Lumberjack Match: QT Marshall	W	AEW Rampage	9:31
Dec 7	Dynamite Diamond Battle Royale	L	AEW Dynamite	13:10
Dec 9	Trent Seven	W	AEW Rampage	11:55
Dec 16	Trent Seven, Kip Sabian, The Butcher & The Blade (w/Dustin Rhodes, Trent Beretta & Chuck Taylor)	W	AEW Rampage	10:42
Dec 23	$300,000 Three Kings Christmas Casino Trios Royale (w/Chuck Taylor & Trent Beretta)	L	AEW Rampage	22:01
Dec 30	Trent Beretta	W	AEW Rampage	14:36

ORO MENSA (AS OLIVER CARTER UNTIL SEPTEMBER 20)

Jan 6	Primate & T-Bone (w/Ashton Smith)	W	NXT UK	9:37
Feb 3	Dave Mastiff & Jack Starz (w/Ashton Smith)	W	NXT UK	12:31
Feb 24	Trent Seven & Tyler Bate (w/Ashton Smith)	L	NXT UK	13:02
Mar 17	Tyler Bate	W	NXT UK	10:07
Apr 21	2/3 Falls: Trent Seven & Tyler Bate (w/Ashton Smith)	L	NXT UK	21:38
May 12	Joe Coffey & Mark Coffey (w/Ashton Smith)	W	NXT UK	10:24
Jun 2	Trent Seven & Tyler Bate, Charlie Dempsey & Rohan Raja (w/Ashton Smith)	W	NXT UK	14:17
Aug 4	Rohan Raja	W	NXT UK	5:25
Aug 11	Charlie Dempsey	W	NXT UK	9:08
Aug 25	Trent Seven	L	NXT UK	9:15
Sep 20	Grayson Waller	W	NXT	5:23
Oct 4	Carmelo Hayes	L	NXT	5:35
Oct 18	Carmelo Hayes & Trick Williams (w/Wes Lee)	L	NXT	2:43
Oct 22	Ladder Match: Carmelo Hayes, Wes Lee, Von Wagner, Nathan Frazer	L	NXT Halloween Havoc '22	22:25

Date	Opponent/Match	W/L	Show	Time
Nov 4	Xyon Quinn	W	NXT Level Up	6:08
Nov 18	Channing Lorenzo	L	NXT Level Up	5:41
Dec 2	Myles Borne	W	NXT Level Up	6:11
Dec 30	Javier Bernal	W	NXT Level Up	6:18

ORTIZ

Date	Opponent/Match	W/L	Show	Time
Jan 7	No DQ, No Holds Barred: Daniel Garcia, Matt Lee & Jeff Parker (w/Eddie Kingston & Santana)	W	AEW Rampage	13:50
Jan 14	Serpentico	W	AEW Dark	4:07
Jan 24	Breaux Keller & Goldy (w/Santana)	W	AEW Dark Elevation	3:10
Jan 26	Daniel Garcia, Matt Lee & Jeff Parker (w/Chris Jericho & Santana)	W	AEW Dynamite: Beach Break	8:52
Feb 16	Chris Jericho & Jake Hager (w/Santana)	W	AEW Dynamite	10:43
Feb 23	Tag Team Battle Royal (w/Santana)	L	AEW Dynamite	5:28
Mar 2	Casino Battle Royale (w/Santana)	L	AEW Dynamite	22:27
Apr 13	Chris Jericho, Jake Hager & Daniel Garcia (w/Eddie Kingston & Santana)	L	AEW Dynamite	11:46
May 29	Anarchy In The Arena: Chris Jericho, Daniel Garcia, Jake Hager, Angelo Parker & Matt Menard (w/Jon Moxley, Eddie Kingston, Santana & Bryan Danielson)	L	AEW Double Or Nothing '22	22:45
Jun 13	Anaya	W	AEW Dark Elevation	1:14
Jun 15	Hair vs. Hair: Chris Jericho	L	AEW Dynamite: Road Rager	11:06
Jun 29	Blood & Guts: Chris Jericho, Daniel Garcia, Jake Hager, Matt Menard, Angelo Parker & Sammy Guevara (w/Jon Moxley, Claudio Castagnoli, Wheeler Yuta, Eddie Kingston & Santana)	W	AEW Dynamite: Blood & Guts	46:45
Aug 22	Mickey Midas & Queen Aminata (w/Ruby Soho)	W	AEW Dark Elevation	1:50
Aug 26	Sammy Guevara & Tay Melo (w/Ruby Soho)	L	AEW Rampage	8:35
Sep 2	Sammy Guevara & Tay Melo (w/Ruby Soho)	W	AEW Rampage	7:40
Sep 3	Baliyan Akki & Emi Sakura (w/Ruby Soho)	W	AEW Dark Elevation	2:20
Sep 4	Sammy Guevara & Tay Melo (w/Ruby Soho)	L	AEW All Out Buy-In	6:00
Sep 26	Serpentico	W	AEW Dark Elevation	3:22
Oct 18	Jake O'Reilly & Mo Jabari (w/Eddie Kingston)	W	AEW Dark	3:56
Oct 24	Russ Myers & T-Money (w/Eddie Kingston)	W	AEW Dark Elevation	1:54
Oct 31	Breaux Keller & Myles Hawkins (w/Eddie Kingston)	W	AEW Dark Elevation	1:30
Nov 7	Joe Keys & Myles Hawkins (w/Eddie Kingston)	W	AEW Dark Elevation	3:25
Nov 8	AR Fox & Caleb Konley (w/Eddie Kingston)	W	AEW Dark	1:49
Nov 18	Jun Akiyama & Konosuke Takeshita (w/Eddie Kingston)	L	AEW Rampage	12:17
Nov 28	Aaron Solo & Nick Comoroto (w/Eddie Kingston)	W	AEW Dark Elevation	4:55
Dec 13	Jeeves Kay & Slim J (w/Eddie Kingston)	W	AEW Dark	6:59
Dec 19	Hagane Shinno & Steven Andrews (w/Eddie Kingston)	W	AEW Dark Elevation	3:50

OTIS

Date	Opponent/Match	W/L	Show	Time
Jan 3	Randy Orton & Riddle (w/Chad Gable)	W	WWE Monday Night RAW	2:40
Jan 10	Randy Orton & Riddle (w/Chad Gable)	W	WWE Monday Night RAW	8:57
Jan 29	Royal Rumble Match	L	WWE Royal Rumble '22	8:52
Jan 31	Riddle	L	WWE Monday Night RAW	7:25
Feb 7	Angelo Dawkins & Montez Ford (w/Chad Gable)	W	WWE Monday Night RAW	5:37
Feb 14	Rey Mysterio & Dominik Mysterio (w/Chad Gable)	L	WWE Monday Night RAW	10:34
Feb 21	Angelo Dawkins & Montez Ford (w/Chad Gable)	W	WWE Monday Night RAW	9:05
Feb 28	Seth Rollins & Kevin Owens (w/Chad Gable)	L	WWE Monday Night RAW	12:50
Mar 7	No DQ: Randy Orton & Riddle, Seth Rollins & Kevin Owens (w/Chad Gable)	L	WWE Monday Night RAW	27:05
Mar 21	Randy Orton & Riddle (w/Chad Gable)	L	WWE Monday Night RAW	7:45
Apr 3	Randy Orton & Riddle, Angelo Dawkins & Montez Ford (w/Chad Gable)	L	WWE WrestleMania XXXVIII	11:30
Apr 4	Angelo Dawkins & Montez Ford (w/Chad Gable)	L	WWE Monday Night RAW	8:25
Apr 11	Randy Orton & Riddle (w/Chad Gable)	L	WWE Monday Night RAW	8:30
May 2	Ezekiel, Angelo Dawkins & Montez Ford (w/Kevin Owens & Chad Gable)	W	WWE Monday Night RAW	9:45
May 30	Ezekiel, Rey Mysterio & Dominik Mysterio (w/Kevin Owens & Chad Gable)	L	WWE Monday Night RAW	8:30
Jun 6	Ezekiel	W	WWE Monday Night RAW	2:20
Jun 20	Gauntlet Match: Bobby Lashley, Chad Gable, Theory	L	WWE Monday Night RAW	16:45
Jun 27	Handicap Match: Bobby Lashley (w/Chad Gable)	L	WWE Monday Night RAW	8:15
Jul 4	Bobby Lashley, Angelo Dawkins & Montez Ford (w/Theory & Chad Gable)	L	WWE Monday Night RAW	10:05
Jul 21	Cedric Alexander & Mustafa Ali (w/Chad Gable)	W	WWE Main Event	8:49
Jul 25	AJ Styles & Dolph Ziggler (w/Chad Gable)	L	WWE Monday Night RAW	6:30
Aug 18	Angelo Dawkins & Montez Ford (w/Chad Gable)	L	WWE Main Event	6:49
Aug 29	Angelo Dawkins & Montez Ford (w/Chad Gable)	L	WWE Monday Night RAW	16:04
Sep 3	Madcap Moss, Angelo Dawkins & Montez Ford (w/Austin Theory & Chad Gable)	L	WWE Clash At The Castle Kickoff	6:29
Sep 5	Angel & Humberto, Xavier Woods & Kofi Kingston, Angelo Dawkins & Montez Ford (w/Chad Gable)	D	WWE Monday Night RAW	14:30
Sep 22	Mustafa Ali & Shelton Benjamin (w/Otis)	W	WWE Main Event	9:52
Sep 23	Braun Strowman	L	WWE SmackDown	5:45
Sep 26	Kevin Owens & Johnny Gargano (w/Chad Gable)	L	WWE Monday Night RAW	13:09
Sep 30	Drew McIntyre, Kevin Owens & Johnny Gargano (w/Austin Theory & Chad Gable)	L	WWE SmackDown	13:38
Oct 3	Johnny Gargano	W	WWE Monday Night RAW	5:40
Oct 17	Luke Gallows & Karl Anderson (w/Chad Gable)	L	WWE Monday Night RAW	8:20
Oct 31	Trick Or Street Fight: Matt Riddle	L	WWE Monday Night RAW	7:39
Nov 7	Elias	W	WWE Monday Night RAW	3:00
Nov 21	Elias & Matt Riddle (w/Chad Gable)	L	WWE Monday Night RAW	16:05
Nov 28	Angelo Dawkins & Montez Ford (w/Chad Gable)	L	WWE Monday Night RAW	12:00
Dec 5	AJ Styles, Luke Gallows & Karl Anderson (w/Baron Corbin & Chad Gable)	L	WWE Monday Night RAW	14:30
Dec 19	Luke Gallows & Karl Anderson (w/Chad Gable)	L	WWE Monday Night RAW	9:05

PAC

Feb 2	Malakai Black & Brody King (w/Penta El Zero M)	L	AEW Dynamite	10:23
Feb 23	Malakai Black & Brody King (w/Penta Oscuro)	W	AEW Dynamite	7:31
Mar 6	Malakai Black, Brody King & Buddy Matthews (w/Penta Oscuro & Erick Redbeard)	L	AEW Revolution Buy-In	17:20
Mar 9	Wheeler Yuta	W	AEW Dynamite	5:40
May 13	Marq Quen, The Butcher & The Blade (w/Penta El Zero M & Rey Fenix)	W	AEW Rampage	10:22
May 28	Aaron Solo, Nick Comoroto & QT Marshall (w/Penta El Zero M & Rey Fenix)	W	AEW Dark	10:32
May 29	Malakai Black, Buddy Matthews & Brody King (w/Penta Oscuro & Rey Fenix)	L	AEW Double Or Nothing '22	15:35
Jun 6	Cezar Bononi, Peter Avalon & Ryan Nemeth (w/Penta Oscuro & Rey Fenix)	W	AEW Dark Elevation	5:04
Jun 8	Buddy Matthews	W	AEW Dynamite	10:46
Jun 26	Clark Connors, Miro, Malakai Black	W	AEW x NJPW Forbidden Door	15:10
Jul 12	Shota Umino	W	AEW Dark	18:43
Jul 26	LJ Cleary	W	AEW Dark	15:15
Aug 2	Connor Mills	W	AEW Dark	18:16
Aug 22	Dean Alexander, Jake Manning & Rosario Grillo (w/Penta Oscuro & Rey Fenix)	W	AEW Dark Elevation	2:36
Aug 24	Will Ospreay, Kyle Fletcher & Mark Davis (w/Penta El Zero M & Rey Fenix)	L	AEW Dynamite	25:18
Sep 4	Kip Sabian	W	AEW All Out Buy-In	10:00
Sep 7	Orange Cassidy, Chuck Taylor & Trent Beretta (w/Penta El Zero M & Rey Fenix)	W	AEW Dynamite	12:58
Sep 21	Orange Cassidy	W	AEW Dynamite: Grand Slam	12:34
Oct 7	Alex Reynolds, John Silver & Ten (w/Penta El Zero M & Rey Fenix)	W	AEW Rampage	21:01
Oct 7	Trent Beretta	W	AEW Battle Of The Belts IV	14:25
Oct 12	Orange Cassidy	L	AEW Dynamite	11:18
Oct 18	Orange Cassidy, Chuck Taylor & Trent Beretta (w/Penta El Zero M & Rey Fenix)	W	AEW Dynamite: Title Tuesday	11:45
Nov 16	AR Fox, Dante Martin & Darius Martin (w/Penta El Zero M & Rey Fenix)	W	AEW Dynamite	11:33
Nov 19	Kenny Omega, Matt Jackson & Nick Jackson (w/Penta El Zero M & Rey Fenix)	W	AEW Full Gear '22	18:40
Nov 23	Kenny Omega, Matt Jackson & Nick Jackson (w/Penta El Zero M & Rey Fenix)	W	AEW Dynamite: Thanksgiving Eve	14:49
Nov 30	Kenny Omega, Matt Jackson & Nick Jackson (w/Penta El Zero M & Rey Fenix)	L	AEW Dynamite	17:20
Dec 14	Kenny Omega, Matt Jackson & Nick Jackson (w/Penta El Zero M & Rey Fenix)	W	AEW Dynamite: Winter Is Coming	14:59
Dec 21	No DQ: Kenny Omega, Matt Jackson & Nick Jackson (w/Penta El Zero M & Rey Fenix)	L	AEW Dynamite: Holiday Bash	13:41
Dec 28	Falls Count Anywhere: Kenny Omega, Matt Jackson & Nick Jackson (w/Penta El Zero M & Rey Fenix)	L	AEW Dynamite	17:16

PAIGE VANZANT

May 29	Frankie Kazarian, Sammy Guevara & Tay Conti (w/Scorpio Sky & Ethan Page)	W	AEW Double Or Nothing '22	12:30

PAOLA BLAZE

Jan 5	Natalia Markova	L	NWA Power	3:57
Mar 22	Allysin Kay & Marti Belle (w/Jennacide)	L	NWA Power	7:24
May 10	Kamille	L	NWA Power	7:48
Aug 16	Angelina Love & Chelsea Green (w/Rylee Rockett)	L	NWA Power	4:00

PARKER BOUDREAUX (AS HARLAND UNTIL AUGUST 2)

Jan 11	Malik Blade & Edris Enofe (w/Joe Gacy)	L	NXT 2.0	3:14
Feb 18	Javier Bernal	W	NXT Level Up	1:55
Feb 25	Ikemen Jiro & Kushida (w/Joe Gacy)	W	NXT Level Up	6:55
Mar 1	Draco Anthony	W	NXT 2.0	2:25
Aug 2	Serpentico	W	AEW Dark	1:47
Aug 8	Casey Carrington	W	AEW Dark Elevation	1:37
Aug 9	Sonny Kiss, Xavier Walker & Zack Clayton (w/Ari Daivari & Slim J)	W	AEW Dark	3:10
Aug 12	Sonny Kiss	W	AEW Rampage: Quake By The Lake	1:10
Aug 19	Orange Cassidy, Trent Beretta & Chuck Taylor (w/Ari Daivari & Slim J)	L	AEW Rampage	11:00
Aug 23	Cash Flo, Omar Amir & Ryan Howe (w/Ari Daivari & Slim J)	W	AEW Dark	2:30
Aug 30	Hermano, Logan Cruz & Tyshaun Perez (w/Ari Daivari & Slim J)	W	AEW Dark	3:35
Sep 20	GKM, Marcus Kross & Mike Magnum (w/Ari Daivari & Slim J)	W	AEW Dark	4:08
Oct 4	Terry Kid	W	AEW Dark	:42
Dec 20	Gus De La Vega	W	AEW Dark	1:21

PARROW

Jan 5	Bestia 666, Mecha Wolf & Homicide (w/Jax Dane & Odinson)	L	NWA Power	6:54
Feb 8	Team War: Jordan Clearwater, Marshe Rockett & Tyrus, Alex Taylor, Jeremiah Plunkett & Rush Freeman, Aaron Stevens, JR Kratos & Judais (w/Odinson & Rodney Mack)	W	NWA Power	11:40
Feb 15	Team War: Chris Adonis, Thom Latimer & El Rudo (w/Odinson & Rodney Mack)	L	NWA Power	11:35
Mar 19	Luke Hawx & PJ Hawx (w/Odinson)	L	NWA Crockett Cup '22	9:20
Mar 29	Bestia 666 & Mecha Wolf (w/Odinson)	L	NWA Power	7:17
May 17	Team War: BLK Jeez, Jordan Clearwater & Marshe Rockett, Alex Taylor, Jeremiah Plunkett & Rush Freeman (w/Jax Dane & Odinson)	W	NWA Power	6:54

PAT MCAFEE

Apr 3	Austin Theory	W	WWE WrestleMania XXXVIII	9:40
Apr 3	Vince McMahon	L	WWE WrestleMania XXXVIII	3:45
Jul 30	Happy Corbin	W	WWE SummerSlam '22	10:40

PAUL WIGHT

Apr 4	Austin Green	W	AEW Dark Elevation	2:04

PCO

Jan 27	Chris Sabin	W	IMPACT Wrestling	15:48
Apr 1	Josh Alexander & Jonah (w/Moose)	L	IMPACT Multiverse Of Matches	12:47
Apr 14	Jonah	L	IMPACT Wrestling	14:00
May 5	Monster's Ball Match: Jonah	W	IMPACT Wrestling	15:09
May 12	Gauntlet For The Gold	L	IMPACT Wrestling	39:00
Jun 2	Moose & Steve Maclin (w/W. Morrissey)	L	IMPACT Wrestling	10:51
Jun 9	Steve Maclin	L	IMPACT Wrestling	8:55
Jun 19	Alex Shelley, Chris Sabin, Davey Richards, Frankie Kazarian & Magnus (w/Eddie Edwards, Matt Taven, Mike Bennett & Vincent)	L	IMPACT Slammiversary XX	18:45
Jun 30	Luke Gallows & Karl Anderson (w/Vincent)	L	IMPACT Wrestling	5:19
Jul 7	Black Taurus	W	IMPACT Wrestling	6:04
Aug 4	Derby City Street Fight: Luke Gallows	W	IMPACT Wrestling	11:59
Sep 22	Street Fight: Heath	L	IMPACT Wrestling	9:12
Sep 29	Heath & Rich Swann (w/Vincent)	L	IMPACT Wrestling	4:32
Oct 7	Call Your Shot Gauntlet	L	IMPACT Bound For Glory '22	29:18

PENELOPE FORD

Jan 14	Red Velvet, Leyla Hirsch & Kris Statlander (w/The Bunny & Nyla Rose)	W	AEW Rampage	8:12
Feb 1	Angelica Risk	W	AEW Dark	4:02
Aug 15	Heather Reckless	W	AEW Dark Elevation	2:46
Aug 19	Athena	L	AEW Rampage	4:00
Sep 7	Toni Storm	L	AEW Dynamite	5:50
Sep 13	Alice Crowley	W	AEW Dark	3:20
Sep 16	Willow Nightingale	W	AEW Rampage	7:28
Sep 26	Shawn Dean & Skye Blue (w/Kip Sabian)	W	AEW Dark Elevation	5:16
Oct 3	Gia Scott & LSG (w/Kip Sabian)	W	AEW Dark Elevation	3:20
Oct 5	Toni Storm, Athena & Willow Nightingale (w/Jamie Hayter & Serena Deeb)	L	AEW Dynamite: Anniversary	9:29
Oct 11	Brittany Blake, Jordan Blade & Trish Adora (w/Jamie Hayter & Serena Deeb)	W	AEW Dark	4:32
Oct 17	Jeremy Prophet & Jessika Neri (w/Kip Sabian)	W	AEW Dark Elevation	3:58

PENTA EL ZERO M

Jan 5	Jungle Boy & Luchasaurus (w/Rey Fenix)	L	AEW Dynamite	14:03
Jan 12	Matt Hardy	W	AEW Dynamite	8:51
Jan 25	Wheeler Yuta	W	AEW Dark	9:43
Jan 31	Serpentico	W	AEW Dark Elevation	5:30
Feb 2	Malakai Black & Brody King (w/Pac)	L	AEW Dynamite	10:23
Feb 19	Dralistico	W	AAA Rey De Reyes '22	13:19
Feb 23	Malakai Black & Brody King (w/Pac)	W	AEW Dynamite	7:31
Mar 6	Malakai Black, Brody King & Buddy Matthews (w/Pac & Erick Redbeard)	L	AEW Revolution Buy-In	17:20
Mar 28	JPH	W	AEW Dark Elevation	1:55
Apr 11	Jora Johl	W	AEW Dark Elevation	3:50
Apr 13	CM Punk	L	AEW Dynamite	13:38
Apr 25	Max Caster	W	AEW Dark Elevation	4:45
Apr 26	QT Marshall	W	AEW Dark	7:15
Apr 30	Ultimo Dragon	L	AAA TripleMania XXX: Monterrey	9:19
May 13	Marq Quen, The Butcher & The Blade (w/Pac & Rey Fenix)	W	AEW Rampage	10:22
May 28	Aaron Solo, Nick Comoroto & QT Marshall (w/Pac & Rey Fenix)	W	AEW Dark	10:32
May 29	Malakai Black, Buddy Matthews & Brody King (w/Pac & Rey Fenix)	L	AEW Double Or Nothing '22	15:35
Jun 3	Matt Jackson & Nick Jackson (w/Rey Fenix)	L	AEW Rampage	14:53
Jun 18	Blue Demon Jr.	L	AAA TripleMania XXX: Tijuana	11:52
Jun 22	Malakai Black	L	AEW Dynamite	9:56
Jul 1	Royal Rampage Match	L	AEW Rampage	22:41
Jul 6	Cezar Bononi, Peter Avalon & Ryan Nemeth (w/Pac & Rey Fenix)	W	AEW Dark Elevation	5:04
Jul 6	Rush	L	AEW Dynamite	11:04
Jul 15	Marq Quen & Isiah Kassidy (w/Rey Fenix)	W	AEW Rampage	11:16
Aug 8	Peter Avalon & Ryan Nemeth (w/Rey Fenix)	W	AEW Dark Elevation	4:50
Aug 10	Tornado Tag: Andrade El Idolo & Rush (w/Rey Fenix)	L	AEW Dynamite: Quake By The Lake	13:45
Aug 22	Dean Alexander, Jake Manning & Rosario Grillo (w/Pac & Rey Fenix)	W	AEW Dark Elevation	2:36
Aug 24	Will Ospreay, Kyle Fletcher & Mark Davis (w/Pac & Rey Fenix)	L	AEW Dynamite	25:18
Sep 4	Casino Ladder Match: MJF, Claudio Castagnoli, Wheeler Yuta, Rey Fenix, Rush, Andrade El Idolo, Dante Martin	L	AEW All Out '22	14:15
Sep 7	Orange Cassidy, Chuck Taylor & Trent Beretta (w/Pac & Rey Fenix)	W	AEW Dynamite	12:58
Sep 14	Swerve Strickland & Keith Lee (w/Rey Fenix)	L	AEW Dynamite	8:15
Sep 23	Golden Ticket Battle Royale	L	AEW Rampage: Grand Slam	12:16
Oct 3	Dante Martin & Tony Deppen (w/Rey Fenix)	W	AEW Dark Elevation	6:20
Oct 7	Alex Reynolds, John Silver & Ten (w/Pac & Rey Fenix)	W	AEW Rampage	21:01
Oct 15	Mask vs. Mask: Villano IV	W	AAA TripleMania XXX: Mexico City	25:30
Oct 18	Orange Cassidy, Chuck Taylor & Trent Beretta (w/Pac & Rey Fenix)	W	AEW Dynamite: Title Tuesday	11:45
Oct 25	Anthony Henry & JD Drake (w/Rey Fenix)	W	AEW Dark	2:55
Oct 26	Jon Moxley	L	AEW Dynamite	12:21
Nov 16	AR Fox, Dante Martin & Darius Martin (w/Pac & Rey Fenix)	W	AEW Dynamite	11:33

Nov 19	Kenny Omega, Matt Jackson & Nick Jackson (w/Pac & Rey Fenix)	W	AEW Full Gear '22	18:40
Nov 23	Kenny Omega, Matt Jackson & Nick Jackson (w/Pac & Rey Fenix)	W	AEW Dynamite: Thanksgiving Eve	14:49
Nov 30	Kenny Omega, Matt Jackson & Nick Jackson (w/Pac & Rey Fenix)	L	AEW Dynamite	17:20
Dec 14	Kenny Omega, Matt Jackson & Nick Jackson (w/Pac & Rey Fenix)	W	AEW Dynamite: Winter Is Coming	14:59
Dec 21	No DQ: Kenny Omega, Matt Jackson & Nick Jackson (w/Pac & Rey Fenix)	L	AEW Dynamite: Holiday Bash	13:41
Dec 28	Falls Count Anywhere Kenny Omega, Matt Jackson & Nick Jackson (w/Pac & Rey Fenix)	L	AEW Dynamite	17:16

PERSIA PIROTTA

Jan 11	Kacy Katanzaro, Kayden Carter & Amari Miller (w/Wendy Choo & Indi Hartwell)	W	NXT 2.0	3:40
Jan 25	Mandy Rose, Gigi Dolin & Jacy Jayne (w/Kay Lee Ray & Indi Hartwell)	W	NXT 2.0	10:25
Feb 15	Gigi Dolin & Jacy Jayne (w/Indi Hartwell)	L	NXT 2.0: Vengeance Day '22	7:54
Mar 1	Wendy Choo & Dakota Kai (w/Indi Hartwell)	L	NXT 2.0	5:21
Mar 15	Indi Hartwell	L	NXT 2.0	2:24

PETER AVALON

Jan 18	Orange Cassidy & Wheeler Yuta (w/JD Drake)	L	AEW Dark	7:32
Feb 21	Brock Anderson, Frankie Kazarian, Jay Lethal, Lee Johnson & Matt Sydal (w/Luther, Serpentico, Cezar Bononi & JD Drake)	L	AEW Dark Elevation	6:06
Feb 22	Caleb Teninity, Karam, Rohit Raju & Sotheara Chhun (w/Cezar Bononi, JD Drake & Ryan Nemeth)	W	AEW Dark	2:29
Mar 2	Casino Battle Royale (w/Ryan Nemeth)	L	AEW Dynamite	18:58
Mar 8	Dante Martin & Darius Martin (w/Ryan Nemeth)	L	AEW Dark	6:25
May 9	Sonny Kiss	L	AEW Dark Elevation	4:12
May 24	Rocky Romero & Trent Beretta (w/Ryan Nemeth)	L	AEW Dark	7:02
May 31	John Silver, Evil Uno & Ten (w/Ryan Nemeth & Serpentico)	L	AEW Dark	5:37
Jun 6	Pac, Penta Oscuro & Rey Fenix (w/Cezar Bononi & Ryan Nemeth)	L	AEW Dark Elevation	5:04
Jun 21	John Silver & Alex Reynolds (w/Cezar Bononi)	L	AEW Dark	5:01
Jul 5	John Silver, Alex Reynolds, Evil Uno & Ten (w/Ryan Nemeth, Cezar Bononi & JD Drake)	L	AEW Dark	7:22
Jul 26	Dante Martin	L	AEW Dark	5:08
Aug 2	Anthony Bowens & Max Caster (w/Ryan Nemeth)	L	AEW Dark	5:00
Aug 8	Penta El Zero M & Rey Fenix (w/Ryan Nemeth)	L	AEW Dark Elevation	4:50
Aug 9	Evil Uno & Ten (w/JD Drake)	L	AEW Dark	4:15
Aug 23	Adrian Alanis & Liam Gray (w/Ryan Nemeth)	W	AEW Dark	2:40
Sep 13	Danhausen	L	AEW Dark	2:15
Sep 17	Adrian Quest	W	NJPW Strong	8:52
Nov 8	Brandon Cutler	W	AEW Dark	6:37
Nov 19	Keita Murray	W	NJPW Strong	8:58
Nov 29	Matt Hardy, Isiah Kassidy & Marq Quen (w/Cezar Bononi & Ryan Nemeth)	L	AEW Dark	7:16
Dec 19	Ethan Page, Isiah Kassidy, Konosuke Takeshita, Matt Hardy, Dante Martin & Darius Martin (w/Jeeves Jay, Slim J, Sonny Kiss, Cezar Bononi & Ryan Nemeth)	L	AEW Dark Elevation	7:45
Dec 20	Jake St. Patrick & Sage Scott (w/Ryan Nemeth)	W	AEW Dark	3:27

PJ BLACK

Nov 3	Yuya Uemura	W	IMPACT Before The Impact	8:33
Nov 17	Black Taurus	L	IMPACT Wrestling	6:18

PJ HAWX

Jan 18	Jordan Clearwater & Marshe Rockett (w/Luke Hawx)	W	NWA Power	6:32
Mar 3	Odinson & Parrow (w/Luke Hawx)	W	NWA Crockett Cup '22	9:20
Mar 3	Handicap Match: Bestia 666 & Mecha Wolf	L	NWA Crockett Cup '22	7:25
Jun 11	Homicide	L	NWA Alwayz Ready '22	10:50
Jun 28	Gustavo Aguilar, Sal The Pal	W	NWA Power	4:00
Aug 23	Dirty Dango & JTG, Gustavo Aguilar & Rhett Titus (w/Luke Hawx)	W	NWA Power	5:56
Aug 27	Bestia 666 & Mecha Wolf (w/Luke Hawx)	L	NWA 74th Anniversary Show	13:10
Aug 28	Tag Team Battle Royal (w/Luke Hawx)	L	NWA 74th Anniversary Show	14:07
Nov 1	Dirty Dango & JTG (w/Luke Hawx)	W	NWA Power	6:22
Nov 12	Bestia 666 & Mecha Wolf (w/Luke Hawx)	L	NWA Hard Times 3	10:48
Dec 6	Damage & Rush Freeman (w/Judais)	W	NWA Power	6:42
Dec 20	Alex Taylor	L	NWA Power	7:11

POWERHOUSE HOBBS

Jan 4	Colt Cabana	W	AEW Dark	4:46
Jan 5	Dante Martin	L	AEW Dynamite	10:07
Jan 10	Ryan Clancy	W	AEW Dark Elevation	1:23
Jan 11	Alexander Moss	W	AEW Dark	:24
Jan 24	Lee Moriarty & Matt Sydal (w/Ricky Starks)	W	AEW Dark Elevation	5:21
Feb 8	Gus De La Vega	W	AEW Dark	2:01
Feb 10	Lee Johnson	W	AEW Dark	7:08
Feb 14	Matt Sydal	W	AEW Dark Elevation	5:19
Feb 18	Dante Martin	W	AEW Rampage: Slam Dunk	9:29
Mar 6	Ladder Match: Christian Cage, Keith Lee, Orange Cassidy, Wardlow, Ricky Starks	W	AEW Revolution '22	17:20
Mar 22	Fuego Del Sol	W	AEW Dark	4:08
Apr 1	Keith Lee	L	AEW Rampage	10:53
Apr 12	Axton Ray	W	AEW Dark	1:17
Apr 13	Keith Lee & Swerve Strickland (w/Ricky Starks)	W	AEW Dynamite	12:32
Apr 19	Evil Uno & Stu Grayson (w/Ricky Starks)	W	AEW Dark	8:48

Date	Opponent(s)	Result	Show	Time
May 3	Jay Lucas & Terry Yaki (w/Ricky Starks)	W	AEW Dark	3:55
May 29	Jungle Boy & Luchasaurus, Keith Lee & Swerve Strickland (w/Ricky Starks)	L	AEW Double Or Nothing '22	17:15
Jun 3	Jordan Cruz & Ju Dizz (w/Ricky Starks)	W	AEW Rampage	:47
Jun 8	Casino Battle Royale	L	AEW Dynamite	24:59
Jun 27	Joey Jett & Jordan Chaos (w/Ricky Starks)	W	AEW Dark Elevation	3:28
Jul 1	Royal Rampage Match	L	AEW Rampage	22:41
Jul 13	Keith Lee & Swerve Strickland, Matt Jackson & Nick Jackson (w/Ricky Starks)	L	AEW Dynamite: Fyter Fest	18:14
Aug 3	Ren Jones	W	AEW Dynamite	:53
Aug 16	Blake Christian	W	AEW Dark	4:45
Aug 26	Ashton Day	W	AEW Rampage	1:02
Sep 4	Ricky Starks	W	AEW All Out '22	5:05
Sep 14	Matt DiMartino	W	AEW Dynamite	:29
Sep 23	Lights Out Match: Ricky Starks	L	AEW Rampage: Grand Slam	11:52
Nov 8	Rico Gonzalez	W	AEW Dark	:54
Nov 19	Wardlow, Samoa Joe	L	AEW Full Gear '22	9:55

PRESTON VANCE (AS TEN UNTIL DECEMBER 23)

Date	Opponent(s)	Result	Show	Time
Jan 10	Isiah Kassidy, Marq Quen & The Blade (w/John Silver & Alex Reynolds)	W	AEW Dark Elevation	4:01
Jan 11	Matt Hardy, Serpentico & Isiah Kassidy (w/Hangman Page & Alan Angels)	W	AEW Dark	14:27
Jan 25	Anthony Bowens, Max Caster, Austin Gunn & Billy Gunn (w/Alan Angels, Alex Reynolds & Evil Uno)	L	AEW Dark	6:15
Feb 1	Ari Daivari & Invictus Khash (w/Alan Angels)	W	AEW Dark	7:44
Feb 15	Luther & Serpentico (w/Alan Angels)	W	AEW Dark	8:16
Feb 18	Adam Cole	L	AEW Rampage	9:52
Feb 22	Ben Bishop	W	AEW Dark	2:49
Feb 23	Ricky Starks	L	AEW Dynamite	5:56
Mar 2	Casino Battle Royale (w/Alan Angels)	L	AEW Dynamite	18:25
Mar 15	Aaron Solo	W	AEW Dark	5:41
Mar 25	Kyle O'Reilly & Bobby Fish (w/Alan Angels)	L	AEW Rampage	7:00
Mar 29	Brandon Bullock, Foxx Vinyer & Jameson Ryan (w/John Silver & Alex Reynolds)	W	AEW Dark	3:20
Apr 5	Aaron Solo & Nick Comoroto (w/Alan Angels)	W	AEW Dark	8:08
Apr 11	Luther, Serpentico, Austin Gunn, Colten Gunn & Billy Gunn (w/John Silver, Alex Reynolds, Alan Angels & Stu Grayson)	W	AEW Dark Elevation	5:20
Apr 25	Bulk Nasty, Jake Omen, Luther, RC Dupree & Tito Ortic (w/Evil Uno, Alex Reynolds, Alan Angels & Stu Grayson)	W	AEW Dark Elevation	3:09
May 2	Anthony Bennett, Bret Waters, Cory Bishop, Eli Isom, Jaden Valo & Mike Law (w/John Silver, Alex Reynolds, Alan Angels, Evil Uno & Colt Cabana)	W	AEW Dark Elevation	1:44
May 9	Brandon Scott, Diego, Josh Fuller & Ryan Mooney (w/Alex Reynolds, Alan Angels & Evil Uno)	W	AEW Dark Elevation	4:27
May 10	Cezar Bononi & Tiger Ruas (w/Evil Uno)	W	AEW Dark	8:30
May 16	Eric James & VSK (w/Evil Uno)	W	AEW Dark Elevation	2:30
May 20	Malakai Black, Brody King & Buddy Matthews (w/Fuego Del Sol & Evil Uno)	L	AEW Rampage	9:25
May 31	Serpentico, Peter Avalon & Ryan Nemeth (w/John Silver & Evil Uno)	W	AEW Dark	5:37
Jun 6	Aaron Solo, Anthony Ogogo, Nick Comoroto & QT Marshall (w/Alan Angels, Evil Uno & John Silver)	L	AEW Dark Elevation	6:28
Jun 7	Max Caster, Austin Gunn & Colten Gunn (w/John Silver & Alex Reynolds)	L	AEW Dark	5:26
Jun 13	Aaron Solo & QT Marshall (w/Evil Uno)	W	AEW Dark Elevation	8:13
Jun 27	Austin Gunn, Colten Gunn & Max Caster (w/Alex Reynolds & Evil Uno)	L	AEW Dark Elevation	4:08
Jun 28	JD Drake & Ryan Nemeth (w/Evil Uno)	W	AEW Dark	8:16
Jul 4	Aaron Solo, Nick Comoroto & QT Marshall (w/Alex Reynolds & Evil Uno)	W	AEW Dark Elevation	7:56
Jul 5	Cezar Bononi, JD Drake, Peter Avalon & Ryan Nemeth (w/John Silver, Alex Reynolds & Evil Uno)	W	AEW Dark	7:22
Jul 18	Terrell Hughes & Terrence Hughes (w/Evil Uno)	W	AEW Dark Elevation	4:44
Jul 25	Aaron Solo & Nick Comoroto (w/Evil Uno)	W	AEW Dark Elevation	6:35
Aug 9	JD Drake & Peter Avalon (w/Evil Uno)	W	AEW Dark	4:15
Aug 15	Adam Grace, Drew System, Rylie Jackson & TUG Cooper (w/John Silver, Alex Reynolds & Evil Uno)	W	AEW Dark Elevation	2:25
Aug 22	Alexander Apollo, D'Mone Solavino & RC Dupree (w/John Silver & Alex Reynolds)	W	AEW Dark Elevation	3:22
Aug 23	DK Vandu, Joey Sweets & Tyshaun Perez (w/John Silver & Alex Reynolds)	W	AEW Dark	3:38
Aug 26	Malakai Black, Brody King & Buddy Matthews (w/John Silver & Alex Reynolds)	W	AEW Rampage	9:03
Sep 23	Golden Ticket Battle Royale	L	AEW Rampage: Grand Slam	12:16
Oct 7	Pac, Penta El Zero M & Rey Fenix (w/Alex Reynolds & John Silver)	L	AEW Rampage	21:01
Oct 18	Jordano, Shayne Hawke, Tyler Tirva & Zak Patterson (w/John Silver, Alex Reynolds & Evil Uno)	W	AEW Dark	6:52
Oct 21	Orange Cassidy, Rush	L	AEW Rampage	11:53
Oct 24	Baron Black	W	AEW Dark Elevation	:47
Nov 14	Jora Johl	W	AEW Dark Elevation	1:30
Nov 25	Rush, The Butcher & The Blade (w/Alex Reynolds & John Silver)	L	AEW Rampage: Black Friday	7:24
Dec 23	$300,000 Three Kings Christmas Casino Trios Royale (w/Dralistico & Rush)	L	AEW Rampage	22:01

PRIMATE

Date	Opponent(s)	Result	Show	Time
Jan 6	Ashton Smith & Oliver Carter (w/T-Bone)	L	NXT UK	9:37
Mar 10	Danny Jones & Josh Morrell (w/T-Bone)	W	NXT UK	6:05
Apr 7	Wild Boar	W	NXT UK	3:37
Apr 28	Mark Andrews & Wild Boar (w/T-Bone)	L	NXT UK	7:26

| Jun 9 | Oli Blake & Tate Mayfairs (w/T-Bone) | W | NXT UK | 4:32 |
| Jul 7 | Josh Morrell | L | NXT UK | 4:05 |

PUMA KING

| Mar 31 | Arez, Gino Medina & Mini Abismo Negro (w/Micro Man & Octagon Jr.) | W | MLW Fusion | 15:42 |
| Apr 14 | Alex Kane, ACH, Juicy Finau, Myron Reed | L | MLW Fusion | 4:28 |

QT MARSHALL

Jan 10	Zack Clayton	W	AEW Dark Elevation	2:53
Jan 11	Jungle Boy & Luchasaurus (w/Nick Comoroto)	L	AEW Dark	8:21
Jan 31	Dante Martin, Lee Moriarty & Matt Sydal (w/Aaron Solo & Nick Comoroto)	L	AEW Dark Elevation	7:46
Feb 1	Toa Liona	W	AEW Dark	4:43
Feb 15	Pat Brink	W	AEW Dark	5:15
Mar 6	Hook	L	AEW Revolution Buy-In	5:00
Mar 11	Keith Lee	L	AEW Rampage	4:05
Mar 21	John Silver, Evil Uno & Stu Grayson (w/Aaron Solo & Nick Comoroto)	L	AEW Dark Elevation	7:27
Mar 28	Rocky Romero & Trent Beretta (w/Aaron Solo)	L	AEW Dark Elevation	5:23
Mar 29	Adam Priest, Gus De La Vega & Invictus Khash (w/Aaron Solo & Nick Comoroto)	W	AEW Dark	4:30
Apr 4	Brock Anderson & Lee Johnson (w/Aaron Solo)	L	AEW Dark Elevation	6:59
Apr 8	Swerve Strickland	L	AEW Rampage	6:08
Apr 16	Karl Fredericks, Clark Connors & Yuya Uemura (w/Aaron Solo & Nick Comoroto)	W	NJPW Windy City Riot	11:56
Apr 25	Minoru Suzuki	L	AEW Dark Elevation	4:12
Apr 26	Penta Oscuro	L	AEW Dark	7:15
Apr 27	Bryan Danielson, Jon Moxley & Wheeler Yuta (w/Nick Comoroto & Aaron Solo)	L	AEW Dynamite	8:49
May 17	Alex Coughlin, Clark Connors, Karl Fredericks, Kevin Knight & Yuya Uemura (w/Aaron Solo, Blake Li, Brick Aldridge & Nick Comoroto)	L	AEW Dark	10:30
May 9	Keith Lee & Swerve Strickland (w/Nick Comoroto)	L	AEW Dark Elevation	6:47
May 28	Pac, Penta El Zero M & Rey Fenix (w/Aaron Solo & Nick Comoroto)	L	AEW Dark	10:32
Jun 6	Alan Angels, Evil Uno, John Silver & Ten (w/Aaron Solo, Anthony Ogogo & Nick Comoroto)	W	AEW Dark Elevation	6:28
Jun 11	Karl Fredericks	L	NJPW Strong	8:24
Jun 13	Evil Uno & Ten (w/Aaron Solo)	L	AEW Dark Elevation	8:13
Jun 14	Alan Angels	W	AEW Dark	3:42
Jun 20	Matt Sydal	L	AEW Dark Elevation	7:28
Jun 26	Hirooki Goto & Yoshi-Hashi (w/Aaron Solo)	L	AEW x NJPW Forbidden Door Buy-In	8:53
Jul 4	Alex Reynolds, Evil Uno & Ten (w/Aaron Solo & Nick Comoroto)	L	AEW Dark Elevation	7:56
Jul 11	Chuck Taylor & Trent Beretta (w/Aaron Solo)	L	AEW Dark Elevation	9:40
Jul 19	Fuego Del Sol	W	AEW Dark	10:48
Aug 1	Bobby Orlando, BRG, Bryce Donovan & TUG Cooper (w/Aaron Solo, Anthony Ogogo & Nick Comoroto)	W	AEW Dark Elevation	3:33
Aug 27	Parker Li	W	NJPW Strong	2:56
Sep 2	Ricky Starks	L	AEW Rampage	7:10
Sep 23	Golden Ticket Battle Royale	L	AEW Rampage: Grand Slam	12:16
Sep 24	Keita Murray	W	NJPW Strong	5:12
Oct 3	Chuck Taylor, Trent Beretta, Danhausen & Rocky Romero (w/Aaron Solo, Cole Karter & Nick Comoroto)	L	AEW Dark Elevation	7:54
Oct 8	Shota Umino	L	NJPW Strong	10:11
Oct 11	Action Andretti	W	AEW Dark	7:01
Oct 12	Samoa Joe & Wardlow (w/Nick Comoroto)	L	AEW Dynamite	2:29
Oct 18	Dante Martin	L	AEW Dark	9:19
Oct 24	Claudio Castagnoli	L	AEW Dark Elevation	9:45
Oct 31	Danhausen	W	AEW Dark Elevation	9:00
Nov 7	Cheeseburger, Logan Easton Laroux & Rhett Titus (w/Cole Karter & Lee Johnson)	W	AEW Dark Elevation	6:45
Nov 8	Brian Pillman Jr. & Griff Garrison (w/Cole Karter)	W	AEW Dark	4:13
Nov 15	Channing Thomas, Man Scout & Teddy Goodz (w/Cole Karter & Lee Johnson)	W	AEW Dark	4:11
Nov 19	Orange Cassidy, Chuck Taylor, Trent Beretta, Rocky Romero & Danhausen (w/Aaron Solo, Lee Johnson, Nick Comoroto & Cole Karter)	L	AEW Full Gear Buy-In	11:55
Nov 29	Justin Corino, Ryan Mooney & Steve Josifi (w/Cole Karter & Lee Johnson)	W	AEW Dark	3:40
Dec 2	Lumberjack Match: Orange Cassidy	L	AEW Rampage	9:31
Dec 13	Chris Steeler, Joe Keys & LSG (w/Cole Karter & Lee Johnson)	W	AEW Dark	3:29
Dec 14	Malakai Black, Brody King & Buddy Matthews (w/Aaron Solo & Cole Karter)	L	AEW Dynamite: Winter Is Coming	:23

QUEEN ZELINA

Jan 3	Rhea Ripley & Nikki A.S.H. (w/Carmella)	W	WWE Monday Night RAW	2:40
Jan 24	Bianca Belair	L	WWE Monday Night RAW	3:45
Jan 29	Royal Rumble Match	L	WWE Royal Rumble '22	17:25
Feb 24	Liv Morgan	L	WWE Main Event	6:53
Mar 7	Rhea Ripley & Liv Morgan (w/Carmella)	L	WWE Monday Night RAW	9:05
Mar 14	Liv Morgan	L	WWE Monday Night RAW	2:55
Mar 25	Sasha Banks, Shayna Baszler, Rhea Ripley	L	WWE Main Event	8:43
Mar 28	Naomi, Sasha Banks, Liv Morgan & Rhea Ripley (w/Carmella, Natalya & Shayna Baszler)	L	WWE Monday Night RAW	8:20
Apr 1	Sasha Banks & Naomi (w/Carmella)	L	WWE Main Event	3:13

Apr 3	Sasha Banks & Naomi, Liv Morgan & Rhea Ripley,	L	WWE WrestleMania XXXVIII	10:50
	Natalya & Shayna Baszler (w/Carmella)			
Apr 11	Bianca Belair	L	WWE Monday Night RAW	2:10

QUESTION MARK II, THE

Mar 25	Mask vs. Mask Match: The Question Mark	W	NWA Hard Times 3	6:00
Aug 30	De'Vin Graves	W	NWA Power	1:43
Sep 13	JR Kratos & Da Pope (w/KC Roxx)	L	NWA Power	6:46
Oct 11	KC Roxx	W	NWA Power	5:37
Oct 18	JR Kratos	W	NWA Power	5:37
Dec 27	Damage	L	NWA Power	4:11

QUINCY ELLIOTT

Mar 25	Joe Gacy	L	NXT Level Up	4:15
Apr 22	Edris Enofe & Malik Blade (w/Damaris Griffin)	L	NXT Level Up	6:36
Apr 29	Andre Chase	L	NXT Level Up	6:19
May 20	Josh Briggs	L	NXT Level Up	7:16
Jun 24	Bryson Montana	W	NXT Level Up	5:07
Jul 15	Ikemen Jiro	L	NXT Level Up	5:05
Jul 29	Edris Enofe & Malik Blade (w/Ikemen Jiro)	L	NXT Level Up	6:01
Aug 5	Xyon Quinn	W	NXT Level Up	4:50
Sep 13	Sean Gallagher	W	NXT 2.0	1:21
Oct 18	Xyon Quinn	W	NXT	2:49

R-TRUTH

Apr 1	Andre The Giant Memorial Battle Royal	L	WWE SmackDown	8:05
Jun 2	T-Bar	W	WWE Main Event	6:02
Jun 27	Battle Royal	L	WWE Monday Night RAW	19:25
Jul 4	Gunther	L	WWE Monday Night RAW	:55
Jul 11	Omos, Jimmy Uso & Jey Uso (w/Angelo Dawkins & Montez Ford)	L	WWE Monday Night RAW	11:30
Sep 1	Shelton Benjamin	L	WWE Main Event	4:42
Sep 15	Akira Tozawa	W	WWE Main Event	4:42
Sep 29	Shelton Benjamin	W	WWE Main Event	8:57
Oct 6	Brooks Jensen & Josh Briggs (w/Shelton Benjamin)	W	WWE Main Event	6:48
Oct 13	Von Wagner	W	WWE Main Event	3:34
Oct 24	The Miz	W	WWE Monday Night RAW	2:45
Nov 1	Grayson Waller	L	NXT	7:13
Nov 3	Duke Hudson & Von Vagner (w/Shelton Benjamin)	W	WWE Main Event	6:31

RACHAEL ELLERING

Jan 6	Tasha Steelz, Lady Frost & Chelsea Green	L	IMPACT Wrestling	7:19
	(w/Rosemary & Jordynne Grace)			
Jul 31	Deonna Purrazzo, Jordynne Grace	L	JCP Ric Flair's Last Match	9:17

RAJ SINGH

Jan 6	Juice Robinson	L	IMPACT Before The Impact	9:12
Jan 13	Jonah	L	IMPACT Wrestling	1:24
Fen 3	Black Taurus	L	IMPACT Before The Impact	9:21
May 12	Gauntlet For The Gold	L	IMPACT Wrestling	39:00
May 26	Bhupinder Gujjar & W. Morrissey (w/Shera)	L	IMPACT Wrestling	5:17
Jun 30	Rich Swann	L	IMPACT Before The Impact	6:30
Aug 4	Sami Callihan	L	IMPACT Wrestling	1:56
Sep 15	Yuya Uemura	L	IMPACT Before The Impact	8:59
Oct 13	Chris Sabin & Alex Shelley (w/Shera)	L	IMPACT Before The Impact	7:16
Oct 27	Joe Hendry	L	IMPACT Wrestling	1:47
Nov 17	Ace Austin & Chris Bey, Kyle Fletcher & Mark Davis,	L	IMPACT Wrestling	13:03
	Alex Shelley & Chris Sabin (w/Shera)			
Nov 24	Yuya Uemura & Delirious (w/Shera)	W	IMPACT Before The Impact	9:22

RANDY ORTON

Jan 1	Angelo Dawkins & Montez Ford (w/Riddle)	W	WWE Day 1	11:15
Jan 3	Chad Gable & Otis (w/Riddle)	L	WWE Monday Night RAW	2:40
Jan 10	Chad Gable & Otis (w/Riddle)	L	WWE Monday Night RAW	8:57
Jan 24	Chad Gable	W	WWE Monday Night RAW	13:55
Jan 29	Royal Rumble Match	L	WWE Royal Rumble '22	2:21
Feb 7	Seth Rollins & Kevin Owens (w/Riddle)	L	WWE Monday Night RAW	8:05
Feb 14	Seth Rollins	L	WWE Monday Night RAW	15:17
Feb 21	Seth Rollins & Kevin Owens (w/Riddle)	L	WWE Monday Night RAW	12:40
Feb 28	Angelo Dawkins & Montez Ford (w/Riddle)	L	WWE Monday Night RAW	8:35
Mar 7	No DQ: Chad Gable & Otis, Seth Rollins & Kevin Owens (w/Riddle)	W	WWE Monday Night RAW	27:05
Mar 21	Chad Gable & Otis (w/Riddle)	W	WWE Monday Night RAW	7:45
Mar 28	Jimmy Uso & Jey Uso (w/Riddle)	W	WWE Monday Night RAW	16:20
Apr 3	Angelo Dawkins & Montez Ford, Chad Gable & Otis (w/Riddle)	W	WWE WrestleMania XXXVIII	11:30
Apr 4	Austin Theory, Jimmy Uso & Jey Uso (w/Riddle & Finn Balor)	L	WWE Monday Night RAW	8:25
Apr 11	Chad Gable & Otis (w/Riddle)	W	WWE Monday Night RAW	8:30
Apr 18	Angelo Dawkins & Montez Ford (w/Riddle)	L	WWE Monday Night RAW	7:50
Apr 25	Seth Rollins, Kevin Owens, Jimmy Uso & Jey Uso	W	WWE Monday Night RAW	14:58
	(w/Riddle, Cody Rhodes & Ezekiel)			
May 8	Roman Reigns, Jey Uso & Jimmy Uso (w/Drew McIntyre & Riddle)	L	WWE WrestleMania Backlash '22	22:20
May 9	Angelo Dawkins & Montez Ford (w/Riddle)	W	WWE Monday Night RAW	9:58
May 20	Jimmy Uso & Jey Uso (w/Riddle)	L	WWE SmackDown	13:13

RAQUEL RODRIGUEZ (AS RAQUEL GONZALEZ UNTIL APR 29)

Jan 4	Mandy Rose, Cora Jade	L	NXT 2.0: New Year's Evil '22	12:32
Feb 1	Cora Jade	W	NXT 2.0	6:02
Mar 1	Yulisa Leon & Valentina Feroz (w/Cora Jade)	W	NXT 2.0	4:47
Mar 8	Wendy Choo & Dakota Kai (w/Cora Jade)	L	NXT 2.0: Roadblock '22	10:42
Apr 2	Gigi Golin & Jacy Jayne (w/Dakota Kai)	W	NXT Stand & Deliver Kickoff	7:53
Apr 5	Gigi Dolin & Jacy Jayne (w/Dakota Kai)	L	NXT 2.0	8:31
Apr 29	Cat Cardoza	W	WWE SmackDown	2:36
May 13	Ronda Rousey	L	WWE SmackDown	6:00
May 20	Shotzi	W	WWE SmackDown	2:46
May 27	Ronda Rousey	D	WWE SmackDown	:55
May 27	Natalya & Shayna Baszler (w/Ronda Rousey)	W	WWE SmackDown	7:35
Jun 3	Natalya, Shotzi, Aliyah, Shayna Baszler, Xia Li	L	WWE SmackDown	5:54
Jun 17	Shayna Baszler	W	WWE SmackDown	3:15
Jun 24	Handicap Match: Sonya Deville (w/Lacey Evans)	W	WWE SmackDown	3:05
Jul 1	Alexa Bliss, Liv Morgan & Asuka (w/Lacey Evans & Shotzi)	L	WWE SmackDown	13:14
Jul 2	Money In The Bank Ladder Match: Alexa Bliss, Asuka, Becky Lynch Lacey Evans, Liv Morgan, Shotzi	L	WWE Money In The Bank '22	16:35
Jul 22	Sonya Deville	W	WWE SmackDown	3:40
Aug 5	Gauntlet Match: Shayna Baszler, Sonya Deville, Aliyah, Shotzi, Xia Li, Natalya	L	WWE SmackDown	21:05
Aug 12	Shotzi & Xia Li (w/Aliyah)	W	WWE SmackDown	9:35
Aug 26	Natalya & Sonya Deville (w/Aliyah)	W	WWE SmackDown	8:00
Aug 29	Dakota Kai & Iyo Sky (w/Aliyah)	W	WWE Monday Night RAW	11:17
Sep 5	Nikki A.S.H. & Doudrop (w/Aliyah)	W	WWE Monday Night RAW	3:45
Sep 9	Jacy Jayne & Gigi Dolin (w/Aliyah)	W	WWE SmackDown	5:00
Sep 12	Dakota Kai & Iyo Sky (w/Aliyah)	L	WWE Monday Night RAW	12:30
Sep 16	Bayley	L	WWE SmackDown	8:20
Sep 23	Dakota Kai	W	WWE SmackDown	2:01
Oct 7	Sonya Deville & Xia Li (w/Shotzi)	W	WWE SmackDown	2:16
Oct 14	Bayley, Dakota Kai & Iyo Sky (w/Shotzi & Roxanne Perez)	L	WWE SmackDown	6:42
Oct 18	Pick Your Poison Match: Cora Jade	L	NXT	2:42
Oct 21	Dakota Kai & Iyo Sky (w/Shotzi)	L	WWE SmackDown	9:58
Nov 11	Six-Pack Challenge: Shotzi, Lacey Evans, Sonya Deville, Liv Morgan, Xia Li	L	WWE SmackDown	11:58
Nov 25	Ronda Rousey & Shayna Baszler (w/Shotzi)	L	WWE SmackDown	3:26
Dec 23	Gauntlet Match: Xia Li, Emma, Liv Morgan, Sonya Deville, Tegan Nox, Shayna Baszler	W	WWE SmackDown	23:58
Dec 30	Ronda Rousey	L	WWE SmackDown	16:43

REAL1 (AS NZO UNTIL JULY 7)

Mar 10	KC Navarro	W	MLW Fusion	2:48
May 19	ACH	W	MLW Fusion	6:21
Jun 2	KC Navarro	L	MLW Fusion	1:50
Jul 7	Lince Dorado	W	MLW Fusion	9:58
Nov 10	Jacob Fatu	L	MLW Fusion	2:01

RED VELVET

Jan 4	Renee Michelle, Sofia Castillo & Marina Tucker (w/Leyla Hirsch & Kris Statlander)	W	AEW Dark	2:43
Jan 10	B3CCA & Notorious Mimi (w/Leyla Hirsch)	W	AEW Dark Elevation	1:50
Jan 11	Shalonce Royal	W	AEW Dark	1:20
Jan 14	Penelope Ford, The Bunny & Nyla Rose (w/Leyla Hirsch & Kris Statlander)	L	AEW Rampage	8:12
Jan 18	Vipress	W	AEW Dark	2:56
Jan 24	Janai Kai	W	AEW Dark Elevation	3:36
Jan 26	Leyla Hirsch	W	AEW Dynamite: Beach Break	8:08
Feb 21	Angelica Risk, Arie Alexander & Freya States (w/Anna Jay & Tay Conti)	W	AEW Dark Elevation	3:42
Feb 28	Skye Blue	W	AEW Dark Elevation	2:24
Mar 8	Kiera Hogan	W	AEW Dark	2:16
Mar 18	Leyla Hirsch	W	AEW Rampage	8:00
Mar 23	Leyla Hirsch	W	AEW Dynamite	6:30
Apr 4	Brittany Jade	W	AEW Dark Elevation	2:20
Apr 8	Willow Nightingale	W	AEW Rampage	5:16
Apr 26	Dulce Tormenta	W	AEW Dark	2:35
Apr 29	Skye Blue, Willow Nightingale & Trish Adora (w/Jade Cargill & Kiera Hogan)	W	AEW Rampage	2:46
May 20	Kris Statlander	L	AEW Rampage	7:50
Jun 10	Kris Statlander	L	AEW Rampage	8:55
Dec 7	Kiera Hogan, Skye Blue & Madison Rayne (w/Jade Cargill & Leila Grey)	W	AEW Dynamite	8:13
Dec 27	Billie Starkz	W	AEW Dark	1:54

REN NARITA

Jan 4	Katsuyori Shibata	L	NJPW Wrestle Kingdom 16 Night #1	11:46
Feb 12	Josh Barnett	L	NJPW Strong	10:15
Mar 19	Buddy Matthews	L	NJPW Strong	15:32
Apr 1	Rocky Romero	W	NJPW Lonestar Shootout	7:42
Apr 16	Royce Isaacs, Jorel Nelson, JR Kratos, Black Tiger & Danny Limelight (w/Fred Rosser, Josh Alexander, Alex Coughlin & Chris Dickinson)	W	NJPW Windy City Riot	13:50
Apr 30	Jay Lethal	L	NJPW Strong	12:17
May 14	Karl Fredericks	L	NJPW Capital Collision	10:32
May 21	Chris Dickinson	D	NJPW Strong	15:00
Jun 11	Luke Gallows, Karl Anderson, Hikuleo, Jay White & Juice Robinson	L	NJPW Strong	12:44

(w/Chuck Taylor, Rocky Romero, Tomohiro Ishii & Mascara Dorada)

Jul 30	Fred Yehi, Shota Umino & Yuya Uemura (w/Kevin Knight & The DKC)	L	NJPW Music City Mayhem	13:12
Aug 27	Anthony Henry & JD Drake (w/Kushida)	W	NJPW Strong	11:18
Sep 24	Jakob Austin Young	W	NJPW Strong	4:48
Oct 8	Juice Robinson	W	NJPW Strong	1:20
Oct 8	No DQ: Juice Robinson	W	NJPW Strong	14:45
Oct 10	El Desperado, Yoshinobu Kanemaru & Douki	W	NJPW Declaration Of Power	7:28
	(w/David Finlay & Robbie Eagles)			
Nov 5	Sanada	W	NJPW Battle Autumn '22	14:31

REY FENIX

Jan 5	Jungle Boy & Luchasaurus (wPenta El Zero M)	L	AEW Dynamite	14:03
Apr 30	Matt Jackson & Nick Jackson (w/El Hijo del Vikingo)	L	AAA TripleMania XXX: Monterrey	15:58
May 4	Dante Martin	W	AEW Dynamite	9:38
May 13	Marq Quen, The Butcher & The Blade (w/Pac & Penta El Zero M)	W	AEW Rampage	10:22
May 18	Kyle O'Reilly	L	AEW Dynamite: Wild Card Wednesday	12:00
May 28	Aaron Solo, Nick Comoroto & QT Marshall (w/Pac & Penta El Zero M)	W	AEW Dark	10:32
May 29	Malakai Black, Buddy Matthews & Brody King (w/Pac & Penta Oscuro)	L	AEW Double Or Nothing '22	15:35
Jun 3	Matt Jackson & Nick Jackson (w/Penta El Zero M)	L	AEW Rampage	14:53
Jun 6	Cezar Bononi, Peter Avalon & Ryan Nemeth (w/Pac & Penta Oscuro)	W	AEW Dark Elevation	5:04
Jun 8	Casino Battle Royale	L	AEW Dynamite	24:59
Jun 18	Bandido, El Hijo del Vikingo, Laredo Kid, Taurus	W	AAA TripleMania XXX: Tijuana	20:37
Jun 24	Andrade El Idolo	L	AEW Rampage	16:29
Jul 15	Marq Quen & Isiah Kassidy (w/Penta El Zero M)	W	AEW Rampage	11:16
Jul 31	Laredo Kid, Black Taurus, Bandido	W	JCP Ric Flair's Last Match	11:45
Aug 8	Peter Avalon & Ryan Nemeth (w/Penta El Zero M)	W	AEW Dark Elevation	4:50
Aug 10	Tornado Tag: Andrade El Idolo & Rush (w/Penta El Zero M)	L	AEW Dynamite: Quake By The Lake	13:45
Aug 22	Dean Alexander, Jake Manning & Rosario Grillo (w/Pac & Penta Oscuro)	W	AEW Dark Elevation	2:36
Aug 24	Will Ospreay, Kyle Fletcher & Mark Davis (w/Pac & Penta El Zero M)	L	AEW Dynamite	25:18
Aug 31	Wheeler Yuta, Dante Martin, Rush	L	AEW Dynamite	8:06
Sep 2	Blake Christian	W	AEW Rampage	2:20
Sep 4	Casino Ladder Match: MJF, Claudio Castagnoli, Penta El Zero M,	L	AEW All Out '22	14:15
	Wheeler Yuta, Rush, Andrade El Idolo, Dante Martin			
Sep 7	Orange Cassidy, Chuck Taylor & Trent Beretta (w/Pac & Penta El Zero M)	W	AEW Dynamite	12:58
Sep 14	Swerve Strickland & Keith Lee (w/Penta El Zero M)	L	AEW Dynamite	8:15
Sep 23	Jungle Boy	L	AEW Rampage: Grand Slam	16:40
Oct 3	Dante Martin & Tony Deppen (w/Penta El Zero M)	W	AEW Dark Elevation	6:20
Oct 7	Alex Reynolds, John Silver & Ten (w/Pac & Penta El Zero M)	W	AEW Rampage	21:01
Oct 15	El Hijo del Vikingo	L	AAA TripleMania XXX: Mexico City	19:27
Oct 18	Orange Cassidy, Chuck Taylor & Trent Beretta (w/Pac & Penta El Zero M)	W	AEW Dynamite: Title Tuesday	11:45
Oct 25	Anthony Henry & JD Drake (w/Penta El Zero M)	W	AEW Dark	2:55
Nov 1	AR Fox	W	AEW Dark	4:52
Nov 2	Orange Cassidy, Luchasaurus	L	AEW Dynamite	9:59
Nov 16	AR Fox, Dante Martin & Darius Martin (w/Pac & Penta El Zero M)	W	AEW Dynamite	11:33
Nov 19	Kenny Omega, Matt Jackson & Nick Jackson	L	AEW Full Gear '22	18:40
	(w/Penta El Zero M & Pac)			
Nov 23	Kenny Omega, Matt Jackson & Nick Jackson (w/Pac & Penta El Zero M)	W	AEW Dynamite: Thanksgiving Eve	14:49
Nov 30	Kenny Omega, Matt Jackson & Nick Jackson (w/Pac & Penta El Zero M)	L	AEW Dynamite	17:20
Dec 14	Kenny Omega, Matt Jackson & Nick Jackson (w/Pac & Penta El Zero M)	W	AEW Dynamite: Winter Is Coming	14:59
Dec 21	No DQ: Kenny Omega, Matt Jackson & Nick Jackson	L	AEW Dynamite: Holiday Bash	13:41
	(w/Pac & Penta El Zero M)			
Dec 28	Falls Count Anywhere: Kenny Omega, Matt Jackson & Nick Jackson	L	AEW Dynamite	17:16
	(w/Pac & Penta El Zero M)			

REY MYSTERIO

Jan 6	Cedric Alexander & Shelton Benjamin (w/Dominik Mysterio)	W	WWE Main Event	5:41
Jan 17	Apollo Crews, Commander Azeez, Dolph Ziggler & Robert Roode	W	WWE Monday Night RAW	8:00
	(w/Dominik Mysterio, Angelo Dawkins & Montez Ford)			
Jan 24	Angelo Dawkins & Montez Ford (w/Dominik Mysterio)	W	WWE Monday Night RAW	8:00
Jan 29	Royal Rumble Match	L	WWE Royal Rumble '22	9:05
Jan 31	AJ Styles	L	WWE Monday Night RAW	11:35
Feb 14	Chad Gable & Otis (w/Dominik Mysterio)	L	WWE Monday Night RAW	10:34
Feb 19	The Miz	W	WWE Elimination Chamber Kickoff	8:20
Feb 28	Cedric Alexander & Shelton Benjamin (w/Dominik Mysterio)	L	WWE Monday Night RAW	4:30
Mar 14	Cedric Alexander & Shelton Benjamin (w/Dominik Mysterio)	W	WWE Monday Night RAW	3:25
Mar 21	Dolph Ziggler & Robert Roode (w/Dominik Mysterio)	W	WWE Monday Night RAW	9:25
Mar 28	The Miz	W	WWE Monday Night RAW	5:30
Apr 2	The Miz & Logan Paul (w/Dominik Mysterio)	L	WWE WrestleMania XXXVIII	11:15
May 30	Kevin Owens, Chad Gable & Otis (w/Ezekiel & Dominik Mysterio)	W	WWE Monday Night RAW	8:30
Jun 13	Veer Mahan	L	WWE Monday Night RAW	3:45
Jun 23	Finn Balor & Damian Priest (w/Dominik Mysterio)	W	WWE Main Event	7:31
Jun 27	Battle Royal	L	WWE Monday Night RAW	19:25
Jul 4	Finn Balor & Damian Priest (w/Dominik Mysterio)	W	WWE Monday Night RAW	11:30
Jul 11	Finn Balor	W	WWE Monday Night RAW	10:15
Jul 18	Damian Priest	L	WWE Monday Night RAW	4:59
Jul 25	Finn Balor & Damian Priest (w/Dominik Mysterio)	W	WWE Monday Night RAW	11:29
Jul 30	Finn Balor & Damian Priest (w/Dominik Mysterio)	L	WWE SummerSlam '22	11:05
Aug 1	Jimmy Uso & Jey Uso (w/Dominik Mysterio)	L	WWE Monday Night RAW	15:50
Aug 8	Finn Balor	L	WWE Monday Night RAW	14:00
Sep 3	Finn Balor & Damian Priest (w/Rey Mysterio)	W	WWE Clash At The Castle	12:35
Sep 5	Damian Priest	L	WWE Monday Night RAW	13:35
Sep 19	Finn Balor & Damian Priest (w/Matt Riddle)	L	WWE Monday Night RAW	17:40

Sep 26	Seth Rollins	L	WWE Monday Night RAW	17:57
Oct 3	Finn Balor & Damian Priest (w/AJ Styles)	L	WWE Monday Night RAW	10:42
Oct 10	Chad Gable	W	WWE Monday Night RAW	7:50
Oct 14	Ricochet, Solo Sikoa, Sheamus	W	WWE SmackDown	16:19
Oct 21	Ludwig Kaiser	W	WWE SmackDown	11:25
Nov 4	Gunther	L	WWE SmackDown	18:18
Dec 23	Angel Garza	W	WWE SmackDown	4:18

RHEA RIPLEY

Jan 3	Queen Zelina & Carmella (w/Nikki A.S.H.)	L	WWE Monday Night RAW	2:40
Jan 24	Carmella, Tamina & Nikki ASH. (w/Dana Brooke & Liv Morgan)	W	WWE Monday Night RAW	2:20
Jan 29	Royal Rumble Match	L	WWE Royal Rumble '22	30:59
Jan 31	Nikki A.S.H.	W	WWE Monday Night RAW	8:10
Feb 14	Gauntlet: Bianca Belair, Nikki A.S.H., Liv Morgan, Doudrop	L	WWE Monday Night RAW	44:04
Feb 19	Elimination Chamber: Bianca Belair, Alexa Bliss, Doudrop, Liv Morgan, Nikki A.S.H	L	WWE Elimination Chamber '22	12:45
Feb 21	Nikki A.S.H.	W	WWE Monday Night RAW	2:35
Feb 28	Becky Lynch, Doudrop & Nikki A.S.H. (w/Bianca Belair & Liv Morgan)	W	WWE Monday Night RAW	12:20
Mar 7	Carmella & Queen Zelina (w/Liv Morgan)	W	WWE Monday Night RAW	9:05
Mar 18	Sasha Banks & Naomi (w/Liv Morgan)	D	WWE SmackDown	12:00
Mar 21	Natalya & Shayna Baszler (w/Liv Morgan)	L	WWE Monday Night RAW	3:55
Mar 25	Sasha Banks, Queen Zelina, Shayna Baszler	L	WWE SmackDown	8:43
Mar 28	Queen Zelina, Carmella, Natalya & Shayna Baszler (w/Liv Morgan, Sasha Banks & Naomi)	W	WWE Monday Night RAW	8:20
Apr 3	Sasha Banks & Naomi, Carmella & Queen Zelina, Natalya & Shayna Baszler (w/Liv Morgan)	L	WWE WrestleMania XXXVIII	10:50
Apr 4	Sasha Banks & Naomi (w/Liv Morgan)	L	WWE Monday Night RAW	9:00
Apr 15	Naomi	W	WWE SmackDown	9:04
Apr 18	Sasha Banks & Naomi (w/Liv Morgan)	L	WWE Monday Night RAW	7:25
May 2	Asuka, Liv Morgan & Bianca Belair (w/Becky Lynch & Sonya Deville)	L	WWE Monday Night RAW	15:15
May 9	Liv Morgan	W	WWE Monday Night RAW	5:40
May 23	AJ Styles & Liv Morgan (w/Damian Priest)	W	WWE Monday Night RAW	11:35
May 30	Liv Morgan	L	WWE Monday Night RAW	10:15
Jun 5	AJ Styles, Finn Balor & Liv Morgan (w/Edge & Damian Priest)	W	WWE Hell In A Cell '22	16:00
Jun 6	Alexa Bliss, Liv Morgan, Doudrop	W	WWE Monday Night RAW	14:35
Oct 18	Pick Your Poison Match: Roxanne Perez	W	NXT	12:46
Nov 21	Asuka	W	WWE Monday Night RAW	17:58
Nov 26	WarGames: Bianca Belair, Alexa Bliss, Asuka, Mia Yim & Becky Lynch (w/Bayley, Dakota Kai, Iyo Sky & Nikki Cross)	L	WWE Survivor Series WarGames	39:40
Nov 28	Mia Yim	D	WWE Monday Night RAW	7:05
Nov 28	AJ Styles, Luke Gallows, Karl Anderson & Mia Yim (w/Finn Balor, Damian Priest & Dominik Mysterio)	W	WWE Monday Night RAW	14:20
Dec 5	Bayley, Asuka	L	WWE Monday Night RAW	15:15
Dec 12	Asuka	W	WWE Monday Night RAW	11:40
Dec 19	Akira Tozawa	W	WWE Monday Night RAW	4:55

RHETT TITUS

Feb 22	2/3 Falls: Colby Corino	L	NWA Power	16:55
Apr 1	Minoru Suzuki	L	ROH Supercard Of Honor XV	6:00
Apr 5	Darius Lockhart	W	NWA Power	7:24
Apr 26	Homicide	L	NWA Power	7:53
May 2	Konosuke Takeshita	L	AEW Dark Elevation	4:40
May 31	Thom Latimer	L	NWA Power	9:25
Aug 23	Luke Hawx & PJ Hawx, Dirty Dango & JTG (w/Gustavo Aguilar)	L	NWA Power	5:56
Oct 4	Bestia 666, Mecha Wolf & Damian 666 (w/Matt Taven & Mike Bennett)	W	NWA Power	8:16
Oct 31	Frankie Kazarian	L	AEW Dark Elevation	3:35
Nov 7	Cole Karter, Lee Johnson & QT Marshall (w/Cheeseburger & Logan Easton Laroux)	L	AEW Dark Elevation	6:45
Dec 13	Dak Draper & Mims (w/Trevor Murdoch)	W	NWA Power	9:14

RHINO

Jan 8	Hardcore War: Luke Gallows, Karl Anderson, Eric Young, Deaner & Joe Doering (w/Eddie Edwards, Rich Swann, Willie Mack & Heath)	W	IMPACT Hard To Kill '22	23:25
Jan 20	Luke Gallows & Joe Doering (w/Heath)	L	IMPACT Wrestling	8:39
Feb 10	Matt Taven & Mike Bennett (w/Rich Swann)	L	IMPACT Wrestling	8:42
Mar 17	Steve Maclin	L	IMPACT Wrestling	9:50
Apr 21	Rich Swann & Willie Mack (w/Heath)	W	IMPACT Before The Impact	7:56
Apr 23	Elimination Challenge Match (w/Heath)	L	IMPACT Rebellion '22	33:02
Apr 28	Jay Briscoe & Mark Briscoe (w/Heath)	L	IMPACT Wrestling	6:35
May 12	Gauntlet For The Gold	L	IMPACT Wrestling	39:00
Jun 2	Matt Taven & Mike Bennett (w/Heath)	L	IMPACT Wrestling	6:15
Oct 7	Call Your Shot Gauntlet	L	IMPACT Bound For Glory '22	29:18
Oct 20	Matt Taven & Mike Bennett (w/Heath)	W	IMPACT Wrestling	10:02
Dec 8	Alex Shelley & Chris Sabin (w/Heath)	D	IMPACT Wrestling	8:34
Dec 15	Alex Shelley & Chris Sabin (w/Heath)	L	IMPACT Wrestling	14:04

RIC FLAIR

| Jul 31 | Jeff Jarrett & Jay Lethal (w/Andrade El Idolo) | W | JCP Ric Flair's Last Match | 26:40 |

RICH SWANN

Jan 8	Hardcore War: Luke Gallows, Karl Anderson, Eric Young, Deaner & Joe Doering (w/Eddie Edwards, Willie Mack, Heath & Rhino)	W	IMPACT Hard To Kill '22	23:25
Feb 10	Matt Taven & Mike Bennett (w/Rhino)	L	IMPACT Wrestling	8:42
Feb 24	Kenny King, Matt Taven & Mike Bennett (w/Chris Sabin & Willie Mack)	L	IMPACT Wrestling	8:58
Mar 10	Eddie Edwards	L	IMPACT Wrestling	17:48
Apr 1	Ultimate X Match: Trey Miguel, Chris Bey, Jordynne Grace, Vincent, Willie Mack	L	IMPACT Multiverse Of Matches	7:27
Apr 21	Heath & Rhino (w/Willie Mack)	L	IMPACT Wrestling	7:56
Apr 23	Elimination Challenge Match (w/Willie Mack)	L	IMPACT Rebellion '22	33:02
May 5	Chris Bey & Jay White (w/Willie Mack)	L	IMPACT Wrestling	6:28
May 12	Gauntlet For The Gold	L	IMPACT Wrestling	39:00
Jun 2	Matthew Rehwoldt	W	IMPACT Wrestling	5:13
Jun 30	Raj Singh	W	IMPACT Wrestling	6:30
Jul 7	Shera	W	IMPACT Wrestling	3:49
Jul 28	Kushida	L	IMPACT Wrestling	15:29
Aug 18	Eddie Edwards, Bandido, Moose, Sami Callihan, Steve Maclin	L	IMPACT Wrestling	18:25
Sep 15	Matt Taven & Mike Bennett (w/Josh Alexander)	L	IMPACT Wrestling	6:54
Sep 29	PCO & Vincent (w/Heath)	W	IMPACT Wrestling	4:32
Oct 7	Call Your Shot Gauntlet	L	IMPACT Bound For Glory '22	29:18
Oct 20	Eric Young	W	IMPACT Wrestling	3:14
Nov 17	Laredo Kid	W	IMPACT Wrestling	3:40
Dec 1	Bully Ray	W	IMPACT Wrestling	5:53
Dec 22	Steve Maclin	D	IMPACT Wrestling	6:27

RICHARD HOLLIDAY

Feb 10	King Muertes	L	MLW Fusion	7:34
Apr 7	Matt Cross	W	MLW Fusion	6:44
May 5	Davey Richards	W	MLW Fusion	9:39
Jun 9	Alexander Hammerstone, Marshall Von Erich & Ross Von Erich (w/King Muertes & Mads Krugger)	W	MLW Fusion	9:31
Jul 14	Alexander Hammerstone	L	MLW Fusion	9:53
Nov 24	Falls Count Anywhere: Alexander Hammerstone	L	MLW Fusion	21:55

RICK BOOGS

Jan 7	Sami Zayn	W	WWE SmackDown	6:30
Jan 28	Jinder Mahal & Shanky (w/Shinsuke Nakamura)	W	WWE SmackDown	3:05
Jan 29	Royal Rumble Match	L	WWE Royal Rumble '22	4:33
Mar 11	Jey Uso	W	WWE SmackDown	2:25
Mar 18	Angel & Humberto (w/Shinsuke Nakamura)	W	WWE SmackDown	4:55
Apr 1	Jimmy Uso	D	WWE SmackDown	3:13
Apr 1	Austin Theory, Jimmy Uso & Jey Uso (w/Finn Balor & Shinsuke Nakamura)	L	WWE SmackDown	11:27
Apr 2	Jimmy Uso & Jey Uso (w/Shinsuke Nakamura)	L	WWE WrestleMania XXXVIII	6:55

RICKY MORTON

Apr 7	Marshall Von Erich & Ross Von Erich (w/Kerry Morton)	L	MLW Fusion	5:27
Jul 31	Brock Anderson & Brian Pillman Jr. (w/Kerry Morton)	L	JCP Ric Flair's Last Match	7:21
Aug 9	Wrecking Ball Legursky	W	NWA Power	3:42
Aug 28	Homicide	L	NWA 74th Anniversary Show	6:12
Dec 27	Jay Bradley & Wrecking Ball Legursky (w/Kerry Morton)	W	NWA Power	6:26

RICKY STARKS

Jan 8	Matt Sydal	W	AEW Battle Of The Belts I	9:00
Jan 24	Lee Moriarty & Matt Sydal (w/Powerhouse Hobbs)	W	AEW Dark Elevation	5:21
Feb 4	Jay Lethal	W	AEW Rampage	12:51
Feb 23	Ten	W	AEW Dynamite	5:56
Mar 6	Ladder Match: Christian Cage, Keith Lee, Orange Cassidy, Powerhouse Hobbs, Wardlow	W	AEW Revolution '22	17:20
Mar 15	Darian Bengston	W	AEW Dark	3:22
Mar 25	Swerve Strickland	W	AEW Rampage	11:27
Apr 13	Keith Lee & Swerve Strickland (w/Powerhouse Hobbs)	W	AEW Dynamite	12:32
Apr 19	Evil Uno & Stu Grayson (w/Powerhouse Hobbs)	W	AEW Dark	8:48
May 3	Jay Lucas & Terry Yaki (w/Powerhouse Hobbs)	W	AEW Dark	3:55
May 11	Jungle Boy	W	AEW Dynamite	10:01
May 25	Swerve Strickland, Jungle Boy	L	AEW Dynamite: 3 Year Anniversary	9:36
May 29	Jungle Boy & Luchasaurus, Keith Lee & Swerve Strickland (w/Powerhouse Hobbs)	L	AEW Double Or Nothing '22	17:15
Jun 3	Jordan Cruz & Ju Dizz (w/Powerhouse Hobbs)	W	AEW Rampage	:47
Jun 8	Casino Battle Royale	L	AEW Dynamite	24:59
Jun 27	Joey Jett & Jordan Chaos (w/Powerhouse Hobbs)	W	AEW Dark Elevation	3:28
Jul 1	Royal Rampage Match	L	AEW Rampage	22:41
Jul 13	Matt Jackson & Nick Jackson, Keith Lee & Swerve Strickland (w/Powerhouse Hobbs)	L	AEW Dynamite: Fyter Fest	18:14
Jul 20	Cole Carter	W	AEW Dynamite: Fyter Fest	6:09
Jul 27	Danhausen	W	AEW Dynamite: Fight For The Fallen	1:31
Jul 27	Hook	L	AEW Dynamite: Fight For The Fallen	1:32
Aug 10	Aaron Solo	W	AEW Dynamite: Quake By The Lake	2:13
Sep 2	QT Marshall	W	AEW Rampage	7:10
Sep 4	Powerhouse Hobbs	L	AEW All Out '22	5:05
Sep 23	Lights Out Match: Powerhouse Hobbs	W	AEW Rampage: Grand Slam	11:52
Sep 28	Eli Isom	W	AEW Dynamite	:51
Oct 25	Nick Comoroto	W	AEW Dark	8:47

Nov 18	Lance Archer	W	AEW Rampage	5:23
Nov 19	Brian Cage	W	AEW Full Gear Buy-In	10:00
Nov 23	Ethan Page	W	AEW Dynamite: Thanksgiving Eve	12:58
Nov 30	Ari Daivari	W	AEW Dynamite	:24
Dec 7	Dynamite Diamond Battle Royale	W	AEW Dynamite	13:10
Dec 14	MJF	L	AEW Dynamite: Winter Is Coming	15:46
Dec 20	Cezar Bononi	W	AEW Dark	1:28

RICOCHET

Jan 1	Sheamus & Ridge Holland (w/Cesaro)	L	WWE Day 1 Kickoff	9:45
Jan 14	Sheamus	L	WWE SmackDown	9:53
Jan 21	Sheamus	L	WWE SmackDown	3:20
Jan 28	Ridge Holland & Sheamus (w/Cesaro)	L	WWE SmackDown	10:45
Jan 29	Royal Rumble Match	L	WWE Royal Rumble '22	4:23
Feb 4	Ridge Holland	W	WWE SmackDown	2:20
Feb 4	Ridge Holland & Sheamus (w/Cesaro)	L	WWE SmackDown	5:34
Feb 18	Sheamus	W	WWE SmackDown	10:55
Mar 4	Sami Zayn	W	WWE SmackDown	8:20
Mar 11	Sami Zayn	W	WWE SmackDown	12:59
Mar 25	Angel	L	WWE SmackDown	2:10
Mar 25	Humberto	L	WWE SmackDown	7:18
Mar 28	Austin Theory	L	WWE Monday Night RAW	1:45
Apr 1	Angel, Humberto	W	WWE SmackDown	11:20
Apr 15	Jinder Mahal	W	WWE SmackDown	3:37
Jun 27	Battle Royal	L	WWE Monday Night RAW	19:25
Apr 29	Shanky	W	WWE SmackDown	3:34
May 27	Gunther & Ludwig Kaiser (w/Drew Gulak)	L	WWE SmackDown	6:45
Jun 10	Gunther	L	WWE SmackDown	8:35
Jun 24	Gunther	L	WWE SmackDown	3:10
Aug 5	Happy Corbin	W	WWE SmackDown	11:50
Aug 19	Sheamus, Happy Corbin, Madcap Moss, Sami Zayn	L	WWE SmackDown	22:33
Aug 26	Happy Corbin	W	WWE SmackDown	12:20
Sep 4	Camelo Hayes	L	NXT Worlds Collide '22	15:57
Sep 6	Trick Williams	W	NXT 2.0	5:13
Sep 16	Sami Zayn	W	WWE SmackDown	13:02
Sep 30	Sami Zayn & Solo Sikoa (w/Madcap Moss)	L	WWE SmackDown	12:44
Oct 7	Solo Sikoa	L	WWE SmackDown	8:16
Oct 14	Rey Mysterio, Solo Sikoa, Sheamus	L	WWE SmackDown	16:19
Nov 4	LA Knight	L	WWE SmackDown	9:54
Nov 18	Mustafa Ali	W	WWE SmackDown	10:45
Nov 25	Braun Strowman	W	WWE SmackDown	3:45
Dec 2	Santos Escobar	W	WWE SmackDown	20:45
Dec 9	Gunther, Ludwig Kaiser & Giovanni Vinci (w/Kofi Kingston & Xavier Woods)	W	WWE SmackDown	18:47
Dec 16	Gunther	L	WWE SmackDown	21:37
Dec 17	Gunther, Giovanni Vinci & Ludwig Kaiser (w/Sheamus & Drew McIntyre)	W	WWE Tribute To The Troops '22	16:34
Dec 23	Miracle On 34th Street Fight: Ludwig Kaiser & Giovanni Vinci (w/Braun Strowman)	W	WWE SmackDown	11:59

RIDGE HOLLAND

Jan 1	Cesaro & Ricochet (w/Sheamus)	W	WWE Day 1 Kickoff	9:45
Jan 28	Cesaro & Ricochet (w/Sheamus)	W	WWE SmackDown	10:45
Jan 29	Royal Rumble Match	L	WWE Royal Rumble '22	19:11
Feb 4	Ricochet	L	WWE SmackDown	2:20
Feb 4	Ricochet & Cesaro (w/Sheamus)	W	WWE SmackDown	5:34
Mar 11	Big E & Kofi Kingston (w/Sheamus)	W	WWE SmackDown	8:49
Mar 18	Kofi Kingston	W	WWE SmackDown	6:00
Mar 25	Xavier Woods	L	WWE SmackDown	:46
Apr 3	Kofi Kingston & Xavier Woods (w/Sheamus)	W	WWE WrestleMania XXXVIII	1:40
Apr 29	Xavier Woods	L	WWE SmackDown	8:47
May 6	Tables Match: Kofi Kingston & Xavier Woods (w/Sheamus)	W	WWE SmackDown	12:30
May 27	Drew McIntyre, Kofi Kingston & Xavier Woods (w/Sheamus & Butch)	L	WWE SmackDown	11:30
Jun 3	Drew McIntyre, Kofi Kingston & Xavier Woods (w/Sheamus & Butch)	W	WWE SmackDown	10:30
Jul 15	Drew McIntyre	L	WWE SmackDown	3:25
Sep 9	Gunther, Ludwig Kaiser & Giovanni Vinci (w/Sheamus & Butch)	L	WWE SmackDown	19:05
Sep 16	Ashante Adonis & Top Dolla, Ludwig Kaiser & Giovanni Vinci, Kofi Kingston & Xavier Woods (w/Butch)	W	WWE SmackDown	18:44
Sep 19	Angelo Dawkins & Montez Ford (w/Butch)	W	WWE Monday Night RAW	12:57
Sep 23	Jimmy Uso & Jey Uso (w/Butch)	L	WWE SmackDown	14:10
Oct 4	Elton Prince & Kit Wilson (w/Butch)	L	NXT	12:27
Oct 8	Good Old Fashioned Donnybrook Match: Gunther, Ludwig Kaiser & Giovanni Vinci (w/Sheamus & Butch)	W	WWE Extreme Rules '22	17:50
Oct 28	Sami Zayn & Solo Sikoa (w/Butch)	W	WWE SmackDown	11:50
Nov 5	Jey Uso & Jimmy Uso (w/Butch)	L	WWE Crown Jewel '22	10:45
Nov 21	Finn Balor, Damian Priest & Dominik Mysterio (w/Sheamus & Butch)	W	WWE Monday Night RAW	14:50
Nov 26	WarGames: Roman Reigns, Solo Sikoa, Sami Zayn, Jey Uso & Jimmy Uso (w/Sheamus, Butch, Drew McIntyre & Kevin Owens)	L	WWE Survivor Series WarGames	38:30

RIHO

Jan 3	Valentina Rossi	W	AEW Dark Elevation	3:33
Jan 7	Dr. Britt Baker D.M.D. & Jamie Hayter (w/Ruby Soho)	W	AEW Rampage	8:10
Jan 8	Dr. Britt Baker D.M.D.	L	AEW Battle Of The Belts I	12:47

May 6	Yuka Sakazaki	W	AEW Rampage	9:18
May 13	Ruby Soho	L	AEW Rampage	9:07
May 28	Diamante, Emi Sakura & Nyla Rose (w/Skye Blue & Yuka Sakazaki)	W	AEW Dark	6:11
Jul 9	Mei Suruga & Suzume (w/Arisa Endo)	L	TJPW Summer Sun Princess '22	14:21
Oct 25	Jungle Kyona	W	AEW Dark	5:20
Oct 26	Jamie Hayter	L	AEW Dynamite	10:52
Nov 14	Emi Sakura & Mei Suruga (w/Willow Nightingale)	W	AEW Dark Elevation	6:14

RIP FOWLER (AS ZACK GIBSON UNTIL JUNE 14)

Jan 25	Andre Chase & Bodhi Hayward (w/James Drake)	W	NXT 2.0	5:11
Feb 8	Julius Creed & Brutus Creed (w/James Drake)	L	NXT 2.0	12:03
Mar 11	Brooks Jensen & Josh Briggs (w/James Drake)	W	NXT Level Up	5:58
Mar 22	Julius Creed & Brutus Creed (w/James Drake)	L	NXT 2.0	4:14
Apr 19	Joaquin Wilde & Raul Mendoza (w/James Drake)	L	NXT 2.0	3:57
Jun 14	Dante Chen & Javier Bernal (w/James Drake)	W	NXT 2.0	3:56
Jun 28	Roderick Strong, Julius Creed & Brutus Creed (w/Joe Gacy & Jagger Reid)	W	NXT 2.0	13:56
Aug 23	Joaquin Wildge & Cruz Del Toro (w/Jagger Reid)	W	NXT 2.0	5:02
Sep 20	Edris Enofe & Malik Blade (w/Jagger Reid)	W	NXT	9:17
Oct 11	Edris Enofe & Malik Blade, Brooks Jensen & Josh Briggs (w/Jagger Reid)	L	NXT	9:10
Oct 18	Cameron Grimes, Luke Gallows & Karl Anderson (w/Joe Gacy & Jagger Reid)	L	NXT	11:56
Nov 15	Josh Briggs & Brooks Jensen (w/Jagger Reid)	W	NXT	4:10
Dec 16	Bronco Nima & Lucien Price (w/Jagger Reid)	W	NXT Level Up	5:39
Dec 27	Edris Enofe, Malik Blade & Odyssey Jones (w/Jagger Reid & Joe Gacy)	W	NXT	11:15

RIVERA

Feb 17	Ladder Match: El Hijo de LA Park & LA Park Jr. (w/Slice Boogie)	W	MLW Fusion	10:18
Mar 31	Calvin Tankman & EJ Nduka (w/Slice Boogie)	W	MLW Fusion	8:08
May 19	Bunkhouse Brawl: Marshall Von Erich & Ross Von Erich (w/Hernandez)	L	MLW Fusion	9:42
Jun 16	Calvin Tankman & EJ Nduka, Marshall Von Erich & Ross Von Erich (w/Slice Boogie)	L	MLW Fusion	9:12

ROBBIE EAGLES

Jan 5	Ryusuke Taguchi & Rocky Romero, Taiji Ishimori & El Phantasmo (w/Tiger Mask)	W	NJPW Wrestle Kingdom 16 Night #2	12:07
Sep 10	Kevin Blackwood	W	NJPW Strong	11:32
Oct 10	El Desperado, Yoshinobu Kanemaru & Douki (w/David Finlay & Ren Narita)	W	NJPW Declaration Of Power	7:28

ROBERT ROODE

Jan 10	Damian Priest, Angelo Dawkins & Montez Ford (w/Dolph Ziggler & Apollo Crews)	W	WWE Monday Night RAW	8:30
Jan 17	Rey Mysterio, Dominik Mysterio, Angelo Dawkins & Montez Ford (w/Dolph Ziggler, Apollo Crews & Commander Azeez)	L	WWE Monday Night RAW	8:00
Jan 29	Royal Rumble Match	L	WWE Royal Rumble '22	:54
Feb 10	Cedric Alexander & Shelton Benjamin (w/Dolph Ziggler)	L	WWE Main Event	7:01
Feb 14	Angelo Dawkins & Montez Ford (w/Dolph Ziggler)	L	WWE Monday Night RAW	2:50
Feb 21	Tommaso Ciampa & Finn Balor (w/Dolph Ziggler)	L	WWE Monday Night RAW	9:15
Feb 28	Tommaso Ciampa	L	WWE Monday Night RAW	2:40
Mar 1	Bron Breakker & Tommaso Ciampa (w/Dolph Ziggler)	L	NXT 2.0	13:05
Mar 7	Tommaso Ciampa & Bron Breakker (w/Dolph Ziggler)	L	WWE Monday Night RAW	9:37
Mar 21	Rey Mysterio & Dominik Mysterio (w/Dolph Ziggler)	L	WWE Monday Night RAW	9:25
Mar 22	Bron Breakker	L	NXT 2.0	15:14
Apr 1	Andre The Giant Memorial Battle Royal	L	WWE SmackDown	8:05

ROBYN RENEGADE

Jan 11	Tay Conti & Anna Jay (w/Charlette Renegade)	L	AEW Dark	3:48
Jan 18	Skye Blue	L	AEW Dark	2:51
Feb 11	Dr. Britt Baker D.M.D.	L	AEW Rampage	6:28
Mar 21	Nyla Rose	L	AEW Dark Elevation	1:24
Mar 28	Anna Jay & Ruby Soho (w/Charlette Renegade)	L	AEW Dark Elevation	2:17
Apr 15	Ruby Soho	L	AEW Rampage	8:22
May 24	Vicky Dreamboat	W	AEW Dark	3:31
Jul 15	Athena & Kris Statlander (w/Charlette Renegade)	L	AEW Rampage	:25
Jul 19	Avery Breaux & Valentina Rossi (w/Charlette Renegade)	W	AEW Dark	4:09
Jul 25	Hikaru Shida	L	AEW Dark	5:33
Aug 16	Willow Nightingale	L	AEW Dark	4:01
Aug 23	Allie Recks & Rocky Radley (w/Charlette Renegade)	W	AEW Dark	3:24
Sep 27	Mila Moore & Mylo (w/Charlette Renegade)	W	AEW Dark	:21
Oct 4	Skye Blue	L	AEW Dark	3:19

ROCKY ROMERO

Jan 4	Kenta, Taiji Ishimori & El Phantasmo (w/Hiroshi Tanahashi & Ryusuke Taguchi)	L	NJPW Wrestle Kingdom 16 Night #1	8:40
Jan 5	Robbie Eagles & Tiger Mask, Taiji Ishimori & El Phantasmo (w/Ryusuke Taguchi)	L	NJPW Wrestle Kingdom 16 Night #2	12:07
Jan 22	Jorel Nelson, Tom Lawlor & Black Tiger (w/Fred Rosser & Taylor Rust)	W	NJPW Strong	11:35
Feb 5	Jorel Nelson & Royce Isaacs (w/Lio Rush)	W	NJPW Strong	10:52
Feb 11	Matt Jackson & Nick Jackson (w/Trent Beretta)	L	AEW Rampage	13:23
Mar 24	Eddie Edwards	L	IMPACT Wrestling	12:45
Mar 26	Black Tiger	L	NJPW Strong	11:02
Mar 28	Aaron Solo & QT Marshall (w/Trent Beretta)	W	AEW Dark Elevation	5:23

Apr 1	Ren Narita	L	NJPW Lonestar Shootout	7:42
Apr 2	Black Tiger & JR Kratos (w/Wheeler Yuta)	L	NJPW Strong	9:50
Apr 14	Jonathan Gresham	L	IMPACT Wrestling	10:45
Apr 18	Aaron Solo & Nick Comoroto (w/Trent Beretta)	W	AEW Dark Elevation	7:25
May 5	Ace Austin	L	IMPACT Wrestling	11:39
May 13	Black Tiger, Danny Limelight & JR Kratos (w/Adrian Quest & Alex Coughlin)	W	NJPW Strong	8:33
May 14	Jay White & Hikuleo (w/Kazuchika Okada)	L	NJPW Capital Collision	15:59
May 24	Peter Avalon & Ryan Nemeth (w/Trent Beretta)	W	AEW Dark	7:02
May 25	Dax Harwood & Cash Wheeler (w/Trent Beretta)	D	AEW Dynamite: 3 Year Anniversary	10:12
Jun 11	Luke Gallows, Karl Anderson, Jay White, Juice Robinson & Hikuleo (w/Chucky Taylor, Tomohiro Ishii, Mascara Dorada & Ren Narita)	L	NJPW Strong	12:44
Jun 22	Will Ospreay, Kyle Fletcher & Mark Davis (w/Trent Beretta & Orange Cassidy)	W	AEW Dynamite	11:37
Jun 26	Dax Harwood & Cash Wheeler, Great-O-Khan & Jeff Cobb (w/Trent Beretta)	L	AEW x NJPW Forbidden Door	16:19
Jul 23	Adrian Quest, Lucas Riley & Negro Casas (w/David Finlay & Mascara Dorada)	W	NJPW Strong	11:03
Jul 30	Davey Richards	L	NJPW Music City Mayhem	11:29
Aug 11	Mike Bailey	L	IMPACT Wrestling	12:04
Aug 20	Dax Harwood	L	NJPW Strong	10:26
Sep 17	Chase Owens, Hikuleo, Jay White & Juice Robinson (w/Kushida, Taylor Rust & Trent Beretta)	L	NJPW Strong	14:46
Oct 3	Aaron Solo, Cole Karter, Nick Comoroto & QT Marshall (w/Chuck Taylor, Trent Beretta & Danhausen)	W	AEW Dark Elevation	7:54
Oct 22	Shingo Takagi	L	NJPW Strong	15:51
Oct 28	Yujiro Takahashi & Sho (w/Yoh)	L	NJPW Rumble On 44th Street	7:42
Nov 5	Christopher Daniels	L	NJPW Strong	9:24
Nov 7	Angelico, The Butcher & The Blade (w/Chuck Taylor & Trent Beretta)	W	AEW Dark Elevation	7:20
Nov 19	QT Marshall, Aaron Solo, Lee Johnson, Nick Comoroto & Cole Karter (w/Orange Cassidy, Chuck Taylor, Trent Beretta & Danhausen)	W	AEW Full Gear Buy-In	11:55
Nov 28	Davey Bang, Freedom Ramsey & Yabo (w/Chuck Taylor & Trent Beretta)	W	AEW Dark Elevation	3:54
Dec 3	Atlantis Jr. & Virus (w/Adrian Quest)	W	NJPW Strong	10:33

RODERICK STRONG

Jan 4	Carmelo Hayes	L	NXT 2.0: New Year's Evil '22	15:30
Jan 18	Walter	L	NXT 2.0	12:15
Jan 27	T-Bar	L	WWE Main Event	5:21
Feb 1	Walter, Marcel Barthel & Fabian Aichner (w/Julius Creed & Brutus Creed)	L	NXT 2.0	12:01
Mar 17	Wolfgang	W	NXT UK	9:51
Mar 22	Ladder Match: Solo Sikoa	L	NXT 2.0	9:18
Mar 29	Ladder Match: Cameron Grimes, A-Kid	L	NXT 2.0	10:55
Apr 7	Ilja Dragunov	L	NXT UK	14:40
May 31	Elton Prince & Kit Wilson (w/Damon Kemp)	L	NXT 2.0	13:17
Jun 21	Cruz Del Toro & Joaquin Wilde (w/Damon Kemp)	W	NXT 2.0	4:57
Jun 28	Joe Gacy, Rip Fowler & Jagger Reid (w/Julius Creed & Brutus Creed)	L	NXT 2.0	13:56
Jul 5	Julius Creed & Brutus Creed (w/Damon Kemp)	L	NXT 2.0: Great American Bash	12:13
Jul 19	Damon Kemp	W	NXT 2.0	5:55
Jul 26	Tony D'Agelo, Channing Lorenzo, Joaquin Wilde & Cruz Del Toro (w/Damon Kemp, Julius Creed & Brutus Creed)	L	NXT 2.0	11:39
Aug 9	Apollo Crews	L	NXT 2.0	11:55

RODNEY MACK (*AS THE QUESTION MARK)

Feb 8	Team War: Jordan Clearwater, Marshe Rockett & Tyrus, Alex Taylor, Jeremiah Plunkett & Rush Freeman, Aaron Stevens, JR Kratos & Judais (w/Odinson & Parrow)	W	NWA Power	11:40
Feb 15	Team War: Chris Adonis, Thom Latimer & El Rudo (w/Odinson & Parrow)	L	NWA Power	11:35
Mar 20	Tyrus	L	NWA Crockett Cup '22	8:14
Mar 29	Jake Dumas	L	NWA Power	4:08
Jun 28	Anthony Andrews	W	NWA Power	4:29
Aug 2	Cyon	L	NWA Power	4:39
Aug 16	BLK Jeez	W	NWA Power	3:28
Aug 28	Missouri Tornado Match: JR Kratos & Da Pope (w/Aron Stevens)	L	NWA 74th Anniversary Show	9:40
Nov 12	Mask vs. Mask Match: The Question Mark II	L	NWA Hard Times 3	6:00*

ROHAN RAJA

Jan 13	Dave Mastiff & Jack Starz (w/Teoman)	L	NXT UK	9:24
Jan 27	Joe Coffey, Mark Coffey & Wolfgang (w/Charlie Dempsey & Teoman)	W	NXT UK	11:18
Feb 24	Danny Jones	W	NXT UK	5:00
Mar 24	A-Kid & Saxon Huxley (w/Charlie Dempsey)	W	NXT UK	8:24
May 19	Dave Mastiff & Jack Starz (w/Charlie Dempsey)	W	NXT UK	8:01
Jun 2	Ashton Smith & Oliver Carter, Trent Seven & Tyler Bate (w/Charlie Dempsey)	L	NXT UK	14:17
Jun 23	Brooks Jensen & Josh Briggs, Dave Mastiff & Jack Starz. Mark Andrews & Wild Boar (w/Charlie Dempsey)	L	NXT UK	18:15
Aug 4	Oliver Carter	L	NXT UK	5:25

ROHIT RAJU

Feb 22	Cezar Bononi, JD Drake, Peter Avalon & Ryan Nemeth (w/Caleb Teninity, Karam & Sotheara Chhun)	L	AEW Dark	2:29
Mar 22	Blake Christian	L	AEW Dark	3:29
Apr 12	Shawn Dean	L	AEW Dark	5:44

May 10	Adam Priest	W	AEW Dark	3:00
Jul 12	Baron Black	W	AEW Dark	4:12
Aug 9	Chuck Taylor & Trent Beretta (w/Ren Jones)	L	AEW Dark	3:28
Aug 16	Invictus Khash	W	AEW Dark	2:43
Oct 4	Josh Woods & Tony Nese (w/Invictus Khash)	L	AEW Dark	2:34

ROLANDO FREEMAN

Aug 27	Matt Cardona	W	NWA 74th Anniversary Show	5:41
Aug 30	No DQ Match: Matt Cardona	W	NWA Power	8:17
Nov 1	Brian Myers, Mike Knox & VSK (w/Brady Pierce & Rush Freeman)	W	NWA Power	6:54
Nov 29	Matt Cardona	L	NWA Power	7:40
Dec 6	Anthony Andrews, Jeremiah Plunkett, Sal The Pal	W	NWA Power	5:36

ROMAN REIGNS

Jan 29	Seth Rollins	L	WWE Royal Rumble '22	14:25
Feb 19	Goldberg	W	WWE Elimination Chamber '22	6:00
Apr 3	Brock Lesnar	W	WWE WrestleMania XXXVIII	12:15
May 8	Drew McIntyre, Randy Orton & Riddle (w/Jey Uso & Jimmy Uso)	W	WWE WrestleMania Backlash '22	22:20
Jun 17	Riddle	W	WWE SmackDown	16:56
Jul 25	Riddle, Angelo Dawkins & Montez Ford (w/Jimmy Uso & Jey Uso)	W	WWE Monday Night RAW	19:25
Jul 30	Last Man Standing: Brock Lesnar	W	WWE SummerSlam '22	23:00
Sep 3	Drew McIntyre	W	WWE Clash At The Castle	30:47
Nov 5	Logan Paul	W	WWE Crown Jewel '22	24:50
Nov 26	WarGames: Sheamus, Butch, Ridge Holland, Drew McIntyre & Kevin Owens (w/Sami Zayn, Solo Sikoa, Jey Uso & Jimmy Uso)	W	WWE Survivor Series WarGames	38:30
Dec 30	John Cena & Kevin Owens (w/Sami Zayn)	L	WWE SmackDown	10:57

RONDA ROUSEY

Jan 29	Royal Rumble Match	W	WWE Royal Rumble '22	10:16
Feb 19	Charlotte Flair & Sonya Deville (w/Naomi)	W	WWE Elimination Chamber '22	9:14
Mar 4	Sonya Deville	W	WWE SmackDown	3:15
Apr 2	Charlotte Flair	L	WWE WrestleMania XXXVIII	18:30
Apr 29	"I Quit" Beat The Clock Challenge: Shotzi	W	WWE SmackDown	1:41
May 8	I Quit Match: Charlotte Flair	W	WWE WrestleMania Backlash '22	16:35
May 13	Raquel Rodriguez	W	WWE SmackDown	6:00
May 27	Raquel Rodriguez	D	WWE SmackDown	:55
May 27	Shayna Baszler & Natalya (w/Raquel Rodriguez)	W	WWE SmackDown	7:35
Jun 10	Shotzi	W	WWE SmackDown	7:20
Jul 2	Natalya	W	WWE Money In The Bank '22	12:30
Jul 2	Liv Morgan	L	WWE Money In The Bank '22	:35
Jul 8	Natalya	W	WWE SmackDown	2:15
Jul 29	Sonya Deville & Natalya (w/Liv Morgan)	W	WWE SmackDown	11:30
Jul 30	Liv Morgan	L	WWE SummerSlam '22	4:35
Sep 9	Sonya Deville, Xia Li, Natalya, Lacey Evans	W	WWE SmackDown	4:40
Sep 30	Natalya	W	WWE SmackDown	4:18
Oct 8	Extreme Rules Match: Liv Morgan	W	WWE Extreme Rules '22	12:05
Oct 28	Emma	W	WWE SmackDown	6:50
Nov 25	Raquel Rodriguez & Shotzi (w/Shayna Baszler)	W	WWE SmackDown	3:26
Nov 26	Shotzi	W	WWE Survivor Series WarGames	7:15
Dec 9	Liv Morgan & Tegan Nox (w/Shayna Baszler)	L	WWE SmackDown	4:07
Dec 17	Emma & Tamina (w/Shayna Baszler)	W	WWE Tribute To The Troops '22	7:34
Dec 30	Raquel Rodriguez	W	WWE SmackDown	16:43
Dec 30	Charlotte Flair	L	WWE SmackDown	:40

ROSEMARY

Jan 6	Tasha Steelz, Lady Frost & Chelsea Green (w/Jordynne Grace & Rachael Ellering)	L	IMPACT Wrestling	7:19
Jan 8	Ultimate X Match: Tasha Steelz, Alisha Edwards, Chelsea Green, Jordynne Grace, Lady Frost	L	IMPACT Hard To Kill '22	9:00
Jan 20	Tenille Dashwood & Madison Rayne (w/Havok)	L	IMPACT Wrestling	3:35
Mar 31	Battle Royal	W	IMPACT Wrestling	7:15
Apr 1	Madison Rayne & Tenille Dashwood, Tasha Steelz & Savannah Evans, Gisele Shaw & Lady Frost (w/Havok)	L	IMPACT Multiverse Of Matches	9:02
Apr 23	Tasha Steelz	L	IMPACT Rebellion '22	11:45
Apr 28	Savannah Evans & Tasha Steelz (w/Havok)	W	IMPACT Wrestling	4:51
Jun 6	Tenille Dashwood	W	IMPACT Wrestling	6:10
Jun 19	Madison Rayne & Tenille Dashwood (w/Taya Valkyrie)	W	IMPACT Slammiversary XX	7:20
Jun 30	Gisele Shaw	L	IMPACT Wrestling	5:51
Aug 4	Deonna Purrazzo	L	IMPACT Wrestling	7:11
Aug 18	Gisele Shaw	L	IMPACT Before The Impact	8:27
Oct 13	Chelsea Green, Deonna Purrazzo & Gisele Shaw (w/Jessicka & Taya Valkyrie)	L	IMPACT Wrestling	5:40
Dec 22	Deonna Purrazzo & Gisele Shaw (w/Jessicka)	W	IMPACT Wrestling	5:39

ROSS VON ERICH

Apr 7	Kerry Morton & Ricky Morton (w/Marshall Von Erich)	W	MLW Fusion	5:27
May 19	Bunkhouse Brawl: Hernandez & Rivera (w/Marshall Von Erich)	W	MLW Fusion	9:42
Jun 9	King Muertes, Mads Krugger & Richard Holliday (w/Marshall Von Erich & Alexander Hammerstone)	L	MLW Fusion	9:31
Jun 16	Calvin Tankman & EJ Nduka, Rivera & Slice Boogie (w/Marshall Von Erich)	L	MLW Fusion	9:12
Jul 31	Jay Briscoe & Mark Briscoe (w/Marshall Von Erich)	L	JCP Ric Flair's Last Match	7:43

ROXANNE PEREZ (AS ROK-C UNTIL APRIL 15)

Jan 13	Deonna Purrazzo	L	IMPACT Wrestling	14:24
Mar 17	Miranda Gordy	L	MLW Fusion	7:38
Apr 15	Sloane Jacobs	W	NXT Level Up	4:18
Apr 19	Jacy Jayne	W	NXT 2.0	2:17
Apr 26	Mandy Rose	L	NXT 2.0	9:58
May 10	Gigi Dolin & Jacy Jayne (w/Wendy Choo)	L	NXT 2.0	10:01
May 17	Kiana James	W	NXT 2.0	5:15
May 24	Lash Legend	W	NXT 2.0	3:19
Jun 7	Tiffany Stratton	W	NXT 2.0	8:48
Jun 14	Mandy Rose, Gigi Dolin & Jacy Jayne (w/Cora Jade & Indi Hartwell)	W	NXT 2.0	13:51
Jun 28	Katana Chance & Kayden Carter (w/Cora Jade)	W	NXT 2.0	13:46
Jul 5	Gigi Dolin & Jacy Jayne (w/Cora Jade)	W	NXT 2.0: Great American Bash	10:29
Jul 12	Mandy Rose	L	NXT 2.0	9:17
Aug 16	Cora Jade	L	NXT 2.0: Heatwave	11:41
Sep 6	Meiko Satomura	L	NXT 2.0	11:19
Oct 14	Bayley, Dakota Kai & Iyo Sky (w/Raquel Rodriguez & Shotzi)	L	WWE SmackDown	6:42
Oct 18	Pick Your Poison Match: Rhea Ripley	L	NXT	12:46
Oct 22	Weapons Wild Match: Cora Jade	W	NXT Halloween Havoc '22	12:25
Nov 29	Indi Hartwell	W	NXT	9:07
Dec 10	Iron Survivor Challenge: Zoey Stark, Cora Jade, Indi Hartwell, Kiana James	W	NXT Deadline	25:00
Dec 13	Mandy Rose	W	NXT	9:37

ROYCE ISAACS

Jan 22	Lucas Riley	W	NJPW Strong	7:24
Feb 5	Lio Rush & Rocky Romero (w/Jorel Nelson)	L	NJPW Strong	10:52
Mar 26	Elimination Match: Adrian Quest, Clark Connors, Fred Rosser, The DKC & Taylor Rust (w/Danny Limelight, Jorel Nelson, JR Kratos & Tom Lawlor)	W	NJPW Strong	16:29
Apr 16	Fred Rosser, Josh Alexander, Alex Coughlin, Ren Narita & Chris Dickinson (w/Jorel Nelson, JR Kratos, Black Tiger & Danny Limelight)	L	NJPW Windy City Riot	13:50
May 7	Alex Coughlin, Fred Rosser & The DKC (w/JR Kratos & Tom Lawlor)	W	NJPW Strong	11:12
May 13	Handicap Match: Fred Rosser (w/Jorel Nelson)	W	NJPW Strong	7:28
May 14	The DKC, Yuya Uemura, David Finlay, Tanga Loa & Fred Rosser (w/Tom Lawlor, Jorel Nelson, JR Kratos & Danny Limelight)	W	NJPW Capital Collision	14:48
Jun 18	Alex Coughlin, Kevin Knight & The DKC (w/Jorel Nelson & JR Kratos)	W	NJPW Strong	9:21
Jul 9	Mikey Nicholls & Shane Haste (w/Jorel Nelson)	L	NJPW Strong	10:21
Sep 10	Kyle Fletcher & Mark Davis (w/Jorel Nelson)	L	NJPW Strong	11:38
Oct 22	Greg Sharpe & Jakob Austin Young (w/Jorel Nelson)	W	NJPW Strong	6:01
Oct 28	Homicide, Wheeler Yuta & Shota Umino (w/Tom Lawlor & Jorel Nelson)	L	NJPW Rumble On 44th Street	12:15
Nov 5	Barrett Brown & Misterioso, Kevin Knight & The DKC, Bad Dude Tito & Shane Haste (w/Jorel Nelson)	L	NJPW Strong	12:36
Dec 10	Alan Angels, David Finlay, Hikuleo & Tama Tonga (w/El Phantasmo, Jay White & Jorel Nelson)	L	NJPW Strong	13:20

RU FENG

Jan 7	Ikemen Jiro	L	WWE 205 Live	6:39
Jun 24	Ikemen Jiro	L	NXT Level Up	5:27
Jul 22	Bryson Montana	L	NXT Level Up	4:40
Sep 30	Javier Bernal	L	NXT Level Up	5:20

RUBY SOHO

Jan 5	Jade Cargill	L	AEW Dynamite	11:13
Jan 7	Dr. Britt Baker D.M.D. & Jamie Hayter (w/Riho)	W	AEW Rampage	8:10
Jan 17	Kenzie Paige	W	AEW Dark Elevation	3:07
Jan 24	Jordan Blake & Leva Bates (w/Thunder Rosa)	W	AEW Dark Elevation	2:52
Jan 31	Joseline Navarro & Megan Meyers (w/Thunder Rosa)	W	AEW Dark Elevation	2:46
Feb 2	Nyla Rose	L	AEW Dynamite	10:48
Feb 14	Emi Sakura, Nyla Rose & The Bunny (w/Anna Jay & Tay Conti)	W	AEW Dark Elevation	3:43
Feb 21	Haley J	W	AEW Dark Elevation	2:00
Mar 7	Session Moth Martina	W	AEW Dark Elevation	3:50
Mar 8	Diamante & Emi Sakura (w/AQA)	W	AEW Dark	5:02
Mar 14	Amber Nova	W	AEW Dark Elevation	3:34
Mar 15	Ashley D'Amboise	W	AEW Dark	2:53
Mar 21	Emi Sakura & The Bunny (w/Anna Jay)	W	AEW Dark Elevation	4:20
Mar 28	Charlette Renegade & Robyn Renegade (w/Anna Jay)	W	AEW Dark Elevation	2:17
Apr 4	Ashley D'Amboise & Diamante (w/Anna Jay)	W	AEW Dark Elevation	4:50
Apr 11	Emi Sakura, LuFisto & The Bunny (w/Anna Jay & Skye Blue)	W	AEW Dark Elevation	3:21
Apr 15	Robyn Renegade	W	AEW Rampage	8:22
Apr 18	Emi Sakura, Raychell Rose & The Bunny (w/Anna Jay & Hikaru Shida)	W	AEW Dark Elevation	3:20
Apr 25	Emi Sakura, Nyla Rose & The Bunny (w/Anna Jay & Skye Blue)	W	AEW Dark Elevation	6:35
May 6	Dr. Britt Baker D.M.D. & Jamie Hayter (w/Toni Storm)	W	AEW Rampage	8:38
May 13	Riho	W	AEW Rampage	9:07
May 27	Kris Statlander	W	AEW Rampage	10:06
May 29	Dr. Britt Baker D.M.D.	L	AEW Double Or Nothing '22	13:20
Jun 1	Jamie Hayter & Dr. Britt Baker D.M.D. (w/Toni Storm)	W	AEW Dynamite	9:48
Jun 13	Heidi Howitzer	W	AEW Dark Elevation	3:17
Jun 14	Diamante, Emi Sakura & Nyla Rose (w/Anna Jay & Kris Statlander)	W	AEW Dark	7:54
Jun 20	Miranda Gordy	W	AEW Dark Elevation	2:05
Jun 27	Missa Kate	W	AEW Dark Elevation	2:39
Jul 29	Anna Jay	L	AEW Rampage	9:48
Aug 8	Megan Myers & Nikki Victory (w/Skye Blue)	W	AEW Dark Elevation	3:11

Aug 9	Emi Sakura, Leva Bates & Serena Deeb (w/Athena & Hikaru Shida)	W	AEW Dark	8:08
Aug 22	Mickey Midas & ueen Aminata (w/Ortiz)	W	AEW Dark Elevation	1:50
Aug 26	Sammy Guevara & Tay Melo (w/Ortiz)	L	AEW Rampage	8:35
Sep 2	Sammy Guevara & Tay Melo (w/Ortiz)	W	AEW Rampage	7:40
Sep 3	Baliyan Akki & Emi Sakura (w/Ortiz)	W	AEW Dark Elevation	2:20
Sep 4	Sammy Guevara & Tay Melo (w/Ortiz)	L	AEW All Out Buy-In	6:00
Dec 14	Tay Melo	W	AEW Dynamite: Winter Is Coming	7:22
Dec 26	Madi Wrenkowski & Vertvixen (w/Willow Nightingale)	W	AEW Dark Elevation	4:47
Dec 28	Tay Melo & Anna Jay (w/Willow Nightingale)	L	AEW Dynamite	11:58

RUSH

Jul 1	Royal Rampage Match	L	AEW Rampage	22:41
Jul 6	Penta Oscuro	W	AEW Dynamite	11:04
Jul 23	Dragon Lee	W	ROH Death Before Dishonor XIX	15:50
Jul 27	Jon Moxley	L	AEW Dynamite: Fight For The Fallen	13:27
Aug 10	Tornado Match: Penta El Zero M & Rey Fenix (w/Andrade El Idolo)	W	AEW Dynamite: Quake By The Lake	13:45
Aug 17	Kenny Omega, Matt Jackson & Nick Jackson (w/Andrade El Idolo & Dragon Lee)	L	AEW Dynamite	20:54
Aug 29	Chase Oliver, Elijah Dean & Zack Nystrom (w/ The Butcher & The Blade)	W	AEW Dark Elevation	3:20
Aug 30	Blake Christian	W	AEW Dark	5:47
Aug 31	Wheeler Yuta, Dante Martin, Rey Fenix	L	AEW Dynamite	8:06
Sep 4	Casino Ladder Match: MJF, Claudio Castagnoli, Penta El Zero M, Rey Fenix, Wheeler Yuta, Andrade El Idolo, Dante Martin	L	AEW All Out '22	14:15
Sep 23	Golden Ticket Battle Royale	L	AEW Rampage: Grand Slam	12:16
Sep 30	John Silver	W	AEW Rampage	10:58
Oct 5	Hangman Page	L	AEW Dynamite: Anniversary	9:05
Oct 7	Claudio Castagnoli, Jon Moxley & Wheeler Yuta (w/Marq Quen & Isiah Kassidy)	L	AEW Rampage	10:16
Oct 21	Orange Cassidy, Ten	L	AEW Rampage	11:53
Nov 11	Bandido	L	AEW Rampage	8:45
Nov 21	Brett Gosselin, Channing Thomas & Doug Love (w/The Butcher & The Blade)	W	AEW Dark Elevation	2:20
Nov 22	Leon Ruffin	W	AEW Dark	1:04
Nov 25	John Silver, Alex Reynolds & Ten (w/The Butcher & The Blade)	W	AEW Rampage: Black Friday	7:24
Dec 10	Blake Christian & AR Fox (w/Dralistico)	L	ROH Final Battle '22	10:35
Dec 23	$300,000 Three Kings Christmas Casino Trios Royale (w/Dralistico & Preston Vance)	L	AEW Rampage	22:01

RUSH FREEMAN

Jan 18	Handicap Match: Dirty Dango & JTG (w/Wrecking Ball Legursky & Jay Bradley)	W	NWA Power	4:29
Feb 1	Handicap Match: Dirty Dango & JTG (w/Alex Taylor & Captain Yuma)	L	NWA Power	4:09
Feb 8	Team War Match: Odinson, Parrow & Rodney Mack, Marshe Rockett, Tyrus & Jordan Clearwater, Aron Stevens, JR Kratos & Judais (w/Alex Taylor & Jeremiah Plunkett)	L	NWA Power	11:40
Mar 8	BLK Jeez, Jordan Clearwater, Marshe Rockett & Tyrus (w/Alex Taylor, Cyon & Mims)	L	NWA Power	6:59
Mar 19	Doug Williams & Harry Smith (w/Alex Taylor)	L	NWA Crockett Cup '22	6:38
Mar 29	Mike Knox & VSK (w/Alex Taylor)	L	NWA Power	4:18
May 17	Team War Match: Jax Dane, Odinson & Parrow, Jordan Clearwater, BLK Jeez & Marshe Rockett (w/Alex Taylor & Jeremiah Plunkett)	L	NWA Power	6:54
Aug 2	Gaagz The Gymp, Judais & Sal The Pal (w/Alex Taylor & Jeremiah Plunkett)	L	NWA Power	8:08
Aug 23	Doug Williams & Harry Smith (w/Brady Pierce)	L	NWA Power	4:48
Aug 28	Tag Team Battle Royal (w/Brady Pierce)	L	NWA 74th Anniversary Show	14:07
Nov 1	Brian Myers, Mike Knox & VSK (w/Rolando Freeman & Brady Pierce)	W	NWA Power	6:54
Nov 12	Jay Bradley & Wrecking Ball Legursky (w/Brady Pierce)	L	NWA Hard Times 3	9:15
Nov 29	Matt Cardona & Mike Knox (w/Brady Pierce)	W	NWA Power	11:19
Dec 6	Judais & PJ Hawx (w/Damage)	L	NWA Power	6:42

RYAN NEMETH

Feb 22	Caleb Teninity, Karam, Rohit Raju & Sotheara Chhun (w/Cezar Bononi, JD Drake & Peter Avalon)	W	AEW Dark	2:29
Mar 2	Casino Battle Royale (w/Peter Avalon)	L	AEW Dynamite	18:59
Mar 8	Dante Martin & Darius Martin (w/Peter Avalon)	L	AEW Dark	6:25
Apr 5	Chandler Hopkins	W	AEW Dark	3:57
May 3	John Silver	L	AEW Dark	6:43
May 17	Trent Beretta	L	AEW Dark	3:30
May 24	Rocky Romero & Trent Beretta (w/Peter Avalon)	L	AEW Dark	7:02
May 30	Konosuke Takeshita	L	AEW Dark Elevation	5:31
May 31	John Silver, Evil Uno & Ten (w/Peter Avalon & Serpentico)	L	AEW Dark	5:37
Jun 6	Pac, Penta Oscuro & Rey Fenix (w/Cezar Bononi & Peter Avalon)	L	AEW Dark Elevation	5:04
Jun 28	Evil Uno & Ten (w/JD Drake)	L	AEW Dark	8:16
Jul 5	John Silver, Alex Reynolds, Evil Uno & Ten (w/Peter Avalon, Cezar Bononi & JD Drake)	L	AEW Dark	7:22
Jul 26	Alex Reynolds	L	AEW Dark	5:56
Aug 2	Anthony Bowens & Max Caster (w/Peter Avalon)	L	AEW Dark	5:00
Aug 5	Konosuke Takeshita	L	AEW Rampage	1:36
Aug 8	Penta El Zero M & Rey Fenix (w/Peter Avalon)	L	AEW Dark Elevation	4:50
Aug 23	Adrian Alanis & Liam Gray (w/Peter Avalon)	W	AEW Dark	2:40
Aug 26	Wardlow	L	AEW Rampage	1:31
Sep 12	John Silver	L	AEW Dark Elevation	3:33

Sep 13	Dante Martin & Matt Sydal (w/Cezar Bononi)	L	AEW Dark	6:19
Sep 27	Arjun Singh	W	AEW Dark	2:37
Oct 4	Chris Pharaoh & Eli Isom (w/Cezar Bononi)	W	AEW Dark	1:58
Nov 8	Claudio Castagnoli & Wheeler Yuta (w/Cezar Bononi)	L	AEW Dark	4:40
Nov 29	Matt Hardy, Isiah Kassidy & Marq Quen (w/Cezar Bononi & Peter Avalon)	L	AEW Dark	7:16
Dec 19	Ethan Page, Isiah Kassidy, Konosuke Takeshita, Matt Hardy, Dante Martin & Darius Martin (w/Jeeves Jay, Slim J, Sonny Kiss, Cezar Bononi & Peter Avalon)	L	AEW Dark Elevation	7:45
Dec 20	Jake St. Patrick & Sage Scott (w/Peter Avalon)	W	AEW Dark	3:27

RYUSUKE TAGUCHI

Jan 4	Kenta, Taiji Ishimori & El Phantasmo (w/Hiroshi Tanahashi & Rocky Romero)	L	NJPW Wrestle Kingdom 16 Night #1	8:40
Jan 5	Robbie Eagles & Tiger Mask, Taiji Ishimori & El Phantasmo (w/Rocky Romero)	L	NJPW Wrestle Kingdom 16 Night #2	12:07
Jan 8	Daisuke Harada, Hajime Ohara, Daiki Inaba, Yoshiaki Inamura & Kinya Okada (w/Tomohiro Ishii, Hirooki Goto, Yoshi-Hashi & Master Wato)	W	NJPW Wrestle Kingdom 16 Night #3	11:42
Mar 1	Hirooki Goto & Yoshi-Hashi (w/Master Wato)	L	NJPW 50th Anniversary Show	15:04
Apr 9	Taiji Ishimori & El Phantasmo (Master Wato)	W	NJPW Hyper Battle '22	15:13
May 1	Yoshinobu Kanemaru & Douki (w/Master Wato)	W	NJPW Wrestling Dontaku '22	9:10
Jun 12	Aaron Henare, TJP & Francesco Akira (w/Master Wato & Hiroyoshi Tenzan)	L	NJPW Dominion '22	10:31
Sep 25	Francesco Akira & TJP (w/Master Wato)	L	NJPW Burning Spirit '22	12:43
Oct 10	Evil, Yujiro Takahashi & Sho (w/Hiroshi Tanahashi & Hikuleo)	W	NJPW Declaration Of Power	7:14

SAL THE PAL

Apr 12	Jay Bradley, Wrecking Ball Legursky & Colby Corino (w/Gaagz The Gymp & Judais)	W	NWA Power	6:27
May 10	Dirty Dango & JTG (w/Gaagz The Gymp)	L	NWA Power	6:37
Aug 27	Beelzebub's Bedlam Match: Danny Dealz, Alex Taylor & Jeremiah Plunkett (w/Judais & Gaagz The Gymp)	W	NWA 74th Anniversary Show	9:41
Jun 28	PJ Hawx, Gustavo Aguilar	L	NWA Power	4:00
Aug 2	Alex Taylor, Jeremiah Plunkett & Rush Freeman (w/Gaagz The Gymp & Judais)	W	NWA Power	8:08
Aug 28	Tag Team Battle Royal (w/Gaagz The Gymp)	L	NWA 74th Anniversary Show	14:07
Dec 6	Rolando Freeman, Anthony Andrews, Jeremiah Plunkett	L	NWA Power	5:36

SAM GRADWELL

Jan 20	Lewis Howley & Sam Stoker (w/Saxon Huxley)	L	NXT UK	9:22
Feb 17	Kenny Williams	W	NXT UK	3:54
Apr 21	Back Alley Brawl: Kenny Williams	W	NXT UK	9:42
Jun 2	Von Wagner	L	NXT UK	6:47
Jul 21	Trent Seven	L	NXT UK	11:01
Aug 11	Teoman	W	NXT UK	5:54

SAMI CALLIHAN

Jun 19	Monster's Ball Match: Moose	L	IMPACT Slammiversary XX	16:00
Jun 23	Jack Price	W	IMPACT Wrestling	1:28
Aug 4	Raj Singh	W	IMPACT Wrestling	1:56
Aug 18	Eddie Edwards, Bandido, Moose, Rich Swann, Steve Maclin	L	IMPACT Wrestling	18:25
Oct 7	Call Your Shot Gauntlet	L	IMPACT Bound For Glory '22	29:18
Nov 3	Eric Young	W	IMPACT Wrestling	6:11
Nov 17	Death Machine's Double Jeopardy Match: Eric Young	W	IMPACT Wrestling	14:04
Dec 8	Big Kon	L	IMPACT Wrestling	5:46
Dec 15	Alan Angels	W	IMPACT Wrestling	6:53

SAMI ZAYN

Jan 7	Rick Boogs	L	WWE SmackDown	6:30
Jan 29	Royal Rumble Match	L	WWE Royal Rumble '22	3:17
Feb 18	Shinsuke Nakamura	W	WWE SmackDown	18:15
Mar 4	Ricochet	L	WWE SmackDown	8:20
Mar 11	Ricochet	L	WWE SmackDown	12:59
Apr 3	Anything Goes Match: Johnny Knoxville	L	WWE WrestleMania XXXVIII	14:25
Apr 8	Drew McIntyre	L	WWE SmackDown	3:40
Apr 15	Drew McIntyre	L	WWE SmackDown	2:39
Apr 22	Lumberjack Match: Drew McIntyre	D	WWE SmackDown	9:00
Apr 29	Steel Cage Match: Drew McIntyre	L	WWE SmackDown	10:36
May 6	Shinsuke Nakamura	W	WWE SmackDown	9:15
May 13	Riddle	L	WWE SmackDown	10:50
May 20	Shinsuke Nakamura	L	WWE SmackDown	10:28
May 23	Riddle, Angelo Dawkins & Montez Ford (w/Jimmy Uso & Jey Uso)	L	WWE Monday Night RAW	12:35
Jun 10	Riddle	L	WWE SmackDown	13:05
Jun 24	Shinsuke Nakamura	W	WWE SmackDown	9:55
Jul 1	Battle Royal	L	WWE SmackDown	14:36
Jul 2	Money In The Bank Ladder Match: Drew McIntyre, Madcap Moss, Theory, Omos, Riddle, Seth Rollins, Sheamus	L	WWE Money In The Bank '22	25:25
Aug 19	Sheamus, Happy Corbin, Madcap Moss, Ricochet	L	WWE SmackDown	22:33
Aug 26	Drew McIntyre	L	WWE SmackDown	10:20
Sep 16	Ricochet	L	WWE SmackDown	13:02
Sep 26	AJ Styles	W	WWE Monday Night RAW	20:02
Sep 30	Ricochet & Madcap Moss (w/Solo Sikoa)	W	WWE SmackDown	12:44
Oct 7	Braun Strowman, Xavier Woods & Kofi Kingston (w/Jimmy Uso & Jey Uso)	L	WWE SmackDown	10:30
Oct 10	Matt Riddle	L	WWE Monday Night RAW	16:15

Oct 14	Kofi Kingston	W	WWE SmackDown		14:50
Oct 28	Ridge Holland & Butch (w/Solo Sikoa)	L	WWE SmackDown		11:50
Nov 18	Butch	L	WWE SmackDown		7:30
Nov 26	WarGames: Shearnus, Butch, Ridge Holland, Drew McIntyre & Kevin Owens (w/Roman Reigns, Solo Sikoa, Jey Uso & Jimmy Uso)	W	WWE Survivor Series WarGames		38:30
Dec 2	Sheamus	W	WWE SmackDown		18:02
Dec 19	AJ Styles	W	WWE Monday Night RAW		12:15
Dec 30	John Cena & Kevin Owens (w/Roman Reigns)	L	WWE SmackDown		10:57

SAMMY GUEVARA

Jan 4	Ho Ho Lun	W	AEW Dark	4:11
Jan 8	Dustin Rhodes	W	AEW Battle Of The Belts I	16:15
Jan 12	Daniel Garcia	W	AEW Dynamite	12:34
Jan 26	Ladder Match: Cody Rhodes	W	AEW Dynamite: Beach Break	22:59
Feb 4	Isiah Kassidy	W	AEW Rampage	9:14
Feb 16	Darby Allin	W	AEW Dynamite	14:51
Feb 25	Andrade El Idolo	W	AEW Rampage	12:23
Mar 4	Darby Allin, Andrade El Idolo	W	AEW Rampage	13:12
Mar 6	Tornado Match: Andrade El Idolo, Matt Hardy & Isiah Kassidy (w/Darby Allin & Sting)	W	AEW Revolution '22	13:20
Mar 9	Scorpio Sky	L	AEW Dynamite	11:50
Apr 16	Scorpio Sky	W	AEW Battle Of The Belts II	12:45
Apr 27	Ladder Match: Scorpio Sky	L	AEW Dynamite	14:06
Apr 30	Komander & Sexy Star, Latigo & Maravilla, Arez & Chik Tormenta (w/Tay Conti)	W	AAA TripleMania XXX: Monterrey	12:35
May 29	Ethan Page, Scorpio Sky & Paige VanZant (w/Frankie Kazarian & Tay Conti)	L	AEW Double Or Nothing '22	12:30
Jun 26	Eddie Kingston, Shota Umino & Wheeler Yuta (w/Chris Jericho & Minoru Suzuki)	W	AEW x NJPW Forbidden Door	18:58
Jun 29	Blood & Guts: Jon Moxley, Claudio Castagnoli, Wheeler Yuta, Eddie Kingston, Santana, Ortiz (w/Chris Jericho, Daniel Garcia, Jake Hager, Angelo Parker, Matt Menard)	L	AEW Dynamite: Blood & Guts	46:45
Jul 27	Dante Martin	W	AEW Dynamite: Fight For The Fallen	8:48
Aug 12	Dante Martin & Skye Blue (w/Tay Conti)	W	AEW Rampage: Quake By The Lake	8:00
Aug 26	Ortiz & Ruby Soho (w/Tay Melo)	W	AEW Rampage	8:35
Sep 2	Ortiz & Ruby Soho (w/Tay Melo)	L	AEW Rampage	7:40
Sep 3	GPA & Laynie Lucky (w/Tay Melo)	W	AEW Dark Elevation	4:27
Sep 4	Ortiz & Ruby Soho (w/Tay Melo)	W	AEW All Out Buy-In	6:00
Sep 9	Darby Allin	W	AEW Rampage	11:06
Sep 14	Jon Moxley	L	AEW Dynamite	13:27
Sep 23	Eddie Kingston	L	AEW Rampage: Grand Slam	8:11
Oct 5	Bryan Danielson & Daniel Garcia (w/Chris Jericho)	W	AEW Dynamite: Anniversary	14:23
Oct 26	Bryan Danielson	L	AEW Dynamite	14:58
Nov 9	2/3 Falls: Bryan Danielson	L	AEW Dynamite	20:33
Nov 16	Claudio Castagnoli & Bryan Danielson (w/Chris Jericho)	L	AEW Dynamite	18:02
Nov 19	Bryan Danielson, Chris Jericho, Claudio Castagnoli	L	AEW Full Gear '22	21:30
Dec 16	Jon Moxley	L	AEW Rampage	15:34

SAMOA JOE

Apr 6	Max Caster	W	AEW Dynamite	2:52
Apr 13	Minoru Suzuki	W	AEW Dynamite	11:37
Apr 29	Trent Beretta	W	AEW Rampage	9:57
May 18	Johnny Elite	W	AEW Dynamite: Wild Card Wednesday	10:25
May 25	Kyle O'Reilly	W	AEW Dynamite: 3 Year Anniversary	12:38
May 29	Adam Cole	L	AEW Double Or Nothing '22	12:30
Jul 23	Jay Lethal	W	ROH Death Before Dishonor XIX	12:20
Sep 16	Josh Woods	W	AEW Rampage	10:10
Sep 23	Tony Nese & Josh Woods (w/Wardlow)	W	AEW Rampage: Grand Slam	2:26
Oct 12	QT Marshall & Nick Comoroto (w/Wardlow)	W	AEW Dynamite	2:29
Nov 2	Brian Cage	W	AEW Dynamite	11:23
Nov 4	Kaun & Toa Liona (w/Wardlow)	W	AEW Rampage	9:10
Nov 19	Wardlow, Powerhouse Hobbs	W	AEW Full Gear '22	9:55
Nov 30	AR Fox	W	AEW Dynamite	6:36
Dec 7	Darby Allin	W	AEW Dynamite	10:29
Dec 10	Juice Robinson	W	ROH Final Battle '22	13:40
Dec 28	Wardlow	W	AEW Dynamite	12:12

SANADA

Jan 4	Will Ospreay, Great-O-Khan & Jeff Cobb (w/Tetsuya Naito & Bushi)	L	NJPW Wrestle Kingdom 16 Night #1	9:27
Jan 5	Great-O-Khan	W	NJPW Wrestle Kingdom 16 Night #2	13:21
Jan 8	Katsuhiko Nakajima, Kenoh, Manabu Soya, Tadasuke & Aleja (w/Tetsuya Naito, Shingo Takagi, Bushi & Hiromu Takahashi)	W	NJPW Wrestle Kingdom 16 Night #3	26:33
Mar 1	Togi Makabe, Tomoaki Honma, Tomohiro Ishii, Shiro Koshinaka & Toru Yano (w/Tetsuya Naito, Shingo Takagi, Bushi & Hiromu Takahashi)	W	NJPW 50th Anniversary Show	12:38
Jun 12	Will Ospreay	L	NJPW Dominion '22	12:48
Sep 25	Taichi & Zack Sabre Jr. (w/Tetsuya Naito)	L	NJPW Buming Spirit '22	9:32
Oct 1	Zack Sabre Jr., El Desperado & Douki (w/Tetsuya Naito & Hiromu Takahashi)	W	NJPW Royal Quest II Night #1	14:29
Oct 2	Ethan Allen & Luke Jacob (w/Hiromu Takahashi)	W	NJPW Royal Quest II Night #2	14:04
Oct 10	Will Ospreay, Aaron Henare, TJP & Francesco Akira (w/Tetsuya Naito, Bushi & Hiromu Takahashi)	W	NJPW Declaration Of Power	8:07
Nov 5	Ren Narita	L	NJPW Battle Autumn '22	14:31

Nov 20	Kyle Fletcher, Mark Davis, Francesco Akira, TJP & Gideon Grey (w/Bushi, Hiromu Takahashi, Shingo Takagi & Tetsuya Naito)	L	NJPW x Stardom Historic X-Over	9:55

SANGA

Feb 8	LA Knight	L	NXT 2.0	3:12
Apr 12	Gauntlet Match: Brooks Jensen & Josh Briggs, Kit Wilson & Elton Prince Joaquin Wilde & Raul Mendoza, Julius Creed & Brutus Creed (w/Grayson Waller)	L	NXT 2.0	27:08
Apr 19	Grayon Waller	L	NXT 2.0	3:28
May 13	Dante Chen	W	NXT Level Up	5:08
May 24	Wes Lee	W	NXT 2.0	3:51
Jun 28	Xyon Quin	W	NXT 2.0	5:08
Jul 12	Duke Hudson	W	NXT 2.0	3:01
Sep 20	Von Wagner	L	NXT	2:52
Nov 15	Ariel Dominguez & George Cannon (w/Veer)	W	NXT	3:26

SANTANA

Jan 14	No DQ, No Holds Barred: Daniel Garcia, Matt Lee & Jeff Parker (w/Eddie Kingston & Ortiz)	W	AEW Rampage	13:50
Jan 24	Breaux Keller & Goldy (w/Ortiz)	W	AEW Dark Elevation	3:10
Jan 26	Daniel Garcia, Matt Lee & Jeff Parker (w/Chris Jericho & Ortiz)	W	AEW Dynamite: Beach Break	8:52
Feb 16	Chris Jericho & Jake Hager (w/Ortiz)	W	AEW Dynamite	10:43
Feb 23	Tag Team Battle Royal (w/Ortiz)	L	AEW Dynamite	14:29
Mar 2	Casino Battle Royale (w/Ortiz)	L	AEW Dynamite	22:26
Apr 13	Chris Jericho, Jake Hager & Daniel Garcia (w/Eddie Kingston & Oriz)	L	AEW Dynamite	11:46
May 4	Chris Jericho	L	AEW Dynamite	9:05
May 29	Anarchy In The Arena: Chris Jericho, Daniel Garcia, Jake Hager, Angelo Parker & Matt Menard (w/Jon Moxley, Eddie Kingston, Bryan Danielson & Ortiz)	L	AEW Double Or Nothing '22	22:45
Jun 29	Blood & Guts: Chris Jericho, Daniel Garcia, Jake Hager, Matt Menard, Angelo Parker & Sammy Guevara (w/Jon Moxley, Claudio Castagnoli, Wheeler Yuta, Eddie Kingston & Ortiz)	W	AEW Dynamite: Blood & Guts	46:45

SANTOS ESCOBAR

Jan 11	Xyon Quinn	W	NXT 2.0	10:38
Feb 15	Bron Breakker	L	NXT 2.0: Vengeance Day '22	12:05
Mar 15	Ladder Match: Cameron Grimes	W	NXT 2.0	11:30
Apr 2	Ladder Match: Cameron Grimes, Carmelo Hayes, Solo Sikoa, Grayson Waller	L	NXT Stand & Deliver '22	21:01
Apr 19	Carmelo Hayes	L	NXT 2.0	13:54
May 17	Tony D'Angelo	W	NXT 2.0	12:49
Jun 4	Tony D'Angelo, Channing Lorenzo & Troy Donovan (w/Cruz del Toro & Joaquin Wilde)	L	NXT In Your House '22	12:45
Jun 7	Nathan Frazer	L	NXT 2.0	11:54
Aug 16	Street Fight: Tony D'Angelo	L	NXT 2.0: Heatwave	12:44
Oct 28	Shinsuke Nakamura, Ashante Adonis & Top Dolla (w/Joaquin Wilde & Cruz Del Toro)	L	WWE SmackDown	4:19
Nov 11	Shinsuke Nakamura	W	WWE SmackDown	8:20
Nov 25	Butch	W	WWE SmackDown	6:41
Dec 2	Ricochet	L	WWE SmackDown	20:45

SARAH LOGAN

Jan 29	Royal Rumble Match	L	WWE Royal Rumble '22	:43

SARAYA

Nov 19	Dr. Britt Baker D.M.D.	W	AEW Full Gear '22	12:30

SARRAY

Feb 1	Kayla Inlay	W	NXT 2.0	3:29
Feb 8	Dakota Kai	W	NXT 2.0	6:20
Feb 25	Elektra Lopez	L	NXT Level Up	3:43
Mar 15	Tiffany Stratton	L	NXT 2.0	:54
Apr 19	Tiffany Stratton	L	NXT 2.0	4:31
May 6	Ivy Nile & Tatum Paxley (w/Erica Yan)	L	NXT Level Up	5:32
May 10	Tiffany Stratton & Grayson Waller (w/Andre Chase)	W	NXT 2.0	7:00
Jun 23	Nina Samuels	W	NXT UK	5:34
Jul 7	Eliza Alexander & Xia Brookside (w/Meiko Satomura)	W	NXY UK	9:27
Aug 2	Mandy Rose	L	NXT 2.0	5:44

SASHA BANKS

Jan 29	Royal Rumble Match	L	WWE Royal Rumble '22	9:44
Feb 25	Shotzi	W	WWE SmackDown	2:10
Mar 11	Shayna Baszler & Natalya (w/Naomi)	W	WWE SmackDown	3:19
Mar 18	Rhea Ripley & Liv Morgan (w/Naomi)	D	WWE SmackDown	12:00
Mar 25	Queen Zelina, Shayna Baszler, Rhea Ripley	W	WWE SmackDown	8:43
Mar 28	Queen Zelina, Carmella, Natalya & Shayna Baszler (w/Naomi, Liv Morgan & Rhea Ripley)	W	WWE Monday Night RAW	8:20
Apr 1	Carmella & Queen Zelina (w/Naomi)	W	WWE SmackDown	3:13
Apr 3	Natalya & Shayna Baszler, Carmella & Queen Zelina, Rhea Ripley & Liv Morgan (w/Naomi)	W	WWE WrestleMania XXXVIII	10:50
Apr 4	Liv Morgan & Rhea Ripley (w/Naomi)	W	WWE Monday Night RAW	9:00
Apr 8	Liv Morgan	L	WWE SmackDown	7:08

Apr 18	Liv Morgan & Rhea Ripley (w/Naomi)	W	WWE Monday Night RAW	7:25
May 6	Shayna Baszler	L	WWE SmackDown	8:05
May 9	Doudrop & Nikki A.S.H. (w/Naomi)	W	WWE Monday Night RAW	4:25
May 13	Natalya & Shayna Baszler (w/Naomi)	W	WWE SmackDown	8:30

SATNAM SINGH

Jun 10	Mat Fitchett & Davey Vega (w/Jay Lethal)	W	AEW Rampage	1:37
Jul 4	Cage Alexander & Ryan Jones (w/Jay Lethal)	W	AEW Dark Elevation	2:30
Jul 5	Darian Bengston & Gus De La Vega (w/Jay Lethal)	W	AEW Dark	4:11
Jul 29	Orange Cassidy, Chuck Taylor & Trent Beretta (w/Jay Lethal & Sonjay Dutt)	L	AEW Rampage	7:29
Oct 17	Dylan Davis & Junior Benito (w/Jay Lethal)	W	AEW Dark Elevation	2:32
Nov 28	GPA & Joe Alonzo (w/Jay Lethal)	W	AEW Dark Elevation	1:44
Dec 6	JCruz & Victor Chase (w/Jay Lethal)	W	AEW Dark	1:54
Dec 20	Dean Alexander & Rosario Grillo (w/Jeff Jarrett)	W	AEW Dark	2:32

SAVANNAH EVANS

Feb 17	Chelsea Green & Mickie James (w/Tasha Steelz)	W	IMPACT Wrestling	12:26
Mar 10	Chelsea Green, Mickie James, Cassie Lee & Jessie McKay (w/Tasha Steelz, Madison Rayne & Tenille Dashwood)	L	IMPACT Wrestling	6:00
Mar 31	Battle Royal	L	IMPACT Wrestling	7:15
Apr 1	Madison Rayne & Tenille Dashwood, Gisele Shaw & Lady Frost, Havok & Rosemary (w/Tasha Steelz)	L	IMPACT Multiverse Of Matches	9:02
Apr 28	Havok & Rosemary (w/Tasha Steelz)	L	IMPACT Wrestling	4:51
May 19	Jordynne Grace, Mia Yim & Taya Valkyrie (w/Deonna Purrazzo & Tasha Steelz)	L	IMPACT Wrestling	12:00
Jun 2	Mia Yim	L	IMPACT Wrestling	7:51
Jun 16	Jordynne Grace & Mia Yim (w/Tasha Steelz)	W	IMPACT Wrestling	6:49
Jun 30	Jordynne Grace	L	IMPACT Wrestling	3:47
Aug 4	Alisha Edwards	W	IMPACT Wrestling	7:33
Aug 18	Killer Kelly	L	IMPACT Wrestling	3:30
Oct 7	Call Your Shot Gauntlet	L	IMPACT Bound For Glory '22	29:18
Nov 3	Jessicka	W	IMPACT Wrestling	7:38
Dec 8	Taya Valkyrie	W	IMPACT Wrestling	6:51
Dec 22	Mickie James & Jordynne Grace (w/Tasha Steel)	L	IMPACT Wrestling	11:08

SAXON HUXLEY

Jan 20	Lewis Howley & Sam Stoker (w/Sam Gradwell)	L	NXT UK	9:22
Feb 10	A-Kid	L	NXT UK	7:03
Mar 24	Charlie Dempsey & Rohan Raja (w/A-Kid)	L	NXT UK	8:24
Apr 28	Von Wagner	L	NXT UK	4:04
May 26	Mark Coffey	L	NXT UK	4:13
Aug 18	Andre Chase & Bodhi Hayward (w/Eddie Dennis)	L	NXT UK	6:49
Sep 1	Kenny Williams	W	NXT UK	5:44

SCARLETT BORDEAUX

| Nov 10 | Clara Carreras | W | MLW Fusion | 1:47 |

SCORPIO SKY

Jan 3	Ray Jaz	W	AEW Dark Elevation	2:41
Jan 24	Logan LaRoux & Mike Fowler (w/Ethan Page)	W	AEW Dark Elevation	3:00
Feb 7	Stephen Wolf	W	AEW Dark Elevation	3:40
Feb 14	Jaden Valo & Steve Pena (w/Ethan Page)	W	AEW Dark Elevation	3:12
Mar 7	Shawn Dean	W	AEW Dark Elevation	5:11
Mar 8	Sonny Kiss	W	AEW Dark	5:42
Mar 9	Sammy Guevara	W	AEW Dynamite	11:50
Mar 16	Wardlow	W	AEW Dynamite: St. Patrick's Day Slam	9:20
Apr 16	Sammy Guevara	L	AEW Battle Of The Belts II	12:45
Apr 27	Steel Cage Match: Sammy Guevara	W	AEW Dynamite	14:06
May 13	Frankie Kazarian	W	AEW Rampage	11:37
May 29	Frankie Kazarian, Sammy Guevara & Tay Conti (w/Ethan Page & Paige VanZant)	W	AEW Double Or Nothing '22	12:30
Jun 3	Dante Martin	W	AEW Rampage	8:10
Jul 6	Street Fight: Wardlow	L	AEW Dynamite	8:29

SCRYPTS (AS REGGIE UNTIL NOVEMBER 22)

Jan 3	Tamina & Akira Tozawa (w/Dana Brooke)	W	WWE Monday Night RAW	1:10
Jan 17	Omos	L	WWE Monday Night RAW	:28
Feb 21	Dana Brooke	L	WWE Monday Night RAW	3:10
Feb 28	Tamina & Akira Tozawa (w/Dana Brooke)	W	WWE Monday Night RAW	1:40
Mar 21	Tamina & Akira Tozawa (w/Dana Brooke)	W	WWE Monday Night RAW	1:05
Apr 1	Andre The Giant Memorial Battle Royal	L	WWE SmackDown	8:05
Apr 25	Tamina & Akira Tozawa (w/Dana Brooke)	L	WWE Monday Night RAW	1:30
May 12	T-Bar	L	WWE Main Event	2:50
May 19	Ciampa	L	WWE Main Event	5:37
Jun 9	Ciampa	L	WWE Main Event	5:29
Jun 16	T-Bar	L	WWE Main Event	6:29
Jun 27	Battle Royal	L	WWE Monday Night RAW	19:25
Jul 21	Akira Tozawa	L	WWE Main Event	6:12
Sep 8	Shelton Benjamin	L	WWE Main Event	6:09
Nov 22	Guru Raaj	W	NXT	1:22
Dec 27	Ikemen Jiro	W	NXT	4:14

SERENA DEEB

Jan 12	Hikaru Shida	W	AEW Dynamite		1:59
Jan 19	Skye Blue	W	AEW Dynamite		2:51
Feb 9	Katie Arquette	W	AEW Dynamite		1:02
Feb 18	Angelica Risk	W	AEW Rampage: Slam Dunk		2:04
Feb 25	Kayla Sparks	W	AEW Rampage		2:29
Mar 4	Leila Gray	W	AEW Rampage		:58
Apr 4	Dani Mo	W	AEW Dark Elevation		2:15
Apr 27	Street Fight: Hikaru Shida	L	AEW Dynamite		11:40
May 29	Thunder Rosa	L	AEW Double Or Nothing '22		16:55
Jun 6	Miyu Yamashita & Skye Blue (w/Nyla Rose)	W	AEW Dark Elevation		7:40
Jun 13	Miranda Gordy & Tootie Lynn (w/Mercedes Martinez)	W	AEW Dark Elevation		4:15
Jun 20	Heather Reckless & Tootie Lynn (w/Mercedes Martinez)	W	AEW Dark Elevation		4:29
Jun 21	Anna Diaz & Yaide (w/Mercedes Martinez)	W	AEW Dark		2:21
Jun 24	Laynie Luck & Sierra (w/Mercedes Martinez)	W	AEW Rampage		3:25
Jul 8	Christina Marie & Kayla Sparks (w/Mercedes Martinez)	W	AEW Rampage		2:23
Jul 13	Anna Jay	W	AEW Dynamite: Fyter Fest		8:22
Jul 19	Viva Van	W	AEW Dark		3:56
Jul 23	Mercedes Martinez	L	ROH Death Before Dishonor XIX		17:20
Aug 9	Athena, Hikaru Shida & Ruby Soho (w/Emi Sakura & Leva Bates)	L	AEW Dark		8:08
Aug 15	Sierra	W	AEW Dark Elevation		2:58
Aug 22	Megan Meyers	W	AEW Dark Elevation		2:57
Aug 29	Katie Arquette	W	AEW Dark Elevation		2:03
Sep 5	Nikki Victory	W	AEW Dark Elevation		3:50
Sep 6	Sierra	W	AEW Dark		4:48
Sep 9	Madison Rayne	W	AEW Rampage		3:56
Sep 14	Toni Storm & Athena (w/Dr. Britt Baker D.M.D.)	W	AEW Dynamite		8:34
Sep 21	Toni Storm, Athena, Dr. Britt Baker D.M.D.	L	AEW Dynamite: Grand Slam		9:50
Sep 28	Lumberjack Match: Toni Storm	L	AEW Dynamite		11:09
Oct 5	Toni Storm, Athena & Willow Nightingale (w/Jamie Hayter & Penelope Ford)	L	AEW Dynamite: Anniversary		9:29
Oct 11	Brittany Blake, Jordan Blade & Trish Adora (w/Jamie Hayter & Penelope Ford)	W	AEW Dark		4:32
Oct 17	Madison Rayne & Skye Blue (w/Emi Sakura)	W	AEW Dark Elevation		6:00
Oct 24	Haley J	W	AEW Dark Elevation		2:01
Oct 25	KC Spinelli & Taylor Rising (w/Emi Sakura)	W	AEW Dark		4:34

SERPENTICO

Jan 3	Jake Atlas	L	AEW Dark Elevation		2:19
Jan 11	Hangman Page, Alan Angels & Ten (w/Matt Hardy & Isiah Kassidy)	L	AEW Dark		14:27
Jan 21	Hook	L	AEW Rampage		1:10
Jan 31	Penta El Zero M	L	AEW Dark Elevation		5:30
Feb 7	Chuck Taylor & Trent Beretta (w/Luther)	L	AEW Dark Elevation		6:42
Feb 8	Fuego Del Sol	L	AEW Dark		5:42
Feb 14	Zack Clayton	L	AEW Dark		3:46
Feb 15	Alan Angels & Ten (w/Luther)	L	AEW Dark		8:16
Feb 21	Brock Anderson, Frankie Kazarian, Jay Lethal, Lee Johnson & Matt Sydal (w/Luther, Cezar Bononi, JD Drake & Peter Avalon)	L	AEW Dark Elevation		6:06
Feb 22	Matt Sydal	L	AEW Dark		6:27
Feb 28	Evil Uno & Stu Grayson (w/Luther)	L	AEW Dark Elevation		4:53
Mar 8	Jay Lethal	L	AEW Dark		5:12
Mar 14	John Silver & Alex Reynolds (w/Luther)	L	AEW Dark Elevation		4:40
Mar 15	John Silver & Alex Reynolds (w/Luther)	L	AEW Dark		4:26
Mar 21	Dante Martin & Darius Martin (w/Luther)	L	AEW Dark Elevation		4:54
Mar 28	Lee Moriarty	L	AEW Dark Elevation		3:59
Apr 11	John Silver, Alex Reynolds, Alan Angels, Stu Grayson & Ten (w/Luther, Austin Gunn, Colten Gunn & Billy Gunn)	L	AEW Dark Elevation		5:20
Apr 22	Lance Archer	L	AEW Rampage		:33
Apr 26	Lee Moriarty	L	AEW Dark		3:50
May 10	Shawn Dean	L	AEW Dark		7:30
May 17	Keith Lee & Swerve Strickland (w/Luther)	L	AEW Dark		6:00
May 27	Matt Jackson & Nick Jackson (w/Taylor Rust)	L	AEW Rampage		2:39
May 31	John Silver, Evil Uno & Ten (w/Peter Avalon & Ryan Nemeth)	L	AEW Dark		5:37
Jun 6	Frankie Kazarian	L	AEW Dark Elevation		5:00
Jun 7	Ortiz	L	AEW Dark		4:07
Jun 21	Vary Morales	W	AEW Dark		3:16
Jun 27	Ethan Page	L	AEW Dark Elevation		1:37
Jun 29	Luchasaurus	L	AEW Dynamite: Blood & Guts		:49
Aug 1	Cole Karter	L	AEW Dark Elevation		4:02
Aug 2	Parker Boudreaux	L	AEW Dark		1:47
Aug 4	Mance Warner	L	AEW Dark Elevation		3:57
Aug 16	Brock Anderson	L	AEW Dark		6:38
Aug 19	Buddy Matthews	L	AEW Rampage		1:33
Aug 30	John Silver	L	AEW Dark		4:10
Sep 6	Zack Clayton	L	AEW Dark		4:37
Sep 12	Dante Martin & Matt Sydal (w/Zack Clayton)	L	AEW Dark Elevation		:57
Sep 19	Mascara Dorada	L	AEW Dark Elevation		2:46
Sep 26	Ortiz	L	AEW Dark Elevation		3:22
Oct 10	Brandon Cutler	L	AEW Dark Elevation		5:45
Oct 25	Aaron Solo	L	AEW Dark		5:13
Oct 28	Keith Lee	L	AEW Rampage		:14
Nov 14	AR Fox	L	AEW Dark Elevation		3:07

Nov 28	Matt Hardy, Isiah Kassidy & Marq Quen (w/Isaia Moore & Luther)	L	AEW Dark Elevation	4:50
Dec 5	Lee Moriarty	L	AEW Dark Elevation	3:23
Dec 12	Ari Daivari, Josh Woods & Tony Nese (w/Brandon Cutler & Luther)	L	AEW Dark Elevation	5:20
Dec 20	Jarett Diaz, Jay Marti & Richard Adonis (w/Angelico & Luther)	W	AEW Dark	4:07
Dec 23	$300,000 Three Kings Christmas Casino Trios Royale (w/Luther & Angelico)	L	AEW Rampage	22:01

SETH ROLLINS

Jan 1	Brock Lesnar, Big E, Kevin Owens, Bobby Lashley	L	WWE Day 1	8:19
Jan 3	Bobby Lashley, Big E, Kevin Owens	L	WWE Monday Night RAW	18:40
Jan 10	Big E	W	WWE Monday Night RAW	18:00
Jan 17	Bobby Lashley	L	WWE Monday Night RAW	13:17
Jan 21	Jimmy Uso & Jey Uso (w/Kevin Owens)	W	WWE SmackDown	15:00
Jan 29	Roman Reigns	W	WWE Royal Rumble '22	14:25
Feb 7	Riddle	L	WWE Monday Night RAW	7:39
Feb 7	Randy Orton & Riddle (w/Kevin Owens)	W	WWE Monday Night RAW	8:05
Feb 14	Randy Orton	W	WWE Monday Night RAW	15:17
Feb 19	Elimination Chamber: AJ Styles, Austin Theory, Riddle, Brock Lesnar	L	WWE Elimination Chamber '22	9:50
Feb 21	Randy Orton & Riddle (w/Kevin Owens)	W	WWE Monday Night RAW	12:40
Feb 28	Chad Gable & Otis (w/Kevin Owens)	W	WWE Monday Night RAW	12:50
Mar 7	No DQ: Randy Orton & Riddle, Chad Gable & Otis (w/Kevin Owens)	L	WWE Monday Night RAW	27:05
Mar 14	Kevin Owens	L	WWE Monday Night RAW	16:20
Mar 21	AJ Styles	L	WWE Monday Night RAW	22:45
Apr 2	Cody Rhodes	L	WWE WrestleMania XXXVIII	21:40
Apr 25	Cody Rhodes, Ezekiel, Randy Orton & Riddle (w/Kevin Owens, Jimmy Uso & Jey Uso)	L	WWE Monday Night RAW	14:58
May 8	Cody Rhodes	L	WWE WrestleMania Backlash '22	20:45
Jun 5	Hell In A Cell: Seth Rollins	L	WWE Hell In A Cell '22	24:20
Jun 13	AJ Styles	W	WWE Monday Night RAW	15:05
Jul 1	Battle Royal	L	WWE SmackDown	14:36
Jul 2	Money In The Bank Ladder Match: Drew McIntyre, Madcap Moss, Theory, Omos, Riddle, Sami Zayn, Sheamus	L	WWE Money In The Bank '22	25:25
Jul 4	Ezekiel	W	WWE Monday Night RAW	10:15
Jul 11	Bobby Lashley & Riddle (w/Theory)	L	WWE Monday Night RAW	13:50
Jul 18	Ezekiel	W	WWE Monday Night RAW	11:55
Aug 1	Montez Ford	W	WWE Monday Night RAW	10:59
Aug 8	Angelo Dawkins	W	WWE Monday Night RAW	8:50
Sep 3	Matt Riddle	W	WWE Clash At The Castle	17:22
Sep 19	Bobby Lashley	L	WWE Monday Night RAW	20:15
Sep 26	Rey Mysterio	W	WWE Monday Night RAW	17:57
Oct 8	Fight Pit Match: Matt Riddle	L	WWE Extreme Rules '22	16:35
Oct 10	Bobby Lashley	W	WWE Monday Night RAW	2:35
Oct 17	Matt Riddle	W	WWE Monday Night RAW	14:50
Oct 31	Austin Theory	W	WWE Monday Night RAW	14:40
Nov 7	Austin Theory	W	WWE Monday Night RAW	5:00
Nov 14	Finn Balor	W	WWE Monday Night RAW	21:10
Nov 26	Austin Theory, Bobby Lashley	L	WWE Survivor Series WarGames	14:50
Dec 12	Bobby Lashley	W	WWE Monday Night RAW	12:55
Dec 19	Jey Uso & Jimmy Uso (w/Kevin Owens)	W	WWE Monday Night RAW	10:50

SHA SAMUELS

Mar 3	Mark Coffey	L	NXT UK	7:41
May 26	Damon Kemp	W	NXT UK	5:42
Jun 16	Damon Kemp & Wolfgang (w/Noam Dar)	L	NXT UK	12:41
Jun 30	Wolfgang	L	NXT UK	10:18
Aug 4	Bodhi Hayward	W	NXT UK	4:43

SHANE HASTE

Apr 2	David Finlay & Juice Robinson (w/Jonah)	L	NJPW Strong	6:34
Apr 16	Chicago Street Fight: David Finlay, Juice Robinson & Brody King (w/Jonah and Bad Dude Tito)	L	NJPW Windy City Riot	24:11
May 14	Aaron Henare, Kyle Fletcher, Mark Davis & Jeff Cobb (w/Mikey Nicholls, Jonah & Bad Dude Tito)	W	NJPW Capital Collision	12:09
May 28	Jeff Cobb, Kyle Fletcher & Mark Davis (w/Bad Dude Tito & Jonah)	L	NJPW Strong	14:39
Jul 2	Aaron Henare, Great-O-Khan, Kyle Fletcher & Mark Davis (w/Bad Dude Tito, Jonah & Mikey Nicholls)	L	NJPW Strong	11:35
Jul 9	Jorel Nelson & Royce Isaacs (w/Mikey Nicholls)	W	NJPW Strong	10:21
Jul 23	Christopher Daniels & Yuya Uemura (w/Mikey Nicholls)	L	NJPW Strong	10:02
Aug 13	Jorel Nelson	L	NJPW Strong	8:16
Sep 24	Christopher Daniels & Yuya Uemura (w/Bad Dude Tito)	W	NJPW Strong	9:10
Sep 25	Togi Makabe, Tomoaki Honma & Kazuchika Okada (w/Bad Dude Tito & Jonah)	W	NJPW Burning Spirit '22	12:09
Oct 10	Taichi & Zack Sabre Jr. (w/Bad Dude Tito)	L	NJPW Declaration Of Power	9:58
Nov 15	Barrett Brown & Misterioso, Kevin Knight & The DKC, Jorel Nelson & Royce Isaacs (w/Bad Dude Tito)	L	NJPW Strong	12:36

SHANE MCMAHON

Jan 29	Royal Rumble Match	L	WWE Royal Rumble '22	5:38

SHANKY

Jan 14	Erik & Ivar, Angel & Humberto, Cesaro & Mansoor (w/Jinder Mahal)	L	WWE SmackDown	13:21
Jan 28	Shinsuke Nakamura & Rick Boogs (w/Jinder Mahal)	L	WWE SmackDown	3:05

Mar 18	Drew McInytre, Erik & Ivar (w/Happy Corbin & Jinder Mahal)	L	WWE SmackDown	7:10
Apr 1	Andre The Giant Memorial Battle Royal	L	WWE SmackDown	8:05
Apr 29	Ricochet	L	WWE SmackDown	3:34
May 27	Angel & Humberto (w/Jinder Mahal)	L	WWE SmackDown	2:15
Jun 17	Xavier Woods & Kofi Kingston (w/Jinder Mahal)	L	WWE SmackDown	3:02
Jun 27	Battle Royal	L	WWE Monday Night RAW	19:25
Jul 8	Erik & Ivar (w/Jinder Mahal)	L	WWE SmackDown	1:15
Jul 22	Erik & Ivar (w/Jinder Mahal)	L	WWE SmackDown	1:30

SHARK BOY

Jan 27	Handicap Match: W. Morrissey (w/VSK, Zicky Dice, D-Ray 3000, David Young, Elix Skipper, Mikey Batts, Lev Lovett & Jerelle Clark	L	IMPACT Wrestling	3:00
May 12	Gauntlet For The Gold	L	IMPACT Wrestling	39:00
Jun 23	Johnny Swinger & Zicky Dice (w/Bhupinder Gujjar)	W	IMPACT Wrestling	3:50

SHAWN DEAN

Jan 5	MJF	W	AEW Dynamite	:47
Jan 11	Liam Cross	W	AEW Dark	2:23
Feb 21	Andrade El Idolo, Isiah Kassidy, Marq Quen, The Butcher & The Blade (w/Baron Black, Carlie Bravo, Chandler Hopkins & Jameson Ryan)	L	AEW Dark Elevation	4:20
Mar 1	Will Austin	W	AEW Dark	2:50
Mar 7	Scorpio Sky	L	AEW Dark Elevation	5:11
Mar 22	The Butcher & The Blade (w/Carlie Bravo)	L	AEW Dark	2:41
Apr 6	Shawn Spears	W	AEW Dynamite	3:50
Apr 12	Rohit Raju	W	AEW Dark	5:44
Apr 13	MJF	W	AEW Dynamite	4:07
May 10	Serpentico	W	AEW Dark	7:30
Jul 12	Conan Lycan	W	AEW Dark	4:48
Aug 2	Jonathan Hudson	W	AEW Dark	2:22
Sep 26	Kip Sabian & Penelope Ford (w/Skye Blue)	L	AEW Dark Elevation	5:16
Dec 7	Dynamite Diamond Battle Royale	L	AEW Dynamite	13:10

SHAWN SPEARS

Jan 17	Andrew Everett	W	AEW Rampage	:57
Jan 19	CM Punk	L	AEW Dynamite	:12
Apr 6	Shawn Dean	L	AEW Dynamite	3:50
May 3	Lord Crewe	W	AEW Dark	3:50
May 13	Bear Boulder	W	AEW Rampage	2:03
May 20	Big Damo	W	AEW Rampage	1:40
May 25	Steel Cage Match: Wardlow	L	AEW Dynamite: 3 Year Anniversary	6:56
Oct 14	Brian Cage, Kaun & Toa Liona (w/Dax Harwood & Cash Wheeler)	L	AEW Rampage	10:29

SHAYNA BASZLER

Jan 29	Royal Rumble Match	L	WWE Royal Rumble '22	5:31
Mar 11	Sasha Banks & Naomi (w/Natalya)	L	WWE SmackDown	3:19
Mar 21	Liv Morgan & Rhea Ripley (w/Natalya)	W	WWE Monday Night RAW	3:55
Mar 25	Sasha Banks, Queen Zelina, Rhea Ripley	L	WWE SmackDown	8:43
Mar 28	Naomi, Sasha Banks, Liv Morgan & Rhea Ripley (w/Queen Zelina, Carmella & Natalya)	L	WWE Monday Night RAW	8:20
Apr 3	Sasha Banks & Naomi, Carmella & Queen Zelina, Rhea Ripley & Liv Morgan (w/Natalya)	L	WWE WrestleMania XXXVIII	10:50
Apr 29	Naomi	L	WWE SmackDown	2:27
May 6	Sasha Banks	W	WWE SmackDown	8:05
May 13	Sasha Banks & Naomi (w/Natalya)	L	WWE SmackDown	8:30
May 27	Ronda Rousey & Raquel Rodriguez (w/Natalya)	L	WWE SmackDown	7:35
Jun 3	Natalya, Raquel Rodriguez, Shotzi, Aliyah, Xia Li	L	WWE SmackDown	5:54
Jun 17	Raquel Rodriguez	L	WWE SmackDown	3:15
Jun 27	Becky Lynch, Doudrop, Nikki A.S.H., Xia Li, Tamina	L	WWE Monday Night RAW	13:20
Aug 5	Gauntlet Match: Sonya Deville, Raquel Rodriguez, Aliyah, Shotzi, Xia Li, Natalya	W	WWE SmackDown	21:05
Sep 3	Liv Morgan	L	WWE Clash At The Castle	11:02
Nov 4	Natalya	W	WWE SmackDown	4:11
Nov 18	Shotzi	L	WWE SmackDown	5:01
Nov 25	Shotzi & Raquel Rodriguez (w/Ronda Rousey)	W	WWE SmackDown	3:26
Dec 2	Emma	W	WWE SmackDown	4:10
Dec 9	Liv Morgan & Tegan Nox (w/Ronda Rousey)	L	WWE SmackDown	4:07
Dec 16	Gauntlet Match: Raquel Rodriguez, Xia Li, Emma, Liv Morgan, Sonya Deville, Tegan Nox		WWE SmackDown	
Dec 17	Emma & Tamina (w/Ronda Rousey)	W	WWE Tribute To The Troops '22	7:34

SHEAMUS

Jan 1	Ricochet & Cesaro (w/Ridge Holland)	W	WWE Day 1 Kickoff	9:45
Jan 14	Ricochet	W	WWE SmackDown	9:53
Jan 21	Ricochet	W	WWE SmackDown	3:20
Jan 28	Ricochet & Cesaro (w/Ridge Holland)	W	WWE SmackDown	10:45
Jan 29	Royal Rumble Match	L	WWE Royal Rumble '22	17:55
Feb 4	Ricochet & Cesaro (w/Ridge Holland)	W	WWE SmackDown	5:34
Feb 18	Ricochet	L	WWE SmackDown	10:55
Mar 11	Big E & Kofi Kingston (w/Ridge Holland)	W	WWE SmackDown	8:49
Apr 3	Kofi Kingston & Xavier Woods (w/Ridge Holland)	W	WWE WrestleMania XXXVIII	1:40
Apr 29	Kofi Kingston	W	WWE SmackDown	2:57
May 6	Tables Match: Xavier Woods & Kofi Kingston (w/Ridge Holland)	W	WWE SmackDown	12:30

May 27	Drew McIntyre, Xavier Woods & Kofi Kingston (w/Ridge Holland & Butch)	L	WWE SmackDown	11:30
Jun 3	Drew McIntyre, Xavier Woods & Kofi Kingston (w/Ridge Holland & Butch)	W	WWE SmackDown	10:30
Jun 10	Drew McIntyre	D	WWE SmackDown	11:50
Jun 24	Jimmy Uso & Jey Uso (w/Drew McIntyre)	W	WWE SmackDown	11:20
Jul 1	Battle Royal	L	WWE SmackDown	14:36
Jul 2	Money In The Bank Ladder Match: Drew McIntyre, Madcap Moss, Theory, Omos, Riddle, Sami Zayn, Seth Rollins	L	WWE Money In The Bank '22	25:25
Jul 25	Drew McIntyre & Bobby Lashley (w/Theory)	L	WWE Monday Night RAW	12:20
Jul 29	Donnybrook Match: Drew McIntyre	L	WWE SmackDown	25:30
Aug 19	Happy Corbin, Madcap Moss, Ricochet, Sami Zayn	W	WWE SmackDown	22:33
Sep 3	Gunther	L	WWE Clash At The Castle	19:33
Sep 9	Gunther, Ludwig Kaiser & Giovanni Vinci (w/Ridge Holland & Butch)	L	WWE SmackDown	19:05
Oct 7	Gunther	L	WWE SmackDown	18:18
Oct 8	Good Old Fashioned Donnybrook Match: Gunther, Ludwig Kaiser & Giovanni Vinci (w/Butch & Ridge Holland)	W	WWE Extreme Rules '22	17:50
Oct 14	Rey Mysterio, Ricochet, Solo Sikoa	L	WWE SmackDown	16:19
Oct 21	Solo Sikoa	L	WWE SmackDown	13:05
Nov 21	Finn Balor, Damian Priest & Dominik Mysterio (w/Ridge Holland & Butch)	W	WWE Monday Night RAW	14:50
Nov 25	Jimmy Uso & Jey Uso (w/Drew McIntyre)	W	WWE SmackDown	14:43
Nov 26	WarGames: Roman Reigns, Sami Zayn, Solo Sikoa, Jey Uso & Jimmy Uso (w/Butch, Ridge Holland, Drew McIntyre & Kevin Owens)	L	WWE Survivor Series WarGames	38:30
Dec 2	Sami Zayn		WWE SmackDown	18:02
Dec 9	Jey Uso & Jimmy Uso (w/Butch)	L	WWE SmackDown	19:20
Dec 17	Gunther, Giovanni Vinci & Ludwig Kaiser (w/Drew McIntyre & Ricochet)	W	WWE Tribute To The Troops '22	16:34
Dec 30	Solo Sikoa	L	WWE SmackDown	11:10

SHELTON BENJAMIN

Jan 6	Rey Mysterio & Dominik Mysterio (w/Cedric Alexander)	L	WWE Main Event	5:41
Feb 10	Dolph Ziggler & Robert Roode (w/Cedric Alexander)	W	WWE Main Event	7:01
Feb 14	Handicap Match: Omos (w/Cedric Alexander)	L	WWE Monday Night RAW	1:25
Feb 21	Damian Priest	L	WWE Monday Night RAW	3:10
Feb 28	Rey Mysterio & Dominik Mysterio (w/Cedric Alexander)	W	WWE Monday Night RAW	4:30
Mar 10	Angelo Dawkins & Montez Ford (w/Cedric Alexander)	L	WWE Main Event	9:23
Mar 14	Rey Mysterio & Dominik Mysterio (w/Cedric Alexander)	L	WWE Monday Night RAW	3:25
Apr 1	Andre The Giant Memorial Battle Royal	L	WWE SmackDown	8:05
Apr 7	T-Bar	W	WWE Main Event	8:36
Apr 14	Apollo Crews & Commander Azeez (w/Cedric Alexander)	L	WWE Main Event	6:59
Apr 28	Angelo Dawkins & Montez Ford (w/Cedric Alexander)	L	WWE Main Event	9:31
Jun 16	Akira Tozawa	W	WWE Main Event	6:16
Jun 27	Battle Royal	L	WWE Monday Night RAW	19:25
Aug 4	T-Bar	W	WWE Main Event	9:23
Aug 11	Cedric Alexander	L	WWE Main Event	4:51
Aug 18	Akira Tozawa	W	WWE Main Event	5:22
Aug 25	Cedric Alexander & Mustafa Ali (w/T-Bar)	L	WWE Main Event	8:30
Sep 1	R-Truth	W	WWE Main Event	4:42
Sep 8	Reggie	W	WWE Main Event	6:09
Sep 15	Cedric Alexander	W	WWE Main Event	8:00
Sep 22	Chad Gable & Otis (w/Mustafa Ali)	L	WWE Main Event	9:52
Sep 29	R-Truth	L	WWE Main Event	8:57
Oct 6	Brooks Jensen & Josh Briggs (w/R-Truth)	L	WWE Main Event	6:48
Nov 3	Duke Hudson & Von Wagner (w/R-Truth)	W	WWE Main Event	6:31
Nov 7	Austin Theory	L	WWE Monday Night RAW	2:40
Nov 14	Dominik Mysterio	L	WWE Monday Night RAW	5:00

SHERA

Mar 24	Crazzy Steve	W	IMPACT Before The Impact	7:15
Apr 21	Gabriel Rodriguez	W	IMPACT Wrestling	:23
May 12	Gauntlet For The Gold	L	IMPACT Wrestling	39:00
May 26	Bhupinder Gujjar & W. Morrissey (w/Raj Singh)	L	IMPACT Wrestling	5:17
Jul 7	Rich Swann	L	IMPACT Wrestling	3:49
Jul 28	Josh Alexander	L	IMPACT Wrestling	3:12
Oct 13	Chris Sabin & Alex Shelley (w/Raj Singh)	L	IMPACT Before The Impact	7:16
Nov 17	Ace Austin & Chris Bey, Kyle Fletcher & Mark Davis, Alex Shelley & Chris Sabin (w/Raj Singh)	L	IMPACT Wrestling	13:03
Nov 24	Yuya Uemura & Delirious (w/Raj Singh)	W	IMPACT Before The Impact	9:22
Dec 15	Jake Price	W	IMPACT Before The Impact	8:24

SHINGO TAKAGI

Jan 4	Kazuchika Okada	L	NJPW Wrestle Kingdom 16 Night #1	35:44
Jan 8	Katsuhiko Nakajima, Kenoh, Manabu Soya, Tadasuke & Aleja (w/Tetsuya Naito, Sanada, Bushi & Hiromu Takahashi)	W	NJPW Wrestle Kingdom 16 Night #3	26:33
Mar 1	Togi Makabe, Tomoaki Honma, Tomohiro Ishii, Shiro Koshinaka & Toru Yano (w/Sanada, Tetsuya Naito, Bushi & Hiromu Takahashi)	W	NJPW 50th Anniversary Show	12:38
Apr 9	Will Ospreay & Aaron Henare (w/Tetsuya Naito)	W	NJPW Hyper Battle '22	9:23
May 1	Taichi, Zack Sabre Jr. & Taka Michinoku (w/Bushi & Shiro Koshinaka)	L	NJPW Wrestling Dontaku '22	10:15
Jun 12	10 Minute Unlimited Pinfall Scramble: Taichi	W	NJPW Dominion '22	10:00
Jun 26	El Phantasmo, Matt Jackson & Nick Jackson (w/Darby Allin & Sting)	W	AEW x NJPW Forbidden Door	13:01
Sep 25	El Phantasmo, Hikuleo & Kenta (w/Bushi & Hiromu Takahashi)	W	NJPW Burning Spirit '22	8:43
Oct 10	Who's Your Daddy Match: El Phantasmo	W	NJPW Declaration Of Power	16:01
Oct 22	Rocky Romero	W	NJPW Strong	15:51
Oct 28	New York City Street Fight: El Phantasmo	W	NJPW Rumble On 44th Street	20:59
Nov 20	Kyle Fletcher, Mark Davis, Francesco Akira, TJP & Gideon Grey (w/Bushi, Hiromu Takahashi, Sanada & Tetsuya Naito)	L	NJPW x Stardom Historic X-Over	9:55

SHINSUKE NAKAMURA

Jan 28	Jinder Mahal & Shanky (w/Rick Boogs)	W	WWE SmackDown	3:05
Jan 29	Royal Rumble Match	L	WWE Royal Rumble '22	5:51
Feb 4	Jinder Mahal	W	WWE SmackDown	3:09
Feb 18	Sami Zayn	L	WWE SmackDown	18:15
Mar 18	Angel & Humberto (w/Rick Boogs)	W	WWE SmackDown	4:55
Mar 25	Jimmy Uso	W	WWE SmackDown	8:48
Apr 1	Austin Theory, Jimmy Uso & Jey Uso (w/Finn Balor & Rick Boogs)	L	WWE SmackDown	11:27
Apr 2	Jimmy Uso & Jey Uso (w/Rick Boogs)	L	WWE WrestleMania XXXVIII	6:55
May 6	Sami Zayn	L	WWE SmackDown	9:15
May 20	Sami Zayn	W	WWE SmackDown	10:28
May 30	Jimmy Uso & Jey Uso (w/Riddle)	W	WWE Monday Night RAW	12:30
Jun 24	Sami Zayn	L	WWE SmackDown	9:55
Jun 27	Battle Royal	L	WWE Monday Night RAW	19:25
Jul 8	Ludwig Kaiser	W	WWE SmackDown	6:40
Jul 22	Ludwig Kaiser	L	WWE SmackDown	9:30
Aug 5	Ludwig Kaiser	W	WWE SmackDown	8:45
Aug 12	Gunther	L	WWE SmackDown	14:20
Sep 2	Happy Corbin	W	WWE SmackDown	2:20
Oct 18	Channing Lorenzo	W	NXT	5:22
Oct 28	Santos Escobar, Joaquin Wilde & Cruz Del Toro (w/Ashante Adonis & Top Dolla)	W	WWE SmackDown	4:19
Nov 11	Santos Escobar	L	WWE SmackDown	8:20

SHO

Jan 4	Yoh	L	NJPW Wrestle Kingdom 16 Night #1	12:32
Jan 5	Hirooki Goto, Yoshi-Hashi & Yoh (w/Evil & Yujiro Takahashi)	W	NJPW Wrestle Kingdom 16 Night #2	9:37
Jan 8	Atsushi Kotoge	W	NJPW Wrestle Kingdom 16 Night #3	8:20
Mar 1	Tiger Mask, Yoh & Ryohei Oiwa (w/Evil & Yujiro Takahashi)	W	NJPW 50th Anniversary Show	6:35
Apr 9	El Desperado	L	NJPW Hyper Battle '22	20:33
Jun 12	Zack Sabre Jr., El Desperado & Yoshinobu Kanemaru (w/Evil & Yujiro Takahashi)	W	NJPW Dominion '22	9:26
Oct 10	Hiroshi Tanahashi, Hikuleo & Ryusuke Taguchi (w/Evil & Yujiro Takahashi)	L	NJPW Declaration Of Power	7:14
Oct 28	Rocky Romero & Yoh (w/Yujiro Takahashi)	W	NJPW Rumble On 44th Street	7:42
Nov 20	Lio Rush, Tomohiro Ishii, Yoh & Yoshi-Hashi (w/Dick Togo, Evil & Yujiro Takahashi)	L	NJPW Historic X-Over	7:05

SHOTA UMINO

Apr 16	Jay White	L	NJPW Windy City Riot	15:45
Jun 26	Chris Jericho, Minoru Suzuki & Sammy Guevara (w/Eddie Kingston & Wheeler Yuta)	L	AEW x NJPW Forbidden Door	18:58
Jul 12	Pac	L	AEW Dark	18:43
Jul 30	Kevin Knight, Ren Narita & The DKC (w/Fred Yehi & Yuya Uemura)	W	NJPW Music City Mayhem	13:12
Oct 1	Will Ospreay	L	NJPW Royal Quest II Night #1	15:30
Oct 2	Will Ospreay, Great-O-Khan, Mark Davis, Kyle Fletcher & Gideon Grey (w/Cash Wheeler, Dax Harwood, Gabriel Kidd & Ricky Knight Jr.)	L	NJPW Royal Quest II Night #2	16:57
Oct 8	QT Marshall	W	NJPW Strong	10:11
Oct 28	Tom Lawlor, Royce Isaacs & Jorel Nelson (w/Homicide & Wheeler Yuta)	W	NJPW Rumble On 44th Street	12:15
Nov 20	Will Ospreay	L	NJPW x Stardom Historic X-Over	23:30

SHOTZI

Jan 29	Royal Rumble Match	L	WWE Royal Rumble '22	2:56
Feb 25	Sasha Banks	L	WWE SmackDown	2:10
Apr 29	"I Quit" Beat The Clock Challenge: Ronda Rousey	L	WWE SmackDown	1:41
May 20	Raquel Rodriguez	L	WWE SmackDown	2:46
Jun 3	Natalya, Raquel Rodriguez, Aliyah, Shayna Baszler, Xia Li	L	WWE SmackDown	5:54
Jun 10	Ronda Rousey	L	WWE SmackDown	7:20
Jun 24	Tamina	W	WWE SmackDown	2:40
Jul 1	Alexa Bliss, Liv Morgan & Asuka (w/Raquel Rodriguez & Lacey Evans)	L	WWE SmackDown	13:14
Jul 2	Money In The Bank Ladder Match: Alexa Bliss, Asuka, Becky Lynch, Lacey Evans, Liv Morgan, Raquel Rodriguez	L	WWE Money In The Bank '22	16:35
Jul 29	Aliyah	W	WWE SmackDown	3:20
Aug 5	Gauntlet Match: Shayna Baszler, Sonya Deville, Raquel Rodriguez, Aliyah, Xia Li, Natalya	L	WWE SmackDown	21:05
Aug 12	Raquel Rodriguez & Aliyah (w/Xia Li)	L	WWE SmackDown	9:35
Aug 19	Liv Morgan	L	WWE SmackDown	6:48
Aug 26	Natalya & Sonya Deville, Nikki A.S.H. & Doudrop, Dana Brooke & Tamina (w/Xia Li)	L	WWE SmackDown	3:10
Sep 30	Bayley	L	WWE SmackDown	6:42
Oct 7	Sonya Deville & Xia Li (w/Raquel Rodriguez)	W	WWE SmackDown	2:16
Oct 14	Bayley, Dakota Kai & Iyo Sky (w/Raquel Rodriguez & Roxanne Perez)	L	WWE SmackDown	6:42
Oct 21	Dakota Kai & Iyo Sky (w/Raquel Rodriguez)	L	WWE SmackDown	9:58
Oct 25	Lash Legend	W	NXT	3:42
Nov 11	Six-Pack Challenge: Lacey Evans, Raquel Rodriguez, Sonya Deville, Liv Morgan, Xia Li	W	WWE SmackDown	11:58
Nov 18	Shayna Baszler	W	WWE SmackDown	5:01
Nov 25	Ronda Rousey & Shayna Baszler (w/Raquel Rodriguez)	L	WWE SmackDown	3:26
Nov 26	Ronda Rousey	L	WWE Survivor Series WarGames	7:15

SIERRA ST. PIERRE

Jun 10	Sloane Jacobs	L	NXT Level Up	4:51

SKYE BLUE

Jan 3	Angelica Risk	W	AEW Dark Elevation		2:56
Jan 10	Emi Sakura & Nyla Rose (w/Tina San Antonio)	L	AEW Dark Elevation		2:44
Jan 11	Jade Cargill	L	AEW Dark		1:59
Jan 18	Robyn Renegade	W	AEW Dark		2:51
Jan 19	Serena Deeb	L	AEW Dynamite		2:51
Feb 7	Diamante, Emi Sakura & The Bunny (w/Heather Reckless & Queen Aminata)	L	AEW Dark Elevation		4:02
Feb 21	Emi Sakura, Leyla Hirsch & Nyla Rose (w/AQA & Kiera Hogan)	L	AEW Dark Elevation		4:48
Feb 22	Ruthie Jay	W	AEW Dark		2:49
Feb 28	Red Velvet	L	AEW Dark Elevation		2:24
Mar 8	Nyla Rose	L	AEW Dark		2:38
Mar 14	Emi Sakura & The Bunny (w/KiLynn King)	L	AEW Dark Elevation		6:00
Mar 21	Julia Hart	L	AEW Dark Elevation		4:00
Apr 1	Jamie Hayter	L	AEW Rampage		5:36
Apr 11	Emi Sakura, LuFisto & The Bunny (w/Anna Jay & Ruby Soho)	W	AEW Dark Elevation		3:21
Apr 13	Marina Shafir	L	AEW Dynamite		2:24
Apr 25	Emi Sakura, Nyla Rose & The Bunny (w/Anna Jay & Ruby Soho)	W	AEW Dark Elevation		6:35
Apr 26	Raychell Rose & The Bunny (w/Anna Jay)	W	AEW Dark		5:07
Apr 29	Jade Cargill, Red Velvet & Kiera Hogan (w/Willow Nightingale & Trish Adora)	L	AEW Rampage		2:46
May 10	Kiera Hogan	L	AEW Dark		4:00
May 17	Amber Nova	W	AEW Dark		3:30
May 23	Emi Sakura & Nyla Rose (w/Yuka Sakazaki)	L	AEW Dark Elevation		6:17
May 28	Diamante, Emi Sakura & Nyla Rose (w/Riho & Yuka Sakazaki)	W	AEW Dark		6:11
Jun 6	Nyla Rose & Serena Deeb (w/Miyu Yamashita)	L	AEW Dark Elevation		7:40
Jun 7	Marina Shafir	L	AEW Dark		3:32
Jul 18	Marina Shafir & Nyla Rose (w/Brittany Jade)	L	AEW Dark Elevation		4:30
Jul 22	Dr. Britt Baker D.M.D. & Jamie Hayter (w/Ashley D'Amboise)	L	AEW Rampage: Fyter Fest		5:00
Aug 8	Megan Myers & Nikki Victory (w/Ruby Soho)	W	AEW Dark Elevation		3:11
Aug 12	Sammy Guevara & Tay Conti (w/Dante Martin)	L	AEW Rampage: Quake By The Lake		8:00
Aug 16	Charlette Renegade	W	AEW Dark		4:44
Aug 22	Emi Sakura & Maki Itoh (w/Hikaru Shida)	L	AEW Dark Elevation		7:15
Aug 29	Marina Shafir & Nyla Rose (w/Queen Aminata)	L	AEW Dark Elevation		3:40
Sep 5	Diamante	W	AEW Dark Elevation		4:37
Sep 13	Diamante & Emi Sakura (w/Queen Aminata)	W	AEW Dark		4:01
Sep 19	Chica Carreras	W	AEW Dark Elevation		2:17
Sep 26	Kip Sabian & Penelope Ford (w/Shawn Dean)	L	AEW Dark Elevation		5:16
Oct 3	Trish Adora	W	AEW Dark Elevation		2:30
Oct 4	Robyn Renegade	W	AEW Dark		3:19
Oct 7	Anna Jay & Tay Melo (w/Madison Rayne)	L	AEW Rampage		7:42
Oct 17	Emi Sakura & Serena Deeb (w/Madison Rayne)	L	AEW Dark Elevation		6:00
Oct 31	Kiera Hogan	L	AEW Dark Elevation		2:05
Nov 4	Dr. Britt Baker D.M.D. & Jamie Hayter (w/Madison Rayne)	L	AEW Rampage		7:18
Nov 9	Jamie Hayter	L	AEW Dynamite		6:48
Nov 15	Paris Van Dale	W	AEW Dark		2:25
Nov 22	Tay Melo	L	AEW Dark		5:54
Dec 7	Jade Cargill, Leila Grey & Red Velvet (w/Kiera Hogan & Madison Rayne)	L	AEW Dynamite		8:13
Dec 16	Dr. Britt Baker D.M.D.	L	AEW Rampage		6:15

SLICE BOOGIE

Feb 17	Ladder Match: El Hijo de LA Park & LA Park Jr. (w/Rivera)	W	MLW Fusion		10:18
Mar 31	Calvin Tankman & EJ Nduka (w/Rivera)	W	MLW Fusion		8:08
Jun 16	Calvin Tankman & EJ Nduka, Marshall Von Erich & Ross Von Erich (w/Rivera)	L	MLW Fusion		9:12

SLIM J

Jul 26	Blake Li	W	AEW Dark		2:53
Aug 2	Logan Cruz & Tyshon Price (w/Ari Daivari)	W	AEW Dark		3:02
Aug 9	Sonny Kiss, Xavier Walker & Zack Clayton (w/Ari Daivari & Parker Boudreaux)	W	AEW Dark		3:10
Aug 19	Orange Cassidy, Trent Beretta & Chuck Taylor (w/Ari Daivari & Parker Boudreaux)	L	AEW Rampage		11:00
Aug 23	Cash Flo, Omar Amir & Ryan Howe (w/Ari Daivari & Parker Boudreaux)	W	AEW Dark		2:30
Aug 30	Hermano, Logan Cruz & Tyshaun Perez (w/Ari Daivari & Parker Boudreaux)	W	AEW Dark		3:35
Sep 20	GKM, Marcus Kross & Mike Magnum (w/Ari Daivari & Parker Boudreaux)	W	AEW Dark		4:08
Oct 4	Blake Christian	W	AEW Dark		6:16
Nov 7	Dalton Castle, Brandon Tate & Brent Tate (w/Ari Daivari & Jeeves Kay)	L	AEW Dark Elevation		5:25
Dec 13	Eddie Kingston & Ortiz (w/Jeeves Kay)	L	AEW Dark		6:59
Dec 19	Ethan Page, Isiah Kassidy, Konosuke Takeshita, Matt Hardy, Dante Martin & Darius Martin (w/Jeeves Kay, Sonny Kiss, Cezar Bononi, Peter Avalon & Ryan Nemeth)	L	AEW Dark Elevation		7:45

SLOANE JACOBS

Jan 5	Leyla Hirsch & Red Velvet (w/B3CCA)	L	AEW Dynamite		1:50
Mar 9	Nikkita Lyons	L	NXT 2.0		1:47
Apr 15	Roxanne Perez	L	NXT Level Up		4:18
May 6	Thea Hail	W	NXT Level Up		5:07
May 10	Fallon Henley	L	NXT 2.0		4:28
Jun 3	Tatum Paxley	L	NXT Level Up		5:48
Jun 10	Sierra St. Pierre	W	NXT Level Up		4:51
Jul 1	Amari Miller	L	NXT Level Up		5:54

Jul 19	Battle Royal	L	NXT 2.0	13:13
Sep 16	Ivy Nile & Tatum Paxley (w/Erica Yan)	L	NXT Level Up	5:21
Oct 7	Indi Hartwell	L	NXT Level Up	3:20

SOL RUCA

Jul 15	Kiana James	L	NXT Level Up	4:20
Jul 29	Fallon Henley	L	NXT Level Up	5:14
Aug 12	Elektra Lopez	L	NXT Level Up	3:56
Sep 9	Valentina Feroz	L	NXT Level Up	5:52
Sep 27	Amari Miller	W	NXT	4:48
Oct 7	Arianna Grace & Kiana James (w/Fallon Henley)	W	NXT Level Up	5:06
Oct 25	Indi Hartwell	L	NXT	1:19
Nov 4	Ivy Nile	L	NXT Level Up	4:51
Nov 8	Elektra Lopez	L	NXT	3:02
Nov 22	Zoey Stark	L	NXT	4:17
Dec 2	Thea Hail	L	NXT Level Up	6:18
Dec 9	Valentina Feroz	W	NXT Level Up	4:30
Dec 23	Dani Palmer	W	NXT Level Up	3:01

SOLO SIKOA

Jan 11	Boa	D	NXT 2.0	3:47
Jan 25	Falls Count Anywhere No DQ Match: Boa	W	NXT 2.0	8:08
Mar 1	Gunther	L	NXT 2.0	7:37
Mar 22	Ladder Match: Roderick Strong	W	NXT 2.0	9:18
Apr 2	Ladder Match: Cameron Grimes, Carmelo Hayes, Santos Escobar, Grayson Waller	L	NXT Stand & Deliver '22	21:01
Apr 12	Cameron Grimes	L	NXT 2.0	13:11
Apr 26	Trick Williams	W	NXT 2.0	5:08
May 3	Cameron Grimes, Carmelo Hayes	L	NXT 2.0: Spring Breakin'	14:06
May 17	Carmelo Hayes & Trick Williams (w/Cameron Grimes)	W	NXT 2.0	9:57
May 31	Duke Hudson	W	NXT 2.0	4:44
Jun 7	Grayson Wallter & Carmelo Hayes (w/Apollo Crews)	W	NXT 2.0	13:45
Jun 21	Grayson Waller	L	NXT 2.0	12:18
Jul 12	Von Wagner	D	NXT 2.0	6:50
Aug 2	Falls Count Anywhere: Von Wagner	W	NXT 2.0	12:25
Sep 9	Drew McIntyre	L	WWE SmackDown	10:35
Sep 13	Carmelo Hayes	W	NXT 2.0	10:02
Sep 16	Madcap Moss	W	WWE SmackDown	10:49
Sep 30	Ricochet & Madcap Moss (w/Sami Zayn)	W	WWE SmackDown	12:44
Oct 3	Angelo Dawkins	W	WWE Monday Night RAW	12:20
Oct 7	Ricochet	W	WWE SmackDown	8:16
Oct 14	Rey Mysterio, Ricochet, Sheamus	L	WWE SmackDown	16:19
Oct 21	Sheamus	W	WWE SmackDown	13:05
Oct 28	Ridge Holland & Butch (w/Sami Zayn)	L	WWE SmackDown	11:50
Nov 7	Matt Riddle, Xavier Woods & Kofi Kingston (w/Jey Uso & Jimmy Uso)	W	WWE Monday Night RAW	20:55
Nov 26	WarGames: Sheamus, Butch, Ridge Holland, Drew McIntyre & Kevin Owens (w/Roman Reigns, Sami Zayn, Jey Uso & Jimmy Uso)	W	WWE Survivor Series WarGames	38:30
Dec 12	Elias	W	WWE Monday Night RAW	8:15
Dec 30	Sheamus	W	WWE SmackDown	11:10

SONNY KISS

Jan 10	Chris Steeler & Jaden Valo (w/Jay Lethal)	W	AEW Dark Elevation	2:32
Feb 10	Aaron Solo	L	AEW Dark	6:53
Mar 1	Ashton Starr	W	AEW Dark	2:29
Mar 8	Scorpio Sky	L	AEW Dark	5:42
Mar 28	Max Caster	L	AEW Dark Elevation	4:17
Apr 5	JP Harlow	W	AEW Dark	1:56
May 9	Peter Avalon	W	AEW Dark Elevation	4:12
May 24	Carlie Bravo	W	AEW Dark	4:29
Jul 5	Lamar Diggs	W	AEW Dark	2:26
Aug 9	Ari Daivari, Parker Boudreaux & Slim J (w/Xavier Walker & Zack Clayton)	L	AEW Dark	3:10
Aug 12	Parker Boudreaux	L	AEW Rampage: Quake By The Lake	1:10
Sep 20	Joe Ocasio	W	AEW Dark	1:30
Nov 1	Orange Cassidy, Chuck Taylor & Trent Beretta (w/Tony Deppen & Ari Daivari)	L	AEW Dark	6:04
Nov 21	Matt Hardy, Isiah Kassidy & Marq Quen (w/Encore & Ari Daivari)	L	AEW Dark Elevation	3:15
Nov 22	John Silver, Alex Reynolds & Evil Uno (w/Ari Daivari & Jeeves Kay)	L	AEW Dark	5:26
Dec 19	Ethan Page, Isiah Kassidy, Konosuke Takeshita, Matt Hardy, Dante Martin & Darius Martin (w/Jeeves Kay, Slim J, Cezar Bononi, Peter Avalon & Ryan Nemeth)	L	AEW Dark Elevation	7:45

SONYA DEVILLE

Jan 28	Naomi	L	WWE SmackDown	11:45
Jan 29	Royal Rumble Match	L	WWE Royal Rumble '22	2:00
Feb 19	Ronda Rousey & Naomi (w/Charlotte Flair)	L	WWE Elimination Chamber '22	9:14
Mar 4	Ronda Rousey	L	WWE SmackDown	3:15
Apr 25	Bianca Belair	L	WWE Monday Night RAW	8:55
May 2	Asuka, Liv Morgan & Bianca Belair (w/Becky Lynch & Rhea Ripley)	L	WWE Monday Night RAW	15:15
May 9	Alexa Bliss	L	WWE Monday Night RAW	:40
May 16	Alexa Bliss	L	WWE Monday Night RAW	4:00
Jun 24	Handicap Match: Lacey Evans & Raquel Rodriguez	L	WWE SmackDown	3:05
Jul 22	Raquel Gonzalez	L	WWE SmackDown	3:40

Date	Opponent(s)	Result	Event	Time
Jul 29	Ronda Rousey & Liv Morgan (w/Natalya)	L	WWE SmackDown	11:30
Aug 5	Gauntlet Match: Shayna Baszler, Raquel Rodriguez, Aliyah, Shotzi Xia Li, Natalya	L	WWE SmackDown	21:05
Aug 19	Jacy Jayne & Gigi Dolin (w/Natalya)	L	WWE SmackDown	8:48
Aug 26	Nikki A.S.H. & Doudrop, Dana Brooke & Tamina, Shotzi & Xia Li (w/Natalya)	W	WWE SmackDown	3:10
Aug 26	Raquel Rodriguez & Aliyah (w/Natalya)	L	WWE SmackDown	8:00
Sep 9	Ronda Rousey, Xia Li, Natalya, Lacey Evans	L	WWE SmackDown	4:40
Sep 12	Bianca Belair	L	WWE Monday Night RAW	12:00
Oct 7	Shotzi & Raquel Rodriguez (w/Xia Li)	L	WWE SmackDown	2:16
Oct 18	Alba Fyre	L	NXT	2:09
Oct 21	Liv Morgan	D	WWE SmackDown	8:50
Nov 4	No DQ: Liv Morgan	L	WWE SmackDown	13:48
Nov 11	Six-Pack Challenge: Shotzi, Raquel Rodriguez, Liv Morgan, Xia Li, Lacey Evans	L	WWE SmackDown	11:58
Dec 23	Gauntlet Match: Raquel Rodriguez, Xia Li, Emma, Liv Morgan, Tegan Nox, Shayna Baszler	L	WWE SmackDown	23:58

STEVE AUSTIN

Date	Opponent(s)	Result	Event	Time
Apr 2	No Holds Barred: Kevin Owens	W	WWE WrestleMania XXXVIII	13:55

STEVE MACLIN

Date	Opponent(s)	Result	Event	Time
Jan 8	Trey Miguel	L	IMPACT Hard To Kill '22	12:50
Jan 20	Jonathan Gresham	L	IMPACT Wrestling	10:20
Feb 3	Jonathan Gresham	W	IMPACT Wrestling	11:52
Mar 3	Eddie Edwards	W	IMPACT Wrestling	6:52
Mar 17	Rhino	W	IMPACT Wrestling	9:50
Mar 24	Heath	W	IMPACT Wrestling	4:50
Apr 14	Alex Shelley	L	IMPACT Wrestling	10:00
Apr 23	Chris Sabin, Jay White	W	IMPACT Rebellion '22	12:07
May 5	Tomohiro Ishii	L	IMPACT Wrestling	13:58
May 12	Gauntlet For The Gold	L	IMPACT Wrestling	39:00
Jun 2	PCO & W. Morrissey (w/Moose)	W	IMPACT Wrestling	10:51
Jun 9	PCO	W	IMPACT Wrestling	8:55
Jun 30	Trey Miguel, Chris Bey, Laredo Kid	L	IMPACT Wrestling	6:12
Jul 14	James Storm	W	IMPACT Wrestling	8:34
Aug 11	Crazzy Steve	W	IMPACT Before The Impact	7:37
Aug 18	Eddie Edwards, Bandido, Moose, Rich Swann, Sami Callihan	L	IMPACT Wrestling	18:25
Sep 15	Black Taurus & Crazzy Steve (w/Moose)	L	IMPACT Wrestling	1:52
Oct 6	Moose	W	IMPACT Wrestling	9:51
Oct 7	Call Your Shot Gauntlet	L	IMPACT Bound For Glory '22	29:18
Nov 17	Old School Rules: Tommy Dreamer	W	IMPACT Wrestling	8:10
Dec 1	Frankie Kazarian	L	IMPACT Wrestling	7:26
Dec 22	Rich Swann	D	IMPACT Wrestling	6:27

STEVIE TURNER

Date	Opponent(s)	Result	Event	Time
Jan 13	Amale	L	NXT UK	3:59
Feb 17	Myla Grace	W	NXT UK	4:34
Mar 17	Aleah James	L	NXT UK	4:10
Apr 21	Emilia McKenzie	L	NXT UK	4:42
Jun 2	Angel Hayze	W	NXT UK	4:04
Jul 14	Amale	L	NXT UK	4:15

STING

Date	Opponent(s)	Result	Event	Time
Jan 19	Anthony Bowens & Max Caster (w/Darby Allin)	W	AEW Dynamite	9:22
Mar 6	Tornado Match: Andrade El Idolo, Matt Hardy & Isiah Kassidy (w/Sammy Guevara & Darby Allin)	W	AEW Revolution '22	13:20
Mar 23	Tornado Match: Isiah Kassidy, Marq Quen, The Butcher & The Blade (w/Darby Allin, Matt Hardy & Jeff Hardy)	W	AEW Dynamite	9:27
Jun 26	El Phantasmo, Matt Jackson & Nick Jackson (w/Darby Allin & Shingo Takagi)	W	AEW x NJPW Forbidden Door	13:01
Sep 4	Malakai Black, Brody King & Buddy Matthews (w/Darby Allin & Miro)	W	AEW All Out '22	12:10
Sep 23	No DQ: Buddy Matthews & Brody King (w/Darby Allin)	W	AEW Rampage: Grand Slam	12:57
Nov 19	No DQ: Jeff Jarrett & Jay Lethal (w/Darby Allin)	W	AEW Full Gear '22	11:00

STU GRAYSON

Date	Opponent(s)	Result	Event	Time
Feb 14	Jeff Parker, Matt Lee, Daniel Garcia, Anthony Bowens & Max Caster (w/John Silver, Alex Reynolds, Evil Uno & Alan Angels)	L	AEW Dark Elevation	5:56
Feb 28	Luther & Serpentico (w/Evil Uno)	W	AEW Dark Elevation	4:53
Mar 2	Casino Battle Royale (w/Evil Uno)	L	AEW Dynamite	19:08
Mar 21	Aaron Solo, Nick Comoroto & QT Marshall (w/John Silver & Evil Uno)	W	AEW Dark Elevation	7:27
Mar 29	Alexander Zane, Jay Marte & Richard King (w/Evil Uno & Alan Angels)	W	AEW Dark	3:09
Apr 1	Malakai Black, Brody King & Buddy Matthews (w/Fuego Del Sol & Evil Uno)	L	AEW Rampage	7:15
Apr 11	Luther, Serpentico, Austin Gunn, Colten Gunn & Billy Gunn (w/John Silver, Alex Reynolds, Alan Angels & Ten)	W	AEW Dark Elevation	5:20
Apr 18	Allen Russell, Dale Springs, Izaiah Zane & Kameron Russell (w/John Silver, Alex Reynolds & Evil Uno)	W	AEW Dark Elevation	2:17
Apr 19	Powerhouse Hobbs & Ricky Starks (w/Evil Uno)	L	AEW Dark	8:48
Apr 25	Bulk Nasty, Jake Omen, Luther, RC Dupree & Tito Ortic (w/Evil Uno, Alex Reynolds, Alan Angels & Ten)	W	AEW Dark Elevation	3:09

SUMMER RAE

Jan 29	Royal Rumble Match		L	WWE Royal Rumble '22	:52

SWERVE STRICKLAND

Mar 11	Tony Nese		W	AEW Rampage	12:58
Mar 12	Jay White		L	NJPW Strong	17:15
Mar 25	Ricky Starks		L	AEW Rampage	11:27
Apr 1	Alex Zayne		W	ROH Supercard Of Honor XV	11:40
Apr 8	QT Marshall		W	AEW Rampage	6:08
Apr 13	Ricky Starks & Powerhouse Hobbs (w/Keith Lee)		L	AEW Dynamite	12:32
Apr 19	Aaron Solo & Nick Comoroto (w/Keith Lee)		W	AEW Dark	8:40
Apr 23	Blake Christian		W	NJPW Strong	11:27
Apr 29	Darby Allin		L	AEW Rampage	10:23
May 9	Nick Comoroto & QT Marshall (w/Keith Lee)		W	AEW Dark Elevation	6:47
May 5	Myron Reed		L	MLW Fusion	7:54
May 17	Luther & Serpentico (w/Keith Lee)		W	AEW Dark	6:00
May 18	JD Drake & Anthony Henry (w/Keith Lee)		W	AEW Dynamite: Wild Card Wednesday	2:24
May 25	Ricky Starks, Jungle Boy		W	AEW Dynamite: 3 Year Anniversary	9:36
May 29	Jungle Boy & Luchasaurus, Powerhouse Hobbs & Ricky Starks (w/Keith Lee)		L	AEW Double Or Nothing '22	17:15
Jun 8	Casino Battle Royale		L	AEW Dynamite	24:59
Jun 20	Davey Vega & Mat Fitchett (w/Keith Lee)		W	AEW Dark Elevation	3:10
Jun 26	El Desperado & Yoshinobu Kanemaru (w/Keith Lee)		W	AEW x NJPW Forbidden Door Buy-In	12:08
Jun 27	GPA & Vic Capri (w/Keith Lee)		W	AEW Dark Elevation	4:07
Jul 1	Royal Rampage Match		L	AEW Rampage	22:41
Jul 6	The Butcher & The Blade (w/Keith Lee)		W	AEW Dynamite	9:38
Jul 13	Matt Jackson & Nick Jackson, Ricky Starks & Powerhouse Hobbs (w/Keith Lee)		W	AEW Dynamite: Fyter Fest	18:14
Jul 27	Handicap Match: Mark Sterling & Tony Nese		W	AEW Dynamite	6:44
Aug 5	Street Fight: Tony Nese & Josh Woods (w/Keith Lee)		W	AEW Rampage	12:53
Aug 19	Marq Quen & Isiah Kassidy (w/Keith Lee)		W	AEW Rampage	7:15
Sep 3	Jah-C & Storm Grayson (w/Keith Lee)		W	AEW Dark Elevation	3:54
Sep 4	Anthony Bowens & Max Caster (w/Keith Lee)		W	AEW All Out '22	22:30
Sep 14	Penta El Zero M & Rey Fenix (w/Keith Lee)		W	AEW Dynamite	8:15
Sep 21	Anthony Bowens & Max Caster (w/Keith Lee)		W	AEW Dynamite: Grand Slam	13:44
Oct 12	Billy Gunn		W	AEW Dynamite	8:48
Oct 26	Dax Harwood & Cash Wheeler (w/Keith Lee)		W	AEW Dynamite	15:06
Nov 9	Anthony Bowens, Max Caster, Dax Harwood & Cash Wheeler (w/Keith Lee, Austin Gunn & Colten Gunn)		L	AEW Dynamite	12:22
Nov 16	Anthony Bowens		W	AEW Dynamite	9:36
Nov 19	Anthony Bowens & Max Caster (w/Keith Lee)		L	AEW Full Gear '22	19:40
Dec 10	Shane Taylor & JD Griffey (w/Keith Lee)		W	ROH Final Battle '22	13:50
Dec 30	Wheeler Yuta		W	AEW Rampage	13:58

T-BONE

Jan 6	Ashton Smith & Oliver Carter (w/Primate)		L	NXT UK	9:37
Mar 10	Danny Jones & Josh Morrell (w/Primate)		W	NXT UK	6:05
Mar 24	Wild Boar		L	NXT UK	4:37
Apr 28	Mark Andrews & Wild Boar (w/Primate)		L	NXT UK	7:26
Jun 9	Oli Blake & Tate Mayfairs (w/Primate)		W	NXT UK	4:32

TAICHI

Jan 4	Hirooki Goto & Yoshi-Hashi (w/Zack Sabre Jr.)		L	NJPW Wrestle Kingdom 16 Night #1	15:27
Jan 8	Takashi Sugiura, Kazushi Sakuraba & Toru Yano (w/Minoru Suzuki & Taka Michinoku)		L	NJPW Wrestle Kingdom 16 Night #3	9:37
Mar 1	Bad Luck Fale, Taiji Ishimori & El Phantasmo (w/Taichi, Taka Michinoku & Minoru Tanaka)		L	NJPW 50th Anniversary Show	9:50
Apr 9	No Rope Ring Out Match: Toru Yano		W	NJPW Hyper Battle '22	4:18
May 1	Shingo Takagi, Bushi & Shiro Koshinaka (w/Zack Sabre Jr. & Taka Michinoku)		W	NJPW Wrestling Dontaku '22	10:15
Jun 12	10 Minute Unlimited Pinfall Scramble Match: Shingo Takagi		L	NJPW Dominion '22	10:00
Sep 25	Sanada & Tetsuya Naito (w/Zack Sabre Jr.)		W	NJPW Burning Spirit '22	9:32
Oct 10	Shane Haste & Bad Dude Tito (w/Zack Sabre Jr.)		W	NJPW Declaration Of Power	9:58
Nov 20	Momo Watanabe, Starlight Kid, El Desperado & Douki (w/Tam Nakano, Natsupoi & Yoshinobu Kanemaru)		W	NJPW x Stardom Historic X-Over	12:01

TAIJI ISHIMORI

Jan 4	Hiroshi Tanahashi, Ryusuke Taguchi & Rocky Romero (w/El Phantasmo & Kenta)		W	NJPW Wrestle Kingdom 16 Night #1	8:40
Jan 5	Robbie Eagles & Tiger Mask, Ryusuke Taguchi & Rocky Romero (w/El Phantasmo)		L	NJPW Wrestle Kingdom 16 Night #2	12:07
Jan 8	Hayata & Seiki Yoshioka (w/Gedo)		L	NJPW Wrestle Kingdom 16 Night #3	5:59
Mar 1	Taichi, Taka Michinoku & Minoru Tanaka (w/Bad Luck Fale & El Phantasmo)	W		NJPW 50th Anniversary Show	9:50
Apr 9	Ryusuke Taguchi & Master Wato (w/El Phantasmo)		L	NJPW Hyper Battle '22	15:13
May 1	El Desperado		W	NJPW Wrestling Dontaku '22	14:40
Jun 12	Tetsuya Naito, Bushi & Hiromu Takahashi (w/El Phantasmo & Ace Austin)		W	NJPW Dominion '22	8:04
Sep 24	Alan Angels		W	NJPW Strong	9:14
Sep 25	Jado & Tama Tonga (w/Jay White)		W	NJPW Burning Spirit '22	10:39
Oct 10	Master Wato		L	NJPW Declaration Of Power '22	14:40
Nov 5	Master Wato & El Desperado (w/Hiromu Takahashi)		L	NJPW Battle Autumn '22	16:48

TAMA TONGA

Feb 3	Jake Something, Mike Bailey, Madman Fulton & Ace Austin (w/Chris Bey, Jay White & Tanga Loa)	W	IMPACT Wrestling	16:49
Feb 17	Eric Young, Deaner & Joe Doering (w/Jay White & Tanga Loa)	W	IMPACT Wrestling	13:19
Mar 3	Chris Bey, Luke Gallows, Karl Anderson & Jay White (w/Tanga Loa, Deaner & Joe Doering)	L	IMPACT Wrestling	9:48
Apr 9	Bad Luck Fale, Chase Owens, Yujiro Takahashi & Gedo (w/Tanga Loa, Jado & Hiroshi Tanahashi)	W	NJPW Hyper Battle '22	10:28
May 1	Evil	W	NJPW Wrestling Dontaku '22	13:25
Jun 12	Karl Anderson	L	NJPW Dominion '12	16:27
Sep 25	Jay White & Taiji Ishimori (w/Jado)	L	NJPW Burning Spirit '22	10:39
Oct 1	Jay White, Karl Anderson, Luke Gallows & Gedo (w/Hiroshi Tanahashi, Hikuleo & Jado)	W	NJPW Royal Quest II Night #1	12:15
Oct 2	Jay White, Luke Gallows & Karl Anderson (w/Hiroshi Tanahashi & Hikuleo)	W	NJPW Royal Quest II Night #2	10:54
Oct 10	Jay White	L	NJPW Declaration Of Power	31:07
Nov 5	Jay White & Kenta (w/Kazuchika Okada)	W	NJPW Battle Autumn '22	17:34
Dec 10	El Phantasmo, Jay White, Jorel Nelson & Royce Isaacs (w/Alan Angels, David Finlay & Hikuleo)	W	NJPW Strong	13:20

TAMINA

Jan 3	Dana Brooke & Reggie (w/Akira Tozawa)	L	WWE Monday Night RAW	1:10
Jan 24	Dana Brooke, Rhea Ripley & Liv Morgan (w/Carmella & Nikki A.S.H.)	L	WWE Monday Night RAW	2:20
Jan 29	Royal Rumble Match	L	WWE Royal Rumble '22	16:41
Feb 28	Dana Brooke & Reggie (w/Akira Tozawa)	L	WWE Monday Night RAW	1:40
Mar 7	Dana Brooke	L	WWE Monday Night RAW	1:45
Mar 21	Dana Brooke & Reggie (w/Akira Tozawa)	L	WWE Monday Night RAW	1:05
Apr 25	Dana Brooke & Reggie (w/Akira Tozawa)	W	WWE Monday Night RAW	1:30
Jun 24	Shotzi	L	WWE SmackDown	2:40
Jun 27	Becky Lynch, Doudrop, Nikki A.S.H., Xia Li, Shayna Baszler	L	WWE Monday Night RAW	13:20
Jul 14	Jazmin Allure	W	WWE Main Event	5:22
Jul 18	Alexa Bliss, Asuka & Dana Brooke (w/Doudrop & Nikki A.S.H.)	L	WWE Monday Night RAW	2:35
Jul 28	Asuka & Dana Brooke (w/Carmella)	L	WWE Main Event	7:09
Aug 8	Iyo Sky & Dakota Kai (w/Dana Brooke)	L	WWE Monday Night RAW	10:00
Aug 25	Doudrop & Nikki A.S.H. (w/Dana Brooke)	L	WWE Main Event	5:14
Aug 26	Natalya & Sonya Deville, Nikki A.S.H. & Doudrop, Shotzi & Xia Li (w/Dana Brooke)	L	WWE SmackDown	3:10
Sep 22	Dana Brooke	L	WWE Main Event	5:00
Nov 10	Wendy Choo	L	WWE Main Event	5:25
Nov 14	Mia Yim	L	WWE Monday Night RAW	2:00
Nov 24	Alba Fyre	L	WWE Main Event	5:21
Dec 8	Katana Chance	L	WWE Main Event	1:47
Dec 17	Ronda Rousey & Shayna Baszler (w/Emma)	L	WWE Tribute To The Troops '22	7:34

TANGA LOA

Feb 3	Jake Something, Mike Bailey, Madman Fulton & Ace Austin (w/Chris Bey, Jay White & Tama Tonga)	W	IMPACT Wrestling	16:49
Feb 17	Eric Young, Deaner & Joe Doering (w/Jay White & Tama Tonga)	W	IMPACT Wrestling	13:19
Mar 3	Chris Bey, Luke Gallows, Karl Anderson & Jay White (w/Tama Tonga, Deaner & Joe Doering)	L	IMPACT Wrestling	9:48
Apr 9	Bad Luck Fale, Chase Owen Yujiro Takahashi & Gedo (w/Hiroshi Tanahashi, Tama Tonga & Jado)	W	NJPW Hyper Battle '22	10:28
May 1	Yujiro Takahashi	W	NJPW Wrestling Dontaku '22	11:33
May 14	Tom Lawlor, Jorel Nelson, Royce Isaacs, JR Kratos & Danny Limelight (w/The DKC, Yuya Uemura, David Finlay & Fred Rosser)	L	NJPW Capital Collision	14:48

TANK LEDGER

Oct 14	Bryson Montana & Duke Hudson (w/Ikemen Jiro)	W	NXT Level Up	6:18
Oct 28	Channing Lorenzo	L	NXT Level Up	5:42
Nov 25	Xyon Quinn	L	NXT Level Up	4:57

TARYN TERRELL

Feb 22	Kamille	L	NWA Power	7:48
Jun 14	Taya Valkyrie	L	NWA Power	6:45
Aug 27	Burke Invitational Gauntlet	L	NWA 74th Anniversary Show	17:24
Oct 11	Allysin Kay & Marti Belle (w/Natalia Markova)	L	NWA Power	5:33

TASHA STEELZ

Jan 6	Rosemary, Jordynne Grace & Rachael Ellering (w/Lady Frost & Chelsea Green)	W	IMPACT Wrestling	7:19
Jan 8	Ultimate X Match: Alisha Edwards, Chelsea Green, Jordynne Grace, Lady Frost, Rosemary	W	IMPACT Hard To Kill '22	9:00
Jan 20	Chelsea Green	W	IMPACT Wrestling	4:24
Feb 17	Chelsea Green & Mickie James (w/Savannah Evans)	W	IMPACT Wrestling	12:26
Mar 3	Chelsea Green	W	IMPACT Wrestling	8:05
Mar 10	Cassie Lee, Jessie McKay, Chelsea Green & Mickie James (w/Madison Rayne, Tenille Dashwood & Savannah Evans)	L	IMPACT Wrestling	6:00
Mar 24	Street Fight: Mickie James	W	IMPACT Wrestling	16:00
Apr 1	Madison Rayne & Tenille Dashwood, Gisele Shaw & Lady Frost, Havok & Rosemark (w/Savannah Evans)	L	IMPACT Multiverse Of Matches	9:02
Apr 23	Rosemary	W	IMPACT Rebellion '22	11:45
Apr 28	Havok & Rosemary (w/Savannah Evans)	L	IMPACT Wrestling	4:51
May 19	Jordynne Grace, Mia Yim & Taya Valkyrie	L	IMPACT Wrestling	12:00

(w/Deonna Purrazzo & Savannah Evans)

Jun 16	Jordynne Grace & Mia Yim (w/Savannah Evans)	W	IMPACT Wrestling	6:49
Jun 19	Queen Of The Mountain: Jordynne Grace, Chelsea Green, Mia Yim, Deonna Purrazzo	L	IMPACT Slammiversary XX	18:15
Oct 7	Call Your Shot Gauntlet	L	IMPACT Bound For Glory '22	29:18
Oct 13	No DQ Match: Killer Kelly	L	IMPACT Wrestling	6:52
Oct 27	Rachelle Scheel	L	IMPACT Wrestling	1:57
Nov 17	Taya Valkyrie	L	IMPACT Wrestling	2:20
Dec 22	Jordynne Grace & Mickie James (w/Savannah Evans)	L	IMPACT Wrestling	11:08

TATE MAYFAIRS

Mar 31	Kenny Williams	W	NXT UK	5:53
May 5	Tiger Turan	L	NXT UK	4:03
Jun 9	Primate & T-Bone (w/Oli Blake)	L	NXT UK	4:32
Jul 7	Trent Seven	L	NXT UK	4:05

TATUM PAXLEY

Feb 18	Fallon Henley & Kayla Inlay (w/Ivy Nile)	W	NXT Level Up	4:18
Feb 22	Kayden Carter & Kacy Catanzaro (w/Ivy Nile)	L	NXT 2.0	3:26
Apr 1	Kayden Carter	L	NXT Level Up	6:01
Apr 15	Kiana James	W	NXT Level Up	3:58
Apr 19	Natalya	L	NXT 2.0	4:52
May 6	Erica Yan & Sarray (w/Ivy Nile)	W	NXT Level Up	5:32
May 17	Lash Legend	L	NXT 2.0	3:50
Jun 3	Sloane Jacobs	W	NXT Level Up	5:48
Jun 7	Alba Fyre	L	NXT 2.0	2:38
Jul 12	Kayden Carter	W	NXT 2.0	3:31
Jul 19	Battle Royal	L	NXT 2.0	13:13
Aug 2	Elimination Match: Kayden Carter & Katana Chance, Valentina Feroz & Yulisa Leon, Gigi Dolin & Jacy Jayne (w/Ivy Nile)	L	NXT 2.0	12:09
Aug 30	Kayden Karter & Katana Chance (w/Ivy Nile)	L	NXT 2.0	4:17
Sep 16	Erica Yan & Sloane Jacobs (w/Ivy Nile)	W	NXT Level Up	5:21
Sep 20	Gigi Dolin & Jacy Jayne (w/Ivy Nile)	L	NXT	3:58
Nov 11	Jakara Jackson & Lash Legend (w/Ivy Nile)	W	NXT Level Up	4:42
Nov 15	Indi Hartwell	L	NXT	4:00
Dec 13	Gigi Dolin & Jacy Jayne (w/Ivy Nile)	L	NXT	2:26
Dec 20	Kayden Carter & Katana Chance, Gigi Dolin & Jacy Jayne (w/Ivy Nile)	L	NXT	6:35

TAY MELO

Jan 11	Charlette Renegade & Robyn Renegade (w/Anna Jay)	W	AEW Dark	3:48
Jan 17	Ameera	W	AEW Dark Elevation	1:57
Feb 14	Emi Sakura, Nyla Rose & The Bunny (w/Anna Jay & Ruby Soho)	W	AEW Dark Elevation	3:43
Feb 21	Angelica Risk, Arie Alexander & Freya States (w/Anna Jay & Red Velvet)	W	AEW Dark Elevation	3:42
Mar 6	Jade Cargill	L	AEW Revolution '22	6:40
Mar 29	Shalonce Royal	W	AEW Dark	2:53
May 29	Ethan Page, Scorpio Sky & Paige VanZant (w/Sammy Guevara & Savannah Evans)	L	AEW Double Or Nothing '22	12:30
Apr 30	Komander & Sexy Star, Latigo & Maravilla, Arez & Chik Tormenta (w/Sammy Guevara)	W	AAA TripleMania XXX: Monterrey	12:35
Aug 26	Ortiz & Ruby Soho (w/Sammy Guevara)	W	AEW Rampage	8:35
Sep 2	Ortiz & Ruby Soho (w/Sammy Guevara)	L	AEW Rampage	7:40
Sep 3	GPA & Laynie Luck (w/Sammy Guevara)	W	AEW Dark Elevation	4:27
Sep 4	Ortiz & Ruby Soho (w/Sammy Guevara)	W	AEW All Out Buy-In	6:00
Oct 7	Madison Rayne & Skye Blue (w/Anna Jay)	W	AEW Rampage	7:42
Oct 28	Madison Rayne	W	AEW Rampage	9:23
Nov 7	Trish Adora	W	AEW Dark Elevation	2:10
Nov 14	Paris Van Dale	W	AEW Dark Elevation	1:33
Nov 22	Skye Blue	W	AEW Dark	5:54
Nov 23	Dr. Britt Baker D.M.D. & Jamie Hayter, Willow Nightingale & Skye Blue (w/Anna Jay)	L	AEW Dynamite: Thanksgiving Eve	8:05
Dec 13	Miranda Vionette	W	AEW Dark	1:07
Dec 14	Ruby Soho	L	AEW Dynamite: Winter Is Coming	7:22
Dec 28	Ruby Soho & Willow Nightingale (w/Anna Jay)	W	AEW Dynamite	11:58

TAYA VALKYRIE

Feb 19	Flammer, Keyra, Lady Shani, Maravilla	W	AAA Rey De Reyes '22	12:20
Apr 23	Deonna Purrazzo	W	IMPACT Rebellion '22	9:03
Apr 30	Andrade El Idolo, Cibernetico & Deonna Purrazzo (w/Pagano & Bandido)	W	AAA TripleMania XXX: Monterrey	18:53
May 19	Deonna Purrazzo, Savannah Evans & Tasha Steelz (w/Jordynne Grace & Mia Yim)	W	IMPACT Wrestling	12:00
Jun 11	Natalia Markova	L	NWA Alwayz Ready '22	8:43
Jun 14	Taryn Terrell	W	NWA Power	6:45
Jun 16	Holidead	W	MLW Fusion	9:00
Jun 19	Madison Rayne & Tenille Dashwood (w/Rosemary)	W	IMPACT Slammiversary XX	7:20
Jun 30	Arez, Holidead & Mini Abismo Negro (w/Lince Dorado & Micro Man)	W	MLW Fusion	6:32
Jul 19	Max The Impaler, Ella Envy	L	NWA Power	6:37
Jul 26	KiLynn King	W	NWA Power	6:50
Aug 27	Kamille	L	NWA 74th Anniversary Show	18:57
Seo 6	Chelsea Green, Jennacide, KiLynn King	W	NWA Power	4:22
Sep 8	Chelsea Green	L	IMPACT Wrestling	6:27
Oct 6	Swingerella #1 & Swingerella #2 (w/Jessicka)	W	IMPACT Wrestling	1:30

Oct 7	Chelsea Green & Deonna Purrazzo (w/Jessicka)	W	IMPACT Bound For Glory '22	7:24
Oct 11	KiLynn King	L	NWA Power	8:57
Oct 13	Chelsea Green, Deonna Purrazzo & Gisele Shaw (w/Jessicka & Rosemary)	L	IMPACT Wrestling	5:40
Oct 15	Kamille	W	AAA TripleMania XXX: Mexico City	15:18
Nov 8	Madi Wrenkowski	W	NWA Power	6:22
Nov 17	Tasha Steelz	W	IMPACT Wrestling	2:20
Nov 24	Brittany Blake	W	MLW Fusion	6:50
Dec 8	Savannah Evans	L	IMPACT Wrestling	6:51
Dec 22	Lady Flammer	W	MLW Fusion	8:48

TAYLOR RUST

Jan 22	Jorel Nelson, Tom Lawlor & Black Tiger (w/Fred Rosser & Rocky Romero)	L	NJPW Strong	11:35
Feb 26	Tom Lawlor	L	NJPW Strong	19:11
Mar 26	Elimination Match: Danny Limelight, Jorel Nelson, JR Kratos, Tom Lawlor & Royce Isaacs (w/Adrian Quest, Clark Connors, Fred Rosser & The DKC)	L	NJPW Strong	16:29
May 21	Aaron Henare, Great-O-Khan & TJP (w/Brody King & Mascara Dorada)	L	NJPW Strong	14:04
May 27	Matt Jackson & Nick Jackson (w/Jon Cruz)	L	AEW Rampage	2:34
Jun 14	Matt Sydal	L	AEW Dark	3:19
Jul 9	Jonah	L	NJPW Strong	12:50
Sep 17	Chase Owens, Hikuleo, Jay White & Juice Robinson (w/Kushida, Trent Beretta & Rocky Romero)	L	NJPW Strong	14:46

TAYLOR WILDE

Oct 7	Call Your Shot Gauntlet	L	IMPACT Bound For Glory '22	29:18
Oct 20	Mia Yim	W	IMPACT Wrestling	9:22
Oct 27	Chelsea Green, Deonna Purrazzo & Gisele Shaw (w/Jordynne Grace & Mickie James)	W	IMPACT Wrestling	13:46
Dec 22	KiLynn King	W	IMPACT Before The Impact	7:20

TEGAN NOX

Dec 9	Ronda Rousey & Shayna Baszler (w/Liv Morgan)	W	WWE SmackDown	4:07
Dec 16	Dakota Kai & Iyo Sky (w/Liv Morgan)	L	WWE SmackDown	14:48
Dec 23	Gauntlet Match: Raquel Rodriguez, Xia Li, Emma, Sonya Deville, Shayna Baszler, Liv Morgan	L	WWE SmackDown	23:58

TEOMAN

Jan 13	Dave Mastiff & Jack Starz (w/Rohan Raja)	L	NXT UK	9:24
Jan 27	Joe Coffey, Mark Coffey & Wolfgang (w/Charlie Dempsey & Rohan Raja)	W	NXT UK	11:18
Feb 10	Nathan Frazer	L	NXT UK	13:15
Apr 14	A-Kid	W	NXT UK	11:23
Jul 14	Ashton Smith	L	NXT UK	7:24
Aug 11	Sam Gradwell	L	NXT UK	5:54

TETSUYA NAITO

Jan 4	Will Ospreay, Great-O-Khan & Jeff Cobb (w/Sanada & Bushi)	L	NJPW Wrestle Kingdom 16 Night #1	9:27
Jan 5	Jeff Cobb	W	NJPW Wrestle Kingdom 16 Night #2	15:34
Jan 8	Katsuhiko Nakajima, Kenoh, Manabu Soya, Tadasuke & Aleja (w/Shingo Takagi, Sanada, Bushi & Hiromu Takahashi)	W	NJPW Wrestle Kingdom 16 Night #3	26:33
Mar 1	Togi Makabe, Tomoaki Honma, Tomohiro Ishii, Shiro Koshinaka & Toru Yano (w/Sanada, Shingo Takagi, Bushi & Hiromu Takahashi)	W	NJPW 50th Anniversary Show	12:38
Apr 9	Will Ospreay & Aaron Henare (w/Shingo Takagi)	W	NJPW Hyper Battle '22	9:23
May 1	Kazuchika Okada	L	NJPW Wrestling Dontaku '22	34:12
Jun 12	Taiji Ishimori, El Phantasmo & Ace Austin (w/Bushi & Hiromu Takahashi)	L	NJPW Dominion '22	8:04
Sep 25	Taichi & Zack Sabre Jr. (w/Sanada)	L	NJPW Burning Spirit '22	9:32
Oct 1	Zack Sabre Jr., El Desperado & Douki (w/Sanada & Hiromu Takahashi)	W	NJPW Royal Quest II Night #1	14:29
Oct 2	Zack Sabre Jr.	W	NJPW Royal Quest II Night #2	21:05
Oct 10	Will Ospreay, Aaron Henare, TJP & Francesco Akira (w/Sanada, Bushi & Hirormu Takahashi)	W	NJPW Declaration Of Power	8:07
Nov 5	Will Ospreay	L	NJPW Battle Autumn '22	30:07
Nov 20	Kyle Fletcher, Mark David, Francesco Akira, TJP & Gideon Grey (w/Bushi, Hiromu Takahashi, Sanada & Shingo Takagi)	L	NJPW x Stardom Historic X-Over	9:55

THEA HAIL

Apr 8	Ivy Nile	L	NXT Level Up	4:08
Apr 22	Fallon Henley	L	NXT Level Up	4:21
May 6	Sloane Jacobs	L	NXT Level Up	5:07
May 13	Elektra Jacobs	L	NXT Level Up	5:08
Jun 17	Arianna Grace	W	NXT Level Up	5:27
Jul 22	Brooklyn Barlow	W	NXT Level Up	5:26
Aug 5	Arianna Grace	L	NXT Level Up	5:03
Aug 9	Arianna Grace	L	NXT 2.0	3:49
Aug 11	Eliza Alexander	L	NXT UK	4:12
Sep 30	Valentina Feroz	W	NXT Level Up	4:38
Oct 11	Kiana James	L	NXT	1:18
Oct 28	Jakara Jackson	W	NXT Level Up	4:25
Nov 1	Kiana James	L	NXT	4:20
Nov 18	Dani Palmer	W	NXT Level Up	4:41
Dec 2	Sol Ruca	W	NXT Level Up	6:18
Dec 6	Isla Dawn	L	NXT	2:51
Dec 30	Amari Miller	W	NXT Level Up	5:53

THOM LATIMER

Jan 11	Matt Cardona & Mike Knox, Tim Storm & Trevor Murdoch (w/Chris Adonis)	L	NWA Power	5:25
Feb 8	Team War Elimination Match: Matt Taven, Mike Bennett & Victor Benjamin, Bestia 666, Mecha Wolf & Homicide, Jay Bradley, Wrecking Ball Legursky & Colby Corino (w/Chris Adonis & El Rudo)	W	NWA Power	11:09
Feb 15	Team War: Odinson, Parrow & Rodney Mack (w/Chris Adonis & El Rudo)	W	NWA Power	11:35
Mar 8	"I Quit" Match: Nick Aldis	L	NWA Power	13:38
Mar 19	Jordan Clearwater & Marshe Rockett	L	NWA Crockett Cup '22	4:18
May 31	Rhett Titus	W	NWA Power	9:25
Jun 11	Cyon	W	NWA Alwayz Ready '22	12:30
Jun 11	Trevor Murdoch, Nick Aldis, Sam Shaw	L	NWA Alwayz Ready '22	18:10
Jun 14	Mike Knox & VSK (w/Chris Adonis)	W	NWA Power	7:23
Jul 12	Chris Adonis	W	NWA Power	6:48
Jul 19	Nick Aldis, Mike Knox, Brian Myers	L	NWA Power	8:47
Aug 28	EC3	D	NWA 74th Anniversary Show	6:42
Aug 30	Chris Sainz	W	NWA Power	2:03
Sep 20	Mike Knox & VSK (w/Bully Ray)	W	NWA Power	5:15
Nov 8	Doug Williams, JR Kratos & Da Pope (w/Trevor Murdoch & Tyrus)	D	NWA Power	6:49
Nov 12	EC3	L	NWA Hard Times 3	8:31
Nov 22	EC3 & Matt Lancie (w/Danny Flamingo)	W	NWA Power	7:43
Dec 6	EC3	D	NWA Power	5:47
Dec 20	Chris Adonis, Dak Draper & Mims (w/Bully Ray & Judais)	W	NWA Power	8:18

THRILLBILLY SILAS

Jul 5	Trevor Murdoch	L	NWA Power	3:09
Aug 28	Davey Richards	L	NWA 74th Anniversary Show	10:24
Oct 11	Dak Draper, Chris Adonis	L	NWA Power	5:15
Nov 12	Odinson	W	NWA Hard Times 3	4:43
Nov 22	Cyon	L	NWA Power	4:56
Dec 6	JR Kratos	W	NWA Power	8:08

THUNDER ROSA

Jan 11	Kasey Fox	W	AEW Dark	2:00
Jan 24	Jordan Blake & Leva Bates (w/Ruby Soho)	W	AEW Dark Elevation	2:52
Jan 31	Joseline Navarro & Megan Meyers (w/Ruby Soho)	W	AEW Dark Elevation	2:46
Feb 4	Riley Shepard	W	AEW Dark Elevation	2:24
Feb 4	Mercedes Martinez	W	AEW Rampage	7:41
Feb 16	No DQ Match: Mercedes Martinez	W	AEW Dynamite	9:31
Mar 2	Dr. Britt Baker D.M.D. & Jamie Hayter (w/Mercedes Martinez)	W	AEW Dynamite	8:32
Mar 6	Dr. Britt Baker D.M.D.	L	AEW Revolution '22	17:25
Mar 9	Leyla Hirsch	W	AEW Dynamite	8:51
Mar 16	Steel Cage Match: Dr. Britt Baker D.M.D.	W	AEW Dynamite: St. Patrick's Day Slam	17:33
Apr 16	Nyla Rose	W	AEW Battle Of The Belts II	14:10
May 29	Serena Deeb	W	AEW Double Or Nothing '22	16:55
Jun 8	Marina Shafir	W	AEW Dynamite	8:26
Jun 26	Toni Storm	W	AEW x NJPW Forbidden Door	10:42
Jul 6	Marina Shafir & Nyla Rose (w/Toni Storm)	W	AEW Dynamite	9:07
Jul 9	Miyu Yamashita	L	TJPW Summer Sun Princess '22	13:39
Jul 27	Miyu Yamashita	W	AEW Dynamite: Fight For The Fallen	10:02
Aug 3	Dr. Britt Baker D.M.D. & Jamie Hayter (w/Toni Storm)	W	AEW Dynamite	12:02
Aug 6	Jamie Hayter	W	AEW Battle Of The Belts III	11:31
Aug 15	Emi Sakura, Marina Shafir & Nyla Rose (w/Toni Storm & Hikaru Shida)	W	AEW Dark Elevation	2:42

TIFFANY STRATTON

Jan 25	Io Shirai	L	NXT 2.0	4:18
Feb 8	Wendy Choo	W	NXT 2.0	3:07
Mar 4	Erica Yan	W	NXT Level Up	3:51
Mar 8	Fallon Henley	L	NXT 2.0: Roadblock '22	2:48
Mar 15	Sarray	W	NXT 2.0	:54
Mar 29	Ivy Nile	L	NXT 2.0	3:32
Apr 19	Sarray	W	NXT 2.0	4:31
May 10	Sarray & Andre Chase (w/Grayson Waller)	L	NXT 2.0	7:00
May 24	Fallon Henley	W	NXT 2.0	5:02
Jun 7	Roxanne Perez	L	NXT 2.0	8:48
Jun 14	Fallon Henley	L	NXT 2.0	3:10
Jul 5	Wendy Choo	W	NXT 2.0: Great American Bash	5:05
Jul 19	Battle Royal	L	NXT 2.0	13:13
Aug 23	Light's Out Match: Wendy Choo	L	NXT 2.0	13:09

TIGER TURAN

May 5	Tate Mayfairs	W	NXT UK	4:03
Jun 16	Josh Morrell	W	NXT UK	3:03
Jul 7	Kenny Williams	W	NXT UK	6:33

TIM STORM

Jan 11	Matt Cardona & Mike Knox, Chris Adonis & Thom Latimer (w/Trevor Murdoch)	L	NWA Power	5:25
Apr 5	Matt Cardona	L	NWA Power	5:21
Jul 12	Nick Aldis	L	NWA Power	8:30
Aug 16	Larry D	W	NWA Power	3:59

TJP

Date	Opponent	W/L	Promotion	Time
Jan 8	The DKC	W	NJPW Strong	8:31
Feb 5	Clark Connors	L	NJPW Strong	18:19
Mar 5	Brogan Finlay	W	NJPW Strong	9:06
Mar 17	Buddy Matthews	W	MLW Fusion	20:21
Apr 7	Myron Reed	L	MLW Fusion	13:39
Apr 14	Matt Cross	L	MLW Fusion	11:07
Apr 16	Hikuleo, Chris Bey, El Phantasmo, Karl Anderson, Luke Gallows & Scott Norton (w/Aaron Henare, Great-O-Khan, Jeff Cobb, Mark Davis & Kyle Fletcher)	W	NJPW Windy City Riot	11:58
Apr 30	Mascara Dorada	L	NJPW Strong	10:50
May 21	Brody King, Mascara Dorada & Taylor Rust (w/Aaron Henare & Great-O-Khan)	W	NJPW Strong	14:04
May 26	Aero Star, El Dragon & Micro Man (w/Arez & Mini Abismo Negro)	L	MLW Fusion	10:36
Jun 12	Ryusuke Taguchi, Master Wato & Hiroshi Tanahashi (w/Aaron Henare & Francesco Akira)	W	NJPW Dominion '22	10:31
Jul 30	Alex Zayne, Cash Wheeler & Dax Harwood (w/Kyle Fletcher & Mark Davis)	W	NJPW Music City Mayhem	14:30
Aug 27	Mascara Dorada	W	NJPW Strong	11:55
Sep 25	Ryusuke Taguchi & Master Wato (w/Francesco Akira)	W	NJPW Burning Spirit '22	12:43
Oct 1	Fred Rosser	L	NJPW Strong	17:20
Oct 10	Tetsuya Naito, Sanada, Bushi & Hiromu Takahashi (w/Will Ospreay, Aaron Henare & Francesco Akira)	L	NJPW Declaration Of Power	8:07
Nov 5	Bushi & Titan (w/Francesco Akira)	W	NJPW Battle Autumn '22	11:36
Nov 20	Bushi, Hiromu Takahashi, Sanada, Shingo Takagi & Tetsuya Naito (w/Kyle Fletcher, Mark Davis, Francesco Akira & Gideon Grey)	W	NJPW x Stardom Historic X-Over	9:55

TOA LIONA

Date	Opponent	W/L	Promotion	Time
Feb 1	QT Marshall	L	AEW Dark	4:43
Jul 8	Jonathan Gresham & Lee Moriarty (w/Kaun)	W	AEW Rampage	7:27
Oct 7	Dax Harwood & Cash Wheeler (w/Kaun)	L	AEW Battle Of The Belts IV	13:26
Oct 14	Shawn Spears, Dax Harwood & Cash Wheeler (w/Brian Cage & Kaun)	L	AEW Rampage	10:29
Nov 1	Fuego Del Sol, Jaylen Brandyn & Traevon Jordan (w/Brian Cage & Kaun)	W	AEW Dark	4:01
Nov 4	Wardlow & Samoa Joe (w/Kaun)	L	AEW Rampage	9:10
Nov 14	Big Cuzzo & Teddy Goodz (w/Kaun)	W	AEW Dark Elevation	1:37
Dec 5	Dan Adams, Facade & Star Rider (w/Brian Cage & Kaun)	W	AEW Dark Elevation	3:43
Dec 10	Dalton Castle, Brandon Tate & Brent Tate (w/Kaun & Brian Cage)	W	ROH Final Battle '22	10:05

TOM LAWLOR

Date	Opponent	W/L	Promotion	Time
Jan 22	Fred Rosser, Rocky Romero & Taylor Rust (w/Jorel Nelson & Black Tiger)	L	NJPW Strong	11:35
Feb 26	Taylor Rust	W	NJPW Strong	19:11
Mar 26	Elimimination Match: Adrian Quest, Clark Connors, Fred Rosser, The DKC & Taylor Rust (w/Danny Limelight, Jorel Nelson, Royce Isaacs & JR Kratos)	W	NJPW Strong	16:29
Apr 2	Clark Connors	W	NJPW Strong	13:58
Apr 16	Yuji Nagata	W	NJPW Windy City Riot	13:57
May 7	Alex Coughlin, Fred Rosser & The DKC (w/JR Kratos & Royce Isaacs)	W	NJPW Strong	11:12
May 14	The DKC, Yuya Uemura, David Finlay, Tanga Loa & Fred Rosser (w/Jorel Nelson, Royce Isaacs, JR Kratos & Danny Limelight)	W	NJPW Capital Collision	14:48
Jun 25	Fred Rosser	L	NJPW Strong	24:19
Jul 16	Bad Dude Tito	W	NJPW Strong	12:09
Sep 17	Cody Chhun & Jordan Cruz (w/JR Kratos)	W	NJPW Strong	9:54
Oct 28	Homicide, Wheeler Yuta & Shota Umino (w/Royce Isaacs & Jorel Nelson)	L	NJPW Rumble On 44th Street	12:15
Oct 29	Tomohiro Ishii	L	NJPW Strong	15:31
Nov 19	Homicide	L	NJPW Strong	13:44
Nov 20	Giulia & Zack Sabre Jr. (w/Syuri)	L	NJPW x Stardom Historic X-Over	10:20

TOMMASO CIAMPA

Date	Opponent	W/L	Promotion	Time
Jan 4	Bron Breakker	L	NXT 2.0: New Year's Evil '22	15:28
Jan 13	T-Bar	W	WWE Main Event	5:28
Jan 20	Akira Tozawa	W	WWE Main Event	5:33
Feb 1	Joaquin Wilde & Raul Mendoza (w/Bron Breakker)	W	NXT 2.0	11:28
Feb 17	T-Bar	W	WWE Main Event	8:29
Feb 21	Dolph Ziggler & Robert Roode (w/Finn Balor)	W	WWE Monday Night RAW	9:15
Feb 22	Dolph Ziggler	L	NXT 2.0	15:37
Feb 28	Robert Roode	W	WWE Monday Night RAW	2:40
Mar 1	Dolph Ziggler & Robert Roode (w/Bron Breakker)	W	NXT 2.0	13:05
Mar 7	Dolph Ziggler & Robert Roode (w/Bron Breakker)	W	WWE Monday Night RAW	9:37
Mar 8	Dolph Ziggler, Bron Breakker	L	NXT 2.0: Roadblock '22	12:24
Mar 17	T-Bar	W	WWE Main Event	5:58
Apr 2	Tony D'Angelo	L	NXT Stand & Deliver '22	13:11
Apr 14	T-Bar	W	WWE Main Event	6:26
Apr 21	Cedric Alexander	W	WWE Main Event	7:42
May 5	Apollo Crews	W	WWE Main Event	7:29
May 9	Mustafa Ali	W	WWE Monday Night RAW	3:55
May 19	Reggie	W	WWE Main Event	5:37
May 30	Mustafa Ali	L	WWE Monday Night RAW	3:24
Jun 9	Reggie	W	WWE Main Event	5:29
Jun 13	Riddle	L	WWE Monday Night RAW	4:30
Jun 20	AJ Styles	L	WWE Monday Night RAW	4:30
Jun 27	Battle Royal	L	WWE Monday Night RAW	19:25
Jun 30	Akira Tozawa	W	WWE Main Event	8:39
Jul 11	AJ Styles & Ezekiel (w/The Miz)	L	WWE Monday Night RAW	11:29

Aug 1	Dolph Ziggler, Chad Gable	W	WWE Monday Night RAW	10:30
Aug 1	AJ Styles	W	WWE Monday Night RAW	13:30
Aug 8	Bobby Lashley	L	WWE Monday Night RAW	13:30
Aug 15	Cedric Alexander & Mustafa Ali (w/The Miz)	W	WWE Monday Night RAW	9:30
Aug 22	AJ Styles & Bobby Lashley (w/The Miz)	W	WWE Monday Night RAW	13:30

TOMMY DREAMER

Oct 7	Call Your Shot Gauntlet	L	IMPACT Bound For Glory '22	29:18
Oct 20	Chris Bey & Juice Robinson (w/Bully Ray)	W	IMPACT Wrestling	6:23
Oct 27	Chris Bey	L	IMPACT Wrestling	6:50
Nov 17	Old School Rules: Steve Maclin	L	IMPACT Wrestling	8:10

TOMOHIRO ISHII

Jan 4	Evil	L	NJPW Wrestle Kingdom 16 Night #1	12:10
Jan 8	Daisuke Harada, Hajime Ohara, Daiki Inaba, Yoshiki Inamura & Kinya Okada (w/Hirooki Goto, Yoshi-Hashi, Master Wato & Ryusuke Taguchi)	W	NJPW Wrestle Kingdom 16 Night #3	11:42
Mar 1	Sanada, Tetsuya Naito, Shingo Takagi, Bushi & Hiromu Takahashi (w/Togi Makabe, Tomoaki Honma, Toru Yano & Shiro Koshinaka)	L	NJPW 50th Anniversary Show	12:38
Apr 1	Eddie Edwards	W	IMPACT Multiverse Of Matches	14:09
Apr 1	Chris Dickinson	W	NJPW Lonestar Shootout	16:11
Apr 16	Minoru Suzuki	W	NJPW Windy City Riot	18:46
Apr 22	Adam Cole	L	AEW Rampage	11:14
Apr 23	Jonah	W	IMPACT Rebellion '22	14:34
May 1	Hiroshi Tanahashi	L	NJPW Wrestling Dontaku '22	23:20
May 5	Steve Maclin	W	IMPACT Wrestling	13:58
May 12	El Phantasmo & Jay White (w/Josh Alexander)	W	IMPACT Wrestling	10:28
May 14	Eddie Kingston	W	NJPW Capital Collision	16:07
Jun 4	Big Damo	W	NJPW Strong	13:02
Jun 11	Luke Gallows, Karl Anderson, Hikuleo, Jay White & Juice Robinson (w/Chuck Taylor, Rocky Romero, Mascara Dorada & Ren Narita)	L	NJPW Strong	12:44
Sep 4	Eddie Kingston	L	AEW All Out Buy-In	13:25
Oct 1	Bad Dude Tito & Zak Knight (w/Kazuchika Okada)	W	NJPW Royal Quest II Night #1	12:47
Oct 2	Yota Tsuji	W	NJPW Royal Quest II Night #2	17:36
Oct 29	Tom Lawlor	W	NJPW Strong	15:31
Nov 20	Dick Togo, Evil, Sho & Yujiro Takahashi (w/Lio Rush, Yoh & Yoshi-Hashi)	W	NJPW x Stardom Historic X-Over	7:05
Nov 23	Chris Jericho	L	AEW Dynamite	15:29

TONI STORM

Mar 30	The Bunny	W	AEW Dynamite	8:41
Apr 19	Gigi Rey	W	AEW Dark	3:10
May 3	Diamante	W	AEW Dark	8:38
May 6	Dr. Britt Baker D.M.D. & Jamie Hayter (w/Ruby Soho)	W	AEW Rampage	8:38
May 11	Jamie Hayter	W	AEW Dynamite	8:32
May 25	Dr. Britt Baker D.M.D.	L	AEW Dynamite	9:02
Jun 1	Jamie Hayter & Dr. Britt Baker D.M.D. (w/Ruby Soho)	W	AEW Dynamite	9:48
Jun 7	Zeda Zhang	W	AEW Dark	3:37
Jun 15	Dr. Britt Baker D.M.D.	W	AEW Dynamite: Road Rager	7:34
Jun 22	Marina Shafir	W	AEW Dynamite	7:22
Jun 26	Thunder Rosa	L	AEW x NJPW Forbidden Door	10:42
Jul 1	Nyla Rose	W	AEW Rampage	9:42
Jul 6	Marina Shafir & Nyla Rose (w/Thunder Rosa)	W	AEW Dynamite	9:07
Jul 25	Emi Sakura	W	AEW Dark Elevation	7:33
Aug 1	Emi Sakura, Marina Shafir & Nyla Rose (w/Hikaru Shida & Willow Nightingale)	W	AEW Dark Elevation	8:05
Aug 3	Jamie Hayter & Dr. Britt Baker D.M.D. (w/Thunder Rosa)	L	AEW Dynamite	12:02
Aug 15	Emi Sakura, Marina Shafir & Nyla Rose (w/Hikaru Shida & Thunder Rosa)	W	AEW Dark Elevation	2:42
Aug 17	KiLynn King	W	AEW Dynamite	6:49
Aug 31	Jamie Hayter & Dr. Britt Baker D.M.D. (w/Hikaru Shida)	W	AEW Dynamite	7:40
Sep 4	Dr. Britt Baker D.M.D., Jamie Hayter, Hikaru Shida	W	AEW All Out '22	14:20
Sep 7	Penelope Ford	W	AEW Dynamite	5:50
Sep 14	Serena Deeb & Dr. Britt Baker D.M.D. (w/Athena)	L	AEW Dynamite	8:34
Sep 21	Athena, Dr. Britt Baker D.M.D., Serena Deeb	W	AEW Dynamite: Grand Slam	9:50
Sep 28	Lumberjack Match: Sereba Deeb	W	AEW Dynamite	11:09
Oct 5	Jamie Hayter, Serena Deeb & Penelope Ford (w/Athena & Willow Nightingale)	W	AEW Dynamite: Anniversary	9:29
Oct 11	Emi Sakura	W	AEW Dark	8:53
Oct 12	Jamie Hayter & Dr. Britt Baker D.M.D. (w/Hikaru Shida)	W	AEW Dynamite	8:18
Oct 18	Hikaru Shida	W	AEW Dynamite: Title Tuesday	8:44
Nov 1	Diamante	W	AEW Dark	6:43
Nov 8	Emi Sakura & Mei Suruga (w/Hikaru Shida)	W	AEW Dark	7:51
Nov 16	Anna Jay	W	AEW Dynamite	7:09
Nov 19	Jamie Hayter	L	AEW Full Gear '22	15:00

TONY D'ANGELO

Jan 11	Crowbar On A Pole Match: Pete Dunne	W	NXT 2.0	13:17
Jan 25	Cameron Grimes	L	NXT 2.0	11:41
Feb 15	Weaponized Steel Cage Match: Pete Dunne	L	NXT 2.0: Vengeance Day '22	9:52
Mar 22	Dexter Lumis	W	NXT 2.0	7:15
Apr 2	Tommaso Ciampa	W	NXT Stand & Deliver '22	13:11
Apr 26	Von Wagner	L	NXT 2.0	10:44
May 17	Santos Escobar	L	NXT 2.0	12:49

Jun 4	Santos Escobar, Cruz del Toro & Joaquin Wilde	W	NXT In Your House '22	12:45
	(w/Channing Lorenzo & Troy Donovan)			
Jun 21	Carmelo Hayes	L	NXT 2.0	10:38
Jul 12	Edris Enofe & Malik Blade (w/Channing Lorenzo)	W	NXT 2.0	5:23
Jul 26	Roderick Strong, Damon Kemp, Julius Creed & Brutus Creed	W	NXT 2.0	11:39
	(w/Channing Lorenzo, Joaquin Wilde & Cruz Del Toro)			
Aug 2	Julius Creed & Brutus Creed (w/Channing Lorenzo)	L	NXT 2.0	10:46
Aug 16	Street Fight: Santos Escobar	W	NXT 2.0: Heatwave	12:44
Sep 13	Cameron Grimes & Joe Gacy (w/Channing Lorenzo)	L	NXT 2.0	5:36
Sep 27	Wes Lee	L	NXT	8:45
Dec 6	Xyon Quinn	W	NXT	1:55
Dec 27	Wes Lee	L	NXT	14:48

TONY DEPPEN

May 9	John Silver	L	AEW Dark Elevation	2:34
Jun 25	Minoru Suzuki	L	NJPW Strong	10:32
Oct 3	Penta El Zero M & Rey Fenix (w/Dante Martin)	L	AEW Dark Elevation	6:20
Nov 1	Orange Cassidy, Chuck Taylor & Trent Beretta (w/Ari Daivari & Sonny Kiss)	L	AEW Dark	6:04
Nov 21	Angelo Parker, Matt Menard & Daniel Garcia	L	AEW Dark Elevation	2:46
	(w/Leon Ruffin & Tracy Williams)			
Nov 29	Brian Cage	L	AEW Dark	3:07
Dec 13	Kip Sabian	L	AEW Dark	5:27

TONY NESE

Jan 4	Alan Angels	W	AEW Dark	6:46
Feb 1	Zack Clayton	W	AEW Dark	5:17
Feb 15	Carlie Bravo	W	AEW Dark	3:51
Mar 11	Swerve Strickland	L	AEW Rampage	12:58
Mar 22	Karam	W	AEW Dark	2:39
Apr 18	J. Spade	W	AEW Dark Elevation	2:35
Apr 19	JD Griffey	W	AEW Dark	1:54
Apr 25	The Steel City Brawler	W	AEW Dark Elevation	2:51
May 2	Cheeseburger	W	AEW Dark Elevation	4:13
May 3	Leon Ruffin	W	AEW Dark	4:11
May 11	Danhausen	W	AEW Dynamite	:32
May 29	Hook & Danhausen (w/Mark Sterling)	L	AEW Double Or Nothing Buy-In	5:20
Jun 8	Casino Battle Royale	L	AEW Dynamite	24:59
Jun 20	Warhorse	L	AEW Dark Elevation	2:53
Jun 21	Pure Rules Match: JDX	W	AEW Dark	3:08
Jun 28	Wheeler Yuta	L	AEW Dark	10:16
Jul 1	Royal Rampage Match	L	AEW Rampage	22:41
Jul 8	Orange Cassidy	L	AEW Rampage	15:01
Jul 18	John Walters	W	AEW Dark Elevation	2:34
Jul 27	Handicap Match: Swerve Strickland (w/Mark Sterling)	L	AEW Dynamite: Fight For The Fallen	6:44
Aug 4	Damian Chambers & Dean Alexander (w/Josh Woods)	W	AEW Dark Elevation	2:52
Aug 5	Street Fight: Keith Lee & Swerve Strickland (w/Josh Woods)	L	AEW Rampage	12:53
Aug 15	Arik Cannon & Travis Titan (w/Josh Woods)	W	AEW Dark Elevation	2:40
Aug 22	Andrea Guercio & Logan James (w/Josh Woods)	W	AEW Dark	2:16
Aug 23	GKM & Oliver Sawyer (w/Josh Woods)	W	AEW Dark	1:25
Sep 5	Jordan Kross & Renny D (w/Josh Woods)	W	AEW Dark Elevation	2:27
Sep 6	Brandon Gore & Storm Grayson (w/Josh Woods)	W	AEW Dark	2:10
Sep 7	Warlow	L	AEW Dynamite	1:24
Sep 20	Baliyan Akki & Ryan Matthews (w/Josh Woods)	W	AEW Dark	4:02
Sep 23	Samoa Joe & Wardlow (w/Josh Woods)	L	AEW Rampage: Grand Slam	2:26
Oct 4	Invictus Khash & Rohit Raju (w/Josh Woods)	W	AEW Dark	2:34
Oct 7	Brian Pillman Jr. & Griff Garrison (w/Josh Woods)	W	AEW Rampage	1:45
Oct 10	Action Andretti & Myles Hawkins (w/Josh Woods)	W	AEW Dark Elevation	5:55
Oct 21	Anthony Bowens & Max Caster (w/Josh Woods)	L	AEW Rampage	8:06
Nov 22	Dean Alexander & Rosario Grillo (w/Josh Woods)	W	AEW Dark	3:32
Dec 12	Brandon Cutler, Luther & Serpentico (w/Ari Daivari & Josh Woods)	W	AEW Dark Elevation	5:20
Dec 23	$300,000 Three Kings Christmas Casino Trios Royale	L	AEW Rampage	22:01
	(w/Josh Woods & Ari Daivari)			

TOOTIE LYNN

Jan 5	Kamille & Missa Kate (w/Kylie Rae)	W	NWA Power	6:44
Feb 15	Marti Belle	W	NWA Power	4:36
Apr 26	Angelina Love	L	NWA Power	5:14
Jun 13	Mercedes Martinez & Serena Deeb (w/Miranda Gordy)	L	AEW Dark Elevation	4:15
Jun 20	Mercedes Martinez & Serena Deeb (w/Heather Reckless)	L	AEW Dark Elevation	4:29
Aug 27	Burke Invitational Gauntlet	L	NWA 74th Anniversary Show	17:24

TOP DOLLA

Aug 12	Trevor Urban & Brandon Scott (w/Ashante Adonis)	W	WWE SmackDown	1:50
Sep 2	Mace & Mansoor (w/Ashante Adonis)	W	WWE SmackDown	3:05
Sep 9	Angel, Humberto, Mace & Mansoor	W	WWE SmackDown	8:35
	(w/Ashante Adonis, Angelo Dawkins & Montez Ford)			
Sep 16	Ridge Holland & Butch, Ludwig Kaiser & Giovanni Vinci,	L	WWE SmackDown	18:44
	Xavier Woods & Kofi Kingston (w/Ashante Adonis)			
Sep 30	Angel & Humberto (w/Ashante Adonis)	W	WWE SmackDown	3:21
Oct 14	Joaquin Wilde & Cruz Del Toro (w/Ashante Adonis)	L	WWE SmackDown	1:22
Oct 28	Santos Escobar, Joaquin Wilde & Cruz Del Toro	W	WWE SmackDown	4:19
	(w/Ashante Adonis & Shinsuke Nakamura)			

Nov 25	Erik & Ivar (w/Ashante Adonis)	L	WWE SmackDown	2:46
Dec 16	Erik & Ivar, Joaquin Wilde & Cruz Del Toro (w/Ashante Adonis)	W	WWE SmackDown	9:20
Dec 23	Jey Uso & Jimmy Uso (w/Ashante Adonis)	L	WWE SmackDown	9:43

TORU YANO

Jan 5	Minoru Suzuki, Chase Owens, Cima	L	NJPW Wrestle Kingdom 16 Night #2	6:08
Jan 8	Taichi, Minoru Suzuki & Taka Michinoku (w/Takashi Sugiura & Kazushi Sakuraba)	W	NJPW Wrestle Kingdom 16 Night #3	9:37
Mar 1	Sanada, Tetsuya Naito, Shingo Takagi, Bushi & Hiromu Takahashi (w/Togi Makabe, Tomoaki Honma, Tomohiro Ishii & Shiro Koshinaka)	L	NJPW 50th Anniversary Show	12:38
Apr 9	No Rope Ring Out Match: Taichi	L	NJPW Hyper Battle '22	4:18
Jun 12	Luke Gallows	W	NJPW Dominion '22	4:05
Sep 25	Luke Gallows	D	NJPW Burning Spirit '22	3:45
Nov 5	Aaron Henare, Gideon Grey, Kyle Fletcher & Mark Davis (w/Hiroshi Tanahashi, David Finlay & Alex Zayne)	L	NJPW Battle Autumn '22	9:50
Nov 20	Great-O-Khan, Jeff Cobb & Aaron Henare (w/Kazuchika Okada & The Great Muta)	W	NJPW x Stardom Historic X-Over	9:48

TRENT BERETTA

Jan 14	Adam Cole	L	AEW Rampage	11:34
Jan 21	Nick Jackson	W	AEW Rampage	13:00
Feb 7	Luther & Serpentico (w/Chuck Taylor)	W	AEW Dark Elevation	6:42
Feb 11	Matt Jackson & Nick Jackson (w/Rocky Romero)	L	AEW Rampage	13:23
Feb 18	Jay White	L	AEW Rampage: Slam Dunk	15:11
Feb 23	Tag Team Battle Royal (w/Chuck Taylor)	L	AEW Dynamite	14:29
Mar 2	Casino Battle Royale (w/Chuck Taylor)	L	AEW Dynamite	22:40
Mar 28	Aaron Solo & QT Marshall (w/Rocky Romero)	W	AEW Dark Elevation	5:23
Apr 4	Anthony Henry & JD Drake (w/Chuck Taylor)	W	AEW Dark Elevation	8:00
Apr 8	Bryan Danielson	L	AEW Rampage	13:39
Apr 18	Aaron Solo & Nick Comoroto (w/Rocky Romero)	W	AEW Dark Elevation	7:25
Apr 29	Samoa Joe	L	AEW Rampage	9:57
May 17	Ryan Nemeth	W	AEW Dark	3:30
May 24	Peter Avalon & Ryan Nemeth (w/Rocky Romero)	W	AEW Dark	7:02
May 25	Dax Harwood & Cash Wheeler (w/Rocky Romero)	D	AEW Dynamite: 3 Year Anniversary	10:12
Jun 10	Will Ospreay, Kyle Fletcher & Mark Davis (w/Dax Harwood & Cash Wheeler)	W	AEW Rampage	13:59
Jun 22	Will Ospreay, Kyle Fletcher & Mark Davis (w/Rocky Romero & Orange Cassidy)	W	AEW Dynamite	11:37
Jun 26	Dax Harwood & Cash Wheeler, Great-O-Khan & Jeff Cobb (w/Rocky Romero)	L	AEW x NJPW Forbidden Door	16:19
Jul 4	GPA & Isaiah Broner (w/Chuck Taylor)	W	AEW Dark Elevation	3:52
Jul 11	Aaron Solo & QT Marshall (w/Chuck Taylor)	W	AEW Dark Elevation	9:40
Jul 20	Jon Moxley & Wheeler Yuta (w/Chuck Taylor)	L	AEW Dynamite: Fyter Fest	11:53
Jul 29	Jay Lethal, Satnam Singh & Sonjay Dutt (w/Orange Cassidy & Chuck Taylor)	W	AEW Rampage	7:29
Aug 9	Ren Jones & Rohit Raju (w/Chuck Taylor)	W	AEW Dark	3:28
Aug 19	Ari Daivari, Parker Boudreaux & Slim J (w/Orange Cassidy & Chuck Taylor)	W	AEW Rampage	11:00
Sep 2	Hangman Page, John Silver & Alex Reynolds (w/Orange Cassidy & Chuck Taylor)	L	AEW Rampage	11:12
Sep 3	Angelico, The Butcher & The Blade (w/Orange Cassidy & Chuck Taylor)	W	AEW Dark Elevation	8:13
Sep 7	Pac, Penta El Zero M & Rey Fenix (w/Orange Cassidy & Chuck Taylor)	L	AEW Dynamite	12:58
Sep 17	Chase Owens, Hikuleo, Jay White & Juice Robinson (w/Kushida, Taylor Rust & Rocky Romero)	L	NJPW Strong	14:46
Sep 23	Golden Ticket Battle Royale	L	AEW Rampage: Grand Slam	12:16
Oct 3	Aaron Solo, Cole Karter, Nick Comoroto & QT Marshall (w/Danhausen, Rocky Romero & Chuck Taylor)	W	AEW Dark Elevation	7:54
Oct 7	Pac	L	AEW Battle Of The Belts IV	14:25
Oct 18	Jessie V, Kobe Durst & Steven Mainz (w/Orange Cassidy & Chuck Taylor)	W	AEW Dark	2:44
Oct 18	Pac, Penta El Zero M & Rey Fenix (w/Orange Cassidy & Chuck Taylor)	L	AEW Dynamite: Title Tuesday	11:45
Oct 31	Anthony Young, Patton & Victor Andrews (w/Orange Cassidy & Chuck Taylor)	W	AEW Dark Elevation	3:30
Nov 1	Tony Deppen, Ari Daivari & Sonny Kiss (w/Orange Cassidy & Chuck Taylor)	W	AEW Dark	6:04
Nov 7	Angelico, The Butcher & The Blade (w/Rocky Romero & Chuck Taylor)	W	AEW Dark Elevation	7:20
Nov 9	Jay Lethal	L	AEW Dynamite	7:17
Nov 19	QT Marshall, Aaron Solo, Lee Johnson, Nick Comoroto & Cole Karter (w/Orange Cassidy, Chuck Taylor, Rocky Romero & Danhausen)	W	AEW Full Gear Buy-In	11:55
Nov 21	Aaron Solo, Cole Karter & Lee Johnson (w/Orange Cassidy & Chuck Taylor)	W	AEW Dark Elevation	3:38
Nov 28	Davey Bang, Freedom Ramsey & Yabo (w/Rocky Romero & Chuck Taylor)	W	AEW Dark Elevation	3:54
Dec 6	Anthony Henry	W	AEW Dark	10:49
Dec 12	Zack Clayton & Zane Valero (w/Chuck Taylor)	W	AEW Dark Elevation	3:00
Dec 16	Trent Seven, Kip Sabian, The Butcher & The Blade (w/Orange Cassidy, Dustin Rhodes & Chuck Taylor)	W	AEW Rampage	10:42
Dec 23	$300,000 Three Kings Christmas Casino Trios Royale (w/Orange Cassidy & Chuck Taylor)	L	AEW Rampage	22:01
Dec 30	Orange Cassidy	L	AEW Rampage	14:36

TRENT SEVEN

Feb 24	Ashton Smith & Oliver Carter (w/Tyler Bate)	W	NXT UK	13:02
Mar 31	Ashton Smith	W	NXT UK	8:50
Apr 21	2/3 Falls: Ashton Smith & Oliver Carter (w/Tyler Bate)	W	NXT UK	21:38

Jun 2	Ashton Smith & Oliver Carter, Charlie Dempsey & Rohan Raja (w/Tyler Bate)	L	NXT UK	14:17
Jul 7	Tate Mayfairs	W	NXT UK	4:05
Jul 21	Sam Gradwell	W	NXT UK	11:01
Aug 11	Wolfgang	W	NXT UK	9:03
Aug 25	Oliver Carter	W	NXT UK	9:15
Sep 1	Tyler Bate	L	NXT UK	20:31
Dec 9	Orange Cassidy	L	AEW Rampage	11:55
Dec 16	Orange Cassidy, Dustin Rhodes, Chuck Taylor & Trent Beretta (w/Kip Sabian, The Butcher & The Blade)	L	AEW Rampage	10:42

TREVOR MURDOCH

Jan 11	Matt Cardona & Mike Knox, Chris Adonis & Thom Latimer (w/Tim Storm)	L	NWA Power	5:25
Feb 1	Matt Cardona	W	NWA Power	5:02
Mar 8	Matt Cardona	L	NWA Power	11:04
Mar 22	Brett Buffshaw	W	NWA Power	1:39
Apr 5	Garrison Creed	W	NWA Power	:39
Apr 26	Aron Stevens	W	NWA Power	5:24
May 24	Mike Knox	W	NWA Power	7:58
Jun 11	Aron Stevens	W	NWA Alwayz Ready '22	4:38
Jun 11	Nick Aldis, Thom Latimer, Sam Shaw	W	NWA Alwayz Ready '22	18:10
Jul 5	Thrillbilly Silas	W	NWA Power	3:09
Aug 9	Da Pope	D	NWA Power	7:30
Aug 28	Tyrus	W	NWA 74th Anniversary Show	13:44
Oct 18	Matt Taven	W	NWA Power	5:39
Nov 8	Doug Williams, JR Kratos & Da Pope (w/Thom Latimer & Tyrus)	D	NWA Power	6:49
Nov 12	Tyrus, Matt Cardona	L	NWA Hard Times 3	10:03
Dec 13	Dak Draper & Mims (w/Rhett Titus)	W	NWA Power	9:14
Dec 20	Jax Dane	D	NWA Power	8:47

TREY MIGUEL

Jan 8	Steve Maclin	W	IMPACT Hard To Kill '22	12:50
Feb 24	Ace Austin & Mike Bailey (w/Jake Something)	L	IMPACT Before The Impact	8:01
Apr 1	Ultimate X Match: Chris Bey, Jordynne Grace, Rich Swann, Vincent, Willie Mack	W	IMPACT Multiverse Of Matches	7:27
Apr 21	Ace Austin & Mike Bailey (w/Laredo Kid)	W	IMPACT Wrestling	6:00
Apr 23	Ace Austin, Mike Bailey	L	IMPACT Rebellion '22	10:25
May 12	Gauntlet For The Gold	L	IMPACT Wrestling	39:00
May 26	Alex Shelley	W	IMPACT Wrestling	12:26
Jun 16	Mike Bailey	W	IMPACT Wrestling	10:42
Jun 19	Ultimate X Match: Mike Bailey, Ace Austin, Alex Zayne, Andrew Everett, Kenny King	L	IMPACT Slammiversary XX	9:50
Jun 30	Chris Bey, Laredo Kid, Steve Maclin	W	IMPACT Wrestling	6:12
Jul 7	Laredo Kid	W	IMPACT Wrestling	7:41
Jul 28	Johnny Swinger & Zicky Dice (w/Laredo Kid)	W	IMPACT Wrestling	4:01
Aug 18	Black Taurus, Laredo Kid, Rey Horus	L	IMPACT Wrestling	7:33
Sep 22	Black Taurus, Alex Zayne, Laredo Kid, Mia Yim	L	IMPACT Wrestling	11:58
Sep 29	Ace Austin & Chris Bey (w/Laredo Kid)	L	IMPACT Wrestling	8:16
Oct 13	Alex Zayne, Black Taurus, Kenny King, Laredo Kid, Yuya Uemura	W	IMPACT Wrestling	5:19
Oct 27	Alan Angels	W	IMPACT Wrestling	8:17
Nov 10	Mike Bailey	W	IMPACT Wrestling	7:02
Dec 8	Jason Hotch	W	IMPACT Wrestling	8:27

TRICK WILLIAMS

Feb 11	Ikemen Jiro	W	WWE 205 Live	5:09
Feb 22	Cameron Grimes	L	NXT 2.0	6:06
Mar 11	Guru Raaj	W	NXT Level Up	4:08
Apr 26	Solo Sikoa	L	NXT 2.0	5:08
May 13	Javier Bernal	W	NXT Level Up	6:20
May 17	Cameron Grimes & Solo Sikoa (w/Carmelo Hayes)	L	NXT 2.0	9:57
May 27	Dante Chen	W	NXT Level Up	6:05
Jun 14	Troy Donovan & Channing Lorenzo (w/Carmelo Hayes)	W	NXT 2.0	4:22
Jul 5	Wes Lee	W	NXT 2.0: Great American Bash	3:46
Aug 9	Rounds Match: Wes Lee	L	NXT 2.0	10:56
Sep 6	Ricochet	L	NXT 2.0	5:13
Sep 20	Andre Chase & Bodhi Hayward (w/Carmelo Hayes)	L	NXT	4:15
Oct 18	Wes Lee & Oro Mensah (w/Carmelo Hayes)	W	NXT	2:43
Oct 28	Brooks Jensen	L	NXT Level Up	6:11
Dec 8	Cedric Alexander	L	WWE Main Event	7:56
Dec 9	Ikemen Jiro	W	NXT Level Up	5:50
Dec 23	Hank Walker	W	NXT Level Up	6:13

TYLER BATE

Feb 24	Ashton Smith & Oliver Carter (w/Trent Seven)	W	NXT UK	13:02
Mar 17	Oliver Carter	L	NXT UK	10:07
Apr 21	2/3 Falls: Ashton Smith & Oliver Carter (w/Trent Seven)	W	NXT UK	21:38
Jun 2	Ashton Smith & Oliver Carter, Charlie Dempsey & Rohan Raja (w/Trent Seven)	L	NXT UK	14:17
Aug 23	Von Wagner	W	NXT 2.0	6:14
Aug 25	Joe Coffey	W	NXT UK	12:00
Sep 1	Trent Seven	W	NXT UK	20:31
Sep 4	Bron Breakker	L	NXT Worlds Collide '22	17:11

| Sep 6 | Mark Coffey & Joe Coffey (w/Bron Breakker) | W | NXT 2.0 | 10:51 |
| Sep 20 | JD McDonagh | L | NXT | 12:54 |

TYRUS

Jan 11	Jaden Roller	W	NWA Power	2:54
Mar 20	Rodney Mack	W	NWA Crockett Cup '22	8:14
Feb 8	Team War: Odinson, Parrow & Rodney Mack, Alex Taylor, Rush Freeman & Jeremiah Plunkett, Aron Stevens, JR Kratos & Judais (w/Jordan Clearwater & Marshe Rockett)	L	NWA Power	11:40
Mar 8	Alex Taylor, Rush Freeman, Cyon & Mims (w/BLK Jeez, Jordan Clearwater & Marshe Rockett)	W	NWA Power	6:59
Apr 5	Slam Challenge Match: Cyon	D	NWA Power	3:09
May 3	Slam Challenge Match: Mims	L	NWA Power	:47
Jun 7	KC Roxx	W	NWA Power	1:10
Jun 11	Mims	W	NWA Alwayz Ready '22	8:37
Jun 21	Alex Taylor & Jeremiah Plunkett (w/Cyon)	W	NWA Power	7:40
Aug 2	Odinson	W	NWA Power	4:04
Aug 28	Trevor Murdoch	L	NWA 74th Anniversary Show	13:44
Sep 13	Mims	W	NWA Power	2:03
Nov 8	Doug Williams, JR Kratos & Da Pope (w/Thom Latimer & Trevor Murdoch)	D	NWA Power	6:49
Nov 12	Trevor Murdoch, Matt Cardona	W	NWA Hard Times 3	10:03
Dec 27	Joe Alonzo, Bestia 666 & Mecha Wolf (w/Cyon & Jordan Clearwater)	W	NWA Power	7:56

VALENTINA FEROZ

Jan 14	Ivy Nile	L	WWE 205 Live	4:39
Jan 28	Amari Miller & Lash Legend (w/Yulisa Leon)	W	WWE 205 Live	6:29
Mar 1	Raquel Gonzalez & Cora Jade (w/Yulisa Leon)	L	NXT 2.0	4:47
Mar 18	Lash Legend	L	NXT Level Up	4:53
Apr 26	Katana Chance & Kayden Carter (w/Yulisa Leon)	L	NXT 2.0	6:01
Jun 10	Arianna Grace	W	NXT Level Up	4:16
Jun 21	Katana Chance & Kayden Carter (w/Yulisa Leon)	L	NXT 2.0	5:15
Jul 19	Battle Royal	L	NXT 2.0	13:13
Aug 2	Elimination Match: Kayden Carter & Katana Chance, Ivy Nile & Tatum Paxley, Gigi Dolin & Jacy Jayne (w/Yulisa Leon)	L	NXT 2.0	12:09
Sep 9	Sol Ruca	W	NXT Level Up	5:52
Sep 23	Indi Hartwell	L	NXT Level Up	4:37
Sep 30	Thea Hail	L	NXT Level Up	4:38
Oct 11	Indi Hartwell	L	NXT	3:33
Nov 1	Cora Jade	L	NXT	3:37
Dec 9	Sol Ruca	L	NXT Level Up	4:30

VEER MAHAAN

Feb 3	Akira Tozawa	W	WWE Main Event	2:14
Feb 10	T-Bar	W	WWE Main Event	5:36
Feb 17	Apollo Crews	W	WWE Main Event	5:04
Feb 24	Apollo Crews	W	WWE Main Event	4:59
Mar 3	Storm Grayson	W	WWE Main Event	3:36
Mar 10	Savion Truitt	W	WWE Main Event	4:50
Mar 17	Gary Heck	W	WWE Main Event	3:28
Mar 24	Joe Alonzo	W	WWE Main Event	4:10
Mar 31	Cedric Alexander	W	WWE Main Event	5:19
Apr 11	Dominik Mysterio	W	WWE Monday Night RAW	2:00
Apr 18	Jeff Brooks	W	WWE Monday Night RAW	1:10
Apr 25	Sam Smothers	W	WWE Monday Night RAW	:38
May 2	Burt Hanson	W	WWE Monday Night RAW	1:30
May 9	Frank Loman	W	WWE Monday Night RAW	1:25
May 16	Mustafa Ali	W	WWE Monday Night RAW	2:50
Jun 6	Dominik Mysterio	W	WWE Monday Night RAW	9:20
Jun 13	Rey Mysterio	W	WWE Monday Night RAW	3:45
Jun 27	Battle Royal	L	WWE Monday Night RAW	19:25
Jul 7	Mustafa Ali	W	WWE Main Event	7:09
Aug 15	Beaux Keller	W	WWE Monday Night RAW	1:50
Nov 15	Ariel Dominguez & George Cannon (w/Sanga)	W	NXT	3:26

VINCE MCMAHON

| Apr 3 | Pat McAfee | W | WWE WrestleMania XXXVIII | 3:45 |

VINCENT

Feb 3	Josh Alexander	L	IMPACT Wrestling	10:28
Mar 3	Heath	L	IMPACT Wrestling	9:34
Apr 1	Ultimate X Match: Trey Miguel, Chris Bey, Jordynne Grace, Rich Swann, Willie Mack	L	IMPACT Multiverse Of Matches	7:27
Apr 21	Chris Bey, Luke Gallows, Karl Anderson & Jay White (w/Kenny King, Matt Taven & Mike Bennett)	L	IMPACT Wrestling	9:22
Apr 28	Crazzy Steve	W	IMPACT Before The Impact	9:20
May 12	Gauntlet For The Gold	L	IMPACT Wrestling	39:00
Jun 16	Garrett Bischoff & Wes Brisco (w/Kenny King)	W	IMPACT Wrestling	3:28
Jun 19	Alex Shelley, Chris Sabin, Davey Richards, Frankie Kazarian & Magnus (w/Eddie Edwards, Matt Taven, Mike Bennett & PCO)	L	IMPACT Slammiversary XX	18:45
Jun 30	Luke Gallows & Karl Anderson (w/PCO)	L	IMPACT Wrestling	5:19
Jul 23	Dalton Castle, Brandon Tate & Brent Tate (w/Bateman & Dutch)	L	ROH Death Before Dishonor XIX	9:40
Jul 28	Bhupinder Gujjar	L	IMPACT Before The Impact	6:12

Aug 25	Josh Alexander		L	IMPACT Wrestling	4:05
Sep 29	Heath & Rich Swann (w/PCO)		L	IMPACT Wrestling	4:32

VON WAGNER

Mar 1	Andre Chase		W	NXT 2.0	4:10
Mar 29	Bodhi Hayward		W	NXT 2.0	3:42
Apr 12	Ikemen Jiro		W	NXT 2.0	2:55
Apr 26	Tony D'Angelo		W	NXT 2.0	10:44
Apr 28	Saxon Huxley		W	NXT UK	4:04
May 24	Ikemen Jiro		W	NXT 2.0	4:13
Jun 2	Sam Gradwell		W	NXT UK	6:47
Jun 7	Josh Briggs		L	NXT 2.0	3:04
Jun 21	Brooks Jensen		W	NXT 2.0	4:45
Jul 12	Solo Sikoa		D	NXT 2.0	6:50
Aug 2	Falls Count Anywhere: Solo Sikoa		L	NXT 2.0	12:25
Aug 23	Tyler Bate		L	NXT 2.0	6:14
Sep 20	Sanga		W	NXT	2:52
Oct 4	Andre Chase		W	NXT	3:36
Oct 13	R-Truth		L	WWE Main Event	3:34
Oct 22	Ladder Match: Carmelo Hayes, Oro Mensa, Wes Lee, Nathan Frazer		L	NXT Halloween Havoc '22	22:25
Oct 27	Cedric Alexander		L	WWE Main Event	8:50
Nov 3	R-Truth & Shelton Benjamin (w/Duke Hudson)		L	WWE Main Event	6:31
Nov 15	Bron Breakker		L	NXT	12:42
Nov 29	Malik Blade		W	NXT	2:43
Dec 6	Axiom, Andre Chase		L	NXT	11:54
Dec 13	Odyssey Jones		L	NXT	2:54

VSK

Jan 20	Handicap Match: W. Morrissey (w/Zicky Dice)		L	IMPACT Wrestling	1:08
Jan 27	Handicap Match: W. Morrissey (w/Zicky Dice, D-Ray 3000, David Young, Elix Skipper, Mikey Batts, Lex Lovett, Jerelle Clarke & Shark Boy)		L	IMPACT Wrestling	3:00
Mar 19	Da Pope & Mims (w/Mike Knox)		W	NWA Crockett Cup '22	9:59
Mar 19	Jay Bradley & Wrecking Ball Legursky (w/Mike Knox)		W	NWA Crockett Cup '22	7:03
Mar 20	Jay Briscoe & Mark Briscoe (w/Mike Knox)		L	NWA Crockett Cup '22	7:45
Mar 29	Alex Taylor & Rush Freeman (w/Mike Knox)		W	NWA Power	4:18
Apr 28	Bhupinder Gujjar		L	IMPACT Wrestling	4:31
May 10	Nick Aldis, Doug Williams & Harry Smith (w/Mike Knox & Matt Cardona)		L	NWA Power	8:15
Jun 14	Chris Adonis & Thom Latimer (w/Mike Knox)		L	NWA Power	7:23
Sep 20	Bully Ray & Thom Latimer (w/Mike Knox)		L	NWA Power	5:15
Nov 1	Rolando Freeman, Brady Pierce & Rush Freeman (w/Brian Myers & Mike Knox)		L	NWA Power	6:54

WARDLOW

Jan 5	Antonio Zambrano		W	AEW Dynamite	1:23
Jan 12	CM Punk		L	AEW Dynamite	14:06
Jan 26	Handicap Match: James Alexander & Elijah Dean		W	AEW Dynamite: Beach Break	1:23
Feb 9	The Blade		W	AEW Dynamite	6:15
Feb 16	Max Caster		W	AEW Dynamite	5:18
Feb 25	Nick Comoroto		W	AEW Rampage	6:25
Mar 2	Cezar Bononi		W	AEW Dynamite	:50
Mar 6	Ladder Match: Christian Cage, Keith Lee, Orange Cassidy, Powerhouse Hobbs, Ricky Starks		W	AEW Revolution '22	17:20
Mar 16	Scorpio Sky		L	AEW Dynamite: St. Patrick's Day Slam	9:20
Apr 20	The Butcher		W	AEW Dynamite	4:20
Apr 27	Lance Archer		W	AEW Dynamite	5:29
May 4	W. Morrissey		W	AEW Dynamite	5:32
May 25	Steel Cage Match: Shawn Spears		W	AEW Dynamite: 3 Year Anniversary	6:56
May 29	MJF		W	AEW Double Or Nothing '22	7:30
Jun 1	JD Drake		W	AEW Dynamite	1:11
Jun 15	Handicap Match: Plaintiff #1, Plaintiff #2, Plaintiff #3, Plaintiff #4 Plaintiff #5, Plaintiff #6, Plaintiff #7, Plaintiff #8, Plaintiff #9, Plaintiff #10 Plaintiff #11, Plaintiff #12, Plaintiff #13, Plaintiff #14, Plaintiff #15, Plaintiff #16, Plaintiff #17, Plaintiff #18, Plaintiff #19, Plaintiff #20		W	AEW Dynamite: Road Rager	4:09
Jul 6	Street Fight: Scorpio Sky		W	AEW Dynamite	8:29
Jul 13	Orange Cassidy		W	AEW Dynamite: Fyter Fest	11:36
Aug 6	Jay Lethal		W	AEW Battle Of The Belts III	7:21
Aug 26	Ryan Nemeth		W	AEW Rampage	1:31
Aug 31	Ren Jones, Vic Capri & Silas Young (w/Cash Wheeler & Dax Harwood)		W	AEW Dynamite	2:02
Sep 4	Jay Lethal, Chris Sabin & Alex Shelley (w/Cash Wheeler & Dax Harwood)		W	AEW All Out '22	16:30
Sep 7	Tony Nese		W	AEW Dynamite	1:24
Sep 23	Tony Nese & Josh Woods (w/Samoa Joe)		W	AEW Rampage: Grand Slam	2:26
Oct 5	Brian Cage		W	AEW Dynamite: Anniversary	10:04
Oct 12	QT Marshall & Nick Comoroto (w/Samoa Joe)		W	AEW Dynamite	2:29
Oct 28	Matt Taven		W	AEW Rampage	8:59
Nov 4	Kaun & Toa Liona (w/Samoa Joe)		W	AEW Rampage	9:10
Nov 9	Ari Daivari		W	AEW Dynamite	1:48
Nov 19	Samoa Joe, Powerhouse Hobbs		L	AEW Full Gear '22	9:55
Dec 16	Exodus Prime		W	AEW Rampage	2:06
Dec 28	Samoa Joe		L	AEW Dynamite	12:12

WENDY CHOO

Jan 11	Kacy Katanzaro, Kayden Carter & Amari Miller (w/Indi Hartwell & Persia Pirotta)	W	NXT 2.0	3:40
Feb 1	Amari Miller	W	NXT 2.0	3:26
Feb 8	Tiffany Stratton	L	NXT 2.0	3:07
Mar 1	Indi Hartwell & Persia Pirotta (w/Dakota Kai)	W	NXT 2.0	5:21
Mar 8	Raquel Gonzalez & Cora Jade (w/Dakota Kai)	W	NXT 2.0: Roadblock '22	10:42
Mar 22	Io Shirai & Kay Lee Ray (w/Dakota Kai)	L	NXT 2.0	10:22
May 10	Gigi Dolin & Jacy Jayne (w/Roxanne Perez)	L	NXT 2.0	10:01
Jun 4	Mandy Rose	L	NXT In Your House '22	11:08
Jul 5	Tiffany Stratton	L	NXT 2.0: Great American Bash	5:05
Jul 19	Battle Royal	L	NXT 2.0	13:13
Aug 23	Lights Out Match: Tiffany Stratton	W	NXT 2.0	13:09
Sep 20	Cora Jade	L	NXT	4:14
Oct 4	Lash Legend	W	NXT	3:50
Nov 10	Tamina	W	WWE Main Event	5:25
Nov 22	Cora Jade	L	NXT	9:08
Dec 6	Indi Hartwell, Fallon Henley	L	NXT	10:15
Dec 27	Cora Jade	W	NXT	6:10

WES LEE

Jan 4	Walter, Marcel Barthel & Fabian Aichner (w/Riddle & Nash Carter)	W	NXT 2.0: New Year's Evil '22	13:52
Jan 25	Kushida & Ikemen Jiro (w/Nash Carter)	W	NXT 2.0	11:32
Feb 8	Malik Blade & Edris Enofe (w/Nash Carter)	W	NXT 2.0	9:29
Feb 15	Julius Creed & Brutus Creed (w/Nash Carter)	L	NXT 2.0: Vengeance Day '22	9:36
Mar 8	Marcel Barthel & Fabian Aichner (w/Nash Carter)	D	NXT 2.0: Roadblock '22	5:33
Mar 29	Gunther, Marcel Barthel & Fabian Aichner (w/LA Knight & Nash Carter)	L	NXT 2.0	12:11
Apr 2	Fabian Aichner & Marcel Barthel, Brutus Creed & Julius Creed (w/Nash Carter)	W	NXT Stand & Deliver '22	11:22
Apr 19	Xyon Quin	L	NXT 2.0	3:29
May 17	Nathan Frazer	D	NXT 2.0	4:21
May 24	Sanga	L	NXT 2.0	3:51
May 31	Xyon Quinn	W	NXT 2.0	3:41
Jun 14	Xyon Quin	W	NXT 2.0	2:50
Jul 5	Trick Williams	L	NXT 2.0: Great American Bash	3:46
Jul 26	Grayson Waller	L	NXT 2.0	10:59
Aug 9	Rounds Match: Trick Williams	W	NXT 2.0	10:56
Sep 6	JD McDonagh	L	NXT 2.0	9:37
Sep 27	Tony D'Angelo	W	NXT	8:45
Oct 11	Channing Lorenzo	W	NXT	3:57
Oct 18	Carmelo Hayes & Trick Williams (w/Oro Mensah)	L	NXT	2:43
Oct 22	Ladder Match: Carmelo Hayes, Oro Mensa, Von Wagner, Nathan Frazer	W	NXT Halloween Havoc '22	22:25
Nov 1	Elton Prince & Kit Wilson (w/Bron Breakker)	L	NXT	11:57
Nov 22	Carmelo Hayes	W	NXT	13:01
Dec 13	Channing Lorenzo	W	NXT	9:52
Dec 27	Tony D'Angelo	W	NXT	14:48

WHEELER YUTA

Jan 18	Peter Avalon & JD Drake (w/Orange Cassidy)	W	AEW Dark	7:32
Jan 25	Penta El Zero M	L	AEW Dark	9:43
Feb 2	Jon Moxley	L	AEW Dynamite	7:29
Feb 8	Aaron Solo	W	AEW Dark	7:00
Mar 1	Aaron Solo & Nick Comoroto (w/Orange Cassidy)	W	AEW Dark	14:17
Mar 7	Aaron Solo	W	AEW Dark Elevation	7:07
Mar 9	Pac	L	AEW Dynamite	5:40
Mar 16	Bryan Danielson & Jon Moxley (w/Chuck Taylor)	L	AEW Dynamite: St. Patrick's Day Slam	11:45
Mar 30	Bryan Danielson	L	AEW Dynamite	10:10
Apr 1	Pure Wrestling Rules: Josh Woods	W	ROH Supercard Of Honor XV	12:55
Apr 2	Black Tiger & JR Kratos (w/Rocky Romero)	L	NJPW Strong	9:50
Apr 8	Jon Moxley	L	AEW Rampage	12:40
Apr 15	Billy Gunn, Austin Gunn & Colten Gunn (w/Bryan Danielson & Jon Moxley)	W	AEW Rampage	9:06
Apr 20	Lee Moriarty, Dante Martin & Brock Anderson (w/Bryan Danielson & Jon Moxley)	W	AEW Dynamite	8:08
Apr 27	QT Marshall, Aaron Solo & Nick Comoroto (w/Bryan Danielson & Jon Moxley)	W	AEW Dynamite	8:49
May 4	Angelico, The Butcher & The Blade (w/Bryan Danielson & Jon Moxley)	W	AEW Dynamite	7:27
May 17	Josh Woods	W	AEW Dark	12:30
Jun 8	Casino Battle Royale	L	AEW Dynamite	24:59
Jun 26	Chris Jericho, Minoru Suzuki & Sammy Guevara (w/Eddie Kingston & Shota Umino)	L	AEW x NJPW Forbidden Door	18:58
Jun 28	Tony Nese	W	AEW Dark	10:16
Jun 29	Blood & Guts: Chris Jericho, Daniel Garcia, Jake Hager, Matt Menard, Angelo Parker & Sammy Guevara (w/Jon Moxley, Claudio Castagnoli, Eddie Kingston, Santana & Ortiz)	W	AEW Dynamite: Blood & Guts	46:45
Jul 19	Bryce Donovan	W	AEW Dark	4:24
Jul 20	Chuck Taylor & Trent Beretta (w/Jon Moxley)	W	AEW Dynamite: Fyter Fest	11:53
Jul 23	Pure Wrestling Rules: Daniel Garcia	W	ROH Death Before Dishonor XIX	15:55
Aug 3	Chris Jericho	L	AEW Dynamite	12:33
Aug 31	Dante Martin, Rush, Rey Fenix	W	AEW Dynamite	8:06
Sep 4	Casino Ladder Match: MJF, Claudio Castagnoli, Penta El Zero M, Rey Fenix, Rush, Andrade El Idolo, Dante Martin	L	AEW All Out '22	14:15

Sep 7	Daniel Garcia	L	AEW Dynamite	16:04
Oct 5	MJF	L	AEW Dynamite: Anniversary	15:06
Oct 7	Rush, Marq Quen & Isiah Kassidy (w/Claudio Castagnoli & Jon Moxley)	W	AEW Rampage	10:16
Oct 8	Jay White & Karl Anderson (w/Homicide)	L	NJPW Strong	14:37
Oct 26	Chris Jericho & Daniel Garcia (w/Claudio Castagnoli)	W	AEW Dynamite	11:40
Oct 28	Tom Lawlor, Royce Isaacs & Jorel Nelson (w/Homicide & Shota Umino)	W	NJPW Rumble On 44th Street	12:15
Nov 8	Cezar Bononi & Ryan Nemeth (w/Claudio Castagnoli)	W	AEW Dark	4:40
Nov 21	Zack Clayton	W	AEW Dark Elevation	1:55
Nov 22	KM	W	AEW Dark	3:21
Dec 7	Jake Hager & Daniel Garcia (w/Claudio Castagnoli)	W	AEW Dynamite	12:42
Dec 10	Pure Wrestling Rules: Daniel Garcia	W	ROH Final Battle '22	14:50
Dec 19	Anthony Henry & JD Drake (w/Claudio Castagnoli)	W	AEW Dark Elevation	7:55
Dec 23	$300,000 Three Kings Christmas Casino Trios Royale (w/Claudio Castagnoli & Jon Moxley)	L	AEW Rampage	22:01
Dec 30	Swerve Strickland	L	AEW Rampage	13:58

WILD BOAR

Mar 24	T-Bone	W	NXT UK	4:37
Apr 7	Primate	L	NXT UK	3:37
Apr 28	Primate & T-Bone (w/Mark Andrews)	W	NXT UK	7:26
May 19	Dog Collar Match: Eddie Dennis	W	NXT UK	10:17
Jun 23	Elimination Match: Brooks Jensen & Josh Briggs, Dave Mastiff & Jack Starz, Charlie Dempsey & Rohan Raja (w/Mark Andrews)	L	NXT UK	18:15
Jul 28	Brooks Jensen & Josh Briggs (w/Mark Andrews)	L	NXT UK	9:03

WILL OSPREAY

Jan 4	Tetsuya Naito, Sanada & Bushi (w/Great-O-Khan & Jeff Cobb)	W	NJPW Wrestle Kingdom 16 Night #1	9:27
Jan 5	Kazuchika Okada	L	NJPW Wrestle Kingdom 16 Night #2	32:52
Mar 1	Satoshi Kojima, Yuji Nagata, Kosei Fujita & Yuto Nakashima (w/Great-O-Khan, Jeff Cobb & Aaron Henare)	W	NJPW 50th Anniversary Show	9:20
Apr 9	Tetsuya Naito & Shingo Takagi (w/Aaron Henare)	L	NJPW Hyper Battle '22	9:23
Apr 16	Jon Moxley	L	NJPW Windy City Riot	21:24
May 14	Juice Robinson, Hiroshi Tanahashi, Jon Moxley	L	NJPW Capital Collision	15:45
Jun 10	Trent Beretta, Dax Harwood & Cash Wheeler (w/Kyle Fletcher & Mark Davis)	L	AEW Rampage	13:59
Jun 12	Sanada	W	NJPW Dominion '22	12:48
Jun 15	Dax Harwood	W	AEW Dynamite: Road Rager	13:43
Jun 22	Orange Cassidy, Trent Beretta & Rocky Romero (w/Kyle Fletcher & Mark Davis)	L	AEW Dynamite	11:37
Jun 26	Orange Cassidy	W	AEW x NJPW Forbidden Door	16:43
Jul 2	Homicide	W	NJPW Strong	20:47
Aug 24	Pac, Penta El Zero M & Rey Fenix (w/Kyle Fletcher & Mark Davis)	W	AEW Dynamite	25:18
Aug 31	Kenny Omega, Matt Jackson & Nick Jackson (w/Kyle Fletcher & Mark Davis)	L	AEW Dynamite	18:54
Sep 25	David Finlay	W	NJPW Burning Spirit '22	28:22
Oct 1	Shota Umino	W	NJPW Royal Quest II Night #1	15:30
Oct 2	Cash Wheeler, Dax Harwood, Shota Umino, Ricky Knight Jr. & Gabriel Kidd (w/Great-O-Khan, Mark Davis, Kyle Fletcher & Gideon Grey)	W	NJPW Royal Quest II Night #2	16:57
Oct 10	Tetsuya Naito, Sanada, Bushi & Hiromu Takahashi (w/Aaron Henare, TJP & Francesco Akira)	L	NJPW Declaration Of Power	8:07
Nov 5	Tetsuya Naito	W	NJPW Battle Autumn '22	30:07
Nov 20	Shota Umino	W	NJPW x Stardom Historic X-Over	23:30

WILLIE MACK

Jan 8	Hardcore War: Luke Gallows, Karl Anderson, Eric Young, Deaner & Joe Doering (w/Eddie Edwards, Rich Swann, Heath & Rhino)	W	IMPACT Hard To Kill '22	23:25
Feb 24	Kenny King, Matt Taven & Mike Bennett (w/Chris Sabin & Rich Swann)	L	IMPACT Wrestling	8:58
Mar 10	Kenny King	W	IMPACT Wrestling	8:32
Mar 24	Mike Bailey, Laredo Kid	L	IMPACT Wrestling	10:09
Apr 1	Ultimate X Match: Trey Miguel, Chris Bey, Jordynne Grace, Vincent, Rich Swann	L	IMPACT Multiverse Of Matches	7:27
Apr 21	Heath & Rhino (w/Rich Swann)	L	IMPACT Before The Impact	7:56
Apr 23	Elimination Challenge Match (w/Rich Swann)	L	IMPACT Rebellion '22	33:02
May 5	Chris Bey & Jay White (w/Rich Swann)	L	IMPACT Wrestling	6:28
Jul 2	Jeff Cobb	L	NJPW Strong	13:13
Oct 15	Dragon Lee & Dralistico, Latigo & Toxin, Komander & Myzteziz Jr. (w/Arez)	L	AAA TripleMania XXX: Mexico City	9:00

WILLOW NIGHTINGALE

Jan 24	Brandi Rhodes	L	AEW Dark Elevation	2:27
Feb 28	Leyla Hirsch	L	AEW Dark Elevation	2:16
Apr 1	Mercedes Martinez	L	ROH Supercard Of Honor XV	12:45
Apr 8	Red Velvet	L	AEW Rampage	5:16
Apr 14	Deonna Purrazzo	L	IMPACT Wrestling	9:32
Apr 29	Jade Cargill, Red Velvet & Kiera Hogan (w/Skye Blue & Trish Adora)	L	AEW Rampage	2:46
May 2	Gia Scott	W	AEW Dark Elevation	1:24
Jun 17	Jade Cargill	L	AEW Rampage: Road Rager	4:58
Jun 28	Ashley D'Amboise	W	AEW Dark	3:41
Jul 12	Mila Moore	W	AEW Dark	3:02
Jul 20	Jade Cargill & Kiera Hogan (w/Athena)	L	AEW Dynamite: Fyter Fest	8:25
Aug 1	Emi Sakura, Marina Shafir & Nyla Rose (w/Toni Storm & Hikaru Shida)	W	AEW Dark Elevation	8:05
Aug 2	Harley Cameron	W	AEW Dark	4:15

Aug 16	Robyn Renegade	W	AEW Dark	4:01
Sep 16	Penelope Ford	L	AEW Rampage	7:28
Sep 30	Jamie Hayter	L	AEW Rampage	7:12
Oct 5	Jamie Hayter, Serena Deeb & Penelope Ford (w/Athena & Toni Storm)	W	AEW Dynamite: Anniversary	9:29
Oct 7	Jade Cargill	L	AEW Battle Of The Belts IV	7:30
Oct 18	Seleziya Sparx	W	AEW Dark	5:25
Oct 21	Leila Grey	W	AEW Rampage	7:51
Nov 14	Emi Sakura & Mei Suruga (w/Riho)	W	AEW Dark Elevation	6:14
Nov 21	Emi Sakura & Leva Bates (w/Hikaru Shida)	W	AEW Dark Elevation	4:28
Nov 22	Marina Shafir	W	AEW Dark	5:00
Nov 23	Dr. Britt Baker D.M.D. & Jamie Hayter, Anna Jay & Tay Melo (w/Skye Blue)	L	AEW Dynamite: Thanksgiving Eve	8:05
Nov 30	Anna Jay	W	AEW Dynamite	7:29
Dec 12	Vertvixen	W	AEW Dark Elevation	2:10
Dec 26	Madi Wrenkowski & Vertvixen (w/Ruby Soho)	W	AEW Dark Elevation	4:47
Dec 28	Tay Melo & Anna Jay (w/Ruby Soho)	L	AEW Dynamite	11:58

WOLFGANG

Jan 27	Charlie Dempsey, Rohan Raja & Teoman (w/Mark Coffey & Joe Coffey)	L	NXT UK	11:18
Feb 17	Jordan Devlin	L	NXT UK	13:40
Mar 17	Roderick Strong	L	NXT UK	9:51
Apr 7	Charlie Dempsey	L	NXT UK	7:20
Jun 16	Noam Dar & Sha Samuels (w/Damon Kemp)	W	NXT UK	12:41
Jun 30	Sha Samuels	W	NXT UK	10:18
Jul 28	Ilja Dragunov	L	NXT UK	15:55
Aug 11	Trent Seven	L	NXT UK	9:03
Aug 23	Josh Briggs & Brooks Jensen (w/Mark Coffey)	L	NXT 2.0	8:46
Aug 30	Damon Kemp, Julius Creed & Brutus Creed (w/Joe Coffey & Mark Coffey)	W	NXT 2.0	10:59
Sep 4	Elimination Match: Elton Prince & Kit Wilson, Brutus Creed & Julius Creed, Brooks Jensen & Josh Briggs (w/Mark Coffey)	L	NXT Worlds Collide '22	15:34
Sep 27	Pub Rules Match: Brooks Jensen & Josh Briggs (w/Mark Coffey)	L	NXT	11:35

WRECKING BALL LEGURSKY

Jan 5	Matt Taven	L	NWA Power	6:29
Jan 18	Handicap Match: Dirty Dango & JTG (w/Jay Bradley & Rush Freeman)	W	NWA Power	4:29
Feb 8	Team War Elimination Match: Chris Adonis, Thom Latimer & El Rudo, Matt Taven, Mike Bennett & Victor Benjamin, Bestia 666, Mecha Wolf & Homicide (w/Jay Bradley & Colby Corino)	L	NWA Power	11:09
Mar 1	Matt Taven & Mike Bennett (w/Jay Bradley)	W	NWA Power	10:47
Mar 19	Mike Knox & VSK (w/Jay Bradley)	L	NWA Crockett Cup '22	7:03
Apr 12	Gaagz The Gymp, Judais & Sal The Pal (w/Jay Bradley & Colby Corino)	L	NWA Power	6:27
May 3	No DQ: El Rudo & Jamie Stanley (w/Jay Bradley)	W	NWA Power	8:33
Aug 9	Ricky Morton	L	NWA Power	3:42
Aug 28	Tag Team Battle Royal (w/Jay Bradley)	W	NWA 74th Anniversary Show	14:07
Nov 12	Brady Pierce & Rush Freeman (w/Jay Bradley)	W	NWA Hard Times 3	9:15
Dec 27	Kerry Morton & Ricky Morton (w/Jay Bradley)	L	NWA Power	6:26

XAVIER WOODS

Jan 1	Jimmy Uso & Jey Uso (w/Kofi Kingston)	L	WWE Day 1	18:05
Jan 7	Jimmy Uso & Jey Uso (w/Kofi Kingston)	L	WWE SmackDown	17:45
Mar 25	Ridge Holland	W	WWE SmackDown	:46
Apr 3	Sheamus & Ridge Holland (w/Kofi Kingston)	L	WWE WrestleMania XXXVIII	1:40
Apr 8	Butch	W	WWE SmackDown	8:35
Apr 22	Butch	W	WWE SmackDown	9:00
Apr 29	Ridge Holland	W	WWE SmackDown	8:47
May 6	Tables Match: Sheamus & Ridge Holland (w/Kofi Kingston)	L	WWE SmackDown	12:30
May 20	Butch	W	WWE SmackDown	3:28
May 27	Sheamus, Ridge Holland & Butch (w/Drew McIntyre & Kofi Kingston)	W	WWE SmackDown	11:30
Jun 3	Sheamus, Ridge Holland & Butch (w/Drew McIntyre & Kofi Kingston)	L	WWE SmackDown	10:30
Jun 17	Jinder Mahal & Shanky (w/Kofi Kingston)	W	WWE SmackDown	3:02
Jul 29	Erik & Ivar (w/Kofi Kingston)	L	WWE SmackDown	9:15
Sep 2	Viking Rules Match: Erik & Ivar (w/Kofi Kingston)	L	WWE SmackDown	22:15
Sep 5	Chad Gable & Otis, Angel & Humberto, Angelo Dawkins & Montez Ford (w/Kofi Kingston)	D	WWE Monday Night RAW	14:30
Sep 16	Ridge Holland & Butch, Ludwig Kaiser & Giovanni Vinci, Ashante Adonis & Top Dolla (w/Kofi Kingston)	L	WWE SmackDown	18:44
Sep 23	Mace & Mansoor (w/Kofi Kingston)	W	WWE SmackDown	3:18
Oct 7	Sami Zayn, Jimmy Uso & Jey Uso (w/Braun Strowman & Kofi Kingston)	W	WWE SmackDown	10:30
Oct 28	Mace & Mansoor (w/Kofi Kingston)	W	WWE SmackDown	3:45
Nov 7	Jimmy Uso, Jey Uso & Solo Sikoa (w/Matt Riddle & Kofi Kingston)	L	WWE Monday Night RAW	20:55
Nov 11	Jey Uso & Jimmy Uso (w/Kofi Kingston)	L	WWE SmackDown	23:50
Nov 18	Gunther, Ludwig Kaiser & Giovanni Vinci (w/Kofi Kingston & Braun Strowman)	W	WWE SmackDown	7:38
Dec 9	Gunther, Ludwig Kaiser & Giovanni Vinci (w/Ricochet & Kofi Kingston)	W	WWE SmackDown	18:47
Dec 10	Elton Prince & Kit Wilson (w/Kofi Kingston)	W	NXT Deadline	14:05
Dec 20	Brooks Jensen & Josh Briggs (w/Kofi Kingston)	W	NXT	11:10

XIA BROOKSIDE

Jan 6	Myla Grace	W	NXT UK	3:51
Feb 24	Amale	L	NXT UK	6:14
Mar 31	Amale	W	NXT UK	5:51
Apr 28	Angel Hayze	W	NXT UK	5:05
May 19	Amale & Angel Hayze (w/Eliza Alexander)	W	NXT UK	5:54
Jul 7	Meiko Satomura & Sarray (w/Eliza Alexander)	L	NXT UK	9:27

XIA LI

Feb 25	Natalya	W	WWE SmackDown	4:00
Jun 3	Natalya, Raquel Rodriguez, Shotzi, Aliyah, Shayna Baszler	L	WWE SmackDown	5:54
Jun 10	Lacey Evans	L	WWE SmackDown	2:30
Jun 27	Becky Lynch, Doudrop, Nikki A.S.H., Shayna Baszler, Tamina	L	WWE Monday Night RAW	13:20
Aug 5	Gauntlet Match: Shayna Baszler, Sonya Deville, Raquel Rodriguez, Aliyah, Shotzi, Natalya			
Aug 12	Raquel Rodriguez & Aliyah (w/Shotzi)	L	WWE SmackDown	9:35
Aug 26	Natalya & Sonya Deville, Nikki A.S.H. & Doudrop, Dana Brooke & Tamina (w/Shotzi)	L	WWE SmackDown	3:10
Sep 9	Ronda Rousey, Sonya Deville, Natalya, Lacey Evans	L	WWE SmackDown	4:40
Oct 7	Shotzi & Raquel Rodriguez (w/Sonya Deville)	L	WWE SmackDown	2:16
Nov 11	Six-Pack Challenge: Shotzi, Raquel Rodriguez, Sonya Deville, Liv Morgan, Lacey Evans	L	WWE SmackDown	11:58
Dec 23	Gauntlet Match: Raquel Rodriguez, Emma, Liv Morgan, Sonya Deville, Tegan Nox, Shayna Baszler	L	WWE SmackDown	23:58

XYON QUINN

Jan 11	Santos Escobar	L	NXT 2.0	10:38
Feb 11	Joe Gacy	L	WWE 205 Live	5:39
Feb 25	James Drake	L	NXT Level Up	4:53
Mar 18	Damon Kemp	W	NXT Level Up	5:24
Apr 1	Dante Chen	W	NXT Level Up	4:48
Apr 12	Draco Anthony	W	NXT 2.0	2:58
Apr 19	Wes Lee	W	NXT 2.0	3:29
May 31	Wes Lee	L	NXT 2.0	3:41
Jun 14	Wes Lee	L	NXT 2.0	2:50
Jun 28	Sanga	L	NXT 2.0	5:08
Jul 26	Apollo Crews	L	NXT 2.0	5:40
Aug 5	Quincy Elliott	L	NXT Level Up	4:50
Aug 19	Axiom	L	NXT Level Up	6:10
Sep 2	Dante Chen	W	NXT Level Up	5:53
Sep 27	Ilja Dragunov	L	NXT	4:55
Oct 4	Hank Walker	W	NXT	2:15
Oct 18	Quincy Elliott	W	NXT	2:49
Nov 4	Oro Mensah	L	NXT Level Up	6:08
Nov 10	Akira Tozawa	W	WWE Main Event	8:34
Nov 11	Edris Enofe, Malik Blade & Odyssey Jones (w/Brono Nima & Lucien Price)	L	NXT Level Up	6:41
Nov 25	Tank Ledger	W	NXT Level Up	4:57
Dec 6	Tony D'Angelo	L	NXT	1:55
Dec 16	Andre Chase & Duke Hudson (w/Javier Bernal)	L	NXT Level Up	7:16

YOH

Jan 4	Sho	W	NJPW Wrestle Kingdom 16 Night #1	12:32
Jan 5	Evil, Yujiro Takahashi & Sho (Hirooki Goto & Yoshi-Hashi)	L	NJPW Wrestle Kingdom 16 Night #2	9:37
Mar 1	Evil, Yujiro Takahashi & Sho (w/Tiger Mask & Ryohei Oiwa)	L	NJPW 50th Anniversary Show	6:35
May 1	Hiromu Takahashi	L	NJPW Wrestling Dontaku '22	9:59
Oct 10	Yujiro Takahashi & Sho (w/Rocky Romero)	L	NJPW Rumble On 44th Street	7:42
Nov 20	Dick Togo, Evil, Sho & Yujiro Takahashi (w/Lio Rush, Tomohiro Ishii & Yoshi-Hashi)	W	NJPW x Stardom Historic X-Over	7:05

YOSHI-HASHI

Jan 4	Taichi & Zack Sabre Jr. (w/Hirooki Goto)	W	NJPW Wrestle Kingdom 16 Night #1	15:27
Jan 5	Evil, Yujiro Takahashi & Sho (w/Hirooki Goto & Yoh)	L	NJPW Wrestle Kingdom 16 Night #2	9:37
Jan 8	Daisuke Harada, Hajime Ohara, Daiki Inaba, Yoshiki Inamura & Kinya Okada (w/Tomohiro Ishii, Hirooki Goto, Master Wato & Ryusuke Taguchi)	W	NJPW Wrestle Kingdom 16 Night #3	11:22
Mar 1	Ryusuke Taguchi & Master Wato (w/Hirooki Goto)	W	NJPW 50th Anniversary Show	15:04
Apr 9	Great-O-Khan & Jeff Cobb (w/Hirooki Goto)	L	NJPW Hyper Battle '22	16:05
May 1	Bad Luck Fale & Chase Owens, Great-O-Khan & Jeff Cobb (w/Hirooki Goto)	L	NJPW Wrestling Dontaku '22	9:43
Jun 26	Aaron Solo & QT Marshall (w/Hirooki Goto)	W	AEW x NJPW Forbidden Door Buy-In	8:53
Jul 1	Matt Jackson & Nick Jackson (w/Hirooki Goto)	L	AEW Rampage	9:31
Oct 10	Great-O-Khan & Jeff Cobb (w/Hirooki Goto)	L	NJPW Declaration Of Power	10:09
Nov 20	Dick Togo, Evil, Sho & Yujiro Takahashi (w/Lio Rush, Tomohiro Ishii & Yoh)	W	NJPW x Stardom Historic X-Over	7:05

YOSHINOBU KANEMARU

Jan 8	Naomichi Marufuji & Yoshinari Ogawa (w/Zack Sabre Jr.)	L	NJPW Wrestle Kingdom 16 Night #1	15:20
Mar 1	Cima, T-Hawk & El Lindaman (w/El Desperado & Douki)	L	NJPW 50th Anniversary Show	9:22
May 1	Ryusuke Taguchi & Master Wato (w/Douki)	L	NJPW Wrestling Dontaku '22	9:10
Jun 12	Evil, Sho & Yujiro Takahashi (w/Zack Sabre Jr. & El Desperado)	L	NJPW Dominion '22	9:26
Jun 26	Keith Lee & Swerve Strickland (w/El Desperado)	L	AEW x NJPW Forbidden Door Buy-In	12:08
Oct 10	David Finlay, Robbie Eagles & Ren Narita (w/El Desperado & Douki)	L	NJPW Declaration Of Power	7:28
Nov 20	Momo Watanabe, Starlight Kid, El Desperado & Douki (w/Tam Nakano, Natsupoi & Taichi)	W	NJPW x Stardom Historic X-Over	12:01

YUJIRO TAKAHASHI

Jan 5	Hirooki Goto, Yoshi-Hashi & Yoh (w/Evil & Sho)	W	NJPW Wrestle Kingdom 16 Night #2	9:37
Mar 1	Tiger Mask, Yoh & Ryohei Oiwa (w/Evil & Sho)	W	NJPW 50th Anniversary Show	6:35
Apr 9	Hiroshi Tanahashi, Tama Tonga, Tanga Loa & Jado (w/Bad Luck Fale, Chase Owens & Gedo)	L	NJPW Hyper Battle '22	10:28
May 1	Tanga Loa	L	NJPW Wrestling Dontaku '22	11:33

Jun 12	Zack Sabre Jr., El Desperado & Yoshinobu Kanemaru (w/Evil & Sho)	W	NJPW Dominion '22	9:26
Oct 10	Hiroshi Tanahashi, Hikuleo & Ryusuke Taguchi (w/Evil & Sho)	L	NJPW Declaration Of Power	7:14
Oct 28	Rocky Romero & Yoh (w/Sho)	W	NJPW Rumble On 44th Street	7:42
Nov 5	Hikuleo	L	NJPW Battle Autumn '22	:28
Nov 20	Lio Rush, Tomohiro Ishii, Yoh & Yoshi-Hashi (w/Dick Togo, Evil & Sho)	W	NJPW x Stardom Historic X-Over	7:05

YUKA SAKAZAKI

Mar 3	Miu Watanabe & Rika Tatsumi (w/Mizuki)	W	TJPW Grand Princess '22	17:05
May 6	Riho	L	AEW Rampage	9:18
May 16	Emi Sakura & Nyla Rose (w/Anna Jay)	W	AEW Dark Elevation	3:32
May 23	Emi Sakura & Nyla Rose (w/Skye Blue)	L	AEW Dark Elevation	6:17
May 28	Diamante, Emi Sakura & Nyla Rose (w/Riho & Skye Blue)	W	AEW Dark	6:11
Jun 12	Shoko Nakajima	L	Cyberfight Festival '22	14:57
Jul 4	Heather Reckless & Laynie Luck (w/Hikaru Shida)	W	AEW Dark Elevation	2:53
Jul 9	Saki Akai & Yuki Arai (w/Mizuki)	L	TJPW Summer Sun Princess '22	24:28

YULISA LEON

Jan 18	Dakota Kai	L	NXT 2.0	4:05
Jan 28	Amari Miller & Lash Legend (w/Valentina Feroz)	W	WWE 205 Live	6:29
Mar 1	Raquel Gonzalez & Cora Jade (w/Valentina Feroz)	L	NXT 2.0	4:47
Apr 26	Katana Chance & Kayden Carter (w/Valentina Feroz)	L	NXT 2.0	6:01
May 20	Ivy Nile	L	NXT Level Up	5:16
Jun 21	Katana Chance & Kayden Carter (w/Valentina Feroz)	L	NXT 2.0	5:15
Jul 8	Arianna Grace	W	NXT Level Up	6:21
Jul 19	Battle Royal	L	NXT 2.0	13:13
Aug 2	Elimination Match: Kayden Carter & Katana Chance, Ivy Nile & Tatum Paxley, Gigi Dolin & Jacy Jayne (w/Valentina Feroz)	L	NXT 2.0	12:09

YUYA UEMURA

Feb 5	Brody King	L	NJPW Strong	12:56
Mar 26	Daniel Garcia	L	NJPW Strong	10:39
Apr 1	David Finlay, Juice Robinson, Daniel Garcia & Kevin Knight (w/Karl Fredericks, Mascara Dorada & Clark Connors)	W	NJPW Lonestar Shootout	10:45
Apr 16	QT Marshall, Aaron Solo & Nick Comoroto (w/Karl Fredericks & Clark Connors)	L	NJPW Windy City Riot	11:56
Apr 23	Buddy Matthews	L	NJPW Strong	9:50
May 3	Angelico	L	AEW Dark	8:55
May 14	Tom Lawlor, Jorel Nelson, Royce Isaacs, JR Kratos & Danny Limelight (w/The DKC, David Finlay, Tanga Loa & Fred Rosser)	L	NJPW Capital Collision	14:48
May 17	Aaron Solo, Blake Li, Brick Aldridge, Nick Comoroto & QT Marshall (w/Alex Coughlin, Clark Connors, Karl Fredericks & Kevin Knight)	W	AEW Dark	10:30
Jun 4	Kevin Blackwood & Lucas Riley (w/Keita Murray)	W	NJPW Strong	8:33
Jun 11	Killer Kross	L	NJPW Strong	7:50
Jun 26	Max Caster, Billy Gunn, Austin Gunn & Colten Gunn (w/The DKC, Kevin Knight & Alex Coughlin)	L	AEW x NJPW Forbidden Door Buy-In	5:35
Jul 9	Aaron Solo & Nick Comoroto (w/Christopher Daniels)	W	NJPW Strong	9:17
Jul 23	Mikey Nicholls & Shane Haste (w/Christopher Daniels)	W	NJPW Strong	10:02
Jul 30	Kevin Knight, Ren Narita & The DKC (w/Fred Yehi & Shota Umino)	W	NJPW Music City Mayhem	13:12
Aug 13	Kyle Fletcher & Mark Davis (w/Christopher Daniels)	L	NJPW Strong	11:57
Sep 8	Kenny King	W	IMPACT Wrestling	9:02
Sep 15	Raj Singh	W	IMPACT Before The Impact	8:59
Sep 24	Bad Dude Tito & Shane Haste (w/Christopher Daniels)	I	NJPW Strong	9:10
Sep 29	Jason Hotch	W	IMPACT Before The Impact	8:30
Oct 13	Trey Miguel, Alex Zayne, Black Taurus, Kenny King, Laredo Kid	L	IMPACT Wrestling	5:19
Oct 22	Christopher Daniels	W	NJPW Strong	9:48
Nov 3	PJ Black	L	IMPACT Before The Impact	8:33
Nov 17	Andrew Everett	W	IMPACT Before The Impact	8:00
Nov 24	Raj Singh & Shera (w/Delirious)	L	IMPACT Before The Impact	9:22
Dec 22	Mike Bailey	L	IMPACT Wrestling	11:16
Dec 29	John Skyler & Jason Hotch (w/Delirious)	W	IMPACT Before The Impact	9:08

ZACK CLAYTON

Jan 10	QT Marshall	L	AEW Dark Elevation	2:53
Feb 1	Tony Nese	L	AEW Dark	5:17
Feb 14	Serpentico	W	AEW Dark Elevation	3:46
May 2	Max Caster	L	AEW Dark Elevation	1:24
May 16	Anthony Bowens, Max Caster, Austin Gunn & Colten Gunn (w/Bryce Donovan, GKM & Lucas Chase)	L	AEW Dark Elevation	1:22
Aug 9	Ari Daivari, Parker Boudreaux & Slim J (w/Sonny Kiss & Xavier Walker)	L	AEW Dark	3:10
Aug 19	Hook	L	AEW Rampage	:30
Sep 6	Serpentico	W	AEW Dark	4:37
Sep 12	Dante Martin & Matt Sydal (w/Serpentico)	L	AEW Dark Elevation	:57
Sep 19	Conan Lycan	W	AEW Dark Elevation	3:34
Sep 20	Vary Morales	W	AEW Dark	3:04
Oct 25	Shane Saber	W	AEW Dark	3:57
Nov 8	Blake Li	W	AEW Dark	1:41
Nov 15	Frankie Kazarian	L	AEW Dark	3:39
Nov 21	Wheeler Yuta	L	AEW Dark Elevation	1:55
Nov 29	Chris Wylde	W	AEW Dark	2:40
Dec 12	Chuck Taylor & Trent Beretta (w/Zane Valero)	L	AEW Dark Elevation	3:00
Dec 13	Steve Pena	W	AEW Dark	2:15

ZACK SABRE JR.

Jan 4	Hirooki Goto & Yoshi-Hashi (w/Taichi)	L	NJPW Wrestle Kingdom 16 Night #1	15:27
Jan 8	Naomichi Marufuji & Yoshinari Ogawa (w/Yoshinobu Kanemaru)	L	NJPW Wrestle Kingdom 16 Night #3	15:20
Mar 1	Kazuchika Okada, Hiroshi Tanahashi & Tatsumi Fujinami (w/Minoru Suzuki & Yoshiaki Fujiwara)	L	NJPW 50th Anniversary Show	18:12
Apr 9	Kazuchika Okada	L	NJPW Hyper Battle '22	28:25
May 1	Shingo Takagi, Bushi & Shiro Koshinaka (w/Taichi & Taka Michinoku)	W	NJPW Wrestling Dontaku '22	10:15
Jun 12	Evil, Sho & Yujiro Takahashi (w/El Desperado & Yoshinobu Kanemaru)	L	NJPW Dominion '22	9:26
Jun 26	Claudio Castagnoli	L	AEW x NJPW Forbidden Door	18:26
Sep 25	Sanada & Tetsuya Naito (w/Taichi)	W	NJPW Burning Spirit '22	9:32
Oct 1	Tetsuya Naito, Sanada & Hiromu Takahashi (w/El Desperado & Douki)	L	NJPW Royal Quest II Night #1	14:29
Oct 2	Tetsuya Naito	L	NJPW Royal Quest II Night #2	21:05
Oct 10	Shane Haste & Bad Dude Tito (w/Taichi)	W	NJPW Declaration Of Power	9:58
Nov 5	Evil	W	NJPW Battle Autumn '22	4:48
Nov 20	Syuri & Tom Lawlor (w/Giulia)	W	NJPW x Stardom Historic X-Over	10:20

ZICKY DICE

Jan 13	Moose	L	IMPACT Wrestling	:16
Jan 20	Handicap Match: W. Morrissey (w/VSK)	L	IMPACT Wrestling	1:08
Jan 27	Handicap Match: W. Morrissey (w/VSK, D-Ray 3000, David Young, Elix Skipper, Mikey Batts, Iex Lovett, Jerelle Clark & Shark Boy)	L	IMPACT Wrestling	3:00
Feb 24	Jonah	L	IMPACT Wrestling	1:00
Mar 17	Jonah	L	IMPACT Wrestling	:30
Mar 31	Luke Gallows & Karl Anderson (w/Johnny Swinger)	L	IMPACT Wrestling	:50
Apr 23	Elimination Challenge Match (w/Johnny Swinger)	L	IMPACT Rebellion '22	33:02
May 19	Crazzy Steve	L	IMPACT Before The Impact	9:13
Jun 9	Crazzy Steve & Black Taurus (w/Johnny Swinger)	L	IMPACT Before The Impact	8:18
Jun 23	Bhupinder Gujjar & Shark Boy (w/Johnny Swinger)	L	IMPACT Wrestling	3:50
Jul 28	Laredo Kid & Trey Miguel (w/Johnny Swinger)	L	IMPACT Wrestling	4:01
Aug 25	Ace Austin & Hikuleo (w/Johnny Swinger)	L	IMPACT Before The Impact	7:46
Sep 22	Jordynne Grace	L	IMPACT Wrestling	:43
Nov 10	Bully Ray	L	IMPACT Wrestling	1:10
Dec 15	Bhupinder Gujjar & Joe Hendry (w/Johnny Swinger)	L	IMPACT Wrestling	3:17

ZOEY STARK

Jul 19	Battle Royal	W	NXT 2.0	13:13
Jul 26	Gigi Dolin	W	NXT 2.0	2:48
Aug 9	Cora Jade	W	NXT 2.0	11:05
Aug 16	Mandy Rose	L	NXT 2.0: Heatwave	11:26
Aug 30	Kiana James	W	NXT 2.0	4:23
Sep 13	Kiana James & Arianna Grace (w/Nikkita Lyons)	W	NXT 2.0	9:04
Oct 4	Gigi Dolin & Jacy Jayne (w/Nikkita Lyons)	W	NXT	10:28
Oct 25	Katana Chance & Kayden Carter (w/Nikkita Lyons)	L	NXT	12:52
Nov 1	Indi Hartwell	L	NXT	6:30
Nov 8	Katana Chance & Kayden Carter (w/Nikkita Lyons)	L	NXT	11:02
Nov 22	Sol Ruca	W	NXT	4:17
Dec 1	Dana Brooke	W	WWE Main Event	5:42
Dec 10	Iron Survivor Challenge: Roxanne Perez, Cora Jade, Indi Hartwell, Kiana James	L	NXT Deadline	25:00
Dec 20	Nikkita Lyons	W	NXT	5:23

WRESTLER CAREER HISTORIES

Within this section is a loose overview of the careers of notable wrestlers in major promotions who were active throughout 2022. The data included for each wrestler shows their primary ring name in 2022, their billed height and weight, their birth city, the year they made their wrestling debut and their age as of December 31, 2022. Besides each year of their career is the acronym of the major promotions they worked for that year (see Promotion Acronym Key) and the approximate number of matches they wrestled for that promotion, based on available records. This is not a definitive number of matches they wrestled for the promotion, due to the inaccuracies in historical record keeping. Only promotions that could reasonably be considered a wrestler's "home" promotion in a given year have been included. Generally this means they were contracted to that promotion or were a regular guest. Due to the sheer amount of independent groups and the unreliable records of their results and matches, these have been grouped together as Indies, without match data.

PROMOTIONS ACRONYM KEY

AAA
Lucha Libre AAA Worldwide
AEW
All Elite Wrestling
AJPW
All Japan Pro Wrestling
AJW
All Japan Women's Pro-Wrestling
AWA
American Wrestling Association
CMLL
Consejo Mundial de Lucha Libre
CSW
Central States Wrestling
CWA
Continental Wrestling Association
CWA (Europe)
Catch Wrestling Association
CWF
Championship Wrestling from Florida
DDT
Dramatic Dream Team
DGUSA
Dragon Gate USA
Diana
World Woman Pro-Wrestling Diana
Dragon Gate
Dragongate Japan Pro-Wrestling
DSW
Deep South Wrestling
ECW
Extreme Championship Wrestling
EVOLVE
Evolve Wrestling
FCW
Florida Championship Wrestling
FMW
Frontier Martial-Arts Wrestling
GAEA Japan
Gaea Japan
Gatoh Move
Gatoh Move Pro Wrestling
GCW
Georgia Championship Wrestling
GFW
Global Force Wrestling
HUSTLE
Hustle
HWA
Heartland Wrestling Association
Ice Ribbon
Ice Ribbon Joshi Pro Wrestling
Impact
Impact Wrestling
IWA Japan
International Wrestling Association of Japan
IWE
International Wrestling Enterprise
JCP
Jim Crockett Promotions
LU
Lucha Underground
MACW
Mid-Atlantic Championship Wrestling
Mid-South
Mid-South Wrestling
MLW
Major League Wrestling
MLW (1980s)
Maple Leaf Wrestling
NEO
NEO Japan Ladies Pro-Wrestling
NJPW
New Japan Pro Wrestling

NOAH
Pro Wrestling NOAH
NWA
National Wrestling Alliance
NWE
New Wrestling Entertainment
OVW
Ohio Valley Wrestling
PNW
Pacific Northwest Wrestling
RKK
Ring Ka King
ROH
Ring Of Honor
SEAdLINNNG
Seadlinng
SECW
Southeastern Championship Wrestling
Sendai Girls
Sendai Girls' Pro Wrestling
SLWC
St. Louis Wrestling Club
SMW
Smoky Mountain Wrestling
Stampede
Stampede Wrestling
Stardom
World Wonder Ring Stardom
USWA
United States Wrestling Association
UWF
Universal Wrestling Federation
WAR
Wrestle Association R
WAVE
Pro Wrestling Wave
WCCW
World Class Championship Wrestling
WCW
World Championship Wrestling
World Japan
Fighting of World Japan Pro-Wrestling
WWA
World Wrestling All-Stars
WWC
World Wrestling Council
WWE
World Wrestling Entertainment
WWF
World Wrestling Federation

AARON HENARE
5'11, 231 lbs, Auckland, New Zealand, 2010, 30
2010	Indies	
2011	Indies	
2012	Indies	
2013	Indies	
2014	Indies	
2015	Indies	
2016	NJPW	37
2017	NJPW	41
2018	NJPW	142
2019	NJPW	144
2020	NJPW	33
2021	NJPW	55
2022	NJPW	97

AARON SOLO
6'1, 205 lbs, San Francisco, California, 2009, 35
2009	Indies	
2010	Indies	
2011	Indies	
2012	Indies	
2013	ROH	2
2014	ROH	2
	TNA	1
	WWE	1
2015	WWE	2
	ROH	1
2016	Indies	
2017	WWE	2
2018	WWE	2
	ROH	1
2019	NJPW	6
2020	AEW	14
2021	AEW	39
2022	AEW	43
	NJPW	7

ABADON
5'0, 178 lbs, Denver, Colorado, 2020, 30
2020	AEW	7
2021	AEW	23
2022	AEW	12

ACE AUSTIN
5'9, 174 lbs, Atlantic City, New Jersey, 2015, 25
2015	Indies	
2016	Indies	
2017	Indies	
2018	Impact	6
2019	Impact	34
2020	Impact	28
2021	Impact	38
2022	NJPW	30
	Impact	28

ACTION ANDRETTI
6'0, 185 lbs, Philadelphia, Pennsylvania, 2019, 24
2019	Indies	
2020	Indies	
2021	Indies	
2022	AEW	6

ADAM COLE
5'11, 210 lbs, Lancaster, Pennsylvania, 2008, 33
2008	Indies	
2009	ROH	4
2010	ROH	16
2011	ROH	25
2012	ROH	33
2013	ROH	31
2014	ROH	38
2015	ROH	37
2016	ROH	35
	NJPW	8
2017	WWE	31

	ROH	18
	NJPW	7
2018	WWE	92
2019	WWE	71
2020	WWE	27
2021	AEW	15
	WWE	9
2022	AEW	19

ADRIAN QUEST
5'8, 145 lbs, Colton, California, 2009, 27
2009	Indies	
2010	Indies	
2011	Indies	
2012	Indies	
2013	Indies	
2014	Indies	
2015	Indies	
2016	Indies	
2017	Indies	
2018	Indies	
2019	Impact	2
2020	NJPW	8
2021	NJPW	13
2022	NJPW	7

AJ STYLES
5'10, 218lbs, Camp Legeune, North Carolina, 1998, 45
1999	Indies	
2000	Indies	
2001	WCW	4
2002	TNA	28
	ROH	8
2003	TNA	44
	ROH	18
2004	TNA	59
	ROH	6
2005	TNA	37
	ROH	11
2006	TNA	56
	ROH	9
2007	TNA	57
2008	TNA	97
2009	TNA	89
2010	TNA	122
2011	TNA	78
2012	TNA	98
2013	TNA	45
2014	NJPW	31
	ROH	13
2015	NJPW	47
	ROH	16
2016	WWE	171
2017	WWE	183
2018	WWE	166
2019	WWE	129
2020	WWE	40
2021	WWE	71
2022	WWE	70

AKIRA TOZAWA
5'7, 156lbs, Kobe, Japan, 2005, 37
2005	Dragon Gate	66
2006	Dragon Gate	142
2007	Dragon Gate	104
2008	Dragon Gate	133
2009	Dragon Gate	150
2010	Dragon Gate	61
2011	Dragon Gate	95
2012	Dragon Gate	157
	DGUSA	9
2013	Dragon Gate	170
	DGUSA	9
2014	Dragon Gate	176
2015	Dragon Gate	190
2016	Dragon Gate	147
	WWE	10
2017	WWE	82
2018	WWE	45

2019	WWE	36
2020	WWE	40
2021	WWE	31
2022	WWE	35

ALAN ANGELS
5'8, 170 lbs, Snelville, Georgia, 2016, 24

2016	Indies	
2017	Indies	
2018	Indies	
2019	Indies	
2020	AEW	22
2021	AEW	43
2022	AEW	20
	NJPW	4
	Impact	3

ALBA FYRE
5'8, 112 lbs, Paisley, Scotland, 2009, 30

2009	Indies	
2010	Indies	
2011	Indies	
2012	Indies	
2013	Indies	
2014	Indies	
2015	Indies	
2016	Stardom	15
2017	Stardom	14
2018	Indies	
2019	WWE	16
2020	WWE	11
2021	WWE	11
2022	WWE	26

ALEAH JAMES
5'1, 100 lbs, Romford, England, 2019, 24

2019	Indies	
2020	WWE	2
2021	WWE	6
2022	WWE	1

ALEX COUGHLIN
6'0, 209 lbs, New York, 2018, 29

2018	NJPW	2
2019	NJPW	30
	ROH	8
2020	NJPW	9
2021	NJPW	21
2022	NJPW	18

ALEX REYNOLDS
5'10, 185 lbs, Southampton, New York, 2007, 34

2007	Indies	
2008	Indies	
2009	Indies	
2010	Indies	
2011	Indies	
2012	Indies	
2013	Indies	
2014	Indies	
2015	Indies	
2016	Indies	
2017	Indies	
2018	Indies	
2019	AEW	4
2020	AEW	21
2021	AEW	41
2022	AEW	46

ALEX SHELLEY
5'10, 205 lbs, Detroit, Michigan, 2002, 39

2002	Indies	
2003	ROH	4
2004	TNA	29
	ROH	21
2005	TNA	21

	ROH	20
2006	TNA	44
	ROH	11
2007	TNA	41
2008	TNA	79
2009	TNA	56
2010	TNA	72
2011	TNA	30
2012	TNA	26
	NJPW	24
2013	NJPW	54
2014	NJPW	50
2015	NJPW	39
2016	ROH	38
	NJPW	5
2017	ROH	26
	NJPW	5
2018	ROH	9
2019	ROH	5
2020	Impact	9
2021	Indies	
2022	Impact	27

ALEX ZAYNE
6'1, 202 lbs, Lexington, Kentucky, 2007, 36

2007	Indies	
2008	Indies	
2009	Indies	
2010	Indies	
2011	Indies	
2012	Indies	
2013	Indies	
2014	Indies	
2015	Indies	
2016	Indies	
2017	Indies	
2018	Indies	
2019	NJPW	1
	Impact	1
2020	NJPW	12
2021	WWE	10
	NJPW	5
2022	NJPW	45
	Impact	8

ALEXA BLISS
5'1, 102lbs, Columbus, Ohio, 2013, 31

2013	WWE	2
2014	WWE	36
2015	WWE	55
2016	WWE	124
2017	WWE	148
2018	WWE	115
2019	WWE	65
2020	WWE	26
2021	WWE	19
2022	WWE	48

ALISHA EDWARDS
5'0, 119 lbs, San Diego, Florida, 2004, 36

2004	Indies	
2005	Indies	
2006	Indies	
2007	Indies	
2008	Indies	
2009	Indies	
2010	Indies	
2011	Indies	
2012	Indies	
2013	Indies	
2014	Indies	
2015	Indies	
2016	Indies	
2017	Impact	6
2018	Impact	11
2019	Impact	9
2020	Impact	13
2021	Impact	11
2022	Impact	14

ALIYAH
5'3, 112lbs, Toronto, Canada, 2013, 28

2015	WWE	13
2016	WWE	76
2017	WWE	60
2018	WWE	72
2019	WWE	61
2020	WWE	20
2021	WWE	21
2022	WWE	48

AMALE
5'4, 135 lbs, Beziers, Occitanie, France, 2012, 29

2012	Indies	
2013	Indies	
2014	Indies	
2015	Indies	
2016	Indies	
2017	Indies	
2018	Indies	
2019	WWE	1
2020	WWE	6
2021	WWE	8
2022	WWE	9

AMARI MILLER
5'8, Kansas City, Missouri, 2017, 26

2017	Indies	
2018	Indies	
2019	WWE	1
2020	Indies	
2021	WWE	15
2022	WWE	18

ANDRADE EL IDOLO
5'11, 209 lbs, Gomez Palacio, Durango, Mexico, 2007, 33

2007	CMLL	66
2008	CMLL	88
2009	CMLL	109
2010	CMLL	130
	NJPW	16
2011	CMLL	123
	NJPW	12
2012	CMLL	106
	NJPW	7
2013	CMLL	115
	NJPW	25
2014	CMLL	113
	NJPW	17
2015	CMLL	91
	NJPW	6
2016	WWE	107
2017	WWE	104
2018	WWE	112
2019	WWE	121
2020	WWE	44
2021	AEW	13
2022	AEW	14

ANDRE CHASE
6'2, 216 lbs, Draper, North Carolina, 2007, 33

2007	Indies	
2008	Indies	
2009	ROH	8
2010	ROH	24
2011	ROH	23
2012	NOAH	25
	ROH	11
2013	NOAH	31
2014	Indies	
2015	Indies	
2016	Indies	
2017	Indies	
2018	Indies	
2019	EVOLVE	19
2020	Indies	
2021	WWE	19
2022	WWE	38

ANDREW EVERETT
5'9, 169 lbs, Burlington, North Carolina, 2007, 30

2007	Indies	
2008	Indies	
2009	Indies	
2010	Indies	
2011	Indies	
2012	Indies	
2013	Indies	
2014	ROH	7
2015	TNA	4
2016	TNA	21
2017	Impact	23
2018	Impact	9
2019	Indies	
2020	ROH	3
2021	Indies	
2022	Impact	4

ANGEL
6'0, 205lbs, Nuevo Leon, Mexico, 2008, 30

2009	Indies	
2010	Indies	
2011	Indies	
2012	Indies	
2013	Indies	
2014	Indies	
2015	Indies	
2016	AAA	14
2017	Impact	19
2018	Indies	
2019	WWE	45
2020	WWE	58
2021	WWE	47
2022	WWE	40

ANGEL HAYZE
5'1, 119 lbs, Glasgow, Scotland, 2016, 21

2016	Indies	
2017	Indies	
2018	Indies	
2019	Indies	
2020	Indies	
2021	WWE	2
2022	WWE	6

ANGELICO
6'3, 213 lbs, Johannesburg, South Africa, 2008, 35

2008	Indies	
2009	Indies	
2010	Indies	
2011	Indies	
2012	Indies	
2013	AAA	23
2014	AAA	25
2015	AAA	26
	LU	19
2016	Indies	
2017	AAA	10
2018	Indies	
2019	AEW	9
2020	AEW	22
2021	AEW	37
2022	AEW	21

ANGELO DAWKINS
6'5, 260lbs, Cincinnati, Ohio, 2012, 32

2013	WWE	16
2014	WWE	30
2015	WWE	53
2016	WWE	82
2017	WWE	86
2018	WWE	78
2019	WWE	86
2020	WWE	42
2021	WWE	59
2022	WWE	88

ANGELO PARKER
5'11, 194 lbs, Montreal, Quebec, Canada, 2002, 38

Year	Promotion	
2002	Indies	
2003	Indies	
2004	Indies	
2005	Indies	
2006	ROH	1
2007	Indies	
2008	Indies	
2009	Indies	
2010	Indies	
2011	Indies	
2012	ROH	1
2013	ROH	1
2014	Indies	
2015	Indies	
2016	WWE	1
2017	Indies	
2018	WWE	1
2019	WWE	46
2020	WWE	29
2021	AEW	19
	WWE	8
2022	AEW	25

ANNA JAY
5'8, 143 lbs, Brunswick, Georgia, 2019, 24

Year	Promotion	
2019	Indies	
2020	AEW	13
2021	AEW	19
2022	AEW	36

ANTHONY BOWENS
5'10, 205 lbs, Nutley, New Jersey, 2013, 32

Year	Promotion	
2013	Indies	
2014	Indies	
2015	Indies	
2016	WWE	1
2017	Impact	1
2018	Impact	2
2019	Impact	1
2020	AEW	12
2021	AEW	47
2022	AEW	28

ANTHONY HENRY
5'10, 180 lbs, Augusta, Georgia, 2003, 39

Year	Promotion	
2003	Indies	
2004	Indies	
2008	Indies	
2009	Indies	
2010	Indies	
2011	Indies	
2012	Indies	
2013	Indies	
2014	Indies	
2015	Indies	
2016	Indies	
2017	EVOLVE	10
2018	EVOLVE	18
2019	EVOLVE	21
2020	Indies	
2021	WWE	11
2022	AEW	23

ANTHONY OGOGO
6'0, 220 lbs, Lowestoft, Suffolk, England, 2019, 34

Year	Promotion	
2019	Indies	
2021	AEW	8
2022	AEW	14

APOLLO CREWS
6'0, 250lbs, Stone Mountain, Georgia, 2009, 35

Year	Promotion	
2010	Indies	
2011	Dragon Gate	15
2012	Indies	
2013	Dragon Gate	105
2014	Dragon Gate	73
2015	WWE	65
	Dragon Gate	13
2016	WWE	154
2017	WWE	129
2018	WWE	127
2019	WWE	70
2020	WWE	32
2021	WWE	48
2022	WWE	38

AR FOX
6'0, 185 lbs, Ansonia, Connecticut, 2009, 35

Year	Promotion	
2009	Indies	
2010	Indies	
2011	DGUSA	14
	Dragon Gate	11
2012	Dragon Gate	12
	EVOLVE	11
2013	DGUSA	10
2014	Indies	
2015	ROH	1
2016	Indies	
2017	Indies	
2018	EVOLVE	21
2019	EVOLVE	24
2020	Indies	
2021	Indies	
2022	AEW	11

ARI DAIVARI
5'10, 191 lbs, Plymouth, Minnesota, 2006, 33

Year	Promotion	
2006	Indies	
2007	Indies	
2008	Indies	
2009	Indies	
2010	Indies	
2011	Indies	
2012	Indies	
2013	WWE	1
2014	Indies	
2015	ROH	2
2016	WWE	15
2017	WWE	64
2018	WWE	27
2019	WWE	27
2020	WWE	23
2021	WWE	19
2022	AEW	29

ARIANNA GRACE
5'7, 138 lbs, Toronto, Ontario, Canada, 2020, 27

Year	Promotion	
2020	Indies	
2021	NWA	1
2022	WWE	20

ASHANTE ADONIS
5'10, 209 lbs, Hammonton, New Jersey, 2018, 32

Year	Promotion	
2018	ROH	1
2019	WWE	14
2020	WWE	31
2021	WWE	13
2022	WWE	24

ASHTON SMITH
6'2, 205 lbs, Kingston, Jamaica, 2007, 34

Year	Promotion	
2007	Indies	
2008	Indies	
2009	Indies	
2010	Indies	
2011	Indies	
2012	Indies	
2013	Indies	
2014	Indies	
2015	ROH	4
2016	Indies	
2017	Indies	
2018	WWE	8
2019	WWE	10
2020	WWE	6
2021	WWE	10
2022	WWE	6

ASUKA
5'3, 137lbs, Osaka, Japan, 2004, 41

Year	Promotion	
2004	Indies	
2005	Indies	
2006	Indies	
2007	Indies	
2008	WAVE	30
	NEO	26
2009	NEO	30
	WAVE	22
2010	WAVE	29
	NEO	11
2011	WAVE	34
2012	WAVE	39
2013	WAVE	48
2014	WAVE	48
2015	WAVE	31
	WWE	23
2016	WWE	117
2017	WWE	93
2018	WWE	158
2019	WWE	120
2020	WWE	65
2021	WWE	27
2022	WWE	63

ATHENA
5'2, 121 lbs, Dallas, Texas, 2007, 34

Year	Promotion	
2007	Indies	
2008	Indies	
2009	Indies	
2010	Indies	
2011	Indies	
2012	Indies	
2013	ROH	6
2014	Indies	
2015	WWE	9
2016	WWE	76
2017	WWE	83
2018	WWE	123
2019	WWE	52
2020	WWE	7
2021	WWE	19
2022	AEW	30

AUSTIN GUNN
5'11, 216 lbs, Orlando, Florida, 2017, 28

Year	Promotion	
2017	Indies	
2018	Indies	
2019	ROH	5
2020	AEW	18
2021	AEW	25
2022	AEW	32

AUSTIN THEORY
6'1, 220lbs, McDonough, Georgia, 2016, 25

Year	Promotion	
2016	Indies	
2017	EVOLVE	20
2018	EVOLVE	22
2019	EVOLVE	22
	WWE	22
2020	WWE	38
2021	WWE	35
2022	WWE	120

AXIOM
5'8, 154 lbs, Madrid, Spain, 2012, 25

Year	Promotion	
2012	Indies	
2013	Indies	
2014	Indies	
2015	Indies	
2016	Indies	
2017	Indies	
2018	Indies	
2019	WWE	6
2020	WWE	10
2021	WWE	10
2022	WWE	28

BAD DUDE TITO
6'1, 255 lbs, Bocas Del Toro, Panama, 2011, ?

Year	Promotion	
2011	Indies	
2012	Indies	
2013	Indies	
2014	Indies	
2015	Indies	
2016	Indies	
2017	Indies	
2018	Indies	
2019	Indies	
2020	Indies	
2021	Indies	
2022	NJPW	42

BAD LUCK FALE
6'4, 308 lbs, Tonga, 2010, 40

Year	Promotion	
2010	NJPW	89
2011	NJPW	94
2012	NJPW	11
2013	NJPW	49
2014	NJPW	98
2015	NJPW	107
2016	NJPW	110
2017	NJPW	97
2018	NJPW	74
2019	NJPW	98
2020	NJPW	23
2021	NJPW	33
2022	NJPW	82

BANDIDO
5'7, 183 lbs, Torreon, Coahuila, Mexico, 2013, 27

Year	Promotion	
2013	Indies	
2014	Indies	
2015	Indies	
2016	Indies	
2017	Indies	
2018	Dragon Gate	72
2019	ROH	29
	NJPW	17
	CMLL	6
2020	CMLL	9
	ROH	5
2021	ROH	23
	CMLL	5
2022	AAA	16

BARON CORBIN
6'8, 285lbs, Lenexa, Kansas, 2012, 38

Year	Promotion	
2012	WWE	3
2013	WWE	29
2014	WWE	60
2015	WWE	113
2016	WWE	165
2017	WWE	173
2018	WWE	159
2019	WWE	153
2020	WWE	50
2021	WWE	58
2022	WWE	48

BATEMAN
6'3, 200 lbs, Moore, Oklahoma, 2002, 42

Year	Promotion	
2002	Indies	
2003	Indies	
2004	Indies	
2005	Indies	
2006	Indies	

Year	Promotion	#
2007	Indies	
2008	Indies	
2009	Indies	
2010	Indies	
2011	Indies	
2012	Indies	
2013	Indies	
2014	Indies	
2015	Indies	
2016	Indies	
2017	Indies	
2018	Indies	
2019	Indies	
2020	ROH	7
2021	NJPW	16
	ROH	7
2022	NJPW	7

BAYLEY
5'7, 119 lbs, Newark, California, 2008, 33

Year	Promotion	#
2008	Indies	
2009	Indies	
2010	Indies	
2011	Indies	
2012	Indies	
2013	WWE	43
2014	WWE	78
2015	WWE	119
2016	WWE	139
2017	WWE	135
2018	WWE	134
2019	WWE	137
2020	WWE	52
2021	WWE	12
2022	WWE	37

BECKY LYNCH
5'6, 135lbs, Limerick, Ireland, 2002, 35

Year	Promotion	#
2004	Indies	
2005	Indies	
2006	Indies	
2008	Indies	
2012	Indies	
2013	WWE	3
2014	WWE	45
2015	WWE	132
2016	WWE	161
2017	WWE	143
2018	WWE	149
2019	WWE	127
2020	WWE	18
2021	WWE	36
2022	WWE	65

BHUPINDER GUJJAR
??, ???lbs, Punjab, India, 2019, 28

Year	Promotion	#
2019	Impact	4
2020	Indies	
2021	Indies	
2022	Impact	22

BIANCA BELAIR
5'7, 115lbs, Knoxville, Tennessee, 2016, 33

Year	Promotion	#
2016	WWE	7
2017	WWE	47
2018	WWE	58
2019	WWE	71
2020	WWE	42
2021	WWE	78
2022	WWE	105

BIG BILL
6'10, 282 lbs, New York City, New York, 2009, 35

Year	Promotion	#
2009	Indies	
2010	Indies	
2011	Indies	
2012	WWE	7

Year	Promotion	#
2013	WWE	44
2014	WWE	73
2015	WWE	93
2016	WWE	149
2017	WWE	86
2018	WWE	24
2019	Indies	
2021	Impact	21
2022	Impact	11
	AEW	2

BIG DAMO
6'3, 310 lbs, Belfast, Northern Ireland, 2005, 37

Year	Promotion	#
2005	Indies	
2006	Indies	
2007	Indies	
2008	Indies	
2009	Indies	
2010	Indies	
2011	Indies	
2012	Indies	
2013	Indies	
2014	Indies	
2015	Indies	
2016	WWE	10
2017	WWE	96
2018	WWE	59
2019	WWE	45
2020	WWE	18
2021	WWE	8
2022	Indies	

BIG E
5'11, 285lbs, Tampa, Florida, 2009, 36

Year	Promotion	#
2010	FCW	52
2011	FCW	53
2012	FCW	35
	WWE	29
2013	WWE	135
2014	WWE	155
2015	WWE	183
2016	WWE	143
2017	WWE	107
2018	WWE	139
2019	WWE	104
2020	WWE	42
2021	WWE	74
2022	WWE	24

BIG KON
6'3, 244 lbs, Boston, Massachusetts, 2003, 42

Year	Promotion	#
2003	Indies	
2004	Indies	
2005	Indies	
2006	WWE	11
2007	WWE	8
2008	Indies	
2009	Indies	
2010	WWE	2
2011	WWE	15
2012	WWE	12
2013	WWE	67
2014	WWE	80
2015	WWE	160
2016	WWE	113
2017	WWE	106
2018	WWE	69
2019	WWE	25
2020	Indies	
2021	Indies	
2022	Impact	4

BILLY GUNN
6'4, 266 lbs, Orlando, Florida, 1989, 59

Year	Promotion	#
1989	Indies	
1990	Indies	
1991	Indies	
1992	Indies	

Year	Promotion	#
1993	WWF	104
1994	WWF	141
1995	WWF	136
1996	WWF	128
1997	WWF	129
1998	WWF	191
1999	WWF	171
2000	WWF	69
2001	WWF	129
2002	WWE	138
2003	WWE	44
2004	WWE	76
2005	TNA	20
2006	TNA	35
2007	TNA	29
2008	TNA	37
2009	TNA	32
2010	Indies	
2011	Indies	
2012	WWE	4
2013	WWE	21
2014	WWE	18
2015	WWE	2
2016	NJPW	17
2017	NJPW	4
2018	Indies	
2019	AEW	2
2020	AEW	23
2021	AEW	34
2022	AEW	7

BLACK TAURUS
5'10, 198 lbs, Torreon, Coahuila, Mexico, 2006, 35

Year	Promotion	#
2006	Indies	
2007	Indies	
2008	CMLL	13
2009	CMLL	29
2010	CMLL	38
2011	CMLL	19
	AAA	2
2012	AAA	19
2013	AAA	11
2014	AAA	8
2015	AAA	14
2016	AAA	11
2017	Indies	
2018	AAA	17
2019	AAA	40
	Impact	4
2020	AAA	5
	Impact	3
2021	Impact	28
	AAA	26
2022	AAA	33
	Impact	24

BLACK TIGER (RICKY REYES)
5'9, 191 lbs, Fontana, California, 2000, 44

Year	Promotion	#
2000	Indies	
2001	Indies	
2002	NJPW	16
2003	CMLL	11
2004	ROH	11
2005	ROH	17
2006	ROH	17
2007	ROH	1
2008	Indies	
2009	WWC	43
	ROH	2
2010	ROH	9
2011	Indies	
2012	Indies	
2013	Indies	
2014	Indies	
2015	Indies	
2016	Indies	
2017	Indies	
2018	Indies	
2019	Indies	
2020	Indies	

Year	Promotion	#
2021	Indies	
2022	NJPW	4

BLADE, THE
6'0, 220 lbs, Buffalo, New York, 2000, 42

Year	Promotion	#
2000	Indies	
2001	Indies	
2002	Indies	
2003	Indies	
2004	Indies	
2005	Indies	
2006	Indies	
2007	Indies	
2008	Indies	
2009	Indies	
2010	Indies	
2011	Indies	
2012	Indies	
2013	Indies	
2014	Indies	
2015	TNA	2
2016	TNA	27
2017	Impact	23
2018	Impact	8
2019	AEW	2
2020	AEW	33
2021	AEW	36
2022	AEW	37

BLAIR DAVENPORT
5'7, 141 lbs, Harrogate, North Yorkshire, England, 2013, 26

Year	Promotion	#
2013	Indies	
2014	Indies	
2015	Indies	
2016	Indies	
2017	Stardom	14
2018	Stardom	33
2019	Stardom	74
	AEW	7
2020	Stardom	39
2021	Stardom	30
	WWE	5
2022	WWE	8

BLAKE CHRISTIAN
5'10, 174 lbs, Missouri, 2019, 25

Year	Promotion	#
2019	Indies	
2020	NJPW	11
2021	WWE	10
	Impact	6
2022	AEW	11
	NJPW	11
	Impact	5
	ROH	3

BOA
6'4, 220 lbs, Beijing, China, 2017, 27

Year	Promotion	#
2017	WWE	7
2018	WWE	26
2019	WWE	29
2021	WWE	11
2022	WWE	2

BOBBY FISH
5'11, 196 lbs, Albany, New York, 2004, 46

Year	Promotion	#
2004	Indies	
2005	Indies	
2006	NOAH	12
2007	NOAH	21
2008	NOAH	19
2009	NOAH	27
2010	NOAH	29
2011	NOAH	44
2012	NOAH	15
	ROH	4
2013	ROH	33
	NOAH	10
2014	ROH	37

	NJPW	14
	NOAH	10
2015	NJPW	47
	ROH	38
2016	ROH	37
	NJPW	37
2017	WWE	30
	ROH	15
2018	WWE	29
2019	WWE	55
2020	WWE	23
2021	AEW	13
	WWE	4
2022	AEW	14

BOBBY LASHLEY
6'3, 273lbs, Junction City, Kansas, 2005, 46

2005	WWE	57
	OVW	27
2006	WWE	139
2007	WWE	76
2008	Indies	
2009	TNA	19
2010	Indies	
2011	Indies	
2012	Indies	
2013	Indies	
2014	TNA	32
2015	TNA	34
2016	TNA	33
2017	TNA	30
2018	WWE	99
	Impact	6
2019	WWE	99
2020	WWE	52
2021	WWE	71
2022	WWE	71

BOULDER
6'6, 339 lbs, Elizabeth, New Jersey, 2012, 32

2012	Indies	
2013	Indies	
2014	Indies	
2015	Indies	
2016	Indies	
2017	Indies	
2018	Indies	
2019	Indies	
2020	AEW	3
2021	AEW	23
2022	AEW	18

BRANDON CUTLER
6'2, 169 lbs, Huntington Beach, California, 2005, 35

2005	Indies	
2006	Indies	
2007	Indies	
2008	Indies	
2009	Indies	
2010	Indies	
2011	Indies	
2018	Indies	
2019	AEW	6
2020	AEW	33
2021	AEW	11
2022	AEW	14

BRANDON TATE
5'9, 169 lbs, Knoxville, Tennessee, 2010, 31

2010	Indies	
2011	Indies	
2012	Indies	
2013	Indies	
2014	Indies	
2015	Indies	
2016	ROH	3
2017	ROH	13
2018	ROH	16
2019	ROH	10
2020	Indies	
2021	AEW	2
2022	AEW	6
	ROH	2

BRAUN STROWMAN
6'8, 340 lbs, Sherrills Ford, North Carolina, 2014, 39

2014	WWE	2
2015	WWE	62
2016	WWE	121
2017	WWE	124
2018	WWE	145
2019	WWE	121
2020	WWE	35
2021	WWE	15
2022	WWE	33

BRENT TATE
5'9, 161 lbs, Knoxville, Tennessee, 2010, 31

2010	Indies	
2011	Indies	
2012	Indies	
2013	Indies	
2014	Indies	
2015	Indies	
2016	ROH	3
2017	ROH	13
2018	ROH	16
2019	ROH	10
2020	Indies	
2021	AEW	2
2022	AEW	6
	ROH	2

BRIAN CAGE
6'0, 264 lbs, Chico, California, 2005, 39

2005	Indies	
2006	Indies	
2007	Indies	
2008	Indies	
2009	Indies	
2010	Indies	
2011	Indies	
2012	Indies	
2013	Indies	
2014	Indies	
2015	AAA	21
2016	AAA	13
2017	NOAH	13
2018	Impact	26
	AAA	6
2019	Impact	29
	AAA	6
2020	AEW	19
2021	AEW	34
2022	AEW	15
	ROH	3

BRIAN MYERS
6'1, 216 lbs, Long Island, New York, 2004, 37

2004	Indies	
2005	Indies	
2006	Indies	
2007	WWE	38
2008	WWE	71
2009	WWE	2
2010	WWE	30
2011	WWE	55
2012	WWE	58
2013	WWE	27
2014	WWE	6
2015	TNA	7
2016	WWE	48
2017	WWE	128
2018	WWE	92
2019	WWE	88
2020	Impact	14
	WWE	7
2021	Impact	27
2022	Impact	18
	NWA	6

BRIAN PILLMAN JR.
6'1, 205 lbs, Cincinnati, Ohio, 2018, 29

2018	MLW	8
2019	MLW	16
	AEW	1
2020	AEW	16
	MLW	4
2021	AEW	45
	MLW	3
2022	AEW	20

BROCK ANDERSON
6'0, 209 lbs, Charlotte, North Carolina, 2021, 25

2021	AEW	16
2022	AEW	17

BROCK LESNAR
6'3, 286lbs, Webster, South Dakota, 2000, 45

2001	WWF	30
	OVW	24
2002	WWE	139
2003	WWE	136
2004	WWE	18
2005	NJPW	3
2006	NJPW	4
2012	WWE	2
2013	WWE	3
2014	WWE	4
2015	WWE	9
2016	WWE	12
2017	WWE	14
2018	WWE	11
2019	WWE	8
2020	WWE	3
2021	WWE	1
2022	WWE	8

BRODY KING
6'5, 285 lbs, Palmdale, California, 2015, 35

2015	Indies	
2016	Indies	
2017	Indies	
2018	MLW	9
2019	ROH	32
	NJPW	12
2020	NJPW	9
	ROH	6
2021	NJPW	21
	ROH	14
2022	AEW	22
	NJPW	6

BRON BREAKKER
6'0, 230lbs, Woodstock, Georgia, 2020, 25

2021	WWE	13
2022	WWE	44

BRONSON
6'2, 260 lbs, East Islip, New York, 2015, 27

2015	Indies	
2016	Indies	
2017	Indies	
2018	Indies	
2019	Indies	
2020	AEW	3
2021	AEW	34
2022	AEW	19

BROOKLYN BARLOW
?, ?, Saint George, Utah, 2022, ?

2022	WWE	4

BROOKS JENSEN
6'5, 243 lbs, Ranburne, Alabama, 2019, 21

2019	Indies	
2020	Indies	
2021	WWE	7
2022	WWE	36

BRUTUS CREED
5'11, 282 lbs, Lexington, Ohio, 2021, 26

2021	WWE	10
2022	WWE	34

BRYAN DANIELSON
5'10, 210 lbs, Aberdeen, Washington, 1999, 41

1999	Indies	
2000	Indies	
2001	Indies	
2002	ROH	16
	NJPW	16
2003	NJPW	30
	WWE	6
	ROH	5
2004	NJPW	66
	ROH	12
2005	ROH	22
2006	ROH	46
	NOAH	10
2007	ROH	29
	NOAH	29
2008	NOAH	54
	ROH	36
2009	ROH	35
	NOAH	10
2010	WWE	77
2011	WWE	193
2012	WWE	213
2013	WWE	228
2014	WWE	53
2015	WWE	58
2018	WWE	87
2019	WWE	90
2020	WWE	38
2021	WWE	19
	AEW	17
2022	AEW	33

BRYSON MONTANA
6'0, 216 lbs, Houston, Texas, 2022, ?

2022	WWE	13

BUDDY MATTHEWS
5'11, 203 lbs, Melbourne, Victoria, Australia, 2007, 34

2007	Indies	
2008	Indies	
2009	Indies	
2010	Indies	
2011	Indies	
2012	Indies	
2013	WWE	2
2014	WWE	35
2015	WWE	90
2016	WWE	78
2017	WWE	47
2018	WWE	66
2019	WWE	59
2020	WWE	50
2021	WWE	3
2022	AEW	15

BULLY RAY
6'4, 326 lbs, New York City, New York, 1991, 51

1991	Indies	
1992	Indies	
1993	Indies	
1995	ECW	11
1996	ECW	64

Year	Promotion	Value
1997	ECW	81
1998	ECW	105
1999	ECW	78
	WWF	55
2000	WWF	173
2001	WWF	164
2002	WWE	152
2003	WWE	130
2004	WWE	112
2005	AJPW	15
	TNA	5
	WWE	3
2006	TNA	31
2007	TNA	42
2008	TNA	49
2009	TNA	63
	NJPW	4
2010	TNA	42
2011	TNA	85
2012	TNA	90
2013	TNA	69
2014	TNA	53
2015	WWE	65
2016	WWE	93
2017	ROH	22
	NJPW	6
2018	ROH	18
	NJPW	4
2019	ROH	7
	NJPW	3
2020	ROH	2
2021	Indies	
2022	Impact	6
	NWA	5

BUNNY, THE
5'5, 125 lbs, Toronto, Ontario, Canada, 2005, 37

Year	Promotion	Value
2005	Indies	
2006	Indies	
2007	Indies	
2008	Indies	
2009	Indies	
2010	Indies	
2011	Indies	
2012	Indies	
2013	Indies	
2014	Indies	
2015	Indies	
2016	TNA	11
2017	Impact	17
2018	Impact	26
2019	Impact	6
	AEW	6
2020	AEW	9
2021	AEW	34
2022	AEW	18

BUSHI
5'6, 183 lbs, Adachi, Tokyo, Japan, 2007, 39

Year	Promotion	Value
2007	AJPW	74
2008	AJPW	73
2009	Indies	
2010	AJPW	109
2011	AJPW	115
2012	NJPW	61
	AJPW	9
2013	NJPW	83
	CMLL	12
2014	NJPW	99
2015	NJPW	6
2016	NJPW	138
2017	NJPW	155
	ROH	9
2018	NJPW	138
	ROH	10
2019	NJPW	141
2020	NJPW	82
2021	NJPW	128
2022	NJPW	135

BUTCH
5'10, 205lbs, Birmingham, England, 2007, 29

Year	Promotion	Value
2008	Indies	
2009	Indies	
2010	Indies	
2011	Indies	
2012	Indies	
2013	Indies	
2014	Indies	
2015	Indies	
2016	Indies	
2017	WWE	38
2018	WWE	38
2019	WWE	49
2020	WWE	27
2021	WWE	21
2022	WWE	66

BUTCHER, THE
6'3, 273 lbs, Buffalo, New York, 2016, 45

Year	Promotion	Value
2016	Indies	
2017	Indies	
2018	Indies	
2019	AEW	2
2020	AEW	33
2021	AEW	22
2022	AEW	35

CALEB KONLEY
6'0, 207 lbs, Cartersville, Georgia, 2005, 39

Year	Promotion	Value
2005	Indies	
2006	Indies	
2007	Indies	
2008	Indies	
2009	Indies	
2010	Indies	
2011	DGUSA	8
	ROH	5
2012	DGUSA	9
	EVOLVE	8
2013	DGUSA	5
	EVOLVE	5
2014	EVOLVE	12
	DGUSA	5
2015	EVOLVE	14
2016	EVOLVE	7
	TNA	4
2017	Impact	37
2018	Impact	19
2019	NWA	6
	Impact	4
2020	NWA	2
	Impact	2
2021	Impact	19
2022	AEW	4
	Impact	2

CAMERON GRIMES
5'11, 210 lbs, Cameron, North Carolina, 2007, 29

Year	Promotion	Value
2007	Indies	
2008	Indies	
2009	Indies	
2010	Indies	
2011	Indies	
2012	Indies	
2013	Indies	
2014	Indies	
2015	EVOLVE	9
	TNA	7
2016	TNA	34
2017	Impact	39
2018	Impact	31
2019	WWE	55
2020	WWE	43
2021	WWE	19
2022	WWE	26

CANDICE LERAE
5'2, 110 lbs, Riverside, California, 2002, 37

Year	Promotion	Value
2002	Indies	
2003	Indies	
2004	Indies	
2005	Indies	
2006	Indies	
2007	Indies	
2008	Indies	
2009	Indies	
2010	Indies	
2011	Indies	
2012	Indies	
2013	Indies	
2014	Indies	
2015	Indies	
2016	Indies	
2017	WWE	5
2018	WWE	79
2019	WWE	50
2020	WWE	31
2021	WWE	11
2022	WWE	8

CARMELLA
5'5, 110lbs, Spencer, Massachusetts, 2014, 35

Year	Promotion	Value
2014	WWE	27
2015	WWE	66
2016	WWE	122
2017	WWE	139
2018	WWE	142
2019	WWE	79
2020	WWE	11
2021	WWE	41
2022	WWE	26

CARMELO HAYES
5'10, 210 lbs, Worcester, Massachusetts, 2014, 28

Year	Promotion	Value
2014	Indies	
2015	Indies	
2016	Indies	
2017	Indies	
2018	Indies	
2019	Indies	
2020	Indies	
2021	WWE	14
2022	WWE	40

CASH WHEELER
5'10, 222 lbs, Raleigh, North Carolina, 2005, 35

Year	Promotion	Value
2005	Indies	
2006	Indies	
2007	Indies	
2008	Indies	
2009	Indies	
2010	Indies	
2011	Indies	
2012	Indies	
2013	Indies	
2014	WWE	44
2015	WWE	95
2016	WWE	101
2017	WWE	54
2018	WWE	115
2019	WWE	150
2020	AEW	16
	WWE	13
2021	AEW	30
2022	AEW	23
	NJPW	5
	ROH	3
	AAA	2

CASSIE LEE
5'8, 132 lbs, Sydney, New South Wales, Australia, 2009, 30

Year	Promotion	Value
2009	Indies	
2010	Indies	

Year	Promotion	Value
2011	Indies	
2012	Indies	
2013	Indies	
2014	Indies	
2015	WWE	37
2016	WWE	89
2017	WWE	66
2018	WWE	62
2019	WWE	67
2020	WWE	26
2021	WWE	6
	Impact	4
2022	Impact	5

CEDRIC ALEXANDER
5'10, 205lbs, Charlotte, North Carolina, 2009, 33

Year	Promotion	Value
2009	Indies	
2010	Indies	
2011	ROH	12
2012	ROH	16
2013	ROH	28
2014	ROH	37
2015	ROH	29
2016	WWE	39
2017	WWE	62
2018	WWE	81
2019	WWE	68
2020	WWE	48
2021	WWE	45
2022	WWE	41

CEZAR BONONI
6'9, 255 lbs, São Paulo, Brazil, 2004, 36

Year	Promotion	Value
2014	Indies	
2015	Indies	
2016	WWE	11
2017	WWE	49
2018	WWE	51
2019	WWE	42
2020	AEW	6
	WWE	4
2021	AEW	33
2022	AEW	21

CHAD GABLE
5'8, 202lbs, Minneapolis, Minnesota, 2012, 36

Year	Promotion	Value
2014	WWE	20
2015	WWE	79
2016	WWE	145
2017	WWE	139
2018	WWE	119
2019	WWE	93
2020	WWE	20
2021	WWE	36
2022	WWE	92

CHARLIE DEMPSEY
?, ?, Blackpool, Lancashire, England, 2018, ?

Year	Promotion	Value
2018	Indies	
2019	Indies	
2021	WWE	5
2022	WWE	14

CHARLOTTE FLAIR
5'10, 144lbs, Charlotte, North Carolina, 2012, 36

Year	Promotion	Value
2012	WWE	4
2013	WWE	31
2014	WWE	65
2015	WWE	143
2016	WWE	160
2017	WWE	168
2018	WWE	148
2019	WWE	136
2020	WWE	35
2021	WWE	81
2022	WWE	35

CHASE OWENS
6'1, 205 lbs, Bristol, Tennessee, 2007, 32

Year	Promotion	Matches
2007	Indies	
2008	Indies	
2009	Indies	
2010	Indies	
2011	Indies	
2012	Indies	
2013	Indies	
2014	Indies	
2015	NJPW	25
2016	NJPW	65
2017	NJPW	76
2018	NJPW	84
2019	NJPW	115
2020	NJPW	39
2021	NJPW	73
2022	NJPW	74

CHELSEA GREEN
5'7, 125 lbs, Victoria, British Columbia, Canada, 2014, 31

Year	Promotion	Matches
2014	Indies	
2015	Indies	
2016	Stardom	11
	TNA	10
2017	Impact	22
2018	WWE	9
	Impact	7
2019	WWE	31
2020	WWE	16
2021	Impact	14
	ROH	6
	NWA	4
2022	Impact	22
	NWA	9

CHRIS BEY
5'9, 165 lbs, Alexandria, Virginia, 2017, 26

Year	Promotion	Matches
2017	Indies	
2018	Indies	
2019	Impact	5
2020	Impact	23
2021	Impact	32
	NJPW	5
2022	Impact	32
	NJPW	19

CHRIS JERICHO
6'0, 227 lbs, Manhasset, New York, 1990, 52

Year	Promotion	Matches
1990	Indies	
1991	Indies	
1992	Indies	
1993	CMLL	39
1994	SMW	49
	CMLL	10
1995	CMLL	23
1996	WCW	47
	ECW	22
1997	WCW	91
	NJPW	38
1998	WCW	152
1999	WCW	52
	WWF	50
2000	WWF	172
2001	WWF	165
2002	WWE	158
2003	WWE	113
2004	WWE	148
2005	WWE	79
2007	WWE	8
2008	WWE	135
2009	WWE	166
2010	WWE	111
2012	WWE	77
2013	WWE	59
2014	WWE	32
2015	WWE	46
2016	WWE	115
2017	WWE	40
2018	NJPW	3
2019	AEW	10
2020	AEW	25
2021	AEW	18
2022	AEW	27

CHRIS SABIN
5'10, 207 lbs, Detroit, Michigan, 2000, 40

Year	Promotion	Matches
2000	Indies	
2001	Indies	
2002	Indies	
2003	TNA	30
	ROH	7
2004	TNA	55
2005	TNA	41
2006	TNA	56
2007	TNA	49
	AJPW	12
2008	TNA	70
2009	TNA	58
2010	TNA	81
2011	TNA	23
2012	TNA	11
2013	TNA	45
2014	TNA	19
2015	ROH	3
2016	ROH	38
2017	ROH	35
2018	NJPW	34
	ROH	20
2019	ROH	1
2020	Impact	13
2021	Impact	33
2022	Impact	34

CHRISTIAN CAGE
6'1, 227 lbs, Kitchener, Ontario, Canada, 1995, 49

Year	Promotion	Matches
1995	Indies	
1996	Indies	
1997	Indies	
1998	WWF	25
1999	WWF	151
2000	WWF	178
2001	WWF	141
2002	WWE	170
2003	WWE	132
2004	WWE	109
2005	WWE	114
	TNA	3
2006	TNA	29
2007	TNA	57
2008	TNA	64
2009	WWE	156
2010	WWE	119
2011	WWE	138
2012	WWE	58
2013	WWE	33
2014	WWE	24
2020	WWE	1
2021	AEW	17
	Impact	5
	WWE	1
2022	AEW	7

CHRISTOPHER DANIELS
5'10, 232 lbs, Fayetteville, North Carolina, 1993, 52

Year	Promotion	Matches
1993	Indies	
1994	Indies	
1995	WWC	4
1996	Indies	
1997	Indies	
1998	WWF	7
1999	WWF	6
	ECW	6
2000	Indies	
2001	Indies	
2002	ROH	16
	NJPW	16
	TNA	3
2003	TNA	35
	NJPW	26
	ROH	18
	MLW	6
2004	TNA	43
	NJPW	30
2005	TNA	31
	ROH	16
2006	TNA	49
	ROH	35
2007	TNA	36
	ROH	10
2008	TNA	51
	NJPW	5
2009	TNA	78
2010	TNA	23
	ROH	22
2011	TNA	40
	ROH	16
2012	TNA	115
2013	TNA	84
2014	ROH	15
	TNA	11
2015	ROH	33
	NJPW	17
2016	ROH	44
2017	ROH	35
	NJPW	6
2018	ROH	43
	NJPW	8
2019	AEW	6
2020	AEW	26
2021	AEW	21
2022	AEW	10
	NJPW	10

CHUCK TAYLOR
6'1, 185 lbs, Murray, Kentucky, 2002, 36

Year	Promotion	Matches
2002	Indies	
2003	Indies	
2004	Indies	
2005	Indies	
2006	Indies	
2007	Indies	
2008	Indies	
2009	Indies	
2010	EVOLVE	6
	DGUSA	5
2011	DGUSA	12
	Dragon Gate	9
2012	EVOLVE	9
	DGUSA	9
2013	DGUSA	9
	EVOLVE	6
2014	EVOLVE	7
	DGUSA	5
2015	Indies	
2016	EVOLVE	12
2017	NJPW	19
	ROH	13
2018	NJPW	52
	ROH	23
2019	AEW	12
	NJPW	5
2020	AEW	36
2021	AEW	35
2022	AEW	28

CLARK CONNORS
5'8, 185 lbs, Snoqualmie, Washington, 2017, 29

Year	Promotion	Matches
2017	Indies	
2018	Indies	
2019	NJPW	54
	ROH	8
2020	NJPW	22
2021	NJPW	24
2022	NJPW	43
	AEW	2

CLAUDIO CASTAGNOLI
6'5, 232lbs, Luzern, Switzerland, 2000, 42

Year	Promotion	Matches
2000	Indies	
2001	Indies	
2002	Indies	
2003	Indies	
2004	Indies	
2005	ROH	12
2006	ROH	35
2007	ROH	36
2008	ROH	32
	NOAH	9
2009	ROH	47
	NOAH	8
2010	ROH	38
	NOAH	20
2011	ROH	16
	FCW	15
	NOAH	12
2012	WWE	108
	FCW	30
2013	WWE	213
2014	WWE	214
2015	WWE	188
2016	WWE	143
2017	WWE	171
2018	WWE	155
2019	WWE	134
2020	WWE	39
2021	WWE	50
2022	AEW	21
	WWE	5

CM PUNK
6'2, 185lbs, Chicago, Illinois, 1999, 44

Year	Promotion	Matches
1999	Indies	
2000	Indies	
2001	Indies	
2002	ROH	3
2003	ROH	21
	TNA	19
	MLW	5
2004	ROH	30
	TNA	7
2005	ROH	21
	WWE	8
2006	WWE	73
	OVW	42
2007	WWE	135
	OVW	9
2008	WWE	176
2009	WWE	192
2010	WWE	115
2011	WWE	187
2012	WWE	178
2013	WWE	112
2014	WWE	13
2021	AEW	9
2022	AEW	14

CODY RHODES
6'2, 218lbs, Marietta, Georgia, 2006, 37

Year	Promotion	Matches
2006	OVW	47
2007	WWE	75
	OVW	38
2008	WWE	150
2009	WWE	155
2010	WWE	162
2011	WWE	153
2012	WWE	171
2013	WWE	168
2014	WWE	187
2015	WWE	148
2016	WWE	71
2017	ROH	39
	NJPW	25
2018	ROH	42
	NJPW	26
2019	AEW	10
2020	AEW	34

Year	Promotion	Rank
2021	AEW	28
2022	WWE	23
	AEW	1

COLE KARTER
6'2, 239 lbs, Charleston, West Virginia, 2019, 22

Year	Promotion	Rank
2019	WWE	1
2020	Indies	
2021	AEW	9
2022	AEW	16
	WWE	6

COLT CABANA
6'1, 233 lbs, Deerfield, Illinois, 1999, 42

Year	Promotion	Rank
1999	Indies	
2000	Indies	
2001	Indies	
2002	Indies	
2003	ROH	18
2004	ROH	18
2005	ROH	33
2006	ROH	40
	WWE	7
2007	OVW	63
	ROH	14
2008	FCW	37
	OVW	12
	WWE	4
2009	ROH	39
2010	ROH	40
2011	ROH	15
	NOAH	9
2012	NOAH	10
2013	NOAH	9
2014	NOAH	20
2015	NOAH	27
2016	ROH	22
2017	ROH	8
2018	Indies	
2019	NJPW	36
	ROH	18
	NWA	9
2020	AEW	28
	NJPW	9
2021	AEW	40
2022	AEW	6
	ROH	2

COLTEN GUNN
?, ?, Orlando, Florida, 2020, 31

Year	Promotion	Rank
2020	AEW	7
2021	AEW	35
2022	AEW	34

COMMANDER AZEEZ
6'9, 350lbs, Olesnica, Poland, 2016, 34

Year	Promotion	Rank
2017	WWE	18
2018	WWE	41
2019	WWE	29
	EVOLVE	14
2020	WWE	9
2021	WWE	10
2022	WWE	11

CORA JADE
5'6, 110 lbs, Chicago, Illinois, 2018, 21

Year	Promotion	Rank
2018	Indies	
2019	Indies	
2020	Indies	
2021	WWE	13
2022	WWE	34

CRAZZY STEVE
5'10, 200 lbs, Montreal, Quebec, Canada, 2003, 38

Year	Promotion	Rank
2003	Indies	
2004	Indies	
2005	Indies	

Year	Promotion	Rank
2006	Indies	
2007	Indies	
2008	Indies	
2009	Indies	
2010	Indies	
2011	Indies	
2012	Indies	
2013	Indies	
2014	TNA	19
2015	TNA	24
2016	TNA	32
2017	Impact	12
2018	Indies	
2019	Indies	
2020	Impact	16
2021	Impact	31
2022	Impact	17

CRUZ DEL TORO
5'5, 178 lbs, Córdoba, Mexico, 2006, 31

Year	Promotion	Rank
2009	Indies	
2010	Indies	
2011	Indies	
2012	Indies	
2013	Indies	
2014	NOAH	25
2015	Indies	
2016	Indies	
2017	WWE	34
2018	WWE	77
2019	WWE	62
2020	WWE	29
2021	WWE	17
2022	WWE	27

DAKOTA KAI
5'6, 121lbs, Auckland, New Zealand, 2007, 34

Year	Promotion	Rank
2007	Indies	
2008	Indies	
2009	Indies	
2010	Indies	
2011	Indies	
2012	Indies	
2013	Indies	
2014	Indies	
2015	Indies	
2016	Indies	
2017	WWE	24
2018	WWE	89
2019	WWE	25
2020	WWE	35
2021	WWE	30
2022	WWE	44

DALTON CASTLE
5'11, 211 lbs, Albany, New York, 2008, 36

Year	Promotion	Rank
2008	Indies	
2009	Indies	
2010	Indies	
2011	Indies	
2012	Indies	
2013	Indies	
2014	Indies	
2015	ROH	35
2016	ROH	48
	NJPW	6
2017	ROH	36
	NJPW	8
2018	ROH	29
	NJPW	5
2019	ROH	31
	NJPW	4
2020	ROH	11
2021	ROH	12
2022	AEW	10
	ROH	3

DAMIAN PRIEST
6'7, 251lbs, New York City, New York, 2004, 40

Year	Promotion	Rank
2004	Indies	
2005	Indies	
2006	Indies	
2007	Indies	
2008	Indies	
2009	Indies	
2010	Indies	
2011	Indies	
2012	Indies	
2013	Indies	
2014	Indies	
2015	Indies	
2016	Indies	
	ROH	14
2017	ROH	33
2018	ROH	29
	WWE	11
2019	WWE	88
2020	WWE	35
2021	WWE	62
2022	WWE	84

DAMON KEMP
6'0, 220 lbs, Apple Valley, Minnesota, 2021, 23

Year	Promotion	Rank
2021	WWE	1
2022	WWE	29

DANA BROOKE
5'3, 125lbs, Seven Hills, Ohio, 2014, 34

Year	Promotion	Rank
2014	WWE	14
2015	WWE	55
2016	WWE	85
2017	WWE	73
2018	WWE	46
2019	WWE	77
2020	WWE	22
2021	WWE	25
2022	WWE	61

DANHAUSEN
5'10, 180 lbs, Detroit, Michigan, 2013, 32

Year	Promotion	Rank
2013	Indies	
2014	Indies	
2015	Indies	
2016	Indies	
2017	Indies	
2018	Indies	
2019	Indies	
2020	ROH	4
2021	ROH	14
2022	AEW	14

DANIEL GARCIA
6'0, 187 lbs, Buffalo, New York, 2017, 24

Year	Promotion	Rank
2017	Indies	
2018	Indies	
2019	Indies	
2020	AEW	2
2021	AEW	21
2022	AEW	36
	NJPW	3
	ROH	2

DANNY JONES
6'3, 194 lbs, Ebbw Vale, Wales, 2012, 27

Year	Promotion	Rank
2012	Indies	
2013	Indies	
2014	Indies	
2015	Indies	
2016	Indies	
2017	AJPW	29
2018	Indies	
2019	Indies	
2020	AJPW	11

DANNY LIMELIGHT
5'8, 161 lbs, New York City, New York, 2014, 31

Year	Promotion	Rank
2014	Indies	
2015	Indies	
2016	Indies	
2017	Indies	
2018	Indies	
2019	Indies	
2020	NJPW	14
	AEW	8
2021	AEW	18
	NJPW	14
	MLW	5
2022	NJPW	9
	MLW	6

DANTE CHEN
6'0, 213 lbs, Singapore, 2013, 26

Year	Promotion	Rank
2013	Indies	
2014	Indies	
2015	Indies	
2016	Indies	
2017	Indies	
2018	Indies	
2019	Indies	
2020	Indies	
2021	WWE	3
2022	WWE	28

DANTE MARTIN
5'1, 187 lbs, St. Paul, Minnesota, 2016, 21

Year	Promotion	Rank
2016	Indies	
2017	Indies	
2018	Indies	
2019	Indies	
2020	AEW	6
2021	AEW	48
2022	AEW	64

DARBY ALLIN
5'8, 170 lbs, Seattle, Washington, 2015, 29

Year	Promotion	Rank
2015	Indies	
2016	EVOLVE	13
2017	EVOLVE	16
2018	EVOLVE	21
2019	AEW	10
	EVOLVE	7
2020	AEW	26
2021	AEW	36
2022	AEW	30

DARIUS LOCKHART
?, 196 lbs, Charlotte, North Carolina, 2014, 27

Year	Promotion	Rank
2014	Indies	
2015	Indies	
2016	Indies	
2017	Indies	
2018	Indies	
2019	Indies	
2020	Indies	
2021	AEW	3
	NWA	2
2022	NWA	2

DARIUS MARTIN
5'10, 189 lbs, Minneapolis, Minnesota, 2016, 23

Year	Promotion	Rank
2016	Indies	
2017	Indies	
2018	Indies	
2019	MLW	9
2020	AEW	7
2021	AEW	6
2022	AEW	18
	ROH	1

DAVE MASTIFF
5'9, 315 lbs, Birmingham, England, 2002, 38

Year	Promotion	Rank
2002	Indies	
2003	Indies	
2004	Indies	
2005	Indies	
2006	Indies	
2007	Indies	
2008	Indies	
2009	Indies	
2010	Indies	
2011	Indies	
2012	Indies	
2013	Indies	
2014	Indies	
2015	Indies	
2016	Indies	
2017	Indies	
2018	WWE	10
2019	WWE	14
2020	WWE	8
2021	WWE	11
2022	WWE	6

DAVID FINLAY
5'9, 194 lbs, Hannover, Germany, 2012, 29

Year	Promotion	Rank
2012	Indies	
2013	Indies	
2014	Indies	
2015	NJPW	76
2016	NJPW	137
2017	NJPW	130
2018	NJPW	114
	CMLL	9
2019	NJPW	27
	ROH	9
2020	NJPW	34
2021	Impact	24
	NJPW	22
2022	NJPW	49

DAX HARWOOD
5'10, 224 lbs, Whiteville, North Carolina, 2004, 38

Year	Promotion	Rank
2004	Indies	
2005	Indies	
2006	Indies	
2007	Indies	
2008	Indies	
2010	ROH	1
2011	Indies	
2012	WWE	1
2013	WWE	42
2014	WWE	41
2015	WWE	96
2016	WWE	100
2017	WWE	31
2018	WWE	116
2019	WWE	152
2020	AEW	16
	WWE	12
2021	AEW	33
2022	AEW	28
	NJPW	6
	ROH	3
	AAA	2

DEANER
6'0, 219 lbs, Port Bruce, Canada, 1999, 40

Year	Promotion	Rank
1999	Indies	
2001	Indies	
2002	Indies	
2003	Indies	
2004	Indies	
2005	Indies	
2006	Indies	
2007	Indies	
2008	Indies	
2009	TNA	11

Year	Promotion	Rank
2010	Indies	
2011	Indies	
2012	Indies	
2013	Indies	
2014	Indies	
2015	Indies	
2016	Indies	
2017	Indies	
2018	Impact	5
2019	Impact	16
2020	Impact	18
2021	Impact	22
2022	Impact	17

DEONNA PURRAZZO
5'3, 138 lbs, Livingston, New Jersey, 2013, 28

Year	Promotion	Rank
2013	Indies	
2014	Indies	
2015	Indies	
2016	ROH	6
	WWE	5
2017	ROH	12
	Stardom	12
2018	WWE	21
	ROH	8
	Stardom	7
2019	WWE	56
2020	WWE	13
	Impact	12
2021	Impact	23
2022	Impact	26

DEXTER LUMIS
6'1, 240 lbs, Jacksonville, Florida, 2007, 38

Year	Promotion	Rank
2007	Indies	
2008	Indies	
2009	Indies	
2010	Indies	
2011	Indies	
2012	OVW	19
	TNA	5
2013	OVW	33
	TNA	6
2014	TNA	31
2015	TNA	10
2016	Indies	
2017	Indies	
2018	NWA	2
2019	WWE	48
2020	WWE	26
2021	WWE	14
2022	WWE	16

DIAMANTE
5'1, 114 lbs, Miami Gardens, Florida, 2008, 31

Year	Promotion	Rank
2008	Indies	
2009	Indies	
2010	Indies	
2011	Indies	
2012	Indies	
2013	Indies	
2014	Indies	
2015	Indies	
2016	Indies	
2017	Impact	4
2018	Impact	1
2019	Indies	
2020	AEW	18
2021	AEW	35
2022	AEW	22

DIJAK
6'7, 275lbs, Luneburg, Massachusetts, 2013, 35

Year	Promotion	Rank
2013	Indies	
2014	Indies	
2015	ROH	25
2016	ROH	28
2017	WWE	18

Year	Promotion	Rank
2018	WWE	73
2019	WWE	59
2020	WWE	22
2021	WWE	36
2022	WWE	30

DKC, THE
5'8, 154 lbs, California, 2018, ?

Year	Promotion	Rank
2018	Indies	
2019	Indies	
2020	NJPW	10
2021	NJPW	24
2022	NJPW	34
	AEW	2

DOLPH ZIGGLER
6'0, 213lbs, Cleveland, Ohio, 2004, 42

Year	Promotion	Rank
2004	OVW	4
2005	OVW	27
	WWE	10
2006	WWE	76
	OVW	8
2007	OVW	34
	FCW	14
	WWE	3
2008	FCW	44
	WWE	25
2009	WWE	139
2010	WWE	153
2011	WWE	186
2012	WWE	191
2013	WWE	187
2014	WWE	194
2015	WWE	167
2016	WWE	166
2017	WWE	142
2018	WWE	139
2019	WWE	71
2020	WWE	37
2021	WWE	60
2022	WWE	48

DOMINIK MYSTERIO
6'1, 200lbs, San Diego, California, 2020, 25

Year	Promotion	Rank
2020	WWE	10
2021	WWE	66
2022	WWE	55

DOUDROP
5'8, 209lbs, Ayr, Scotland, 2008, 31

Year	Promotion	Rank
2009	Indies	
2010	Indies	
2011	Indies	
2012	Indies	
2013	Indies	
2014	Indies	
2015	Indies	
2016	Stardom	18
2017	Stardom	21
2018	Stardom	14
2019	WWE	14
	Stardom	12
2020	WWE	6
2021	WWE	27
2022	WWE	44

DOUKI
5'7, 187 lbs, Yokohama, Japan, 2011, 31

Year	Promotion	Rank
2011	Indies	
2012	Indies	
2013	Indies	
2014	Indies	
2015	Indies	
2016	Indies	
2017	Indies	
2018	Indies	
2019	NJPW	54
2020	NJPW	68

Year	Promotion	Rank
2021	NJPW	94
2022	NJPW	97

DR. BRITT BAKER D.M.D
5'7, 121 lbs, Punxsutawney, Pennsylvania, 2015, 31

Year	Promotion	Rank
2015	Indies	
2016	Indies	
2017	Indies	
2018	ROH	5
2019	AEW	12
2020	AEW	16
2021	AEW	30
2022	AEW	27

DRAGON LEE
5'7, 165 lbs, Tala, Mexico, 2012, 27

Year	Promotion	Rank
2012	Indies	
2013	Indies	
2014	CMLL	69
2015	CMLL	100
2016	CMLL	83
	NJPW	6
	ROH	4
2017	CMLL	96
	NJPW	41
	ROH	4
2018	CMLL	55
	NJPW	25
2019	CMLL	56
	NJPW	47
	ROH	10
2020	ROH	5
	NJPW	3
2021	ROH	24
2022	AAA	15

DREW GULAK
6'1, 193lbs, Philadelphia, Pennsylvania, 2005, 35

Year	Promotion	Rank
2005	Indies	
2006	Indies	
2007	Indies	
2008	Indies	
2009	Indies	
2010	Indies	
2011	Indies	
2012	Indies	
2013	Indies	
2014	Indies	
2015	EVOLVE	12
2016	EVOLVE	24
	WWE	16
2017	WWE	57
2018	WWE	59
2019	WWE	45
2020	WWE	42
2021	WWE	38
2022	WWE	27

DREW MCINTYRE
6'5, 250lbs, Ayr, Scotland, 2001, 37

Year	Promotion	Rank
2001	Indies	
2002	Indies	
2003	Indies	
2004	Indies	
2005	Indies	
2006	Indies	
2007	WWE	19
2008	FCW	47
	OVW	13
	WWE	7
2009	WWE	76
	FCW	41
2010	WWE	171
2011	WWE	119
2012	WWE	90
2013	WWE	124
2014	WWE	56
2015	TNA	32

Year	Promotion	#
2016	TNA	31
2017	WWE	68
2018	WWE	103
2019	WWE	127
2020	WWE	54
2021	WWE	97
2022	WWE	99

DUKE HUDSON
6'5, 253 lbs, Adelaide, Australia, 2008, 33

Year	Promotion	#
2006	Indies	
2007	Indies	
2008	Indies	
2009	Indies	
2010	Indies	
2011	Indies	
2012	Indies	
2013	Indies	
2014	Indies	
2015	Indies	
2016	Indies	
2017	Indies	
2018	NJPW	4
2019	WWE	39
2020	WWE	17
2021	WWE	7
2022	WWE	33

DUSTIN RHODES
6'6, 232lbs, Austin, Texas, 1988, 53

Year	Promotion	#
1988	JCP	11
1989	USWA	67
	NWA	20
	AJPW	17
	PWF	10
1990	WWF	68
	AJPW	23
	USWA	14
	WCCW	7
1991	WCW	198
	WWF	6
1992	WCW	208
1993	WCW	155
1994	WCW	81
1995	WWF	50
	WCW	20
1996	WWF	181
1997	WWF	161
1998	WWF	143
1999	WWF	69
	WCW	11
2000	WCW	34
2001	WCW	11
2002	WWE	139
2003	WWE	48
2004	TNA	4
2005	TNA	12
2006	WWE	44
	WWC	6
2007	TNA	12
2008	TNA	14
	WWE	2
2009	WWE	99
2010	WWE	110
2011	WWE	0
2012	Indies	
2013	WWE	48
2014	WWE	179
2015	WWE	61
2016	WWE	123
2017	WWE	113
2018	WWE	41
2019	AEW	6
2020	AEW	25
2021	AEW	18
2022	AEW	7

EDDIE DENNIS
6'5, 218 lbs, Swansea, Wales, 2008, 36

Year	Promotion	#
2008	Indies	
2009	Indies	
2010	Indies	
2011	Indies	
2012	Indies	
2013	Indies	
2014	Indies	
2015	Indies	
2016	Indies	
2017	Indies	
2018	WWE	8
2019	WWE	4
2020	WWE	3
2021	WWE	6
2022	WWE	2

EDDIE EDWARDS
5'11, 223 lbs, Boston, Massachusetts, 2000, 39

Year	Promotion	#
2002	Indies	
2003	Indies	
2004	Indies	
2005	NOAH	14
2006	NOAH	23
2007	NOAH	20
	ROH	8
2008	NOAH	21
	ROH	16
2009	ROH	38
	NOAH	20
2010	ROH	41
	NOAH	30
2011	ROH	25
	NOAH	21
2012	NOAH	29
	ROH	24
2013	ROH	33
	NOAH	19
2014	TNA	70
2015	TNA	39
2016	TNA	51
2017	NOAH	36
	Impact	32
2018	Impact	23
2019	Impact	55
2020	Impact	24
2021	Impact	32
2022	Impact	27

EDDIE KINGSTON
6'2, 245 lbs, Yonkers, New York, 2001, 41

Year	Promotion	#
2001	Indies	
2002	Indies	
2003	Indies	
2004	Indies	
2005	Indies	
2006	Indies	
2007	Indies	
2008	Indies	
2009	ROH	13
2010	ROH	5
2011	Indies	
2012	Indies	
2013	ROH	6
2014	ROH	4
2015	Indies	
2016	Indies	
2017	Impact	13
2018	Impact	2
2019	EVOLVE	21
	NWA	6
2020	AEW	11
2021	AEW	43
2022	AEW	26
	NJPW	7

EDGE
6'5, 240lbs, Ontario, Canada, 1992, 49

Year	Promotion	#
1996	Indies	
1997	Indies	
1998	WWF	67
1999	WWF	177
2000	WWF	172
2001	WWF	143
2002	WWE	159
2003	WWE	19
2004	WWE	91
2005	WWE	129
2006	WWE	162
2007	WWE	87
2008	WWE	108
2009	WWE	100
2010	WWE	136
2011	WWE	47
2020	WWE	3
2021	WWE	10
2022	WWE	9

EDRIS ENOFE
?, ?, Nigeria, 2021, ?

Year	Promotion	#
2021	WWE	5
2022	WWE	40

EL DESPERADO
5'10, 220 lbs, Nagaoka, Niigata, Japan, 2010, 39

Year	Promotion	#
2010	NJPW	48
2011	NJPW	75
2012	CMLL	66
2013	CMLL	83
2014	NJPW	96
2015	NOAH	88
2016	NOAH	112
2017	NJPW	128
2018	NJPW	112
2019	NJPW	61
2020	NJPW	80
2021	NJPW	98
2022	NJPW	109

EL PHANTASMO
6'1, 196 lbs, Vancouver, Canada, 2005, 36

Year	Promotion	#
2005	Indies	
2006	Indies	
2007	Indies	
2008	Indies	
2009	Indies	
2010	Indies	
2011	Indies	
2012	Indies	
2013	Indies	
2014	Indies	
2015	Indies	
2016	Indies	
2017	Indies	
2018	Indies	
2019	NJPW	68
2020	NJPW	14
2021	NJPW	86
	Impact	7
2022	NJPW	79

ELEKTRA LOPEZ
?, ?, Bergen County, New Jersey, 2017, 30

Year	Promotion	#
2017	Indies	
2018	Indies	
2019	ROH	4
2021	WWE	7
2022	WWE	18

ELIAS
6'1, 222lbs, Pittsburgh, Pennsylvania, 2008, 35

Year	Promotion	#
2008	Indies	
2009	Indies	

Year	Promotion	#
2010	Indies	
2011	Indies	
2012	Indies	
2013	Indies	
2014	WWE	23
2015	WWE	56
2016	WWE	77
2017	WWE	108
2018	WWE	124
2019	WWE	70
2020	WWE	17
2021	WWE	24
2022	WWE	31

ELIZA ALEXANDER
5'5, 139 lbs, Liverpool, England, 2013, 34

Year	Promotion	#
2013	Indies	
2014	Indies	
2015	Indies	
2016	Stardom	3
2017	Indies	
2018	Indies	
2019	Indies	
2020	Indies	
2021	Indies	
2022	WWE	6

ELTON PRINCE
6'1, 172 lbs, Grays, Essex, England, 2014, 25

Year	Promotion	#
2014	Indies	
2015	Indies	
2016	Indies	
2017	Indies	
2018	Indies	
2019	WWE	5
2020	WWE	8
2021	WWE	10
2022	WWE	30

EMI SAKURA
5'1, 154 lbs, Kimitsu, Chiba, Japan, 1995, 46

Year	Promotion	#
1995	IWA Japan	29
1996	IWA Japan	64
1997	AJW	55
	IWA Japan	43
1998	AJW	123
	IWA Japan	14
1999	FMW	29
2000	FMW	76
2001	FMW	52
2002	Indies	
2003	AJW	15
2004	NEO	16
2005	NEO	20
2006	NEO	11
2007	Ice Ribbon	55
2008	Ice Ribbon	78
2009	Ice Ribbon	84
2010	Ice Ribbon	128
2011	Ice Ribbon	116
2012	Gatoh Move	36
2013	Gatoh Move	85
2014	Gatoh Move	86
2015	Gatoh Move	49
2016	Gatoh Move	67
2017	Gatoh Move	64
2018	Gatoh Move	56
2019	Gatoh Move	58
	AEW	7
2020	Gatoh Move	88
2021	Gatoh Move	46
	AEW	29
2022	AEW	49
	Gatoh Move	23

EMILIA MCKENZIE
5'6, 128 lbs, Coventry, England, 2015, 22

Year	Promotion	#
2015	Indies	

Year	Promotion	Rank
2016	Indies	
2017	Indies	
2018	Indies	
2019	Indies	
2020	Indies	
2021	WWE	9
2022	WWE	6

EMMA
5'5, 132 lbs, Melbourne, Australia, 2005, 33

Year	Promotion	Rank
2005	Indies	
2008	Indies	
2009	Indies	
2010	Indies	
2011	Indies	
2012	WWE	13
2013	WWE	54
2014	WWE	100
2015	WWE	124
2016	WWE	44
2017	WWE	54
2018	ROH	18
2019	Impact	9
2020	Impact	11
2021	Impact	31
2022	Impact	13
	WWE	12

ERIC YOUNG
5'11, 225 lbs, Florence, Ontario, Canada, 1998, 43

Year	Promotion	Rank
1998	Indies	
1999	Indies	
2000	Indies	
2001	Indies	
2002	Indies	
2003	WWE	4
	TNA	2
2004	TNA	34
2005	TNA	29
2006	TNA	48
2007	TNA	48
2008	TNA	79
2009	TNA	84
2010	TNA	68
2011	TNA	48
2012	TNA	39
2013	TNA	30
2014	TNA	55
2015	TNA	40
2016	TNA	19
	WWE	16
2017	WWE	78
2018	WWE	53
2019	WWE	45
2020	Impact	10
	WWE	6
2021	Impact	8
2022	Impact	18

ERICA YAN
?, ?, Shanghai, China, 2021, ?

Year	Promotion	Rank
2021	WWE	5
2022	WWE	7

ERIK
6'1, 247lbs, Cleveland, Ohio, 2003, 38

Year	Promotion	Rank
2003	Indies	
2004	Indies	
2005	Indies	
2006	Indies	
2007	Indies	
2008	Indies	
2009	Indies	
2010	Indies	
2011	Indies	
2012	Indies	
2013	Indies	
2014	ROH	14
2015	ROH	35
2016	ROH	34
	NJPW	21
2017	NJPW	72
	ROH	25
2018	WWE	61
2019	WWE	112
2020	WWE	36
2021	WWE	31
2022	WWE	44

ETHAN PAGE
6'2, 230 lbs, Hamilton, Ontario, Canada, 2006, 33

Year	Promotion	Rank
2006	Indies	
2007	Indies	
2008	Indies	
2009	Indies	
2010	Indies	
2011	Indies	
2012	Indies	
2013	Indies	
2014	ROH	8
2015	EVOLVE	11
2016	EVOLVE	24
2017	EVOLVE	19
2018	Impact	5
2019	Impact	36
2020	Impact	26
2021	AEW	29
2022	AEW	21

EVIL
5'10, 198 lbs, Mishima, Shizuoka, Japan, 2011, 35

Year	Promotion	Rank
2011	NJPW	45
2012	NJPW	51
2013	NJPW	53
	NOAH	10
2014	ROH	9
	NJPW	2
2015	NJPW	25
	ROH	16
2016	NJPW	138
	ROH	4
2017	NJPW	155
	ROH	9
2018	NJPW	114
	ROH	14
2019	NJPW	132
	ROH	6
2020	NJPW	85
2021	NJPW	127
2022	NJPW	121

EVIL UNO
6'0, 220 lbs, Quebec, Canada, 2004, 35

Year	Promotion	Rank
2004	Indies	
2005	Indies	
2006	Indies	
2007	Indies	
2008	Indies	
2009	ROH	11
2010	ROH	5
2011	Indies	
2012	DGUSA	5
	EVOLVE	4
2013	Indies	
2014	Indies	
2015	Indies	
2016	Indies	
2017	Indies	
2018	Indies	
2019	AEW	6
2020	AEW	25
2021	AEW	52
2022	AEW	38

FALLON HENLEY
5'7, ?, Tampa, Florida, 2017, 28

Year	Promotion	Rank
2017	Indies	
2018	WWE	2
2019	Indies	
2020	AEW	8
2021	AEW	13
	WWE	5
2022	WWE	31

FINN BALOR
5'11, 190lbs, Bray, Ireland, 2000, 41

Year	Promotion	Rank
2002	Indies	
2003	Indies	
2004	Indies	
2005	Indies	
2006	NJPW	73
2007	NJPW	69
2008	NJPW	65
2009	NJPW	107
2010	NJPW	102
2011	NJPW	93
2012	NJPW	56
	CMLL	15
2013	NJPW	91
2014	NJPW	21
	WWE	11
2015	WWE	125
2016	WWE	73
2017	WWE	127
2018	WWE	171
2019	WWE	83
2020	WWE	23
2021	WWE	61
2022	WWE	75

FRANCESCO AKIRA
5'9, 154 lbs, Bergamo, Italy, 2015, 23

Year	Promotion	Rank
2015	Indies	
2016	Indies	
2017	Indies	
2018	Indies	
2019	AJPW	53
2020	AJPW	59
2021	AJPW	47
2022	NJPW	60

FRANKIE KAZARIAN
6'1, 215 lbs, Palm Springs, California, 1998, 45

Year	Promotion	Rank
2000	Indies	
2001	WWF	3
2002	Indies	
2003	TNA	16
2004	TNA	47
2005	TNA	5
	WWE	5
2006	TNA	17
2007	TNA	34
2008	TNA	45
2009	TNA	75
2010	TNA	69
2011	TNA	73
2012	TNA	90
2013	TNA	75
2014	TNA	16
	ROH	15
2015	ROH	31
	NJPW	17
2016	ROH	44
	NJPW	5
2017	ROH	36
	NJPW	6
2018	ROH	40
	NJPW	8
2019	AEW	14
2020	AEW	39
2021	AEW	41
2022	AEW	23
	Impact	10

FRED ROSSER
6'1, 239 lbs, Union City, New Jersey, 2002, 39

Year	Promotion	Rank
2002	Indies	
2003	Indies	
2004	Indies	
2005	Indies	
2006	WWE	6
2007	Indies	
2008	Indies	
2009	FCW	19
2010	WWE	29
	FCW	26
2011	WWE	34
2012	WWE	112
2013	WWE	137
2014	WWE	34
2015	WWE	136
2016	WWE	104
2017	WWE	21
2018	Indies	
2019	Indies	
2020	NJPW	9
2021	NJPW	22
	NWA	7
2022	NJPW	18

FRED YEHI
5'9, 185 lbs, Daytona Beach, Florida, 2012, 29

Year	Promotion	Rank
2012	Indies	
2013	Indies	
2014	Indies	
2015	Indies	
	EVOLVE	1
2016	EVOLVE	23
2017	EVOLVE	23
2018	MLW	8
	EVOLVE	4
2019	Indies	
2020	ROH	3
2021	NJPW	10
	ROH	7
2022	NJPW	7

FUEGO DEL SOL
?, 169 lbs, Oklahoma City, Oklahoma, 2014, 27

Year	Promotion	Rank
2014	Indies	
2015	Indies	
2016	Indies	
2017	Indies	
2018	Indies	
2019	Indies	
2020	AEW	16
2021	AEW	41
2022	AEW	20

GABRIEL KIDD
6'0, 198 lbs, Nottingham, England, 2011, 25

Year	Promotion	Rank
2011	Indies	
2012	Indies	
2013	Indies	
2014	Indies	
2015	Indies	
2016	Indies	
2017	Indies	
2018	Indies	
2019	Indies	
2020	NJPW	70
2021	NJPW	34
2022	NJPW	15

GIGI DOLIN
5'5, 114 lbs, Douglasville, Georgia, 2015, 25

Year	Promotion	Rank
2015	Indies	
2016	Indies	
2017	Indies	
2018	EVOLVE	3
2019	EVOLVE	3
2020	Indies	
2021	WWE	12
2022	WWE	29

GIOVANNI VINCI
6'0, 220 lbs, Trentino-Alto Adige, Italy, 2011, 32

Year	Promotion	No.
2011	Indies	
2012	Indies	
2013	Indies	
2014	Indies	
2015	Indies	
2016	Indies	
2017	WWE	35
2018	WWE	78
	EVOLVE	4
2019	WWE	62
	EVOLVE	2
2020	WWE	20
2021	WWE	12
2022	WWE	46

GISELE SHAW
5'7, 130 lbs, Toledo, Philippines, 2015, 34

Year	Promotion	No.
2015	Indies	
2016	Indies	
2017	Indies	
2018	Indies	
2019	Indies	
2020	Indies	
2021	Indies	
2022	Impact	25

GOLDBERG
6'4, 283lbs, Tulsa, Oklahoma, 1997, 56

Year	Promotion	No.
1997	WCW	19
1998	WCW	139
1999	WCW	90
2000	WCW	50
2001	WCW	3
2002	AJPW	3
2003	WWE	47
	AJPW	1
2004	WWE	7
	HUSTLE	1
2016	WWE	1
2017	WWE	3
2019	WWE	2
2020	WWE	2
2021	WWE	3
2022	WWE	1

GRAYSON WALLER
6'3, 224 lbs, Sydney, Australia, 2017, 32

Year	Promotion	No.
2017	Indies	
2018	Indies	
2019	Indies	
2020	Indies	
2021	WWE	21
2022	WWE	39

GREAT-O-KHAN
6'1, 254 lbs, Maebashi, Japan, 2016, 31

Year	Promotion	No.
2016	NJPW	2
2017	NJPW	112
2018	NJPW	70
2019	NJPW	2
2020	NJPW	29
2021	NJPW	113
2022	NJPW	111

GRIFF GARRISON
6'3, 202 lbs, Winston-Salem, North Carolina, 2016, 25

Year	Promotion	No.
2016	Indies	
2017	Indies	
2018	Indies	
2019	ROH	6
2020	AEW	23
	ROH	2
2021	AEW	42
2022	AEW	18

GUNTHER
6'4, 297lbs, Wien, Austria, 2005, 35

Year	Promotion	No.
2005	Indies	
2006	Indies	
2007	Indies	
2008	Indies	
2009	Indies	
2010	Indies	
2011	Indies	
2012	Indies	
2013	Indies	
2014	Indies	
2015	Indies	
2016	Indies	
2017	Indies	
2018	Indies	
2019	WWE	25
2020	WWE	8
2021	WWE	10
2022	WWE	85

GURU RAAJ
5'9, 209 lbs, Bandia, Uttarakhand, India, 2020, ?

Year	Promotion	No.
2020	WWE	1
2021	WWE	7
2022	WWE	12

HANGMAN ADAM PAGE
5'10, 214 lbs, Aaron's Creek, Virginia, 2008, 31

Year	Promotion	No.
2008	Indies	
2009	Indies	
2010	Indies	
2011	ROH	1
2012	ROH	3
	EVOLVE	3
2013	ROH	15
2014	ROH	24
2015	ROH	28
2016	ROH	31
	NJPW	30
2017	ROH	42
	NJPW	37
2018	NJPW	54
	ROH	46
2019	AEW	15
2020	AEW	28
2021	AEW	21
2022	AEW	22

HEATH
6'2, 216 lbs, Pineville, West Virginia, 2004, 39

Year	Promotion	No.
2004	Indies	
2005	Indies	
2006	DSW	24
2007	DSW	15
	FCW	14
2008	FCW	57
2009	FCW	53
	WWE	5
2010	WWE	72
	FCW	28
2011	WWE	134
2012	WWE	119
2013	WWE	143
2014	WWE	118
2015	WWE	132
2016	WWE	126
2017	WWE	117
2018	WWE	82
2019	WWE	19
2020	Impact	5
	WWE	3
2021	Impact	4
2022	Impact	26

HIKARU SHIDA
5'5, 125 lbs, Samukawa, Kanagawa, Japan, 2008, 34

Year	Promotion	No.
2008	Indies	
2009	Indies	
2010	Indies	
2011	Indies	
2012	Indies	
2013	Indies	
2014	Indies	
2015	Indies	
2016	Indies	
2017	Indies	
2018	Indies	
2019	AEW	7
2020	AEW	29
2021	AEW	29
2022	AEW	28

HIKULEO
6'8, 280 lbs, ?, 2016, 31

Year	Promotion	No.
2016	NJPW	1
2017	NJPW	45
2018	NJPW	16
	ROH	2
2019	NJPW	37
	ROH	7
2020	NJPW	8
2021	NJPW	21
	Impact	8
	AEW	2
2022	NJPW	47
	Impact	3
	AEW	1

HIROMU TAKAHASHI
5'7, 181lbs, Tokyo, Japan, 2010, 33

Year	Promotion	No.
2010	NJPW	38
2011	NJPW	88
2012	NJPW	71
2013	NJPW	40
2014	CMLL	69
2015	CMLL	68
2016	ROH	26
	CMLL	10
	NJPW	6
2017	NJPW	152
2018	NJPW	84
2019	NJPW	3
2020	NJPW	73
2021	NJPW	59
2022	NJPW	121

HIROOKI GOTO
5'11, 227 lbs, Kuwana, Mie, Japan, 2003, 43

Year	Promotion	No.
2003	NJPW	52
2004	NJPW	107
2005	NJPW	115
2006	NJPW	59
	CMLL	9
	TNA	3
2007	NJPW	35
	CMLL	21
2008	NJPW	106
2009	NJPW	110
2010	NJPW	123
2011	NJPW	106
	CMLL	13
2012	NJPW	114
2013	NJPW	64
2014	NJPW	101
2015	NJPW	137
	ROH	2
2016	NJPW	135
	ROH	3
2017	NJPW	132
	ROH	6
2018	NJPW	112
2019	NJPW	116
	ROH	6
2020	NJPW	75
2021	NJPW	119
2022	NJPW	111
	AEW	2

HIROSHI TANAHASHI
5'9, 227lbs, Ogaki, Japan, 1999, 46

Year	Promotion	No.
1999	NJPW	31
2000	NJPW	80
2001	NJPW	86
2002	NJPW	110
2003	NJPW	114
2004	NJPW	141
2005	NJPW	98
	CMLL	11
2006	NJPW	128
2007	NJPW	86
2008	NJPW	59
	TNA	8
	AJPW	7
2009	NJPW	93
2010	NJPW	119
	CMLL	7
2011	NJPW	107
	CMLL	11
2012	NJPW	111
	CMLL	8
2013	NJPW	108
	CMLL	9
2014	NJPW	110
2015	NJPW	144
2016	NJPW	125
	ROH	11
2017	NJPW	134
2018	NJPW	108
2019	NJPW	117
2020	NJPW	87
2021	NJPW	121
2022	NJPW	141

HOOK
5'10, 201 lbs, Massapequa, New York, 2021, 23

Year	Promotion	No.
2021	AEW	2
2022	AEW	16

HUMBERTO
6'1, 198lbs, Nuevo Leon, Mexico, 2007, 27

Year	Promotion	No.
2007	Indies	
2008	Indies	
2012	Indies	
2013	Indies	
2014	Indies	
2015	Indies	
2016	Indies	
2017	Indies	
2018	WWE	26
2019	WWE	72
2020	WWE	44
2021	WWE	39
2022	WWE	42

IKEMEN JIRO
5'11, 176 lbs, Adachi, Tokyo, Japan, 2011, 30

Year	Promotion	No.
2011	Indies	
2012	Indies	
2013	Indies	
2014	Indies	
2015	Indies	
2016	Indies	
2017	Indies	
2018	Indies	
2019	AJPW	8
2020	AJPW	16
2021	WWE	21
2022	WWE	30

ILJA DRAGUNOV
5'10, 187 lbs, Orenburg, Russia, 2012, 29

Year	Promotion	#
2012	Indies	
2013	Indies	
2014	Indies	
2015	Indies	
2016	Indies	
2017	Indies	
2018	Indies	
2019	WWE	13
2020	WWE	11
2021	WWE	13
2022	WWE	8

INDI HARTWELL
5'9, 139 lbs, Melbourne, Australia, 2016, 26

Year	Promotion	#
2016	Indies	
2017	Indies	
2018	Indies	
2019	WWE	3
2020	WWE	20
2021	WWE	18
2022	WWE	38

ISIAH KASSIDY
6'0, 215 lbs, New York City, New York, 2015, 25

Year	Promotion	#
2015	Indies	
2016	Indies	
2017	Indies	
2018	Indies	
2019	AEW	13
2020	AEW	30
2021	AEW	44
2022	AEW	41

ISLA DAWN
5'7, 150 lbs, Glasgow, Scotland, 2013, 28

Year	Promotion	#
2013	Indies	
2014	Indies	
2015	Indies	
2016	Stardom	6
2017	WWE	1
2018	WWE	10
2019	WWE	11
2020	WWE	8
2021	WWE	11
2022	WWE	12

IVAR
6'2, 305lbs, Lynn, Massachusetts, 2001, 38

Year	Promotion	#
2001	Indies	
2002	Indies	
2003	Indies	
2004	Indies	
2005	Indies	
2006	Indies	
2007	Indies	
2008	Indies	
2009	Indies	
2010	Indies	
2011	Indies	
2012	Indies	
2013	Indies	
2014	ROH	24
2015	ROH	44
2016	ROH	34
	NJPW	21
2017	NJPW	72
	ROH	28
2018	WWE	59
2019	WWE	111
2020	WWE	32
2021	WWE	30
2022	WWE	42

IVY NILE
5'2, 125 lbs, Knoxville, Tennessee, 2020, 30

Year	Promotion	#
2020	WWE	4
2021	WWE	5
2022	WWE	41

IYO SKY
5'1, 119lbs, Kanagawa, Japan, 2007, 32

Year	Promotion	#
2007	Indies	
2008	WAVE	12
2009	WAVE	22
	NEO	11
	Ice Ribbon	10
2010	WAVE	25
2011	WAVE	23
	Stardom	12
2012	Stardom	32
2013	Stardom	44
2014	Stardom	46
2015	Stardom	65
2016	Stardom	65
2017	Stardom	68
2018	Stardom	57
	WWE	24
2019	WWE	68
2020	WWE	21
2021	WWE	16
2022	WWE	42

JACK EVANS
5'8, 165 lbs, Fountain Valley, California, 2000, 40

Year	Promotion	#
2000	Indies	
2001	Indies	
2002	Indies	
2003	Indies	
2004	ROH	19
2005	ROH	20
	Dragon Gate	5
2006	Dragon Gate	97
	ROH	15
2007	Dragon Gate	38
	ROH	29
2008	AAA	31
	ROH	9
	Dragon Gate	7
2009	AAA	42
2010	AAA	28
	NOAH	10
2011	AAA	29
	NOAH	11
2012	AAA	23
2013	AAA	24
2014	AAA	23
2015	AAA	29
2016	AAA	8
2017	Indies	
2018	AAA	12
2019	AEW	11
	AAA	6
2020	AEW	19
2021	AEW	32
2022	AAA	3
	AEW	2

JACK STARZ
5'6, 172 lbs, Leicester, Leicestershire, England, 2010, ?

Year	Promotion	#
2010	Indies	
2012	Indies	
2013	Indies	
2014	Indies	
2015	Indies	
2016	Indies	
2017	WWE	1
2018	WWE	5
2019	WWE	9
2020	WWE	4
2021	WWE	11
2022	WWE	6

JACY JAYNE
5'6, 114 lbs, Tampa, Florida, 2018, 26

Year	Promotion	#
2018	Indies	
2019	Indies	
2020	EVOLVE	4
	WWE	1
2021	WWE	10
2022	WWE	30

JADE CARGILL
5'10, 160 lbs, Vero Beach, Florida, 2021, 30

Year	Promotion	#
2021	AEW	23
2022	AEW	24

JAGGER REID
5'11, 178 lbs, Blackpool, Lancashire, England, 2010, 29

Year	Promotion	#
2010	Indies	
2011	Indies	
2012	Indies	
2013	Indies	
2014	Indies	
2015	Indies	
2016	Indies	
2017	WWE	11
2018	WWE	15
2019	WWE	19
2020	WWE	10
2021	WWE	18
2022	WWE	28

JAKARA JACKSON
5'5, 124 lbs, Albuquerque, New Mexico, 2022, 27

Year	Promotion	#
2022	WWE	9

JAKE HAGER
6'7, 275lbs, Perry, Oklahoma, 2006, 40

Year	Promotion	#
2006	DSW	11
2007	OVW	40
	FCW	15
2008	WWE	42
	FCW	34
2009	WWE	163
2010	WWE	186
2011	WWE	173
2012	WWE	137
2013	WWE	159
2014	WWE	171
2015	WWE	126
2016	WWE	141
2017	WWE	9
2018	Indies	
2019	Indies	
2020	AEW	18
2021	AEW	12
2022	AEW	12

JAKE SOMETHING
6'2, 235 lbs, Midland, Michigan, 2010, 33

Year	Promotion	#
2010	Indies	
2011	Indies	
2012	Indies	
2013	Indies	
2014	Indies	
2015	Indies	
2016	Indies	
2017	Impact	3
2018	Impact	5
2019	Impact	17
2020	Impact	19
2021	Impact	33
2022	Impact	9
	NJPW	4
	AEW	3

JAMES STORM
6'0, 230 lbs, Franklin, Tennessee, 1997, 45

Year	Promotion	#
1997	Indies	
1998	Indies	
1999	Indies	
2000	WCW	5
2001	Indies	
2002	TNA	23
2003	TNA	45
2004	TNA	50
2005	TNA	34
2006	TNA	50
	WWC	6
2007	TNA	53
2008	TNA	97
2009	TNA	101
2010	TNA	100
2011	TNA	99
2012	TNA	112
2013	TNA	92
2014	TNA	64
2015	TNA	27
	WWE	2
2016	TNA	30
2017	Impact	26
2018	Indies	
2019	NWA	8
2020	NWA	4
	Impact	2
2021	Impact	10
	NWA	3
2022	Impact	3

JAMIE HAYTER
5'5, 159 lbs, Southampton, England, 2015, 27

Year	Promotion	#
2015	Indies	
2016	Indies	
2017	Indies	
2018	Stardom	12
2019	Stardom	59
	AEW	2
2020	Stardom	16
2021	AEW	16
2022	AEW	24

JAVIER BERNAL
6'0, 191 lbs, Ave Maria, Florida, 2022, ?

Year	Promotion	#
2022	WWE	34

JAY BRISCOE
5'11, 195 lbs, Laurel, Delaware, 2000, 38

Year	Promotion	#
2000	Indies	
2001	Indies	
2002	ROH	12
	TNA	3
2003	ROH	13
2004	ROH	16
2005	Indies	
2006	ROH	35
2007	ROH	43
	NOAH	22
2008	ROH	39
	NOAH	20
2009	ROH	45
2010	ROH	40
2011	ROH	30
2012	ROH	33
2013	ROH	20
2014	ROH	44
	NJPW	2
2015	ROH	47
	NJPW	3
2016	ROH	48
	NJPW	18
2017	ROH	36
	NJPW	10
2018	ROH	40
	NJPW	6

	CMLL	3
	WWC	2
2019	ROH	40
	CMLL	6
	NJPW	6
	NWA	2
2020	ROH	10
2021	ROH	17
2022	Impact	8
	NWA	6
	ROH	3

JAY LETHAL
5'10, 190 lbs, Elizabeth, New Jersey, 2001, 37

2001	Indies	
2002	ROH	1
2003	ROH	15
2004	ROH	21
2005	ROH	29
	TNA	1
2006	TNA	54
	ROH	7
2007	TNA	52
2008	TNA	65
2009	TNA	71
2010	TNA	70
2011	ROH	12
	TNA	9
2012	ROH	34
2013	ROH	36
2014	ROH	38
	NJPW	2
2015	ROH	47
	NJPW	3
2016	ROH	47
	NJPW	13
2017	ROH	42
	NJPW	10
2018	ROH	45
	NJPW	9
2019	ROH	38
	NJPW	8
	CMLL	3
2020	ROH	10
2021	ROH	19
	AEW	4
2022	AEW	36
	ROH	2
	NJPW	2

JAY WHITE
6'1, 198lbs, Auckland, New Zealand, 2013, 30

2013	Indies	
2014	Indies	
2015	NJPW	103
2016	NJPW	60
	ROH	23
2017	ROH	31
	NJPW	8
2018	NJPW	105
2019	NJPW	113
2020	NJPW	49
2021	NJPW	44
2022	NJPW	46
	Impact	14

JD DRAKE
6'2, 302 lbs, Shelby, North Carolina, 2002, 39

2013	Indies	
2014	Indies	
2015	Indies	
2016	Indies	
2017	EVOLVE	8
2018	EVOLVE	16
2019	EVOLVE	23
2020	EVOLVE	2
2021	AEW	29
2022	AEW	28

JD MCDONAGH
5'10, 180 lbs, Bray, Wicklow, Ireland, 2006, 32

2006	Indies	
2007	Indies	
2008	Indies	
2009	Indies	
2010	Indies	
2011	Indies	
2012	Indies	
2013	Indies	
2014	Indies	
2015	Indies	
2016	Indies	
2017	WWE	4
2018	WWE	13
2019	WWE	21
2020	WWE	14
2021	WWE	13
2022	WWE	25

JEFF COBB
5'10, 263 lbs, Honolulu, Hawaii, 2009, 40

2009	Indies	
2010	Indies	
2011	Indies	
2012	Indies	
2013	Indies	
2014	Indies	
2015	Indies	
2016	Indies	
2017	NJPW	19
	EVOLVE	6
2018	NJPW	32
	ROH	11
2019	NJPW	53
	ROH	38
2020	NJPW	44
	ROH	5
2021	NJPW	87
2022	NJPW	86
	AEW	2
	ROH	1

JEFF HARDY
6'1, 225lbs, Cameron, North Carolina, 1993, 45

1993	Indies	
1994	WWF	5
1995	WWF	8
1996	WWF	6
1997	WWF	8
1998	WWF	32
1999	WWF	133
2000	WWF	180
2001	WWF	162
2002	WWF	124
	ROH	1
2003	WWE	23
2004	TNA	20
2005	TNA	21
2006	WWE	62
	TNA	7
2007	WWE	148
2008	WWE	137
2009	WWE	107
2010	TNA	70
2011	TNA	56
2012	TNA	115
2013	TNA	68
2014	TNA	30
2015	TNA	9
2016	TNA	35
2017	WWE	58
	TNA	8
	ROH	4
2018	WWE	122
2019	WWE	42
2020	WWE	29
2021	WWE	49
2022	AEW	9

JEFF JARRETT
6'0, 230lbs, Hendersonville, Tennessee, 1986, 55

1986	CWA	118
1987	CWA	146
1988	CWA	145
1989	USWA	145
	WCCW	57
1990	USWA	109
	WCCW	35
1991	USWA	94
1992	USWA	67
	WWF	6
1993	USWA	125
	WWF	17
1994	WWF	201
	USWA	2
1995	WWF	105
	USWA	9
1996	USWA	25
	WCW	24
	WWF	19
1997	WCW	102
	WWF	9
1998	WWF	158
1999	WWF	149
	WCW	21
2000	WCW	118
2001	WCW	19
	WWA	16
2002	TNA	20
	WWA	6
2003	TNA	27
2004	TNA	29
2005	TNA	17
2006	TNA	29
2007	TNA	3
2008	TNA	1
2009	TNA	39
2010	TNA	91
2011	TNA	94
	AAA	5
2012	AAA	4
	RKK	4
2013	AAA	2
2014	AAA	5
2015	TNA	2
	GFW	2
	NJPW	1
2016	GFW	15
2017	GFW	1
	AAA	1
2018	AAA	7
2019	AAA	2
	WWE	2
2022	AEW	5
	JCP	1

JESSICKA
6'0, 250 lbs, Canton, Ohio, 2004, 36

2004	Indies	
2005	Indies	
2006	Indies	
2007	Indies	
2008	Indies	
2009	Indies	
2010	Indies	
2011	Indies	
2012	Indies	
2013	Indies	
2014	TNA	7
2015	TNA	9
2016	Indies	
2017	Stardom	13
2018	Indies	
2019	Impact	27
2020	Impact	20
2021	Impact	31
2022	Impact	17

JESSIE MCKAY
5'8, 132 lbs, Sydney, Australia, 2007, 33

2007	Indies	
2008	Indies	
2009	Indies	
2010	Indies	
2011	Indies	
2012	Indies	
2013	Indies	
2014	Indies	
2015	WWE	39
2016	WWE	79
2017	WWE	58
2018	WWE	62
2019	WWE	65
2020	WWE	24
2021	Impact	5
	WWE	2
2022	Impact	6

JEY USO
6'1, 228lbs, San Francisco, California, 2007, 38

2010	WWE	57
	FCW	42
2011	WWE	78
2012	WWE	91
2013	WWE	145
2014	WWE	188
2015	WWE	65
2016	WWE	168
2017	WWE	144
2018	WWE	121
2019	WWE	66
2020	WWE	30
2021	WWE	79
2022	WWE	135

JIMMY USO
6'2, 251lbs, San Francisco, California, 2007, 38

2009	FCW	10
2010	WWE	56
	FCW	45
2011	WWE	78
2012	WWE	92
2013	WWE	145
2014	WWE	189
2015	WWE	120
2016	WWE	152
2017	WWE	145
2018	WWE	129
2019	WWE	64
2020	WWE	15
2021	WWE	70
2022	WWE	135

JINDER MAHAL
6'5, 220lbs, Calgary, Canada, 2003, 36

2003	Indies	
2004	Indies	
2005	Stampede	36
2006	Stampede	16
2007	Stampede	14
2008	Indies	
2009	Indies	
2010	FCW	24
2011	WWE	74
	FCW	24
2012	WWE	135
2013	WWE	116
2014	WWE	51
2015	Indies	
2016	WWE	41
2017	WWE	179
2018	WWE	157
2019	WWE	41
2020	WWE	3
2021	WWE	38
2022	WWE	33

JINNY
5'6, 128lbs, London, England, 2014, 33

2014	Indies	
2015	Indies	
2015	Indies	
2016	Indies	
2017	WWE	2
2018	WWE	7
2019	WWE	12
2020	WWE	4
2021	WWE	12
2022	WWE	1

JOAQUIN WILDE
5'8, 170 lbs, Los Angeles, California, 2004, 36

2004	Indies	
2005	Indies	
2006	Indies	
2007	Indies	
2008	Indies	
2009	Indies	
2010	Indies	
2011	TNA	9
2012	TNA	68
2013	TNA	23
2014	TNA	58
2015	TNA	32
2016	TNA	36
2017	Impact	11
	EVOLVE	4
2018	EVOLVE	9
	Impact	9
2019	WWE	9
	EVOLVE	2
2020	WWE	26
	EVOLVE	1
2021	WWE	17
2022	WWE	27

JOE COFFEY
5'11, 242 lbs, Glasgow, Scotland, 2009, 34

2009	Indies	
2010	Indies	
2011	Indies	
2012	Indies	
2013	Indies	
2014	Indies	
2015	Indies	
2016	Indies	
2017	Indies	
2018	WWE	16
2019	WWE	19
2020	WWE	9
2021	WWE	13
2022	WWE	9

JOE DOERING
6'5, 297 lbs, Windsor, Canada, 2004, 40

2004	Indies	
2005	Indies	
2006	WWC	12
2007	AJPW	50
2008	AJPW	81
2009	AJPW	76
2010	FCW	19
	AJPW	10
2011	AJPW	83
2012	AJPW	69
2013	AJPW	104
2014	AJPW	71
2015	AJPW	55
2016	Indies	
2017	AJPW	82
2018	AJPW	97
2019	AJPW	63
2020	Indies	
2021	Impact	20
2022	Impact	14

JOE HENDRY
6'2, 225lbs, Edinburgh, Scotland, 2013, 34

2013	Indies	
2014	Indies	
2015	Indies	
2016	Indies	
2017	Indies	
2018	Impact	7
	ROH	4
2019	ROH	13
2020	ROH	4
2021	ROH	1
2022	Impact	6
	ROH	1

JOHN CENA
6'1, 240lbs, West Newbury, Massachusetts, 1999, 45

1999	UPW	3
2000	UPW	25
2001	OVW	13
2002	WWE	91
	OVW	23
2003	WWE	135
2004	WWE	113
2005	WWE	165
2006	WWE	176
2007	WWE	128
2008	WWE	89
2009	WWE	177
2010	WWE	182
2011	WWE	204
2012	WWE	176
2013	WWE	134
2014	WWE	164
2015	WWE	135
2016	WWE	45
2017	WWE	69
2018	WWE	29
2019	WWE	7
2020	WWE	1
2021	WWE	15
2022	WWE	1

JOHN SILVER
5'4, 178lbs, Wantagh, New York, 2007, 32

2007	Indies	
2008	Indies	
2009	Indies	
2010	Indies	
2011	Indies	
2012	Indies	
2013	Indies	
2014	Indies	
2015	Indies	
2016	Indies	
2017	Indies	
2018	Indies	
2019	EVOLVE	8
	AEW	3
2020	AEW	26
2021	AEW	36
2022	AEW	52

JOHNNY GARGANO
5'10, 198lbs, Lakewood, Ohio, 2005, 35

2005	Indies	
2006	Indies	
2007	Indies	
2008	Indies	
2009	DGUSA	3
2010	DGUSA	6
	EVOLVE	6
2011	DGUSA	15
	Dragon Gate	9
	EVOLVE	3
2012	Dragon Gate	12
	EVOLVE	9
	DGUSA	8

2013	DGUSA	10
	EVOLVE	7
2014	DGUSA	4
2015	EVOLVE	13
	WWE	6
2016	WWE	47
	EVOLVE	16
2017	WWE	78
2018	WWE	65
2019	WWE	31
2020	WWE	28
2021	WWE	19
2022	WWE	19

JOHNNY SWINGER
5'10, 216lbs, Niagara Falls, New York, 1993, 47

1993	Indies	
1994	Indies	
1995	WWF	3
	WCW	3
1996	WCW	1
1997	WCW	31
1998	WCW	27
1999	WCW	21
2000	ECW	50
2001	XWF	4
	WWF	2
	WCW	2
	ECW	1
2002	WWA	9
2003	TNA	23
2004	TNA	27
2005	DSW	10
	WWE	10
2006	DSW	13
	WWE	2
2007	Indies	
2008	Indies	
2009	Indies	
2010	Indies	
2011	Indies	
2012	Indies	
2013	TNA	2
2014	Indies	
2015	Indies	
2016	Indies	
2017	Indies	
2018	Impact	1
2019	Impact	8
2020	Impact	25
2021	Impact	15
2022	Impact	20

JON MOXLEY
6'4, 225lbs, Cincinnati, Ohio, 2004, 37

2004	Indies	
2005	Indies	
2006	Indies	
2007	Indies	
2008	Indies	
2009	ROH	2
2010	DGUSA	11
	EVOLVE	4
2011	FCW	35
	DGUSA	6
	WWE	5
2012	WWE	53
	FCW	22
2013	WWE	218
2014	WWE	168
2015	WWE	218
2016	WWE	204
2017	WWE	171
2018	WWE	45
2019	WWE	49
	NJPW	20
	AEW	9
2020	AEW	25
	NJPW	5
2021	AEW	34

	NJPW	4
2022	AEW	47
	NJPW	5

JONAH
6'0, 352lbs, Adelaide, Australia, 2007, 34

2007	Indies	
2008	Indies	
2009	Indies	
2010	Indies	
2011	Indies	
2012	Indies	
2013	NOAH	21
2014	NOAH	22
2015	NOAH	21
2016	Indies	
2017	Indies	
2018	NJPW	4
2019	WWE	58
2020	WWE	32
2021	WWE	16
	NJPW	2
2022	NJPW	44
	Impact	14

JONATHAN GRESHAM
5'4, 180lbs, Atlanta, Georgia, 2005, 34

2005	Indies	
2006	Indies	
2007	Indies	
2008	Indies	
2009	Indies	
2010	Indies	
2011	Indies	
2012	Indies	
2013	Indies	
2014	Indies	
2015	ROH	5
2016	ROH	10
2017	ROH	27
2018	ROH	31
2019	ROH	32
	NJPW	25
2020	ROH	11
2021	ROH	23
2022	Impact	7
	ROH	4
	AEW	4

JORDYNNE GRACE
5'1, 150lbs, St. Louis, Missouri, 2011, 26

2011	Indies	
2012	Indies	
2013	Indies	
2014	Indies	
2015	Indies	
2016	Indies	
2017	Indies	
2018	Impact	3
2019	Impact	40
2020	Impact	22
2021	Impact	32
2022	Impact	28

JOSH ALEXANDER
6'1, 240lbs, Bolton, Canada, 2005, 35

2005	Indies	
2006	Indies	
2007	Indies	
2008	Indies	
2009	Indies	
2010	Indies	
2011	Indies	
2012	Indies	
2013	Indies	
2014	Indies	
2015	Indies	
2016	Indies	

2017	Indies	
2018	Impact	5
2019	Impact	31
2020	Impact	28
2021	Impact	32
	NJPW	4
2022	Impact	30
	NJPW	2

JOSH BRIGGS
6'8, 268lbs, Bullhead City, Arizona, 2016, 29

2016	Indies	
2017	Indies	
2018	EVOLVE	15
2019	EVOLVE	24
2020	EVOLVE	4
2021	WWE	13
2022	WWE	38

JOSH MORRELL
??, ???lbs, Egremont, England, 2014, 24

2016	Indies	
2017	Indies	
2018	WWE	2
2019	WWE	1
2020	WWE	3
2021	WWE	7
2022	WWE	7

JOSH WOODS
6'0, 220lbs, Dallas, Texas, 2015, 33

2015	WWE	10
2016	WWE	24
2017	ROH	19
2018	ROH	12
2019	ROH	16
2020	ROH	11
2021	ROH	13
	AEW	1
2022	AEW	24
	ROH	1

JR KRATOS
6'1, 286lbs, Pacifica, California, 2012, 40

2012	Indies	
2013	Indies	
2014	Indies	
2015	GFW	2
2016	Indies	
2017	Indies	
2018	Indies	
2019	Indies	
2020	AJPW	11
	NJPW	5
2021	NJPW	21
	NWA	17
2022	NJPW	14
	NWA	7

JUICE ROBINSON
6'3, 220lbs, Joliet, Illinois, 2008, 33

2008	Indies	
2009	Indies	
2010	Indies	
2011	FCW	29
2012	FCW	34
	WWE	17
2013	WWE	40
2014	WWE	68
2015	NJPW	47
	WWE	18
2016	NJPW	140
2017	NJPW	141
	CMLL	11
2018	NJPW	123
2019	NJPW	105
	ROH	12

2020	NJPW	41
2021	NJPW	22
	Impact	22
2022	NJPW	34
	Impact	5
	AEW	2
	ROH	1

JULIA HART
5'7, 149lbs, Cambridge, Minnesota, 2019, 21

2019	Indies	
2020	Indies	
2021	AEW	19
2022	AEW	23

JULIUS CREED
6'3, 229lbs, Lexington, Ohio, 2021, 28

2021	WWE	11
2022	WWE	34

JUN AKIYAMA
6'2, 242lbs, Osaka, Japan, 1992, 53

1992	AJPW	36
1993	AJPW	128
1994	AJPW	132
1995	AJPW	139
1996	AJPW	129
1997	AJPW	139
1998	AJPW	123
1999	AJPW	123
2000	AJPW	65
	NOAH	43
2001	NOAH	109
2002	NOAH	105
2003	NOAH	109
	NJPW	8
2004	NOAH	106
2005	NOAH	108
2006	NOAH	101
2007	NOAH	100
2008	NOAH	99
2009	NOAH	73
2010	NOAH	72
2011	NOAH	114
	AJPW	11
2012	NOAH	111
	AJPW	8
2013	AJPW	104
2014	AJPW	102
2015	AJPW	106
2016	AJPW	87
2017	AJPW	125
2018	AJPW	114
2019	AJPW	127
2020	DDT	37
2021	DDT	67
2022	DDT	75
	AEW	2

JUNGLE BOY
5'10, 167lbs, Los Angeles, California, 2015, 25

2015	Indies	
2016	Indies	
2017	Indies	
2018	Indies	
2019	AEW	11
2020	AEW	48
2021	AEW	54
2022	AEW	23

KARL ANDERSON
6'0, 213lbs, Detroit, Michigan, 2002, 43

2002	Indies	
2003	Indies	
2004	Indies	
2005	Indies	
2006	Indies	

2007	ROH	2
2008	NJPW	72
2009	NJPW	101
2010	NJPW	98
2011	NJPW	83
2012	NJPW	94
2013	NJPW	93
	ROH	4
2014	NJPW	100
2015	NJPW	109
	GFW	7
2016	WWE	122
	NJPW	13
2017	WWE	138
2018	WWE	122
2019	WWE	106
2020	WWE	15
	Impact	11
2021	Impact	29
	AEW	12
	NJPW	4
2022	Impact	22
	WWE	17
	NJPW	12

KARL FREDERICKS
6'1, 222lbs, Reno, Nevada, 2015, 32

2015	Indies	
2016	Indies	
2017	Indies	
2018	NJPW	2
2019	NJPW	66
	ROH	8
2020	NJPW	18
2021	NJPW	21
2022	NJPW	8
	AEW	1

KARRION KROSS
6'4, 264lbs, New York City, New York, 2014, 37

2014	Indies	
2015	GFW	3
	TNA	3
2016	LU	12
2017	AAA	8
2018	AAA	12
	Impact	11
	LU	2
2019	AAA	14
	Impact	14
2020	WWE	8
	MLW	2
2021	WWE	32
2022	WWE	28
	MLW	3
	NJPW	2
	JCP	1

KATANA CHANCE
5'0, 100lbs, Glen Ridge, New Jersey, 2018, 32

2018	WWE	23
2019	WWE	31
2020	WWE	18
2021	WWE	18
2022	WWE	24

KATSUYORI SHIBATA
6'0, 209lbs, Kuwana, Japan, 1999, 43

1999	NJPW	33
2000	NJPW	77
2001	NJPW	92
2002	NJPW	48
2003	NJPW	66
2004	NJPW	95
2005	Indies	
2006	Indies	
2011	Indies	
2012	NJPW	6

2013	NJPW	20
2014	NJPW	62
2015	NJPW	123
2016	NJPW	123
	ROH	5
2017	NJPW	37
2021	NJPW	1
2022	AEW	1
	NJPW	1

KAUN
6'0, 235lbs, Minneapolis, Minnesota, 2017, ??

2017	Indies	
2018	ROH	1
2019	ROH	10
2020	ROH	4
2021	ROH	16
	AEW	2
2022	AEW	8
	ROH	3

KAYDEN CARTER
5'2, 120lbs, Winter Park, Florida, 2016, 34

2016	Indies	
2017	Indies	
2018	WWE	17
2019	WWE	59
2020	WWE	35
2021	WWE	15
2022	WWE	28

KAZUCHIKA OKADA
6'3, 235lbs, Aichi, Japan, 2004, 35

2004	Indies	
2005	Indies	
2006	Indies	
2007	NJPW	1
2008	NJPW	84
2009	NJPW	107
2010	TNA	14
	NJPW	6
2011	NJPW	4
	TNA	4
2012	NJPW	111
2013	NJPW	110
2014	NJPW	111
2015	NJPW	141
2016	NJPW	143
	ROH	5
2017	NJPW	139
2018	NJPW	135
2019	NJPW	126
2020	NJPW	76
2021	NJPW	101
2022	NJPW	106
	AEW	1

KEITH LEE
6'2, 332lbs, Wichita Falls, Texas, 2005, 38

2005	Indies	
2006	Indies	
2007	Indies	
2008	Indies	
2009	Indies	
2010	Indies	
2011	Indies	
2012	Indies	
2013	Indies	
2014	Indies	
2015	ROH	4
2016	ROH	18
2017	EVOLVE	22
2018	WWE	40
	EVOLVE	8
2019	WWE	79
2020	WWE	51
2021	WWE	27
2022	AEW	31

KENNY KING
6'0, 229lbs, Orlando, Florida, 2002, 41

Year	Promotion	Rank
2002	Indies	
2003	Indies	
2004	Indies	
2005	TNA	3
2006	TNA	6
2007	ROH	3
2008	ROH	12
2009	ROH	43
2010	ROH	40
2011	ROH	27
2012	ROH	18
	TNA	11
2013	TNA	32
2014	TNA	29
2015	TNA	32
	ROH	16
2016	ROH	37
2017	ROH	30
2018	ROH	32
2019	ROH	28
	CMLL	5
2020	ROH	8
2021	ROH	20
2022	Impact	24
	CMLL	10

KENNY OMEGA
6'0, 218lbs, Transcona, Canada, 2000, 39

Year	Promotion	Rank
2000	Indies	
2001	Indies	
2002	Indies	
2003	Indies	
2004	Indies	
2005	DSW	1
2006	DSW	14
2007	Indies	
2008	ROH	8
	DDT	7
2009	ROH	24
	DDT	14
2010	DDT	34
	NJPW	15
	ROH	6
2011	DDT	27
	NJPW	18
	AJPW	11
2012	DDT	38
	AJPW	11
2013	DDT	45
	NJPW	10
2014	DDT	49
	NJPW	8
2015	NJPW	67
2016	NJPW	117
	ROH	6
2017	NJPW	73
	ROH	10
2018	NJPW	54
	ROH	4
2019	AEW	16
	AAA	3
	NJPW	1
2020	AEW	32
2021	AEW	23
	Impact	8
2022	AEW	10

KENNY WILLIAMS
5'9, 180lbs, Glasgow, Scotland, 2012, 29

Year	Promotion	Rank
2013	Indies	
2014	Indies	
2015	Indies	
2016	Indies	
2017	Indies	
2018	WWE	13
2019	WWE	14
2020	WWE	7
2021	WWE	13
2022	WWE	9

KENTA
5'9, 187lbs, Saitama, Japan, 2000, 41

Year	Promotion	Rank
2000	NOAH	31
	AJPW	12
2001	NOAH	57
2002	NOAH	97
2003	NOAH	105
2004	NOAH	104
2005	NOAH	110
2006	NOAH	102
	ROH	10
2007	NOAH	108
	ROH	6
2008	NOAH	117
2009	NOAH	79
	ROH	10
2010	NOAH	61
2011	NOAH	120
2012	NOAH	50
2013	NOAH	108
2014	NOAH	37
	WWE	25
2015	WWE	39
2016	WWE	29
2017	WWE	73
2018	WWE	31
2019	NJPW	64
	WWE	4
2020	NJPW	49
2021	NJPW	61
2022	NJPW	59

KEVIN OWENS
5'10, 266lbs, Quebec, Canada, 2000, 38

Year	Promotion	Rank
2000	Indies	
2001	Indies	
2002	Indies	
2003	Indies	
2004	Indies	
2005	Indies	
2006	Dragon Gate	26
2007	ROH	23
2008	ROH	37
2009	ROH	46
2010	ROH	38
2011	Indies	
2012	ROH	28
2013	ROH	31
2014	ROH	19
2015	WWE	152
2016	WWE	191
2017	WWE	155
2018	WWE	108
2019	WWE	78
2020	WWE	46
2021	WWE	55
2022	WWE	75

KIANA JAMES
5'10, 154lbs, Sioux City, Iowa, 2021, 25

Year	Promotion	Rank
2021	AEW	4
2022	WWE	38

KIERA HOGAN
4'11, 114lbs, Decatur, Georgia, 2015, 28

Year	Promotion	Rank
2015	Indies	
2016	Indies	
2017	Indies	
2018	Impact	21
2019	Impact	22
2020	Impact	22
2021	Impact	20
	AEW	10
	NWA	8
2022	AEW	19

KILLER KELLY
5'5, 128lbs, Lisbon, Portugal, 2016, 30

Year	Promotion	Rank
2016	Indies	
2017	Indies	
2018	WWE	11
2019	WWE	7
2020	Impact	2
2021	Indies	
2022	Impact	7

KIP SABIAN
5'11, 180lbs, Great Yarmouth, England, 2010, 30

Year	Promotion	Rank
2010	Indies	
2011	Indies	
2012	Indies	
2013	Indies	
2014	Indies	
2015	Indies	
2016	Indies	
2017	Indies	
2018	ROH	3
2019	AEW	8
2020	AEW	30
2021	AEW	6
2022	AEW	16

KIT WILSON
5'11, 175lbs, London, England, 2014, 28

Year	Promotion	Rank
2014	Indies	
2015	Indies	
2016	Indies	
2017	Indies	
2018	Indies	
2019	WWE	5
2020	WWE	8
2021	WWE	9
2022	WWE	30

KOFI KINGSTON
6'0, 218lbs, Kumasi, Ghana, 2006, 41

Year	Promotion	Rank
2006	Indies	
2007	FCW	16
	WWE	11
2008	WWE	149
2009	WWE	185
2010	WWE	189
2011	WWE	194
2012	WWE	200
2013	WWE	157
2014	WWE	147
2015	WWE	178
2016	WWE	135
2017	WWE	112
2018	WWE	124
2019	WWE	145
2020	WWE	46
2021	WWE	57
2022	WWE	90

KONOSUKE TAKESHITA
6'2, 231lbs, Osaka, Japan, 2012, 27

Year	Promotion	Rank
2012	DDT	12
2013	DDT	29
2014	DDT	71
2015	DDT	89
2016	DDT	106
2017	DDT	108
2018	DDT	105
2019	DDT	114
2020	DDT	83
2021	DDT	88
	AEW	3
2022	DDT	35
	AEW	25

KRIS STATLANDER
5'8, 143lbs, West Islip, New York, 2016, 27

Year	Promotion	Rank
2016	Indies	
2017	Indies	
2018	Indies	
2019	Indies	
2020	AEW	12
2021	AEW	35
2022	AEW	18

KUSHIDA
5'9, 176lbs, Tokyo, Japan, 2006, 39

Year	Promotion	Rank
2006	HUSTLE	6
2007	HUSTLE	21
	AJPW	16
2008	HUSTLE	24
	AJPW	8
2009	HUSTLE	4
2010	NJPW	32
2011	NJPW	105
2012	NJPW	104
2013	NJPW	100
2014	NJPW	84
2015	NJPW	134
2016	NJPW	117
	ROH	16
	CMLL	10
2017	NJPW	108
	ROH	20
2018	NJPW	114
2019	WWE	49
	NJPW	10
2020	WWE	35
2021	WWE	24
2022	NJPW	30
	WWE	6
	Impact	4

KYLE FLETCHER
6'3, 205lbs, Sydney, Australia, 2014, 24

Year	Promotion	Rank
2014	Indies	
2015	Indies	
2016	Indies	
2017	Indies	
2018	Indies	
2019	ROH	3
2020	Indies	
2021	Indies	
2022	NJPW	29
	Impact	4
	AEW	4

KYLE O'REILLY
5'11, 200lbs, Surrey, Canada, 2005, 35

Year	Promotion	Rank
2005	Indies	
2006	Indies	
2007	Indies	
2008	Indies	
2009	ROH	5
2010	ROH	13
2011	ROH	29
2012	ROH	26
2013	ROH	34
2014	ROH	36
	NJPW	14
2015	NJPW	49
	ROH	45
2016	ROH	37
	NJPW	36
2017	WWE	30
	EVOLVE	4
2018	WWE	94
2019	WWE	57
2020	WWE	22
2021	WWE	21
	AEW	1
2022	AEW	14

LA KNIGHT
6'1, 240lbs, Hagerstown, Maryland, 2002, 40

2002	Indies	
2003	HWA	3
2004	HWA	41
2005	HWA	18
2006	HWA	23
2007	HWA	7
2008	HWA	16
2009	HWA	10
2010	Indies	
2011	Indies	
2012	Indies	
2013	WWE	7
2014	WWE	3
2015	TNA	22
2016	TNA	36
2017	Impact	32
2018	Impact	34
2019	Impact	10
	NWA	7
2020	NWA	4
2021	WWE	21
2022	WWE	14

LACEY EVANS
5'8, 130lbs, Marietta, Georgia, 2014, 32

2016	WWE	11
2017	WWE	66
2018	WWE	67
2019	WWE	113
2020	WWE	36
2021	WWE	7
2022	WWE	14

LADY FROST
??, ??lbs, Pittsburgh, Pennsylvania, 2018, 37

2018	Indies	
2019	ROH	3
2020	AEW	2
2021	NWA	7
	Impact	5
2022	Impact	10
	CMLL	9

LANCE ARCHER
6'8, 270lbs, Hearne, Texas, 2000, 45

2000	Indies	
2001	Indies	
2002	Indies	
2003	TNA	1
2004	TNA	29
2005	TNA	34
2006	TNA	26
2007	TNA	27
2008	TNA	59
2009	FCW	32
	WWE	13
	AJPW	5
	TNA	1
2010	WWE	34
	FCW	31
2011	NJPW	38
2012	NJPW	68
2013	NJPW	46
2014	NJPW	39
2015	NOAH	65
	NJPW	2
2016	NOAH	82
2017	NJPW	44
2018	NJPW	61
2019	NJPW	69
2020	AEW	18
	NJPW	7
2021	AEW	34
2022	NJPW	39
	AEW	23

LASH LEGEND
5'11, 176lbs, Atlanta, Georgia, 2021, 25

| 2021 | WWE | 2 |
| 2022 | WWE | 41 |

LEE JOHNSON
5'10, 180lbs, Gary, Indiana, 2017, 25

2017	Indies	
2018	Indies	
2019	Indies	
2020	AEW	27
2021	AEW	40
2022	AEW	19

LEE MORIARTY
5'11, 185lbs, Pittsburgh, Pennsylvania, 2015, 27

2015	Indies	
2016	Indies	
2017	Indies	
2018	Indies	
2019	Indies	
2020	Indies	
2021	AEW	12
2022	AEW	27
	ROH	1

LEILA GREY
5'3, ??lbs, New York City, New York, 2020, 32

2020	Indies	
2021	AEW	13
2022	AEW	11
	WWE	1

LEON RUFFIN
5'7, 156lbs, Pensacola, Florida, 2017, 26

2017	Indies	
2018	EVOLVE	10
2019	EVOLVE	25
	WWE	1
2020	WWE	17
	EVOLVE	4
2021	WWE	10
2022	AEW	13

LEVA BATES
5'2, 114lbs, Madinsonville, Kentucky, 2007, 39

2007	Indies	
2008	TNA	1
2009	Indies	
2010	Indies	
2011	TNA	1
2012	Indies	
2013	Indies	
2014	WWE	3
2015	WWE	7
2016	Indies	
2017	Indies	
2018	Indies	
2019	AEW	6
2020	AEW	6
2021	AEW	3
2022	AEW	9

LEYLA HIRSCH
4'11, 125lbs, Moscow, Russia, 2017, 26

2017	Indies	
2018	Indies	
2019	Indies	
2020	Stardom	14
	AEW	6
2021	AEW	31
2022	AEW	15

LIV MORGAN
5'4, 125lbs, Paramus, New Jersey, 2015, 28

2015	WWE	22
2016	WWE	84
2017	WWE	85
2018	WWE	110
2019	WWE	44
2020	WWE	41
2021	WWE	39
2022	WWE	113

LOGAN PAUL
6'2, 205lbs, Westlake, Ohio, 2022, 27

| 2022 | WWE | 3 |

LUCHASAURUS
6'5, 275lbs, Los Angeles, California, 2009, 37

2009	Indies	
2010	Indies	
2011	Indies	
2012	WWE	4
2013	WWE	6
2016	LU	4
2017	Indies	
2018	ROH	3
	LU	1
2019	AEW	7
	ROH	3
2020	AEW	42
2021	AEW	36
2022	AEW	20

LUCIEN PRICE
6'3, 245lbs, Beltsville, Maryland, 2022, ??

| 2022 | WWE | 9 |

LUDWIG KAISER
6'2, 220lbs, Pinneberg, Germany, 2008, 32

2008	Indies	
2009	Indies	
2010	Indies	
2011	Indies	
2012	Indies	
2013	Indies	
2014	Indies	
2015	Indies	
2016	Indies	
2017	WWE	23
2018	WWE	67
2019	WWE	58
2020	WWE	18
2021	WWE	13
2022	WWE	41

LUKE GALLOWS
6'8, 304lbs, Cumberland, Maryland, 2003, 39

2003	Indies	
2004	Indies	
2005	DSW	11
	WWE	6
2006	DSW	20
	WWE	4
2007	WWE	48
	OVW	22
	DSW	8
2008	WWE	66
2009	WWE	17
2010	WWE	82
2011	TNA	1
2012	TNA	13
	NOAH	7
2013	TNA	28
	NJPW	14
2014	NJPW	99
2015	NJPW	109
	GFW	11

(TNA continued)

	TNA	1
2016	WWE	113
	NJPW	13
	ROH	3
2017	WWE	120
2018	WWE	111
2019	WWE	104
2020	WWE	18
	Impact	9
2021	Impact	30
	AEW	11
	NJPW	4
2022	Impact	20
	WWE	13
	NJPW	12

LUTHER
6'1, 251lbs, Calgary, Canada, 1988, 54

1988	Indies	
1989	Indies	
1990	Indies	
1991	Indies	
1992	FMW	61
1993	FMW	56
1994	FMW	43
1995	WAR	13
1996	IWA Japan	15
	WAR	12
1997	IWA Japan	5
1998	ECW	2
1999	Indies	
2000	WCW	1
2001	Indies	
2002	Indies	
2003	Indies	
2009	Indies	
2011	Indies	
2016	Indies	
2017	Indies	
2020	AEW	19
2021	AEW	36
2022	AEW	15

LYRA VALKYRIA
5'6, 130lbs, Dublin, Ireland, 2015, 26

2015	Indies	
2016	Indies	
2017	Indies	
2018	Indies	
2019	Indies	
2020	WWE	9
2021	WWE	6
2022	WWE	3

MACE
6'6, 314lbs, North Easton, Massachusetts, 2016, 31

2016	WWE	3
2017	WWE	27
2018	WWE	51
2019	WWE	39
2020	WWE	15
2021	WWE	26
2022	WWE	20

MADCAP MOSS
6'3, 245lbs, Edina, Minnesota, 2014, 33

2014	WWE	2
2015	WWE	57
2016	WWE	70
2017	WWE	75
2018	WWE	28
2019	WWE	75
2020	WWE	13
2021	WWE	19
2022	WWE	64

MADISON RAYNE
5'3, 114lbs, Columbus, Ohio, 2005, 37

Year	Promotion	#
2005	Indies	
2006	Indies	
2007	Indies	
2008	TNA	1
2009	TNA	46
2010	TNA	103
2011	TNA	68
2012	TNA	35
2013	TNA	4
2014	TNA	57
2015	TNA	17
2016	TNA	26
2017	Impact	4
2018	ROH	11
	Impact	8
2019	Impact	32
	ROH	4
2020	Impact	5
2021	Impact	13
2022	AEW	15
	Impact	14

MADMAN FULTON
6'8, 317lbs, Toledo, Ohio, 2009, 32

Year	Promotion	#
2009	Indies	
2010	Indies	
2011	Indies	
2012	WWE	3
2013	WWE	24
2014	WWE	40
2015	WWE	48
2016	WWE	71
2017	WWE	12
2018	MLW	2
2019	Impact	30
2020	Impact	25
2021	Impact	21
2022	Impact	4
	AEW	2

MALAKAI BLACK
6'0, 215lbs, Alkmaar, Netherlands, 2002, 37

Year	Promotion	#
2002	Indies	
2003	Indies	
2004	Indies	
2005	Indies	
2006	Indies	
2007	Indies	
2008	Indies	
2009	Indies	
2010	Indies	
2011	Indies	
2012	Indies	
2013	Indies	
2014	Indies	
2015	Indies	
2016	WWE	5
2017	WWE	97
2018	WWE	73
2019	WWE	91
2020	WWE	44
2021	AEW	10
2022	AEW	17

MALIK BLADE
6'0, 180lbs, Orlando, Florida, 2018, 24

Year	Promotion	#
2018	Indies	
2019	Indies	
2020	Indies	
2021	WWE	13
2022	WWE	41

MANDY ROSE
5'4, 120lbs, Westchester County, New York, 2015, 32

Year	Promotion	#
2015	WWE	1
2016	WWE	68
2017	WWE	77
2018	WWE	86
2019	WWE	97
2020	WWE	17
2021	WWE	24
2022	WWE	32

MANSOOR
6'0, 190lbs, Riad, Saudi Arabia, 2015, 27

Year	Promotion	#
2015	Indies	
2016	Indies	
2017	Indies	
2018	WWE	13
2019	WWE	71
2020	WWE	15
2021	WWE	45
2022	WWE	23

MARINA SHAFIR
5'7, 145lbs, Soroca, Moldova, 2018, 34

Year	Promotion	#
2018	WWE	24
2019	WWE	55
2020	WWE	7
2021	AEW	2
	WWE	1
2022	AEW	37

MARK ANDREWS
5'8, 161lbs, Cardiff, Wales, 2006, 31

Year	Promotion	#
2006	Indies	
2007	Indies	
2008	Indies	
2009	Indies	
2010	Indies	
2011	Indies	
2012	Indies	
2013	Indies	
2014	TNA	3
2015	TNA	18
2016	TNA	24
2017	WWE	24
2018	WWE	32
2019	WWE	20
2020	WWE	4
2021	WWE	10
2022	WWE	6

MARK BRISCOE
6'0, 229lbs, Salisbury, Maryland, 2000, 38

Year	Promotion	#
2000	Indies	
2001	Indies	
2002	ROH	2
2003	ROH	13
2004	ROH	17
2005	Indies	
2006	ROH	35
2007	ROH	37
	NOAH	22
2008	ROH	33
	NOAH	18
2009	ROH	21
2010	ROH	38
2011	ROH	30
2012	ROH	31
2013	ROH	28
2014	ROH	43
	NJPW	2
2015	ROH	44
	NJPW	3
2016	ROH	47
	NJPW	18
2017	ROH	37
	NJPW	10
2018	ROH	39
	NJPW	6
2019	ROH	40
	NJPW	6
	NWA	2
2020	ROH	10
2021	ROH	19
2022	Impact	8
	NWA	6
	ROH	3

MARK COFFEY
6'2, 238lbs, Glasgow, Scotland, 2010, 32

Year	Promotion	#
2010	Indies	
2011	Indies	
2012	Indies	
2013	Indies	
2014	Indies	
2015	Indies	
2016	Indies	
2017	Indies	
2018	WWE	12
2019	WWE	18
2020	WWE	8
2021	WWE	8
2022	WWE	14

MARK DAVIS
6'3, 242lbs, Queensland, Australia, 2007, 33

Year	Promotion	#
2007	Indies	
2008	Indies	
2009	Indies	
2010	Indies	
2011	Indies	
2012	Indies	
2013	Indies	
2014	Indies	
2015	Indies	
2016	Indies	
2017	Indies	
2018	Indies	
2019	NJPW	1
2020	Indies	
2021	Indies	
2022	NJPW	29
	Impact	4
	AEW	4

MARQ QUEN
5'10, 209lbs, New York City, New York, 2012, 28

Year	Promotion	#
2012	Indies	
2013	Indies	
2014	Indies	
2015	Indies	
2016	Indies	
2017	Indies	
2018	Indies	
2019	AEW	13
2020	AEW	30
2021	AEW	35
2022	AEW	37

MARYSE
5'8, 115lbs, Montreal, Canada, 2006, 39

Year	Promotion	#
2007	OVW	18
	WWE	5
2008	WWE	69
2009	WWE	77
2010	WWE	128
2011	WWE	33
2017	WWE	1
2018	WWE	2
2022	WWE	1

MASCARA DORADA
5'9, 189lbs, Guadalajara, Mexico, 2005, 34

Year	Promotion	#
2005	Indies	
2006	Indies	
2007	CMLL	13
2008	CMLL	66
2009	CMLL	107
2010	CMLL	119
	NJPW	6
2011	CMLL	100
	NJPW	28
2012	CMLL	86
	NJPW	15
2013	CMLL	116
	NJPW	8
2014	CMLL	84
	NJPW	43
2015	NJPW	133
	CMLL	3
2016	CMLL	90
	WWE	13
	NJPW	9
2017	WWE	45
2018	WWE	51
2019	WWE	71
2020	WWE	27
2021	WWE	22
2022	NJPW	13
	AEW	2
	Impact	2
	ROH	1

MASHA SLAMOVICH
5'3, 136lbs, Moscow, Russia, 2016, 24

Year	Promotion	#
2016	Indies	
2017	Indies	
2018	Indies	
2019	Indies	
2020	Indies	
2021	AEW	2
	Impact	1
	NWA	1
2022	Impact	19

MASTER WATO
5'9, 176lbs, Osaka, Japan, 2016, 25

Year	Promotion	#
2016	NJPW	55
2017	NJPW	127
2018	CMLL	78
	NJPW	10
2019	CMLL	67
2020	NJPW	42
	CMLL	13
2021	NJPW	91
2022	NJPW	116

MATT CARDONA
6'1, 213lbs, North Merrick, New York, 2004, 37

Year	Promotion	#
2004	Indies	
2005	Indies	
2006	DSW	23
2007	OVW	45
	WWE	37
2008	WWE	74
2009	WWE	55
2010	WWE	119
2011	WWE	151
2012	WWE	163
2013	WWE	156
2014	WWE	61
2015	WWE	133
2016	WWE	172
2017	WWE	56
2018	WWE	73
2019	WWE	87
2020	WWE	6
	AEW	2
2021	Impact	29
	NWA	2
2022	Impact	13
	NWA	10

MATT HARDY
6'2, 236lbs, Cameron, North Carolina, 1992, 48

Year	Promotion	#
1992	Indies	

Year	Promotion	Matches
1993	Indies	
1994	WWF	5
1995	WWF	11
1996	WWF	8
1997	WWF	8
1998	WWF	39
1999	WWF	133
2000	WWF	178
2001	WWF	158
2002	WWE	148
2003	WWE	136
2004	WWE	74
2005	WWE	45
	ROH	3
2006	WWE	127
2007	WWE	123
2008	WWE	139
2009	WWE	114
2010	WWE	86
2011	TNA	48
2012	Indies	
2013	ROH	11
2014	TNA	11
	ROH	5
2015	TNA	38
2016	TNA	35
2017	WWE	88
	TNA	6
	ROH	4
2018	WWE	96
2019	WWE	39
2020	AEW	12
	WWE	1
2021	AEW	38
2022	AEW	24

MATT JACKSON
5'10, 172lbs, Rancho Cucamonga, California, 2004, 37

Year	Promotion	Matches
2004	Indies	
2005	Indies	
2006	Indies	
2007	Indies	
2008	Dragon Gate	31
2009	ROH	19
	Dragon Gate	17
	DGUSA	3
2010	TNA	49
	ROH	5
	DGUSA	3
2011	TNA	21
	ROH	9
2012	ROH	11
2013	NJPW	11
	DGUSA	9
	EVOLVE	6
	ROH	3
2014	NJPW	40
	ROH	10
	EVOLVE	2
2015	NJPW	41
	ROH	26
2016	ROH	40
	NJPW	36
2017	ROH	45
	NJPW	24
2018	ROH	47
	NJPW	30
2019	AEW	14
	AAA	3
	NJPW	1
2020	AEW	33
2021	AEW	31
2022	AEW	25

MATT MENARD
5'10, 202lbs, Montreal, Canada, 2002, 39

Year	Promotion	Matches
2002	Indies	
2003	Indies	
2004	Indies	
2005	Indies	
2006	Indies	
2007	Indies	
2008	Indies	
2009	Indies	
2010	Indies	
2011	Indies	
2012	Indies	
2013	Indies	
2014	Indies	
2015	Indies	
2016	Indies	
2017	Indies	
2018	Indies	
2019	WWE	36
2020	WWE	25
2021	AEW	19
	WWE	7
2022	AEW	25

MATT RIDDLE
6'1, 170lbs, Allentown, Pennsylvania, 2015, 36

Year	Promotion	Matches
2015	Indies	
2016	EVOLVE	23
2017	EVOLVE	20
2018	WWE	28
	EVOLVE	14
2019	WWE	96
2020	WWE	50
2021	WWE	81
2022	WWE	110

MATT SYDAL
5'9, 165lbs, St. Louis, Missouri, 2000, 39

Year	Promotion	Matches
2000	Indies	
2001	Indies	
2002	Indies	
2003	TNA	9
2004	ROH	8
2005	ROH	13
2006	Dragon Gate	38
	ROH	36
2007	Dragon Gate	55
	ROH	21
	OVW	17
2008	WWE	41
	OVW	13
	FCW	9
2009	WWE	123
2010	WWE	127
2011	WWE	142
2012	WWE	10
2013	WWE	1
2014	ROH	7
2015	ROH	28
	NJPW	17
	Dragon Gate	12
2016	NJPW	36
	ROH	14
2017	Impact	19
2018	Impact	39
2019	EVOLVE	4
2020	AEW	16
	ROH	2
2021	AEW	46
2022	AEW	24

MATT TAVEN
6'2, 218lbs, Derry, New Hampshire, 2008, 37

Year	Promotion	Matches
2008	Indies	
2009	ROH	2
2010	Indies	
2011	ROH	1
2012	ROH	8
2013	ROH	32
2014	ROH	23
2015	ROH	42
	NJPW	25
2016	CMLL	9
	ROH	4
2017	ROH	35
	CMLL	20
	NJPW	3
2018	ROH	37
	CMLL	36
	NJPW	6
2019	ROH	33
	CMLL	8
	NJPW	6
2020	ROH	2
2021	ROH	15
	NWA	5
2022	Impact	25
	NWA	9
	CMLL	8
	AEW	2

MATTHEW REHWOLDT
6'3, 216lbs, Chicago, Illinois, 2009, 35

Year	Promotion	Matches
2009	Indies	
2010	Indies	
2011	Indies	
2012	FCW	22
	WWE	18
2013	WWE	55
2014	WWE	76
2015	WWE	97
2016	WWE	132
2017	WWE	136
2018	WWE	77
2019	WWE	11
2020	Indies	
2021	Impact	11
	NJPW	2
2022	Impact	3
	NJPW	1

MAX CASTER
6'1, 229lbs, Long Island, New York, 2014, 33

Year	Promotion	Matches
2014	Indies	
2015	Indies	
2016	Indies	
2017	Indies	
2018	Indies	
2019	Indies	
2020	AEW	13
2021	AEW	52
2022	AEW	46

MEIKO SATOMURA
5'2, 150lbs, Niigata, Japan, 1995, 43

Year	Promotion	Matches
1995	GAEA Japan	15
1996	GAEA Japan	26
	WCW	4
1997	GAEA Japan	48
	WCW	1
1998	GAEA Japan	44
1999	GAEA Japan	43
2000	GAEA Japan	31
2001	GAEA Japan	50
2002	GAEA Japan	35
2003	GAEA Japan	39
2004	GAEA Japan	29
2005	GAEA Japan	2
2006	Sendai Girls	4
2007	Sendai Girls	14
2008	Sendai Girls	5
2009	Sendai Girls	8
2010	Sendai Girls	11
2011	Sendai Girls	11
2012	Sendai Girls	14
2013	Sendai Girls	26
2014	Sendai Girls	21
2015	Sendai Girls	25
2016	Sendai Girls	35
2017	Sendai Girls	37
2018	Sendai Girls	36
	WWE	4
2019	Sendai Girls	49
2020	Sendai Girls	13
2021	Sendai Girls	3
	WWE	12
2022	WWE	7

MERCEDES MARTINEZ
5'7, 147lbs, Waterbury, Connecticut, 2000, 42

Year	Promotion	Matches
2000	Indies	
2001	Indies	
2002	TNA	1
2003	Indies	
2004	Indies	
2005	Indies	
2006	ROH	3
2007	Indies	
2008	Indies	
2009	Indies	
2010	EVOLVE	5
2011	Indies	
2012	Indies	
2013	Indies	
2014	DGUSA	1
2016	Indies	
2017	WWE	6
2018	WWE	3
	Impact	1
2019	AEW	2
2020	WWE	12
2021	WWE	10
	Impact	6
2022	AEW	18
	ROH	3
	Impact	1

MIA YIM "MICHIN"
5'7, 132lbs, Fontana, California, 2009, 33

Year	Promotion	Matches
2009	Indies	
2010	Indies	
2011	Indies	
2012	Indies	
2013	TNA	1
2014	TNA	2
2015	TNA	11
2016	TNA	38
2017	Impact	5
	WWE	2
2018	WWE	21
2019	WWE	74
2020	WWE	36
2022	Impact	16
	WWE	13

MICKIE JAMES
5'4, 121lbs, Richmond, Virginia, 1999, 43

Year	Promotion	Matches
1999	Indies	
2000	Indies	
2001	Indies	
2002	ROH	4
2003	ROH	6
	TNA	5
2004	OVW	14
2005	OVW	13
	WWE	9
2006	WWE	102
2007	WWE	105
2008	WWE	114
2009	WWE	117
2010	WWE	22
	TNA	11
2011	TNA	81
2012	TNA	41
2013	TNA	33
2014	Indies	
2015	TNA	2
2016	WWE	1
2017	WWE	92
2018	WWE	70
2019	WWE	17

2020	WWE	5
2021	Impact	5
	NWA	4
	WWE	1
2022	Impact	20
	NWA	2
	WWE	1

MIKE BAILEY
5'8, 174lbs, Quebec, Canada, 2006, 32

2006	Indies	
2007	Indies	
2008	Indies	
2009	Indies	
2010	Indies	
2011	Indies	
2012	Indies	
2013	Indies	
2014	Indies	
2015	Indies	
2016	DDT	28
2017	DDT	56
2018	DDT	72
2019	DDT	36
2020	DDT	5
2021	Indies	
2022	Impact	33

MIKE BENNETT
6'1, 218lbs, Carver, Massachusetts, 2001, 37

2001	Indies	
2002	Indies	
2003	Indies	
2004	Indies	
2005	Indies	
2006	Indies	
2007	ROH	1
2008	ROH	3
2009	Indies	
2010	ROH	10
2011	ROH	27
2012	ROH	26
2013	ROH	21
2014	ROH	28
	NJPW	15
2015	ROH	40
	NJPW	25
2016	TNA	41
2017	WWE	42
	Impact	7
2018	WWE	61
2019	WWE	27
2020	WWE	9
	ROH	2
2021	ROH	16
	NWA	4
2022	Impact	24
	NWA	10
	AEW	1
	ROH	1

MIKEY NICHOLLS
6'1, 229lbs, Perth, Australia, 2001, 37

2001	Indies	
2002	Indies	
2003	Indies	
2004	Indies	
2005	Indies	
2006	NJPW	1
2007	Indies	
2008	Indies	
2009	ROH	4
2010	Indies	
2011	NOAH	40
2012	NOAH	48
	ROH	3
2013	NOAH	79
2014	NOAH	91
2015	NOAH	61

	NJPW	1
2016	NJPW	50
	NOAH	5
2017	WWE	22
2018	WWE	72
2019	NJPW	58
2020	Indies	
2021	Indies	
2022	NJPW	15

MINORU SUZUKI
5'10, 220lbs, Yokohama, Japan, 1987, 54

1987	Indies	
1988	NJPW	43
1989	NJPW	26
	UWF	10
1990	UWF	12
1991	PWFG	7
1992	PWFG	11
2003	NJPW	15
2004	NJPW	93
2005	NJPW	32
	NOAH	31
2006	AJPW	67
	NOAH	11
2007	AJPW	86
2008	AJPW	83
2009	AJPW	101
2010	AJPW	114
2011	NJPW	72
	AJPW	69
2012	NJPW	98
2013	NJPW	96
2014	NJPW	98
2015	NOAH	100
2016	NJPW	114
2017	NJPW	119
	ROH	6
2018	NJPW	131
2019	NJPW	127
2020	NJPW	68
2021	NJPW	72
	Impact	3
	AEW	3
2022	NJPW	63
	AJPW	4
	AEW	3

MIRO
6'0, 280lbs, Plovdiv, Bulgaria, 2008, 37

2008	Indies	
2009	Indies	
2010	Indies	
2011	FCW	7
2012	FCW	21
2013	WWE	51
2014	WWE	153
2015	WWE	148
2016	WWE	168
2017	WWE	120
2018	WWE	166
2019	WWE	68
2020	WWE	8
	AEW	5
2021	AEW	20
2022	AEW	4

MISTERIOSO
5'11, 218lbs, Los Angeles, California, 2011, ??

2011	Indies	
2012	Indies	
2013	Indies	
2014	Indies	
2015	Indies	
2016	Indies	
2017	Dragon Gate	9
2018	Indies	
2019	Dragon Gate	11
	NJPW	2

2020	NJPW	16
2021	NJPW	17
	AEW	1
2022	NJPW	10

MISTICO
5'7, 175lbs, Ciudad de Mexico, Mexico, 1998, 40

1998	Indies	
1999	Indies	
2000	CMLL	1
2001	CMLL	1
2002	Indies	
2003	CMLL	7
2004	CMLL	46
2005	CMLL	93
2006	CMLL	125
2007	CMLL	191
2008	CMLL	137
2009	CMLL	171
	NJPW	5
2010	CMLL	176
2011	WWE	68
	CMLL	11
2012	WWE	97
2013	WWE	48
2014	AAA	55
2015	AAA	30
	CMLL	2
2016	CMLL	45
2017	CMLL	120
2018	CMLL	133
2019	CMLL	165
	NJPW	11
	ROH	5
2020	CMLL	44
	NJPW	8
2021	CMLL	76
2022	CMLL	79
	NJPW	2

MIZ, THE
6'2, 220lbs, Parma, Ohio, 2003, 42

2005	WWE	25
	DSW	15
2006	OVW	33
	WWE	30
2007	WWE	70
2008	WWE	142
2009	WWE	164
2010	WWE	181
2011	WWE	194
2012	WWE	150
2013	WWE	146
2014	WWE	133
2015	WWE	131
2016	WWE	144
2017	WWE	124
2018	WWE	137
2019	WWE	71
2020	WWE	52
2021	WWE	25
2022	WWE	68

MJF
5'11, 216lbs, Plainview, New York, 2015, 26

2015	Indies	
2016	Indies	
2017	MLW	2
2018	MLW	12
2019	MLW	11
2020	AEW	23
	MLW	2
2021	AEW	17
2022	AEW	9

MONTEZ FORD
6'1, 232lbs, Chicago, Illinois, 2015, 32

2015	WWE	1

2016	WWE	38
2017	WWE	89
2018	WWE	77
2019	WWE	86
2020	WWE	43
2021	WWE	58
2022	WWE	93

MOOSE
6'5, 300lbs, Seabrook, Maryland, 2013, 38

2013	Indies	
2014	ROH	18
2015	ROH	38
2016	ROH	26
	TNA	14
2017	Impact	32
	NOAH	12
2018	Impact	27
2019	Impact	48
2020	Impact	25
2021	Impact	31
	NJPW	2
2022	Impact	21

MT NAKAZAWA
5'9, 198lbs, Kawasaki, Japan, 2005, 47

2005	DDT	9
2006	DDT	60
2007	DDT	60
2008	DDT	76
	ROH	2
2009	DDT	51
2010	DDT	40
2011	DDT	64
2012	DDT	76
	AJPW	7
2013	DDT	76
2014	DDT	77
2015	DDT	4
2016	DDT	1
2017	DDT	1
2018	DDT	4
2019	DDT	5
	AEW	4
	AAA	2
2020	AEW	14
2021	AEW	7
2022	AEW	3
	DDT	3

MUSTAFA ALI
5'10, 182lbs, Bolingbrook, Illinois, 2003, 36

2003	Indies	
2004	Indies	
2005	Indies	
2006	Indies	
2007	Indies	
2008	Indies	
2009	Indies	
2010	Indies	
2011	Indies	
2012	Indies	
2013	Indies	
2014	Indies	
2015	Indies	
2016	WWE	6
2017	WWE	64
2018	WWE	46
2019	WWE	112
2020	WWE	24
2021	WWE	30
2022	WWE	41

MVP
6'0, 252lbs, Miami, Florida, 2001, 49

2001	Indies	
2002	Indies	
2003	TNA	1

2004	TNA	3
2005	WWE	2
2006	WWE	33
	DSW	30
2007	WWE	148
2008	WWE	143
2009	WWE	166
2010	WWE	157
2011	NJPW	56
2012	NJPW	25
2013	Indies	
2014	TNA	28
2015	TNA	17
2016	Indies	
2017	Indies	
2018	Indies	
2019	Indies	
2020	WWE	25
2021	WWE	12
2022	WWE	6

MYLES BORNE
??, ???lbs, Wilmington, North Carolina, 2022, ??

2022	WWE	18

NAOMI
5'5, 125lbs, Sanford, Florida, 2009, 35

2009	FCW	6
2010	FCW	56
	WWE	13
2011	FCW	35
2012	WWE	3
2013	WWE	84
2014	WWE	93
2015	WWE	146
2016	WWE	86
2017	WWE	130
2018	WWE	134
2019	WWE	55
2020	WWE	17
2021	WWE	31
2022	WWE	47

NASH CARTER
5'10, 175lbs, Lima, Ohio, 2014, 28

2014	Indies	
2015	Indies	
2016	Indies	
2017	Impact	2
2018	Dragon Gate	32
	Impact	6
	EVOLVE	2
2019	Impact	39
2020	Impact	29
2021	WWE	16
2022	WWE	7

NATALYA
5'5, 135lbs, Calgary, Canada, 2000, 40

2003	Stampede	22
2004	Stampede	29
2005	Stampede	24
2006	Indies	
2007	FCW	9
	OVW	7
	WWE	5
2008	WWE	67
	FCW	11
2009	WWE	73
2010	WWE	56
2011	WWE	114
2012	WWE	119
2013	WWE	114
2014	WWE	132
2015	WWE	98
2016	WWE	145
2017	WWE	160
2018	WWE	123
2019	WWE	106
2020	WWE	39
2021	WWE	55
2022	WWE	80

NATHAN FRAZER
5'10, 180lbs, Jersey, 2018, 24

2018	Indies	
2019	Indies	
2020	AEW	3
2021	WWE	14
2022	WWE	20

NICK ALDIS
6'4, 240lbs, King's Lynn, England, 2003, 36

2003	Indies	
2004	Indies	
2005	Indies	
2006	Indies	
2007	Indies	
2008	Indies	
2009	TNA	68
2010	TNA	39
2011	TNA	49
2012	TNA	64
2013	TNA	73
2014	TNA	65
2015	TNA	12
	GFW	13
2016	GFW	9
2017	Impact	4
2018	ROH	3
	NWA	1
2019	NWA	8
	ROH	2
2020	NWA	4
	ROH	1
2021	NWA	15
2022	NWA	13
	Impact	2

NICK COMOROTO
6'3, 273lbs, Blackwood, New Jersey, 2013, 31

2013	Indies	
2014	Indies	
2015	Indies	
2016	Indies	
2017	Indies	
2018	Indies	
2019	WWE	36
2020	WWE	6
	AEW	5
2021	AEW	33
2022	AEW	36
	NJPW	4

NICK JACKSON
5'10, 178lbs, Hesperia, California, 2004, 33

2004	Indies	
2005	Indies	
2006	Indies	
2007	Indies	
2008	Dragon Gate	31
2009	ROH	19
	Dragon Gate	17
	DGUSA	3
2010	TNA	48
	ROH	5
	DGUSA	3
2011	TNA	18
	ROH	9
2012	ROH	10
	TNA	3
2013	NJPW	11
	DGUSA	9
	EVOLVE	4
	ROH	3
2014	NJPW	41
	ROH	10
	EVOLVE	3
2015	NJPW	53
	ROH	23
2016	ROH	39
	NJPW	34
2017	ROH	46
	NJPW	24
2018	ROH	47
	NJPW	30
2019	AEW	15
	AAA	3
	NJPW	1
2020	AEW	32
2021	AEW	30
2022	AEW	26

NIKKI CROSS
5'1, 117lbs, Glasgow, Scotland, 2008, 33

2008	Indies	
2009	Indies	
2010	Indies	
2011	Indies	
2012	Indies	
2013	Indies	
2014	Indies	
2015	Stardom	15
2016	WWE	29
2017	WWE	70
2018	WWE	85
2019	WWE	107
2020	WWE	31
2021	WWE	44
2022	WWE	57

NIKKITA LYONS
5'8, 154lbs, Las Vegas, Nevada, 2018, 23

2018	Indies	
2019	Indies	
2020	Indies	
2021	WWE	1
2022	WWE	26

NINA SAMUELS
5'7, 150lbs, London, England, 2014, 34

2014	Indies	
2015	Indies	
2016	Indies	
2017	Indies	
2018	WWE	7
2019	WWE	10
2020	WWE	6
2021	WWE	5
2022	WWE	6

NOAM DAR
5'9, 178lbs, Be'er Ja'akow, Israel, 2008, 29

2008	Indies	
2009	Indies	
2010	Indies	
2011	Indies	
2012	Indies	
2013	Indies	
2014	Indies	
2015	TNA	3
2016	WWE	19
2017	WWE	56
2018	WWE	12
2019	WWE	17
2020	WWE	7
2021	WWE	9
2022	WWE	6

NYLA ROSE
5'9, 170lbs, Washington, D.C., 2012, 40

2012	Indies	
2013	Indies	
2014	Indies	
2015	Indies	
2016	Indies	
2017	Indies	
2018	Indies	
2019	AEW	8
2020	AEW	24
2021	AEW	50
2022	AEW	41

OBA FEMI
6'4, 275lbs, Lagos, Nigeria, 2022, 21

2022	WWE	3

ODYSSEY JONES
6'5, 405lbs, Coram, New York, 2019, 28

2019	WWE	3
2020	WWE	3
2021	WWE	18
2022	WWE	12

OMOS
7'3, 400lbs, Lagos, Nigeria, 2019, 28

2019	WWE	5
2020	WWE	1
2021	WWE	37
2022	WWE	72

ORANGE CASSIDY
5'10, 160lbs, West Orange, New Jersey, 2004, 38

2004	Indies	
2005	Indies	
2006	Indies	
2007	Indies	
2008	Indies	
2009	ROH	4
2010	Indies	
2011	Indies	
2012	DGUSA	4
2013	DGUSA	6
	EVOLVE	3
2014	DGUSA	9
	EVOLVE	7
2015	Indies	
2016	Indies	
2017	Indies	
2018	Indies	
2019	AEW	4
	EVOLVE	3
2020	AEW	25
2021	AEW	50
2022	AEW	40

ORO MENSAH
5'11, 198lbs, Zurich, Switzerland, 2012, 27

2012	Indies	
2013	Indies	
2014	Indies	
2015	Indies	
2016	Indies	
2017	Indies	
2018	Indies	
2019	WWE	8
2020	WWE	7
2021	WWE	8
2022	WWE	26

ORTIZ
5'8, 192lbs, New York City, New York, 2008, 31

2008	Indies	
2009	Indies	
2010	Indies	
2011	Indies	
2012	Indies	
2013	Indies	
2014	Indies	
2015	Indies	

Year	Promotion	#
2016	Indies	
2017	Impact	21
2018	Impact	22
2019	Impact	20
	AEW	8
	AAA	3
2020	AEW	30
2021	AEW	29
2022	AEW	28

OTIS
5'10, 310lbs, Duluth, Minnesota, 2015, 31

Year	Promotion	#
2016	WWE	41
2017	WWE	80
2018	WWE	88
2019	WWE	79
2020	WWE	29
2021	WWE	38
2022	WWE	78

PAC
5'10, 194lbs, Newcastle, England, 2004, 36

Year	Promotion	#
2004	Indies	
2005	Indies	
2006	Indies	
2007	Dragon Gate	43
	NWE	8
	ROH	4
	TNA	2
2008	Dragon Gate	80
	NWE	15
2009	Dragon Gate	81
	NWE	9
2010	Dragon Gate	112
	DGUSA	2
2011	Dragon Gate	112
	DGUSA	15
2012	Dragon Gate	44
	WWE	9
	NJPW	9
	DGUSA	4
2013	WWE	72
2014	WWE	108
2015	WWE	188
2016	WWE	105
2017	WWE	115
2018	Dragon Gate	33
2019	Dragon Gate	45
	AEW	9
2020	AEW	10
2021	AEW	29
2022	AEW	26

PARKER BOUDREAUX
6'4, 300lbs, Winter Garden, Florida, 2021, 24

Year	Promotion	#
2021	WWE	2
2022	AEW	5
	WWE	4

PAT MCAFEE
6'1, 235lbs, Plum, Pennsylvania, 2009, 35

Year	Promotion	#
2020	WWE	2
2022	WWE	3

PAUL WIGHT
7'0, 383lbs, Aiken, South Carolina, 1994, 50

Year	Promotion	#
1994	Indies	
1995	WCW	11
1996	WCW	94
1997	WCW	81
1998	WCW	109
1999	WWF	155
	WCW	4
2000	WWF	66
2001	WWF	130
2002	WWE	137
2003	WWE	114
2004	WWE	71
2005	WWE	141
2006	WWE	121
2008	WWE	108
2009	WWE	170
2010	WWE	172
2011	WWE	124
2012	WWE	208
2013	WWE	124
2014	WWE	126
2015	WWE	123
2016	WWE	77
2017	WWE	37
2018	WWE	4
2020	WWE	6
2021	AEW	3
2022	AEW	1

PCO
6'1, 300lbs, Quebec, Canada, 1987, 55

Year	Promotion	#
1987	Indies	
1988	Indies	
1989	Indies	
1990	Indies	
1991	Indies	
1992	CWA (Europe)	44
1993	WWF	70
	WWC	10
1994	WWF	135
1995	WWF	93
1996	WCW	15
1997	CWA	41
	WCW	30
1998	WWF	42
1999	AJPW	13
	WWF	1
2000	ECW	5
	WCW	3
2001	Indies	
2002	Indies	
2003	TNA	6
2004	Indies	
2005	Indies	
2006	Indies	
2007	Indies	
2008	Indies	
2009	Indies	
2010	Indies	
2016	Indies	
2017	Indies	
2018	MLW	5
	ROH	1
2019	ROH	44
2020	ROH	6
2021	ROH	12
2022	Impact	20

PENELOPE FORD
5'4, 119lbs, Phoenix, Arizona, 2014, 30

Year	Promotion	#
2014	Indies	
2015	Indies	
2016	Indies	
2017	Indies	
2018	Indies	
2019	AEW	3
2020	AEW	24
2021	AEW	28
2022	AEW	11

PENTA EL ZERO M
5'11, 207lbs, Ciudad de Mexico, Mexico, 2007, 37

Year	Promotion	#
2007	Indies	
2008	Indies	
2009	CMLL	2
2010	CMLL	2
	AAA	2
2011	AAA	29
2012	AAA	66
2013	AAA	96
2014	AAA	94
	LU	8
2015	AAA	29
	LU	15
2016	AAA	23
	LU	19
2017	Indies	
2018	Impact	23
	MLW	10
	AAA	6
	LU	3
2019	AEW	14
	Impact	11
	AAA	10
	MLW	5
	CMLL	2
2020	AEW	24
	AAA	10
2021	AEW	47
	AAA	4
2022	AEW	41
	AAA	11

PERSIA PIROTTA
5'11, 187lbs, Sydney, Australia, 2017, 25

Year	Promotion	#
2017	Indies	
2018	Indies	
2019	Indies	
2020	Indies	
2021	WWE	6
2022	WWE	5

PETER AVALON
5'10, 170lbs, Rancho Cucamonga, California, 2008, 33

Year	Promotion	#
2008	Indies	
2009	Indies	
2010	Indies	
2011	Indies	
2012	Indies	
2013	TNA	6
2014	TNA	3
2015	TNA	2
2016	Indies	
2017	Indies	
2018	Indies	
2019	AEW	6
	Impact	2
2020	AEW	32
2021	AEW	20
2022	AEW	21
	NJPW	3

PJ BLACK
6'1, 225lbs, Cape Town, South Africa, 1997, 41

Year	Promotion	#
1997	Indies	
1998	Indies	
1999	Indies	
2000	Indies	
2001	Indies	
2002	Indies	
2003	Indies	
2004	Indies	
2005	Indies	
2006	Indies	
2007	Indies	
2008	Indies	
2009	FCW	55
2010	WWE	77
	FCW	38
2011	WWE	127
2012	WWE	117
2013	WWE	128
2014	WWE	66
2015	WWE	9
	LU	6
	EVOLVE	3
	TNA	3
2016	LU	22
	EVOLVE	2
2017	Indies	
2018	ROH	3
2019	ROH	25
2020	NJPW	9
	ROH	7
2021	ROH	11
	NJPW	1
2022	Impact	2

POWERHOUSE HOBBS
6'1, 252lbs, East Palo Alto, California, 2009, 32

Year	Promotion	#
2009	Indies	
2010	Indies	
2011	Indies	
2012	Indies	
2013	Indies	
2014	Indies	
2015	Indies	
2016	Indies	
2017	Indies	
2018	Indies	
2019	Indies	
2020	AEW	19
2021	AEW	37
2022	AEW	28

PRESTON VANCE
6'2, 240lbs, Clare, Michigan, 2015, 30

Year	Promotion	#
2015	Indies	
2016	Indies	
2017	Indies	
2018	Indies	
2019	Indies	
2020	AEW	20
2021	AEW	47
2022	AEW	43

PRIMATE
5'11, 209lbs, Newcastle, England, 2014, 38

Year	Promotion	#
2014	Indies	
2015	Indies	
2016	Indies	
2017	Indies	
2018	WWE	2
2019	WWE	12
2020	WWE	7
2021	WWE	9
2022	WWE	6

QT MARSHALL
6'1, 238lbs, Newark, New Jersey, 2004, 37

Year	Promotion	#
2004	Indies	
2005	Indies	
2006	Indies	
2007	Indies	
2008	Indies	
2009	Indies	
2010	Indies	
2011	Indies	
2012	ROH	8
2013	ROH	17
2014	ROH	4
2015	ROH	2
2016	ROH	1
2017	ROH	2
2018	ROH	1
2019	AEW	3
2020	AEW	28
2021	AEW	41
2022	AEW	39
	NJPW	7

QUEEN ZELINA
4'11, 105lbs, New York City, New York, 2008, 32

Year	Promotion	#
2010	Indies	
2011	TNA	22

Year	Promotion	Count
2012	TNA	11
2013	Indies	
2014	Indies	
2015	TNA	2
2016	Indies	
2017	Indies	
2018	WWE	45
2019	WWE	17
2020	WWE	11
2021	WWE	28
2022	WWE	17

QUINCY ELLIOTT
??, ??lbs, California, 2018, ??

Year	Promotion	Count
2018	Indies	
2019	Indies	
2020	Indies	
2021	Indies	
2022	WWE	19

R-TRUTH
6'1, 230lbs, Atlanta, Georgia, 1997, 50

Year	Promotion	Count
1997	Indies	
1998	Indies	
1999	Indies	
2000	WWF	34
2001	WWF	52
2002	TNA	19
2003	TNA	34
2004	TNA	52
2005	TNA	28
2006	TNA	59
2007	TNA	8
2008	WWE	71
2009	WWE	104
2010	WWE	126
2011	WWE	145
2012	WWE	147
2013	WWE	134
2014	WWE	112
2015	WWE	137
2016	WWE	118
2017	WWE	94
2018	WWE	55
2019	WWE	89
2020	WWE	42
2021	WWE	22
2022	WWE	35

RAJ SINGH
5'11, 213lbs, Calgary, Canada, 2003, 38

Year	Promotion	Count
2003	Indies	
2004	Stampede	1
2005	Stampede	32
2006	Stampede	10
2007	Stampede	14
2008	Stampede	4
2009	Indies	
2010	Indies	
2011	Indies	
2012	Indies	
2013	Indies	
2014	Indies	
2015	Indies	
2016	Indies	
2017	Indies	
2018	Impact	3
2019	Impact	18
2021	Impact	3
2022	Impact	17

RANDY ORTON
6'4, 245lbs, Knoxville, Tennessee, 2000, 42

Year	Promotion	Count
2000	OVW	18
2001	OVW	30
	WWF	23
2002	WWE	108
2003	WWE	83
2004	WWE	154
2005	WWE	96
2006	WWE	118
2007	WWE	145
2008	WWE	85
2009	WWE	178
2010	WWE	176
2011	WWE	204
2012	WWE	119
2013	WWE	202
2014	WWE	126
2015	WWE	93
2016	WWE	57
2017	WWE	139
2018	WWE	80
2019	WWE	79
2020	WWE	29
2021	WWE	56
2022	WWE	26

RAQUEL RODRIGUEZ
6'0, 176lbs, La Feria, Texas, 2014, 31

Year	Promotion	Count
2017	WWE	15
2018	WWE	65
2019	WWE	56
2020	WWE	26
2021	WWE	25
2022	WWE	64

REBEL
5'8, ??lbs, Owasso, Oklahoma, 2014, 44

Year	Promotion	Count
2014	TNA	4
2015	TNA	7
2016	TNA	8
2017	TNA	4
2018	TNA	5
2019	WWE	1
2020	AEW	2
2021	AEW	9
2022	AEW	1

RED VELVET
5'1, ??lbs, Miami, Florida, 2016, 30

Year	Promotion	Count
2016	Indies	
2017	Indies	
2018	Indies	
2019	Indies	
2020	AEW	17
2021	AEW	43
2022	AEW	20

REN NARITA
6'0, 183lbs, Aomori, Japan, 2017, 25

Year	Promotion	Count
2017	NJPW	28
2018	NJPW	93
2019	NJPW	112
2020	NJPW	6
2021	NJPW	20
	AEW	2
2022	NJPW	35

REY FENIX
5'10, 176lbs, Ciudad de Mexico, Mexico, 2005, 32

Year	Promotion	Count
2005	Indies	
2006	Indies	
2007	Indies	
2008	Indies	
2009	Indies	
2010	CMLL	6
2011	AAA	37
2012	AAA	72
2013	AAA	94
	NOAH	11
2014	AAA	89
	LU	10
2015	AAA	31
	LU	16
2016	LU	24
	AAA	8
2017	Indies	
2018	Impact	17
	CMLL	13
	MLW	9
	AAA	5
	LU	2
2019	AEW	13
	Impact	11
	AAA	9
	MLW	5
	CMLL	2
2020	AEW	32
	AAA	5
2021	AEW	39
	AAA	3
2022	AEW	33
	AAA	7

REY MYSTERIO
5'3, 175lbs, Chula Visa, California, 1989, 48

Year	Promotion	Count
1989	Indies	
1990	Indies	
1991	Indies	
1992	AAA	24
1993	AAA	31
1994	AAA	53
1995	AAA	64
	ECW	6
1996	WCW	43
	AAA	18
	WAR	10
	ECW	4
1997	WCW	79
1998	WCW	42
1999	WCW	133
2000	WCW	64
2001	WCW	20
	CMLL	10
2002	WWE	79
2003	WWE	136
2004	WWE	146
2005	WWE	132
2006	WWE	112
2007	WWE	55
2008	WWE	70
2009	WWE	138
2010	WWE	145
2011	WWE	93
2012	WWE	51
2013	WWE	19
2014	WWE	19
2015	AAA	17
2016	LU	14
2017	Indies	14
2018	WWE	29
2019	WWE	53
2020	WWE	22
2021	WWE	66
2022	WWE	50

RHEA RIPLEY
5'8, 137lbs, Adelaide, Australia, 2013, 26

Year	Promotion	Count
2013	Indies	
2014	Indies	
2015	Indies	
2016	Indies	
2017	WWE	16
2018	WWE	33
2019	WWE	59
2020	WWE	33
2021	WWE	55
2022	WWE	64

RHINO
5'10, 295lbs, Detroit, Michigan, 1994, 47

Year	Promotion	Count
1994	Indies	
1995	Indies	
1996	Indies	
1997	Indies	
1998	Indies	
1999	ECW	56
2000	ECW	79
2001	WWE	99
	ECW	3
2003	WWE	116
2004	WWE	150
2005	WWE	28
	TNA	19
2006	TNA	47
2007	TNA	43
2008	TNA	65
	NJPW	4
2009	TNA	51
2010	TNA	50
2011	NJPW	3
	ROH	2
2012	ROH	11
2013	ROH	11
2014	TNA	6
2015	WWE	25
2016	WWE	64
2017	WWE	118
2018	WWE	91
2019	Impact	16
	WWE	8
2020	Impact	24
2021	Impact	19
2022	Impact	17

RIC FLAIR
6'1, 243lbs, Memphis, Tennessee, 1972, 73

Year	Promotion	Count
1973	AWA	88
1974	MACW	148
	AWA	41
	IWE	20
1975	MACW	216
1976	MACW	245
1977	MACW	239
	GCW	11
1978	MACW	232
	GCW	20
	AJPW	10
1979	MACW	263
	MLW	11
	GCW	10
1980	MACW	269
1981	MACW	228
	GCW	37
	CWF	24
	SLWC	15
	MACW	14
	MLW	13
1982	MACW	96
	CWF	69
	GCW	35
	CSW	14
	WCCW	13
	PNW	10
1983	JCP	136
	CWF	29
	GCW	28
	WCCW	13
	SLWC	13
	CSW	10
1984	JCP	77
	CWF	46
	WCCW	26
	CSW	22
	PNW	12
	GCW	11
1985	JCP	131
	CWF	35
	Mid-South	22
	CSW	13
	SECW	11
1986	JCP	225
	CWF	19
	CSW	13
1987	JCP	266

1988	JCP	207
1989	WCW	140
1990	WCW	196
1991	WCW	106
	WWF	75
1992	WWF	211
1993	WCW	73
	WWF	36
1994	WCW	71
1995	WCW	54
	NJPW	8
1996	WCW	109
1997	WCW	45
1998	WCW	28
1999	WCW	81
2000	WCW	44
2001	WCW	2
2002	WWE	47
2003	WWE	54
2004	WWE	76
2005	WWE	80
2006	WWE	81
2007	WWE	61
2008	WWE	21
2010	TNA	8
2011	TNA	4
2022	JCP	1

RICH SWANN
5'6, 170lbs, Balitmore, Maryland, 2008, 31

2008	Indies	
2009	Indies	
2010	DGUSA	5
	EVOLVE	3
2011	Dragon Gate	100
	DGUSA	16
	EVOLVE	2
2012	Dragon Gate	62
	DGUSA	8
	EVOLVE	4
2013	Dragon Gate	63
	DGUSA	9
	EVOLVE	3
2014	EVOLVE	16
	DGUSA	9
2015	EVOLVE	11
	WWE	4
2016	WWE	62
2017	WWE	74
2018	MLW	9
2019	Impact	50
	MLW	5
	AAA	3
2020	Impact	10
2021	Impact	27
2022	Impact	30

RICK BOOGS
6'1, 276lbs, Franklin, Wisconsin, 2017, 35

2017	WWE	5
2018	WWE	5
2019	WWE	53
2020	WWE	9
2021	WWE	28
2022	WWE	18

RICKY STARKS
6'0, 195lbs, New Orleans, Louisiana, 2011, 32

2011	Indies	
2012	Indies	
2013	Indies	
2014	Indies	
2015	Indies	
2016	WWE	2
2017	Indies	
2018	NWA	1
2019	NWA	9
2020	AEW	24
	NWA	7

2021	AEW	24
2022	AEW	34

RICOCHET
5'10, 170lbs, Paducah, Kentucky, 2003, 34

2003	Indies	
2004	Indies	
2005	Indies	
2006	Indies	
2007	Indies	
2008	Indies	
2009	Indies	
2010	Dragon Gate	11
2011	Dragon Gate	124
	DGUSA	14
2012	Dragon Gate	67
2013	Dragon Gate	72
	NJPW	10
2014	Dragon Gate	43
	EVOLVE	13
	NJPW	10
2015	LU	18
	NJPW	15
	Dragon Gate	14
2016	NJPW	38
	LU	21
2017	NJPW	47
2018	WWE	80
2019	WWE	152
2020	WWE	55
2021	WWE	53
2022	WWE	98

RIDGE HOLLAND
6'1, 251lbs, Liversedge, England, 2016, 34

2016	Indies	
2017	Indies	
2018	WWE	27
2019	WWE	49
2020	WWE	16
2021	WWE	19
2022	WWE	72

RIHO
5'1, 93lbs, Tokyo, Japan, 2006, 25

2006	Ice Ribbon	16
2007	Ice Ribbon	56
2008	Ice Ribbon	68
2009	Ice Ribbon	47
2010	Ice Ribbon	63
2011	Ice Ribbon	41
2012	Ice Ribbon	16
	Gatoh Move	15
2013	Gatoh Move	65
2014	Gatoh Move	68
2015	Gatoh Move	60
2016	Gatoh Move	53
2017	Gatoh Move	56
2018	Gatoh Move	66
2019	Gatoh Move	32
	Stardom	20
	AEW	10
2020	Stardom	38
	AEW	8
2021	AEW	23
2022	AEW	9

RIP FOWLER
6'3, 220lbs, Liverpool, England, 2007, 32

2007	Indies	
2008	Indies	
2009	Indies	
2010	Indies	
2011	Indies	
2012	Indies	
2013	Indies	
2014	Indies	
2015	Indies	

2016	Indies	
2017	Indies	
2018	WWE	27
2019	WWE	17
2020	WWE	10
2021	WWE	18
2022	WWE	26

ROBBIE EAGLES
5'9, 176lbs, Sydney, Australia, 2008, 32

2008	Indies	
2009	Indies	
2010	Indies	
2011	Indies	
2012	Indies	
2013	Indies	
2014	Indies	
2015	Indies	
2016	Indies	
2017	Indies	
2018	NJPW	16
2019	NJPW	55
2020	NJPW	21
2021	NJPW	50
2022	NJPW	33
	CMLL	8

ROBERT ROODE
6'0, 235lbs, Ontario, Canada, 1998, 45

1998	Indies	
1999	Indies	
2000	Indies	
2001	Indies	
2002	Indies	
2003	WWE	13
2004	TNA	47
2005	TNA	24
2006	TNA	45
2007	TNA	57
2008	TNA	98
2009	TNA	112
2010	TNA	98
2011	TNA	102
2012	TNA	108
2013	TNA	94
2014	TNA	52
2015	TNA	41
2016	WWE	55
	TNA	16
2017	WWE	123
2018	WWE	144
2019	WWE	99
2020	WWE	23
2021	WWE	51
2022	WWE	25

ROCKY ROMERO
5'7, 175lbs, La Habana, Cuba, 1997, 40

2000	Indies	
2001	Indies	
2002	NJPW	17
2003	CMLL	26
2004	NJPW	18
	ROH	14
2005	NJPW	31
	ROH	11
2006	NJPW	41
2007	NOAH	34
	ROH	32
2008	CMLL	43
	NJPW	11
	ROH	10
	NOAH	9
	AAA	6
2009	AAA	47
	NJPW	10
2010	AAA	14
	NJPW	6
2011	NJPW	37

2012	NJPW	72
2013	NJPW	49
	ROH	7
2014	NJPW	53
	ROH	8
2015	NJPW	72
	ROH	12
2016	NJPW	74
	ROH	8
2017	NJPW	56
	ROH	9
2018	NJPW	76
	ROH	3
2019	NJPW	80
	ROH	6
2020	NJPW	23
	ROH	2
2021	NJPW	30
	AEW	4
	Impact	3
	ROH	3
2022	NJPW	24
	AEW	11
	CMLL	5
	Impact	4

RODERICK STRONG
5'10, 200lbs, Eau Claire, Wisconsin, 2000, 39

2000	Indies	
2001	Indies	
2002	Indies	
2003	Indies	
2004	ROH	19
	TNA	10
2005	ROH	36
	TNA	11
2006	ROH	43
	TNA	10
2007	ROH	42
2008	ROH	34
2009	ROH	43
	NOAH	17
2010	ROH	39
	NOAH	11
2011	ROH	27
	NOAH	11
2012	ROH	33
2013	ROH	36
	NOAH	10
2014	ROH	33
2015	ROH	47
2016	ROH	24
	WWE	18
2017	WWE	95
2018	WWE	103
2019	WWE	73
2020	WWE	31
2021	WWE	19
2022	WWE	20

ROHAN RAJA
6'1, 210lbs, Crawley, England, 2015, 31

2015	Indies	
2016	Indies	
2017	Indies	
2018	Impact	10
2019	Indies	
2021	WWE	5
2022	WWE	8

ROHIT RAJU
5'8, 163lbs, Saginaw, Michigan, 2008, 42

2008	Indies	
2009	Indies	
2010	Indies	
2011	Indies	
2012	Indies	
2013	ROH	2
2014	ROH	2

2015	ROH	2
2016	Indies	
2017	Impact	4
2018	Impact	27
2019	Impact	32
2020	Impact	27
2021	Impact	33
2022	AEW	7

ROMAN REIGNS
6'3, 265lbs, Pensacola, Florida, 2010, 37

2010	FCW	12
2011	FCW	55
2012	WWE	25
	FCW	15
2013	WWE	203
2014	WWE	151
2015	WWE	210
2016	WWE	158
2017	WWE	142
2018	WWE	134
2019	WWE	100
2020	WWE	33
2021	WWE	58
2022	WWE	47

RONDA ROUSEY
5'7, 135lbs, Riverside, California, 2018, 35

2018	WWE	50
2019	WWE	21
2022	WWE	55

ROSEMARY
5'8, 123lbs, Winnipeg, Canada, 2008, 39

2008	Indies	
2009	Indies	
2010	Indies	
2011	Indies	
2012	Indies	
2013	Indies	
2014	Indies	
2015	Indies	
2016	TNA	11
2017	Impact	23
2018	Impact	5
2019	Impact	22
2020	Impact	17
2021	Impact	27
2022	Impact	16

ROXANNE PEREZ
5'1, 115lbs, Laredo, Texas, 2018, 21

2018	Indies	
2019	Indies	
2020	Indies	
2021	ROH	13
2022	WWE	32
	Impact	1
	MLW	1

ROYCE ISAACS
6'1, 243lbs, Denver, Colorado, 2014, 33

2014	Indies	
2015	Indies	
2016	Indies	
2017	Indies	
2018	Indies	
2019	NWA	14
	ROH	5
2020	NWA	3
2021	NJPW	16
	AEW	8
2022	NJPW	28

RUBY SOHO
5'2, 125lbs, Edwardsburg, Michigan, 2010, 31

2010	Indies	
2011	Indies	
2012	Indies	
2013	Indies	
2014	Indies	
2015	Stardom	12
2016	Indies	
2017	WWE	98
2018	WWE	108
2019	WWE	44
2020	WWE	32
2021	AEW	13
	WWE	8
2022	AEW	39

RUSH
6'0, 216lbs, Tala, Mexico, 2007, 34

2007	Indies	
2008	Indies	
2009	CMLL	36
2010	CMLL	94
2011	CMLL	155
2012	CMLL	134
	NJPW	20
2013	CMLL	155
	NJPW	3
2014	CMLL	134
	NJPW	5
2015	CMLL	65
2016	CMLL	71
	NJPW	17
2017	CMLL	91
	NJPW	7
2018	CMLL	107
	NJPW	8
	MLW	3
	ROH	1
2019	CMLL	72
	ROH	31
	NJPW	5
	AAA	2
2020	ROH	6
	AAA	4
2021	ROH	9
	AAA	1
2022	AEW	18
	ROH	2

RYAN NEMETH
6'0, 203lbs, Cleveland, Ohio, 2010, 38

2010	OVW	10
2011	FCW	20
	OVW	9
2012	FCW	9
	WWE	6
2013	WWE	16
2014	Indies	
2015	Indies	
2016	Indies	
2017	Indies	
2018	Indies	
2019	Indies	
2020	Indies	
2021	AEW	34
2022	AEW	26

RYUSUKE TAGUCHI
5'11, 201lbs, Iwanuma, Japan, 2002, 43

2002	NJPW	5
2003	NJPW	109
2004	NJPW	123
2005	CMLL	56
	NJPW	30
2006	NJPW	117
2007	NJPW	92
2008	NJPW	104

2009	NJPW	110
2010	NJPW	124
2011	NJPW	119
2012	NJPW	102
2013	NJPW	48
2014	NJPW	90
2015	NJPW	135
2016	NJPW	133
2017	NJPW	120
2018	NJPW	105
2019	NJPW	120
2020	NJPW	65
2021	NJPW	78
2022	NJPW	107

SAM GRADWELL
6'1, 212lbs, Blackpool, England, 2009, 31

2009	Indies	
2010	Indies	
2011	Indies	
2012	Indies	
2013	Indies	
2014	Indies	
2015	Indies	
2016	Indies	
2017	WWE	6
2018	WWE	5
2020	WWE	2
2021	WWE	12
2022	WWE	6

SAMI CALLIHAN
5'10, 200lbs, Bellefontaine, Ohio, 2006, 35

2006	Indies	
2007	Indies	
2008	ROH	4
2009	ROH	10
2010	DGUSA	4
	EVOLVE	3
	ROH	2
2011	DGUSA	16
	EVOLVE	5
2012	DGUSA	7
	EVOLVE	7
2013	DGUSA	5
	EVOLVE	3
	WWE	2
2014	WWE	25
2015	WWE	83
2016	LU	14
	EVOLVE	8
2017	NJPW	19
	Impact	3
2018	Impact	25
	MLW	12
	LU	2
	ROH	2
2019	Impact	45
	MLW	5
2020	Impact	16
2021	Impact	25
2022	Impact	15

SAMI ZAYN
5'11, 180lbs, Montreal, Canada, 2002, 38

2002	Indies	
2003	Indies	
2004	Indies	
2005	Indies	
2006	Indies	
2007	ROH	25
2008	ROH	35
	Dragon Gate	21
2009	ROH	36
	Dragon Gate	10
2010	ROH	33
2011	ROH	27
2012	DDT	15
	PWG	10

2013	WWE	57
2014	WWE	101
2015	WWE	32
2016	WWE	179
2017	WWE	180
2018	WWE	74
2019	WWE	61
2020	WWE	17
2021	WWE	54
2022	WWE	79

SAMMY GUEVARA
5'11, 189lbs, Houston, Texas, 2013, 29

2013	Indies	
2014	Indies	
2015	Indies	
2016	Indies	
2017	EVOLVE	2
	Impact	2
	MLW	1
2018	AAA	4
	MLW	4
	LU	1
	NWA	1
2019	AEW	10
	AAA	6
2020	AEW	32
2021	AEW	20
2022	AEW	29

SAMOA JOE
6'2, 282lbs, Huntington Beach, California, 1999, 43

1999	Indies	
2000	Indies	
2001	Indies	
2002	ROH	5
2003	ROH	23
2004	ROH	25
2005	ROH	36
2006	TNA	45
	ROH	33
2007	TNA	52
	ROH	8
2008	TNA	88
2009	TNA	86
2010	TNA	58
2011	TNA	60
2012	TNA	74
2013	TNA	63
2014	TNA	59
2015	WWE	47
	TNA	6
	ROH	5
2016	WWE	96
2017	WWE	116
2018	WWE	108
2019	WWE	96
2020	WWE	12
2021	WWE	1
2022	AEW	15
	ROH	2

SANADA
6'0, 216lbs, Niigata, Japan, 2007, 35

2007	AJPW	81
2008	AJPW	108
2009	AJPW	101
2010	AJPW	113
2011	AJPW	127
2012	AJPW	108
2013	AJPW	45
2014	TNA	39
2015	TNA	8
2016	NJPW	102
2017	NJPW	155
2018	NJPW	131
2019	NJPW	138
2020	NJPW	87
2021	NJPW	134
2022	NJPW	108

SANGA
6'8, 300lbs, Dabra, India, 2011, 38

Year	Promotion	#
2011	Indies	
2012	Indies	
2013	Indies	
2014	Indies	
2015	Indies	
2016	Indies	
2017	Indies	
2018	WWE	7
2019	WWE	27
2020	WWE	10
2021	WWE	1
2022	WWE	20

SANTANA
5'10, 197lbs, New York City, New York, 2007, 31

Year	Promotion	#
2007	Indies	
2008	Indies	
2009	Indies	
2009	Indies	
2010	Indies	
2011	Indies	
2012	Indies	
2013	Indies	
2014	Indies	
2015	Indies	
2016	Indies	
2017	Impact	21
2018	Impact	24
2019	Impact	19
	AEW	8
	AAA	3
2020	AEW	29
2021	AEW	29
2022	AEW	10

SANTOS ESCOBAR
5'11, 205lbs, Ciudad de Mexico, Mexico, 2000, 38

Year	Promotion	#
2000	Indies	
2001	Indies	
2002	Indies	
2003	Indies	
2004	Indies	
2005	Indies	
2006	Indies	
2007	CMLL	6
2008	CMLL	73
2009	CMLL	112
2010	CMLL	117
2011	CMLL	119
2012	CMLL	107
2013	CMLL	67
	AAA	12
2014	AAA	53
	LU	9
2015	AAA	27
	LU	19
2016	AAA	12
	LU	8
2017	AAA	24
	Impact	10
	LU	2
2018	AAA	27
	Impact	14
	LU	1
2019	AAA	4
2020	WWE	23
2021	WWE	16
2022	WWE	18

SARAYA
5'8, 135lbs, Norwich, England, 2005, 30

Year	Promotion	#
2005	Indies	
2006	Indies	
2007	Indies	
2008	Indies	
2008	Indies	
2010	Indies	
2011	Indies	
2012	FCW	33
	WWE	25
2013	WWE	54
2014	WWE	131
2015	WWE	131
2016	WWE	44
2017	WWE	7
2022	AEW	1

SARRAY
5'2, 106lbs, Tokyo, Japan, 2011, 26

Year	Promotion	#
2011	Diana	19
2012	Diana	29
2013	Diana	37
2014	Diana	31
2015	Diana	28
2016	Diana	38
2017	SEAdLINNNG	12
	Diana	6
2018	Diana	29
2019	Diana	25
2020	Diana	12
2021	WWE	13
2022	WWE	10

SASHA BANKS
5'5, 115lbs, Fairfield, California, 2010, 30

Year	Promotion	#
2010	Indies	
2011	Indies	
2012	WWE	11
2013	WWE	49
2014	WWE	65
2015	WWE	149
2016	WWE	134
2017	WWE	162
2018	WWE	133
2019	WWE	71
2020	WWE	38
2021	WWE	46
2022	WWE	33

SATNAM SINGH
7'4, 304lbs, Punjab, India, 2022, 27

Year	Promotion	#
2022	AEW	8

SAVANNAH EVANS
5'10, 172lbs, Charlotte, North Carolina, 2014, 35

Year	Promotion	#
2014	Indies	
2015	Indies	
2016	Indies	
2017	Indies	
2018	Indies	
2019	EVOLVE	1
2020	AEW	1
2021	Impact	9
	AEW	1
2022	Impact	18

SAXON HUXLEY
6'3, 220lbs, Durham, England, 2010, 35

Year	Promotion	#
2010	Indies	
2011	Indies	
2012	Indies	
2013	Indies	
2014	Indies	
2015	Indies	
2016	Indies	
2017	WWE	6
2018	WWE	9
2019	WWE	12
2020	WWE	9
2021	WWE	8
2022	WWE	9

SCORPIO SKY
5'10, 183lbs, Los Angeles, California, 2002, 39

Year	Promotion	#
2002	Indies	
2003	Indies	
2004	Indies	
2005	Indies	
2006	Indies	
2007	Indies	
2008	Indies	
2009	Indies	
2010	ROH	3
2011	Indies	
2012	TNA	4
2013	TNA	2
2014	Indies	
2015	Indies	
2016	LU	2
	ROH	1
2017	ROH	7
2018	ROH	36
2019	AEW	16
2020	AEW	33
2021	AEW	27
2022	AEW	13

SCRYPTS
5'8, 176lbs, Memphis, Tennessee, 2020, 29

Year	Promotion	#
2021	WWE	20
2022	WWE	26

SERENA DEEB
5'4, 130lbs, Oakton, Virginia, 2005, 36

Year	Promotion	#
2005	OVW	3
2006	OVW	28
2007	OVW	34
	ROH	2
2008	OVW	16
	ROH	1
2009	FCW	12
	OVW	2
2010	FCW	15
	WWE	3
	ROH	1
2011	ROH	1
2013	TNA	1
2014	Indies	
2015	TNA	1
2017	WWE	2
2020	AEW	7
2021	AEW	10
2022	AEW	30
	ROH	1

SERPENTICO
5'6, 174lbs, Bayamon, Puerto Rico, 2004, 38

Year	Promotion	#
2004	Indies	
2005	Indies	
2006	Indies	
2007	Indies	
2008	Indies	
2009	Indies	
2010	TNA	3
2011	ROH	1
2012	DGUSA	1
	TNA	1
2013	EVOLVE	3
2014	EVOLVE	4
2015	TNA	2
2016	WWE	1
2017	WWE	1
2018	Impact	2
	ROH	1
2019	Indies	1
2020	AEW	33
2021	AEW	55
2022	AEW	46

SETH ROLLINS
6'1, 217lbs, Davenport, Iowa, 2005, 36

Year	Promotion	#
2005	Indies	
2006	Indies	
2007	ROH	11
2008	ROH	42
2009	ROH	46
2010	ROH	32
	FCW	16
2011	FCW	60
	WWE	6
2012	WWE	40
	FCW	39
2013	WWE	213
2014	WWE	193
2015	WWE	175
2016	WWE	115
2017	WWE	153
2018	WWE	164
2019	WWE	142
2020	WWE	54
2021	WWE	53
2022	WWE	118

SHA SAMUELS
6'1, 235lbs, London, England, 2004, 37

Year	Promotion	#
2004	Indies	
2005	Indies	
2006	Indies	
2007	Indies	
2008	Indies	
2009	Indies	
2010	Indies	
2011	Indies	
2012	Indies	
2013	Indies	
2014	Indies	
2015	Indies	
2016	Indies	
2017	Indies	
2018	Indies	
2019	WWE	1
2020	Indies	
2021	WWE	9
2022	WWE	6

SHANE HASTE
6'1, 220lbs, Perth, Australia, 2003, 37

Year	Promotion	#
2003	Indies	
2004	Indies	
2005	Indies	
2006	Indies	
2007	Indies	
2008	Indies	
2009	Indies	
2010	Indies	
2011	NOAH	41
2012	NOAH	48
	ROH	3
	TNA	1
2013	NOAH	79
2014	NOAH	99
2015	NOAH	37
	NJPW	1
2016	WWE	52
	NOAH	5
2017	WWE	12
2018	WWE	75
2019	WWE	55
2020	WWE	38
2021	WWE	10
2022	NJPW	36

SHANE MCMAHON
6'2, 230lbs, Greenwich, Connecticut, 1998, 52

Year	Promotion	#
1998	WWF	1
1999	WWF	22
2000	WWF	17

Year	Promotion	Count
2001	WWF	11
2003	WWE	24
2006	WWE	10
2007	WWE	8
2009	WWE	9
2016	WWE	2
2017	WWE	3
2018	WWE	6
2019	WWE	15
2021	WWE	1
2022	WWE	1

SHANKY
7'1, 342lbs, Haryana, India, 2015, ??

Year	Promotion	Count
2021	WWE	10
2022	WWE	14

SHAWN DEAN
??, 194lbs, Chicago, Illinois, 2017, 41

Year	Promotion	Count
2017	Indies	
2018	EVOLVE	1
2019	Indies	
2020	AEW	26
2021	AEW	20
2022	AEW	14

SHAWN SPEARS
6'3, 225lbs, Ontario, Canada, 2002, 41

Year	Promotion	Count
2002	Indies	
2003	Indies	
2004	Indies	
2005	WWE	1
2006	Indies	
2007	OVW	84
	WWE	2
2008	FCW	37
	OVW	15
	WWE	5
2009	FCW	1
	TNA	1
2010	TNA	8
2011	AJPW	7
	TNA	3
2012	TNA	1
2013	WWE	7
	TNA	1
2014	WWE	45
2015	WWE	93
2016	WWE	101
2017	WWE	137
2018	WWE	84
2019	AEW	11
	WWE	5
2020	AEW	28
2021	AEW	23
2022	AEW	8

SHAYNA BASZLER
5'7, 136lbs, Sioux Falls, South Dakota, 2015, 42

Year	Promotion	Count
2015	Indies	
2016	Indies	
2017	WWE	24
	Stardom	13
2018	WWE	91
2019	WWE	80
2020	WWE	42
2021	WWE	67
2022	WWE	77

SHEAMUS
6'4, 267lbs, Clonsilla, Ireland, 2002, 44

Year	Promotion	Count
2002	Indies	
2003	Indies	
2004	Indies	
2005	Indies	
2006	Indies	
2007	Indies	
2008	FCW	60
2009	WWE	83
	FCW	40
2010	WWE	184
2011	WWE	182
2012	WWE	218
2013	WWE	134
2014	WWE	168
2015	WWE	144
2016	WWE	165
2017	WWE	169
2018	WWE	152
2019	WWE	44
2020	WWE	43
2021	WWE	66
2022	WWE	84

SHELTON BENJAMIN
6'2, 245lbs, Orangeburg, South Carolina, 2000, 47

Year	Promotion	Count
2000	OVW	23
2001	OVW	27
2002	WWE	80
	OVW	27
2003	WWE	144
2004	WWE	141
2005	WWE	153
2006	WWE	140
2007	WWE	88
2008	WWE	151
2009	WWE	127
2010	WWE	13
2011	ROH	22
2012	ROH	21
	NJPW	20
2013	NJPW	45
2014	NJPW	29
2015	NOAH	65
2016	NOAH	58
2017	WWE	36
2018	WWE	125
2019	WWE	49
2020	WWE	44
2021	WWE	35
2022	WWE	26

SHERA
6'4, 242lbs, Punjab, India, 2011, 32

Year	Promotion	Count
2011	Indies	
2012	Indies	
2013	Indies	
2014	Indies	
2015	TNA	25
2016	TNA	24
2017	Impact	24
2018	WWE	10
2019	Impact	13
2020	Impact	7
2021	Impact	16
2022	Impact	13

SHINGO TAKAGI
5'10, 209lbs, Yamanashi, Japan, 2004, 40

Year	Promotion	Count
2004	Dragon Gate	42
2005	Dragon Gate	196
2006	Dragon Gate	55
	ROH	9
2007	Dragon Gate	111
	ROH	15
2008	Dragon Gate	158
	ROH	3
2009	Dragon Gate	154
	DGUSA	3
2010	Dragon Gate	164
	DGUSA	10
2011	Dragon Gate	130
2012	Dragon Gate	165
2013	Dragon Gate	168
2014	Dragon Gate	168
2015	Dragon Gate	169
2016	Dragon Gate	184
2017	Dragon Gate	170
2018	Dragon Gate	99
	NJPW	26
2019	NJPW	156
2020	NJPW	88
2021	NJPW	116
2022	NJPW	116
	AEW	1

SHINSUKE NAKAMURA
6'2, 229lbs, Kyoto, Japan, 2002, 42

Year	Promotion	Count
2002	NJPW	1
2003	NJPW	68
2004	NJPW	76
2005	NJPW	98
	CMLL	11
2006	NJPW	47
2007	NJPW	79
2008	NJPW	106
2009	NJPW	110
2010	NJPW	109
2011	NJPW	109
	CMLL	13
2012	NJPW	114
2013	NJPW	100
	CMLL	11
2014	NJPW	110
2015	NJPW	141
2016	WWE	96
	NJPW	10
2017	WWE	165
2018	WWE	170
2019	WWE	121
2020	WWE	44
2021	WWE	63
2022	WWE	70

SHO
5'8, 205lbs, Uwajima, Japan, 2012, 33

Year	Promotion	Count
2012	NJPW	5
2013	NJPW	60
2014	NJPW	60
2015	NJPW	113
	NOAH	13
2016	CMLL	26
	ROH	11
	NJPW	8
2017	NJPW	21
	ROH	15
2018	NJPW	131
2019	NJPW	113
2020	NJPW	64
2021	NJPW	115
2022	NJPW	118

SHOTA UMINO
6'0, 205lbs, Tokyo, Japan, 2017, 25

Year	Promotion	Count
2017	NJPW	79
2018	NJPW	132
2019	NJPW	105
2020	Indies	
2021	Indies	
2022	NJPW	10

SHOTZI
5'6, 125lbs, Los Angeles, California, 2014, 30

Year	Promotion	Count
2014	Indies	
2015	Indies	
2016	Indies	
2017	Indies	
2018	Indies	
2019	Indies	
2020	WWE	34
2021	WWE	35
2022	WWE	46

SKYE BLUE
5'8, 110lbs, Chicago, Illinois, 2017, 23

Year	Promotion	Count
2017	Indies	
2018	Indies	
2019	Indies	
2020	Indies	
2021	AEW	14
	NWA	10
2022	AEW	45

SLIM J
5'9, 187lbs, Detroit, Michigan, 2001, 37

Year	Promotion	Count
2001	Indies	
2002	TNA	1
	ROH	1
2003	ROH	4
2004	ROH	1
2005	Indies	
2006	Indies	
2007	Indies	
2008	Indies	
2009	Indies	
2010	Indies	
2011	Indies	
2012	Indies	
2013	Indies	
2014	Indies	
2015	Indies	
2016	ROH	1
2017	ROH	1
2018	ROH	1
2019	EVOLVE	2
	ROH	1
2020	Indies	
2021	Indies	
2022	AEW	7
	ROH	1

SLOANE JACOBS
5'8, 148lbs, West Chester, Pennsylvania, 2019, 19

Year	Promotion	Count
2019	Indies	
2020	Indies	
2021	AEW	3
2022	WWE	13
	AEW	1

SOL RUCA
5'8, ???lbs, Ontario, California, 2022, 23

Year	Promotion	Count
2022	WWE	22

SOLO SIKOA
5'11, 220lbs, Sacramento, California, 2018, 29

Year	Promotion	Count
2018	Indies	
2019	Indies	
2020	Indies	
2021	WWE	7
2022	WWE	48

SONJAY DUTT
5'8, 185lbs, Washington, D.C., 2000, 40

Year	Promotion	Count
2000	Indies	
2001	Indies	
2002	Indies	
2003	TNA	10
2004	TNA	36
2005	TNA	22
2006	TNA	59
2007	TNA	42
2008	TNA	81
2009	ROH	16
	TNA	5
2010	ROH	4
2011	Indies	
2012	TNA	12
2013	TNA	13
2014	TNA	4

2015	TNA	10
2016	Indies	
2017	Impact	19
2022	AEW	1

SONNY KISS
5'8, 188lbs, Jersey City, New Jersey, 2013, 29

2013	Indies	
2014	Indies	
2015	Indies	
2016	Indies	
2017	Indies	
2018	Indies	
2019	AEW	6
2020	AEW	34
2021	AEW	26
2020	AEW	15

SONYA DEVILLE
5'7, 130lbs, Los Angeles, California, 2015, 29

2015	WWE	2
2016	WWE	74
2017	WWE	95
2018	WWE	88
2019	WWE	81
2020	WWE	10
2021	WWE	2
2022	WWE	48

STEVE AUSTIN
6'2, 252lbs, Victoria, Texas, 1989, 58

1989	USWA	6
	WCCW	5
1990	USWA	41
	WCCW	39
1991	WCW	125
	USWA	20
1992	WCW	177
1993	WCW	145
1994	WCW	104
1995	WCW	25
	WWF	2
	ECW	2
1996	WWF	180
1997	WWF	120
1998	WWF	142
1999	WWF	78
2000	WWF	27
2001	WWF	109
2002	WWE	56
2003	WWE	3
2022	WWE	1

STEVE MACLIN
6'1, 226lbs, Rutherford, New Jersey, 2012, 35

2012	Indies	
2013	Indies	
2014	WWE	16
2015	WWE	29
2016	WWE	46
2017	WWE	62
2018	WWE	62
2019	WWE	82
2020	WWE	15
2021	Impact	15
2022	Impact	30

STEVIE TURNER
5'5, 110lbs, Hitchin, England, 2016, 26

2016	Indies	
2017	Indies	
2018	Indies	
2019	Stardom	43
2020	Indies	
2021	WWE	7
2022	WWE	6

STING
6'3, 252lbs, Omaha, Nebraska, 1985, 63

1985	CWA	17
1986	Mid-South	94
	CWA	16
1987	JCP	157
	UWF	30
1988	JCP	251
1989	WCW	157
1990	WCW	106
1991	WCW	208
1992	WCW	173
1993	WCW	143
1994	WCW	89
1995	WCW	97
1996	WCW	94
1997	WCW	3
1998	WCW	81
1999	WCW	95
2000	WCW	66
2001	WCW	1
2002	WWA	8
2003	TNA	4
	WWA	3
2004	Indies	
2005	Indies	
2006	TNA	16
2007	TNA	24
2008	TNA	16
2009	TNA	26
2010	TNA	13
2011	TNA	22
2012	TNA	13
2013	TNA	27
2014	TNA	4
2015	WWE	4
2021	AEW	6
2022	AEW	7

STU GRAYSON
5'11, 160lbs, Quebec, Canada, 2005, 33

2005	Indies	
2006	Indies	
2007	Indies	
2008	ROH	2
2009	ROH	10
2010	ROH	7
2011	Indies	
2012	DGUSA	5
	EVOLVE	4
2013	DGUSA	2
2014	Indies	
2015	Indies	
2016	Indies	
2017	Indies	
2018	Indies	
2019	AEW	6
2020	AEW	25
2021	AEW	41
2022	AEW	10

SWERVE STRICKLAND
6'0, 201lbs, Tacoma, Washington, 2011, 32

2011	Indies	
2012	EVOLVE	1
2013	EVOLVE	5
	DGUSA	4
2014	DGUSA	2
2015	LU	17
	EVOLVE	2
2016	LU	14
2017	MLW	2
2018	MLW	13
	EVOLVE	9
	LU	2
2019	WWE	49
	EVOLVE	6
2020	WWE	39
2021	WWE	13

| 2022 | AEW | 32 |
| | ROH | 2 |

T-BONE
6'0, 245lbs, Worcester, England, 2006, 41

2006	Indies	
2007	Indies	
2008	Indies	
2009	Indies	
2010	Indies	
2011	Indies	
2012	Indies	
2013	Indies	
2014	Indies	
2015	Indies	
2016	Indies	
2017	WWE	8
2018	WWE	9
2019	WWE	8
2020	WWE	4
2021	WWE	9
2022	WWE	5

TAICHI
5'8, 187lbs, Ishikari, Japan, 2002, 42

2002	AJPW	3
2003	AJPW	90
2004	AJPW	89
	TNA	3
2005	AJPW	55
2006	NJPW	14
2007	NJPW	66
2008	NJPW	79
2009	NJPW	96
2010	CMLL	54
	NJPW	44
2011	NJPW	108
2012	NJPW	88
	CMLL	11
2013	NJPW	78
	CMLL	9
2014	NJPW	81
2015	NOAH	100
	NJPW	3
2016	NOAH	113
	NJPW	3
2017	NJPW	110
2018	NJPW	93
2019	NJPW	123
2020	NJPW	83
2021	NJPW	90
2022	NJPW	113

TAIJI ISHIMORI
5'8, 165lbs, Tagajo, Japan, 2002, 39

2002	Indies	
2003	Indies	
2004	NJPW	27
2005	AJPW	26
	NJPW	19
2006	NOAH	44
	AJPW	20
2007	NOAH	88
2008	NOAH	118
2009	NOAH	94
2010	NOAH	107
	NJPW	10
2011	NOAH	112
2012	NOAH	111
2013	NOAH	124
2014	NOAH	97
2015	NOAH	106
2016	NOAH	122
	NJPW	13
2017	NOAH	104
2018	NJPW	56
	NOAH	18
	Impact	12
2019	NJPW	118

2020	NJPW	54
2021	NJPW	107
2022	NJPW	113

TAMA TONGA
6'0, 210lbs, Kissimmee, Florida, 2008, 40

2008	Indies	
2009	Indies	
2010	NJPW	77
	WWC	26
2011	NJPW	67
2012	NJPW	70
	CMLL	26
2013	NJPW	60
	CMLL	20
2014	NJPW	78
2015	NJPW	106
	CMLL	13
2016	NJPW	110
2017	NJPW	96
2018	NJPW	77
2019	NJPW	92
2020	NJPW	38
2021	NJPW	73
2022	NJPW	54

TAMINA
5'9, 170lbs, Vancouver, Washington, 2009, 44

2009	Indies	
2010	WWE	19
	FCW	14
2011	WWE	48
2012	WWE	44
2013	WWE	97
2014	WWE	47
2015	WWE	60
2016	WWE	41
2017	WWE	107
2018	WWE	30
2019	WWE	53
2020	WWE	12
2021	WWE	46
2022	WWE	50

TANGA LOA
6'2, 230lbs, Kissimmee, Florida, 2008, 39

2008	Indies	
2009	FCW	29
2010	FCW	60
2011	FCW	46
2012	WWE	36
2013	WWE	25
2014	WWE	15
2015	TNA	18
2016	NJPW	69
	CMLL	11
	ROH	6
2017	NJPW	80
2018	NJPW	86
2019	NJPW	92
2020	NJPW	37
2021	NJPW	73
2022	NJPW	24

TASHA STEELZ
5'4, ???lbs, Bloomfield, New Jersey, 2015, 34

2015	Indies	
2016	Indies	
2017	Indies	
2018	Indies	
2019	ROH	4
2020	Impact	15
2021	Impact	32
2022	Impact	24

TATUM PAXLEY
??, ???lbs, ???, 2022, 26

| 2022 | WWE | 29 |

TAY MELO
5'5, 126lbs, Rio de Janiero, Brazil, 2017, 27

2017	WWE	11
2018	WWE	42
2019	WWE	45
2020	WWE	8
	AEW	8
2021	AEW	53
2022	AEW	20

TAYLOR WILDE
5'3, 115lbs, Toronto, Canada, 2003, 36

2003	Indies	
2004	Indies	
2005	Indies	
2006	DSW	6
2007	WWE	3
2008	TNA	41
2009	TNA	78
2010	TNA	45
2011	Indies	
2021	TNA	9
2022	TNA	6

TEGAN NOX
5'6, 141lbs, Bargoed, Wales, 2013, 28

2013	Indies	
2014	Indies	
2015	Indies	
2016	Stardom	3
2017	Stardom	5
2018	WWE	20
2019	WWE	30
2020	WWE	26
2021	WWE	11
2022	WWE	4

TEOMAN
6'0, 198lbs, Berlin, Germany, 2008, 29

2008	Indies	
2009	Indies	
2010	Indies	
2011	Indies	
2012	Indies	
2013	Indies	
2014	Indies	
2015	Indies	
2016	Indies	
2017	Indies	
2018	Indies	
2019	Indies	
2020	Indies	
2021	WWE	9
2022	WWE	8

THEA HAIL
??, ???lbs, Pittsburgh, Pennsylvania, 2021, 19

2021	AEW	2
2022	WWE	26

THUNDER ROSA
5'3, 119lbs, Tijuana, Mexico, 2014, 36

2014	Indies	
2015	Stardom	14
	LU	3
2016	Stardom	13
	LU	5
2017	Indies	
2018	ROH	5
2019	NWA	7
	ROH	3
2020	AEW	8
	NWA	3
2021	AEW	45
	NWA	6
2022	AEW	19

TIFFANY STRATTON
5'7, 143lbs, Prior Lake, Minnesota, 2021, 23

2021	WWE	2
2022	WWE	22

TIGER TURAN
5'10, 189lbs, Pakistan, 2015, 25

2015	Indies	
2016	Indies	
2017	Indies	
2018	WWE	9
2019	WWE	5
2020	WWE	7
2021	WWE	6
2022	WWE	3

TJP
5'10, 175lbs, Los Angeles, California, 1998, 38

1998	Indies	
1999	Indies	
2000	Indies	
2001	Indies	
2002	CMLL	12
	NJPW	3
2003	Indies	
2004	NJPW	8
2005	NJPW	10
	ROH	4
2006	TNA	5
2007	ROH	3
2008	Indies	
2009	Indies	
2010	DGUSA	3
2011	ROH	10
	NJPW	9
2012	ROH	10
2013	TNA	20
2014	TNA	19
2015	TNA	35
	EVOLVE	12
2016	WWE	32
	EVOLVE	16
2017	WWE	61
2018	WWE	41
2019	NJPW	22
	Impact	11
	WWE	3
2020	Impact	29
	NJPW	15
2021	Impact	23
	NJPW	21
	MLW	8
2022	NJPW	67
	MLW	4

TOA LIONA
6'4, 301lbs, San Jose, California, 2020, 31

2020	Indies	
2021	AEW	3
2022	AEW	7
	ROH	3

TOM LAWLOR
6'0, 185lbs, Fall River, Massachusetts, 2005, 40

2005	Indies	
2006	Indies	
2017	MLW	2
2018	MLW	13
2019	MLW	12
2020	MLW	6
	NJPW	5
2021	NJPW	21
	MLW	6
2022	NJPW	35

TOMMASO CIAMPA
5'11, 201lbs, Boston, Massachusetts, 2005, 37

2005	Indies	
2006	Indies	
2007	OVW	23
2008	Indies	
2009	Indies	
2010	Indies	
2011	ROH	16
2012	ROH	18
2013	ROH	18
2014	ROH	34
2015	ROH	9
	WWE	6
2016	WWE	48
2017	WWE	31
2018	WWE	49
2019	WWE	19
2020	WWE	29
2021	WWE	26
2022	WWE	48

TOMMY DREAMER
6'3, 265lbs, Yonkers, New York, 1989, 51

1989	Indies	
1990	Indies	
1991	Indies	
1992	Indies	
1993	ECW	9
1994	ECW	47
1995	ECW	49
	AJPW	20
1996	ECW	62
1997	ECW	89
1998	ECW	105
1999	ECW	84
2000	ECW	67
2001	WWF	46
	ECW	3
2002	WWE	134
2003	WWE	101
2004	WWE	1
2005	WWE	1
2006	WWE	67
2007	WWE	120
2008	WWE	85
2009	WWE	103
2010	TNA	19
2011	TNA	26
2012	DGUSA	1
	WWE	1
2013	TNA	4
2014	TNA	6
2015	WWE	14
	TNA	7
2016	WWE	4
2017	ROH	1
2018	Impact	8
	MLW	6
2019	Impact	18
2020	Impact	13
2021	Impact	10
2022	Impact	4

TOMOHIRO ISHII
5'6, 220lbs, Kawasaki, Japan, 1996, 47

1996	WAR	2
1997	WAR	44
1998	WAR	24
1999	WAR	9
2000	Indies	
2001	Indies	
2002	Indies	
2003	World Japan	68
2004	World Japan	11
2005	Indies	
2006	NJPW	98
2007	NJPW	102
2008	NJPW	102

2009	NJPW	107
2010	NJPW	110
2011	NJPW	103
2012	NJPW	105
2013	NJPW	98
2014	NJPW	100
2015	NJPW	136
2016	NJPW	137
2017	NJPW	130
2018	NJPW	128
2019	NJPW	130
2020	NJPW	67
2021	NJPW	106
2022	NJPW	77

TONI STORM
5'5, 152lbs, Auckland, New Zealand, 2009, 27

2009	Indies	
2010	Indies	
2011	Indies	
2012	Indies	
2013	Indies	
2014	Indies	
2015	Indies	
2016	Stardom	23
2017	Stardom	36
	WWE	6
2018	WWE	16
	Stardom	14
2019	WWE	11
	Stardom	9
2020	WWE	13
2021	WWE	21
2022	AEW	30

TONY D'ANGELO
6'0, 196lbs, Oak Park, Illinois, 2021, 27

2021	WWE	6
2022	WWE	25

TONY NESE
5'9, 196lbs, New York City, New York, 2005, 37

2005	Indies	
2006	Indies	
2007	Indies	
2008	Indies	
2009	ROH	2
2010	Indies	
2011	TNA	6
	DGUSA	3
	EVOLVE	3
2012	EVOLVE	4
2013	Dragon Gate	6
	DGUSA	6
	EVOLVE	5
2014	EVOLVE	12
	DGUSA	5
2015	EVOLVE	16
2016	WWE	19
	EVOLVE	17
2017	WWE	75
2018	WWE	54
2019	WWE	47
2020	WWE	42
2021	WWE	17
	AEW	8
2022	AEW	35

TOP DOLLA
6'5, 330lbs, Washington, D.C., 2019, 32

2019	Indies	
2021	WWE	7
2022	WWE	24

TORU YANO
6'1, 243lbs, Tokyo, Japan, 2002, 44

2002	NJPW	69

Year	Promotion	Rank
2003	NJPW	103
2004	NJPW	107
2005	NJPW	75
2006	NJPW	130
2007	NJPW	116
2008	NJPW	108
2009	NJPW	107
2010	NJPW	121
2011	NJPW	114
2012	NJPW	114
2013	NJPW	97
	NOAH	19
2014	NJPW	98
2015	NJPW	135
2016	NOAH	59
	NJPW	58
	ROH	6
2017	NJPW	130
2018	NJPW	125
2019	NJPW	102
2020	NJPW	76
2021	NJPW	113
2022	NJPW	110

TRENT BERETTA
6'1, 203lbs, Mount Sinai, New York, 2004, 35

Year	Promotion	Rank
2004	Indies	
2005	Indies	
2006	Indies	
2007	Indies	
2008	FCW	41
2009	FCW	67
	WWE	5
2010	WWE	49
	FCW	47
2011	WWE	77
	FCW	11
2012	WWE	28
2013	NJPW	19
	DGUSA	7
2014	EVOLVE	11
	DGUSA	9
2015	NJPW	70
	ROH	12
	EVOLVE	6
2016	NJPW	75
	ROH	9
2017	NJPW	84
	ROH	15
2018	NJPW	51
	ROH	14
2019	AEW	14
	NJPW	5
2020	AEW	37
2021	AEW	6
2022	AEW	44

TRENT SEVEN
5'10, 204lbs, Wolverhampton, England, 2009, 41

Year	Promotion	Rank
2010	Indies	
2011	Indies	
2012	Indies	
2013	Indies	
2014	Indies	
2015	Indies	
2016	Indies	
2017	WWE	29
2018	WWE	31
2019	WWE	16
2020	WWE	13
2021	WWE	10
2022	WWE	9
	AEW	2

TREY MIGUEL
5'9, 136lbs, Toledo, Ohio, 2009, 28

Year	Promotion	Rank
2009	Indies	
2010	Indies	
2011	Indies	
2012	Indies	
2013	Indies	
2014	Indies	
2015	Indies	
2016	Indies	
2017	Indies	
2018	Impact	4
	MLW	3
2019	Impact	35
2020	Impact	26
2021	Impact	33
2022	Impact	26

TRICK WILLIAMS
6'4, 205lbs, Columbia, South Carolina, 2021, 28

Year	Promotion	Rank
2021	WWE	4
2022	WWE	29

TYLER BATE
5'7, 172lbs, Netherton, England, 2012, 25

Year	Promotion	Rank
2012	Indies	
2013	Indies	
2014	Indies	
2015	Indies	
2016	Indies	
2017	WWE	34
2018	WWE	31
2019	WWE	24
2020	WWE	10
2021	WWE	14
2022	WWE	11

VALENTINA FEROZ
??, ??lbs, Brazil, 2019, 27

Year	Promotion	Rank
2019	WWE	3
2020	WWE	9
2021	WWE	15
2022	WWE	21

VEER MAHAAN
6'3, 256lbs, Lucknow, India, 2018, 34

Year	Promotion	Rank
2018	WWE	15
2019	WWE	31
2020	WWE	10
2021	WWE	17
2022	WWE	49

VINCENT
5'8, 189lbs, Warwick, Rhode Island, 2009, 36

Year	Promotion	Rank
2009	Indies	
2010	Indies	
2011	Indies	
2012	ROH	3
2013	ROH	5
2014	ROH	2
2015	ROH	1
2016	ROH	5
2017	ROH	31
2018	ROH	30
2019	ROH	29
2020	ROH	6
2021	ROH	5
2022	ROH	1

VON WAGNER
6'4, 250lbs, Osseo, Minnesota, 2019, 28

Year	Promotion	Rank
2019	WWE	23
2020	WWE	11
2021	WWE	10
2022	WWE	33

WARDLOW
6'3, 267lbs, Middlefield, Ohio, 2014, 34

Year	Promotion	Rank
2014	Indies	
2015	Indies	
2016	Indies	
2017	Indies	
2018	Indies	
2019	Indies	
2020	AEW	15
2021	AEW	34
2022	AEW	32

WENDY CHOO
5'2, ???lbs, New York City, New York, 2014, 30

Year	Promotion	Rank
2014	Indies	
2015	Indies	
2016	Indies	
2017	ROH	7
2018	ROH	8
	WWE	2
2019	WWE	25
2021	WWE	3
2022	WWE	26

WES LEE
5'7, 190lbs, Dayton, Ohio, 2011, 28

Year	Promotion	Rank
2011	Indies	
2012	Indies	
2013	Indies	
2014	Indies	
2015	Indies	
2016	Indies	
2017	Impact	17
2018	Impact	12
2019	Impact	36
2020	Impact	23
2021	WWE	16
2022	WWE	39

WHEELER YUTA
6'0, 191lbs, Philadelphia, Pennsylvania, 2015, 26

Year	Promotion	Rank
2015	Indies	
2016	Indies	
2017	MLW	2
2018	MLW	10
2019	MLW	4
2020	ROH	3
2021	AEW	29
	NJPW	11
	ROH	3
2022	AEW	37
	NJPW	20
	ROH	3

WILL OSPREAY
6'1, 225lbs, London, England, 2012, 29

Year	Promotion	Rank
2012	Indies	
2013	Indies	
2014	Indies	
2015	Indies	
2016	NJPW	50
	ROH	5
	Impact	5
2017	NJPW	94
	ROH	14
2018	NJPW	77
2019	NJPW	99
2020	NJPW	44
2021	NJPW	61
2022	NJPW	56
	AEW	6

WILLIE MACK
5'11, 275lbs, Los Angeles, California, 2006, 35

Year	Promotion	Rank
2006	Indies	
2007	Indies	
2008	Indies	
2009	Indies	
2010	Indies	
2011	Indies	
2012	Indies	
2013	AAA	1
2014	Indies	
2015	LU	16
2016	LU	22
2017	Indies	
2018	Dragon Gate	27
	Impact	5
2019	Impact	41
	AAA	7
	ROH	6
2020	Impact	31
2021	Impact	28
2022	AAA	14
	Impact	9

WILLOW NIGHTINGALE
??, ???lbs, Franklin Square, New York, 2015, 28

Year	Promotion	Rank
2015	Indies	
2016	Indies	
2017	Indies	
2018	Indies	
2019	Indies	
2020	Indies	
2021	ROH	10
	AEW	6
2022	AEW	24

WOLFGANG
6'1, 255lbs, Glasgow, Scotland, 2003, 36

Year	Promotion	Rank
2003	Indies	
2004	Indies	
2005	Indies	
2006	Indies	
2007	Indies	
2008	Indies	
2009	Indies	
2010	Indies	
2011	Indies	
2012	Indies	
2013	Indies	
2014	Indies	
2015	Indies	
2016	Indies	
2017	WWE	21
2018	WWE	24
2019	WWE	13
2020	WWE	8
2021	WWE	9
2022	WWE	12

XAVIER WOODS
5'9, 205lbs, Marietta, Georgia, 2005, 36

Year	Promotion	Rank
2005	Indies	
2006	Indies	
2007	Indies	
2008	TNA	61
2009	TNA	71
2010	FCW	33
2011	FCW	32
2012	FCW	24
	WWE	20
2013	WWE	52
2014	WWE	79
2015	WWE	114
2016	WWE	104
2017	WWE	53
2018	WWE	76
2019	WWE	68
2020	WWE	13
2021	WWE	65
2022	WWE	68

XIA BROOKSIDE
5'3, 110lbs, Leicester, England, 2015, 23

Year	Promotion	Rank
2015	Indies	
2016	Indies	
2017	Stardom	17
2018	Stardom	18
	WWE	7

2019	WWE	12
	Stardom	10
2020	WWE	6
2021	WWE	7
2022	WWE	6

XIA LI
5'3, 136lbs, Chongqing, China, 2017, 34

2017	WWE	1
2018	WWE	23
2019	WWE	53
2020	WWE	16
2021	WWE	21
2022	WWE	26

XYON QUINN
6'2, 246lbs, Brisbane, Australia, 2018, 31

2018	WWE	1
2019	WWE	23
2020	WWE	6
2021	WWE	12
2022	WWE	33

YOH
5'8, 187lbs, Kurihara, Japan, 2012, 34

2012	NJPW	5
2013	NJPW	64
2014	NJPW	60
2015	NJPW	132
2016	CMLL	29
	ROH	10
	NJPW	8
2017	NJPW	21
	ROH	15
2018	NJPW	133
2019	NJPW	114
2020	NJPW	20
2021	NJPW	67
2022	NJPW	97

YOSHI-HASHI
5'11, 198lbs, Aichi, Japan, 2008, 40

2008	NJPW	44
2009	NJPW	86
2010	NJPW	41
	CMLL	32
2011	CMLL	72
2012	NJPW	107
2013	NJPW	99
2014	NJPW	92
2015	NJPW	138
2016	NJPW	140
2017	NJPW	137
	ROH	6
2018	NJPW	108
2019	NJPW	128
2020	NJPW	68
2021	NJPW	117
2022	NJPW	108

YOSHINOBU KANEMARU
5'7", 187lbs, Kofu, Japan, 1996, 46

1996	AJPW	39
1997	AJPW	69
1998	AJPW	107
1999	AJPW	114
2000	AJPW	67
	NOAH	43
2001	NOAH	109
2002	NOAH	107
2003	NOAH	117
2004	NOAH	107
2005	NOAH	108
2006	NOAH	95
2007	NOAH	102
2008	NOAH	101
2009	NOAH	92

2010	NOAH	111
2011	NOAH	120
2012	NOAH	109
2013	AJPW	102
2014	AJPW	91
2015	AJPW	105
2016	NOAH	114
2017	NJPW	100
2018	NJPW	107
2019	NJPW	110
2020	NJPW	69
2021	NJPW	100
2022	NJPW	103

YUJIRO TAKAHASHI
5'10", 225lbs, Niigata, Japan, 2004, 41

2004	NJPW	35
2005	NJPW	80
2006	NJPW	89
2007	NJPW	112
2008	NJPW	107
2009	CMLL	73
	NJPW	10
2010	NJPW	124
2011	NJPW	115
2012	NJPW	98
	CMLL	19
2013	NJPW	100
	NOAH	13
2014	NJPW	94
2015	NJPW	96
2016	NJPW	126
2017	NJPW	118
2018	NJPW	92
2019	NJPW	88
2020	NJPW	65
2021	NJPW	121
2022	NJPW	110

YUKA SAKAZAKI
5'2", ??lbs, Tokyo, Japan, 2013, ??

2013	Indies	
2014	Indies	
2015	DDT	11
2016	DDT	6
2017	DDT	6
2018	DDT	5
2019	DDT	5
	AEW	2
2020	AEW	3
2021	AEW	7
2022	AEW	8

YULISA LEON
??, ??lbs, Monterrey, Mexico, 2021, ??

| 2021 | WWE | 6 |
| 2022 | WWE | 10 |

YUYA UEMURA
5'11, 181lbs, Imabari, Japan, 2018, 28

2018	NJPW	54
2019	NJPW	100
2020	NJPW	83
2021	NJPW	68
2022	NJPW	16
	Impact	11

ZACK CLAYTON
6'3, 256lbs, Albany, New York, 2015, ??

2015	Indies	
2016	Indies	
2017	Indies	
2018	Indies	
2019	Indies	
2020	AEW	2
2021	AEW	5
2022	AEW	17

ZACK SABRE JR.
6'0, 181lbs, Sittingbourne, England, 2002, 35

2002	Indies	
2003	Indies	
2004	Indies	
2005	Indies	
2006	Indies	
2007	Indies	
2008	NOAH	2
2009	Dragon Gate	2
2010	Indies	
2011	NOAH	34
2012	NOAH	51
2013	NOAH	48
2014	NOAH	62
2015	NOAH	82
2016	EVOLVE	19
	WWE	4
	NJPW	2
2017	NJPW	35
	EVOLVE	21
2018	NJPW	69
	EVOLVE	5
2019	NJPW	112
	ROH	5
2020	NJPW	78
2021	NJPW	105
2022	NJPW	92

ZICKY DICE
??, ?? lbs, California, 2015, ??

2015	Indies	
2016	Indies	
2017	Indies	
2018	Indies	
2019	NWA	2
2020	NWA	4
2021	Impact	6
2022	Impact	18

ZOEY STARK
5'7, 140lbs, Utah, 2013, 28

2013	Indies	
2014	Indies	
2018	Indies	
2019	Indies	
2020	Indies	
2021	WWE	17
2022	WWE	23

TITLE
HISTORIES

Within this section is what we consider the definitive history of notable active titles in major promotions. In many cases the dates and reign length will differ from promotions' official records, due to inaccurate record keeping on their part. Where a title change took place on television, we have used the air date rather than the taping date. In some cases we have recognised title changes that a promotion does not. In these cases we feel there is strong enough justification to recognise the title change, usually because it was widely known and accepted at the time prior to history being rewrote.

WWE CHAMPIONSHIP

DATE	WON BY	DAYS
11-04-63	**Buddy Rogers**	22
	(Awarded)	
17-05-63	**Bruno Sammartino**	2,803
	(House Show, New York)	
18-01-71	**Ivan Koloff**	21
	(House Show, New York)	
08-02-71	**Pedro Morales**	1,027
	(House Show, New York)	
01-12-73	**Stan Stasiak**	9
	(House Show, Philadelphia)	
10-12-73	**Bruno Sammartino²**	1,237
	(House Show, New York)	
30-04-77	**Superstar Billy Graham**	296
	(House Show, Baltimore)	
20-02-78	**Bob Backlund**	648
	(WWF On MSG Network, New York)	
30-11-79	**Antonio Inoki**	6
	(Toukon Series, Tokushima, Japan)	
06-12-79	**VACANT**	
17-12-79	**Bob Backlund²**	1,470
	(WWF On MSG Network, New York)	
26-12-83	**The Iron Sheik**	28
	(WWF On MSG Network, New York)	
23-01-84	**Hulk Hogan**	1,474
	(WWF On MSG Network, New York)	
05-02-88	**Andre The Giant**	<1
	(The Main Event I, Indianapolis)	
13-02-88	**VACANT**	
27-03-88	**Randy Savage**	371
	(WrestleMania IV, Atlantic City)	
02-04-89	**Hulk Hogan²**	364
	(WrestleMania V, Atlantic City)	
01-04-90	**Ultimate Warrior**	293
	(WrestleMania VI, Toronto, Canada)	
19-01-91	**Sgt. Slaughter**	64
	(Royal Rumble '91, Miami)	
24-03-91	**Hulk Hogan³**	248
	(WrestleMania VII, Los Angeles)	
27-11-91	**The Undertaker**	6
	(Survivor Series '91, Detroit)	
03-12-91	**Hulk Hogan⁴**	4
	(This Tuesday In Texas, San Antonio)	
07-12-91	**VACANT**	
19-01-92	**Ric Flair**	77
	(Royal Rumble '92, Albany)	
05-04-92	**Randy Savage²**	149
	(WrestleMania VIII, Indianapolis)	
01-09-92	**Ric Flair²**	41
	(Prime Time Wrestling, Hershey)	
12-10-92	**Bret Hart**	174
	(House Show, Saskatoon, Canada)	
04-04-93	**Yokozuna**	<1
	(WrestleMania IX, Paradise)	
04-04-93	**Hulk Hogan⁵**	70
	(WrestleMania IX, Paradise)	
13-06-93	**Yokozuna²**	280
	(King Of The Ring '93, Dayton)	
20-03-94	**Bret Hart²**	248
	(WrestleMania X, New York)	
23-11-94	**Bob Backlund³**	3
	(Survivor Series '94, San Antonio)	
26-11-94	**Diesel**	358
	(House Show, New York)	
19-11-95	**Bret Hart³**	133
	(Survivor Series '95, Landover)	
31-03-96	**Shawn Michaels**	231
	(WrestleMania XII, Anaheim)	
17-11-96	**Sycho Sid**	63
	(Survivor Series '96, New York)	
19-01-97	**Shawn Michaels²**	25
	(Royal Rumble '97, San Antonio)	
13-02-97	**VACANT**	
16-02-97	**Bret Hart⁴**	1
	(In Your House 13, Chattanooga)	
17-02-97	**Sycho Sid²**	34
	(Monday Night RAW, Nashville)	
23-03-97	**The Undertaker²**	133
	(WrestleMania XIII, Rosemont)	
03-08-97	**Bret Hart⁵**	98
	(SummerSlam '97, East Rutherford)	
09-11-97	**Shawn Michaels³**	140
	(Survivor Series '97, Montreal, Canada)	
29-03-98	**Steve Austin**	91
	(WrestleMania XIV, Boston)	
28-06-98	**Kane**	1
	(King Of The Ring '98, Pittsburgh)	
29-06-98	**Steve Austin²**	90
	(Monday Night RAW, Cleveland)	
27-09-98	**VACANT**	
15-11-98	**The Rock**	50
	(Survivor Series '98, St. Louis)	
04-01-99	**Mankind**	20
	(Monday Night RAW, Worcester)	
24-01-99	**The Rock²**	7
	(Royal Rumble '99, Anaheim)	
31-01-99	**Mankind²**	15
	(Halftime Heat, Tucson)	
15-02-99	**The Rock³**	41
	(Monday Night RAW, Birmingham)	
28-03-99	**Steve Austin³**	56
	(WrestleMania XV, Philadelphia)	
23-05-99	**The Undertaker³**	36
	(Over The Edge '99, Kansas City)	
28-06-99	**Steve Austin⁴**	55
	(Monday Night RAW, Charlotte)	
22-08-99	**Mankind³**	1
	(SummerSlam '99, Minneapolis)	
23-08-99	**Triple H**	24
	(Monday Night RAW, Ames)	
16-09-99	**Vince McMahon**	4
	(SmackDown, Las Vegas)	
20-09-99	**VACANT**	
26-09-99	**Triple H²**	49
	(Unforgiven '99, Charlotte)	
14-11-99	**The Big Show**	50
	(Survivor Series '99, Detroit)	
03-01-00	**Triple H³**	118
	(Monday Night RAW, Miami)	
30-04-00	**The Rock⁴**	21
	(Backlash '00, Washington)	
21-05-00	**Triple H⁴**	35
	(Judgment Day '00, Louisville)	
25-06-00	**The Rock⁵**	119
	(King Of The Ring '00, Boston)	
22-10-00	**Kurt Angle**	126
	(No Mercy '00, Albany)	
25-02-01	**The Rock⁶**	35
	(No Way Out '01, Las Vegas)	
01-04-01	**Steve Austin⁵**	175
	(WrestleMania XVII, Houston)	
23-09-01	**Kurt Angle²**	15
	(Unforgiven '01, Pittsburgh)	
08-10-01	**Steve Austin⁶**	62
	(Monday Night RAW, Indianapolis)	
09-12-01	**Chris Jericho**	98
	(Vengeance '01, San Diego)	
17-03-02	**Triple H⁵**	35
	(WrestleMania XVIII, Toronto)	

21-04-02	**Hulk Hogan**[6] (Backlash '02, Kansas City)	28
19-05-02	**The Undertaker**[4] (Judgment Day '02, Nashville)	63
21-07-02	**The Rock**[7] (Vengeance '02, Detroit)	35
25-08-02	**Brock Lesnar** (SummerSlam '02, Uniondale)	84
17-11-02	**The Big Show**[2] (Survivor Series '02, New York)	28
15-12-02	**Kurt Angle**[3] (Armageddon '02, Sunrise)	105
30-03-03	**Brock Lesnar**[2] (WrestleMania XIX, Seattle)	119
27-07-03	**Kurt Angle**[4] (Vengeance '03, Denver)	53
18-09-03	**Brock Lesnar**[3] (SmackDown, Raleigh)	150
15-02-04	**Eddie Guerrero** (No Way Out '04, Daly City)	133
27-06-04	**John Bradshaw Layfield** (Great American Bash '04, Norfolk)	280
03-04-05	**John Cena** (WrestleMania XXI, Los Angeles)	280
08-01-06	**Edge** (New Year's Revolution '06, Albany)	21
29-01-06	**John Cena**[2] (Royal Rumble '06, Miami)	133
11-06-06	**Rob Van Dam** (ECW One Night Stand '06, New York)	22
03-07-06	**Edge**[2] (Monday Night RAW, Philadelphia)	76
17-09-06	**John Cena**[3] (Unforgiven '06, Toronto)	380
02-10-07	**VACANT**	
07-10-07	**Randy Orton** (No Mercy '07, Rosemont)	<1
07-10-07	**Triple H**[6] (No Mercy '07, Rosemont)	<1
07-10-07	**Randy Orton**[2] (No Mercy '07, Rosemont)	203
27-04-08	**Triple H**[7] (Backlash '08, Baltimore)	210
23-11-08	**Edge**[3] (Survivor Series '08, Boston)	21
14-12-08	**Jeff Hardy** (Armageddon '08, Buffalo)	42
25-01-09	**Edge**[4] (Royal Rumble '09, Detroit)	21
15-02-09	**Triple H**[8] (No Way Out '09, Seattle)	70
26-04-09	**Randy Orton**[3] (Backlash '09, Providence)	42
07-06-09	**Batista** (Extreme Rules '09, New Orleans)	2
09-06-09	**VACANT**	
15-06-09	**Randy Orton**[4] (Monday Night RAW, Charlotte)	90
13-09-09	**John Cena**[4] (Breaking Point '09, Montreal, Canada)	21
04-10-09	**Randy Orton**[5] (Hell In A Cell '09, Newark)	21
25-10-09	**John Cena**[5] (Bragging Rights '09, Pittsburgh)	49
13-12-09	**Sheamus** (TLC '09, San Antonio)	70
21-02-10	**John Cena**[6] (Elimination Chamber '10, St. Louis)	<1
21-02-10	**Batista**[2] (Elimination Chamber '10, St. Louis)	35
28-03-10	**John Cena**[7]	84
	(WrestleMania XXVI, Glendale)	
20-06-10	**Sheamus**[2] (Fatal 4-Way '10, Uniondale)	91
19-09-10	**Randy Orton**[6] (Night Of Champions '10, Rosemont)	64
22-11-10	**The Miz** (Monday Night RAW, Orlando)	160
01-05-11	**John Cena**[8] (Extreme Rules '11, Tampa)	77
17-07-11	**CM Punk** (Money In The Bank '11, Rosemont)	28
25-07-11	*Rey Mysterio (acting)* (Monday Night RAW, Hampton)	<1
25-07-11	**John Cena**[9] *(acting)* (Monday Night RAW, Hampton)	20
14-08-11	**Alberto Del Rio** (SummerSlam '11, Los Angeles)	35
18-09-11	**John Cena**[10] (Night Of Champions '11, Buffalo)	14
02-10-11	**Alberto Del Rio**[2] (Hell In A Cell '11, New Orleans)	49
20-11-11	**CM Punk**[2] (Survivor Series '11, New York)	434
27-01-13	**The Rock**[8] (Royal Rumble '13, Phoenix)	70
07-04-13	**John Cena**[11] (WrestleMania XXIX, East Rutherford)	133
18-08-13	**Daniel Bryan** (SummerSlam '13, Los Angeles)	<1
18-08-13	**Randy Orton**[7] (SummerSlam '13, Los Angeles)	28
15-09-13	**Daniel Bryan**[2] (Night Of Champions '13, Detroit)	1
16-09-13	**VACANT**	
27-10-13	**Randy Orton**[8] (Hell In A Cell '13, Miami)	161
06-04-14	**Daniel Bryan**[3] (WrestleMania XXX, New Orleans)	65
09-06-14	**VACANT**	
29-06-14	**John Cena**[12] (Money In The Bank '14, Boston)	49
17-08-14	**Brock Lesnar**[4] (SummerSlam '14, Los Angeles)	224
29-03-15	**Seth Rollins** (WrestleMania XXXI, Santa Clara)	221
05-11-15	**VACANT**	
22-11-15	**Roman Reigns** (Survivor Series '15, Atlanta)	<1
22-11-15	**Sheamus**[3] (Survivor Series '15, Atlanta)	22
14-12-15	**Roman Reigns**[2] (Monday Night RAW, Philadelphia)	41
24-01-16	**Triple H**[9] (Royal Rumble '16, Orlando)	70
03-04-16	**Roman Reigns**[3] (WrestleMania XXXII, Arlington)	77
19-06-16	**Seth Rollins**[2] (Money In The Bank '16, Las Vegas)	<1
19-06-16	**Dean Ambrose** (Money In The Bank '16, Las Vegas)	84
11-09-16	**AJ Styles** (Backlash '16, Richmond)	140
29-01-17	**John Cena**[13] (Royal Rumble '17, San Antonio)	14
12-02-17	**Bray Wyatt** (Elimination Chamber '17, Phoenix)	49
02-04-17	**Randy Orton**[9] (WrestleMania XXXIII, Orlando)	49
21-05-17	**Jinder Mahal** (Backlash '17, Rosemont)	170
07-11-17	**AJ Styles**[2]	371

(SmackDown, Manchester)

13-11-18	**Daniel Bryan**[4]	145

(SmackDown, St. Louis)

07-04-19	**Kofi Kingston**	180

(WrestleMania XXXV, East Rutherford)

04-10-19	**Brock Lesnar**[5]	184

(SmackDown, Los Angeles)

05-04-20	**Drew McIntyre**	203

(WrestleMania XXXVI, Orlando)

25-10-20	**Randy Orton**[10]	22

(Hell In A Cell '20, Orlando)

16-11-20	**Drew McIntyre**[2]	97

(Monday Night RAW, Orlando)

21-02-21	**The Miz**[2]	8

(Elimination Chamber '21, St. Petersburg)

01-03-21	**Bobby Lashley**	196

(Monday Night RAW, St. Petersburg)

13-09-21	**Big E**	110

(Monday Night RAW, Boston)

01-01-22	**Brock Lesnar**[6]	28

(Day 1 '22, Atlanta)

29-01-22	**Bobby Lashley**[2]	21

(Royal Rumble '22, St. Louis)

19-02-22	**Brock Lesnar**[7]	43

(Elimination Chamber '22, Jeddah, S. Arabia)

03-04-22	**Roman Reigns**[4]	272*

(WrestleMania XXXVIII, Arlington)

Most Reigns

1.	John Cena	13
2.	Randy Orton	10
3.	Triple H	9
4.	The Rock	8
5.	Brock Lesnar	7

Longest Reigns

1.	Bruno Sammartino	2,803
2.	Hulk Hogan	1,474
3.	Bob Backlund	1,470
4.	Bruno Sammartino	1,237
5.	Pedro Morales	1,027

Longest Cumulative Reigns

1.	Bruno Sammartino	4,040
2.	Hulk Hogan	2,185
3.	Bob Backlund	2,121
4.	John Cena	1,254
5.	Pedro Morales	1,027

WWE UNIVERSAL CHAMPIONSHIP

DATE	WON BY	DAYS
21-08-16	**Finn Balor**	1

(SummerSlam '16, Brooklyn)

22-08-16	**VACANT**	
29-08-16	**Kevin Owens**	188

(Monday Night RAW, Houston)

05-03-17	**Goldberg**	28

(Fastlane '17, Milwaukee)

02-04-17	**Brock Lesnar**	504

(WrestleMania XXXIII, Orlando)

19-08-18	**Roman Reigns**	64

(SummerSlam '18, Brooklyn)

22-10-18	**VACANT**	
02-11-18	**Brock Lesnar**[2]	156

(Crown Jewel '18, Riyadh, Saudi Arabia)

07-04-19	**Seth Rollins**	98

(WrestleMania XXXV, East Rutherford)

14-07-19	**Brock Lesnar**[3]	28

(Extreme Rules '19, Philadelphia)

11-08-19	**Seth Rollins**[2]	81

(SummerSlam '19, Toronto, Canada)

31-10-19	**The Fiend**	119

(Crown Jewel '19, Riyadh, Saudi Arabia)

27-02-20	**Goldberg**[2]	37

(Super Showdown '20, Riyadh, Saudi Arabia)

04-04-20	**Braun Strowman**	141

(WrestleMania XXXVI, Orlando)

23-08-20	**The Fiend**[2]	7

(SummerSlam '20, Orlando)

30-08-20	**Roman Reigns**[2]	852*

(Payback '20, Orlando)

Most Reigns

1.	Brock Lesnar	3
2.	Seth Rollins	2
3.	Goldberg	2
4.	The Fiend	2
5.	Roman Reigns	2

Longest Reigns

1.	Roman Reigns	852*
2.	Brock Lesnar	504
3.	Kevin Owens	188
4.	Brock Lesnar	156
5.	Braun Strowman	141

Longest Cumulative Reigns

1.	Roman Reigns	916*
2.	Brock Lesnar	687
3.	Kevin Owens	188
4.	Seth Rollins	179
5.	Braun Strowman	141

WWE INTERCONTINENTAL CHAMPIONSHIP

DATE	WON BY	DAYS
01-09-79	**Pat Patterson**	233

(Awarded)

21-04-80	**Ken Patera**	231

(House Show, New York)

08-12-80	**Pedro Morales**	194

(House Show, New York)

20-06-81	**Don Muraco**	156

(House Show, Philadelphia)

23-11-81	**Pedro Morales**[2]	425

(House Show, New York)

22-01-83	**Don Muraco**[2]	385

(House Show, New York)

11-02-84	**Tito Santana**	245

(House Show, Boston)

13-10-84	**Greg Valentine**	266

(Maple Leaf Wrestling, Ontario)

06-07-85	**Tito Santana**[2]	217

(House Show, Baltimore)

08-02-86	**Randy Savage**	414

(House Show, Boston)

29-03-87	**Ricky Steamboat**	76

(WrestleMania III, Pontiac)

13-06-87	**The Honky Tonk Man**	443

(Superstars Of Wrestling, Buffalo)

29-08-88	**Ultimate Warrior**	216

(SummerSlam '88, New York)

02-04-89	**Rick Rude**	148

	(WrestleMania V, Atlantic City)	
28-08-89	**Ultimate Warrior**[2]	218
	(SummerSlam '89, East Rutherford)	
03-04-90	**VACANT**	
19-05-90	**Mr. Perfect**	100
	(Superstars Of Wrestling, Austin)	
27-08-90	**The Texas Tornado**	110
	(SummerSlam '90, Philadelphia)	
15-12-90	**Mr. Perfect**[2]	254
	(Superstars Of Wrestling, Rochester)	
26-08-91	**Bret Hart**	144
	(SummerSlam '91, New York)	
17-01-92	**The Mountie**	2
	(House Show, Springfield)	
19-01-92	**Roddy Piper**	77
	(Royal Rumble '92, Albany)	
05-04-92	**Bret Hart**[2]	146
	(WrestleMania VIII, Indianapolis)	
29-08-92	**The British Bulldog**	77
	(SummerSlam '92, London, England)	
14-11-92	**Shawn Michaels**	184
	(Saturday Night's Main Event, Terre Haute)	
17-05-93	**Marty Jannetty**	20
	(Monday Night RAW, New York)	
06-06-93	**Shawn Michaels**[2]	113
	(House Show, Albany)	
27-09-93	**VACANT**	
11-10-93	**Razor Ramon**	201
	(Monday Night RAW, New Haven)	
30-04-94	**Diesel**	121
	(Superstars, Rochester)	
29-08-94	**Razor Ramon**[2]	146
	(SummerSlam '94, Chicago)	
22-01-95	**Jeff Jarrett**	98
	(Royal Rumble '95, Tampa)	
30-04-95	**VACANT**	
07-05-95	**Jeff Jarrett**[2]	12
	(Action Zone, Moline)	
19-05-95	**Razor Ramon**[3]	2
	(House Show, Montreal, Canada)	
21-05-95	**Jeff Jarrett**[3]	63
	(House Show, Trois-Rivieres, Canada)	
23-07-95	**Shawn Michaels**[3]	91
	(In Your House 2, Nashville)	
22-10-95	**Dean Douglas**	<1
	(In Your House 4, Winnipeg, Canada)	
22-10-95	**Razor Ramon**[4]	91
	(In Your House 4, Winnipeg, Canada)	
21-01-96	**Goldust**	85
	(Royal Rumble '96, Fresno)	
15-04-96	**VACANT**	
22-04-96	**Goldust**[2]	63
	(Monday Night RAW, San Bernardino)	
23-06-96	**Ahmed Johnson**	58
	(King of the Ring '96, Milwaukee)	
12-08-96	**VACANT**	
23-09-96	**Marc Mero**	28
	(Monday Night RAW, Hershey)	
21-10-96	**Hunter Hearst Helmsley**	115
	(Monday Night RAW, Fort Wayne)	
13-02-97	**Rocky Maivia**	73
	(Thursday RAW Thursday, Lowell)	
28-04-97	**Owen Hart**	97
	(Monday Night RAW, Omaha)	
03-08-97	**Steve Austin**	36
	(SummerSlam '97, East Rutherford)	
08-09-97	**VACANT**	
05-10-97	**Owen Hart**[2]	35
	(In Your House 18, St. Louis)	
09-11-97	**Steve Austin**[2]	29
	(Survivor Series '97, Montreal, Canada)	
08-12-97	**The Rock**[2]	264
	(Monday Night RAW, Portland)	
30-08-98	**Triple H**[2]	40
	(SummerSlam '98, New York)	
09-10-98	**VACANT**	
12-10-98	**Ken Shamrock**	125
	(Monday Night RAW, Uniondale)	
14-02-99	**Val Venis**	29
	(St. Valentine's Day Massacre, Memphis)	
15-03-99	**Road Dogg**	14
	(Monday Night RAW, San Jose)	
29-03-99	**Goldust**[3]	14
	(Monday Night RAW, East Rutherford)	
12-04-99	**The Godfather**	43
	(Monday Night RAW, Detroit)	
31-05-99	**Jeff Jarrett**[4]	54
	(Monday Night RAW, Moline)	
24-07-99	**Edge**	1
	(House Show, Toronto, Canada)	
25-07-99	**Jeff Jarrett**[5]	8
	(Fully Loaded '99, Buffalo)	
02-08-99	**D'Lo Brown**	20
	(Monday Night RAW, Columbus)	
22-08-99	**Jeff Jarrett**[6]	56
	(SummerSlam '99, Minneapolis)	
17-10-99	**Chyna**	56
	(No Mercy '99, Cleveland)	
12-12-99	**Chris Jericho**	22
	(Armageddon '99, Sunrise)	
03-01-00	**VACANT**	
23-01-00	**Chris Jericho**[2]	35
	(Royal Rumble '00, New York)	
27-02-00	**Kurt Angle**	35
	(No Way Out '00, Hartford)	
02-04-00	**Chris Benoit**	32
	(WrestleMania XVI, Anaheim)	
04-05-00	**Chris Jericho**[3]	4
	(SmackDown, Richmond)	
08-05-00	**Chris Benoit**[2]	43
	(Monday Night RAW, Uniondale)	
22-06-00	**Rikishi**	14
	(SmackDown, Memphis)	
06-07-00	**Val Venis**[2]	52
	(SmackDown, Sunrise)	
27-08-00	**Chyna**[2]	8
	(SummerSlam '00, Raleigh)	
04-09-00	**Eddie Guerrero**	80
	(Monday Night RAW, Lexington)	
23-11-00	**Billy Gunn**	17
	(SmackDown, Sunrise)	
10-12-00	**Chris Benoit**[3]	42
	(Armageddon '00, Birmingham)	
21-01-01	**Chris Jericho**[4]	74
	(Royal Rumble '01, New Orleans)	
05-04-01	**Triple H**[3]	7
	(SmackDown, Oklahoma City)	
12-04-01	**Jeff Hardy**	4
	(SmackDown, Philadelphia)	
16-04-01	**Triple H**[4]	34
	(Monday Night RAW, Knoxville)	
20-05-01	**Kane**	39
	(Judgment Day '01, Sacramento)	
28-06-01	**Albert**	25
	(SmackDown, New York)	
23-07-01	**Lance Storm**	27
	(Monday Night RAW, Buffalo)	
19-08-01	**Edge**[2]	35
	(SummerSlam '01, San Jose)	
23-09-01	**Christian**	28
	(Unforgiven '01, Pittsburgh)	
21-10-01	**Edge**[3]	15

(No Mercy '01, St. Louis)

Date	Wrestler	
05-11-01	**Test**	13
	(Monday Night RAW, Uniondale)	
18-11-01	**Edge**[4]	63
	(Survivor Series '01, Greensboro)	
20-01-02	**William Regal**	56
	(Royal Rumble '02, Atlanta)	
17-03-02	**Rob Van Dam**	35
	(WrestleMania XVIII, Toronto, Canada)	
21-04-02	**Eddie Guerrero**[2]	36
	(Backlash '02, Kansas City)	
27-05-02	**Rob Van Dam**[2]	63
	(Monday Night RAW, Edmonton, Canada)	
29-07-02	**Chris Benoit**[4]	27
	(Monday Night RAW, Greensboro)	
25-08-02	**Rob Van Dam**[3]	22
	(SummerSlam '02, Uniondale)	
16-09-02	**Chris Jericho**[5]	14
	(Monday Night RAW, Denver)	
30-09-02	**Kane**[2]	20
	(Monday Night RAW, Houston)	
20-10-02	**Triple H**[5]	<1
	(No Mercy '02, Little Rock)	
20-10-02	**DEACTIVATED**	
18-05-03	**Christian**[2]	50
	(Judgment Day '03, Charlotte)	
07-07-03	**Booker T**	34
	(Monday Night RAW, Montreal, Canada)	
10-08-03	**Christian**[3]	50
	(House Show, Des Moines)	
29-09-03	**Rob Van Dam**[3]	28
	(Monday Night RAW, Rosemont)	
27-10-03	**Chris Jericho**[6]	<1
	(Monday Night RAW, Fayetteville)	
27-10-03	**Rob Van Dam**[4]	48
	(Monday Night RAW, Fayetteville)	
14-12-03	**Randy Orton**	210
	(Armageddon '03, Orlando)	
11-07-04	**Edge**[5]	57
	(Vengeance '04, Hartford)	
06-09-04	**VACANT**	
12-09-04	**Chris Jericho**[7]	37
	(Unforgiven '04, Portland)	
19-10-04	**Shelton Benjamin**	244
	(Taboo Tuesday '04, Milwaukee)	
20-06-05	**Carlito**	90
	(Monday Night RAW, Phoenix)	
18-09-05	**Ric Flair**	155
	(Unforgiven '05, Oklahoma City)	
20-02-06	**Shelton Benjamin**[2]	69
	(Monday Night RAW, Trenton)	
30-04-06	**Rob Van Dam**[5]	15
	(Backlash '06, Lexington)	
15-05-06	**Shelton Benjamin**[3]	41
	(Monday Night RAW, Lubbock)	
25-06-06	**Johnny Nitro**	99
	(Vengeance '06, Charlotte)	
02-10-06	**Jeff Hardy**[2]	35
	(Monday Night RAW, Topeka)	
06-11-06	**Johnny Nitro**[2]	7
	(Monday Night RAW, Columbus)	
13-11-06	**Jeff Hardy**[3]	98
	(Monday Night RAW, Manchester, England)	
19-02-07	**Umaga**	56
	(Monday Night RAW, Bakersfield)	
16-04-07	**Santino Marella**	77
	(Monday Night RAW, Milan, Italy)	
02-07-07	**Umaga**[2]	63
	(Monday Night RAW, Dallas)	
03-09-07	**Jeff Hardy**[4]	189
	(Monday Night RAW, Columbus)	
10-03-08	**Chris Jericho**[8]	111
	(Monday Night RAW, Milwaukee)	
29-06-08	**Kofi Kingston**	49
	(Night Of Champions '08, Dallas)	
17-08-08	**Santino Marella**[2]	85
	(SummerSlam '08, Indianapolis)	
10-11-08	**William Regal**[2]	70
	(Monday Night RAW, Manchester, England)	
19-01-09	**CM Punk**	49
	(Monday Night RAW, Rosemont)	
09-03-09	**John Bradshaw Layfield**	27
	(Monday Night RAW, Jacksonville)	
05-04-09	**Rey Mysterio**	63
	(WrestleMania XXV, Houston)	
07-06-09	**Chris Jericho**[9]	21
	(Extreme Rules '09, New Orleans)	
28-06-09	**Rey Mysterio**[2]	68
	(The Bash '09, Sacramento)	
04-09-09	**John Morrison**[3]	100
	(SmackDown, Cleveland)	
13-12-09	**Drew McIntyre**	161
	(TLC '09, San Antonio)	
23-05-10	**Kofi Kingston**[2]	74
	(Over The Limit '10, Detroit)	
06-08-10	**Dolph Ziggler**	154
	(SmackDown, Laredo)	
07-01-11	**Kofi Kingston**[3]	77
	(SmackDown, Tucson)	
25-03-11	**Wade Barrett**	86
	(SmackDown, Columbus)	
19-06-11	**Ezekiel Jackson**	54
	(Capitol Punishment '11, Washington)	
12-08-11	**Cody Rhodes**	234
	(SmackDown, Sacramento)	
01-04-12	**Big Show**	28
	(WrestleMania XXVIII, Miami)	
29-04-12	**Cody Rhodes**[2]	21
	(Extreme Rules '12, Rosemont)	
20-05-12	**Christian**[4]	64
	(Over The Limit '12, Raleigh)	
23-07-12	**The Miz**	86
	(Monday Night RAW, St. Louis)	
17-10-12	**Kofi Kingston**[4]	75
	(Main Event, Memphis)	
31-12-12	**Wade Barrett**[2]	97
	(Monday Night RAW, Washington)	
07-04-13	**The Miz**[2]	1
	(WrestleMania XXIX, East Rutherford)	
08-04-13	**Wade Barrett**[3]	69
	(Monday Night RAW, East Rutherford)	
16-06-13	**Curtis Axel**	156
	(Payback '13, Rosemont)	
18-11-13	**Big E**	167
	(Monday Night RAW, Nashville)	
04-05-14	**Bad News Barrett**[4]	58
	(Extreme Rules '14, East Rutherford)	
30-06-14	**VACANT**	
20-07-14	**The Miz**[3]	28
	(Battleground '14, Tampa)	
17-08-14	**Dolph Ziggler**[2]	35
	(SummerSlam '14, Los Angeles)	
21-09-14	**The Miz**[4]	1
	(Night Of Champions '14, Nashville)	
22-09-14	**Dolph Ziggler**[3]	56
	(Monday Night RAW, Memphis)	
17-11-14	**Luke Harper**	27
	(Monday Night RAW, Roanoke)	
14-12-14	**Dolph Ziggler**[4]	22
	(TLC '14, Cleveland)	
05-01-15	**Bad News Barrett**[5]	83
	(Monday Night RAW, Corpus Christi)	

29-03-15	**Daniel Bryan**	43
	(WrestleMania XXXI, Santa Clara)	
11-05-15	**VACANT**	
31-05-15	**Ryback**	112
	(Elimination Chamber '15 , Corpus Christi)	
20-09-15	**Kevin Owens**	84
	(Night Of Champions '15, Houston)	
13-12-15	**Dean Ambrose**	64
	(TLC '15, Boston)	
15-02-16	**Kevin Owens²**	48
	(Monday Night RAW, Anaheim)	
03-04-16	**Zack Ryder**	1
	(WrestleMania XXXII, Dallas)	
04-04-16	**The Miz⁵**	188
	(Monday Night RAW, Dallas)	
09-10-16	**Dolph Ziggler⁵**	37
	(No Mercy '16, Sacramento)	
15-11-16	**The Miz⁶**	49
	(SmackDown, Wilkes-Barre)	
03-01-17	**Dean Ambrose²**	152
	(SmackDown, Jacksonville)	
04-06-17	**The Miz⁷**	169
	(Extreme Rules '17, Baltimore)	
20-11-17	**Roman Reigns**	63
	(Monday Night RAW, Houston)	
22-01-18	**The Miz⁸**	76
	(Monday Night RAW, Brooklyn)	
08-04-18	**Seth Rollins**	71
	(WrestleMania XXXIV, New Orleans)	
18-06-18	**Dolph Ziggler⁶**	62
	(Monday Night RAW, Grand Rapids)	
19-08-18	**Seth Rollins²**	119
	(SummerSlam '18, Brooklyn)	
16-12-18	**Dean Ambrose³**	29
	(TLC '18, San Jose)	
14-01-19	**Bobby Lashley**	34
	(Monday Night RAW, Memphis)	
17-02-19	**Finn Balor**	22
	(Elimination Chamber '19, Houston)	
11-03-19	**Bobby Lashley²**	27
	(Monday Night RAW, Pittsburgh)	
07-04-19	**Finn Balor²**	98
	(WrestleMania XXXV, East Rutherford)	
14-07-19	**Shinsuke Nakamura**	201
	(Extreme Rules '19, Philadelphia)	
31-01-20	**Braun Strowman**	37
	(SmackDown, Tulsa)	
08-03-20	**Sami Zayn**	65
	(Elimination Chamber '20, Philadelphia)	
12-05-20	**VACANT**	
12-06-20	**AJ Styles**	71
	(SmackDown, Orlando)	
21-08-20	**Jeff Hardy⁵**	37
	(SmackDown, Orlando)	
27-09-20	**Sami Zayn²**	89
	(Clash Of Champions '20, Orlando)	
25-12-20	**Big E²**	107
	(SmackDown, St. Petersburg)	
11-04-21	**Apollo Crews**	124
	(WrestleMania XXXVII, Tampa)	
13-08-21	**Shinsuke Nakamura²**	189
	(SmackDown, Tulsa)	
18-02-22	**Sami Zayn³**	14
	(SmackDown, New Orleans)	
04-03-22	**Ricochet**	98
	(SmackDown, Miami)	
10-06-22	**Gunther**	204*
	(SmackDown, Baton Rouge)	

Most Reigns

1.	Chris Jericho	9
2.	The Miz	8
3.	Dolph Ziggler	6
4.	Jeff Jarrett	6
5.	Rob Van Dam	6

Longest Reigns

1.	The Honky Tonk Man	443
2.	Pedro Morales	425
3.	Randy Savage	414
4.	Don Muraco	385
5.	Greg Valentine	266

Longest Cumulative Reigns

1.	Pedro Morales	617
2.	The Miz	598
3.	Don Muraco	541
4.	Tito Santana	462
5.	The Honky Tonk Man	443

WWE UNITED STATES CHAMPIONSHIP

DATE	WON BY	DAYS
01-01-75	**Harley Race**	183
	(House Show, Tallahassee)	
03-07-75	**Johnny Valentine**	93
	(House Show, Greensboro)	
04-10-75	**VACANT**	
09-11-75	**Terry Funk**	18
	(House Show, Greensboro)	
27-11-75	**Paul Jones**	107
	(House Show, Greensboro)	
13-03-76	**Blackjack Mulligan**	217
	(House Show, Greensboro)	
16-10-76	**Paul Jones²**	43
	(House Show, Greensboro)	
15-12-76	**Blackjack Mulligan²**	204
	(House Show, Raleigh)	
07-07-77	**Bobo Brazil**	22
	(House Show, Norfolk)	
29-07-77	**Ric Flair**	84
	(House Show, Richmond)	
21-10-77	**Ricky Steamboat**	72
	(House Show, Charleston)	
01-01-78	**Blackjack Mulligan³**	78
	(House Show, Greensboro)	
19-03-78	**Mr. Wrestling**	21
	(House Show, Greensboro)	
09-04-78	**Ric Flair²**	253
	(House Show, Charlotte)	
17-12-78	**Ricky Steamboat²**	105
	(House Show, Toronto, Canada)	
01-04-79	**Ric Flair³**	133
	(House Show, Greensboro)	
12-08-79	**VACANT**	
01-09-79	**Jimmy Snuka**	231
	(House Show, Charlotte)	
19-04-80	**Ric Flair⁴**	283
	(House Show, Greensboro)	
27-01-81	**Roddy Piper**	193
	(House Show, Raleigh)	
08-08-81	**Wahoo McDaniel**	31
	(House Show, Greensboro)	
08-09-81	**VACANT**	
04-10-81	**Sgt. Slaughter**	229
	(House Show, Charlotte)	

Date	Name	Days
21-05-82	**Wahoo McDaniel**[2] (House Show, Richmond)	17
07-06-82	**Sgt. Slaughter**[2] (House Show, Greenville)	76
22-08-82	**Wahoo McDaniel**[3] (House Show, Charlotte)	74
04-11-82	**Greg Valentine** (House Show, Norfolk)	163
16-04-83	**Roddy Piper**[2] (House Show, Greensboro)	14
30-04-83	**Greg Valentine**[2] (House Show, Greensboro)	228
14-12-83	**Dick Slater** (House Show, Shelby)	129
21-04-84	**Ricky Steamboat**[3] (House Show, Greensboro)	64
24-06-84	**Wahoo McDaniel**[4] (House Show, Greensboro)	7
01-07-84	**VACANT**	
07-10-84	**Wahoo McDaniel**[5] (House Show, Charlotte)	167
23-03-85	**Magnum T.A.** (Worldwide Wrestling, Charlotte)	120
21-07-85	**Tully Blanchard** (House Show, Charlotte)	130
28-11-85	**Magnum T.A.**[2] (Starrcade '85, Greensboro)	182
29-05-86	**VACANT**	
17-08-86	**Nikita Koloff** (House Show, Charlotte)	328
11-07-87	**Lex Luger** (Great American Bash '87, Greensboro)	138
26-11-87	**Dusty Rhodes** (Starrcade '87, Chicago)	141
15-04-88	**VACANT**	
13-05-88	**Barry Windham** (House Show, Houston)	283
20-02-89	**Lex Luger**[2] (Chi-Town Rumble '89, Chicago)	76
07-05-89	**Michael Hayes** (WrestleWar '89, Nashville)	15
22-05-89	**Lex Luger**[3] (House Show, Bluefield)	523
27-10-90	**Stan Hansen** (Halloween Havoc '90, Chicago)	50
16-12-90	**Lex Luger**[4] (Starrcade '90, St. Louis)	210
14-07-91	**VACANT**	
25-08-91	**Sting** (House Show, Atlanta)	86
19-11-91	**Rick Rude** (Clash Of The Champions XVII, Savannah)	378
01-12-92	**VACANT**	
16-01-93	**Dustin Rhodes** (Saturday Night, Atlanta)	133
29-05-93	**VACANT**	
11-09-93	**Dustin Rhodes**[2] (Saturday Night, Atlanta)	107
27-12-93	**Steve Austin** (Starrcade '93, Charlotte)	240
24-08-94	**Ricky Steamboat**[4] (COTC XXVIII, Cedar Rapids)	25
18-09-94	**Steve Austin**[2] (Fall Brawl '94, Roanoke)	<1
18-09-94	**Jim Duggan** (Fall Brawl '94, Roanoke)	100
27-12-94	**Big Van Vader** (Starrcade '94, Nashville)	88
25-03-95	**VACANT**	
18-06-95	**Sting**[2] (The Great American Bash '95, Dayton)	148

Date	Name	Days
13-11-95	**Kensuke Sasaki** (WCW World In Japan, Tokyo, Japan)	44
27-12-95	**One Man Gang** (Starrcade '95, Nashville)	33
29-01-96	**Konnan** (Main Event, Canton)	160
07-07-96	**Ric Flair**[5] (Bash At The Beach '96, Daytona Beach)	141
25-11-96	**VACANT**	
29-12-96	**Eddie Guerrero** (Starrcade '96, Nashville)	77
16-03-97	**Dean Malenko** (Uncensored '97, North Charleston)	85
09-06-97	**Jeff Jarrett** (Monday Nitro, Boston)	73
21-08-97	**Steve McMichael** (Clash Of The Champions XXXV, Nashville)	25
15-09-97	**Curt Hennig** (Monday Nitro, Charlotte)	104
28-12-97	**Diamond Dallas Page** (Starrcade '97, Washington)	112
19-04-98	**Raven** (Spring Stampede '98, Denver)	1
20-04-98	**Goldberg** (Monday Nitro, Colorado Springs)	75
06-07-98	**VACANT**	
20-07-98	**Bret Hart** (Monday Nitro, Salt Lake City)	21
10-08-98	**Lex Luger**[5] (Monday Nitro, Rapid City)	3
13-08-98	**Bret Hart**[2] (Thunder, Fargo)	74
26-10-98	**Diamond Dallas Page**[2] (Monday Nitro, Phoenix)	35
30-11-98	**Bret Hart**[3] (Monday Nitro, Chattanooga)	70
08-02-99	**Roddy Piper**[3] (Monday Nitro, Buffalo)	13
21-02-99	**Scott Hall** (SuperBrawl IX, Oakland)	25
18-03-99	**VACANT**	
11-04-99	**Scott Steiner** (Spring Stampede '99, Tacoma)	85
05-07-99	**VACANT**	
05-07-99	**David Flair** (Monday Nitro, Atlanta)	35
09-08-99	**Chris Benoit** (Monday Nitro, Boise)	34
12-09-99	**Sid Vicious** (Fall Brawl '99, Winston-Salem)	42
24-10-99	**Goldberg**[2] (Halloween Havoc '99, Paradise)	1
25-10-99	**Bret Hart**[4] (Monday Nitro, Phoenix)	14
08-11-99	**Scott Hall** (Monday Nitro, Indianapolis)	41
19-12-99	**Chris Benoit**[2] (Starrcade '99, Washington)	1
20-12-99	**Jeff Jarrett**[2] (Monday Nitro, Baltimore)	27
16-01-00	**VACANT**	
17-01-00	**Jeff Jarrett**[3] (Monday Nitro, Columbus)	84
10-04-00	**VACANT**	
16-04-00	**Scott Steiner**[2] (Spring Stampede '00, Chicago)	84
09-07-00	**VACANT**	
18-07-00	**Lance Storm** (Monday Nitro, Auburn Hills)	66
22-09-00	**Terry Funk** (House Show, Amarillo)	1

23-09-00	**Lance Storm²** (House Show, Lubbock)	36
29-10-00	**General Rection** (Halloween Havoc '00, Paradise)	12
10-11-00	**Lance Storm³** (Monday Nitro, London, England)	13
26-11-00	**General Rection²** (Mayhem '00, Milwaukee)	49
14-01-01	**Shane Douglas** (Sin '01, Indianapolis)	22
05-02-01	**Rick Steiner** (Monday Nitro, Tupelo)	41
18-03-01	**Booker T** (Greed '01, Jacksonville)	128
26-07-01	**Kanyon** (SmackDown, Pittsburgh)	46
10-09-01	**Tajiri** (Monday Night RAW, San Antonio)	13
23-09-01	**Rhyno** (Unforgiven '01, Pittsburgh)	29
22-10-01	**Kurt Angle** (Monday Night RAW, Kansas City)	21
12-11-01	**Edge** (Monday Night RAW, Boston)	6
18-11-01	**DEACTIVATED**	
27-07-03	**Eddie Guerrero²** (Vengeance '03, Denver)	84
19-10-03	**Big Show** (No Mercy '03, Baltimore)	147
14-03-04	**John Cena** (WrestleMania XX, New York)	116
08-07-04	**VACANT**	
29-07-04	**Booker T²** (SmackDown, Cincinnati)	66
03-10-04	**John Cena²** (No Mercy '04, East Rutherford)	4
07-10-04	**Carlito** (SmackDown, Boston)	42
18-11-04	**John Cena³** (SmackDown, Dayton)	105
03-03-05	**Orlando Jordan** (SmackDown, Albany)	171
21-08-05	**Chris Benoit³** (SummerSlam '05, Washington)	61
21-10-05	**Booker T³** (SmackDown, Reno)	35
25-11-05	**VACANT**	
13-01-06	**Booker T⁴** (SmackDown, Philadelphia)	37
19-02-06	**Chris Benoit⁴** (No Way Out '06, Baltimore)	42
02-04-06	**John Bradshaw Layfield** (WrestleMania XXII, Rosemont)	54
26-05-06	**Bobby Lashley** (SmackDown, Bakersfield)	48
14-07-06	**Finlay** (SmackDown, Minneapolis)	48
01-09-06	**Mr. Kennedy** (SmackDown, Reading)	42
13-10-06	**Chris Benoit⁵** (SmackDown, Jacksonville)	219
20-05-07	**MVP** (Judgment Day '07, St. Louis)	343
27-04-08	**Matt Hardy** (Backlash '08, Baltimore)	84
20-07-08	**Shelton Benjamin** (The Great American Bash '08, Uniondale)	246
20-03-09	**MVP²** (SmackDown, Corpus Christi)	73
01-06-09	**Kofi Kingston** (Monday Night RAW, Birmingham)	126
05-10-09	**The Miz** (Monday Night RAW, Wilkes-Barre)	224
17-05-10	**Bret Hart⁵** (Monday Night RAW, Toronto, Canada)	7
24-05-10	**VACANT**	
24-05-10	**R-Truth** (Monday Night RAW, Toledo)	21
14-06-10	**The Miz²** (Monday Night RAW, Charlotte)	97
19-09-10	**Daniel Bryan** (Night Of Champions '10, Rosemont)	176
14-03-11	**Sheamus** (Monday Night RAW, St. Louis)	48
01-05-11	**Kofi Kingston²** (Extreme Rules '11, Tampa)	49
19-06-11	**Dolph Ziggler** (Capitol Punishment '11, Washington)	182
18-12-11	**Zack Ryder** (TLC '11, Baltimore)	29
16-01-12	**Jack Swagger** (Monday Night RAW, Anaheim)	49
05-03-12	**Santino Marella** (Monday Night RAW, Boston)	167
19-08-12	**Cesaro** (SummerSlam '12, Los Angeles)	239
15-04-13	**Kofi Kingston³** (Monday Night RAW, Greenville)	34
19-05-13	**Dean Ambrose** (Extreme Rules '13, St. Louis)	351
05-05-14	**Sheamus²** (Monday Night RAW, Albany)	182
03-11-14	**Rusev** (RAW Backstage Pass, Buffalo)	146
29-03-15	**John Cena⁴** (WrestleMania XXXI, Santa Clara)	147
23-08-15	**Seth Rollins** (SummerSlam '15, Brooklyn)	28
20-09-15	**John Cena⁵** (Night Of Champions '15, Houston)	35
25-10-15	**Alberto Del Rio** (Hell In A Cell '15, Los Angeles)	78
11-01-16	**Kalisto** (Monday Night RAW, New Orleans)	3
14-01-16	**Alberto Del Rio²** (SmackDown, Lafayette)	10
24-01-16	**Kalisto²** (Royal Rumble '16, Orlando)	119
22-05-16	**Rusev²** (Extreme Rules '16, Newark)	126
25-09-16	**Roman Reigns** (Clash Of Champions '16, Indianapolis)	106
09-01-17	**Chris Jericho** (Monday Night RAW, New Orleans)	83
02-04-17	**Kevin Owens** (WrestleMania XXXIII, Orlando)	28
30-04-17	**Chris Jericho²** (Payback '17, San Jose)	2
02-05-17	**Kevin Owens²** (SmackDown, Fresno)	66
07-07-17	**AJ Styles** (House Show, New York)	16
23-07-17	**Kevin Owens³** (Battleground '17, Philadelphia)	2
25-07-17	**AJ Styles²** (SmackDown, Richmond)	75
08-10-17	**Baron Corbin** (Hell In A Cell '17, Detroit)	70
17-12-17	**Dolph Ziggler²** (Clash Of Champions '17, Boston)	9
26-12-17	**VACANT**	
16-01-18	**Bobby Roode**	54

(SmackDown, Laredo)

Date	Won By	Days
11-03-18	**Randy Orton**	28
	(Fastlane '18, Columbus)	
08-04-18	**Jinder Mahal**	8
	(WrestleMania XXXIV, New Orleans)	
16-04-18	**Jeff Hardy**	90
	(Monday Night RAW, Hartford)	
15-07-18	**Shinsuke Nakamura**	163
	(Extreme Rules '18, Pittsburgh)	
25-12-18	**Rusev**²	32
	(SmackDown, Fresno)	
27-01-19	**Shinsuke Nakamura**²	2
	(Royal Rumble '19, Phoenix)	
29-01-19	**R-Truth**²	35
	(SmackDown, Phoenix)	
05-03-19	**Samoa Joe**	75
	(SmackDown, Wilkes-Barre)	
19-05-19	**Rey Mysterio**	15
	(Money In The Bank '19, Hartford)	
03-06-19	**Samoa Joe**²	20
	(Monday Night RAW, Austin)	
23-06-19	**Ricochet**	21
	(Stomping Grounds '19, Tacoma)	
14-07-19	**AJ Styles**³	134
	(Extreme Rules '19, Philadelphia)	
25-11-19	**Rey Mysterio**²	31
	(Monday Night RAW, Rosemont)	
26-12-19	**Andrade**	151
	(House Show, New York)	
25-05-20	**Apollo Crews**	97
	(Monday Night RAW, Orlando)	
30-08-20	**Bobby Lashley**²	175
	(Payback '20, Orlando)	
21-02-21	**Matt Riddle**	49
	(Elimination Chamber '21, St. Petersburg)	
11-04-21	**Sheamus**³	132
	(WrestleMania XXXVII, Tampa)	
21-08-21	**Damian Priest**	191
	(SummerSlam '21, Paradise)	
28-02-22	**Finn Balor**	49
	(Monday Night RAW, Columbus)	
18-04-22	**Austin Theory**	75
	(Monday Night RAW, Buffalo)	
02-07-22	**Bobby Lashley**³	100
	(Money In The Bank '22, Paradise)	
10-10-22	**Seth Rollins**²	47
	(Monday Night RAW, Brooklyn)	
26-11-22	**Austin Theory**²	36*
	(Survivor Series '22, Boston)	

Most Reigns
1.	Ric Flair	5
2.	Lex Luger	5
3.	John Cena	5
4.	Chris Benoit	5
5.	Wahoo McDaniel	5
6.	Bret Hart	5

Longest Reigns
1.	Lex Luger	523
2.	Rick Rude	378
3.	Dean Ambrose	351
4.	MVP	343
5.	Nikita Koloff	328

Longest Cumulative Reigns
1.	Lex Luger	950
2.	Ric Flair	984
3.	Blackjack Mulligan	499
4.	MVP	416
5.	John Cena	407

WWE RAW TAG TEAM CHAMPIONSHIP

DATE	WON BY	DAYS
20-10-02	**Chris Benoit & Kurt Angle**	18
	(No Mercy '02, Little Rock)	
07-11-02	**Edge & Rey Mysterio**	10
	(SmackDown, Manchester)	
17-11-02	**Eddie Guerrero & Chavo Guerrero**	81
	(Survivor Series '02, New York)	
06-02-03	**Charlie Haas & Shelton Benjamin**	101
	(SmackDown, Philadelphia)	
18-05-03	**Eddie Guerrero² & Tajiri**	46
	(Judgment Day '03, Charlotte)	
03-07-03	**Charlie Haas² & Shelton Benjamin²**	77
	(SmackDown, Rochester)	
18-09-03	**Eddie Guerrero³ & Chavo Guerrero²**	35
	(SmackDown, Raleigh)	
23-10-03	**Danny Basham & Doug Basham**	105
	(SmackDown, Albany)	
05-02-04	**Rikishi & Scotty 2 Hotty**	77
	(SmackDown, Cleveland)	
22-04-04	**Charlie Haas³ & Rico**	56
	(SmackDown, Kelowna, Canada)	
17-06-04	**Bubba Ray Dudley & D-Von Dudley**	21
	(SmackDown, Rosemont)	
08-07-04	**Billy Kidman & Paul London**	63
	(SmackDown, Winnipeg, Canada)	
09-09-04	**Kenzo Suzuki & Rene Dupree**	91
	(SmackDown, Tulsa)	
09-12-04	**Rey Mysterio² & Rob Van Dam**	35
	(SmackDown, Greenville)	
13-01-05	**Danny Basham² & Doug Basham²**	38
	(SmackDown, Tampa)	
20-02-05	**Eddie Guerrero⁴ & Rey Mysterio³**	60
	(No Way Out '05, Pittsburgh)	
21-04-05	**Joey Mercury & Johnny Nitro**	95
	(SmackDown, New York)	
24-07-05	**Animal & Heidenreich**	95
	(The Great American Bash '05, Buffalo)	
28-10-05	**Joey Mercury² & Johnny Nitro²**	49
	(SmackDown, Daly City)	
16-12-05	**Batista & Rey Mysterio⁴**	14
	(SmackDown, Springfield)	
30-12-05	**Joey Mercury³ & Johnny Nitro³**	142
	(SmackDown, Uncasville)	
21-05-06	**Brian Kendrick & Paul London²**	334
	(Judgment Day '06, Phoenix)	
20-04-07	**Deuce & Domino**	133
	(SmackDown, Milan, Italy)	
31-08-07	**Matt Hardy & MVP**	77
	(SmackDown, Albany)	
16-11-07	**John Morrison⁴ & The Miz**	247
	(SmackDown, Wichita)	
20-07-08	**Curt Hawkins & Zack Ryder**	68
	(The Great American Bash '08, Uniondale)	
26-09-08	**Primo Colon & Carlito Colon**	275
	(SmackDown, Columbus)	
28-06-09	**Edge² & Chris Jericho**	28
	(The Bash '09, Sacramento)	
26-07-09	**The Big Show & Chris Jericho²**	140
	(Night Of Champions '09, Philadelphia)	

13-12-09	**Triple H & Shawn Michaels** (TLC '09, San Antonio)	57	
08-02-10	**The Big Show**[2] **& The Miz**[2] (Monday Night RAW, Lafayette)	77	
26-04-10	**David Hart Smith & Tyson Kidd** (Monday Night RAW, Richmond)	146	
19-09-10	**Cody Rhodes & Drew McIntyre** (Night Of Champions '10, Rosemont)	35	
24-10-10	**David Otunga & John Cena** (Bragging Rights '10, Minneapolis)	1	
25-10-10	**Heath Slater & Justin Gabriel** (Monday Night RAW, Green Bay)	42	
06-12-10	**Santino Marella & Vladimir Kozlov** (Monday Night RAW, Louisville)	76	
20-02-11	**Heath Slater**[2] **& Justin Gabriel**[2] (Elimination Chamber '11, Oakland)	1	
21-02-11	**John Cena**[2] **& The Miz**[3] (Monday Night RAW, Fresno)	<1	
21-02-11	**Heath Slater**[3] **& Justin Gabriel**[3] (Monday Night RAW, Fresno)	59	
22-04-11	**The Big Show**[3] **& Kane** (SmackDown, London, England)	31	
23-05-11	**David Otunga**[2] **& Michael McGillicutty** (Monday Night RAW, Portland)	91	
22-08-11	**Evan Bourne & Kofi Kingston** (Monday Night RAW, Edmonton, Canada)	146	
15-01-12	**Primo Colon**[2] **& Epico Colon** (House Show, Oakland)	106	
30-04-12	**Kofi Kingston**[2] **& R-Truth** (Monday Night RAW, Dayton)	139	
16-09-12	**Kane**[2] **& Daniel Bryan** (Night Of Champions '12, Boston)	245	
19-05-13	**Roman Reigns & Seth Rollins** (Extreme Rules '13, St. Louis)	148	
14-10-13	**Cody Rhodes**[2] **& Goldust** (Monday Night RAW, St. Louis)	104	
26-01-14	**Billy Gunn & Road Dogg** (Royal Rumble '14, Pittsburgh)	36	
03-03-14	**Jimmy Uso & Jey Uso** (Monday Night RAW, Rosemont)	202	
21-09-14	**Goldust**[2] **& Stardust**[3] (Night Of Champions '14, Nashville)	63	
23-11-14	**The Miz**[4] **& Damien Mizdow** (Survivor Series '14, St. Louis)	36	
29-12-14	**Jimmy Uso**[2] **& Jey Uso**[2] (Monday Night RAW, Washington)	55	
22-02-15	**Tyson Kidd**[2] **& Cesaro** (Fastlane '15, Memphis)	63	
26-04-15	**Big E, Kofi Kingston**[3] **& Xavier Woods** (Extreme Rules '15, Rosemont)	49	
14-06-15	**Titus O'Neil & Darren Young** (Money In The Bank '15, Columbus)	70	
23-08-15	**Big E**[2], **Kofi Kingston**[4] **& Xavier Woods**[2] (SummerSlam '15, Brooklyn)	483	
18-12-16	**Sheamus & Cesaro**[2] (Roadblock '16, Pittsburgh)	42	
29-01-17	**Luke Gallows & Karl Anderson** (Royal Rumble '17, San Antonio)	64	
02-04-17	**Jeff Hardy & Matt Hardy**[2] (WrestleMania XXXIII, Orlando)	63	
04-06-17	**Sheamus**[2] **& Cesaro**[3] (Extreme Rules '17, Baltimore)	77	
20-08-17	**Dean Ambrose & Seth Rollins**[2] (SummerSlam '17, Brooklyn)	78	
06-11-17	**Sheamus**[3] **& Cesaro**[4] (Monday Night RAW, Manchester, England)	49	
25-12-17	**Seth Rollins**[3] **& Jason Jordan**	34	

	(Monday Night RAW, Rosemont)		
28-01-18	**Sheamus**[4] **& Cesaro**[5] (Royal Rumble '18, Philadelphia)	70	
08-04-18	**Braun Strowman & Nicholas** (WrestleMania XXXIV, New Orleans)	1	
09-04-18	**VACANT**		
27-04-18	**Matt Hardy**[3] **& Bray Wyatt** (Greatest Royal Rumble, Saudi Arabia)	79	
15-07-18	**Bo Dallas & Curtis Axel**[2] (Extreme Rules '18, Pittsburgh)	50	
03-09-18	**Drew McIntyre**[2] **& Dolph Ziggler** (Monday Night RAW, Columbus)	49	
22-10-18	**Dean Ambrose**[2] **& Seth Rollins**[4] (Monday Night RAW, Providence)	14	
05-11-18	**Akam & Rezar** (Monday Night RAW, Manchester, England)	35	
10-12-18	**Bobby Roode & Chad Gable** (Monday Night RAW, San Diego)	63	
11-02-19	**Dash Wilder & Scott Dawson** (Monday Night RAW, Grand Rapids)	55	
07-04-19	**Curt Hawkins**[2] **& Zack Ryder**[2] (WrestleMania XXXV, East Rutherford)	64	
10-06-19	**Dash Wilder**[2] **& Scott Dawson**[2] (Monday Night RAW, San Jose)	49	
29-07-19	**Luke Gallows**[2] **& Karl Anderson**[2] (Monday Night RAW, Little Rock)	21	
19-08-19	**Braun Strowman**[2] **& Seth Rollins**[5] (Monday Night RAW, St. Paul)	27	
15-09-19	**Dolph Ziggler**[2] **& Robert Roode**[2] (Clash Of Champions '19, Charlotte)	29	
14-10-19	**Erik & Ivar** (Monday Night RAW, Denver)	98	
20-01-20	**Seth Rollins**[6] **& Murphy** (Monday Night RAW, Wichita)	42	
02-03-20	**Montez Ford & Angelo Dawkins** (Monday Night RAW, Brooklyn)	224	
12-10-20	**Kofi Kingston**[5] **& Xavier Woods**[3] (Monday Night RAW, Orlando)	69	
20-12-20	**Cedric Alexander & Shelton Benjamin**[3] (TLC '20, St. Petersburg)	85	
15-03-21	**Kofi Kingston**[6] **& Xavier Woods**[4] (Monday Night RAW, St. Petersburg)	26	
10-04-21	**AJ Styles & Omos** (WrestleMania XXXVII, Tampa)	133	
21-08-21	**Randy Orton & Matt Riddle** (SummerSlam '21, Paradise)	142	
10-01-22	**Chad Gable**[2] **& Otis** (Monday Night RAW, Philadelphia)	56	
07-03-22	**Randy Orton**[2] **& Matt Riddle**[2] (Monday Night RAW, Cleveland)	74	
20-05-22	**Jimmy Uso**[3] **& Jey Uso**[3] (SmackDown, Grand Rapids)	225*	

Most Reigns

1.	Seth Rollins	6
2.	Kofi Kingston	6
3.	Cesaro	5
4.	Xavier Woods	4

Longest Reigns

1.	Kofi Kingston, Big E & Xavier Woods	504
2.	Paul London & Brian Kendrick	334
3.	Carlito & Primo	275
4.	John Morrison & The Miz	247
5.	Daniel Bryan & Kane	245

Longest Cumulative Reigns

1.	Kofi Kingston	912
2.	Xavier Woods	627

3.	John Morrison	533
4.	Big E	532
5.	Jey Uso	482*
6.	Jimmy Uso	482*

WWE SMACKDOWN TAG TEAM CHAMPIONSHIP

DATE	WON BY	DAYS
11-09-16	**Heath Slater & Rhyno** (Backlash '16, Richmond)	18
04-12-16	**Bray Wyatt, Luke Harper & Randy Orton** (TLC '16, Dallas)	23
27-12-16	**Chad Gable & Jason Jordan** (SmackDown, Rosemont)	83
21-03-17	**Jey Uso & Jimmy Uso** (SmackDown, Uncasville)	124
23-07-17	**Big E, Kofi Kingston & Xavier Woods** (Battleground '17, Philadelphia)	28
20-08-17	**Jey Uso[2] & Jimmy Uso[2]** (SummerSlam '17, Brooklyn)	23
12-09-17	**Big E[2], Kofi Kingston[2] & Xavier Woods[2]** (SmackDown, Las Vegas)	26
08-10-17	**Jey Uso[3] & Jimmy Uso[3]** (Hell In A Cell '17, Detroit)	182
08-04-18	**Harper[2] & Rowan** (WrestleMania XXXIV, New Orleans)	135
21-08-18	**Big E[3], Kofi Kingston[3] & Xavier Woods[3]** (SmackDown, Brooklyn)	56
16-10-18	**Sheamus & Cesaro** (SmackDown, Washington)	103
27-01-19	**Shane McMahon & The Miz** (Royal Rumble '19, Phoenix)	21
17-02-19	**Jey Uso[4] & Jimmy Uso[4]** (Elimination Chamber '19, Houston)	51
09-04-19	**Matt Hardy & Jeff Hardy** (SmackDown, Brooklyn)	21
30-04-19	**VACANT**	
07-05-19	**Rowan[2] & Daniel Bryan** (SmackDown, Louisville)	68
14-07-19	**Big E[4], Kofi Kingston[4] & Xavier Woods[4]** (Extreme Rules '19, Philadelphia)	63
15-09-19	**Dash Wilder & Scott Dawson** (Clash Of Champions '19, Charlotte)	54
08-11-19	**Big E[5], Kofi Kingston[5] & Xavier Woods[5]** (SmackDown, Manchester, England)	111
27-02-20	**The Miz[2] & John Morrison** (Super ShowDown '20, Riyadh, Saudi Arabia)	50
17-04-20	**Big E[6], Kofi Kingston[6] & Xavier Woods[6]** (SmackDown, Orlando)	93
19-07-20	**Cesaro[2] & Shinsuke Nakamura** (Extreme Rules '20, Orlando)	82
09-10-20	**Kofi Kingston[7] & Xavier Woods[7]** (SmackDown, Orlando)	3
12-10-20	**Montez Ford & Angelo Dawkins** (Monday Night RAW, Orlando)	88
08-01-21	**Dolph Ziggler & Robert Roode** (SmackDown, St. Petersburg)	128
16-05-21	**Rey Mysterio & Dominik Mysterio** (WrestleMania Backlash '21, Tampa)	63
18-07-21	**Jey Uso[5] & Jimmy Uso[5]**	531*

(Money In The Bank '21, Fort Worth)

Most Reigns

1.	Kofi Kingston	7
2.	Xavier Woods	7
3.	Big E	6
4.	Jimmy Uso	5
5.	Jey Uso	5

Longest Reigns

1.	Jey Uso & Jimmy Uso	531*
2.	Jey Uso & Jimmy Uso	182
3.	Harper & Rowan	135
4.	Dolph Ziggler & Robert Roode	128
5.	Jey Uso & Jimmy Uso	124

Longest Cumulative Reigns

1.	Jey Uso	911
2.	Jimmy Uso	911
3.	Kofi Kingston	380
4.	Xavier Woods	380
5.	Big E	377

WWE RAW WOMEN'S CHAMPIONSHIP

DATE	WON BY	DAYS
03-04-16	**Charlotte Flair** (WrestleMania XXXII, Dallas)	113
25-07-16	**Sasha Banks** (Monday Night RAW, Pittsburgh)	27
21-08-16	**Charlotte Flair[2]** (SummerSlam '16, Brooklyn)	43
03-10-16	**Sasha Banks[2]** (Monday Night RAW, Los Angeles)	27
30-10-16	**Charlotte Flair[3]** (Hell In A Cell '16, Boston)	29
28-11-16	**Sasha Banks[3]** (Monday Night RAW, Charlotte)	20
18-12-16	**Charlotte Flair[4]** (Roadblock '16, Pittsburgh)	57
13-02-17	**Bayley** (Monday Night RAW, Las Vegas)	76
30-04-17	**Alexa Bliss** (Payback '17, San Jose)	112
20-08-17	**Sasha Banks[4]** (SummerSlam '17, Brooklyn)	8
28-08-17	**Alexa Bliss[2]** (Monday Night RAW, Memphis)	223
08-04-18	**Nia Jax** (WrestleMania XXXIV, New Orleans)	70
17-06-18	**Alexa Bliss[3]** (Money In The Bank '18, Rosemont)	63
19-08-18	**Ronda Rousey** (SummerSlam '18, Brooklyn)	232
08-04-19	**Becky Lynch** (WrestleMania XXXV, East Rutherford)	398
10-05-20	**Asuka** (Money In The Bank '20, Stamford)	78
27-07-20	**Sasha Banks[5]** (Monday Night RAW, Orlando)	27
23-08-20	**Asuka[2]** (SummerSlam '20, Orlando)	231
11-04-21	**Rhea Ripley** (WrestleMania XXXVII, Tampa)	98
18-07-21	**Charlotte Flair[5]** (Money In The Bank '21, Fort Worth)	1
19-07-21	**Nikki A.S.H.**	33

	(Monday Night RAW, Dallas)	
21-08-21	**Charlotte Flair**[6]	62
	(SummerSlam '21, Paradise)	
22-10-21	**Becky Lynch**[2]	162
	(SmackDown, Wichita)	
02-04-22	**Bianca Belair**	273*
	(WrestleMania XXXVIII, Arlington)	

Most Reigns

1.	Charlotte Flair	6
2.	Sasha Banks	5
3.	Alexa Bliss	3
4.	Asuka	2
5.	Becky Lynch	2

Longest Reigns

1.	Becky Lynch	398
2.	Bianca Belair	273*
3.	Ronda Rousey	232
4.	Asuka	231
5.	Alexa Bliss	223

Longest Cumulative Reigns

1.	Becky Lynch	560
2.	Alexa Bliss	398
3.	Charlotte Flair	305
4.	Bianca Belair	273*
5.	Ronda Rousey	232

WWE SMACKDOWN WOMEN'S CHAMPIONSHIP

DATE	WON BY	DAYS
11-09-16	**Becky Lynch**	84
	(Backlash '16, Richmond)	
04-12-16	**Alexa Bliss**	70
	(TLC '16, Dallas)	
12-02-17	**Naomi**	9
	(Elimination Chamber '17, Phoenix)	
21-02-17	**VACANT**	
21-02-17	**Alexa Bliss**[2]	40
	(SmackDown, Ontario)	
02-04-17	**Naomi**[2]	140
	(WrestleMania XXXIII, Orlando)	
20-08-17	**Natalya**	86
	(SummerSlam '17, Brooklyn)	
14-11-17	**Charlotte Flair**	147
	(SmackDown, Charlotte)	
10-04-18	**Carmella**	131
	(SmackDown, New Orleans)	
19-08-18	**Charlotte Flair**[2]	28
	(SummerSlam '18, Brooklyn)	
16-09-18	**Becky Lynch**[2]	91
	(Hell In A Cell '18, San Antonio)	
16-12-18	**Asuka**	100
	(TLC '18, San Jose)	
26-03-19	**Charlotte Flair**[3]	13
	(SmackDown, Uncasville)	
08-04-19	**Becky Lynch**[3]	41
	(WrestleMania XXXV, East Rutherford)	
19-05-19	**Charlotte Flair**[4]	<1
	(Money In The Bank '19, Hartford)	
19-05-19	**Bayley**	140
	(Money In The Bank '19, Hartford)	
06-10-19	**Charlotte Flair**[5]	5
	(Hell In A Cell '19, Sacramento)	
11-10-19	**Bayley**[2]	380
	(SmackDown, Paradise)	

25-10-20	**Sasha Banks**	167
	(Hell In A Cell '20, Orlando)	
10-04-21	**Bianca Belair**	133
	(WrestleMania XXXVII, Tampa)	
21-08-21	**Becky Lynch**[4]	62
	(SummerSlam '21, Paradise)	
22-10-21	**Charlotte Flair**[6]	198
	(SmackDown, Wichita)	
08-05-22	**Ronda Rousey**	55
	(WrestleMania Backlash '22, Providence)	
02-07-22	**Liv Morgan**	98
	(Money In The Bank '22, Paradise)	
08-10-22	**Ronda Rousey**[2]	83
	(Extreme Rules '22, Philadelphia)	
30-12-22	**Charlotte Flair**[7]	1*
	(SmackDown, Tampa)	

Most Reigns

1.	Charlotte Flair	7
2.	Becky Lynch	4
3.	Alexa Bliss	2
4.	Bayley	2
5.	Naomi	2
6.	Ronda Rousey	2

Longest Reigns

1.	Bayley	380
2.	Charlotte Flair	198
3.	Sasha Banks	167
4.	Charlotte Flair	147
5.	Bayley	140
6.	Naomi	140

Longest Cumulative Reigns

1.	Bayley	520
2.	Charlotte Flair	391
3.	Becky Lynch	278
4.	Sasha Banks	167
5.	Naomi	149

WWE WOMEN'S TAG TEAM CHAMPIONSHIP

DATE	WON BY	DAYS
17-02-19	**Bayley & Sasha Banks**	49
	(Elimination Chamber '19, Houston)	
07-04-19	**Billie Kay & Peyton Royce**	120
	(WrestleMania XXXV, East Rutherford)	
05-08-19	**Alexa Bliss & Nikki Cross**	62
	(Monday Night RAW, Pittsburgh)	
06-10-19	**Asuka & Kairi Sane**	180
	(Hell In A Cell '19, Sacramento)	
04-04-20	**Alexa Bliss**[2] **& Nikki Cross**[2]	62
	(WrestleMania XXXVI, Orlando)	
05-06-20	**Bayley**[2] **& Sasha Banks**[2]	85
	(SmackDown, Orlando)	
30-08-20	**Nia Jax & Shayna Baszler**	112
	(Payback '20, Orlando)	
20-12-20	**Asuka**[2] **& Charlotte Flair**	42
	(TLC '20, St. Petersburg)	
31-01-21	**Nia Jax**[2] **& Shayna Baszler**[2]	103
	(Royal Rumble '21, St. Petersburg)	
14-05-21	**Tamina & Natalya**	129
	(SmackDown, Tampa)	
20-09-21	**Nikki A.S.H.**[3] **& Rhea Ripley**	63
	(Monday Night RAW, Raleigh)	
22-11-21	**Carmella & Queen Zelina**	132
	(Monday Night RAW, Brooklyn)	

03-04-22	**Sasha Banks[3] & Naomi**	47
	(WrestleMania XXXVIII, Arlington)	
20-05-22	**VACANT**	
29-08-22	**Aliyah & Raquel Rodriguez**	14
	(Monday Night RAW, Pittsburgh)	
12-09-22	**Dakota Kai & Iyo Sky**	49
	(Monday Night RAW, Portland)	
31-10-22	**Alexa Bliss[3] & Asuka[3]**	5
	(Monday Night RAW, Dallas)	
05-11-22	**Dakota Kai[2] & Iyo Sky[2]**	57*
	(Crown Jewel '22, Riyadh, Saudi Arabia)	

Most Reigns

1.	Nikki Cross/A.S.H.	3
2.	Sasha Banks	3
3.	Alexa Bliss	3
4.	Asuka	3

Longest Reigns

1.	Asuka & Kairi Sane	180
2.	Carmella & Queen Zelina	132
3.	Tamina & Natalya	129
4.	Billie Kay & Peyton Royce	120
5.	Nia Jax & Shayna Baszler	112

Longest Cumulative Reigns

1.	Asuka	227
2.	Shayna Baszler	215
3.	Nia Jax	215
4.	Sasha Banks	181
5.	Nikki Cross/A.S.H.	187

WWE 24/7 CHAMPIONSHIP

DATE	WON BY	DAYS
20-05-19	**Titus O'Neil**	‹1
	(Monday Night RAW, Albany)	
20-05-19	**Robert Roode**	‹1
	(Monday Night RAW, Albany)	
20-05-19	**R-Truth**	8
	(Monday Night RAW, Albany)	
28-05-19	**Elias**	‹1
	(SmackDown, Tulsa)	
28-05-19	**R-Truth[2]**	5
	(SmackDown, Tulsa)	
02-06-19	**Jinder Mahal**	‹1
	(Golf Course)	
02-06-19	**R-Truth[3]**	2
	(Golf Course)	
04-06-19	**Elias[2]**	‹1
	(SmackDown, Laredo)	
04-06-19	**R-Truth[4]**	2
	(SmackDown, Laredo)	
06-06-19	**Jinder Mahal[2]**	‹1
	(Frankfurt, Germany)	
06-06-19	**R-Truth[5]**	12
	(Red Sea)	
18-06-19	**Drake Maverick**	3
	(SmackDown, Ontario)	
21-06-19	**R-Truth[6]**	3
	(Orlando)	
24-06-19	**Heath Slater**	‹1
	(Monday Night RAW, Everett)	
24-06-19	**R-Truth[7]**	‹1
	(Monday Night RAW, Everett)	
24-06-19	**Cedric Alexander**	‹1
	(Monday Night RAW, Everett)	
24-06-19	**EC3**	‹1
	(Monday Night RAW, Everett)	
24-06-19	**R-Truth[8]**	7
	(Monday Night RAW, Everett)	
01-07-19	**Drake Maverick[2]**	14
	(Monday Night RAW, Dallas)	
15-07-19	**R-Truth[9]**	7
	(Monday Night RAW, Uniondale)	
22-07-19	**Drake Maverick[3]**	‹1
	(Monday Night RAW, Tampa)	
22-07-19	**Pat Patterson**	‹1
	(Monday Night RAW, Tampa)	
22-07-19	**Gerald Brisco**	‹1
	(Monday Night RAW, Tampa)	
22-07-19	**Kelly Kelly**	‹1
	(Monday Night RAW, Tampa)	
22-07-19	**Candice Michelle**	‹1
	(Monday Night RAW, Tampa)	
22-07-19	**Alundra Blayze**	‹1
	(Monday Night RAW, Tampa)	
22-07-19	**Ted DiBiase**	‹1
	(Monday Night RAW, Tampa)	
22-07-19	**Drake Maverick[4]**	‹1
	(Monday Night RAW, Tampa)	
22-07-19	**R-Truth[10]**	7
	(Monday Night RAW, Tampa)	
29-07-19	**Mike Kanellis**	‹1
	(Monday Night RAW, Little Rock)	
29-07-19	**Maria Kanellis**	7
	(Monday Night RAW, Little Rock)	
05-08-19	**Mike Kanellis[2]**	‹1
	(Monday Night RAW, Pittsburgh)	
05-08-19	**R-Truth[11]**	7
	(Monday Night RAW, Pittsburgh)	
12-08-19	**Dash Wilder & Scott Dawson**	‹1
	(Monday Night RAW, Toronto, Canada)	
12-08-19	**R-Truth[12]**	‹1
	(Monday Night RAW, Toronto, Canada)	
12-08-19	**Elias[3]**	12
	(Monday Night RAW, Toronto, Canada)	
24-08-19	**R-Truth[13]**	‹1
	(Los Angeles)	
24-08-19	**Rob Stone**	‹1
	(Los Angeles)	
24-08-19	**Elias[4]**	‹1
	(Los Angeles)	
27-08-19	**Drake Maverick[5]**	7
	(SmackDown, Baton Rouge)	
03-09-19	**Bo Dallas**	‹1
	(SmackDown, Norfolk)	
03-09-19	**Drake Maverick[6]**	‹1
	(SmackDown, Norfolk)	
03-09-19	**R-Truth[14]**	6
	(SmackDown, Norfolk)	
09-09-19	**Enes Kanter**	‹1
	(Main Event, New York)	
09-09-19	**R-Truth[15]**	7
	(Main Event, New York)	
16-09-19	**Glenn Jacobs**	‹1
	(Monday Night RAW, Knoxville)	
16-09-19	**R-Truth[16]**	4
	(Monday Night RAW, Knoxville)	
20-09-19	**EC3[2]**	‹1
	(House Show, Quezon City, Philippines)	
20-09-19	**R-Truth[17]**	1
	(House Show, Quezon City, Philippines)	
21-09-19	**EC3[3]**	‹1
	(House Show, Shanghai, China)	
21-09-19	**R-Truth[18]**	1
	(House Show, Shanghai, China)	
22-09-19	**EC3[4]**	‹1
	(House Show, Honolulu)	
22-09-19	**R-Truth[19]**	1

	(House Show, Honolulu)	
23-09-19	**Carmella**	11
	(Monday Night RAW, San Francisco)	
04-10-19	**Marshmello**	<1
	(SmackDown, Los Angeles)	
04-10-19	**Carmella**[2]	2
	(SmackDown, Los Angeles)	
06-10-19	**Tamina**	<1
	(Hell In A Cell '19, Sacramento)	
06-10-19	**R-Truth**[20]	15
	(Hell In A Cell '19, Sacramento)	
21-10-19	**Sunil Singh**	10
	(Monday Night RAW, Cleveland)	
31-10-19	**R-Truth**[21]	<1
	(Crown Jewel '19, Riyadh, Saudi Arabia)	
31-10-19	**Samir Singh**	18
	(Crown Jewel '19, Riyadh, Saudi Arabia)	
18-11-19	**R-Truth**[22]	1
	(Monday Night RAW, Boston)	
19-11-19	**Michael Giaccio**	<1
	(Stamford)	
19-11-19	**R-Truth**[23]	13
	(Stamford)	
02-12-19	**Kyle Busch**	<1
	(Monday Night RAW, Nashville)	
02-12-19	**R-Truth**[24]	20
	(Monday Night RAW, Nashville)	
22-12-19	**Akira Tozawa**	<1
	(New York)	
22-12-19	**Santa Claus**	<1
	(New York)	
22-12-19	**R-Truth**[25]	4
	(New York)	
26-12-19	**Samir Singh**[2]	<1
	(House Show, New York)	
26-12-19	**Sunil Singh**[2]	<1
	(House Show, New York)	
26-12-19	**R-Truth**[26]	1
	(House Show, New York)	
27-12-19	**Samir Singh**[3]	<1
	(House Show, Pittsburgh)	
27-12-19	**Mike Rome**	<1
	(House Show, Pittsburgh)	
27-12-19	**Sunil Singh**[3]	<1
	(House Show, Pittsburgh)	
27-12-19	**R-Truth**[27]	1
	(House Show, Pittsburgh)	
28-12-19	**Samir Singh**[4]	<1
	(House Show, Baltimore)	
28-12-19	**R-Truth**[28]	1
	(House Show, Baltimore)	
29-12-19	**Samir Singh**[5]	<1
	(House Show, Hershey)	
29-12-19	**Sunil Singh**[4]	<1
	(House Show, Hershey)	
29-12-19	**R-Truth**[29]	2
	(House Show, Hershey)	
31-12-19	**Mojo Rawley**	<1
	(New York)	
31-12-19	**R-Truth**[30]	13
	(New York)	
13-01-20	**Mojo Rawley**[2]	4
	(Monday Night RAW, Lexington)	
17-01-20	**R-Truth**[31]	<1
	(House Show, Lafayette)	
17-01-20	**Mojo Rawley**[3]	1
	(House Show, Lafayette)	
18-01-20	**R-Truth**[32]	<1
	(House Show, Jackson)	
18-01-20	**Mojo Rawley**[4]	1
	(House Show, Jackson)	
19-01-20	**R-Truth**[33]	<1
	(House Show, Topeka)	
19-01-20	**Mojo Rawley**[5]	8
	(House Show, Topeka)	
27-01-20	**R-Truth**[34]	<1
	(Monday Night RAW, San Antonio)	
27-01-20	**Mojo Rawley**[6]	14
	(Monday Night RAW, San Antonio)	
10-02-20	**Riddick Moss**	41
	(Monday Night RAW, Ontario)	
22-03-20	**R-Truth**[35]	13
	(Orlando)	
04-04-20	**Mojo Rawley**[7]	1
	(WrestleMania XXXVI, Orlando)	
05-04-20	**Rob Gronkowski**	57
	(WrestleMania XXXVI, Orlando)	
01-06-20	**R-Truth**[36]	21
	(Foxborough)	
22-06-20	**Akira Tozawa**[2]	7
	(Monday Night RAW, Orlando)	
29-06-20	**R-Truth**[37]	21
	(Monday Night RAW, Orlando)	
20-07-20	**Shelton Benjamin**	14
	(Monday Night RAW, Orlando)	
03-08-20	**Akira Tozawa**[3]	7
	(Monday Night RAW, Orlando)	
10-08-20	**R-Truth**[38]	7
	(Monday Night RAW, Orlando)	
17-08-20	**Shelton Benjamin**[2]	<1
	(Monday Night RAW, Orlando)	
17-08-20	**Cedric Alexander**[2]	<1
	(Monday Night RAW, Orlando)	
17-08-20	**Shelton Benjamin**[3]	7
	(Monday Night RAW, Orlando)	
24-08-20	**Akira Tozawa**[4]	7
	(Monday Night RAW, Orlando)	
31-08-20	**R-Truth**[39]	27
	(Monday Night RAW, Orlando)	
27-09-20	**Drew Gulak**	<1
	(Clash Of Champions '20, Orlando)	
27-09-20	**R-Truth**[40]	1
	(Clash Of Champions '20, Orlando)	
28-09-20	**Akira Tozawa**[5]	<1
	(Monday Night RAW, Orlando)	
28-09-20	**Drew Gulak**[2]	<1
	(Monday Night RAW, Orlando)	
28-09-20	**R-Truth**[41]	7
	(Monday Night RAW, Orlando)	
05-10-20	**Drew Gulak**[3]	<1
	(Monday Night RAW, Orlando)	
05-10-20	**R-Truth**[42]	28
	(Monday Night RAW, Orlando)	
02-11-20	**Drew Gulak**[4]	7
	(Monday Night RAW, Orlando)	
09-11-20	**R-Truth**[43]	<1
	(Monday Night RAW, Orlando)	
09-11-20	**Akira Tozawa**[6]	<1
	(Monday Night RAW, Orlando)	
09-11-20	**Erik**	<1
	(Monday Night RAW, Orlando)	
09-11-20	**Drew Gulak**[5]	<1
	(Monday Night RAW, Orlando)	
09-11-20	**Tucker**	<1
	(Monday Night RAW, Orlando)	
09-11-20	**Drew Gulak**[6]	<1
	(Monday Night RAW, Orlando)	
09-11-20	**Tucker**[2]	<1
	(Monday Night RAW, Orlando)	
09-11-20	**Gran Metalik**	<1
	(Monday Night RAW, Orlando)	
09-11-20	**Lince Dorado**	<1

Date	Name	#	Venue
			(Monday Night RAW, Orlando)
09-11-20	R-Truth[44]	13	
			(Monday Night RAW, Orlando)
22-11-20	The Gobbledy Gooker	<1	
			(Survivor Series '20, Orlando)
22-11-20	Akira Tozawa[7]	<1	
			(Survivor Series '20, Orlando)
22-11-20	R-Truth[45]	39	
			(Survivor Series '20, Orlando)
31-12-20	Angel Garza	4	
			(N/A)
04-01-21	R-Truth[46]	28	
			(Monday Night RAW, St. Petersburg)
31-01-21	Alicia Fox	<1	
			(Royal Rumble '21, St. Petersburg)
31-01-21	R-Truth[47]	<1	
			(Royal Rumble '21, St. Petersburg)
31-01-21	Peter Rosenberg	1	
			(Royal Rumble '21, St. Petersburg)
01-02-21	R-Truth[48]	5	
			(The Michael Kay Show)
06-02-21	Doug Flutie	<1	
			(Celebrity Flag Football Game, Clearwater)
06-02-21	R-Truth[49]	9	
			(Celebrity Flag Football Game, Clearwater)
15-02-21	Akira Tozawa[8]	<1	
			(Monday Night RAW, St. Petersburg)
15-02-21	Bad Bunny	28	
			(Monday Night RAW, St. Petersburg)
15-03-21	R-Truth[50]	6	
			(Monday Night RAW, St. Petersburg)
21-03-21	Joseph Average	<1	
			(Fastlane '21, St. Petersburg)
21-03-21	R-Truth[51]	29	
			(Fastlane '21, St. Petersburg)
19-04-21	Akira Tozawa[9]	<1	
			(St. Petersburg)
19-04-21	Joseph Average[2]	<1	
			(St. Petersburg)
19-04-21	R-Truth[52]	28	
			(St. Petersburg)
17-05-21	Akira Tozawa[10]	42	
			(Monday Night RAW, Tampa)
28-06-21	Drew Gulak[7]	<1	
			(Monday Night RAW, Tampa)
28-06-21	R-Truth[53]	<1	
			(Monday Night RAW, Tampa)
28-06-21	Akira Tozawa[11]	21	
			(Monday Night RAW, Tampa)
19-07-21	Reggie	112	
			(Monday Night RAW, Dallas)
08-11-21	Drake Maverick[7]	<1	
			(Monday Night RAW, Louisville)
08-11-21	Akira Tozawa[12]	<1	
			(Monday Night RAW, Louisville)
08-11-21	Corey Graves	<1	
			(Monday Night RAW, Louisville)
08-11-21	Byron Saxton	<1	
			(Monday Night RAW, Louisville)
08-11-21	Drake Maverick[8]	<1	
			(Monday Night RAW, Louisville)
08-11-21	Reggie[2]	14	
			(Monday Night RAW, Louisville)
22-11-21	Cedric Alexander[3]	<1	
			(Monday Night RAW, Brooklyn)
22-11-21	Dana Brooke	84	
			(Monday Night RAW, Brooklyn)
14-02-22	Reggie[3]	7	
			(Monday Night RAW, Indianapolis)
21-02-22	Dana Brooke[2]	56	
			(Monday Night RAW, Columbia)
18-04-22	Reggie[4]	<1	
			(Monday Night RAW, Buffalo)
18-04-22	Tamina[2]	<1	
			(Monday Night RAW, Buffalo)
18-04-22	Akira Tozawa[13]	<1	
			(Monday Night RAW, Buffalo)
18-04-22	Dana Brooke[3]	14	
			(Monday Night RAW, Buffalo)
02-05-22	Nikki A.S.H.	<1	
			(Monday Night RAW, Greensboro)
02-05-22	Dana Brooke[4]	28	
			(Monday Night RAW, Greensboro)
30-05-22	Tamina[3]	<1	
			(Monday Night RAW, Des Moines)
30-05-22	Akira Tozawa[14]	7	
			(Monday Night RAW, Des Moines)
06-06-22	Dana Brooke[5]	17	
			(Monday Night RAW, Green Bay)
23-06-22	Doudrop	<1	
			(Main Event, Lincoln)
23-06-22	Akira Tozawa[15]	<1	
			(Main Event, Lincoln)
23-06-22	R-Truth[54]	<1	
			(Main Event, Lincoln)
23-06-22	Nikki A.S.H.[2]	<1	
			(Main Event, Lincoln)
23-06-22	Dana Brooke[6]	15	
			(Main Event, Lincoln)
09-07-22	Carmella[3]	<1	
			(House Show, Bossier City)
09-07-22	Dana Brooke[7]	1	
			(House Show, Bossier City)
10-07-22	Carmella[4]	<1	
			(House Show, Waco)
10-07-22	Dana Brooke[8]	8	
			(House Show, Waco)
18-07-22	Akira Tozawa[16]	<1	
			(Monday Night RAW, Tampa)
18-07-22	Nikki A.S.H.[3]	<1	
			(Monday Night RAW, Tampa)
18-07-22	Alexa Bliss	<1	
			(Monday Night RAW, Tampa)
18-07-22	Doudrop[2]	<1	
			(Monday Night RAW, Tampa)
18-07-22	Tamina[4]	<1	
			(Monday Night RAW, Tampa)
18-07-22	Dana Brooke[9]	33	
			(Monday Night RAW, Tampa)
20-08-22	Nikki A.S.H.[4]	<1	
			(House Show, Kingston, Canada)
20-08-22	Tamina[5]	<1	
			(House Show, Kingston, Canada)
20-08-22	Dana Brooke[10]	1	
			(House Show, Kingston, Canada)
21-08-22	Nikki A.S.H.[5]	<1	
			(House Show, London, Canada)
21-08-22	Shawn Bennett	<1	
			(House Show, London, Canada)
21-08-22	Tamina[6]	<1	
			(House Show, London, Canada)
21-08-22	Dana Brooke[11]	20	
			(House Show, London, Canada)
10-09-22	Nikki A.S.H.[6]	<1	
			(House Show, Colorado Springs)
10-09-22	Eddie Orengo	<1	
			(House Show, Colorado Springs)
10-09-22	Tamina[7]	<1	
			(House Show, Colorado Springs)
10-09-22	Dana Brooke[12]	14	
			(House Show, Colorado Springs)
24-09-22	Nikki A.S.H.[7]	<1	

	(House Show, Vancouver, Canada)	
24-09-22	**Daphanie LaShaunn**	‹1
	(House Show, Vancouver, Canada)	
24-09-22	**Nikki A.S.H.**[8]	‹1
	(House Show, Vancouver, Canada)	
24-09-22	**Dana Brooke**[13]	35
	(House Show, Vancouver, Canada)	
29-10-22	**Nikki Cross**[9]	‹1
	(House Show, Monterrey, Mexico)	
29-10-22	**Tamina**[8]	‹1
	(House Show, Monterrey, Mexico)	
29-10-22	**Dana Brooke**[14]	1
	(House Show, Monterrey, Mexico)	
30-10-22	**Nikki Cross**[10]	‹1
	(House Show, Mexico City, Mexico)	
30-10-22	**Tamina**[9]	‹1
	(House Show, Mexico City, Mexico)	
30-10-22	**Dana Brooke**[15]	8
	(House Show, Mexico City, Mexico)	
07-11-22	**Nikki Cross**[11]	‹1
	(Monday Night RAW, Wilkes-Barre)	
07-11-22	**DEACTIVATED**	

NXT CHAMPIONSHIP

DATE	WON BY	DAYS
29-08-12	**Seth Rollins**	133
	(NXT, Winter Park)	
09-01-13	**Big E Langston**	153
	(NXT, Winter Park)	
12-06-13	**Bo Dallas**	260
	(NXT, Winter Park)	
27-02-14	**Adrian Neville**	287
	(Arrival, Winter Park)	
11-12-14	**Sami Zayn**	62
	(TakeOver: R Evolution, Winter Park)	
11-02-15	**Kevin Owens**	143
	(TakeOver: Rival, Winter Park)	
04-07-15	**Finn Balor**	292
	(WWE The Beast In The East, Tokyo, Japan)	
21-04-16	**Samoa Joe**	121
	(House Show, Lowell)	
20-08-16	**Shinsuke Nakamura**	91
	(TakeOver: Brooklyn II, Brooklyn)	
19-11-16	**Samoa Joe**[2]	14
	(TakeOver: Toronto, Toronto, Canada)	
03-12-16	**Shinsuke Nakamura**[2]	56
	(NXT, Osaka, Japan)	
28-01-17	**Bobby Roode**	203
	(TakeOver: San Antonio, San Antonio)	
19-08-17	**Drew McIntyre**	91
	(TakeOver: Brooklyn III, Brooklyn)	
18-11-17	**Andrade Cien Almas**	140
	(TakeOver: WarGames, Houston)	
07-04-18	**Aleister Black**	108
	(TakeOver: New Orleans, New Orleans)	
25-07-18	**Tommaso Ciampa**	238
	(NXT, Winter Park)	
20-03-19	**VACANT**	
05-04-19	**Johnny Gargano**	57
	(TakeOver: New York, Brooklyn)	
01-06-19	**Adam Cole**	403
	(TakeOver XXV, Bridgeport)	
08-07-20	**Keith Lee**	45
	(The Great American Bash '20, Winter Park)	
22-08-20	**Karrion Kross**	4
	(TakeOver XXX, Winter Park)	
26-08-20	**VACANT**	
08-09-20	**Finn Balor**[2]	212

	(Super Tuesday II, Winter Park)	
08-04-21	**Karrion Kross**[2]	136
	(TakeOver: Stand & Deliver, Orlando)	
22-08-21	**Samoa Joe**[3]	36
	(TakeOver 36, Orlando)	
12-09-21	**VACANT**	
14-09-21	**Tommaso Ciampa**[2]	112
	(NXT 2.0, Orlando)	
04-01-22	**Bron Breakker**	63
	(New Year's Evil, Orlando)	
08-03-22	**Dolph Ziggler**	27
	(Roadblock, Orlando)	
04-04-22	**Bron Breakker**[2]	271*
	(WWE Monday Night RAW, Dallas)	

Most Reigns
1.	Samoa Joe	3
2.	Shinsuke Nakamura	2
3.	Finn Balor	2
4.	Tommaso Ciampa	2
5.	Karrion Kross	2
6.	Bron Breakker	2

Longest Reigns
1.	Adam Cole	403
2.	Finn Balor	292
3.	Adrian Neville	287
4.	Bron Breakker	271*
5.	Bo Dallas	260

Longest Cumulative Reigns
1.	Finn Balor	504
2.	Adam Cole	403
3.	Tommaso Ciampa	350
4.	Bron Breakker	334*
5.	Adrian Neville	287

NXT NORTH AMERICAN CHAMPIONSHIP

DATE	WON BY	DAYS
07-04-18	**Adam Cole**	133
	(TakeOver: New Orleans, New Orleans)	
18-08-18	**Ricochet**	161
	(TakeOver: Brooklyn IV, Brooklyn)	
26-01-19	**Johnny Gargano**	25
	(TakeOver: Phoenix, Phoenix)	
20-02-19	**Velveteen Dream**	210
	(NXT, Winter Park)	
18-09-19	**Roderick Strong**	126
	(NXT, Winter Park)	
22-01-20	**Keith Lee**	182
	(NXT, Winter Park)	
22-07-20	**VACANT**	
22-08-20	**Damian Priest**	67
	(TakeOver XXX, Winter Park)	
28-10-20	**Johnny Gargano**[2]	14
	(Halloween Havoc, Orlando)	
11-11-20	**Leon Ruff**	25
	(NXT, Orlando)	
06-12-20	**Johnny Gargano**[3]	163
	(TakeOver: WarGames, Orlando)	
18-05-21	**Bronson Reed**	42
	(NXT, Orlando)	
29-06-21	**Isaiah "Swerve" Scott**	105
	(NXT, Orlando)	
12-10-21	**Carmelo Hayes**	172
	(NXT 2.0, Orlando)	

DATE	WON BY	DAYS
02-04-22	**Cameron Grimes** (Stand & Deliver '22, Dallas)	63
04-06-22	**Carmelo Hayes**[2] (In Your House '22, Orlando)	101
13-09-22	**Solo Sikoa** (NXT 2.0 One Year Anniversary, Orlando)	7
20-09-22	**VACANT**	
22-10-22	**Wes Lee** (Halloween Havoc, Orlando)	70*

Most Reigns
1. Johnny Gargano — 3
2. Carmelo Hayes — 2

Longest Reigns
1. Velveteen Dream — 210
2. Keith Lee — 182
3. Carmelo Hayes — 172
4. Johnny Gargano — 163
5. Ricochet — 161

Longest Cumulative Reigns
1. Carmelon Hayes — 273
2. Velveteen Dream — 210
3. Johnny Gargano — 202
4. Keith Lee — 182
5. Ricochet — 161

NXT TAG TEAM CHAMPIONSHIP

DATE	WON BY	DAYS
13-02-13	**Adrian Neville & Oliver Grey** (NXT, Winter Park)	84
08-05-13	**Luke Harper & Erick Rowan** (NXT, Winter Park)	70
17-07-13	**Adrian Neville[2] & Corey Graves** (NXT, Winter Park)	77
02-10-13	**Konnor & Viktor** (NXT, Winter Park)	344
11-09-14	**Kalisto & Sin Cara** (TakeOver: Fatal 4-Way, Winter Park)	139
28-01-15	**Wesley Blake & Buddy Murphy** (NXT, Winter Park)	206
22-08-15	**Simon Gotch & Aiden English** (TakeOver: Brooklyn, Brooklyn)	81
11-11-15	**Scott Dawson & Dash Wilder** (NXT, Winter Park)	142
01-04-16	**Chad Gable & Jason Jordan** (TakeOver: Dallas, Dallas)	68
08-06-16	**Scott Dawson[2] & Dash Wilder[2]** (TakeOver: The End, Winter Park)	164
19-11-16	**Johnny Gargano & Tommaso Ciampa** (TakeOver: Toronto, Toronto)	70
28-01-17	**Akam & Rezar** (TakeOver: San Antonio, San Antonio)	203
19-08-17	**Eric Young & Alexander Wolfe** (TakeOver: Brooklyn III, Brooklyn)	123
20-12-17	**Roderick Strong, Bobby Fish, Adam Cole & Kyle O'Reilly** (NXT, Winter Park)	188
26-06-18	**Trent Seven & Tyler Bate** (UK Tournament, London, England)	15
11-07-18	**Kyle O'Reilly[2] & Roderick Strong[2]** (NXT, Winter Park)	199
26-01-19	**Hanson & Rowe** (TakeOver: Phoenix, Phoenix)	109

DATE	WON BY	DAYS
15-05-19	**VACANT**	
01-06-19	**Montez Ford & Angelo Dawkins** (TakeOver XXV, Bridgeport)	88
28-08-19	**Bobby Fish & Kyle O'Reilly[3]** (NXT, Winter Park)	172
16-02-20	**Pete Dunne & Matt Riddle** (TakeOver: Portland, Portland)	87
13-05-20	**Fabian Aichner & Marcel Barthel** (NXT, Winter Park)	105
26-08-20	**Tyler Breeze & Fandango** (NXT, Winter Park)	56
21-10-20	**Danny Burch & Oney Lorcan** (NXT, Orlando)	153
23-03-21	**VACANT**	
07-04-21	**Wes Lee & Nash Carter** (TakeOver: Stand & Deliver, Orlando)	202
26-10-21	**Fabian Aichner[2] & Marcel Barthel[2]** (Halloween Havoc '21, Orlando)	158
02-04-22	**Wes Lee & Nash Carter** (Stand & Deliver '22, Dallas)	6
08-04-22	**VACANT**	
12-04-22	**Elton Prince & Kit Wilson** (NXT 2.0, Orlando)	53
04-06-22	**Brutus Creed & Julius Creed** (In Your House '22, Orlando)	92
04-09-22	**Elton Prince[2] & Kit Wilson[2]** (Worlds Collide, Orlando)	97
10-12-22	**Kofi Kingston & Xavier Woods** (Deadline, Orlando)	21*

Most Reigns
1. Kyle O'Reilly — 3
2. Bobby Fish — 2
3. Roderick Strong — 2
4. Adrian Neville — 2
5. Scott Dawson — 2
6. Dash Wilder — 2
7. Fabian Aichner — 2
8. Marcel Barthel — 2
9. Elton Prince — 2
10. Kit Wilson — 2

Longest Reigns
1. Konnor & Viktor — 344
2. Blake & Murphy — 206
3. Akam & Rezar — 203
4. Wes Lee & Nash Carter — 202
5. Kyle O'Reilly & Roderick Strong — 199

Longest Cumulative Reigns
1. Kyle O'Reilly — 559
2. Bobby Fish — 360
3. Viktor — 344
4. Konnor — 344
5. Dash Wilder — 306
6. Scott Dawson — 306

NXT WOMEN'S CHAMPIONSHIP

DATE	WON BY	DAYS
24-07-13	**Paige** (NXT, Winter Park)	273
24-04-14	**VACANT**	
29-05-14	**Charlotte Flair** (TakeOver, Winter Park)	258
11-02-15	**Sasha Banks**	192

	(TakeOver: Rival, Winter Park)	
22-08-15	**Bayley**	223
	(TakeOver: Brooklyn, Brooklyn)	
01-04-16	**Asuka**	523
	(TakeOver: Dallas, Dallas)	
06-09-17	**VACANT**	
18-11-17	**Ember Moon**	140
	(TakeOver: WarGames, Houston)	
07-04-18	**Shayna Baszler**	133
	(TakeOver: New Orleans, New Orleans)	
18-08-18	**Kairi Sane**	71
	(TakeOver: Brooklyn IV, Brooklyn)	
28-10-18	**Shayna Baszler**[2]	416
	(WWE Evolution, Uniondale)	
18-12-19	**Rhea Ripley**	109
	(NXT, Winter Park)	
05-04-20	**Charlotte Flair**[2]	63
	(WWE WrestleMania XXXVI, Orlando)	
07-06-20	**Io Shirai**	304
	(In Your House, Winter Park)	
07-04-21	**Raquel Gonzalez**	202
	(TakeOver: Stand & Deliver, Orlando)	
26-10-21	**Mandy Rose**	413
	(Halloween Havoc '21, Orlando)	
13-12-22	**Roxanne Perez**	18*
	(NXT, Orlando)	

Most Reigns
1. Charlotte Flair — 2
2. Shayna Baszler — 2

Longest Reigns
1. Asuka — 523
2. Shayna Baszler — 416
3. Mandy Rose — 413
4. Io Shirai — 304
5. Paige — 273

Longest Cumulative Reigns
1. Shayna Baszler — 549
2. Asuka — 523
3. Mandy Rose — 413
4. Charlotte Flair — 321
5. Io Shirai — 304

NXT WOMEN'S TAG TEAM CHAMPIONSHIP

DATE	WON BY	DAYS
10-03-21	**Dakota Kai & Raquel Gonzalez**	<1
	(NXT, Orlando)	
10-03-21	**Ember Moon & Shotzi Blackheart**	55
	(NXT, Orlando)	
04-05-21	**Candice LeRae & Indi Hartwell**	63
	(NXT, Orlando)	
06-07-21	**Io Shirai & Zoey Stark**	112
	(Great American Bash '21, Orlando)	
26-10-21	**Gigi Dolin & Jacy Jayne**	158
	(Halloween Havoc '21, Orlando)	
02-04-22	**Dakota Kai**[2] **& Raquel Gonzalez**[2]	3
	(Stand & Deliver '22, Dallas)	
05-04-22	**Gigi Dolin**[2] **& Jacy Jayne**[2]	91
	(NXT 2.0, Orlando)	
05-07-22	**Cora Jade & Roxanne Perez**	
	(Great American Bash '22, Orlando)	
19-07-22	**Roxanne Perez**[2]	7
	(NXT 2.0, Orlando)	
26-07-22	**VACANT**	

02-08-22	**Katana Chance & Kayden Carter**	151*
	(NXT 2.0, Orlando)	

Most Reigns
1. Gigi Dolin — 2
2. Jacy Jayne — 2
3. Dakota Kai — 2
4. Raquel Rodriguez — 2
5. Roxanne Perez — 2

Longest Reigns
1. Gigi Dolin & Jacy Jayne — 158
2. Katana Chance & Kayden Carter — 151*
3. Io Shirai & Zoe Stark — 112

Longest Cumulative Reigns
1. Gigi Dolin — 249
2. Jacy Jayne — 249
3. Katana Chance — 151*
4. Kayden Carter — 151*

NXT UNITED KINGDOM CHAMPIONSHIP

DATE	WON BY	DAYS
15-01-17	**Tyler Bate**	125
	(UK Championship Tourn., Blackpool)	
20-05-17	**Pete Dunne**	685
	(NXT TakeOver: Chicago, Rosemont)	
05-04-19	**Walter**	807
	(NXT TakeOver: New York, Brooklyn)	
22-08-21	**Ilja Dragunov**	347
	(NXT TakeOver 36, Orlando)	
04-08-22	**VACANT**	
01-09-22	**Tyler Bate**[2]	3
	(NXT UK, London, England)	
04-09-22	**Bron Breakker**	<1
	(NXT Worlds Collide, Orlando)	
04-09-22	**UNIFIED**	

NXT UK HERITAGE CUP

DATE	WON BY	DAYS
26-11-20	**A-Kid**	174
	(NXT UK, London, England)	
20-05-21	**Tyler Bate**	161
	(NXT UK, London, England)	
28-10-21	**Noam Dar**	259
	(NXT UK, London, England)	
14-07-22	**Mark Coffey**	42
	(NXT UK, London, England)	
25-08-22	**Noam Dar**[2]	128*
	(NXT UK, London, England)	

NXT UK TAG TEAM CHAMPIONSHIP

DATE	WON BY	DAYS
12-01-19	**James Drake & Zack Gibson**	231
	(TakeOver: Blackpool, Blackpool, England)	
31-08-19	**Flash Morgan Webster & Mark Andrews**	47

(TakeOver: Cardiff, Cardiff)

DATE	WON BY	DAYS
17-10-19	**Mark Coffey & Wolfgang**	497
	(NXT UK, Brentwood, England)	
25-02-21	**Lewis Howley & Sam Stoker**	297
	(NXT UK, London, England)	
09-12-21	**Tyler Bate & Trent Seven**	175
	(NXT UK, London, England)	
02-06-22	**Ashton Smith & Oliver Carter**	21
	(NXT UK, London, England)	
23-06-22	**VACANT**	
23-06-22	**Brooks Jensen & Josh Briggs**	73
	(NXT UK, London, England)	
04-09-22	**Elton Prince² & Kit Wilson²**	<1
	(NXT Worlds Collide, Orlando)	
04-09-22	**UNIFIED**	

NXT UK WOMEN'S CHAMPIONSHIP

DATE	WON BY	DAYS
28-11-18	**Rhea Ripley**	45
	(NXT UK, Birmingham, England)	
12-01-19	**Toni Storm**	231
	(TakeOver: Blackpool, Blackpool)	
31-08-19	**Kay Lee Ray**	649
	(TakeOver: Cardiff, Cardiff)	
10-06-21	**Meiko Satomura**	451
	(NXT UK, London, England)	
04-09-22	**Mandy Rose**	<1
	(NXT Worlds Collide, Orlando)	
04-09-22	**UNIFIED**	

AEW WORLD CHAMPIONSHIP

DATE	WON BY	DAYS
31-08-19	**Chris Jericho**	182
	(All Out '19, Hoffman Estates)	
29-02-20	**Jon Moxley**	277
	(Revolution '20, Chicago)	
02-12-20	**Kenny Omega**	346
	(Dynamite: Winter Is Coming, Jacksonville)	
13-11-21	**Adam Page**	197
	(Full Gear '21, Minneapolis)	
29-05-22	**CM Punk**	87
	(Double Or Nothing '22, Paradise)	
26-06-22	*Jon Moxley (interim)*	59
	(Forbidden Door, Chicago)	
24-08-22	**Jon Moxley²**	11
	(Dynamite, Cleveland)	
04-09-22	**CM Punk²**	3
	(All Out '22, Hoffman Estates)	
07-09-22	**VACANT**	
21-09-22	**Jon Moxley³**	59
	(Dynamite: Grand Slam, Flushing)	
19-11-22	**MJF**	42*
	(Full Gear '22, Newark)	

Most Reigns
1. Jon Moxley 3
2. CM Punk 2

Longest Reigns
1. Kenny Omega 346
2. Jon Moxley 277
3. Adam Page 197

Longest Cumulative Reigns
1. Jon Moxley 347

DATE	WON BY	DAYS
2.	Kenny Omega	346
3.	Adam Page	197

AEW TNT CHAMPIONSHIP

DATE	WON BY	DAYS
23-05-20	**Cody Rhodes**	91
	(Double Or Nothing '20, Jacksonville)	
22-08-20	**Mr. Brodie Lee**	46
	(Dynamite, Jacksonville)	
07-10-20	**Cody Rhodes²**	31
	(Dynamite, Jacksonville)	
07-11-20	**Darby Allin**	186
	(Full Gear '20, Jacksonville)	
12-05-21	**Miro**	140
	(Dynamite, Jacksonville)	
29-09-21	**Sammy Guevara**	88
	(Dynamite, Rochester)	
25-15-21	**Cody Rhodes³**	32
	(Rampage: Holiday Bash, Greensboro)	
08-01-22	*Sammy Guevara (interim)*	18
	(Battle Of The Belts I, Charlotte)	
26-01-22	**Sammy Guevara²**	42
	(Dynamite: Beach Break, Cleveland)	
09-03-22	**Scorpio Sky**	38
	(Dynamite, Estero)	
15-04-22	**Sammy Guevara³**	11
	(Battle Of The Belts II, Garland)	
27-04-22	**Scorpio Sky²**	70
	(Dynamite, Philadelphia)	
06-07-22	**Wardlow**	136
	(Dynamite, Rochester, NY)	
19-11-22	**Samoa Joe**	42*
	(Full Gear '22, Newark)	

Most Reigns
1. Cody Rhodes 3
2. Sammy Guevara 3
3. Scorpio Sky 2

Longest Reigns
1. Darby Allin 186
2. Miro 140
3. Wardlow 136

Longest Cumulative Reigns
1. Darby Allin 186
2. Cody Rhodes 155
3. Sammy Guevara 141

AEW ALL-ATLANTIC CHAMPIONSHIP

DATE	WON BY	DAYS
26-06-22	**Pac**	108
	(Forbidden Door, Chicago)	
12-10-22	**Orange Cassidy**	90*
	(Dynamite, Toronto, Canada)	

FTW CHAMPIONSHIP (AEW)

DATE	WON BY	DAYS
14-05-98	**Taz**	219
	(ECW It Ain't Seinfeld, Queens)	

23-12-98	**Sabu**	88
	(ECW Hardcore TV, Philadelphia)	
21-03-99	**Taz²**	<1
	(ECW Living Dangerously '99, Asbury Park)	
21-03-99	DEACTIVATED	
08-07-20	**Brian Cage**	371
	(Dynamite: Fyter Fest, Jacksonville)	
14-07-21	**Ricky Starks**	378
	(Dynamite: Fyter Fest, Cedar Park)	
27-07-22	**Hook**	157*
	(Dynamite: Fight For The Fallen, Worcester)	

AEW WORLD TAG TEAM CHAMPIONSHIP

DATE	WON BY	DAYS
30-10-19	**Frankie Kazarian & Scorpio Sky**	84
	(Dynamite, Charleston)	
22-01-20	**Adam Page & Kenny Omega**	227
	(Dynamite, Nassau, Bahamas)	
05-09-20	**Cash Wheeler & Dax Harwood**	63
	(All Out '20, Jacksonville)	
07-11-20	**Matt Jackson & Nick Jackson**	302
	(Full Gear '20, Jacksonville)	
05-09-21	**Penta El Zero Miedo & Rey Fenix**	122
	(All Out '21, Hoffman Estates)	
05-01-22	**Jungle Boy & Luchasaurus**	161
	(Dynamite, Newark)	
15-06-22	**Matt Jackson² & Nick Jackson²**	28
	(Dynamite: Road Rager, St. Louis)	
13-07-22	**Keith Lee & Swerve Strickland**	70
	(Dynamite: Fyter Fest, Savannah)	
21-09-22	**Anthony Bowens & Max Caster**	101*
	(Dynamite: Grand Slam, Flushing)	

Most Reigns

1.	Matt Jackson	2
2.	Nick Jackson	2

Longest Reigns

1.	Matt Jackson & Nick Jackson	302
2.	Adam Page & Kenny Omega	227
3.	Jungle Boy & Luchasaurus	161

Longest Cumulative Reigns

1.	Matt Jackson & Nick Jackson	330
2.	Adam Page & Kenny Omega	227
3.	Jungle Boy & Luchasaurus	161

AEW WORLD TRIOS CHAMPIONSHIP

DATE	WON BY	DAYS
04-09-22	**Kenny Omega, Matt Jackson & Nick Jackson**	3
	(All Out '22, Hoffman Estates)	
07-09-22	VACANT	
07-09-22	**Pac, Penta El Zero Miedo & Rey Fenix**	115*
	(Dynamite, Buffalo)	

AEW WOMEN'S WORLD CHAMPIONSHIP

DATE	WON BY	DAYS
02-10-19	**Riho**	133
	(Dynamite, Washington)	
12-02-20	**Nyla Rose**	101
	(Dynamite, Cedar Park)	
23-05-20	**Hikaru Shida**	372
	(Double Or Nothing '20, Jacksonville)	
30-05-21	**Dr. Britt Baker, D.M.D.**	290
	(Double Or Nothing '21, Jacksonville)	
16-03-22	**Thunder Rosa**	172
	(Dynamite: St. Patrick's Day Slam, San Ant.)	
04-09-22	VACANT	
04-09-22	**Toni Storm**	76
	(All Out '22, Hoffman Estates)	
19-11-22	**Jamie Hayter**	42*
	(Full Gear '22, Newark)	

AEW TBS CHAMPIONSHIP

DATE	WON BY	DAYS
05-01-22	**Jade Cargill**	360*
	(Dynamite, Newark)	

IMPACT WORLD CHAMPIONSHIP

DATE	WON BY	DAYS
13-05-07	**Kurt Angle**	4
	(Sacrifice '07, Orlando)	
17-05-07	VACANT	
17-06-07	**Kurt Angle²**	119
	(Slammiversary '07, Nashville)	
14-10-07	**Sting**	11
	(Bound For Glory '07, Duluth)	
25-10-07	**Kurt Angle³**	171
	(Impact!, Orlando)	
13-04-08	**Samoa Joe**	182
	(Lockdown '08, Lowell)	
12-10-08	**Sting²**	189
	(Bound For Glory IV, Hoffman Estates)	
19-04-09	**Mick Foley**	63
	(Lockdown '09, Philadelphia)	
21-06-09	**Kurt Angle⁴**	91
	(Slammiversary '09, Auburn Hills)	
20-09-09	**AJ Styles**	211
	(No Surrender '09, Orlando)	
19-04-10	**Rob Van Dam**	122
	(Impact!, Orlando)	
19-08-10	VACANT	
10-10-10	**Jeff Hardy**	91
	(Bound For Glory '10, Daytona Beach)	
09-01-11	**Mr. Anderson**	35
	(Genesis '11, Orlando)	
13-02-11	**Jeff Hardy²**	18
	(Against All Odds '11, Orlando)	
03-03-11	**Sting³**	101
	(Impact!, Fayetteville)	
12-06-11	**Mr. Anderson²**	32
	(Slammiversary IX, Orlando)	
14-07-11	**Sting⁴**	24

	(Impact!, Orlando)	
07-08-11	**Kurt Angle**[5]	74
	(Hardcore Justice '11, Orlando)	
20-10-11	**James Storm**	14
	(Impact!, Orlando)	
03-11-11	**Bobby Roode**	248
	(Impact!, Macon)	
08-07-12	**Austin Aries**	98
	(Destination X '12, Orlando)	
14-10-12	**Jeff Hardy**[3]	147
	(Bound For Glory '12, Phoenix)	
10-03-13	**Bully Ray**	140
	(Lockdown '13, San Antonio)	
18-07-13	**Chris Sabin**	28
	(Destination X '13, Louisville)	
15-08-13	**Bully Ray**[2]	66
	(Hardcore Justice '13, Norfolk)	
20-10-13	**AJ Styles**[2]	9
	(Bound For Glory '13, San Diego)	
29-10-13	**VACANT**	
19-12-13	**Magnus**	112
	(Impact!, Orlando)	
10-04-14	**Eric Young**	70
	(Impact!, Orlando)	
19-06-14	**Bobby Lashley**	132
	(Impact!, Bethlehem)	
29-10-14	**Bobby Roode**[2]	70
	(Impact!, Bethlehem)	
07-01-15	**Bobby Lashley**[2]	72
	(Impact!, New York)	
20-03-15	**Kurt Angle**[6]	103
	(Impact!, London, England)	
01-07-15	**Ethan Carter III**	95
	(Impact!, Orlando)	
04-10-15	**Matt Hardy**	2
	(Bound For Glory '15, Concord)	
06-10-15	**VACANT**	
05-01-16	**Ethan Carter III**[2]	14
	(Impact!, Bethlehem)	
19-01-16	**Matt Hardy**[2]	56
	(Impact!, Bethlehem)	
15-03-16	**Drew Galloway**	89
	(Impact!, Orlando)	
12-06-16	**Bobby Lashley**[3]	116
	(Slammiversary '16, Orlando)	
06-10-16	**Eddie Edwards**	112
	(Impact!, Orlando)	
26-01-17	**Bobby Lashley**[4]	157
	(Impact!, Orlando)	
02-07-17	**Alberto El Patron**	43
	(Slammiversary XV, Orlando)	
14-08-17	**VACANT**	
18-09-17	**Eli Drake**	136
	(Impact!, Orlando)	
01-02-18	**Austin Aries**[2]	80
	(Impact!, Orlando)	
22-04-18	**Pentagon Jr.**	39
	(Redemption '18, Orlando)	
31-05-18	**Austin Aries**[3]	136
	(Impact!, Orlando)	
14-10-18	**Johnny Impact**	196
	(Bound For Glory '18, New York)	
28-04-19	**Brian Cage**	184
	(Rebellion '19, Toronto, Canada)	
29-10-19	**Sami Callihan**	75
	(Impact!, Windsor, Canada)	
12-01-20	**Tessa Blanchard**	165
	(Hard To Kill '20, Dallas)	
25-06-20	**VACANT**	
18-07-20	**Eddie Edwards**[2]	45
	(Slammiversary XVIII, Nashville)	

01-09-20	**Eric Young**[2]	53
	(Impact!, Nashville)	
24-10-20	**Rich Swann**	183
	(Bound For Glory '20, Nashville)	
25-04-21	**Kenny Omega**	110
	(Rebellion '21, Nashville)	
13-08-21	**Christian Cage**	71
	(AEW Rampage, Pittsburgh)	
23-10-21	**Josh Alexander**	<1
	(Bound For Glory '21, Sunrise Manor)	
23-10-21	**Moose**	182
	(Bound For Glory '21, Sunrise Manor)	
23-04-22	**Josh Alexander**[2]	253*
	(Rebellion '22, Poughkeepsie)	

Most Reigns

1.	Kurt Angle	6
2.	Bobby Lashley	4
3.	Sting	4
4.	Austin Aries	3
5.	Jeff Hardy	3

Longest Reigns

1.	Josh Alexander	253*
2.	Bobby Roode	248
3.	AJ Styles	211
4.	Johnny Impact	196
5.	Sting	189

Longest Cumulative Reigns

1.	Kurt Angle	562
2.	Bobby Lashley	477
3.	Sting	325
4.	Bobby Roode	318
5.	Austin Aries	314

IMPACT X-DIVISION CHAMPIONSHIP

DATE	WON BY	DAYS
26-06-02	**AJ Styles**	42
	(Total Nonstop Action, Huntsville)	
07-08-02	**Low Ki**	14
	(Total Nonstop Action, Nashville)	
28-08-02	**Jerry Lynn**	42
	(Total Nonstop Action, Nashville)	
09-10-02	**VACANT**	
09-10-02	**Syxx-Pac**	14
	(Total Nonstop Action, Nashville)	
23-10-02	**AJ Styles**[2]	14
	(Total Nonstop Action, Nashville)	
06-11-02	**Jerry Lynn**[2]	35
	(Total Nonstop Action, Nashville)	
11-12-02	**Sonny Siaki**	63
	(Total Nonstop Action, Nashville)	
12-02-03	**Kid Kash**	77
	(Total Nonstop Action, Nashville)	
30-04-03	**Amazing Red**	14
	(Total Nonstop Action, Nashville)	
14-05-03	**Chris Sabin**	98
	(Total Nonstop Action, Nashville)	
20-08-03	**Michael Shane**	140
	(Total Nonstop Action, Nashville)	
07-01-04	**Chris Sabin**[2]	84
	(Total Nonstop Action, Nashville)	
31-03-04	**VACANT**	
31-03-04	**Frankie Kazarian**	70
	(Total Nonstop Action, Nashville)	

Date	Champion	Days
09-06-04	**AJ Styles[3]** (Total Nonstop Action, Nashville)	49
28-07-04	**Frankie Kazarian[2]** (Total Nonstop Action, Nashville)	14
28-07-04	**Michael Shane[2]** (Total Nonstop Action, Nashville)	14
11-08-04	**Petey Williams** (Total Nonstop Action, Nashville)	158
16-01-05	**AJ Styles[4]** (Final Resolution '05, Orlando)	56
13-03-05	**Christopher Daniels** (Destination X '05, Orlando)	182
11-09-05	**AJ Styles[5]** (Unbreakable '05, Orlando)	91
11-12-05	**Samoa Joe** (Turning Point '05, Orlando)	91
12-03-06	**Christopher Daniels[2]** (Destination X '06, Orlando)	32
13-04-06	**Samoa Joe[2]** (Impact!, Orlando)	70
22-06-06	**Senshi[2]** (Impact!, Orlando)	122
22-10-06	**Chris Sabin[3]** (Bound For Glory '06, Plymouth Township)	11
02-11-06	**AJ Styles[6]** (Impact!, Orlando)	14
16-11-06	**Christopher Daniels[3]** (Impact!, Orlando)	59
14-01-07	**Chris Sabin[4]** (Final Resolution '07, Orlando)	154
17-06-07	**Jay Lethal** (Slammiversary '07, Nashville)	4
21-06-07	**Samoa Joe[3]** (Impact!, Orlando)	52
12-08-07	**Kurt Angle** (Hard Justice '07, Orlando)	28
09-09-07	**Jay Lethal[2]** (No Surrender '07, Orlando)	137
24-01-08	**Johnny Devine** (Impact!, Orlando)	17
10-02-08	**Jay Lethal[3]** (Against All Odds '08, Greenville)	67
17-04-08	**Petey Williams[2]** (Impact!, Orlando)	150
14-09-08	**Sheik Abdul Bashir** (No Surrender '08, Oshawa, Canada)	84
07-12-08	**Eric Young** (Final Resolution '08, Orlando)	<1
07-12-08	**VACANT**	
11-01-09	**Alex Shelley** (Genesis '09, Charlotte)	63
15-03-09	**Suicide** (Destination X '09, Orlando)	123
16-07-09	**Homicide** (Impact!, Orlando)	31
16-08-09	**Samoa Joe[4]** (Hard Justice '09, Orlando)	53
08-10-09	**Amazing Red[2]** (Impact!, Orlando)	112
28-01-10	**Douglas Williams** (Impact!, Orlando)	80
18-04-10	**VACANT**	
18-04-10	**Frankie Kazarian[3]** (Lockdown '10, St. Charles)	28
16-05-10	**Douglas Williams[2]** (Sacrifice '10, Orlando)	123
16-09-10	**Jay Lethal[4]** (Impact!, Orlando)	7
23-09-10	**Amazing Red[3]** (House Show, New York)	2
25-09-10	**Jay Lethal[5]**	43
	(House Show, Rahway)	
07-11-10	**Robbie E** (Turning Point '10, Orlando)	39
16-12-10	**Jay Lethal[6]** (Impact!, Orlando)	24
09-01-11	**Frankie Kazarian[4]** (Genesis '11, Orlando)	130
19-05-11	**Abyss** (Impact!, Orlando)	52
10-07-11	**Brian Kendrick** (Destination X '11, Orlando)	63
11-09-11	**Austin Aries** (No Surrender '11, Orlando)	301
08-07-12	**VACANT**	
08-07-12	**Zema Ion** (Destination X '12, Orlando)	98
14-10-12	**Rob Van Dam** (Bound For Glory '12, Phoenix)	137
28-02-13	**Kenny King** (Impact!, Orlando)	94
02-06-13	**Chris Sabin[5]** (Slammiversary XI, Boston)	25
27-06-13	**Austin Aries[2]** (Impact!, Peoria)	7
04-07-13	**Chris Sabin[6]** (Impact!, Las Vegas)	7
11-07-13	**VACANT**	
25-07-13	**Manik[2]** (Impact!, Louisville)	87
20-10-13	**Chris Sabin[7]** (Bound For Glory '13, San Diego)	53
12-12-13	**Austin Aries[3]** (Impact!, Orlando)	21
02-01-14	**Chris Sabin[8]** (Impact!, Orlando)	21
23-01-14	**Austin Aries[4]** (Impact!, Huntsville)	38
02-03-14	**Sanada** (Kaisen: Outbreak, Tokyo, Japan)	130
10-07-14	**Austin Aries[5]** (Impact!, Bethlehem)	14
24-07-14	**VACANT**	
07-08-14	**Samoa Joe[5]** (Impact!, New York)	97
12-11-14	**VACANT**	
19-11-14	**Low Ki[3]** (Impact!, Bethlehem)	49
07-01-15	**Austin Aries[6]** (Impact!, New York)	9
16-01-15	**Low Ki[4]** (Impact!, New York)	63
20-03-15	**Rockstar Spud** (Impact!, London, England)	42
01-05-15	**Kenny King[2]** (Impact!, Orlando)	28
29-05-15	**Rockstar Spud[2]** (Impact!, Orlando)	12
10-06-15	**VACANT**	
24-06-15	**Tigre Uno** (Impact!, Orlando)	223
02-02-16	**Trevor Lee** (Impact!, Bethlehem)	131
12-06-16	**Eddie Edwards** (Slammiversary XIV, Orlando)	9
21-06-16	**Mike Bennett** (Impact!, Orlando)	14
05-07-16	**Eddie Edwards[2]** (Impact!, Orlando)	16
21-07-16	**Bobby Lashley** (Impact!, Orlando)	28
18-08-16	**VACANT**	

01-09-16	**DJZ²**	154
	(Impact!, Orlando)	
02-02-17	**Trevor Lee²**	77
	(Impact!, Orlando)	
20-04-17	**Low Ki⁵**	56
	(Impact!, Orlando)	
15-06-17	**Sonjay Dutt**	91
	(Impact!, Mumbai, India)	
14-09-17	**Trevor Lee³**	112
	(Impact!, Orlando)	
04-01-18	**Taiji Ishimori**	63
	(Impact!, Ottawa, Canada)	
08-03-18	**Matt Sydal**	136
	(Impact!, Orlando)	
22-07-18	**Brian Cage**	116
	(Slammiversary XVI, Toronto, Canada)	
15-11-18	**VACANT**	
06-01-19	**Rich Swann**	201
	(Homecoming, Nashville)	
26-07-19	**Jake Crist**	86
	(Impact!, Windsor, Canada)	
20-10-19	**Ace Austin**	184
	(Bound For Glory '19, Villa Park)	
21-04-20	**Willie Mack**	89
	(Rebellion, Nashville)	
18-07-20	**Chris Bey**	31
	(Slammiversary XVIII, Nashville)	
18-08-20	**Rohit Raju**	116
	(Emergence, Nashville)	
12-12-20	**Manik³**	91
	(Final Resolution '20, Nashville)	
13-03-21	**Ace Austin²**	43
	(Sacrifice '21, Nashville)	
25-04-21	**Josh Alexander**	151
	(Rebellion '21, Nashville)	
23-09-21	**VACANT**	
23-10-21	**Trey Miguel**	182
	(Bound For Glory '21, Sunrise Manor)	
23-04-22	**Ace Austin³**	57
	(Rebellion '22, Poughkeepsie)	
19-06-22	**Mike Bailey**	110
	(Slammiversary XX, Nashville)	
07-10-22	**Frankie Kazarian⁵**	13
	(Bound For Glory '22, Albany)	
20-10-22	**VACANT**	
18-11-22	**Trey Miguel²**	43*
	(Over Drive, Louisville)	

Most Reigns

1.	Chris Sabin	8
2.	Austin Aries	6
3.	Jay Lethal	6
4.	AJ Styles	6
5.	Frankie Kazarian	5

Longest Reigns

1.	Austin Aries	301
2.	Tigre Uno	223
3.	Rich Swann	201
4.	Ace Austin	184
5.	Christopher Daniels	182
6.	Trey Miguel	182

Longest Cumulative Reigns

1.	Chris Sabin	453
2.	Austin Aries	390
3.	Samoa Joe	363
4.	Trevor Lee	320
5.	Petey Williams	308

IMPACT DIGITAL MEDIA CHAMPIONSHIP

DATE	WON BY	DAYS
23-10-21	**Jordynne Grace**	103
	(Bound For Glory '21, Sunrise Manor)	
03-02-22	**Matt Cardona**	114
	(Impact!, Pembroke Pines)	
28-05-22	**Rich Swann**	34
	(REVOLVER Vegas Vacation, Las Vegas)	
01-07-22	**Brian Myers**	132
	(Against All Odds '22, Atlanta)	
10-11-22	**Joe Hendry**	51*
	(Impact!, Sunrise Manor)	

IMPACT WORLD TAG TEAM CHAMPIONSHIP

DATE	WON BY	DAYS
17-05-07	**Brother Ray & Brother Devon**	59
	(TNA Today, Orlando)	
15-07-07	**Samoa Joe**	28
	(Victory Road '07, Orlando)	
12-08-07	**Kurt Angle**	18
	(Hard Justice '07, Orlando)	
30-08-07	**Kurt Angle & Sting**	10
	(Impact!, Orlando)	
09-09-07	**Pacman Jones & Ron Killings**	35
	(No Surrender '07, Orlando)	
14-10-07	**AJ Styles & Tomko**	186
	(Bound For Glory '07, Duluth)	
17-04-08	**Frankie Kazarian & Eric Young**	‹1
	(Impact!, Orlando)	
17-04-08	**VACANT**	
11-05-08	**Homicide & Hernandez**	91
	(Sacrifice '08, Orlando)	
10-08-08	**James Storm & Bobby Roode**	154
	(Hard Justice '08, Trenton)	
08-01-09	**Jay Lethal & Consequences Creed**	3
	(Impact!, Orlando)	
11-01-09	**James Storm² & Bobby Roode²**	98
	(Genesis '09, Charlotte)	
19-04-09	**Brother Ray² & Brother Devon²**	63
	(Lockdown '09, Philadelphia)	
21-06-09	**James Storm³ & Bobby Roode³**	28
	(Slammiversary VII, Auburn Hills)	
19-07-09	**Booker T & Scott Steiner**	91
	(Victory Road '09, Orlando)	
18-10-09	**Brutus Magnus & Doug Williams**	91
	(Bound For Glory '09, Irvine)	
17-01-10	**Hernandez² & Matt Morgan**	78
	(Genesis '10, Orlando)	
05-04-10	**Matt Morgan**	38
	(Impact!, Orlando)	
13-05-10	**Eric Young², Kevin Nash & Scott Hall**	35
	(Impact!, Orlando)	
17-06-10	**VACANT**	
11-07-10	**Alex Shelley & Chris Sabin**	182
	(Victory Road '10, Orlando)	
09-01-11	**James Storm⁴ & Bobby Roode⁴**	221
	(Genesis '11, Orlando)	
18-08-11	**Hernandez³ & Anarquia**	84
	(Impact!, Orlando)	
17-11-11	**Crimson & Matt Morgan²**	87

(Impact!, Orlando)

Date	Champion	Days
12-02-12	**Magnus[2] & Samoa Joe[2]** (Against All Odds '12, Orlando)	91
13-05-12	**Christopher Daniels & Kazarian[2]** (Sacrifice '12, Orlando)	28
10-06-12	**AJ Styles[2] & Kurt Angle[2]** (Slammiversary X, Arlington)	18
28-06-12	**Christopher Daniels[2] & Kazarian[3]** (Impact!, Orlando)	108
14-10-12	**Chavo Guerrero & Hernandez[4]** (Bound For Glory '12, Phoenix)	116
07-02-13	**Bobby Roode[5] & Austin Aries** (Impact!, Manchester, England)	63
11-04-13	**Chavo Guerrero[2] & Hernandez[5]** (Impact!, Corpus Christi)	52
02-06-13	**Gunner & James Storm[5]** (Slammiversary XI, Boston)	140
20-10-13	**Robbie E & Jessie Godderz** (Bound For Glory '13, San Diego)	126
23-02-14	**Davey Richards & Eddie Edwards** (House Show, Morgantown)	7
02-03-14	**Robbie E[2] & Jessie Godderz[2]** (Kaisen: Outbreak, Tokyo, Japan)	56
27-04-14	**Davey Richards[2] & Eddie Edwards[2]** (Sacrifice '14, Orlando)	199
12-11-14	**Abyss & James Storm[6]** (Impact!, Bethlehem)	114
06-03-15	**Davey Richards[3] & Eddie Edwards[3]** (Impact!, Manchester, England)	28
03-04-15	**VACANT**	
17-04-15	**Jeff Hardy & Matt Hardy** (Impact!, Orlando)	21
08-05-15	**VACANT**	
01-07-15	**Davey Richards[4] & Eddie Edwards[4]** (Impact!, Orlando)	63
02-09-15	**Brian Myers & Trevor Lee** (Impact!, Orlando)	7
09-09-15	**Davey Richards[5] & Eddie Edwards[5]** (Impact!, Orlando)	181
08-03-16	**James Storm[7] & Bobby Roode[6]** (Impact!, Birmingham, England)	49
26-04-16	**Abyss[2] & Crazzy Steve** (Impact!, Orlando)	159
02-10-16	**Jeff Hardy[2] & Matt Hardy[2]** (Bound For Glory '16, Orlando)	165
16-03-17	**VACANT**	
30-03-17	**Ortiz & Santana** (Impact!, Orlando)	182
28-09-17	**Dave Crist & Jake Crist** (Impact!, Orlando)	98
04-01-18	**Ortiz[2] & Santana[2]** (Impact!, Ottawa, Canada)	108
22-04-18	**Eli Drake & Scott Steiner[2]** (Redemption, Orlando)	25
17-05-18	**Andrew Everett & DJZ** (Impact!, Orlando)	35
21-06-18	**Ortiz[3] & Santana[3]** (Impact!, Orlando)	232
08-02-19	**Pentagon Jr. & Rey Fenix** (Impact!, Mexico City, Mexico)	79
28-04-19	**Ortiz[4] & Santana[4]** (Rebellion, Toronto, Canada)	68
05-07-19	**Ethan Page & Josh Alexander** (Bash At The Brewery, San Antonio)	382
21-07-20	**Alex Shelley[2] & Chris Sabin[2]** (Impact!, Nashville)	95
24-10-20	**Ethan Page[2] & Josh Alexander[2]** (Bound For Glory '20, Nashville)	21
14-11-20	**Luke Gallows & Karl Anderson** (Turning Point '20, Nashville)	119
13-03-21	**David Finlay & Juice Robinson**	68
	(Sacrifice '21, Nashville)	
20-05-21	**Eric Young[3], Rhino, Joe Doering & Deaner** (Impact!, Nashville)	58
17-07-21	**Luke Gallows[2] & Karl Anderson[2]** (Slammiversary XIX, Nashville)	231
05-03-22	**Eric Young[4], Joe Doering[2] & Deaner** (Sacrifice '22, Louisville)	63
07-05-22	**Jay Briscoe & Mark Briscoe** (Under Siege, Newport)	43
19-06-22	**Luke Gallows[3] & Karl Anderson[3]** (Slammiversary XX, Nashville)	73
01-09-22	**Mike Bennett & Matt Taven** (Impact!, Dallas)	49
20-10-22	**Heath & Rhino[2]** (Impact!, Albany)	56
15-12-22	**Alex Shelley[3] & Chris Sabin[3]** (Impact!, Pembroke Pines)	16*

Most Reigns
1.	James Storm	7
2.	Bobby Roode	6
3.	Hernandez	5
4.	Davey Richards	5
5.	Eddie Edwards	5
6.		

Longest Reigns
1.	Ethan Page & Josh Alexander	382
2.	Ortiz & Santana	232
3.	Luke Gallows & Karl Anderson	231
4.	James Storm & Bobby Roode	221
5.	Davey Richards & Eddie Edwards	199
6.		

Longest Cumulative Reigns
1.	James Storm	804
2.	Bobby Roode	613
3.	Ortiz	590
4.	Santana	590
5.	Davey Richards	478
6.	Eddie Edwards	478

IMPACT KNOCKOUTS CHAMPIONSHIP

DATE	WON BY	DAYS
14-10-07	**Gail Kim** (Bound For Glory '07, Duluth)	88
10-01-08	**Awesome Kong** (Impact!, Orlando)	182
10-07-08	**Taylor Wilde** (Impact!, Orlando)	105
23-10-08	**Awesome Kong[2]** (Impact!, Las Vegas)	178
19-04-09	**Angelina Love** (Lockdown '09, Philadelphia)	81
09-07-09	**Tara** (Impact!, Orlando)	10
19-07-09	**Angelina Love[2]** (Victory Road '09, Orlando)	28
16-08-09	**ODB** (Hard Justice '09, Orlando)	11
27-08-09	**VACANT**	
20-09-09	**ODB[2]** (No Surrender '09, Orlando)	91
20-12-09	**Tara[2]** (Final Resolution '09, Orlando)	15

04-01-10	**ODB**[3]	13
	(Impact!, Orlando)	
17-01-10	**Tara**[3]	78
	(Genesis '10, Orlando)	
05-04-10	**Angelina Love**[3]	13
	(Impact!, Orlando)	
18-04-10	**Madison Rayne**	84
	(Lockdown '10, St. Charles)	
11-07-10	**Angelina Love**[4]	21
	(Victory Road '10, Orlando)	
22-07-10	**Madison Rayne**[2]	21
	(Impact!, Orlando)	
12-08-10	**Angelina Love**[5]	59
	(Impact!, Orlando)	
10-10-10	**Tara**[4]	4
	(Bound For Glory '10, Daytona Beach)	
14-10-10	**Madison Rayne**[3]	185
	(Impact!, Orlando)	
17-04-11	**Mickie James**	113
	(Lockdown '11, Cincinnati)	
07-08-11	**Winter**	25
	(Hardcore Justice '11, Orlando)	
01-09-11	**Mickie James**[2]	10
	(Impact!, Huntsville)	
11-09-11	**Winter**[2]	35
	(No Surrender '11, Orlando)	
16-10-11	**Velvet Sky**	28
	(Bound For Glory '11, Philadelphia)	
13-11-11	**Gail Kim**[2]	210
	(Turning Point '11, Orlando)	
10-06-12	**Miss Tessmacher**	63
	(Slammiversary X, Arlington)	
12-08-12	**Madison Rayne**[4]	4
	(Hardcore Justice '12, Orlando)	
16-08-12	**Miss Tessmacher**[2]	59
	(Impact!, Orlando)	
14-10-12	**Tara**[5]	130
	(Bound For Glory '12, Phoenix)	
21-02-13	**Velvet Sky**[2]	91
	(Impact!, London, England)	
23-05-13	**Mickie James**[3]	119
	(Impact!, Tampa)	
19-09-13	**ODB**[4]	31
	(Impact!, St. Louis)	
20-10-13	**Gail Kim**[3]	88
	(Bound For Glory '13, San Diego)	
16-01-14	**Madison Rayne**[5]	101
	(Impact!, Huntsville)	
27-04-14	**Angelina Love**[6]	67
	(Sacrifice '14, Orlando)	
03-07-14	**Gail Kim**[4]	90
	(Impact!, Bethlehem)	
01-10-14	**Havok**	49
	(Impact!, Bethlehem)	
19-11-14	**Taryn Terrell**	238
	(Impact!, Bethlehem)	
15-07-15	**Brooke**[3]	63
	(Impact!, Orlando)	
16-09-15	**Gail Kim**[5]	202
	(Impact!, Orlando)	
05-04-16	**Jade**	78
	(Impact!, Orlando)	
12-06-16	**Sienna**	74
	(Slammiversary XIV, Orlando)	
25-08-16	**Allie**	7
	(Impact!, Orlando)	
01-09-16	**Maria Kanellis-Bennett**	31
	(Impact!, Orlando)	
02-10-16	**Gail Kim**[6]	46
	(Bound For Glory '16, Orlando)	
17-11-16	**VACANT**	

01-12-16	**Rosemary**	213
	(Impact!, Orlando)	
02-07-17	**Sienna**[2]	126
	(Slammiversary XV, Orlando)	
05-11-17	**Gail Kim**[7]	11
	(Bound For Glory '17, Ottawa, Canada)	
16-11-17	**VACANT**	
14-12-17	**Laurel Van Ness**	94
	(Impact!, Ottawa, Canada)	
08-03-18	**Allie**[2]	84
	(Impact!, Orlando)	
31-05-18	**Su Yung**	91
	(Impact!, Orlando)	
30-08-18	**Tessa Blanchard**	129
	(Impact!, Toronto, Canada)	
06-01-19	**Taya Valkyrie**	402
	(Homecoming, Nashville)	
11-02-20	**Jordynne Grace**	158
	(Impact!, Mexico City, Mexico)	
18-07-20	**Deonna Purrazzo**	98
	(Slammiversary XVII, Nashville)	
24-10-20	**Su Yung**[2]	21
	(Bound For Glory '20, Nashville)	
14-11-20	**Deonna Purrazzo**[2]	343
	(Turning Point '20, Nashville)	
23-10-21	**Mickie James**[4]	133
	(Bound For Glory '21, Sunrise Manor)	
05-03-22	**Tasha Steelz**	106
	(Sacrifice '22, Louisville)	
19-06-22	**Jordynne Grace**[2]	195*
	(Slammiversary XX, Nashville)	

Most Reigns

1.	Gail Kim	7
2.	Angelina Love	6
3.	Madison Rayne	5
4.	Tara	5
5.	ODB	4
6.	Mickie James	4

Longest Reigns

1.	Taya Valkyrie	402
2.	Deonna Purrazzo	343
3.	Taryn Terrell	238
4.	Rosemary	213
5.	Gail Kim	210

Longest Cumulative Reigns

1.	Gail Kim	735
2.	Deonna Purrazzo	441
3.	Taya Valkyrie	402
4.	Madison Rayne	395
5.	Mickie James	375

IMPACT KNOCKOUTS TAG TEAM CHAMPIONSHIP

DATE	WON BY	DAYS
20-09-09	**Sarita & Taylor Wilde**	106
	(No Surrender '09, Orlando)	
04-01-10	**Awesome Kong & Hamada**	63
	(Impact!, Orlando)	
08-03-10	**VACANT**	
08-03-10	**Lacey Von Erich, Madison Rayne & Velvet Sky**	150
	(Impact!, Orlando)	
05-08-10	**Hamada**[2] **& Taylor Wilde**	126
	(Impact!, Orlando)	

09-12-10	**VACANT**	
23-12-10	**Angelina Love & Winter**	80
	(Impact!, Orlando)	
13-03-11	**Sarita² & Rosita**	130
	(Victory Road '11, Orlando)	
21-07-11	**Brooke Tessmacher & Tara**	105
	(Impact!, Orlando)	
03-11-11	**Gail Kim & Madison Rayne²**	126
	(Impact!, Macon)	
08-03-12	**Eric Young & ODB**	477
	(Impact!, Orlando)	
20-06-13	**VACANT**	
27-06-13	**DEACTIVATED**	
16-01-21	**Kiera Hogan & Tasha Steelz**	99
	(Hard To Kill '21, Nashville)	
25-04-21	**Jordynne Grace**	20
	& Rachael Ellering	
	(Rebellion '21, Nashville)	
15-05-21	**Kiera Hogan² & Tasha Steelz²**	63
	(Under Siege, Nashville)	
17-07-21	**Havok & Rosemary**	63
	(Slammiversary XIX Pre-Show, Nashville)	
23-10-21	**Jessie McKay & Cassie Lee**	133
	(Bound For Glory '21, Sunrise Manor)	
05-03-22	**Madison Rayne³**	106
	& Tenille Dashwood	
	(Sacrifice '22, Louisville)	
19-06-22	**Rosemary² & Taya Valkyrie**	54
	(Slammiversary XX, Nashville)	
12-08-22	**Chelsea Green**	56
	& Deonna Purrazzo	
	(Emergence Pre-Show, Cicero)	
07-10-22	**Jessicka², Rosemary³**	85*
	& Taya Valkyrie²	
	(Bound For Glory '22, Albany)	

ROH WORLD CHAMPIONSHIP

DATE	WON BY	DAYS
27-02-02	**Low Ki**	56
	(Crowning A Champion, Philadelphia)	
21-09-02	**Xavier**	182
	(Unscripted, Philadelphia)	
22-03-03	**Samoa Joe**	645
	(Night Of Champions, Philadelphia)	
26-12-04	**Austin Aries**	174
	(Final Battle '04, Philadelphia)	
18-06-05	**CM Punk**	55
	(Death Before Dishonor III, Morristown)	
12-08-05	**James Gibson**	36
	(Redemption, Dayton)	
17-09-05	**Bryan Danielson**	462
	(Glory By Honor IV, Lake Grove)	
23-12-06	**Homicide**	56
	(Final Battle '06, New York)	
17-02-07	**Takeshi Morishima**	231
	(Fifth Year Festival: Philly, Philadelphia)	
06-10-07	**Nigel McGuinness**	545
	(Undeniable, Edison)	
03-04-09	**Jerry Lynn**	71
	(Supercard Of Honor IV, Houston)	
13-06-09	**Austin Aries²**	245
	(Manhattan Mayhem III, New York)	
13-02-10	**Tyler Black**	210
	(8th Anniversary Show, New York)	
11-09-10	**Roderick Strong**	189
	(Glory By Honor IX, New York)	
19-03-11	**Eddie Edwards**	99
	(Manhattan Mayhem IV, New York)	

26-06-11	**Davey Richards**	321
	(Best In The World '11, New York)	
12-05-12	**Kevin Steen**	328
	(Border Wars, Toronto, Canada)	
05-04-13	**Jay Briscoe**	89
	(Supercard Of Honor VII, New York_	
03-07-13	**VACANT**	
20-09-13	**Adam Cole**	275
	(Death Before Dishonor XI, Philadelphia)	
22-06-14	**Michael Elgin**	76
	(Best In The World '14, Nashville)	
06-09-14	**Jay Briscoe²**	286
	(All Star Extravaganza VI, Toronto, Canada)	
19-06-15	**Jay Lethal**	427
	(Best In The World '15, New York)	
19-08-16	**Adam Cole²**	105
	(Death Before Dishonor XIV, Las Vegas)	
02-12-16	**Kyle O'Reilly**	33
	(Final Battle '16, New York)	
04-01-17	**Adam Cole³**	65
	(Wrestle Kingdom 11, Tokyo, Japan)	
10-03-17	**Christopher Daniels**	105
	(15th Anniversary Show, Las Vegas)	
23-06-17	**Cody Rhodes**	175
	(Best In The World '17, Lowell)	
15-12-17	**Dalton Castle**	220
	(Final Battle '17, New York)	
23-07-18	**Jay Lethal²**	257
	(Ring Of Honor Wrestling, Fairfax)	
06-04-19	**Matt Taven**	175
	(G1 Supercard, New York)	
27-09-19	**Rush**	77
	(Death Before Dishonor XVII, Las Vegas)	
13-12-19	**PCO**	78
	(Final Battle '19, Baltimore)	
29-02-20	**Rush²**	498
	(Gateway To Honor, St. Charles)	
11-07-21	**Bandido**	153
	(Best In The World '21, Baltimore)	
10-12-21	**VACANT**	
11-12-21	**Jonathan Gresham**	224
	(Final Battle '21, Baltimore)	
23-07-22	**Claudio Castagnoli**	60
	(Death Before Dishonor '22, Lowell)	
21-09-22	**Chris Jericho**	80
	(AEW Dynamite: Grand Slam, Flushing)	
10-12-22	**Claudio Castagnoli²**	21*
	(Final Battle '22, Arlington)	

Most Reigns

1.	Adam Cole	3
2.	Austin Aries	2
3.	Jay Briscoe	2
4.	Jay Lethal	2
5.	Rush	2
6.	Claudio Castagnoli	2

Longest Reigns

1.	Samoa Joe	645
2.	Nigel McGuinness	545
3.	Rush	498
4.	Bryan Danielson	462
5.	Jay Lethal	427

Longest Cumulative Reigns

1.	Jay Lethal	684
2.	Samoa Joe	645
3.	Rush	575
4.	Nigel McGuinness	545
5.	Bryan Danielson	462

ROH WORLD TELEVISION CHAMPIONSHIP

DATE	WON BY	DAYS
26-04-10	**Eddie Edwards**	280
	(Ring Of Honor Wrestling, Philadelphia)	
31-01-11	**Christopher Daniels**	146
	(Ring Of Honor Wrestling, Louisville)	
26-06-11	**El Generico**	97
	(Best In The World '11, New York)	
01-10-11	**Jay Lethal**	182
	(Ring Of Honor Wrestling, Chicago Ridge)	
31-03-12	**Roderick Strong**	119
	(Showdown In The Sun, Fort Lauderdale)	
28-07-12	**Adam Cole**	217
	(Ring Of Honor Wrestling, Baltimore)	
02-03-13	**Matt Taven**	287
	(11th Anniversary Show, Chicago Ridge)	
14-12-13	**Tommaso Ciampa**	111
	(Final Battle '13, New York)	
04-04-14	**Jay Lethal**[2]	567
	(Supercard Of Honor VIII, Westwego)	
23-10-15	**Roderick Strong**[2]	119
	(Glory By Honor XIV, Kalamazoo)	
19-02-16	**Tomohiro Ishii**	79
	(Honor Rising: Japan '16, Tokyo, Japan)	
08-05-16	**Bobby Fish**	194
	(Global Wars '16, Chicago Ridge)	
18-11-16	**Will Ospreay**	2
	(Reach For The Sky Tour, Liverpool, England)	
20-11-16	**Marty Scurll**	175
	(Reach For The Sky Tour, London, England)	
14-05-17	**Kushida**	131
	(War Of The Worlds '17, Philadelphia)	
22-09-17	**Kenny King**	84
	(Death Before Dishonor XV, Las Vegas)	
15-12-17	**Silas Young**	72
	(Final Battle '17, New York)	
25-02-18	**Kenny King**[2]	41
	(Ring Of Honor Wrestling, Atlanta)	
07-04-18	**Silas Young**[2]	70
	(Supercard Of Honor XII, New Orleans)	
16-06-18	**Punishment Martinez**	125
	(State Of The Art '18, Dallas)	
19-10-18	**Jeff Cobb**	202
	(Ring of Honor Wrestling, Las Vegas)	
09-05-19	**Shane Taylor**	218
	(War Of The Worlds '19, Toronto, Canada)	
13-12-19	**Dragon Lee**	469
	(Final Battle '19, Baltimore)	
26-03-21	**Tracy Williams**	36
	(19th Anniversary Show, Baltimore)	
01-05-21	**Tony Deppen**	71
	(Ring Of Honor Wrestling, Baltimore)	
11-07-21	**Dragon Lee**[2]	133
	(Best In The World '21, Baltimore)	
21-11-21	**Dalton Castle**	20
	(Ring Of Honor Wrestling, Baltimore)	
11-12-21	**Rhett Titus**	111
	(Final Battle '21, Baltimore)	
01-04-22	**Minoru Suzuki**	12
	(Supercard Of Honor XV, Garland)	
13-04-22	**Samoa Joe**	262*
	(AEW Dynamite, New Orleans)	

Most Reigns

1.	Jay Lethal	2
2.	Roderick Strong	2
3.	Kenny King	2
4.	Silas Young	2
5.	Dragon Lee	2

Longest Reigns

1.	Jay Lethal	567
2.	Dragon Lee	469
3.	Matt Taven	287
4.	Eddie Edwards	280
5.	Samoa Joe	262

Longest Cumulative Reigns

1.	Jay Lethal	749
2.	Dragon Lee	602
3.	Matt Taven	287
4.	Eddie Edwards	280
5.	Samoa Joe	262

ROH PURE CHAMPIONSHIP

DATE	WON BY	DAYS
14-02-04	**AJ Styles**	70
	(Second Anniversary Show, Braintree)	
24-04-04	**VACANT**	
17-07-04	**Doug Williams**	42
	(Reborn: Completion, Elizabeth)	
28-08-04	**John Walters**	189
	(Scramble Cage Melee, Elizabeth)	
05-03-05	**Jay Lethal**	63
	(Trios Tournament 2005, Philadelphia)	
07-05-05	**Samoa Joe**	112
	(Manhattan Mayhem I, New York)	
27-08-05	**Nigel McGuinness**	350
	(Dragon Gate Invasion, Buffalo)	
12-08-06	**Bryan Danielson**	<1
	(Unified, Liverpool, England)	
12-08-06	**DEACTIVATED**	
31-10-20	**Jonathan Gresham**	317
	(Ring Of Honor Wrestling, Baltimore)	
12-09-21	**Josh Woods**	201
	(Death Before Dishonor XVIII, Philadelphia)	
01-04-22	**Wheeler Yuta**	159
	(Supercard Of Honor XV, Garland)	
07-09-22	**Daniel Garcia**	94
	(AEW Dynamite, Buffalo)	
10-12-22	**Wheeler Yuta**[2]	21*
	(Final Battle '22, Arlington)	

ROH WORLD TAG TEAM CHAMPIONSHIP

DATE	WON BY	DAYS
21-09-02	**Christopher Daniels**	175
	& Donovan Morgan	
	(Unscripted, Philadelphia)	
15-03-03	**AJ Styles & Amazing Red**	175
	(Expect The Unexpected, Cambridge)	
06-09-03	**VACANT**	
20-09-03	**Johnny Kashmere & Trent Acid**	26
	(Glory By Honor II, Philadelphia)	
16-10-03	**Dixie & Izzy**	16
	(Tradition Continues, Glen Burnie)	
01-11-03	**Mark Briscoe & Jay Briscoe**	175

(Main Event Spectacles, Elizabeth)

24-04-04 **CM Punk & Colt Cabana** 21
(Reborn: Stage Two, Chicago Ridge)

15-05-04 **BJ Whitmer & Dan Maff** <1
(Round Robin Challenge III, Lexington)

15-05-04 **Mark Briscoe² & Jay Briscoe²** <1
(Round Robin Challenge III, Lexington)

15-05-04 **CM Punk² & Colt Cabana²** 84
(Round Robin Challenge III, Lexington)

07-08-04 **Ricky Reyes & Rocky Romero** 196
(Testing The Limit, Philadelphia)

19-02-05 **BJ Whitmer² & Dan Maff²** 42
(Third Anniversary Show, Elizabeth)

28-03-05 **VACANT**

02-04-05 **BJ Whitmer³ & Jimmy Jacobs** 98
(Best Of American Super J, Asbury Park)

09-07-05 **HC Loc & Tony DeVito** 14
(Escape From New York, New York)

23-07-05 **BJ Whitmer⁴ & Jimmy Jacobs²** 70
(The Homecoming, Philadelphia)

01-10-05 **Sal Rinauro & Tony Mamaluke** 77
(Joe vs Kobashi, New York)

17-12-05 **Austin Aries & Roderick Strong** 273
(Final Battle '05, Edison)

16-09-06 **Chris Hero & Claudio Castagnoli** 70
(Glory By Honor V, New York)

25-11-06 **Christopher Daniels² & Matt Sydal** 91
(Dethroned, Edison)

24-02-07 **Mark Briscoe³ & Jay Briscoe³** 7
(Fifth Year Festival, Chicago)

03-03-07 **Naruki Doi & Shingo Takagi** 27
(Fifth Year Festival, Liverpool, England)

30-03-07 **Mark Briscoe⁴ & Jay Briscoe⁴** 275
(All-Star Extravaganza III, Detroit)

30-12-07 **Jimmy Jacobs³ & Tyler Black** 27
(Final Battle '07, New York)

26-01-08 **Davey Richards & Rocky Romero²** 77
(Without Remorse, Chicago Ridge)

12-04-08 **Mark Briscoe⁵ & Jay Briscoe⁵** 28
(Injustice, Edison)

10-05-08 **VACANT**

06-06-08 **Jimmy Jacobs⁴ & Tyler Black²** 105
(Up For Grabs, Hartford)

19-09-08 **El Generico & Kevin Steen** 253
(Driven '08, Boston)

30-05-09 **Davey Richards² & Eddie Edwards** 203
(Ring Of Honor Wrestling, Philadelphia)

19-12-09 **Mark Briscoe⁶ & Jay Briscoe⁶** 105
(Final Battle '09, New York)

03-04-10 **Chris Hero² Claudio Castagnoli²** 363
(The Big Bang!, Charlotte)

01-04-11 **Charlie Haas & Shelton Benjamin** 266
(Honor Takes Center Stage, Atlanta)

23-12-11 **Mark Briscoe⁷ & Jay Briscoe⁷** 141
(Final Battle '11, New York)

12-05-12 **Charlie Haas²** 43
& Shelton Benjamin²
(Border Wars, Toronto, Canada)

24-06-12 **Rhett Titus & Kenny King** 16
(Best In The World '12, New York)

10-07-12 **VACATED**

15-09-12 **Jimmy Jacobs⁵ & Steve Corino** 92
(Death Before Dishonor X, Chicago Ridge)

16-12-12 **Mark Briscoe⁸ & Jay Briscoe⁸** 76
(Final Battle '12, New York)

02-03-13 **Bobby Fish & Kyle O'Reilly** 154
(11th Anniversary Show, Chicago Ridge)

03-08-13 **Alex Koslov & Rocky Romero³** <1
(Ring Of Honor Wrestling, Providence)

03-08-13 **Davey Richards³ & Eddie Edwards²** 14
(All-Star Extravaganza V, Toronto, Canada)

17-08-13 **Bobby Fish² & Kyle O'Reilly²** 203
(Manhattan Mayhem V, New York)

08-03-14 **Matt Jackson & Nick Jackson** 70
(Raising The Bar: Night 2, Chicago Ridge)

17-05-14 **Bobby Fish³ & Kyle O'Reilly³** 343
(War Of The Worlds '14, New York)

25-04-15 **Christopher Daniels³** 146
& Frankie Kazarian
(Ring Of Honor Wrestling, San Antonio)

18-09-15 **Matt Taven & Mike Bennett** 91
(All Star Extravaganza VII, San Antonio)

18-12-15 **Hanson & Raymond Rowe** 143
(Final Battle '15, Philadelphia)

09-05-16 **Christopher Daniels⁴** 144
& Frankie Kazarian²
(War Of The Worlds '16, Dearborn)

30-09-16 **Matt Jackson² & Nick Jackson²** 155
(All Star Extravaganza VIII, Lowell)

04-03-17 **Jeff Hardy & Matt Hardy** 28
(Manhattan Mayhem VI, New York)

01-04-17 **Matt Jackson³ & Nick Jackson³** 174
(Supercard Of Honor XI, Lakeland)

22-09-17 **Alex Shelley & Chris Sabin** 168
(Death Before Dishonor XV, Las Vegas)

09-03-18 **Mark Briscoe⁹ & Jay Briscoe⁹** 252
(16th Anniversary Show, Sunrise Manor)

16-11-18 **Frankie Kazarian³ & Scorpio Sky** 28
(Glory By Honor XVI, Philadelphia)

14-12-18 **Mark Briscoe¹⁰ & Jay Briscoe¹⁰** 91
(Final Battle '18, New York)

15-03-19 **Brody King & PCO** 22
(17th Anniversary Show, Sunrise Manor)

06-04-19 **Tama Tonga & Tanga Loa** 105
(G1 Supercard, New York)

20-07-19 **Mark Briscoe¹¹ & Jay Briscoe¹¹** 146
(Manhattan Mayhem, New York)

13-12-19 **Jay Lethal & Jonathan Gresham** 442
(Final Battle '19, Baltimore)

27-02-21 **Dragon Lee & Kenny King²** 28
(Ring Of Honor Wrestling, Baltimore)

26-03-21 **Rhett Titus² & Tracy Williams** 107
(19th Anniversary Show, Baltimore)

11-07-21 **Chris Dickinson & Homicide** 62
(Best In The World '21, Baltimore)

11-09-21 **Dragon Lee² & Kenny King³** 64
(Ring Of Honor Wrestling, Baltimore)

14-11-21 **Matt Taven² & Mike Bennett²** 27
(Honor For All, Baltimore)

11-12-21 **Mark Briscoe¹² & Jay Briscoe¹²** 111
(Final Battle '21, Baltimore)

01-04-22 **Cash Wheeler & Dax Harwood** 253
(Supercard Of Honor XV, Garland)

10-12-22 **Mark Briscoe¹³ & Jay Briscoe¹³** 21
(Final Battle '22, Arlington)

Most Reigns
1.   Mark Briscoe   13
2.   Jay Briscoe   13
3.   Jimmy Jacobs   5
4.   Christopher Daniels   4
5.   BJ Whitmer   4

Longest Reigns
1.   Jay Lethal &   442
     Jonathan Gresham
2.   Claudio Castagnoli   363
     & Chris Hero
3.   Bobby Fish & Kyle O'Reilly 343
4.   Jay Briscoe & Mark Briscoe 275
5.   Austin Aries & Roderick Strong 273

Longest Cumulative Reigns

1.	Mark Briscoe	1,428*
2.	Jay Briscoe	1,428*
3.	Bobby Fish	700
4.	Kyle O'Reilly	700
5.	Christopher Daniels	556

ROH WORLD SIX MAN TAG TEAM CHAMPIONSHIP

DATE	WON BY	DAYS
02-12-16	Matt Taven, TK O'Ryan & Vinny Marseglia (Final Battle '16, New York)	130
11-04-17	Bully Ray, Jay Briscoe & Mark Briscoe (Ring Of Honor Wrestling, Las Vegas)	73
23-06-17	Dalton Castle, Boy 1 & Boy 2 (Best In The World '17, Lowell)	58
20-08-17	Hangman Page, Matt Jackson & Nick Jackson (War Of The Worlds UK, Edinburgh, Scotland)	201
09-03-18	Christopher Daniels, Scorpio Sky & Frankie Kazarian (16th Anniversary Show, Las Vegas)	61
09-05-18	Matt Taven[2], TK O'Ryan[2] & Vinny Marseglia[2] (War Of The Worlds Tour, Lowell)	73
21-07-18	Cody Rhodes, Matt Jackson[2] & Nick Jackson[2] (Ring Of Honor Wrestling, Atlanta)	106
04-11-18	Matt Taven[3], TK O'Ryan[3] & Vinny Marseglia[3] (Survival Of The Fittest '18, Columbus)	132
30-03-19	Brody King, Marty Scurll & PCO (Ring Of Honor Wrestling, Sunrise Manor)	287
11-01-20	Bandido, Flamita & Rey Horus (Saturday Night at Centre Stage, Atlanta)	405
20-02-21	Shane Taylor, Moses & Kaun (Ring Of Honor Wrestling, Baltimore)	295
11-12-21	Vincent[4], Bateman & Dutch (Final Battle '21, Baltimore)	224
23-07-22	Dalton Castle[2], Boy 1[2] and Boy 2[2] (Death Before Dishonor, Lowell)	140
10-12-22	Brian Cage, Kaun[2] & Toa Liona (Final Battle '22, Arlington)	21*

ROH WORLD WOMEN'S CHAMPIONSHIP

DATE	WON BY	DAYS
12-09-21	Rok-C (Death Before Dishonor XVIII, Philadelphia)	123
13-01-22	Deonna Purrazzo (Impact!, Dallas)	111
01-04-22	Mercedes Martinez (interim) (Supercard Of Honor XV, Garland)	33
04-05-22	Mercedes Martinez (AEW Dynamite, Baltimore)	220
10-12-22	Athena (Final Battle '22, Arlington)	21*

NWA WORLDS HEAVYWEIGHT CHAMPIONSHIP

DATE	WON BY	DAYS
14-07-48	Orville Brown (House Show, Des Moines)	501
27-11-49	Lou Thesz (N/A)	2,300
15-03-56	Whipper Billy Watson (House Show, Toronto, Canada)	239
09-11-56	Lou Thesz[2] (House Show, St. Louis)	370
14-11-57	Dick Hutton (House Show, Toronto, Canada)	421
09-01-59	Pat O'Connor (House Show, St. Louis)	903
30-06-61	Buddy Rogers (House Show, Chicago)	573
24-01-63	Lou Thesz[3] (House Show, Toronto, Canada)	1,079
07-01-66	Gene Kiniski (House Show, St. Louis)	1,131
11-02-69	Dory Funk Jr. (House Show, Tampa)	1,563
24-05-73	Harley Race (House Show, Kansas City)	57
20-07-73	Jack Brisco (House Show, Houston)	500
02-12-74	Giant Baba (House Show, Kagoshima, Japan)	7
09-12-74	Jack Brisco[2] (House Show, Toyohashi, Japan)	366
10-12-75	Terry Funk (House Show, Miami Beach)	424
06-02-77	Harley Race[2] (House Show, Toronto, Canada)	926
21-08-79	Dusty Rhodes (House Show, Tampa)	5
26-08-79	Harley Race[3] (House Show, Orlando)	66
31-10-79	Giant Baba[2] (House Show, Nagoya, Japan)	7
07-11-79	Harley Race[4] (House Show, Amagasaki, Japan)	302
04-09-80	Giant Baba[3] (House Show, Saga, Japan)	5
09-09-80	Harley Race[5] (House Show, Otsu, Japan)	230
27-04-81	Tommy Rich (House Show, Augusta)	4
01-05-81	Harley Race[6] (House Show, Gainesville)	51
21-06-81	Dusty Rhodes[2] (House Show, Atlanta)	88
17-09-81	Ric Flair (House Show, Kansas City)	631
10-06-83	Harley Race[7] (House Show, St. Louis)	167
24-11-83	Ric Flair[2] (Starrcade '83, Greensboro)	117
20-03-84	Harley Race[8] (House Show, Wellington, New Zealand)	3
23-03-84	Ric Flair[3] (House Show, Kallang, Singapore)	44
06-05-84	Kerry Von Erich (WCCW Parade of Champions '84, Irving)	18
24-05-84	Ric Flair[4]	793

(House Show, Yokosuka, Japan)

26-07-86	**Dusty Rhodes³**	14
	(NWA Great American Bash '86, Greensbor.)	
09-08-86	**Ric Flair⁵**	412
	(House Show, St. Louis)	
25-09-87	**Ron Garvin**	62
	(NWA World Wide Wrestling, Detroit)	
26-11-87	**Ric Flair⁶**	452
	(NWA Starrcade '87, Chicago)	
20-02-89	**Ricky Steamboat**	76
	(NWA Chi-Town Rumble '89, Chicago)	
07-05-89	**Ric Flair⁷**	426
	(NWA WrestleWar '89, Nashville)	
07-07-90	**Sting**	188
	(WCW Great American Bash '90, Baltimore)	
11-01-91	**Ric Flair⁸**	69
	(House Show, East Rutherford)	
21-03-91	**Tatsumi Fujinami**	59
	(WCW Japan Supershow I, Tokyo, Japan)	
19-05-91	**Ric Flair⁹**	112
	(WCW SuperBrawl I, St. Petersburg)	
08-09-91	**VACANT**	
12-08-92	**Masahiro Chono**	145
	(NJPW G1 Climax '92 Day 5, Tokyo, Japan)	
04-01-93	**The Great Muta**	48
	(WCW Japan Supershow III, Tokyo, Japan)	
21-02-93	**Barry Windham**	147
	(WCW SuperBrawl III, Asheville)	
18-07-93	**Ric Flair¹⁰**	59
	(WCW Beach Blast '93, Biloxi)	
15-09-93	**VACANT**	
27-08-94	**Shane Douglas**	<1
	(NWA World Title Tournament, Philadelphia)	
27-08-94	**VACANT**	
19-11-94	**Chris Candido**	97
	(NWA World Hvt Title Tourn, Cherry Hill)	
24-02-95	**Dan Severn**	1,479
	(House Show, Erlanger)	
14-03-99	**Naoya Ogawa**	195
	(House Show, Yokohama, Japan)	
25-09-99	**Gary Steele**	7
	(NWA 51st Anniversary Show, Charlotte)	
02-10-99	**Naoya Ogawa²**	274
	(House Show, Thomaston)	
02-07-00	**VACANT**	
19-09-00	**Mike Rapada**	56
	(House Show, Tampa)	
14-11-00	**Sabu**	38
	(House Show, Tampa)	
22-12-00	**Mike Rapada²**	123
	(House Show, Nashville)	
24-04-01	**Steve Corino**	172
	(House Show, Tampa)	
13-10-01	**VACANT**	
15-12-01	**Shinya Hashimoto**	84
	(NWA Clash Of Champions, McKeesport)	
09-03-02	**Dan Severn²**	80
	(Vast Energy, Tokyo, Japan)	
28-05-02	**VACANT**	
19-06-02	**Ken Shamrock**	49
	(Total Nonstop Action, Huntsville)	
07-08-02	**Ron Killings**	105
	(Total Nonstop Action, Nashville)	
20-11-02	**Jeff Jarrett**	203
	(Total Nonstop Action, Nashville)	
11-06-03	**AJ Styles**	133
	(Total Nonstop Action, Nashville)	
22-10-03	**Jeff Jarrett²**	182
	(Total Nonstop Action, Nashville)	
21-04-04	**AJ Styles²**	28
	(Total Nonstop Action, Nashville)	
19-05-04	**Ron Killings²**	14
	(Total Nonstop Action, Nashville)	
02-06-04	**Jeff Jarrett³**	347
	(Total Nonstop Action, Nashville)	
15-05-05	**AJ Styles³**	35
	(TNA Hard Justice '05, Orlando)	
19-06-05	**Raven**	88
	(TNA Slammiversary III, Orlando)	
15-09-05	**Jeff Jarrett⁴**	38
	(BCW International Incident, Canada)	
23-10-05	**Rhino**	11
	(TNA Bound For Glory '05, Orlando)	
03-11-05	**Jeff Jarrett⁵**	101
	(TNA Impact!, Orlando)	
12-02-06	**Christian Cage**	126
	(TNA Against All Odds '06, Orlando)	
18-06-06	**Jeff Jarrett⁶**	126
	(TNA Slammiversary IV, Orlando)	
22-10-06	**Sting²**	28
	(TNA Bound For Glory '06, Plymouth)	
19-11-06	**Abyss**	56
	(TNA Genesis '06, Orlando)	
14-01-07	**Christian Cage²**	119
	(TNA Final Resolution '07, Orlando)	
13-05-07	**VACANT**	
01-09-07	**Adam Pearce**	336
	(House Show, Bayamon, Puerto Rico)	
02-08-08	**Brent Albright**	49
	(ROH Death Before Dishonor VI, New York)	
20-09-08	**Adam Pearce²**	35
	(ROH Glory By Honor VII, Philadelphia)	
25-10-08	**Blue Demon Jr.**	505
	(House Show, Mexico City, Mexico)	
14-03-10	**Adam Pearce³**	357
	(House Show, Charlotte)	
06-03-11	**Colt Cabana**	48
	(NWA Championship Wrestling From Hollywood, West Hollywood)	
23-04-11	**The Sheik**	79
	(NWA Florida Subtle Hustle, Jacksonville)	
11-07-11	**VACANT**	
31-07-11	**Adam Pearce⁴**	252
	(NWA At The Ohio State Fair, Columbus)	
08-04-12	**Colt Cabana²**	104
	(NWA Championship Wrestling From Hollywood, Glendale)	
21-07-12	**Adam Pearce⁵**	98
	(Metro Pro Wrestling, Kansas City)	
27-10-12	**VACANT**	
02-11-12	**Kahagas**	134
	(NWA Wrath Of Champions, Clayton)	
16-03-13	**Rob Conway**	294
	(NWA A Monster's Ball, San Antonio)	
04-01-14	**Satoshi Kojima**	149
	(NJPW Wrestle Kingdom 8, Tokyo, Japan)	
02-06-14	**Rob Conway²**	257
	(Cauliflower Alley Club Reunion, Las Vegas)	
14-02-15	**Hiroyoshi Tenzan**	196
	(NJPW The New Beginning In Sendai, Sendai, Japan)	
29-08-15	**Jax Dane**	419
	(NWA World War Gold, San Antonio)	
21-10-16	**Tim Storm**	414
	(House Show, Sherman)	
09-12-17	**Nick Aldis**	266
	(CZW Cage Of Death 19, Sewell)	
01-09-18	**Cody Rhodes**	50
	(All In, Hoffman Estates)	
21-10-18	**Nick Aldis²**	1,043
	(NWA 70th Anniversary Show, Nashville)	
29-08-21	**Trevor Murdoch**	191

(NWA 73rd Anniversary Show, St. Louis)

DATE	WON BY	DAYS
08-03-22	**Matt Cardona**	95
	(NWA PowerrrTrip, Oak Grove)	
11-06-22	**VACANT**	
11-06-22	**Trevor Murdoch**[2]	154
	(NWA Alwayz Ready, Knoxville)	
12-11-22	**Tyrus**	49*
	(NWA Hard Times 3, Chalmette)	

Most Reigns

1.	Ric Flair	10
2.	Harley Race	8
3.	Jeff Jarrett	6
4.	Adam Pearce	5
5.	Lou Thesz	3
6.	AJ Styles	3
7.	Dusty Rhodes	3
8.	Giant Baba	3

Longest Reigns

1.	Lou Thesz	2,300
2.	Dory Funk Jr.	1,563
3.	Dan Severn	1,479
4.	Gene Kiniski	1,131
5.	Lou Thesz	1,079

Longest Cumulative Reigns

1.	Lou Thesz	3,749
2.	Ric Flair	3,116
3.	Harley Race	1,803
4.	Dory Funk Jr.	1,563
5.	Dan Severn	1,559

NWA NATIONAL HEAVYWEIGHT CHAMPIONSHIP

DATE	WON BY	DAYS
12-01-80	**Austin Idol**	221
	(N/A, Atlanta)	
20-08-80	**VACANT**	
09-10-80	**Jack Brisco**	58
	(House Show, Atlanta)	
12-12-80	**Mongolian Stomper**	107
	(House Show, Atlanta)	
29-03-81	**Steve Olsonoski**	139
	(House Show, Atlanta)	
15-08-81	**The Masked Superstar**	44
	(House Show, Columbus)	
28-09-81	**Tommy Rich**	58
	(House Show, Augusta)	
25-11-81	**The Masked Superstar**[2]	53
	(House Show, Atlanta)	
17-01-82	**Tommy Rich**[2]	57
	(House Show, Atlanta)	
15-03-82	**Ron Bass**	35
	(House Show, Augusta)	
19-04-82	**Tommy Rich**[3]	13
	(House Show, Augusta)	
02-05-82	**Buzz Sawyer**	49
	(House Show, Atlanta)	
20-06-82	**Paul Orndorff**	40
	(House Show, Atlanta)	
30-07-82	**VACANT**	
29-08-82	**The Super Destroyer**	35
	(House Show, Atlanta)	
03-10-82	**Paul Orndorff**[2]	14

DATE	WON BY	DAYS
	(House Show, Atlanta)	
17-10-82	**The Masked Superstar**[3]	21
	(House Show, Atlanta)	
07-11-82	**Paul Orndorff**[3]	133
	(House Show, Atlanta)	
20-03-83	**Killer Tim Brooks**	<1
	(House Show, Atlanta)	
20-03-83	**Larry Zbyszko**	41
	(House Show, Atlanta)	
30-04-83	**VACANT**	
05-06-83	**Larry Zbyszko**[2]	14
	(House Show, Atlanta)	
19-06-83	**Mr. Wrestling II**	28
	(House Show, Atlanta)	
17-07-83	**Larry Zbyszko**[3]	70
	(House Show, Huntington)	
25-09-83	**Brett Wayne**	54
	(House Show, Atlanta)	
18-11-83	**Ted DiBiase**	92
	(House Show, Cleveland)	
18-02-84	**Brad Armstrong**	54
	(World Championship Wrestling, Atlanta)	
12-04-84	**The Spoiler**	22
	(House Show, Wheeling)	
04-05-84	**Brad Armstrong**[2]	58
	(House Show, Marietta)	
01-07-84	**The Spoiler**[2]	13
	(House Show, Atlanta)	
14-07-84	**Ted DiBiase**[2]	89
	(N/A, Macon)	
11-10-84	**Ron Garvin**	233
	(NWA Night Of Champions, Baltimore)	
01-06-85	**Black Bart**	113
	(World Championship Wrestling, Atlanta)	
22-09-85	**Terry Taylor**	67
	(House Show, Atlanta)	
28-11-85	**Buddy Landel**	21
	(NWA Starrcade '85, Greensboro)	
19-12-85	**Dusty Rhodes**	75
	(N/A, Albuquerque)	
04-03-86	**Tully Blanchard**	177
	(MACW TV Taping, Spartanburg)	
28-08-86	**Wahoo McDaniel**	31
	(House Show, Los Angeles)	
28-09-86	**Nikita Koloff**	<1
	(House Show, Atlanta)	
28-09-86	**DEACTIVATED**	
17-05-97	**Big Slam**	62
	(N/A)	
18-07-97	**Salvatore Sincere**	85
	(House Show, Raeford)	
11-10-97	**VACANT**	
27-03-98	**Doug Gilbert**	148
	(House Show, Mount Holly)	
22-08-98	**Stevie Richards**	63
	(House Show, Mount Holly)	
24-10-98	**Doug Gilbert**[2]	448
	(NWA 50th Anniversary, Cherry Hill)	
15-01-00	**Don Brodie**	90
	(House Show, Memphis)	
14-04-00	**Kevin Northcutt**	152
	(NWA Southwest Parade of Champions, North Richland Hills)	
13-09-00	**Stone Mountain**	52
	(House Show, Athens)	
04-11-00	**Terry Knight**	69
	(House Show, Cornelia)	
12-01-01	**Don Brodie**[2]	222
	(House Show, Greenville)	
10-08-01	**VACANT**	
22-08-01	**Kevin Northcutt**[2]	52

	(N/A)	
13-10-01	**Hotstuff Hernandez**	455
	(NWA 53rd Anniversary, St. Petersburg)	
11-01-03	**Ricky Murdock**	643
	(House Show, Greenville)	
15-10-04	**Spyder**	358
	(NWA 56th Anniversary, Winnipeg, Canada)	
08-10-05	**VACANT**	
08-10-05	**Ricky Murdock**[2]	174
	(NWA 57th Anniversary, Nashville)	
31-03-06	**VACANT**	
01-04-06	**Big Bully Douglas**	182
	(House Show, Columbia)	
30-09-06	**Kory Williams**	217
	(House Show, Lebanon)	
05-05-07	**Chance Prophet**	160
	(House Show, Salyersville)	
12-10-07	**VACANT**	
20-10-07	**Pepper Parks**	181
	(House Show, Lebanon)	
18-04-08	**Crusher Hansen**	239
	(NWA Crossfire, McKeesport)	
13-12-08	**Brandon K**	4
	(NWA Christmas Chaos 2, McKeesport)	
17-12-08	**Crusher Hansen**[2]	31
	(House Show, McKeesport)	
17-01-09	**Phil Shatter**	763
	(NWA Genesis 2, McKeesport)	
19-02-11	**Chance Prophet**[2]	404
	(NWA Vintage, Franklinville)	
29-03-12	**Kahagas**	230
	(NWA Battle Of The Belts, Miami)	
14-11-12	**VACANT**	
05-01-13	**Damien Wayne**	160
	(NWA Edge, Nashville)	
14-06-13	**Vordell Walker**	49
	(NWA Gathering Of Champions, Millersville)	
02-08-13	**Damien Wayne**[2]	43
	(House Show, Millersville)	
14-09-13	**Phil Monahan**	168
	(House Show, Toledo)	
01-03-14	**Lou Marconi**	21
	(House Show, Williamston)	
22-03-14	**Phil Monahan**[2]	1
	(NWA WrestleRama 13, Hillsdale)	
23-03-14	**Lou Marconi**[2]	13
	(House Show, Oregon)	
05-04-14	**Phil Monahan**[3]	98
	(House Show, Carolina Beach)	
12-07-14	**Lou Marconi**[3]	209
	(NWA Smoky Mountain Steel Cage Showdown, Carolina Beach)	
06-02-15	**Jax Dane**	111
	(House Show, Millersville)	
28-05-15	**VACANT**	
11-07-15	**Arrick Andrews**	175
	(House Show, Cookeville)	
02-01-16	**VACANT**	
09-01-16	**John Saxon**	21
	(House Show, Dyersburg)	
30-01-16	**Greg Anthony**	154
	(House Show, Dyersburg)	
02-07-16	**Mustang Mike**	7
	(House Show, Morgan City)	
09-07-16	**Greg Anthony**[2]	70
	(House Show, Dyersburg)	
17-09-16	**Jake Logan**	42
	(House Show, Amarillo)	
29-10-16	**Greg Anthony**[3]	21
	(House Show, Dyersburg)	
19-11-16	**Damien Wayne**	76

	(House Show, Gallatin)	
03-02-17	**Kahagas**[2]	239
	(House Show, Franklin)	
30-09-17	**VACANT**	
21-10-18	**Willie Mack**	188
	(NWA 70th Anniversary, Nashville)	
27-04-19	**Colt Cabana**	76
	(NWA Crockett Cup '19, Concord)	
12-07-19	**James Storm**	116
	(Ring of Honor Wrestling, Philadelphia)	
05-11-19	**Colt Cabana**[2]	39
	(NWA Power, Atlanta)	
14-12-19	**Aron Stevens**	290
	(NWA Into The Fire, Atlanta)	
29-09-20	**Trevor Murdoch**	182
	(UWN Primetime Live, Long Beach)	
30-03-21	**Chris Adonis**	56
	(NWA Power, Atlanta)	
25-05-21	**VACANT**	
06-07-21	**Chris Adonis**[2]	237
	(NWA SuperPowerrr, Atlanta)	
01-03-22	**Anthony Mayweather**	19
	(NWA PowerrrTrip, Oak Grove)	
20-03-22	**Jax Dane**[2]	160
	(NWA Crockett Cup '22, Nashville)	
27-08-22	**Cyon**	126*
	(NWA 74th Anniversary, St. Louis)	

Most Reigns

1.	Damien Wayne	3
2.	Phil Monahan	3
3.	Greg Anthony	3
4.	Lou Marconi	3
5.	Paul Orndorff	3
6.	Tommy Rich	3

Longest Reigns

1.	Phil Shatter	763
2.	Ricky Murdock	643
3.	Hotstuff Hernandez	455
4.	Doug Gilbert	448
5.	Chance Prophet	404

Longest Cumulative Reigns

1.	Ricky Murdock	817
2.	Phil Shatter	763
3.	Doug Gilbert	596
4.	Chance Prophet	564
5.	Kahagas	469

NWA WORLD TELEVISION CHAMPIONSHIP

DATE	WON BY	DAYS
24-01-20	**Ricky Starks**	39
	(NWA Hard Times, Atlanta)	
03-03-20	**Zicky Dice**	231
	(NWA Power, Atlanta)	
20-10-20	**Elijah Burke**	290
	(UWN Primetime Live, Long Beach)	
06-08-21	**Tyrus**	414
	(NWA Power, Atlanta)	
24-09-22	**VACANT**	
12-11-22	**Jordan Clearwater**	49*
	(NWA Hard Times 3, New Orleans)	

NWA WORLD JUNIOR HEAVYWEIGHT CHAMPIONSHIP

DATE	WON BY	DAYS
15-05-45	Ken Fenelon	15
	(Awarded)	
30-05-45	Marshall Esteppe	216
	(House Show, Toronto)	
10-01-46	Larry Tillman	69
	(House Show, Des Moines)	
11-03-46	Ken Fenelon[2]	301
	(House Show, Des Moines)	
06-01-47	Marshall Esteppe[2]	77
	(House Show, Des Moines)	
24-03-47	Ray Steele	35
	(House Show, Des Moines)	
28-04-47	Marshall Esteppe[3]	323
	(House Show, Des Moines)	
16-03-48	Billy Goelz	159
	(House Show, Des Moines)	
22-08-48	Al Williams	14
	(House Show, Waterloo)	
05-09-48	Billy Goelz[2]	114
	(House Show, Waterloo)	
28-12-48	Leroy McGuirk	406
	(House Show, Des Moines)	
07-02-50	VACANT	
13-11-50	Verne Gagne	371
	(House Show, Tulsa)	
19-11-51	Danny McShain	637
	(House Show, Memphis)	
17-08-53	Baron Michele Leone	602
	(House Show, Memphis)	
11-04-55	Ed Francis	365
	(House Show, Tulsa)	
10-04-56	Mike Clancy	350
	(House Show, Oklahoma City)	
26-03-57	Fred Blassie	<1
	(House Show, Nashville)	
26-03-57	VACANT	
09-04-57	Mike Clancy[2]	217
	(House Show, Nashville)	
12-11-57	VACANT	
19-11-57	Mike Clancy[3]	101
	(House Show, Nashville)	
28-02-58	Angelo Savoldi	97
	(House Show, Oklahoma City)	
05-06-58	Dory Funk	36
	(House Show, Amarillo)	
11-07-58	Angelo Savoldi[2]	224
	(N/A)	
20-02-59	Ivan The Terrible	14
	(House Show, Oklahoma City)	
06-03-59	Angelo Savoldi[3]	84
	(House Show, Oklahoma City)	
29-05-59	Mike DiBiase	84
	(N/A)	
21-08-59	Angelo Savoldi[4]	336
	(N/A)	
22-07-60	Danny Hodge	1,450
	(House Show, Oklahoma City)	
11-07-64	Hiro Matsuda	125
	(House Show, Tampa)	
13-11-64	Angelo Savoldi[5]	161
	(House Show, Oklahoma City)	
23-04-65	Danny Hodge[2]	214

DATE	WON BY	DAYS
	(House Show, Oklahoma City)	
23-11-65	Lorenzo Parente	42
	(N/A)	
04-01-66	Danny Hodge[3]	10
	(House Show, Little Rock)	
14-01-66	Lorenzo Parente[2]	29
	(House Show, Oklahoma City)	
12-02-66	Joe McCarthy	80
	(House Show, Oklahoma City)	
03-05-66	Danny Hodge[4]	1,361
	(House Show, Little Rock)	
13-07-70	Sputnik Monroe	28
	(House Show, Shreveport)	
10-08-70	Danny Hodge[5]	283
	(House Show, Tulsa)	
20-05-71	Roger Kirby	113
	(House Show, New Orleans)	
10-09-71	Ramon Torres	84
	(House Show, Oklahoma City)	
03-12-71	Dr. X	108
	(House Show, Oklahoma City)	
20-03-72	Danny Hodge[6]	639
	(House Show, Shreveport)	
19-12-73	Ken Mantell	542
	(House Show, Jackson)	
14-06-75	Hiro Matsuda[2]	262
	(House Show, St. Petersburg)	
02-03-76	Danny Hodge[7]	13
	(House Show, Shreveport)	
15-03-76	VACANT	
28-09-76	Pat Barrett	65
	(N/A)	
02-12-76	Ron Starr	4
	(House Show, New Orleans)	
06-12-76	Nelson Royal	566
	(House Show, New Orleans)	
24-02-78	Chavo Guerrero Sr.	42
	(N/A)	
07-04-78	Nelson Royal[2]	79
	(N/A)	
25-06-78	Al Madril	398
	(House Show, Houston)	
28-07-79	Nelson Royal[3]	134
	(N/A)	
09-12-79	VACANT	
11-02-80	Ron Starr[2]	19
	(House Show, Tulsa)	
01-03-80	Les Thornton	331
	(N/A)	
26-01-81	Jerry Stubbs	5
	(House Show, Mobile)	
31-01-81	Les Thornton[2]	127
	(House Show, Dothan)	
07-06-81	Terry Taylor	13
	(House Show, Roanoke)	
20-06-81	Les Thornton[3]	88
	(House Show, Roanoke)	
16-09-81	Gerald Brisco	30
	(House Show, Miami)	
16-10-81	Les Thornton[4]	22
	(House Show, Knoxville)	
07-11-81	Joe Lightfoot	7
	(House Show, Bayamon, Puerto Rico)	
14-11-81	Les Thornton[5]	192
	(House Show, San Juan, Puerto Rico)	
25-05-82	Tiger Mask	313
	(NJPW Big Fight Series '82, Shizuoka, Japan)	
03-04-83	VACANT	
02-06-83	Tiger Mask[2]	71
	(N/A)	
12-08-83	VACANT	

Date	Name	Days
03-11-83	**The Cobra** (N/A)	633
28-07-85	**Hiro Saito** (House Show, Osaka, Japan)	<1
28-07-85	**The Cobra²** (House Show, Osaka, Japan)	4
01-08-85	**VACANT**	
01-08-85	**Denny Brown** (N/A)	14
15-08-85	**Gary Royal** (House Show, Kansas City)	31
15-09-85	**Denny Brown²** (House Show, Atlanta)	321
02-08-86	**Steve Regal** (House Show, Atlanta)	30
01-09-86	**Denny Brown³** (House Show, Greenville)	187
07-03-87	**Lazer Tron** (House Show, Atlanta)	215
08-10-87	**VACANT**	
16-10-87	**Nelson Royal⁴** (House Show, Columbia)	280
22-07-88	**Scott Armstrong** (House Show, Knoxville)	1
23-07-88	**Nelson Royal⁵** (House Show, Hazard)	7
30-07-88	**Scott Armstrong²** (House Show, Chattanooga)	3
02-08-88	**Nelson Royal⁶** (House Show, Knoxville)	108
18-11-88	**Les Anderson** (N/A)	209
15-06-89	**Rock The Hunter** (N/A)	193
25-12-89	**Les Anderson²** (N/A)	1
26-12-89	**DEACTIVATED**	
30-08-95	**Masayoshi Motegi** (WYF, Tokyo, Japan)	338
02-08-96	**The Great Sasuke** (NJPW G1 Climax '96, Tokyo, Japan)	70
11-10-96	**Ultimo Dragon** (WAR Osaka Crush, Osaka, Japan)	85
04-01-97	**Jushin Thunder Liger** (NJPW Wrestling World '97, Tokyo, Japan)	183
06-07-97	**El Samurai** (NJPW Summer Struggle '97, Sapporo, Jap)	35
10-08-97	**Shinjiro Otani** (NJPW The Four Heaven, Nagoya, Japan)	87
05-11-97	**VACANT**	
05-03-99	**Logan Caine** (House Show, Parkersburg)	237
28-10-99	**VACANT**	
28-10-99	**Vince Kaplack** (House Show, Pittsburgh)	78
14-01-00	**Tony Kozina** (House Show, North Versailles)	190
22-07-00	**Rockford 2000** (House Show, Surrey, Canada)	35
30-08-00	**Tony Kozina²** (N/A)	39
14-10-00	**Vince Kaplack²** (NWA 52nd Anniversary, Nashville)	175
07-04-01	**Rocky Reynolds** (House Show, Pennsboro)	27
04-05-01	**Mike Thunder** (House Show, North Richland)	109
21-08-01	**Lex Lovett** (House Show, Tampa)	53
13-10-01	**Jason Rumble** (NWA 53rd Anniversary, St. Petersburg)	112
02-02-02	**Rocky Reynolds²** (House Show, Titusville)	14
16-02-02	**Jason Rumble²** (House Show, Malden)	49
06-04-02	**Rocky Reynolds³** (House Show, Parkersburg)	56
29-06-02	**Jimmy Rave** (House Show, Cornelia)	42
10-08-02	**Star** (House Show, Columbia)	7
17-08-02	**Jimmy Rave²** (House Show, Columbia)	154
18-01-03	**Brother Love** (House Show, Greenville)	140
07-06-03	**Rocky Reynolds⁴** (House Show, Parkersburg)	56
02-08-03	**Chris Draven** (House Show, Parkersburg)	161
10-01-04	**Jerrelle Clark** (House Show, St. Petersburg)	281
17-10-04	**Jason Rumble³** (NWA 56th Anniversary, Winnipeg, Canada)	312
25-08-05	**Black Tiger IV** (House Show, Columbia)	178
19-02-06	**Tiger Mask IV** (NJPW Circuit Acceleration, Tokyo, Japan)	446
11-05-07	**Mike Quackenbush** (FSM Chapter Two, Portage)	1,275
06-11-10	**Craig Classic** (NWA November Coming Fire, Fort Pierce)	247
20-09-11	**VACANT**	
07-10-11	**Kevin Douglas** (House Show, Charlotte)	372
13-10-12	**VACANT**	
13-10-12	**Chase Owens** (House Show, Kingsport)	301
10-08-13	**Jason Kincaid** (House Show, Kingsport)	69
18-10-13	**Chase Owens²** (House Show, Houston)	78
04-01-14	**Ricky Morton** (House Show, Kingsport)	62
07-03-14	**Chase Owens³** (House Show, Church Hill)	246
08-11-14	**Jushin Thunder Liger²** (NJPW Power Struggle, Osaka)	156
13-04-15	**Steve Anthony** (VPW Casino Royale, Las Vegas)	163
23-09-15	**Tiger Mask IV²** (NJPW Destruction, Okayama)	178
19-03-16	**Steve Anthony²** (NJPW Road To Invasion Attack, Nagoya)	112
09-07-16	**John Saxon** (House Show, Pensacola)	275
08-04-17	**Arrick Andrews** (House Show, Dyersburg)	41
19-05-17	**Mr. USA** (House Show, Franklin)	85
12-08-17	**Barrett Brown** (House Show, Dyersburg)	49
30-09-17	**VACANT**	
20-03-22	**Homicide** (NWA Crockett Cup '22, Nashville)	237
12-11-22	**Kerry Morton** (NWA Hard Times 3, New Orleans)	49*

Most Reigns

1.	Danny Hodge	7
2.	Nelson Royal	6
3.	Les Thornton	6
4.	Angelo Savoldi	5

| 5. | Rocky Reynolds | 4 |

Longest Reigns

1.	Danny Hodge	1,450
2.	Danny Hodge	1,361
3.	Mike Quackenbush	1,275
4.	Danny Hodge	639
5.	Danny McShain	637

Longest Cumulative Reigns

1.	Danny Hodge	3,970
2.	Mike Quackenbush	1,275
3.	Nelson Royal	1,174
4.	Angelo Savoldi	902
5.	Les Thornton	760

NWA WORLD TAG TEAM CHAMPIONSHIP

DATE	WON BY	DAYS
11-04-95	Ricky Morton & Robert Gibson	76
	(House Show, Dallas)	
26-06-95	VACANT	
03-07-95	Ricky Morton[2] & Robert Gibson[2]	32
	(House Show, Memphis)	
04-08-95	VACANT	
09-12-95	Mr. Gannosuke & Tarzan Goto	236
	(House Show, Saitama, Japan)	
20-08-96	VACANT	
14-09-96	C.W. Anderson & Pat Anderson	389
	(House Show, Goldston)	
08-10-97	VACANT	
12-01-98	Ricky Morton[3] & Robert Gibson[3]	36
	(N/A, State College)	
17-02-98	Mosh & Thrasher	41
	(WWF Monday Night RAW, Waco)	
30-03-98	Bart Gunn & Bob Holly	137
	(WWF Monday Night RAW, Albany)	
14-08-98	Agent Gunn & Agent Maxx	29
	(House Show, Greenville)	
12-09-98	Barry Windham & Tully Blanchard	28
	(House Show, Lincolnton)	
10-10-98	Agent Gunn[2] & Agent Maxx[2]	14
	(House Show, Cameron)	
24-10-98	Eric Sbraccia & Knuckles Nelson	130
	(NWA 50th Anniversary, Cherry Hill)	
03-03-99	VACANT	
10-06-99	Knuckles Nelson[2] & Rick Fuller	7
	(House Show, Dallas)	
17-06-99	Johnny Grunge & Rocco Rock	2
	(House Show, Bolton)	
19-06-99	Knuckles Nelson[3] & Dukes Dalton	98
	(House Show, Dorchester)	
25-09-99	Khris Germany & Kit Carson	62
	(NWA 51st Anniversary, Charlotte)	
26-11-99	Jimmy James & Kevin Northcutt	21
	(House Show, North Richland Hills)	
17-12-99	Khris Germany[2] & Kit Carson[2]	78
	(House Show, North Richland Hills)	
04-03-00	Curtis Thompson & Drake Dawson	34
	(House Show, Cornelia)	
07-04-00	Reno Riggins & Steven Dunn	5
	(House Show, Eskan, Saudi Arabia)	
12-04-00	Ricky Morton[4] & Robert Gibson[4]	5
	(House Show, Waegwan, South Korea)	
17-04-00	Big Bubba Pain & L.A. Stephens	2
	(House Show, Osan, South Korea)	
19-04-00	Curtis Thompson[2]	118

	& Drake Dawson[2]	
	(House Show, Okinawa, Japan)	
15-08-00	David Young & Rick Michaels	172
	(House Show, Tampa)	
03-02-01	Christian York & Joey Matthews	14
	(House Show, Nashville)	
17-02-01	David Young[2] & Rick Michaels[2]	33
	(House Show, Cornelia)	
22-03-01	Dan Factor & David Flair	1
	(House Show, Athens)	
23-03-01	David Young[3] & Rick Michaels[3]	32
	(House Show, Toccoa)	
24-04-01	Chris Nelson & Vito DeNucci	248
	(House Show, Tampa)	
28-12-01	Glacier & Jason Sugarman	1
	(House Show, DeLand)	
29-12-01	Chris Nelson[2] & Vito DeNucci[2]	28
	(House Show, Live Oak)	
26-01-02	Jeff Daniels & Tim Renesto	81
	(House Show, Columbia)	
17-04-02	Chris Nelson[3] & Vito DeNucci[3]	52
	(House Show, Winter Haven)	
08-06-02	Mike Shane & Todd Shane	20
	(House Show, Lima, Peru)	
28-06-02	VACANT	
03-07-02	AJ Styles & Jerry Lynn	42
	(Total Nonstop Action, Nashville)	
14-08-02	VACANT	
18-09-02	Chris Harris & James Storm	56
	(Total Nonstop Action, Nashville)	
13-11-02	Brian Lee & Slash	56
	(Total Nonstop Action, Nashville)	
08-01-03	Chris Harris[2] & James Storm[2]	14
	(Total Nonstop Action, Nashville)	
22-01-03	Chris Daniels, Low Ki	14
	& Elix Skipper	
	(Total Nonstop Action, Nashville)	
05-02-03	VACANT	
12-03-03	Chris Daniels[2], Low Ki[2]	35
	& Elix Skipper[2]	
	(Total Nonstop Action, Nashville)	
16-04-03	The Amazing Red & Jerry Lynn[2]	21
	(Total Nonstop Action, Nashville)	
07-05-03	Chris Daniels[3], Low Ki[3]	49
	& Elix Skipper[3]	
	(Total Nonstop Action, Nashville)	
25-06-03	Chris Harris[3] & James Storm[3]	63
	(Total Nonstop Action, Nashville)	
27-08-03	Johnny Swinger	91
	& Simon Diamond	
	(Total Nonstop Action, Nashville)	
26-11-03	B.G. James, Konnan	63
	& Ron Killings	
	(Total Nonstop Action, Nashville)	
28-01-04	Joe Legend & Kevin Northcutt[2]	7
	(Total Nonstop Action, Nashville)	
04-02-04	Abyss & AJ Styles[2]	28
	(Total Nonstop Action, Nashville)	
03-03-04	VACANT	
31-03-04	Dallas & Kid Kash	14
	(Total Nonstop Action, Nashville)	
14-04-04	D'Lo Brown & El Gran Apolo	7
	(Total Nonstop Action, Nashville)	
21-04-04	Dallas[2] & Kid Kash[2]	44
	(Total Nonstop Action, Nashville)	
04-06-04	Chris Harris[4] & James Storm[4]	33
	(Impact Wrestling, Nashville)	
07-07-04	Andy Douglas & Chase Stevens	63
	(Total Nonstop Action, Nashville)	
08-09-04	Chris Harris[5] & Elix Skipper[4]	16
	(Total Nonstop Action, Nashville)	

24-09-04	Chris Daniels[4] & James Storm[5] (TNA Impact!, Orlando)	21
15-10-04	Bobby Roode & Eric Young (TNA Impact!, Orlando)	23
07-11-04	B.G. James[2], Konnan[2] & Ron Killings[2] (TNA Victory Road '04, Orlando)	28
05-12-04	Bobby Roode[2] & Eric Young[2] (TNA Turning Point '04, Orlando)	42
16-01-05	Chris Harris[6] & James Storm[6] (TNA Final Resolution '05, Orlando)	100
26-04-05	Andy Douglas[2] & Chase Stevens[2] (TNA Impact!, Orlando)	162
05-10-05	VACANT	
08-10-05	Andy Douglas[3] & Chase Stevens[3] (NWA 57th Anniversary, Nashville)	14
22-10-05	Chris Harris[7] & James Storm[7] (TNA Impact!, Orlando)	239
18-06-06	AJ Styles[3] & Christopher Daniels[5] (TNA Slammiversary IV, Orlando)	67
24-08-06	Homicide & Hernandez (TNA Impact!, Orlando)	31
24-09-06	AJ Styles[3] & Christopher Daniels[6] (TNA No Surrender '06, Orlando)	28
22-10-06	Homicide[2] & Hernandez[2] (TNA Bound For Glory '06, Plymouth Town.)	175
15-04-07	Brother Devon & Brother Ray (TNA Lockdown '07, St. Charles)	28
13-05-07	VACANT	
08-07-07	Joey Ryan & Karl Anderson (House Show, McAllen)	217
10-02-08	Phoenix Star & Zokre (House Show, Las Vegas)	237
04-10-08	Keith Walker & Rasche Brown (House Show, Robstown)	777
20-11-10	Jon Davis & Kory Chavis (House Show, Milwaukee)	162
01-05-11	AJ Steele & Murder One (NWA Memorial Mayhem '11, Warner Rob.)	14
15-05-11	Jon Davis[2] & Kory Chavis[2] (House Show, Warner Robins)	580
15-12-12	Ryan Genesis & Scot Summers (NWA December To Remember, San Ant.)	126
20-04-13	Davey Boy Smith Jr. & Lance Archer[3] (NWA Parade Of Champions, Houston)	203
09-11-13	Jax Dane & Rob Conway (NJPW Power Struggle '13, Osaka, Japan)	148
06-04-14	Hiroyoshi Tenzan & Satoshi Kojima (NJPW Invasion Attack '14, Tokyo, Japan)	190
13-10-14	Davey Boy Smith Jr.[2] & Lance Archer[4] (NJPW King of Pro-Wrestling '14, Tokyo, Jap.)	362
10-10-15	Elliott Russell & Sigmon (NWA Glory Lasts Forever, Dyersburg)	55
04-12-15	Matt Riviera & Rob Conway[2] (NWA Wrestling At The Resorts Casino, Robinsonville)	280
09-09-16	Elliott Russell[2] & Sigmon[2] (House Show, Ripley)	1
10-09-16	Matt Riviera[2] & Rob Conway[3] (House Show, Dyersburg)	90
09-12-16	Elliott Russell[3] & Sigmon[3] (House Show, Ripley)	28
06-01-17	Matt Riviera[3] & Rob Conway[4] (House Show, Ripley)	48
23-02-17	Kazushi Miyamoto & Rob Terry (Diamond Stars Wrestling, Tokyo, Japan)	114
17-06-17	Elliott Russell[4] & Sigmon[4] (House Show, Dyersburg)	105
30-09-17	VACANT	

27-04-19	Brody King & PCO (NWA Crockett Cup '19, Concord)	133
07-09-19	Royce Isaacs & Thomas Latimer (ROH Global Wars Espectacular, Villa Park)	87
03-12-19	Ricky Morton[5] & Robert Gibson[5] (NWA Power, Atlanta)	52
24-01-20	Eli Drake & James Storm[8] (NWA Hard Times '20, Atlanta)	291
10-11-20	Aron Stevens & JR Kratos (UWN Primetime Live #9, Long Beach)	292
29-08-21	Bestia 666 & Mecha Wolf (NWA 73rd Anniversary, St. Louis)	286
11-06-22	Doug Williams & Harry Smith[2] (NWA Alwayz Ready, Knoxville)	77
27-08-22	VACANT	
27-08-22	Bestia 666[2] & Mecha Wolf[2] (NWA 74th Anniversary, St. Louis)	126*

Most Reigns

1.	James Storm	8
2.	Chris Harris	7
3.	Christopher Daniels	6
4.	Ricky Morton	5
5.	Robert Gibson	5

Longest Reigns

1.	Keith Walker & Rasche Brown	777
2.	Jon Davis & Kory Chavis	580
3.	C.W. Anderson & Pat Anderson	389
4.	Davey Boy Smith Jr. & Lance Archer	362
5.	Eli Drake & James Storm	291

Longest Cumulative Reigns

1.	James Storm	828
2.	Keith Walker	777
3.	Rasche Brown	777
4.	Jon Davis	742
5.	Kory Chavis	742

NWA UNITED STATES TAG TEAM CHAMPIONSHIP

DATE	WON BY	DAYS
28-08-22	Wrecking Ball Legursky & Jay Bradley (NWA 74th Anniversary Show, St. Louis)	125*

NWA WORLD WOMEN'S CHAMPIONSHIP

DATE	WON BY	DAYS
1937	Mildred Burke (House Show, N/A)	??
20-08-54	June Byers (House Show, Atlanta)	757
18-09-56	The Fabulous Moolah (House Show, Baltimore)	3,651
17-09-66	Bette Boucher (House Show, Seattle)	16
10-10-66	The Fabulous Moolah[2] (House Show, Vancouver, Canada)	524
10-03-68	Yukiko Tomoe (House Show, Osaka, Japan)	23
02-04-68	The Fabulous Moolah[3]	3,841

(House Show, Hamamatsu, Japan)

Date	Name	Days
08-10-78	**Evelyn Stevens**	1
	(House Show, Dallas)	
09-10-78	**The Fabulous Moolah**[4]	1,909
	(House Show, Fort Worth)	
31-12-83	**VACANT**	
12-02-86	**Debbie Combs**	??
	(House Show, Honolulu)	
1987	**VACANT**	
10-04-87	**Debbie Combs**[2]	??
	(House Show, Kansas City)	
25-07-94	**Bambi**	‹1
	(House Show, Gadsden)	
25-07-94	**Peggy Lee Leather**	1
	(House Show, Gadsden)	
26-07-94	**Bambi**[2]	654
	(NWA TV Tapings, East Ridge)	
09-08-96	**Malia Hosaka**	1
	(House Show, Johnson City)	
10-05-96	**Debbie Combs**[3]	156
	(House Show, Fall Branch)	
Oct 1996	**VACANT**	
14-10-00	**Strawberry Fields**	17
	(NWA 52nd Anniversary, Nashville)	
Nov 2000	**VACANT**	
23-08-02	**Madison**	64
	(House Show, Surrey, Canada)	
26-10-02	**Char Starr**	41
	(NWA 54th Anniversary, Corpus Christie)	
06-12-02	**Madison**[2]	96
	(House Show, Port Coquitlam, Canada)	
12-03-03	**Leilani Kai**	465
	(House Show, Nashville)	
19-06-04	**VACANT**	
19-06-04	**Kiley McLean**	308
	(House Show, Richmond)	
23-04-05	**Lexie Fyfe**	168
	(House Show, Richmond)	
08-10-05	**Christie Ricci**	476
	(NWA 57th Anniversary, Nashville)	
27-01-17	**MsChif**	98
	(House Show, Lebanon)	
05-05-07	**Amazing Kong**	358
	(House Show, Streamwood)	
27-04-08	**MsChif**[2]	818
	(House Show, Cape Girardeau)	
27-07-10	**Tasha Simone**	70
	(House Show, Lebanon)	
02-10-10	**La Reina de Corazones**	35
	(House Show, Altus)	
06-11-10	**VACANT**	
06-11-10	**Tasha Simone**[2]	365
	(House Show, Lebanon)	
06-11-11	**Tiffany Roxx**	49
	(House Show, Lebanon)	
25-12-11	**Tasha Simone**[3]	300
	(House Show, Lebanon)	
20-10-12	**Kacee Carlisle**	462
	(House Show, Lebanon)	
25-01-14	**Barbi Hayden**	378
	(House Show, Cypress)	
07-02-15	**Santana Garrett**	314
	(House Show, Plant City)	
18-12-15	**Amber Gallows**	273
	(House Show, Sherman)	
16-09-16	**Jazz**	948
	(House Show, Sherman)	
22-04-19	**VACANT**	
27-04-19	**Allysin Kay**	272
	(NWA Crockett Cup '19, Concord)	
24-01-20	**Thunder Rosa**	278

(NWA Hard Times '20, Atlanta)

28-10-20	**Serena Deeb**	221
	(UWN Primetime Live, Long Beach)	
06-06-21	**Kamille**	573*
	(NWA When Our Shadows Fall, Atlanta)	

NWA WORLD WOMEN'S TAG TEAM CHAMPIONSHIP

DATE	WON BY	DAYS
N/A	**Ella Waldek & Mae Young**	??
	(N/A)	
11-09-52	**June Byers & Millie Stafford**	134
	(House Show, Mexico City, Mexico)	
23-01-53	**June Byers**[2] **& Mary Jane Mull**	??
	(House Show, Nebraska)	
??	**Daisy Mae & Golden Venus**	??
	(N/A)	
??	**Carol Cook & Ruth Boatcallie**	??
	(N/A)	
14-12-53	**June Byers**[3] **& Mary Jane Mull**[2]	249
	(House Show, Birmingham)	
20-08-54	**VACANT**	
07-12-54	**June Byers**[4] **& Millie Stafford**[2]	??
	(N/A)	
??	**Lorraine Johnson & Penny Banner**	??
	(House Show, Ohio)	
??	**Daisy Mae & Golden Venus**	??
	(House Show, West Virginia)	
30-07-56	**Bonnie Watson & Penny Banner**[2]	??
	(N/A)	
??	**June Byers**[5] **& Mars Bennett**	??
	(N/A)	
??	**Betty Jo Hawkins & Penny Banner**[3]	??
	(N/A)	
13-02-57	**June Byers**[6] **& Barbara Baker**	??
	(House Show, Vancouver, Canada)	
??	**Betty Jo Hawkins**[2] **& Penny Banner**[4]	??
	(N/A)	
09-07-57	**June Byers**[7] **& Ethel Johnson**	208
	(N/A)	
02-02-58	**Lorraine Johnson**[2] **& Millie Stafford**[3]	??
	(House Show, Joplin)	
16-06-58	**Lorraine Johnson**[3] **& Penny Banner**[5]	171
	(N/A)	
04-12-58	**Kay Noble & Lolita Martinez**	??
	(House Show, Amarillo)	
23-11-61	**Adrienne Ames & Pat Lyda**	??
	(House Show, Harvey)	
02-11-67	**The Fabulous Moolah & Patty Nelson**	??
	(N/A)	
??	**The Fabulous Moolah**[2] **& Toni Rose**	??
	(N/A)	
15-05-70	**Donna Christanello & Kathy O'Day**	21
	(House Show, Los Angeles)	
05-06-70	**The Fabulous Moolah**[3] **& Toni Rose**[2]	??
	(House Show, Bakersfield)	
02-10-70	**Donna Christanello**[2] **& Toni Rose**[3]	415
	(N/A)	
21-11-71	**Sandy Parker & Susan Green**	6
	(House Show, Honolulu)	

27-11-71	**Donna Christanello[3] & Toni Rose[4]** (House Show, Honolulu)	688
15-10-73	**Joyce Grable & Vicki Williams** (House Show, New York City)	677
23-08-75	**Donna Christanello[4] & Toni Rose[5]** (House Show, Boston)	554
27-02-77	**Joyce Grable[2] & Vicki Williams[2]** (House Show, St. Petersburg)	??
??	**Beverly Shade & Natasha Hatchet Lady** (House Show, Memphis)	??
23-08-78	**Judy Martin & Leilani Kai** (House Show, Key West)	2
25-08-78	**Joyce Grable[3] & Vicki Williams[3]** (House Show, St. Petersburg)	??
26-12-79	**Judy Martin[2] & Leilani Kai[2]** (N/A)	126
30-04-80	**Joyce Grable[4] & Wendi Richter** (House Show, Springfield)	729
29-04-82	**Princess Victoria & Sabrina** (House Show, Kansas City)	7
06-05-82	**Joyce Grable[5] & Wendi Richter[2]** (House Show, Kansas City)	372
13-05-83	**Penny Mitchell & Velvet McIntyre** (House Show, Calgary, Canada)	10
23-05-83	**Joyce Grable[6] & Wendi Richter[3]** (House Show, Vancouver, Canada)	317
04-04-84	**DEACTIVATED**	
28-08-21	**Allysin Kay & Marti Belle** (NWA EmPowerrr, St. Louis)	287
11-06-22	**Ella Envy & Kenzie Paige** (NWA Alwayz Ready, Knoxville)	203*

MLW WORLD HEAVYWEIGHT CHAMPIONSHIP

DATE	WON BY	DAYS
15-06-02	**Shane Douglas** (Genesis, New York)	90
13-09-02	**VACANT**	
26-09-02	**Satoshi Kojima** (Reload, New York)	267
20-06-03	**Mike Awesome** (Hybrid Hell, Fort Lauderdale)	‹1
20-06-03	**Steve Corino** (Hybrid Hell, Fort Lauderdale)	235
10-02-04	**DEACTIVATED**	
12-04-18	**Shane Strickland** (The World Championship Finals, Orlando)	99
20-07-18	**Low Ki** (Fusion, Orlando)	197
02-02-19	**Tom Lawlor** (SuperFight, Philadelphia)	154
06-07-19	**Jacob Fatu** (Kings Of Colosseum, Cicero)	819
02-10-21	**Alexander Hammerstone** (Fightland '21, Philadelphia)	455*

MLW NATIONAL OPENWEIGHT CHAMPIONSHIP

DATE	WON BY	DAYS
01-06-19	**Alexander Hammerstone** (Fury Road, Waukesha)	865
13-10-21	**VACANT**	

06-11-21	**Alex Kane** (War Chamber, Philadelphia)	229
23-06-22	**Davey Richards** (Battle Riot IV, New York)	191*

MLW WORLD MIDDLEWEIGHT CHAMPIONSHIP

DATE	WON BY	DAYS
27-07-18	**MJF** (Battle Riot I, New York)	133
07-12-18	**VACANT**	
14-12-18	**Teddy Hart** (Fusion Live, Miami)	330
09-11-19	**Myron Reed** (Blood and Thunder, Orlando)	424
06-01-21	**Lio Rush** (Kings of Colosseum, Orlando)	119
05-05-21	**Myron Reed[2]** (Fusion Live, Orlando)	150
02-10-21	**Tajiri** (Fightland '21, Philadelphia)	111
21-01-22	**Myron Reed[3]** (Blood And Thunderm North Richland Hills)	240
18-09-22	**Shun Skywalker** (Super Series, Norcross)	42
30-10-22	**Lince Dorado** (Fightland, Philadelphia)	62*

MLW WORLD TAG TEAM CHAMPIONSHIP

DATE	WON BY	DAYS
09-05-03	**CW Anderson & Simon Diamond** (Revolutions, Orlando)	277
10-02-04	**VACANT**	
15-06-18	**Pentagon Jr. & Rey Fenix** (Fusion, Orlando)	232
02-02-19	**Teddy Hart & David Boy Smith Jr.** (SuperFight, Philadelphia)	161
13-07-19	**MJF & Richard Holliday** (Fusion, Cicero)	112
02-11-19	**Marshall Von Erich & Ross Von Erich** (Saturday Night SuperFight, Cicero)	438
13-01-21	**El Hijo de L.A. Park & L.A. Park** (Fusion, Orlando)	297
06-11-21	**Danny Rivera & Slice Boogie** (War Chamber, Philadelphia)	112
26-02-22	**EJ Nduka & Calvin Tankman** (SuperFight, Charlotte)	308*

MLW WOMEN'S FEATHERWEIGHT CHAMPIONSHIP

DATE	WON BY	DAYS
13-05-22	**Taya Valkyrie** (Kings Of Colosseum, Philadelphia)	232*

IWGP WORLD HEAVYWEIGHT CHAMPIONSHIP

DATE	WON BY	DAYS
04-03-21	**Kota Ibushi** (49th Anniversary Show, Tokyo)	31
04-04-21	**Will Ospreay** (Sakura Genesis '21, Tokyo)	46
20-05-21	**VACANT**	
07-06-21	**Shingo Takagi** (Dominion '21, Osaka)	211
04-01-22	**Kazuchika Okada** (Wrestle Kingdom 16, Tokyo)	159
12-06-22	**Jay White** (Dominion '22, Osaka)	202*

IWGP UNITED STATES CHAMPIONSHIP

DATE	WON BY	DAYS
02-07-17	**Kenny Omega** (G1 Special In USA, Long Beach)	210
28-01-18	**Jay White** (The New Beginning in Sapporo, Sapporo)	160
07-07-18	**Juice Robinson** (G1 Special in San Francisco, Daly City)	85
30-09-18	**Cody Rhodes** (Fighting Spirit Unleashed, Long Beach)	96
04-01-19	**Juice Robinson²** (Wrestle Kingdom 13, Tokyo)	152
05-06-19	**Jon Moxley** (Best Of The Super Juniors 26, Tokyo)	130
14-10-19	**VACANT**	
14-10-19	**Lance Archer** (King Of Pro-Wrestling '19, Tokyo)	82
04-01-20	**Jon Moxley²** (Wrestle Kingdom 14, Tokyo)	564
21-07-21	**Lance Archer²** (AEW Fyter Fest '21, Garland)	24
14-08-21	**Hiroshi Tanahashi** (Resurgence, Los Angeles)	84
06-11-21	**Kenta** (Power Struggle '21, Osaka)	60
05-01-22	**Hiroshi Tanahashi²** (Wrestle Kingdom 16, Tokyo)	45
19-02-22	**Sanada** (New Years Golden Series, Sapporo)	49
09-04-22	**VACANT**	
01-05-22	**Hiroshi Tanahashi³** (Wrestling Dontaku, Fukuoka)	13
14-05-22	**Juice Robinson³** (Capital Collision, Washington)	28
11-06-22	**VACANT**	
12-06-22	**Will Ospreay** (Dominion '22, Osaka)	202*

IWGP JUNIOR HEAVYWEIGHT CHAMPIONSHIP

DATE	WON BY	DAYS
06-02-86	**Shiro Koshinaka** (New Year Dash '86, Tokyo)	102
19-05-86	**Nobuhiko Takada** (IWGP Champion Series '86, Tokyo)	123
19-09-86	**Shiro Koshinaka²** (Challenge Spirit '86, Fukuoka)	317
02-08-87	**VACANT**	
20-08-87	**Kuniyaki Kobayashi** (Summer Night Fever in Kokugikan, Tokyo)	129
27-12-87	**Hiroshi Hase** (Year End in Kokugikan, Tokyo)	152
27-05-87	**Owen Hart** (IWGP Champion Series '88, Sendai)	28
24-06-88	**Shiro Koshinaka³** (IWGP Champion Series '88, Osaka)	265
16-03-89	**Hiroshi Hase²** (Big Fight Series, Yokohama)	70
25-05-89	**Jushin Liger** (Battle Satellite '89, Osaka)	77
10-08-89	**Naoki Sano** (Fighting Satellite '89, Tokyo)	174
31-01-90	**Jushin Liger²** (New Spring Gold Series '90, Osaka)	200
19-08-90	**Pegasus Kid** (Summer Night Fever II, Tokyo)	74
01-11-90	**Jushin Liger³** (Dream Tour '90, Tokyo)	165
15-04-91	**VACANT**	
30-04-91	**Norio Honaga** (Explosion Tour '91, Tokyo)	43
12-06-91	**Jushin Liger⁴** (Fighting Connection, Tokyo)	58
09-08-91	**Akira Nogami** (Violent Storm in Kokugikan, Tokyo)	88
05-11-91	**Norio Honaga²** (Tokyo 3 Days Battle, Tokyo)	95
08-02-92	**Jushin Liger⁵** (Fighting Spirit '92, Sapporo)	139
26-06-92	**El Samurai** (Masters Of Wrestling, Tokyo)	149
22-11-92	**Ultimo Dragon** (Wrestling Scramble '92, Tokyo)	43
04-01-93	**Jushin Liger⁶** (Fantastic Story in Tokyo Dome, Tokyo)	628
24-09-94	**VACANT**	
27-09-94	**Norio Honaga³** (G1 Climax Special '94, Osaka)	145
19-02-95	**Koji Kanemoto** (Fighting Spirit '95, Tokyo)	73
03-05-95	**Sabu** (Wrestling Dontaku '95, Fukuoka)	42
14-06-95	**Koji Kanemoto²** (Spirit Legend, Tokyo)	204
04-01-96	**Jushin Liger⁷** (Wrestling World '96, Tokyo)	116
29-04-96	**The Great Sasuke** (Battle Formation, Tokyo)	165
11-10-96	**Ultimo Dragon²** (Osaka Crush Night, Osaka)	85
04-01-97	**Jushin Liger⁸** (Wrestling World '97, Tokyo)	183
06-07-97	**El Samurai²** (Summer Struggle '97, Sapporo)	35
10-08-97	**Shinjiro Otani** (The Four Heaven in Nagoya Dome)	181
07-02-98	**Jushin Liger⁹** (Fighting Spirit '98, Sapporo)	403
17-03-99	**Koji Kanemoto³** (Hyper Battle '99, Hiroshima)	164
28-08-99	**Kendo Kashin** (Jingu Climax, Tokyo)	44
11-10-99	**Jushin Liger¹⁰** (Final Dome, Tokyo)	49

29-11-99	**Juventud Guerrera**	7
	(WCW Nitro, Denver)	
06-12-99	**Jushin Liger**[11]	227
	(WCW Nitro, Milwaukee)	
20-07-00	**Tatsuhito Takaiwa**	101
	(Summer Struggle '00, Sapporo)	
29-10-00	**Minoru Tanaka**	264
	(Get A Right!!, Kobe)	
20-07-01	**Masayuki Naruse**	80
	(Dome Quake, Sapporo)	
08-10-01	**Kendo Kashin**[2]	116
	(Indicate Of Next, Tokyo)	
01-02-02	**VACANT**	
16-02-02	**Minoru Tanaka**[2]	153
	(Fighting Spirit '02, Tokyo)	
19-07-02	**Koji Kanemoto**[4]	278
	(Summer Fight Series '02, Sapporo)	
23-04-03	**Tiger Mask**	153
	(Strong Energy '03, Hiroshima)	
23-09-03	**VACANT**	
13-10-03	**Jado**	62
	(Ultimate Crush II, Tokyo)	
14-12-03	**Heat**[3]	387
	(Battle Final '03, Nagoya)	
04-01-05	**Tiger Mask**[2]	277
	(Toukon Festival: Wrestling World, Tokyo)	
08-10-05	**Black Tiger**	134
	(Toukon Souzou New Chapter, Tokyo)	
19-02-06	**Tiger Mask**[3]	73
	(Acceleration, Tokyo)	
03-05-06	**Koji Kanemoto**[5]	235
	(New Japan Cup '06, Fukuoka)	
24-12-06	**Minoru**[4]	194
	(Battle Xmas! Catch the Victory, Tokyo)	
06-07-07	**Ryusuke Taguchi**	155
	(Soul C.T.U Farewell Tour, Tokyo)	
08-12-07	**Wataru Inoue**	191
	(New Japan Alive, Osaka)	
16-06-08	**VACANT**	
08-07-08	**Tiger Mask**[4]	75
	(New Japan Trill, Tokyo)	
21-09-08	**Low Ki**	105
	(New Japan Generation, Kobe)	
04-01-09	**Tiger Mask**[5]	223
	(Wrestle Kingdom 3, Tokyo)	
15-08-09	**Mistico**	85
	(G1 Climax '09, Tokyo)	
08-11-09	**Tiger Mask**[6]	57
	(Destruction '09, Tokyo)	
04-01-10	**Naomichi Marufuji**	166
	(Wrestle Kingdom 4, Tokyo)	
19-06-10	**Prince Devitt**	364
	(Dominion '10, Osaka)	
18-06-11	**Kota Ibushi**	85
	(Dominion '11, Osaka)	
12-09-11	**VACANT**	
19-09-11	**Prince Devitt**[2]	227
	(Kantaro Hoshino Memorial Show, Kobe)	
03-05-12	**Low Ki**[2]	87
	(Wrestling Dontaku '12, Fukuoka)	
29-07-12	**Kota Ibushi**[2]	71
	(Last Rebellion, Tokyo)	
08-10-12	**Low Ki**[3]	34
	(King Of Pro-Wrestling '12, Tokyo)	
11-11-12	**Prince Devitt**[3]	419
	(Power Struggle '12, Osaka)	
04-01-14	**Kota Ibushi**[3]	181
	(Wrestle Kingdom 8, Tokyo)	
04-07-14	**Kushida**	79
	(Kizuna Road '14, Tokyo)	
21-09-14	**Ryusuke Taguchi**[2]	105

	(Destruction In Kobe '14, Kobe)	
04-01-15	**Kenny Omega**	182
	(Wrestle Kingdom 9, Tokyo)	
05-07-15	**Kushida**[2]	80
	(Dominion '15, Osaka)	
23-09-15	**Kenny Omega**[2]	103
	(Destruction In Okayama '15, Okayama)	
04-01-16	**Kushida**[3]	257
	(Wrestle Kingdom 10, Tokyo)	
17-09-16	**Bushi**	49
	(Destruction In Tokyo '16, Tokyo)	
05-11-16	**Kushida**[4]	60
	(Power Struggle '16, Osaka)	
04-01-17	**Hiromu Takahashi**	158
	(Wrestle Kingdom 11, Tokyo)	
11-06-17	**Kushida**[5]	120
	(Dominion '17, Osaka)	
09-10-17	**Will Ospreay**	27
	(King Of Pro-Wrestling '17, Tokyo)	
05-11-17	**Marty Scurll**	60
	(Power Struggle '17, Osaka)	
04-01-18	**Will Ospreay**[2]	156
	(Wrestle Kingdom 12, Tokyo)	
09-06-18	**Hiromu Takahashi**[2]	72
	(Dominion '18, Osaka)	
20-08-18	**VACANT**	
08-10-18	**Kushida**[6]	88
	(King Of Pro-Wrestling '18, Tokyo)	
04-01-19	**Taiji Ishimori**	92
	(Wrestle Kingdom 13, Tokyo)	
06-04-19	**Dragon Lee**	64
	(G1 Supercard, New York)	
09-06-19	**Will Ospreay**[3]	209
	(Dominion '19, Osaka)	
04-01-20	**Hiromu Takahashi**[3]	238
	(Wrestle Kingdom 14, Tokyo)	
29-08-20	**Taiji Ishimori**[2]	129
	(Summer Struggle In Jingu, Tokyo)	
05-01-21	**Hiromu Takahashi**[4]	51
	(Wrestle Kingdom 15, Tokyo)	
25-02-21	**VACANT**	
28-02-21	**El Desperado**	147
	(Castle Attack, Osaka)	
25-07-21	**Robbie Eagles**	104
	(Wrestle Grand Slam In Tokyo Dome, Tokyo)	
06-11-21	**El Desperado**[2]	176
	(Power Struggle '21, Osaka)	
01-05-22	**Taiji Ishimori**[3]	244*
	(Wrestling Dontaku, Fukuoka)	

Most Reigns
1.	Jushin Liger	11
2.	Tiger Mask	6
3.	Kushida	6
4.	Koji Kanemoto	5
5.	Minoru Tanaka	4
6.	Hiromu Takahashi	4

Longest Reigns
1.	Jushin Liger	628
2.	Prince Devitt	419
3.	Jushin Liger	403
4.	Heat	387
5.	Prince Devitt	364

Longest Cumulative Reigns
1.	Jushin Liger	2,245
2.	Prince Devitt	1,010
3.	Minoru Tanaka/Heat	998
4.	Koji Kanemoto	954
5.	Tiger Mask	858

IWGP TAG TEAM CHAMPIONSHIP

DATE	WON BY	DAYS
12-12-85	Kengo Kimura & Tatsumi Fujinami (IWGP Tag Team League, Sendai)	236
05-08-86	Akira Maeda & Osamu Kido (Burning Spirit In Summer, Tokyo)	49
23-09-86	Kengo Kimura[2] & Tatsumi Fujinami[2] (Challenge Spirit '86, Tokyo)	135
05-02-87	VACANT	
20-03-87	Keiji Mutoh & Shiro Koshinaka (Spring Flare Up '87, Tokyo)	6
26-03-87	Akira Maeda[2] & Nobuhiko Takada (Inoki Toukon Live II, Osaka)	159
01-09-87	Kazuo Yamazaki & Yoshiaki Fujiwara (Sengoku Battle Series '87, Fukuoka)	139
18-01-88	Kengo Kimura[3] & Tatsumi Fujinami[3] (New Year Golden Series '88, Takuyuma)	144
10-06-88	Masa Saito & Riki Choshu (Champion Series '88, Hiroshima)	282
19-03-89	George Takano & Super Strong Machine (Big Fight Series, Yokohama)	116
13-07-89	Riki Choshu[2] & Takayuki Iizuka (Super Fight Series, Tokyo)	69
20-09-89	Masa Saito[2] & Shinya Hashimoto (Bloody Fight Series '89, Osaka)	219
27-04-90	Keiji Mutoh[2] & Masahiro Chono (Shintou Station Bay NK, Tokyo)	189
01-11-90	Hiroshi Hase & Kensuke Sasaki (Dream Tour '90, Tokyo)	55
26-12-90	Hiro Saito & Super Strong Machine[2] (King Of Kings, Hamamatsu)	70
06-03-91	Hiroshi Hase[2] & Kensuke Sasaki[2] (Big Fight Series '91, Nagasaki)	15
21-03-91	Rick Steiner & Scott Steiner (Starrcade '91 In Tokyo Dome, Tokyo)	229
05-11-91	Hiroshi Hase[3] & Keiji Mutoh[3] (Tokyo 3Days Battle, Tokyo)	117
01-03-92	Big Van Vader & Bam Bam Bigelow (Big Fight Series '92, Yokohama)	117
26-06-92	Rick Steiner[2] & Scott Steiner[2] (Masters Of Wrestling, Tokyo)	149
22-11-92	Scott Norton & Tony Halme (Wrestling Scramble '92, Tokyo)	22
14-12-92	Hawk Warrior & Power Warrior[3] (Battle Final '92, Tokyo)	234
05-08-93	Hercules Hernandez & Scott Norton[2] (G1 Climax '93, Tokyo)	152
04-01-94	Hawk Warrior[2] & Power Warrior[4] (Battlefield, Tokyo)	325
25-11-94	Hiroshi Hase[4] & Keiji Mutoh[4] (Battle Final '94, Iwate)	162
06-05-95	VACANT	
10-06-95	Hiroyoshi Tenzan & Masahiro Chono[2] (Fighting Spirit Legend, Osaka)	27
07-07-95	VACANT	
13-07-95	Junji Hirata[3] & Shinya Hashimoto[2] (Best Of The Super Juniors II, Sapporo)	335
12-06-96	Kazuo Yamazaki[2] & Takashi Iizuka[2] (Best Of The Super Juniors III, Osaka)	34
16-07-96	Hiroyoshi Tenzan[2] & Masahiro Chono[3] (Summer Struggle '96, Sapporo)	172
04-01-97	Kengo Kimura[4] & Tatsumi Fujinami[4] (Wrestling World '97, Tokyo)	98
12-04-97	Kensuke Sasaki[5] & Riki Choshu[3] (Battle Formation '97, Tokyo)	21
03-05-97	Manabu Nakanishi & Satoshi Kojima (Strong Style Evolution, Osaka)	99
10-08-97	Kazuo Yamazaki[3] & Kensuke Sasaki[6] (Four Heaven in Nagoya Dome, Nagoya)	70
19-10-97	Keiji Mutoh[5] & Masahiro Chono[4] (nWo Typhoon '97, Kobe)	184
21-04-98	VACANT	
05-06-98	Hiroyoshi Tenzan[3] & Masahiro Chono[5] (Best Of The Super Juniors V, Tokyo)	40
15-07-98	Genichiro Tenryu & Shiro Koshinaka[2] (Summer Struggle '98, Sapporo)	173
04-01-99	Hiroyoshi Tenzan[4] & Satoshi Kojima[2] (Wrestling World '99, Tokyo)	77
22-03-99	Kensuke Sasaki[7] & Shiro Koshinaka[3] (Hyper Battle '99, Amagasaki)	97
27-06-99	Michiyoshi Ohara & Tatsuhito Goto (Summer Struggle '99, Shizuoka)	62
28-08-99	Manabu Nakanishi[2] & Yuji Nagata (Jingu Climax, Shizuoka)	327
20-07-00	Hiroyoshi Tenzan[5] & Satoshi Kojima[3] (Summer Struggle '00, Tokyo)	430
23-09-01	Osamu Nishimura & Tatsumi Fujinami[5] (G1 World '01, Osaka)	35
28-10-01	Keiji Mutoh[6] & Taiyo Kea (Survival '01, Fukuoka)	97
02-02-02	VACANT	
24-03-02	Hiroyoshi Tenzan[6] & Masahiro Chono[6] (Hyper Battle '02, Hyogo)	446
13-06-03	Hiroshi Tanahashi & Yutaka Yoshie (Crush, Tokyo)	184
14-12-03	Hiroyoshi Tenzan[7] & Osamu Nishimura (Battle Final '03, Nagoya)	49
01-02-04	Minoru Suzuki & Yoshihiro Takayama (Fighting Spirit '04, Sapporo)	294
21-11-04	VACANT	
11-12-04	Hiroshi Tanahashi[2] & Shinsuke Nakamura (Battle Final '04, Osaka)	323
30-10-05	Hiroyoshi Tenzan[8] & Masahiro Chono[7] (Toukon Series '05, Kobe)	325
28-09-06	Manabu Nakanishi[3] & Takao Omori (Circuit 2006 Final: Next Progress, Sapporo)	164
11-03-07	Giant Bernard & Travis Tomko	343

	(35th Anniversary Tour Circuit, Nagoya)	
17-02-08	**Togi Makabe & Toru Yano**	322
	(Circuit 2008 New Japan Ism, Tokyo)	
04-01-09	**Brother Devon & Brother Ray**	198
	(Wrestle Kingdom 3, Tokyo)	
21-07-09	**Brutus Magnus & Doug Williams**	89
	(TNA Impact Wrestling, Orlando)	
18-10-09	**Brother Devon[2] & Brother Ray[2]**	78
	(TNA Bound For Glory '09, Irvine)	
04-01-10	**Tetsuya Naito & Yujiro Takahashi**	119
	(Wrestle Kingdom 4, Tokyo)	
03-05-10	**Wataru Inoue & Yuji Nagata[2]**	47
	(Wrestling Dontaku '10, Fukuoka)	
19-06-10	**Giant Bernard[2] & Karl Anderson**	564
	(Dominion '10, Osaka)	
04-01-12	**Hiroyoshi Tenzan[9]**	120
	& Satoshi Kojima[4]	
	(Wrestle Kingdom 6, Tokyo)	
03-05-12	**Takashi Iizuka[3] & Toru Yano[2]**	48
	(Wrestling Dontaku '12, Fukuoka)	
20-06-12	**VACANT**	
22-07-12	**Hiroyoshi Tenzan[10]**	78
	& Satoshi Kojima[5]	
	(Kizuna Road, Yamagata)	
08-10-12	**Davey Boy Smith Jr.**	207
	& Lance Archer	
	(King Of Pro-Wrestling '12, Tokyo)	
03-05-13	**Hiroyoshi Tenzan[11]**	190
	& Satoshi Kojima[6]	
	(Wrestling Dontaku '13, Fukuoka)	
09-11-13	**Davey Boy Smith Jr.[2]**	56
	& Lance Archer[2]	
	(Power Struggle '13, Osaka)	
04-01-14	**Luke Gallows & Karl Anderson[2]**	365
	(Wrestle Kingdom 8, Tokyo)	
04-01-15	**Hirooki Goto & Katsuyori Shibata**	38
	(Wrestle Kingdom 9, Tokyo)	
11-02-15	**Luke Gallows[2] & Karl Anderson[3]**	53
	(The New Beginning In Osaka '15, Osaka)	
05-04-15	**Matt Taven & Mike Bennett**	91
	(Invasion Attack '15, Tokyo)	
05-07-15	**Luke Gallows[3] & Karl Anderson[4]**	183
	(Dominion '15, Osaka)	
04-01-16	**Togi Makabe[2] & Tomoaki Honma**	97
	(Wrestle Kingdom 10, Tokyo)	
10-04-16	**Tama Tonga & Tanga Loa**	70
	(Invasion Attack '16, Tokyo)	
19-06-16	**Jay Briscoe & Mark Briscoe**	113
	(Dominion '16, Osaka)	
10-10-16	**Tama Tonga[2] & Tanga Loa[2]**	86
	(King Of Pro-Wrestling '16, Tokyo)	
04-01-17	**Tomohiro Ishii & Toru Yano[3]**	61
	(Wrestle Kingdom 11, Tokyo)	
06-03-17	**Hiroyoshi Tenzan[12]**	34
	& Satoshi Kojima[7]	
	(Hataage Kinebi, Tokyo)	
09-04-17	**Hanson & Raymond Rowe**	63
	(Sakura Genesis '17, Tokyo)	
11-06-17	**Tama Tonga[3] & Tanga Loa[3]**	20
	(Dominion '17, Osaka)	
01-07-17	**Hanson[2] & Raymond Rowe[2]**	85
	(G1 Special in USA, Long Beach)	
24-09-17	**Davey Boy Smith Jr.[3]**	102
	& Lance Archer[3]	
	(Destruction In Kobe '17, Kobe)	
04-01-18	**Evil & Sanada**	156
	(Wrestle Kingdom 12, Tokyo)	
09-06-18	**Matt Jackson & Nick Jackson**	113
	(Dominion '18, Osaka)	
30-09-18	**Tama Tonga[4] & Tanga Loa[4]**	96
	(Fighting Spirit Unleashed, Long Beach)	

04-01-19	**Evil[2] & Sanada[2]**	50
	(Wrestle Kingdom 13, Tokyo)	
23-02-19	**Tama Tonga[5] & Tanga Loa[5]**	31
	(Honor Rising: Japan '19, Tokyo)	
04-01-20	**David Finlay & Juice Robinson**	28
	(Wrestle Kingdom 14, Tokyo)	
01-02-20	**Tama Tonga[6] & Tanga Loa[6]**	20
	(The New Beginning USA, Atlanta)	
21-02-20	**Hiroshi Tanahashi[3] & Kota Ibushi**	142
	(New Japan Road, Tokyo)	
12-07-20	**Taichi & Zack Sabre Jr.**	176
	(Dominion '20, Osaka)	
04-01-21	**Tama Tonga[7] & Tanga Loa[7]**	148
	(Wrestle Kingdom 15, Tokyo)	
01-06-21	**Taichi[2] & Zack Sabre Jr.[2]**	40
	(Road To Dominion, Tokyo)	
11-07-21	**Tetsuya Naito[2] & Sanada[3]**	14
	(Summer Struggle In Sapporo, Tokyo)	
25-07-21	**Taichi[3] & Zack Sabre Jr.[3]**	163
	(Wrestle Grand Slam In Tokyo Dome, Tokyo)	
04-01-22	**Hirooki Goto[2] & Yoshi-Hashi**	95
	(Wrestle Kingdom 16, Tokyo)	
09-04-22	**Great-O-Khan & Jeff Cobb**	22
	(Hyper Battle '22, Tokyo)	
01-05-22	**Bad Luck Fale & Chase Owens**	42
	(Wrestle Dontaku '22, Fukuoka)	
12-06-22	**Great-O-Khan[2] & Jeff Cobb[2]**	14
	(Dominion '22, Osaka)	
26-06-22	**Cash Wheeler & Dax Harwood**	188
	(AEW x NJPW Forbidden Door, Chicago)	

Most Reigns

1.	Hiroyoshi Tenzan	12
2.	Masahiro Chono	7
3.	Satoshi Kojima	7
4.	Kensuke Sasaki	7
5.	Tama Tonga	7
6.	Tanga Loa	7

Longest Reigns

1.	Giant Bernard	564
	& Karl Anderson	
2.	Hiroyoshi Tenzan	446
	& Masa Chono	
3.	Hiroyoshi Tenzan	430
	& Satoshi Kojima	
4.	Luke Gallows	365
	& Karl Anderson	
5.	Giant Bernard	343
	& Tyson Tomko	

Longest Cumulative Reigns

1.	Hiroyoshi Tenzan	1,988
2.	Masahiro Chono	1,383
3.	Karl Anderson	1,165
4.	Satoshi Kojima	1,028
5.	Giant Bernard	907

IWGP JUNIOR HEAVYWEIGHT TAG TEAM CHAMPIONSHIP

DATE	WON BY	DAYS
08-09-98	**Shinjiro Otani &**	149
	Tatsuhito Takaiwa	
	(Rising The Next Generations, Osaka)	
04-01-99	**Dr. Wagner Jr. & Kendo Kashin**	96
	(Wrestling World '99, Tokyo)	
10-04-99	**The Great Sasuke & Jushin Liger**	94

(Strong Style Symphony, Tokyo)

13-07-99 **Shinjiro Otani^2 &** 348
Tatsuhito Takaiwa^2
(Summer Struggle '99, Morioka)

25-06-00 **Koji Kanemoto & Minoru Tanaka** 254
(Summer Struggle '00, Tokyo)

06-03-01 **El Samurai & Jushin Liger^2** 136
(Hyper Battle '01, Tokyo)

20-07-01 **Gedo & Jado** 286
(Dome Quake, Sapporo)

02-05-02 **Jushin Liger^3 & Minoru Tanaka^2** 119
(Toukon Memorial Day, Tokyo)

29-08-02 **Tsuyoshi Kikuchi &** 150
Yoshinobu Kanemaru
(Cross Road, Tokyo)

26-01-03 **Jushin Liger^4 & Koji Kanemoto^2** 282
(The First Navigation '03, Kobe)

04-11-03 **VACANT**

29-11-03 **Gedo^2 & Jado^2** 104
(Battle Final '03, Miyagi)

12-03-04 **American Dragon & Curry Man** 85
(Hyper Battle '04, Tokyo)

05-06-04 **Gedo^3 & Jado^3** 272
(Best Of The Super Juniors XI, Osaka)

04-03-05 **Koji Kanemoto^3 & Wataru Inoue** 71
(Big Fight Series '05, Tokyo)

14-05-05 **Hirooki Goto & Minoru^3** 281
(Nexess VI, Tokyo)

19-02-06 **El Samurai^2 & Ryusuke Taguchi** 139
(Circuit2006 Acceleration, Tokyo)

08-07-06 **Gedo^4 & Jado^4** 298
(Circuit2006 Turbulance, Shizuoka)

02-05-07 **Dick Togo & Taka Michinoku** 270
(35th Anniversary Show, Tokyo)

27-01-08 **Minoru^4 & Prince Devitt** 21
(Circuit2008 New Japan Ism, Tokyo)

17-02-08 **Akira & Jushin Liger^5** 155
(Circuit2008 New Japan Ism, Tokyo)

21-07-08 **Minoru^5 & Prince Devitt^2** 84
(Circuit2008: New Japan Soul, Sapporo)

13-10-08 **Tetsuya Naito & Yujiro** 83
(Destruction '08, Tokyo)

04-01-09 **Alex Shelley & Chris Sabin** 182
(Wrestle Kingdom 3, Tokyo)

05-07-09 **Prince Devitt^3 & Ryusuke Taguchi^2** 290
(Circuit2009 New Japan Soul, Tokyo)

21-04-10 **VACANT**

08-05-10 **El Samurai^3 & Koji Kanemoto^4** 72
(Super J Tag Tournament 1st, Tokyo)

19-07-10 **Prince Devitt^4 & Ryusuke Taguchi^3** 84
(Circuit2010 New Japan Soul, Sapporo)

11-10-10 **Kenny Omega & Kota Ibushi** 104
(Destruction '10, Tokyo)

23-01-11 **Prince Devitt^5 & Ryusuke Taguchi^4** 260
(Fantastica Mania '11, Tokyo)

10-10-11 **Davey Richards & Rocky Romero** 86
(Destruction '11, Tokyo)

04-01-12 **Prince Devitt^6 & Ryusuke Taguchi^5** 39
(Wrestle Kingdom 6, Tokyo)

12-02-12 **Davey Richards^2 & Rocky Romero^2** 80
(The New Beginning '12, Osaka)

02-05-12 **VACANT**

16-06-12 **Jushin Liger^6 & Tiger Mask** 36
(Dominion '12, Osaka)

22-07-12 **Alex Koslov & Rocky Romero^3** 112
(Kizuna Road, Yamagata)

11-11-12 **Alex Shelley^2 & Kushida** 173
(Power Struggle '12, Tokyo)

03-05-13 **Alex Koslov^2 & Rocky Romero^4** 164
(Wrestling Dontaku '13, Fukuoka)

14-10-13 **Taichi & Taka Michinoku^2** 26

(King Of Pro-Wrestling '13, Tokyo)

09-11-13 **Matt Jackson & Nick Jackson** 224
(Power Struggle '13, Osaka)

21-06-14 **Alex Shelley^3 & Kushida^2** 140
(Dominion '14, Osaka)

08-11-14 **Bobby Fish & Kyle O'Reilly** 95
(Power Struggle '14, Osaka)

11-02-15 **Matt Jackson^2 & Nick Jackson^2** 53
(The New Beginning In Osaka '15, Osaka)

05-04-15 **Trent Beretta & Rocky Romero^5** 28
(Invasion Attack '15, Tokyo)

03-05-15 **Matt Jackson^3 & Nick Jackson^3** 105
(Wrestling Dontaku '15, Fukuoka)

16-08-15 **Bobby Fish^2 & Kyle O'Reilly^2** 141
(G1 Climax 25, Tokyo)

04-01-16 **Matt Jackson^4 & Nick Jackson^4** 38
(Wrestle Kingdom 10, Tokyo)

11-02-16 **Matt Sydal & Ricochet** 59
(The New Beginning In Osaka '16, Osaka)

10-04-16 **Trent Beretta^2 & Rocky Romero^6** 23
(Invasion Attack '16, Tokyo)

03-05-16 **Matt Sydal^2 & Ricochet^2** 47
(Wrestling Dontaku '16, Fukuoka)

19-06-16 **Matt Jackson^5 & Nick Jackson^5** 199
(Dominion '16, Osaka)

04-01-17 **Trent Beretta^3 & Rocky Romero^7** 61
(Wrestle Kingdom 11, Tokyo)

06-03-17 **Taichi^2 & Yoshinobu Kanemaru^2** 52
(Hataage Kinenbi, Tokyo)

27-04-17 **Trent Beretta^4 & Rocky Romero^8** 45
(Road To Wrestling Dontaku '17, Hiroshima)

11-06-17 **Matt Jackson^6 & Nick Jackson^6** 63
(Dominion '17, Osaka)

13-08-17 **Ricochet^3 & Ryusuke Taguchi^6** 57
(G1 Climax 27, Tokyo)

09-10-17 **Sho & Yoh** 87
(King Of Pro-Wrestling '17, Tokyo)

04-01-18 **Matt Jackson^7 & Nick Jackson^7** 24
(Wrestle Kingdom 12, Tokyo)

28-01-18 **Sho^2 & Yoh^2** 37
(New Beginning in Sapporo '18, Sapporo)

06-03-18 **El Desperado &** 304
Yoshinobu Kanemaru^3
(46th Anniversary Show, Tokyo)

04-01-19 **Bushi & Shingo Takagi** 61
(Wrestle Kingdom 13, Tokyo)

06-03-19 **Sho^3 & Yoh^3** 102
(47th Anniversary Show, Tokyo)

16-06-19 **El Phantasmo & Taiji Ishimori** 203
(Kizuna Road, Tokyo)

04-01-20 **Sho^4 & Yoh^4** 239
(Wrestle Kingdom 14, Tokyo)

31-08-20 **VACANT**

11-09-20 **El Desperado^2 &** 134
Yoshinobu Kanemaru^4
(New Japan Road, Tokyo)

23-01-21 **El Phantasmo^2 & Taiji Ishimori^2** 33
(Road To The New Beginning, Tokyo)

25-02-21 **El Desperado^3 &** 38
Yoshinobu Kanemaru^5
(Road To Castle Attack, Tokyo)

04-04-21 **Sho^5 & Yoh^5** 80
(Sakura Genesis '21, Tokyo)

23-06-21 **El Phantasmo^3 & Taiji Ishimori^3** 74
(Kizuna Road '21, Tokyo)

05-09-21 **El Desperado^4 &** 51
Yoshinobu Kanemaru^6
(Wrestle Grand Slam, Tokorozawa)

26-10-21 **Robbie Eagles & Tiger Mask^2** 116
(Road To Power Struggle, Tokyo)

19-02-22 **Ryusuke Taguchi^7 & Master Wato** 121

	(New Years Golden Series, Sapporo)	
20-06-22	**TJP & Francesco Akira**	194*
	(New Japan Road '22, Tokyo)	

Most Reigns

1.	Rocky Romero	8
2.	Matt Jackson	7
3.	Nick Jackson	7
4.	Ryusuke Taguchi	7
5.	Jushin Liger	6
6.	Prince Devitt	6
7.	Yoshinobu Kanemaru	6

Longest Reigns

1.	Shinjiro Otani &	348
	Tatsuhito Takaiwa	
2.	El Desperado &	304
	Yoshinobu Kanemaru	
3.	Gedo & Jado	298
4.	Prince Devitt &	290
	Ryusuke Taguchi	
5.	Gedo & Jado	286

Longest Cumulative Reigns

1.	Ryusuke Taguchi	990
2.	Gedo	960
3.	Jado	960
4.	Jushin Liger	822
5.	Prince Devitt	778

IWGP WOMEN'S CHAMPIONSHIP

DATE	WON BY	DAYS
20-11-22	**Kairi**	41*
	(Historic X-Over, Tokyo)	

NEVER OPENWEIGHT CHAMPIONSHIP

DATE	WON BY	DAYS
19-12-12	**Masato Tanaka**	314
	(NEVER Tournament, Tokyo)	
29-09-13	**Tetsuya Naito**	135
	(Destruction '13, Kobe)	
11-02-14	**Tomohiro Ishii**	138
	(The New Beginning In Osaka '14, Osaka)	
29-06-14	**Yujiro Takahashi**	106
	(Kizuna Road '14, Tokyo)	
13-10-14	**Tomohiro Ishii**[2]	83
	(King Of Pro-Wrestling '14, Tokyo)	
04-01-15	**Togi Makabe**	41
	(Wrestle Kingdom 9, Tokyo)	
14-02-15	**VACANT**	
14-02-15	**Tomohiro Ishii**[3]	74
	(The New Beginning In Sendai '15, Sendai)	
29-04-15	**Togi Makabe**[2]	166
	(Wrestling Hinokuni '15, Mashiki)	
12-10-15	**Tomohiro Ishii**[4]	84
	(King Of Pro-Wrestling '15, Tokyo)	
04-01-16	**Katsuyori Shibata**	120
	(Wrestle Kingdom 10, Tokyo)	
03-05-16	**Yuji Nagata**	47
	(Wrestling Dontaku '16, Fukuoka)	
19-06-16	**Katsuyori Shibata**[2]	139

	(Dominion '16, Osaka)	
05-11-16	**Evil**	10
	(Power Struggle '16, Osaka)	
15-11-16	**Katsuyori Shibata**[3]	50
	(Wrestling World '16, Singapore)	
04-01-17	**Hirooki Goto**	113
	(Wrestle Kingdom 11, Tokyo)	
27-04-17	**Minoru Suzuki**	252
	(Road To Wrestling Dontaku '17, Hiroshima)	
04-01-18	**Hirooki Goto**[2]	156
	(Wrestle Kingdom 12, Tokyo)	
09-06-18	**Michael Elgin**	8
	(Dominion '18, Osaka)	
17-06-18	**Hirooki Goto**[3]	92
	(Kizuna Road '18, Tokyo)	
17-09-18	**Taichi**	47
	(Destruction In Beppu '18, Beppu)	
03-11-18	**Hirooki Goto**[4]	36
	(Power Struggle '18, Osaka)	
09-12-18	**Kota Ibushi**	26
	(World Tag League '18, Iwate)	
04-01-19	**Will Ospreay**	92
	(Wrestle Kingdom 13, Tokyo)	
06-04-19	**Jeff Cobb**	27
	(G1 Supercard, New York)	
03-05-19	**Taichi**[2]	37
	(Wrestling Dontaku '19, Fukuoka)	
09-06-19	**Tomohiro Ishii**[5]	83
	(Dominion '19, Osaka)	
31-08-19	**Kenta**	127
	(Royal Quest, London, England)	
04-01-20	**Hirooki Goto**[5]	27
	(Wrestle Kingdom 14, Tokyo)	
01-02-20	**Shingo Takagi**	210
	(New Beginning In Sapporo '20, Sapporo)	
29-08-20	**Minoru Suzuki**[2]	70
	(Summer Struggle In Jingu, Tokyo)	
07-11-20	**Shingo Takagi**[2]	84
	(Power Struggle '20, Osaka)	
30-01-21	**Hiroshi Tanahashi**	93
	(The New Beginning in Nagoya '21, Nagoya)	
03-05-21	**Jay White**	194
	(Wrestling Dontaku '21, Fukuoka)	
13-11-21	**Tomohiro Ishii**[6]	52
	(Battle In The Valley, San Jose)	
04-01-22	**Evil**[2]	117
	(Wrestle Kingdom 16)	
01-05-22	**Tama Tonga**	42
	(Wrestling Dontaku '22, Fukuoka)	
12-06-22	**Karl Anderson**	202*
	(Wrestle Kingdom 17)	

Most Reigns

1.	Tomohiro Ishii	6
2.	Hirooki Goto	5
3.	Katsuyori Shibata	3

Longest Reigns

1.	Masato Tanaka	314
2.	Minoru Suzuki	252
3.	Shingo Takagi	210
4.	Karl Anderson	202*
5.	Jay White	194

Longest Cumulative Reigns

1.	Tomohiro Ishii	514
2.	Hirooki Goto	424
3.	Minoru Suzuki	322
4.	Masato Tanaka	314

5.   Katsuyori Shibata   309

NEVER OPENWEIGHT 6-MAN TAG TEAM CHAMPIONSHIP

DATE	WON BY	DAYS
04-01-16	Jay Briscoe, Mark Briscoe & Toru Yano (Wrestle Kingdom 10, Tokyo)	38
11-02-16	Bad Luck Fale, Tama Tonga & Yujiro Takahashi (The New Beginning In Osaka, Osaka)	3
14-02-16	Jay Briscoe[2], Mark Briscoe[2] & Toru Yano[2] (The New Beginning In Niigata, Nagaoka)	6
20-02-16	Kenny Omega, Matt Jackson & Nick Jackson (Honor Rising '16: Japan, Tokyo)	50
10-04-16	Hiroshi Tanahashi, Michael Elgin & Yoshitatsu (Invasion Attack '16, Tokyo)	23
03-05-16	Kenny Omega[2], Matt Jackson[2] & Nick Jackson[2] (Wrestling Dontaku '16, Fukuoka)	61
03-07-16	Matt Sydal, Ricochet & Satoshi Kojima (Kizuna Road '16, Takizawa)	84
25-09-16	VACANT	
25-09-16	David Finlay, Ricochet[2] & Satoshi Kojima[2] (Destruction In Kobe '16, Kobe)	101
04-01-17	Bushi, Evil & Sanada (Wrestle Kingdom 11, Tokyo)	1
05-01-17	Hiroshi Tanahashi[2], Manabu Nakanishi & Ryusuke Taguchi (New Year Dash!! '17, Tokyo)	37
11-02-17	Bushi[2], Evil[2] & Sanada[2] (New Beginning in Osaka '17, Osaka)	52
04-04-17	Hiroshi Tanahashi[3], Ricochet[3] & Ryusuke Taguchi[2] (Road to Sakura Genesis '17, Tokyo)	29
03-05-17	Bushi[3], Evil[3] & Sanada[3] (Wrestling Dontaku '17, Fukuoka)	228
17-12-17	Bad Luck Fale[2], Tama Tonga[2] & Tanga Loa (Road To Tokyo Dome, Tokyo)	18
04-01-18	Trent Beretta, Tomohiro Ishii & Toru Yano[3] (Wrestle Kingdom 12, Tokyo)	1
05-01-18	Bad Luck Fale[3], Tama Tonga[3] & Tanga Loa[2] (New Year Dash! '18, Tokyo)	118
03-05-18	Marty Scurll, Matt Jackson[3] & Nick Jackson[3] (Wrestling Dontaku '18, Fukuoka)	101
12-08-18	Tama Tonga[4], Tanga Loa[3] & Taiji Ishimori (G1 Climax 28, Tokyo)	171
30-01-19	Ryusuke Taguchi[3], Toki Makabe & Toru Yano[4] (Road To The New Beginning, Miyagi)	340
04-01-20	Bushi[4], Evil[4] & Shingo Takagi (Wrestle Kingdom 14, Tokyo)	208
31-07-20	VACANT	
09-08-20	Hirooki Goto, Tomohiro Ishii[2] & Yoshi-Hashi (Summer Struggle '20, Tokyo)	454
06-11-21	Evil[5], Sho & Yujiro Takahashi[2]	241

(Power Struggle '21, Tokyo)

05-07-22	Hirooki Goto[2], Yoh & Yoshi-Hashi[2] (New Japan Road, Tokyo)	80
23-09-22	Evil[6], Sho[2] & Yujiro Takahashi[2] (New Japan Burning Spirit, Tokyo)	99*

STRONG OPENWEIGHT CHAMPIONSHIP

DATE	WON BY	DAYS
23-04-21	Tom Lawlor (New Japan Cup USA, Port Hueneme)	428
25-06-22	Fred Rosser (New Japan Strong, Philadelphia)	189*

STRONG OPENWEIGHT TAG TEAM CHAMPIONSHIP

DATE	WON BY	DAYS
13-08-22	Kyle Fletcher & Mark Davis (New Japan Strong, Charlotte)	76
28-10-22	Alex Shelley & Chris Sabin (Rumble On 44th Street, New York)	64*

TOURNAMENT
RECORDS

AAA REY DE REYES

YEAR	WON BY
1997	**Latin Lover**
	(Runners Up: Heavy Metal, Hector Garza, Octagon)
1998	**Octagon**
	(Runners Up: Latin Lover, Perro Aguayo, Cibemetico)
1999	**Cibernetico**
	(Runners Up: Octagon, Latin Lover, Electroshock)
2000	**Abismo Negro**
	(Runners Up: El Alebrije, Charly Manson, Cibemetico)
2001	**La Parka Jr.**
	(Runners Up: Latin Lover, Abismo Negro, Heavy Metal)
2002	**El Canek**
	(Runners Up: Pirata Morgan, Cibernetico, Octagon)
2003	**La Parka Jr.[2]**
	(Runners Up: Abismo Negro)
2004	**Jeff Jarrett**
	(Runners Up: Latin Lover)
2005	**La Parka[3]**
	(Runners Up: Latin Lover, Abismo Negro, Chessman, Jeff Jarrett, Konnan, Cibernetico)
2006	**Vampiro**
	(Runners Up: La Sectra Cibernetico, Team TNA, Los Guapos VIP)
2007	**La Parka[4]**
	(Runners Up: Octagon, Abismo Negro, Rhino, Fuerza Guerrera, Latin Lover)
2008	**El Zorro**
	(Runners Up: Abismo Negro, Mr. Niebla, Alan Stone)
2009	**Electroshock**
	(Runners Up: La Parka, Silver King, Latin Lover)
2010	**Chessman**
	(Runners Up: Hernandez, Marco Corleone)
2011	**Extreme Tiger**
	(Runners Up: Carlito, L.A. Park, El Mesias)
2012	**El Hijo del Perro Aguayo**
	(Runners Up: Hector Garza, Jack Evans, L.A. Park)
2013	**El Mesias**
	(Runners Up: Canek, L.A. Park)
2014	**La Parka[5]**
	(Runners Up: Black Warrior, El Zorro, El Hijo del Perro Aguayo)
2015	**El Texano Jr.**
	(Runners Up: Aero Star, Psycho Clown, El Mesias)
2016	**Pentagon Jr.**
	(Runners Up: La Parka, Villano IV)
2017	**Argenis**
	(Runners Up: Averno, Bengala, Chessman, El Elegido, Joe Liger, Nino Hamburguesa, La Parka, Pimpinela Escarlata)
2018	**Rey Escorpion**
	(Runners Up: Bengala, El Hijo del Vikingo, La Parka)
2019	**Aero Star**
	(Runners Up: Laredo Kid, El Hijo del Vikingo, Jack Evans, Sammy Guevara, Australian Suicide, Taurus, Golden Magic, Myzteziz Jr.)
2021	**Laredo Kid**
	(Runners Up: Texano Jr., Murder Clown, Abismo Negro Jr., Vikingo, Myzteziz Jr., Aerostar)
2022	**Psycho Clown**
	(Runners Up: Cibernetico, Laredo Kid, Bandido, Heavy Metal)

1997

SF	Latin Lover def. Jerry Estrada, The Killer and Máscara Sagrada Jr.
SF	Heavy Metal def. Blue Demon Jr., Maniaco and May Flowers
SF	Héctor Garza def. Abismo Negro, La Parka Jr. and Perro Aguayo Jr.
SF	Octagón def. Fuerza Guerrera, El Pantera and Pentagón
F	Latin Lover def. Heavy Metal, Héctor Garza and Octagón

1998

SF	Perro Aguayo def. El Cobarde #2, Electroshock and La Parka Jr.
SF	Latin Lover def. Black Demon, Blue Demon Jr. and The Killer
SF	Cibernético def. Máscara Sagrada, Perro Aguayo Jr. and Shiiba
SF	Octagón def. Fuerza Guerrera, Hong Kong Lee and Máscara Sagrada Jr.
F	Octagón def. Cibernético, Latin Lover and Perro Aguayo

1999

SF	Octagón def. El Alebrije, Espectro Jr. and El Hijo del Solitario
SF	Cibernético def. Abismo Negro, Dos Caras and Máscara Sagrada
SF	Latin Lover def. Gran Apache, Óscar Sevilla and The Panther
SF	Electroshock def. Blue Demon Jr., El Canek and Pentagón
F	Cibernético def. Electroshock, Latin Lover and Octagón

2000

SF	Abismo Negro def. Dos Caras, The Killer and Psicosis
SF	El Alebrije def. Electroshock, Maniaco and Óscar Sevilla
SF	Charly Manson def. Histeria, Máscara Sagrada Jr. and Path Finder
SF	Cibernético def. Blue Demon Jr., Espectro Jr. and El Mexicano
F	Abismo Negro def. El Alebrije, Charly Manson and Cibernético

2001

SF	Latin Lover def. Cibernético, El Cobarde #2 and El Hijo del Solitario
SF	Abismo Negro def. Héctor Garza, Óscar Sevilla and El Texano
SF	La Parka Jr. def. Electroshock, Perro Aguayo Jr. and Pirata Morgan
SF	Heavy Metal def. Blue Demon Jr., Espectro Jr. and Pimpinela Escarlata
F	La Parka Jr. def. Abismo Negro, Heavy Metal and Latin Lover

2002

SF	Octagón def. Máscara Maligna, Máscara Sagrada and Pentagon
SF	Cibernético def. Dos Caras, El Oriental and El Texano
SF	Pirata Morgan def. Gronda, Loco Zandokan #2 and Pimpinela Escarlata

SF	El Canek def. El Hijo del Solitario, El Picudo and Septiembre Negro Jr.
F	El Canek def. Cibernético, Octagón and Pirata Morgan

2003

SF	Abismo Negro and La Parka Jr. def. El Canek, Cibernético, Latin Lover and Octagón
F	La Parka Jr. def. Abismo Negro

2004

F	Jeff Jarrett def. Latin Lover

2005

F	La Parka Jr. def. Abismo Negro, Chessman, Jeff Jarrett, Konnan and Latin Lover

2006

F	Vampiro survived a Team Elimination Match to win the Tournament. It was Team AAA (La Parka, Octagón and Vampiro) vs. La Secta Cibernetica (Chessman, Cibernético and Muerte Cibernetica) vs. Team TNA (Konnan, Ron Killings and Samoa Joe) vs.Los Guapos (Scorpio Jr., Shocker and Zumbido)

2007

F	La Parka Jr. def. Abismo Negro, Fuerza Guerrera, Latin Lover, Octagón and Rhyno

2008

R1	Decnis and Scorpio Jr. def. Charly Manson and Chessman, Extreme Tiger and Halloween and Laredo Kid and Octagón
R1	Pirata Morgan, Pirata Morgan Jr. and El Hijo del Piratá Morgan def. Argenis, Chiva Rayada #1 and El Gato Eveready
R1	Aero Star, El Ángel, Pegasso and Rey Cometa def. Jesse, Nygma, Polvo de Estrellas and Yuriko
R1	Histeria, Mr. Niebla and Psicosis def. Alan Stone, Chris Stone and Súper Caló
R1	Abismo Negro, Electroshock and Head Hunter A def. Joe Líder, Juventud Guerrera and Último Gladiador
R1	El Alebrije, Laredo Kid and Máscara Divina def. Extreme Tiger, Halloween and TJ Extreme
R1	Electroshock, Kenzo Suzuki and El Zorro def. Charly Manson, Chessman and El Intocable
R1	Alan Stone, Brazo de Plata, El Elegido and Zumbido def. Electroshock, Escoria, El Intocable and Kenzo Suzuki
R1	Abismo Negro and Psicosis def. El Alebrije and Gronda #2 and Nygma and Polvo de Estrellas
R1	Billy Boy and Súper Fly def. Antifaz del Norte and Histeria and Chris Stone and Súper Caló
SF	Mr. Niebla def. El Elegido, Máscara Divina and Zumbido
SF	Alan Stone def. Decnis, Head Hunter A and Pirata Morgan
SF	Abismo Negro def. Aero Star, Brazo de Plata and Psicosis
SF	El Zorro def. Billy Boy, Scorpio Jr. and Súper Fly
F	El Zorro def. Abismo Negro, Alan Stone and Mr. Niebla

2009

SF	Latin Lover def. Abismo Negro, Black Abyss and Ozz
SF	Silver King def. Alan Stone, El Elegido and Joe Líder

SF	Electroshock def. Nicho el Millonario, Octagón and Súper Fly
SF	La Parka Jr. def. Brazo de Plata, Escoria and Kenzo Suzuki
F	Electroshock def. Latin Lover, La Parka Jr. and Silver King

2010

SF	Chessman def. Octagón, La Parka Jr. and El Zorro
SF	Hernandez def. Crazy Boy, El Elegido and Kenzo Suzuki
SF	Marco Corleone def. Decnis, Jack Evans and Ozz
F	Chessman def. Hernandez and Marco Corleone

2011

F	Extreme Tiger def. Carlito Caribbean Cool, L.A. Park and El Mesías

2012

SF	Héctor Garza def. Heavy Metal, Joe Líder and Toscano
SF	Perro Aguayo Jr. def. Cibernético, Juventud Guerrera and Máscara Año Dos Mil Jr.
SF	Jack Evans def. Chessman, Nicho el Millonario and El Texano Jr.
SF	L.A. Park def. Electroshock, La Parka Jr. and Silver Caín
F	Perro Aguayo Jr. def. Héctor Garza, Jack Evans and L.A. Park

2013

SF	El Mesías def. Heavy Metal, Octagón, La Parka Jr., La Parka Negra and Pentagón Jr.
SF	L.A. Park def. Chessman, Drago, Jack Evans, Psicosis and Villano IV
SF	El Canek def. Cibernético, Electroshock, Perro Aguayo Jr., Silver Caín and Toscano
F	El Mesías def. El Canek and L.A. Park

2014

SF	El Zorro def. Fénix, El Mesías and Silver Caín
SF	La Parka Jr. def. Blue Demon Jr., Chessman and La Parka Negra
SF	Perro Aguayo Jr. def. Cibernético, Electroshock and El Elegido
SF	Black Warrior def. Psicosis, Psycho Clown and El Texano Jr.
F	La Parka Jr. def. Black Warrior, Perro Aguayo Jr. and El Zorro

2015

SF	Aero Star def. El Hijo del Pirata Morgan, Monster Clown and Súper Fly
SF	El Mesías def. Cibernético, La Parka Jr. and La Parka Negra
SF	Psycho Clown def. Cuervo, Electroshock and El Zorro
SF	El Texano Jr. def. Bengala, Machine Rocker and Murder Clown
F	El Texano Jr. def. Aero Star, El Mesías and Psycho Clown

2016

SF	Blue Demon Jr. def. Dr. Wagner Jr., Garza Jr. and Taurus
SF	Villano IV def. Chessman, Electroshock and Jack Evans
SF	La Parka Jr. def. El Averno, Psycho Clown and El Zorro
SF	Pentagón Jr. def. Fénix, El Hijo del Fantasma

and Octagón Jr.

F Pentagón Jr. def. La Parka Jr. and Villano IV

2017

F Argenis def. El Averno, Bengala, Chessman, El Elegido, Joe Líder, El Niño Hamburguesa, La Parka Jr. and Pimpinela Escarlata

2018

R1 Dinastía, Pimpinela Escarlata and Venum def. Chicano, Black Mamba and Villano III Jr.

R1 Ángel Mortal Jr. and Máscara de Bronce def. Raptor and Tiger Boy

R1 Dave the Clown and La Parka Jr. def. Monster Clown and Murder Clown

R1 Angelikal and Bengala defeated Histeria and Psicosis

R1 Cuervo, Escoria and El Hijo del Vikingo def. El Averno, Chessman and Súper Fly

SF Rey Escorpión def. Angelikal, Dave the Clown and Pimpinela Escarlata

SF Bengala def. Argenis, Escoria and Máscara de Bronce

SF El Hijo del Vikingo def. Ángel Mortal Jr., Cuervo and Pagano

SF La Parka Jr. def. Dinastía, El Mesías and Venum

F Rey Escorpión def. Bengala, El Hijo del Vikingo and La Parka Jr.

2019

F Aero Star def. Eclipse Vengador Jr., Golden Magic, El Hijo del Vikingo, Jack Evans, Laredo Kid, Myzteziz Jr., Sammy Guevara and Taurus

2021

F Laredo Kid def. Abismo Negro Jr., Aero Star, Drago, El Hijo del Vikingo, Murder Clown, Myzteziz Jr. and El Texano Jr.

2022

F Psycho Clown def. El Bandido, Cibernético, Heavy Metal and Laredo Kid

---

AEW MEN'S OWEN HART CUP

YEAR	WON BY
2022	**Adam Cole**
	(Runner Up: Samoa Joe)

2022

R1	Samoa Joe def. Max Caster
R1	Rey Fenix def. Dante Martin
R1	Kyle O'Reilly def. Jungle Boy
R1	Adam Cole def. Tomohiro Ishii
R1	Dax Harwood def. Cash Wheeler
R1	Darby Allin def. Swerve Strickland
R1	Jeff Hardy def. Bobby Fish
QF	Samoa Joe def. Johnny Elite
QF	Kyle O'Reilly def. Rey Fenix
QF	Adam Cole def. Dax Harwood
QF	Jeff Hardy def. Darby Allin
SF	Samoa Joe def. Kyle O'Reilly
SF	Adam Cole def. Jeff Hardy
F	Adam Cole def. Samoa Joe

AEW WOMEN'S OWEN HART CUP

YEAR	WON BY
2022	**Dr. Britt Baker D.M.D.**
	(Runner Up: Ruby Soho)

2022

R1	Toni Storm def. The Bunny
R1	Jamie Hayter def. Skye Blue
R1	Dr. Britt Baker D.M.D. def. Danielle Kamela
R1	Riho def. Yuka Sakazaki
R1	Ruby Soho def. Robyn Renegade
R1	Red Velvet def. Willow Nightingale
R1	Hikaru Shida def. Julia Hart
QF	Toni Storm def. Jamie Hayter
QF	Dr. Britt Baker D.M.D. def. Maki Itoh
QF	Ruby Soho def. Riho
QF	Kris Statlander def. Red Velvet
SF	Dr. Britt Baker D.M.D. def. Toni Storm
SF	Ruby Soho def. Kris Statlander
F	Dr. Britt Baker D.M.D. def. Ruby Soho

AJPW CHAMPION CARNIVAL

YEAR	WON BY
1973	**Giant Baba**
	(Runner Up: Mark Lewin)
1974	**Giant Baba[2]**
	(Runner Up: Mr. Wrestling)
1975	**Giant Baba[3]**
	(Runner Up: Gene Kiniski)
1976	**Abdullah The Butcher**
	(Runner Up: Giant Baba)
1977	**Giant Baba[4]**
	(Runner Up: Jumbo Tsuruta)
1978	**Giant Baba[5]**
	(Runner Up: Abdullah The Butcher)
1979	**Abdullah The Butcher[2]**
	(Runner Up: Jumbo Tsuruta)
1980	**Jumbo Tsuruta**
	(Runner Up: Dick Slater)
1981	**Giant Baba[6]**
	(Runner Up: Jumbo Tsuruta)
1982	**Giant Baba[7]**
	(Runner Up: Bruiser Brody)
1991	**Jumbo Tsuruta**
	(Runner Up: Stan Hansen)
1992	**Stan Hansen**
	(Runner Up: Mitsuharu Misawa)
1993	**Stan Hansen[2]**
	(Runner Up: Mitsuharu Misawa)
1994	**Toshiaki Kawada**
	(Runner Up: Steve Williams)
1995	**Mitsuharu Misawa**
	(Runner Up: Akira Taue)
1996	**Akira Taue**
	(Runner Up: Steve Williams)
1997	**Toshiaki Kawada[2]**
	(Runner Up: Kenta Kobashi)
1998	**Mitsuharu Misawa[2]**
	(Runner Up: Jun Akiyama)
1999	**Vader**
	(Runner Up: Kenta Kobashi)
2000	**Kenta Kobashi**

(Runner Up: Takao Omori)

Year	Won By
2001	**Genichiro Tenryu** (Runner Up: Taiyo Kea)
2002	**Keiji Mutoh** (Runner Up: Mike Barton)
2003	**Satoshi Kojima** (Runner Up: Arashi)
2004	**Keiji Mutoh²** (Runner Up: Kensuke Sasaki)
2005	**Kensuke Sasaki** (Runner Up: Jamal)
2006	**Taiyo Kea** (Runner Up: Suwama)
2007	**Keiji Mutoh³** (Runner Up: Toshiaki Kawada)
2008	**Suwama** (Runner Up: Hiroshi Tanahashi)
2009	**Minoru Suzuki** (Runner Up: Kaz Hayashi)
2010	**Minoru Suzuki²** (Runner Up: Masakatsu Funaki)
2011	**Yuji Nagata** (Runner Up: Sanada)
2012	**Taiyo Kea²** (Runner Up: Suwama)
2013	**Jun Akiyama** (Runner Up: Kai)
2014	**Takao Omori** (Runner Up: Jun Akiyama)
2015	**Akebono** (Runner Up: Suwama)
2016	**Daisuke Sekimoto** (Runner Up: Zeus)
2017	**Shuji Ishikawa** (Runner Up: Joe Doering)
2018	**Naomichi Marufuji** (Runner Up: Kento Miyahara)
2019	**Kento Miyahara** (Runner Up: Jake Lee)
2020	**Zeus** (Runner Up: Kento Miyahara)
2021	**Jake Lee** (Runner Up: Kento Miyahara)
2022	**Yuma Aoyagi** (Runner Up: Jake Lee)

AJPW JUNIOR LEAGUE

YEAR	WON BY
1983	**Chavo Guerrero** (Runner Up: Ultra Seven)
1998	**Yoshinari Ogawa** (Runner Up: Satoru Asako)
2003	**Carl Contini** (Runner Up: Jimmy Yang)
2006	**Kaz Hayashi** (Runner Up: Katsuhiko Nakajima)
2007	**Chris Sabin** (Runner Up: Shuji Kondo)
2008	**Kai** (Runner Up: Silver King)
2009	**Shuji Kondo** (Runner Up: Super Crazy)
2010	**Jimmy Yang** (Runner Up: Kai)
2011	**Kai²** (Runner Up: Koji Kanemoto)
2012	**Hiroshi Yamato** (Runner Up: Shuji Kondo)

Year	Won By
2014	**Kotaro Suzuki** (Runner Up: Masaaki Mochizuki)
2015	**Kotaro Suzuki²** (Runner Up: Atsushi Aoki)
2016	**Atsushi Aoki** (Runner Up: Hikaru Sato)
2017	**Koji Iwamoto** (Runner Up: Hikaru Sato)
2018	**Shuji Kondo** (Runner Up: Koji Iwamoto)
2019	**Koji Iwamoto²** (Runner Up: Seiki Yoshioka)
2021	**Akira Francesco** (Runner Up: El Lindaman)
2022	**Atsuki Aoyagi** (Runner Up: Dan Tamura)

AJPW JUNIOR TAG LEAGUE

YEAR	WON BY
1984	**Gran Hamada & Mighty Inoue** (Runners Up: Chavo Guerrero & Hector Guerrero)
2002	**Jimmy Yang & Kaz Hayashi** (Runners Up: Kendo Kashin & Robbie Brookside)
2006	**Mazada & Nosawa Rongai** (Runners Up: Yasshi & Shuji Kondo)
2008	**Katsuhiko Nakajima & Ryuji Hijikata** (Runners Up: El Samurai & Kaz Hayashi)
2009	**Minoru & Toshizo** (Runners Up: Shuji Kondo & Kaz Hayashi)
2010	**Bushi & Super Crazy** (Runners Up: Shuji Kondo & Hiroshi Yamato)
2011	**Kai & Kaz Hayashi²** (Runners Up: Koji Kanemoto & Minoru)
2012	**Kaz Hayashi³ & Shuji Kondo** (Runners Up: Bushi & Sushi)
2013	**Atsushi Aoki & Kotaro Suzuki** (Runners Up: Hikaru Sato & Hiroshi Yamato)
2014	**Atsushi Aoki² & Hikaru Sato** (Runners Up: Ultimo Dragon & Yoshinobu Kanemaru)
2015	**Atsushi Aoki³ & Hikaru Sato²** (Runners Up: Isami Kodaka & Yuko Miyamoto)
2016	**Atsushi Aoki⁴ & Hikaru Sato³** (Runners Up: Soma Takao & Yuma Aoyagi)
2017	**Atsushi Maruyama & Masashi Takeda** (Runners Up: Black Tiger VII & Black Spider VII)
2018	**Koji Iwamoto & Yoshihiro Tajiri** (Runners Up: Atsushi Aoki & Hikaru Sato)
2019	**Hikaru Sato⁴ & Yusuke Okada** (Runners Up: Kagetora & Yosuke Santa Maria)
2020	**Dan Tamura & Hikaru Sato⁵** (Runners Up: Atsuki Aoyagi & Rising Hayato)
2021	**Hokuto Omori & Yusuke Kodama** (Runners Up: Dan Tamura & Hikaru Sato)

AJPW ODO TOURNAMENT

YEAR	WON BY
2013	**Akebono** (Runner Up: Go Shiozaki)
2014	**Go Shiozaki** (Runner Up: Suwama)
2015	**Jun Akiyama** (Runner Up: Akebono)

2016	**Suwama**
	(Runner Up: Zeus)
2017	**Suwama**[2]
	(Runner Up: Shuji Ishikawa)
2018	**Kento Miyahara**
	(Runner Up: Kengo Mashimo)
2019	**Jake Lee**
	(Runner Up: Kento Miyahara)
2021	**Suwama**[3]
	(Runner Up: Shotaro Ashino)
2022	**Kento Miyahara**[2]
	(Runner Up: Jake Lee)

AJPW REAL WORLD TAG LEAGUE

YEAR	WON BY
1977	**Dory Funk Jr. & Terry Funk**
	(Runners Up: Giant Baba & Jumbo Tsuruta)
1978	**Giant Baba & Jumbo Tsuruta**
	(Runners Up: Dory Funk Jr. & Terry Funk)
1979	**Dory Funk Jr.[2] & Terry Funk[2]**
	(Runners Up: Giant Baba & Jumbo Tsuruta)
1980	**Giant Baba[2] & Jumbo Tsuruta[2]**
	(Runners Up: Dory Funk Jr. & Terry Funk)
1981	**Bruiser Brody & Jimmy Snuka**
	(Runners Up: Giant Baba & Jumbo Tsuruta)
1982	**Dory Funk Jr.[3] & Terry Funk[3]**
	(Runners Up: Bruiser Brody & Stan Hansen)
1983	**Stan Hansen & Bruiser Brody[2]**
	(Runners Up: Dory Funk Jr. & Giant Baba)
1984	**Genichiro Tenryu & Jumbo Tsuruta[3]**
	(Runners Up: Bruiser Brody & Stan Hansen)
1985	**Stan Hansen[2] & Ted DiBiase**
	(Runners Up: Genichiro Tenryu & Jumbo Tsuruta)
1986	**Genichiro Tenryu[2] & Jumbo Tsuruta[4]**
	(Runners Up: Stan Hansen & Ted DiBiase)
1987	**Jumbo Tsuruta[5] & Yoshiaki Yatsu**
	(Runners Up: Dory Funk Jr. & Dory Funk)
1988	**Stan Hansen[3] & Terry Gordy**
	(Runners Up: Jumbo Tsuruta & Yoshiaki Yatsu)
1989	**Stan Hansen[4] & Genichiro Tenryu[3]**
	(Runners Up: Jumbo Tsuruta & Yoshiaki Yatsu)
1990	**Terry Gordy[2] & Steve Williams**
	(Runners Up: Stan Hansen & Dan Spivey)
1991	**Terry Gordy[3] & Steve Williams[2]**
	(Runners Up: Stan Hansen & Dan Spivey)
1992	**Mitsuharu Misawa & Toshiaki Kawada**
	(Runners Up: Terry Gordy & Steve Williams)
1993	**Mitsuharu Misawa[2] & Kenta Kobashi**
	(Runners Up: Giant Baba & Stan Hansen)
1994	**Mitsuharu Misawa[3] & Kenta Kobashi[2]**
	(Runners Up: Giant Baba & Stan Hansen)
1995	**Mitsuharu Misawa[4] & Kenta Kobashi[3]**
	(Runners Up: Toshiaki Kawada & Akira Taue)
1996	**Toshiaki Kawada[2] & Akira Taue**
	(Runners Up: Jun Akiyama & Mitsuharu Misawa)
1997	**Toshiaki Kawada[3] & Akira Taue[2]**
	(Runners Up: Jun Akiyama & Mitsuharu Misawa)
1998	**Jun Akiyama & Kenta Kobashi[4]**
	(Runners Up: Stan Hansen & Vader)
1999	**Jun Akiyama[2] & Kenta Kobashi[5]**
	(Runners Up: Stan Hansen & Akira Taue)
2000	**Mike Rotundo & Steve Williams[3]**
	(Runners Up: Masanobu Fuchi

	& Toshiaki Kawada)
2001	**Taiyo Kea & Keiji Mutoh**
	(Runners Up: Toshiaki Kawada & Mitsuya Nagai)
2002	**Taiyo Kea[2] & Satoshi Kojima**
	(Runners Up: Genichiro Tenryu & John Tenta)
2003	**Kaz Hayashi & Satoshi Kojima[2]**
	(Runners Up: Justin Credible & Jamal)
2004	**Taiyo Kea[3] & Jamal**
	(Runners Up: Kaz Hayashi & Satoshi Kojima)
2005	**Bubba Ray Dudley & D-Von Dudley**
	(Runners Up: Akebono & Keiji Mutoh)
2006	**Satoshi Kojima[3] & Hiroyoshi Tenzan**
	(Runners Up: Suwama & RO'Z)
2007	**Joe Doering & Keiji Mutoh[2]**
	(Runners Up: Suwama & Satoshi Kojima)
2008	**Satoshi Kojima[4] & Hiroyoshi Tenzan[2]**
	(Runners Up: Suwama & Shuji Kondo)
2009	**Masakatsu Funaki & Keiji Mutoh[3]**
	(Runners Up: Suwama & Masayuki Kono)
2010	**Kenso & Masayuki Kono**
	(Runners Up: Suwama & Ryoto Hama)
2011	**Kai & Sanada**
	(Runners Up: Masakatsu Funaki & Masayuki Kono)
2012	**Takao Omori & Manabu Soya**
	(Runners Up: Suwama & Joe Doering)
2013	**Suwama & Joe Doering[2]**
	(Runners Up: Go Shiozaki & Kento Miyahara)
2014	**Jun Akiyama[3] & Takao Omori[2]**
	(Runners Up: Go Shiozaki & Kento Miyahara)
2015	**Suwama[2] & Kento Miyahara**
	(Runners Up: The Bodyguard & Zeus)
2016	**Takao Omori[3] & Manabu Soya[2]**
	(Runners Up: Jake Lee & Kento Miyahara)
2017	**Suwama[3] & Shuji Ishikawa**
	(Runners Up: Daichi Hashimoto & Hideyoshi Kamitani)
2018	**Joe Doering[3] & Dylan James**
	(Runners Up: Jun Akiyama & Daisuke Sekimoto)
2019	**Suwama[4] & Shuji Ishikawa[2]**
	(Runners Up: Jake Lee & Naoya Nomura)
2020	**Kento Miyahara[2] & Yuma Aoyagi**
	(Runners Up: Suwama & Shuji Ishikawa)
2021	**Kento Miyahara[3] & Yuma Aoyagi[2]**
	(Runners Up: Kuma Arashi & Koji Doi)
2022	**Kento Miyahara[4] & Takuya Nomura**
	(Runners Up: Shuji Ishikawa & Cyrus)

COW PALACE BATTLE ROYAL

YEAR	WON BY
1967	**Bearcat Wright**
1968	**Big Bill Miller**
1969	**Ray Stevens**
1970	N/A
1971	N/A
1972	**Ray Stevens[2]**
1973	**The Great Mephisto**
1974	**Peter Maivia**
1975	**Pat Patterson**
1976	**Mr. Fuji**
1977	**Andre the Giant**
1978	**Don Muraco**
1979	**Ron Starr**
1980	**Ray Stevens[3]**
1981	**Pat Patterson[2]**

ECWA SUPER 8

YEAR	WON BY
1997	**Ace Darling** (Runner Up: Cheetah Master)
1998	**Lance Diamond** (Runner Up: Inferno Kid)
1999	**Steve Bradley** (Runner Up: Christopher Daniels)
2000	**Christopher Daniels** (Runner Up: Scoot Andrews)
2001	**Low Ki** (Runner Up: Bryan Danielson)
2002	**Donovan Morgan** (Runner Up: AJ Styles)
2003	**Paul London** (Runner Up: Chance Beckett)
2004	**Christopher Daniels²** (Runner Up: Austin Aries)
2005	**Petey Williams** (Runner Up: Puma)
2006	**Davey Richards** (Runner Up: Charlie Haas)
2007	**Jerry Lynn** (Runner Up: Sonjay Dutt)
2008	**Aden Chambers** (Runner Up: Alex Koslov)
2009	**Nick Logan** (Runner Up: Tommaso Ciampa)
2010	**Austin Creed** (Runner Up: Tommaso Ciampa)
2011	**Tommaso Ciampa** (Runner Up: Adam Cole)
2012	**Papadon** (Runner Up: Bandido Jr.)
2013	**Damian Dragon** (Runner Up: Papadon)
2014	**Matt Cross** (Runner Up: John Skyler)
2015	**Jason Kincaid** (Runner Up: Corey Hollis)
2016	**Napalm Bomb** (Runner Up: John Skyler)
2017	**Sean Carr** (Runner Up: Lio Rush)
2018	**Richard Holliday** (Runner Up: Chase Owens)
2019	**Lance Anoa'i** (Runner Up: Brian Pillman Jr.)
2020	**A Very Good Professional Wrestler** (Runner Up: KTB)
2021	**Killian McMurphy** (Runner Up: A Very Good Professional Wrestler)
2022	**Darius Carter** (Runner Up: Erica Leigh)

2022	
QF	Travis Huckabee def. Encore
QF	Erica Leigh def. Eric Corvis
QF	Eel O'Neal def. Ryan Clancy
QF	Darius Carter def. Ricky Morton
SF	Erica Leigh def. Eel O'Neal
SF	Darius Carter def. Travis Huckabee
F	Darius Carter def. Erica Leigh

ECWA WOMEN'S SUPER 8

YEAR	WON BY
2014	**Tessa Blanchard** (Runner Up: Jenny Rose)
2015	**Deonna Purrazzo** (Runner Up: Tessa Blanchard)
2016	**Deonna Purrazzo²** (Runner Up: Karen Q)
2017	**Karen Q** (Runner Up: Deonna Purrazzo, Santana Garrett)
2019	**Quinn McKay** (Runner Up: Gabby Ortiz)
2021	**Megan Bayne** (Runner Up: Ashley D'Amboise)
2022	**Erica Leigh** (Runner Up: Jordan Blade)

2022	
QF	Kennedi Copeland def. Bonesaw Brooks
QF	Jordan Blade def. Cosmic
QF	Mother Endless def. Abby Jane
QF	Erica Leigh def. Adena Steele
SF	Jordan Blade def. Kennedi Copeland
SF	Erica Leigh def. Mother Endless
F	Eric Leigh def. Jordan Blade

MLW OPERA CUP

YEAR	WON BY
2019	**Davey Boy Smith Jr.** (Runner Up: Brian Pillman Jr.)
2020	**Tom Lawlor** (Runner Up: Low Ki)
2021	**Davey Richards** (Runner Up: TJP)

2019	
QF	Davey Boy Smith Jr. def. Low Ki
QF	Alexander Hammerstone def. MJF
QF	Timothy Thatcher def. Richard Holliday
QF	Brian Pillman Jr. def. TJP
SF	Davey Boy Smith Jr. def. Alexander Hammerstone
SF	Brian Pillman Jr. def. Timothy Thatcher
F	Davey Boy Smith Jr. def. Brian Pillman Jr.

2020	
QF	Tom Lawlor def. Rocky Romero
QF	ACH def. Laredo Kid
QF	Low Ki def. Davey Boy Smith Jr.
QF	Richard Holliday def. TJP
SF	Tom Lawlor def. ACH
SF	Low Ki def. Richard Holliday
F	Tom Lawlor def. Low Ki

2021	
QF	Calvin Tankman def. Matt Cross
QF	TJP def. Alex Shelley
QF	Bobby Fish def. Lee Moriarty
QF	Davey Richards def. Tom Lawlor
SF	TJP def. Calvin Tankman
SF	Davey Richards def. Bobby Fish
F	Davey Richards def. TJP

NJPW BEST OF THE SUPER JUNIORS

YEAR	WON BY
1988	**Shiro Koshinaka**
	(Runner Up: Hiroshi Hase)
1991	**Norio Honaga**
	(Runner Up: Jushin Liger)
1992	**Jushin Liger**
	(Runner Up: El Samurai)
1993	**Pegasus Kid**
	(Runner Up: El Samurai)
1994	**Jushin Liger²**
	(Runner Up: Super Delfin)
1995	**Wild Pegasus²**
	(Runner Up: Shinjiro Otani)
1996	**Black Tiger II**
	(Runner Up: Jushin Liger)
1997	**El Samurai**
	(Runner Up: Koji Kanemoto)
1998	**Koji Kanemoto**
	(Runner Up: Dr. Wagner Jr.)
1999	**Kendo Kashin**
	(Runner Up: Koji Kanemoto)
2000	**Tatsuhito Takaiwa**
	(Runner Up: Shinjiro Otani)
2001	**Jushin Liger³**
	(Runner Up: Minoru Tanaka)
2002	**Koji Kanemoto²**
	(Runner Up: Minoru Tanaka)
2003	**Masahito Kakihara**
	(Runner Up: Koji Kanemoto)
2004	**Tiger Mask**
	(Runner Up: Koji Kanemoto)
2005	**Tiger Mask²**
	(Runner Up: Gedo)
2006	**Minoru**
	(Runner Up: Tiger Mask)
2007	**Milano Collection AT**
	(Runner Up: Wataru Inoue)
2008	**Wataru Inoue**
	(Runner Up: Koji Kanemoto)
2009	**Koji Kanemoto³**
	(Runner Up: Prince Devitt)
2010	**Prince Devitt**
	(Runner Up: Kota Ibushi)
2011	**Kota Ibushi**
	(Runner Up: Ryusuke Taguchi)
2012	**Ryusuke Taguchi**
	(Runner Up: Low Ki)
2013	**Prince Devitt²**
	(Runner Up: Alex Shelley)
2014	**Ricochet**
	(Runner Up: Kushida)
2015	**Kushida**
	(Runner Up: Kyle O'Reilly)
2016	**Will Ospreay**
	(Runner Up: Ryusuke Taguchi)
2017	**Kushida²**
	(Runner Up: Will Ospreay)
2018	**Hiromu Takahashi**
	(Runner Up: Taiji Ishimori)
2019	**Will Ospreay²**
	(Runner Up: Shingo Takagi)
2020	**Hiromu Takahashi²**
	(Runner Up: El Desperado)
2021	**Hiromu Takahashi³**
	(Runner Up: Yoh)
2022	**Hiromu Takahashi⁴**
	(Runner Up: El Desperado)

1988
Block Standings: Shiro Koshinaka 41, Hiroshi Hase 41, Nobuhiko Takada 40, Owen Hart 39, Kazuo Yamazaki 38, Keiichi Yamada 31, Kuniaki Kobayashi 24, Hiro Saito 24, Tony St. Clair 14, Tatsutoshi Goto 9, Masakatsu Funaki 8, Norio Honaga 0

1991
Block Standings: Norio Honaga 8, Jushin Liger 8, Pegasus Kid 8, Negro Casas 8, Owen Hart 6, David Finlay 4, Flyin' Scorpio 0

1992
Block Standings: El Samurai 14, **Jushin Liger 12**, Norio Honaga 12, Negro Casas 10, Pegasus Kid 10, David Finlay 6, Eddie Guerrero 4, Flyin 'Scorpio 2, Koji Kanemoto 2

1993
Block Standings: Pegasus Kid 14, El Samurai 12, Dean Malenko 12, Flyin' Scorpio 12, Black Tiger II 12, Jushin Liger 12, David Finlay 10, Norio Honaga 10, Lightning Kid 8, Shinjiro Otani 4, Masao Orihara 4

1994
Block Standings: Jushin Liger 14, Super Delfin 14, El Samurai 12, Wild Pegasus 12, Black Tiger II 12, Dean Malenko 12, Shinjiro Otani 10, Tokimitsu Ishizawa 8, David Finlay 8, Taka Michinoku 4, Masayoshi Motegi 2

1995
Block Standings: Wild Pegasus 10, Shinjiro Otani 10, Black Tiger II 10, Koji Kanemoto 10, Dean Malenko 8, Gran Hamada 8, Brian Pillman 8, El Samurai 8, Alex Wright 8, Norio Honaga 4

1996
Block A: El Samurai 10, Wild Pegasus 10, Tatsuhito Takaiwa 4, Franz Schumann 2, Emilio Charles Jr. 2, Mr. JL 2, Koji Kanemoto 2 **Block B: Black Tiger II 10**, Jushin Liger 8, Shinjiro Otani 6, Dean Malenko 6, Norio Honaga 4, Tokimitsu Ishizawa 4, Villano IV 2

1997
Block A: Koji Kanemoto 5, Jushin Liger 4, Tatsuhito Takaiwa 4, Gran Naniwa 3, Dr. Wagner Jr. 2, Doc Dean 2, Chavo Guerrero Jr. 1 **Block B: El Samurai 5**, Shinjiro Otani 4, Chris Jericho 4, Hanzo Nakajima 3, Yoshihiro Tajiri 3, Scorpio Jr. 1, Robbie Brookside 1

1998
Block A: Dr. Wagner Jr. 4, Jushin Liger 3, El Samurai 3, Shinjiro Otani 2, Tatsuhito Takaiwa 2, Masakazu Fukuda 1 **Block B: Koji Kanemoto 4**, Shiryu 3, Kendo Kashin 3, El Felino 2, Nanjyo Hayato 2, Yuji Yasuraoka 1

1999
Block A: Koji Kanemoto 8, Gran Hamada 6, Jushin Liger 6, Masaaki Mochizuki 4, Tatsuhito Takaiwa 4, Super Shocker 2 **Block B: Kendo Kashin 8**, Shinjiro Otani 7, El Samurai 5, Dr. Wagner Jr. 4, Minoru Tanaka 4, Masao Orihara 2

2000
Block A: Tatsuhito Takaiwa 8, Gran Hamada 6, Koji Kanemoto 6, El Samurai 4, Dr. Wagner Jr. 4, Shinya Makabe 2 **Block B:** Shinjiro Otani 10, Minoru Tanaka 6,

Kendo Kashiin 6, Katsumi Usuda 4, Kid Romeo 2, Minoru Fujita 2

2001

Block A: Jushin Liger 10, El Samurai 6, Silver King 6, Chris Candido 4, Gran Naniwa 4, Wataru Inoue 0 **Block B:** Minoru Tanaka 8, Akira 6, Super Shocker 6, Dr. Wagner Jr. 6, Shinya Makabe 4, Katsuyori Shibata 0

2002

Block A: Koji Kanemoto 4, Jushin Liger 4, Katsuyori Shibata 3, Black Tiger III 3, Masahito Kakihara 3, Curry Man 2, Jado 1 **Block B:** Minoru Tanaka 4, El Samurai 4, Gedo 3, Masayuki Naruse 3, Akira 3, Tiger Mask IV 3, Wataru Inoue 2

2003

Block A: Akira 10, Takashi Sugiura 8, Jushin Liger 8, Minoru Fujita 8, Ebessan 4, Gedo 4, Ryusuke Taguchi 0 **Block B:** Koji Kanemoto 8, **Masahito Kakihara 8**, Tiger Mask IV 8, Masayuki Naruse 6, Stampede Kid 4, El Samurai 4, Jado 4

2004

Block A: Jushin Liger 9, American Dragon 9, Masahito Kakihara 9, Koji Kanemoto 7, El Samurai 7, Big Boss Ma-g-ma 7, Wataru Inoue 4, Ryusuke Taguchi 4 **Block B: Tiger Mask IV 12**, Ultimo Dragon 11, Heat 10, Masayuki Naruse 10, Rocky Romero 7, Garuda 3, Katsuhiko Nakajima 2, Curry Man 1

2005

Block A: Minoru 8, Koji Kanemoto 8, Hirooki Goto 6, El Samurai 6, Masahito Kakihara 6, Stampede Kid 4, Jado 4 **Block B:** Gedo 10, **Tiger Mask IV 8**, Jushin Liger 8, Wataru Inoue 6, Black Tiger IV 4, Katsushi Takemura 4, Akiya Anzawa 2

2006

Block A: Jushin Liger 10, **Minoru 8**, El Samurai 7, Ryusuke Taguchi 7, Jado 6, Sangre Azteca 2, Fuego 2 **Block B:** Wataru Inoue 10, Tiger Mask IV 8, Koji Kanemoto 7, Gedo 5, Black Tiger IV 4, Hirooki Goto 4, Gentaro 4

2007

Block A: Wataru Inoue 10, **Milano Collecton A.T. 8**, Tiger Mask IV 8, Jushin Liger 8, Taichi Ishikari 4, Yujiro 4, Prince Devitt 0 **Block B:** Ryusuke Taguchi 10, Minoru 8, Koji Kanemoto 7, Gedo 5, BxB Hulk 4, El Samurai 4, Tetsuya Naito 4

2008

Block A: Ryusuke Taguchi 8, **Wataru Inoue 8**, Minoru 4, Jushin Liger 4, Tatsuhito Takaiwa 4, Yujiro 2 **Block B:** Tiger Mask IV 10, Koji Kanemoto 6, Jimmy Rave 6, Tetsuya Naito 4, Akira 4, Prince Devitt 0

2009

Block A: Prince Devitt 8, Atsushi Aoki 8, Akira 6, Jado 6, Milano Collection A.T. 6, Tiger Mask IV 6, Black Tiger V 2 **Block B: Koji Kanemoto 8**, Kota Ibushi 8, Jushin Liger 6, Ryusuke Taguchi 6, Tsuyoshi Kikuchi 6, Taichi 4, Yamato 4

2010

Block A: Kota Ibushi 12, **Prince Devitt 10**, Davey Richards 10, Jushin Liger 8, Kushida 8, La Sombra 6, Gedo 2, Tiger Mask IV 0 **Block B:** Taiji Ishimori 10, Ryusuke Taguchi 10, Akira 8, Kenny Omega 8, Koji Kanemoto 6, Fujita Hayato 6, Tama Tonga 4, Nobuo Yoshihashi 2

2011

Block A: Prince Devitt 14, Davey Richards 12, Kenny Omega 10, Koji Kanemoto 8, Tiger Mask IV 8, Fujita Hayato 6, TJP 6, Taichi 4, Jado 4 **Block B: Kota Ibushi 12**, Ryusuke Taguchi 10, Great Sasuke 10, Kushida 10, Taka Michinoku 8, Mascara Dorada 8, Jushin Liger 8, Gedo 4, Daisuke Sasaki 2

2012

Block A: Pac 10, Prince Devitt 10, Angel de Oro 8, Jushin Liger 8, Rocky Romero 8, Taichi 8, Kushida 8, Bushi 6, Gedo 6 **Block B:** Low Ki 16, **Ryusuke Taguchi 10**, Brian Kendrick 10, Alex Koslov 10, Tiger Mask IV 8, Taka Michinoku 8, Daisuke Sasaki 4, Jado 4, Hiromu Takahashi 2

2013

Block A: Prince Devitt 16, Alex Shelley 10, Ricochet 10, Taichi 8, Rocky Romero 8, Jushin Liger 8, Beretta 6, Titan 6, Hiromu Takahashi 0 **Block B:** Ryusuke Taguchi 10, Kenny Omega 10, Taka Michinoku 8, Kushida 8, Alex Koslov 8, Brian Kendrick 8, Tiger Mask IV 8, Bushi 6, Jado 6

2014

Block A: Kushida 10, **Ricochet 10**, Taka Michinoku 8, Matt Jackson 8, Bushi 8, Mascara Dorada 6, Jushin Liger 6, Alex Koslov 0 **Block B:** Alex Shelley 8, Ryusuke Taguchi 8, Taichi 8, Nick Jackson 8, Kenny Omega 6, Tiger Mask IV 6, El Desperado 6, Rocky Romero 6

2015

Block A: Kyle O'Reilly 12, Ryusuke Taguchi 10, Beretta 8, Chase Owens 8, Jushin Liger 8, Barbaro Cavernario 6, Gedo 4, Yohei Komatsu 0 **Block B: Kushida 12**, Bobby Fish 10, Mascara Dorada 10, Rocky Romero 8, Tiger Mask IV 8, Nick Jackson 6, Alex Shelley 2, David Finlay Jr.

2016

Block A: Ryusuke Taguchi 10, Matt Sydal 10, Bushi 8, Kyle O'Reilly 8, Kushida 8, David Finlay Jr. 2, Gedo 2 **Block B: Will Ospreay 8**, Bobby Fish 8, Ricochet 8, Volador Jr. 8, Jushin Liger 6, Tiger Mask IV 6, Chase Owens 6, Beretta 6

2017

Block A: Will Ospreay 10, Dragon Lee 8, Ricochet 8, Hiromu Takahashi 8, Taichi 8, Marty Scurll 8, Taka Michinoku 4, Jushin Liger 4 **Block B: Kushida 8**, Bushi 8, Ryusuke Taguchi 8, Yoshinobu Kanemaru 8, Volador Jr. 6, Tiger Mask 6, ACH 6, El Desperado 6

2018

Block A: Taiji Ishimori 10, Will Ospreay 10, ACH 6, Bushi 6, Flip Gordon 6, Tiger Mask 6, Yoh 6, Yoshinobu Kanemaru 6 **Block B: Hiromu Takahashi 10**, Kushida 8, Marty Scurll 8, Chris Sabin 6, Dragon Lee 6, El Desperado 6, Ryusuke Taguchi 6, Sho 6

2019

Block A: Shingo Takagi 18, Taiji Ishimori 14, Dragon Lee 14, Sho 10, Marty Scurll 10, Jonathan Gresham 8, Titan 6, Yoshinobu Kanemaru 6, Tiger Mask 4, Taka Michinoku 0 **Block B: Will Ospreay 14**, Ryusuke Taguchi 12, El Phantasmo 12, Bushi 12, Yoh 12, Bandido 10, Robbie Eagles 10, Rocky Romero 6, Douki 2, Ren Narita 0

2020

Block Standings: El Desperado 14, **Hiromu Takahashi 14**, Taiji Ishimori 14, Sho 12, Bushi 8, Master Wato 8, Robbie Eagles 8, Ryusuke Taguchi 8, Douki 4, Yuya Uemura 0

2021
Block Standings: Hiromu Takahashi 15, Yoh 14, El Desperado 13, Taiji Ishimori 12, Robbie Eagles 12, El Phantasmo 12, Sho 12, Bushi 10, Ryusuke Taguchi 10, Master Wato 8, Yoshinobu Kanemaru 8, Douki 6

2022
Block A: Hiromu Takahashi 12, Taiji Ishimori 12, Sho 10, Ace Austin 10, Yoh 8, Clark Connors 8, Alex Zayne 8, Francesco Akira 8, Yoshinobu Kanemaru 8, Ryusuke Taguchi 6 **Block B:** El Desperado 12, El Phantasmo 12, Robbie Eagles 10, Wheeler Yuta 10, El Lindaman 8, Titan 8, TJP 8, Bushi 8, Master Wato 8, Douki 6

NJPW G1 CLIMAX

YEAR	WON BY
1991	**Masahiro Chono**
	(Runner Up: Keiji Mutoh)
1992	**Masahiro Chono**[2]
	(Runner Up: Rick Rude)
1993	**Tatsumi Fujinami**
	(Runner Up: Hiroshi Hase)
1994	**Masahiro Chono**[3]
	(Runner Up: Power Warrior)
1995	**Keiji Mutoh**
	(Runner Up: Shinya Hashimoto)
1996	**Riki Choshu**
	(Runner Up: Masahiro Chono)
1997	**Kensuke Sasaki**
	(Runner Up: Hiroyoshi Tenzan)
1998	**Shinya Hashimoto**
	(Runner Up: Kazuo Yamazaki)
1999	**Manabu Nakanishi**
	(Runner Up: Keiji Mutoh)
2000	**Kensuke Sasaki**[2]
	(Runner Up: Manabu Nakanishi)
2001	**Yuji Nagata**
	(Runner Up: Keiji Mutoh)
2002	**Masahiro Chono**[4]
	(Runner Up: Yoshihiro Takayama)
2003	**Hiroyoshi Tenzan**
	(Runner Up: Jun Akiyama)
2004	**Hiroyoshi Tenzan**[2]
	(Runner Up: Hiroshi Tanahashi)
2005	**Masahiro Chono**[5]
	(Runner Up: Kazuyuki Fujita)
2006	**Hiroyoshi Tenzan**[3]
	(Runner Up: Satoshi Kojima)
2007	**Hiroshi Tanahashi**
	(Runner Up: Yuji Nagata)
2008	**Hirooki Goto**
	(Runner Up: Togi Makabe)
2009	**Togi Makabe**
	(Runner Up: Shinsuke Nakamura)
2010	**Satoshi Kojima**
	(Runner Up: Hiroshi Tanahashi)
2011	**Shinsuke Nakamura**
	(Runner Up: Tetsuya Naito)
2012	**Kazuchika Okada**
	(Runner Up: Karl Anderson)
2013	**Tetsuya Naito**
	(Runner Up: Hiroshi Tanahashi)
2014	**Kazuchika Okada**[2]
	(Runner Up: Shinsuke Nakamura)
2015	**Hiroshi Tanahashi**[2]
	(Runner Up: Shinsuke Nakamura)
2016	**Kenny Omega**
	(Runner Up: Hirooki Goto)

2017	**Tetsuya Naito**[2]
	(Runner Up: Kenny Omega)
2018	**Hiroshi Tanahashi**[3]
	(Runner Up: Kota Ibushi)
2019	**Kota Ibushi**
	(Runner Up: Jay White)
2020	**Kota Ibush**[2]
	(Runner Up: Sanada)
2021	**Kazuchika Okada**[3]
	(Runner Up: Kota Ibushi)
2022	**Kazuchika Okada**[4]
	(Runner Up: Will Ospreay)

1991
Block A: Keiji Mutoh 4, Tatsumi Fujinami 3, Scott Norton 3, Big Van Vader 3 **Block B: Masahiro Chono 5**, Shinya Hashimoto 5, Bam Bam Bigelow 2, Riki Choshu 0

1992

R1	Steve Austin def. Arn Anderson
R1	Keiji Mutoh def. Barry Windham
R1	Masahiro Chono def. Tony Halme
R1	Scott Norton def. Bam Bam Bigelow
R1	Kensuke Sasaki def. Jim Neidhart
R1	Terry Taylor def. Hiroshi Hase
R1	Shinya Hashimoto def. The Barbarian
R1	Rick Rude def. Super Strong Machine
QF	Keiji Mutoh def. Steve Austin
QF	Masahiro Chono def. Scott Norton
QF	Kensuke Sasaki def. Terry Taylor
QF	Rick Rude def. Shinya Hashimoto
SF	Masahiro Chono def. Keiji Mutoh
SF	Rick Rude def. Kensuke Sasaki
F	Masahiro Chono def. Rick Rude

1993

R1	Hiroshi Hase def. Shinya Hashimoto
R1	Kengo Kimura def. Michiyoshi Ohara
R1	Hiromichi Fuyuki def. Takayuki Iizuka
R1	Masahiro Chono def. Ashura Hara
R1	Tatsumi Fujinami def. Yoshiaki Fujiwara
R1	Osamu Kido def. Takashi Ishikawa
R1	Super Strong Machine def. Shiro Koshinaka
R1	Keiji Mutoh def. The Great Kabuki
QF	Hiroshi Hase def. Kengo Kimura
QF	Masahiro Chono def. Hiromichi Fuyuki
QF	Tatsumi Fujinami def. Osamu Kido
QF	Keiji Mutoh def. Super Strong Machine
SF	Hiroshi Hase def. Masahiro Chono
SF	Tatsumi Fujinami def. Keiji Mutoh
F	Tatsumi Fujinami def. Hiroshi Hase

1994
Block A: Masahiro Chono 8, Keiji Mutoh 6, Riki Choshu 6, Yoshiaki Yatsu 4, Yoshiaki Fujiwara 4, Osamu Kido 2 **Block B:** Power Warrior 7, Hiroshi Hase 6, Shinya Hashimoto 6, Tatsumi Fujinami 6, Shiro Koshinaka 5, Takayuki Iizuka 0

1995
Block A: Keiji Mutoh 4, Masahiro Chono 3, Ric Flair 3, Shiro Koshinaka 2 **Block B:** Shinya Hashimoto 4, Scott Norton 4, Hiroyoshi Tenzan 2, Kensuke Sasaki 2

1996
Block A: Riki Choshu 8, Kensuke Sasaki 6, Hiroyoshi Tenzan 4, Shinya Hashimoto 2, Junji Hirata 0 **Block B:** Masahiro Chono 6, Shiro Koshinaka 4, Keiji Mutoh 4, Kazuo Yamazaki 4, Satoshi Kojima 2

1997

R1	Satoshi Kojima def. Steven Regal
R1	Hiroyoshi Tenzan def. Tadao Yasuda
R1	Masahiro Chono def. Michiyoshi Ohara
R1	Shinya Hashimoto def. Kazuo Yamazaki
R1	Scott Norton def. Junji Hirata
R1	The Great Muta def. Manabu Nakanishi
QF	Hiroyoshi Tenzan def. Satoshi Kojima
QF	Shinya Hashimoto def. Masahiro Chono
QF	Scott Norton def. The Great Muta
QF	Kensuke Sasaki def. Buff Bagwell
SF	Hiroyoshi Tenzan def. Shinya Hashimoto
SF	Kensuke Sasaki def. Scott Norton
F	Kensuke Sasaki def. Hiroyoshi Tenzan

1998

R1	Tadao Yasuda def. Big Titan
R1	Satoshi Kojima def. Hiroyoshi Tenzan
R1	Shinya Hashimoto def. Tatsutoshi Goto
R1	Genichiro Tenryu def. Keiji Mutoh
R1	Shiro Koshinaka def. Osamu Nishimura
R1	Masahiro Chono def. Manabu Nakanishi
R1	Kensuke Sasaki def. Michiyoshi Ohara
R1	Kazuo Yamazaki def. Tatsumi Fujinami
QF	Satoshi Kojima def. Tadao Yasuda
QF	Shinya Hashimoto def. Genichiro Tenryu
QF	Masahiro Chono def. Shiro Koshinaka
QF	Kazuo Yamazaki def. Kensuke Sasaki
SF	Shinya Hashimoto def. Satoshi Kojima
SF	Kazuo Yamazaki def. Masahiro Chono
F	Shinya Hashimoto def. Kazuo Yamazaki

1999

Block A: Keiji Mutoh 8, Yuji Nagata 8, Kensuke Sasaki 6, Tatsumi Fujinami 6, Satoshi Kojima 2, Tadao Yasuda 0 **Block B: Manabu Nakanishi 8**, Hiroyoshi Tenzan 6, Shiro Koshinaka 6, Masahiro Chono 6, Shinya Hashimoto 4, Kazuo Yamazaki 0

2000

Block A: Yuji Nagata 3, Takashi Iizuka 3, Tatsumi Fujinami 2, Jushin Liger 1, Tatsutoshi Goto 1 **Block B: Kensuke Sasaki 3**, Satoshi Kojima 2, Brian Johnston 2, Osamu Kido 0, Hiro Saito 0 **Block C:** Manabu Nakanishi 3, Hiroyoshi Tenzan 3, Tadao Yasuda 2, Osamu Nishimura 2, Kenzo Suzuki 0 **Block D:** Masahiro Chono 3, Junji Hirata 2, Shiro Koshinaka 2, Yutaka Yoshie 2, Tatsuhito Takaiwa 1

2001

Block A: Yuji Nagata 7, Tadao Yasuda 6, Manabu Nakanishi 6, Kazunari Murakami 5, Tatsumi Fujinami 4, Minoru Tanaka 2 **Block B:** Keiji Mutoh 8, Masahiro Chono 6, Hiroyoshi Tenzan 6, Satoshi Kojima 4, Jushin Liger 3, Osamu Nishimura 3

2002

Block A: Yoshihiro Takayama 8, Hiroyoshi Tenzan 6, Kensuke Sasaki 6, Hiroshi Tanahashi 4, Shiro Koshinaka 4, Yutaka Yoshie 2 **Block B: Masahiro Chono 7**, Osamu Nishimura 5, Manabu Nakanishi 5, Yuji Nagata 5, Kenzo Suzuki 4, Tadao Yasuda 4

2003

Block A: Jun Akiyama 7, **Hiroyoshi Tenzan 6**, Masahiro Chono 5, Manabu Nakanishi 4, Osamu Nishimura 4, Hiroshi Tanahashi 4 **Block B:** Yoshihiro Takayama 8, Yuji Nagata 5, Katsuyori Shibata 5, Yutaka Yoshie 4, Shinsuke Nakamura 4, Tadao Yasuda 4

2004

Block A: Katsuyori Shibata 8, Genichiro Tenryu 8, Shinsuke Nakamura 8, Masahiro Chono 8, Minoru Suzuki 8, Yuji Nagata 8, Blue Wolf 4, Yutaka Yoshie 2 **Block B: Hiroshi Tanahashi 12**, Hiroyoshi Tenzan 11, Kensuke Sasaki 9, Koji Kanemoto 6, Manabu Nakanishi 6, Osamu Nishimura 6, Togi Makabe 4, Yoshihiro Takayama 2

2005

Block A: Masahiro Chono 10, Toshiaki Kawada 10, Yuji Nagata 8, Hiroyoshi Tenzan 8, Minoru Suzuki 6, Kendo Kashin 5, Osamu Nishimura 5, Tatsumi Fujinami 4 **Block B:** Kazuyuki Fujita 14, Shinsuke Nakamura 11, Manabu Nakanishi 10, Hiroshi Tanahashi 7, Yutaka Yoshie 6, Tatsutoshi Goto 4, Toru Yano 4, Togi Makabe 0

2006

Block A: Satoshi Kojima 7, Giant Bernard 5, Hiroshi Tanahashi 4, Jushin Liger 2, Manabu Nakanishi 2 **Block B: Hiroyoshi Tenzan 8**, Koji Kanemoto 5, Yuji Nagata 4, Togi Makabe 3, Naofumi Yamamoto 0

2007

Block A: Togi Makabe 6, Yuji Nagata 6, Akebono 5, Giant Bernard 5, Hiroyoshi Tenzan 4, Masahiro Chono 4 **Block B:** Shinsuke Nakamura 7, **Hiroshi Tanahashi 6**, Toru Yano 5, Shiro Koshinaka 4, Milano Collection A.T. 4, Manabu Nakanishi 4

2008

Block A: Togi Makabe 8, Satoshi Kojima 7, Shinjiro Otani 7, Manabu Nakanishi 6, Giant Bernard 6, Hiroshi Tanahashi 4, Wataru Inoue 4 **Block B: Hirooki Goto 8**, Shinsuke Nakamura 8, Toshiaki Kawada 7, Yutaka Yoshie 7, Yuji Nagata 6, Toru Yano 4, Hiroyoshi Tenzan 2

2009

Block A: Togi Makabe 7, Hiroshi Tanahashi 7, Masato Tanaka 7, Toru Yano 6, Takao Omori 6, Giant Bernard 5, Tajiri 4 **Block B:** Shinsuke Nakamura 12, Takashi Sugiura 7, Hirooki Goto 6, Manabu Nakanishi 6, Yuji Nagata 5, Hiroyoshi Tenzan 4, Takashi Iizuka 2

2010

Block A: Hiroshi Tanahashi 9, Togi Makabe 8, Manabu Nakanishi 8, Toru Yano 8, Prince Devitt 8, Tetsuya Naito 7, Strong Man 4, Karl Anderson 4 **Block B: Satoshi Kojima 10**, Shinsuke Nakamura 9, Go Shiozaki 9, Hirooki Goto 8, Yuji Nagata 8, Giant Bernard 6, Yujiro Takahashi 4, Wataru Inoue 2

2011

Block A: Tetsuya Naito 12, Hiroshi Tanahashi 12, Yoshihiro Takayama 10, Togi Makabe 10, Giant Bernard 10, Toru Yano 10, Yuji Nagata 10, Lance Archer 8, Yujiro Takahashi 6, Hideo Saito 2 **Block B: Shinsuke Nakamura 14**, Satoshi Kojima 12, Minoru Suzuki 12, MVP 12, Hirooki Goto 12, Karl Anderson 8, Hiroyoshi Tenzan 8, La Sombra 4, Wataru Inoue 4, Strong Man 4

2012

Block A: Karl Anderson 10, Hiroshi Tanahashi 10, Shelton Benjamin 8, Yuji Nagata 8, Minoru Suzuki 8, Satoshi Kojima 8, Naomichi Marufuji 8, Toru Yano 6, Yujiro Takahashi 6 **Block B: Kazuchika Okada 10**, Lance Archer 8, Hirooki Goto 8, Togi Makabe 8, MVP 8, Tetsuya Naito 8, Hiroyoshi Tenzan 8, Shinsuke Nakamura 8, Rush 6

2013

Block A: Hiroshi Tanahashi 11, Katsuyori Shibata 10, Davey Boy Smith Jr. 10, Prince Devitt 10, Togi Makabe 10, Kazuchika Okada 9, Hirooki Goto 8, Lance Archer 8, Satoshi Kojima 8, Tomohiro Ishii 6 **Block B: Tetsuya Naito 10**, Minoru Suzuki 10, Karl Anderson 10, Shelton Benjamin 10, Shinsuke Nakamura 10, Yuji Nagata 10, Kota Ibushi 8, Toru Yano 8, Yujiro Takahashi 8, Hiroyoshi Tenzan 6

2014

Block A: Shinsuke Nakamura 16, Hiroshi Tanahashi 14, Bad Luck Fale 12, Katsuyori Shibata 12, Shelton Benjamin 10, Tomohiro Ishii 10, Satoshi Kojima 10, Davey Boy Smith Jr. 10, Luke Gallows 8, Yuji Nagata 8, Tomoaki Honma 0 **Block B: Kazuchika Okada 16**, AJ Styles 16, Karl Anderson 10, Minoru Suzuki 10, Tetsuya Naito 10, Lance Archer 8, Yujiro Takahashi 8, Hiroyoshi Tenzan 8, Toru Yano 8, Hirooki Goto 8, Togi Makabe 8

2015

Block A: Hiroshi Tanahashi 14, AJ Styles 12, Tetsuya Naito 10, Bad Luck Fale 10, Toru Yano 8, Katsuyori Shibata 8, Kota Ibushi 8, Togi Makabe 8, Hiroyoshi Tenzan 6, Luke Gallows 6 **Block B:** Shinsuke Nakamura 14, Kazuchika Okada 14, Karl Anderson 12, Hirooki Goto 12, Tomohiro Ishii 10, Michael Elgin 8, Yujiro Takahashi 6, Yuji Nagata 6, Satoshi Kojima 6, Tomoaki Honma 2

2016

Block A: Hirooki Goto 12, Kazuchika Okada 11, Hiroshi Tanahashi 11, Bad Luck Fale 10, Naomichi Marufuji 10, Togi Makabe 8, Tama Tonga 8, Sanada 8, Tomohiro Ishii 8, Hiroyoshi Tenzan 4 **Block B: Kenny Omega 12**, Tetsuya Naito 12, Katsuhiko Nakajima 10, Toru Yano 10, Michael Elgin 10, Katsuyori Shibata 10, Evil 8, Tomoaki Honma 6, Yuji Nagata 6, Yoshi-Hashi 6

2017

Block A: Tetsuya Naito 14, Hiroshi Tanahashi 12, Bad Luck Fale 12, Hirooki Goto 10, Kota Ibushi 10, Zack Sabre Jr. 10, Tomohiro Ishii 8, Togi Makabe 8, Yoshi-Hashi 4, Yuji Nagata 2 **Block B:** Kenny Omega 14, Kazuchika Okada 13, Evil 12, Minoru Suzuki 9, Tama Tonga 8, Sanada 8, Juice Robinson 8, Toru Yano 8, Michael Elgin 8, Satoshi Kojima 2

2018

Block A: Hiroshi Tanahashi 15, Kazuchika Okada 13, Jay White 12, Minoru Suzuki 10, Evil 10, Yoshi-Hashi 6, Michael Elgin 6, Togi Makabe 6, Hangman Page 6, Bad Luck Fale 6 **Block B:** Kota Ibushi 12, Kenny Omega 12, Zack Sabre Jr. 12, Tetsuya Naito 12, Tomohiro Ishii 10, Sanada 8, Juice Robinson 6, Hirooki Goto 6, Toru Yano 6, Tama Tonga 6

2019

Block A: Kota Ibushi 14, Kazuchika Okada 14, Bad Luck Fale 8, Evil 8, Hiroshi Tanahashi 8, Kenta 8, Sanada 8, Zack Sabre Jr. 8, Will Ospreay 8, Lance Archer 6 **Block B:** Jay White 12, Hirooki Goto 10, Jon Moxley 10, Tetsuya Naito 10, Jeff Cobb 8, Juice Robinson 8, Shingo Takagi 8, Taichi 8, Tomohiro Ishii 8, Toru Yano 8

2020

Block A: Kota Ibushi 14, Will Ospreay 12, Jay White 12, Kazuchika Okada 12, Taichi 8, Jeff Cobb 8, Tomohiro Ishii 8, Shingo Takagi 8, Minoru Suzuki 6, Yujiro Takahashi 6 **Block B:** Sanada 12, Evil 12, Tetsuya Naito 12, Kenta 10, Zack Sabre Jr. 10, Hirooki Goto 8, Hiroshi Tanahashi 8, Juice Robinson 8, Toru Yano 6, Yoshi-Hashi 4

2021

Block A: Kota Ibushi 14, Shingo Takagi 13, Kenta 12, Zack Sabre Jr. 12, Toru Yano 10, Tomohiro Ishii 10, Great-O-Khan 8, Tanga Loa 6, Yujiro Takahashi 5, Tetsuya Naito 0 **Block B: Kazuchika Okada 16**, Jeff Cobb 16, Evil 14, Hiroshi Tanahashi 10, Sanada 8, Hirooki Goto 6, Yoshi-Hashi 6, Tama Tonga 6, Taichi 6, Chase Owens 4

2022

Block A: Kazuchika Okada 10, Jonah 8, Lance Archer 6, Tom Lawlor 6, Jeff Cobb 6, Bad Luck Fale 4, Toru Yano 2 **Block B:** Tama Tonga 10, Jay White 10, Sanada 6, Taichi 4, Great-O-Khan 4, Chase Owens 4, Tomohiro Ishii 4 **Block C:** Tetsuya Naito 8, Zack Sabre Jr. 8, Evil 6, Kenta 6, Hirooki Goto 6, Hiroshi Tanahashi 6, Aaron Henare 2 **Block D:** Will Ospreay 8, El Phantasmo 6, Shingo Takagi 6, Yujiro Takahashi 6, Yoshi-Hashi 6, David Finlay 6, Juice Robinson 4

NJPW NEW JAPAN CUP

YEAR	WON BY
2005	**Hiroshi Tanahashi** (Runner Up: Manabu Nakanishi)
2006	**Giant Bernard** (Runner Up: Yuji Nagata)
2007	**Yuji Nagata** (Runner Up: Togi Makabe)
2008	**Hiroshi Tanahashi**[2] (Runner Up: Giant Bernard)
2009	**Hirooki Goto** (Runner Up: Giant Bernard)
2010	**Hirooki Goto**[2] (Runner Up: Togi Makabe)
2011	**Yuji Nagata**[2] (Runner Up: Shinsuke Nakamura)
2012	**Hirooki Goto**[3] (Runner Up: Hiroshi Tanahashi)
2013	**Kazuchika Okada** (Runner Up: Hirooki Goto)
2014	**Shinsuke Nakamura** (Runner Up: Bad Luck Fale)
2015	**Kota Ibushi** (Runner Up: Hirooki Goto)
2016	**Tetsuya Naito** (Runner Up: Hirooki Goto)
2017	**Katsuyori Shibata** (Runner Up: Bad Luck Fale)
2018	**Zack Sabre Jr.** (Runner Up: Hiroshi Tanahashi)
2019	**Kazuchika Okada**[2] (Runner Up: Sanada)
2020	**Evil** (Runner Up: Kazuchika Okada)
2021	**Will Ospreay** (Runner Up: Shingo Takagi)
2022	**Zack Sabre Jr.**[2] (Runner Up: Tetsuya Naito)

2005

R1	Hiroshi Tanahashi def. Yuji Nagata
R1	Koji Kanemoto def. Ryushi Yanagisawa
R1	Minoru def. Osamu Nishimura
R1	Hiroyoshi Tenzan def. Jushin Liger
R1	Kendo Kashin def. Shinsuke Nakamura
R1	Yutaka Yoshie def. Scott Norton
R1	Masahiro Chono def. Tiger Mask
R1	Manabu Nakanishi def. Hirooki Goto
QF	Hiroshi Tanahashi def. Koji Kanemoto

QF	Hiroyoshi Tenzan def. Osamu Nishimura
QF	Kendo Kashin def. Yutaka Yoshie
QF	Manabu Nakanishi def. Masahiro Chono
SF	Hiroshi Tanahashi def. Hiroyoshi Tenzan
SF	Manabu Nakanishi def. Kendo Kashin
F	Hiroshi Tanahashi def. Manabu Nakanishi

2006

R1	Giant Bernard def. Toru Yano
R1	Riki Choshu def. Black Strong Machine
R1	Manabu Nakanishi def. Takashi Iizuka
R1	Ryoji Sai def. Naofumi Yamamoto
R1	Hiroshi Tanahashi def. Masahiro Chono
R1	Hiroyoshi Tenzan def. Scott Norton
R1	Togi Makabe def. Tatsutoshi Goto
R1	Yuji Nagata def. Tomohiro Ishii
QF	Giant Bernard def. Riki Choshu
QF	Manabu Nakanishi def. Ryoji Sai
QF	Hiroshi Tanahashi def. Hiroyoshi Tenzan
QF	Yuji Nagata def. Togi Makabe
SF	Giant Bernard def. Manabu Nakanishi
SF	Yuji Nagata def. Hiroshi Tanahashi
F	Giant Bernard def. Yuji Nagata

2007

R1	Togi Makabe def. Travis Tomko
R1	Takashi Iizuka def. Tomoaki Honma
R1	Shinsuke Nakamura def. Toru Yano
R1	Yuji Nagata def. Tomohiro Ishii
R1	Masahiro Chono def. Riki Choshu
R1	Manabu Nakanishi def. Shiro Koshinaka
QF	Togi Makabe def. Takashi Iizuka
QF	Hiroyoshi Tenzan def. Shinsuke Nakamura
QF	Yuji Nagata def. Masahiro Chono
QF	Giant Bernard def. Manabu Nakanishi
SF	Togi Makabe def. Hiroyoshi Tenzan
SF	Yuji Nagata def. Giant Bernard
F	Yuji Nagata def. Togi Makabe

2008

R1	Hiroyoshi Tenzan def. Tomohiro Ishii
R1	Togi Makabe def. Takashi Iizuka
R1	Hiroshi Tanahashi def. Hirooki Goto
R1	Ryusuke Taguchi def. Jushin Liger
R1	Koji Kanemoto def. Karl Anderson
R1	Giant Bernard def. Tomoaki Honma
R1	Toru Yano def. Milano Collection A.T.
R1	Rhino def. Manabu Nakanishi
QF	Togi Makabe def. Hiroyoshi Tenzan
QF	Hiroshi Tanahashi def. Ryusuke Taguchi
QF	Giant Bernard def. Koji Kanemoto
QF	Toru Yano def. Rhino
SF	Hiroshi Tanahashi def. Togi Makabe
SF	Giant Bernard def. Toru Yano
F	Hiroshi Tanahashi def. Giant Bernard

2009

R1	Hirooki Goto def. Karl Anderson
R1	Shinsuke Nakamura def. Togi Makabe
R1	Takashi Iizuka def. Tomoaki Honma
R1	Milano Collection A.T. def. Toru Yano
R1	Yutaka Yoshie def. Manaby Nakanishi
R1	Tomohiro Ishii def. Wataru Inoue
QF	Hirooki Goto def. Shinsuke Nakamura
QF	Yuji Nagata def. Takashi Iizuka
QF	Giant Bernard def. Milano Collection A.T.
QF	Yutaka Yoshi def. Tomohiro Ishii
SF	Hirooki Goto def. Yuji Nagata
SF	Giant Bernard def. Yutaka Yoshie
F	Hirooki Goto def. Giant Bernard

2010

R1	Yujiro Takahashi def. Yuji Nagata
R1	Wataru Inoue def. Giant Bernard
R1	Masata Tanaka def. Manabu Nakanishi
R1	Togi Makabe def. Tomohiro Ishii
R1	Toru Yano def. Tomoaki Honma
R1	Hiroshi Tanahashi def. Strong Man
R1	Tetsuya Naito def. Karl Anderson
QF	Hirooki Goto def. Yujiro Takahashi
QF	Masato Tanaka def. Wataru Inoue
QF	Togi Makabe def. Toru Yano
QF	Tetsuya Naito def. Hiroshi Tanahashi
SF	Hirooki Goto def. Masata Tanaka
SF	Togi Makabe def. Tetsuya Naito
F	Hirooki Goto def. Togi Makabe

2011

R1	Manabu Nakanishi def. Yujiro Takahashi
R1	Shinsuke Nakamura def. Hirooki Goto
R1	MVP def. Karl Anderson
R1	Togi Makabe def. Satoshi Kojima
R1	Toru Yano def. Wataru Inoue
R1	Hiroyoshi Tenzan def. Takashi Iizuka
R1	Masata Tanaka def. Tetsuya Naito
R1	Yuji Nagata def. Giant Bernard
QF	Shinsuke Nakamura def. Manabu Nakanishi
QF	Togi Makabe def. MVP
QF	Toru Yano def. Hiroyoshi Tenzan
QF	Yuji Nagata def. Masato Tanaka
SF	Shinsuke Nakamura def. Togi Makabe
SF	Yuji Nagata def. Toru Yano
F	Yuji Nagata def. Shinsuke Nakamura

2012

R1	Hiroshi Tanahashi def. Toru Yano
R1	Tetsuya Naito def. Satoshi Kojima
R1	Karl Anderson def. Hiroyoshi Tenzan
R1	Shinsuke Nakamura def. MVP
R1	Togi Makabe def. Lance Archer
R1	Minoru Suzuki def. Yuji Nagata
R1	Hirooki Goto def. Yujiro Takahashi
R1	La Sombra def. Yoshi-Hashi
QF	Hiroshi Tanahashi def. Tetsuya Naito
QF	Karl Anderson def. Shinsuke Nakamura
QF	Togi Makabe def. Minoru Suzuki
QF	Hirooki Goto def. La Sombra
SF	Hiroshi Tanahashi def. Karl Anderson
SF	Hirooki Goto def. Togi Makabe
F	Hirooki Goto def. Hiroshi Tanahashi

2013

R1	Yujiro Takahashi def. Togi Makabe
R1	Davey Boy Smith Jr. def. Shinsuke Nakamura
R1	Tomohiro Ishii def. Satoshi Kojima
R1	Hirooki Goto def. Tama Tonga
R1	Karl Anderson def. Hiroyoshi Tenzan
R1	Kazuchika Okada def. Lance Archer
R1	Minoru Suzuki def. Yuji Nagata
R1	Toru Yano def. Manabu Nakanishi
QF	Davey Boy Smith Jr. def. Yujiro Takahashi
QF	Hirooki Goto def. Tomohiro Ishii
QF	Kazuchika Okada def. Karl Anderson
QF	Toru Yano def. Minoru Suzuki
SF	Hirooki Goto def. Davey Boy Smith Jr.
SF	Kazuchika Okada def. Toru Yano
F	Kazuchika Okada def. Hirooki Goto

2014

R1	Bad Luck Fale def. Togi Makabe
R1	Tetsuya Naito def. Tomohiro Ishii
R1	Katsuyori Shibata def. Karl Anderson

R1	Shelton Benjamin def. Yujiro Takahashi
R1	Hirooki Goto def. Luke Gallows
R1	Minoru Suzuki def. Toru Yano
R1	Shinsuke Nakamura def. Davey Boy Smith Jr.
R1	Prince Devitt def. Lance Archer
QF	Bad Luck Fale def. Tetsuya Naito
QF	Shelton Benjamin def. Katsuyori Shibata
QF	Minoru Suzuki def. Hirooki Goto
QF	Shinsuke Nakamura def. Prince Devitt
SF	Bad Luck Fale def. Shelton Benjamin
SF	Shinsuke Nakamura def. Minoru Suzuki
F	Shinsuke Nakamura def. Bad Luck Fale

2015

R1	Toru Yano def. Hiroshi Tanahashi
R1	Kota Ibushi def. Luke Gallows
R1	Tetsuya Naito def. Karl Anderson
R1	Bad Luck Fale def. Kazuchika Okada
R1	Togi Makabe def. Tomoaki Honma
R1	Yujiro Takahashi def. Yoshi-Hashi
R1	Hirooki Goto def. Yuji Nagata
R1	Katsuyori Shibata def. Satoshi Kojima
QF	Kota Ibushi def. Toru Yano
QF	Tetsuya Naito def. Bad Luck Fale
QF	Togi Makabe def. Yujiro Takahashi
QF	Hirooki Goto def. Katsuyori Shibata
SF	Kota Ibushi def. Tetsuya Naito
SF	Hirooki Goto def. Togi Makabe
F	Kota Ibushi def. Hirooki Goto

2016

R1	Bad Luck Fale def. Hiroshi Tanahashi
R1	Michael Elgin def. Hiroyoshi Tenzan
R1	Tama Tonga def. Togi Makabe
R1	Hirooki Goto def. Yuji Nagata
R1	Satoshi Kojima def. Tomoaki Honma
R1	Toru Yano def. Yujiro Takahashi
R1	Tomohiro Ishii def. Evil
R1	Tetsuya Naito def. Yoshi-Hashi
QF	Michael Elgin def. Bad Luck Fale
QF	Hirooki Goto def. Tama Tonga
QF	Toru Yano def. Satoshi Kojima
QF	Tetsuya Naito def. Tomohiro Ishii
SF	Hirooki Goto def. Michael Elgin
SF	Tetsuya Naito def. Toru Yano
F	Tetsuya Naito def. Hirooki Goto

2017

R1	Evil def. Hiroshi Tanahashi
R1	Yuji Nagata def. Tanga Loa
R1	Bad Luck Fale def. Michael Elgin
R1	Toru Yano def. Tama Tonga
R1	Katsuyori Shibata def. Minoru Suzuki
R1	Jucie Robinson def. Yujiro Takahashi
R1	Tomohiro Ishii def. Kenny Omega
R1	Sanada def. Yoshi-Hashi
QF	Evil def. Yuji Nagata
QF	Bad Luck Fale def. Toru Yano
QF	Katsuyori Shibata def. Juice Robinson
QF	Tomohiro Ishii def. Sanada
SF	Bad Luck Fale def. Evil
SF	Katsuyori Shibata def. Tomohiro Ishii
F	Katsuyori Shibata def. Bad Luck Fale

2018

R1	Michael Elgin def. Tomohiro Ishii
R1	Juice Robinson def. Yujiro Takahashi
R1	Hiroshi Tanahashi def. Taichi
R1	Bad Luck Fale def. Lance Archer
R1	Kota Ibushi def. Yoshi-Hashi
R1	Zack Sabre Jr. def. Tetsuya Naito

R1	Toru Yano def. Davey Boy Smith Jr.
R1	Sanada def. Chuckie T.
QF	Juice Robinson def. Michael Elgin
QF	Hiroshi Tanahashi def. Bad Luck Fale
QF	Zack Sabre Jr. def. Kota Ibushi
QF	Sanada def. Toru Yano
SF	Hiroshi Tanahashi def. Juice Robinson
SF	Zack Sabre Jr. def. Sanada
F	Zack Sabre Jr. def. Hiroshi Tanahashi

2019

R1	Tomohiro Ishii def. Yuji Nagata
R1	Taichi def. Tomoaki Honma
R1	Yoshi-Hashi def. Manabu Nakanishi
R1	Chase Owens def. Juice Robinson
R1	Kazuchika Okada def. Michael Elgin
R1	Mikey Nicholls def. Hikuleo
R1	Will Ospreay def. Bad Luck Fale
R1	Lance Archer def. Toa Henare
R1	Hiroshi Tanahashi def. Shota Umino
R1	Ryusuke Taguchi def. Hiroyoshi Tenzan
R1	Kota Ibushi def. Tetsuya Naito
R1	Zack Sabre Jr. def. Evil
R1	Colt Cabana def. Togi Makabe
R1	Toru Yano def. Davey Boy Smith Jr.
R1	Minoru Suzuki def. Satoshi Kojima
R1	Sanada def. Hirooki Goto
R2	Tomohiro Ishii def. Taichi
R2	Yoshi-Hashiu def. Chase Owens
R2	Kazuchika Okada def. Mikey Nicholls
R2	Will Ospreay def. Lance Archer
R2	Hiroshi Tanahashi def. Ryusuke Taguchi
R2	Zack Sabre Jr. def. Kota Ibushi
R2	Colt Cabana def. Toru Yano
R2	Sanada def. Minoru Suzuki
QF	Tomohiro Ishii def. Yoshi-Hashi
QF	Kazuchika Okada def. Will Ospreay
QF	Hiroshi Tanahashi def. Zack Sabre Jr.
QF	Sanada def. Colt Cabana
SF	Kazuchika Okada def. Tomohiro Ishii
SF	Sanada def. Hiroshi Tanahashi
F	Kazuchika Okada def. Sanada

2020

R1	Togi Makabe def. Yota Tsuji
R1	Tomohiro Ishii def. El Desperado
R1	Toru Yano def. Jado
R1	Hiromu Takahashi def. Tomoaki Honma
R1	Kazuchika Okada def. Gedo
R1	Yuji Nagata def. Minoru Suzuki
R1	Yoshinobu Kanemaru def. Yuya Uemura
R1	Taiji Ishimori def. Gabriel Kiss
R1	Taichi def. Hiroshi Tanahashi
R1	Kota Ibushi def. Zack Sabre Jr.
R1	Sanada def. Ryusuke Taguchi
R1	Sho def. Shingo Takagi
R1	Yoshi-Hashi def. Hiroyoshi Tenzan
R1	Bushi def. Yoh
R1	Evil def. Satoshi Kojima
R1	Hirooki Goto def. Yujiro Takahashi
R2	Tomohiro Ishii def. Togi Makabe
R2	Hiromu Takahashi def. Toru Yano
R2	Kazuchika Okada def. Yuji Nagata
R2	Taiji Ishimori def. Yoshinobu Kamemaru
R2	Taichi def. Kota Ibushi
R2	Sanada def. Sho
R2	Yoshi-Hashi def. Bushi
R2	Evil def. Hirooki Goto
QF	Hiromu Takahashi def. Tomohiro Ishii
QF	Kazuchika Okada def. Taiji Ishimori
QF	Sanada def. Taichi

QF	Evil def. Yoshi-Hashi
SF	Kazuchika Okada def. Hiromu Takahashi
SF	Evil def. Sanada
F	Evil def. Kazuchika Okada

2021

R1	Jeff Cobb def. Satoshi Kojima
R1	Great-O-Khan def. Tetsuya Naito
R1	Toru Yano def. Bad Luck Fale
R1	Hirooki Goto def. Taichi
R1	Shingo Takagi def. Kazuchika Okada
R1	Minoru Suzuzki def. Tomoaki Honma
R1	Kenta def. Juice Robinson
R1	Will Ospreay def. Hiroyoshi Tenzan
R1	Zack Sabre Jr. def. Gabriel Kidd
R1	Yuji Nagata def. Yota Tsuji
R1	Sanada def. Tomohiro Ishii
R1	David Finlay def. Chase Owens
R1	Yoshi-Hashi def. Yujiro Takahashi
R1	Jay White def. Toa Henare
R2	Evil def. Jeff Cobb
R2	Toru Yano def. Great-O-Khan
R2	Shingo Takagi def. Hirooki Goto
R2	Kenta def. Minoru Suzuki
R2	WIll Ospreay def. Zack Sabre Jr.
R2	Sanada def. Yuji Nagata
R2	David Finlay def. Yoshi-Hashi
R2	Jay White def. Hiroshi Tanahashi
QF	Evil def. Toru Yano
QF	Shingo Takagi def. Kenta
QF	Will Ospreay def. Sanada
QF	David Finlay def. Jay White
SF	Shingo Takagi def. Evil
SF	Will Ospreay def. David Finlay
F	Will Ospreay def. Shingo Takagi

2022

R1	Kazuchika Okada def. El Desperado
R1	Taichi def. Toru Yano
R1	Hirooki Goto def. Yuji Nagata
R1	Cima def. Taka Michinoku
R1	Hiroshi Tanahashi def. Yoh
R1	Tetsuya Naito def. Yujiro Takahashi
R1	Jeff Cobb def. Togi Makabe
R1	Yoshi-Hashi def. Tomoaki Honma
R1	Great-O-Khan def. Kota Ibushi
R1	Zack Sabre Jr. def. Ryohei Oiwa
R1	Aaron Henare def. Yuto Nakashima
R1	Will Ospreay def. Bushi
R1	Shingo Takagi def. Tomohiro Ishii
R1	Chase Owens def. Jado
R1	Evil def. Ryusuke Taguchi
R1	Hiromu Takakashi def. Sho
R2	Kazuchika Okada def. Master Wato
R2	Taichi def. Hiroyoshi Tenzan
R2	Hirooki Goto def. Dick Togo
R2	Cima def. Yoshinobu Kanemaru
R2	Hiroshi Tanahashi def. Bad Luck Fale
R2	Tetsuya Naito def. Gedo
R2	Jeff Cobb def. Satoshi Kojima
R2	Yoshi-Hashi def. Kosei Fujita
R2	Great-O-Khan def. Taiji Ishimori
R2	Zack Sabre Jr. def. Douki
R2	Sanada def. Aaron Henare
R2	Will Ospreay def. El Phantasmo
R2	Shingo Takagi def. Tanga Loa
R2	Chase Owens def. Tiger Mask
R2	Evil def. Tama Tonga
R2	Hiromu Takahashi def. Minoru Suzuki
R3	Kazuchika Okada def. Taichi
R3	Cima def. Hirooki Goto

R3	Tetsuya Naito def. Hiroshi Tanahashi
R3	Jeff Cobb def. Yoshi-Hashi
R3	Zack Sabre Jr. def. Great-O-Khan
R3	Will Ospreay def. Sanada
R3	Shingo Takagi def. Chase Owens
R3	Hiromu Takahashi def. Evil
QF	Kazuchika Okada def. Cima
QF	Tetsuya Naito def. Jeff Cobb
QF	Zack Sabre Jr. def. Will Ospreay
QF	Shingo Takagi def. Hiromu Takahashi
SF	Tetsuya Naito def. Kazuchika Okada
SF	Zack Sabre Jr. def. Shingo Takagi
F	Zack Sabre Jr. def. Tetsuya Naito

NJPW SUPER J-CUP

YEAR	WON BY
1994	**Wild Pegasus**
	(Runner Up: The Great Sasuke)
1995	**Jushin Liger**
	(Runner Up: Gedo)
2000	**Jushin Liger**[2]
	(Runner Up: Cima)
2004	**Naomichi Marufuji**
	(Runner Up: Takehiro Murahama)
2009	**Naomichi Marufuji**[2]
	(Runner Up: Prince Devitt)
2016	**Kushida**
	(Runner Up: Yoshinobu Kanemaru)
2019	**El Phantasmo**
	(Runner Up: Dragon Lee)
2020	**El Phantasmo**[2]
	(Runner Up: ACH)

1994

R1	Black Tiger def. Taka Michinoku
R1	Gedo def. Dean Malenko
R1	Super Delfin def. Shinjiro Otani
R1	Ricky Fuji def. Negro Casas
R1	Jushin Liger def. Hayabusa
R1	El Samurai def. Masayoshi Motegi
QF	Wild Pegasus def. Black Tiger
QF	Gedo def. Super Delfin
QF	Jushin Liger def. Ricky Fuji
QF	The Great Sasuke def. El Samurai
SF	Wild Pegasus def. Gedo
SF	The Great Sasuke def. Jushin Liger
F	Wild Pegasus def. The Great Sasuke

1995

R1	Gran Naniwa def. Damian 666
R1	Shinjiro Otani def. Masaaki Mochizuki
R1	Ultimo Dragon def. Shoichi Funaki
R1	Gedo def. Masayoshi Motegi
R1	Dos Caras def. El Samurai
R1	Lionheart def. Hanzo Nakajima
QF	Jushin Liger def. Gran Naniwa
QF	Ultimo Dragon def. Shinjiro Otani
QF	Gedo def. Dos Caras
QF	Wild Pegasus def. Lionheart
SF	Jushin Liger def. Ultimo Dragon
SF	Gedo def. Wild Pegasus
F	Jushin Liger def. Gedo

2000

R1	Cima def. Ricky Marvin
R1	Onryo def. Curry Man
R1	Naoki Sano def. Judo Suwa
R1	The Great Sasuke def. Kaz Hayashi
R1	Jushin Liger def. Tiger Mask IV

R1	Men's Teioh def. Katsumi Usada
R1	Gran Hamada def. Shinya Makabe
R1	Ricky Fuji def. Sasuke The Great
QF	Cima def. Onryo
QF	Naoki Sano def. The Great Sasuke
QF	Jushin Liger def. Men's Teioh
QF	Gran Hamada def. Ricky Fuji
SF	Cima def. Naoki Sano
SF	Jushin Liger def. Gran Hamada
F	Jushin Liger def. Cima

2004

QF	Naomichi Marufuji def. Jun Kasai
QF	Garudo def. Goa
QF	Wataru Inoue def. Kazuya Yuasa
QF	Takehiro Murahama def. Taichi Ishikari
SF	Naomichi Marufuji def. Garuda
SF	Takehiro Muraham def. Wataru Inoue
F	Naomichi Marufuji def. Takehiro Murahama

2009

R1	Prince Devitt def. Atsushi Aoki
R1	Danshoku Dino def. Jado
R1	Gedo def. Kota Ibushi
R1	Yamato def. Akira
R1	Naomichi Marufuji def. Jushin Liger
R1	Tigers Mask def. Taichi
R1	Koji Kanemoto def. Hayato Fujita
R1	Ryusuke Taguchi def. Gentaro
QF	Prince Devitt def. Danshoku Dino
QF	Yamato def. Gedo
QF	Naomichi Marufuji def. Tigers Mask
QF	Ryusuke Taguchi def. Koji Kanemoto
SF	Prince Devitt def. Yamato
SF	Naomichi Marufuji def. Ryusuke Taguchi
F	Naomichi Marufuji def. Prince Devitt

2016

R1	Jushin Liger def. Eita
R1	Taichi def. Yuma Aoyagi
R1	Kushida def. Taiji Ishimori
R1	Kenoh def. Gurukun Mask
R1	Ryusuke Taguchi def. Daisuke Harada
R1	Yoshinobu Kanemaru def. Bushi
R1	Will Ospreay def. Titan
R1	Matt Sydal def. Kaji Tomato
QF	Taichi def. Jushin Liger
QF	Kushida def. Kenoh
QF	Yoshinobu Kanemaru def. Ryusuke Taguchi
QF	Matt Sydal def. Will Ospreay
SF	Kushida def. Taichi
SF	Yoshinobu Kanemaru def. Matt Sydal
F	Kushida def. Yoshinobu Kanemaru

2019

R1	Will Ospreay def. Amazing Red
R1	Sho def. Taiji Ishimoro
R1	TJP def. Clark Connors
R1	El Phantasmo def. Robbie Eagles
R1	Ryusuke Taguchi def. Jonathan Gresham
R1	Dragon Lee def. Yoh
R1	Caristico def. Bushi
R1	Soberano Jr. def. Rocky Romero
QF	Will Ospreay def. Yoh
QF	El Phantasmo def. TJP
QF	Dragon Lee def. Ryusuke Taguchi
QF	Caristico def. Soberano Jr.
SF	El Phantasmo def. Will Ospreay
SF	Dragon Lee def. Caristico
F	El Phantasmo def. Caristico

2020

QF	Chris Bey def. Clark Connors
QF	ACH def. TJP
QF	Blake Christian def. Rey Horus
QF	El Phantasmo def. Lio Rush
SF	ACH def. Chris Bey
SF	El Phantasmo def. Blake Christian
F	El Phantasmo def. ACH

NJPW SUPER JUNIOR TAG LEAGUE

YEAR	WON BY
2010	**El Samurai & Koji Kanemoto** (Runners Up: Prince Devitt & Ryusuke Taguchi)
2012	**Alex Shelley & Kushida** (Runners Up: Prince Devitt & Ryusuke Taguchi)
2013	**Matt Jackson & Nick Jackson** (Runners Up: Alex Koslov & Rocky Romero)
2014	**Bobby Fish & Kyle O'Reilly** (Runners Up: Matt Jackson & Nick Jackson)
2015	**Matt Sydal & Ricochet** (Runners Up: Trent Beretta & Rocky Romero)
2016	**Trent Beretta & Rocky Romero** (Runners Up: ACH & Taiji Ishimori)
2017	**Sho & Yoh** (Runners Up: ACH & Ryusuke Taguchi)
2018	**Sho[2] & Yoh[2]** (Runners Up: Yoshinobu Kanemaru & El Desperado
2019	**Sho[3] & Yoh[3]** (Runners Up: Yoshinobu Kanemaru & El Desperado)
2021	**El Desperado & Yoshinobu Kanemaru** (Runners Up: Taiji Ishimori & El Phantasmo)
2022	**Lio Rush & Yoh[4]** (Runners Up: Ace Austin & Chris Bey)

2010

QF	Fujita Hayato & Taro Nohashi def. Jushin Liger & Nobuo Yoshihashi
QF	El Samurai & Koji Kanemoto def. Davey Richards & Tama Tonga
QF	Gedo & Kushida def. Austin Creed & Kota Ibushi
QF	Prince Devitt & Ryusuke Taguchi def. Mascara Dorado & Valiente
SF	El Samurai & Koji Kanemoto def. Fujita Hayato & Taro Nohashi
SF	Prince Devitt & Ryusuke Taguchi def. Gedo & Kushida
F	El Samurai & Koji Kanemoto def. Prince Devitt & Ryusuke Taguchi

2012

QF	Alex Koslov & Rocky Romero def. Jushin Liger & Tiger Mask
QF	Prince Devitt & Ryusuke Taguchi def. Brian Kendrick & Low Ki
QF	Alex Shelley & Kushida def. Jado & Gedo
QF	Taichi & Taka Michinoku def. Bushi & Negro Casas
SF	Prince Devitt & Ryusuke Taguchi def. Alex Koslov & Rocky Romero
SF	Alex Shelley & Kushida def. Taichi & Taka Michinoku
F	Alex Shelley & Kushida def. Prince Devitt & Ryusuke Taguchi

2013

QF	Jado & Gedo def. Jushin Liger & Tiger Mask
QF	Matt Jackson & Nick Jackson def. Trent Beretta & Brian Kendrick
QF	Bushi & Valiente def. Kushida & Yohei Komatsu
QF	Alex Koslov & Rocky Romero def. Taichi & Taka Michinoku
SF	Matt Jackson & Nick Jackson def. Jado & Gedo
SF	Alex Koslov & Rocky Romero def. Bushi & Valiente
F	Matt Jackson & Nick Jackson def. Alex Koslov & Rocky Romero

2014

QF	Matt Jackson & Nick Jackson def. Jushin Liger & Tiger Mask
QF	El Desperado & Taichi def. Fuego & Ryusuke Taguchi
QF	Alex Koslov & Rocky Romero def. Kushida & Alex Shelley
QF	Kyle O'Reilly & Bobby Fish def. Bushi & Mascara Dorada
SF	Mat Jackson & Nick Jackson def. El Desperado & Taichi
SF	Kyle O'Reilly & Bobby Fish def. Alex Koslov & Rocky Romero
F	Kyle O'Reilly & Bobby Fish def. Matt Jackson & Nick Jackson

2015

QF	Kyle O'Reilly & Bobby Fish def. Jushin Liger & Tiger Mask
QF	Trent Beretta & Rocky Romero def. Chase Owens & Kenny Omega
QF	Matt Jackson & Nick Jackson def. Mascara Dorada & Ryusuke Taguchi
QF	Matt Sydal & Ricochet def. Kushida & Alex Shelley
SF	Trent Beretta & Rocky Romero def. Kyle O'Reilly & Bobby Fish
SF	Mat Sydal & Ricochet def. Matt Jackson & Nick Jackson
F	Matt Sydal & Ricochet def. Trent Beretta & Rocky Romero

2016

QF	Fuego & Ryusuke Taguchi def. Jushin Liger & Tiger Mask
QF	Trent Beretta & Rocky Romero def. Angel de Oro & Titan
QF	David Finlay & Ricochet def. Gedo & Will Ospreay
QF	ACH & Taiji Ishimori def. Matt Jackson & Nick Jackson
SF	Trent Beretta & Rocky Romero def. Fuego & Ryusuke Taguchi
SF	ACH & Taiji Ishimori def. David Finlay & Ricochet
F	Trent Beretta & Rocky Romero def. ACH & Taiji Ishimori

2017

QF	Sho & Yoh def. Hirai Kawato & Kushida
QF	Bushi & Hiromu Takahashi def. Dragon Lee & Titan
QF	El Desperado & Yoshinobu Kanemaru def. Jushin Liger & Tiger Mask
QF	ACH & Ryusuke Taguchi def. Taichi & Taka Michinoku
SF	Sho & Yoh def. Bushi & Hiromu Takahashi
SF	ACH & Ryusuke Taguchi def. El Desperado & Yoshinobu Kanemaru
F	Sho & Yoh & ACH & Ryusuke Taguchi

2018

Block Standings: El Desperado & Yoshinobu Kanemaru 10, Bushi & Shingo Takagi 10, **Sho & Yoh 10**, Taiji Ishimori & Robbie Eagles 6, Kushida & Chris Sabin 6, Ryusuke Taguchi & ACH 6, Jushin Liger & Tiger Mask 4, Volador Jr. & Soberano Jr. 4

2019

Block Standings: El Desperado & Yoshinobu Kanemaru 10, **Sho & Yoh 10**, Taiji Ishimori & El Phantasmo 10, Will Ospreay & Robbie Eagles 8, Volador & Titan 8, Ryusuke Taguchi & Rocky Romero 8, TJ Perkins & Clark Connors 2, Tiger Mask & Yuya Uemura 0

2021

Block Standings: El Desperado & Yoshinobu Kanemaru 8, Taiji Ishimori & El Phantasmo 8, Ryusuke Taguchi & Master Wato 6, Tiger Mask & Robbie Eagles 6, Sho & Yoh 0, Gedo & Dick Togo 0

2022

Block Standings: Ace Austin & Chris Bey 14, **Lio Rush & Yoh 14**, TJP & Francesco Akira 12, Alex Zayne & El Lindaman 12, Bushi & Titan 12, Yoshinobu Kanemaru & Douki 8, Ryusuke Taguchi & Clark Connors 6, Robbie Eagles & Tiger Mask 4, Kushida & Kevin Knight 4, Sho & Dick Togo 4

NJPW WORLD TAG LEAGUE

YEAR	WON BY
1980	**Antonio Inoki & Bob Backlund** (Runners Up: Hulk Hogan & Stan Hansen)
1981	**Andre The Giant & Rene Goulet** (Runners Up: Antonio Inoki & Tatsumi Fujinami)
1982	**Antonio Inoki[2] & Hulk Hogan** (Runners Up: Killer Khan & Tiger Toguchi)
1983	**Antonio Inoki[3] & Hulk Hogan[2]** (Runners Up: Adrian Adonis & Dick Murdoch)
1984	**Antonio Inoki[4] & Tatsumi Fujinami** (Runners Up: Adrian Adonis & Dick Murdoch)
1985	**Tatsumi Fujinami[2] & Kengo Kimura** (Runners Up: Antonio Inoki & Seiji Sakaguchi)
1986	**Antonio Inoki[5] & Yoshiaki Fujiwara** (Runners Up: Osamu Kido & Akira Maeda)
1987	**Tatsumi Fujinami[3] & Kengo Kimura[2]** (Runners Up: Antonio Inoki & Dick Murdoch)
1991	**Tatsumi Fujinami[4] & Big Van Vader** (Runners Up: Riki Choshu & Masa Saito)
1992	**Riki Choshu & Shinya Hashimoto** (Runners Up: Hiroshi Hase & Kensuke Sasaki)
1993	**Hiroshi Hase & Keiji Mutoh** (Runners Up: Hercules & Scott Norton)
1994	**Hiroshi Hase[2] & Keiji Mutoh[2]** (Runners Up: Masahiro Chono & Super Strong Machine)
1995	**Masahiro Chono & Hiroyoshi Tenzan** (Runners Up: Osamu Kido & Kazuo Yamazaki)
1996	**Shinya Hashimoto[2] & Scott Norton** (Runners Up: Keiji Mutoh & Rick Steiner)
1997	**Masahiro Chono[2] & Keiji Mutoh[3]** (Runners Up: Shinya Hashimoto & Manabu Nakanishi)
1998	**Satoshi Kojima & Keiji Mutoh[4]**

(Runners Up: Shinya Hashimoto
& Tatsumi Fujinami)

1999	**Keiji Mutoh[5] & Scott Norton**

(Runners Up: Yuji Nagata
& Manabu Nakanishi)

2000	**Takashi Iizuka & Yuji Nagata**

(Runners Up: Satoshi Kojima
& Hiroyoshi Tenzan)

2001	**Satoshi Kojima[2] & Hiroyoshi Tenzan[2]**

(Runners Up: Mike Barton & Jim Steele)

2003	**Osamu Nishimura & Hiroyoshi Tenzan[3]**

(Runners Up: Yoshihiro Takayama & TOA)

2006	**Masahiro Chono[3] & Shinsuke Nakamura**

(Runners Up: Koji Kanamoto
& Hiroshi Tanahashi)

2007	**Giant Bernard & Travis Tomko**

(Runners Up: Koji Kanemoto
& Hiroshi Tanahashi)

2008	**Satoshi Kojima[3] & Hiroyshi Tenzan[4]**

(Runners Up: Togi Makabe & Toru Yano)

2009	**Karl Anderson & Giant Bernard[2]**

(Runners Up: Prince Devitt & Ryusuke Taguchi)

2010	**Yuji Nagata[2] & Wataru Inoue**

(Runners Up: Tetsuya Naito & Yujiro Takahashi)

2011	**Lance Archer & Minoru Suzuki**

(Runners Up: Giant Bernard & Karl Anderson)

2012	**Hirooki Goto & Karl Anderson[2]**

(Runners Up: Davey Boy Smith Jr.
& Lance Archer)

2013	**Luke Gallows & Karl Anderson[3]**

(Runners Up: Satoshi Kojima
& Hiroyoshi Tenzan)

2014	**Hirooki Goto[2] & Katsuyori Shibata**

(Runners Up: Luke Gallows & Karl Anderson)

2015	**Togi Makabe & Tomoaki Honma**

(Runners Up: Evil & Tetsuya Naito)

2016	**Togi Makabe[2] & Tomoaki Honma[2]**

(Runners Up: Tama Tonga & Tanga Loa)

2017	**Evil & Sanada**

(Runners Up: Tama Tonga & Tanga Loa)

2018	**Evil[2] & Sanada[2]**

(Runners Up: Tama Tonga & Tanga Loa)

2019	**Juce Robinson & David Finlay**

(Runners Up: Evil & Sanada)

2020	**Tama Tonga & Tanga Loa**

(Runners Up: Juice Robinson & David Finlay)

2021	**Hirooki Goto[3] & Yoshi-Hashi**

(Runners Up: Evil & Yujiro Takahashi)

2022	**Hirooki Goto[4] & Yoshi-Hashi[2]**

(Runners Up: Kyle Fletcher & Mark Davis)

1980
Block Standings: Antonio Inoki & Bob Backlund 34,
Stan Hansen & Hulk Hogan 32, Andre the Giant & The
Hangman 28, Tiger Jeet Singh and Umanosuke Ueda 24,
Seiji Sakaguchi & Strong Kobayashi 20, Tatsumi Fujinami
& Kengo Kimura 15, Willem Ruska & Bad News Allen 10,
Kantaro Hoshino & Riki Choshu 9, Ox Baker & Johnny
Powers 0

1981
Block Standings: Andre the Giant & Rene Goulet 10,
Antonio Inoki & Tatsumi Fujinami 8, Stan Hansen & Dick
Murdoch 8, Tiger Toguchi & Killer Khan 6, Seiji Sakaguchi
& Kengo Kimura 6, Rusher Kimura & Animal Hamaguchi
2, Riki Choshu & Yoshiaki Yatsu 2. Bad News Allen & Pat
Patterson 2, Afa & Sika 2, El Canek & Super Maquina 2

1982
Block Standings: Antonio Inoki & Hulk Hogan 28,
Killer Khan & Tiger Toguchi 23, Seiji Sakaguchi & Tatsumi

Fujinami 22, Dick Murdoch & Masked Superstar 21, Andre
the Giant & Rene Goulet 20, Adrian Adonis & Dino Bravo
9, El Canek & Perro Aguayo 4, Wayne Bridges & Young
Samson 0

1983
Block Standings: Andre the Giant & Swede Hanson 32,
Antonio Inoki & Hulk Hogan 28.5, Adrian Adonis & Dick
Murdoch 27.5, Riki Choshu & Animal Hamaguchi 26.5,
Tatsumi Fujinami & Akira Maeda 24, Killer Khan & Tiger
Toguchi 16.5m Seiji Sakaguchi & Kengo Kimura 14, Bobby
Duncum & Curt Hennig 5, Wayne Bridges & Otto Wanz 5

1984
Block Standings: Adrian Adonis & Dick Murdoch 23,
Antonio Inoki & Tatsumi Fujinami 22.5, Andre the Giant
& Gerry Morrow 21.5, Seiji Sakaguchi & Kengo Kimura
13, Tiger Toguchi & Kerry Brown 8, Strong Machine #1 &
Strong Machine #2 8, Hulk Hogan & The Wild Samoan 0

1985
Block Standings: Bruiser Brody & Jimmy Snuka 29,
Tatsumi Fujinami & Kengo Kimura 23, Antonio Inoki &
Seiji Sakaguchi 21, Dick Murdoch & Masked Superstar 19,
Hacksaw Higgins & Nord the Barbarian 19, El Canek &
Dos Caras 9, Mr. Pogo & Kendo Nagasaki 7, Mike Kelly
& Pat Kelly 0

1986
Block Standings: Antonio Inoki & Yoshiaki Fujiwara,
Osamu Kido & Akira Maeda, Dick Murdoch & Masked
Superstar, Nobuhiko Takada & Shiro Koshinaka, Keiji
Mutoh & Tatsumi Fujinami, Kengo Kimura & George
Takano, Tonga Kid & The Wild Samoan, Seiji Sakaguchi &
Umanosuke Ueda

1987
Block Standings: Antonio Inoki & Dick Murdoch 29,
Tatsumi Fujinami & Kengo Kimura 26, Masa Saito &
Yoshiaki Fujiwara 26, Seiji Sakaguchi & Scott Hall 17, Keiji
Mutoh & Nobuhiko Takada 13, Akira Maeda & Super
Strong Machine 10, Kendo Nagasaki & Mr. Pogo 9, Ron
Starr & Ron Ritchie 0

1991
Block Standings: Riki Choshu & Masa Saito 10, Tatsumi
Fujinami & Big Van Vader 8, Bam Bam Bigelow &
Masahiro Chono 8, Hiroshi Hase & Keiji Mutoh 6, Shinya
Hashimoto & Scott Norton 6, The Great Kokina & The
Wild Samoan 2, Kim Duk & Tiger Jeet Singh 2

1992
Block Standings: Riki Choshu & Shinya Hashimoto 9,
Hiroshi Hase & Kensuke Sasaki 9, Bam Bam Bigelow &
Keiji Mutoh 8, Masahiro Chono & Tony Halme 8, Scott
Norton & Super Strong Machine 6, Tatsumi Fujinami &
Manabu Nakanishi 2, Tom Zenk & Jim Neidhart 0

1993
Block Standings: Hercules Hernandez & Scott Norton
14, **Hiroshi Hase & Keiji Mutoh 14,** Masahiro Chono &
Shinya Hashimoto 13, Tatsumi Fujinami & Osamu Kido
13, Hawk Warrior & Power Warrior 10, Shiro Koshinaka
& Michiyoshi Ohara 8, Takayuki Iizuka & Akira Nogami
6, The Barbarian & Masa Saito 4, Jushin Liger & Wild
Pegasus 4, Brad Armstrong & Sean Royal 0

1994
Block Standings: Masahiro Chono & Super Strong
Machine 14, **Hiroshi Hase & Keiji Mutoh 14,** Hawk
Warrior & Power Warrior 14, Tatsumi Fujinami & Yoshiaki

Fujiwara 10, Osamu Kido & Scott Norton 10, Shinya Hashimoto & Manabu Nakanishi 8, Takayuki Iizuka & Akira Nogami 6, Riki Choshu & Yoshiaki Yatsu 6, Mike Enos & Steven Regal 6, Nailz & Ron Simmons 4

1995
Block Standings: Osamu Kido & Kazuo Yamazaki 8, **Masahiro Chono & Hiroyoshi Tenzan 7,** Shinya Hashimoto & Junji Hirata 7, Tatsutoshi Goto & Shiro Koshinaka 6, Keiji Mutoh & Osamu Nishimura 6, Takashi Iizuka & Akira Nogami 4, Masa Saito/Riki Choshu & Kensuke Sasaki 4

1996
Block Standings: Keiji Mutoh & Rick Steiner 5, **Shinya Hashimoto & Scott Norton 5,** Takashi Iizuka & Kazuo Yamazaki 4, Riki Choshu & Kensuke Sasaki 4, Masahiro Chono & Hiroyoshi Tenzan 3, Satoshi Kojima & Manabu Nakanishi 3, Tatsumi Fujinami & Shiro Koshinaka 2, Steve Regal & David Taylor 1

1997
Block Standings: Masahiro Chono & Keiji Mutoh 6, Shinya Hashimoto & Manabu Nakanishi 5, Kensuke Sasaki & Kazuo Yamazaki 5, Tatsumi Fujinami & Kengo Kimura 4, nWo Sting & Hiroyoshi Tenzan 3, Satoshi Kojima & Tadao Yasuda 2, Kenny Kaos & Rob Rage 2, Tatsutoshi Goto & Michiyoshi Ohara 1

1998
Block Standings: Keiji Mutoh & Satoshi Kojima 8, Tatsumi Fujinami & Shinya Hashimoto 8, Kensuke Sasaki & Kazuo Yamazaki 8, Shiro Koshinaka & Genichiro Tenryu 8, Yuji Nagata & Manabu Nakanishi 6, nWo Sting & Hiroyoshi Tenzan 4, David Finlay & Jerry Flynn 0

1999
Block Standings: Scott Norton & Keiji Mutoh 14, Yuji Nagata & Manabu Nakanishi 10, Satoshi Kojima & Hiroyoshi Tenzan 10, Junji Hirata & Shiro Koshinaka 8, Shinya Hashimoto & Meng 8, Masahiro Chono & Don Frye 6, Tatsutoshi Goto & Michiyoshi Ohara 6, Takashi Iizuka & Brian Johnston 6, Kazuyuki Fujita & Kensuke Sasaki 4

2000
Block Standings: Takashi Iizuka & Yuji Nagata 8, Satoshi Kojima & Hiroyoshi Tenzan 8, Manabu Nakanishi & Yutaka Yoshie 8, Masahiro Chono & Scott Norton 8, Jushin Liger & Super Strong Machine 4, Shiro Koshinaka & Kensuke Sasaki 4, T2000 Machine #1 & T2000 Machine #2 2

2001
Block Standings: Mike Barton & Jim Steele 9, **Satoshi Kojima & Hiroyoshi Tenzan 8,** Yuji Nagata & Manabu Nakanishi 8, Dan Devine & Kensuke Sasaki 8, Scott Norton & Super J 7, Jushin Liger & Osamu Nishimura 6, Masahiro Chono & Giant Silva 6, Kenzo Suzuki & Hiroshi Tanahashi 4

2003
Block Standings: Yoshihiro Takayama & TOA 10, **Osamu Nishimura & Hiroyoshi Tenzan 9,** Yuji Nagata & Manabu Nakanishi 9, Hiroshi Tanahashi & Yutaka Yoshie 7, Makai #1 & Tadao Yasuda 7, Mike Barton & Jim Steele 6, Blue Wolf & Shinsuke Nakamura 6, Masahiro Chono & Jushin Liger 2

2006
Block A: Takashi Iizuka & Yuji Nagata 6, **Masahiro Chono & Shinsuke Nakamura 4,** Akebono & Riki Choshu 4, Gedo & Jado 4, Shiro Koshinaka & Togi Makabe 2
Block B: Giant Bernard & Travis Tomko 6, Koji Kanemoto & Hiroshi Tanahashi 4, Jushin Liger & Hiroyoshi Tenzan 4, Tomohiro Ishii & Toru Yano 3, Manabu Nakanishi & Naofumi Yamamoto 3

2007
Block Standings: Giant Bernard & Travis Tomko 8, Hirooki Goto & Milano Collection A.T. 8, Koji Kanemoto & Hiroshi Tanahashi 8, Togi Makabe & Toru Yano 8, Takashi Iizuka & Naofumi Yamamoto 6, Gedo & Jado 6, Yuji Nagata & Manabu Nakanishi 6, Akebono & Masahiro Chono 6

2008
Block A: Satoshi Kojima & Hiroyoshi Tenzan 8, Hirooki Goto & Shinsuke Nakamura 7, Giant Bernard & Rick Fuller 7, Wataru Inoue & Koji Kanemoto 4, Taichi Ishikari & Milano Collection A.T. 4, Takashi Iizuka & Tomohiro Ishii 2
Block B: Togi Makabe & Toru Yano 8, Manabu Nakanishi & Yutaka Yoshie 7, Gedo & Jado 6, Tetsuya Naito & Yujiro 4, Negro Casas & Rocky Romero 4, Mitsuhide Hirasawa & Yuji Nagata 1

2009
Block A: Shinsuke Nakamura & Toru Yano 6, Manabu Nakanishi & Takao Omori 6, Wataru Inoue & Yuji Nagata 4, Tomohiro Ishii & Masato Tanaka 4, Hirooki Goto & Kazuchika Okada 0 **Block B: Karl Anderson & Giant Bernard 8,** Prince Devitt & Ryusuke Taguchi 4, Togi Makabe & Tomoaki Honma 4, Masahiro Chono & Akira 2, Gedo & Jado 2

2010
Block A: Yuji Nagata & Wataru Inoue 8, Manabu Nakanishi & Strong Man 8, Masato Tanaka & Tomohiro Ishii 6, Hirooki Goto & Tama Tonga 4, Togi Makabe & Tomoaki Honma 4, King Fale & Super Strong Machine 0 **Block B:** Tetsuya Naito & Yujiro Takahashi 6, Giant Bernard & Karl Anderson 6, Hiroshi Tanahashi & Tajiri 6, Daniel Puder & Shinsuke Nakamura 4, Terrible & El Texano Jr. 4, Takashi Iizuka & Toru Yano 4

2011
Block A: Giant Bernard & Karl Anderson 8, **Lance Archer & Minoru Suzuki 8,** Masato Tanaka & Yujiro Takahashi 6, Tetsuya Naito & Tomoaki Honma 4, Strong Man & Tama Tonga 2, King Fale & Yuji Nagata 2 **Block B:** Shinsuke Nakamura & Toru Yano 10, Hirooki Goto & Hiroshi Tanahashi 6, Satoshi Kojima & Togi Makabe 6, Don Fujii & Tomohiro Ishii 4, Hiroyoshi Tenzan & Wataru Inoue 4, Hideo Saito & Takashi Iizuka 0

2012
Block A: Togi Makabe & Wataru Inoue 8, **Hirooki Goto & Karl Anderson 8,** Masaaki Mochizuki & Yuji Nagata 8, Shinsuke Nakamura & Tomohiro Ishii 6, Kazuchika Okada & Yoshi-Hashi 6, Kengo Mashimo & Minoru Suzuki 6, Captain New Japan & Hiroshi Tanahashi 0 **Block B:** Hiroyoshi Tenzan & Satoshi Kojima 8, Davey Boy Smith Jr. & Lance Archer 8, Masato Tanaka & Yujiro Takahashi 6, Takashi Iizuka & Toru Yano 6, MVP & Shelton Benjamin 6, Manabu Nakanishi & Strong Man 4, Diamante Azul & Rush 4

2013
Block A: Davey Boy Smith Jr. & Lance Archer 10, Togi Makabe & Tomoaki Honma 8, Bad Luck Fale & Prince

Devitt 6, Masato Tanaka & Yujiro Takahashi 6, Shinsuke Nakamura & Tomohiro Ishii 6, Manabu Nakanishi & Strong Man 4, Captain New Japan & Hiroshi Tanahashi 2 **Block B: Luke Gallows & Karl Anderson 8**, Hiroyoshi Tenzan & Satoshi Kojima 8, Jax Dane & Rob Conway 6, Minoru Suzuki & Shelton Benjamin 6, La Sombra & Tetsuya Naito 6, Kazuchika Okada & Yoshi-Hashi 4, Takashi Iizuka & Toru Yano 4

2014

Block A: Luke Gallows & Karl Anderson 10, Kazuchika Okada & Yoshi-Hashi 8, Matt Taven & Mike Bennett 8, AJ Styles & Yujiro Takahashi 8, La Sombra & Tetsuya Naito 8, Hiroyoshi Tenzan & Satoshi Kojima 8, Jax Dane & Rob Conway 6, Hiroshi Tanahashi & Yoshitatsu 0 **Block B: Hirooki Goto & Katsuyori Shibata 8**, Shinsuke Nakamura & Tomohiro Ishii 8, Davey Boy Smith Jr. & Lance Archer 8, Kazushi Sakuraba & Toru Yano 7, Minoru Suzuki & Takashi Iizuka 7, Bad Luck Fale & Tama Tonga 6, Manabu Nakanishi & Yuji Nagata 6, Togi Makabe & Tomoaki Honma 6

2015

Block A: Togi Makabe & Tomoaki Honma 8, Hiroshi Tanahashi & Michael Elgin 8, Christopher Daniels & Frankie Kazarian 6, Kazuchika Okada & Yoshi-Hashi 6, Kazushi Sakuraba & Toru Yano 6, Bad Luck Fale & Tama Tonga 4, Manabu Nakanishi & Yuji Nagata 4 **Block B:** Evil & Tetsuya Naito 10, Hirooki Goto & Katsuyori Shibata 8, Luke Gallows & Karl Anderson 8, Shinsuke Nakamura & Tomohiro Ishii 6, Matt Taven & Mike Bennett 4, Hiroyoshi Tenzan & Satoshi Kojima 4, AJ Styles & Yujiro Takahashi 2

2016

Block A: Tama Tonga & Tanga Loa 12, Hangman Page & Yujiro Takahashi 8, Hanson & Raymond Rowe 8, Hiroyoshi Tenzan & Satoshi Kojima 8, Rush & Tetsuya Naito 8, Hiroshi Tanahashi & Juice Robinson 6, Brian Breaker & Leland Race 6, Henare & Manabu Nakanishi 6 **Block B: Togi Makabe & Tomoaki Honma 10**, Evil & Sanada 10, Kazuchika Okada & Yoshi-Hashi 8, Katsuyori Shibata & Yuji Nagata 8, Hirooki Goto & Tomohiro Ishii 8, Billy Gunn & Yoshitatsu 6, Chase Owens & Kenny Omega 6, Bad Luck Fale & Bone Soldier 0

2017

Block A: Evil & Sanada 10, Juice Robinson & Sami Callihan 8, Hangman Page & Yujiro Takahashi 8, Hirooki Goto & Yoshi-Hashi 8, Bad Luck Fale & Chase Owens 6, Hiroyoshi Tenzan & Satoshi Kojima 6, Minoru Suzuki & Takashi Iizuka 6, Manabu Nakanishi & Yuji Nagata 4 **Block B:** Tama Tonga & Tanga Loa 10, Hanson & Raymond Rowe 10, Davey Boy Smith Jr. & Lance Archer 10, Beretta & Chuckie T 8, Jeff Cobb & Michael Elgin 8, Tomohiro Ishii & Toru Yano 8, Henare & Togi Makabe 2, David Finlay & Katsuya Kitamura 0

2018

Block Standings: Tama Tonga & Tanga Loa 20, **Evil & Sanada 20**, Tomohiro Ishii & Toru Yano 18, Davey Boy Smith Jr. & Lance Archer 18, Michael Elgin & Jeff Cobb 16, Zack Sabre Jr. & Taichi 16, Juice Robinson & David Finlay 16, Beretta & Chuckie T 14, Minoru Suzuki & Takashi Iizuka 10, Hangman Page & Yujiro Takahashi 10, Hiroyoshi Tenzan & Satoshi Kojima 10, Togi Makabe & Toa Henare 8, Yuji Nagata & Manabu Nakanishi 6, Ayato Yoshida & Shota Umino 0

2019

Block Standings: Juice Robinson & David Finlay 26, Evil & Sanada 26, Tama Tonga & Tanga Loa 24, Tomohiro Ishii & Yoshi-Hashi 22, Zack Sabre Jr. & Taichi 18, Minoru Suzuki & Lance Archer 18, Toru Yano & Colt Cabana 18, Kenta & Yujiro Takahashi 16, Jeff Cobb & Mikey Nicholls 16, Shingo Takagi & Terrible 12, Bad Luck Fale & Chase Owens 12, Hiroyoshi Tenzan & Satoshi Kojima 8, Togi Makabe & Tomoaki Honma 8, Hirooki Goto & Karl Fredericks 6, Hiroshi Tanahashi & Toa Henare 6, Yuji Nagata & Manabu Nakanishi 4

2020

Block Standings: Juice Robinson & David Finlay 12, **Tama Tonga & Tanga Loa 12**, Zack Sabre Jr. & Taichi 12, Shingo Takagi & Sanada 10, Tomohiro Ishii & Toru Yano 10, Hirooki Goto & Yoshi-Hashi 10, Great-O-Khan & Jeff Cobb 10, Bad Luck Fale & Chase Owens 6, Evil & Yujiro Takahashi 6, Hiroshi Tanahashi & Toa Henare 2

2021

Standings: Hirooki Goto & Yoshi-Hashi 18, Evil & Yujiro Takahashi 16, Taichi & Zack Sabre Jr. 16, Tetsuya Naito & Sanada 16, Tama Tonga & Tanga Loa 14, Hiroshi Tanahashi & Toru Yano 14, Great-O-Khan & Aaron Henare 14, Bad Luck Fale & Chase Owens 12, Hiroyoshi Tenzan & Satoshi Kojima 6, Togi Makabe & Tomoaki Honma 4, Yuji Nagata & Tiger Mask 2, Minoru Suzuki & Taka Michinoku 0.

NOAH GLOBAL JUNIOR HEAVYWEIGHT LEAGUE

YEAR	WON BY
2009	**Yoshinobu Kanemaru** (Runner Up: Jushin Liger)
2015	**Daisuke Harada** (Runner Up: Atsushi Kotoge)
2018	**Kotaro Suzuki** (Runner Up: Yo-Hey)
2019	**Hayata** (Runner Up: Tadasuke)
2020	**Daisuke Harada[2]** (Runner Up: Dick Togo)

NOAH GLOBAL JUNIOR HEAVYWEIGHT TAG LEAGUE

YEAR	WON BY
2007	**Kenta & Taiji Ishimori** (Runner Up: Jay Briscoe & Mark Briscoe)
2008	**Kenta[2] & Taiji Ishimori[2]** (Runner Up: Kotaru Suzuki & Yoshinobu Kanemaru)
2009	**Kotaro Suzuki & Yoshinobu Kanemaru** (Runner Up: Atsushi Aoki & Kota Ibushi)
2010	**Kenta[3] & Atsushi Aoki** (Runner Up: Eddie Edwards & Roderick Strong)
2011	**Kotaro Suzuki[2] & Atsushi Aoki[2]** (Runner Up: Kenta & Yoshinobu Kanemaru)
2012	**Atsushi Kotoge & Taiji Ishimori** (Runner Up: Daichi Hashimoto & Ikuto Hidaka)
2013	**Jushin Liger & Tiger Mask**

(Runner Up: Atsushi Kotoge & Taiji Ishimori)

2014 **Hajime Ohara & Kenoh**
(Runner Up: Daisuke Harada & Quiet Storm)

2015 **Atsushi Kotoge^2 & Daisuke Harada**
(Runner Up: El Desperado & Taka Michinoku)

2016 **ACH & Taiji Ishimori^2**
(Runner Up: Daisuke Harada & Atsushi Kotoge)

2017 **Hayata & Yo-Hey**
(Runner Up: Hi69 & Taiji Ishimori)

2018 **Hayata^2 & Yo-Hey^2**
(Runner Up: Hajime Ohara & Hitoshi Kumano)

2019 **Kotaru Suzuki^2 & Yoshinari Ogawa**
(Runner Up: Hayata & Yo-Hey)

2021 **Tadasuke, Aleja, Haoh & Nioh**
(Runner Up: Daisuke Harada, Atsushi Kotoge, Hajime Ohara & Junta Miyawaki)

2022 **Daisuke Harada, Atsushi Kotoge^3, Hajime Ohara & Junta Miyawaki**
(Runner Up: Tadasuke, Aleja, Haoh & Nioh)

NOAH GLOBAL TAG LEAGUE

YEAR	WON BY
2008	**Akitoshi Saito & Bison Smith**
	(Runner Up: Jun Akiyama & Takeshi Rikio)
2009	**Mitsuharu Misawa & Go Shiozaki**
	(Runner Up: Takeshi Morishima & Kensuke Sasaki)
2010	**Takuma Sano & Yoshihiro Takayama**
	(Runner Up: Takashi Sugiura & Shuhei Taniguchi)
2011	**Akitoshi Saito^2 & Jun Akiyama**
	(Runner Up: Takuma Sano & Yoshihiro Takayama)
2012	**Naomichi Marufuji & Muhammad Yone**
	(Runner Up: Takeshi Morishima & Katsuhiko Nakajima)
2013	**Kenta & Yoshihiro Takayama^2**
	(Runner Up: Sasaki/Nakajima)
2014	**Masato Tanaka & Takashi Sugiura**
	(Runner Up: Naomichi Marufuji & Katsuhiko Nakajima)
2015	**Masato Tanaka^2 & Takashi Sugiura^2**
	(Runner Up: Davey Boy Smith Jr & Lance Archer)
2016	**Naomichi Marufuji^2 & Toru Yano**
	(Runner Up: Davey Boy Smith Jr & Lance Archer)
2017	**Naomichi Marufuji^3 & Maybach Taniguchi**
	(Runner Up: Atsushi Kotoge & Go Shiozaki)
2018	**Go Shiozaki^2 & Kaito Kiyomiya**
	(Runner Up: Kenoh & Takashi Sugiura)
2019	**Kazma Sakamoto & Takashi Sugiura^3**
	(Runner Up: Go Shiozaki & Katsuhiko Nakajima)
2020	**El Hijo de Dr. Wagner Jr & Rene Dupree**
	(Runner Up: Go Shiozaki & Katsuhiko Nakajima)

NOAH N-1 VICTORY

YEAR	WON BY
2010	**Yoshihiro Takayama**
	(Runner Up: Jun Akiyama)
2011	**Takeshi Morishima**
	(Runner Up: Kenta)

2012	**Kenta**
	(Runner Up: Takashi Sugiura)
2013	**Yuji Nagata**
	(Runner Up: Takeshi Morishima)
2014	**Takashi Sugiura**
	(Runner Up: Daisuke Sekimoto)
2015	**Naomichi Marufuji**
	(Runner Up: Shelton Benjamin)
2016	**Minoru Suzuki**
	(Runner Up: Masa Kitamiya)
2017	**Kenoh**
	(Runner Up: Go Shiozaki)
2018	**Kaito Kiyomiya**
	(Runner Up: Katsuhiko Nakajima)
2019	**Kenoh^2**
	(Runner Up: Takashi Sugiura)
2020	**Katsuhiko Nakajima**
	(Runner Up: Kaito Kiyomiya)
2021	**Katsuhiko Nakajima^2**
	(Runner Up: Kenoh)
2022	**Kaito Kiyomya^2**
	(Runner Up: Hideki Suzuki)

NWA CROCKETT CUP

YEAR	WON BY
1986	**Animal & Hawk**
	(Runner Up: Magnum T.A. & Ronnie Garvin)
1987	**Dusty Rhodes & Nikita Koloff**
	(Runner Up: Lex Luger & Tully Blanchard)
1988	**Lex Luger & Sting**
	(Runner Up: Arn Anderson & Tully Blanchard)
2019	**Brody King & PCO**
	(Runner Up: Royce Isaacs & Thom Latimer)
2022	**Jay Briscoe & Mark Briscoe**
	(Runner Up: Doug Williams & Harry Smith)

1986	
R1	Mark Youngblood & Wahoo McDaniel def. Bobby Jaggers & Mike Miller
R1	Nelson Royal & Sam Houston def. Bart Batten & Brad Batten
R1	Jimmy Valiant & Manny Fernandez def. Baron von Raschke & The Barbarian
R1	Steve Williams & Terry Taylor def. Bill Dundee and Buddy Landel
R1	Butch Miller & Luke Williams def. Chavo Guerrero & Hector Guerrero
R1	Bobby Fulton & Tommy Rogers def. Stan Lane & Steve Keirn
R1	Buzz Sawyer & Rick Steiner def. Koko Ware & The Italian Stallion
R1	Black Bart & Jimmy Garvin def. Brett Sawyer & David Peterson
R2	Animal & Hawk def. Mark Youngblood & Wahoo McDaniel
R2	Bobby Eaton & Dennis Condrey def. Nelson Royal & Sam Houston
R2	Bobby Fulton & Tommy Rogers def. Arn Anderson & Tully Blanchard
R2	Butch Miller & Luke Williams def. Ricky Morton & Robert Gibson
R2	Ivan Koloff & Nikita Koloff def. Jimmy Valiant & Manny Fernandez
R2	Steve Williams & Terry Taylor def. Dino Bravo & Rick Martel (forfeit)
R2	Magnum T.A. & Ronnie Garvin def. Buzz Sawyer & Rick Steiner
R2	Giant Baba & Tiger Mask

	def. Black Bart & Jimmy Garvin
QF	Animal & Hawk
	def. Bobby Eaton & Dennis Condrey
QF	Bobby Fulton & Tommy Rogers vs.
	Butch Miller & Luke Williams ended in a draw
QF	Ivan Koloff & Nikita Koloff vs.
	Steve Williams & Terry Taylor ended in a draw
QF	Magnum T.A. & Ronnie Garvin
	def. Giant Baba & Tiger Mask
SF	Animal & Hawk received a bye
SF	Magnum T.A. & Ronnie Garvin received a bye
F	Animal & Hawk
	def. Magnum T.A. & Ronnie Garvin

1987

R1	Brad Armstong & Bob Armstrong
	def. Ivan Koloff & Vladimir Petrov
R1	Basher & Spike def.
	Baron von Raschke & Wahoo McDaniel
R1	Chris Champion & Denny Brown
	def. Bill Mulkey & Randy Mulkey
R1	George South & Steve Keim vs. Mike Graham
	& Nelson Royal ended in a draw
R1	Shaska Wahtley & Teijho Khan
	def. Jimmy Valiant & LazerTron
R1	Jimmy Garvin & Ronnie Garvin
	def. Ricky Lee Jones & The Italian Stallion
R1	Thunderfoot #1 & Thunderfoot #2
	def. Bobby Jaggers & Rocky King
R1	Bill Dundee & The Barbarian
	def. Mike Rotunda & Tim Horner
R2	Brad Armstrong & Bob Armstrong
	def. Arn Anderson & Kevin Sullivan
RD2	Lex Luger & Tully Blanchard
	def. Basher & Spike
RD2	Isao Takagi & Giant Baba
	def. Chris Champion & Denny Brown
RD2	Ricky Morton & Robert Gibson received a bye
RD2	Animal & Hawk
	def. Shaska Whatley & Teijho Khan
RD2	Bobby Eaton & Stan Lane
	def. Jimmy Garvin & Ronnie Garvin
RD2	Manny Fernandez & Rick Rude
	def. Thunderfoot #1 & Thunderfoot #2
RD2	Dusty Rhodes & Nikita Koloff
	def. Bill Dundee & The Barbarian
QF	Lex Luger & Tully Blanchard
	def. Brad Armstrong & Brad Armstrong
QF	Isao Takagi & Giant Baba
	def. Ricky Morton & Robert Gibson
QF	Bobby Eaton & Stan Lane
	def. Animal & Hawk
QF	Dusty Rhodes & Nikita Koloff
	def. Manny Fernandez & Rick Rude
SF	Lex Luger & Tully Blanchard
	def. Isao Takagi & Giant Baba
SF	Dusty Rhodes & Nikita Koloff
	def. Bobby Eaton & Stan Lane
F	Dusty Rhodes & Nikita Koloff
	def. Lex Luger & Tully Blanchard

1988

R1	Bobby Eaton & Stan Lane
	def. Johnny Ace & John Savage
R1	Butch Miller & Luke Williams def.
	Cruel Connection #1 & Cruel Connection #2
R1	Dick Murdoch & Ivan Koloff
	def. Jimmy Valiant & Mighty Wilbur
R1	Chris Champion & Mark Starr
	def. Twin Devil #1 & Twin Devil #2
R1	Shaska Whatley & Tiger Conway Jr.

	def. Nelson Royal & Rocky King
R1	Kendall Windham & The Italian Stallion
	def. Green Machine & The Terminator
R1	Al Perez & Larry Zbyszko
	def. Joe Cruz & Ricky Santana
R2	Bobby Eaton & Stan Lane
	def. Butch Miller & Luke Williams
R2	Lex Luger & Sting def.
	Dick Murdoch & Ivan Koloff
R2	The Barbarian & The Warlord
	def. Chris Champion & Mark Starr
R2	Animal & Hawk def.
	Shaska Whatley & Tiger Conway Jr.
R2	Arn Anderson & Tully Blanchard def.
	Kendall Windham & The Italian Stallion
R2	Bobby Fulton & Tommy Rogers
	def. Al Perez & Larry Zbyszko
R2	Mike Rotunda & Rick Steiner
	def. Ron Simmons & Steve Williams
QF	Lex Luger & Sting def.
	Bobby Eaton & Stan Lane
QF	The Barbarian & The Warlord
	def. Animal & Hawk
QF	Arn Anderson & Tully Blanchard received bye
QF	Bobby Fulton & Tommy Rogers
	def. Mike Rotunda & Rick Steiner
SF	Lex Luger & Sting def.
	The Barbarian & The Warlord
SF	Arn Anderson & Tully Blanchard
	def. Bobby Fulton & Tommy Rogers
F	Lex Luger & Sting def.
	Arn Anderson & Tully Blanchard

2019

QF	Jay Briscoe & Mark Briscoe def.
	Ricky Morton & Robert Gibson
QF	Brody King & PCO def.
	Satoshi Kojima & Yuji Nagata
QF	Bandido & Flip Gordon def.
	Guerrero Maya Jr. & Stuka Jr.
QF	Royce Isaacs & Thomas Latimer
	def. Crimson & Jax Dane
SF	Brody King & PCO def.
	Jay Briscoe & Mark Briscoe
SF	Royce Isaacs & Thomas Latimer
	def. Bandido & Flip Gordon
F	Brody King & PCO def.
	Royce Isaacs & Thomas Latimer

2022

R1	Bestia 666 & Mecha Wolf
	def. Brandon Tate & Brent Tate
R1	Luke Hawx & PJ Hawx
	def. Odinson & Parrow
R1	Jordan Clearwater & Marshe Rockett
	def. Chris Adonis & Thom Latimer
R1	Doug Williams & Harry Smith
	def. Alex Taylor & Rush Freeman
R1	Mike Knox & VSK def.
	Mims & The Pope
R1	Jay Bradley & Wrecking Ball Legursky
	def. Matt Taven & Mike Bennett
R1	Dirty Dango & JTG def.
	Aron Stevens & The Blue Meanie
R1	Jay Briscoe & Mark Briscoe
	def. Hale Collins & Vik Dalishus
QF	Bestia 666 & Mecha Wolf def. PJ Hawx
QF	Doug Williams & Harry Smith def.
	Jordan Clearwater & Marshe Rockett
QF	Mike Knox & VSK def.
	Jay Bradley & Wrecking Ball Legursky

QF	Jay Briscoe & Mark Briscoe def. Dirty Dango & JTG
SF	Doug Williams & Harry Smith def. Bestia 666 & Mecha Wolf
SF	Jay Briscoe & Mark Briscoe def. Mike Knox & VSK
F	Jay Briscoe & Mark Briscoe def. Doug Williams & Harry Smith

---

NXT DUSTY RHODES TAG TEAM CLASSIC (MEN)

YEAR	WON BY
2015	**Finn Balor & Samoa Joe** (Runner Up: Baron Corbin & Rhyno)
2016	**Akam & Rezar** (Runner Up: Nick Miller & Shane Thorne)
2017	**N/A**
2018	**Adam Cole & Kyle O'Reilly** (Runner Up: Akam & Rezar, Pete Dunne & Roderick Strong)
2019	**Aleister Black & Ricochet** (Runner Up: Steve Cutler & Wesley Blake)
2020	**Pete Dunne & Matt Riddle** (Runner Up: James Drake & Zack Gibson)
2021	**Wes Lee & Nash Carter** (Runner Up: James Drake & Zack Gibson)
2022	**Brutus Creed & Julius Creed** (Runner Up: Wes Lee & Nash Carter)

2015

R1	Enzo Amore & Colin Cassady def. Angelo Dawkins & Sawyer Fulton
R1	Finn Balor & Samoa Joe def. Kalisto & Sin Cara
R1	Aiden English & Simon Gotch def. Blake & Murphy
R1	Scott Dawson & Dash Wilder def. Tucker Knight & Elias Samson
R1	Zack Ryder & Mojo Rawley def. Noah Kekoa & Alexander Wolfe
R1	Jason Jordan & Chad Gable def. Neville & Solomon Crowe
R1	Baron Corbin & Rhyno def. Konnor & Viktor
R1	Johnny Gargano & Tommaso Ciampa def. Tyler Breeze & Bull Dempsey
QF	Finn Balor & Samoa Joe def. Enzo Amore & Colin Cassady
QF	Scott Dawson & Dash Wilder def. Aiden English & Simon Gotch
QF	Jason Jordan & Chad Gable def. Zack Ryder & Mojo Rawley
QF	Baron Corbin & Rhyno def. Johnny Gargano & Tommaso Ciampa
SF	Finn Balor & Samoa Joe def. Scott Dawson & Dash Wilder
SF	Baron Corbin & Rhyno def. Jason Jordan & Chad Gable
F	Finn Balor & Samoa Joe def. Baron Corbin & Rhyno

2016

R1	Nick Miller & Shane Thorne def. Tino Sabbatelli & Riddick Moss
R1	Austin Aries & Roderick Strong def. Tucker Knight & Otis
R1	Kota Ibushi & TJ Perkins def.

	Lince Dorado & Mustafa ALi
R1	Alexander Wolfe & Sawyer Fulton def. Bobby Roode & Tye Dillinger
R1	Akam & Rezar def. Gurv Sihra & Harv Sihra
R1	No Way Jose & Rich Swann def. Tony Nese & Drew Gulak
R1	Scott Dawson & Dash Wilder def. Andrade Almas & Cedric Alexander
R1	Johnny Gargano & Tommaso Ciampa def. Ho Ho Lun & Tian Bing
QF	Nick Miller & Shane Thorne def. Austin Aries & Roderick Strong
QF	Alexander Wolfe & Sawyer Fulton def. Kota Ibushi & TJ Perkins
QF	Akam & Rezar def. No Way Jose & Rich Swann
QF	Johnny Gargano & Tommaso Ciampa def. Scott Dawson & Dash Wilder
SF	Nick Miller & Shane Thorne def. Alexander Wolfe & Sawyer Fulton
SF	Akam & Rezar def. Johnny Gargano & Tommaso Ciampa
F	Akam & Rezar def. Nick Miller & Shane Thorne

2018

QF	Angelo Dawkins & Montez Ford def. Otis Dozovic & Tucker Knight
QF	Akam & Rezar def. Nick Miller & Shane Thorne
QF	Alexander Wolfe & Eric Young def. Riddick Moss & Tino Sabbatelli
QF	Pete Dunne & Roderick Strong def. Danny Burch & Oney Lorcan
SF	Akam & Rezar def. Angelo Dawkins & Montez Ford
SF	Pete Dunne & Roderick Strong def. Alexander Wolfe & Eric Young
F	Adam Cole & Kyle O'Reilly def. Pete Dunne & Roderick Strong and Akam & Rezar

2019

QF	Trent Seven & Tyler Bate def. Angelo Dawkins & Montez Ford
QF	Steve Cutler & Wesley Blake def. Danny Burch & Oney Lorcan
QF	Johnny Gargano & Tommaso Ciampa def. Kyle O'Reilly & Bobby Fish
QF	Aleister Black & Ricochet def. Fabian Aichner & Marcel Barthel
SF	Steve Cutler & Wesley Blake def. Trent Seven & Tyler Bate
SF	Aleister Black & Ricochet def. Johnny Gargano & Tommaso Ciampa
F	Aleister Black & Ricochet def. Steve Cutler & Wesley Blake

2020

QF	Fabian Aichner & Marcel Barthel def. Steve Cutler & Wesley Blake
QF	Matt Riddle & Pete Dunne def. Mark Andrews & Flash Morgan Webster
QF	James Drake & Zack Gibson def. Alex Shelley & Kushida
QF	Bobby Fish & Kyle O'Reilly def. Mark Coffey & Wolfgang
SF	Matt Riddle & Pete Dunne def. Fabian Aichner & Marcel Barthel
SF	James Drake & Zack Gibson def. Bobby Fish & Kyle O'Reilly

F	Matt Riddle & Pete Dunne def. James Drake & Zack Gibson

2021

R1	Adam Cole & Roderick Strong def. Tyler Breeze & Fandango
R1	Tommaso Ciampa & Timothy Thatcher def. Ari Daivari & Tony Nese
R1	Kushida & Leon Ruff def. Johnny Gargano & Austin Theory
R1	James Drake & Zack Gibson def. Chase Parker & Matt Martel
R1	Nash Carter & Wes Lee def. Jake Atlas & Isaiah "Swerve" Scott
R1	Drake Maverick & Killian Dain def. August Grey & Curt Stallion
R1	Gran Metalik & Lince Dorado def. Fabian Aichner & Marcel Barthel
R1	Joaquin Wilde & Raul Mendoza def. Samir Singh & Sunil Singh
QF	Tommaso Ciampa & Timothy Thatcher def. Adam Cole & Roderick Strong
QF	James Drake & Zack Gibson def. Kushida & Leon Ruff
QF	Nash Carter & Wes Lee def. Drake Maverick & Killian Dain
QF	Joaquin Wilde & Raul Mendoza def. Gran Metalik & Lince Dorado
SF	James Drake & Zack Gibson def. Tommaso Ciampa & Timothy Thatcher
SF	Nash Carter & Wes Lee def. Joaquin Wilde & Raul Mendoza
F	Nash Carter & Wes Lee def. James Drake & Zack Gibson

2022

QF	Wes Lee & Nash Carter def. Ikemen Jiro & Kushida
QF	Edris Enofe & Malik Blade def. Joaquin Wilde & Raul Mendoza
QF	Brutus Creed & Julius Creed def. Brooks Jensen & Josh Briggs
QF	James Drake & Zack Gibson def. Andre Chase & Bodhi Hayward
SF	Wes Lee & Nash Carter def. Edris Enofe & Malik Blade
SF	Brutus Creed & Julius Creed def. James Drake & Zack Gibson
F	Brutus Creed & Julius Creed def. Wes Lee & Nash Carter

NXT DUSTY RHODES TAG TEAM CLASSIC (WOMEN)

YEAR	WON BY
2021	**Dakota Kai & Raquel Gonzalez** (Runner Up: Ember Moon & Shotzi Blackheart)
2022	**Io Shirai & Kay Lee Ray** (Runner Up: Dakota Kai & Wendy Choo)

2021

QF	Candice LeRae & Indi Hartwell def. Cora Jade & Gigi Dolin
QF	Ember Moon & Shotzi Blackheart def. Marina Shafir & Zoey Stark
QF	Kacy Catanzaro & Kayden Carter def. Mercedes Martinez & Toni Storm
QF	Dakota Kai & Raquel Gonzalez def. Aliyah & Jessi Kamea
SF	Ember Moon & Shotzi Blackheart def. Candice LeRae & Indi Hartwell
SF	Dakota Kai & Raquel Gonzalez def. Kacy Katanzaro & Kayden Carter
F	Dakota Kai & Raquel Gonzalez def. Ember Moon & Shotzi Blackheart

2022

QF	Io Shirai & Kay Lee Ray def. Amari Miller & Lash Legend
QF	Kacy Katanzaro & Kayden Carter def. Ivy Nile & Tatum Paxley
QF	Wendy Choo & Dakota Kai def. Indi Hartwell & Persia Pirotta
QF	Cora Jade & Raquel Gonzalez def. Valentina Feroz & Yulisa Leon
SF	Io Shirai & Kay Lee Ray def. Kacy Katanzaro & Kayden Carter
SF	Wendy Choo & Dakota Kai def. Cora Jade & Raquel Gonzalez
F	Io Shirai & Kay Lee Ray def. Wendy Choo & Dakota Kai

PWG BATTLE OF LOS ANGELES

YEAR	WON BY
2005	**Chris Bosh** (Runner Up: AJ Styles)
2006	**Davey Richards** (Runner Up: Cima)
2007	**Cima** (Runner Up: Roderick Strong, El Generico)
2008	**Low Ki** (Runner Up: Chris Hero)
2009	**Kenny Omega** (Runner Up: Roderick Strong)
2010	**Joey Ryan** (Runner Up: Chris Hero)
2011	**El Generico** (Runner Up: Kevin Steen)
2012	**Adam Cole** (Runner Up: Michael Elgin)
2013	**Kyle O'Reilly** (Runner Up: Michael Elgin)
2014	**Ricochet** (Runner Up: Roderick Strong, Johnny Gargano)
2015	**Zack Sabre Jr.** (Runner Up: Chris Hero, Mike Bailey)
2016	**Marty Scurll** (Runner Up: Will Ospreay, Trevor Lee)
2017	**Ricochet[2]** (Runner Up: Jeff Cobb, Keith Lee)
2018	**Jeff Cobb** (Runner Up: Bandido, Shingo Takagi)
2019	**Bandido** (Runner Up: David Starr, Jonathan Gresham)
2022	**Daniel Garcia** (Runner Up: Mike Bailey)

2022

R1	Daniel Garcia def. Kevin Blackwood
R1	Alex Shelley def. Lee Moriarty
R1	Aramis def. Rey Horus
R1	Black Taurus def. JD Drake
R1	Mike Bailey def. Bandido
R1	Wheeler Yuta def. Blake Christian
R1	Buddy Matthews def. Jonah

R1	Lio Rush def. Jack Cartwheel
QF	Daniel Garcia def. Alex Shelley
QF	Black Taurus def. Aramis
QF	Mike Bailey def. Wheeler Yuta
QF	Lio Rush def. Buddy Matthews
SF	Daniel Garcia def. Black Taurus
SF	Mike Bailey def. Buddy Matthews
F	Daniel Garcia def. Mike Bailey

STARDOM 5STAR GRAND PRIX

YEAR	WON BY
2012	**Yuzuki Aikawa**
	(Runner Up: Kyoko Kimura)
2013	**Nanae Takahashi**
	(Runner Up: Alpha Female)
2014	**Io Shirai**
	(Runner Up: Yoshiko)
2015	**Kairi Hojo**
	(Runner Up: Hudson Envy)
2016	**Yoko Bito**
	(Runner Up: Tessa Blanchard)
2017	**Toni Storm**
	(Runner Up: Yoko Bito)
2018	**Mayu Iwatani**
	(Runner Up: Utami Hayashishita)
2019	**Hana Kimura**
	(Runner Up: Konami)
2020	**Utami Hayashishita**
	(Runner Up: Himeka)
2021	**Syuri**
	(Runner Up: Momo Watanabe)
2022	**Giulia**
	(Runner Up: Tam Nakano)

STARDOM CINDERELLA TOURNAMENT

YEAR	WON BY
2015	**Mayu Iwatani**
	(Runner Up: Koguma)
2016	**Mayu Iwatani**[2]
	(Runner Up: Hiroyo Matsumoto)
2017	**Toni Storm**
	(Runner Up: Mayu Iwatani)
2018	**Momo Watanabe**
	(Runner Up: Bea Priestley)
2019	**Arisa Hoshiki**
	(Runner Up: Konami)
2020	**Giulia**
	(Runner Up: Natsuko Tora)
2021	**Saya Kamitani**
	(Runner Up: Maika)
2022	**Mirai**
	(Runner Up: Koguma)

STARDOM GODDESSES OF STARDOM TAG LEAGUE

YEAR	WON BY
2011	**Yoko Bito & Yuzuki Aikawa**
	(Runners Up: Natsuki Taiyo & Yoshiko)
2012	**Natsuki Taiyo & Yoshiko**
	(Runners Up: Natsumi Showzuki & Kairi Hojo)
2013	**Kyoko Kimura & Act Yasukawa**
	(Runners Up: Alpha Female & Female Predator Amazon)
2014	**Nanae Takahashi & Kairi Hojo**
	(Runners Up: Mayu Iwatani & Io Shirai)
2015	**Mayu Iwatani & Io Shirai**
	(Runners Up: Santana Garrett & Hiroyo Matsumoto)
2016	**Yoko Bito**[2] **& Kairi Hojo**[2]
	(Runners Up: Mayu Iwatani & Io Shirai)
2017	**Bea Priestley & Kelly Klein**
	(Runners Up: Yoko Bito & Jungle Kyona)
2018	**Utami Hayashishita & Momo Watanabe**
	(Runners Up: Bea Priestley & Chardonnay)
2019	**Arisa Hoshiki & Tam Nakano**
	(Runners Up: Bea Priestley & Jamie Hayter)
2020	**AZM & Momo Watanabe**[2]
	(Runners Up: Giulia & Maika)
2021	**Hazuki & Koguma**
	(Runners Up: AZM & Momo Watanabe)
2022	**Nanae Takahashi & Yuu**
	(Runners Up: Utami Hayashishita & Saya Kamitani)

WWE ANDRE THE GIANT MEMORIAL BATTLE ROYAL

YEAR	WON BY
2014	**Cesaro**
	(Runner Up: Big Show)
2015	**Big Show**
	(Runner Up: Damien Mizdow)
2016	**Baron Corbin**
	(Runner Up: Kane)
2017	**Mojo Rawley**
	(Runner Up: Jinder Mahal)
2018	**Matt Hardy**
	(Runner Up: Baron Corbin)
2019	**Braun Strowman**
	(Runner Up: Colin Jost)
2020	N/A
2021	**Jey Uso**
	(Runner Up: Shinsuke Nakamura)
2022	**Madcap Moss**
	(Runner Up: Finn Balor)

WWE KING OF THE RING

YEAR	WON BY
1985	**Don Muraco**
	Runner Up: The Iron Sheik
1986	**Harley Race**
	Runner Up: Pedro Morales
1987	**Randy Savage**
	Runner Up: King Kong Bundy
1988	**Ted DiBiase**
	Runner Up: Randy Savage
1989	**Tito Santana**
	Runner Up: Rick Martel
1991	**Bret Hart**
	Runner Up: IRS
1993	**Bret Hart**[2]
	Runner Up: Bam Bam Bigelow
1994	**Owen Hart**
	Runner Up: Razor Ramon
1995	**Mabel**

	Runner Up: Savio Vega
1996	**Steve Austin**
	Runner Up: Jake Roberts
1997	**Triple H**
	Runner Up: Mankind
1998	**Ken Shamrock**
	Runner Up: The Rock
1999	**Billy Gunn**
	Runner Up: X-Pac
2000	**Kurt Angle**
	Runner Up: Rikishi
2001	**Edge**
	Runner Up: Kurt Angle
2002	**Brock Lesnar**
	Runner Up: Rob Van Dam
2006	**Booker T**
	Runner Up: Bobby Lashley
2008	**William Regal**
	Runner Up: CM Punk
2010	**Sheamus**
	Runner Up: John Morrison
2015	**Bad News Barrett**
	Runner Up: Neville
2019	**Baron Corbin**
	Runner Up: Chad Gable
2021	**Xavier Woods**
	Runner Up: Finn Balor

1985

R1	Don Muraco def. Junkyard Dog
R1	Les Thornton def. Steve Lombardi
R1	Paul Orndorff vs. Bob Orton ended in a draw
R1	Pedro Morales def. Johnny V
R1	Tito Santana def. Terry Funk by DQ
R1	Jim Brunzell def. The Spoiler
R1	Ricky Steamboat def. Greg Valentine
R1	The Iron Sheik def. B. Brian Blair
QF	Don Muraco def. Les Thornton
QF	Pedro Morales received a bye
QF	Jim Brunzell def. Tito Santana
QF	The Iron Sheik def. Ricky Steamboat
SF	Don Muraco def. Pedro Morales
SF	The Iron Sheik def. Jim Brunzell
F	Don Muraco def. The Iron Sheik

1986

R1	Billy Jack Haynes def. The Iron Sheik
R1	Harley Race def. George Steele by DQ
R1	Don Muraco vs. Roddy Piper ended in draw
R1	Nikolai Volkoff def. Dan Spivey
R1	Junkyard Dog def. Paul Orndorff by DQ
R1	Pedro Morales def. Rudy Diamond
QF	Billy Jack Haynes def. Mr. X
QF	Harley Race received a bye
QF	Nikolai Volkoff def. Junkyard Dog
QF	Pedro Morales def. Mike Rotundo
SF	Harley Race def. Billy Jack Haynes
SF	Pedro Morales def. Nikolai Volkoff
F	Harley Race def. Pedro Morales

1987

R1	Haku def. Brutus Beefcake
R1	Rick Martel def. Dan Spivey
R1	King Kong Bundy def. One Man Gang
R1	SD Jones def. Sika
R1	Danny Davis def. Tito Santana
R1	Junkyard Dog def. Tama
R1	Jim Brunzell def. Ron Bass
R1	Randy Savage def. Nikolai Volkoff
QF	Haku vs. Rick Martel ended in a draw
QF	King Kong Bundy def. SD Jones

QF	Danny Davis def. Junkyard Dog
QF	Randy Savage def. Jim Brunzell
SF	King Kong Bundy received a bye
SF	Randy Savage def. Danny Davis
F	Randy Savage def. King Kong Bundy

1988

R1	Ken Patera def. Nikolai Volkoff
R1	Ted DiBiase def. Brutus Beefcake
R1	Ron Bass def. The Barbarian
R1	Shawn Michaels def. Danny Davis
R1	Bad News Brown vs. Hercules ended in draw
R1	Randy Savage def. Virgil
R1	The Red Rooster def. Marty Jannetty
R1	Iron Mike Sharpe def. Boris Zhukov
QF	Ted DiBiase def. Ken Patera
QF	Ron Bass def. Shawn Michaels
QF	Randy Savage received a bye
QF	The Red Rooster def. Iron Mike Sharpe
SF	Ted DiBiase def. Ron Bass
SF	Randy Savage def. The Red Rooster
F	Ted DiBiase def. Randy Savage

1989

R1	Akeem def. Brutus Beefcake
R1	Hercules vs. Jim Neidhart ended in a draw
R1	The Warlord def. Butch
R1	Tito Santana def. Bad News Brown
R1	Rick Martel def. Bill Woods
R1	Luke def. Nikolai Volkoff
R1	Jimmy Snuka def. The Barbarian
R1	Haku def. The Red Rooster
QF	Akeem received a bye
QF	Tito Santana def. The Warlord
QF	Rick Martel def. Luke
QF	Jimmy Snuka def. Haku
SF	Tito Santana def. Akeem
SF	Rick Martel def. Jimmy Snuka
F	Tito Santana def. Rick Martel

1991

R1	Jerry Sags def. Hawk
R1	Rick Steamboat vs Ted DiBiase went to draw
R1	Jim Duggan def. Brian Knobbs
R1	IRS def. The Berzerker
R1	Bret Hart def. Pete Doherty
R1	Skinner def. Virgil
R1	Sid Justice def. The Warlord
R1	The Undertaker def. Animal
QF	Jerry Sags received a bye
QF	IRS def. Jim Duggan
QF	Bret Hart def. Skinner
QF	The Undertaker vs. Sid Justice ended in draw
SF	IRS def. Jerry Sags
SF	Bret Hart received a bye
F	Bret Hart def. IRS

1993

R1	Bret Hart received a bye
R1	Razor Ramon def. Tito Santana
R1	Mr. Perfect def. Doink the Clown
R1	Mr. Hughes def. Kamala
R1	Jim Duggan def. Papa Shango
R1	Bam Bam Bigelow def. Typhoon
R1	Lex Luger def. Bob Backlund
R1	Tatanka def. Giant Gonzalez
QF	Bret Hart def. Razor Ramon
QF	Mr. Perfect def. Mr. Hughes
QF	Bam Bam Bigelow def. Jim Neidhart
QF	Lex Luger vs. Tatanka ended in a draw
SF	Bret Hart def. Mr. Perfect

SF	Bam Bam Bigelow received a bye	
F	Bret Hart def. Bam Bam Bigelow	

1994

R1	Razor Ramon def. Kwang
R1	Bam Bam Bigelow def. Sparky Plugg
R1	IRS def. Scott Steiner
R1	Mabel def. Quebecer Pierre
R1	Owen Hart def. Doink the Clown
R1	Tatanka def. Crush
R1	1-2-3 Kid def. Adam Bomb
R1	Jeff Jarrett def. Lex Luger
QF	Razor Ramon def. Bam Bam Bigelow
QF	IRS def. Mabel
QF	Owen Hart def. Tatanka
QF	1-2-3 Kid def. Jeff Jarrett
SF	Razor Ramon def. IRS
SF	Owen Hart def. 1-2-3 Kid
F	Owen Hart def. Razor Ramon

1995

R1	Mabel def. Adam Bomb
R1	The Undertaker def. Jeff Jarrett
R1	Kama def. Duke Droese
R1	Shawn Michaels def. King Kong Bundy
R1	Bob Holly def. Mantaur
R1	Roadie def. Doink the Clown
R1	Owen Hart vs. British Bulldog ended in draw
R1	Yokozuna def. Lex Luger
R1	Razor Ramon def. Jacob Blu
R1	Savio Vega def. IRS
QF	Mabel def. The Undertaker
QF	Kama vs. Shawn Michaels ended in a draw
QF	Roadie def. Bob Holly
QF	Savio Vega def. Yokozuna
SF	Mabel received a bye
SF	Savio Vega def. Roadie
F	Mabel def. Savio Vega

1996

R1	Vader def. Ahmed Johnson
R1	Ultimate Warrior vs. Goldust ended in a draw
R1	Jake Roberts def. Hunter Hearst Helmsley
R1	Justin Bradshaw def. Henry Godwinn
R1	Steve Austin def. Bob Holly
R1	Savio Vega def. Marty Jannetty
R1	Marc Mero def. Skip
R1	Owen Hart def. Yokozuna
QF	Vader received a bye
QF	Jake Roberts def. Justin Bradshaw
QF	Steve Austin def. Savio Vega
QF	Marc Mero def. Owen Hart
SF	Jake Roberts def. Vader
SF	Steve Austin def. Marc Mero
F	Steve Austin def. Jake Roberts

1997

QF	Ahmed Johnson def. Triple H
QF	Triple H def. Crush
QF	Jerry Lawler def. Goldust
QF	Mankind def. Savio Vega
SF	Triple H def. Ahmed Johnson
SF	Mankind def. Jerry Lawler
F	Triple H def. Mankind

1998

R1	The Rock def. Vader
R1	Triple H def. X-Pac
R1	Owen Hart def. Scorpio
R1	Dan Severn def. D'Lo Brown
R1	Ken Shamrock def. Kama Mustafa
R1	Mark Henry def. Terry Funk
R1	Jeff Jarrett def. Faarooq
R1	Marc Mero def. Steve Blackman
QF	The Rock def. Triple H
QF	Dan Severn def. Owen Hart
QF	Ken Shamrock def. Mark Henry
QF	Jeff Jarrett def. Marc Mero
SF	The Rock def. Dan Severn
SF	Ken Shamrock def. Jeff Jarrett
F	Ken Shamrock def. The Rock

1999

R1	Billy Gunn def. Viscera
R1	Ken Shamrock def. Jeff Jarrett
R1	Big Show def. Droz
R1	Kane def. Test
R1	Road Dogg def. The Godfather
R1	Chyna def. Val Venis
R1	Hardcore Holly def. Al Snow
R1	X-Pac def. The Big Boss Man
QF	Billy Gunn def. Ken Shamrock
QF	Kane def. Big Show
QF	Road Dogg def. Chyna
QF	X-Pac def. Hardcore Holly
SF	Billy Gunn def. Kane
SF	X-Pac def. Road Dogg
F	Billy Gunn def. X-Pac

2000

R1	Kurt Angle def. Bradshaw
R1	Bubba Ray Dudley def. The Big Boss Man
R1	Chris Jericho def. Test
R1	Edge def. Grandmaster Sexay
R1	Crash Holly def. Albert
R1	Hardcore Holly def. Faarooq
R1	Bull Buchanan def. Steve Blackman
R1	Perry Saturn def. D-Von Dudley
R1	Rikishi def. Shane McMahon
R1	Scotty 2 Hotty def. D'Lo Brown
R1	Chris Benoit def. Road Dogg
R1	X-Pac def. Dean Malenko
R1	Val Venis def. Al Snow
R1	Jeff Hardy def. Christian
R1	Eddie Guerrero def. Matt Hardy
R1	Chyna def. The Godfather
R2	Kurt Angle def. Bubba Ray Dudley
R2	Chris Jericho def. Edge
R2	Crash Holly def. Hardcore Holly
R2	Bull Buchanan def. Perry Saturn
R2	Rikishi def. Scotty 2 Hotty
R2	Chris Benoit def. X-Pac
R2	Val Venis def. Jeff Hardy
R2	Eddie Guerrero def. Chyna
QF	Kurt Angle def. Chris Jericho
QF	Crash Holly def. Bull Buchanan
QF	Rikishi def. Chris Benoit
QF	Val Venis def. Eddie Guerrero
SF	Kurt Angle def. Crash Holly
SF	Rikishi def. Val Venis
F	Kurt Angle def. Rikishi

2001

R1	Kurt Angle def. Hardcore Holly
R1	Jeff Hardy def. Matt Hardy
R1	Christian def. Kane
R1	Big Show def. Raven
R1	Edge def. Test
R1	Perry Saturn def. Steve Blackman
R1	Tajiri def. Crash Holly
R1	Rhyno def. Tazz
QF	Kurt Angle def. Jeff Hardy

QF	Christian def. Big Show
QF	Edge def. Perry Saturn
QF	Rhyno def. Tajiri
SF	Kurt Angle def. Christian
SF	Edge def. Rhyno
F	Edge def. Kurt Angle

2002

R1	Brock Lesnar def. Bubba Ray Dudley
R1	Booker T def. William Regal
R1	Hardcore Holly def. Tajiri
R1	Test def. The Hurricane
R1	Chris Jericho def. Edge
R1	The Big Valbowski def. Christian
R1	X-Pac def. Goldust
R1	Rob Van Dam def. Eddie Guerrero
QF	Brock Lesnar def. Booker T
QF	Test def. Hardcore Holly
QF	Chris Jericho def. The Big Valbowski
QF	Rob Van Dam def. X-Pac
SF	Brock Lesnar def. Test
SF	Rob Van Dam def. Chris Jericho
F	Brock Lesnar def. Rob Van Dam

2006

QF	Kurt Angle def. Randy Orton
QF	Booker T def. Matt Hardy
QF	Finlay def. Chris Benoit
QF	Bobby Lashley def. Mark Henry
SF	Booker T received a bye
SF	Bobby Lashley def. Finlay
F	Booker T def. Bobby Lashley

2008

QF	Chris Jericho def. MVP
QF	CM Punk def. Matt Hardy
QF	Finlay def. The Great Khali
QF	William Regal def. Hornswoggle
SF	CM Punk def. Chris Jericho
SF	William Regal def. Finlay
F	William Regal def. CM Punk

2010

R1	Sheamus def. R-Truth
R1	Kofi Kingston def. Jack Swagger
R1	Drew McIntyre def. MVP
R1	Ezekiel Jackson def. Alex Riley
R1	John Morrison def. Tyson Kidd
R1	Cody Rhodes def. Rey Mysterio
R1	Alberto Del Rio def. Big Show
R1	Daniel Bryan def. Ted DiBiase
QF	Sheamus def. Kofi Kingston
QF	Drew McIntyre vs Ezekiel Jackson drew
QF	John Morrison def. Cody Rhodes
QF	Alberto Del Rio def. Daniel Bryan
SF	Sheamus received a bye
SF	John Morrison def. Alberto Del Rio
F	Sheamus def. John Morrison

2015

QF	Bad News Barrett def. Dolph Ziggler
QF	R-Truth def. Stardust
QF	Sheamus def. Dean Ambrose
QF	Neville def. Luke Harper
SF	Bad News Barrett def. R-Truth
SF	Neville def. Sheamus
F	Bad News Barrett def. Neville

2019

R1	Samoa Joe def. Cesaro
R1	Ricochet def. Drew McIntyre
R1	Cedric Alexander def. Sami Zayn
R1	Baron Corbin def. The Miz
R1	Elias def. Kevin Owens
R1	Ali def. Buddy Murphy
R1	Chad Gable def. Shelton Benjamin
R1	Andrade def. Apollo Crews
QF	Samoa Joe vs. Ricochet drew
QF	Baron Corbin def. Cedric Alexander
QF	Elias def. Ali
QF	Chad Gable def. Andrade
SF	Baron Corbin def. Ricochet & Samoa Joe
SF	Chad Gable def. Shane McMahon
F	Baron Corbin def. Chad Gable

2021

QF	Sami Zayn def. Rey Mysterio
QF	Finn Balor def. Cesaro
QF	Xavier Woods def. Ricochet
QF	Jinder Mahal def. Kofi Kingston
SF	Finn Balor def. Sami Zayn
SF	Xavier Woods def. Jinder Mahal
F	Xavier Woods def. Finn Balor

WWE MONEY IN THE BANK BRIEFCASE (MEN)

YEAR	WON BY
2005	**Edge**
	(Cash In: Successful)
2006	**Rob Van Dam**
	(Cash In: Successful)
2007	**Mr. Kennedy**
	(Cash In: N/A)
2007	**Edge²**
	(Cash In: Successful)
2008	**CM Punk**
	(Cash In: Successful)
2009	**CM Punk²**
	(Cash In: Successful)
2010	**Jack Swagger**
	(Cash In: Successful)
2010	**Kane**
	(Cash In: Successful)
2010	**The Miz**
	(Cash In: Successful)
2011	**Daniel Bryan**
	(Cash In: Successful)
2011	**Alberto Del Rio**
	(Cash In: Successful)
2012	**Dolph Ziggler**
	(Cash In: Successful)
2012	**John Cena**
	(Cash In: Failed)
2013	**Damien Sandow**
	(Cash In: Failed)
2013	**Randy Orton**
	(Cash In: Successful)
2014	**Seth Rollins**
	(Cash In: Successful)
2015	**Sheamus**
	(Cash In: Successful)
2016	**Dean Ambrose**
	(Cash In: Successful)
2017	**Baron Corbin**
	(Cash In: Failed)
2018	**Braun Strowman**
	(Cash In: Failed)
2019	**Brock Lesnar**

		(Cash In: Successful)
2020	**Otis**	
	(Cash In: N/A)	
2020	**The Miz**[2]	
	(Cash In: Successful)	
2021	**Big E**	
	(Cash In: Successful)	
2022	**Austin Theory**	
	(Cash In: Failed)	

WWE MONEY IN THE BANK BRIEFCASE (WOMEN)

YEAR	WON BY
2017	**Carmella**
	(Cash In: Successful)
2018	**Alexa Bliss**
	(Cash In: Successful)
2019	**Bayley**
	(Cash In: Successful)
2020	**Asuka**
	(Cash In: N/A)
2021	**Nikki A.S.H.**
	(Cash In: Successful)
2022	**Liv Morgan**
	(Cash In: Successful)

WWE QUEEN'S CROWN

YEAR	WON BY
2021	**Zelina Vega**
	(Runner Up: Doudrop)

2021

QF	Zelina Vega def. Toni Storm
QF	Carmella def. Liv Morgan
QF	Shayna Baszler def. Dana Brooke
QF	Doudrop def. Natalya
SF	Zelina Vega def. Carmella
SF	Doudrop def. Shayna Baszler
F	Zelina Vega def. Doudrop

WWE ROYAL RUMBLE (MEN)

YEAR	WON BY
1988	**Jim Duggan**
	(Runner Up: One Man Gang)
1989	**Big John Studd**
	(Runner Up: Ted DiBiase)
1990	**Hulk Hogan**
	(Runner Up: Mr. Perfect)
1991	**Hulk Hogan**[2]
	(Runner Up: Earthquake)
1992	**Ric Flair**
	(Runner Up: Sid Justice)
1993	**Yokozuna**
	(Runner Up: Randy Savage)
1994	**Bret Hart / Lex Luger**
	(Runner Up: Bret Hart / Lex Luger)
1995	**Shawn Michaels**
	(Runner Up: The British Bulldog)
1996	**Shawn Michaels**[2]
	(Runner Up: Diesel)
1997	**Steve Austin**

		(Runner Up: Bret Hart)
1998	**Steve Austin**[2]	
	(Runner Up: The Rock)	
1999	**Vince McMahon**	
	(Runner Up: Steve Austin)	
2000	**The Rock**	
	(Runner Up: Big Show)	
2001	**Steve Austin**[3]	
	(Runner Up: Kane)	
2002	**Triple H**	
	(Runner Up: Kurt Angle)	
2003	**Brock Lesnar**	
	(Runner Up: The Undertaker)	
2004	**Chris Benoit**	
	(Runner Up: Big Show)	
2005	**Batista**	
	(Runner Up: John Cena)	
2006	**Rey Mysterio**	
	(Runner Up: Randy Orton)	
2007	**The Undertaker**	
	(Runner Up: Shawn Michaels)	
2008	**John Cena**	
	(Runner Up: Triple H)	
2009	**Randy Orton**	
	(Runner Up: Triple H)	
2010	**Edge**	
	(Runner Up: John Cena)	
2011	**Alberto Del Rio**	
	(Runner Up: Santino Marella)	
2012	**Sheamus**	
	(Runner Up: Chris Jericho)	
2013	**John Cena**[2]	
	(Runner Up: Ryback)	
2014	**Batista**[2]	
	(Runner Up: Roman Reigns)	
2015	**Roman Reigns**	
	(Runner Up: Rusev)	
2016	**Triple H**[2]	
	(Runner Up: Dean Ambrose)	
2017	**Randy Orton**[2]	
	(Runner Up: Roman Reigns)	
2018	**Shinsuke Nakamura**	
	(Runner Up: Roman Reigns)	
2018*	**Braun Strowman**	
	(Runner Up: Big Cass)	
2019	**Seth Rollins**	
	(Runner Up: Braun Strowman)	
2020	**Drew McIntyre**	
	(Runner Up: Roman Reigns)	
2021	**Edge**[2]	
	(Runner Up: Randy Orton)	
2022	**Brock Lesnar**[2]	
	(Runner Up: Drew McIntyre)	

Greatest Royal Rumble

1988

Order Of Entry: 1. Bret Hart **(25:42)** 2. Tito Santana 3. Butch Reed 4. Jim Neidhart 5. Jake Roberts 6. Harley Race 7. Jim Brunzell 8. Sam Houston 9. Danny Davis 10. Boris Zhukov 11. Don Muraco 12. Nikolai Volkoff **13. Hacksaw Jim Duggan** 14. Ron Bass 15. B. Brian Blair 16. Hillbilly Jim 17. Dino Bravo 18. The Ultimate Warrior 19. One Man Gang 20. Junkyard Dog

Eliminations: 6 - One Man Gang, 3 - Don Muraco, Jim Duggan, 2 - Jake Roberts, Ron Bass, Dino Bravo, 1 - Bret Hart, Jim Neidhart, Jim Brunzell, Nikolai Volkoff, Hillbilly Jim

1989

Order Of Entry: 1. Ax 2. Smash 3. Andre the Giant 4. Mr.

Perfect **(27:58)** 5. Ronnie Garvin 6. Greg Valentine 7. Jake Roberts 8. Ron Bass 9. Shawn Michaels 10. Bushwhacker Butch 11. Honky Tonk Man 12. Tito Santana 13. Bad News Brown 14. Marty Jannetty 15. Randy Savage 16. Arn Anderson 17. Tully Blanchard 18. Hulk Hogan 19. Bushwhacker Luke 20. Koko B. Ware 21. The Warlord 22. Big Boss Man 23. Akeem 24. Brutus Beefcake 25. The Red Rooster 26. The Barbarian **27. Big John Studd** 28. Hercules 29. Rick Martel 30. Ted DiBiase

Eliminations: 10 - Hulk Hogan, 3 - Andre the Giant, Randy Savage, Ted DiBiase, 2 - Arn Anderson, Akeem, The Barbarian, Big John Studd, 1 - Mr. Perfect, Shawn Michaels, Bushwhacker Butch, Tito Santana, Bad News Brown, Marty Jannetty, Tully Blanchard, Big Boss Man, Rick Martel

1990
Order Of Entry: 1. Ted DiBiase **(44:47)** 2. Koko B. Ware 3. Marty Jannetty 4. Jake Roberts 5. Randy Savage 6. Roddy Piper 7. The Warlord 8. Bret Hart 9. Bad News Brown 10. Dusty Rhodes 11. Andre the Giant 12. The Red Rooster 13. Ax 14. Haku 15. Smash 16. Akeem 17. Jimmy Snuka 18. Dino Bravo 19. Earthquake 20. Jim Neidhart 21. Ultimate Warrior 22. Rick Martel 23. Tito Santana 24. Honky Tonk Man **25. Hulk Hogan** 26. Shawn Michaels 27. The Barbarian 28. Rick Rude 29. Hercules 30. Mr. Perfect

Eliminations: 6 - Hulk Hogan, The Ultimate Warrior, 3 - Ted DiBiase, 2 - Dusty Rhodes, Andre the Giant, Haku, Smash, Jimmy Snuka, Earthquake, Rick Martel, Rick Rude, 1 - Randy Savage, Roddy Piper, Bad News Brown, Ax, Jim Neidhart, The Barbarian, Hercules, Mr. Perfect

1991
Order Of Entry: 1. Bret Hart 2. Dino Bravo 3. Greg Valentine 4. Paul Roma 5. The Texas Tornado 6. Rick Martel **(52:17)** 7. Saba Simba 8. Bushwhacker Butch 9. Jake Roberts 10. Hercules 11. Tito Santana 12. The Undertaker 13. Jimmy Snuka 14. British Bulldog 15. Smash 16. Hawk 17. Shane Douglas 18. Randy Savage 19. Animal 20. Crush 21. Jim Duggan 22. Earthquake 23. Mr. Perfect **24. Hulk Hogan** 25. Haku 26. Jim Neidhart 27. Bushwhacker Luke 28. Brian Knobbs 29. The Warlord 30. Tugboat

Eliminations: 7 - Hulk Hogan, 4 - Rick Martel, Earthquake, 3 - The Undertaker, The British Bulldog, Brian Knobbs, 2 - Hawk, 1 - Greg Valentine, Jake Roberts, Hercules, Animal, Mr. Perfect

1992
Order Of Entry: 1. British Bulldog 2. Ted DiBiase **3. Ric Flair (60:02)** 4. Jerry Sags 5. Haku 6. Shawn Michaels 7. Tito Santana 8. The Barbarian 9. The Texas Tornado 10. Repo Man 11. Greg Valentine 12. Nikolai Volkoff 13. Big Boss Man 14. Hercules 15. Roddy Piper 16. Jake Roberts 17. Jim Duggan 18. IRS 19. Jimmy Snuka 20. The Undertaker 21. Randy Savage 22. The Berzerker 23. Virgil 24. Col. Mustafa 25. Rick Martel 26. Hulk Hogan 27. Skinner 28. Sgt. Slaughter 29. Sid Justice 30. The Warlord

Eliminations: 6 - Sid Justice, 5 - Ric Flair, 4 - Hulk Hogan, 3 - The British Bulldog, 2 - Repo Man, Big Boss Man, Randy Savage, 1 - Shawn Michaels, Tito Santana, Hercules, Roddy Piper, Jim Duggan, The Undertaker, Virgil, Rick Martel

1993
Order Of Entry: 1. Ric Flair 2. Bob Backlund **(61:10)** 3. Papa Shango 4. Ted DiBiase 5. Brian Knobbs 6. Virgil 7.

Jerry Lawler 8. Max Moon 9. Genichiro Tenryu 10. Mr. Perfect 11. Skinner 12. Koko B. Ware 13. Samu 14. The Berzerker 15. The Undertaker 16. Terry Taylor 17. Damien Demento 18. IRS 19. Tatanka 20. Jerry Sags 21. Typhoon 22. Fatu 23. Earthquake 24. Carlos Colon 25. Tito Santana 26. Rick Martel **27. Yokozuna** 28. Owen Hart 29. Repo Man 30. Randy Savage

Eliminations: 7 - Yokozuna, 4 - Ted DiBiase, The Undertaker, 3 - Mr. Perfect, 2 - Bob Backlund, Jerry Lawler, Earthquake, 1 - Ric Flair, Koko B. Ware, The Berzerker, Carlos Colon, Owen Hart, Randy Savage

1994
Order Of Entry: 1. Scott Steiner 2. Samu 3. Rick Steiner 4. Kwang 5. Owen Hart 6. Bart Gunn 7. Diesel 8. Bob Backlund 9. Billy Gunn 10. Virgil 11. Randy Savage 12. Jeff Jarrett 13. Crush 14. Doink the Clown 15. Bam Bam Bigelow **(30:12)** 16. Mabel 17. Thurman Plugg 18. Shawn Michaels 19. Mo 20. Greg Valentine 21. Tatanka 22. The Great Kabuki **23. Lex Luger** 24. Genichiro Tenryu 25. Bastion Booger 26. Rick Martel **27. Bret Hart** 28. Fatu 29. Marty Jannetty 30. Adam Bomb

Eliminations: 7 - Diesel, 6 - Lex Luger, 5 - Bam Bam Bigelow, 4 - Shawn Michaels, Bret Hart, 3 - Crush, Thurman Plugg, 2 - Tatanka, 1 - Scott Steiner, Owen Hart, Randy Savage, Mabel, Greg Valentine, The Great Kabuki, Rick Martel, Fatu

1995
Order Of Entry: 1. Shawn Michaels (38:41) 2. British Bulldog **(38:41)** 3. Eli Blu 4. Duke Droese 5. Jimmy Del Ray 6. Sione 7. Tom Prichard 8. Doink the Clown 9. Kwang 10. Rick Martel 11. Owen Hart 12. Timothy Well 13. Bushwhacker Luke 14. Jacob Blu 15. King Kong Bundy 16. Mo 17. Mabel 18. Bushwhacker Butch 19. Lex Luger 20. Mantaur 21. Aldo Montoya 22. Henry O. Godwinn 23. Billy Gunn 24. Bart Gunn 25. Bob Backlund 26. Steven Dunn 27. Dick Murdoch 28. Adam Bomb 29. Fatu 30. Crush

Eliminations: 8 - Shawn Michaels, 5 - Crush, 4 - The British Bulldog, Lex Luger, 3 - Sione, 2 - Dick Murdoch, 1 - Eli Blu, Kwang, King Kong Bundy, Mabel, Aldo Montoya, Henry O. Godwinn

1996
Order Of Entry: 1. Hunter Hearst Helmsley **(48:04)** 2. Henry O. Godwinn 3. Bob Backlund 4. Jerry Lawler 5. Bob Holly 6. King Mabel 7. Jake Roberts 8. Dory Funk Jr. 9. Yokozuna 10. The 1-2-3 Kid 11. Takao Omori 12. Savio Vega 13. Vader 14. Doug Gilbert 15. Squat Teamer #1 16. Squat Teamer #2 17. Owen Hart **18. Shawn Michaels** 19. Hakushi 20. Tatanka 21. Aldo Montoya 22. Diesel 23. Kama 24. The Ringmaster 25. Barry Horowitz 26. Fatu 27. Isaac Yankem DDS 28. Marty Jannetty 29. British Bulldog 30. Duke Droese

Eliminations: 8 - Shawn Michaels, 5 - Diesel, 4 - Vader, 3 - Yokozuna, 2 - Jake Roberts, Owen Hart, 1 - Hunter Hearst Helmsley, Savio Vega, Tatanka, Kama, The Ringmaster, Fatu, Isaac Yankem DDS, The British Bulldog

1997
Order Of Entry: 1. Crush 2. Ahmed Johnson 3. Razor Ramon 4. Phineas Godwinn **5. Steve Austin (45:07)** 6. Bart Gunn 7. Jake Roberts 8. British Bulldog 9. Pierroth 10. The Sultan 11. Mil Mascaras 12. Hunter Hearst Helmsley 13. Owen Hart 14. Goldust 15. Cibernetico 16. Marc Mero 17. Latin Lover 18. Faarooq 19. Savio Vega 20. Jesse

James 21. Bret Hart 22. Jerry Lawler 23. Diesel 24. Terry Funk 25. Rocky Maivia 26. Mankind 27. Flash Funk 28. Vader 29. Henry Godwinn 30. The Undertaker

Eliminations: 10 - Steve Austin, 2 - Ahmed Johnson, Mil Mascaras, Owen Hart, Bret Hart, Mankind, The Undertaker, 1 - Phineas Godwinn, The British Bulldog, Pierroth, Goldust, Faarooq, Vader

1998

Order Of Entry: 1. Cactus Jack 2. Chainsaw Charlie 3. Tom Brandi 4. The Rock **(51:32)** 5. Mosh 6. Phineas Godwinn 7. 8-Ball 8. Bradshaw 9. Owen Hart 10. Steve Blackman 11. D'Lo Brown 12. Kurrgan 13. Marc Mero 14. Ken Shamrock 15. Thrasher 16. Mankind 17. Goldust 18. Jeff Jarrett 19. Honky Tonk Man 20. Ahmed Johnson 21. Mark Henry 22. Skull 23. Kama Mustafa 24. **Steve Austin** 25. Henry Godwinn 26. Savio Vega 27. Faarooq 28. Dude Love 29. Chainz 30. Vader

Eliminations: 7 - Steve Austin, 3 - The Rock, Faarooq, 2 - Chainsaw Charlie, Kurrgan, Goldust, Mark Henry, Dude Love, 1 - Cactus Jack, Phineas Godwinn, 8-Ball, Bradshaw, Owen Hart, D'Lo Brown, Ken Shamrock, Mankind, Chainz, Vader

1999

Order Of Entry: 1. Steve Austin **(56:38) 2. Vince McMahon (56:38)** 3. Golga 4. Droz 5. Edge 6. Gillberg 7. Steve Blackman 8. Dan Severn 9. Tiger Ali Singh 10. The Blue Meanie 11. Mabel 12. Road Dogg 13. Gangrel 14. Kurrgan 15. Al Snow 16. Goldust 17. The Godfather 18. Kane 19. Ken Shamrock 20. Billy Gunn 21. Test 22. Mark Henry 27. Jeff Jarrett 28. D'Lo Brown 29. Owen Hart 30. Chyna

Eliminations: 8 - Steve Austin, 5 - Mabel, 4 - Kane, 3 - Road Dogg, 2 - Big Boss Man, Triple H, 1 - Vince McMahon, Edge, Chyna

2000

Order Of Entry: 1. D'Lo Brown 2. Grand Master Sexay 3. Mosh 4. Christian 5. Rikishi 6. Scotty 2 Hotty 7. Steve Blackman 8. Viscera 9. Big Boss Man 10. Test **(26:17)** 11. British Bulldog 12. Gangrel 13. Edge 14. Bob Backlund 15. Chris Jericho 16. Crash Holly 17. Chyna 18. Faarooq 19. Road Dogg 20. Al Snow 21. Val Venis 22. Prince Albert 23. Hardcore Holly **24. The Rock** 25. Billy Gunn 26. Big Show 27. Bradshaw 28. Kane 29. The Godfather 30. X-Pac

Eliminations: 7 - Rikishi, 4 - The Rock, The Big Show, 3 - Big Boss Man, Kane, 2 - Road Dogg, Al Snow, Billy Gunn, 1 - Test, The British Bulldog, Gangrel, Edge, Bob Backlund, Chris Jericho, Chyna, Val Venis, X-Pac

2001

Order Of Entry: 1. Jeff Hardy 2. Bull Buchanan 3. Matt Hardy 4. Faarooq 5. Drew Carey 6. Kane **(53:46)** 7. Raven 8. Al Snow 9. Perry Saturn 10. Steve Blackman 11. Grand Master Sexay 12. Honky Tonk Man 13. The Rock 14. The Godfather 15. Tazz 16. Bradshaw 17. Albert 18. Hardcore Holly 19. K-Kwik 20. Val Venis 21. William Regal 22. Test 23. Big Show 24. Crash Holly 25. The Undertaker 26. Scotty 2 Hotty 27. **Steve Austin** 28. Billy Gunn 29. Haku 30. Rikishi

Eliminations: 11 - Kane, 4 - The Undertaker, 3 - Jeff Hardy, Matt Hardy, The Rock, Steve Austin, 2 - The Big Show, 1 - Test, Rikishi

2002

Order Of Entry: 1. Rikishi 2. Goldust 3. Big Boss Man 4. Bradshaw 5. Lance Storm 6. Al Snow 7. Billy 8. The Undertaker 9. Matt Hardy 10. Jeff Hardy 11. Maven 12. Scotty 2 Hotty 13. Christian 14. Diamond Dallas Page 15. Chuck 16. The Godfather 17. Albert 18. Perry Saturn 19. Steve Austin **(26:46)** 20. Val Venis 21. Test **22. Triple H** 23. The Hurricane 24. Faarooq 25. Mr. Perfect 26. Kurt Angle 27. Big Show 28. Kane 29. Rob Van Dam 30. Booker T

Eliminations: 7 - The Undertaker, Steve Austin, 4 - Triple H, 3 - Christian, 2 - Chuck Palumbo, Kurt Angle, 1 - Rikishi, Al Snow, Billy Gunn, Maven, Diamond Dallas Page, Mr. Perfect, Kane, Booker T

2003

Order Of Entry: 1. Shawn Michaels 2. Chris Jericho **(39:00)** 3. Christopher Nowinski 4. Rey Mysterio 5. Edge 6. Christian 7. Chavo Guerrero 8. Tajiri 9. Bill DeMott 10. Tommy Dreamer 11. B   12. Rob Van Dam 13. Matt Hardy 14. Eddie Guerrero 15. Jeff Hardy 16. Rosey 17. Test 18. John Cena 19. Charlie Haas 20. Rikishi 21. Jamal 22. Kane 23. Shelton Benjamin 24. Booker T 25. A-Train 26. Maven 27. Goldust 28. Batista **29. Brock Lesnar** 30. The Undertaker

Eliminations: 6 - Chris Jericho, 5 - The Undertaker, 4 - Brock Lesnar, 3 - Edge, Kane, 2 - Rob Van Dam, Charlie Haas, Shelton Benjamin, Batista, 1 - Rey Mysterio, Christian, Test, Booker T

2004

Order Of Entry: 1. Chris Benoit (61:35) 2. Randy Orton 3. Mark Henry 4. Tajiri 5. Bradshaw 6. Rhyno 7. Matt Hardy 8. Scott Steiner 9. Matt Morgan 10. The Hurricane 11. Booker T 12. Kane 13. Spike Dudley 14. Rikishi 15. Rene Dupree 16. A-Train 17. Shelton Benjamin 18. Ernest Miller 19. Kurt Angle 20. Rico 21. Mick Foley 22. Christian 23. Nunzio 24. Big Show 25. Chris Jericho 26. Charlie Haas 27. Billy Gunn 28. John Cena 29. Rob Van Dam 30. Goldberg

Eliminations: 6 - Chris Benoit, 5 - Randy Orton, 4 - The Big Show, 3 - Goldberg, 2 - Booker T, 1 - Mark Henry, Rhyno, Matt Morgan, Rikishi, Rene Dupree, Kurt Angle, Mick Foley, Chris Jericho

2005

Order Of Entry: 1. Eddie Guerrero 2. Chris Benoit **(47:26)** 3. Daniel Puder 4. Hardcore Holly 5. The Hurricane 6. Kenzo Suzuki 7. Edge 8. Rey Mysterio 9. Shelton Benjamin 10. Booker T 11. Chris Jericho 12. Luther Reigns 13. Muhammad Hassan 14. Orlando Jordan 15. Scotty 2 Hotty 16. Charlie Haas 17. Rene Dupree 18. Simon Dean 19. Shawn Michaels 20. Kurt Angle 21. Jonathan Coachman 22. Mark Jindrak 23. Viscera 24. Paul London 25. John Cena 26. Gene Snitsky 27. Kane **28. Batista** 29. Christian 30. Ric Flair

Eliminations: 6 - Batista, 5 - Edge, 4 - Eddie Guerrero, 3 - Booker T, Shawn Michaels, John Cena, 2 - Chris Benoit, Chris Jericho, Ric Flair, 1 - Hardcore Holly, Rey Mysterio, Shelton Benjamin, Luther Reigns, Kurt Angle, Gene Snitsky, Kane

2006

Order Of Entry: 1. Triple H **2. Rey Mysterio (62:12)** 3. Simon Dean 4. Psicosis 5. Ric Flair 6. Big Show 7. Jonathan Coachman 8. Bobby Lashley 9. Kane 10. Sylvan 11. Carlito 12. Chris Benoit 13. Booker T 14. Joey Mercury 15. Tatanka 16. Johnny Nitro 17. Trevor Murdoch 18. Eugene

19. Animal 20. Rob Van Dam 21. Orlando Jordan 22. Chavo Guerrero 23. Matt Hardy 24. Super Crazy 25. Shawn Michaels 26. Chris Masters 27. Viscera 28. Shelton Benjamin 29. Goldust 30. Randy Orton

Eliminations: 6 - Triple H, Rey Mysterio, 4 - Rob Van Dam, Shawn Michaels, 2 - The Big Show, Carlito, Chris Benoit, Johnny Nitro, Randy Orton, 1 - Bobby Lashley, Kane, Joey Mercury, Chris Masters, Viscera

2007
Order Of Entry: 1. Ric Flair 2. Finlay 3. Kenny Dykstra 4. Matt Hardy 5. Edge **(44:02)** 6. Tommy Dreamer 7. Sabu 8. Gregory Helms 9. Shelton Benjamin 10. Kane 11. CM Punk 12. King Booker 13. Super Crazy 14. Jeff Hardy 15. The Sandman 16. Randy Orton 17. Chris Benoit 18. Rob Van Dam 19. Viscera 20. Johnny Nitro 21. Kevin Thorn 22. Hardcore Holly 23. Shawn Michaels 24. Chris Masters 25. Chavo Guerrero 26. Montel Vontavious Porter 27. Carlito 28. The Great Khali 29. The Miz **30. The Undertaker**

Eliminations: 7 - The Great Khali, 5 - Edge, 4 - Shawn Michaels, 3 - Kane, King Booker, Chris Benoit, The Undertaker, 2 - Randy Orton, Rob Van Dam, 1 - Kenny Dykstra, Shelton Benjamin, CM Punk, Johnny Nitro, Kevin Thorn, Hardcore Holly

2008
Order Of Entry: 1. The Undertaker 2. Shawn Michaels 3. Santino Marella 4. The Great Khali 5. Hardcore Holly 6. John Morrison 7. Tommy Dreamer 8. Batista **(37:46)** 9. Hornswoggle 10. Chuck Palumbo 11. Jamie Noble 12. CM Punk 13. Cody Rhodes 14. Umaga 15. Snitsky 16. The Miz 17. Shelton Benjamin 18. Jimmy Snuka 19. Roddy Piper 20. Kane 21. Carlito 22. Mick Foley 23. Mr. Kennedy 24. Big Daddy V 25. Mark Henry 26. Chavo Guerrero 27. Finlay 28. Elijah Burke 29. Triple H **30. John Cena**

Eliminations: 6 - Triple H, 4 - Batista, John Cena, 3 - The Undertaker, Kane, 2 - Shawn Michaels, 1 - Hornswoggle, Chuck Palumbo, CM Punk, Umaga, Mick Foley, Mr. Kennedy, Chavo Guerrero

2009
Order Of Entry: 1. Rey Mysterio 2. John Morrison 3. Carlito 4. Montel Vontavious Porter 5. The Great Khali 6. Vladimir Kozlov 7. Triple H **(50:00) 8. Randy Orton** 9. JTG 10. Ted DiBiase Jr. 11. Chris Jericho 12. Mike Knox 13. The Miz 14. Finlay 15. Cody Rhodes 16. The Undertaker 17. Goldust 18. CM Punk 19. Mark Henry 20. Shelton Benjamin 21. William Regal 22. Kofi Kingston 23. Kane 24. R-Truth 25. Rob Van Dam 26. The Brian Kendrick 27. Dolph Ziggler 28. Santino Marella 29. Jim Duggan 30. Big Show

Eliminations: 6 - Triple H, The Big Show, 4 - The Undertaker, 3 - Vladimir Kozlov, Randy Orton, Kane, 2- Cody Rhodes, 1 - Rey Mysterio, Ted DiBiase, Chris Jericho, CM Punk, The Brian Kendrick

2010
Order Of Entry: 1. Dolph Ziggler 2. Evan Bourne 3. CM Punk 4. JTG 5. The Great Khali 6. Beth Phoenix 7. Zack Ryder 8. Triple H 9. Drew McIntyre 10. Ted DiBiase Jr. 11. John Morrison 12. Kane 13. Cody Rhodes 14. MVP 15. Carlito 16. The Miz 17. Matt Hardy 18. Shawn Michaels 19. John Cena **(27:11)** 20. Shelton Benjamin 21. Yoshi Tatsu 22. Big Show 23. Mark Henry 24. Chris Masters 25. R-Truth 26. Jack Swagger 27. Kofi Kingston 28. Chris Jericho **29. Edge** 30. Batista

Eliminations: 6 - Shawn Michaels, 5 - CM Punk, 4 - John

Cena, 3 - Triple H, 2 - R-Truth, Kofi Kingston, Edge, 1 - Beth Phoenix, Kane, MVP, The Big Show, Batista

2011
Order Of Entry: 1. CM Punk **(35:21)** 2. Daniel Bryan 3. Justin Gabriel 4. Zack Ryder 5. William Regal 6. Ted DiBiase Jr. 7. John Morrison 8. Yoshi Tatsu 9. Husky Harris 10. Chavo Guerrero 11. Mark Henry 12. JTG 13. Michael McGillicutty 14. Chris Masters 15. David Otunga 16. Tyler Reks 17. Vladimir Kozlov 18. R-Truth 19. The Great Khali 20. Mason Ryan 21. Booker T 22. John Cena 23. Hornswoggle 24. Tyson Kidd 25. Heath Slater 26. Kofi Kingston 27. Jack Swagger 28. Sheamus 29. Rey Mysterio 30. Wade Barrett 31. Dolph Ziggler 32. Diesel 33. Drew McIntyre 34. Alex Riley 35. Big Show 36. Ezekiel Jackson 37. Santino Marella **38. Alberto Del Rio** 39. Randy Orton 40. Kane

Eliminations: 7 - CM Punk, John Cena, 4 - Michael McGillicutty, 3 - Husky Harris, Randy Orton, 2 - Daniel Bryan, Mark Henry, David Otunga, Mason Ryan, Rey Mysterio, Wade Barrett, The Big Show, Alberto Del Rio, 1 - Ted DiBiase, The Great Khali, Kofi Kingston, Sheamus, Ezekiel Jackson, Kane

2012
Order Of Entry: 1. The Miz **(45:39)** 2. Alex Riley 3. R-Truth 4. Cody Rhodes 5. Justin Gabriel 6. Primo 7. Mick Foley 8. Ricardo Rodriguez 9. Santino Marella 10. Epico 11. Kofi Kingston 12. Jerry Lawler 13. Ezekiel Jackson 14. Jinder Mahal 15. The Great Khali 16. Hunico 17. Booker T 18. Dolph Ziggler 19. Jim Duggan 20. Michael Cole 21. Kharma **22. Sheamus** 23. Road Dogg 24. Jey Uso 25. Jack Swagger 26. Wade Barrett 27. David Otunga 28. Randy Orton 29. Chris Jericho 30. Big Show

Eliminations: 6 - Cody Rhodes, 4 - The Big Show, 3 - Mick Foley, Sheamus, Randy Orton, 2 - The Miz, The Great Khali, Dolph Ziggler, Chris Jericho, 1 - Ricardo Rodriguez, Santino Marella, Jerry Lawler, Booker T, Kharma, Wade Barrett

2013
Order Of Entry: 1. Dolph Ziggler **(49:47)** 2. Chris Jericho 3. Cody Rhodes 4. Kofi Kingston 5. Santino Marella 6. Drew McIntyre 7. Titus O'Neil 8. Goldust 9. David Otunga 10. Heath Slater 11. Sheamus 12. Tensai 13. Brodus Clay 14. Rey Mysterio 15. Darren Young 16. Bo Dallas 17. The Godfather 18. Wade Barrett **19. John Cena** 20. Damien Sandow 21. Daniel Bryan 22. Antonio Cesaro 23. The Great Khali 24. Kane 25. Zack Ryder 26. Randy Orton 27. Jinder Mahal 28. The Miz 29. Sin Cara 30. Ryback

Eliminations: 5 - Sheamus, Ryback, 4 - Cody Rhodes, John Cena, 2 - Dolph Ziggler, Chris Jericho, Kofi Kingston, Wade Barrett, Daniel Bryan, Kane, 1 - Heath Slater, Darren Young, Bo Dallas, Antonio Cesaro, Randy Orton

2014
Order Of Entry: 1. CM Punk **(49:12)** 2. Seth Rollis 3. Damien Sandow 4. Cody Rhodes 5. Kane 6. Alexander Rusev 7. Jack Swagger 8. Kofi Kingston 9. Jimmy Uso 10. Goldust 11. Dean Ambrose 12. Dolph Ziggler 13. R-Truth 14. Kevin Nash 15. Roman Reigns 16. The Great Khali 17. Sheamus 18. The Miz 19. Fandango 20. El Torito 21. Antonio Cesaro 22. Luke Harper 23. Jey Uso 24. JBL 25. Erick Rowan 26. Ryback 27. Alberto Del Rio **28. Batista** 29. Big E Langston 30. Rey Mysterio

Eliminations: 12 - Roman Reigns, 4 - Batista, 3 - CM Punk, Seth Rollins, Dean Ambrose, 2 - Luke Harper, 1 -

Cody Rhodes, Kane, Kofi Kingston, Goldust, Kevin Nash, Sheamus, El Torito

2015

Order Of Entry: 1. The Miz 2. R-Truth 3. Bubba Ray Dudley 4. Luke Harper 5. Bray Wyatt **(46:50)** 6. Curtis Axel 7. The Boogeyman 8. Sin Cara 9. Zack Ryder 10. Daniel Bryan 11. Fandango 12. Tyson Kidd 13. Stardust 14. Diamond Dallas Page 15. Rusev 16. Goldust 17. Kofi Kingston 18. Adam Rose **19. Roman Reigns** 20. Big E 21. Damien Mizdow 22. Jack Swagger 23. Ryback 24. Kane 25. Dean Ambrose 26. Titus O'Neil 27. Bad News Barrett 28. Cesaro 29. Big Show 30. Dolph Ziggler

Eliminations: 6 - Roman Reigns, Bray Wyatt, Rusev, 5 - The Big Show, 4 - Kane, 2 - Bubba Ray Dudley, Dolph Ziggler, 1 - Daniel Bryan, Kofi Kingston, Dean Ambrose

2016

Order Of Entry: 1. Roman Reigns **(59:48)** 2. Rusev 3. AJ Styles 4. Tyler Breeze 5. Curtis Axel 6. Chris Jericho 7. Kane 8. Goldust 9. Ryback 10. Kofi Kingston 11. Titus O'Neil 12. R-Truth 13. Luke Harper 14. Stardust 15. Big Show 16. Neville 17. Braun Strowman 18. Kevin Owens 19. Dean Ambrose 20. Sami Zayn 21. Erick Rowan 22. Mark Henry 23. Brock Lesnar 24. Jack Swagger 25. The Miz 26. Alberto Del Rio 27. Bray Wyatt 28. Dolph Ziggler 29. Sheamus **30. Triple H**

Eliminations: 5 - Roman Reigns, Braun Strowman, 4 - Luke Harper, Brock Lesnar, Triple H, 2 - AJ Styles, The Big Show, Erick Rowan, 1 - Chris Jericho, Kane, Titus O'Neil, Kevin Owens, Dean Ambrose, Sami Zayn, Sheamus

2017

Order Of Entry: 1. Big Cass 2. Chris Jericho **(60:13)** 3. Kalisto 4. Mojo Rawley 5. Jack Gallagher 6. Mark Henry 7. Braun Strowman 8. Sami Zayn 9. Big Show 10. Tye Dillinger 11. James Ellsworth 12. Dean Ambrose 13. Baron Corbin 14. Kofi Kingston 15. The Miz 16. Sheamus 17. Big E 18. Rusev 19. Cesaro 20. Xavier Woods 21. Bray Wyatt 22. Apollo Crews **23. Randy Orton** 24. Dolph Ziggler 25. Luke Harper 26. Brock Lesnar 27. Enzo Amore 28. Goldberg 29. The Undertaker 30. Roman Reigns

Eliminations: 7 - Braun Strowman, 4 - The Undertaker, 3 - Sheamus, Cesaro, Brock Lesnar, Goldberg, Roman Reigns, 2 - Chris Jericho, 1 - Mark Henry, Baron Corbin, Randy Orton, Luke Harper

2018

Order Of Entry: 1. Rusev 2. Finn Balor **(57:38)** 3. Rhyno 4. Baron Corbin 5. Heath Slater 6. Elias 7. Andrade Almas 8. Bray Wyatt 9. Big E 10. Sami Zayn 11. Sheamus 12. Xavier Woods 13. Apollo Crews **14. Shinsuke Nakamura** 15. Cesaro 16. Kofi Kingston 17. Jinder Mahal 18. Seth Rollins 19. Matt Hardy 20. John Cena 21. The Hurricane 22. Aiden English 23. Adam Cole 24. Randy Orton 25. Titus O'Neil 26. The Miz 27. Rey Mysterio 28. Roman Reigns 29. Goldust 30. Dolph Ziggler

Eliminations: 4 - Finn Balor, Roman Reigns, 3 - Shinsuke Nakamura, John Cena, 2 - Bray Wyatt, Jinder Mahal, Seth Rollins, Matt Hardy, 1 - Baron Corbin, Heath Slater, Andrade Almas, Cesaro, Kofi Kingston, Randy Orton, Rey Mysterio, Dolph Ziggler

2018 (Greatest Royal Rumble)

Order Of Entry: 1. Daniel Bryan **(76:05)** 2. Dolph Ziggler 3. Sin Cara 4. Curtis Axel 5. Mark Henry 6. Mike Kanellis 7. Hiroki Sumi 8. Viktor 9. Kofi Kingston 10. Tony Nese 11.

Dash Wilder 12. Hornswoggle 13. Primo Colon 14. Xavier Woods 15. Bo Dallas 16. Kurt Angle 17. Scott Dawson 18. Goldust 19. Konnor 20. Elias 21. Luke Gallows 22. Rhyno 23. Drew Gulak 24. Tucker Knight 25. Bobby Roode 26. Fandango 27. Chad Gable 28. Rey Mysterio 29. Mojo Rawley 30. Tyler Breeze 31. Big E 32. Karl Anderson 33. Apollo Crews 34. Roderick Strong 35. Randy Orton 36. Heath Slater 37. Babatunde 38. Baron Corbin 39. Titus O'Neil 40. Dan Matha **41. Braun Strowman** 42. Tye Dillinger 43. Curt Hawkins 44. Bobby Lashley 45. The Great Khali 46. Kevin Owens 47. Shane McMahon 48. Shelton Benjamin 49. Big Cass 50. Chris Jericho

Eliminations: 13 - Braun Strowman, 5 - Elias, 4 - Randy Orton, 3 - Daniel Bryan, Mark Henry, Kurt Angle, Baron Corbin, 2 - Dolph Ziggler, Bobby Roode, Mojo Rawley, Bobby Lashley, 1 - Kofi Kingston, Tony Nese, Hornswoggle, Xavier Woods, Tucker Knight, Rey Mysterio, Big E, Apollo Crews, Roderick Strong, Big Cass, Chris Jericho

2019

Order Of Entry: 1. Elias 2. Jeff Jarrett 3. Shinsuke Nakamura 4. Kurt Angle 5. Big E 6. Johnny Gargano 7. Jinder Mahal 8. Samoa Joe 9. Curt Hawkins **10. Seth Rollins (43:00)** 11. Titus O'Neil 12. Kofi Kingston 13. Mustafa Ali 14. Dean Ambrose 15. No Way Jose 16. Drew McIntyre 17. Xavier Woods 18. Pete Dunne 19. Andrade 20. Apollo Crews 21. Aleister Black 22. Shelton Benjamin 23. Baron Corbin 24. Jeff Hardy 25. Rey Mysterio 26. Bobby Lashley 27. Braun Strowman 28. Dolph Ziggler 29. Randy Orton 30. Nia Jax

Eliminations: 6 - Braun Strowman, 4 - Drew McIntyre, 3 - Samoa Joe, Seth Rollins, 2 - Mustafa Ali, Baron Corbin, 1 - Elias, Shinsuke Nakamura, Johnny Gargano, Curt Hawkins, Dean Ambrose, Andrade, Aleister Black, Rey Mysterio, Dolph Ziggler, Randy Orton, Nia Jax

2020

Order Of Entry: 1. Brock Lesnar 2. Elias 3. Erick Rowan 4. Robert Roode 5. John Morrison 6. Kofi Kingston 7. Rey Mysterio 8. Big E 9. Cesaro 10. Shelton Benjamin 11. Shinsuke Nakamura 12. MVP 13. Keith Lee 14. Braun Strowman 15. Ricochet **16. Drew McIntyre (34:11)** 17. The Miz 18. AJ Styles 19. Dolph Ziggler 20. Karl Anderson 21. Edge 22. King Corbin 23. Matt Riddle 24. Luke Gallows 25. Randy Orton 26. Roman Reigns 27. Kevin Owens 28. Aleister Black 29. Samoa Joe 30. Seth Rollins

Eliminations: 13 - Brock Lesnar, 6 - Drew McIntyre, 3 - Edge, Seth Rollins, 2 - Roman Reigns, 1 - Keith Lee, Braun Strowman, King Corbin, Randy Orton

2021

Order Of Entry: 1. Edge (58:30) 2. Randy Orton 3. Sami Zayn 4. Mustafa Ali 5. Jeff Hardy 6. Dolph Ziggler 7. Shinsuke Nakamura 8. Carlito 9. Xavier Woods 10. Big E 11. John Morrison 12. Ricochet 13. Elias 14. Damian Priest 15. The Miz 16. Riddle 17. Daniel Bryan 18. Kane 19. King Corbin 20. Otis 21. Dominik Mysterio 22. Bobby Lashley 23. Hurricane Helms 24. Christian 25. AJ Styles 26. Rey Mysterio 27. Sheamus 28. Cesaro 29. Seth Rollins 30. Braun Strowman

Eliminations: 4 - Big E, Damian Priest, Seth Rollins, 3 - Edge, Bobby Lashley, Braun Strowman, 2 - Kane, King Corbin, Christian, 1 - Mustafa Ali, Dolph Ziggler, Elias, Riddle, Daniel Bryan, Dominik Mysterio

2022

Order Of Entry: 1. AJ Styles **(29:06)** 2. Shinsuke

Nakamura 3. Austin Theory 4. Robert Roode 5. Ridge Holland 6. Montez Ford 7. Damian Priest 8. Sami Zayn 9. Johnny Knoxville 10. Angelo Dawkins 11. Omos 12. Ricochet 13. Chad Gable 14. Dominik Mysterio 15. Happy Corbin 16. Dolph Ziggler 17. Sheamus 18. Rick Boogs 19. Madcap Moss 20. Riddle 21. Drew McIntyre 22. Kevin Owens 23. Rey Mysterio 24. Kofi Kingston 25. Otis 26. Big E 27. Bad Bunny 28. Shane McMahon 29. Randy Orton 30. **Brock Lesnar**

Eliminations: 6 - AJ Styles, 5 - Brock Lesnar, 3 - Omos, Happy Corbin, 2 - Riddle, Drew McIntyre, Bad Bunny, Randy Orton, 1 - Austin Theory, Ridge Holland, Sami Zayn, Ricochet, Chad Gable, Dominik Mysterio, Rick Boogs, Madcap Moss, Kevin Owens, Rey Mysterio, Otis, Shane McMahon

WWE ROYAL RUMBLE (WOMEN)

YEAR	WON BY
2018	**Asuka**
	(Runner Up: Nikki Bella)
2019	**Becky Lynch**
	(Runner Up: Charlotte Flair)
2020	**Charlotte Flair**
	(Runner Up: Shayna Baszler)
2021	**Bianca Belair**
	(Runner Up: Rhea Ripley)
2022	**Ronda Rousey**
	(Runner Up: Charlotte Flair)

2018
Order Of Entry: 1. Sasha Banks **(54:46)** 2. Becky Lynch 3. Sarah Logan 4. Mandy Rose 5. Lita 6. Kairi Sane 7. Tamina 8. Dana Brooke 9. Torrie Wilson 10. Sonya Deville 11. Liv Morgan 12. Molly Holly 13. Lana 14. Michelle McCool 15. Ruby Riott 16. Vickie Guerrero 17. Carmella 18. Natalya 19. Kelly Kelly 20. Naomi 21. Jacqueline 22. Nia Jax 23. Ember Moon 24. Beth Phoenix **25. Asuka** 26. Mickie James 27. Nikki Bella 28. Brie Bella 29. Bayley 30. Trish Stratus

Eliminations: 5 - Michelle McCool, 4 - Nia Jax, Nikki Bella, 3 - Sasha Banks, Natalya, Asuka, Trish Stratus, 2 - Becky Lynch, Lita, Ruby Riott, Brie Bella, 1 - Dana Brooke, Torrie Wilson, Sonya Deville, Molly Holly, Bayley

2019
Order Of Entry: 1. Lacey Evans 2. Natalya **(56:01)** 3. Mandy Rose 4. Liv Morgan 5. Mickie James 6. Ember Moon 7. Billie Kay 8. Nikki Cross 9. Peyton Royce 10. Tamina 11. Xia Li 12. Sarah Logan 13. Charlotte Flair 14. Kairi Sane 15. Maria Kanellis 16. Naomi 17. Candice LeRae 18. Alicia Fox 19. Kacy Catanzaro 20. Zelina Vega 21. Ruby Riott 22. Dana Brooke 23. Io Shirai 24. Rhea Ripley 25. Sonya Deville 26. Alexa Bliss 27. Bayley **28. Becky Lynch** 29. Nia Jax 30. Carmella

Eliminations: 5 - Charlotte Flair, 3 - Ruby Riott, Rhea Ripley, Bayley, Nia Jax, 2 - Lacey Evans, Natalya, Alexa Bliss, Becky Lynch, 1 - Mandy Rose, Billie Kay, Peyton Royce, Tamina, Kairi Sane, Naomi, Alicia Fox, Carmella

2020
Order Of Entry: 1. Alexa Bliss 2. Bianca Belair **(33:20)** 3. Molly Holly 4. Nikki Cross 5. Lana 6. Mercedes Martinez 7. Liv Morgan 8. Mandy Rose 9. Candice LeRae 10. Sonya

Deville 11. Kairi Sane 12. Mia Yim 13. Dana Brooke 14. Tamina 15. Dakota Kai 16. Chelsea Green **17. Charlotte Flair** 18. Naomi 19. Beth Phoenix 20. Toni Storm 21. Kelly Kelly 22. Sarah Logan 23. Natalya 24. Xia Li 25. Zelina Vega 26. Shotzi Blackheart 27. Carmella 28. Tegan Nox 29. Santina Marella 30. Shayna Baszler

Eliminations: 8 - Bianca Belair, Shayna Baszler, 4 - Alexa Bliss, Charlotte Flair, 1 - Lana, Liv Morgan, Mandy Rose, Sonya Deville, Chelsea Green, Beth Phoenix, Shotzi Blackheart, Santina Marella

2021
Order Of Entry: 1. Bayley 2. Naomi **3. Bianca Belair (56:52)** 4. Billie Kay 5. Shotzi Blackheart 6. Shayna Baszler 7. Toni Storm 8. Jillian Hall 9. Ruby Riott 10. Victoria 11. Peyton Royce 12. Santana Garrett 13. Liv Morgan 14. Rhea Ripley 15. Charlotte Flair 16. Dana Brooke 17. Torrie Wilson 18. Lacey Evans 19. Mickie James 20. Nikki Cross 21. Alicia Fox 22. Mandy Rose 23. Dakota Kai 24. Carmella 25. Tamina 26. Lana 27. Alexa Bliss 28. Ember Moon 29. Nia Jax 30. Natalya

Eliminations: 7 - Rhea Ripley, 6 - Shayna Baszler, 4 - Bianca Belair, Nia Jax, 1 - Bayley, Billie Kay, Ruby Riott, Peyton Royce, Liv Morgan, Charlotte Flair, Lacey Evans, Mandy Rose, Carmella, Tamina, Lana, Natalya

2022
Order Of Entry: 1. Sasha Banks 2. Melina 3. Tamina 4. Kelly Kelly 5. Aliyah 6. Liv Morgan 7. Queen Zelina 8. Bianca Belair **(47:30)** 9. Dana Brooke 10. Michelle McCool 11. Sonya Deville 12. Natalya 13. Cameron 14. Naomi 15. Carmella 16. Rhea Ripley 17. Charlotte Flair 18. Ivory 19. Brie Bella 20. Mickie James 21. Alicia Fox 22. Nikki A.S.H. 23. Summer Rae 24. Nikki Bella 25. Sarah Logan 26. Lita 27. Mighty Molly **28. Ronda Rousey** 29. Shotzi 30. Shayna Baszler

Eliminations: 5 - Charlotte Flair, 4 - Ronda Rousey, 3 - Rhea Ripley, Brie Bella, 2 - Sasha Banks, Sonya Deville, Natalya, Nikki Bella, 1 - Queen Zelina, Bianca Belair, Michelle McCool, Naomi, Mickie James, Nikki A.S.H., Lita

ROYAL RUMBLE WINNING NUMBERS		
ENTRANT	**WINNERS**	**YEARS**
#1	3	(1995, 2004, 2021)
#2	2	(1999, 2006)
#3	2	(1992, 2021)
#4	N/A	
#5	1	(1997)
#6	N/A	
#7	N/A	
#8	1	(2009)
#9	N/A	
#10	1	(2019)
#11	N/A	
#12	N/A	
#13	1	(1988)
#14	1	(2018)
#15	N/A	
#16	1	(2020)
#17	1	(2020)
#18	1	(1996)
#19	2	(2003, 2017)
#20	N/A	
#21	N/A	
#22	2	(2002, 2012)
#23	2	(1994, 2017)

#24	3	(1991, 1998, 2000)
#25	2	(1990, 2018)
#26	N/A	
#27	4	(1989, 1992, 1994, 2001)
#28	4	(2005, 2014, 2019, 2022)
#29	2	(2003, 2010)
#30	4	(2007, 2008, 2016, 2022)
#38	1	(2011)
#41	1	(GRR)

LONGEST TIME SPENT IN A ROYAL RUMBLE MATCH

POS	WRESTLER	TIME	YEAR
1.	Daniel Bryan	1:16:05	GRR
2.	Rey Mysterio	1:02:12	2006
3.	Chris Benoit	1:01:30	2004
4.	Bob Backlund	1:01:10	1993
5.	Triple H	1:00:16	2006
6.	Chris Jericho	1:00:13	2017
7.	Ric Flair	1:00:02	1992
8.	Roman Reigns	59:48	2016
=9.	Edge	58:30	2021
=9.	Randy Orton	58:30	2021

SHORTEST TIME SPENT IN A ROYAL RUMBLE MATCH

POS	WRESTLER	TIME	YEAR
1.	Santino Marella	0:00:01	2009
=2.	The Warlord	0:00:02	1989
=2.	Sheamus	0:00:02	2018
=2.	No Way Jose	0:00:02	2019
=5.	Mo	0:00:03	1995
=5.	Owen Hart	0:00:03	1995
=5.	Mike Kanellis	0:00:03	GRR
=5.	Xavier Woods	0:00:03	2019
=9.	Bushwhacker Luke	0:00:04	1991
=9.	Jerry Lawler	0:00:04	1997
=9.	Titus O'Neil	0:00:04	2015

LONGEST CUMULATIVE TIME IN ROYAL RUMBLES

POS	WRESTLER	TIME
1.	Chris Jericho	4:59:33
2.	Randy Orton	4:34:08
3.	Rey Mysterio	4:14:46
4.	Triple H	4:00:50
5.	Shawn Michaels	3:47:32
6.	Edge	3:31:51
7.	Kane	3:19:40
8.	Dolph Ziggler	3:08:39
9.	Cody Rhodes	3:06:45
10.	John Cena	2:48:32

MOST ELIMINATIONS IN A SINGLE ROYAL RUMBLE

POS	WRESTLER	AMOUNT	YEAR
=1.	Brock Lesnar	13	2020
=1.	Braun Strowman	13	GRR
3.	Roman Reigns	12	2014
4.	Kane	11	2001
=5.	Hulk Hogan	10	1989
=5.	Steve Austin	10	1997
=7.	Shawn Michaels	8	1995
=7.	Shawn Michaels	8	1996
=7.	Steve Austin	8	1999
=7.	Shayna Baszler	8	2020
=7.	Bianca Belair	8	2020

MOST ROYAL RUMBLE ELIMINATIONS

POS	WRESTLER	AMOUNT	RUMBLES
1.	Kane	46	20
2.	Shawn Michaels	41	12
3.	The Undertaker	40	11
4.	Steve Austin	36	6
5.	Braun Strowman	35	6
6.	Triple H	33	9
=7.	Roman Reigns	32	6
=7.	The Big Show	32	12
=9.	Brock Lesnar	29	5
=9.	Randy Orton	29	14

MOST ROYAL RUMBLE APPEARANCES

POS	WRESTLER	RUMBLES
1.	Kane	20
2.	Dolph Ziggler	15
=3.	Kofi Kingston	14
=3.	Randy Orton	14
=5.	The Miz	13
=5.	Goldust	13
=5.	Rey Mysterio	13
=8.	The Big Show	12
=8.	Shawn Michaels	12
=10.	Chris Jericho	11
=10.	Shelton Benjamin	11
=10.	The Undertaker	11

ROYAL RUMBLE MATCH LENGTHS

POS	YEAR	LENGTH
1.	2018 (GRR)	77:20
2.	2019 (W)	72:00
3.	2011	69:51
4.	2002	69:22
5.	1993	66:35
6.	2018 (M)	65:27
7.	1991	65:17
8.	1989	64:53
9.	2006	62:12
10.	2017	62:06
11.	1992	62:02
12.	2001	61:52
13.	2016	61:42
14.	2004	61:37
15.	2020 (M)	60:50
16.	2022 (W)	59:40
17.	2009	59:37
18.	2015	59:31
19.	2018 (W)	58:57
20.	2021 (W)	58:50
21.	1996	58:49
22.	1990	58:46
23.	2021 (M)	58:30
24.	2019 (M)	57:35
25.	1999	56:38
26.	2007	56:18
27.	1998	55:25
28.	2014	55:08
29.	2013	55:05
30.	1994	55:04
31.	2012	54:32
32.	2020 (W)	54:20
33.	2003	53:47
34.	2000	51:48
35.	2008	51:25

36.	2022 (M)	51:10
37.	2005	51:07
38.	1997	50:30
39.	2010	49:24
40.	1995	38:41
41.	1988	33:00

WXW 16 CARAT GOLD TOURNAMENT

YEAR	WON BY
2006	**Baron von Hagen**
	(Runner Up: Murat Bosporus)
2007	**Chris Hero**
	(Runner Up: Ares)
2008	**Bad Bones**
	(Runner Up: Bryan Danielson)
2009	**Shingo Takagi**
	(Runner Up: Drake Younger)
2010	**Walter**
	(Runner Up: Chris Hero)
2011	**Sami Callihan**
	(Runner Up: Walter)
2012	**El Generico**
	(Runner Up: Tommy End)
2013	**Tommy End**
	(Runner Up: Zack Sabre Jr.)
2014	**Chris Hero**[2]
	(Runner Up: Axel Tischer)
2015	**Tommy End**[2]
	(Runner Up: Axel Dieter Jr.)
2016	**Zack Sabre Jr.**
	(Runner Up: Axel Dieter Jr.)
2017	**Ilja Dragunov**
	(Runner Up: Walter)
2018	**Absolute Andy**
	(Runner Up: David Starr)
2019	**Lucky Kid**
	(Runner Up: Walter)
2020	**Cara Noir**
	(Runner Up: Mike Bailey)
2022	**Jonathan Gresham**
	(Runner Up: Robert Dreissker)

2006

R1	Rocky Romero def. Tengkwa
R1	Murat Bosporus def. Vries Kastelein
R1	Adam Polak def. HATE
R1	Ian Rotten def. Ares
R1	Tommy End def. Bad Bones
R1	Steve Douglas def. Steve Allison
R1	Doug Williams def. Bernard Vandamme
R1	Baron von Hagen def. Iceman
QF	Murat Bosporus def. Adam Polak
QF	Steve Douglas def. Tommy End
QF	Baron von Hagen def. Ian Rotten
QF	Doug Williams defeated Rocky Romero
SF	Murat Bosporus def. Steve Douglas
SF	Baron von Hagen def. Doug Williams
F	Baron von Hagen def. Murat Bosporus

2007

R1	Go Shiozaki def. Davey Richards
R1	Nigel McGuinness def. Doug Williams
R1	Ares def. Tommy End
R1	El Generico def. Pac
R1	Ryo Saito def. Matt Sydal
R1	Bad Bones def. Emil Sitoci
R1	Murat Bosporus def. Steve Douglas
R1	Chris Hero def. Claudio Castagnoli
QF	El Generico def. Bad Bones
QF	Ares def. Nigel McGuinness
QF	Chris Hero def. Ryo Saito
QF	Murat Bosporus def. Go Shiozaki
SF	Ares def. El Generico
SF	Chris Hero def. Murat Bosporus
F	Chris Hero def. Ares

2008

R1	Ares def. Big Van Walter
R1	Tommy End def. Jimmy Jacobs
R1	Chris Hero def. Absolute Andy
R1	El Generico def. Taiji Ishimori
R1	Bad Bones def. Pierre Carl Ouellet
R1	Emil Sitoci def. Chuck Taylor
R1	Bryan Danielson def. Mike Quackenbush
R1	Naomichi Marufuji def. Doug Williams
QF	Chris Hero def. Emil Sitoci
QF	Bad Bones def. El Generico
QF	Ares def. Tommy End
QF	Bryan Danielson def. Naomichi Marufuji
SF	Bryan Danielson def. Chris Hero
SF	Bad Bones def. Ares
F	Bad Bones def. Bryan Danielson

2009

R1	Daisuke Sekimoto def. Martin Stone
R1	Drake Younger def. Adam Polak
R1	Steve Douglas def. Tatsuhito Takaiwa
R1	Bryan Danielson def. Doug Williams
R1	Zack Sabre Jr. def. Terry Frazier
R1	Big Van Walter def. Erick Stevens
R1	SHINGO def. Absolute Andy
R1	Tyler Black def. Chris Sabin
QF	Zack Sabre Jr. def. Bryan Danielson
QF	Steve Douglas def. Daisuke Sekimoto
QF	Drake Younger def. Big Van Walter
QF	SHINGO def. Tyler Black
SF	SHINGO def. Zack Sabre Jr.
SF	Drake Younger def. Steve Douglas
F	SHINGO def. Drake Younger

2010

R1	Ares def. Matt Jackson
R1	Munenori Sawa def. Paul Tracey
R1	Martin Stone def. Yuji Okabayashi
R1	Claudio Castagnoli def. Johnny Kidd
R1	KAGETORA def. Nick Jackson and Tommy End
R1	Erick Stevens def. Adam Polak
R1	Big Van Walter def. Daisuke Sekimoto
R1	Chris Hero def. Bad Bones
QF	Big Van Walter def. Munenori Sawa
QF	Erick Stevens def. KAGETORA
QF	Ares def. Claudio Castagnoli
QF	Chris Hero def. Martin Stone
SF	Big Van Walter def. Erick Stevens
SF	Chris Hero def. Ares
F	Big Van Walter def. Chris Hero

2011

R1	Yoshihito Sasaki def. Carnage
R1	Zack Sabre Jr. def. Colt Cabana
R1	Mark Haskins def. Adam Cole
R1	Go Shiozaki def. Johnny Moss
R1	Big Van Walter def. Rico Bushido
R1	Davey Richards def. Jon Ryan
R1	Sami Callihan def. Tommy End
R1	Kotaro Suzuki def. El Generico
QF	Big Van Walter def. Mark Haskins

QF	Sami Callihan def. Yoshihito Sasaki
QF	Go Shiozaki def. Kotaro Suzuki
QF	Davey Richards def. Zack Sabre Jr.
SF	Sami Callihan def. Davey Richards
SF	Big Van Walter def. Go Shiozaki
F	Sami Callihan def. Big Van Walter

2012

R1	Yoshihito Sasaki def. Bad Bones
R1	Karsten Beck def. Drake Younger
R1	Ricky Marvin def. Axeman
R1	Johnny Moss def. Doug Williams
R1	Tommy End def. Emil Sitoci
R1	Zack Sabre Jr. def. Jon Ryan
R1	El Generico def.Marty Scurll
R1	Fit Finlay def. Sami Callihan
QF	Tommy End def. Ricky Marvin
QF	Zack Sabre Jr. def. Yoshihito Sasaki
QF	El Generico def. Karsten Beck
QF	Johnny Moss def. Fit Finlay
SF	El Generico def. Johnny Moss
SF	Tommy End def. Zack Sabre Jr.
F	El Generico def. Tommy End

2013

R1	Shinobu def. Bad Bones
R1	Karsten Beck def. Paul Tracey
R1	Tommy End def. Ricochet
R1	Robert Dreissker def. Yuji Okabayashi
R1	Eddie Kingston def. Chuck Taylor
R1	Super Crazy def. MASADA
R1	Jonathan Gresham def. Ricky Marvin
R1	Zack Sabre Jr. def. Johnny Moss
QF	Shinobu def. Eddie Kingston
QF	Zack Sabre Jr. def. Robert Dreissker
QF	Karsten Beck def. Super Crazy
QF	Tommy End def. Jonathan Gresham
SF	Zack Sabre Jr. def. Karsten Beck
SF	Tommy End def. Shinobu
F	Tommy End def. Zack Sabre Jr.

2014

R1	Bad Bones def. Tommaso Ciampa
R1	Robert Dreissker def. Ryuichi Kawakami
R1	Big Daddy Walter def. Sasa Keel
R1	Johnny Gargano def. Toby Blunt
R1	Axel Tischer def. KUSHIDA
R1	Karsten Beck def. Matt Striker
R1	Adam Cole def. Trent Barreta
R1	Chris Hero def. Freddy Stahl
QF	Big Daddy Walter def. Johnny Gargano
QF	Adam Cole def. Robert Dreissker
QF	Chris Hero def. Karsten Beck
QF	Axel Tischer def. Bad Bones
SF	Chris Hero def. Adam Cole
SF	Axel Tischer def. Big Daddy Walter
F	Chris Hero def. Axel Tischer

2015

R1	Marty Scurll def. Cedric Alexander
R1	Absolute Andy def. Mr. Sha Samuels
R1	Axel Dieter Jr. def. Timothy Thatcher
R1	Tommy End def. Chris Sabin
R1	Sasa Keel def. Uhaa Nation
R1	Daisuke Harada def. Kim Ray
R1	Andrew Everett def. Robert Dreissker
R1	Zack Sabre Jr. def. Axel Tischer
QF	Tommy End def. Andrew Everett
QF	Axel Dieter Jr. def. Marty Scurll
QF	Absolute Andy def. Sasa Keel
QF	Zack Sabre Jr. def. Daisuke Harada

SF	Axel Dieter Jr. def. Zack Sabre Jr.
SF	Tommy End def. Absolute Andy
F	Tommy End def. Axel Dieter Jr.

2016

R1	Zack Sabre Jr. def. Big Daddy Walter
R1	Timothy Thatcher def. Sasa Keel
R1	Ilja Dragunov def. Mike Bailey
R1	Will Ospreay def. Shane Strickland
R1	Angélico def. Trevor Lee
R1	Drew Galloway def. Silas Young
R1	Sami Callihan def. Kim Ray
R1	Axel Dieter Jr. def. Marty Scurll
QF	Axel Dieter Jr. def. Ilja Dragunov
QF	Zack Sabre Jr. def. Will Ospreay
QF	Sami Callihan def. Timothy Thatcher
QF	Drew Galloway def. Angélico
SF	Axel Dieter Jr. def. Drew Galloway
SF	Zack Sabre Jr. def. Sami Callihan
F	Zack Sabre Jr. def. Axel Dieter Jr.

2017

R1	Cody Rhodes def. Da Mack
R1	Marius Al-Ani def. JT Dunn
R1	Timothy Thatcher def. Koji Kanemoto
R1	Ilja Dragunov def. Robert Dreissker
R1	Matt Riddle def. Donovan Dijak
R1	John Klinger def. Paul London
R1	Mike Bailey def. ACH
R1	Walter def. David Starr
QF	Matt Riddle def. Mike Bailey
QF	Ilja Dragunov def. Timothy Thatcher
QF	Walter def. Marius Al-Ani
QF	John Klinger def. Cody Rhodes
SF	Ilja Dragunov def. John Klinger
SF	Walter def. Matt Riddle
F	Ilja Dragunov def. Walter

2018

R1	Keith Lee def. The Avalanche
R1	Chris Brookes def. Alexander James
R1	Lucky Kid def. Matt Sydal
R1	David Starr def. Emil Sitoci
R1	Matt Riddle def. Da Mack
R1	Travis Banks def. Mark Haskins
R1	Timothy Thatcher def. Jonah Rock
R1	Absolute Andy def. Marius Al-Ani
QF	Keith Lee def. Chris Brookes
QF	Timothy Thatcher def. Lucky Kid
QF	David Starr def. Travis Banks
QF	Absolute Andy def. Matt Riddle
SF	David Starr def. Keith Lee
SF	Absolute Andy def. Timothy Thatcher
F	Absolute Andy def. David Starr

2019

R1	Axel Dieter Jr. def. Marius Al-Ani
R1	Fénix def. Rey Horus
R1	Shigehiro Irie def. Chris Brookes
R1	Lucky Kid def. Timothy Thatcher
R1	The Avalanche def. Jurn Simmons
R1	Pentagón Jr. def. Mark Davis
R1	Ilja Dragunov def. Daisuke Sekimoto
R1	Walter def. David Starr
QF	Ilja Dragunov def. Pentagón Jr.
QF	The Avalanche def. Shigehiro Irie
QF	Walter def. Fénix
QF	Lucky Kid def. Axel Dieter Jr.
SF	Lucky Kid def. Ilja Dragunov
SF	Walter def. The Avalanche
F	Lucky Kid def. Walter

2020

R1	Mike Bailey def. Chris Ridgeway
R1	Jurn Simmons def. Lucky Kid
R1	The Rotation def. Puma King
R1	Eddie Kingston def. Daniel Makabe
R1	El Bandido def. Julian Pace
R1	Shigehiro Irie def. Black Taurus
R1	Jeff Cobb def. Alexander James
R1	Cara Noir def. Marius Al-Ani
QF	Cara Noir def. Jeff Cobb
QF	Eddie Kingston def. The Rotation
QF	Mike Bailey def. El Bandido
QF	Jurn Simmons def. Shigehiro Irie
SF	Mike Bailey def. Jurn Simmons
SF	Cara Noir def. Eddie Kingston
F	Cara Noir def. Mike Bailey

2022

R1	Robert Dreissker def. Fuminori Abe
R1	Cara Noir def. Heisenberg
R1	Péter Tihanyi def. Aigle Blanc
R1	LuFisto def. Dennis Dullnig
R1	Marius Al-Ani def. Michael Knight
R1	Maggot def. Ace Romero
R1	Shigehiro Irie def. Senza Volto
R1	Jonathan Gresham def. Bobby Gunns
QF	Shigehiro Irie def. Hektor Invictus
QF	Jonathan Gresham def. Péter Tihanyi
QF	LuFisto def. Maggot
QF	Robert Dreissker def. Cara Noir
SF	Robert Dreissker def. LuFisto
SF	Jonathan Gresham def. Shigehiro Irie
F	Jonathan Gresham def. Robert Dreissker

HISTORICAL
PS50 & ITR50
RANKINGS

The PS 50 was PowerSlam Magazine's annual ranking of the top 50 wrestlers on the planet, which ran uninterrupted from 1994 to 2013. Over the years, it became one of pro wrestling's most respected and prestigeous ranking lists. Inside The Ropes Magazine took up the mantle with the inaugural ITR 50 in 2020 (which, unlike the PS 50, included men and women on the same list). The list expanded to 100 entrants with the 2021 edition, before settling on two lists of 50 - one for men and one for women - in 2022. On the pages that follow are the complete 50 listings for each year from both the PS 50 and ITR 50 and the cover of the magazine they featured in.

#	1994 (PS50)	#	1995 (PS50)	#	1996 (PS50)
1	Shawn Michaels	1	Mitsuharu Misawa	1	Shawn Michaels
2	Chris Benoit	2	Chris Benoit	2	Kenta Kobashi
3	Toshiaki Kawada	3	Shawn Michaels	3	Dean Malenko
4	Mitsuharu Misawa	4	Eddy Guerrero	4	Sabu
5	Jushin Liger	5	Toshiaki Kawada	5	Mankind
6	Bret Hart	6	Bret Hart	6	Rey Misterio Jr.
7	Steve Williams	7	Sabu	7	The Great Sasuke
8	Sabu	8	Kenta Kobashi	8	Mitsuharu Misawa
9	Nobuhiko Takada	9	Keiji Muto	9	Steve Austin
10	Vader	10	Ken Shamrock	10	Jushin Liger
11	Steve Austin	11	Jushin Liger	11	Akira Taue
12	Kenta Kobashi	12	Koji Kanemoto	12	Shinya Hashimoto
13	2 Cold Scorpio	13	2 Cold Scorpio	13	Steve Williams
14	Art Barr	14	Dean Malenko	14	Chris Benoit
15	Hiro Hase	15	Hakushi	15	Bret Hart
16	1-2-3 Kid	16	Nobuhiko Takada	16	Ultimo Dragon
17	Shane Douglas	17	Rey Misterio Jr.	17	Nobuhiko Takada
18	Terry Funk	18	Akira Taue	18	Toshiaki Kawada
19	The Great Sasuke	19	Marty Jannetty	19	2 Cold Scorpio
20	Keiji Muto	20	Cactus Jack	20	Shinjiro Otani
21	Eddy Guerrero	21	Johnny Ace	21	Davey Boy Smith
22	Owen Hart	22	Vader	22	Perry Saturn
23	Cactus Jack	23	1-2-3 Kid	23	Shane Douglas
24	Stan Hansen	24	Mikey Whipwreck	24	Jun Akiyama
25	Brian Pillman	25	Alex Wright	25	Chris Jericho
26	Jimmy Del Ray	26	Davey Boy Smith	26	Eddy Guerrero
27	Tracy Smothers	27	Psicosis	27	Keiji Muto
28	Dan Kroffat	28	Brian Pillman	28	Johnny B. Badd
29	Ultimo Dragon	29	Owen Hart	29	Owen Hart
30	Sting	30	Rocco Rock	30	Mikey Whipwreck
31	Rey Misterio Jr.	31	Al Snow	31	Johnny Ace
32	Tom Prichard	32	The Great Sasuke	32	Hunter Hearst Helmsley
33	Jinsei Shinzaki	33	Raven	33	Steven Regal
34	Psicosis	34	Terry Funk	34	Psicosis
35	Bam Bam Bigelow	35	Hunter Hearst Helmsley	35	Pitbull #2
36	Ricky Steamboat	36	Ultimo Dragon	36	Diamond Dallas Page
37	Scott Steiner	37	Razor Ramon	37	Kevin Nash
38	Diesel	38	Johnny B. Badd	38	Shiro Koshinaka
39	Chris Candido	39	Arn Anderson	39	John Kronus
40	Arn Anderson	40	Steve Austin	40	Rob Van Dam
41	Super Delfin	41	Ric Flair	41	Raven
42	Heavy Metal	42	Skip	42	Goldust
43	The Patriot	43	Bam Bam Bigelow	43	Taz
44	Billy Gunn	44	Hayabusa	44	Stevie Richards
45	Dustin Rhodes	45	Scott Steiner	45	Scott Hall
46	Razor Ramon	46	The Sandman	46	Riki Choshu
47	Rocco Rock	47	The Headhunters	47	Booker T
48	Mike Awesome	48	Diesel	48	Vader
49	Hulk Hogan	49	Dean Douglas	49	Ric Flair
50	Steven Regal	50	La Parka	50	The Sandman

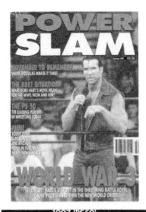 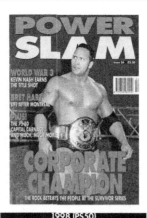 

	1997 (PS50)		1998 (PS50)		1999 (PS50)
1	Bret Hart	1	Steve Austin	1	Chris Benoit
2	Jushin Liger	2	Koji Kanemoto	2	Keiji Muto
3	Shawn Michaels	3	Mankind	3	Kenta Kobashi
4	Shinjiro Otani	4	Chris Benoit	4	The Rock
5	Eddy Guerrero	5	Jun Akiyama	5	Steve Austin
6	Ultimo Dragon	6	Shinjiro Otani	6	Jerry Lynn
7	The Undertaker	7	Chris Jericho	7	Yuji Nagata
8	Steve Austin	8	Ken Shamrock	8	Shinjiro Otani
9	Mitsuharu Misawa	9	Jushin Liger	9	Rey Misterio Jr.
10	Diamond Dallas Page	10	Billy Kidman	10	Koji Kanemoto
11	El Samurai	11	Kenta Kobashi	11	Billy Kidman
12	Dean Malenko	12	Jerry Lynn	12	Mitsuharu Misawa
13	Rey Misterio Jr.	13	The Rock	13	Triple H
14	Kenta Kobashi	14	Diamond Dallas Page	14	Diamond Dallas Page
15	Toshiaki Kawada	15	Raven	15	Justin Credible
16	Shinya Hashimoto	16	Mitsuharu Misawa	16	Jushin Liger
17	Randy Savage	17	Shinya Hashimoto	17	Juventud Guerrera
18	Chris Benoit	18	Satoshi Kojima	18	Jun Akiyama
19	Koji Kanemoto	19	Juventud Guerrera	19	Super Crazy
20	Sabu	20	Masato Tanaka	20	Mankind
21	Ken Shamrock	21	El Samurai	21	Yoshihiro Tajiri
22	Mankind	22	Bam Bam Bigelow	22	Jeff Hardy
23	Akira Taue	23	Owen Hart	23	Tatsuhito Takaiwa
24	Davey Boy Smith	24	Booker T	24	Sabu
25	Curt Hennig	25	Tatsuhito Takaiwa	25	Satoshi Kojima
26	Owen Hart	26	Triple H	26	Vader
27	Jun Akiyama	27	Dean Malenko	27	Christian
28	Kensuke Sasaki	28	Toshiaki Kawada	28	Toshiaki Kawada
29	Vader	29	X-Pac	29	Dean Malenko
30	Shane Douglas	30	Rob Van Dam	30	Raven
31	Hiroyoshi Tenzan	31	Ultimo Dragon	31	Yoshinari Ogawa
32	Jeff Jarrett	32	Eddy Guerrero	32	Edge
33	Syxx	33	Justin Credible	33	Lance Storm
34	Taka Michinoku	34	Bret Hart	34	The Great Sasuke
35	Keiji Muto	35	Lance Storm	35	Rob Van Dam
36	The Great Sasuke	36	Chavo Guerrero Jr.	36	Bill Goldberg
37	Taz	37	Genichiro Tenryu	37	Matt Hardy
38	Booker T	38	Terry Funk	38	Bam Bam Bigelow
39	Scott Steiner	39	Rey Misterio Jr.	39	Masato Tanaka
40	Bam Bam Bigelow	40	The Undertaker	40	Jeff Jarrett
41	Chris Candido	41	Disco Inferno	41	X-Pac
42	Masa Chono	42	D-Lo Brown	42	D-Lo Brown
43	Hunter Hearst Helmsley	43	Sting	43	Taz
44	Buff Bagwell	44	Chris Candido	44	Perry Saturn
45	Chris Jericho	45	Billy Gunn	45	Bret Hart
46	The Rock	46	Saturn	46	Shane McMahon
47	Rob Van Dam	47	The Great Sasuke	47	Mike Awesome
48	Brian Christopher	48	Kanyon	48	Eddy Guerrero
49	D-Von Dudley	49	Road Dogg	49	Test
50	Scott Hall	50	Sabu	50	Hardcore Holly

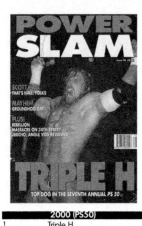

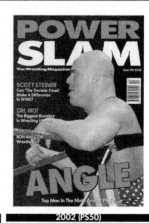

	2000 (PS50)		2001 (PS50)		2002 (PS50)
1	Triple H	1	Steve Austin	1	Kurt Angle
2	Chris Benoit	2	Keiji Muto	2	Yuji Nagata
3	The Rock	3	Kurt Angle	3	Low Ki
4	Tajiri	4	Rob Van Dam	4	Eddie Guerrero
5	Kenta Kobashi	5	Yuji Nagata	5	Satoshi Kojima
6	Chris Jericho	6	The Rock	6	Jerry Lynn
7	Jeff Hardy	7	Minoru Tanaka	7	Keiji Muto
8	Shinjiro Otani	8	Jun Akiyama	8	Rob Van Dam
9	Rob Van Dam	9	Triple H	9	Edge
10	Jun Akiyama	10	Chris Jericho	10	Genichiro Tenryu
11	Kid Kash	11	Satoshi Kojima	11	AJ Styles
12	Minoru Tanaka	12	Booker T	12	Jun Akiyama
13	Kurt Angle	13	Chris Benoit	13	The Rock
14	Justin Credible	14	Jeff Hardy	14	Chris Benoit
15	Toshiaki Kawada	15	Hiroyoshi Tenzan	15	Bryan Danielson
16	Edge	16	Edge	16	Yoshinobu Kanemaru
17	Mike Awesome	17	Toshiaki Kawada	17	Christopher Daniels
18	Little Guido	18	Genichiro Tenryu	18	Koji Kanemoto
19	Tatsuhito Takaiwa	19	Bubba Ray Dudley	19	Rey Mysterio
20	Scott Steiner	20	Rhyno	20	Triple H
21	Matt Hardy	21	Tatsuhito Takaiwa	21	Doug Williams
22	Mitsuharu Misawa	22	Matt Hardy	22	Hiroyoshi Tenzan
23	Jeff Jarrett	23	Christian	23	Chris Jericho
24	Christian	24	D-Von Dudley	24	Shinjiro Otani
25	Jerry Lynn	25	Tajiri	25	Minoru Tanaka
26	Lance Storm	26	Shinjiro Otani	26	Yoshihiro Takayama
27	X-Pac	27	Kensuke Sasaki	27	Booker T
28	Booker T	28	Jushin Liger	28	Manabu Nakanishi
29	Kensuke Sasaki	29	Shinya Hashimoto	29	Jushin Liger
30	Bubba Ray Dudley	30	Mitsuharu Misawa	30	Jamie Noble
31	Vader	31	Test	31	Matt Hardy
32	Diamond Dallas Page	32	Taiyo Kea	32	Mitsuharu Misawa
33	Super Crazy	33	Kanyon	33	Jody Fleisch
34	Koji Kanemoto	34	El Samurai	34	Jeff Hardy
35	Dean Malenko	35	The Hurricane	35	Steve Austin
36	Rhino	36	Doug Williams	36	Chavo Guerrero Jr.
37	Eddie Guerrero	37	Christopher Daniels	37	Brock Lesnar
38	Masato Tanaka	38	Bryan Danielson	38	Jonny Storm
39	Jushin Liger	39	Scott Steiner	39	Christian
40	Genichiro Tenryu	40	William Regal	40	Masa Chono
41	Scotty 2 Hotty	41	Jonny Storm	41	Spanky
42	D-Von Dudley	42	Vader	42	Masato Tanaka
43	Mick Foley	43	Alex Shane	43	Tajiri
44	Keiji Muto	44	Lance Storm	44	Kenta Kobashi
45	Kanyon	45	E.Z. Money	45	Magnum Tokyo
46	Grandmaster Sexay	46	Kaz Hayashi	46	The Undertaker
47	Terry Funk	47	Billy Kidman	47	Trent Acid
48	Val Venis	48	Low Ki	48	Dragon Kid
49	Steve Corino	49	Kane	49	The Amazing Red
50	Crash Holly	50	X-Pac	50	Lance Storm

2003 (PS50)		2004 (PS50)		2005 (PS50)	
1	Kenta Kobashi	1	Chris Benoit	1	AJ Styles
2	Kurt Angle	2	Kenta Kobashi	2	Shawn Michaels
3	Eddie Guerrero	3	AJ Styles	3	Samoa Joe
4	Yuji Nagata	4	Samoa Joe	4	Kenta Kobashi
5	Brock Lesnar	5	Shawn Michaels	5	Kurt Angle
6	KENTA	6	Randy Orton	6	KENTA
7	AJ Styles	7	KENTA	7	Christopher Daniels
8	Jun Akiyama	8	Jushin Liger	8	Naomichi Marafuji
9	Chris Benoit	9	Kensuke Sasaki	9	Eddie Guerrero
10	Naomichi Marafuji	10	Eddie Guerrero	10	Kensuke Sasaki
11	Paul London	11	Hiroshi Tanahashi	11	Chris Benoit
12	Koji Kanemoto	12	Low Ki	12	Rey Mysterio
13	Shawn Michaels	13	Naomichi Marafuji	13	Satoshi Kojima
14	Rey Mysterio	14	CM Punk	14	Edge
15	Hiroyoshi Tenzan	15	Triple H	15	Jamie Noble
16	Christopher Daniels	16	Rey Mysterio	16	Triple H
17	Shinjiro Otani	17	Hiroyoshi Tenzan	17	Toshiaki Kawada
18	Jushin Liger	18	Kurt Angle	18	Austin Aries
19	Low Ki	19	Christopher Daniels	19	Chris Jericho
20	Tajiri	20	Doug Williams	20	Jun Akiyama
21	Yoshihiro Takayama	21	Yuji Nagata	21	Yoshinobu Kanemaru
22	Rob Van Dam	22	Bryan Danielson	22	Koji Kanemoto
23	Juventud Guerrera	23	Yoshihiro Takayama	23	CM Punk
24	Samoa Joe	24	Yoshinobu Kanemaru	24	Chris Harris
25	Chris Jericho	25	Shinsuke Nakamura	25	Suwa
26	Christian	26	Toshiaki Kawada	26	Bryan Danielson
27	Toshiaki Kawada	27	Mitsuharu Misawa	27	Hiroshi Tanahashi
28	Shelton Benjamin	28	Koji Kanemoto	28	James Storm
29	Doug Williams	29	Christian	29	Roderick Strong
30	Satoshi Kojima	30	Jun Akiyama	30	Chris Sabin
31	Charlie Haas	31	Homicide	31	Shelton Benjamin
32	The Undertaker	32	Mick Foley	32	Doug Williams
33	Jerry Lynn	33	Edge	33	Alex Shelley
34	Booker T	34	Shelton Benjamin	34	Christian
35	Cima	35	Minoru Tanaka	35	Low Ki
36	Bryan Danielson	36	Chris Jericho	36	Petey Williams
37	Raven	37	Susuma Yokosuka	37	Hiroyoshi Tenzan
38	Chris Sabin	38	Chris Sabin	38	Milano Collection A.T.
39	Randy Orton	39	Chavo Guerrero Jr.	39	Takashi Sugiura
40	Chris Harris	40	Paul London	40	Randy Orton
41	Jonny Storm	41	Chris Hero	41	Eric Young
42	Yossino	42	Alex Shane	42	Jay Lethal
43	CM Punk	43	Petey Williams	43	Matt Hardy
44	Chavo Guerrero Jr.	44	James Tighe	44	Homicide
45	Jeff Jarrett	45	Tajiri	45	Nigel McGuinness
46	Matt Hardy	46	Jonny Storm	46	Jeff Jarrett
47	Jay Briscoe	47	Jeff Jarrett	47	Abyss
48	John Cena	48	The Undertaker	48	Booker T
49	Goldberg	49	Colt Cabana	49	Batista
50	James Tighe	50	Paul Burchill	50	Sabu

2006 (PS50)		2007 (PS50)		2008 (PS50)
1	Edge	1	Kurt Angle	1	Shawn Michaels
2	Bryan Danielson	2	Nigel McGuinness	2	KENTA
3	KENTA	3	KENTA	3	Nigel McGuinness
4	Samoa Joe	4	Yuji Nagata	4	Kurt Angle
5	Naomichi Marafuji	5	Randy Orton	5	Edge
6	AJ Styles	6	Samoa Joe	6	The Undertaker
7	Takeshi Morishima	7	Bryan Danielson	7	Hiroshi Tanahashi
8	Christopher Daniels	8	Shawn Michaels	8	Naomichi Marafuji
9	Yuji Nagata	9	Naomichi Marafuji	9	Jeff Hardy
10	Rey Mysterio	10	Hiroshi Tanahashi	10	Bryan Danielson
11	Cima	11	Takeshi Morishima	11	Triple H
12	Senshi	12	Christian Cage	12	Katsuhiko Nakajima
13	Homicide	13	The Undertaker	13	Kota Ibushi
14	Shuji Kondo	14	Jay Briscoe	14	Keiji Muto
15	Kurt Angle	15	Mark Briscoe	15	Shingo Takagi
16	Takashi Sugiura	16	AJ Styles	16	Masato Tanaka
17	Satoshi Kojima	17	Ricky Marvin	17	AJ Styles
18	Hiroshi Tanahashi	18	Katsuhiko Nakajima	18	Daisuke Sekimoto
19	Chris Benoit	19	Cima	19	Kensuke Sasaki
20	Randy Orton	20	Kensuke Sasaki	20	Samoa Joe
21	Austin Aries	21	Edge	21	CM Punk
22	Rob Van Dam	22	Kotaru Suzuki	22	Takeshi Morishima
23	Shawn Michaels	23	Jeff Hardy	23	Matt Hardy
24	Nigel McGuinness	24	Jay Lethal	24	Chris Jericho
25	Finlay	25	Batista	25	Christian Cage
26	Katsuhiko Nakajima	26	Austin Aries	26	Yuji Nagata
27	Kenta Kobashi	27	Umaga	27	Batista
28	Koji Kanemoto	28	Chris Sabin	28	Shinjiro Otani
29	Kensuke Sasaki	29	John Cena	29	Randy Orton
30	Roderick Strong	30	Matt Hardy	30	BxB Hulk
31	Jun Akiyama	31	Matt Sydal	31	Tyler Black
32	Davey Richards	32	Go Shiozaki	32	Prince Devitt
33	Jay Briscoe	33	Delirious	33	Austin Aries
34	Chris Sabin	34	CM Punk	34	Shinsuke Nakamura
35	Mark Briscoe	35	Roderick Strong	35	Chris Sabin
36	Triple H	36	Christopher Daniels	36	Jay Briscoe
37	Booker T	37	Finlay	37	Kevin Steen
38	Petey Williams	38	Homicide	38	Hirooki Goto
39	Abyss	39	Booker T	39	Mark Briscoe
40	Rhino	40	Kevin Steen	40	Jay Lethal
41	Brian Kendrick	41	Abyss	41	Homicide
42	Hiroyoshi Tenzan	42	Claudio Castagnoli	42	El Generico
43	Paul London	43	Rhino	43	Jimmy Jacobs
44	CM Punk	44	El Generico	44	John Morrison
45	The Undertaker	45	John Morrison	45	Alex Shelley
46	Matt Sydal	46	Triple H	46	Kenta Kobashi
47	Matt Hardy	47	James Storm	47	Robert Roode
48	Johnny Nitro	48	Rob Van Dam	48	Rey Mysterio
49	Gregory Helms	49	Rey Mysterio	49	Martin Stone
50	Pac	50	Doug Williams	50	Claudio Castagnoli

	2009 (PS50)		2010 (PS50)		2011 (PS50)
1	Rey Mysterio	1	Kurt Angle	1	Hiroshi Tanahashi
2	KENTA	2	Davey Richards	2	Randy Orton
3	Hiroshi Tanahashi	3	Hiroshi Tanahashi	3	Davey Richards
4	Davey Richards	4	Prince Devitt	4	Prince Devitt
5	AJ Styles	5	Takashi Sugiura	5	Shingo Takagi
6	CM Punk	6	Shingo Takagi	6	Christian
7	Randy Orton	7	Go Shiozaki	7	Kurt Angle
8	Bryan Danielson	8	Naomichi Marafuji	8	CM Punk
9	Kurt Angle	9	Chris Sabin	9	Kota Ibushi
10	Jeff Hardy	10	Seth Rollins	10	Takashi Sugiura
11	Takashi Sugiura	11	Alex Shelley	11	KENTA
12	Kota Ibushi	12	Shinsuke Nakamura	12	Go Shiozaki
13	Katsuhiko Nakajima	13	Cima	13	Pac
14	Naruki Doi	14	Hirooki Goto	14	Akira Tozawa
15	Masato Yoshino	15	Rey Mysterio	15	Hirooki Goto
16	Triple H	16	BxB Hulk	16	Eddie Edwards
17	Hirooki Goto	17	AJ Styles	17	BxB Hulk
18	Chris Jericho	18	Kota Ibushi	18	Tetsuya Naito
19	Austin Aries	19	Randy Orton	19	AJ Styles
20	Christian	20	KENTA	20	Shinsuke Nakamura
21	Shingo Takagi	21	El Generico	21	Masaaki Mochizuki
22	BxB Hulk	22	Naruki Doi	22	Bobby Roode
23	Edge	23	Chris Jericho	23	Rey Mysterio
24	Go Shiozaki	24	Chris Hero	24	Kenny Omega
25	Shinsuke Nakamura	25	Pac	25	Sheamus
26	Desmond Wolfe	26	Daniel Bryan	26	Antonio Cesaro
27	Cima	27	Claudio Castagnoli	27	Cima
28	Yoshinobu Kanemaru	28	Daisuke Sekimoto	28	Katsuhiko Nakajima
29	Kaz Hayashi	29	Christian	29	Masato Yoshino
30	Masato Tanaka	30	Kevin Steen	30	Chris Hero
31	Dragon Kid	31	Kenny Omega	31	Dragon Kid
32	Eddie Edwards	32	Yamato	32	Jay Briscoe
33	Prince Devitt	33	Satoshi Kojima	33	Ricochet
34	Kotaru Suzuki	34	Robert Roode	34	Mark Briscoe
35	Chris Sabin	35	Togi Makabe	35	Kevin Steen
36	Yuji Nagata	36	Mark Briscoe	36	Yuji Nagata
37	Alex Shelley	37	Roderick Strong	37	James Storm
38	Shawn Michaels	38	James Storm	38	Dolph Ziggler
39	Jerry Lynn	39	Kaz Hayashi	39	Daniel Bryan
40	The Undertaker	40	Jay Briscoe	40	El Generico
41	Ted DiBiase Jr.	41	Sheamus	41	Alberto Del Rio
42	Tyler Black	42	The Miz	40	Ryusuke Taguchi
43	John Morrison	43	Eddie Edwards	43	Austin Aries
44	Pac	44	CM Punk	44	Jeff Jarrett
45	Samoa Joe	45	Jeremy Buck	45	Kofi Kingston
46	Nick Jackson	46	Shawn Michaels	46	Bully Ray
47	Tyson Kidd	47	Edge	47	Christopher Daniels
48	Matt Jackson	48	Max Buck	48	The Miz
49	The Miz	49	Jeff Hardy	49	John Morrison
50	Kofi Kingston	50	Jack Swagger	50	Kenny King

2012 (PS50)		2013 (PS50)		2020 (ITR50)	
1	Hiroshi Tanahashi	1	Kazuchika Okada	1	Drew McIntyre
2	Austin Aries	2	Hiroshi Tanahashi	2	Bayley
3	CM Punk	3	Daniel Bryan	3	Cody Rhodes
4	Kazuchika Okada	4	Shinsuke Nakamura	4	Chris Jericho
5	Prince Devitt	5	Tomohiro Ishii	5	Randy Orton
6	Daniel Bryan	6	Randy Orton	6	Kota Ibushi
7	Cima	7	CM Punk	7	Jon Moxley
8	Tetsuya Naito	8	Prince Devitt	8	Hangman Page
9	Kevin Owens	9	Katsuyori Shibata	9	Sasha Banks
10	AJ Styles	10	Kota Ibushi	10	Will Ospreay
11	Shingo Takagi	11	Austin Aries	11	Shingo Takagi
12	Low Ki	12	Shingo Takagi	12	Roman Reigns
13	Akira Tozawa	13	Hirooki Goto	13	Kenny Omega
14	Kurt Angle	14	Bully Ray	14	Minoru Suzuki
15	Davey Richards	15	Ricochet	15	Kazuchika Okada
16	Christopher Daniels	16	Kurt Angle	16	The Young Bucks
17	Shinsuke Nakamura	17	Akira Tozawa	17	Io Shirai
18	Jun Akiyama	18	Masato Yoshino	18	Asuka
19	Bobby Roode	19	Cima	19	Adam Cole
20	Hirooki Goto	20	Seth Rollins	20	MJF
21	El Generico	21	Minoru Suzuki	21	Tomohiro Ishii
22	Dolph Ziggler	22	Tetsuya Naito	22	Orange Cassidy
23	Sheamus	23	Naruki Doi	23	AJ Styles
24	Adrian Neville	24	Bobby Roode	24	Rhea Ripley
25	Kenny Omega	25	Matt Jackson	25	Tetsuya Naito
26	Yamato	26	Nick Jackson	26	Darby Allin
27	Randy Orton	27	Kevin Steen	27	Jey Uso
28	Samoa Joe	28	Dean Ambrose	28	Hiroshi Tanahashi
29	Ryusuke Taguchi	29	Masato Tanaka	29	Sammy Guevara
30	Kota Ibushi	30	Antonio Cesaro	30	FTR
31	Suwama	31	AJ Styles	31	Johnny Gargano
32	Jeff Hardy	32	Roman Reigns	32	Finn Balor
33	Naomichi Marafuji	33	Yuji Nagata	33	Mayu Iwatani
34	Karl Anderson	34	BxB Hulk	34	Hiromu Takahashi
35	Masaaki Mochizuki	35	KENTA	35	Jungle Boy
36	Ricochet	36	Karl Anderson	36	Walter
37	Alberto Del Rio	37	Dolph Ziggler	37	Daniel Bryan
38	Kazarian	38	Jeff Hardy	38	Candice LeRae
39	Michael Elgin	39	Alberto Del Rio	39	Riddle
40	Matt Jackson	40	Michael Elgin	40	The Fiend
41	Eddie Edwards	41	Brock Lesnar	41	Ilja Dragunov
42	KENTA	42	Adam Cole	42	Seth Rollins
43	Nick Jackson	43	Davey Richards	43	Dr. Britt Baker D.M.D.
44	Minoru Suzuki	44	Kenny Omega	44	Hikaru Shida
45	James Storm	45	Kris Travis	45	Rey Mysterio
46	Rockstar Spud	46	Jay Briscoe	46	Deonna Purrazzo
47	Noam Dar	47	El Ligero	47	Zack Sabre Jr.
48	Bully Ray	48	Christopher Daniels	48	Sanada
49	El Ligero	49	Sami Zayn	49	Keith Lee
50	Kofi Kingston	50	Cody Rhodes	50	Pac

#	2021 (ITR100)	#	2022 (ITR50)	#	2022 (ITR WOMEN'S 50)
1	Roman Reigns	1	Roman Reigns	1	Bianca Belair
2	Kenny Omega	2	Jon Moxley	2	Syuri
3	Bryan Danielson	3	Will Ospreay	3	Giulia
4	Shingo Takagi	4	CM Punk	4	Becky Lynch
5	Dr. Britt Baker D.M.D.	5	MJF	5	Jamie Hayter
6	Bianca Belair	6	Seth Rollins	6	Mandy Rose
7	Darby Allin	7	Bryan Danielson	7	Yuka Sakazaki
8	Hangman Page	8	Dax Harwood	8	Rhea Ripley
9	Edge	9	Cody Rhodes	9	Mayu Iwatani
10	The Young Bucks	10	Brock Lesnar	10	Jordynne Grace
11	Jon Moxley	11	Kazuchika Okada	11	Tam Nakano
12	Will Ospreay	12	Gunther	12	Miyu Yamashita
13	Utami Hayashishita	13	Cash Wheeler	13	Taya Valkyrie
14	Bobby Lashley	14	Chris Jericho	14	Saya Kamitani
15	Kazuchika Okada	15	Sami Zayn	15	Dr. Britt Baker D.M.D.
16	MJF	16	Sheamus	16	Asuka
17	Kota Ibushi	17	Adam Page	17	Shoko Nakajima
18	Drew McIntyre	18	Matt Riddle	18	Iyo Sky
19	Big E	19	The Usos	19	Dakota Kai
20	Sasha Banks	20	Shingo Takagi	20	Starlight Kid
21	Seth Rollins	21	Bobby Lashley	21	Thunder Rosa
22	Chris Jericho	22	Rey Fenix	22	Toni Storm
23	Adam Cole	23	The Young Bucks	23	Serena Deeb
24	The Lucha Brothers	24	Eddie Kingston	24	Roxanne Perez
25	Zack Sabre Jr.	25	Tomohiro Ishii	25	Masha Slamovich
26	CM Punk	26	Logan Paul	26	Mickie James
27	Minoru Suzuki	27	The Acclaimed	27	Hikaru Shida
28	Eddie Kingston	28	Zack Sabre Jr.	28	Maki Itoh
29	Sting	29	Daniel Garcia	29	Cora Jade
30	Raquel Gonzalez	30	Drew McIntyre	30	Mei Sugura
31	Riddle	31	Pac	31	Suzu Suzuki
32	Christian Cage	32	Penta El Zero Miedo	32	Tasha Steelz
33	Randy Orton	33	Hiroshi Tanahashi	33	Kairi
34	Sammu Guevara	34	Bron Breakker	34	Liv Morgan
35	Hiroshi Tanahashi	35	El Hijo Del Vikingo	35	Willow Nightingale
36	Syuri	36	Kevin Owens	36	Rina Yamashita
37	Charlotte Flair	37	Austin Theory	37	Bayley
38	Walter	38	Wheeler Yuta	38	Alex Windsor
39	Jungle Boy	39	Josh Alexander	39	Allie Katch
40	Thunder Rosa	40	El Desperado	40	Miu Watanabe
41	Io Shirai	41	Randy Orton	41	Ronda Rousey
42	The Usos	42	Konosuke Takeshita	42	KiLynn King
43	Tomohiro Ishii	43	Kenny Omega	43	Billie Starkz
44	Finn Balor	44	Warlow	44	Tay Melo
45	Cesaro	45	Adam Cole	45	Kamille
46	Malakai Black	46	Sammy Guevara	46	Deonna Purrazzo
47	Rhea Ripley	47	Hiromu Takahashi	47	Charlotte Flair
48	Giulia	48	Darby Allin	48	Raquel Rodriguez
49	Jeff Cobb	49	Claudio Castagnoli	49	Alba Fyre
50	Cody Rhodes	50	Nick Wayne	50	Jade Cargill

END OF YEAR AWARDS

In this section you will find a list of the the winners of year end awards from a number of respected publications, both historic and current. Some of these are awarded by the staff at the publications in question, others are voted on by the readers. The publications included are: Inside The Ropes Magazine, Power Slam Magazine, Pro Wrestling Illustrated, and The Wrestling Observer Newsletter.

INSIDE THE ROPES MAGAZINE EDITORIAL AWARDS

MALE WRESTLER OF THE YEAR
2020 Drew McIntyre
2021 Roman Reigns
2022 Roman Reigns[2]

FEMALE WRESTLER OF THE YEAR
2020 Bayley
2021 Dr. Britt Baker D.M.D.
2022 Bianca Belair

TAG TEAM OF THE YEAR
2020 The Young Bucks
2021 The Young Bucks[2]
2022 FTR

COMMENTATOR OF THE YEAR
2020 Tony Schiavone
2021 Pat McAfee
2022 Taz

MANAGER OF THE YEAR
2020 Paul Heyman
2021 Paul Heyman[2]
2022 Paul Heyman[3]

PROMOTION OF THE YEAR
2020 All Elite Wrestling
2021 All Elite Wrestling[2]
2022 World Wrestling Entertainment

BABYFACE OF THE YEAR
2020 Drew McIntyre
2021 Hangman Page
2022 Sami Zayn

HEEL OF THE YEAR
2020 MJF
2021 Roman Reigns
2022 MJF[2]

RIVALRY OF THE YEAR
2020 Roman Reigns vs. Jey Uso
2021 Hangman Page vs. The Elite
2022 CM Punk vs. MJF

MATCH OF THE YEAR
2020 Stadium Stampede
(AEW Double Or Nothing)
2021 Bryan Danielson vs. Kenny Omega[2]
(AEW Dynamite)
2022 Cody Rhodes vs. Seth Rollins
(WWE Hell In A Cell)

CHARACTER OF THE YEAR
2020 The Fiend
2021 Roman Reigns
2022 Sami Zayn

BEST INTERVIEWS OF THE YEAR
2020 Cody Rhodes
2021 Eddie Kingston
2022 MJF

MOST IMPROVED WRESTLER
2020 Jey Uso
2021 Tay Conti
2022 Logan Paul

BILL APTER ACTIVE LEGEND
2020 Dustin Rhodes
2021 Sting
2022 Billy Gunn

TELEVISION SHOW OF THE YEAR
2020 AEW Dynamite
2021 AEW Dynamite[2]
2022 WWE SmackDown

SUPERCARD OF THE YEAR
2020 AEW Revolution '20
2021 AEW All Out '21
2022 WWE WrestleMania XXXVIII

INSIDE THE ROPES MAGAZINE READER AWARDS

MALE WRESTLER OF THE YEAR
2020 Drew McIntyre
2021 Roman Reigns
2022 Roman Reigns[2]

FEMALE WRESTLER OF THE YEAR
2020 Bayley
2021 Dr. Britt Baker D.M.D.
2022 Bianca Belair

TAG TEAM OF THE YEAR
2020 The Young Bucks
2021 The Young Bucks[2]
2022 FTR

MATCH OF THE YEAR
2020 Stadium Stampede
(AEW Double Or Nothing)
2021 Bryan Danielson vs. Kenny Omega[2]
(AEW Dynamite)
2022 Gunther vs. Sheamus
(WWE Clash At The Castle)

MANAGER OF THE YEAR
2020 Paul Heyman
2021 Paul Heyman[2]
2022 Paul Heyman[3]

RIVALRY OF THE YEAR
2020 Roman Reigns vs. Jey Usp
2021 Hangman Page vs. Kenny Omega
2022 CM Punk vs. MJF

BABYFACE OF THE YEAR
2020 Drew McIntyre
2021 Hangman Page
2022 Cody Rhodes

HEEL OF THE YEAR
2020 MJF
2021 Roman Reigns
2022 MJF[2]

COMMENTATOR OF THE YEAR

2020	Tony Schiavone
2021	Pat McAfee
2022	Pat McAfee[2]

CHARACTER OF THE YEAR

2020	The Fiend
2021	Roman Reigns
2022	Sami Zayn

BEST INTERVIEWS OF THE YEAR

2020	Cody Rhodes
2021	MJF
2022	MJF[2]

MOST UNDERRATED

2020	Bianca Belair
2021	Cesaro
2022	Ricky Starks

MOST IMPROVED

2020	Jey Uso
2021	Jungle Boy
2022	The Acclaimed

BEST TELEVISION SHOW OF THE YEAR

2020	AEW Dynamite
2021	AEW Dynamite[2]
2022	WWE SmackDown

SUPERCARD OF THE YEAR

2020	AEW Revolution
2021	AEW All Out
2022	WWE WrestleMania XXXVIII

PROMOTION OF THE YEAR

2020	AEW
2021	AEW[2]
2022	WWE

POWER SLAM MAGAZINE READER AWARDS

WRESTLER OF THE YEAR

1993	Vader
1994	Diesel
1995	Shawn Michaels
1996	Shawn Michaels[2]
1997	Steve Austin
1998	Steve Austin[2]
1999	The Rock
2000	Triple H
2001	Kurt Angle
2002	Kurt Angle[2]
2003	Kurt Angle[3]
2004	Chris Benoit
2005	Shawn Michaels[3]
2006	Edge
2007	Bryan Danielson
2008	Edge[2]
2009	CM Punk
2010	Kurt Angle[4]
2011	Randy Orton
2012	CM Punk[2]
2013	Daniel Bryan[2]

TAG TEAM OF THE YEAR

1995	The Public Enemy
1996	Owen Hart & The British Bulldog
1997	Owen Hart[2] & The British Bulldog[2]
1998	The New Age Outlaws
1999	The Hardy Boyz
2000	Edge & Christian
2001	The Dudley Boyz
2002	Los Guerreros
2003	Shelton Benjamin & Charlie Haas
2004	Rob Van Dam & Rey Mysterio
2005	MNM
2006	Latin American Xchange
2007	The Briscoe Brothers
2008	The Miz & John Morrison
2009	Chris Jericho & The Big Show
2010	The Motor City Machine Guns
2011	Air Boom
2012	Bad Influence
2013	Seth Rollins & Roman Reigns

COMMENTATOR OF THE YEAR

1995	Joey Styles
1996	Jim Ross
1997	Jim Ross[2]
1998	Jim Ross[3]
1999	Jim Ross[4]
2000	Jerry Lawler
2001	Paul Heyman
2002	Jim Ross[5]
2003	Tazz
2004	Tazz[2]
2005	Joey Styles[2]
2006	John Bradshaw Layfield
2007	John Bradshaw Layfield[2]
2008	Matt Striker
2009	Matt Striker[2]
2010	Michael Cole
2011	Michael Cole[2]
2012	John Bradshaw Layfield[3]
2013	John Bradshaw Layfield[4]

PROMOTION OF THE YEAR

1995	WWF
1996	WWF[2]
1997	WWF[3]
1998	WWF[4]
1999	WWF[5]
2000	WWF[6]
2001	WWF[7]
2002	WWE[8]
2003	WWE[9]
2004	WWE[10]
2005	TNA
2006	TNA[2]
2007	WWE[11]
2008	WWE[12]
2009	WWE[13]
2010	WWE[14]
2011	WWE[15]
2012	WWE[16]
2013	WWE[17]

BABYFACE OF THE YEAR

1993	Bret Hart
1994	Bret Hart[2]
1995	Shawn Michaels
1996	Shawn Michaels[2]
1997	Steve Austin
1998	Steve Austin[2]
1999	The Rock

2000	The Rock[2]
2001	The Rock[3]
2002	Rob Van Dam
2003	Eddie Guerrero
2004	Eddie Guerrero[2]
2005	Shawn Michaels[3]
2006	Shawn Michaels[4]
2007	Jeff Hardy
2008	Jeff Hardy[2]
2009	Jeff Hardy[3]
2010	Daniel Bryan
2011	CM Punk
2012	Jeff Hardy[4]

HEEL OF THE YEAR

1993	Vader
1994	Owen Hart
1995	The British Bulldog
1996	Steve Austin
1997	Bret Hart
1998	Vince McMahon
1999	Triple H
2000	Triple H[2]
2001	Steve Austin[2]
2002	Kurt Angle
2003	Brock Lesnar
2004	Triple H[3]
2005	Kurt Angle[2]
2006	Edge
2007	Randy Orton
2008	Edge[2]
2009	CM Punk
2010	The Miz
2011	Christian
2012	CM Punk[2]

RIVALRY OF THE YEAR

1993	Bret Hart vs. Jerry Lawler
1994	Bret Hart[2] vs. Owen Hart
1995	Razor Ramon vs. Jeff Jarrett
1996	The Undertaker vs. Mankind
1997	Bret Hart[3] vs. Shawn Michaels
1998	Steve Austin vs. Vince McMahon
1999	Triple H vs. Vince McMahon[2]
2000	Triple H[2] vs. The Rock
2001	Steve Austin[2] vs. Kurt Angle
2002	Kurt Angle[2] vs. Edge
2003	Kurt Angle[3] vs. Brock Lesnar
2004	Mick Foley[2] vs. Randy Orton
2005	Rey Mysterio vs.Eddie Guerrero
2006	Edge[2] vs. John Cena
2007	The Undertaker[2] vs. Batista
2008	Chris Jericho vs. Shawn Michaels[2]
2009	CM Punk vs. Jeff Hardy
2010	CM Punk[2] vs. Rey Mysterio[2]
2011	Randy Orton[2] vs. Christian
2012	CM Punk[3] vs. Daniel Bryan
2013	CM Punk[4] vs. Paul Heyman

MATCH OF THE YEAR

1993	Shawn Michaels vs. Marty Jannetty (Monday Night RAW)
1994	Shawn Michaels[2] vs. Razor Ramon (WrestleMania X)
1995	Shawn Michaels[3] vs. Razor Ramon[2] (SummerSlam '95)
1996	Shawn Michaels[4] vs. Mankind (IYH10 Mind Games)
1997	Shawn Michaels[5] vs. The Undertaker (IYH18 Bad Blood)
1998	The Undertaker[2] vs. Mankind[2] (King Of The Ring '98)

1999	The Hardy Boyz vs. Edge & Christian (No Mercy '99)
2000	The Hardy Boyz[2] vs. Edge & Christian[2] vs. The Dudley Boyz (SummerSlam '00)
2001	Steve Austin vs. The Rock (WrestleMania XVII)
2002	Shawn Michaels[6] vs. Triple H (SummerSlam '02)
2003	Kurt Angle vs. Chris Benoit (Royal Rumble '03)
2004	Shawn Michaels[7] vs. Triple H[2] vs. Chris Benoit[2] (WrestleMania XX)
2005	Shawn Michaels[8] vs. Kurt Angle[2] (WrestleMania XXI)
2006	The Undertaker[2] vs. Kurt Angle[3] (No Way Out '06)
2007	The Undertaker[3] vs. Batista (WrestleMania XXIII)
2008	The Undertaker[4] vs. Edge[3] (WrestleMania XXIV)
2009	The Undertaker[5] vs. Shawn Michaels[9] (WrestleMania XXV)
2010	The Undertaker[6] vs. Shawn Michaels[10] (WrestleMania XXVI)
2011	CM Punk vs. John Cena (Money In The Bank '11)
2012	The Undertaker[7] vs. Triple H[3] (WrestleMania XXVIII)
2013	The Undertaker[8] vs. CM Punk[2] (WrestleMania XXIX)

CHARACTER OF THE YEAR

1995	The Undertaker
1996	Goldust
1997	Steve Austin
1998	Chris Jericho
1999	The Rock
2000	Kurt Angle
2001	Steve Austin[2]
2002	Kurt Angle[2]
2003	John Cena
2004	John Bradshaw Layfield
2005	Mr. Kennedy
2006	Mr. Kennedy[2]
2007	Santino Marella
2008	Santino Marella[2]
2009	CM Punk
2010	The Miz
2011	CM Punk[2]
2012	Daniel Bryan
2013	Daniel Bryan[2]

BEST INTERVIEWS OF THE YEAR

2013	Paul Heyman

TELEVISION SHOW OF THE YEAR

2013	WWE Monday Night RAW

SUPERCARD OF THE YEAR

1994	ECW The Night The Line Was Crossed
1995	WWF SummerSlam
1996	WWF King Of The Ring
1997	WWF In Your House 16
1998	WWF SummerSlam
1999	WWF No Mercy
2000	WWF Backlash
2001	WWF WrestleMania XVII
2002	WWE SummerSlam
2003	WWE WrestleMania XIX
2004	WWE WrestleMania XX

2005	ECW One Night Stand
2006	WWE WrestleMania XXII
2007	WWE WrestleMania XXIII
2008	WWE WrestleMania XXIV
2009	TNA Turning Point
2010	WWE WrestleMania XXVI
2011	WWE Money In The Bank
2012	WWE Extreme Rules
2013	WWE SummerSlam

PRO WRESTLING ILLUSTRATED READER AWARDS

WRESTLER OF THE YEAR

1972	Pedro Morales
1973	Jack Brisco
1974	Bruno Sammartino
1975	Mr. Wrestling II
1976	Terry Funk
1977	Dusty Rhodes
1978	Dusty Rhodes^2
1979	Harley Race
1980	Bob Backlund
1981	Ric Flair
1982	Bob Backlund^2
1983	Harley Race^2
1984	Ric Flair^2
1985	Ric Flair^3
1986	Ric Flair^4
1987	Hulk Hogan
1988	Randy Savage
1989	Ric Flair^5
1990	Sting
1991	Hulk Hogan^2
1992	Ric Flair^6
1993	Big Van Vader
1994	Hulk Hogan^3
1995	Diesel
1996	The Giant
1997	Lex Luger
1998	Steve Austin
1999	Steve Austin^2
2000	The Rock
2001	Steve Austin^3
2002	Brock Lesnar
2003	Kurt Angle
2004	Chris Benoit
2005	Batista
2006	John Cena
2007	John Cena^2
2008	Triple H
2009	Randy Orton
2010	Randy Orton^2
2011	CM Punk
2012	CM Punk^2
2013	Daniel Bryan
2014	Brock Lesnar^2
2015	Seth Rollins
2016	AJ Styles
2017	AJ Styles^2
2018	AJ Styles^3
2019	Adam Cole
2020	Jon Moxley
2021	Kenny Omega

WOMAN OF THE YEAR

1972	Marie LaVerne
1973	Nick Bockwinkel & Ray Stevens
1974	Rachel Dubois
1975	Ann Casey
1976	Sue Green
2000	Stephanie McMahon
2001	Lita
2002	Trish Stratus
2003	Trish Stratus^2
2004	Victoria
2005	Trish Stratus^3
2006	Trish Stratus^4
2007	Candice Michelle
2008	Awesome Kong
2009	Mickie James
2010	Michelle McCool
2011	Mickie James^2
2012	AJ Lee
2013	AJ Lee^2
2014	AJ Lee^3
2015	Sasha Banks
2016	Charlotte Flair
2017	Asuka
2018	Becky Lynch
2019	Becky Lynch^2
2021	Dr. Britt Baker D.M.D.

TAG TEAM OF THE YEAR

1972	Dick The Bruiser & The Crusher
1973	Nick Bockwinkel & Ray Stevens
1974	Jimmy & Johnny Valiant
1975	Gene & Ole Anderson
1976	The Executioners
1977	Gene & Ole Anderson (2)
1978	Ricky Steamboat & Paul Jones
1979	Ivan Putski & Tito Santana
1980	Jimmy Snuka & Ray Stevens^2
1981	The Fabulous Freebirds
1982	The High Flyers
1983	The Road Warriors
1984	The Road Warriors^2
1985	The Road Warriors^3
1986	The Rock 'n' Roll Express
1987	The Midnight Express
1988	The Road Warriors^4
1989	The Brain Busters
1990	The Steiner Brothers
1991	The Enforcers
1992	The Miracle Violence Connection
1993	The Steiner Brothers^2
1994	The Nasty Boys
1995	Harlem Heat
1996	Harlem Heat^2
1997	The Outsiders
1998	The New Age Outlaws
1999	Kane and X-Pac
2000	The Hardy Boyz
2001	The Dudley Boyz
2002	Billy & Chuck
2003	The World's Greatest Tag Team
2004	America's Most Wanted
2005	MNM
2006	AJ Styles & Christopher Daniels
2007	Paul London & Brian Kendrick
2008	Beer Money Inc.
2009	Team 3D^2
2010	Motor City Machine Guns
2011	Beer Money Inc.^{2}
2012	Kofi Kingston and R-Truth
2013	The Shield

2014	The Usos
2015	The New Day
2016	The New Day[2]
2017	The Young Bucks
2018	The Young Bucks[2]
2019	The Undisputed Era
2020	Golden Role Models
2021	The Young Bucks[3]

FACTION OF THE YEAR

| 2021 | The Innter Circle |

MATCH OF THE YEAR

1972	Battle Royal
	(Battle Royal In Los Angeles)
1973	Dory Funk Jr. vs. Harley Race
	(24-05-73)
1974	Jack Brisco vs. Dory Funk Jr.[2]
	(19-04-74)
1975	Bruno Sammartino vs. Spiros Arion
	(17-03-75)
1976	Bruno Sammartino[2] vs. Stan Hansen
	(26-04-76)
1977	Bruno Sammartino[3] vs.
	Superstar Billy Graham
	(30-04-77)
1978	Superstar Billy Graham[2] vs. Bob Backlund
	(20-02-78)
1979	Harley Race[2] vs. Dusty Rhodes
	(21-08-79)
1980	Bruno Sammartino[4] vs. Larry Zbyszko
	(Showdown at Shea '80)
1981	Andre the Giant vs. Killer Khan
	(24-08-81)
1982	Bob Backlund[2] vs. Jimmy Snuka
	(28-06-82)
1983	Ric Flair vs. Harley Race[3]
	(10-06-83)
1984	Ric Flair[2] vs.Kerry Von Erich
	(Parade of Champions)
1985	Hulk Hogan & Mr. T vs. Roddy Piper &
	Paul Orndorff
	(WrestleMania)
1986	Ric Flair[3] vs. Dusty Rhodes[2]
	(The Great American Bash '86)
1987	Randy Savage vs. Ricky Steamboat
	(WrestleMania III)
1988	Hulk Hogan[2] vs. Andre the Giant[2]
	(The Main Event I)
1989	Ricky Steamboat[2] vs. Ric Flair[4]
	(WrestleWar '89)
1990	Hulk Hogan[3] vs. The Ultimate Warrior
	(WrestleMania VI)
1991	The Steiner Brothers vs. Sting & Lex Luger
	(SuperBrawl I)
1992	Bret Hart vs. The British Bulldog
	(SummerSlam '92)
1993	Shawn Michaels vs. Marty Jannetty
	(Monday Night RAW)
1994	Razor Ramon vs. Shawn Michaels[2]
	(WrestleMania X)
1995	Diesel vs. Shawn Michaels[3]
	(WrestleMania XI)
1996	Bret Hart[2] vs. Shawn Michaels[4]
	(WrestleMania XII)
1997	Bret Hart[3] vs. Steve Austin
	(WrestleMania XIII)
1998	The Undertaker vs. Mankind
	(King of the Ring '98)
1999	The Rock vs. Mankind[2]
	(Royal Rumble '99)

2000	The Dudley Boyz vs. The Hardy Boyz
	vs. Edge & Christian
	(WrestleMania XVI)
2001	The Dudley Boyz[2] vs. The Hardy Boyz[2] vs.
	Edge & Christian[2]
	(WrestleMania XVII)
2002	The Rock[2] vs. Hollywood Hogan[4]
	(WrestleMania XVIII)
2003	Kurt Angle vs. Brock Lesnar
	(SmackDown)
2004	Triple H vs. Chris Benoit vs. Shawn Michaels[5]
	(WrestleMania XX)
2005	Shawn Michaels[6] vs. Kurt Angle[2]
	(WrestleMania XXI)
2006	Shawn Michaels[7] vs. Vince McMahon
	(WrestleMania XXII)
2007	John Cena vs. Shawn Michaels[8]
	(Monday Night RAW)
2008	Shawn Michaels[9] vs. Ric Flair[5]
	(WrestleMania XXIV)
2009	The Undertaker[2] vs. Shawn Michaels[10]
	(WrestleMania XXV)
2010	The Undertaker[3] vs. Shawn Michaels[11]
	(WrestleMania XXVI)
2011	John Cena[2] vs. CM Punk
	(Money In The Bank '11)
2012	The Undertaker[4] vs. Triple H[2]
	(WrestleMania XXVIII)
2013	John Cena[3] vs. Daniel Bryan
	(SummerSlam '13)
2014	John Cena[4] vs. Bray Wyatt
	(Payback '14)
2015	Bayley vs. Sasha Banks
	(TakeOver: Respect)
2016	AJ Styles vs. John Cena[5]
	(SummerSlam '16)
2017	Kazuchika Okada vs. Kenny Omega
	(Wrestle Kingdom 11)
2018	Kazuchika Okada[2] vs. Kenny Omega[2]
	(Dominion '18)
2019	Cody Rhodes vs. Dustin Rhodes
	(Double Or Nothing '19)
2020	Adam Page & Kenny Omega[3]
	vs. Young Bucks
	(Revolution '20)
2021	Dr. Britt Baker D.M.D. vs. Thunder Rosa
	(Dynamite: St. Patrick's Day Slam)

FEUD OF THE YEAR

1986	Hulk Hogan vs. Paul Orndorff
1987	The Four Horsemen vs.
	The Super Powers & The Road Warriors
1988	Ric Flair[2] vs. Lex Luger
1989	Ric Flair[3] vs. Terry Funk
1990	Ric Flair[4] vs. Lex Luger[2]
1991	The Ultimate Warrior vs. The Undertaker
1992	The Moondogs vs. Jerry Lawler & Jeff Jarrett
1993	Bret Hart vs. Jerry Lawler[2]
1994	Bret Hart[2] vs. Owen Hart
1995	Axl Rotten vs. Ian Rotten
1996	Eric Bischoff vs. Vince McMahon
1997	Diamond Dallas Page vs. Randy Savage
1998	Vince McMahon[2] vs. Steve Austin
1999	Vince McMahon[3] vs. Steve Austin[2]
2000	Triple H vs. Kurt Angle
2001	Shane McMahon vs. Vince McMahon[4]
2002	Eric Bischoff[2] vs. Stephanie McMahon
2003	Brock Lesnar vs. Kurt Angle
2004	Triple H[2] vs. Chris Benoit
2005	Matt Hardy vs. Edge & Lita
2006	John Cena vs. Edge[2]

2007	Kurt Angle vs. Samoa Joe
2008	Chris Jericho vs. Shawn Michaels
2009	Randy Orton vs. Triple H[3]
2010	The Nexus vs. WWE
2011	CM Punk vs. John Cena[2]
2012	Aces & Eights vs. TNA
2013	Daniel Bryan vs. Triple H[4] & Stephanie[2]
2014	Seth Rollins vs. Dean Ambrose
2015	Brock Lesnar[2] vs. The Undertaker
2016	Sasha Banks vs. Charlotte Flair
2017	Kazuchika Okada vs. Kenny Omega
2018	Johnny Gargano vs. Tommaso Ciampa
2019	Johnny Gargano[2] vs. Adam Cole
2020	Bayley vs. Sasha Banks[2]
2021	Chris Jericho[2] vs. MJF

MOST POPULAR WRESTLER

1972	Jack Brisco
	Fred Curry
1973	Chief Jay Strongbow
1974	Billy Robinson
1975	Mil Mascaras
1976	Wahoo McDaniel
1977	Andre the Giant
1978	Dusty Rhodes
1979	Dusty Rhodes[2]
1980	Mr. Wrestling II
1981	Tommy Rich
1982	Andre the Giant[2]
1983	Jimmy Snuka
1984	Kerry Von Erich
1985	Hulk Hogan
1986	Roddy Piper
1987	Dusty Rhodes[3]
1988	Randy Savage
1989	Hulk Hogan[2]
1990	Hulk Hogan[3]
1991	Sting
1992	Sting[2]
1993	Lex Luger
1994	Sting[3]
1995	Shawn Michaels
1996	Shawn Michaels[2]
1997	Sting[4]
1998	Steve Austin
1999	The Rock
2000	The Rock[2]
2001	Rob Van Dam
2002	Rob Van Dam[2]
2003	Kurt Angle
2004	John Cena
2005	John Cena[2]
2006	Samoa Joe
2007	John Cena[3]
2008	Jeff Hardy
2009	Jeff Hardy[2]
2010	Randy Orton
2011	CM Punk
2012	John Cena[4]
2013	Daniel Bryan
2014	Dean Ambrose
2015	Dean Ambrose[2]
2016	Shinsuke Nakamura
2017	AJ Styles
2018	AJ Styles[2]
2019	Becky Lynch
2020	Orange Cassidy
2021	CM Punk[2]

MOST HATED WRESTLER

1972	The Sheik

1973	Superstar Billy Graham
1974	The Great Mephisto
1975	Greg Valentine
1976	Stan Hansen
1977	Ken Patera
1978	Ric Flair
1979	Greg Valentine[2]
1980	Larry Zbyszko
1981	Ken Patera[2]
1982	Ted DiBiase
1983	Greg Valentine[3]
1984	Roddy Piper
1985	Roddy Piper[2]
1986	Paul Orndorff
1987	Ric Flair[2]
1988	Andre the Giant
1989	Randy Savage
1990	Earthquake
1991	Sgt. Slaughter
1992	Rick Rude
1993	Jerry Lawler
1994	Bob Backlund
1995	Jerry Lawler[2]
1996	Hollywood Hogan
1997	Bret Hart
1998	Hollywood Hogan[2]
1999	Diamond Dallas Page
2000	Kurt Angle
2001	Steve Austin
2002	Chris Jericho
2003	Triple H
2004	Triple H[2]
2005	Triple H[3]
2006	Edge
2007	Randy Orton
2008	Chris Jericho[2]
2009	Randy Orton[2]
2010	The Nexus
2011	The Miz
2012	CM Punk
2013	Triple H[4] & Stephanie
2014	Triple H[5] & Stephanie[2]
2015	Seth Rollins
2016	Roman Reigns
2017	Jinder Mahal
2018	Brock Lesnar
2019	Baron Corbin
2020	Seth Rollins[2]
2021	MJF

COMEBACK OF THE YEAR

1992	The Ultimate Warrior
1993	Lex Luger
1994	Hulk Hogan
1995	Randy Savage
1996	Sycho Sid
1997	Bret Hart
1998	X-Pac
1999	Eddie Guerrero
2000	Rikishi
2001	Rob Van Dam
2002	Hollywood Hogan[2]
2003	Kurt Angle
2004	Edge
2005	Road Warrior Animal
2006	Sting
2007	Jeff Hardy
2008	Chris Jericho
2009	Jerry Lynn
2010	Rob Van Dam[2]
2011	Sting[2]

2012	Jeff Hardy[2]
2013	Goldust
2014	Sting[3]
2015	The Undertaker
2016	Goldberg
2017	The Hardy Boyz
2018	Daniel Bryan
2019	Roman Reigns
2020	MVP
2021	CM Punk

MOST IMPROVED WRESTLER

1978	Dino Bravo
1979	Tommy Rich
1980	Tony Atlas
1981	Kevin Sullivan
1982	Barry Windham
1983	Brett Wayne Sawyer
1984	Billy Jack Haynes
1985	Steve Williams
1986	Terry Gordy
1987	Curt Hennig
1988	Sting
1989	Scott Steiner
1990	Paul Roma
1991	Dustin Rhodes
1992	Razor Ramon
1993	Yokozuna
1994	Diesel
1995	Diamond Dallas Page
1996	Ahmed Johnson
1997	Ken Shamrock
1998	Booker T
1999	Jerry Lynn
2000	Steve Corino
2001	Edge
2002	Brock Lesnar
2003	John Cena
2004	Randy Orton
2005	Batista
2006	Bobby Lashley
2007	Candice Michelle
2008	Cody Rhodes
2009	John Morrison
2010	D'Angelo Dinero
2011	Mark Henry
2012	Ryback
2013	Magnus
2014	Rusev
2015	Roman Reigns
2016	The Miz
2017	Jinder Mahal
2018	Velveteen Dream
2019	Brian Cage
2020	Drew McIntyre
2021	Dr. Britt Baker D.M.D.

INDIE WRESTLER OF THE YEAR

2020	Warhorse
2021	Nick Gage

MOST INSPIRATIONAL WRESTLER

1972	Lord Alfred Hayes
1973	Johnny Valentine
1974	Dick Murdoch
1975	Mike McCord
1976	Bruno Sammartino
1977	Bob Backlund
1978	Blackjack Mulligan
1979	Chief Jay Strongbow
1980	Junkyard Dog

1981	Bob Backlund[2]
1982	Roddy Piper
1983	Hulk Hogan
1984	Sgt. Slaughter
1985	Mike Von Erich
1986	Chris Adams
1987	Nikita Koloff
1988	Jerry Lawler
1989	Eric Embry
1990	Sting
1991	The Patriot
1992	Ron Simmons
1993	Cactus Jack
1994	Bret Hart
1995	Barry Horowitz
1996	Jake Roberts
1997	Terry Funk
1998	Goldberg
1999	Hulk Hogan[2]
2000	Booker T
2001	Kurt Angle
2002	Eddie Guerrero
2003	Zach Gowen
2004	Eddie Guerrero[2]
2005	Chris Candido
2006	Matt Cappotelli
2007	Jeff Jarrett
2008	Ric Flair
2009	Ricky Steamboat
2010	Shawn Michaels
2011	Rosita
2012	Jerry Lawler[2]
2013	Darren Young
2014	Daniel Bryan
2015	Bayley
2016	Bayley[2]
2017	Christopher Daniels
2018	Roman Reigns
2019	Roman Reigns[2]
2020	Shad Gaspard
2021	Edge

ROOKIE OF THE YEAR

1972	Mike Graham
1973	Bob Orton Jr.
	Tony Garea
1974	Larry Zbyszko
1975	Ric Flair
1976	Bob Backlund
1977	Ricky Steamboat
1978	Tommy Rich
1979	Sweet Brown Sugar
1980	Terry Taylor
1981	David Sammartino
1982	Brad Armstrong
1983	Angelo Mosca, Jr.
1984	Mike Von Erich
1985	Nord the Barbarian
1986	Lex Luger
1987	Owen Hart
1988	Madusa Miceli
1989	The Destruction Crew
1990	Steve Austin
1991	Johnny B. Badd
1992	Erik Watts
1993	Vampire Warrior
1994	Bob Holly
1995	Alex Wright
1996	The Giant
1997	Prince Iaukea
1998	Bill Goldberg

1999	Shane McMahon
2000	Kurt Angle
2001	Randy Orton
2002	Maven
2003	Zach Gowen
2004	Monty Brown
2005	Bobby Lashley
2006	The Boogeyman
2007	Hornswoggle
2008	Joe Hennig
2009	Mike Sydal
2010	David Otunga
2011	Ace Hawkins
2012	Veda Scott
2013	Tim Zbyszko
2014	Charlotte Flair
2015	Moose
2016	Nia Jax
2017	Otis Dozovic
2018	Ronda Rousey
2019	Brian Pillman Jr.
2020	Dominik Mysterio
2021	Jade Cargill

STANLEY WESTON AWARD

1981	Bruno Sammartino
1982	Lou Thesz
1983	The Grand Wizard
1984	David Von Erich
1985	Dan Shocket
1986	Verne Gagne
1987	Paul Boesch
1988	Bruiser Brody
1989	Gordon Solie
1990	Buddy Rogers
1991	The Fabulous Moolah
1992	Stanley Weston
1993	Andre the Giant
1994	Captain Lou Albano
1995	Ricky Steamboat
1996	Danny Hodge
1997	Arn Anderson
1998	Bobo Brazil
1999	Owen Hart
2000	Freddie Blassie
2001	Johnny Valentine
2002	Jim Ross
2003	Bret Hart
2004	Pat Patterson
2005	Eddie Guerrero
2006	Harley Race
2007	Nick Bockwinkel
2008	Ric Flair
2009	Vince McMahon
2010	Killer Kowalski
2011	Randy Savage
2012	Bobby Heenan
2013	Dusty Rhodes
2014	Dory Funk Jr.
2015	Roddy Piper
2016	Dick Beyer
2017	Jack Brisco
2018	Antonio Inoki
2019	Steve Austin
2020	Madusa
	Stu Saks
2021	Ron Simmons
	Terry Funk

WRESTLING OBSERVER NEWSLETTER READER AWARDS

WRESTLER OF THE YEAR

1980	Harley Race
1981	Harley Race[2]
1982	Ric Flair
1983	Ric Flair[2]
1984	Ric Flair[3]
1985	Ric Flair[4]
1986	Ric Flair[5]
1987	Riki Choshu
1988	Akira Maeda
1989	Ric Flair[6]
1990	Ric Flair[7]
1991	Jumbo Tsuruta
1992	Ric Flair[8]
1993	Big Van Vader
1994	Toshiaki Kawada
1995	Mitsuharu Misawa
1996	Kenta Kobashi
1997	Mitsuharu Misawa[2]
1998	Steve Austin
1999	Mitsuharu Misawa[3]
2000	Triple H
2001	Keiji Mutoh
2002	Kurt Angle
2003	Kenta Kobashi[2]
2004	Kenta Kobashi[3]
2005	Kenta Kobashi[4]
2006	Místico
2007	John Cena
2008	Chris Jericho
2009	Chris Jericho[2]
2010	John Cena[2]
2011	Hiroshi Tanahashi
2012	Hiroshi Tanahashi[2]
2013	Hiroshi Tanahashi[3]
2014	Shinsuke Nakamura
2015	AJ Styles
2016	AJ Styles[2]
2017	Kazuchika Okada
2018	Kenny Omega
2019	Chris Jericho[3]
2020	Jon Moxley
2021	Kenny Omega[2]
2022	Jon Moxley[2]

MOST OUTSTANDING WRESTLER

1986	Ric Flair
1987	Ric Flair[2]
1988	Tatsumi Fujinami
1989	Ric Flair[3]
1990	Jushin Liger
1991	Jushin Liger[2]
1992	Jushin Liger[3]
1993	Kenta Kobashi
1994	Kenta Kobashi[2]
1995	Manami Toyota
1996	Rey Misterio Jr.
1997	Mitsuharu Misawa
1998	Koji Kanemoto
1999	Mitsuharu Misawa[2]
2000	Chris Benoit

2001	Kurt Angle
2002	Kurt Angle[2]
2003	Kurt Angle[3]
2004	Chris Benoit[2]
2005	Samoa Joe
2006	Bryan Danielson
2007	Bryan Danielson[2]
2008	Bryan Danielson[3]
2009	Bryan Danielson[4]
2010	Bryan Danielson[5]
2011	Davey Richards
2012	Hiroshi Tanahashi
2013	Hiroshi Tanahashi[2]
2014	AJ Styles
2015	AJ Styles[2]
2016	AJ Styles[3]
2017	Kazuchika Okada
2018	Kenny Omega
2019	Will Ospreay
2020	Kenny Omega[2]
2021	Shingo Takagi
2022	Will Ospreay[2]

TAG TEAM OF THE YEAR

1980	The Fabulous Freedbirds
1981	Jimmy Snuka & Terry Gordy[2]
1982	Stan Hansen & Ole Anderson
1983	Ricky Steamboat & Jay Youngblood
1984	The Road Warriors
1985	The British Bulldogs
1986	The Midnight Express
1987	The Midnight Express[2]
1988	The Midnight Express[3]
1989	The Rockers
1990	The Steiner Brothers
1991	Mitsuharu Misawa & Toshiaki Kawada
1992	Miracle Violence Connection
1993	The Hollywood Blonds
1994	Los Gringos Locos
1995	Mitsuharu Misawa[2] & Kenta Kobashi
1996	Mitsuharu Misawa[3] & Jun Akiyama
1997	Mitsuharu Misawa[4] & Jun Akiyama[2]
1998	Shinjiro Otani & Tatsuhito Takaiwa
1999	Kenta Kobashi[2] & Jun Akiyama[3]
2000	Edge & Christian
2001	Tencozy
2002	Los Guerreros
2003	Kenta & Naomichi Marufuji
2004	Kenta[2] & Naomichi Marufuji[2]
2005	America's Most Wanted
2006	LAX
2007	The Briscoe Brothers
2008	John Morrison & The Miz
2009	The American Wolves
2010	The Kings of Wrestling
2011	Bad Intentions
2012	Bad Influence
2013	The Shield
2014	The Young Bucks
2015	The Young Bucks[2]
2016	The Young Bucks[3]
2017	The Young Bucks[4]
2018	The Young Bucks[5]
2019	The Lucha Brothers
2020	The Young Bucks[6]
2021	The Young Bucks[7]
2022	FTR

BEST ON INTERVIEWS

1981	Lou Albano
	Roddy Piper
1982	Roddy Piper[2]
1983	Roddy Piper[3]
1984	Jimmy Hart
1985	Jim Cornette
1986	Jim Cornette[2]
1987	Jim Cornette[3]
1988	Jim Cornette[4]
1989	Terry Funk
1990	Arn Anderson
1991	Ric Flair
1992	Ric Flair[2]
1993	Jim Cornette[5]
1994	Ric Flair[3]
1995	Cactus Jack
1996	Steve Austin
1997	Steve Austin[2]
1998	Steve Austin[3]
1999	The Rock
2000	The Rock[2]
2001	Steve Austin[4]
2002	Kurt Angle
2003	Chris Jericho
2004	Mick Foley[2]
2005	Eddie Guerrero
2006	Mick Foley[3]
2007	John Cena
2008	Chris Jericho
2009	Chris Jericho[2]
2010	Chael Sonnen
2011	CM Punk
2012	CM Punk[2]
2013	Paul Heyman
2014	Paul Heyman[2]
2015	Conor McGregor
2016	Conor McGregor[2]
2017	Conor McGregor[3]
2018	Daniel Bryan
2019	Chris Jericho[3]
2020	Eddie Kingston
2021	MJF
2022	MJF[2]

PROMOTION OF THE YEAR

1983	JCP
1984	NJPW
1985	AJPW
1986	UWF
1987	NJPW[2]
1988	NJPW[3]
1989	UWF[2]
1990	AJPW[2]
1991	AJPW[3]
1992	NJPW[4]
1993	AJPW[4]
1994	AAA
1995	NJPW[5]
1996	NJPW[6]
1997	NJPW[7]
1998	NJPW[8]
1999	WWF
2000	WWF[2]
2001	Pride
2002	Pride[2]
2003	Pride[3]
2004	NOAH
2005	NOAH[2]
2006	UFC
2007	UFC[2]
2008	UFC[3]
2009	UFC[4]
2010	UFC[5]

2011	UFC[6]
2012	NJPW[9]
2013	NJPW[10]
2014	NJPW[11]
2015	NJPW[12]
2016	NJPW[13]
2017	NJPW[14]
2018	NJPW[15]
2019	NJPW[16]
2020	AEW
2021	AEW[2]
2022	AEW[3]

BEST WEEKLY TV SHOW

1983	NJPW World Pro Wrestling
1984	NJPW World Pro Wrestling[2]
1985	MSW Mid-South Wrestling
1986	UWF Universal Wrestling Federation
1987	CWA 90 Minute Memphis Live Wrestling
1988	NJPW World Pro Wrestling[3]
1989	AJPW All Japan Pro Wrestling
1990	AJPW All Japan Pro Wrestling[2]
1991	AJPW All Japan Pro Wrestling[3]
1992	AJPW All Japan Pro Wrestling[4]
1993	AJPW All Japan Pro Wrestling[5]
1994	ECW Hardcore TV
1995	ECW Hardcore TV[2]
1996	ECW Hardcore TV[3]
1997	NJPW World Pro Wrestling[4]
1998	WWF Monday Night RAW
1999	WWF Monday Night RAW[2]
2000	WWF Monday Night RAW[3]
2001	NJPW World Pro Wrestling[5]
2002	WWE SmackDown
2003	NOAH Power Hour
2004	WWE Monday Night RAW[4]
2005	UFC The Ultimate Fighter
2006	UFC The Ultimate Fighter[2]
2007	UFC The Ultimate Fighter[3]
2008	UFC The Ultimate Fighter[4]
2009	WWE SmackDown[2]
2010	ROH Ring of Honor Wrestling
2011	WWE SmackDown[3]
2012	TNA Impact Wrestling
2013	WWE NXT
2014	WWE NXT[2]
2015	WWE NXT[3]
2016	NJPW New Japan on AXS
2017	NJPW New Japan on AXS[2]
2018	WWE NXT[4]
2019	AEW Dynamite
2020	AEW Dynamite[2]
2021	AEW Dynamite[3]
2022	AEW Dynamite[4]

PRO WRESTLING MATCH OF THE YEAR

1980	Bob Backlund vs. Ken Patera
1981	Pat Patterson vs. Sgt Slaughter
1982	Tiger Mask vs. Dynamite Kid
1983	Ricky Steamboat & Jay Youngblood vs. Sgt. Slaughter & Don Kernodle
1984	The Freebirds vs. The Von Erichs
1985	Tiger Mask II vs. Kuniaki Kobayashi
1986	Ric Flair vs. Barry Windham
1987	Ricky Steamboat[2] vs. Randy Savage
1988	Sting vs. Ric Flair[2]
1989	Ricky Steamboat[3] vs. Ric Flair[3]
1990	Jushin Liger vs. Naoki Sano
1991	Hiroshi Hase & Kensuke Sasaki vs. The Steiners
1992	Kenta Kobashi & Tsuyoshi Kikuchi

	vs. Doug Furnas & Dan Kroffat
1993	Manami Toyota & Toshiyo Yamada vs. Dynamite Kansai & Mayumi Ozaki
1994	Shawn Michaels vs. Razor Ramon
1995	Manami Toyota[2] vs. Kyoko Inoue
1996	Mitsuharu Misawa & Jun Akiyama vs. Steve Williams & Johnny Ace
1997	Bret Hart vs. Steve Austin
1998	Kenta Kobashi[2] vs. Mitsuharu Misawa[2]
1999	Kenta Kobashi[3] vs. Mitsuharu Misawa[3]
2000	Atlantis vs. Villano III
2001	Keiji Mutoh vs. Genichiro Tenryu
2002	Kurt Angle & Chris Benoit vs. Edge & Rey Mysterio
2003	Kenta Kobashi[4] vs. Mitsuharu Misawa[4]
2004	Kenta Kobashi[6] vs. Jun Akiyama[2]
2005	Kenta Kobashi[6] vs. Samoa Joe
2006	Dragon Kid, Ryo Saito & Genki Horiguchi vs. Cima, Masato Yoshino and Naruki Doi
2007	Takeshi Morishima vs. Bryan Danielson
2008	Chris Jericho vs. Shawn Michaels[2]
2009	The Undertaker vs. Shawn Michaels[3]
2010	The Undertaker[2] vs. Shawn Michaels[4]
2011	CM Punk vs. John Cena
2012	Hiroshi Tanahashi vs. Minoru Suzuki
2013	Hiroshi Tanahashi[2] vs. Kazuchika Okada
2014	AJ Styles vs. Minoru Suzuki[2]
2015	Shinsuke Nakamura vs. Kota Ibushi
2016	Kazuchika Okada[2] vs. Hiroshi Tanahashi[3]
2017	Kazuchika Okada[3] vs. Kenny Omega
2018	Kazuchika Okada[4] vs. Kenny Omega[2]
2019	Will Ospreay vs. Shingo Takagi
2020	Kenny Omega[5] & Adam Page vs. Young Bucks
2021	The Young Bucks[2] vs. The Lucha Brothers
2022	Kazuchika Okada[5] vs. Will Ospreay[2]

US/CANADA MVP

2018	AJ Styles
2019	Chris Jericho
2020	Jon Moxley
2021	Kenny Omega
2022	Jon Moxley[2]

JAPAN MVP

2018	Kenny Omega
2019	Kazuchika Okada
2020	Tetsuya Naito
2021	Shingo Takagi
2022	Kazuchika Okada[2]

MEXICO MVP

2018	LA. Park
2019	Rey Fenix
2020	Rey Fenix[2]
2021	El Hijo del Vikingo
2022	El Hijo del Vikingo[2]

EUROPE MVP

2018	Walter
2019	Walter[2]
2020	Walter[3]
2021	Will Ospreay
2022	Will Ospreay[2]

NON-HEAVYWEIGHT MVP

2018	Will Ospreay
2019	Will Ospreay[2]
2020	Hiromu Takahashi
2021	Darby Allin
2022	El Hijo del Vikingo

WOMENS WRESTLING MVP

2018	Becky Lynch
2019	Becky Lynch[2]
2020	Bayley
2021	Utami Hayashishita
2022	Syuri[2]

BEST BOX OFFICE DRAW

1997	Hulk Hogan
1998	Steve Austin
1999	Steve Austin
2000	The Rock
2001	Kazushi Sakuraba
2002	Bob Sapp
2003	Bob Sapp[2]
2004	Kenta Kobashi
2005	Kenta Kobashi[2]
2006	Mistico
2007	John Cena
2008	Brock Lesnar
2009	Brock Lesnar[2]
2010	Brock Lesnar[3]
2011	The Rock[2]
2012	The Rock[3]
2013	Georges St-Pierre
2014	Ronda Rousey
2015	Ronda Rousey[2]
2016	Conor McGregor
2017	Conor McGregor[2]
2018	Conor McGregor[3]
2019	Chris Jericho
2020	Conor McGregor[4]
2021	CM Punk
	Conor McGregor[5]
2022	Roman Reigns

FEUD OF THE YEAR

1980	Bruno Sammartino vs. Larry Zbyszko
1981	Andre The Giant vs. Killer Khan
1982	Ted DiBiase vs. Junkyard Dog
1983	The Freebirds vs. The Von Erichs
1984	The Freebirds[2] vs. The Von Erichs[2]
1985	Ted DiBiase[2] vs. Jim Duggan
1986	Hulk Hogan vs. Paul Orndorff
1987	Jerry Lawler vs. Austin Idol & Tommy Rich
1988	The Fantastics vs. The Midnight Express
1989	Ric Flair vs. Terry Funk
1990	Mitsuharu Misawa vs. Jumbo Tsuruta
1991	Misuharu Misawa[2] (& co) vs. Jumbo Tsuruta[2] (& co)
1992	Jarrett & Lawler[2] vs. The Moondogs
1993	Bret Hart vs. Jerry Lawler[3]
1994	Los Gringos Locos vs. AAA
1995	Eddie Guerrero[2] vs. Dean Malenko
1996	NWO vs. WCW
1997	Steve Austin vs. The Hart Foundation
1998	Steve Austin[2] vs. Vince McMahon
1999	Steve Austin[3] vs. Vince McMahon
2000	Mick Foley vs. Triple H
2001	Kazushi Sakuruba vs. Wanderlei Silva
2002	Tito Ortiz vs. Ken Shamrock
2003	Kurt Angle vs. Brock Lesnar
2004	Chris Benoit vs. Shawn Michaels vs. Triple H[2]
2005	Batista vs. Triple H[3]
2006	Tito Ortiz[2] vs. Ken Shamrock[2]
2007	Batista[2] vs. The Undertaker
2008	Chris Jericho vs. Shawn Michaels[2]
2009	Jeff Hardy vs. CM Punk
2010	El Generico vs. Kevin Steen
2011	John Cena vs. CM Punk[2]
2012	Hiroshi Tanahashi vs. Kazuchika Okada
2013	Hiroshi Tanahashi[2] vs. Kazuchika Okada[2]
2014	Jon Jones vs. Daniel Cormier
2015	Jose Aldo vs. Conor McGregor
2016	Conor McGregor[2] vs. Nate Diaz
2017	Kazuchika Okada[3] vs. Kenny Omega
2018	Johnny Gargano vs. Tommaso Ciampa
2019	Johnny Gargano[2] vs. Adam Cole
2020	Jon Moxley vs. Eddie Kingston
2021	Kenny Omega[2] vs. Adam Page
2022	FTR vs. The Briscoes

MOST IMPROVED

1980	Larry Zbyszko
1981	Adrian Adonis
1982	Jim Duggan
1983	Curt Hennig
1984	The Cobra
1985	Steve Williams
1986	Rick Steiner
1987	Big Bubba Rogers
1988	Sting
1989	Lex Luger
1990	Kenta Kobashi
1991	Dustin Rhodes
1992	El Samurai
1993	Tracy Smothers
1994	Diesel
1995	Johnny B. Badd
1996	Diamond Dallas Page
1997	Tatsuhito Takaiwa
1998	The Rock
1999	Vader
2000	Kurt Angle
2001	Keiji Mutoh
2002	Brock Lesnar
2003	Brock Lesnar[2]
2004	Randy Orton
2005	Roderick Strong
2006	Takeshi Morishima
2007	Montel Vontavious Porter
2008	The Miz
2009	The Miz[2]
2010	Sheamus
2011	Dolph Ziggler
2012	Kazuchika Okada
2013	Roman Reigns
2014	Rusev
2015	Bayley
2016	Matt Riddle
2017	Braun Strowman
2018	Hangman Page
2019	Lance Archer
2020	Dr. Britt Baker D.M.D.
2021	Tay Conti
2022	The Acclaimed

MOST CHARISMATIC

1980	Ric Flair
1981	Michael Hayes
1982	Ric Flair[2]
	Dusty Rhodes
1983	Ric Flair[3]
1984	Ric Flair[4]
1985	Hulk Hogan
1986	Hulk Hogan[2]
1987	Hulk Hogan[3]
1988	Sting
1989	Hulk Hogan[4]
1990	Hulk Hogan[5]
1991	Hulk Hogan[6]
1992	Sting[2]

1993	Ric Flair[5]
1994	Atsushi Onita
1995	Shawn Michaels
1996	Shawn Michaels[2]
1997	Steve Austin
1998	Steve Austin[2]
1999	The Rock
2000	The Rock[2]
2001	The Rock[3]
2002	The Rock[4]
2003	Bob Sapp
2004	Eddie Guerrero
2005	Eddie Guerrero[2]
2006	John Cena
2007	John Cena[2]
2008	John Cena[3]
2009	John Cena[4]
2010	John Cena[5]
2011	The Rock[5]
2012	The Rock[6]
2013	Hiroshi Tanahashi
2014	Shinsuke Nakamura
2015	Shinsuke Nakamura[2]
2016	Conor McGregor
2017	Tetsuya Naito
2018	Tetsuya Naito[2]
2019	Chris Jericho
2020	MJF
2021	CM Punk
2022	MJF[2]

BEST TECHNICAL WRESTLER

1980	Bob Backlund
1981	Ted DiBiase
1982	Tiger Mask
1983	Tiger Mask[2]
1984	Dynamite Kid
	Masa Saito
1985	Tatsumi Fujinami
1986	Tatsumi Fujinami[2]
1987	Nobuhiko Takada
1988	Tatsumi Fujinami[3]
1989	Jushin Liger
1990	Jushin Liger[2]
1991	Jushin Liger[3]
1992	Jushin Liger[4]
1993	Hiroshi Hase
1994	Chris Benoit
1995	Chris Benoit[2]
1996	Dean Malenko
1997	Dean Malenko[2]
1998	Kiyoshi Tamura
1999	Shinjiro Otani
2000	Chris Benoit[3]
2001	Minoru Tanaka
2002	Kurt Angle
2003	Chris Benoit[4]
2004	Chris Benoit[5]
2005	Bryan Danielson
2006	Bryan Danielson[2]
2007	Bryan Danielson[3]
2008	Bryan Danielson[4]
2009	Bryan Danielson[5]
2010	Bryan Danielson[6]
2011	Daniel Bryan[7]
2012	Daniel Bryan[8]
2013	Daniel Bryan[9]
2014	Zack Sabre Jr.
2015	Zack Sabre Jr.[2]
2016	Zack Sabre Jr.[3]
2017	Zack Sabre Jr.[4]
2018	Zack Sabre Jr.[5]
2019	Zack Sabre Jr.[6]
2020	Zack Sabre Jr.[7]
2021	Bryan Danielson[10]
2022	Bryan Danielson[11]

BEST BRAWLER

1980	Bruiser Brody
1981	Bruiser Brody[2]
1982	Bruiser Brody[3]
1983	Bruiser Brody[4]
1984	Bruiser Brody[5]
1985	Stan Hansen
1986	Terry Gordy
1987	Bruiser Brody[6]
1988	Bruiser Brody[7]
1989	Terry Funk
1990	Stan Hansen
1991	Cactus Jack
1992	Cactus Jack[2]
1993	Cactus Jack[3]
1994	Cactus Jack[4]
1995	Cactus Jack[5]
1996	Cactus Jack/Mankind[6]
1997	Mankind/Dude Love/Cactus Jack[7]
1998	Mankind/Dude Love/Cactus Jack[8]
1999	Mankind/Cactus Jack[9]
2000	Mankind/Cactus Jack[10]
2001	Steve Austin
2002	Yoshihiro Takayama
2003	Brock Lesnar
2004	Chris Benoit
2005	Samoa Joe
2006	Samoa Joe[2]
2007	Takeshi Morishima
2008	Necro Butcher
2009	Necro Butcher[2]
2010	Kevin Steen
2011	Kevin Steen[2]
2012	Kevin Steen[3]
2013	Katsuyori Shibata
2014	Tomohiro Ishii
2015	Tomohiro Ishii[2]
2016	Tomohiro Ishii[3]
2017	Tomohiro Ishii[4]
2018	Tomohiro Ishii[5]
2019	Tomohiro Ishii[6]
2020	Jon Moxley
2021	Jon Moxley[2]
2022	Jon Moxley[3]

BEST FLYER

1981	Jimmy Snuka
1982	Tiger Mask
1983	Tiger Mask[2]
1984	Dynamite Kid
1985	Tiger Mask II
1986	Tiger Mask II[2]
1987	Owen Hart
1988	Owen Hart[2]
1989	Jushin Liger
1990	Jushin Liger[2]
1991	Jushin Liger[3]
1992	Jushin Liger[4]
1993	Jushin Liger[5]
1994	The Great Sasuke
1995	Rey Misterio Jr
1996	Rey Misterio Jr[2]
1997	Rey Misterio Jr[3]
1998	Juventud Guerrera
1999	Juventus Guerrera[2]

2000	Jeff Hardy
2001	Dragon Kid
2002	Rey Mysterio⁴
2003	Rey Mysterio⁵
2004	Rey Mysterio⁶
2005	AJ Styles
2006	Mistico
2007	Mistico²
2008	Evan Bourne
2009	Kota Ibushi
2010	Kota Ibushi²
2011	Ricochet
2012	Kota Ibushi³
2013	Kota Ibushi⁴
2014	Ricochet²
2015	Ricochet³
2016	Will Ospreay
2017	Will Ospreay²
2018	Will Ospreay³
2019	Will Ospreay⁴
2020	Rey Fenix
2021	Rey Fenix²
2022	El Hijo del Vikingo

MOST OVERRATED

1980	Mr. Wrestling II
1981	Pedro Morales
1982	Pedro Morales²
1983	Bob Backlund
1984	Big John Studd
1985	Hulk Hogan
1986	Hulk Hogan²
1987	Dusty Rhodes
1988	Dusty Rhodes²
1989	The Ultimate Warrior
1990	The Ultimate Warrior²
1991	The Ultimate Warrior³
1992	Erik Watts
1993	Sid Vicious
1994	Hulk Hogan³
1995	Hulk Hogan⁴
1996	Hulk Hogan⁵
1997	Hulk Hogan⁶
1998	Hulk Hogan⁷
1999	Kevin Nash
2000	Kevin Nash²
2001	The Undertaker
2002	Triple H
2003	Triple H²
2004	Triple H³
2005	Jeff Jarrett
2006	Batista
2007	The Great Khali
2008	Vladimir Kozlov
2009	Triple H⁴
2010	Kane
2011	Crimson
2012	Ryback
2013	Randy Orton
2014	Kane²
2015	Kane³
2016	Roman Reigns
2017	Jinder Mahal
2018	Baron Corbin
2019	Baron Corbin²
2020	Bray Wyatt
2021	Evil
2022	Ronda Rousey

MOST UNDERRATED

1980	Hossein Arab
1981	Buzz Sawyer
1982	Adrian Adonis
1983	Dynamite Kid
1984	B. Brian Blair
1985	Bobby Eaton
1986	Bobby Eaton²
1987	Brad Armstrong
1988	Tiger Mask II
1989	Dan Kroffat
1990	Bobby Eaton³
1991	Terry Taylor
1992	Terry Taylor²
1993	Bobby Eaton⁴
1994	Brian Pillman
1995	Skip
1996	Leif Cassidy
1996	Flash Funk
1998	Chris Benoit
1999	Chris Jericho
2000	Chris Jericho²
2001	Lance Storm
2002	Booker T
2003	Ultimo Dragon
2004	Paul London
2005	Shelton Benjamin
2006	Shelton Benjamin²
2007	Shelton Benjamin³
2008	MVP
2009	Evan Bourne
2010	Kaval
2011	Dolph Ziggler
2012	Tyson Kidd
2013	Cesaro
2014	Cesaro²
2015	Cesaro³
2016	Cesaro⁴
2017	Rusev
2018	Finn Balor
2019	Shorty G
2020	Ricochet
2021	Ricochet²
2022	Konosuke Takeshita

ROOKIE OF THE YEAR

1980	Barry Windham
1981	Brad Armstrong
	Brad Rheingans
1982	Steve Williams
1983	The Road Warriors
1984	Tom Zenk
	Keiichi Yamada
1985	Jack Victory
1986	Bam Bam Bigelow
1987	Brian Pillman
1988	Gary Albright
1989	Dustin Rhodes
1990	Steve Austin
1991	Johnny B. Badd
1992	Rey Misterio Jr.
1993	Jun Akiyama
1994	Mikey Whipwreck
1995	Perro Aguayo Jr.
1996	The Giant
1997	Mr. Aguila
1998	Goldberg
1999	Blitzkrieg
2000	Sean O'Haire
2001	El Hombre Sin Nombre
2002	Bob Sapp

2003	Chris Sabin
2004	Petey Williams
2005	Shingo Takagi
2006	Atsushi Aoki
2007	Erick Stevens
2008	Kai
2009	Frightmare
2010	Adam Cole
2011	Daichi Hashimoto
2012	Dinastía
2013	Yohei Komatsu
2014	Dragon Lee
2015	Chad Gable
2016	Matt Riddle
2017	Katsuya Kitamura
2018	Ronda Rousey
2019	Jungle Boy
2020	Pat McAfee
2021	Jade Cargill
2022	Bron Breakker

BEST NON WRESTLER

1999	Vince McMahon
2000	Vince McMahon[2]
2001	Paul Heyman
2002	Paul Heyman[2]
2003	Steve Austin
2004	Paul Heyman[3]
2005	Eric Bischoff
2006	Jim Cornette
2007	Larry Sweeney
2008	Larry Sweeney[2]
2009	Vickie Guerrero
2010	Vickie Guerrero[2]
2011	Ricardo Rodriguez
2012	Paul Heyman[4]
2013	Paul Heyman[5]
2014	Paul Heyman[6]
2015	Dario Cueto
2016	Dario Cueto[2]
2017	Daniel Bryan
2018	Paul Heyman[7]
2019	Paul Heyman[8]
2020	Taz
2021	Paul Heyman[9]
2022	Paul Heyman[10]

BEST TV ANNOUNCER

1981	Gordon Solie
1982	Gordon Solie[2]
1983	Gordon Solie[3]
1984	Lance Russell
1985	Lance Russell[2]
1986	Lance Russell[3]
1987	Lance Russell[4]
1988	Jim Ross
1989	Jim Ross[2]
1990	Jim Ross[3]
1991	Jim Ross[4]
1992	Jim Ross[5]
1993	Jim Ross[6]
1994	Joey Styles
1995	Joey Styles[2]
1996	Joey Styles[3]
1997	Mike Tenay
1998	Jim Ross[7]
1999	Jim Ross[8]
2000	Jim Ross[9]
2001	Jim Ross[10]
2002	Mike Tenay[2]
2003	Mike Tenay[3]

2004	Mike Tenay[4]
2005	Mike Tenay[5]
2006	Jim Ross[11]
2007	Jim Ross[12]
2008	Matt Striker
2009	Jim Ross[13]
2010	Joe Rogan
2011	Joe Rogan[2]
2012	Jim Ross[14]
2013	William Regal
2014	William Regal[2]
2015	Mauro Ranallo
2016	Mauro Ranallo[2]
2017	Mauro Ranallo[3]
2018	Kevin Kelly
2019	Kevin Kelly[2]
2020	Excalibur
2021	Excalibur[2]
2022	Kevin Kelly[3]

WORST TV ANNOUNCER

1984	Angelo Mosca
1985	Gorilla Monsoon
1986	David Crockett
1987	David Crockett[2]
1988	David Crockett[3]
1989	Ed Whalen
1990	Herb Abrams
1991	Gorilla Monsoon[2]
1992	Gorilla Monsoon[3]
1993	Gorilla Monsoon[4]
1994	Gorilla Monsoon[5]
1995	Gorilla Monsoon[6]
1996	Steve McMichael
1997	Dusty Rhodes
1998	Lee Marshall
1999	Tony Schiavone
2000	Tony Schiavone[2]
2001	Michael Cole
2002	Jerry Lawler
2003	Jonathan Coachman
2004	Todd Grisham
2005	Jonathan Coachman[2]
2006	Todd Grisham[2]
2007	Don West
2008	Mike Adamle
2009	Michael Cole[2]
2010	Michael Cole[3]
2011	Michael Cole[4]
2012	Michael Cole[5]
2013	Taz
2014	John Bradshaw Layfield
2015	John Bradshaw Layfield[2]
2016	David Otunga
2017	Booker T
2018	Jonathan Coachman[3]
2019	Corey Graves
2020	Michael Cole[6]
2021	Corey Graves[2]
2022	Corey Graves[3]

BEST MAJOR WRESTLING SHOW

1989	WCW The Great American Bash '89
1990	WWF/NJPW/AJPW Wrestling Summit
1991	WCW WrestleWar '91
1992	AJW Wrestlemarinpiad '92
1993	AJW Dream Slam I
1994	NJPW Super J-Cup '94
1995	WPW Bridge of Dreams
1996	WAR Super J-Cup '96: 2nd Stage
1997	WWF In Your House 16: Canadian Stampede

1998	ECW Heat Wave '98		1985	Tiger Mask II
1999	ECW Anarchy Rulz '99			*Tope con Giro*
2000	CMLL Juicio Final		1986	Chavo Guerrero
2001	WWF WrestleMania XVII			*Moonsault block*
2002	WWF SummerSlam '02		1987	Keiichi Yamada
2003	Pride Final Conflict '03			*Shooting star press*
2004	NOAH Departure '04		1988	Keiichi Yamada[2]
2005	NOAH Destiny '05			*Shooting star press*
2006	ROH Glory By Honor V: N2		1989	Scott Steiner
2007	ROH Man Up '07			*Frankensteiner*
2008	WWE WrestleMania XXIV		1990	Scott Steiner[2]
2009	DG:USA Open the Historic Gate '09			*Frankensteiner*
2010	UFC UFC 116		1991	Masao Orihara
2011	WWE Money in the Bank '11			*Moonsault to the outside of the ring*
2012	NJPW King of Pro-Wrestling '12		1992	2 Cold Scorpio
2013	NJPW G1 Climax 23: Day 4			*450 splash*
2014	NJPW G1 Climax 24: Day 7		1993	Vader
2015	NJPW Wrestle Kingdom 9			*Moonsault*
2016	NJPW Wrestle Kingdom 10		1994	The Great Sasuke
2017	NJPW Wrestle Kingdom 11			*Sasuke Special*
2018	NJPW Dominion 6.9		1995	Rey Misterio Jr.
2019	AEW Double or Nothing '19			*Flip dive into a frankensteiner on the floor*
2020	AEW Revolution '20		1996	Último Dragón
2021	AEW All Out '21			*Running Liger bomb*
2022	AEW x NJPW Forbidden Door		1997	Diamond Dallas Page
				Diamond Cutter

WORST MAJOR WRESTLING SHOW

			1998	Kenta Kobashi
1989	WWF WrestleMania V			*Burning Hammer*
1990	WCW Clash Of The Champions XII		1999	Dragon Kid
1991	WCW The Great American Bash '91			*Dragonrana*
1992	WCW Halloween Havoc '92		2000	Dragon Kid[2]
1993	WCW Fall Brawl '93			*Dragonrana*
1994	UWF Blackjack Brawl '94		2001	Keiji Mutoh/Great Muta
1995	WCW Uncensored '95			*Shining Wizard/Sensou Yojutsu*
1996	WCW Uncensored '96		2002	Brock Lesnar
1997	WCW Souled Out '97			*F-5*
1998	WCW Fall Brawl '98		2003	AJ Styles
1999	HOW Heroes of Wrestling			*Styles Clash*
2000	WCW Halloween Havoc '00		2004	Petey Williams
2001	WOW Unleashed '01			*Canadian Destroyer*
2002	WWE King Of The Ring '02		2005	Petey Williams[2]
2003	WWE Backlash '03			*Canadian Destroyer*
2004	WWE The Great American Bash '04		2006	Kenta
2005	WWE The Great American Bash '05			*Go 2 Sleep*
2006	UFC UFC 61		2007	Kenta[2]
2007	ECW December To Dismember '06			*Go 2 Sleep*
2008	WWE Survivor Series '08		2008	Evan Bourne
2009	TNA Victory Road '09			*Shooting star press*
2010	TNA Hardcore Justice '10		2009	The Young Bucks
2011	TNA Victory Road '11			*More Bang for Your Buck*
2012	UFC UFC 149		2010	Ricochet
2013	WWE Battleground '13			*Double rotation moonsault*
2014	WWE Battleground '14		2011	Ricochet[2]
2015	AAA Triplemania XXIII			*Double rotation moonsault*
2016	WWE WrestleMania XXXII		2012	Kazuchika Okada
2017	WWE Battleground '17			*Rainmaker*
2018	WWE Crown Jewel '18		2013	Kazuchika Okada[2]
2019	WWE Super ShowDown '19			*Rainmaker*
2020	WWE Super ShowDown '20		2014	The Young Bucks[2]
2021	WWE Survivor Series '21			*Meltzer Driver*
2022	WWE Royal Rumble '22		2015	AJ Styles[2]
				Styles Clash

BEST WRESTLING MANEUVER

			2016	Kenny Omega
1981	Jimmy Snuka			*One-Winged Angel*
	Superfly splash		2017	Kenny Omega[2]
1982	Super Destroyer			*One-Winged Angel*
	Superplex		2018	Kenny Omega[3]
1983	Jimmy Snuka[2]			*One-Winged Angel*
	Superfly splash		2019	Will Ospreay
1984	The British Bulldogs			*Storm Breaker*
	Military press followed by a missile dropkick		2020	Kenny Omega[4]

	One-Winged Angel		day of London bombings
2021	Adam Page	2006	WWE
	Buckshot Lariat		Exploitation of the death of Eddie Guerrero
2022	Will Ospreay	2007	TNA
	Hidden Blade		Signing of Pacman Jones and having him
			"Make It Rain" on television when his doing
MOST DISGUSTING PROMOTIONAL TACTIC			so in a strip club led to the paralysis of a
1981	LeBelle Promotions		wrestler
	Monster character (Tony Hernandez)	2008	WWE
1982	WWF		Teasing a Jeff Hardy drug overdose to
	Bob Backlund as WWF Champion		garner late interest in a PPV show
1983	WWE	2009	WWE
	Eddie Gilbert re-breaking his neck in an		Mickie James' "Piggy James" angle making
	angle after having done so		fun of her weight
	legitimately	2010	WWE
1984	CWF		Stand Up For WWE campaign launched in
	Blackjack Mulligan fake heart attack		coincidence with Linda McMahon's US
1985	WCCW		Senate run
	Usage of Mike Von Erich's near-death to sell	2011	WWE
	tickets		Promoting an anti-bullying campaign despite
1986	WCCW		blatant mistreatment of Jim Ross
	Comparing Chris Adams' blindness angle	2012	WWE
	with the death of Gino Hernandez		CM Punk and Paul Heyman exploiting Jerry
1987	WCCW		Lawler's real-life heart attack
	Exploitation of the death of Mike Von Erich	2013	WWE
1988	WCCW		Exploitation of the death of Bill Moody
	Fritz Von Erich's fake heart attack		(Paul Bearer)
1989	WWC/CSP	2014	WWE
	José González babyface push one year		WWE Insulting fans who purchased PPVs
	after Bruiser Brody stabbing case	2015	WWE
1990	FMW		Using Reid Fliehr's death in an angle
	Atsushi Onita stabbing José González two	2016	Bellator
	years after Bruiser Brody stabbing case		Kimbo vs. Dada 5000 fight
1991	WWF	2017	WWE
	Exploiting the Persian Gulf War (Sgt.		Promoting Jimmy Snuka as a hero in death
	Slaughter Iraqi sympathizer angle)		not long after his trial over the death of
1992	WCW		Nancy Argentino
	Pushing Erik Watts	2018	WWE
1993	WCW		Relationship with Saudi Arabia
	Cactus Jack gets amnesia	2019	WWE
1994	WCW		Relationship with Saudi Arabia[2]
	Ric Flair retirement angle	2020	WWE
1995	WCW		Firing people during a pandemic in a year
	Gene Okerlund's 900 hotline advertisements		where they were setting profit records
1996	WWF	2021	WWE
	Fake Diesel and Razor Ramon		Firing people during a pandemic in a year
1997	WWF		where they were setting profit records[2]
	Melanie Pillman interview on Raw the day	2022	Vince McMahon
	after Brian Pillman's death		Appearing on television for a crowd pop
1998	WCW		after sexual misconduct allegations came
	Exploiting Scott Hall's alcoholism		out.
1999	WWF		
	Over the Edge pay-per-view continuing after		**WORST TELEVISION SHOW**
	the death of Owen Hart	1984	WWF All-Star Wrestling
2000	WCW	1985	CWF Championship Wrestling From Florida
	David Arquette wins the WCW World	1986	CCW California Championship Wrestling
	Heavyweight Championship	1987	WCCW World Class Championship Wrestling
2001	WWF	1988	AWA Championship Wrestling
	Stephanie McMahon comparing her father's	1989	ICW ICW Wrestling
	indictment to 9/11 attacks	1990	AWA Championship Wrestling[2]
2002	WWE	1991	UWF Fury Hour
	Triple H accusing Kane of murder and	1992	GWF Global Wrestling Federation on ESPN
	necrophilia (Katie Vick)	1993	GWF Global Wrestling Federation on ESPN[2]
2003	WWE	1994	WCW Saturday Night
	McMahons all over the product	1995	WCW Saturday Night[2]
2004	WWE	1996	AWF Warriors of Wrestling
	Kane and Lita pregnancy/ wedding/	1997	USWA United States Wrestling Association
	miscarriage	1998	WCW Monday Nitro
2005	WWE	1999	WCW Thunder
	Not editing out a terrorist angle that aired	2000	WCW Thunder[2]
on		2001	WWF Excess

2002	WWE Monday Night RAW
2003	WWE Monday Night RAW[2]
2004	WWE SmackDown!
2005	WWE SmackDown![2]
2006	WWE Monday Night RAW[3]
2007	TNA Impact Wrestling
2008	TNA Impact Wrestling[2]
2009	TNA Impact Wrestling[3]
2010	TNA Impact Wrestling[4]
2011	TNA Impact Wrestling[5]
2012	WWE Monday Night RAW[4]
2013	TNA Impact Wrestling[6]
2014	WWE Monday Night RAW[5]
2015	WWE Monday Night RAW[6]
2016	WWE Monday Night RAW[7]
2017	WWE Monday Night RAW[8]
2018	WWE Monday Night RAW[9]
2019	WWE Monday Night RAW[10]
2020	WWE Monday Night RAW[11]
2021	WWE Monday Night RAW[12]
2022	WWE Monday Night RAW[13]

WORST MATCH OF THE YEAR

1984	Wendi Richter vs. Fabulous Moolah
1985	Freddie Blassie vs. Lou Albano
1986	Mr. T vs. Roddy Piper
1987	Hulk Hogan vs. Andre the Giant
1988	Hiroshi Wajima vs. Tom Magee
1989	Andre the Giant[2] vs. The Ultimate Warrior
1990	Sid Vicious vs. The Nightstalker
1991	Bobby Eaton & P.N. News vs. Terry Taylor & Steve Austin
1992	Rick Rude vs. Masahiro Chono
1993	The Bushwhackers & Men on a Mission vs. Bam Bam Bigelow, Bastion Booger & The Headshrinkers
1994	The Royal Court vs. Clowns R' Us
1995	Sting vs. Tony Palmora
1996	Hulk Hogan[2] & Randy Savage vs. Ric Flair, Arn Anderson, Meng, The Barbarian, The Taskmaster, Ze Gangsta, The Ultimate Solution & Lex Luger
1997	Hulk Hogan[3] vs. Roddy Piper[2]
1998	Hulk Hogan[4] vs. The Warrior[2]
1999	Al Snow vs. The Big Boss Man
2000	Pat Patterson vs. Gerald Brisco
2001	Kane & The Undertaker vs. Kronik[2]
2002	Bradshaw & Trish Stratus vs. Chris Nowinski & Jackie Gayda
2003	Triple H vs. Scott Steiner
2004	Tyson Tomko vs. Stevie Richards
2005	Eric Bischoff vs. Theodore Long
2006	Reverse Battle Royal
2007	James Storm vs. Chris Harris
2008	Edge vs. Triple H[2] vs. Vladimir Kozlov
2009	Jenna Morasca vs. Sharmell
2010	Kaitlyn vs. Maxine
2011	Sting[2] vs. Jeff Hardy
2012	John Cena vs. John Laurinaitis
2013	Total Divas vs. True Divas
2014	John Cena[2] vs. Bray Wyatt
2015	Los Psycho Circus vs. Los Villanos
2016	Shelly Martinez vs. Rebel
2017	Bray Wyatt[2] vs. Randy Orton
2018	Shawn Michaels & Triple H[3] vs. Kane[2] & The Undertaker[2]
2019	Seth Rollins vs. The Fiend[3]
2020	Braun Strowman vs. The Fiend[4]
2021	The Miz vs. Damian Priest
2022	Pat McAfee vs. Vince McMahon

WORST FEUD OF THE YEAR

1984	Andre the Giant vs. Big John Studd
1985	Sgt. Slaughter vs. Boris Zhukov
1986	The Machines vs. King Kong Bundy & Big John Studd[2]
1987	George Steele vs. Danny Davis
1988	The Midnight Rider vs. Tully Blanchard
1989	Andre the Giant[3] vs. The Ultimate Warrior
1990	Ric Flair vs. The Junkyard Dog
1991	Hulk Hogan vs. Sgt. Slaughter[2]
1992	The Ultimate Warrior[2] vs. Papa Shango
1993	The Undertaker vs. Giant Gonzalez
1994	Jerry Lawler vs. Doink the Clown
1995	Hulk Hogan[2] vs. The Dungeon of Doom
1996	Big Bubba vs. John Tenta
1997	D.O.A. vs. Los Boricuas
1998	Hulk Hogan[3] vs. The Warrior[3]
1999	Big Boss Man[2] vs. Big Show
2000	Hulk Hogan[4] vs. Billy Kidman
2001	WWF vs. The Alliance
2002	Triple H vs. Kane
2003	Kane[2] vs. Shane McMahon
2004	Kane[3] vs. Matt Hardy and Lita
2005	McMahon Family vs. Jim Ross
2006	McMahon Family[2] vs. Triple H[2] & Michaels
2007	Kane[4] vs. Big Daddy V
2008	Kane[5] vs. Rey Mysterio
2009	Homswoggle vs. Chavo Guerrero
2010	Edge vs. Kane[6]
2011	Triple H[3] vs. Kevin Nash
2012	John Cena vs. Kane[7]
2013	Big Show[2] vs. Triple H[4] & Stephanie[3]
2014	Brie Bella vs. Nikki Bella
2015	Team PCB vs. Team B.A.D. vs. Team Bella[2]
2016	Titus O'Neil vs. Darren Young
2017	Bray Wyatt vs. Randy Orton
2018	Sasha Banks[2] vs. Bayley
2019	Seth Rollins vs. The Fiend[2]
2020	Braun Strowman vs. Bray Wyatt[3]
2021	Randy Orton[2] vs. The Fiend[4] & Alexa Bliss
2022	The Mix vs. Dexter Lumis

WORST PROMOTION OF THE YEAR

1986	AWA
1987	WCCW
1988	AWA[2]
1989	AWA[3]
1990	AWA[4]
1991	UWF
1992	GWF
1993	WCW
1994	WCW[2]
1995	WCW[3]
1996	AWF
1997	USWA
1998	WCW[4]
1999	WCW[5]
2000	WCW[6]
2001	WCW[7]
2002	XPW
2003	World Japan
2004	NJPW
2005	NJPW[2]
2006	WWE
2007	TNA
2008	TNA[2]
2009	TNA[3]
2010	TNA[4]
2011	TNA[5]
2012	TNA[6]
2013	TNA[7]

2014	TNA[8]
2015	TNA[9]
2016	TNA[10]
2017	Impact Wrestling[11]
2018	WWE[2]
2019	WWE[3]
2020	WWE[4]
2021	WWE[5]
2022	WWE[6]

BEST BOOKER OF THE YEAR

1986	Dusty Rhodes
1987	Vince McMahon
1988	Eddie Gilbert
1989	Shohei Baba
1990	Shohei Baba[2]
1991	Shohei Baba[3]
1992	Riki Choshu
1993	Jim Cornette
1994	Paul Heyman
1995	Paul Heyman[2]
1996	Paul Heyman[3]
1997	Paul Heyman[4]
1998	Vince McMahon[2]
1999	Vince McMahon[3]
2000	Vince McMahon[4]
2001	Jim Cornette[2]
2002	Paul Heyman[5]
2003	Jim Cornette[3]
2004	Gabe Sapolsky
2005	Gabe Sapolsky[2]
2006	Gabe Sapolsky[3]
2007	Gabe Sapolsky[4]
2008	Joe Silva
2009	Joe Silva[2]
2010	Joe Silva[3]
2011	Gedo and Jado
2012	Gedo[2] and Jado[2]
2013	Gedo[3] and Jado[3]
2014	Gedo[4] and Jado[4]
2015	Triple H and Ryan Ward
2016	Gedo[5]
2017	Gedo[6]
2018	Gedo[7]
2019	Gedo[8]
2020	Tony Khan
2021	Tony Khan[2]
2022	Tony Khan[3]

PROMOTER OF THE YEAR

1988	Vince McMahon
1989	Akira Maeda
1990	Shohei Baba
1991	Shohei Baba[2]
1992	Shohei Baba[3]
1993	Shohei Baba[4]
1994	Shohei Baba[5]
1995	Riki Choshu
1996	Riki Choshu[2]
1997	Riki Choshu[3]
1998	Vince McMahon[2]
1999	Vince McMahon[3]
2000	Vince McMahon[4]
2001	Antonio Inoki
2002	Kazuyoshi Ishii
2003	Nobuyuki Sakakibara
2004	Nobuyuki Sakakibara[2]
2005	Dana White
2006	Dana White[2]
2007	Dana White[3]
2008	Dana White[4]

2009	Dana White[5]
2010	Dana White[6]
2011	Dana White[7]
2012	Dana White[8]
2013	Dana White[9]
2014	Takaaki Kidani
2015	Dana White[10]
2016	Dana White[11]
2017	Takaaki Kidani[2]
2018	Takaaki Kidani[3]
2019	Tony Khan
2020	Tony Khan[2]
2021	Tony Khan[3]
2022	Tony Khan[4]

BEST GIMMICK OF THE YEAR

1986	Adrian Street
1987	Ted DiBiase
1988	Rick Steiner
1989	Jushin Liger
1990	The Undertaker
1991	The Undertaker[2]
1992	The Undertaker[3]
1993	The Undertaker[4]
1994	The Undertaker[5]
1995	Disco Inferno
1996	nWo
1997	Steve Austin
1998	Steve Austin[2]
1999	The Rock
2000	Kurt Angle
2001	The Hurricane
2002	Matt Hardy
2003	John Cena
2004	John Bradshaw Layfield
2005	Mr. Kennedy
2006	Latin American Xchange
2007	Santino Marella
2008	Santino Marella[2]
2009	CM Punk
2010	Alberto Del Rio
2011	CM Punk[2]
2012	Joseph Park
2013	The Wyatt Family
2014	Rusev and Lana
2015	The New Day
2016	Broken Matt Hardy
2017	LIJ
2018	Velveteen Dream
2019	The Fiend
2020	Orange Cassidy
2021	Roman Reigns
2022	Sami Zayn

WORST GIMMICK OF THE YEAR

1986	Adrian Adonis
1987	Adrian Adonis[2]
1988	Midnight Rider
1989	The Ding Dongs
1990	The Gobbledy Gooker
1991	Oz
1992	Papa Shango
1993	The Shockmaster
1994	Dave Sullivan
1995	Goldust
1996	Fake Diesel
	Fake Razor Ramon
	Real Double J
1997	TAFKA Goldust
1998	The Oddities
1999	The Powers That Be

2000	Mike Awesome
2001	Diamond Dallas Page
2002	The Johnsons
2003	Rico Constantino
2004	Mordecai
2005	Jillian Hall
2006	Vito
2007	Black Reign
2008	The Great Khali
2009	Hornswoggle
2010	Orlando Jordan
2011	Michael Cole
2012	Aces & Eights
2013	Aces & Eights[2]
2014	Adam Rose
2015	Stardust
2016	Bone Soldier
2017	Bray Wyatt/Sister Abigail
2018	Constable Corbin
2019	Shorty G
2020	The Fiend/Bray Wyatt[2]
2021	Alexa Bliss
2022	Maxiumum Male Models

SHAD GASPARD / JON HUBER MEMORIAL AWARD

2020	Big E
	Margaret Stalvey
	Megha Parekh
	Sami Zayn
	Shad Gaspard
	Tracy Smothers
2021	Jon Moxley
	Titus O'Neil

BEST PRO WRESTLING BOOK

2005	The Death of WCW
	Bryan Alvarez & R.D. Reynolds
2006	Tangled Ropes
	Superstar Billy Graham
	& Keith Elliot Greenberg
2007	Hitman: My Real Life in the Cartoon
	World of Wrestling
	Bret Hart
2008	Gorgeous George: The Bad Boy Wrestler . . .
	John Capouya
2009	Midnight Express 25th Anniversary
	Scrapbook
	Jim Cornette
2010	Countdown to Lockdown
	Mick Foley
2011	Undisputed: How to Become the World
	Champion in 1,372 Easy Steps
	Chris Jericho
2012	Shooters: The Toughest Men in
	Professional Wrestling
	Jonathan Snowden
2013	Mad Dogs, Midgets and Screw Jobs
	Pat Laprade & Bertrand Hébert
2014	The Death of WCW – 10th Anniversary
	Edition
	Bryan Alvarez & R.D. Reynolds
2015	Yes!: My Improbable Journey to the Main
	Event of WrestleMania
	Daniel Bryan & Craig Tello
2016	Ali vs. Inoki
	Josh Gross
2017	Crazy Like a Fox: The Definitive Chronicle
	of Brian Pillman
	Liam O'Rourke
2018	Eggshells: Pro Wrestling in the Tokyo Dome
	Chris Charlton

2019	100 Things a WWE Fan Should Know & Do
	Before They Die
	Bryan Alvarez
2020	Young Bucks: Killing The Business - From The
	Backyard To The Big Leagues
	Matt Jackson & Nick Jackson
2021	Mox
	Jon Moxley
2022	Blood and Fire
	Brian Solomon

BEST PRO WRESTLING DVD/STREAMING DOCUMENTARY

2005	The Rise and Fall of ECW
2006	Bret "Hit Man" Hart:
	The Best There Is, The Best There Was . . .
2007	Ric Flair And The Four Horsemen
2008	"Nature Boy" Ric Flair: The Definitive
	Collection
2009	Macho Madness: The Randy Savage
	Ultimate Collection
2010	Breaking the Code: Behind the Walls of
	Chris Jericho
2011	Shawn Michaels vs. Bret Hart: WWE's
	Greatest Rivalries
2012	CM Punk: Best in the World
2013	Jim Crockett Promotions: The Good Old Days
2014	Ladies and Gentlemen, My Name Is Paul
	Heyman
2015	Daniel Bryan: Just Say Yes! Yes! Yes!
2016	WWE 24: Seth Rollins
2017	30 for 30: Nature Boy
2018	André the Giant
2019	Dark Side of the Ring
2020	Dark Side of the Ring[2]: Owen Hart
2021	Dark Side Of The Ring[3]: Brian Pillman
2022	Tales From The Territories: Lawler/Kaufmann

WRESTLING HALLS OF FAME

WRESTLING OBSERVER NEWSLETTER HALL OF FAME

1996 Inductees:
Abdullah the Butcher
Al Costello
Akira Maeda
Alfonso Dantés
André the Giant
Antonino Rocca
Antonio Inoki
Antonio Peña
Atsushi Onita
Bert Assirati
Big Van Vader
Bill Watts
Billy Graham
Billy Robinson
Billy Sandow
Blue Demon
Bobo Brazil
Bobby Heenan
Bronko Nagurski
Bruiser Brody
Bruno Sammartino
Bret Hart
Buddy Rogers
Cavernario Galindo
Danny Hodge
Danny McShain
Dara Singh
Devil Masami
Dick Lane
Dick the Bruiser
Don Kent
Don Leo Jonathan
Dory Funk
Dory Funk, Jr.
Dump Matsumoto
Dusty Rhodes
Dynamite Kid
Earl McCready
Ed Don George
Ed Lewis
Eddie Graham
El Canek
El Santo
El Solitario
Ernie Ladd
Frank Gotch
Frank Tunney
Fred Kohler
Freddie Blassie
Fritz Von Erich
Gene Kiniski
Genichiro Tenryu
Georg Hackenschmidt
Gordon Solie
Gorgeous George
Gory Guerrero
Harley Race
Hisashi Shinma
Hulk Hogan
Jack Brisco

Jackie Fargo
Jackie Sato
Jaguar Yokota
Jerry Lawler
Jim Barnett
Jim Cornette
Jim Londos
Joe Stecher
Joe Toots Mondt
John Pesek
Johnny Valentine
Jumbo Tsuruta
Karl Gotch
Killer Kowalski
Kintaro Oki
Lance Russell
Leroy McGuirk
Lou Thesz
Maurice Vachon
Mil Máscaras
Mildred Burke
Mitsuharu Misawa
Negro Casas
Nick Bockwinkel
Nobuhiko Takada
Pat O'Connor
Pat Patterson
Paul Boesch
Perro Aguayo
Randy Savage
Ray Mendoza
Ray Steele
Ray Stevens
Rayo de Jalisco, Sr.
Red Berry
René Guajardo
Ric Flair
Ricky Steamboat
Riki Choshu
Rikidozan
Roadwarrior Animal
Roadwarrior Hawk
Roddy Piper
Roy Heffernan
Sam Muchnick
Shohei Giant Baba
Salvador Lutteroth
Satoru Sayama
Stan Hansen
Stanislaus Zbyszko
Stu Hart
Tatsumi Fujinami
Ted DiBiase
Terry Funk
The Crusher
The Destroyer
The Dusek Family
The Sheik
Tom Jenkins
Tony Stecher
Verne Gagne
Vincent J. McMahon
Vincent K. McMahon
Whipper Billy Watson
Yvon Robert

1997 Inductees:
Chigusa Nagayo
Edouard Carpentier
Jimmy Lennon
Toshiaki Kawada

William Muldoon

1998 Inductees:
Dos Caras

1999 Inductees:
Jim Ross
Jushin Liger
Keiji Muto
Lioness Asuka

2000 Inductees:
Akira Hokuto
Bill Longson
Frank Sexton
Mick Foley
Sandor Szabo
Shinya Hashimoto
Steve Austin

2001 Inductees:
Black Shadow
Bull Nakano
Diablo Velasco
El Satanico
Lizmark

2002 Inductees:
Farmer Burns
Jack Curley
Kenta Kobashi
Manami Toyota
Wahoo McDaniel

2003 Inductees:
Chris Benoit
Earl Caddock
Francisco Flores
Shawn Michaels

2004 Inductees:
Bob Backlund
Kazushi Sakuraba
Kurt Angle
Masahiro Chono
Tarzan Lopez
The Undertaker
Último Dragon

2005 Inductees:
Buddy Roberts
Michael Hayes
Paul Heyman
Terry Gordy
Triple H

2006 Inductees:
Aja Kong
Eddie Guerrero
Hiroshi Hase
Masakatsu Funaki
Paul Bowser

2007 Inductees:
Evan Lewis
The Rock
Tom Packs

2008 Inductees:
Martín Karadagian
Paco Alonso

2009 Inductees:
Bill Miller
Bobby Eaton
Dennis Condrey
Everett Marshall
Konnan
Masa Saito
Roy Shire
Stan Lane

2010 Inductees:
Chris Jericho
Rey Mysterio, Jr.
Wladek Zbyszko

2011 Inductees:
Curtis Iaukea
Kent Walton
Steve Williams

2012 Inductees:
Alfonso Morales
Gus Sonnenberg
Hans Schmidt
John Cena
Lou Albano
Mick McManus

2013 Inductees:
Atlantis
Dr. Wagner Sr.
Henri Deglane
Hiroshi Tanahashi
Kensuke Sasaki
Takashi Matsunaga

2014 Inductees:
Ray Fabiani
Ricky Morton
Robert Gibson

2015 Inductees:
Brock Lesnar
Carlos Colón
Eddie Quinn
Ivan Koloff
Jody Hamilton
Perro Aguayo, Jr.
Shinsuke Nakamura
Tom Renesto

2016 Inductees:
Bryan Danielson
Gene Okerlund
James McLaughlin
Sting

2017 Inductees:
AJ Styles
Ben Sharpe
Mark Lewin
Mike Sharpe
Minoru Suzuki
Pedro Morales

2018 Inductees:
Bill Apter
Gary Hart
Howard Finkel
Jerry Jarrett
Jimmy Hart

L.A. Park
Yuji Nagata

2019 Inductees:
Bearcat Wright
Dr. Wagner Jr.
Gedo
El Signo
El Texano
Jim Crockett Sr.
Negro Navarro
Paul Pons
Ultimo Guerrero
Villano III

2020 Inductees:
Dan Koloff
Jun Akiyama
Karloff Lagarde
Kenny Omega
Medico Asesino

2021 Inductees:
Brazo de Oro
Brazo de Plata
Don Owen
El Brazo
Jim Crockett Jr.
Kazuchika Okada

2022 Inductees:
Akira Taue
Johnny Doyle
Kota Ibushi
Lou Daro
Mark "Rollerball" Rocco
Mistico
Tetsuya Naito
Toshiaki Kawada
Villano I
Villano II
Villano III
Villano IV
Villano V

PRO WRESTLING HALL OF FAME

2002 Inductees:
Andre the Giant
Bruno Sammartino
Buddy Rogers
Ed Lewis
Frank Gotch
George Hackenschmidt
Gorgeous George
Jim Londos
Joe Stecher
Lou Thesz
Mildred Burke
Ricky Steamboat
Sky Low Low

2003 Inductees:
Al Costello

Antonino Rocca
The Destroyer
The Fabulous Moolah
Farmer Burns
Hulk Hogan
Ilio DiPaolo
Killer Kowalski
Little Beaver
Nick Bockwinkel
Roy Heffernan
Sam Muchnick
Stanislaus Zbyszko

2004 Inductees:
Angelo Savoldi
Butcher Vachon
Freddie Blassie
Gordon Solie
Harley Race
John J. Bonica
Len Rossi
Lord Littlebrook
Mad Dog Vachon
Mae Young
Terry Funk
Verne Gagne
Vincent J. McMahon
William Muldoon

2005 Inductees:
Crusher
The Destroyer
Dick the Bruiser
Dory Funk Jr.
Fuzzy Cupid
George Steele
Jack Brisco
John Pesek
Mike Mazurki
Orville Brown
Paul Boesch
Penny Banner
Ray Stern

2006 Inductees:
Bobby Heenan
Don Leo Jonathan
Ed Don George
Ida Mae Martinez
Johnny Valentine
June Byers
Pat Patterson
Ray Stevens
Ric Flair
Rikidozan
Wild Bill Longson

2007 Inductees:
Billy Darnell
Chris Tolos
Cora Combs
Danny Hodge
Earl Caddock
Gus Sonnenberg
Jack Pfefer
John Tolos
Karl Gotch
Pat O'Connor
Roddy Piper
Ted DiBiase

2008 Inductees:
Betty Niccoli
Bob Backlund
Bobo Brazil
Bret Hart
Emil Dusek
Ernie Dusek
Gene Kiniski
Giant Baba
Ray Steele
Tom Drake
Tom Jenkins
Toots Mondt

2009 Inductees:
Antonio Inoki
Captain Lou Albano
Chief Jay Strongbow
Don Curtis
Donna Christanello
Evan Lewis
Hank Garrett
Mark Lewin
Paul Orndorff
Randy Savage
Superstar Billy Graham
Wladek Zbyszko

2010 Inductees:
Ben Sharpe
Danny McShain
Dusty Rhodes
Edouard Carpentier
Gorilla Monsoon
Kay Noble
Mike Sharpe
Mil Mascaras
Stan Hansen
Wahoo McDaniel
Wild Red Berry

2011 Inductees:
Billy Robinson
Bronko Nagurski
Dick the Bruiser
Everett Marshall
Ivan Koloff
Jerry Lawler
Judy Grable
Paul Ellering
Road Warrior Animal
Road Warrior Hawk
The Sheik
Vincent K. McMahon

2012 Inductees:
Abe Coleman
Afa
Dominic DeNucci
The French Angel
Fritz Von Erich
George Gordienko
Jim Cornette
Jimmy Snuka
Junkyard Dog
Sika
Wendi Richter

2013 Inductees:
Baron von Raschke
Bill Watts

Dick Murdoch
Dick Shikat
El Santo
J.J. Dillon
Jody Hamilton
Joyce Grable
Sandor Szabo
Tito Santana
Tom Renesto

2014 Inductees:
Bruiser Brody
Don Fargo
Don Muraco
Gary Hart
Jackie Fargo
Leroy McGuirk
Lord Alfred Hayes
The Masked Superstar
Mr. Wrestling II
Sensational Sherri
Stu Hart

2015 Inductees:
Billy Watson
Buddy Roberts
The Great Gama
Jim Crockett Sr.
Joe Malcewicz
Jumbo Tsuruta
Michael Hayes
Mr. Perfect
Pedro Morales
Rick Martel
Terry Gordy
Vivian Vachon

2016 Inductees:
Blackjack Lanza
Blackjack Mulligan
Earl McCready
Gene Okerlund
Greg Valentine
Hans Schmidt
Joe Panzandak
Leilani Kai
Peter Maivia
Sgt. Slaughter
Steve Austin

2017 Inductees:
Dick Raines
George Napolitano
Harley Race
Larry Hennig
Luther Lindsay
Mick Foley
Shawn Michaels
Sputnik Monroe
Tatsumi Fujinami
Sue Green
Yvon Robert

2018 Inductees:
Billy Red Lyons
Eddie Graham
Ernie Ladd
Fred Beell
Hiro Matsuda
Jim Duggan
Joe Higuchi

Pampero Firpo
Ralph Silverstein
Red Bastien
Sting
Toni Rose

2019 Inductees:
Abdullah the Butcher
Ann LaVerne
Baron Michele Leone
Beverly Shade
Bob Roop
Bobby Eaton
Charley Fox
Dennis Condrey
Gory Guerrero
Johnny Dugan
Lord James Blears
Owen Hart
Randy Rose
Ronnie Garvin
Wally Karbo

2020 Inductees:
Bobby Managoff
Butch Miller
Debbie Combs
Dick Woehrle
Dory Funk
George Zaharias
The Great Kabuki
Jake Roberts
Karl Kox
King Curtis
Luke Williams
Luna Vachon
Magnum T.A.
Tim Brooks

2021 Inductees:
Don Owen
Jose Lothario
Juanita Coffman
Judy Martin
Leo Burke
Man Mountain Dean
Paul Bowser
Ricky Morton
Robert Gibson
Ronnie West
Skandor Akbar
Tiger Conway Sr.
Tommy Rich
Tony Atlas

WWE HALL OF FAME

1993 Inductees:
Andre the Giant

1994 Inductees:
Arnold Skaaland
Bobo Brazil
Buddy Rogers
Chief Jay Strongbow
Freddie Blassie

Gorilla Monsoon
James Dudley

1995 Inductees:
Antonino Rocca
Ernie Ladd
George Steele
Ivan Putski
Pedro Morales
The Fabulous Moolah
The Grand Wizard
1996 Inductees:
Jimmy Valiant
Jimmy Snuka
Johnny Rodz
Johnny Valiant
Killer Kowalski
Lou Albano
Mikel Scicluna
Pat Patterson
Vincent J. McMahon

2004 Inductees:
Big John Studd
Bobby Heenan
Don Muraco
Greg Valentine
Harley Race
Jesse Ventura
Junkyard Dog
Pete Rose
Sgt. Slaughter
Superstar Billy Graham
Tito Santana

2005 Inductees:
Bob Orton Jr.
Hulk Hogan
Iron Sheik
Jimmy Hart
Nikolai Volkoff
Paul Orndorff
Roddy Piper

2006 Inductees:
Blackjack Mulligan
Blackjack Lanza
Bret Hart
Eddie Guerrero
Gene Okerlund
Sensational Sherri
Tony Atlas
Verne Gagne
William Perry

2007 Inductees:
Afa
Dusty Rhodes
Jerry Lawler
Jim Ross
Mr. Fuji
Mr. Perfect
Nick Bockwinkel
Sika
The Sheik

2008 Inductees:
Eddie Graham
Gerald Brisco
Gordon Solie
Jack Brisco

Mae Young
Peter Maivia
Ric Flair
Rocky Johnson

2009 Inductees:
Bill Watts
Chris Von Erich
David Von Erich
Dory Funk Jr.
Fritz Von Erich
Howard Finkel
Kerry Von Erich
Kevin Von Erich
Koko B. Ware
Mike Von Erich
Ricky Steamboat
Steve Austin
Terry Funk

2010 Inductees:
Antonio Inoki
Bob Uecker
Gorgeous George
Mad Dog Vachon
Stu Hart
Ted DiBiase
Wendi Richter

2011 Inductees:
Abdullah the Butcher
Bob Armstrong
Drew Carey
Jim Duggan
Paul Ellering
Roadwarrior Animal
Roadwarrior Hawk
Shawn Michaels
Sunny

2012 Inductees:
Arn Anderson
Barry Windham
Edge
JJ Dillon
Mike Tyson
Mil Mascaras
Ric Flair
Ron Simmons
Tully Blanchard
Yokozuna

2013 Inductees:
Bob Backlund
Booker T
Bruno Sammartino
Donald Trump
Mick Foley
Trish Stratus

2014 Inductees:
Carlos Colon Sr.
Jake Roberts
Lita
Mr. T
Paul Bearer
Razor Ramon
The Ultimate Warrior

2015 Inductees:
Alundra Blayze

Arnold Schwarzenegger
Bushwhacker Butch
Bushwhacker Luke
Connor Michalek
Kevin Nash
Larry Zbyszko
Randy Savage
Rikishi
Tatsumi Fujinami

2016 Inductees:
Art Thomas
Big Boss Man
Buddy Roberts
Ed Lewis
Frank Gotch
George Hackenschmidt
The Godfather
Jacqueline
Jimmy Garvin
Joan Lunden
Lou Thesz
Michael Hayes
Mildred Burke
Pat O'Connor
Snoop Dogg
Stan Hansen
Sting
Terry Gordy

2017 Inductees:
Bearcat Wright
Beth Phoenix
Diamond Dallas Page
Eric LeGrand
Farmer Burns
Haystacks Calhoun
Jerry Graham
Judy Grable
June Byers
Kurt Angle
Luther Lindsay
Rick Rude
Ricky Morton
Rikidozan
Robert Gibson
Teddy Long
Toots Mondt

2018 Inductees:
Boris Malenko
Bubba Ray Dudley
Cora Combs
Dara Singh
D-Von Dudley
El Santo
Goldberg
Hillbilly Jim
Hiro Matsuda
Ivory
Jarrius Robertson
Jeff Jarrett
Jim Londos
Kid Rock
Lord Alfred Hayes
Mark Henry
Rufus R. Jones
Sputnik Monroe
Stan Stasiak

2019 Inductees:
Billy Gunn
Booker T
Bret Hart
Bruiser Brody
Brutus Beefcake
Buddy Rose
Chyna
Hisashi Shinma
Honky Tonk Man
Jim Barnett
Jim Neidhart
Joseph Cohen
Luna Vachon
Primo Carnera
Road Dogg
S.D. Jones
Shawn Michaels
Stevie Ray
Sue Aitchison
Torrie Wilson
Toru Tanaka
Triple H
Wahoo McDaniel
X-Pac

2020 Inductees:
Baron Michele Leone
Brickhouse Brown
Brie Bella
Gary Hart
Hollywood Hogan
John Bradshaw Layfield
Jushin Thunder Liger
Kevin Nash
Nikki Bella
Ray Stevens
Scott Hall
Sean Waltman
Steve Williams
The British Bulldog
Titus O'Neil
William Shatner

2021 Inductees:
Buzz Sawyer
Dick the Bruiser
Eric Bischoff
Ethel Johnson
Kane
Molly Holly
Ozzy Osbourne
Paul Boesch
Pez Whatley
Rob Van Dam
Rich Hering
The Great Khali

2022 Inductees:
Queen Sharmell
Rick Steiner
Scott Steiner
Shad Gaspard
The Undertaker
Vader

GEORGE TRAGOS / LOU THESZ PRO WRESTLING HALL OF FAME

1999 Inductees:
Ed "Strangler" Lewis
Frank Gotch
George Tragos
Lou Thesz
Verne Gagne

2000 Inductees:
Danny Hodge
Dick Hutton
Earl Caddock
Joe Stecher

2001 Inductees:
Farmer Burns
Jack Brisco
Tim Woods
William Muldoon

2002 Inductees:
Baron von Raschke
Bob Geigel
Ed Don George
Peter Sauer
The Destroyer

2003 Inductees:
Billy Robinson
George Hackenschmidt
Joe Scarpello
Mad Dog Vachon

2004 Inductees:
Brad Rheingans
Gene Kiniski
Leroy McGuirk
Pat O'Connor

2005 Inductees:
Antonio Inoki
Dr. Bill Miller
Earl McCready
Gerald Brisco
Harley Race
John Pesek

2006 Inductees:
Bob Roop
Bret Hart
Dory Funk
Larry Hennig
Mike DiBiase
Tom Jenkins

2007 Inductees:
Bill Murdock

Curt Hennig
Dale Lewis
Red Bastien
Steve Williams
Ted DiBiase
The Great Gama

2008 Inductees:
Abe Jacobs
Father Jason Sanderson
Leo Nomellini
Masa Saito
Ray Gunkel
Roddy Piper
Stu Hart

2009 Inductees:
Bill Kersten
Bronko Nagurski
Fritz Von Goering
Karl Gotch
Luther Lindsay
Nick Bockwinkel
Ricky Steamboat

2010 Inductees:
Butcher Vachon
George Gordienko
Rene Goulet
Stanislaus Zbyszko
Terry Funk
Warren Bockwinkel

2011 Inductees:
Dory Funk Jr.
Gorilla Monsoon
Jim Ross

2012 Inductees:
Don Curtis
John Bradshaw Layfield
Kurt Angle

2013 Inductees:
Bill Watts
Chris Taylor
Edge
Ric Flair

2014 Inductees:
Larry Hennig
Rick Steiner
Scott Steiner
Wilbur Snyder

2015 Inductees:
Brian Blair
Jim Londos
The Great Wojo

2016 Inductees:
Bob Backlund
Iron Sheik
J. J. Dillon
Joe Blanchard

2017 Inductees:
Dusty Rhodes
Magnum T.A.
Paul Orndorff

2018 Inductees:
Booker T
Dan Severn
Owen Hart

2019 Inductees:
Beth Phoenix
Bruno Sammartino
Thunderbolt Patterson

2021 Inductees:
Adnan Al-Kaissie
Don Kernodle
Earl Wampler
Gordon Solie
Trish Stratus

2022 Inductees:
Dan Spivey
Dick Bourne
Jim Ross
Mike Rotunda

NWA HALL OF FAME

2005 Inductees:
Gordon Solier
Harley Race
Jim Barnett
Jim Cornette
Lou Thesz
Sam Muchnick

2006 Inductees:
Dory Funk Jr.
Eddie Graham
Lance Russell
Leilani Kai
Ricky Morton
Robert Gibson
Saul Weingeroff

2008 Inductees:
Bobby Eaton
Corsica Jean
Corsica Joe
Dennis Condrey
Iron Sheik
Nikita Koloff
Ric Flair
Tommy Rich

2009 Inductees:
Dennis Coralluzzo
Gene Kiniski
Jerry Jarrett
Mil Mascaras
Paul Orndorff
Terry Funk
Tully Blanchard

2010 Inductees:
Buddy Rogers
Dan Severn
Danny Hodge
Ed Chuman
Gene Anderson

Jack Brisco
Lars Anderson
Nick Gulas
Ole Anderson
Shinya Hashimoto
The Sheik

2011 Inductees:
Aileen LeBell Eaton
Angelo Savoldi
Bill Apter
Dusty Rhodes
Freddie Blassie
Gene LeBell
Johnny Valentine
Mike LeBell
Pat O'Connor
Rikidozan
Sue Green
Wahoo McDaniel

2012 Inductees:
Fabulous Moolah
John Tolos
Joyce Grable
Little Beaver
Misty Blue
Mr. Wrestling II
Paul Boesch
Ricky Steamboat
Road Warrior Animal
Road Warrior Hawk
Sputnik Monroe
Teddy Long

2013 Inductees:
Al Costello
Bobo Brazil
Dory Funk Sr.
Ernie Ladd
Jackie Fargo
Ray Stevens
Roy Heffernan
Salvador Lutteroth

2014 Inductees:
Cowboy Bob Kelly
Giant Baba
J.J. Dillon
Kevin Sullivan
Ox Baker
Pinkie George

2015 Inductees:
Adam Pearce
Don Wright
Leroy McGuirk
Mike Sircy
Ron Wright

2016 Inductees:
Boris Malenko
Gary Hart
Jim Ross
Len Rossi
Nick Bockwinkel

2017 Inductees:
Everett Marshall
Jose Lothario

IMPACT WRESTLING HALL OF FAME

2012 Inductees:
Sting

2013 Inductees:
Kurt Angle

2014 Inductees:
Bully Ray
Devon

2015 Inductees:
Earl Hebner
Jeff Jarrett

2016 Inductees:
Gail Kim

2018 Inductees:
Abyss

2020 Inductees:
Ken Shamrock

2021 Inductees:
Awesome Kong

2022 Inductees:
Raven

WCW HALL OF FAME

1993 Inductees:
Eddie Graham
Lou Thesz
Mr. Wrestling II
Verne Gagne

1994 Inductees:
Dick the Bruiser
Ernie Ladd
Harley Race
Masked Assassin
Ole Anderson
The Crusher

1995 Inductees:
Angelo Poffo
Antonio Inoki
Big John Studd
Dusty Rhodes
Gordon Solie
Terry Funk
Wahoo McDaniel

INTERNATIONAL PROFESSIONAL WRESTLING HALL OF FAME

2021 Inductees:
Andre the Giant
Antonio Inoki
Bruno Sammartino
Buddy Rogers
Danny Hodge
Ed 'Strangler' Lewis
Evan 'Strangler' Lewis
Frank Gotch
George Hackenschmidt
Giant Baba
Great Gama
Hulk Hogan
Lou Thesz
Martin 'Farmer' Burns
Mil Mascaras
Paul Pons
Ric Flair
Rikidozan
Satoru Sayama
Stanislaus Zbyszko
Tatsumi Fujinami
Terry Funk
William Muldoon
Yusuf Ismail

2022 Inductees:
Aleksander Aberg
Billy Robinson
Dory Funk Jr.
Fred Beell
Genichiro Tenryu
Jim Londos
Joe Stecher
Karl Gotch
Mildred Burke
Riki Choshu
Steve Austin
Tom Cannon
Tom Jenkins

NWA WRESTLING LEGENDS HALL OF HEROES

2007 Inductees:
Bob Caudle
Gene Anderson
George Scott
Ole Anderson
Penny Banner
Rip Hawk
Swede Hanson

2008 Inductees:
Buddy Roberts

Grizzly Smith
Ivan Koloff
Johnny Weaver
Paul Jones
Sandy Scott
Thunderbolt Patterson

2009 Inductees:
Blackjack Mulligan
Don Fargo
Gary Hart
Jackie Fargo
Lance Russell
Nelson Royal
Sonny Fargo
Wahoo McDaniel

2010 Inductees:
Billy Robinson
Danny Hodge
Greg Valentine
Joe Blanchard
Johnny Valentine
Mr. Wrestling
Mr. Wrestling II

2011 Inductees:
Gordon Solie
Jody Hamilton
Masked Superstar
Ray Stevens
Ron Garvin
Sir Oliver Humperdink
Ted Turner
Tom Renesto

2013 Inductees:
Bobby Eaton
Danny Miller
Dennis Condrey
Jim Cornette
Lars Anderson
Les Thatcher
Magnum T.A.
Ricky Morton
Robert Gibson
Stan Lane

2014 Inductees:
Angelo Poffo
Arn Anderson
Boris Malenko
James J. Dillon
Jerry Brisco
Lanny Poffo
Ox Baker
Randy Savage
Tommy Young
Tully Blanchard

2015 Inductees:
Jay Youngblood
Jim Crockett Sr.
Ricky Steamboat
2016 Inductees:
Animal
Baby Doll
Dusty Rhodes
Hawk
Jimmy Valiant
Paul Ellering

GCW INDIE WRESTLING HALL OF FAME

2022 Inductees:
Dave Prazak
Homicide
Jerry Lynn
LuFisto
Ruckus
Tracy Smothers

ROH HALL OF FAME

2022 Inductees:
Bryan Danielson
Cary Silkin
CM Punk
Jay Briscoe
Mark Briscoe
Samoa Joe

HARDCORE HALL OF FAME

2002 Inductees:
Rocco Rock

2005 Inductees:
Terry Funk

2007 Inductees:
Johnny Grunge
The Sandman

2008 Inductees:
John Zandig

2009 Inductees:
Chris Candido
Eddie Gilbert
Sabu
Tod Gordon

2010 Inductees:
Jerry Lynn
Tommy Dreamer
Trent Acid

2011 Inductees:
ECW Arena Fans

2014 Inductees:
2 Cold Scorpio
Pitbull #1
Pitbull #2
Shane Douglas
The Blue Meanie

2015 Inductees:

Dean Malenko
Eddie Guerrero

2021 Inductees:
Animal
Charlie Bruzzese
Hawk

2022 Inductees:
Rob Van Dam

WRESTLING OBSERVER FIVE-STAR MATCHES

DATE	FED	EVENT	MATCH
07-04-82	CWF	Miami Beach Show	Ric Flair vs. Butch Reed
21-04-83	NJPW	Big Fight Series II	Dynamite Kid vs. Tiger Mask I
05-12-84	UWF	Year-End Special	Kazuo Yamazaki vs. Nobuhiko Takada
12-12-84	AJPW	Real World Tag League	Bruiser Brody & Stan Hansen vs. Dory Funk Jr. & Terry Funk
09-03-85	AJPW	85 Gekitoh! Exciting Wars	Kuniaki Kobayashi vs. Tiger Mask II
22-08-85	AJW	Summer Night Festival in Budokan	Jaguar Yokota vs. Lioness Asuka
28-01-86	AJPW	New Years War Super Battle	Genichiro Tenryu & Jumbo Tsuruta vs. Riki Choshu & Yoshiaki Yatsu
14-02-86	CWF	Battle Of The Belts 2	Barry Windham vs. Ric Flair^2
19-04-86	JCP	Crockett Cup '86	Butch Miller & Luke Williams vs. Bobby Fulton & Tommy Rogers
20-01-87	JCP	World Wide Wrestling	Barry Windham^2 vs. Ric Flair^3
26-02-87	AJW	Kawasaki Show	Chigusa Nagoyo vs. Lioness Asuka^2
20-03-87	NJPW	Spring Flare Up	Akira Maeda & Nobuhiko Takada^2 vs. Keiji Mutoh & Shiro Koshinaka
11-04-87	JCP	Crockett Cup '87	Barry Windham^3 vs. Ric Flair^4
04-07-87	JCP	The Great American Bash '87	Paul Ellering, Hawk, Animal, Dusty Rhodes & Nikita Koloff vs. Arn Anderson, Lex Luger, Ric Flair^5, Tully Blanchard & J. J. Dillon
31-07-87	JCP	The Great American Bash '87	Animal^2, Dusty Rhodes^2, Hawk^2, Nikita Koloff^2 & Paul Ellering^2 vs. Arn Anderson^2, Ric Flair^6, Lex Luger^2, The War Machine & Tully Blanchard^2
16-12-87	AJW	House Show	Chigusa Nagoyo^2, Mika Suzuki, Mika Takahashi, Yachiya Hirata, Yumi Ogura & Yumiko Hotta vs. Etsuko Mita, Kazue Nagahori, Lioness Asuka^3, Mika Komatsu, Mitsuko Nishiwaki & Sachiko Nakamura
16-12-88	AJPW	Real World Tag League	Stan Hansen^2 & Terry Gordy vs. Genichiro Tenryu^2 & Toshiaki Kawada
28-01-89	AJPW	New Year Giant Series	Genichiro Tenryu^3, Samson Fuyuki & Toshiaki Kawada^2 vs. Jumbo Tsuruta^2, Masanobu Fuchi & Yoshiaki Yatsu^2
20-02-89	NWA	Chi-Town Rumble '89	Ric Flair^7 vs. Ricky Steamboat
18-03-89	NWA	House Show	Ric Flair^8 vs. Ricky Steamboat^2
02-04-89	NWA	Clash Of The Champions VI	Ric Flair^9 vs. Ricky Steamboat^3
07-05-89	NWA	WrestleWar '89	Ric Flair^{10} vs. Ricky Steamboat^4
05-06-89	AJPW	Super Power Series	Genichiro Tenryu^4 vs. Jumbo Tsuruta^3
15-11-89	NWA	Clash Of The Champions IX	Ric Flair^{11} vs. Terry Funk^2
31-01-90	NJPW	New Spring Gold Series	Jushin Liger vs. Naoki Sano
08-06-90	AJPW	Super Power Series	Jumbo Tsuruta^4 vs. Mitsuharu Misawa^2
30-09-90	AJPW	October Giant Series	Akira Taue & Jumbo Tsuruta^5 vs. Mitsuharu Misawa^3 & Toshiaki Kawada^3
19-10-90	AJPW	October Giant Series	Kenta Kobashi, Mitsuharu Misawa^4 & Toshiaki Kawada^4 vs. Akira Taue^2, Jumbo Tsuruta^6 & Masanobu Fuchi^2
04-01-91	AJW	House Show	Akira Hokuto vs. Bull Nakano
24-02-91	WCW	WrestleWar '91	Barry Windham^4, Larry Zbyszko, Ric Flair^{12} & Sid Vicious vs. Brian Pillman, Rick Steiner, Scott Steiner & Sting
20-04-91	AJPW	Fan Appreciation Day	Kenta Kobashi^2, Mitsuharu Misawa^5 & Toshiaki Kawada^5 vs. Akira Taue^3, Jumbo Tsuruta^7 & Masanobu Fuchi^3
09-08-91	NJPW	Violent Storm In Kokugikan	Big Van Vader vs. Keiji Mutoh^2
24-04-92	AJW	Wrestlemarinepiad '92	Kyoko Inoue vs. Manami Toyota
30-04-92	NJPW	Explosion Tour	El Samurai vs. Jushin Liger^2
17-05-92	WCW	WrestleWar '92	Barry Windham^5, Dustin Rhodes, Nikita Koloff^3, Ricky Steamboat^5 & Sting^2 vs. Arn Anderson^3, Bobby Eaton, Larry Zbyszko^2, Rick Rude & Steve Austin
22-05-92	AJPW	Super Power Series	Kenta Kobashi^3, Mitsuharu Misawa^6 & Toshiaki Kawada^6 vs. Akira Taue^4, Jumbo Tsuruta^8 & Masanobu Fuchi^4
25-05-92	AJPW	Super Power Series	Kenta Kobashi^4 & Tsuyoshi Kikuchi vs. Dan Kroffat & Doug Furnas
05-07-92	AJPW	Summer Action Series	Kenta Kobashi^5 & Tsuyoshi Kikuchi^2 vs. Masanobu Fuchi^5 & Yoshinari Ogawa
15-08-92	AJW	Mid Summer Typhoon	Manami Toyota^2 vs. Toshiyo Yamada
02-04-93	AJW	Dream Slam I	Kyoko Inoue^2 & Takako Inoue vs. Cutie Suzuki & Mayumi Ozaki
02-04-93	AJW	Dream Slam I	Akira Hokuto^2 vs. Shonobu Kandori
11-04-93	AJW	Dream Slam II	Manami Toyota^3 & Toshiyo Yamada^2 vs. Dynamite Kansai & Mayumi Ozaki^2
18-04-93	JWP	House Show	Bull Nakano^2 vs. Devil Masami
25-04-93	AJPW	Champion Carnival	Kenta Kobashi^6 vs. Toshiaki Kawada^7
09-05-93	SMW	Volunteer Slam II: Rage In A Cage	Robert Gibson, Robert Fuller, Ricky Morton, Jimmy Golden & Brian Lee vs. Tom Prichard, The Tazmaniac, Stan Lane, Killer Kyle & Kevin Sullivan
02-07-93	AJPW	Summer Action Series	Jun Akiyama, Kenta Kobashi^7 & Mitsuharu Misawa^7 vs. Akira Taue^5, Toshiaki Kawada^8 & Yoshinari Ogawa^2
29-07-93	AJPW	Summer Action Series	Kenta Kobashi^8 vs. Stan Hansen^3
31-07-93	JWP	Thunder Queen Battle in Yokohama	Aja Kong, Kyoko Inoue^3, Sakie Hasegawa & Takako Inoue^2 vs. Cutie Suzuki^2, Dynamite Kansai^2, Hikari Fukuoka & Mayumi Ozaki^3
31-08-93	AJPW	Summer Action Series II	Kenta Kobashi^9 vs. Steve Williams
03-12-93	AJPW	Real World Tag League	Kenta Kobashi^{10} & Mitsuharu Misawa^8 vs. Akira Taue^6 & Toshiaki Kawada^9
06-12-93	AJW	St. Battle Final	Manami Toyota^4 & Toshiyo Yamada^3 vs. Cutie Suzuki^3 & Mayumi Ozaki^4
10-12-93	AJW	Tag League The Best	Akira Hokuto^3 & Manami Toyota^5 vs. Kyoko Inoue^4 & Toshiyo Yamada^4
10-12-93	AJW	Tag League The Best	Akira Hokuto^4 & Manami Toyota^6 vs. Kyoko Inoue^5 & Toshiyo Yamada^5

Date	Promotion	Event	Match
29-01-94	AJPW	New Year Giant Series	Giant Baba, Kenta Kobashi[11] & Mitsuharu Misawa[9] vs. Akira Taue[7], Masanobu Fuchi[6] & Toshiaki Kawada[10]
20-03-94	WWF	WrestleMania X	Razor Ramon vs. Shawn Michaels
16-04-94	NJPW	Super J Cup '94	The Great Sasuke vs. Wild Pegasus
21-05-94	AJPW	Super Power Series	Mitsuharu Misawa[10] & Kenta Kobashi[12] vs. Akira Taue[8] & Toshiaki Kawada[11]
03-06-94	AJPW	Budokan Hall Show	Mitsuharu Misawa[11] vs. Toshiaki Kawada[12]
08-07-94	NJPW	Summer Struggle	The Great Sasuke[2] vs. Jushin Liger[3]
29-08-94	WWF	SummerSlam '94	Bret Hart vs. Owen Hart
09-10-94	AJW	Wrestlemarinepiad '94	Kyoko Inoue[6] & Takako Inoue[3] vs. Manami Toyota[7] & Toshiyo Yamada[6]
06-11-94	AAA	When Worlds Collide	El Hijo Del Santo & Octagon vs. Art Barr & Eddy Guerrero
20-11-94	AJW	Doumu Super Woman Great War	Aja Kong[2] vs. Manami Toyota[8]
30-11-94	AAA	House Show	Juventud Guerrera vs. Rey Misterio Jr.
19-01-95	AJPW	New Year Giant Series	Kenta Kobashi[13] vs. Toshiaki Kawada[13]
24-01-95	AJPW	New Year Giant Series	Kenta Kobashi[14] & Mitsuharu Misawa[12] vs. Akira Taue[9] & Toshiaki Kawada[14]
04-03-95	AJPW	Excite Series	Kenta Kobashi[15] & Mitsuharu Misawa[13] vs. Johnny Ace & Steve Williams[2]
15-04-95	AJPW	Champion Carnival	Akira Taue[10] vs. Mitsuharu Misawa[14]
07-05-95	AJW	G*Top 2nd	Kyoko Inoue[7] vs. Manami Toyota[9]
09-06-95	AJPW	Super Power Series	Akira Taue[11] & Toshiaki Kawada[15] vs. Kenta Kobashi[16] & Mitsuharu Misawa[15]
27-06-95	AJW	Zenjo Movement	Aja Kong[3] vs. Manami Toyota[10]
30-06-95	AJPW	Summer Action Series	Kenta Kobashi[17], Mitsuharu Misawa[16] & Satoru Asako vs. Akira Taue[12], Tamon Honda & Toshiaki Kawada[16]
23-07-95	AJW	Japan Grand Prix	Manami Toyota[11] vs. Mima Shimoda
30-08-95	AJW	WWWA Champions Night	Kyoko Inoue[8] & Takako Inoue[4] vs. Manami Toyota[12] & Sakie Hasegawa[2]
02-09-95	AJW	Destiny	Akira Hokuto[5] vs. Manami Toyota[13]
22-09-95	AAA	House Show	Psicosis vs. Rey Misterio Jr.[2]
09-03-96	ECW	Big Ass Extreme Bash '96	Juventus Guerrera[2] vs. Rey Misterio Jr.[3]
23-05-96	AJPW	Super Power Series	Jun Akiyama[2] & Mitsuharu Misawa[17] vs. Akira Taue[13] & Toshiaki Kawada[17]
07-06-96	AJPW	Super Power Series	Jun Akiyama[3] & Mitsuharu Misawa[18] vs. Johnny Ace[2] & Steve Williams[3]
10-10-96	MPW	3rd Anniversary	Dick Togo, Men's Teioh, Shiryu, Shoichi Funaki & Taka Michinoku vs. Gran Hamada, Gran Naniwa, Masato Yakushiji, Super Delfin & Tiger Mask IV
06-12-96	AJPW	Real World Tag League	Akira Taue[14] & Toshiaki Kawada[18] vs. Jun Akiyama[4] & Mitsuharu Misawa[19]
23-03-97	WWF	WrestleMania XIII	Bret Hart[2] vs. Steve Austin[2]
05-06-97	NJPW	Best Of The Super Juniors IV	El Samurai[2] vs. Koji Kanemoto
06-06-97	AJPW	Super Power Series	Mitsuharu Misawa[20] vs. Toshiaki Kawada[19]
05-10-97	WWF	In Your House 18: Badd Blood	Shawn Michaels[2] vs. The Undertaker
05-12-97	AJPW	Real World Tag League	Akira Taue[15] & Toshiaki Kawada[20]
27-06-98	RINGS	Fourth Fighting Integration	Kiyoshi Tamura vs. Tsuyoshi Kohsaka
31-10-98	AJPW	26th Anniversary Show	Kenta Kobashi[18] vs. Mitsuharu Misawa[21]
11-06-99	AJPW	Super Power Series	Kenta Kobashi[19] & Mitsuharu Misawa[22] vs. Jun Akiyama[5] & Mitsuharu Misawa[23]
23-10-99	AJPW	October Giant Series	Jun Akiyama[6] & Kenta Kobashi[20] vs. Yoshinari Ogawa[3] & Mitsuharu Misawa[24]
14-12-00	NJPW	The 2nd Judgement!!	Masanobu Fuchi[7] & Toshiaki Kawada[21] vs. Takashi Iizuka & Yuji Nagata
01-03-03	NOAH	Navigate For Evolution '03	Kenta Kobashi[21] vs. Mitsuharu Misawa[25]
10-07-04	NOAH	Departure '04	Jun Akiyama[7] vs. Kenta Kobashi[22]
16-10-04	ROH	Joe Vs. Punk II	CM Punk vs. Samoa Joe
11-09-05	TNA	Unbreakable '05	AJ Styles vs. Christopher Daniels vs. Samoa Joe[2]
01-10-05	ROH	Joe Vs. Kobashi	Kenta Kobashi[23] vs. Samoa Joe[3]
31-03-06	ROH	Supercard Of Honor '06	Dragon Kid, Genki Horiguchi & Ryo Saito vs. CIMA, Masato Yoshino & Naruki Doi
17-07-11	WWE	Money In The Bank '11	CM Punk[2] vs. John Cena0
31-03-12	ROH	Showdown In The Sun	Davey Richards vs. Michael Elgin
08-10-12	NJPW	King Of Pro Wrestling	Hiroshi Tanahashi vs. Minoru Suzuki
06-04-13	NJPW	Invasion Attack	Hiroshi Tanahashi[2] vs. Kazuchika Okada[2]
03-08-13	NJPW	G1 Climax 23	Katsuyori Shibata vs. Tomohiro Ishii
14-10-13	NJPW	King Of Pro Wrestling '13	Hiroshi Tanahashi[3] vs. Kazuchika Okada[3]
21-09-14	NJPW	Destruction In Kobe '14	Hiroshi Tanahashi[4] vs. Katsuyori Shibata[2]
04-01-15	NJPW	Wrestle Kingdom 9	Kota Ibushi vs. Shinsuke Nakamura
14-02-15	NJPW	The New Beginning In Sendai '15	Tomoaki Honma vs. Tomohiro Ishii[2]
16-08-15	NJPW	G1 Climax 25	Hiroshi Tanahashi[5] vs. Shinsuke Nakamura[2]
01-11-15	DG	Gate Of Destiny '15	Masaaki Mochizuki vs. Shingo Takagi
04-01-16	NJPW	Wrestle Kingdom 10	Hiroshi Tanahashi[6] vs. Kazuchika Okada[4]
06-08-16	NJPW	G1 Climax 26	Kazuchika Okada[4] vs. Tomohiro Ishii[3]
13-08-16	NJPW	G1 Climax 26	Kenny Omega vs. Tetsuya Naito
03-09-16	PWG	Battle Of Los Angeles '16	Matt Sydal, Ricochet & Will Ospreay vs. Adam Cole, Matt Jackson & Nick Jackson
04-01-17	NJPW	Wrestle Kingdom XI	Kazuchika Okada[5] vs. Kenny Omega[2]
11-02-17	NJPW	The New Beginning In Osaka '17	Michael Elgin[2] vs. Tetsuya Naito[2]
09-04-17	NJPW	Sakura Genesis '17	Katsuyori Shibata[3] vs. Kazuchika Okada[6]
03-06-17	NJPW	Best Of The Super Juniors XXIV	KUSHIDA vs. Will Ospreay[2]
11-06-17	NJPW	Dominion '17	Kazuchika Okada[7] vs. Kenny Omega[3]

Date	Promotion	Event	Match
11-08-17	NJPW	G1 Climax 27	Hiroshi Tanahashi[7] vs. Tetsuya Naito[3]
12-08-17	NJPW	G1 Climax 27	Kazuchika Okada[8] vs. Kenny Omega[4]
13-08-17	NJPW	G1 Climax 27	Kenny Omega[5] vs. Tetsuyta Naito[4]
03-09-17	PWG	Battle Of Los Angeles 2017	Donovan Dijak vs. Keith Lee
21-10-17	PWG	All Star Weekend 13	Walter vs. Zack Sabre Jr.
04-01-18	NJPW	WrestleKingdom 12	Chris Jericho vs. Kenny Omega[6]
27-01-18	NXT	TakeOver: Philadelphia	Andrade Almas vs. Johnny Gargano
25-03-18	NJPW	Strong Style Evolved	Kenny Omega[7] & Kota Ibushi[2] vs. Matt Jackson[2] & Nick Jackson[2]
01-04-18	NJPW	Sakura Genesis '18	Marty Scurll vs. Will Ospreay[3]
07-04-18	NXT	Takeover: New Orleans	Adam Cole[2] vs. EC3 vs. Killian Dain vs. Lars Sullivan vs. Ricochet[2] vs. Velveteen Dream
07-04-18	NXT	Takeover: New Orleans	Johnny Gargano[2] vs. Tommaso Ciampa
14-04-18	WWW	Total Rumble 8	A-Kid vs. Zack Sabre Jr.[2]
04-05-18	NJPW	Wrestling Dontaku '18	Hiroshi Tanahashi[8] vs. Kazuchika Okada[9]
04-06-18	NJPW	Best Of The Super Juniors XXV	Hiromu Takahashi vs. Taiji Ishimori
09-06-18	NJPW	Dominion '18	Kazuchika Okada[10] vs. Kenny Omega[8]
11-07-18	NXT	NXT TV	Roderick Strong, Kyle O'Reilly vs. Trent Seven & Tyler Bate
15-07-18	NJPW	G1 Climax 28	Kenny Omega[9] vs. Tetsuya Naito[5]
19-07-18	NJPW	G1 Climax 28	Hirooki Goto vs. Kenny Omega[10]
21-07-18	NJPW	G1 Climax 28	Hirooki Goto[2] vs. Tomohiro Ishii[4]
04-08-18	NJPW	G1 Climax 28	Kenny Omega[11] vs. Tomohiro Ishii[5]
10-08-18	NJPW	G1 Climax 28	Hiroshi Tanahashi[9] vs. Kazuchika Okada[11]
11-08-18	NJPW	G1 Climax 28	Kenny Omega[12] vs. Kota Ibushi[3]
12-08-18	NJPW	G1 Climax 28	Hiroshi Tanahashi[10] vs. Kota Ibushi[4]
23-09-18	NJPW	Destruction In Kobe '18	Hiroshi Tanahashi[11] vs. Kazuchika Okada[12]
30-09-18	NJPW	Fighting Spirit Unleashed	Kenny Omega[13] & Kota Ibushi[5] vs. Kazuchika Okada[13] & Tomohiro Ishii[6]
15-12-18	NJPW	Road To Tokyo Dome '19	Kenny Omega[14] & Kota Ibushi[6] vs. Hiroshi Tanahashi[12] & Will Ospreay[4]
04-01-19	NJPW	WrestleKingdom 13	Hiroshi Tanahashi[13] vs. Kenny Omega[15]
24-03-19	NJPW	New Japan Cup '19	Kazuchika Okada[14] vs. SANADA
05-04-19	NXT	TakeOver: New York	Adam Cole[3] vs. Johnny Gargano[3]
23-05-19	NJPW	Best Of The Super Juniors XXVI	Bandido vs. Will Ospreay[5]
25-05-19	AEW	Double Or Nothing '19	Cody Rhodes vs. Dustin Rhodes[2]
01-06-19	NXT	TakeOver XXV	Adam Cole[4] vs. Johnny Gargano[4]
05-06-19	NJPW	Best Of The Super Juniors XXVI	Shingo Takagi[2] vs. Will Ospreay[6]
09-06-19	NJPW	Dominion '19	Dragon Lee vs. Will Ospreay[7]
18-07-19	NJPW	G1 Climax 29	Kota Ibushi[7] vs. Will Ospreay[8]
19-07-19	NJPW	G1 Climax 29	Jon Moxley vs. Tomohiro Ishii[7]
20-07-19	NJPW	G1 Climax 29	Kazuchika Okada[15] vs. Will Ospreay[9]
26-07-19	PWG	Sixteen	Bandido[2], Flamita & Rey Horus vs. Black Taurus, Laredo Kid & Puma King
03-08-19	NJPW	G1 Climax 29	Kazuchika Okada[16] vs. SANADA[2]
04-08-19	NJPW	G1 Climax 29	Shingo Takagi[3] vs. Tetsuya Naito[6]
08-08-19	NJPW	G1 Climax 29	Shingo Takagi[4] vs. Tomohiro Ishii[8]
10-08-19	NJPW	G1 Climax 29	Kazuchika Okada[17] vs. Kota Ibushi[8]
12-08-19	NJPW	G1 Climax 29	Jay White vs. Kota Ibushi[9]
31-08-19	NXT UK	TakeOver: Cardiff	Tyler Bate[2] vs. Walter[2]
31-08-19	AEW	All Out '19	Penta El Zero Miedo & Rey Fenix vs. Matt Jackson[3] & Nick Jackson[3]
22-09-19	PWG	Battle Of Los Angeles '19	Bandido[3] vs. Dragon Lee[2]
26-10-19	OTT	Fifth Year Anniversary	David Starr vs. Jordan Devlin
04-01-20	NJPW	Wrestle Kingdom 14	Hiromu Takahashi[2] vs. Will Ospreay[10]
04-01-20	NJPW	Wrestle Kingdom 14	Kazuchika Okada[18] vs. Kota Ibushi[10]
05-01-20	NJPW	Wrestle Kingdom 14	Kazuchika Okada[19] vs. Tetsuya Naito[7]
14-02-20	RevPro	High Stakes '20	Will Ospreay[11] vs. Zack Sabre Jr.[3]
29-02-20	AEW	Revolution '20	Hangman Page & Kenny Omega[16] vs. Matt Jackson[4] & Nick Jackson[4]
19-09-20	AEW	Dynamite	Chuck Taylor & Trent vs. Ortiz & Santana
27-09-20	NJPW	G1 Climax 30	Shingo Takagi[5] vs. Will Ospreay[12]
10-10-20	NJPW	G1 Climax 30	Kazuchika Okada[20] vs. Shingo Takagi[6]
10-10-20	NJPW	G1 Climax 30	Kota Ibushi[11] vs. Minoru Suzuki[2]
29-10-20	NXT UK	NXT UK TV	Ilja Dragunov vs. Walter[3]
07-11-20	AEW	Full Gear '20	Cash Wheeler & Dax Harwood vs. Matt Jackson[5] & Nick Jackson[5]
06-12-20	NOAH	The BEST ~ Final Chronicle '20 ~	Go Shiozaki vs. Takashi Sugiura
04-01-21	NJPW	Wrestle Kingdom 15	Kazuchika Okada[21] vs. Will Ospreay[13]
04-12-21	NJPW	Wrestle Kingdom 15	Kota Ibushi[12] vs. Tetsuya Naito[8]
05-01-21	NJPW	Wrestle Kingdom 15	Shingo Takagi[7] vs. Jeff Cobb
05-01-21	NJPW	Wrestle Kingdom 15	Kota Ibushi[13] vs. Jay White[2]
06-01-21	AEW	Dynamite	Kenny Omega[17] vs. Rey Fenix[2]
30-01-21	NJPW	The New Beginning In Nagoya '21	Hiroshi Tanahashi[14] vs. Shingo Takagi[8]
14-03-21	NJPW	New Japan Cup '21	Will Ospreay[14] vs. Zack Sabre Jr.[4]
21-03-21	NJPW	New Japan Cup '21	Will Ospreay[15] vs. Shingo Takagi[9]
14-04-21	AEW	Dynamite	Matt Jackson[6] & Nick Jackson[6] vs. Pac & Rey Fenix[3]
04-05-21	NJPW	Wrestling Dontaku '21	Will Ospreay[16] vs. Shingo Takagi[10]
12-06-21	STARDOM	Tokyo Dream Cinderella Special Edition	Utami Hayashishita vs. Syuri
25-07-21	NJPW	Wrestle Grand Slam In Tokyo Dome	Shingo Takagi[11] vs. Hiroshi Tanahashi[15]
22-08-21	NXT	TakeOver 36	Walter[4] vs. Ilja Dragunov[2]
05-09-21	AEW	All Out '21	Matt Jackson[7] & Nick Jackson[7] vs. Penta El Zero Miedo[2] & Rey Fenix[4]
18-09-21	NJPW	G1 Climax 31	Shingo Takagi[12] vs. Tomohiro Ishii[9]

22-09-21	AEW	Dynamite	Bryan Danielson vs. Kenny Omega[18]
09-10-21	AAA	Heroes Inmortales XIV	Pentagon Jr.[3] & Rey Fenix[5] vs. El Hijo del Vikingo & Laredo Kid[2]
13-11-21	AEW	Full Gear '21	Jungle Boy, Luchasaurus & Christian Cage vs. Adam Cole[5], Matt Jackson[8] & Nick Jackson[9]
13-11-21	AEW	Full Gear '21	Kenny Omega[19] vs. Hangman Page[2]
15-12-21	AEW	Dynamite: Winter Is Coming	Bryan Danielson[2] vs. Hangman Page[3]
05-01-22	NJPW	Wrestle Kingdom 16	Kazuchika Okada[22] vs. Will Ospreay[17]
26-01-22	AEW	Dynamite: Beach Break	Cody Rhodes[2] vs. Sammy Guevara
29-01-22	RevPro	High Stakes '22	Will Ospreay[18] vs. Michael Oku
21-03-22	NJPW	New Japan Cup '22	Will Ospreay[19] vs. Zack Sabre Jr.[5]
26-03-22	NJPW	New Japan Cup '22	Shingo Takagi[13] vs. Zack Sabre Jr.[6]
01-04-22	ROH	Supercard Of Honor '22	Cash Wheeler[2] & Dax Harwood[2] vs. Jay Briscoe & Mark Briscoe
29-05-22	AEW	Double Or Nothing '22	Bryan Danielson[3], Jon Moxley[2], Eddie Kingston, Santana[2] & Ortiz[2] vs. Chris Jericho[2], Daniel Garcia, Jake Hager, Angelo Parker & Matt Menard
03-06-22	AEW	Rampage	Matt Jackson[9] & Nick Jackson[9] vs. Penta Oscuro[4] & Rey Fenix[6]
05-06-22	WWE	Hell In A Cell '22	Cody Rhodes[3] vs. Seth Rollins
23-07-22	ROH	Death Before Dishonor '22	Cash Wheeler[3] & Dax Harwood[3] vs. Jay Briscoe[2] & Mark Briscoe[2]
06-08-22	NJPW	G1 Climax 32	Will Ospreay[20] vs. Shingo Takagi[14]
18-08-22	NJPW	G1 Climax 32	Will Ospreay[21] vs. Kazuchika Okada[23]
21-08-22	RevPro	Tenth Anniversary	Will Ospreay[22] vs. Ricky Knight Jr.
24-08-22	AEW	Dynamite	Will Ospreay[23], Kyle Fletcher & Mark Davis vs. Pac[2], Penta El Zero Miedo[5] & Rey Fenix[7]
03-09-22	WWE	Clash At The Castle	Gunther[5] vs. Sheamus
02-10-22	NJPW	Royal Quest II	Cash Wheeler[4] & Dax Harwood[4] vs. Kyle Fletcher[2] & Mark Davis[2]
15-10-22	AAA	TripleMania XXX	Rey Fenix[8] vs. El Hijo del Vikingo[2]
23-10-22	AAA	Showcenter Championship Round	Laredo Kid[3] vs. El Hijo del Vikingo[3]
05-11-22	NJPW	Battle Autumn '22	Will Ospreay[24] vs. Tetsuya Naito[9]
10-12-22	ROH	Final Battle '22	Cash Wheeler[5] & Dax Harwood[5] vs. Jay Briscoe[3] & Mark Briscoe[3]
19-12-22	JTO	50th Anniversary For TAKATaichi Together	Shingo Takagi[15] vs. Taichi

PROMOTION

1.	NJPW	80
2.	AJPW	35
3.	AJW	19
4.	WWF/WWE	16
5.	AEW	16
6.	WCW	7
7.	ROH	7
8.	AAA	6
9.	JCP	5
10.	PWG	5
11.	RevPro	3
12.	NOAH	3
13.	Stardom	1
14.	Impact/TNA	1
15.	JTO	1
16.	OTT	1
17.	ECW	1
18.	WWW	1
19.	RINGS	1
20.	CWF	1
21.	UWF	1

WRESTLER

1.	Mitsuharu Misawa	25
2.	Will Ospreay	24
3.	Kazuchika Okada	23
4.	Kenta Kobashi	23
5.	Toshiaki Kawada	21
6.	Kenny Omega	19
7.	Hiroshi Tanahashi	15
8.	Akira Taue	15
9.	Shingo Takagi	15
10.	Kota Ibushi	13
11.	Manami Toyota	13
12.	Ric Flair	12
13.	Matt Jackson	9
14.	Nick Jackson	9
15.	Tetsuya Naito	9
16.	Tomohiro Ishii	9
17.	Jumbo Tsuruta	8
18.	Kyoko Inoue	8
19.	Rey Fenix	8
20.	Jun Akiyama	7
21.	Masanobu Fuchi	7
22.	Zack Sabre Jr.	6
23.	Toshiyo Yamada	6
24.	Ricky Steamboat	5
25.	Penta El Zero M	5
26.	Cash Wheeler	5
27.	Dax Harwood	5
28.	Adam Cole	5
29.	Gunther	5
30.	Akira Hokuto	5
31.	Barry Windham	5

EVENTS DIRECTORY

In this section you will find results and match times from over 1,500 major wrestling supercards and television specials from the past 50 years, with show and match ratings given to every one of them based on the ITR Star Ratings Key above. We only have five ratings, we do not award negative stars or fractions. We consider both one star and five star ratings to be exceedingly rare and neither is ever awarded without serious consideration. The date listed is when the show aired (be it on television, closed circuit, pay-per-view or via a streaming service such as the WWE Network) rather than the live event date. "NA Buys" is the estimated number of pay-per-view buys the event generated in North America (not worldwide) where applicable. The PPV buy rate data in this section is amassed from a number of reputable sources and may differ considerably from numbers erroneously repeated online (which are often sourced from early estimates rather than final numbers), but thanks to the considerable research, we believe it to be the most accurate list of PPV buy rates ever assembled.

ITR STAR RATINGS KEY

Legendary
Excellent
Good/Average
Bad/Throwaway
Offensive

DATE	FED	EVENT	LOCATION	NA BUYS	RATING
03-06-73	WWWF	WWWF at Madison Square Garden (30-06-73)	New York City, NY	-	★★
29-04-74	WWWF	WWWF at Madison Square Garden (29-04-74)	New York City, NY	-	★★★
17-02-75	WWWF	WWWF at Madison Square Garden (17-02-75)	New York City, NY	-	★★★
17-03-75	WWWF	WWWF at Madison Square Garden (17-03-75)	New York City, NY	-	★★★
14-04-75	WWWF	WWWF at Madison Square Garden (14-04-75)	New York City, NY	-	★★
16-06-75	WWWF	WWWF at Madison Square Garden (16-06-75)	New York City, NY	-	★★
13-10-75	WWWF	WWWF at Madison Square Garden (13-10-75)	New York City, NY	-	★★★
02-02-76	WWWF	WWWF at Madison Square Garden (02-02-76)	New York City, NY	-	★★
01-03-76	WWWF	WWWF at Madison Square Garden (01-03-76)	New York City, NY	-	★★
07-08-76	WWWF	WWWF at Madison Square Garden (07-08-76)	New York City, NY	-	★★★
25-10-76	WWWF	WWWF at Madison Square Garden (25-10-76)	New York City, NY	-	★★★
07-03-77	WWWF	WWWF at Madison Square Garden (07-03-77)	New York City, NY	-	★★★
27-06-77	WWWF	WWWF at Madison Square Garden (27-06-77)	New York City, NY	-	★★
29-08-77	WWWF	WWWF at Madison Square Garden (29-08-77)	New York City, NY	-	★★
26-09-77	WWWF	WWWF at Madison Square Garden (26-09-77)	New York City, NY	-	★★★
24-10-77	WWWF	WWWF at Madison Square Garden (24-10-77)	New York City, NY	-	★★
19-12-77	WWWF	WWWF at Madison Square Garden (19-12-77)	New York City, NY	-	★★
18-02-78	WWWF	WWWF at Spectrum (18-02-78)	Philadelphia, PA	-	★★
20-03-78	WWWF	WWWF at Madison Square Garden (20-03-78)	New York City, NY	-	★★★
25-03-78	WWWF	WWWF at Spectrum (25-03-78)	Philadelphia, PA	-	★★★
28-08-78	WWWF	WWWF at Madison Square Garden (28-08-78)	New York City, NY	-	★★★
23-10-78	WWWF	WWWF at Madison Square Garden (23-10-78)	New York City, NY	-	★★★
16-12-78	WWWF	WWWF at Spectrum (16-12-78)	Philadelphia, PA	-	★★★
18-12-78	WWWF	WWWF at Madison Square Garden (18-12-78)	New York City, NY	-	★★★
17-03-79	WWWF	WWWF at Spectrum (17-03-79)	Philadelphia, PA	-	★★★
26-03-79	WWWF	WWWF at Madison Square Garden (26-03-79)	New York City, NY	-	★★★
28-04-79	WWF	WWF at Spectrum (28-04-79)	Philadelphia, PA	-	★★★★
26-05-79	WWF	WWF at Spectrum (26-05-79)	Philadelphia, PA	-	★★★
04-06-79	WWF	WWF at Madison Square Garden (04-06-79)	New York City, NY	-	★★★
23-06-79	WWF	WWF at Spectrum (23-06-79)	Philadelphia, PA	-	★★
21-07-79	WWF	WWF at Spectrum (21-07-79)	Philadelphia, PA	-	★★★
18-08-79	WWF	WWF at Spectrum (18-08-79)	Philadelphia, PA	-	★★
27-08-79	WWF	WWF at Madison Square Garden (27-08-79)	New York City, NY	-	★★★
24-09-79	WWF	WWF at Madison Square Garden (04-06-79)	New York City, NY	-	★★
20-10-79	WWF	WWF at Spectrum (20-10-79)	Philadelphia, PA	-	★★
22-10-79	WWF	WWF at Madison Square Garden (22-10-79)	New York City, NY	-	★★★
17-11-79	WWF	WWF at Spectrum (17-11-79)	Philadelphia, PA	-	★★
17-12-79	WWF	WWF at Madison Square Garden (17-12-79)	New York City, NY	-	★★★
12-01-80	WWF	WWF at Spectrum (12-01-80)	Philadelphia, PA	-	★★
21-01-80	WWF	WWF at Madison Square Garden (21-01-80)	New York City, NY	-	★★★
01-03-80	WWF	WWF at Spectrum (01-03-80)	Philadelphia, PA	-	★★★
24-03-80	WWF	WWF at Madison Square Garden (24-03-80)	New York City, NY	-	★★★
12-04-80	WWF	WWF at Spectrum (12-04-80)	Philadelphia, PA	-	★★★★
21-04-80	WWF	WWF at Madison Square Garden (21-04-80)	New York City, NY	-	★★★
10-05-80	WWF	WWF at Spectrum (10-05-80)	Philadelphia, PA	-	★★★
19-05-80	WWF	WWF at Madison Square Garden (19-05-80)	New York City, NY	-	★★★★
21-06-80	WWF	WWF at Spectrum (21-06-80)	Philadelphia, PA	-	★★★
26-07-80	WWF	WWF at Spectrum (26-07-80)	Philadelphia, PA	-	★★★
02-08-80	MSW	SuperDome Extravaganza	New Orleans, LA	-	★★★
03-08-80	CWF	Last Tangle In Tampa	Tampa, FL	-	★★★
09-08-80	WWF	Showdown At Shea '80	Flushing, NY	-	★★
23-08-80	WWF	WWF at Spectrum (23-08-80)	Philadelphia, PA	-	★★★
22-09-80	WWF	WWF at Madison Square Garden (22-09-80)	New York City, NY	-	★★
11-10-80	WWF	WWF at Spectrum (11-10-80)	Philadelphia, PA	-	★★★
20-10-80	WWF	WWF at Madison Square Garden (20-10-80)	New York City, NY	-	★★★
08-11-80	WWF	WWF at Spectrum (08-11-80)	Philadelphia, PA	-	★★
08-12-80	WWF	WWF at Madison Square Garden (08-12-80)	New York City, NY	-	★★★
13-12-80	WWF	WWF at Spectrum (13-12-80)	Philadelphia, PA	-	★★★
29-12-80	WWF	WWF at Madison Square Garden (29-12-80)	New York City, NY	-	★★★
10-01-81	WWF	WWF at Spectrum (10-01-81)	Philadelphia, PA	-	★★★
14-02-81	WWF	WWF at Spectrum (14-02-81)	Philadelphia, PA	-	★★
16-02-81	WWF	WWF at Madison Square Garden (16-02-81)	New York City, NY	-	★★★
22-02-81	WCCW	Wrestling Star Wars (February '81)	Dallas, TX	-	★★
16-03-81	WWF	WWF at Madison Square Garden (16-03-81)	New York City, NY	-	★★
21-03-81	WWF	WWF at Spectrum (21-03-81)	Philadelphia, PA	-	★★★
06-04-81	WWF	WWF at Madison Square Garden (06-04-81)	New York City, NY	-	★★
18-04-81	WWF	WWF at Spectrum (18-04-81)	Philadelphia, PA	-	★★
04-05-81	WWF	WWF at Madison Square Garden (04-05-81)	New York City, NY	-	★★★
23-05-81	WWF	WWF at Spectrum (23-05-81)	Philadelphia, PA	-	★★
04-06-81	WCCW	Wrestling Star Wars (June '81)	Dallas, TX	-	★★★
08-06-81	WWF	WWF at Madison Square Garden (08-06-81)	New York City, NY	-	★★★
20-06-81	WWF	WWF at Spectrum (20-06-81)	Philadelphia, PA	-	★★★
27-06-81	WWF	WWF at Capital Centre (27-06-81)	Landover, MD	-	★★

DATE	FED	EVENT	LOCATION	NA BUYS	RATING
20-07-81	WWF	WWF at Madison Square Garden (20-07-81)	New York City, NY	-	★★★
24-08-81	WWF	WWF at Madison Square Garden (24-08-81)	New York City, NY	-	★★★
21-09-81	WWF	WWF at Madison Square Garden (21-09-81)	New York City, NY	-	★★★
17-10-81	WWF	WWF at Spectrum (17-10-81)	Philadelphia, PA	-	★★★★
19-10-81	WWF	WWF at Madison Square Garden (19-10-81)	New York City, NY	-	★★★
14-11-81	WWF	WWF at Spectrum (14-11-81)	Philadelphia, PA	-	★★★
23-11-81	WWF	WWF at Madison Square Garden (23-11-81)	New York City, NY	-	★★
29-11-81	WWF	WWF at Capital Centre (29-11-81)	Landover, MD	-	★★
12-12-81	WWF	WWF at Spectrum (12-12-81)	Philadelphia, PA	-	★★
26-12-81	WCCW	Christmas Star Wars '81	Dallas, Texas	-	★★
16-01-82	WWF	WWF at Spectrum (16-01-82)	Philadelphia, PA	-	★★
18-01-82	WWF	WWF at Madison Square Garden (18-01-82)	New York City, NY	-	★★★
20-02-82	WWF	WWF at Spectrum (20-02-82)	Philadelphia, PA	-	★★★
14-03-82	WWF	WWF at Madison Square Garden (14-03-82)	New York City, NY	-	★★
20-03-82	WWF	WWF at Spectrum (20-03-82)	Philadelphia, PA	-	★★★
28-03-82	WWF	WWF at Capital Centre (28-03-82)	Landover, MD	-	★★★
17-04-82	WWF	WWF at Spectrum (17-04-82)	Philadelphia, PA	-	★★
22-05-82	WWF	WWF at Spectrum (22-05-82)	Philadelphia, PA	-	★★
05-06-82	WWF	WWF at Madison Square Garden (05-06-82)	New York City, NY	-	★★
06-06-82	WCCW	Star Wars - Superbowl Of Wrestling	Irving, TX	-	★★★
26-06-82	WWF	WWF at Spectrum (26-06-82)	Philadelphia, PA	-	★★
28-06-82	WWF	WWF at Madison Square Garden (28-06-82)	New York City, NY	-	★★★
31-07-82	WWF	WWF at Spectrum (31-07-82)	Philadelphia, PA	-	★★
02-08-82	WWF	WWF at Madison Square Garden (02-08-82)	New York City, NY	-	★★
15-08-82	WCCW	Wrestling Star Wars (August '82)	Dallas, TX	-	★★★★
30-08-82	WWF	WWF at Madison Square Garden (30-08-82)	New York City, NY	-	★★
18-09-82	WWF	WWF at Spectrum (18-09-82)	Philadelphia, PA	-	★★★
04-10-82	WWF	WWF at Madison Square Garden (04-10-82)	New York City, NY	-	★★
16-10-82	WWF	WWF at Spectrum (16-10-82)	Philadelphia, PA	-	★★
22-11-82	WWF	WWF at Madison Square Garden (22-11-82)	New York City, NY	-	★★
25-11-82	WWF	WWF at Spectrum (25-11-82)	Philadelphia, PA	-	★★★
25-12-82	AWA	Christmas Night '82	St. Paul, MN	-	★★★★
25-12-82	WCCW	Christmas Star Wars '82	Dallas, TX	-	★★★★
28-12-82	WWF	WWF at Madison Square Garden (28-11-82)	New York City, NY	-	★★
22-01-83	WWF	WWF at Madison Square Garden (22-01-83)	New York City, NY	-	★★
18-02-83	WWF	WWF at Madison Square Garden (18-02-83)	New York City, NY	-	★★★
19-02-83	WWF	WWF at Spectrum (19-02-83)	Philadelphia, PA	-	★★★
12-03-83	NWA/MACW	Final Conflict	Greensboro, NC	-	★★★★
19-03-83	WWF	WWF at Spectrum (19-03-83)	Philadelphia, PA	-	★★
20-03-83	WWF	WWF at Madison Square Garden (20-03-83)	New York City, NY	-	★★★
24-04-83	AWA	Super Sunday	St. Paul, MN	-	★★★
25-04-83	WWF	WWF at Madison Square Garden (25-04-83)	New York City, NY	-	★★★
30-04-83	WWF	WWF at Spectrum (30-04-83)	Philadelphia, PA	-	★★★
23-05-83	WWF	WWF at Madison Square Garden (23-05-83)	New York City, NY	-	★★★
28-05-83	WWF	WWF at Capital Centre (28-05-83)	Landover, MD	-	★★
04-06-83	WWF	WWF at Spectrum (04-06-83)	Philadelphia, PA	-	★★★
17-06-83	WCCW	Wrestling Star Wars '83	Dallas, TX	-	★★
16-07-83	WWF	WWF at Spectrum (16-07-83)	Philadelphia, PA	-	★★
23-07-83	WWF	WWF at Capital Centre (23-07-83)	Landover, MD	-	★★
30-07-83	WWF	WWF at Madison Square Garden (30-07-83)	New York City, NY	-	★★
13-08-83	WWF	WWF at Spectrum (13-08-83)	Philadelphia, PA	-	★★★
17-09-83	WWC	Aniversario	San Juan, Puerto Rico	-	★★★
24-09-83	WWF	WWF at Spectrum (24-09-83)	Philadelphia, PA	-	★★★
17-10-83	WWF	WWF at Madison Square Garden (17-10-83)	New York City, NY	-	★★★
22-10-83	WWF	WWF at Spectrum (22-10-83)	Philadelphia, PA	-	★★★
23-10-83	NWA	The Last Battle Of Atlanta	Atlanta, GA	-	★★★★
24-11-83	WWF	WWF at Spectrum (24-11-83)	Philadelphia, PA	-	★★★
24-11-83	WCCW	Thanksgiving Star Wars	Dallas, TX	-	★★★★
24-11-83	NWA	Starrcade '83	Greensboro, NC	-	★★★★★
04-12-83	GCW	NWA at The Omni (04-12-83)	Atlanta, GA	-	★★★
25-12-83	AWA	Christmas Night '83	St. Paul, MN	-	★★★
25-12-83	WCCW	Christmas Star Wars '83	Dallas, TX	-	★★★★
26-12-83	WWF	WWF at Madison Square Garden (26-12-83)	New York City, NY	-	★★★
21-04-84	WWF	WWF at Spectrum (21-04-84)	Philadelphia, PA	-	★★★
23-01-84	WWF	WWF at Madison Square Garden (23-01-84)	New York City, NY	-	★★★
18-02-84	WWF	WWF at Spectrum (18-02-84)	Philadelphia, PA	-	★★
20-02-84	WWF	WWF at Madison Square Garden (20-02-84)	New York City, NY	-	★★★★
17-03-84	NWA	Boogie Jam	Greensboro, NC	-	★★★★
25-03-84	WWF	WWF at Madison Square Garden (25-03-84)	New York City, NY	-	★★★
31-03-84	WWF	WWF at Spectrum (31-03-84)	Philadelphia, PA	-	★★
23-04-84	WWF	WWF at Madison Square Garden (23-04-84)	New York City, NY	-	★★★
05-05-84	WWF	WWF at Spectrum (05-05-84)	Philadelphia, PA	-	★★
06-05-84	WCCW	1st David Von Erich Memorial Parade of Champions	Irving, TX	-	★★★

DATE	FED	EVENT	LOCATION	NA BUYS	RATING
19-05-84	WWF	WWF at Capital Centre (19-05-84)	Landover, MD	-	★★
21-05-84	WWF	WWF at Madison Square Garden (21-05-84)	New York City, NY	-	★★★
02-06-84	WWF	WWF at Spectrum (02-06-84)	Philadelphia, PA	-	★★
09-06-84	WWF	WWF at Capital Centre (09-06-84)	Landover, MD	-	★★
16-06-84	WWF	WWF at Madison Square Garden (16-06-84)	New York City, NY	-	★★★★
07-07-84	WWF	WWF at Spectrum (07-07-84)	Philadelphia, PA	-	★★
15-07-84	WWF	WWF at Meadowlands Arena (15-07-84)	East Rutherford, NJ	-	★★★
23-07-84	WWF	The Brawl To End It All	New York City, NY	-	★★★
28-07-84	WWF	WWF at Capital Centre (28-07-84)	Landover, MD	-	★★★
04-08-84	WWF	WWF at Spectrum (04-08-84)	Philadelphia, PA	-	★★
10-08-84	WWF	WWF at Kiel Auditorium (10-08-84)	St. Louis, MO	-	★★
25-08-84	WWF	WWF at Madison Square Garden (25-08-84)	New York City, NY	-	★★
01-09-84	WWF	WWF at Spectrum (01-09-84)	Philadelphia, PA	-	★★
22-09-84	WWF	WWF at Madison Square Garden (22-09-84)	New York City, NY	-	★★
23-09-84	WWF	WWF at Maple Leaf Gardens (23-09-84)	Toronto, Canada	-	★★★
13-10-84	WWF	WWF at Spectrum (13-10-84)	Philadelphia, PA	-	★★
14-10-84	WWF	WWF at Meadowlands Arena (14-10-84)	East Rutherford, NJ	-	★★★
21-10-84	WWF	WWF at Maple Leaf Gardens (21-10-84)	Toronto, Canada	-	★★
22-10-84	WWF	WWF at Maple Leaf Gardens (22-10-84)	Toronto, Canada	-	★★
27-10-84	WCCW	1st Cotton Bowl Extravaganza	Dallas, TX	-	★★
10-11-84	WWF	WWF at Spectrum (10-11-84)	Philadelphia, PA	-	★★
22-11-84	WCCW	Thanksgiving Star Wars '84	Dallas, TX	-	★★★
22-11-84	NWA	Starrcade '84	Greensboro, NC	-	★★
26-11-84	WWF	WWF at Madison Square Garden (26-11-84)	New York City, NY	-	★★★
01-12-84	WWF	WWF at Spectrum (01-12-84)	Philadelphia, PA	-	★★
10-12-84	WWF	WWF at Meadowlands Arena (10-12-84)	East Rutherford, NJ	-	★★
25-12-84	AWA	Christmas Night '84	St. Paul, MN	-	★★★★
25-12-84	WCCW	Christmas Star Wars '84	Dallas, TX	-	★★
28-12-84	WWF	WWF at Madison Square Garden (28-12-84)	New York City, NY	-	★★★★
12-01-85	WWF	WWF at Spectrum (12-01-85)	Philadelphia, PA	-	★★
21-01-85	WWF	WWF at Madison Square Garden (21-01-85)	New York City, NY	-	★★
16-02-85	WWF	WWF at Spectrum (16-02-85)	Philadelphia, PA	-	★★
18-02-85	WWF	The War To Settle The Score	New York City, NY	-	★★
24-02-85	AWAWCCW	Star Wars (February '85)	East Rutherford, NJ	-	★★★
17-03-85	WWF	WWF at Madison Square Garden (17-03-85)	New York City, NY	-	★★
17-03-85	WWF	WWF at Spectrum (17-03-85)	Philadelphia, PA	-	★★★
31-03-85	WWF	WrestleMania	New York, NY	23,000	★★
19-04-85	AWA	Meadowlands Mayhem	East Rutherford, NJ	-	★★
21-04-85	AWA	StarCage '85	St. Paul, MN	-	★★★
21-04-85	WWF	WWF at Maple Leaf Gardens (21-04-85)	Toronto, Canada	-	★★★
22-04-85	WWF	WWF at Madison Square Garden (22-04-85)	New York City, NY	-	★★★★
27-04-85	WWF	WWF at Spectrum (27-04-85)	Philadelphia, PA	-	★★★
05-05-85	WCCW	2nd David Von Erich Memorial Parade Of Champions	Irving, TX	-	★★★
11-05-85	WWF	Saturday Night's Main Event I	Uniondale, NY	-	★★
18-05-85	WWF	WWF at Boston Garden (18-05-85)	Boston, MA	-	★★
20-05-85	WWF	WWF at Madison Square Garden (20-05-85)	New York City, NY	-	★★
25-05-85	WWF	WWF at Spectrum (25-05-85)	Philadelphia, PA	-	★★★
21-06-85	WWF	WWF at Madison Square Garden (21-06-85)	New York City, NY	-	★★
22-06-85	WWF	WWF at Boston Garden (22-06-85)	Boston, MA	-	★★
29-06-85	WWF	WWF at Spectrum (29-06-85)	Philadelphia, PA	-	★★
06-07-85	NWA	Great American Bash '85	Charlotte, NC	-	★★★
13-07-85	WWF	WWF at Madison Square Garden (13-07-85)	New York City, NY	-	★★★
27-07-85	WWF	WWF at Spectrum (27-07-85)	Philadelphia, PA	-	★★
28-07-85	WWF	WrestleFest '85	Tulsa, OK	-	★★★
03-08-85	WWF	WWF at Boston Garden (03-08-85)	Boston, MA	-	★★
03-08-85	PPW	Hot Summer Night	Honolulu, HI	-	★★★
10-08-85	WWF	WWF at Madison Square Garden (10-08-85)	New York City, NY	-	★★★★
17-08-85	WWF	WWF at Capital Centre (17-08-85)	Landover, MD	-	★★
18-08-85	WWF	WWF at Maple Leaf Gardens (18-08-85)	Toronto, Canada	-	★★
24-08-85	WWF	WWF at Spectrum (24-08-85)	Philadelphia, PA	-	★★
26-08-85	AWA	Wrestling For A Cure	Boston, MA	-	★★
02-09-85	CWF	Battle Of The Belts I	Tampa, FL	-	★★★
07-09-85	WWF	WWF at Boston Garden (07-09-85)	Boston, MA	-	★★
22-09-85	WWF	WWF at Maple Leaf Gardens (22-09-85)	Toronto, Canada	-	★★
23-09-85	WWF	WWF at Madison Square Garden (23-09-85)	New York City, NY	-	★★★
28-09-85	WWF	WWF at Spectrum (28-09-85)	Philadelphia, PA	-	★★★
28-09-85	AWA	SuperClash '85	Chicago, IL	-	★★
05-10-85	WWF	Saturday Night's Main Event II	East Rutherford, NJ	-	★★
06-10-85	WCCW	2nd Cotton Bowl Extravaganza	Dallas, TX	-	★★
12-10-85	WWF	WWF at Boston Garden (12-10-85)	Boston, MA	-	★★
13-10-85	WWF	WWF at Maple Leaf Gardens (13-10-85)	Toronto, Canada	-	★★
19-10-85	WWF	WWF at Hiram Bithorn Stadium	San Juan, Puerto Rico	-	★
21-10-85	WWF	WWF at Madison Square Garden (21-10-85)	New York City, NY	-	★★

DATE	FED	EVENT	LOCATION	NA BUYS	RATING
26-10-85	WWF	WWF at Spectrum (26-10-85)	Philadelphia, PA	-	★★
02-11-85	WWF	Saturday Night's Main Event III	Hershey, PA	-	★★
07-11-85	WWF	The Wrestling Classic	Rosemont, IL	52,000	★★
09-11-85	WWF	WWF at Boston Garden (09-11-85)	Boston, MA	-	★★★
22-11-85	WWF	WWF at Spectrum (22-11-85)	Philadelphia, PA	-	★★
25-11-85	WWF	WWF at Madison Square Garden (25-11-85)	New York City, NY	-	★★★
28-11-85	WCCW	Thanksgiving Star Wars '85	Dallas, TX	-	★★★
28-11-85	NWA	Starrcade '85	Greensboro/Atlanta	-	★★★★★
07-12-85	WWF	WWF at Boston Garden (07-12-85)	Boston, MA	-	★★★
07-12-85	WWF	WWF at Spectrum (07-12-85)	Philadelphia, PA	-	★★★
15-12-85	WWF	WWF at Maple Leaf Gardens (15-12-85)	Toronto, Canada	-	★★
25-12-85	WWF	Christmas Star Wars '85	Dallas, TX	-	★★
29-12-85	NWA/AWA	Nite Of Champions II	East Rutherford, NJ	-	★★★
30-12-85	WWF	WWF at Madison Square Garden (30-12-85)	New York City, NY	-	★★
04-01-86	WWF	Saturday Night's Main Event IV	Tampa, FL	-	★★★
11-01-86	WWF	WWF at Boston Garden (11-01-86)	Boston, MA	-	★★★★
11-01-86	WWF	WWF at Spectrum (11-01-86)	Philadelphia, PA	-	★★
27-01-86	WWF	WWF at Madison Square Garden (27-01-86)	New York City, NY	-	★★★
02-02-86	NWA	Superstars On The Superstation	Atlanta, GA	-	★★★★
08-02-86	WWF	WWF at Boston Garden (08-02-86)	Boston, MA	-	★★★★
08-02-86	WWF	WWF at Spectrum (08-02-86)	Philadelphia, PA	-	★★★
14-02-86	CWF/NWA	Battle Of The Belts II	Orlando, FL	-	★★★★
17-02-86	WWF	WWF at Madison Square Garden (17-02-86)	New York City, NY	-	★★★
28-02-86	WWF	WWF at Sydney Entertainment Centre	Sydney, Australia	-	★★
01-03-86	WWF	Saturday Night's Main Event V	Phoenix, AZ	-	★★
08-03-86	WWF	WWF at Boston Garden (08-03-86)	Boston, MA	-	★★★
16-03-86	WWF	WWF at Madison Square Garden (16-03-86)	New York City, NY	-	★★★
23-03-86	WWF	WWF at Maple Leaf Gardens (23-03-86)	Toronto, Canada	-	★★
30-03-86	WWF	WWF at Spectrum (30-03-86)	Philadelphia, PA	-	★★
07-04-86	WWF	WrestleMania II	Uniondale/Rosemont/LA	382,000	★★
19-04-86	NWA	Crockett Cup '86	New Orleans, LA	-	★★★
20-04-86	AWA	WrestleRock '86	Minneapolis, MN	-	★★★
22-04-86	WWF	WWF at Madison Square Garden (22-04-86)	New York City, NY	-	★★★
26-04-86	WWF	WWF at Joe Louis Arena (26-04-86)	Detroit, MI	-	★★
26-04-86	WWF	WWF at Boston Garden (26-04-86)	Boston, MA	-	★★
03-05-86	WWF	Saturday Night's Main Event VI	Providence, RI	-	★★★★
04-05-86	WCCW	3rd David Von Erich Memorial Parade Of Champions	Irving, Texas	-	★★★
04-05-86	WWF	WWF at Maple Leaf Gardens (04-05-86)	Toronto, Canada	-	★★★
19-05-86	WWF	WWF at Madison Square Garden (19-05-86)	New York City, NY	-	★★
24-05-86	WWF	WWF at Boston Garden (24-05-86)	Boston, MA	-	★★
31-05-86	WWF	WWF at Spectrum (31-05-86)	Philadelphia, PA	-	★★★
14-06-86	WWF	WWF at Madison Square Garden (14-06-86)	New York City, NY	-	★★
27-06-86	WWF	WWF at Boston Garden (27-06-86)	Boston, MA	-	★★
28-06-86	AWA	Battle By The Bay	Oakland, CA	-	★★
28-06-86	WWF	WWF at Spectrum (28-06-86)	Philadelphia, PA	-	★★
05-07-86	NWA	Great American Bash '86 (Charlotte)	Charlotte, NC	-	★★★
12-07-86	WWF	WWF at Madison Square Garden (12-07-86)	New York City, NY	-	★★★
26-07-86	WWF	WWF at Spectrum (26-07-86)	Philadelphia, PA	-	★★★
26-07-86	NWA	Great American Bash '86 (Greensboro)	Greensboro, NC	-	★★★
27-07-86	WWF	WWF at Maple Leaf Gardens (27-07-86)	Toronto, Canada	-	★★★
09-08-86	WWF	WWF at Boston Garden (09-08-86)	Boston, MA	-	★★★
23-08-86	WWF	WWF at Spectrum (23-08-86)	Philadelphia, PA	-	★★
25-08-86	WWF	WWF at Madison Square Garden (25-08-86)	New York City, NY	-	★★
28-08-86	WWF	The Big Event	Toronto, Canada	-	★★
01-09-86	WCCW	Labor Day Star Wars '86	Fort Worth, TX	-	★★
01-09-86	CWF/NWA	Battle Of The Belts III	Daytona Beach, FL	-	★★★
06-09-86	WWF	WWF at Boston Garden (06-09-86)	Boston, MA	-	★★
22-09-86	WWF	WWF at Madison Square Garden (22-09-86)	New York City, NY	-	★★★
04-10-86	WWF	WWF at Boston Garden (04-10-86)	Boston, MA	-	★★
04-10-86	WWF	Saturday Night's Main Event VII	Richfield, OH	-	★★★
12-10-86	WCCW	3rd Cotton Bowl Extravaganza	Dallas, TX	-	★★★
18-10-86	WWF	WWF at Spectrum (18-10-86)	Philadelphia, PA	-	★★
19-10-86	WWF	WWF at Houston Summit (19-10-86)	Houston, TX	-	★★
20-10-86	WWF	WWF at Madison Square Garden (20-10-86)	New York City, NY	-	★★★
01-11-86	WWF	WWF at Boston Garden (01-11-86)	Boston, MA	-	★★★★
08-11-86	WWF	WWF at Spectrum (08-11-86)	Philadelphia, PA	-	★★
16-11-86	WWF	WWF at Maple Leaf Gardens (16-11-86)	Toronto, Canada	-	★★
24-11-86	WWF	WWF at Madison Square Garden (24-11-86)	New York City, NY	-	★★
26-11-86	WWF	WWF at Houston Summit (26-11-86)	Houston, TX	-	★★
27-11-86	NWA	Starrcade '86	Grensboro, NC	-	★★★
29-11-86	WWF	Saturday Night's Main Event VIII	Los Angeles, CA	-	★★★
06-12-86	WWF	WWF at Boston Garden (06-12-86)	Boston, MA	-	★★
13-12-86	WWF	WWF at Spectrum (13-12-86)	Philadelphia, PA	-	★★

DATE	FED	EVENT	LOCATION	NA BUYS	RATING
25-12-86	AWA	Brawl In St. Paul	St. Paul, MN	-	★★★★
26-12-86	WWF	WWF at Madison Square Garden (26-12-86)	New York City, NY	-	★★
03-01-87	WWF	WWF at Boston Garden (03-01-87)	Boston, MA	-	★★
03-01-87	WWF	Saturday Night's Main Event IX	Hartford, CT	-	★★★
10-01-87	WWF	WWF at Spectrum (10-01-87)	Philadelphia, PA	-	★★★
11-01-87	WWF	WWF at Maple Leaf Gardens (11-01-87)	Toronto, Canada	-	★★
19-01-87	WWF	WWF at Madison Square Garden (19-01-87)	New York City, NY	-	★★
07-02-87	WWF	WWF at Boston Garden (07-02-87)	Boston, MA	-	★★
14-02-87	WWF	WWF at Spectrum (14-02-87)	Philadelphia, PA	-	★★
15-02-87	WWF	WWF at Maple Leaf Gardens (15-02-87)	Toronto, Canada	-	★★★
23-02-87	WWF	WWF at Madison Square Garden (23-02-87)	New York City, NY	-	★★★
07-03-87	WWF	WWF at Boston Garden (07-03-87)	Boston, MA	-	★★
14-03-87	WWF	WWF at Spectrum (14-03-87)	Philadelphia, PA	-	★★★
14-03-87	WWF	Saturday Night's Main Event X	Detroit, MI	-	★★★
15-03-87	WWF	WWF at Maple Leaf Gardens (15-03-87)	Toronto, Canada	-	★★★
16-03-87	WWF	WWF at London Gardens (16-03-87)	London, Canada	-	★★
29-03-87	WWF	WrestleMania III	Pontiac, MI	663,000	★★★★★
10/11-04-87	NWA	Crockett Cup '87	Baltimore, MD	-	★★★
02-05-87	WWF	WWF at Boston Garden (02-05-87)	Boston, MA	-	★★
02-05-87	WWF	Saturday Night's Main Event XI	Notre Dame, IN	-	★★★★
02-05-87	AWA	SuperClash II	San Francisco, CA	-	★★
03-05-87	WCCW	4th David Von Erich Memorial Parade Of Champions	Irving, TX	-	★
09-05-87	WWF	WWF at Spectrum (09-05-87)	Philadelphia, PA	-	★★★
17-05-87	WWF	WWF at Maple Leaf Gardens (17-05-87)	Toronto, Canada	-	★★
18-05-87	WWF	WWF at Madison Square Garden (18-05-87)	New York City, NY	-	★★
06-06-87	WWF	WWF at Boston Garden (06-06-87)	Boston, MA	-	★★
14-06-87	WWF	WWF at Madison Square Garden (14-06-87)	New York City, NY	-	★★★
20-06-87	WWF	WWF at Spectrum (20-06-87)	Philadelphia, PA	-	★★
11-07-87	WWF	WWF at Boston Garden (11-07-87)	Boston, MA	-	★★
18-07-87	WWF	WWF at Spectrum (18-07-87)	Philadelphia, PA	-	★★
25-07-87	WWF	WWF at Madison Square Garden (25-07-87)	New York City, NY	-	★★★
31-07-87	NWA	Great American Bash '87 (Miami)	Miami, FL	-	★★★
15-08-87	WWF	WWF at Boston Garden (15-08-87)	Boston, MA	-	★★
15-08-87	WWF	WWF at Spectrum (15-08-87)	Philadelphia, PA	-	★★
22-08-87	WWF	WWF at Madison Square Garden (22-08-87)	New York City, NY	-	★★★
28-08-87	WWF	WWF at Sam Houston Coliseum	Houston, TX	-	★★★
12-09-87	WWF	WWF at Boston Garden (12-09-87)	Boston, MA	-	★★★
18-09-87	WWF	WWF at Spectrum (18-09-87)	Philadelphia, PA	-	★★★
21-09-87	WWF	WWF at Madison Square Garden (21-09-87)	New York City, NY	-	★★★
03-10-87	WWF	WWF at Boston Garden (03-10-87)	Boston, MA	-	★★
03-10-87	WWF	Saturday Night's Main Event XII	Hershey, PA	-	★★★★
09-10-87	WWF	WWF at Sam Houston Coliseum (09-10-87)	Houston, TX	-	★★★
10-10-87	WWF	WWF at Spectrum (10-10-87)	Philadelphia, PA	-	★★
16-10-87	WWF	WWF at Madison Square Garden (16-10-87)	New York City, NY	-	★★★
17-10-87	WCCW	4th Cotton Bowl Extravaganza	Dallas, TX	-	★★
23-10-87	WWF	WWF at Bercy Stadium (23-10-87)	Paris, France	-	★★
01-11-87	WWF	WWF at Maple Leaf Gardens (01-11-87)	Toronto, Canada	-	★★
06-11-87	WWF	WWF at Sam Houston Coliseum (06-11-87)	Houston, TX	-	★★
07-11-87	WWF	WWF at Boston Garden (07-11-87)	Boston, MA	-	★★
07-11-87	WWF	WWF at Spectrum (07-11-87)	Philadelphia, PA	-	★★
24-11-87	WWF	WWF at Madison Square Garden (24-11-87)	New York City, NY	-	★★★
26-11-87	NWA	Starrcade '87	Chicago, IL	20,000	★★
26-11-87	WWF	Survivor Series '87	Richfield, OH	525,000	★★★★
28-11-87	WWF	Saturday Night's Main Event XIII	Seattle, WA	-	★★★★
05-12-87	WWF	WWF at Spectrum (05-12-87)	Philadelphia, PA	-	★★
11-12-87	WWF	WWF at Sam Houston Coliseum (11-12-87)	Houston, TX	-	★★
12-12-87	WWF	WWF at Boston Garden (12-12-87)	Boston, MA	-	★★
25-12-87	AWA	Christmas Night '87	Minneapolis, MN	-	★★
25-12-87	WCCW	Christmas Star Wars '87	Dallas, TX	-	★★
26-12-87	WWF	WWF at Madison Square Garden (26-12-87)	New York City, NY	-	★★★
29-12-87	WWF	WWF at Copps Coliseum (29-12-87)	Hamilton, Canada	-	★★
02-01-88	WWF	Saturday Night's Main Event XIV	Landover, MD	-	★★
09-01-88	WWF	WWF at Spectrum (09-01-88)	Philadelphia, PA	-	★★★
09-01-88	WWF	WWF at Boston Garden (09-01-88)	Boston, MA	-	★★★
24-01-88	NWA	Bunkhouse Stampede '88	Uniondale, NY	200,000	★★
24-01-88	WWF	Royal Rumble '88	Hamilton, Canada	-	★★
25-01-88	WWF	WWF at Madison Square Garden (25-01-88)	New York City, NY	-	★★
05-02-88	WWF	The Main Event I	Indianapolis, IN	-	★★★★★
06-02-88	WWF	WWF at Boston Garden (06-02-88)	Boston, MA	-	★★★
06-02-88	WWF	WWF at Spectrum (06-02-88)	Philadelphia, PA	-	★★
22-02-88	WWF	WWF at Madison Square Garden (22-02-88)	New York City, NY	-	★★
05-03-88	WWF	WWF at Boston Garden (05-03-88)	Boston, MA	-	★★★
12-03-88	WWF	WWF at Spectrum (12-03-88)	Philadelphia, PA	-	★★★

DATE	FED	EVENT	LOCATION	NA BUYS	RATING
12-03-88	WWF	Saturday Night's Main Event XV	Nashville, TN	-	★★★★
13-03-88	WWF	WWF at Copps Coliseum (13-03-88)	Hamilton, Canada	-	★★★
27-03-88	NWA	Clash Of The Champions I	Greensboro, NC	-	★★★★★
27-03-88	WWF	WrestleMania IV	Atlantic City, NJ	909,000	★★★
02-04-88	WWF	WWF at Palatrussardi (02-04-88)	Milan, Italy	-	★★
22/23-04-88	NWA	Crockett Cup '88	Greenville/Greensboro, NC	-	★★
24-04-88	WWF	WWF at Maple Leaf Gardens (24-04-88)	Toronto, Canada	-	★★
25-04-88	WWF	WWF at Madison Square Garden (25-04-88)	New York City, NY	-	★★★
30-04-88	WWF	Saturday Night's Main Event XVI	Springfield, MA	-	★★
07-05-88	WWF	WWF at Boston Garden (07-05-88)	Boston, MA	-	★★★
21-05-88	WWF	WWF at Spectrum (21-05-88)	Philadelphia, PA	-	★★★
27-05-88	WWF	WWF at Madison Square Garden (27-05-88)	New York City, NY	-	★★
04-06-88	WWF	WWF at Boston Garden (04-06-88)	Boston, MA	-	★★
08-06-88	NWA	Clash Of The Champions II: Miami Mayhem	Miami, FL	-	★★
18-06-88	WWF	WWF at Spectrum (18-06-88)	Philadelphia, PA	-	★★
25-06-88	WWF	WWF at Madison Square Garden (25-06-88)	New York City, NY	-	★★
09-07-88	WWF	WWF at Boston Garden (09-07-88)	Boston, MA	-	★★★
10-07-88	NWA	Great American Bash '88	Baltimore, MD	190,000	★★★
15-07-88	WWF	WWF at LA Sports Arena (15-07-88)	Los Angeles, CA	-	★★
16-07-88	NWA	Great American Bash '88 (Greensboro)	Greensboro, NC	-	★★★★
23-07-88	WWF	WWF at Spectrum (23-07-88)	Philadelphia, PA	-	★★
24-07-88	WWF	WWF at Maple Leaf Gardens (24-07-88)	Toronto, Canada	-	★★
25-07-88	WWF	WWF at Madison Square Garden (25-07-88)	New York City, NY	-	★★★
31-07-88	WWF	WrestleFest '88	Milwaukee, WI	-	★★
06-08-88	WWF	WWF at Boston Garden (06-08-88)	Boston, MA	-	★★★
13-08-88	WWF	WWF at LA Sports Arena (13-08-88)	Los Angeles, CA	-	★★★
27-08-88	WWF	WWF at Spectrum (27-08-88)	Philadelphia, PA	-	★★★
29-08-88	WWF	SummerSlam '88	New York, NY	880,000	★★★
07-09-88	NWA	Clash Of The Champions III: Fall Brawl	Albany, GA	-	★★★
10-09-88	WWF	WWF at Boston Garden (10-09-88)	Boston, MA	-	★★
10-09-88	WWC	Aniversario '88 - A Hot Night In Bayamon	Bayamon, Puerto Rico	-	★★★
11-09-88	WWF	WWF at Meadowlands Arena	East Rutherford, NJ	-	★★★
18-09-88	WWF	WWF at Maple Leaf Gardens (18-09-88)	Toronto, Canada	-	★★★
18-09-88	AWA	The Road To SuperClash III	Louisville, KY	-	★★
24-09-88	WWF	WWF at Spectrum (24-09-88)	Philadelphia, PA	-	★★★
29-09-88	WWF	WWF at Madison Square Garden (29-09-88)	New York City, NY	-	★★
07-10-88	WWF	WWF at Bercy Stadium (07-10-88)	Paris, France	-	★★
09-10-88	WWF	WWF at Maple Leaf Gardens (09-10-88)	Toronto, Canada	-	★★
10-10-88	WWF	WWF at Boston Garden (10-10-88)	Boston, MA	-	★★
15-10-88	WWF	WWF at Palatrussardi (15-10-88)	Milan, Italy	-	★★
16-10-88	WWF	WWF at Palaeur (16-10-88)	Rome, Italy	-	★★
16-10-88	WWF	WWF at LA Sports Arena (16-10-88)	Los Angeles, CA	-	★★
24-10-88	WWF	WWF at Madison Square Garden (24-10-88)	New York City, NY	-	★★★
29-10-88	WWF	Saturday Night's Main Event XVII	Baltimore, MD	-	★★★
05-11-88	WWF	WWF at Boston Garden (05-11-88)	Boston, MA	-	★★
06-11-88	WWF	WWF at Maple Leaf Gardens (06-11-88)	Toronto, Canada	-	★★★
12-11-88	WWF	WWF at Spectrum (12-11-88)	Philadelphia, PA	-	★★
17-11-88	WWF	WWF at LA Sports Arena (17-11-88)	Los Angeles, CA	-	★★
24-11-88	WWF	Survivor Series '88	Richfield, OH	310,000	★★★★
26-11-88	WWF	WWF at Madison Square Garden (26-11-88)	New York City, NY	-	★★
26-11-88	WWF	Saturday Night's Main Event XVIII	Sacramento, CA	-	★★
03-12-88	WWF	WWF at Boston Garden (03-12-88)	Boston, MA	-	★★
04-12-88	WWF	WWF at Copps Coliseum (04-12-88)	Hamilton, Canada	-	★★
07-12-88	NWA	Clash Of The Champions IV: Season's Beatings	Chattanooga, TN	-	★★★
13-12-88	AWA	SuperClash III	Chicago, IL	45,000	★★
17-12-88	WWF	WWF at Spectrum (17-12-88)	Philadelphia, PA	-	★★
17-12-88	WWF	WWF at LA Sports Arena (17-12-88)	Los Angeles, CA	-	★★
26-12-88	NWA	Starrcade '88	Norfolk, VA	150,000	★★★★
30-12-88	WWF	WWF at Madison Square Garden (30-12-88)	New York City, NY	-	★★★
07-01-89	WWF	Saturday Night's Main Event XIX	Tampa, FL	-	★★★
13-01-89	WWF	WWF at Boston Garden (13-01-89)	Boston, MA	-	★★
14-01-89	WWF	WWF at Spectrum (14-01-89)	Philadelphia, PA	-	★★
15-01-89	WWF	Royal Rumble '89	Houston, TX	420,000	★★
23-01-89	WWF	WWF at Madison Square Garden (23-01-89)	New York City, NY	-	★★★
29-01-89	WWF	WWF at LA Sports Arena (29-01-89)	Los Angeles, CA	-	★★
03-02-89	WWF	The Main Event II	Milwaukee, WI	-	★★★★★
11-02-89	WWF	WWF at Boston Garden (11-02-89)	Boston, MA	-	★★
11-02-89	WWF	WWF at Spectrum (11-02-89)	Philadelphia, PA	-	★★
15-02-89	NWA	Clash Of The Champions V: St. Valentine's Massacre	Cleveland, OH	-	★
20-02-89	WWF	WWF at Madison Square Garden (20-02-89)	New York City, NY	-	★★★
20-02-89	NWA	Chi-Town Rumble	Chicago, IL	130,000	★★★★
11-03-89	WWF	Saturday Night's Main Event XX	Hershey, PA	-	★★★★★
18-03-89	WWF	WWF at Madison Square Garden (18-03-89)	New York City, NY	-	★★★★

DATE	FED	EVENT	LOCATION	NA BUYS	RATING
18-03-89	WWF	WWF at Boston Garden (18-03-89)	Boston, MA	-	★★★★
02-04-89	NWA	Clash Of The Champions VI: Ragin' Cajun	New Orleans, LA	-	★★★★
02-04-89	WWF	WrestleMania V	Atlantic City, NJ	915,000	★★★
08-04-89	WWF	WWF at Palatrussardi (08-04-89)	Milan, Italy	-	★★★
22-04-89	WWF	WWF at Boston Garden (22-04-89)	Boston, MA	-	★★
23-04-89	WWF	WWF at Maple Leaf Gardens (23-04-89)	Toronto, Canada	-	★★
24-04-89	WWF	WWF at Madison Square Garden (24-04-89)	New York City, NY	-	★★★
01-05-89	WWF	WWF at Copps Coliseum (01-05-89)	Hamilton, Canada	-	★★★
06-05-89	AWA	Rage In Rochester	Rochester, MN	-	★★
07-05-89	NWA	WrestleWar '89	Nashville, TN	120,000	★★★
08-05-89	WWF	WWF at Meadowlands Arena (08-05-89)	East Rutherford, NJ	-	★★★
13-05-89	WWF	WWF at Boston Garden (13-05-89)	Boston, MA	-	★★
27-05-89	WWF	Saturday Night's Main Event XXI	Des Moines, IA	-	★★★★★
03-06-89	WWF	WWF at Boston Garden (03-06-89)	Boston, MA	-	★★★
10-06-89	WWF	WWF at Nassau Coliseum (10-06-89)	Long Island, NY	-	★★
14-06-89	NWA	Clash Of The Champions VII: Guts and Glory	Fort Bragg, NC	-	★★★
23-06-89	AWA	War In The Windy City	Chicago, IL	-	★★
10-07-89	WWF	WWF at Nassau Coliseum (10-07-89)	Long Island, NY	-	★★
23-07-89	NWA	Great American Bash '89	Baltimore, MD	140,000	★★★★★
29-07-89	WWF	Saturday Night's Main Event XXII	Worcester, MA	-	★★★★
28-08-89	WWF	SummerSlam '89	East Rutherford, NJ	812,000	★★★★
12-09-89	NWA	Clash Of The Champions VIII: Fall Brawl '89	Columbia, SC	-	★★★★
30-09-89	WWF	WWF at Madison Square Garden (30-09-89)	New York City, NY	-	★★
08-10-89	WWF	WWF at Maple Leaf Gardens (08-10-89)	Toronto, Canada	-	★★
10-10-89	WWF	WWF On Sky One	London, England	-	★★
13-10-89	WWF	WWF at Bercy Stadium (13-10-89)	Paris, France	-	★★★
14-10-89	WWF	Saturday Night's Main Event XXIII	Cincinnati, OH	-	★★★
28-10-89	NWA	Halloween Havoc '89	Philadelphia, PA	177,000	★★★★
28-10-89	WWF	WWF at Madison Square Garden (28-10-89)	New York City, NY	-	★★
12-11-89	WWF	Survivor Series Showdown (1989)	Wichita, KS	-	★★★
15-11-89	NWA	Clash Of The Champions IX: New York Knockout	Troy, NY	-	★★★★★
23-11-89	WWF	Survivor Series '89	Rosemont, IL	264,000	★★★
25-11-89	WWF	Saturday Night's Main Event XXIV	Topeka, KS	-	★★★
25-11-89	WWF	WWF at Madison Square Garden (25-11-89)	New York City, NY	-	★★★
13-12-89	NWA	Starrcade '89	Atlanta, GA	156,000	★★★
27-12-89	WWF	No Holds Barred: The Match/The Movie	Nashville, TN	440,000	★★
28-12-89	WWF	WWF at Madison Square Garden (28-12-89)	New York City, NY	-	★★
15-01-90	WWF	WWF at Madison Square Garden (15-01-90)	New York City, NY	-	★★★
21-01-90	WWF	Royal Rumble '90	Orlando, FL	260,000	★★★
27-01-90	WWF	Saturday Night's Main Event XXV	Chattanooga, TN	-	★★★
06-02-90	NWA	Clash Of The Champions X: Texas Shootout	Corpus Christi, TX	-	★★★
19-02-90	WWF	WWF at Madison Square Garden (19-02-90)	New York City, NY	-	★★
23-02-90	WWF	The Main Event III	Detroit, MI	-	★★
25-02-90	NWA	WrestleWar '90	Greensboro, NC	175,000	★★★
19-03-90	WWF	WWF at Madison Square Garden (19-03-90)	New York City, NY	-	★
25-03-90	WWF	The Ultimate Challenge	San Francisco, CA	-	★★
01-04-90	WWF	WrestleMania VI	Toronto, Canada	550,000	★★★
13-04-90	Various	Wrestling Summit	Tokyo, Japan	-	★★★
28-04-90	WWF	Saturday Night's Main Event XXVI	Austin, TX	-	★★★
30-04-90	WWF	WWF at Madison Square Garden (30-04-90)	New York City, NY	-	★★
19-05-90	NWA	Capital Combat '90	Washington, D.C.	160,000	★★★★
13-06-90	NWA	Clash Of The Champions XI: Coastal Crush	Charleston, SC	-	★★★
07-07-90	WWC	Aniversario '90	Bayamon, Puerto Rico	-	★★★
07-07-90	NWA	Great American Bash '90	Baltimore, MD	200,000	★★★★
28-07-90	WWF	Saturday Night's Main Event XXVII	Omaha, NE	-	★★★★
27-08-90	WWF	SummerSlam '90	Philadelphia, PA	507,000	★★★
05-09-90	NWA	Clash Of The Champions XII: Mountain Madness	Asheville, NC	-	★★
21-09-90	WWF	WWF at Madison Square Garden (21-09-90)	New York City, NY	-	★★
13-10-90	WWF	Saturday Night's Main Event XXVIII	Toledo, OH	-	★★
19-10-90	WWF	WWF at Madison Square Garden (19-10-90)	New York City, NY	-	★★
27-10-90	NWA	Halloween Havoc '90	Chicago, IL	160,000	★★★
18-11-90	WWF	Survivor Series Showdown (1990)	Indianapolis, IN	-	★★
20-11-90	NWA	Clash Of The Champions XIII: Thanksgiving Thunder	Jacksonville, FL	-	★
22-11-90	WWF	Survivor Series '90	Hartford, CT	400,000	★★★
23-11-90	WWF	The Main Event IV	Fort Wayne, IN	-	★★★
24-11-90	WWF	WWF at Madison Square Garden (24-11-90)	New York City, NY	-	★★
16-12-90	NWA	Starrcade '90	St. Louis, MO	165,000	★★★
28-12-90	WWF	WWF at Madison Square Garden (28-12-90)	New York City, NY	-	★★
19-01-91	WWF	Royal Rumble '91	Miami, FL	440,000	★★★★
21-01-91	WWF	WWF at Madison Square Garden (21-01-91)	New York City, NY	-	★★
30-01-91	WCW	Clash Of The Champions XIV: Dixie Dynamite	Gainesville, GA	-	★★
01-02-91	WWF	The Main Event V	Macon, GA	-	★★
24-02-91	WCW	WrestleWar '91	Phoenix, AZ	160,000	★★★★
15-03-91	WWF	WWF at Madison Square Garden (15-03-91)	New York City, NY	-	★★★
21-03-91	WCW/NJPW	Japan Supershow I	Tokyo, Japan	-	★★★★
24-03-91	WWF	WrestleMania VII	Los Angeles, CA	400,000	★★★★

DATE	FED	EVENT	LOCATION	NA BUYS	RATING
30-03-91	SWS/WWF	WrestleFest In Tokyo Dome	Tokyo, Japan	-	★★★
22-04-91	WWF	WWF at Madison Square Garden (22-04-91)	New York City, NY	-	★★
24-04-91	WWF	UK Rampage '91	London, England	-	★★
27-04-91	WWF	Saturday Night's Main Event XXIX	Omaha, NE	-	★★★
19-05-91	WCW	SuperBrawl I	St. Petersburg, FL	150,000	★★★
03-06-91	WWF	WWF at Madison Square Garden (03-06-91)	New York City, NY	-	★★
09-06-91	UWF	Beach Brawl	Palmetto, FL	3,000	★★
12-06-91	WCW	Clash Of The Champions XV: Knocksville USA	Knoxville, TN	-	★★★★
01-07-91	WWF	WWF at Madison Square Garden (01-07-91)	New York City, NY	-	★★
14-07-91	WCW	Great American Bash '91	Balitmore, MD	145,000	★
18-08-91	WWF	SummerSlam Spectacular (1991)	Worcester, MA	-	★★
26-08-91	WWF	SummerSlam '91	New York, NY	405,000	★★★★
05-09-91	WCW	Clash Of The Champions XVI: Fall Brawl	Augusta, GA	-	★★
03-10-91	WWF	Battle Royal At The Albert Hall	London, England	-	★★
05-10-91	WWF	WWF at Palau Sant Jordi (05-10-91)	Barcelona, Spain	-	★★★
27-10-91	WCW	Halloween Havoc '91	Chattanooga, TN	120,000	★★
28-10-91	WWF	WWF at Madison Square Garden (28-10-91)	New York City, NY	-	★★
19-11-91	WCW	Clash Of The Champions XVII	Savannah, GA	-	★★★
24-11-91	WWF	Survivor Series Showdown (1991)	Utica, NY	-	★★
27-11-91	WWF	Survivor Series '91	Detroit, MI	300,000	★★★
30-11-91	WWF	WWF at Madison Square Garden (30-11-91)	New York City, NY	-	★★★
03-12-91	WWF	This Tuesday In Texas	San Antonio, TX	140,000	★★★
12-12-91	SWS/WWF	SuperWrestle '91	Tokyo, Japan	-	★★
29-12-91	WWF	WWF at Madison Square Garden (29-12-91)	New York City, NY	-	★★
29-12-91	WCW	Starrcade '91	Norfolk, VA	155,000	★★
04-01-92	WCW/NJPW	Japan Supershow II	Tokyo, Japan	-	★★★
19-01-92	WWF	Royal Rumble '92	Albany, NY	260,000	★★★★★
21-01-92	WCW	Clash Of The Champions XVIII	Topeka, KS	-	★★★★
31-01-92	WWF	WWF at Madison Square Garden (31-01-92)	New York City, NY	-	★★
08-02-92	WWF	Saturday Night's Main Event XXX	Lubbock, TX	-	★★★
23-02-92	WWF	WWF at Madison Square Garden (23-02-92)	New York City, NY	-	★★
23-02-92	LPWA	Super Ladies Showdown	Rochester, MN	1,500	★★
29-02-92	WCW	SuperBrawl II	Milwaukee, WI	160,000	★★★★
23-03-92	WWF	WWF at Madison Square Garden (23-03-92)	New York City, NY	-	★★
29-03-92	WWF	March To WrestleMania VIII	Biloxi, MS	-	★★★
05-04-92	WWF	WrestleMania VIII	Indianapolis, IN	390,000	★★★★
04-04-92	WWF	European Rampage '92 (Munich)	Munich, Germany	-	★★
19-04-92	WWF	UK Rampage '92	Sheffield, England	-	★★
17-05-92	WCW	WrestleWar '92	Jacksonville, FL	105,000	★★★★★
22-05-92	SMW	Volunteer Slam I	Knoxville, TN	-	★★
20-06-92	WCW	Beach Blast '92	Mobile, AL	70,000	★★★★
22-06-92	WCW	Clash Of The Champions XIX	Charleston, NC	-	★★★
12-07-92	WCW	Great American Bash '92	Albany, GA	70,000	★★★
08-08-92	SMW	Fire On The Mountain '92	Johnson City, TN	-	★★★
23-08-92	WWF	SummerSlam Spectacular (1992)	Nashville, TN	-	★★★
29-08-92	WWF	SummerSlam '92	London, England	280,000	★★★★
02-09-92	WCW	Clash Of The Champions XX: 20th Anniversary	Atlanta, GA	-	★★★
25-10-92	WCW	Halloween Havoc '92	Philadelphia, PA	165,000	★★
14-11-92	WWF	Saturday Night's Main Event XXXI	Terre Haute, IN	-	★★★
18-11-92	WCW	Clash Of The Champions XXI	Macon, GA	-	★★★★
22-11-92	WWF	Survivor Series Showdown (1992)	Springfield, IL	-	★★
25-11-92	WWF	Survivor Series '92	Richfield, OH	250,000	★★★
28-12-92	WCW	Starrcade '92	Atlanta, GA	95,000	★★★
04-01-93	WCW	Japan Supershow III	Tokyo, Japan	-	★★★★
13-01-93	WCW	Clash Of The Champions XXII	Milwaukee, WI	-	★★★★
23-01-93	ECW	Battle Of The Belts	Philadelphia, PA	-	★★
24-01-93	WWF	Royal Rumble '93	Sacramento, CA	300,000	★★★
21-02-93	WCW	SuperBrawl III	Asheville, NC	95,000	★★★★★
05-03-93	GLOW	Reunion	Las Vegas, NV	-	★
28-03-93	WWF	March To WrestleMania IX	Fayeteville, NC	-	★★
02-04-93	SMW	Bluegrass Brawl '93	Pikeville, KY	-	★★★
04-04-93	WWF	WrestleMania IX	Paradise, NV	430,000	★★
08-04-93	WWF	Rampage Bercy '93	Paris, France	-	★★
11-04-93	WWF	UK Rampage '93	Sheffield, England	-	★
24-04-93	WWF	European Rampage '93 (Barcelona)	Barcelona, Spain	-	★★★
25-04-93	WWF	European Rampage '93 (Milan)	Milan, Italy	-	★★★
23-05-93	WCW	Slamboree '93	Atlanta, GA	100,000	★★★★
13-06-93	WWF	King Of The Ring '93	Dayton, OH	245,000	★★★★
16-06-93	WCW	Clash Of The Champions XXIII	Norfolk, VA	-	★★★
19-06-93	ECW	Super Summer Sizzler Spectacular	Philadelphia, PA	-	★★
18-07-93	WCW	Beach Blast '93	Biloxi, MS	100,000	★★
14-08-93	SMW	Fire On The Mountain '93	Johnson City, TN	-	★★★★
18-08-93	WCW	Clash Of The Champions XXIV	Daytona Beach, FL	-	★★★★
22-08-93	WWF	SummerSlam Spectacular (1993)	Poughkeepsie, NY	-	★★★★
30-08-93	WWF	SummerSlam '93	Auburn Hills, MI	195,000	★★★
18-09-93	ECW	Ultra Clash '93	Philadelphia, PA	-	★★
19-09-93	WCW	Fall Brawl '93	Houston, TX	95,000	★★
24-10-93	WCW	Halloween Havoc '93	New Orleans, LA	100,000	★★★
10-11-93	WCW	Clash Of The Champions XXV	St. Petersburgh, FL	-	★★★
20-11-93	WCW	Battlebowl '93	Pensacola, FL	55,000	★★

DATE	FED	EVENT	LOCATION	NA BUYS	RATING
21-11-93	WWF	Survivor Series Showdown (1993)	Bushkill, PA/Delhi, NY	-	★★
24-11-93	WWF	Survivor Series '93	Boston, MA	128,000	★★★
25-11-93	SMW	Thanksgiving Thunder '93	Hazard, KY	-	★★
27-12-93	WCW	Starrcade '93	Charlotte, NC	115,000	★★
22-01-94	WWF	Royal Rumble '94	Providence, RI	146,000	★★★★
27-01-94	WCW	Clash Of The Champions XXVI	Baton Rouge, LA	-	★★★
05-02-94	ECW	The Night The Line Was Crossed	Philadelphia, PA	-	★★
20-02-94	WCW	SuperBrawl IV	Albany, GA	110,000	★★
13-03-94	WWF	March To WrestleMania X	Poughkeepsie, NY	-	★★★
20-03-94	WWF	WrestleMania X	New York, NY	283,000	★★★★★
17-04-94	WCW	Spring Stampede '94	Chicago, IL	115,000	★★★★★
14-05-94	ECW	When Worlds Collide	Philadelphia, PA	-	★★
22-05-94	WCW	Slamboree '94	Philadelphia, PA	105,000	★★★★
19-06-94	WWF	King Of The Ring '94	Baltimore, MD	148,000	★★★
23-06-94	WCW	Clash Of The Champions XXVII	Charleston, SC	-	★★★
24-06-94	ECW	Hostile City Showdown '94	Philadelphia, PA	-	★★
16-07-94	ECW	Heat Wave '94	Philadelphia, PA	-	★★★
17-07-94	WCW	Bash At The Beach '94	Orlando, FL	225,000	★★★
05-08-94	SMW	Night Of Legends '94	Knoville, TN	-	★★★★
13-08-94	ECW	Hardcore Heaven '94	Philadelphia, PA	-	★★★
21-08-94	WWF	Sunday Night Slam I	Youngstown, OH	-	★★
24-08-94	WCW	Clash Of The Champions XXVIII	Cedar Rapids, IA	-	★★★
29-08-94	WWF	SummerSlam '94	Chicago, IL	235,000	★★★★
18-09-94	WCW	Fall Brawl '94	Roanoke, VA	115,000	★★★
23-09-94	UWF	Blackjack Brawl	Las Vegas, NV	-	★
23-10-94	WCW	Halloween Havoc '94	Detroit, MI	210,000	★★★
05-11-94	ECW	November To Remember '94	Philadelphia, PA	-	★★
06-11-94	AAA	When Worlds Collide	Los Angeles, CA	75,000	★★★★★
16-11-94	WCW	Clash Of The Champions XXIX	Jacksonville, FL	-	★★
20-11-94	WWF	Sunday Night Slam II	Bushkill, PA	-	★★★
23-11-94	WWF	Survivor Series '94	San Antonio, TX	169,000	★★★
27-12-94	WCW	Starrcade '94	Nashville, TN	130,000	★
22-01-95	WWF	Royal Rumble '95	Tampa, FL	194,000	★★★
25-01-95	WCW	Clash Of The Champions XXX	Paradise, NV	-	★★
04-02-95	ECW	Double Tables	Philadelpia, PA	-	★★★★
19-02-95	WCW	SuperBrawl V	Baltimore, MD	180,000	★★
25-02-95	ECW	Return Of The Funker	Philadelphia, PA	-	★★★★
19-03-95	WCW	Uncensored '95	Tupelo, MS	180,000	★
26-03-95	WWF	Sunday Night Slam III	Stockton, CA	-	★★
02-04-95	WWF	WrestleMania XI	Hartford, CT	261,000	★★
08-04-95	ECW	Three Way Dance	Philadelphia, PA	-	★★★
15-04-95	ECW	Hostile City Showdown '95	Philadelphia, PA	-	★★★
13-05-95	ECW	Enter Sandman	Philadelphia, PA	-	★★
14-05-95	WWF	In Your House 1: Premiere	Syracuse, NY	172,000	★★
21-05-95	WCW	Slamboree '95	St. Petersburg, FL	110,000	★★
17-06-95	ECW	Barbed Wire, Hoodies & Chokeslams	Philadelphia, PA	-	★
18-06-95	WCW	Great American Bash '95	Dayton, OH	100,000	★★★
25-06-95	WWF	King Of The Ring '95	Philadelphia, PA	139,000	★★
15-07-95	ECW	Heat Wave '95	Philadelphia, PA	-	★★★
16-07-95	WCW	Bash At The Beach '95	Huntington Beach, CA	160,000	★
23-07-95	WWF	In Your House 2: The Lumberjacks	Nashville, TN	155,000	★★★
04-08-95	WCW	Collision In Korea	Pyongyang, North Korea	-	★★★
05-08-95	ECW	Wrestlepalooza '95	Philadelphia, PA	-	★★
06-08-95	WCW	Clash Of The Champions XXXI	Daytona Beach, FL	-	★
27-08-95	WWF	SummerSlam '95	Pittsburgh, PA	205,000	★★★
16-09-95	ECW	Gangstas Paradise	Philadelphia, PA	-	★★★
17-09-95	WCW	Fall Brawl '95	Asheville, NC	95,000	★★★
24-09-95	WWF	In Your House 3: Triple Header	Saginaw, MI	162,000	★★★
22-10-95	WWF	In Your House 4: Great White North	Winnipeg, Canada	94,000	★★
29-10-95	WCW	Halloween Havoc '95	Detroit, MI	120,000	★★
18-11-95	ECW	November To Remember '95	Philadelphia, PA	-	★★★★
19-11-95	WWF	Survivor Series '95	Landover, MD	135,000	★★★★
26-11-95	WCW	World War 3 '95	Norfolk, VA	90,000	★★★
17-12-95	WWF	In Your House 5: Seasons Beatings	Hershey, PA	84,000	★★
27-12-95	WCW	Starrcade '95	Nashville, TN	75,000	★★★
29-12-95	ECW	Holiday Hell '95	New York City, NY	-	★★★
05-01-96	ECW	House Party '96	Philadelphia, PA	-	★★★
21-01-96	WWF	Royal Rumble '96	Fresno, CA	269,000	★★★
23-01-96	WCW	Clash Of The Champions XXXII	Paradise, NV	-	★★
03-02-96	ECW	Big Apple Blizzard Blast	New York City, NY	-	★★
11-02-96	WCW	SuperBrawl VI	St. Petersburg, FL	210,000	★★★
17-02-96	ECW	Cyberslam '96	Philadelphia, PA	-	★★★
18-02-96	WWF	In Your House 6: Rage In The Cage	Louisville, KY	186,000	★★★
23-02-96	ECW	Just Another Night	Glenolden, PA	-	★★★
24-03-96	WCW	Uncensored '96	Tupelo, MS	250,000	★
31-03-96	WWF	WrestleMania XII	Anaheim, CA	301,000	★★★
13-04-96	ECW	Massacre On Queens BLVD	New York City, NY	-	★★★
20-04-96	ECW	Hostile City Showdown	Philadelphia, PA	-	★★
28-04-96	WWF	In Your House 7: Good Friends, Better Enemies	Omaha, NE	165,000	★★★
11-05-96	ECW	A Matter Of Respect	Philadelphia, PA	-	★★★★
19-05-96	WCW	Slamboree '96	Baton Rouge, LA	155,000	★★

DATE	FED	EVENT	LOCATION	NA BUYS	RATING
26-05-96	WWF	In Your House 8: Beware Of Dog	Florence, SC	116,000	★★★
01-06-96	Various	World Wrestling Peace Festival	Los Angeles, CA	-	★★★
16-06-96	WCW	Great American Bash '96	Baltimore, MD	170,000	★★★★
22-06-96	ECW	Hardcore Heaven '96	Philadelphia, PA	-	★★★
23-06-96	WWF	King Of The Ring '96	Milwaukee, WI	158,000	★★★★
07-07-96	WCW	Bash At The Beach '96	Daytona Beach, FL	250,000	★★★★
13-07-96	ECW	Heatwave '96	Philadelphia, PA	-	★★★★
21-07-96	WWF	In Your House 9: International Incident	Vancouver, BC	99,000	★★★
03-08-96	ECW	The Doctor Is In	Philadelphia, PA	-	★★★
10-08-96	WCW	Hog Wild '96	Sturgis, SD	220,000	★★★
15-08-96	WCW	Clash Of The Champions XXXIII	Denver, CO	-	★★
18-08-96	WWF	SummerSlam '96	Cleveland, OH	157,000	★★★★
24-08-96	ECW	Natural Born Killaz	Philadelphia, PA	-	★★
15-09-96	WCW	Fall Brawl '96	Winston-Salem, NC	230,000	★★★★
22-09-96	WWF	In Your House 10: Mind Games	Philadelphia, PA	131,000	★★★
20-10-96	WWF	In Your House 11: Buried Alive	Indianapolis, IN	110,000	★★★
27-10-96	WCW	Halloween Havoc '96	Paradise, NV	250,000	★★★
16-11-96	ECW	November To Remember '96	Philadelphia, PA	-	★★
17-11-96	WWF	Survivor Series '96	New York, NY	160,000	★★★★
24-11-96	WCW	World War 3 '96	Norfolk, VA	200,000	★★★
15-12-96	WWF	In Your House 12: It's Time	West Palm Beach, FL	97,000	★★★
29-12-96	WCW	Starrcade '96	Nashville, TN	345,000	★★★★
19-01-97	WWF	Royal Rumble '97	San Antonio, TX	196,000	★★
21-01-97	WCW	Clash Of The Champions XXXIV	Milwaukee, WI	-	★★
25-01-97	WCW	Souled Out '97	Cedar Rapids, IA	170,000	★
01-02-97	ECW	Crossing The Line Again	Philadelphia, PA	-	★★
16-02-97	WWF	In Your House 13: Final Four	Chattanooga, TN	141,000	★★★
22-02-97	ECW	Cyberslam '97	Philadelphia, PA	-	★★
23-02-97	WCW	SuperBrawl VII	San Francisco, CA	275,000	★★★
16-03-97	WWF	WWF at Madison Square Garden (16-03-97)	New York City, NY	-	★★
16-03-97	WCW	Uncensored '97	North Charleston, NC	325,000	★★★
23-03-97	WWF	WrestleMania XIII	Rosemont, IL	218,000	★★★
06-04-97	ECW	Barely Legal	Philadelphia, PA	45,000	★★★★
13-04-97	WWF	In Your House 14: Revenge Of Taker	Rochester, NY	142,000	★★
20-04-97	WWF	In Your House 15: A Cold Day In Hell	Richmond, VA	163,000	★★★
11-05-97	WCW	Slamboree '97	Charlotte, NC	220,000	★★★
18-05-97	ECW	Wrestlepalooza '97	Philadelphia, PA	-	★★
06-06-97	WWF	King Of The Ring '97	Providence, RI	144,000	★★
08-06-97	WCW	Great American Bash '97	Moline, IL	220,000	★★★
15-06-97	WCW	nWo vs. WCW Takeover '97	Oberhausen, Germany	-	★★★
21-06-97	WWF	In Your House 16: Canadian Stampede	Calgary, Canada	171,000	★★★★★
06-07-97	WCW	Bash At The Beach '97	Daytona Beach, FL	325,000	★★★★
13-07-97	WWF	SummerSlam '97	East Rutherford, NJ	235,000	★★★
03-08-97	WCW	Road Wild '97	Sturgis, SD	240,000	★★
09-08-97	ECW	Born To Be Wired '97	Philadelphia, PA	-	★★★
09-08-97	ECW	Hardcore Heaven '97	Fort Lauderdale, FL	36,000	★★★
17-08-97	WCW	Clash Of The Champions XXXV	Nashville, TN	-	★★★
21-08-97	WWF	In Your House 17: Ground Zero	Louisville, KY	136,000	★★★
07-09-97	ECW	Terry Funk's WrestleFest	Amarillo, TX	-	★★★
11-09-97	WCW	Fall Brawl '97	Winston-Salem, NC	195,000	★★★
14-09-97	WWF	One Night Only	Birmingham, England	-	★★★★
20-09-97	WWF	In Your House 18: Badd Blood	St. Louis, MO	186,000	★★
05-10-97	WCW	Halloween Havoc '97	Paradise, NV	405,000	★★★★
26-10-97	WWF	Survivor Series '97	Montreal, Canada	284,000	★★★
09-11-97	WCW	World War 3 '97	Auburn Hills, MI	205,000	★★★
23-11-97	ECW	November To Remember '97	Monaca, PA	40,000	★★★
30-11-97	WWF	In Your House 19: DeGeneration X	Springfield, MA	144,000	★★
07-12-97	WCW	Starrcade '97	Washington, D.C.	700,000	★
28-12-97	WWF	Royal Rumble '98	San Jose, CA	325,000	★★★★
18-01-98	WCW	Souled Out '98	Trotwood, OH	380,000	★★★★
24-01-98	WWF	No Way Out Of Texas	Houston, TX	179,000	★★★★
15-02-98	ECW	Cyberslam '98	Philadelphia, PA	-	★★
21-02-98	WCW	SuperBrawl VIII	San Francisco, CA	415,000	★★★
22-02-98	ECW	Living Dangerously '98	Asbury Park, NJ	53,000	★★
01-03-98	WCW	Uncensored '98	Mobile, AL	415,000	★★★
15-03-98	WWF	WrestleMania XIV	Boston, MA	809,000	★★★★★
29-03-98	WCW	Spring Stampede '98	Denver, CO	275,000	★★★
19-04-98	WWF	Unforgiven '98	Greensboro, NC	306,000	★★★
26-04-98	ECW	Wrestlepalooza '98	Marietta, GA	75,000	★
03-05-98	WCW	Slamboree '98	Worcester, MA	275,000	★★★
17-05-98	WWF	Over The Edge '98	Milwaukee, WI	214,000	★★★
31-05-98	WCW	Great American Bash '98	Baltimore, MD	290,000	★★★
14-06-98	WWF	King Of The Ring '98	Pittsburgh, PA	320,000	★★★★
28-06-98	WCW	Bash At The Beach '98	San Diego, CA	580,000	★★
12-07-98	WWF	Fully Loaded '98	Fresno, CA	347,000	★★★
26-07-98	ECW	Heat Wave '98	Dayton, OH	70,000	★★★★
02-08-98	WCW	Road Wild '98	Sturgis, SD	365,000	★
08-08-98	WWF	SummerSlam '98	New York, NY	655,000	★★★★
30-08-98	WCW	Fall Brawl '98	Winston-Salem, NC	275,000	★
13-09-98	WWF	Breakdown '98	Hamilton, Canada	342,000	★★★

DATE	FED	EVENT	LOCATION	NA BUYS	RATING
18-10-98	WWF	Judgment Day '98	Rosemont, IL	350,000	★★
25-10-98	WCW	Halloween Havoc '98	Paradise, NV	310,000	★★
01-11-98	ECW	November To Remember '98	New Orleans, LA	75,000	★★
15-11-98	WWF	Survivor Series '98	St. Louis, MO	506,000	★★★★
22-11-98	WCW	World War 3 '98	Auburn Hills, MI	250,000	★
06-12-98	WWF	Capital Carnage '98	London, England	-	★★
13-12-98	WWF	Rock Bottom '98	Vancouver, Canada	300,000	★★
27-12-98	WCW	Starrcade '98	Washington, D.C.	460,000	★★
10-01-99	ECW	Guilty As Charged '99	Kissimmee, FL	75,000	★★★
17-01-99	WCW	Souled Out '99	Charleston, WV	330,000	★★
24-01-99	WWF	Royal Rumble '99	Anaheim, CA	716,000	★★★
14-02-99	WWF	St. Valentine's Day Massacre	Memphis, TN	455,000	★★★
21-02-99	WCW	SuperBrawl IX	Oakland, CA	485,000	★★
21-03-99	ECW	Living Dangerously '99	Asbury Park, NJ	70,000	★★★
14-03-99	WCW	Uncensored '99	Louisville, KY	325,000	★★
28-03-99	WWF	WrestleMania XV	Philadelphia, PA	863,000	★★
03-04-99	ECW	Cyberslam '99	Philadelphia, PA	-	★★★
11-04-99	WCW	Spring Stampede '99	Tacoma, WA	255,000	★★★★
25-04-99	WWF	Backlash '99	Providence, RI	390,000	★★★
29-04-99	WWF	SmackDown Pilot	New Haven, CT	-	★★★
09-05-99	WCW	Slamboree '99	St. Louis, MO	195,000	★★
16-05-99	WWF	No Mercy (UK) '99	Manchester, England	-	★
16-05-99	ECW	Hardcore Heaven '99	Poughkeepsie, PA	75,000	★★★
23-05-99	WWF	Over The Edge '99	Kansas City, MO	400,000	★★
13-06-99	WCW	Great American Bash '99	Baltimore, MD	185,000	★
27-06-99	WWF	King Of The Ring '99	Greensboro, NC	406,000	★★
11-07-99	WCW	Bash At The Beach '99	Sunrise, FL	175,000	★
18-07-99	ECW	Heat Wave '99	Dayton, OH	99,000	★★★
25-07-99	WWF	Fully Loaded '99	Buffalo, NY	334,000	★★★
14-08-99	WCW	Road Wild '99	Sturgis, SD	235,000	★★
22-08-99	WWF	SummerSlam '99	Minneapolis, MN	565,000	★★★
12-09-99	WCW	Fall Brawl '99	Winston-Salem, NC	130,000	★★
19-09-99	ECW	Anarchy Rulz '99	Villa Park, IL	85,000	★★★★
26-09-99	WWF	Unforgiven '99	Charlotte, NC	300,000	★★★
02-10-99	WWF	Rebellion '99	Birmingham, England	-	★★
10-10-99		Heroes Of Wrestling	Bay St. Louis, MS	29,000	★
17-10-99	WWF	No Mercy '99	Cleveland, OH	298,000	★★★★
24-10-99	WCW	Halloween Havoc '99	Las Vegas, NV	230,000	★★
07-11-99	ECW	November To Remember '99	Buffalo, NY	80,000	★★★
14-11-99	WWF	Survivor Series '99	Detroit, MI	406,000	★★
21-11-99	WCW	Mayhem '99	Toronto, Canada	200,000	★★
12-12-99	WWF	Armageddon '99	Sunrise, FL	337,000	★★
19-12-99	WCW	Starrcade '99	Washington, D.C.	145,000	★★
09-01-00	ECW	Guilty As Charged '00	Birmingham, AL	80,000	★★★
16-01-00	WCW	Souled Out '00	Cincinnati, OH	115,000	★★
23-01-00	WWF	Royal Rumble '00	New York, NY	569,000	★★★★★
12-02-00	WCW	Millennium Tour	Oberhausen, Germany	-	★★
20-02-00	WCW	SuperBrawl X	San Francisco, CA	70,000	★★
27-02-00	WWF	No Way Out '00	Hartford, CT	435,000	★★★★
12-03-00	ECW	Living Dangerously '00	Danbury, CT	95,000	★★
19-03-00	WCW	Uncensored '00	Miami, FL	60,000	★★
02-04-00	WWF	WrestleMania XVI	Anaheim, CA	757,000	★★★
16-04-00	WCW	Spring Stampede '00	Chicago, IL	115,000	★★
30-04-00	WWF	Backlash '00	Washington, D.C.	593,000	★★★★★
06-05-00	WWF	Insurrextion '00	London, England	-	★★★
07-05-00	WCW	Slamboree '00	Kansas City, MO	65,000	★★★
14-05-00	ECW	Hardcore Heaven '00	Milwaukee, WI	-	★★★
21-05-00	WWF	Judgment Day '00	Louisville, KY	386,000	★★★★★
11-06-00	WCW	Great American Bash '00	Baltimore, MD	85,000	★★
25-06-00	WWF	King Of The Ring '00	Boston, MA	440,000	★★
09-07-00	WCW	Bash At The Beach '00	Daytona Beach, FL	100,000	★★
16-07-00	ECW	Heat Wave '00	Los Angeles, CA	-	★★★
23-07-00	WWF	Fully Loaded '00	Dallas, TX	386,000	★★★★
30-07-00	IGW	Superstars Of Wrestling: Rodman Down Under	Sydney, Australia	-	★
13-08-00	WCW	New Blood Rising '00	British Columbia, Canada	85,000	★★
27-08-00	WWF	SummerSlam '00	Raleigh, NC	520,000	★★★★
17-09-00	WCW	Fall Brawl '00	Buffalo, NY	75,000	★★★
24-09-00	WWF	Unforgiven '00	Philadelphia, PA	564,000	★★
01-10-00	ECW	Anarchy Rulz '00	Saint Paul, MN	-	★★★
22-10-00	WWF	No Mercy '00	Albany, NY	499,000	★★★
29-10-00	WCW	Halloween Havoc '00	Las Vegas, NV	70,000	★
05-11-00	ECW	November To Remember '00	Villa Park, IL	-	★★
16-11-00	WCW	Millennium Final	Oberhausen, Germany	-	★★
19-11-00	WWF	Survivor Series '00	Tampa, FL	385,000	★★
26-11-00	WCW	Mayhem '00	Milwaukee, WI	55,000	★★
02-12-00	WWF	Rebellion '00	Sheffield, England	-	★★
03-12-00	ECW	Massacre On 34th Street	New York, NY	-	★★★
10-12-00	WWF	Armageddon '00	Birmingham, AL	449,000	★★
17-12-00	WCW	Starrcade '00	Washington, D.C.	50,000	★★
07-01-01	ECW	Guilty As Charged '01	New York, NY	-	★★
14-01-01	WCW	Sin '01	Indianapolis, IN	80,000	★★★

DATE	FED	EVENT	LOCATION	NA BUYS	RATING
21-01-01	WWF	Royal Rumble '01	New Orleans, LA	533,000	★★★★★
04-02-01	WOW	Unleashed	Inglewood, CA	6,000	★
18-02-01	WCW	SuperBrawl Revenge	Nashville, TN	70,000	★★★
25-02-01	WWF	No Way Out '01	Paradise, NV	523,000	★★★★
18-03-01	WCW	Greed '01	Jacksonville, FL	50,000	★★★
01-04-01	WWF	WrestleMania XVII	Houston, TX	970,000	★★★★★
29-04-01	WWF	Backlash '01	Rosemont, IL	382,000	★★★
05-05-01	WWF	Insurrextion '01	London, England	-	★★★
20-05-01	WWF	Judgment Day '01	Sacramento, CA	302,000	★★★
24-06-01	WWF	King Of The Ring '01	East Rutherford, NJ	345,000	★★★
22-07-01	WWF	Invasion '01	Cleveland, OH	590,000	★★★
19-08-01	WWF	SummerSlam '01	San Jose, CA	435,000	★★★★
23-09-01	WWF	Unforgiven '01	Pittsburgh, PA	340,000	★★★
21-10-01	WWF	No Mercy '01	St. Louis, MO	333,000	★★★★
03-11-01	WWF	Rebellion '01	Manchester, England	-	★★★
18-11-01	WWF	Survivor Series '01	Greensboro, NC	471,000	★★★
09-12-01	WWF	Vengeance '01	San Diego, CA	326,000	★★★
06-01-02	WWA	The Inception	Sydney, Australia	-	★★★
20-01-02	WWF	Royal Rumble '02	Atlanta, GA	708,000	★★★★
17-02-02	WWF	No Way Out '02	Milwaukee, WI	462,000	★★
23-02-02	ROH	The Era Of Honor Begins	Philadelpha, PA	-	★★
24-02-02	WWA	The Revolution	Las Vegas, NV	-	★★
17-03-02	WWF	WrestleMania XVIII	Toronto, Canada	707,000	★★★
30-03-02	ROH	Round Robin Challenge	Philadelphia, PA	-	★★★
14-04-02	WWA	The Eruption	Melbourne, Australia	-	★★
21-04-02	WWF	Backlash '02	Kansas City, MO	379,000	★★★
04-05-02	WWF	Insurrextion '02	London, England	-	★★
19-05-02	WWE	Judgment Day '02	Nashville, TN	313,000	★★★★
19-06-02	NWA-TNA	Total Nonstop Action (19-06-02)	Huntsville, AL	-	★★★
22-06-02	ROH	Road To The Title	Philadelphia, PA	-	★★★
23-06-02	WWE	King Of The Ring '02	Columbus, OH	271,000	★★
26-06-02	NWA-TNA	Total Nonstop Action (26-06-02)	Huntsville, AL	-	★★★
03-07-02	NWA-TNA	Total Nonstop Action (03-07-02)	Nashville, TN	-	★★
10-07-02	NWA-TNA	Total Nonstop Action (10-07-02)	Nashville, TN	-	★★★
17-07-02	NWA-TNA	Total Nonstop Action (17-07-02)	Nashville, TN	-	★★
21-07-02	WWE	Vengeance '02	Detroit, MI	318,000	★★★
24-07-02	NWA-TNA	Total Nonstop Action (24-07-02)	Nashville, TN	-	★★
27-07-02	ROH	Crowning A Champion	Philadelphia, PA	-	★★★
31-07-02	NWA-TNA	Total Nonstop Action (31-07-02)	Nashville, TN	-	★★
07-08-02	NWA-TNA	Total Nonstop Action (07-08-02)	Nashville, TN	-	★★
10-08-02	WWE	Global Warning Tour	Melbourne, Australia	-	★★★
14-08-02	NWA-TNA	Total Nonstop Action (14-08-02)	Nashville, TN	-	★★
21-08-02	NWA-TNA	Total Nonstop Action (21-08-02)	Nashville, TN	-	★★★
25-08-02	WWE	SummerSlam '02	Uniondale, NY	425,000	★★★★★
28-08-02	NWA-TNA	Total Nonstop Action (28-08-02)	Nashville, TN	-	★★★
18-09-02	NWA-TNA	Total Nonstop Action (18-09-02)	Nashville, TN	-	★★
21-09-02	ROH	Unscripted	Philadelphia, PA	-	★★★
22-09-02	WWE	Unforgiven '02	Los Angeles, CA	240,000	★★★
25-09-02	NWA-TNA	Total Nonstop Action (25-09-02)	Nashville, TN	-	★★
02-10-02	NWA-TNA	Total Nonstop Action (02-10-02)	Nashville, TN	-	★★★
05-10-02	ROH	Glory By Honor I	Philadelphia, PA	-	★★★
09-10-02	NWA-TNA	Total Nonstop Action (09-10-02)	Nashville, TN	-	★★
16-10-02	NWA-TNA	Total Nonstop Action (16-10-02)	Nashville, TN	-	★★
20-10-02	WWE	No Mercy '02	Little Rock, AR	242,000	★★★★
23-10-02	NWA-TNA	Total Nonstop Action (23-10-02)	Nashville, TN	-	★★
26-10-02	WWE	Rebellion '02	Manchester, England	-	★★★
30-10-02	NWA-TNA	Total Nonstop Action (30-10-02)	Nashville, TN	-	★★
06-11-02	NWA-TNA	Total Nonstop Action (06-11-02)	Nashville, TN	-	★★
09-11-02	ROH	All Star Extravaganza I	Philadelphia, PA	-	★★★★
13-11-02	NWA-TNA	Total Nonstop Action (13-11-02)	Nashville, TN	-	★★
17-11-02	WWE	Survivor Series '02	New York, NY	276,000	★★★★
20-11-02	NWA-TNA	Total Nonstop Action (20-11-02)	Nashville, TN	-	★★★
27-11-02	NWA-TNA	Total Nonstop Action (27-11-02)	Nashville, TN	-	★★
04-12-02	NWA-TNA	Total Nonstop Action (04-12-02)	Nashville, TN	-	★★
11-12-02	NWA-TNA	Total Nonstop Action (11-12-02)	Nashville, TN	-	★★★
15-12-02	WWE	Armageddon '02	Sunrise, FL	265,000	★★★
18-12-02	NWA-TNA	Total Nonstop Action (18-12-02)	Nashville, TN	-	★★★
28-12-02	ROH	Final Battle '02	Philadelphia, PA	-	★★★
08-01-03	NWA-TNA	Total Nonstop Action (08-01-03)	Nashville, TN	-	★★
15-01-03	NWA-TNA	Total Nonstop Action (15-01-03)	Nashville, TN	-	★★
19-01-03	WWE	Royal Rumble '03	Boston, MA	400,000	★★★
22-01-03	NWA-TNA	Total Nonstop Action (22-01-03)	Nashville, TN	-	★★
29-01-03	NWA-TNA	Total Nonstop Action (29-01-03)	Nashville, TN	-	★
05-02-03	NWA-TNA	Total Nonstop Action (05-02-03)	Nashville, TN	-	★★
08-02-03	ROH	One Year Anniversary Show	New York City, NY	-	★★★
09-02-03	WWA	The Retribution	Glasgow, Scotland	-	★★
12-02-03	NWA-TNA	Total Nonstop Action (12-02-03)	Nashville, TN	-	★★
19-02-03	NWA-TNA	Total Nonstop Action (19-02-03)	Nashville, TN	-	★★
23-02-03	WWE	No Way Out '03	Montreal, Canada	348,000	★★★
26-02-03	NWA-TNA	Total Nonstop Action (26-02-03)	Nashville, TN	-	★★
05-03-03	NWA-TNA	Total Nonstop Action (05-03-03)	Nashville, TN	-	★★

DATE	FED	EVENT	LOCATION	NA BUYS	RATING
12-03-03	NWA-TNA	Total Nonstop Action (12-03-03)	Nashville, TN	-	★★
15-03-03	ROH	Expect The Unexpected	Boston, MA	-	★★★
19-03-03	NWA-TNA	Total Nonstop Action (19-03-03)	Nashville, TN	-	★★
22-03-03	ROH	Night Of Champions	Philadelphia, PA	-	★★★★
26-03-03	NWA-TNA	Total Nonstop Action (26-03-03)	Nashville, TN	-	★★
30-03-03	WWE	WrestleMania XIX	Seattle, WA	427,000	★★★★★
02-04-03	NWA-TNA	Total Nonstop Action (02-04-03)	Nashville, TN	-	★★
09-04-03	NWA-TNA	Total Nonstop Action (09-04-03)	Nashville, TN	-	★★★
16-04-03	NWA-TNA	Total Nonstop Action (16-04-03)	Nashville, TN	-	★★★
23-04-03	NWA-TNA	Total Nonstop Action (23-04-03)	Nashville, TN	-	★★★
26-04-03	ROH	Retribution: Round Robin Challenge II	West Miffin, PA	-	★★★
27-04-03	WWE	Backlash '03	Worcester, MA	262,000	★★
30-04-03	NWA-TNA	Total Nonstop Action (30-04-03)	Nashville, TN	-	★★★
07-05-03	NWA-TNA	Total Nonstop Action (07-05-03)	Nashville, TN	-	★★
14-05-03	NWA-TNA	Total Nonstop Action (14-05-03)	Nashville, TN	-	★★
18-05-03	WWE	Judgment Day '03	Charlotte, NC	240,000	★★
21-05-03	NWA-TNA	Total Nonstop Action (21-05-03)	Nashville, TN	-	★★
28-05-03	NWA-TNA	Total Nonstop Action (28-05-03)	Nashville, TN	-	★
04-06-03	NWA-TNA	Total Nonstop Action (04-06-03)	Nashville, TN	-	★
07-06-03	WWE	Insurrextion '03	Newcastle, England	-	★★
08-06-03	WWA	The Reckoning	Auckland, New Zealand	-	★★
11-06-03	NWA-TNA	Total Nonstop Action (11-06-03)	Nashville, TN	-	★★
15-06-03	WWE	Bad Blood '03	Houston, TX	287,000	★★★
18-06-03	NWA-TNA	Total Nonstop Action (18-06-03)	Nashville, TN	-	★★★
25-06-03	NWA-TNA	Total Nonstop Action (25-06-03)	Nashville, TN	-	★★★★
02-07-03	NWA-TNA	Total Nonstop Action (02-07-03)	Nashville, TN	-	★★
09-07-03	NWA-TNA	Total Nonstop Action (09-07-03)	Nashville, TN	-	★★
16-07-03	NWA-TNA	Total Nonstop Action (16-07-03)	Nashville, TN	-	★
19-07-03	ROH	Death Before Dishonor '03	Elizabeth, NJ	-	★★★★
23-07-03	NWA-TNA	Total Nonstop Action (23-07-03)	Nashville, TN	-	★★
27-07-03	WWE	Vengeance '03	Denver, CO	261,000	★★★★
30-07-03	NWA-TNA	Total Nonstop Action (30-07-03)	Nashville, TN	-	★★
06-08-03	NWA-TNA	Total Nonstop Action (06-08-03)	Nashville, TN	-	★★★
13-08-03	NWA-TNA	Total Nonstop Action (13-08-03)	Nashville, TN	-	★★★★
20-08-03	NWA-TNA	Total Nonstop Action (20-08-03)	Nashville, TN	-	★★★★
24-08-03	WWE	SummerSlam '03	Phoenix, AZ	326,000	★★★
27-08-03	NWA-TNA	Total Nonstop Action (27-08-03)	Nashville, TN	-	★★★
03-09-03	NWA-TNA	Total Nonstop Action (03-09-03)	Nashville, TN	-	★★★★
17-09-03	NWA-TNA	Total Nonstop Action (17-09-03)	Nashville, TN	-	★★
21-09-03	WWE	Unforgiven '03	Hershey, PA	216,000	★★
24-09-03	NWA-TNA	Total Nonstop Action (24-09-03)	Nashville, TN	-	★★
20-09-03	ROH	Glory By Honor II	Philadelphia, PA	-	★★
01-10-03	NWA-TNA	Total Nonstop Action (01-10-03)	Nashville, TN	-	★★
08-10-03	NWA-TNA	Total Nonstop Action (08-10-03)	Nashville, TN	-	★★
15-10-03	NWA-TNA	Total Nonstop Action (15-10-03)	Nashville, TN	-	★★
19-10-03	WWE	No Mercy '03	Baltimore, MD	188,000	★★
22-10-03	NWA-TNA	Total Nonstop Action (22-10-03)	Nashville, TN	-	★★
29-10-03	NWA-TNA	Total Nonstop Action (29-10-03)	Nashville, TN	-	★★
01-11-03	ROH	Main Event Spectacles	Elizabeth, NJ	-	★★★★
05-11-03	NWA-TNA	Total Nonstop Action (05-11-03)	Nashville, TN	-	★★
12-11-03	NWA-TNA	Total Nonstop Action (12-11-03)	Nashville, TN	-	★★
16-11-03	WWE	Survivor Series '03	Dallas, TX	276,000	★★★
19-11-03	NWA-TNA	Total Nonstop Action (19-11-03)	Nashville, TN	-	★★
26-11-03	NWA-TNA	Total Nonstop Action (26-11-03)	Nashville, TN	-	★★
03-12-03	NWA-TNA	Total Nonstop Action (03-12-03)	Nashville, TN	-	★★
10-12-03	NWA-TNA	Total Nonstop Action (10-12-03)	Nashville, TN	-	★★
14-12-03	WWE	Armageddon '03	Orlando, FL	171,000	★★
17-12-03	NWA-TNA	Total Nonstop Action (17-12-03)	Nashville, TN	-	★★
20-12-03	WWE	Tribute To The Troops '03	Baghdad, Iraq	-	★★
27-12-03	ROH	Final Battle '03	Philadelphia, PA	-	★★★★
07-01-04	NWA-TNA	Total Nonstop Action (07-01-04)	Nashville, TN	-	★★
14-01-04	NWA-TNA	Total Nonstop Action (14-01-04)	Nashville, TN	-	★★
21-01-04	NWA-TNA	Total Nonstop Action (21-01-04)	Nashville, TN	-	★★
25-01-04	WWE	Royal Rumble '04	Philadelphia, PA	403,000	★★★
28-01-04	NWA-TNA	Total Nonstop Action (28-01-04)	Nashville, TN	-	★★★
04-02-04	NWA-TNA	Total Nonstop Action (04-02-04)	Nashville, TN	-	★★
11-02-04	NWA-TNA	Total Nonstop Action (11-02-04)	Nashville, TN	-	★★
14-02-04	ROH	Second Anniversary Show	Braintree, MA	-	★★★
15-02-04	WWE	No Way Out '04	Daly City, CA	193,000	★★★
18-02-04	NWA-TNA	Total Nonstop Action (18-02-04)	Nashville, TN	-	★★
25-02-04	NWA-TNA	Total Nonstop Action (25-02-04)	Nashville, TN	-	★★
03-03-04	NWA-TNA	Total Nonstop Action (03-03-04)	Nashville, TN	-	★★
10-03-04	NWA-TNA	Total Nonstop Action (10-03-04)	Nashville, TN	-	★★
14-03-04	WWE	WrestleMania XX	New York City, NY	618,000	★★★
17-03-04	NWA-TNA	Total Nonstop Action (17-03-04)	Nashville, TN	-	★★★
24-03-04	NWA-TNA	Total Nonstop Action (24-03-04)	Nashville, TN	-	★★
31-03-04	NWA-TNA	Total Nonstop Action (31-03-04)	Nashville, TN	-	★★
07-04-04	NWA-TNA	Total Nonstop Action (07-04-04)	Nashville, TN	-	★
14-04-04	NWA-TNA	Total Nonstop Action (14-04-04)	Nashville, TN	-	★★
18-04-04	WWE	Backlash '04	Edmonton, Canada	215,000	★★★★
21-04-04	NWA-TNA	Total Nonstop Action (21-04-04)	Nashville, TN	-	★★

DATE	FED	EVENT	LOCATION	NA BUYS	RATING
28-04-04	NWA-TNA	Total Nonstop Action (28-04-04)	Nashville, TN	-	★★
05-05-04	NWA-TNA	Total Nonstop Action (05-05-04)	Nashville, TN	-	★★
12-05-04	NWA-TNA	Total Nonstop Action (12-05-04)	Nashville, TN	-	★★
15-05-04	ROH	Round Robin Challenge III	Lexington, MA	-	★★
16-05-04	WWE	Judgment Day '04	Los Angeles, CA	165,000	★★
19-05-04	NWA-TNA	Total Nonstop Action (19-05-04)	Nashville, TN	-	★★
26-05-04	NWA-TNA	Total Nonstop Action (26-05-04)	Nashville, TN	-	★★★
02-06-04	NWA-TNA	Total Nonstop Action (02-06-04)	Nashville, TN	-	★★
09-06-04	NWA-TNA	Total Nonstop Action (09-06-04)	Nashville, TN	-	★★
13-06-04	WWE	Bad Blood '04	Columbus, OH	194,000	★★★
16-06-04	NWA-TNA	Total Nonstop Action (16-06-04)	Nashville, TN	-	★★
23-06-04	NWA-TNA	Total Nonstop Action (23-06-04)	Nashville, TN	-	★★
27-06-04	WWE	Great American Bash '04	Norfolk, VA	172,000	★★
30-06-04	NWA-TNA	Total Nonstop Action (30-06-04)	Nashville, TN	-	★★
07-07-04	NWA-TNA	Total Nonstop Action (07-07-04)	Nashville, TN	-	★★★
11-07-04	WWE	Vengeance '04	Hartford, CT	173,000	★★★★
14-07-04	NWA-TNA	Total Nonstop Action (14-07-04)	Nashville, TN	-	★★★
17-07-04	ROH	Reborn: Completion	Elizabeth, NJ	-	★★★
21-07-04	NWA-TNA	Total Nonstop Action (21-07-04)	Nashville, TN	-	★★
23-07-04	ROH	Death Before Dishonor II Night #1	Wauwatosa, WI	-	★★★★
24-07-04	ROH	Death Before Dishonor II Night #2	Chicago Ridge, IL	-	★★★★
28-07-04	NWA-TNA	Total Nonstop Action (28-07-04)	Nashville, TN	-	★★★
04-08-04	NWA-TNA	Total Nonstop Action (04-08-04)	Nashville, TN	-	★★★
07-08-04	ROH	Testing The Limit	Essington, PA	-	★★★
11-08-04	NWA-TNA	Total Nonstop Action (11-08-04)	Nashville, TN	-	★★★
15-08-04	WWE	SummerSlam '04	Toronto, Canada	279,000	★★
18-08-04	NWA-TNA	Total Nonstop Action (18-08-04)	Nashville, TN	-	★★★
25-08-04	NWA-TNA	Total Nonstop Action (25-08-04)	Nashville, TN	-	★★★
01-09-04	NWA-TNA	Total Nonstop Action (01-09-04)	Nashville, TN	-	★★★
08-09-04	NWA-TNA	Total Nonstop Action (08-09-04)	Nashville, TN	-	★★
11-09-04	ROH	Glory By Honor III	Elizabeth, NJ	-	★★★
12-09-04	WWE	Unforgiven '04	Portland, OR	177,000	★★
03-10-04	WWE	No Mercy '04	East Rutherford, NJ	140,000	★★
16-10-04	ROH	Joe vs. Punk II	Chicago, IL	-	★★★★
19-10-04	WWE	Taboo Tuesday '04	Milwaukee, WI	123,000	★★
07-11-04	TNA	Victory Road '04	Orlando, FL	25,000	★★
14-11-04	WWE	Survivor Series '04	Cleveland, OH	233,000	★★
04-12-04	ROH	All Star Extravaganza II	Elizabeth, NJ	-	★★★★
05-12-04	TNA	Turning Point '04	Orlando, FL	20,000	★★★★
12-12-04	WWE	Armageddon '04	Atlanta, GA	169,000	★★
18-12-04	WWE	Tribute To The Troops '04	Tikrit, Iraq	-	★★
26-12-04	ROH	Final Battle '04	Philadelphia, PA	-	★★★
09-01-05	WWE	New Year's Revolution '05	San Juan, Puerto Rico	192,000	★★
16-01-05	TNA	Final Resolution '05	Orlando, FL	20,000	★★★★
30-01-05	WWE	Royal Rumble '05	Fresno, CA	397,000	★★★
13-02-05	TNA	Against All Odds '05	Orlando, FL	20,000	★★★
20-02-05	WWE	No Way Out '05	Pittsburgh, PA	108,000	★★
13-03-05	TNA	Destination X '05	Orlando, FL	20,000	★
03-04-05	WWE	WrestleMania XXI	Los Angeles, CA	650,000	★★★★★
24-04-05	TNA	Lockdown '05	Orlando, FL	30,000	★★★★
01-05-05	WWE	Backlash '05	Manchester, NH	205,000	★★★
07-05-05	ROH	Manhattan Mayhem	New York City, NY	-	★★★★
15-05-05	TNA	Hard Justice '05	Orlando, FL	20,000	★★★
22-05-05	WWE	Judgment Day '05	Minneapolis, MN	163,000	★★★★
10-06-05	HH	An Extreme Reunion	Philadelphia, PA	-	★★★
12-06-05	ECW	One Night Stand '05	New York City, NY	333,000	★★★★★
18-06-05	ROH	Death Before Dishonor III	Morristown, NJ	-	★★★
19-06-05	TNA	Slammiversary III	Orlando, FL	20,000	★★
26-06-05	WWE	Vengeance '05	Las Vegas, NV	260,000	★★★★
17-07-05	TNA	No Surrender '05	Orlando, FL	15,000	★★★★
24-07-05	WWE	Great American Bash '05	Buffalo, NY	173,000	★★
13-08-05	ROH	Punk: The Final Chapter	Chicago Ridge, IL	-	★★★
14-08-05	TNA	Sacrifice '05	Orlando, FL	15,000	★★★★
21-08-05	WWE	SummerSlam '05	Washington, D.C.	480,000	★★★
11-09-05	TNA	Unbreakable '05	Orlando, FL	15,000	★★★★
17-09-05	ROH	Glory By Honor IV	Long Island, NY	-	★★★
18-09-05	WWE	Unforgiven '05	Oklahoma City, OK	155,000	★★★
24-09-05	ROH	Survival Of The Fittest '05	Dorchester, MA	-	★★★
01-10-05	ROH	Joe vs. Kobashi	New York City, NY	-	★★★
09-10-05	WWE	No Mercy '05	Houston, TX	142,000	★★
23-10-05	TNA	Bound For Glory '05	Orlando, FL	35,000	★★★
01-11-05	WWE	Taboo Tuesday '05	San Diego, CA	155,000	★★★
05-11-05	HH	November Reign	Philadelphia, PA	-	★★
13-11-05	TNA	Genesis '05	Orlando, FL	20,000	★★★
27-11-05	WWE	Survivor Series '05	Detroit, MI	247,000	★★★
11-12-05	TNA	Turning Point '05	Orlando, FL	30,000	★★★★
17-12-05	ROH	Final Battle '05	Edison, NJ	-	★★★★
18-12-05	WWE	Armageddon '05	Providence, RI	198,000	★★★
19-12-05	WWE	Tribute To The Troops '05	Bagram, Afghanistan	-	★★
08-01-06	WWE	New Year's Revolution '06	Albany, NY	214,000	★★
15-01-06	TNA	Final Resolution '06	Orlando, FL	45,000	★★★

DATE	FED	EVENT	LOCATION	NA BUYS	RATING
29-01-06	WWE	Royal Rumble '06	Miami, FL	357,000	★★
12-02-06	TNA	Against All Odds '06	Orlando, FL	35,000	★★★★
19-02-06	WWE	No Way Out '06	Baltimore, MD	133,000	★★★
25-02-06	ROH	Fourth Anniversary Show	Edison, NJ	-	★★★
12-03-06	TNA	Destination X '06	Orlando, FL	30,000	★★★
18-03-06	WWE	Saturday Night's Main Event XXXII	Detroit, MI	-	★★
25-03-06	ROH	Best In The World '06	New York City, NY	-	★★★
31-03-06	ROH	Supercard Of Honor '06	Chicago Ridge, IL	-	★★★★
02-04-06	WWE	WrestleMania XXII	Rosemont, IL	636,000	★★★
23-04-06	TNA	Lockdown '06	Orlando, FL	45,000	★★★
30-04-06	WWE	Backlash '06	Lexington, KY	143,000	★★★★
14-05-06	TNA	Sacrifice '06	Orlando, FL	25,000	★★
21-05-06	WWE	Judgment Day '06	Phoenix, AZ	154,000	★★★
07-06-06	ECW	WWE vs. ECW Head To Head	Dayton, OH	-	★★★
11-06-06	ECW	One Night Stand '06	New York City, NY	185,000	★★★★
18-06-06	TNA	Slammiversary IV	Orlando, FL	35,000	★★★
25-06-06	WWE	Vengeance '06	Charlotte, NC	270,000	★★★
15-07-06	WWE	Saturday Night's Main Event XXXIII	Dallas, TX	-	★★
15-07-06	ROH	Death Before Dishonor IV	Philadelphia, PA	-	★★★★
16-07-06	TNA	Victory Road '06	Orlando, FL	25,000	★★
23-07-06	WWE	Great American Bash '06	Indianapolis, IN	141,000	★★
13-08-06	TNA	Hard Justice '06	Orlando, FL	35,000	★★★
20-08-06	WWE	SummerSlam '06	Boston, MA	330,000	★★★
15-09-06	ROH	Glory By Honor V Night #1	East Windsor, CT	-	★★★★
16-09-06	ROH	Glory By Honor V Night #2	New York City, NY	-	★★★★★
17-09-06	WWE	Unforgiven '06	Toronto, Canada	187,000	★★★
24-09-06	TNA	No Surrender '06	Orlando, FL	30,000	★★★
06-10-06	ROH	Survival Of The Fittest '06	Cleveland, OH	-	★★★
08-10-06	WWE	No Mercy '06	Raleigh, NC	114,000	★★★
22-10-06	TNA	Bound For Glory '06	Plymouth, MI	60,000	★★★★
05-11-06	WWE	Cyber Sunday '06	Cincinnati, OH	139,000	★★
19-11-06	TNA	Genesis '06	Orlando, FL	60,000	★★★
26-11-06	WWE	Survivor Series '06	Philadelphia, PA	234,000	★★
03-12-06	ECW	December To Dismember '06	Augusta, GA	52,000	★
10-12-06	TNA	Turning Point '06	Orlando, FL	35,000	★★★
17-12-06	WWE	Armageddon '06	Richmond, VA	139,000	★★
23-12-06	ROH	Final Battle '06	New York City, NY	-	★★★★★
25-12-06	WWE	Tribute To The Troops '06	Baghdad, Iraq	-	★★
07-01-07	WWE	New Year's Revolution '07	Kansas City, MO	149,000	★★★
14-01-07	TNA	Final Resolution '07	Orlando, FL	35,000	★★★
28-01-07	WWE	Royal Rumble '07	San Antonio, TX	347,000	★★★★
11-02-07	TNA	Against All Odds '07	Orlando, FL	25,000	★★★
18-02-07	WWE	No Way Out '07	Los Angeles, CA	135,000	★★
11-03-07	TNA	Destination X '07	Orlando, FL	30,000	★★★
30-03-07	ROH	All Star Extravaganza III	Detroit, MI	-	★★★
31-03-07	ROH	Supercard Of Honor II	Detroit, MI	-	★★★★
01-04-07	WWE	WrestleMania XXIII	Detroit, MI	825,000	★★★★
15-04-07	TNA	Lockdown '07	St. Louis, MO	35,000	★★★
29-04-07	WWE	Backlash '07	Atlanta, GA	139,000	★★★★
13-05-07	TNA	Sacrifice '07	Orlando, FL	25,000	★★★★
20-05-07	WWE	Judgment Day '07	St. Louis, MO	158,000	★★
02-06-07	WWE	Saturday Night's Main Event XXXIV	Toronto, Canada	-	★★
03-06-07	WWE	One Night Stand '07	Jacksonville, FL	124,000	★★★
17-06-07	TNA	Slammiversary V	Nashville, TN	25,000	★★
24-06-07	WWE	Vengeance '07	Houston, TX	168,000	★★
01-07-07	ROH	Respect Is Earned	New York, NY	-	★★★★
15-07-07	TNA	Victory Road '07	Orlando, FL	20,000	★★★
22-07-07	WWE	Great American Bash '07	San Jose, CA	165,000	★★★
10-08-07	ROH	Death Before Dishonor V Night #1	Boston, MA	-	★★★★
11-08-07	ROH	Death Before Dishonor V Night #2	Philadelphia, PA	-	★★★★
12-08-07	TNA	Hard Justice '07	Orlando, FL	25,000	★★
18-08-07	WWE	Saturday Night's Main Event XXXV	New York City, NY	-	★★
25-08-07	ROH	Manhattan Mayhem II	New York City, NY	-	★★★★
26-08-07	WWE	SummerSlam '07	East Rutherford, NJ	360,000	★★
09-09-07	TNA	No Surrender '07	Orlando, FL	20,000	★★★
16-09-07	WWE	Unforgiven '07	Memphis, TN	134,000	★★
21-09-07	ROH	Driven '07	Chicago Ridge, IL	-	★★★★
07-10-07	WWE	No Mercy '07	Rosemont, IL	171,000	★★
14-10-07	TNA	Bound For Glory '07	Duluth, GA	40,000	★★★
19-10-07	ROH	Survival Of The Fittest '07	Las Vegas, NV	-	★★★
28-10-07	WWE	Cyber Sunday '07	Washington, D.C.	122,000	★★★
02-11-07	ROH	Glory By Honor VI Night #1	Philadelphia, PA	-	★★★
03-11-07	ROH	Glory By Honor VI Night #2	New York City, NY	-	★★★
11-11-07	TNA	Genesis '07	Orlando, FL	25,000	★★★
18-11-07	WWE	Survivor Series '07	Miami, FL	215,000	★★★
30-11-07	ROH	Man Up	Chicago Ridge, IL	-	★★★★
02-12-07	TNA	Turning Point '07	Orlando, FL	20,000	★★
16-12-07	WWE	Armageddon '07	Pittsburgh, PA	149,000	★★★
24-12-07	WWE	Tribute To The Troops '07	Baghdad, Iraq	-	★★
30-12-07	ROH	Final Battle '07	New York City, NY	-	★★★
06-01-08	TNA	Final Resolution '08 (January)	Orlando, FL	25,000	★★

DATE	FED	EVENT	LOCATION	NA BUYS	RATING
18-01-08	ROH	Undeniable	Edison, NJ	-	★★★
27-01-08	WWE	Royal Rumble '08	New York, NY	403,000	★★★
10-02-08	TNA	Against All Odds '08	Greenville, SC	25,000	★★
17-02-08	WWE	No Way Out '08	Las Vegas, NV	256,000	★★★
23-02-08	ROH	Sixth Anniversary Show	New York City, NY	-	★★★★
07-03-08	ROH	Rising Above '08	New York, NY	-	★★★
09-03-08	TNA	Destination X '08	Norfolk, VA	20,000	★★
30-03-08	WWE	WrestleMania XXIV	Orlando, FL	697,000	★★★★
13-04-08	TNA	Lockdown '08	Lowell, MA	55,000	★★★
27-04-08	WWE	Backlash '08	Baltimore, MD	141,000	★★★
11-05-08	TNA	Sacrifice '08	Orlando, FL	25,000	★★
18-05-08	WWE	Judgment Day '08	Omaha, NE	169,000	★★★
30-05-08	ROH	Take No Prisoners '08	Philadelphia, PA	-	★★★★
01-06-08	WWE	One Night Stand '08	San Diego, CA	134,000	★★
08-06-08	TNA	Slammiversary VI	Southaven, MS	30,000	★★★
29-06-08	WWE	Night Of Champions '08	Dallas, TX	191,000	★★
13-07-08	TNA	Victory Road '08	Houston, TX	25,000	★★★
20-07-08	WWE	Great American Bash '08	Uniondale, NY	135,000	★★★
01-08-08	ROH	Respect Is Earned II	Philadelphia, PA	-	★★★★
02-08-08	WWE	Saturday Night's Main Event XXXVI	Washington, D.C.	-	★★
02-08-08	ROH	Death Before Dishonor VI	New York City, NY	-	★★★★
10-08-08	TNA	Hard Justice '08	Trenton, NJ	35,000	★★★
17-08-08	WWE	SummerSlam '08	Indianapolis, IN	329,000	★★★★
07-09-08	WWE	Unforgiven '08	Cleveland, OH	146,000	★★★
14-09-08	TNA	No Surrender '08	Oshawa, Canada	20,000	★★★
20-09-08	ROH	Glory By Honor VII	Philadelphia, PA	-	★★★
26-09-08	ROH	New Horizons	Detroit, MI	-	★★★★
05-10-08	WWE	No Mercy '08	Portland, OR	157,000	★★★★
12-10-08	TNA	Bound For Glory '08	Hoffman Estates, IL	40,000	★★★
26-10-08	WWE	Cyber Sunday '08	Phoenix, AZ	92,000	★★★
09-11-08	TNA	Turning Point '08	Orlando, FL	35,000	★★★★
14-11-08	ROH	Driven '08	Boston, MA	-	★★★
23-11-08	WWE	Survivor Series '08	Boston, MA	191,000	★★
07-12-08	TNA	Final Resolution '08 (December)	Orlando, FL	20,000	★★
14-12-08	WWE	Armageddon '08	Buffalo, NY	116,000	★★★
20-12-08	WWE	Tribute To The Troops '08	Baghdad, Iraq	-	★★
26-12-08	ROH	All Star Extravaganza IV	Philadelphia, PA	-	★★★★
27-12-08	ROH	Final Battle '08	New York City, NY	-	★★★★
11-01-09	TNA	Genesis '09	Charlotte, NC	30,000	★★★
16-01-09	ROH	Rising Above '09	Chicago Ridge, IL	-	★★★★
25-01-09	WWE	Royal Rumble '09	Detroit, MI	288,000	★★★
08-02-09	TNA	Against All Odds '09	Orlando, FL	20,000	★★
15-02-09	WWE	No Way Out '09	Seattle, WA	174,000	★★★★
15-03-09	TNA	Destination X '09	Orlando, FL	30,000	★★
21-03-09	ROH	7th Anniversary Show	New York City, NY	-	★★★★
03-04-09	ROH	Supercard Of Honor IV	Houston, TX	-	★★★★
05-04-09	WWE	WrestleMania XXV	Houston, TX	605,000	★★★
17-04-09	ROH	Caged Collision	Chicago Ridge, IL	-	★★★
19-04-09	TNA	Lockdown '09	Philadelphia, PA	40,000	★★
26-04-09	WWE	Backlash '09	Providence, RI	116,000	★★★
17-05-09	WWE	Judgment Day '09	Rosemont, IL	146,000	★★★★
24-05-09	TNA	Sacrifice '09	Orlando, FL	20,000	★★★
07-06-09	WWE	Extreme Rules '09	New Orleans, LA	136,000	★★★
12-06-09	ROH	Take No Prisoners '09	Houston, TX	-	★★★
13-06-09	ROH	Manhattan Mayhem III	New York City, NY	-	★★★
21-06-09	TNA	Slammiversary VII	Auburn Hills, MI	35,000	★★★
28-06-09	WWE	The Bash '09	Sacramento, CA	114,000	★★
19-07-09	TNA	Victory Road '09	Orlando, FL	35,000	★
24-07-09	ROH	Death Before Dishonor VII Day #1	Toronto, Canada	-	★★★
25-07-09	ROH	Death Before Dishonor VII Day #2	Toronto, Canada	-	★★★
26-07-09	WWE	Night Of Champions '09	Philadelphia, PA	166,000	★★★
16-08-09	TNA	Hard Justice '09	Orlando, FL	20,000	★★
23-08-09	WWE	SummerSlam '09	Los Angeles, CA	229,000	★★★
13-09-09	WWE	Breaking Point '09	Montreal, Canada	105,000	★★
20-09-09	TNA	No Surrender '09	Orlando, FL	8,000	★★★
26-09-09	ROH	Glory By Honor VIII	New York City, NY	-	★★★★
04-10-09	WWE	Hell In A Cell '09	Newark, NJ	164,000	★★★
10-10-09	ROH	Survival Of The Fittest '09	Indianapolis, IN	-	★★★
18-10-09	TNA	Bound For Glory '09	Irvine, CA	38,000	★★★
25-10-09	WWE	Bragging Rights '09	Pittsburgh, PA	105,000	★★★
15-11-09	TNA	Turning Point '09	Orlando, FL	20,000	★★★★
22-11-09	WWE	Survivor Series '09	Washington, D.C.	136,000	★★★
13-12-09	WWE	TLC '09	San Antonio, TX	132,000	★★★
19-12-09	WWE	Tribute To The Troops '09	Baghdad, Iraq	-	★★
19-12-09	ROH	Final Battle '09	New York, NY	1,200	★★★
20-12-09	TNA	Final Resolution '09	Orlando, FL	7,500	★★★★
17-01-10	TNA	Genesis '10	Orlando, FL	15,000	★★
31-01-10	WWE	Royal Rumble '10	Atlanta, GA	259,000	★★★
13-02-10	ROH	8th Anniversary Show	New York City, NY	-	★★★
14-02-10	TNA	Against All Odds '10	Orlando, FL	15,000	★★
21-02-10	WWE	Elimination Chamber '10	St. Louis, MO	160,000	★★★

DATE	FED	EVENT	LOCATION	NA BUYS	RATING
21-03-10	TNA	Destination X '10	Orlando, FL	15,000	★★
28-03-10	WWE	WrestleMania XXVI	Glendale, AZ	495,000	★★★
03-04-10	ROH	The Big Bang!	Charlotte, NC	950	★★★
18-04-10	TNA	Lockdown '10	St. Charles, MO	15,000	★★★
25-04-10	WWE	Extreme Rules '10	Baltimore, MD	112,000	★★★
05-05-10	ROH	Supercard Of Honor V	New York City, NY	-	★★★
16-05-10	TNA	Sacrifice '10	Orlando, FL	15,000	★★
23-05-10	WWE	Over The Limit '10	Detroit, MI	121,000	★★
13-06-10	TNA	Slammiversary VIII	Orlando, FL	15,000	★★★
19-06-10	ROH	Death Before Dishonor VIII	Toronto, Canada	1,500	★★★★
20-06-10	WWE	Fatal 4-Way	Uniondale, NY	88,000	★★★
11-07-10	TNA	Victory Road '10	Orlando, FL	15,000	★★★
18-07-10	WWE	Money In The Bank '10	Kansas City, MO	98,000	★★★
08-08-10	TNA	Hardcore Justice '10	Orlando, FL	20,000	★★
15-08-10	WWE	SummerSlam '10	Los Angeles, CA	209,000	★★
05-09-10	TNA	No Surrender '10	Orlando, FL	15,000	★★★
11-09-10	ROH	Glory By Honor IX	New York, NY	-	★★★
19-09-10	WWE	Night Of Champions '10	Rosemont, IL	99,000	★★
03-10-10	WWE	Hell In A Cell '10	Dallas, TX	109,000	★★
10-10-10	TNA	Bound For Glory '10	Daytona Beach, FL	30,000	★★★
24-10-10	WWE	Bragging Rights '10	Minneapolis, MN	71,000	★★
07-11-10	TNA	Turning Point '10	Orlando, FL	15,000	★★
21-11-10	WWE	Survivor Series '10	Miami, FL	127,000	★★
05-12-10	TNA	Final Resolution '10	Orlando, FL	15,000	★★★
18-12-10	ROH	Final Battle '10	New York, NY	-	★★★★
19-12-10	WWE	TLC '10	Houston, TX	101,000	★★★
22-12-10	WWE	Tribute To The Troops '10	Fort Hood, TX	-	★★
09-01-11	TNA	Genesis '11	Orlando, FL	17,000	★★★
30-01-11	WWE	Royal Rumble '11	Boston, MA	281,000	★★★
13-02-11	TNA	Against All Odds '11	Orlando, FL	15,500	★★★
20-02-11	WWE	Elimination Chamber '11	Oakland, CA	145,000	★★★★
26-02-11	ROH	9th Anniversary Show	Chicago Ridge, IL	-	★★★
13-03-11	TNA	Victory Road '11	Orlando, FL	17,000	★
19-03-11	ROH	Manhattan Mayhem IV	New York City, NY	-	★★★
01-04-11	ROH	Honor Takes Center Stage Day #1	Atlanta, GA	-	★★★★
02-04-11	ROH	Honor Takes Center Stage Day #2	Atlanta, GA	-	★★★★
03-04-11	WWE	WrestleMania XXVII	Atlanta, GA	679,000	★★
17-04-11	TNA	Lockdown '11	Cincinnati, OH	23,000	★★
01-05-11	WWE	Extreme Rules '11	Tampa, FL	108,000	★★★
15-05-11	TNA	Sacrifice '11	Orlando, FL	20,000	★★
22-05-11	WWE	Over The Limit '11	Seattle, WA	72,000	★★
12-06-11	TNA	Slammiversary IX	Orlando, FL	30,000	★★★
19-06-11	WWE	Capitol Punishment	Washington, D.C.	85,000	★★★
26-06-11	ROH	Best In The World '11	New York, NY	-	★★★★
10-07-11	TNA	Destination X '11	Orlando, FL	40,000	★★★★
17-07-11	WWE	Money In The Bank '11	Rosemont, IL	146,000	★★★★★
07-08-11	TNA	Hardcore Justice '11	Orlando, FL	8,500	★★
12-08-11	JCW	Legends & Icons	Cave-In-Rock, IL	-	★
14-08-11	WWE	SummerSlam '11	Los Angeles, CA	180,000	★★★
11-09-11	TNA	No Surrender '11	Orlando, FL	9,000	★★
17-09-11	ROH	Death Before Dishonor IX	New York, NY	-	★★★
18-09-11	WWE	Night Of Champions '11	Buffalo, NY	109,000	★★★
02-10-11	WWE	Hell In A Cell '11	New Orleans, LA	98,000	★★★
16-10-11	TNA	Bound For Glory '11	Philadelphia, PA	25,000	★★★
23-10-11	WWE	Vengeance '11	San Antonio, TX	65,000	★★★
13-11-11	TNA	Turning Point '11	Orlando, FL	10,000	★★
20-11-11	WWE	Survivor Series '11	New York City, NY	179,000	★★
11-12-11	TNA	Final Resolution '11	Orlando, FL	7,000	★★★
13-12-11	WWE	Tribute To The Troops '11	Fayeteville, NC	-	★★
18-12-11	WWE	TLC '11	Baltimore, MD	98,000	★★★
23-12-11	ROH	Final Battle '11	New York, NY	-	★★★
08-01-12	TNA	Genesis '12	Orlando, FL	13,000	★★
29-01-12	WWE	Royal Rumble '12	St. Louis, MO	299,000	★★
12-02-12	TNA	Against All Odds '12	Orlando, FL	8,000	★★
19-02-12	WWE	Elimination Chamber '12	Milwaukee, WI	138,000	★★★
04-03-12	ROH	10th Anniversary Show	New York, NY	-	★★★
18-03-12	TNA	Victory Road '12	Orlando, FL	7,000	★★★
30-03-12	ROH	Showdown In The Sun '12 Day #1	Fort Lauderdale, FL	-	★★★
31-03-12	ROH	Showdown In The Sun '12 Day #2	Fort Lauderdale, FL	-	★★★★
01-04-12	WWE	WrestleMania XXVIII	Miami, FL	715,000	★★★★
15-04-12	TNA	Lockdown '12	Nashville, TN	17,000	★★
29-04-12	WWE	Extreme Rules '12	Rosemont, IL	159,000	★★★★
12-05-12	ROH	Border Wars '12	Toronto, Canada	-	★★★★
13-05-12	TNA	Sacrifice '12	Orlando, FL	9,000	★★★
20-05-12	WWE	Over The Limit '12	Raleigh, NC	124,000	★★★
10-06-12	TNA	Slammiversary X	Arlington, TX	15,000	★★★
17-06-12	WWE	No Way Out '12	East Rutherford, NJ	110,000	★★
24-06-12	ROH	Best In The World '12	New York, NY	-	★★★
08-07-12	TNA	Destination X '12	Orlando, FL	9,000	★★★★
15-07-12	WWE	Money In The Bank '12	Phoenix, AZ	114,000	★★★★
11-08-12	ROH	Boiling Point '12	Providence, RI	-	★★★

DATE	FED	EVENT	LOCATION	NA BUYS	RATING
12-08-12	TNA	Hardcore Justice '12	Orlando, FL	8,000	★★
19-08-12	WWE	SummerSlam '12	Los Angeles, CA	296,000	★★
09-09-12	TNA	No Surrender '12	Orlando, FL	7,000	★★
15-09-12	ROH	Death Before Dishonor X	Chicago Ridge, IL	-	★★★
16-09-12	WWE	Night Of Champions '12	Boston, MA	112,000	★★★
13-10-12	ROH	Glory By Honor XI	Mississauga, Canada	-	★★★★
14-10-12	TNA	Bound For Glory '12	Phoenix, AZ	20,000	★★★★
28-10-12	WWE	Hell In A Cell '12	Atlanta, GA	157,000	★★
11-11-12	TNA	Turning Point '12	Orlando, FL	11,000	★★★★
18-11-12	WWE	Survivor Series '12	Indianapolis, IN	125,000	★★
09-12-12	TNA	Final Resolution '12	Orlando, FL	11,000	★★
16-12-12	ROH	Final Battle '12	New York, NY	-	★★★
16-12-12	WWE	TLC '12	Brooklyn, NY	75,000	★★★
19-12-12	WWE	Tribute To The Troops '12	Brooklyn, NY	-	★★
13-01-13	TNA	Genesis '13	Orlando, FL	13,000	★★
27-01-13	WWE	Royal Rumble '13	Phoenix, AZ	364,000	★★★
17-02-13	WWE	Elimination Chamber '13	New Orleans, LA	181,000	★★★
02-03-13	ROH	11th Anniversary Show	Chicago Ridge, IL	-	★★★★
10-03-13	TNA	Lockdown '13	San Antonio, TX	17,000	★★★
05-04-13	ROH	Supercard Of Honor VII	New York, NY	-	★★★★
07-04-13	WWE	WrestleMania XXIX	East Rutherford, NJ	662,000	★★
04-05-13	ROH	Border Wars '13	Toronto, Canada	-	★★★
19-05-13	WWE	Extreme Rules '13	St. Louis, MO	137,000	★★
02-06-13	TNA	Slammiversary XI	Boston, MA	15,000	★★★
16-06-13	WWE	Payback '13	Rosemont, IL	108,000	★★★
22-06-13	ROH	Best In The World '13	Baltimore, MD	-	★★★
14-07-13	WWE	Money In The Bank '13	Philadelphia, PA	169,000	★★★★
18-08-13	WWE	SummerSlam '13	Los Angeles, CA	207,000	★★★★★
15-09-13	WWE	Night Of Champions '13	Detroit, MI	103,000	★★
20-09-13	ROH	Death Before Dishonor XI	Philadelphia, PA	-	★★★
06-10-13	WWE	Battleground '13	Buffalo, NY	84,000	★★
20-10-13	TNA	Bound For Glory '13	San Diego, CA	17,000	★★
27-10-13	WWE	Hell In A Cell '13	Miami, FL	135,000	★★★
24-11-13	WWE	Survivor Series '13	Boston, MA	98,000	★★
14-12-13	ROH	Final Battle '13	Manhattan, NY	-	★★★
15-12-13	WWE	TLC '13	Houston, TX	146,000	★★★
28-12-13	WWE	Tribute To The Troops '13	Tacoma, WA	-	★★
26-01-14	WWE	Royal Rumble '14	Pittsburgh, PA	337,000	★★★
23-02-14	WWE	Elimination Chamber '14	Minneapolis, MN	159,000	★★★
27-02-14	NXT	Arrival	Winter Park, FL	-	★★★
09-03-14	TNA	Lockdown '14	Coral Gables, FL	17,000	★★
06-04-14	WWE	WrestleMania XXX	New Orleans, LA	420,000	★★★★★
27-04-14	TNA	Sacrifice '14	Orlando, FL	13,000	★★
04-05-14	WWE	Extreme Rules '14	East Rutherford, NJ	45,000	★★★
10-05-14	ROH	Global Wars '14	Toronto, Canada	-	★★★
17-05-14	ROH/NJPW	War Of The Worlds '14	New York, NY	-	★★★★
29-05-14	NXT	TakeOver	Winter Park, FL	-	★★★★
01-06-14	WWE	Payback '14	Rosemont, IL	29,000	★★★★
15-06-14	TNA	Slammiversary XII	Arlington, TX	15,000	★★★
22-06-14	ROH	Best In The World '14	Nashville, TN	8,000	★★★
29-06-14	WWE	Money In The Bank '14	Boston, MA	53,000	★★★
20-07-14	WWE	Battleground '14	Tampa, FL	36,000	★★
17-08-14	WWE	SummerSlam '14	Los Angeles, CA	74,000	★★★
06-09-14	ROH	All Star Extravaganza VI	Toronto, Canada	-	★★★
11-09-14	NXT	TakeOver: Fatal 4-Way	Winter Park, FL	-	★★★
21-09-14	WWE	Night Of Champions '14	Nashville, TN	35,000	★★★
12-10-14	TNA	Bound For Glory '14	Tokyo, Japan	10,000	★★
26-10-14	WWE	Hell In A Cell '14	Dallas, TX	23,000	★★★
23-11-14	WWE	Survivor Series '14	St. Louis, MO	32,000	★★
07-12-14	ROH	Final Battle '14	New York, NY	8,000	★★★★
11-12-14	NXT	TakeOver: R Evolution	Winter Park, FL	-	★★★★
14-12-14	WWE	TLC '14	Cleveland, OH	17,000	★★
17-12-14	WWE	Tribute To The Troops '14	Columbus, GA	-	★★
25-01-15	WWE	Royal Rumble '15	Philadelphia, PA	50,000	★★
11-02-15	NXT	TakeOver: Rival	Winter Park, FL	-	★★★★
22-02-15	WWE	Fastlane '15	Memphis, TN	26,000	★★
01-03-15	ROH	13th Anniversary Show	Las Vegas, NV	10,000	★★★
29-03-15	WWE	WrestleMania XXXI	Santa Clara, CA	103,000	★★★★★
26-04-15	WWE	Extreme Rules '15	Rosemont, IL	31,000	★★★
28-04-15	WWE	King Of The Ring '15	Moline, IL	-	★★
15-05-15	ROH	Global Wars '15	Toronto, Canada	-	★★★
17-05-15	WWE	Payback '15	Baltimore, MD	19,000	★★★
20-05-15	NXT	TakeOver: Unstoppable	Winter Park, FL	-	★★★
31-05-15	WWE	Elimination Chamber '15	Corpus Christi, TX	41,000	★★★
14-06-15	WWE	Money In The Bank '15	Columbus, OH	24,000	★★★
19-06-15	ROH	Best In The World '15	New York, NY	-	★★★
28-06-15	TNA	Slammiversary XIII	Orlando, FL	-	★★★
04-07-15	WWE	Beast In The East '15	Tokyo, Japan	-	★★★★
19-07-15	WWE	Battleground '15	St. Louis, MO	25,000	★★
22-08-15	NXT	TakeOver: Brooklyn	Brooklyn, NY	-	★★★★★
23-08-15	WWE	SummerSlam '15	Brooklyn, NY	36,000	★★★

DATE	FED	EVENT	LOCATION	NA BUYS	RATING
18-09-15	ROH	All Star Extravaganza VII	San Antonio, TX	-	★★★
20-09-15	WWE	Night Of Champions '15	Houston, TX	31,000	★★★
03-10-15	WWE	Live From Madison Square Garden	New York City, NY	-	★★
04-10-15	TNA	Bound For Glory '15	Orlando, FL	-	★★
07-10-15	NXT	TakeOver: Respect	Winter Park, FL	-	★★★★
25-10-15	WWE	Hell In A Cell '15	Los Angeles, CA	23,000	★★★
22-11-15	WWE	Survivor Series '15	Atlanta, GA	19,000	★★
13-12-15	WWE	TLC '15	Boston, MA	14,000	★★★
16-12-15	NXT	TakeOver: London	London, England	-	★★★
18-12-15	ROH	Final Battle '15	Philadelphia, PA	-	★★★
23-12-15	WWE	Tribute To The Troops '15	Jacksonville, FL	-	★★
24-01-16	WWE	Royal Rumble '16	Orlando, FL	32,000	★★★
21-02-16	WWE	Fastlane '16	Cleveland, OH	18,000	★★
26-02-16	ROH	14th Anniversary Show	Las Vegas, NV	-	★★★
12-03-16	WWE	Roadblock '16	Toronto, ON	-	★★★
01-04-16	NXT	TakeOver: Dallas	Dallas, TX	-	★★★★★
03-04-16	WWE	WrestleMania XXXII	Arlington, TX	-	★★
01-05-16	WWE	Payback '16	Rosemont, IL	-	★★★★
08-05-16	ROH/NJPW	Global Wars '16	Chicago Ridge, IL	-	★★
22-05-16	WWE	Extreme Rules '16	Newark, NJ	-	★★★★
08-06-16	NXT	TakeOver: The End	Winter Park, FL	-	★★★★
12-06-16	TNA	Slammiversary XIV	Orlando, FL	-	★★
19-06-16	WWE	Money In The Bank '16	Paradise, NV	-	★★★
24-06-16	ROH	Best In The World '16	Concord, NC	-	★★★
24-07-16	WWE	Battleground '16	Washington, D.C.	-	★★★
19-08-16	ROH	Death Before Dishonor XIV	Las Vegas, NV	-	★★★
20-08-16	NXT	TakeOver: Brooklyn II	Brooklyn, NY	-	★★★★
21-08-16	WWE	SummerSlam '16	Brooklyn, NY	-	★★★
11-09-16	WWE	Backlash '16	Richmond, VA	-	★★★
14-09-16	WWE	Cruiserweight Classic Finale	Winter Park, FL	-	★★★★
25-09-16	WWE	Clash Of Champions '16	Indianapolis, IN	-	★★★
30-09-16	ROH	All Star Extravaganza VIII	Lowell, MA	-	★★★
02-10-16	TNA	Bound For Glory '16	Orlando, FL	-	★★
09-10-16	WWE	No Mercy '16	Sacramento, CA	-	★★★
30-10-16	WWE	Hell In A Cell '16	Boston, MA	-	★★
19-11-16	NXT	TakeOver: Toronto	Toronto, Canada	-	★★★★
20-11-16	WWE	Survivor Series '16	Toronto, Canada	-	★★★
02-12-16	ROH	Final Battle '16	New York, NY	-	★★★
04-12-16	WWE	TLC '16	Dallas, TX	-	★★★
14-12-16	WWE	Tribute To The Troops '16	Washington, D.C.	-	★★
18-12-16	WWE	Roadblock: End Of The Line '16	Pittsburgh, PA	-	★★★
14-01-17	WWE	UK Championship Tournament Night 1	Blackpool, England	-	★★
15-01-17	WWE	UK Championship Tournament Night 2	Blackpool, England	-	★★★
28-01-17	NXT	TakeOver: San Antonio	San Antonio, TX	-	★★★
29-01-17	WWE	Royal Rumble '17	San Antonio, TX	-	★★★★
12-02-17	WWE	Elimination Chamber '17	Phoenix, AZ	-	★★
05-03-17	WWE	Fastlane '17	Milwaukee, WI	-	★★
10-03-17	ROH	15th Anniversary Show	Las Vegas, NV	-	★★★★
01-04-17	NXT	TakeOver: Orlando	Orlando, FL	-	★★★
01-04-17	ROH	Supercard Of Honor XI	Lakeland, FL	-	★★★
02-04-17	WWE	WrestleMania XXXIII	Orlando, FL	-	★★★
30-04-17	WWE	Payback '17	San Jose, CA	-	★★★
12-05-17	ROH/NJPW	War Of The Worlds '17	New York, NY	-	★★★
19-05-17	WWE	UK Championship Special '17	Norwich, England	-	★★★
20-05-17	NXT	TakeOver: Chicago	Rosemont, IL	-	★★★
21-05-17	WWE	Backlash '17	Rosemont, IL	-	★★
04-06-17	WWE	Extreme Rules '17	Baltimore, MD	-	★★★
18-06-17	WWE	Money In The Bank '17	St. Louis, MO	-	★★
23-06-17	ROH	Best In The World '17	Lowell, MA	-	★★★
02-07-17	Impact	Slammiversary XV	Orlando, FL	-	★★
09-07-17	WWE	Great Balls Of Fire '17	Dallas, TX	-	★★★
23-07-17	WWE	Battleground '17	Philadelphia, PA	-	★★
19-08-17	ROH/NJPW	War Of The Worlds UK '17	Liverpool, England	-	★★
19-08-17	NXT	TakeOver: Brooklyn III	Brooklyn, NY	-	★★★★
20-08-17	WWE	SummerSlam '17	Brooklyn, NY	-	★★
22-09-17	ROH	Death Before Dishonor XV	Las Vegas, NV	-	★★★
24-09-17	WWE	No Mercy '17	Los Angeles, CA	-	★★★
08-10-17	WWE	Hell In A Cell '17	Detroit, MI	-	★★★
15-10-17	ROH/NJPW	Global Wars '17	Villa Park, IL	-	★★★
22-10-17	WWE	TLC '17	Minneapolis, MN	-	★★★
05-11-17	Impact	Bound For Glory '17	Ottawa, Canada	-	★★
18-11-17	NXT	TakeOver: WarGames	Houston, TX	-	★★★★
19-11-17	WWE	Survivor Series '17	Houston, TX	-	★★★
14-12-17	WWE	Tribute To The Troops '17	San Diego, CA	-	★★
15-12-17	ROH	Final Battle '17	New York, NY	-	★★
17-12-17	WWE	Clash Of Champions '17	Boston, MA	-	★★
27-01-18	NXT	TakeOver: Philadelphia	Philadelphia, PA	-	★★★★
28-01-18	WWE	Royal Rumble '18	Philadelphia, PA	-	★★★★
09-02-18	ROH	Honor Reigns Supreme '18	Condord, NC	-	★★
25-02-18	WWE	Elimination Chamber '18	Paradise, NV	-	★★
09-03-18	ROH	16th Anniversary Show	Las Vegas, NV	-	★★★

DATE	FED	EVENT	LOCATION	NA BUYS	RATING
11-03-18	WWE	Fastlane '18	Columbus, OH	-	★★★
07-04-18	NXT	TakeOver: New Orleans	New Orleans, LA	-	★★★★★
07-04-18	ROH	Supercard Of Honor XII	New Orleans, LA	-	★★★
08-04-18	WWE	WrestleMania XXXIV	New Orleans, LA	-	★★★
22-04-18	Impact	Redemption	Orlando, FL	-	★★★
27-04-18	WWE	Greatest Royal Rumble '18	Jeddah, Saudi Arabia	-	★★★
06-05-18	WWE	Backlash '18	Newark, NJ	-	★★
16-06-18	NXT	TakeOver: Chicago II	Rosemont, IL	-	★★★★
17-06-18	WWE	Money In The Bank '18	Rosemont, IL	-	★★★
25-06-18	NXT UK	United Kingdom Championship Tournament '18	London, England	-	★★★
26-06-18	NXT	U.K. Championship	London, England	-	★★★
29-06-18	ROH	Best In The World '18	Baltimore, MD	-	★★★
15-07-18	WWE	Extreme Rules '18	Pittsburgh, PA	-	★★
22-07-18	Impact	Slammiversary XVI	Toronto, Canada	1,500	★★★★
18-08-18	NXT	TakeOver: Brooklyn IV	Brooklyn, NY	-	★★★★
19-08-18	WWE	SummerSlam '18	Brooklyn, NY	29,900	★★★
01-09-18		All In	Hoffman Estates, IL	45,000	★★★★
16-09-18	WWE	Hell In A Cell '18	San Antonio, TX	16,300	★★★
28-09-18	ROH	Death Before Dishonor XVI	Las Vegas, NV	-	★★★
06-10-18	WWE	Super Show-Down '18	Melbourne, Australia	-	★★★
14-10-18	Impact	Bound For Glory '18	New York, NY	-	★★★
21-10-18	NWA	70th Anniversary Show	Nashville, TN	-	★★★
28-10-18	WWE	Evolution	Uniondale, NY	14,100	★★★
02-11-18	WWE	Crown Jewel '18	Riyadh, Saudi Arabia	-	★
17-11-18	NXT	TakeOver: WarGames II	Los Angeles, CA	-	★★★★
18-11-18	WWE	Survivor Series '18	Los Angeles, CA	-	★★★★
25-11-18	WWE	Starrcade '18	Cincinnati, Ohio	-	★★
14-12-18	ROH	Final Battle '18	Manhattan, NY	3,700	★★★★
16-12-18	WWE	TLC '18	San Jose, CA	-	★★★
20-12-18	WWE	Tribute To The Troops '18	Killeen, TX	-	★★
06-01-19	Impact	Homecoming	Nashville, TN	3,100	★★★
12-01-19	NXT UK	TakeOver: Blackpool	Blackpool, England	-	★★★
26-01-19	NXT	TakeOver: Phoenix	Phoenix, AZ	-	★★★★
27-01-19	WWE	Royal Rumble '19	Phoenix, AZ	-	★★★
02-02-19	WWE	Worlds Collide '19	Phoenix, AZ	-	★★
17-02-19	WWE	Elimination Chamber '19	Houston, TX	-	★★★
10-03-19	WWE	Fastlane '19	Cleveland, OH	-	★★★
15-03-19	ROH	17th Anniversary Show	Las Vegas, NV	2,800	★★★
04-04-19	Impact	United We Stand	Rahway, NJ	-	★★
05-04-19	NXT	TakeOver: New York	Brooklyn, NY	-	★★★★★
06-04-19	ROH/NJPW	G1 Supercard	New York City, NY	5,300	★★★
07-04-19	WWE	WrestleMania XXXV	East Rutherford, NJ	64,100	★★★
14-04-19	WWE	Worlds Collide: NXT vs. NXT Alumni	Brooklyn, NY	-	★★★
17-04-19	WWE	Worlds Collide: Cruiserweights Collide	Brooklyn, NY	-	★★★
27-04-19	NWA	Crockett Cup '19	Concord, NC	2,600	★★★
28-04-19	Impact	Rebellion '19	Toronto, Canada	2,000	★★★
19-05-19	WWE	Money In The Bank '19	Hartford, CT	15,700	★★★
25-05-19	AEW	Double Or Nothing '19	Paradise, NV	98,000	★★★★
01-06-19	NXT	TakeOver: XXV	Bridgeport, CT	-	★★★★
07-06-19	WWE	Super ShowDown '19	Jeddah, Saudi Arabia	11,000	★
23-06-19	WWE	Stomping Grounds '19	Tacoma, WA	9,800	★★
28-06-19	ROH	Best In The World '19	Baltimore, MD	1,500	★★
29-06-19	AEW	Fyter Fest '19	Daytona Beach, FL	-	★★★
07-07-19	Impact	Slammiversary XVII	Dallas, TX	1,500	★★★
13-07-19	AEW	Fight For The Fallen '19	Jacksonville, FL	-	★★
14-07-19	WWE	Extreme Rules '19	Philadelphia, PA	13,500	★★★
10-08-19	NXT	TakeOver: Toronto	Toronto, Canada	-	★★★★
11-08-19	WWE	SummerSlam '19	Toronto, Canada	22,300	★★★
31-08-19	NXT UK	TakeOver: Cardiff	Cardiff, Wales	-	★★★★
31-08-19	AEW	All Out '19	Hoffman Estates, IL	88,000	★★★
15-09-19	AAA	Lucha Invades NY	New York, NY	-	★★★
15-09-19	WWE	Clash Of Champions '19	Charlotte, NC	12,800	★★
27-09-19	ROH	Death Before Dishonor XVII	Las Vegas, NV	800	★★★
06-10-19	WWE	Hell In A Cell '19	Sacramento, CA	12,500	★★
20-10-19	Impact	Bound For Glory '19	Villa Park, IL	-	★★★
31-10-19	WWE	Crown Jewel '19	Riyadh, Saudi Arabia	-	★★
02-11-19	MLW	Saturday Night SuperFight '19	Cicero, IL	-	★★★★
09-11-19	AEW	Full Gear '19	Baltimore, MD	80,000	★★★★
23-11-19	NXT	TakeOver: WarGames III	Rosemont, IL	-	★★★★
24-11-19	WWE	Survivor Series '19	Rosemont, IL	-	★★★
01-12-19	WWF	Starrcade '19	Duluth, GA	-	★★
13-12-19	ROH	Final Battle '19	Baltimore, MD	-	★★★
14-12-19	NWA	Into The Fire	Atlanta, GA	-	★★★
15-12-19	WWE	TLC '19	Minneapolis, MN	-	★★
12-01-20	NXT UK	TakeOver: Blackpool II	Blackpool, England	-	★★★
12-01-20	Impact	Hard To Kill	Dallas, TX	-	★★★
24-01-20	NWA	Hard Times	Atlanta, GA	-	★★★
25-01-20	NXT	Worlds Collide '20	Houston, TX	-	★★★
26-01-20	WWE	Royal Rumble '20	Houston, TX	-	★★★★
16-02-20	NXT	TakeOver: Portland	Portland, OR	-	★★★★
27-02-20	WWE	Super Showdown '20	Riyadh, Saudi Arabia	-	★

DATE	FED	EVENT	LOCATION	NA BUYS	RATING
29-02-20	AEW	Revolution '20	Chicago, IL	90,000	★★★★★
08-03-20	WWE	Elimination Chamber '20	Philadelphia, PA	-	★★
04-04-20	WWE	WrestleMania XXXVI Night #1	Orlando, FL	-	★★★
05-04-20	WWE	WrestleMania XXXVI Night #2	Orlando, FL	-	★★★
10-05-20	WWE	Money In The Bank '20	Orlando, FL	-	★★★
23-05-20	AEW	Double Or Nothing '20	Jacksonville, FL	105,000	★★★★
07-06-20	NXT	TakeOver: In Your House	Winter Park, FL	-	★★★
14-06-20	WWE	Backlash '20	Orlando, FL	-	★★★
18-07-20	Impact	Slammiversary XVIII	Nashville, TN	-	★★★
19-07-20	WWE	The Horror Show At Extreme Rules '20	Orlando, FL	-	★★
22-08-20	NXT	TakeOver XXX	Winter Park, FL	-	★★★
23-08-20	WWE	SummerSlam '20	Orlando, FL	-	★★★★
30-08-20	WWE	Payback '20	Orlando, FL	-	★★★
05-09-20	AEW	All Out '20	Jacksonville, FL	90,000	★★★
27-09-20	WWE	Clash Of Champions '20	Orlando, FL	-	★★★★
04-10-20	NXT	TakeOver 31	Orlando, FL	-	★★★
24-10-20	Impact	Bound For Glory '20	Nashville, TN	-	★★
25-10-20	WWE	Hell In A Cell '20	Orlando, FL	-	★★★★
07-11-20	AEW	Full Gear '20	Jacksonville, FL	85,000	★★★★
22-11-20	WWE	Survivor Series '20	Orlando, FL	-	★★★
06-12-20	WWE	Tribute To The Troops '20	Orlando, FL	-	★★
06-12-20	NXT	TakeOver: WarGames IV	Orlando, FL	-	★★★
18-12-20	ROH	Final Battle '20	Baltimore, MD	-	★★★
20-12-20	WWE	TLC '20	St. Petersburg, FL	-	★★★★
16-01-21	Impact	Hard To Kill '21	Nashville, TN	-	★★★
26-01-21	WWE	Superstar Spectacle	St. Petersburg, FL	-	★★
31-01-21	WWE	Royal Rumble '21	St. Petersburg, FL	6,400	★★★
14-02-21	NXT	TakeOver Vengeance Day	Orlando, FL	-	★★★★
21-02-21	WWE	Elimination Chamber '21	St. Petersburg, FL	2,600	★★★
07-03-21	AEW	Revolution '21	Jacksonville, FL	135,000	★★★
21-03-21	NWA	Back For The Attack	Atlanta, GA	-	★★★
21-03-21	WWE	Fastlane '21	St. Petersburg, FL	3,800	★★★
26-03-21	ROH	19th Anniversary Show	Baltimore, MD	-	★★
08-04-21	NXT	Takeover Stand & Deliver '21	Orlando, FL	-	★★
10-04-21	WWE	WrestleMania XXXVII Night #1	Tampa, FL	6,000	★★★★
11-04-21	WWE	WrestleMania XXXVII Night #2	Tampa, FL	6,000	★★★
25-04-21	Impact	Rebellion '21	Nashville, TN	-	★★★
16-05-21	WWE	WrestleMania Backlash '21	Tampa, FL	5,500	★★★
30-05-21	AEW	Double Or Nothing '21	Jacksonville, FL	115,000	★★★★
06-06-21	NWA	When Our Shadows Fall	Atlanta, FA	-	★★★
13-06-21	NXT	Takeover In Your House '21	Orlando, FL	-	★★★
20-06-21	WWE	Hell In A Cell '21	Tampa, FL	-	★★★
11-07-21	ROH	Best In The World '21	Baltimore, MD	-	★★★
17-07-21	Impact	Slammiversary XIX	Nashville, TN	-	★★★
18-07-21	WWE	Money In The Bank '21	Fort Worth, TX	-	★★★★
20-08-21	ROH	Glory By Honor XVIII Night #1	Philadelphia, PA	-	★★
21-08-21	ROH	Glory By Honor XVIII Night #2	Philadelphia, PA	-	★★★
21-08-21	WWE	SummerSlam '21	Paradise, NV	-	★★★
22-08-21	NXT	Takeover 36	Orlando, FL	-	★★★
28-08-21	NWA	Empowerrr	St. Louis, MO	-	★★
29-08-21	NWA	73rd Anniversary Show	St. Louis, MO	-	★★★
05-09-21	AEW	All Out '21	Hoffman Estates, IL	205,000	★★★★★
12-09-21	ROH	Death Before Hishonor XVIII	Philadelphia, PA	-	★★★
26-09-21	WWE	Extreme Rules '21	Columbus, OH	-	★★★
21-10-21	WWE	Crown Jewel '21	Riyadh, Saudi Arabia	-	★★★★
23-10-21	Impact	Bound For Glory '21	Las Vegas, NV	-	★★★
13-11-21	AEW	Full Gear '21	Minneapolis, MN	145,000	★★★★★
14-11-21	ROH	Honor For All '21	Baltimore, MD	-	★★
14-11-21	WWE	Tribute To The Troops '21	Ontario, CA	-	★★
21-11-21	WWE	Survivor Series '21	Brooklyn, NY	-	★★
04-12-21	NWA	Hard Times 2	Atlanta, GA	-	★★
05-12-21	NXT 2.0	WarGames V	Orlando, FL	-	★★★
11-12-21	ROH	Final Battle '21	Baltimore, MD	-	★★★
01-01-22	WWE	Day 1	Atlanta, GA	-	★★★
08-01-22	AEW	Battle Of The Belts I	Charlotte, NC	-	★★
08-01-22	Impact	Hard To Kill '22	Dallas, TX	-	★★★★
29-01-22	WWE	Royal Rumble '22	St. Louis, MO	-	★★
19-02-22	WWE	Elimination Chamber '22	Jeddah, Saudi Arabia	-	★★
06-03-22	AEW	Revolution '22	Orlando, FL	-	★★★★
19-03-22	NWA	Crockett Cup '22 Night #1	Nashville, TN	-	★★
20-03-22	NWA	Crockett Cup '22 Night #2	Nashville, TN	-	★★★
01-04-22	Impact	Multiverse Of Matches	Dallas, TX	-	★★★
01-04-22	ROH	Supercard Of Honor XV	Garland, TX	-	★★★
02-04-22	NXT	Stand & Deliver '22	Dallas, TX	-	★★★
02-04-22	WWE	WrestleMania XXXVIII Night #1	Dallas, TX	-	★★★★★
03-04-22	WWE	WrestleMania XXXVIII Night #2	Dallas, TX	-	★★★
16-04-22	AEW	Battle Of The Belts II	Garland, TX	-	★★
23-04-22	Impact	Rebellion '22	Poughkeepsie, NY	-	★★★
08-05-22	WWE	WrestleMania Backlash '22	Providence, RI	-	★★★
29-05-22	AEW	Double Or Nothing '22	Paradise, NV	-	★★★
04-06-22	NXT	In Your House '22	Orlando, FL	-	★★

DATE	FED	EVENT	LOCATION	NA BUYS	RATING
05-06-22	WWE	Hell In A Cell '22	Rosemont, IL	-	★★★★
11-06-22	NWA	Alwayz Ready '22	Knoxville, TN	-	★★★
19-06-22	Impact	Slammiversary XX	Nashville, TN	-	★★★
26-06-22	AEW/NJPW	Forbidden Door	Chicago, IL	-	★★★★
02-07-22	WWE	Money In The Bank '22	Paradise, NV	-	★★
23-07-22	ROH	Death Before Dishonor XIX	Lowell, MA	-	★★★★
30-07-22	WWE	SummerSlam '22	Nashville, TN	-	★★★★
31-07-22	JCP	Ric Flair's Last Match	Nashville, TN	-	★★
06-08-22	AEW	Battle Of The Belts III	Grand Rapids, MI	-	★★★
27-08-22	NWA	74th Anniversary Show Night #1	St. Louis, MO	-	★★
28-08-22	NWA	74th Anniversary Show Night #2	St. Louis, MO	-	★★
03-09-22	WWE	Clash At The Castle	Cardiff, Wales	-	★★★★
04-09-22	NXT	Worlds Collide '22	Orlando, FL	-	★★★
04-09-22	AEW	All Out '22	Hoffman Estates, IL	-	★★★
07-10-22	Impact	Bound For Glory '22	Albany, NY	-	★★★★
07-10-22	AEW	Battle Of The Belts IV	Washington, D.C.	-	★★
08-10-22	WWE	Extreme Rules '22	Philadelphia, PA	-	★★★
22-10-22	NXT	Halloween Havoc '22	Orlando, FL	-	★★★
05-11-22	WWE	Crown Jewel '22	Riyadh, Saudi Arabia	-	★★★
12-11-22	NWA	Hard Times 3	Chalmette, LA	-	★★★
19-11-22	AEW	Full Gear '22	Newark, NJ	-	★★★★
26-11-22	WWE	Survivor Series WarGames	Boston, MA	-	★★★
10-12-22	NXT	Deadline	Orlando, FL	-	★★★
10-12-22	ROH	Final Battle '22	Arlington, TX	-	★★★
17-12-22	WWE	Tribute To The Troops '22	Indianapolis, IN	-	★★

HISTORIC
EVENT
RESULTS

WWWF at Madison Square Garden (30-06-73) ★★

03-06-73, New York City, New York **WWWF**

Blackjack Lanza defeated Lee Wong in 5:05 (★★); Professor Toru Tanaka defeated El Olympico in 9:34 (★★); Gorilla Monsoon defeated Captain Lou Albano in 2:58 (★★); Victor Rivera defeated Black Gordman in 11:34 (★★★); Joyce Grable and Jan Sheridan defeated Peggy Patterson and Dottie Downs 2-1 in a Best Two Out Of Three Falls Match in 20:47 (★); Pedro Morales defeated George Steele in 8:16 (★★★); Chief Jay Strongbow defeated Mr. Fuji in 13:58 (★★); Haystacks Calhoun defeated Moondog Mayne in 6:03 (★★).

WWWF at Madison Square Garden (29-04-74) ★★★

29-04-74, New York City, New York **WWWF**

Jose Gonzalez vs. Larry Zbyszko ended in a draw in 20:00 (★★★); Tony Garea defeated Mike Conrad in 17:09 (★★★); Nikolai Volkoff defeated Dean Ho in 5:22 (★★); Robert Fuller defeated Ed Sullivan in 10:39 (★★); Bruno Sammartino vs. Killer Kowalski ended in a no contest in 24:15 (★★★★); Pedro Morales defeated Mr. Fuji in 10:29 (★★★); Chief Jay Strongbow and Andre The Giant defeated Otto Von Heller and Don Leo Jonathan 2-0 in a Best Two Out Of Three Falls Match in 10:08 (★★).

WWWF at Madison Square Garden (17-02-75) ★★★

17-02-75, New York City, New York **WWWF**

Manuel Soto and Pete Sanchez defeated Jack Evans and Johnny Rodz in a Best Two Out Of Three Falls Match in 7:59 (★★); Butcher Nova defeated Bill White in 15:02 (★★★); Victor Rivera defeated Hans Schroeder in 9:17 (★★); Dean Ho and Tony Garea defeated Killer Kowalski and Bobby Duncum by DQ in 14:17 (★★★); The Wolfman defeated El Olympico in 3:14 (★★); Pedro Morales defeated Butcher Vachon in 4:59 (★★★); Spiros Arion defeated Bruno Sammartino by DQ in 18:14 (★★★); The Valiant Brothers (Jimmy Valiant and Johnny Valiant) vs. Gorilla Monsoon and Chief Jay Strongbow ended in a draw in 19:09 (★★★).

WWWF at Madison Square Garden (17-03-75) ★★★

17-03-75, New York City, New York **WWWF**

Johnny Rodz defeated Bill White in 11:31 (★★); Mike Paidousis defeated Jack Evans in 5:43 (★★); Manuel Soto and Pete Sanchez defeated Joe Nova and Hans Schroeder in a Best Two Out Of Three Falls Match in 22:05 (★★★); Chief Jay Strongbow defeated Butcher Vachon in 9:10 (★★); Bruno Sammartino defeated Spiros Arion in a Texas Death Match in 14:51 (★★★); Victor Rivera defeated Killer Kowalski by DQ in 15:58 (★★); Ivan Putski defeated The Wolfman in 6:45 (★★); Dean Ho and Tony Garea vs. The Valiant Brothers (Johnny Valiant and Jimmy Valiant) ended in a draw in a Best Two Out Of Three Falls Match in 12:13 (★★★).

WWWF at Madison Square Garden (14-04-75) ★★

14-04-75, New York City, New York **WWWF**

Mike Paidousis defeated Tony Altimore in 13:05 (★★); Greg Valentine defeated El Olympico in 7:49 (★★); Waldo Von Erich defeated Chief Jay Strongbow via count out in :39 (★★); Little Tokyo and Lord Littlebrook defeated Little Louie and Sonny Boy Hayes 2-1 in a Best Two Out Of Three Falls Match in 18:49 (★★); Bruno Sammartino defeated Spiros Arion in a Greek Death Match in 14:58 (★★★★); Edouard Carpentier defeated Joe Nova in 9:16 (★★★); Bobby Duncum vs. Victor Rivera ended in a draw in 15:53 (★★).

WWWF at Madison Square Garden (16-06-75) ★★

16-06-75, New York City, New York **WWWF**

The Fabulous Moolah defeated Susan Green in 10:16 (★★); Pete Sanchez defeated Johnny Rodz in 12:09 (★★); Jack Evans defeated Bill White in 13:55 (★★); Baron Mikel Scicluna defeated Mike Paidousis in 11:02 (★★); Dominic DeNucci and Victor Rivera defeated Bobby Duncum and Butcher Vachon 2-1 in a Best Two Out Of Three Falls Match in 22:23 (★★★); Ivan Putski defeated Johnny Valiant in 4:30 (★★); Chief Jay Strongbow defeated Jimmy Valiant in 15:50 (★★★); Bruno Sammartino defeated Waldo Von Erich in 4:12 (★★).

WWWF at Madison Square Garden (13-10-75) ★★★

13-10-75, New York City, New York **WWWF**

Manuel Soto defeated Jack Evans in 14:55 (★★★); Francisco Flores defeated Johnny Rodz in 11:36 (★★★); Pete Sanchez vs. Frank Monte ended in a draw in 20:00 (★★); Louis Cerdan and Tony Parisi defeated Spiros Arion and Waldo Von Erich 2-0 in a Best Two Out Of Three Falls Match in 12:16 (★★★); Dominic DeNucci defeated Baron Mikel Scicluna in 7:05 (★★); Bruno Sammartino vs. Ivan Koloff ended in a draw in 21:59 (★★★); Gorilla Monsoon, Ivan Putski and Haystacks Calhoun vs. Bugsy McGraw and The Blackjacks (Blackjack Mulligan and Blackjack Lanza) ended in a draw in a Best Three Out Of Five Falls Match in 14:37 (★★★).

WWWF at Madison Square Garden (02-02-76) ★★

02-02-76, New York City, New York **WWWF**

Frank Monte defeated Pete Sanchez in 9:21 (★★); Louis Cyr defeated Francisco Flores in 9:16 (★★); Spiros Arion defeated Kevin Sullivan in 6:44 (★★); Ernie Ladd defeated Dominic DeNucci in 11:55 (★★); Ivan Putski vs. Ivan Koloff ended in a draw in 10:40 (★★); Little Louie and The Cocoa Kid defeated Billy The Kid and Little Johnny 2-0 in a Best Two Out Of Three Falls Match in 18:29 (★★); Bruno Sammartino defeated Superstar Billy Graham in 17:55 (★★★); Baron Mikel Scicluna defeated Pat Barrett in 6:44 (★★); Bobo Brazil and Tony Parisi defeated Crusher Blackwell and Bugsy McGraw 2-0 in a Best Two Out Of Three Falls Match in 11:34 (★★).

WWWF at Madison Square Garden (01-03-76) ★★★

01-03-76, New York City, New York **WWWF**

Rocky Tomayo defeated Johnny Rivera in 14:58 (★★★); Dominic DeNucci defeated Baron Mikel Scicluna in 16:02 (★★); Ric Flair defeated Pete Sanchez in 10:05 (★★); Louis Cyr defeated Pat Barrett in 11:05 (★★); Superstar Billy Graham and Ivan Koloff defeated Tony Parisi and Louis Cerdan by DQ in a Best Two Out Of Three Falls Match in 19:07 (★★★); Bruno Sammartino defeated Ernie Ladd in 11:25 (★★); Susan Green defeated Kitty Adams in 9:21 (★★); Bobo Brazil defeated Crusher Blackwell in 8:22 (★★).

WWWF at Madison Square Garden (07-08-76) ★★★

07-08-76, New York City, New York **WWWF**

Manuel Soto vs. Pete Sanchez ended in a draw in 15:00 (★★); Johnny Rivera defeated Jose Cadiz in 10:41 (★★); SD Jones defeated Johnny Rodz in 8:12 (★★); The Executioners (Executioner #1 and Executioner #2) defeated Jose Gonzalez and Dominic DeNucci 2-1 in a Best Two Out Of Three Falls Match in 22:54 (★★★); Bruiser Brody defeated Kevin Sullivan in 2:29 (★★); Chief Jay Strongbow and Billy White Wolf defeated Baron Mikel Scicluna and Rocky Tomayo in 5:58 (★); Bruno Sammartino defeated Stan Hansen in a Steel Cage Match in 11:11 (★★★★); Bobo Brazil defeated Doug Gilbert in :35 (★); Ivan Putski defeated General Skandor Akbar in 2:56 (★★).

WWWF at Madison Square Garden (25-10-76) ★★★

25-10-76, New York City, New York **WWWF**

Manuel Soto defeated Johnny Rodz in 11:45 (★★); Kevin Sullivan vs. Pete Sanchez ended in a draw in 20:00 (★★★); Bobo Brazil defeated Doug Gilbert in 8:04 (★★); Tor Kamata defeated Jose Gonzalez in 11:36 (★★); Ivan Putski defeated Stan Hansen in 6:26 (★★); Bruno Sammartino defeated Nikolai Volkoff in 19:44 (★★★★); Victor Rivera defeated Baron Mikel Scicluna in 6:15 (★★); Andre The Giant, Chief Jay Strongbow and Billy White Wolf defeated Bruiser Brody and The Executioners (Executioner #1 and Executioner #2) 3-1 in a Best Three Out Of Five Falls Match in 20:34 (★★).

WWWF at Madison Square Garden (07-03-77) ★★★

07-03-77, New York City, New York **WWWF**

Don Kent vs. Jose Gonzalez ended in a draw in 20:00 (★★★); Gino Hernandez defeated Johnny Rodz in 8:24 (★★); Carlos Rocha defeated Executioner #1 in 8:04 (★★); Ivan Putski defeated Executioner #2 in 9:35 (★★★); Larry Zbyszko defeated Doug Gilbert in 12:18 (★★★); Bruno Sammartino defeated Ken Patera in 17:29 (★★★); Bobo Brazil defeated Jan Nelson in 3:18 (★★); Dusty Rhodes defeated Pete Doherty in 2:59 (★★); Tony Garea defeated Baron Mikel Scicluna in 4:58 (★★); Chief Jay Strongbow and Billy White Wolf defeated Stan Stasiak and Tor Kamata 2-1 in a Best Two Out Of Three Falls Match in 11:41 (★★★).

WWWF at Madison Square Garden (27-06-77) ★★
27-06-77, New York City, New York **WWWF**
Jose Gonzalez defeated Jan Nelson in 9:46 (★★); Larry Zbyszko defeated Rocky Tomayo in 7:31 (★★); Tony Garea defeated George Steele by DQ in 7:28 (★★); Andre the Giant and Chief Jay Strongbow defeated Nikolai Volkoff and Ken Patera 2-0 in a Best Two Out Of Three Falls Match in 16:25 (★★★); Stan Stasiak defeated Lenny Hurst in 8:21 (★★); Superstar Billy Graham vs. Bruno Sammartino ended in a Double DQ in 18:39 (★★★); Ivan Putski vs. Baron Von Raschke ended in a draw in 19:13 (★★); Peter Maivia defeated Baron Mikel Scicluna in 2:09 (★★); Professor Toru Tanaka and Mr. Fuji defeated Haystacks Calhoun and Dominic DeNucci in a Best Two Out Of Three Falls Match in 4:44 (★★).

WWWF at Madison Square Garden (29-08-77) ★★
29-08-77, New York City, New York **WWWF**
Johnny Rivera defeated Joe Turco in 10:51 (★★); SD Jones defeated Jack Evans in 8:19 (★★); Peter Maivia defeated Stan Stasiak via count out in 7:35 (★★); Tony Garea and Larry Zbyszko defeated George Steele and Baron Mikel Scicluna 2-0 in a Best Two Out Of Three Falls Match in 10:34 (★★); Superstar Billy Graham defeated Ivan Putski via count out in 18:01 (★★); Verne Gagne defeated Nikolai Volkoff in 7:10 (★★); Bruno Sammartino defeated Ken Patera in a Texas Death Match in 12:13 (★★★); Chief Jay Strongbow vs. Mr. Fuji ended in a draw in 6:18 (★★).

WWWF at Madison Square Garden (26-09-77) ★★★
26-09-77, New York City, New York **WWWF**
Cowboy Lang and Haiti Kid defeated Little John and Little Tokyo 2-0 on a Best Two Out Of Three Falls Match in 16:42 (★★★); Professor Toru Tanaka defeated Johnny Rivera in 10:09 (★★); Baron Mikel Scicluna vs. Jack Evans ended in a double DQ in 7:29 (★★); Mr. Fuji defeated Lenny Hurst in 6:19 (★★); Bob Backlund defeated Larry Sharpe in 9:04 (★★★); Dusty Rhodes defeated Superstar Billy Graham via count out in 15:55 (★★★); Peter Maivia defeated George Steele via count out in 13:19 (★★); Chief Jay Strongbow, Tony Garea and Larry Zbyszko defeated Ken Patera, Stan Stasiak and Captain Lou Albano in a Best Three Out Of Five Falls Match in 23:24 (★★★).

WWWF at Madison Square Garden (24-10-77) ★★
24-10-77, New York City, New York **WWWF**
Larry Zbyszko defeated Johnny Rodz in 9:29 (★★); Tony Garea defeated Baron Mikel Scicluna; Larry Sharpe defeated Johnny Rivera in 10:22 (★★); Butcher Vachon defeated Lenny Hurst in 5:59 (★★); Kitty Adams and Leilani Kai defeated Winona Little Heart and Vivian St. John in 10:43 (★★); Superstar Billy Graham defeated Dusty Rhodes in a Texas Death Match in 9:12 (★★★); Mil Mascaras defeated Jack Evans in 8:17 (★★★); Professor Toru Tanaka and Mr. Fuji vs. Peter Maivia and Chief Jay Strongbow ended in a draw in a Best Two Out Of Three Falls Match in 23:06 (★★★); Ivan Putski defeated Stan Stasiak via count out in 2:03 (★).

WWWF at Madison Square Garden (19-12-77) ★★
19-12-77, New York City, New York **WWWF**
Baron Mikel Scicluna vs. SD Jones ended in a Draw in 14:49 (★★); Butcher Vachon defeated Johnny Rivera in 6:04 (★★); Arnold Skaaland defeated Captain Lou Albano via count out in 4:35 (★); Bob Backlund defeated Mr. Fuji in 11:40 (★★); Mil Mascaras defeated Superstar Billy Graham in 16:24 (★★★); Dusty Rhodes defeated Stan Stasiak in 11:22 (★★); Chief Jay Strongbow defeated Professor Toru Tanaka by DQ in 11:23 (★★); Tony Garea and Larry Zbyszko defeated Larry Sharpe and Jack Evans in a Best Two Out Of Three Falls Match in 13:16 (★★).

WWWF at Spectrum (18-02-78) ★★
18-02-78, Philadelphia, Pennsylvania **WWWF**
Ted Adams defeated Joe Turco in 10:32 (★★); Davey O'Hannon defeated Steve King in 13:23 (★★); Wee Willie Wilson and Hillbilly Pete defeated Little Johnny and Billy The Kid 2-1 in a Best Two Out Of Three Falls Match in 21:10 (★★); SD Jones defeated Nikolai Volkoff in 10:43 (★★★); Spiros Arion defeated Dominic DeNucci in 8:16 (★★); Superstar Billy Graham defeated Bruno Sammartino in a Steel Cage Match in 7:43 (★★); Peter Maivia defeated Baron Mikel Scicluna in 4:45 (★★); Mr. Fuji and Professor Toru Tanaka defeated Gorilla Monsoon and Chief Jay Strongbow 2-1 in a Best Two Out Of Three Falls Match in 12:09 (★★).

WWWF at Madison Square Garden (20-03-78) ★★★
20-03-78, New York City, New York **WWWF**
Dick Slater defeated Baron Mikel Scicluna in 5:43 (★★); Steve Keirn and Mike Graham defeated Butcher Vachon and The Golden Terror 2-0 in a Best Two Out Of Three Falls Match in 24:00 (★★★); Spiros Arion defeated Larry Zbyszko in 13:20 (★★★); Peter Maivia defeated Stan Stasiak in 9:30 (★★★); Superstar Billy Graham defeated Bob Backlund in 18:31 (★★★); Seiji Sakaguchi defeated Wilhelm Ruska in a Judo Match in 10:45 (★★); Tatsumi Fujinami defeated Frank Rodriguez in 8:43 (★★★); Dusty Rhodes, Mil Mascaras and Andre The Giant defeated Mr. Fuji, Professor Toru Tanaka and Ken Patera 2-0 in a Best Two Out Of Three Falls Match in 6:42 (★★★).

WWWF at Spectrum (25-03-78) ★★★
25-03-78, Philadelphia, Pennsylvania **WWWF**
Joe Turco defeated Pete Reeves in 10:17 (★); Gypsy Rodriguez defeated Pete Austin in 10:57 (★★); Dominic DeNucci defeated Davey O'Hannon in 10:31 (★★); Gorilla Monsoon defeated The Golden Terror in 4:42 (★★); Bob Backlund vs. Spiros Arion ended in a double DQ in 17:49 (★★★★); Bruno Sammartino vs. Ken Patera ended in a double count out in 16:24 (★★★); Haystacks Calhoun defeated Nikolai Volkoff in 2:39 (★★); Peter Maivia and Chief Jay Strongbow defeated Stan Stasiak and Baron Mikel Scicluna 2-1 in a Best Two Out Of Three Falls Match in 8:38 (★★).

WWWF at Madison Square Garden (28-08-78) ★★★
28-08-78, New York City, New York **WWWF**
Stan Stasiak vs. Dominic DeNucci ended in a draw in 19:48 (★★★); Haystacks Calhoun defeated Baron Mikel Scicluna in 7:12 (★★); Victor Rivera defeated SD Jones in 10:21 (★★); Ivan Koloff defeated Bob Backlund in 30:11 (★★★★); Peter Maivia defeated Luke Graham by DQ in 14:02 (★); Dusty Rhodes defeated Superstar Billy Graham in a No DQ Bullrope Match in 6:28 (★★); The Fabulous Moolah defeated Vicki Williams in 5:20 (★★); Andre The Giant, Tony Garea and Dino Bravo defeated Spiros Arion and The Yukon Lumberjacks (Lumberjack Eric and Lumberjack Pierre) 2-0 in a Best Two Out Of Three Falls Match in 6:14 (★★).

WWWF at Madison Square Garden (23-10-78) ★★★
23-10-78, New York City, New York **WWWF**
Johnny Rodz defeated Del Adams in 9:39 (★); Baron Mikel Scicluna vs. SD Jones ended in a draw in 20:00 (★★); The Yukon Lumberjacks (Lumberjack Eric and Lumberjack Pierre) defeated Peter Maivia and Chief Jay Strongbow in 3:57 (★★); Crusher Blackwell defeated Tony Russo in 4:39 (★★); Bob Backlund defeated Ernie Ladd in 17:24 (★★★); Larry Zbyszko defeated Spiros Arion in 6:12 (★★★); Bruno Sammartino defeated Superstar Billy Graham in 12:19 (★★★); Ivan Koloff defeated Tony Garea in 2:39 (★★); Victor Rivera defeated Dominic DeNucci in 4:11 (★★); Dino Bravo defeated Luke Graham in 3:46 (★★).

WWWF at Spectrum (16-12-78) ★★★
16-12-78, Philadelphia, Pennsylvania **WWWF**
SD Jones defeated Moose Monroe in 8:46 (★★); Mike Paidousis defeated Gypsy Rodriguez in 8:22 (★★); Victor Rivera and Spiros Arion defeated Larry Zbyszko and Tony Garea in 11:36 (★★★); Frankie Williams defeated Tony Russo in 7:36 (★★); Ivan Koloff defeated Bob Backlund in 22:33 (★★★★); Dino Bravo defeated Johnny Rodz in 6:28 (★★); Gorilla Monsoon defeated Crusher Blackwell in :19 (★); Bruno Sammartino defeated George Steele in 10:46 (★★★).

WWWF at Madison Square Garden (18-12-78) ★★★
18-12-78, New York City, New York **WWWF**
SD Jones defeated Crusher Blackwell in 7:09 (★★); Chief Jay Strongbow vs. Spiros Arion ended in a draw in 20:00 (★★★); Antonio Inoki defeated Texas Red in 16:27 (★★★); Harley Race defeated Tony Garea in 8:57 (★★★); Bob Backlund vs. Peter Maivia ended in a double count out in 21:45 (★★★); Ernie Ladd defeated Larry Zbyszko in 3:47 (★★); Tatsumi Fujinami defeated Jose Estrada in 10:59 (★★★); Ivan Koloff, Victor Rivera and Lumberjack Pierre defeated Dino Bravo, Dominic DeNucci and Dusty Rhodes in 5:54 (★★★).

WWWF at Spectrum (17-03-79) ★★★
17-03-79, Philadelphia, Pennsylvania **WWWF**
Allen Coage defeated Johnny Rodz in 11:36 (★ ★ ★); Victor Rivera defeated Baron Mikel Scicluna in 6:31 (★ ★); Ivan Koloff defeated Dusty Rhodes in 7:31 (★ ★ ★); Greg Valentine defeated Steve Travis in 15:47 (★ ★); Bob Backlund defeated Peter Maivia in 20:53 (★ ★ ★ ★); Ernie Ladd defeated Dominic DeNucci in 4:32 (★ ★); Bulldog Brower defeated SD Jones in 2:31 (★ ★); Captain Lou Albano and The Valiant Brothers (Jerry Valiant and Johnny Valiant) defeated Ivan Putski, Tony Garea and Larry Zbyszko 2-1 in a Best Two Out Of Three Falls Match in 11:59 (★ ★ ★).

WWWF at Madison Square Garden (26-03-79) ★★★
26-03-79, New York City, New York **WWWF**
Dominic DeNucci defeated Baron Mikel Scicluna in 4:35 (★ ★); Allen Coage defeated SD Jones in 4:02 (★ ★); Steve Travis defeated Mike Hall in 5:32 (★ ★); Dick Murdoch defeated Johnny Rodz in 1:20 (★ ★); Bob Backlund defeated Greg Valentine in a No Time Limit Match in 30:56 (★ ★ ★ ★); Fred Curry defeated Victor Rivera in 6:04 (★ ★); Bruno Sammartino defeated Ivan Koloff in 12:14 (★ ★ ★); Captain Lou Albano and The Valiant Brothers (Johnny Valiant and Jerry Valiant) defeated Dusty Rhodes, Larry Zbyszko and Tony Garea 2-1 in a Best Two Out Of Three Falls Match in 18:04 (★ ★ ★); Ivan Putski defeated Peter Maivia in 9:13 (★ ★).

WWF at Spectrum (28-04-79) ★★★★
28-04-79, Philadelphia, Pennsylvania **WWF**
Nikolai Volkoff defeated Baron Mikel Scicluna in 9:18 (★ ★ ★); Allen Coage defeated Mr. X in 11:31 (★ ★ ★); Johnny Valiant defeated Dominic DeNucci in 12:42 (★ ★); Ted DiBiase defeated Jerry Valiant in 11:53 (★ ★ ★); Greg Valentine defeated Bob Backlund in 23:35 (★ ★ ★ ★); Tiny Tom and Cowboy Lang defeated Little Tokyo and Butch Cassidy in 8:46 (★ ★); Bruno Sammartino defeated Ivan Koloff in 15:56 (★ ★ ★).

WWF at Spectrum (26-05-79) ★★★
26-05-79, Philadelphia, Pennsylvania **WWF**
Johnny Rivera vs. Mr. X ended in a time limit draw in 20:00 (★ ★); Dominic DeNucci defeated Johnny Rodz in 4:32 (★ ★); Nikolai Volkoff defeated Frank Williams in 4:41 (★ ★); Bulldog Brower defeated SD Jones in 9:27 (★ ★); Bob Backlund defeated Greg Valentine in 22:13 (★ ★ ★); The Valiant Brothers (Johnny Valiant and Jerry Valiant) defeated Steve Travis and Gorilla Monsoon in 11:21 (★ ★ ★); The Great Hossein Arab defeated Jose Estrada in 4:23 (★ ★); Tito Santana defeated Baron Mikel Scicluna in 4:16 (★ ★); Ted DiBiase vs. Jimmy Valiant ended in a draw in 14:12 (★ ★ ★).

WWWF at Madison Square Garden (04-06-79) ★★★
04-06-79, New York City, New York **WWWF**
The Great Hossein Arab won a 20-Man Battle Royal in 8:17 (★ ★); Nikolai Volkoff defeated SD Jones in 6:50 (★ ★); Greg Valentine defeated Dominic DeNucci in 9:07 (★ ★ ★); Bulldog Brower defeated Mr. X in 3:00 (★ ★); Bob Backlund defeated The Great Hossein Arab in 30:40 (★ ★ ★ ★); Ivan Putski defeated Baron Mikel Scicluna in 4:28 (★ ★); Ted DiBiase vs. Jimmy Valiant ended in a draw in 15:00 (★ ★ ★); The Valiant Brothers (Johnny Valiant and Jerry Valiant) defeated Haystacks Calhoun and Steve Travis in 6:25 (★ ★).

WWF at Spectrum (23-06-79) ★★
23-06-79, Philadelphia, Pennsylvania **WWWF**
Johnny Rivera defeated Jose Estrada in 11:04 (★ ★); Nikolai Volkoff defeated Johnny Rodz in 7:13 (★ ★); Steve Travis defeated Baron Mikel Scicluna in 9:13 (★ ★); The Great Hossein Arab defeated SD Jones in 4:09 (★ ★); Ivan Putski defeated Captain Lou Albano in 4:13 (★ ★); Bob Backlund defeated Bulldog Brower in 15:33 (★ ★ ★); Tito Santana defeated Mr. X in 7:43 (★ ★); The Valiant Brothers (Jimmy Valiant, Jerry Valiant and Johnny Valiant) defeated Ted DiBiase, Dominic DeNucci and Gorilla Monsoon 2-1 in a Best Two Out Of Three Falls Match in 14:23 (★ ★ ★); Greg Valentine defeated Haystacks Calhoun in 5:42 (★ ★).

WWF at Spectrum (21-07-79) ★★★
21-07-79, Philadelphia, Pennsylvania **WWF**
Tito Santana defeated Johnny Rodz in 9:37 (★ ★); Baron Mikel Scicluna defeated Jose Estrada in 5:22 (★ ★); SD Jones defeated Joe Mascara in 4:58 (★ ★); Greg Valentine defeated Chief Jay Strongbow in 10:43 (★ ★ ★ ★); Bulldog Brower defeated Johnny Rivera in 13:14 (★ ★); The Valiant Brothers (Johnny Valiant and Jerry Valiant) defeated Bob Backlund and Ivan Putski 2-0 in a Best Two Out Of Three Falls Match in 15:41 (★ ★ ★); The Great Hossein Arab defeated Dominic DeNucci in 2:51 (★ ★); Jimmy Valiant defeated Steve Travis in 6:03 (★ ★); Pat Patterson defeated Ted DiBiase in 11:34 (★ ★ ★).

WWF at Spectrum (18-08-79) ★★
18-08-79, Philadelphia, Pennsylvania **WWF**
Steve King defeated Joe Mascara in 9:22 (★ ★); Bulldog Brower defeated Pete Sanchez in 9:41 (★ ★); SD Jones defeated The Columbian Jaguar in 8:29 (★ ★); Chief Jay Strongbow vs. Greg Valentine went to a double count out in a Indian Strap Match in 10:28 (★ ★ ★); Tito Santana defeated Gypsy Rodriguez in 7:48 (★ ★); Andre the Giant defeated Jerry Valiant in 7:34 (★ ★); Bob Backlund defeated Johnny Valiant in 20:13 (★ ★ ★).

WWF at Madison Square Garden (27-08-79) ★★★
27-08-79, New York City, New York **WWF**
SD Jones defeated Frank Rodriguez in 6:02 (★ ★); Johnny Valiant defeated Dominic DeNucci in 8:31 (★ ★); Greg Valentine defeated Steve Travis in 11:39 (★ ★); Ivan The Terrible and Billy The Kid defeated Butch Cassidy and Tiny Tom in 6:56 (★ ★); Pat Patterson defeated Bob Backlund in 14:29 (★ ★ ★); Tito Santana vs. The Great Hossein Arab ended in a draw in 20:00 (★ ★ ★); Bruno Sammartino defeated Nikolai Volkoff in 6:21 (★ ★ ★); Ted DiBiase vs. Jimmy Valiant ended in a double count out in 6:19 (★ ★); Andre The Giant defeated Jerry Valiant in 3:43 (★ ★); Chief Jay Strongbow defeated Bulldog Brower in 4:53 (★ ★).

WWF at Madison Square Garden (24-09-79) ★★
24-09-79, New York City, New York **WWF**
Johnny Rivera defeated Gypsy Rodriguez in 10:23 (★ ★); Johnny Rodz defeated Steve King in 8:08 (★ ★); Baron Mikel Scicluna defeated SD Jones via count out in 7:09 (★ ★); Ted DiBiase defeated Jose Estrada in 9:42 (★ ★ ★); The Great Hossein Arab defeated Pete Sanchez in 3:57 (★ ★); Bob Backlund defeated Pat Patterson in a Steel Cage Match in 16:43 (★ ★ ★ ★); Andre the Giant and Tito Santana defeated The Valiant Brothers (Jimmy Valiant and Jerry Valiant) in 6:04 (★ ★); Greg Valentine defeated Dominic DeNucci in 10:46 (★ ★ ★); Ivan Putski defeated Johnny Valiant by DQ in 6:53 (★ ★); Nikolai Volkoff vs. Chief Jay Strongbow ended in a draw in 4:42 (★ ★).

WWF at Spectrum (20-10-79) ★★
20-10-79, Philadelphia, Pennsylvania **WWF**
Joe Mascara defeated Davey O'Hannon in 10:26 (★ ★); Larry Zbyszko defeated Johnny Ringo in 8:53 (★ ★); Tito Santana defeated Moose Monroe in 8:47 (★ ★); Bulldog Brower defeated Mike Masters in 6:03 (★ ★); Pat Patterson defeated Bob Backlund in 17:41 (★ ★ ★); Dominic DeNucci vs. Johnny Valiant ended in a double count out in 28:05 (★ ★ ★); Gorilla Monsoon defeated Jerry Valiant in 3:31 (★ ★); Bruno Sammartino defeated Nikolai Volkoff in 8:37 (★ ★ ★).

WWF at Madison Square Garden (22-10-79) ★★★
22-10-79, New York City, New York **WWF**
Johnny Rivera vs. Johnny Rodz ended in a draw in 20:00 (★ ★ ★); Ivan Putski and Tito Santana defeated The Valiant Brothers (Johnny Valiant and Jerry Valiant) to win the WWF World Tag Team Title in 13:39 (★ ★ ★); Nikolai Volkoff defeated Moose Monroe in 3:56 (★ ★); Bob Backlund defeated Swede Hanson in 16:28 (★ ★ ★); The Great Hossein Arab defeated Dominic DeNucci by count out in 6:31 (★ ★); Bruno Sammartino defeated Greg Valentine in 15:10 (★ ★ ★); Dusty Rhodes defeated Jimmy Valiant in 5:27 (★ ★); Larry Zbyszko defeated Bulldog Brower in 3:49 (★ ★); Pat Patterson defeated Ted DiBiase in 7:54 (★ ★ ★).

WWF at Spectrum (17-11-79) ★★

17-11-79, Philadelphia, Pennsylvania **WWF**

Ivan Putski won an 18-Man Battle Royal in 12:27 (★★★); Johnny Rodz vs. Johnny Rivera ended in a time limit draw in 15:00 (★★★); Gorilla Monsoon defeated Moose Monroe in :36 (★★); The Great Hossein Arab defeated Jose Estrada in 3:24 (★★); Bobby Duncum defeated Chief Jay Strongbow in 6:07 (★★); Swede Hanson defeated Ted DiBiase in 9:25 (★★); Bob Backlund defeated Pat Patterson in 18:02 (★★★); Tito Santana defeated Bulldog Brower in 7:26 (★★); Larry Zbyszko defeated Jerry Valiant in 4:43 (★★); Ivan Putski defeated Jimmy Valiant in 5:42 (★★).

WWF at Madison Square Garden (17-12-79) ★★★

17-12-79, New York City, New York **WWF**

Larry Zbyszko defeated Bulldog Brower in 4:43 (★★); Riki Choshu and Seiji Sakaguchi defeated Bad News Allen Coage and Jo Jo Andrews in 9:44 (★★); Mike Graham defeated Johnny Rodz in 5:03 (★★); Hulk Hogan defeated Ted DiBiase in 11:12 (★★★); Bob Backlund defeated Bobby Duncum in a Texas Death Match to win the vacant WWF World Heavyweight Title in 17:18 (★★); Antonio Inoki defeated The Great Hossein Arab in 14:59 (★★★); Harley Race defeated Dusty Rhodes in 13:18 (★★★); Pat Patterson defeated Dominic DeNucci in 6:31 (★★); Tatsumi Fujinami defeated Johnny Rivera in 10:17 (★★★); Ivan Putski and Tito Santana defeated Victor Rivera and Swede Hanson in 6:57 (★★).

WWF at Spectrum (12-01-80) ★★

12-01-80, Philadelphia, Pennsylvania **WWF**

Rene Goulet defeated Johnny Rodz in 13:57 (★★); Davey O'Hannon defeated Jose Estrada in 14:51 (★★); Bulldog Brower defeated Mike Masters in 14:21 (★★); Bobby Duncum defeated Bob Backlund in 16:09 (★★★); Hulk Hogan defeated Tito Santana in 6:10 (★★★); Pat Patterson defeated Captain Lou Albano in 3:22 (★★); Larry Zbyszko defeated The Great Hossein Arab in 20:00 (★★); Gorilla Monsoon defeated Swede Hanson in 1:08 (★); Ken Patera defeated Ivan Putski in 1:40 (★).

WWF at Madison Square Garden (21-01-80) ★★★

21-01-80, New York City, New York **WWF**

Davey O'Hannon defeated Angelo Gomez in 10:21 (★★); Kevin Von Erich defeated Johnny Rodz in 8:28 (★★); Larry Zbyszko defeated The Great Hossein Arab in 10:29 (★★★); Hulk Hogan defeated Dominic DeNucci in 7:34 (★★★); The Wild Samoans (Afa and Sika) defeated Ivan Putski and Tito Santana via count out in 12:46 (★★); Rene Goulet defeated Baron Mikel Scicluna in 4:59 (★★); Bob Backlund vs. Ken Patera ended in a draw in 25:52 (★★★★); Pat Patterson defeated Captain Lou Albano via count out in 6:11 (★★★); Bobby Duncum defeated Mike Masters in 1:29 (★); Tony Atlas defeated Swede Hanson in 2:17 (★★).

WWF at Spectrum (01-03-80) ★★★

01-03-80, Philadelphia, Pennsylvania **WWF**

Johnny Rodz defeated Mike Masters in 6:44 (★★); Vivian St. John and Joyce Grable defeated Winonah Littleheart and Cindy Majors in 19:55 (★★★); Ken Patera defeated Dominic DeNucci in 12:06 (★★★); Larry Zbyszko defeated Bruno Sammartino in 18:32 (★★★); Gorilla Monsoon defeated Baron Mikel Scicluna in 8:31 (★★); Sika defeated Tito Santana in 14:05 (★★); Bob Backlund defeated Afa in 19:18 (★★★); Pat Patterson defeated Bulldog Brower in 4:06 (★★).

WWF at Madison Square Garden (24-03-80) ★★★

24-03-80, New York City, New York **WWF**

Bulldog Brower defeated Frank Williams in 8:53 (★★); Kerry Von Erich defeated Jose Estrada in 10:49 (★★★); Tor Kamata defeated Mike Masters in 5:46 (★★); Bruno Sammartino by DQ in 15:31 (★★★★); Afa defeated Dominic DeNucci in 9:42 (★); Bob Backlund defeated Sika in 18:32 (★★); Andre The Giant and Pat Patterson defeated Bobby Duncum and Ken Patera in 11:04 (★★★); Rene Goulet defeated Baron Mikel Scicluna in 6:11 (★★); Hulk Hogan defeated Tito Santana in 8:12 (★★).

WWF at Spectrum (12-04-80) ★★★★

12-04-80, Philadelphia, Pennsylvania **WWF**

Baron Mikel Scicluna defeated Tony Altimore in 6:42 (★★); Larry Sharpe defeated Jose Estrada in 8:37 (★★); Tor Kamata defeated Johnny Rodz in 5:01 (★★); Ken Patera defeated Rene Goulet in 9:26 (★★★); Hulk Hogan defeated Bob Backlund via count out in 29:00 (★★★★); Bruno Sammartino defeated Larry Zbyszko in 11:09 (★★★★); Dominic DeNucci defeated Davey O'Hannon in 8:02 (★★★); The Wild Samoans (Afa and Sika) defeated Tito Santana and Ivan Putski to win the WWF World Tag Team Title in 7:36 (★★★).

WWF at Madison Square Garden (21-04-80) ★★★

21-04-80, New York City, New York **WWF**

Larry Sharpe defeated Mike Masters in 8:11 (★★); Greg Gagne defeated Jose Estrada in 8:53 (★★); Ken Patera defeated Pat Patterson to win the WWF Intercontinental Title in 20:38 (★★); Sika defeated Dominic DeNucci in 9:27 (★★); Bruno Sammartino defeated Larry Zbyszko in 11:53 (★★); Ricky Steamboat and Jay Youngblood defeated Tor Kamata and Bulldog Brower in 15:11 (★★★); Bob Backlund defeated Afa in 16:34 (★★); Hulk Hogan defeated Rene Goulet in 3:14 (★★); Andre The Giant defeated Bobby Duncum in 13:11 (★★).

WWF at Spectrum (10-05-80) ★★★

10-05-80, Philadelphia, Pennsylvania **WWF**

Davey O'Hannon defeated Manuel Soto in 13:22 (★★★); Dominic DeNucci defeated Jose Estrada in 10:21 (★★★); Rick McGraw defeated Mark Pole in 4:32 (★★); Bobby Duncum defeated Tony Atlas in 12:41 (★★★); El Olympico defeated Joe Mascara in 7:18 (★★); Bob Backlund defeated Hulk Hogan in 17:48 (★★★); Larry Sharpe defeated Mike Masters in 8:16 (★★); Ken Patera defeated Ivan Putski in 10:51 (★★★).

WWF at Madison Square Garden (19-05-80) ★★★★

19-05-80, New York City, New York **WWF**

Rick McGraw defeated Jose Estrada in 10:38 (★★); Larry Zbyszko won a 16-Man Battle Royal in 11:25 (★★★); Larry Sharpe defeated Frankie Williams in 7:02 (★★); Larry Zbyszko defeated Dominic DeNucci in 7:08 (★★★); Tor Kamata defeated Johnny Rodz in 7:58 (★★★); Bob Backlund defeated Ken Patera in a Texas Death Match in 22:56 (★★★★★); Gorilla Monsoon defeated Baron Mikel Scicluna in 3:11 (★★); Bobby Duncum defeated Rene Goulet in 5:42 (★★); Tony Atlas, Ivan Putski and Pat Patterson defeated Peter Maivia and The Wild Samoans (Afa and Sika) 2-1 in a Best Two Out Of Three Falls Match in 16:25 (★★★).

WWF at Spectrum (21-06-80) ★★★

21-06-80, Philadelphia, Pennsylvania **WWF**

Rick McGraw defeated Frank Savage in 8:51 (★★); Larry Sharpe defeated Johnny Rodz in 4:31 (★★); Rene Goulet defeated Tor Kamata in 5:57 (★★); Ken Patera defeated Bob Backlund in 25:28 (★★★★); The Wild Samoans (Afa and Sika) and Captain Lou Albano defeated Gorilla Monsoon, Pat Patterson and Dominic DeNucci 2-1 in a Best Two Out Of Three Falls Match in 16:57 (★★★); Tony Atlas defeated Bobby Duncum in a Texas Death Match in 9:23 (★★★).

WWF at Spectrum (26-07-80) ★★★

26-07-80, Philadelphia, Pennsylvania **WWF**

Larry Sharpe defeated Rick McGraw in 12:32 (★★★); Tor Kamata vs. Angel Marvilla ended in a draw in 18:14 (★★★); Sika defeated Rene Goulet in 6:19 (★★); Larry Zbyszko defeated Ivan Putski in 5:19 (★★); Bob Backlund defeated Ken Patera in 14:58 (★★★); Andre The Giant defeated Hulk Hogan in 7:23 (★★★); Pedro Morales defeated Afa in 5:35 (★★).

SuperDome Extravaganza ★★★

02-08-80, New Orleans, Louisiana **MSW**

Terry Latham defeated Tommy Right in 9:15 (★★); Terry Orndorff and Mike Miller defeated Johnny Mantel and Ron Cheatham in 12:00 (★★); King Cobra defeated Frank Dusek in 10:15 (★★); The Assassin defeated Steven Little Bear in 12:00 (★★); Ray Candy defeated Killer Khan in 9:47 (★★); The Grappler defeated Wahoo McDaniel by DQ in 11:00 (★★★★); Paul Orndorff defeated Ken Mantel by DQ in 14:00 (★★★); Andre the Giant vs. Hulk Hogan went to a double count out in 13:00 (★★★); Ted DiBiase defeated Mr. Wrestling II in 14:00 (★★★★); Dusty Rhodes and Buck Robley defeated The Fabulous Freebirds (Buddy Roberts and Terry Gordy) in a Double Bullrope Match in 5:00 (★★★); **Junkyard Dog** defeated **Michael Hayes** in a Steel Cage Dog Collar Match in 11:20 (★★★★).

Last Tangle In Tampa ★★★
03-08-80, Tampa, Florida **CWF**
Scott McGhee defeated **Bill White** (★★); **Jimmy Garvin** defeated **Bobby Jaggers** in 10:21 (★★★); **Bugsy McGraw** and **Dick Murdoch** defeated **Ivan Koloff** and **Nikolai Volkoff** in 14:52 (★★★); **Dick Slater** defeated **Barry Windham** via count out to win the vacant Southern Heavyweight Title in 11:03 (★★★★); **Jack Brisco** defeated **Mr. Saito** in 9:18 (★★); **Wendi Richter** won a Battle Royal in 10:34 (★); **Jerry Brisco** defeated **Lord Alfred Hayes** in 8:23 (★★★); **The Super Destroyer** defeated **Mr. Florida** in 11:33 (★★); **Andre the Giant** defeated **The Super Destroyer** in 8:19 (★★★); **Les Thornton** defeated **Mike Graham** by DQ in 15:31 (★★★); **Bob Backlund** defeated **Don Muraco** by DQ (★★★★); **Harley Race** vs. **Dusty Rhodes** went to a time limit draw in 60:00 in a Best Two Out of Three Falls Match (★★★★★).

Showdown At Shea '80 ★★★
09-08-80, Flushing, New York **WWF**
Angel Maravilla defeated **Jose Estrada** in 7:26 (★★); **Dominic DeNucci** defeated **Baron Mikel Scicluna** in 5:56 (★★); **Tatsumi Fujinami** defeated **Chavo Guerrero** in 10:28 (★★★★); **Antonio Inoki** defeated **Larry Sharpe** in 9:41 (★★); **Bob Backlund** and **Pedro Morales** defeated **The Wild Samoans** (Afa and Sika) 2-0 in a Best Two Out Of Three Falls Match to win the WWF World Tag Team Title in 13:06 (★★★); **Pat Patterson** defeated **Tor Kamata** by DQ in 2:09 (★★); **Beverly Shade** and **The Fabulous Moolah** defeated **Kandi Malloy** and **Peggy Lee** in 6:03 (★★); **Greg Gagne** defeated **Rick McGraw** in 14:33 (★★); **Tony Atlas** defeated **Ken Patera** via count out in 8:13 (★★★); **Ivan Putski** defeated **Johnny Rodz** in 4:47 (★★); **The Hangman** defeated **Rene Goulet** in 8:28 (★); **Andre The Giant** defeated **Hulk Hogan** in 7:48 (★★); **Bruno Sammartino** defeated **Larry Zbyszko** in a Steel Cage Match in 14:10 (★★★★).

WWF at Spectrum (23-08-80) ★★★
23-08-80, Philadelphia, Pennsylvania **WWF**
Baron Mikel Scicluna defeated **Johnny Rodz** in 8:46 (★★); **Rick McGraw** defeated **Jose Estrada** in 13:18 (★★); **The Hangman** defeated **Dominic DeNucci** in 8:46 (★★); **Larry Zbyszko** defeated **Ivan Putski** in 10:48 in a Texas Death Match (★★★★); **Andre The Giant** and **Pedro Morales** defeated **Captain Lou Albano** and **Afa** in 9:22 (★★★); **Ken Patera** defeated **Gorilla Monsoon** in a Title vs. Career Match in 11:54 (★★★); **Hulk Hogan** defeated **Rene Goulet** in 5:36 (★★); **Pat Patterson** defeated **Tor Kamata** in :21 (★).

WWF at Madison Square Garden (22-09-80) ★★
22-09-80, New York City, New York **WWF**
Les Thornton defeated **Jose Estrada** in 7:41 (★★★); **Pat Patterson** defeated **Johnny Rodz** in 8:38 (★★); **The Hangman** defeated **Dominic DeNucci** in 10:15 (★★); **Larry Zbyszko** defeated **Tony Garea** by DQ in 13:39 (★★★); **Rick Martel** defeated **Rick McGraw** in 6:47 (★★★); **Pedro Morales** defeated **Afa** in 1:04 (★★); **Ken Patera** defeated **Rene Goulet** in 5:32 (★★); **Tony Atlas** defeated **Sika** in 5:32 (★★).

WWF at Spectrum (11-10-80) ★★★
11-10-80, Philadelphia, Pennsylvania **WWF**
The Hangman defeated **Rene Goulet** in 8:11 (★★); **Dominic DeNucci** defeated **Baron Mikel Scicluna** in 9:51 (★★); **Tony Garea** defeated **Sika** in 8:57 (★★); **Pedro Morales** defeated **Afa** in 11:21 (★★); **Andre The Giant** defeated **Ken Patera** in 9:17 (★★); **Larry Zbyszko** defeated **Bob Backlund** in 20:13 (★★★); **Rick McGraw** and **Rick Martel** defeated **Jose Estrada** and **Johnny Rodz** 2-1 in a Best Two Out Of Three Falls Match in 26:43 (★★★); **Pat Patterson** defeated **Larry Sharpe** in 4:15 (★★).

WWF at Madison Square Garden (20-10-80) ★★★
20-10-80, New York City, New York **WWF**
Terry Taylor defeated **Jose Estrada** in 9:59 (★★★); **Rene Goulet** defeated **Johnny Rodz** in 8:41 (★★); **The Hangman** defeated **Rick McGraw** in 7:19 (★★); **Pedro Morales** vs. **Ken Patera** ended in a double DQ in 16:19 (★★★★); **Dominic DeNucci** defeated **Larry Sharpe** in 8:38 (★★); **Sgt. Slaughter** defeated **Bob Backlund** by DQ in 16:33 (★★★); **Rick Martel**

defeated **Baron Mikel Scicluna** in 3:34 (★★); **Tony Garea** defeated **Larry Zbyszko** by DQ in 4:58 (★★); **Dusty Rhodes** and **Pat Patterson** defeated **The Wild Samoans** (Afa and Sika) in a Best Two Out Of Three Falls Match in 18:34 (★★★).

WWF at Spectrum (08-11-80) ★★
08-11-80, Philadelphia, Pennsylvania **WWF**
Rene Goulet vs. **Larry Sharpe** ended in a draw in 20:00 (★★); **Rick McGraw** defeated **Jose Estrada** in 10:53 (★★); **Johnny Rodz** defeated **Charlie Brown** in 4:47 (★★); **Bruno Sammartino** defeated **Ken Patera** by DQ 14:57 (★★★); **Sgt. Slaughter** defeated **Angel Marvilla** in 4:06 (★★); **Bob Backlund** defeated **Larry Zbyszko** in 14:47 (★★★); **Pedro Morales** defeated **The Hangman** in 11:02 (★★); **Rick Martel** and **Tony Garea** defeated **The Wild Samoans** (Afa and Sika) to win the WWF World Tag Team Title in 14:29 (★★).

WWF at Madison Square Garden (08-12-80) ★★★
08-12-80, New York City, New York **WWF**
Johnny Rodz defeated **Sylvano Sousa** in 10:49 (★★); **The Moondogs** (Moondog King and Moondog Rex) defeated **Rick McGraw** and **Angel Marvilla** in 11:37 (★★★); **Larry Zbyszko** defeated **Dominic DeNucci** in 12:42 (★★★); **Rick Martel** and **Tony Garea** defeated **The Wild Samoans** (Afa and Sika) 2-1 in a Best Two Out Of Three Falls Match in 26:27 (★★★); **Ernie Ladd** vs. **Tony Atlas** ended in a double count out in 5:24 (★★); **Pedro Morales** defeated **Ken Patera** to win the WWF Intercontinental Title in 18:51 (★★★); **Bruno Sammartino** defeated **Sgt. Slaughter** in 18:38 (★★★).

WWF at Spectrum (13-12-80) ★★★
13-12-80, Philadelphia, Pennsylvania **WWF**
Johnny Rodz defeated **Rick Stallone** in 9:32 (★★); **The Moondogs** (Moondog King and Moondog Rex) defeated **Rick McGraw** and **Steve King** in 14:12 (★★★); **Sgt. Slaughter** defeated **Dominic DeNucci** in 9:17 (★★); **Tony Atlas** vs. **Larry Zbyszko** ended in a double DQ in 11:14 (★★★); **Tony Garea** and **Rick Martel** defeated **The Wild Samoans** (Afa and Sika) 2-0 in a Best Two Out Of Three Falls Match in 13:34 (★★); **Pedro Morales** defeated **Ernie Ladd** by DQ in 9:44 (★★); **Bruno Sammartino** defeated **Ken Patera** in 7:51 (★★).

WWF at Madison Square Garden (29-12-80) ★★★
29-12-80, New York City, New York **WWF**
Yoshiaki Yatsu defeated **Jose Estrada** in 8:47 (★★); **Seiji Sakaguchi** vs. **Sika** ended in a draw in 5:34 (★★); **Tatsumi Fujinami** defeated **Don Diamond** in 10:28 (★★★); **Tony Garea** and **Rick Martel** defeated **The Moondogs** (Moondog King and Moondog Rex) by DQ in 13:16 (★★); **Hulk Hogan** defeated **Dominic DeNucci** in 4:38 (★★); **Bob Backlund** defeated **Killer Khan** in 12:23 (★★★); **Antonio Inoki** defeated **Bobby Duncum** in 12:47 (★★★); **The Fabulous Moolah** and **Joyce Grable** defeated **Candy Malloy** and **Peggy Lee** in 5:09 (★★); **Pedro Morales** defeated **The Hangman** in 7:07 (★★); **Pat Patterson** defeated **Ken Patera** by DQ in 8:12 (★★).

WWF at Spectrum (10-01-81) ★★★
10-01-81, Philadelphia, Pennsylvania **WWF**
Frank Savage vs. **Jim Duggan** ended in a draw in 20:00 (★★★); **SD Jones** defeated **The Black Demon** in 13:22 (★★★); **Larry Sharpe** defeated **Rick Stallone** in 8:15 (★★); **Pat Patterson** defeated **Bulldog Brower** in 7:37 (★★); **The Moondogs** (Moondog King and Moondog Rex) defeated **Rick Martel** and **Tony Garea** in 25:17 (★★★); **Tony Atlas** defeated **Larry Zbyszko** in 7:06 (★★); **Sgt. Slaughter** defeated **Bob Backlund** in 23:27 (★★★).

WWF at Spectrum (14-02-81) ★★
14-02-81, Philadelphia, Pennsylvania **WWF**
Bulldog Brower defeated **Angelo Gomez** in 5:23 (★★); **Larry Sharpe** defeated **Steve King** in 3:27 (★★); **Yoshiaki Yatsu** defeated **Frank Savage** in 8:52 (★); **Hulk Hogan** defeated **Dominic DeNucci** in 8:31 (★★); **Pedro Morales** vs. **Stan Hansen** ended in a double DQ in 11:10 (★★★); **Killer Khan** defeated **Rick McGraw** in 5:34 (★★); **Sgt. Slaughter** vs. **Bob Backlund** ended in a double count out in 16:48 (★★★); **The Hangman** defeated **Johnny Rodz** in 6:57 (★★); **SD Jones** defeated **Baron Mikel Scicluna** in 4:24 (★★); **Tony Garea** and **Rick Martel** defeated **The Moondogs** (Moondog King and Moondog Rex) in a Texas Death Match in 13:27 (★★★).

WWF at Madison Square Garden (16-02-81) ★★★

16-02-81, New York City, New York **WWF**

Yoshiaki Yatsu defeated Johnny Rodz in 11:12 (★★); The Hangman defeated Frank Savage in 10:58 (★★); SD Jones defeated Baron Mikel Scicluna in 8:44 (★★); Pedro Morales defeated Sgt. Slaughter in 22:40 (★★★★); Hulk Hogan defeated Rick McGraw in 1:31 (★★); Bob Backlund vs. Stan Hansen ended in a draw in 18:22 (★★★★); Killer Khan defeated Dominic DeNucci in 7:46 (★★); Pat Patterson, Rick Martel and Tony Garea defeated The Moondogs (Moondog King and Moondog Rex) and Captain Lou Albano 2-1 in a Best Two Out Of Three Falls Match in 9:47 (★★★).

Wrestling Star Wars (February '81) ★★

22-02-81, Dallas, Texas **WCCW**

Mil Mascaras defeated Tim Brooks in 9:56 (★★★); Fritz Von Erich defeated The Great Kabuki in a Texas Death Match in 10:15 (★★); Harley Race vs. Kerry Von Erich ended in a double count out in 16:28 (★★★); David Von Erich and Kevin Von Erich defeated Hercules Ayala and Ali Mustafa to win the WCWA Tag Team Title in 16:40 (★★); Bruiser Brody won an 11-Man Battle Royal in 5:49 (★★).

WWF at Madison Square Garden (16-03-81) ★★

16-03-81, New York City, New York **WWF**

Yoshiaki Yatsu defeated Baron Mikel Scicluna in 8:39 (★★); SD Jones defeated Johnny Rodz in 9:41 (★★); Moondog Rex defeated Rick McGraw in 6:38 (★★); Dominic DeNucci defeated Larry Sharpe in 6:53 (★★); Stan Hansen defeated Bob Backlund by count out in 12:02 (★★); Pedro Morales defeated Moondog King in 4:48 (★★); Andre The Giant defeated Sgt. Slaughter by DQ in 7:58 (★★★); Rick Martel defeated The Hangman in 15:37 (★★); Tony Garea defeated Bulldog Brower in 10:56 (★★); Tony Atlas defeated Hulk Hogan in 7:08 (★★★).

WWF at Spectrum (21-03-81) ★★★

21-03-81, Philadelphia, Pennsylvania **WWF**

The Great Yatsu defeated Baron Mikel Scicluna in 9:45 (★★); Dominic DeNucci defeated Johnny Rodz in 9:40 (★★); Larry Sharpe defeated Frank Savage in 6:50 (★★); Rick Martel defeated The Hangman in 4:21 (★★); SD Jones vs. Bulldog Brower ended in a Double DQ in 5:00 (★); Stan Hansen defeated Tony Garea in 8:20 (★★); Bob Backlund defeated Sgt. Slaughter in a Steel Cage Match in 17:19 (★★★★); Moondog King defeated Rick McGraw in 8:10 (★★); Pedro Morales defeated Moondog Rex in 9:12 (★★); Andre the Giant defeated Hulk Hogan in 12:51 (★★★).

WWF at Madison Square Garden (06-04-81) ★★★

06-04-81, New York City, New York **WWF**

Yoshiaki Yatsu defeated Terry Gunn in 5:11 (★); Killer Khan defeated Dominic DeNucci in 5:10 (★★); Pedro Morales defeated Moondog Rex in 9:33 (★★); Pat Patterson vs. Sgt. Slaughter ended in a double DQ in 13:36 (★★★); Mil Mascaras defeated Moondog King in 8:14 (★★); Bob Backlund defeated Stan Hansen in a Steel Cage Match in 8:59 (★★★); SD Jones defeated Baron Mikel Scicluna in 8:53 (★★); The Fabulous Moolah and Leilani Kai defeated Jill Fontaine and Suzette Ferrara in 7:08 (★★); Tony Garea and Rick Martel defeated Johnny Rodz and Larry Sharpe in 14:04 (★★).

WWF at Spectrum (18-04-81) ★★

18-04-81, Philadelphia, Pennsylvania **WWF**

Johnny Rodz defeated Frank Savage in 9:56 (★★); Tony Garea and Andre The Giant defeated Moondog Rex and Sgt. Slaughter in 13:51 (★★★); Larry Sharpe defeated Tony Altimore in 4:44 (★★); Yoshiaki Yatsu vs. The Hangman ended in a draw in 18:01 (★★); Bob Backlund defeated Killer Khan in 16:09 (★★★); Pat Patterson defeated Sgt. Slaughter in 15:00 (★★★); Dominic DeNucci defeated Baron Mikel Scicluna in 4:23 (★★); Leilani Kai and The Fabulous Moolah defeated Jill Fontaine and Suzette Ferreira in 8:35 (★★); Tony Atlas defeated Hulk Hogan in 13:02 (★★★).

WWF at Madison Square Garden (04-05-81) ★★★

04-05-81, New York City, New York **WWF**

SD Jones defeated Johnny Rodz in 15:36 (★★); Yoshiaki Yatsu defeated The Hangman in 10:31 (★★); Dominic DeNucci defeated Baron Mikel Scicluna in 6:53 (★★); Peter Maivia defeated Rick McGraw in 7:08 (★★); Angelo Mosca defeated Bob Backlund by DQ in 15:51 (★★★); Pat Patterson defeated

Sgt. Slaughter in an Alley Fight in 14:13 (★★★★★★); Tony Garea, Rick Martel and Gorilla Monsoon defeated Stan Hansen, Moondog Rex and Captain Lou Albano 2-0 in a Best Two Out Of Three Falls Match in 14:01 (★★); The Carolina Kid and Farmer Jerome defeated Sky Low Low and Kid Chocolate in 11:23 (★★).

WWF at Spectrum (23-05-81) ★★

23-05-81, Philadelphia, Pennsylvania **WWF**

Rick McGraw defeated Johnny Rodz in 17:42 (★★); Yoshiaki Yatsu defeated Ron Shaw in 4:15 (★★); SD Jones defeated Frank Savage in 3:55 (★★); Tony Garea, Rick Martel and Pedro Morales defeated The Moondogs (Moondog Rex and Moondog Spot) and Captain Lou Albano 2-1 in a Best Two Out Of Three Falls Match in 28:13 (★★★); Bob Backlund defeated Angelo Mosca in 16:06 (★★★); Baron Mikel Scicluna defeated Chris Canyon in 4:49 (★★); The Carolina Kid and Farmer Jerome defeated Sky Low Low and Kid Chocolate in 10:53 (★★); Killer Khan defeated Dominic DeNucci in 4:48 (★★).

Wrestling Star Wars (June '81) ★★★

04-06-81, Dallas, Texas **WCCW**

Kerry Von Erich defeated Ernie Ladd to win the NWA American Heavyweight Title in 17:36 (★★★★); Bruiser Brody defeated The Great Kabuki in a Texas Death Steel Cage Match in 10:55 (★★★); Fritz Von Erich defeated Gary Hart in 4:49 (★).

WWF at Madison Square Garden (08-06-81) ★★★

08-06-81, New York City, New York **WWF**

Larry Sharpe defeated Rick McGraw in 9:06 (★★); Curt Hennig defeated Johnny Rodz in 9:45 (★★); Don Muraco defeated Rick Martel by count out in 10:27 (★★); SD Jones defeated Frank Savage in 6:17 (★★); Dusty Rhodes defeated Killer Khan by DQ in 11:45 (★★★); Tony Garea defeated Man Mountain Cannon in 6:23 (★★); Bob Backlund defeated Angelo Mosca in 10:31 (★★); Yoshiaki Yatsu and Tatsumi Fujinami defeated The Moondogs (Moondog Rex and Moondog Spot) 2-0 in a Best Two Out Of Three Falls Match in 22:15 (★★★); Pedro Morales defeated Sgt. Slaughter by DQ in 6:53 (★★).

WWF at Spectrum (20-06-81) ★★★

20-06-81, Philadelphia, Pennsylvania **WWF**

Johnny Rodz vs. Curt Hennig ended in a draw in 20:00 (★★★); Larry Sharpe defeated Tony Altimore in 5:11 (★★); Strong Kobayashi defeated Baron Mikel Scicluna in 4:38 (★★); Angelo Mosca defeated Tony Garea in 12:56 (★★★); Don Muraco defeated Pedro Morales to win the WWF Intercontinental Title in 15:21 (★★★★); Sgt. Slaughter defeated Rick McGraw in 5:03 (★★); Bob Backlund defeated George Steele in 13:19 (★★★); The Moondogs (Moondog Rex and Moondog Spot) defeated Dominic DeNucci and SD Jones in 11:29 (★★★); Rick Martel defeated Captain Lou Albano in 4:05 (★★).

WWF at Capital Centre (27-06-81) ★★

27-06-81, Landover, Maryland **WWF**

Johnny Rodz defeated Steve King in 10:51 (★★); Curt Hennig defeated Jack Carson in 8:01 (★★); Don Muraco defeated SD Jones in 11:55 (★★★); Bob Backlund defeated Angelo Mosca in 14:01 (★★); Tony Garea, Rick Martel and Andre the Giant defeated Captain Lou Albano and The Moondogs (Moondog Rex and Moondog Spot) 2-1 in a Best Two Out Of Three Falls Match in 15:45 (★★★); Rick McGraw defeated Chris Canyon in 4:38 (★★); Mil Mascaras defeated Sgt. Slaughter in 10:13 (★★).

WWF at Madison Square Garden (20-07-81) ★★★

20-07-81, New York City, New York **WWF**

Johnny Rodz defeated Terry Gunn in 9:31 (★★); SD Jones defeated Baron Mikel Scicluna in 9:18 (★★); Curt Hennig defeated Strong Kobayashi in 5:44 (★★★); Sgt. Slaughter defeated Dominic DeNucci in 8:39 (★★★); Bob Backlund defeated George Steele in 7:11 (★★); Pat Patterson defeated Angelo Mosca in 11:08 (★★★); Don Muraco vs. Pedro Morales ended in a draw in 20:00 (★★★); Andre The Giant vs. Killer Khan ended in a double DQ in 24:32 (★★★); Tony Garea and Rick Martel defeated The Moondogs (Moondog Rex and Moondog Spot) 2-0 in a Best Two Out Of Three Falls Match in 5:35 (★★★).

WWF at Madison Square Garden (24-08-81) ★★★
24-08-81, New York City, New York WWF

Curt Hennig defeated Baron Mikel Scicluna in 6:42 (★★); Dominic DeNucci defeated Frank Savage in 5:16 (★★); SD Jones defeated Johnny Rodz in 5:53 (★★); El Canek defeated Jose Estrada in 14:31 (★★★); Bob Backlund vs. Don Muraco ended in a draw in 60:00 (★★★★); Pedro Morales defeated Angelo Mosca by DQ in 10:49 (★★); Andre The Giant defeated Killer Khan in a Texas Death Match in 6:48 (★★★); Tony Garea defeated Bulldog Brower in 5:16 (★★); Rick Martel defeated Moondog Spot in 3:27 (★★); Tony Atlas defeated Moondog Rex in 5:02 (★★)

WWF at Madison Square Garden (21-09-81) ★★★
21-09-81, New York City, New York WWF

Yoshiaki Yatsu defeated Baron Mikel Scicluna in 9:37 (★); Mr. Saito and Mr. Fuji co-won a $10,000 20-Man Battle Royal in 18:24 (★★★); Steve O defeated Ron Shaw in 6:52 (★★); Mr. Fuji defeated Curt Hennig in 7:14 (★★); Killer Khan defeated Dominic DeNucci in 4:03 (★★); Mr. Saito defeated Roberto Soto in 6:54 (★★); Bob Backlund defeated Don Muraco in a Texas Death Match in 31:35 (★★★★); Pedro Morales defeated Larry Sharpe in 6:28 (★★); Mil Mascaras defeated Bulldog Brower in 2:41 (★); Tony Garea and Rick Martel defeated Johnny Rodz and Jose Estrada in 12:15 (★★)

WWF at Spectrum (17-10-81) ★★★★
17-10-81, Philadelphia, Pennsylvania WWF

Curt Hennig defeated Baron Mikel Scicluna in 6:58 (★★); Mr. Fuji and Mr. Saito defeated Johnny Rodz and Jose Estrada in 10:24 (★★); Pedro Morales defeated Angelo Mosca by DQ in 11:13 (★★); Bob Backlund vs. Don Muraco ended in a draw in 60:00 (★★★★); Tony Atlas defeated George Steele (★★); Andre The Giant vs. Killer Khan ended in a double count out in 17:43 (★★★★); Tony Garea and Rick Martel defeated Larry Sharpe and Bulldog Brower in 12:39 (★★)

WWF at Madison Square Garden (19-10-81) ★★★
19-10-81, New York City, New York WWF

Curt Hennig defeated Joe Cox in 9:14 (★★); Tony Garea and Rick Martel defeated Mr. Fuji and Mr. Saito by DQ in 11:44 (★★★); Pedro Morales defeated Don Muraco in 18:46 (★★★★); Dusty Rhodes defeated Ron Shaw in 1:28 (★); Bob Backlund vs. Greg Valentine ended in a no contest in 19:32 (★★★); Pat Patterson defeated Angelo Mosca in 9:18 (★★); Dominic DeNucci and SD Jones defeated Jose Estrada and Johnny Rodz in 11:29 (★★★); Tony Atlas defeated Killer Khan by count out in 9:49 (★★)

WWF at Spectrum (14-11-81) ★★★
14-11-81, Philadelphia, Pennsylvania WWF

The Haiti Kid defeated Little Boy Blue in 7:36 (★★); Pedro Morales defeated The Executioner in 5:11 (★★); Greg Valentine defeated Tony Garea in 12:47 (★★★); Mr. Fuji and Mr. Saito defeated Tony Atlas and SD Jones in 22:31 (★★★); Baron Mikel Scicluna defeated Tony Altimore in 7:16 (★★); Curt Hennig defeated Jose Estrada in 11:26 (★★); Johnny Rodz defeated Jerry Johnson in 6:29 (★★); Angelo Mosca defeated Dominic DeNucci in 3:25 (★★); Andre The Giant defeated Killer Khan in a Stretcher Match in 9:57 (★★); Bob Backlund defeated Don Muraco in 21:25 (★★★)

WWF at Madison Square Garden (23-11-81) ★★
23-11-81, New York City, New York WWF

Mr. Saito defeated SD Jones in 7:37 (★★); Rick Martel defeated Hans Schroeder in 13:11 (★★); Tony Garea defeated Baron Mikel Scicluna in 11:39 (★★); Dominic DeNucci and Curt Hennig defeated Johnny Rodz and Jose Estrada in 11:26 (★★★); Pedro Morales defeated Don Muraco in a Texas Death Match to win the WWF Intercontinental Title (★★★); The Haiti Kid defeated Little Boy Blue in 8:33 (★★); Bob Backlund defeated Greg Valentine in 15:36 (★★★); Dusty Rhodes defeated Angelo Mosca by count out in 7:24 (★★); Mil Mascaras defeated The Executioner in 2:36 (★★); Tony Atlas defeated Mr. Fuji in 8:16 (★★)

WWF at Capital Centre (29-11-81) ★★
29-11-81, Landover, Maryland WWF

Dominic DeNucci vs. Larry Sharpe went to a time limit draw in 20:00 (★★); Johnny Rodz defeated Hans Schroeder in 8:23 (★★); Curt Hennig defeated Bulldog Brower in 7:58 (★★); Tony Atlas defeated Angelo Mosca in 16:10 (★★★); The Haiti

Kid defeated Little Boy Blue in 11:22 (★★); Bob Backlund defeated Don Muraco in a Texas Death Match in 13:26 (★★★); Greg Valentine defeated SD Jones in 8:47 (★★); Tony Garea and Rick Martel defeated Mr. Fuji and Mr. Saito by DQ in 13:14 (★★★)

WWF at Spectrum (12-12-81) ★★
12-12-81, Philadelphia, Pennsylvania WWF

Johnny Rodz defeated Ron Shaw in 11:41 (★★); SD Jones defeated Jose Estrada in 10:37 (★★); Bulldog Brower defeated Curt Hennig in 5:29 (★★); Rick Martel defeated Larry Sharpe in 11:49 (★★); Killer Khan defeated Tony Garea in 11:57 (★★); Greg Valentine defeated Bob Backlund in 19:48 (★★★); Andre The Giant and Tony Atlas defeated Mr. Fuji, Mr. Saito and Captain Lou Albano in a Handicap Match in 8:14 (★★★); Pedro Morales defeated Don Muraco in 3:41 (★★); Pat Patterson defeated Angelo Mosca in 7:25 (★★)

Christmas Star Wars '81 ★★
26-12-81, Dallas, Texas WCCW

Jose Lothario defeated Ernie Ladd to win the WCCW Brass Knuckles Title in 6:14 (★★); El Solitario defeated Tim Brooks in 5:22 (★★); The Great Kabuki defeated Fritz Von Erich in a Texas Death Match in 18:02 (★★★); David Von Erich, Kerry Von Erich and Kevin Von Erich defeated Bill Irwin, Frank Dusek and Ten Gu in 10:54 (★★★); Big Daddy Bundy won a 16-Man Battle Royal in 11:58 (★★)

WWF at Spectrum (16-01-82) ★★
16-01-82, Philadelphia, Pennsylvania WWF

Charlie Fulton defeated Tony Altimore in 6:01 (★); Bulldog Brower defeated Baron Mikel Scicluna via count out in 7:38 (★); Davey O'Hannon defeated Johnny Rodz in 12:19 (★); Jesse Ventura defeated Jeff Craney in 4:59 (★★); Pedro Morales defeated Killer Khan in 12:35 (★★); Bob Backlund defeated Greg Valentine in a Steel Cage Match in 20:23 (★★★); Tony Garea and Rick Martel defeated Mr. Fuji and Mr. Saito by DQ in 10:27 (★★★); Adrian Adonis defeated Dominic DeNucci in 7:49 (★★); Larry Sharpe defeated Jose Estrada in 6:30 (★★); Steve Travis defeated Hans Schroeder in 6:56 (★)

WWF at Madison Square Garden (18-01-82) ★★★
18-01-82, New York City, New York WWF

Davey O'Hannon defeated Manuel Soto in 9:52 (★★); Larry Sharpe defeated Jose Estrada in 8:41 (★★); Charlie Fulton defeated Johnny Rodz in 9:28 (★★); Greg Valentine defeated Pedro Morales by DQ in 14:43 (★★★); Jesse Ventura defeated Dominic DeNucci in 10:26 (★★★); Adrian Adonis defeated Bob Backlund in 30:54 (★★★★); Rick Martel and Tony Garea defeated Mr. Fuji and Mr. Saito by DQ in 8:58 (★★★); Tony Atlas defeated The Executioner in 2:57 (★★); Ivan Putski defeated Killer Khan in 2:29 (★★)

WWF at Spectrum (20-02-82) ★★★
20-02-82, Philadelphia, Pennsylvania WWF

Charlie Fulton defeated Jeff Craney in 10:19 (★★); Adrian Adonis defeated SD Jones in 10:48 (★★★); Captain Lou Albano, Mr. Fuji and Mr. Saito defeated Tony Garea, Rick Martel and Tony Atlas 2-1 in a Best Two Out Of Three Falls Match in 16:28 (★★★); Greg Valentine defeated Pedro Morales in 14:51 (★★★); Bob Backlund defeated Jesse Ventura in 17:43 (★★★); Ivan Putski defeated Killer Khan in 6:33 (★★); Steve Travis and Rick McGraw vs. Jose Estrada and Johnny Rodz ended in a draw in 11:53 (★★)

WWF at Madison Square Garden (14-03-82) ★★
14-03-82, New York City, New York WWF

Steve Travis defeated Jose Estrada in 10:06 (★); The Fabulous Moolah and Wendi Richter defeated Velvet McIntyre and Princess Victoria in 11:56 (★★★); Greg Valentine defeated SD Jones in 9:48 (★); Rick McGraw and Andre The Giant defeated Mr. Saito and Mr. Fuji 2-0 in a Best Two Out Of Three Falls Match in 13:02 (★★); Bob Backlund defeated Jesse Ventura in 9:21 (★★★); Pedro Morales defeated Adrian Adonis in 10:47 (★★★); Pat Patterson defeated Captain Lou Albano via count out in 1:59 (★★); Tony Garea and Rick Martel defeated Charlie Fulton and The Executioner in 7:28 (★★)

WWF at Spectrum (20-03-82) ★★★

20-03-82, Philadelphia, Pennsylvania **WWF**

Johnny Rodz vs. Davey O'Hannon ended in a draw in 20:00 (★★★); Steve Travis defeated Jose Estrada in 9:47 (★★); Ivan Putski defeated Mr. Fuji in 8:23 (★★); Bob Backlund defeated Adrian Adonis in 21:50 (★★★★); The Fabulous Moolah and Wendi Richter defeated Velvet McIntyre and Princess Victoria 2-1 in a Best Two Out Of Three Falls Match in 15:09 (★★★); Pedro Morales defeated Greg Valentine in 9:11 (★★); Jesse Ventura defeated Tony Garea in 6:21 (★★); Rick Martel vs. Mr. Saito ended in a double DQ in 5:28 (★★); SD Jones defeated Charlie Fulton in 5:38 (★).

WWF at Capital Centre (28-03-82) ★★★

28-03-82, Landover, Maryland **WWF**

Steve Travis defeated Johnny Rodz in 12:47 (★★); Princess Victoria defeated Wendi Richter in 11:02 (★★★); Greg Valentine defeated Pedro Morales by DQ in 15:18 (★★★); Mr. Saito defeated Jose Estrada in 11:11 (★★); Bob Backlund defeated Adrian Adonis in a Lumberjack Match in 16:04 (★★★); Rick McGraw defeated Charlie Fulton in 8:52 (★★); Jesse Ventura defeated Tony Garea in 14:06 (★★★); Ivan Putski defeated Mr. Fuji in 4:12 (★★).

WWF at Spectrum (17-04-82) ★★

17-04-82, Philadelphia, Pennsylvania **WWF**

Larry Sharpe defeated Jose Estrada in 8:18 (★★); Tony Garea defeated Johnny Rodz in 9:49 (★); Bob Orton defeated SD Jones in 7:03 (★★); Jesse Ventura defeated Tony Atlas in 15:47 (★★★); Greg Valentine defeated Steve Travis in 10:57 (★★); Bob Backlund defeated Blackjack Mulligan in 11:15 (★★); Pedro Morales defeated Adrian Adonis in 11:05 (★★★); Ivan Putski defeated The Black Demon in 3:00 (★★); Andre The Giant and Rick McGraw defeated Mr. Saito and Mr. Fuji 2-1 in a Best Two Out Of Three Falls Match in 11:56 (★★).

WWF at Spectrum (22-05-82) ★★

22-05-82, Philadelphia, Pennsylvania **WWF**

Larry Sharpe defeated Charlie Fulton in 6:53 (★★); Baron Mikel Scicluna defeated Pete Sanchez in 7:31 (★★); Swede Hanson defeated Laurent Soucie in 5:49 (★★); Mr. Saito defeated Johnny Rodz in 6:45 (★★); Jimmy Snuka defeated Pedro Morales in 15:21 (★★); Blackjack Mulligan defeated Steve Travis in 6:46 (★★); Bob Orton defeated Bob Backlund via count out in 16:12 (★★); Tony Atlas defeated Jesse Ventura in a Steel Cage Match in 10:37 (★★★★); Rick McGraw defeated Mr. Fuji by DQ in 4:09 (★★); Ivan Putski defeated Adrian Adonis in 7:24 (★★).

WWF at Madison Square Garden (05-06-82) ★★

05-06-82, New York City, New York **WWF**

Jose Estrada defeated Laurent Soucie in 10:28 (★★); Ivan Putski defeated Mr. Saito in 8:37 (★★); Tony Atlas vs. Greg Valentine went to a double count out in 8:24 (★★); Bob Orton defeated Steve Travis in 9:42 (★★); Tony Garea defeated Swede Hanson by DQ in 7:31 (★★); Jimmy Snuka defeated Bob Backlund via count out in 20:53 (★★★); Pedro Morales defeated Mr. Fuji in 5:39 (★★); Chief Jay Strongbow and Jules Strongbow defeated The East-West Connection (Jesse Ventura and Adrian Adonis) in 11:19 (★★★); Rick McGraw defeated Charlie Fulton in 2:21 (★★); The Fabulous Moolah and Sherri Martel defeated Judy Martin and Penny Mitchell in 3:30 (★★); Andre The Giant vs. Blackjack Mulligan went to a double count out in 9:34 (★★).

Star Wars - Superbowl Of Wrestling ★★★

06-06-82, Irving, Texas **WCCW**

Bill Irwin defeated Ken Mantell in 13:39 (★★★); Lola Gonzalez defeated Irma Gonzalez in 10:00 (★★); El Solitario defeated Rene Guajardo in 10:07 (★★★); Andre the Giant won a 7-Man Battle Royal in 5:44 (★★); The Magic Dragon and The Great Kabuki defeated Kevin Von Erich and David Von Erich by DQ in 15:01 (★★★); Kerry Von Erich defeated Harley Race in 15:27 (★★★★); Fritz Von Erich defeated King Kong Bundy in a No DQ Falls Count Anywhere Match to win the WCCW American Heavyweight Title in 7:40 (★★★).

WWF at Spectrum (26-06-82) ★★

26-06-82, Philadelphia, Pennsylvania **WWF**

Tony Atlas won a 20-Man Battle Royal in 18:25 (★★★); Baron Mikel Scicluna defeated Laurent Soucie in 7:22 (★★); Chief Jay Strongbow defeated Jose Estrada in 7:21 (★); Jimmy Snuka defeated Steve Travis in 18:38 (★★); Ivan Putski defeated Charlie Fulton in 6:09 (★★); Pedro Morales defeated Mr. Saito in 15:17 (★★); Blackjack Mulligan defeated SD Jones in 2:47 (★★); Tony Atlas defeated Adrian Adonis in 6:33 (★★★); Mr. Fuji defeated Tony Garea in :49 (★); Bob Backlund defeated Bob Orton in a Lumberjack Match in 12:12 (★★★).

WWF at Madison Square Garden (28-06-82) ★★★

28-06-82, New York City, New York **WWF**

Johnny Rodz defeated Rick McGraw in 10:32 (★★); Swede Hanson defeated Laurent Soucie in 3:24 (★★); Salvatore Bellomo defeated Baron Mikel Scicluna in 4:19 (★★); Bob Orton defeated Pedro Morales by DQ in 14:38 (★★★); Blackjack Mulligan defeated SD Jones in 7:44 (★★); Steve Travis defeated Charlie Fulton in 5:41 (★); Bob Backlund defeated Jimmy Snuka in a Steel Cage Match in 15:10 (★★★★); Chief Jay Strongbow and Jules Strongbow defeated Mr. Fuji and Mr. Saito to win the WWF World Tag Team Title in 9:48 (★★); Tony Garea defeated Adrian Adonis by DQ in 8:35 (★★); Tony Atlas defeated Greg Valentine via count out in 3:02 (★).

WWF at Spectrum (31-07-82) ★★

31-07-82, Philadelphia, Pennsylvania **WWF**

Tony Garea vs. Steve Travis ended in a draw in 10:26 (★★); The Fabulous Moolah and Leilani Kai defeated Vivian St. John and Peggy Lee in 9:47 (★★); Salvatore Bellomo defeated Pete Sanchez in 11:12 (★★); Mr. Fuji and Mr. Saito defeated Chief Jay Strongbow and Jules Strongbow in 10:49 (★★★); Bob Backlund vs. Jimmy Snuka ended in a double DQ in 21:06 (★★★); Andre The Giant defeated Blackjack Mulligan in 9:16 (★★★); Ivan Putski defeated Bob Orton in 2:14 (★★); Pedro Morales defeated Swede Hanson in 1:33 (★); Ivan Putski defeated The Masked Demon #2 in 1:36 (★).

WWF at Madison Square Garden (02-08-82) ★★

02-08-82, New York City, New York **WWF**

The Fabulous Moolah and Leilani Kai defeated Vivian St. John and Peggy Lee in 7:13 (★★); Johnny Rodz vs. Pete Sanchez ended in a double DQ in 9:37 (★★); Tony Garea vs. Steve Travis ended in a draw in 13:32 (★★); Salvatore Bellomo defeated Jose Estrada in 4:14 (★★); SD Jones defeated Swede Hanson in 2:36 (★★); Ivan Putski defeated Mr. Saito in 10:18 (★★); Ivan Putski defeated Mr. Fuji by DQ in 2:58 (★★); Chief Jay Strongbow and Jules Strongbow defeated The Masked Demons (The Masked Demon #1 and The Masked Demon #2) in 5:06 (★★); Jimmy Snuka defeated Pedro Morales via count out in 9:18 (★★★); Andre The Giant defeated Blackjack Mulligan in a Texas Death Match in 14:41 (★★★); Bob Backlund defeated Bob Orton in 23:38 (★★★).

Wrestling Star Wars (August '82) ★★★★

15-08-82, Dallas, Texas **WCCW**

Kevin Von Erich and David Von Erich defeated The Magic Dragon and The Great Kabuki to win the All Asia Tag Team Title in 13:39 (★★★★); King Kong Bundy vs. Harley Race ended in a double count out in 12:23 (★★★); Ric Flair defeated Kerry Von Erich 2-1 in a Best Two Out Of Three Falls Match in 35:20 (★★★★★).

WWF at Madison Square Garden (30-08-82) ★★

30-08-82, New York City, New York **WWF**

Tony Garea defeated Charlie Fulton in 6:39 (★★); Killer Khan defeated Steve Travis in 5:31 (★★); Bob Orton defeated Pat Patterson via count out in 9:28 (★★); Tiger Mask defeated Dynamite Kid in 6:34 (★★★); Pedro Morales vs. Jimmy Snuka went to a double DQ in 17:55 (★★); Tiger Jackson and Little Beaver defeated Sky Low Low and Sonny Boy 2-0 in a Best Two Out Of Three Falls Match in 6:03 (★★); Tatsumi Fujinami defeated Gino Brito to win the WWF International Champion in 11:34 (★★★); Salvatore Bellomo defeated Swede Hanson in 3:26 (★); Bob Backlund defeated Buddy Rose in 20:24 (★★); The Fabulous Moolah defeated Penny Mitchell in 4:49 (★★); Andre The Giant, Chief Jay Strongbow and Jules Strongbow defeated Blackjack Mulligan, Mr. Fuji and Mr. Saito 2-1 in a Best Two Out Of Three Falls Match in 14:03 (★★★).

WWF at Spectrum (18-09-82) ★★★
18-09-82, Philadelphia, Pennsylvania **WWF**

Salvatore Bellomo defeated Swede Hanson in 11:52 (★★); Pat Patterson defeated Bob Orton in 9:23 (★★★); Charlie Fulton defeted Jeff Craney in 6:07 (★★); Johnny Rodz and Jose Estrada defeated Steve Travis and Tony Garea 2-1 in a Best Two Out Of Three Falls Match in 21:13 (★★★); Bob Backlund defeated Jimmy Snuka in 21:33 (★★★★); Buddy Rose defeated Pedro Morales in 14:38 (★★★); Andre The Giant, Chief Jay Strongbow and Jules Strongbow defeated Blackjack Mulligan, Mr. Fuji and Mr. Saito 2-1 in a Best Two Out Of Three Falls Match in 17:53 (★★★).

WWF at Madison Square Garden (04-10-82) ★★
04-10-82, New York City, New York **WWF**

Baron Mikel Scicluna defeated Pete Sanchez in 9:23 (★★); SD Jones defeated Mac Rivera in 5:41 (★★); Salvatore Bellomo defeated Johnny Rodz in 9:54 (★★); Ivan Putski defeated Swede Hanson in 10:43 (★★); Tony Garea and Curt Hennig defeated The Black Demon and The White Angel in 13:36 (★★); Chief Jay Strongbow and Jules Strongbow defeated Mr. Saito and Mr. Fuji 2-1 in a Best Two Out Of Three Falls Match in 8:58 (★★★); Andre The Giant defeated Bob Orton in 9:26 (★★★); Buddy Rose vs. Pedro Morales ended in a draw in 20:00 (★★); Superstar Billy Graham defeated Bob Backlund by DQ in 15:10 (★★★).

WWF at Spectrum (16-10-82) ★★★
16-10-82, Philadelphia, Pennsylvania **WWF**

Curt Hennig defeated Johnny Rodz in 11:52 (★★); Pat Patterson defeated Mr. Fuji in 7:03 (★★); Jules Strongbow defeated Swede Hanson in 7:11 (★★); Buddy Rose defeated Bob Backlund in 17:35 (★★★); Salvatore Bellomo defeated The Blue Demon in 5:22 (★★); Joyce Grable defeated Penny Mitchell in 9:11 (★★); Tony Garea defeated The White Angel in 8:03 (★★); Pete Sanchez defeated Mac Rivera in 5:08 (★★); Chief Jay Strongbow defeated Mr. Saito in 6:00 (★★); Superstar Billy Graham defeated Pedro Morales in 15:09 (★★★).

WWF at Madison Square Garden (22-11-82) ★★
22-11-82, New York City, New York **WWF**

Curt Hennig vs. Eddie Gilbert ended in a draw in 14:22 (★★★); SD Jones defeated Swede Hanson by DQ in 9:20 (★★); Tiger Mask defeated Jose Estrada in 9:42 (★★★); Little Beaver and Sonny Boy Hayes defeated Sky Low Low and Butch Cassidy 2-0 in a Best Two Out Of Three Falls Match in 8:27 (★★); Bob Backlund vs. Superstar Billy Graham ended in a double DQ in 10:14 (★★); Salvatore Bellomo defeated Mr. Fuji by DQ in 7:11 (★★); Pedro Morales defeated Buddy Rose in 11:29 (★★); Jimmy Snuka defeated Captain Lou Albano in 5:59 (★★); Ray Stevens defeated Chief Jay Strongbow in 1:02 (★★); Jules Strongbow defeated Charlie Fulton in 4:36 (★); Rocky Johnson and Tony Garea defeated Riki Choshu and Mr. Saito 2-1 in a Best Two Out Of Three Falls Match in 9:13 (★★★).

WWF at Spectrum (25-11-82) ★★★
25-11-82, Philadelphia, Pennsylvania **WWF**

Tiger Mask defeated Eddie Gilbert in 11:36 (★★★); Chin Kobiashi defeated Johnny Rodz in 10:15 (★★★); Little Brutus and Sonny Boy Blue defeated Sky Low Low and Butch Cassidy in 8:11 (★★); Jose Estrada defeated Curt Hennig in 8:47 (★★★); Superstar Billy Graham defeated Chief Jay Strongbow via count out in 9:46 (★★★); Tony Garea defeated Swede Hanson in 5:26 (★★); Bob Backlund defeated Buddy Rose in a Lumberjack Match in 13:02 (★★★); Pedro Morales and Salvatore Bellomo defeated Mr. Saito and Riki Choshu 2-1 in a Best Two Out Of Three Falls Match in 12:11 (★★); Jules Strongbow defeated Baron Mikel Scicluna in 1:22 (★); Jimmy Snuka and Buddy Rogers defeated Captain Lou Albano and Ray Stevens via count out in 9:48 (★★★); Rocky Johnson defeated Mr. Fuji in 1:51 (★★).

Christmas Night '82 ★★★★
25-12-82, St. Paul, Minnesota **AWA**

Baron Von Raschke defeated Jacques Goulet in 11:52 (★★); Ken Patera defeated Steve Olsonoski in 10:16 (★★★); Rick Martel defeated Bobby Heenan in 7:58 (★★★★); Nick Bockwinkel defeated Billy Robinson in 16:22 (★★★★); Bobby Duncum and Ken Patera defeated Hulk Hogan and Tito Santana by DQ in 11:02 (★★★★).

Christmas Star Wars '82 ★★★★
25-12-82, Dallas, Texas **WCCW**

The Fabulous Freebirds (Michael Hayes and Terry Gordy) and David Von Erich defeated Mike Sharpe, Ben Sharpe and Tom Steele to win the inaugural WCCW Six-Man Tag Team Title in 17:55 (★★★★); Kevin Von Erich defeated King Kong Bundy by DQ in 8:37 (★★); Ric Flair defeated Kerry Von Erich in a Steel Cage Match in 24:33 (★★★★); Ken Mantell won a 15-Man Pole Battle Royal in 10:48 (★★).

WWF at Madison Square Garden (28-12-82) ★★
28-12-82, New York City, New York **WWF**

SD Jones vs. Eddie Gilbert ended in a draw in 13:44 (★★); Tony Garea defeated Johnny Rodz in 9:04 (★★); Buddy Rose defeated Ivan Putski via count out in 8:33 (★★); Pedro Morales vs. Don Muraco ended in a double DQ in 14:25 (★★★); Salvatore Bellomo defeated Jose Estrada in 8:46 (★★); Bob Backlund defeated Superstar Billy Graham in a Lumberjack Match in 12:33 (★★★★); Wendi Richter and The Fabulous Moolah defeated Elizabeth Chase and Princess Victoria in 9:11 (★★); Jimmy Snuka defeated Ray Stevens via count out in 6:50 (★★); Rocky Johnson defeated The Black Demon in 5:13 (★★); Chief Jay Strongbow and Jules Strongbow defeated Mr. Fuji and Mr. Saito in a Texas Death Match in 8:47 (★★★).

WWF at Madison Square Garden (22-01-83) ★★
22-01-83, New York City, New York **WWF**

Johnny Rodz defeated Pete Sanchez in 8:42 (★★); SD Jones defeated Baron Mikel Scicluna in 6:36 (★); Superstar Billy Graham defeated Swede Hanson in 3:29 (★★); Don Muraco defeated Pedro Morales to win the WWF Intercontinental Title in 11:34 (★★★); The Wild Samoans (Afa and Sika) defeated Tony Garea and Eddie Gilbert in 9:23 (★★); Ray Stevens defeated Jules Strongbow in 7:51 (★★★); Bob Backlund defeated Big John Studd in 7:17 (★★); Curt Hennig defeated Mac Rivera in 8:29 (★★); Jimmy Snuka defeated Buddy Rose in 15:26 (★★); Salvatore Bellomo defeated Charlie Fulton in 3:33 (★★); Rocky Johnson defeated Mr. Fuji in 6:28 (★★).

WWF at Madison Square Garden (18-02-83) ★★★
18-02-83, New York City, New York **WWF**

Jose Estrada defeated Curt Hennig in 13:25 (★★★); Johnny Rodz defeated Baron Mikel Scicluna in 4:59 (★★); Mr. Fuji defeated Tony Garea in 8:26 (★★); Big John Studd defeated Jules Strongbow in 2:40 (★★); Ray Stevens defeated Chief Jay Strongbow in 9:26 (★★★); Don Muraco defeated Bob Backlund by DQ in 21:19 (★★★★); Rocky Johnson defeated Superstar Billy Graham via count out in 3:46 (★★); Andre the Giant and Jimmy Snuka defeated The Wild Samoans (Afa and Sika) in 12:51 (★★★★); Eddie Gilbert defeated Charlie Fulton in 9:20 (★★); Salvatore Bellomo defeated Swede Hanson in 4:51 (★★); Pedro Morales defeated Buddy Rose in 11:36 (★★).

WWF at Spectrum (19-02-83) ★★★
19-02-83, Philadelphia, Pennsylvania **WWF**

Jose Estrada defeated Curt Hennig in 9:24 (★★★); Johnny Rodz defeated Mac Luis Rivera in 8:07 (★★); Tony Garea defeated Charlie Fulton in 11:42 (★★); Swede Hanson defeated SD Jones in 9:59 (★★); Eddie Gilbert defeated Baron Mikel Scicluna in 4:20 (★★); Big John Studd defeated Bob Backlund via count out in 11:13 (★★★); The Wild Samoans (Afa and Sika) defeated Chief Jay Strongbow and Jules Strongbow 2-0 in a Best Two Out Of Three Falls Match in 14:16 (★★★); Andre The Giant, Rocky Johnson, Salvatore Bellomo, Jimmy Snuka and Pedro Morales defeated Mr. Fuji, Ray Stevens, Don Muraco, Buddy Rose and Superstar Billy Graham 3-1 in a Best Three Out Of Five Falls Match in 17:05 (★★★★).

Final Conflict ★★★★
12-03-83, Grensboro, North Carolina **NWA/MACW**

Jerry Brisco defeated Ken Timbs in 3:50 (★★); Mike Rotundo defeated Rick Harris in 4:44 (★★); Jim Nelson and Johnny Weaver defeated Gene Anderson and Red Dog Lane in 6:29 (★★); Roddy Piper defeated Dick Slater in 14:25 (★★★); Jay Youngblood and Ricky Steamboat defeated Don Kernodle and Sgt. Slaughter in a Steel Cage Match to win the NWA World Tag Team Title in 32:43 (★★★★★★).

WWF at Spectrum (19-03-83) ★★
19-03-83, Philadelphia, Pennsylvania **WWF**
SD Jones defeated Baron Mikel Scicluna in 7:49 (★★); Jose Estrada defeated Pete Sanchez in 9:29 (★★); Sonny Boy and Pancho Boy defeated Tiger Jackson and Butch Cassidy in 7:40 (★★); Ray Stevens vs. Jules Strongbow ended in a double count out in 8:03 (★★); Tony Garea defeated Johnny Rodz in 9:47 (★★); Don Muraco defeated Rocky Johnson in 13:42 (★★); Salvatore Bellomo defeated Superstar Billy Graham in 7:14 (★★); Andre The Giant, Jimmy Snuka and Bob Backlund defeated Big John Studd, Afa and Captain Lou Albano 3-0 in a Best Three Out Of Five Falls Match in 13:26 (★★).

WWF at Madison Square Garden (20-03-83) ★★★
20-03-83, New York City, New York **WWF**
Mac Rivera defeated Baron Mikel Scicluna in 8:46 (★★); Swede Hanson defeated Pete Sanchez in 6:35 (★★); Tony Garea defeated Johnny Rodz in 10:09 (★★); Superstar Billy Graham defeated Jules Strongbow in 9:42 (★★); Salvatore Bellomo vs. Ray Stevens ended in a double count out in 9:28 (★★); Bob Backlund defeated Don Muraco in a Texas Death Match in 19:51 (★★); Andre the Giant, Rocky Johnson and Jimmy Snuka defeated Big John Studd, Afa and Captain Lou Albano 3-0 in a Best Three Out Of Five Falls Match in 9:36 (★★★); SD Jones defeated Jose Estrada in 4:14 (★); Sonny Boy Hayes and Pancho Boy defeated Tiger Jackson and Butch Cassidy in 7:40 (★★).

Super Sunday ★★★
24-04-83, St. Paul, Minnesota **AWA**
Brad Rheingans defeated Rocky Stone in 9:34 (★★); Buck Zumhoffe defeated Steve Regal in 11:05 (★★); Jerry Lawler defeated John Tolos in 8:24 (★★); Joyce Grable and Wendi Richter defeated Judy Martin and Velvet McIntyre in 15:28 (★★★); Wahoo McDaniel defeated Eddie Boulder in 9:04 (★); Jesse Ventura, Ken Patera and Blackjack Lanza defeated Rick Martel and The High Flyers (Greg Gagne and Jim Brunzell) in 17:03 (★★); Nick Bockwinkel defeated Hulk Hogan by reverse decision in 18:12 (★★★); Verne Gagne and Mad Dog Vachon defeated Jerry Blackwell and Sheik Adnan Al-Kaissie in 13:28 (★★★).

WWF at Madison Square Garden (25-04-83) ★★★
25-04-83, New York City, New York **WWF**
Salvatore Bellomo defeated Baron Mikel Scicluna in 9:43 (★★); Mr. Fuji defeated SD Jones in 11:34 (★★); Iron Mike Sharpe defeated Johnny Rodz in 9:31 (★★); Ray Stevens defeated Tony Garea in 10:17 (★★); The Wild Samoans (Samula and Afa defeated Chief Jay Strongbow and Jules Strongbow) 2-1 in a Best Two Out Of Three Falls Match in 11:55 (★★); Rocky Johnson defeated Don Muraco via count out in 14:20 (★★); Bob Backlund defeated Ivan Koloff in 28:36 (★★★); Jimmy Snuka defeated Superstar Billy Graham in 3:28 (★★); Pedro Morales defeated Swede Hanson in 4:39 (★★); Eddie Gilbert defeated Jose Estrada in 5:58 (★★); Andre the Giant defeated Big John Studd via count out in 8:22 (★★).

WWF at Spectrum (30-04-83) ★★★
30-04-83, Philadelphia, Pennsylvania **WWF**
Eddie Gilbert defeated Baron Mikel Scicluna in 10:03 (★★); Ray Stevens defeated Tony Garea in 11:14 (★★); Andre The Giant and Rocky Johnson defeated Don Muraco and Big John Studd in 17:01 (★★); Ivan Koloff defeated SD Jones in 12:47 (★★); Bob Backlund defeated Iron Mike Sharpe in 19:14 (★★); Mr. Fuji defeated Johnny Rodz in 7:46 (★★); Samula and Afa defeated Chief Jay Strongbow and Jules Strongbow in 10:19 (★★).

WWF at Madison Square Garden (23-05-83) ★★★
23-05-83, New York City, New York **WWF**
Don Kernodle defeated Baron Mikel Scicluna in 10:57 (★★); Mac Rivera defeated Pete Doherty in 10:39 (★★); Ivan Koloff defeated Jules Strongbow in 11:23 (★★); Salvatore Bellomo defeated Swede Hanson in 10:28 (★★); Chief Jay Strongbow vs. Iron Mike Sharpe ended in a double DQ in 6:48 (★★); Bob Backlund defeated Sgt. Slaughter by DQ in 16:53 (★★★); Dusty Rhodes defeated Samula in 9:10 (★★); Susan Starr defeated Leilani Kai in 6:04 (★★); Jimmy Snuka defeated Afa in 3:02 (★★); The Fabulous Moolah defeated Princess Victoria in 5:27 (★★); Rocky Johnson vs. Don Muraco ended in a draw in 17:20 (★★★★).

WWF at Capital Centre (28-05-83) ★★
28-05-83, Landover, Maryland **WWF**
Mac Rivera defeated Barry Hart in 11:13 (★★); Princess Victoria and Susan Starr defeated The Fabulous Moolah and Leilani Kai in 14:53 (★★★); Ivan Koloff defeated Salvatore Bellomo in 12:33 (★★); Jimmy Snuka defeated Sika in 6:05 (★★); Iron Mike Sharpe defeated Baron Mikel Scicluna in 9:57 (★★); Don Muraco vs. Rocky Johnson ended in a double DQ in 17:43 (★★); Samula defeated Bob Bradley in 9:18 (★★); Sgt. Slaughter defeated Chief Jay Strongbow in 11:45 (★★); Bob Backlund defeated Afa in 14:53 (★★).

WWF at Spectrum (04-06-83) ★★★
04-06-83, Philadelphia, Pennsylvania **WWF**
Butcher Vachon defeated Jeff Craney in 5:38 (★★); Samula defeated Don Kernodle in 9:12 (★★); Sgt. Slaughter defeated Chief Jay Strongbow in 11:53 (★★); Don Muraco defeated Swede Hanson in 13:26 (★★); Jimmy Snuka defeated Afa in 3:00 (★★); Bob Backlund defeated Iron Koloff in 16:45 (★★★); Andre The Giant defeated Big John Studd in 17:50 (★★★); Salvatore Bellomo defeated Iron Mike Sharpe in 5:36 (★★); Rocky Johnson defeated Sika in 3:08 (★★).

Wrestling Star Wars '83 ★★
17-06-83, Dallas, Texas **WCCW**
Jose Lothario, Chris Adams and Chavo Guerrero defeated Bill Irwin, The Fishman and The Mongol in 7:37 (★★); Jimmy Garvin defeated David Von Erich in 11:28 (★★); Buddy Roberts defeated Iceman King Parsons in a Hair vs. Hair Match in 7:48 (★★); Kamala defeated Tola Yatsu, Mike Bond and Armand Hussein in a Handicap Elimination Match in 3:21 (★); Harley Race defeated Kevin Von Erich by DQ in 14:01 (★★★); Kerry Von Erich and Bruiser Brody defeated The Fabulous Freebirds (Terry Gordy and Michael Hayes) to win the WCCW American Tag Team Title in 4:41 (★★).

WWF at Spectrum (16-07-83) ★★
16-07-83, Philadelphia, Pennsylvania **WWF**
Swede Hanson defeated Jeff Craney in 7:21 (★★); Iron Mike Sharpe defeated Tony Garea in 13:44 (★★); Tito Santana defeated Don Kernodle in 15:18 (★★); Don Muraco defeated Jimmy Snuka in 8:21 (★★); Sgt. Slaughter defeated SD Jones in 7:56 (★★); Bob Backlund defeated George Steele in :58 (★); The Invaders (Invader #1 and Invader #2) defeated Mr. Fuji and Frank Williams in 8:01 (★★); Ivan Koloff defeated Salvatore Bellomo in 4:26 (★★); Andre The Giant, Ivan Putski, Chief Jay Strongbow and Rocky Johnson defeated Big John Studd and The Wild Samoans (Afa, Sika and Samula) 3-1 in a Best Three Out Of Five Falls Match in 9:08 (★★).

WWF at Capital Centre (23-07-83) ★★
23-07-83, Landover, Maryland **WWF**
Bob Bradley defeated Steve King in 12:55 (★★); Jeff Craney defeated Jack Carson in 11:08 (★★); George Steele defeated Salvatore Bellomo in 8:22 (★★); Don Muraco vs. Jimmy Snuka ended in a double DQ in 15:46 (★★); Rocky Johnson defeated Mr. Fuji in 13:08 (★★★); Pete Sanchez defeated Israel Matia in 5:55 (★★); Swede Hanson defeated Tony Colon in 1:32 (★); Andre the Giant defeated Big John Studd in a Steel Cage Match in 15:21 (★★★).

WWF at Madison Square Garden (30-07-83) ★★
30-07-83, New York City, New York **WWF**
Tony Garea vs. Iron Mike Sharpe ended in a draw in 12:06 (★★); Ivan Koloff defeated SD Jones in 5:31 (★★); The Invaders (Invader #1 and Invader #2) defeated Jeff Craney and Gypsy Rodriguez in 11:27 (★★); Big John Studd defeated Salvatore Bellomo in 5:09 (★★); Don Muraco vs. Jimmy Snuka ended in a double DQ in 12:29 (★★★); Sgt. Slaughter defeated Swede Hanson in 9:44 (★★); George Steele defeated Bob Backlund by DQ in 10:52 (★★); Andre the Giant, Dusty Rhodes and Ivan Putski defeated The Wild Samoans (Afa, Sika and Samula) in 12:46 (★★); Rocky Johnson defeated Don Kernodle in 6:15 (★★); Tito Santana defeated Mr. Fuji in 5:39 (★★).

WWF at Spectrum (13-08-83) ★★★
13-08-83, Philadelphia, Pennsylvania **WWF**
Pete Sanchez defeated Israel Matia in 10:19 (★★); Tito Santana defeated Mr. Fuji in 11:04 (★★); Big John Studd defeated Chief Jay Strongbow in 6:48 (★★); Jimmy Snuka defeated Don Muraco in 11:24 (★★); Tiger Chung Lee

defeated **Tony Garea** in 11:12 (★★); **The Wild Samoans** (**Afa** and **Sika**) defeated **Rocky Johnson** and **Salvatore Bellomo** in 10:26 (★★★); **Pat Patterson** defeated **Iron Mike Sharpe** in 3:32 (★★); **Bob Backlund** defeated **Sgt. Slaughter** in 11:26 (★★★); **The Invaders** (**Invader #1** and **Invader #2**) defeated **Ivan Koloff** and **Don Kernodle** in 6:42 (★★); **Ivan Putski** defeated **George Steele** in 3:05 (★★).

Aniversario ★★★
17-09-83, San Juan, Puerto Rico **WWC**
Miguel Perez defeated **Barrabas** in 3:42 (★★); **Pete Sanchez** defeated **Assassin #2** in :21 (★); **Bob Sweetan** defeated **Gama Singh** in 6:27 (★★); **Hercules Ayala** defeated **The Iron Sheik** in 4:10 (★★★); **Pierre Martel** defeated **Don Kent** in 8:28 (★★★); **Abdullah Tamba** defeated **Gorilla Monsoon** in 1:11 (★); **The Medics** (**Medic #1** and **Medic #2**) defeated **Chief Thundercloud** and **Chuy Little Fox** in 6:02 (★★★); **Pedro Morales** defeated **Ric Flair** by DQ in 11:28 (★★★★); **King Tonga** defeated **Dory Funk Jr.** in 15:59 (★★★); **Invader #1** defeated **Ox Baker** in 8:32 (★★); **El Gran Apollo** vs. **Kendo Nagasaki** went to a time limit draw in 20:00 (★★★); **Harley Race** vs. **Carlos Colon** went to a time limit draw in 60:00 (★★★); **Mil Mascaras** and **Dos Carras** defeated **The Infernos** (**Gypsy Joe** and **Tim Tall**) in 8:20 (★★★★); **Andre the Giant** vs. **Abdullah the Butcher** went to a double count out in 9:42 (★★★).

WWF at Spectrum (24-09-83) ★★★
24-09-83, Philadelphia, Pennsylvania **WWF**
Salvatore Bellomo defeated **Butcher Vachon** in 4:16 (★★); **Don Kernodle** defeated **Israel Matia** in 6:39 (★★); **The Invaders** (**Invader #1** and **Invader #2**) defeated **Swede Hanson** and **Iron Mike Sharpe** in 12:46 (★★); **Don Muraco** defeated **Chief Jay Strongbow** in 7:12 (★★); **Bob Backlund** defeated **Sgt. Slaughter** in a Texas Death Match in 14:06 (★★★★); **Andre The Giant** defeated **Big John Studd** in a Steel Cage Match in 10:04 (★★★); **Tiger Chung Lee** defeated **Rene Goulet** in 4:25 (★★); **Penny Mitchell** and **Susan Starr** defeated **Judy Martin** and **The Fabulous Moolah** in 7:09 (★★); **Jimmy Snuka**, **Tito Santana** and **Rocky Johnson** defeated **Ivan Koloff** and **The Wild Samoans** (**Afa** and **Sika**) 2-0 in a Best Two Out Of Three Falls Match in 13:25 (★★★).

WWF at Madison Square Garden (17-10-83) ★★★
17-10-83, New York City, New York **WWF**
Tony Garea defeated **Rene Goulet** in 12:33 (★★★); **Tiger Chung Lee** defeated **SD Jones** in 8:41 (★★); **Sgt. Slaughter** defeated **Ivan Putski** by DQ in 10:29 (★★★); **Tito Santana** vs. **Iron Mike Sharpe** ended in a draw in 18:02 (★★★); **The Masked Superstar** defeated **Bob Backlund** via count out in 16:13 (★★★); **Mike Graham** defeated **Bob Bradley** in 4:53 (★★); **Don Muraco** defeated **Jimmy Snuka** in a Steel Cage Match in 6:46 (★★★★); **Rocky Johnson** defeated **Sika** in 1:46 (★★); **The Invaders** (**Invader #1** and **Invader #2**) defeated **Israel Matia** and **Butcher Vachon** in 6:58 (★★); **Andre the Giant** defeated **Afa** in 1:07 (★).

WWF at Spectrum (22-10-83) ★★★
22-10-83, Philadelphia, Pennsylvania **WWF**
Tony Garea defeated **Butcher Vachon** in 6:52 (★★); **Tiger Chung Lee** defeated **SD Jones** in 12:04 (★★); **Tito Santana** defeated **Sika** in 9:38 (★★★); **Iron Mike Sharpe** defeated **Swede Hanson** in 11:07 (★★); **Bob Backlund** defeated **Sgt. Slaughter** in a Sicilian Stretcher Match in 12:39 (★★★); **Don Muraco** defeated **Jimmy Snuka** in a Fijian Strap Match in 8:44 (★★★★); **Rocky Johnson** defeated **Afa** in 10:05 (★★★); **The Invaders** (**Invader #1** and **Invader #2**) defeated **Rene Goulet** and **Don Kernodle** in 11:57 (★★★).

The Last Battle Of Atlanta ★★★★
23-10-83, Atlanta, Georgia **NWA**
Les Thornton defeated **Joe Lightfoot** in 9:36 (★★★); **Bruno Sammartino Jr.** defeated **Pat Rose** in 6:02 (★★); **Mr. Wrestling II** defeated **Bob Roop** in a Mask vs. Mask Match in 10:58 (★★★★); **Brett Wayne** vs. **Jake Roberts** ended in a no contest in 21:50 (★★★); **The Great Kabuki** defeated **Ronnie Garvin** in 16:46 (★★★); **The Road Warriors** (**Hawk** and **Animal**) vs. **Jimmy Valiant** and **Pez Whatley** ended in a double DQ in 4:02 (★★); **Tommy Rich** defeated **Buzz Sawyer** in a Steel Cage Match in 12:05 (★★★★); **Ole Anderson** defeated **Paul Ellering** in a Steel Cage Match in 9:26 (★★).

WWF at Spectrum (24-11-83) ★★★
24-11-83, Philadelphia, Pennsylvania **WWF**
The Invaders (**Invader #1** and **Invader #2**) defeated **Iron Mike Sharpe** and **Mr. Fuji** in 4:48 (★★); **Tony Garea** defeated **Rene Goulet** in 11:08 (★★); **The Tonga Kid** defeated **Charlie Fulton** in 6:57 (★★); **SD Jones** defeated **Butcher Vachon** in 5:07 (★★); **Tito Santana** defeated **Big John Studd** in 6:54 (★★★); **Sgt. Slaughter** vs. **Tony Atlas** ended in a double DQ in 16:02 (★★★); **Jimmy Snuka** and **Arnold Skaaland** defeated **Don Muraco** and **Captain Lou Albano** in 13:11 (★★★); **Rocky Johnson** defeated **Bob Bradley** in 4:21 (★); **Pat Patterson** defeated **Ivan Koloff** in 5:37 (★★★); **Bob Backlund** defeated **The Iron Sheik** in 16:49 (★★).

Thanksgiving Star Wars ★★★★
24-11-83, Dallas, Texas **WCCW**
Jose Lothario, **Mike Reed** and **Johnny Mantell** defeated **Black Gordman**, **Tonga John** and **Boris Zhukov** in 9:31 (★★★); **Kevin Von Erich** defeated **Terry Gordy** in 11:28 (★★★); **David Von Erich** defeated **Kimala** by DQ in 6:53 (★★★); **Mike Von Erich** defeated **Skandor Akbar** in 5:06 (★★); **The Super Destroyers** (**Super Destroyer #1** and **Super Destroyer #2**) defeated **Iceman King Parsons** and **Junkyard Dog** by DQ in 10:23 (★★★); **Chris Adams** defeated **Jimmy Garvin** to win the WCCW American Heavyweight Title in 7:16 (★★★); **Kerry Von Erich** defeated **Michael Hayes** in a Loser Leaves Town Steel Cage Match in 7:42 (★★★★).

Starrcade '83 ★★★★★
24-11-83, Greensboro, North Carolina **NWA**
The Assassins (**Assassin #1** and **Assassin #2**) defeated **Bugsy McGraw** and **Rufus R. Jones** in 8:11 (★★); **Kevin Sullivan** and **Mark Lewin** defeated **Johnny Weaver** and **Scott McGhee** in 6:43 (★★★); **Abdullah the Butcher** defeated **Carlos Colon** in 4:30 (★★); **Bob Orton** and **Dick Slater** defeated **Wahoo McDaniel** and **Mark Youngblood** in 14:48 (★★★); **Charlie Brown** defeated **The Great Kabuki** to win the NWA Television Title in 10:35 (★★); **Roddy Piper** defeated **Greg Valentine** in a Dog Collar Match in 16:08 (★★★★★); **Ricky Steamboat** and **Jay Youngblood** defeated **The Brisco Brothers** (**Jack Brisco** and **Jerry Brisco**) to win the NWA World Tag Team Title in 13:24 (★★★★); **Ric Flair** defeated **Harley Race** in a Steel Cage Match to win the NWA World Heavyweight Title in 23:49 (★★★★★).

NWA at The Omni (04-12-83) ★★★
04-12-83, Atlanta, Georgia **GCW**
Bob Roop defeated **Mike Jackson** in 5:54 (★★); **Johnny Rich** defeated **Chic Donovan** in 10:17 (★★★); **Ron Garvin** defeated **Cy Jernigan** in 4:48 (★★); **Jake Roberts** vs. **Pez Whatley** ended in a draw in 30:09 (★★★); **Ted DiBiase** vs. **Buzz Sawyer** ended in a double DQ in 15:08 (★★★); **Brett Sawyer** and **Buzz Sawyer** defeated **The Road Warriors** (**Animal** and **Hawk**) in 11:20 (★★★); **Ric Flair** defeated **Tommy Rich** in 24:30 (★★★).

Christmas Night '83 ★★★
25-12-83, St. Paul, Minnesota **AWA**
Billy Robinson vs. **Brad Rheingans** ended in a draw in 13:30 (★★★); **Jesse Ventura** defeated **Steve Olsonoski** in 8:34 (★★★); **Rick Martel** defeated **Superstar Billy Graham** by DQ in 6:51 (★★); **Baron Von Raschke**, **Ray Stevens** and **The High Flyers** (**Greg Gagne** and **Jim Brunzell**) defeated **Jerry Blackwell**, **Ken Patera**, **Mr. Saito** and **Sheik Adnan Al-Kassie** in 10:36 (★★★); **Mad Dog Vachon** defeated **Nick Bockwinkel** by DQ in 8:20 (★★★).

Christmas Star Wars '83 ★★★★
25-12-83, Dallas, Texas **WCCW**
The Missing Link defeated **Johnny Mantell** in 6:09 (★★); **Brian Adias** and **Iceman King Parsons** defeated **The Super Destroyers** (**Super Destroyer #1** and **Super Destroyer #2**) to win the WCCW American Tag Team Title in 15:28 (★★★★); **Kerry Von Erich** defeated **Kimala** by DQ in 5:09 (★★★); **David Von Erich** defeated **Ric Flair** by DQ in 10:23 (★★★★); **Jose Lothario** defeated **Black Gordman** in 7:21 (★★); **Mike Von Erich** and **Kevin Von Erich** defeated **The Fabulous Freebirds** (**Buddy Roberts** and **Terry Gordy**) in an Anything Goes Loser Leaves Town Match in 10:49 (★★★★); **Jimmy Garvin** defeated **Chris Adams** to win the WCCW American Heavyweight Title in 4:45 (★★★).

WWF at Madison Square Garden (26-12-83) ★★★
26-12-83, New York City, New York **WWF**
Jose Luis Rivera defeated Rene Goulet in 10:05 (★★); Salvatore Bellomo vs. Tiger Chung Lee ended in a time limit draw in 19:30 (★★); Jimmy Snuka and Arnold Skaaland defeated Don Muraco and Captain Lou Albano in 10:07 (★★★); Sgt. Slaughter defeated Chief Jay Strongbow in 7:42 (★★); The Masked Superstar vs. Ivan Putski ended in a double DQ in 7:00 (★★); The Iron Sheik defeated Bob Backlund to win the WWF World Title in 11:50 (★★); The Wild Samoans (Afa, Sika and Samula) defeated SD Jones, Rocky Johnson and Tony Atlas 2-1 in a Best Two Out Of Thre Falls Match in 20:15 (★★★); Tito Santana defeated Ivan Koloff in 15:46 (★★★); The Invaders (Invader #1 and Invader #2) defeated Iron Mike Sharpe and Butcher Vachon in 4:45 (★★).

WWF at Spectrum (21-01-84) ★★★
21-01-84, Philadelphia, Pennsylvania **WWF**
Eddie Gilbert vs. Rene Goulet ended in a draw in 18:58 (★★); Swede Hanson defeated Butcher Vachon in 3:58 (★); The Invaders (Invader #1 and Invader #2) defeated Mr. Fuji and Charlie Fulton in 9:28 (★★); The Iron Sheik vs. Tito Santana ended in a double DQ in 10:54 (★★★); Don Muraco defeated Salvatore Bellomo in 10:04 (★★★); The Masked Superstar defeated Bob Backlund via count out in 17:20 (★★★); Haiti Kid and Tiger Jackson defeated Pancho Boy and Dana Carpenter in 5:10 (★★); Andre The Giant, Jimmy Snuka, Tony Atlas and Rocky Johnson defeated The Wild Samoans (Afa, Sika and Samula) and Sgt. Slaughter 2-1 in a Best Two Out Of Three Falls Match in 9:16 (★★).

WWF at Madison Square Garden (23-01-84) ★★★
23-01-84, New York City, New York **WWF**
Tony Garea defeated Jose Luis Rivera in 6:46 (★★); The Invaders (Invader #1 and Invader #2) vs. Mr. Fuji and Tiger Chung Lee ended in a draw in 20:23 (★★★); The Masked Superstar defeated Chief Jay Strongbow in 7:26 (★★); Sgt. Slaughter defeated Ivan Putski via count out in 11:29 (★★); Paul Orndorff defeated Salvatore Bellomo in 14:06 (★★); Don Muraco vs. Tito Santana ended in a double DQ in 16:03 (★★); Haiti Kid and Tiger Jackson defeated Dana Carpenter and Pancho Boy 2-0 in a Best Two Out Of Three Falls Match in 6:53 (★★); Hulk Hogan defeated The Iron Sheik to win the WWF World Title in 5:40 (★★★); Jimmy Snuka defeated Rene Goulet in 3:54 (★★); Andre the Giant, Rocky Johnson and Tony Atlas defeated The Wild Samoans (Afa, Sika and Samula) in 5:29 (★★).

WWF at Spectrum (18-02-84) ★★
18-02-84, Philadelphia, Pennsylvania **WWF**
B. Brian Blair vs. Rene Goulet ended in a draw in 18:05 (★★); Jose Luis Rivera defeated Steve Lombardi in 7:14 (★★); Tony Atlas and Rocky Johnson defeated Roddy Piper and Don Muraco in 10:03 (★★★); Tito Santana vs. The Iron Sheik ended in a double count out in 9:13 (★★); Mr. Fuji and Tiger Chung Lee defeated Eddie Gilbert and Tony Garea in 11:47 (★★); Hulk Hogan defeated The Masked Superstar in 10:43 (★★★); Salvatore Bellomo defeated Butcher Vachon in 1:09 (★); Andre The Giant and Jimmy Snuka defeated Sgt. Slaughter and David Schultz in 3:43 (★★).

WWF at Madison Square Garden (20-02-84) ★★★★
20-02-84, New York City, New York **WWF**
Jose Luis Rivera defeated Charlie Fulton in 7:14 (★★); Iron Mike Sharpe defeated B. Brian Blair in 9:35 (★★★); Afa defeated Tony Garea in 11:37 (★★); The Iron Sheik defeated Eddie Gilbert in 5:48 (★★★); Roddy Piper and David Schultz defeated The Invaders (Invader #1 and Invader #2) in 11:17 (★★★); Tito Santana defeated Don Muraco via count out in 17:20 (★★★); Andre the Giant defeated The Masked Superstar in 7:46 (★★★); Hulk Hogan defeated Paul Orndorff via count out in 12:24 (★★★); Jimmy Snuka defeated Samula in 9:32 (★★); Ivan Putski, Rocky Johnson and Tony Atlas defeated Sgt. Slaughter, Mr. Fuji and Tiger Chung Lee in 6:20 (★★).

Boogie Jam ★★★★
17-03-84, Greensboro, North Carolina **NWA**
Tully Blanchard defeated Dory Funk Jr. in 13:48 (★★★); Rufus R. Jones defeated Ernie Ladd in 6:06 (★★); Wahoo McDaniel and Mark Youngblood defeated Don Kernodle and Bob Orton Jr. in 11:31 (★★★); Angelo Mosca Sr., Angelo Mosca Jr. and

Junkyard Dog defeated Gary Hart, The Great Kabuki and Ivan Koloff in 10:04 (★★); Dick Slater defeated Greg Valentine in a Steel Cage Match in 23:38 (★★★); Ric Flair vs. Ricky Steamboat ended in a draw in 56:38 (★★★); Jimmy Valiant defeated Assassin #2 in a Hair vs. Mask Match in 6:49 (★★).

WWF at Madison Square Garden (25-03-84) ★★★
25-03-84, New York City, New York **WWF**
SD Jones defeated Rene Goulet in 9:23 (★★); B. Brian Blair defeated Charlie Fulton in 9:30 (★★); The Iron Sheik defeated Ivan Putski in 3:53 (★★); Akira Maeda defeated Pierre Lefebvre in 4:55 (★★); Sgt. Slaughter defeated Mr. Fuji and Tiger Chung Lee in a Handicap Match in 4:18 (★★); Roddy Piper and David Schultz defeated Andre the Giant and Jimmy Snuka by DQ in 21:42 (★★★★); Tony Garea defeated Iron Mike Sharpe by DQ in 8:37 (★★); Bob Backlund vs. Greg Valentine ended in a double count out in 9:30 (★★); Tito Santana vs. Paul Orndorff ended in a time limit draw in 18:34 (★★★★); Tony Atlas and Rocky Johnson vs. The Wild Samoans (Afa and Sika) ended in a double DQ in 10:02 (★★★).

WWF at Spectrum (31-03-84) ★★
31-03-84, Philadelphia, Pennsylvania **WWF**
Tito Santana vs. Greg Valentine ended in a draw in 16:50 (★★★); Paul Orndorff defeated Chief Jay Strongbow in 6:02 (★★); Sgt. Slaughter vs. David Schultz ended in a double DQ in 6:26 (★★); Andre the Giant, Jimmy Snuka and Tony Garea defeated The Wild Samoans (Afa and Sika) and Rene Goulet 2-0 in a Best Two Out Of Three Falls Match in 15:12 (★★★); The Iron Sheik defeated Bob Backlund in 4:26 (★★); Princess Victoria and Velvet McIntyre defeated Wendi Richter and Peggy Lee in 6:28 (★★); Rocky Johnson and Tony Atlas defeated Mr. Fuji and Tiger Chung Lee in 5:36 (★★).

WWF at Madison Square Garden (23-04-84) ★★★
23-04-84, New York City, New York **WWF**
Tiger Chung Lee defeated Tonga Kid in 8:02 (★★); Rene Goulet defeated Jose Luis Rivera in 7:36 (★★); Tito Santana defeated JJ Dillon in 7:46 (★★); The Iron Sheik defeated Sgt. Slaughter by DQ in 8:31 (★★★★); Salvatore Bellomo defeated Ron Shaw in 7:53 (★★); Roddy Piper, Paul Orndorff and David Schultz defeated Ivan Putski, Rocky Johnson and Tony Atlas in 17:43 (★★); Princess Victoria and Velvet McIntyre defeated Peggy Lee and Wendi Richter in 19:02 (★★★); Bob Backlund defeated Greg Valentine in 25:34 (★★★★).

WWF at Spectrum (05-05-84) ★★
05-05-84, Philadelphia, Pennsylvania **WWF**
Rene Goulet defeated Akira Maeda in 8:36 (★★); B. Brian Blair defeated Ron Shaw in 7:04 (★★); Afa defeated Salvatore Bellomo in 7:49 (★★); Sgt. Slaughter defeated David Schultz in 6:36 (★★); Tiger Chung Lee defeated Jose Luis Rivera in 8:29 (★); Buzz Sawyer defeated The Tonga Kid in 4:27 (★★); Hulk Hogan vs. The Iron Sheik ended in a double count out in 10:47 (★★★★); Tito Santana defeated Greg Valentine in 12:04 (★★★); Terry Daniels defeated Rene Goulet in 7:35 (★); Susan Starr and Donna Christianello defeated Wendi Richter and Peggy Lee in 6:31 (★★); Rocky Johnson defeated Samula in 7:27 (★★).

1st David Von Erich Memorial Parade Of Champions ★★★
06-05-84, Irving, Texas **WCCW**
Chris Adams and Sunshine defeated Jimmy Garvin and Precious in 4:40 (★★); Butch Reed defeated Chick Donovan in 4:23 (★); Kimala vs. The Great Kabuki went to a double DQ in 8:06 (★★); Junkyard Dog defeated The Missing Link by DQ in 3:11 (★★); Rock and Soul (Buck Zumhofe and Iceman King Parsons) defeated The Super Destroyers (Bill Irwin and Scott Irwin) to win the WCCW American Tag Team Title in 8:12 (★★); Kevin Von Erich, Mike Von Erich and Fritz Von Erich defeated The Fabulous Freebirds (Michael Hayes, Terry Gordy and Buddy Roberts) to win the WCCW World Six-Man Tag Team Title in 7:37 (★★★); Kerry Von Erich defeated Ric Flair to win the NWA World Heavyweight Title in 18:35 (★★★★)

WWF at Capital Centre (19-05-84) ★★
19-05-84, Landover, Maryland **WWF**
B. Brian Blair defeated Rene Goulet in 15:00 (★★★); George Steele defeated Akira Maeda in 3:13 (★★); Jesse Ventura defeated Chief Jay Strongbow in 4:51 (★★); Greg Valentine

defeated **Tony Garea** in 4:50 (★★); **Tiger Chung Lee** defeated **Jose Luis Rivera** in 5:04 (★★); **Sgt. Slaughter** vs. **The Iron Sheik** ended in a double DQ in 10:24 (★★★); **Roddy Piper, Paul Orndorff** and **David Schultz** defeated **Rocky Johnson, SD Jones** and **Bobo Brazil** in 9:32 (★★★); **Bob Backlund** defeated **Mr. Fuji** in 5:51 (★★).

WWF at Madison Square Garden (21-05-84) ★★★
21-05-84, New York City, New York **WWF**
Akira Maeda defeated **Rene Goulet** in 9:47 (★★); **Jimmy Snuka** defeated **Greg Valentine** by DQ in 10:05 (★★★); **Paul Orndorff** defeated **Tito Santana** via count out in 22:26 (★★★); **Jesse Ventura** defeated **Salvatore Bellomo** in 4:31 (★★); **Sgt. Slaughter** vs. **The Iron Sheik** ended in a double DQ in 14:47 (★★★★); **The Wild Samoans (Afa, Sika** and **Samula)** defeated **Bobo Brazil, Rocky Johnson** and **SD Jones** in 7:25 (★); **The Fabulous Moolah** defeated **Wendi Richter** by DQ in 12:20 (★★); **Mr. Fuji** and **Tiger Chung Lee** defeated **B. Brian Blair** and **Tony Garea** in 18:04 (★★); **Hulk Hogan** defeated **David Schultz** in 5:46 (★★); **George Steele** defeated **Terry Daniels** in 2:57 (★); **Roddy Piper** defeated **Ivan Putski** by DQ in 4:07 (★★).

WWF at Spectrum (02-06-84) ★★
02-06-84, Philadelphia, Pennsylvania **WWF**
Samula defeated **Steve Lombardi** in 7:45 (★★); **Tony Garea** defeated **Israel Matia** in 7:44 (★); **Tito Santana** defeated **David Schultz** in 7:44 (★★★); **Salvatore Bellomo** defeated **Ron Shaw** in 6:43 (★); **Hulk Hogan** defeated **The Iron Sheik** in 7:56 (★★★); **Paul Orndorff** defeated **Sgt. Slaughter** in 12:04 (★★★); **Jose Luis Rivera** defeated **Tony Colon** in 2:40 (★★); **Bob Backlund** defeated **Samula** in 5:04 (★★).

WWF at Capital Centre (09-06-84) ★★
09-06-84, Landover, Maryland **WWF**
SD Jones defeated **Tiger Chung Lee** in 13:36 (★★); **Jesse Ventura** defeated **Tony Garea** in 5:40 (★★); **Greg Valentine** defeated **Salvatore Bellomo** in 3:34 (★★); **Jimmy Snuka** defeated **David Schultz** in 9:38 (★★); **Sgt. Slaughter** defeated **The Iron Sheik** in a Boot Camp Match in 13:10 (★★★); **Roddy Piper** defeated **Rocky Johnson** in 5:57 (★★); **Terry Daniels** defeated **Samula** in 6:46 (★★); **Ivan Putski** defeated **Bob Orton** by DQ in 8:36 (★★).

WWF at Madison Square Garden (16-06-84) ★★★★
16-06-84, New York City, New York **WWF**
Don Muraco defeated **Tony Garea** in 4:49 (★★); **George Steele** defeated **Jose Luis Rivera** in 2:24 (★); **Dick Murdoch** and **Adrian Adonis** vs. **The Wild Samoans (Afa** and **Sika)** ended in a double DQ in a Best Two Out Of Three Falls Match in 19:51 (★★★); **Jesse Ventura** defeated **SD Jones** in 4:58 (★★); **Greg Valentine** defeated **Tito Santana** via count out in 14:02 (★★★★); **Andre The Giant** defeated **David Schultz** in 7:05 (★★); **Mad Dog Vachon** defeated **Steve Lombardi** in 3:18 (★★); **Paul Orndorff** defeated **Salvatore Bellomo** in 9:01 (★★★); **Bob Orton** defeated **Chief Jay Strongbow** in 9:46 (★★); **Sgt. Slaughter** defeated **The Iron Sheik** in a Boot Camp Match in 16:02 (★★★★★).

WWF at Spectrum (07-07-84) ★★
07-07-84, Philadelphia, Pennsylvania **WWF**
Salvatore Bellomo defeated **Moondog Rex** in 6:44 (★★); **Big John Studd** defeated **Bobo Brazil** in 5:44 (★★); **Greg Valentine** defeated **Pat Patterson** in 5:50 (★★); **Hulk Hogan** and **Paul Orndorff** in 12:02 (★★★); **The Wild Samoans (Afa** and **Sika)** defeated **Mr. Fuji** and **Tiger Chung Lee** in 21:58 (★); **Jimmy Snuka** defeated **Roddy Piper** in 4:37 (★★★); **George Steele** defeated **Steve Lombardi** in 6:10 (★★); **Adrian Adonis** and **Dick Murdoch** defeated **Bob Backlund** and **B. Brian Blair** in 17:39 (★★★).

WWF at Meadowlands Arena (15-07-84) ★★★
15-07-84, East Rutherford, New Jersey **WWF**
The Moondogs (Moondog Rex and **Moondog Spot)** defeated **SD Jones** and **Jose Luis Rivera** in 12:13 (★★); **Salvatore Bellomo** defeated **Tony Colon** in 5:20 (★★); **Paul Orndorff** defeated **B. Brian Blair** in 17:08 (★★★); **The Wild Samoans (Afa** and **Sika)** defeated **Mr. Fuji** and **Tiger Chung Lee** in 6:34 (★★); **Ivan Putski** defeated **Rene Goulet** in 5:34 (★★); **Roddy Piper** defeated **Jimmy Snuka** via count out in 8:33 (★★★); **Haiti Kid** defeated **Dana Carpenter** in 8:12 (★); **Mil Mascaras** defeated **Pete Doherty** in 10:18 (★★); **Hulk Hogan** and **Andre the Giant** defeated **Big John Studd, Adrian Adonis** and **Dick Murdoch** in a Handicap Match in 22:21 (★★★★).

The Brawl To End It All ★★★
23-07-84, New York City, New York **WWF**
Sika defeated **Ron Shaw** in 5:12 (★★); **The Iron Sheik** defeated **Tony Garea** in 5:35 (★★★); **Tito Santana** vs. **Bob Orton** ended in a draw in 20:00 (★★★★); **Bob Backlund** defeated **Butcher Vachon** in 2:40 (★★); **Hulk Hogan** defeated **Greg Valentine** in 10:33 (★★★); **Antonio Inoki** defeated **Charlie Fulton** in 4:10 (★★); **Adrian Adonis** and **Dick Murdoch** defeated **Sgt. Slaughter** and **Terry Daniels** in 16:52 (★★★); **Wendi Richter** defeated **The Fabulous Moolah** to win the WWF Women's Title in 11:20 (★★); **Paul Orndorff** defeated **Chief Jay Strongbow** in 6:05 (★★); **Afa** defeated **Rene Goulet** in 5:26 (★★); **Antonio Inoki** won a 20-Man Battle Royal in 13:23 (★★★).

WWF at Capital Centre (28-07-84) ★★★
28-07-84, Landover, Maryland **WWF**
Charlie Fulton defeated **Jose Luis Rivera** in 9:26 (★); **Tony Garea** defeated **Iron Mike Sharpe** in 5:39 (★★); **Sika** vs. **George Steele** ended in a double count out in 5:30 (★★); **Princess Victoria** and **Velvet McIntyre** defeated **Peggy Lee** and **Peggy Patterson** in 13:15 (★★); **Sgt. Slaughter** defeated **Greg Valentine** by DQ in 10:36 (★★★); **Paul Orndorff** defeated **Hulk Hogan** by DQ in 12:12 (★★★); **Roddy Piper** defeated **Jimmy Snuka** via count out in 6:17 (★★★); **The Iron Sheik** defeated **Billy Travis** in 3:30 (★).

WWF at Spectrum (04-08-84) ★★
04-08-84, Philadelphia, Pennsylvania **WWF**
Bob Backlund defeated **Salvatore Bellomo** in 10:56 (★★); **Gama Singh** defeated **Dave Barbie** in 5:46 (★★); **Mr. Fuji** defeated **Tiger Chung Lee** in 14:33 (★★); **Andre The Giant** defeated **Big John Studd** in 9:47 (★★★); **Hulk Hogan** defeated **Greg Valentine** in 11:18 (★★★); **The Freebirds (Michael Hayes, Terry Gordy** and **Buddy Roberts)** defeated **Ron Shaw, Rene Goulet** and **Charlie Fulton** in 5:12 (★★); **The Haiti Kid** defeated **Dana Carpenter** in 3:51 (★★); **Iron Mike Sharpe** defeated **Rocky Johnson** in 4:46 (★★); **Kamala** defeated **Fred Marzino** in 3:10 (★★); **Ken Patera** defeated **Steve Lombardi** in 5:43 (★★); **Tito Santana** defeated **The Iron Sheik** in 7:51 (★★★).

WWF at Kiel Auditorium (10-08-84) ★★
10-08-84, St. Louis, Missouri **WWF**
Don Muraco defeated **Brian Madden** in 5:15 (★★); **Big John Studd, Adrian Adonis** and **Dick Murdoch** defeated **The Wild Samoans (Afa, Sika** and **Samu)** in 14:47 (★★★); **Junkyard Dog** defeated **Max Blue** in 4:17 (★★); **Nikolai Volkoff** defeated **Johnny Phillips** in 3:51 (★★); **George Steele** defeated **Hulk Hogan** via count out in 9:17 (★★★); **Ken Patera** defeated **Tony Garea** in 6:22 (★★); **The Spoiler** defeated **Billy Travis** in 7:07 (★★); **Bob Orton** defeated **Pat Patterson** in 6:12 (★★); **The Fabulous Freebirds (Michael Hayes, Terry Gordy** and **Buddy Roberts)** defeated **Jerry Valiant, Alexis Smirnoff** and **Max Blue** in 3:49 (★★); **Kamala** defeated **Salvatore Bellomo** in 3:18 (★★).

WWF at Madison Square Garden (25-08-84) ★★
25-08-84, New York City, New York **WWF**
Kamala defeated **Chief Jay Strongbow** in 2:50 (★★); **B. Brian Blair** vs. **Iron Mike Sharpe** ended in a double count out in 13:02 (★★★); **Rick McGraw** vs. **Salvatore Bellomo** ended in a time limit draw in 18:07 (★★); **The North-South Connection (Dick Murdoch** and **Adrian Adonis)** defeated **The Wild Samoans (Afa** and **Sika)** by DQ in 12:00 (★★); **Ken Patera** defeated **Pat Patterson** in 9:04 (★★); **Jesse Ventura** defeated **Ivan Putski** via count out in 11:40 (★★★); **The Fabulous Freebirds (Michael Hayes, Terry Gordy** and **Buddy Roberts)** defeated **Butcher Vachon, Ron Shaw** and **Pete Doherty** 2-0 in a Best Two Out Of Three Falls Match in 8:58 (★★); **Roddy Piper** defeated **Jimmy Snuka** via count out in 7:05 (★★); **Terry Daniels** defeated **Fred Marzino** in 3:55 (★); **Tito Santana** defeated **Greg Valentine** in 7:23 (★★).

WWF at Spectrum (01-09-84) ★★
01-09-84, Philadelphia, Pennsylvania **WWF**
Iron Mike Sharpe defeated **Steve Lombardi** in 11:39 (★★★); **David Schultz** defeated **AJ Petruzzi** in 5:12 (★); **Velvet McIntyre** and **Princess Victoria** defeated **Leilani Kai** and **Despina Montagas** in 13:47 (★★★); **Jesse Ventura** defeated **Ivan Putski** in 14:07 (★★★); **Greg Valentine** vs. **Rocky Johnson** ended in a draw in 18:50 (★★); **Andre The Giant** defeated **Roddy Piper** via count out in 4:44 (★★); **Nikolai Volkoff** defeated **Rick McGraw** in 7:19 (★★); **The Wild Samoans (Afa** and **Sika)** defeated **Adrian Adonis** and **Dick Murdoch** in 11:00 (★★★).

WWF at Madison Square Garden (22-09-84) ★ ★

22-09-84, New York City, New York **WWF**

Brutus Beefcake defeated Salvatore Bellomo in 9:56 (★ ★); Nikolai Volkoff defeated Chief Jay Strongbow in 6:48 (★ ★); David Schultz defeated SD Jones in 6:35 (★ ★); Greg Valentine defeated Jose Luis Rivera in 7:19 (★ ★); Big John Studd defeated Hulk Hogan via count out in 11:09 (★ ★ ★); Ken Patera defeated Rick McGraw in 7:40 (★ ★); Sgt. Slaughter and The Wild Samoans (Afa and Sika) defeated Captain Lou Albano, Dick Murdoch and Adrian Adonis in 20:16 (★ ★ ★); B. Brian Blair defeated Iron Mike Sharpe by DQ in 19:46 (★ ★ ★); Kamala defeated Pat Patterson in 5:21 (★ ★).

WWF at Maple Leaf Gardens (23-09-84) ★ ★ ★

23-09-84, Toronto, Canda **WWF**

Bret Hart defeated Butcher Vachon in 9:14 (★ ★ ★); Brutus Beefcake defeated Nick DeCarlo in 11:16 (★ ★); Davey Boy Smith defeated Goldie Rogers in 13:38 (★ ★); Ivan Putski defeated Greg Valentine in 14:32 (★ ★ ★); Nikolai Volkoff defeated Richard Cummings in 1:29 (★); Kamala defeated Andre the Giant via count out in 7:45 (★ ★); Ken Patera defeated Rick McGraw in 10:40 (★ ★ ★); Dynamite Kid defeated Jerry Valiant in 5:41 (★ ★ ★); Iron Mike Sharpe defeated B. Brian Blair in 11:12 (★ ★); Sgt. Slaughter defeated The Iron Sheik by DQ in 9:02 (★ ★ ★).

WWF at Spectrum (13-10-84) ★ ★

13-10-84, Philadelphia, Pennsylvania **WWF**

Rene Goulet defeated Bob Bradley in 11:17 (★ ★); Ron Shaw defeated Steve Lombardi in 9:38 (★); Moondog Rex defeated Dave Barbie in 3:30 (★); David Sammartino defeated Moondog Spot in 11:34 (★ ★); Sgt. Slaughter and Junkyard Dog vs. Nikolai Volkoff and The Iron Sheik ended in a double DQ in 16:12 (★ ★ ★); Brutus Beefcake defeated Salvatore Bellomo in 10:40 (★ ★); Ken Patera defeated Tony Garea in 6:33 (★ ★); Greg Valentine defeated SD Jones in 4:44 (★ ★); Hulk Hogan defeated Big John Studd in 9:13 (★ ★ ★).

WWF at Meadowlands Arena (14-10-84) ★ ★ ★

14-10-84, East Rutherford, New Jersey **WWF**

Rene Goulet defeated Salvatore Bellomo in 15:49 (★ ★); Brutus Beefcake defeated Rick McGraw in 15:29 (★ ★ ★); David Sammartino defeated Mr. Fuji in 12:11 (★ ★); The Brisco Brothers (Jack Brisco and Jerry Brisco) defeated Rene Goulet and Steve Lombardi in 6:31 (★ ★); Rocky Johnson defeated Moondog Spot in 11:38 (★ ★); Adrian Adonis and Dick Murdoch vs. The Wild Samoans (Afa and Sika) ended in a double DQ in 12:09 (★ ★); Big John Studd defeated SD Jones in 11:02 (★ ★); Andre the Giant and Sgt. Slaughter defeated The Iron Sheik and Nikolai Volkoff in 14:39 (★ ★ ★).

WWF at Maple Leaf Gardens (21-10-84) ★ ★

21-10-84, Toronto, Canada **WWF**

Rene Goulet defeated Nick DeCarlo in 11:16 (★ ★); David Sammartino defeated Moondog Rex in 11:28 (★ ★); David Schultz defeated Rick McGraw in 3:50 (★ ★); Greg Valentine defeated SD Jones in 9:02 (★ ★); Nikolai Volkoff defeated Rocky Johnson in 8:06 (★ ★); Angelo Mosca defeated The Iron Sheik in 6:40 (★ ★); The British Bulldogs (Davey Boy Smith and Dynamite Kid) defeated Bobby Bass and Goldie Rogers in 9:31; Andre the Giant defeated Kamala in a Steel Cage Match in 13:56 (★ ★).

WWF at Madison Square Garden (22-10-84) ★ ★

22-10-84, New York City, New York **WWF**

David Schultz defeated Salvatore Bellomo in 4:02 (★ ★); Afa vs. Dick Murdoch ended in a draw in 19:15 (★); Mad Dog Vachon defeated Rick McGraw in 7:24 (★ ★); David Sammartino defeated Moondog Spot in 12:23 (★ ★); Greg Valentine defeated Tito Santana by DQ in 12:23 (★ ★ ★); Ken Patera defeated Rocky Johnson in 13:08 (★ ★); Sika defeated Adrian Adonis by DQ in 9:29 (★ ★); Nikolai Volkoff defeated Sgt. Slaughter via count out in 15:40 (★ ★); Brutus Beefcake defeated Tony Garea in 5:20 (★ ★); Hulk Hogan defeated Big John Studd in 10:48 (★ ★).

1st Cotton Bowl Extravaganza ★ ★

27-10-84, Dallas, Texas **WCCW**

Butch Reed vs. Iceman King Parsons ended in a draw in 8:16 (★ ★); The Missing Link defeated George Wengroff in 2:25 (★ ★); The Fantastics (Tommy Rogers and Bobby Fulton) defeated Kelly Kiniski and El Diablo in 9:21 (★ ★); Mike Von

Erich and Stella Mae French defeated Gino Hernandez and Nickla Roberts in 6:20 (★ ★); Kevin Von Erich defeated Chris Adams in 10:07 (★ ★ ★); Gino Hernandez, Jake Roberts and Chris Adams defeated Bobby Fulton, Kerry Von Erich and Mike Von Erich to win the WCCW World Six-Man Tag Team Title in 13:19 (★ ★ ★).

WWF at Spectrum (10-11-84) ★ ★

10-11-84, Philadelphia, Pennsylvania **WWF**

Rick McGraw vs. Rene Goulet ended in a draw in 14:48 (★ ★); Terry Gibbs defeated Jose Luis Rivera in 7:17 (★ ★); Mike Rotundo defeated Johnny Rodz in 12:51 (★ ★); Brutus Beefcake defeated Samula in 12:45 (★ ★); David Sammartino defeated Charlie Fulton in 7:04 (★ ★); The Tonga Kid defeated Moondog Spot in 4:31 (★ ★); Blackjack Mulligan defeated Moondog Rex in 4:04 (★ ★); Barry Windham defeated Jerry Valiant in 2:07 (★ ★); Andre The Giant vs. Big John Studd ended in a double count out in 8:20 (★ ★ ★); Sgt. Slaughter and Junkyard Dog defeated The Iron Sheik and Nikolai Volkoff in a Texas Tornado Match in 11:21 (★ ★ ★).

Thanksgiving Star Wars '84 ★ ★ ★

22-11-84, Dallas, Texas **WCCW**

The Missing Link defeated Buck Zumhofe in 1:39 (★); Stella Mae French defeated Nickla Roberts in 3:23 (★); Chic Donovan defeated Skandar Akbar by DQ in 8:15 (★ ★); The Fantastics (Tommy Rogers and Bobby Fulton) defeated The Pretty Young Things (Koko Ware and Norvell Austin) in 14:05 (★ ★ ★); Iceman King Parsons and Kerry Von Erich defeated Jake Roberts and Kelly Kiniski in 6:04 (★ ★ ★); Mike Von Erich defeated Gino Hernandez by DQ in 4:13 (★ ★); Terry Gordy defeated Killer Khan in a Texas Death Match in 15:41 (★ ★ ★); Chris Adams defeated Kevin Von Erich in a No DQ Match in 3:28 (★ ★).

Starrcade '84 ★ ★

22-11-84, Greensboro, North Carolina **NWA**

Denny Brown defeated Mike Davis to win the NWA World Junior Heavyweight Title in 5:35 (★ ★); Brian Adidas defeated Mr. Ito in 3:11 (★); Jesse Barr defeated Mike Graham in 11:46 (★ ★ ★); Buzz Tyler and The Assassin defeated The Zambuie Express (Elijah Akeem and Kareem Muhammad) in a Tag Team Elimination Match in 4:54 (★ ★); Manny Fernandez defeated Black Bart to win the Mid-Atlantic Brass Knuckles Title in 7:35 (★ ★ ★); Paul Jones defeated Jimmy Valiant in a Loser Leaves Town Tuxedo Street Fight in 5:22 (★); Ron Bass defeated Dick Slater by DQ in 9:07 (★ ★); The Russians (Ivan Koloff and Nikita Koloff) defeated Keith Larson and Ole Anderson in 15:20 (★ ★); Tully Blanchard defeated Ricky Steamboat in 13:15 (★ ★ ★ ★); Wahoo McDaniel defeated Superstar Billy Graham in 4:14 (★); Ric Flair defeated Dusty Rhodes by referee's decision in 12:09 (★ ★).

WWF at Madison Square Garden (26-11-84) ★ ★ ★

26-11-84, New York City, New York **WWF**

SD Jones defeated Charlie Fulton in 10:40 (★ ★); Moondog Spot defeated Jose Luis Rivera in 9:16 (★ ★ ★); Bobby Heenan defeated Salvatore Bellomo in 8:56 (★ ★); Angelo Mosca defeated Mr. Fuji by DQ in 8:01 (★ ★); Bob Orton defeated Swede Hanson in 8:51 (★); Roddy Piper vs. The Tonga Kid ended in a double DQ in 7:03 (★ ★ ★); Barry Windham defeated Moondog Rex in 12:11 (★ ★); Tony Atlas defeated The Executioner in 1:48 (★ ★); David Schultz defeated Rocky Johnson in 9:25 (★ ★); David Sammartino defeated Ken Patera by DQ in 12:24 (★ ★); Tito Santana vs. Greg Valentine ended in a draw in 22:23 (★ ★ ★ ★).

WWF at Spectrum (01-12-84) ★ ★

01-12-84, Philadelphia, Pennsylvania **WWF**

Mr. Fuji defeated Salvatore Bellomo in 8:13 (★ ★); Gama Singh defeated Johnny Rodz in 11:17 (★ ★); David Schultz defeated Swede Hanson in 5:33 (★ ★); Bob Orton vs. Mike Rotundo ended in a draw in 19:12 (★ ★ ★); The Iron Sheik defeated Dave Barbie in 2:43 (★ ★); Ken Patera defeated Jose Luis Rivera in 6:20 (★ ★); Roddy Piper defeated The Tonga Kid in 6:15 (★ ★); Wendi Richter defeated Judy Martin in 7:29 (★ ★); Junkyard Dog defeated Brutus Beefcake in 6:28 (★ ★ ★); Sgt. Slaughter vs. Nikolai Volkoff ended in a double count out in 8:05 (★ ★ ★); Barry Windham defeated Buddy Rose in 4:29 (★ ★).

WWF at Meadowlands Arena (10-12-84) ★★
10-12-84, East Rutherford, New Jersey **WWF**

Buddy Rose defeated Jose Luis Rivera in 11:45 (★★); Johnny V defeated Steve Lombardi in 7:01 (★★); George Wells defeated Charlie Fulton in 13:07 (★★); Ken Patera defeated Jim Powers in 8:08 (★★); Bobby Heenan defeated SD Jones in 11:27 (★★); Velvet McIntyre and Desiree Patterson defeated Penny Mitchell and Peggy Patterson in 17:17 (★★); Junkyard Dog defeated Paul Orndorff in 17:35 (★★★); Jimmy Snuka vs. Bob Orton ended in a double count out in 2:33 (★★); Brutus Beefcake defeated Salvatore Bellomo in 7:32 (★★); Hulk Hogan defeated Big John Studd via count out in a $15,000 Bodyslam Match in 10:01 (★★).

Christmas Night '84 ★★★★
25-12-84, St. Paul, Minnesota **AWA**

Billy Robinson defeated Steve Olsonoski in 12:58 (★★★); Baron von Raschke defeated Steve Regal in 17:14 (★★★); Jim Brunzell vs. Mr. Saito ended in a draw in 14:16 (★★★); Curt Hennig defeated Nick Bockwinkel in 14:19 (★★★★); King Kong Brody and The Masked Superstar defeated Greg Gagne and Jerry Blackwell in 10:49 (★★★); Rick Martel defeated Jimmy Garvin by DQ in 17:02 (★★★).

Christmas Star Wars '84 ★★
25-12-84, Dallas, Texas **WCCW**

Rip Oliver defeated Iceman King Parsons in 8:22 (★★); The Fantastics (Tommy Rogers and Bobby Fulton) defeated The Midnight Express (Bobby Eaton and Dennis Condrey) in 12:49 (★★★); Kerry Von Erich defeated Ric Flair by DQ in 18:17 (★★★); Kevin Von Erich defeated Chris Adams in a Lumberjack Match in 5:01 (★★); The Fabulous Freebirds (Terry Gordy and Buddy Roberts) and Chic Donovan defeated Skandor Akbar, The Missing Link and Mr. X in a Loser Leaves The Area Elimination Match (★★); Mike Von Erich and Billy Jack Haynes defeated Jake Roberts and Gino Hernandez in 3:34 (★★).

WWF at Madison Square Garden (28-12-84) ★★★★
28-12-84, New York City, New York **WWF**

Brutus Beefcake defeated SD Jones in 13:22 (★★); Salvatore Bellomo defeated Johnny Rodz in 5:36 (★★); Antonio Inoki defeated David Schultz in 5:16 (★★); Junkyard Dog defeated Paul Kelly in 3:05 (★★); The Cobra defeated The Black Tiger to win the vacant WWF Jr. Heavyweight Title in 12:29 (★★★★); Jimmy Snuka and The Tonga Kid vs. Roddy Piper and Bob Orton ended in a double DQ in 14:58 (★★★); Mike Rotundo defeated Rene Goulet in 10:38 (★★); The North-South Connection (Dick Murdoch and Adrian Adonis) vs. The Brisco Brothers (Jack Brisco and Jerry Brisco) ended in a double count out in 26:46 (★★★★★); Barry Windham defeated Mr. Fuji in :19 (★★); Hulk Hogan defeated The Iron Sheik in 3:31 (★★).

WWF at Spectrum (12-01-85) ★★
12-01-85, Philadelphia, Pennsylvania **WWF**

Rick McGraw defeated Johnny Rodz in 13:19 (★★); David Schultz defeated Dave Barbie in 5:45 (★★); The Spoiler vs. George Wells ended in a draw in 18:13 (★★); Brutus Beefcake defeated Salvatore Bellomo in 6:16 (★★); David Sammartino defeated Paul Orndorff by DQ in 10:15 (★★★); Adrian Adonis and Dick Murdoch defeated The Brisco Brothers (Jack Brisco and Jerry Brisco) in 14:11 (★★★); Don Muraco defeated Swede Hanson in 3:02 (★★); Roddy Piper and Bob Orton vs. Jimmy Snuka and Tony Atlas ended in a double count out in 9:30 (★★★).

WWF at Madison Square Garden (21-01-85) ★★
21-01-85, New York City, New York **WWF**

Moondog Rex defeated Terry Gibbs in 10:14 (★★); Bret Hart defeated Rene Goulet in 14:32 (★★); Jim Neidhart defeated Tony Garea in 12:05 (★★); Don Muraco defeated Swede Hanson in 10:54 (★); Blackjack Mulligan defeated Moondog Spot in 6:40 (★★); Andre The Giant defeated Ken Patera by DQ in 7:44 (★★★); Big John Studd defeated George Wells in 7:19 (★); Roddy Piper and Bob Orton defeated Jimmy Snuka and Junkyard Dog in a Texas Tornado Match in 8:45 (★★); The Spoiler defeated Rick McGraw in 8:59 (★); Tito Santana defeated Greg Valentine via count out in 20:21 (★★★).

WWF at Spectrum (16-02-85) ★★
16-02-85, Philadelphia, Pennsylvania **WWF**

Moondog Rex defeated Tony Garea in 10:38 (★★); AJ Petruzzi defeated Jim Powers in 3:16 (★★); Dave Barbie defeated Carl Fury in 3:27 (★); Swede Hanson defeated Charlie Fulton in 3:27 (★★); Nikolai Volkoff defeated George Wells in 6:10 (★★); Barry Windham defeated Dick Murdoch in 13:38 (★★★); Bruno Sammartino and David Sammartino defeated Paul Orndorff and Bobby Heenan in 11:39 (★★★); Mike Rotundo defeated Mr. X in 5:35 (★★); Tony Atlas defeated Moondog Spot in 7:40 (★★); Hillbilly Jim defeated Rene Goulet in 5:18 (★★); Hulk Hogan defeated Brutus Beefcake in 9:45 (★★★).

The War To Settle The Score ★★
18-02-85, New York City, New York **WWF**

Rick McGraw vs. Moondog Spot ended in a draw in 14:32 (★★); Johnny Rodz defeated Jose Luis Rivera in 11:14 (★★); Hillbilly Jim defeated Rene Goulet in 7:29 (★★); Leilani Kai defeated Wendi Richter to win the WWF Women's Title in 11:49 (★★); David Sammartino defeated Moondog Rex in 12:27 (★); Nikolai Volkoff defeated Swede Hanson in 5:48 (★); Jimmy Snuka defeated Bob Orton in 9:59 (★★); Paul Orndorff defeated Tony Atlas in 6:08 (★★); The US Express (Barry Windham and Mike Rotundo) defeated The Spoiler and The Assassin in :36 (★); Don Muraco defeated Salvatore Bellomo in 2:41 (★★); Hulk Hogan defeated Roddy Piper by DQ in 7:40 (★★★).

Star Wars (February '85) ★★★
24-02-85, East Rutherford, New Jersey **AWA/WCCW**

Ivan Koloff and Nikita Koloff defeated Jimmy Valiant and Steve Keirn in 9:34 (★★★); Jimmy Garvin defeated Rick Martel by DQ in 7:37 (★★★); The Road Warriors (Animal and Hawk) defeated Baron Von Raschke and Jerry Lawler in 9:40 (★★); Ric Flair defeated Harley Race in 15:18 (★★★); Sgt Slaughter won a 23-Man Tag Team Battle Royal in 12:01 (★★★).

WWF at Madison Square Garden (17-03-85) ★★
17-03-85, New York City, New York **WWF**

Rocky Johnson defeated Charlie Fulton in 3:51 (★★); Barry O defeated Rene Goulet in 8:50 (★★); Jim Neidhart defeated SD Jones in 6:52 (★★); King Kong Bundy defeated Jose Luis Rivera in 2:30 (★★); The Iron Sheik and Nikolai Volkoff defeated George Wells and Bret Hart in 8:45 (★★); David Sammartino defeated Matt Borne in 8:36 (★★); Andre The Giant, Jimmy Snuka and Junkyard Dog defeated Big John Studd, Jesse Ventura and Ken Patera in 11:55 (★★); Ricky Steamboat defeated Terry Gibbs in 4:36 (★★); Greg Valentine defeated Tito Santana in a Lumberjack Match in 10:22 (★★★).

WWF at Spectrum (17-03-85) ★★★
17-03-85, Philadelphia, Pennsylvania **WWF**

Rocky Johnson defeated Moondog Spot in 9:24 (★); Tito Santana defeated Mr. X in 7:01 (★★); Don Muraco defeated The Cobra in 11:14 (★★★); King Kong Bundy defeated Swede Hanson in 8:16 (★★); Jimmy Snuka vs. Roddy Piper ended in a double count out in 6:55 (★★★); Ricky Steamboat defeated Matt Borne in 11:02 (★★); Greg Valentine defeated Junkyard Dog in 12:26 (★★★); Bruno Sammartino and David Sammartino defeated Paul Orndorff and Bobby Heenan in a Lumberjack Match in 8:16 (★★★).

WrestleMania ★★
31-03-85, New York City, New York **WWF**

Tito Santana defeated The Executioner in 4:49 (★★); King Kong Bundy defeated SD Jones in :25 (★★); Ricky Steamboat defeated Matt Borne in 4:39 (★★); Brutus Beefcake vs. David Sammartino went to a double DQ in 11:43 (★★); Junkyard Dog defeated Greg Valentine via count out in 6:55 (★★); Nikolai Volkoff and The Iron Sheik defeated The US Express (Barry Windham and Mike Rotundo) to win the WWF World Tag Team Title in 6:55 (★★); Andre the Giant defeated Big John Studd in a $15,000 Bodyslam Match in 5:53 (★★); Wendi Richter defeated Leilani Kai to win the WWF World Women's Title in 6:14 (★); Hulk Hogan and Mr. T defeated Paul Orndorff and Roddy Piper in 13:34 (★★★).

Meadowlands Mayhem ★★
19-04-85, East Rutherford, New Jersey **AWA**

Bobby Duncum defeated Larry Sharpe in 3:59 (★★); The Wild Samoans (Afa and Sika) defeated Steve Olsonoski and Tom Zenk in 5:21 (★★); Jim Duggan defeated Kendo Nagasaki in 2:43 (★ ★); **Jimmy Garvin** defeated **Baron von Raschke** in 7:09 (★ ★); **The Fabulous Freebirds (Buddy Roberts, Michael Hayes** and **Terry Gordy)** vs. **The High Flyers (Greg Gagne** and **Jim Brunzell)** and **The Tonga Kid** ended in a double DQ in 19:22 (★ ★ ★ ★); **Rick Martel** defeated **King Tonga** in 13:34 (★ ★); **Kamala** defeated **Sgt. Slaughter** in a Ugandan Death Match in 13:04 (★ ★); **Bob Backlund** defeated **Larry Zbyszko** by DQ in 14:11 (★ ★ ★).

StarCage '85 ★ ★ ★
21-04-85, St. Paul, Minnesota **AWA**

Steve Olsonoski and **Tom Zenk** defeated **The Alaskans (Alaskan #1** and **Alaskan #2)** in 12:01 (★ ★); **Baron von Raschke** and **Buck Zumhofe** defeated **Jimmy Garvin** and **Steve Regal** in 14:21 (★ ★); **Bob Backlund** and **Brad Rheingans** defeated **Butch Reed** and **Larry Zbyszko** in 15:46 (★ ★ ★ ★); **Jim Brunzell** and **The Tonga Kid** defeated **Billy Robinson** and **Bobby Duncum** in 11:19 (★ ★); **Greg Gagne** and **Verne Gagne** defeated **Mr. Saito** and **Nick Bockwinkel** in 13:42 (★ ★); **The Road Warriors (Animal** and **Hawk)** defeated **Curt Hennig** and **Larry Hennig** by DQ in 12:16 (★ ★); **Jerry Blackwell** and **Sgt. Slaughter** defeated **King Tonga, Sheik Adnan Al-Kassie** and **The Masked Superstar** in a Handicap Steel Cage Match in 15:12 (★ ★).

WWF at Maple Leaf Gardens (21-04-85) ★ ★ ★
21-04-85, Toronto, Canada **WWF**

Jim Neidhart defeated **Rick McGraw** in 7:47 (★ ★); **Don Muraco** defeated **Steve Lombardi** in 6:09 (★ ★); **Ivan Putski** defeated **Jerry Valiant** in 5:23 (★ ★); **Bret Hart** defeated **George Wells** in 9:11 (★ ★ ★); **The British Bulldogs (Davey Boy Smith** and **Dynamite Kid)** defeated **Moondog Spot** and **Barry O** in 16:31 (★ ★ ★); **Ricky Steamboat** and **Tito Santana** defeated **The Dream Team (Greg Valentine** and **Brutus Beefcake)** in 15:31 (★ ★ ★ ★); **Hulk Hogan** defeated **Paul Orndorff** in 10:03 (★ ★ ★).

WWF at Madison Square Garden (22-04-85) ★ ★ ★ ★
22-04-85, New York, New York **WWF**

The Cobra defeated **Barry O** in 13:20 (★ ★ ★ ★); **Tatsumi Fujinami** defeated **Matt Borne** in 11:25 (★ ★); **King Kong Bundy** defeated **Swede Hanson** in 4:27 (★ ★); **The British Bulldogs (Davey Boy Smith** and **Dynamite Kid)** defeated **Rene Goulet** and **Johnny Rodz** in 8:16 (★ ★); **Ricky Steamboat** defeated **Moondog Spot** in 7:24 (★ ★ ★); **Don Muraco** defeated **Hulk Hogan** via count out in 13:35 (★ ★); **Mike Rotundo** defeated **The Iron Sheik** in 14:16 (★ ★ ★ ★); **Barry Windham** defeated **Nikolai Volkoff** by DQ in 12:11 (★ ★); **Tito Santana** and **Junkyard Dog** defeated **The Dream Team (Brutus Beefcake** and **Greg Valentine)** in 16:03 (★ ★ ★).

WWF at Spectrum (27-04-85) ★ ★ ★
27-04-85, Philadelphia, Pennsylvania **WWF**

The British Bulldogs (Davey Boy Smith and **Dynamite Kid)** vs. **The Hart Foundation (Bret Hart** and **Jim Neidhart)** ended in a draw in 20:00 (★ ★); **Tito Santana** and **David Sammartino** defeated **Greg Valentine** and **Brutus Beefcake** in 11:04 (★ ★); **Roddy Piper** and **Bob Orton** defeated **SD Jones** and **George Wells** in 2:24 (★ ★); **Barry Windham** and **Mike Rotundo** defeated **The Iron Sheik** and **Nikolai Volkoff** in 14:07 (★ ★ ★); **Ricky Steamboat** and **Jimmy Snuka** defeated **Charlie Fulton** and **Moondog Spot** in 16:06 (★ ★); **Hulk Hogan** defeated **Paul Orndorff** in 10:06 (★ ★); **Ricky Steamboat** and **Jimmy Snuka** won a Tag Team Battle Royal in 8:37 (★ ★ ★).

2nd David Von Erich Memorial Parade Of Champions ★ ★ ★
05-05-85, Irving, Texas **WCCW**

Mike Von Erich defeated **Rip Oliver** in 7:52 (★ ★); **The Fantastics (Tommy Rogers** and **Bobby Fulton)** defeated **The Midnight Express (Bobby Eaton** and **Dennis Condrey)** in a Two Ring No DQ Match to win the vacant WCCW American Tag Team Title in 8:36 (★ ★); **Mike Von Erich, Kerry Von Erich, Kevin Von Erich** and **The Fabulous Freebirds (Michael Hayes, Terry Gordy** and **Buddy Roberts)** defeated **One Man Gang, Rip Oliver, Kimala, Steve Williams, Chris Adams** and **Gino Hernandez** 3-2 in a Best Three Out Of Five Falls Match in 18:41 (★ ★); **Ric Flair** vs. **Kevin Von Erich** ended in a double count out in 20:37 (★ ★ ★ ★); **Kerry Von Erich** defeated **One Man Gang** in a Hair vs. Hair Match in 8:15 (★ ★ ★).

Saturday Night's Main Event I ★ ★
11-05-85, Uniondale, New York **WWF**

The US Express (Barry Windham and **Mike Rotundo)** and **Ricky Steamboat** defeated **The Iron Sheik, Nikolai Volkoff** and **George Steele** in 6:30 (★ ★); **Hulk Hogan** defeated **Bob Orton** by DQ in 6:54 (★ ★); **Wendi Richter** defeated **The Fabulous Moolah** in 4:00 (★ ★); **Junkyard Dog** defeated **Pete Doherty** in 3:15 (★ ★).

WWF at Boston Garden (18-05-85) ★ ★
18-05-85, Boston, Massachusetts **WWF**

Moondog Spot defeated **Salvatore Bellomo** in 7:43 (★ ★); **Swede Hanson** defeated **Steve Lombardi** in 9:41 (★ ★); **Big John Studd** defeated **Rocky Johnson** in 4:09 (★ ★); **Tito Santana** defeated **Brutus Beefcake** in 12:52 (★ ★ ★); **Ken Patera** defeated **Tony Garea** in 7:56 (★ ★); **Greg Valentine** defeated **Junkyard Dog** in 10:33 (★ ★ ★); **Ivan Putski** defeated **Barry O** in 3:53 (★ ★); **Pete Doherty** defeated **Mario Mancini** in 2:10 (★); **Hulk Hogan** and **Jimmy Snuka** defeated **Don Muraco** and **Bob Orton** in 9:32 (★ ★ ★).

WWF at Madison Square Garden (20-05-85) ★ ★
20-05-85, New York City, New York **WWF**

Rocky Johnson defeated **Rene Goulet** in 10:19 (★ ★ ★); **Jim Neidhart** defeated **Ivan Putski** in 6:04 (★ ★); **Pedro Morales** defeated **Terry Gibbs** in 12:15 (★ ★); **Hulk Hogan** defeated **Don Muraco** by DQ in 6:12 (★ ★ ★); **Bret Hart** defeated **Rick McGraw** in 8:31 (★ ★); **Ken Patera** defeated **Tony Atlas** in 10:50 (★ ★); **The US Express (Barry Windham** and **Mike Rotundo)** defeated **Nikolai Volkoff** and **The Iron Sheik** via count out in 11:21 (★ ★ ★); **The Missing Link** defeated **SD Jones** in 1:55 (★ ★); **Jesse Ventura** defeated **Tony Garea** in 10:31 (★ ★); **Bruno Sammartino** and **David Sammartino** defeated **Brutus Beefcake** and **Johnny V** in 9:07 (★ ★).

WWF at Spectrum (25-05-85) ★ ★ ★
25-05-85, Philadelphia, Pennsylvania **WWF**

The Spoiler defeated **Salvatore Bellomo** in 9:58 (★ ★); **Paul Roma** defeated **Johnny Rodz** in 14:50 (★ ★ ★); **Bob Orton** defeated **Paul Orndorff** in a Bounty Match 11:41 (★ ★ ★); **Charlie Fulton** defeated **Jim Powers** in 8:24 (★ ★); **Hulk Hogan** defeated **Ken Patera** in 11:41 (★ ★ ★); **Big John Studd** defeated **Steve Lombardi** in 6:33 (★ ★); **George Steele** defeated **Barry O** in 3:25 (★ ★); **The Iron Sheik** and **Nikolai Volkoff** defeated **Barry Windham** and **Mike Rotundo** in 12:26 (★ ★ ★).

WWF at Madison Square Garden (21-06-85) ★ ★
21-06-85, New York City, New York **WWF**

Lanny Poffo defeated **Terry Gibbs** in 6:34 (★ ★ ★); **Tony Atlas** defeated **Matt Borne** in 7:02 (★ ★); **The Missing Link** defeated **Jose Luis Rivera** in 1:42 (★); **Jim Brunzell** defeated **Moondog Spot** in 12:22 (★ ★); **Randy Savage** defeated **Rick McGraw** in 12:51 (★ ★); **Adrian Adonis, Big John Studd** and **Bobby Heenan** defeated **George Steele** and **The US Express (Barry Windham** and **Mike Rotundo)** by DQ in 9:59 (★ ★); **Desiree Peterson** defeated **Judy Martin** in 16:05 (★ ★); **King Kong Bundy** defeated **Tony Garea** in 6:17 (★ ★); **Ricky Steamboat** defeated **Greg Valentine** via count out in 14:20 (★ ★ ★ ★); **B. Brian Blair** defeated **Barry O** in 8:13 (★ ★); **Hulk Hogan** defeated **Don Muraco** in a Steel Cage Match in 9:05 (★ ★ ★).

WWF at Boston Garden (22-06-85) ★ ★
22-06-85, Boston, Massachusetts **WWF**

Steve Lombardi defeated **Jack Armstrong** in 7:31 (★ ★); **George Steele** defeated **Moondog Spot** in 4:20 (★); **Randy Savage** defeated **SD Jones** in 7:23 (★ ★ ★); **Adrian Adonis** defeated **Swede Hanson** in 6:39 (★ ★); **The Missing Link** defeated **Tony Garea** in 3:01 (★); **Junkyard Dog** defeated **Greg Valentine** in 8:02 (★ ★); **Lanny Poffo** defeated **Barry O** in 12:02 (★ ★); **Nikolai Volkoff** and **The Iron Sheik** defeated **The US Express (Barry Windham** and **Mike Rotundo)** in 12:39 (★ ★ ★); **Desiree Peterson** defeated **Judy Martin** in 9:13 (★ ★); **Hulk Hogan** defeated **Big John Studd** in 13:42 (★ ★ ★).

WWF at Spectrum (29-06-85) ★ ★
29-06-85, Philadelphia, Pennsylvania **WWF**

Lanny Poffo defeated **Barry O** in 15:55 (★ ★ ★); **The Missing Link** defeated **Jose Luis Rivera** in 6:47 (★ ★); **David Sammartino** defeated **Bobby Heenan** in 17:55 (★ ★); **Randy Savage** defeated **Swede Hanson** in 11:10 (★ ★); **Ricky Steamboat** defeated **Don Muraco** in 1:08 (★ ★); **Big John Studd** defeated **George Wells** in 7:02 (★ ★); **B. Brian Blair** defeated **Steve Lombardi** in 9:51 (★ ★); **Hulk Hogan** and **Paul Orndorff** defeated **Roddy Piper** and **Bob Orton** in 5:02 (★ ★ ★).

Great American Bash '85 ★★★
06-07-85, Charlotte, North Carolina **NWA**

Buddy Landel vs. Ron Bass went to a time limit draw in 20:00 (★★); The Minnesota Wrecking Crew (Arn Anderson and Ole Anderson) defeated Buzz Sawyer and Dick Slater (★★★); Buzz Tyler, Manny Fernandez and Sam Houston defeated Abdullah The Butcher, Konga The Barbarian and Superstar Billy Graham (★★); Jimmy Valiant defeated Paul Jones in a Dog Collar Match (★★); The Road Warriors (Hawk and Animal) vs. The Russians (Ivan Koloff and Krusher Kruschev) went to a double DQ (★★★); Magnum TA defeated Kamala by DQ (★★★); Ric Flair and Nikita Koloff in 23:12 (★★★★★); Dusty Rhodes defeated Tully Blanchard in a Steel Cage Match to win the NWA World Television Title in 11:30 (★★★★).

WWF at Madison Square Garden (13-07-85) ★★★
13-07-85, New York City, New York **WWF**

Ivan Putski defeated Moondog Spot in 12:58 (★★★); The Missing Link defeated Rick McGraw in 2:25 (★★); Pedro Morales defeated Rene Goulet in 12:56 (★★); Adrian Adonis defeated Jose Luis Rivera in 10:29 (★); Junkyard Dog defeated Bob Orton by DQ in 14:40 (★★); Terry Funk defeated Lanny Poffo in 13:02 (★★★★); Paul Orndorff defeated Roddy Piper by DQ in 8:43 (★★★★); The Iron Sheik defeated Swede Hanson in 2:24 (★); George Steele vs. Nikolai Volkoff ended in a double count out in 4:18 (★); Brutus Beefcake defeated George Wells in 7:26 (★★); The British Bulldogs (Davey Boy Smith and Dynamite Kid) vs. The Hart Foundation (Bret Hart and Jim Neidhart) ended in a draw in 13:12 (★★★).

WWF at Spectrum (27-07-85) ★★
27-07-85, Philadelphia, Pennsylvania **WWF**

Jim Neidhart defeated Tony Garea in 9:25 (★★); Bret Hart defeated Swede Hanson in 8:53 (★★); The Missing Link defeated Salvatore Bellomo in 4:16 (★★); Pedro Morales defeated Rene Goulet in 12:38 (★); Paul Orndorff vs. Roddy Piper ended in a double DQ in 5:31 (★★); Brutus Beefcake defeated George Wells in 9:01 (★★); Spider Lady defeated Susan Starr in 9:08 (★); George Steele defeated Big John Studd in 3:57 (★★); Terry Funk defeated SD Jones in 10:13 (★★); Andre The Giant and Ricky Steamboat defeated Don Muraco and Mr. Fuji in 4:32 (★★).

WrestleFest '85 ★★★★
28-07-85, Tulsa, Oklahoma **MSW**

Al Perez defeated Mark Ragin in 5:55 (★★); One Man Gang defeated Wendell Cooley in 4:48 (★★); Nord the Barbarian defeated Brickhouse Brown in 4:50 (★★); The Fantastics (Bobby Fulton and Tommy Rogers) defeated Eddie Gilbert and Jerry Grey in 12:36 (★★★★); Jake Roberts defeated Ted DiBiase in 13:12 (★★★★); Butch Reed defeated Dutch Mantel in 10:01 (★★); Bill Watts, Dick Murdoch and Jim Duggan defeated Kamala, Kareem Muhammad and Skandor Akbar in 9:27 (★★); Ric Flair defeated Dusty Rhodes by DQ in 15:20 (★★); Wahoo McDaniel defeated The Champion (Moondog Rex) by DQ in 4:44 (★★).

WWF at Boston Garden (03-08-85) ★★
03-08-85, Boston, Massachusetts **WWF**

Les Thornton defeated Jose Luis Rivera in 12:34 (★★); George Steele defeated Tiger Chung Lee in 4:37 (★); Brutus Beefcake defeated George Wells in 10:20 (★★); Pedro Morales defeated Mr. X in 7:49 (★★); Paul Orndorff vs. Roddy Piper ended in a double count out in 7:51 (★★★); Randy Savage defeated Salvatore Bellomo in 9:17 (★★); Terry Funk defeated Rick McGraw in 13:40 (★★); Ricky Steamboat and Junkyard Dog defeated Mr. Fuji and Don Muraco in 12:02 (★★★).

Hot Summer Night ★★★
03-08-85, Honolulu, Hawaii **PPW**

The Cobra defeated Super Fly Tui Selinga in 7:13 (★★★); Seiji Sakaguchi defeated Matt Borne in 3:16 (★★★★); Kengo Kimura and Tatsumi Fujinami defeated Gary Fulton and Gary Lewis in 11:38 (★★★); Jimmy Snuka defeated Larry Sharpe (★★★); Manny Fernandez defeated Black Bart by DQ in 14:17 (★★); Steve Regal vs. Mighty Milo went to a time-limit draw (★★); Debbie Combs defeated The Fallen Angel by DQ in a Women's Street Fight (★); The Samoan Connection (Farmer Boy Ipo and Leroy Brown) defeated The Deaton Brothers (Joel Deaton and Vernon Deaton) (★); Little Kevin defeated Pancho Boy (★★); Richie Magnett defeated Gypsy Joe (★★); Dusty Rhodes and Magnum T.A. defeated Nikita Koloff and Krusher Khrushchev

(★★★); Andre the Giant, Angelo Mosca and Steve Collins defeated King Kong Bundy, Mark Lewin and Kevin Sullivan (★★); Lars Anderson defeated Bad News Allen to win the Polynesian Heavyweight Championship in 4:56 (★★); Ricky Johnson and Rocky Johnson defeated The Dirty White Boys (Len Denton and Tony Anthony) to win the Polynesian Tag Team Championship (★★); Antonio Inoki vs. Bruiser Brody ended in a double count out in 8:40 (★★★★★); Ric Flair vs. Sivi Afi ended in a double DQ in 26:18 (★★★★).

WWF at Madison Square Garden (10-08-85) ★★★★
10-08-85, New York City, New York **WWF**

Paul Roma defeated Charlie Fulton in 10:45 (★★); Lanny Poffo vs. Iron Mike Sharpe ended in a draw in 20:00 (★★★); The Missing Link defeated Tony Garea in 4:09 (★★); Pedro Morales defeated Barry O in 5:02 (★★); Uncle Elmer defeated Big John Studd by DQ in 2:40 (★); Tony Atlas defeated Les Thornton in 11:32 (★★); Andre The Giant and Paul Orndorff defeated Roddy Piper and Bob Orton in 8:25 (★★★★); Randy Savage defeated Jose Luis Rivera in 16:14 (★★★); The US Express (Barry Windham and Mike Rotundo) defeated The Dream Team (Greg Valentine and Brutus Beefcake) in 24:02 (★★★★).

WWF at Capital Centre (17-08-85) ★★
17-08-85, Landover, Maryland **WWF**

Johnny Valiant defeated Steve Lombardi in 5:04 (★★); Cousin Junior defeated Moondog Spot in 12:46 (★★); Adrian Adonis defeated Tony Garea in 9:57 (★★); Terry Funk defeated Salvatore Bellomo in 10:47 (★★); Junkyard Dog and Ricky Steamboat defeated Don Muraco and Mr. Fuji in 13:33 (★★★); The Hart Foundation (Bret Hart and Jim Neidhart) defeated Swede Hanson and Lanny Poffo in 10:37 (★★); Randy Savage defeated Rick McGraw in 9:16 (★★★); Hulk Hogan defeated Brutus Beefcake in 12:35 (★★★).

WWF at Maple Leaf Gardens (18-08-85) ★★
18-08-85, Toronto, Canada **WWF**

Adrian Adonis defeated Lanny Poffo in 6:55 (★★); Dino Bravo defeated Richard Charland in 3:41 (★★); Randy Savage defeated Bob Marcus in 3:38 (★★); King Kong Bundy defeated Jose Luis Rivera in 2:45 (★★); Cousin Junior defeated Tito Senza in 3:41 (★★); Andre The Giant defeated Big John Studd by DQ in 13:01 (★★★); Rick McGraw defeated Ted Grizzly in 2:04 (★★); The Hart Foundation (Bret Hart and Jim Neidhart) defeated The Killer Bees (B. Brian Blair and Jim Brunzell) in 9:05 (★★★); Junkyard Dog vs. Terry Funk ended in a double count out in 9:28 (★★★); Ricky Steamboat defeated Don Muraco by DQ in 13:04 (★★★).

WWF at Spectrum (24-08-85) ★★
24-08-85, Philadelphia, Pennsylvania **WWF**

Steve Gatorwolf defeated Terry Gibbs in 4:24 (★★); Corporal Kirchner defeated AJ Petruzzi in 7:38 (★★); Bob Orton defeated Lanny Poffo in 14:07 (★★); Paul Orndorff defeated Roddy Piper by DQ in 8:09 (★★★); The Missing Link defeated Tony Garea in 8:08 (★); Cousin Junior defeated Big John Studd by DQ in 3:44 (★★); The Dream Team (Brutus Beefcake and Greg Valentine) defeated The US Express (Barry Windham and Mike Rotundo) to win the WWF World Tag Team Title in 19:08 (★★); Bret Hart defeated Rick McGraw in 5:32 (★★).

Wrestling For A Cure ★★
26-08-85, Boston, Massachusetts **AWA**

Bob Backlund defeated Larry Zbyszko by DQ in 6:47 (★★★); The Road Warriors (Animal and Hawk) defeated The Long Riders (Bill Irwin and Scott Irwin) in 7:22 (★★); Greg Gagne defeated Steve Regal in 5:49 (★★); Brad Rheingans defeated Billy Robinson in 4:07 (★★); Rick Martel vs. Nick Bockwinkel ended in a draw in 8:07 (★★★); Sgt. Slaughter defeated Boris Zhukov in 9:11 (★★).

Battle Of The Belts I ★★★
02-09-85, Tampa, Florida **CWF/NWA**

Chavo Guerrero and Hector Guerrero defeated The Grappler and Rip Oliver in 15:40 (★★★); Cocoa Samoa defeated Rip Rogers in 10:49 (★★★); Kendall Windham defeated Jack Hart to win the Florida Heavyweight Title in 11:16 (★★★); Rick Rude defeated Billy Jack Haynes in 14:16 (★★★); The Road Warriors (Hawk and Animal) vs. Harley Race and Stan Hansen went to a double count-out in 9:25 (★★); Nick Bockwinkel defeated Frankie Lane in 3:54 (★★); Ric Flair defeated Wahoo McDaniel 2-1 in Best Two Out Of Three Falls Match in 44:53 (★★★★).

WWF at Boston Garden (07-09-85) ★★
07-09-85, Boston, Massachusetts **WWF**
Lanny Poffo vs. **Iron Mike Sharpe** ended in a draw in 17:40 (★★); King Tonga defeated **Rene Goulet** in 9:21 (★★); Corporal Kirchner defeated **Moondog Spot** in 14:48 (★★); The Missing Link defeated **Swede Hanson** in 5:34 (★★); Hulk Hogan defeated **King Kong Bundy** in 8:48 (★★★); Adrian Adonis defeated **SD Jones** in 9:33 (★★); Terry Funk defeated **George Wells** in 12:23 (★★); Desiree Peterson defeated **Leilani Kai** in 10:10 (★★); Pedro Morales, Ivan Putski and Uncle Elmer defeated **Johnny V, Brutus Beefcake and Greg Valentine** in 12:47 (★★).

WWF at Maple Leaf Gardens (22-09-85) ★★
22-09-85 Toronto, Canada **WWF**
Scott McGhee defeated **Rene Goulet** in 11:56 (★★); Dino Bravo defeated **Frank Marconi** in 2:20 (★★); King Kong Bundy defeated **Swede Hanson** in 5:16 (★★); The Killer Bees (B. Brian Blair and Jim Brunzell) defeated **Iron Mike Sharpe and Tiger Chung Lee** in 12:47 (★★); Ricky Steamboat defeated **Don Muraco** in a Lumberjack Match in 9:48 (★★★); King Tonga defeated **Barry O** in 5:58 (★★); The Dream Team (Greg Valentine and Brutus Beefcake) defeated **Uncle Elmer and Cousin Junior** in 11:15 (★★); Bob Orton defeated **Lanny Poffo** in 7:18 (★★); Tito Santana vs. **Jesse Ventura** ended in a double count out in 11:36 (★★★).

WWF at Madison Square Garden (23-09-85) ★★★
23-09-85, New York City, New York **WWF**
Scott McGhee defeated **Les Thornton** in 18:20 (★★); Adrian Adonis defeated **Rick McGraw** in 10:06 (★★); Randy Savage defeated **Paul Roma** in 6:57 (★★★); Andre The Giant defeated **King Kong Bundy** by DQ in 13:50 (★★); Bob Orton defeated **SD Jones** in 12:07 (★★); The British Bulldogs (Davey Boy Smith and Dynamite Kid) defeated **The Hart Foundation (Bret Hart and Jim Neidhart)** in 18:31 (★★★); The Missing Link defeated **Lanny Poffo** in 5:59 (★★); Ricky Steamboat defeated **Don Muraco** by DQ in 12:45 (★★★); Corporal Kirchner defeated **Moondog Spot** in 2:45 (★★); Junkyard Dog defeated **Terry Funk** in 3:34 (★★).

WWF at Spectrum (28-09-85) ★★★
28-09-85, Philadelphia, Pennsylvania **WWF**
Moondog Spot defeated **Rick McGraw** in 16:24 (★★); SD Jones defeated **AJ Petruzzi** in 6:49 (★★); King Kong Bundy defeated **Steve Gatorwolf** in 4:09 (★★); Scott McGhee defeated **Rene Goulet** in 14:31 (★★); Roddy Piper and Bob Orton defeated **Paul Orndorff and Bruno Sammartino** via count out in 7:52 (★★); Don Muraco defeated **Ricky Steamboat** by DQ in 16:05 (★★); King Tonga defeated **Barry O** in 5:42 (★★); Hulk Hogan defeated **Randy Savage** in 11:17 (★★★).

SuperClash '85 ★★
28-09-85, Chicago, Illinois **AWA**
Steve Regal defeated **Brad Rheingans** in 8:19 (★★); Sherri Martel defeated **Candi Devine** to win the AWA World Women's Title in 11:44 (★★); Mil Mascaras defeated **Buddy Roberts** in 6:57 (★★); Curt Hennig, Scott Hall and Greg Gagne defeated **Nick Bockwinkel, Ray Stevens and Larry Zbyszko** in 12:20 (★★); Little Tokyo defeated **Little Mr. T** in 6:54 (★); Giant Baba, Jumbo Tsuruta and Genichiro Tenryu defeated **Harley Race, Bill Irwin and Scott Irwin** in 10:57 (★★); Kerry Von Erich defeated **Jimmy Garvin** in 6:57 (★★); Ivan Koloff, Nikita Koloff and Krusher Khrushchev defeated **The Crusher, Dick the Bruiser and Baron Von Raschke** in 9:40 (★★); Jerry Blackwell defeated **Kamala** in a Bodyslam Match in 6:50 (★); The Road Warriors (Hawk and Animal) defeated **The Fabulous Freebirds (Michael Hayes and Terry Gordy)** via reverse decision in 10:05 (★★★); Sgt. Slaughter defeated **Boris Zhukov** by DQ in 8:24 (★★); Rick Martel vs. **Stan Hansen** ended in a double DQ at 2:30 (★★); Ric Flair defeated **Magnum T.A.** in 25:48 (★★★★).

Saturday Night's Main Event II ★★
05-10-85, East Rutherford, New Jersey **WWF**
Hulk Hogan defeated **Nikolai Volkoff** in a Flag Match in 5:17 (★); Uncle Elmer defeated **Jerry Valiant** in :12 (★); Paul Orndorff vs. **Roddy Piper** went to a double count out in 4:01 (★★★); Andre the Giant and Tony Atlas defeated **King Kong Bundy and Big John Studd** by DQ in 4:26 (★★); The Dream Team (Brutus Beefcake and Greg Valentine) defeated **Lanny Poffo and Tony Garea** in 3:30 (★★).

2nd Cotton Bowl Extravaganza ★★
06-10-85, Dallas, Texas **WCCW**
Tim Brooks defeated **Scott Casey** in 4:18 (★★); Kelly Kiniski defeated **Tommy Montana** in 8:26 (★★); The Fantastics (Tommy Rogers and Bobby Fulton) defeated **John Tatum and David Peterson** in 12:16 (★★); The Great Kabuki defeated **Mark Lewin** by DQ in 5:37 (★★); Brian Adias defeated **Jack Victory** in 9:17 (★★); Iceman King Parsons defeated **One Man Gang** in a Taped Fist Match in 10:33 (★★); Kerry Von Erich and Kevin Von Erich defeated **The Dynamic Duo (Chris Adams and Gino Hernandez)** in an Anything Goes Hair vs Hair Match in 11:45 (★★★★).

WWF at Boston Garden (12-10-85) ★★
12-10-85, Boston, Massachusetts **WWF**
King Tonga defeated **Mr. X** in 10:16 (★★); Corporal Kirchner defeated **Rene Goulet** in 10:26 (★★); David Sammartino defeated **Tiger Chung Lee** in 7:26 (★★); Barry Windham and SD Jones defeated **Iron Mike Sharpe and Barry O** in 8:03 (★★); Paul Orndorff defeated **The Missing Link** in 4:23 (★★); Terry Funk defeated **Junkyard Dog** in 13:28 (★★); The Dream Team (Greg Valentine and Brutus Beefcake) defeated **The British Bulldogs (Davey Boy Smith and Dynamite Kid)** in 17:47 (★★★); Randy Savage defeated **Scott McGhee** in 6:13 (★★); Hulk Hogan defeated **King Kong Bundy** in 6:11 (★★).

WWF at Maple Leaf Gardens (13-10-85) ★★
13-10-85, Toronto, Canada **WWF**
Scott McGhee defeated **Barry O** in 10:22 (★★); Tony Parisi defeated **Rene Goulet** in 11:55 (★★); Nikolai Volkoff and The Iron Sheik defeated **George Steele and Corporal Kirchner** by DQ in 16:33 (★★); Iron Mike Sharpe defeated **SD Jones** in 5:24 (★★); Terry Funk defeated **Steve Gatorwolf** in 7:00 (★★); The Dream Team (Brutus Beefcake and Greg Valentine) defeated **The British Bulldogs (Davey Boy Smith and Dynamite Kid)** in 19:00 (★★★); Dino Bravo defeated **Mr. X** in 3:50 (★★); Hulk Hogan defeated **Randy Savage** in 14:00 (★★★).

WWF at Hiram Bithorn Stadium (19-10-85) ★
19-10-85, San Juan, Puerto Rico **WWF**
Tony Atlas defeated **Steve Lombardi** in 5:45 (★★); Corporal Kirchner defeated **Tiger Chung Lee** in 7:07 (★★); Ricky Steamboat defeated **Moondog Spot** in 4:29 (★★); Wendi Richter defeated **Spider Lady** in 6:08 (★★); Hulk Hogan defeated **Big John Studd** via count out in 7:23 (★★); The Killer Bees (B. Brian Blair and Jim Brunzell) defeated **Iron Mike Sharpe and Barry O** in 4:10 (★); Tito Santana defeated **Randy Savage** in 8:08 (★); Pedro Morales defeated **The Spoiler** in 1:14 (★).

WWF at Madison Square Garden (21-10-85) ★★
21-10-85, New York City, New York **WWF**
Steve Gatorwolf defeated **Terry Gibbs** in 7:17 (★★); Adrian Adonis defeated **SD Jones** in 6:51 (★★); Mike Rotundo and Tony Atlas defeated **Barry O and Iron Mike Sharpe** in 16:45 (★★★); King Tonga defeated **Ron Shaw** in 9:25 (★★); Pedro Morales defeated **Rene Goulet** in 14:03 (★★); Andre The Giant and Hillbilly Jim vs. **Big John Studd and King Kong Bundy** ended in a double DQ in 14:08 (★★★); Paul Orndorff defeated **The Spoiler** in 12:35 (★★); The British Bulldogs (Davey Boy Smith and Dynamite Kid) defeated **The Iron Sheik and Nikolai Volkoff** in 6:46 (★★★).

WWF at Spectrum (26-10-85) ★★
26-10-85, Philadelphia, Pennsylvania **WWF**
Tony Garea defeated **Dave Barbie** in 9:34 (★★); David Sammartino defeated **Steve Lombardi** in 9:43 (★★); Dan Spivey defeated **Terry Gibbs** in 6:54 (★★); Pedro Morales defeated **Tiger Chung Lee** in 10:03 (★★); Tito Santana defeated **Don Muraco** in 13:47 (★★★); Wendi Richter defeated **Spider Lady** in 11:40 (★★); Junkyard Dog defeated **Terry Funk** in 11:18 (★★★); Hillbilly Jim and Cousin Junior defeated **Moondog Spot and Iron Mike Sharpe** in 8:12 (★★); Bruno Sammartino and Paul Orndorff defeated **Roddy Piper and Bob Orton** in a Steel Cage Match in 7:25 (★★★).

Saturday Night's Main Event III ★★
02-11-85, Hershey, Pennsylvania **WWF**
Terry Funk defeated **Junkyard Dog** in 5:16 (★★); Hulk Hogan and Andre the Giant defeated **King Kong Bundy and Big John Studd** by DQ in 8:00 (★★); Randy Savage vs. **Tito Santana** went to a double count out in 4:08 (★★); Ricky Steamboat defeated **Mr. Fuji** in a Kung Fu Challenge in 3:16 (★★).

The Wrestling Classic ★★

07-11-85, Rosemont, Illinois **WWF**

Adrian Adonis defeated Corporal Kirchner in 3:20 (★★); Dynamite Kid defeated Nikolai Volkoff in :09 (★); Randy Savage defeated Ivan Putski in 2:45 (★★); Ricky Steamboat defeated Davey Boy Smith in 2:53 (★★★); Junkyard Dog defeated The Iron Sheik in 3:25 (★★); Moondog Spot defeated Terry Funk in :27 (★); Tito Santana defeated Don Muraco in 4:17 (★★★); Paul Orndorff defeated Bob Orton by DQ in 6:28 (★★); Dynamite Kid defeated Adrian Adonis in 6:00 (★★★); Randy Savage defeated Ricky Steamboat in 4:00 (★★); Junkyard Dog defeated Moondog Spot in :45 (★); Paul Orndorff vs. Tito Santana went to a double count out in 8:06 (★★); Hulk Hogan defeated Roddy Piper by DQ in 7:14 (★★); Randy Savage defeated Dynamite Kid in 4:52 (★★); Junkyard Dog defeated Randy Savage via count out in 9:44 (★★).

WWF at Boston Garden (09-11-85) ★★★

09-11-85, Boston, Massachusetts **WWF**

Bret Hart defeated Lanny Poffo in 8:22 (★★); The British Bulldogs (Davey Boy Smith and Dynamite Kid) defeated Moondog Spot and Barry O in 9:55 (★★); Corporal Kirchner defeated Rene Goulet in 10:29 (★★); Jim Neidhart defeated Tony Garea in 7:17 (★★); Bob Orton defeated Pedro Morales in 11:34 (★★); Don Muraco defeated Ricky Steamboat by DQ in 15:33 (★★★); Randy Savage defeated Tony Atlas in 6:08 (★★); The Dream Team (Brutus Beefcake and Greg Valentine) defeated The US Express (Mike Rotundo and Dan Spivey) in 12:36 (★★★); Junkyard Dog defeated Terry Funk in 8:23 (★★★).

WWF at Spectrum (22-11-85) ★★

22-11-85, Philadelphia, Pennsylvania **WWF**

King Tonga defeated Moondog Spot in 13:53 (★★); Hercules defeated Jose Luis Rivera in 8:09 (★★); Hillbilly Jim defeated Big John Studd in 10:34 (★★); Corporal Kirchner defeated Barry O in 11:01 (★★); Ricky Steamboat and Tito Santana defeated Don Muraco and Mr. Fuji in 12:41 (★★★); The Hart Foundation (Bret Hart and Jim Neidhart) defeated Uncle Elmer and Cousin Junior in 10:07 (★★★); Ron Shaw defeated David Sammartino in 2:03 (★); Andre The Giant defeated King Kong Bundy in 7:52 (★★).

WWF at Madison Square Garden (25-11-85) ★★★

25-11-85, New York City, New York **WWF**

Dan Spivey defeated Terry Gibbs in 10:10 (★★); King Tonga defeated Mr. X in 8:48 (★★); Jesse Ventura defeated Barry O in 10:21 (★★); Hercules defeated Cousin Junior in 11:33 (★★); Spider Lady defeated Wendi Richter to win the WWF Women's Title in 6:38 (★); Tito Santana and Pedro Morales defeated The Dream Team (Greg Valentine and Brutus Beefcake) by DQ in 15:17 (★★); Don Muraco defeated Ricky Steamboat by DQ in 16:37 (★★); Terry Funk defeated Mr. Wrestling II in 13:54 (★★); Andre The Giant, Hillbilly Jim and Captain Lou Albano defeated Big John Studd, King King Bundy and Bobby Heenan in 12:18 (★★★).

Thanksgiving Star Wars '85 ★★★

28-11-85, Dallas, Texas **WCCW**

The Grappler and The Missing Link defeated David Peterson and Johnny Mantell in 12:31 (★★); Lance Von Erich defeated Tim Brooks in 2:10 (★★); One Man Gang vs. Kimala ended in a double DQ in 3:24 (★); Brian Adias defeated Jack Victory in 7:06 (★★★); Rick Rude defeated Iceman King Parsons in 11:07 (★★★); John Tatum defeated Scott Casey in a Texas Death Steel Cage Match in 8:33 (★★★); Gino Hernandez and Chris Adams defeated Kevin Von Erich and Kerry Von Erich in a Steel Cage Match to win the vacant WCCW American Tag Team Title in 7:16 (★★★★).

Starrcade '85 ★★★★★

28-11-85, Greensboro/Atlanta **NWA**

Krusher Khruschev defeated Sam Houston to win the vacant NWA Mid-Atlantic Heavyweight Title in 9:30 (★★); Manny Fernandez defeated Abdullah The Butcher in a Mexican Death Match in 9:07 (★★); Ron Bass defeated Black Bart in a Texas Bullrope Match in 8:34 (★★); James J. Dillon defeated Ron Bass in a Texas Bullrope Match in 3:29 (★); Superstar Billy Graham defeated The Barbarian by DQ in an Arm Wrestling Match; Superstar Billy Graham defeated The Barbarian by DQ in 3:02 (★); Buddy Landel defeated Terry Taylor to win the NWA National Heavyweight Title in 10:30 (★★); The Minnesota

Wrecking Crew (Ole Anderson and Arn Anderson) defeated Wahoo McDaniel and Billy Jack Haynes in 9:28 (★★); Magnum T.A. defeated Tully Blanchard in an "I Quit" Steel Cage Match to win the NWA United States Heavyweight Title in 14:43 (★★★★★); Jimmy Valiant and Miss Atlanta Lively defeated The Midnight Express (Bobby Eaton and Dennis Condrey) in an Atlanta Street Fight in 6:36 (★★); The Rock 'n' Roll Express (Ricky Morton and Robert Gibson) defeated Ivan Koloff and Nikita Koloff in a Steel Cage Match to win the NWA World Tag Team Title in 12:22 (★★★★); Dusty Rhodes defeated Ric Flair by DQ in 22:06 (★★★★★).

WWF at Boston Garden (07-12-85) ★★★

07-12-85, Boston, Massachusetts **WWF**

Paul Roma vs. Barry O ended in a draw in 18:08 (★★); Tony Atlas defeated Moondog Spot in 7:24 (★★); Pedro Morales defeated Bob Orton in 6:45 (★★★★); Randy Savage defeated Ricky Steamboat in 11:15 (★★★); Bruno Sammartino defeated Roddy Piper by DQ in 5:05 (★★★); Jesse Ventura defeated Tito Santana via count out in 8:13 (★★); Hercules defeated Scott McGhee in 8:22 (★); Adrian Adonis defeated Lanny Poffo in 2:51 (★); The Dream Team (Greg Valentine and Brutus Beefcake) defeated The Killer Bees (B. Brian Blair and Jim Brunzell) in 9:48 (★★).

WWF at Spectrum (07-12-85) ★★★

07-12-85, Philadelphia, Pennsylvania **WWF**

Dan Spivey defeated Tiger Chung Lee in 10:44 (★★); King Tonga defeated Iron Mike Sharpe in 6:40 (★★); Hercules defeated Scott McGhee in 12:26 (★); Brutus Beefcake defeated Lanny Poffo in 11:42 (★★); Hulk Hogan defeated Terry Funk in 10:39 (★★); Mike Rotundo defeated Greg Valentine in 9:24 (★★); Ricky Steamboat vs. Don Muraco endd in a double count out in 10:33 (★★); Tito Santana and Tony Atlas defeated Randy Savage and Jesse Ventura in 8:42 (★★★).

WWF at Maple Leaf Gardens (15-12-85) ★★

15-12-85, Toronto, Canada **WWF**

Tony Parisi defeated Johnny K-9 in 7:55 (★★); Hercules defeated Bob Marcus in 5:09 (★★); Ron Shaw defeated Rene Goulet in 6:57 (★★); Dino Bravo defeated Tiger Chung Lee in 8:49 (★★); Hillbilly Jim and Uncle Elmer defeated The Hart Foundation (Bret Hart and Jim Neidhart) via count out in 8:55 (★★); King Tonga defeated Bob Orton by DQ in 7:59 (★★); Paul Orndorff defeated Ted Grizzly in :51 (★); Hulk Hogan defeated Terry Funk in 8:42 (★★★); The Dream Team (Greg Valentine and Brutus Beefcake) vs. The British Bulldogs (Davey Boy Smith and Dynamite Kid) ended in a draw in 13:34 (★★★★).

Christmas Star Wars '85 ★★

25-12-85, Dallas, Texas **WCCW**

Brian Adias and Iceman King Parsons defeated The Grappler and The Great Kabuki in 12:11 (★★); Tatsumi Fujinami defeated Bob Sweetan in 2:59 (★★); Lance Von Erich defeated Rick Rude by DQ in 6:09 (★★); The Fabulous Freebirds (Terry Gordy and Buddy Roberts) defeated Mark Youngblood and David Peterson in 7:03 (★★); The Missing Link defeated Jack Victory in 3:09 (★★); Kevin Von Erich and Kerry Von Erich defeated Gino Hernandez and Chris Adams by DQ in 14:17 (★★); Scott Casey and Sunshine defeated John Tatum and Missy Hyatt in 9:28 (★★★); Antonio Inoki defeated Steve Williams in 8:13 (★★★); Kerry Von Erich, Kevin Von Erich and Lance Von Erich defeated The Fabulous Freebirds (Michael Hayes, Terry Gordy and Buddy Roberts) in 7:30 (★★★).

Nite Of Champions II ★★★

29-12-85, East Rutherford, New Jersey **NWA/AWA**

Ron Bass defeated JJ Dillon in 5:28 (★); Little Tokyo defeated Cowboy Lang in 6:54 (★★); Sherri Martel defeated Debbie Combs in 10:23 (★★); Carlos Colon defeated Konga the Barbarian in 6:38 (★★); Buddy Roberts defeated Paul Ellering by DQ in 4:50 (★★); The Rock 'n' Roll Express (Ricky Morton and Robert Gibson) defeated The Long Riders (Bill Irwin and Scott Irwin) in 11:04 (★★★); Sgt. Slaughter defeated Boris Zhukov and Chris Markoff in a Russian Handicap Death Match in 12:54 (★); Magnum TA defeated Tully Blanchard in 11:12 (★★★); Ric Flair defeated Dusty Rhodes by DQ in 14:50 (★★); The Road Warriors (Hawk and Animal) defeated The Russians (Ivan Koloff and Krusher Kruschev) by DQ in 10:46 (★★); Stan Hansen defeated Rick Martel to win the AWA World Heavyweight Title in 14:01 (★★★★).

WWF at Madison Square Garden (30-12-85) ★★

30-12-85, New York City, New York **WWF**

SD Jones defeated Ron Shaw in 18:36 (★); Jim Neidhart vs. B. Brian Blair ended in a draw in 15:00 (★★); Hercules defeated Jose Luis Rivera in 9:51 (★); Adrian Adonis defeated Lanny Poffo in 9:02 (★); Randy Savage defeated Hulk Hogan via count out in 9:55 (★★); Big John Studd defeated Tony Atlas in 12:15 (★); Haiti Kid defeated Butch Cassidy in 10:32 (★); Jim Brunzell defeated Bret Hart in 13:55 (★★); The Dream Team (Brutus Beefcake and Greg Valentine) defeated Uncle Elmer and Hillbilly Jim in 4:29 (★★).

Saturday Night's Main Event IV ★★★

04-01-86, Tampa, Florida **WWF**

Jesse Ventura, Roddy Piper and Bob Orton defeated Hillbilly Jim, Uncle Elmer and Cousin Luke in 8:00 (★★); Hulk Hogan defeated Terry Funk in 8:30 (★★); Randy Savage defeated George Steele in 4:05 (★); Nikolai Volkoff defeated Corporal Kirchner in a Peace Match in 4:22 (★); Junkyard Dog and Ricky Steamboat defeated Mr. Fuji and Don Muraco in 5:19 (★★).

WWF at Boston Garden (11-01-86) ★★★★

11-01-86, Boston, Massachusetts **WWF**

Lanny Poffo defeated Terry Gibbs in 9:13 (★★); Scott McGhee defeated Moondog Spot in 12:51 (★★); Cousin Luke defeated Les Thornton in 3:28 (★); Randy Savage defeated Tito Santana via count out in 13:01 (★★★); Roddy Piper and Bob Orton defeated Paul Orndorff and Bruno Sammartino via count out in 8:40 (★★★); Terry Funk defeated Pedro Morales in 11:14 (★★★★); George Wells defeated Iron Mike Sharpe in 9:37 (★); Nikolai Volkoff and The Iron Sheik defeated Junkyard Dog and Corporal Kirchner in 11:47 (★★).

WWF at Spectrum (11-01-86) ★★

11-01-86, Philadelphia, Pennsylvania **WWF**

Dan Spivey defeated Ron Shaw in 8:34 (★); Jim Neidhart vs. B. Brian Blair ended in a draw in 16:19 (★★); Hercules defeated SD Jones in 8:37 (★★); Adrian Adonis defeated Tony Atlas in 10:30 (★★); King Tonga defeated Tiger Chung Lee in 8:11 (★★); Hulk Hogan and Andre The Giant defeated King Kong Bundy, Big John Studd and Bobby Heenan in a Handicap Match in 12:17 (★★★); Bret Hart defeated Ivan Putski in 5:49 (★★); Ricky Steamboat defeated Don Muraco in a Martial Arts Match in 14:18 (★★★); The British Bulldogs (Davey Boy Smith and Dynamite Kid) defeated The Dream Team (Greg Valentine and Brutus Beefcake) by DQ in 7:48 (★★★).

WWF at Madison Square Garden (27-01-86) ★★★

27-01-86, New York City, New York **WWF**

Dan Spivey defeated Rene Goulet in 12:50 (★★); Iron Mike Sharpe vs. George Wells ended in a draw in 18:37 (★★); Ted Arcidi defeated Tiger Chung Lee in 4:05 (★); Paul Orndorff defeated Big John Studd by DQ in 5:26 (★★); Terry Funk defeated Scott McGhee in 9:44 (★★★); Randy Savage defeated Hulk Hogan via count out in 8:33 (★★★); Pedro Morales defeated Moondog Spot in 7:38 (★★); Sivi Afi defeated Ron Shaw in 6:27 (★); Adrian Adonis defeated Junkyard Dog by DQ in 6:11 (★); George Steele defeated Barry O in 1:18 (★); The Dream Team (Greg Valentine and Brutus Beefcake) defeated The British Bulldogs (Davey Boy Smith and Dynamite Kid) in 7:46 (★★★).

Superstars On The Superstation ★★★★

02-02-86, Atlanta, Georgia **NWA**

The Midnight Express (Bobby Eaton and Dennis Condrey) defeated The Rock 'n' Roll Express (Ricky Morton and Robert Gibson) to win the NWA World Tag Team Title in 17:29 (★★★★); The Road Warriors (Animal and Hawk) defeated Ivan Koloff and Nikita Koloff by DQ in 6:54 (★★); Dusty Rhodes vs. Tully Blanchard ended in a draw in 16:38 (★★); Ric Flair defeated Ron Garvin in 14:28 (★★★★).

WWF at Boston Garden (08-02-86) ★★★★

08-02-86, Boston, Massachusetts **WWF**

Lanny Poffo defeated Paul Christy in 9:56 (★★); Sivi Afi defeated Barry O in 7:41 (★★); George Steele defeated Tiger Chung Lee in 5:24 (★★); Hillbilly Jim defeated Big John Studd via count out in 7:26 (★★); Randy Savage defeated Tito Santana to win the WWF Intercontinental Title in 10:29

(★★★★); The Hart Foundation (Bret Hart and Jim Neidhart) defeated The Killer Bees (B. Brian Blair and Jim Brunzell) in 15:41 (★★★); Ricky Steamboat defeated Don Muraco in a Martial Arts Match in 17:20 (★★★★); Bruno Sammartino defeated Roddy Piper in a Steel Cage Match in 8:40 (★★★★).

WWF at Spectrum (08-02-86) ★★★

08-02-86, Philadelphia, Pennsylvania **WWF**

George Skaaland defeated Ron Shaw in 8:58 (★★); Pedro Morales defeated Rene Goulet in 11:56 (★★); Hercules defeated Scott McGhee in 8:44 (★★); Corporal Kirchner defeated The Iron Sheik in 7:47 (★★); Adrian Adonis defeated George Wells in 10:23 (★★); Junkyard Dog defeated Terry Funk in 13:05 (★★); The Dream Team (Brutus Beefcake and Greg Valentine) defeated The British Bulldogs (Davey Boy Smith and Dynamite Kid) in 15:35 (★★); Dan Spivey defeated Iron Mike Sharpe in 5:32 (★★); Hulk Hogan defeated King Kong Bundy by DQ in 9:15 (★★★).

Battle Of The Belts II ★★★★

14-02-86, Orlando, Florida **CWF/NWA**

Tyree Pride defeated Ron Slinker in 3:31 (★★); Kendall Windham defeated Prince Iaukea in 3:44 (★★); Denny Brown defeated The White Ninja in 13:36 (★★); Lex Luger defeated Jesse Barr to win the NWA Florida Southern Heavyweight Title in 20:34 (★★); Bruiser Brody vs. Wahoo McDaniel ended in a double count out in 5:21 (★★★); The Road Warriors (Animal and Hawk) and Blackjack Mulligan defeated Kevin Sullivan, Bob Roop and The Purple Haze in 6:19 (★★); Ric Flair vs. Barry Windham ended in a double count out in 41:44 (★★★★★★).

WWF at Madison Square Garden (17-02-86) ★★★

17-02-86, New York City, New York **WWF**

Lanny Poffo defeated Rene Goulet in 12:42 (★★); King Tonga defeated Les Thornton in 9:18 (★★); The Hart Foundation (Bret Hart and Jim Neidhart) vs. The Killer Bees (B. Brian Blair and Jim Brunzell) ended in a draw in 18:48 (★★★); King Kong Bundy defeated George Wells in 3:17 (★★); Ricky Steamboat defeated Don Muraco in a Martial Arts Match in 12:47 (★★★); Tony Atlas defeated Barry O in 4:27 (★★); Adrian Adonis defeated George Steele by DQ in 4:04 (★★); The Iron Sheik and Nikolai Volkoff defeated Corporal Kirchner and Dan Spivey in 9:41 (★★); Ted Arcidi defeated Terry Gibbs in 2:37 (★★); Hulk Hogan defeated Randy Savage in a Lumberjack Match in 7:36 (★★★★).

WWF at Sydney Entertainment Centre ★★

28-02-86, Sydney, Australia **WWF**

The Tiger defeated Mr. X in 10:40 (★★); Ted Arcidi defeated Matt Borne in 2:31 (★★); Tiger Chung Lee defeated Paul Roma in 9:02 (★★); The Rougeau Brothers (Jacques Rougeau and Raymond Rougeau) defeated The Moondogs (Moondog Spot and Moondog Rex) in 18:12 (★★★); Don Muraco and Mr. Fuji defeated SD Jones and King Tonga in 14:35 (★★); Andre the Giant defeated Big John Studd in 8:09 (★★).

Saturday Night's Main Event V ★★

01-03-86, Phoenix, Arizona **WWF**

Mr. T defeated Bob Orton via count out in a Boxing Match in 5:00; King Kong Bundy defeated Steve Gatorwolf in :41 (★★); Hulk Hogan defeated Don Muraco by DQ in 6:53 (★★); The Dream Team (Brutus Beefcake and Greg Valentine) defeated The British Bulldogs (Davey Boy Smith and Dynamite Kid) in 12:00 (★★★); Junkyard Dog defeated Adrian Adonis in 8:45 (★★).

WWF at Boston Garden (08-03-86) ★★★

08-03-86, Boston, Massachusetts **WWF**

Sivi Afi defeated Rene Goulet in 11:06 (★★); Jake Roberts defeated Jose Luis Rivera in 10:30 (★★); The Crush Girls (Chigusa Nagayo and Lioness Asuka) defeated Judy Martin and Donna Christianello in 15:33 (★★); Jim Neidhart defeated Scott McGhee in 5:59 (★★); Ricky Steamboat defeated Bret Hart in 15:08 (★★★); Randy Savage defeated Tito Santana by DQ in 7:17 (★★); Velvet McIntyre and Dawn Marie defeated Bull Nakano and Dump Matsumoto in 8:27 (★★); Corporal Kirchner defeated Iron Mike Sharpe in 9:56 (★★); Ted Arcidi defeated Barry O in 3:13 (★★); Hulk Hogan and Junkyard Dog defeated The Funk Brothers (Terry Funk and Hoss Funk) in 11:32 (★★★).

WWF at Madison Square Garden (16-03-86) ★★★
16-03-86, New York City, New York **WWF**

Sivi Afi defeated Moondog Spot in 7:07 (★★); Hercules defeated George Wells in 4:11 (★★); Dump Matsumoto and Bull Nakano defeated Linda Gonzalez and Velvet McIntyre in 10:02 (★★★); Pedro Morales defeated Bob Orton by DQ in 9:19 (★★★); Don Muraco defeated King Tonga in 8:05 (★★); The Crush Gals (Lioness Asuka and Chigusa Nagayo) defeated Leilani Kai and Penny Mitchell in 7:05 (★★★); King Kong Bundy defeated Hillbilly Jim in 6:03 (★★); Ricky Steamboat defeated Mr. Fuji in 6:09 (★★); Jake Roberts defeated Lanny Poffo in 6:49 (★★); Tito Santana defeated Randy Savage by DQ in 9:28 (★★★★); Haiti Kid defeated Dana Carpenter in 6:51 (★★); The British Bulldogs (Davey Boy Smith and Dynamite Kid) and Captain Lou Albano defeated Johnny V and The Dream Team (Brutus Beefcake and Greg Valentine) in 13:30 (★★).

WWF at Maple Leaf Gardens (23-03-86) ★★
23-03-86, Toronto, Canada **WWF**

King Tonga defeated Paul Christy in 9:32 (★★); The Rougeau Brothers (Jacques Rougeau and Raymond Rougeau) defeated The Moondogs (Moondog Spot and Moondog Rex) in 16:02 (★★★); Bob Orton defeated Lanny Poffo in 12:17 (★★★); Ricky Steamboat defeated Don Muraco in a Martial Arts Match in 16:22 (★★★); The Hart Foundation (Bret Hart and Jim Neidhart) defeated The Killer Bees (B. Brian Blair and Jim Brunzell) in 15:02 (★★★); Corporal Kirchner defeated Iron Mike Sharpe in 7:54 (★★); Jake Roberts defeated George Wells in 8:53 (★★); Andre the Giant and Junkyard Dog defeated Jimmy Hart and The Funk Brothers (Hoss Funk and Terry Funk) by DQ in a Handicap Match in 12:44 (★★).

WWF at Spectrum (30-03-86) ★★
30-03-86, Philadelphia, Pennsylvania **WWF**

King Tonga defeated Iron Mike Sharpe in 10:47 (★★); Hercules defeated Lanny Poffo in 13:17 (★★); Nikolai Volkoff defeated Tony Atlas in 3:33 (★★); Paul Orndorff defeated Bob Orton via count out in 14:30 (★★★); Hulk Hogan and Ricky Steamboat defeated Don Muraco, Johnny V and Mr. Fuji in a Handicap Match in 10:12 (★★); Sivi Afi defeated Tiger Chung Lee in 5:33 (★★); The Hart Foundation (Bret Hart and Jim Neidhart) defeated Tony Garea and B. Brian Blair in 11:19 (★★); Jake Roberts defeated SD Jones in 4:50 (★★); King Kong Bundy defeated Hillbilly Jim in 5:25 (★★).

WrestleMania II ★★
07-04-86, Uniondale/Rosemont/Los Angeles **WWF**

Don Muraco vs. Paul Orndorff went to a double count out in 4:10 (★★); Randy Savage defeated George Steele in 5:10 (★★); Jake Roberts defeated George Wells in 3:15 (★★); Mr. T defeated Roddy Piper by DQ in a Boxing Match in 13:14 (★); The Fabulous Moolah defeated Velvet McIntyre in 1:25 (★★); Corporal Kirchner defeated Nikolai Volkoff in a Flag Match in 2:05 (★★); Andre the Giant won a WWF vs. NFL Battle Royal in 9:13 (★★★); The British Bulldogs (Davey Boy Smith and Dynamite Kid) defeated The Dream Team (Brutus Beefcake and Greg Valentine) to win the WWF World Tag Team Title in 13:03 (★★★★); Ricky Steamboat defeated Hercules in 7:27 (★★); Adrian Adonis defeated Uncle Elmer in 3:01 (★★); Hoss Funk and Terry Funk defeated Junkyard Dog and Tito Santana in 11:42 (★★★★); Hulk Hogan defeated King Kong Bundy in a Steel Cage Match in 10:15 (★★).

Crockett Cup '86 ★★★
19-04-86, New Orleans, Louisiana **NWA**

Mark Youngblood and Wahoo McDaniel defeated Bobby Jaggers and Mike Miller in 1:51 [shown] (★★); Nelson Royal and Sam Houston defeated The Batten Twins (Bart Batten and Brad Batten) in 1:56 [shown] (★★); Jimmy Valiant and Manny Fernandez defeated Baron Von Raschke and The Barbarian in 2:35 [shown] (★); Steve Williams and Terry Taylor defeated Bill Dundee and Buddy Landel in 1:56 [shown] (★★); The Sheepherders (Luke Williams and Butch Miller) defeated The Guerrero Brothers (Chavo Guerrero and Hector Guerrero) in 2:34 [shown] (★★); The Fantastics (Bobby Fulton and Tommy Rogers) defeated The Fabulous Ones (Steve Keirn and Stan Lane) in 14:20 (★★★); Buzz Sawyer and Rick Steiner defeated Koko B. Ware and The Italian Stallion in 15:14 (★★); Jimmy Garvin and Black Bart defeated Brett Wayne and D.J. Peterson in 6:11 (★★); The Midnight Express (Dennis Condrey and Bobby Eaton) defeated Nelson Royal and Sam Houston in 1:48

(★★); Ronnie Garvin and Magnum T.A. defeated Buzz Sawyer and Rick Steiner in 5:19 (★★); The Road Warriors (Hawk and Animal) defeated Mark Youngblood and Wahoo McDaniel in 4:21 (★★); The Russian Team (Ivan Koloff and Nikita Koloff) defeated Jimmy Valiant and Manny Fernandez in 9:00 (★★★); The Sheepherders (Luke Williams and Butch Miller) defeated The Rock 'n' Roll Express (Ricky Morton and Robert Gibson) by DQ in 8:43 (★★★); The Fantastics (Bobby Fulton and Tommy Rogers) defeated Arn Anderson and Tully Blanchard in 11:29 (★★★★); Giant Baba and Tiger Mask defeated Black Bart and Jimmy Garvin in 7:53 (★★); The Road Warriors (Hawk and Animal) defeated The Midnight Express (Dennis Condrey and Bobby Eaton) by DQ in 8:06 (★★); Steve Williams and Terry Taylor vs. The Russian Team (Ivan Koloff and Nikita Koloff) ended in a draw in 20:00 (★★★★); The Fantastics (Bobby Fulton and Tommy Rogers) vs. The Sheepherders (Luke Williams and Butch Miller) ended in a double DQ in 14:25 (★★★★); Magnum T.A. and Ronnie Garvin defeated Giant Baba and Tiger Mask in 9:54 (★★); Ric Flair defeated Dusty Rhodes by DQ in 20:13 (★★★); The Road Warriors (Hawk and Animal) defeated Magnum T.A. and Ronnie Garvin to win the Crockett Cup in 9:49 (★★★).

WrestleRock '86 ★★★
20-04-86, Irving, Texas **AWA**

Brad Rheingans defeated Boris Zhukov in 8:35 (★★); Little Mr. T and Cowboy Lang defeated Lord Littlebrook and Little Tokyo in 10:02 (★★); Colonel DeBeers defeated Wahoo McDaniel by DQ in 5:01 (★★); Buddy Rose and Doug Somers defeated The Midnight Rockers (Shawn Michaels and Marty Jannetty) in 12:05 (★★★★); Tiger Mask defeated Buck Zumhofe in 10:57 (★★); Barry Windham and Mike Rotundo defeated The Fabulous Ones (Stan Lane and Steve Keirn) in 14:05 (★★★); Giant Baba defeated Bulldog Bob Brown in 5:42 (★); Harley Race vs. Rick Martel went to a double count out in 17:35 (★★); Sherri Martel won a Battle Royal in 7:34 (★★); Sgt. Slaughter defeated Kamala by DQ in 9:44; (★★); Scott Hall and Curt Hennig defeated The Long Riders (Scott Irwin and Bill Irwin) in 13:04 (★★★); Scott LeDoux defeated Larry Zbyszko by DQ in a Martial Arts Match in 12:19 (★★); Nick Bockwinkel defeated Stan Hansen by DQ in 10:12 (★★★); Greg Gagne and Jimmy Snuka defeated King Kong Brody and The Barbarian in a Steel Cage Match in 11:29 (★★★); Verne Gagne defeated Sheik Adnan El Kassey in a Steel Cage Match in 4:25 (★★); The Road Warriors (Hawk and Animal) defeated The Fabulous Freebirds (Michael Hayes and Jimmy Garvin) in a Steel Cage Match in 6:48 (★★★).

WWF at Madison Square Garden (22-04-86) ★★★
22-04-86, New York City, New York **WWF**

Lanny Poffo defeated Rene Goulet in 13:16 (★★); Nikolai Volkoff defeated Tony Garea in 6:54 (★★); King Tonga defeated Paul Christy in 5:57 (★★); Sivi Afi defeated Iron Mike Sharpe via count out in 13:51 (★★); Dynamite Kid defeated Brutus Beefcake in 11:18 (★★★); Randy Savage defeated Tito Santana in a No DQ Match in 18:52 (★★★★); Greg Valentine defeated Davey Boy Smith in 9:12 (★★); Corporal Kirchner defeated The Iron Sheik by DQ in 4:56 (★★); Pedro Morales defeated Tiger Chung Lee in 3:10 (★★); Jake Roberts defeated Scott McGhee in 4:07 (★★); Hulk Hogan and Hillbilly Jim defeated Big John Studd and King Kong Bundy by DQ in 10:48 (★★★).

WWF at Joe Louis Arena (26-04-86) ★★
26-04-86, Detroit, Michigan **WWF**

Bret Hart defeated Sivi Afi in 10:33 (★★); Tony Atlas defeated Hercules in 9:31 (★★); George Steele defeated Jim Neidhart in 3:52 (★★); Corporal Kirchner defeated Iron Mike Sharpe in 10:28 (★★); Hillbilly Jim defeated Adrian Adonis by DQ in 8:51 (★★); Tito Santana defeated Bob Orton in 9:51 (★★★); The Iron Sheik and Nikolai Volkoff defeated The Killer Bees (B. Brian Blair and Jim Brunzell) in 11:41 (★★★); Jake Roberts defeated Scott McGhee in 7:02 (★★); Hulk Hogan defeated Randy Savage in 11:46 (★★★).

WWF at Boston Garden (26-04-86) ★★
26-04-86, Boston, Massachusetts **WWF**

Tony Garea defeated Mr. X in 14:20 (★★); Moondog Spot defeated Jose Luis Rivera in 12:20 (★★); Don Muraco defeated Dan Spivey in 9:02 (★★★); The Dream Team (Greg Valentine and Brutus Beefcake) defeated Pedro Morales and Davey Boy Smith in 13:35 (★★★); King Tonga defeated Tiger Chung Lee in 10:37 (★★); **Lanny Poffo** defeated **Psycho Capone** in 6:59 (★★); **Ted Arcidi** vs. **Big John Studd** ended in a double count out in 10:23 (★★); **Jimmy Hart, Jimmy Jack Funk** and **Hoss Funk** defeated **Ricky Steamboat, Junkyard Dog** and **Haiti Kid** in 11:33 (★★).

Saturday Night's Main Event VI ★★★★
03-05-86, Providence, Rhode Island **WWF**
Hulk Hogan and **Junkyard Dog** defeated **Terry Funk** and **Hoss Funk** in 13:30 (★★★); **King Kong Bundy** defeated **Uncle Elmer** in 2:35 (★); **Adrian Adonis** defeated **Paul Orndorff** by DQ in 12:00 (★★); **Ricky Steamboat** vs. **Ricky Steamboat** went to a no contest; **The British Bulldogs** (**Davey Boy Smith** and **Dynamite Kid**) defeated **Nikolai Volkoff** and **The Iron Sheik** in a Two Out Of Three Falls Match in 16:36 (★★★).

3rd David Von Erich Memorial Parade Of Champions ★★★
04-05-86, Irving, Texas **WCCW**
The Great Kabuki defeated **Mark Youngblood** in 3:22 (★★); **The Great Kabuki** defeated **Jerry Allen** in 1:56 (★★); **Steve Simpson** defeated **The Great Kabuki** in 4:04 (★★); **Brian Adias** defeated **Steve Regal** in 8:26 (★★); **Chris Adams** and **Brickhouse Brown** defeated **John Tatum** and **The Grappler** in 9:30 (★★); **Bruiser Brody** defeated **Terry Gordy** in a Barbed Wire Match in 8:51 (★★★); **Rick Rude** defeated **Bruiser Brody** by DQ in 7:47 (★★); **Kerry Von Erich, Lance Von Erich** and **Steve Simpson** defeated **The Fabulous Freebirds** (**Michael Hayes, Terry Gordy** and **Buddy Roberts**) in a Lumberjack Strap Elimination Match to win the WCCW Six Man Tag Team Title (★★★).

WWF at Maple Leaf Gardens (04-05-86) ★★★
04-05-86, Toronto, Canada **WWF**
Tiger Chung Lee defeated **Don Kolov** in 5:34 (★★); **Scott McGhee** defeated **Johnny K-9** in 5:22 (★★); **Bret Hart** defeated **Bret Hart** by DQ in 9:08 (★★★); **B. Brian Blair** defeated **Jim Neidhart** in 7:14 (★★); **Randy Savage** defeated **Tito Santana** in a No DQ Match in 13:56 (★★★★); **The Funk Brothers** (**Jimmy Jack Funk** and **Hoss Funk**) defeated **Lanny Poffo** and **George Wells** in 13:31 (★★); **Harley Race** defeated **SD Jones** in 4:45 (★★); **Adrian Adonis** defeated **Danny Spivey** in 8:18 (★★); **Hulk Hogan** and **Junkyard Dog** defeated **Big John Studd** and **King Kong Bundy** by DQ in 9:37 (★★★).

WWF at Madison Square Garden (19-05-86) ★★
19-05-86, New York City, New York **WWF**
Lanny Poffo defeated **Tiger Chung Lee** in 11:15 (★★); **Bret Hart** defeated **SD Jones** in 10:15 (★★); **Hercules** defeated **Sivi Afi** in 13:07 (★★); **Nikolai Volkoff** defeated **Corporal Kirchner** in 11:30 (★★); **Tito Santana** defeated **Randy Savage** by DQ in 9:59 (★★); **King Kong Bundy** defeated **Tony Atlas** in 8:04 (★); **Jake Roberts** vs. **Ricky Steamboat** ended in a double DQ in 7:03 (★★★); **Dan Spivey** defeated **Paul Christy** in 4:41 (★★); **Jim Neidhart** vs. **Jim Brunzell** ended in a draw in 20:00 (★★); **The British Bulldogs** (**Davey Boy Smith** and **Dynamite Kid**) defeated **The Dream Team** (**Greg Valentine** and **Brutus Beefcake**) in 11:54 (★★★).

WWF at Boston Garden (24-05-86) ★★
24-05-86, Boston, Massachusetts **WWF**
David Sammartino defeated **Tiger Chung Lee** in 12:27 (★); **Iron Mike Sharpe** defeated **Tony Garea** in 11:35 (★★); **Jim Neidhart** defeated **Lanny Poffo** in 5:29 (★★); **Bret Hart** defeated **Sivi Afi** in 10:20 (★★); **King Kong Bundy** defeated **Tony Atlas** in 6:18 (★★); **Hercules** defeated **Scott McGhee** in 8:05 (★★); **Corporal Kirchner** defeated **Nikolai Volkoff** in 7:26 (★★); **Pedro Morales, Davey Boy Smith** and **Dan Spivey** defeated **The Dream Team** (**Greg Valentine** and **Brutus Beefcake**) and **Johnny V** in 11:20 (★★); **Randy Savage** defeated **Hulk Hogan** via count out in 13:58 (★★★).

WWF at Spectrum (31-05-86) ★★★
31-05-86, Philadelphia, Pennsylvania **WWF**
David Sammartino defeated **Les Thornton** in 11:36 (★★); **Bob Orton** defeated **Lanny Poffo** in 6:40 (★★); **Adrian Adonis** defeated **Sivi Afi** in 5:45 (★★); **Dan Spivey** defeated **Iron Mike Sharpe** in 9:58 (★); **Paul Orndorff** defeated **Don Muraco** in 16:19 (★★★); **Randy Savage** defeated **Tito Santana** in a No DQ Match in 11:47 (★★★); **The Killer Bees** (**B. Brian Blair** and **Jim Brunzell**) defeated **The Hart Foundation** (**Bret Hart** and **Jim Neidhart**) in 16:44 (★★★); **Ricky Steamboat** vs. **Jake Roberts** ended in a double DQ in 9:13 (★★★).

WWF at Madison Square Garden (14-06-86) ★★
14-06-86, New York City, New York **WWF**
Jimmy Jack Funk defeated **Tony Garea** in 10:06 (★★); **Pedro Morales** defeated **The Iron Sheik** by DQ in 11:16 (★★); **The US Express** (**Mike Rotundo** and **Dan Spivey**) defeated **The Moondogs** (**Moondog Rex** and **Moondog Spot**) in 11:37 (★★); **Nikolai Volkoff** defeated **George Steele** by DQ in 6:21 (★★); **Cowboy Lang** defeated **Lord Littlebrook** in 10:01 (★★); **Randy Savage** and **Adrian Adonis** defeated **Bruno Sammartino** and **Tito Santana** via count out in 9:40 (★★★); **Hoss Funk** defeated **George Wells** in 9:54 (★★); **Big John Studd** vs. **King Tonga** ended in a double count out in 3:50 (★★); **Harley Race** defeated **Lanny Poffo** in 10:56 (★★★); **Junkyard Dog** defeated **King Kong Bundy** by DQ in 8:43 (★★).

WWF at Boston Garden (27-06-86) ★★
27-06-86, Boston, Massachusetts **WWF**
The US Express (**Mike Rotundo** and **Dan Spivey**) defeated **Les Thornton** and **Tiger Chung Lee** in 12:16 (★★); **Harley Race** defeated **Tony Atlas** in 8:27 (★); **King Tonga** defeated **Pete Doherty** in 4:20 (★★); **Pedro Morales** defeated **Moondog Spot** in 7:25 (★★); **Jake Roberts** defeated **Ricky Steamboat** in 13:28 (★★★); **Hulk Hogan** defeated **Randy Savage** in 7:12 (★★); **Billy Jack Haynes** defeated **Moondog Rex** in 5:38 (★); **King Kong Bundy** defeated **Junkyard Dog** in 7:21 (★); **Paul Orndorff** defeated **Don Muraco** in 15:00 (★★).

Battle By The Bay ★★
28-06-86, Oakland, California **AWA**
Earthquake Ferris defeated **Ali Khan** in 5:58 (★★); **Sherri Martel** defeated **Candi Devine** to win the AWA Ladies Title in 8:39 (★★); **Jimmy Snuka** defeated **Jay York** in 8:53 (★★); **Nord The Barbarian** defeated **Nick Bockwinkel** in 12:20 (★★); **Stan Hansen** defeated **Jerry Blackwell** by DQ in 8:44 (★★); **Curt Hennig** and **The Midnight Rockers** (**Marty Jannetty** and **Shawn Michaels**) defeated **Alexis Smirnoff, Buddy Rose** and **Doug Somers** in 11:41 (★★★★).

WWF at Spectrum (28-06-86) ★★
28-06-86, Philadelphia, Pennsylvania **WWF**
Brickhouse Brown defeated **Moondog Rex** in 6:29 (★★); **The US Express** (**Dan Spivey** and **Mike Rotundo**) defeated **Hercules** and **Tiger Chung Lee** in 12:26 (★★); **Adrian Adonis** defeated **Tito Santana** in 11:38 (★★); **Billy Jack Haynes** defeated **Moondog Spot** in 10:34 (★★); **Junkyard Dog** defeated **Don Muraco** in 6:20 (★); **Hulk Hogan** defeated **King Kong Bundy** in 7:09 (★★★); **Harley Race** defeated **George Wells** in 6:05 (★★); **King Tonga** defeated **Les Thornton** in 4:14 (★★); **Paul Orndorff** defeated **Randy Savage** in 8:20 (★★★).

Great American Bash '86 (Charlotte) ★★★
05-07-86, Charlotte, North Carolina **NWA**
Denny Brown vs. **Steve Regal** went to a time limit draw in 15:00 (★★); **Robert Gibson** defeated **Black Bart** in 7:42 (★★★); **The Minnesota Wrecking Crew** (**Ole Anderson** and **Arn Anderson**) defeated **Sam Houston** and **Nelson Royal** in 12:20 (★★); **Manny Fernandez** defeated **Baron von Raschke** in a Bunkhouse Match in 9:00 (★★); **Wahoo McDaniel** defeated **Jimmy Garvin** in an Indian Strap Match in 10:23 (★★); **Ron Garvin** defeated **Tully Blanchard** in a Taped Fist Match in 15:20 (★★); **The Road Warriors** (**Hawk** and **Animal**) defeated **The Russian Team** (**Ivan Koloff** and **Nikita Koloff**) in a Russian Chain Match in 5:48 (★★); **Jimmy Valiant** defeated **Shaska Whatley** in a Hair vs. Hair Match in 10:40 (★★); **Dusty Rhodes, Magnum T.A.** and **Baby Doll** defeated **The Midnight Express** (**Bobby Eaton** and **Dennis Condrey**) and **Jim Cornette** in a Steel Cage Match in 10:03 (★★); **Ric Flair** defeated **Ricky Morton** in a Steel Cage Match in 23:10 (★★★★).

WWF at Madison Square Garden (12-07-86) ★★★
12-07-86, New York City, New York **WWF**
Tony Atlas defeated **Lanny Poffo** in 12:35 (★★★); **Jimmy Hart** won a 22-Man Battle Royal in 12:53 (★★★); **The British Bulldogs** (**Davey Boy Smith** and **Dynamite Kid**) defeated **The Moondogs** (**Moondog Rex** and **Moondog Spot**) in 18:23 (★★★); **Pedro Morales** defeated **Iron Mike Sharpe** in 5:54 (★★); **Billy Jack Haynes** defeated **Brutus Beefcake** by DQ in 6:26 (★★); **King Kong Bundy** and **Big John Studd** defeated **King Tonga** and **Sivi Afi** in 8:33 (★★); **Harley Race** defeated **Tony Garea** in 2:05 (★★); **Junkyard Dog** vs. **Greg Valentine** ended in a double count out in 13:32 (★★); **Bruno Sammartino** and **Tito Santana** defeated **Randy Savage** and **Adrian Adonis** in a Steel Cage Match in 9:51 (★★★★).

WWF at Spectrum (26-07-86) ★★★
26-07-86, Philadelphia, Pennsylvania WWF
Hercules defeated Lanny Poffo in 9:08 (★★); Tito Santana vs. Bob Orton ended in a draw in 18:22 (★★★); Harley Race defeated Cousin Luke in 7:16 (★★); The Iron Sheik and Nikolai Volkoff defeated The Funk Brothers (Jimmy Jack Funk and Hoss Funk) in 7:59 (★★); Junkyard Dog defeated Don Muraco in a Dog Collar Match in 6:09 (★★); The US Express (Danny Spivey and Mike Rotundo) defeated The Moondogs (Moondog Rex and Moondog Spot) in 19:44 (★★★); Randy Savage defeated George Steele by DQ in 5:29 (★★); Hulk Hogan defeated Adrian Adonis in 9:13 (★★★).

Great American Bash '86 (Greensboro) ★★★
26-07-86, Greensboro, North Carolina NWA
Steve Regal defeated Sam Houston in 8:00 (★★); Black Bart and Konga the Barbarian defeated Denny Brown and Italian Stallion in 7:58 (★★); Manny Fernandez and Baron von Raschke in a Loaded Glove on a Pole Match in 8:24 (★★); Wahoo McDaniel defeated Jimmy Garvin in an Indian Strap Match in 8:27 (★★★); Tully Blanchard defeated Ron Garvin in a Taped Fist Match in 11:38 (★★); The Rock 'n' Roll Express (Ricky Morton and Robert Gibson) vs. The Minnesota Wrecking Crew (Arn Anderson and Ole Anderson) went to a time limit draw in 20:00 (★★★★); Paul Jones defeated Jimmy Valiant in a Hair vs. Hair Match in 4:30 (★★); Magnum T.A. defeated Nikita Koloff in 13:38 (★★); The Road Warriors (Hawk and Animal) and Baby Doll defeated The Midnight Express (Bobby Eaton and Dennis Condrey) and Jim Cornette in a Steel Cage Match in 9:22 (★★); Dusty Rhodes defeated Ric Flair in a Steel Cage Match to win the NWA World Heavyweight Title in 21:10 (★★).

WWF at Maple Leaf Gardens (27-07-86) ★★★
27-07-86, Toronto, Canada WWF
Hercules defeated Scott McGhee in 6:59 (★★); The Rougeau Brothers (Jacques Rougeau and Raymond Rougeau) defeated The Moondogs (Moondog Rex and Moondog Spot) in 11:25 (★★★); Billy Jack Haynes defeated The Iron Sheik in 5:27 (★★); The Funk Brothers (Jimmy Jack Funk and Hoss Funk) defeated The US Express (Mike Rotundo and Danny Spivey) in 15:25 (★★★); Corporal Kirchner defeated Nikolai Volkoff in a Boot Camp Match in 11:22 (★★★); Junkyard Dog defeated King Kong Bundy by DQ in 6:16 (★★); Ricky Steamboat defeated Randy Savage via count out in 15:25 (★★★★).

WWF at Boston Garden (09-08-86) ★★★
09-08-86, Boston, Massachusetts WWF
Tito Santana vs. Bob Orton ended in a draw in 28:50 (★★★★); Lanny Poffo defeated Mr. X in 7:17 (★★); Dick Slater defeated Pete Doherty in 6:45 (★); Nikolai Volkoff and The Iron Sheik defeated The Hart Foundation (Bret Hart and Jim Neidhart) in 6:39 (★★★); Tony Atlas vs. Ted Arcidi ended in a double count out in 7:28 (★); Ricky Steamboat defeated Jake Roberts in 17:21 (★★★★); Cowboy Lang defeated Lord Littlebrook in 7:53 (★★); Hulk Hogan and George Steele defeated Randy Savage and Adrian Adonis in 10:28 (★★).

WWF at Spectrum (23-08-86) ★★
23-08-86, Philadelphia, Pennsylvania WWF
Paul Roma defeated Les Thornton in 12:13 (★★); Jose Luis Rivera defeated Ron Shaw in 8:38 (★★); Paul Orndorff defeated Junkyard Dog in 12:39 (★★); The Machines (Big Machine and Super Machine) vs. Big John Studd and King Kong Bundy ended in a double DQ in 8:05 (★★★); The Dream Team (Greg Valentine and Brutus Beefcake) vs. The US Express (Mike Rotundo and Dan Spivey) ended in a draw in 16:17 (★★); Jake Roberts defeated Cousin Luke in 9:44 (★★); The British Bulldogs (Davey Boy Smith and Dynamite Kid) defeated Nikolai Volkoff and The Iron Sheik in 12:48 (★★★).

WWF at Madison Square Garden (25-08-86) ★★
25-08-86, New York City, New York WWF
Nick Kiniski defeated Les Thornton in 9:49 (★★); Jake Roberts defeated Sivi Afi in 16:46 (★★); Billy Jack Haynes defeated Hercules via count out in 21:29 (★★); Paul Orndorff defeated Corporal Kirchner in 9:42 (★★); King Kong Bundy and Big John Studd defeated The Machines (Big Machine and Super Machine) by DQ in 9:07 (★★); Adrian Adonis defeated Tony Atlas in 7:20 (★★); Nikolai Volkoff and The Iron Sheik defeated The US Express (Dan Spivey and Mike Rotundo) in 12:46 (★★); Pedro Morales defeated Randy Savage via count out in 7:19

(★★); The British Bulldogs (Davey Boy Smith and Dynamite Kid) defeated The Funks (Jimmy Jack Funk and Hoss Funk) in 5:27 (★★★).

The Big Event ★★
28-08-86, Toronto, Ontario WWF
The Killer Bees (Jim Brunzell and B. Brian Blair) defeated Jimmy Jack Funk and Hoss Funk in 6:53 (★★); Don Muraco vs. King Tonga went to a time limit draw in 15:00 (★★); Ted Arcidi defeated Tony Garea in 2:41 (★); Junkyard Dog defeated Adrian Adonis via count out in 4:15 (★★); Dick Slater defeated Iron Mike Sharpe in 6:24 (★★); Bobby Heenan, King Kong Bundy and Big John Studd defeated Lou Albano and The Machines (Super Machine and Big Machine) in 7:49 (★★); Ricky Steamboat defeated Jake Roberts in a Snake Pit Match in 10:17 (★★★★); Billy Jack Haynes defeated Hercules in 6:08 (★★); The Fabulous Rougeaus (Jacques Rougeau and Raymond Rougeau) defeated The Dream Team (Brutus Beefcake and Greg Valentine in 14:51 (★★★); Harley Race defeated Pedro Morales in 3:23 (★★); Hulk Hogan defeated Paul Orndorff by DQ in 11:05 (★★★).

Labor Day Star Wars '86 ★★
01-09-86, Fort Worth, Texas WCCW
Mark Lewin and Kevin Sullivan defeated The Batten Twins (Brad Batten and Bart Batten) in 11:59 (★★); The Youngblood Brothers (Chris Youngblood and Mark Youngblood) defeated Rick Rude and Jos LeDuc by DQ in 7:42 (★★); Abdullah The Butcher defeated Bruiser Brody by DQ in 5:38 (★★★); The Dingo Warrior and Socko defeated Tim Brooks and The Grappler in 5:26 (★★); Buzz Sawyer and Matt Borne defeated Kevin Von Erich and Mike Von Erich via count out in 7:43 (★★★); The Youngbloods Brothers (Chris Youngblood and Mark Youngblood) defeated Ted Oates and Jerry Oates in 10:19 (★★★); Buzz Sawyer and Matt Borne defeated Mark Lewin and Kevin Sullivan in 12:00 (★★★).

Battle Of The Belts III ★★★
01-09-86, Daytona Beach, Florida CWF/NWA
Tyree Pride defeated The Cuban Assassin in 15:20 (★★); The Fabulous Ones (Stan Lane and Steve Keirn) defeated The Sheepherders (Butch Miller and Luke Williams) in 7:37 (★★★); The Ninja defeated Tim Horner to win the NWA US Junior Heavyweight Title in 10:29 (★★★★); Nick Bockwinkel defeated Kendo Nagasaki by DQ in 7:03 (★★); The Road Warriors (Animal and Hawk) vs. The Shock Troops (Ed Gantner and Kareem Muhammad) ended in a double DQ in 6:35 (★★); Kendall Windham defeated Chris Champion by DQ in 3:35 (★★); Ric Flair vs. Lex Luger ended in a 1-1 draw in a Best Two Out Of Three Falls Match in 32:21 (★★★); Barry Windham defeated Ron Bass to win the NWA Florida Heavyweight Title in 2:34 (★★) (ended in progress).

WWF at Boston Garden (06-09-86) ★★
06-09-86, Boston, Massachusetts WWF
Sivi Afi defeated Pete Doherty in 7:02 (★★); The Hart Foundation (Bret Hart and Jim Neidhart) vs. The US Express (Dan Spivey and Mike Rotundo) ended in a time limit draw in 18:30 (★★★★); Randy Savage defeated George Steele in 5:25 (★★); Pedro Morales defeated Rene Goulet in 10:41 (★★); The Machines (Big Machine and Super Machine) defeated King Kong Bundy and Big John Studd in 9:07 (★★); Harley Race defeated Corporal Kirchner in 13:40 (★★); Bob Orton defeated Cousin Luke in 4:12 (★★); The British Bulldogs (Davey Boy Smith and Dynamite Kid) defeated Nikolai Volkoff and The Iron Sheik in 7:44 (★★).

WWF at Madison Square Garden (22-09-86) ★★★
22-09-86, New York City, New York WWF
The Islanders (Haku and Tama) defeated The Moondogs (Moondog Rex and Moondog Spot) in 13:17 (★★★); Nick Kiniski defeated Steve Lombardi in 8:57 (★★); Bob Orton defeated Billy Jack Haynes in 9:31 (★★); The Rougeau Brothers (Jacques Rougeau and Raymond Rougeau) defeated The Hart Foundation (Bret Hart and Jim Neidhart) in 14:52 (★★★★); Ted Arcidi defeated Tony Garea in 4:30 (★★); Steve Regal defeated Jose Luis Rivera in 7:53 (★★); SD Jones defeated Mr. X in 8:09 (★★); Harley Race defeated Tito Santana in 12:43 (★★★); Sika defeated Lanny Poffo in 7:28 (★★); The Machines (Hulk Machine, Big Machine and Super Machine) defeated King Kong Bundy, Big John Studd and Bobby Heenan in 8:45 (★★★).

WWF at Boston Garden (04-10-86) ★★
04-10-86, Boston, Massachusetts **WWF**

Mr. X defeated Rudy Diamond in 7:29 (★★); Bob Orton defeated Pedro Morales in 10:41 (★★); Randy Savage defeated George Steele in a No DQ Match in 3:46 (★★); The Machines (Big Machine, Super Machine and Piper Machine) defeated King Kong Bundy, Big John Studd and Bobby Heenan in 10:15 (★★); The Islanders (Haku and Tama) defeated Jimmy Jack Funk and Mr. X in 11:14 (★★); Sika defeated Jerry Allen in 6:08 (★); Tito Santana defeated Harley Race in 12:05 (★★).

Saturday Night's Main Event VII ★★★
04-10-86, Richfield, Ohio **WWF**

Hulk Hogan defeated Paul Orndorff by DQ in 10:00 (★★★); Ricky Steamboat defeated Jake Roberts in 6:19 (★★★); Roddy Piper defeated The Iron Sheik in :43 (★★); The British Bulldogs (Davey Boy Smith and Dynamite Kid) defeated The Dream Team (Brutus Beefcake and Greg Valentine) in a Two Out Of Three Falls Match in 13:09 (★★★); Kamala defeated Lanny Poffo in 1:44 (★★).

3rd Cotton Bowl Extravaganza ★★★
12-10-86, Dallas, Texas **WCCW**

Scott Casey defeated The Grappler in 5:31 (★★); Buzz Sawyer and Matt Borne defeated Steve Simpson and The Dingo Warrior by DQ in 10:21 (★★★); Crusher Yurkoff defeated Brian Adias in 8:04 (★★★); Mike Von Erich defeated Spike Johnson in 5:50 (★); The Youngblood Brothers (Mark Youngblood and Chris Youngblood) defeated The US Express (Brad Batten and Bart Batten) in 8:09 (★★★); Kevin Von Erich defeated Black Bart to win the WCCW World Heavyweight Title in 6:58 (★★★); Bruiser Brody defeated Abdullah The Butcher in a Steel Cage Match in 8:04 (★★★).

WWF at Spectrum (18-10-86) ★★
18-10-86, Philadelphia, Pennsylvania **WWF**

Corporal Kirchner defeated Tiger Chung Lee in 12:07 (★★); Pedro Morales defeated Steve Lombardi in 6:11 (★★); Billy Jack Haynes vs. Hercules ended in a draw in 20:00 (★★); Koko B. Ware defeated The Red Demon in 5:35 (★★); Randy Savage defeated The Honky Tonk Man via count out in 7:04 (★★★); Hillbilly Jim defeated Mr. Fuji in a Tuxedo Match in 5:06 (★); Kamala defeated Lanny Poffo in 3:35 (★★); Hulk Hogan defeated Paul Orndorff via count out in 16:23 (★★★★).

WWF at Houston Summit (19-10-86) ★★
19-10-86, Houston, Texas **WWF**

Mike Rotundo vs. Jim Brunzell ended in a draw in 13:55 (★★★); Bret Hart defeated Raymond Rougeau in 8:34 (★★★); Brutus Beefcake defeated SD Jones in 5:35 (★★); Big John Studd defeated Big Machine in 2:57 (★); Greg Valentine defeated Steve Gatorwolf in 8:30 (★); Davey Boy Smith defeated The Iron Sheik by DQ in 6:04 (★★); Hulk Hogan defeated Paul Orndorff via count out in 6:05 (★★); Nikolai Volkoff defeated Tama in 5:52 (★); Dynamite Kid defeated Moondog Rex in 8:15 (★★★); Nikolai Volkoff and The Iron Sheik won a 12-Team Battle Royal in 9:10 (★★).

WWF at Madison Square Garden (20-10-86) ★★★
20-10-86, New York City, New York **WWF**

SD Jones defeated Moondog Spot in 9:33 (★★); Tama defeated Moondog Rex in 8:18 (★★); Brutus Beefcake defeated B. Brian Blair in 9:24 (★★); King Kong Bundy defeated Super Machine in 3:17 (★); Dynamite Kid defeated Jim Neidhart in 5:49 (★★★); Jacques Rougeau defeated The Iron Sheik in 7:29 (★★★); Mike Rotundo vs. Jim Brunzell ended in a double count out in 9:10 (★★); Greg Valentine defeated Davey Boy Smith in 12:57 (★★★★); Haku defeated Nikolai Volkoff in 4:51 (★★); Bret Hart defeated Raymond Rougeau in 8:34 (★★); The Islanders (Haku and Tama) won a Tag Team Battle Royal in 10:20 (★★★).

WWF at Boston Garden (01-11-86) ★★★★
01-11-86, Boston, Massachusetts **WWF**

Raymond Rougeau and Lanny Poffo defeated The Moondogs (Moondog Rex and Moondog Spot) in 10:54 (★★★); Koko B. Ware defeated Jimmy Jack Funk by DQ in 12:03 (★★); Ricky Steamboat defeated Randy Savage via count out in 14:47 (★★★★); Hercules defeated Salvatore Bellomo in 3:41 (★); Leilani Kai and Judy Martin defeated Penny Mitchell and Candice Pardue in 9:35 (★★); Billy Jack Haynes vs. Bob Orton ended in a draw in 21:47 (★★★); The British Bulldogs (Davey

Boy Smith and Dynamite Kid) defeated The Hart Foundation (Bret Hart and Jim Neidhart) in 13:44 (★★★★); Sika defeated Scott McGhee in 4:39 (★★); Roddy Piper defeated Don Muraco in 7:23 (★★★).

WWF at Spectrum (08-11-86) ★★
08-11-86, Philadelphia, Pennsylvania **WWF**

Dick Slater defeated Moondog Rex in 7:29 (★★); Mike Rotundo defeated Iron Mike Sharpe in 6:03 (★★); Harley Race defeated George Steele in 7:03 (★★); Pedro Morales defeated Sika in 8:29 (★★); The Hart Foundation (Bret Hart and Jim Neidhart) defeated The Islanders (Haku and Tama) in 15:18 (★★★); Moondog Spot defeated Jerry Allen in 12:45 (★★); Ricky Steamboat defeated Randy Savage in 12:53 (★★★); Judy Martin and Leilani Kai defeated Candice Pardue and Penny Mitchell in 8:35 (★★); Roddy Piper defeated Bob Orton in 8:54 (★★★).

WWF at Maple Leaf Gardens (16-11-86) ★★
16-11-86, Toronto, Canada **WWF**

Jose Luis Rivera defeated Frankie Lane in 10:37 (★); Dino Bravo defeated Pedro Morales via count out in 9:23 (★★); Kamala defeated George Steele in 4:30 (★); Tito Santana vs. Butch Reed ended in a draw in 21:23 (★★★); Paul Roma defeated Steve Lombardi in 7:04 (★★); The Hart Foundation (Bret Hart and Jim Neidhart) defeated The Islanders (Haku and Tama) in 11:17 (★★★); The Honky Tonk Man defeated Mr. X in 6:34 (★★); Roddy Piper defeated Don Muraco in 7:05 (★★★).

WWF at Madison Square Garden (24-11-86) ★★
24-11-86, New York City, New York **WWF**

Billy Jack Haynes vs. Bob Orton ended in a double count out in 13:43 (★★★); Hercules defeated Pedro Morales in 9:07 (★★); Kamala defeated George Steele in 3:16 (★); Lanny Poffo defeated Steve Lombardi in 9:58 (★★); Hillbilly Jim defeated Don Muraco by DQ in 7:06 (★); Hulk Hogan and Roddy Piper defeated Paul Orndorff and Harley Race in 8:15 (★★★); Karate Kid and Pepe Gomez defeated Lord Littlebrook and Little Tokyo in 13:30 (★★); Koko B. Ware defeated Jimmy Jack Funk in 8:46 (★★); The Dream Team (Greg Valentine and Brutus Beefcake) defeated The Islanders (Haku and Tama) in 13:13 (★★).

WWF at Houston Summit (26-11-86) ★★
26-11-86, Houston, Texas **WWF**

Dan Spivey defeated Moondog Spot in 9:36 (★★); Butch Reed defeated Steve Gatorwolf in 5:43 (★★); Jake Roberts vs. Tito Santana ended in a draw in 17:25 (★★); Dick Slater defeated Dino Bravo in 9:54 (★★); The British Bulldogs (Davey Boy Smith and Dynamite Kid) defeated Nikolai Volkoff and The Iron Sheik in 12:43 (★★★); Mike Rotundo defeated Moondog Rex in 9:34 (★★); Randy Savage defeated Junkyard Dog via count out in 6:29 (★★).

Starrcade '86 ★★★
27-11-86, Toronto, Ontario **NWA**

Tim Horner and Nelson Royal defeated Rocky Kernodle and Don Kernodle in 6:12 (★★); Brad Armstrong vs. Jimmy Garvin went to a time limit draw in 15:00 (★★★); Hector Guerrero and Baron Von Raschke defeated Shaska Whatley and The Barbarian in 6:18 (★★); The Russian Team (Ivan Koloff and Krusher Khruschev) defeated The Kansas Jayhawks (Bobby Jaggers and Dutch Mantel) in 7:54 (★★); Wahoo McDaniel defeated Rick Rude in an Indian Strap Match in 8:11 (★★); Sam Houston defeated Bill Dundee by DQ in 10:24 (★★); Jimmy Valiant defeated Paul Jones in a Hair vs. Hair Match in 4:23 (★); Big Bubba Rogers defeated Ron Garvin in a Street Fight in 11:50 (★★★); Tully Blanchard defeated Dusty Rhodes in a First Blood Match to win the NWA World Television Title in 8:28 (★★); The Road Warriors (Hawk and Animal) defeated The Midnight Express (Bobby Eaton and Dennis Condrey) in a Skywalkers Match in 7:10 (★★); The Rock 'n' Roll Express (Ricky Morton and Robert Gibson) defeated The Minnesota Wrecking Crew (Arn Anderson and Ole Anderson) in a Steel Cage Match in 18:49 (★★★★); Ric Flair vs. Nikita Koloff went to a double DQ in 19:10 (★★★★).

Saturday Night's Main Event VIII ★★★
29-11-86, Los Angeles, California **WWF**

Randy Savage vs. Jake Roberts went to a double DQ in 12:40 (★★★); Hulk Hogan defeated Hercules in 6:22 (★★); Roddy Piper defeated Bob Orton in 3:48 (★★); The Killer Bees (Jim

Brunzell and B. Brian Blair) defeated The Hart Foundation (Bret Hart and Jim Neidhart) in 8:30 (★★★); Koko B. Ware defeated Nikolai Volkoff in 2:30 (★★); Don Muraco defeated Dick Slater in 2:05 (★★).

WWF at Boston Garden (06-12-86) ★★
06-12-86, Boston, Massachusetts **WWF**

SD Jones defeated Iron Mike Sharpe in 8:25 (★★); The Rougeau Brothers (Jacques Rougeau and Raymond Rougeau) vs. The US Express (Mike Rotundo and Dan Spivey) ended in a double DQ in 12:01 (★★); Harley Race defeated Pedro Morales in 8:43 (★★); Dick Slater defeated Steve Lombardi in 6:20 (★★); Lord Littlebrook and Little Tokyo defeated The Karate Kid and Pepe Gomez in 8:18 (★★); Junkyard Dog defeated Adrian Adonis via count out in 7:34 (★★); Blackjack Mulligan defeated Jimmy Jack Funk in 5:30 (★★); The Dream Team (Greg Valentine and Brutus Beefcake) vs. The Islanders (Haku and Tama) ended in a draw in 20:00 (★★★); Dino Bravo defeated Corporal Kirchner in 3:32 (★★); Hulk Hogan defeated Kamala in 7:45 (★★★).

WWF at Spectrum (13-12-86) ★★
13-12-86, Philadelphia, Pennsylvania **WWF**

Steve Lombardi defeated Tony Garea in 5:42 (★★); Butch Reed defeated Sivi Afi in 6:01 (★★); Brutus Beefcake defeated Mike Rotundo in 9:25 (★★); The Honky Tonk Man defeated SD Jones in 7:32 (★★); Dan Spivey defeated Greg Valentine in 6:28 (★★★); Blackjack Mulligan defeated Jimmy Jack Funk in :51 (★); The Hart Foundation (Bret Hart and Jim Neidhart) defeated Pedro Morales and Tito Santana in 10:18 (★★); Junkyard Dog vs. Harley Race ended in a double count out in 7:47 (★★); Hercules defeated Billy Jack Haynes by DQ in 7:23 (★★); Jose Luis Rivera defeated Iron Mike Sharpe in 1:43 (★★); Kamala defeated Corporal Kirchner in 2:42 (★★); Hulk Hogan defeated Paul Orndorff in a Steel Cage Match in 8:04 (★★★★).

Brawl In St. Paul ★★★★
25-12-86, St. Paul, Minnesota **AWA**

Earthquake Ferris defeated Brian Knobbs in 4:25 (★★); Boris Zhukov defeated Steve Olsonoski in 13:09 (★★); Greg Gagne, Leon White and Scott Hall vs. Larry Zbyszko, Mr. Saito and The Super Ninja ended in a no contest in 16:08 (★★★); Nick Bockwinkel defeated Curt Hennig by DQ in 19:22 (★★★★); Col. DeBeers defeated Jimmy Snuka by DQ in 3:45 (★★); The Midnight Rockers (Marty Jannetty and Shawn Michaels) defeated Buddy Rose and Doug Somers in a Steel Cage Match in 17:21 (★★★★).

WWF at Madison Square Garden (26-12-86) ★★
26-12-86, New York City, New York **WWF**

Paul Roma defeated Terry Gibbs in 9:22 (★★); The Hart Foundation (Bret Hart and Jim Neidhart) defeated Corporal Kirchner and Dick Slater in 12:36 (★★★); The Fabulous Moolah defeated Leilani Kai in 10:10 (★★); Pedro Morales defeated Dino Bravo by DQ in 14:24 (★★); Hulk Hogan defeated Kamala by DQ in 6:39 (★★); Jose Luis Rivera defeated Steve Lombardi in 2:37 (★★); Hillbilly Jim defeated Mr. Fuji in a Tuxedo Match in 4:00 (★); The Honky Tonk Man defeated Sivi Afi in 7:02 (★★); Hercules defeated Tito Santana in 15:40 (★★★★); Blackjack Mulligan defeated Nikolai Volkoff in :33 (★).

WWF at Boston Garden (03-01-87) ★★
03-01-87, Boston, Massachusetts **WWF**

Dan Spivey defeated Jimmy Jack Funk in 7:05 (★★); Don Muraco defeated Lanny Poffo in 6:47 (★★); Greg Valentine defeated Dick Slater in 13:05 (★★★); Tama defeated Scott McGhee in 8:48 (★★); Randy Savage defeated Bruno Sammartino via count out in 6:01 (★★★); Sika defeated Corporal Kirchner in 7:47 (★★); Mike Rotundo defeated Pete Doherty in 5:43 (★★); Blackjack Mulligan defeated Brutus Beefcake in 2:17 (★★); Hillbilly Jim defeated Jim Neidhart by DQ in 6:56 (★★); Blackjack Mulligan won a Bunkhouse Battle Royal in 7:46 (★★★).

Saturday Night's Main Event IX ★★★★
03-01-87, Hartford, Connecticut **WWF**

Hulk Hogan defeated Paul Orndorff in a Steel Cage Match in 15:10 (★★★★); Randy Savage defeated George Steele in 10:00 (★★); Junkyard Dog defeated Harley Race by DQ in 4:33 (★★); Adrian Adonis defeated Roddy Piper via count out in 3:35 (★★); Blackjack Mulligan defeated Jimmy Jack Funk in 2:31 (★★).

WWF at Spectrum (10-01-87) ★★★
10-01-87, Philadelphia, Pennsylvania **WWF**

Scott McGhee defeated Terry Gibbs in 8:56 (★★); Koko B. Ware vs. Don Muraco ended in a draw in 16:50 (★★★); The Dream Team (Greg Valentine and Brutus Beefcake) defeated The US Express (Dan Spivey and Mike Rotundo) in 15:43 (★★★); The Honky Tonk Man defeated George Steele in 6:14 (★★); Dino Bravo defeated Paul Roma in 6:10 (★★); King Kong Bundy and Jake Roberts ended in a double count out in 6:58 (★★★); Davey Boy Smith and Junkyard Dog defeated The Hart Foundation (Bret Hart and Jim Neidhart) in 14:48 (★★★); Jose Luis Rivera defeated Barry O in 3:49 (★★); Randy Savage defeated Ricky Steamboat in 6:10 (★★★).

WWF at Maple Leaf Gardens (11-01-87) ★★
11-01-87, Toronto, Canada **WWF**

Jose Luis Rivera defeated Terry Gibbs in 7:57 (★★); Don Muraco vs. Koko B. Ware ended in a draw in 20:00 (★★★); The Dream Team (Greg Valentine and Brutus Beefcake) defeated The US Express (Mike Rotundo and Dan Spivey) in 17:21 (★★★); George Steele defeated Johnny V by DQ in 1:59 (★); Dino Bravo defeated Scott McGhee in 5:54 (★★); Jake Roberts vs. King Kong Bundy ended in a double count out in 6:43 (★★); Paul Roma defeated Barry O in 6:28 (★★); Davey Boy Smith and Junkyard Dog defeated The Hart Foundation (Bret Hart and Jim Neidhart) in 14:44 (★★★); Hulk Hogan defeated Kamala in a Steel Cage Match in 6:20 (★★★★).

WWF at Madison Square Garden (19-01-87) ★★
19-01-87, New York City, New York **WWF**

Brad Rheingans defeated Frenchy Martin in 16:49 (★★); The Can-Am Connection (Rick Martel and Tom Zenk) defeated The Dream Team (Greg Valentine and Brutus Beefcake) in 18:36 (★★★); Ron Bass defeated SD Jones in 6:56 (★★); Paul Orndorff defeated George Steele by DQ in 6:00 (★★); Tiger Chung Lee defeated Jerry Allen in 7:34 (★★); Hulk Hogan defeated Kamala in a No DQ Match in 7:56 (★★★); Lanny Poffo defeated The Red Demon in 14:38 (★★); Junkyard Dog defeated Harley Race via count out in 5:27 (★★); Billy Jack Haynes and Davey Boy Smith defeated The Hart Foundation (Bret Hart and Jim Neidhart) in 9:26 (★★★).

WWF at Boston Garden (07-02-87) ★★
07-02-87, Boston, Massachusetts **WWF**

Tama defeated Frenchy Martin in 4:42 (★★); Koko B. Ware defeated The Red Demon in 9:52 (★★); Hercules defeated Billy Jack Haynes in 10:19 (★★); Haku defeated Terry Gibbs in 4:28 (★★); The Rougeau Brothers (Jacques Rougeau and Raymond Rougeau) defeated The Hart Foundation (Bret Hart and Jim Neidhart) in 11:37 (★★★); King Kong Bundy defeated Pete Doherty by DQ in 3:02 (★); Ricky Steamboat defeated Sika in 4:06 (★★); Dino Bravo defeated SD Jones in 7:29 (★★); Bruno Sammartino defeated Randy Savage by DQ in a Lumberjack Match in 4:14 (★★★).

WWF at Spectrum (14-02-87) ★★
14-02-87, Philadelphia, Pennsylvania **WWF**

Paul Roma vs. Steve Lombardi ended in a draw in 18:43 (★★); Dino Bravo defeated Pedro Morales in 8:41 (★★); Billy Jack Haynes vs. Hercules ended in a double count out in 7:59 (★★); The Islanders (Haku and Tama) defeated The Rougeau Brothers (Jacques Rougeau and Raymond Rougeau) in 7:53 (★★★); Hulk Hogan defeated Kamala by DQ in 6:23 (★★★); Sika defeated SD Jones in 3:41 (★★); The Honky Tonk Man defeated Koko B. Ware in 5:14 (★★); Brad Rheingans defeated Moondog Spot in 4:03 (★★); Randy Savage defeated Ricky Steamboat in 7:42 (★★★).

WWF at Maple Leaf Gardens (15-02-87) ★★★
15-02-87, Toronto, Canada **WWF**

Ron Bass defeated SD Jones in 6:53 (★★); Sika defeated Moondog Spot in 6:56 (★★); Corporal Kirchner defeated Johnny K-9 in 11:11 (★★); Roddy Piper defeated Adrian Adonis by DQ in 10:07 (★★★); Paul Orndorff defeated Pedro Morales in 4:29 (★★); Harley Race defeated Junkyard Dog in 6:08 (★★★); Randy Savage defeated Ricky Steamboat in 13:39 (★★★★); The Killer Bees (B. Brian Blair and Jim Brunzell) defeated The Hart Foundation (Bret Hart and Jim Neidhart) in 7:37 (★★★).

WWF at Madison Square Garden (23-02-87) ★★★
23-02-87, New York City, New York **WWF**
Paul Roma defeated Salvatore Bellomo in 12:23 (★★); Demolition (Ax and Smash) defeated The Islanders (Haku and Tama) in 9:13 (★★★); Koko B. Ware defeated Sika in 4:51 (★★); Tito Santana vs. Butch Reed ended in a double DQ in 12:10 (★★★); The Hart Foundation (Bret Hart and Jim Neidhart) defeated The Killer Bees (B. Brian Blair and Jim Brunzell) in 13:52 (★★★); Outback Jack defeated Barry O in 3:33 (★★); Jake Roberts defeated King Kong Bundy via count out in 9:17 (★★); The Honky Tonk Man defeated Pedro Morales in 11:58 (★★★); Roddy Piper, Junkyard Dog and Ricky Steamboat defeated Randy Savage, Adrian Adonis and Harley Race in an Elimination Match in 20:22 (★★★★).

WWF at Boston Garden (07-03-87) ★★
07-03-87, Boston, Massachusetts **WWF**
Pedro Morales defeated Jimmy Jack Funk in 7:26 (★★); Jim Duggan defeated Moondog Spot in 6:22 (★★); Don Muraco and Bob Orton defeated Dan Spivey and Jerry Allen in 11:46 (★★); Ron Bass defeated SD Jones in 10:59 (★★); The Hart Foundation (Bret Hart and Jim Neidhart) defeated The Rougeau Brothers (Jacques Rougeau and Raymond Rougeau) in 14:50 (★★); Outback Jack defeated Jimmy Jack Funk in :58 (★); Hulk Hogan, Roddy Piper and Billy Jack Haynes defeated Adrian Adonis, Paul Orndorff and Hercules in an Elimination Match in 18:04 (★★★).

WWF at Spectrum (14-03-87) ★★★
14-03-87, Philadelphia, Pennsylvania **WWF**
Paul Roma defeated Steve Lombardi in 9:53 (★★); Butch Reed defeated Dick Slater in 8:17 (★★); Outback Jack defeated Frenchy Martin in 4:58 (★★); Dino Bravo defeated SD Jones in 3:02 (★★); The Hart Foundation (Bret Hart and Jim Neidhart) defeated The Islanders (Haku and Tama) in 18:22 (★★★); Tom Zenk defeated Greg Valentine by DQ in 11:39 (★★); Rick Martel vs. Brutus Beefcake ended in a double count out in 15:35 (★★★); Hulk Hogan and Roddy Piper defeated Kamala and Paul Orndorff in 8:53 (★★★).

Saturday Night's Main Event X ★★★
14-03-87, Detroit, Michigan **WWF**
Randy Savage defeated George Steele via count out in 4:20 (★★); Hercules won a Battle Royal in 11:22 (★★); King Kong Bundy defeated Jake Roberts by DQ in 6:14 (★★); The Hart Foundation (Bret Hart and Jim Neidhart) defeated Tito Santana and Dan Spivey in 5:31 (★★); Ricky Steamboat defeated The Iron Sheik in 3:29 (★★).

WWF at Maple Leaf Gardens (15-03-87) ★★★
15-03-87, Toronto, Canada **WWF**
Sivi Afi defeated The Red Demon in 4:45 (★★); Hillbilly Jim defeated Dino Bravo by DQ in 5:35 (★★); The Killer Bees (B. Brian Blair and Jim Brunzell) defeated Kamala and Sika in 7:32 (★★); The Can-Am Connection (Rick Martel and Tom Zenk) defeated Jerry Allen and Danny Spivey in 10:31 (★★); Demolition (Ax and Smash) defeated The British Bulldogs (Davey Boy Smith and Dynamite Kid) by DQ in 4:50 (★★); Paul Orndorff and King Kong Bundy defeated Don Muraco and Bob Orton in 6:20 (★★); Demolition (Ax and Smash) defeated The Can-Am Connection (Rick Martel and Tom Zenk) via count out in 9:21 (★★); The Killer Bees (B. Brian Blair and Jim Brunzell) defeated Paul Orndorff and King Kong Bundy in 4:22 (★★); The Killer Bees (B. Brian Blair and Jim Brunzell) defeated Demolition (Ax and Smash) to win the Frank Tunney Sr. Memorial Tournament in 6:16 (★★★); The Hart Foundation (Bret Hart and Jim Neidhart) defeated The Killer Bees (B. Brian Blair and Jim Brunzell) in 9:01 (★★★).

WWF at London Gardens (16-03-87) ★★
16-03-87, London, Canada **WWF**
SD Jones defeated The Red Demon in 8:11 (★★); Sivi Afi defeated Ivan McDonald in 5:55 (★★); Jose Luis Rivera defeated Johnny K-9 in 5:23 (★★); Tom Magee defeated Terry Gibbs in 5:14 (★★); Ron Bass defeated Lanny Poffo in 14:09 (★★★); Demolition (Ax and Smash) defeated Jerry Allen and Danny Spivey in 10:48 (★★); Koko B. Ware vs. Danny Davis ended in a draw in 16:58 (★★); The British Bulldogs (Davey Boy Smith and Dynamite Kid) defeated The Hart Foundation (Bret Hart and Jim Neidhart) by DQ in 6:19 (★★★).

WrestleMania III ★★★★★
29-03-87, Pontiac, Michigan **WWF**
The Can-Am Connection (Rick Martel and Tom Zenk) defeated Bob Orton and Don Muraco in 5:37 (★★); Billy Jack Haynes vs. Hercules went to a double count out in 7:44 (★★); Hillbilly Jim, Haiti Kid and Little Beaver defeated King Kong Bundy, Little Tokyo and Lord Littlebrook by DQ in 4:20 (★★); Harley Race defeated Junkyard Dog in a Loser Must Bow Match in 3:22 (★★); The Dream Team (Greg Valentine and Brutus Beefcake) defeated The Rougeau Brothers (Jacques Rougeau and Raymond Rougeau) in 4:11 (★★); Roddy Piper defeated Adrian Adonis in a Hair vs. Hair Match in 6:55 (★★★); Danny Davis and The Hart Foundation (Bret Hart and Jim Neidhart) defeated Tito Santana and The British Bulldogs (Davey Boy Smith and Dynamite Kid) in 8:52 (★★★); Butch Reed defeated Koko B. Ware in 3:39 (★★); Ricky Steamboat defeated Randy Savage to win the WWF Intercontinental Title in 14:35 (★★★★★); The Honky Tonk Man defeated Jake Roberts in 7:23 (★★★); The Iron Sheik and Nikolai Volkoff defeated The Killer Bees (B. Brian Blair and Jim Brunzell) in 5:44 (★★); Hulk Hogan defeated Andre the Giant in 11:34 (★★★★).

Crockett Cup '87 ★★★
10-04-87/11-04-87, Baltimore, Maryland **NWA**
Bill Dundee and The Barbarian defeated Tim Horner and Mike Rotundo in 3:05 [shown] (★★); Shaska Whatley and Teijho Khan defeated Jimmy Valiant and LazorTron by DQ in 3:11 (★★); Brad Armstrong and Bob Armstrong defeated The Russians (Ivan Koloff and Vladimir Petrov) by DQ in 1:58 [aired] (★★); The Road Warriors (Hawk and Animal) defeated Shaska Whatley and Teijho Khan in 3:47 [aired] (★★); The Midnight Express (Bobby Eaton and Stan Lane) defeated Jimmy Garvin and Ronnie Garvin via count out in 6:27 (★★★); Brad Armstrong and Bob Armstrong defeated Kevin Sullivan and Arn Anderson in 5:25 (★★); Tully Blanchard and Lex Luger defeated The MOD Squad (Basher and Spike) in 6:35 (★★); Ole Anderson defeated Big Bubba Rogers in a Last Man Standing Steel Cage Match in 5:10 [aired] (★★); Tully Blanchard and Lex Luger defeated Brad Armstrong and Bob Armstrong in 17:47 (★★★★); The Midnight Express (Bobby Eaton and Stan Lane) defeated The Road Warriors (Hawk and Animal) by DQ in 11:04 (★★★★); The Super Powers (Dusty Rhodes and Nikita Koloff) defeated Manny Fernandez and Rick Rude in 9:37 (★★); Tully Blanchard and Lex Luger defeated Giant Baba and Isao Takagi in 8:32 (★★★); The Super Powers (Dusty Rhodes and Nikita Koloff) defeated The Midnight Express (Bobby Eaton and Stan Lane) in 9:56 (★★); Ric Flair defeated Barry Windham in 25:50 (★★★★★); The Super Powers (Dusty Rhodes and Nikita Koloff) defeated Tully Blanchard and Lex Luger to win the Crockett Cup in 17:14 (★★★).

WWF at Boston Garden (02-05-87) ★★
02-05-87, Boston, Massachusetts **WWF**
Nick Kiniski defeated Frenchy Martin in 11:31 (★★); Demolition (Ax and Smash) defeated The Islanders (Haku and Tama) in 9:32 (★★); Iron Mike Sharpe defeated Sivi Afi in 9:37 (★★); Hulk Hogan defeated Harley Race in 9:17 (★★★); Sika defeated Pete Doherty in 3:07 (★); Brutus Beefcake defeated Johnny V in 3:24 (★★); Ken Patera defeated The Honky Tonk Man in 9:22 (★★); The Hart Foundation (Bret Hart and Jim Neidhart) defeated The British Bulldogs (Davey Boy Smith and Dynamite Kid) in 7:47 (★★).

Saturday Night's Main Event XI ★★★★
02-05-87, Notre Dame, Indiana **WWF**
Kamala defeated Jake Roberts in 4:25 (★★); Randy Savage defeated George Steele in a Lumberjack Match in 6:44 (★★); The British Bulldogs (Davey Boy Smith and Dynamite Kid) defeated The Hart Foundation (Bret Hart and Jim Neidhart) by DQ in a Two Out Of Three Falls Match in 9:48 (★★★★); Ricky Steamboat defeated Hercules by DQ in 6:42 (★★★); The Can-Am Connection (Rick Martel and Tom Zenk) defeated Nikolai Volkoff and The Iron Sheik in 4:45 (★★★).

SuperClash II ★★
02-05-87, San Francisco, California **AWA**
Sheik Adnan El-Kaissey defeated Buck Zumhofe in 10:45 (★★); DJ Peterson vs. The Super Ninja went to a time limit draw in 15:00 (★★); Sherri Martel defeated Madusa Micelli in 11:45 (★★); Curt Hennig defeated Nick Bockwinkel to win the AWA World Heavyweight Title in 24:00 (★★★★); Ray Stevens and The Midnight Rockers (Shawn Michaels and Marty Jannetty)

defeated **Buddy Wolfe**, **Kevin Kelly** and **Doug Somers** in 18:00 (★★); **Jerry Blackwell** defeated **Boris Zhukov** in 12:30 (★); **Jimmy Snuka** and **Russ Francis** defeated **The Terrorist** and **The Mercenary** in 11:26 (★★).

4th David Von Erich Memorial Parade Of Champions ★
03-05-87, Irving, Texas WCCW
Matt Borne and **Scott Casey** defeated **Black Bart** and **Jack Victory** in 7:02 (★★); **Steve Doll** defeated **Tim Brooks** in 7:39 (★★); **Cousin Junior** defeated **The Grappler** in 4:47 (★★); **Red River Jack** and **Spike Huber** defeated **Abdullah the Butcher** and **Eli The Eliminator** in 6:28 (★★); **Red River Jack** vs. **Gary Hart** ended in a double count out in 1:56 (★); **Mil Mascaras** defeated **Al Madril** in 7:04 (★★); **Kevin Von Erich** vs. **Nord the Barbarian** ended in a double count out in 5:11 (★★); **The Fantastics** (**Tommy Rogers** and **Bobby Fulton**) and **Steve Simpson** defeated **The Rock-n-Roll RPMs** (**Mike Davis** and **Tommy Lane**) and **Eric Embry** in a Scaffold Match in 5:20 (★); **Bruiser Brody** defeated **Jeep Swenson** in 4:26 (★★).

WWF at Spectrum (09-05-87) ★★★
09-05-87, Philadelphia, Pennsylvania WWF
Pedro Morales defeated **Steve Lombardi** in 5:44 (★★); **The Young Stallions** (**Paul Roma** and **Jim Powers**) defeated **The Shadows** (**Shadow #1** and **Shadow #2**) in 16:53 (★★★); **Kamala** defeated **George Steele** via count out in 6:00 (★★); **Hulk Hogan** defeated **Harley Race** in 8:47 (★★★); **Billy Jack Haynes** defeated **The Honky Tonk Man** in 13:28 (★★★); **Nikolai Volkoff** defeated **Corporal Kirchner** in 10:17 (★★); **Danny Davis** defeated **Koko B. Ware** in 14:15 (★★★); **The Rougeau Brothers** (**Jacques Rougeau** and **Raymond Rougeau**) defeated **The Dream Team** (**Greg Valentine** and **Dino Bravo**) in 10:23 (★★).

WWF at Maple Leaf Gardens (17-05-87) ★★
17-05-87, Toronto, Canada WWF
Sam Houston defeated **Johnny K-9** in 7:41 (★★); **Bob Orton** defeated **Frankie Lane** in 4:42 (★★); **Outback Jack** defeated **Frenchy Martin** in 4:21 (★★); **Don Muraco** defeated **Lanny Poffo** in 6:50 (★★★); **Nikolai Volkoff** defeated **Corporal Kirchner** in 13:05 (★★); **Hulk Hogan** defeated **Harley Race** in 7:33 (★★★).

WWF at Madison Square Garden (18-05-87) ★★
18-05-87, New York City, New York WWF
Sam Houston defeated **Terry Gibbs** in 7:53 (★★); **The Young Stallions** (**Jim Powers** and **Paul Roma**) defeated **Bob Orton** and **Don Muraco** in 10:31 (★★★); **Danny Davis** defeated **Koko B. Ware** in 13:15 (★★); **Lanny Poffo** defeated **Dave Barbie** in 8:05 (★); **Hulk Hogan** defeated **Harley Race** in 7:54 (★★★); **Debbie Combs** defeated **The Fabulous Moolah** via count out in 8:49 (★★); **Demolition** (**Ax** and **Smash**) defeated **The Killer Bees** (**B. Brian Blair** and **Jim Brunzell**) in 16:09 (★★★); **Ron Bass** defeated **Jose Luis Rivera** in 9:37 (★★); **Ken Patera** defeated **The Honky Tonk Man** by DQ in 9:56 (★★★).

WWF at Boston Garden (06-06-87) ★★
06-06-87, Boston, Massachusetts WWF
Jose Estrada defeated **Sivi Afi** in 9:45 (★★); **The Can-Am Connection** (**Tom Zenk** and **Rick Martel**) defeated **Demolition** (**Ax** and **Smash**) in 12:43 (★★★); **SD Jones** defeated **Pete Doherty** in 6:42 (★★); **The Honky Tonk Man** defeated **Koko B. Ware** in 9:32 (★★); **Tiger Chung Lee** defeated **Brad Rheingans** in 5:51 (★★); **George Steele** defeated **Danny Davis** in 9:43 (★★); **Lanny Poffo** defeated **Frenchy Martin** in 4:42 (★★); **Hulk Hogan** defeated **Harley Race** in a Texas Death Match in 9:46 (★★★).

WWF at Madison Square Garden (14-06-87) ★★★
14-06-87, New York City, New York WWF
The Can-Am Connection (**Rick Martel** and **Tom Zenk**) defeated **The Shadows** (**Shadow #1** and **Shadow #2**) in 18:56 (★★); **Hercules** vs. **Billy Jack Haynes** ended in a draw in 22:55 (★★); **The Islanders** (**Haku** and **Tama**) defeated **The Young Stallions** (**Paul Roma** and **Jim Powers**) in 19:02 (★★★); **Paul Orndorff** defeated **Junkyard Dog** in 9:47 (★★★); **Hulk Hogan** defeated **Harley Race** in a Texas Death Match in 9:56 (★★★★); **Outback Jack** defeated **Jose Estrada** in 4:47 (★★); **Billy Jack Haynes** and **The British Bulldogs** (**Davey Boy Smith** and **Dynamite Kid**) defeated **Danny Davis** and **The Hart Foundation** (**Bret Hart** and **Jim Neidhart**) in 18:08 (★★★).

WWF at Spectrum (20-06-87) ★★
20-06-87, Philadelphia, Pennsylvania WWF
Jerry Allen defeated **Terry Gibbs** in 10:53 (★★); **Outback Jack** defeated **Jose Estrada** in 8:24 (★★); **The Young Stallions** (**Paul Roma** and **Jim Powers**) defeated **The Shadows** (**Shadow #1** and **Shadow #2**) in 14:28 (★★); **Tito Santana** defeated **Ron Bass** by DQ in 11:20 (★★★); **Paul Orndorff** vs. **Billy Jack Haynes** ended in a draw in 21:01 (★★★); **The Fabulous Moolah** defeated **Debbie Combs** in 6:37 (★★); **Kamala** defeated **Ricky Steamboat** in 6:01 (★★); **Hulk Hogan** and **Ken Patera** defeated **Harley Race** and **Hercules** in 11:24 (★★★).

WWF at Boston Garden (11-07-87) ★★
11-07-87, Boston, Massachusetts WWF
Jim Powers defeated **Shadow #2** in 11:07 (★★); **Dino Bravo** defeated **Scott Casey** in 5:59 (★★); **Bob Orton** defeated **Jerry Allen** in 6:26 (★★); **Tito Santana** defeated **Don Muraco** in 8:22 (★★); **Bruno Sammartino** defeated **The Honky Tonk Man** via count out in 11:17 (★★★); **One Man Gang** defeated **Jose Luis Rivera** in 4:11 (★★); **Paul Roma** defeated **Shadow #1** in 8:54 (★★); **Brutus Beefcake** defeated **Johnny V** in 3:26 (★★); **Rick Martel** and **Junkyard Dog** defeated **The Islanders** (**Haku** and **Tama**) in 11:22 (★★★).

WWF at Spectrum (18-07-87) ★★
18-07-87, Philadelphia, Pennsylvania WWF
Brady Boone defeated **Barry Horowitz** in 11:36 (★★); **Rick Rude** defeated **Scott Casey** in 11:44 (★★); **Koko B. Ware** defeated **Nikolai Volkoff** in 11:11 (★★); **One Man Gang** defeated **Outback Jack** in 6:04 (★★); **Rick Martel** defeated **Tama** in 15:25 (★★); **Danny Davis** defeated **George Steele** by DQ in 4:58 (★); **Killer Khan** defeated **Lanny Poffo** in 7:02 (★★); **Bruno Sammartino** defeated **The Honky Tonk Man** via count out in 10:55 (★★★).

WWF at Madison Square Garden (25-07-87) ★★★
25-07-87, New York City, New York WWF
Dino Bravo defeated **Brady Boone** in 10:46 (★★); **Rick Martel** defeated **Tama** in 19:47 (★★★); **Butch Reed** defeated **Hillbilly Jim** in 10:58 (★★); **Ricky Steamboat** defeated **The Honky Tonk Man** via count out in 11:39 (★★★★); **Tito Santana** defeated **Nikolai Volkoff** in 8:21 (★★); **Ron Bass** defeated **Outback Jack** in 3:51 (★★); **Brutus Beefcake** defeated **Greg Valentine** by DQ in 13:11 (★★); **Rick Rude** defeated **Jerry Allen** in 7:12 (★★); **The Hart Foundation** (**Bret Hart** and **Jim Neidhart**) defeated **The British Bulldogs** (**Davey Boy Smith** and **Dynamite Kid**) in 10:26 (★★★).

Great American Bash '87 (Miami) ★★★
31-07-87, Miami, Florida NWA
Steve Keirn and **Bugsy McGraw** defeated **The Cuban Connection** (**Ricky Santana** and **The Cuban Assassin**) in 2:28 (★★); **Manny Fernandez** defeated **The Mulkey Brothers** (**Randy Mulkey** and **Bill Mulkey**) in a Handicap Match in 2:16 (★★); **Barry Windham** defeated **Incubus** in 4:01 (★★); **The Sheepherders** (**Butch Miller** and **Luke Williams**) vs. **Jimmy Garvin** and **Ron Garvin** ended in a double DQ in 7:40 (★★★); **Mike Rotundo** defeated **Ivan Koloff** in 2:32 (★★); **Kevin Sullivan** defeated **Dory Funk Jr.** in a Texas Death Match in 5:22 (★★★); **The Rock 'n' Roll Express** (**Ricky Morton** and **Robert Gibson**) defeated **The Midnight Express** (**Bobby Eaton** and **Stan Lane**) by DQ in 6:42 (★★★); **Dusty Rhodes**, **Nikita Koloff**, **The Road Warriors** (**Hawk** and **Animal**) and **Paul Ellering** defeated **Ric Flair**, **Arn Anderson**, **Tully Blanchard**, **Lex Luger** and **The War Machine** in a Wargames Match in 20:07 (★★★★★).

WWF at Boston Garden (15-08-87) ★★
15-08-87, Boston, Massachusetts WWF
The Dingo Warrior defeated **Barry Horowitz** in 4:42 (★★); **Paul Orndorff** defeated **Nikolai Volkoff** in 8:57 (★★); **Ted DiBiase** defeated **Sivi Afi** in 6:28 (★★); **Bruno Sammartino**, **Jake Roberts** and **Tito Santana** defeated **The Honky Tonk Man** and **The Hart Foundation** (**Bret Hart** and **Jim Neidhart**) in an Elimination Match in 15:05 (★★★★); **Iron Mike Sharpe** defeated **Brady Boone** in 9:34 (★★); **Hillbilly Jim** defeated **One Man Gang** via count out in 12:47 (★★); **The Rougeau Brothers** (**Jacques Rougeau** and **Raymond Rougeau**) defeated **Johnny V** and **Dino Bravo** in 8:28 (★★).

WWF at Spectrum (15-08-87) ★★
15-08-87, Philadelphia, Pennsylvania **WWF**

Jerry Allen defeated Jose Estrada in 11:59 (★★); Rick Rude defeated SD Jones in 10:22 (★★); Brutus Beefcake defeated Greg Valentine by DQ in 12:55 (★★); Koko B. Ware defeated Kamala via count out in 6:07 (★★); Haku defeated Rick Martel in 14:31 (★★★); Brad Rheingans defeated Terry Gibbs in 5:23 (★★); Superstar Billy Graham defeated Hercules in a Whipping Match in 6:50 (★★).

WWF at Madison Square Garden (22-08-87) ★★★
22-08-87, New York City, New York **WWF**

Tama defeated Scott Casey in 11:23 (★★); Tito Santana vs. Ron Bass ended in a draw in 19:45 (★★★★); Sensational Sherri defeated Velvet McIntyre in 14:21 (★★★); Haku defeated Rick Martel in 9:19 (★★★); The Honky Tonk Man defeated Ricky Steamboat in a Lumberjack Match in 11:06 (★★★); Superstar Billy Graham vs. Butch Reed ended in a double DQ in 8:56 (★★); Lanny Poffo defeated Jose Estrada in 7:42 (★★); Demolition (Ax and Smash) defeated Junkyard Dog and George Steele by DQ in 6:10 (★★).

WWF at Sam Houston Coliseum (28-08-87) ★★★
28-08-87, Houston, Texas **WWF**

Sam Houston defeated Steve Lombardi in 13:56 (★★); Bruno Sammartino defeated Hercules via count out in 6:47 (★★); Brutus Beefcake defeated Johnny V in a Hair vs. Hair Match in 6:36 (★★); Tom Prichard defeated Mark Lewin in 2:58 (★★); Hulk Hogan defeated One Man Gang in 10:13 (★★★); Sensational Sherri defeated The Fabulous Moolah in 6:47 (★★); Junkyard Dog and Tony Atlas defeated Sika and Kamala in 5:41 (★★); Ted Dibiase defeated Jim Duggan in 8:30 (★★★); Mil Mascaras and Tito Santana defeated Demolition (Ax and Smash) by DQ in 5:56 (★★★).

WWF at Boston Garden (12-09-87) ★★★
12-09-87, Boston, Massachusetts **WWF**

Pete Doherty defeated Lanny Poffo in 10:07 (★★★); Scott Casey and SD Jones defeated The Shadows (Shadow #1 and Shadow #2) in 11:39 (★★); Steve Lombardi defeated Sivi Afi in 8:32 (★★); Hulk Hogan defeated Killer Khan in 9:39 (★★★); Hercules defeated Davey Boy Smith in 10:35 (★★★); Ted DiBiase defeated Brutus Beefcake in 14:04 (★★★); The Hart Foundation (Bret Hart and Jim Neidhart) defeated Mr. Fuji and Sika in 7:04 (★★); George Steele defeated Harley Race in 7:02 (★★★).

WWF at Spectrum (18-09-87) ★★★
18-09-87, Philadelphia, Pennsylvania **WWF**

Barry Horowitz defeated Lanny Poffo in 12:34 (★★★); Frenchy Martin defeated SD Jones in 9:46 (★★); Randy Savage defeated Harley Race in 8:24 (★★★); Scott Casey defeated Iron Mike Sharpe in 9:01 (★★); Brutus Beefcake defeated Rick Rude in 12:45 (★★★); Ted DiBiase defeated Junkyard Dog in 8:49 (★★★); The Hart Foundation (Bret Hart and Jim Neidhart) defeated The Killer Bees (B. Brian Blair and Jim Brunzell) in 13:28 (★★★); Outback Jack defeated Tiger Chung Lee in 3:06 (★★); Hulk Hogan defeated Killer Khan in 9:15 (★★★).

WWF at Madison Square Garden (21-09-87) ★★★
21-09-87, New York City, New York **WWF**

Scott Casey defeated Steve Lombardi in 11:32 (★★); Don Muraco defeated Bob Orton in 11:42 (★★★); The Islanders (Haku and Tama) defeated Strike Force (Rick Martel and Tito Santana) in 13:58 (★★★); Tiger Chung Lee defeated Brad Rheingans in 5:01 (★★); Hulk Hogan vs. One Man Gang ended in a double count out in 9:09 (★★); The Rougeau Brothers (Jacques Rougeau and Raymond Rougeau) vs. The Dream Team (Greg Valentine and Dino Bravo) ended in a draw in 17:07 (★★★); George Steele defeated Sika by DQ in 3:00 (★★); Harley Race defeated Hillbilly Jim in 8:37 (★★); Randy Savage defeated The Honky Tonk Man in 11:56 (★★★★),

WWF at Boston Garden (03-10-87) ★★
03-10-87, Boston, Massachusetts **WWF**

Jerry Allen defeated Pete Doherty by DQ in 7:23 (★); Dan Spivey defeated SD Jones in 7:08 (★★); Butch Reed defeated Superstar Billy Graham in 7:56 (★★); Don Muraco defeated Bob Orton in 8:15 (★★); Brady Boone defeated Jose Estrada in 9:44 (★★); Bam Bam Bigelow defeated Sika in 6:48 (★★); Nikolai Volkoff defeated Outback Jack in 4:28 (★); Randy Savage defeated Hercules in 7:25 (★★); The Islanders (Haku and Tama) defeated Strike Force (Rick Martel and Tito Santana) in 10:45 (★★★).

Saturday Night's Main Event XII ★★★★
03-10-87, Hershey, Pennsylvania **WWF**

Randy Savage defeated The Honky Tonk Man by DQ in 15:18 (★★★); Hulk Hogan defeated Sika in 10:00 (★★); King Kong Bundy defeated Paul Orndorff in 10:00 (★★); The Hart Foundation (Bret Hart and Jim Neidhart) defeated The Young Stallions (Paul Roma and Jim Powers) in 4:35 (★★).

WWF at Sam Houston Coliseum (09-10-87) ★★★
09-10-87, Houston, Texas **WWF**

Sam Houston defeated Barry Horowitz in 8:12 (★★); Bam Bam Bigelow defeated Nikolai Volkoff in 3:35 (★★); Boris Zhukov defeated SD Jones in 5:28 (★★); Ted DiBiase defeated Hulk Hogan via count out in 9:52 (★★★); The Honky Tonk Man defeated Hillbilly Jim in 7:20 (★★); Brutus Beefcake defeated Greg Valentine in 8:30 (★★); Randy Savage defeated Killer Khan in 4:40 (★★); Demolition (Ax and Smash) defeated The Killer Bees (B. Brian Blair and Jim Brunzell) 2-1 in a Best Two Out Of Three Falls Match in 17:49 (★★★★).

WWF at Spectrum (10-10-87) ★★
10-10-87, Philadelphia, Pennsylvania **WWF**

Sam Houston defeated Barry Horowitz in 13:06 (★★); Brutus Beefcake defeated Danny Davis in 11:11 (★★); Butch Reed defeated Superstar Billy Graham in 7:08 (★★); Bob Orton defeated Sivi Afi in 11:20 (★★); Nikolai Volkoff defeated Jim Powers in 10:32 (★★); Boris Zhukov defeated Hillbilly Jim in 9:07 (★★); Bam Bam Bigelow defeated King Kong Bundy in 5:25 (★★); Jerry Allen defeated Frenchy Martin in 5:35 (★★); The Islanders (Haku and Tama) defeated Strike Force (Tito Santana and Rick Martel) in 16:21 (★★★).

WWF at Madison Square Garden (16-10-87) ★★★
16-10-87, New York City, New York **WWF**

Outback Jack defeated Jose Estrada in 9:44 (★★); The Killer Bees (B. Brian Blair and Jim Brunzell) defeated The Dream Team (Dino Bravo and Greg Valentine) in 10:57 (★★★); Ivan Putski defeated Iron Mike Sharpe in 5:34 (★★); Rick Rude defeated Paul Orndorff via count out in 10:41 (★★); Don Muraco defeated Sika in 8:20 (★★); Randy Savage defeated Killer Khan in 10:14 (★★); Superstar Billy Graham defeated Butch Reed in a Steel Cage Match in 10:59 (★★★); Billy Jack Haynes defeated Nikolai Volkoff in 5:27 (★★); Strike Force (Rick Martel and Tito Santana) defeated The Islanders (Haku and Tama) 2-1 in a Best Two Out Of Three Falls Match in 10:27 (★★★★).

4th Cotton Bowl Extravaganza ★★
17-10-87, Dallas, Texas **WCCW**

Mil Mascaras, Al Madril and Manuel Villalobos defeated The Thumper, Cowboy Tony and Vince Apollo in 3:43 (★★); Matt Borne vs. The Iron Sheik ended in a double count out in 9:08 (★★); Eric Embry defeated Shaun Simpson by DQ in 1:52 (★★); Kerry Von Erich vs. Matt Borne ended in a no decision in a Workout Match in 2:04 (★★); Kerry Von Erich vs. Frankie Lancaster ended in a no decision in a Workout Match in 2:02 (★★); Kerry Von Erich defeated Tim Brooks in a Workout Match in 1:44 (★★); Kevin Von Erich defeated Al Perez to win the WCCW World Heavyweight Title in 9:52 (★★★).

WWF at Bercy Stadium (23-10-87) ★★
23-10-87, Paris, France **WWF**

SD Jones defeated Sika in 4:04 (★★); Sensational Sherri defeated Velvet McIntyre in 14:31 (★★★); Jim Duggan defeated The Iron Sheik in 5:54 (★★); King Harley Race defeated Junkyard Dog by DQ in 14:32 (★★); Cowboy Lang defeated Lord Littlebrook in 12:20 (★★); Outback Jack defeated Nikolai Volkoff in 4:29 (★★); The Rougeau Brothers (Jacques Rougeau and Raymond Rougeau) defeated The Dream Team (Greg Valentine and Dino Bravo) in 22:34 (★★★).

WWF at Maple Leaf Gardens (01-11-87) ★★
01-11-87, Toronto, Canada **WWF**

Frenchy Martin defeated Lanny Poffo in 4:17 (★★); Jake Roberts defeated Sika in 7:33 (★★); The Dream Team (Greg Valentine and Dino Bravo) defeated The Young Stallions (Paul Roma and Jim Powers) in 15:19 (★★★); The British Bulldogs (Davey Boy Smith and Dynamite Kid) defeated The Bolsheviks (Nikolai Volkoff and Boris Zhukov) in 13:59 (★★★); Sensational Sherri defeated Debbie Combs in 12:13 (★★); Harley Race defeated Junkyard Dog in 7:52 (★★★); Jim Duggan defeated Bob Orton in 4:42 (★★); Paul Orndorff defeated Rick Rude in a Steel Cage Match in 7:29 (★★).

WWF at Sam Houston Coliseum (06-11-87) ★★
06-11-87, Houston, Texas **WWF**
Danny Spivey defeated Sam Houston in 7:51 (★★); Scott Casey defeated Barry Horowitz in 6:12 (★★); Butch Reed defeated Superstar Billy Graham in 5:39 (★); The Hart Foundation (Bret Hart and Jim Neidhart) defeated The British Bulldogs (Davey Boy Smith and Dynamite Kid) in 9:37 (★★★); Don Muraco defeated Sika in 3:06 (★); Rick Rude defeated Paul Omdorff in 7:11 (★★★); The Ultimate Warrior defeated Rip Oliver in 4:58 (★★); Jim Duggan defeated Harley Race in 7:21 (★★); Strike Force (Rick Martel and Tito Santana) defeated The Islanders (Haku and Tama) in 12:44 (★★); Koko B. Ware defeated Danny Davis in 3:48 (★★); The Honky Tonk Man defeated Randy Savage by DQ in 6:39 (★★★).

WWF at Boston Garden (07-11-87) ★★
07-11-87, Boston, Massachusetts **WWF**
Dino Bravo defeated Brady Boone in 5:07 (★★); The Bolsheviks (Nikolai Volkoff and Boris Zhukov) defeated The Young Stallions (Jim Powers and Paul Roma) in 11:24 (★★); Brutus Beefcake defeated Greg Valentine in 10:11 (★★); Bam Bam Bigelow defeated Killer Khan in 7:24 (★★); The Honky Tonk Man defeated Randy Savage in 7:26 (★★); Demolition (Ax and Smash) vs. Ken Patera and Billy Jack Haynes ended in a double DQ in 7:21 (★); Hercules defeated Ivan Putski in 5:45 (★); Virgil defeated Junkyard Dog in 2:53 (★); Strike Force (Rick Martel and Tito Santana) defeated The Islanders (Haku and Tama) in 10:09 (★★).

WWF at Spectrum (07-11-87) ★★
07-11-87, Philadelphia, Pennsylvania **WWF**
Dino Bravo defeated Brady Boone in 6:31 (★★); The Bolsheviks (Nikolai Volkoff and Boris Zhukov) defeated The Young Stallions (Jim Powers and Paul Roma) in 12:43 (★★★); Bam Bam Bigelow defeated Killer Khan in 7:26 (★★); Hercules defeated Junkyard Dog in 7:57 (★); Strike Force (Rick Martel and Tito Santana) vs. The Islanders (Haku and Tama) ended in a double DQ in 9:41 (★★★); Brutus Beefcake defeated Virgil in 2:57 (★★); Demolition (Ax and Smash) defeated Ken Patera and Billy Jack Haynes in 8:02 (★★); Greg Valentine defeated Ivan Putski in 8:14 (★★); The Honky Tonk Man defeated Randy Savage via count out in 8:18 (★★★).

WWF at Madison Square Garden (24-11-87) ★★★
24-11-87, New York City, New York **WWF**
The Ultimate Warrior defeated Frenchy Martin in 4:38 (★★); The Glamour Girls (Judy Martin and Leilani Kai) defeated The Jumping Bomb Angels (Noriyo Tateno and Itsuki Yamazaki) in 13:59 (★★★★); Rick Rude defeated Paul Omdorff in 8:44 (★★); The Killer Bees (B. Brian Blair and Jim Brunzell) defeated The Bolsheviks (Boris Zhukov and Nikolai Volkoff) in 20:26 (★★); The Honky Tonk Man defeated Randy Savage via count out in 13:24 (★★★); Jake Roberts defeated Danny Davis in 7:22 (★★); Strike Force (Tito Santana and Rick Martel) defeated The Hart Foundation (Bret Hart and Jim Neidhart) by DQ in 18:18 (★★★★); Ted DiBiase defeated Ivan Putski in 3:00 (★); Bam Bam Bigelow defeated King Kong Bundy in 3:22 (★★).

Starrcade '87 ★★
26-11-87, Chicago, Illinois **NWA**
Eddie Gilbert, Larry Zbyszko and Rick Steiner vs. Jimmy Garvin, Michael Hayes and Sting went to a time limit draw in 15:00 (★); Steve Williams defeated Barry Windham in 6:50 (★★); The Rock 'n' Roll Express (Ricky Morton and Robert Gibson) defeated The Midnight Express (Bobby Eaton and Stan Lane) in a Skywalkers Match in 10:23 (★★); Nikita Koloff defeated Terry Taylor to unify the NWA World Television Title and UWF World Television Title in 18:58 (★★★); Arn Anderson and Tully Blanchard defeated The Road Warriors (Hawk and Animal) by DQ in 13:27 (★★★); Dusty Rhodes defeated Lex Luger in a Steel Cage Match to win the NWA United States Heavyweight Title in 16:28 (★★); Ric Flair defeated Ron Garvin in a Steel Cage Match to win the NWA World Heavyweight Title in 17:38 (★★★).

Survivor Series '87 ★★★★
26-11-87, Richfield Township, Ohio **WWF**
Brutus Beefcake, Jake Roberts, Jim Duggan, Randy Savage and Ricky Steamboat defeated Danny Davis, Harley Race, Hercules, The Honky Tonk Man and Ron Bass in an Elimination Match in 23:38 (★★★); The Fabulous Moolah, The Jumping Bomb

Angels (Itsuki Yamazaki and Noriyo Tateno), Rockin Robin and Velvet McIntyre defeated Dawn Marie Johnston, Donna Christanello, The Glamour Girls (Leilani Kai and Judy Martin) and Sensational Sherri in an Elimination Match in 20:18 (★★★); The British Bulldogs (Davey Boy Smith and Dynamite Kid), The Killer Bees (B. Brian Blair and Jim Brunzell), The Fabulous Rougeaus (Jacques Rougeau and Raymond Rougeau), Strike Force (Rick Martel and Tito Santana) and The Young Stallions (Jim Powers and Paul Roma) defeated The Bolsheviks (Boris Zhukov and Nikolai Volkoff), Demolition (Ax and Smash), The Dream Team (Dino Bravo and Greg Valentine), The Hart Foundation (Bret Hart and Jim Neidhart) and The Islanders (Haku and Tama) in an Elimination Match in 37:14 (★★★★); Andre the Giant, Butch Reed, King Kong Bundy, One Man Gang and Rick Rude defeated Bam Bam Bigelow, Don Muraco, Hulk Hogan, Ken Patera and Paul Orndorff in an Elimination Match in 24:21 (★★★★).

Saturday Night's Main Event XIII ★★★★
28-11-87, Seattle, Washington **WWF**
George Steele defeated Danny Davis by DQ in 3:49 (★★); Randy Savage defeated Bret Hart in 14:00 (★★★★); King Kong Bundy defeated Hulk Hogan via count out in 14:45 (★★★); Bam Bam Bigelow defeated Hercules in 9:10 (★★).

WWF at Spectrum (05-12-87) ★★
05-12-87, Philadelphia, Pennsylvania **WWF**
Outback Jack defeated Barry Horowitz in 8:08 (★★); The Ultimate Warrior defeated Iron Mike Sharpe in 7:49 (★★); The British Bulldogs (Davey Boy Smith and Dynamite Kid) defeated The Bolsheviks (Nikolai Volkoff and Boris Zhukov) in 13:06 (★★★); Dino Bravo defeated Hillbilly Jim in 9:27 (★★); Jake Roberts defeated Sika in 3:39 (★★); Hulk Hogan defeated One Man Gang in 11:13 (★★★); Strike Force (Rick Martel and Tito Santana) defeated The Islanders (Haku and Tama) in 13:29 (★★); Hercules defeated Junkyard Dog via count out in 5:53 (★); Bam Bam Bigelow defeated King Kong Bundy in 4:48 (★★).

WWF at Sam Houston Coliseum (11-12-87) ★★
11-12-87, Houston, Texas **WWF**
Sam Houston defeated Dusty Wolfe in 8:36 (★★); Hercules defeated Junkyard Dog in 8:15 (★); Demolition (Ax and Smash) defeated Billy Jack Haynes and Brady Boone in 10:22 (★★); Rick Rude defeated Paul Orndorff in 8:59 (★★★); One Man Gang defeated Brutus Beefcake in 9:17 (★); Strike Force (Rick Martel and Tito Santana) defeated The Hart Foundation (Bret Hart and Jim Neidhart) by DQ in 16:19 (★★★); The Ultimate Warrior defeated Iron Mike Sharpe in 5:31 (★★); Ricky Steamboat defeated Ron Bass in 9:26 (★★★); Greg Valentine defeated Ken Johnson in 3:04 (★★); Hulk Hogan defeated Ted Dibiase in 9:30 (★★★).

WWF at Boston Garden (12-12-87) ★★
12-12-87, Boston, Massachusetts **WWF**
The Young Stallions (Jim Powers and Paul Roma) defeated The Conquistadors (Conquistador #1 and Conquistador #2) in 15:41 (★★★); Koko B. Ware defeated Pete Doherty in 7:19 (★★); One Man Gang defeated Brutus Beefcake in 9:38 (★★); Bam Bam Bigelow defeated King Kong Bundy in 4:27 (★★); Jake Roberts defeated Sika in 3:58 (★★); Don Muraco vs. Butch Reed ended in a draw in 18:23 (★★★); The British Bulldogs (Davey Boy Smith and Dynamite Kid) defeated The Bolsheviks (Nikolai Volkoff and Boris Zhukov) in 7:39 (★★★); Jim Duggan defeated Harley Race in 4:40 (★★); Randy Savage defeated The Honky Tonk Man in 6:20 (★★★).

Christmas Night '87 ★★
25-12-87, Minneapolis, Minnesota **AWA**
Nick Kiniski defeated Mitch Snow in 7:10 (★★); Kevin Kelly defeated Alan West in 10:54 (★★); Nord the Barbarian defeated Soldat Ustinov in 5:42 (★★); The Original Midnight Express (Dennis Condrey and Randy Rose) vs. The Midnight Rockers (Marty Jannetty and Shawn Michaels) ended in a draw in 18:11 (★★★); Adrian Adonis defeated Wahoo McDaniel by DQ in 5:50 (★★); Greg Gagne defeated Curt Hennig by DQ in 18:33 (★★★).

Christmas Star Wars '87 ★★

25-12-87, Dallas, Texas **WCCW**

The Missing Link defeated Vince Apollo in 1:17 (★); The Fantastics (Tommy Rogers and Bobby Fulton) defeated Jack Victory and John Tatum in 6:53 (★★); Kerry Von Erich won a 24-Man Pole Battle Royal in 3:23 (★); Steve Simpson, Chris Adams and Kevin Von Erich defeated The Fabulous Freebirds (Terry Gordy and Buddy Roberts) and King Parsons in a Steel Cage Match to win the vacant WCCW Six-Man Tag Team Title in 12:09 (★★★); Al Perez defeated Kerry Von Erich in a Steel Cage Match in 8:04 (★★★).

WWF at Madison Square Garden (26-12-87) ★★★

26-12-87, New York City, New York **WWF**

Iron Mike Sharpe defeated SD Jones in 7:33 (★★); The Rougeau Brothers (Jacques Rougeau and Raymond Rougeau) defeated The Conquistadors (Conquistador #1 and Conquistador #2) in 13:07 (★★★); Jim Duggan defeated Sika in 9:16 (★★); Sensational Sherri defeated Rockin Robin in 7:30 (★★★); Greg Valentine defeated Brutus Beefcake via count out in 11:53 (★★); Ricky Steamboat vs. Rick Rude ended in a draw in 20:28 (★★★★); Dino Bravo defeated Koko B. Ware in 6:38 (★★); The Islanders (Haku and Tama) defeated The Killer Bees (B. Brian Blair and Jim Brunzell) in 10:45 (★★★); Cowboy Lang and Chris Dube defeated Little Tokyo and Lord Littlebrook in 3:19 (★★); Randy Savage defeated The Honky Tonk Man by DQ in 9:29 (★★★).

WWF at Copps Coliseum (29-12-87) ★★

29-12-87, Hamilton, Canada **WWF**

Dan Spivey defeated Lanny Poffo in 8:41 (★★); The Ultimate Warrior defeated Steve Lombardi in 7:43 (★★); Jim Duggan defeated Harley Race in 8:51 (★★★); Bret Hart defeated Paul Roma in 12:59 (★★★); Koko B. Ware defeated Iron Mike Sharpe in 6:03 (★★); Dino Bravo defeated Hillbilly Jim in 4:45 (★★); Demolition (Ax and Smash) defeated Billy Jack Haynes and Ken Patera in 8:23 (★★); Hulk Hogan defeated Butch Reed in 4:02 (★★★).

Saturday Night's Main Event XIV ★★

02-01-88, Landover, Maryland **WWF**

Strike Force (Tito Santana and Rick Martel) defeated The Bolsheviks (Nikolai Volkoff and Boris Zhukov) in a Two Out Of Three Falls Match in 8:40 (★★); Jake Roberts defeated Sika in 3:35 (★★); Hulk Hogan defeated King Kong Bundy in 12:09 (★★); Greg Valentine defeated Koko B. Ware in 7:20 (★★).

WWF at Spectrum (09-01-88) ★★★

09-01-88, Philadelphia, Pennsylvania **WWF**

Dino Bravo defeated SD Jones in 8:19 (★★); The Ultimate Warrior vs. Rick Rude ended in a double count out in 16:25 (★★); Greg Valentine defeated Brutus Beefcake in 11:06 (★★); The Glamour Girls (Judy Martin and Leilani Kai) defeated The Jumping Bomb Angels (Itsuki Yamazaki and Noriyo Tateno) in 15:34 (★★★); The Honky Tonk Man defeated Randy Savage in a Steel Cage Match in 9:13 (★★); The British Bulldogs (Davey Boy Smith and Dynamite Kid) defeated The Conquistadors (Conquistador #1 and Conquistador #2) in 8:07 (★★★); Ted DiBiase defeated Jake Roberts in 8:33 (★★★); Strike Force (Tito Santana and Rick Martel) defeated The Hart Foundation (Bret Hart and Jim Neidhart) by DQ in 11:01 (★★★).

WWF at Boston Garden (09-01-88) ★★★

09-01-88, Boston, Massachusetts **WWF**

Iron Mike Sharpe defeated SD Jones in 8:22 (★★); The British Bulldogs (Davey Boy Smith and Dynamite Kid) defeated The Conquistadors (Conquistador #1 and Conquistador #2) in 13:55 (★★); Ted DiBiase defeated Jake Roberts in 10:58 (★★★); Dino Bravo defeated Jerry Allen in 3:36 (★★); Hulk Hogan defeated Rick Rude in 11:40 (★★★); The Glamour Girls (Judy Martin and Leilani Kai) defeated The Jumping Bomb Angels (Itsuki Yamazaki and Noriyo Tateno) in 10:56 (★★★); Greg Valentine defeated Brutus Beefcake via count out in 8:02 (★★); Strike Force (Rick Martel and Tito Santana) defeated The Hart Foundation (Bret Hart and Jim Neidhart) by DQ in 12:37 (★★★).

Bunkhouse Stampede '88 ★★

24-01-88, Uniondale, New York **NWA**

Nikita Koloff vs. Bobby Eaton went to a time limit draw in 20:00 (★); Larry Zbyszko defeated Barry Windham to win the UWF Western States Title in 19:16 (★★); Hawk defeated Ric Flair by DQ in 21:39 (★★★★); Dusty Rhodes defeated Arn Anderson, The Barbarian, Ivan Koloff, Lex Luger, Animal, Tully Blanchard and The Warlord in a Steel Cage Bunkhouse Stampede in 26:21 (★★).

Royal Rumble '88 ★★

24-01-88, Hamilton, Ontario **WWF**

Ricky Steamboat defeated Rick Rude by DQ in 17:39 (★★); The Jumping Bomb Angels (Noriyo Tateno and Itsuki Yamazaki) defeated The Glamour Girls (Judy Martin and Leilani Kai) in a Two Out Of Three Falls Match to win the WWF Women's Tag Team Title in 15:00 (★★★); Jim Duggan won the 20-Man Royal Rumble Match in 33:00 (★★★); The Islanders (Haku and Tama) defeated The Young Stallions (Paul Roma and Jim Powers) in a Two Out Of Three Falls Match in 14:00 (★★).

WWF at Madison Square Garden (25-01-88) ★★

25-01-88, New York City, New York **WWF**

Scott Casey defeated Jose Estrada in 10:06 (★★); Sam Houston defeated Danny Davis in 8:08 (★★); Butch Reed defeated Junkyard Dog in 5:26 (★★); Omar Atlas defeated Dusty Wolfe in 7:29 (★★); One Man Gang defeated Don Muraco in 8:29 (★★); Hulk Hogan and Bam Bam Bigelow defeated Ted DiBiase and Virgil in 9:26 (★★); The Young Stallions (Paul Roma and Jim Powers) defeated Steve Lombardi and Barry Horowitz in 13:33 (★★); Jim Duggan defeated Harley Race in 10:50 (★★★); Ron Bass defeated Hillbilly Jim in 5:32 (★★); The Islanders (Haku and Tama) defeated The British Bulldogs (Davey Boy Smith and Dynamite Kid) by DQ in 15:35 (★★★).

The Main Event I ★★★★★

05-02-88, Indianapolis, Indiana **WWF**

Randy Savage defeated The Honky Tonk Man via count out in 8:20 (★★★); Andre the Giant defeated Hulk Hogan to win the WWF World Heavyweight Title in 9:05 (★★★★); Strike Force (Tito Santana and Rick Martel) defeated The Hart Foundation (Bret Hart and Jim Neidhart) in 10:03 (★★★).

WWF at Boston Garden (06-02-88) ★★★

06-02-88, Boston, Massachusetts **WWF**

Lanny Poffo defeated Terry Gibbs in 9:48 (★★); The Rougeau Brothers (Jacques Rougeau and Raymond Rougeau) defeated Steve Lombardi and Barry Horowitz in 11:20 (★★); Sam Houston defeated Iron Mike Sharpe in 11:37 (★★★); Sensational Sherri defeated Rockin Robin in 5:32 (★★); Hulk Hogan and Bam Bam Bigelow defeated Ted DiBiase and Andre The Giant in 7:59 (★★); Ricky Steamboat vs. Dino Bravo ended in a double count out in 12:23 (★★★); Danny Davis defeated Brady Boone in 7:59 (★★); One Man Gang defeated George Steele in 4:24 (★★); The Islanders (Haku and Tama) defeated The British Bulldogs (Davey Boy Smith and Dynamite Kid) by DQ in 12:36 (★★★).

WWF at Spectrum (06-02-88) ★★

06-02-88, Philadelphia, Pennsylvania **WWF**

Lanny Poffo defeated Terry Gibbs in 8:59 (★★); One Man Gang defeated George Steele in 4:32 (★★); Ricky Steamboat vs. Dino Bravo ended in a draw in 13:31 (★★★); Danny Davis defeated Sam Houston in 9:41 (★★); Hulk Hogan and Bam Bam Bigelow defeated Andre The Giant and Ted DiBiase in 9:56 (★★★); The Rougeau Brothers (Jacques Rougeau and Raymond Rougeau) defeated Steve Lombardi and Barry Horowitz in 9:08 (★★); Sensational Sherri defeated Rockin Robin in 7:35 (★★); Iron Mike Sharpe defeated Brady Boone in 9:05 (★★); The Islanders (Haku and Tama) defeated The British Bulldogs (Davey Boy Smith and Dynamite Kid) in 13:03 (★★★).

WWF at Madison Square Garden (22-02-88) ★★

22-02-88, New York City, New York **WWF**

The Rougeau Brothers (Jacques Rougeau and Raymond Rougeau) defeated Harley Race and Iron Mike Sharpe in 9:26 (★★); George Steele defeated Sika in 2:49 (★); Ax defeated Ken Patera in 7:27 (★★); Junkyard Dog defeated Smash in 3:44 (★★); Jake Roberts vs. Dino Bravo ended in a draw in 19:23 (★★); Ted DiBiase defeated Bam Bam Bigelow via count out in 11:04 (★★); Jim Duggan vs. Ron Bass ended in a double count out in 15:16 (★); Don Muraco and The Ultimate Warrior defeated Butch Reed and King Kong Bundy in 14:48 (★★).

WWF at Boston Garden (05-03-88) ★★★
05-03-88, Boston, Massachusetts WWF
Steve Lombardi defeated SD Jones in 8:02 (★★); Danny Davis defeated Sam Houston in 9:23 (★★); Demolition (Ax and Smash) defeated The Rougeau Brothers (Jacques Rougeau and Raymond Rougeau) in 8:14 (★★★); The Ultimate Warrior defeated Harley Race in 4:54 (★★); Dino Bravo defeated David Sammartino in 5:38 (★★); Jake Roberts defeated Ron Bass via count out in 10:57 (★★★); The Jumping Bomb Angels (Itsuki Yamazaki and Noriyo Tateno) defeated The Glamour Girls (Judy Martin and Leilani Kai) in 11:47 (★★★★); Randy Savage and Strike Force (Rick Martel and Tito Santana) defeated The Honky Tonk Man and The Hart Foundation (Bret Hart and Jim Neidhart) in a Steel Cage Match in 8:20 (★★★).

WWF at Spectrum (12-03-88) ★★★
12-03-88, Philadelphia, Pennsylvania WWF
SD Jones defeated Johnny V in 6:09 (★★); The Jumping Bomb Angels (Itsuki Yamazaki and Noriyo Tateno) defeated The Glamour Girls (Judy Martin and Leilani Kai) in 8:01 (★★★); Dino Bravo defeated Koko B. Ware in 8:34 (★★); Bam Bam Bigelow and Don Muraco defeated One Man Gang and Butch Reed in 14:11 (★★★); The Killer Bees (B. Brian Blair and Jim Brunzell) defeated The Bolsheviks (Nikolai Volkoff and Boris Zhukov) in 10:42 (★★); Brutus Beefcake defeated Greg Valentine in 10:25 (★★★); Hulk Hogan defeated Ted DiBiase in a Lumberjack Match in 6:05 (★★★).

Saturday Night's Main Event XV ★★★★
12-03-88, Nashville, Tennessee WWF
Brutus Beefcake defeated Greg Valentine in 9:48 (★★★); Hulk Hogan defeated Harley Race in 7:24 (★★★); Ted DiBiase defeated Randy Savage via count out in 11:42 (★★★★); The Islanders (Haku and Tama) defeated The Killer Bees (Jim Brunzell and B. Brian Blair) in a Two Out Of Three Falls Match in 3:38 (★★); One Man Gang defeated Ken Patera in 3:07 (★★).

WWF at Copps Coliseum (13-03-88) ★★★
13-03-88, Hamilton, Canada WWF
SD Jones defeated Johnny V in 6:55 (★★); The Bolsheviks (Nikolai Volkoff and Boris Zhukov) defeated The Killer Bees (B. Brian Blair and Jim Brunzell) in 11:15 (★★); Dino Bravo defeated Koko B. Ware in 7:47 (★★); Noriyo Tateno defeated Leilani Kai in 13:12 (★★★); Brutus Beefcake defeated Greg Valentine by DQ in 9:03 (★★★); Don Muraco and George Steele defeated Butch Reed and One Man Gang in 17:52 (★★); Bam Bam Bigelow and Hulk Hogan defeated Ted DiBiase and Virgil in 10:06 (★★★).

Clash Of The Champions I ★★★★★
27-03-88, Greensboro, North Carolina NWA
Mike Rotunda defeated Jimmy Garvin in a College Rules Match in 6:10 (★★); The Midnight Express (Bobby Eaton and Stan Lane) defeated The Fantastics (Bobby Fulton and Tommy Rogers) by DQ in 10:15 (★★★★); The Road Warriors (Hawk and Animal) and Dusty Rhodes defeated The Powers Of Pain (The Warlord and The Barbarian) and Ivan Koloff in a Barbed Wire Rope Chicago Street Fight in 3:39 (★★); Lex Luger and Barry Windham defeated Arn Anderson and Tully Blanchard in 9:35 (★★★★); Ric Flair vs. Sting ended in a time limit draw in 45:00 (★★★★).

WrestleMania IV ★★★
27-03-88, Atlantic City, New Jersey WWF
Bad News Brown won a Battle Royal in 9:44 (★★★); Ted DiBiase defeated Jim Duggan in 5:02 (★★); Don Muraco defeated Dino Bravo by DQ in 4:53 (★★); Greg Valentine defeated Ricky Steamboat in 9:12 (★★); Randy Savage defeated Butch Reed in 5:07 (★★); One Man Gang and Bam Bam Bigelow via count out in 2:56 (★★); Jake Roberts vs. Rick Rude went to a time limit draw in 15:00 (★★); The Ultimate Warrior defeated Hercules in 4:29 (★★); Andre the Giant vs. Hulk Hogan went to a double DQ in 5:52 (★★); Ted DiBiase defeated Don Muraco in 5:44 (★★); Randy Savage defeated Greg Valentine in 6:06 (★★★); Brutus Beefcake defeated The Honky Tonk Man by DQ in 6:30 (★★); The Islanders (Haku and Tama) and Bobby Heenan defeated The British Bulldogs (Davey Boy Smith and Dynamite Kid) and Koko B. Ware in 7:30 (★★★); Randy Savage defeated One Man Gang by DQ in 4:05 (★★); Demolition (Ax and Smash) defeated Strike Force (Rick Martel and Tito Santana) to win the WWF World Tag Team Title in 12:33 (★★★); Randy Savage defeated Ted DiBiase to win the vacant WWF World Heavyweight Title in 9:27 (★★★).

WWF at Palatrussardi (02-04-88) ★★
02-04-88, Milan, Italy WWF
Demolition (Ax and Smash) defeated The Young Stallions (Paul Roma and Jim Powers) in 7:47 (★★★); Brutus Beefcake defeated Greg Valentine in 8:06 (★★★); Koko B. Ware defeated Ron Bass in 9:10 (★★); The Ultimate Warrior vs. Hercules ended in a double count out in 4:24 (★★); Andre the Giant defeated Jim Duggan in 6:55 (★★).

Crockett Cup '88 ★★
22-04-88/23-04-88, Greenville/Greensboro NWA
Dick Murdoch and Ivan Koloff defeated Jimmy Valiant and Wilbur in 2:26 [shown] (★★); The Varsity Club (Mike Rotundo and Rick Steiner) defeated Steve Williams and Ron Simmons via count out in 4:28 [shown] (★★); Tully Blanchard and Arn Anderson defeated Kendall Windham and The Italian Stallion in 3:29 [shown] (★★); The Road Warriors (Hawk and Animal) defeated The Jive Tones (Pez Whatley and Tiger Conway) in 2:24 [shown] (★★); The Fantastics (Bobby Fulton and Tommy Rogers) defeated Larry Zbyszko and Al Perez in 3:36 [shown] (★★); Lex Luger and Sting defeated Dick Murdoch and Ivan Koloff in 5:19 (★★); The Midnight Express (Bobby Eaton and Stan Lane) defeated The Sheepherders (Butch Miller and Luke Williams) in 2:48 (★); Jimmy Garvin defeated Kevin Sullivan in a Prince Of Darkness Death Match in 2:33 [shown] (★); Dusty Rhodes won a Bunkhouse Stampede in 14:19 (★★★); The Powers Of Pain (The Barbarian and The Warlord) defeated The Road Warriors (Hawk and Animal) by DQ in 8:40 (★★); The Midnight Rider defeated James J. Dillon in a Bullrope Match in 4:10 (★); Lex Luger and Sting defeated The Powers Of Pain (The Barbarian and The Warlord) in 5:35 [shown] (★★★); Tully Blanchard and Arn Anderson defeated The Fantastics (Bobby Fulton and Tommy Rogers) in 7:02 (★★★); Nikita Koloff defeated Ric Flair by DQ in 8:53 (★★★); Lex Luger and Sting defeated Tully Blanchard and Arn Anderson to win the Crockett Cup in 11:34 (★★★★).

WWF at Maple Leaf Gardens (24-04-88) ★★
24-04-88, Toronto, Canada WWF
Scott Casey defeated Iron Mike Sharpe in 9:42 (★); The Fabulous Rougeaus (Jacques Rougeau and Raymond Rougeau) defeated The Killer Bees (B. Brian Blair and Jim Brunzell) in 16:03 (★★★); Rick Rude defeated Don Muraco in 7:37 (★★); Jake Roberts defeated Greg Valentine in 14:01 (★★); Andre The Giant defeated Jim Duggan via count out in 9:17 (★★); The Islanders (Haku and Tama) and Bobby Heenan defeated The British Bulldogs (Davey Boy Smith and Dynamite Kid) and Koko B. Ware in 14:42 (★★★); The Honky Tonk Man defeated Brutus Beefcake via count out in 7:50 (★★).

WWF at Madison Square Garden (25-04-88) ★★★
25-04-88, New York City, New York WWF
Brady Boone defeated Steve Lombardi in 14:57 (★★★). Bret Hart vs. Bad News Brown ended in a draw in 18:19 (★★★); One Man Gang defeated Bam Bam Bigelow by DQ in 9:12 (★★★); Ted DiBiase defeated Randy Savage via count out in 11:59 (★★★); Barry Horowitz defeated Jose Luis Rivera in 10:39 (★★); Sensational Sherri defeated Desiree Peterson in 7:29 (★★); The Ultimate Warrior defeated Hercules in 12:48 (★★); Demolition (Ax and Smash) defeated Strike Force (Rick Martel and Tito Santana) in 7:22 (★★★).

Saturday Night's Main Event XVI ★★
30-04-88, Springfield, Massachusetts WWF
Jim Duggan defeated Hercules by DQ in 9:31 (★★); Brutus Beefcake defeated Danny Davis in 3:10 (★★); Randy Savage defeated One Man Gang in 6:10 (★★); Demolition (Ax and Smash) defeated The British Bulldogs (Davey Boy Smith and Dynamite Kid) by DQ in 7:00 (★★); Ted DiBiase defeated Don Muraco in 4:12 (★★); Rick Rude defeated Koko B. Ware in 3:44 (★★).

WWF at Boston Garden (07-05-88) ★★★
07-05-88, Boston, Massachusetts WWF
Scott Casey defeated Iron Mike Sharpe in 7:49 (★★); Jake Roberts defeated Greg Valentine in 12:50 (★★★); The Rougeau Brothers (Jacques Rougeau and Raymond Rougeau) defeated The Killer Bees (B. Brian Blair and Jim Brunzell) in 15:21 (★★★); Frenchy Martin defeated Jerry Allen in 3:08 (★★); Pete Doherty defeated SD Jones in 5:23 (★★); Rick Rude defeated Koko B. Ware in 9:25 (★★); Andre The Giant defeated Jim Duggan via count out in 10:39 (★★); Bret Hart

vs. **Bad News Brown** ended in a draw in 16:40 (★★★); **Demolition** (**Ax** and **Smash**) defeated **Strike Force** (**Rick Martel** and **Tito Santana**) in 10:06 (★★★); **The Honky Tonk Man** defeated **Brutus Beefcake** via count out in 9:37 (★★).

WWF at Spectrum (21-05-88) ★★★
21-05-88, Philadelphia, Pennsylvania **WWF**
Jerry Allen defeated **Steve Lombardi** in 11:06 (★★); **The Rougeau Brothers** (**Jacques Rougeau** and **Raymond Rougeau**) defeated **The Young Stallions** (**Jim Powers** and **Paul Roma**) in 13:32 (★★); **Bret Hart** vs. **Bad News Brown** ended in a draw in 17:47 (★★★★); **Andre The Giant** defeated **Jim Duggan** via count out in 11:04 (★★); **Haku, High Chief Afi** and **Bobby Heenan** defeated **The British Bulldogs** (**Davey Boy Smith** and **Dynamite Kid**) and **Koko B. Ware** in 17:12 (★★★); **Don Muraco** defeated **Greg Valentine** by DQ in 9:46 (★★★); **Jake Roberts** defeated **Rick Rude** in 11:54 (★★★).

WWF at Madison Square Garden (27-05-88) ★★
27-05-88, New York City, New York **WWF**
The Conquistador defeated **SD Jones** in 9:13 (★★); **Greg Valentine** defeated **George Steele** by DQ in 5:54 (★★); **The Rougeau Brothers** (**Jacques Rougeau** and **Raymond Rougeau**) defeated **The Young Stallions** (**Jim Powers** and **Paul Roma**) in 14:26 (★★); **Brutus Beefcake** vs. **One Man Gang** ended in a double count out in 10:20 (★★); **Haku, High Chief Afi** and **Bobby Heenan** defeated **Koko B. Ware** and **The British Bulldogs** (**Davey Boy Smith** and **Dynamite Kid**) in 14:10 (★★); **Iron Mike Sharpe** defeated **Jerry Allen** in 6:26 (★); **Randy Savage** defeated **Ted Dibiase** by DQ in 11:55 (★★); **Jim Neidhart** defeated **Don Muraco** in 6:22 (★★); **Dino Bravo** defeated **Ken Patera** in 7:15 (★★); **Junkyard Dog** defeated **Ron Bass** in 8:15 (★★).

WWF at Boston Garden (04-06-88) ★★
04-06-88, Boston, Massachusetts **WWF**
Conquistador #1 defeated **Jerry Allen** in 10:39 (★★); **Don Muraco** defeated **One Man Gang** via count out in 11:27 (★★); **Bad News Brown** defeated **Bret Hart** in 11:09 (★★); **Bam Bam Bigelow** defeated **Hercules** in 8:39 (★★); **Jake Roberts** vs. **Rick Rude** ended in a double count out in 11:24 (★★★); **Andre The Giant** defeated **Jim Duggan** in 9:20 (★★); **The Ultimate Warrior** and **Strike Force** (**Rick Martel** and **Tito Santana**) defeated **Mr. Fuji** and **Demolition** (**Ax** and **Smash**) in 16:11 (★★★).

Clash Of The Champions II: Miami Mayhem ★★
08-06-88, Miami, Florida **NWA**
Barry Windham defeated **Brad Armstrong** in 13:45 (★★); **The Fantastics** (**Bobby Fulton** and **Tommy Rogers**) defeated **The Sheepherders** (**Luke Williams** and **Butch Miller**) in 17:03 (★★★); **Jimmy Garvin** and **Ronnie Garvin** defeated **The Varsity Club** (**Rick Steiner** and **Mike Rotunda**) in 13:11 (★★); **Nikita Koloff** defeated **Al Perez** by DQ in 12:04 (★★); **Arn Anderson** and **Tully Blanchard** vs. **Sting** and **Dusty Rhodes** ended in a double DQ in 10:58 (★★).

WWF at Spectrum (18-06-88) ★★
18-06-88, Philadelphia, Pennsylvania **WWF**
Hercules defeated **SD Jones** in 8:07 (★★); **Dino Bravo** defeated **Ken Patera** in 6:03 (★★); **The Bolsheviks** (**Nikolai Volkoff** and **Boris Zhukov**) defeated **The Young Stallions** (**Paul Roma** and **Jim Powers**) in 18:25 (★★); **The Ultimate Warrior** defeated **Bobby Heenan** in a Weasel Suit Match in 2:24 (★★); **The Honky Tonk Man** defeated **Brutus Beefcake** in 12:05 (★★); **Sam Houston** defeated **Iron Mike Sharpe** in 13:11 (★★); **Bam Bam Bigelow** defeated **One Man Gang** in 9:21 (★★); **Junkyard Dog** defeated **Ron Bass** in 11:06 (★★); **Andre The Giant** defeated **Jim Duggan** in 6:31 (★★).

WWF at Madison Square Garden (25-06-88) ★★
25-06-88, New York City, New York **WWF**
The Big Boss Man defeated **Scott Casey** in 7:45 (★★); **The Rougeau Brothers** (**Jacques Rougeau** and **Raymond Rougeau**) defeated **The Conquistadors** (**Conquistador #1** and **Conquistador #2**) in 11:35 (★★); **Greg Valentine** via count out in a No DQ match in 6:35 (★); **Don Muraco** defeated **Danny Davis** by DQ in 7:06 (★★); **Andre The Giant** defeated **Bam Bam Bigelow** in 9:09 (★★); **Bad News Brown** defeated **Jim Neidhart** via count out in 16:23 (★★); **Jim Duggan** defeated **One Man Gang** in 9:49 (★★); **The Ultimate Warrior** defeated **Bobby Heenan** in a Weasel Suit Match in 5:30 (★★); **Randy Savage** defeated **Ted DiBiase** in a Steel Cage Match in 12:20 (★★★★).

WWF at Boston Garden (09-07-88) ★★★
09-07-88, Boston, Massachusetts **WWF**
The Iron Sheik defeated **Scott Casey** in 9:44 (★★); **The British Bulldogs** (**Davey Boy Smith** and **Dynamite Kid**) defeated **The Bolsheviks** (**Nikolai Volkoff** and **Boris Zhukov**) in 15:01 (★★); **The Big Boss Man** defeated **Sam Houston** in 7:54 (★★); **Greg Valentine** defeated **Don Muraco** in 15:42 (★★★); **The Rockers** (**Shawn Michaels** and **Marty Jannetty**) defeated **The Conquistadors** (**Conquistador #1** and **Conquistador #2**) in 10:01 (★★★); **Randy Savage** defeated **Ted DiBiase** in 13:39 (★★★); **Jake Roberts** defeated **Rick Rude** in 17:21 (★★★).

Great American Bash '88 ★★★
10-07-88, Baltimore, Maryland **NWA**
Arn Anderson and **Tully Blanchard** vs. **Nikita Koloff** and **Sting** went to a time limit draw in 20:00 (★★★); **The Midnight Express** (**Bobby Eaton** and **Stan Lane**) defeated **The Fantastics** (**Bobby Fulton** and **Tommy Rogers**) to win the NWA United States Tag Team Title in 16:23 (★★★★); **The Road Warriors** (**Hawk** and **Animal**), **Steve Williams**, **Ron Garvin** and **Jimmy Garvin** defeated **Al Perez, Ivan Koloff, Kevin Sullivan, Mike Rotunda** and **Russian Assassin #1** in a Tower Of Doom Match in 19:13 (★★); **Barry Windham** defeated **Dusty Rhodes** in 15:55 (★★); **Ric Flair** defeated **Lex Luger** in 23:13 (★★★).

WWF at LA Sports Arena (15-07-88) ★★
15-07-88, Los Angeles, California **WWF**
The Big Boss Man defeated **Scott Casey** in 7:21 (★★); **The Rockers** (**Shawn Michaels** and **Marty Jannetty**) defeated **The Conquistadors** (**Conquistador #1** and **Conquistador #2**) in 14:37 (★★); **Andre the Giant** defeated **Jim Duggan** in 13:03 (★★); **The Ultimate Warrior** defeated **Bobby Heenan** in a Weasel Suit Match in 7:25 (★★); **Bad News Brown** defeated **Jim Neidhart** in 12:40 (★★★); **Rick Rude** defeated **Jake Roberts** via count out in 17:46 (★★★).

Great American Bash '88 (Greensboro) ★★★★
16-07-88, Greensboro, North Carolina **NWA**
Bugsy McGraw and **Tim Horner** defeated **Larry Zbyszko** and **Rip Morgan** in 8:08 (★★★); **Ron Garvin** defeated **The Italian Stallion** in 1:13 (★★); **Dick Murdoch** defeated **Gary Royal** in 7:01 (★★); **Jimmy Garvin** defeated **Rick Steiner** in 1:27 (★★); **The Rock 'n' Roll Express** (**Ricky Morton** and **Robert Gibson**) defeated **The New Zealand Sheepherders** (**Butch Miller** and **Luke Williams**) in 14:04 (★★★); **Al Perez** defeated **Brad Armstrong** in 11:16 (★★★); **The Fantastics** (**Bobby Fulton** and **Tommy Rogers**) defeated **Jim Cornette** and **The Midnight Express** (**Bobby Eaton** and **Stan Lane**) in a Bunkhouse Handicap Match in 15:08 (★★★★); **Sting** defeated **Mike Rotunda** by DQ in 10:16 (★★★); **The Road Warriors** (**Animal** and **Hawk**) defeated **Ivan Koloff** and **The Russian Assassin** in a Scaffold Match in 5:33 (★★★); **Dusty Rhodes, Lex Luger, Nikita Koloff, Paul Ellering** and **Steve Williams** defeated **The Four Horsemen** (**Arn Anderson, Barry Windham, JJ Dillon, Ric Flair** and **Tully Blanchard**) in a War Games Match in 21:07 (★★★★).

WWF at Spectrum (23-07-88) ★★
23-07-88, Philadelphia, Pennsylvania **WWF**
The Big Boss Man defeated **Sam Houston** in 7:07 (★★); **Greg Valentine** defeated **Don Muraco** in 11:06 (★★★); **The Bolsheviks** (**Nikolai Volkoff** and **Boris Zhukov**) defeated **The British Bulldogs** (**Davey Boy Smith** and **Dynamite Kid**) in 12:49 (★★); **Terry Taylor** defeated **Scott Casey** in 10:12 (★★); **Ted DiBiase** defeated **Randy Savage** via count out in 12:42 (★★★); **The Powers Of Pain** (**The Barbarian** and **The Warlord**) defeated **Demolition** (**Ax** and **Smash**) via count out in 9:37 (★★); **The Honky Tonk Man** defeated **Brutus Beefcake** in 10:35 (★★); **The Ultimate Warrior** defeated **Hercules** in 3:22 (★★).

WWF at Maple Leaf Gardens (24-07-88) ★★
24-07-88, Toronto, Canada **WWF**
Terry Taylor defeated **Scott Casey** in 12:07 (★★); **King Haku** defeated **SD Jones** in 8:20 (★★); **Greg Valentine** defeated **Don Muraco** in 13:53 (★★★); **Randy Savage** defeated **Ted DiBiase** by DQ in 12:18 (★★★); **Terry Taylor** defeated **Richard Charland** in 5:48 (★★); **The Powers Of Pain** (**The Barbarian** and **The Warlord**) defeated **The Bolsheviks** (**Nikolai Volkoff** and **Boris Zhukov**) in 11:38 (★★); **The Ultimate Warrior** and **The British Bulldogs** (**Davey Boy Smith** and **Dynamite Kid**) defeated **Mr. Fuji** and **Demolition** (**Ax** and **Smash**) in 7:37 (★★★).

WWF at Madison Square Garden (25-07-88) ★★★
25-07-88, New York City, New York **WWF**
Terry Taylor defeated Lanny Poffo in 9:52 (★★); The Rougeau Brothers (Jacques Rougeau and Raymond Rougeau) defeated The Rockers (Shawn Michaels and Marty Jannetty) in 14:59 (★★★); Bret Hart defeated Danny Davis in 9:35 (★★★); Don Muraco vs. Greg Valentine ended in a draw in 18:41 (★★★); Demolition (Ax and Smash) defeated The British Bulldogs (Davey Boy Smith and Dynamite Kid) in 20:25 (★★★★); The Powers Of Pain (The Barbarian and The Warlord) defeated The Bolsheviks (Nikolai Volkoff and Boris Zhukov) in 7:37 (★★); King Haku defeated SD Jones in 7:06 (★★); Andre The Giant defeated Jim Duggan in a Lumberjack Match in 12:38 (★★★).

WrestleFest '88 ★★
31-07-88, Milwaukee, Wisconsin **WWF**
The Big Boss Man defeated Scott Casey in 4:15 (★★); Brutus Beefcake defeated Hercules in 9:37 (★★); The Fabulous Rougeaus (Jacques Rougeau and Raymond Rougeau) defeated The Killer Bees (B. Brian Blair and Jim Brunzell) in 13:59 (★★); Bad News Brown defeated Bret Hart in 6:26 (★★★); Jim Duggan defeated The Honky Tonk Man in 4:38 (★★); The Powers Of Pain (The Warlord and The Barbarian) defeated The Bolsheviks (Boris Zhukov and Nikolai Volkoff) in 6:47 (★); Jim Neidhart defeated Lanny Poffo in 2:35 (★★); Randy Savage defeated Ted DiBiase in 14:52 (★★★); Mr. Perfect defeated The Red Rooster in 4:52 (★★); Jake Roberts vs. Rick Rude ended in a double count out in 15:44 (★★); King Haku defeated Sam Houston in 5:04 (★★); The Ultimate Warrior defeated Bobby Heenan in a Loser Wears A Weasel Suit Match in 4:59 (★★★); Demolition (Ax and Smash) defeated The British Bulldogs (Davey Boy Smith and Dynamite Kid) in 7:08 (★★★); Dino Bravo defeated Ken Patera in 3:28 (★★); Hulk Hogan defeated Andre the Giant in a Steel Cage Match in 9:52 (★★).

WWF at Boston Garden (06-08-88) ★★★
06-08-88, Boston, Massachusetts **WWF**
Ron Bass defeated Koko B. Ware in 8:52 (★★); The Fabulous Rougeaus (Jacques Rougeau and Raymond Rougeau) defeated The Hart Foundation (Bret Hart and Jim Neidhart) in 12:01 (★★★); DJ Peterson defeated Lanny Poffo in 5:52 (★★); The Honky Tonk Man defeated Brutus Beefcake in 6:02 (★★); Demolition (Ax and Smash) defeated The British Bulldogs (Davey Boy Smith and Dynamite Kid) in 9:01 (★★★); Bad News Brown defeated Scott Casey in 11:30 (★★); Randy Savage defeated Ted DiBiase via count out in 6:47 (★★★); Andre the Giant defeated Jim Duggan in a Lumberjack Match in 7:51 (★★★).

WWF at LA Sports Arena (13-08-88) ★★★
13-08-88, Los Angeles, California **WWF**
Sam Houston defeated Black Jack in 5:47 (★★); The Blue Angel defeated Barry Horowitz in 14:31 (★★★); The Powers Of Pain (The Barbarian and The Warlord) defeated The Bolsheviks (Nikolai Volkoff and Boris Zhukov) in 9:08 (★★); Curt Hennig defeated SD Jones in 13:06 (★★); Randy Savage vs. Andre the Giant ended in a double count out in 10:24 (★★); The Fabulous Rougeau Brothers (Jacques Rougeau and Raymond Rougeau) defeated The Hart Foundation (Bret Hart and Jim Neidhart) in 17:41 (★★★); Ron Bass defeated DJ Peterson in 10:57 (★★); Jake Roberts defeated Rick Rude in 13:24 (★★★).

WWF at Spectrum (27-08-88) ★★★
27-08-88, Philadelphia, Pennsylvania **WWF**
Ron Bass defeated Lanny Poffo in 5:36 (★★); The Fabulous Rougeaus (Jacques Rougeau and Raymond Rougeau) defeated The Hart Foundation (Bret Hart and Jim Neidhart) in 17:46 (★★★); The Blue Blazer defeated Barry Horowitz in 9:55 (★★★); Randy Savage defeated Ted DiBiase by DQ in 12:41 (★★★); Tito Santana vs. King Haku ended in a draw in 15:31 (★★); The Powers Of Pain (The Barbarian and The Warlord) defeated The Bolsheviks (Nikolai Volkoff and Boris Zhukov) in 8:50 (★★); Rick Rude defeated Jake Roberts via count out in 18:45 (★★★).

SummerSlam '88 ★★★
29-08-88, New York City, New York **WWF**
The British Bulldogs (Davey Boy Smith and Dynamite Kid) vs. The Fabulous Rougeaus (Jacques Rougeau and Raymond Rougeau) ended in a time limit draw in 20:00 (★★★); Bad News Brown defeated Ken Patera in 6:33 (★★); Rick Rude defeated Junkyard Dog by DQ in 6:18 (★★); The Powers Of

Pain (The Barbarian and The Warlord) defeated The Bolsheviks (Boris Zhukov and Nikolai Volkoff) in 5:27 (★★); The Ultimate Warrior defeated The Honky Tonk Man to win the WWF Intercontinental Title in :31 (★★★★); Dino Bravo defeated Don Muraco in 5:28 (★★); Demolition (Ax and Smash) defeated The Hart Foundation (Bret Hart and Jim Neidhart) in 10:49 (★★★); The Big Boss Man defeated Koko B. Ware in 5:57 (★★); Jake Roberts defeated Hercules in 10:06 (★★); The Mega Powers (Hulk Hogan and Randy Savage) defeated The Mega Bucks (Andre the Giant and Ted DiBiase) in 14:43 (★★★★).

Clash Of The Champions III: Fall Brawl ★★★
07-09-88, Albany, Georgia **NWA**
Mike Rotunda vs. Brad Armstrong went to a time limit draw in 20:00 (★★★); Nikita Koloff and Steve Williams defeated The Sheepherders (Luke Williams and Butch Miller) in 16:53 (★★★); Dusty Rhodes defeated Kevin Sullivan in 6:59 (★★); Ricky Morton defeated Ivan Koloff in a Russian Chain Match in 9:52 (★★); Sting defeated Barry Windham by DQ in 21:14 (★★★★).

WWF at Boston Garden (10-09-88) ★★
10-09-88, Boston, Massachusetts **WWF**
The Blue Blazer defeated Barry Horowitz in 12:27 (★★★); Paul Roma defeated Danny Davis in 7:59 (★★); The Hart Foundation (Bret Hart and Jim Neidhart) defeated The Fabulous Rougeaus (Jacques Rougeau and Raymond Rougeau) by DQ in 12:45 (★★); Bad News Brown defeated Junkyard Dog in 7:12 (★★); The Honky Tonk Man defeated The Ultimate Warrior via count out in 3:03 (★★); Mr. Perfect defeated Jim Brunzell in 7:22 (★★); The Big Boss Man defeated Ken Patera in 8:42 (★★); Hulk Hogan defeated Ted DiBiase in 13:30 (★★★).

Aniversario '88 - A Hot Night In Bayamon ★★★
10-09-88, Bayamon, Puerto Rico **WWC**
Jimmy Valiant and Rufus R. Jones defeated The Wild Samoans (Afa and Sika) by DQ in 10:21 (★★); Ricky Santana defeated Mr. Pogo in 13:42 (★★); The Batten Twins (Bart Batten and Brad Batten) defeated The New Zealand Sheepherders (Butch Miller and Luke Williams) by DQ in 14:08 (★★★); Wahoo McDaniel defeated Danny Spivey in 5:59 (★★); Chicky Starr defeated Invader #3 in 10:29 (★★★); Ronnie Garvin defeated The Iron Sheik via count out in 7:57 (★★); Huracan Castillo and Miguel Perez Jr. defeated Bobby Jaggers and Dan Kroffat in a Hair vs Hair Match in 13:19 (★★★); Carlos Colon defeated Hercules Ayala in a Fire Match in 9:01 (★★).

WWF at Meadowlands Arena (11-09-88) ★★★
11-09-88, East Rutherford, New Jersey **WWF**
Mr. Perfect defeated Jim Brunzell in 13:01 (★★); Greg Valentine vs. Don Muraco ended in a draw in 19:18 (★★★); Hercules defeated Junkyard Dog in 9:38 (★★); Hulk Hogan defeated Bad News Brown in 9:21 (★★★); The Blue Blazer defeated Barry Horowitz in 11:15 (★★★); Ted DiBiase defeated Jim Duggan by DQ in 12:03 (★★); The Fabulous Rougeaus (Jacques Rougeau and Raymond Rougeau) defeated The Hart Foundation (Bret Hart and Jim Neidhart) in 12:17 (★★★); Jake Roberts defeated Rick Rude in 11:50 (★★★★).

WWF at Maple Leaf Gardens (18-09-88) ★★★
18-09-88, Toronto, Canada **WWF**
Mr. Perfect defeated Jim Brunzell in 9:53 (★★★); Iron Mike Sharpe defeated Tommy Angel in 10:21 (★★); Brutus Beefcake defeated Ron Bass by DQ in 10:20 (★★); The Powers Of Pain (The Barbarian and The Warlord) defeated The Bolsheviks (Nikolai Volkoff and Boris Zhukov) in 12:09 (★★); Jake Roberts defeated Rick Rude in 15:23 (★★★★); The Big Boss Man defeated Jim Powers in 4:11 (★★); Hulk Hogan defeated King Haku in 12:42 (★★★).

The Road To SuperClash III ★★
18-09-88, Louisville, Kentucky **AWA**
The Top Guns (John Paul and Ricky Rice) defeated Terry Adonis and The Beast in 3:25 (★★); Ronnie Garvin defeated Scott Steiner in 1:46 (★★); Kerry Von Erich defeated Gary Young in 1:34 (★★); Greg Gagne defeated Mike Enos in 3:36 (★★); Magnificent Mimi and Wendi Richter defeated Madusa Miceli and Sylvia in 7:38 (★); The Badd Company (Pat Tanaka and Paul Diamond) defeated Natures Best (Bill Justin and Darryl Justin) in 4:39 (★★); The Rock 'n' Roll Express (Ricky Morton and Robert Gibson) defeated Terry Adonis and The Hangman in 1:45 (★★); Michael Hayes defeated Iceman King Parsons

by DQ in 4:12 (★★); **Steve Cox** defeated **Terry Garvin** in 1:42 (★★); **Soldat Ustinov** and **Teijo Khan** defeated **Keith Eric** and **Sgt. Slaughter** via count out in 6:16 (★★); **Manny Fernandez** vs. **Wahoo McDaniel** ended in a double count out in 7:04 (★★★); **The Guerrero Brothers (Chavo Guerrero, Hector Guerrero** and **Mando Guerrero)** defeated **The Hangman** and **The Rock 'N' Roll RPM's (Mike Davis** and **Tommy Lane)** in 5:20 (★★); **Col. DeBeers** defeated **Alan Reynolds** in 1:37 (★★); **The SST (Fatu** and **Samu)** defeated **Ray Odyssey** and **Shawn Baxter** in 4:11 (★★); **Jerry Lawler** defeated **Terry Adonis** in 1:54 (★★); **Bill Dundee** and **Brickhouse Brown** defeated **The Stud Stable** (**Jimmy Golden** and **Robert Fuller**) by DQ in 7:26 (★★); **Jeff Jarrett, The Rock 'n' Roll Express (Ricky Morton** and **Robert Gibson)** and **The Top Guns (John Paul** and **Ricky Rice)** defeated **Cactus Jack, The Badd Company (Pat Tanaka** and **Paul Diamond)** and **The Rock 'N' Roll RPM's (Mike Davis** and **Tommy Lane)** in 10:20 (★★); **Jerry Lawler** and **Jimmy Valiant** vs. **Kerry Von Erich** and **Michael Hayes** ended in a double count out in 7:59 (★★★).

WWF at Spectrum (24-09-88) ★★★
24-09-88, Philadelphia, Pennsylvania **WWF**

Mr. Perfect defeated **B. Brian Blair** in 14:35 (★★); **Barry Horowitz** defeated **DJ Peterson** in 10:13 (★★); **The Big Boss Man** defeated **Ken Patera** in 8:05 (★★); **The Honky Tonk Man** defeated **The Ultimate Warrior** via count out in 3:47 (★★); **Demolition (Ax** and **Smash)** defeated **The British Bulldogs (Davey Boy Smith** and **Dynamite Kid)** in 14:51 (★★★); **Bad News Brown** defeated **Junkyard Dog** in 9:25 (★★); **The Hart Foundation (Bret Hart** and **Jim Neidhart)** defeated **The Fabulous Rougeaus (Jacques Rougeau** and **Raymond Rougeau)** by DQ in 13:05 (★★); **Jim Powers** defeated **Iron Mike Sharpe** in 4:37 (★★); **Randy Savage** defeated **Ted DiBiase** in a Steel Cage Match in 12:31 (★★★★).

WWF at Madison Square Garden (29-09-88) ★★
29-09-88, New York City, New York **WWF**

Terry Taylor defeated **Sam Houston** in 8:19 (★★); **The Rockers (Shawn Michaels** and **Marty Jannetty)** defeated **The Conquistadors (Conquistador #1** and **Conquistador #2)** in 14:30 (★★★); **Junkyard Dog** defeated **King Haku** by DQ in 14:45 (★★); **Dino Bravo** defeated **B. Brian Blair** in 13:45 (★★); **Randy Savage** vs. **Andre the Giant** ended in a double count out in 9:57 (★★); **Scott Casey** defeated **Sandy Beach** in 6:06 (★★); **Brutus Beefcake** defeated **Ron Bass** in 10:50 (★★); **Bad News Brown** defeated **Tito Santana** in 7:44 (★★★); **The Honky Tonk Man** defeated **The Ultimate Warrior** via count out in 3:48 (★★).

WWF at Bercy Stadium (07-10-88) ★★
07-10-88, Paris, France **WWF**

Greg Valentine defeated **Don Muraco** in 11:57 (★★★); **Andre the Giant** defeated **Junkyard Dog** in 7:09 (★★); **Rockin Robin** defeated **Sensational Sherri** to win the WWF Women's Title in 12:32 (★★★); **Lanny Poffo** defeated **Barry Horowitz** in 13:03 (★★); **Demolition (Ax** and **Smash)** defeated **The British Bulldogs (Davey Boy Smith** and **Dynamite Kid)** in 23:21 (★★★); **Randy Savage** defeated **Akeem** in 10:13 (★★).

WWF at Maple Leaf Gardens (09-10-88) ★★
09-10-88, Toronto, Canada **WWF**

Scott Casey defeated **Richard Charland** in 13:41 (★★); **B. Brian Blair** defeated **Iron Mike Sharpe** in 8:23 (★★); **The Blue Blazer** defeated **Steve Lombardi** in 8:18 (★★★); **Bad News Brown** defeated **Koko B. Ware** in 10:31 (★★); **Dino Bravo** defeated **Randy Savage** via count out in 11:08 (★★); **The Hart Foundation (Bret Hart** and **Jim Neidhart)** defeated **The Rougeau Brothers (Jacques Rougeau** and **Raymond Rougeau)** in 12:10 (★★★); **King Haku** defeated **Hillbilly Jim** in 8:04 (★★); **The Ultimate Warrior** defeated **The Honky Tonk Man** by DQ in 4:01 (★★).

WWF at Boston Garden (10-10-88) ★★
10-10-88, Boston, Massachusetts **WWF**

B. Brian Blair defeated **Iron Mike Sharpe** in 9:27 (★★); **Scott Casey** defeated **Pete Doherty** in 6:43 (★★); **The Blue Blazer** defeated **Steve Lombardi** in 7:25 (★★); **King Haku** defeated **Hillbilly Jim** in 12:07 (★★); **Bad News Brown** defeated **Randy Savage** via count out in 8:51 (★★★); **Dino Bravo** defeated **Koko B. Ware** in 3:37 (★★); **The Ultimate Warrior** defeated **The Honky Tonk Man** by DQ in 3:56 (★★); **The Hart Foundation (Bret Hart** and **Jim Neidhart)** defeated **The Fabulous Rougeaus (Jacques Rougeau** and **Raymond Rougeau)** in 11:27 (★★★).

WWF at Palatrussardi (15-10-88) ★★
15-10-88, Milan, Italy **WWF**

Lanny Poffo defeated **Barry Horowitz** in 7:05 (★★); **Andre the Giant** defeated **Tito Santana** in 6:59 (★★); **Greg Valentine** defeated **Don Muraco** in 7:07 (★★★); **Rockin Robin** defeated **Sensational Sherri** in 14:25 (★★★); **The British Bulldogs (Davey Boy Smith** and **Dynamite Kid)** defeated **Demolition (Ax** and **Smash)** in 8:05 (★★★).

WWF at Palaeur (16-10-88) ★★
16-10-88, Rome, Italy **WWF**

Don Muraco defeated **Barry Horowitz** in 4:18 (★★); **Andre the Giant** defeated **Tito Santana** in 6:27 (★★); **Akeem** and **Harley Race** defeated **B. Brian Blair** and **Junkyard Dog** in 4:27 (★★); **Demolition (Ax** and **Smash)** defeated **The British Bulldogs (Davey Boy Smith** and **Dynamite Kid)** in 9:30 (★★★).

WWF at LA Sports Arena (16-10-88) ★★
16-10-88, Los Angeles, California **WWF**

Paul Roma defeated **Steve Lombardi** in 14:08 (★★); **The Blue Blazer** defeated **Jose Estrada** in 11:00 (★★); **The Ultimate Warrior** defeated **The Honky Tonk Man** by DQ in 3:57 (★★); **Mr. Perfect** defeated **Jim Brunzell** in 12:15 (★★); **Hulk Hogan** defeated **King Haku** in 8:50 (★★★); **The Big Boss Man** defeated **Koko B. Ware** in 5:55 (★★); **The Hart Foundation (Bret Hart** and **Jim Neidhart)** defeated **The Fabulous Rougeaus (Jacques Rougeau** and **Raymond Rougeau)** by DQ in 21:17 (★★★); **Jake Roberts** defeated **Rick Rude** in 20:34 (★★★).

WWF at Madison Square Garden (24-10-88) ★★★
24-10-88, New York City, New York **WWF**

Paul Roma defeated **Danny Davis** in 12:22 (★★); **The Big Boss Man** defeated **Koko B. Ware** in 7:03 (★★); **Demolition (Ax** and **Smash)** defeated **The Rockers (Shawn Michaels** and **Marty Jannetty)** in 12:24 (★★★); **Hercules** defeated **Virgil** in 2:15 (★★); **The Blue Blazer** defeated **Steve Lombardi** in 8:09 (★★); **Randy Savage** defeated **Andre The Giant** by DQ in 6:59 (★★★); **Dino Bravo** defeated **Jim Duggan** via count out in 8:16 (★★); **The Hart Foundation (Bret Hart** and **Jim Neidhart)** vs. **The Fabulous Rougeaus (Jacques Rougeau** and **Raymond Rougeau)** ended in a draw in 22:32 (★★★); **Jake Roberts** defeated **Rick Rude** in 12:24 (★★★).

Saturday Night's Main Event XVII ★★★
29-10-88, Baltimore, Maryland **WWF**

Jake Roberts defeated **Rick Rude** by DQ in 9:40 (★★★); **Demolition (Ax** and **Smash)** defeated **The Hart Foundation (Bret Hart** and **Jim Neidhart)** in 5:58 (★★); **Hulk Hogan** defeated **King Haku** in 6:16 (★★★); **Dino Bravo** defeated **Ken Patera** in 3:03 (★★); **The Big Boss Man** defeated **Jim Powers** in 2:34 (★★).

WWF at Boston Garden (05-11-88) ★★
05-11-88, Boston, Massachusetts **WWF**

Lanny Poffo defeated **Barry Horowitz** in 6:28 (★★); **The Red Rooster** defeated **Ken Patera** in 8:25 (★★); **Jim Neidhart** defeated **Raymond Rougeau** in 2:27 (★★); **King Haku** defeated **Jim Brunzell** in 8:03 (★★); **Jacques Rougeau** defeated **Bret Hart** in 11:51 (★★★); **Dino Bravo** defeated **Jim Duggan** via count out in 8:48 (★★); **Sensational Sherri** defeated **Rockin Robin** in 9:37 (★★); **Ted DiBiase** defeated **Hercules** in 8:23 (★★★); **Randy Savage** defeated **Bad News Brown** in 7:40 (★★★).

WWF at Maple Leaf Gardens (06-11-88) ★★★
06-11-88, Toronto, Canada **WWF**

B. Brian Blair defeated **Iron Mike Sharpe** in 10:20 (★★); **Koko B. Ware** defeated **Steve Lombardi** in 7:09 (★★); **The Brain Busters (Arn Anderson** and **Tully Blanchard)** defeated **The Young Stallions (Jim Powers** and **Paul Roma)** in 12:14 (★★★); **The Blue Blazer** defeated **Danny Davis** in 5:44 (★★); **Hulk Hogan** defeated **The Big Boss Man** via count out in 9:29 (★★★); **Demolition (Ax** and **Smash)** defeated **The British Bulldogs (Davey Boy Smith** and **Dynamite Kid)** in 9:52 (★★★); **Dino Bravo** defeated **Jim Duggan** in 6:50 (★★★); **The Ultimate Warrior** defeated **The Honky Tonk Man** in a No DQ Match in 4:25 (★★★).

WWF at Spectrum (12-11-88) ★★
12-11-88, Philadelphia, Pennsylvania WWF

The Blue Blazer defeated Danny Davis in 7:51 (★★); The Brain Busters (Arn Anderson and Tully Blanchard) defeated The Young Stallions (Paul Roma and Jim Powers) in 16:43 (★★★); Dino Bravo defeated Jim Duggan in 8:56 (★★); Brutus Beefcake defeated Ron Bass in 10:54 (★★); The Ultimate Warrior defeated The Honky Tonk Man by DQ in 4:55 (★★); The Hart Foundation (Bret Hart and Jim Neidhart) defeated The Fabulous Rougeaus (Jacques Rougeau and Raymond Rougeau) in 11:41 (★★); Akeem defeated SD Jones in 4:35 (★★); Hulk Hogan defeated The Big Boss Man via count out in 9:30 (★★★).

WWF at Los Angeles Sports Arena (17-11-88) ★★
17-11-88, Los Angeles, California WWF

The Blue Blazer defeated Danny Davis in 10:54 (★★); The Rockers (Shawn Michaels and Marty Jannetty) defeated The Conquistadors (Conquistador #1 and Conquistador #2) in 15:35 (★★★); Bad News Brown defeated Ken Patera in 5:58 (★★); Brutus Beefcake defeated Ron Bass in 9:09 (★★); Hulk Hogan defeated The Big Boss Man via count out in 9:17 (★★★); The Brainbusters (Arn Anderson and Tully Blanchard) defeated The Young Stallions (Paul Roma and Jim Powers) in 13:59 (★★★); Hercules defeated Virgil in 3:22 (★★); The Ultimate Warrior defeated The Honky Tonk Man in a No DQ, No Count Out Match in 8:46 (★★★).

Survivor Series '88 ★★★★
24-11-88, Richfield Township, Ohio WWF

The Blue Blazer, Brutus Beefcake, Jim Brunzell, Sam Houston and The Ultimate Warrior defeated The Honky Tonk Man, Ron Bass, Danny Davis, Bad News Brown and Greg Valentine in an Elimination Match in 17:50 (★★★); The Powers Of Pain (The Barbarian and The Warlord), The Rockers (Marty Jannetty and Shawn Michaels), The Hart Foundation (Bret Hart and Jim Neidhart), The Young Stallions (Jim Powers and Paul Roma) and The British Bulldogs (Davey Boy Smith and Dynamite Kid) defeated Demolition (Ax and Smash), The Brain Busters (Arn Anderson and Tully Blanchard), The Bolsheviks (Boris Zhukov and Nikolai Volkoff), The Fabulous Rougeaus (Jacques Rougeau and Raymond Rougeau) and The Conquistadors (Uno and Dos) in an Elimination Match in 42:18 (★★★★); Andre the Giant, Dino Bravo, Mr. Perfect, Rick Rude and Harley Race defeated Jake Roberts, Jim Duggan, Ken Patera, Scott Casey and Tito Santana in an Elimination Match in 32:08 (★★★); Hercules, Hillbilly Jim, Koko B. Ware, Hulk Hogan and Randy Savage defeated Akeem, The Big Boss Man, Haku, The Red Rooster and Ted DiBiase in an Elimination Match in 29:10 (★★★★).

WWF at Madison Square Garden (26-11-88) ★★
26-11-88, New York City, New York WWF

Lanny Poffo defeated Barry Horowitz in 12:33 (★★); Mr. Perfect defeated Paul Roma in 8:35 (★★★); Ted DiBiase defeated Hercules in 9:06 (★★★); Akeem defeated SD Jones in 4:42 (★★); Demolition (Ax and Smash) vs. The Powers Of Pain (The Barbarian and The Warlord) ended in a double DQ in 5:59 (★★); Nikolai Volkoff defeated Iron Mike Sharpe in 5:27 (★★); Tito Santana vs. Greg Valentine ended in a draw in 18:13 (★★); Rockin Robin defeated Sensational Sherri in 8:25 (★★); Hulk Hogan defeated The Big Boss Man via count out in 10:57 (★★★).

Saturday Night's Main Event XVIII ★★
26-11-88, Sacramento, California WWF

The Ultimate Warrior defeated Super Ninja in 2:11 (★★); Hercules defeated Virgil in 3:20 (★★); Randy Savage vs. Andre the Giant went to a double DQ in 11:00 (★★); Jim Duggan defeated Boris Zhukov in a Flag Match in 2:27 (★); The Fabulous Rougeaus (Jacques Rougeau and Raymond Rougeau) defeated The Young Stallions (Paul Roma and Jim Powers) in 3:05 (★★).

WWF at Boston Garden (03-12-88) ★★
03-12-88, Boston, Massachusetts WWF

Jim Powers defeated Jose Estrada in 13:15 (★★); King Haku defeated SD Jones in 5:47 (★★); Mr. Perfect defeated Tim Horner in 9:44 (★★★); Iron Mike Sharpe defeated Barry Horowitz in 11:46 (★★); Koko B. Ware vs. The Red Rooster ended in a draw in 19:02 (★★★); Demolition (Ax and Smash) vs. The Powers Of Pain (The Barbarian and The Warlord) ended in a double DQ in 5:40 (★★); Akeem defeated Pete Doherty in 3:30 (★); Brutus Beefcake defeated Ron Bass in 9:29 (★★); Hulk Hogan defeated The Big Boss Man via count out in 10:17 (★★★).

WWF at Copps Coliseum (04-12-88) ★★
04-12-88, Hamilton, Canada WWF

Tim Horner defeated Johnny K-9 in 15:54 (★★); Hulk Hogan defeated The Big Boss Man by DQ in 16:01 (★★★); Ted DiBiase defeated Koko B. Ware in 6:16 (★★); Virgil defeated Hercules in 3:36 (★★); Tito Santana defeated Greg Valentine via count out in 8:55 (★★★); Mr. Perfect defeated Jose Luis Rivera in 6:11 (★★); Jim Duggan defeated Dino Bravo in 6:38 (★★).

Clash Of The Champions IV: Season's Beatings ★★★
07-12-88, Chattanooga, Tennessee NWA

The Fantastics (Bobby Fulton and Tommy Rogers) defeated Eddie Gilbert and Ron Simmons in 26:53 (★★); Steve Williams defeated The Italian Stallion in 15:20 (★★); Ivan Koloff defeated Paul Jones in 8:21 (★); Animal defeated Dusty Rhodes by DQ in 2:54 (★★); Ric Flair and Barry Windham defeated The Midnight Express (Bobby Eaton and Stan Lane) in 17:41 (★★★★).

SuperClash III ★★
13-12-88, Chicago, Illinois AWA

Chavo Guerrero, Mando Guerrero and Hector Guerrero defeated Cactus Jack and The Rock 'n' Roll RPMs (Mike Davis and Tommy Lance) in 6:35 (★★); Eric Embry defeated Jeff Jarrett to win the WCCW World Light Heavyweight Title in 4:13; (★★); Jimmy Valiant defeated Wayne Bloom in :24 (★★); Iceman King Parsons defeated Brickhouse Brown in 5:41 (★); Wendi Richter and The Top Guns (Ricky Rice and Derrick Dukes) defeated Madusa Miceli and Badd Company (Paul Diamond and Pat Tanaka) in 5:43 (★★); Greg Gagne defeated Ron Garvin via count out to win the vacant AWA International Television Title in 5:52 (★★); The Syrian Terrorist won a Street Fight Lingerie Battle Royal in 8:36 (★); Sgt. Slaughter defeated Colonel DeBeers by DQ in a Boot Camp Match in 5:42 (★); The Samoan Swat Team (Samu and Fatu) defeated Michael Hayes and Steve Cox in 7:53 (★★★); Wahoo McDaniel defeated Manny Fernandez in an Indian Strap Match in 7:48 (★★); Jerry Lawler defeated Kerry Von Erich by referee stoppage to unify the AWA World Heavyweight Title and WCCW World Heavyweight Title in 18:53 (★★★★); The Rock 'n' Roll Express (Ricky Morton and Robert Gibson) vs. Stud Stable (Robert Fuller and Jimmy Golden) ended in a double DQ in 7:03 (★★).

WWF at Spectrum (17-12-88) ★★
17-12-88, Philadelphia, Pennsylvania WWF

The Red Rooster defeated Sam Houston in 5:09 (★★); Mr. Perfect defeated Paul Roma in 8:00 (★★); Brutus Beefcake vs. Rick Rude ended in a double count out in 8:59 (★★); The Brain Busters (Arn Anderson and Tully Blanchard) defeated The Rockers (Shawn Michaels and Marty Jannetty) in 11:34 (★★★★); The Ultimate Warrior defeated The Honky Tonk Man in 6:50 (★★); Harley Race defeated Danny Davis in 3:14 (★★); Randy Savage defeated King Haku in 9:22 (★★); Jim Duggan defeated Frenchy Martin in 5:02 (★★); Andre The Giant defeated Jake Roberts by DQ in 6:20 (★★).

WWF at LA Sports Arena (17-12-88) ★★
17-12-88, Los Angeles, California WWF

Boris Zhukov defeated Lanny Poffo in 12:06 (★★); Tito Santana vs. Greg Valentine ended in a draw in 20:01 (★★★★); Bad News Brown defeated Jim Powers in 10:52 (★★); Demolition (Ax and Smash) vs. The Powers Of Pain (The Barbarian and The Warlord) ended in a double DQ in 6:01 (★★); Ted DiBiase defeated Hercules in 8:38 (★★); Akeem defeated Koko B. Ware in 11:17 (★★); Rockin Robin defeated Sensational Sherri in 10:16 (★★★); Hulk Hogan defeated The Big Boss Man in 9:12 (★★★).

Starrcade '88 ★★★★
26-12-88, Norfolk, Virginia NWA

The Varsity Club (Kevin Sullivan and Steve Williams) defeated The Fantastics (Bobby Fulton and Tommy Rogers) to win the NWA United States Tag Team Title in 15:50 (★★★); The Midnight Express (Bobby Eaton and Stan Lane) defeated The Original Midnight Express (Dennis Condrey and Randy Rose) in 17:46 (★★★); The Russian Assassins (Russian Assassin #1 and Russian Assassin #2) defeated Junkyard Dog and Ivan Koloff in 6:47 (★★); Rick Steiner defeated Mike Rotunda to win the NWA World Television Title in 17:59 (★★); Barry Windham defeated Bam Bam Bigelow via count out in 16:17 (★★★); Sting and Dusty Rhodes defeated The Road Warriors (Hawk and Animal) by DQ in 11:20 (★★★); Ric Flair defeated Lex Luger in 30:59 (★★★★).

WWF at Madison Square Garden (30-12-88) ★★★
30-12-88, New York City, New York **WWF**

The Blue Blazer vs. The Red Rooster ended in a draw in 20:00 (★★★); Mr. Perfect defeated Koko B. Ware in 11:42 (★★★); The Bushwackers (Butch and Luke) defeated The Bolsheviks (Nikolai Volkoff and Boris Zhukov) in 9:23 (★★); Jim Duggan defeated Dino Bravo in a Flag Match in 7:26 (★★); Tim Horner defeated Barry Horowitz in 8:20 (★★★); The Powers Of Pain (The Barbarian and The Warlord) defeated Demolition (Ax and Smash) via count out in a No DQ Match in 6:55 (★★); Greg Valentine defeated Ronnie Garvin in 17:09 (★★★); Randy Savage defeated Bad News Brown in 9:54 (★★★★).

Saturday Night's Main Event XIX ★★★
07-01-89, Tampa, Florida **WWF**

Brutus Beefcake defeated Ron Bass in a Hair vs. Hair Match in 7:38 (★★); Hulk Hogan defeated Akeem by DQ in 10:38 (★★); The Ultimate Warrior defeated The Honky Tonk Man in 5:07 (★★); Tito Santana defeated The Red Rooster in 9:43 (★★); Mr. Perfect defeated Koko B. Ware in 3:07 (★★).

WWF at Boston Garden (13-01-89) ★★
13-01-89, Boston, Massachusetts **WWF**

Steve Lombardi defeated Lanny Poffo in 6:32 (★★); The Bushwackers (Luke and Butch) defeated The Bolsheviks (Nikolai Volkoff and Boris Zhukov) in 9:29 (★★); Akeem defeated The Blue Blazer in 8:06 (★★); Ronnie Garvin vs. Greg Valentine ended in a double count out in 13:51 (★★★); The Brain Busters (Arn Anderson and Tully Blanchard) defeated The Rockers (Shawn Michaels and Marty Jannetty) in 15:11 (★★★★); Jim Duggan defeated Dino Bravo in a Flag Match in 8:35 (★★); Hercules defeated Virgil in 3:04 (★★); The Big Boss Man defeated Hulk Hogan by DQ in 11:28 (★★).

WWF at Spectrum (14-01-89) ★★
14-01-89, Philadelphia, Pennsylvania **WWF**

Tim Horner defeated Jose Estrada in 9:36 (★★★); The Bushwackers (Luke and Butch) defeated The Bolsheviks (Nikolai Volkoff and Boris Zhukov) in 9:47 (★★); Akeem defeated The Blue Blazer in 8:03 (★★); Hercules defeated Ted DiBiase by DQ in 8:02 (★★★); Jim Duggan defeated Dino Bravo in a Flag Match in 5:55 (★★); The Powers Of Pain (The Warlord and The Barbarian) vs. Demolition (Ax and Smash) ended in a double DQ in 6:45 (★★); Greg Valentine defeated Ronnie Garvin in 12:10 (★★★); Paul Roma defeated Iron Mike Sharpe in 3:48 (★★); Randy Savage defeated Bad News Brown in 5:36 (★★★).

Royal Rumble '89 ★★
15-01-89, Houston, Texas **WWF**

Jim Duggan and The Hart Foundation (Bret Hart and Jim Neidhart) defeated Dino Bravo and The Fabulous Rougeaus (Jacques Rougeau and Raymond Rougeau) in a Two Out Of Three Falls Match in 15:42 (★★); Rockin Robin defeated Judy Martin in 6:24 (★★); Haku defeated King Harley Race to win the King Of The Ring Crown and Cape in 9:01 (★★); Big John Studd won the 30-Man Royal Rumble Match in 64:53 (★★).

WWF at Madison Square Garden (23-01-89) ★★★
23-01-89, New York City, New York **WWF**

Sam Houston defeated Danny Davis in 9:39 (★★); Mr. Perfect defeated Brutus Beefcake via count out in 9:29 (★★★); Tim Horner defeated Jose Estrada in 8:15 (★★); Bret Hart vs. The Honky Tonk Man went to a double count out in 12:04 (★★★); The Brain Busters (Arn Anderson and Tully Blanchard) defeated The Rockers (Shawn Michaels and Marty Jannetty) in 16:14 (★★★★); Rick Rude defeated Hillbilly Jim in 8:00 (★★); Hercules defeated Ted DiBiase in 12:41 (★★★); Tito Santana defeated Ron Bass in 6:35 (★★); The Big Boss Man defeated Hulk Hogan by DQ in 9:29 (★★).

WWF at LA Sports Arena (29-01-89) ★★
29-01-89, Los Angeles, California **WWF**

Sam Houston defeated Barry Horowitz in 18:15 (★★); Rick Rude defeated Brutus Beefcake in 8:16 (★★); The Ultimate Warrior defeated King Haku in 7:15 (★★); Andre the Giant defeated Jake Roberts by DQ in 7:31 (★★); The Red Rooster defeated Danny Davis in 6:47 (★); Greg Valentine defeated Jim Neidhart in 10:11 (★★); The Brain Busters (Arn Anderson and Tully Blanchard) defeated The Rockers (Shawn Michaels and Marty Jannetty) in 18:21 (★★★★).

The Main Event II ★★★★★
03-02-89, Milwaukee, Wisconsin **WWF**

The Mega Powers (Hulk Hogan and Randy Savage) defeated The Twin Towers (Akeem and The Big Boss Man) in 22:00 (★★★); Ted DiBiase defeated Hercules in 7:12 (★★).

WWF at Boston Garden (11-02-89) ★★
11-02-89, Boston, Massachusetts **WWF**

Jim Powers defeated Iron Mike Sharpe in 11:06 (★★); Koko B. Ware defeated Boris Zhukov in 8:58 (★★); Big John Studd vs. Akeem went to a double count out in 8:06 (★); Bad News Brown defeated Pete Doherty in 4:58 (★★); The Fabulous Rougeaus (Jacques Rougeau and Raymond Rougeau) defeated The Bushwackers (Luke and Butch) by DQ in 14:04 (★★); Ron Bass defeated Paul Roma in 8:50 (★★); Rick Rude defeated Tito Santana in 16:43 (★★★); Randy Savage defeated The Ultimate Warrior via count out in 10:32 (★★).

WWF at Spectrum (11-02-89) ★★
11-02-89, Philadelphia, Pennsylvania **WWF**

The Red Rooster defeated The Brooklyn Brawler in 10:53 (★★); Sam Houston defeated Barry Horowitz in 10:26 (★★); Brutus Beefcake defeated Ted DiBiase in 10:54 (★★★); Greg Valentine defeated Jim Neidhart in 6:38 (★★); Hulk Hogan defeated The Big Boss Man in 9:09 (★★★); Rockin Robin defeated Sensational Sherri in 9:22 (★★); The Fabulous Rougeaus (Jacques Rougeau and Raymond Rougeau) defeated King Haku by DQ in 13:22 (★★); Demolition (Ax and Smash) defeated The Powers Of Pain (The Warlord and The Barbarian) via count out in a No DQ Match in 7:29 (★★).

Clash Of The Champions V: St. Valentine's Massacre ★
15-02-89, Cleveland, Ohio **NWA**

The Midnight Express (Bobby Eaton and Stan Lane) defeated The Russian Assassins (Russian Assassin #1 and Russian Assassin #2) in 13:14 (★★); Butch Reed defeated Steve Casey in 17:36 (★); Lex Luger defeated The Blackmailer in 12:53 (★★); The Varsity Club (Mike Rotunda and Steve Williams) defeated The Fantastics (Bobby Fulton and Tommy Rogers) in 13:25 (★★); Ricky Steamboat defeated Bob Bradley in 6:23 (★★); Rick Steiner defeated Rip Morgan in 4:40 (★★); The Road Warriors (Hawk and Animal) and Genichiro Tenryu vs. The Varsity Club (Mike Rotunda, Kevin Sullivan and Steve Williams) went to a double DQ in 5:53 (★★).

WWF at Madison Square Garden (20-02-89) ★★★
20-02-89, New York City, New York **WWF**

Jim Powers defeated Iron Mike Sharpe in 12:14 (★★); The Brooklyn Brawler defeated The Red Rooster in 14:40 (★★); Big John Studd vs. Akeem went to a double count out in 7:49 (★★); The Bushwackers (Luke and Butch) defeated The Fabulous Rougeaus (Jacques Rougeau and Raymond Rougeau) in 12:15 (★★); Brutus Beefcake defeated Rick Rude in 14:38 (★★★); Rick Martel vs. King Haku ended in a time limit draw in 20:00 (★★★); Greg Valentine defeated Jim Neidhart in 8:06 (★★); Randy Savage defeated The Ultimate Warrior via count out in 9:34 (★★★).

Chi-Town Rumble ★★★★
20-02-89, Chicago, Illinois **NWA**

Michael Hayes defeated Russian Assassin #1 in 15:48 (★★); Sting defeated Butch Reed in 20:07 (★★); The Midnight Express (Bobby Eaton and Stan Lane) defeated The Original Midnight Express (Jack Victory and Randy Rose) in a Loser Leaves NWA Match in 15:51 (★★★); Mike Rotunda defeated Rick Steiner to win the NWA World Television Title in 16:21 (★★); Lex Luger defeated Barry Windham to win the NWA United States Heavyweight Title in 10:43 (★★★★); The Road Warriors (Hawk and Animal) defeated The Varsity Club (Kevin Sullivan and Steve Williams) in 8:27 (★★); Ricky Steamboat defeated Ric Flair to win the NWA World Heavyweight Title in 23:18 (★★★★★).

Saturday Night's Main Event XX ★★★★★
11-03-89, Hershey, Pennsylvania **WWF**

Brutus Beefcake defeated Rick Rude by DQ in 5:45 (★★); Hulk Hogan defeated Bad News Brown in 9:44 (★★★★); Ted DiBiase defeated The Blue Blazer in 3:57 (★★★); The Brain Busters (Arn Anderson and Tully Blanchard) vs. The Rockers (Shawn Michaels and Marty Jannetty) ended in a double count out in 9:19 (★★★★); The Red Rooster defeated The Brooklyn Brawler in 1:05 (★★).

WWF at Madison Square Garden (18-03-89) ★★★★
18-03-89, New York City, New York **WWF**

The Young Stallions (Paul Roma and Jim Powers) defeated The Conquistadors (Conquistador #1 and Conquistador #2) in 13:19 (★★★); Rockin Robin defeated Judy Martin in 9:59 (★★★); Mr. Perfect defeated Ronnie Garvin in 12:21 (★★★★); Hulk Hogan defeated The Big Boss Man in a Steel Cage Match in 11:14 (★★★★); The Rockers (Shawn Michaels and Marty Jannetty) defeated The Brain Busters (Arn Anderson and Tully Blanchard) by DQ in 13:53 (★★★★); The Red Rooster defeated The Brooklyn Brawler in 11:50 (★★); Hercules vs. Bad News Brown ended in a double count out in 14:48 (★★); Jim Duggan and The Bushwhackers (Luke and Butch) defeated Dino Bravo and The Fabulous Rougeaus (Jacques Rougeau and Raymond Rougeau) in 15:00 (★★).

WWF at Boston Garden (18-03-89) ★★★★
18-03-89, Boston, Massachusetts **WWF**

The Young Stallions (Paul Roma and Jim Powers) defeated The Conquistadors (Conquistador #1 and Conquistador #2) in 14:56 (★★); Rockin Robin defeated Judy Martin in 7:45 (★★); Mr. Perfect defeated Ronnie Garvin in 14:21 (★★); The Rockers (Shawn Michaels and Marty Jannetty) defeated The Brain Busters (Arn Anderson and Tully Blanchard) by DQ in 22:25 (★★★★); The Red Rooster defeated The Brooklyn Brawler in 11:16 (★★); Hercules vs. Bad News Brown ended in a double count out in 14:48 (★★); Jim Duggan and The Bushwhackers (Luke and Butch) defeated Dino Bravo and The Fabulous Rougeaus (Jacques Rougeau and Raymond Rougeau) in 11:38 (★★); Hulk Hogan defeated The Big Boss Man in a Steel Cage Match in 9:09 (★★★★).

Clash Of The Champions VI: Ragin' Cajun ★★★★
02-04-89, New Orleans, Louisiana **NWA**

The Samoan Swat Team (Samu and Fatu) defeated The Midnight Express (Bobby Eaton and Stan Lane) in 20:32 (★★★); The Great Muta defeated Steve Casey in 8:11 (★★★); Junkyard Dog defeated Butch Reed in 9:56 (★★); Bob Orton defeated Dick Murdoch in :33 (★★); The Varsity Club (Mike Rotunda and Steve Williams) defeated The Road Warriors (Hawk and Animal) to win the NWA World Tag Team Title in 11:40 (★★); Ranger Ross defeated The Iron Sheik by DQ in 1:56 (★★); Eddie Gilbert and Rick Steiner defeated The Varsity Club (Dan Spivey and Kevin Sullivan) in 3:51 (★★); Ricky Steamboat defeated Ric Flair in a Two Out Of Three Falls Match in 55:32 (★★★★★).

WrestleMania V ★★★
02-04-89, Atlantic City, New Jersey **WWF**

Hercules defeated King Haku in 6:57 (★★); The Twin Towers (Akeem and The Big Boss Man) defeated The Rockers (Shawn Michaels and Marty Jannetty) in 8:02 (★★); Brutus Beefcake vs. Ted DiBiase ended in a double count out in 10:01 (★★); The Bushwhackers (Luke and Butch) defeated The Fabulous Rougeaus (Jacques Rougeau and Raymond Rougeau) in 9:10 (★★); Mr. Perfect defeated The Blue Blazer in 5:38 (★★★); Demolition (Ax and Smash) defeated The Powers Of Pain (The Warlord and The Barbarian) and Mr. Fuji in a Handicap Match in 8:20 (★★); Dino Bravo defeated Ronnie Garvin in 3:06 (★★); The Brain Busters (Arn Anderson and Tully Blanchard) defeated Strike Force (Rick Martel and Tito Santana) in 9:17 (★★★); Jake Roberts defeated Andre the Giant by DQ in 9:44 (★★); The Hart Foundation (Bret Hart and Jim Neidhart) defeated Rhythm and Blues (Greg Valentine and The Honky Tonk Man) in 7:40 (★★); Rick Rude defeated The Ultimate Warrior to win the WWF Intercontinental Title in 9:36 (★★★); Bad News Brown vs. Jim Duggan ended in a double DQ in 3:49 (★★); The Red Rooster defeated Bobby Heenan in :31 (★★); Hulk Hogan defeated Randy Savage to win the WWF World Heavyweight Title in 17:54 (★★★★).

WWF at Palatrussardi (08-04-89) ★★★
08-04-89, Milan, Italy **WWF**

Mr. Perfect defeated The Blue Blazer in 15:42 (★★★★); Andre the Giant defeated Bret Hart in 7:28 (★★); King Haku defeated Rick Martel in 12:12 (★★★); The Big Boss Man defeated Koko B. Ware in 9:04 (★★); The Ultimate Warrior defeated Rick Rude by DQ in 9:30 (★★★); Demolition (Ax and Smash) defeated The Powers of Pain (The Barbarian and The Warlord) by DQ in 9:50 (★★★).

WWF at Boston Garden (22-04-89) ★★
22-04-89, Boston, Massachusetts **WWF**

Greg Valentine defeated The Blue Blazer in 11:03 (★★★); The Barbarian defeated Jim Neidhart in 8:36 (★★); The Honky Tonk Man defeated Hillbilly Jim in 7:33 (★★); Demolition (Ax and Smash) defeated The Twin Towers (The Big Boss Man and Akeem) by DQ in 13:45 (★★); The Genius defeated Jim Powers in 10:31 (★★); Brutus Beefcake defeated Bad News Brown in 7:37 (★★); Rick Martel defeated Tito Santana in 3:03 (★★); The Ultimate Warrior defeated Rick Rude via count out in 10:15 (★★★).

WWF at Maple Leaf Gardens (23-04-89) ★★
23-04-89, Toronto, Canada **WWF**

Greg Valentine defeated The Blue Blazer in 12:28 (★★★); Dino Bravo defeated Hercules in 15:43 (★★); Hillbilly Jim defeated The Honky Tonk Man by DQ in :27 (★); Jake Roberts defeated Ted DiBiase in 15:04 (★★); Paul Roma defeated Boris Zhukov in 11:33 (★★); Randy Savage defeated Hulk Hogan via count out in 10:15 (★★); Mr. Perfect vs. Bret Hart ended in a time limit draw in 19:53 (★★★★); The Bushwhackers (Luke and Butch) defeated The Brain Busters (Arn Anderson and Tully Blanchard) in 11:22 (★★).

WWF at Madison Square Garden (24-04-89) ★★★
24-04-89, New York City, New York **WWF**

Greg Valentine defeated The Blue Blazer in 10:57 (★★★); Hillbilly Jim defeated The Honky Tonk Man by DQ in :24 (★); Dino Bravo defeated Hercules in 16:26 (★★); Paul Roma defeated Boris Zhukov in 12:21 (★★); Jake Roberts defeated Ted DiBiase in 16:16 (★★★); Mr. Perfect vs. Bret Hart went to a time limit draw in 20:00 (★★★); The Bushwhackers (Luke and Butch) defeated The Brain Busters (Arn Anderson and Tully Blanchard) in 10:02 (★★★); Randy Savage defeated Hulk Hogan via count out in 10:36 (★★★).

WWF at Copps Coliseum (01-05-89) ★★★
01-05-89, Hamilton, Canada **WWF**

The Honky Tonk Man defeated Jim Powers in 12:19 (★★); The Blue Blazer defeated The Brooklyn Brawler in 9:19 (★★★); Greg Valentine defeated Hillbilly Jim in 7:45 (★★); Demolition (Ax and Smash) vs. The Twin Towers (The Big Boss Man and Akeem) ended in a double DQ in 8:57 (★★★); The Red Rooster defeated Richard Charland in 9:44 (★★★); Rick Martel defeated Bret Hart in 11:07 (★★★); Mr. Perfect defeated Tito Santana in 10:40 (★★★); The Ultimate Warrior defeated Rick Rude via count out in 12:04 (★★★); Bret Hart won a Battle Royal in 10:52 (★★).

Rage In Rochester ★★
06-05-89, Rochester, Minnesota **AWA**

Akio Sato defeated Jim Evans in 3:56 (★★); Scott Norton defeated Tom Stone in 4:04 (★★); Col. DeBeers defeated Eddie Slater in 2:27 (★★); Greg Gagne defeated Tony Leone in 2:56 (★★); Mike George defeated Jake Milliman in 2:04 (★★); Derrick Dukes and Tommy Jammer defeated The Badd Company (Pat Tanaka and Paul Diamond) in 13:43 (★★★); Akio Sato defeated Greg Gagne by DQ in 10:31 (★★); Tom Zenk defeated Paul Diamond in 9:42 (★★★); Scott Norton and Wahoo McDaniel vs. The Destruction Crew (Mike Enos and Wayne Bloom) ended in a no contest in 5:56 (★★).

WrestleWar '89 ★★★
07-05-89, Nashville, Tennessee **NWA**

The Great Muta defeated Doug Gilbert in 3:03 (★★); Butch Reed defeated Ranger Ross in 6:59 (★★); Dick Murdoch defeated Bob Orton in a Bullrope Match in 4:54 (★★); The Dynamic Dudes (Johnny Ace and Shane Douglas) defeated The Samoan Swat Team (Samu and Fatu) in 11:02 (★★); Michael Hayes defeated Lex Luger to win the NWA United States Heavyweight Title in 16:06 (★★★); Sting defeated The Iron Sheik in 2:12 (★★); Ric Flair defeated Ricky Steamboat to win the NWA World Heavyweight Title in 31:37 (★★★★★); The Road Warriors (Hawk and Animal) defeated The Varsity Club (Mike Rotunda and Steve Williams) by DQ in 6:06; Eddie Gilbert and Rick Steiner defeated The Varsity Club (Dan Spivey and Kevin Sullivan) in 6:41 (★★★).

WWF at Meadowlands Arena (08-05-89) ★★★
08-05-89, East Rutherford, New Jersey **WWF**
Mr. Perfect defeated The Blue Blazer in 10:59 (★★★); Bret Hart vs. Greg Valentine ended in a draw in 19:34 (★★★); The Honky Tonk Man defeated Hillbilly Jim in 9:15 (★★); The Ultimate Warrior defeated Rick Rude via count out in 10:02 (★★★); Jim Powers defeated Iron Mike Sharpe in 10:34 (★★); The Red Rooster defeated The Brooklyn Brawler in 10:10 (★★); Rick Martel defeated Tito Santana in 3:24 (★★); Demolition (Ax and Smash) defeated The Twin Towers (The Big Boss Man and Akeem) by DQ in 15:12 (★★★).

WWF at Boston Garden (13-05-89) ★★
13-05-89, Boston, Massachusetts **WWF**
The Red Rooster defeated The Brooklyn Brawler in 12:16 (★★); Barry Horowitz defeated Dusty Wolfe in 10:20 (★★); Tom Magee defeated Tim Horner in 6:51 (★★); The Warlord defeated Koko B. Ware in 10:35 (★★); The Rockers (Shawn Michaels and Marty Jannetty) defeated The Fabulous Rougeaus (Jacques Rougeau and Raymond Rougeau) in 17:31 (★★★); King Duggan defeated Haku in 10:06 (★); Big John Studd defeated Andre the Giant by DQ in 6:38 (★).

Saturday Night's Main Event XXI ★★★★★
27-05-89, Des Moines, Iowa **WWF**
King Duggan defeated Rick Rude via count out in 7:15 (★★★); Randy Savage defeated Jim Neidhart in 5:54 (★★★); Hulk Hogan defeated The Big Boss Man in a Steel Cage Match in 10:01 (★★★★); The Brain Busters (Arn Anderson and Tully Blanchard) defeated Demolition (Ax and Smash) by DQ in 9:15 (★★★★); Jimmy Snuka defeated Boris Zhukov in 1:11 (★★).

WWF at Boston Garden (03-06-89) ★★★
03-06-89, Boston, Massachusetts **WWF**
Tim Horner defeated Barry Horowitz in 11:55 (★★★); The Warlord defeated Jim Neidhart in 4:35 (★★); Dusty Rhodes defeated Ted DiBiase in 8:30 (★★★); Paul Roma defeated Boris Zhukov in 11:36 (★★); Randy Savage defeated Hulk Hogan via count out in 12:56 (★★★); Bret Hart vs. Mr. Perfect ended in a time limit draw in 18:53 (★★★★); Dino Bravo defeated Hercules in 8:42 (★★); Demolition (Ax and Smash) defeated The Twin Towers (The Big Boss Man and Akeem) in 10:33 (★★).

WWF at Nassau Coliseum (10-06-89) ★★
10-06-89, Long Island, New York **WWF**
The Genius defeated Jim Powers in 14:02 (★★★); The Fabulous Rougeaus (Jacques Rougeau and Raymond Rougeau) defeated The Rockers (Shawn Michaels and Marty Jannetty) in 23:14 (★★★); Brutus Beefcake defeated Greg Valentine in 14:47 (★★); Hillbilly Jim defeated Andre the Giant by DQ in 8:04 (★); King Duggan defeated Haku in 10:32 (★); Jimmy Snuka defeated Boris Zhukov in 7:20 (★); The Hart Foundation (Bret Hart and Jim Neidhart) defeated The Powers Of Pain (The Warlord and The Barbarian) via count out in 13:34 (★★★).

Clash Of The Champions VII: Guts And Glory ★★★
14-06-89, Fort Bragg, North Carolina **NWA**
The Fabulous Freebirds (Michael Hayes and Jimmy Garvin) defeated The Dynamic Dudes (Johnny Ace and Shane Douglas) in 7:14 (★★★); Ranger Ross defeated The Terrorist in 1:25 (★★); The Ding Dongs (Ding Dong #1 and Ding Dong #2) defeated Cougar Jay and George South in 3:00 (★★); The Midnight Express (Bobby Eaton and Stan Lane) defeated The Samoan Swat Team (Samu and Fatu) in 6:00 (★★); Terry Gordy vs. Steve Williams went to a double count out in 6:26 (★★★); Norman the Lunatic defeated Mike Justice in :47 (★★); The Varsity Club (Mike Rotunda and Kevin Sullivan) defeated The Steiner Brothers (Rick Steiner and Scott Steiner) in 8:36 (★★★); Sting defeated Bill Irwin in 3:14 (★★); The Fabulous Freedbirds (Michael Hayes and Jimmy Garvin) defeated The Midnight Express (Bobby Eaton and Stan Lane) to win the vacant NWA World Tag Team Title in 10:03 (★★); Ricky Steamboat defeated Terry Funk by DQ in 14:00 (★★★★).

War In The Windy City ★★
23-06-89, Chicago, Illinois **AWA**
Tommy Jammer defeated Johnnie Stewart in 3:11 (★★); Akio Sato defeated Paul Diamond by DQ in 4:39 (★★); Ken Patera and Scott Norton defeated The Destruction Crew (Mike Enos and Wayne Bloom) by DQ in 6:06 (★★); Mike George defeated Rockin' Randy in 1:56 (★★); Wendi Richter defeated Candi

Devine in 3:51 (★★); Larry Zbyszko vs. Greg Gagne ended in a draw in 12:24 (★★★).

WWF at Nassau Coliseum (10-07-89) ★★
10-07-89, Long Island, New York **WWF**
Tim Horner defeated Iron Mike Sharpe in 11:27 (★★); The Warlord defeated Koko B. Ware in 6:55 (★★); Mr. Perfect vs. Hercules went to a time limit draw in 16:54 (★★★); The Genius defeated Jose Luis Rivera in 13:07 (★); Hillbilly Jim and Jim Duggan defeated The Colossal Connection (Andre the Giant and Haku) in 14:13 (★★); Paul Roma defeated Sandy Beach in 11:02 (★★); Brutus Beefcake defeated Randy Savage by DQ in 12:44 (★★★); Demolition (Ax and Smash) defeated The Twin Towers (The Big Boss Man and Akeem) in 11:06 (★★).

Great American Bash '89 ★★★★★
23-07-89, Baltimore, Maryland **NWA**
The Skyscrapers (Sid Vicious and Dan Spivey) won a King Of The Hill Double Ring Battle Royal in 10:20 (★★★); Brian Pillman defeated Bill Irwin in 10:18 (★★); The Skyscrapers (Sid Vicious and Dan Spivey) defeated The Dynamic Dudes (Johnny Ace and Shane Douglas) in 9:14 (★★); Jim Cornette defeated Paul E. Dangerously in a Tuxedo Match in 6:22 (★★★); The Steiner Brothers (Rick Steiner and Scott Steiner) defeated The Varsity Club (Kevin Sullivan and Mike Rotunda) in a Texas Tornado Match in 4:22 (★★★); Sting vs. The Great Muta ended in a double pinfall in 8:40 (★★★★); Lex Luger defeated Ricky Steamboat by DQ in 10:26 (★★★★); The Road Warriors (Hawk and Animal), The Midnight Express (Bobby Eaton and Stan Lane) and Steve Williams defeated The Fabulous Freebirds (Michael Hayes, Jimmy Garvin and Terry Gordy) and The Samoan Swat Team (Samu and Fatu) in a War Games Match in 22:18 (★★★★); Ric Flair defeated Terry Funk in 17:23 (★★★★).

Saturday Night's Main Event XXII ★★★★
29-07-89, Worcester, Massachusetts **WWF**
Hulk Hogan defeated The Honky Tonk Man in 6:14 (★★★); Jimmy Snuka defeated Greg Valentine in 3:14 (★★); Brutus Beefcake defeated Randy Savage by DQ in 11:30 (★★★); The Brain Busters (Arn Anderson and Tully Blanchard) defeated Demolition (Ax and Smash) in a Two Out Of Three Falls Match to win the WWF World Tag Team Title in 12:33 (★★★).

SummerSlam '89 ★★★★
28-08-89, East Rutherford, New Jersey **WWF**
The Brain Busters (Arn Anderson and Tully Blanchard) defeated The Hart Foundation (Bret Hart and Jim Neidhart) in 16:23 (★★★★); Dusty Rhodes defeated The Honky Tonk Man in 9:36 (★★); Mr. Perfect defeated The Red Rooster in 3:21 (★★); Rick Martel and The Fabulous Rougeaus (Jacques Rougeau and Raymond Rougeau) defeated Tito Santana and The Rockers (Shawn Michaels and Marty Jannetty) in 14:58 (★★); The Ultimate Warrior defeated Rick Rude to win the WWF Intercontinental Title in 16:02 (★★★★); Jim Duggan and Demolition (Ax and Smash) defeated Andre the Giant and The Twin Towers (Akeem and The Big Boss Man) in 7:23 (★★★); Greg Valentine defeated Hercules in 3:08 (★★); Ted DiBiase defeated Jimmy Snuka via count out in 6:27 (★★); Hulk Hogan and Brutus Beefcake defeated Randy Savage and Zeus in 15:04 (★★★★).

Clash Of The Champions VIII: Fall Brawl '89 ★★★★
12-09-89, Columbia, South Carolina **NWA**
The Road Warriors (Hawk and Animal) defeated The Samoan Swat Team (Samu and Fatu) in 6:46 (★★★); Tom Zenk defeated The Cuban Assassin in 3:36 (★★); Sid Vicious defeated Ranger Ross in 1:08 (★★); The Fabulous Freebirds (Michael Hayes and Jimmy Garvin) defeated The Steiner Brothers (Rick Steiner and Scott Steiner) in 10:27 (★★★); Brian Pillman defeated Norman the Lunatic in 3:38 (★★★★); Steve Williams defeated Mike Rotunda in 7:04 (★★); Lex Luger defeated Tommy Rich in 10:36 (★★★); Sting and Ric Flair defeated Dick Slater and The Great Muta by DQ in 19:16 (★★★★).

WWF at Madison Square Garden (30-09-89) ★★
30-09-89, New York City, New York **WWF**
The Genius defeated Koko B. Ware in 13:01 (★★); Jimmy Snuka defeated The Honky Tonk Man in 10:27 (★★); Mr. Perfect defeated The Red Rooster in 9:38 (★★); Mark Young defeated Barry Horowitz in 10:58 (★★); The Ultimate Warrior

defeated **Andre the Giant** by DQ in 9:28 (★ ★); **Demolition** (Ax and Smash) defeated **The Brain Busters** (Arn Anderson and Tully Blanchard) by DQ in 12:51 (★ ★); **Greg Valentine** defeated **Ronnie Garvin** in 17:05 (★ ★ ★ ★); **Roddy Piper** vs. **Rick Rude** ended in a double count out in 11:00 (★ ★ ★).

WWF at Maple Leaf Gardens (08-10-89) ★ ★
08-10-89, Toronto, Canada **WWF**
Paul Roma defeated **Boris Zhukov** in 14:14 (★); **Greg Valentine** defeated **Ronnie Garvin** in 13:23 (★ ★ ★); **The Bushwhackers** (Luke and Butch) defeated **The Powers Of Pain** (The Warlord and The Barbarian) in 8:59 (★ ★); **Randy Savage** defeated **Jimmy Snuka** in 11:52 (★ ★); **The Genius** defeated **Hillbilly Jim** via count out in 3:51 (★); **Jim Duggan** defeated **Akeem** in 5:49 (★ ★); **Richard Charland** defeated **Barry Horowitz** in 6:22 (★); **Rick Rude** defeated **Roddy Piper** by DQ in 12:07 (★ ★ ★).

WWF On Sky One ★ ★
10-10-89, London, England **WWF**
Koko B. Ware defeated **Boris Zhukov** in 10:59; **Dino Bravo** defeated **Bret Hart** in 16:09 (★ ★); **King Duggan** defeated **The Honky Tonk Man** in 9:06 (★); **The Rockers** (Shawn Michaels and Marty Jannetty) defeated **The Fabulous Rougeaus** (Jacques Rougeau and Raymond Rougeau) in 24:16 (★ ★ ★ ★); **The Brooklyn Brawler** defeated **Paul Roma** in 6:13 (★ ★); **Hulk Hogan** defeated **Randy Savage** in 14:04 (★ ★ ★).

WWF at Bercy Stadium (13-10-89) ★ ★ ★
13-10-89, Paris, France **WWF**
Bret Hart defeated **The Honky Tonk Man** by DQ in 15:25 (★ ★ ★); **King Duggan** defeated **Dino Bravo** in 8:35 (★ ★); **The Rockers** (Shawn Michaels and Marty Jannetty) defeated **The Rougeau Brothers** (Jacques Rougeau and Raymond Rougeau) in 12:56 (★ ★ ★); **Hulk Hogan** defeated **Randy Savage** in 12:01 (★ ★ ★).

Saturday Night's Main Event XXIII ★ ★ ★
14-10-89, Cincinatti, Ohio **WWF**
Randy Savage defeated **Jimmy Snuka** in 5:37 (★ ★); **Hulk Hogan** defeated **Ted DiBiase** in 8:24 (★ ★); **Roddy Piper** defeated **Haku** in 3:02 (★ ★); **Tito Santana** vs. **Rick Martel** ended in a double DQ in 9:41 (★ ★ ★); **The Bushwhackers** (Luke and Butch) defeated **The Fabulous Rougeaus** (Jacques Rougeau and Raymond Rougeau) in 3:15 (★ ★).

Halloween Havoc '89 ★ ★ ★ ★
28-10-89, Philadelphia, Pennsylvania **NWA**
Tom Zenk defeated **Mike Rotunda** in 13:23 (★ ★ ★); **The Samoan Swat Team** (Samu, Fatu and The Samoan Savage) defeated **The Midnight Express** (Bobby Eaton and Stan Lane) and **Steve Williams** in 18:23 (★ ★ ★ ★); **Tommy Rich** defeated **The Cuban Assassin** in 8:29 (★ ★); **The Fabulous Freebirds** (Michael Hayes and Jimmy Garvin) defeated **The Dynamic Dudes** (Johnny Ace and Shane Douglas) in 11:28 (★ ★); **Doom** (Ron Simmons and Butch Reed) defeated **The Steiner Brothers** (Rick Steiner and Scott Steiner) in 15:32 (★ ★); **Lex Luger** defeated **Brian Pillman** in 16:49 (★ ★ ★ ★); **The Road Warriors** (Hawk and Animal) defeated **The Skyscrapers** (Sid Vicious and Dan Spivey) by DQ in 11:39 (★ ★); **Ric Flair** and **Sting** defeated **Terry Funk** and **The Great Muta** in a Thunderdome Match in 23:46 (★ ★ ★ ★).

WWF at Madison Square Garden (28-10-89) ★ ★
28-10-89, New York City, New York **WWF**
Tito Santana defeated **Boris Zhukov** in 12:46 (★ ★); **Al Perez** defeated **Conquistador #1** in 10:15 (★ ★); **Bret Hart** vs. **Dino Bravo** went to a time limit draw in 20:00 (★ ★); **The Brooklyn Brawler** defeated **Jose Luis Rivera** in 7:34 (★); **Randy Savage** defeated **Jim Duggan** in 16:04 (★ ★ ★ ★); **Hercules** defeated **Akeem** via count out in 11:19 (★ ★); **Mr. Perfect** defeated **Jimmy Snuka** in 10:36 (★ ★); **The Ultimate Warrior** defeated **Andre the Giant** in :20 (★); **The Bushwhackers** (Luke and Butch) defeated **The Powers of Pain** (The Warlord and The Barbarian) by DQ in 7:55 (★ ★).

Survivor Series Showdown (1989) ★ ★ ★
12-11-89, Wichita, Kansas **WWF**
Tito Santana defeated **The Big Boss Man** in 11:35 (★ ★ ★); **Mr. Perfect** defeated **Butch** in 6:55 (★ ★); **Randy Savage** defeated **Hercules** in 10:54 (★ ★ ★); **The Ultimate Warrior** defeated **Tully Blanchard** by DQ in 6:00 (★ ★); **Ted DiBiase** defeated **Smash** in 10:11 (★ ★).

Clash Of The Champions IX: New York Knockout ★ ★ ★ ★ ★
15-11-89, Troy, New York **NWA**
The Fabulous Freebirds (Michael Hayes and Jimmy Garvin) defeated **The Road Warriors** (Hawk and Animal) by DQ in 5:18 (★ ★); **Doom** (Ron Simmons and Butch Reed) defeated **Eddie Gilbert** and **Tommy Rich** in 5:15 (★ ★); **The Midnight Express** (Bobby Eaton and Stan Lane) defeated **The Dynamic Dudes** (Johnny Ace and Shane Douglas) in 9:22 (★ ★ ★); **Steve Williams** defeated **The Super Destroyer** in 1:41 (★ ★); **The Steiner Brothers** (Rick Steiner and Scott Steiner) defeated **The Skyscrapers** (Dan Spivey and Sid Vicious) by DQ in 6:08 (★ ★); **Lex Luger** defeated **Brian Pillman** in 12:38 (★ ★ ★ ★); **Ric Flair** defeated **Terry Funk** in an "I Quit" Match in 18:33 (★ ★ ★ ★ ★).

Survivor Series '89 ★ ★ ★
23-11-89, Rosemont, Illinois **WWF**
The Dream Team (Dusty Rhodes, Brutus Beefcake, The Red Rooster and Tito Santana) defeated **The Enforcers** (The Big Boss Man, Bad News Brown, Rick Martel and The Honky Tonk Man) in an Elimination Match in 22:02 (★ ★ ★); **The King's Court** (Randy Savage, Canadian Earthquake, Dino Bravo and Greg Valentine) defeated **The 4x4s** (Jim Duggan, Bret Hart, Ronnie Garvin and Hercules) in an Elimination Match in 23:25 (★ ★); **The Hulkamaniacs** (Hulk Hogan, Jake Roberts, Ax and Smash) defeated **The Million Dollar Team** (Ted DiBiase, Zeus, The Warlord and The Barbarian) in an Elimination Match in 27:32 (★ ★ ★ ★); **The Rude Brood** (Rick Rude, Mr. Perfect, Jacques Rougeau and Raymond Rougeau) defeated **Roddy's Rowdies** (Roddy Piper, Jimmy Snuka, Luke and Butch) in an Elimination Match in 21:27 (★ ★ ★); **The Ultimate Warriors** (The Ultimate Warrior, Jim Neidhart, Shawn Michaels and Marty Jannetty) defeated **The Heenan Family** (Bobby Heenan, Andre the Giant, Haku and Arn Anderson) in an Elimination Match in 20:28 (★ ★ ★).

Saturday Night's Main Event XXIV ★ ★ ★
25-11-89, Topeka, Kansas **WWF**
The Ultimate Warrior defeated **Andre the Giant** by DQ in 7:46 (★); **The Genius** defeated **Hulk Hogan** via count out in 7:34 (★ ★); **Dusty Rhodes** defeated **The Big Boss Man** in 4:47 (★ ★); **Mr. Perfect** defeated **The Red Rooster** in 4:13 (★ ★); **The Rockers** (Shawn Michaels and Marty Jannetty) defeated **The Brain Busters** (Arn Anderson and Tully Blanchard) in a Two Out Of Three Falls Match in 7:32 (★ ★ ★ ★).

WWF at Madison Square Garden (25-11-89) ★ ★ ★
25-11-89, New York City, New York **WWF**
Haku defeated **Paul Roma** in 10:08 (★ ★ ★); **The Hart Foundation** (Bret Hart and Jim Neidhart) vs. **The Rockers** (Shawn Michaels and Marty Jannetty) went to a time limit draw in 19:39 (★ ★ ★ ★); **Al Perez** defeated **The Brooklyn Brawler** in 8:33 (★ ★); **Jake Roberts** defeated **Ted DiBiase** in 15:09 (★ ★); **Tito Santana** vs. **Bad News Brown** ended in a count out in 15:53 (★ ★ ★); **Dino Bravo** defeated **Hercules** in 9:11 (★); **Jim Duggan** defeated **Randy Savage** via count out in 7:33 (★ ★).

Starrcade '89 ★ ★ ★
13-12-89, Atlanta, Georgia **NWA**
The Steiner Brothers (Rick Steiner and Scott Steiner) defeated **Doom** (Ron Simmons and Butch Reed) via count out in 12:24 (★ ★); **Lex Luger** defeated **Sting** in 11:31 (★ ★); **The Road Warriors** (Hawk and Animal) defeated **Doom** (Ron Simmons and Butch Reed) in 8:31 (★ ★); **Ric Flair** defeated **The Great Muta** in 1:55 (★ ★); **The Steiner Brothers** (Rick Steiner and Scott Steiner) defeated **The Road Warriors** (Hawk and Animal) in 7:27 (★ ★ ★); **Sting** defeated **The Great Muta** in 8:41 (★ ★ ★ ★); **The New Wild Samoans** (Fatu and The Samoan Savage) defeated **Doom** (Ron Simmons and Butch Reed) in 8:22 (★ ★); **Ric Flair** vs. **Lex Luger** ended in a time limit draw in 17:15 (★ ★ ★ ★); **The New Wild Samoans** (Fatu and The Samoan Savage) defeated **The Steiner Brothers** (Rick Steiner and Scott Steiner) by DQ in 14:05 (★ ★ ★); **Lex Luger** defeated **The Great Muta** by DQ in 14:14 (★ ★); **The Road Warriors** (Hawk and Animal) defeated **The New Wild Samoans** (Fatu and The Samoan Savage) in 5:18 (★); **Sting** defeated **Ric Flair** in 14:30 (★ ★ ★ ★).

No Holds Barred: The Match/The Movie ★★
27-12-89, Nashville, Tennessee **WWF**

Dark: **Dusty Rhodes** defeated **The Big Boss Man**; Dark: **The Ultimate Warrior** defeated **Dino Bravo**; Dark: **The Colossal Connection** (**Andre the Giant** and **Haku**) defeated **Demolition** (**Ax** and **Smash**) via count out; Dark: **Mr. Perfect** defeated **Ronnie Garvin**; **Hulk Hogan** and **Brutus Beefcake** defeated **Randy Savage** and **Zeus** in a Steel Cage Match in 10:27 (★★).

WWF at Madison Square Garden (28-12-89) ★★
28-12-89, New York City, New York **WWF**

Tito Santana defeated **Bob Bradley** in 14:24 (★★); **Little Cocoa** and **Karate Chris Dube** defeated **Cowboy Cottrell** and **Little Tokyo** in 11:55 (★★); **Rick Martel** defeated **Brutus Beefcake** in 14:48 (★★); **Tugboat Thomas** defeated **Dale Wolfe** in 2:28 (★); **Jake Roberts** defeated **Ted DiBiase** in a No DQ Match in 18:37 (★★); **Koko B. Ware** defeated **Iron Mike Sharpe** in 12:07 (★★); **The Colossal Connection** (**Andre the Giant** and **Haku**) defeated **Demolition** (**Ax** and **Smash**) via count out in 11:12 (★★★); **Roddy Piper** defeated **Rick Rude** in a Steel Cage Match in 12:55 (★★★★).

WWF at Madison Square Garden (15-01-90) ★★★
15-01-90, New York City, New York **WWF**

The Genius defeated **Jim Neidhart** in 9:21 (★★); **The Powers Of Pain** (**The Barbarian** and **The Warlord**) defeated **The Rockers** (**Shawn Michaels** and **Marty Jannetty**) in 9:59 (★★★★); **Al Perez** defeated **Paul Roma** in 11:18 (★★); **Mr. Perfect** defeated **Hulk Hogan** by DQ in 13:36 (★★★); **Akeem** defeated **Bret Hart** in 8:30 (★★); **Jimmy Snuka** and **Ronnie Garvin** vs. **Rhythm & Blues** (**The Honky Tonk Man** and **Greg Valentine**) ended in a draw in 19:39 (★★); **Ted DiBiase** defeated **Jake Roberts** via count out in 20:31 (★★★).

Royal Rumble '90 ★★★★
21-01-90, Orlando, Florida **WWF**

The Bushwhackers (**Luke** and **Butch**) defeated **The Fabulous Rougeaus** (**Jacques Rougeau** and **Raymond Rougeau**) in 13:35 (★★); **Brutus Beefcake** vs. **The Genius** ended in a double DQ in 11:07 (★★); **Ronnie Garvin** defeated **Greg Valentine** in a Submission Match in 16:55 (★★★★); **Jim Duggan** defeated **The Big Boss Man** by DQ in 6:13 (★★); **Hulk Hogan** won the 30-Man Royal Rumble Match in 58:46 (★★★★).

Saturday Night's Main Event XXV ★★★★
27-01-90, Chattanooga, Tennessee **WWF**

Randy Savage defeated **Jim Duggan** in 7:55 (★★★); **Hulk Hogan** and **The Ultimate Warrior** defeated **Mr. Perfect** and **The Genius** in 7:50 (★★★); **Jake Roberts** defeated **Greg Valentine** by DQ in 5:16 (★★); **Dusty Rhodes** vs. **Rick Rude** ended in a double count out in 8:38 (★★); **Dino Bravo** defeated **Ronnie Garvin** in 3:15 (★★).

Clash Of The Champions X: Texas Shootout ★★★★
06-02-90, Corpus Christi, Texas **NWA**

Steve Williams defeated **The Samoan Savage** in 7:55 (★★); **Brian Pillman** and **Tom Zenk** defeated **The MOD Squad** (**Spike** and **Basher**) in 9:53 (★★); **Mil Mascaras** defeated **Cactus Jack** in 5:00 (★★); **Norman the Lunatic** defeated **Kevin Sullivan** in a Falls Count Anywhere Match in 7:26 (★★★); **The Road Warriors** (**Hawk** and **Animal**) defeated **The Skyscrapers** (**Dan Spivey** and **Mark Callous**) by DQ in 7:26 (★★); **The Steiner Brothers** (**Rick Steiner** and **Scott Steiner**) defeated **Doom** (**Ron Simmons** and **Butch Reed**) in a Title vs. Mask Match in 13:04 (★★★); **The Four Horsemen** (**Ric Flair**, **Arn Anderson** and **Ole Anderson**) defeated **Gary Hart International** (**Buzz Sawyer**, **The Great Muta** and **The Dragon Master**) in 6:10 (★★).

WWF at Madison Square Garden (19-02-90) ★★
19-02-90, New York City, New York **WWF**

Tito Santana defeated **Buddy Rose** in 16:55 (★★); **Earthquake** defeated **Ronnie Garvin** in 7:35 (★★); **Rick Martel** defeated **The Red Rooster** in 21:00 (★★★); **Hulk Hogan** and **Brutus Beefcake** defeated **Mr. Perfect** and **The Genius** in 15:27 (★★★); **Bad News Brown** defeated **Jim Brunzell** in 14:39 (★★); **Dusty Rhodes** defeated **Akeem** via count out in 9:04 (★); **Jim Duggan** and **The Rockers** (**Shawn Michaels** and **Marty Jannetty**) defeated **Mr. Fuji** and **The Powers Of Pain** (**The Barbarian** and **The Warlord**) in 16:38 (★★).

The Main Event III ★★
23-02-90, Detroit, Michigan **WWF**

Hulk Hogan defeated **Randy Savage** in 9:55 (★★); **The Ultimate Warrior** defeated **Dino Bravo** in 4:11 (★★).

WrestleWar '90 ★★★
25-02-90, Greensboro, North Carolina **NWA**

Kevin Sullivan and **Buzz Sawyer** defeated **The Dynamic Dudes** (**Johnny Ace** and **Shane Douglas**) in 10:15 (★★); **Norman the Lunatic** defeated **Cactus Jack** in 9:33 (★★); **The Rock 'n' Roll Express** (**Ricky Morton** and **Robert Gibson**) defeated **The Midnight Express** (**Bobby Eaton** and **Stan Lane**) in 19:31 (★★★★); **The Road Warriors** (**Hawk** and **Animal**) defeated **The Skyscrapers** (**Mark Callous** and **The Masked Skyscraper**) in a Chicago Street Fight in 4:59 (★★); **Brian Pillman** and **Tom Zenk** defeated **The Fabulous Freebirds** (**Michael Hayes** and **Jimmy Garvin**) in 24:32 (★★); **The Steiner Brothers** (**Rick Steiner** and **Scott Steiner**) defeated **Arn Anderson** and **Ole Anderson** in 16:05 (★★★★); **Ric Flair** defeated **Lex Luger** via count out in 38:08 (★★★★).

WWF at Madison Square Garden (19-03-90) ★
19-03-90, New York City, New York **WWF**

Jim Powers defeated **Iron Mike Sharpe** in 13:00 (★★); **Hercules** defeated **Black Bart** in 12:06 (★); **Koko B. Ware** defeated **Frenchy Martin** in 12:40 (★); **The Orient Express** (**Sato** and **Tanaka**) defeated **Demolition** (**Ax** and **Smash**) via count out in 10:58 (★★); **Earthquake** defeated **Jim Duggan** in 6:30 (★); **Bret Hart** vs. **Rick Martel** ended in a draw in 21:36 (★★★); **Dino Bravo** defeated **Brutus Beefcake** via count out in 11:27 (★★); **Tugboat** defeated **Pez Whatley** in 5:51 (★); **The Ultimate Warrior** defeated **Mr. Perfect** in 10:02 (★★).

The Ultimate Challenge ★★
25-03-90, San Francisco, California **WWF**

Ted DiBiase defeated **The Red Rooster** in 8:00 (★★); **The Big Boss Man** defeated **Boris Zhukov** in 7:24 (★★); **Rhythm & Blues** (**Greg Valentine** and **The Honky Tonk Man**) defeated **Jerry Monti** and **Jim Gorman** in 1:47 (★★); **Dusty Rhodes** defeated **Randy Savage** by DQ in 7:30 (★★); **Earthquake** defeated **Ronnie Garvin** in 4:59 (★★★); **The Colossal Connection** (**Andre the Giant** and **Haku**) defeated **The Rockers** (**Marty Jannetty** and **Shawn Michaels**) by DQ in 3:38 (★★).

WrestleMania VI ★★★
01-04-90, Toronto, Ontario **WWF**

Rick Martel defeated **Koko B. Ware** in 3:51 (★★); **Demolition** (**Ax** and **Smash**) defeated **The Colossal Connection** (**Andre the Giant** and **Haku**) to win the WWF World Tag Team Title in 9:30 (★★); **Earthquake** defeated **Hercules** in 4:52 (★★); **Brutus Beefcake** defeated **Mr. Perfect** in 7:48 (★★); **Bad News Brown** vs. **Roddy Piper** ended in a double count out in 6:48 (★★); **The Hart Foundation** (**Bret Hart** and **Jim Neidhart**) defeated **The Bolsheviks** (**Nikolai Volkoff** and **Boris Zhukov**) in :19 (★★); **The Barbarian** defeated **Tito Santana** in 4:33 (★★); **Dusty Rhodes** and **Sapphire** defeated **Randy Savage** and **Queen Sherri** in 7:52 (★★); **The Orient Express** (**Sato** and **Tanaka**) defeated **The Rockers** (**Shawn Michaels** and **Marty Jannetty**) via count out in 7:38 (★★); **Jim Duggan** defeated **Dino Bravo** in 4:15 (★★); **Ted DiBiase** defeated **Jake Roberts** via count out in 11:50 (★★); **The Big Boss Man** defeated **Akeem** in 1:49 (★★); **Rick Rude** defeated **Jimmy Snuka** in 3:59 (★★); **The Ultimate Warrior** defeated **Hulk Hogan** to win the WWF World Heavyweight Title in 24:51 (★★★★).

Wrestling Summit ★★★
13-04-90, Tokyo, Japan **WWF/NJPW/AJPW**

Jimmy Snuka and **Tito Santana** defeated **Kenta Kobashi** and **Masanobu Fuchi** in 8:26 (★★); **Bret Hart** vs. **Tiger Mask** ended in a time limit draw in 20:16 (★★); **The Great Kabuki** defeated **Greg Valentine** in 7:17 (★★); **Jake Roberts** defeated **The Big Boss Man** in 10:26 (★★); **Jumbo Tsuruta** and **King Haku** defeated **Mr. Perfect** and **Rick Martel** in 10:53 (★★★); **Genichiro Tenryu** defeated **Randy Savage** in 10:49 (★★★★); **The Ultimate Warrior** defeated **Ted DiBiase** in 6:13 (★★); **Andre the Giant** and **Giant Baba** defeated **Demolition** (**Ax** and **Smash**) in 6:38 (★★); **Hulk Hogan** defeated **Stan Hansen** in 12:31 (★★★★).

Saturday Night's Main Event XXVI ★★★
28-04-90, Austin, Texas **WWF**
Hulk Hogan defeated **Mr. Perfect** in 7:55 (★★); Earthquake defeated **Hillbilly Jim** in 1:53 (★★); The Hart Foundation (Bret Hart and Jim Neidhart) vs. The Rockers (Shawn Michaels and Marty Jannetty) ended in a double DQ in 11:31 (★★★★); The Ultimate Warrior defeated **Haku** in 4:45 (★★); The Big Boss Man defeated **Akeem** by DQ in 3:18 (★★).

WWF at Madison Square Garden (30-04-90) ★★
30-04-90, New York City, New York **WWF**
Hercules defeated **Haku** in 11:51 (★★); Paul Diamond defeated **Jim Powers** in 9:53 (★★); Jake Roberts defeated **Bad News Brown** in 12:55 (★★★); Nikolai Volkoff defeated **Jose Luis Rivera** in 5:23 (★); Rhythm & Blues (The Honky Tonk Man and Greg Valentine) defeated **The Bushwhackers** (Butch and Luke) via count out in 13:01 (★★); Dino Bravo defeated **The Red Rooster** in 4:45 (★★); The Big Boss Man defeated **Ted DiBiase** in 11:18 (★★); The Barbarian defeated **Jimmy Snuka** in 6:40 (★★); Hulk Hogan defeated **Earthquake** by DQ in 8:39 (★★).

Capital Combat '90 ★★★★
19-05-90, Washington, D.C. **NWA**
Norman the Lunatic and The Road Warriors (Hawk and Animal) defeated **Bam Bam Bigelow, Cactus Jack and Kevin Sullivan** in 9:38 (★★★); Mean Mark defeated **Johnny Ace** in 10:41 (★★); The Samoan SWAT Team (Fatu and The Samoan Savage) defeated **Mike Rotunda and Tommy Rich** in 17:54 (★★); Paul Ellering defeated **Teddy Long** in a Hair vs. Hair Match in 1:57 (★); The Midnight Express (Bobby Eaton and Stan Lane) defeated **Brian Pillman and Tom Zenk** to win the NWA United States Tag Team Title in 20:20 (★★★★); The Rock 'n' Roll Express (Ricky Morton and Robert Gibson) defeated **The Fabulous Freebirds** (Michael Hayes and Jimmy Garvin) in a Corporal Punishment Match in 18:33 (★★★); Doom (Ron Simmons and Butch Reed) defeated **The Steiner Brothers** (Rick Steiner and Scott Steiner) to win the NWA World Tag Team Title in 19:14 (★★★★); Lex Luger defeated **Ric Flair** by DQ in a Steel Cage Match in 17:21 (★★★).

Clash Of The Champions XI: Coastal Crush ★★★
13-06-90, Charleston, South Carolina **NWA**
The Southern Boys (Steve Armstrong and Tracy Smothers) defeated **The Fabulous Freebirds** (Michael Hayes and Jimmy Garvin) in 7:29 (★★); Tommy Rich defeated **Bam Bam Bigelow** by DQ in 3:46 (★★); Tom Zenk and Mike Rotunda defeated **The Samoan SWAT Team** (Fatu and The Samoan Savage) in 5:25 (★★); Mean Mark defeated **Brian Pillman** in 5:40 (★★); The Rock 'n' Roll Express (Ricky Morton and Robert Gibson) defeated **The Midnight Express** (Bobby Eaton and Stan Lane) by DQ in 12:08 (★★★); Barry Windham defeated **Doug Furnas** in 5:40 (★★); Lex Luger defeated **Sid Vicious** in :26 (★★); Doom (Ron Simmons and Butch Reed) defeated **The Steiner Brothers** (Rick Steiner and Scott Steiner) in 11:19 (★★★); Paul Orndorff defeated **Arn Anderson** in 11:39 (★★); Junkyard Dog defeated **Ric Flair** by DQ in 6:37 (★★).

Aniversario '90 ★★★
07-07-90, Bayamon, Puerto Rico **WWC**
Chris Youngblood defeated **Chicky Starr** in 10:26 (★★★); Espectrito and Piratita Morgan defeated **Aguilita Solitaria and Mascarita Sagrada** in 6:42 (★); Scott Hall defeated **Atkie Malumba** by DQ in 4:57 (★★); Invader #1 defeated **Leo Burke** in a Boxing Match to win the WWC Caribbean Heavyweight Title in 11:47 (★★); Abdullah The Butcher vs. Zeus ended in a double count out in 9:52 (★); The Caribbean Express (Huracan Castillo and Miguel Perez Jr.) defeated **Ron Starr and The Cuban Assassin** to win the WWC Caribbean Tag Team Title in 7:01 (★★★); Super Medicos (Super Medic I and Super Medic II) defeated **The Rougeau Brothers** (Jacques Rougeau and Raymond Rougeau) in 11:10 (★★★); Monster Ripper defeated **Candi Devine** to win the vacant WWC Womens Title in 5:14 (★★); Carlos Colon vs. TNT ended in a draw in 60:00 (★★★★).

Great American Bash '90 ★★★★
07-07-90, Baltimore, Maryland **NWA**
Brian Pillman defeated **Buddy Landel** in 9:29 (★★★); Mike Rotunda defeated **The Iron Sheik** in 6:46 (★★); Doug Furnas defeated **Dutch Mantel** in 11:18 (★★); Harley Race defeated **Tommy Rich** in 6:32 (★★); The Midnight Express (Bobby Eaton and Stan Lane) defeated **The Southern Boys** (Steve Armstrong

and Tracy Smothers) in 18:14 (★★★★★); Big Van Vader defeated **Tom Zenk** in 2:16 (★★); The Steiner Brothers (Rick Steiner and Scott Steiner) defeated **The Fabulous Freebirds** (Michael Hayes and Jimmy Garvin) in 13:45 (★★★); El Gigante, Junkyard Dog and Paul Orndorff defeated **Arn Anderson, Barry Windham and Sid Vicious** by DQ in 8:53 (★★); Lex Luger defeated **Mark Callous** in 12:10 (★★); Doom (Ron Simmons and Butch Reed) defeated **The Rock 'n' Roll Express** (Ricky Morton and Robert Gibson) in 15:40 (★★); Sting defeated **Ric Flair** to win the NWA World Heavyweight Title in 16:06 (★★★★).

Saturday Night's Main Event XXVII ★★★★
28-07-90, Omaha, Nebraska **WWF**
The Ultimate Warrior defeated **Rick Rude** by DQ in 9:45 (★★★); Demolition (Smash and Crush) defeated **The Rockers** (Shawn Michaels and Marty Jannetty) in 9:34 (★★★); Mr. Perfect defeated **Tito Santana** in 12:19 (★★★★); The Texas Tornado defeated **Buddy Rose** in 3:09 (★★).

SummerSlam '90 ★★★
27-08-90, Philadelphia, Pennsylvania **WWF**
Power and Glory (Hercules and Paul Roma) defeated **The Rockers** (Shawn Michaels and Marty Jannetty) in 6:00 (★★); The Texas Tornado defeated **Mr. Perfect** to win the WWF Intercontinental Title in 5:15 (★★); Queen Sherri defeated **Sapphire** via forfeit (★); The Warlord defeated **Tito Santana** in 5:28 (★★★); The Hart Foundation (Bret Hart and Jim Neidhart) defeated **Demolition** (Smash and Crush) in a Two Out Of Three Falls Match to win the WWF World Tag Team Title in 14:24 (★★★); Jake Roberts defeated **Bad News Brown** by DQ in 4:44 (★); Jim Duggan and Nikolai Volkoff defeated **The Orient Express** (Sato and Tanaka) in 3:22 (★★); Randy Savage defeated **Dusty Rhodes** in 2:15 (★★); Hulk Hogan defeated **Earthquake** via count out in 13:16 (★★); The Ultimate Warrior defeated **Rick Rude** in a Steel Cage Match in 10:05 (★★★).

Clash Of The Champions XII: Mountain Madness ★★
05-09-90, Asheville, North Carolina **NWA**
The Southern Boys (Steve Armstrong and Tracy Smothers) defeated **The Fabulous Freebirds** (Michael Hayes and Jimmy Garvin) in 8:34 (★★); Mike Rotunda defeated **Buddy Landel** in 5:39 (★★); The Master Blasters (Iron and Steel) defeated **Brad Armstrong and Tim Horner** in 4:52 (★★); The Nasty Boys (Brian Knobbs and Jerry Sags) defeated **Jackie Fulton and Terry Taylor** in 7:11 (★★); Tommy Rich defeated **Bill Irwin** in 3:59 (★★); Susan Sexton defeated **Bambi** in 4:11 (★★); The Steiner Brothers (Rick Steiner and Scott Steiner) defeated **Maximum Overdrive** (Tim Hunt and Jeff Warner) in 6:23 (★); Stan Hansen defeated **Tom Zenk** in 3:19 (★★); Lex Luger defeated **Ric Flair** by DQ in 15:28 (★★★★); Sting defeated **The Black Scorpion** in 8:13 (★★).

WWF at Madison Square Garden (21-09-90) ★★
21-09-90, New York City, New York **WWF**
Dustin Rhodes defeated **Paul Diamond** in 13:04 (★★); Sgt. Slaughter defeated **Nikolai Volkoff** in 8:40 (★); The Barbarian defeated **Tito Santana** in 13:28 (★★); Paul Roma defeated **Marty Jannetty** in 13:43 (★★); Ronnie Garvin defeated **Bob Bradley** in 12:21 (★); Jim Duggan defeated **Rick Rude** by DQ in 9:10 (★★); The Ultimate Warrior and The Legion of Doom (Animal and Hawk) defeated **Demolition** (Ax, Smash and Crush) in 12:59 (★★).

Saturday Night's Main Event XXVIII ★★
13-10-90, Toledo, Ohio **WWF**
The Ultimate Warrior and The Legion Of Doom (Hawk and Animal) defeated **Demolition** (Ax, Smash and Crush) in 5:33 (★★); Randy Savage defeated **Dusty Rhodes** via count out in 12:22 (★★); Hulk Hogan and Tugboat defeated **Rhythm and Blues** (Greg Valentine and The Honky Tonk Man) by DQ in 11:11 (★★); The Texas Tornado defeated **Haku** in 4:09 (★★); Sgt. Slaughter defeated **Koko B. Ware** in 5:18 (★★).

WWF at Madison Square Garden (19-10-90) ★★
19-10-90, New York City, New York **WWF**
Shane Douglas defeated **The Brooklyn Brawler** in 10:19 (★★); The Warlord defeated **Koko B. Ware** in 8:07 (★★); Mr. Perfect vs. The Texas Tornado ended in a double count out in 8:50 (★★); Iron Mike Sharpe defeated **SD Jones** in 10:56 (★); Ted DiBiase defeated **Dusty Rhodes** by DQ in 8:46 (★★); The British

Bulldog defeated **Haku** in 19:34 (★ ★); **Tugboat** defeated **Dino Bravo** by DQ in 8:28 (★); **The Hart Foundation** (Bret Hart and Jim Neidhart) defeated **Rhythm & Blues** (Greg Valentine and The Honky Tonk Man) in 6:10 (★ ★).

Halloween Havoc '90 ★ ★ ★
27-10-90, Chicago, Illinois **NWA**

Tommy Rich and **Ricky Morton** defeated **The Midnight Express** (Bobby Eaton and Stan Lane) in 20:49 (★ ★); **Terry Taylor** defeated **Bill Irwin** in 11:47 (★ ★); **Brad Armstrong** defeated **J.W. Storm** in 5:04 (★ ★); **The Master Blasters** (Blade and Steel) defeated **The Southern Boys** (Steve Armstrong and Tracy Smothers) in 7:17 (★ ★); **The Fabulous Freebirds** (Michael Hayes and Jimmy Garvin) defeated **The Renegade Warriors** (Chris Youngblood and Mark Youngblood) in 17:28 (★); **The Steiner Brothers** (Rick Steiner and Scott Steiner) defeated **The Nasty Boys** (Brian Knobbs and Jerry Sags) in 15:24 (★ ★ ★ ★); **Junkyard Dog** defeated **Moondog Rex** in 3:15 (★ ★); **Doom** (Ron Simmons and Butch Reed) vs. **Ric Flair** and **Arn Anderson** went to a double count out in 18:20 (★ ★ ★ ★); **Stan Hansen** defeated **Lex Luger** to win the NWA United States Heavyweight Title in 9:30 (★ ★); **Sting** defeated **Sid Vicious** in 12:38 (★ ★).

Survivor Series Showdown (1990) ★ ★
18-11-90, Indianapolis, Indiana **WWF**

Sgt. Slaughter defeated **Tito Santana** in 11:30 (★ ★); **Rick Martel** defeated **Marty Jannetty** in 10:49 (★ ★ ★); **Earthquake** defeated **The Big Boss Man** via count out in 10:59 (★ ★); **Bret Hart** defeated **The Honky Tonk Man** in 10:25 (★ ★); **The Texas Tornado** defeated **Smash** by DQ in 7:44 (★ ★).

Clash Of The Champions XIII: Thanksgiving Thunder ★
20-11-90, Jacksonville, Florida **NWA**

The Fabulous Freebirds (Michael Hayes and Jimmy Garvin) defeated **The Southern Boys** (Steve Armstrong and Tracy Smothers) in 4:50 (★ ★); **Brian Pillman** defeated **Buddy Landel** in 5:52 (★ ★); **The Big Cat** defeated **Brad Armstrong** in 4:31 (★ ★); **Tom Zenk** defeated **Brian Lee** in 3:10 (★ ★); **Michael Wallstreet** defeated **The Starblazer** in 4:15 (★ ★); **Sgt. Krueger** and **Col. DeKlerk** defeated **The Botswana Beast** and **Kaluha** in 4:48 (★); **Lex Luger** defeated **The Motor City Madman** in 2:35 (★); **The Renegade Warriors** (Chris Youngblood and Mark Youngblood) defeated **The Nasty Boys** (Brian Knobbs and Jerry Sags) by DQ in 4:49 (★ ★); **Sid Vicious** defeated **The Nightstalker** in 3:30 (★); **The Steiner Brothers** (Rick Steiner and Scott Steiner) defeated **Magnum Force** (Magnum Force #1 and Magnum Force #2) in 1:57 (★ ★); **Ric Flair** defeated **Butch Reed** in 14:13 (★ ★ ★).

Survivor Series '90 ★ ★ ★
22-11-90, Hartford, Connecticut **WWF**

The Warriors (The Ultimate Warrior, The Texas Tornado, Hawk and Animal) defeated **The Perfect Team** (Mr. Perfect, Ax, Smash and Crush) in an Elimination Match in 14:20 (★ ★); **The Million Dollar Team** (Ted DiBiase, The Undertaker, The Honky Tonk Man and Greg Valentine) defeated **The Dream Team** (Dusty Rhodes, Bret Hart, Jim Neidhart and Koko B. Ware) in an Elimination Match in 13:54 (★ ★ ★); **The Visionaries** (Rick Martel, The Warlord, Hercules and Paul Roma) defeated **The Vipers** (Jake Roberts, Jimmy Snuka, Shawn Michaels and Paul Roma) in an Elimination Match in 17:42 (★ ★ ★); **The Hulkamaniacs** (Hulk Hogan, The Big Boss Man, Jim Duggan and Tugboat) defeated **The Natural Disasters** (Earthquake, Dino Bravo, The Barbarian and Haku) in an Elimination Match in 14:49 (★ ★ ★); **The Alliance** (Tito Santana, Nikolai Volkoff, Luke and Butch) defeated **The Mercenaries** (Sgt. Slaughter, Boris Zhukov, Sato and Tanaka) in an Elimination Match in 10:52 (★ ★); **Hulk Hogan, Tito Santana** and **The Ultimate Warrior** defeated **Ted DiBiase, Hercules, Paul Roma, Rick Martel** and **The Warlord** in an Elimination Handicap Match in 9:07 (★ ★).

The Main Event IV ★ ★ ★
23-11-90, Fort Wayne, Indiana **WWF**

The Ultimate Warrior defeated **Ted DiBiase** by DQ in 12:07 (★ ★ ★ ★); **Mr. Perfect** defeated **The Big Boss Man** via count out in 8:22 (★ ★); **Rick Martel** defeated **Tito Santana** in 6:55 (★ ★ ★).

WWF at Madison Square Garden (24-11-90) ★ ★
24-11-90, New York City, New York **WWF**

The British Bulldog defeated **Buddy Rose** in 8:48 (★ ★ ★); **Tugboat** defeated **Boris Zhukov** in 5:57 (★); **Earthquake** defeated **Hulk Hogan** via count out in 8:33 (★ ★); **Shane Douglas** defeated **Haku** in 7:48 (★ ★); **The Texas Tornado** defeated **Mr. Perfect** in 11:38 (★ ★); **Ted DiBiase** and **Virgil** defeated **Dusty Rhodes** and **Dustin Rhodes** in 8:51 (★ ★); **Sgt. Slaughter** defeated **Jim Duggan** in 9:10 (★ ★); **Bret Hart** defeated **The Barbarian** in 4:09 (★ ★); **The Rockers** (Shawn Michaels and Marty Jannetty) defeated **Demolition** (Crush and Smash) by DQ in 10:53 (★ ★ ★).

Starrcade '90 ★ ★ ★
16-12-90, St. Louis, Missouri **NWA**

Bobby Eaton defeated **Tom Zenk** in 8:45 (★ ★ ★); **The Steiner Brothers** (Rick Steiner and Scott Steiner) defeated **Colonel DeKlerk** and **Sgt. Krueger** in 2:12 (★ ★); **Konnan** and **Rey Misterio** defeated **Chris Adams** and **Norman Smiley** in 5:29 (★ ★ ★); **Mr. Saito** and **The Great Muta** defeated **The Royal Family** (Jack Victory and Rip Morgan) in 5:41 (★ ★); **Salman Hashimikov** and **Victor Zangiev** defeated **Danny Johnson** and **Troy Montour** in 3:54 (★ ★); **Michael Wallstreet** defeated **Terry Taylor** in 6:52 (★ ★); **The Skyscrapers** (Sid Vicious and Dan Spivey) defeated **The Big Cat** and **The Motor City Madman** in 1:01 (★ ★); **Tommy Rich** and **Ricky Morton** defeated **The Fabulous Freebirds** (Michael Hayes and Jimmy Garvin) in 6:13 (★ ★); **The Steiner Brothers** (Rick Steiner and Scott Steiner) defeated **Konnan** and **Rey Mistero** in 2:51 (★ ★); **Mr. Saito** and **The Great Muta** defeated **Salman Hashimikov** and **Victor Zangiev** in 3:08 (★ ★); **Lex Luger** defeated **Stan Hansen** in a Texas Bullrope Match to win the NWA United States Heavyweight Title in 10:13 (★ ★); **Doom** (Ron Simmons and Butch Reed) vs. **Arn Anderson** and **Barry Windham** in a Street Fight went to a no contest in 7:19 (★ ★ ★ ★); **The Steiner Brothers** (Rick Steiner and Scott Steiner) defeated **Mr. Saito** and **The Great Muta** in 10:52 (★ ★); **Sting** defeated **The Black Scorpion** in a Steel Cage Match in 18:31 (★ ★).

WWF at Madison Square Garden (28-11-90) ★ ★
28-12-90, New York City, New York **WWF**

Koko B. Ware defeated **Black Bart** in 10:07 (★ ★); **Jimmy Snuka** defeated **The Warlord** by DQ in 8:28 (★); **The Rockers** (Shawn Michaels and Marty Jannetty) vs. **Power and Glory** (Paul Roma and Hercules) ended in a draw in 21:11 (★ ★ ★); **Saba Simba** defeated **Greg Valentine** by DQ in 8:29 (★); **Hulk Hogan** and **Tugboat** defeated **Earthquake** and **Dino Bravo** in 9:24 (★ ★); **The Texas Tornado** defeated **Virgil** in 7:55 (★ ★); **Sgt. Slaughter** and **General Adnan** defeated **Dusty Rhodes** and **Jim Duggan** in 9:10 (★ ★); **Roddy Piper** defeated **Mr. Perfect** via count out in 12:38 (★ ★ ★ ★).

Royal Rumble '91 ★ ★ ★ ★
19-01-91, Miami, Florida **WWF**

The Rockers (Shawn Michaels and Marty Jannetty) defeated **The Orient Express** (Kato and Tanaka) in 19:15 (★ ★ ★ ★); **The Big Boss Man** defeated **The Barbarian** in 14:15 (★ ★ ★ ★); **Sgt. Slaughter** defeated **The Ultimate Warrior** to win the WWF World Heavyweight Title in 12:47 (★ ★ ★); **The Mountie** defeated **Koko B. Ware** in 9:12 (★ ★); **Ted DiBiase** and **Virgil** defeated **Dusty Rhodes** and **Dustin Rhodes** in 9:57 (★ ★); **Hulk Hogan** won the 30-Man Royal Rumble Match in 65:17 (★ ★ ★).

WWF at Madison Square Garden (21-01-91) ★ ★
21-01-91, New York City, New York **WWF**

Paul Roma defeated **Shane Douglas** in 10:01 (★ ★); **Tito Santana** defeated **Koko B. Ware** in 10:10 (★ ★ ★); **The Undertaker** defeated **Jimmy Snuka** in 7:14 (★ ★); **The Legion Of Doom** (Animal and Hawk) defeated **Demolition** (Crush and Smash) in 2:58 (★ ★); **The Big Boss Man** defeated **Hercules** by DQ in 7:16 (★ ★); **Greg Valentine** defeated **Dino Bravo** in 8:53 (★ ★); **The Nasty Boys** (Brian Knobbs and Jerry Sags) defeated **The Bushwhackers** (Butch and Luke) in 7:49 (★ ★); **Randy Savage** defeated **The Ultimate Warrior** in a Steel Cage Match in 10:33 (★ ★ ★).

Clash Of The Champions XIV: Dixie Dynamite ★ ★
30-01-91, Gainesville, Georgia **WCW**

Sting and **Lex Luger** defeated **Doom** (Ron Simmons and Butch Reed) by DQ in 10:33 (★ ★); **Tom Zenk** defeated **Bobby Eaton** in 7:08 (★ ★); **The Fabulous Freebirds** (Michael Hayes and Jimmy Garvin) defeated **Tommy Rich** and **Allen Iron Eagle** in 5:53 (★);

Sid Vicious defeated Joey Maggs in 1:11 (★★); Terry Taylor defeated Ricky Morton in 11:53 (★★); Ranger Ross defeated El Cubano in 3:05 (★★); Arn Anderson and Barry Windham defeated The Renegade Warriors (Chris Youngblood and Mark Youngblood) in 7:30 (★★); Brian Pillman defeated Buddy Lee Parker in 3:17 (★★); Missy Hyatt defeated Paul E. Dangerously in an Arm Wrestling Match; Ric Flair vs. Scott Steiner ended in a draw in 24:39 (★★★★).

The Main Event V ★★
01-02-91, Macon, Georgia WWF

Hulk Hogan and Tugboat defeated Earthquake and Dino Bravo in 13:02 (★★); Jim Duggan defeated Sgt. Slaughter by DQ in 7:00 (★★); The Legion Of Doom (Hawk and Animal) defeated The Orient Express (Kato and Tanaka) in 5:11.

WrestleWar '91 ★★★★
24-02-91, Phoenix, Arizona WCW

Ricky Morton, Tommy Rich and Junkyard Dog defeated Big Cat and The State Patrol (Lt. James Earl Wright and Sgt. Buddy Lee Parker) in 9:54 (★★); Bobby Eaton defeated Brad Armstrong in 12:51 (★★★); Istuki Yamazaki and Mami Kitamura defeated Miki Handa and Miss A in 6:47 (★★★); Dustin Rhodes defeated Buddy Landel in 6:33 (★★); The Young Pistols (Steve Armstrong and Tracy Smothers) defeated The Royal Family (Jack Victory and Rip Morgan) in 12:05 (★★); Terry Taylor defeated Tom Zenk in a No DQ Match in 10:59 (★★★); Big Van Vader vs. Stan Hansen went to a double DQ in 6:21 (★★★); Lex Luger defeated Dan Spivey in 12:52 (★★★★); The Fabulous Freebirds (Michael Hayes and Jimmy Garvin) defeated Doom (Ron Simmons and Butch Reed) to win the WCW World Tag Team Title in 6:56 (★★); Ric Flair, Barry Windham, Sid Vicious and Larry Zbyszko defeated Sting, Brian Pillman and The Steiner Brothers (Rick Steiner and Scott Steiner) in a War Games Match in 21:50 (★★★★★★).

WWF at Madison Square Garden (15-03-91) ★★★
15-03-91, New York City, New York WWF

Marty Jannetty defeated Pat Tanaka in 10:52 (★★★); The Mountie defeated Koko B. Ware in 4:43 (★★); The British Bulldog defeated The Warlord in 10:34 (★★★); The Undertaker defeated Tugboat in 3:23 (★★); The Hart Foundation (Bret Hart and Jim Neidhart) defeated Earthquake and Dino Bravo in 10:24 (★★); The Barbarian defeated Jim Brunzell in 7:13 (★★); The Texas Tornado defeated Ted DiBiase in 4:50 (★★); Kato defeated Shawn Michaels in 12:50 (★★★); Jim Duggan defeated Sgt. Slaughter by DQ in a Flag Match in 14:12 (★★).

Japan Supershow I ★★★★
21-03-91, Tokyo, Japan WCW/NJPW

Kengo Kimura, Kantaro Hoshino, Osamu Kido and Animal Hamaguchi defeated Hiro Saito, Norio Honaga, Tatsutoshi Goto and Super Strong Machine in 12:08 (★★★); Shiro Koshinaka, Kuniaki Kobayashi and Takayuki Iizuka defeated Tim Horner, Brian Pillman and Tom Zenk in 12:10 (★★★); Scott Norton defeated Equalizer in 2:23 (★); Jushin Thunder Liger defeated Akira Nogami in 16:08 (★★★★); Arn Anderson and Barry Windham defeated Masa Saito and Masahiro Chono in 9:17 (★★★); The Steiner Brothers (Rick Steiner and Scott Steiner) defeated Hiroshi Hase and Kensuke Sasaki to win the IWGP Tag Team Title in 9:49 (★★★★); El Gigante defeated Big Cat Hughes in 2:16 (★★); Big Van Vader and Bam Bam Bigelow defeated Doom (Butch Reed and Ron Simmons) in 13:17 (★★★); The Great Muta defeated Sting in 12:41 (★★★); Riki Choshu defeated Tiger Jeet Singh in a No DQ, No Referee, No Count Out Match to win the Greatest 18 Club Title in 11:07 (★★); Tatsumi Fujinami defeated Ric Flair to win the NWA World Heavyweight Title in 23:06 (★★★).

WrestleMania VII ★★★★
24-03-91, Los Angeles, California WWF

The Rockers (Shawn Michaels and Marty Jannetty) defeated Haku and The Barbarian in 10:33 (★★★★); The Texas Tornado defeated Dino Bravo in 3:11 (★★); The British Bulldog defeated The Warlord in 8:15 (★★★); The Nasty Boys (Brian Knobbs and Jerry Sags) defeated The Hart Foundation (Bret Hart and Jim Neidhart) to win the WWF World Tag Team Title in 12:10 (★★★★); Jake Roberts defeated Rick Martel in a Blindfold Match in 8:34 (★); The Undertaker defeated Jimmy Snuka in 4:20 (★★); The Ultimate Warrior defeated Randy Savage in a Retirement Match in 20:47 (★★★★★★); Genichiro Tenryu and Koji Kitao defeated Demolition (Smash and Crush) in 4:44 (★★); The Big Boss Man defeated Mr. Perfect by DQ in 10:46 (★★★★); Earthquake defeated Greg Valentine in 3:15 (★★); The Legion Of Doom (Hawk and Animal) defeated Power and Glory (Hercules and Paul Roma) in :59 (★); Virgil defeated Ted DiBiase via count out in 7:41 (★★); The Mountie defeated Tito Santana in 1:21 (★); Hulk Hogan defeated Sgt. Slaughter to win the WWF World Heavyweight Title in 20:26 (★★★).

WrestleFest In Tokyo Dome ★★★
30-03-91, Tokyo, Japan SWS/WWF

The Hart Foundation (Bret Hart and Jim Neidhart) defeated The Rockers (Shawn Michaels and Marty Jannetty) in 14:41 (★★★); Earthquake defeated Koji Kitao in 6:10 (★★); Haku and Ted DiBiase defeated Takashi Ishikawa and The Great Kabuki in 15:16 (★★); Apollo Sugawara, Masao Orihara, Samson Fuyuki and Tatsumi Kitihara defeated Don Arakawa, Fumihiro Niikura, Goro Tsurumi and Kenichi Oya in 5:37 (★★); Kendo Nagasaki defeated Jim Duggan in 2:50 (★); Demolition (Crush and Smash) defeated Shinichi Nakano and Shunji Takano in 5:22 (★★); The Ultimate Warrior defeated Sgt. Slaughter in 6:14 (★★); Masa Funaki defeated Naoki Sano in 10:23 (★★); Kerry Von Erich defeated Mr. Perfect by DQ in 6:59 (★★); Koji Ishinriki and Yoshiaki Yatsu defeated Jimmy Snuka and The Barbarian in 10:00 (★★★); Randy Savage defeated George Takano in 13:42 (★★); The Legion Of Doom (Hawk and Animal) defeated Hulk Hogan and Genichiro Tenryu via count out in 14:03 (★★★★).

WWF at Madison Square Garden (22-04-91) ★★
22-04-91, New York City, New York WWF

Ricky Steamboat defeated Haku in 9:35 (★★); Power and Glory (Paul Roma and Hercules) defeated The Bushwhackers (Butch and Luke) in 8:34 (★); The Big Boss Man defeated The Mountie in 7:56 (★★); Sgt. Slaughter defeated Hulk Hogan by DQ in 16:00 (★★★); Irwin R Schyster defeated Jimmy Snuka in 6:33 (★★); The Texas Tornado vs. The Warlord ended in a double count out in 9:15 (★); The Rockers (Shawn Michaels and Marty Jannetty) and Virgil defeated The Orient Express (Kato and Tanaka) and Mr. Fuji in 10:33 (★★★); Ted DiBiase defeated Roddy Piper in 7:33 (★★).

UK Rampage '91 ★★
24-04-91, London, England WWF

Jim Neidhart defeated The Warlord in 13:31 (★★); Ted DiBiase defeated The Texas Tornado via count out in 14:05 (★★); Greg Valentine defeated Haku in 8:41 (★★); The Rockers defeated The Orient Express (Kato and Tanaka) in 15:46 (★★★); Jimmy Snuka defeated The Barbarian in 15:56 (★★); The British Bulldog defeated The Berzerker in 16:03 (★★); Earthquake defeated Jake Roberts by DQ in 11:11 (★★); Hulk Hogan defeated Sgt. Slaughter in 16:01 (★★).

Saturday Night's Main Event XXIX ★★★
27-04-91, Omaha, Nebraska WWF

The Ultimate Warrior defeated Sgt. Slaughter by DQ in 7:30 (★★); The Nasty Boys (Brian Knobbs and Jerry Sags) defeated The Bushwhackers (Luke and Butch) in 4:56 (★★); Mr. Perfect won a Battle Royal in 12:30 (★★★); Ted DiBiase vs. Bret Hart ended in a double count out in 9:37 (★★★★); The Mountie defeated Tito Santana in 4:29 (★★).

SuperBrawl I ★★★
19-05-91, St. Petersburg, Florida WCW

The Fabulous Freebirds (Michael Hayes and Jimmy Garvin) defeated The Young Pistols (Steve Armstrong and Tracy Smothers) to win the vacant WCW United States Tag Team Title in 10:19 (★★★); Dan Spivey defeated Ricky Morton in 3:11 (★★); Nikita Koloff defeated Tommy Rich in 4:27 (★★); Dustin Rhodes defeated Terrance Taylor in 8:05 (★★); Big Josh defeated Black Bart in 3:46 (★★); Oz defeated Tim Parker in :26 (★); Barry Windham defeated Brian Pillman in a Taped Fist Match in 6:07 (★★); El Gigante defeated Sid Vicious in a Stretcher Match in 2:13 (★); Ron Simmons defeated Butch Reed in a Steel Cage Match in 9:39 (★★); The Steiner Brothers (Rick Steiner and Scott Steiner) defeated Sting and Lex Luger in 11:09 (★★★★★★); Bobby Eaton defeated Arn Anderson to win the WCW World Television Title in 11:50 (★★★); Ric Flair defeated Tatsumi Fujinami to win the NWA World Heavyweight Title in 18:39 (★★★).

WWF at Madison Square Garden (03-06-91) ★★
03-06-91, New York City, New York **WWF**

Ricky Steamboat defeated Smash in 10:14 (★★); The Warlord defeated Koko B. Ware in 10:33 (★); Colonel Mustafa defeated Jim Duggan via count out in 5:47 (★); Bret Hart defeated The Barbarian in 12:09 (★★); Jimmy Snuka defeated Bob Bradley in 4:02 (★★); Earthquake defeated Jake Roberts by DQ in 10:56 (★★); Tugboat defeated The Brooklyn Brawler in 2:40 (★★); The Mountie defeated The Big Boss Man in 5:50 (★★); Animal defeated Paul Roma in 5:00 (★★); Hulk Hogan defeated Sgt. Slaughter in a Desert Storm Match in 15:34 (★★★★).

Beach Brawl ★★
09-06-91, Palmetto, Florida **UWF**

The Blackhearts (Apocalypse and Destruction) defeated Fire Cat and Jim Cooper in 7:45 (★★); Terry Gordy vs. Johnny Ace in a Street Fight ended in a double count out in 6:08 (★★); Masked Confusion (B. Brian Blair and Jim Brunzell) defeated The Power Twins (Larry Power and David Power) in 12:23 (★★); Rockin Robin defeated Candi Devine to win the vacant UWF Women's World Title in 6:05 (★★); Paul Orndorff defeated Colonel DeBeers in a Strap Match in 4:15 (★★); Bob Backlund defeated Ivan Koloff in 2:23 (★★); Wet'N'Wild (Steve Ray and Sunny Beach) defeated Cactus Jack and Bob Orton in 4:02 (★★); Steve Williams defeated Bam Bam Bigelow to win the vacant UWF SportsChannel Television Title in 7:11 (★★★).

Clash Of The Champions XV: Knocksville USA ★★★★
12-06-91, Knoxville, Tennessee **WCW**

The Young Pistols (Tracy Smothers and Steve Armstrong) and Tom Zenk defeated The Fabulous Freebirds (Michael Hayes, Jimmy Garvin and Badstreet) in 4:49 (★★); Oz defeated Johnny Rich in 1:29 (★★); Dan Spivey defeated Big Josh in 2:49 (★★); Dustin Rhodes defeated Terrance Taylor by DQ in 4:27 (★★); Sting defeated Nikita Koloff in 9:33 (★★★); Barry Windham and Arn Anderson defeated Brian Pillman and El Gigante in a Loser Leaves WCW Match in 3:08 (★★); The Steiner Brothers (Rick Steiner and Scott Steiner) defeated Masahiro Chono and Hiroshi Hase in 8:14 (★★★★); The Diamond Studd defeated Tommy Rich in 1:59 (★★); Lex Luger defeated The Great Muta in 3:43 (★★); Steve Austin defeated Joey Maggs in :25 (★★); Ric Flair defeated Bobby Eaton 2-1 in a Two Out Of Three Falls Match in 14:26 (★★★★).

WWF at Madison Square Garden (01-07-91) ★★
01-07-91, New York City, New York **WWF**

Dino Bravo defeated Shane Douglas in 5:32 (★★); Ricky Steamboat defeated Paul Roma in 11:05 (★★★); The Berzerker defeated Jimmy Snuka in 7:16 (★★); The Nasty Boys (Brian Knobbs and Jerry Sags) defeated The Hart Foundation (Bret Hart and Jim Neidhart) by DQ in 13:46 (★★); The Warlord defeated Greg Valentine in 10:19 (★★); Jake Roberts defeated Earthquake in 10:30 (★★★); Haku and The Barbarian defeated Mr. Fuji and Kato in 7:32 (★★); The Ultimate Warrior defeated The Undertaker in a Bodybag Match in 9:29 (★★★).

Great American Bash '91 ★
14-07-91, Baltimore, Maryland **WCW**

P.N. News and Bobby Eaton defeated Steve Austin and Terrance Taylor in a Capture The Flag Scaffold Match in 6:19 (★); The Diamond Studd defeated Tom Zenk in 9:00 (★★); Ron Simmons defeated Oz in 7:55 (★★); Richard Morton defeated Robert Gibson in 17:03 (★★); Dustin Rhodes and The Young Pistols (Steve Armstrong and Tracy Smothers) defeated The Fabulous Freebirds (Michael Hayes, Jimmy Garvin and Badstreet) in an Elimination Match in 17:10 (★★); The Yellow Dog defeated Johnny B. Badd by DQ in a Bounty Match in 6:00 (★★); Big Josh defeated Black Blood in a Lumberjack Match in 5:39 (★★); El Gigante defeated One Man Gang in 6:13 (★); Nikita Koloff defeated Sting in a Russian Chain Match in 11:38 (★★); Lex Luger defeated Barry Windham in a Steel Cage Match to win the vacant WCW World Heavyweight Title in 12:25 (★★★); Rick Steiner defeated Arn Anderson and Paul E. Dangerously in a Steel Cage Match in 2:08 (★★).

SummerSlam Spectacular (1991) ★★
18-08-91, Worcester, Massachusetts **WWF**

Hawk defeated Brian Knobbs in 9:12 (★★); Bret Hart defeated The Barbarian in 12:00 (★★); Irwin R. Schyster defeated Mark Thomas in 2:01 (★★); The British Bulldog, Ricky Steamboat and The Texas Tornado defeated The Orient Express (Kato,

Pat Tanaka and Sato) in 10:31 (★★); Hulk Hogan defeated Sgt. Slaughter by DQ in 6:42 (★★); The Natural Disasters (Earthquake and Typhoon) defeated Roy Garcia and Russ Greenberg in 2:15 (★★); Virgil defeated Masked Wrestler in 4:52 (★).

SummerSlam '91 ★★★★
26-08-91, New York City, New York **WWF**

The British Bulldog, Ricky Steamboat and The Texas Tornado defeated Power and Glory (Hercules and Paul Roma) and The Warlord in 10:43 (★★); Bret Hart defeated Mr. Perfect to win the WWF Intercontinental Title in 18:04 (★★★★★★); The Natural Disasters (Earthquake and Typhoon) defeated The Bushwhackers (Luke and Butch) in 6:27 (★★); Virgil defeated Ted DiBiase to win the Million Dollar Title in 13:11 (★★★★); The Big Boss Man defeated The Mountie in a Jailhouse Match in 9:38 (★★★); The Legion Of Doom (Hawk and Animal) defeated The Nasty Boys (Brian Knobbs and Jerry Sags) in a Street Fight to win the WWF World Tag Team Title in 7:45 (★★★); Irwin R. Schyster defeated Greg Valentine in 7:07 (★★); Hulk Hogan and The Ultimate Warrior defeated Sgt. Slaughter, Colonel Mustafa and General Adnan in a Handicap Match in 12:40 (★★).

Clash Of The Champions XVI: Fall Brawl ★★
05-09-91, Augusta, Georgia **WCW**

El Gigante won a 20-man Battle Royal in 9:33 (★★); Brian Pillman defeated Badstreet in 6:52 (★★★); Sting defeated Johnny B. Badd in 6:11 (★★); Richard Morton defeated Mike Graham in 7:40 (★★); The Fabulous Freebirds (Michael Hayes and Jimmy Garvin) defeated The Patriots (Todd Champion and Firebreaker Chip) in 5:42 (★★); Ron Simmons defeated The Diamond Studd in 2:25 (★★); Van Hammer defeated Terrance Taylor in 1:07 (★★); Steve Austin defeated Tom Zenk in 9:07 (★★); The Enforcers (Arn Anderson and Larry Zbyszko) defeated Rick Steiner and Bill Kazmaier to win the vacant WCW World Tag Team Title in 3:33 (★★).

Battle Royal At The Albert Hall ★★
03-10-91, London, England **WWF**

The Nasty Boys (Brian Knobbs and Jerry Sags) defeated The Rockers (Shawn Michaels and Marty Jannetty) in 16:21 (★★); Ric Flair defeated Tito Santana in 16:14 (★★★★); Earthquake defeated The Big Boss Man in 15:47 (★★); The Undertaker defeated Jim Duggan by DQ in 6:18 (★★); The Mountie defeated The Texas Tornado in 13:46 (★★); The British Bulldog defeated The Barbarian in 10:07 (★★); The Legion Of Doom (Hawk and Animal) defeated Power and Glory (Hercules and Paul Roma) in 9:08 (★★); The British Bulldog won a 20-Man Battle Royal in 14:40 (★★).

WWF at Palau Sant Jordi (05-10-91) ★★★
05-10-91, Barcelona, Spain **WWF**

The Rockers (Shawn Michaels and Marty Jannetty) defeated Power and Glory (Paul Roma and Hercules) in 10:54 (★★★); The Mountie defeated The Big Boss Man via count out in 9:17 (★★); Roddy Piper defeated The Barbarian in 6:31 (★★); The British Bulldog defeated Earthquake in 8:15 (★★); Typhoon defeated Jim Duggan by DQ in 8:43 (★★); The Legion Of Doom (Animal and Hawk) defeated The Nasty Boys (Brian Knobbs and Jerry Sags) in 11:40 (★★★); Ric Flair defeated Kerry Von Erich in 15:15 (★★★★); Tito Santana defeated The Undertaker in 13:53 (★★★).

Halloween Havoc '91 ★★
27-10-91, Chattanooga, Tennessee **WCW**

Sting, El Gigante and The Steiner Brothers (Rick Steiner and Scott Steiner) defeated Big Van Vader, Cactus Jack, Abdullah the Butcher and The Diamond Studd in a Chamber Of Horrors Match in 12:33 (★); Big Josh and P.N. News defeated The Creatures (Creature #1 and Creature #2) in 5:16 (★★); Bobby Eaton defeated Terrance Taylor in 16:00 (★★★); Johnny B. Badd defeated Jimmy Garvin in 8:16 (★★); Steve Austin vs. Dustin Rhodes went to a time limit draw in 15:00 (★★★); Bill Kazmaier defeated Oz in 3:59 (★); Van Hammer defeated Doug Somers in 1:13 (★); Brian Pillman defeated Richard Morton to win the vacant WCW Light Heavyweight Title in 12:45 (★★); The Halloween Phantom defeated Tom Zenk in 1:27 (★★); The Enforcers (Arn Anderson and Larry Zbyszko) defeated The Patriots (Firebreaker Chip and Todd Champion) in 9:51 (★★); Lex Luger defeated Ron Simmons in a Two Out Of Three Falls Match in 18:59 (★★★).

WWF at Madison Square Garden (28-10-91) ★★
28-10-91, New York City, New York **WWF**

The Texas Tornado defeated Big Bully Busick in 7:47 (★★); The British Bulldog vs. Irwin R. Schyster ended in a draw in 20:05 (★★); The Mountie defeated Jim Neidhart in 11:19 (★★); Ric Flair defeated Roddy Piper in 11:59 (★★★★); The Big Boss Man defeated Colonel Mustafa in 4:52 (★★); Bret Hart defeated The Berzerker in 10:17 (★★); Tito Santana defeated Hercules in 9:11 (★★); The Legion Of Doom (Animal and Hawk) defeated The Natural Disasters (Earthquake and Typhoon) by DQ in 8:02 (★★).

Clash Of The Champions XVII ★★★
19-11-91, Savannah, Georgia **WCW**

Big Josh defeated Thomas Rich in a Lumberjack Match in 6:03 (★★); Bobby Eaton defeated Firebreaker Chip in 4:52 (★★); Tom Zenk defeated The Diamond Studd in 1:24 (★★); Steve Austin defeated P.N. News in 4:21 (★★); Cactus Jack defeated Van Hammer in 4:03 (★★); Dustin Rhodes and Ricky Steamboat defeated The Enforcers (Arn Anderson and Larry Zbyszko) to win the WCW World Tag Team Title in 14:48 (★★★★★); Brian Pillman defeated Johnny B. Badd in 4:19 (★★); Rick Rude defeated Sting in 4:50 (★★★); Lex Luger defeated Rick Steiner in 11:30 (★★).

Survivor Series Showdown (1991) ★★
24-11-91, Utica, New York **WWF**

The Big Boss Man defeated Earthquake in 10:00 (★★); Luke defeated Blake Beverly in 6:25 (★★); Ted DiBiase defeated Virgil to win the Million Dollar Title in 9:46 (★★); Tito Santana defeated Skinner in 11:27 (★★); Roddy Piper defeated Hercules in 5:09 (★★).

Survivor Series '91 ★★★
27-11-91, Detroit, Michigan **WWF**

Ric Flair, The Mountie, Ted DiBiase and The Warlord defeated Bret Hart, Roddy Piper, The British Bulldog and Virgil in an Elimination Match in 22:48 (★★★★); Sgt. Slaughter, Jim Duggan, The Texas Tornado and Tito Santana defeated Colonel Mustafa, The Berzerker, Skinner and Hercules in an Elimination Match in 14:19 (★★); The Undertaker defeated Hulk Hogan to win the WWF World Heavyweight Title in 12:45 (★★★); The Nasty Boys (Brian Knobbs and Jerry Sags) and The Beverly Brothers (Beau Beverly and Blake Beverly) defeated The Rockers (Shawn Michaels and Marty Jannetty) and The Bushwhackers (Luke and Butch) in an Elimination Match in 23:06 (★★); The Big Boss Man and The Legion Of Doom (Hawk and Animal) defeated Irwin R. Schyster and The Natural Disasters (Earthquake and Typhoon) in an Elimination Match in 15:21 (★★).

WWF at Madison Square Garden (30-11-91) ★★★
30-11-91, New York City, New York **WWF**

Tito Santana defeated Kato in 10:04 (★★); The Texas Tornado defeated The Berzerker via count out in 2:00 (★); Virgil defeated Skinner in 6:07 (★★); Hulk Hogan defeated Ric Flair in 9:25 (★★★); Jim Duggan defeated The Barbarian in 7:51 (★★); Bret Hart defeated The Mountie in 12:58 (★★★); Irwin R. Schyster defeated The Big Boss Man in 13:46 (★★★); The Nasty Boys (Brian Knobbs and Jerry Sags) defeated The Rockers (Shawn Michaels and Marty Jannetty) in 16:20 (★★).

This Tuesday In Texas ★★★
03-12-91, San Antonio, Texas **WWF**

Bret Hart defeated Skinner in 13:46 (★★★); Randy Savage defeated Jake Roberts in 6:25 (★★); The British Bulldog defeated The Warlord in 12:45 (★★); Ted DiBiase and Repo Man defeated Virgil and Tito Santana in 11:28 (★★★); Hulk Hogan defeated The Undertaker to win the WWF World Heavyweight Title in 13:09 (★★).

SuperWrestle '91 ★★
12-12-91, Tokyo, Japan **SWS/WWF**

Masakatsu Funaki defeated Jerry Flynn in 5:18 (★★); Ultimo Dragon defeated Jerry Estrada in 10:15 (★★); Ashura Hara and The British Bulldog defeated Haku and Yoshiaki Yatsu in 16:57 (★★); George Takano and Shunji Takano defeated The Rockers (Marty Jannetty and Shawn Michaels) in 10:55 (★★); Ted DiBiase defeated Kerry Von Erich in 9:18 (★★); Naoki Sano defeated Rick Martel to win the vacant SWS Light Heavyweight

Title in 7:29 (★★★); Yoshiaki Fujiwara defeated Ishinriki in 11:22 (★★★); The Legion Of Doom (Hawk and Animal) defeated The Natural Disasters (Earthquake and Typhoon) in 9:15 (★★); Hulk Hogan defeated Genichiro Tenryu in 13:57 (★★★).

WWF at Madison Square Garden (29-12-91) ★★
29-12-91, New York City, New York **WWF**

The British Bulldog defeated The Berzerker in 5:05 (★★); Sgt. Slaughter defeated General Adnan and Colonel Mustafa in a Handicap Flag Match in 3:27 (★); Hercules defeated Greg Valentine in 7:44 (★); The Nasty Boys (Brian Knobbs and Jerry Sags) defeated The Bushwhackers (Butch and Luke) in 10:21 (★★); Skinner defeated Jim Powers in 6:51 (★★); Chris Walker defeated The Brooklyn Brawler in 4:02 (★★); Virgil defeated Repo Man by DQ in 9:35 (★★); Bret Hart vs. Ted DiBiase ended in a draw in 19:06 (★★★★); Hulk Hogan defeated Ric Flair via count out in 10:09 (★★★).

Starrcade '91 ★★
29-12-91, Norfolk, Virginia **WCW**

Marcus Bagwell and Jimmy Garvin defeated Michael Hayes and Tracy Smothers in 12:45 (★★); Steve Austin and Rick Rude defeated Van Hammer and Big Josh in 12:56 (★★); Dustin Rhodes and Richard Morton defeated Larry Zbyszko and El Gigante in 12:45 (★); Bill Kazmaier and Jushin Thunder Liger defeated Diamond Dallas Page and Mike Graham in 13:08 (★★); Lex Luger and Arn Anderson defeated Terry Taylor and Tom Zenk in 10:25 (★★★★); Ricky Steamboat and Todd Champion defeated Cactus Jack and Buddy Lee Parker in 7:48 (★★); Sting and Abdullah the Butcher defeated Brian Pillman and Bobby Eaton in 5:55 (★★★); Big Van Vader and Mr. Hughes defeated Rick Steiner and The Nightstalker in 5:05 (★★); Scott Steiner and Firebreaker Chip defeated Arachnaman and Johnny B. Badd in 11:16 (★★); Ron Simmons and Thomas Rich defeated Steve Armstrong and P.N. News in 12:01 (★★); Sting won a Battlebowl Battle Royal in 25:10 (★★★).

Japan Supershow II ★★★
04-01-92, Tokyo, Japan **WCW/NJPW**

Jushin Thunder Liger, Masashi Aoyagi and Akira Nogami defeated Hiro Saito, Super Strong Machine and Norio Honaga in 15:12 (★★); The Enforcers (Arn Anderson and Larry Zbyszko) defeated Michiyoshi Ohara and Shiro Koshinaka in 12:32 (★★); Dusty Rhodes and Dustin Rhodes defeated Masa Saito and Kim Duk in 14:23 (★★); Big Van Vader vs. El Gigante ended in a double DQ in 4:49 (★★); Lex Luger defeated Masahiro Chono in 15:09 (★★); Riki Choshu defeated Tatsumi Fujinami to win the IWGP Heavyweight Title in 12:11 (★★★); Sting and The Great Muta defeated The Steiner Brothers (Rick Steiner and Scott Steiner) in 11:03 (★★★).

Royal Rumble '92 ★★★★★
19-01-92, Albany, New York **WWF**

The New Foundation (Owen Hart and Jim Neidhart) defeated The Orient Express (Kato and Tanaka) in 17:18 (★★); Roddy Piper defeated The Mountie to win the WWF Intercontinental Title in 5:22 (★★); The Beverly Brothers (Beau Beverly and Blake Beverly) defeated The Bushwhackers (Luke and Butch) in 14:56 (★); The Natural Disasters (Earthquake and Typhoon) defeated The Legion Of Doom (Hawk and Animal) via count out in 9:24 (★★); Ric Flair won the 30-Man Royal Rumble Match in 62:02 (★★★★★).

Clash Of The Champions XVIII ★★★★
21-01-92, Topeka, Kansas **WCW**

The Steiner Brothers (Rick Steiner and Scott Steiner) defeated Big Van Vader and Mr. Hughes in 9:02 (★★★); Marcus Alexander Bagwell and Brian Pillman defeated Terry Taylor and Tracy Smothers in 7:49 (★★★); Johnny B. Badd defeated Richard Morton in 3:20 (★★); P.N. News defeated Diamond Dallas Page in 3:25 (★); Cactus Jack defeated Van Hammer in a Falls Count Anywhere Match in 10:08 (★★★); The Fabulous Freebirds (Michael Hayes and Jimmy Garvin) defeated Brad Armstrong and Big Josh in 3:03 (★★); Vinnie Vegas defeated Thomas Rich in :56 (★★); Dustin Rhodes, Barry Windham and Ron Simmons defeated The Dangerous Alliance (Arn Anderson, Bobby Eaton and Larry Zbyszko) in 9:28 (★★★★); Sting and Ricky Steamboat defeated Steve Austin and Rick Rude in 11:21 (★★★★).

WWF at Madison Square Garden (31-01-92) ★★
31-01-92, New York City, New York **WWF**

Rick Martel defeated The Texas Tornado in 9:39 (★★); Shawn Michaels defeated Jimmy Snuka in 12:17 (★★); Sid Justice defeated The Mountie in 4:26 (★); The Warlord defeated Hercules in 5:39 (★); Sgt. Slaughter and Jim Duggan defeated The Nasty Boys (Brian Knobbs and Jerry Sags) via count out in 10:26 (★★); Chris Walker defeated Kato in 9:44 (★★); The Undertaker defeated Bret Hart in 12:27 (★★★); Repo Man defeated Virgil in 11:04 (★★); Randy Savage defeated Jake Roberts in 6:07 (★★).

Saturday Night's Main Event XXX ★★★
08-02-92, Lubbock, Texas **WWF**

Roddy Piper defeated The Mountie in 3:40 (★★); Hulk Hogan and Sid Justice defeated Ric Flair and The Undertaker by DQ in 10:58 (★★★); Sgt. Slaughter and Jim Duggan defeated The Beverly Brothers (Beau Beverly and Blake Beverly) in 2:38 (★★); Randy Savage defeated Jake Roberts in 7:26 (★★).

WWF at Madison Square Garden (23-02-92) ★★
23-02-92, New York City, New York **WWF**

The Berzerker defeated Jim Brunzell in 8:44 (★★); The Nasty Boys (Brian Knobbs and Jerry Sags) defeated The Bushwackers (Butch and Luke) in 12:38 (★); The Warlord defeated Chris Walker in 11:14 (★★); Sid Justice defeated Hercules in :25 (★); Roddy Piper defeated Repo Man in 3:31 (★★); The Undertaker defeated The British Bulldog in 5:19 (★★); Rick Martel defeated The Big Boss Man in 13:49 (★★); Sid Justice won a 20-Man Battle Royal in 16:37 (★★★).

Super Ladies Showdown ★★
23-02-92, Rochester, Minnesota **LPWA**

Mami Kitamura and Miki Handa defeated Allison Royal and Lisa Starr in 3:46 (★★); Denise Storm defeated Susan Green in 6:02 (★★); Reggie Bennett defeated Yukari Osawa in 6:19 (★★); Shinobu Kandori defeated Desiree Petersen in 4:31 (★★); Harley Saito defeated Mizuki Endoh in 7:06 (★★); Eagle Sawai defeated Midori Saito in 5:43 (★★); Black Venus defeated Rockin Robin in 5:39 (★★); Denise Storm defeated Reggie Bennett by DQ in 8:27 (★★); Harley Saito defeated Eagle Sawai on points in 10:00 (★★); The Glamour Girls (Judy Martin and Leilani Kai) defeated Bambi and Malia Hosaka in 8:47 (★★); Harley Saito defeated Denise Storm to win the vacant LPWA Japanese Title in 8:07 (★★); Terri Power defeated Lady X to win the LPWA Title in 8:36 (★★).

SuperBrawl II ★★★★
29-02-92, Milwaukee, Wisconsin **WCW**

Brian Pillman defeated Jushin Thunder Liger to win the WCW Light Heavyweight Title in 17:00 (★★★★★); Marcus Alexander Bagwell defeated Terry Taylor in 7:38 (★★); Ron Simmons defeated Cactus Jack in 6:34 (★★); Van Hammer and Tom Zenk defeated Richard Morton and Vinnie Vegas in 12:01 (★★★); Barry Windham and Dustin Rhodes defeated Steve Austin and Larry Zbyszko in 18:23 (★★★★); Arn Anderson and Bobby Eaton defeated The Steiner Brothers (Rick Steiner and Scott Steiner) by DQ in 20:06 (★★); Rick Rude defeated Ricky Steamboat in 20:02 (★★★); Sting defeated Lex Luger to win the WCW World Heavyweight Title in 13:02 (★★).

WWF at Madison Square Garden (23-03-92) ★★
23-03-92, New York City, New York **WWF**

Tatanka defeated Colonel Mustafa in 8:45 (★★); Irwin R. Schyster vs. Tito Santana ended in a draw in 20:34 (★★); Rick Martel defeated JW Storm in 9:33 (★★); Bret Hart and The Bushwackers (Butch and Luke) defeated The Mountie and The Nasty Boys (Brian Knobbs and Jerry Sags) in 13:22 (★★); The Warlord defeated Jim Brunzell in 10:18 (★); Shawn Michaels defeated Virgil in 12:13 (★★); Hulk Hogan and Roddy Piper defeated Ric Flair and Sid Justice in 18:02 (★★★).

March To WrestleMania VIII ★★★
29-03-92, Biloxi, Mississippi **WWF**

Shawn Michaels defeated Roddy Piper by DQ in 8:00 (★★★★); Ric Flair defeated Jim Brunzell in 3:59 (★★); Jake Roberts defeated Jim Powers in 3:07 (★★); The Natural Disasters (Earthquake and Typhoon) defeated Kato and Barry Horowitz in 1:57 (★★).

WrestleMania VIII ★★★★
05-04-92, Indianapolis, Indiana **WWF**

Shawn Michaels defeated Tito Santana in 10:38 (★★★); The Undertaker defeated Jake Roberts in 6:36 (★★); Bret Hart defeated Roddy Piper to win the WWF Intercontinental Title in 13:51 (★★★★★); The Big Boss Man, Virgil, Sgt. Slaughter and Jim Duggan defeated The Mountie, Repo Man and The Nasty Boys (Brian Knobbs and Jerry Sags) in 6:33 (★★); Randy Savage defeated Ric Flair to win the WWF World Heavyweight Title in 18:04 (★★★★); Tatanka defeated Rick Martel in 4:33 (★★); The Natural Disasters (Earthquake and Typhoon) defeated Money Inc. (Ted DiBiase and Irwin R. Schyster) via count out in 8:38 (★★); Owen Hart defeated Skinner in 1:36 (★★); Hulk Hogan defeated Sid Justice by DQ in 12:28 (★★).

European Rampage '92 (Munich) ★★
14-04-92, Munich, Germany **WWF**

Bret Hart defeated Dino Bravo in 14:16 (★★★); Jim Duggan def. Colonel Mustafa in 8:09 (★★); Repo Man defeated Sgt. Slaughter in 14:10 (★★); The British Bulldog and The Legion Of Doom (Hawk and Animal) defeated The Mountie and The Nasty Boys (Brian Knobbs and Jerry Sags) in 12:24 (★★); Papa Shango defeated Tito Santana in 9:49 (★★); Randy Savage defeated Shawn Michaels in 14:28 (★★★); The British Bulldog won a 15-Man Battle Royal (★★).

UK Rampage '92 ★★
19-04-92, Sheffield, England **WWF**

Tatanka defeated Skinner in 11:53 (★★); The Legion Of Doom (Hawk and Animal) defeated Colonel Mustafa and Dino Bravo in 4:29 (★★); Sid Justice defeated The Undertaker via count out in 5:15 (★★); Randy Savage defeated Shawn Michaels in 16:21 (★★); The Mountie defeated Virgil in 8:57 (★★); Bret Hart defeated Rick Martel in 13:02 (★★); Jim Duggan defeated Repo Man by DQ in 7:14 (★★); The British Bulldog defeated Irwin R. Schyster in 12:48 (★★).

WrestleWar '92 ★★★★★
17-05-92, Jacksonville, Florida **WCW**

The Fabulous Freebirds (Michael Hayes and Jimmy Garvin) defeated Terry Taylor and Greg Valentine to win the WCW United States Tag Team Title in 16:02 (★★); Johnny B. Badd defeated Tracy Smothers in 7:03 (★★); Scotty Flamingo defeated Marcus Alexander Bagwell in 7:11 (★★); Ron Simmons defeated Mr. Hughes in 5:22 (★★); The Super Invader defeated Todd Champion in 5:26 (★); Big Josh defeated Richard Morton in 7:33 (★★); Brian Pillman defeated Tom Zenk in 15:30 (★★★); The Steiner Brothers (Rick Steiner and Scott Steiner) defeated Tatsumi Fujinami and Takayuki Iizuka in 18:17 (★★★★); Sting's Squadron (Sting, Barry Windham, Dustin Rhodes, Ricky Steamboat and Nikita Koloff) defeated The Dangerous Alliance (Steve Austin, Rick Rude, Arn Anderson, Bobby Eaton and Larry Zbyszko) in a War Games Match in 23:27 (★★★★★).

Volunteer Slam I ★★
22-05-92, Knoxville, Tennessee **SMW**

The Dirty White Boy defeated Dixie Dynamite in 7:59 (★★); Brian Lee defeated Buddy Landell in 3:17 (★★); Paul Orndorff defeated Tim Horner in 13:51 (★★★); Robert Gibson defeated Jimmy Golden in 7:47 (★★); Brian Lee defeated The Dirty White Boy in 10:13 (★★); Paul Orndorff defeated Robert Gibson in 3:41 (★★); The Heavenly Bodies (Stan Lane and Tom Prichard) defeated The Party Patrol (Davey Rich and Johnny Rich) in 10:19 (★★★); Brian Lee defeated Paul Orndorff to win the vacant SMW Heavyweight Title in 6:28 (★★).

Beach Blast '92 ★★★★
20-06-92, Mobile, Alabama **WCW**

Scotty Flamingo defeated Brian Pillman to win the WCW Light Heavyweight Title in 17:29 (★★★★); Ron Simmons defeated Terry Taylor in 7:10 (★★); Greg Valentine defeated Marcus Alexander Bagwell in 7:17 (★★★); Sting defeated Cactus Jack in a Falls Count Anywhere Match in 11:24 (★★★★); Ricky Steamboat defeated Rick Rude 4-3 in an Iron Man Match in 30:00 (★★★★★); Dustin Rhodes, Barry Windham and Nikita Koloff defeated Arn Anderson, Steve Austin and Bobby Eaton by DQ in 15:32 (★★); The Steiner Brothers (Rick Steiner and Scott Steiner) vs. The Miracle Violence Connection (Steve Williams and Terry Gordy) ended in a time limit draw in 30:00 (★★★).

Clash Of The Champions XIX ★★★
22-06-92, Charleston, South Carolina **WCW**
Ricky Steamboat and Nikita Koloff defeated Joe Malenko and Dean Malenko in 9:50 (★★); Rick Rude and Steve Austin defeated Marcus Alexander Bagwell and Tom Zenk in 7:54 (★★); Terry Gordy and Steve Williams defeated Larry O'Day and Jeff O'Day in 2:35 (★★); The Steiner Brothers (Rick Steiner and Scott Steiner) defeated Miguel Perez Jr. and Ricky Santana via forfeit; Barry Windham and Dustin Rhodes defeated Arn Anderson and Bobby Eaton in 10:23 (★★★); The Fabulous Freebirds (Michael Hayes and Jimmy Garvin) defeated The Silver Kings (Silver King I and Silver King II) in 6:28 (★★); Jushin Thunder Liger and Brian Pillman defeated Chris Benoit and Biff Wellington in 11:30 (★★★★); Akira Nagami and Hiroshi Hase defeated The Headhunters (Headhunter #1 and Headhunter #2) in 5:19 (★★); Terry Gordy and Steve Williams defeated The Steiner Brothers (Rick Steiner and Scott Steiner) in 15:01 (★★★).

Great American Bash '92 ★★★
12-07-92, Albany, Georgia **WCW**
Nikita Koloff and Ricky Steamboat defeated Jushin Thunder Liger and Brian Pillman in 19:26 (★★★★); Hiroshi Hase and Shinya Hashimoto defeated The Fabulous Freebirds (Michael Hayes and Jimmy Garvin) in 9:16 (★★); Dustin Rhodes and Barry Windham defeated Steve Austin and Rick Rude in 19:15 (★★★); The Miracle Violence Connection (Steve Williams and Terry Gordy) defeated Nikita Koloff and Ricky Steamboat in 21:39 (★); Dustin Rhodes and Barry Windham defeated Hiroshi Hase and Shinya Hashimoto in 14:55 (★★); Big Van Vader defeated Sting to win the WCW World Heavyweight Title in 17:17 (★★★★); The Miracle Violence Connection (Steve Williams and Terry Gordy) defeated Dustin Rhodes and Barry Windham to win the vacant NWA World Tag Team Title in 21:10 (★★).

Fire On The Mountain '92 ★★★
08-08-92, Johnson City, Tennessee **SMW**
Tim Horner defeated Buddy Landell in an "I Quit" Match in 15:15 (★★★); Ronnie Garvin defeated Paul Orndorff in a Piledriver Match in 18:47 (★★); The Rock 'n' Roll Express (Robert Gibson and Ricky Morton) defeated Robert Fuller and Jimmy Golden in 14:38 (★★); The Dirty White Boy defeated Brian Lee to win the SMW Heavyweight Title in 13:18 (★★); The Fantastics (Bobby Fulton and Jackie Fulton) defeated The Heavenly Bodies (Stan Lane and Tom Prichard) in a Barbed Wire Cage Match to win the SMW Tag Team Title in 13:04 (★★★★).

SummerSlam Spectacular (1992) ★★★
23-08-92, Nashville, Tennessee **WWF**
Ric Flair defeated Tito Santana in 16:30 (★★★); Tatanka defeated Kato in 8:40 (★★); Nailz defeated Ken Wayne in 3:48 (★★); The Nasty Boys (Brian Knobbs and Jerry Sags) defeated Randy Savage and The Ultimate Warrior via count out in 12:00 (★★★); Rick Martel defeated Joey Maggs in 2:43 (★★); Kamala defeated Burt Stiles in 2:31 (★★); Money Inc. (Ted DiBiase and Irwin R. Schyster) defeated The Bushwhackers (Luke and Butch) in 5:50 (★★); Bret Hart defeated Skinner in 5:51 (★★).

SummerSlam '92 ★★★★
31-08-92, London, England **WWF**
Jim Duggan and The Bushwhackers (Luke and Butch) defeated The Mountie and The Nasty Boys (Brian Knobbs and Jerry Sags) in 12:33 (★★); Papa Shango defeated Tito Santana in 6:00 (★★); The Legion Of Doom (Hawk and Animal) defeated Money Inc. (Ted DiBiase and Irwin R. Schyster) in 15:10 (★★); Nailz defeated Virgil in 3:55 (★★); Rick Martel vs. Shawn Michaels ended in a double count out in 8:06 (★★★); The Natural Disasters (Earthquake and Typhoon) defeated The Beverly Brothers (Beau Beverly and Blake Beverly) in 10:30 (★★); Crush defeated Repo Man in 5:41 (★★); The Ultimate Warrior defeated Randy Savage via count out in 28:00 (★★★★); The Undertaker defeated Kamala by DQ in 3:27 (★★); Tatanka defeated The Berzerker in 5:46 (★★); The British Bulldog defeated Bret Hart to win the WWF Intercontinental Title in 25:40 (★★★★★★★).

Clash Of The Champions XX: 20th Anniversary ★★★
02-09-92, Atlanta, Georgia **WCW**
Ricky Steamboat defeated Steve Austin in a No DQ Match to win the WCW World Television Title in 10:43 (★★★); Arn Anderson and Bobby Eaton defeated Dick Slater and Greg Valentine in 5:42 (★★); Ron Simmons defeated Cactus Jack in 8:51 (★★); The Barbarian and Butch Reed defeated Barry Windham and Dustin Rhodes in 8:13 (★★★); Rick Rude, Jake Roberts, Super Invader and Big Van Vader defeated Sting, Nikita Koloff and The Steiner Brothers (Rick Steiner and Scott Steiner) in an Elimination Match in 15:57 (★★★).

Halloween Havoc '92 ★★
25-10-92, Philadelphia, Pennsylvania **WCW**
Tom Zenk, Johnny Gunn and Shane Douglas defeated Arn Anderson, Bobby Eaton and Michael Hayes in 11:02 (★★); Ricky Steamboat defeated Brian Pillman in 10:25 (★★★); Big Van Vader defeated Nikita Koloff in 11:35 (★★); Barry Windham and Dustin Rhodes vs. Steve Williams and Steve Austin went to a time limit draw in 30:00 (★★★★); Rick Rude defeated Masahiro Chono by DQ in 22:23 (★★); Ron Simmons defeated The Barbarian in 12:41 (★); Sting defeated Jake Roberts in a Coal Miner's Glove Match in 10:34 (★).

Saturday Night's Main Event XXXI ★★★
14-11-92, Terre Haute, Indiana **WWF**
The Ultimate Maniacs (The Ultimate Warrior and Randy Savage) defeated Money Inc. (Ted DiBiase and Irwin R. Schyster) via count out in 6:11 (★★); Shawn Michaels defeated The British Bulldog to win the WWF Intercontinental Title in 10:28 (★★★); Bret Hart defeated Papa Shango in 7:13 (★★).

Clash Of The Champions XXI ★★★★
18-11-92, Macon, Georgia **WCW**
Erik Watts and Kensuke Sasaki defeated Arn Anderson and Bobby Eaton in a Bounty Match in 6:06 (★★); Scotty Flamingo defeated Johnny B. Badd in a Boxing Match in 3:01 (★★★); Ron Simmons and Too Cold Scorpio defeated Tony Atlas, The Barbarian and Cactus Jack in a Handicap Match in 5:52 (★★); Madusa vs. Paul E. Dangerously ended in a time limit draw in 5:00 (★★); Sting defeated Rick Rude in 20:00 (★★★★); Shane Douglas and Ricky Steamboat defeated Barry Windham and Dustin Rhodes to win the NWA and WCW World Tag Team Title in 15:52 (★★★★).

Survivor Series Showdown (1992) ★★
22-11-92, Springfield, Illinois **WWF**
Tatanka defeated Repo Man in 7:42 (★★); Marty Jannetty defeated The Brooklyn Brawler in 4:58 (★★); Kamala defeated Red Tyler in 3:27 (★★); Earthquake defeated Irwin R. Schyster by DQ in 11:01 (★★); The Big Boss Man defeated Barry Horowitz in 3:27 (★★); The Headshrinkers (Samu and Fatu) defeated Red Fox and Royce Royal in 2:42 (★★).

Survivor Series '92 ★★★
25-11-92, Richfield Township, Ohio **WWF**
The Headshrinkers (Samu and Fatu) defeated High Energy (Owen Hart and Koko B. Ware) in 7:40 (★★★); The Big Boss Man defeated Nailz in a Nightstick On A Pole Match in 5:44 (★★); Tatanka defeated Rick Martel in 11:07 (★★); Randy Savage and Mr. Perfect defeated Ric Flair and Razor Ramon by DQ in 16:38 (★★★); Yokozuna defeated Virgil in 3:34 (★★); The Natural Disasters (Earthquake and Typhoon) and The Nasty Boys (Brian Knobbs and Jerry Sags) defeated Money Inc. (Ted DiBiase and Irwin R. Schyster) and The Beverly Brothers (Beau Beverly and Blake Beverly) in an Elimination Match in 15:50 (★★); The Undertaker defeated Kamala in a Coffin Match in 5:27 (★★); Bret Hart defeated Shawn Michaels in 26:40 (★★★★).

Starrcade '92 ★★★
28-12-92, Atlanta, Georgia **WCW**
Van Hammer and Dan Spivey defeated Johnny B. Badd and Cactus Jack in 6:51 (★★); Big Van Vader and Dustin Rhodes defeated Kensuke Sasaki and The Barbarian in 6:56 (★★★); The Great Muta and Barry Windham defeated Brian Pillman and Too Cold Scorpio in 6:59 (★★★); Steve Williams and Sting defeated Jushin Thunder Liger and Erik Watts in 9:08 (★★); Masahiro Chono defeated The Great Muta in 12:49 (★★); Ron Simmons defeated Steve Williams by DQ in 15:12 (★★); Shane Douglas and Ricky Steamboat defeated Barry Windham and Brian Pillman in 20:02 (★★★★); Sting defeated Big Van Vader in 16:50 (★★★★); The Great Muta won Battlebowl II in 14:01 (★★).

Japan Supershow III ★★★★
04-01-93, Tokyo, Japan WCW/NJPW

Jushin Thunder Liger defeated Ultimo Dragon to win the IWGP Junior Heavyweight Title in 20:09 (★★★); Ron Simmons defeated Tony Halme in 6:10 (★★); Masa Saito and Shinya Hashimoto defeated Scott Norton and Dustin Rhodes in 13:57 (★★); The Great Muta defeated Masahiro Chono to win the NWA World Heavyweight Title in 19:48 (★★★★); Takayuki Iizuka, Akira Nogami and El Samurai defeated Nobukazu Hirai, Masao Orihara and Koki Kitahara in 15:11 (★★); Sting defeated Hiroshi Hase in 15:31 (★★).

Clash Of The Champions XXII ★★★★
13-01-93, Milwaukee, Wisconsin WCW

Cactus Jack defeated Johnny B. Badd in 2:50 (★); Too Cold Scorpio defeated Scotty Flamingo in 4:13 (★★); Chris Benoit defeated Brad Armstrong in 9:13 (★★★); The Wrecking Crew (Rage and Fury) defeated Johnny Gunn and Tom Zenk in 6:06 (★★); Shane Douglas and Ricky Steamboat defeated Brian Pillman and Steve Austin in 13:39 (★★★★); Dustin Rhodes, Sting and Cactus Jack defeated Big Van Vader, Barry Windham and Paul Orndorff in a Thundercage Match in 11:22 (★★★).

Battle Of The Belts ★★
23-01-93, Philadelphia, Pennsylvania ECW

Ray Odyssey defeated Chris Evans in 9:22 (★★); The Super Destroyers (Super Destroyer #1 and Super Destroyer #2) defeated The Lords Of Darkness (Agony and Pain) to unify the WWA Tag Team Title in 8:11 (★★); Kerry Von Erich vs. Salvatore Bellomo ended in a double DQ in 5:53 (★★); Johnny Hot Body defeated Tony Stetson in a Brass Knuckles Bullrope Cowbell Match in 4:39 (★★); Davey Boy Smith defeated The Masked Superstar in 1:42 (★★); The Sandman vs. The Spider ended in a double DQ in 11:55 (★★); Terry Funk defeated Eddie Gilbert in an "I Quit" Texas Death Match in 23:24 (★★★).

Royal Rumble '93 ★★★★
24-01-93, Sacramento, California WWF

The Steiner Brothers (Rick Steiner and Scott Steiner) defeated The Beverly Brothers (Beau Beverly and Blake Beverly) in 10:34 (★★); Shawn Michaels defeated Marty Jannetty in 14:20 (★★★); Bam Bam Bigelow defeated The Big Boss Man in 10:10 (★★); Bret Hart defeated Razor Ramon in 17:52 (★★★); Yokozuna won the 30-Man Royal Rumble Match in 66:35 (★★★).

SuperBrawl III ★★★★★
21-02-93, Asheville, North Carolina WCW

The Hollywood Blonds (Brian Pillman and Steve Austin) defeated Erik Watts and Marcus Alexander Bagwell in 16:34 (★★★); Too Cold Scorpio defeated Chris Benoit in 19:59 (★★★★); The British Bulldog defeated Bill Irwin in 5:49 (★★); Cactus Jack defeated Paul Orndorff in a Falls Count Anywhere Match in 12:17 (★★★); The Rock 'n' Roll Express (Ricky Morton and Robert Gibson) defeated The Heavenly Bodies (Tom Prichard and Stan Lane) in 12:52 (★★★★); Dustin Rhodes defeated Maxx Payne by DQ in 11:28 (★★); Barry Windham defeated The Great Muta to win the NWA World Heavyweight Title in 24:10 (★★); Big Van Vader defeated Sting in a White Castle Of Fear Strap Match in 20:54 (★★★★).

Reunion ★
05-03-93, Las Vegas, Nevada GLOW

Babe defeated The Party Animal in 2:11 (★); Liberty defeated MTV by DQ in 6:40 (★); Zelda defeated Beastie by DQ in 2:46 (★); Daisy defeated Ninotchka in 9:49 (★); Hollywood defeated Tulsa to win the inaugural US Title in 11:32 (★); Mt. Fiji defeated Big Bad Mama in a Sumo Circle Ring Match in 3:42 (★).

March To WrestleMania IX ★★
28-03-93, Fayetteville, North Carolina WWF

Yokozuna defeated Randy Savage in 6:36 (★★); Mr. Perfect defeated Skinner in 5:27 (★★); Kamala defeated Kim Chee in 2:10 (★); Money Inc. (Ted DiBiase and Irwin R. Schyster) defeated Jerry Sabin and Reno Riggins in 2:55 (★★); Tatanka defeated George South in 3:16 (★★); The Bushwhackers (Luke and Butch) and Tiger Jackson defeated The Beverly Brothers (Beau Beverly and Blake Beverly) and Little Louie in 9:57 (★★); The Undertaker defeated Bam Bam Bigelow via count out in 7:39 (★★★).

Bluegrass Brawl '93 ★★★
02-04-93, Pikeville, Kentucky SMW

The Mongolian Stomper defeated Rob Morgan in 1:24 (★); Tim Horner defeated The Nightstalker in 13:12 (★); Brian Lee defeated Kevin Sullivan in a Singapore Spike Match in 7:06 (★★); Tracy Smothers defeated The Dirty White Boy in a Chain Match to win the SMW Heavyweight Title in 26:05 (★★★★); The Heavenly Bodies (Stan Lane and Tom Prichard) and Bobby Eaton defeated The Stud Stable (Jimmy Golden and Robert Fuller) and Dutch Mantell, and The Rock 'n' Roll Express (Robert Gibson and Ricky Morton) and Arn Anderson in a Three Way Street Fight Elimination Match in 13:24 (★★★).

WrestleMania IX ★★
04-04-93, Paradise, Nevada WWF

Tatanka defeated Shawn Michaels via count out in 18:13 (★★★); The Steiner Brothers (Rick Steiner and Scott Steiner) defeated The Headshrinkers (Samu and Fatu) in 14:22 (★★★); Doink the Clown defeated Crush in 8:28 (★★); Razor Ramon defeated Bob Backlund in 3:45 (★★); Money Inc. (Ted DiBiase and Irwin R. Schyster) defeated The Mega Maniacs (Hulk Hogan and Brutus Beefcake) by DQ in 18:27 (★★); Lex Luger defeated Mr. Perfect in 10:56 (★★); The Undertaker defeated Giant Gonzalez by DQ in 7:33 (★★); Yokozuna defeated Bret Hart to win the WWF World Heavyweight Title in 8:55 (★★); Hulk Hogan defeated Yokozuna to win the WWF World Heavyweight Title in :22 (★).

Rampage Bercy '93 ★★
08-04-93, Paris, France WWF

Shawn Michaels defeated Bob Backlund in 13:10 (★★★); Crush defeated Doink the Clown via count out in 8:10 (★★); The Nasty Boys (Brian Knobbs and Jerry Sags) vs. The Headshrinkers (Samu and Fatu) went to a double DQ in 11:33 (★★); Mr. Perfect defeated Lex Luger in 6:44 (★★); Kamala defeated Kimchee in 6:45 (★★); Typhoon defeated Damien Demento in 6:25 (★★); Yokozuna defeated Jim Duggan in 7:31 (★★).

UK Rampage '93 ★
11-04-93, Sheffield, England WWF

Fatu defeated Brian Knobbs in 9:43 (★★); Doink the Clown defeated Kamala in 5:54 (★★); Mr. Perfect defeated Samu in 13:34 (★★); Bob Backlund defeated Damien Demento in 7:56 (★); Typhoon defeated The Brooklyn Brawler in 9:49 (★); Crush defeated Shawn Michaels via count out in 8:51 (★★); Lex Luger defeated Jim Duggan via DQ in 6:42 (★★).

European Rampage '93 (Barcelona) ★★★
24-04-93, Barcelona, Spain WWF

Virgil defeated Terry Taylor in 12:30 (★★★); Tatanka defeated Papa Shango in 6:27 (★★); The Steiner Brothers (Rick Steiner and Scott Steiner) defeated Money Inc. (Ted DiBiase and Irwin R Schyster) in 10:15 (★★★); Tito Santana defeated Doink the Clown in 2:54 (★★); Bret Hart defeated Bam Bam Bigelow in 11:56 (★★★).

European Rampage '93 (Milan) ★★★
25-04-93, Milan, Italy WWF

Doink the Clown defeated Tito Santana in 8:43 (★★★); The Steiner Brothers (Rick Steiner and Scott Steiner) defeated Money Inc. (Ted DiBiase and Irwin R Schyster) in 15:07 (★★★); The Undertaker defeated Yokozuna in 5:43 (★★); Tatanka defeated Papa Shango in 6:03 (★★★); The Bushwhackers (Butch and Luke) defeated The Beverly Brothers (Beau Beverly and Blake Beverly) in 14:36 (★★★); Bret Hart defeated Bam Bam Bigelow in 20:38 (★★★★).

Slamboree '93 ★★★★★
23-05-93, Atlanta, Georgia WCW

Too Cold Scorpio and Marcus Alexander Bagwell defeated Bobby Eaton and Chris Benoit in 9:22 (★★); Sid Vicious defeated Van Hammer in :35 (★★); Dick Murdoch, Don Muraco and Jimmy Snuka vs. Wahoo McDaniel, Blackjack Mulligan and Jim Brunzell ended in a no contest in 9:06 (★★); Thunderbolt Patterson and Brad Armstrong defeated Ivan Koloff and Baron von Raschke in 4:39 (★★); Dory Funk Jr. vs. Nick Bockwinkel went to a time limit draw in 15:00 (★★★); Rick Rude and Paul Orndorff defeated Dustin Rhodes and Kensuke Sasaki in 9:25 (★★); Sting defeated The Prisoner in 5:16 (★★); The Hollywood Blonds (Brian Pillman and Steve Austin) defeated Ricky Steamboat and Tom Zenk in a Steel Cage Match in 16:08

(★★★★); Barry Windham defeated Arn Anderson in 10:55 (★★★★); The British Bulldog defeated Big Van Vader by DQ in 16:16 (★★★).

King Of The Ring '93 ★★★★
13-06-93, Dayton, Ohio **WWF**
Bret Hart defeated Razor Ramon in 10:25 (★★★); Mr. Perfect defeated Mr. Hughes by DQ in 6:02 (★★); Bam Bam Bigelow defeated Jim Duggan in 4:59 (★★); Lex Luger vs. Tatanka ended in a time limit draw in 15:00 (★★); Bret Hart defeated Mr. Perfect in 18:56 (★★★★); Yokozuna defeated Hulk Hogan to win the WWF World Heavyweight Title in 13:08 (★★); The Steiner Brothers (Rick Steiner and Scott Steiner) and The Smoking Gunns (Billy Gunn and Bart Gunn) defeated Money Inc. (Ted DiBiase and Irwin R. Schyster) and The Headshrinkers (Samu and Fatu) in 6:49 (★★); Shawn Michaels defeated Crush in 11:14 (★★); Bret Hart defeated Bam Bam Bigelow in 18:11 (★★★★).

Clash Of The Champions XXIII ★★★
16-06-93, Norfolk, Virginia **WCW**
Ron Simmons defeated Dick Slater in 3:56 (★★); Lord Steven Regal defeated Marcus Alexander Bagwell in 6:18 (★★); Barry Windham defeated Too Cold Scorpio in 12:53 (★★★); Big Van Vader, Sid Vicious and Rick Rude defeated Dustin Rhodes, Sting and The British Bulldog in 10:59 (★★); Ric Flair and Arn Anderson defeated The Hollywood Blondes (Brian Pillman and Steve Austin) 2-0 in a Two Out Of Three Falls Match in 20:45 (★★★★).

Super Summer Sizzler Spectacular ★★
19-06-93, Philadelphia, Pennsylvania **ECW**
Don E. Allen vs. Herve Renesto ended in a no contest in 1:27 (★); Jimmy Snuka defeated JT Smith in 5:57 (★★); Tony Stetson defeated Larry Winters in a First Blood Match in 5:36 (★★); Peaches defeated Tigra in a Loser Gets Stripped Match in 3:22 (★); Jimmy Snuka defeated Tommy Cairo in 6:05 (★★); The Rockin' Rebel defeated The Sandman in a Philadelphia Street Fight in 5:11 (★★); Dick Murdoch defeated The Dark Patriot II in 5:36 (★★); Salvatore Bellomo, Stevie Wonderful and Super Destroyer #1 defeated Hunter Q. Robbins III and The Suicide Blondes (Jonathan Hot Body and Richard Michaels) in 10:08 (★★); Eddie Gilbert defeated Terry Funk in a Texas Chain Match in 17:13 (★★★).

Beach Blast '93 ★★
18-07-93, Biloxi, Mississippi **WCW**
Paul Orndorff defeated Ron Simmons by DQ in 11:15 (★★); Too Cold Scorpio and Marcus Alexander Bagwell defeated Tex Slazenger and Shanghai Pierce in 12:48 (★★); Lord Steven Regal defeated Erik Watts in 7:31 (★★); Johnny B. Badd defeated Maxx Payne in 4:50 (★★); The Hollywood Blonds (Brian Pillman and Steve Austin) defeated Arn Anderson and Paul Roma in 26:14 (★★); Dustin Rhodes vs. Rick Rude in an Iron Man Match ended in a 1-1 draw in 30:00 (★★); Ric Flair defeated Barry Windham to win the NWA World Heavyweight Title in 11:15 (★★); Sting and The British Bulldog defeated Big Van Vader and Sid Vicious in 16:44 (★★★).

Fire On The Mountain '93 ★★★★
14-08-93, Johnson City, Tennessee **SMW**
Jimmy Del Rey defeated Steve Armstrong in 4:48 (★★★); The Dirty White Boy vs. The Mongolian Stomper ended in a double DQ in 5:07 (★★); The Big Boss Man defeated Kevin Sullivan in 8:56 (★★★); Chris Candido defeated Tim Horner in a Loser Must Drink From a Baby Bottle Match in 18:39 (★★★); Brian Lee defeated Tracy Smothers in a Coal Miner's Glove Match in 20:02 (★★★★); The Rock 'n' Roll Express (Ricky Morton and Robert Gibson), Bob Armstrong, Steve Armstrong and Scott Armstrong defeated The Heavenly Bodies (Jimmy Del Rey and Tom Prichard), The Bruise Brothers (Ron Harris and Don Harris) and Jim Cornette in a Rage In A Cage Match in 21:29 (★★★★).

Clash Of The Champions XXIV ★★★★
18-08-93, Daytona Beach, Florida **WCW**
Arn Anderson and Paul Roma defeated Steve Austin and Lord Steven Regal to win the NWA and WCW World Tag Team Title in 9:52 (★★★); Too Cold Scorpio defeated Bobby Eaton in 5:26 (★★); Johnny B. Badd defeated Maxx Payne in a Mask vs. Guitar Match in 2:41 (★★); Ricky Steamboat defeated Paul

Orndorff to win the WCW World Television Title in 8:31 (★★); Sting and Ric Flair defeated The Colossal Kongs (Awesome Kong and King Kong) in 2:14 (★★); Hawk and Dustin Rhodes defeated The Equalizer and Rick Rude in 7:41 (★★); Big Van Vader defeated The British Bulldog in 11:11 (★★★).

SummerSlam Spectacular (1993) ★★★★
22-08-93, Poughkeepsie, New York **WWF**
Yokozuna defeated Jim Duggan in 8:27 (★★); Razor Ramon defeated Blake Beverly in 6:11 (★★); Tatanka and The Smoking Gunns (Billy Gunn and Bart Gunn) defeated Barry Horowitz, Reno Riggins and The Brooklyn Brawler in 7:04 (★★★); Shawn Michaels defeated Bob Backlund in 6:23 (★★); Marty Jannetty defeated Dwayne Gill in 3:21 (★★); The Steiner Brothers (Rick Steiner and Scott Steiner) defeated Money Inc. (Ted DiBiase and Irwin R. Schyster) in a Steel Cage Match in 18:00 (★★★★).

SummerSlam '93 ★★★
30-08-93, Auburn Hill, Michigan **WWF**
Razor Ramon defeated Ted DiBiase in 7:32 (★★); The Steiner Brothers (Rick Steiner and Scott Steiner) defeated The Heavenly Bodies (Jimmy Del Ray and Tom Prichard) in 9:28 (★★★); Shawn Michaels defeated Mr. Perfect via count out in 11:20 (★★★); Irwin R. Schyster defeated 1-2-3 Kid in 5:44 (★★); Bret Hart defeated Doink the Clown by DQ in 9:05 (★★); Jerry Lawler defeated Bret Hart by DQ in 6:32 (★★); Ludvig Borga defeated Marty Jannetty in 5:15 (★★); The Undertaker defeated Giant Gonzalez in a Rest In Peace Match in 8:04 (★★); The Smoking Gunns (Billy Gunn and Bart Gunn) and Tatanka defeated The Headshrinkers (Samu and Fatu) and Bam Bam Bigelow in 11:15 (★★★); Lex Luger defeated Yokozuna via count out in 17:58 (★★★★).

Ultra Clash '93 ★★
18-09-93, Philadelphia, Pennsylvania **ECW**
Public Enemy (Johnny Grunge and Rocco Rock) defeated Ian Rotten and Jason Knight in 4:37 (★★); Tony Stetson defeated Tommy Cairo in 7:30 (★★); Super Destroyer #1 defeated Super Destroyer #2 in a Mask vs. Mask Match in 6:24 (★★); The Dark Patriot defeated JT Smith in a Scaffold Match in 6:32 (★); Stan Hansen and Terry Funk defeated Abdullah the Butcher and Kevin Sullivan by DQ in a Bunkhouse Match in 7:32 (★★★); Tigra defeated Angel, Don E. Allen, Hunter Q. Robbins III, Jay Sulli and Sherri Martel in a Battle Royal in 3:45 (★); Sal Bellomo defeated Richard Michaels in a Strap Match in 7:18 (★★); Shane Douglas defeated The Sandman in 8:14 (★★); The Headhunters (Headhunter A and Headhunter B) defeated Crash The Terminator and Miguelito Perez in a Baseball Bat Match in 9:01 (★★).

Fall Brawl '93 ★★
19-09-93, Houston, Texas **WWF**
Lord Steven Regal defeated Ricky Steamboat to win the WCW World Television Title in 17:05 (★★); Charlie Norris defeated Big Sky in 4:34 (★★); Too Cold Scorpio and Marcus Alexander Bagwell defeated The Equalizer and Paul Orndorff in 10:46 (★★); Ice Train defeated Shanghai Pierce in 3:27 (★); The Nasty Boys (Brian Knobbs and Jerry Sags) defeated Arn Anderson and Paul Roma to win the WCW World Tag Team Title in 23:58 (★★); Cactus Jack defeated Yoshi Kwan in 3:38 (★★); Rick Rude defeated Ric Flair to win the WCW International World Heavyweight Title in 30:47 (★★); Sting, The British Bulldog, Dustin Rhodes and The Shockmaster defeated Sid Vicious, Big Van Vader and Harlem Heat (Kole and Kane) in a War Games Match in 16:39 (★★).

Halloween Havoc '93 ★★★
24-10-93, New Orleans, Louisiana **WCW**
Ice Train, Charlie Norris and The Shockmaster defeated The Equalizer and Harlem Heat (Kane and Kole) in 9:45 (★★); Paul Orndorff defeated Ricky Steamboat via count out in 18:35 (★★★); Lord Steven Regal vs. The British Bulldog ended in a time limit draw in 15:00 (★★); Dustin Rhodes defeated Steve Austin in 14:23 (★★); The Nasty Boys (Brian Knobbs and Jerry Sags) defeated Marcus Alexander Bagwell and Too Cold Scorpio in 14:38 (★★★); Sting defeated Sid Vicious in 10:41 (★★); Rick Rude defeated Ric Flair by DQ in 19:22 (★★); Big Van Vader defeated Cactus Jack in a Texas Death Match in 15:59 (★★★★).

Clash Of The Champions XXV ★★★
10-11-93, St. Petersburg, Florida **WCW**

Rick Rude vs. Hawk wended in a double count out in 5:23 (★); The Shockmaster defeated The Equalizer in 2:29 (★); Lord Steven Regal defeated Johnny B. Badd in 6:33 (★ ★); Steve Austin defeated Brian Pillman in 9:12 (★ ★ ★); Dustin Rhodes defeated Paul Orndorff in 11:57 (★ ★); The Nasty Boys (Brian Knobbs and Jerry Sags) defeated Sting and The British Bulldog in 8:30 (★ ★); Ric Flair defeated Big Van Vader by DQ in 9:24 (★ ★ ★).

Battlebowl '93 ★★
20-11-93, Pensacola, Florida **WCW**

Big Van Vader and Cactus Jack defeated Charlie Norris and Kane in 7:34 (★ ★); Brian Knobbs and Johnny B. Badd defeated Erik Watts and Paul Roma in 12:56 (★ ★); The Shockmaster and Paul Orndorff defeated Ricky Steamboat and Lord Steven Regal in 12:26 (★ ★ ★); King Kong and Dustin Rhodes defeated The Equalizer and Awesome Kong in 5:55 (★); Sting and Jerry Sags defeated Ron Simmons and Keith Cole in 13:14 (★ ★); Ric Flair and Steve Austin defeated Too Cold Scorpio and Maxx Payne in 14:31 (★ ★ ★); Rick Rude and Shanghai Pierce defeated Tex Slazenger and Marcus Alexander Bagwell in 14:50 (★); Hawk and Rip Rogers defeated The British Bulldog and Kole in 7:55 (★ ★); Big Van Vader won a Battlebowl Battle Royal in 25:33 (★ ★).

Survivor Series Showdown (1993) ★★
21-11-93, Bushkill, Pennsylvania/Delhi, New York **WWF**

Doink the Clown defeated Bastion Booger in 7:37 (★); Crush defeated Virgil in 7:55 (★ ★); Irwin R. Schyster defeated Marty Jannetty in 12:36 (★ ★); Yokozuna defeated Bret Hart by DQ in 17:00 (★ ★ ★).

Survivor Series '93 ★★★
24-11-93, Boston, Massachusetts **WWF**

1-2-3 Kid, Marty Jannetty, Randy Savage and Razor Ramon defeated Adam Bomb, Diesel, Irwin R. Schyster and Rick Martel in an Elimination Match in 26:58 (★ ★ ★); Bret Hart, Bruce Hart, Keith Hart and Owen Hart defeated Shawn Michaels, The Black Knight, The Blue Knight and The Red Knight in an Elimination Match in 30:57 (★ ★); The Heavenly Bodies (Jimmy Del Ray and Tom Prichard) defeated The Rock 'n' Roll Express (Ricky Morton and Robert Gibson) to win the SMW Tag Team Title in 13:41 (★ ★ ★); The Bushwhackers (Luke and Butch) and Men On A Mission (Mabel and Mo) defeated Bam Bam Bigelow, Bastion Booger and The Headshrinkers (Samu and Fatu) in an Elimination Match in 10:38 (★); The All-Americans (Lex Luger, The Undertaker, Rick Steiner and Scott Steiner) defeated The Foreign Fanatics (Yokozuna, Ludvig Borga, Crush and Jacques) in 27:59 (★ ★).

Thanksgiving Thunder '93 ★★
25-11-93, Hazard, Kentucky **SMW**

Chris Candido defeated Bobby Blaze in a Loser Gets Tarred and Feathered Match in 18:07 (★ ★ ★); Prince Kharis defeated Tim Horner in 7:53 (★); The Bullet defeated Kevin Sullivan in a Prince Of Darkness Match in 2:50 (★ ★); The Rock 'n' Roll Express (Ricky Morton and Robert Gibson) vs. The Moondogs (Moondog Rex and Moondog Spot) ended in a no contest in 6:24 (★ ★); Brian Lee defeated The Dirty White Boy in 9:18 (★ ★); The Bruise Brothers (Ron Harris and Don Harris) defeated The Heavenly Bodies (Jimmy Del Rey and Tom Prichard) in a Gang Fight Match in 13:12 (★ ★ ★).

Starrcade '93 ★★
27-12-93, Charlotte, North Carolina **WCW**

Pretty Wonderful (Paul Orndorff and Paul Roma) defeated Too Cold Scorpio and Marcus Alexander Bagwell in 11:45 (★ ★); The Shockmaster defeated Awesome Kong in 1:34 (★); Lord Steven Regal vs. Ricky Steamboat went to a time limit draw in 15:14 (★ ★); Cactus Jack and Maxx Payne defeated Tex Slazenger and Shanghai Pierce in 7:48 (★ ★); Steve Austin defeated Dustin Rhodes in a Two Out Of Three Falls Match to win the WCW United States Heavyweight Title in 23:56 (★ ★); Rick Rude defeated The Boss in 9:08 (★ ★); Sting and Hawk defeated The Nasty Boys (Brian Knobbs and Jerry Sags) by DQ in 29:11 (★ ★); Ric Flair defeated Big Van Vader to win the WCW World Heavyweight Title in 21:18 (★ ★ ★ ★).

Royal Rumble '94 ★★★★
22-01-94, Providence, Rhode Island **WWF**

Tatanka defeated Bam Bam Bigelow in 8:12 (★ ★ ★); The Quebecers (Jacques and Pierre) defeated Bret Hart and Owen Hart in 16:48 (★ ★ ★ ★); Razor Ramon defeated Irwin R. Schyster in 11:30 (★ ★); Yokozuna defeated The Undertaker in a Casket Match in 14:20 (★ ★); Bret Hart and Lex Luger co-won the 30-Man Royal Rumble Match in 55:04 (★ ★ ★ ★).

Clash Of The Champions XXVI ★★★
27-01-94, Baton Rouge, Louisiana **WCW**

Marcus Alexander Bagwell and Too Cold Scorpio defeated Pretty Wonderful (Paul Roma and Paul Orndorff) in 12:39 (★ ★); Ron Simmons defeated Ice Train in 3:32 (★); Lord Steven Regal vs. Dustin Rhodes ended in a time draw in 15:00 (★ ★); Cactus Jack and Maxx Payne defeated The Nasty Boys (Brian Knobbs and Jerry Sags) in 6:46 (★ ★); Brian Pillman defeated Col. Robert Parker in a Loser Wears A Chicken Suit Match in 5:41 (★ ★); Sting and Ric Flair defeated Big Van Vader and Rick Rude in 22:07 (★ ★ ★).

The Night The Line Was Crossed ★★
05-02-94, Philadelphia, Pennsylvania **ECW**

Mr. Hughes defeated Sal Bellomo in 3:17 (★ ★); The Sandman and Tommy Cairo defeated The Pitbull and The Rockin' Rebel in a Double Dog Collar Chain Match in 4:49 (★ ★); Public Enemy (Johnny Grunge and Rocco Rock) defeated The Bruise Brothers (Don Harris and Ron Harris) in a No Rules Match in 7:59 (★ ★ ★); Jimmy Snuka defeated Tommy Dreamer in 10:15 (★ ★); Pat Tanaka and The Original Sheik defeated Kevin Sullivan and The Tazmaniac in 3:15 (★ ★); JT Smith defeated Mike Awesome in 2:00 (★ ★ ★); Terry Funk vs. Sabu vs. Shane Douglas ended in a draw in a Three Way Dance in 57:35 (★ ★ ★).

SuperBrawl IV ★★
20-02-94, Albany, Georgia **WCW**

Harlem Heat (Kane and Kole) defeated Thunder and Lightning in 9:47 (★ ★); Jim Steele defeated The Equalizer in 6:31 (★); Terry Taylor defeated Diamond Dallas Page in 11:45 (★ ★); Johnny B. Badd defeated Jimmy Garvin in 10:48 (★ ★); Lord Steven Regal defeated Arn Anderson in 29:54 (★ ★); Cactus Jack and Maxx Payne defeated The Nasty Boys (Brian Knobbs and Jerry Sags) by DQ in 12:37 (★ ★ ★); Sting, Brian Pillman and Dustin Rhodes defeated Steve Austin, Rick Rude and Paul Orndorff in a Thundercam Match in 14:36 (★ ★ ★); Ric Flair defeated Big Van Vader in a Thundercage Match in 11:32 (★ ★).

March To WrestleMania X ★★★
13-03-94, Poughkeepsie/Loch Sheldrake, New York **WWF**

Lex Luger defeated Jimmy Del Ray in 8:36 (★ ★); Bam Bam Bigelow defeated Ben Jordan in 3:37 (★ ★); Razor Ramon defeated Tony DeVito in 4:11 (★ ★); Earthquake defeated The Executioner in 1:58 (★ ★); Crush defeated Bret Hart in 12:41 (★ ★ ★); The Quebecers (Jacques and Pierre) defeated Mike Bell and PJ Walker in 4:11 (★ ★); Yokozuna defeated Tatanka in 9:20 (★ ★ ★).

WrestleMania X ★★★★★
20-03-94, New York City, New York **WWF**

Owen Hart defeated Bret Hart in 20:21 (★ ★ ★ ★ ★); Bam Bam Bigelow and Luna Vachon defeated Doink the Clown and Dink the Clown in 6:09 (★ ★); Randy Savage defeated Crush in a Falls Count Anywhere Match in 9:49 (★ ★); Alundra Blayze defeated Leilani Kai in 3:20 (★ ★); Men On A Mission (Mabel and Mo) defeated The Quebecers (Jacques and Pierre) via count out in 7:41 (★ ★); Yokozuna defeated Lex Luger by DQ in 14:40 (★ ★); Earthquake defeated Adam Bomb in :35 (★ ★); Razor Ramon defeated Shawn Michaels in a Ladder Match in 18:47 (★ ★ ★ ★ ★); Bret Hart defeated Yokozuna to win the WWF World Heavyweight Title in 10:38 (★ ★).

Spring Stampede '94 ★★★★★
17-04-94, Chicago, Illinois **WCW**

Johnny B. Badd defeated Diamond Dallas Page in 5:55 (★ ★); Lord Steven Regal vs. Brian Pillman ended in a time limit draw in 15:00 (★ ★); The Nasty Boys (Brian Knobbs and Jerry Sags) defeated Cactus Jack and Maxx Payne in a Chicago Street Fight in 8:54 (★ ★ ★ ★ ★); Steve Austin defeated The Great Muta by DQ in 16:20 (★ ★); Sting defeated Rick Rude to win the WCW International World Heavyweight Title in 12:50 (★ ★); Bunkhouse Buck defeated Dustin Rhodes in a Bunkhouse Match in 14:11 (★★★★); Big Van Vader defeated The Boss in 9:02 (★★★★); Ric Flair vs. Ricky Steamboat ended in a draw in 32:19 (★★★★).

When Worlds Collide ★★
14-05-94, Philadelphia, Pennsylvania ECW

Tommy Dreamer defeated The Rockin' Rebel in 6:21 (★★); Mikey Whipwreck defeated 911 by DQ in 1:42 (★★); Jimmy Snuka defeated Kevin Sullivan in 4:30 (★★); Peaches and Tommy Cairo defeated The Sandman and Woman in a Singapore Canes Match in 5:02 (★★); The Pitbull defeated The Tazmaniac in 8:45 (★★); JT Smith and The Bruise Brothers (Don Harris and Ron Harris) defeated Mr. Hughes, Shane Douglas and Public Enemy (Johnny Grunge and Rocco Rock) in a Handicap Elimination Match in 24:51 (★★); Bobby Eaton and Sabu defeated Arn Anderson and Terry Funk in 19:34 (★★★★).

Slamboree '94 ★★★★
22-05-94, Philadelphia, Pennsylvania WCW

Steve Austin defeated Johnny B. Badd in 16:12 (★★★); Terry Funk vs. Tully Blanchard ended in a double DQ in 7:15 (★★★★); Larry Zbyszko defeated Lord Steven Regal in 11:30 (★★★); Dustin Rhodes defeated Bunkhouse Buck in a Bullrope Match in 12:47 (★★); Ric Flair defeated Barry Windham in 13:21 (★★★); Cactus Jack and Kevin Sullivan defeated The Nasty Boys (Brian Knobbs and Jerry Sags) in a Broad Street Bully Match to win the WCW World Tag Team Title in 9:56 (★★★★); Sting defeated Big Van Vader in to win the vacant WCW International World Heavyweight Title in 13:54 (★★★).

King Of The Ring '94 ★★★
19-06-94, Baltimore, Maryland WWF

Razor Ramon defeated Bam Bam Bigelow in 8:24 (★★★); Irwin R. Schyster defeated Mabel in 5:34 (★★); Owen Hart defeated Tatanka in 8:18 (★★★); 1-2-3 Kid defeated Jeff Jarrett in 4:39 (★★★); Diesel defeated Bret Hart by DQ in 22:51 (★★★★); Razor Ramon defeated Irwin R. Schyster in 5:13 (★★); Owen Hart defeated 1-2-3 Kid in 3:37 (★★★★); The Headshrinkers (Samu and Fatu) defeated Crush and Yokozuna in 9:16 (★★); Owen Hart defeated Razor Ramon in 6:35 (★★); Roddy Piper defeated Jerry Lawler in 12:30 (★).

Clash Of The Champions XXVII ★★★
23-06-94, Charleston, South Carolina WCW

Cactus Jack and Kevin Sullivan defeated The Nasty Boys (Brian Knobbs and Jerry Sags) in 10:35 (★★); The Guardian Angel defeated Tex Slazenger in 1:44 (★★); Lord Steven Regal defeated Larry Zbyszko to win the WCW World Television Title in 9:25 (★★★); Johnny B. Badd defeated Steve Austin by DQ in 10:25 (★★); Ric Flair defeated Sting to unify the WCW World Heavyweight Title and WCW International Title in 17:17 (★★★★).

Hostile City Showdown '94 ★★
24-06-94, Philadelphia, Pennsylvania ECW

Tommy Dreamer defeated Hack Myers in 6:48 (★★); The Tazmaniac defeated The Pitbull in a Dog Collar Match in 7:37 (★★); The Bruise Brothers (Don Harris and Ron Harris) defeated Mr. Hughes and Shane Douglas in 8:39 (★★); The Sandman vs. Tommy Cairo ended in a no contest in a Singapore Cane On A Pole Match in 5:31 (★★); The Funk Brothers (Dory Funk Jr. and Terry Funk) vs. Public Enemy (Johnny Grunge and Rocco Rock) ended in a no contest in 13:24 (★★); Mikey Whipwreck defeated The Rockin' Rebel by DQ in 3:23 (★★); Sabu defeated Cactus Jack in 13:02 (★★★★).

Heat Wave '94 ★★★★
16-07-94, Philadelphia, Pennsylvania ECW

The Bad Breed (Axl Rotten and Ian Rotten) defeated Hack Myers and The Rockin' Rebel in 9:38 (★★); Mikey Whipwreck defeated Chad Austin by DQ in 9:11 (★★); Tommy Dreamer defeated Steve Richards in 7:44 (★★); Mr. Hughes defeated Tommy Dreamer in 3:00 (★★); Sabu and The Tazmaniac defeated The Pitbulls (Pitbull #1 and Pitbull #2) in 5:23 (★★★); The Sandman defeated Tommy Cairo in a Dueling Singapore Canes Match in 8:47 (★★); Shane Douglas defeated Sabu via count out in 19:38 (★★★); Public Enemy (Johnny Grunge and Rocco Rock) defeated The Funk Brothers (Dory Funk Jr. and Terry Funk) in a No Ropes Barbed Wire Match in 11:50 (★★).

Bash At The Beach '94 ★★★
17-07-94, Orlando, Florida WCW

Lord Steven Regal defeated Johnny B. Badd in 10:40 (★★); Big Van Vader defeated The Guardian Angel by DQ in 7:58 (★★); Terry Funk and Bunkhouse Buck defeated Dustin Rhodes and Arn Anderson in 11:15 (★★); Steve Austin defeated Ricky Steamboat in 20:06 (★★★★); Pretty Wonderful (Paul Roma and Paul Orndorff) defeated Cactus Jack and Kevin Sullivan to win the WCW World Tag Team Title in 20:21 (★★); Hulk Hogan defeated Ric Flair to win the WCW World Heavyweight Title in 21:54 (★★★).

Night Of Legends '94 ★★★★
05-08-94, Knoxville, Tennessee SMW

Doug Furnas defeated Killer Kyle in 8:46 (★★★); Bob Orton and Dick Slater vs. Ronnie Garvin and The Mongolian Stomper ended in a double DQ in 11:50 (★★★); The Rock 'n' Roll Express (Ricky Morton and Robert Gibson) defeated Brian Lee and Chris Candido to win the SMW Tag Team Title in 12:51 (★★★★); The Thrillseekers (Chris Jericho and Lance Storm) defeated The Heavenly Bodies (Jimmy Del Ray and Tom Prichard) in a Street Fight in 15:34 (★★★★); The Dirty White Boy defeated Terry Gordy in 10:26 (★★); Bob Armstrong, Tracy Smothers and Road Warrior Hawk defeated Bruiser Bedlam, Terry Funk and Dory Funk Jr. in a Coward Waves the Flag Match in 8:45 (★★★★).

Hardcore Heaven '94 ★★★
13-08-94, Philadelphia, Pennsylvania ECW

Hack Myers defeated The Rockin' Rebel in 4:41 (★★); Chad Austin defeated Tommy Cairo in 4:30 (★★); Jason defeated Mikey Whipwreck to win the ECW Television Title in 12:08 (★★); Jimmy Snuka and The Tazmaniac defeated The Pitbulls (Pitbull #1 and Pitbull #2) in :39 (★); 911 defeated Mr. Hughes in 3:31 (★★); The Sandman defeated Tommy Dreamer in a Singapore Cane Match in :53 (★); Public Enemy (Johnny Grunge and Rocco Rock) defeated The Bad Breed (Axl Rotten and Ian Rotten) in a Base Brawl Match in 19:09 (★★★); Sabu defeated Too Cold Scorpio in 18:27 (★★★★); Cactus Jack vs. Terry Funk ended in a no contest in 10:58 (★★★).

Sunday Night Slam I ★★
21-08-94, Youngstown, Ohio WWF

Lex Luger defeated Crush in 12:30 (★★); Bam Bam Bigelow and Irwin R. Schyster defeated Bob Holly and 1-2-3 Kid in 10:13 (★★★); Razor Ramon defeated Todd Becker in 3:45 (★★); Bull Nakano defeated Heidi Lee Morgan in 7:32 (★★); Diesel defeated Typhoon in 5:01 (★); The Undertaker defeated Sonny Rogers in 1:21 (★★).

Clash Of The Champions XXVIII ★★★
24-08-94, Cedar Rapids, Iowa WCW

The Nasty Boys (Brian Knobbs and Jerry Sags) defeated Pretty Wonderful (Paul Roma and Paul Orndorff) in 9:33 (★★); Ricky Steamboat defeated Steve Austin to win the WCW United States Heavyweight Title in 16:02 (★★★★); Dusty Rhodes and Dustin Rhodes defeated Terry Funk and Bunkhouse Buck by DQ in 7:27 (★★); Antonio Inoki defeated Lord Steven Regal in 8:26 (★★); Ric Flair defeated Hulk Hogan via count out in 14:26 (★★★).

SummerSlam '94 ★★★★
29-08-94, Chicago, Illinois WWF

Bam Bam Bigelow and Irwin R. Schyster defeated The Headshrinkers (Samu and Fatu) by DQ in 7:20 (★★); Alundra Blayze defeated Bull Nakano in 8:10 (★★★); Razor Ramon defeated Diesel to win the WWF Intercontinental Title in 15:03 (★★★); Tatanka defeated Lex Luger in 6:02 (★★); Jeff Jarrett defeated Mabel in 5:45 (★★); Bret Hart defeated Owen Hart in a Steel Cage Match in 32:22 (★★★★★); The Undertaker defeated The Undertaker in 8:57 (★).

Fall Brawl '94 ★★★
18-09-94, Roanoke, Virginia WCW

Johnny B. Badd defeated Lord Steven Regal to win the WCW World Television Title in 11:08 (★★★); Kevin Sullivan defeated Cactus Jack in a Loser Leaves WCW match in 6:08 (★★); Jim Duggan defeated Steve Austin to win the WCW United States Heavyweight Title in :35 (★); Pretty Wonderful (Paul Roma and Paul Orndorff) defeated Stars and Stripes (The Patriot and Marcus Alexander Bagwell) in 12:54 (★★); Big Van Vader defeated Sting and The Guardian Angel in a Triangle Elimination Match in 30:22 (★★★★); Dusty Rhodes, Dustin Rhodes and

The Nasty Boys (Brian Knobbs and Jerry Sags) defeated The Stud Stable (Terry Funk, Arn Anderson, Bunkhouse Buck and Col. Robert Parker) in a War Games Match in 19:05 (★★).

Blackjack Brawl ★
23-09-94, Las Vegas, Nevada **UWF**
Dan Spivey defeated Johnny Ace to win the vacant UWF Americas Title in 7:17 (★★); Jack Armstrong defeated Mando Guerrero to win the vacant UWF Junior Heavyweight Title in 4:24 (★★); Sunny Beach defeated Dr. Feelgood to win the vacant UWF SportsChannel Television Title in 5:24 (★); Bob Orton vs. Finland Thor ended in a double DQ in 5:16 (★★); Little Tokyo defeated The Karate Kid to win the vacant UWF Midget World Title in 7:07 (★★); Samson defeated The Irish Assassin in 4:30 (★); Tyler Mane defeated Steve Ray to win the vacant UWF MGM Grand Title in 6:27 (★★); Candi Devine defeated Tina Moretti to win the vacant UWF Women's World Title in 3:24 (★); The Killer Bees (B. Brian Blair and Jim Brunzell) defeated The New Powers Of Pain (Power Warrior and The Warlord) to win the vacant UWF World Tag Team Title in 11:30 (★★); Cactus Jack vs. Jimmy Snuka ended in a double count out in a Lumberjack Match in 8:40 (★★); Steve Williams defeated Sid Vicious by DQ in 10:45 (★★).

Halloween Havoc '94 ★★★
23-10-94, Detroit, Michigan **WCW**
Johnny B. Badd vs. The Honky Tonk Man ended in a time limit draw in 10:00 (★★); Pretty Wonderful (Paul Roma and Paul Orndorff) defeated Stars and Stripes (The Patriot and Marcus Alexander Bagwell) to win the WCW World Tag Team Title in 13:47 (★★); Dave Sullivan defeated Kevin Sullivan via count out in 5:17 (★★); Dustin Rhodes defeated Arn Anderson in 9:50 (★★); Jim Duggan defeated Steve Austin by DQ in 8:02 (★★); Big Van Vader defeated The Guardian Angel in 8:17 (★★★); The Nasty Boys (Brian Knobbs and Jerry Sags) defeated Terry Funk and Bunkhouse Buck in 7:56 (★); Hulk Hogan defeated Ric Flair in a Steel Cage Retirement Match in 19:25 (★★★★).

November To Remember '94 ★★
05-11-94, Philadelphia, Pennsylvania **ECW**
JT Smith defeated Hack Myers in 4:02 (★★); The Pitbulls (Pitbull #1 and Pitbull #2) defeated The Bad Breed (Axl Rotten and Ian Rotten) in 3:11 (★★); Too Cold Scorpio defeated Mr. Hughes in 7:09 (★★); Tommy Dreamer defeated Tommy Cairo in 7:09 (★★); Dean Malenko defeated The Tazmaniac in 5:13 (★★); Shane Douglas defeated Ron Simmons in 6:34 (★★); Public Enemy (Johnny Grunge and Rocco Rock) defeated Cactus Jack and Mikey Whipwreck in a Brawl Game Match to win the ECW Tag Team Title in 12:34 (★★★); Chris Benoit vs. Sabu ended in a no contest in :37 (★); 911 defeated Chris Benoit in :27 (★); Chris Benoit vs. Too Cold Scorpio ended in a double count out in 5:34 (★★).

When World Collide ★★★★★
06-11-94, Los Angeles, California **AAA**
Mascarita Sagrada and Octagoncito defeated Espectrito and Jerrito Estrada in 8:30 (★★★); Fuerza Guerrera, Madonna's Boyfriend and Psicosis defeated Rey Mysterio Jr., Heavy Metal and Latin Lover in 12:46 (★★★★); The Pegasus Kid, Too Cold Scorpio and Tito Santana defeated Jerry Estrada, La Parka and Blue Panther in 14:58 (★★★); Octagon and El Hijo del Santo defeated Los Gringos Locos (Art Bart and Eddy Guerrero) in a Two Out Of Three Falls Mask vs. Hair Match in 22:29; (★★★★★) Perro Aguayo defeated Konnan in a Steel Cage Match in 17:50 (★★★).

Clash Of The Champions XXIX ★★
16-11-94, Jacksonville, Florida **WCW**
Stars And Stripes (The Patriot and Marcus Alexander Bagwell) defeated Pretty Wonderful (Paul Roma and Paul Orndorff) to win the WCW World Tag Team Title in 9:20 (★★); Johnny B. Badd defeated The Honky Tonk Man by DQ in 6:10 (★★); Harlem Heat (Booker T and Stevie Ray) defeated The Nasty Boys (Brian Knobbs and Jerry Sags) in 10:36 (★★); Big Van Vader defeated Dustin Rhodes in 11:43 (★★★); Jim Duggan defeated Steve Austin by DQ in :54 (★); Hulk Hogan, Sting and Dave Sullivan defeated The Three Faces Of Fear (The Butcher, Avalanche and Kevin Sullivan) in 10:55 (★★).

Sunday Night Slam II ★★★
20-11-94, Bushkill, Pennsylvania **WWF**
The Smoking Gunns (Bart Gunn and Billy Gunn) defeated The Heavenly Bodies (Jimmy Del Ray and Tom Prichard) in 14:00 (★★★); Yokozuna defeated John Chrystal in 1:06 (★★); The British Bulldog defeated Owen Hart by DQ in 11:00 (★★★).

Survivor Series '94 ★★★
23-11-94, San Antonio, Texas **WWF**
The Bad Guys (Razor Ramon, 1-2-3 Kid, The British Bulldog, Fatu and Seone) defeated The Teamsters (Diesel, Shawn Michaels, Jeff Jarrett, Jim Neidhart and Owen Hart) in an Elimination Match in 21:45 (★★★); The Royal Family (Jerry Lawler, Cheesy, Queasy and Sleazy) defeated Clowns R' Us (Doink the Clown, Dink the Clown, Pink the Clown and Wink the Clown) in an Elimination Match in 16:05 (★★); Bob Backlund defeated Bret Hart in a Submission Match to win the WWF World Heavyweight Title in 35:11 (★★★); The Million Dollar Team (Bam Bam Bigelow, Jimmy Del Ray, Tom Prichard, King Kong Bundy and Tatanka) defeated Guts and Glory (Adam Bomb, Bart Gunn, Billy Gunn, Mabel and Lex Luger) in an Elimination Match in 23:21 (★★★); The Undertaker defeated Yokozuna in a Casket Match in 15:24 (★★).

Starrcade '94 ★
27-12-94, Nashville, Tennessee **WCW**
Big Van Vader defeated Jim Duggan to win the WCW United States Heavyweight Title in 12:06 (★★); Alex Wright defeated Jean-Paul Levesque in 14:03 (★★); Johnny B. Badd defeated Arn Anderson in 12:11 (★★); The Nasty Boys (Brian Knobbs and Jerry Sags) defeated Harlem Heat (Booker T and Stevie Ray) by DQ in 17:49 (★★); Mr. T defeated Kevin Sullivan in 3:50 (★); Sting vs. Avalanche by DQ in 15:26 (★★); Hulk Hogan defeated The Butcher in 12:07 (★★).

Royal Rumble '95 ★★★
22-01-95, Tampa, Florida **WWF**
Jeff Jarrett defeated Razor Ramon to win the WWF Intercontinental Title in 18:06 (★★★); The Undertaker defeated Irwin R. Schyster in 12:21 (★★); Diesel vs. Bret Hart ended in a draw in 27:19 (★★★★); 1-2-3 Kid and Bob Holly defeated Bam Bam Bigelow and Tatanka to win the vacant WWF World Tag Team Title in 15:32 (★★); Shawn Michaels won the 30-Man Royal Rumble Match in 38:41 (★★).

Clash Of The Champions XXX ★★
25-01-95, Paradise, Nevada **WCW**
Arn Anderson defeated Johnny B. Badd in 7:38 (★★); Alex Wright defeated Bobby Eaton in 7:38 (★★); Harlem Heat (Booker T and Stevie Ray) defeated Stars And Stripes (Marcus Alexander Bagwell and The Patriot) in 9:45 (★★); Sting defeated Avalanche in 5:22 (★★); Hulk Hogan and Randy Savage defeated Kevin Sullivan and The Butcher in 11:04 (★★).

Double Tables ★★★★
04-02-95, Philadelphia, Pennsylvania **ECW**
Jason The Terrible and The Pitbulls (Pitbull #1 and Pitbull #2) defeated Hack Myers and The Young Dragons (Young Dragon #1 & Young Dragon #2) in 11:22 (★★); Tommy Dreamer defeated Stevie Richards in 7:38 (★★); Mikey Whipwreck defeated Paul Lauria in 9:17 (★★); Ian Rotten defeated Axl Rotten in 6:41 (★★); Chris Benoit defeated Al Snow in 14:36 (★★★★); Shane Douglas defeated Tully Blanchard in 10:27 (★★); Cactus Jack defeated The Sandman in a Texas Death Match in 15:47 (★★★); Sabu and The Tazmaniac defeated Public Enemy (Johnny Grunge and Rocco Rock) in a Double Tables Match to win the ECW Tag Team Title in 12:48 (★★★★).

SuperBrawl V ★★
19-02-95, Baltimore, Maryland **WCW**
Alex Wright defeated Paul Roma in 13:21 (★★); Jim Duggan defeated Bunkhouse Buck in 11:58 (★); Kevin Sullivan defeated Dave Sullivan in 7:18 (★); Harlem Heat (Booker T and Stevie Ray) defeated The Nasty Boys (Brian Knobbs and Jerry Sags) by DQ in 17:07 (★★); The Blacktop Bully defeated Dustin Rhodes in 16:10 (★★); Sting and Randy Savage defeated Avalanche and Big Bubba Rogers in 10:18 (★★); Hulk Hogan defeated Big Van Vader by DQ in 15:09 (★★).

Return Of The Funker ★★★★

25-02-95, Philadelphia, Pennsylvania **ECW**

The Pitbulls (Pitbull #1 and Pitbull #2) defeated Chad Austin and Joel Hartgood in 4:21 (★★); Jason Knight and Paul Lauria defeated Hack Myers and Mikey Whipwreck in 15:00 (★★); Too Cold Scorpio defeated Hector Guerrero in 11:19 (★★); Axl Rotten defeated Ian Rotten in a Barbed Wire Baseball Bat Match in 12:22 (★★); Shane Douglas defeated Marty Jannetty in 18:19 (★★★★); Chris Benoit and Dean Malenko defeated Sabu and The Tazmaniac to win the ECW Tag Team Title in 10:28 (★★★★); Cactus Jack defeated DC Drake in 4:07 (★★).

Uncensored '95 ★

19-03-95, Tupelo, Mississippi **WCW**

The Blacktop Bully defeated Dustin Rhodes in a King Of The Road Match in 13:06 (★★); Meng defeated Jim Duggan in a Martial Arts Match in 7:04 (★); Johnny B. Badd defeated Arn Anderson in a Boxing Match in 9:22 (★★★); Randy Savage defeated Avalanche by DQ in 11:44 (★★); Big Bubba Rogers defeated Sting in 13:43 (★★); The Nasty Boys (Brian Knobbs and Jerry Sags) defeated Harlem Heat (Booker T and Stevie Ray) in a Falls Count Anywhere Match in 8:43 (★★); Hulk Hogan defeated Big Van Vader in a Leather Strap Match in 18:21 (★).

Sunday Night Slam III ★★

26-03-95, Stockton, California **WWF**

Bob Backlund defeated Jeff Jarrett by DQ in 5:00 (★★); Bam Bam Bigelow defeated Seone in 2:54 (★★); Lex Luger defeated Tatanka in a Steel Cage Match in 9:00 (★★).

WrestleMania XI ★★

02-04-95, Hartford, Connecticut **WWF**

The Allied Powers (Lex Luger and The British Bulldog) defeated The Blu Brothers (Jacob Blu and Eli Blu) in 6:34 (★★); Razor Ramon defeated Jeff Jarrett by DQ in 13:32 (★★); The Undertaker defeated King Kong Bundy in 6:36 (★); Owen Hart and Yokozuna defeated The Smoking Gunns (Billy Gunn and Bart Gunn) to win the WWF World Tag Team Title in 9:42 (★★); Bret Hart defeated Bob Backlund in an "I Quit" Match in 9:34 (★★); Diesel defeated Shawn Michaels in 20:35 (★★★★); Lawrence Taylor defeated Bam Bam Bigelow in 11:42 (★★★).

Three Way Dance ★★★

08-04-95, Philadelphia, Pennsylvia **ECW**

The Pitbulls (Pitbull #1 and Pitbull #2) defeated Johnny Hot Body and Tony Stetson in :59 (★); Raven defeated Tommy Dreamer in 8:43 (★★); Mikey Whipwreck defeated Ron Simmons by DQ in 4:18 (★); Eddie Guerrero defeated Too Cold Scorpio to win the ECW Television Title in 14:49 (★★★★); Axl Rotten defeated Ian Rotten in a Hair vs. Hair Match in 9:49 (★); Hack Myers defeated Dino Sandoff in 4:14 (★★); Shane Douglas defeated The Sandman in 10:02 (★★★); Public Enemy (Johnny Grunge and Rocco Rock) defeated Chris Benoit and Dean Malenko, and Rick Steiner and The Tazmaniac in a Three Way Dance to win the ECW Tag Team Title in 19:56 (★★).

Hostile City Showdown '95 ★★★

15-04-95, Philadelphia, Pennsylvania **ECW**

Mikey Whipwreck defeated Stevie Richards in 7:34 (★★); Tsubo Genjin defeated Tony Stetson in 4:48 (★★); Axl Rotten defeated Ian Rotten in a Barbed Wire Baseball Bat Match in 9:08 (★★★); Raven vs. Tommy Dreamer ended in a no contest in 7:30 (★★); Eddie Guerrero vs. Dean Malenko ended in a draw in 25:57 (★★★★); The Sandman defeated Shane Douglas to win the ECW World Title in 7:52 (★★); Public Enemy (Johnny Grunge and Rocco Rock) defeated The Pitbulls (Pitbull #1 and Pitbull #2) in 16:47 (★★★); 911 defeated Ron Simmons in 5:31 (★★); Cactus Jack defeated Terry Funk in 12:57 (★★★★).

Enter Sandman ★★

13-05-95, Philadelphia, Pennsylvania **ECW**

Hack Myers defeated Tony Stetson in 5:32 (★★); 911 and The Tazmaniac defeated Hiroshi Itakura and Tsubo Genjin in 2:51 (★★); Axl Rotten defeated Ian Rotten in a Barbed Wire Baseball Bat Barbed Wire Chair Match in 6:18 (★★); Raven and Stevie Richards defeated Mikey Whipwreck and Tommy Dreamer by DQ in 8:51 (★★); Eddie Guerrero vs. Dean Malenko ended in a draw in 30:00 (★★★★); The Sandman defeated Cactus Jack in 11:28 (★★); The Sandman defeated Shane Douglas in 10:41 (★); Public Enemy (Johnny Grunge and Rocco Rock) defeated The Pitbulls (Pitbull #1 and Pitbull #2) in a Double Dog Collar Match in 16:41 (★★).

In Your House 1: Premiere ★★

14-05-95, Syracuse, New York **WWF**

Bret Hart defeated Hakushi in 14:39 (★★★★); Razor Ramon defeated Jeff Jarrett and The Roadie in a Handicap Match in 12:36 (★★); Mabel defeated Adam Bomb in 1:54 (★★); Owen Hart and Yokozuna defeated The Smoking Gunns (Billy Gunn and Bart Gunn) in 5:44 (★★); Jerry Lawler defeated Bret Hart in 5:01 (★★); Diesel defeated Sycho Sid by DQ in 11:31 (★★).

Slamboree '95 ★★

21-05-95, St. Petersburg, Florida **WCW**

The Nasty Boys (Brian Knobbs and Jerry Sags) defeated Harlem Heat (Booker T and Stevie Ray) to win the WCW World Tag Team Title in 10:52 (★★); Kevin Sullivan defeated The Man With No Name in 5:24 (★); Wahoo McDaniel defeated Dick Murdoch in 6:18 (★); The Great Muta defeated Paul Orndorff in 14:11 (★★); Arn Anderson defeated Alex Wright in 11:36 (★★); Meng vs. Hawk ended in a double count out in 4:41 (★★); Sting defeated Big Bubba Rogers in 9:29 (★★); Hulk Hogan and Randy Savage defeated Ric Flair and Vader in 18:57 (★★★).

Barbed Wire, Hoodies & Chokeslams ★

17-06-95, Philadelphia, Pennsylvania **ECW**

The Broad Street Bully defeated The New Jersey Devil in :16 (★); Mikey Whipwreck defeated Val Puccio in 3:11 (★★); The Vampire Warrior defeated Hack Myers in 2:36 (★★); Tommy Dreamer defeated The Vampire Warrior in 7:18 (★★); 911 defeated Jim Steele in :34 (★); Beulah McGillicutty defeated Luna Vachon in :03 (★); Taz and Too Cold Scorpio defeated Raven and The Pitbulls (Pitbull #1 and Pitbull #2) in a Handicap Match in 12:50 (★★); The Sandman defeated Cactus Jack in a Barbed Wire Match in 19:48 (★★★).

Great American Bash '95 ★★★

18-06-95, Dayton, Ohio **WCW**

Alex Wright defeated Brian Pillman in 15:42 (★★★★); Jim Duggan defeated Sgt. Craig Pittman by DQ in 8:13 (★★); Harlem Heat (Booker T and Stevie Ray) defeated Dick Slater and Bunkhouse Buck in 8:39 (★★); The Renegade defeated Arn Anderson to win the WCW World Television Title in 9:07 (★); The Nasty Boys (Brian Knobbs and Jerry Sags) defeated The Blue Bloods (Earl Robert Eaton and Lord Steven Regal) in 15:03 (★★); Sting defeated Meng to win the vacant WCW United States Heavyweight Title in 13:34 (★★★); Ric Flair defeated Randy Savage in 14:42 (★★★★).

King Of The Ring '95 ★

25-06-95, Philadelphia, Pennsylvania **WWF**

Savio Vega defeated Yokozuna via count out in 8:24 (★★); The Roadie defeated Bob Holly in 7:11 (★★); Kama vs. Shawn Michaels ended in a time limit draw in 15:00 (★★); Mabel defeated The Undertaker in 10:44 (★); Savio Vega defeated The Roadie in 6:36 (★★); Bret Hart defeated Jerry Lawler in a Kiss My Foot Match in 9:20 (★★); Mabel defeated Savio Vega in 8:32 (★); Bam Bam Bigelow and Diesel defeated Sycho Sid and Tatanka in 17:35 (★★).

Heat Wave '95 ★★★★

15-07-95, Philadelphia, Pennsylvia **ECW**

Mikey Whipwreck defeated Mike Norman in 6:41 (★★); Don E. Allen and Tony Stetson defeated Raven and Stevie Richards via count out in 2:10 (★★); Hack Myers defeated Val Puccio in 6:15 (★); The Pitbulls (Pitbull #1 and Pitbull #2) and Tommy Dreamer defeated Raven and The Dudleys (Dudley Dudley and Snot Dudley) in 5:33 (★★); Dean Malenko and Too Cold Scorpio defeated Eddie Guerrero and Taz in 20:00 (★★★★); The Sandman defeated Axl Rotten in 10:35 (★★); Luna Vachon defeated Stevie Richards in a Steel Cage Match in 7:45 (★★★); The Gangstas (Mustafa and New Jack) defeated Public Enemy (Johnny Grunge and Rocco Rock) in 14:23 (★★★).

Bash At The Beach '95 ★

16-07-95, Huntington Beach, California **WCW**

Sting defeated Meng in 15:28 (★★); The Renegade defeated Paul Orndorff in 6:41 (★); Kamala defeated Jim Duggan in 6:06 (★); Diamond Dallas Page defeated Dave Sullivan in 4:23 (★); Harlem Heat (Booker T and Stevie Ray) defeated The Nasty Boys (Brian Knobbs and Jerry Sags) and The Blue Bloods (Earl Robert Eaton and Lord Steven Regal) in a Triangle Match in 13:08 (★); Randy Savage defeated Ric Flair in a Lifeguard Match in 13:56 (★★); Hulk Hogan defeated Big Van Vader in a Steel Cage Match in 13:23 (★★).

In Your House 2: The Lumberjacks ★★★
23-07-95, Nashville, Tennessee **WWF**
The Roadie defeated 1-2-3 Kid in 7:26 (★★★); Men On A Mission (Mabel and Mo) defeated Razor Ramon and Savio Vega in 10:09 (★★); Bam Bam Bigelow defeated Henry O. Godwinn in 5:33 (★★); Shawn Michaels defeated Jeff Jarrett to win the WWF Intercontinental Title in 20:01 (★★★★★★); Owen Hart and Yokozuna defeated The Allied Powers (Lex Luger and The British Bulldog) in 10:54 (★★); Diesel defeated Sycho Sid in a Lumberjack Match in 10:06 (★★).

Collision In Korea ★★★
04-08-95, Pyongyang, North Korea **WCW/NJPW**
Wild Pegasus defeated Too Cold Scorpio in 6:03 (★★★); Yuji Nagata defeated Tokimitsu Ishizawa in 4:28 (★★); Masahiro Chono and Hiro Saito defeated El Samurai and Tadao Yasuda in 8:06 (★★); Bull Nakano and Akira Hokuta defeated Manami Toyota and Mariko Yoshida in 8:35 (★★★); Shinya Hashimoto vs. Scott Norton ended in a time limit draw in 20:00 (★★); Hawk defeated Tadao Yasuda in 2:22 (★★); The Steiner Brothers (Rick Steiner and Scott Steiner) defeated Kensuke Sasaki and Hiroshi Hase in 11:48 (★★); Antonio Inoki defeated Ric Flair in 14:53 (★★★).

Wrestlepalooza '95 ★★
05-08-95, Philadelphia, Pennsylvania **ECW**
JT Smith defeated Hack Myers in 6:33 (★); Big Val Puccio defeated Tony Stetson by DQ in 1:23 (★); Big Dick Dudley, Raven, Snot Dudley and Stevie Richards defeated Cactus Jack, The Pitbulls (Pitbull #1 and Pitbull #2) and Tommy Dreamer in 4:49 (★); Cactus Jack, Dean Malenko and Too Cold Scorpio defeated Eddie Guerrero and The Steiner Brothers (Rick Steiner and Scott Steiner) in 21:59 (★★★★); Mikey Whipwreck defeated The Sandman in a Singapore Cane Match in 5:51 (★★); The Gangstas (Mustafa and New Jack) defeated Public Enemy (Johnny Grunge and Rocco Rock) in a Stretcher Match in 17:51 (★★★).

Clash Of The Champions XXXI ★
06-08-95, Daytona Beach, Florida **WCW**
Sting and Hawk defeated Meng and Kurasawa in 7:23 (★); Diamond Dallas Page defeated Alex Wright in 8:14 (★★); The Renegade defeated Paul Orndorff in 3:59 (★); Harlem Heat (Booker T and Stevie Ray) and Sister Sherri defeated Bunkhouse Buck, Dick Slater and Col. Robert Parker in 11:01 (★); Big Van Vader defeated Arn Anderson and Ric Flair in a Handicap Match in 8:05 (★★).

SummerSlam '95 ★★★
27-08-95, Pittsburgh, Pennsylvania **WWF**
Hakushi defeated 1-2-3 Kid in 9:27 (★★★); Hunter Hearst Helmsley defeated Bob Holly in 7:10 (★★); The Smoking Gunns (Billy Gunn and Bart Gunn) defeated The Blu Brothers (Jacob Blu and Eli Blu) in 6:09 (★★); Barry Horowitz defeated Skip in 11:21 (★); Bertha Faye defeated Alundra Blayze to win the WWF Women's Title in 4:14 (★★); The Undertaker defeated Kama in a Casket Match in 16:26 (★★); Bret Hart defeated Isaac Yankem DDS by DQ in 16:07 (★★); Shawn Michaels defeated Razor Ramon in a Ladder Match in 25:04 (★★★★★★); Diesel defeated King Mabel in 9:14 (★★).

Gangstas Paradise ★★★
16-09-95, Philadelphia, Pennsylvania **ECW**
Bull Pain defeated Tony Stetson in 8:12 (★★); Dances With Dudley and Dudley Dudley defeated Chad Austin and Don E. Allen in 4:16 (★★); Hack Myers defeated JT Smith via count out in 4:57 (★★); Jason Knight and The Eliminators (John Kronus and Perry Saturn) defeated Taz and The Steiner Brothers (Rick Steiner and Scott Steiner) in 3:18 (★★); The Pitbulls (Pitbull #1 and Pitbull #2) defeated Raven and Stevie Richards in a Best Two Out Of Three Falls Double Dog Collar Match to win the ECW Tag Team Title in 19:47 (★★★★); Rey Misterio Jr. defeated Psicosis in 10:19 (★★★★); Mikey Whipwreck and Public Enemy (Johnny Grunge and Rocco Rock) defeated New Jack, The Sandman and Too Cold Scorpio in a Steel Cage Match in 14:51 (★★).

Fall Brawl '95 ★★★
17-09-95, Asheville, North Carolina **WCW**
Johnny B. Badd defeated Brian Pillman in 29:14 (★★★★★); Craig Pittman defeated Cobra in 1:22 (★★); Diamond Dallas Page defeated The Renegade to win the WCW World Television

Title in 8:07 (★★); Harlem Heat (Booker T and Stevie Ray) defeated Bunkhouse Buck and Dick Slater to win the WCW World Tag Team Title in 16:49 (★★); Arn Anderson defeated Ric Flair in 22:37 (★★★★); Hulk Hogan, Randy Savage, Lex Luger and Sting defeated The Dungeon Of Doom (Kamala, The Zodiac, The Shark and Meng) in a War Games Match in 18:47 (★★).

In Your House 3: Triple Header ★★★
24-09-95, Saginaw, Michigan **WWF**
Savio Vega defeated Waylon Mercy in 7:06 (★★); Sycho Sid defeated Henry O. Godwinn in 7:23 (★★); The British Bulldog defeated Bam Bam Bigelow in 12:00 (★★); Dean Douglas defeated Razor Ramon in 14:53 (★★); Bret Hart defeated Jean-Pierre Lafitte in 16:37 (★★★★); Diesel and Shawn Michaels defeated Yokozuna and The British Bulldog to win the WWF World Tag Team Title in 15:42 (★★).

In Your House 4: Great White North ★★
22-10-95, Winnipeg, Manitoba **WWF**
Hunter Hearst Helmsley defeated Fatu in 8:06 (★★); The Smoking Gunns (Billy Gunn and Bart Gunn) defeated 1-2-3 Kid and Razor Ramon in 12:46 (★★); Goldust defeated Marty Jannetty in 11:15 (★★); King Mabel vs. Yokozuna went to a double count out in 5:12 (★★); Razor Ramon defeated Dean Douglas to win the WWF Intercontinental Title in 11:01 (★★); The British Bulldog defeated Diesel by DQ in 18:14 (★★).

Halloween Havoc '95 ★★
29-10-95, Detroit, Michigan **WCW**
Johnny B. Badd defeated Diamond Dallas Page to win the WCW World Television Title in 17:01 (★★); Randy Savage defeated The Zodiac in 1:30 (★★); Kurasawa defeated Hawk in 3:15 (★★); Sabu defeated Mr. JL in 3:25 (★★); Lex Luger defeated Meng by DQ in 13:14 (★★); Sting and Ric Flair defeated Brian Pillman and Ric Flair by DQ in 17:09 (★★★); Hulk Hogan defeated The Giant in a Sumo Monster Truck Match in 5:00 (★); Randy Savage defeated Lex Luger in 5:23 (★★); The Giant defeated Hulk Hogan by DQ to win the WCW World Heavyweight Title in 14:30 (★★).

November To Remember '95 ★★★★
18-11-95, Philadelphia, Pennsylvania **ECW**
Buh Buh Ray Dudley defeated The Broad Street Bully in :48 (★); Konnan defeated Jason Knight in :14 (★); Stevie Richards defeated El Puerto Riqueno in 3:03 (★★); The Pitbulls (Pitbull #1 and Pitbull #2) defeated The Eliminators (John Kronus and Perry Saturn) in 10:37 (★★★); Rey Misterio Jr. defeated Psicosis in a Mexican Death Match in 14:47 (★★★★); The Sandman and Too Cold Scorpio defeated Public Enemy (Johnny Grunge and Rocco Rock) in 16:03 (★★); Bill Alfonso defeated Tod Gordon in 6:37 (★★★); Mikey Whipwreck defeated Steve Austin in 4:38 (★★★); Sabu defeated Hack Myers in 12:55 (★★); Terry Funk and Tommy Dreamer defeated Cactus Jack and Raven in 13:36 (★★★★).

Survivor Series '95 ★★★★
19-11-95, Landover, Maryland **WWF**
The BodyDonnas (Skip, Rad Radford, Tom Prichard and 1-2-3 Kid) defeated The Underdogs (Marty Jannetty, Hakushi, Barry Horowitz and Bob Holly) in an Elimination Match in 18:45 (★★★★); Bertha Faye, Aja Kong, Tomoko Watanabe and Lioness Asuka defeated Alundra Blayze, Kyoko Inoue, Sakie Hasegawa and Chaparita Asari in an Elimination Match in 10:01 (★★★); Goldust defeated Bam Bam Bigelow in 8:18 (★★); The Darkside (The Undertaker, Savio Vega, Fatu and Henry O. Godwinn) defeated The Royals (King Mabel, Jerry Lawler, Hunter Hearst Helmsley and Isaac Yankem DDS) in an Elimination Match in 14:21 (★★); Shawn Michaels, Ahmed Johnson, The British Bulldog and Sycho Sid defeated Yokozuna, Owen Hart, Razor Ramon and Dean Douglas in an Elimination Match in 27:24 (★★★); Bret Hart defeated Diesel in a No DQ Match to win the WWF World Heavyweight Title in 24:54 (★★★★).

World War 3 '95 ★★★
26-11-95, Norfolk, Virginia **WCW**
Johnny B. Badd defeated Diamond Dallas Page in 12:35 (★★★★); Big Bubba Rogers defeated Jim Duggan in a Taped Fist Match in 10:08 (★★); Bull Nakano and Akira Hokuto defeated Mayumi Ozaki and Cutie Suzuki in 9:16 (★★★★); Kensuke Sasaki defeated Chris Benoit in 10:00 (★★); Lex

Luger defeated **Randy Savage** in 5:28 (★★); **Sting** defeated **Ric Flair** in 14:30 (★★★); **Randy Savage** won the 60-Man World War 3 Match to win the vacant WCW World Heavyweight Title in 29:40 (★★).

In Your House 5: Seasons Beatings ★★
17-12-95, Hershey, Pennsylvania **WWF**

Razor Ramon and **Marty Jannetty** defeated **1-2-3 Kid** and **Sycho Sid** in 12:22 (★★); **Ahmed Johnson** defeated **Buddy Landel** in :45 (★★); **Hunter Hearst Helmsley** defeated **Henry O. Godwinn** in an Arkansas Hog Pen Match in 8:58 (★★); **Owen Hart** defeated **Diesel** by DQ in 4:34 (★★); **The Undertaker** defeated **King Mabel** in a Casket Match in 6:11 (★★); **Bret Hart** defeated **The British Bulldog** in 21:09 (★★★★).

Starrcade '95 ★★★
27-12-95, Nashville, Tennessee **WCW**

Jushin Thunder Liger defeated **Chris Benoit** in 10:29 (★★★); **Koji Kanemoto** defeated **Alex Wright** in 11:44 (★★★); **Lex Luger** defeated **Masahiro Chono** in 6:41 (★★); **Johnny B. Badd** defeated **Masa Saito** by DQ in 5:52 (★★); **Shinjiro Otani** defeated **Eddy Guerrero** in 13:43 (★★★★); **Randy Savage** defeated **Hiroyoshi Tenzan** in 6:55 (★★); **Sting** defeated **Kensuke Sasaki** in 6:52 (★★); **Ric Flair** defeated **Lex Luger** and **Sting** via count out in a Triangle Match in 28:03 (★★★); **Ric Flair** defeated **Randy Savage** to win the WCW World Heavyweight Title in 8:41 (★★).

Holiday Hell '95 ★★★
29-12-95, New York City, New York **ECW**

Taz defeated **Koji Nakagawa** in 2:34 (★★); **JT Smith** defeated **Hack Myers** in 4:39 (★★); **Mikey Whipwreck** defeated **Too Cold Scorpio** to win the ECW Television Title and ECW Tag Team Title in 11:54 (★★); **The Eliminators** (**John Kronus** and **Perry Saturn**) defeated **The Pitbulls** (**Pitbull #1** and **Pitbull #2**) in 16:13 (★★★); **Tommy Dreamer** defeated **The Blue Meanie** in :13 (★); **Tommy Dreamer** defeated **Stevie Richards** in :11 (★); **Raven** defeated **Tommy Dreamer** in 11:36 (★★★); **Bruiser Mastino** defeated **El Puerto Ricano** in 3:12 (★★); **Buh Buh Ray Dudley** defeated **The Blue Meanie** in 1:10 (★); **The Sandman** defeated **Raven** in 13:16 (★★); **The Gangstas** (**Mustafa** and **New Jack**) defeated **Public Enemy** (**Johnny Grunge** and **Rocco Rock**) in 8:26 (★★); **Sabu** defeated **Cactus Jack** in 12:59 (★★★).

House Party '96 ★★★
05-01-96, Philadelphia, Pennsylvania **ECW**

911 and **Rey Misterio Jr.** defeated **The Eliminators** (**John Kronus** and **Perry Saturn**) in 7:31 (★★); **Rob Van Dam** defeated **Axl Rotten** in 6:11 (★★); **Too Cold Scorpio** defeated **Mikey Whipwreck** to win the ECW World Television Title in 16:47 (★★★); **Taz** defeated **Hack Myers** in 3:41 (★★); **Buh Buh Ray Dudley** defeated **Jimmy Del Ray** in 2:59 (★★); **The Sandman** defeated **Konnan** in 14:01 (★★); **Sabu** defeated **Stevie Richards** in 14:31 (★★★★); **Public Enemy** (**Johnny Grunge** and **Rocco Rock**) defeated **The Gangstas** (**Mustafa** and **New Jack**) in a Street Fight in 13:41 (★★★).

Royal Rumble '96 ★★★
21-01-96, Fresno, California **WWF**

Ahmed Johnson defeated **Jeff Jarrett** by DQ in 6:40 (★★); **The Smoking Gunns** (**Billy Gunn** and **Bart Gunn**) defeated **The Bodydonnas** (**Skip** and **Zip**) in 11:14 (★★); **Goldust** defeated **Razor Ramon** to win the WWF Intercontinental Title in 14:17 (★★); **Shawn Michaels** won the 30-Man Royal Rumble Match in 58:49 (★★★); **The Undertaker** defeated **Bret Hart** by DQ in 28:31 (★★★).

Clash Of The Champions XXXII ★★
23-01-96, Paradise, Nevada **WCW**

Public Enemy (**Rocco Rock** and **Johnny Grunge**) vs. **The Nasty Boys** (**Brian Knobbs** and **Jerry Sags**) ended in a double DQ in 4:02 (★★); **Dean Malenko** defeated **Alex Wright** in 5:31 (★★★); **Brian Pillman** defeated **Eddie Guerrero** in 5:50 (★★); **Sting** and **Lex Luger** defeated **The Blue Bloods** (**Lord Steven Regal** and **Robert Eaton**) in 7:46 (★★★); **Konnan** defeated **Psychosis** in 5:26 (★★); **Ric Flair** and **The Giant** defeated **Hulk Hogan** and **Randy Savage** in 9:51 (★★).

Big Apple Blizzard Blast ★★
03-02-96, New York City, New York **ECW**

Taz defeated **The Shark Attack Kid** in 3:55 (★★); **The Headhunters** (**Headhunter A** and **Headhunter B**) defeated **Axl Rotten** and **El Puerto Riqueno** in 6:45 (★★); **The Eliminators** (**John Kronus** and **Perry Saturn**) defeated **Cactus Jack** and **Mikey Whipwreck** to win the ECW Tag Team Title in 12:10 (★★); **Shane Douglas** and **Tommy Dreamer** defeated **Raven** and **Stevie Richards** in 19:34 (★★★); **Rey Misterio Jr.** defeated **Juventud Guerrera** in 8:46 (★★★); **Chris Jericho** defeated **Rob Van Dam** in 10:58 (★★★); **Buh Buh Ray Dudley** defeated **JT Smith** in :45 (★); **Sabu** defeated **Mr. Hughes** in 12:30 (★★); **The Sandman** and **Too Cold Scorpio** defeated **The Gangstas** (**Mustafa** and **New Jack**) in 8:53 (★★).

SuperBrawl VI ★★★
11-02-96, St. Petersburg, Florida **WCW**

The Nasty Boys (**Brian Knobbs** and **Jerry Sags**) defeated **Public Enemy** (**Rocco Rock** and **Johnny Grunge**) in a Street Fight in 7:49 (★★); **Johnny B. Badd** defeated **Diamond Dallas Page** in 14:59 (★★★); **Sting** and **Lex Luger** defeated **Harlem Heat** (**Booker T** and **Stevie Ray**) in 11:49 (★★); **Konnan** defeated **One Man Gang** in 7:27 (★); **The Taskmaster** defeated **Brian Pillman** in a Strap Match in 1:36 (★★); **Arn Anderson** vs. **The Taskmaster** ended in a no contest in 3:45 (★★); **Sting** and **Lex Luger** vs. **The Road Warriors** (**Hawk** and **Animal**) ended in a double count out in 13:56 (★★); **Ric Flair** defeated **Randy Savage** in a Steel Cage Match to win the WCW World Heavyweight Title in 18:52 (★★★); **Hulk Hogan** defeated **The Giant** in a Steel Cage Match in 15:04 (★).

Cyberslam '96 ★★★
17-02-96, Philadelphia, Pennsylvania **ECW**

Judge Dredd and **The Bad Crew** (**Dog** and **Rose**) defeated **Dino Sandoff**, **Don E. Allen** and **The Dirtbike Kid** in 2:03 (★★); **Spiros Greco** defeated **El Puerto Riqueno** in 4:27 (★★); **Taz** defeated **Joel Hartgood** in 1:54 (★★); **Buh Buh Ray Dudley** defeated **Mr. Hughes** in :36 (★); **The Bruise Brothers** (**Don Harris** and **Ron Harris**) defeated **The Headhunters** (**Headhunter A** and **Headhunter B**) in 3:58 (★); **JT Smith** defeated **Axl Rotten** in 6:12 (★★★); **Francine** and **The Pitbulls** (**Pitbull #1** and **Pitbull #2**) defeated **Stevie Richards** and **The Eliminators** (**John Kronus** and **Perry Saturn**) in a Triple Dog Collar Match in 14:03 (★★); **Too Cold Scorpio** vs. **Sabu** ended in a draw in 30:00 (★★★★); **Shane Douglas** defeated **Cactus Jack** in 15:37 (★★★); **Raven** defeated **The Sandman** in 8:21 (★★).

In Your House 6: Rage In The Cage ★★★
18-02-96, Louisville, Kentucky **WWF**

Razor Ramon defeated **1-2-3 Kid** in a Crybaby Match in 12:01 (★★★); **Hunter Hearst Helmsley** defeated **Duke Droese** in 9:40 (★★); **Yokozuna** defeated **The British Bulldog** by DQ in 5:05 (★★); **Shawn Michaels** defeated **Owen Hart** in 15:57 (★★★★); **Bret Hart** defeated **Diesel** in a Steel Cage Match in 19:13 (★★).

Just Another Night ★★★
23-02-96, Glenolden, Pennsylvania **ECW**

The Bad Crew (**Dog** and **Rose**) defeated **Joel Hartgood** and **JT Smith** in 3:27 (★★); **The Pitbulls** (**Pitbull #1** and **Pitbull #2**) defeated **Stevie Richards** and **The Blue Meanie** in 9:07 (★★); **Bill Alfonso** defeated **Tod Gordon** in 2:36 (★); **The Eliminators** (**John Kronus** and **Perry Saturn**) defeated **Buh Buh Ray Dudley** and **Hack Myers** in 6:26 (★★); **The Sandman** defeated **Axl Rotten** in 16:09 (★★★); **Bam Bam Bigelow** defeated **Cactus Jack** in 3:48 (★★); **Sabu** vs. **Too Cold Scorpio** ended in a draw in 20:00 (★★★); **Raven** defeated **Shane Douglas** in 12:31 (★★★).

Uncensored '96 ★
24-03-96, Tupelo, Mississippi **WCW**

Konnan defeated **Eddie Guerrero** in 18:27 (★★★); **The Belfast Bruiser** defeated **Lord Steven Regal** by DQ in 17:33 (★★★); **Col. Robert Parker** defeated **Madusa** in 3:47 (★); **The Booty Man** defeated **Diamond Dallas Page** in 16:00 (★); **The Giant** defeated **Loch Ness** in 2:34 (★★); **Sting** and **Booker T** defeated **The Road Warriors** (**Hawk** and **Animal**) in a Chicago Street Fight in 29:33 (★★★); **Hulk Hogan** and **Randy Savage** defeated **Ric Flair**, **Arn Anderson**, **Meng**, **The Barbarian**, **Lex Luger**, **The Taskmaster**, **Z-Gangsta** and **The Ultimate Solution** in a Handicap Doomsday Cage Match in 25:16 (★).

WrestleMania XII ★★★
31-03-96, Anaheim, California **WWF**
The British Bulldog, Owen Hart and Vader defeated Ahmed Johnson, Jake Roberts and Yokozuna in 13:08 (★★); Roddy Piper defeated Goldust in a Hollywood Backlot Brawl in 16:47 (★★★); Steve Austin defeated Savio Vega in 10:05 (★★★); The Ultimate Warrior defeated Hunter Hearst Helmsley in 1:39 (★★); The Undertaker defeated Diesel in 16:46 (★★★); Shawn Michaels defeated Bret Hart 1-0 in an Iron Man Match in 61:56 (★★★).

Massacre On Queens BLVD ★★★
13-04-96, New York City, New York **ECW**
Little Guido and JT Smith defeated The Dudleys (Big Dick Dudley and Buh Buh Ray Dudley) by DQ in 3:46 (★★); Hack Myers defeated Billy Black in 6:01 (★★); The Eliminators (John Kronus and Perry Saturn) defeated El Puerto Riqueno and Joel Hartgood in 2:08 (★★); Raven defeated Damian 666 in 8:30 (★★); Shane Douglas defeated Axl Rotten in 6:55 (★★★); Taz defeated Chris Jericho in 3:17 (★★); Brian Lee and The Bruise Brothers (Don Harris and Ron Harris) defeated The Pitbulls (Pitbull #1 and Pitbull #2) and Tommy Dreamer in 11:45 (★★★); Sabu defeated Mikey Whipwreck in 15:21 (★★); The Gangstas (Mustafa and New Jack) defeated The Headhunters (Headhunter A and Headhunter B) and The Sandman and Too Cold Scorpio in a Three Way Elimination Match in 18:57 (★★★).

Hostile City Showdown '96 ★★
20-04-96, Philadelphia, Pennsylvania **ECW**
El Puerto Ricano vs. Super Nova ended in a no contest in 2:07 (★★); Mikey Whipwreck defeated Billy Black in 7:09 (★★); The Dudley Boyz (Buh Buh Ray Dudley and D-Von Dudley) vs. The Pitbulls (Pitbull #1 and Pitbull #2) ended in a no contest in 9:00 (★★); Taz defeated Devon Storm via count out in 4:51 (★★); Axl Rotten defeated Little Guido in 6:21 (★★); The Sandman and Too Cold Scorpio defeated The Bruise Brothers (Don Harris and Ron Harris) in 8:25 (★★); Brian Lee defeated Tommy Dreamer in 6:49 (★★); Sabu defeated Rob Van Dam in 18:57 (★★★★); Raven defeated Shane Douglas in 16:40 (★★★).

In Your House 7: Good Friends, Better Enemies ★★★
28-04-96, Omaha, Nebraska **WWF**
Owen Hart and The British Bulldog defeated Ahmed Johnson and Jake Roberts in 13:47 (★★); The Ultimate Warrior defeated Goldust via count out in 7:38 (★); Vader defeated Razor Ramon in 14:49 (★★★); The Bodydonnas (Skip and Zip) defeated The Godwinns (Henry O. Godwinn and Phineas I. Godwinn) in 7:17 (★★); Shawn Michaels defeated Diesel in a No Holds Barred Match in 17:53 (★★★★).

A Matter Of Respect ★★★★
11-05-96, Philadelphia, Pennsylvania **ECW**
Damian 666 vs. El Puerto Riqueno ended in a no contest in :36 (★); Damien Kane and Devon Storm defeated The Dudley Boyz (Buh Buh Ray Dudley and D-Von Dudley) by DQ in 14:01 (★★); The F.B.I. (JT Smith and Little Guido) defeated Axl Rotten and Hack Myers in 10:55 (★★); Raven defeated Pitbull #2 and The Sandman in a Three Way Match in 18:26 (★★★); Chris Jericho defeated Mikey Whipwreck in 14:21 (★★★); Shane Douglas defeated Too Cold Scorpio to win the ECW World Television Title in 26:31 (★★★★); Rob Van Dam defeated Sabu in a Respect Match in 18:47 (★★★★); The Gangstas (Mustafa and New Jack) and Tommy Dreamer defeated Brian Lee and The Eliminators (John Kronus and Perry Saturn) in 20:46 (★★).

Slamboree '96 ★★
19-05-96, Baton Rouge, Louisiana **WCW**
Animal and Booker T vs. Hawk and Lex Luger ended in a double count out in 6:54 (★★); Public Enemy (Rocco Rock and Johnny Grunge) defeated Chris Benoit and The Taskmaster in 4:44 (★★); Rick Steiner and The Booty Man defeated Sgt. Craig Pittman and Scott Steiner in 8:21 (★★); VK Wallstreet and Jim Duggan defeated The Blue Bloods (Lord Steven Regal and Squire David Taylor) in 3:46 (★★); Dick Slater and Earl Robert Eaton defeated Disco Inferno and Alex Wright in 2:56 (★★); Diamond Dallas Page and The Barbarian defeated Meng and Hugh Morrus in 5:15 (★★); Fire and Ice (Scott Norton and Ice Train) defeated Big Bubba Rogers and Stevie Ray in 3:32 (★★); Ric Flair and Randy Savage defeated Arn Anderson and

Eddie Guerrero in 4:04 (★★★); Dean Malenko defeated Brad Armstrong in 8:29 (★★); Dick Slater and Earl Robert Eaton defeated VK Wallstreet and Jim Duggan in 4:08 (★★); Public Enemy (Rocco Rock and Johnny Grunge) defeated Ric Flair and Randy Savage via forfeit; Diamond Dallas Page and The Barbarian defeated Rick Steiner and The Booty Man in 5:05 (★★); Konnan defeated Jushin Thunder Liger in 9:30 (★★★); Diamond Dallas Page won the Battlebowl Match in 9:33 (★★); The Giant defeated Sting in 10:41 (★★).

In Your House 8: Beware Of Dog ★★★
26-05-96, Florence/Charleston, South Carolina **WWF**
Marc Mero defeated Hunter Hearst Helmsley in 16:23 (★★★); Shawn Michaels vs. The British Bulldog ended in a no contest in 17:21 (★★★); Savio Vega defeated Steve Austin in a Caribbean Strap Match in 21:27 (★★★); Vader defeated Yokozuna in 8:53 (★★); Goldust defeated The Undertaker in a Casket Match in 12:36 (★★).

World Wrestling Peace Festival ★★★
01-06-96, Los Angeles, California **Various**
Sgt. Craig Pittman defeated KGB in 6:11 (★★); Jim Neidhart defeated Bobby Bradley Jr. in 5:00 (★★); Akira Hokuto and Lady Apache defeated Bull Nakano and Neftali in 8:24 (★★★); Chris Benoit defeated Alex Wright in 9:54 (★★★); Rey Misterio Jr. and Ultimo Dragon defeated Heavy Metal and Psychosis in 11:40 (★★★★); Lex Luger defeated Masa Saito in 5:53 (★★); Negro Casas defeated El Hijo del Santo in 5:54 (★★★); Atlantis, Dos Caras and Hector Garza defeated Silver King, Dr. Wagner Jr. and Gran Markus Jr. in 10:35 (★★★); Tatsumi Fujinami defeated Black Cat in 5:15 (★★); Perro Aguayo and La Parka defeated Pierroth Jr. and Cibernetico in 9:38 (★★); Chris Jericho defeated Konnan and Bam Bam Bigelow in a Triangle Match in 7:31 (★★); Jushin Thunder Liger defeated The Great Sasuke in 12:47 (★★★★); The Giant defeated Sting in 5:09 (★★); Antonio Inoki and Dan Severn defeated Yoshiaki Fujiwara and Oleg Taktarov in 9:15 (★★).

Great American Bash '96 ★★★★
16-06-96, Baltimore, Maryland **WCW**
The Steiner Brothers (Rick Steiner and Scott Steiner) defeated Fire and Ice (Scott Norton and Ice Train) in 10:29 (★★★); Konnan defeated El Gato in 6:03 (★★); Diamond Dallas Page defeated Marcus Alexander Bagwell in 9:39 (★★); Dean Malenko defeated Rey Misterio Jr. in 17:50 (★★★★); John Tenta defeated Big Bubba Rogers in 5:24 (★★); Chris Benoit defeated Kevin Sullivan in a Falls Count Anywhere Match in 9:58 (★★★★); Sting defeated Lord Steven Regal in 16:30 (★★★★); Ric Flair and Arn Anderson defeated Kevin Greene and Steve McMichael in 20:51 (★★★); The Giant defeated Lex Luger in 9:21 (★★).

Hardcore Heaven '96 ★★★
22-06-96, Philadelphia, Pennsylvania **ECW**
Shane Douglas defeated Mikey Whipwreck in 11:33 (★★★); The F.B.I. (JT Smith and Little Guido) defeated The Dudleys (Big Dick Dudley and Buh Buh Ray Dudley) by DQ in 10:10 (★★); Taz defeated Paul Varelans in a Shoot Fight Rules Match in 2:24 (★★); Raven defeated Terry Gordy in 12:45 (★★★); The Eliminators (John Kronus and Perry Saturn) vs. The Bruise Brothers (Don Harris and Ron Harris) ended in a no contest in 8:16 (★★); Axl Rotten and Hack Myers vs. The Samoan Gangsta Party (Mack Daddy Kane and Sammy Silk) ended in a no contest in 2:00 (★★); Chris Jericho defeated Pitbull #2 to win the ECW Television Title in 12:09 (★★★); Tommy Dreamer defeated Brian Lee in a Weapons Match in 9:02 (★★★); Sabu defeated Rob Van Dam in 19:40 (★★★).

King Of The Ring '96 ★★★★
23-06-96, Milwaukee, Wisconsin **WWF**
Steve Austin defeated Marc Mero in 16:49 (★★★★); Jake Roberts defeated Vader by DQ in 3:34 (★★); The Smoking Gunns (Billy Gunn and Bart Gunn) defeated The Godwinns (Henry O. Godwinn and Phineas I. Godwinn) in 10:10 (★★); The Ultimate Warrior defeated Jerry Lawler in 3:50 (★★); Mankind defeated The Undertaker in 18:21 (★★★); Ahmed Johnson defeated Goldust to win the WWF Intercontinental Title in 15:34 (★★); Steve Austin defeated Jake Roberts in 4:28 (★★); Shawn Michaels defeated The British Bulldog in 26:24 (★★★★).

Bash At The Beach '96 ★★★★
07-07-96, Daytona Beach, Florida **WCW**

Rey Misterio Jr. defeated Psychosis in 15:18 (★★★★); John Tenta defeated Big Bubba in a Carson City Silver Dollar Match in 8:53 (★); Diamond Dallas Page defeated Jim Duggan in a Taped Fist Match in 5:39 (★★); The Nasty Boys (Brian Knobbs and Jerry Sags) defeated Public Enemy (Rocco Rock and Johnny Grunge) in a Double Dog Collar Match in 11:25 (★★★); Dean Malenko defeated Disco Inferno in 12:04 (★★★★); Steve McMichael defeated Joe Gomez in 6:44 (★★); Ric Flair defeated Konnan to win the WCW United States Heavyweight Title in 15:39 (★★); The Giant and The Taskmaster defeated Arn Anderson and Chris Benoit in 7:59 (★★); The Outsiders (Kevin Nash and Scott Hall) and Hulk Hogan defeated Randy Savage, Sting and Lex Luger in 16:55 (★★★★).

Heat Wave '96 ★★★★
13-07-96, Philadelphia, Pennsylvania **ECW**

The Gangstas (Mustafa and New Jack) defeated The Samoan Gangsta Party (Mack Daddy Kane and Sammy Silk) in 2:55 (★★); Mikey Whipwreck defeated Paul Lauria in 1:32 (★); The Eliminators (John Kronus and Perry Saturn) defeated Mikey Whipwreck and Sabu in 12:02 (★★); The Dudleys (Big Dick Dudley and Buh Buh Ray Dudley) defeated The F.B.I. (JT Smith and Little Guido) in 6:38 (★★); Tarzan Goto defeated Axl Rotten in 7:02 (★★); Shane Douglas defeated Chris Jericho, Pitbull #2 and Too Cold Scorpio in a Four Way Elimination Match to win the ECW Television Title in 39:37 (★★★★); Louie Spicolli defeated El Puerto Ricano in 1:10 (★); Sabu defeated Louie Spicolli in 11:36 (★★); Terry Gordy, The Sandman and Tommy Dreamer defeated Brian Lee, Raven and Stevie Richards in a Rage In A Cage Match in 16:42 (★★★).

In Your House 9: International Incident ★★★
21-07-96, Vancouver, British Columbia **WWF**

The Bodydonnas (Skip and Zip) defeated The Smoking Gunns (Billy Gunn and Bart Gunn) in 13:05 (★★); Mankind defeated Henry O. Godwinn in 6:54 (★★); Steve Austin defeated Marc Mero in 10:48 (★★★); The Undertaker defeated Goldust by DQ in 12:07 (★★); Camp Cornette (Vader, The British Bulldog and Owen Hart) defeated Shawn Michaels, Sycho Sid and Ahmed Johnson in 24:32 (★★★★).

The Doctor Is In ★★★
03-08-96, Philadelphia, Pennsylvania **ECW**

Mikey Whipwreck defeated Devon Storm in 12:25 (★★); Johnny Smith defeated Louie Spicolli in 5:39 (★★); Axl Rotten vs. D-Von Dudley ended in a no contest in 3:16 (★); Stevie Richards defeated The Sandman in 7:12 (★★★); Too Cold Scorpio defeated Chris Jericho in 19:56 (★★★); Shane Douglas defeated Pitbull #2 in 15:26 (★★★); Brian Lee and Taz defeated Steve Williams and Tommy Dreamer in 6:57 (★★); The Gangstas (Mustafa and New Jack) defeated The Eliminators (John Kronus and Perry Saturn), The Bruise Brothers (Don Harris and Ron Harris) and The Samoan Gangsta Party (Mack Daddy Kane and Sammy Silk) in a Four Way Elimination Match to win the ECW Tag Team Title in 11:01 (★★★); Sabu defeated Rob Van Dam in a Stretcher Match in 23:22 (★★★).

Hog Wild '96 ★★★
10-08-96, Sturgis, South Dakota **WCW**

Rey Misterio Jr. defeated Ultimo Dragon in 11:35 (★★★); Scott Norton defeated Ice Train in 5:05 (★★); Madusa defeated Bull Nakano in 5:21 (★★); Chris Benoit defeated Dean Malenko in 26:55 (★★★★); Harlem Heat (Booker T and Stevie Ray) defeated The Steiner Brothers (Rick Steiner and Scott Steiner) in 17:53 (★★); Ric Flair defeated Eddie Guerrero in 14:17 (★★★); The Outsiders (Kevin Nash and Scott Hall) and Sting and Lex Luger in 14:36 (★★); Hollywood Hogan defeated The Giant to win the WCW World Heavyweight Title in 14:56 (★).

Clash Of The Champions XXXIII ★★
15-08-96, Denver, Colorado **WCW**

Rey Misterio Jr. defeated Dean Malenko in 12:07 (★★★★); VK Wallstreet defeated Jim Duggan in 3:48 (★★); Konnan defeated Ultimo Dragon in 2:57 (★★); Madusa defeated Bull Nakano in 2:42 (★★); Eddie Guerrero defeated Diamond Dallas Page in 4:20 (★★); The Giant defeated Chris Benoit in :23 (★); Harlem Heat (Booker T and Stevie Ray) vs. The Steiner Brothers (Rick Steiner and Scott Steiner) vs. Sting and Lex Luger ended in a no contest in 13:22 (★★); Ric Flair defeated Hollywood Hogan in 8:23 (★★).

SummerSlam '96 ★★★★
18-08-96, Cleveland, Ohio **WWF**

Owen Hart defeated Savio Vega in 13:23 (★★★); The Smoking Gunns (Billy Gunn and Bart Gunn) defeated The New Rockers (Marty Jannetty and Leif Cassidy), The Godwinns (Henry O. Godwinn and Phineas I. Godwinn) and The Bodydonnas (Skip and Zip) in a Four Way Elimination Match in 12:18 (★★); Sycho Sid defeated The British Bulldog in 6:24 (★★); Goldust defeated Marc Mero in 11:01 (★★); Jerry Lawler defeated Jake Roberts in 4:07 (★); Mankind defeated The Undertaker in Boiler Room Brawl in 26:40 (★★★); Shawn Michaels defeated Vader in 22:58 (★★★★).

Natural Born Killaz ★★
24-08-96, Philadelphia, Pennsylvania **ECW**

Louie Spicolli defeated Devon Storm in 5:22 (★★); Mikey Whipwreck defeated Little Guido in 8:57 (★★); The Dudleys (Big Dick Dudley and Buh Buh Ray Dudley) defeated Axl Rotten and D-Von Dudley in 8:54 (★★); Terry Gordy defeated Brian Lee in a Badstreet Match in 5:12 (★★); Rob Van Dam defeated Doug Furnas in 13:07 (★★★); Taz vs. Tommy Dreamer ended in a no contest in 12:36 (★★); Pitbull #2 and The Sandman defeated Raven and Shane Douglas in a Dog Collar Match in 15:22 (★★★); The Gangstas (Mustafa and New Jack) defeated The Eliminators (John Kronus and Perry Saturn) in a Steel Cage Weapons Match in 15:03 (★★).

Fall Brawl '96 ★★★★
15-09-96, Winston-Salem, North Carolina **WCW**

Diamond Dallas Page defeated Chavo Guerrero Jr. in 13:07 (★★★); Ice Train defeated Scott Norton in a Submission Match in 7:08 (★★); Konnan defeated Juventud Guerrera in 13:45 (★★★); Chris Benoit defeated Chris Jericho in 14:36 (★★★★); Rey Misterio Jr. defeated Super Calo in 15:47 (★★★★); Harlem Heat (Booker T and Stevie Ray) defeated The Nasty Boys (Brian Knobbs and Jerry Sags) in 15:31 (★★★); The Giant defeated Randy Savage in 7:47 (★★); Hollywood Hogan, nWo Sting and The Outsiders (Kevin Nash and Scott Hall) defeated Sting, Lex Luger, Ric Flair and Arn Anderson in a War Games Match in 18:15 (★★★).

In Your House 10: Mind Games ★★★
22-09-96, Philadelphia, Pennsylvania **WWF**

Savio Vega defeated Justin Hawk Bradshaw in a Caribbean Strap Match in 7:07 (★★); Jose Lothario defeated Jim Cornette in :56 (★★); Owen Hart and The British Bulldog defeated The Smoking Gunns (Billy Gunn and Bart Gunn) to win the WWF World Tag Team Title in 10:59 (★★★); Mark Henry defeated Jerry Lawler in 5:13 (★★); The Undertaker defeated Goldust in a Final Curtain Match in 10:23 (★★); Shawn Michaels defeated Mankind by DQ in 26:25 (★★★★★★).

In Your House 11: Buried Alive ★★★
20-10-96, Indianapolis, Indiana **WWF**

Steve Austin defeated Hunter Hearst Helmsley in 15:30 (★★★); Owen Hart and The British Bulldog defeated The Smoking Gunns (Billy Gunn and Bart Gunn) in 9:17 (★★); Marc Mero defeated Goldust in 11:38 (★★); Sycho Sid defeated Vader in 8:00 (★★); The Undertaker defeated Mankind in a Buried Alive Match in 18:25 (★★★★).

Halloween Havoc '96 ★★★
27-10-96, Las Vegas, Nevada **WCW**

Dean Malenko defeated Rey Misterio Jr. to win the WCW Cruiserweight Title in 18:32 (★★★★); Diamond Dallas Page defeated Eddie Guerrero in 13:44 (★★★); The Giant defeated Jeff Jarrett by DQ in 9:55 (★★★); Syxx defeated Chris Jericho in 9:49 (★★); Lex Luger defeated Arn Anderson in 12:22 (★★); Steve McMichael and Chris Benoit defeated The Faces of Fear (Meng and The Barbarian) in 9:23 (★★); The Outsiders (Kevin Nash and Scott Hall) defeated Harlem Heat (Booker T and Stevie Ray) to win the WCW World Tag Team Title in 13:07 (★★★); Hollywood Hogan defeated Randy Savage in 18:37 (★★).

November To Remember '96 ★★
16-11-96, Philadelphia, Pennsylvania **ECW**

Big Stevie Cool defeated Davey Morton Tyler Jericho in 9:25 (★★★); Axl Rotten defeated Hack Myers in 4:25 (★); Buh Buh Ray Dudley defeated D-Von Dudley in 10:20 (★★); Rob Van Dam and Sabu vs. The Eliminators (John Kronus and Perry Saturn) ended in a draw in 26:55 (★★); Chris Candido defeated **Mikey Whipwreck** in 11:54 (★★); **The Gangstas (Mustafa** and **New Jack)** defeated **Rob Van Dam** and **Sabu** and **The Eliminators (John Kronus** and **Perry Saturn)** in a Three Way Elimination Match in 8:54 (★); **Too Cold Scorpio** defeated **Devon Storm** in a Loser Leaves Town Match in 1:00 (★); **Too Cold Scorpio** defeated **JT Smith** in a Loser Leaves Town Match in :32 (★); **Too Cold Scorpio** defeated **Hack Myers** in a Loser Leaves Town Match in 1:15 (★); **Louie Spicolli** defeated **Too Cold Scorpio** in a Loser Leaves Town Match in 2:14 (★★); **The Sandman** defeated **Raven** in 15:07 (★★); **Terry Funk** and **Tommy Dreamer** defeated **Brian Lee** and **Shane Douglas** in 26:12 (★★).

Survivor Series '96 ★★★★
17-11-96, New York City, New York **WWF**
Doug Furnas, Phil LaFon and **The Godwinns (Henry O. Godwin** and **Phineas I. Godwin)** defeated **The British Bulldog, Owen Hart** and **The New Rockers (Marty Jannetty** and **Leif Cassidy)** in an Elimination Match in 20:41 (★★★); **The Undertaker** defeated **Mankind** in 14:54 (★★★); **Jake Roberts, Marc Mero, Rocky Maivia** and **The Stalker** defeated **Crush, Goldust, Jerry Lawler** and **Hunter Hearst Helmsley** in an Elimination Match in 23:44 (★★); **Bret Hart** defeated **Steve Austin** in 28:36 (★★★★★); **Diesel, Razor Ramon, Vader** and **Faarooq** vs. **Flash Funk, Jimmy Snuka, Savio Vega** and **Yokozuna** ended in a no contest in 9:48 (★★); **Sycho Sid** defeated **Shawn Michaels** to win the WWF World Heavyweight Title in 20:02 (★★★★).

World War 3 '96 ★★★
24-11-96, Norfolk, Virginia **WCW**
Ultimo Dragon defeated **Rey Misterio Jr.** in 13:48 (★★★★); **Chris Jericho** defeated **Nick Patrick** in 8:02 (★★); **The Giant** defeated **Jeff Jarrett** in 6:05 (★★); **Harlem Heat (Booker T** and **Stevie Ray)** defeated **The Amazing French-Canadians (Jacques Rougeau** and **Carl Ouellet)** in 9:14 (★★★); **Sister Sherri** defeated **Col. Robert Parker** via count out in 1:30 (★); **Dean Malenko** defeated **Psychosis** in 14:33 (★★★); **The Outsiders (Kevin Nash** and **Scott Hall)** defeated **The Faces of Fear (Meng** and **The Barbarian)** and **The Nasty Boys (Brian Knobbs** and **Jerry Sags)** in a Triangle Match in 16:11 (★★★); **The Giant** won the 60-Man World War 3 Match in 28:21 (★★★).

In Your House 12: It's Time ★★★
15-12-96, West Palm Beach, Florida **WWF**
Flash Funk defeated **Leif Cassidy** in 10:34 (★★★); **Owen Hart** and **The British Bulldog** defeated **Razor Ramon** and **Diesel** in 10:45 (★★); **Marc Mero** defeated **Hunter Hearst Helmsley** via count out in 13:12 (★★★); **The Undertaker** defeated **The Executioner** in an Armageddon Rules Match in 11:32 (★★); **Sycho Sid** defeated **Bret Hart** in 17:04 (★★★).

Starrcade '96 ★★★★
29-12-96, Nashville, Tennessee **WCW**
Ultimo Dragon defeated **Dean Malenko** to win the WCW Cruiserweight Title in 18:30 (★★★★); **Akira Hokuto** defeated **Madusa** in 7:06 (★★); **Jushin Thunder Liger** defeated **Rey Misterio Jr.** in 14:16 (★★★★); **Jeff Jarrett** defeated **Chris Benoit** in a No DQ Match in 13:48 (★★★★); **The Outsiders (Kevin Nash** and **Scott Hall)** defeated **The Faces of Fear (Meng** and **The Barbarian)** in 11:55 (★★); **Eddie Guerrero** defeated **Diamond Dallas Page** to win the vacant WCW United States Heavyweight Title in 15:20 (★★★); **Lex Luger** defeated **The Giant** in 13:23 (★★); **Roddy Piper** defeated **Hollywood Hogan** in 15:27 (★★).

Royal Rumble '97 ★★
19-01-97, San Antonio, Texas **WWF**
Hunter Hearst Helmsley defeated **Goldust** in 16:50 (★★); **Ahmed Johnson** defeated **Faarooq** by DQ in 8:48 (★★); **Vader** defeated **The Undertaker** in 13:19 (★★); **Canek, Hector Garza** and **Perro Aguayo** defeated **Fuerza Guerrera, Heavy Metal** and **Jerry Estrada** in 10:56 (★★); **Steve Austin** won the 30-Man Royal Rumble Match in 50:30 (★★★); **Shawn Michaels** defeated **Sycho Sid** to win the WWF World Heavyweight Title in 13:49 (★★).

Clash Of The Champions XXXIV ★★
21-01-97, Milwaukee, Wisconsin **WCW**
Dean Malenko defeated **Ultimo Dragon** in 15:07 (★★★★); **Scotty Riggs** defeated **Mike Enos** in 2:26 (★★); **Chris Jericho, Super Calo** and **Chavo Guerrero Jr.** defeated **Konnan, La Parka** and **Mr. JL** in 5:27 (★★); **Harlem Heat (Booker T** and **Stevie**

Ray) defeated **The Renegade** and **Joe Gomez** in 3:44 (★★); **Masahiro Chono** defeated **Alex Wright** in 4:30 (★★); **Eddie Guerrero** defeated **Scott Norton** in 5:36 (★★); **Chris Benoit** defeated **The Taskmaster** in a Falls Count Anywhere Match in 5:04 (★★); **The Steiner Brothers (Rick Steiner** and **Scott Steiner)** defeated **The Amazing French-Canadians (Jacques Rougeau** and **Carl Ouellet)** in 6:55 (★★); **Lex Luger** defeated **Scott Hall** by DQ in 10:29 (★★).

Souled Out '97 ★
25-01-97, Cedar Rapids, Iowa **WCW**
Masahiro Chono defeated **Chris Jericho** in 11:08 (★★); **Big Bubba Rogers** defeated **Hugh Morrus** in a Mexican Death Match in 9:03 (★★); **Jeff Jarrett** defeated **Michael Wallstreet** in 9:22 (★); **Buff Bagwell** defeated **Scotty Riggs** in 13:51 (★★); **Scott Norton** defeated **Diamond Dallas Page** via count out in 9:39 (★★); **The Steiner Brothers (Rick Steiner** and **Scott Steiner)** defeated **The Outsiders (Kevin Nash** and **Scott Hall)** to win the WCW World Tag Team Title in 14:43 (★★); **Eddie Guerrero** defeated **Syxx** in a Ladder Match in 13:50 (★★); **Hollywood Hogan** vs. **The Giant** went to a no contest in 10:52 (★).

Crossing The Line Again ★★
01-02-97, Philadelphia, Pennsylvania **ECW**
Lance Storm defeated **Balls Mahoney** in 5:32 (★★); **Big Stevie Cool** defeated **Ricky Morton** in 5:22 (★★); **Steve Williams** defeated **Axl Rotten** in 1:52 (★★); **Raven** defeated **Steve Williams** in 8:27 (★★); **The Sandman** defeated **D-Von Dudley** in 5:33 (★★); **The Eliminators (John Kronus** and **Perry Saturn)** defeated **Rob Van Dam** and **Sabu** in 20:02 (★★); **Terry Funk** defeated **Tommy Rich** in 10:45 (★★); **The Pitbulls (Pitbull #1** and **Pitbull #2)** and **Tommy Dreamer** defeated **The Triple Threat (Brian Lee, Chris Candido** and **Shane Douglas)** in 16:22 (★★).

In Your House 13: Final Four ★★★
16-02-97, Chattanooga, Tennessee **WWF**
Marc Mero defeated **Leif Cassidy** in 9:31 (★★); **The Nation of Domination (Faarooq, Crush** and **Savio Vega)** defeated **Bart Gunn, Flash Funk** and **Goldust** in 6:43 (★★); **Rocky Maivia** defeated **Hunter Hearst Helmsley** in 12:30 (★★); **Doug Furnas** and **Phil LaFon** defeated **Owen Hart** and **The British Bulldog** by DQ in 10:30 (★★); **Bret Hart** defeated **Steve Austin, Vader** and **The Undertaker** in a Four Corners Elimination Match to win the vacant WWF World Heavyweight Title in 24:06 (★★★).

Cyberslam '97 ★★
22-02-97, Philadelphia, Pennsylvania **ECW**
The Eliminators (John Kronus and **Perry Saturn)** defeated **Rob Van Dam** and **Sabu** in a Tables And Ladders Match in 20:18 (★★); **Chris Chetti** defeated **Little Guido** in 5:46 (★★); **Stevie Richards** defeated **Balls Mahoney** in 12:26 (★★); **Axl Rotten** defeated **Spike Dudley** in 4:06 (★★); **The Dudley Boyz (Buh Buh Ray Dudley** and **D-Von Dudley)** defeated **The Gangstas (Mustafa** and **New Jack)** in 14:22 (★★); **Taz** defeated **Tracy Smothers** in 3:21 (★★); **Brian Lee** and **Raven** vs. **Terry Funk** and **Tommy Dreamer** ended in a no contest in 14:00 (★★); **Sabu** defeated **Chris Candido** in 18:22 (★★★).

SuperBrawl VII ★★★
23-02-97, San Francisco, California **WCW**
Syxx defeated **Dean Malenko** to win the WCW Cruiserweight Title in 12:02 (★★★); **Konnan, La Parka** and **Villano IV** defeated **Juventud Guerrera, Super Calo** and **Ciclope** in 9:51 (★★★); **Prince Iaukea** defeated **Rey Misterio Jr.** in 8:56 (★★★); **Diamond Dallas Page** defeated **Buff Bagwell** by DQ in 9:46 (★★★); **Eddie Guerrero** defeated **Chris Jericho** in 12:02 (★★★); **Public Enemy (Rocco Rock** and **Johnny Grunge)** defeated **Harlem Heat (Booker T** and **Stevie Ray)** and **The Faces of Fear (Meng** and **The Barbarian)** in a Three Way Match in 7:43 (★★); **Jeff Jarrett** defeated **Steve McMichael** in 8:12 (★★); **Chris Benoit** defeated **The Taskmaster** in a San Francisco Death Match in 8:35 (★★★); **Lex Luger** and **The Giant** defeated **The Outsiders (Kevin Nash** and **Scott Hall)** to win the WCW World Tag Team Title in 8:53 (★★); **Hollywood Hogan** defeated **Roddy Piper** in 10:59 (★★).

WWF at Madison Square Garden (16-03-97) ★★
16-03-97, New York City, New York **WWF**
The Sultan defeated **Flash Funk** in 7:42 (★★); **The New Blackjacks (Blackjack Windham** and **Blackjack Bradshaw)** defeated **The Godwinns (Henry Godwinn** and **Phineas Godwinn)** in 8:13 (★★); **Crush** defeated **Aldo Montoya** in 1:46 (★★);

Ahmed Johnson defeated Savio Vega by DQ in 8:56 (★★);
Davey Boy Smith and Owen Hart defeated Phil LaFon and Doug
Furnas in 13:33 (★★★); Hunter Hearst Helmsley defeated
Rocky Maivia by DQ in 14:45 (★★★); Faarooq defeated
Goldust in 8:26 (★★); Vader defeated The Undertaker in a
Casket Match in 7:26 (★★).

Uncensored '97 ★★★
16-03-97, North Charleston, South Carolina WCW

Dean Malenko defeated Eddie Guerrero to win the WCW
United States Heavyweight Title in 19:14 (★★★★); Ultimo
Dragon defeated Psychosis in 13:17 (★★★); Glacier defeated
Mortis in 9:04 (★★★); Buff Bagwell defeated Scotty Riggs in a
Strap Match in 12:27 (★★); Harlem Heat (Booker T and Stevie
Ray) defeated Public Enemy (Rocco Rock and Johnny Grunge) in
a Texas Tornado Match in 13:17 (★★); Prince Iaukea defeated
Rey Misterio Jr. in 15:00 (★★); Team nWo (Hollywood Hogan,
Randy Savage, Kevin Nash and Scott Hall) defeated Team Piper
(Roddy Piper, Chris Benoit, Steve McMichael and Jeff Jarrett)
and Team WCW (Lex Luger, The Giant and Scott Steiner) in a
Triangle Elimination Match in 19:22 (★★).

WrestleMania XIII ★★★
23-03-97, Rosemont, Illinois WWF

The Headbangers (Mosh and Thrasher) defeated Doug Furnas
and Phil LaFon, The Godwinns (Henry O. Godwinn and Phineas
I. Godwinn) and The New Blackjacks (Blackjack Bradshaw and
Blackjack Windham) in a Four Way Elimination Match in 10:39
(★★); Rocky Maivia defeated The Sultan in 9:47 (★★); Hunter
Hearst Helmsley defeated Goldust in 14:29 (★★); Owen
Hart and The British Bulldog vs. Vader and Mankind went to
a double count out in 16:08 (★★); Bret Hart defeated Steve
Austin in a No DQ Submission Match in 22:04 (★★★★★);
Ahmed Johnson and The Legion of Doom (Hawk and Animal)
defeated The Nation of Domination (Faarooq, Crush and
Savio Vega) in a Chicago Street Fight in 10:46 (★★★); The
Undertaker defeated Sycho Sid in a No DQ Match to win the
WWF World Heavyweight Title in 21:19 (★★).

Spring Stampede '97 ★★
06-04-97, Tupelo, Mississippi WCW

Rey Misterio Jr. defeated Ultimo Dragon in 14:55 (★★★); Akira
Hokuto defeated Madusa in 5:14 (★★); Prince Iaukea defeated
Lord Steven Regal in 10:00 (★★); Public Enemy (Rocco Rock
and Johnny Grunge) defeated Steve McMichael and Jeff
Jarrett in 10:42 (★★); Dean Malenko vs. Chris Benoit went to a
no contest in 17:53 (★★★); Kevin Nash defeated Rick Steiner
in 10:25 (★★); Lex Luger defeated The Giant, Booker T and
Stevie Ray in a Four Corners Match in 18:18 (★★); Diamond
Dallas Page defeated Randy Savage in a No DQ Match in 15:38
(★★★★).

Barely Legal ★★★★
13-04-97, Philadelphia, Pennsylvania ECW

The Eliminators (Perry Saturn and John Kronus) defeated The
Dudley Boyz (Buh Buh Ray Dudley and D-Von Dudley) to win
the ECW World Tag Team Title in 6:11 (★★★); Rob Van Dam
defeated Lance Storm in 10:10 (★★); The Great Sasuke, Gran
Hamada and Masato Yakushiji defeated Taka Michinoku, Dick
Togo and Terry Boy in 16:55 (★★★★★); Shane Douglas
defeated Pitbull #2 in 20:43 (★★); Taz defeated Sabu in 17:49
(★★); Terry Funk defeated The Sandman and Stevie Richards in
a Three Way Match in 19:10 (★★); Terry Funk defeated Raven to
win the ECW World Heavyweight Title in 7:20 (★★).

In Your House 14: Revenge Of The 'Taker ★★
20-04-97, Rochester, New York WWF

The Legion of Doom (Hawk and Animal) defeated Owen Hart
and The British Bulldog by DQ in 12:16 (★★); Savio Vega
defeated Rocky Maivia via count out in 8:33 (★★); Jesse James
defeated Rockabilly in 6:46 (★); The Undertaker defeated
Mankind in 17:26 (★★★); Steve Austin defeated Bret Hart by
DQ in 21:09 (★★★).

In Your House 15: A Cold Day In Hell ★★★
11-05-97, Richmond, Virginia WWF

Hunter Hearst Helmsley defeated Flash Funk in 10:05 (★★★);
Mankind defeated Rocky Maivia in 8:46 (★★★); The Nation of
Domination (Faarooq, Crush and Savio Vega) defeated Ahmed
Johnson in a Gauntlet Match in 13:25 (★★); Ken Shamrock
defeated Vader in a No Holds Barred Match in 13:21 (★★★★);
The Undertaker defeated Steve Austin in 20:27 (★★★).

Slamboree '97 ★★★
18-05-97, Charlotte, North Carolina WCW

Lord Steven Regal defeated Ultimo Dragon to win the WCW
World Television Title in 16:04 (★★★★); Madusa defeated
Luna Vachon in 5:09 (★★); Rey Misterio Jr. defeated Yuji
Yasuraoka in 14:58 (★★★); Glacier defeated Mortis by DQ
in 1:51 (★★); Dean Malenko defeated Jeff Jarrett in 15:03
(★★★); Meng defeated Chris Benoit in a Death Match in 14:54
(★★); The Steiner Brothers (Rick Steiner and Scott Steiner)
defeated Konnan and Hugh Morrus in 9:35 (★★); Steve
McMichael defeated Reggie White in 15:17 (★); Ric Flair, Roddy
Piper and Kevin Greene defeated Kevin Nash, Scott Hall and
Syxx in 17:20 (★★★).

Wrestlepalooza '97 ★★
06-06-97, Philadelphia, Pennsylvania ECW

Shane Douglas defeated Chris Chetti in 6:51 (★★); The Pitbulls
(Pitbull #1 and Pitbull #2) defeated The F.B.I. (Little Guido and
Tracy Smothers) in 7:14 (★★); The Dudley Boyz (Buh Buh Ray
Dudley and D-Von Dudley) defeated Balls Mahoney and The
Sandman in 7:26 (★★); Terry Funk defeated Chris Candido in
12:54 (★); Tommy Dreamer defeated Raven in a Loser Leaves
Town Match in 15:06 (★★★); Sabu defeated Taz in 8:14 (★★);
Taz defeated Shane Douglas to win the ECW World Television
Title in 2:51 (★★); The Eliminators (John Kronus and Perry
Saturn) defeated The Dudley Boyz (Buh Buh Ray Dudley and
D-Von Dudley) in 7:34 (★★).

King Of The Ring '97 ★★
08-06-97, Providence, Rhode Island WWF

Hunter Hearst Helmsley defeated Ahmed Johnson in 7:42
(★★); Mankind defeated Jerry Lawler in 10:24 (★★); Goldust
defeated Crush in 9:56 (★★); The Hart Foundation (The British
Bulldog, Owen Hart and Jim Neidhart) defeated Sycho Sid
and The Legion of Doom (Hawk and Animal) in 13:37 (★★);
Hunter Hearst Helmsley defeated Mankind in 19:26 (★★);
Shawn Michaels vs. Steve Austin ended in a double DQ in 22:29
(★★★★); The Undertaker defeated Faarooq in 13:44 (★★).

Great American Bash '97 ★★★
15-06-97, Moline, Illinois WCW

Ultimo Dragon defeated Psychosis in 14:20 (★★★); Harlem
Heat (Booker T and Stevie Ray) defeated The Steiner Brothers
(Rick Steiner and Scott Steiner) by DQ in 12:02 (★★); Konnan
defeated Hugh Morrus in 10:34 (★); Glacier defeated Wrath in
12:02 (★★); Akira Hokuto defeated Madusa in 11:41 (★★);
Chris Benoit defeated Meng in a Death Match in 14:59 (★★★);
Kevin Greene defeated Steve McMichael in 9:21 (★★); The
Outsiders (Kevin Nash and Scott Hall) defeated Ric Flair and
Roddy Piper in 10:02 (★★); Randy Savage defeated Diamond
Dallas Page in a Falls Count Anywhere Match in 16:56 (★★★).

nWo vs. WCW Takeover '97 ★★★
21-06-97, Oberhausen, Germany WCW

Alex Wright defeated Hugh Morrus in 10:59 (★★★); Madusa
defeated Luna Vachon in 7:34 (★★); The Steiner Brothers
(Rick Steiner and Scott Steiner) defeated Harlem Heat (Booker
T and Stevie Ray) in 15:06 (★★★); Rey Misterio Jr. defeated
Dean Malenko in 17:57 (★★★★); Diamond Dallas Page
defeated M. Wallstreet in 9:55 (★★); Chris Benoit defeated
Meng in 17:51 (★★★); Lex Luger and The Giant defeated The
Outsiders (Kevin Nash and Scott Hall) in 16:29 (★★★).

In Your House 16: Canadian Stampede ★★★★★
06-07-97, Calgary, Alberta WWF

Hunter Hearst Helmsley vs. Mankind ended in a double count
out in 13:14 (★★★); The Great Sasuke defeated Taka
Michinoku in 10:00 (★★★★); The Undertaker defeated Vader
in 12:39 (★★★★); The Hart Foundation (Bret Hart, Brian
Pillman, Owen Hart, The British Bulldog and Jim Neidhart)
defeated Steve Austin, Ken Shamrock, Goldust and The Legion
of Doom (Hawk and Animal) in 24:31 (★★★★★).

Bash At The Beach '97 ★★★★
13-07-97, Daytona Beach, Florida WCW

Mortis and Wrath defeated Glacier and Ernest Miller in 9:47
(★★); Chris Jericho defeated Ultimo Dragon in 12:55
(★★★★); The Steiner Brothers (Rick Steiner and Scott Steiner)
defeated The Great Muta and Masahiro Chono in 11:37
(★★★); Juventud Guerrera, Hector Garza and Lizmark Jr.
defeated La Parka, Psychosis and Villano IV in 10:08 (★★★★);
Chris Benoit defeated The Taskmaster in a Retirement Match in

13:11 (★★★); Jeff Jarrett defeated Steve McMichael in 6:56 (★★); Scott Hall and Randy Savage defeated Diamond Dallas Page and Curt Hennig in 9:35 (★★); Roddy Piper defeated Ric Flair in 13:26 (★★★); Lex Luger and The Giant defeated Hollywood Hogan and Dennis Rodman in 22:19 (★★★).

SummerSlam '97 ★★★
03-08-97, East Rutherford, New Jersey **WWF**

Mankind defeated Hunter Hearst Helmsley in a Steel Cage Match in 16:26 (★★★); Goldust defeated Brian Pillman in 7:17 (★★); The Legion of Doom (Hawk and Animal) defeated The Godwinns (Henry O. Godwinn and Phineas I. Godwinn) in 9:15 (★★); The British Bulldog defeated Ken Shamrock by DQ in 7:26 (★★); Los Boricuas (Jesus Castillo, Jose Estrada Jr., Miguel Perez Jr. and Savio Vega) defeated The Disciples of Apocalypse (Crush, Chainz, Skull and 8-Ball) in 9:08 (★★); Steve Austin defeated Owen Hart to win the WWF Intercontinental Title in 16:16 (★★★); Bret Hart defeated The Undertaker to win the WWF World Heavyweight Title in 28:09 (★★★★).

Road Wild '97 ★★
09-08-97, Sturgis, South Dakota **WCW**

Harlem Heat (Booker T and Stevie Ray) defeated Vicious and Delicious (Buff Bagwell and Scott Norton) in 10:20 (★★); Konnan defeated Rey Misterio Jr. in a Mexican Death Match in 10:20 (★★★); Steve McMichael and Chris Benoit defeated Jeff Jarrett and Dean Malenko in an Elimination Match in 9:36 (★★); Alex Wright defeated Chris Jericho in 13:03 (★★★); Ric Flair defeated Syxx in 11:06 (★★); Curt Hennig defeated Diamond Dallas Page in 9:41 (★★); The Giant defeated Randy Savage in 6:05 (★★); The Steiner Brothers (Rick Steiner and Scott Steiner) defeated The Outsiders (Kevin Nash and Scott Hall) by DQ in 15:29 (★★); Hollywood Hogan defeated Lex Luger to win the WCW World Heavyweight Title in 16:15 (★★).

Born To Be Wired '97 ★★★
09-08-97, Philadelphia, Pennsylvania **ECW**

Little Guido defeated Pablo Marquez in 6:05 (★★); Mikey Whipwreck defeated Louie Spicolli in 6:56 (★★); Spike Dudley defeated Bam Bam Bigelow in 6:37 (★★★); Chris Candido defeated Chris Chetti in 10:43 (★★★); Shane Douglas defeated Lance Storm in 9:02 (★★★); Taz defeated Al Snow in 10:15 (★★); The Dudleys (Big Dick Dudley, Buh Buh Ray Dudley and D-Von Dudley) defeated Axl Rotten, Balls Mahoney and Hack Myers in 12:00 (★★); Rob Van Dam defeated Tommy Dreamer in 9:49 (★★★); Sabu defeated Terry Funk in a No Rope Barbed Wire Match to win the ECW World Title in 20:38 (★★★).

Hardcore Heaven '97 ★★★
17-08-97, Fort Lauderdale, Florida **ECW**

Taz defeated Chris Candido in 10:52 (★★); Bam Bam Bigelow defeated Spike Dudley in 5:05 (★★); Rob Van Dam defeated Al Snow in 13:43 (★★★); The Dudley Boyz (Buh Buh Ray Dudley and D-Von Dudley) defeated PG-13 (Jamie Dundee and Wolfie D) in 10:58 (★★); Tommy Dreamer defeated Jerry Lawler in 18:57 (★★★); Shane Douglas defeated Sabu and Terry Funk in a Three Way Match to win the ECW World Heavyweight Title in 26:37 (★★★).

Clash Of The Champions XXXV ★★★★
21-08-97, Nashville, Tennessee **WCW**

Steve McMichael defeated Jeff Jarrett to win the WCW United States Title in 8:07 (★★); Raven defeated Stevie Richards in a No DQ Match in 5:01 (★★); Alex Wright defeated Ultimo Dragon to win the WCW World Television Title in 13:55 (★★★); Chris Jericho defeated Eddie Guerrero in 6:41 (★★★★); Psychosis, Silver King, Villano IV and Villano V defeated Juventud Guerrera, Super Calo, Hector Garza and Lizmark Jr. in 4:52 (★★★); Ric Flair and Curt Hennig defeated Konnan and Syxx in 5:09 (★★); Scott Hall and Randy Savage defeated Diamond Dallas Page and Lex Luger in 9:55 (★★).

In Your House 17: Ground Zero ★★★★
07-09-97, Louisville, Kentucky **WWF**

Brian Pillman defeated Goldust in 11:06 (★★); Brian Christopher defeated Scott Putski via count out in 4:45 (★★); Savio Vega defeated Faarooq and Crush in a Three Way Match in 11:37 (★★); Max Mini defeated El Torito in 9:21 (★★★); The Headbangers (Mosh and Thrasher) defeated The Godwinns (Henry O. Godwinn and Phineas I. Godwinn), The Legion of Doom (Hawk and Animal) and Owen Hart and The British

Bulldog to win the vacant WWF World Tag Team Title in 17:19 (★★); Bret Hart defeated The Patriot in 19:19 (★★★); Shawn Michaels vs. The Undertaker ended in a no contest in 16:20 (★★★★).

Terry Funk's WrestleFest ★★★
11-09-97, Amarillo, Texas **ECW**

Wing Kanemura defeated Roadkill in 6:01 (★★); Taz defeated Chris Candido in 7:22 (★★); Shark Tsuchiya defeated Lady Cooga in 6:54 (★); The Youngbloods (Chris Youngblood and Mark Youngblood) defeated The Bushwhackers (Butch and Luke) in 10:22 (★); Balls Mahoney defeated Buh Buh Ray Dudley in a No DQ Match in 6:54 (★★); Shane Douglas defeated Tommy Dreamer in 10:02 (★★★); Dory Funk Jr. defeated Rob Van Dam in 11:31 (★★); Mankind defeated Sabu by DQ in 8:55 (★★★); Hakushi, Hayabusa and Masato Tanaka defeated Jake Roberts and The Headhunters (Headhunter A and Headhunter B) in 12:03 (★★); Bret Hart defeated Terry Funk in a No DQ Match in 25:10 (★★★★).

Fall Brawl '97 ★★★★
14-09-97, Winston-Salem, North Carolina **WCW**

Eddie Guerrero defeated Chris Jericho to win the WCW Cruiserweight Title in 17:19 (★★★★); The Steiner Brothers (Rick Steiner and Scott Steiner) defeated Harlem Heat (Booker T and Stevie Ray) in 11:44 (★★★); Alex Wright defeated Ultimo Dragon in 18:43 (★★★); Jeff Jarrett defeated Dean Malenko in 14:53 (★★★); Wrath and Mortis defeated The Faces of Fear (Meng and The Barbarian) in 12:22 (★★★); The Giant defeated Scott Norton in 5:27 (★★); Lex Luger and Diamond Dallas Page defeated Scott Hall and Randy Savage in a No DQ Match in 10:19 (★★); nWo (Kevin Nash, Buff Bagwell, Syxx and Konnan) defeated The Four Horsemen (Ric Flair, Chris Benoit, Steve McMichael and Curt Hennig) in a War Games Match in 19:38 (★★★).

One Night Only ★★★★
20-09-97, Birmingham, England **WWF**

Hunter Hearst Helmsley defeated Dude Love in 12:51 (★★★★); Tiger Ali Singh defeated Leif Cassidy in 4:06 (★); The Headbangers (Mosh and Thrasher) defeated Los Boricuas (Miguel Perez Jr. and Savio Vega) in 13:34 (★★); The Patriot defeated Flash Funk in 8:47 (★★); The Legion of Doom (Hawk and Animal) defeated The Godwinns (Henry O. Godwinn and Phineas I. Godwinn) in 10:42 (★★); Vader defeated Owen Hart in 12:14 (★★★); Bret Hart defeated The Undertaker by DQ in 28:34 (★★★★); Shawn Michaels defeated The British Bulldog to win the WWF European Title in 22:53 (★★★★).

In Your House 18: Badd Blood ★★
05-10-97, St. Louis, Missouri **WWF**

The Nation of Domination (D-Lo Brown, Kama Mustafa and Rocky Maivia) defeated The Legion of Doom (Hawk and Animal) in a Handicap Match in 12:20 (★★); Max Mini and Nova defeated Mosaic and Tarantula in 6:43 (★★); The Godwinns (Henry O. Godwinn and Phineas I. Godwinn) defeated The Headbangers (Mosh and Thrasher) to win the WWF World Tag Team Title in 12:18 (★★); Owen Hart defeated Faarooq to win the vacant WWF Intercontinental Title in 7:16 (★★); The Disciples of Apocalypse (Crush, Chainz, Skull and 8-Ball) defeated Los Boricuas (Savio Vega, Jesus Castillo Jr., Jose Estrada Jr. and Miguel Perez Jr.) in 9:11 (★★); Bret Hart and The British Bulldog defeated The Patriot and Vader in a Flag Match in 23:13 (★★); Shawn Michaels defeated The Undertaker in a Hell In A Cell Match in 29:59 (★★★★★).

Halloween Havoc '97 ★★★★
26-10-97, Las Vegas, Nevada **WCW**

Yuji Nagata defeated Ultimo Dragon in 9:42 (★★★★); Chris Jericho defeated Gedo in 7:18 (★★★); Rey Misterio Jr. defeated Eddie Guerrero to win the WCW Cruiserweight Title in 13:51 (★★★★★); Alex Wright defeated Steve McMichael in 6:31 (★★); Jacqueline defeated Disco Inferno in 9:39 (★); Curt Hennig defeated Ric Flair by DQ in 13:57 (★★★); Lex Luger defeated Scott Hall in 13:02 (★★); Randy Savage defeated Diamond Dallas Page in a Las Vegas Sudden Death Match in 18:07 (★★★★); Roddy Piper defeated Hollywood Hogan in a Steel Cage Match in 13:37 (★).

Survivor Series '97 ★★★
09-11-97, Montreal, Quebec **WWF**

The Godwinns (Henry O. Godwinn and Phineas I. Godwinn) and The New Age Outlaws (Billy Gunn and Road Dogg) defeated The Headbangers (Mosh and Thrasher) and The New Blackjacks (Blackjack Bradshaw and Blackjack Windham) in an Elimination Match in 15:25 (★★); The Truth Commission (The Interrogator, Jackyl, Recon and Sniper) defeated The Disciples of Apocalypse (Crush, Chainz, Skull and 8-Ball) in an Elimination Match in 9:59 (★★); Team Canada (The British Bulldog, Jim Neidhart, Doug Furnas and Phil LaFon) defeated Team USA (Goldust, Marc Mero, Steve Blackman and Vader) in an Elimination Match in 17:05 (★★); Kane defeated Mankind in 9:27 (★★); Ken Shamrock, Ahmed Johnson and The Legion of Doom (Hawk and Animal) defeated The Nation of Domination (Faarooq, Rocky Maivia, D-Lo Brown and Kama Mustafa) in an Elimination Match in 20:28 (★★★); Steve Austin defeated Owen Hart to win the WWF Intercontinental Title in 4:03 (★★); Shawn Michaels defeated Bret Hart to win the WWF World Heavyweight Title in 12:19 (★★★).

World War 3 '97 ★★★
23-11-97, Auburn Hills, Michigan **WCW**

The Faces of Fear (Meng and The Barbarian) defeated Glacier and Ernest Miller in 9:09 (★★★); Perry Saturn defeated Disco Inferno in 8:19 (★★); Yuji Nagata defeated Ultimo Dragon in 12:45 (★★★); The Steiner Brothers (Rick Steiner and Scott Steiner) defeated The Blue Bloods (Lord Steven Regal and Squire David Taylor) in 9:45 (★★); Raven defeated Scotty Riggs in a Raven's Rules Match in 9:43 (★★); Steve McMichael defeated Alex Wright in 3:36 (★); Eddie Guerrero defeated Rey Misterio Jr. in 12:42 (★★★★); Curt Hennig defeated Ric Flair in a No DQ Match in 17:57 (★★★); Scott Hall won the 60-Man World War 3 Match in 29:48 (★).

November To Remember '97 ★★
30-11-97, Monaca, Pennsylvania **ECW**

Chris Candido vs. Tommy Rogers ended in a no contest in 13:20 (★★); Chris Candido and Lance Storm defeated Tommy Rogers and Jerry Lynn in 3:23 (★★); Mikey Whipwreck defeated Justin Credible in 7:15 (★★); Taz defeated Pitbull #2 in 1:29 (★★); The F.B.I. (Tracy Smothers and Little Guido) defeated The Dudley Boyz (Buh Buh Ray Dudley and D-Von Dudley), The Hardcore Chair Swingin' Freaks (Balls Mahoney and Axl Rotten) and The Gangstanators (New Jack and John Kronus) in a Four Way Dance in 14:32 (★★); Rob Van Dam vs. Tommy Dreamer went to a no contest in a Flag Match in 16:02 (★★★); Sabu defeated The Sandman in a Tables and Ladders Match in 20:55 (★); Shane Douglas defeated Bam Bam Bigelow to win the ECW World Heavyweight Title in 25:02 (★★).

In Your House 19: DeGeneration X ★★
07-12-97, Springfield, Massachusetts **WWF**

Taka Michinoku defeated Brian Christopher to win the vacant WWF Light Heavyweight Title in 12:02 (★★★); Los Boricuas (Jesus Castillo Jr., Jose Estrada Jr. and Miguel Perez Jr.) defeated The Disciples of Apocalypse (Chainz, Skull and 8-Ball) in 7:58 (★★); Butterbean defeated Marc Mero by DQ in a Toughman Match in 10:20 (★★); The New Age Outlaws (Billy Gunn and Road Dogg) defeated The Legion of Doom (Hawk and Animal) by DQ in 10:32 (★★); Triple H defeated Sgt. Slaughter in a Boot Camp Match in 17:39 (★); Jeff Jarrett defeated The Undertaker by DQ in 6:54 (★★); Steve Austin defeated The Rock in 5:28 (★★★); Ken Shamrock defeated Shawn Michaels by DQ in 18:27 (★★★).

Starrcade '97 ★
28-12-97, Washington, D.C. **WCW**

Eddie Guerrero defeated Dean Malenko in 14:57 (★★); Scott Norton, Vincent and Randy Savage defeated Ray Traylor and The Steiner Brothers (Rick Steiner and Scott Steiner) in 11:06 (★★); Goldberg defeated Steve McMichael in 5:59 (★); Perry Saturn defeated Chris Benoit in a Raven's Rules Match 10:50 (★★); Buff Bagwell defeated Lex Luger in 16:36 (★★); Diamond Dallas Page defeated Curt Hennig to win the WCW United States Heavyweight Title in 10:52 (★★★); Larry Zbyszko defeated Eric Bischoff by DQ in 11:12 (★); Sting defeated Hollywood Hogan to win the WCW World Heavyweight Title in 12:53 (★).

Royal Rumble '98 ★★★★
18-01-98, San Jose, California **WWF**

Vader defeated TAFKA Goldust in 7:51 (★); Max Mini, Mosaic and Nova defeated Battalion, El Torito and Tarantula in 7:48 (★★); The Rock defeated Ken Shamrock by DQ in 10:53 (★★★); The Legion of Doom (Hawk and Animal) defeated The New Age Outlaws (Billy Gunn and Road Dogg) by DQ in 7:56 (★★); Steve Austin won the 30-Man Royal Rumble Match in 55:25 (★★★); Shawn Michaels defeated The Undertaker in a Casket Match in 20:30 (★★★★).

Souled Out '98 ★★★★
24-01-98, Trotwood, Ohio **WCW**

Juventud Guerrera, Super Calo, Lizmark Jr. and Chavo Guerrero Jr. defeated La Parka, Psychosis, Silver King and El Dandy in 9:30 (★★★★); Chris Benoit defeated Raven in a Raven's Rules Match in 10:36 (★★★★); Chris Jericho defeated Rey Mysterio Jr. to win the WCW Cruiserweight Title in 8:22 (★★); Booker T defeated Rick Martel in 10:50 (★★★); Larry Zbyszko defeated Scott Hall by DQ in 8:09 (★★); Ray Traylor and The Steiner Brothers (Rick Steiner and Scott Steiner) defeated Konnan, Scott Norton and Buff Bagwell in 12:20 (★★); Kevin Nash defeated The Giant in 10:47 (★★); Bret Hart defeated Ric Flair in 18:06 (★★★★); Lex Luger defeated Randy Savage in 7:07 (★★).

No Way Out Of Texas ★★★★
15-02-98, Houston, Texas **WWF**

The Headbangers (Mosh and Thrasher) defeated TAFKA Goldust and Marc Mero in 13:27 (★★); Taka Michinoku defeated Pantera in 10:09 (★★★); The Godwinns (Henry O. Godwinn and Phineas I. Godwinn) defeated The Quebecers (Jacques and Pierre) in 11:15 (★★); Justin Bradshaw defeated Jeff Jarrett by DQ in 8:33 (★★); Ahmed Johnson, Ken Shamrock and The Disciples of Apocalypse (Chainz, Skull and 8-Ball) defeated The Nation of Domination (The Rock, Faarooq, D-Lo Brown, Kama Mustafa and Mark Henry) in a War Of Attrition Match in 13:44 (★★★); Kane defeated Vader in 11:00 (★★); Cactus Jack, Chainsaw Charlie, Owen Hart and Steve Austin defeated Triple H, Savio Vega and The New Age Outlaws (Billy Gunn and Road Dogg) in a Non Sanctioned Match in 17:37 (★★★★).

Cyberslam '98 ★★
21-02-98, Philadelphia, Pennsylvania **ECW**

Jerry Lynn defeated Danny Doring in 9:57 (★★); Al Snow defeated Tracy Smothers in 22:07 (★); Chris Chetti defeated Doug Furnas in 4:07 (★★); Lance Storm defeated Chris Candido in 8:46 (★★★); Taz defeated Brakus in 2:37 (★★); Justin Credible defeated Tommy Dreamer in a First Blood Match in 11:11 (★★); Axl Rotten, Balls Mahoney and The Sandman defeated Spike Dudley and The Gangstanators (John Kronus and New Jack) and The Dudleys (Big Dick Dudley, Buh Buh Ray Dudley and D-Von Dudley) in a Three Way Elimination Match in 18:25 (★★); Bam Bam Bigelow and Shane Douglas defeated Rob Van Dam and Sabu in 23:10 (★★).

SuperBrawl VIII ★★★
22-02-98, San Francisco, California **WCW**

Booker T defeated Rick Martel to win the WCW World Television Title in 10:33 (★★★); Booker T defeated Perry Saturn in 14:23 (★★★); Disco Inferno defeated La Parka in 11:41 (★★); Goldberg defeated Brad Armstrong in 2:23 (★★); Chris Jericho defeated Juventud Guerrera in a Title vs. Mask Match in 13:29 (★★★★); The British Bulldog defeated Steve McMichael in 6:10 (★★); Diamond Dallas Page defeated Chris Benoit in 15:47 (★★★); Lex Luger defeated Randy Savage in a No DQ Match in 7:26 (★★); The Outsiders (Kevin Nash and Scott Hall) defeated The Steiner Brothers (Rick Steiner and Scott Steiner) to win the WCW World Tag Team Title in 4:18 (★★); Sting defeated Hollywood Hogan to win the vacant WCW World Heavyweight Title in 16:33 (★★).

Living Dangerously '98 ★★
01-03-98, Asbury Park, New Jersey **ECW**

Jerry Lynn and Chris Chetti defeated The F.B.I. (Little Guido and Tracy Smothers) in 8:19 (★★); Masato Tanaka defeated Doug Furnas in 5:46 (★★); Rob Van Dam defeated Too Cold Scorpio in 27:10 (★★); New Jack and Spike Dudley defeated The Dudley Boyz (Buh Buh Ray Dudley and D-Von Dudley) and The Hardcore Chair Swingin' Freaks (Balls Mahoney and Axl Rotten) in a Three Way Match in 13:25 (★★); Tommy Dreamer defeated Justin Credible in 8:58 (★★); Bam Bam Bigelow defeated Taz to win the ECW World Television Title in 13:37 (★★); **Sabu** defeated **The Sandman** in a Dueling Canes Match in 9:21 (★★); **Al Snow** and **Lance Storm** defeated **Shane Douglas** and **Chris Candido** in 4:49 (★★).

Uncensored '98 ★★★
15-03-98, Mobile, Alabama **WCW**
Booker T defeated **Eddie Guerrero** in 11:08 (★★★); **Juventud Guerrera** defeated **Konnan** in 10:21 (★★); **Chris Jericho** defeated **Dean Malenko** in 14:42 (★★★); **Lex Luger** defeated **Scott Steiner** in 3:53 (★★); **Diamond Dallas Page** defeated **Raven** in a Three Way Match in 15:53 (★★★★); **The Giant** defeated **Kevin Nash** by DQ in 6:36 (★★); **Bret Hart** defeated **Curt Hennig** in 13:51 (★★); **Sting** defeated **Scott Hall** in 8:28 (★★); **Hollywood Hogan** vs. **Randy Savage** went to a no contest in a Steel Cage Match in 15:20 (★).

WrestleMania XIV ★★★★★
29-03-98, Boston, Massachusetts **WWF**
LOD 2000 (Hawk and **Animal)** won a Tag Team Battle Royal in 8:19 (★★); **Taka Michinoku** defeated **Aguila** in 5:57 (★★); **Triple H** defeated **Owen Hart** in 11:29 (★★★); **Marc Mero** and **Sable** defeated **TAFKA Goldust** and **Luna Vachon** in 9:11 (★★★); **The Rock** defeated **Ken Shamrock** by DQ in 4:49 (★★★★); **Cactus Jack** and **Chainsaw Charlie** defeated **The New Age Outlaws (Billy Gunn** and **Road Dogg)** in a Dumpster Match to win the WWF World Tag Team Title in 10:01 (★★★★); **The Undertaker** defeated **Kane** in 17:05 (★★★); **Steve Austin** defeated **Shawn Michaels** to win the WWF World Heavyweight Title in 20:08 (★★★★).

Spring Stampede '98 ★★★
19-04-98, Denver, Colorado **WCW**
Goldberg defeated **Perry Saturn** in 8:10 (★★★); **Ultimo Dragon** defeated **Chavo Guerrero Jr.** in 11:49 (★★); **Booker T** defeated **Chris Benoit** in 14:11 (★★★); **Curt Hennig** defeated **The British Bulldog** in 4:48 (★); **Chris Jericho** defeated **Prince Iaukea** in 9:55 (★★); **Rick Steiner** and **Lex Luger** defeated **Scott Steiner** and **Buff Bagwell** in 5:58 (★★); **Psychosis** defeated **La Parka** in 6:59 (★★★); **Hollywood Hogan** and **Kevin Nash** defeated **Roddy Piper** and **The Giant** in a Baseball Bat On A Pole Match in 13:23 (★); **Raven** defeated **Diamond Dallas Page** in a Raven's Rules Match to win the WCW United States Heavyweight Title in 11:52 (★★★); **Randy Savage** defeated **Sting** in a No DQ Match to win the WCW World Heavyweight Title in 10:08 (★★).

Unforgiven '98 ★★★
26-04-98, Greensboro, North Carolina **WWF**
Faarooq, Ken Shamrock and **Steve Blackman** defeated **The Nation of Domination (The Rock, D-Lo Brown** and **Mark Henry)** in 13:32 (★★); **Triple H** defeated **Owen Hart** in 12:26 (★★★); **The Midnight Express (Bodacious Bart** and **Bombastic Bob)** defeated **The Rock 'n' Roll Express (Ricky Morton** and **Robert Gibson)** in 7:12 (★★); **Luna Vachon** defeated **Sable** in an Evening Gown Match in 2:50 (★); **The New Age Outlaws (Billy Gunn** and **Road Dogg)** defeated **LOD 2000 (Hawk** and **Animal)** in 12:13 (★★); **The Undertaker** defeated **Kane** in an Inferno Match in 16:00 (★★★); **Dude Love** defeated **Steve Austin** by DQ in 18:49 (★★★★).

Wrestlepalooza '98 ★
03-05-98, Marietta, Georgia **ECW**
The bWo (The Blue Meanie and **Super Nova)** defeated **The F.B.I. (Little Guido** and **Tracy Smothers)** in 9:28 (★★); **Justin Credible** defeated **Mikey Whipwreck** in 9:53 (★★); **Chris Candido** and **Lance Storm** defeated **The Hardcore Chair Swingin' Freaks (Balls Mahoney** and **Axl Rotten)** in 12:04 (★★); **Bam Bam Bigelow** defeated **New Jack** in 8:27 (★); **Tommy Dreamer** and **The Sandman** defeated **The Dudley Boyz (Buh Buh Ray Dudley** and **D-Von Dudley)** in 11:19 (★★); **Rob Van Dam** vs. **Sabu** went to a time limit draw in 30:00; **Shane Douglas** defeated **Al Snow** in 13:05 (★★).

Slamboree '98 ★★★
17-05-98, Worcester, Massachusetts **WCW**
Fit Finlay defeated **Chris Benoit** in 14:53 (★★★); **Lex Luger** defeated **Brian Adams** in 5:05 (★★); **Ciclope (Dean Malenko)** won a Battle Royal in 8:27 (★★); **Dean Malenko** defeated **Chris Jericho** to win the WCW Cruiserweight Title in 7:02 (★★★); **Diamond Dallas Page** defeated **Raven** in a Bowery Death Match in 14:35 (★★); **Eddie Guerrero** defeated **Ultimo Dragon** in

11:09 (★★); **Goldberg** defeated **Perry Saturn** in 7:01 (★★); **Bret Hart** defeated **Randy Savage** by DQ in 16:38 (★★); **Sting** and **The Giant** defeated **The Outsiders (Kevin Nash** and **Scott Hall)** to win the WCW World Tag Team Title in 14:46 (★★).

Over The Edge '98 ★★★
31-05-98, Milwaukee, Wisconsin **WWF**
LOD 2000 (Hawk and **Animal)** defeated **The Disciples of Apocalypse (Skull** and **8-Ball)** in 9:57 (★★); **Jeff Jarrett** defeated **Steve Blackman** in 10:15 (★★); **Marc Mero** defeated **Sable** in :30 (★★); **Kaientai (Dick Togo, Men's Teioh** and **Sho Funaki)** defeated **Justin Bradshaw** and **Taka Michinoku** in a Handicap Match in 9:52 (★★); **The Rock** defeated **Faarooq** in 5:07 (★★); **Kane** defeated **Vader** in a Mask vs. Mask Match in 7:20 (★★); **The Nation of Domination (Owen Hart, Kama Mustafa** and **D-Lo Brown)** defeated **D-Generation X (Triple H, Billy Gunn** and **Road Dogg)** in 18:33 (★★); **Steve Austin** defeated **Dude Love** in a Falls Count Anywhere Match in 22:27 (★★★★★).

Great American Bash '98 ★★★
14-06-98, Baltimore, Maryland **WCW**
Booker T defeated **Chris Benoit** in 16:20 (★★★★); **Chris Kanyon** defeated **Perry Saturn** in 14:46 (★★★); **Chris Jericho** defeated **Dean Malenko** by DQ to win the vacant WCW Cruiserweight Title in 13:52 (★★★); **Juventud Guerrera** defeated **Reese** in 8:45 (★★); **Chavo Guerrero Jr.** defeated **Eddie Guerrero** in 14:46 (★★★); **Booker T** defeated **Fit Finlay** to win the WCW World Television Title in 13:13 (★★); **Goldberg** defeated **Konnan** in 1:57 (★★); **Hollywood Hogan** and **Bret Hart** defeated **Roddy Piper** and **Randy Savage** in 11:40 (★★); **Roddy Piper** defeated **Randy Savage** in 1:37 (★); **Sting** defeated **The Giant** to win control of the WCW World Tag Team Title in 6:40 (★★).

King Of The Ring '98 ★★★★
28-06-98, Pittsburgh, Pennsylvania **WWF**
The Headbangers (Mosh and **Thrasher)** and **Taka Michinoku** defeated **Kaientai (Funaki, Men's Teioh** and **Dick Togo)** in 6:44 (★★); **Ken Shamrock** defeated **Jeff Jarrett** in 5:29 (★★); **The Rock** defeated **Dan Severn** in 4:25 (★★); **Too Much (Brian Christopher** and **Scott Taylor)** defeated **Al Snow** and **Head** in 8:26 (★★); **X-Pac** defeated **Owen Hart** in 8:30 (★★★); **The New Age Outlaws (Billy Gunn** and **Road Dogg)** defeated **The Midnight Express (Bodacious Bart** and **Bombastic Bob)** in 9:34 (★★); **Ken Shamrock** defeated **The Rock** in 14:09 (★★★); **The Undertaker** defeated **Mankind** in a Hell In A Cell Match in 17:00 (★★★★★★); **Kane** defeated **Steve Austin** in a First Blood Match to win the WWF World Heavyweight Title in 15:58 (★★★).

Bash At The Beach '98 ★★
12-07-98, San Diego, California **WCW**
Raven defeated **Perry Saturn** in a Raven's Rules Match in 10:40 (★★); **Juventud Guerrera** defeated **Billy Kidman** in 9:55 (★★★); **Stevie Ray** defeated **Chavo Guerrero Jr.** in 1:35 (★); **Eddie Guerrero** defeated **Chavo Guerrero Jr.** in a Hair vs. Hair Match in 11:54 (★★★); **Konnan** defeated **Disco Inferno** in 2:16 (★★); **The Giant** defeated **Kevin Greene** in 6:58 (★★); **Rey Misterio Jr.** defeated **Chris Jericho** in a No DQ Match to win the WCW Cruiserweight Title in 6:00 (★★); **Booker T** defeated **Bret Hart** by DQ in 8:28 (★★); **Goldberg** defeated **Curt Hennig** in 3:50 (★★); **Hollywood Hogan** and **Dennis Rodman** defeated **Diamond Dallas Page** and **Karl Malone** in 23:47 (★★).

Fully Loaded '98 ★★★
26-07-98, Fresno, California **WWF**
Val Venis defeated **Jeff Jarrett** in 7:45 (★★★); **D-Lo Brown** defeated **X-Pac** in 8:26 (★★); **Faarooq** and **Too Cold Scorpio** defeated **Justin Bradshaw** and **Terry Funk** in 6:49 (★★); **Mark Henry** defeated **Vader** in 5:03 (★★); **The Disciples of Apocalypse (Skull** and **8-Ball)** defeated **LOD 2000 (Hawk** and **Animal)** in 8:50 (★★); **Owen Hart** defeated **Ken Shamrock** in a Dungeon Match in 4:46 (★★★); **The Rock** vs. **Triple H** went to a time limit draw in a Two Out Of Three Falls Match in 30:00 (★★★); **Jacqueline** defeated **Sable** in a Bikini Contest; **Steve Austin** and **The Undertaker** defeated **Kane** and **Mankind** to win the WWF World Tag Team Title in 18:08 (★★).

Heat Wave '98 ★★★★
02-08-98, Dayton, Ohio **ECW**
Justin Credible defeated Jerry Lynn in 14:36 (★★★); Chris Candido defeated Lance Storm in 11:00 (★★★); Masato Tanaka defeated Mike Awesome in 11:49 (★★★★); Rob Van Dam and Sabu defeated Hayabusa and Jinsei Shinzaki in 20:51 (★★★); Taz defeated Bam Bam Bigelow in a Falls Count Anywhere Match in 13:21 (★★★★); Tommy Dreamer, The Sandman and Spike Dudley defeated The Dudley Boyz (Buh Buh Ray Dudley, D-Von Dudley and Big Dick Dudley) in a Street Fight in 14:26 (★★★).

Road Wild '98 ★
08-08-98, Sturgis, South Dakota **WCW**
Meng defeated The Barbarian in 4:48 (★★); Public Enemy (Rocco Rock and Johnny Grunge) defeated The Dancing Fools (Disco Inferno and Alex Wright) in 15:27 (★★); Perry Saturn defeated Raven and Chris Kanyon in a Raven's Rules Match in 12:26 (★★); Rey Misterio Jr. defeated Psychosis in 13:38 (★★); Stevie Ray defeated Chavo Guerrero Jr. in 2:38 (★); Steve McMichael defeated Brian Adams in 6:32 (★); Juventud Guerrera defeated Chris Jericho to win the WCW Cruiserweight Title in 16:24 (★★★); Goldberg won a Battle Royal in 7:58 (★); Diamond Dallas Page and Jay Leno defeated Hollywood Hogan and Eric Bischoff in 14:31 (★★).

SummerSlam '98 ★★★★
30-08-98, New York City, New York **WWF**
D-Lo Brown defeated Val Venis by DQ in 15:24 (★★★★); The Oddities (Giant Silva, Golga and Kurrgan) defeated Kaientai (Dick Togo, Men's Teioh, Funaki and Taka Michinoku) in a Handicap Match in 10:10 (★★); X-Pac defeated Jeff Jarrett in a Hair vs. Hair Match in 11:11 (★★★); Edge and Sable defeated Marc Mero and Jacqueline in 8:26 (★★); Ken Shamrock defeated Owen Hart in a Lion's Den Match in 9:15 (★★★★); The New Age Outlaws (Billy Gunn and Road Dogg) defeated Mankind in a Falls Count Anywhere Handicap Match in 5:17 (★★); Triple H defeated The Rock in a Ladder Match to win the WWF Intercontinental Title in 25:58 (★★★★); Steve Austin defeated The Undertaker in 20:52 (★★★).

Fall Brawl '98 ★
13-09-98, Winston-Salem, North Carolina **WCW**
The British Bulldog and Jim Neidhart defeated The Dancing Fools (Alex Wright and Disco Inferno) in 11:03 (★★); Chris Jericho defeated "Goldberg" in 1:15 (★); Ernest Miller defeated Norman Smiley in 5:04 (★★); Rick Steiner vs. Scott Steiner ended in a no contest in 5:30 (★); Juventud Guerrera defeated Silver King in 8:36 (★★); Perry Saturn defeated Raven in a Raven's Rules Match 14:04 (★★); Dean Malenko defeated Curt Hennig by DQ in 7:38 (★★); Konnan defeated Scott Hall in 12:03 (★); Team WCW (Diamond Dallas Page, Roddy Piper and The Warrior) defeated nWo Hollywood (Hollywood Hogan, Bret Hart and Stevie Ray) and nWo Wolfpac (Sting, Lex Luger and Kevin Nash) in a War Games Match in 20:06 (★).

Breakdown ★★★
27-09-98, Hamilton, Ontario **WWF**
Owen Hart defeated Edge in 9:16 (★★★); Al Snow and Too Cold Scorpio defeated Too Much (Brian Christopher and Scott Taylor) in 8:03 (★★); Marc Mero defeated Droz in 5:12 (★★); Bradshaw defeated Vader in a Falls Count Anywhere Match in 7:56 (★★★); D-Lo Brown defeated Gangrel in 7:46 (★★); The Rock defeated Ken Shamrock and Mankind in a Triple Threat Steel Cage Match in 18:47 (★★★★); Val Venis defeated Dustin Runnels in 9:09 (★★); D-Generation X (X-Pac, Billy Gunn and Road Dogg) defeated Jeff Jarrett and Southern Justice (Dennis Knight and Mark Canterbury) in 11:17 (★★); Kane and The Undertaker defeated Steve Austin in a Three Way Match to co-win the WWF World Heavyweight Title in 22:05 (★★).

Judgment Day '98 ★★
18-10-98, Rosemont, Illinois **WWF**
Al Snow defeated Marc Mero in 7:12 (★★); LOD 2000 (Hawk, Animal and Droz) defeated The Disciples of Apocalypse (Skull, 8-Ball and Paul Ellering) in 5:04 (★★); Christian defeated Taka Michinoku to win the WWF Light Heavyweight Title in 8:35 (★★★); Goldust defeated Val Venis in 12:05 (★★★); X-Pac defeated D-Lo Brown to win the WWF European Title in 14:37 (★★★); The Headbangers (Mosh and Thrasher) defeated The New Age Outlaws (Billy Gunn and Road Dogg) by DQ in 14:00 (★★); Ken Shamrock defeated Mankind in 14:36 (★★★); Mark Henry defeated The Rock in 5:06 (★★); Kane vs. The Undertaker ended in a draw in 17:39 (★).

Halloween Havoc '98 ★★
25-10-98, Las Vegas, Nevada **WCW**
Chris Jericho defeated Raven in 7:50 (★★★); Wrath defeated Meng in 4:23 (★); Disco Inferno defeated Juventud Guerrera in 9:39 (★); Alex Wright defeated Fit Finlay in 5:09 (★★); Perry Saturn defeated Lodi in 3:50 (★★); Billy Kidman defeated Disco Inferno in 10:49 (★★); Rick Steiner and Buff Bagwell defeated The Giant and Scott Steiner to win the WCW World Tag Team Title in 8:24 (★★); Rick Steiner defeated Scott Steiner in 5:10 (★★); Scott Hall defeated Kevin Nash via count out in 14:19 (★); Bret Hart defeated Sting in 15:05 (★★); Hollywood Hogan defeated The Warrior in 14:18 (★); Goldberg defeated Diamond Dallas Page in 10:29 (★★★★).

November To Remember '98 ★★
01-11-98, New Orleans, Louisiana **ECW**
The bWo (The Blue Meanie and Super Nova) defeated Danny Doring and Roadkill in 10:54 (★★); Tommy Rogers defeated Tracy Smothers in 7:51 (★★); Spike Dudley defeated Mabel in :05; Lance Storm defeated Jerry Lynn in 16:48 (★★★★); Masato Tanaka and Balls Mahoney defeated The Dudley Boyz (Buh Buh Ray Dudley and D-Von Dudley) to win the ECW World Tag Team Title in 15:01 (★★★); Tommy Dreamer and Jake Roberts defeated Justin Credible and Jack Victory in 12:26 (★); Sabu, Rob Van Dam and Taz defeated The Triple Threat (Shane Douglas, Bam Bam Bigelow and Chris Candido) in 12:57 (★★).

Survivor Series '98 ★★★★
15-11-98, St. Louis, Missouri **WWF**
Mankind defeated Duane Gill in :30 (★★); Al Snow defeated Jeff Jarrett in 3:31 (★★); Steve Austin defeated The Big Boss Man by DQ in 3:20 (★★); Steven Regal vs. X-Pac ended in a double count out in 8:10 (★★); Ken Shamrock defeated Goldust in 5:56 (★★); The Rock defeated The Big Boss Man in :03 (★★); The Undertaker defeated Kane in 7:16 (★★); Mankind defeated Al Snow in 3:55 (★★); The Rock defeated Ken Shamrock in 8:20 (★★); Sable defeated Jacqueline to win the WWF Women's Title in 3:14 (★★); Mankind defeated Steve Austin in 10:27 (★★★); The Rock defeated The Undertaker by DQ in 8:24 (★★); The New Age Outlaws (Billy Gunn and Road Dogg) defeated D-Lo Brown and Mark Henry, and The Headbangers (Mosh and Thrasher) in a Three Way Match in 10:10 (★★); The Rock defeated Mankind to win the vacant WWF World Heavyweight Title in 17:17 (★★★).

World War 3 '98 ★
22-11-98, Auburn Hills, Michigan **WCW**
Wrath defeated Glacier in 8:22 (★★); Stevie Ray defeated Konnan by DQ in 6:55 (★); Ernest Miller and Sonny Onoo defeated Perry Saturn and Kaz Hayashi in 8:04 (★); Billy Kidman defeated Juventud Guerrera to win the WCW Cruiserweight Title in 15:27 (★★★); Rick Steiner vs. Scott Steiner ended in a no contest (★); Chris Jericho defeated Bobby Duncum Jr. in 13:22 (★★); Kevin Nash won the 60-Man World War 3 Match in 23:28 (★★); Diamond Dallas Page defeated Bret Hart in 18:31 (★★).

Capital Carnage ★★
06-12-98, London, England **WWF**
Gangrel defeated Al Snow in 5:51 (★★); The Headbangers (Mosh and Thrasher) defeated The Legion of Doom (Animal and Droz) in 3:21 (★★); Val Venis defeated Goldust in 5:33 (★★); Tiger Ali Singh defeated Edge in 2:51 (★★); Christian and Sable defeated Marc Mero and Jacqueline in 4:49 (★★); Ken Shamrock defeated Steve Blackman in 6:51 (★★); Triple H defeated Jeff Jarrett in 6:55 (★★); The New Age Outlaws (Billy Gunn and Road Dogg) defeated D-Lo Brown and Mark Henry in 12:34 (★★); The Rock defeated X-Pac by DQ in 12:34 (★★★); Steve Austin defeated Kane, Mankind and The Undertaker in a Four Way Match in 16:12 (★★).

Rock Bottom ★★
13-12-98, Vancouver, British Columbia **WWF**
D-Lo Brown and Mark Henry defeated Supply and Demand (The Godfather and Val Venis) in 5:54 (★★); The Headbangers (Mosh and Thrasher) defeated The Oddities (Golga and Kurrgan) in 6:29 (★★); Steve Blackman defeated Owen Hart by count out in 10:26 (★★★); The Brood (Edge, Christian and Gangrel) defeated The J.O.B. Squad (Al Snow, Bob Holly and Too Cold Scorpio) in 9:08 (★★); Goldust defeated Jeff Jarrett by DQ in a Strip Tease Match in 8:06 (★★); The New Age Outlaws (Billy Gunn and Road Dogg) defeated The Corporation

(Ken Shamrock and The Big Boss Man) in 16:10 (★★); Mankind defeated The Rock in 13:35 (★★★); Steve Austin defeated The Undertaker in a Buried Alive Match in 21:33 (★).

Starrcade '98 ★★
27-12-98, Washington, D.C. **WCW**
Billy Kidman defeated Rey Mysterio Jr. and Juventud Guerrera in a Three Way Match in 14:56 (★★★★); Billy Kidman defeated Eddie Guerrero in 10:48 (★★★); Norman Smiley defeated Prince Iaukea in 11:31 (★★); Perry Saturn defeated Ernest Miller in 7:07 (★★); Brian Adams and Scott Norton defeated Fit Finlay and Jerry Flynn in 8:56 (★★); Konnan defeated Chris Jericho in 7:28 (★★); Eric Bischoff defeated Ric Flair in 7:08 (★★); Diamond Dallas Page defeated The Giant in 12:45 (★★); Kevin Nash defeated Goldberg in a No DQ Match to win the WCW World Heavyweight Title in 11:20 (★★).

Guilty As Charged '99 ★★★
10-01-99, Kissimmee, Florida **ECW**
The Hardcore Chair Swingin' Freaks (Balls Mahoney and Axl Rotten) defeated The F.B.I. (Little Guido and Tracy Smothers) and Danny Doring and Roadkill in a Three Way Match in 10:43 (★★); Yoshihiro Tajiri defeated Super Crazy in 11:37 (★★★); Sid Vicious defeated John Kronus in 1:31 (★★★); The Dudley Boyz (Buh Buh Ray Dudley and D-Von Dudley) defeated New Jack and Spike Dudley in 10:01 (★★); Rob Van Dam defeated Lance Storm in 18:50 (★★★); Justin Credible defeated Tommy Dreamer in a Stairway To Hell Match in 18:45 (★★); Taz defeated Shane Douglas to win the ECW World Heavyweight Title in 22:15 (★★★).

Souled Out '99 ★★
17-01-99, Charleston, West Virginia **WCW**
Chris Benoit defeated Mike Enos in 10:34 (★★★); Norman Smiley defeated Chavo Guerrero Jr. in 15:44 (★★★); Fit Finlay defeated Van Hammer in 7:54 (★★); Bam Bam Bigelow defeated Wrath in 9:23 (★★); Lex Luger defeated Konnan in 9:31 (★★); Chris Jericho defeated Perry Saturn in a Loser Must Wear A Dress Match in 11:44 (★★); Billy Kidman defeated Rey Mysterio Jr., Juventud Guerrera and Psychosis in a Four Way Match in 14:25 (★★★); Ric Flair and David Flair defeated Curt Hennig and Barry Windham in 13:56 (★★); Goldberg defeated Scott Hall in a Stun Gun Ladder Match in 17:45 (★★).

Royal Rumble '99 ★★★
24-01-99, Anaheim, Califomia **WWF**
The Big Boss Man defeated Road Dogg in 11:52 (★★); Ken Shamrock defeated Billy Gunn in 14:23 (★★); X-Pac defeated Gangrel in 5:53 (★★); Sable defeated Luna Vachon in a Strap Match in 4:43 (★★); The Rock defeated Mankind in an "I Quit" Match to win the WWF World Heavyweight Title in 21:47 (★★★★); Vince McMahon won the 30-Man Royal Rumble Match in 56:38 (★★★).

St. Valentine's Day Massacre ★★★
14-02-99, Memphis, Tennessee **WWF**
Goldust defeated Bluedust in 3:04 (★★); Bob Holly defeated Al Snow in a Hardcore Match to win the vacant WWF Hardcore Title in 9:58 (★★); The Big Boss Man defeated Mideon in 6:19 (★); Jeff Jarrett and Owen Hart defeated D-Lo Brown and Mark Henry in 9:34 (★★); Val Venis defeated Ken Shamrock to win the WWF Intercontinental Title in 15:53 (★★); Chyna and Kane defeated Triple H and X-Pac in 14:46 (★★★); Mankind vs. The Rock went to a draw in a Last Man Standing Match in 22:00 (★★★); Steve Austin defeated Vince McMahon in a Steel Cage Match in 7:55 (★★★).

SuperBrawl IX ★★
21-02-99, Oakland, Califomia **WCW**
Booker T defeated Disco Inferno in 9:19 (★★★); Chris Jericho defeated Perry Saturn via count out in 11:17 (★★); Billy Kidman defeated Chavo Guerrero Jr. in 8:26 (★★); Curt Hennig and Barry Windham defeated Chris Benoit and Dean Malenko in a Two Out Of Three Falls Match to win the vacant WCW World Tag Team Title in 20:37 (★★); The Outsiders (Kevin Nash and Scott Hall) defeated Konnan and Rey Misterio Jr. in a Hair vs. Mask Match in 11:00 (★★★); Scott Steiner defeated Diamond Dallas Page in 13:54 (★★); Scott Hall defeated Roddy Piper to win the WCW United States Heavyweight Title in 8:21 (★); Goldberg defeated Bam Bam Bigelow in 11:39 (★★); Hollywood Hogan defeated Ric Flair in 12:01 (★★).

Living Dangerously '99 ★★★
21-03-99, Asbury Park, New Jersey **ECW**
Super Crazy defeated Yoshihiro Tajiri in 9:55 (★★★); Balls Mahoney defeated Steve Corino in 3:56 (★★); Little Guido defeated Antifaz del Norte in 5:37 (★★); Rob Van Dam defeated Jerry Lynn in 22:18 (★★★★); New Jack defeated Mustafa in 9:27 (★); Spike Dudley and Sid Vicious defeated The Dudley Boyz (Buh Buh Ray Dudley and D-Von Dudley) in 11:00 (★★); Tommy Dreamer and Shane Douglas defeated The Impact Players (Justin Credible and Lance Storm) in 18:58 (★★); Taz defeated Sabu in an Extreme Death Match to win the FTW World Heavyweight Title in 18:28 (★★★).

Uncensored '99 ★★
14-03-99, Louisville, Kentucky **WCW**
Billy Kidman defeated Mikey Whipwreck in 14:57 (★★★); Stevie Ray defeated Vincent in a Harlem Street Fight in 6:30 (★★); Kevin Nash defeated Rey Misterio Jr. in 6:19 (★★); Jerry Flynn defeated Ernest Miller and Sonny Onoo in a Handicap Match in 7:08 (★★); Hak defeated Bam Bam Bigelow and Raven in a Falls Count Anywhere Three Way Match in 14:29 (★★★); Chris Benoit and Dean Malenko defeated Curt Hennig and Barry Windham in a Lumberjack Match to win the WCW World Tag Team Title in 15:58 (★★); Perry Saturn defeated Chris Jericho in a Dog Collar Match in 11:50 (★★); Booker T defeated Scott Steiner to win the WCW World Television Title in 13:30 (★★); Ric Flair defeated Hollywood Hogan in a Barbed Wire Steel Cage First Blood Match to win the WCW World Heavyweight Title in 14:19 (★★).

WrestleMania XV ★★
28-03-99, Philadelphia, Pennsylvania **WWF**
Hardcore Holly defeated Al Snow and Billy Gunn in a Triple Threat Hardcore Match to win the WWF Hardcore Title in 7:06 (★★); Owen Hart and Jeff Jarrett defeated D-Lo Brown and Test in 3:58 (★★); Butterbean defeated Bart Gunn in a Brawl For All Match in :35 (★); Mankind defeated The Big Show by DQ in 6:50 (★); Road Dogg defeated Goldust, Ken Shamrock and Val Venis in a Four Corners Elimination Match in 9:47 (★★); Kane defeated Triple H by DQ in 11:33 (★★); Sable defeated Tori by 5:06 (★); Shane McMahon defeated X-Pac in 8:41 (★★★); The Undertaker defeated The Big Boss Man in a Hell In A Cell Match in 9:46 (★); Steve Austin defeated The Rock in a No DQ Match to win the WWF World Heavyweight Title in 16:52 (★★★).

Cyberslam '99 ★★★
03-04-99, Philadelphia, Pennsylvania **ECW**
Jerry Lynn defeated Yoshihiro Tajiri in 8:52 (★★★); Chris Chetti and Super Nova defeated Rod Price and Skull Von Krush in 4:22 (★★); Super Crazy defeated Mosco de la Merced in 9:51 (★★); Taka Michinoku defeated Papi Chulo in 6:42 (★★★); Rob Van Dam defeated Too Cold Scorpio in 16:43 (★★★); Taz defeated Chris Candido in a Falls Count Anywhere Match in 11:46 (★★★); Shane Douglas defeated Justin Credible in 14:49 (★★); Mustafa and The Dudley Boyz (Buh Buh Ray Dudley and D-Von Dudley) defeated Axl Rotten, Balls Mahoney and New Jack in a Steel Cage Match in 14:23 (★★).

Spring Stampede '99 ★★★★
11-04-99, Tacoma, Washington **WCW**
Juventud Guerrera defeated Blitzkrieg in 11:11 (★★★★); Bam Bam Bigelow defeated Hak in a Hardcore Match in 11:33 (★★★); Scott Riggs defeated Mikey Whipwreck in 7:03 (★★); Konnan defeated Disco Inferno in 9:17 (★★); Rey Misterio Jr. defeated Billy Kidman in 15:32 (★★★); Chris Benoit and Dean Malenko defeated Raven and Perry Saturn in 14:11 (★★★); Scott Steiner defeated Booker T to win the vacant WCW United States Heavyweight Title in 16:00 (★★); Goldberg defeated Kevin Nash in 7:44 (★★); Diamond Dallas Page defeated Ric Flair, Hollywood Hogan and Sting in a Four Corners Match to win the WCW World Heavyweight Title in 17:27 (★★).

Backlash '99 ★★★
25-04-99, Providence, Rhode Island **WWF**
The Ministry of Darkness (Mideon, Faarooq and Bradshaw) defeated The Brood (Edge, Christian and Gangrel) in 11:38 (★★); Al Snow defeated Hardcore Holly in a Hardcore Match to win the WWF Hardcore Title in 15:27 (★★); The Godfather defeated Goldust in 5:22 (★★); The New Age Outlaws (Billy Gunn and Road Dogg) defeated Jeff Jarrett and Owen Hart in 10:33 (★★★); Mankind defeated The Big Show in a Boiler Room Brawl in 7:40 (★★★); Triple H defeated X-Pac in 19:19

(★★★); The Undertaker defeated Ken Shamrock in 18:50 (★★); Steve Austin defeated The Rock in a No Holds Barred Match in 17:07 (★★★★).

SmackDown Pilot ★★★
29-04-99, New Haven, Connecticut WWF
The Blue Blazer defeated Val Venis in 2:19 (★★); The Big Show defeated Test in :47 (★); D-Lo Brown defeated Droz by DQ in 3:16 (★); Kane and X-Pac defeated The New Age Outlaws (Billy Gunn and Road Dogg) in 7:02 (★★★); Ken Shamrock defeated Bradshaw in a No Holds Barred Street Fight in 4:08 (★★); Mankind defeated The Big Boss Man in 1:36 (★★); Steve Austin and The Rock defeated The Undertaker and Triple H by DQ in 5:28 (★★★).

Slamboree '99 ★★
09-05-99, St. Louis, Missouri WCW
Raven and Perry Saturn defeated Rey Misterio Jr. and Billy Kidman, and Dean Malenko and Chris Benoit in a Three Way Match to win the WCW World Tag Team Title in 17:28 (★★★★); Konnan defeated Stevie Ray in 6:10 (★★); Bam Bam Bigelow defeated Brian Knobbs in a Hardcore Match in 11:29 (★★); Rick Steiner defeated Booker T to win the WCW World Television Title in 11:08 (★★); Gorgeous George defeated Charles Robinson in 10:39 (★★); Scott Steiner defeated Buff Bagwell in 7:11 (★★); Roddy Piper defeated Ric Flair by DQ in 12:10 (★★); Sting vs. Goldberg ended in a no contest in 8:17 (★★); Kevin Nash defeated Diamond Dallas Page to win the WCW World Heavyweight Title in 18:23 (★★).

No Mercy (UK) ★
16-05-99, Manchester, England WWF
Tiger Ali Singh defeated Gillberg in 1:05 (★); The Ministry of Darkness (Viscera, Faarooq and Bradshaw) defeated The Brood (Edge, Christian and Gangrel) in 13:49 (★★); Steve Blackman defeated Droz in 7:43 (★★); Kane defeated Mideon by DQ in 4:34 (★); Nicole Bass defeated Tori in :27 (★); Shane McMahon defeated X-Pac in 8:26 (★★); Billy Gunn defeated Mankind in 12:17 (★★); Steve Austin defeated Triple H and The Undertaker in an Anything Goes Three Way Match in 18:27 (★★).

Hardcore Heaven '99 ★★★
16-05-99, Poughkeepsie, New York ECW
Taz defeated Chris Candido in 1:10 (★★); The Dudley Boyz (Buh Buh Ray Dudley and D-Von Dudley) defeated Balls Mahoney and Spike Dudley in 7:48 (★★); Super Crazy defeated Taka Michinoku in 8:28 (★★); Yoshihiro Tajiri defeated Little Guido in 11:06 (★★★); Lance Storm defeated Tommy Dreamer in 13:40 (★★); Rob Van Dam defeated Jerry Lynn in 26:57 (★★★★); Sid Vicious vs. Justin Credible went to a no contest in 2:01 (★★); Taz defeated Buh Buh Ray Dudley in a Falls Count Anywhere Match in 12:17 (★★).

Over The Edge '99 ★★
23-05-99, Kansas City, Missouri WWF
Kane and X-Pac defeated D-Lo Brown and Mark Henry in 14:45 (★); Al Snow defeated Hardcore Holly in a Hardcore Match in 12:53 (★★); Nicole Bass and Val Venis defeated Debra and Jeff Jarrett in 6:07 (★★); Billy Gunn defeated Road Dogg in 11:14 (★★); The Union (The Big Show, Ken Shamrock, Mankind and Test) defeated The Corporate Ministry (The Big Boss Man, Viscera, Faarooq and Bradshaw) in an Elimination Match in 14:59 (★★); The Rock defeated Triple H by DQ in 11:41 (★★); The Undertaker defeated Steve Austin to win the WWF World Heavyweight Title in 22:58 (★★).

Great American Bash '99 ★
13-06-99, Baltimore, Maryland WCW
Hak defeated Brian Knobbs in a Hardcore Match in 5:41 (★★); Van Hammer defeated Mikey Whipwreck in 8:35 (★★); Buff Bagwell defeated Disco Inferno in 10:33 (★★); The No Limit Soldiers (Konnan and Rey Misterio Jr.) defeated The West Texas Rednecks (Curt Hennig and Bobby Duncum Jr.) in 10:44 (★★); Ernest Miller defeated Horace Hogan in 5:10 (★); Ric Flair defeated Roddy Piper by DQ in 8:16 (★); Rick Steiner defeated Sting in a Falls Count Anywhere Match in 10:35 (★); The Jersey Triad (Diamond Dallas Page and Chris Kanyon) defeated Chris Benoit and Perry Saturn to win the WCW World Tag Team Title in 19:13 (★★); Kevin Nash defeated Randy Savage by DQ in 7:29 (★).

King Of The Ring '99 ★★
27-06-99, Greensboro, North Carolina WWF
X-Pac defeated Hardcore Holly by DQ in 3:02 (★★); Kane defeated The Big Show in 6:36 (★); Billy Gunn defeated Ken Shamrock in 3:37 (★★); Road Dogg defeated Chyna in 13:21 (★★); The Hardy Boyz (Jeff Hardy and Matt Hardy) defeated The Brood (Edge and Christian) in 4:49 (★★); Billy Gunn defeated Kane in 5:25 (★★); X-Pac defeated Road Dogg in 3:08 (★★); The Undertaker defeated The Rock in 19:11 (★★); Billy Gunn defeated X-Pac in 5:33 (★★); Vince McMahon and Shane McMahon defeated Steve Austin in a Handicap Ladder Match in 17:13 (★★).

Bash At The Beach '99 ★
11-07-99, Fort Lauderdale, Florida WCW
Ernest Miller defeated Disco Inferno in 8:07 (★★); Rick Steiner defeated Van Hammer in 3:05 (★★); David Flair defeated Dean Malenko in 3:05 (★); The No Limit Soldiers (Konnan, Rey Misterio Jr., Swoll and B.A.) defeated The West Texas Rednecks (Curt Hennig, Bobby Duncum Jr., Barry Windham and Kendall Windham) in an Elimination Match in 15:35 (★★); Fit Finlay won a Junkyard Invitational Match in 13:51 (★); The Jersey Triad (Diamond Dallas Page, Chris Kanyon and Bam Bam Bigelow) defeated Perry Saturn and Chris Benoit in a Handicap Match in 23:16 (★★★★); Buff Bagwell defeated Roddy Piper in a Boxing Match in 6:36 (★); Randy Savage and Sid Vicious defeated Kevin Nash and Sting in 13:20. As a result, Randy Savage won the WCW World Heavyweight Title (★).

Heat Wave '99 ★★★
18-07-99, Dayton, Ohio ECW
Chris Chetti and Nova defeated Danny Doring and Roadkill in 7:03; (★★) Jazz defeated Jason Knight in 6:33 (★★); Super Crazy defeated Little Guido in 12:31 (★★★); Spike Dudley and Balls Mahoney defeated The Dudley Boyz (Buh Buh Ray Dudley and D-Von Dudley) to win the ECW World Tag Team Title in 15:41 (★★); Taz defeated Yoshihiro Tajiri in 10:06 (★★); Rob Van Dam and Jerry Lynn defeated The Impact Players (Lance Storm and Justin Credible) in 21:07 (★★★).

Fully Loaded '99 ★★★
25-07-99, Buffalo, New York WWF
Jeff Jarrett defeated Edge to win the WWF Intercontinental Title in 13:23 (★★); The Acolytes (Faarooq and Bradshaw) defeated The Hardy Boyz (Jeff Hardy and Matt Hardy) and Michael Hayes in an Acolytes Rules Handicap Match to win the WWF World Tag Team Title in 9:35 (★★★); D-Lo Brown defeated Mideon to win the WWF European Title in 7:12 (★★); The Big Boss Man defeated Al Snow in a Hardcore Match to win the WWF Hardcore Title in 10:13 (★★★); The Big Show defeated Kane in 8:13 (★★); Ken Shamrock defeated Steve Blackman in an Iron Circle Match in 4:19 (★★); Road Dogg and X-Pac defeated Billy Gunn and Chyna in 11:44 (★★); Triple H defeated The Rock in a Strap Match in 19:23 (★★★); Steve Austin defeated The Undertaker in a First Blood Match in 15:58 (★★★).

Road Wild '99 ★★
14-08-99, Sturgis, South Dakota WCW
Rey Misterio Jr., Billy Kidman and Eddie Guerrero defeated Vampiro and Insane Clown Posse (Violent J and Shaggy 2 Dope) in 12:22 (★★★); Harlem Heat (Booker T and Stevie Ray) defeated Chris Kanyon and Bam Bam Bigelow to win the WCW World Tag Team Title in 13:06 (★★); The Revolution (Perry Saturn, Shane Douglas and Dean Malenko) defeated The West Texas Redneck (Curt Hennig, Barry Windham and Bobby Duncum Jr.) in 10:57 (★★); Buff Bagwell defeated Ernest Miller in 7:24 (★★); Chris Benoit defeated Diamond Dallas Page in 12:14 (★★★); Sid Vicious defeated Sting in 10:40 (★★); Goldberg defeated Rick Steiner in 5:39 (★★); Randy Savage defeated Dennis Rodman in 11:30 (★★); Hulk Hogan defeated Kevin Nash in a Retirement Match in 12:18 (★★).

SummerSlam '99 ★★★
22-08-99, Minneapolis, Minnesota WWF
Jeff Jarrett defeated D-Lo Brown to win the WWF Intercontinental Title and WWF European Title in 7:27 (★★★); The Acolytes (Faarooq and Bradshaw) won a Tag Team Turmoil Match in 16:13 (★★); Al Snow defeated The Big Boss Man in a Hardcore Match to win the WWF Hardcore Title in 7:27 (★★★); Ivory defeated Tori in 4:08 (★★); Ken Shamrock defeated Steve Blackman in a Lion's Den Weapons Match in 9:06 (★★); Test defeated Shane

McMahon in a Greenwich Street Fight in 12:04 (★ ★); **The Unholy Alliance (The Big Show** and **The Undertaker)** defeated **Kane** and **X-Pac** to win the WWF World Tag Team Title in 12:01 (★ ★ ★); **The Rock** defeated **Billy Gunn** in a Kiss My Ass Match in 10:12 (★ ★); **Mankind** defeated **Steve Austin** and **Triple H** in a Three Way Match to win the WWF World Heavyweight Title in 16:23 (★ ★ ★).

Fall Brawl '99 ★ ★
12-09-99, Winston-Salem, North Carolina **WCW**
The Filthy Animals (Rey Misterio Jr., Eddie Guerrero and **Billy Kidman)** defeated **Vampiro** and **Insane Clown Posse (Violent J** and **Shaggy 2 Dope)** in 14:14 (★ ★ ★); **Lenny Lane** defeated **Kaz Hayashi** in 12:09 (★ ★ ★); **The First Family (Hugh Morrus** and **Brian Knobbs)** defeated **The Revolution (Dean Malenko** and **Shane Douglas)** in a No DQ Match in 9:26 (★ ★); **Rick Steiner** defeated **Perry Saturn** in 9:23 (★); **Berlyn** defeated **Jim Duggan** in 7:58 (★); **Harlem Heat (Booker T** and **Stevie Ray)** defeated **The West Texas Rednecks (Barry Windham** and **Kendall Windham)** to win the WCW World Tag Team Title in 13:05 (★ ★); **Sid Vicious** defeated **Chris Benoit** to win the WCW United States Heavyweight Title in 11:48 (★ ★); **Goldberg** defeated **Diamond Dallas Page** in 9:04 (★ ★); **Sting** defeated **Hulk Hogan** to win the WCW World Heavyweight Title in 15:21 (★ ★).

Anarchy Rulz '99 ★ ★ ★ ★
19-09-99, Villa Park, Illinois **ECW**
Lance Storm defeated **Jerry Lynn** in 16:38 (★ ★ ★ ★); **Jazz** defeated **The Prodigy** by DQ in :58 (★ ★); **Chris Chetti** and **Nova** vs. **Simon Diamond** and **Tony DeVito** went to a no contest in 3:52 (★); **Yoshihiro Tajiri** defeated **Super Crazy** and **Little Guido** in a Three Way Match in 14:38 (★ ★ ★); **Justin Credible** defeated **Sabu** in 14:06 (★ ★ ★); **Mike Awesome** defeated **Masato Tanaka** and **Taz** in a Three Way Match to win the ECW World Heavyweight Title in 13:48 (★ ★ ★ ★); **Tommy Dreamer** and **Raven** defeated **Rhino** and **Steve Corino** in 3:24 (★ ★); **Rob Van Dam** defeated **Balls Mahoney** in 19:39 (★ ★).

Unforgiven '99 ★ ★ ★
26-09-99, Charlotte, North Carolina **WWF**
Val Venis defeated **Steve Blackman** in 6:33 (★ ★); **D-Lo Brown** defeated **Mark Henry** to win the WWF European Title in 9:11 (★ ★); **Jeff Jarrett** defeated **Chyna** by DQ in 11:52 (★ ★ ★); **The Acolytes (Faarooq** and **Bradshaw)** defeated **The Dudley Boyz (Bubba Ray Dudley** and **D-Von Dudley)** in 7:28 (★ ★); **Ivory** defeated **Luna Vachon** in a Hardcore Match in 3:37 (★ ★); **The New Age Outlaws (Billy Gunn** and **Road Dogg)** defeated **Edge** and **Christian** in 11:09 (★ ★ ★); **Al Snow** defeated **The Big Boss Man** in a Kennel From Hell Match in 11:42 (★); **X-Pac** defeated **Chris Jericho** by DQ in 13:10 (★ ★ ★ ★); **Triple H** defeated **The Big Show, The British Bulldog, Kane, Mankind** and **The Rock** in a Six Pack Challenge to win the vacant WWF World Heavyweight Title in 20:28 (★ ★ ★ ★).

Rebellion '99 ★ ★
02-10-99, Birmingham, England **WWF**
Jeff Jarrett defeated **D-Lo Brown** in 6:12 (★ ★); **The Godfather** defeated **Gangrel** in 6:19 (★ ★); **Val Venis** defeated **Mark Henry** in 3:47 (★ ★); **Ivory** defeated **Jacqueline, Luna Vachon** and **Tori** in a Four Corners Match in 6:51 (★ ★); **Chris Jericho** defeated **Road Dogg** in 11:58 (★ ★); **Chyna** defeated **Jeff Jarrett** by DQ in 4:28 (★ ★); **Kane** defeated **The Big Show** in a No DQ Match in 8:38 (★ ★); **The British Bulldog** defeated **X-Pac** in 5:23 (★ ★); **Edge** and **Christian** defeated **The Acolytes (Faarooq** and **Bradshaw)** and **The Hollys (Bob Holly** and **Crash Holly)** in a Triangle Match in 8:42 (★ ★); **Triple H** defeated **The Rock** in a Steel Cage Match in 20:33 (★ ★ ★ ★).

Heroes Of Wrestling ★
10-10-99, Bay St. Louis, Mississippi
The Samoan Swat Team (Samu and **The Samoan Savage)** defeated **Marty Jannetty** and **Tommy Rogers** in 10:00 (★ ★); **Greg Valentine** defeated **George Steele** in 6:37 (★); **Too Cold Scorpio** defeated **Julio Fantastico** in 9:37 (★ ★); **The Bushwhackers (Luke** and **Butch)** defeated **The Iron Sheik** and **Nikolai Volkoff** in 8:42 (★); **Tully Blanchard** defeated **Stan Lane** in 7:04 (★ ★); **Abdullah the Butcher** vs. **One Man Gang** went to a double count out in 7:34 (★); **Jimmy Snuka** defeated **Bob Orton** in 11:46 (★); **Jim Neidhart** and **King Kong Bundy** defeated **Jake Roberts** and **Yokozuna** in 16:34 (★).

No Mercy '99 ★ ★ ★ ★
17-10-99, Cleveland, Ohio **WWF**
The Godfather defeated **Mideon** in 7:31 (★ ★); **The Fabulous Moolah** defeated **Ivory** to win the WWF Women's Title in 3:01 (★); **The Hollys (Hardcore Holly** and **Crash Holly)** defeated **The New Age Outlaws (Billy Gunn** and **Road Dogg)** by DQ in 10:11 (★ ★); **Chyna** defeated **Jeff Jarrett** in a Good Housekeeping Match to win the WWF Intercontinental Title in 8:37 (★ ★ ★); **The Rock** defeated **The British Bulldog** in 6:20 (★ ★); **The New Brood (Jeff Hardy** and **Matt Hardy)** defeated **Edge** and **Christian** in a Ladder Match in 16:30 (★ ★ ★ ★ ★ ★ ★); **Val Venis** defeated **Mankind** in 9:26 (★ ★); **X-Pac** defeated **Bradshaw, Faarooq** and **Kane** in a Four Corners Elimination Match in 10:08 (★ ★ ★); **Triple H** defeated **Steve Austin** in an Anything Goes Match in 21:53 (★ ★ ★ ★).

Halloween Havoc '99 ★ ★
24-10-99, Paradise, Nevada **WCW**
Disco Inferno defeated **Lash LeRoux** in 7:35 (★ ★); **Harlem Heat (Booker T** and **Stevie Ray)** defeated **The Filthy Animals (Billy Kidman** and **Konnan)** and **The First Family (Hugh Morrus** and **Brian Knobbs)** in a Three Way Street Fight to win the vacant WCW World Tag Team Title in 5:02 (★ ★); **Eddie Guerrero** defeated **Perry Saturn** by DQ in 11:12 (★ ★); **Brad Armstrong** defeated **Berlyn** in 4:23 (★ ★); **Rick Steiner** defeated **Chris Benoit** to win the WCW World Television Title in 12:50 (★ ★); **Lex Luger** defeated **Bret Hart** in 7:46 (★ ★); **Sting** defeated **Hulk Hogan** in :03 (★); **Goldberg** defeated **Sid Vicious** to win the WCW United States Heavyweight Title in 7:11 (★ ★); **Diamond Dallas Page** defeated **Ric Flair** in a Strap Match in 12:49 (★ ★); **Goldberg** defeated **Sting** in 3:08 (★ ★).

November To Remember '99 ★ ★ ★
07-11-99, Buffalo, New York **ECW**
Spike Dudley defeated **Simon Diamond** in 2:59 (★ ★); **Little Guido** defeated **Nova** in 4:20 (★); **Jerry Lynn** defeated **Yoshihiro Tajiri** and **Super Crazy** in a Three Way Match in 10:59 (★ ★ ★); **Da Baldies (Spanish Angel, Tony DeVito, Vito LoGrasso** and **P.N. News)** defeated **New Jack** and **The Hardcore Chair Swingin' Freaks (Balls Mahoney** and **Axl Rotten)** in a Handicap Match in 8:21 (★ ★); **Sabu** defeated **Chris Candido** in 17:42 (★ ★ ★); **Mike Awesome** defeated **Masato Tanaka** in 12:26 (★ ★ ★ ★); **Rob Van Dam** defeated **Taz** in 14:34 (★ ★); **Rhino** and **The Impact Players (Justin Credible** and **Lance Storm)** defeated **Raven, Tommy Dreamer** and **The Sandman** in 9:19 (★ ★).

Survivor Series '99 ★ ★
14-11-99, Detroit, Michigan **WWF**
D-Lo Brown, The Godfather and **The Headbangers (Mosh** and **Thrasher)** defeated **The Acolytes (Faarooq** and **Bradshaw)** and **The Dudley Boyz (Bubba Ray Dudley** and **D-Von Dudley)** in an Elimination Match in 9:36 (★ ★); **Kurt Angle** defeated **Shawn Stasiak** in 5:57 (★ ★); **Gangrel, Mark Henry, Steve Blackman** and **Val Venis** defeated **The British Bulldog** and **The Mean Street Posse (Joey Abs, Pete Gas** and **Rodney)** in an Elimination Match in 9:08 (★ ★); **Debra, The Fabulous Moolah, Mae Young** and **Tori** defeated **Ivory, Jacqueline, Luna** and **Terri Runnels** in 1:50 (★); **Kane** defeated **X-Pac** by DQ in 4:15 (★ ★); **The Big Show** defeated **The Big Boss Man, Mideon, Prince Albert** and **Viscera** in a Handicap Elimination Match in 1:26 (★); **Chyna** defeated **Chris Jericho** in 13:34 (★ ★ ★); **The Hollys (Hardcore Holly** and **Crash Holly)** and **Too Cool (Grandmaster Sexay** and **Scotty 2 Hotty)** defeated **Edge** and **Christian** and **The Hardy Boyz (Jeff Hardy** and **Matt Hardy)** in an Elimination Match in 14:27 (★ ★ ★); **The New Age Outlaws (Billy Gunn** and **Road Dogg)** defeated **Al Snow** and **Mankind** in 13:59 (★ ★); **The Big Show** defeated **Triple H** and **The Rock** in a Three Way Match to win the WWF World Heavyweight Title in 16:13 (★ ★).

Mayhem '99 ★ ★
21-11-99, Toronto, Ontario **WCW**
Chris Benoit defeated **Jeff Jarrett** in 9:27 (★ ★ ★ ★); **Evan Karagias** defeated **Disco Inferno** to win the WCW Cruiserweight Title in 8:28 (★); **Norman Smiley** defeated **Brian Knobbs** in a Hardcore Match to win the vacant WCW Hardcore Title in 7:27 (★ ★); **The Revolution (Perry Saturn, Dean Malenko** and **Asya)** defeated **The Filthy Animals (Eddie Guerrero, Billy Kidman** and **Torrie Wilson)** in 10:55 (★ ★); **Buff Bagwell** defeated **Curt Hennig** in a Retirement Match in 7:47 (★ ★); **Bret Hart** defeated **Sting** in 9:27 (★ ★); **Vampiro** defeated **Berlyn** in a Dog Collar Match in 4:57 (★); **Meng** defeated **Lex Luger** in 5:23 (★); **Scott**

Hall defeated **Booker T** in 6:04 (★★); **David Flair** vs. **Kimberly Page** went to a no contest in 4:55 (★); **Goldberg** defeated **Sid Vicious** in an "I Quit" Match in 5:30 (★★); **Bret Hart** defeated **Chris Benoit** to win the vacant WCW World Heavyweight Title in 17:44 (★★★).

Armageddon '99 ★★
12-12-99, Sunrise, Florida **WWF**

The Acolytes (Faarooq and Bradshaw) won a Battle Royal in 10:57 (★★); **Kurt Angle** defeated **Steve Blackman** in 6:42 (★★); **Miss Kitty** defeated **B.B.**, **Ivory** and **Jacqueline** in an Evening Gown Pool Match to win the WWF Women's Title in 2:53 (★★); **The Hollys** (Hardcore Holly and Crash Holly) defeated **Rikishi** and **Viscera** in 4:23 (★★); **Val Venis** defeated **The British Bulldog** and **D-Lo Brown** in a Three Way Match to win the WWF European Title in 9:15 (★★); **Kane** defeated **X-Pac** in a Steel Cage Match in 9:00 (★★★); **Chris Jericho** defeated **Chyna** to win the WWF Intercontinental Title in 10:19 (★★★); **The Rock 'n' Sock Connection** (Mankind and The Rock) defeated **The New Age Outlaws** (Billy Gunn and Road Dogg) by DQ in 16:00 (★★★); **The Big Show** defeated **The Big Boss Man** in 3:00 (★★); **Triple H** defeated **Vince McMahon** in a No Holds Barred Match in 29:45 (★★).

Starrcade '99 ★★
19-12-99, Washington, D.C. **WCW**

The Mamalukes (Big Vito and Johnny the Bull) defeated **Disco Inferno** and **Lash LeRoux** in 9:40 (★★); **Madusa** defeated **Evan Karagias** to win the WCW Cruiserweight Title in 3:32 (★★); **Norman Smiley** defeated **Meng** in a Hardcore Match in 4:29 (★★); **The Revolution** (Shane Douglas, Dean Malenko, Perry Saturn and Asya) defeated **Jim Duggan** and **The Varsity Club** (Kevin Sullivan, Mike Rotunda and Rick Steiner) in 4:53 (★); **Vampiro** defeated **Steve Williams** by DQ in 5:02 (★★); **Vampiro** defeated **Oklahoma** in 2:52 (★); **Creative Control** (Gerald and Patrick) and **Curt Hennig** defeated **Harlem Heat** (Booker T and Stevie Ray) and **Midnight** in 7:52 (★★); **Jeff Jarrett** defeated **Dustin Rhodes** in a Bunkhouse Brawl in 11:18 (★★); **Diamond Dallas Page** defeated **David Flair** in a Crowbar On A Pole Match in 3:53 (★★); **Sting** defeated **Lex Luger** by DQ in 5:31 (★★); **Kevin Nash** defeated **Sid Vicious** in a Powerbomb Match in 6:58 (★); **Chris Benoit** defeated **Jeff Jarrett** in a Ladder Match in 10:15 (★★★); **Bret Hart** defeated **Goldberg** in a No DQ Match in 12:07 (★★★).

Guilty As Charged '00 ★★★
09-01-00, Birmingham, Alabama **ECW**

C.W. Anderson defeated **Mikey Whipwreck** in 3:42 (★★); **Danny Doring**, **Roadkill** and **Simon Diamond** defeated **Nova**, **Kid Kash** and **Jazz** in 9:58 (★★); **Yoshihiro Tajiri** and **Super Crazy** defeated **Little Guido** and **Jerry Lynn** in 12:48 (★★★); **Angel** defeated **New Jack** in 8:48 (★★); **Rob Van Dam** defeated **Sabu** in 14:37 (★★★); **The Impact Players** (Lance Storm and Justin Credible) defeated **Tommy Dreamer** and **Raven** to win the ECW World Tag Team Title in 9:23 (★★★); **Mike Awesome** defeated **Spike Dudley** in 14:10 (★★★).

Souled Out '00 ★★
16-01-00, Cincinnati, Ohio **WCW**

Billy Kidman defeated **Dean Malenko** in a Catch-as-Catch Can Match in 2:36 (★★); **Vampiro** defeated **David Flair** and **Crowbar** in a Three Way Match in 10:32 (★★); **Big Vito** and **Johnny the Bull** defeated **The Harris Brothers** (Ron Harris and Don Harris) in 9:33 (★★); **Oklahoma** defeated **Madusa** to win the WCW Cruiserweight Title in 2:56 (★); **Brian Knobbs** defeated **Fit Finlay**, **Norman Smiley** and **Meng** in a Four Way Hardcore Match in 6:11 (★★); **Billy Kidman** defeated **Perry Saturn** in a Bunkhouse Brawl in 10:05 (★★); **Booker T** defeated **Stevie Ray** by DQ in 6:30 (★★); **Tank Abbott** defeated **Jerry Flynn** in 1:39 (★); **Buff Bagwell** defeated **Diamond Dallas Page** in a Last Man Standing Match in 11:19 (★★); **The Wall** defeated **Billy Kidman** in a Caged Heat Match in 5:03 (★★); **Kevin Nash** defeated **Terry Funk** in a Hardcore Match in 7:59 (★★); **Chris Benoit** defeated **Sid Vicious** to win the vacant WCW World Heavyweight Title in 14:53 (★★★).

Royal Rumble '00 ★★★★★
23-01-00, New York City, New York **WWF**

Tazz defeated **Kurt Angle** in 3:16 (★★★); **The Hardy Boyz** (Jeff Hardy and Matt Hardy) defeated **The Dudley Boyz** in a Tables Match in 10:17 (★★★★); **Chris Jericho** defeated **Chyna** and **Hardcore Holly** in a Three Way Match to become the undisputed

WWF Intercontinental Champion in 7:30 (★★); **The New Age Outlaws** (Billy Gunn and Road Dogg) defeated **The Acolytes** (Faarooq and Bradshaw) in 2:35 (★★); **Triple H** defeated **Cactus Jack** in a Street Fight in 26:55 (★★★★★); **The Rock** won the 30-Man Royal Rumble Match in 51:48 (★★★).

Millennium Tour ★★
12-02-00, Oberhausen, Germany **WCW**

Booker T defeated **Stevie Ray** in 7:27 (★★); **Jim Duggan** defeated **The Wall** in 8:07 (★); **The Harris Brothers** (Ron Harris and Don Harris) defeated **The Mamalukes** (Big Vito and Johnny the Bull) to win the WCW World Tag Team Title in 10:40 (★★★); **Vampiro** defeated **David Flair** in 8:59 (★★); **Norman Smiley** defeated **Dustin Rhodes** in 8:58 (★); **Terry Funk** and **Norman Smiley** defeated **Dustin Rhodes** and **Brian Knobbs** in a Hardcore Match in 9:29 (★★); **Scott Hall** defeated **Fit Finlay** in 14:44 (★★★); **Berlyn** defeated **Tom Gerhardt** in 4:02 (★); **Sid Vicious** defeated **Jeff Jarrett** in 10:15 (★★★).

SuperBrawl X ★★
20-02-00, Daly City, California **WCW**

TAFKA Prince Iaukea defeated **Lash LeRoux** to win the vacant WCW Cruiserweight Title in 5:47 (★); **Brian Knobbs** defeated **Bam Bam Bigelow** in a Hardcore Match to win the WCW Hardcore Title in 4:44 (★★); **3 Count** (Evan Karagias, Shannon Moore and Shane Helms) defeated **Norman Smiley** in a Handicap Match in 4:06 (★★); **The Wall** defeated **The Demon** in 3:37 (★); **Tank Abbott** defeated **Big Al** in a Leather Jacket On A Pole Match in 4:34 (★); **Big T** defeated **Booker** in 5:23 (★); **Billy Kidman** defeated **Vampiro** in 7:20 (★★); **The Mamalukes** (Big Vito and Johnny the Bull) defeated **David Flair** and **Crowbar** in a Sicilian Stretcher Match in 11:22 (★★); **Ric Flair** and **Terry Funk** in a Texas Death Match in 15:40 (★★★); **Hulk Hogan** defeated **Lex Luger** in 8:10 (★★); **Sid Vicious** defeated **Scott Hall** and **Jeff Jarrett** in a Three Way Match in 7:40 (★★).

No Way Out '00 ★★★★
27-02-00, Hartford, Connecticut **WWF**

Kurt Angle defeated **Chris Jericho** to win the WWF Intercontinental Title in 8:02 (★★★); **The Dudley Boyz** (Bubba Ray Dudley and D-Von Dudley) defeated **The New Age Outlaws** (Billy Gunn and Road Dogg) to win the WWF World Tag Team Title in 5:16 (★★); **Mark Henry** defeated **Viscera** in 3:48 (★★); **Edge** and **Christian** defeated **The Hardy Boyz** (Matt Hardy and Jeff Hardy) in 16:55 (★★★★); **Tazz** defeated **The Big Boss Man** by DQ in :47 (★★); **X-Pac** defeated **Kane** in a No Holds Barred Match in 7:46 (★★★); **Too Cool** (Grandmaster Sexay, Scotty 2 Hotty and Rikishi) defeated **The Radicalz** (Chris Benoit, Dean Malenko and Perry Saturn) in 12:38 (★★★★); **The Big Show** defeated **The Rock** in 8:55 (★★); **Triple H** defeated **Cactus Jack** in a Hell In A Cell Match in 24:00 (★★★★).

Living Dangerously '00 ★★
12-03-00, Danbury, Connecticut **ECW**

Dusty Rhodes defeated **Steve Corino** in a Texas Bullrope Match in 10:13 (★★); **The New Dangerous Alliance** (C.W. Anderson and Bill Wiles) defeated **Danny Doring** and **Roadkill** in 7:23 (★★); **Mike Awesome** defeated **Kid Kash** in 4:44 (★★★); **Nova** and **Chris Chetti** defeated **Jado** and **Gedo** in 7:33 (★★); **Rhino** defeated **The Sandman** via forfeit; **Super Crazy** defeated **Little Guido** in 7:47 (★★★); **Balls Mahoney** defeated **Kintaro Kanemura** in 1:58 (★★); **New Jack** vs. **Vic Grimes** ended in a no contest (★); **The Impact Players** (Lance Storm and Justin Credible) defeated **Raven** and **Mike Awesome**, and **Tommy Dreamer** and **Masato Tanaka** in a Three Way Match to win the ECW World Tag Team Title in 9:06 (★★); **Super Crazy** defeated **Rhino** to win the vacant ECW World Television Title in 7:56 (★★).

Uncensored '00 ★★
19-03-00, Miami, Florida **WCW**

The Artist defeated **Psychosis** in 7:22 (★★); **Norman Smiley** and **The Demon** defeated **Lane** and **Rave** in 3:41 (★); **Bam Bam Bigelow** defeated **The Wall** by DQ in 3:26 (★★); **Brian Knobbs** defeated **3 Count** (Evan Karagias, Shannon Moore and Shane Helms) in a Handicap Elimination Match to win the WCW Hardcore Title in 6:51 (★★); **Billy Kidman** and **Booker T** defeated **Harlem Heat 2000** (Big T and Stevie Ray) in 6:59 (★★); **Vampiro** defeated **Fit Finlay** in a Falls Count Anywhere Match in 8:38 (★★); **The Harris Brothers** (Ron Harris and Don Harris) defeated **The Mamalukes** (Big Vito and Johnny the Bull) to win the WCW World Tag Team Title in 8:45 (★★); **Dustin Rhodes** defeated **Terry Funk** in a Bullrope Match in 9:01 (★★);

Sting defeated **Lex Luger** in a Lumberjack Match in 7:01 (★★); **Sid Vicious** defeated **Jeff Jarrett** in 7:36 (★★); **Hulk Hogan** defeated **Ric Flair** in a Yappapi Indian Strap Match in 14:28 (★★).

WrestleMania XVI ★★★
02-04-00, Anaheim, California **WWF**
The Big Boss Man and **Bull Buchanan** defeated **The Godfather** and **D-Lo Brown** in 9:08 (★★); **Hardcore Holly** won a Hardcore Battle Royal to win the WWF Hardcore Title in 15:00 (★★); **T&A** (Test and Albert) defeated **Head Cheese** (Al Snow and Steve Blackman) in 7:04 (★★); **Edge** and **Christian** defeated **The Dudley Boyz** (Bubba Ray Dudley and D-Von Dudley) and **The Hardy Boyz** (Jeff Hardy and Matt Hardy) in a Triangle Ladder Match to win the WWF World Tag Team Title in 23:30 (★★★★★); **Terri Runnels** defeated **The Kat** in a Catfight in 2:24 (★); **Chyna** and **Too Cool** (Grandmaster Sexay and Scotty 2 Hotty) defeated **The Radicalz** (Perry Saturn, Dean Malenko and Eddie Guerrero) in 9:38 (★★★); **Chris Benoit** defeated **Chris Jericho** and **Kurt Angle** to win the WWF Intercontinental Title in a Three Way Match, **Chris Jericho** defeated **Chris Benoit** and **Kurt Angle** to win the WWF European Title in a Three Way Match in 13:42 (★★★); **Kane** and **Rikishi** defeated **X-Pac** and **Road Dogg** 4:16 (★★); **Triple H** defeated **The Rock, Mick Foley** and **The Big Show** in a Fatal Four Way Elimination Match in 38:28 (★★★).

Spring Stampede '00 ★★
16-04-00, Chicago, Illinois **WCW**
Ric Flair and **Lex Luger** defeated **The Harris Brothers** (Ron Harris and Don Harris) and **The Mamalukes** (Big Vito and Johnny the Bull) in a Three Way Match in 6:11 (★); **Mancow** defeated **Jimmy Hart** in 2:48 (★); **Scott Steiner** defeated **The Wall** by DQ in 3:53 (★★); **Mike Awesome** defeated **Ernest Miller** in 4:00 (★★); **Shane Douglas** and **Buff Bagwell** defeated **Harlem Heat 2000** (Big T and Stevie Ray) in 2:41 (★); **Sting** defeated **Booker T** in 6:34 (★★); **Vampiro** defeated **Billy Kidman** in 8:28 (★★); **Terry Funk** defeated **Norman Smiley** in a Hardcore Match to win the vacant WCW Hardcore Title in 8:02 (★★); **Scott Steiner** defeated **Mike Awesome** in 3:14 (★); **Sting** defeated **Vampiro** in 5:59 (★★); **Chris Candido** defeated **The Artist, Juventud Guerrera, Shannon Moore, Lash LeRoux** and **Crowbar** in a Six Way Match to win the vacant WCW Cruiserweight Title in 5:12 (★★); **Shane Douglas** and **Buff Bagwell** defeated **Ric Flair** and **Lex Luger** to win the vacant WCW World Tag Team Title in 8:29 (★★); **Scott Steiner** defeated **Sting** to win the vacant WCW United States Heavyweight Title in 5:33 (★★); **Jeff Jarrett** defeated **Diamond Dallas Page** to win the vacant WCW World Heavyweight Title in 15:02 (★★★).

Backlash '00 ★★★★★
30-04-00, Washington, D.C. **WWF**
Edge and **Christian** defeated **X-Pac** and **Road Dogg** in 8:37 (★★); **Dean Malenko** defeated **Scotty 2 Hotty** in 11:47 (★★★); **The Big Boss Man** and **Bull Buchanan** defeated **The APA** (Faarooq and Bradshaw) in 8:37 (★★); **Crash Holly** defeated **Matt Hardy, Jeff Hardy, Hardcore Holly, Perry Saturn** and **Tazz** in a Six Pack Hardcore Match in 12:18 (★★★); **The Big Show** defeated **Kurt Angle** in 2:35 (★★★); **T&A** (Test and Albert) defeated **The Dudley Boyz** (Bubba Ray Dudley and D-Von Dudley) in 11:06 (★★); **Eddie Guerrero** defeated **Essa Rios** in 8:38 (★★★); **Chris Benoit** defeated **Chris Jericho** in 15:03 (★★★★); **The Rock** defeated **Triple H** to win the WWF World Heavyweight Title in 19:22 (★★★★★).

Insurrextion '00 ★★★
06-05-00, London, England **WWF**
Too Cool (Grandmaster Sexay and Scotty 2 Hotty) defeated **The Radicalz** (Dean Malenko and Perry Saturn) in 7:00 (★★); **Kane** defeated **Bull Buchanan** in 3:31 (★★); **Road Dogg** defeated **Bradshaw** in 5:58 (★★); **The Kat** defeated **Terri Runnels** in an Arm Wrestling Match in :34 (★); **Rikishi** and **The Big Show** defeated **The Dudley Boyz** (Bubba Ray Dudley and D-Von Dudley) in 7:10 (★★); **Kurt Angle** defeated **Chris Benoit** in 6:04 (★★★); **The British Bulldog** defeated **Crash Holly** in a Hardcore Match to win the WWF Hardcore Title in 3:37 (★★); **The Hardy Boyz** (Jeff Hardy and Matt Hardy) defeated **Edge** and **Christian** by DQ in 12:53 (★★★); **Eddie Guerrero** defeated **Chris Jericho** in 12:56 (★★★); **The Rock** defeated **Triple H** and **Shane McMahon** in a Three Way Match in 15:37 (★★★).

Slamboree '00 ★★★
07-05-00, Kansas City, Missouri **WCW**
Chris Candido defeated **The Artist** in 7:59 (★★); **Terry Funk** defeated **Norman Smiley** and **Ralphus** in a Three Way Hardcore Match in 10:03 (★★★); **Shawn Stasiak** defeated **Curt Hennig** in 7:54 (★★); **Scott Steiner** defeated **Captain Hugh G. Rection** in 9:24 (★); **Mike Awesome** vs. **Chris Kanyon** ended in a no contest in 12:11 (★★★); **Lex Luger** defeated **Buff Bagwell** in 9:30 (★★); **Shane Douglas** defeated **Ric Flair** in 8:46 (★★★); **Sting** defeated **Vampiro** in 6:49 (★★); **Hulk Hogan** defeated **Billy Kidman** in 13:31 (★★); **Jeff Jarrett** defeated **David Arquette** and **Diamond Dallas Page** in a Three Way Ready To Rumble Cage Match to win the WCW World Heavyweight Title in 15:29 (★★★).

Hardcore Heaven '00 ★★★
14-05-00, Milwaukee, Wisconsin **ECW**
Masato Tanaka defeated **Balls Mahoney** in 9:15 (★★★); **Little Guido** defeated **Mikey Whipwreck** and **Simon Diamond** in a Three Way Match in 7:15 (★★); **Kid Kash** defeated **C.W. Anderson** in 5:57 (★★); **Nova** and **Chris Chetti** defeated **Da Baldies** (Angel and Tony DeVito) and **Danny Doring** and **Roadkill** in a Three Way Match in 6:32 (★★); **New Jack** defeated **Angel** in 9:00 (★★); **Yoshihiro Tajiri** defeated **Steve Corino** in 10:22 (★★); **Rhino** defeated **The Sandman** in 6:15 (★★); **Jerry Lynn** defeated **Rob Van Dam** in 19:54 (★★★★); **Justin Credible** defeated **Lance Storm** in 12:28 (★★★).

Judgment Day '00 ★★★★★
21-05-00, Louisville, Kentucky **WWF**
Too Cool (Grandmaster Sexay, Scotty 2 Hotty and Rikishi) defeated **Team ECK** (Edge, Christian and Kurt Angle) in 9:47 (★★★★); **Eddie Guerrero** defeated **Dean Malenko** and **Perry Saturn** in a Three Way Match in 7:56 (★★★); **Shane McMahon** defeated **The Big Show** in a Falls Count Anywhere Match in 7:11 (★★); **Chris Benoit** defeated **Chris Jericho** in a Submission Match in 13:22 (★★★★); **Road Dogg** and **X-Pac** defeated **The Dudley Boyz** (Bubba Ray Dudley and D-Von Dudley) in a Tables Match in 10:55 (★★); **Triple H** defeated **The Rock** 6-5 in an Iron Man Match in 60:00 (★★★★).

Great American Bash '00 ★★
11-06-00, Baltimore, Maryland **WCW**
Lieutenant Loco defeated **Disqo** in 4:57 (★★); **KroniK** (Brian Adams and Bryan Clark) defeated **The Mamalukes** (Big Vito and Johnny the Bull) in 9:20 (★★★); **Mike Awesome** defeated **Diamond Dallas Page** in an Ambulance Match in 9:41 (★★); **GI Bro** defeated **Shawn Stasiak** in a Boot Camp Match in 13:58 (★★); **Shane Douglas** defeated **The Wall** in a Tables Match in 8:12 (★★); **Scott Steiner** defeated **Rick Steiner** and **Tank Abbott** in a Handicap Asylum Match in 3:46 (★); **Hollywood Hogan** defeated **Billy Kidman** in 11:39 (★★); **Ric Flair** defeated **David Flair** in 10:16 (★★★); **Vampiro** defeated **Sting** in a Human Torch Match in 7:23 (★); **Jeff Jarrett** defeated **Kevin Nash** in 17:22 (★★).

King Of The Ring '00 ★★
25-06-00, Boston, Massachusetts **WWF**
Rikishi defeated **Chris Benoit** by DQ in 3:25 (★★); **Val Venis** defeated **Eddie Guerrero** in 8:04 (★★); **Crash Holly** defeated **Bull Buchanan** in 4:07 (★★); **Kurt Angle** defeated **Chris Jericho** in 9:50 (★★★); **Edge** and **Christian** defeated **Too Cool** (Grandmaster Sexay and Scotty 2 Hotty), **The Hardy Boyz** (Jeff Hardy and Matt Hardy) and **T&A** (Test and Albert) in a Fatal Four Way Elimination Match to win the WWF World Tag Team Title in 14:11 (★★★); **Rikishi** defeated **Val Venis** in 3:15 (★★); **Kurt Angle** defeated **Crash Holly** in 3:58 (★★); **Pat Patterson** vs. **Gerald Brisco** went to a no contest in a Hardcore Evening Gown Match in 3:07 (★); **Road Dogg, X-Pac** and **Tori** defeated **The Dudley Boyz** (Bubba Ray Dudley and D-Von Dudley) in a Handicap Tables Dumpster Match in 9:45 (★★); **Kurt Angle** defeated **Rikishi** in 5:56 (★★); **The Rock** and **The Brothers of Destruction** (Kane and The Undertaker) defeated **Vince McMahon, Shane McMahon** and **Triple H**. As a result The Rock won the WWF World Heavyweight Title in 17:54 (★★).

Bash At The Beach '00 ★★
09-07-00, Daytona Beach, Florida **WCW**
Lieutenant Loco defeated **Juventud Guerrera** in 12:07 (★★); **Big Vito** defeated **Norman Smiley** and **Ralphus** in a Three Way Hardcore Match in 5:56 (★★); **Daffney** defeated **Ms. Hancock** in a Wedding Gown Match in 4:14 (★); **KroniK** (Brian Adams

and **Bryan Clark**) defeated **The Perfect Event** (**Shawn Stasiak** and **Chuck Palumbo**) to win the WCW World Tag Team Title in 13:34 (★); **Chris Kanyon** defeated **Booker T** in 10:04 (★★★); **Mike Awesome** defeated **Scott Steiner** by DQ in 9:09 (★★); **Vampiro** defeated **The Demon** in a Graveyard Match in 8:07 (★); **Shane Douglas** defeated **Buff Bagwell** in 7:52 (★★); **Hollywood Hogan** defeated **Jeff Jarrett** to win the WCW World Heavyweight Title in 1:19 (★); **Goldberg** defeated **Kevin Nash** in 5:27 (★); **Booker T** defeated **Jeff Jarrett** to win the WCW World Heavyweight Title in 13:41 (★★★).

Heatwave '00 ★★★
16-07-00, Los Angeles, California **ECW**
Sal E. Graziano defeated **Balls Mahoney** in 2:30 (★); **Kid Kash**, **Danny Doring** and **Roadkill** defeated **Simon Diamond**, **C.W. Anderson** and **Johnny Swinger** in 11:01 (★★★); **Jerry Lynn** defeated **Steve Corino** in 15:23 (★★★); **Chris Chetti** and **Nova** defeated **Da Baldies** (**Tony DeVito** and **Angel**) in 5:00 (★); **Yoshihiro Tajiri** defeated **Mikey Whipwreck**, **Little Guido** and **Psicosis** in a Four Way Dance in 9:12 (★★★); **Rhino** defeated **The Sandman** in 8:38 (★★); **Rob Van Dam** defeated **Scotty Anton** in 9:42 (★★); **Justin Credible** defeated **Tommy Dreamer** in a Stairway To Hell Match in 12:20 (★★).

Fully Loaded '00 ★★★★
23-07-00, Dallas, Texas **WWF**
The Hardy Boyz (**Jeff Hardy** and **Matt Hardy**) and **Lita** defeated **T&A** (**Test** and **Albert**) and **Trish Stratus** in 13:12 (★★★); **Tazz** defeated **Al Snow** in 5:20 (★); **Perry Saturn** defeated **Eddie Guerrero** to win the WWF European Title in 8:10 (★); **The APA** (**Faarooq** and **Bradshaw**) defeated **Edge** and **Christian** by DQ in 5:29 (★★); **Val Venis** defeated **Rikishi** in a Steel Cage Match in 14:10 (★★★); **The Undertaker** defeated **Kurt Angle** in 7:34 (★); **Triple H** defeated **Chris Jericho** in a Last Man Standing Match in 23:11 (★★★★); **The Rock** defeated **Chris Benoit** in 22:09 (★★★★).

Superstars Of Wrestling: Rodman Down Under ★
30-07-00, Sydney, Australia **iGW**
The Road Warriors (**Hawk** and **Animal**) defeated **Public Enemy** (**Rocco Rock** and **Johnny Grunge**) in a Tables Match to win the i-Generation Tag Team Title in 8:59 (★); **The Barbarian** defeated **Brute Force** in a Hardcore Match in 11:13 (★); **Sweet Destiny** defeated **Brandi Wine** in 10:27 (★★); **One Man Gang** defeated **Tatanka** to win the i-Generation Australasian Title in 16:12 (★★); **Curt Hennig** defeated **Dennis Rodman** by DQ in an Australian Outback Match in 8:46 (★★).

New Blood Rising ★★
13-08-00, Vancouver, British Columbia **WCW**
3 Count (**Evan Karagias**, **Shannon Moore** and **Shane Helms**) defeated **The Jung Dragons** (**Kaz Hayashi**, **Jamie-San** and **Yun Yang**) in a Gold Record Ladder Match in 11:32 (★★★); **Ernest Miller** defeated **The Great Muta** in 6:47 (★★); **Buff Bagwell** defeated **Chris Kanyon** in a Judy Bagwell On A Forklift Match in 6:45 (★); **KroniK** (**Brian Adams** and **Bryan Clark**) defeated **The Perfect Event** (**Shawn Stasiak** and **Chuck Palumbo**), **Sean O'Haire** and **Mark Jindrak**, and **The Misfits In Action** (**General Rection** and **Corporal Cajun**) in a Four Corners Match in 12:22 (★★); **Billy Kidman** defeated **Shane Douglas** in a Strap Match in 8:22 (★★); **Major Gunns** defeated **Ms. Hancock** in a Mud Rip Off The Clothes Match in 6:43 (★); **Sting** defeated **The Demon** in :52 (★); **Lance Storm** defeated **Mike Awesome** in a Canadian Rules Match in 11:28 (★); **The Dark Carnival** (**Vampiro** and **The Great Muta**) defeated **KroniK** (**Brian Adams** and **Bryan Clark**) to win the WCW World Tag Team Title in 9:06 (★★); **Kevin Nash** defeated **Goldberg** and **Scott Steiner** in a Three Way Match in 10:48 (★★); **Booker T** defeated **Jeff Jarrett** in 14:54 (★★).

SummerSlam '00 ★★★★
27-08-00, Raleigh, North Carolina **WWF**
Right To Censor (**Bull Buchanan**, **The Goodfather** and **Steven Richards**) defeated **Too Cool** (**Grandmaster Sexay**, **Scotty 2 Hotty** and **Rikishi**) in 4:57 (★★); **X-Pac** defeated **Road Dogg** in 4:31 (★★); **Eddie Guerrero** and **Chyna** defeated **Val Venis** and **Trish Stratus** in 7:04. As a result Chyna won the WWF Intercontinental Title (★★); **Jerry Lawler** defeated **Tazz** in 4:21 (★★); **Steve Blackman** defeated **Shane McMahon** in a Hardcore Match to win the WWF Hardcore Title in 10:17 (★★★); **Chris Benoit** defeated **Chris Jericho** in a Two Out Of Three Falls Match in 13:01 (★★★★); **Edge** and **Christian** defeated **The Dudley Boyz** (**Bubba Ray Dudley** and **D-Von Dudley**) and **The**

Hardy Boyz (**Jeff Hardy** and **Matt Hardy**) in a Tables, Ladders and Chairs Match in 18:38 (★★★★★); **The Kat** defeated **Terri** in a Stinkface Match in 3:07 (★); **Kane** vs. **The Undertaker** ended in a no contest in a No DQ Match in 7:33 (★★); **The Rock** defeated **Triple H** and **Kurt Angle** in a Three Way Match in 20:11 (★★★★).

Fall Brawl '00 ★★★
17-09-00, Buffalo, New York **WCW**
Elix Skipper defeated **Kwee Wee** in 11:03 (★★); **The Misfits In Action** (**Corporal Cajun**, **Lt. Loco** and **Sgt. AWOL**) defeated **3 Count** (**Shannon Moore**, **Evan Karagias** and **Shane Helms**) in 10:25 (★★); **The Harris Brothers** (**Ron Harris** and **Don Harris**) defeated **KroniK** (**Brian Adams** and **Bryan Clark**) in a First Blood Chain Match in 6:37 (★); **Lance Storm** defeated **Gen. Rection** in 6:46 (★); **The Filthy Animals** (**Disqo**, **Rey Misterio Jr.**, **Juventud Guerrera**, **Konnan** and **Tygress**), **Big Vito** and **Paul Orndorff** vs. **The Natural Born Thrillers** (**Mark Jindrak**, **Sean O'Haire**, **Mike Sanders**, **Chuck Palumbo**, **Shawn Stasiak**, **Reno** and **Johnny the Bull**) went to a no contest in an Elimination Match in 16:34 (★★★); **Shane Douglas** and **Torrie Wilson** defeated **Billy Kidman** and **Madusa** in a Scaffold Match in 5:01 (★); **Sting** defeated **The Great Muta** and **Vampiro** in a Three Way Match in 5:12 (★); **Mike Awesome** defeated **Jeff Jarrett** in a Bunkhouse Brawl in 9:04 (★); **Scott Steiner** defeated **Goldberg** in a No DQ Match in 13:50 (★★★); **Booker T** defeated **Kevin Nash** in a Caged Heat Match to win the WCW World Heavyweight Title in 9:02 (★★).

Unforgiven '00 ★★
24-09-00, Philadelphia, Pennsylvania **WWF**
Right To Censor (**Bull Buchanan**, **The Goodfather**, **Steven Richards** and **Val Venis**) defeated **The APA** (**Faarooq** and **Bradshaw**) and **The Dudley Boyz** (**Bubba Ray Dudley** and **D-Von Dudley**) in 6:05 (★★); **Tazz** defeated **Jerry Lawler** in a Strap Match in 5:07 (★); **Steve Blackman** won a Hardcore Battle Royal to win the WWF Hardcore Title in 10:00 (★★); **Chris Jericho** defeated **X-Pac** in 9:05 (★); **The Hardy Boyz** (**Jeff Hardy** and **Matt Hardy**) defeated **Edge** and **Christian** in a Steel Cage Match to win the WWF World Tag Team Title in 14:00 (★★★); **Eddie Guerrero** defeated **Rikishi** by DQ in 6:10 (★★); **Triple H** defeated **Kurt Angle** in a No DQ Match in 17:28 (★★★); **The Rock** defeated **Chris Benoit**, **Kane** and **The Undertaker** in a Four Way Match in 16:03 (★★★).

Anarchy Rulz '00 ★★★
01-10-00, Saint Paul, Minnesota **ECW**
Danny Doring and **Roadkill** defeated **The Bad Street Boys** (**Christian York** and **Joey Matthews**) in 7:14 (★); **Kid Kash** defeated **EZ Money** in 9:39 (★★); **Joel Gertner** defeated **Cyrus** in 2:34 (★); **Da Baldies** (**Angel** and **Tony DeVito**) defeated **Balls Mahoney** and **Chilly Willy** in 7:39 (★★); **Steve Corino** defeated **C.W. Anderson** in 12:47 (★); **The F.B.I.** (**Little Guido** and **Tony Mamaluke**) defeated **The Unholy Alliance** (**Mikey Whipwreck** and **Yoshihiro Tajiri**) in 8:38 (★★); **Rhino** defeated **Rob Van Dam** in 12:41 (★★); **Jerry Lynn** defeated **Justin Credible** to win the ECW World Heavyweight Title in 19:36 (★★★).

No Mercy '00 ★★★
22-10-00, Albany, New York **WWF**
The Dudley Boyz (**Bubba Ray Dudley** and **D-Von Dudley**) won a Dudley Boyz Invitational Tables Match 12:18 (★★); **The APA** (**Faarooq** and **Bradshaw**) and **Lita** vs. **T&A** (**Test** and **Albert**) and **Trish Stratus** ended in a no contest; **Chris Jericho** defeated **X-Pac** in a Steel Cage Match in 10:40 (★★★); **Right To Censor** (**Steven Richards** and **Val Venis**) defeated **Billy Gunn** and **Chyna** in 7:10 (★★); **Rikishi** vs. **Steve Austin** went to a no contest in a No Holds Barred Match in 10:30 (★); **William Regal** defeated **Naked Mideon** in 6:02 (★★); **Los Conquistadores** (**Uno** and **Dos**) defeated **The Hardy Boyz** (**Jeff Hardy** and **Matt Hardy**) to win the WWF World Tag Team Title in 10:58 (★★★); **Triple H** defeated **Chris Benoit** in 18:44 (★★★); **Kurt Angle** defeated **The Rock** in a No DQ Match to win the WWF World Heavyweight Title in 21:45 (★★★★).

Halloween Havoc '00 ★
29-10-00, Las Vegas, Nevada **WCW**
The Natural Born Thrillers (**Mark Jindrak** and **Sean O'Haire**) defeated **The Filthy Animals** (**Billy Kidman** and **Rey Misterio Jr.**) and **The Boogie Knights** (**Disqo** and **Alex Wright**) in a Three Way Match in 10:04 (★★★); **Reno** defeated **Sgt. AWOL** in a

Hardcore Match in 10:55 (★★); **The Misfits In Action** (Lt. Loco and Corporal Cajun) defeated **The Perfect Event** (Shawn Stasiak and Chuck Palumbo) in 9:21 (★★); **The Filthy Animals** (Konnan and Tygress) defeated **Shane Douglas** and **Torrie Wilson** in 8:38 (★); **Buff Bagwell** defeated **David Flair** in a First Blood DNA Match in 5:40 (★); **Mike Sanders** defeated **Ernest Miller** by count out in a Kickboxing Match in 8:32 (★); **Mike Awesome** defeated **Vampiro** in 9:50 (★); **Gen. Rection** defeated **Lance Storm** and **Jim Duggan** in a Handicap Match to capture the WCW United States Heavyweight Title in 10:07 (★★); **Jeff Jarrett** defeated **Sting** in 14:30 (★★); **Booker T** defeated **Scott Steiner** by DQ in 13:00 (★★); **Goldberg** defeated **KroniK** (Brian Adams and Bryan Clark) in a Handicap Elimination Match in 3:43 (★★).

November To Remember '00 ★★
05-11-00, Villa Park, Illinois **ECW**
Simon Diamond and **Johnny Swinger** defeated **The Bad Street Boys** (Christian York and Joey Matthews) in 5:21 (★★); **Kid Kash** defeated **C.W. Anderson** in 10:47 (★★); **Spike Dudley**, **Danny Doring** and **Roadkill** defeated **Hot Commodity** (Chris Hamrick, Julio Dinero and E.Z. Money) in 8:23 (★★); **Nova** defeated **Chris Chetti** in a Loser Leaves Town Match in 9:48 (★★); **Balls Mahoney** and **Chilly Willy** defeated **Da Baldies** (Angel and Tony DeVito) in a Flaming Tables Match in 12:17 (★★); **Rhino** defeated **New Jack** in 7:56 (★★); **The F.B.I.** (Little Guido and Tony Mamaluke) defeated **The Unholy Alliance** (Mikey Whipwreck and Yoshihiro Tajiri) in 15:47 (★★★); **Steve Corino** defeated **Justin Credible, The Sandman** and **Jerry Lynn** in a Double Jeopardy Match to win the ECW World Heavyweight Title in 24:21 (★★).

Millennium Final ★★
16-11-00, Oberhausen, Germany **WCW**
KroniK (Brian Adams and Bryan Clark) defeated **The Filthy Animals** (Billy Kidman and Rey Misterio Jr.) in 10:15 (★★); **Mike Awesome** won a Battle Royal in 19:07 (★★); **Kwee Wee** defeated **Elix Skipper** in 10:28 (★★); **Ernest Miller** defeated **Mike Sanders** in 5:32 (★★); **Gen. Rection** defeated **Lance Storm** by DQ in 7:34 (★★); **Norman Smiley** defeated **Fit Finlay** in an Oktoberfest Hardcore Match in 10:27 (★★); **The Boogie Knights** (Alex Wright and Disqo) defeated **The Natural Born Thrillers** (Mark Jindrak and Sean O'Haire) in 11:26 (★★); **Kevin Nash** defeated **Alex Wright** and **Mike Awesome** in a Three Way Match in 7:24 (★★); **Booker T** defeated **Scott Steiner** in 11:34 (★★); **Sting** defeated **Kevin Nash** in 5:45 (★★).

Survivor Series '00 ★★
19-11-00, Tampa, Florida **WWF**
Steve Blackman, Crash Holly and **Molly Holly** defeated **T&A** (Test and Albert) and **Trish Stratus** in 5:06 (★★); **The Radicalz** (Eddie Guerrero, Chris Benoit, Dean Malenko and Perry Saturn) defeated **Billy Gunn, Chyna, K-Kwik** and **Road Dogg** in an Elimination Match in 12:41 (★★); **Kane** defeated **Chris Jericho** in 12:35 (★★); **William Regal** defeated **Hardcore Holly** by DQ in 5:06 (★★); **The Rock** defeated **Rikishi** in 13:00 (★★★); **Ivory** defeated **Lita** in 4:55 (★★); **Kurt Angle** defeated **The Undertaker** in 16:15 (★★); **The Dudley Boyz** (Bubba Ray Dudley and D-Von Dudley) and **The Hardy Boyz** (Jeff Hardy and Matt Hardy) defeated **Edge** and **Christian** and **Right to Censor** (Bull Buchanan and The Goodfather) in an Elimination Match in 10:04 (★★); **Steve Austin** vs. **Triple H** went to a no contest in a No DQ Match in 25:09 (★★).

Mayhem '00 ★★
26-11-00, Milwaukee, Wisconsin **WCW**
Mike Sanders defeated **Kwee Wee** in 7:50 (★★); **3 Count** (Shane Helms and Shannon Moore) defeated **Evan Karagias** and **Jamie Noble**, and **The Jung Dragons** (Kaz Hayashi and Yun Yang) in a Triple Threat Tag Match in 10:53 (★★); **Mancow** defeated **Jimmy Hart** in 1:38 (★); **Crowbar** defeated **Big Vito** and **Reno** in a Hardcore Match in 7:50 (★★); **The Filthy Animals** (Billy Kidman and Rey Misterio Jr.) defeated **KroniK** (Brian Adams and Bryan Clark) and **Alex Wright** in a Handicap Match in 7:46 (★★); **Ernest Miller** defeated **Shane Douglas** in 8:00 (★★); **Bam Bam Bigelow** defeated **Sgt. AWOL** in 5:41 (★★); **Gen. Rection** defeated **Lance Storm** to win the WCW United States Heavyweight Title in 6:25 (★★); **Jeff Jarrett** defeated **Buff Bagwell** in 11:10 (★★); **The Insiders** (Diamond Dallas Page and Kevin Nash) defeated **The Perfect Event** (Chuck Palumbo and Shawn Stasiak) to win the WCW World Tag Team Title in 14:55 (★★); **Goldberg** defeated **Lex Luger** in 5:53 (★★); **Scott Steiner** defeated **Booker T** in a Straitjacket Caged Heat Match to win the WCW World Heavyweight Title in 13:10 (★★★).

Rebellion '00 ★★
02-12-00, Sheffield, England **WWF**
The Dudley Boyz (Bubba Ray Dudley and D-Von Dudley) defeated **Edge** and **Christian**, and **T&A** (Test and Albert) in an Elimination Tables Match in 9:55 (★★); **Ivory** defeated **Lita** in 2:57 (★★); **Steve Blackman** defeated **Perry Saturn** in a Hardcore Match in 6:02 (★★); **Crash Holly** defeated **William Regal** to win the WWF European Title in 4:59 (★★); **Billy Gunn** and **Chyna** defeated **Dean Malenko** and **Eddie Guerrero** in 7:26 (★★); **Kane** defeated **Chris Jericho** in 8:06 (★★); **Right to Censor** (Bull Buchanan and The Goodfather) defeated **The Hardy Boyz** (Jeff Hardy and Matt Hardy) in 8:08 (★★); **The Undertaker** defeated **Chris Benoit** in 12:18 (★★); **Kurt Angle** defeated **Rikishi, The Rock** and **Steve Austin** in a Four Way Match in 8:51 (★★★).

Massacre On 34th Street ★★★
03-12-00, New York City, New York **ECW**
The Bad Street Boys (Christian York and Joey Matthews) defeated **Simon** and **Swinger** in 5:38 (★★); **EZ Money** defeated **Balls Mahoney** in 7:52 (★★); **Nova** defeated **Julio Dinero** in 5:57 (★★); **Danny Doring** and **Roadkill** defeated **The F.B.I.** (Little Guido and Tony Mamaluke) to win the ECW World Tag Team Title in 9:01 (★★); **C.W. Anderson** defeated **Tommy Dreamer** in 16:47 (★★); **Rhino** defeated **Spike Dudley** in 9:51 (★★); **The Unholy Alliance** (Mikey Whipwreck and Yoshihiro Tajiri) defeated **Super Crazy** and **Kid Kash** in 18:24 (★★); **Steve Corino** defeated **Jerry Lynn** and **Justin Credible** in a Three Way Match in 22:51 (★★).

Armageddon '00 ★★
10-12-00, Birmingham, Alabama **WWF**
The Radicalz (Dean Malenko, Eddie Guerrero and Perry Saturn) defeated **The Hardy Boyz** (Jeff Hardy and Matt Hardy) and **Lita** in an Elimination Match in 8:06 (★★); **William Regal** defeated **Hardcore Holly** in 5:00 (★★); **Val Venis** defeated **Chyna** in 4:59 (★★); **Chris Jericho** defeated **Kane** in a Last Man Standing Match in 17:16 (★★); **Edge** and **Christian** defeated **The Dudley Boyz** (Bubba Ray Dudley and D-Von Dudley), **K-Kwik** and **Road Dogg**, and **Right to Censor** (Bull Buchanan and The Goodfather) in a Four Way Match to win the WWF World Tag Team Title in 9:42 (★★); **Chris Benoit** defeated **Billy Gunn** to win the WWF Intercontinental Title in 10:03 (★★); **Ivory** defeated **Molly Holly** and **Trish Stratus** in a Three Way Match in 2:12 (★★); **Kurt Angle** defeated **The Rock, Steve Austin, Triple H, The Undertaker** and **Rikishi** in a Six Way Hell In A Cell Match in 32:12 (★★★★★★).

Starrcade '00 ★★
17-12-00, Washington, D.C. **WCW**
3 Count (Shane Helms and Shannon Moore) defeated **The Jung Dragons** (Kaz Hayashi and Yun Yang), and **Evan Karagias** and **Jamie Noble** in a Three Way Ladder Match in 13:49 (★★★★); **Lance Storm** defeated **Ernest Miller** in 7:25 (★★); **Terry Funk** defeated **Crowbar** in a Hardcore Match to win the WCW Hardcore Title in 10:21 (★★); **Big Vito** and **Reno** vs. **KroniK** (Brian Adams and Bryan Clark) ended in a no contest in 8:18 (★★); **Mike Awesome** defeated **Bam Bam Bigelow** in an Ambulance Match in 7:56 (★★); **Gen. Rection** defeated **Shane Douglas** by DQ in 9:46 (★★); **The Harris Brothers** (Don Harris and Ron Harris) and **Jeff Jarrett** defeated **The Filthy Animals** (Billy Kidman, Konnan and Rey Misterio Jr.) in a Bunkhouse Brawl in 12:31 (★★★); **The Insiders** (Diamond Dallas Page and Kevin Nash) defeated **The Perfect Event** (Chuck Palumbo and Shawn Stasiak) to win the WCW World Tag Title in 12:04 (★★); **Goldberg** defeated **Lex Luger** in a No Holds Barred Match in 7:17 (★★); **Scott Steiner** defeated **Sid Vicious** in 10:12 (★★).

Guilty As Charged '01 ★★
07-01-01, New York City, New York **ECW**
Cyrus and **Jerry Lynn** defeated **The Bad Street Boys** (Christian York and Joey Matthews) in 2:41 (★★); **Danny Doring** and **Roadkill** defeated **Hot Commodity** (Julio Dinero and EZ Money) in 10:06 (★★); **Nova** defeated **Chris Hamrick** in 5:30 (★★); **Tommy Dreamer** defeated **C.W. Anderson** in an "I Quit" Match in 14:11 (★★★); **The Unholy Alliance** (Yoshihiro Tajiri and Mikey Whipwreck) defeated **Kid Kash** and **Super Crazy**, and **The F.B.I.** (Little Guido and Tony Mamaluke) in a Three Way Match in 13:31 (★★★); **Simon** and **Swinger** vs. **Balls Mahoney** and **Chilly Willy** went to a no contest in :48 (★); **The Sandman** defeated **Steve Corino** and **Justin Credible** in a Three Way Tables, Ladders, Chairs and Canes Match to win the ECW World Heavyweight Title in 13:20 (★★); **Rhino** defeated **The Sandman** to win the ECW World Heavyweight Title in 1:00 (★★); **Rob Van Dam** defeated **Jerry Lynn** in 24:30 (★★★).

Sin ★★★
14-01-01, Indianapolis, Indiana WCW

Chavo Guerrero Jr. defeated Shane Helms in 11:14 (★★★); Reno defeated Big Vito in 8:41 (★★); The Jung Dragons (Kaz Hayashi and Yun Yang) defeated Evan Karagias and Jamie Noble in 9:21 (★★★★); Ernest Miller defeated Mike Sanders in 5:44 (★★); Team Canada (Elix Skipper, Lance Storm and Mike Awesome) defeated The Filthy Animals (Billy Kidman, Konnan and Rey Misterio Jr.) in a Penalty Box Match in 13:07 (★★); Meng defeated Crowbar and Terry Funk in a Triple Threat Hardcore Match to win the WCW Hardcore Title in 11:41 (★★★); The Natural Born Thrillers (Chuck Palumbo and Sean O'Haire) defeated The Insiders (Diamond Dallas Page and Kevin Nash) to win the WCW World Tag Team Title in 11:16 (★★); Shane Douglas defeated Gen. Rection in a First Blood Chain Match to win the WCW United States Heavyweight Title in 11:36 (★★); Totally Buffed (Lex Luger and Buff Bagwell) defeated Goldberg and DeWayne Bruce in a No DQ Match in 11:53 (★★); Scott Steiner defeated Jeff Jarrett, Sid Vicious and Animal in a Four Corners Match in 7:53 (★★).

Royal Rumble '01 ★★★★★
21-01-01, New Orleans, Louisiana WWF

The Dudley Boyz (Bubba Ray Dudley and D-Von Dudley) defeated Edge and Christian to win the WWF Tag Team Title in 9:58 (★★★★); Chris Jericho defeated Chris Benoit in a Ladder Match to win the WWF Intercontinental Title in 18:43 (★★★★★); Ivory defeated Chyna in 3:27 (★); Kurt Angle defeated Triple H in 24:18 (★★★); Steve Austin won the 30-Man Royal Rumble Match in 61:52 (★★★★).

Unleashed ★
04-02-01, Inglewood, California WOW

Randi Rah Rah defeated Jacklyn Hyde in 2:15 (★★); The Beach Patrol (Sandy and Summer) vs. Farah and Paradise went to a no contest in 2:30 (★★); Tanja The Warrior Woman defeated Jane Blond in 2:47 (★); Nicki Law defeated Heather Steele in 2:02 (★★); Boom Boom and Caliente defeated The Asian Invasion (Jade and Lotus) in 4:43 (★★); Bronco Billie defeated The Disciplinarian in 3:55 (★★); Roxy Powers vs. Slam Dunk ended in a double DQ in 6:16 (★); Riot defeated Wendi Wheels in a Hardcore Match in 9:40 (★★); Jungle Grrrl defeated Beckie in a Splash Match in 9:45 (★★); Caged Heat (Delta Lotta Pain and Loca) defeated Harley's Angels (Charlie Davidson and EZ Rider) to win the vacant WOW World Tag Team Title in 5:52 (★★); Terry Gold defeated Danger to win the WOW World Title in 4:20 (★); Lana Star and Patti Pizzazz defeated Ice Cold and Poison in a Hair vs. Hair Match in 5:16 (★); Thug defeated Selina Majors in a Steel Cage Match in 15:01 (★).

SuperBrawl Revenge ★★★
18-02-01, Nashville, Tennessee WCW

Shane Helms defeated Evan Karagias, Kaz Hayashi, Jamie Noble, Shannon Moore and Yun Yang in a Six Way Elimination Match in 17:30 (★★★); Hugh Morrus defeated The Wall in 9:43 (★★); The Natural Born Thrillers (Sean O'Haire and Chuck Palumbo) defeated Mark Jindrak and Shawn Stasiak in 11:37 (★★★); Chavo Guerrero Jr. defeated Rey Misterio Jr. in 15:54 (★★★); Rick Steiner defeated Dustin Rhodes in 9:11 (★★); Totally Buffed (Lex Luger and Buff Bagwell) defeated Brian Adams in a Handicap Match in 6:25 (★★); Ernest Miller defeated Lance Storm in 8:07 (★★); Chris Kanyon defeated Diamond Dallas Page in 8:15 (★★★); Diamond Dallas Page defeated Jeff Jarrett in 8:30 (★★★); Scott Steiner defeated Kevin Nash in a Two Out Of Three Falls Loser Leaves WCW Match in 11:04 (★★).

No Way Out '01 ★★★★
25-02-01, Paradise, Nevada WWF

The Big Show defeated Raven in a Hardcore Match to win the WWF Hardcore Title in 4:20 (★★); Chris Jericho defeated Chris Benoit, Eddie Guerrero and X-Pac in a Four Way Match in 12:17 (★★★★); Stephanie McMahon-Helmsley defeated Trish Stratus in 8:29 (★★★); Triple H defeated Steve Austin in a Three Stages Of Hell Match in 39:26 (★★★★★); Steven Richards defeated Jerry Lawler in 5:32 (★★); The Dudley Boyz (Bubba Ray Dudley and D-Von Dudley) defeated The Brothers Of Destruction (Kane and The Undertaker) and Edge and Christian in a Triple Threat Tables Match in 12:04 (★★★); The Rock defeated Kurt Angle to win the WWF World Heavyweight Title in 16:53 (★★★★).

Greed ★★★
18-03-01, Jacksonville, Florida WCW

Jason Jett defeated Kwee Wee in 12:17 (★★★★); Elix Skipper and Kid Romeo defeated The Filthy Animals (Billy Kidman and Rey Misterio Jr.) to win the vacant WCW Cruiserweight Tag Team Title in 13:46 (★★★); Shawn Stasiak defeated Bam Bam Bigelow in 5:55 (★★); Team Canada (Lance Storm and Mike Awesome) defeated Hugh Morrus and Konnan in 11:28 (★★); Shane Helms defeated Chavo Guerrero Jr. to win the WCW Cruiserweight Title in 13:57 (★★★); The Natural Born Thrillers (Chuck Palumbo and Sean O'Haire) defeated Totally Buffed (Lex Luger and Buff Bagwell) in :54 (★); Ernest Miller defeated Chris Kanyon in 10:31 (★★); Booker T defeated Rick Steiner to win the WCW United States Heavyweight Title in 7:31 (★★); Dustin Rhodes and Dusty Rhodes defeated Ric Flair and Jeff Jarrett in 9:58 (★★); Scott Steiner defeated Diamond Dallas Page in a Falls Count Anywhere Match in 14:14 (★★★).

WrestleMania XVII ★★★★★★
01-04-01, Houston, Texas WWF

Chris Jericho defeated William Regal in 7:40 (★★★); Tazz and The APA (Faarooq and Bradshaw) defeated Right To Censor (Bull Buchanan, The Goodfather and Val Venis) in 3:56 (★★); Kane defeated Raven and The Big Show in a Triple Threat Hardcore Match to win the WWF Hardcore Title in 9:28 (★★★); Eddie Guerrero defeated Test to win the WWF European Title in 8:32 (★★); Kurt Angle defeated Chris Benoit in 14:10 (★★★★); Chyna defeated Ivory to win the WWF Women's Title in 2:38 (★★); Shane McMahon defeated Vince McMahon in a Street Fight in 14:11 (★★★★); Edge and Christian defeated The Dudley Boyz (Bubba Ray Dudley and D-Von Dudley) and The Hardy Boyz (Jeff Hardy and Matt Hardy) in a Tables, Ladders and Chairs Match in 15:50 (★★★★★); The Iron Sheik won a Battle Royal in 3:50 (★★★); The Undertaker defeated Triple H in 18:27 (★★★★); Steve Austin defeated The Rock in a No DQ Match to win the WWF World Heavyweight Title in 28:08 (★★★★★).

Backlash '01 ★★★
29-04-01, Rosemont, Illinois WWF

X-Factor (X-Pac, Justin Credible and Albert) defeated The Dudley Boyz (Bubba Ray Dudley, D-Von Dudley and Spike Dudley) in 8:00 (★★); Rhyno defeated Raven in a Hardcore Match in 8:11 (★★★★); William Regal defeated Chris Jericho in a Duchess Of Queensbury Rules Match in 12:34 (★★); Chris Benoit defeated Kurt Angle 4-3 in an Ultimate Submission Match in 31:33 (★★★★); Shane McMahon defeated The Big Show in a Last Man Standing Match in 11:55 (★★★); Matt Hardy defeated Christian and Eddie Guerrero in a Three Way Match in 6:37 (★★); The Two-Man Power Trip (Steve Austin and Triple H) defeated The Brothers Of Destruction (Kane and The Undertaker) to win the WWF World Tag Team Title in 25:02 (★★).

Insurrextion '01 ★★★
05-05-01, London, England WWF

Eddie Guerrero defeated Grandmaster Sexay in 4:30 (★★); The Radicalz (Perry Saturn and Dean Malenko) defeated The Hollys (Crash Holly, Hardcore Holly and Molly Holly) in a Handicap Match in 5:37 (★★); Bradshaw defeated The Big Show in 3:20 (★★); Edge and Christian defeated The Dudley Boyz (Bubba Ray Dudley and D-Von Dudley), The Hardy Boyz (Jeff Hardy and Matt Hardy) and X-Factor (Justin Credible and X-Pac) in a Four Way Elimination Match in 13:20 (★★★); Chris Benoit defeated Kurt Angle in a Best Two Out Of Three Falls Match in 14:23 (★★); Chris Jericho defeated William Regal in 14:46 (★★★); The Undertaker defeated The Two-Man Power Trip (Triple H and Steve Austin) in a Handicap Match in 17:12 (★★★).

Judgment Day '01 ★★★
20-05-01, Sacramento, California WWF

William Regal defeated Rikishi in 3:56 (★★); Kurt Angle defeated Chris Benoit in a Best Two Out Of Three Falls Match in 23:58 (★★★★); Rhyno defeated The Big Show and Test in a Triple Threat Hardcore Match in 9:13 (★★); Chyna defeated Lita in 6:30 (★★); Kane defeated Triple H in a Chain Match to win the WWF Intercontinental Title in 12:24 (★★); Chris Benoit and Chris Jericho won a Tag Team Turmoil Match in 25:53 (★★★); Steve Austin defeated The Undertaker in a No Holds Barred Match in 23:06 (★★★).

King Of The Ring '01 ★★★
24-06-01, East Rutherford, New Jersey **WWF**

Kurt Angle defeated Christian in 8:51 (★★); Edge defeated Rhyno in 10:20 (★★); The Dudley Boyz (Bubba Ray Dudley and D-Von Dudley) defeated Kane and Spike Dudley in 8:24 (★★); Edge defeated Kurt Angle in 10:20 (★★); Jeff Hardy defeated X-Pac in 7:10 (★★); Kurt Angle defeated Shane McMahon in a Street Fight in 25:58 (★★★); Steve Austin defeated Chris Benoit and Chris Jericho in a Three Way Match in 27:52 (★★★★).

Invasion ★★★
22-07-01, Cleveland, Ohio **WWF**

Edge and Christian defeated Lance Storm and Mike Awesome in 10:10 (★★); Earl Hebner defeated Nick Patrick in 2:48 (★); The APA (Faarooq and Bradshaw) defeated Chuck Palumbo and Sean O'Haire in 6:48 (★★); Billy Kidman defeated X-Pac in 7:07 (★★); Raven defeated William Regal in 6:35 (★★); Chris Kanyon, Hugh Morrus and Shawn Stasiak defeated Albert, The Big Show and Billy Gunn in 4:20 (★★); Tajiri defeated Tazz in 5:30 (★★); Rob Van Dam defeated Jeff Hardy in a Hardcore Match to win the WWF Hardcore Title in 12:40 (★★★★); Trish Stratus and Lita defeated Torrie Wilson and Stacy Keibler in a Bra and Panties Match in 5:03 (★★); Booker T, Diamond Dallas Page, Rhyno and The Dudley Boyz (Bubba Ray Dudley and D-Von Dudley) defeated Chris Jericho, Kane, Kurt Angle, Steve Austin and The Undertaker in 29:05 (★★).

SummerSlam '01 ★★★★
19-08-01, San Jose, California **WWF**

Edge defeated Lance Storm to win the WWF Intercontinental Title in 11:16 (★★★); The Dudley Boyz (Bubba Ray Dudley and D-Von Dudley) and Test defeated The APA (Faarooq and Bradshaw) and Spike Dudley in 7:18 (★★); X-Pac defeated Tajiri to win the WWF Light Heavyweight Title in 7:33 (★★★); Chris Jericho defeated Rhyno in 12:34 (★★★); Rob Van Dam defeated Jeff Hardy in a Ladder Match to win the WWF Hardcore Title in 16:33 (★★★★); The Brothers Of Destruction (Kane and The Undertaker) defeated Diamond Dallas Page and Chris Kanyon in a Steel Cage Match to win the WWF World Tag Team Title in 10:17 (★★); Kurt Angle defeated Steve Austin by DQ in 22:11 (★★★★); The Rock defeated Booker T to win the WCW World Heavyweight Title in 15:18 (★★).

Unforgiven '01 ★★★
23-09-01, Pittsburgh, Pennsylvania **WWF**

The Dudley Boyz (Bubba Ray Dudley and D-Von Dudley) defeated The Big Show and Spike Dudley, The Hurricane and Lance Storm, and The Hardy Boyz (Jeff Hardy and Matt Hardy) in a Four Way Elimination Match in 14:22 (★★); Perry Saturn defeated Raven in 5:07 (★★); Christian defeated Edge to win the WWF Intercontinental Title in 11:53 (★★); The Brothers Of Destruction (The Undertaker and Kane) defeated Kronik (Brian Adams and Bryan Clark) in 10:21 (★); Rob Van Dam defeated Chris Jericho in a Hardcore Match in 16:33 (★★★); The Rock defeated Booker T and Shane McMahon in a Handicap Match in 15:24 (★★); Rhyno defeated Tajiri to win the WCW United States Heavyweight Title in 4:50 (★★); Kurt Angle defeated Steve Austin to win the WWF World Heavyweight Title in 23:54 (★★★★).

No Mercy '01 ★★★★
21-10-01, St. Louis, Missouri **WWF**

The Hardy Boyz (Jeff Hardy and Matt Hardy) defeated The Hurricane and Lance Storm in 7:41 (★★★); Test defeated Kane in 10:05 (★★★); Torrie Wilson defeated Stacy Keibler in a Lingerie Match in 3:09 (★★); Edge defeated Christian in a Ladder Match to win the WWF Intercontinental Title in 22:12 (★★★); The Dudley Boyz (Bubba Ray Dudley and D-Von Dudley) defeated The Big Show and Tajiri in 9:30 (★★); The Undertaker defeated Booker T in 12:10 (★★); Chris Jericho defeated The Rock to win the WCW World Heavyweight Title in 23:44 (★★★); Steve Austin defeated Kurt Angle and Rob Van Dam in a Three Way Match in 15:16 (★★★★).

Rebellion '01 ★★★
03-11-01, Manchester, England **WWF**

Edge defeated Christian in a Steel Cage Match in 20:49 (★★★); Scotty 2 Hotty defeated The Hurricane in 8:55 (★★); The Big Show defeated Diamond Dallas Page in 3:15 (★★); The Dudley Boyz (Bubba Ray Dudley and D-Von Dudley) defeated The APA (Faarooq and Bradshaw) and The Hardy Boyz (Matt

Hardy and Jeff Hardy) in a Three Way Match in 12:01 (★★); William Regal defeated Tajiri in 5:55 (★★); Chris Jericho defeated Kurt Angle in 14:55 (★★★); Lita and Torrie Wilson defeated Mighty Molly and Stacy Keibler in 4:16 (★★); Steve Austin defeated The Rock in 22:09 (★★★★).

Survivor Series '01 ★★★
18-11-01, Greensboro, North Carolina **WWF**

Christian defeated Al Snow in 6:30 (★★); William Regal defeated Tajiri in 2:59 (★★); Edge defeated Test to win the WWF Intercontinental Title in 11:19 (★★★); The Dudley Boyz (Bubba Ray Dudley and D-Von Dudley) defeated The Hardy Boyz (Matt Hardy and Jeff Hardy) to win the WWF World Tag Team Title in 15:44 (★★★); Test won a Battle Royal in 7:37 (★★); Trish Stratus defeated Ivory, Jazz, Jacqueline, Lita and Mighty Molly in a Six Pack Challenge to win the vacant WWF Women's Title in 4:23 (★★); Team WWF (The Rock, Chris Jericho, The Undertaker, Kane and The Big Show) defeated The Alliance (Steve Austin, Kurt Angle, Rob Van Dam, Booker T and Shane McMahon) in an Elimination Match in 44:57 (★★★★).

Vengeance '01 ★★★
09-12-01, San Diego, California **WWF**

Scotty 2 Hotty and Albert defeated Christian and Test in 6:12 (★★); Edge defeated William Regal in 9:06 (★★); Jeff Hardy defeated Matt Hardy in 12:30 (★★); The Dudley Boyz (Bubba Ray Dudley and D-Von Dudley) defeated The Big Show and Kane in 6:50 (★); The Undertaker defeated Rob Van Dam in a Hardcore Match to win the WWF Hardcore Title in 11:08 (★★★); Trish Stratus defeated Jacqueline in 3:34 (★★); Steve Austin defeated Kurt Angle in 14:55 (★★★); Chris Jericho defeated The Rock to win the World Title in 19:05 (★★★); Chris Jericho defeated Steve Austin to win the Undisputed WWF Title in 12:31 (★★★).

The Inception ★★★
06-01-02, Sydney, Australia **WWA**

Juventud Guerrera defeated Psicosis in a Ladder Match to win the vacant WWA International Cruiserweight Title in 8:11 (★★★); Road Dogg defeated Konnan in a Dog Collar Match in 3:39 (★★); Norman Smiley defeated Crowbar in a Hardcore Match in 9:54 (★★★); Buff Bagwell won a Battle Royal in 6:15 (★★); Jeff Jarrett defeated Nathan Jones in a Guitar On A Pole Match in 4:07 (★★); Road Dogg defeated Lenny Lane and Lodi in a Three Way Match in 3:56 (★★); Jeff Jarrett defeated Buff Bagwell in a Tits, Whips and Buff Match in 4:05 (★★); Gangrel defeated Luna Vachon in a Black Wedding Match in 5:16 (★★); Jeff Jarrett defeated Road Dogg in a Steel Cage Match to win the vacant WWA World Heavyweight Title in 10:26 (★★★).

Royal Rumble '02 ★★★★
20-01-02, Atlanta, Georgia **WWF**

Spike Dudley and Tazz defeated The Dudley Boyz (Bubba Ray Dudley and D-Von Dudley) in 5:06 (★★); William Regal defeated Edge to win the WWF Intercontinental Title in 9:45 (★★); Trish Stratus defeated Jazz in 3:43 (★★); Ric Flair defeated Vince McMahon in a Street Fight in 14:55 (★★★); Chris Jericho defeated The Rock in 18:48 (★★★); Triple H won the 30-Man Royal Rumble Match in 69:22 (★★★★).

No Way Out '02 ★★
17-02-02, Milwaukee, Wisconsin **WWF**

The APA (Faarooq and Bradshaw) won a Tag Team Turmoil Match in 16:38 (★★); Rob Van Dam defeated Goldust in 11:08 (★★); Tazz and Spike Dudley defeated Booker T and Test in 7:16 (★★); William Regal defeated Edge in a Brass Knuckles On A Pole Match in 10:22 (★★); The Rock defeated The Undertaker in 17:25 (★★); Kurt Angle defeated Triple H in 14:39 (★★); Chris Jericho defeated Steve Austin in 21:33 (★★★).

The Era Of Honor Begins ★★
23-02-02, Philadelphia, Pennsylvania **ROH**

Da Hit Squad (Mafia and Monsta Mack) defeated The Christopher Street Connection (Buff-E and Mace) in 1:12 (★); The Amazing Red defeated Jay Briscoe in 8:31 (★★); Xavier defeated Scoot Andrews in 10:02 (★★); The Boogie Knights (Danny Drake and Mike Tobin) defeated The Natural Born Sinners (Boogalou and Homicide) by DQ in 7:43 (★★); Quiet Storm defeated Brian XL, Chris Divine, Joel Maximo, Jose Maximo and The Amazing Red in a Ultimate Aerial Elimination Match in 14:55 (★★); Prince Nana defeated Eric Tuttle in :53

(★); Ikaika Loa and Spanky defeated Michael Shane and Oz in 12:31 (★★); Super Crazy defeated Eddie Guerrero to win the vacant IWA Puerto Rico Intercontinental Title in 10:42 (★★★); Low Ki defeated The American Dragon and Christopher Daniels in a Three Way Match in 20:04 (★★★★).

The Revolution ★★
24-02-02, Paradise, Nevada **WWA**
Nova defeated Low Ki, Shark Boy, AJ Styles, Tony Mamaluke and Christopher Daniels in a Six Way Elimination Match in 19:42 (★★★); The Funkster defeated Reno in 7:34 (★★); KroniK (Brian Adams and Bryan Clark) defeated Native Blood (The Navajo Warrior and Ghost Walker) in 4:51 (★); Puppet the Midget Killer defeated Teo in a Falls Count Anywhere Match in 7:38 (★★); Eddie Guerrero defeated Psicosis and Juventud Guerrera in a Three Way Match to win the WWA International Cruiserweight Title in 12:40 (★★); Devon Storm defeated Sabu in a No DQ Match in 20:39 (★★); Rick Steiner and The Cat defeated The West Hollywood Blondes (Lenny Lane and Lodi) in :58 (★★); Jeff Jarrett defeated Brian Christopher in 13:17 (★★).

WrestleMania XVIII ★★★
17-03-02, Toronto, Ontario **WWF**
Rob Van Dam defeated William Regal to win the WWF Intercontinental Title in 6:19 (★★); Diamond Dallas Page defeated Christian in 6:08 (★★); Maven vs. Goldust went to a no contest in a Hardcore Match in 3:17 (★★); Kurt Angle defeated Kane in 10:45 (★★★); The Undertaker defeated Ric Flair in a No DQ Match in 18:47 (★★★); Edge defeated Booker T in 6:32 (★★); Steve Austin defeated Scott Hall in 9:51 (★★); Billy and Chuck defeated The APA (Faarooq and Ron Simmons), The Dudley Boyz (Bubba Ray Dudley and D-Von Dudley), and The Hardy Boyz (Jeff Hardy and Matt Hardy) in a Four Corners Elimination Match in 13:50 (★★); The Rock defeated Hulk Hogan in 16:23 (★★★★); Jazz defeated Trish Stratus and Lita in a Three Way Match in 6:16 (★★); Triple H defeated Chris Jericho to win the Undisputed WWF Title in 18:41 (★★).

Round Robin Challenge ★★★
30-03-02, Philadelphia, Pennsylvania **ROH**
Christopher Daniels defeated The American Dragon in 14:23 (★★★); Da Hit Squad (Mafia and Monsta Mack) defeated Eric Tuttle and Prince Nana in 1:51 (★); Christian York and Joey Matthews defeated CW Anderson and Elax in 7:05 (★★); Xavier defeated James Maritato in 7:13 (★★); The Natural Born Sinners (Boogalou and Homicide) defeated The Boogie Knights (Danny Drake and Mike Tobin) in 2:49 (★★); Low Ki defeated Christopher Daniels in 11:02 (★★); Paul London defeated Chris Marvel in 2:08 (★★); Spanky defeated Jay Briscoe in 11:23 (★★★); The SAT (Joel Maximo and Jose Maximo) defeated Brian XL and The Amazing Red, and Divine Storm (Chris Divine and Quiet Storm) in a Three Way Elimination Match in 12:13 (★★); The American Dragon defeated Low Ki in 32:07 (★★★★).

The Eruption ★★
13-04-02, Melbourne, Australia **WWA**
AJ Styles defeated Nova in 4:11 (★★); Jerry Lynn defeated Chuckie Chaos in 1:10 (★★); Tio defeated Puppet the Psycho Dwarf in a Hardcore Match in 5:22 (★★); Brian Christopher and Ernest Miller defeated Buff Bagwell and Stevie Ray in 8:06 (★★); The Funkster defeated Pierre Ouellet in 6:15 (★★); AJ Styles defeated Jerry Lynn to win the vacant WWA International Cruiserweight Title in 11:30 (★★); Sabu defeated Devon Storm in a Steel Cage Match in 17:02 (★★★); Midajah defeated Queen Bea in an Evening Gown Match in 2:20 (★★); Scott Steiner defeated Nathan Jones to win the WWA World Heavyweight Title in 14:40 (★★).

Backlash '02 ★★★
21-04-02, Kansas City, Missouri **WWF**
Tajiri defeated Billy Kidman to win the WWF Cruiserweight Title in 9:08 (★★); Scott Hall defeated Bradshaw in 5:43 (★★); Jazz defeated Trish Stratus in 4:29 (★★); Brock Lesnar defeated Jeff Hardy in 5:32 (★★); Kurt Angle defeated Edge in 13:25 (★★★★); Eddie Guerrero defeated Rob Van Dam to win the WWF Intercontinental Title in 11:43 (★★★); The Undertaker defeated Steve Austin in 27:03 (★★); Billy and Chuck defeated Maven and Al Snow in 5:58 (★★); Hulk Hogan defeated Triple H to win the Undisputed WWF Title in 22:04 (★★★).

Insurrextion '02 ★★
04-05-02, London, England **WWF**
Rob Van Dam defeated Eddie Guerrero by DQ in 11:24 (★★); Jacqueline and Trish Stratus defeated Jazz and Molly Holly in 7:43 (★★); X-Pac defeated Bradshaw in 8:49 (★★); Booker T defeated Steven Richards in a Hardcore Match to win the WWF Hardcore Title in 9:50 (★★); The Hardy Boyz (Jeff Hardy and Matt Hardy) defeated Brock Lesnar and Shawn Stasiak in 6:42 (★★); Spike Dudley defeated William Regal in 4:56 (★★); Steve Austin defeated The Big Show in 15:00 (★★); Triple H defeated The Undertaker in 14:31 (★★).

Judgment Day '02 ★★★★
19-05-02, Nashville, Tennessee **WWE**
Eddie Guerrero defeated Rob Van Dam in 10:17 (★★★★); Trish Stratus defeated Stacy Keibler in 2:54 (★★); Brock Lesnar and Paul Heyman defeated The Hardy Boyz (Jeff Hardy and Matt Hardy) in 4:47 (★★); Steve Austin defeated The Big Show and Ric Flair in a Handicap Match in 15:36 (★★★); Edge defeated Kurt Angle in a Hair vs. Hair Match in 15:30 (★★★); Triple H defeated Chris Jericho in a Hell In A Cell Match in 24:31 (★★★★); Rico and Rikishi defeated Billy and Chuck to win the WWE World Tag Team Title in 3:50 (★★); The Undertaker defeated Hulk Hogan to win the WWE Undisputed Title in 11:17 (★★).

Total Nonstop Action (19-06-02) ★★★
19-06-02, Huntsville, Alabama **NWA-TNA**
The Flying Elvises (Jimmy Yang, Jorge Estrada and Sonny Siaki) defeated AJ Styles, Low Ki and Jerry Lynn in 6:25 (★★★); Teo defeated Hollywood in 2:49 (★★); The Johnsons (Richard Johnson and Rod Johnson) defeated Psicosis and James Storm in 4:51 (★★); The Dupps (Stan Dupp and Bo Dupp) defeated Christian York and Joey Matthews in 3:41 (★★); Ken Shamrock and Malice won the 21-Man Gauntlet For The Gold Battle Royal in 31:00 (★★★); Ken Shamrock defeated Malice to win the vacant NWA World Heavyweight Title in 5:51 (★★).

Road To The Title ★★★
22-06-02, Philadelphia, Pennsylvania **ROH**
The American Dragon defeated Bio-Hazard in 2:33 (★★); Spanky defeated Paul London in 9:57 (★★★★); Doug Williams defeated Jay Briscoe in 6:18 (★★); Jody Fleisch defeated Jonny Storm in 7:01 (★★); Low Ki defeated Prince Nana in 3:54 (★★); The Amazing Red defeated Xavier in 4:21 (★★); Christopher Daniels defeated Scoot Andrews in 2:29 (★★); AJ Styles defeated Jerry Lynn in 15:30 (★★★); Spanky defeated Jody Fleisch in 5:14 (★★); Doug Williams defeated The American Dragon in 13:27 (★★★); Low Ki defeated The Amazing Red in 11:14 (★★★★); Christopher Daniels defeated AJ Styles in 21:47 (★★★★).

King Of The Ring '02 ★★
23-06-02, Columbus, Ohio **WWE**
Rob Van Dam defeated Chris Jericho in 14:31 (★★★); Brock Lesnar defeated Test in 8:12 (★★); Jamie Noble defeated The Hurricane to win the WWE Cruiserweight Title in 11:58 (★★); Ric Flair defeated Eddie Guerrero in 17:00 (★★); Molly Holly defeated Trish Stratus to win the WWE Women's Title in 5:05 (★★★); Kurt Angle defeated Hulk Hogan in 12:05 (★★); Brock Lesnar defeated Rob Van Dam in 5:36 (★★); The Undertaker defeated Triple H in 23:00 (★★).

Total Nonstop Action (26-06-02) ★★★
26-06-02, Huntsville, Alabama **NWA-TNA**
Scott Hall defeated Jeff Jarrett in 7:02 (★★); Cheex defeated Frank Parker in 2:10 (★); Brian Christopher defeated K-Krush in 4:46 (★★); Taylor Vaughn won a Lingerie Battle Royal in 4:45 (★); Apolo defeated David Young in 5:26 (★★); Chris Harris and James Storm defeated The Rainbow Express (Lenny and Bruce) in 4:48 (★★); AJ Styles defeated Psicosis, Low Ki and Jerry Lynn in a Four Way Double Elimination Match to win the inaugural NWA-TNA X-Division Title in 25:59 (★★★★).

Total Nonstop Action (03-07-02) ★★
03-07-02, Nashville, Tennessee **NWA-TNA**
Chris Harris and James Storm defeated The Johnsons (Richard Johnson and Rod Johnson) in 4:42 (★★); Monty Brown defeated Anthony Ingram in 1:31 (★★); The Rainbow Express (Lenny and Bruce) defeated Buff Bagwell and Apolo in 5:48 (★★); Puppet The Psycho Dwarf defeated Todd Stone in a Hardcore Match in 1:55 (★★); Francine defeated Taylor Vaughn

by DQ in 1:00 (★★); **Ken Shamrock** defeated **Malice** in 5:53 (★★); **AJ Styles** defeated **David Young** in 8:46 (★★); **Jerry Lynn** and **AJ Styles** defeated **The Rainbow Express** (**Lenny** and **Bruce**) to win the vacant NWA World Tag Team Title in 12:24 (★★★); **K-Krush** and **Jeff Jarrett** defeated **Brian Christopher** and **Scott Hall** in 11:42 (★★).

Total Nonstop Action (10-07-02) ★★★
10-07-02, Nashville, Tennessee NWA-TNA
AJ Styles and **Jerry Lynn** defeated **The Disciples Of The New Church** (**Slash** and **Tempest**) in 10:35 (★★★); **Brian Lawler** defeated **Norman Smiley** in 4:45 (★★); **Hermie Sadler** defeated **K-Krush** in 5:08 (★★); **The Briscoe Brothers** (**Jay Briscoe** and **Mark Briscoe**) vs. **The Hot Shots** (**Cassidy** and **Chase**) ended in a no contest in 2:10 (★★); **The Flying Elvises** (**Jorge Estrada** and **Sonny Siaki**) defeated **The Dupps** (**Bo Dupp** and **Stan Dupp**) in 5:03 (★★); **Ken Shamrock** vs. **Takao Omori** ended in a no contest in 7:51 (★★); **Low Ki** defeated **Elix Skipper, Kid Romeo, Tony Mamaluke, Christopher Daniels** and **Jerry Lynn** in a Six Way Elimination Match in 21:44 (★★★★).

Total Nonstop Action (17-07-02) ★★
17-07-02, Nashville, Tennessee NWA-TNA
Sabu defeated **Malice** in a Ladder Match in 13:25 (★★★); **K-Krush** defeated **Norman Smiley** in 3:22 (★★); **The Flying Elvises** (**Jorge Estrada** and **Sonny Siaki**) defeated **Elix Skipper** and **Christopher Daniels** in 9:47 (★★); **Puppet The Psycho Dwarf** defeated **Meatball** in a Hardcore Match in 6:14 (★★); **Jasmine St. Claire** vs. **Francine** ended in a no contest in 1:22 (★★); **AJ Styles** defeated **Low Ki** in 10:38 (★★); **Scott Hall** defeated **Brian Lawler** in 8:21 (★★).

Vengeance '02 ★★★
21-07-02, Detroit, Michigan WWE
The Dudley Boyz (**Bubba Ray Dudley** and **D-Von Dudley**) defeated **Chris Benoit** and **Eddie Guerrero** in a Tag Team Elimination Tables Match in 15:01 (★★★); **Jamie Noble** defeated **Billy Kidman** in 7:27 (★★); **Jeff Hardy** defeated **William Regal** in 4:16 (★★); **John Cena** defeated **Chris Jericho** in 6:16 (★★); **Rob Van Dam** defeated **Brock Lesnar** by DQ in 9:21 (★★); **Booker T** defeated **The Big Show** in a No DQ Match in 6:14 (★★); **The Un-Americans** (**Christian** and **Lance Storm**) defeated **Edge** and **Hulk Hogan** to win the WWE World Tag Team Title in 9:48 (★★); **The Rock** defeated **The Undertaker** and **Kurt Angle** in a Three Way Match to win the WWE Undisputed Title in 19:47 (★★★★).

Total Nonstop Action (24-07-02) ★★
24-07-02, Nashville, Tennessee NWA-TNA
Low Ki defeated **Amazing Red** in 7:27 (★★★★); **Chris Harris** and **James Storm** defeated **The Hot Shots** (**Cassidy O'Reilly** and **Chase Stevens**) in 5:26 (★★); **Apolo** defeated **Brian Lawler** in 7:05 (★★); **AJ Styles** and **Jerry Lynn** defeated **The Flying Elvises** (**Jimmy Yang** and **Jorge Estrada**) in 16:14 (★★); **Monty Brown** and **Elix Skipper** defeated **Simon Diamond** and **Johnny Swinger** in 5:38 (★★); **Ian Harrison** defeated **Bo Dupp** by DQ in 2:58 (★★); **Ken Shamrock** vs. **Sabu** went to a no contest in a Submissions or Ladder Match in 9:03 (★).

Crowning A Champion ★★★
27-07-02, Philadelphia, Pennsylvania ROH
Tony Mamaluke defeated **Jeremy Lopez** in 7:22 (★★); **Christian York** and **Joey Matthews** defeated **Jacob Ladder** and **Prince Nana** in 1:45 (★★); **Bio-Hazard** and **Michael Shane** defeated **Don Juan** and **Paul London** in 8:29 (★★); **Da Hit Squad** (**Mafia** and **Monsta Mack**) defeated **Divine Storm** (**Chris Divine** and **Quiet Storm**) in 4:33 (★★); **James Maritato** defeated **Jay Briscoe** in 8:33 (★★★); **The Natural Born Sinners** (**Boogalou** and **Homicide**) defeated **The Carnage Crew** (**DeVito** and **Loc**) in a Bunkhouse Match in 9:35 (★★★); **AJ Styles** defeated **Adam Jacobs** and **David Young** in an Elimination Match in 8:01 (★★); **Scoot Andrews** defeated **Xavier** in 5:03 (★★); **Low Ki** defeated **Christopher Daniels, Doug Williams** and **Spanky** in a Final Four Iron Man Match to win the inaugural ROH World Title in 60:00 (★★★★).

Total Nonstop Action (31-07-02) ★★
31-07-02, Nashville, Tennessee NWA-TNA
AJ Styles defeated **Elix Skipper** in 12:38 (★★★); **Slash** defeated **Sonny Siaki** in 7:40 (★★); **Apolo** defeated **Malice** in 6:34 (★★); **Bruce** defeated **Taylor Vaughn** in 2:09 to win the Miss TNA Title (★★); **Low Ki** vs. **Jerry Lynn** went to a no contest in 14:11 (★★★); **Jeff Jarrett** defeated **Scott Hall** in a Stretcher Match in 12:10 (★★).

Total Nonstop Action (07-08-02) ★★
07-08-02, Nashville, Tennessee NWA-TNA
The Flying Elvises (**Jimmy Yang, Jorge Estrada** and **Sonny Siaki**) defeated **The S.A.T.** (**Amazing Red, Joel Maximo** and **Jose Maximo**) in 11:42 (★★); **Ron Killings** defeated **Ken Shamrock** to win the NWA World Heavyweight Title in 9:19 (★★); **Bo Dupp** defeated **Ed Ferrara** in a Dupp Cupp Invitational Match in 5:43 (★); **Malice** defeated **Don Harris** in a First Blood Match in 6:31 (★); **Jeff Jarrett** defeated **Apolo** in 10:15 (★★); **Miss TNA Bruce** defeated **Taylor Vaughn** in an Evening Gown Match in 2:02 (★); **Low Ki** defeated **Jerry Lynn** and **AJ Styles** in a Three Way Match to win the NWA-TNA X Division Title in 16:19 (★★★★).

Global Warning Tour ★★★
10-08-02, Melbourne, Australia WWE
Rikishi defeated **Rico** in a Kiss My Ass Match in 2:32 (★★); **Jamie Noble** defeated **The Hurricane** in 8:45 (★★); **The Un-Americans** (**Christian** and **Lance Storm**) defeated **Billy Kidman** and **Rey Mysterio** in 9:10 (★★★); **Edge** defeated **Chris Jericho** in 12:49 (★★★); **Torrie Wilson** defeated **Stacy Keibler** in a Bra and Panties Match in 4:45 (★★); **The Rock** defeated **Triple H** and **Brock Lesnar** in a Three Way Match in 14:35 (★★★).

Total Nonstop Action (14-08-02) ★★
14-08-02, Nashville, Tennessee NWA-TNA
The S.A.T. (**Amazing Red, Joel Maximo** and **Jose Maximo**) defeated **Kid Kash, Shark Boy** and **Slim J** in 10:36 (★★★); **Miss TNA Bruce** defeated **Tina Hamilton** in 1:52 (★★); **Don Harris** defeated **Malice** in a Last Man Standing Match in 7:05 (★★); **Teo** defeated **Bo Dupp** in 4:24 (★); **Monty Brown** defeated **Elix Skipper** in a Detroit Street Fight in 5:45 (★★); **Low Ki** defeated **Jimmy Yang, Jorge Estrada** and **Sonny Siaki** in a Four Way Elimination Match in 9:25 (★★); **AJ Styles** and **Jerry Lynn** vs. **Jeff Jarrett** and **Ron Killings** ended in a no contest in 12:25 (★★).

Total Nonstop Action (21-08-02) ★★★
21-08-02, Nashville, Tennessee NWA-TNA
Jerry Lynn defeated **AJ Styles** in a Falls Count Anywhere Match in 9:56 (★★★); **Chris Harris** and **James Storm** defeated **Ron Harris** and **Brian Lee** in 9:00 (★★); **Sonny Siaki** defeated **Jimmy Yang** 2-1 in a Best Two Out Of Three Falls Match in 14:08 (★★★); **Brian Lawler** defeated **Slash** in 5:56 (★★); **Low Ki** defeated **Amazing Red, Joel Maximo** and **Jose Maximo** in a Four Way Elimination Match in 12:05 (★★★); **Ron Killings** defeated **Monty Brown** in 10:11 (★★); **AJ Styles** defeated **Jerry Lynn** in a No Disqualification Match in 11:39 (★★); **Jerry Lynn** vs. **AJ Styles** ended in a 3-3 draw in a 10-Minute Iron Man Match in 10:00 (★★★).

SummerSlam '02 ★★★★★
25-08-02, Uniondale, New York WWE
Kurt Angle defeated **Rey Mysterio** in 9:20 (★★★); **Ric Flair** defeated **Chris Jericho** in 10:22 (★★); **Edge** defeated **Eddie Guerrero** in 11:47 (★★★); **The Un-Americans** (**Christian** and **Lance Storm**) defeated **Booker T** and **Goldust** in 9:37 (★★); **Rob Van Dam** defeated **Chris Benoit** to win the WWF Intercontinental Title in 16:30 (★★★★); **The Undertaker** defeated **Test** in 8:18 (★★); **Shawn Michaels** defeated **Triple H** in an Unsanctioned Street Fight in 27:20 (★★★★★); **Brock Lesnar** defeated **The Rock** to win the WWE Undisputed Title in 16:01 (★★★★).

Total Nonstop Action (28-08-02) ★★★
28-08-02, Nashville, Tennessee NWA-TNA
Kid Kash defeated **Amazing Red** in 9:26 (★★); **Sonny Siaki** defeated **Monty Brown** in 10:13 (★★); **Chris Harris** and **James Storm** defeated **The Backseat Boys** (**Johnny Kashmere** and **Trent Acid**), **The Disciples Of The New Church** (**Cobain** and **Slash**) and **The Hot Shots** (**Cassidy O'Reilly** and **Chase Stevens**) in a Four Way Tag Team Elimination Match in 12:52 (★★); **Miss TNA Bruce** defeated **April Hunter** in 3:02 (★★); **The Flying Elvises** (**Jimmy Yang** and **Jorge Estrada**) defeated **The S.A.T.** (**Jose Maximo** and **Joel Maximo**) in 14:21 (★★); **Jeff Jarrett** fought **The Bullet** to a no contest in 3:42 (★★); **Jerry Lynn** defeated **Low Ki** and **AJ Styles** in a Three Way Ladder Match to win the NWA-TNA X Division Title in 20:06 (★★★★).

Total Nonstop Action (18-09-02) ★★
18-09-02, Nashville, Tennessee NWA-TNA
AJ Styles defeated **Kid Kash** in 9:57 (★★); **Dustin Diamond** defeated **Tiny the Bellkeeper** in a Boxing Match in :44 (★★); **CM Punk** and **Ace Steel** defeated **Derek Wylde** and **Jimmy**

Rave, and **The Hot Shots** (Cassidy O'Reilly and Chase Stevens) in a Handicap Match in 7:13 (★); **Miss TNA Bruce** defeated **Christie Ricci** in 1:10 (★); **Brian Lee** and **Chris Harris** won the 20-Man Gauntlet For The Gold Battle Royal in 23:09 (★★★); **Chris Harris** and **James Storm** defeated **Brian Lee** and **Ron Harris** to win the vacant NWA World Tag Team Title in 4:32 (★★); **Ron Killings** defeated **Jerry Lynn** in 12:30 (★★).

Unscripted ★★★
21-09-02, Philadelphia, Pennsylvania **ROH**
The Prophecy (Christopher Daniels and Donovan Morgan) defeated **The SAT** (Joel Maximo and Jose Maximo) in 7:21 (★★); **Dick Togo** and **Ikuto Hidaka** defeated **James Maritato** and **Tony Mamaluke** in 9:42 (★★★); **Tony Mamaluke** defeated **James Maritato** in 2:55 (★★); **The American Dragon** and **Michael Modest** defeated **Divine Storm** (Chris Divine and Quiet Storm) in 6:22 (★★); **The Prophecy** (Christopher Daniels and Donovan Morgan) defeated **Dick Togo** and **Ikuto Hidaka** in 13:55 (★★★); **Alex Arion** defeated **Dunn** in 1:35 (★); **Xavier** defeated **Low Ki** to win the ROH World Title in 25:42 (★★★); **Takao Omori** defeated **Sonny Siaki** in 7:28 (★★); **Jay Briscoe** defeated **The Amazing Red** in 7:47 (★★★); **Paul London** defeated **Michael Shane** in a Street Fight in 20:38 (★★★★); **The Prophecy** (Christopher Daniels and Donovan Morgan) defeated **The American Dragon** and **Michael Modest** to win the inaugural ROH Tag Team Title in 14:42 (★★★).

Unforgiven '02 ★★★
22-09-02, Los Angeles, California **WWE**
Booker T, **Bubba Ray Dudley**, **Goldust** and **Kane** defeated **The Un-Americans** (Christian, Lance Storm, William Regal and Test) in 9:59 (★★); **Chris Jericho** defeated **Ric Flair** in 6:16 (★★); **Eddie Guerrero** defeated **Edge** in 11:55 (★★★★); **3-Minute Warning** (Rosey and Jamal) defeated **Billy** and **Chuck** in 6:38 (★★); **Triple H** defeated **Rob Van Dam** in 18:17 (★★); **Trish Stratus** defeated **Molly Holly** to win the WWE Women's Title in 5:46 (★★); **Chris Benoit** defeated **Kurt Angle** in 13:55 (★★★★); **Brock Lesnar** vs. **The Undertaker** went to a double DQ in 20:27 (★★).

Total Nonstop Action (25-09-02) ★★
25-09-02, Nashville, Tennessee **NWA-TNA**
Sonny Siaki defeated **Amazing Red** in 7:23 (★★); **Chris Harris** and **James Storm** defeated **Brian Lee** and **Ron Harris** in a Tables Match in 6:41 (★★); **AJ Styles** defeated **Low Ki** 2-1 in a Best Two Out Of Three Falls Match in 14:47 (★★★); **Scott Hall** and **Syxx-Pac** defeated **Brian Lawler** and **Elix Skipper** in 9:13 (★★); **Jorge Estrada** defeated **Kid Kash** in 6:06 (★★); **Jerry Lynn** defeated **Ron Killings** in a Lumberjack Match in 9:03 (★★); **BG James** defeated **Jeff Jarrett** by DQ in 9:10 (★★).

Total Nonstop Action (02-10-02) ★★★
02-10-02, Nashville, Tennessee **NWA-TNA**
Amazing Red defeated **Shark Boy** in 6:54 (★★); **Ron Killings** defeated **Low Ki** in 12:59 (★★★); **The S.A.T.** (Jose Maximo and Joel Maximo) defeated **The Flying Elvises** (Jimmy Yang and Jorge Estrada) in 8:47 (★★); **Sonny Siaki** defeated **David Young** in 6:12 (★★); **Chris Harris** and **James Storm** defeated **Ashley Hudson** and **Ron Harris** in 7:03 (★★); **Jerry Lynn** defeated **AJ Styles** in a Ladder Match in 17:27 (★★★★); **BG James** and **Syxx-Pac** defeated **Jeff Jarrett** and **Brian Lawler** in 9:39 (★★).

Glory By Honor I ★★★
05-10-02, Philadelphia, Pennsylvania **ROH**
Homicide defeated **Divine Storm** (Chris Divine and Quiet Storm), **Special K** (Dixie and Izzy) and **The SAT** (Joel Maximo and Jose Maximo) in a Scramble Match in 13:52 (★★★); **The Backseat Boyz** (Johnny Kashmere and Trent Acid) defeated **Homicide** and **Steve Corino** in 6:44 (★★); **The Christopher Street Connection** (Allison Danger, Buff-E and Mace) defeated **Alexis Laree**, **Christian York** and **Joey Matthews** in 4:47 (★★); **Tony Mamaluke** defeated **James Maritato** in a Winner Earns Rights Of FBI Gimmick Match in 8:29 (★★); **The Amazing Red** defeated **Ikuto Hidaka** in 13:43 (★★★★); **Fast Eddie** defeated **Don Juan** in 3:22 (★★); **Steve Corino** defeated **Rudy Boy Gonzales** in a Texas Death Match in 8:04 (★★); **Low Ki** defeated **Samoa Joe** in a Fight Without Honor Match in 16:25 (★★★★); **Prince Nana** defeated **Elax** in :55 (★); **Jay Briscoe** defeated **Xavier** in 13:19 (★★); **The Carnage Crew** (DeVito and Loc) vs. **Da Hit Squad** (Mafia and Monsta Mack) ended in a no contest in a Philadelphia Street Fight in 6:50 (★★); **Michael Shane** defeated **Paul London** and **Spanky** in a Three Way Elimination Match in 19:45 (★★★); **Christopher Daniels** defeated **Doug Williams** in 12:25 (★★).

Total Nonstop Action (09-10-02) ★★
09-10-02, Nashville, Tennessee **NWA-TNA**
Syxx-Pac, **BG James** and **Curt Hennig** defeated **Ron Killings**, **Jeff Jarrett** and **Brian Lawler** in 14:23 (★★); **Chris Harris** and **James Storm** defeated **The S.A.T.** (Jose Maximo and Joel Maximo) in 10:27 (★★); **Ace Steel** defeated **Kid Kash**, **Tony Mamaluke** and **Low Ki** in a Four Way 15-Minute Iron Man Match in 15:06 (★★); **Chris Michaels** and **Rick Michaels** defeated **Ron Harris** and **Sonny Siaki** in 7:22 (★★); **Low Ki** defeated **Ace Steel** by DQ in 1:30 (★); **Syxx-Pac** defeated **Ace Steel**, **Jose Maximo**, **Joel Maximo**, **Kid Kash**, **Tony Mamaluke** and **AJ Styles** in a Ladder Match to win the vacant NWA-TNA X-Division Title in 15:45 (★★★).

Total Nonstop Action (16-10-02) ★★
16-10-02, Nashville, Tennessee **NWA-TNA**
Brian Lawler defeated **David Young** in 5:52 (★★); **Sonny Siaki** defeated **Jorge Estrada** in 5:18 (★★); **Ace Steel** defeated **Derek Wylde** in 3:54 (★★); **BG James** and **Hermie Sadler** defeated **Jeff Jarrett** and **Miss TNA Bruce** in 6:56 (★★); **Ron Harris** defeated **Norman Smiley** in 4:50 (★★); **Chris Harris** and **James Storm** defeated **Chris Michaels** and **Rick Michaels** in 6:49 (★★); **AJ Styles** defeated **Syxx-Pac** by DQ in 13:54 (★★★); **Ron Killings** defeated **Curt Hennig** in 8:58 (★).

No Mercy '02 ★★★★
20-10-02, North Little Rock, Arkansas **WWE**
Chris Jericho and **Christian** defeated **Booker T** and **Goldust** in 8:46 (★★); **Torrie Wilson** defeated **Dawn Marie** in 4:40 (★★); **Rob Van Dam** defeated **Ric Flair** in 7:59 (★★); **Jamie Noble** defeated **Tajiri** in 8:15 (★★★); **Triple H** defeated **Kane** to win the WWE Intercontinental Title in 16:13 (★★); **Chris Benoit** and **Kurt Angle** defeated **Edge** and **Rey Mysterio** to win the vacant WWE Tag Team Title in 22:03 (★★★★★); **Trish Stratus** defeated **Victoria** in 5:31 (★★); **Brock Lesnar** defeated **The Undertaker** in a Hell In A Cell Match in 27:18 (★★★★).

Total Nonstop Action (23-10-02) ★★
23-10-02, Nashville, Tennessee **NWA-TNA**
Amazing Red defeated **Kid Kash**, **Joel Maximo**, **Jose Maximo** and **Elix Skipper** in a Five Way Elimination Match in 12:23 (★★); **Chris Harris** and **James Storm** defeated **The Hot Shots** (Cassidy O'Reilly and Chase Stevens) in 7:23 (★★); **Jerry Lynn** defeated **Sonny Siaki** in 5:48 (★★); **Scott Hall** defeated **Jeff Jarrett** in 11:39 (★★); **BG James** defeated **Brian Lawler** in 4:41 (★★); **AJ Styles** defeated **Syxx-Pac** to win the NXT-TNA X Division Title in a No DQ Match in 8:58 (★★★); **Jorge Estrada** defeated **Ace Steel** in 6:27 (★★); **Ron Killings** defeated **Curt Hennig** in 8:33 (★★).

Rebellion '02 ★★★
26-10-02, Manchester, England **WWE**
Booker T defeated **Matt Hardy** in 11:57 (★★); **Billy Kidman** and **Torrie Wilson** defeated **John Cena** and **Dawn Marie** in 5:20 (★★); **Funaki** defeated **Crash Holly** in 5:37 (★★); **Jamie Noble** defeated **Rey Mysterio** and **Tajiri** in a Three Way Match in 12:30 (★★★); **Reverend D-Von** and **Ron Simmons** defeated **Chuck Palumbo** and **The Big Valbowski** in 4:03 (★★); **Rikishi** defeated **Albert** in a Kiss My Ass Match in 7:13 (★★); **Chris Benoit** and **Kurt Angle** defeated **Los Guerreros** (Eddie Guerrero and Chavo Guerrero) in 16:33 (★★★★); **Brock Lesnar** and **Paul Heyman** defeated **Edge** in a Handicap Match in 18:33 (★★★).

Total Nonstop Action (30-10-02) ★★
30-10-02, Nashville, Tennessee **NWA-TNA**
Kid Kash defeated **Tony Mamaluke** in 8:33 (★★); **Ron Killings** defeated **Scott Hall** in 6:44 (★★); **Chris Harris** and **James Storm** defeated **The Hot Shots** (Cassidy O'Reilly and Chase Stevens), and **Chris Michaels** and **Rick Michaels** in a Three Way Match in 6:22 (★★); **BG James** defeated **Ron Harris** in 5:38 (★★); **Ace Steel** and **Miss TNA Bruce** defeated **Jorge Estrada** and **Priscilla** in 5:52 (★★); **Jeff Jarrett** defeated **Curt Hennig** in 1:13 (★); **Sonny Siaki** defeated **Jerry Lynn** in 15:01 (★★); **AJ Styles** defeated **Amazing Red** in 12:39 (★★★★).

Total Nonstop Action (06-11-02) ★★
06-11-02, Nashville, Tennessee **NWA-TNA**
Jorge Estrada defeated **Miss TNA Bruce** via count out in 8:49 (★★); **BG James** defeated **Sonny Siaki** in 7:08 (★★); **Chris Harris** and **James Storm** defeated **The Disciples Of The New Church** (Brian Lee and Slash) by DQ in 7:46 (★★); **Syxx-Pac** defeated **Brian Lawler** in 5:02 (★★); **Kid Kash** defeated **Joel**

Maximo, Jose Maximo, Tony Mamaluke and Ace Steel in a Five Way Tables Elimination Match in 12:54 (★★); Jeff Jarrett defeated Curt Hennig by DQ in 4:32 (★★); Jerry Lynn defeated AJ Styles to win the NWA-TNA X Division Title in 21:01 (★★★★).

All Star Extravaganza I ★★★★
09-11-02, Philadelphia, Pennsylvania ROH

The SAT (Joel Maximo and Jose Maximo) defeated Da Hit Squad (Mafia and Monsta Mack), Divine Storm (Chris Divine and Quiet Storm) and Special K (Dixie and Joey Matthews) in a Four Way Scramble Match in 10:12 (★★); Michael Shane defeated CM Punk in 13:04 (★★★); Paul London defeated Michael Shane in 4:38 (★★); Paul London defeated The Amazing Red in 5:50 (★★); The American Dragon defeated Paul London in 9:17 (★★★); Samoa Joe and The Prophecy (Christopher Daniels and Donovan Morgan) defeated Doug Williams, Homicide and Low Ki in 23:07 (★★★★); Alexis Laree defeated Allison Danger in 3:21 (★★); The Carnage Crew (DeVito and Loc) defeated The Ring Crew Express (Dunn and Marcos) in a Bunkhouse Match in 2:27 (★★); Xavier defeated Jay Briscoe in 20:49 (★★★); AJ Styles defeated The American Dragon in 22:30 (★★★★); Masato Tanaka and Shinjiro Otani defeated Low Ki and Steve Corino in 15:42 (★★★).

Total Nonstop Action (13-11-02) ★★
13-11-02, Nashville, Tennessee NWA-TNA

EZ Money defeated Tony Mamaluke in 4:53 (★★); Sonny Siaki defeated Chris Vaughn in 2:06 (★★); Malice defeated Kaos in 2:57 (★★); Brian Lawler defeated Jorge Estrada in 3:21 (★); Amazing Red defeated Jimmy Yang in 9:39 (★★); The S.A.T. (Jose Maximo and Joel Maximo) defeated The Rainbow Express (Lenny and Miss TNA Bruce) in 7:20 (★★); The Harris Brothers (Ron Harris and Don Harris) defeated The Hot Shots (Cassidy O'Reilly and Chase Stevens) in 3:56 (★★); Jeff Jarrett defeated BG James in 7:18 (★★); The Disciples Of The New Church (Brian Lee and Slash) defeated Chris Harris and James Storm to win the NWA World Tag Team Title in 9:06 (★★★); Jerry Lynn defeated AJ Styles and Kid Kash in a Three Way Match in 10:50 (★★★).

Survivor Series '02 ★★★★
17-11-02, New York City, New York WWE

The Dudley Boyz (Bubba Ray Dudley and D-Von Dudley) and Jeff Hardy defeated 3-Minute Warning (Rosey and Jamal) and Rico in an Elimination Tables Match in 14:22 (★★); Billy Kidman defeated Jamie Noble to win the WWE Cruiserweight Title in 7:29 (★★★); Victoria defeated Trish Stratus in a Hardcore Match to win the WWE Women's Title in 7:01 (★★★); The Big Show defeated Brock Lesnar to win the WWE Title in 4:19 (★★★); Los Guerreros (Eddie Guerrero and Chavo Guerrero) defeated Edge and Rey Mysterio, and Kurt Angle and Chris Benoit in a Triple Threat Elimination Match to win the WWE Tag Team Title in 19:25 (★★★); Shawn Michaels defeated Triple H, Chris Jericho, Kane, Booker T and Rob Van Dam in an Elimination Chamber Match to win the World Heavyweight Title in 39:20 (★★★★).

Total Nonstop Action (20-11-02) ★★★
20-11-02, Nashville, Tennessee NWA-TNA

EZ Money and Sonny Siaki defeated Divine Storm (Chris Divine and Quiet Storm) in 5:47 (★★); Malice defeated Kory Williams in 1:59 (★★); The Harris Brothers (Ron Harris and Don Harris) defeated The S.A.T. (Jose Maximo and Joel Maximo) in 6:07 (★★); BG James defeated Lenny Lane in 2:55 (★★); AJ Styles defeated Jorge Estrada and Crimson Dragon a Three Way Match in 11:00 (★★); The Disciples Of The New Church (Brian Lee and Slash) defeated America's Most Wanted (Chris Harris and James Storm) by DQ in 10:44 (★★★); Jerry Lynn defeated Amazing Red in 10:02 (★★★); Jeff Jarrett defeated Ron Killings to win the NWA World Heavyweight Title in 17:36 (★★★).

Total Nonstop Action (27-11-02) ★★
27-11-02, Nashville, Tennessee NWA-TNA

Divine Storm (Chris Divine and Quiet Storm) defeated The Briscoe Brothers (Jay Briscoe and Mark Briscoe) in 6:08 (★★); The Hot Shots (Cassidy O'Reilly and Chase Stevens) defeated America's Most Wanted (Chris Harris and James Storm) via count out in 5:17 (★★); The Disciples Of The New Church (Brian Lee and Slash) defeated BG James and Curt Hennig by DQ in 10:34 (★★); EZ Money defeated Alex Winters in 3:19 (★★); Sonny Siaki defeated Crimson Dragon in 5:17 (★★); Jerry Lynn defeated AJ Styles in 12:37 (★★); Jeff Jarrett defeated Ron Killings in 14:17 (★★★).

Total Nonstop Action (04-12-02) ★★
04-12-02, Nashville, Tennessee NWA-TNA

Divine Storm (Chris Divine and Quiet Storm) defeated The S.A.T. (Jose Maximo and Joel Maximo) in 7:33 (★★); Chris Harris defeated Brian Lee in 5:13 (★★); James Storm defeated Slash in 6:25 (★★); EZ Money defeated Kid Kash, AJ Styles and Joel Maximo in a Four Way Double Elimination Match in 20:36 (★★★); America's Most Wanted (Chris Harris and James Storm) defeated Belladonna in a Handicap Bullrope Match in 2:00 (★); Jeff Jarrett defeated The Harris Brothers (Big Ron and Heavy D) in a Handicap Match in 5:13 (★★).

Total Nonstop Action (11-12-02) ★★★
11-12-02, Nashville, Tennessee NWA-TNA

Tony Mamaluke defeated Jason Cross in 6:30 (★★); Kid Kash defeated Jorge Estrada in 5:15 (★★); Divine Storm (Chris Divine and Quiet Storm) defeated America's Most Wanted (Chris Harris and James Storm) in 6:55 (★★); Amazing Red defeated AJ Styles in 12:07 (★★); The Disciples Of The New Church (Brian Lee and Slash) defeated The Harris Brothers (Big Ron and Heavy D) by DQ in 4:17 (★★); Sonny Siaki defeated Jerry Lynn to win the NWA-TNA X Division Title in 11:57 (★★); Ron Killings defeated BG James in a Chairs and Chains Match in 4:03 (★★); Jeff Jarrett defeated Curt Hennig in 8:10 (★★).

Armageddon '02 ★★★
15-12-02, Sunrise, Florida WWE

Booker T and Goldust defeated Chris Jericho and Christian, The Dudley Boyz (Bubba Ray Dudley and D-Von Dudley), and Lance Storm and William Regal in a Fatal Four Way Elimination Match to win the World Tag Team Title in 16:43 (★★★); Edge defeated A-Train by DQ in 7:12 (★★); Chris Benoit defeated Eddie Guerrero in 16:47 (★★★★); Batista defeated Kane in 6:38 (★★); Victoria defeated Trish Stratus and Jacqueline in a Three Way Match in 4:28 (★★); Kurt Angle defeated The Big Show to win the WWE Title in 12:36 (★★); Triple H defeated Shawn Michaels in a Three Stages Of Hell Match to win the World Heavyweight Title in 35:25 (★★).

Total Nonstop Action (18-12-02) ★★★
18-12-02, Nashville, Tennessee NWA-TNA

Jason Cross won a 10-Man Gauntlet For The Gold Battle Royal in 22:11 (★★★); America's Most Wanted (Chris Harris and James Storm) defeated The Disciples Of The New Church (Brian Lee and Slash) and The Harris Brothers (Big Ron and Heavy D) in a Three Way Match in 7:38 (★★); Sonny Siaki defeated EZ Money and Jerry Lynn in a Three Way Match in 7:45 (★★★); BG James defeated Ron Killings in a Street Fight in 4:36 (★★); Christopher Daniels, Elix Skipper and Low Ki defeated The S.A.T. (Amazing Red, Jose Maximo and Joel Maximo) in 21:03 (★★★★).

Final Battle '02 ★★★
28-12-02, Philadelphia, Pennsylvania ROH

CM Punk defeated Colt Cabana in 9:24 (★★★); Simply Luscious defeated Alexis Laree in :41 (★); Special K (Angel Dust and Deranged) defeated Da Hit Squad (Mafia and Monsta Mack) and The Backseat Boyz (Johnny Kashmere and Trent Acid) in a Three Way Scramble Match in 10:24 (★★); The Prophecy (Christopher Daniels and Donovan Morgan) defeated The SAT (Joel Maximo and Jose Maximo) 2-1 in a Best Two Out Of Three Falls Match in 19:02 (★★★); Eddie Guapo and Mace defeated The Carnage Crew (DeVito and Loc) by DQ in 2:00 (★★); Jody Reisch defeated The Amazing Red in 6:14 (★★); Xavier defeated Paul London in 17:05 (★★★); The American Dragon vs. Low Ki vs. Samoa Joe vs. Steve Corino ended in a draw in a Four Way Match in 45:00 (★★★★).

Total Nonstop Action (08-01-03) ★★
08-01-03, Nashville, Tennessee NWA-TNA

David Young and Tony Mamaluke defeated EZ Money and Kid Kash in 7:42 (★★); Sonny Siaki defeated Jason Cross in 8:11 (★★); Jerry Lynn and Ron Killings defeated BG James and Don Harris by DQ in 6:29 (★★); America's Most Wanted (Chris Harris and James Storm) defeated The Disciples Of The New Church (Brian Lee and Slash) to win the NWA World Tag Team Title in 14:15 (★★★); Curt Hennig defeated David Flair in an Axehandle On A Pole Match in 2:39 (★); Jeff Jarrett defeated Christopher Daniels in 4:45 (★★); Jeff Jarrett defeated Elix Skipper in 5:55 (★★); Jeff Jarrett defeated Low Ki by DQ in 7:50 (★★).

Total Nonstop Action (15-01-03) ★★
15-01-03, Nashville, Tennessee **NWA-TNA**
America's Most Wanted (Chris Harris and James Storm) defeated Divine Storm (Chris Divine and Quiet Storm) in 7:07 (★★); AJ Styles defeated Ron Killings in 8:48 (★★); Desire defeated April Hunter in 2:58 (★); Jerry Lynn defeated Mike Sanders in 7:48 (★★); David Young defeated Jason Cross in 5:20 (★★); Sonny Siaki defeated Kid Kash in 4:50 (★★); Christopher Daniels, Elix Skipper, Low Ki and Vince Russo defeated The Road Warriors (Hawk and Animal), Dusty Rhodes and Jeff Jarrett in 11:40 (★★★).

Royal Rumble '03 ★★★
19-01-03, Boston, Massachusetts **WWE**
Brock Lesnar defeated The Big Show in 6:15 (★★); The Dudley Boyz (Bubba Ray Dudley and D-Von Dudley) defeated Lance Storm and William Regal to win the World Tag Team Title in 7:26 (★★); Torrie Wilson defeated Dawn Marie Wilson in 3:35 (★); Scott Steiner defeated Triple H by DQ in 17:00 (★); Kurt Angle defeated Chris Benoit in 17:18 (★★★★★); Brock Lesnar won the 30-Man Royal Rumble Match in 53:47 (★★★).

Total Nonstop Action (22-01-03) ★★
22-01-03, Nashville, Tennessee **NWA-TNA**
The S.A.T. (Amazing Red, Jose Maximo and Joel Maximo) defeated Jimmy Yang, David Young and Shark Boy in 12:29 (★★★); Ashley Hudson defeated Jorge Estrada in 5:00 (★); AJ Styles defeated Larry Zbyszko in 5:49 (★★); Mike Sanders and David Flair defeated Ron Killings and Jerry Lynn in 7:50 (★★); Elix Skipper and Low Ki defeated America's Most Wanted (Chris Harris and James Storm) to win the NWA World Tag Team Title in 15:19 (★★★); Sonny Siaki defeated Athena and Chris Vaughn in a Three Way Match in 1:37 (★★); Jeff Jarrett defeated BG James, Christopher Daniels and Don Harris in a Gauntlet Elimination Match in 10:26 (★★).

Total Nonstop Action (29-01-03) ★
29-01-03, Nashville, Tennessee **NWA-TNA**
Amazing Red defeated Jorge Estrada in 6:20 (★★); David Flair defeated Jerry Lynn in 5:11 (★); Mike Sanders defeated Ron Killings in 7:32 (★★); Larry Zbyszko defeated AJ Styles in a 10-Minute Challenge Match in 10:02 (★★); Kid Kash and Trinity defeated Sonny Siaki and Desire in 6:17 (★★); The Rock 'n' Roll Express (Ricky Morton and Robert Gibson) defeated America's Most Wanted (Chris Harris and James Storm) in 8:48 (★★).

Total Nonstop Action (05-02-03) ★★
05-02-03, Nashville, Tennessee **NWA-TNA**
Jorge Estrada defeated Glenn Gilbertti in 6:54 (★); Sonny Siaki defeated Amazing Red in 9:46 (★★★); Tenacious Z defeated BG James in 3:55 (★★); Ron Killings defeated Jerry Lynn, Mike Sanders and David Flair in a Four Way Elimination Match in 9:09 (★); Trinity defeated Desire in 8:24 (★); Elix Skipper and Low Ki vs. The Disciples Of The New Church (Brian Lee and Slash) ended in a double pinfall draw in 15:33 (★★★).

One Year Anniversary Show ★★★
08-02-03, New York City, New York **ROH**
EZ Money defeated Chad Collyer, Colt Cabana and Michael Shane in a Four Corner Survival Match in 15:18 (★★); The Texas Wrestling Academy (Don Juan, Fast Eddie and Hotstuff Hernandez) defeated The Carnage Crew (DeVito, Loc and Masada) by DQ in a Three Way Match in 9:42 (★★); Jay Briscoe defeated Mark Briscoe in 16:40 (★★★); Steve Corino defeated Homicide in 12:17 (★★); CM Punk defeated CW Anderson in 9:42 (★★); Bryan Danielson defeated Samoa Joe in 15:21 (★★★); Paul London defeated AJ Styles and Low Ki in a Three Way Match in 19:12 (★★★★); Xavier defeated Paul London in 19:33 (★★★); Da Hit Squad (Mafia and Monsta Mack), Divine Storm (Chris Divine and Quiet Storm), Mikey Whipwreck and The SAT (Joel Maximo and Jose Maximo) defeated Special K (Angel Dust, Brian XL, Deranged, Dixie, Hydro, Izzy, Jody Fleisch, Slim J, Slugger and Yeyo) in a Handicap Scramble Match in 33:37 (★).

The Retribution ★★
09-02-03, Glasgow, Scotland **WWA**
Shark Boy defeated Frankie Kazarian in 10:03 (★★); Konnan defeated Nate Webb in :03 (★); Buff Bagwell and Johnny Swinger defeated Norman Smiley and Malice in 9:54 (★★); Teo defeated Puppet in a Hardcore Match in 3:20 (★★); Mike Sanders defeated Joe E. Legend in 9:12 (★★); Jeff Jarrett

defeated Nathan Jones in 5:42 (★★); Sabu defeated Simon Diamond and Perry Saturn in a Three Way Match in 16:20 (★★★); Lex Luger defeated Sting to win the vacant WWA World Heavyweight Title in 7:09 (★★).

Total Nonstop Action (12-02-03) ★★
12-02-03, Nashville, Tennessee **NWA-TNA**
America's Most Wanted (Chris Harris and James Storm) defeated The Rock 'n' Roll Express (Ricky Morton and Robert Gibson) in 4:58 (★★); The Harris Brothers (Big Ron and Heavy D) defeated The Disciples Of The New Church (Brian Lee and Slash) in 4:49 (★★); Kid Kash defeated Sonny Siaki to win the NWA-TNA X Division Title in 7:09 (★★); Ron Killings, Jorge Estrada and Tenacious Z defeated S.E.X. (Mike Sanders, Glenn Gilbertti and BG James) in 7:41 (★★); Steve Corino defeated Low Ki by DQ in 6:55 (★★); Jerry Lynn defeated Shark Boy, Joel Maximo, Jose Maximo, Jimmy Rave, Tony Mamaluke, David Young and Paul London in an Eight Man Elimination Match in 15:54 (★★★); Raven defeated The Sandman in a Falls Count Anywhere Match in 7:41 (★★).

Total Nonstop Action (19-02-03) ★★
19-02-03, Nashville, Tennessee **NWA-TNA**
America's Most Wanted (Chris Harris and James Storm) defeated The Harris Brothers (Big Ron and Heavy D) in 7:02 (★★); Jerry Lynn defeated Joel Maximo and Jose Maximo in a Three Way Match in 6:38 (★★); Disgraceland defeated Shark Boy in 3:08 (★); Kid Kash defeated Paul London in 8:17 (★★); Mike Sanders defeated Jonah in 5:31 (★★); Raven and Low Ki defeated The Sandman and Steve Corino in 8:09 (★★); Jeff Jarrett defeated AJ Styles in 16:05 (★★★★).

No Way Out '03 ★★★
23-02-03, Montreal, Quebec **WWE**
Chris Jericho defeated Jeff Hardy in 12:59 (★★★); Lance Storm and William Regal defeated Kane and Rob Van Dam in 9:20 (★★); Matt Hardy defeated Billy Kidman to win the WWE Cruiserweight Title in 9:31 (★★); The Undertaker defeated The Big Show in 14:08 (★★); Brock Lesnar and Chris Benoit defeated Kurt Angle and Team Angle (Shelton Benjamin and Charlie Haas) in a Handicap Match in 13:19 (★★★); Triple H defeated Scott Steiner in 13:01 (★); Steve Austin defeated Eric Bischoff in 4:26 (★★); The Rock defeated Hulk Hogan in 12:20 (★★).

Total Nonstop Action (26-02-03) ★★
26-02-03, Nashville, Tennessee **NWA-TNA**
Kid Kash defeated Jason Cross in 6:38 (★★); The Disciples Of The New Church (Brian Lee and Slash) defeated Simon Diamond and Johnny Swinger in 6:33 (★★); America's Most Wanted (Chris Harris and James Storm) defeated The Hot Shots (Cassidy O'Reilly and Chase Stevens) in 8:12 (★★★); Raven defeated Julio Dinero in 6:00 (★★); Jerry Lynn defeated Juventud Guerrera in 9:10 (★★★); AJ Styles defeated The Sandman in 6:12 (★★); Dusty Rhodes and Vader defeated The Harris Brothers (Big Ron and Heavy D) by DQ in 5:44 (★★).

Total Nonstop Action (05-03-03) ★★
05-03-03, Nashville, Tennessee **NWA-TNA**
Jerry Lynn defeated Super Crazy in 9:10 (★★★); The Disciples Of The New Church (Brian Lee and Slash) defeated The Hot Shots (Cassidy O'Reilly and Chase Stevens) in 6:18 (★★); Jorge Estrada defeated Disgraceland in 3:35 (★★); Kid Kash defeated Amazing Red in 9:40 (★★★); Mike Sanders and Glenn Gilbertti defeated America's Most Wanted (Chris Harris and James Storm) in 8:49 (★★); Raven defeated The Sandman in a Clockwork Orange House of Fun Match in 8:19 (★★).

Total Nonstop Action (12-03-03) ★★
12-03-03, Nashville, Tennessee **NWA-TNA**
Jerry Lynn and David Young defeated Halloween and Damien in 4:24 (★★); Kid Kash defeated Jonny Storm and Amazing Red in a Three Way Match in 9:37 (★★★); The Harris Brothers (Big Ron and Heavy D) defeated The Sandman and Steve Corino in :29 (★); Jim Duggan defeated Mike Sanders in 5:58 (★); Triple X (Christopher Daniels and Low Ki) defeated America's Most Wanted (Chris Harris and James Storm) to win the vacant NWA World Tag Team Title in 11:52 (★★★); Raven vs. AJ Styles ended in a double pinfall draw in 10:03 (★★).

Expect The Unexpected ★★★
15-03-03, Boston, Massachusetts ROH

Chad Collyer defeated Matt Stryker in 15:05 (★★★); The Amazing Red defeated Slim J in 12:03 (★★); AJ Styles defeated The Backseat Boyz (Johnny Kashmere and Trent Acid), The Carnage Crew (DeVito and Loc) and The SAT (Joel Maximo and Jose Maximo) in a Scramble Match in 12:15 (★★★); Da Hit Squad (Mafia and Monsta Mack) and Low Ki defeated Special K (Angel Dust, Deranged and Dixie) in 18:12 (★★★); Ghost Shadow and Quiet Storm defeated The Ring Crew Express (Dunn and Marcos) in 3:37 (★★); CM Punk defeated Raven in a Ravens Rules Match in 28:52 (★★★★); Samoa Joe defeated BJ Whitmer, EZ Money and Homicide in a Four Way Match in 16:34 (★★★); AJ Styles and The Amazing Red defeated The Prophecy (Christopher Daniels and Xavier) to win the ROH Tag Team Titles in 21:11 (★★★).

Total Nonstop Action (19-03-03) ★★
19-03-03, Nashville, Tennessee NWA-TNA

Triple X (Elix Skipper and Low Ki) defeated The Disciples Of The New Church (Brian Lee and Slash) by DQ in 8:50 (★★★); Konnan and Juventud Guerrera defeated Jerry Lynn and Jason Cross in 9:24 (★★); Jim Duggan and Moondog Spot defeated S.E.X. (Glenn Gilbertti and Mike Sanders) in 1:56 (★); Kid Kash defeated Amazing Red and Trinity in a Three Way Match in 5:56 (★★); D-Lo Brown, Dusty Rhodes and Jeff Jarrett defeated Erik Watts, Brian Lawler and David Flair in 8:27 (★★); Raven defeated AJ Styles in a Hardcore Ladder Match in 11:12 (★★★).

Night Of Champions ★★★★
22-03-03, Philadelphia, Pennsylvania ROH

BJ Whitmer defeated Alex Arion, Dixie and Matt Stryker in a Four Corner Survival Match in 11:26 (★★); Special K (Angel Dust, Deranged and Izzy) defeated Quiet Storm and The SAT (Joel Maximo and Jose Maximo) in a Scramble Match in 6:25 (★★); The Backseat Boyz (Johnny Kashmere and Trent Acid) defeated The Ring Crew Express (Dunn and Marcos) in 5:19 (★★); Doug Williams defeated Christopher Daniels in the FWA British Heavyweight Title in 19:14 (★★★★); Da Hit Squad (Mafia and Monsta Mack) and Homicide defeated The Group (CW Anderson, Jack Victory and Samoa Joe) by DQ in 7:12 (★★); The Carnage Crew (DeVito and Loc) defeated Hotstuff Hernandez and Mace Mendoza in 6:22 (★★); AJ Styles and The Amazing Red defeated The Briscoe Brothers (Jay Briscoe and Mark Briscoe) in 16:34 (★★★★); Low Ki defeated Jody Fleisch in 19:38 (★★★); Colt Cabana and Raven defeated Ace Steel and CM Punk in a Ravens Rules Match 21:16 (★★★); Samoa Joe defeated Xavier to win the ROH World Title in 11:55 (★★★).

Total Nonstop Action (26-03-03) ★★
26-03-03, Nashville, Tennessee NWA-TNA

AJ Styles defeated Mike Sanders in 8:12 (★★); Jerry Lynn defeated Konnan in 5:31 (★★); David Young vs. Sonny Siaki went to a no contest in 5:47 (★★); Dusty Rhodes defeated David Flair in a Bunkhouse Stampede Match in 2:26 (★); Kid Kash and Trinity defeated Alexis Laree and Amazing Red in 7:33 (★★); D-Lo Brown defeated Chris Harris in 6:48 (★★); The Disciples Of The New Church (Brian Lee and Slash), The Sandman and Perry Saturn defeated The Harris Brothers (Big Ron and Heavy D) and Triple X (Christopher Daniels and Elix Skipper) in a Sadistic Madness Match in 11:22 (★★).

WrestleMania XIX ★★★★★
30-03-03, Seattle, Washington WWE

Matt Hardy defeated Rey Mysterio in 5:37 (★★); The Undertaker defeated The Big Show and A-Train in a Handicap Match in 9:42 (★★); Trish Stratus defeated Victoria and Jazz in a Three Way Match to win the WWE Women's Title in 7:17 (★★); Team Angle (Charlie Haas and Shelton Benjamin) defeated Chris Benoit and Rhyno, and Los Guerreros (Eddie Guerrero and Chavo Guerrero) in a Three Way Match in 8:48 (★★★); Shawn Michaels defeated Chris Jericho in 22:34 (★★★★); Triple H defeated Booker T in 18:45 (★★); Hulk Hogan defeated Vince McMahon in a Street Fight in 20:47 (★★★); The Rock defeated Steve Austin in 17:55 (★★★★); Brock Lesnar defeated Kurt Angle to win the WWE Title in 21:07 (★★★★).

Total Nonstop Action (02-04-03) ★★
02-04-03, Nashville, Tennessee NWA-TNA

Brian Lawler defeated Chris Harris in 6:55 (★★); Trinity defeated Alexis Laree in 6:40 (★★); Perry Saturn, The Sandman and New Jack defeated Christopher Daniels and The Harris Brothers (Big Ron and Heavy D) in 5:12 (★★); David Young defeated Sonny Siaki in 4:33 (★★★); Ron Killings defeated Elix Skipper in 9:02 (★★); Kid Kash defeated Jerry Lynn in 11:43 (★★★); Jeff Jarrett defeated D-Lo Brown in 10:03 (★★).

Total Nonstop Action (09-04-03) ★★★
09-04-03, Nashville, Tennessee NWA-TNA

The Harris Brothers (Big Ron and Heavy D) defeated The Sandman and New Jack, and The Disciples Of The New Church (Brian Lee and Slash) in a Three Way Armed Asylum Match in 8:32 (★★); Dusty Rhodes defeated Brian Lawler in a Ladder Match in 8:23 (★★); AJ Styles defeated Glenn Gilbertti in 7:24 (★★); Sonny Siaki and Desire defeated David Young and Athena in :41 (★); Perry Saturn defeated Mike Barton in 7:24 (★★★); D-Lo Brown defeated Mike Sanders in 7:05 (★★); Raven defeated Kid Kash in 7:28 (★★); Jerry Lynn and Amazing Red defeated Triple X (Christopher Daniels and Elix Skipper), Shark Boy and Jason Cross, and Jonny Storm and Chris Sabin in a Four Way Elimination Match in 13:37 (★★★★).

Total Nonstop Action (16-04-03) ★★★
16-04-03, Nashville, Tennessee NWA-TNA

Raven defeated D-Lo Brown in 5:54 (★★★); Glenn Gilbertti defeated AJ Styles in a Falls Count Anywhere Street Match in 7:49 (★★); Kid Kash defeated Mike Sanders in 7:09 (★★); Mike Awesome defeated Perry Saturn by DQ in 7:55 (★★); David Young defeated James Storm in 5:55 (★★); The Disciples Of The New Church (Brian Lee and Slash) defeated The Sandman and New Jack in 6:17 (★★); Jerry Lynn and Amazing Red defeated Triple X (Christopher Daniels and Elix Skipper) to win the NWA World Tag Team Title in 14:16 (★★★★); Julio Dinero and Alexis Laree defeated Jeff Jarrett in a Handicap Clockwork Orange House of Fun Match in 6:10 (★★).

Total Nonstop Action (23-04-03) ★★★
23-04-03, Nashville, Tennessee NWA-TNA

AJ Styles and D-Lo Brown defeated Glenn Gilbertti and Mike Sanders by DQ in 6:31 (★★); Triple X (Christopher Daniels and Elix Skipper) defeated America's Most Wanted (Chris Harris and James Storm) in 11:06 (★★★); Team Extreme (New Jack, Perry Saturn and The Sandman) defeated The Disciples Of The New Church (Mike Awesome, Brian Lee and Slash) in an Ultimate Sin Match in 9:35 (★★); Trinity defeated Kid Kash in 6:34 (★★); Slash vs. Justin Credible ended in a no contest in 4:32 (★★); Amazing Red defeated Jerry Lynn in 14:05 (★★★).

Retribution: Round Robin Challenge II ★★★
26-04-03, West Mifflin, Pennsylvania ROH

Christopher Daniels defeated The Amazing Red in 11:10 (★★); The Second City Saints (Ace Steel and Colt Cabana) defeated Da Hit Squad (Dan Maff and Monsta Mack) in 8:12 (★★); The SAT (Joel Maximo and Jose Maximo) defeated EZ Money and Sterling James Keenan, and Special K (Brian XL and Hydro), and The Ring Crew Express (Dunn and Marcos) in a Four Way Scramble Match in 9:14 (★★); Homicide defeated CM Punk in 15:27 (★★★); The Carnage Crew (DeVito, Loc and Masada) defeated The Texas Wrestling Academy (Don Juan, Fast Eddie and Hotstuff Hernandez) in a No DQ Match in 9:12 (★★); Paul London defeated The Amazing Red in 10:09 (★★★); Alexis Laree defeated Persephone in 5:28 (★★); Matt Stryker defeated BJ Whitmer, Chad Collyer, Donovan Morgan and Michael Shane in a Five Way Match in 19:11 (★★★); Christopher Daniels defeated Paul London in 24:54 (★★★); Samoa Joe defeated Doug Williams in 11:45 (★★★).

Backlash '03 ★★
27-04-03, Worcester, Massachusetts WWE

Team Angle (Charlie Haas and Shelton Benjamin) defeated Los Guerreros (Eddie Guerrero and Chavo Guerrero) in 15:03 (★★); Sean O'Haire defeated Rikishi in 4:52 (★★); Kane and Rob Van Dam defeated The Dudley Boyz (Bubba Ray Dudley and D-Von Dudley) in 13:01 (★★); Trish Stratus defeated Jazz to win the WWE Women's Title in 5:50 (★★); The Big Show defeated Rey Mysterio in 3:47 (★★); Brock Lesnar defeated John Cena in 15:14 (★★); Triple H, Ric Flair and Chris Jericho defeated Shawn Michaels, Kevin Nash and Booker T in 17:51 (★★); Goldberg defeated The Rock in 13:03 (★★).

Total Nonstop Action (30-04-03) ★★★

30-04-03, Nashville, Tennessee **NWA-TNA**

Justin Credible and Perry Saturn defeated The Disciples Of The New Church (Brian Lee and Slash), The Harris Brothers (Big Ron and Heavy D) and America's Most Wanted (Chris Harris and James Storm) in a Four Way Match in 8:07 (★★); Jerry Lynn defeated Christopher Daniels in 7:05 (★★★); AJ Styles and D-Lo Brown defeated David Young and Sonny Siaki in 9:10 (★★★); Chris Sabin defeated Jason Cross, Shark Boy and Jimmy Rave in a Four Way Elimination Match in 8:13 (★★); Amazing Red defeated Kid Kash to win the NWA-TNA X Division Title in 9:17 (★★); Jeff Jarrett defeated Raven in 17:31 (★★★).

Total Nonstop Action (07-05-03) ★★

07-05-03, Nashville, Tennessee **NWA-TNA**

AJ Styles and D-Lo Brown defeated Triple X (Low Ki and Elix Skipper) in 9:04 (★★★); Sabu defeated New Jack and The Sandman in a Three Way Match in 6:10 (★★); James Storm defeated Chris Harris in 7:35 (★★); Traci defeated Desire in 2:40 (★); Christopher Daniels defeated Jerry Lynn and Amazing Red by DQ in a Handicap Match to win the NWA World Tag Team Title (★★); Glenn Gilbertti and Sabu co-won an Anarchy In The Asylum Battle Royal in 28:13 (★★); Glenn Gilbertti defeated Sabu in 1:38 (★★).

Total Nonstop Action (14-05-03) ★★

14-05-03, Nashville, Tennessee **NWA-TNA**

Chris Sabin defeated Jerry Lynn and Amazing Red to win the NWA-TNA X Division Title in a Three Way Match in 10:49 (★★★); Mike Sanders defeated Mike Awesome in a Tables Match in 5:31 (★); Ron Killings defeated Kid Kash in 9:08 (★★); Chris Harris defeated David Young in 11:35 (★★); Glenn Gilbertti defeated Perry Saturn in 6:28 (★★); Triple X (Christopher Daniels and Elix Skipper) defeated AJ Styles and D-Lo Brown in 8:57 (★★★).

Judgment Day '03 ★★

18-05-03, Charlotte, North Carolina **WWE**

John Cena and The F.B.I. (Chuck Palumbo and Johnny Stamboli) defeated Chris Benoit, Rhyno and Spanky in 3:55 (★★); La Resistance (Sylvain Grenier and Rene Dupree) defeated Scott Steiner and Test in 6:20 (★★); Eddie Guerrero and Tajiri defeated Team Angle (Charlie Haas and Shelton Benjamin) in a Ladder Match to win the WWE Tag Team Title in 14:10 (★★★); Christian won a Battle Royal to win the vacant WWF Intercontinental Title in 11:55 (★★); Mr. America defeated Roddy Piper in 4:50 (★★); Kevin Nash defeated Triple H by DQ in 7:22 (★★); Jazz defeated Jacqueline, Trish Stratus and Victoria in a Four Way Match in 4:47 (★★); Brock Lesnar defeated The Big Show in a Stretcher Match in 15:27 (★★).

Total Nonstop Action (21-05-03) ★★

21-05-03, Nashville, Tennessee **NWA-TNA**

Paul London defeated Jason Cross, CM Punk and Kid Romeo in a Four Way Elimination Match in 11:15 (★★★); Slash, Justin Credible and Amazing Red defeated Triple X (Christopher Daniels and Elix Skipper) in a Handicap Match in 12:11 (★★★); Mike Sanders defeated Brian Lee 10-8 in a Hard Ten Tournament Match in 5:49 (★); Ron Killings and Don Harris defeated New Jack and Shark Boy in 3:13 (★★); David Young and Traci defeated Trinity and Kid Kash in 7:45 (★★); America's Most Wanted (Chris Harris and James Storm) defeated AJ Styles and D-Lo Brown in 9:07 (★★); Sonny Siaki vs. The Sandman went to a no contest in a Clockwork Orange House of Fun match in 9:34 (★).

Total Nonstop Action (28-05-03) ★

28-05-03, Nashville, Tennessee **NWA-TNA**

AJ Styles and D-Lo Brown defeated Jason Cross and CM Punk in 4:31 (★★); BG James and Konnan defeated The Sandman and Sonny Siaki in 2:41 (★★); New Jack defeated Slash 18-13 in a Hard Ten Tournament Match in 7:09 (★); Triple X (Christopher Daniels and Elix Skipper) defeated The S.A.T. (Jose Maximo and Joel Maximo) in 6:20 (★★); Kid Kash defeated Trinity in 2:30 (★); Chris Harris and Chris Sabin defeated Jerry Lynn and Justin Credible in 9:04 (★★); Glenn Gilbertti defeated Raven in 15:46 (★★).

Total Nonstop Action (04-06-03) ★

04-06-03, Nashville, Tennessee **NWA-TNA**

CM Punk, Matt Stryker and Frankie Kazarian defeated Kid Romeo, Damien Dothart and Johnny Swinger in 11:10 (★★); Sonny Siaki defeated The Vampire Warrior 12-5 in a Hard Ten Tournament Match in 3:51 (★); David Young and Traci defeated Ron Killings in a Handicap Match in 6:53 (★); America's Most Wanted (Chris Harris and James Storm) defeated BG James and Konnan in 5:27 (★★); AJ Styles defeated D-Lo Brown in 9:07 (★★); Jeff Jarrett defeated Glenn Gilbertti in 13:43 (★★).

Insurrextion '03 ★★

07-06-03, Newcastle, England **WWE**

Jazz defeated Trish Stratus in 10:45 (★★); Christian defeated Booker T in 15:12 (★★★); Kane and Rob Van Dam defeated La Resistance (Sylvain Grenier and Rene Dupree) in 9:03 (★★); Goldust defeated Rico in 9:53 (★★); The Dudley Boyz (Bubba Ray Dudley, D-Von Dudley and Spike Dudley) defeated Christopher Nowinski, Rodney Mack and Theodore Long in 9:15 (★★); Scott Steiner defeated Test in 6:49 (★★); Triple H defeated Kevin Nash in a Street Fight in 16:33 (★★).

The Reckoning ★★

08-06-03, Auckland, New Zealand **WWA**

Rick Steiner defeated Mark Mercedes in 3:49 (★★); Teo defeated Meatball and Puppet in a Triangle Match in 3:14 (★★); Devon Storm defeated Konnan in a Hardcore Match in 10:07 (★★); Chris Sabin defeated Jerry Lynn, Frankie Kazarian and Johnny Swinger in a Four Way Match to win the WWA International Cruiserweight Title in 14:16 (★★★★); Sabu defeated Joe E. Legend in 17:23 (★★); Jeff Jarrett defeated Sting to win the WWA World Heavyweight Title in 13:41 (★★).

Total Nonstop Action (11-06-03) ★★

11-06-03, Nashville, Tennessee **NWA-TNA**

D-Lo Brown defeated Julio Dinero in 6:36 (★★); Chris Sabin defeated Shark Boy in 6:19 (★★); Ron Killings and Konnan defeated The Harris Brothers (Big Ron and Heavy D) in 6:53 (★★); Kid Kash defeated Goldylocks and Trinity in a Handicap Match in 5:01 (★★); The Sandman defeated Devon Storm 11-7 in a Hard Ten Tournament Match in 6:48 (★★); America's Most Wanted (Chris Harris and James Storm) defeated Traci and David Young to win the Asylum Alliance Tournament in 6:41 (★); AJ Styles defeated Raven and Jeff Jarrett in a Three Way Match to win the NWA World Heavyweight Title in 13:59 (★★★).

Bad Blood '03 ★★★

15-06-03, Houston, Texas **WWE**

Christopher Nowinski and Rodney Mack defeated The Dudley Boyz (Bubba Ray Dudley and D-Von Dudley) in 7:07 (★★); Scott Steiner defeated Test in 6:23 (★★); Booker T defeated Christian by DQ in 7:53 (★★); La Resistance (Sylvain Grenier and Rene Dupree) defeated Kane and Rob Van Dam to win the World Tag Team Title in 5:47 (★★); Goldberg defeated Chris Jericho in 10:53 (★★★); Ric Flair defeated Shawn Michaels in 14:18 (★★★); Triple H defeated Kevin Nash in a Hell In A Cell Match in 21:01 (★★★).

Total Nonstop Action (18-06-03) ★★★

18-06-03, Nashville, Tennessee **NWA-TNA**

Frankie Kazarian, D-Lo Brown and The Sandman defeated Sonny Siaki, Don Harris and David Young in 3:53 (★★); Chris Sabin defeated Paul London in 7:53 (★★); New Jack defeated Mike Sanders 10-7 in a Hard Ten Tournament Match in 5:33 (★★); Justin Credible defeated Jerry Lynn in 2:43 (★★); Kenzo Suzuki vs. Perry Saturn ended in a no contest in 4:35 (★★); Triple X (Christopher Daniels and Elix Skipper) defeated America's Most Wanted (Chris Harris and James Storm) in 7:04 (★★★); Jeff Jarrett and Sting defeated AJ Styles and Sean Waltman in 11:49 (★★★).

Total Nonstop Action (25-06-03) ★★★★

25-06-03, Nashville, Tennessee **NWA-TNA**

America's Most Wanted (Chris Harris and James Storm) defeated Triple X (Christopher Daniels and Elix Skipper) in a Steel Cage Match to win the NWA World Tag Team Title in 17:49 (★★★★★); D-Lo Brown defeated AJ Styles by DQ in a Steel Cage Match in 4:55 (★★); Jerry Lynn defeated Justin Credible in a Lights Out Match in 3:33 (★★); Frankie Kazarian defeated Chris Sabin in 11:55 (★★★★); Kid Kash defeated Erik Watts in 8:35 (★★); The Sandman defeated Sonny Siaki 11-9 in a Hard Ten Tournament Match in 4:54 (★★); Raven and Jeff Jarrett defeated Glenn Gilbertti and Shane Douglas by DQ in 11:05 (★★).

Total Nonstop Action (02-07-03) ★★
02-07-03, Nashville, Tennessee NWA-TNA

Shane Douglas defeated CM Punk in a Clockwork Orange House of Fun Match in 6:00 (★★); America's Most Wanted (Chris Harris and James Storm) defeated David Young and Sonny Siaki in 8:52 (★★); Abyss defeated Erik Watts in 6:26 (★★); Jerry Lynn defeated Justin Credible in a Russian Chain Match in 7:09 (★★); Shark Boy defeated Mike Sanders in 4:04 (★★); The Sandman defeated New Jack 12-7 in 5:11 to win the Hard Ten Tournament in 5:11 (★); AJ Styles defeated Frankie Kazarian in 13:23 (★★★).

Total Nonstop Action (09-07-03) ★★
09-07-03, Nashville, Tennessee NWA-TNA

America's Most Wanted (Chris Harris and James Storm) defeated Simon Diamond and Johnny Swinger in 8:54 (★★★); Frankie Kazarian defeated Kid Romeo, Matt Sydal, Altar Boy Luke, Delirious and Matt Stryker in a Six Way Elimination Match in 9:52 (★★); Chris Sabin defeated Frankie Kazarian in 3:04 (★★); Shane Douglas defeated Julio Dinero in 5:54 (★); Don Harris defeated Shark Boy in 5:24 (★★); Kid Kash defeated Jerry Lynn in 7:06 (★★); AJ Styles defeated D-Lo Brown in 7:22 (★★).

Total Nonstop Action (16-07-03) ★
16-07-03, Nashville, Tennessee NWA-TNA

D-Lo Brown defeated Sonny Siaki in 4:28 (★); Jerry Lynn defeated Justin Credible in a Last Man Standing Match in 11:29 (★★); Chris Sabin defeated Frankie Kazarian by DQ in 7:57 (★★); The Harris Brothers (Big Ron and Heavy D) defeated New Jack and Shark Boy in 4:11 (★); Elix Skipper defeated Amazing Red in 4:59 (★★); Edward Chastain defeated Norman Smiley in 3:08 (★); Joe Legend defeated Jeff Jarrett in 2:21 (★★); D-Lo Brown vs. Vince Russo ended in a no contest in 2:47 (★).

Death Before Dishonor '03 ★★★★
19-07-03, Elizabeth, New Jersey ROH

Low Ki defeated Deranged in 6:34 (★★); Matt Stryker defeated Jimmy Rave in 8:46 (★★★); The Texas Wrestling Academy (Don Juan, Fast Eddie, Hotstuff Hernandez and Rudy Boy Gonzales) defeated The Carnage Crew (DeVito, Justin Credible, Loc and Masada) in a Weapons Match in 12:05 (★★★); The Purists (John Walters and Tony Mamaluke) defeated The Outcast Killaz (Diablo Santiago and Oman Tortuga) in 9:31 (★★); Tom Carter defeated Doug Williams in 14:22 (★★★); BJ Whitmer defeated Colt Cabana, Dan Maff and Homicide in a Four Corner Survival Match in 13:45 (★★★★); Special K (Angel Dust, Dixie, Hydro and Mikey Whipwreck) defeated The Backseat Boyz (Johnny Kashmere and Trent Acid) and The SAT (Joel Maximo and Jose Maximo) in a Scramble Match in 8:21 (★★); Jeff Hardy defeated Joey Matthews and Krazy K in a Three Way Match in 6:35 (★); CM Punk defeated Raven in a Dog Collar Match in 18:43 (★★★★); AJ Styles and The Amazing Red defeated The Briscoe Brothers (Jay Briscoe and Mark Briscoe) in 14:29 (★★★); Samoa Joe defeated Paul London in 14:13 (★★★).

Total Nonstop Action (23-07-03) ★★
23-07-03, Nashville, Tennessee NWA-TNA

AJ Styles defeated D-Lo Brown in a Pinfalls Only Match in 7:46 (★★); Elix Skipper defeated Mad Mikey in 6:34 (★★); Joe Legend defeated Altar Boy Luke and Matt Sydal in a Handicap Match in 3:38; D-Lo Brown defeated AJ Styles in a Submissions Only Match in 5:50 (★★); America's Most Wanted (Chris Harris and James Storm) defeated Simon Diamond and Johnny Swinger by DQ in 9:15 (★★); The Disciples Of The New Church (Brian Lee and Slash) and Shane Douglas defeated Julio Dinero, CM Punk and Raven in 9:22 (★★); AJ Styles vs. D-Lo Brown ended in a draw in a Ladder Match in 10:59 (★★).

Vengeance '03 ★★★★
27-07-03, Denver, Colorado WWE

Eddie Guerrero defeated Chris Benoit to win the vacant WWE United States Title in 21:54 (★★★★); Jamie Noble defeated Billy Gunn in 4:59 (★★); Bradshaw won an APA Invitational Bar Room Brawl in 4:33 (★★); The World's Greatest Tag Team (Charlie Haas and Shelton Benjamin) defeated Billy Kidman and Rey Mysterio in 15:01 (★★★★); Sable defeated Stephanie McMahon in a No Count Out Match in 6:32 (★★); The Undertaker defeated John Cena in 16:06 (★★★); Vince McMahon defeated Zach Gowen in 14:22 (★★); Kurt Angle defeated Brock Lesnar and The Big Show in a Three Way Match to win the WWE Title in 17:38 (★★★★).

Total Nonstop Action (30-07-03) ★★
30-07-03, Nashville, Tennessee NWA-TNA

Jerry Lynn defeated Elix Skipper 2-0 in a Best Two Out Of Three Falls Match in 6:34 (★★); The Sandman defeated Edward Chastain in 2:11 (★); Simon Diamond and Johnny Swinger defeated Shark Boy and Norman Smiley in 5:06 (★★); Chris Sabin defeated Michael Shane in 9:02 (★★★); Kid Kash defeated Ricky Morton in 6:11 (★★★); Shane Douglas and The Disciples Of The New Church (Brian Lee and Slash) defeated Julio Dinero, Alexis and Raven in a Falls Count Anywhere Clockwork Orange House of Fun Match in 9:49 (★★); Jeff Jarrett defeated Joe Legend in a Guitar and Baseball Bat On A Pole Match in 9:03 (★★).

Total Nonstop Action (06-08-03) ★★★
06-08-03, Nashville, Tennessee NWA-TNA

America's Most Wanted (Chris Harris and James Storm) defeated Simon Diamond and Johnny Swinger in a Rawhide Strap Match in 11:04 (★★★); Michael Shane defeated Joey Matthews, Danny Doring and Shark Boy in a Four Way Elimination Match in 8:12 (★); Kid Kash defeated Larry Zbyszko in 6:02 (★★); Chris Sabin vs. Frankie Kazarian ended in a no contest in 7:18 (★★); AJ Styles defeated D-Lo Brown in a Steel Cage Match in 10:21 (★★).

Total Nonstop Action (13-08-03) ★★★★
13-08-03, Nashville, Tennessee NWA-TNA

3 Live Krew (BG James, Ron Killings and Konnan) defeated Devon Storm, The Vampire Warrior and Sinn in 5:22 (★★); Jerry Lynn defeated Elix Skipper in 3:59 (★★); Frankie Kazarian vs. Michael Shane ended in a no contest in a Ladder Match in 8:14 (★★★); Kid Kash defeated Bobby Eaton in 3:37 (★★); Raven defeated Shane Douglas in 10:55 (★★★); America's Most Wanted (Chris Harris and James Storm) and Dusty Rhodes defeated Glenn Gilbertti, Simon Diamond and Johnny Swinger in 8:43 (★★★); AJ Styles defeated Low Ki in 14:53 (★★★★).

Total Nonstop Action (20-08-03) ★★★★
20-08-03, Nashville, Tennessee NWA-TNA

Michael Shane defeated Frankie Kazarian and Chris Sabin in an Ultimate X Match to win the NWA-TNA X-Division Title in 13:48 (★★★★); Simon Diamond and Johnny Swinger defeated America's Most Wanted (Chris Harris and James Storm) in a Double Bullrope Match in 8:35 (★★★); The Disciples Of The New Church (Sinn and Slash) defeated The Gathering (Julio Dinero and CM Punk) in 7:05 (★★★); Erik Watts and Jeff Jarrett defeated Joe Legend and Christopher Daniels in 8:19 (★★★); Raven won a Gauntlet Battle Royal in 22:24 (★★★★).

SummerSlam '03 ★★★
24-08-03, Phoenix, Arizona WWE

La Resistance (Sylvain Grenier and Rene Dupree) defeated The Dudley Boyz (Bubba Ray Dudley and D-Von Dudley) in 7:51 (★★); The Undertaker defeated A-Train in 9:10 (★★); Shane McMahon defeated Eric Bischoff in a Falls Count Anywhere Match in 10:36 (★★); Eddie Guerrero defeated Chris Benoit, Rhyno and Tajiri in a Four Way Match in 10:50 (★★★); Kurt Angle defeated Brock Lesnar in 21:18 (★★★); Kane defeated Rob Van Dam in a No Holds Barred Match in 12:49 (★★); Triple H defeated Goldberg, Chris Jericho, Shawn Michaels, Randy Orton and Kevin Nash in an Elimination Chamber Match in 19:16 (★★★).

Total Nonstop Action (27-08-03) ★★★
27-08-03, Nashville, Tennessee NWA-TNA

Shane Douglas and The Disciples Of The New Church (Sinn and Slash) vs. 3 Live Krew (BG James, Ron Killings and Konnan) ended in a no contest in 7:08 (★★); Sonny Siaki defeated D-Lo Brown in 4:55 (★★); Michael Shane defeated Jerry Lynn in 12:24 (★★); Abyss defeated The Sandman in 3:44 (★); Simon Diamond and Johnny Swinger defeated America's Most Wanted (Chris Harris and James Storm) to win the NWA World Tag Team Title in 9:14 (★★★); Glenn Gilbertti defeated Dusty Rhodes in a Bullrope Match in 4:11 (★★); AJ Styles defeated Raven in 15:02 (★★★★).

Total Nonstop Action (03-09-03) ★★★★
03-09-03, Nashville, Tennessee NWA-TNA

Mad Mikey defeated Lazz in 1:53 (★★); Juventud Guerrera defeated Nosawa in 4:31 (★★); Teddy Hart defeated Jonny Storm in 2:49 (★★); Chris Sabin defeated Jerry Lynn in 3:30

(★★); Frankie Kazarian defeated Michael Shane in 3:25 (★★); Juventud Guerrera defeated Teddy Hart in 9:59 (★★★★); Chris Sabin defeated Frankie Kazarian in 7:32 (★★★★); Chris Sabin defeated Juventud Guerrera to win the Super X Cup in 14:46 (★★★★); Jeff Jarrett, Chris Harris, D-Lo Brown, James Storm and Raven defeated Christopher Daniels, AJ Styles, Simon Diamond, Shane Douglas and Johnny Swinger in a Wednesday Bloody Wednesday Steel Cage Match in 20:42 (★★).

Total Nonstop Action (17-09-03) ★★
17-09-03, Nashville, Tennessee NWA-TNA
3 Live Krew (BG James and Ron Killings) defeated Kid Kash and Abyss, The Disciples Of The New Church (Sinn and Slash) and America's Most Wanted (Chris Harris and James Storm) in a Four Way Match in 7:20 (★★); Sonny Siaki defeated D-Lo Brown in a Casket Match in 5:24 (★★); Nosawa, Chris Sabin and Michael Shane defeated Eric Young, Frankie Kazarian and Juventud Guerrera in 9:14 (★★); Simon Diamond and Johnny Swinger defeated Shark Boy and Mad Mikey in 4:56 (★★); AJ Styles defeated Jerry Lynn in 9:04 (★★★); Shane Douglas defeated Raven in a Hair vs. Hair Match in 17:02 (★★).

Unforgiven '03 ★★
21-09-03, Hershey, Pennsylvania WWE
The Dudley Boyz (Bubba Ray Dudley and D-Von Dudley) defeated La Resistance (Sylvain Grenier, Rene Dupree and Rob Conway) in a Handicap Tables Match to win the World Tag Team Title in 10:17 (★★); Test defeated Scott Steiner in 6:56 (★★); Randy Orton defeated Shawn Michaels in 18:47 (★★★); Lita and Trish Stratus defeated Gail Kim and Molly Holly in 6:46 (★★★); Kane defeated Shane McMahon in a Last Man Standing Match in 19:42 (★★); Christian defeated Chris Jericho and Rob Van Dam in a Three Way Match in 19:03 (★★); Al Snow and Jonathan Coachman defeated Jerry Lawler and Jim Ross in 8:16 (★); Goldberg defeated Triple H to win the World Heavyweight Title in 14:57 (★★).

Total Nonstop Action (24-09-03) ★★
24-09-03, Nashville, Tennessee NWA-TNA
Jerry Lynn defeated Nosawa, Frankie Kazarian, Juventud Guerrera and Chris Sabin in a Five Way Elimination Match in 15:09 (★★); Black Shirt Security (Rick Santel and Chris Vaughn) defeated Red Shirt Security (Ryan Wilson and Kevin Northcutt) in 6:24 (★★); Terry Taylor defeated Kid Kash in 6:11 (★★); Jeff Jarrett defeated Christopher Daniels in 7:19 (★★); Glenn Gilbertti, Simon Diamond and David Young defeated 3 Live Kru (BG James, Ron Killings and Konnan) in 10:01 (★★); AJ Styles vs. Dusty Rhodes went to a no contest in a Bunkhouse Match in 4:24 (★★); The Gathering (CM Punk, Julio Dinero and Raven) defeated Shane Douglas and The Disciples Of The New Church (Sinn and Slash) in 7:51 in a Dog Collar Match (★★).

Glory By Honor II ★★
20-09-03, Philadelphia, Pennsylvania ROH
BJ Whitmer defeated Jimmy Rave in 9:25 (★★); Xavier defeated John Walters in 10:45 (★★); Teddy Hart defeated TJ Wilson in 7:42 (★★); Steve Corino defeated Raven in a Ravens Rules Match in 13:08 (★★); Colt Cabana defeated AJ Styles, Chris Sabin and Matt Stryker in a Four Corner Survival Match in 18:55 (★★★); Special K (Angel Dust, Deranged and Hydro) defeated The Carnage Crew (Justin Credible, DeVito and Loc) by DQ in 9:06 (★★); The Briscoe Brothers (Jay Briscoe and Mark Briscoe) defeated Special K (Deranged and Hydro) in 2:46 (★★); The Briscoe Brothers (Jay Briscoe and Mark Briscoe) defeated The Ring Crew Express (Dunn and Marcos) in 1:42 (★★); Special K (Dixie and Izzy) defeated The Briscoe Brothers (Jay Briscoe and Mark Briscoe) in 5:16 (★★); The Backseat Boyz (Johnny Kashmere and Trent Acid) defeated Special K (Dixie and Izzy) to win the vacant ROH Tag Team Title in 3:52 (★★); Alexis Laree defeated Hijinx in 1:15 (★★); Terry Funk defeated CM Punk by DQ in 15:46 (★★★); Samoa Joe defeated Christopher Daniels in 15:01 (★★★★).

Total Nonstop Action (01-10-03) ★★
01-10-03, Nashville, Tennessee NWA-TNA
Kid Kash and Abyss defeated America's Most Wanted (Chris Harris and James Storm) in 11:25 (★★); Michael Shane defeated Jerry Lynn in 9:54 (★★); Christopher Daniels defeated D-Lo Brown in 8:00 (★★); Sonny Siaki and Ekmo defeated Mad Mikey and Shark Boy in 4:41 (★★); The Sandman defeated David Young in 4:14 (★); 3 Live Kru (BG James, Ron Killings and

Konnan) defeated The Disciples Of The New Church (Sinn and Slash) and Vampiro by DQ in 7:05 (★★); Jeff Jarrett and Dusty Rhodes defeated AJ Styles and Vince Russo in 9:33 (★★).

Total Nonstop Action (08-10-03) ★★
08-10-03, Nashville, Tennessee NWA-TNA
Red Shirt Security (Ryan Wilson and Kevin Northcutt) defeated Chris Vaughn and D-Lo Brown in 4:43 (★★); Michael Shane defeated Chris Sabin to win the Super X Cup Trophy in 7:32 (★★★); Glenn Gilbertti, Simon Diamond and Johnny Swinger defeated 3 Live Kru (BG James, Ron Killings and Konnan) in an Elimination Match in 11:12 (★★); Christopher Daniels defeated Frankie Kazarian in 6:00 (★★); America's Most Wanted (Chris Harris and James Storm) defeated Kid Kash and Abyss in 7:51 (★★); Raven defeated Sinn in 2:55 (★★); AJ Styles defeated Dusty Rhodes in 15:42 (★★).

Total Nonstop Action (15-10-03) ★★
15-10-03, Nashville, Tennessee NWA-TNA
America's Most Wanted (Chris Harris and James Storm) and Dusty Rhodes defeated Legend, Ekmo and Sonny Siaki in 8:41 (★★); Michael Shane defeated Christopher Daniels in 9:56 (★★); Kevin Northcutt defeated Erik Watts in 4:28 (★★); Eric Young and Sonjay Dutt defeated El Fuego and Jerelle Clark in 7:02 (★★★); Danny Doring and Roadkill defeated Johnny Swinger and Simon Diamond in 6:12 (★★); Abyss defeated Kid Kash in 5:37 (★★); Slash and Vampiro defeated The Gathering (CM Punk and Julio Dinero) in 4:18 (★★).

No Mercy '03 ★★
19-10-03, Baltimore, Maryland WWE
Tajiri defeated Rey Mysterio in 11:40 (★★★); Chris Benoit defeated A-Train in 12:24 (★★); Zach Gowen defeated Matt Hardy in 5:33 (★★); The Basham Brothers (Doug Basham and Danny Basham) defeated The APA (Faarooq and Bradshaw) in 8:55 (★★); Vince McMahon defeated Stephanie McMahon in an "I Quit" Loser Gets Fired Match in 9:24 (★★); Kurt Angle defeated John Cena in 18:28 (★★★★); The Big Show defeated Eddie Guerrero to win the WWE United States Title in 11:27 (★★); Brock Lesnar defeated The Undertaker in a Biker Chain Match in 24:14 (★★).

Total Nonstop Action (22-10-03) ★★
22-10-03, Nashville, Tennessee NWA-TNA
3 Live Kru (BG James, Ron Killings and Konnan) defeated Legend, Ekmo and Sonny Siaki in 5:47 (★★); Kid Kash defeated Sonjay Dutt in 4:40 (★★); Simon Diamond and Johnny Swinger defeated Danny Doring and Roadkill in 7:00 (★★); Michael Shane defeated Christopher Daniels and Chris Sabin in a Three Way Match in 10:12 (★★★); Raven defeated Slash in a Dog Collar Match in 4:25 (★★); America's Most Wanted (Chris Harris and James Storm) defeated The Naturals (Andy Douglas and Chase Stevens) in 6:04 (★★); Jeff Jarrett defeated AJ Styles to win the NWA World Heavyweight Title in 12:12 (★★).

Total Nonstop Action (29-10-03) ★★
29-10-03, Nashville, Tennessee NWA-TNA
America's Most Wanted (Chris Harris and James Storm) defeated David Young and Glenn Gilbertti in 11:30 (★★); Michael Shane defeated Sonjay Dutt in 7:05 (★★); Erik Watts and Don Harris defeated Red Shirt Security (Ryan Wilson and Kevin Northcutt) in 4:55 (★★); Sonny Siaki and Ekmo defeated Danny Doring and Roadkill in 6:00 (★★); Kid Kash defeated Abyss in a Chair On A Pole First Blood Match in 6:37 (★★); Raven defeated Vampiro in a Blood Gallows Of Retribution Match in 12:47 (★★); Jeff Jarrett defeated Jim Duggan in 3:40 (★); Rick Steiner defeated Jeff Jarrett by DQ in 3:04 (★).

Main Event Spectacles ★★★★
01-11-03, Elizabeth, New Jersey ROH
Dan Maff defeated Colt Cabana in 7:26 (★★); Nigel McGuinness and Xavier defeated The Purists (John Walters and Tony Mamaluke) in a Pure Rules Match in 11:30 (★★★); Matt Stryker defeated Justin Credible in 10:36 (★★); The Briscoe Brothers (Jay Briscoe and Mark Briscoe) defeated Special K (Dixie and Izzy) to win the ROH Tag Team Title in 9:55 (★★); Homicide defeated BJ Whitmer in 19:20 (★★★★); The Backseat Boyz (Johnny Kashmere and Trent Acid) defeated Special K (Angel Dust and Hydro), The Carnage Crew (DeVito and Loc), The Next Generation Hart Foundation (Jack Evans and Teddy Hart) and The SAT (Joel Maximo and Jose Maximo) in a Five Way Scramble Cage Match in 14:14 (★★★★); CM Punk

and **Steve Corino** co-defeated **Christopher Daniels** and **Samoa Joe** in a Four Corner Survival Match in 22:58 (★★★); **AJ Styles** defeated **Bryan Danielson** in 24:16 (★★★★).

Total Nonstop Action (05-11-03) ★★
*05-11-03, Nashville, Tennessee **NWA-TNA***
The Gathering (CM Punk and Julio Dinero) defeated **Kid Kash** and **Lazz** in 7:22 (★); **Shane Douglas** defeated **The Sandman** in 4:51 (★); **Sonny Siaki** and **Ekmo** defeated **America's Most Wanted** (Chris Harris and James Storm) in 9:09 (★★); **X** won an 8-Man Battle Royal in 10:17 (★★★); **3 Live Kru** (BG James and Ron Killings) defeated **Glenn Gilbertti** and **David Young** in 4:15 (★); **Raven** defeated **Father James Mitchell** in a Last Man Standing Match in 5:14 (★); **Sting** defeated **Jeff Jarrett** by DQ in 8:45 (★★).

Total Nonstop Action (12-11-03) ★★
*12-11-03, Nashville, Tennessee **NWA-TNA***
Ron Killings won a 10-Man Gauntlet Battle Royal in 13:03 (★★); **Christopher Daniels** defeated **Low Ki** in 9:46 (★★); **Sonjay Dutt** defeated **Chad Collyer** in 6:22 (★★); **Abyss** defeated **Don Harris** in 7:08 (★★); **Red Shirt Security** (Ryan Wilson and Kevin Northcutt) defeated **Raven** and **The Sandman** in 7:48 (★★); **Sting** and **AJ Styles** defeated **Jeff Jarrett** and **Lex Luger** in 10:35 (★★).

Survivor Series '03 ★★★
*16-11-03, Dallas, Texas **WWE***
Team Angle (Kurt Angle, Bradshaw, Chris Benoit, Hardcore Holly and John Cena) defeated **Team Lesnar** (Brock Lesnar, A-Train, The Big Show, Matt Morgan and Nathan Jones) in an Elimination Match in 13:15 (★★★); **Molly Holly** defeated **Lita** in 6:48 (★★); **Kane** defeated **Shane McMahon** in an Ambulance Match in 13:34 (★★★); **The Basham Brothers** (Doug Basham and Danny Basham) defeated **Los Guerreros** (Eddie Guerrero and Chavo Guerrero) in 7:31 (★); **Team Bischoff** (Chris Jericho, Christian, Mark Henry, Randy Orton and Scott Steiner) defeated **Team Austin** (Booker T, Bubba Ray Dudley, D-Von Dudley, Rob Van Dam and Shawn Michaels) in an Elimination Match in 27:27 (★★★★); **Vince McMahon** defeated **The Undertaker** in a Buried Alive Match in 11:59 (★★); **Goldberg** defeated **Triple H** in 11:44 (★★).

Total Nonstop Action (19-11-03) ★★
*19-11-03, Nashville, Tennessee **NWA-TNA***
Erik Watts, **The Sandman** and **Raven** defeated **Red Shirt Security** (Ryan Wilson, Kevin Northcutt and Legend) in a Clockwork Orange House Of Fun Match in 8:22 (★★); **Kid Kash** defeated **Shark Boy** in 3:56 (★); **Julio Dinero** and **CM Punk** defeated **Ekmo Fatu** and **Sonny Siaki** in 5:15 (★★); **Chris Sabin** defeated **David Young** in 2:22 (★★); **Simon Diamond** and **Johnny Swinger** vs. **3 Live Kru** (BG James and Ron Killings) ended in a no contest in 8:56 (★★); **Sonjay Dutt** defeated **X** and **Christopher Daniels** in 10:41 (★★); **AJ Styles** defeated **Abyss** in 13:53 (★★★).

Total Nonstop Action (26-11-03) ★★
*26-11-03, Nashville, Tennessee **NWA-TNA***
Kid Kash defeated **Low Ki** in 9:26 (★★★); **Abyss** defeated **Shark Boy** in 3:34 (★★); **Chris Sabin** defeated **X** in 6:21 (★★); **Raven** defeated **Legend** in 4:53 (★); **Raven** vs. **Kevin Northcutt** ended in a no contest in 1:56 (★); **Michael Shane** defeated **Sonjay Dutt** in 6:23 (★★); **3 Live Kru** (BG James, Ron Killings and Konnan) defeated **Glenn Gilbertti, Simon Diamond** and **Johnny Swinger** to win the vacant NWA World Tag Team Title in 8:59 (★★); **Jeff Jarrett** vs. **Dusty Rhodes** ended in a no contest in a Fan's Revenge Lumberjack Match in 6:18 (★).

Total Nonstop Action (03-12-03) ★★
*03-12-03, Nashville, Tennessee **NWA-TNA***
Low Ki defeated **Kid Kash** and **Christopher Daniels** in a Three Way Match in 9:54 (★★★); **Shane Douglas** and **Michael Shane** defeated **Chris Sabin** and **Sonjay Dutt** in 8:11 (★★); **X** defeated **Don Harris** in 4:15 (★★); **America's Most Wanted** (Chris Harris and James Storm) defeated **David Young** and **Glenn Gilbertti**, and **Simon Diamond** and **Johnny Swinger** in a Three Way Match in 8:54 (★★); **Red Shirt Security** (Legend and Kevin Northcutt) and **Abyss** defeated **The Gathering** (CM Punk, Julio Dinero and Raven) in 6:24 (★★); **Jeff Jarrett** defeated **AJ Styles** in 19:29 (★★★).

Total Nonstop Action (10-12-03) ★★
*10-12-03, Nashville, Tennessee **NWA-TNA***
Kid Kash defeated **Don Harris** in 2:41 (★★); **Michael Shane** defeated **Christopher Daniels** by DQ in 10:17 (★★); **3 Live Kru** (BG James and Ron Killings) defeated **America's Most Wanted** (Chris Harris and James Storm) in 8:06 (★★); **The Gathering** (Julio Dinero and CM Punk) defeated **Red Shirt Security** (Legend and Kevin Northcutt) in 7:29 (★★); **Chris Sabin** defeated **Shane Douglas** in 4:46 (★★); **Raven** defeated **Abyss** by DQ in 11:05 (★★); **AJ Styles** and **D-Lo Brown** defeated **Jeff Jarrett** and **Kid Kash** in 12:56 (★★).

Armageddon '03 ★★
*14-12-03, Orlando, Florida **WWE***
Booker T defeated **Mark Henry** in 10:20 (★★); **Randy Orton** defeated **Rob Van Dam** to win the WWF Intercontinental Title in 17:59 (★★); **Chris Jericho** and **Christian** defeated **Lita** and **Trish Stratus** in 6:37 (★★★); **Shawn Michaels** defeated **Batista** in 12:28 (★★); **Evolution** (Batista and Ric Flair) won a Tag Team Turmoil Match to win the World Tag Team Title in 20:48 (★★); **Molly Holly** defeated **Ivory** in 4:23 (★); **Triple H** defeated **Goldberg** and **Kane** in a Three Way Match to win the World Heavyweight Title in 19:28 (★★).

Total Nonstop Action (17-12-03) ★★
*17-12-03, Nashville, Tennessee **NWA-TNA***
Sting defeated **Jeff Jarrett** in 8:08 (★★); **Christopher Daniels** defeated **Chris Sabin** in 7:29 (★★); **America's Most Wanted** (Chris Harris and James Storm) defeated **David Young** and **Glenn Gilbertti** in a Street Fight in 10:01; **Simon Diamond** and **Johnny Swinger** defeated **AJ Styles** and **D-Lo Brown** in 10:57 (★★); **Michael Shane** defeated **Low Ki** in 11:20 (★★); **Abyss** and **Red Shirt Security** (Legend and Kevin Northcutt) defeated **The Gathering** (CM Punk, Julio Dinero and Raven) in a Steel Cage Match in 12:43 (★★).

Tribute To The Troops '03 ★★
*20-12-03, Baghdad, Iraq **WWE***
The APA (Bradshaw and Faarooq) defeated **The World's Greatest Tag Team** (Charlie Haas and Shelton Benjamin) in 4:38 (★★); **Rikishi** defeated **Rhyno** in 2:28 (★★); **Eddie Guerrero** defeated **Chris Benoit** in 11:38 (★★★); **John Cena** defeated **The Big Show** in 4:12 (★★).

Final Battle '03 ★★★★
*27-12-03, Philadelphia, Pennsylvania **ROH***
Bryan Danielson defeated **Jay Briscoe** in 13:36 (★★★); **John Walters** defeated **Xavier** in 18:44 (★★★); **Matt Stryker** defeated **BJ Whitmer** to win the Field Of Honor Tournament in 18:08 (★★★); **Samoa Joe** defeated **Mark Briscoe** in 14:44 (★★★); **The Second City Saints** (CM Punk and Colt Cabana) defeated **Turmeric Storm** (Kazushi Miyamoto and Tomoaki Honma) in 16:34 (★★★); **AJ Styles** defeated **Kaz Hayashi** in 14:49 (★★★); **Satoshi Kojima** defeated **Homicide** in 13:11 (★★); **Arashi** and **The Great Muta** defeated **The Prophecy** (Christopher Daniels and Dan Maff) in 16:06 (★★).

Total Nonstop Action (07-01-04) ★★
*07-01-04, Nashville, Tennessee **TNA***
Red Shirt Security (Legend and Kevin Northcutt) and **Abyss** defeated **America's Most Wanted** (Chris Harris and James Storm) and **AJ Styles** in 8:13 (★★); **3 Live Kru** (BG James and Ron Killings) defeated **Simon Diamond** and **Johnny Swinger** in 3:36 (★★); **Chris Vaughn** defeated **Kid Kash** in 1:34 (★★); **The Gathering** (CM Punk and Julio Dinero) defeated **Raven** and **The Sandman** in 7:24 (★★); **Chris Sabin** defeated **Low Ki, Christopher Daniels** and **Michael Shane** in an Ultimate X Match to win NWA X Division Title in 15:10 (★★★★).

Total Nonstop Action (14-01-04) ★★
*14-01-04, Nashville, Tennessee **TNA***
America's Most Wanted (Chris Harris and James Storm) defeated **Red Shirt Security** (Legend and Kevin Northcutt) in a Rawhide Strap Match in 8:39 (★★); **Michael Shane** defeated **Low Ki** and **Christopher Daniels** in a Three Way Match in 10:25 (★); **David Young** defeated **Simon Diamond** in 6:08 (★★); **Shane Douglas** defeated **Elix Skipper** in 3:16 (★★); **Kid Kash** defeated **Chris Vaughn** in 6:35 (★★); **The Gathering** (CM Punk and Julio Dinero) defeated **The Sandman** in a Singapore Cane on a Pole Handicap Match in 5:06 (★★); **AJ Styles** and **Erik Watts** defeated **Jeff Jarrett** and **Abyss** in 9:39 (★★).

Total Nonstop Action (21-01-04) ★★

21-01-04, Nashville, Tennessee **TNA**

The Gathering (CM Punk and Julio Dinero) defeated The Sandman and Balls Mahoney in 3:41 (★★); Simon Diamond and Johnny Swinger defeated Glenn Gilbertti and David Young in 4:45 (★★); D-Lo Brown defeated Sonny Siaki in 5:27 (★★); Shane Douglas and Michael Shane defeated Christopher Daniels and Elix Skipper in 10:12 (★★); Red Shirt Security (Legend and Kevin Northcutt) defeated America's Most Wanted (Chris Harris and James Storm) in 11:59 (★★); Jeff Jarrett vs. El Leon ended in a no contest in a Street Fight in 7:50 (★★).

Royal Rumble '04 ★★★

25-01-04, Philadelphia, Pennsylvania **WWE**

Evolution (Batista and Ric Flair) defeated The Dudley Boyz (Bubba Ray Dudley and D-Von Dudley) in a Tables Match in 5:29 (★); Rey Mysterio defeated Jamie Noble in 3:06 (★★); Eddie Guerrero defeated Chavo Guerrero in 8:02 (★★); Brock Lesnar defeated Hardcore Holly in 6:22 (★★); Triple H vs. Shawn Michaels went to a draw in a Last Man Standing Match in 23:05 (★★★); Chris Benoit won the 30-Man Royal Rumble Match in 61:37 (★★★★).

Total Nonstop Action (28-01-04) ★★★

28-01-04, Nashville, Tennessee **TNA**

Abyss defeated D-Lo Brown in 7:40 (★★★); Chris Sabin defeated Michael Shane in 10:11 (★★★); The Gathering (CM Punk and Julio Dinero) defeated The Sandman and Mikey Whipwreck in 3:22 (★★); Juventud Guerrera, Abismo Negro, Hector Garza and Mr. Aguila defeated Eric Young, Shark Boy, Matt Stryker and Chad Collyer in 9:08 (★★); Red Shirt Security (Legend and Kevin Northcutt) defeated 3 Live Kru (BG James and Ron Killings) to win the NWA World Tag Team Title in 7:05 (★★); Don Callis defeated Erik Watts in a No DQ Match in 9:53 (★★).

Total Nonstop Action (04-02-04) ★★

04-02-04, Nashville, Tennessee **TNA**

Insane Clown Posse (Violent J and Shaggy 2 Dope) defeated David Young and Glenn Gilbertti in 6:46 (★★); Sonny Siaki defeated Kid Kash in 5:23 (★★); Abyss defeated El Leon by DQ in 7:51 (★★); The Gathering (CM Punk and Julio Dinero) defeated The Sandman and Terry Funk in 5:06 (★★); AJ Styles and Abyss defeated The Red Shirts (Joe Legend and Kevin Northcutt) to win the NWA World Tag Team Title in 11:17 (★★); Jeff Jarrett defeated Dustin Rhodes in 7:08 (★★).

Total Nonstop Action (11-02-04) ★★

11-02-04, Nashville, Tennessee **TNA**

Juventud Guerrera defeated Chris Sabin in 10:02 (★★); Hector Garza defeated Sonjay Dutt in 4:50 (★★); Jerry Lynn defeated Mr. Aguila in 7:47 (★★); Abismo Negro defeated Elix Skipper in 6:54 (★); Juventud Guerrera and Abismo Negro defeated Jerry Lynn and Sonjay Dutt in 11:40 (★★); Chris Sabin and Elix Skipper defeated Hector Garza and Mr. Aguila in 10:52 (★★); Juventud Guerrera, Hector Garza, Mr. Aguila and Abismo Negro defeated Chris Sabin, Sonjay Dutt, Jerry Lynn and Elix Skipper in an Elimination Match to win the America's X Cup in 22:19 (★★★).

Second Anniversary Show ★★★

14-02-04, Braintree, Massachusetts **ROH**

CM Punk defeated John Walters in 13:01 (★★★); Doug Williams defeated Chris Sabin in 8:18 (★★★); Matt Stryker defeated Josh Daniels in 8:29 (★★); AJ Styles defeated Jimmy Rave in 7:35 (★★★); Special K (Dixie, Hydro and Izzy) defeated The Carnage Crew (DeVito, Justin Credible and Loc) in a Country Whipping Match in 8:46 (★★); CM Punk defeated Doug Williams in 10:44 (★★★); AJ Styles defeated Matt Stryker in 20:46 (★★); The Briscoe Brothers (Jay Briscoe and Mark Briscoe) defeated The Backseat Boyz (Johnny Kashmere and Trent Acid) in 8:00 (★★★); Samoa Joe defeated BJ Whitmer, Dan Maff and Low Ki in a Four Corner Survival Match in 23:01 (★★★★); AJ Styles defeated CM Punk to win the vacant ROH Pure Wrestling Title in 16:37 (★★★).

No Way Out '04 ★★★

15-02-04, Daly City, California **WWE**

Too Cool (Rikishi and Scotty 2 Hotty) defeated The Basham Brothers (Doug Basham and Danny Basham) and Shaniqua in a Handicap Match in 7:38 (★★); Jamie Noble defeated Nidia in 4:25 (★★); The World's Greatest Tag Team (Charlie Haas and Shelton Benjamin) defeated The APA (Faarooq and Bradshaw) in 7:20 (★★); Hardcore Holly defeated Rhyno in 9:50 (★★); Chavo Guerrero defeated Rey Mysterio to win the WWE Cruiserweight Title in 17:21 (★★★); Kurt Angle defeated John Cena and The Big Show in a Three Way Match in 12:19 (★★★); Eddie Guerrero defeated Brock Lesnar to win the WWE Title in 29:55 (★★★★).

Total Nonstop Action (18-02-04) ★★

18-02-04, Nashville, Tennessee **TNA**

Jerry Lynn, Sonjay Dutt, Elix Skipper and Chris Sabin defeated Jason Cross, Jimmy Rave, Roderick Strong and Shark Boy in 7:15 (★★); Michael Shane defeated Ron Killings in 7:00 (★★); Dustin Rhodes and El Leon defeated The Red Shirts (Joe Legend and Kevin Northcutt) in 9:08 (★); AJ Styles defeated Abyss by DQ in 9:51 (★★); Insane Clown Posse (Violent J and Shaggy 2 Dope) defeated Glenn Gilbertti and Kid Kash in a Street Fight in 5:31 (★★); Raven and Terry Funk defeated The Gathering (CM Punk and Julio Dinero) in 7:15 (★★); Jeff Jarrett defeated Chris Harris in 11:17 (★★).

Total Nonstop Action (25-02-04) ★★

25-02-04, Nashville, Tennessee **TNA**

Petey Williams defeated Juventud Guerrera and Jerry Lynn in a Three Way Match in 8:10 (★★); Simon Diamond defeated Johnny Swinger by DQ in 6:46 (★★); Shane Douglas and Michael Shane defeated 3 Live Kru (Konnan and Ron Killings) in 6:56 (★★); Chris Harris defeated Chase Stevens in 4:36 (★★); Chris Harris defeated Andy Douglas in 2:41 (★★); Chris Harris defeated The Naturals (Andy Douglas and Chase Stevens) in a Handicap Match in 6:34; Raven and Sabu defeated The Gathering (CM Punk and Julio Dinero) in 6:05 (★★); Abyss defeated AJ Styles in a Tables Match to win the NWA World Tag Team Title in 13:53 (★★★).

Total Nonstop Action (03-03-04) ★★

03-03-04, Nashville, Tennessee **TNA**

Chris Harris defeated Kevin Northcutt in 9:10 (★★); Sonny Siaki, D-Lo Brown, Simon Diamond, Konnan and Ron Killings defeated Kid Kash, Michael Shane, David Young, Johnny Swinger and Glenn Gilbertti in 10:11 (★★); Frankie Kazarian defeated Jerry Lynn in 9:08 (★★); Team NWA (Sonjay Dutt, Elix Skipper and Chris Sabin) defeated Team Japan (Kuishinbo Kamen, Ebessan and Nosawa) in 6:58 (★★); Abyss vs. AJ Styles went to a no contest in a Falls Count Anywhere Match in 14:42 (★★★); Chris Harris defeated Shane Douglas in 10:08 (★★).

Total Nonstop Action (10-03-04) ★★

10-03-04, Nashville, Tennessee **TNA**

Teddy Hart defeated Mr. Aguila in 9:14 (★★); Juventud Guerrera defeated Petey Williams in 9:02 (★★); Johnny Devine defeated Abismo Negro in 6:02 (★★); Hector Garza defeated Jack Evans in 6:35 (★★); Abismo Negro and Juventud Guerrera defeated Jack Evans and Teddy Hart in 7:18 (★★★); Petey Williams and Johnny Devine defeated Hector Garza and Mr. Aguila in 8:55 (★★★); Juventud Guerrera, Hector Garza, Mr. Aguila and Abismo Negro defeated Teddy Hart, Petey Williams, Johnny Devine and Jack Evans in an Elimination Match in 15:43 (★★★); Kid Kash, David Young and Glenn Gilbertti defeated Insane Clown Posse (Violent J and Shaggy 2 Dope) and 2 Tuff Tony in a Dark Carnival Match in 11:58 (★★)

WrestleMania XX ★★★

14-03-04, New York City, New York **WWE**

John Cena defeated The Big Show to win the WWE United States Title in 9:13 (★★); Booker T and Rob Van Dam defeated The Dudley Boyz (Bubba Ray Dudley and D-Von Dudley), Garrison Cade and Mark Jindrak, and La Resistance (Rene Dupree and Rob Conway) in a Four Way Match in 7:55 (★★); Christian defeated Chris Jericho in 14:56 (★★★); Evolution (Batista, Ric Flair and Randy Orton) defeated The Rock 'n' Sock Connection (The Rock and Mick Foley) in a Handicap Match in 17:09 (★★★★); Torrie Wilson and Sable defeated Miss Jackie and Stacy Keibler in a Playboy Evening Gown Match in 2:41 (★★); Chavo Guerrero won a Cruiserweight Open Match in 10:38 (★★); Goldberg defeated Brock Lesnar in 13:48 (★); Too Cool (Rikishi and Scotty 2 Hotty) defeated The APA (Faarooq and Bradshaw), The Basham Brothers (Doug Basham and Danny Basham), and The World's Greatest Tag Team (Charlie Haas and Shelton Benjamin) in a Four Way Match in 6:05 (★★); Victoria defeated Molly Holly in a Hair vs. Title Match in 4:52 (★★); Eddie Guerrero defeated Kurt Angle in 21:30 (★★★★);

The Undertaker defeated Kane in 6:56 (★ ★ ★); Chris Benoit defeated Triple H and Shawn Michaels in a Three Way Match to win the World Heavyweight Title in 24:07 (★ ★ ★ ★ ★).

Total Nonstop Action (17-03-04) ★ ★ ★
17-03-04, Nashville, Tennessee TNA

Frankie Kazarian defeated Elix Skipper in 6:16 (★ ★); Monty Brown defeated Chris Vaughn in 4:55 (★ ★); James Storm defeated Shane Douglas in 5:09 (★ ★); Ron Killings won a 10-Man Gauntlet Match in 12:25 (★ ★); Abyss defeated AJ Styles in a Ladder Match in 13:01 (★ ★ ★); Jeff Jarrett defeated Chris Harris in 19:47 (★ ★ ★).

Total Nonstop Action (24-03-04) ★ ★
24-03-04, Nashville, Tennessee TNA

Christopher Daniels and Low Ki defeated The New Franchise (Shane Douglas and Michael Shane) in 9:17 (★ ★); Slash and Sinn defeated Glenn Gilbertti and David Young in 7:00 (★ ★); Kid Kash and Dallas defeated Simon Diamond and Sonny Siaki in 10:10 (★ ★); The Naturals (Andy Douglas and Chase Stevens) defeated 3 Live Kru (BG James and Konnan) in 6:35 (★ ★); Abyss vs. Ron Killings ended in a no contest in 9:14 (★ ★); Amazing Red defeated Petey Williams, Nosawa, Frankie Kazarian, Elix Skipper and Jerry Lynn in an Elimination Match in 12:09 (★ ★).

Total Nonstop Action (31-03-04) ★ ★
31-03-04, Nashville, Tennessee TNA

Christopher Daniels and Low Ki defeated The Naturals (Andy Douglas and Chase Stevens) in 12:11 (★ ★); Dallas and Kid Kash defeated Slash and Sinn in 8:46 (★ ★); Sabu vs. Monty Brown went to a no contest in 10:31 (★ ★); D-Lo Brown and Apolo defeated Sonny Siaki and Simon Diamond, Glenn Gilbertti and David Young and The New Franchise (Shane Douglas and Michael Shane) in a Four Corners Match in 9:51 (★ ★); Frankie Kazarian defeated Amazing Red in 9:16 (★ ★); Raven defeated Abyss, Ron Killings and AJ Styles in a Four Way Match in 11:13 (★ ★).

Total Nonstop Action (07-04-04) ★
07-04-04, Nashville, Tennessee TNA

Mr. Aguila defeated Xtreme Dean in 6:16 (★ ★); Heavy Metal defeated Robbie Dynamite in 3:39 (★); Hector Garza defeated Frankie Sloan in 9:28 (★); James Mason defeated Abismo Negro in 5:40 (★ ★); Robbie Dynamite and Frankie Sloan defeated Mr. Aguila and Hector Garza in 9:35 (★); Xtreme Dean and James Mason defeated Abismo Negro and Heavy Metal in 7:27 (★ ★); Heavy Metal, Hector Garza, Mr. Aguila and Abismo Negro defeated Xtreme Dean, Robbie Dynamite, Frankie Sloan and James Mason in an Elimination Match in 12:22 (★); Dallas and Kid Kash defeated Low Ki and Christopher Daniels to win the vacant NWA World Tag Team Title in 14:25 (★ ★).

Total Nonstop Action (14-04-04) ★ ★
14-04-04, Nashville, Tennessee TNA

Jeff Jarrett defeated James Storm in 11:53 (★ ★); Frankie Kazarian defeated Sonjay Dutt in 11:57 (★ ★ ★); Simon Diamond defeated Johnny Swinger in 8:00 (★ ★); Monty Brown defeated Sabu in a Falls Count Anywhere Match in 8:38 (★ ★); Apolo and D-Lo Brown defeated Dallas and Kid Kash by DQ to win the NWA World Tag Team Title in 8:22 (★ ★); Chris Harris defeated Raven in 17:14 (★ ★).

Backlash '04 ★ ★ ★ ★
18-04-04, Edmonton, Alberta WWE

Shelton Benjamin defeated Ric Flair in 9:29 (★ ★); Jonathan Coachman defeated Tajiri in 6:25 (★ ★); Chris Jericho defeated Christian and Trish Stratus in a Handicap Match in 11:12 (★ ★); Victoria defeated Lita in 7:22 (★ ★); Randy Orton defeated Cactus Jack in a Hardcore Match in 23:03 (★ ★ ★ ★ ★); The Hurricane and Rosey defeated La Resistance (Sylvain Grenier and Robert Conway) in 5:02 (★ ★); Edge defeated Kane in 6:25 (★ ★); Chris Benoit defeated Shawn Michaels and Triple H in a Three Way Match in 30:12 (★ ★ ★ ★).

Total Nonstop Action (21-04-04) ★ ★
21-04-04, Nashville, Tennessee TNA

Monty Brown and Abyss defeated Sabu in a Handicap Match in 7:30 (★ ★); Shark Boy defeated David Young in 4:10 (★); Glenn Gilbertti and Johnny Swinger defeated Sonny Siaki and Simon Diamond in 10:17 (★ ★); Christopher Daniels defeated

Michael Shane in 13:25 (★ ★); Kid Kash and Dallas defeated D-Lo Brown and Apolo by DQ to win the NWA World Tag Team Title in 6:28 (★ ★); AJ Styles defeated Jeff Jarrett in a Steel Cage Match to win the NWA World Heavyweight Title in 13:39 (★ ★).

Total Nonstop Action (28-04-04) ★ ★
28-04-04, Nashville, Tennessee TNA

Team NWA (Jerry Lynn, Chris Sabin, Christopher Daniels and Elix Skipper) defeated Team AAA (Heavy Metal, Hector Garza, Mr. Aguila and Abismo Negro) in 11:17 (★ ★); Kid Kash and Dallas defeated D-Lo Brown and Apolo in a Nightstick On A Pole Match in 7:27 (★ ★); Sabu defeated Abyss by DQ in 7:48 (★ ★); Desire, Sonny Siaki and Pat Kenney defeated Glenn Gilbertti, Johnny Swinger and Trinity in 8:21 (★ ★); Raven defeated James Storm in 9:56 (★ ★); AJ Styles defeated Ron Killings in 9:41 (★ ★).

Total Nonstop Action (05-05-04) ★ ★
05-05-04, Nashville, Tennessee TNA

Sonjay Dutt defeated Amazing Red in 9:37 (★ ★); Shane Douglas defeated Michael Shane in 8:24 (★ ★); Team Canada (Bobby Roode, Eric Young, Johnny Devine and Petey Williams) defeated Team NWA (Elix Skipper, Christopher Daniels, Chris Sabin and Jerry Lynn) in 10:48 (★ ★ ★); Trinity defeated Desire in 2:51 (★); Abyss defeated Erik Watts in 6:00 (★ ★); AJ Styles defeated Raven in 16:02 (★ ★).

Total Nonstop Action (12-05-04) ★ ★
12-05-04, Nashville, Tennessee TNA

James Storm defeated Kid Kash in 9:08 (★ ★ ★); Monty Brown defeated BG James in 6:42 (★ ★); Amazing Red defeated Sonjay Dutt in 7:25 (★ ★); Shane Douglas defeated Michael Shane in a Corporal Punishment Match in 9:08 (★ ★); Team Canada (Petey Williams and Bobby Roode) defeated Team Mexico (Abismo Negro and Hector Garza) in 8:13 (★ ★); AJ Styles defeated Chris Harris in 15:40 (★ ★).

Round Robin Challenge III ★ ★
15-05-04, Lexington, Massachusetts ROH

The Prophecy (BJ Whitmer and Dan Maff) defeated The Second City Saints (CM Punk and Colt Cabana) to win the ROH Tag Team Title in 6:51 (★ ★ ★); Alex Shelley defeated Matt Stryker in 7:05 (★ ★); The Carnage Crew (DeVito and Loc) and The Ring Crew Express (Dunn and Marcos) defeated The Embassy (Diablo Santiago, Josh Daniels, Oman Tortuga and Prince Nana) in 7:59 (★ ★); Samoa Joe defeated Ricky Reyes in 9:43 (★ ★ ★); The Briscoe Brothers (Jay Briscoe and Mark Briscoe) defeated The Prophecy (BJ Whitmer and Dan Maff) to win the ROH Tag Team Title in 13:26 (★ ★); Josh Daniels defeated Dixie in 5:07 (★ ★); John Walters defeated Hydro, Izzy, Masada, Roderick Strong and Trent Acid in a Six Man Mayhem Match in 12:32 (★ ★); Homicide defeated Spanky in 16:13 (★ ★ ★); The Second City Saints (CM Punk and Colt Cabana) defeated The Briscoe Brothers (Jay Briscoe and Mark Briscoe) to win the ROH Tag Team Title in 19:16 (★ ★ ★).

Judgment Day '04 ★ ★
16-05-04, Los Angeles, California WWE

Rey Mysterio and Rob Van Dam defeated The Dudley Boyz (Bubba Ray Dudley and D-Von Dudley) in 15:19 (★ ★ ★); Torrie Wilson defeated Dawn Marie in 6:14 (★); Mordecai defeated Scotty 2 Hotty in 3:01 (★ ★); Charlie Haas and Rico defeated Billy Gunn and Hardcore Holly in 10:26 (★ ★); Chavo Guerrero defeated Jacqueline to win the WWE Cruiserweight Title in 4:47 (★ ★); John Cena defeated Rene Dupree in 9:54 (★ ★); The Undertaker defeated Booker T in 11:25 (★ ★); John Bradshaw Layfield defeated Eddie Guerrero by DQ in 23:15 (★ ★ ★ ★).

Total Nonstop Action (19-05-04) ★ ★
19-05-04, Nashville, Tennessee TNA

Jerry Lynn defeated Bobby Roode in 9:22 (★ ★); Jerry Lynn defeated Scott D'Amore by DQ in 4:05 (★ ★); D-Ray 3000 defeated David Young in 4:33 (★); Team Mexico (Abismo Negro, Mr. Aguila and Heavy Metal) defeated Team All Japan (Ryuji Hijikata, Mitsu Hirai Jr. and Nosawa) in 7:05 (★ ★); Amazing Red defeated Sonjay Dutt in 9:13 (★ ★ ★); Dusty Rhodes and James Storm defeated Kid Kash and Dallas in a Bunkhouse Brawl in 11:36 (★ ★); Ron Killings defeated AJ Styles, Chris Harris and Raven in a Deadly Draw Match to win the NWA World Tag Team Title in 19:14 (★ ★).

Total Nonstop Action (26-05-04) ★★★
26-05-04, Nashville, Tennessee TNA
Hector Garza won a 16-Man Gauntlet Match in 18:47 (★★); Elix Skipper and Christopher Daniels defeated Bobby Roode and Johnny Devine in 11:34 (★★); Ryuji Hijikata and Mitsu Hirai Jr. defeated Abismo Negro and Heavy Metal in 7:59 (★★); Eric Young defeated Taichi Ishikari, Mr. Aguila and Jerry Lynn in a Four Way Ladder Match in 18:44 (★★); Chris Sabin defeated Petey Williams and Frankie Kazarian in Three Way Ultimate X Match to win the World-X-Cup for Team NWA in 13:48 (★★★).

Total Nonstop Action (02-06-04) ★★
02-06-04, Nashville, Tennessee TNA
Team Canada (Petey Williams and Bobby Roode) defeated Jerry Lynn and Heavy Metal in 9:00 (★★); Monty Brown defeated Sonny Siaki in 7:11 (★); Frankie Kazarian defeated Amazing Red in 9:46 (★★); Abyss defeated D-Ray 3000 in 3:09 (★★); Kid Kash and Dallas defeated Dusty Rhodes and James Storm in 11:00 (★); Jeff Jarrett defeated Chris Harris, Raven, AJ Styles and Ron Killings in a King Of The Mountain Match to win the NWA World Heavyweight Title in 20:12 (★★★).

Total Nonstop Action (09-06-04) ★★
09-06-04, Nashville, Tennessee TNA
America's Most Wanted (Chris Harris and James Storm) defeated The NYC (Johnny Swinger and Glenn Gilbertti) in 7:12 (★★); Michael Shane defeated Chris Sabin in 5:58 (★★); Sonjay Dutt defeated David Young, Shark Boy and D-Ray 3000 in a Four Way Match in 3:58 (★★); Team Canada (Petey Williams, Eric Young and Bobby Roode) defeated Heavy Metal, Hector Garza and Jerry Lynn in 7:07 (★★); Jeff Jarrett defeated Konnan in a Barrio Strap Match in 2:03 (★); Jeff Jarrett defeated BG James in a Trailer Park Trash Match in 3:19 (★★); Ron Killings defeated Jeff Jarrett in a Ghetto Justice Match in 4:23 (★★); AJ Styles defeated Frankie Kazarian to win the NWA X Division Title in 19:16 (★★).

Bad Blood '04 ★★★
13-06-04, Columbus, Ohio WWE
Chris Benoit and Edge defeated La Resistance (Sylvain Grenier and Robert Conway) by DQ in 10:17 (★★); Chris Jericho defeated Tyson Tomko in 6:03 (★★); Randy Orton defeated Shelton Benjamin in 15:03 (★★); Trish Stratus defeated Victoria, Gail Kim and Lita in a Four Way Match to win the WWE Women's Title in 4:43 (★★); Eugene defeated Jonathan Coachman in 7:38 (★); Chris Benoit defeated Kane in 18:20 (★★); Triple H defeated Shawn Michaels in a Hell In A Cell Match in 47:26 (★★★).

Total Nonstop Action (16-06-04) ★★
16-06-04, Nashville, Tennessee TNA
3 Live Kru (BG James, Ron Killings and Konnan) defeated The Elite Guard (Onyx, Collyer and Hernandez) in 5:42 (★★); Trinity defeated Angel Williams in 4:01 (★★); Sonny Siaki and Pat Kenney defeated The NYC (Johnny Swinger and Glenn Gilbertti) in an Ultimate Humiliation Match in 8:03 (★★); Raven defeated Sonjay Dutt in a No DQ Match in 4:53 (★★); AJ Styles defeated Dallas in 10:54 (★); America's Most Wanted (Chris Harris and James Storm) defeated Abyss and Monty Brown by DQ in 13:56 (★); Team Canada (Petey Williams, Eric Young and Bobby Roode) defeated Team NWA (Jerry Lynn, Chris Sabin and Elix Skipper) in a Flag Match in 12:51 (★★★).

Total Nonstop Action (23-06-04) ★★
23-06-04, Nashville, Tennessee TNA
America's Most Wanted (Chris Harris and James Storm) defeated Nosawa and Miyamoto in 7:14 (★★); Trinity defeated Desire in a Stretcher Match in 9:52 (★★); Jerry Lynn defeated Scott D'Amore in 15:20 (★); Mascarita Sagrada defeated Mini Pierroth in 8:12 (★★); AJ Styles vs. Jeff Hardy ended in a no contest in 6:58 (★★); Jeff Jarrett vs. Ron Killings ended in a no contest in 14:02 (★★★).

Great American Bash '04 ★★
27-06-04, Norfolk, Virginia WWE
John Cena defeated Booker T, Rene Dupree and Rob Van Dam in a Four Way Match in 15:52 (★★); Luther Reigns defeated Charlie Haas in 7:11 (★★); Rey Mysterio defeated Chavo Guerrero in 19:40 (★★); Kenzo Suzuki defeated Billy Gunn in 8:06 (★); Sable defeated Torrie Wilson in 6:06 (★); Mordecai defeated Hardcore Holly in 6:31 (★★); John Bradshaw Layfield defeated Eddie Guerrero in a Bullrope Match to win the WWE

Title in 21:06 (★★★); The Undertaker defeated The Dudley Boyz (Bubba Ray Dudley and D-Von Dudley) in a Handicap Concrete Crypt Match in 14:42 (★★).

Total Nonstop Action (30-06-04) ★★
30-06-04, Nashville, Tennessee TNA
Sonjay Dutt and Sabu defeated Team Canada (Petey Williams and Bobby Roode) in 10:25 (★★); D-Lo Brown vs. Monty Brown ended in a double count out in 4:54 (★); Sonny Siaki and Pat Kenney defeated The New York Connection (Johnny Swinger and Glenn Gilbertti) in a Double Or Nothing Humiliation Match in 6:35 (★); Abyss defeated Erik Watts in 7:27 (★★); The Naturals (Andy Douglas and Chase Stevens) defeated America's Most Wanted (Chris Harris and James Storm) in 11:04 (★★); AJ Styles defeated Michael Shane, Frankie Kazarian, Elix Skipper, Amazing Red and Chris Sabin in a Six Way Match in 15:44 (★★★).

Total Nonstop Action (07-07-04) ★★★
07-07-04, Nashville, Tennessee TNA
Frankie Kazarian and Michael Shane defeated Shark Boy and D-Ray 3000 in 6:25 (★★★); Monty Brown defeated D-Lo Brown in 7:24 (★); Trinity and Big Vito defeated Sonny Siaki and Desire in 6:32 (★★); The Naturals (Andy Douglas and Chase Stevens) defeated America's Most Wanted (Chris Harris and James Storm) to win NWA World Tag Team Title in :18 (★); Triple X (Christopher Daniels and Elix Skipper) defeated Team Canada (Bobby Roode and Petey Williams), and Chris Sabin and Amazing Red in a Three Way Tornado Match in 11:55 (★★★★); Jeff Jarrett won an 8-Man Gauntlet Match in 13:33 (★★).

Vengeance '04 ★★★★
11-07-04, Hartford, Connecticut WWE
Rhyno and Tajiri defeated Garrison Cade and Jonathan Coachman in 7:30 (★); Batista defeated Chris Jericho in 12:19 (★★); La Resistance (Sylvain Grenier and Robert Conway) defeated Eugene and Ric Flair by DQ in 12:30 (★★); Matt Hardy defeated Kane in a No DQ Match in 10:34 (★★); Edge defeated Randy Orton to win the WWE Intercontinental Title in 26:36 (★★★★); Victoria defeated Molly Holly in 6:22 (★★); Chris Benoit defeated Triple H in 29:06 (★★★★).

Total Nonstop Action (14-07-04) ★★★
14-07-04, Nashville, Tennessee TNA
Michael Shane defeated AJ Styles in 11:12 (★★★); Alex Shelley and Abyss defeated Sonjay Dutt and Sabu in 8:21 (★★); Chris Sabin, Amazing Red and Triple X (Christopher Daniels and Elix Skipper) defeated Team Canada (Petey Williams, Eric Young, Johnny Devine and Bobby Roode) in 9:08 (★★); 3 Live Kru (BG James, Ron Killings and Konnan), Larry Zbyszko and Dusty Rhodes defeated The Elite Guard (Onyx, Chad Collyer and Hotstuff Hernandez), Ken Shamrock and Jeff Jarrett in a Guitar On A Pole Match in 8:00 (★); Frankie Kazarian defeated AJ Styles in 9:42 (★★); America's Most Wanted (Chris Harris and James Storm) defeated The Naturals (Andy Douglas and Chase Stevens) in a Ladder Match in 13:21 (★★★).

Reborn: Completion ★★★
17-07-07, Elizabeth, New Jersey ROH
Generation Next (Jack Evans and Roderick Strong) defeated Special K (Dixie and Izzy) in 8:59 (★★★); Doug Williams defeated Jay Lethal, John Walters and Nigel McGuinness in 18:39 (★★); The Carnage Crew (DeVito and Loc) defeated The New And Improved Carnage Crew (Danny Daniels and Masada) in a Losing Team Must Break Up Weapons Match in 10:12 (★★); Alex Shelley defeated Austin Aries, CM Punk and Matt Stryker in a Four Corner Survival Match in 19:34 (★★); BJ Whitmer and Dan Maff defeated The Second City Saints (Ace Steel and Colt Cabana) in a Falls Count Anywhere Match in 10:52 (★★); Jimmy Rave defeated Trent Acid in 10:04 (★★); Doug Williams defeated Alex Shelley to win the vacant ROH Pure Title in 19:21 (★★★); Samoa Joe and The Briscoe Brothers (Jay Briscoe and Mark Briscoe) defeated The Rottweilers (Homicide, Ricky Reyes and Rocky Romero) by DQ in 32:01 (★★★).

Total Nonstop Action (21-07-04) ★★
21-07-04, Nashville, Tennessee TNA
Triple X (Christopher Daniels and Elix Skipper) defeated Team Mexico (Abismo Negro and Mr. Aguila) in 8:56 (★★); Big Vito defeated Pat Kenney in a Sicilian Street Fight in 7:21 (★);

Shark Boy, D-Ray 3000 and **Mike Posey** defeated **Johnny Swinger** and **David Young** in a Handicap Match in 7:24 (★★); **Abyss** defeated **Sabu** in a No DQ Falls Count Anywhere Match in 11:37 (★★); **Jerry Lynn** and **Chris Sabin** defeated **Frankie Kazarian** and **Michael Shane** in 7:23 (★★); **The Naturals** (**Andy Douglas** and **Chase Stevens**) defeated **America's Most Wanted** (**Chris Harris** and **James Storm**) in a Steel Cage Match in 15:30 (★★★).

Death Before Dishonor II Night #1 ★★★★
23-07-04, Wauwatosa, Wisconsin **ROH**
Trent Acid defeated **Ace Steel, Delirious** and **Matt Sydal** in a Four Corner Survival Match in 9:21 (★★); **Doug Williams** defeated **Alex Shelley** in 16:47 (★★★); **The Rottweilers** (**Low Ki** and **Rocky Romero**) defeated **BJ Whitmer** and **Dan Maff** in 16:56 (★★★); **Chad Collyer** defeated **Danny Daniels** in 8:28 (★★); **Jimmy Jacobs, John Walters** and **Matt Stryker** defeated **Generation Next** (**Austin Aries, Jack Evans** and **Roderick Strong**) in 16:47 (★★★); **Samoa Joe** defeated **Homicide** in 24:01 (★★★★); **The Second City Saints** (**CM Punk** and **Colt Cabana**) defeated **The Briscoe Brothers** (**Jay Briscoe** and **Mark Briscoe**) 2-1 in a Best Two Out Of Three Falls Match in 37:29 (★★★★).

Death Before Dishonor II Night #2 ★★★★
24-07-04, Chicago Ridge, Illinois **ROH**
Rocky Romero defeated **Chad Collyer** in 11:31 (★★★); **Alex Shelley** defeated **Jimmy Jacobs** in a Grudge Match in 14:29 (★★★); **Generation Next** (**Jack Evans** and **Roderick Strong**) defeated **John Walters** and **Matt Stryker** in 10:43 (★★★); **Trent Acid** defeated **Danny Daniels, Delirious, Matt Sydal, Shawn Daivari** and **The Great Kazushi** in a Six Man Mayhem Match in 8:45 (★★); **Doug Williams** defeated **Austin Aries** in 14:13 (★★★); **Low Ki** defeated **Mark Briscoe** in 16:49 (★★★); **Homicide** defeated **Jay Briscoe** in 11:23 (★★); **Samoa Joe** defeated **Colt Cabana** in 17:29 (★★★); **The Second City Saints** (**Ace Steel** and **CM Punk**) defeated **BJ Whitmer** and **Dan Maff** in an Unsanctioned Chicago Street Fight in 27:42 (★★★★).

Total Nonstop Action (28-07-04) ★★★
28-07-04, Nashville, Tennessee **TNA**
America's Most Wanted (**Chris Harris** and **James Storm**) defeated **Team Canada** (**Bobby Roode** and **Petey Williams**) in 9:17 (★★); **Alex Shelley** and **Abyss** defeated **D-Ray 3000** and **Shark Boy** in 5:26 (★★); **Mike Posey** defeated **David Young** in 5:05 (★); **The Naturals** (**Andy Douglas** and **Chase Stevens**) defeated **Triple X** (**Christopher Daniels** & **Elix Skipper**) in 12:23 (★★); **Jeff Hardy** defeated **Monty Brown** in 9:23 (★★); **Frankie Kazarian** and **Michael Shane** defeated **AJ Styles** in an Ultimate X Match to co-win the NWA X Division Title in 14:57 (★★★).

Total Nonstop Action (04-08-04) ★★★
04-08-04, Nashville, Tennessee **TNA**
Raven defeated **Sabu** in a No DQ Match in 11:56 (★★★); **Abyss** defeated **Sonny Siaki** in 7:37 (★★); **Michael Shane** and **Frankie Kazarian** defeated **Jerry Lynn** and **Chris Sabin** in 8:15 (★★); **Pat Kenney** defeated **Big Vito** in a Luck Of The Irish Weapons Match in 6:54 (★); **America's Most Wanted** (**Chris Harris** and **James Storm**) defeated **Team Canada** (**Bobby Roode** and **Petey Williams**) in a Country Whipping Match in 8:37 (★★★); **AJ Styles** defeated **Kid Kash** in 14:23 (★★★).

Testing The Limit ★★★
07-08-04, Essington, Pennsylvania **ROH**
John Walters defeated **Nigel McGuinness** in 8:02 (★★); **Roderick Strong** defeated **Izzy** in 6:31 (★★); **The Carnage Crew** (**DeVito** and **Loc**) defeated **BJ Whitmer** and **Dan Maff** in 9:17 (★★); **Alex Shelley** defeated **Ace Steel, Jay Lethal** and **Too Cold Scorpio** in a Four Corner Survival Match in 18:09 (★★★); **The Briscoe Brothers** (**Jay Briscoe** and **Mark Briscoe**) defeated **Homicide** and **Low Ki** in 12:43 (★★★); **The Havana Pitbulls** (**Ricky Reyes** and **Rocky Romero**) defeated **The Second City Saints** (**CM Punk** and **Colt Cabana**) to win the ROH Tag Team Title in 19:08 (★★★); **Samoa Joe** defeated **Trent Acid** in 8:04 (★★★); **Austin Aries** defeated **Bryan Danielson** 2-1 in a Best Two Out Of Three Falls Match in 74:12 (★★★★).

Total Nonstop Action (11-08-04) ★★★
11-08-04, Nashville, Tennessee **TNA**
3 Live Kru (**Konnan** and **BG James**) defeated **Team Canada** (**Eric Young** and **Johnny Devine**) in 9:12 (★★); **Alex Shelley** defeated **Ekmo** in 5:14 (★★); **David Young** defeated **Glenn Gilbertti** in a Loser Gets Fired Match in 8:18 (★★); **America's Most Wanted**

(**Chris Harris** and **James Storm**) defeated **Triple X** (**Christopher Daniels** and **Elix Skipper**) in 9:18 (★★★); **Petey Williams** won a Gauntlet For The Gold Match to win the vacant NWA X Division Title in 31:03 (★★★).

SummerSlam '04 ★★
15-08-04, Toronto, Ontario **WWE**
The Dudley Boyz (**Bubba Ray Dudley, D-Von Dudley** and **Spike Dudley**) defeated **Billy Kidman, Paul London** and **Rey Mysterio** in 8:06 (★★); **Kane** defeated **Matt Hardy** in a "Till Death Do Us Part" Match in 6:08 (★★); **John Cena** defeated **Booker T** to win the WWE United States Title in 6:25 (★★); **Edge** defeated **Batista** and **Chris Jericho** in a Three Way Match in 8:26 (★★); **Kurt Angle** defeated **Eddie Guerrero** in 13:38 (★★★); **Triple H** defeated **Eugene** in 14:06 (★★); **John Bradshaw Layfield** defeated **The Undertaker** by DQ in 17:37 (★★); **Randy Orton** defeated **Chris Benoit** to win the World Heavyweight Title in 20:08 (★★★).

Total Nonstop Action (18-08-04) ★★★
18-08-04, Nashville, Tennessee **TNA**
Sonjay Dutt defeated **Raven** in a Hangman's Horror Match in 10:04 (★★★); **Petey Williams** defeated **Chris Sabin** in 9:11 (★★★); **Triple X** (**Christopher Daniels** and **Elix Skipper**) defeated **America's Most Wanted** (**Chris Harris** and **James Storm**) in 9:08 (★★★); **Monty Brown** defeated **Ron Killings** in 8:03 (★★); **The Naturals** (**Andy Douglas** and **Chase Stevens**) defeated **3 Live Kru** (**Konnan** and **BG James**) by DQ in 10:14 (★★); **AJ Styles** defeated **Kid Kash** in a Street Fight in 15:19 (★★★).

Total Nonstop Action (25-08-04) ★★★
25-08-04, Nashville, Tennessee **TNA**
Michael Shane and **Frankie Kazarian** defeated **LA Park** and **Psicosis** in 9:26 (★★★); **Erik Watts** defeated **Alex Shelley** in :52 (★); **Sonjay Dutt** defeated **Jason Cross, Joey Matthews** and **Chris Sabin** in a Four Way Match in 8:44 (★★★); **Triple X** (**Christopher Daniels** and **Elix Skipper**) vs. **America's Most Wanted** (**Chris Harris** and **James Storm**) ended in a no contest in 13:01 (★★★); **Team Canada** (**Eric Young, Johnny Devine** and **Scott D'Amore**) defeated **3 Live Kru** (**Konnan** and **BG James**) by DQ in a Handicap Match in 10:16 (★★); **Jeff Hardy, AJ Styles** and **Ron Killings** defeated **Monty Brown, Kid Kash** and **Dallas** in 14:01 (★★).

Total Nonstop Action (01-09-04) ★★★
01-09-04, Nashville, Tennessee **TNA**
The Naturals (**Andy Douglas** and **Chase Stevens**) defeated **America's Most Wanted** (**Chris Harris** and **James Storm**), and **Triple X** (**Christopher Daniels** and **Elix Skipper**) in a Three Way Match in 12:15 (★★★); **Michael Shane** and **Frankie Kazarian** defeated **Amazing Red** and **Chris Sabin** in 8:07 (★★★); **Petey Williams** defeated **Sonjay Dutt** in 8:03 (★★★); **3 Live Kru** (**Konnan** and **BG James**) and **The Midnight Rider** defeated **Team Canada** (**Bobby Roode, Eric Young** and **Johnny Devine**) in 6:05 (★★); **Sonny Siaki** and **Erik Watts** defeated **Abyss** and **Alex Shelley** in 5:58 (★★); **AJ Styles** and **Ron Killings** defeated **Kid Kash** and **Dallas** in an Asylum Streetfight in 14:36 (★★).

Total Nonstop Action (08-09-04) ★★
08-09-04, Nashville, Tennessee **TNA**
Mikey Batts and **Jerelle Clark** won a Tag Team Dominance Battle Royal in 12:16 (★★); **Desire, Sonny Siaki** and **Erik Watts** defeated **Goldylocks, Alex Shelley** and **Abyss** in 7:45 (★★); **AJ Styles** defeated **Kid Kash** in a Tables Match in 12:44 (★★★); **Dusty Rhodes** defeated **Scott D'Amore** in 6:40 (★); **Elix Skipper** and **Chris Harris** defeated **The Naturals** (**Andy Douglas** and **Chase Stevens**) to win the NWA World Tag Team Title in 12:25 (★★); **Jeff Jarrett** defeated **Jeff Hardy** in 11:16 (★★).

Glory By Honor III ★★★
11-09-04, Elizabeth, New Jersey **ROH**
Jimmy Rave defeated **Dixie** in 5:39 (★★); **Jay Lethal** defeated **Matt Stryker** in 4:23 (★★); **Trent Acid** defeated **Ace Steel, Angel Dust, Fast Eddie, Izzy** and **Kahagas** in a Six Man Mayhem Match in 7:52 (★★); **CM Punk** defeated **Austin Aries** in 18:57 (★★★); **BJ Whitmer** and **Dan Maff** defeated **Chicano** and **Slash Venom** in 3:06 (★★); **Bryan Danielson** defeated **Alex Shelley** in 19:21 (★★★); **John Walters** defeated **Nigel McGuinness** in 16:13 (★★★); **Samoa Joe** defeated **Doug Williams** in 17:54 (★★★); **The Havana Pitbulls** (**Ricky Reyes** and **Rocky Romero**) defeated **BJ Whitmer** and **Dan Maff, Generation Next** (**Jack Evans** and

Roderick Strong), and **The Carnage Crew (DeVito and Loc)** in a Ultimate Endurance Four Way Elimination Match in 20:25 (★★★).

Unforgiven '04 ★★
12-09-04, Portland, Oregon **WWE**

Chris Benoit and **William Regal** defeated **Evolution (Batista and Ric Flair)** in 15:07 (★★); **Trish Stratus** defeated **Victoria** in 8:21 (★★); **Tyson Tomko** defeated **Steven Richards** in 6:24 (★); **Chris Jericho** defeated **Christian** in a Ladder Match to win the vacant WWE Intercontinental Title in 22:29 (★★★); **Shawn Michaels** defeated **Kane** in a No DQ Match in 18:02 (★★★); **La Resistance (Sylvain Grenier and Robert Conway)** defeated **Rhyno** and **Tajiri** in 9:40 (★★); **Triple H** defeated **Randy Orton** to win the World Heavyweight Title in 24:47 (★★★).

No Mercy '04 ★★
03-10-04, East Rutherford, New Jersey **WWE**

Eddie Guerrero defeated **Luther Reigns** in 13:13 (★★); **Spike Dudley** defeated **Nunzio** in 8:44 (★★); **Billy Kidman** defeated **Paul London** in 10:33 (★★★); **Kenzo Suzuki** and **Rene Dupree** defeated **Rey Mysterio** and **Rob Van Dam** in 9:09 (★★); **The Big Show** defeated **Kurt Angle** in 15:07 (★★); **John Cena** defeated **Booker T** to win the WWE United States Title in 10:32 (★★); **Charlie Haas, Miss Jackie** and **Rico** defeated **Dawn Marie** and **The Dudley Boyz (Bubba Ray Dudley** and **D-Von Dudley)** in 8:44 (★★★); **John Bradshaw Layfield** defeated **The Undertaker** in a Last Ride Match in 20:01 (★★).

Joe vs. Punk II ★★★★
16-10-04, Chicago Ridge, Illinois **ROH**

Jay Lethal defeated **Delirious** in 8:19 (★★★); **Traci Brooks** defeated **Daizee Haze** in 3:42 (★★); **Matt Stryker** defeated **Dixie** in 3:10 (★★); **Josh Daniels** defeated **Angel Dust, Matt Sydal** and **Trent Acid** in a Four Corner Survival Match in 6:33 (★★); **Chad Collyer** and **Nigel McGuinness** defeated **BJ Whitmer** and **Dan Maff** in a Hardcore Match in 11:39 (★★); **The Carnage Crew (DeVito and Loc)** defeated **Davey Andrews** and **TJ Dalton** in 4:22 (★); **Generation Next (Jack Evans** and **Roderick Strong)** defeated **The Rottweilers (Homicide and Rocky Romero)** in 17:29 (★★★); **Alex Shelley** defeated **Jimmy Jacobs** in a "I Quit" Match in 16:47 (★★★★); **Samoa Joe** vs. **CM Punk** ended in a draw in 60:00 (★★★★★).

Taboo Tuesday '04 ★★
19-10-04, Milwaukee, Wisconsin **WWE**

Shelton Benjamin defeated **Chris Jericho** to win the WWE Intercontinental Title in 10:55 (★★★); **Trish Stratus** won a Fulfil Your Fantasy Battle Royal in 5:30 (★★); **Gene Snitsky** defeated **Kane** in a Weapon Of Choice Match in 14:17 (★★); **Eugene** defeated **Eric Bischoff** in a "Choose The Loser's Fate" Match in 2:01 (★★); **Chris Benoit** and **Edge** defeated **La Resistance (Sylvain Grenier** and **Robert Conway)** to win the World Tag Team Title in 16:15 (★★); **Christy Hemme** defeated **Carmella** in a Lingerie Pillow Fight in 1:48 (★); **Triple H** defeated **Shawn Michaels** in 14:05 (★★★); **Randy Orton** defeated **Ric Flair** in a Steel Cage Match in 10:35 (★★★).

Victory Road '04 ★★
07-11-04, Orlando, Florida **TNA**

Hector Garza won a 20-Man Gauntlet Match to win the X Division Cup in 26:25 (★★★); **Ron Killings, Erik Watts, Johnny B. Badd** and **Pat Kenney** defeated **The Naturals (Andy Douglas** and **Chase Stevens), Kid Kash** and **Dallas** in 4:37 (★★); **Mascarita Sagrada** defeated **Piratita Morgan** in 2:58 (★★); **3Live Kru (B.G. James** and **Konnan)** defeated **Team Canada (Eric Young** and **Bobby Roode)** to win the NWA World Tag Team Title in 6:57 (★★); **Stephanie Trinity** defeated **Jacqueline** in 1:50 (★★); **Monty Brown** defeated **Raven** and **Abyss** in a Three Way Monster's Ball Match in 9:05 (★★); **Petey Williams** defeated **AJ Styles** in 9:48 (★★★); **America's Most Wanted (James Storm** and **Chris Harris)** defeated **Triple X (Christopher Daniels** and **Elix Skipper)** in an Elimination Last Team Standing Match in 11:31 (★★); **Jeff Jarrett** defeated **Jeff Hardy** in a Ladder Match in 18:37 (★★).

Survivor Series '04 ★★
14-11-04, Cleveland, Ohio **WWE**

Spike Dudley defeated **Billy Kidman, Chavo Guerrero** and **Rey Mysterio** in a Four Way Match in 9:09 (★★★); **Shelton Benjamin** defeated **Christian** in 13:23 (★★★); **Team Guerrero (Eddie Guerrero, The Big Show, John Cena** and **Rob Van Dam)**

---

defeated **Team Angle (Kurt Angle, Carlito, Luther Reigns** and **Mark Jindrak)** in an Elimination Match in 12:26 (★★); **The Undertaker** defeated **Heidenreich** in 15:58 (★★); **Trish Stratus** defeated **Lita** by DQ in 1:24 (★★); **John Bradshaw Layfield** defeated **Booker T** in 14:43 (★★); **Team Orton (Randy Orton, Chris Benoit, Chris Jericho** and **Maven)** defeated **Team Triple H (Triple H, Batista, Edge** and **Gene Snitsky)** in an Elimination Match in 24:31 (★★★).

All Star Extravaganza II ★★★★
04-12-04, Elizabeth, New Jersey **ROH**

Anthony Franco, Davey Andrews, Matt Turner and **Shane Hagadorn** defeated **Special K (Angel Dust, Deranged, Dixie** and **Izzy)** in 4:54 (★★); **Jay Lethal** defeated **The Weapon Of Mask Destruction** in 6:39 (★★); **The Outcast Killaz (Diablo Santiago** and **Oman Tortuga)** defeated **BJ Whitmer** and **Dan Maff, The Carnage Crew (DeVito and Loc)** and **The Ring Crew Express (Dunn** and **Marcos)** in a Four Way Scramble Match in 9:21 (★★); **John Walters** defeated **Jimmy Rave** via count out in 16:51 (★★★★); **Austin Aries** vs. **Low Ki** ended in a draw in 20:00 (★★★★★); **The Havana Pitbulls (Ricky Reyes** and **Rocky Romero)** defeated **Chad Collyer** and **Nigel McGuinness** in 16:25 (★★); **Trent Acid** defeated **Jerk Jackson** in 3:26 (★); **Colt Cabana** and **Jimmy Jacobs** defeated **Generation Next (Jack Evans** and **Roderick Strong)** in 17:34 (★★★); **Bryan Danielson** defeated **Homicide** in 25:29 (★★★★); **Samoa Joe** defeated **CM Punk** in 31:33 (★★★★).

Turning Point '04 ★★★★
05-12-04, Orlando, Florida **TNA**

Team Canada (Eric Young and **Bobby Roode)** defeated **3Live Kru (B.G. James** and **Ron Killings)** to win the NWA World Tag Team Title in 8:30 (★★); **Sonny Siaki, Hector Garza** and **Sonjay Dutt** defeated **Kid Kash, Michael Shane** and **Kazarian** in 11:01 (★★★); **Monty Brown** defeated **Abyss** in a Serengeti Survival Match in 12:17 (★★★); **Pat Kenney** and **Johnny B. Badd** defeated **The New York Connection (Johnny Swinger** and **Glenn Gilbertti)** in 7:50 (★★); **Diamond Dallas Page** defeated **Raven** in 12:03 (★★★); **Petey Williams** defeated **Chris Sabin** in 18:11 (★★★★); **AJ Styles, Jeff Hardy** and **Randy Savage** defeated **Jeff Jarrett, Kevin Nash** and **Scott Hall** in 17:52 (★★); **America's Most Wanted (Chris Harris** and **James Storm)** defeated **Triple X (Christopher Daniels** and **Elix Skipper)** in a Six Sides Of Steel Match in 21:01 (★★★★★).

Armageddon '04 ★★
12-12-04, Duluth, Georgia **WWE**

Rob Van Dam and **Rey Mysterio** defeated **Rene Dupree** and **Kenzo Suzuki** in 17:12 (★★★); **Kurt Angle** defeated **Santa Claus** in :25 (★★); **Daniel Puder** defeated **Mike Mizanin** in a Dixie Dog Fight in 3:00 (★); **The Basham Brothers (Doug Basham** and **Danny Basham)** defeated **Hardcore Holly** and **Charlie Haas** in 6:50 (★★); **John Cena** defeated **Jesus** in a Street Fight in 7:50 (★★); **Dawn Marie** defeated **Miss Jackie** in 1:04 (★★); **The Big Show** defeated **Kurt Angle, Mark Jindrak** and **Luther Reigns** in a Handicap Match in 9:55 (★★); **Funaki** defeated **Spike Dudley** to win the WWE Cruiserweight Title in 9:29 (★★); **John Bradshaw Layfield** defeated **Eddie Guerrero, Booker T** and **The Undertaker** in a Four Way Match in 25:37 (★★★).

Tribute To The Troops '04 ★★
18-12-04, Tikrit, Iraq **WWE**

Booker T defeated **Rene Dupree** in 3:41 (★★); **The Undertaker** defeated **Heidenreich** via count out in 7:34 (★★); **Hardcore Holly** defeated **Kenzo Suzuki** in 2:38 (★★); **Eddie Guerrero** and **Rey Mysterio** defeated **Kurt Angle** and **Luther Reigns** in 6:01 (★★).

Final Battle '04 ★★★
26-12-04, Philadelphia, Pennsylvania **ROH**

Jimmy Jacobs defeated **Trent Acid** in 6:01 (★★); **Deranged** and **Lacey** defeated **Angel Dust** and **Becky Bayless** in 7:39 (★★); **Rockin' Rebel** defeated **Devon Moore** in 4:24 (★★); **Homicide** defeated **Josh Daniels** in 11:20 (★★); **John Walters** defeated **Jimmy Rave** in 11:31 (★★★); **BJ Whitmer** and **Dan Maff** defeated **The Carnage Crew (DeVito and Loc)** in a Fight Without Honor Match in 16:42 (★★★); **Jay Lethal** defeated **The Weapon Of Mask Destruction #2** in 6:32 (★★); **CM Punk** and **Steve Corino** defeated **Generation Next (Alex Shelley** and **Roderick Strong)** in 17:32 (★★★); **Bryan Danielson** defeated **Low Ki** by DQ in 20:57 (★★★); **Austin Aries** defeated **Samoa Joe** to win the ROH World Title in 17:34 (★★★★).

New Years Revolution '05 ★★

09-01-05, San Juan, Puerto Rico **WWE**

Eugene and **William Regal** defeated **Christian** and **Tyson Tomko** in 12:22 (★ ★); **Trish Stratus** defeated **Lita** to win the WWE Women's Title in 3:46 (★ ★); **Shelton Benjamin** defeated **Maven** in 6:08 (★); **Shelton Benjamin** defeated **Maven** in :05 (★); **Muhammad Hassan** defeated **Jerry Lawler** in 10:51 (★); **Kane** defeated **Gene Snitsky** in 11:38 (★ ★); **Triple H** defeated **Randy Orton**, **Batista**, **Chris Jericho**, **Chris Benoit** and **Edge** in an Elimination Chamber Match in 35:01 (★ ★ ★ ★).

Final Resolution '05 ★★★★

16-01-05, Orlando, Florida **TNA**

3Live Kru (**Ron Killings**, **Konnan** and **B.G. James**) defeated **Christopher Daniels**, **Michael Shane** and **Kazarian** in 8:21 (★ ★ ★); **Elix Skipper** defeated **Sonjay Dutt** in 10:12 (★ ★); **Dustin Rhodes** defeated **Kid Kash** in 10:50 (★ ★ ★); **Erik Watts** defeated **Raven** in 10:19 (★ ★); **Jeff Jarrett** defeated **Scott Hall** in 5:42 (★ ★); **Monty Brown** defeated **Diamond Dallas Page** and **Kevin Nash** in a Triple Threat Elimination Match in 9:40 (★ ★); **America's Most Wanted** (**Chris Harris** and **James Storm**) defeated **Team Canada** (**Eric Young** and **Bobby Roode**) to win the NWA World Tag Team Title in 19:12 (★ ★ ★ ★); **AJ Styles** defeated **Petey Williams** and **Chris Sabin** in a Three Way Ultimate X Match to win the TNA X Division Title in 19:55 (★ ★ ★ ★); **Jeff Jarrett** defeated **Monty Brown** in 16:17 (★ ★ ★).

Royal Rumble '05 ★★★

30-01-05, Fresno, California **WWE**

Edge defeated **Shawn Michaels** in 18:32 (★ ★ ★); **The Undertaker** defeated **Heidenreich** in a Casket Match in 13:20 (★ ★); **John Bradshaw Layfield** defeated **The Big Show** and **Kurt Angle** in a Three Way Match in 12:04 (★ ★ ★); **Triple H** defeated **Randy Orton** in 21:28 (★ ★ ★); **Batista** won the 30-Man Royal Rumble Match in 51:07 (★ ★ ★ ★).

Against All Odds '05 ★★★

13-02-05, Orlando, Florida **TNA**

Elix Skipper defeated **Petey Williams** in 7:58 (★ ★); **B.G. James** and **Jeff Hammond** defeated **Michael Shane** and **Kazarian** in 5:33 (★); **Raven** defeated **Dustin Rhodes** in 8:20 (★ ★); **America's Most Wanted** (**Chris Harris** and **James Storm**) defeated **Kid Kash** and **Lance Hoyt** in 12:25 (★ ★ ★); **Abyss** defeated **Jeff Hardy** in a Full Metal Mayhem Match in 15:21 (★ ★ ★); **Diamond Dallas Page** and **Monty Brown** defeated **Team Canada** (**Eric Young** and **Bobby Roode**) in 9:43 (★ ★ ★); **AJ Styles** defeated **Christopher Daniels** 2-1 in an Iron Man Match in 31:42 (★ ★ ★ ★); **Jeff Jarrett** defeated **Kevin Nash** in 19:45 (★ ★).

No Way Out '05 ★★

20-02-05, Pittsburgh, Pennsylvania **WWE**

Eddie Guerrero and **Rey Mysterio** defeated **The Basham Brothers** (**Doug Basham** and **Danny Basham**) to win the WWE Tag Team Title in 14:50 (★ ★); **Booker T** defeated **Heidenreich** by DQ in 6:49 (★); **Chavo Guerrero** won a Cruiserweight Open to win the WWE Cruiserweight Title in 9:43 (★ ★); **The Undertaker** defeated **Luther Reigns** in 11:44 (★ ★); **John Cena** defeated **Kurt Angle** in 19:22 (★ ★ ★); **John Bradshaw Layfield** defeated **The Big Show** in a Barbed Wire Steel Cage Match in 15:11 (★ ★).

Destination X '05 ★

13-03-05, Orlando, Florida **TNA**

Team Canada (**Petey Williams**, **Eric Young**, **Bobby Roode** and **A-1**) defeated **3Live Kru** (**Konnan** and **B.G. James**) and **America's Most Wanted** (**Chris Harris** and **James Storm**) in 8:53 (★ ★); **Chris Sabin** defeated **Chase Stevens** in 6:18 (★ ★); **Dustin Rhodes** defeated **Raven** in a Texas Bullrope Match in 6:10 (★ ★); **The Disciples Of Destruction** (**Don Harris** and **Ron Harris**) defeated **Phi Delta Slam** (**Bruno Sassi** and **Big Tilly**) in 10:18 (★); **Monty Brown** vs. **Trytan** ended in a no contest in 5:26 (★); **Jeff Hardy** defeated **Abyss** in a Falls Count Anywhere Match in 15:48 (★ ★); **The Outlaw** defeated **Kevin Nash** in a First Blood Match in 11:20 (★); **Christopher Daniels** defeated **AJ Styles**, **Ron Killings** and **Elix Skipper** in a Four Way Ultimate X Challenge to win the TNA X Division Title in 25:19 (★ ★ ★); **Jeff Jarrett** defeated **Diamond Dallas Page** in a Ringside Revenge Match in 21:40 (★ ★).

WrestleMania XXI ★★★★★

03-04-05, Los Angeles, California **WWE**

Rey Mysterio defeated **Eddie Guerrero** in 12:39 (★ ★ ★); **Edge** defeated **Chris Benoit**, **Chris Jericho**, **Christian**, **Kane** and **Shelton Benjamin** in a Money In The Bank Ladder Match in 15:17 (★ ★ ★ ★ ★); **The Undertaker** defeated **Randy Orton** in 14:14 (★ ★ ★); **Trish Stratus** defeated **Christy Hemme** in 4:11 (★ ★); **Kurt Angle** defeated **Shawn Michaels** in 27:27 (★ ★ ★ ★ ★); **Akebono** defeated **The Big Show** in a Sumo Match in 1:02 (★ ★); **John Cena** defeated **John Bradshaw Layfield** to win the WWE Title in 11:26 (★ ★); **Batista** defeated **Triple H** to win the World Heavyweight Title in 21:34 (★ ★ ★).

Lockdown '05 ★★★★

24-04-05, Orlando, Florida **TNA**

Apolo and **Sonny Siaki** defeated **Chris Candido** and **Lance Hoyt** in a Six Sides Of Steel Cage Match in 6:58 (★ ★); **Dustin Rhodes** defeated **Bobby Roode** 2-1 in a Prince Of Darkness Match in 15:20 (★ ★); **Shocker** defeated **Chris Sabin**, **Matt Bentley** and **Sonjay Dutt** in a Four-Way Xscape Match in 16:14 (★ ★); **Jeff Hardy** defeated **Raven** in a Six Sides Of Steel Tables Match in 11:51 (★ ★ ★); **America's Most Wanted** (**Chris Harris** and **James Storm**) defeated **Team Canada** (**Eric Young** and **Petey Williams**) in a Six Sides Of Steel Strap Match in 14:00 (★ ★ ★); **Christopher Daniels** defeated **Elix Skipper** in a Six Sides Of Steel Cage Match in 15:28 (★ ★ ★); **Team Nash** (**B.G. James**, **Diamond Dallas Page** and **Sean Waltman**) defeated **Team Jarrett** (**Jeff Jarrett**, **Monty Brown** and **The Outlaw**) in a Lethal Lockdown Match in 15:35 (★ ★); **AJ Styles** defeated **Abyss** in a Six Sides Of Steel Match in 18:00 (★ ★ ★ ★).

Backlash '05 ★★★

01-05-05, Manchester, New Hampshire **WWE**

Shelton Benjamin defeated **Chris Jericho** in 14:31 (★ ★ ★ ★); **The Hurricane** and **Rosey** won a Tag Team Turmoil Match to win the World Tag Team Title in 13:43 (★ ★); **Edge** defeated **Chris Benoit** in a Last Man Standing Match in 18:47 (★ ★ ★ ★); **Kane** defeated **Viscera** in 6:09 (★ ★); **Hulk Hogan** and **Shawn Michaels** defeated **Daivari** and **Muhammad Hassan** in 15:05 (★ ★); **Batista** defeated **Triple H** in 16:26 (★ ★).

Manhattan Mayhem ★★★★

07-05-05, New York City, New York **ROH**

Lacey's Angels (**Deranged** and **Izzy**) defeated **Azrieal** and **Dixie** in a Losing Team Must Disband Match in 10:17 (★ ★ ★); **Nigel McGuinness** defeated **Colt Cabana** in 11:52 (★ ★ ★); **James Gibson** defeated **Black Tiger IV** in 15:58 (★ ★ ★); **BJ Whitmer** and **Jimmy Jacobs** defeated **Generation Next** (**Jack Evans** and **Roderick Strong**) in 14:45 (★ ★ ★); **Samoa Joe** defeated **Jay Lethal** to win the ROH Pure Title in 16:34 (★ ★ ★ ★); **Jimmy Rave** defeated **CM Punk** in a Dog Collar Match in 13:33 (★ ★ ★); **Austin Aries** defeated **Alex Shelley** in 19:33 (★ ★ ★ ★); **The Rottweilers** (**Homicide** and **Low Ki**) defeated **Jay Lethal** and **Samoa Joe** in 9:17 (★ ★ ★).

Hard Justice '05 ★★★

15-05-05, Orlando, Florida **TNA**

Team Canada (**Eric Young** and **Petey Williams**) defeated **Apolo** and **Sonny Siaki** in 8:06 (★ ★); **Michael Shane** and **Trinity** defeated **Chris Sabin** and **Traci** in 10:19 (★ ★); **Raven** defeated **Sean Waltman** in a Clockwork Orange House Of Fun Match in 13:00 (★ ★ ★); **Monty Brown** and **The Outlaw** defeated **Diamond Dallas Page** and **Ron Killings** in 8:55 (★ ★); **The Naturals** (**Andy Douglas** and **Chase Stevens**) defeated **America's Most Wanted** (**Chris Harris** and **James Storm**) in 14:10 (★ ★ ★); **Christopher Daniels** defeated **Shocker** in 11:58 (★ ★ ★); **Abyss** won a 20-Man Gauntlet For The Gold in 26:45 (★ ★ ★); **AJ Styles** defeated **Jeff Jarrett** to win the NWA World Heavyweight Title in 19:30 (★ ★ ★).

Judgment Day '05 ★★★★★

22-05-05, Minneapolis, Minnesota **WWE**

MNM (**Joey Mercury** and **Johnny Nitro**) defeated **Charlie Haas** and **Hardcore Holly** in 8:06 (★ ★ ★); **Carlito** defeated **The Big Show** in 4:41 (★ ★); **Paul London** defeated **Chavo Guerrero** in 10:41 (★ ★ ★); **Booker T** defeated **Kurt Angle** in 14:10 (★ ★ ★); **Orlando Jordan** defeated **Heidenreich** in 4:54 (★); **Rey Mysterio** defeated **Eddie Guerrero** by DQ in 18:30 (★ ★ ★ ★); **John Cena** defeated **John Bradshaw Layfield** in an "I Quit" Match in 22:45 (★ ★ ★ ★).

An Extreme Reunion ★★★
10-06-05, Philadelphia, Pennsylvania **Hardcore Homecoming**

Chris Chetti and Mikey Whipwreck defeated CW Anderson and Simon Diamond in 9:49 (★★); Tracy Smothers defeated The Blue Meanie in 8:12 (★★); Too Cold Scorpio defeated Kid Kash in 17:01 (★★); The Bad Breed (Axl Rotten and Ian Rotten) vs. John Kronus and New Jack ended in a no contest in 8:28 (★★); Jerry Lynn defeated Justin Credible in 20:23 (★★); Raven defeated The Sandman in 9:56 (★★); Sabu defeated Shane Douglas and Terry Funk in a Three Way No Rope Barbed Wire Match in 21:08 (★★★).

One Night Stand '05 ★★★★★
12-06-05, New York City, New York **ECW**

Lance Storm defeated Chris Jericho in 7:22 (★★★); Super Crazy defeated Little Guido and Tajiri in a Three Way Match in 6:12 (★★★); Rey Mysterio Jr. defeated Psicosis in 6:22 (★★); Sabu defeated Rhyno in 6:30 (★★★); Chris Benoit defeated Eddie Guerrero in 10:37 (★★★★); Mike Awesome defeated Masato Tanaka in 9:52 (★★★★); The Dudley Boyz (Bubba Ray Dudley and D-Von Dudley) defeated Tommy Dreamer and The Sandman in 10:52 (★★★★).

Death Before Dishonor III ★★★
18-06-05, Morristown, New Jersey **ROH**

BJ Whitmer and Jimmy Jacobs defeated The Embassy (Fast Eddie and Jimmy Rave) in 10:03 (★★★); The Carnage Crew (DeVito and Loc) defeated The Ring Crew Express (Dunn and Marcos) in an Anything Goes Match in 8:36 (★★); Samoa Joe defeated Colt Cabana in 14:06 (★★★); AJ Styles defeated Petey Williams in 16:37 (★★★); Lacey's Angels (Deranged and Izzy) defeated Generation Next (Jack Evans and Roderick Strong) in 12:32 (★★); Nigel McGuinness defeated Azrieal, Homicide and James Gibson in a Four Corner Survival Match in 20:28 (★★★); Jay Lethal vs. Low Ki ended in a no contest in 15:11 (★★★); CM Punk defeated Austin Aries to win the ROH World Title in 30:28 (★★★★).

Slammiversary III ★★
19-06-05, Orlando, Florida **TNA**

Shark Boy defeated Amazing Red, Delirious, Elix Skipper, Jerrelle Clark and Zach Gowen in a Six Way Match in 6:25 (★★★); Shocker defeated Alex Shelley in 10:13 (★★★★); Ron Killings defeated The Outlaw in 7:30 (★★); The Naturals (Andy Douglas and Chase Stevens) defeated Team Canada (Eric Young and Petey Williams) in 15:22 (★★); Samoa Joe defeated Sonjay Dutt in 6:22 (★★); Bobby Roode defeated Lance Hoyt in 7:24 (★★); America's Most Wanted (Chris Harris and James Storm) defeated 3Live Kru (B.G. James and Konnan) in 6:54 (★★); Christopher Daniels defeated Chris Sabin and Michael Shane in a Three Way Elimination Match in 17:10 (★★★); Raven defeated AJ Styles, Abyss, Monty Brown and Sean Waltman in a King Of The Mountain Match to win the NWA World Heavyweight Title in 14:17 (★★★).

Vengeance '05 ★★★★
26-06-05, Las Vegas, Nevada **WWE**

Carlito defeated Shelton Benjamin in 12:50 (★★); Victoria defeated Christy Hemme in 5:06 (★★); Kane defeated Edge in 11:11 (★★); Shawn Michaels defeated Kurt Angle in 26:13 (★★★★); John Cena defeated Chris Jericho and Christian in a Three Way Match in 15:08 (★★★★); Batista defeated Triple H in a Hell In A Cell Match in 26:55 (★★★★).

No Surrender '05 ★★★★
17-07-05, Orlando, Florida **TNA**

America's Most Wanted (Chris Harris and James Storm) defeated Alex Shelley and Matt Bentley in 11:47 (★★★); Sonjay Dutt defeated Elix Skipper, Mikey Batts and Shark Boy in a Four Way Match in 8:22 (★★★★); Apolo and Sonny Siaki defeated David Young and Simon Diamond in 5:32 (★★); Samoa Joe defeated Chris Sabin in 14:02 (★★★★); Team Canada (A-1, Bobby Roode and Eric Young) defeated The Naturals (Andy Douglas and Chase Stevens) and Lance Hoyt in 14:44 (★★★); Monty Brown and Kip James defeated 3Live Kru (Konnan and Ron Killings) in a Street Fight in 5:20 (★★); AJ Styles defeated Sean Waltman in 14:37 (★★★); Christopher Daniels defeated Petey Williams in 16:24 (★★★); Raven defeated Abyss in a Dog Collar Match in 19:17 (★★★).

Great American Bash '05 ★★
24-07-05, Buffalo, New York **WWE**

The Legion Of Doom (Animal and Heidenreich) defeated MNM (Joey Mercury and Johnny Nitro) to win the WWE Tag Team Title in 6:45 (★★); Booker T defeated Christian in 11:52 (★★); Orlando Jordan defeated Chris Benoit in 14:23 (★★); The Undertaker defeated Muhammad Hassan in 8:04 (★★); The Mexicools (Super Crazy, Juventud Guerrera and Psicosis) defeated The bWo (Big Stevie Cool, The Blue Meanie and Hollywood Nova) in 4:53 (★★); Rey Mysterio defeated Eddie Guerrero in 15:39 (★★); Melina defeated Torrie Wilson in a Bra and Panties Match in 3:53 (★★); John Bradshaw Layfield defeated Batista by DQ in 19:47 (★★).

Punk: The Final Chapter ★★★
13-08-05, Chicago Ridge, Illinois **ROH**

Nigel McGuinness defeated Alex Shelley, Delirious and Matt Sydal in a Four Corner Survival Match in 10:53 (★★★); Chad Collyer defeated Ace Steel in 10:28 (★★); Austin Aries defeated Jimmy Rave in 13:29 (★★★); Jay Lethal and Samoa Joe defeated The Rottweilers (Homicide and Low Ki) by DQ in 17:34 (★★★); BJ Whitmer and Jimmy Jacobs defeated James Gibson and Spanky in 17:29 (★★★); Roderick Strong defeated Matt Hardy in 23:52 (★★★); Colt Cabana defeated CM Punk 2-1 in a Best Two Out Of Three Falls Match in 27:44 (★★★).

Sacrifice '05 ★★★★
14-08-05, Orlando, Florida **TNA**

Chris Sabin, Shark Boy and Sonjay Dutt defeated Elix Skipper, Simon Diamond and David Young in 7:21 (★★); Alex Shelley defeated Shocker in 8:50 (★★); Abyss defeated Lance Hoyt in 9:09 (★★); 3Live Kru (Ron Killings and Konnan) defeated Kip James and Monty Brown in 7:45 (★★); Christopher Daniels defeated Austin Aries in 9:35 (★★★); Sean Waltman in 15:31 (★★★★); Team Canada (A-1, Bobby Roode, Eric Young and Petey Williams) defeated America's Most Wanted (Chris Harris and James Storm) and The Naturals (Andy Douglas and Chase Stevens) in 11:11 (★★★); Samoa Joe defeated AJ Styles in 15:15 (★★★★); Jeff Jarrett and Rhino defeated Raven and Sabu in 16:23 (★★★).

SummerSlam '05 ★★★
21-08-05, Washington, D.C. **WWE**

Chris Benoit defeated Orlando Jordan to win the WWE United States Title in :25 (★); Edge defeated Matt Hardy in 4:50 (★★); Rey Mysterio defeated Eddie Guerrero in a Ladder Match in 20:19 (★★★); Kurt Angle defeated Eugene in 4:31 (★★); Randy Orton defeated The Undertaker in 17:17 (★★); John Cena defeated Chris Jericho in 14:49 (★★★); Batista defeated John Bradshaw Layfield in a No Holds Barred Match in 9:05 (★★); Hulk Hogan defeated Shawn Michaels in 21:24 (★★★★).

Unbreakable '05 ★★★★
11-09-05, Orlando, Florida **TNA**

3Live Kru (B.G. James, Konnan and Ron Killings) defeated The Diamonds In The Rough (David Young, Elix Skipper and Simon Diamond) in 4:20 (★★); Austin Aries defeated Roderick Strong in 8:00 (★★★); Kip James and Monty Brown defeated Apolo and Lance Hoyt in 9:58 (★★); Chris Sabin defeated Petey Williams in 12:34 (★★★); Abyss defeated Sabu in a No DQ Match in 11:30 (★★★); Bobby Roode defeated Jeff Hardy in 9:07 (★★); The Naturals (Andy Douglas and Chase Stevens) defeated Alex Shelley and Johnny Candido, America's Most Wanted (Chris Harris and James Storm), and Team Canada (A-1 and Eric Young) in a Four Way Elimination Match in 18:01 (★★★); Raven defeated Rhino in a Raven's Rules Match in 14:28 (★★★); AJ Styles defeated Christopher Daniels and Samoa Joe in a Three Way Match to win the TNA X Division Title in 22:50 (★★★★★).

Glory By Honor IV ★★★
17-09-05, Long Island, New York **ROH**

Low Ki defeated Jay Lethal in a Fight Without Honor Match in 16:22 (★★★); Austin Aries defeated Azrieal in 11:17 (★★); Nigel McGuinness defeated Roderick Strong in 12:14 (★★★); Colt Cabana defeated Homicide by DQ in 14:30 (★★); Jay Lethal defeated Low Ki in 9:20 (★★); Davey Andrews defeated Eric Matlock in 2:28 (★★); Samoa Joe defeated Adam Pearce, BJ Whitmer and Ricky Reyes in a Four Corner Survival Match in 18:38 (★★); Bryan Danielson defeated James Gibson to win the ROH World Title in 32:25 (★★★★); AJ Styles defeated Jimmy Rave in a Finisher's Match in 18:41 (★★★).

Unforgiven '05 ★★★
18-09-05, Oklahoma City, Oklahoma **WWE**

Ric Flair defeated Carlito to win the WWE Intercontinental Title in 11:46 (★★); Ashley Massaro and Trish Stratus defeated The Ladies In Pink (Torrie Wilson and Victoria) in 7:05 (★★); The Big Show defeated Snitsky in 6:11 (★★); Shelton Benjamin defeated Kerwin White in 8:06 (★★); Matt Hardy defeated Edge in a Steel Cage Match in 21:33 (★★★★); Lance Cade and Trevor Murdoch defeated The Hurricane and Rosey to win the World Tag Team Title in 7:40 (★★); Shawn Michaels defeated Chris Masters in 16:44 (★★★); Kurt Angle defeated John Cena by DQ in 17:15 (★★★).

Survival Of The Fittest '05 ★★★★
24-09-05, Dorchester, Massachussets **ROH**

Jay Lethal defeated Salvatore Rinauro in 11:36 (★★); Colt Cabana defeated Ricky Reyes in 4:26 (★★); Roderick Strong defeated Jerrelle Clark in 11:13 (★★); Austin Aries defeated Jimmy Rave by DQ in 12:51 (★★★); Samoa Joe defeated Milano Collection AT in 14:21 (★★); Christopher Daniels defeated James Gibson in 26:02 (★★★★); Nigel McGuinness defeated BJ Whitmer in 14:14 (★★); Roderick Strong defeated Austin Aries, Christopher Daniels, Colt Cabana, Jay Lethal and Samoa Joe in an Elimination Match to win the Survival Of The Fittest Tournament in 50:31 (★★★★).

Joe vs. Kobashi ★★★
01-10-05, New York City, New York **ROH**

Claudio Castagnoli defeated Colt Cabana in 7:51 (★★); Christopher Daniels defeated Azrieal and Matt Sydal in a Three Way Elimination Match in 13:01 (★★); Sal Rinauro and Tony Mamaluke defeated BJ Whitmer and Jimmy Jacobs to win the ROH Tag Team Title in 13:48 (★★); Nigel McGuinness defeated Jay Lethal in 10:59 (★★★); Roderick Strong defeated Jimmy Rave in a Grudge Match in 13:46 (★★★); Ricky Reyes defeated Pelle Primeau in :48 (★); James Gibson defeated Jimmy Yang in 15:48 (★★★); Jack Evans defeated Homicide in 13:37 (★★); Kenta Kobashi defeated Samoa Joe in 22:16 (★★★★★).

No Mercy '05 ★★
09-10-05, Houston, Texas **WWE**

Christy Hemme and The Legion Of Doom (Animal and Heidenreich) defeated MNM (Joey Mercury, Johnny Nitro and Melina) in 6:28 (★★); Bobby Lashley defeated Simon Dean in 1:55 (★★); Chris Benoit defeated Booker T, Christian and Orlando Jordan in a Four Way Match in 10:22 (★★); Mr. Kennedy defeated Hardcore Holly in 8:49 (★★); John Bradshaw Layfield defeated Rey Mysterio in 13:34 (★★★); Randy Orton and Bob Orton defeated The Undertaker in a Handicap Casket Match in 19:16 (★★); Juventud Guerrera defeated Nunzio to win the WWE Cruiserweight Title in 6:38 (★★); Batista defeated Eddie Guerrero in 18:40 (★★).

Bound For Glory '05 ★★★
23-10-05, Orlando, Florida **TNA**

Samoa Joe defeated Jushin Thunder Liger in 7:27 (★★); The Diamonds In The Rough (David Young, Elix Skipper and Simon Diamond) defeated Apolo, Shark Boy and Sonny Siaki in 7:03 (★★); Monty Brown defeated Lance Hoyt in 6:29 (★★); Team Canada (A-1, Bobby Roode and Eric Young) defeated 3Live Kru (B.G. James, Konnan and Ron Killings) in 6:08 (★★); Petey Williams defeated Chris Sabin and Matt Bentley in an Ultimate X Match in 13:13 (★★★); America's Most Wanted (James Storm and Chris Harris) defeated The Naturals (Andy Douglas and Chase Stevens) in 10:37 (★★★); Rhino defeated Abyss, Jeff Hardy and Sabu in a Monster's Ball Match in 12:20 (★★★); AJ Styles defeated Christopher Daniels 1-0 in an Iron Man Match in 30:00 (★★★★); Rhino won a 10-Man Gauntlet Match in 14:12 (★★); Rhino defeated Jeff Jarrett to win the NWA World Heavyweight Title in 5:30 (★★).

Taboo Tuesday '05 ★★★
01-11-05, San Diego, California **WWE**

Matt Hardy and Rey Mysterio defeated Chris Masters and Snitsky in 13:46 (★★★); Eugene and Jimmy Snuka defeated Rob Conway and Tyson Tomko in 6:21 (★★); Mankind defeated Carlito in 7:22 (★★); The Big Show and Kane defeated Lance Cade and Trevor Murdoch to win the World Tag Team Title in 7:59 (★★); Batista defeated Jonathan Coachman, Vader and Goldust in a Street Fight in 4:22 (★★); Trish Stratus won a Fulfil Your Fantasy Battle Royal in 5:23 (★); Ric Flair defeated Triple H in a Steel Cage Match in 23:47 (★★★★); John Cena defeated Kurt Angle and Shawn Michaels in a Three Way Match in 16:42 (★★★).

November Reign ★★
05-11-05, Philadelphia, Pennsylvania **Hardcore Homecoming**

The Blue Meanie defeated Danny Doring in 3:57 (★★); Balls Mahoney defeated John Kronus in 8:38 (★★); Matt Hyson defeated CW Anderson in 6:27 (★★); Axl Rotten defeated Ian Rotten in a Taipei Death Match in 9:30 (★★); Gary Wolfe defeated Shane Douglas in a Dog Collar Match in 8:45 (★★); PJ Polaco defeated Jerry Lynn in a Steel Cage Match in 15:34 (★★★).

Genesis '05 ★★★
13-11-05, Orlando, Florida **TNA**

Raven defeated P.J. Polaco in 5:45 (★★); 3Live Kru (B.G. James, Konnan and Ron Killings) defeated Team Canada (A-1, Bobby Roode and Eric Young) in a Hockey Stick Fight in 10:23 (★★); Monty Brown defeated Jeff Hardy in 8:43 (★★); Team Ministry (Alex Shelley, Christopher Daniels, Roderick Strong and Samoa Joe) defeated Austin Aries, Chris Sabin, Matt Bentley and Sonjay Dutt in an Elimination X Match in 23:15 (★★★); Abyss defeated Sabu in a No DQ Match in 10:48 (★★★); AJ Styles defeated Petey Williams in 18:20 (★★★); Rhino and Team 3D (Brother Ray and Brother Devon) defeated Jeff Jarrett and America's Most Wanted (Chris Harris and James Storm) in 15:48 (★★★★).

Survivor Series '05 ★★★
27-11-05, Detroit, Michigan **WWE**

Booker T defeated Chris Benoit in 14:39 (★★★); Trish Stratus defeated Melina in 6:30 (★★); Triple H defeated Ric Flair in a Last Man Standing Match in 27:01 (★★★); John Cena defeated Kurt Angle in 13:56 (★★★); Teddy Long defeated Eric Bischoff in 5:23 (★); Team SmackDown (Batista, Bobby Lashley, John Bradshaw Layfield, Randy Orton and Rey Mysterio) defeated Team Raw (The Big Show, Carlito, Chris Masters, Kane and Shawn Michaels) in an Elimination Match in 24:01 (★★★).

Turning Point '05 ★★★★
11-12-05, Orlando, Florida **TNA**

Sabu defeated Abyss in a Barbed Wire Massacre in 10:59 (★★★); Austin Aries and Matt Bentley defeated Alex Shelley and Roderick Strong in 8:04 (★★★); Raven defeated Chris K in 5:45 (★★); Team Canada (A-1, Bobby Roode, Eric Young and Petey Williams) defeated 4Live Kru (B.G. James, Kip James, Konnan and Ron Killings) in 7:18 (★★); Chris Sabin, Dale Torborg and Sonjay Dutt defeated The Diamonds In The Rough (David Young, Elix Skipper and Simon Diamond) in 7:57 (★★); Christian Cage defeated Monty Brown in 12:32 (★★★); Team 3D (Brother Ray and Brother Devon) defeated America's Most Wanted (Chris Harris and James Storm) in a Tables Match in 9:40 (★★); Samoa Joe defeated AJ Styles to win the TNA X Division Title in 18:58 (★★★★★); Jeff Jarrett defeated Rhino in 17:30 (★★★).

Final Battle '05 ★★★★
17-12-05, Edison, New Jersey **ROH**

Jimmy Rave defeated Milano Collection AT in 12:45 (★★★); Colt Cabana defeated Azrieal in 7:18 (★★); Nigel McGuinness defeated Claudio Castagnoli by DQ in 14:37 (★★★); Alex Shelley defeated Steve Corino in 11:05 (★★★); Jay Lethal defeated BJ Whitmer, Christopher Daniels and Samoa Joe in a Four Corner Survival Match in 15:01 (★★★); Generation Next (Austin Aries and Roderick Strong) defeated Sal Rinauro and Tony Mamaluke to win the ROH Tag Team the Title in 18:18 (★★★); Bryan Danielson defeated Naomichi Marufuji in 23:44 (★★★★); KENTA defeated Low Ki in 24:59 (★★★★).

Armageddon '05 ★★★
18-12-05, Providence, Rhode Island **WWE**

John Bradshaw Layfield defeated Matt Hardy in 6:20 (★★); MNM (Joey Mercury and Johnny Nitro) defeated The Mexicools (Super Crazy and Psicosis) in 8:50 (★★★); Chris Benoit defeated Booker T in 20:11 (★★★); Bobby Lashley defeated William Regal and Paul Burchill in a Handicap Match in 3:30 (★★); Kid Kash defeated Juventud Guerrera to win the WWE Cruiserweight Title in 9:00 (★★★); The Big Show and Kane defeated Rey Mysterio and Batista in 8:33 (★★); The Undertaker defeated Randy Orton in a Hell In A Cell Match in 30:30 (★★★★).

Tribute To The Troops '05 ★★
19-12-05, Bagram, Afghanistan WWE

The Big Show defeated Carlito in 1:09 (★★); Good Santa (Mick Foley) defeated Bad Santa (John Bradshaw Layfield) in a No Holds Barred Match in 1:58; Snitsky defeated Shelton Benjamin in 1:52 (★★); John Cena defeated Chris Masters in 4:53 (★★); Ric Flair defeated Jonathan Coachman in 2:01 (★★); Candice Michelle and Maria defeated Ashley Massaro and Trish Stratus in 4:16 (★★); Shawn Michaels defeated Triple H in a Boot Camp Match in 13:35 (★★★).

New Year's Revolution '06 ★★
08-01-06, Albany, New York WWE

Ric Flair defeated Edge by DQ in 7:17 (★★); Trish Stratus defeated Mickie James in 7:18 (★★★); Jerry Lawler defeated Gregory Helms in 9:32 (★★); Triple H defeated The Big Show in 16:11 (★★); Shelton Benjamin defeated Viscera in 7:48 (★★); Ashley Massaro defeated Candice Michelle, Maria, Torrie Wilson and Victoria in a Bra and Panties Gauntlet Match in 11:01 (★); John Cena defeated Carlito, Chris Masters, Shawn Michaels, Kane and Kurt Angle in an Elimination Chamber Match in 28:23 (★★★); Edge defeated John Cena to win the WWE Title in 1:46 (★★★).

Final Resolution '06 ★★★
15-01-06, Orlando, Florida TNA

Alex Shelley, Austin Aries and Roderick Strong defeated Chris Sabin, Matt Bentley and Sonjay Dutt in 10:32 (★★★); The James Gang (B.G. James and Kip James) defeated The Diamonds In The Rough (David Young and Elix Skipper) in 7:47 (★); AJ Styles defeated Hiroshi Tanahashi in 11:03 (★★★); Sean Waltman defeated Raven in a No DQ Match in 10:00 (★★); Bobby Roode defeated Ron Killings in 9:53 (★★★); Abyss defeated Rhino in 9:18 (★★); America's Most Wanted (Chris Harris and James Storm) defeated Team 3D (Brother Ray and Brother Devon) in 12:41 (★★★); Samoa Joe defeated Christopher Daniels in 15:30 (★★★); Christian Cage and Sting defeated Jeff Jarrett and Monty Brown in 15:35 (★★).

Royal Rumble '06 ★★
29-01-06, Miami, Florida WWE

Gregory Helms won a Cruiserweight Open to win the WWE Cruiserweight Title in 7:40 (★★★); Mickie James defeated Ashley Massaro in 7:44 (★); The Boogeyman defeated John Bradshaw Layfield in 1:54 (★); Rey Mysterio won the 30-Man Royal Rumble Match in 62:12 (★★★); John Cena defeated Edge to win the WWE Title in 15:01 (★★); Kurt Angle defeated Mark Henry in 9:29 (★★).

Against All Odds '06 ★★★★
12-02-06, Orlando, Florida TNA

The Naturals (Andy Douglas and Chase Stevens) defeated Austin Aries and Roderick Strong in 10:28 (★★); Jay Lethal defeated Matt Bentley, Alex Shelley and Petey Williams in a Four Way Match in 10:37 (★★★); The James Gang (B.G. James and Kip James) defeated The Latin American Exchange (Homicide and Machete) in 6:00 (★★); America's Most Wanted (Chris Harris and James Storm) defeated Chris Sabin and Sonjay Dutt in 10:26 (★★★); Rhino defeated Abyss in a Falls Count Anywhere Match in 15:25 (★★★★); Samoa Joe defeated AJ Styles and Christopher Daniels in a Three Way Match in 16:02 (★★★★); Team 3D (Brother Ray and Brother Devon) defeated Team Canada (Eric Young and Bobby Roode) in 13:55 (★★★); Christian Cage defeated Jeff Jarrett to win the NWA World Heavyweight Title in 16:23 (★★★).

No Way Out '06 ★★★★
19-02-06, Baltimore, Maryland WWE

Gregory Helms won a Cruiserweight Open in 9:42 (★★); John Bradshaw Layfield defeated Bobby Lashley in 10:58 (★★); Matt Hardy and Tatanka defeated MNM (Joey Mercury and Johnny Nitro) in 10:28 (★★); Chris Benoit defeated Booker T to win the WWE United States Title in 18:13 (★★★); Randy Orton defeated Rey Mysterio in 17:28 (★★); Kurt Angle defeated The Undertaker in 29:38 (★★★★).

Fourth Anniversary Show ★★★
25-02-06, Edison, New Jersey ROH

The Briscoe Brothers (Jay Briscoe and Mark Briscoe) defeated Jason Blade and Kid Mikaze, and Sal Rinauro and Tony Mamaluke in a Three Way Match in 6:44 (★★); Adam Pearce defeated Azrieal, Claudio Castagnoli and Jay Fury in a Four

Corner Survival Match in 11:12 (★★); Samoa Joe defeated Jay Lethal in 14:20 (★★★); BJ Whitmer vs. Christopher Daniels ended in a no contest in 5:30 (★★); Homicide defeated Colt Cabana in a Ghetto Street Fight in 18:56 (★★★); Bryan Danielson defeated Jimmy Rave in 32:03 (★★★); Ricky Reyes defeated Jack Evans in 7:57 (★★); Generation Next (Austin Aries and Roderick Strong) defeated AJ Styles and Matt Sydal in 23:11 (★★★★).

Destination X '06 ★★★
12-03-06, Orlando, Florida TNA

Alex Shelley defeated Jay Lethal in 9:58 (★★★); Lance Hoyt defeated Matt Bentley in 8:01 (★★); Team Canada (Eric Young and Bobby Roode) defeated The Naturals (Chase Stevens and Andy Douglas) in 13:05 (★★); The James Gang (B.G. James and Kip James) and Bob Armstrong defeated The Latin American Exchange (Homicide, Machete and Konnan) in 6:40 (★); Chris Sabin defeated Petey Williams, Sonjay Dutt and Puma in a Four Way Match in 14:55 (★★★★); Abyss, Jeff Jarrett and America's Most Wanted (Chris Harris and James Storm) defeated Rhino, Ron Killings and Team 3D (Brother Ray and Brother Devon) in an Eight Man War in 20:12 (★★★); Christopher Daniels defeated Samoa Joe and AJ Styles in an Ultimate X Match to win the TNA X Division Title in 13:30 (★★); Christian Cage defeated Monty Brown in 17:07 (★★★).

Saturday Night's Main Event XXXII ★★
18-03-06, Detroit, Michigan WWE

John Cena and Triple H defeated Kurt Angle, Rey Mysterio and Randy Orton in a Handicap Match in 11:40 (★★); Mickie James and Trish Stratus defeated Candice Michelle and Victoria in 2:40 (★★); Shane McMahon defeated Shawn Michaels in a Street Fight in 16:42 (★★★).

Best In The World '06 ★★★
25-03-06, New York City, New York ROH

Jimmy Rave defeated Pelle Primeau in 1:57 (★★); Jimmy Yang defeated Jimmy Rave in 6:32 (★★); Allison Danger defeated Daizee Haze, Lacey and Mercedes Martinez in a Four Corner Survival Match in 10:31 (★★★); Chris Hero and Necro Butcher defeated Jason Blade and Kid Mikaze in :47 (★); Adam Pearce vs. Chris Hero ended in a no contest in 3:10 (★★); Christopher Daniels defeated Alex Shelley in 14:34 (★★★); Nigel McGuinness defeated Claudio Castagnoli in 12:57 (★★★); Austin Aries defeated Ricky Reyes by DQ in 11:27 (★★); Generation Next (Jack Evans and Roderick Strong) defeated The Briscoe Brothers (Jay Briscoe and Mark Briscoe) in 19:30 (★★★); Kenta and Naomichi Marufuji defeated Bryan Danielson and Samoa Joe in 33:34 (★★★★).

Supercard Of Honor '06 ★★★★
31-03-06, Chicago Ridge, Illinois ROH

Adam Pearce and Samoa Joe defeated Hardcore Wrestler #1 and Hardcore Wrestler #2 in :58 (★); Ricky Reyes defeated Delirious, Flash Flanagan and Shane Hagadorn in a Four Corner Survival Match in 6:54 (★★); The Embassy (Alex Shelley and Jimmy Rave) defeated Claudio Castagnoli and Jimmy Yang in 16:03 (★★★); Ace Steel defeated Chad Collyer in a First Blood Match in 11:53 (★★); AJ Styles and Matt Sydal defeated Generation Next (Austin Aries and Jack Evans) in 17:47 (★★★★); Do FIXER (Dragon Kid, Genki Horiguchi and Ryo Saito) defeated Blood Generation (Cima, Masato Yoshino and Naruki Doi) in 20:34 (★★★★★); MsChif defeated Allison Danger, Cheerleader Melissa, Daizee Haze, Lacey and Rain in a Six Way Mayhem Match in 8:44 (★★); Homicide defeated Mitch Franklin in 2:35 (★★); Samoa Joe defeated Jimmy Jacobs and Christopher Daniels in a Three Way Match in 9:14 (★★★); Bryan Danielson defeated Roderick Strong in 56:04 (★★★★).

WrestleMania XXII ★★★
02-04-06, Rosemont, Illinois WWE

The Big Show and Kane defeated Carlito and Chris Masters in 6:42 (★★); Rob Van Dam defeated Bobby Lashley, Finlay, Matt Hardy, Ric Flair and Shelton Benjamin in a Money In The Bank Ladder Match in 12:14 (★★★★); John Bradshaw Layfield defeated Chris Benoit to win the WWE United States Title in 9:48 (★★); Edge defeated Mick Foley in a Hardcore Match in 14:36 (★★★★); The Boogeyman defeated Booker T and Sharmell in a Handicap Match in 3:43 (★); Mickie James defeated Trish Stratus to win the WWE Women's Title in 8:48 (★★★); The Undertaker defeated Mark Henry in a Casket Match in 9:28 (★★); Shawn Michaels defeated Vince McMahon in a No

Holds Barred Match in 18:22 (★ ★ ★); **Rey Mysterio** defeated **Randy Orton** and **Kurt Angle** in a Three Way Match to win the World Heavyweight Title in 9:19 (★ ★ ★); **Torrie Wilson** defeated **Candice Michelle** in a Playboy Pillow Fight Match in 3:54 (★ ★); **John Cena** defeated **Triple H** in 22:02 (★ ★ ★ ★).

Lockdown '06 ★ ★ ★
23-04-06, Orlando, Florida TNA
Team Japan (Black Tiger, Minoru Tanaka and Hirooki Goto) defeated **Team USA** (Sonjay Dutt, Jay Lethal and Alex Shelley) in a Six Sides Of Steel Match in 12:03 (★ ★ ★); **Senshi** defeated **Christopher Daniels** in a Six Sides Of Steel Match in 12:05 (★ ★ ★); **Chris Sabin** defeated **Elix Skipper, Petey Williams, Chase Stevens, Shark Boy** and **Puma** in an Xscape Match in 12:52 (★ ★ ★); **Samoa Joe** defeated **Sabu** in a Six Sides Of Steel Match in 6:10 (★ ★); **Team 3D** (Brother Ray, Brother Devon and Brother Runt) defeated **Team Canada** (Bobby Roode, Eric Young and A-1) in a Six Sides Of Steel Anthem Match in 8:47 (★ ★); **Christian Cage** defeated **Abyss** in a Six Sides Of Steel Match in 14:07 (★ ★ ★ ★); **Sting's Warriors** (Sting, AJ Styles, Ron Killings and Rhino) defeated **Jarrett's Army** (Jeff Jarrett, Scott Steiner, Chris Harris and James Storm) in a Lethal Lockdown Match in 25:23 (★ ★ ★).

Backlash '06 ★ ★ ★ ★
30-04-06, Lexington, Kentucky WWE
Carlito defeated **Chris Masters** in 9:58 (★ ★ ★); **Umaga** defeated **Ric Flair** in 3:29 (★ ★); **Trish Stratus** defeated **Mickie James** by DQ in 4:03 (★ ★); **Rob Van Dam** defeated **Shelton Benjamin** to win the WWE Intercontinental Title in 18:42 (★ ★ ★); **The Big Show** vs. **Kane** ended in a no contest in 9:30 (★); **Vince McMahon** and **Shane McMahon** defeated **Shawn Michaels** and **Kane** in a No Holds Barred Match in 19:57 (★ ★ ★); **John Cena** defeated **Triple H** and **Edge** in a Three Way Match in 17:33 (★ ★ ★ ★).

Sacrifice '06 ★ ★
14-05-06, Orlando, Florida TNA
Jushin Thunder Liger defeated **Petey Williams** in 8:30 (★ ★); **America's Most Wanted** (Chris Harris and James Storm) defeated **AJ Styles** and **Christopher Daniels** in 15:40 (★ ★ ★ ★); **Raven** defeated **A-1** in 5:30 (★ ★); **Bobby Roode** defeated **Rhino** in 12:16 (★ ★); **The James Gang** (B.G. James and Kip James) defeated **Team 3D** (Brother Ray and Brother Devon) in 9:40 (★ ★); **Petey Williams** won a World X Cup Gauntlet Match in 18:13 (★ ★ ★); **Sting** and **Samoa Joe** defeated **Jeff Jarrett** and **Scott Steiner** in 14:30 (★ ★ ★); **Christian Cage** defeated **Abyss** in a Full Metal Mayhem Match in 16:14 (★ ★ ★).

Judgment Day '06 ★ ★ ★
21-05-06, Phoenix, Arizona WWE
Brian Kendrick and **Paul London** defeated **MNM** (Joey Mercury and Johnny Nitro) in 13:43 (★ ★ ★); **Chris Benoit** defeated **Finlay** in 21:10 (★ ★ ★ ★); **Jillian Hall** defeated **Melina** in 4:18 (★ ★); **Gregory Helms** defeated **Super Crazy** in 9:55 (★ ★); **Mark Henry** defeated **Kurt Angle** via count out in 9:11 (★ ★); **Booker T** defeated **Bobby Lashley** to win the King Of The Ring Tournament in 9:15 (★ ★); **The Great Khali** defeated **The Undertaker** in 8:31 (★ ★); **Rey Mysterio** defeated **John Bradshaw Layfield** in 15:56 (★ ★ ★).

WWE vs. ECW Head To Head ★ ★ ★
07-06-06, Dayton, Ohio ECW
Rob Van Dam defeated **Rey Mysterio** in a No DQ Match in 7:42 (★ ★ ★); **Mickie James** defeated **Jazz** in 2:01 (★ ★); **The Big Show** won a 20-Man Battle Royal in 8:06 (★ ★); **Edge** defeated **Tommy Dreamer** in an ECW Rules Match in 6:46 (★ ★); **John Cena** defeated **Sabu** by DQ in an ECW Rules Match in 6:04 (★ ★).

One Night Stand '06 ★ ★ ★ ★
11-06-06, Manhattan, New York ECW
Tazz defeated **Jerry Lawler** in :35 (★ ★); **Kurt Angle** defeated **Randy Orton** in 15:07 (★ ★ ★); **The F.B.I.** (Little Guido and Tony Mamaluke) defeated **Super Crazy** and **Tajiri** in 12:24 (★ ★ ★); **Rey Mysterio** vs. **Sabu** went to a no contest in 9:10 (★ ★); **Edge, Mick Foley** and **Lita** defeated **Terry Funk, Tommy Dreamer** and **Beulah McGillicutty** in a Hardcore Match in 18:45 (★ ★ ★ ★); **Balls Mahoney** defeated **Masato Tanaka** in 5:03 (★ ★); **Rob Van Dam** defeated **John Cena** to win the WWE Title in 20:40 (★ ★ ★ ★).

Slammiversary IV ★ ★ ★
18-06-06, Orlando, Florida TNA
Team 3D (Brother Ray and Brother Devon) defeated **The James Gang** (B.G. James and Kip James) in a Bingo Hall Brawl in 10:19 (★ ★ ★); **Rhino** defeated **Team Canada** (Bobby Roode and Coach D'Amore) in a Handicap Match in 11:00 (★ ★); **Senshi** defeated **Sonjay Dutt, Alex Shelley, Shark Boy, Petey Williams** and **Jay Lethal** in an Elimination Match in 19:29 (★ ★ ★); **Kevin Nash** defeated **Chris Sabin** in 8:20 (★ ★); **AJ Styles** and **Christopher Daniels** defeated **America's Most Wanted** (Chris Harris and James Storm) to win the NWA World Tag Team Title in 17:44 (★ ★ ★ ★); **Samoa Joe** defeated **Scott Steiner** in 13:04 (★ ★ ★); **Jeff Jarrett** defeated **Christian Cage, Abyss, Ron Killings** and **Sting** in a King Of The Mountain Match to win the NWA World Heavyweight Title in 23:00 (★ ★ ★).

Vengeance '06 ★ ★ ★
25-06-06, Charlotte, North Carolina WWE
Randy Orton defeated **Kurt Angle** in 12:50 (★ ★); **Umaga** defeated **Eugene** in 1:26 (★ ★); **Ric Flair** defeated **Mick Foley** in a Best Two Out Of Three Falls Match in 7:32 (★ ★); **Johnny Nitro** defeated **Shelton Benjamin** and **Carlito** in a Three Way Match to win the WWE Intercontinental Title in 12:01 (★ ★ ★); **Rob Van Dam** defeated **Edge** in 17:55 (★ ★ ★); **Imposter Kane** defeated **Kane** in 7:08 (★); **John Cena** defeated **Sabu** in an Extreme Lumberjack Match in 6:38 (★ ★ ★); **D-Generation X** (Shawn Michaels and Triple H) defeated **The Spirit Squad** (Kenny, Johnny, Mitch, Nicky and Mikey) in a Handicap Match in 17:45 (★ ★).

Saturday Night's Main Event XXXIII ★ ★
15-07-06, Dallas, Texas WWE
Batista, Rey Mysterio and **Bobby Lashley** defeated **Mark Henry, Finlay** and **King Booker** in 10:07 (★ ★); **Carlito** and **Trish Stratus** defeated **Johnny Nitro** and **Melina** in 2:36 (★ ★); **D-Generation X** (Triple H and Shawn Michaels) defeated **The Spirit Squad** (Kenny, Mitch, Nicky, Johnny and Mikey) in a Handicap Elimination Match in 8:52 (★); **Sabu** defeated **Stevie Richards** in an Extreme Rules Match in 2:02 (★); **John Cena** defeated **Edge** by DQ in 7:54 (★ ★).

Death Before Dishonor IV ★ ★ ★ ★
15-07-06, Philadelphia, Pennsylvania ROH
Delirious defeated **Seth Delay** in 4:47 (★ ★); **The Embassy** (Jimmy Rave and Sal Rinauro) defeated **Colt Cabana** and **Jay Lethal** in 11:38 (★ ★ ★); **Nigel McGuinness** defeated **Roderick Strong** via count out in 15:48 (★ ★ ★ ★); **The Briscoe Brothers** (Jay Briscoe and Mark Briscoe) defeated **Irish Airborne** (Dave Crist and Jake Crist) in 15:08 (★ ★ ★); **AJ Styles** defeated **Davey Richards** in 17:02 (★ ★); **Bryan Danielson** defeated **Sonjay Dutt** in 18:48 (★ ★); **Team ROH** (Ace Steel, Adam Pearce, BJ Whitmer, Bryan Danielson, Homicide and Samoa Joe) defeated **Team CZW** (Chris Hero, Claudio Castagnoli, Eddie Kingston, Nate Webb and Necro Butcher) in a Cage Of Death Match in 40:37 (★ ★ ★ ★).

Victory Road '06 ★ ★
16-07-06, Orlando, Florida TNA
The Naturals (Chase Stevens and Andy Douglas) defeated **The Diamonds In The Rough** (Elix Skipper and David Young) in 5:27 (★ ★); **Monty Brown** vs. **Rhino** went to a no contest in 4:56 (★ ★); **The Latin American Xchange** (Homicide and Hernandez) defeated **Sonjay Dutt** and **Ron Killings** in 10:07 (★ ★ ★); **Senshi** defeated **Kazarian** in 11:19 (★ ★); **Raven** defeated **Larry Zbyszko** in a Hair vs. Hair Match in 3:48 (★); **Chris Sabin** and **Jay Lethal** defeated **The Paparazzi** (Kevin Nash and Alex Shelley) in 9:07 (★ ★); **The James Gang** (B.G. James and Kip James) and **Abyss** defeated **Team 3D** (Brother Ray, Brother Devon and Brother Runt) in 10:24 (★ ★); **Sirelda, AJ Styles** and **Christopher Daniels** defeated **Gail Kim** and **America's Most Wanted** (Chris Harris and James Storm) in 11:52 (★ ★); **Sting** defeated **Christian Cage, Samoa Joe** and **Scott Steiner** in a Road To Victory Match in 14:09 (★ ★).

Great American Bash '06 ★ ★
23-07-06, Indianapolis, Indiana WWE
Paul London and **Brian Kendrick** defeated **The Pit Bulls** (Jamie Noble and Kid Kash) in 13:28 (★ ★ ★); **Finlay** defeated **William Regal** in 13:49 (★ ★); **Gregory Helms** defeated **Matt Hardy** in 11:43 (★ ★); **The Undertaker** defeated **The Big Show** in a Punjabi Prison Match in 21:35 (★); **Ashley Massaro** defeated **Kristal Marshall, Jillian Hall** and **Michelle McCool** in a Four Way

Bra and Panties Match in 5:17 (★); **Mr. Kennedy** defeated **Batista** by DQ in 8:38 (★★); **King Booker** defeated **Rey Mysterio** to win the World Heavyweight Title in 16:46 (★★★).

Hard Justice '06 ★★★
13-08-06, Orlando, Florida TNA
Eric Young defeated **Johnny Devine** in 5:46 (★★); **Chris Sabin** defeated **Alex Shelley** in 8:19 (★★); **Abyss** defeated **Brother Runt** in 6:17 (★★); **Samoa Joe** defeated **Rhino** and **Monty Brown** in a Three Way Falls Count Anywhere Match in 13:37 (★★★★); **Gail Kim** defeated **Sirelda** in 4:01 (★★); **Senshi** defeated **Petey Williams** and **Jay Lethal** in a Three Way Match in 10:35 (★★); **AJ Styles** and **Christopher Daniels** defeated **The Latin American Xchange** (**Homicide** and **Hernandez**) in 14:37 (★★★★); **Jeff Jarrett** defeated **Sting** in 15:09 (★★).

SummerSlam '06 ★★★
20-08-06, Boston, Massachusetts WWE
Chavo Guerrero defeated **Rey Mysterio** in 11:01 (★★★); The **Big Show** defeated **Sabu** in an Extreme Rules Match in 8:31 (★★); **Hulk Hogan** defeated **Randy Orton** in 10:56 (★★); **Ric Flair** defeated **Mick Foley** in an "I Quit" Match in 13:14 (★★★); **Batista** defeated **King Booker** by DQ in 10:26 (★★); **D-Generation X** (**Shawn Michaels** and **Triple H**) defeated **Vince McMahon** and **Shane McMahon** in 13:01 (★★★); **Edge** defeated **John Cena** in 15:41 (★★★).

Glory By Honor V Night #1 ★★★★★
15-09-06, East Windsor, Connecticut ROH
The Ring Crew Express (**Dunn** and **Marcos**) defeated **Pelle Primeau** and **Rhett Titus** in 2:03 (★★); **The Kings Of Wrestling** (**Chris Hero** and **Claudio Castagnoli**) defeated **The Ring Crew Express** (**Dunn** and **Marcos**) in 5:20 (★★); **Jack Evans** defeated **Colt Cabana**, **Jimmy Jacobs** and **Ricky Reyes** in a Four Corner Survival Match in 13:05 (★★); **Nigel McGuinness** defeated **Christopher Daniels** in 16:44 (★★★); **Austin Aries** and **Davey Richards** in 17:07 (★★); **Delirious** defeated **Shane Hagadorn** in 6:22 (★★); **Samoa Joe** defeated **Roderick Strong** in 19:14 (★★★★); **Kenta** and **Naomichi Marufuji** defeated **The Briscoe Brothers** (**Jay Briscoe** and **Mark Briscoe**) in 20:25 (★★★★).

Glory By Honor V Night #2 ★★★★★
16-09-06, New York City, New York ROH
Davey Richards defeated **Jack Evans** in 7:35 (★★★); **Adam Pearce** defeated **Delirious** in 8:18 (★★); **Jimmy Jacobs** defeated **Christopher Daniels** and **Colt Cabana** in a Three Way Match in 11:06 (★★★); **Homicide** and **Samoa Joe** defeated **The Briscoe Brothers** (**Jay Briscoe** and **Mark Briscoe**) in 18:00 (★★★★); **The Kings Of Wrestling** (**Chris Hero** and **Claudio Castagnoli**) defeated **Austin Aries** and **Roderick Strong** to win the ROH Tag Team Title in 21:34 (★★★★); **Naomichi Marufuji** defeated **Nigel McGuinness** in 23:32 (★★★★); **Bryan Danielson** defeated **Kenta** in 23:01 (★★★★★★★).

Unforgiven '06 ★★★
17-09-06, Toronto, Ontario WWE
Johnny Nitro defeated **Jeff Hardy** in 17:36 (★★★); **Kane** vs. **Umaga** went to a double count out in 7:03 (★★); The **Spirit Squad** (**Kenny** and **Mikey**) defeated **The Highlanders** (**Robbie McAllister** and **Rory McAllister**) in 8:59 (★★); **D-Generation X** (**Shawn Michaels** and **Triple H**) defeated **The Big Show**, **Vince McMahon** and **Shane McMahon** in a Handicap Hell In A Cell Match in 25:04 (★★★); **Trish Stratus** defeated **Lita** to win the WWE Women's Title in 11:34 (★★★); **Randy Orton** defeated **Carlito** in 8:41 (★★); **John Cena** defeated **Edge** in a TLC Match to win the WWE Title in 25:28 (★★★★).

No Surrender '06 ★★★
24-09-06, Orlando, Florida TNA
Eric Young defeated **A-1** in 6:20 (★★); **Jay Lethal** defeated **Petey Williams** in 7:25 (★★); **Abyss** defeated **Raven** and **Brother Runt** in a Three Way No DQ Match in 11:30 (★★); The **Naturals** (**Chase Stevens** and **Andy Douglas**) won a Battle Royal in 14:25 (★★); **Senshi** defeated **Chris Sabin** in 17:15 (★★★); **Christian Cage** defeated **Rhino** in 16:30 (★★); **AJ Styles** and **Christopher Daniels** defeated **The Latin American Xchange** (**Homicide** and **Hernandez**) in an Ultimate X Match to win the NWA World Tag Team Title in 15:30 (★★★★); **Samoa Joe** defeated **Jeff Jarrett** in a Fan's Revenge Lumberjack Match in 11:06 (★★).

Survival Of The Fittest '06 ★★★
06-10-06, Cleveland, Ohio ROH
Matt Sydal defeated **Davey Richards** in 12:23 (★★); **Delirious** defeated **Jimmy Rave** in 10:22 (★★); **Austin Aries** defeated **Christopher Daniels** in 17:09 (★★★); **The Briscoe Brothers** (**Jay Briscoe** and **Mark Briscoe**) defeated **Homicide** and **Roderick Strong** in 19:50 (★★★); **Bryan Danielson** vs. **Samoa Joe** ended in a draw in 20:00 (★★★); **The Kings Of Wrestling** (**Chris Hero** and **Claudio Castagnoli**) defeated **Colt Cabana** and **Jimmy Jacobs** in 17:28 (★★); **Delirious** defeated **Austin Aries**, **Jay Briscoe**, **Mark Briscoe** and **Matt Sydal** in the Survival of the Fittest Final Elimination Match in 34:51 (★★★★).

No Mercy '06 ★★★
08-10-06, Raleigh, North Carolina WWE
Matt Hardy defeated **Gregory Helms** in 13:07 (★★★); **Paul London** and **Brian Kendrick** defeated **K.C. James** and **Idol Stevens** in 9:35 (★★); **MVP** defeated **Marty Garner** in 2:28 (★★); **Mr. Kennedy** defeated **The Undertaker** by DQ in 20:34 (★★); **Rey Mysterio** defeated **Chavo Guerrero** in a Falls Count Anywhere Match in 12:10 (★★); **Chris Benoit** defeated **William Regal** in 11:16 (★★★); **King Booker** defeated **Bobby Lashley**, **Batista** and **Finlay** in a Four Way Match in 16:52 (★★).

Bound For Glory '06 ★★★
22-10-06, Plymouth Township, Michigan TNA
Austin Starr won a Gauntlet Battle Royal in 17:24 (★★★); **Team 3D** (**Brother Ray** and **Brother Devon**) defeated **America's Most Wanted** (**Chris Harris** and **James Storm**), **The James Gang** (**B.G. James** and **Kip James**), and **The Naturals** (**Chase Stevens** and **Andy Douglas**) in a Four Way Match in 7:02 (★★); **Samoa Joe** defeated **Abyss**, **Brother Runt** and **Raven** in a Monster's Ball Match in 11:51 (★★); **Eric Young** defeated **Larry Zbyszko** in a Loser Gets Fired Match in 3:35 (★★); **Chris Sabin** defeated **Senshi** to win the TNA X Division Title in 13:00 (★★★★); **Christian Cage** defeated **Rhino** in an 8 Mile Street Fight in 14:44 (★★★); **The Latin American Xchange** (**Homicide** and **Hernandez**) defeated **AJ Styles** and **Christopher Daniels** in a Six Sides Of Steel Match to win the NWA World Tag Team Title in 14:50 (★★★★); **Sting** defeated **Jeff Jarrett** to win the NWA World Heavyweight Title in 15:11 (★★).

Cyber Sunday '06 ★★
05-11-06, Cincinnati, Ohio WWE
Umaga defeated **Kane** in 8:39 (★★); **Cryme Tyme** (**JTG** and **Shad Gaspard**) defeated **The Highlanders** (**Robbie McAllister** and **Rory McAllister**), **Charlie Haas** and **Viscera**, and **Lance Cade** and **Trevor Murdoch** in a Texas Tornado Match in 4:28 (★★); **Jeff Hardy** defeated **Carlito** in 13:21 (★★); **Rated-RKO** (**Randy Orton** and **Edge**) defeated **D-Generation X** (**Shawn Michaels** and **Triple H**) in 18:11 (★★); **Lita** defeated **Mickie James** in a Lumberjill Match to win the vacant WWE Women's Title in 11:07 (★); **Ric Flair** and **Roddy Piper** defeated **The Spirit Squad** (**Kenny** and **Mikey**) to win the World Tag Team Title in 6:55 (★★); **King Booker** defeated **The Big Show** and **John Cena** in a Three Way Match in 21:05 (★★).

Genesis '06 ★★★
19-11-06, Orlando, Florida TNA
The Voodoo Kin Mafia (**B.G. James** and **Kip James**) defeated **Kazarian**, **Maverick Matt** and **Johnny Devine** in a Handicap Match in 3:39 (★★); **The Naturals** (**Chase Stevens** and **Andy Douglas**) defeated **Sonjay Dutt** and **Jay Lethal** in 8:20 (★★); **Christopher Daniels** defeated **Chris Sabin** in 13:26 (★★); **Ron Killings** and **Lance Hoyt** defeated **The Paparazzi** (**Austin Starr** and **Alex Shelley**) in 11:07 (★★); **Christian Cage** defeated **AJ Styles** in 15:50 (★★★); **The Latin American Xchange** (**Homicide** and **Hernandez**) defeated **America's Most Wanted** (**Chris Harris** and **James Storm**) in 9:20 (★★); **Abyss** defeated **Sting** by DQ in 15:10 (★★); **Kurt Angle** defeated **Samoa Joe** in 13:35 (★★★★).

Survivor Series '06 ★★★
26-11-06, Philadelphia, Pennsylvania WWE
Team WWE Legends (**Dusty Rhodes**, **Ric Flair**, **Ron Simmons** and **Sgt. Slaughter**) defeated **The Spirit Squad** (**Johnny**, **Kenny**, **Mikey** and **Nicky**) in an Elimination Match in 10:31 (★★); **Chris Benoit** defeated **Chavo Guerrero** in 8:19 (★★); **Mickie James** defeated **Lita** to win the WWE Women's Title in 8:18 (★★); **Team DX** (**Shawn Michaels**, **Triple H**, **CM Punk**, **Matt Hardy** and **Jeff Hardy**) defeated **Team Rated-RKO** (**Randy Orton**, **Edge**, **Gregory Helms**, **Johnny Nitro** and **Mike Knox**) in an Elimination Match in 11:30

(★★); Mr. Kennedy defeated The Undertaker in a First Blood Match in 9:15 (★★); Team Cena (John Cena, Bobby Lashley, Kane, Rob Van Dam and Sabu) defeated Team Big Show (The Big Show, Finlay, MVP, Test and Umaga) in an Elimination Match in 12:35 (★★); Batista defeated King Booker to win the World Heavyweight Title in 13:58 (★★).

December To Dismember '06 ★
03-12-06, Augusta, Georgia **ECW**
The Hardy Boyz (Matt Hardy and Jeff Hardy) defeated MNM (Joey Mercury and Johnny Nitro) in 22:33 (★★★); Balls Mahoney defeated Matt Striker in a Striker's Rules Match in 7:12 (★); Elijah Burke and Sylvester Terkay defeated The F.B.I. (Little Guido and Tony Mamaluke) in 6:41 (★); Daivari defeated Tommy Dreamer in 7:22 (★); Ariel and Kevin Thorn defeated Kelly Kelly and Mike Knox in 7:43 (★); Bobby Lashley defeated The Big Show, Test, Rob Van Dam, Hardcore Holly and CM Punk in an Extreme Elimination Chamber Match to win the ECW World Title in 24:42 (★★).

Turning Point '06 ★★★
10-12-06, Orlando, Florida **TNA**
Senshi defeated Alex Shelley, Sonjay Dutt, Austin Starr and Jay Lethal in a Five Way Elimination Match in 14:37 (★★); Christopher Daniels defeated Chris Sabin in 13:30 (★★); AJ Styles defeated Rhino in 7:28 (★★); The Latin American Xchange (Homicide and Hernandez) defeated America's Most Wanted (Chris Harris and James Storm) in a Flag Match in 10:45 (★★★); Abyss defeated Sting and Christian Cage in a Three Way Match in 11:59 (★★); Samoa Joe defeated Kurt Angle in 19:17 (★★★★).

Armageddon '06 ★★
17-12-06, Richmond, Virginia **WWE**
Kane defeated MVP in an Inferno Match in 8:14 (★★); Paul London and Brian Kendrick defeated William Regal and Dave Taylor, MNM (Joey Mercury and Johnny Nitro) and The Hardy Boyz (Matt Hardy and Jeff Hardy) in a Four Way Ladder Match in 20:13 (★★★★); The Boogeyman defeated The Miz in 2:51 (★); Chris Benoit defeated Chavo Guerrero in 12:14 (★★★); Gregory Helms defeated Jimmy Wang Yang in 10:51 (★★★); The Undertaker defeated Mr. Kennedy in a Last Ride Match in 19:49 (★★); John Cena and Batista defeated King Booker and Finlay in 11:29 (★★).

Final Battle '06 ★★★★★
23-12-06, New York City, New York **ROH**
Jimmy Rave defeated Christopher Daniels, Davey Richards and El Generico in a Four Corner Survival Match in 17:48 (★★★); Adam Pearce defeated Ricky Reyes in 3:22 (★★); Brent Albright and Jimmy Jacobs defeated BJ Whitmer and Colt Cabana in 13:49 (★★); The Briscoe Brothers (Jay Briscoe and Mark Briscoe) defeated The Kings Of Wrestling (Chris Hero and Claudio Castagnoli) in 16:03 (★★★★); Jimmy Rave defeated Nigel McGuinness in 16:59 (★★★); Cima, Matt Sydal and Shingo defeated Austin Aries, Delirious and Roderick Strong in a Dragon Gate Rules Match in 24:03 (★★★★); Homicide defeated Bryan Danielson to win the ROH World Title in 30:38 (★★★★).

Tribute To The Troops '06 ★★
25-12-06, Baghdad, Iraq **WWE**
John Cena defeated Edge in 16:33 (★★★); CM Punk defeated Shelton Benjamin in 4:47 (★★); The Undertaker defeated Johnny Nitro in 3:57 (★); Bobby Lashley defeated Hardcore Holly in 6:28 (★); Umaga defeated Jeff Hardy in 5:53 (★); Carlito defeated Randy Orton in 5:09 (★★).

New Year's Revolution '07 ★★★
07-01-07, Kansas City, Missouri **WWE**
Jeff Hardy defeated Johnny Nitro in a Steel Cage Match in 14:50 (★★★); Cryme Tyme (JTG and Shad Gaspard) won a Tag Team Turmoil Match in 19:03 (★★); Kenny Dykstra defeated Ric Flair in 10:02 (★★); Mickie James defeated Victoria in 6:50 (★★); Rated-RKO (Randy Orton and Edge) vs. D-Generation X (Triple H and Shawn Michaels) went to a no contest in 23:20 (★★★); Chris Master defeated Carlito in 5:55 (★★); John Cena defeated Umaga in 17:20 (★★★).

Final Resolution '07 ★★★
14-01-07, Orlando, Florida **TNA**
Rhino defeated AJ Styles in a Last Man Standing Match in 15:06 (★★★); Chris Sabin defeated Christopher Daniels and Jerry Lynn in a Three Way Match to win the TNA X Division Title in 11:50 (★★★); Alex Shelley defeated Austin Starr in 14:59 (★★★); James Storm defeated Petey Williams in 6:50 (★★); The Latin American Xchange (Homicide and Hernandez) defeated Team 3D (Brother Ray and Brother Devon) by DQ in 10:21 (★★); Kurt Angle defeated Samoa Joe in an Iron Man Match in 30:00 (★★★★); Christian Cage defeated Abyss and Sting in a Three Way Elimination Match to win the NWA World Heavyweight Title in 13:18 (★★★).

Royal Rumble '07 ★★★★
28-01-07, San Antonio, Texas **WWE**
The Hardy Boyz (Matt Hardy and Jeff Hardy) defeated MNM (Joey Mercury and Johnny Nitro) in 15:27 (★★); Bobby Lashley defeated Test via count out in 7:18 (★★); Batista defeated Mr. Kennedy in 10:29 (★★); John Cena defeated Umaga in a Last Man Standing Match in 23:09 (★★★); The Undertaker won the 30-Man Royal Rumble Match in 56:18 (★★★★).

Against All Odds '07 ★★★
11-02-07, Orlando, Florida **TNA**
The Latin American Xchange (Homicide and Hernandez) defeated Team 3D (Brother Ray and Brother Devon) in a Little Italy Street Fight in 9:26 (★★★); Senshi defeated Austin Starr in 8:21 (★★); Christy Hemme defeated Big Fat Oily Guy in a Tuxedo Match in 2:29 (★); Lance Hoyt defeated Dale Torborg in a Basebrawl Match in 5:04 (★★); AJ Styles defeated Rhino in a Motor City Chain Match in 15:07 (★★); Chris Sabin defeated Jerry Lynn in 13:33 (★★★); James Storm and Jacqueline Moore defeated Petey Williams and Gail Kim in 8:49 (★★); Sting defeated Abyss in a Prison Yard Match in 11:57 (★★★); Christian Cage defeated Kurt Angle in 19:04 (★★★).

No Way Out '07 ★★
18-02-07, Los Angeles, California **WWE**
Chris Benoit and The Hardy Boyz (Matt Hardy and Jeff Hardy) defeated MVP and MNM (Joey Mercury and Johnny Nitro) in 14:19 (★★★); Chavo Guerrero won a Cruiserweight Open to win the WWE Cruiserweight Title in 14:11 (★★); Finlay and Little Bastard defeated The Boogeyman and Little Boogeyman in 6:44 (★); Kane defeated King Booker in 12:38 (★★); Brian Kendrick and Paul London defeated Deuce and Domino in 8:07 (★★); Mr. Kennedy defeated Bobby Lashley by DQ in 15:27 (★★); Ashley Massaro defeated Jillian Hall, Kelly Kelly, Layla and Brooke Adams in a Diva Talent Invitational Match in 9:40 (★); John Cena and Shawn Michaels defeated Batista and The Undertaker in 22:09 (★★★).

Destination X '07 ★★★
11-03-07, Orlando, Florida **TNA**
The Latin American Xchange (Homicide and Hernandez) defeated Team 3D (Brother Ray and Brother Devon) in a Ghetto Brawl in 14:50 (★★); James Storm and Jacqueline Moore defeated Petey Williams and Gail Kim in a Double Bullrope Match in 8:05 (★★); Senshi defeated Austin Starr in a Crossface Chickenwing Match in 11:10 (★★); The Voodoo Kin Mafia (B.G. James and Kip James) defeated The Heartbreakers (Antonio Thomas and Romeo Roselli) in 9:07 (★★); Chris Sabin defeated Jerry Lynn 2-1 in a Two Out Of Three Falls Match in 13:30 (★★★); Rhino defeated AJ Styles in an Elevation X Match in 12:40 (★★★); Kurt Angle defeated Scott Steiner in 12:00 (★★); Sting defeated Abyss in a Last Rites Match in 9:51 (★); Christian Cage defeated Samoa Joe in 17:10 (★★★★).

All Star Extravaganza III ★★★
30-03-07, Detroit, Michigan **ROH**
Adam Pearce defeated Chris Hero, Colt Cabana and Matt Sydal in a Four Corner Survival Match in 11:15 (★★); Erick Stevens defeated Alex Payne in a Do Or Die Match in :21 (★); Masaaki Mochizuki defeated Davey Richards in 10:40 (★★★); Jimmy Jacobs and Lacey defeated BJ Whitmer and Daizee Haze in a Anything Goes Match in 9:47 (★★); The Briscoe Brothers (Jay Briscoe and Mark Briscoe) defeated Naruki Doi and Shingo to win the ROH Tag Team Title in 16:22 (★★); Yamato defeated Pelle Primeau in 2:20 (★★); Brent Albright defeated Nigel McGuinness in 11:36 (★★); Homicide defeated Christopher Daniels in 15:00 (★★); Roderick Strong defeated

Jack Evans in 21:45 (★ ★); Cima, Dragon Kid, Ryo Saito and Susumu Yokosuka defeated Austin Aries, Claudio Castagnoli, Delirious and Rocky Romero in a Dragon Gate Rules Match in 27:56 (★ ★ ★ ★).

Supercard Of Honor II ★ ★ ★ ★
31-03-07, Detroit, Michigan ROH

Delirious and Jay Briscoe defeated Christopher Daniels and Matt Sydal in 18:07 (★ ★ ★); Claudio Castagnoli defeated Yamato in 6:55 (★ ★); Erick Stevens defeated Mitch Franklin in a Do Or Die Match in :40 (★); Nigel McGuinness defeated Chris Hero in 9:41 (★ ★); Jack Evans and Naruki Doi defeated No Remorse Corps (Davey Richards and Rocky Romero) in 14:22 (★ ★); Homicide defeated Brent Albright by DQ in 1:20 (★); Colt Cabana and Homicide defeated Adam Pearce and Brent Albright in 12:33 (★ ★); Jimmy Jacobs defeated BJ Whitmer in a Pin Or Submission Only Cage Match in 24:34 (★ ★ ★); Roderick Strong defeated Austin Aries in 21:56 (★ ★ ★ ★); Cima, Shingo and Susumu Yokosuka defeated Dragon Kid, Masaaki Mochizuki and Ryo Saito in 27:18 (★ ★ ★ ★).

WrestleMania XXIII ★ ★ ★ ★
01-04-07, Detroit, Michigan WWE

Mr. Kennedy defeated CM Punk, Edge, Finlay, Jeff Hardy, King Booker, Matt Hardy and Randy Orton in a Money In The Bank Ladder Match in 24:10 (★ ★ ★ ★); The Great Khali defeated Kane in 5:30 (★ ★); Chris Benoit defeated MVP in 9:15 (★ ★ ★); The Undertaker defeated Batista to win the World Heavyweight Title in 15:46 (★ ★ ★ ★); The ECW Originals (Rob Van Dam, Sabu, The Sandman and Tommy Dreamer) defeated The New Breed (Elijah Burke, Kevin Thorn, Marcus Cor Von and Matt Striker) in 7:27 (★ ★); Bobby Lashley defeated Umaga in a Hair vs. Hair Battle Of The Billionaires Match in 13:00 (★ ★ ★); Melina defeated Ashley Massaro in a Lumberjill Match in 3:40; (★) John Cena defeated Shawn Michaels in 28:20 (★ ★ ★ ★).

Lockdown '07 ★ ★ ★
15-04-07, St. Charles, Missouri TNA

Chris Sabin defeated Jay Lethal, Sonjay Dutt, Alex Shelley and Shark Boy in an Xscape Match in 15:50 (★ ★); Robert Roode defeated Petey Williams in a Six Sides Of Steel Match in 10:14 (★ ★); Gail Kim defeated Jacqueline Moore in a Six Sides Of Steel Match in 7:13 (★ ★); Senshi defeated Austin Starr in a Six Sides Of Steel Match in 9:57 (★ ★ ★); James Storm defeated Chris Harris in a Six Sides Of Steel Blindfold Match in 9:05 (★); Christopher Daniels defeated Jerry Lynn in a Six Sides Of Steel Match in 13:29 (★ ★ ★); Team 3D (Brother Ray and Brother Devon) defeated The Latin American Xchange (Homicide and Hernandez) in an Electrified Six Sides Of Steel Match to win the NWA World Tag Team Title in 15:36 (★ ★); Team Angle (Kurt Angle, Samoa Joe, Rhino, Sting and Jeff Jarrett) defeated Team Cage (Christian Cage, AJ Styles, Scott Steiner, Abyss and Tomko) in a Lethal Lockdown Match in 28:04 (★ ★ ★ ★).

Backlash '07 ★ ★ ★ ★
29-04-07, Atlanta, Georgia WWE

The Hardy Boyz (Matt Hardy and Jeff Hardy) defeated Lance Cade and Trevor Murdoch in 14:18 (★ ★); Melina defeated Mickie James in 9:02 (★ ★ ★); Chris Benoit defeated MVP in 13:10 (★ ★); Vince McMahon, Shane McMahon and Umaga defeated Bobby Lashley in a Handicap Match in 15:45. As a result Vince McMahon won the ECW World Title in 7:49 (★); The Undertaker vs. Batista went to a draw in a Last Man Standing Match in 20:23 (★ ★ ★ ★); John Cena defeated Randy Orton, Edge and Shawn Michaels in a Four Way Match in 19:21 (★ ★ ★ ★).

Sacrifice '07 ★ ★ ★ ★
13-05-07, Orlando, Florida TNA

Chris Sabin defeated Jay Lethal and Sonjay Dutt in a Three Way Match in 13:01 (★ ★ ★); Robert Roode defeated Jeff Jarrett in 11:22 (★ ★); Christopher Daniels defeated Rhino in 9:57 (★ ★); Basham and Damaja defeated Kip James in a Handicap Match in 4:27 (★ ★); Chris Harris defeated James Storm in a Texas Death Match in 17:12 (★ ★ ★ ★ ★); Jerry Lynn defeated Tiger Mask, Alex Shelley and Senshi in a Four Corners Match in 10:45 (★ ★ ★); Team 3D (Brother Ray and Brother Devon) defeated Scott Steiner and Tomko, and The Latin American Xchange (Homicide and Hernandez) in a Three Way Match in 12:40 (★ ★ ★); Samoa Joe defeated AJ Styles in 12:40 (★ ★ ★); Kurt Angle defeated Sting and Christian Cage in a Three Way Match to win the NWA World Heavyweight Title in 10:44 (★ ★ ★).

Judgment Day '07 ★ ★
20-05-07, St. Louis, Missouri WWE

Ric Flair defeated Carlito in 15:34 (★ ★); Bobby Lashley defeated Vince McMahon, Shane McMahon and Umaga in a Handicap Match in 1:13 (★ ★); CM Punk defeated Elijah Burke in 16:50 (★ ★ ★); Randy Orton defeated Shawn Michaels in 4:32 (★ ★); The Hardy Boyz (Matt Hardy and Jeff Hardy) defeated Lance Cade and Trevor Murdoch in 15:02 (★ ★ ★); Edge defeated Batista in 10:37 (★ ★); MVP defeated Chris Benoit 2-0 in a Two Out Of Three Falls Match to win the WWE United States Title in 12:46 (★ ★); John Cena defeated The Great Khali in 8:15 (★ ★).

Saturday Night's Main Event XXXIV ★ ★
02-06-07, Toronto, Canada WWE

The Great Khali defeated John Cena in 6:20 (★ ★); Batista and Chris Benoit defeated Edge and MVP in 10:37 (★ ★); Finlay and Hornswoggle defeated The Boogeyman and Little Boogeyman in 3:49 (★); Kane, Doink the Clown and Eugene defeated Kevin Thorn, Viscera and Umaga in 10:55 (★ ★).

One Night Stand '07 ★ ★ ★
03-06-07, Jacksonville, Florida WWE

Rob Van Dam defeated Randy Orton in a Stretcher Match in 14:31 (★ ★); CM Punk, The Sandman and Tommy Dreamer defeated Elijah Burke, Matt Striker and Marcus Cor Von in a Tables Match in 7:18 (★ ★); The Hardy Boyz (Matt Hardy and Jeff Hardy) defeated The World's Greatest Tag Team (Charlie Haas and Shelton Benjamin) in a Ladder Match in 17:17 (★ ★ ★ ★); Mark Henry defeated Kane in a Lumberjack Match in 9:07 (★ ★); Bobby Lashley defeated Vince McMahon in a Street Fight to win the ECW World Title in 12:23 (★ ★); Candice Michelle defeated Melina in a Pudding Match in 2:55 (★); Edge defeated Batista in a Steel Cage Match in 15:39 (★ ★ ★); John Cena defeated The Great Khali in a Falls Count Anywhere Match in 10:30 (★ ★).

Slammiversary V ★ ★
17-06-07, Nashville, Tennessee TNA

Rhino and Senshi defeated The Latin American Xchange (Homicide and Hernandez) in 8:25 (★ ★ ★); Jay Lethal defeated Chris Sabin to win the TNA X Division Title in 8:52 (★ ★ ★); Frank Wycheck and Jerry Lynn defeated James Storm and Ron Killings in 8:52 (★ ★); Bob Backlund defeated Alex Shelley in 3:46 (★ ★); The Voodoo Kin Mafia (B.G. James and Kip James) defeated Basham and Damaja in 2:47 (★ ★); Eric Young defeated Robert Roode in 9:09 (★ ★ ★); Team 3D (Brother Ray and Brother Devon) defeated Rick Steiner and Animal in 6:39 (★ ★); Sting defeated Christopher Daniels in 6:33 (★ ★); Abyss defeated Tomko in a No DQ Match in 13:54 (★ ★); Kurt Angle defeated Samoa Joe, AJ Styles, Christian Cage and Chris Harris in a King Of The Mountain Match to win the vacant TNA World Heavyweight Title in 19:21 (★ ★ ★ ★).

Vengeance '07 ★ ★
24-06-07, Houston, Texas WWE

Lance Cade and Trevor Murdoch defeated The Hardy Boyz (Matt Hardy and Jeff Hardy) in 8:55 (★ ★); Chavo Guerrero defeated Jimmy Wang Yang in 10:16 (★ ★ ★); Johnny Nitro defeated CM Punk to win the vacant ECW World Title in 8:00 (★ ★); Santino Marella defeated Umaga by DQ in 2:34 (★); MVP defeated Ric Flair in 8:43 (★ ★); Deuce and Domino defeated Jimmy Snuka and Sgt. Slaughter in 6:34 (★); Edge defeated Batista via count out in 16:50 (★ ★); Candice Michelle defeated Melina to win the WWE Women's Title in 4:07 (★ ★); John Cena defeated Bobby Lashley, King Booker, Mick Foley and Randy Orton in a Five Pack Challenge in 10:08 (★ ★ ★).

Respect Is Earned ★ ★ ★ ★
01-07-07, Manhattan, New York ROH

Takeshi Morishima defeated B.J. Whitmer in 2:50 (★ ★); Naomichi Marufuji defeated Rocky Romero in 16:04 (★ ★ ★); The Briscoe Brothers (Jay Briscoe and Mark Briscoe) defeated Claudio Castagnoli and Matt Sydal in 20:11 (★ ★ ★ ★); Roderick Strong defeated Delirious in 21:38 (★ ★ ★); Takeshi Morishima and Bryan Danielson defeated Nigel McGuinness and Kenta in 26:31 (★ ★ ★ ★).

Victory Road '07 ★★★
15-07-07, Orlando, Florida **TNA**

Christopher Daniels won an Ultimate X Gauntlet Match in 18:48 (★★★); The Voodoo Kin Mafia (B.G. James and Kip James) defeated Basham and Damaja in 7:03 (★★); James Storm defeated Rhino in 10:26 (★★); The Motor City Machine Guns (Chris Sabin and Alex Shelley) defeated Jerry Lynn and Bob Backlund in 8:44 (★★); Eric Young and Gail Kim defeated Robert Roode and Ms. Brooks in 8:17 (★★★); Christian Cage defeated Chris Harris in 13:58 (★★★); Sting and Abyss defeated AJ Styles and Tomko in 15:33 (★★); Kurt Angle and Samoa Joe defeated Team 3D (Brother Ray and Brother Devon) to win the TNA World Tag Team Title in 18:25 (★★★).

Great American Bash '07 ★★★
22-07-07, San Jose, California **WWE**

MVP defeated Matt Hardy in 12:55 (★★); Hornswoggle won a Cruiserweight Open to win the WWE Cruiserweight Title in 6:59 (★★); Carlito defeated The Sandman in a Singapore Cane On A Pole Match in 5:31 (★★); Candice Michelle defeated Melina in 6:22 (★★); Umaga defeated Jeff Hardy in 11:20 (★★★); John Morrison defeated CM Punk in 7:50 (★★); Randy Orton defeated Dusty Rhodes in a Texas Bullrope Match in 5:40 (★★); The Great Khali defeated Batista and Kane in a Three Way Match in 10:04 (★★); John Cena defeated Bobby Lashley in 14:52 (★★★).

Death Before Dishonor V Night #1 ★★★★
10-08-07, Boston, Massachusetts **ROH**

Jack Evans defeated Davey Richards by DQ in 11:19 (★★); Lacey defeated Daizee Haze in 8:10 (★★); Chris Hero defeated Nigel McGuinness in a Pure Wrestling Rules Match in 19:59 (★★★); Matt Cross defeated Brent Albright, Delirious, Eddie Edwards, Jigsaw and Pelle Primeau in a Six Man Mayhem Match in 10:44 (★★); The Resilience (Austin Aries and Erick Stevens) defeated No Remorse Corps (Rocky Romero and Roderick Strong) in 18:05 (★★); Bryan Danielson defeated Matt Sydal in 16:40 (★★★); Takeshi Morishima defeated Claudio Castagnoli in 15:30 (★★★★); El Generico and Kevin Steen defeated The Briscoe Brothers (Jay Briscoe and Mark Briscoe) in a Boston Street Fight in 22:13 (★★★★).

Death Before Dishonor V Night #2 ★★★★
11-08-07, Philadelphia, Pennsylvania **ROH**

El Generico defeated Mark Briscoe in a Falls Count Anywhere Match in 8:19 (★★★); Jack Evans defeated Deranged in 6:42 (★★); Chris Hero and Jigsaw defeated Claudio Castagnoli and Nigel McGuinness in 14:59 (★★); Sara Del Rey defeated Lacey in 12:37 (★★★); Bryan Danielson defeated Mike Quackenbush in 17:08 (★★★★); Kevin Steen defeated Jay Briscoe in a Last Man Standing Match in 14:11 (★★); Takeshi Morishima defeated Brent Albright in 15:15 (★★★); No Remorse Corps (Davey Richards, Rocky Romero and Roderick Strong) and Matt Sydal defeated The Resilience (Austin Aries, Erick Stevens and Matt Cross) and Delirious in a Philadelphia Street Fight in 33:51 (★★★★).

Hard Justice '07 ★★
12-08-07, Orlando, Florida **TNA**

Jay Lethal and Sonjay Dutt defeated The Motor City Machine Guns (Chris Sabin and Alex Shelley) and Triple X (Christopher Daniels and Senshi) in a Three Way Match in 15:50 (★★★); Kaz defeated Raven in 5:41 (★★); James Storm defeated Rhino in a Bar Room Brawl in 13:15 (★★); The Latin American Xchange (Homicide and Hernandez) defeated The Voodoo Kin Mafia (B.G. James and Kip James) in 5:50 (★★); Robert Roode defeated Eric Young in a Humiliation Match in 9:31 (★★); Chris Harris defeated Black Reign by DQ in 4:50 (★★); The Steiner Brothers (Rick Steiner and Scott Steiner) defeated Team 3D (Brother Ray and Brother Devon) in 11:00 (★★); Abyss, Andrew Martin and Sting defeated Christian's Coalition (Christian Cage, AJ Styles and Tomko) in a Doomsday Chamber Of Blood Match in 10:51 (★★); Kurt Angle defeated Samoa Joe to win the TNA X Division Title in 18:34 (★★★).

Saturday Night's Main Event XXXV ★★
18-08-07, New York City, New York **WWE**

Batista and Kane defeated Finlay and The Great Khali in 8:25 (★★); John Cena defeated Carlito in 5:37 (★★); Evander Holyfield vs. Matt Hardy went to a no contest in a Boxing Match in 2:44 (★★★); CM Punk and The Boogeyman defeated John Morrison and Big Daddy V in 6:40 (★★).

Manhattan Mayhem II ★★★★
25-08-07, New York City, New York **ROH**

The Resilience (Erick Stevens and Matt Cross) defeated Jigsaw and Mike Quackenbush in 12:26 (★★★); Jimmy Jacobs defeated Mitch Franklin in 5:15 (★★); Adam Pearce, BJ Whitmer and Brent Albright defeated Delirious, Nigel McGuinness and Pelle Primeau in 11:34 (★★★); Davey Richards defeated Pac in 12:39 (★★); Austin Aries defeated Jack Evans and Roderick Strong in a Three Way Match in 14:41 (★★); Ruckus defeated Eddie Edwards in 6:10 (★★); Claudio Castagnoli defeated Chris Hero in 15:58 (★★★); Takeshi Morishima defeated Bryan Danielson in 20:17 (★★★★); The Briscoe Brothers (Jay Briscoe and Mark Briscoe) defeated El Generico and Kevin Steen 2-0 in a Best Two Out Of Three Falls Match in 24:44 (★★★★).

SummerSlam '07 ★★
26-08-07, East Rutherford, New Jersey **WWE**

Kane defeated Finlay in 8:54 (★★); Umaga defeated Carlito and Mr. Kennedy in a Three Way Match in 7:35 (★★); Rey Mysterio defeated Chavo Guerrero in 12:06 (★★); Beth Phoenix won a Battle Royal in 7:09 (★); John Morrison defeated CM Punk in 7:09 (★★★); Triple H defeated King Booker in 7:58 (★★); Batista defeated The Great Khali by DQ in 6:51 (★); John Cena defeated Randy Orton in 21:20 (★★).

No Surrender '07 ★★★
09-09-07, Orlando, Florida **TNA**

Pacman Jones and Ron Killings defeated AJ Styles and Sting to win the TNA World Tag Team Title in 5:30 (★★); Rhino defeated James Storm in 13:20 (★★★); Robert Roode defeated Kaz in 13:50 (★★★); Jay Lethal defeated Kurt Angle to win the TNA X Division Title in 12:30 (★★); Chris Harris defeated Black Reign in a No DQ Match in 5:30 (★★); AJ Styles and Tomko won a Gauntlet Match in 25:50 (★★); Christian Cage defeated Samoa Joe by DQ in 15:15 (★★); Kurt Angle defeated Abyss in 19:30 (★★★).

Unforgiven '07 ★★
16-09-07, Memphis, Tennessee **WWE**

CM Punk defeated Elijah Burke in 11:52 (★★); Matt Hardy and MVP defeated Deuce and Domino in 9:19 (★★); Triple H defeated Carlito in a No DQ Match in 10:40 (★★); Candice Michelle defeated Beth Phoenix in 7:17 (★★); Batista defeated The Great Khali and Rey Mysterio in a Three Way Match to win the World Heavyweight Title in 8:01 (★★); Lance Cade and Trevor Murdoch defeated Brian Kendrick and Paul London in 11:48 (★★); Randy Orton defeated John Cena by DQ in 7:22 (★★); The Undertaker defeated Mark Henry in 11:25 (★★).

Driven '07 ★★★★
21-09-07, Chicago Ridge, Illinois **ROH**

No Remorse Corps (Roderick Strong, Davey Richards and Rocky Romero) defeated Delirious and The Resilience (Matt Cross and Erick Stevens) in 11:23 (★★★); Claudio Castagnoli defeated Matt Sydal in 8:18 (★★★); Naomichi Marufuji defeated B.J. Whitmer in 10:56 (★★); Brent Albright defeated Pelle Primeau in 1:41 (★★); Takeshi Morishima defeated Jimmy Rave in 3:56 (★★); The Briscoe Brothers (Jay Briscoe and Mark Briscoe) defeated Kevin Steen and El Generico in 16:06 (★★★★); Bryan Danielson defeated Nigel McGuinness in 25:33 (★★★★★).

No Mercy '07 ★★
07-10-07, Rosemont, Illinois **WWE**

Triple H defeated Randy Orton to win the WWE Title in 11:07 (★★); Mr. Kennedy, Lance Cade and Trevor Murdoch defeated Jeff Hardy, Brian Kendrick and Paul London in 8:05 (★★); CM Punk defeated Big Daddy V by DQ in 1:37 (★★); Triple H defeated Umaga in 6:33 (★★); Finlay vs. Rey Mysterio went to a no contest in 9:00 (★★); Beth Phoenix defeated Candice Michelle to win the WWE Women's Title in 4:32 (★★); Batista defeated The Great Khali in a Punjabi Prison Match in 14:47 (★★); Randy Orton defeated Triple H in a Last Man Standing Match to win the WWE Title in 20:26 (★★★★).

Bound For Glory '07 ★★★★
14-10-07, Duluth, Georgia **TNA**

The Latin American Xchange (Homicide and Hernandez) defeated Triple X (Senshi and Elix Skipper) in an Ultimate X Match in 11:59 (★★★); Eric Young won a Reverse Battle Royal in 11:51 (★★); AJ Styles and Tomko defeated Ron Killings and

Consequences Creed to win the TNA World Tag Team Title in 8:48 (★★); **Jay Lethal** defeated **Christopher Daniels** in 11:02 (★★★); **The Steiner Brothers** (Rick Steiner and Scott Steiner) defeated **Team 3D** (Brother Ray and Brother Devon) in a Two Out Of Three Falls Tables Match in 12:43 (★★); **Gail Kim** won a Gauntlet For The Gold Match to win the vacant TNA Knockouts Title in 12:12 (★★); **Samoa Joe** defeated **Christian Cage** in 15:48 (★★★★); **Abyss** defeated **Raven, Rhino** and **Black Reign** in a Monster's Ball Match in 9:07 (★★); **Sting** defeated **Kurt Angle** to win the TNA World Heavyweight Title in 18:20 (★★★).

Survival Of The Fittest '07 ★★★
19-10-07, Las Vegas, Nevada **ROH**

Roderick Strong defeated **Brent Albright** in 9:01 (★★); **Chris Hero** defeated **Karl Anderson** in 7:02 (★★); **Rocky Romero** defeated **TJ Perkins** in 6:29 (★★★); **Austin Aries** defeated **Delirious** in 12:17 (★★★); **Claudio Castagnoli** defeated **Davey Richards** in 8:02 (★★); **Bryan Danielson** vs. **Nigel McGuinness** ended in a draw in 20:00 (★★★); **Human Tornado** defeated **Shane Hagadorn** and **Tony Kozina** in a Three Way Match in 3:27 (★★); **The Age Of The Fall** (Jimmy Jacobs and Necro Butcher) defeated **The Briscoe Brothers** (Jay Briscoe and Mark Briscoe) in a Street Fight in 12:43 (★★★); **Chris Hero** defeated **Austin Aries, Claudio Castagnoli, Human Tornado, Rocky Romero** and **Roderick Strong** in the Survival of the Fittest Final Elimination Match in 27:43 (★★★).

Cyber Sunday '07 ★★★
28-10-07, Washington, D.C. **WWE**

Rey Mysterio defeated **Finlay** in a Stretcher Match in 9:41 (★★); **CM Punk** defeated **The Miz** in 8:48 (★★); **Mr. Kennedy** defeated **Jeff Hardy** in 9:05 (★★); **Kane** defeated **MVP** via count out in 6:38 (★★); **Shawn Michaels** defeated **Randy Orton** by DQ in 15:53 (★★★); **Triple H** defeated **Umaga** in a Street Fight in 17:21 (★★★); **Batista** defeated **The Undertaker** in 17:22 (★★★★).

Glory By Honor VI Night #1 ★★★
02-11-07, Philadelphia, Pennsylvania **ROH**

El Generico and **Kevin Steen** defeated **The Hangmen Three** (BJ Whitmer and Brent Albright) in 8:52 (★★); **Claudio Castagnoli** defeated **Hallowicked** in 5:57 (★★); **Davey Richards** defeated **Delirious** in 13:33 (★★★); **The Briscoe Brothers** (Jay Briscoe and Mark Briscoe) defeated **No Remorse Corps** (Rocky Romero and Roderick Strong) in 17:59 (★★★); **The Age Of The Fall** (Jimmy Jacobs, Necro Butcher and Tyler Black) defeated **The Vulture Squad** (Jack Evans, Jigsaw and Ruckus) in 6:28 (★★); **Ernie Osiris** defeated **Mitch Franklin** in the ROH Top Of The Class Trophy in 2:58 (★★); **Austin Aries** defeated **Bryan Danielson** in 17:20 (★★★★); **Nigel McGuinness** defeated **Chris Hero** in 9:05 (★★); **Kenta** and **Mitsuharu Misawa** vs. **Naomichi Marufuji** and **Takeshi Morishima** ended in a draw in 30:00 (★★★).

Glory By Honor VI Night #2 ★★★
03-11-07, New York City, New York **ROH**

Chris Hero defeated **El Generico** in 14:24 (★★); **The Hangmen Three** (BJ Whitmer and Brent Albright) defeated **Delirious** and **Kevin Steen** in 10:53 (★★); **Austin Aries** defeated **Shane Hagadorn** in 1:12 (★★); **Claudio Castagnoli** defeated **Naomichi Marufuji** in 18:38 (★★★); **The Briscoe Brothers** (Jay Briscoe and Mark Briscoe) vs. **The Age Of The Fall** (Jimmy Jacobs and Necro Butcher) ended in a double DQ in :38 (★★); **Tyler Black** defeated **Alex Payne** in 1:07 (★★); **Takeshi Morishima** defeated **Bryan Danielson** by DQ in 11:38 (★★★); **No Remorse Corps** (Davey Richards, Rocky Romero and Roderick Strong) defeated **The Vulture Squad** (Jack Evans, Jigsaw and Ruckus) in 14:35 (★★); **Austin Aries** defeated **Chris Hero** in 16:06 (★★★); **Mitsuharu Misawa** defeated **Kenta** in 18:32 (★★★); **The Briscoe Brothers** (Jay Briscoe and Mark Briscoe) defeated **The Age Of The Fall** (Jimmy Jacobs and Necro Butcher) in a Street Fight in 17:45 (★★).

Genesis '07 ★★★★
11-11-07, Orlando, Florida **TNA**

Abyss defeated **Black Reign** in a Shop Of Horrors Match in 10:13 (★★); **The Motor City Machine Guns** (Alex Shelley and Chris Sabin) defeated **Team 3D** (Brother Ray and Brother Devon) in 17:37 (★★★); **Gail Kim** defeated **Roxxi Laveaux, ODB** and **Angel Williams** in a Four Way Match in 9:01 (★★); **Jay Lethal** defeated **Sonjay Dutt** in 12:01 (★★★); **Christian's Coalition** (AJ Styles and Tomko) defeated **The Steiner Brothers** (Rick Steiner

and **Scott Steiner**) in 10:43 (★★); **Samoa Joe** defeated **Robert Roode** in 15:43 (★★); **Kaz** defeated **Christian Cage** in a Ladder Match in 15:13 (★★★★); **Kurt Angle** and **Kevin Nash** defeated **Sting** and **Booker T** in 13:41 (★★).

Survivor Series '07 ★★★
18-11-07, Miami, Florida **WWE**

CM Punk defeated **John Morrison** and **The Miz** in a Three Way Match in 7:56 (★★★); **Kelly Kelly, Maria, Michelle McCool, Mickie James** and **Torrie Wilson** defeated **Beth Phoenix, Jillian Hall, Layla, Melina** and **Victoria** in 4:42 (★★); **Lance Cade** and **Trevor Murdoch** defeated **Cody Rhodes** and **Hardcore Holly** in 7:18 (★★); **Team Triple H** (Triple H, Jeff Hardy, Kane and Rey Mysterio) defeated **Team Umaga** (Umaga, Big Daddy V, Finlay, Mr. Kennedy and MVP) in a Handicap Elimination Match in 22:08 (★★); **The Great Khali** defeated **Hornswoggle** by DQ in 3:16 (★); **Randy Orton** defeated **Shawn Michaels** in 17:48 (★★★); **Batista** defeated **The Undertaker** in a Hell In A Cell Match in 21:24 (★★★★).

Man Up ★★★★★
30-11-07, Chicago Ridge, Illinois **ROH**

Nigel McGuinness defeated **Claudio Castagnoli, Chris Hero** and **Naomichi Marufuji** in a Four Corner Survival Match in 18:00 (★★★★); **Rocky Romero** defeated **Matt Cross** in 4:45 (★★); **Austin Aries** defeated **Davey Richards** in 13:23 (★★★); **Roderick Strong** defeated **Erick Stevens** in 16:26 (★★★); **Takeshi Morishima** defeated **Bryan Danielson** in 12:43 (★★★★); **The Briscoe Brothers** (Jay Briscoe and Mark Briscoe) defeated **Kevin Steen** and **El Generico** in a Ladder War in 27:23 (★★★★).

Turning Point '07 ★★
02-12-07, Orlando, Florida **TNA**

Johnny Devine and **Team 3D** (Brother Ray and Brother Devon) defeated **Jay Lethal** and **The Motor City Machine Guns** (Alex Shelley and Chris Sabin) in a Tables Match in 14:59 (★★★); **Velvet-Love Entertainment** (Angelina Love and Velvet Sky) defeated **ODB** and **Roxxi Laveaux** in 6:02 (★★); **Eric Young** defeated **James Storm** in 12:21 (★★); **Petey Williams, B.G. James, Senshi** and **Scott Steiner** defeated **on a Feast Or Fired Match in 11:55 (★★); **Gail Kim** defeated **Awesome Kong** by DQ in 8:23 (★★★); **Abyss** and **Raven** defeated **Rellik** and **Black Reign** in a Match Of 10,000 Tacks in 14:41 (★★); **Kaz** and **Booker T** defeated **Christian Cage** and **Robert Roode** in 15:50 (★★★★); **Samoa Joe, Kevin Nash** and **Eric Young** defeated **The Angle Alliance** (Kurt Angle, AJ Styles and Tomko) in 9:31 (★★).

Armageddon '07 ★★★
16-12-07, Pittsburgh, Pennsylvania **WWE**

Rey Mysterio defeated **MVP** via count out in 11:29 (★★★); **Big Daddy V** and **Mark Henry** defeated **CM Punk** and **Kane** in 10:33 (★★); **Shawn Michaels** defeated **Mr. Kennedy** in 15:16 (★★★); **Jeff Hardy** defeated **Triple H** in 15:23 (★★★); **Finlay** defeated **The Great Khali** in 6:02 (★★); **Chris Jericho** defeated **Randy Orton** by DQ in 15:05 (★★★); **Beth Phoenix** defeated **Mickie James** in 4:45 (★★); **Edge** defeated **Batista** and **The Undertaker** in a Three Way Match to win the World Heavyweight Title in 13:00 (★★★).

Tribute To The Troops '07 ★★
24-12-07, Baghdad, Iraq **WWE**

Chris Jericho defeated **Randy Orton** by DQ in 14:19 (★★★); **Jeff Hardy** defeated **Carlito** in 6:34 (★★); **Maria** and **Mickie James** vs. **Kelly Kelly** and **Layla** ended in a no contest in 4:00 (★★); **Rey Mysterio** defeated **Mark Henry** in 4:17 (★★); **D-Generation X** (Shawn Michaels and Triple H) defeated **Mr. Kennedy** and **Umaga** in 11:00 (★★).

Final Battle '07 ★★★
30-12-07, New York City, New York **ROH**

The Vulture Squad (Jigsaw and Ruckus) defeated **Bobby Fish** and **Matt Cross** in 8:01 (★★); **Larry Sweeney** defeated **Claudio Castagnoli** in 2:30 (★★); **Jack Evans** defeated **Necro Butcher** in a No DQ Match in 11:15 (★★); **Naomichi Marufuji** defeated **Davey Richards** in 15:12 (★★★); **The Hangmen Three** (Adam Pearce, BJ Whitmer and Brent Albright) defeated **Delirious, El Generico** and **Kevin Steen** in a Tables Are Legal Match in 18:24 (★★★); **Rocky Romero** defeated **Ernie Osiris** in 1:09 (★★); **Erick Stevens** defeated **Roderick Strong** to win the FIP World Heavyweight Title in 20:54 (★★★); **Bryan Danielson** defeated **Austin Aries, Chris Hero** and **Takeshi Morishima** in a Four Way

Four Way Elimination Match in 22:49 (★★★); The Age Of The Fall (Jimmy Jacobs and Tyler Black) defeated The Briscoe Brothers (Jay Briscoe and Mark Briscoe) to win the ROH Tag Team Title in 18:54 (★★★).

Final Resolution '08 (January) ★★
06-01-08, Orlando, Florida TNA

The Latin American Xchange (Homicide and Hernandez) defeated The Rock 'n' Rave Infection (Jimmy Rave and Lance Hoyt) in 6:48 (★★); Kaz defeated Black Reign in 7:28 (★★); Gail Kim defeated Awesome Kong in a No DQ Match in 12:44 (★★★); Judas Mesias defeated Abyss in 11:03 (★★); Booker T and Sharmell defeated Robert Roode and Ms. Brooks in 10:47 (★★); Team 3D (Brother Ray and Brother Devon) and Johnny Devine defeated The Motor City Machine Guns (Alex Shelley and Chris Sabin) and Jay Lethal in an Ultimate X Match in 12:02 (★★); AJ Styles and Tomko defeated Kevin Nash and Samoa Joe in 12:10 (★★); Kurt Angle defeated Christian Cage in 18:45 (★★★).

Undeniable ★★★
18-01-08, Edison, New Jersey ROH

The Age Of The Fall (Jimmy Jacobs and Tyler Black) defeated The Vulture Squad (Jack Evans and Ruckus) in 5:38 (★★); Daizee Haze defeated Sara Del Rey in 3:52 (★★); Bryan Danielson defeated Chris Hero in 11:08 (★★); The Hangmen 3 (Adam Pearce, BJ Whitmer and Brent Albright) defeated Delirious, Kevin Steen and El Generico in 11:04 (★★); Austin Aries defeated Roderick Strong in 20:57 (★★★★); The Briscoe Brothers (Jay Briscoe and Mark Briscoe) defeated No Remorse Corps (Davey Richards and Rocky Romero) in 18:15 (★★★); Nigel McGuinness defeated Takeshi Morishima to win the ROH World Title in 14:16 (★★★).

Royal Rumble '08 ★★★
27-01-08, New York, New York WWE

Ric Flair defeated MVP in 7:48 (★★); John Bradshaw Layfield defeated Chris Jericho by DQ in 9:23 (★★); Edge defeated Rey Mysterio in 12:34 (★★); Randy Orton defeated Jeff Hardy in 14:03 (★★); John Cena won the 30-Man Royal Rumble Match in 51:25 (★★).

Against All Odds '08 ★★
10-02-08, Greenville, South Carolina TNA

AJ Styles and Tomko defeated B.G. James and Bob Armstrong in 7:45 (★★); Traci Brooks defeated Payton Banks in 5:07 (★★); Scott Steiner defeated Petey Williams in 9:24 (★★); Eric Young defeated James Storm in 7:49 (★★); Awesome Kong defeated ODB in 6:54 (★★); Abyss defeated Judas Mesias in a Barbed Wire Massacre in 14:51 (★★★); Booker T vs. Robert Roode went to a double count out in 9:17 (★★); The Motor City Machine Guns (Alex Shelley and Chris Sabin) and Jay Lethal defeated Team 3D (Brother Ray and Brother Devon) and Johnny Devine in a Street Fight in 12:30. As a result, Jay Lethal won the TNA X Division Title (★★★); Kurt Angle defeated Christian Cage in 20:40 (★★★).

No Way Out '08 ★★★
17-02-08, Las Vegas, Nevada WWE

Chavo Guerrero defeated CM Punk in 7:06 (★★); The Undertaker defeated Batista, Finlay, MVP, The Great Khali and Big Daddy V in an Elimination Chamber Match in 29:28 (★★★); Ric Flair defeated Mr. Kennedy in 7:13 (★★); Edge defeated Rey Mysterio in 5:27 (★★); John Cena defeated Randy Orton by DQ in 15:51 (★★★); Triple H defeated Jeff Hardy, Shawn Michaels, Chris Jericho, Umaga and John Bradshaw Layfield in an Elimination Chamber Match in 23:54 (★★★).

Sixth Anniversary Show ★★★★
23-02-08, New York City, New York ROH

Delirious vs. Human Tornado ended in a no contest in 1:44 (★); The Age Of The Fall (Jimmy Jacobs and Tyler Black) defeated Delirious and Human Tornado in 9:54 (★★); Brent Albright defeated El Generico in 13:12 (★★); Kevin Steen defeated Joey Matthews in 11:08 (★★); Austin Aries defeated Go Shiozaki in 20:03 (★★★★); Sara Del Rey defeated Daizee Haze in 8:30 (★★); No Remorse Corps (Davey Richards and Rocky Romero) defeated The Vulture Squad (Jigsaw and Ruckus) in 11:12 (★★★); Roderick Strong defeated Erick Stevens and Necro Butcher in a Three Way No DQ Match in 17:37 (★★★); Nigel McGuinness defeated Bryan Danielson in 30:05 (★★★★).

Rising Above '08 ★★★
07-03-08, New York, New York ROH

Delirious defeated Brent Albright in 6:11 (★★); Kevin Steen and El Generico defeated The Age Of The Fall (Jimmy Jacobs and Tyler Black), The Hangmen 3 (Adam Pearce and B.J. Whitmer), and The Vulture Squad (Jack Evans and Ruckus) in a Scramble Match in 7:31 (★★); Daizee Haze defeated Lacey and Sara Del Rey in a Three Way Match in 6:26 (★★); Davey Richards defeated Erick Stevens in 9:52 (★★); Claudio Castagnoli defeated Chris Hero in 9:20 (★★★); Bryan Danielson defeated Takeshi Morishima by DQ in 8:20 (★★); The Briscoe Brothers (Jay Briscoe and Mark Briscoe) defeated No Remorse Corps (Roderick Strong and Rocky Romero) in a Two Out Of Three Falls Match in 21:45 (★★★); Nigel McGuiness defeated Austin Aries in 23:16 (★★★★).

Destination X '08 ★★
09-03-08, Norfolk, Virginia TNA

The Latin American Xchange (Homicide and Hernandez) defeated The Motor City Machine Guns (Alex Shelley and Chris Sabin) and The Rock 'n' Rave Infection (Jimmy Rave and Lance Hoyt) in a Three Way Match in 10:26 (★★★); Jay Lethal defeated Petey Williams in 11:39 (★★); Eric Young and Kaz defeated Black Reign and Rellik in 10:03 (★★); Awesome Kong defeated Gail Kim and ODB in a Three Way Match in 11:27 (★★★); Curry Man and Shark Boy defeated Team 3D (Brother Ray and Brother Devon) in a Fish Market Street Fight in 13:13 (★★★); Robert Roode defeated Booker T in a Strap Match in 7:56 (★★); Rhino defeated James Storm in an Elevation X Match in 13:13 (★★); The Unlikely Alliance (Christian Cage, Kevin Nash and Samoa Joe) defeated The Angle Alliance (AJ Styles, Kurt Angle and Tomko) in 12:26 (★★).

WrestleMania XXIV ★★★★
30-03-08, Orlando, Florida WWE

John Bradshaw Layfield defeated Finlay in a Belfast Brawl in 8:43 (★★); CM Punk defeated Carlito, Chris Jericho, John Morrison, Mr. Kennedy, MVP and Shelton Benjamin in a Money In The Bank Ladder Match in 15:12 (★★★); Batista defeated Umaga in 7:03 (★★); Kane defeated Chavo Guerrero to win the ECW World Title in :11 (★); Shawn Michaels defeated Ric Flair in 20:34 (★★★); Beth Phoenix and Melina defeated Ashley Massaro and Maria in a Playboy BunnyMania Lumberjill Match in 5:00 (★); Randy Orton defeated John Cena and Triple H in a Three Way Match in 14:10 (★★★); Floyd Mayweather defeated The Big Show in a No DQ Match in 11:40 (★★★); The Undertaker defeated Edge to win the World Heavyweight Title in 24:03 (★★★★).

Lockdown '08 ★★★
13-04-08, Lowell, Massachusetts TNA

Jay Lethal defeated Consequences Creed, Curry Man, Johnny Devine, Shark Boy and Sonjay Dutt in a Six Man Xscape Match in 10:45 (★★★); Roxxi Laveaux defeated Angelina Love, Christy Hemme, Jacqueline Moore, Rhaka Khan, Salinas, Traci Brooks and Velvet Sky in a Queen Of The Cage Match in 5:30 (★); B.G. James defeated Kip James in a Six Sides Of Steel Match in 8:00 (★★); Kaz and Super Eric won a Cuffed In The Cage Match in 10:45 (★★); Gail Kim and ODB defeated Awesome Kong and Raisha Saeed in a Six Sides Of Steel Match in 8:30 (★★); Booker T and Sharmell defeated Robert Roode and Payton Banks in a Six Sides Of Steel Match in 7:45 (★★); Team Cage (Christian Cage, Kevin Nash, Matt Morgan, Rhino and Sting) defeated Team Tomko (AJ Styles, James Storm, Tomko, Brother Ray and Brother Devon) in a Lethal Lockdown Match in 26:45 (★★★★); Samoa Joe defeated Kurt Angle in a Six Sides Of Steel Match to win the TNA World Heavyweight Title in 17:45 (★★★★).

Backlash '08 ★★★
27-04-08, Baltimore, Maryland WWE

Matt Hardy defeated MVP to win the WWE United States Title in 11:24 (★★); Kane defeated Chavo Guerrero in 8:49 (★★); The Big Show defeated The Great Khali in 8:05 (★★); Shawn Michaels defeated Batista in 15:00 (★★★); Beth Phoenix, Jillian Hall, Layla, Melina, Natalya and Victoria defeated Ashley Massaro, Cherry, Kelly Kelly, Maria, Michelle McCool and Mickie James in 6:31 (★); The Undertaker defeated Edge in 18:23 (★★★); Triple H defeated Randy Orton, John Cena and John Bradshaw Layfield in a Four Way Match to win the WWE Title in 28:11 (★★).

Sacrifice '08 ★★
11-05-08, Orlando, Florida TNA

Team 3D (Brother Ray and Brother Devon) defeated James Storm and Sting in 8:50 (★★); Christian Cage and Rhino defeated Booker T and Robert Roode in 7:05 (★★); The Latin American Xchange (Homicide and Hernandez) defeated Kip James and Matt Morgan in 4:20 (★★); AJ Styles and Super Eric defeated Awesome Kong and B.G. James in 5:45 (★★); Kaz won a TerrorDome Match in 10:45 (★★★); Team 3D (Brother Ray and Brother Devon) defeated Christian Cage and Rhino in 10:00 (★★); The Latin American Xchange (Homicide and Hernandez) defeated AJ Styles and Super Eric in 7:40 (★★★); Gail Kim and Roxxi Laveaux co-won a Battle Royal in 3:43 (★); Gail Kim defeated Roxxi Laveaux in a Ladder Match in 4:46 (★★); The Latin American Xchange (Homicide and Hernandez) defeated Team 3D (Brother Ray and Brother Devon) to win the vacant TNA World Tag Team Title in 11:30 (★★★); Samoa Joe defeated Kaz and Scott Steiner in a Three Way Match in 14:30 (★★★).

Judgment Day '08 ★★★
18-05-08, Omaha, Nebraska WWE

John Cena defeated John Bradshaw Layfield in 15:03 (★★); John Morrison and The Miz defeated Kane and CM Punk in 7:12 (★★); Shawn Michaels defeated Chris Jericho in 15:56 (★★★★); Mickie James defeated Beth Phoenix and Melina in a Three Way Match in 6:14 (★★); The Undertaker defeated Edge via count out in 16:15 (★★★); Jeff Hardy defeated MVP in 9:42 (★★); Triple H defeated Randy Orton in a Steel Cage Match in 21:12 (★★★).

Take No Prisoners '08 ★★★★
30-05-08, Philadelphia, Pennsylvania ROH

Tyler Black defeated Go Shiozaki, Delirious and Claudio Castagnoli in a Four Corners Survival Match in 9:35 (★★★); Kevin Steen defeated Roderick Strong in 11:12 (★★); The Briscoe Brothers (Jay Briscoe and Mark Briscoe) defeated The Age Of The Fall (Joey Matthews and Necro Butcher) in a Philadelphia Street Fight in 14:32 (★★★); Brent Albright defeated Erick Stevens in 6:17 (★★); No Remorse Corps (Davey Richards and Rocky Romero) defeated The Vulture Squad (Ruckus and Jigsaw) in 9:15 (★★★); Bryan Danielson defeated Austin Aries in 17:21 (★★★★); Nigel McGuinness defeated Tyler Black in 21:24 (★★★★).

One Night Stand '08 ★★
01-06-08, San Diego, California WWE

Jeff Hardy defeated Umaga in a Falls Count Anywhere Match in 9:27 (★★); The Big Show defeated Chavo Guerrero, CM Punk, John Morrison and Tommy Dreamer in a Singapore Cane Match in 8:35 (★★); John Cena defeated John Bradshaw Layfield in a First Blood Match in 14:30 (★★); Beth Phoenix defeated Melina in an "I Quit" Match in 9:14 (★★); Batista defeated Shawn Michaels in a Stretcher Match in 17:03 (★★★); Triple H defeated Randy Orton in a Last Man Standing Match in 13:15 (★★); Edge defeated The Undertaker in a TLC Match to win the vacant World Heavyweight Title in 23:50 (★★★).

Slammiversary VI ★★★
08-06-08, Southaven, Mississippi TNA

Petey Williams defeated Kaz in 15:19 (★★★); Gail Kim, ODB and Roxxi defeated The Beautiful People (Angelina Love and Velvet Sky) and Moose in 10:14 (★★); The Latin American Xchange (Homicide and Hernandez) defeated Team 3D (Brother Ray and Brother Devon) in 15:00 (★★); Awesome Kong defeated Serena Deeb in 2:26 (★★); Awesome Kong defeated Josie Robinson in 1:42 (★★); AJ Styles defeated Kurt Angle in 22:44 (★★★); Samoa Joe defeated Booker T, Christian Cage, Rhino and Robert Roode in a King Of The Mountain Match in 19:49 (★★★).

Night Of Champions '08 ★★★
29-06-08, Dallas, Texas WWE

John Morrison and The Miz defeated Finlay and Hornswoggle in 8:46 (★★); Matt Hardy defeated Chavo Guerrero in 9:22 (★★); Mark Henry defeated Kane and The Big Show in a Three Way Match to win the ECW World Title in 8:18 (★★); Cody Rhodes and Ted DiBiase defeated Hardcore Holly in a Handicap Match to win the World Tag Team Title in 1:28 (★); Kofi Kingston defeated Chris Jericho to win the WWE Intercontinental Title in 13:28 (★★); Mickie James defeated Katie Lea Burchill in 7:17 (★); Edge defeated Batista in 17:10 (★★); Triple H defeated John Cena in 21:38 (★★★).

Victory Road '08 ★★★
13-07-08, Houston, Texas TNA

Team TNA (Alex Shelley, Chris Sabin and Curry Man) defeated Team Japan (Masato Yoshino, Milano Collection A.T. and Puma), Team Mexico (Averno, Rey Bucanero and Ultimo Guerrero), and Team International (Alex Koslov, Doug Williams and Tyson Dux) in a Four Corners Elimination Match in 24:16; (★★★★); Gail Kim defeated Angelina Love in 6:13 (★★); Sonjay Dutt defeated Jay Lethal in 8:24 (★★); The Latin American Xchange (Homicide and Hernandez) defeated Beer Money Inc. (James Storm and Robert Roode) in a Fans Revenge Lumberjack Match in 10:06 (★★); Taylor Wilde defeated Awesome Kong in 4:51 (★★); Volador Jr. defeated Daivari, Kaz and Naruki Doi in a Four Way Ultimate X Match in 10:58 (★★★); Kurt Angle and Team 3D (Brother Ray and Brother Devon) defeated AJ Styles, Christian Cage and Rhino in a Full Metal Mayhem Match in 15:55 (★★★★); Samoa Joe vs. Booker T went to a no contest in 15:14 (★★★).

Great American Bash '08 ★★★
20-07-08, Uniondale, New York WWE

Curt Hawkins and Zack Ryder defeated John Morrison and The Miz, Jesse and Festus, and Finlay and Hornswoggle in a Four Way Match to win the WWE Tag Team Title in 9:05 (★★); Shelton Benjamin defeated Matt Hardy to win the WWE United States Title in 9:33 (★★★); Mark Henry defeated Tommy Dreamer in 5:29 (★★); Chris Jericho defeated Shawn Michaels in 18:18 (★★★); Michelle McCool defeated Natalya to win the vacant WWE Divas Title in 4:14 (★★); CM Punk vs. Batista went to a double DQ in 11:10 (★★★); John Bradshaw Layfield defeated John Cena in a New York City Parking Lot Brawl in 14:36 (★★); Triple H defeated Edge in 16:48 (★★★).

Respect Is Earned II ★★★★
01-08-08, Philadelphia, Pennsylvania ROH

Kevin Steen and El Generico defeated The Vulture Squad (Ruckus and Jigsaw) in 8:05 (★★); Claudio Castagnoli defeated Davey Richards in 9:15 (★★); Brent Albright, Delirious and Pelle Primeau defeated Sweet and Sour Inc. (Chris Hero, Adam Pearce and Eddie Edwards) in 11:21 (★★★); Roderick Strong defeated Erick Stevens in a Fight Without Honor Match in 20:54 (★★★★); Nigel McGuinness defeated Go Shiozaki in 17:00 (★★★); The Age Of The Fall (Jimmy Jacobs and Tyler Black) defeated TeamWork (Austin Aries and Bryan Danielson) in 23:45 (★★★★).

Saturday Night's Main Event XXXVI ★★
02-08-08, Washington, D.C. WWE

John Bradshaw Layfield, Kane and The Legacy (Cody Rhodes and Ted DiBiase) defeated John Cena, Batista and Cryme Tyme (Shad Gaspard and JTG) in 11:20 (★★); The Great Khali defeated Jimmy Wang Yang in 1:30 (★); Edge defeated Jeff Hardy in 12:00 (★★).

Death Before Dishonor VI ★★★★
02-08-08, New York City, New York ROH

The Briscoe Brothers (Jay Briscoe and Mark Briscoe) defeated The Vulture Squad (Jigsaw and Ruckus) in 6:00 (★★★); Chris Hero defeated Delirious in 8:23 (★★); Eddie Edwards defeated Roderick Strong in 9:42 (★★); Brent Albright defeated Adam Pearce to win the NWA World Heavyweight Title in 19:42 (★★★★); Austin Aries defeated Jimmy Jacobs and Necro Butcher in a Three Way Match in 11:47 (★★★); Naomichi Marufuji defeated Go Shiozaki in 23:02 (★★★★); El Generico and Kevin Steen defeated The Motor City Machine Guns (Alex Shelley and Chris Sabin) in 19:51 (★★★★); Nigel McGuinness defeated Bryan Danielson, Claudio Castagnoli and Tyler Black in a Four Way Elimination Match in 30:45 (★★★★).

Hard Justice '08 ★★★
10-08-08, Trenton, New Jersey TNA

Petey Williams defeated Consequences Creed in 12:30 (★★★); Gail Kim, ODB and Taylor Wilde defeated Awesome Kong and The Beautiful People (Angelina Love and Velvet Sky) in 11:27 (★★); Beer Money Inc. (James Storm and Robert Roode) defeated The Latin American Xchange (Homicide and Hernandez) to win the TNA World Tag Team Title in 14:15 (★★★); Jay Lethal defeated Sonjay Dutt in a Black Tie Brawl and Chain Match in 11:14 (★★); Christian Cage and Rhino defeated Team 3D (Brother Ray and Brother Devon) in a New Jersey Street Fight in 15:22 (★★); AJ Styles defeated Kurt Angle in a Last Man Standing Match in 24:50 (★★★★); Samoa Joe defeated Booker T in a Six Sides Of Steel Weapons Match in 12:44 (★★).

SummerSlam '08 ★★★★
17-08-08, Indianapolis, Indiana WWE

MVP defeated Jeff Hardy in 10:10 (★★★); Glamarella (Santino Marella and Beth Phoenix) defeated Kofi Kingston and Mickie James in 5:25. As a result, Santino Marella won the WWE Intercontinental Title and Beth Phoenix won the WWE Women's Title (★★); Matt Hardy defeated Mark Henry by DQ in :33 (★); CM Punk defeated John Bradshaw Layfield in 10:29 (★★★); Triple H defeated The Great Khali in 10:00 (★★); Batista defeated John Cena in 14:10 (★★★★); The Undertaker defeated Edge in a Hell In A Cell Match in 26:44 (★★★★).

Unforgiven '08 ★★★
07-09-08, Cleveland, Ohio WWE

Matt Hardy defeated Chavo Guerrero, Finlay, Mark Henry and The Miz in a Championship Scramble Match to win the ECW World Title in 16:44 (★★★★); Cody Rhodes and Ted DiBiase defeated Cryme Tyme (JTG and Shad Gaspard) in 11:35 (★★); Shawn Michaels defeated Chris Jericho in an Unsanctioned Match in 26:53 (★★★★); Triple H defeated The Brian Kendrick, Jeff Hardy, MVP and Shelton Benjamin in a Championship Scramble Match in 20:15 (★★); Michelle McCool defeated Maryse in 5:42 (★★); Chris Jericho defeated Batista, Kane, John Bradshaw Layfield and Rey Mysterio in a Championship Scramble Match to win the vacant World Heavyweight Title in 17:08 (★★).

No Surrender '08 ★★★
14-09-08, Oshawa, Ontario TNA

The Prince Justice Brotherhood (Curry Man, Shark Boy and Super Eric) defeated The Rock 'n' Rave Infection (Christy Hemme, Jimmy Rave and Lance Rock) in 7:35 (★★); Awesome Kong defeated ODB in a Falls Count Anywhere Match in 10:23 (★★★); Abyss and Matt Morgan defeated Team 3D (Brother Ray and Brother Devon) in 11:33 (★★); Sheik Abdul Bashir defeated Consequences Creed and Petey Williams in a Three Way Match to win the TNA X Division Title in 8:15 (★★★); Taylor Wilde defeated Angelina Love in 6:22 (★★); Sonjay Dutt defeated Jay Lethal in a Ladder Of Love Match in 13:19 (★★★); Beer Money Inc. (James Storm and Robert Roode) defeated The Latin American Xchange (Homicide and Hernandez) in 8:42 (★★); AJ Styles vs. Frank Trigg went to a no contest in a Mixed Martial Arts Match in 6:07 (★); Samoa Joe defeated Christian Cage and Kurt Angle in a Three Way Match in 15:27 (★★★).

Glory By Honor VII ★★★
20-09-08, Philadelphia, Pennsylvania ROH

Jerry Lynn defeated Kenny King in 10:19 (★★★); Adam Pearce defeated Brent Albright to win the NWA World Heavyweight Title in 13:56 (★★★); Go Shiozaki defeated Kevin Steen in 15:21 (★★); Bryan Danielson defeated Katsuhiko Nakajima in 23:04 (★★★★); Erick Stevens defeated Rhett Titus in 3:24 (★★); Sweet 'n' Sour Inc. (Chris Hero, Eddie Edwards and Shane Hagadorn) defeated Roderick Strong and The Vulture Squad (Jigsaw and Ruckus) in 11:08 (★★); Kensuke Sasaki defeated Claudio Castagnoli in 14:44 (★★); Nigel McGuinness defeated El Generico in 20:59 (★★★); Austin Aries and The Briscoe Brothers (Jay Briscoe and Mark Briscoe) defeated Necro Butcher and The Age Of The Fall (Delirious, Jimmy Jacobs and Tyler Black) in a Steel Cage Warfare Match in 29:11 (★★★).

New Horizons ★★★★
26-09-08, Detroit, Michigan ROH

The Briscoe Brothers (Jay Briscoe and Mark Briscoe) defeated Silas Young and Mitch Franklin in 1:44 (★★); Erick Stevens defeated Ruckus, Delirious and Shane Hagadorn in a Four Corner Survival Match in 4:49 (★★); Kevin Steen defeated Necro Butcher in a No DQ Match in 8:41 (★★); Roderick Strong and Naomichi Marufuji defeated Chris Hero and Go Shiozaki in 11:53 (★★★); Nigel McGuinness defeated Claudio Castagnoli in 19:22 (★★★★); Bryan Danielson defeated Tyler Black in 24:30 (★★★★).

No Mercy '08 ★★★★
05-10-08, Portland, Oregon WWE

Matt Hardy defeated Mark Henry in 8:08 (★★); Beth Phoenix defeated Candice Michelle in 4:40 (★★); Rey Mysterio defeated Kane by DQ in 10:10 (★★); Batista defeated John Bradshaw Layfield in 5:18 (★★); The Big Show defeated The Undertaker in 10:04 (★★★); Triple H defeated Jeff Hardy in 17:02 (★★★★); Chris Jericho defeated Shawn Michaels in a Ladder Match in 22:20 (★★★★★).

Bound For Glory '08 ★★★
12-10-08, Hoffman Estates, Illinois TNA

Jay Lethal won a Steel Asylum Match in 12:07 (★★★); ODB, Rhaka Khan and Rhino defeated The Beautiful People (Angelina Love, Cute Kip and Velvet Sky) in a Bimbo Brawl Match in 6:15 (★); Sheik Abdul Bashir defeated Consequences Creed in 9:18 (★★); Taylor Wilde defeated Awesome Kong and Roxxi in a Three Way Match in 5:11 (★★); Beer Money Inc. (James Storm and Robert Roode) defeated Abyss and Matt Morgan, The Latin American Xchange (Homicide and Hernandez), Team 3D (Brother Ray and Brother Devon) in a Monster's Ball Match in 20:20 (★★★); Booker T defeated AJ Styles and Christian Cage in a Three Way War Match in 13:05 (★★★); Jeff Jarrett defeated Kurt Angle in 20:07 (★★★); Sting defeated Samoa Joe to win the TNA World Heavyweight Title in 16:54 (★★).

Cyber Sunday '08 ★★★
26-10-08, Phoenix, Arizona WWE

Rey Mysterio defeated Kane in a No Holds Barred Match in 10:17 (★★); Matt Hardy defeated Evan Bourne in 11:01 (★★★); John Morrison and The Miz defeated Cryme Tyme (JTG and Shad Gaspard) in 10:22 (★★); The Honky Tonk Man defeated Santino Marella by DQ in 1:06 (★★); The Undertaker defeated The Big Show in a Last Man Standing Match in 19:23 (★★); Triple H defeated Jeff Hardy in 15:37 (★★★); Batista defeated Chris Jericho to win the World Heavyweight Title in 17:06 (★★★).

Turning Point '08 ★★★★
09-11-08, Orlando, Florida TNA

Eric Young defeated Consequences Creed, Doug Williams, Homicide, Jay Lethal, Jimmy Rave, Petey Williams, Sonjay Dutt, Hiroshi Tanahashi and Volador in a Ten Man Elimination Match in 17:15 (★★★); Roxxi and Taylor Wilde defeated Awesome Kong and Raisha Saeed in 16:30 (★★); Sheik Abdul Bashir in 8:20 (★★); Beer Money Inc. (James Storm and Robert Roode) defeated The Motor City Machine Guns (Alex Shelley and Chris Sabin) in 16:30 (★★★); Booker T defeated Christian Cage in 12:00 (★★); Kurt Angle defeated Abyss in a Falls Count Anywhere Match in 17:00 (★★★★); Kevin Nash defeated Samoa Joe in 11:30 (★★); Sting defeated AJ Styles in 14:45 (★★★).

Driven '08 ★★★
14-11-08, Boston, Massachusetts ROH

Austin Aries defeated Delirious in 6:45 (★★); Sara Del Rey defeated Jessie McKay in :40 (★); Brent Albright and Erick Stevens defeated Sweet and Sour Inc. (Adam Pearce and Eddie Edwards) in 4:04 (★★); Chris Hero defeated Jerry Lynn in 9:20 (★★★); Bryan Danielson defeated Claudio Castagnoli and Go Shiozaki in a Three Way Elimination Match in 14:25 (★★★); The Briscoe Brothers (Jay Briscoe and Mark Briscoe) defeated The Vulture Squad (Ruckus and Jigsaw), The YRR (Jason Blade and Kenny King), and Necro Butcher in a Scramble Match in 6:20 (★★); Nigel McGuinness defeated Roderick Strong in 24:19 (★★★★); Kevin Steen and El Generico defeated The Age Of The Fall (Jimmy Jacobs and Tyler Black) to win the ROH World Tag Team Title in 20:27 (★★★★).

Survivor Series '08 ★★
23-11-08, Boston, Massachusetts WWE

Team HBK (Shawn Michaels, The Great Khali, Rey Mysterio, JTG and Shad Gaspard) defeated Team JBL (John Bradshaw Layfield, John Morrison, Kane, The Miz and MVP) in an Elimination Match in 18:13 (★★★); Team Raw (Beth Phoenix, Candice Michelle, Jillian Hall, Kelly Kelly and Mickie James) defeated Team SmackDown (Maria, Maryse, Michelle McCool, Natalya and Victoria) in an Elimination Match in 9:39 (★); The Undertaker defeated The Big Show in a Casket Match in 12:45 (★★); Team Orton (Randy Orton, Cody Rhodes, Mark Henry, Shelton Benjamin and William Regal) defeated Team Batista (Batista, CM Punk, Kofi Kingston, Matt Hardy and R-Truth) in an Elimination Match in 16:13 (★★★); Edge defeated Vladimir Kozlov and Triple H in a Three Way Match to win the WWE Title in 14:22 (★★); John Cena defeated Chris Jericho to win the World Heavyweight Title in 21:19 (★★★).

Final Resolution '08 (December) ★★
07-12-08, Orlando, Florida TNA

Curry Man, Hernandez, Homicide and Jay Lethal won a Feast Or Fired Battle Royal in 12:10 (★★★); ODB, Roxxi and Taylor Wilde defeated The Beautiful People (Angelina Love and Velvet

Sky) and Sharmell in 7:27 (★★); Eric Young defeated Sheik Abdul Bashir to win the TNA X Division Title in 8:05 (★★); Christy Hemme defeated Awesome Kong by DQ in 5:05 (★★); Beer Money Inc. (James Storm and Robert Roode) defeated Abyss and Matt Morgan in 11:35 (★★); Kurt Angle defeated Rhino in 14:34 (★★); The Main Event Mafia (Booker T, Kevin Nash, Scott Steiner and Sting) defeated The TNA Front Line (AJ Styles, Brother Ray, Brother Devon and Samoa Joe) in 21:24 (★★★).

Armageddon '08 ★★★
14-12-08, Buffalo, New York **WWE**

Vladimir Kozlov defeated Matt Hardy in 9:02 (★★); CM Punk defeated Rey Mysterio in 12:15 (★★★); Finlay defeated Mark Henry in a Belfast Brawl in 9:38 (★★); Batista and Randy Orton in 16:41 (★★); Michelle McCool, Maria, Kelly Kelly and Mickie James defeated Maryse, Jillian Hall, Victoria and Natalya in a Santa's Little Helper Match in 4:33 (★★); John Cena defeated Chris Jericho in 12:43 (★★); Jeff Hardy defeated Edge and Triple H in a Three Way Match to win the WWE Title in 17:19 (★★★★).

Tribute To The Troops '08 ★★
20-12-08, Baghdad, Iraq **WWE**

CM Punk, Jeff Hardy and R-Truth defeated John Bradshaw Layfield, John Morrison and The Miz in 7:41 (★★); Batista, John Cena and Rey Mysterio defeated The Big Show, Chris Jericho and Randy Orton in 9:50 (★★).

All Star Extravaganza IV ★★★★
26-12-08, Philadelphia, Pennsylvania **ROH**

Kenny Omega defeated Rhett Titus in 7:42 (★★); Chris Hero defeated Erick Stevens in 9:39 (★★); Kensuke Office (Katsuhiko Nakajima and Kensuke Sasaki) defeated Brent Albright and Roderick Strong in 16:02 (★★★★); Takeshi Morishima defeated Go Shiozaki in 11:31 (★★★); The Briscoe Brothers (Jay Briscoe and Mark Briscoe) defeated The American Wolves (Davey Richards and Eddie Edwards), and Claudio Castagnoli and Nigel McGuinness in a Three Way Elimination Match in 18:58 (★★★); Naomichi Marufuji defeated Austin Aries in 20:07 (★★★★); The Age Of The Fall (Delirious, Jimmy Jacobs and Tyler Black) defeated El Generico, Kevin Steen and Necro Butcher in 16:22 (★★★); Bryan Danielson defeated Jerry Lynn in 27:28 (★★★★).

Final Battle '08 ★★★★★
27-12-08, New York City, New York **ROH**

Kenny Omega defeated Claudio Castagnoli in 6:59 (★★★); Jerry Lynn defeated Chris Hero, Necro Butcher and Rhett Titus in a Four Corner Survival Match in 12:50 (★★★); El Generico and Kevin Steen defeated The Age Of The Fall (Delirious and Jimmy Jacobs) in 13:39 (★★); Brent Albright, Erick Stevens and Roderick Strong defeated The Sweet 'n' Sour Inc. (Davey Richards, Eddie Edwards and Go Shiozaki) in a Street Fight in 14:33 (★★); The Briscoe Brothers (Jay Briscoe and Mark Briscoe) defeated Kensuke Office (Katsuhiko Nakajima and Kensuke Sasaki) in 16:49 (★★★); Austin Aries defeated Tyler Black in 17:09 (★★★); Nigel McGuinness defeated Naomichi Marufuji in 18:16 (★★★★); Bryan Danielson defeated Takeshi Morishima in a Fight Without Honor in 18:55 (★★★★★).

Genesis '09 ★★★
11-01-09, Charlotte, North Carolina **TNA**

Eric Young and The Latin American Xchange (Homicide and Hernandez) defeated Jimmy Rave, Kiyoshi and Sonjay Dutt in an Elimination Match in 13;43 (★★); Alex Shelley defeated Chris Sabin to win the vacant TNA X Division Title in 16:38 (★★★★); Shane Sewell defeated Sheik Abdul Bashir in 10:18 (★★); Beer Money Inc. (James Storm and Robert Roode) defeated Consequences Creed and Jay Lethal, and Abyss and Matt Morgan in a Three Way Match to win the TNA World Tag Team Title in 15:19 (★★); ODB, Roxxi and Taylor Wilde defeated The Kongtourage (Raisha Saeed, Rhaka Khan and Sojournor Bolt) in 7:44 (★); Kurt Angle defeated Jeff Jarrett in a No DQ Match in 21:59 (★★★); Sting defeated Rhino in 8:18 (★★); Mick Foley, AJ Styles and Brother Devon defeated Cute Kip and The Main Event Mafia (Booker T and Scott Steiner) in a Hardcore Match in 14:02 (★★).

Rising Above '09 ★★★★
16-01-09, Chicago Ridge, Illinois **ROH**

Kevin Steen and El Generico defeated The Briscoe Brothers (Jay Briscoe and Mark Briscoe) in 6:39 (★★); MsChif defeated Sara Del Rey in 9:11 (★★); Claudio Castagnoli defeated Sami Callihan, Silas Young and Alex Payne in a Four Corner Survival Match in 8:54 (★★); Sweet and Sour Inc. (Chris Hero, Go Shiozaki and Davey Richards) defeated Roderick Strong, Brent Albright and Ace Steel in 16:15 (★★★); Austin Aries defeated Jimmy Jacobs in an "I Quit" Match in 22:08 (★★★★); Nigel McGuinness defeated Bryan Danielson in 28:16 (★★★★).

Royal Rumble '09 ★★★
25-01-09, Detroit, Michigan **WWE**

Jack Swagger defeated Matt Hardy in 10:27 (★★★); Melina defeated Beth Phoenix to win the WWE Women's Title in 5:56 (★★); John Cena defeated John Bradshaw Layfield in 15:29 (★★); Edge defeated Jeff Hardy in a No DQ Match to win the WWE Title in 19:23 (★★★); Randy Orton won the 30-Man Royal Rumble Match in 58:37 (★★★).

Against All Odds '09 ★★
08-02-09, Orlando, Florida **TNA**

Alex Shelley defeated Eric Young in 13:01 (★★); Scott Steiner defeated Petey Williams in 11:17 (★★); Brutus Magnus defeated Chris Sabin in 6:38 (★★); Awesome Kong defeated ODB in 5:39 (★★); Booker T defeated Shane Sewell in 6:01 (★★); Abyss defeated Matt Morgan in 15:37 (★★); Beer Money Inc. (James Storm and Robert Roode) defeated Lethal Consequences (Consequences Creed and Jay Lethal) in 15:41 (★★★); Sting defeated Brother Ray, Brother Devon and Kurt Angle in a Four Way Match in 14:34 (★★).

No Way Out '09 ★★★★
15-02-09, Seattle, Washington **WWE**

Triple H defeated The Undertaker, Jeff Hardy, The Big Show, Vladimir Kozlov and Edge in an Elimination Chamber Match to win the WWE Title in 35:55 (★★★★); Randy Orton defeated Shane McMahon in a No Holds Barred Match in 18:16 (★★★); Jack Swagger defeated Finlay in 7:53 (★★); Shawn Michaels defeated John Bradshaw Layfield in 13:17 (★★); Edge defeated Rey Mysterio, Chris Jericho, John Cena, Mike Knox and Kane in an Elimination Chamber Match to win the World Heavyweight Title in 29:46 (★★★★).

Destination X '09 ★★
15-03-09, Orlando, Florida **TNA**

The Governor, Roxxi and Taylor Wilde defeated The Beautiful People (Angelina Love, Madison Rayne and Velvet Sky) in 5:04 (★★); Brutus Magnus defeated Eric Young in 4:45 (★★); Matt Morgan defeated Abyss in a Match Of 10,000 Tacks in 8:48 (★★); Awesome Kong defeated Sojourner Bolt in 4:17 (★★); Scott Steiner defeated Samoa Joe by DQ in 1:30 (★); AJ Styles defeated Booker T to win the TNA Legends Title in 9:14 (★★★); Team 3D (Brother Ray and Brother Devon) defeated Beer Money Inc. (James Storm and Robert Roode) via count out in a No DQ Off The Wagon Challenge Match in 11:20 (★★); Suicide defeated Alex Shelley, Chris Sabin, Consequences Creed and Jay Lethal in an Ultimate X Match to win the TNA X Division Title in 14:10 (★★★); Sting defeated Kurt Angle in 13:50 (★).

7th Anniversary Show ★★★★
21-03-09, New York City, New York **ROH**

Erick Stevens and Roderick Strong defeated Kenny King and Rhett Titus in 8:51 (★★); Brent Albright defeated Claudio Castagnoli by DQ in 17:41 (★★★); Bobby Dempsey defeated Adam Pearce in :25 (★); Jerry Lynn defeated Mike Quackenbush in 9:35 (★★); Delirious, Necro Butcher and Tyler Black defeated Austin Aries and The Age Of The Fall (Brodie Lee and Jimmy Jacobs) in a Endurance Elimination Match in 20:53 (★★★); Bryan Danielson and Colt Cabana defeated The Embassy (Bison Smith and Jimmy Rave) in 10:04 (★★★); D-Lo Brown defeated Jay Briscoe in 12:44 (★★); El Generico and Kevin Steen defeated The American Wolves (Davey Richards and Eddie Edwards) in a No DQ Match in 15:14 (★★★); Nigel McGuinness defeated Kenta in 25:19 (★★★★).

Supercard Of Honor IV ★★★★
03-04-09, Houston, Texas **ROH**

Erick Stevens defeated Rhett Titus in 6:46 (★★); Incognito and Sweet 'n' Sour Inc. (Chris Hero and Eddie Edwards) defeated Jay Briscoe, Kevin Steen and Magno in 15:22 (★★); Roderick

Strong defeated Katsuhiko Nakajima in 9:31 (★ ★); Claudio Castagnoli defeated Blue Demon Jr., Brent Albright and El Generico in a Four Corner Survival Match in 9:14 (★ ★); Bryan Danielson defeated Alex Koslov in 15:16 (★ ★ ★); D-Lo Brown defeated Colt Cabana in 11:03 (★ ★); Kenta defeated Davey Richards in 18:18 (★ ★ ★ ★); Austin Aries and Jimmy Jacobs defeated Necro Butcher and Tyler Black in 10:58 (★ ★ ★); Jerry Lynn defeated Nigel McGuinness to win the NWA World Heavyweight title in 19:08 (★ ★ ★ ★).

WrestleMania XXV ★ ★ ★
05-04-09, Houston, Texas WWE
CM Punk defeated Christian, Finlay, Kane, Kofi Kingston, Mark Henry, MVP and Shelton Benjamin in a Money In The Bank Ladder Match in 14:30 (★ ★ ★); Santina Marella won a Battle Royal in 7:30 (★); Chris Jericho defeated Jimmy Snuka, Roddy Piper and Ricky Steamboat in a Handicap Elimination Match in 8:30 (★ ★); Matt Hardy defeated Jeff Hardy in an Extreme Rules Match in 13:33 (★ ★); Rey Mysterio defeated John Bradshaw Layfield to win the WWE Intercontinental Title in :22 (★); The Undertaker defeated Shawn Michaels in 30:30 (★ ★ ★ ★ ★); John Cena defeated The Big Show and Edge in a Three Way Match to win the World Heavyweight Title in 14:14 (★ ★); Triple H defeated Randy Orton in 24:24 (★ ★).

Caged Collision ★ ★ ★
17-04-09, Chicago Ridge, Illinois ROH
Alex Payne defeated Kenny King and Silas Young in a Three Way Match in 7:11 (★ ★); Claudio Castagnoli defeated Kevin Steen in 9:05 (★ ★); Jerry Lynn and Necro Butcher defeated The Age Of The Fall (Brodie Lee and Delirious) in 11:39 (★ ★); Tyler Black defeated Austin Aries, Bryan Danielson and Jimmy Jacobs in a Four Corner Survival Match in 19:51 (★ ★ ★); Nigel McGuinness defeated El Generico in 17:06 (★ ★ ★ ★); Ace Steel, Brent Albright, Erick Stevens, Jay Briscoe and Roderick Strong defeated Sweet and Sour Inc. (Adam Pearce, Bobby Dempsey, Davey Richards, Eddie Edwards and Tank Toland) in a Steel Cage Warfare Match in 17:24 (★ ★ ★).

Lockdown '09 ★ ★
19-04-09, Philadelphia, Pennsylvania TNA
Suicide defeated Consequences Creed, Kiyoshi, Jay Lethal and Sheik Abdul Bashir in an Xscape Match in 11:37 (★ ★); ODB defeated Daffney, Madison Rayne and Sohournor Bolt in a Queen Of The Cage Match in 6:05 (★ ★); The Motor City Machine Guns (Alex Shelley and Chris Sabin) defeated The Latin American Xchange (Homicide and Hernandez) and No Limit (Naito and Yujiro) in a Three Way Six Sides Of Steel Match in 11:49 (★ ★); Matt Morgan defeated Abyss in a Doomsday Chamber Of Blood Match in 12:26 (★ ★); Angelina Love defeated Awesome Kong and Taylor Wilde in a Three Way Six Sides Of Steel Match to win the TNA Knockouts Title in 6:53 (★ ★); Team 3D (Brother Ray and Brother Devon) defeated Beer Money Inc. (James Storm and Robert Roode) in a Philadelphia Street Fight to win the TNA World Tag Team Title in 14:59 (★ ★ ★); Team Jarrett (Jeff Jarrett, AJ Styles, Christopher Daniels and Samoa Joe) defeated Team Angle (Kurt Angle, Booker T, Kevin Nash and Scott Steiner) in a Lethal Lockdown Match in 23:01 (★ ★); Mick Foley defeated Sting in a Six Sides Of Steel Match to win the TNA World Heavyweight Title in 15:54 (★ ★).

Backlash '09 ★ ★ ★
26-04-09, Providence, Rhode Island WWE
Christian defeated Jack Swagger to win the ECW World Title in 11:01 (★ ★ ★); Chris Jericho defeated Ricky Steamboat in 12:32 (★ ★ ★); Kane defeated CM Punk in 9:25 (★ ★); Jeff Hardy defeated Matt Hardy in an "I Quit" Match in 19:08 (★ ★ ★); Santino Marella defeated Beth Phoenix in :03 (★ ★); Legacy (Cody Rhodes, Randy Orton and Ted DiBiase) defeated Batista, Shane McMahon and Triple H in 22:50. As a result, Randy Orton won the WWE Title (★ ★ ★); Edge defeated John Cena in a Last Man Standing Match in 28:26 (★ ★ ★ ★).

Judgment Day '09 ★ ★ ★ ★
17-05-09, Rosemont, Illinois WWE
Umaga defeated CM Punk in 11:52 (★ ★); Christian defeated Jack Swagger in 9:33 (★ ★); John Morrison defeated Shelton Benjamin in 10:10 (★ ★ ★); Rey Mysterio defeated Chris Jericho in 12:39 (★ ★ ★ ★); Batista defeated Randy Orton by DQ in 14:44 (★ ★ ★); John Cena defeated The Big Show in 14:57 (★ ★); Edge defeated Jeff Hardy in 19:56 (★ ★ ★ ★).

Sacrifice '09 ★ ★ ★
24-05-09, Orlando, Florida TNA
Eric Young and Lethal Consequences (Jay Lethal and Consequences Creed) defeated The Motor City Machine Guns (Alex Shelley and Chris Sabin) and Sheik Abdul Bashir in 13:54 (★ ★); Taylor Wilde defeated Daffney in a Monster's Ball Match in 3:33 (★ ★); Suicide vs. Christopher Daniels ended in a draw in 17:06 (★ ★); Angelina Love defeated Awesome Kong in 5:56 (★ ★); Samoa Joe defeated Kevin Nash in 8:01 (★ ★); Beer Money Inc. (James Storm and Robert Roode) defeated The British Invasion (Brutus Magnus and Doug Williams) in 10:44 (★ ★ ★); AJ Styles defeated Booker T in an "I Quit" Match in 14:56 (★ ★ ★); Sting defeated Jeff Jarrett, Kurt Angle and Mick Foley in a Four Way Ultimate Sacrifice Match in 14:56 (★ ★).

Extreme Rules '09 ★ ★ ★
07-06-09, New Orleans, Louisiana WWE
Kofi Kingston defeated MVP, William Regal and Matt Hardy in a Four Way Match in 6:42 (★ ★); Chris Jericho defeated Rey Mysterio in a No Holds Barred Match to win the WWE Intercontinental Title in 14:43 (★ ★ ★ ★); CM Punk defeated Umaga in a Samoan Strap Match in 8:59 (★ ★); Tommy Dreamer defeated Jack Swagger and Christian in a Three Way Hardcore Match to win the ECW World Title in 9:38 (★ ★); Santina Marella defeated Chavo Guerrero and Vickie Guerrero in a Handicap Hog Pen Match in 2:43 (★); Batista defeated Randy Orton in a Steel Cage Match to win the WWE Title in 7:03 (★ ★); John Cena defeated The Big Show in a Submission Match in 19:06 (★ ★); Jeff Hardy defeated Edge in a Ladder Match to win the World Heavyweight Title in 20:07 (★ ★ ★ ★); CM Punk defeated Jeff Hardy to win the World Heavyweight Title in 1:02 (★ ★).

Take No Prisoners '09 ★ ★ ★
12-06-09, Houston, Texas ROH
Colt Cabana defeated Ace Steel in 9:20 (★ ★); El Generico, Kevin Steen, Jay Briscoe and Magno defeated Sweet and Sour Inc. (Chris Hero, Davey Richards and Eddie Edwards) and Incognito 9:27 (★ ★ ★); Necro Butcher defeated Jimmy Jacobs in a No DQ Match in 14:53 (★ ★); Brent Albright defeated Blue Demon Jr. and Claudio Castagnoli in a Three Way Match in 5:38 (★ ★); Roderick Strong defeated Alex Koslov in 7:40 (★ ★); Jerry Lynn defeated Bryan Danielson, D-Lo Brown and Erick Stevens in a Four Way Match in 8:10 (★ ★ ★); Kenta and Tyler Black defeated Austin Aries and Katsuhiko Nakajima in 22:15 (★ ★ ★ ★).

Manhattan Mayhem III ★ ★ ★
13-06-09, New York City, New York ROH
The Young Bucks (Matt Jackson and Nick Jackson) defeated Kenny King and Rhett Titus in 8:51 (★ ★); Necro Butcher defeated Jimmy Rave in 6:04 (★ ★); Roderick Strong defeated Sonjay Dutt in 12:52 (★ ★); Jimmy Jacobs defeated Tyler Black in a First Blood Match in :12 (★); Colt Cabana defeated Bryan Danielson, Claudio Castagnoli and D-Lo Brown in a Four Corner Survival Match in 9:48 (★ ★); The American Wolves (Davey Richards and Eddie Edwards) defeated El Generico and Kevin Steen in a Submission Match in 18:42 (★ ★ ★ ★); Jay Briscoe defeated Guido Maritato in 7:29 (★ ★); Austin Aries defeated Jerry Lynn and Tyler Black in a Three Way Elimination Match to win the ROH World Title in 20:02 (★ ★ ★ ★).

Slammiversary VII ★ ★ ★
21-06-09, Auburn Hills, Michigan TNA
Suicide defeated Consequences Creed, Alex Shelley, Chris Sabin and Jay Lethal in a King Of The Mountain Match in 23:46 (★ ★ ★); Christopher Daniels defeated Shane Douglas in 8:12 (★ ★); Angelina Love defeated Tara in 6:51 (★ ★); Abyss and Taylor Wilde defeated Daffney and Raven in a Monster's Ball Match in 14:07 (★ ★ ★); Sting defeated Matt Morgan in 8:59 (★ ★); Beer Money Inc. (James Storm and Robert Roode) defeated Team 3D (Brother Ray and Brother Devon) to win the TNA World Tag Team Title in 16:55 (★ ★); Kurt Angle defeated Mick Foley, AJ Styles, Jeff Jarrett and Samoa Joe in a King Of The Mountain Match to win the TNA World Heavyweight Title in 22:04 (★ ★ ★).

The Bash '09 ★ ★
28-06-09, Sacramento, California WWE
Tommy Dreamer defeated Christian, Finlay, Jack Swagger and Mark Henry in a Championship Scramble Match in 14:46 (★ ★); Rey Mysterio defeated Chris Jericho in a Title vs. Mask Match to

win the WWE Intercontinental Title in 15:42 (★★★); Dolph Ziggler defeated The Great Khali in a No DQ Match in 4:59 (★★); Chris Jericho and Edge defeated The Colons (Carlito and Primo) and Legacy (Cody Rhodes and Ted DiBiase) in a Three Way Match to win the Unified WWE Tag Team Title in 9:37 (★★); Michelle McCool defeated Melina to win the WWE Women's Title in 6:34 (★★); Jeff Hardy defeated CM Punk by DQ in 15:01 (★★); John Cena defeated The Miz in 5:39 (★★); Randy Orton defeated Triple H in a Three Stages Of Hell Match in 21:23 (★★).

Victory Road '09 ★
19-07-09, Orlando, Florida TNA
Angelina Love defeated Tara to win the TNA Knockouts Title in 7:02 (★★); Matt Morgan defeated Christopher Daniels in 10:31 (★★); Abyss defeated Dr. Stevie in a No DQ Match in 9:51 (★); Team 3D (Brother Ray and Brother Devon) defeated The British Invasion (Brutus Magnus and Doug Williams) in 10:16 (★★); Jenna Morasca defeated Sharmell in 5:49 (★); Kevin Nash defeated AJ Styles to win the TNA Legends Title in 14:07 (★★); The Main Event Mafia (Booker T and Scott Steiner) defeated Beer Money Inc. (James Storm and Robert Roode) to win the TNA World Tag Team Title in 12:29 (★★); Samoa Joe defeated Sting in 11:36 (★★); Kurt Angle defeated Mick Foley in 14:06 (★★).

Death Before Dishonor VII Day #1 ★★★
24-07-09, Toronto, Canada ROH
El Generico vs. Sonjay Dutt ended in a draw in 15:00 (★★★); The Briscoe Brothers (Jay Briscoe and Mark Briscoe) defeated The Super Smash Brothers (Player Dos and Player Uno) in 12:38 (★★); D-Lo Brown defeated Franky The Mobster in 6:18 (★★); The Embassy (Bison Smith, Claudio Castagnoli, Jimmy Rave and Joey Ryan) defeated Brent Albright, Colt Cabana, Grizzly Redwood and Necro Butcher in an Elimination Match in 30:29 (★★); Kenny Omega defeated Kenny King in 11:39 (★★★); Kevin Steen and Lance Storm defeated Chris Hero and Davey Richards in 20:02 (★★★); Austin Aries defeated Jerry Lynn, Nigel McGuinness and Tyler Black in a Four Corner Survival Match in 16:08 (★★★).

Death Before Dishonor VII Day #2 ★★★
25-07-09, Toronto, Canada ROH
The Super Smash Brothers (Player Dos and Player Uno) defeated El Generico and Kevin Steen in 14:01 (★★★); Franky The Mobster defeated Bison Smith by DQ in 8:09 (★★); Davey Richards defeated Jerry Lynn, D-Lo Brown, Sonjay Dutt, Jimmy Rave and Necro Butcher in a Gauntlet Match in 21:19 (★★★); Claudio Castagnoli defeated Brent Albright in a European Rules Match in 11:24 (★★); Tyler Black defeated Tyson Dux in 9:13 (★★); Colt Cabana defeated Joey Ryan in a No Rules Match in 12:32 (★★); Kenny Omega and The Briscoe Brothers (Jay Briscoe and Mark Briscoe) defeated Austin Aries, Kenny King and Rhett Titus in 16:10 (★★★); Chris Hero defeated Lance Storm in 16:46 (★★★).

Night Of Champions '09 ★★★
26-07-09, Philadelphia, Pennsylvania WWE
Jeri-Show (The Big Show and Chris Jericho) defeated Legacy (Cody Rhodes and Ted DiBiase) in 9:32 (★★); Christian defeated Tommy Dreamer to win the ECW World Title in 8:28 (★★); Kofi Kingston defeated Carlito, Jack Swagger, The Miz, MVP and Primo in a Six Pack Challenge in 8:35 (★★★); Michelle McCool defeated Melina in 6:12 (★★); Randy Orton defeated John Cena and Triple H in a Three Way Match in 22:19 (★★); Mickie James defeated Maryse to win the WWE Divas Title in 8:36 (★★); Rey Mysterio defeated Dolph Ziggler in 14:20 (★★★); Jeff Hardy defeated CM Punk to win the World Heavyweight Title in 14:56 (★★★★).

Hard Justice '09 ★★
16-08-09, Orlando, Florida TNA
Christopher Daniels won a Steel Asylum Match in 16:33 (★★★); Abyss defeated Jethro Holliday in a $50,000 Bounty Challenge in 8:49 (★★); Hernandez defeated Rob Terry in :09 (★); The British Invasion (Brutus Magnus and Doug Williams) defeated Beer Money Inc. (James Storm and Robert Roode) in 8:45 (★★); Cody Deaner and ODB defeated The Beautiful People (Angelina Love and Velvet Sky) in 7:26 (★★); Samoa Joe defeated Homicide to win the TNA X Division Title in 8:56 (★★); The Main Event Mafia (Booker T and Scott Steiner) defeated Team 3D (Brother Ray and Brother Devon) in a Falls Count Anywhere Match in 13:08 (★★); Kevin Nash defeated

Mick Foley to win the TNA Legends Title in 10:38 (★★); Kurt Angle defeated Matt Morgan and Sting in a Three Way Match in 11:22 (★★).

SummerSlam '09 ★★★
23-08-09, Los Angeles, California WWE
Rey Mysterio defeated Dolph Ziggler in 12:25 (★★★); MVP defeated Jack Swagger in 6:23 (★★); Jeri-Show (Chris Jericho and The Big Show) defeated Cryme Tyme and Shad Gaspard) in 9:45 (★★); Kane defeated The Great Khali in 6:00 (★); D-Generation X (Shawn Michaels and Triple H) defeated Legacy (Cody Rhodes and Ted DiBiase) in 20:00 (★★★★); Christian defeated William Regal in :07 (★); Randy Orton defeated John Cena in 20:45 (★★); CM Punk defeated Jeff Hardy in a TLC Match to win the World Heavyweight Title in 21:35 (★★★★).

Breaking Point '09 ★★
13-09-09, Montreal, Quebec WWE
Jeri-Show (Chris Jericho and The Big Show) defeated The World's Strongest Tag Team (Mark Henry and MVP) in 12:13 (★★); Kofi Kingston defeated The Miz in 11:56 (★★); Legacy (Cody Rhodes and Ted DiBiase) defeated D-Generation X (Shawn Michaels and Triple H) in a Submissions Count Anywhere Match in 21:40 (★★★); Kane defeated The Great Khali in a Singapore Cane Match in 5:50 (★); Christian defeated William Regal in 10:15 (★); John Cena defeated Randy Orton in an "I Quit" Match to win the WWE Title in 19:46 (★★★); CM Punk defeated The Undertaker in 8:52 (★★).

No Surrender '09 ★★★
20-09-09, Orlando, Florida TNA
Sarita and Taylor Wilde defeated The Beautiful People (Madison Rayne and Velvet Sky) to win the vacant TNA Knockouts Tag Team Title in 4:55 (★★); Hernandez defeated Eric Young in :48 (★); Samoa Joe defeated Christopher Daniels in 13:47 (★★★); D'Angelo Dinero defeated Suicide in 12:14 (★★); ODB defeated Cody Deaner to win the vacant TNA Knockouts Title in 7:14 (★★); Kevin Nash defeated Abyss in a $50,000 Bounty Challenge in 8:23 (★★); Beer Money Inc. (James Storm and Robert Roode) and Team 3D (Brother Ray and Brother Devon) defeated The Main Event Mafia (Booker T and Scott Steiner) and The British Invasion (Brutus Magnus and Doug Williams) in a Lethal Lockdown Match in 21:27 (★★★); Bobby Lashley defeated Rhino in 7:04 (★★); AJ Styles defeated Hernandez, Kurt Angle, Matt Morgan and Sting in a Five Way Dance to win the TNA World Heavyweight Title in 15:10 (★★★).

Glory By Honor VIII ★★★★
26-09-09, New York City, New York ROH
Colt Cabana defeated Rhett Titus in 6:24 (★★); The Dark City Fight Club (Jon Davis and Kory Chavis) defeated Up In Smoke (Cheech and Cloudy) in 9:43 (★★); Claudio Castagnoli defeated Kenny Omega in 9:36 (★★★); Roderick Strong defeated Delirious, Grizzly Redwood and Sonjay Dutt in a Four Corner Survival Match in 11:53 (★★★); The American Wolves (Davey Richards and Eddie Edwards) defeated El Generico and Kevin Steen in a Ladder War in 25:05 (★★★★); Chris Hero defeated Eddie Kingston in 16:09 (★★); Austin Aries defeated Petey Williams via count out in 19:52 (★★★); The Young Bucks (Matt Jackson and Nick Jackson) defeated The Briscoe Brothers (Jay Briscoe and Mark Briscoe) in 17:04 (★★★); Bryan Danielson defeated Nigel McGuinness in 28:25 (★★★★).

Hell In A Cell '09 ★★★
04-10-09, Newark, New Jersey WWE
The Undertaker defeated CM Punk in a Hell In A Cell Match to win the World Heavyweight Title in 10:24 (★★); John Morrison defeated Dolph Ziggler in 15:41 (★★★); Mickie James defeated Alicia Fox in 5:20 (★★); Jeri-Show (Chris Jericho and The Big Show) defeated Batista and Rey Mysterio in 13:41 (★★); Randy Orton defeated John Cena in a Hell In A Cell Match to win the WWE Title in 21:24 (★★★); Drew McIntyre defeated R-Truth in 4:38 (★★); Kofi Kingston defeated Jack Swagger and The Miz in a Three Way Match in 7:53 (★★); D-Generation X (Shawn Michaels and Triple H) defeated Legacy (Cody Rhodes and Ted DiBiase) in a Hell In A Cell Match in 17:54 (★★★★).

Survival Of The Fittest '09 ★★★
10-10-09, Indianapolis, Indiana **ROH**

The Young Bucks (Matt Jackson and Nick Jackson) defeated The House Of Truth (Christin Able and Josh Raymond) in 12:07 (★★); Colt Cabana defeated Kevin Steen in 6:48 (★★); Roderick Strong defeated Rhett Titus in 8:29 (★★); Tyler Black defeated Kenny King in 12:32 (★★); Claudio Castagnoli defeated Petey Williams in 9:48 (★★); Chris Hero defeated Kenny Omega in 12:48 (★★); The Briscoe Brothers (Jay Briscoe and Mark Briscoe) defeated Austin Aries and Davey Richards in 18:31 (★★★); Tyler Black defeated Chris Hero, Claudio Castagnoli, Colt Cabana, Delirious and Roderick Strong win the Survival Of The Fittest Tournament in 39:56 (★★★).

Bound For Glory '09 ★★★
18-10-09, Irvine, California **TNA**

Amazing Red defeated Alex Shelley, Chris Sabin, Christopher Daniels, Homicide and Suicide in an Ultimate X Match in 15:17 (★★★); Sarita and Taylor Wilde defeated The Beautiful People (Madison Rayne and Velvet Sky) in 2:58 (★★); Eric Young defeated Kevin Nash and Hernandez in a Three Way Match to win the TNA Legends Title in 8:50 (★★); The British Invasion (Brutus Magnus and Doug Williams) defeated Team 3D (Brother Ray and Brother Devon), The Main Event Mafia (Booker T and Scott Steiner), and Beer Money Inc. (James Storm and Robert Roode) in a Full Metal Mayhem Match to win the TNA World Tag Team Title in 17:13 (★★); ODB defeated Awesome Kong and Tara in a Three Way Match in 7:29 (★★); Bobby Lashley defeated Samoa Joe in 8:07 (★★); Abyss defeated Mick Foley in a Monster's Ball Match in 11:03 (★★★); Kurt Angle defeated Matt Morgan in 14:45 (★★★); AJ Styles defeated Sting in 13:52 (★★).

Bragging Rights '09 ★★★
25-10-09, Pittsburgh, Pennsylvania **WWE**

The Miz defeated John Morrison in 10:54 (★★★); Beth Phoenix, Michelle McCool and Natalya defeated Gail Kim, Kelly Kelly and Melina in 6:54 (★★); The Undertaker defeated Batista, CM Punk and Rey Mysterio in a Four Way Match in 9:55 (★★★); Team SmackDown (Chris Jericho, David Hart Smith, Finlay, Kane, Matt Hardy, R-Truth and Tyson Kidd) defeated Team Raw (The Big Show, Cody Rhodes, Jack Swagger, Kofi Kingston, Mark Henry, Shawn Michaels and Triple H) in 15:34 (★★★); John Cena defeated Randy Orton 6-5 in an Iron Man Match in 60:00 (★★★).

Turning Point '09 ★★★★
15-11-09, Orlando, Florida **TNA**

Amazing Red defeated Homicide in 10:08 (★★★); ODB, Sarita and Taylor Wilde defeated The Beautiful People (Lacey Von Erich, Madison Rayne and Velvet Sky) in 5:54 (★★); The British Invasion (Brutus Magnus and Doug Williams) defeated The Motor City Machine Guns (Alex Shelley and Chris Sabin) and Beer Money Inc. (James Storm and Robert Roode) in a Three Way Match in 10:20 (★★★); Tara defeated Awesome Kong in a Six Sides Of Steel Match in 7:53 (★★★); Team 3D (Brother Ray and Brother Devon) and Rhino defeated D'Angelo Dinero, Hernandez and Matt Morgan in a Street Fight in 14:27 (★★★); Scott Steiner defeated Bobby Lashley in a Falls Count Anywhere Match in 11:27 (★★); Kurt Angle defeated Desmond Wolfe in 16:21 (★★★); AJ Styles defeated Christopher Daniels and Samoa Joe in a Three Way Match in 21:50 (★★★★★).

Survivor Series '09 ★★★
22-11-09, Washington, D.C. **WWE**

Team Miz (The Miz, Dolph Ziggler, Drew McIntyre, Jack Swagger and Sheamus) defeated Team Morrison (John Morrison, Evan Bourne, Finlay, Matt Hardy and Shelton Benjamin) in an Elimination Match in 20:52 (★★); Batista defeated Rey Mysterio in 6:50 (★★); Team Kingston (Kofi Kingston, Christian, Mark Henry, MVP and R-Truth) defeated Team Orton (Randy Orton, CM Punk, Cody Rhodes, Ted DiBiase and William Regal) in an Elimination Match in 20:47 (★★★); The Undertaker defeated Chris Jericho and The Big Show in a Three Way Match in 13:37 (★★★); Team Mickie (Mickie James, Eve Torres, Gail Kim, Kelly Kelly and Melina) defeated Team Michelle (Michelle McCool, Alicia Fox, Beth Phoenix, Jillian Hall and Layla) in an Elimination Match in 10:38 (★★); John Cena defeated Triple H and Shawn Michaels in a Three Way Match in 21:19 (★★).

TLC '09 ★★★
13-12-09, San Antonio, Texas **WWE**

Christian defeated Shelton Benjamin in a Ladder Match in 18:04 (★★★); Drew McIntyre defeated John Morrison to win the WWE Intercontinental Title in 10:19 (★★); Michelle McCool defeated Mickie James in 7:31 (★★); Sheamus defeated John Cena in a Tables Match to win the WWE Title in 16:20 (★★★); The Undertaker defeated Batista in a Chairs Match in 13:14 (★★); Randy Orton defeated Kofi Kingston in 13:11 (★★); D-Generation X (Shawn Michaels and Triple H) defeated Jeri-Show (Chris Jericho and The Big Show) in a TLC Match to win the Unified WWE Tag Team Title in 22:33 (★★★).

Tribute To The Troops '09 ★★
19-12-09, Balad, Iraq **WWE**

Mark Henry and Rey Mysterio defeated Carlito and CM Punk in 3:02 (★★); The Miz defeated John Morrison in 2:57 (★★); John Cena defeated Chris Jericho in 7:53 (★★).

Final Battle '09 ★★★
19-12-09, New York, New York **ROH**

Claudio Castagnoli defeated Colt Cabana, Kenny Omega and Rhett Titus in a Four Corner Survival Match in 6:10 (★★★); The Embassy (Bison Smith and Erick Stevens) defeated Bobby Dempsey and Delirious in 10:12 (★★); Eddie Kingston defeated Chris Hero in a Fight Without Honor in 15:00 (★★★); The Young Bucks (Matt Jackson and Nick Jackson) defeated Kevin Steen and El Generico in 17:11 (★★★); Kenny King defeated Roderick Strong in 10:33 (★★); Rocky Romero defeated Alex Koslov in 11:24 (★★); The Briscoe Brothers (Jay Briscoe and Mark Briscoe) defeated The American Wolves (Davey Richards and Eddie Edwards) to win the ROH World Tag Team Title in 22:50 (★★★); Jack Evans defeated Teddy Hart in an Unsanctioned Match in 5:31 (★★★); Austin Aries vs. Tyler Black went to a time limit draw in 60:00 (★★★).

Final Resolution '09 ★★★★
20-12-09, Orlando, Florida **TNA**

The British Invasion (Brutus Magnus and Doug Williams) defeated The Motor City Machine Guns (Alex Shelley and Chris Sabin) in 11:47 (★★★); Tara defeated ODB to win the TNA Knockouts Title in 5:39 (★★); Kevin Nash, Rob Terry, Samoa Joe and Sheik Abdul Bashir won a Feast Or Fired Match in 11:00 (★★); D'Angelo Dinero, Hernandez, Matt Morgan and Suicide defeated Jesse Neal, Rhino and Team 3D (Brother Ray and Brother Devon) in an Elimination Match in 16:30 (★★); Bobby Lashley defeated Scott Steiner in a Last Man Standing Match in 9:13 (★★); Abyss and Mick Foley defeated Dr. Stevie and Raven in a Foley's Funhouse Rules Match in 9:31 (★★★); Kurt Angle defeated Desmond Wolfe in a Three Degrees Of Pain Match in 26:14 (★★★★); AJ Styles defeated Christopher Daniels in 21:02 (★★★★).

Genesis '10 ★★
17-01-10, Orlando, Florida **TNA**

Amazing Red defeated Brian Kendrick in 9:04 (★★); Sean Morley defeated Christopher Daniels in 9:07 (★★); Tara defeated ODB in a Two Out Of Three Falls Match to win the TNA Knockouts Title in 9:20 (★★); Hernandez and Matt Morgan defeated The British Invasion (Brutus Magnus and Doug Williams) to win the TNA World Tag Team Title in 8:45 (★★); Desmond Wolfe defeated D'Angelo Dinero in 13:32 (★★); Beer Money Inc. (James Storm and Robert Roode) defeated The Band (Kevin Nash and Syxx-Pac) in 9:43 (★★); Mr. Anderson defeated Abyss in 10:35 (★★); AJ Styles defeated Kurt Angle in 28:48 (★★★★).

Royal Rumble '10 ★★★
31-01-10, Atlanta, Georgia **WWE**

Christian defeated Ezekiel Jackson in 11:59 (★★★); The Miz defeated MVP in 7:30 (★★); Sheamus defeated Randy Orton by DQ in 12:24 (★★); Mickie James defeated Michelle McCool to win the WWE Women's Title in :20 (★★); The Undertaker defeated Rey Mysterio in 11:09 (★★★); Edge won the 30-Man Royal Rumble Match in 49:24 (★★★★).

8th Anniversary Show ★★★
13-02-10, New York City, New York **ROH**

Roderick Strong defeated Brian Kendrick in 10:25 (★★); The Kings Of Wrestling (Chris Hero and Claudio Castagnoli) defeated The Bravado Brothers (Harlem Bravado and Lance Bravado) in 5:22 (★★); Eddie Kingston and Necro Butcher defeated **The Embassy** (Erick Stevens and Joey Ryan) in an Unsanctioned Match in 8:05 (★★); **Davey Richards** defeated **El Generico** in 21:15 (★★★★); **The Briscoe Brothers** (Jay Briscoe and Mark Briscoe) defeated **The Dark City Fight Club** (Jon Davis and Kory Chavis) in 9:58 (★★); **Delirious** defeated **Kenny King, Rasche Brown** and **Steve Corino** in a Four Corner Survival Match in 9:11 (★★); **Colt Cabana** defeated **Kevin Steen** by DQ in 8:58 (★★★); **Tyler Black** defeated **Austin Aries** to win the ROH World Title in 22:24 (★★★).

Against All Odds '10 ★★
14-02-10, Orlando, Florida TNA

D'Angelo Dinero defeated **Desmond Wolfe** in 7:39 (★★); **Matt Morgan** defeated **Hernandez** in 8:50 (★★); **Mr. Anderson** defeated **Kurt Angle** in 9:44 (★★); **Abyss** defeated **Mick Foley** in a No DQ Match in 7:40 (★★); **The Nasty Boys** (Brian Knobbs and Jerry Sags) defeated **Team 3D** (Brother Ray and Brother Devon) in 10:39 (★★); **D'Angelo Dinero** defeated **Matt Morgan** in 8:20 (★★); **Mr. Anderson** defeated **Abyss** in 8:07 (★★); **AJ Styles** defeated **Samoa Joe** in a No DQ Match in 21:26 (★★★); **D'Angelo Dinero** defeated **Mr. Anderson** in 15:56 (★★).

Elimination Chamber '10 ★★★
21-02-10, St. Louis, Missouri WWE

John Cena defeated **Triple H, Sheamus, Kofi Kingston, Ted DiBiase** and **Randy Orton** in an Elimination Chamber Match to win the WWE Title in 30:30 (★★★); **Batista** defeated **John Cena** to win the WWE Title in :32 (★★); **Drew McIntyre** defeated **Kane** in 10:06 (★★); **LayCool** (Layla and Michelle McCool) defeated **Gail Kim** and **Maryse** in 3:35 (★★); **The Miz** defeated **MVP** in 13:02 (★★); **Chris Jericho** defeated **The Undertaker, John Morrison, Rey Mysterio, CM Punk** and **R-Truth** in an Elimination Chamber Match to win the World Heavyweight Title in 35:40 (★★★).

Destination X '10 ★★
21-03-10, Orlando, Florida TNA

Kazarian defeated **Amazing Red, Brian Kendrick** and **Christopher Daniels** in a Ladder Match in 13:38 (★★★); **Tara** defeated **Daffney** in 6:42 (★★); **Rob Terry** defeated **Magnus** in 1:23 (★); **The Motor City Machine Guns** (Alex Shelley and Chris Sabin) defeated **Generation Me** (Jeremy Buck and Max Buck) in an Ultimate X Match in 12:03 (★★★); **The Band** (Scott Hall and Syxx-Pac) defeated **Eric Young** and **Kevin Nash** in 7:56 (★★); **Doug Williams** defeated **Shannon Moore** in 6:19 (★★); **Hernandez** and **Matt Morgan** defeated **Beer Money Inc.** (James Storm and Robert Roode) in 11:22 (★★); **Kurt Angle** defeated **Mr. Anderson** in 17:36 (★★); **AJ Styles** vs. **Abyss** went to a no contest in 14:56 (★★).

WrestleMania XXVI ★★★
28-03-10, Glendale, Arizona WWE

ShoMiz (The Miz and The Big Show) defeated **John Morrison** and **R-Truth** in 3:20 (★★); **Randy Orton** defeated **Cody Rhodes** and **Ted DiBiase** in a Three Way Match in 9:01 (★★); **Jack Swagger** defeated **Christian, Dolph Ziggler, Drew McIntyre, Evan Bourne, Kane, Kofi Kingston, Matt Hardy, MVP** and **Shelton Benjamin** in a Money In The Bank Ladder Match in 13:44 (★★★); **Triple H** defeated **Sheamus** in 12:06 (★★); **Rey Mysterio** defeated **CM Punk** in 6:28 (★★); **Bret Hart** defeated **Vince McMahon** in a No Holds Barred Lumberjack Match in 11:09 (★); **Chris Jericho** defeated **Edge** in 15:45 (★★★); **Alicia Fox, Layla, Maryse, Michelle McCool** and **Vickie Guerrero** defeated **Beth Phoenix, Eve Torres, Gail Kim, Kelly Kelly** and **Mickie James** in 3:20 (★); **John Cena** defeated **Batista** to win the WWE Title in 13:30 (★★★★); **The Undertaker** defeated **Shawn Michaels** in a No DQ Match in 24:00 (★★★★★).

The Big Bang! ★★★
03-04-10, Charlotte, North Carolina ROH

Phill Shatter defeated **Zack Salvation** in 7:25 (★★); **Davey Richards** defeated **Kenny King** in 16:56 (★★★); **Necro Butcher** defeated **Erick Stevens** in a Butcher's Rules Match in 8:41 (★★); **Cassandro el Exotico** defeated **Rhett Titus** in 9:03 (★★★); **Colt Cabana** and **El Generico** defeated **Kevin Steen** and **Steve Corino** by DQ in 9:57 (★★); **The Kings Of Wrestling** (Chris Hero and Claudio Castagnoli) defeated **The Briscoe Brothers** (Jay Briscoe and Mark Briscoe) to win the ROH World Tag Team Title in 30:19 (★★★★); **Tyler Black** defeated **Austin Aries** and **Roderick Strong** in a Three Way Elimination Match in 31:37 (★★★★); **Blue Demon Jr.** and **Magno** defeated **Misterioso** and **Super Parka** in 15:36 (★★).

Lockdown '10 ★★★
18-04-10, Saint Charles, Missouri TNA

Rob Van Dam defeated **James Storm** in a Steel Cage Match in 6:40 (★★); **Homicide** defeated **Alex Shelley, Brian Kendrick** and **Chris Sabin** in an Xscape Match in 4:58 (★★); **Kevin Nash** defeated **Eric Young** in a Steel Cage Match in 4:50 (★); **The Beautiful People** (Madison Rayne and Velvet Sky) defeated **Angelina Love** and **Tara** in a Steel Cage Match in 5:10. As a result, Madison Rayne won the TNA Knockouts Title (★★); **Kazarian** defeated **Homicide** and **Shannon Moore** in a Three Way Steel Cage Match to win the vacant TNA X Division Title in 9:07 (★★★); **Team 3D** (Brother Ray and Brother Devon) defeated **The Band** (Kevin Nash and Scott Hall) in a Steel Cage Match in 6:45 (★★★); **Kurt Angle** defeated **Mr. Anderson** in a Steel Cage Match in 20:55 (★★★★); **AJ Styles** defeated **D'Angelo Dinero** in a Steel Cage Match in 15:43 (★★★); **Team Hogan** (Abyss, Jeff Hardy, Jeff Jarrett and Rob Van Dam) defeated **Team Flair** (Desmond Wolfe, James Storm, Robert Roode and Sting) in a Lethal Lockdown Match in 30:15 (★★★).

Extreme Rules '10 ★★★
25-04-10, Baltimore, Maryland WWE

The Hart Dynasty (Tyson Kidd and David Hart Smith) won a Gauntlet Match in 5:18 (★); **CM Punk** defeated **Rey Mysterio** in a Hair Match in 15:57 (★★★); **JTG** defeated **Shad Gaspard** in a Strap Match in 4:41 (★★); **Jack Swagger** defeated **Randy Orton** in an Extreme Rules Match in 13:59 (★★); **Sheamus** defeated **Triple H** in a Street Fight in 15:46 (★★★); **Beth Phoenix** defeated **Michelle McCool** in an Extreme Makeover Match in 6:32 (★★); **Edge** defeated **Chris Jericho** in a Steel Cage Match in 19:59 (★★★); **John Cena** defeated **Batista** in a Last Man Standing Match in 24:34 (★★★★).

Supercard Of Honor V ★★★
08-05-10, New York City, New York ROH

The Briscoe Brothers (Jay Briscoe and Mark Briscoe) defeated **Kenny King** and **Rhett Titus** in 12:53 (★★★); **Erick Stevens** defeated **Grizzly Redwood** in 6:47 (★★); **Sara Del Rey** defeated **Amazing Kong** in 7:16 (★★★); **Christopher Daniels** defeated **Eddie Edwards** in 17:54 (★★★★); **Austin Aries** defeated **Delirious** by DQ in 2:21 (★★); **Kevin Steen** defeated **Colt Cabana** in a 34th Street Death Match in 13:44 (★★★); **The Kings Of Wrestling** (Chris Hero and Claudio Castagnoli) defeated **The Motor City Machine Guns** (Alex Shelley and Chris Sabin) by DQ in 22:07 (★★★★); **Tyler Black** defeated **Roderick Strong** in 27:11 (★★★).

Sacrifice '10 ★★
16-05-10, Orlando, Florida TNA

The Motor City Machine Guns (Alex Shelley and Chris Sabin) defeated **Beer Money Inc.** (James Storm and Robert Roode) and **Team 3D** (Brother Ray and Brother Devon) in a Three Way Match in 13:13 (★★★); **Rob Terry** defeated **Orlando Jordan** in 7:45 (★★); **Douglas Williams** defeated **Kazarian** to win the TNA X Division Title in 13:50 (★★); **Madison Rayne** defeated **Tara** in 6:28 (★★); **The Band** (Kevin Nash and Scott Hall) defeated **Ink Inc.** (Jesse Neal and Shannon Moore) in 8:47 (★★); **Abyss** defeated **Desmond Wolfe** in 9:27 (★★); **Jeff Hardy** defeated **Mr. Anderson** in 13:57 (★★); **Sting** defeated **Jeff Jarrett** in :14 (★); **Rob Van Dam** defeated **AJ Styles** in 24:47 (★★★).

Over The Limit '10 ★★
23-05-10, Detroit, Michigan WWE

Kofi Kingston defeated **Drew McIntyre** to win the WWE Intercontinental Title in 6:24 (★★); **R-Truth** defeated **Ted DiBiase** in 7:46 (★★); **Rey Mysterio** defeated **CM Punk** in a Straight Edge Society Pledge vs. Hair Match in 13:49 (★★★); **The Hart Dynasty** (Tyson Kidd and David Hart Smith) defeated **Chris Jericho** and **The Miz** in 10:44 (★★); **Edge** vs. **Randy Orton** went to a double count out in 12:58 (★★); **The Big Show** defeated **Jack Swagger** by DQ in 5:05 (★★); **Eve Torres** defeated **Maryse** in 5:03 (★); **John Cena** defeated **Batista** in an "I Quit" Match in 20:33 (★★★).

Slammiversary VIII ★★★
13-06-10, Orlando, Florida TNA

Kurt Angle defeated **Kazarian** in 14:15 (★★★★); **Douglas Williams** defeated **Brian Kendrick** in 9:33 (★★★); **Madison Rayne** defeated **Roxxi** in 4:42 (★★); **Jesse Neal** defeated **Brother Ray** in 5:51 (★★); **Matt Morgan** defeated **Hernandez** in 5:18 (★★); **Abyss** defeated **Desmond Wolfe** in a Monster's Ball Match in 11:45 (★★); **Jay Lethal** defeated **AJ Styles** in 16:45

(★★★); Jeff Hardy and Mr. Anderson defeated Beer Money Inc. (James Storm and Robert Roode) in 13:55 (★★★); Rob Van Dam defeated Sting in 10:58 (★★).

Death Before Dishonor VIII ★★★★
19-06-10, Toronto, Ontario **ROH**
Kevin Steen defeated El Generico in 17:42 (★★★); The All Night Express (Kenny King and Rhett Titus) defeated Cheech and Cloudy in 8:42 (★★); Delirious defeated Austin Aries by DQ in 13:04 (★★); Roderick Strong defeated Colt Cabana, Eddie Edwards, Shawn Daivari, Steve Corino and Tyson Dux in a Gauntlet Match in 28:24 (★★★); Christopher Daniels defeated Kenny Omega in 16:12 (★★★★); The Kings Of Wrestling (Chris Hero and Claudio Castagnoli) defeated The Briscoe Brothers (Jay Briscoe and Mark Briscoe) in a No DQ Match in 18:11 (★★★★); Tyler Black defeated Davey Richards in 34:44 (★★★★).

Fatal 4-Way ★★★
20-06-10, Uniondale, New York **WWE**
Kofi Kingston defeated Drew McIntyre in 16:29 (★★); Alicia Fox defeated Eve Torres, Gail Kim and Maryse in a Four Way Match to win the WWE Divas Title in 5:42 (★★); Evan Bourne defeated Chris Jericho in 12:04 (★★★★); Rey Mysterio defeated Jack Swagger, The Big Show and CM Punk in a Four Way Match to win the World Heavyweight Title in 10:28 (★★★); The Miz defeated R-Truth in 13:23 (★★); The Hart Dynasty (Tyson Kidd, David Hart Smith and Natalya) defeated The Usos (Jey Uso and Jimmy Uso) and Tamina in 9:29 (★★); Sheamus defeated John Cena, Edge and Randy Orton in a Four Way Match to win the WWE Title in 17:25 (★★★).

Victory Road '10 ★★★
11-07-10, Orlando, Florida **TNA**
Douglas Williams defeated Brian Kendrick in an Ultimate X Submission Match in 10:08 (★★); Brother Ray defeated Brother Devon and Jesse Neal in a Three Way Match in 6:01 (★★); Angelina Love defeated Madison Rayne by DQ in 4:43 (★★); Fortune (AJ Styles and Kazarian) defeated Rob Terry and Samoa Joe in 8:12 (★★★); Hernandez defeated Matt Morgan in a Steel Cage Match in 10:52 (★★); Jay Lethal defeated Ric Flair in 12:06 (★★★); The Motor City Machine Guns (Alex Shelley and Chris Sabin) defeated Beer Money Inc. (James Storm and Robert Roode) to win the vacant TNA World Tag Team Title in 15:50 (★★★★); Kurt Angle defeated D'Angelo Dinero in 12:10 (★★★); Rob Van Dam defeated Abyss, Jeff Hardy and Mr. Anderson in a Four Way Match in 13:34 (★★).

Money In The Bank '10 ★★★
18-07-10, Kansas City, Missouri **WWE**
Kane defeated The Big Show, Christian, Cody Rhodes, Dolph Ziggler, Drew McIntyre, Kofi Kingston and Matt Hardy in a Money In The Bank Ladder Match in 26:18 (★★★); Alicia Fox defeated Eve Torres in 5:52 (★★); The Hart Dynasty (Tyson Kidd and David Hart Smith) defeated The Usos (Jey Uso and Jimmy Uso) in 5:53 (★★); Rey Mysterio defeated Jack Swagger in 10:43 (★★★); Kane defeated Rey Mysterio to win the World Heavyweight Title in :54 (★); Layla defeated Kelly Kelly in 3:56 (★); The Miz defeated Chris Jericho, Edge, Evan Bourne, John Morrison, Mark Henry, Randy Orton and Ted DiBiase in a Money In The Bank Ladder Match in 20:26 (★★★); Sheamus defeated John Cena in a Steel Cage Match in 23:19 (★★).

Hardcore Justice '10 ★★
08-08-10, Orlando, Florida **TNA**
The F.B.I. (Guido Maritato, Tony Luke and Tracy Smothers) defeated Kid Kash, Johnny Swinger and Simon Diamond in 10:45 (★★); Too Cold Scorpio defeated C.W. Anderson in 6:48 (★★); Stevie Richards defeated P.J. Polaco in 6:33 (★★); Rhino defeated Al Snow and Brother Runt in a Three Way Match in 6:01 (★★); Team 3D (Brother Ray and Brother Devon) defeated Axl Rotten and Kahoneys in a South Philadelphia Street Fight in 11:54 (★★); Raven defeated Tommy Dreamer in 16:59 (★★); Rob Van Dam defeated Sabu in a Hardcore Match in 17:15 (★★★).

SummerSlam '10 ★★
15-08-10, Los Angeles, California **WWE**
Dolph Ziggler vs. Kofi Kingston ended in a no contest in 7:05 (★★); Melina defeated Alicia Fox to win the WWE Divas Title in 5:20 (★★); The Big Show defeated The Straight Edge Society (CM Punk, Joseph Mercury and Luke Gallows) in a Handicap

Match in 6:45 (★★); Randy Orton defeated Sheamus by DQ in 18:55 (★★★); Kane defeated Rey Mysterio in 13:31 (★★); Team WWE (John Cena, John Morrison, R-Truth, Bret Hart, Edge, Chris Jericho and Daniel Bryan) defeated The Nexus (Wade Barrett, David Otunga, Justin Gabriel, Heath Slater, Darren Young, Skip Sheffield and Michael Tarver) in an Elimination Match in 35:15 (★★★).

No Surrender '10 ★★★
05-09-10, Orlando, Florida **TNA**
The Motor City Machine Guns (Alex Shelley and Chris Sabin) defeated Generation Me (Jeremy Buck and Max Buck) in 12:51 (★★★); Douglas Williams defeated Sabu in 11:13 (★★); Velvet Sky defeated Madison Rayne in 4:43 (★); Abyss defeated Rhino in a Falls Count Anywhere Match in 12:40 (★★); Jeff Jarrett and Samoa Joe defeated Kevin Nash and Sting in 6:12 (★★); AJ Styles defeated Tommy Dreamer in an "I Quit" Match in 16:30 (★★★); Jeff Hardy vs. Kurt Angle ended in a time limit draw in 30:00 (★★★★); Mr. Anderson defeated D'Angelo Dinero in 17:22 (★★).

Glory By Honor IX ★★★
11-09-10, New York, New York **ROH**
Kenny King defeated Jay Briscoe in 7:39 (★★★); Mark Briscoe defeated Rhett Titus in 9:30 (★★); The Embassy (Erick Stevens and Necro Butcher) defeated Grizzly Redwood and Ballz Mahoney in 7:44 (★★); Colt Cabana and El Generico defeated Kevin Steen and Steve Corino in a Double Chain Match in 19:43 (★★★); Eddie Edwards defeated Shawn Daivari in 7:43 (★★); Christopher Daniels defeated Austin Aries in 13:07 (★★★); The Kings Of Wrestling (Claudio Castagnoli and Chris Hero) defeated Wrestling's Greatest Tag Team (Charlie Haas and Shelton Benjamin) in 20:43 (★★★★); Roderick Strong defeated Tyler Black in a No DQ Match to win the ROH World Title in 15:00 (★★★).

Night Of Champions '10 ★★
19-09-10, Rosemont, Illinois **WWE**
Dolph Ziggler defeated Kofi Kingston in 12:42 (★★); The Big Show defeated CM Punk in 4:43 (★★); Daniel Bryan defeated The Miz to win the WWE United States Title in 12:29 (★★★); Michelle McCool defeated Melina in a Lumberjill Match to win the WWE Diva's Title in 6:34 (★); Kane defeated The Undertaker in a No Holds Barred Match in 18:29 (★★); Cody Rhodes and Drew McIntyre won a Tag Team Turmoil Match to win the WWE Tag Team Title in 11:42 (★★); Randy Orton defeated Sheamus, Wade Barrett, John Cena, Edge and Chris Jericho in a Six Pack Elimination Match to win the WWE Title in 21:28 (★★★).

Hell In A Cell '10 ★★
03-10-10, Dallas, Texas **WWE**
Daniel Bryan defeated John Morrison and The Miz in a Three Way Submissions Count Anywhere Match in 13:33 (★★★); Randy Orton defeated Sheamus in a Hell In A Cell Match in 22:51 (★★); Edge defeated Jack Swagger in 11:31 (★★); Wade Barrett defeated John Cena in 17:47 (★★★); Natalya defeated Michelle McCool by DQ in 5:00 (★★); Kane defeated The Undertaker in a Hell In A Cell Match in 21:38 (★★).

Bound For Glory '10 ★★★
10-10-10, Daytona Beach, Florida **TNA**
The Motor City Machine Guns (Alex Shelley and Chris Sabin) defeated Generation Me (Jeremy Buck and Max Buck) in 12:54 (★★★★); Tara defeated Angelina Love, Madison Rayne and Velvet Sky in a Four Corners Match to win the TNA Knockouts Title in 5:58 (★★); Ink Inc. (Jesse Neal and Shannon Moore) defeated Eric Young and Orlando Jordan in 6:38 (★★); Jay Lethal defeated Douglas Williams in 8:16 (★★); Rob Van Dam defeated Abyss in a Monster's Ball Match in 12:58 (★★★); The Band (D'Angelo Dinero, Kevin Nash and Sting) defeated Jeff Jarrett and Samoa Joe in a Handicap Match in 7:45 (★★); EV 2.0 (Raven, Rhino, Sabu, Stevie Richards and Tommy Dreamer) defeated Fortune (AJ Styles, James Storm, Kazarian, Matt Morgan and Robert Roode) in a Lethal Lockdown Match in 23:38 (★★); Jeff Hardy defeated Kurt Angle and Mr. Anderson in a Three Way Match to win the vacant TNA World Heavyweight Title in 18:37 (★★★★).

Bragging Rights '10 ★★
24-10-10, Minneapolis, Minnesota **WWE**
Daniel Bryan defeated Dolph Ziggler in 16:14 (★★★); The Nexus (David Otunga and John Cena) defeated Cody Rhodes and Drew McIntyre to win the WWE Tag Team Title in 6:29 (★★); Ted DiBiase defeated Goldust in 7:29 (★★); Layla defeated Natalya in 5:23 (★★); Kane defeated The Undertaker in a Buried Alive Match in 16:59 (★); Team SmackDown (Alberto Del Rio, The Big Show, Edge, Jack Swagger, Kofi Kingston, Rey Mysterio and Tyler Reks) defeated Team Raw (CM Punk, Ezekiel Jackson, John Morrison, The Miz, R-Truth, Santino Marella and Sheamus) in an Elimination Match in 27:40 (★★★); Wade Barrett defeated Randy Orton by DQ in 14:34 (★★).

Turning Point '10 ★★
07-11-10, Orlando, Florida **TNA**
Robbie E defeated Jay Lethal to win the TNA X Division Title in 10:42 (★★); Mickie James defeated Tara in 10:17 (★★); The Motor City Machine Guns (Alex Shelley and Chris Sabin) defeated Team 3D (Brother Ray and Brother Devon) in 18:08 (★★★); Rob Van Dam defeated Tommy Dreamer in a No DQ Match in 16:53 (★★); Fortune (AJ Styles, Douglas Williams, James Storm, Kazarian and Robert Roode) defeated EV 2.0 (Brian Kendrick, Raven, Rhino, Sabu and Stevie Richards) in 12:05 (★★); Abyss defeated D'Angelo Dinero in a Lumberjack Match in 13:02 (★★); Jeff Jarrett defeated Samoa Joe in 10:32 (★★); Jeff Hardy defeated Matt Morgan in 13:06 (★★).

Survivor Series '10 ★★
21-11-10, Miami, Florida **WWE**
Daniel Bryan defeated Ted DiBiase in 9:58 (★★★); John Morrison defeated Sheamus in 11:11 (★★); Dolph Ziggler defeated Kaval in 9:32 (★★); Team Mysterio (The Big Show, Chris Masters, Kofi Kingston, MVP and Rey Mysterio) defeated Team Del Rio (Alberto Del Rio, Cody Rhodes, Drew McIntyre, Jack Swagger and Tyler Reks) in an Elimination Match in 18:12 (★★★); Natalya defeated LayCool (Michelle McCool and Layla) in a Handicap Match to win the WWE Divas Title in 3:38 (★★); Kane vs. Edge ended in a draw in 12:50 (★★); The Nexus (Heath Slater and Justin Gabriel) defeated Santino Marella and Vladimir Kozlov in 5:11 (★★); Randy Orton defeated Wade Barrett in a Pinfall Or Submission Only Match in 15:10 (★★).

Final Resolution '10 ★★★
05-12-10, Orlando, Florida **TNA**
Beer Money Inc. (James Storm and Robert Roode) defeated Ink Inc. (Jesse Neal and Shannon Moore) in 10:45 (★★★); Tara defeated Mickie James in a Falls Count Anywhere Match in 10:25 (★★); Robbie E defeated Jay Lethal by DQ in 8:11 (★★); Rob Van Dam defeated Rhino in a First Blood Match in 12:24 (★★★); Douglas Williams defeated AJ Styles to win the TNA Television Title in 14:50 (★★★★); The Motor City Machine Guns (Alex Shelley and Chris Sabin) defeated Generation Me (Jeremy Buck and Max Buck) in a Full Metal Mayhem Match in 16:27 (★★); Abyss defeated D'Angelo Dinero in a Casket Match in 11:40 (★★); Jeff Jarrett defeated Samoa Joe in a Submission Match in 9:05 (★★); Jeff Hardy defeated Matt Morgan in a No DQ Match in 12:31 (★★).

Final Battle '10 ★★★★
18-12-10, New York, New York **ROH**
The All Night Express (Kenny King and Rhett Titus) defeated Adam Cole and Kyle O'Reilly in 9:23 (★★); Colt Cabana defeated TJ Perkins in 7:56 (★★); Sara Del Rey and Serena Deeb defeated Amazing Kong and Daizee Haze in 8:18 (★★); Eddie Edwards defeated Sonjay Dutt in 10:41 (★★★); Homicide defeated Christopher Daniels in 10:32 (★★); The Briscoe Brothers (Jay Briscoe and Mark Briscoe) and Mike Briscoe defeated The Kings Of Wrestling (Chris Hero and Claudio Castagnoli) and Shane Hagadorn in 15:58 (★★★); Roderick Strong defeated Davey Richards in 30:28 (★★★★); El Generico defeated Kevin Steen in an Unsanctioned Fight Without Honor in 31:13 (★★★★★).

TLC '10 ★★★
19-12-10, Houston, Texas **WWE**
Dolph Ziggler defeated Jack Swagger and Kofi Kingston in a Three Way Ladder Match in 8:56 (★★); Beth Phoenix and Natalya defeated LayCool (Layla and Michelle McCool) in a Tag Team Tables Match in 9:20 (★★); Santino Marella and Vladimir Kozlov defeated The Nexus (Heath Slater and Justin Gabriel)

by DQ in 6:28 (★★); John Morrison defeated King Sheamus in a Ladder Match in 19:08 (★★★★); The Miz defeated Randy Orton in a Tables Match in 13:40 (★★); Edge defeated Kane, Alberto Del Rio and Rey Mysterio in a Fatal Four Way TLC Match to win the World Heavyweight Title in 22:45 (★★★); John Cena defeated Wade Barrett in a Chairs Match in 19:10 (★★★).

Tribute To The Troops '10 ★★
22-12-10, Fort Hood, Texas **WWE**
Mark Henry won a 15-man Battle Royal in 12:00 (★★★); Kofi Kingston and The Big Show defeated Dolph Ziggler and Jack Swagger in 5:00 (★★); R-Truth defeated Ted DiBiase in 3:00 (★★); Natalya, Kelly Kelly and The Bella Twins (Brie Bella and Nikki Bella) defeated Melina, Alicia Fox and Lay Cool (Layla and Michelle McCool) in a Santa's Little Helper Match in 3:00 (★★); John Cena, Rey Mysterio and Randy Orton defeated Alberto Del Rio, Wade Barrett and The Miz in 11:00 (★★).

Genesis '11 ★★★
09-01-11, Orlando, Florida **TNA**
Kazarian defeated Jay Lethal to win the TNA X Division Title in 11:40 (★★); Madison Rayne defeated Mickie James in 10:30 (★★); Beer Money Inc. (James Storm and Robert Roode) defeated The Motor City Machine Guns (Alex Shelley and Chris Sabin) to win the TNA World Tag Team Title in 18:00 (★★★); Bully Ray defeated Brother Devon by DQ in 8:50 (★★); Abyss defeated Douglas Williams to win the TNA Television Title in 9:45 (★★); Matt Hardy defeated Rob Van Dam in 11:55 (★★); Jeff Jarrett vs. Kurt Angle went to a no contest in a Double J Double M A Exhibition Match in 4:30 (★★); Mr. Anderson defeated Matt Morgan in 15:25 (★★); Mr. Anderson defeated Jeff Hardy to win the TNA World Heavyweight Title in 9:05 (★★★).

Royal Rumble '11 ★★★
30-01-11, Boston, Massachusetts **WWE**
Edge defeated Dolph Ziggler in 20:45 (★★★★); The Miz defeated Randy Orton in 19:50 (★★); Eve Torres defeated Layla, Michelle McCool and Natalya in a Four Way Match to win the WWE Divas Title in 5:12 (★★); Alberto Del Rio won the 40-Man Royal Rumble Match in 69:51 (★★★).

Against All Odds '11 ★★★
13-02-11, Orlando, Florida **TNA**
Kazarian defeated Robbie E in 7:11 (★★★); Beer Money Inc. (James Storm and Robert Roode) and Scott Steiner defeated Immortal (Gunner, Murphy and Rob Terry) in 10:13 (★★); Samoa Joe defeated D'Angelo Dinero in 8:31 (★★); Madison Rayne defeated Mickie James in a Last Woman Standing Match in 8:28 (★★); Rob Van Dam defeated Matt Hardy in 13:18 (★★); Bully Ray defeated Brother Devon in a Street Fight in 9:24 (★★); Jeff Jarrett defeated Kurt Angle in 16:13 (★★★); Jeff Hardy defeated Mr. Anderson in a Ladder Match to win the TNA World Heavyweight Title in 18:15 (★★★).

Elimination Chamber '11 ★★★★
20-02-11, Oakland, California **WWE**
Alberto Del Rio defeated Kofi Kingston in 10:30 (★★★); Edge defeated Rey Mysterio, Kane, Drew McIntyre, The Big Show and Wade Barrett in an Elimination Chamber Match in 31:30 (★★★★); The Corre (Heath Slater and Justin Gabriel) defeated Santino Marella and Vladimir Kozlov to win the WWE Tag Team Title in 5:08 (★★); The Miz defeated Jerry Lawler in 12:10 (★★★); John Cena defeated CM Punk, John Morrison, King Sheamus, Randy Orton and R-Truth in an Elimination Chamber Match in 33:12 (★★★★).

9th Anniversary Show ★★★
26-02-11, Chicago, Illinois **ROH**
Davey Richards defeated Colt Cabana in 12:13 (★★); Mike Bennett defeated Grizzly Redwood, Kyle O'Reilly and Steve Corino in a Four Way Match in 10:51 (★★); El Generico defeated Michael Elgin in 10:33 (★★); Roderick Strong defeated Homicide in a No Holds Barred Match in 14:57 (★★); Sara Del Rey defeated MsChif in 3:57 (★★); The Kings Of Wrestling (Chris Hero and Claudio Castagnoli) defeated The All Night Express (Kenny King and Rhett Titus) in 15:50 (★★★); Christopher Daniels vs. Eddie Edwards went to a time limit draw in a Two Out Of Three Falls Match in 30:00 (★★★★); Wrestling's Greatest Tag Team (Charlie Haas and Shelton Benjamin) defeated The Briscoe Brothers (Jay Briscoe and Mark Briscoe) in 22:16 (★★★★).

Victory Road '11 ★
13-03-11, Orlando, Florida **TNA**
Tommy Dreamer defeated Bully Ray in a Falls Count Anywhere Match in 10:45 (★★); Rosita and Sarita defeated Angelina Love and Winter to win the TNA Knockouts Tag Team Title in 4:58 (★); Hernandez defeated Matt Morgan in a First Blood Match in 8:35 (★); Kazarian defeated Jeremy Buck, Max Buck and Robbie E in an Ultimate X Match in 14:22 (★★); Beer Money Inc. (James Storm and Robert Roode) defeated Ink Inc. (Jesse Neal and Shannon Moore) in 12:30 (★★); AJ Styles defeated Matt Hardy in 17:38 (★★★); Mr. Anderson vs. Rob Van Dam went to a double count out in 12:54 (★★); Sting defeated Jeff Hardy in a No DQ Match in 1:28 (★).

Manhattan Mayhem IV ★★★
19-03-11, New York City, New York **ROH**
Adam Cole and Kyle O'Reilly defeated Michael Elgin and Mike Mondo in 12:22 (★★★); Tommaso Ciampa defeated Grizzly Redwood in 7:53 (★★); Mike Bennett defeated Steve Corino in 9:37 (★★); The All-Night Express (Kenny King and Rhett Titus) defeated The Briscoe Brothers (Jay Briscoe and Mark Briscoe) in 14:03 (★★); El Generico defeated TJ Perkins in 7:31 (★★★); The Kings Of Wrestling (Chris Hero and Claudio Castagnoli) defeated The Latin American Exchange (Hernandez and Homicide) in 17:12 (★★★); Davey Richards defeated Christopher Daniels in a Pure Wrestling Rules Match in 21:47 (★★★); Eddie Edwards defeated Roderick Strong to win the ROH World Title in 25:36 (★★★★).

Honor Takes Center Stage Day #1 ★★★★
01-04-11, Atlanta, Georgia **ROH**
Michael Elgin defeated El Generico in 9:13 (★★★); Homicide defeated Colt Cabana, Tommaso Ciampa and Caleb Konley in a Four Corner Survival Match in 9:23 (★★★); Ayumi Kurihara and Hiroyo Matsumoto defeated Sara Del Rey and Serena Deeb in 9:01 (★★★); The Briscoe Brothers (Jay Briscoe and Mark Briscoe) defeated Adam Cole and Kyle O'Reilly in 13:23 (★★★); Davey Richards defeated Roderick Strong in 27:06 (★★★★); Wrestling's Greatest Tag Team (Charlie Haas and Shelton Benjamin) defeated The Kings Of Wrestling (Chris Hero and Claudio Castagnoli) to win the ROH World Tag Team Title in 23:00 (★★★★); Eddie Edwards defeated Christopher Daniels in 30:12 (★★★★).

Honor Takes Center Stage Day #2 ★★★★
02-04-11, Atlanta, Georgia **ROH**
The Kings Of Wrestling (Chris Hero and Claudio Castagnoli) defeated Adam Cole and Kyle O'Reilly in 9:17 (★★★★); Colt Cabana defeated Dave Taylor in 6:31 (★★); Tommaso Ciampa defeated Homicide in 9:47 (★★); Christopher Daniels defeated Michael Elgin in 10:18 (★★); Daizee Haze and Tomoka Nakagawa defeated Ayumi Kurihara and Hiroyo Matsumoto in 7:40 (★★); The Briscoe Brothers (Jay Briscoe and Mark Briscoe) defeated The All Night Express (Rhett Titus and Kenny King) in 16:03 (★★★★); El Generico defeated Roderick Strong in 16:12 (★★★); Wrestling's Greatest Tag Team (Charlie Haas and Shelton Benjamin) defeated The American Wolves (Davey Richards and Eddie Edwards) in 32:00 (★★★★).

WrestleMania XXVII ★★
03-04-11, Atlanta, Georgia **WWE**
Edge defeated Alberto Del Rio in 11:09 (★★); Cody Rhodes defeated Rey Mysterio in 11:58 (★★); The Big Show, Kane, Kofi Kingston and Santino Marella defeated The Corre (Ezekiel Jackson, Heath Slater, Justin Gabriel and Wade Barrett) in 1:32 (★★); Randy Orton defeated CM Punk in 14:46 (★★); Michael Cole defeated Jerry Lawler in 13:45 (★); The Undertaker defeated Triple H in a No Holds Barred Match in 29:23 (★★★★); John Morrison, Trish Stratus and Snooki defeated Dolph Ziggler and LayCool (Layla and Michelle McCool) in 3:16 (★★); The Miz defeated John Cena in 15:21 (★★).

Lockdown '11 ★★
17-04-11, Orlando, Florida **TNA**
Max Buck defeated Amazing Red, Brian Kendrick, Chris Sabin, Jay Lethal, Jeremy Buck, Robbie E and Suicide in an Xscape Match in 13:33 (★★); Ink Inc. (Jesse Neal and Shannon Moore) defeated The British Invasion (Douglas Williams and Magnus), Crimson and Scott Steiner, and Eric Young and Orlando Jordan in a Four Way Tornado Steel Cage Match in 8:51 (★★); Mickie James defeated Madison Rayne in a Steel Cage Title vs. Hair Match to win the TNA Knockouts Title in :36 (★); Samoa Joe defeated D'Angelo Dinero in a Steel Cage Match in 10:25 (★★); Matt Morgan defeated Hernandez in a Steel Cage Match in 8:13 (★★); Jeff Jarrett defeated Kurt Angle in a Two Out Of Three Falls Steel Cage Match in 22:37 (★★★★); Sting defeated Mr. Anderson and Rob Van Dam in a Three Way Steel Cage Match in 8:55 (★★); Fortune (Christopher Daniels, James Storm, Kazarian and Robert Roode) defeated Immortal (Bully Ray, Abyss, Matt Hardy and Ric Flair) in a Lethal Lockdown Match in 22:52 (★★★).

Extreme Rules '11 ★★★
01-05-11, Tampa, Florida **WWE**
Randy Orton defeated CM Punk in a Last Man Standing Match in 20:06 (★★★★); Kofi Kingston defeated Sheamus in a Tables Match to win the WWE United States Title in 9:09 (★★); Jack Swagger and Michael Cole defeated Jerry Lawler and Jim Ross in a Country Whipping Match in 7:04 (★★); Rey Mysterio defeated Cody Rhodes in a Falls Count Anywhere Match in 11:43 (★★); Layla defeated Michelle McCool in a No DQ, No Count Out Loser Leaves WWE Match in 5:24 (★★); Christian defeated Alberto Del Rio in a Ladder Match to win the vacant World Heavyweight Title in 21:05 (★★★★); The Big Show and Kane defeated The Corre (Ezekiel Jackson and Wade Barrett) in a Lumberjack Match in 4:15 (★★); John Cena defeated The Miz and John Morrison in a Three Way Steel Cage Match to win the WWE Title in 19:50 (★★★).

Sacrifice '11 ★★
15-05-11, Orlando, Florida **TNA**
Mexican America (Anarquia and Hernandez) defeated Ink Inc. (Jesse Neal and Shannon Moore) in 9:39 (★★); Brian Kendrick defeated Robbie E in 6:41 (★★); Mickie James defeated Madison Rayne in 6:57 (★★); Kazarian defeated Max Buck in 11:21 (★★); Crimson defeated Abyss in 10:43 (★★); Beer Money Inc. (James Storm and Robert Roode) defeated Immortal (Chris Harris and Matt Hardy) in 13:51 (★★); Tommy Dreamer defeated AJ Styles in a No DQ Match in 13:04 (★★); Chyna and Kurt Angle defeated Jeff Jarrett and Karen Jarrett in 10:19 (★★★); Sting defeated Rob Van Dam in 12:43 (★★).

Over The Limit '11 ★★
22-05-11, Seattle, Washington **WWE**
R-Truth defeated Rey Mysterio in 8:12 (★★); Ezekiel Jackson defeated Wade Barrett by DQ in 7:27 (★★); Sin Cara defeated Chavo Guerrero in 7:23 (★★); The Big Show and Kane defeated The New Nexus (CM Punk and Mason Ryan) in 9:06 (★★); Brie Bella defeated Kelly Kelly in 4:03 (★★); Randy Orton defeated Christian in 16:52 (★★★★); Jerry Lawler defeated Michael Cole in a Kiss My Foot Match in 3:01 (★★); John Cena defeated The Miz in an "I Quit" Match in 24:56 (★★).

Slammiversary IX ★★★★
12-06-11, Orlando, Florida **TNA**
Gun Money (Alex Shelly and James Storm) defeated The British Invasion (Douglas Williams and Magnus) in 10:57 (★★★); Matt Morgan defeated Scott Steiner in 9:20 (★★); Abyss defeated Brian Kendrick and Kazarian in a Three Way Match in 12:05 (★★); Crimson defeated Samoa Joe in 10:33 (★★★); Mickie James defeated Angelina Love in 8:03 (★★); Bully Ray defeated AJ Styles in a Last Man Standing Match in 20:18 (★★★★); Mr. Anderson defeated Sting to win the TNA World Heavyweight Title in 15:52 (★★); Kurt Angle defeated Jeff Jarrett in 17:42 (★★★).

Capitol Punishment ★★★
19-06-11, Washington, D.C. **WWE**
Dolph Ziggler defeated Kofi Kingston to win the WWE United States Title in 11:06 (★★★); Alex Riley defeated The Miz in 10:13 (★★★); Alberto Del Rio defeated The Big Show in 4:57 (★★); Ezekiel Jackson defeated Wade Barrett to win the WWE Intercontinental Title in 6:36 (★★); CM Punk defeated Rey Mysterio in 15:00 (★★★); Randy Orton defeated Christian in 14:06 (★★★); Evan Bourne defeated Jack Swagger in 7:12 (★★); John Cena defeated R-Truth in 14:45 (★★).

Best In The World '11 ★★★★
26-06-11, New York, New York **ROH**
Tommaso Ciampa defeated Colt Cabana in 6:59 (★★); Jay Lethal defeated Mike Bennett in 9:43 (★★); Homicide defeated Rhino in a No Holds Barred Match in 10:16 (★★); Michael Elgin

defeated **Steve Corino** in 8:29 (★★); **El Generico** defeated **Christopher Daniels** to win the ROH World Television Title in 19:30 (★★★★); Wrestling's Greatest Tag Team (**Charlie Haas** and **Shelton Benjamin**) defeated The Briscoe Brothers (**Jay Briscoe** and **Mark Briscoe**), The All Night Express (**Rhett Titus** and **Kenny King**), and The Kings Of Wrestling (**Chris Hero** and **Claudio Castagnoli**) in a Four Way Elimination Match in 40:09 (★★★); **Davey Richards** defeated **Eddie Edwaards** to win the ROH World Title in 36:01 (★★★★★).

Destination X '11 ★★★★
10-07-11, Orlando, Florida **TNA**
Kazarian defeated **Samoa Joe** in 11:19 (★★★); **Douglas Williams** defeated **Mark Haskins** in 7:40 (★★); **Eric Young** and **Shark Boy** defeated Generation Me (**Jeremy Buck** and **Max Buck**) in 7:22 (★★); **Alex Shelley** defeated **Amazing Red**, **Robbie E** and **Shannon Moore** in an Ultimate X Match in 10:30 (★★★); **Rob Van Dam** defeated **Jerry Lynn** in 16:51 (★★★); **Austin Aries** defeated **Jack Evans**, **Low Ki** and **Zema Ion** in a Four Way Match in 13:30 (★★★★); **Brian Kendrick** defeated **Abyss** to win the TNA X Division Title in 10:39 (★★); **AJ Styles** defeated **Christopher Daniels** in 28:27 (★★★★).

Money In The Bank '11 ★★★★★
17-07-11, Rosemont, Illinois **WWE**
Daniel Bryan defeated **Cody Rhodes**, **Heath Slater**, **Justin Gabriel**, **Kane**, **Sin Cara**, **Sheamus** and **Wade Barrett** in a Money In The Bank Ladder Match in 24:27 (★★★★); **Kelly Kelly** defeated **Brie Bella** in 4:54 (★); **Mark Henry** defeated The Big Show in 6:00 (★★); **Alberto Del Rio** defeated **Alex Riley**, **Evan Bourne**, **Jack Swagger**, **Kofi Kingston**, **The Miz**, **R-Truth** and **Rey Mysterio** in a Money In The Bank Ladder Match in 15:54 (★★★★); **Christian** defeated **Randy Orton** by DQ in 12:20 (★★★); **CM Punk** defeated **John Cena** to win the WWE Title in 33:44 (★★★★★).

Hardcore Justice '11 ★★
07-08-11, Orlando, Florida **TNA**
Brian Kendrick defeated **Alex Shelley** and **Austin Aries** in a Three Way Match in 13:10 (★★); **Ms. Tessmacher** and **Tara** defeated Mexican America (**Rosita** and **Sarita**) in 7:08 (★★); **D'Angelo Dinero** defeated **Devon** in 9:33 (★★); **Winter** defeated **Mickie James** to win the TNA Knockouts Title in 8:58 (★); **Crimson** defeated **Rob Van Dam** by DQ in 8:40 (★★); Fortune (**AJ Styles**, **Christopher Daniels** and **Kazarian**) defeated Immortal (**Abyss**, **Gunner** and **Scott Steiner**) in 14:42 (★★★); **Bully Ray** defeated **Mr. Anderson** in 10:04 (★★); Beer Money Inc. (**James Storm** and **Bobby Roode**) defeated Mexican America (**Anarquia** and **Hernandez**) in 10:41 (★★★); **Kurt Angle** defeated **Sting** to win the TNA World Heavyweight Title in 15:22 (★★★).

Legends & Icons ★
12-08-11, Cave-In-Rock, Illinois **JCW**
Greg Valentine defeated **Tito Santana** in a Steel Cage Match in 3:43 (★); **Zach Gowen** won a 15 Man Legends Battle Royal in 28:44 (★); The Rock 'n' Roll Express (**Ricky Morton** and **Robert Gibson**) defeated The Midnight Express (**Bobby Eaton** and **Dennis Condrey**) in :33 (★★); **Rhino** defeated **Too Cold Scorpio**, **Al Snow**, **Balls Mahoney**, **Raven**, **Sabu** and **Shane Douglas** in a Seven Way Philly Madness Match in 3:46 (★★); **Bob Backlund** defeated **Ken Patera** in 6:12 (★); **Austin Idol** defeated **Brickhouse Brown**, **Doug Gilbert**, **Dutch Mantel** and **Koko B. Ware** in a Five Way Memphis Madness Match in 2:42 (★); **Tracy Smothers** defeated **Tommy Rich** in :36 (★); **Kevin Nash** and **X-Pac** defeated The New Age Outlaws (**Billy Gunn** and **Road Dogg**) in 6:27 (★★); **Bob Orton** and **Roddy Piper** defeated **Mick Foley** and **Terry Funk** in 4:14 (★).

SummerSlam '11 ★★★
14-08-11, Los Angeles, California **WWE**
Kofi Kingston, **John Morrison** and **Rey Mysterio** defeated The Miz, **R-Truth** and **Alberto Del Rio** in 9:40 (★★); **Mark Henry** defeated **Sheamus** via count out in 9:22 (★★★); **Kelly Kelly** defeated **Beth Phoenix** in 6:48 (★★); **Wade Barrett** defeated **Daniel Bryan** in 11:48 (★★★); **Randy Orton** defeated **Christian** in a No Holds Barred Match to win the World Heavyweight Title in 23:43 (★★★★); **CM Punk** defeated **John Cena** to win the Undisputed WWE Title in 24:14 (★★★★); **Alberto Del Rio** defeated **CM Punk** to win the WWE Title in :11 (★★).

No Surrender '11 ★★
11-09-11, Orlando, Florida **TNA**
Jesse Sorensen defeated **Kid Kash** in 7:55 (★★); **Bully Ray** defeated **James Storm** by DQ in 11:48 (★★); **Winter** defeat **Mickie James** to win the TNA Knockouts Title in 8:36 (★★); Mexican America (**Anarquia** and **Hernandez**) defeated **D'Angelo Dinero** and **Devon** in 9:45 (★★); **Matt Morgan** defeated **Samoa Joe** in 11:35 (★★); **Bobby Roode** defeated **Gunner** in 11:58 (★★★); **Austin Aries** defeated **Brian Kendrick** to win the TNA X Division Title in 13:24 (★★★); **Bobby Roode** defeated **Bully Ray** in 12:30 (★★); **Kurt Angle** defeated **Mr. Anderson** and **Sting** in a Three Way Match in 15:28 (★★).

Death Before Dishonor IX ★★★
17-09-11, New York, New York **ROH**
The Embassy (**Rhino** and **Tommaso Ciampa**) defeated **Homicide** and **Jay Lethal** in 10:15 (★★); **Shelton Benjamin** defeated **Mike Bennett** in 10:54 (★★); The Young Bucks (**Matt Jackson** and **Nick Jackson**) defeated Future Shock (**Adam Cole** and **Kyle O'Reilly**) and Bravado Brothers (**Harlem Bravado** and **Lancelot Bravado**) in a Three Way Elimination Match in 10:51 (★★★); **El Generico** vs. **Jimmy Jacobs** went to a no contest in 12:00 (★★); **Charlie Haas** defeated **Michael Elgin** in 12:42 (★★); **Eddie Edwards** defeated **Roderick Strong** 2-1 in a Best Two Out Of Three Falls Match in 42:45 (★★★); The All Night Express (**Rhett Titus** and **Kenny King**) defeated The Briscoe Brothers (**Jay Briscoe** and **Mark Briscoe**) in a Ladder War in 27:54 (★★★★).

Night Of Champions '11 ★★★
18-09-11, Buffalo, New York **WWE**
Air Boom (**Evan Bourne** and **Kofi Kingston**) defeated Awesome Truth (**The Miz** and **R-Truth**) in 9:50 (★★); **Cody Rhodes** defeated **Ted DiBiase** in 9:43 (★★); **Dolph Ziggler** defeated **Alex Riley**, **Jack Swagger** and **John Morrison** in a Four Way Match in 8:19 (★★★); **Mark Henry** defeated **Randy Orton** to win the World Heavyweight Title in 13:06 (★★★); **Kelly Kelly** defeated **Beth Phoenix** in 6:26 (★★); **John Cena** defeated **Alberto Del Rio** to win the WWE Title in 17:32 (★★★); **Triple H** defeated **CM Punk** in a No DQ Match in 24:10 (★★★).

Hell In A Cell '11 ★★★
02-10-11, New Orleans, Louisiana **WWE**
Sheamus defeated **Christian** in 13:42 (★★★); **Sin Cara (Azul)** defeated **Sin Cara (Negro)** in 9:46 (★★); Air Boom (**Evan Bourne** and **Kofi Kingston**) defeated **Dolph Ziggler** and **Jack Swagger** in 10:47 (★★); **Mark Henry** defeated **Randy Orton** in a Hell In A Cell Match in 15:58 (★★); **Cody Rhodes** defeated **John Morrison** in 7:20 (★★); **Beth Phoenix** defeated **Kelly Kelly** to win the WWE Divas Title in 8:41 (★); **Alberto Del Rio** defeated **CM Punk** and **John Cena** in a Triple Threat Hell In A Cell Match to win the WWE Title in 24:09 (★★★).

Bound For Glory '11 ★★★
16-10-11, Philadelphia, Pennsylvania **TNA**
Austin Aries defeated **Brian Kendrick** in 10:27 (★★); **Crimson** defeated **Matt Morgan** and **Samoa Joe** in a Three Way Match in 7:14 (★★); **Rob Van Dam** defeated **Jerry Lynn** in a Full Metal Mayhem Match in 13:14 (★★★); **Mr. Anderson** defeated **Bully Ray** in a Falls Count Anywhere Philadelphia Street Fight in 14:33 (★★★); **Velvet Sky** defeated **Madison Rayne**, **Mickie James** and **Winter** in a Four Way Match to win the TNA Knockouts Title in 8:31 (★); **AJ Styles** defeated **Christopher Daniels** in an "I Quit" Match in 13:42 (★★); **Sting** defeated **Hulk Hogan** in 10:43 (★★★); **Kurt Angle** defeated **Bobby Roode** in 14:15 (★★★).

Vengeance '11 ★★★
23-10-11, San Antonio, Texas **WWE**
Air Boom (**Evan Bourne** and **Kofi Kingston**) defeated **Dolph Ziggler** and **Jack Swagger** in 13:24 (★★★); **Dolph Ziggler** defeated **Zack Ryder** in 6:04 (★★); **Beth Phoenix** defeated **Eve Torres** in 7:18 (★★); **Sheamus** defeated **Christian** in 10:37 (★★★); The Miz and **R-Truth** defeated **CM Punk** and **Triple H** in 15:24 (★★); **Randy Orton** defeated **Cody Rhodes** in 12:11 (★★★); **Mark Henry** vs. **The Big Show** went to a no contest in 13:19 (★★★); **Alberto Del Rio** defeated **John Cena** in a Last Man Standing Match in 27:04 (★★★).

Turning Point '11 ★★
13-11-11, Orlando, Florida **TNA**
Robbie E defeated **Eric Young** to win the TNA Television Title in 7:50 (★★); Mexican America (**Anarquia**, **Hernandez** and **Sarita**) defeated Ink Inc. (**Jesse Neal**, **Shannon Moore** and **Toxxin**) in

8:28 (★★); **Austin Aries** defeated **Jesse Sorensen** and **Kid Kash** in a Three Way Match in 12:54 (★★); **Rob Van Dam** defeated **Christopher Daniels** in a No DQ Match in 11:17 (★★); **Crimson** vs. **Matt Morgan** went to a double DQ in 12:06 (★★); **Abyss** and **Mr. Anderson** defeated **Immortal** (**Bully Ray** and **Scott Steiner**) in 12:35 (★★); **Gail Kim** defeated **Velvet Sky** to win the TNA Knockouts Title in 5:52 (★★); **Jeff Hardy** defeated **Jeff Jarrett** in 6:00 (★★); **Bobby Roode** defeated **AJ Styles** in 19:33 (★★).

Survivor Series '11 ★★
20-11-11, New York City, New York **WWE**
Dolph Ziggler defeated **John Morrison** in 10:42 (★★); **Beth Phoenix** defeated **Eve Torres** in a Lumberjill Match in 4:35 (★★); **Team Barrett** (**Wade Barrett**, **Cody Rhodes**, **Dolph Ziggler**, **Hunico** and **Jack Swagger**) defeated **Team Orton** (**Randy Orton**, **Kofi Kingston**, **Mason Ryan**, **Sheamus** and **Sin Cara**) in an Elimination Match in 22:10 (★★); **The Big Show** defeated **Mark Henry** by DQ in 13:04 (★★); **CM Punk** defeated **Alberto Del Rio** to win the WWE Title in 17:14 (★★★); **John Cena** and **The Rock** defeated **The Awesome Truth** (**The Miz** and **R-Truth**) in 21:22 (★★).

Final Resolution '11 ★★★
11-12-11, Orlando, Florida **TNA**
Rob Van Dam defeated **Christopher Daniels** in 9:45 (★★); **Robbie E** defeated **Eric Young** in 7:30 (★★); **Crimson** and **Matt Morgan** defeated **D'Angelo Dinero** and **Devon** in 9:45 (★★); **Austin Aries** defeated **Kid Kash** in 12:45 (★★); **Gail Kim** defeated **Mickie James** in 7:45 (★★); **James Storm** defeated **Kurt Angle** in 17:30 (★★★); **Jeff Hardy** defeated **Jeff Jarrett** in a Steel Cage Match in 9:45 (★★★); **Bobby Roode** vs. **AJ Styles** ended in a 3-3 draw in an Iron Man Match in 30:00 (★★★).

Tribute To The Troops '11 ★★★
13-12-11, Fayetteville, North Carolina **WWE**
Randy Orton vs. **Wade Barrett** ended in a double count out in 5:57 (★★); **Zack Ryder** defeated **Jack Swagger** in 3:45 (★★); **Alicia Fox**, **Eve Torres**, **Kelly Kelly** and **Maria Menounos** defeated **The Divas Of Doom** (**Natalya** and **Beth Phoenix**) and **The Bella Twins** (**Brie Bella** and **Nikki Bella**) in 2:42 (★★); **Daniel Bryan** defeated **Cody Rhodes** in 4:35 (★★); **Primo** and **Epico** defeated **Air Boom** (**Evan Bourne** and **Kofi Kingston**) in 2:59 (★★); **Sheamus** defeated **Drew McIntyre** in 2:15 (★★); **The Big Show**, **CM Punk** and **John Cena** defeated **Mark Henry**, **The Miz** and **Alberto Del Rio** in 9:20 (★★).

TLC '11 ★★★★
18-12-11, Baltimore, Maryland **WWE**
Zack Ryder defeated **Dolph Ziggler** to win the WWE United States Title in 10:21 (★★★); **Air Boom** (**Evan Bourne** and **Kofi Kingston**) defeated **Primo** and **Epico** in 7:32 (★★); **Randy Orton** defeated **Wade Barrett** in a Tables Match in 10:16 (★★★); **Beth Phoenix** defeated **Kelly Kelly** in 5:36 (★★); **Triple H** defeated **Kevin Nash** in a Sledgehammer Ladder Match in 18:18 (★★); **Sheamus** defeated **Jack Swagger** in 5:05 (★★); **The Big Show** defeated **Mark Henry** in a Chairs Match to win the World Heavyweight Title in 5:30 (★★); **Daniel Bryan** defeated **The Big Show** to win the World Heavyweight Title in :07 (★★); **Cody Rhodes** defeated **Booker T** in 9:16 (★★); **CM Punk** defeated **Alberto Del Rio** and **The Miz** in a Triple Threat TLC Match in 18:22 (★★★★).

Final Battle '11 ★★★★
23-12-11, New York, New York **ROH**
Michael Elgin defeated **TJ Perkins** in 7:25 (★★); **Tommaso Ciampa** defeated **Jimmy Rave** in 8:33 (★★); **Jay Lethal** defeated **El Generico** and **Mike Bennett** in a Three Way Match in 18:17 (★★★); **Kevin Steen** defeated **Steve Corino** in a No DQ Match in 23:13 (★★★★); **The Young Bucks** (**Matt Jackson** and **Nick Jackson**) won a Gauntlet Match in 29:36 (★★); **Roderick Strong** defeated **Chris Hero** in 16:37 (★★★); **The Briscoe Brothers** (**Jay Briscoe** and **Mark Briscoe**) defeated **Wrestling's Greatest Tag Team** (**Charlie Haas** and **Shelton Benjamin**) to win the ROH World Tag Team Title in 13:24 (★★); **Davey Richards** defeated **Eddie Edwards** to win the ROH World Title in 41:21 (★★★).

Genesis '12 ★★
08-01-12, Orlando, Florida **TNA**
Austin Aries defeated **Kid Kash**, **Jesse Sorensen** and **Zema Ion** in a Four Corners Elimination Match in 9:50 (★★★); **Devon** defeated **D'Angelo Dinero** in 10:19 (★★); **Gunner** defeated **Rob Van Dam** in 6:51 (★★); **Gail Kim** defeated **Mickie James** in 6:19 (★★); **Abyss** defeated **Bully Ray** in a Monster's Ball Match in 15:28 (★★); **Crimson** and **Matt Morgan** defeated **Magnus** and **Samoa Joe** in 9:22 (★★); **Kurt Angle** defeated **James Storm** in 13:40 (★★); **Jeff Hardy** defeated **Bobby Roode** by DQ in 19:28 (★★).

Royal Rumble '12 ★★
29-01-12, St. Louis, Missouri **WWE**
Daniel Bryan defeated **The Big Show** and **Mark Henry** in a Three Way Steel Cage Match in 9:08 (★★); **Beth Phoenix**, **Natalya**, and **The Bella Twins** (**Brie Bella** and **Nikki Bella**) defeated **Kelly Kelly**, **Eve Torres**, **Alicia Fox** and **Tamina Snuka** in 5:29 (★★); **Kane** vs. **John Cena** went to a double count out in 10:56 (★★); **Brodus Clay** defeated **Drew McIntyre** in 1:05 (★); **CM Punk** defeated **Dolph Ziggler** in 14:30 (★★★); **Sheamus** won the 30-Man Royal Rumble Match in 54:52 (★★★).

Against All Odds '12 ★★
12-02-12, Orlando, Florida **TNA**
Zema Ion defeated **Jesse Sorensen** via count out in 4:35 (★★); **Robbie E** defeated **Shannon Moore** in 9:31 (★★); **Gail Kim** defeated **Tara** in 6:46 (★★); **Samoa Joe** and **Magnus** defeated **Crimson** and **Matt Morgan** to win the TNA World Tag Team Title in 9:59 (★★); **Austin Aries** defeated **Alex Shelley** in 14:25 (★★★); **Kazarian** defeated **AJ Styles** in 18:17 (★★★); **Gunner** defeated **Garett Bischoff** in 12:50 (★★); **Bobby Roode** defeated **James Storm**, **Bully Ray** and **Jeff Hardy** in a Four Way Match in 15:12 (★★).

Elimination Chamber '12 ★★★
19-02-12, Milwaukee, Wisconsin **WWE**
CM Punk defeated **The Miz**, **Chris Jericho**, **Kofi Kingston**, **Dolph Ziggler** and **R-Truth** in an Elimination Chamber Match in 32:39 (★★★); **Beth Phoenix** defeated **Tamina Snuka** in 7:19 (★★); **Daniel Bryan** defeated **Santino Marella**, **Wade Barrett**, **Cody Rhodes**, **The Big Show** and **The Great Khali** in an Elimination Chamber Match in 34:04 (★★★); **Jack Swagger** defeated **Justin Gabriel** in 3:48 (★★); **John Cena** defeated **Kane** in an Ambulance Match in 21:21 (★★).

10th Anniversary Show ★★★
04-03-12, New York City, New York **ROH**
The All Night Express (**Kenny King** and **Rhett Titus**) defeated **Wrestling's Greatest Tag Team** (**Charlie Haas** and **Shelton Benjamin**) in 13:34 (★★★); **Mike Bennett** defeated **Homicide** in 10:47 (★★); **The House Of Truth** (**Michael Elgin** and **Roderick Strong**) defeated **Amazing Red** and **TJ Perkins** in 11:10 (★★★); **Jay Lethal** vs. **Tommaso Ciampa** went to a time limit draw in 15:00 (★★★); **The Briscoe Brothers** (**Jay Briscoe** and **Mark Briscoe**) defeated **The Young Bucks** (**Matt Jackson** and **Nick Jackson**) in 13:12 (★★★); **Kevin Steen** defeated **Jimmy Jacobs** in a No Holds Barred Match in 14:56 (★★★); **Adam Cole** and **Eddie Edwards** defeated **Team Ambition** (**Davey Richards** and **Kyle O'Reilly**) in 39:35 (★★★).

Victory Road '12 ★★★
18-03-12, Orlando, Florida **TNA**
James Storm defeated **Bully Ray** in 1:10 (★★); **Austin Aries** defeated **Zema Ion** in 11:08 (★★); **Magnus** and **Samoa Joe** defeated **Crimson** and **Matt Morgan** in 10:12 (★★); **Devon** defeated **Robbie E** to win the TNA Television Title in 3:00 (★★); **Gail Kim** defeated **Madison Rayne** in 7:09 (★★); **AJ Styles** and **Mr. Anderson** defeated **Christopher Daniels** and **Kazarian** in 13:59 (★★★); **Kurt Angle** defeated **Jeff Hardy** in 19:07 (★★★★); **Bobby Roode** defeated **Sting** in a No Holds Barred Match in 16:40 (★★★).

Showdown In The Sun Day #1 ★★★★
30-03-12, Fort Lauderdale, Florida **ROH**
The Briscoe Brothers (**Jay Briscoe** and **Mark Briscoe**) defeated **TMDK** (**Mikey Nicholls** and **Shane Haste**) in 11:00 (★★★); **Adam Cole** defeated **Adam Pearce** in 4:35 (★★); **The All Night Express** (**Kenny King** and **Rhett Titus**) defeated **The Young Bucks** (**Matt Jackson** and **Nick Jackson**) in a Tornado Match in 8:33 (★★); **Jay Lethal** defeated **Kyle O'Reilly** in 11:28 (★★); **Wrestling's Greatest Tag Team** (**Charlie Haas** and **Shelton**

Benjamin) defeated **Caprice Coleman** and **Cedric Alexander** in 11:19 (★★); **Mike Bennett** defeated **Lance Storm** in 16:20 (★★); **Kevin Steen** defeated **El Generico** in a Last Man Standing Match in 24:07 (★★★); **Davey Richards** defeated **Eddie Edwards** and **Roderick Strong** in a Three Way Elimination Match in 21:03 (★★★).

Showdown In The Sun Day #2 ★★★★
31-03-12, Fort Lauderdale, Florida **ROH**
Jimmy Jacobs defeated **El Generico** in 8:01 (★★); **Tommaso Ciampa** defeated **Cedric Alexander** in 5:30 (★★); **TJ Perkins** defeated **Fire Ant** in 8:21 (★★); **Kyle O'Reilly** defeated **Adam Cole** in 8:00 (★★); **The Young Bucks** (**Matt Jackson** and **Nick Jackson**) defeated **The All Night Express** (**Kenny King** and **Rhett Titus**) in a Street Fight in 12:00 (★★★); **The Briscoe Brothers** (**Jay Briscoe** and **Mark Briscoe**) defeated **Wrestling's Greatest Tag Team** (**Charlie Haas** and **Shelton Benjamin**) in 15:19 (★★★); **Kevin Steen** defeated **Eddie Edwards** in 11:00 (★★); **Roderick Strong** defeated **Jay Lethal** to win the ROH World Television Title in 13:20 (★★★); **Davey Richards** defeated **Michael Elgin** in 26:33 (★★★★★).

WrestleMania XXVIII ★★★★
01-04-12, Miami Gardens, Florida **WWE**
Sheamus defeated **Daniel Bryan** to win the World Heavyweight Title in :18 (★); **Kane** defeated **Randy Orton** in 10:58 (★★); **The Big Show** defeated **Cody Rhodes** to win the WWE Intercontinental Title in 5:19 (★★); **Kelly Kelly** and **Maria Menounos** defeated **Beth Phoenix** and **Eve Torres** in 6:22 (★★); **The Undertaker** defeated **Triple H** in a Hell In A Cell Match in 30:47 (★★★★★); **Team Johnny** (**David Otunga**, **Dolph Ziggler**, **Drew McIntyre**, **Jack Swagger**, **Mark Henry** and **The Miz**) defeated **Team Teddy** (**Booker T**, **Kofi Kingston**, **The Great Khali**, **R-Truth**, **Santino Marella** and **Zack Ryder**) in 10:32 (★★); **CM Punk** defeated **Chris Jericho** in 22:23 (★★★); **The Rock** defeated **John Cena** in 30:35 (★★★★).

Lockdown '12 ★★
15-04-12, Nashville, Tennessee **TNA**
Team Garett (**Garett Bischoff**, **AJ Styles**, **Austin Aries**, **Mr. Anderson** and **Rob Van Dam**) defeated **Team Eric** (**Eric Bischoff**, **Bully Ray**, **Christopher Daniels**, **Gunner** and **Kazarian**) in a Lethal Lockdown Match in 26:10 (★★); **Magnus** and **Samoa Joe** defeated **The Motor City Machine Guns** (**Alex Shelley** and **Chris Sabin**) in a Steel Cage Match in 11:20 (★★); **Devon** defeated **Robbie E** in a Steel Cage Match in 3:25 (★★); **Gail Kim** defeated **Velvet Sky** in a Steel Cage Match in 7:30 (★★); **Crimson** defeated **Matt Morgan** in a Steel Cage Match in 8:00 (★★); **Jeff Hardy** defeated **Kurt Angle** in a Steel Cage Match in 14:52 (★★); **Eric Young** and **ODB** defeated **Mexican America** (**Rosita** and **Sarita**) in a Steel Cage Match in 4:17 (★★); **Bobby Roode** defeated **James Storm** in a Steel Cage Match in 20:09 (★★★).

Extreme Rules '12 ★★★★
29-04-12, Rosemont, Illinois **WWE**
Randy Orton defeated **Kane** in a Falls Count Anywhere Match in 16:45 (★★★); **Brodus Clay** defeated **Dolph Ziggler** in 4:17 (★★); **Cody Rhodes** defeated **The Big Show** in a Tables Match to win the WWE Intercontinental Title in 4:37 (★★); **Sheamus** defeated **Daniel Bryan** 2-1 in a Best Two Out Of Three Falls Match in 22:55 (★★★★); **Ryback** defeated **Aaron Relic** and **Jay Hatton** in a Handicap Match in 1:51 (★★); **CM Punk** defeated **Chris Jericho** in a Chicago Street Fight in 25:15 (★★★); **Layla** defeated **Nikki Bella** to win the WWE Divas Title in 2:45 (★); **John Cena** defeated **Brock Lesnar** in an Extreme Rules Match in 17:43 (★★★★).

Border Wars '12 ★★★★
12-05-12, Toronto, Ontario **ROH**
Eddie Edwards defeated **Rhino** in 11:01 (★★★); **The All Night Express** (**Kenny King** and **Rhett Titus**) and **TJ Perkins** defeated **The Young Bucks** (**Matt Jackson** and **Nick Jackson**) and **Mike Mondo** in 12:58 (★★); **Jay Lethal** defeated **Tommaso Ciampa** in 10:52 (★★★); **Lance Storm** defeated **Mike Bennett** in 12:35 (★★); **Michael Elgin** defeated **Adam Cole** in 13:55 (★★★); **Roderick Strong** defeated **Fit Finlay** in 17:16 (★★★); **Wrestling's Greatest Tag Team** (**Charlie Haas** and **Shelton Benjamin**) defeated **The Briscoe Brothers** (**Jay Briscoe** and **Mark Briscoe**) in a Fight Without Honor to win the ROH World Tag Team Title in 14:31 (★★★); **Kevin Steen** defeated **Davey Richards** to win the ROH World Title in 24:45 (★★★★).

Sacrifice '12 ★★★
13-05-12, Orlando, Florida **TNA**
Bad Influence (**Christopher Daniels** and **Kazarian**) defeated **Magnus** and **Samoa Joe** to win the TNA World Tag Team Title in 10:52 (★★); **Gail Kim** defeated **Brooke Tessmacher** in 7:15 (★★); **Devon** defeated **Robbie E** and **Robbie T** in a Three Way Match in 5:25 (★★); **Mr. Anderson** defeated **Jeff Hardy** in 11:38 (★★); **Crimson** defeated **Eric Young** in 6:04 (★★); **Austin Aries** defeated **Bully Ray** in 13:18 (★★★); **Kurt Angle** defeated **AJ Styles** in 20:43 (★★★★); **Bobby Roode** defeated **Rob Van Dam** in a Ladder Match in 15:27 (★★★).

Over The Limit '12 ★★★
20-05-12, Raleigh, North Carolina **WWE**
Christian won a Battle Royal in 12:24 (★★); **Kofi Kingston** and **R-Truth** defeated **Dolph Ziggler** and **Jack Swagger** in 13:44 (★★); **Layla** defeated **Beth Phoenix** in 7:50 (★★); **Sheamus** defeated **Alberto Del Rio**, **Chris Jericho** and **Randy Orton** in a Four Way Match in 16:06 (★★★); **Brodus Clay** defeated **The Miz** in 5:48 (★★); **Christian** defeated **Cody Rhodes** to win the WWE Intercontinental Title in 8:35 (★★); **CM Punk** defeated **Daniel Bryan** in 24:04 (★★★★); **Ryback** defeated **Camacho** in :54 (★★); **John Laurinaitis** defeated **John Cena** in a No DQ Match in 17:02 (★).

Slammiversary X ★★★
10-06-12, Arlington, Texas **TNA**
Austin Aries defeated **Samoa Joe** in 11:44 (★★); **Hernandez** defeated **Kid Kash** in 5:52 (★★); **Devon** and **Garett Bischoff** defeated **Robbie E** and **Robbie T** in 5:56 (★★); **Mr. Anderson** defeated **Jeff Hardy** and **Rob Van Dam** in a Three Way Match in 11:25 (★★); **James Storm** defeated **Crimson** in 2:11 (★★); **Miss. Tessmacher** defeated **Gail Kim** to win the TNA Knockouts Title in 6:44 (★★); **Joseph Park** defeated **Bully Ray** in a No DQ Match in 10:25 (★★); **AJ Styles** and **Kurt Angle** defeated **Bad Influence** (**Christopher Daniels** and **Kazarian**) to win the TNA World Tag Team Title in 14:25 (★★★★); **Bobby Roode** defeated **Sting** in 10:55 (★★).

No Way Out '12 ★★
17-06-12, East Rutherford, New Jersey **WWE**
Sheamus defeated **Dolph Ziggler** in 15:10 (★★★); **Santino Marella** defeated **Ricardo Rodriguez** in a Tuxedo Match in 4:25 (★); **Christian** defeated **Cody Rhodes** in 11:30 (★★★); **The Prime Time Players** (**Darren Young** and **Titus O'Neil**) defeated **Justin Gabriel** and **Tyson Kidd**, **The Usos** (**Jimmy Uso** and **Jey Uso**) and **Primo** and **Epico** in a Four Way Match in 9:30 (★★★); **Layla** defeated **Beth Phoenix** in 6:57 (★★); **Sin Cara** defeated **Hunico** in 5:48 (★★); **CM Punk** defeated **Daniel Bryan** and **Kane** in a Three Way Match in 18:17 (★★★); **Ryback** defeated **Dan Delaney** and **Rob Grymes** in a Handicap Match in 1:38 (★★); **John Cena** defeated **The Big Show** in a Steel Cage Match in 24:43 (★★).

Best In The World '12 ★★★
24-06-12, New York, New York **ROH**
The Briscoe Brothers (**Jay Briscoe** and **Mark Briscoe**) defeated **The Guardians Of Truth** (**Guardian #1** and **Guardian #2**) in 6:00 (★★); **Homicide** defeated **Eddie Edwards** in 12:45 (★★★); **Adam Cole** defeated **Kyle O'Reilly** in a Hybrid Fighting Rules Match in 12:38 (★★★★); **Michael Elgin** defeated **Fit Finlay** in 19:15 (★★); **Mike Mondo** defeated **Mike Bennett** in 4:12 (★★); **Roderick Strong** defeated **Jay Lethal** and **Tommaso Ciampa** in a Three Way Elimination Match in 13:08 (★★); **The All Night Express** (**Kenny King** and **Rhett Titus**) defeated **Wrestling's Greatest Tag Team** (**Charlie Haas** and **Shelton Benjamin**) to win the ROH World Tag Team Title in 22:51 (★★★); **Kevin Steen** defeated **Davey Richards** in an Anything Goes Match in 21:23 (★★★★).

Destination X '12 ★★★★
08-07-12, Orlando, Florida **TNA**
Mason Andrews defeated **Dakota Darsow**, **Lars Only** and **Rubix** in a Four Way Match in 8:22 (★★); **Mason Andrews** defeated **Kid Kash** in 8:10 (★★); **Kenny King** defeated **Douglas Williams** in 10:35 (★★); **Sonjay Dutt** defeated **Rashad Cameron** in 7:16 (★★); **Zema Ion** defeated **Flip Cassanova** in 3:55 (★★); **Samoa Joe** defeated **Kurt Angle** in 14:38 (★★★★); **AJ Styles** defeated **Christopher Daniels** in a Last Man Standing Match in 17:41 (★★★★); **Zema Ion** defeated **Kenny King**, **Mason Andrews** and **Sonjay Dutt** in an Ultimate X Match to win the vacant TNA X Division Title in 8:50 (★★★); **Austin Aries** defeated **Bobby Roode** to win the TNA World Heavyweight Title in 22:42 (★★★★).

Money In The Bank '12 ★★★★
15-07-12, Phoenix, Arizona **WWE**

Dolph Ziggler defeated Christian, Cody Rhodes, Damien Sandow, Santino Marella, Sin Cara, Tensai and Tyson Kidd in a Money In The Bank Ladder Match in 18:29 (★★★); Sheamus defeated Alberto Del Rio in 14:24 (★★★); Primo and Epico defeated The Prime Time Players (Darren Young and Titus O'Neil) in 7:31 (★★); CM Punk defeated Daniel Bryan in a No DQ Match in 27:48 (★★★); Ryback defeated Curt Hawkins and Tyler Reks in a Handicap Match in 4:22 (★★); Kaitlyn, Layla and Tamina Snuka defeated Beth Phoenix, Eve Torres and Natalya in 3:23 (★★); John Cena defeated The Big Show, Chris Jericho, Kane and The Miz in a Money In The Bank Ladder Match in 20:03 (★★★★).

Boiling Point '12 ★★★★
11-08-12, Providence, Rhode Island **ROH**

Roderick Strong defeated Mike Mondo in 12:39 (★★★); QT Marshall defeated Matt Taven, Antonio Thomas and Vinny Marseglia in a Four Corner Survival Match in 11:00 (★★); Adam Cole defeated Bob Evans in 10:02 (★★); Charlie Haas defeated Michael Elgin in 14:41 (★★); The Briscoe Brothers (Jay Briscoe and Mark Briscoe) defeated S.C.U.M. (Jimmy Jacobs and Steve Corino) in 12:45 (★★★); Jay Lethal defeated Tommaso Ciampa in a Best Two Out Of Three Falls Match in 15:14 (★★★); Eddie Edwards and Sara Del Rey defeated Mike Bennett and Maria Kanellis in 13:06 (★★★); Kevin Steen defeated Eddie Kingston in an Anything Goes Match in 18:46 (★★★).

Hardcore Justice '12 ★★
12-08-12, Orlando, Florida **TNA**

Chavo Guerrero and Hernandez defeated Gunner and Kid Kash in 9:24 (★★); Rob Van Dam defeated Magnus and Mr. Anderson in a Three Way Falls Count Anywhere Match in 9:14 (★★★); Devon defeated Kazarian in 8:33 (★★); Madison Rayne defeated Miss. Tessmacher to win the TNA Knockouts Title in 5:56 (★★); Bully Ray defeated James Storm, Jeff Hardy and Robbie E in a Four Way Tables Match in 13:45 (★★); Zema Ion defeated Kenny King in 11:06 (★★); AJ Styles defeated Christopher Daniels, Kurt Angle and Samoa Joe in a Four Way Ladder Match in 16:22 (★★); Austin Aries defeated Bobby Roode in a Last Chance Match in 24:36 (★★★★).

SummerSlam '12 ★★
19-08-12, Los Angeles, California **WWE**

Chris Jericho defeated Dolph Ziggler in 13:07 (★★★★); Daniel Bryan defeated Kane in 8:02 (★★); The Miz defeated Rey Mysterio in 9:09 (★★); Sheamus defeated Alberto Del Rio in 11:22 (★★); Kofi Kingston and R-Truth defeated The Prime Time Players (Darren Young and Titus O'Neil) in 7:06 (★★); CM Punk defeated The Big Show and John Cena in a Three Way Match in 12:34 (★★); Brock Lesnar defeated Triple H in a No DQ Match in 18:45 (★★).

No Surrender '12 ★★
09-09-12, Orlando, Florida **TNA**

Jeff Hardy defeated Samoa Joe in 12:34 (★★); Bully Ray defeated James Storm in 13:54 (★★); Miss. Tessmacher defeated Tara in 6:55 (★★); Austin Aries defeated The Armbreaker in an Unsanction Match in 6:33 (★★); Zema Ion defeated Sonjay Dutt in 11:32 (★★); Rob Van Dam defeated Magnus in 10:07 (★★); Bad Influence (Christopher Daniels and Kazarian) defeated AJ Styles and Kurt Angle in 19:30 (★★); Jeff Hardy defeated Bully Ray in 12:23 (★★).

Death Before Dishonor X ★★
15-09-12, Chicago Ridge, Illinois **ROH**

S.C.U.M. (Jimmy Jacobs and Steve Corino) defeated Caprice Coleman and Cedric Alexander in 12:16 (★★); TaDarius Thomas defeated Silas Young in 6:27 (★★); Kyle O'Reilly defeated ACH in 9:34 (★★★); Charlie Haas and Rhett Titus defeated The Briscoe Brothers (Jay Briscoe and Mark Briscoe) in 10:47 (★★); Jay Lethal defeated Homicide in 14:33 (★★★); The House Of Truth (Roderick Strong and Michael Elgin) defeated The Irish Airborne (Jake Crist and Dave Crist) in 8:44 (★★); Adam Cole defeated Mike Mondo in 19:30 (★★★); S.C.U.M. (Jimmy Jacobs and Steve Corino) defeated Charlie Haas and Rhett Titus to win the vacant ROH World Tag Team Title in 12:26 (★★); Kevin Steen defeated Rhino in a No DQ Match in 16:18 (★★★).

Night Of Champions '12 ★★★
16-09-12, Boston, Massachusetts **WWE**

The Miz defeated Cody Rhodes, Rey Mysterio and Sin Cara in a Four Way Match in 12:05; (★★★) Daniel Bryan and Kane defeated Kofi Kingston and R-Truth to win the WWE Tag Team Title in 8:30 (★★); Antonio Cesaro defeated Zack Ryder in 6:40 (★★); Randy Orton defeated Dolph Ziggler in 18:24 (★★★); Eve Torres defeated Layla to win the WWE Divas Title in 7:05 (★★); Sheamus defeated Alberto Del Rio in 14:25 (★★★); CM Punk vs. John Cena ended in a draw in 26:55 (★★★★).

Glory By Honor XI ★★★★
13-10-12, Ontario, Canada **ROH**

Caprice Coleman and Cedric Alexander defeated The Bravado Brothers (Harlem Bravado and Lance Bravado) in 10:26 (★★★); Mike Bennett defeated Mike Mondo in 12:30 (★★★); Wrestling's Greatest Tag Team (Charlie Haas and Shelton Benjamin) defeated B.J. Whitmer and Rhett Titus in 11:48 (★★); Jay Lethal defeated Davey Richards in 24:08 (★★★★); TaDarius Thomas defeated Rhino in 7:49 (★★); Adam Cole defeated Eddie Edwards in 19:57 (★★★); S.C.U.M. (Jimmy Jacobs and Steve Corino) defeated The Briscoe Brothers (Jay Briscoe and Mark Briscoe) in 14:05 (★★★); Kevin Steen defeated Michael Elgin in 31:46 (★★★★).

Bound For Glory '12 ★★★★
14-10-12, Phoenix, Arizona **TNA**

Rob Van Dam defeated Zema Ion to win the TNA X Division Title in 8:04 (★★); Samoa Joe defeated Magnus in 9:15 (★★★); James Storm defeated Bobby Roode in a Street Fight in 17:35 (★★★★); Joey Ryan defeated Al Snow in 8:32 (★); Chavo Guerrero and Hernandez defeated Bad Influence (Christopher Daniels and Kazarian) and AJ Styles and Kurt Angle in a Three Way Match to win the TNA World Tag Team Title in 15:39 (★★★); Tara defeated Miss Tessmacher to win the TNA Knockouts Title in 6:21 (★★★); Aces and Eights (D.O.C. and Knux) defeated Bully Ray and Sting in a No DQ Match in 10:51 (★★); Jeff Hardy defeated Austin Aries to win the TNA Heavyweight Title in 23:03 (★★★★).

Hell In A Cell '12 ★★★
28-10-12, Atlanta, Georgia **WWE**

Randy Orton defeated Alberto Del Rio in 13:40 (★★); Team Rhodes Scholars (Cody Rhodes and Damien Sandow) defeated Team Hell No (Daniel Bryan and Kane) by DQ in 11:11 (★★); Kofi Kingston defeated The Miz in 10:21 (★★); Antonio Cesaro defeated Justin Gabriel in 7:22 (★★); Rey Mysterio and Sin Cara defeated The Prime Time Players (Darren Young and Titus O'Neil) in 12:27 (★★); The Big Show defeated Sheamus to win the World Heavyweight Title in 20:26 (★★★); Eve Torres defeated Kaitlyn and Layla in a Three Way Match in 7:33 (★); CM Punk defeated Ryback in a Hell In A Cell Match in 11:21 (★★★).

Turning Point '12 ★★★★
11-11-12, Orlando, Florida **TNA**

Samoa Joe defeated Magnus in a No DQ Match in 12:29 (★★★); Eric Young and ODB defeated Jesse and Tara in 8:32 (★★); Rob Van Dam defeated Joey Ryan in 7:43 (★★); D.O.C. defeated Joseph Park in 11:02 (★★); Chavo Guerrero and Hernandez defeated Bad Influence (Christopher Daniels and Kazarian) in 13:17 (★★★); James Storm defeated AJ Styles and Bobby Roode in a Three Way Match in 16:34 (★★★); Kurt Angle defeated Devon in 11:47 (★★); Jeff Hardy defeated Austin Aries in a Ladder Match in 20:58 (★★★★).

Survivor Series '12 ★★
18-11-12, Indianapolis, Indiana **WWE**

Brodus Clay, Justin Gabriel, Rey Mysterio, Sin Cara and Tyson Kidd defeated Tensai, Darren Young, Titus O'Neil, Primo and Epico in an Elimination Match in 18:27 (★★); Eve Torres defeated Kaitlyn in 7:01 (★); Antonio Cesaro defeated R-Truth in 6:57 (★); Sheamus defeated The Big Show by DQ in 14:44 (★★); Team Ziggler (Dolph Ziggler, Alberto Del Rio, Damien Sandow, David Otunga and Wade Barrett) defeated Team Foley (Daniel Bryan, Kane, Kofi Kingston, The Miz and Randy Orton) in an Elimination Match in 23:43 (★★★); CM Punk defeated John Cena and Ryback in a Three Way Match in 17:58 (★★★).

Final Resolution '12 ★★
09-12-12, Orlando, Florida TNA
James Storm defeated Kazarian in 6:09 (★★); Rob Van Dam defeated Kenny King in 9:22 (★★); Chavo Guerrero and Hernandez defeated Joey Ryan and Matt Morgan by DQ in 10:36 (★★); Austin Aries defeated Bully Ray in 13:08 (★★); Tara defeated Mickie James in 7:53 (★★); Garett Bischoff, Kurt Angle, Samoa Joe and Wes Brisco defeated Aces and Eights (Devon, D.O.C., Knux and C.J. O'Doyle) in 11:22 (★★); Christopher Daniels defeated AJ Styles in 21:37 (★★); Jeff Hardy defeated Bobby Roode in 23:00 (★★).

Final Battle '12 ★★★
16-12-12, New York, New York ROH
Roderick Strong defeated Michael Elgin in 11:30 (★★★); Jay Lethal defeated Rhino in 9:33 (★★); R.D. Evans defeated Prince Nana in 6:12 (★★); Wrestling's Greatest Tag Team (Charlie Haas and Shelton Benjamin) defeated B.J. Whitmer and Rhett Titus in a New York Street Fight in 15:26 (★★); Mike Bennett defeated Jerry Lynn in 10:06 (★★); The American Wolves (Davey Richards and Eddie Edwards) defeated reDRagon (Bobby Fish and Kyle O'Reilly) in 12:24 (★★); Matt Hardy defeated Adam Cole in 11:40 (★★★); The Briscoe Brothers (Jay Briscoe and Mark Briscoe) defeated S.C.U.M. (Jimmy Jacobs and Steve Corino) and C&C Wrestle Factory (Caprice Coleman and Cedric Alexander) in a Three Way Match to win the ROH World Tag Team Title in 7:06 (★★); Kevin Steen defeated El Generico in a Ladder War in 28:07 (★★★★).

TLC '12 ★★★
16-12-12, Brooklyn, New York WWF
Team Rhodes Scholars (Cody Rhodes and Damien Sandow) defeated Rey Mysterio and Sin Cara in a Tables Match in 9:29 (★★★); Antonio Cesaro defeated R-Truth in 6:40 (★★); Kofi Kingston defeated Wade Barrett in 8:13 (★★★); The Shield (Roman Reigns, Dean Ambrose and Seth Rollins) defeated Ryback and Team Hell No (Daniel Bryan and Kane) in a TLC Match in 22:44 (★★★★); Eve Torres defeated Naomi in 2:58 (★★); The Big Show defeated Sheamus in a Chairs Match in 14:17 (★★); The Brooklyn Brawler, The Miz and Alberto Del Rio defeated 3MB (Drew McIntyre, Heath Slater and Jinder Mahal) in 3:23 (★★); Dolph Ziggler defeated John Cena in a Ladder Match in 23:16 (★★★★).

Tribute To The Troops '12 ★★
19-12-12, Norfolk, Virginia WWE
Randy Orton and Sheamus defeated The Big Show and Dolph Ziggler in 12:05 (★★); Ryback defeated Alberto Del Rio by DQ in 1:30 (★★); The Miz defeated Damien Sandow in 3:30 (★★); R-Truth and Team Hell No (Kane and Daniel Bryan) defeated 3MB (Heath Slater, Drew McIntyre and Jinder Mahal) in 3:26 (★); John Cena defeated Antonio Cesaro in 5:10 (★★).

Genesis '13 ★★
13-01-13, Orlando, Florida TNA
Chavo Guerrero and Hernandez defeated Joey Ryan and Matt Morgan in 11:30 (★★); Mr. Anderson defeated Samoa Joe in 10:45 (★★); Christian York defeated Kenny King in 10:12 (★★); Rob Van Dam defeated Christian York in 5:30 (★★); Devon defeated Joseph Park in 11:17 (★★); Velvet Sky defeated Gail Kim, Mickie James, Miss Tessmacher and ODB in a Gauntlet Match in 11:55 (★★); Christopher Daniels defeated James Storm in 13:25 (★★★); Sting defeated D.O.C. in 5:53 (★★); Jeff Hardy defeated Austin Aries and Bobby Roode in a Three Way Elimination Match in 20:32 (★★).

Royal Rumble '13 ★★★
27-01-13, Phoenix, Arizona WWE
Alberto Del Rio defeated The Big Show in a Last Man Standing Match in 16:57 (★★★); Team Hell No (Daniel Bryan and Kane) defeated Team Rhodes Scholars (Cody Rhodes and Damien Sandow) in 9:25 (★★); John Cena won the 30-Man Royal Rumble Match in 55:05 (★★★); The Rock defeated CM Punk to win the WWE Title in 23:20 (★★★).

Elimination Chamber '13 ★★★
17-02-13, New Orleans, Louisiana WWE
Alberto Del Rio defeated The Big Show in 13:05 (★★★); Antonio Cesaro defeated The Miz by DQ in 8:21 (★★); Jack Swagger defeated Randy Orton, Chris Jericho, Mark Henry,

Kane and Daniel Bryan in an Elimination Chamber Match in 31:18 (★★); The Shield (Roman Reigns, Dean Ambrose and Seth Rollins) defeated John Cena, Ryback and Sheamus in 14:49 (★★★); Dolph Ziggler defeated Kofi Kingston in 3:55 (★★); Kaitlyn defeated Tamina Snuka in 3:15 (★); The Rock defeated CM Punk in 20:55 (★★★).

11th Anniversary Show ★★★★
02-03-13, Chicago Ridge, Illinois ROH
ACH defeated QT Marshall, Adam Page, Silas Young, Mike Sydal and TaDarius Thomas in a Six Man Mayhem Match in 7:03 (★★★); S.C.U.M. (Jimmy Jacobs and Steve Corino) defeated Caprice Coleman and Cedric Alexander in 8:33 (★★★); B.J. Whitmer defeated Charlie Haas in a No Holds Barred Match in 12:03 (★★★); The American Wolves (Davey Richards and Eddie Edwards) defeated The Forever Hooligans (Alex Koslov and Rocky Romero) in 15:40 (★★★★); Michael Elgin defeated Roderick Strong in a Best Two Out Of Three Falls Match in 17:38 (★★★); Matt Taven defeated Adam Cole to win the ROH World Television Title in 13:35 (★★★); reDRagon (Bobby Fish and Kyle O'Reilly) defeated The Briscoe Brothers (Jay Briscoe and Mark Briscoe) to win the ROH World Tag Team Title in 15:14 (★★★★); Kevin Steen defeated Jay Lethal in 20:50 (★★★★).

Lockdown '13 ★★★
10-03-13, San Antonio, Texas TNA
Kenny King defeated Christian York and Zema Ion in a Three Way Match in 11:01 (★★); Joseph Park defeated Joey Ryan in 5:42 (★★); Velvet Sky defeated Gail Kim in 7:26 (★★); Robbie T defeated Robbie E in 5:42 (★); Austin Aries and Bobby Roode defeated Bad Influence (Christopher Daniels and Kazarian) and Chavo Guerrero and Hernandez in a Three Way Match in 17:01 (★★★); Wes Brisco defeated Kurt Angle in a Steel Cage Match in 11:44 (★★★); Team TNA (Eric Young, James Storm, Magnus, Samoa Joe and Sting) defeated Aces and Eights (Devon, D.O.C., Garett Bischoff, Knux and Mr. Anderson) in a Lethal Lockdown Match in 25:25 (★★★); Bully Ray defeated Jeff Hardy in a Steel Cage Match to win the TNA World Heavyweight Title in 17:11 (★★★).

Supercard Of Honor VII ★★★★
05-04-13, New York, New York ROH
ACH and TaDarius Thomas defeated QT Marshall and R.D. Evans in 9:52 (★★); Mike Bennett defeated Shelton Benjamin in 7:42 (★★); Michael Elgin defeated Jay Lethal in 18:50 (★★★★); S.C.U.M. (Cliff Compton, Jimmy Jacobs, Jimmy Rave, Rhett Titus and Rhino) defeated Team ROH (B.J. Whitmer, Caprice Coleman, Cedric Alexander, Mark Briscoe and Mike Mondo) in a Ten Man War in 11:37 (★★★); Karl Anderson defeated Roderick Strong in 12:33 (★★★); Matt Taven defeated Adam Cole and Matt Hardy in a Three Way Elimination Match in 11:20 (★★); reDRagon (Bobby Fish and Kyle O'Reilly) defeated The American Wolves (Davey Richards and Eddie Edwards) in 21:08 (★★★★); Jay Briscoe defeated Kevin Steen to win the ROH World Title in 18:27 (★★★★).

WrestleMania XXIX ★★
07-04-13, East Rutherford, New Jersey WWE
The Shield (Roman Reigns, Dean Ambrose and Seth Rollins) defeated The Big Show, Randy Orton and Sheamus in 10:33 (★★); Mark Henry defeated Ryback in 8:02 (★); Team Hell No (Daniel Bryan and Kane) defeated Big E Langston and Dolph Ziggler in 6:17 (★★); Fandango defeated Chris Jericho in 9:11 (★★); Alberto Del Rio defeated Jack Swagger in 10:30 (★★); The Undertaker defeated CM Punk in 22:07 (★★★★); Triple H defeated Brock Lesnar in a No Holds Barred Match in 23:58 (★★); John Cena defeated The Rock to win the WWE Title in 23:59 (★★★).

Border Wars '13 ★★★
04-05-13, Toronto, Canada ROH
Caprice Coleman and Cedric Alexander defeated ACH and TaDarius Thomas in 10:54 (★★★); Roderick Strong defeated Mike Bennett in 12:45 (★★); B.J. Whitmer defeated Rhett Titus in an "I Quit" Match in 11:32 (★); S.C.U.M. (Cliff Compton and Jimmy Jacobs) defeated Jay Lethal and Michael Elgin in 20:14 (★★★); Eddie Edwards defeated Taiji Ishimori in 15:40 (★★★); Matt Taven defeated Mark Briscoe in 13:44 (★★); Davey Richards defeated Paul London in 18:07 (★★★); Jay Briscoe defeated Adam Cole in 20:08 (★★★).

Extreme Rules '13 ★★
19-05-13, St. Louis, Missouri **WWE**

Chris Jericho defeated Fandango in 8:36 (★ ★); Dean Ambrose defeated Kofi Kingston to win the WWE United States Title in 6:49 (★ ★); Sheamus defeated Mark Henry in a Strap Match in 7:59 (★ ★); Alberto Del Rio defeated Jack Swagger in an "I Quit" Match in 11:20 (★ ★); The Shield (Roman Reigns and Seth Rollins) defeated Team Hell No (Daniel Bryan and Kane) in a Tornado Match to win the WWE Tag Team Title in 7:22 (★ ★); Randy Orton defeated The Big Show in an Extreme Rules Match in 13:00 (★ ★); John Cena vs. Ryback ended in a no contest in a Last Man Standing Match in 21:14 (★ ★); Brock Lesnar defeated Triple H in a Steel Cage Match in 20:10 (★ ★).

Slammiversary XI ★★★
02-06-13, Boston, Massachusetts **TNA**

Chris Sabin defeated Kenny King and Suicide in an Ultimate X Match to win the TNA X Division Title in 15:25 (★ ★ ★); Jeff Hardy, Magnus and Samoa Joe defeated Aces and Eights (Garett Bischoff, Mr. Anderson and Wes Brisco) in 10:08 (★ ★); Jay Bradley defeated Sam Shaw in 4:57 (★ ★); Devon defeated Joseph Park via count out in :32 (★); Abyss defeated Devon to win the TNA Television Title in 4:50 (★); Gunner and James Storm defeated Austin Aries and Bobby Roode, Bad Influence (Christopher Daniels and Kazarian), and Chavo Guerrero and Hernandez in a Four Way Elimination Match to win the TNA World Tag Team Title in 16:42 (★ ★ ★); Taryn Terrell defeated Gail Kim in a Last Woman Standing Match in 9:21 (★ ★ ★); Kurt Angle defeated AJ Styles in 15:45 (★ ★ ★ ★); Bully Ray defeated Sting in a No Holds Barred Match in 14:23 (★ ★ ★).

Payback '13 ★★★★
16-06-13, Rosemont, Illinois **WWE**

Curtis Axel defeated Wade Barrett and The Miz in a Three Way Match to win the WWE Intercontinental Title in 10:34 (★ ★ ★); AJ Lee defeated Kaitlyn to win the WWE Divas Title in 9:52 (★ ★); Dean Ambrose defeated Kane via count out in 9:33 (★ ★); Alberto Del Rio defeated Dolph Ziggler to win the World Heavyweight Title in 13:48 (★ ★); CM Punk defeated Chris Jericho in 21:19 (★ ★ ★ ★); The Shield (Roman Reigns and Seth Rollins) defeated Daniel Bryan and Randy Orton in 12:08 (★ ★ ★); John Cena defeated Ryback in a Three Stages Of Hell Match in 24:50 (★ ★ ★).

Best In The World '13 ★★★★
22-06-13, Baltimore, Maryland **ROH**

B.J. Whitmer defeated Mike Bennett in 9:05 (★ ★); The American Wolves (Davey Richards and Eddie Edwards) defeated Adrenaline Rush (ACH and TaDarius Thomas) in 12:49 (★ ★ ★); Adam Cole defeated Roderick Strong via count out in 15:33 (★ ★); Michael Elgin defeated Tommaso Ciampa in 20:06 (★ ★ ★); Matt Taven defeated Jimmy Jacobs and Jay Lethal in a Three Way Match in 11:35 (★ ★ ★); reDRagon (Bobby Fish and Kyle O'Reilly) defeated C&C Wrestle Factory (Caprice Coleman and Cedric Alexander) and S.C.U.M. (Cliff Compton and Rhett Titus) in a Three Way Match in 7:13 (★ ★); Matt Hardy defeated Kevin Steen in a No DQ Match in 14:13 (★ ★ ★); Jay Briscoe defeated Mark Briscoe in 21:27 (★ ★ ★).

Money In The Bank '13 ★★★★
14-07-13, Philadelphia, Pennsylvania **WWE**

Damien Sandow defeated Antonio Cesaro, Cody Rhodes, Dean Ambrose, Fandango, Jack Swagger and Wade Barrett in a Money In The Bank Ladder Match in 16:24 (★ ★ ★ ★); Curtis Axel defeated The Miz in 9:19 (★ ★); AJ Lee defeated Kaitlyn in 7:01 (★ ★); Ryback defeated Chris Jericho in 11:19 (★ ★); Alberto Del Rio defeated Dolph Ziggler by DQ in 14:29 (★ ★ ★); John Cena defeated Mark Henry in 14:42 (★ ★ ★); Randy Orton defeated Christian, CM Punk, Daniel Bryan, Rob Van Dam and Sheamus in a Money In The Bank Ladder Match in 26:38 (★ ★ ★ ★).

SummerSlam '13 ★★★★★
18-08-13, Los Angeles, California **WWE**

Bray Wyatt defeated Kane in a Ring Of Fire Match in 7:49 (★ ★); Cody Rhodes defeated Damien Sandow in 6:40 (★ ★ ★); Alberto Del Rio defeated Christian in 12:30 (★ ★ ★); Natalya defeated Brie Bella in 5:19 (★ ★); Brock Lesnar defeated CM Punk in a No DQ Match in 25:17 (★ ★ ★ ★ ★); Dolph Ziggler and Kaitlyn defeated Big E Langston and AJ Lee in 6:45 (★ ★); Daniel Bryan defeated John Cena to win the WWE Title in 26:55 (★ ★ ★ ★ ★); Randy Orton defeated Daniel Bryan to win the WWE Title in :08 (★).

Night Of Champions '13 ★★
15-09-13, Detroit, Michigan **WWE**

Curtis Axel defeated Kofi Kingston in 13:56 (★ ★); AJ Lee defeated Brie Bella, Naomi and Natalya in a Four Way Match in 5:40 (★ ★); Rob Van Dam defeated Alberto Del Rio by DQ in 13:07 (★ ★); The Miz defeated Fandango in 7:49 (★ ★); Curtis Axel and Paul Heyman defeated CM Punk in a No DQ Handicap Elimination Match in 15:22 (★ ★ ★); Dean Ambrose defeated Dolph Ziggler in 9:37 (★ ★); The Shield (Roman Reigns and Seth Rollins) defeated The Prime Time Players (Darren Young and Titus O'Neil) in 6:59 (★ ★); Daniel Bryan defeated Randy Orton to win the WWE Title in 17:38 (★ ★ ★).

Death Before Dishonor XI ★★★
20-09-13, Philadelphia, Pennsylvania **ROH**

Jay Lethal defeated Silas Young in 9:20 (★ ★); Adam Cole defeated Tommaso Ciampa in 13:54 (★ ★ ★); Michael Elgin defeated Kevin Steen in 19:24 (★ ★ ★); The Forever Hooligans (Rocky Romero and Alex Koslov) defeated The American Wolves (Davey Richards and Eddie Edwards) in 19:44 (★ ★ ★); Adam Page defeated R.D. Evans in 2:02 (★ ★); Roderick Strong defeated Ricky Marvin in 12:46 (★ ★); Adrenaline Rush (ACH and TaDarius Thomas) and C&C Wrestle Factory (Caprice Coleman and Cedric Alexander) defeated reDRagon (Bobby Fish and Kyle O'Reilly), Matt Taven and Michael Bennett in 12:11 (★ ★ ★); Adam Cole defeated Michael Elgin to win the ROH World Title in 26:33 (★ ★ ★ ★).

Battleground '13 ★★
06-10-13, Buffalo, New York **WWE**

Alberto Del Rio defeated Rob Van Dam in a Hardcore Match in 17:08 (★ ★); The Real Americans (Jack Swagger and Antonio Cesaro) defeated Santino Marella and The Great Khali in 7:11 (★); Curtis Axel defeated R-Truth in 7:36 (★ ★); AJ Lee defeated Brie Bella in 6:37 (★ ★); Cody Rhodes and Goldust defeated The Shield (Roman Reigns and Seth Rollins) in 13:54 (★ ★ ★ ★); Bray Wyatt defeated Kofi Kingston in 8:27 (★ ★); CM Punk defeated Ryback in 14:47 (★ ★); Daniel Bryan vs. Randy Orton went to a no contest in 25:00 (★ ★).

Bound For Glory '13 ★★
20-10-13, San Diego, California **TNA**

Chris Sabin defeated Manik, Austin Aries, Jeff Hardy and Samoa Joe in an Ultimate X Match to win the TNA X Division Title in 11:58 (★ ★); The BroMans (Jessie Godderz and Robbie E) defeated Gunner and James Storm to win the TNA World Tag Team Title in 11:41 (★ ★); Gail Kim defeated Brooke Tessmacher and ODB in a Three Way Match to win the TNA Knockouts Title in 10:19 (★ ★); Bobby Roode defeated Kurt Angle in 20:58 (★ ★ ★); Ethan Carter III defeated Norv Fernum in 3:26 (★); Magnus defeated Sting in 11:05 (★ ★); AJ Styles defeated Bully Ray in a No DQ Match to win the TNA World Heavyweight Title in 28:31 (★ ★ ★).

Hell In A Cell '13 ★★★
27-10-13, Miami, Florida **WWE**

Cody Rhodes and Goldust defeated The Usos (Jimmy Uso and Jey Uso) and The Shield (Roman Reigns and Seth Rollins) in a Three Way Match in 14:38 (★ ★ ★ ★); Fandango and Summer Rae defeated The Great Khali and Natalya in 4:50 (★); Big E Langston defeated Dean Ambrose via count out in 8:43 (★ ★); CM Punk defeated Ryback and Paul Heyman in a Handicap Hell In A Cell Match in 13:49 (★ ★); Los Matadores (Diego and Fernando) defeated The Real Americans (Jack Swagger and Antonio Cesaro) in 5:52 (★ ★); John Cena defeated Alberto Del Rio to win the World Heavyweight Title in 15:17 (★ ★ ★); AJ Lee defeated Brie Bella in 5:40 (★ ★); Randy Orton defeated Daniel Bryan in a Hell In A Cell Match in 22:04 (★ ★ ★).

Survivor Series '13 ★★
24-11-13, Boston, Massachusetts **WWE**

The Shield (Dean Ambrose, Seth Rollins and Roman Reigns) and The Real Americans (Antonio Cesaro and Jack Swagger) defeated Cody Rhodes, Goldust, Rey Mysterio and The Usos (Jimmy Uso and Jey Uso) in an Elimination Match in 23:23 (★ ★ ★); Big E Langston defeated Curtis Axel in 7:02 (★ ★); Total Divas (Brie Bella, Nikki Bella, Eva Marie, Cameron, Naomi, JoJo and Natalya) defeated True Divas (AJ Lee, Aksana, Alicia Fox, Kaitlyn, Rosa Mendes, Summer Rae and Tamina Snuka) in an Elimination Match in 11:29 (★); Mark Henry defeated Ryback in 4:46 (★ ★); John Cena defeated Alberto Del Rio in 18:49 (★ ★); CM Punk and Daniel Bryan defeated The Wyatt Family (Erick Rowan and Luke Harper) in 16:51 (★ ★ ★); Randy Orton defeated The Big Show in 11:10 (★ ★).

Final Battle '13 ★★★
15-12-13, Manhattan, New York **ROH**
Matt Hardy defeated Adam Page in 7:20 (★★); Silas Young defeated Mark Briscoe in a Strap Match in 9:15 (★★); The Young Bucks (Matt Jackson and Nick Jackson) defeated Adrenaline Rush (ACH and TaDarius Thomas) in 12:29 (★★★); Kevin Steen defeated Michael Bennett in a Stretcher Match in 16:44 (★★★★); reDRagon (Bobby Fish and Kyle O'Reilly) defeated Outlaw Inc. (Eddie Kingston and Homicide) in 15:07 (★★); Tommaso Ciampa defeated Matt Taven to win the ROH World Television Title in 4:22 (★★); B.J. Whitmer and Eddie Edwards defeated Jay Lethal and Roderick Strong in 16:20 (★★★); Adam Cole defeated Michael Elgin and Jay Briscoe in a Three Way Match in 33:39 (★★★).

TLC '13 ★★★
15-12-13, Houston, Texas **WWE**
CM Punk defeated The Shield (Dean Ambrose, Seth Rollins and Roman Reigns) in a Handicap Match in 13:42 (★★★); AJ Lee defeated Natalya in 6:35 (★★★); Big E Langston defeated Damien Sandow in 6:28 (★★); Cody Rhodes and Goldust defeated The Big Show and Rey Mysterio, The Real Americans (Jack Swagger and Antonio Cesaro), and RybAxel (Ryback and Curtis Axel) in a Four Way Elimination Match in 21:05 (★★★); R-Truth defeated Brodus Clay in 6:02 (★); Kofi Kingston defeated The Miz in a No DQ Match in 8:02 (★★); The Wyatt Family (Bray Wyatt, Luke Harper and Erick Rowan) defeated Daniel Bryan in a Handicap Match in 12:24 (★★); Randy Orton defeated John Cena in a TLC Match in 24:36 (★★★).

Tribute To The Troops '13 ★★
28-12-13, Tacoma, Washington **WWE**
Daniel Bryan defeated Bray Wyatt by DQ in 1:43 (★★); CM Punk and Daniel Bryan defeated Luke Harper and Erick Rowan by DQ in 5:50 (★★); CM Punk, Daniel Bryan and John Cena defeated The Wyatt Family (Bray Wyatt, Luke Harper and Erick Rowan) in 7:00 (★★★); R-Truth defeated Fandango in 1:47 (★★); The Big Show defeated Damien Sandow in 2:05 (★★).

Royal Rumble '14 ★★★
26-01-14, Pittsburgh, Pennsylvania **WWE**
Bray Wyatt defeated Daniel Bryan in 21:30 (★★★★); Brock Lesnar defeated The Big Show in 2:02 (★★); Randy Orton defeated John Cena in 20:54 (★★); Batista won the 30-Man Royal Rumble Match in 55:08 (★★★).

Elimination Chamber '14 ★★★
23-02-14, Minneapolis, Minnesota **WWE**
Big E defeated Jack Swagger in 11:50 (★★★); The New Age Outlaws (Road Dogg and Billy Gunn) defeated The Usos (Jimmy Uso and Jey Uso) in 8:34 (★★); Titus O'Neil defeated Darren Young in 8:17 (★); The Wyatt Family (Bray Wyatt, Erick Rowan and Luke Harper) defeated The Shield (Dean Ambrose, Roman Reigns and Seth Rollins) in 22:42 (★★★★); Cameron defeated AJ Lee by DQ in 4:30 (★); Batista defeated Alberto Del Rio in 7:11 (★★); Randy Orton defeated Daniel Bryan, John Cena, Cesaro, Christian and Sheamus in an Elimination Chamber Match in 37:30 (★★★).

Arrival ★★★
27-02-14, Winter Park, Florida **NXT**
Cesaro defeated Sami Zayn in 22:55 (★★★★); Mojo Rawley defeated CJ Parker in 3:25 (★★); The Ascension (Konnor and Viktor) defeated Too Cool (Grandmaster Sexay and Scotty 2 Hotty) in 6:40 (★★); Paige defeated Emma in 12:54 (★★★); Tyler Breeze vs. Xavier Woods went to a no contest in :35 (★); Adrian Neville defeated Bo Dallas in a Ladder Match to win the NXT Title in 16:02 (★★★).

Lockdown '14 ★★
09-03-14, Coral Gables, Florida **TNA**
The Great Muta, Sanada and Yasu defeated Bad Influence (Christopher Daniels and Kazarian) and Chris Sabin in a Steel Cage Match in 9:25 (★★★); Samuel Shaw defeated Mr. Anderson in a Steel Cage Match in 10:09 (★★); Tigre Uno defeated Manik in a Steel Cage Match in 7:42 (★★); Gunner defeated James Storm in a Last Man Standing Steel Cage Match in 12:25 (★★★); Madison Rayne defeated Gail Kim in a Steel Cage Match in 6:30 (★★★); Magnus defeated Samoa Joe in a Steel Cage Match in 19:21 (★★); Team MVP (MVP, Davey Richards, Eddie Edwards and Willow) defeated Team Dixie (Bobby Roode, Jessie Godderz, Robbie E and Austin Aries) in a Lethal Lockdown Match in 26:09 (★★).

WrestleMania XXX ★★★★★
06-04-14, New Orleans, Louisiana **WWE**
Daniel Bryan defeated Triple H in 25:58 (★★★★); The Shield (Dean Ambrose, Roman Reigns and Seth Rollins) defeated Kane and The New Age Outlaws (Road Dogg and Billy Gunn) in 2:56 (★★); Cesaro won the Andre the Giant Memorial Battle Royal in 13:25 (★★); John Cena defeated Bray Wyatt in 22:25 (★★★); Brock Lesnar defeated The Undertaker in 25:12 (★★★); AJ Lee won a 14-Woman Invitational Match in 6:48 (★); Daniel Bryan defeated Batista and Randy Orton in a Three Way Match to win the WWE World Heayweight Title in 23:20 (★★★★).

Sacrifice '14 ★★
27-04-14, Orlando, Florida **TNA**
The Wolves (Davey Richards and Eddie Edwards) defeated The BroMans (DJZ, Jessie Godderz and Robbie E) in a No DQ Handicap Match to win the TNA World Tag Team Title in 10:14 (★★); Mr. Anderson defeated Samuel Shaw in a Committed Match in 10:30 (★★); Kurt Angle and Willow defeated Ethan Carter III and Rockstar Spud in 9:04 (★★); Sanada defeated Tigre Uno in 9:29 (★★); Gunner defeated James Storm in an "I Quit" Match in 18:50 (★★★); Angelina Love defeated Madison Rayne to win the TNA Knockouts Title in 8:08 (★★); Bobby Roode defeated Bully Ray in a Tables Match in 13:42 (★★); Eric Young defeated Magnus in 15:50 (★★).

Extreme Rules '14 ★★★
04-05-14, East Rutherford, New Jersey **WWE**
Cesaro defeated Rob Van Dam and Jack Swagger in a Three Way Elimination Match in 12:34 (★★); Alexander Rusev defeated R-Truth and Xavier Woods in a Handicap Match in 2:53 (★★); Bad News Barrett defeated Big E to win the WWE Intercontinental Title in 7:55 (★★★); The Shield (Dean Ambrose, Roman Reigns and Seth Rollins) defeated Evolution (Triple H, Batista and Randy Orton) in 19:52 (★★★★); Bray Wyatt defeated John Cena in a Steel Cage Match in 21:12 (★★); Paige defeated Tamina Snuka in 6:18 (★★); Daniel Bryan defeated Kane in an Extreme Rules Match in 22:27 (★★★).

Global Wars '14 ★★★
10-05-14, Toronto, Canada **ROH**
Michael Bennett defeated ACH in 7:51 (★★); Michael Elgin defeated Takaaki Watanabe in 6:40 (★★); The Briscoe Brothers (Jay Briscoe and Mark Briscoe) defeated The Decade (B.J. Whitmer and Jimmy Jacobs) and reDRagon (Bobby Fish and Kyle O'Reilly) in a Three Way Match in 7:35 (★★★); Cedric Alexander defeated Roderick Strong in 14:20 (★★★); The Young Bucks (Matt Jackson and Nick Jackson) defeated Forever Hooligans (Alex Koslov and Rocky Romero) and Time Splitters (Alex Shelley and Kushida) in a Three Way Match in 12:38 (★★★); Hiroshi Tanahashi and Jushin Thunder Liger defeated Jado and Shinsuke Nakamura in 11:28 (★★); Jay Lethal defeated Matt Taven, Silas Young and Tommaso Ciampa in a Four Corner Survival Match in 7:25 (★★); AJ Styles and Karl Anderson defeated Gedo and Kazuchika Okada in 11:22 (★★★); Adam Cole defeated Kevin Steen in 19:13 (★★★★).

War Of The Worlds '14 ★★★★★
17-05-14, New York City, New York **ROH**
ACH, Matt Taven and Tommaso Ciampa defeated Forever Hooligans (Alex Koslov and Rocky Romero) and Takaaki Watanabe in 4:30 (★★); The Decade (B.J. Whitmer and Roderick Strong) defeated Gedo and Jado in 8:40 (★★); Jay Lethal defeated Kushida in 11:40 (★★★); Luke Gallows and Karl Anderson defeated The Briscoe Brothers (Jay Briscoe and Mark Briscoe) in 10:40 (★★); Shinsuke Nakamura defeated Kevin Steen in 12:48 (★★★★); Hiroshi Tanahashi defeated Michael Bennett in 13:44 (★★); reDRagon (Bobby Fish and Kyle O'Reilly) defeated The Young Bucks (Matt Jackson and Nick Jackson) to win the ROH World Tag Team Title in 12:47 (★★★★); Adam Cole defeated Jushin Thunder Liger in 13:14 (★★★); AJ Styles defeated Kazuchika Okada and Michael Elgin in a Three Way Match in 18:02 (★★★★).

Takeover ★★★★
29-05-14, Winter Park, Florida **NXT**
Adam Rose defeated Camacho in 5:07 (★★); The Ascension (Konnor and Viktor) defeated El Local and Kalisto in 6:18 (★★); Tyler Breeze defeated Sami Zayn in 15:55 (★★★★); Charlotte Flair defeated Natalya to win the vacant NXT Women's Title in 16:49 (★★★★); Adrian Neville defeated Tyson Kidd in 20:55 (★★★).

Payback '14 ★★★★
01-06-14, Rosemont, Illinois **WWE**

Sheamus defeated Cesaro in 11:38 (★★); RybAxel (Curtis Axel and Ryback) defeated Cody Rhodes and Goldust in 7:49 (★★); Rusev defeated Big E in 3:40 (★); Bo Dallas vs. Kofi Kingston went to a no contest in :32 (★); Bad News Barrett defeated Rob Van Dam in 9:32 (★★); John Cena defeated Bray Wyatt in a Last Man Standing Match in 24:24 (★★★); Paige defeated Alicia Fox in 6:37 (★★); The Shield (Dean Ambrose, Roman Reigns and Seth Rollins) defeated Evolution (Batista, Randy Orton and Triple H) in a No Holds Barred Elimination Match in 30:56 (★★★★).

Slammiversary XII ★★★
15-06-14, Arlington, Texas **TNA**

Sanada defeated Manik, Tigre Uno, Davey Richards, Eddie Edwards and Crazzy Steve in a Ladder Match in 9:41 (★★★); Bobby Lashley defeated Samoa Joe in 8:54 (★★★); Magnus defeated Willow in 10:01 (★★); Austin Aries defeated Kenny King in 10:01 (★★); The Von Erichs (Marshall Von Erich and Ross Von Erich) defeated The BroMans (Jessie Godderz and DJ Z) by DQ in 5:13 (★★); Angelina Love defeated Gail Kim in 6:43 (★★); Ethan Carter III defeated Bully Ray in a Texas Death Match in 17:12 (★★★); Mr. Anderson defeated James Storm in 5:30 (★★); Eric Young defeated Bobby Lashley and Austin Aries in a Three Way Steel Cage Match in 12:11 (★★★).

Best In The World '14 ★★★
22-06-14, Nashville, Tennessee **ROH**

ACH defeated TaDarius Thomas, Caprice Coleman, B.J. Whitmer, Takaaki Watanabe and Tommaso Ciampa in a Six Man Mayhem Match in 12:07 (★★★); Jay Lethal defeated Matt Taven in 10:56 (★★); Cedric Alexander defeated Roderick Strong in a Submission Match in 16:17 (★★); The Briscoe Brothers (Jay Briscoe and Mark Briscoe) defeated Matt Hardy and Michael Bennett in a No DQ Match in 17:27 (★★★); Kevin Steen defeated Silas Young in 15:02 (★★); reDRagon (Bobby Fish and Kyle O'Reilly) defeated Christopher Daniels and Frankie Kazarian in 17:00 (★★★★); Michael Elgin defeated Adam Cole to win the ROH World Title in 23:00 (★★★★).

Money In The Bank '14 ★★★★
29-06-14, Boston, Massachusetts **WWE**

The Usos (Jimmy Uso and Jey Uso) defeated The Wyatt Family (Erick Rowan and Luke Harper) in 13:53 (★★★); Paige defeated Naomi in 7:02 (★★); Adam Rose defeated Damien Sandow in 5:12 (★★); Seth Rollins defeated Dean Ambrose, Dolph Ziggler, Jack Swagger, Kofi Kingston and Rob Van Dam in a Money In The Bank Ladder Match in 23:10 (★★★★); Goldust and Stardust defeated RybAxel (Curtis Axel and Ryback) in 8:16 (★★); Rusev defeated Big E in 8:19 (★★); Layla defeated Summer Rae in 3:07 (★); John Cena defeated Alberto Del Rio, Bray Wyatt, Cesaro, Kane, Randy Orton, Roman Reigns and Sheamus in a Ladder Match to win the vacant WWE World Heavyweight Title in 26:20 (★★★).

Battleground '14 ★★
20-07-14, Tampa, Florida **WWE**

The Usos (Jimmy Uso and Jey Uso) defeated The Wyatt Family (Erick Rowan and Luke Harper) in a Best Two Out Of Three Falls Match in 18:50 (★★★★); AJ Lee defeated Paige in 7:10 (★★); Rusev defeated Jack Swagger via count out in 9:47 (★★); Chris Jericho defeated Bray Wyatt in 15:01 (★★); The Miz won a Battle Royal to win the vacant WWE Intercontinental Title in 14:10 (★★); John Cena defeated Kane, Randy Orton and Roman Reigns in a Four Way Match in 18:15 (★★★).

SummerSlam '14 ★★★★
17-08-14, Los Angeles, California **WWE**

Dolph Ziggler defeated The Miz to win the WWE Intercontinental Title in 7:57 (★★); Paige defeated AJ Lee in 4:55 (★★); Rusev defeated Jack Swagger in a Flag Match in 9:01 (★★); Seth Rollins defeated Dean Ambrose in a Lumberjack Match in 10:55 (★★★); Bray Wyatt defeated Chris Jericho in 12:53 (★★); Stephanie McMahon defeated Brie Bella in 11:06 (★★); Roman Reigns defeated Randy Orton in 16:30 (★★); Brock Lesnar defeated John Cena to win the WWE World Heavyweight Title in 16:05 (★★★★).

All Star Extravaganza VI ★★★
06-09-14, Toronto, Canada **ROH**

Mark Briscoe defeated Hanson in 8:45 (★★); Moose and R.D. Evans defeated The Decade (Adam Cole and B.J. Whitmer), Caprice Coleman and Takaaki Watanabe, and The Monster Mafia (Ethan Gabriel Owens and Josh Alexander) in a Four Corner Survival Match in 9:31 (★★); The Addiction (Christopher Daniels and Frankie Kazarian) defeated The Decade (Jimmy Jacobs and Roderick Strong) in 10:59 (★★); AJ Styles defeated Adam Cole in 23:18 (★★★★); Jay Lethal defeated Cedric Alexander in 15:39 (★★); Jay Briscoe defeated Michael Elgin to win the ROH World Title in 24:01 (★★★); reDRagon (Bobby Fish and Kyle O'Reilly) defeated The Young Bucks (Matt Jackson and Nick Jackson) in a Best Two Out Of Three Falls Match in 18:20 (★★★★).

Takeover: Fatal 4-Way ★★★
11-09-14, Winter Park, Florida **NXT**

The Lucha Dragons (Kalisto and Sin Cara) defeated The Ascension (Konnor and Viktor) to win the NXT Tag Team Title in 7:48 (★★★); Baron Corbin defeated CJ Parker in :29 (★); Enzo Amore defeated Sylvester Lefort in a Hair vs. Hair Match in 5:38 (★★); Bull Dempsey defeated Mojo Rawley in 1:10 (★); Charlotte Flair defeated Bayley in 10:40 (★★); Adrian Neville defeated Tyson Kidd, Tyler Breeze and Sami Zayn in a Four Way Match in 24:12 (★★★★).

Night Of Champions '14 ★★★
21-09-14, Nashville, Tennessee **WWE**

Goldust and Stardust defeated The Usos (Jimmy Uso and Jey Uso) to win the WWE Tag Team Title in 12:47 (★★★); Sheamus defeated Cesaro in 13:06 (★★★); The Miz defeated Dolph Ziggler to win the WWE Intercontinental Title in 8:25 (★★); Rusev defeated Mark Henry in 7:20 (★★); Randy Orton defeated Chris Jericho in 16:23 (★★★); AJ Lee defeated Nikki Bella and Paige in a Three Way Match to win the WWE Divas Title in 8:41 (★★); John Cena defeated Brock Lesnar by DQ in 14:21 (★★★).

Bound For Glory '14 ★★
12-10-14, Tokyo, Japan **TNA**

Minoru Tanaka defeated Manik in 9:53 (★★); Ethan Carter III defeated Ryota Hama in 5:50 (★★); MVP defeated Kazma Sakamoto in 8:07 (★★); Samoa Joe defeated Kaz Hayashi and Low Ki in a Three Way Match in 10:32 (★★★); Novus (Jiro Kuroshio and Yusuke Kodama) defeated Andy Wu and El Hijo del Pantera in 9:15 (★★); Team 3D (Bully Ray and Devon) defeated Abyss and Tommy Dreamer in a Hardcore Match in 12:53 (★★); Havok defeated Velvet Sky in 6:00 (★★); The Great Muta and Tajiri defeated The Revolution (The Great Sanada and James Storm) in 14:00 (★★).

Hell In A Cell '14 ★★★
26-10-14, Dallas, Texas **WWE**

Dolph Ziggler defeated Cesaro in a Best Two Out Of Three Falls Match in 12:18 (★★★); Nikki Bella defeated Brie Bella in 6:22 (★); Goldust and Stardust defeated The Usos (Jimmy Uso and Jey Uso) in 10:21 (★★); John Cena defeated Randy Orton in a Hell In A Cell Match in 25:52 (★★★); Sheamus defeated The Miz in 8:20 (★★); Rusev defeated The Big Show in 7:55 (★★); AJ Lee defeated Paige in 6:50 (★★); Seth Rollins defeated Dean Ambrose in a Hell In A Cell Match in 14:03 (★★★).

Survivor Series '14 ★★
23-11-14, St. Louis, Missouri **WWE**

Damien Mizdow and The Miz defeated Goldust and Stardust, Los Matadores (Diego and Fernando), and The Usos (Jimmy Uso and Jey Uso) in a Four Way Match to win the WWE Tag Team Title in 15:25 (★★); Team Natalya (Natalya, Alicia Fox, Emma and Naomi) defeated Team Paige (Paige, Cameron, Layla and Summer Rae) in an Elimination Match in 14:35 (★★); Bray Wyatt defeated Dean Ambrose by DQ in 14:00 (★★); Adam Rose and The Bunny defeated Slater-Gator (Heath Slater and Titus O'Neil) in 2:36 (★); Nikki Bella defeated AJ Lee to win the WWE Divas Title in :33 (★); Team Cena (John Cena, Dolph Ziggler, Erick Rowan, The Big Show and Ryback) defeated Team Authority (Seth Rollins, Kane, Luke Harper, Mark Henry and Rusev) in an Elimination Match in 43:28 (★★★★).

Final Battle '14 ★★★★
07-12-14, New York City, New York **ROH**
Hanson defeated Jimmy Jacobs, Mark Briscoe and Caprice Coleman in a Four Corner Survival Match in 10:44 (★★); Roderick Strong defeated Adam Page in 12:06 (★★); Michael Elgin defeated Tommaso Ciampa in 13:21 (★★); The Young Bucks (Matt Jackson and Nick Jackson) and ACH defeated The Addition (Christopher Daniels and Frankie Kazarian) and Cedric Alexander in 12:43 (★★★★); Moose defeated R.D. Evans in 7:34 (★★); Jay Lethal defeated Matt Sydal in 15:03 (★★★); reDRagon (Bobby Fish and Kyle O'Reilly) defeated Time Splitters (Alex Shelley and Kushida) in 18:09 (★★★★); Jay Briscoe defeated Adam Cole in a Fight Without Honor in 21:19 (★★★★).

Takeover: R Evolution ★★★★
11-12-14, Winter Park, Florida **NXT**
Kevin Owens defeated CJ Parker in 3:14 (★★); The Lucha Dragons (Kalisto and Sin Cara) defeated The Vaudevillains (Aiden English and Simon Goch) in 6:40 (★★); Baron Corbin defeated Tye Dillinger in :41 (★★); Finn Balor and Hideo Itami defeated The Ascension (Konnor and Viktor) in 11:38 (★★★); Charlotte Flair defeated Sasha Banks in 12:12 (★★); Sami Zayn defeated Adrian Neville to win the NXT Title in 23:18 (★★★★).

TLC '14 ★★
14-12-14, Cleveland, Ohio **WWE**
Dolph Ziggler defeated Luke Harper in a Ladder Match to win the WWE Intercontinental Title in 16:40 (★★★); The Usos (Jimmy Uso and Jey Uso) defeated Damien Mizdow and The Miz by DQ in 7:17 (★★); The Big Show defeated Erick Rowan in a Stairs Match in 11:14 (★); John Cena defeated Seth Rollins in a Tables Match in 23:35 (★★); Nikki Bella defeated AJ Lee in 7:38 (★★); Ryback defeated Kane in a Chairs Match in 9:50 (★); Rusev defeated Jack Swagger in 4:50 (★★); Bray Wyatt defeated Dean Ambrose in a TLC Match in 26:58 (★★★).

Tribute To The Troops '14 ★★
17-12-14, Columbus, Georgia **WWE**
The Usos (Jimmy Uso and Jey Uso) defeated Goldust and Stardust in 8:19 (★★); Naomi won a 10-woman Santa's Little Helper Battle Royal in 4:01 (★); Dean Ambrose defeated Bray Wyatt in a Boot Camp Match in 11:25 (★★); John Cena, Dolph Ziggler, Erick Rowan and Ryback defeated The Big Show, Kane, Luke Harper and Seth Rollins in 9:48 (★★).

Royal Rumble '15 ★★
25-01-15, Philadelphia, Pennsylvania **WWE**
The Ascension (Konnor and Viktor) defeated The New Age Outlaws (Road Dogg and Billy Gunn) in 5:25 (★★); The Usos (Jimmy Uso and Jey Uso) defeated Damien Mizdow and The Miz in 9:20 (★★); The Bella Twins (Nikki Bella and Brie Bella) defeated Paige and Natalya in 8:05 (★★); Brock Lesnar defeated Seth Rollins and John Cena in a Three Way Match in 22:42 (★★★★); Roman Reigns won the 30-Man Royal Rumble Match in 59:31 (★★).

Takeover Rival ★★★★
11-02-15, Winter Park, Florida **NXT**
Hideo Itami defeated Tyler Breeze in 8:13 (★★★); Baron Corbin defeated Bull Dempsey in a No DQ Match in 4:15 (★★); Buddy Murphy and Wesley Blake defeated The Lucha Dragons (Kalisto and Sin Cara) in 8:10 (★★★); Finn Balor defeated Adrian Neville in 13:25 (★★★★); Sasha Banks defeated Charlotte Flair, Bayley and Becky Lynch in a Four Way Match to win the NXT Women's Title in 12:28 (★★★★); Kevin Owens defeated Sami Zayn to win the NXT Title in 23:27 (★★★★).

Fastlane '15 ★★
22-02-15, Memphis, Tennessee **WWE**
The Authority (The Big Show, Kane and Seth Rollins) defeated Dolph Ziggler, Erick Rowan and Ryback in 13:01 (★★); Goldust defeated Stardust in 8:55 (★★); Cesaro and Tyson Kidd defeated The Usos (Jimmy Uso and Jey Uso) to win the WWE Tag Team Title in 9:33 (★★); Nikki Bella defeated Paige in 5:24 (★★); Bad News Barrett defeated Dean Ambrose by DQ in 7:58 (★★); Rusev defeated John Cena in 18:42 (★★★); Roman Reigns defeated Daniel Bryan in 20:10 (★★★★).

13th Anniversary Show ★★★
01-03-15, Paradise, Nevada **ROH**
Matt Sydal defeated Cedric Alexander in 9:38 (★★★); Moose defeated Mark Briscoe in 5:15 (★★); The Kingdom (Michael Bennett and Matt Taven) defeated Karl Anderson and Luke Gallows, and The Addiction (Christopher Daniels and Frankie Kazarian) in a Three Way Match in 11:58 (★★); Roderick Strong defeated B.J. Whitmer in 10:57 (★★); ODB defeated Maria Kanellis in 5:20 (★★); AJ Styles defeated ACH in 15:30 (★★★); reDRagon (Bobby Fish and Kyle O'Reilly) defeated The Young Bucks (Matt Jackson and Nick Jackson) in 15:40 (★★★★); Jay Lethal defeated Alberto El Patron in 12:33 (★★★); Jay Briscoe defeated Hanson, Michael Elgin and Tommaso Ciampa in a Four Corner Survival Match in 16:21 (★★).

WrestleMania XXXI ★★★★★
29-03-15, Santa Clara, California **WWE**
Daniel Bryan defeated Bad News Barrett, Dean Ambrose, Dolph Ziggler, Luke Harper, Stardust and R-Truth in a Ladder Match to win the WWE Intercontinental Title in 13:47 (★★★★); Randy Orton defeated Seth Rollins in 13:15 (★★★★); Triple H defeated Sting in a No DQ Match in 18:36 (★★★★); AJ Lee and Paige defeated The Bella Twins (Brie Bella and Nikki Bella) in 6:42 (★★); John Cena defeated Rusev to win the WWE United States Title in 14:31 (★★★); The Undertaker defeated Bray Wyatt in 15:12 (★★★); Seth Rollins defeated Brock Lesnar and Roman Reigns in a Three Way Match to win the WWE World Heavyweight Title in 16:43 (★★★★).

Extreme Rules '15 ★★
26-04-15, Rosemont, Illinois **WWE**
Dolph Ziggler defeated Sheamus in a Kiss Me Arse Match in 9:16 (★★); The New Day (Big E and Kofi Kingston) defeated Cesaro and Tyson Kidd to win the WWE Tag Team Title in 9:36 (★★★); Dean Ambrose defeated Luke Harper in a Chicago Street Fight in 56:10 (★); John Cena defeated Rusev in a Russian Chain Match in 13:35 (★★); Nikki Bella defeated Naomi in 7:18 (★★); Roman Reigns defeated The Big Show in a Last Man Standing Match in 19:46 (★★★); Seth Rollins defeated Randy Orton in a Steel Cage Match in 21:02 (★★).

King Of The Ring '15 ★★
28-04-15, Moline, Illinois **WWE**
Neville defeated Sheamus in 5:44 (★★); Bad News Barrett defeated R-Truth in 4:38 (★★); Bad News Barrett defeated Neville in 7:06 (★★).

Global Wars '15 ★★★
15-05-15, Toronto, Ontario **ROH**
Gedo and Moose defeated Silas Young and Takaaki Watanabe in 8:01 (★★); Kushida defeated Chris Sabin and Kyle O'Reilly in a Three Way Match in 9:58 (★★); Matt Taven and Michael Bennett defeated Jushin Thunder Liger and Matt Sydal in 9:12 (★★); Kazuchika Okada defeated Cedric Alexander in 12:15 (★★★); The Addiction (Christopher Daniels and Frankie Kazarian) defeated The Decade (Adam Page and B.J. Whitmer) and Roppongi Vice (Beretta and Rocky Romero) in a Three Way Match in 14:39 (★★); Shinsuke Nakamura defeated ACH in 12:39 (★★★); Jay Lethal defeated Tetsuya Naito in 12:18 (★★★); Hiroshi Tanahashi defeated Michael Elgin in 17:08 (★★); ROH All Stars (Hanson, Jay Briscoe, Mark Briscoe, Raymond Rowe and Roderick Strong) defeated Bullet Club (AJ Styles, Luke Gallows, Karl Anderson, Matt Jackson and Nick Jackson) in 16:48 (★★★★).

Payback '15 ★★★
17-05-15, Baltimore, Maryland **WWE**
Sheamus defeated Dolph Ziggler in 12:20 (★★★); The New Day (Big E and Kofi Kingston) defeated Cesaro and Tyson Kidd in a Best Two Out Of Three Falls Match in 12:40 (★★★); Bray Wyatt defeated Ryback in 10:54 (★★); John Cena defeated Rusev in an "I Quit" Match in 27:58 (★★★); Naomi and Tamina defeated The Bella Twins (Brie Bella and Nikki Bella) in 6:13 (★); Neville defeated King Barrett via count out in 7:22 (★★); Seth Rollins defeated Randy Orton, Dean Ambrose and Roman Reigns in a Four Way Match in 21:06 (★★★).

Takeover Unstoppable ★★★
20-05-15, Winter Park, Florida **NXT**

Finn Balor defeated Tyler Breeze in 11:30 (★★★★); Bayley and Charlotte Flair defeated Dana Brooke and Emma in 6:51 (★★); Baron Corbin defeated Rhyno in 7:15 (★★); Buddy Murphy and Wesley Blake defeated Colin Cassady and Enzo Amore in 8:50 (★★); Sasha Banks defeated Becky Lynch in 15:33 (★★★★); Kevin Owens vs. Sami Zayn went to a no contest in 13:00 (★★★).

Elimination Chamber '15 ★★★
31-05-15, Corpus Christi, Texas **WWE**

The New Day (Big E, Kofi Kingston and Xavier Woods) defeated The Prime Time Players (Darren Young and Titus O'Neil), Tyson Kidd and Cesaro, The Ascension (Konnor and Viktor), The Lucha Dragons (Kalisto and Sin Cara), and Los Matadores (Diego and Fernando) in an Elimination Chamber Match in 23:40 (★★); Nikki Bella defeated Naomi and Paige in a Three Way Match in 6:04 (★★); Kevin Owens defeated John Cena in 20:15 (★★★★★); Neville defeated Bo Dallas in 8:46 (★★); Ryback defeated Sheamus, Dolph Ziggler, Mark Henry, R-Truth and King Barrett in an Elimination Chamber Match to win the vacant WWE Intercontinental Title in 25:12 (★★); Dean Ambrose defeated Seth Rollins by DQ in 21:49 (★★★).

Money In The Bank '15 ★★★
14-06-15, Columbus, Ohio **WWE**

Sheamus defeated Dolph Ziggler, Kane, Kofi Kingston, Neville, Randy Orton and Roman Reigns in a Money In The Bank Ladder Match in 20:50 (★★); Nikki Bella defeated Paige in 11:18 (★★); The Big Show defeated Ryback by DQ in 5:28 (★); John Cena defeated Kevin Owens in 19:15 (★★★★); The Prime Time Players (Darren Young and Titus O'Neil) defeated The New Day (Big E and Xavier Woods) to win the WWE Tag Team Title in 5:48 (★★); Seth Rollins defeated Dean Ambrose in a Ladder Match in 35:40 (★★★).

Best In The World '15 ★★★
19-06-15, New York City, New York **ROH**

Mark Briscoe defeated Donovan Dijak in 8:57 (★★); The Decade (B.J. Whitmer and Adam Page) defeated Matt Sydal and ACH in 9:07 (★★); Dalton Castle defeated Silas Young in 11:02 (★★); War Machine (Hanson and Raymond Rowe) defeated C&C Wrestle Factory (Caprice Coleman and Cedric Alexander) in 3:37 (★★); Roderick Strong defeated Michael Elgin and Moose in a Three Way Match in 13:02 (★★★); Bullet Club (AJ Styles, Matt Jackson and Nick Jackson) defeated The Kingdom (Adam Cole, Michael Bennett and Matt Taven) in 14:47 (★★★); The Addiction (Christopher Daniels and Frankie Kazarian) defeated reDRagon (Bobby Fish and Kyle O'Reilly) in a No DQ Match in 14:50 (★★); Jay Lethal defeated Jay Briscoe to win the ROH World Title in 27:13 (★★★★).

Slammiversary XIII ★★★
28-06-15, Orlando, Florida **TNA**

Tigre Uno defeated DJ Z and Manik in a Three Way Elimination Match in 12:06 (★★★); Robbie E defeated Jessie Godderz in 11:20 (★★); Bram defeated Matt Morgan in a Street Fight in 9:30 (★★); Austin Aries defeated Davey Richards in 17:15 (★★★); Brooke and Awesome Kong defeated The Dollhouse (Jade, Marti Bell and Taryn Terrell) in a Handicap Match in 8:05 (★★); James Storm defeated Magnus in a Non Sanctioned Match in 16:40 (★★★); Ethan Carter III and Tyrus defeated Bobby Lashley and Mr. Anderson in 10:10 (★★); Jeff Jarrett defeated Bobby Roode, Matt Hardy, Eric Young and Drew Galloway in a King Of The Mountain Match to win the vacant TNA King Of The Mountain Title in 20:25 (★★★).

Beast In The East ★★★★
04-07-15, Tokyo, Japan **WWE**

Chris Jericho defeated Neville in 16:20 (★★★★); Nikki Bella defeated Tamina and Paige in a Three Way Match in 7:03 (★★); Brock Lesnar defeated Kofi Kingston in 2:36 (★★); Finn Balor defeated Kevin Owens to win the NXT Title in 19:25 (★★★★); Dolph Ziggler and John Cena defeated Kane and King Barrett in 23:50 (★★).

Battleground '15 ★★
19-07-15, St. Louis, Missouri **WWE**

Randy Orton defeated Sheamus in 16:54 (★★); The Prime Time Players (Darren Young and Titus O'Neil) defeated The New Day (Big E and Kofi Kingston) in 8:50 (★★); Bray Wyatt defeated

Takeover Brooklyn ★★★★★★
22-08-15, Brooklyn, New York **NXT**

Jushin Thunder Liger defeated Tyler Breeze in 8:42 (★★); The Vaudevillains (Aiden English and Simon Gotch) defeated Buddy Murphy and Wesley Blake to win the NXT Tag Team Title in 10:16 (★★★); Apollo Crews defeated Tye Dillinger in 4:43 (★★); Samoa Joe defeated Baron Corbin in 10:21 (★★★); Bayley defeated Sasha Banks to win the NXT Women's Title in 18:22 (★★★★★★); Finn Balor defeated Kevin Owens in a Ladder Match in 21:45 (★★★★).

SummerSlam '15 ★★★
23-08-15, Brooklyn, New York **WWE**

Sheamus defeated Randy Orton in 12:28 (★★); The New Day (Big E and Kofi Kingston) defeated The Prime Time Players (Darren Young and Titus O'Neil), Los Matadores (Diego and Fernando), and The Lucha Dragons (Kalisto and Sin Cara) in a Four Way Match to win the WWE Tag Team Title in 11:20 (★★); Dolph Ziggler vs. Rusev went to a double count out in 11:50 (★★); Neville and Stephen Amell defeated King Barrett and Stardust in 7:35 (★★); Ryback defeated The Miz and The Big Show in a Three Way Match in 5:33 (★★); Dean Ambrose and Roman Reigns defeated The Wyatt Family (Bray Wyatt and Luke Harper) in 10:55 (★★★); Seth Rollins defeated John Cena to win the WWE United States Title in 19:44 (★★★); Team PCB (Becky Lynch, Charlotte Flair and Paige) defeated Team B.A.D. (Naomi, Sasha Banks and Tamina) and Team Bella (Alicia Fox, Brie Bella and Nikki Bella) in a Three Way Elimination Match in 15:20 (★★); Kevin Owens defeated Cesaro in 14:18 (★★★); The Undertaker defeated Brock Lesnar in 17:50 (★★★★).

All Star Extravaganza VII ★★★
18-09-15, San Antonio, Texas **ROH**

Jay Lethal defeated Bobby Fish in 14:09 (★★★); Silas Young defeated Dalton Castle in 12:25 (★★); The All Night Express (Kenny King and Rhett Titus) defeated The Briscoe Brothers (Jay Briscoe and Mark Briscoe) in 8:32 (★★★); Moose defeated Cedric Alexander in a No DQ Match in 13:08 (★★★); ACH defeated Matt Sydal in 16:28 (★★★); The Kingdom (Matt Taven and Michael Bennett) defeated The Addiction (Christopher Daniels and Frankie Kazarian) and The Young Bucks (Matt Jackson and Nick Jackson) in a Three Way Match to win the ROH World Tag Team Title in 13:50 (★★★); AJ Styles defeated Roderick Strong, Adam Cole and Michael Elgin in a Four Corner Survival Match in 14:30 (★★★); Jay Lethal defeated Kyle O'Reilly in 14:00 (★★★).

Night Of Champions '15 ★★★
20-09-15, Houston, Texas **WWE**

Kevin Owens defeated Ryback to win the WWE Intercontinental Title in 9:32 (★★★); Dolph Ziggler defeated Rusev in 13:47 (★★★); The Dudley Boyz (Bubba Ray Dudley and D-Von Dudley) defeated The New Day (Big E and Kofi Kingston) to win the WWE Tag Team Title in 9:57 (★★); Charlotte Flair defeated Nikki Bella to win the WWE Divas Title in 12:41 (★★); The Wyatt Family (Bray Wyatt, Braun Strowman and Luke Harper) defeated Chris Jericho, Dean Ambrose and Roman Reigns in 13:04 (★★); John Cena defeated Seth Rollins to win the WWE United States Title in 16:01 (★★★★); Seth Rollins defeated Sting in 14:56 (★★★).

Live From Madison Square Garden ★★
03-10-15, New York, New York **WWE**

Dolph Ziggler and Randy Orton defeated Rusev and Sheamus in 9:00 (★★); Neville defeated Stardust in 7:20 (★★); Team Bella (Alicia Fox, Brie Bella and Nikki Bella) defeated Team PCB (Becky Lynch, Charlotte Flair and Paige) in 8:35 (★★); Kevin Owens defeated Chris Jericho in 8:10 (★★); The Dudley Boyz (Bubba Ray Dudley and D-Von Dudley) defeated The New Day (Big E and Kofi Kingston) by DQ in 6:40 (★★); Brock Lesnar defeated The Big Show in 4:05 (★★); John Cena defeated Seth Rollins in a Steel Cage Match in 23:43 (★★★).

Bound For Glory '15 ★★
04-10-15, Concord, North Carolina **TNA**

Tigre Uno defeated Andrew Everett, DJ Z and Manik in an Ultimate X Match in 10:02 (★★★); Tyrus won a 12-Man Bound For Gold Gauntlet Match in 24:20 (★); The Wolves (Davey Richards and Eddie Edwards) defeated Brian Myers and Trevor Lee in 11:23 (★★★); Bobby Roode defeated Bobby Lashley in 14:17 (★★); Gail Kim defeated Awesome Kong in 10:05 (★★); Kurt Angle defeated Eric Young in 13:10 (★★); Matt Hardy defeated Ethan Carter III and Drew Galloway in a Three Way Match to win the TNA World Heavyweight Title in 20:04 (★★).

Takeover Respect ★★★★
07-10-15, Winter Park, Florida **NXT**

Finn Balor and Samoa Joe defeated The Mechanics (Dash Wilder and Scott Dawson) in 9:05 (★★★); Baron Corbin and Rhyno defeated American Alpha (Chad Gable and Jason Jordan) in 10:28 (★★★); Asuka defeated Dana Brooke in 5:07 (★★); Apollo Crews defeated Tyler Breeze in 9:41 (★★★); Finn Balor and Samoa Joe defeated Baron Corbin and Rhyno in 10:57 (★★★); Bayley defeated Sasha Banks 3-2 in an Iron Man Match in 30:00 (★★★★).

Hell In A Cell '15 ★★★
25-10-15, Los Angeles, California **WWE**

Alberto Del Rio defeated John Cena to win the WWE United States Title in 7:48 (★★); Roman Reigns defeated Bray Wyatt in a Hell In A Cell Match in 23:03 (★★★); The New Day (Kofi Kingston and Big E) defeated The Dudley Boyz (Bubba Ray Dudley and D-Von Dudley) in 8:24 (★★); Charlotte Flair defeated Nikki Bella in 10:39 (★★); Seth Rollins defeated Kane in 14:35 (★★); Kevin Owens defeated Ryback in 5:35 (★★); Brock Lesnar defeated The Undertaker in a Hell In A Cell Match in 18:10 (★★★★).

Survivor Series '15 ★★
22-11-15, Atlanta, Georgia **WWE**

Roman Reigns defeated Alberto Del Rio in 14:05 (★★★); Dean Ambrose defeated Kevin Owens in 11:20 (★★★); The Usos (Jimmy Uso and Jey Uso), The Lucha Dragons (Kalisto and Sin Cara) and Ryback defeated King Barrett, Sheamus and The New Day (Big E, Kofi Kingston and Xavier Woods) in an Elimination Match in 17:33 (★★); Charlotte Flair defeated Paige in 14:18 (★★); Tyler Breeze defeated Dolph Ziggler in 6:41 (★★); The Brothers Of Destruction (Kane and The Undertaker) defeated The Wyatt Family (Bray Wyatt and Luke Harper) in 10:18 (★★); Roman Reigns defeated Dean Ambrose to win the vacant WWE World Heavyweight Title in 9:02 (★★); Sheamus defeated Roman Reigns to win the WWE World Heavyweight Title in :37 (★★).

TLC '15 ★★★
13-12-15, Boston, Massachusetts **WWE**

The New Day (Big E and Kofi Kingston) defeated The Lucha Dragons (Kalisto and Sin Cara) and The Usos (Jimmy Uso and Jey Uso) in a Three Way Ladder Match in 17:40 (★★★); Rusev defeated Ryback in 7:56 (★★); Alberto Del Rio defeated Jack Swagger in a Chairs Match in 11:11 (★★); The Wyatt Family (Bray Wyatt, Braun Strowman, Erick Rowan and Luke Harper) defeated Tommy Dreamer, Rhyno and The Dudley Boyz (Bubba Ray Dudley and D-Von Dudley) in an Elimination Tables Match in 12:29 (★★); Dean Ambrose defeated Kevin Owens to win the WWE Intercontinental Title in 9:52 (★★★); Charlotte Flair defeated Paige in 10:39 (★★); Sheamus defeated Roman Reigns in a TLC Match in 23:58 (★★★).

Takeover London ★★★
16-12-15, London, England **NXT**

Asuka defeated Emma in 14:49 (★★★); The Mechanics (Dash Wilder and Scott Dawson) defeated Colin Cassady and Enzo Amore in 14:57 (★★★); Baron Corbin defeated Apollo Crews in 11:40 (★★); Bayley defeated Nia Jax in 13:17 (★★★); Finn Balor defeated Samoa Joe in 18:22 (★★★★).

Final Battle '15 ★★★
18-12-15, Philadelphia, Pennsylvania **ROH**

The All Night Express (Kenny King and Rhett Titus) defeated The Briscoe Brothers (Jay Briscoe and Mark Briscoe) and The Young Bucks (Matt Jackson and Nick Jackson) in a Three Way Match in 9:15 (★★★); Silas Young defeated Dalton Castle in 10:40 (★★); Michael Elgin defeated Moose in 11:47 (★★); Adam

Tribute To The Troops '15 ★★
23-12-15, Jacksonville, Florida **WWE**

Jack Swagger defeated Rusev in a Boot Camp Match in 11:02 (★★); Mark Henry defeated Bo Dallas in :45 (★); Ryback defeated Kevin Owens via count out in 3:05 (★★); Paige and Team B.A.D. (Naomi, Tamina and Sasha Banks) defeated Becky Lynch, Charlotte Flair and Team Bella (Brie Bella and Alicia Fox) in 4:37 (★★); Dean Ambrose, Kane, Roman Reigns, Ryback, The Usos (Jimmy Uso and Jey Uso) and The Dudley Boyz (Bubba Ray Dudley and D-Von Dudley) defeated The League Of Nations (Sheamus, Alberto Del Rio, King Barrett and Rusev) and The Wyatt Family (Bray Wyatt, Braun Strowman, Erick Rowan and Luke Harper) in 13:28 (★★).

Royal Rumble '16 ★★★
24-01-16, Orlando, Florida **WWE**

Dean Ambrose defeated Kevin Owens in a Last Man Standing Match in 20:50 (★★★★); The New Day (Big E and Kofi Kingston) defeated The Usos (Jimmy Uso and Jey Uso) in 10:53 (★★); Kalisto defeated Alberto Del Rio to win the WWE United States Title in 11:30 (★★); Charlotte Flair defeated Becky Lynch in 11:40 (★★); Triple H won the 30-Man Royal Rumble Match to win the WWE World Heavyweight Title in 61:42 (★★★).

Fastlane '16 ★★
21-02-16, Cleveland, Ohio **WWE**

Becky Lynch and Sasha Banks defeated Team B.A.D. (Naomi and Tamina) in 9:50 (★★); Kevin Owens defeated Dolph Ziggler in 15:10 (★★★); The Big Show, Kane and Ryback defeated The Wyatt Family (Braun Strowman, Erick Rowan and Luke Harper) in 10:37 (★★); Charlotte Flair defeated Brie Bella in 12:30 (★★); AJ Styles defeated Chris Jericho in 16:25 (★★★); Curtis Axel defeated R-Truth in 2:23 (★); Roman Reigns defeated Dean Ambrose and Brock Lesnar in a Three Way Match in 16:49 (★★★).

14th Anniversary Show ★★★
26-02-16, Sunrise Manor, Nevada **ROH**

Tomohiro Ishii defeated Roderick Strong and Bobby Fish in a Three Way Match in 8:35 (★★★); B.J. Whitmer defeated Adam Page in 9:12 (★★); Hirooki Goto defeated Dalton Castle in 9:49 (★★); Alex Shelley defeated Christopher Daniels in 9:41 (★★); Hiroshi Tanahashi and Michael Elgin defeated The Briscoe Brothers (Jay Briscoe and Mark Briscoe) in 14:50 (★★★); Kazuchika Okada defeated Moose in 10:30 (★★); The Elite (Kenny Omega, Matt Jackson and Nick Jackson) defeated Kushida, ACH and Matt Sydal in 14:50 (★★★★); War Machine (Hanson and Raymond Rowe) defeated The All Night Express (Kenny King and Rhett Titus) in a No DQ Match in 11:20 (★★); Jay Lethal defeated Adam Cole and Kyle O'Reilly in a Three Way Match in 13:44 (★★★).

Roadblock ★★★
12-03-16, Toronto, Ontario **WWE**

The New Day (Big E and Kofi Kingston) defeated The League Of Nations (Sheamus and King Barrett) in 9:49 (★★); Chris Jericho defeated Jack Swagger in 7:54 (★★); The Revival (Dash Wilder and Scott Dawson) defeated Enzo Amore and Big Cass in 10:17 (★★★); Charlotte Flair defeated Natalya in 13:37 (★★★); Brock Lesnar defeated The Wyatt Family (Bray Wyatt and Luke Harper) in a Handicap Match in 4:03 (★★); Sami Zayn defeated Stardust in 12:33 (★★); Triple H defeated Dean Ambrose in 24:43 (★★★★).

Takeover Dallas ★★★★★
01-04-16, Dallas, Texas **NXT**

American Alpha (Chad Gable and Jason Jordan) defeated The Revival (Dash Wilder and Scott Dawson) to win the NXT Tag Team Title in 15:11 (★★★★); Austin Aries defeated Baron Corbin in 10:43 (★★); Shinsuke Nakamura defeated Sami Zayn in 20:07 (★★★★★); Asuka defeated Bayley in 15:25 (★★★); Finn Balor defeated Samoa Joe in 16:22 (★★★).

Cole defeated Kyle O'Reilly in 16:08 (★★★); ACH, Alex Shelley and Matt Sydal defeated Chris Sabin and The Addiction (Christopher Daniels and Frankie Kazarian) in 15:38 (★★★); Roderick Strong defeated Bobby Fish in 15:17 (★★★); War Machine (Hanson and Raymond Rowe) defeated The Kingdom (Michael Bennett and Matt Taven) to win the ROH World Tag Team Title in 3:10 (★★); Jay Lethal defeated AJ Styles in 22:09 (★★★★).

WrestleMania XXXII ★★
03-04-16, Arlington, Texas **WWE**
Zack Ryder defeated Kevin Owens, Dolph Ziggler, The Miz, Sami Zayn, Sin Cara and Goldust in a Ladder Match to win the WWE Intercontinental Title in 15:23 (★★★); Chris Jericho defeated AJ Styles in 17:10 (★★); The League Of Nations (Alberto Del Rio, Rusev and Sheamus) defeated The New Day (Big E, Kofi Kingston and Xavier Woods) in 10:03 (★★); Brock Lesnar defeated Dean Ambrose in a No Holds Barred Street Fight in 13:06 (★★); Charlotte Flair defeated Becky Lynch and Sasha Banks in a Three Way Match to win the vacant WWE Women's Title in 16:03 (★★★); The Undertaker defeated Shane McMahon in a Hell In A Cell Match in 30:05 (★★); Baron Corbin won the Andre the Giant Memorial Battle Royal in 9:41 (★★); The Rock defeated Erick Rowan in :06 (★); Roman Reigns defeated Triple H to win the WWE World Heavyweight Title in 27:11 (★★).

Payback '16 ★★★★
01-05-16, Rosemont, Illinois **WWE**
The Vaudevillains (Aiden English and Simon Gotch) defeated Enzo Amore and Big Cass in 3:58 (★★); Kevin Owens defeated Sami Zayn in 14:30 (★★★★); The Miz defeated Cesaro in 11:20 (★★); Dean Ambrose defeated Chris Jericho in 18:28 (★★★★); Charlotte Flair defeated Natalya in 13:04 (★★); Roman Reigns defeated AJ Styles in a No DQ Match in 25:55 (★★★).

Global Wars '16 ★★
08-05-16, Chicago Ridge, Illinois **ROH**
Dalton Castle defeated ACH, Adam Page and Roderick Strong in a Four Corner Survival Match in 8:26 (★★); Cheeseburger and Jushin Thunder Liger defeated The Addiction (Christopher Daniels and Frankie Kazarian) in 7:02 (★★); War Machine (Hanson and Raymond Rowe) defeated The Briscoe Brothers (Jay Briscoe and Mark Briscoe) in 15:15 (★★★); Tetsuya Naito defeated Kyle O'Reilly in 12:00 (★★★); Kazuchika Okada and Moose defeated Hiroshi Tanahashi and Michael Elgin in 13:46 (★★★); Bobby Fish defeated Tomohiro Ishii to win the ROH World Television Title in 15:30 (★★); Bullet Club (Matt Jackson, Nick Jackson, Tama Tonga and Tanga Loa) defeated Alex Shelley, Chris Sabin, Kushida and Matt Sydal in 13:08 (★★★); Jay Lethal vs. Colt Cabana went to a no contest in 22:30 (★★).

Extreme Rules '16 ★★★★
22-05-16, Newark, New Jersey **WWE**
Luke Gallows and Karl Anderson defeated The Usos (Jimmy Uso and Jey Uso) in a Tornado Match in 8:37 (★★); Rusev defeated Kalisto to win the WWE United States Title in 9:31 (★★); The New Day (Big E and Xavier Woods) defeated The Vaudevillains (Aiden English and Simon Gotch) in 6:20 (★★); The Miz defeated Cesaro, Sami Zayn and Kevin Owens in a Four Way Match in 18:18 (★★★★); Dean Ambrose defeated Chris Jericho in an Asylum Match in 26:21 (★); Charlotte Flair defeated Natalya in a Submission Match in 9:30 (★★); Roman Reigns defeated AJ Styles in an Extreme Rules Match in 22:13 (★★★★).

Takeover The End ★★★★
08-06-16, Winter Park, Florida **NXT**
Andrade Almas defeated Tye Dillinger in 5:22 (★★); The Revival (Dash Wilder and Scott Dawson) defeated American Alpha (Chad Gable and Jason Jordan) to win the NXT Tag Team Title in 16:00 (★★★); Shinsuke Nakamkura defeated Austin Aries in 17:05 (★★★★); Asuka defeated Nia Jax in 9:12 (★★★); Samoa Joe defeated Finn Balor in a Steel Cage Match in 16:10 (★★★).

Slammiversary XIV ★★
12-06-16, Orlando, Florida **TNA**
Eddie Edwards defeated Trevor Lee, Andrew Everett and DJ Z in a Four Way Match to win the TNA X Division Title in 10:09 (★★★); The Tribunal (Baron Dax and Basile Baraka) defeated Grado and Mahabali Shera in 6:53 (★); Sienna defeated Gail Kim and Jade in a Three Way Match to win the TNA Knockouts Title in 7:34 (★); James Storm defeated Braxton Sutter in 6:40 (★); Eli Drake defeated Bram in 8:35 (★★); Ethan Carter III defeated Mike Bennett in 15:01 (★★); Jeff Hardy defeated Broken Matt in a Full Metal Mayhem Match in 16:55 (★★★); Decay (Abyss and Crazzy Steve) defeated The BroMans (Jessie Godderz and Robbie E) in 9:19; Bobby Lashley defeated Drew Galloway to win the TNA World Heavyweight Title in 17:03 (★★★).

Money In The Bank '16 ★★★
19-06-16, Paradise, Nevada **WWE**
The New Day (Big E and Kofi Kingston) defeated Enzo Amore and Big Cass, Luke Gallows and Karl Anderson, and The Vaudevillains (Aiden English and Simon Gotch) in a Four Way Match in 11:43 (★★); Baron Corbin defeated Dolph Ziggler in 12:25 (★★); Charlotte Flair and Dana Brooke defeated Becky Lynch and Natalya in 7:00 (★★); Apollo Crews defeated Sheamus in 8:36 (★★); AJ Styles defeated John Cena in 24:10 (★★★); Dean Ambrose defeated Alberto Del Rio, Cesaro, Chris Jericho, Kevin Owens and Sami Zayn in a Money In The Bank Ladder Match in 21:38 (★★★); Rusev defeated Titus O'Neil in 8:30 (★★); Seth Rollins defeated Roman Reigns to win the WWE World Heavyweight Title in 26:02 (★★★); Dean Ambrose defeated Seth Rollins to win the WWE World Heavyweight Title in :09 (★★★).

Best In The World '16 ★★★
24-06-16, Concord, North Carolina **ROH**
Kyle O'Reilly defeated Kamaitachi in 13:45 (★★★); ACH defeated Silas Young in 11:09 (★★); Mark Briscoe defeated Roderick Strong in 15:37 (★★★); Bullet Club (Adam Cole, Matt Jackson and Nick Jackson) defeated War Machine (Hanson and Raymond Rowe) and Moose in a Tornado Match in 12:59 (★★★); The Addiction (Christopher Daniels and Frankie Kazarian) defeated The Motor City Machine Guns (Alex Shelley and Chris Sabin) in 12:11 (★★); B.J. Whitmer defeated Steve Corino in a Non Sanctioned Fight Without Honor in 15:00 (★★★); Bobby Fish defeated Dalton Castle in 16:50 (★★); Jay Lethal defeated Jay Briscoe in 12:55 (★★★).

Battleground '16 ★★★
24-07-16, Washington, D.C. **WWE**
Bayley and Sasha Banks defeated Charlotte Flair and Dana Brooke in 7:25 (★★★); The Wyatt Family (Bray Wyatt, Erick Rowan and Braun Strowman) defeated The New Day (Big E, Kofi Kingston and Xavier Woods) in 8:47 (★★); Rusev defeated Zack Ryder in 7:01 (★★); Sami Zayn defeated Kevin Owens in 18:22 (★★★★); Natalya defeated Becky Lynch in 9:04 (★★); The Miz vs. Darren Young went to a double DQ in 8:41 (★); Big Cass, Enzo Amore and John Cena defeated The Club (AJ Styles, Luke Gallows and Karl Anderson) in 14:30 (★★); Dean Ambrose defeated Roman Reigns and Seth Rollins in a Three Way Match in 18:03 (★★★).

Death Before Dishonor XIV ★★★
19-08-16, Sunrise Manor, Nevada **ROH**
Donovan Dijak defeated Lio Rush, Jay White and Kamaitachi in a Four Corner Survival Match in 8:10 (★★); Katsuyori Shibata defeated Silas Young in 9:20 (★★); Beretta, Rocky Romero and Toru Yano defeated Yujiro Takahashi, Tama Tonga and Tanga Loa in 11:17 (★★); Hangman Page defeated Jay Briscoe in an Anything Goes Match in 17:40 (★★★); Kazuchika Okada defeated Dalton Castle in 13:53 (★★); Bobby Fish defeated Mark Briscoe in 16:04 (★★); The Addiction (Christopher Daniels and Frankie Kazarian) defeated Tetsuya Naito and Evil, and Hiroshi Tanahashi and Michael Elgin in a Three Way Match in 14:48 (★★★); Adam Cole defeated Jay Lethal to win the ROH World Title in 24:00 (★★★).

Takeover Brooklyn II ★★★★
20-08-16, Brooklyn, New York **NXT**
Austin Aries defeated No Way Jose in 10:42 (★★★); Ember Moon defeated Billie Kay in 4:35 (★★); Bobby Roode defeated Andrade Almas in 10:22 (★★★); The Revival (Dash Wilder and Scott Dawson) defeated DIY (Johnny Gargano and Tommaso Ciampa) in 19:10 (★★★★); Asuka defeated Bayley in 14:07 (★★★); Shinsuke Nakamura defeated Samoa Joe to win the NXT Title in 21:14 (★★★).

SummerSlam '16 ★★★
21-08-16, Brooklyn, New York **WWE**
Chris Jericho and Kevin Owens defeated Enzo Amore and Big Cass in 12:08 (★★); Charlotte Flair defeated Sasha Banks to win the WWE Women's Title in 13:51 (★★★); The Miz defeated Apollo Crews in 5:45 (★★); AJ Styles defeated John Cena in 23:10 (★★★★); Luke Gallows and Karl Anderson defeated The New Day (Kofi Kingston and Xavier Woods) by DQ in 9:09 (★★); Dean Ambrose defeated Dolph Ziggler in 15:18 (★★); Nikki Bella, Natalya and Alexa Bliss defeated Becky Lynch, Naomi and Carmella in 11:04 (★); Finn Balor defeated Seth Rollins to win the inaugural WWE Universal Title in 19:24 (★★★); Brock Lesnar defeated Randy Orton in 11:45 (★★★★).

Backlash '16 ★★★
11-09-16, Richmond, Virginia **WWE**
Becky Lynch defeated Alexa Bliss, Carmella, Naomi, Natalya and Nikki Bella in a Six Pack Elimination Match to win the inaugural WWE SmackDown Women's Title in 14:40 (★★★); The Usos (Jimmy Uso and Jey Uso) defeated The Hype Bros (Mojo Rawley and Zack Ryder) in 10:11 (★★); The Miz defeated Dolph Ziggler in 18:22 (★★★); Kane defeated Bray Wyatt in a No Holds Barred Match in 10:55 (★★); Heath Slater and Rhyno defeated The Usos (Jimmy Uso and Jey Uso) to win the inaugural WWE SmackDown Tag Team Title in 10:02 (★★★); AJ Styles defeated Dean Ambrose to win the WWE World Title in 25:01 (★★★★).

Cruiserweight Classic Finale ★★★★
14-09-16, Winter Park, Florida **WWE**
Gran Metalik defeated Zack Sabre Jr. in 13:13 (★★★); TJ Perkins defeated Kota Ibushi in 14:52 (★★★★); DIY (Johnny Gargano and Tommaso Ciampa) defeated Cedric Alexander and Noam Dar in 9:49 (★★★); TJ Perkins defeated Gran Metalik to win the inaugural WWE Cruiserweight Title in 17:47 (★★★★).

Clash Of Champions '16 ★★★
25-09-16, Indianapolis, Indiana **WWE**
The New Day (Big E and Kofi Kingston) defeated Luke Gallows and Karl Anderson in 6:45 (★★); TJ Perkins defeated The Brian Kendrick in 10:31 (★★★); Cesaro vs. Sheamus went to a no contest in 16:36 (★★★); Chris Jericho defeated Sami Zayn in 15:22 (★★★); Charlotte Flair defeated Sasha Banks and Bayley in a Three Way Match in 15:28 (★★); Roman Reigns defeated Rusev to win the WWE United States Title in 17:07 (★★★); Kevin Owens defeated Seth Rollins in 25:07 (★★★).

All Star Extravaganza VIII ★★★
30-09-16, Lowell, Massachusetts **ROH**
Bobby Fish defeated Donovan Dijak in 11:44 (★★); Colt Cabana and Dalton Castle defeated The All Night Express (Kenny King and Rhett Titus), Keith Lee and Shane Taylor, and War Machine (Hanson and Raymond Rowe) in a Four Corner Survival Match in 8:50 (★★); Dragon Lee defeated Kamaitachi in 16:06 (★★★); Kyle O'Reilly defeated Hangman Page in 9:51 (★★); ACH, Jay White and Kushida defeated Toru Yano and The Briscoe Brothers (Jay Briscoe and Mark Briscoe) in 14:11 (★★); Jay Lethal defeated Tetsuya Naito in 13:06 (★★★); Adam Cole defeated Michael Elgin in 14:07 (★★★); The Young Bucks (Matt Jackson and Nick Jackson) defeated The Addiction (Christopher Daniels and Frankie Kazarian) and The Motor City Machine Guns (Alex Shelley and Chris Sabin) in a Ladder War to win the ROH World Tag Team Title in 23:45 (★★★★).

Bound For Glory '16 ★★
02-10-16, Orlando, Florida **TNA**
DJ Z defeated Trevor Lee in 11:12 (★★★); Eli Drake won a 10-Man Gauntlet Match in 15:19 (★★); Moose defeated Mike Bennett in 10:09 (★★); Aron Rex defeated Eddie Edwards to win the vacant Impact Grand Title in 15:03 (★★); The Broken Hardys (Brother Nero and Broken Matt) defeated Decay (Abyss and Crazzy Steve) in The Great War to win the TNA World Tag Team Title in 22:28 (★★★★); Gail Kim defeated Maria to win the TNA Knockouts Title in 5:19 (★); Bobby Lashley defeated Ethan Carter III in a No Holds Barred Match in 16:11 (★★).

No Mercy '16 ★★★
09-10-16, Sacramento, California **WWE**
AJ Styles defeated Dean Ambrose and John Cena in a Three Way Match in 21:15 (★★★★); Nikki Bella defeated Carmella in 8:05 (★★); Heath Slater and Rhyno defeated The Usos (Jimmy Uso and Jey Uso) in 10:17 (★★); Baron Corbin defeated Jack Swagger in 7:30 (★★); Dolph Ziggler defeated The Miz to win the WWE Intercontinental Title in 19:42 (★★★★); Naomi defeated Alexa Bliss in 5:25 (★); Bray Wyatt defeated Randy Orton in 15:40 (★★).

Hell In A Cell '16 ★★★
30-10-16, Boston, Massachusetts **WWE**
Roman Reigns defeated Rusev in a Hell In A Cell Match in 24:35 (★★); Bayley defeated Dana Brooke in 6:30 (★★); Luke Gallows and Karl Anderson defeated Enzo Amore and Big Cass in 6:45 (★★); Kevin Owens defeated Seth Rollins in a Hell In A Cell Match in 23:15 (★★★); The Brian Kendrick defeated TJ Perkins to win the WWE Cruiserweight Title in 10:35 (★★);

Sheamus and Cesaro defeated The New Day (Big E and Xavier Woods) by DQ in 11:15 (★★); Charlotte Flair defeated Sasha Banks in a Hell In A Cell Match to win the WWE Raw Women's Title in 22:25 (★★★).

Takeover Toronto ★★★★
19-11-16, Toronto, Ontario **NXT**
Bobby Roode defeated Tye Dillinger in 16:28 (★★★); The Authors Of Pain (Akam and Rezar) defeated TM-61 (Nick Miller and Shane Thorne) in 8:20 (★★); DIY (Johnny Gargano and Tommaso Ciampa) defeated The Revival (Dash Wilder and Scott Dawson) in a Best Two Out Of Three Falls Match to win the NXT Tag Team Title in 22:18 (★★★★★); Asuka defeated Mickie James in 13:07 (★★★); Samoa Joe defeated Shinsuke Nakamura to win the NXT Title in 20:12 (★★★★).

Survivor Series '16 ★★★
20-11-16, Toronto, Ontario **WWE**
Team Raw (Charlotte Flair, Bayley, Nia Jax, Alicia Fox and Sasha Banks) defeated Team SmackDown (Becky Lynch, Alexa Bliss, Carmella, Naomi and Natalya) in an Elimination Match in 17:30 (★★); The Miz defeated Sami Zayn in 14:05 (★★); Team Raw (Sheamus, Cesaro, Enzo Amore, Big Cass, Luke Gallows, Karl Anderson, Big E, Kofi Kingston, Epico and Primo) defeated Team SmackDown (Chad Gable, Jason Jordan, Fandango, Tyler Breeze, Heath Slater, Rhyno, Mojo Rawley, Zack Ryder, Jimmy Uso and Jey Uso) in an Elimination Match in 18:55 (★★★); The Brian Kendrick defeated Kalisto by DQ in 12:25 (★★); Team SmackDown (AJ Styles, Bray Wyatt, Dean Ambrose, Randy Orton and Shane McMahon) defeated Team Raw (Braun Strowman, Chris Jericho, Kevin Owens, Roman Reigns and Seth Rollins) in an Elimination Match in 52:55 (★★★★); Goldberg defeated Brock Lesnar in 1:26 (★★★).

Final Battle '16 ★★★
02-12-16, New York City, New York **ROH**
The Rebellion (Caprice Coleman, Kenny King and Rhett Titus) defeated Donovan Dijak and The Motor City Machine Guns (Alex Shelley and Chris Sabin) in 12:22 (★★); Silas Young defeated Jushin Thunder Liger in 11:04 (★★); Dalton Castle defeated Colt Cabana in 10:22 (★★); Cody Rhodes defeated Jay Lethal in 13:15 (★★); The Kingdom (Matt Taven, TK O'Ryan and Vinny Marseglia) defeated Kushida, Lio Rush and Jay White in 15:25 (★★); Marty Scurll defeated Dragon Lee and Will Ospreay in a Three Way Match in 10:46 (★★★); The Young Bucks (Matt Jackson and Nick Jackson) defeated The Briscoe Brothers (Jay Briscoe and Mark Briscoe) in 15:37 (★★★); Kyle O'Reilly defeated Adam Cole in a No DQ Match to win the ROH World Title in 18:48 (★★★).

TLC '16 ★★★
04-12-16, Dallas, Texas **WWE**
The Wyatt Family (Bray Wyatt and Randy Orton) defeated Heath Slater and Rhyno to win the WWE SmackDown Tag Team Title in 5:55 (★★); Nikki Bella defeated Carmella in a No DQ Match in 8:00 (★★); The Miz defeated Dolph Ziggler in a Ladder Match in 24:25 (★★★); Baron Corbin defeated Kalisto in a Chairs Match in 12:50 (★★); Alexa Bliss defeated Becky Lynch in a Tables Match to win the WWE SmackDown Women's Title in 15:10 (★★); AJ Styles defeated Dean Ambrose in a TLC Match in 30:50 (★★★★).

Tribute To The Troops '16 ★★
14-12-16, Washington, D.C. **WWE**
Sheamus and Cesaro defeated The Shining Stars (Primo and Epico), Luke Gallows and Karl Anderson, and The Golden Truth (Goldust and R-Truth) in a Four Way Match in 9:35 (★★); Apollo Crews defeated The Miz in 2:30 (★★); The Wyatt Family (Bray Wyatt, Luke Harper and Randy Orton) defeated Dolph Ziggler and American Alpha (Chad Gable and Jason Jordan) in 10:15 (★★★); Bayley defeated Dana Brooke in 2:30 (★★); Jack Gallagher, Rich Swann and T.J. Perkins defeated The Brian Kendrick, Drew Gulak and Tony Nese in 5:30 (★★); Roman Reigns and Big Cass defeated Kevin Owens and Rusev in 13:00 (★★★).

Roadblock End Of The Line ★★★
18-12-16, Pittsburgh, Pennsylvania **WWE**
Sheamus and Cesaro defeated The New Day (Big E and Kofi Kingston) to win the WWE Raw Tag Team Title in 10:10 (★★★); Sami Zayn defeated Braun Strowman in 10:00 (★★); Seth Rollins defeated Chris Jericho in 17:22 (★★★); Rich Swann

defeated **The Brian Kendrick** and **TJ Perkins** in a Three Way Match in 6:00 (★★); **Charlotte Flair** defeated **Sasha Banks** 3-2 in an Iron Man Match in 34:45 (★★★); **Kevin Owens** defeated **Roman Reigns** by DQ in 23:20 (★★).

United Kingdom Championship Tournament '17 Night #1 ★★
14-01-17, Blackpool, England **WWE**
Trent Seven defeated **HC Dyer** in 5:25 (★★); **Jordan Devlin** defeated **Danny Burch** in 8:55 (★★); **Sam Gradwell** defeated **Saxon Huxley** in 6:00 (★★); **Pete Dunne** defeated **Roy Johnson** in 7:30 (★★); **Wolfgang** defeated **Tyson T-Bone** in 6:20 (★★); **Joseph Conners** defeated **James Drake** in 7:12 (★★); **Mark Andrews** defeated **Dan Moloney** in 5:35 (★★); **Tyler Bate** defeated **Tucker** in 10:34 (★★★).

United Kingdom Championship Tournament '17 Night #2 ★★★
15-01-17, Blackpool, England **WWE**
Pete Dunne defeated **Sam Gradwell** in 4:49 (★★); **Mark Andrews** defeated **Joseph Conners** in 8:12 (★★); **Wolfgang** defeated **Trent Seven** in 6:43 (★★); **Tyler Bate** defeated **Jordan Devlin** in 6:07 (★★); **Pete Dunne** defeated **Mark Andrews** in 10:39 (★★★★); **Tyler Bate** defeated **Wolfgang** in 6:00 (★★); **Neville** defeated **Tommy End** in 8:42 (★★); **Tyler Bate** defeated **Pete Dunne** to win the vacant WWE United Kingdom Title in 15:12 (★★★★).

Takeover San Antonio ★★★
28-01-17, San Antonio, Texas **NXT**
Eric Young defeated **Tye Dillinger** in 10:55 (★★); **Roderick Strong** defeated **Andrade Almas** in 11:40 (★★★); **The Authors Of Pain** (Akam and Rezar) defeated **DIY** (Johnny Gargano and Tommaso Ciampa) to win the NXT Tag Team Title in 14:30 (★★); **Asuka** defeated **Billie Kay, Peyton Royce** and **Nikki Cross** in a Four Way Match in 9:55 (★★); **Bobby Roode** defeated **Shinsuke Nakamura** to win the NXT Title in 27:15 (★★★★).

Royal Rumble '17 ★★★★★
29-01-17, San Antonio, Texas **WWE**
Charlotte Flair defeated **Bayley** in 13:05 (★★★); **Kevin Owens** defeated **Roman Reigns** in a No DQ Match in 22:55 (★★★★★); **Neville** defeated **Rich Swann** to win the WWE Cruiserweight Title in 14:00 (★★★); **John Cena** defeated **AJ Styles** to win the WWE Title in 24:10 (★★★★★); **Randy Orton** won the 30-Man Royal Rumble Match in 62:06 (★★★).

Elimination Chamber '17 ★★
12-02-17, Phoenix, Arizona **WWE**
Becky Lynch defeated **Mickie James** in 11:40 (★★); **Apollo Crews** and **Kalisto** defeated **Dolph Ziggler** in a Handicap Match in 7:20 (★); **American Alpha** (Chad Gable and Jason Jordan) won a Tag Team Turmoil Match in 21:10 (★★); **Natalya** vs. **Nikki Bella** went to a double count out in 13:40 (★★); **Randy Orton** defeated **Luke Harper** in 17:15 (★★★); **Naomi** defeated **Alexa Bliss** to win the WWE SmackDown Women's Title in 8:20 (★★); **Bray Wyatt** defeated **John Cena, AJ Styles, The Miz, Dean Ambrose** and **Baron Corbin** in an Elimination Chamber Match to win the WWE Title in 34:20 (★★★★).

Fastlane '17 ★★
05-03-17, Milwaukee, Wisconsin **WWE**
Samoa Joe defeated **Sami Zayn** in 9:45 (★★); **Luke Gallows** and **Karl Anderson** defeated **Enzo Amore** and **Big Cass** in 8:40 (★★); **Sasha Banks** defeated **Nia Jax** in 8:15 (★★); **Cesaro** defeated **Jinder Mahal** in 8:12 (★★); **The Big Show** defeated **Rusev** in 8:40 (★); **Neville** defeated **Jack Gallagher** in 12:08 (★★★); **Roman Reigns** defeated **Braun Strowman** in 17:13 (★★★); **Bayley** defeated **Charlotte Flair** in 16:49 (★★); **Goldberg** defeated **Kevin Owens** to win the WWE Universal Title in :22 (★).

15th Anniversary Show ★★★★
10-03-17, Sunrise Manor, Nevada **ROH**
Jay White defeated **Kenny King** in 9:58 (★★); **Frankie Kazarian** defeated **Cheeseburger, Chris Sabin, Hangman Page, Punishment Martinez** and **Silas Young** in a Six Man Mayhem Match in 10:16 (★★); **Jay Lethal** defeated **Bobby Fish** in 15:12 (★★★★); **The Kingdom** (Matt Taven, TK O'Ryan and Vinny Marseglia) defeated **Dalton Castle** and **The Boys** (Boy 1 and Boy 2) in 7:55 (★★); **Marty Scurll** defeated **Lio Rush** in 18:37 (★★★); **The Briscoe Brothers** (Jay Briscoe and Mark Briscoe)

and **Bully Ray** defeated **War Machine** (Hanson and Raymond Rowe) and **Davey Boy Smith Jr.** in 11:49 (★); **The Hardy Boyz** (Matt Hardy and Jeff Hardy) defeated **Roppongi Vice** (Beretta and Rocky Romero) and **The Young Bucks** (Matt Jackson and Nick Jackson) in a Three Way Las Vegas Street Fight in 17:17 (★★★★); **Christopher Daniels** defeated **Adam Cole** to win the ROH World Title in 21:55 (★★★).

Takeover Orlando ★★★
01-04-17, Orlando, Florida **NXT**
Sanity (Alexander Wolfe, Eric Young, Killian Dain and Nikki Cross) defeated **Kassius Ohno, Roderick Strong, Tye Dillinger** and **Ruby Riott** in 12:23 (★★); **Aleister Black** defeated **Andrade Almas** in 9:35 (★★); **The Authors Of Pain** (Akam and Rezar) defeated **DIY** (Johnny Gargano and Tommaso Ciampa) and **The Revival** (Dash Wilder and Scott Dawson) in a Three Way Elimination Match in 23:50 (★★★); **Asuka** defeated **Ember Moon** in 12:10 (★★★); **Bobby Roode** defeated **Shinsuke Nakamura** in 28:20 (★★★).

Supercard Of Honor XI ★★★
01-04-17, Lakeland, Florida **ROH**
Marty Scurll defeated **Adam Cole** in 13:01 (★★★); **Silas Young** and **Beer City Bruiser** defeated **The Kingdom** (Matt Taven and Vinny Marseglia) in 6:57 (★★); **The Briscoe Brothers** (Jay Briscoe and Mark Briscoe) and **Bully Ray** defeated **Bullet Club** (Hangman Page, Tama Tonga and Tanga Loa) in 13:31 (★★); **Jay Lethal** defeated **Cody Rhodes** in a Texas Bullrope Match in 17:26 (★★); **The Motor City Machine Guns** (Alex Shelley and Chris Sabin) defeated **Cheeseburger** and **Will Ferrara**, and **The Rebellion** (Rhett Titus and Shane Taylor) in a Three Match Match in 9:24 (★★); **Punishment Martinez** defeated **Frankie Kazarian** in 6:03 (★★); **Bobby Fish** defeated **Silas Young** by DQ in 2:25 (★★); **Volador Jr.** and **Will Ospreay** defeated **Dragon Lee** and **Jay White** in 13:57 (★★★★); **Christopher Daniels** defeated **Dalton Castle** in 15:43 (★★); **The Young Bucks** (Matt Jackson and Nick Jackson) defeated **The Hardy Boyz** (Matt Hardy and Jeff Hardy) in a Ladder War to win the ROH World Tag Team Title in 25:25 (★★★★).

WrestleMania XXXIII ★★★
02-04-17, Orlando, Florida **WWE**
AJ Styles defeated **Shane McMahon** in 20:31 (★★★); **Kevin Owens** defeated **Chris Jericho** to win the WWE United States Title in 16:51 (★★); **Bayley** defeated **Charlotte Flair, Nia Jax** and **Sasha Banks** in a Four Way Elimination Match in 12:41 (★★); **The Hardy Boyz** (Matt Hardy and Jeff Hardy) defeated **Luke Gallows** and **Karl Anderson, Sheamus** and **Cesaro**, and **Enzo Amore** and **Big Cass** in a Fatal Four Way Ladder Match to win the WWE Raw Tag Team Title in 11:06 (★★★); **John Cena** and **Nikki Bella** defeated **The Miz** and **Maryse** in 5:51 (★★); **Seth Rollins** defeated **Triple H** in a Non Sanctioned Match in 25:20 (★★); **Randy Orton** defeated **Bray Wyatt** to win the WWE Title in 10:13 (★); **Brock Lesnar** defeated **Goldberg** to win the WWE Universal Title in 5:55 (★★★★); **Naomi** defeated **Alexa Bliss, Becky Lynch, Carmella, Mickie James** and **Natalya** in a Six Pack Challenge to win the WWE SmackDown Women's Title in 4:15 (★★); **Roman Reigns** defeated **The Undertaker** in a No Holds Barred Match in 25:30 (★).

Payback '17 ★★★
30-04-17, San Jose, California **WWE**
Chris Jericho defeated **Kevin Owens** to win the WWE United States Title in 14:00 (★★★); **Austin Aries** defeated **Neville** by DQ in 11:20 (★★★); **The Hardy Boyz** (Matt Hardy and Jeff Hardy) defeated **Sheamus** and **Cesaro** in 12:45 (★★); **Alexa Bliss** defeated **Bayley** to win the WWE Raw Women's Title in 11:15 (★★); **Bray Wyatt** defeated **Randy Orton** in a House Of Horrors Match in 17:10 (★); **Seth Rollins** defeated **Samoa Joe** in 15:55 (★★); **Braun Strowman** defeated **Roman Reigns** in 11:50 (★★★).

War Of The Worlds '17 ★★★
12-05-17, New York City, New York **ROH**
Dalton Castle defeated **Bobby Fish, Kushida** and **Silas Young** in a Four Way Match in 8:30 (★★); **Hangman Page** defeated **Frankie Kazarian** in 6:00 (★★); **War Machine** (Hanson and Raymond Rowe) defeated **Evil** and **Sanada**, and **Search And Destroy** (Chris Sabin and Jonathan Gresham) in a Three Way Match in 8:47 (★★); **Will Ospreay** defeated **Jay White** in 13:25 (★★★★); **The Briscoe Brothers** (Jay Briscoe and Mark Briscoe) and **Bully Ray** defeated **Beretta, Hirooki Goto** and

Rocky Romero in a No DQ Match in 12:45 (★★); Marty Scurll defeated Matt Sydal in 11:24 (★★); The Young Bucks (Matt Jackson and Nick Jackson) defeated Bushi and Tetsuya Naito in 13:35 (★★★); Hiroshi Tanahashi defeated Adam Cole in 13:32 (★★★); Christopher Daniels defeated Cody Rhodes and Jay Lethal in a Three Way Match in 13:31 (★★).

United Kingdom Championship Special ★★★
19-05-17, Norwich, England WWE

Wolfgang defeated Joseph Conners in 11:00 (★★); The Brian Kendrick and TJP defeated Dan Moloney and Rich Swann in 11:30 (★★); Pete Dunne defeated Trent Seven in 15:55 (★★★); Tyler Bate defeated Mark Andrews in 24:20 (★★★★).

Takeover Chicago ★★★
20-05-17, Rosemont, Illinois NXT

Roderick Strong defeated Eric Young in 13:42 (★★★); Pete Dunne defeated Tyler Bate to win the WWE United Kingdom Title in 15:27 (★★★★★); Asuka defeated Nikki Cross and Ruby Riott in a Three Way Match in 12:30 (★★); Bobby Roode defeated Hideo Itami in 17:50 (★★★); The Authors Of Pain (Akam and Rezar) defeated DIY (Johnny Gargano and Tommaso Ciampa) in a Ladder Match in 20:06 (★★★).

Backlash '17 ★★
21-05-17, Rosemont, Illinois WWE

Shinsuke Nakamura defeated Dolph Ziggler in 15:50 (★★); The Usos (Jimmy Uso and Jey Uso) defeated Breezango (Fandango and Tyler Breeze) in 9:15 (★★); Sami Zayn defeated Baron Corbin in 14:35 (★★); The Welcoming Committee (Natalya, Tamina and Carmella) defeated Becky Lynch, Charlotte Flair and Naomi in 10:05 (★★); Kevin Owens defeated AJ Styles via count out in 21:10 (★★★); Luke Harper defeated Erick Rowan in 8:53 (★★); Jinder Mahal defeated Randy Orton to win the WWE Title in 15:45 (★★).

Extreme Rules '17 ★★★
04-06-17, Baltimore, Maryland WWE

The Miz defeated Dean Ambrose to win the WWE Intercontinental Title in 20:00 (★★★★); Rich Swann and Sasha Banks defeated Noam Dar and Alicia Fox in 6:20 (★★); Alexa Bliss defeated Bayley in a Kendo Stick On A Pole Match in 5:10 (★); Sheamus and Cesaro defeated The Hardy Boyz (Matt Hardy and Jeff Hardy) in a Steel Cage Match to win the WWE Raw Tag Team Title in 15:00 (★★); Neville defeated Austin Aries in 17:35 (★★); Samoa Joe defeated Finn Balor, Roman Reigns, Seth Rollins and Bray Wyatt in a Fatal Five Way Extreme Rules Match in 29:15 (★★★).

Money In The Bank '17 ★★
18-06-17, St. Louis, Missouri WWE

Carmella defeated Becky Lynch, Charlotte Flair, Natalya and Tamina in a Money In The Bank Ladder Match in 13:22 (★★); The New Day (Big E and Kofi Kingston) defeated The Usos (Jimmy Uso and Jey Uso) via count out in 12:13 (★★); Naomi defeated Lana in 7:30 (★); Jinder Mahal defeated Randy Orton in 21:11 (★★); Breezango (Fandango and Tyler Breeze) defeated The Ascension (Konnor and Viktor) in 3:50 (★★); Baron Corbin defeated AJ Styles, Dolph Ziggler, Kevin Owens, Sami Zayn and Shinsuke Nakamura in a Money In The Bank Ladder Match in 29:50 (★★★★).

Best In The World '17 ★★★
23-06-17, Lowell, Massachusetts ROH

El Terrible and Ultimo Guerrero defeated The Kingdom (Matt Taven and Vinny Marseglia) in 11:10 (★★); Frankie Kazarian defeated Hangman Page in a Strap Match in 12:06 (★★★); Search And Destroy (Alex Shelley, Chris Sabin, Jay White and Jonathan Gresham) defeated The Rebellion (Caprice Coleman, Kenny King, Rhett Titus and Shane Taylor) in 12:45 (★★★); Jay Lethal defeated Silas Young in 16:40 (★★); Dalton Castle and The Boys (Boy 1 and Boy 2) defeated Bully Ray and The Briscoe Brothers (Jay Briscoe and Mark Briscoe) to win the ROH World Six Man Tag Team Title in 13:45 (★★); Kushida defeated Marty Scurll in 14:54 (★★★); The Young Bucks (Matt Jackson and Nick Jackson) defeated War Machine (Hanson and Raymond Rowe) and Best Friends (Beretta and Chuckie T) in a Three Way Tornado Match in 12:27 (★★★★); Cody Rhodes defeated Christopher Daniels to win the ROH World Title in 19:18 (★★★).

Slammiversary XV ★★
02-07-17, Orlando, Florida GFW

The Latin American Xchange (Santana and Ortiz) defeated Drago and El Hijo del Fantasma, Garza Jr. and Laredo Kid, and Naomichi Marufuji and Taiji Ishimori in a Four Way Match in 14:40 (★★★); DeAngelo Williams and Moose defeated Chris Adonis and Eli Drake in 10:40 (★★); Ethan Carter III defeated James Storm in a Strap Match in 10:50 (★★★); Jeremy Borash and Joseph Park defeated Josh Matthews and Scott Steiner in a No DQ Match in 10:52 (★★); Alisha Edwards and Eddie Edwards defeated Angelina Love and Davey Richards in a Full Metal Mayhem Match in 8:30 (★★); Sonjay Dutt defeated Low Ki in a Best Two Out Of Three Falls Match in 18:20 (★★★); Sienna defeated Rosemary to win the Impact Knockouts Title in 10:31 (★★); Alberto El Patron defeated Bobby Lashley to win the Impact World Heavyweight Title in 18:05 (★★★).

Great Balls Of Fire ★★
09-07-17, Dallas, Texas WWE

Bray Wyatt defeated Seth Rollins in 12:10 (★★); Big Cass defeated Enzo Amore in 5:25 (★); Sheamus and Cesaro defeated The Hardy Boyz (Matt Hardy and Jeff Hardy) 4-3 in an Iron Man Match in 30:00 (★★★); Sasha Banks defeated Alexa Bliss via count out in 11:40 (★★); The Miz defeated Dean Ambrose in 11:20 (★★); Braun Strowman defeated Roman Reigns in an Ambulance Match in 16:35 (★★); Heath Slater defeated Curt Hawkins in 2:10 (★); Brock Lesnar defeated Samoa Joe in 6:25 (★★★).

Battleground '17 ★★
23-07-17, Philadelphia, Pennsylvania WWE

The New Day (Kofi Kingston and Xavier Woods) defeated The Usos (Jimmy Uso and Jey Uso) to win the WWE SmackDown Tag Team Title in 13:50 (★★★★); Shinsuke Nakamura defeated Baron Corbin by DQ in 12:25 (★★); Natalya defeated Becky Lynch, Charlotte Flair, Lana and Tamina in a Five Way Elimination Match in 10:54 (★★); Kevin Owens defeated AJ Styles to win the WWE United States Title in 17:50 (★★); John Cena defeated Rusev in a Flag Match in 21:10 (★★); Sami Zayn defeated Mike Kanellis in 7:15 (★); Jinder Mahal defeated Randy Orton in a Punjabi Prison Match in 27:40 (★).

War Of The Worlds UK '17 ★★
19-08-17, Liverpool, England ROH

Kenny King defeated Hangman Page in 8:44 (★★); Ultimo Guerrero and Rey Bucanero defeated Mistico and Titan in 11:35 (★★★); Jay Lethal defeated Josh Bodom in 9:17 (★★); Bully Ray and The Briscoe Brothers (Jay Briscoe and Mark Briscoe) defeated Tetsuya Naito, Evil and Bushi in 13:37 (★★); Mark Haskins defeated Silas Young in 10:03 (★★); Kushida defeated Dalton Castle, Hiromu Takahashi and Marty Scurll in a Four Corner Survival Match in 11:22 (★★); The Young Bucks (Matt Jackson and Nick Jackson) defeated The Addiction (Christopher Daniels and Frankie Kazarian) in 13:40 (★★★); Cody Rhodes defeated Sanada in 19:51 (★★).

Takeover Brooklyn III ★★★★
19-08-17, Brooklyn, New York NXT

Andrade Almas defeated Johnny Gargano in 13:13 (★★★★); Sanity (Alexander Wolfe and Eric Young) defeated The Authors Of Pain (Akam and Rezar) to win the NXT Tag Team Title in 12:04 (★★); Aleister Black defeated Hideo Itami in 12:24 (★★★); Asuka defeated Ember Moon in 14:50 (★★★★); Drew McIntyre defeated Bobby Roode to win the NXT Title in 22:25 (★★★).

SummerSlam '17 ★★★
20-08-17, Brooklyn, New York WWE

John Cena defeated Baron Corbin in 10:15 (★★); Natalya defeated Naomi to win the WWE SmackDown Women's Title in 11:10 (★★); Big Cass defeated The Big Show in 10:30 (★); Randy Orton defeated Rusev in :10 (★); Sasha Banks defeated Alexa Bliss in 13:10 (★★); Finn Balor defeated Bray Wyatt in 10:40 (★★); Dean Ambrose and Seth Rollins defeated Sheamus and Cesaro to win the WWE Raw Tag Team Title in 18:35 (★★★); AJ Styles defeated Kevin Owens in 17:20 (★★); Jinder Mahal defeated Shinsuke Nakamura in 11:25 (★); Brock Lesnar defeated Braun Strowman, Roman Reigns and Samoa Joe in a Four Way Match in 20:52 (★★★★).

Death Before Dishonor XV ★★★
22-09-17, Sunrise Manor, Nevada **ROH**
Bully Ray and The Briscoe Brothers (Jay Briscoe and Mark Briscoe) defeated The Kingdom (Matt Taven, TK O'Ryan and Vinny Marseglia) in 12:08 (★★); Marty Scurll defeated Chuckie T in 12:07 (★★★); Punishment Martinez defeated Jay White in a Las Vegas Street Fight in 13:46 (★★★); The Young Bucks (Matt Jackson and Nick Jackson) and Hangman Page defeated Bully Ray and The Briscoe Brothers (Jay Briscoe and Mark Briscoe) in 5:06 (★★); Kenny King defeated Kushida to win the ROH World Television Title in 16:25 (★★★); Silas Young defeated Jay Lethal in a Last Man Standing Match in 21:20 (★★★); The Motor City Machine Guns (Alex Shelley and Chris Sabin) defeated The Young Bucks (Matt Jackson and Nick Jackson) to win the ROH World Tag Team Title in 15:43 (★★★); Cody Rhodes defeated Minoru Suzuki in 12:30 (★★).

No Mercy '17 ★★★
24-09-17, Los Angeles, California **WWE**
The Miz defeated Jason Jordan in 10:15 (★★); Finn Balor defeated Bray Wyatt in 11:35 (★★); Dean Ambrose and Seth Rollins defeated Sheamus and Cesaro in 15:55 (★★★); Alexa Bliss defeated Bayley, Emma, Nia Jax and Sasha Banks in a Five Way Match in 9:40 (★★★); Roman Reigns defeated John Cena in 22:05 (★★★); Enzo Amore defeated Neville to win the WWE Cruiserweight Title in 10:40 (★); Brock Lesnar defeated Braun Strowman in 10:20 (★★).

Hell In A Cell '17 ★★★
08-10-17, Detroit, Michigan **WWE**
The Usos (Jimmy Uso and Jey Uso) defeated The New Day (Big E and Xavier Woods) in a Hell In A Cell Match to win the WWE SmackDown Tag Team Title in 22:00 (★★★★); Randy Orton defeated Rusev in 11:40 (★); Baron Corbin defeated AJ Styles and Tye Dillinger in a Three Way Match to win the WWE United States Title in 19:20 (★★); Charlotte Flair defeated Natalya by DQ in 12:15 (★★); Jinder Mahal defeated Shinsuke Nakamura in 12:10 (★★); Bobby Roode defeated Dolph Ziggler in 11:35 (★★); Kevin Owens defeated Shane McMahon in a Falls Count Anywhere Hell In A Cell Match in 39:00 (★★★★).

Global Wars '17 ★★★
15-10-17, Villa Park, Illinois **ROH**
Beer City Bruiser and Silas Young defeated Best Friends (Beretta and Chuckie T) in 13:10 (★★); Marty Scurll defeated Hiromu Takahashi in 14:30 (★★★); The Addiction (Christopher Daniels and Frankie Kazarian) defeated Cheeseburger and Kushida in 8:21 (★★); Bullet Club (Cody Rhodes, Hangman Page, Matt Jackson and Nick Jackson) defeated Search And Destroy (Alex Shelley, Chris Sabin, Jay White and Jonathan Gresham) in 14:40 (★★★); The Dawgs (Rhett Titus and Will Ferrara) defeated Brian Johnson and Justin Pusser in 5:11 (★★); Davey Boy Smith Jr., Lance Archer and Minoru Suzuki defeated Jay Lethal, Kenny King and Shane Taylor in 16:30 (★★); Colt Cabana defeated Toru Yano and 8:39 (★★); Will Ospreay defeated Flip Gordon in 15:19 (★★★); Kenny Omega defeated Yoshi-Hashi in 25:24 (★★).

TLC '17 ★★★
22-10-17, Minneapolis, Minnesota **WWE**
Asuka defeated Emma in 9:25 (★★); Rich Swann and Cedric Alexander defeated Jack Gallagher and The Brian Kendrick in 8:00 (★★★); Alexa Bliss defeated Mickie James in 11:25 (★★); Enzo Amore defeated Kalisto to win the WWE Cruiserweight Title in 8:45 (★★); Finn Balor defeated AJ Styles in 18:20 (★★★★); Jason Jordan defeated Elias in 8:50 (★★); Kurt Angle, Seth Rollins and Dean Ambrose defeated Braun Strowman, The Miz, Kane, Sheamus and Cesaro in a Handicap TLC Match in 35:25 (★★★).

Bound For Glory '17 ★★
05-11-17, Ottawa, Ontario **Impact**
Trevor Lee defeated Dezmond Xavier, Garza Jr., Matt Sydal, Petey Williams and Sonjay Dutt in a Six Way Match in 12:25 (★★★); Taiji Ishimori defeated Tyson Dux in 4:50 (★★); Abyss defeated Grado in a Monster's Ball Match in 10:40 (★); Team Impact (Ethan Carter III, Eddie Edwards and James Storm) defeated Team AAA (El Hijo del Fantasma, Pagano and Texano) in 15:30 (★★); Ohio Versus Everything (Dave Crist and Jake Crist) defeated The Latin American Xchange (Santana and Ortiz) in a 5150 Street Fight in 10:35 (★★★); Gail Kim defeated Sienna and Allie in a Three Way Match to win the

Impact Knockouts Title in 9:40 (★★); Bobby Lashley and King Mo defeated Moose and Stephan Bonnar in a Six Sides Of Steel Match in 10:40 (★); Eli Drake defeated Johnny Impact in 19:30 (★★).

Takeover WarGames '17 ★★★★
18-11-17, Houston, Texas **NXT**
Lars Sullivan defeated Kassius Ohno in 5:11 (★★); Aleister Black defeated Velveteen Dream in 14:37 (★★★); Ember Moon defeated Kairi Sane, Nikki Cross and Peyton Royce in a Four Way Match to win the vacant NXT Women's Title in 9:52 (★★★); Andrade Almas defeated Drew McIntyre to win the NXT Title in 14:52 (★★★); The Undisputed Era (Adam Cole, Bobby Fish and Kyle O'Reilly) defeated The Authors Of Pain (Akam and Rezar) and Roderick Strong, and Sanity (Alexander Wolfe, Eric Young and Killian Dain) in a Three Way WarGames Match in 36:37 (★★★★).

Survivor Series '17 ★★★
19-11-17, Houston, Texas **WWE**
The Shield (Dean Ambrose, Roman Reigns and Seth Rollins) defeated The New Day (Big E, Kofi Kingston and Xavier Woods) in 21:20 (★★★); Team Raw (Alicia Fox, Sasha Banks, Bayley, Asuka and Nia Jax) defeated Team SmackDown (Becky Lynch, Naomi, Carmella, Natalya and Tamina) in an Elimination Match in 18:35 (★★); Baron Corbin defeated The Miz in 9:35 (★★); The Usos (Jimmy Uso and Jey Uso) defeated Sheamus and Cesaro in 15:55 (★★★); Charlotte Flair defeated Alexa Bliss in 15:53 (★★); Brock Lesnar defeated AJ Styles in 15:25 (★★★★); Team Raw (Kurt Angle, Braun Strowman, Finn Balor, Samoa Joe and Triple H) defeated Team SmackDown (Shane McMahon, Randy Orton, Bobby Roode, Shinsuke Nakamura and John Cena) in an Elimination Match in 33:20 (★★).

Tribute To The Troops '17 ★★
14-12-17, San Diego, California **WWE**
The Shield (Dean Ambrose, Roman Reigns and Seth Rollins) defeated Samoa Joe and The Bar (Cesaro and Sheamus) in 9:57 (★★); Charlotte Flair defeated Carmella and Ruby Riott in a Three Way Match in 10:08 (★★); The New Day (Big E and Xavier Woods) and The Usos (Jimmy Uso and Jey Uso) defeated Chad Gable, Shelton Benjamin and Rusev Day (Aiden English and Rusev) in 8:06 (★★); Absolution (Paige, Mandy Rose and Sonya Deville) defeated Mickie James, Bayley and Sasha Banks in 10:07 (★★); AJ Styles, Randy Orton and Shinsuke Nakamura defeated Jinder Mahal, Kevin Owens and Sami Zayn in 10:21 (★★).

Final Battle '17 ★★
15-12-17, New York City, New York **ROH**
Matt Taven defeated Will Ospreay in 10:58 (★★★); War Machine (Hanson and Raymond Rowe) defeated The Addiction (Christopher Daniels and Frankie Kazarian) in 9:35 (★★); Jay Lethal defeated Marty Scurll in 15:55 (★★); The Motor City Machine Guns (Alex Shelley and Chris Sabin) defeated Best Friends (Beretta and Chuckie T) in 10:20 (★★); Silas Young defeated Kenny King, Punishment Martinez and Shane Taylor in a Four Way Elimination Match to win the ROH World Television Title in 17:25 (★★); The Briscoe Brothers (Jay Briscoe and Mark Briscoe) defeated Bully Ray and Tommy Dreamer in a New York Street Fight in 16:30 (★★); Hangman Page and The Young Bucks (Matt Jackson and Nick Jackson) defeated Dragon Lee, Flip Gordon and Titan in 15:11 (★★★); Dalton Castle defeated Cody Rhodes to win the ROH World Title in 12:55 (★★).

Clash Of Champions '17 ★★
17-12-17, Boston, Massachusetts **WWE**
Dolph Ziggler defeated Baron Corbin and Bobby Roode in a Three Way Match to win the WWE United States Title in 12:45 (★★★); The Usos (Jimmy Uso and Jey Uso) defeated The New Day (Big E and Kofi Kingston), Chad Gable and Shelton Benjamin, and Rusev Day (Rusev and Aiden English) in a Four Way Match in 12:00 (★★★); Charlotte Flair defeated Natalya in a Lumberjack Match in 10:35 (★★); The Bludgeon Brothers (Harper and Rowan) defeated Breezango (Fandango and Tyler Breeze) in 1:55 (★); Kevin Owens and Sami Zayn defeated Randy Orton and Shinsuke Nakamura in 21:40 (★★); AJ Styles defeated Jinder Mahal in 23:00 (★★).

Takeover Philadelphia ★★★★
27-01-18, Philadelphia, Pennsylvania NXT
The Undisputed Era (Bobby Fish and Kyle O'Reilly) defeated The Authors Of Pain (Akam and Rezar) in 14:50 (★★★); Velveteen Dream defeated Kassius Ohno in 10:45 (★★); Ember Moon defeated Shayna Baszler in 10:06 (★★★); Aleister Black defeated Adam Cole in an Extreme Rules Match in 22:02 (★★★★); Andrade Almas defeated Johnny Gargano in 32:19 (★★★★★).

Royal Rumble '18 ★★★★
28-01-18, Philadelphia, Pennsylvania WWE
AJ Styles defeated Kevin Owens and Sami Zayn in a Handicap Match in 15:55 (★★★); The Usos (Jimmy Uso and Jey Uso) defeated Chad Gable and Shelton Benjamin 2-0 in a Best Two Out of Three Falls Match in 13:55 (★★); Shinsuke Nakamura won the 30-Man Royal Rumble Match in 65:27 (★★★★); Sheamus and Cesaro defeated Seth Rollins and Jason Jordan to win the WWE Raw Tag Team Title in 12:50 (★★★); Brock Lesnar defeated Kane and Braun Strowman in a Three Way Match in 10:55 (★★); Asuka won the 30-Woman Royal Rumble Match in 58:57 (★★★★).

Honor Reigns Supreme '18 ★★
09-02-18, Concord, North Carolina ROH
Punishment Martinez defeated Flip Gordon in 9:32 (★★); Kenny King defeated Shane Taylor in 10:17 (★★); Silas Young defeated Josh Woods in 10:52 (★★); SoCal Uncensored (Christopher Daniels, Frankie Kazarian and Scorpio Sky) defeated Dalton Castle and The Boys (Boy 1 and Boy 2) in 13:52 (★★); Mandy Leon and Tenille Dashwood defeated Kelly Klein and Stacy Shadows in 6:43 (★★); Jay Lethal defeated Jonathan Gresham in 17:54 (★★★); The Kingdom (Matt Taven, TK O'Ryan and Vinny Marseglia) defeated Cody Rhodes, Hangman Page and Marty Scurll in 16:31 (★★); The Young Bucks (Matt Jackson and Nick Jackson) defeated Best Friends (Beretta and Chuckie T) in 25:07 (★★★).

Elimination Chamber '18 ★★
25-02-18, Paradise, Nevada WWE
Alexa Bliss defeated Sasha Banks, Bayley, Mickie James, Sonya Deville and Mandy Rose in an Elimination Chamber Match in 29:35 (★★★); Sheamus and Cesaro defeated Titus Worldwide (Apollo Crews and Titus O'Neil) in 10:05 (★★); Asuka defeated Nia Jax in 8:15 (★★★); Matt Hardy defeated Bray Wyatt in 9:55 (★★); Roman Reigns defeated Braun Strowman, Seth Rollins, Finn Balor, John Cena, Elias and The Miz in an Elimination Chamber Match in 40:15 (★★).

16th Anniversary Show ★★★
09-03-18, Sunrise Manor, Nevada ROH
Hiromu Takahashi defeated Flip Gordon in 12:21 (★★); Marty Scurll defeated Punishment Martinez in 10:43 (★★★); Kenny King defeated Silas Young in 14:39 (★★); SoCal Uncensored (Christopher Daniels, Frankie Kazarian and Scorpio Sky) defeated Hangman Page and The Young Bucks (Matt Jackson and Nick Jackson) in a Las Vegas Street Fight to win the ROH World Six Man Tag Team Title in 18:50 (★★★★); Cody Rhodes defeated Matt Taven in 14:14 (★★); The Briscoe Brothers (Jay Briscoe and Mark Briscoe) defeated The Motor City Machine Guns (Alex Shelley and Chris Sabin) to win the ROH World Tag Team Title in 13:41 (★★★); Dalton Castle defeated Jay Lethal in 26:04 (★★★).

Fastlane '18 ★★★
11-03-18, Columbus, Ohio WWE
Shinsuke Nakamura defeated Rusev in 14:50 (★★★); Randy Orton defeated Bobby Roode to win the WWE United States Title in 19:15 (★★); Natalya and Carmella defeated Becky Lynch and Naomi in 8:55 (★★); The Usos (Jimmy Uso and Jey Uso) vs. The New Day (Kofi Kingston and Xavier Woods) in a no contest in 9:00 (★★); Charlotte Flair defeated Ruby Riott in 13:45 (★★); AJ Styles defeated Baron Corbin, Dolph Ziggler, John Cena, Kevin Owens and Sami Zayn in a Six Pack Challenge in 22:55 (★★★).

Takeover New Orleans ★★★★★
07-04-18, New Orleans, Louisiana NXT
Adam Cole defeated EC3, Killian Dain, Lars Sullivan, Ricochet and Velveteen Dream in a Ladder Match to win the vacant NXT North American Title in 31:24 (★★★★); Shayna Baszler defeated Ember Moon to win the NXT Women's Title in 12:56

(★★★); The Undisputed Era (Adam Cole and Kyle O'Reilly) defeated The Authors Of Pain (Akam and Rezar) and Pete Dunne and Roderick Strong in a Three Way Match in 11:38 (★★★); Aleister Black defeated Andrade Almas to win the NXT Title in 18:30 (★★★★); Johnny Gargano defeated Tommaso Ciampa in an Unsanctioned Match in 37:06 (★★★★★).

Supercard Of Honor XII ★★★
07-04-18, New Orleans, Louisiana ROH
Chuckie T defeated Jonathan Gresham in 8:33 (★★); Punishment Martinez defeated Tomohiro Ishii in 8:12 (★★★); Kota Ibushi defeated Hangman Page in 14:36 (★★★★); Sumie Sakai defeated Kelly Klein to win the vacant Women Of Honor Title in 7:38 (★★); SoCal Uncensored (Christopher Daniels, Frankie Kazarian and Scorpio Sky) defeated Flip Gordon and The Young Bucks (Matt Jackson and Nick Jackson) in a Ladder War in 24:08 (★★★★); The Briscoe Brothers (Jay Briscoe and Mark Briscoe) defeated Jay Lethal and Hiroshi Tanahashi in 19:39 (★★★); Silas Young defeated Kenny King in a Last Man Standing Match to win the ROH World Television Title in 16:04 (★★); Cody Rhodes defeated Kenny Omega in 37:15 (★★★); Dalton Castle defeated Marty Scurll in 31:37 (★).

WrestleMania XXXIV ★★★
08-04-18, New Orleans, Louisiana WWE
Seth Rollins defeated The Miz and Finn Balor in a Three Way Match to win the WWE Intercontinental Title in 15:30 (★★★); Charlotte Flair defeated Asuka in 13:05 (★★★★); Jinder Mahal defeated Randy Orton, Bobby Roode and Rusev in a Four Way Match to win the WWE United States Title in 8:15 (★★); Kurt Angle and Ronda Rousey defeated Triple H and Stephanie McMahon in 20:40 (★★★★); The Bludgeon Brothers (Harper and Rowan) defeated The Usos (Jimmy Uso and Jey Uso) and The New Day (Big E and Kofi Kingston) in a Three Way Match to win the WWE SmackDown Tag Team Title in 5:50 (★★); The Undertaker defeated John Cena in 2:45 (★); Daniel Bryan and Shane McMahon defeated Kevin Owens and Sami Zayn in 15:25 (★★); Nia Jax defeated Alexa Bliss to win the WWE Raw Women's Title in 10:15 (★★); AJ Styles defeated Shinsuke Nakamura in 20:20 (★★★); Braun Strowman and Nicholas defeated Sheamus and Cesaro to win the WWE Raw Tag Team Title in 4:00 (★); Brock Lesnar defeated Roman Reigns in 15:55 (★★).

Redemption ★★★
22-04-18, Orlando, Florida Impact
Aerostar defeated Drago in 11:45 (★★★); Eli Drake and Scott Steiner defeated The Latin American Xchange (Santana and Ortiz) to win the Impact World Tag Team Title in 7:55 (★★); Brian Cage defeated Dezmond Xavier, DJ Z, El Hijo del Fantasma, Taiji Ishimori and Trevor Lee in a Six Way Match in 12:50 (★★★); Taya Valkyrie defeated Kiera Hogan in 8:05 (★★); Matt Sydal defeated Petey Williams in 11:35 (★★★); Ohio Versus Everything (Dave Crist, Jake Crist and Sami Callihan) defeated Eddie Edwards, Moose and Tommy Dreamer in a House Of Hardcore Match in 12:55 (★★★); Allie defeated Su Yung in 7:15 (★★); Pentagon Jr. defeated Austin Aries and Fenix in a Three Way Match to win the Impact World Title in 16:20 (★★★).

Greatest Royal Rumble ★★★
27-04-18, Jeddah, Saudi Arabia WWE
John Cena defeated Triple H in 15:45 (★★★); Cedric Alexander defeated Kalisto in 10:15 (★★); Bray Wyatt and Matt Hardy defeated Sheamus and Cesaro to win the vacant WWE Raw Tag Team Title in 8:50 (★★); Jeff Hardy defeated Jinder Mahal in 6:10 (★★); The Bludgeon Brothers (Harper and Rowan) defeated The Usos (Jimmy Uso and Jey Uso) in 5:05 (★★); Seth Rollins defeated The Miz, Finn Balor and Samoa Joe in a Four Way Ladder Match in 15:05 (★★★); AJ Styles vs. Shinsuke Nakamura ended in a double count out in 14:25 (★★★); The Undertaker defeated Rusev in a Casket Match in 9:40 (★★); Brock Lesnar defeated Roman Reigns in a Steel Cage Match in 9:15 (★★); Braun Strowman won a 50-Man Royal Rumble Match to win the WWE Greatest Royal Rumble Trophy in 77:20 (★★★).

Backlash '18 ★★
06-05-18, Newark, New Jersey WWE
Seth Rollins defeated The Miz in 20:30 (★★★★); Nia Jax defeated Alexa Bliss in 10:46 (★★); Jeff Hardy defeated Randy Orton in 11:42 (★★); Daniel Bryan defeated Big Cass in 7:45

(★★); Carmella defeated Charlotte Flair in 10:01 (★★); AJ Styles vs. Shinsuke Nakamura ended in a draw in a No DQ Match in 21:05 (★★★); Braun Strowman and Bobby Lashley defeated Kevin Owens and Sami Zayn in 8:40 (★); Roman Reigns defeated Samoa Joe in 18:10 (★★).

Takeover Chicago II ★★★★
16-06-18, Rosemont, Illinois **NXT**
The Undisputed Era (Kyle O'Reilly and Roderick Strong) defeated Danny Burch and Oney Lorcan in 16:00 (★★★★); Ricochet defeated Velveteen Dream in 22:10 (★★★★); Shayna Baszler defeated Nikki Cross in 9:25 (★★★); Aleister Black defeated Lars Sullivan in 14:07 (★★★); Tommaso Ciampa defeated Johnny Gargano in a Chicago Street Fight in 35:29 (★★★★).

Money In The Bank '18 ★★★
17-06-18, Rosemont, Illinois **WWE**
Daniel Bryan defeated Big Cass in 16:20 (★★★); Bobby Lashley defeated Sami Zayn in 6:35 (★★); Seth Rollins defeated Elias in 17:07 (★★★); Alexa Bliss defeated Becky Lynch, Charlotte Flair, Ember Moon, Lana, Naomi, Natalya and Sasha Banks in a Money In The Bank Ladder Match in 18:30 (★★★); Roman Reigns defeated Jinder Mahal in 15:45 (★★); Carmella defeated Asuka in 11:10 (★); AJ Styles defeated Shinsuke Nakamura in a Last Man Standing Match in 31:15 (★★★); Ronda Rousey defeated Nia Jax in 11:05 (★★★); Alexa Bliss defeated Nia Jax to win the WWE Raw Women's Title in :35 (★); Braun Strowman defeated Bobby Roode, Finn Balor, Kevin Owens, Kofi Kingston, Rusev, Samoa Joe and The Miz in a Money In The Bank Ladder Match in 19:55 (★★★).

United Kingdom Championship Tournament '18 ★★★
25-06-18, London, England **NXT UK**
Zack Gibson defeated Jack Gallagher in 13:37 (★★★); Joe Coffey defeated Dave Mastiff in 7:35 (★★); Flash Morgan Webster defeated Jordan Devlin in 7:10 (★★); Travis Banks defeated Ashton Smith in 6:25 (★★); Toni Storm defeated Isla Dawn and Killer Kelly in a Three Way Match in 4:20 (★★); Zack Gibson defeated Flash Morgan Webster in 4:30 (★★); Travis Banks defeated Joe Coffey in 9:30 (★★); British Strong Style (Pete Dunne, Trent Seven and Tyler Bate) defeated The Undisputed Era (Adam Cole, Kyle O'Reilly and Roderick Strong) in 12:22 (★★★★); Zack Gibson defeated Travis Banks in 17:05 (★★★).

U.K. Championship ★★★
26-06-18, London, England **NXT**
Moustache Mountain (Trent Seven and Tyler Bate) defeated The Undisputed Era (Kyle O'Reilly and Roderick Strong) to win the NXT Tag Team Title in 11:50 (★★★★); Charlie Morgan defeated Killer Kelly in 7:05 (★★); Noam Dar defeated Flash Morgan Webster, Mark Andrews and Travis Banks in a Four Way Match in 9:00 (★★★); Adam Cole defeated Wolfgang in 10:15 (★★); Aleister Black and Ricochet defeated EC3 and Velveteen Dream in 15:55 (★★); Shayna Baszler defeated Toni Storm via count out in 12:18 (★★★); Pete Dunne defeated Zack Gibson in 17:55 (★★★★).

Best In The World '18 ★★★
29-06-18, Catonsville, Maryland **ROH**
The Kingdom (Matt Taven, TK O'Ryan and Vinny Marseglia) defeated Bushi, Evil and Sanada in 11:09 (★★); Flip Gordon defeated Bully Ray by DQ in 5:24 (★★); Sumie Sakai, Jenny Rose, Mayu Iwatani and Tenille Dashwood defeated Kelly Klein, Hazuki, Kagetsu and Hana Kimura in 10:27 (★★); Austin Aries defeated Kenny King in 15:34 (★★); Jay Lethal defeated Kushida in 17:36 (★★★); Punishment Martinez defeated Hangman Page in a Baltimore Street Fight in 15:04 (★★★); The Briscoe Brothers (Jay Briscoe and Mark Briscoe) defeated The Young Bucks (Matt Jackson and Nick Jackson) in 17:02 (★★★★); Dalton Castle defeated Cody Rhodes and Marty Scurll in a Three Way Match in 14:25 (★★).

Extreme Rules '18 ★★
15-07-18, Pittsburgh, Pennsylvania **WWE**
The B-Team (Bo Dallas and Curtis Axel) defeated Matt Hardy and Bray Wyatt to win the WWE Raw Tag Team Title in 8:00 (★★); Finn Balor defeated Baron Corbin in 8:20 (★★);

Carmella defeated Asuka in 5:25 (★); Shinsuke Nakamura defeated Jeff Hardy to win the WWE United States Title in :10 (★); Kevin Owens defeated Braun Strowman in a Steel Cage Match in 8:05 (★★); The Bludgeon Brothers (Harper and Rowan) defeated Team Hell No (Daniel Bryan and Kane) in 8:20 (★★); Bobby Lashley defeated Roman Reigns in 14:50 (★★★); Alexa Bliss defeated Nia Jax in an Extreme Rules Match in 7:30 (★★); AJ Styles defeated Rusev in 18:18 (★★★); Dolph Ziggler defeated Seth Rollins 5-4 in an Iron Man Match in 30:14 (★★★).

Slammiversary XVI ★★★★
22-07-18, Toronto, Ontario **Impact**
Johnny Impact, Fenix, Taiji Ishimori and Petey Williams in a Four Way Match in 12:30 (★★★); Tessa Blanchard defeated Allie in 11:00 (★★); Eddie Edwards defeated Tommy Dreamer in a House Of Hardcore Match in 11:10 (★★); Brian Cage defeated Matt Sydal to win the Impact X Division Title in 9:45 (★★★); Su Yung defeated Madison Rayne in 6:50 (★★); The Latin American Xchange (Santana and Ortiz) defeated The OGz (Homicide and Hernandez) in a 5150 Street Fight in 13:40 (★★★★); Pentagon Jr. defeated Sami Callihan in a Mask vs. Hair Match in 18:15 (★★★); Austin Aries defeated Moose in 15:50 (★★★★).

Takeover Brooklyn IV ★★★★
18-08-18, Brooklyn, New York **NXT**
The Undisputed Era (Kyle O'Reilly and Roderick Strong) defeated Moustache Mountain (Trent Seven and Tyler Bate) in 18:06 (★★★★); Velveteen Dream defeated EC3 in 15:03 (★★★); Ricochet defeated Adam Cole to win the NXT North American Title in 15:19 (★★★★); Kairi Sane defeated Shayna Baszler to win the NXT Women's Title in 13:37 (★★); Tommaso Ciampa defeated Johnny Gargano in a Last Man Standing Match in 33:42 (★★★★★★★).

SummerSlam '18 ★★★
19-08-18, Brooklyn, New York **WWE**
Seth Rollins defeated Dolph Ziggler to win the WWE Intercontinental Title in 22:00 (★★★); The New Day (Big E and Xavier Woods) defeated The Bludgeon Brothers (Harper and Rowan) to win the WWE SmackDown Tag Team Title in 9:45 (★★★); Braun Strowman defeated Kevin Owens in 1:50 (★★); Charlotte Flair defeated Carmella and Becky Lynch in a Three Way Match to win the WWE SmackDown Women's Title in 15:15 (★★★); Samoa Joe defeated AJ Styles by DQ in 22:45 (★★★); The Miz defeated Daniel Bryan in 23:30 (★★); Finn Balor defeated Baron Corbin in 1:35 (★★); Shinsuke Nakamura defeated Jeff Hardy in 11:00 (★★); Ronda Rousey defeated Alexa Bliss to win the WWE Raw Women's Title in 4:00 (★★); Roman Reigns defeated Brock Lesnar to win the WWE Universal Title in 6:10 (★★).

All In ★★★★
01-09-18, Hoffman Estates, Illinois **N/A**
Matt Cross defeated MJF in 9:23 (★★); Christopher Daniels defeated Stephen Amell in 12:30 (★★); Tessa Blanchard defeated Dr. Britt Baker D.M.D., Chelsea Green and Madison Rayne in a Four Corner Survival Match in 12:41 (★★★); Cody Rhodes defeated Nick Aldis to win the NWA World Heavyweight Title in 22:01 (★★★★); Hangman Page defeated Joey Janela in a Chicago Street Fight in 20:08 (★★★); Jay Lethal defeated Flip Gordon in 14:21 (★★★); Kenny Omega defeated Penta El Zero Miedo in 17:47 (★★★★); Kazuchika Okada defeated Marty Scurll in 26:05 (★★★★); The Golden Elite (Kota Ibushi, Matt Jackson and Nick Jackson) defeated Rey Mysterio, Bandido and Rey Fenix in 11:48 (★★★★).

Hell In A Cell '18 ★★★
16-09-18, San Antonio, Texas **WWE**
Randy Orton defeated Jeff Hardy in a Hell In A Cell Match in 24:50 (★★★); Becky Lynch defeated Charlotte Flair to win the WWE SmackDown Women's Title in 13:50 (★★★); Dolph Ziggler and Drew McIntyre defeated Dean Ambrose and Seth Rollins in 24:52 (★★★★); AJ Styles defeated Samoa Joe in 19:00 (★★★); The Miz and Maryse defeated Daniel Bryan and Brie Bella in 13:00 (★★); Ronda Rousey defeated Alexa Bliss in 12:02 (★★); Roman Reigns vs. Braun Strowman went to a no contest in a Hell In A Cell Match in 24:10 (★★).

Death Before Dishonor XVI ★★★
28-09-18, Paradise, Nevada ROH

Kenny King defeated Jushin Thunder Liger in 12:06 (★★); The Briscoe Brothers (Jay Briscoe and Mark Briscoe) defeated The Addiction (Christopher Daniels and Frankie Kazarian) in 17:42 (★★); Sumie Sakai defeated Tenille Dashwood in 12:35 (★★); Punishment Martinez defeated Chris Sabin in 8:01 (★★); Bully Ray and Silas Young defeated Flip Gordon and Colt Cabana in a Tables Match in 13:40 (★★★); Bullet Club Elite (Cody Rhodes, Hangman Page, Marty Scurll, Matt Jackson and Nick Jackson) defeated Chaos (Kazuchika Okada, Chuckie T, Beretta, Rocky Romero and Tomohiro Ishii) in 21:00 (★★★); Jay Lethal defeated Will Ospreay in 22:55 (★★★★).

Super Show-Down '18 ★★★
06-10-18, Melbourne, Australia WWE

The New Day (Kofi Kingston and Xavier Woods) defeated The Bar (Sheamus and Cesaro) in 9:38 (★★); Charlotte Flair defeated Becky Lynch by DQ in 10:50 (★★); John Cena and Bobby Lashley defeated Elias and Kevin Owens in 10:05 (★★); The IIconics (Billie Kay and Peyton Royce) defeated Asuka and Naomi in 5:45 (★★); AJ Styles defeated Samoa Joe in a No Count Out No DQ Match in 23:45 (★★★); Ronda Rousey and The Bella Twins (Nikki Bella and Brie Bella) defeated The Riott Squad (Ruby Riott, Liv Morgan and Sarah Logan) in 10:05 (★★); Buddy Murphy defeated Cedric Alexander to win the WWE Cruiserweight Title in 10:35 (★★★); The Shield (Dean Ambrose, Roman Reigns and Seth Rollins) defeated Braun Strowman, Dolph Ziggler and Drew McIntyre in 19:40 (★★★); Daniel Bryan defeated The Miz in 2:25 (★★); Triple H defeated The Undertaker in a No DQ Match in 27:35 (★).

Bound For Glory '18 ★★★
14-10-18, Queens, New York Impact

Rich Swann and Willie Mack defeated Matt Sydal and Ethan Page in 12:20 (★★★); Eli Drake defeated James Ellsworth in 2:10 (★★); Tessa Blanchard defeated Taya Valkyrie in 10:36 (★★★); Eddie Edwards defeated Moose by DQ in :53 (★); Eddie Edwards and Tommy Dreamer defeated Moose and Killer Kross in a No DQ Match in 9:30 (★★); Ohio Versus Everything (Dave Crist, Jake Crist and Sami Callihan) defeated Brian Cage, Pentagon Jr. and Fenix in an oVe Rules Match in 13:31 (★★★); The Latin American Xchange (Konnan, Santana and Ortiz) defeated The OGz (Homicide, Hernandez and Eddie Kingston) in a Concrete Jungle Death Match in 9:29 (★★★); Johnny Impact defeated Austin Aries to win the Impact World Title in 21:03 (★★★★).

70th Anniversary Show ★★★
21-10-18, Nashville, Tennessee NWA

Sam Shaw defeated Colt Cabana, Sammy Guevara and Scorpio Sky in a Four Way Elimination Match in 7:05 (★★); Barrett Brown defeated Laredo Kid in 10:05 (★★★); Willie Mack defeated Jay Bradley, Mike Parrow and Ricky Starks in a Four Way Elimination Match in 7:35 (★★); Tim Storm defeated Peter Avalon in a Kiss My Foot Match in 5:45 (★★); Jazz defeated Penelope Ford in 7:30 (★★); Willie Mack defeated Sam Shaw to win the vacant NWA National Heavyweight Title in 9:55 (★★★); Crimson and Jax Dane defeated The Kingdom Of Jocephus (Crazzy Steve and Shannon Moore) in 4:35 (★); Nick Aldis defeated Cody Rhodes in a Two Out Of Three Falls Match to win the NWA World Heavyweight Title in 36:40 (★★★).

Evolution ★★★
28-10-18, Uniondale, New York WWE

Trish Stratus and Lita defeated Mickie James and Alicia Fox in 11:05 (★★); Nia Jax won a Battle Royal in 16:10 (★★); Toni Storm defeated Io Shirai in 10:20 (★★); Sasha Banks, Bayley and Natalya defeated The Riott Squad (Ruby Riott, Liv Morgan and Sarah Logan) in 13:10 (★★); Shayna Baszler defeated Kairi Sane to win the NXT Women's Title in 12:10 (★★★); Becky Lynch defeated Charlotte Flair in a Last Woman Standing Match in 28:40 (★★★★); Ronda Rousey defeated Nikki Bella in 14:15 (★★★).

Crown Jewel '18 ★
02-11-18, Riyadh, Saudi Arabia WWE

Rey Mysterio defeated Randy Orton in 5:30 (★★); The Miz defeated Jeff Hardy in 7:05 (★★); Seth Rollins defeated Bobby Lashley in 5:30 (★★); Dolph Ziggler defeated Kurt Angle in 8:10 (★★); The Bar (Sheamus and Cesaro) defeated The New

Day (Big E and Kofi Kingston) in 10:30 (★★); The Miz defeated Rey Mysterio in 11:15 (★★); Dolph Ziggler defeated Seth Rollins in 13:05 (★★★); AJ Styles defeated Samoa Joe in 11:15 (★★★); Brock Lesnar defeated Braun Strowman to win the vacant WWE Universal Title in 3:15 (★); Shane McMahon defeated Dolph Ziggler in 2:30 (★); D-Generation X (Triple H and Shawn Michaels) defeated The Brothers Of Destruction (Kane and The Undertaker) in 27:45 (★).

Takeover WarGames II ★★★★
17-11-18, Los Angeles, California NXT

Matt Riddle defeated Kassius Ohno in :06 (★); Shayna Baszler defeated Kairi Sane 2-1 in a Best Two Out Of Three Falls Match in 10:55 (★★); Aleister Black defeated Johnny Gargano in 18:10 (★★★★); Tommaso Ciampa defeated Velveteen Dream in 22:25 (★★★★); Pete Dunne, Ricochet and War Raiders (Hanson and Rowe) defeated The Undisputed Era (Adam Cole, Bobby Fish, Kyle O'Reilly and Roderick Strong) in a WarGames Match in 47:10 (★★★).

Survivor Series '18 ★★★★
18-11-18, Los Angeles, California WWE

Team Raw (Mickie James, Nia Jax, Tamina, Bayley and Sasha Banks) defeated Team SmackDown (Naomi, Carmella, Sonya Deville, Asuka and Mandy Rose) in an Elimination Match in 18:50 (★★); Seth Rollins defeated Shinsuke Nakamura in 21:50 (★★); AOP (Akam and Rezar) defeated The Bar (Sheamus and Cesaro) in 9:00 (★★); Buddy Murphy defeated Mustafa Ali in 12:20 (★★★); Team Raw (Dolph Ziggler, Drew McIntyre, Braun Strowman, Finn Balor and Bobby Lashley) defeated Team SmackDown (The Miz, Shane McMahon, Rey Mysterio, Samoa Joe and Jeff Hardy) in an Elimination Match in 24:00 (★★★★); Ronda Rousey defeated Charlotte Flair by DQ in 14:40 (★★★★); Brock Lesnar defeated Daniel Bryan in 18:50 (★★★★).

Starrcade '18 ★★
25-11-18, Cincinnati, Ohio WWE

Bayley, Dana Brooke, Ember Moon and Sasha Banks defeated Alicia Fox, Mickie James, Nia Jax and Tamina in 6:50 (★★); Rey Mysterio defeated Shinsuke Nakamura by DQ in 24:11 (★★); Rey Mysterio and Rusev defeated The Miz and Shinsuke Nakamura in 6:10 (★★); AJ Styles defeated Samoa Joe in a Steel Cage Match in 11:58 (★★).

Final Battle '18 ★★★
14-12-18, New York City, New York ROH

Kenny King defeated Eli Isom in 8:55 (★★); Jeff Cobb defeated Hangman Page in 13:35 (★★★★); Kelly Klein defeated Sumie Saakai, Madison Rayne and Karen Q in a Four Corner Survival Match to win the Women Of Honor Title in 13:40 (★★); Zack Sabre Jr. defeated Jonathan Gresham in 11:50 (★★★); Matt Taven defeated Dalton Castle in 15:50 (★★); Marty Scurll defeated Christopher Daniels in 17:30 (★★★); Flip Gordon defeated Bully Ray in an "I Quit" Match in 14:25 (★★); Jay Lethal defeated Cody Rhodes in 23:45 (★★); The Briscoe Brothers (Jay Briscoe and Mark Briscoe) defeated SoCal Uncensored (Frankie Kazarian and Scorpio Sky) in a Ladder War to win the ROH World Tag Team Title in 22:40 (★★★★).

TLC '18 ★★★
16-12-18, San Jose, California WWE

Fabulous Truth (R-Truth and Carmella) defeated Mahalicia (Jinder Mahal and Alicia Fox) in 5:50 (★); The Bar (Sheamus and Cesaro) defeated The New Day (Kofi Kingston and Xavier Woods) and The Usos (Jimmy Uso and Jey Uso) in a Three Way Match in 12:15 (★★★); Braun Strowman defeated Baron Corbin in a TLC Match in 2:31 (★); Natalya defeated Ruby Riott in a Tables Match in 12:40 (★★); Finn Balor defeated Drew McIntyre in 12:20 (★★); Rey Mysterio defeated Randy Orton in a Chairs Match in 11:30 (★★); Ronda Rousey defeated Nia Jax in 10:50 (★★★); Daniel Bryan defeated AJ Styles in 23:55 (★★★★); Dean Ambrose defeated Seth Rollins to win the WWE Intercontinental Title in 23:00 (★★); Asuka defeated Becky Lynch and Charlotte Flair in a Triple Threat TLC Match to win the WWE SmackDown Women's Title in 21:45 (★★★★).

Tribute To The Troops '18 ★★
20-12-18, Killeen, Texas WWE

Natalya and Ronda Rousey defeated The Riott Squad (Liv Morgan and Sarah Lorgan) and Nia Jax and Tamina in a Three Way Match in 6:35 (★★); Finn Balor and Elias defeated Drew

McIntyre and **Bobby Lashley** in 6:55 (★★); **Becky Lynch** and **Charlotte Flair** defeated **Fire and Desire** (**Mandy Rose** and **Sonya Deville**) in 6:10 (★★); **AJ Styles** and **Seth Rollins** defeated **Daniel Bryan** and **Dean Ambrose** in 10:18 (★★★).

Homecoming '19 ★★★
06-01-19, Nashville, Tennessee **Impact**
Rich Swann defeated **Ethan Page, Jake Crist** and **Trey Miguel** in an Ultimate X Match to win the vacant Impact X Division Title in 13:40 (★★★); **Allie** and **Su Yung** defeated **Jordynne Grace** and **Kiera Hogan** in 8:53 (★★); **Eddie Edwards** defeated **Moose** in a Falls Count Anywhere Match in 13:20 (★★); **Sami Callihan** defeated **Willie Mack** in 10:15 (★★); **Eli Drake** defeated **Abyss** in a Monster's Ball Match in 12:15 (★★); **The Latin American Xchange** (**Santana** and **Ortiz**) defeated **The Lucha Bros** (**Fenix** and **Pentagon Jr.**) in 11:20 (★★★); **Taya Valkyrie** defeated **Tessa Blanchard** to win the Impact Knockouts Title in 10:25 (★★); **Johnny Impact** defeated **Brian Cage** in 20:15 (★★★).

Takeover Blackpool ★★★
12-01-19, Blackpool, England **NXT UK**
The Grizzled Young Veterans (**Zack Gibson** and **James Drake**) defeated **Moustache Mountain** (**Trent Seven** and **Tyler Bate**) to win the vacant NXT UK Tag Team Title in 23:45 (★★★★); **Finn Balor** defeated **Jordan Devlin** in 11:45 (★★★); **Dave Mastiff** defeated **Eddie Dennis** in a No DQ Match in 10:50 (★★); **Toni Storm** defeated **Rhea Ripley** to win the NXT UK Women's Title in 14:50 (★★); **Pete Dunne** defeated **Joe Coffey** in 34:15 (★★).

Takeover Phoenix ★★★★
26-01-19, Phoenix, Arizona **NXT**
War Raiders (**Hanson** and **Rowe**) defeated **The Undisputed Era** (**Kyle O'Reilly** and **Roderick Strong**) to win the NXT Tag Team Title in 16:57 (★★★); **Matt Riddle** defeated **Kassius Ohno** in 9:20 (★); **Johnny Gargano** defeated **Ricochet** to win the NXT North American Title in 23:36 (★★★★); **Shayna Baszler** defeated **Bianca Belair** in 15:26 (★★); **Tommaso Ciampa** defeated **Aleister Black** in 26:30 (★★★).

Royal Rumble '19 ★★★
27-01-19, Phoenix, Arizona **WWE**
Asuka defeated **Becky Lynch** in 17:10 (★★★★); **The Miz** and **Shane McMahon** defeated **The Bar** (**Sheamus** and **Cesaro**) to win the WWE SmackDown Tag Team Title in 13:20 (★★); **Ronda Rousey** defeated **Sasha Banks** in 13:55 (★★★); **Becky Lynch** won the 30-Woman Royal Rumble Match in 72:00 (★★); **Daniel Bryan** defeated **AJ Styles** in 24:35 (★★); **Brock Lesnar** defeated **Finn Balor** in 8:40 (★★★); **Seth Rollins** won the 30-Man Royal Rumble Match in 57:35 (★★★).

Worlds Collide '19 ★★
02-02-19, Phoenix, Arizona **WWE**
Jordan Devlin won a 15-man Battle Royal in 19:29 (★★); **Humberto Carrillo** defeated **Zack Gibson** in 6:19 (★★); **Jordan Devlin** defeated **Drew Gulak** in 11:43 (★★); **Tyler Bate** defeated **Adam Cole** in 10:30 (★★); **Velveteen Dream** defeated **Jordan Devlin** in 12:23 (★★); **Velveteen Dream** defeated **Tyler Bate** in 16:09 (★★★).

Elimination Chamber '19 ★★★★
17-02-19, Houston, Texas **WWE**
The Boss 'n' Hug Connection (**Bayley** and **Sasha Banks**) defeated **Carmella** and **Naomi, Mandy Rose** and **Sonya Deville, The IIconics** (**Billie Kay** and **Peyton Royce**), **Nia Jax** and **Tamina**, and **The Riott Squad** (**Liv Morgan** and **Sarah Logan**) in an Elimination Chamber Match to win the vacant WWE Women's Tag Team Title in 33:00 (★★); **The Usos** (**Jimmy Uso** and **Jey Uso**) defeated **The Miz** and **Shane McMahon** to win the WWE SmackDown Tag Team Title in 14:10 (★★); **Finn Balor** defeated **Bobby Lashley** and **Lio Rush** in a Handicap Match to win the WWE Intercontinental Title in 9:30 (★★); **Ronda Rousey** defeated **Ruby Riott** in 1:40 (★); **Baron Corbin** defeated **Braun Strowman** in a No DQ Match in 10:50 (★); **Daniel Bryan** defeated **AJ Styles, Jeff Hardy, Kofi Kingston, Randy Orton** and **Samoa Joe** in an Elimination Chamber Match in 36:40 (★★★★).

Fastlane '19 ★★★★
10-03-19, Cleveland, Ohio **WWE**
The Usos (**Jimmy Uso** and **Jey Uso**) defeated **The Miz** and **Shane McMahon** in 14:10 (★★★); **Asuka** defeated **Mandy Rose** in 6:40 (★★); **The Bar** (**Sheamus** and **Cesaro**) defeated **Kofi Kingston** in a Handicap Match in 5:15 (★); **The Revival** (**Dash**

Wilder and **Scott Dawson**) defeated **Aleister Black** and **Ricochet**, and **Bobby Roode** and **Chad Gable** in a Three Way Match in 10:50 (★★★); **Samoa Joe** defeated **Andrade, R-Truth** and **Rey Mysterio** in a Four Way Match in 10:50 (★★★); **The Boss 'n' Hug Connection** (**Bayley** and **Sasha Banks**) defeated **Nia Jax** and **Tamina** in 7:05 (★★); **Daniel Bryan** defeated **Mustafa Ali** and **Kevin Owens** in a Three Way Match in 18:45 (★★★★); **Becky Lynch** defeated **Charlotte Flair** by DQ in 8:45 (★★); **The Shield** (**Dean Ambrose, Roman Reigns** and **Seth Rollins**) defeated **Baron Corbin, Bobby Lashley** and **Drew McIntyre** in 24:50 (★★★).

17th Anniversary Show ★★★
15-03-19, Sunrise Manor, Nevada **ROH**
Marty Scurll defeated **Kenny King** in 12:45 (★★); **Jeff Cobb** defeated **Shane Taylor** in 13:30 (★★★); **Mayu Iwatani** defeated **Kelly Klein** in 9:00 (★★); **Jay Lethal** vs. **Matt Taven** went to a time limit draw in 60:00 (★★★); **Rush** defeated **Bandido** in 15:00 (★★★); **Villain Enterprises** (**Brody King** and **PCO**) defeated **The Briscoe Brothers** (**Jay Briscoe** and **Mark Briscoe**) in a Las Vegas Street Fight to win the ROH World Tag Team Title in 19:44 (★★).

United We Stand ★★
04-04-19, Rahway, New Jersey **Impact**
Johnny Impact defeated **Ace Austin, Dante Fox, Jake Crist** and **Pat Buck** in an Ultimate X Match in 12:25 (★★★); **Team Lucha Underground** (**Aerostar, Daga, Drago** and **Marty The Moth Martinez**) defeated **Team Impact** (**Brian Cage, Eddie Edwards, Moose** and **Tommy Dreamer**) in 10:30 (★★); **Taya Valkyrie** defeated **Jordynne Grace, Katie Forbes** and **Rosemary** in a Four Way Match in 9:00 (★★); **The Latin American Xchange** (**Santana** and **Ortiz**) defeated **Promociones Dorado** (**Low Ki** and **Ricky Martinez**) in 12:40 (★★); **Tessa Blanchard** defeated **Joey Ryan** in 10:30 (★); **Rich Swann** defeated **Flamita** in 7:50 (★★★); **Sami Callihan** defeated **Jimmy Havoc** in a Monster's Ball Match (★★★); **The Lucha Bros** (**Fenix** and **Pentagon Jr.**) defeated **Rob Van Dam** and **Sabu** in an Extreme Rules Match in 8:05 (★★).

Takeover New York ★★★★★
05-04-19, Brooklyn, New York **NXT**
War Raiders (**Hanson** and **Rowe**) defeated **Aleister Black** and **Ricochet** in 18:50 (★★★★); **Velveteen Dream** defeated **Matt Riddle** in 17:35 (★★★); **Walter** defeated **Pete Dunne** to win the WWE United Kingdom Title in 25:40 (★★★★); **Shayna Baszler** defeated **Bianca Belair, Io Shirai** and **Kairi Sane** in a Four Way Match in 15:41 (★★); **Johnny Gargano** defeated **Adam Cole** 2-1 in a Best Two Out Of Three Falls Match to win the vacant NXT Title in 38:25 (★★★★★).

G1 Supercard ★★★
06-04-19, New York City, New York **ROH/NJPW**
Jeff Cobb defeated **Will Ospreay** to win the NEVER Openweight Title in 12:52 (★★); **Rush** defeated **Dalton Castle** in :15 (★); **Kelly Klein** defeated **Mayu Iwatani** to win the Women Of Honor Title in 10:38 (★★); **Flip Gordon** and **Lifeblood** (**Juice Robinson** and **Mark Haskins**) defeated **Bully Ray, Shane Taylor** and **Silas Young** in a New York City Street Fight in 15:01 (★★); **Dragon Lee** defeated **Taiji Ishimori** and **Bandido** in a Three Way Match to win the IWGP Junior Heavyweight Title in 8:54 (★★★); **Guerrillas Of Destiny** (**Tama Tonga** and **Tanga Loa**) defeated **Villain Enterprises** (**PCO** and **Brody King**), **Evil** and **Sanada**, and **The Briscoe Brothers** (**Jay Briscoe** and **Mark Briscoe**) in a Four Way Match to win the ROH World Tag Team Title in 9:45 (★★★); **Zack Sabre Jr.** defeated **Hiroshi Tanahashi** in 15:14 (★★★); **Kota Ibushi** defeated **Tetsuya Naito** to win the IWGP Intercontinental Title in 20:53 (★★★★); **Matt Taven** defeated **Jay Lethal** and **Marty Scurll** in a Three Way Ladder Match to win the ROH World Title in 29:35 (★★); **Kazuchika Okada** defeated **Jay White** to win the IWGP Heavyweight Title in 32:33 (★★★★).

WrestleMania XXXV ★★★★
07-04-19, East Rutherford, New Jersey **WWE**
Seth Rollins defeated **Brock Lesnar** to win the WWE Universal Title in 2:30 (★★); **AJ Styles** defeated **Randy Orton** in 16:20 (★★★); **The Usos** (**Jimmy Uso** and **Jey Uso**) defeated **Aleister Black** and **Ricochet, Rusev** and **Shinsuke Nakamura**, and **The Bar** (**Sheamus** and **Cesaro**) in a Four Way Match in 10:10 (★★★); **Shane McMahon** defeated **The Miz** in a Falls Count Anywhere Match in 15:30 (★★); **The Iiconics** (**Billie Kay** and

Peyton Royce) defeated **The Boss 'n' Hug Connection** (**Bayley** and **Sasha Banks**), **Nia Jax** and **Tamina**, and **Beth Phoenix** and **Natalya** in a Four Way Match to win the WWE Women's Tag Team Title in 10:45 (★★); **Kofi Kingston** defeated **Daniel Bryan** to win the WWE Title in 23:45 (★★★★); **Samoa Joe** defeated **Rey Mysterio** in :58 (★); **Roman Reigns** defeated **Drew McIntyre** in 10:10 (★★); **Triple H** defeated **Batista** in a No Holds Barred Match in 24:45 (★★); **Baron Corbin** defeated **Kurt Angle** in 6:05 (★); **Finn Balor** defeated **Bobby Lashley** to win the WWE Intercontinental Title in 4:05 (★★); **Becky Lynch** defeated **Ronda Rousey** and **Charlotte Flair** in a Three Way Match to win the WWE Raw Women's Title and the WWE SmackDown Women's Title in 21:30 (★★★★).

Worlds Collide: NXT vs. NXT Alumni ★★★
14-04-19, Brooklyn, New York **WWE**
Kassius Ohno defeated **Aiden English** in 6:00 (★★); **Harper** defeated **Dominik Dijakovic** in 11:55 (★★★); The Undisputed Era (**Bobby Fish** and **Kyle O'Reilly**) defeated **Sanity** (**Alexander Wolfe** and **Killian Dain**) in 9:07 (★★); **Tyler Breeze** defeated **Roderick Strong** in 13:15 (★★★).

Worlds Collide: Cruiserweights Collide ★★★
17-04-19, Brooklyn, New York **WWE**
Tyler Bate defeated **The Brian Kendrick** in 14:00 (★★★); **Flash Morgan Webster** and **Mark Andrews** defeated **Ari Daivari** and **Mike Kanellis** in 13:20 (★★); **Ligero** defeated **Albert Hardie Jr.** and **Gran Metalik** in 11:20 (★★); **Jordan Devlin** defeated **Akira Tozawa** in 13:15 (★★★).

Crockett Cup '19 ★★★
27-04-19, Concord, North Carolina **NWA**
Royce Isaacs and **Thomas Latimer** won a Battle Royal in 6:40 (★★); **Bandido** and **Flip Gordon** defeated **Guerrero Maya Jr.** and **Stuka Jr.** in 12:30 (★★★); **Royce Isaacs** and **Thomas Latimer** defeated **The War Kings** (**Crimson** and **Jax Dane**) in 7:50 (★★); **The Briscoe Brothers** (**Jay Briscoe** and **Mark Briscoe**) defeated **The Rock 'n' Roll Express** (**Ricky Morton** and **Robert Gibson**) in 6:55 (★★★); **Villain Enterprises** (**Brody King** and **PCO**) defeated **Satoshi Kojima** and **Yuji Nagata** in 11:50 (★★★); **Allysin Kay** defeated **Santana Garrett** to win the vacant NWA Women's Title in 8:55 (★★); **Royce Isaacs** and **Thomas Latimer** defeated **Bandido** and **Flip Gordon** in 7:15 (★★); **Villain Enterprises** (**Brody King** and **PCO**) defeated **The Briscoe Brothers** (**Jay Briscoe** and **Mark Briscoe**) by DQ in 9:50 (★★★); **Colt Cabana** defeated **Willie Mack** to win the NWA National Title in 8:45 (★★★); **Villain Enterprises** (**Brody King** and **PCO**) defeated **The Wild Cards** (**Royce Isaacs** and **Thomas Latimer**) to win the vacant NWA World Tag Team Title in 6:40 (★★); **Nick Aldis** defeated **Marty Scurll** in 23:45 (★★★).

Rebellion '19 ★★★
28-04-19, Toronto, Ontario **Impact**
Ace Austin defeated **Aiden Prince**, **Eddie Edwards**, **Jake Crist**, **Cousin Jake** and **Petey Williams** in a Six Way Match in 5:17 (★★); **Scarlett Bordeaux** defeated **Rohit Raju** in 5:01 (★★); **Moose** and **The North** (**Ethan Page** and **Josh Alexander**) defeated **The Rascalz** (**Dezmond Xavier**, **Trey Miguel** and **Zachary Wentz**) in 9:30 (★★); **Taya Valkyrie** defeated **Jordynne Grace** in 9:00 (★★); **Rich Swann** defeated **Sami Callihan** in an oVe Rules Match in 16:20 (★★★); **Tessa Blanchard** defeated **Gail Kim** in 13:10 (★★★); **Brian Cage** defeated **Johnny Impact** to win the Impact World Title in 13:20 (★★★); **The Latin American Xchange** (**Santana** and **Ortiz**) defeated **The Lucha Bros** (**Fenix** and **Pentagon Jr.**) in a Full Metal Mayhem Match to win the Impact World Tag Team Title in 20:30 (★★★★).

Money In The Bank '19 ★★★
19-05-19, Hartford, Connecticut **WWE**
Bayley defeated **Carmella**, **Dana Brooke**, **Ember Moon**, **Mandy Rose**, **Naomi**, **Natalya** and **Nikki Cross** in a Money In The Bank Ladder Match in 13:50 (★★); **Rey Mysterio** defeated **Samoa Joe** to win the WWE United States Title in 1:40 (★); **Shane McMahon** defeated **The Miz** in a Steel Cage Match in 13:00 (★★); **Tony Nese** defeated **Ari Daivari** in 9:25 (★★); **Becky Lynch** defeated **Lacey Evans** in 8:40 (★★); **Charlotte Flair** defeated **Becky Lynch** to win the WWE SmackDown Women's Title in 6:15 (★★); **Bayley** defeated **Charlotte Flair** to win the WWE SmackDown Women's Title in :20 (★★); **Roman Reigns** defeated **Elias** in :08 (★); **Seth Rollins** defeated **AJ Styles** in 19:45 (★★★★); **Kofi Kingston** defeated **Kevin Owens** in 14:10 (★★); **Brock Lesnar** defeated

Mustafa Ali, **Andrade**, **Baron Corbin**, **Drew McIntyre**, **Finn Balor**, **Randy Orton** and **Ricochet** in a Money In The Bank Ladder Match in 19:00 (★★★★).

Double Or Nothing '19 ★★★★
25-05-19, Paradise, Nevada **AEW**
SoCal Uncensored (**Christopher Daniels**, **Frankie Kazarian** and **Scorpio Sky**) defeated **Strong Hearts** (**Cima**, **T-Hawk** and **El Lindaman**) in 13:40 (★★★); **Dr. Britt Baker D.M.D.** defeated **Nyla Rose**, **Kylie Rae** and **Awesome Kong** in a Four Way Match in 11:10 (★★); **Best Friends** (**Chuck Taylor** and **Trent**) defeated **Angelico** and **Jack Evans** in 12:35 (★★★); **Hikaru Shida**, **Riho** and **Ryo Mizunami** defeated **Aja Kong**, **Emi Sakura** and **Yuka Sakazaki** in 13:10 (★★★); **Cody Rhodes** defeated **Dustin Rhodes** in 22:30 (★★★★★★★); **The Young Bucks** (**Matt Jackson** and **Nick Jackson**) defeated **The Lucha Brothers** (**Rey Fenix** and **Pentagon Jr.**) in 24:55 (★★★★); **Chris Jericho** defeated **Kenny Omega** in 27:00 (★★★★).

Takeover XXV ★★★★
01-06-19, Bridgeport, Connecticut **NXT**
Matt Riddle defeated **Roderick Strong** in 14:45 (★★★); **Street Profits** (**Angelo Dawkins** and **Montez Ford**) defeated **Oney Lorcan** and **Danny Burch**, **The Undisputed Era** (**Kyle O'Reilly** and **Bobby Fish**), and **The Forgotten Sons** (**Wesley Blake** and **Steve Cutler**) in a Ladder Match to win the vacant NXT Tag Team Title in 21:30 (★★★★); **Velveteen Dream** defeated **Tyler Breeze** in 16:50 (★★★); **Shayna Baszler** defeated **Io Shirai** in 12:15 (★★★); **Adam Cole** defeated **Johnny Gargano** to win the NXT Title in 31:45 (★★★★).

Super Showdown '19 ★
07-06-19, Jeddah, Saudi Arabia **WWE**
Seth Rollins defeated **Baron Corbin** in 11:15 (★★); **Finn Balor** defeated **Andrade** in 11:35 (★★); **Shane McMahon** defeated **Roman Reigns** in 9:15 (★); **Lars Sullivan** defeated **Lucha House Party** (**Kalisto**, **Gran Metalik** and **Lince Dorado**) by DQ in a Handicap Match in 5:15 (★); **Randy Orton** defeated **Triple H** in 23:45 (★★); **Braun Strowman** defeated **Bobby Lashley** in 8:20 (★★); **Kofi Kingston** defeated **Dolph Ziggler** in 10:15 (★★); **Mansoor** won a Battle Royal in 17:58 (★); **The Undertaker** defeated **Goldberg** in 9:35 (★).

Stomping Grounds ★★
23-06-19, Tacoma, Washington **WWE**
Becky Lynch defeated **Lacey Evans** in 11:30 (★★); **Kevin Owens** and **Sami Zayn** defeated **The New Day** (**Big E** and **Xavier Woods**) in 11:05 (★★★); **Ricochet** defeated **Samoa Joe** to win the WWE United States Title in 12:25 (★★); **Daniel Bryan** and **Rowan** defeated **Heavy Machinery** (**Otis** and **Tucker**) in 14:25 (★★); **Bayley** defeated **Alexa Bliss** in 10:35 (★★); **Roman Reigns** defeated **Drew McIntyre** in 17:20 (★★); **Kofi Kingston** defeated **Dolph Ziggler** in a Steel Cage Match in 20:00 (★★); **Seth Rollins** defeated **Baron Corbin** in a No Count Out, No DQ Match in 18:25 (★★).

Best In The World '19 ★★
28-06-19, Baltimore, Maryland **ROH**
Rush defeated **Flip Gordon** in 10:20 (★★); **Dalton Castle** defeated **Dragon Lee** in 14:20 (★★★); **The Allure** (**Angelina Love** and **Mandy Leon**) defeated **Jenny Rose** and **Kelly Klein** in 9:30 (★★); **Kenny King** defeated **Jay Lethal** in 14:35 (★★); **Jonathan Gresham** defeated **Silas Young** in a Pure Rules Match in 17:55 (★★); **The Briscoe Brothers** (**Jay Briscoe** and **Mark Briscoe**) vs. **Eli Drake** and **Nick Aldis** went to a double count out in 11:00 (★★); **Shane Taylor** defeated **Bandido** in 12:40 (★★★); **Villain Enterprises** (**Marty Scurll**, **PCO** and **Brody King**) defeated **Lifeblood** (**Mark Haskins**, **PJ Black** and **Tracy Williams**) in 17:01 (★★); **Matt Taven** defeated **Jeff Cobb** in 9:50 (★★).

Fyter Fest '19 ★★★
29-06-19, Daytona Beach, Florida **AEW**
Cima defeated **Christopher Daniels** in 9:40 (★★); **Riho** defeated **Yuka Sakazaki** and **Nyla Rose** in a Three Way Match in 12:30 (★★★); **Hangman Page** defeated **Jimmy Havoc**, **Jungle Boy** and **Luchasaurus** in a Four Way Match 10:50 (★★★); **Cody Rhodes** vs. **Darby Allin** went to a time limit draw in 20:00 (★★★); **The Elite** (**Kenny Omega**, **Matt Jackson** and **Nick Jackson**) defeated **The Lucha Brothers** (**Rey Fenix** and **Pentagon Jr.**) and **Laredo Kid** in 20:50 (★★★★); **Jon Moxley** defeated **Joey Janela** in an Unsanctioned Match in 20:00 (★★★★).

Slammiversary XVII ★★★
07-07-19, Dallas, Texas Impact

Willie Mack defeated Jake Crist, TJP and Trey Miguel in a Four Way Match in 9:51 (★★★); The North (Ethan Page and Josh Alexander) defeated The Latin American Xchange (Santana and Ortiz) and The Rascalz (Dezmond Xavier and Zachary Wentz) in a Three Way Match in 7:20 (★★); Eddie Edwards defeated Killer Kross in a First Blood Match in 11:30 (★★); Moose defeated Rob Van Dam in 13:50 (★★); Taya Valkyrie defeated Jessicka Havok, Rosemary and Su Yung in a Four Way Monster's Ball Match in 11:45 (★★★); Rich Swann defeated Johnny Impact in 14:55 (★★★); Brian Cage defeated Michael Elgin in 14:10 (★★★★); Sami Callihan defeated Tessa Blanchard in 15:00 (★★★).

Fight For The Fallen '19 ★★
13-07-19, Jacksonville, Florida AEW

MJF, Sammy Guevara and Shawn Spears defeated Darby Allin, Jimmy Havoc and Joey Janela in 13:15 (★★); Brandi Rhodes defeated Allie in 10:10 (★); The Dark Order (Evil Uno and Stu Grayson) defeated Angelico and Jack Evans and A Boy And His Dinosaur (Jungle Boy and Luchasaurus) in a Three Way Match in 15:15 (★★); Hangman Page defeated Kip Sabian in 19:05 (★★); The Lucha Brothers (Rey Fenix and Pentagon Jr.) defeated SoCal Uncensored (Frankie Kazarian and Scorpio Sky) in 15:10 (★★★); Kenny Omega defeated Cima in 22:30 (★★★); The Young Bucks (Matt Jackson and Nick Jackson) defeated The Brotherhood (Cody Rhodes and Dustin Rhodes) in 31:25 (★★★).

Extreme Rules '19 ★★★
14-07-19, Philadelphia, Pennsylvania WWE

The Undertaker and Roman Reigns defeated Shane McMahon and Drew McIntyre in a No Holds Barred Match in 17:00 (★★★★); The Revival (Dash Wilder and Scott Dawson) defeated The Usos (Jimmy Uso and Jey Uso) in 12:35 (★★★); Aleister Black defeated Cesaro in 9:45 (★★★); Bayley defeated Nikki Cross and Alexa Bliss in a Handicap Match in 10:30 (★★); Braun Strowman defeated Bobby Lashley in a Last Man Standing Match in 17:30 (★★★); The New Day (Big E and Xavier Woods) defeated Daniel Bryan and Rowan, and Heavy Machinery (Tucker and Otis) in a Three Way Match to win the WWE SmackDown Tag Team Title in 16:30 (★★); AJ Styles defeated Ricochet to win the WWE United States Title in 16:30 (★★★); Kevin Owens defeated Dolph Ziggler in :17 (★); Kofi Kingston defeated Samoa Joe in 9:45 (★★); Seth Rollins and Becky Lynch defeated Baron Corbin and Lacey Evans in 19:55 (★★); Brock Lesnar defeated Seth Rollins to win the WWE Universal Title in :16 (★★).

Takeover Toronto '19 ★★★★
10-08-19, Toronto, Ontario NXT

The Street Profits (Angelo Dawkins and Montez Ford) defeated The Undisputed Era (Kyle O'Reilly and Bobby Fish) in 16:55 (★★★); Io Shirai defeated Candice LeRae in 15:00 (★★★★); Velveteen Dream defeated Pete Dunne and Roderick Strong in a Three Way Match in 17:32 (★★★); Shayna Baszler defeated Mia Yim in 14:35 (★★); Adam Cole defeated Johnny Gargano in a Three Stages Of Hell Match in 52:26 (★★★★).

SummerSlam '19 ★★★
11-08-19, Toronto, Ontario WWE

Becky Lynch defeated Natalya in a Submission Match in 12:24 (★★★); Goldberg defeated Dolph Ziggler in 1:50 (★★★); AJ Styles defeated Ricochet in 12:50 (★★); Bayley defeated Ember Moon in 10:08 (★★); Kevin Owens defeated Shane McMahon in 9:20 (★★); Charlotte Flair defeated Trish Stratus in 16:45 (★★★); Kofi Kingston vs. Randy Orton went to a double count out in 16:40 (★★); The Fiend defeated Finn Balor in 3:25 (★★★); Seth Rollins defeated Brock Lesnar to win the WWE Universal Title in 13:25 (★★★).

Takeover Cardiff ★★★★
31-08-19, Cardiff, Wales NXT UK

Noam Dar defeated Travis Banks in 13:55 (★★); Cesaro defeated Ilja Dragunov in 12:26 (★★★); Mark Andrews and Flash Morgan Webster defeated The Grizzled Young Veterans (Zack Gibson and James Drake) and Gallus (Mark Coffey and Wolfgang) in a Three Way Match to win the NXT UK Tag Team Title in 20:17 (★★★); Joe Coffey defeated Dave Mastiff in a Last Man Standing Match in 16:03 (★★); Kay Lee Ray defeated Toni Storm to win the NXT UK Women's Title in 9:52 (★★); Walter defeated Tyler Bate in 42:12 (★★★★★).

All Out '19 ★★★
31-08-19, Hoffman Estates, Illinois AEW

SoCal Uncensored (Christopher Daniels, Frankie Kazarian and Scorpio Sky) defeated Jurassic Express (Jungle Boy, Luchasaurus and Marko Stunt) in 11:45 (★★); Pac defeated Kenny Omega in 23:20 (★★★★); Jimmy Havoc defeated Darby Allin and Joey Janela in a Three Way Cracker Barrel Clash in 15:00 (★★★); The Dark Order (Evil Uno and Stu Grayson) defeated Best Friends (Chuck Taylor and Trent) in 13:40 (★★); Riho defeated Hikaru Shida in 13:35 (★★★); Cody Rhodes defeated Shawn Spears in 16:20 (★★); The Lucha Brothers (Rey Fenix and Pentagon Jr.) defeated The Young Bucks (Matt Jackson and Nick Jackson) in a Ladder Match in 24:10 (★★★★); Chris Jericho defeated Hangman Page to win the vacant AEW World Title in 26:25 (★★).

Lucha Invades NY ★★★
15-09-19, New York City, New York AAA

Chris Dickinson and Mascarita Dorada defeated Dave the Clown and Demus in 8:38 (★★); Josh Alexander, Michael Elgin and Sami Callihan defeated Drago, Faby Apache and Murder Clown in 13:53 (★★★); Daga defeated Puma King, Aerostar and Flamita in a Four Way Match in 10:29 (★★★); Taya Valkyrie defeated Tessa Blanchard to win the AAA Reina de Reinas Title in 10:45 (★★); The Lucha Brothers (Rey Fenix and Pentagon Jr.) defeated The Latin American Xchange (Ortiz and Santana) in 13:46 (★★★★); Brian Cage, Cain Velasquez and Psycho Clown defeated Los Mercenarios (Rey Escorpion, Texano Jr. and Taurus) in 13:51 (★★★); Dr. Wagner Jr. defeated Blue Demon Jr. in a No DQ Match in 10:32 (★★).

Clash Of Champions '19 ★★
15-09-19, Charlotte, North Carolina WWE

Robert Roode and Dolph Ziggler defeated Seth Rollins and Braun Strowman to win the WWE Raw Tag Team Title in 9:32 (★★); Bayley defeated Charlotte Flair in 3:44 (★★); The Revival (Dash Wilder and Scott Dawson) defeated The New Day (Big E and Xavier Woods) to win the WWE SmackDown Tag Team Title in 10:05 (★★); Alexa Bliss and Nikki Cross defeated Fire and Desire (Mandy Rose and Sonya Deville) in 8:07 (★★); Shinsuke Nakamura defeated The Miz in 9:29 (★★); Sasha Banks defeated Becky Lynch by DQ in 20:00 (★★★); Kofi Kingston defeated Randy Orton in 20:50 (★★); Erick Rowan defeated Roman Reigns in a No DQ Match in 17:23 (★★); Seth Rollins defeated Braun Strowman in 10:45 (★★★).

Death Before Dishonor XVII ★★★
27-09-19, Sunrise Manor, Nevada ROH

Marty Scurll defeated Colt Cabana in 14:25 (★★★); PCO defeated Kenny King in a No DQ Match in 11:48 (★★); Angelina Love defeated Kelly Klein to win the Women Of Honor Title in 9:06 (★★); Jonathan Gresham defeated Jay Lethal in 17:20 (★★★); The Bouncers (Beer City Bruiser and Brawler Milonas) defeated Vinny Marseglia and Silas Young in a Bar Room Brawl in 14:30 (★★); Shane Taylor defeated Flip Gordon, Tracy Williams and Dragon Lee in a Four Corner Survival Match in 8:26 (★★); The Briscoe Brothers (Jay Briscoe and Mark Briscoe) defeated Lifeblood (Bandido and Mark Haskins) in 20:16 (★★); Rush defeated Matt Taven to win the ROH World Title in 16:05 (★★★).

Hell In A Cell '19 ★★
06-10-19, Sacramento, California WWE

Becky Lynch defeated Sasha Banks in a Hell In A Cell Match in 21:50 (★★★★); Daniel Bryan and Roman Reigns defeated Erick Rowan and Luke Harper in a Tornado Match in 16:44 (★★★); Randy Orton defeated Mustafa Ali in 12:10 (★★); The Kabuki Warriors (Asuka and Kairi Sane) defeated Alexa Bliss and Nikki Cross to win the WWE Women's Tag Team Title in 10:32 (★★); Braun Strowman and The Viking Raiders (Erik and Ivar) defeated The O.C. (AJ Styles, Luke Gallows and Karl Anderson) by DQ in 8:20 (★★); Chad Gable defeated King Corbin in 12:48 (★★); Charlotte Flair defeated Bayley to win the WWE SmackDown Women's Title in 10:13 (★★); Seth Rollins vs. The Fiend went to a no contest in a Hell In A Cell Match in 17:10 (★).

Bound For Glory '19 ★★★
20-10-19, Villa Park, Illinois Impact

Eddie Edwards won a Call Your Shot Gauntlet Match in 33:05 (★★); Taya Valkyrie defeated Tenille Dashwood in 11:50 (★★); The North (Ethan Page and Josh Alexander) defeated Rich

Swann and Willie Mack, and Rhino and Rob Van Dam in a Three Way Match in 14:25 (★★★); Michael Elgin defeated Naomichi Marufuji in 17:55 (★★★); Ace Austin defeated Jake Crist, Acey Romero, Daga and Tessa Blanchard in a Ladder Match to win the Impact X Division Title in 17:45 (★★★); Moose defeated Ken Shamrock in 10:35 (★★); Brian Cage defeated Sami Callihan in a No DQ Match in 16:40 (★★★).

Crown Jewel '19 ★★
31-10-19, Riyadh, Saudi Arabia **WWE**
Brock Lesnar defeated Cain Velasquez in 1:28 (★); The O.C. (Luke Gallows and Karl Anderson) won a Tag Team Turmoil Match in 32:08 (★★); Mansoor defeated Cesaro in 12:45 (★★); Tyson Fury defeated Braun Strowman via count out in 8:04 (★); AJ Styles defeated Humberto Carrillo in 12:34 (★★); Natalya defeated Lacey Evans in 7:21 (★★); Team Hogan (Roman Reigns, Rusev, Ricochet, Shorty G and Mustafa Ali) defeated Team Flair (Randy Orton, King Corbin, Bobby Lashley, Shinsuke Nakamura and Drew McIntyre) in 19:55 (★★★); The Fiend defeated Seth Rollins in a Falls Count Anywhere Match to win the WWE Universal Title in 21:21 (★★).

Saturday Night SuperFight '19 ★★★★
02-11-19, Cicero, Illinois **MLW**
The Von Erichs (Marshall Von Erich and Ross Von Erich) defeated The Dynasty (MJF and Richard Holliday) in a Texas Tornado Match to win the MLW World Tag Team Title in 9:44 (★★★); Injustice (Jordan Oliver, Kotto Brazil and Myron Reed) defeated Gringo Loco, Puma King and Septimo Dragon in 10:18 (★★★); Teddy Hart defeated Austin Aries in 18:33 (★★★★); Low Ki defeated Brian Pillman Jr. in 8:12 (★★★); Tom Lawlor defeated Timothy Thatcher in 15:27 (★★★★); Mance Warner defeated Bestia 666 and Jimmy Havoc in a Three Way Stairway To Hell Ladder Match in 14:01 (★★★★); Alexander Hammerstone defeated Davey Boy Smith Jr. in 13:27 (★★★); Jacob Fatu defeated LA Park in a No DQ Match in 19:58 (★★★★).

Full Gear '19 ★★★★
09-11-19, Baltimore, Maryland **AEW**
Santana and Ortiz defeated The Young Bucks (Matt Jackson and Nick Jackson) in 21:00 (★★★); Hangman Page defeated Pac in 18:44 (★★★); Shawn Spears defeated Joey Janela in 11:38 (★★); SoCal Uncensored (Frankie Kazarian and Scorpio Sky) defeated The Lucha Brothers (Rey Fenix and Pentagon Jr.) and Private Party (Isiah Kassidy and Marq Quen) in a Three Way Match in 13:01 (★★★); Riho defeated Emi Sakura in 13:11 (★★★); Chris Jericho defeated Cody Rhodes in 29:41 (★★★★); Jon Moxley defeated Kenny Omega in an Unsanctioned Lights Out Match in 38:45 (★★★★).

Takeover WarGames III ★★★★
23-11-19, Rosemont, Illinois **NXT**
Team Ripley (Rhea Ripley, Candice LeRae, Tegan Nox and Dakota Kai) defeated Team Baszler (Shayna Baszler, Bianca Belair, Io Shirai and Kay Lee Ray) in a WarGames Match in 27:32 (★★★★); Pete Dunne defeated Damian Priest and Killian Dain in a Three Way Match in 19:56 (★★); Finn Balor defeated Matt Riddle in 14:30 (★★★); Team Ciampa (Tommaso Ciampa, Keith Lee, Dominik Dijakovic and Kevin Owens) defeated The Undisputed Era (Adam Cole, Bobby Fish, Kyle O'Reilly and Roderick Strong) in a WarGames Match in 38:33 (★★★★).

Survivor Series '19 ★★★★
24-11-19, Rosemont, Illinois **WWE**
Team NXT (Rhea Ripley, Bianca Belair, Candice LeRae, Io Shirai and Toni Storm) defeated Team Raw (Charlotte Flair, Natalya, Asuka, Kairi Sane and Sarah Logan) and Team SmackDown (Sasha Banks, Carmella, Dana Brooke, Lacey Evans and Nikki Cross) in a Three Way Elimination Match in 28:00 (★★★); Roderick Strong defeated AJ Styles and Shinsuke Nakamura in a Three Way Match in 16:45 (★★); Adam Cole defeated Pete Dunne in 14:10 (★★★★); The Fiend defeated Daniel Bryan in 10:10 (★★★); Team SmackDown (Roman Reigns, Braun Strowman, King Corbin, Mustafa Ali and Shorty G) defeated Team Raw (Seth Rollins, Drew McIntyre, Kevin Owens, Randy Orton and Ricochet) and Team NXT (Tommaso Ciampa, Damian Priest, Matt Riddle, Keith Lee and Walter) in a Three Way Elimination Match in 29:14 (★★); Brock Lesnar defeated Rey Mysterio in a No Holds Barred Match in 6:51 (★★); Shayna Baszler defeated Becky Lynch and Bayley in a Three Way Match in 18:06 (★★).

Starrcade '19 ★★
01-12-19, Duluth, Georgia **WWE**
The Street Profits (Angelo Dawkins and Montez Ford) defeated The O.C. (Luke Gallows and Karl Anderson) in 8:30 (★★); The Kabuki Warriors (Asuka and Kairi Sane) defeated Becky Lynch and Charlotte Flair, Bayley and Sasha Banks, and Alexa Bliss and Nikki Cross in a Four Way Match in 13:30 (★★); Bobby Lashley defeated Kevin Owens by DQ in 9:30 (★★).

Final Battle '19 ★★★
13-12-19, Baltimore, Maryland **ROH**
Bandido and Flamita defeated Villain Enterprises (Marty Scurll and Flip Gordon) in 13:51 (★★★); Vincent defeated Matt Taven in 13:32 (★★★); Mark Haskins defeated Bully Ray in 16:30 (★★); Alex Shelley defeated Colt Cabana in 6:31 (★★); Maria Manic defeated Angelina Love in 6:24 (★); Dragon Lee defeated Shane Taylor to win the ROH World Television Title in 14:34 (★★★); Jay Lethal and Jonathan Gresham defeated The Briscoe Brothers (Jay Briscoe and Mark Briscoe) to win the ROH World Tag Team Title in 21:54 (★★★); PCO defeated Rush in a Friday The 13th Massacre No DQ Match to win the ROH World Title in 22:23 (★★).

Into The Fire ★★★
14-12-19, Atlanta, Georgia **NWA**
Eli Drake defeated Ken Anderson in 9:15 (★★★); Thunder Rosa defeated Tasha Steelz in 4:15 (★★); The Question Mark defeated Trevor Murdoch in 5:55 (★★); The Rock 'n' Roll Express (Ricky Morton and Robert Gibson) defeated The Wild Cards (Royce Isaacs and Thomas Latimer) in 5:15 (★★); Allysin Kay and ODB defeated Melina and Marti Belle in 7:25 (★★); Aron Stevens defeated Colt Cabana and Ricky Starks in a Three Way Match to win the NWA National Title in 12:20 (★★★); Nick Aldis defeated James Storm in a Two Out Of Three Falls Match in 21:50 (★★★).

TLC '19 ★★
15-12-19, Minneapolis, Minnesota **WWE**
The New Day (Big E and Kofi Kingston) defeated The Revival (Dash Wilder and Scott Dawson) in a Ladder Match in 19:20 (★★); Aleister Black defeated Buddy Murphy in 13:45 (★★★); The Viking Raiders (Erik and Ivar) vs. The O.C. (Luke Gallows and Karl Anderson) ended in a double count out in 8:30 (★★); King Corbin defeated Roman Reigns in a TLC Match in 22:20 (★★); Bray Wyatt defeated The Miz in 6:40 (★); Bobby Lashley defeated Rusev in a Tables Match in 13:30 (★★); The Kabuki Warriors (Asuka and Kairi Sane) defeated Becky Lynch and Charlotte Flair in a TLC Match in 26:00 (★★).

TakeOver Blackpool II ★★★
12-01-20, Blackpool, England **NXT UK**
Eddie Dennis defeated Trent Seven in 8:20 (★★); Kay Lee Ray defeated Toni Storm and Piper Niven in a Three Way Match in 13:10 (★★); Tyler Bate defeated Jordan Devlin in 22:30 (★★★★); Gallus (Mark Coffey and Wolfgang) defeated Imperium (Fabian Aichner and Marcel Barthel), The Grizzled Young Veterans (Zack Gibson and James Drake), and Mark Andrews and Flash Morgan Webster in a Fatal Four Way Ladder Match in 24:56 (★★); Walter defeated Joe Coffey in 27:35 (★★).

Hard To Kill '20 ★★★
12-01-20, Dallas, Texas **Impact**
Ken Shamrock defeated Madman Fulton in 9:19 (★★); Ace Austin defeated Trey Miguel in 12:55 (★★); Taya Valkyrie defeated Jordynne Grace and ODB in a Three Way Match in 11:37 (★★); Rob Van Dam defeated Brian Cage in 5:18 (★★); Rob Van Dam defeated Daga in 4:11 (★★); Eddie Edwards defeated Michael Elgin in 19:53 (★★★); Moose defeated Rhino in a No DQ Match in 13:00 (★★★); Ethan Page and Josh Alexander defeated Willie Mack in a Handicap Match in 10:32 (★★★); Tessa Blanchard defeated Sami Callihan to win the Impact World Title in 23:49 (★★★★).

Hard Times '20 ★★★
24-01-20, Atlanta, Georgia **NWA**
Trevor Murdoch defeated The Question Mark in 3:08 (★★); Dan Maff defeated Zicky Dice in 2:35 (★★★); Ricky Starks defeated Matt Cross in 3:50 (★★★); Eli Drake and James Storm defeated The Rock 'n' Roll Express (Ricky Morton and Robert Gibson), and Royce Isaacs and Thom Latimer in a Three Way Match to win the NWA World Tag Team Title in 8:14

(★★★); **Thunder Rosa** defeated **Allysin Kay** to win the NWA World Women's Title in 18:05 (★★★); **Trevor Murdoch** defeated **Dan Maff** in 3:27 (★★); **Ricky Starks** defeated **Tim Storm** in 4:43 (★★); **Scott Steiner** defeated **Aron Stevens** via DQ in 6:30 (★); **Nick Aldis** defeated **Flip Gordon** in 15:20 (★★★); **Ricky Starks** defeated **Trevor Murdoch** to win the vacant NWA World Television Title in 9:20 (★★★).

Worlds Collide '20 ★★★
25-01-20, Houston, Texas **NXT/NXT UK**

Finn Balor defeated **Ilja Dragunov** in 14:00 (★★★); **Jordan Devlin** defeated **Angel Garza, Isaiah Scott** and **Travis Banks** in a Fatal 4-Way in 12:05 (★★★); **DIY (Johnny Gargano** and **Tommaso Ciampa)** defeated **Moustache Mountain (Trent Seven** and **Tyler Bate)** in 22:55 (★★★); **Rhea Ripley** defeated **Toni Storm** in 10:15 (★★); **Imperium (Walter, Fabian Aichner, Marcel Barthel** and **Alexander Wolfe)** defeated **The Undisputed Era (Adam Cole, Kyle O'Reilly, Bobby Fish** and **Roderick Strong)** in 29:50 (★★★★).

Royal Rumble '20 ★★★★
26-01-20, Houston, Texas **WWE**

Roman Reigns defeated **King Corbin** in a Falls Count Anywhere Match in 21:20 (★★★); **Charlotte Flair** won the 30-Woman Royal Rumble Match in 54:20 (★★★); **Bayley** defeated **Lacey Evans** in 9:20 (★★); **The Fiend** defeated **Daniel Bryan** in a Strap Match in 17:35 (★★★); **Becky Lynch** defeated **Asuka** in 16:25 (★★★); **Drew McIntyre** won the 30-Man Royal Rumble Match in 1:00:50 (★★★★).

Takeover Portland ★★★★
16-02-20, Portland, Oregon **NXT**

Keith Lee defeated **Dominik Dijakovic** in 20:20 (★★★); **Dakota Kai** defeated **Tegan Nox** in a Street Fight in 13:24 (★★★); **Finn Balor** defeated **Johnny Gargano** in 27:22 (★★★★); **Rhea Ripley** defeated **Bianca Belair** in 13:30 (★★★); **Matt Riddle** and **Pete Dunne** defeated **Bobby Fish** and **Kyle O'Reilly** to win the NXT Tag Team Title in 16:58 (★★★★); **Adam Cole** defeated **Tommaso Ciampa** in 33:23 (★★★★).

Super Showdown '20 ★
27-02-20, Riyadh, Saudi Arabia **WWE**

The Undertaker defeated **AJ Styles, Andrade, Bobby Lashley, Erick Rowan** and **R-Truth** in a Gauntlet Match to win the Prestigious Tuwaiq Mountain Trophy in 21:44 (★); **The Miz** and **John Morrison** defeated **The New Day (Big E** and **Kofi Kingston)** to win the WWE SmackDown Tag Team Title in 13:17 (★★★); **Angel Garza** defeated **Humberto Carrillo** in 9:13 (★★); **Seth Rollins** and **Murphy** defeated **The Street Profits (Angelo Dawkins** and **Montez Ford)** in 10:35 (★★); **Mansoor** defeated **Dolph Ziggler** in 9:21 (★★); **Brock Lesnar** defeated **Ricochet** in 1:34 (★); **Roman Reigns** defeated **King Corbin** in a Steel Cage Match in 12:59 (★★); **Bayley** defeated **Naomi** in 11:33 (★★); **Goldberg** defeated **The Fiend** to win the WWE Universal Title in 2:56 (★).

Revolution '20 ★★★★★
29-02-20, Chicago, Illinois **AEW**

Jake Hager defeated **Dustin Rhodes** in 14:40 (★★); **Darby Allin** defeated **Sammy Guevara** in 4:58 (★★★); **Kenny Omega** and **Hangman Page** defeated **The Young Bucks (Matt Jackson** and **Nick Jackson)** in 30:05 (★★★★★★); **Nyla Rose** defeated **Kris Statlander** in 12:45 (★★); **MJF** defeated **Cody Rhodes** in 24:40 (★★★★); **Pac** defeated **Orange Cassidy** in 13:00 (★★★★); **Jon Moxley** defeated **Chris Jericho** to win the AEW World Title in 22:20 (★★★).

Elimination Chamber '20 ★★
08-03-20, Philadelphia, Pennsylvania **WWE**

Daniel Bryan defeated **Drew Gulak** in 14:20 (★★★); **Andrade** defeated **Humberto Carrillo** in 12:20 (★★); **The Miz** and **John Morrison** defeated **The New Day (Big E** and **Kofi Kingston), The Usos (Jey Uso** and **Jimmy Uso), Heavy Machinery (Otis** and **Tucker), Lucha House Party (Gran Metalik** and **Lince Dorado),** and **Dolph Ziggler** and **Robert Roode** in an Elimination Chamber Match in 32:55 (★★); **Aleister Black** defeated **AJ Styles** in a No DQ Match in 23:15 (★★); **The Street Profits (Angelo Dawkins** and **Montez Ford)** defeated **Seth Rollins** and **Buddy Murphy** to win the WWE RAW Tag Team Title in 18:30 (★★); **Sami Zayn, Shinsuke Nakamura** and **Cesaro** defeated **Braun Strowman** in a Handicap Match in 8:30. As a result, **Sami Zayn** won the WWE Intercontinental Title (★); **Shayna Baszler** defeated **Natalya, Liv Morgan, Asuka, Ruby Riott** and **Sarah Logan** in an Elimination Chamber Match in 21:00 (★★).

WrestleMania XXXVI Night #1 ★★★
04-04-20, Orlando, Florida **WWE**

Alexa Bliss and **Nikki Cross** defeated **Asuka** and **Kairi Sane** in 15:05 (★★★); **Elias** defeated **King Corbin** in 9:00 (★★); **Becky Lynch** defeated **Shayna Baszler** in 8:30 (★★★); **Sami Zayn** defeated **Daniel Bryan** in 9:20 (★★); **John Morrison** defeated **Jimmy Uso** and **Kofi Kingston** in a Triple Threat Ladder Match in 18:30 (★★★); **Kevin Owens** defeated **Seth Rollins** in a No DQ Match in 17:20 (★★★★); **Braun Strowman** defeated **Goldberg** to win the WWE Universal Title in 2:10 (★★); **The Undertaker** defeated **AJ Styles** in a Boneyard Match in 24:00 (★★★★★★).

WrestleMania XXXVI Night #2 ★★★
04-04-20, Orlando, Florida **WWE**

Charlotte Flair defeated **Rhea Ripley** to win the NXT Women's Title in 20:30 (★★★★); **Aleister Black** defeated **Bobby Lashley** in 7:20 (★★★); **Otis** defeated **Dolph Ziggler** in 8:15 (★★); **Edge** defeated **Randy Orton** in a Last Man Standing Match in 36:35 (★★); **The Street Profits (Angelo Dawkins** and **Montez Ford)** defeated **Angel Garza** and **Austin Theory** in 6:20 (★★); **Bayley** defeated **Lacey Evans, Naomi, Sasha Banks** and **Tamina** in a Fatal 5-Way Match in 19:20 (★★); **The Fiend** defeated **John Cena** in a Firefly Fun House Match in 13:00 (★★★★★★); **Drew McIntyre** defeated **Brock Lesnar** to win the WWE Title in 4:35 (★★★).

Money In The Bank '20 ★★★
10-05-20, Orlando, Florida **WWE**

The New Day (Big E and **Kofi Kingston)** defeated **The Forgotten Sons (Steve Cutler** and **Wesley Blake), John Morrison** and **The Miz,** and **Lucha House Party (Gran Metalik** and **Lince Dorado)** in a Fatal 4-Way Match in 12:00 (★★★); **Bobby Lashley** defeated **R-Truth** in 1:30 (★★); **Bayley** defeated **Tamina** in 10:30 (★★); **Braun Strowman** defeated **Bray Wyatt** in 10:55 (★★); **Drew McIntyre** defeated **Seth Rollins** in 19:20 (★★★★); **Asuka** and **Otis** defeated **Carmella, Dana Brooke, Lacey Evans, Nia Jax, Shayna Baszler, AJ Styles, Aleister Black, Daniel Bryan, King Corbin** and **Rey Mysterio** in a Money In The Bank Ladder Match in 27:15 (★★★★).

Double Or Nothing '20 ★★★★
23-05-20, Jacksonville, Florida **AEW**

Brian Cage defeated **Darby Allin, Colt Cabana, Orange Cassidy, Joey Janela, Scorpio Sky, Kip Sabian, Frankie Kazarian** and **Luchasaurus** in a Casino Ladder Match in 28:30 (★★★); **MJF** defeated **Jungle Boy** in 17:20 (★★★★); **Cody Rhodes** defeated **Lance Archer** to win the vacant AEW TNT Title in 22:00 (★★★); **Kris Statlander** defeated **Penelope Ford** in 5:30 (★★); **Dustin Rhodes** defeated **Shawn Spears** in 3:20 (★); **Hikaru Shida** defeated **Nyla Rose** to win the AEW Women's World Title in a No DQ, No Count Out Match in 16:40 (★★★); **Jon Moxley** defeated **Mr. Brodie Lee** in 15:30 (★★★★); **Matt Hardy, Hangman Page, Kenny Omega, Nick Jackson** and **Matt Jackson** defeated **Chris Jericho, Jake Hager, Sammy Guevara, Santana** and **Ortiz** in a Stadium Stampede Match in 34:00 (★★★★★★).

Takeover In Your House '20 ★★★
07-06-20, Winter Park, Florida **NXT**

Mia Yim, Shotzi Blackheart and **Tegan Nox** defeated **Candice LeRae, Dakota Kai** and **Raquel Gonzalez** in 9:50 (★★★); **Finn Balor** defeated **Damian Priest** in 13:07 (★★★); **Keith Lee** defeated **Johnny Gargano** in 20:35 (★★★); **Adam Cole** defeated **Velveteen Dream** in a Backlot Brawl in 14:57 (★★); **Karrion Kross** defeated **Tommaso Ciampa** in 6:13 (★★); **Io Shirai** defeated **Charlotte Flair** and **Rhea Ripley** in a Three Way Match to win the NXT Women's Title in 17:36 (★★★).

Backlash '20 ★★★
14-06-20, Orlando, Florida **WWE**

Bayley and **Sasha Banks** defeated **Alexa Bliss** and **Nikki Cross,** and **The Ilconics (Billie Kay** and **Peyton Royce)** in a Three Way Match in 8:50 (★★); **Sheamus** defeated **Jeff Hardy** in 16:50 (★★); **Asuka** vs. **Nia Jax** went to a double count out in 8:25 (★★); **Braun Strowman** defeated **The Miz** and **John Morrison** in a Handicap Match in 7:20 (★); **Drew McIntyre** defeated **Bobby Lashley** in 13:15 (★★★); **Randy Orton** defeated **Edge** in 44:45 (★★★★).

Slammiversary XVIII ★★★
18-07-20, Nashville, Tennessee **Impact**
The Motor City Machine Guns (Alex Shelley and Chris Sabin) defeated The Rascalz (Dez and Wentz) in 14:17 (★★); Moose defeated Tommy Dreamer in an Old School Rules Match in 11:18 (★); Kylie Ray won a Gauntlet For The Gold Match in 19:20 (★); Chris Bey defeated Willie Mack to win the Impact X Division Title in 10:01 (★★); The North (Ethan Page and Josh Alexander) defeated Ken Shamrock and Sami Callihan in 15:56 (★★★); Deonna Purrazzo defeated Jordynne Grace to win the Impact Knockouts Title in 15:12 (★★★); Eddie Edwards defeated Ace Austin, Trey, Eric Young and Rich Swann in a Five Way Elimination Match to win the vacant Impact World Title in 24:25 (★★★).

The Horror Show At Extreme Rules ★★
19-07-20, Orlando, Florida **WWE**
Cesaro and Shinsuke Nakamura defeated The New Day (Big E and Kofi Kingston) in a Tables Match to win the WWE SmackDown Tag Team Title in 10:25 (★); Bayley defeated Nikki Cross in 12:20 (★★); Seth Rollins defeated Rey Mysterio in an Eye For An Eye Match in 18:05 (★★); Asuka vs. Sasha Banks went to a no contest in 20:15 (★★★); Drew McIntyre defeated Dolph Ziggler in an Extreme Rules Match in 15:25 (★★★); Bray Wyatt defeated Braun Strowman in a Swamp Fight in 18:00 (★).

Takeover XXX ★★★
22-08-20, Orlando, Florida **NXT**
Finn Balor defeated Timothy Thatcher in 13:32 (★★★); Damian Priest defeated Bronson Reed, Cameron Grimes, Johnny Gargano and Velveteen Dream in a Ladder Match to win the vacant NXT North American Title in 21:24 (★★★★); Adam Cole defeated Pat McAfee in 16:12 (★★★); Io Shirai defeated Dakota Kai in 17:13 (★★★); Karrion Kross defeated Keith Lee to win the NXT Title in 21:51 (★★).

SummerSlam '20 ★★★★
23-08-20, Orlando, Florida **WWE**
Bayley defeated Asuka in 11:35 (★★★); The Street Profits (Angelo Dawkins and Montez Ford) defeated Andrade and Angel Garza in 7:52 (★★); Mandy Rose defeated Sonya Deville in a No DQ Loser Leaves WWE Match in 10:03 (★★★); Seth Rollins defeated Dominik Mysterio in 22:25 (★★★★); Asuka defeated Sasha Banks to win the WWE RAW Women's Title in 11:30 (★★★); Drew McIntyre defeated Randy Orton in 20:35 (★★★★); The Fiend defeated Braun Strowman in a Falls Count Anywhere Match to win the WWE Universal Title in 11:58 (★★).

Payback '20 ★★★
30-08-20, Orlando, Florida **WWE**
Bobby Lashley defeated Apollo Crews to win the WWE United States Title in 9:30 (★★); Big E defeated Sheamus in 12:20 (★★); Matt Riddle defeated King Corbin in 10:55 (★★); Shayna Baszler and Nia Jax defeated Bayley and Sasha Banks to win the WWE Women's Tag Team Title in 10:20 (★★★); Keith Lee defeated Randy Orton in 6:40 (★★); The Mysterios (Dominik Mysterio and Rey Mysterio) defeated Seth Rollins and Murphy in 15:58 (★★★); Roman Reigns defeated The Fiend and Braun Strowman in a No Holds Barred Three Way Match to win the WWE Universal Title in 12:46 (★★).

All Out '20 ★★★
05-09-20, Orlando, Florida **AEW**
Big Swole defeated Dr. Britt Baker D.M.D. in a Tooth and Nail Match in 6:18 (★★★); The Young Bucks (Matt Jackson and Nick Jackson) defeated Jurassic Express (Jungle Boy and Luchasaurus) in 15:24 (★★★); Lance Archer won a 21-Man Casino Battle Royale in 21:48 (★★); Matt Hardy defeated Sammy Guevara in a Broken Rules Match in 6:05 (★); Hikaru Shida defeated Thunder Rosa in 16:57; Matt Cardona, Scorpio Sky, Dustin Rhodes and QT Marshall defeated The Dark Order (Mr. Brodie Lee, Colt Cabana, Evil Uno and Stu Grayson) in 15:10 (★★★); FTR (Cash Wheeler and Dax Harwood) defeated Kenny Omega and Hangman Page to win the AEW World Tag Team Title in 29:40 (★★★); Orange Cassidy defeated Chris Jericho in a Mimosa Mayhem Match in 15:15 (★★★); Jon Moxley defeated MJF in 23:40 (★★★).

Clash Of Champions '20 ★★★★
27-09-20, Orlando, Florida **WWE**
Sami Zayn defeated Jeff Hardy and AJ Styles in a Triple Threat Ladder Match to win the WWE Intercontinental Title in 26:35 (★★★★); Asuka defeated Zelina Vega in 7:05 (★★); Bobby Lashley defeated Apollo Crews in 8:15 (★★); The Street Profits (Angelo Dawkins and Montez Ford) defeated Andrade and Angel Garza in 8:15 (★★); Asuka defeated Bayley by DQ in 3:45 (★★); Drew McIntyre defeated Randy Orton in an Ambulance Match in 21:35 (★★★); Roman Reigns defeated Jey Uso in 22:55 (★★★).

Takeover 31 ★★★
04-10-20, Orlando, Florida **NXT**
Damian Priest defeated Johnny Gargano in 18:39 (★★); Kushida defeated Velveteen Dream in 13:00 (★★★); Santos Escobar defeated Isaiah Scott in 15:14 (★★★); Io Shirai defeated Candice LeRae in 16:45 (★★★); Finn Balor defeated Kyle O'Reilly in 28:28 (★★★★).

Bound For Glory '20 ★★
24-10-20, Nashville, Tennessee **Impact**
Rohit Raju defeated Chris Bey, Jordynne Grace, TJP, Willie Mack and Trey in a Six Way Scramble Match in 13:20 (★★★); Rhino won a Call Your Shot Gauntlet Match in 25:22 (★★); Moose defeated EC3 in 9:49 (★★★); Ken Shamrock defeated Eddie Edwards in 12:32 (★★); The North (Ethan Page and Josh Alexander) defeated The Motor Ciy Machine Guns (Alex Shelley and Chris Sabin), The Good Brothers (Luke Gallows and Karl Anderson), and Ace Austin and Madman Fulton in a Four Way Match to win the Impact World Tag Team Title in 14:26 (★★★); Su Yung defeated Deonna Purrazzo to win the Impact Knockouts Title in 15:05 (★★); Rich Swann defeated Eric Young to win the Impact World Title in 21:31 (★★★).

Hell In A Cell '20 ★★★★
25-10-20, Orlando, Florida **WWE**
Roman Reigns defeated Jey Uso in a Hell In A Cell Match in 29:06 (★★★★); Elias defeated Jeff Hardy by DQ in 7:49 (★★); The Miz defeated Otis to win the Money In The Bank Contract in 7:28 (★★); Sasha Banks defeated Bayley in a Hell In A Cell Match to win the WWE SmackDown Women's Title in 26:29 (★★★★); Bobby Lashley defeated Slapjack in 3:50 (★★); Randy Orton defeated Drew McIntyre in a Hell In A Cell Match to win the WWE Title in 30:35 (★★★★).

Full Gear '20 ★★★★
07-11-20, Jacksonville, Florida **AEW**
Kenny Omega defeated Hangman Page in 16:25 (★★★★); Orange Cassidy defeated John Silver in 9:40 (★★); Darby Allin defeated Cody Rhodes to win the AEW TNT Title in 17:00 (★★★); Hikaru Shida defeated Nyla Rose in 14:10 (★★); The Young Bucks (Matt Jackson and Nick Jackson) defeated FTR (Cash Wheeler and Dax Harwood) to win the AEW World Tag Team Title in 28:35 (★★★★); Matt Hardy defeated Sammy Guevara in an Elite Deletion Match in 19:39 (★★★); MJF defeated Chris Jericho in 16:10 (★★★); Jon Moxley defeated Eddie Kingston in an "I Quit" Match in 17:35 (★★★).

Survivor Series '20 ★★★
22-11-20, Orlando, Florida **WWE**
AJ Styles, Keith Lee, Sheamus, Braun Strowman and Riddle defeated Kevin Owens, Jey Uso, King Corbin, Seth Rollins and Otis in an Elimination Match in 19:25 (★★); The Street Profits (Angelo Dawkins and Montez Ford) defeated The New Day (Kofi Kingston and Xavier Woods) in 13:40 (★★★); Bobby Lashley defeated Sami Zayn in 7:50 (★); Sasha Banks defeated Asuka in 13:05 (★★); Nia Jax, Shayna Baszler, Lana, Lacey Evans and Peyton Royce defeated Bianca Belair, Ruby Riott, Liv Morgan, Bayley and Natalya in an Elimination Match in 23:20 (★★); Roman Reigns defeated Drew McIntyre in 24:50 (★★★★).

Tribute To The Troops '20 ★★
06-12-20, Orlando, Florida **WWE**
Daniel Bryan, Jeff Hardy, Rey Mysterio and The Street Profits (Angelo Dawkins and Montez Ford) defeated Elias, King Corbin, Sami Zayn, Dolph Ziggler and Robert Roode in 11:20 (★★); Bianca Belair and Sasha Banks defeated Bayley and Natalya in 8:13 (★★); Drew McIntyre defeated The Miz in 3:49 (★★).

Takeover WarGames IV ★★★
06-12-20, Orlando, Florida NXT

Candice LeRae, Dakota Kai, Raquel Gonzalez and Toni Storm defeated Shotzi Blackheart, Ember Moon, Rhea Ripley and Io Shirai in a WarGames Match in 35:22 (★★★); Tommaso Ciampa defeated Timothy Thatcher in 16:46 (★★★); Dexter Lumis defeated Cameron Grimes in a Strap Match in 12:52 (★★); Johnny Gargano defeated Damian Priest and Leon Ruff in a Three Way Match to win the NXT North American Title in 17:28 (★★); The Undisputed Era (Adam Cole, Kyle O'Reilly, Bobby Fish and Roderick Strong) defeated Pat McAfee, Pete Dunne, Danny Burch and Oney Lorcan in a WarGames Match in 45:01 (★★).

Final Battle '20 ★★★
18-12-20, Baltimore, Maryland ROH

Jay Lethal and Jonathan Gresham defeated Mark Briscoe and PCO in 12:40 (★★); Rey Horus defeated Dalton Castle in 9:10 (★★); Matt Taven and Mike Bennett defeated Bateman and Vincent in 16:19 (★★); Danhausen defeated Brian Johnson by DQ in 8:44 (★); Dragon Lee defeated Tony Deppen in 11:50 (★★); Shane Taylor defeated Jay Briscoe in 13:49 (★★); Jonathan Gresham defeated Flip Gordon in 24:37 (★★★); Rush defeated Brody King in 16:35 (★★★).

TLC '20 ★★★★
20-12-20, St. Petersburg, Florida WWE

Drew McIntyre defeated AJ Styles and The Miz in a Triple Threat TLC Match in 27:01 (★★★); Sasha Banks defeated Carmella in 12:42 (★★); The Hurt Business (Cedric Alexander and Shelton Benjamin) defeated The New Day (Kofi Kingston and Xavier Woods) to win the WWE RAW Tag Team Title in 9:54 (★★); Asuka and Charlotte Flair defeated Nia Jax and Shayna Baszler to win the WWE Women's Tag Team Title in 10:00 (★★★); Roman Reigns defeated Kevin Owens in a TLC Match in 24:45 (★★★★); Randy Orton defeated The Fiend in a Firefly Inferno Match in 12:00 (★★).

Hard To Kill '21 ★★★
16-01-21, Nashville, Tennessee Impact

Decay (Rosemary and Crazzy Steve) defeated Tenille Dashwood and Kaleb with a K in 8:55 (★★); Violent By Design (Eric Young, Deaner and Joe Doering) defeated Cousin Jake, Rhino and Tommy Dreamer in an Old School Rules Match in 9:55 (★★); Fire 'N Flava (Kiera Hogan and Tasha Steelz) defeated Havok and Nevaeh to win the vacant Impact Knockouts Tag Team Title in 8:40 (★★); Matt Cardona defeated Ace Austin by DQ in 2:30 (★); Manik defeated Chris Bey and Rohit Raju in a Three Way Match in 13:50 (★★); Deonna Purrazzo defeated Taya Valkyrie in 11:40 (★★); The Karate Man defeated Ethan Page (★★★); Eddie Edwards defeated Sami Callihan in a Barbed Wire Massacre in 18:50 (★★★); Kenny Omega and The Good Brothers (Luke Gallows and Karl Anderson) defeated Rich Swann, Chris Sabin and Moose in 20:30 (★★★).

Superstar Spectacle ★★
26-01-21, St. Petersburg, Florida WWE

Finn Balor defeated Guru Raaj in 7:08 (★★); Dilsher Shanky, Giant Zanjeer, Rey Mysterio and Ricochet defeated Cesaro, Dolph Ziggler, King Corbin and Shinsuke Nakamura in 6:25 (★★); AJ Styles defeated Jeer Rama in 3:14 (★★); Charlotte Flair and Sareena Sandhu defeated Bayley and Natalya in 6:06 (★★); Drew McIntyre and The Indus Sher (Rinku and Saurav) defeated Jinder Mahal and The Bollywood Boyz (Samir Singh and Sunil Singh) in 9:03 (★★).

Royal Rumble '21 ★★★
31-01-21, St. Petersburg, Florida WWE

Drew McIntyre defeated Goldberg in 2:32 (★★); Sasha Banks defeated Carmella in 10:21 (★★); Bianca Belair won the 30-Woman Royal Rumble Match in 58:48 (★★★); Roman Reigns defeated Kevin Owens in a Last Man Standing Match in 24:54 (★★★); Edge won the 30-Man Royal Rumble Match in 58:28 (★★★).

Takeover Vengeance Day ★★★★
14-02-21, Orlando, Florida NXT

Dakota Kai and Raquel Gonzalez defeated Ember Moon and Shotzi Blackheart in 17:40 (★★★); Johnny Gargano defeated Kushida in 24:51 (★★★★); MSK (Wes Lee and Nash Carter) defeated Grizzled Young Veterans (James Drake and Zack Gibson) in 18:28 (★★★★); Io Shirai defeated Toni Storm and Mercedes Martinez in a Three Way Match in 12:15 (★★); Finn Balor defeated Pete Dunne in 25:11 (★★★★).

Elimination Chamber '21 ★★★
21-02-21, St. Petersburg, Florida WWE

Daniel Bryan defeated Cesaro, Jey Uso, Kevin Owens, King Corbin and Sami Zayn in an Elimination Chamber Match in 34:27 (★★★); Roman Reigns defeated Daniel Bryan in 1:36 (★★); Riddle defeated Bobby Lashley and John Morrison in a Three Way Match to win the WWE United States Title in 8:49 (★★★); Nia Jax and Shayna Baszler defeated Bianca Belair and Sasha Banks in 9:34 (★★); Drew McIntyre defeated AJ Styles, Jeff Hardy, Kofi Kingston, Randy Orton and Sheamus in an Elimination Chamber Match in 31:15 (★★★); The Miz defeated Drew McIntyre to win the WWE Title in :28 (★★).

Revolution '21 ★★★
07-03-21, Jacksonville, Florida AEW

The Young Bucks (Matt Jackson and Nick Jackson) defeated The Inner Circle (Chris Jericho and MJF) in 17:50 (★★★); Rey Fenix won a Battle Royal in 26:45 (★★★); Hikaru Shida defeated Ryo Mizunami in 15:10 (★★★); Kip Sabian and Miro defeated Best Friends (Chuck Taylor and Orange Cassidy) in 7:50 (★★); Hangman Page defeated Matt Hardy in a Big Money Match in 14:40 (★★★); Scorpio Sky defeated Cody Rhodes, Ethan Page, Lance Archer, Max Caster and Penta El Zero Miedo in a Ladder Match in 23:15 (★★★); Darby Allin and Sting defeated Team Taz (Brian Cage and Ricky Starks) in a Street Fight in 13:40 (★★★★); Kenny Omega defeated Jon Moxley in an Exploding Barbed Wire Death Match in 23:15 (★★★★).

Back For The Attack ★★★
21-03-21, Atlanta, Georgia NWA

Slice Boogie defeated Crimson, Jax Dane and Jordan Clearwater in a Four Way Match in 5:41 (★★); Tyrus defeated JR Kratos in 7:27 (★★); Da Pope vs. Thom Latimer went to a time limit draw in 10:00 (★★★); Kamille defeated Thunder Rosa in 14:04 (★★★); Trevor Murdoch defeated Chris Adonis in 8:38 (★★); Nick Aldis defeated Aron Stevens in 21:29 (★★★).

Fastlane '21 ★★★
21-03-21, St. Petersburg, Florida WWE

Nia Jax and Shayna Baszler defeated Bianca Belair and Sasha Banks in 9:45 (★★); Big E defeated Apollo Crews in 5:45 (★★); Braun Strowman defeated Elias in 3:55 (★★); Seth Rollins defeated Shinsuke Nakamura in 12:55 (★★); Drew McIntyre defeated Sheamus in a No Holds Barred Match in 19:40 (★★★★); Alexa Bliss defeated Randy Orton in 4:45 (★★); Roman Reigns defeated Daniel Bryan in 30:00 (★★★★).

19th Anniversary Show ★★
26-03-21, Baltimore, Maryland ROH

Tracy Williams defeated Kenny King to win the vacant ROH World Television Title in 7:16 (★★); Flip Gordon defeated Mark Briscoe in 7:48 (★★); Dalton Castle defeated Josh Woods in 10:19 (★★); Jay Briscoe defeated EC3 in a Grudge Match in 20:55 (★★★); Bandido defeated Flamita and Rey Horus in a Three Way Match in 10:47 (★★★★); Vincent vs. Matt Taven went to a no contest in an Unsanctioned Match in 13:40 (★★); Jonathan Gresham defeated Dak Draper in a Pure Rules Match in 20:29 (★★★); The Foundation (Rhett Titus and Tracy Williams) defeated La Faccion Ingobernable (La Bestia del Ring and Kenny King) to win the ROH World Tag Team Title in 10:29 (★★); Rush defeated Jay Lethal in 18:31 (★★★).

Takeover Stand & Deliver '21 ★★
08-04-21, Orlando, Florida NXT

Santos Escobar defeated Jordan Devlin in a Ladder Match to win the NXT Cruiserweight Title in 18:08 (★★★); Ember Moon and Shotzi Blackheart defeated The Way (Candice LeRae and Indi Hartwell) in 10:34 (★★); Johnny Gargano defeated Bronson Reed in 16:23 (★★★); Karrion Kross defeated Finn Balor to win the NXT Title in 17:05 (★★); Kyle O'Reilly defeated Adam Cole in an Unsanctioned Match in 40:19 (★★).

WrestleMania XXXVII Night #1 ★★★★
10-04-21, Tampa, Florida WWE

Bobby Lashley defeated Drew McIntyre in 18:20 (★★★); Natalya and Tamina won a Tag Team Turmoil Match in 14:15 (★); Cesaro defeated Seth Rollins in 11:35 (★★★★); AJ Styles and Omos defeated The New Day (Kofi Kingston and Xavier Woods) to win the WWE Raw Tag Team Title in 9:45 (★★); Braun Strowman defeated Shane McMahon in a Steel Cage Match in 11:25 (★★★); Bad Bunny and Damian Priest defeated The Miz and John Morrison in 15:05 (★★★); Bianca Belair defeated Sasha Banks to win the WWE SmackDown Women's Title in 17:15 (★★★★).

WrestleMania XXXVII Night #2 ★★★
11-04-21, Tampa, Florida **WWE**
Randy Orton defeated The Fiend in 5:50 (★); Nia Jax and Shayna Baszler defeated Natalya and Tamina in 14:20 (★★); Kevin Owens defeated Sami Zayn in 9:20 (★★★); Sheamus defeated Riddle to win the WWE United States Title in 10:50 (★★★); Apollo Crews defeated Big E in a Nigerian Drum Fight to win the WWE Intercontinental Title in 6:50 (★★); Rhea Ripley defeated Asuka to win the WWE Raw Women's Title in 13:30 (★★★); Roman Reigns defeated Edge and Daniel Bryan in a Three Way Match in 22:40 (★★★★).

Rebellion '21 ★★★
25-04-21, Nashville, Tennessee **Impact**
Josh Alexander defeated Ace Austin and TJP in the Three Way Match to win the Impact X Divison Title in 11:15 (★★★); Violent By Design (Deaner, Joe Doering and Rhyno) and W. Morrissey defeated Chris Sabin, Eddie Edwards, James Storm and Willie Mack in 10:05 (★★★); Brian Myers defeated Matt Cardona in 9:45 (★★); Jordynne Grace and Rachael Ellering defeated Fire 'N Flava (Kiera Hogan and Tasha Steelz) to win the Impact Knockouts Tag Team Title in 9:20 (★★); Trey Miguel defeated Sami Callihan in a Last Man Standing Match in 15:25 (★★★); FinJuice (David Finlay and Juice Robinson) defeated The Good Brothers (Luke Gallows and Karl Anderson) in 10:35 (★★★); Deonna Purrazzo defeated Tenille Dashwood in 9:45 (★★); Kenny Omega defeated Rich Swann to win the Impact World Title in 23:00 (★★★★).

WrestleMania Backlash '21 ★★★
16-05-21, Tampa, Florida **WWE**
Rhea Ripley defeated Asuka and Charlotte Flair in a Three Way Match in 15:22 (★★★); Rey Mysterio and Dominik Mysterio defeated The Dirty Dawgs (Dolph Ziggler and Robert Roode) to win the WWE SmackDown Tag Team Title in 17:02 (★★★); Damian Priest defeated The Miz in a Lumberjack Match in 6:57 (★); Bianca Belair defeated Bayley in 16:05 (★★★); Bobby Lashley defeated Braun Strowman and Drew McIntyre in a Three Way Match in 14:12 (★★★); Roman Reigns defeated Cesaro in 27:35 (★★★★).

Double Or Nothing '21 ★★★★
30-05-21, Jacksonville, Florida **AEW**
Hangman Page defeated Brian Cage in 12:00 (★★★★); The Young Bucks (Matt Jackson and Nick Jackson) defeated Jon Moxley and Eddie Kingston in 21:00 (★★★★); Jungle Boy won a Casino Battle Royal in 23:30 (★★★); Cody Rhodes defeated Anthony Ogogo in 10:55 (★★); Miro defeated Lance Archer in 9:50 (★★★); Dr. Britt Baker D.M.D. defeated Hikaru Shida to win the AEW Women's World Title in 17:20 (★★★); Darby Allin and Sting defeated The Men Of The Year (Ethan Page and Scorpio Sky) in 12:30 (★★★★); Kenny Omega defeated Orange Cassidy and Pac in a Three Way Match in 27:00 (★★★★); The Inner Circle (Chris Jericho, Jake Hager, Sammy Guevara, Santana and Ortiz) defeated The Pinnacle (MJF, Shawn Spears, Wardlow, Cash Wheeler and Dax Harwood) in a Stadium Stampede Match in 31:30 (★★★★).

When Our Shadows Fall ★★★
06-06-21, Atlanta, Georgia **NWA**
La Rebelion Amarilla (Mecha Wolf and Bestia 666) defeated The End (Odinson and Parrow), Slice Boogie and Marshe Rockett, and Sal Rinauro and El Rudo in a Four Way Match in 8:45 (★★★); Tyrus defeated The Pope in a Grudge Match in 10:25 (★); Taryn Terrell and Kylie Rae defeated Thunder Rosa and Melina in 8:55 (★★★); JTG defeated Fred Rosser in 9:30 (★★★); Aron Stevens and JR Kratos defeated The War Kings (Jax Dane and Crimson) and Strictly Business (Thom Latimer and Chris Adonis) in a Three Way Match in 14:15 (★★); Kamille defeated Serena Deeb to win the NWA World Women's Title in 14:20 (★★★★); Nick Aldis defeated Trevor Murdoch by DQ in 12:55 (★★).

Takeover In Your House '21 ★★★
13-06-21, Orlando, Florida **NXT**
Bronson Reed and MSK (Nash Carter and Wes Lee) defeated Legado Del Fantasma (Santos Escobar, Joaquin Wilde and Raul Mendoza) in 13:40 (★★★); Xia Li defeated Mercedes Martinez in 7:40 (★★); LA Knight defeated Cameron Grimes in a Ladder Match to win the vacant Million Dollar Title in 19:30 (★★★); Raquel Gonzalez defeated Ember Moon in 12:40 (★★★); Karrion Kross defeated Kyle O'Reilly, Adam Cole, Johnny Gargano and Pete Dunne in a Fatal Five Way Match in 26:15 (★★★).

Hell In A Cell '21 ★★★
20-06-21, Tampa, Florida **WWE**
Bianca Belair defeated Bayley in a Hell In A Cell Match in 19:45 (★★); Seth Rollins defeated Cesaro in 16:15 (★★★); Alexa Bliss defeated Shayna Baszler in 7:00 (★★); Sami Zayn defeated Kevin Owens in 12:40 (★★★); Charlotte Flair defeated Rhea Ripley by DQ in 14:10 (★★★); Bobby Lashley defeated Drew McIntyre in a Hell In A Cell Match in 25:45 (★★★).

Best In The World '21 ★★★
11-07-21, Baltimore, Maryland **ROH**
The Briscoe Brothers (Jay Briscoe and Mark Briscoe) defeated Brian Johnson and PJ Black in 8:10 (★★); EC3 defeated Flip Gordon in 11:15 (★★); Shane Taylor Promotions (Shane Taylor, Moses and Kaun) defeated Dalton Castle, Eli Isom and Dak Draper in 10:50 (★★); Josh Woods defeated Silas Young in a Last Man Standing Match in 13:45 (★★); Brody King defeated Jay Lethal in 10:45 (★★★); Jonathan Gresham defeated Mike Bennett in a Pure Rules Match in 19:21 (★★★★); Dragon Lee defeated Tony Deppen to win the ROH World Television Title in 10:10 (★★★★); VLNCE UNLTD (Chris Dickinson and Homicide) defeated The Foundation (Jonathan Gresham and Rhett Titus) in a Fight Without Honor to win the ROH World Tag Team Title in 11:45 (★★★); Bandido defeated Rush to win the ROH World Title in 16:00 (★★★★).

Slammiversary XIX ★★★
17-07-21, Nashville, Tennessee **Impact**
Josh Alexander defeated Ace Austin, Chris Bey, Petey Williams, Rohit Raju and Trey Miguel in an Ultimate X Match in 15:45 (★★★★); Matt Cardona and Chelsea Green defeated Brian Myers and Tenille Dashwood in 6:05 (★★); W. Morrissey defeated Eddie Edwards in 11:00 (★★); FinJuice (David Finlay and Juice Robinson) defeated Madman Fulton and Shera in 1:15 (★★); Chris Sabin defeated Moose in 12:00 (★★★); The Good Brothers (Luke Gallows and Karl Anderson) defeated Violent By Design (Joe Doering and Rhino), Rich Swann and Willie Mack, and Fallah Bahh and No Way in a Four Way Match to win the Impact World Tag Team Title in 10:10 (★★); Deonna Purrazzo defeated Thunder Rosa in 10:30 (★★★); Kenny Omega defeated Sami Callihan in a No DQ Match in 27:45 (★★★★).

Money In The Bank '21 ★★★★
18-07-21, Fort Worth, Texas **WWE**
Nikki A.S.H. defeated Alexa Bliss, Asuka, Liv Morgan, Naomi, Natalya, Tamina and Zelina Vega in a Money In The Bank Ladder Match in 15:45 (★★★); AJ Styles and Omos defeated The Viking Raiders (Erik and Ivar) in 12:55 (★★★); Bobby Lashley defeated Kofi Kingston in 7:35 (★★); Charlotte Flair defeated Rhea Ripley to win the WWE Raw Women's Title in 16:50 (★★★★); Big E defeated Drew McIntyre, John Morrison, Kevin Owens, King Nakamura, Ricochet, Riddle and Seth Rollins in a Money In The Bank Ladder Match in 17:40 (★★★★); Roman Reigns defeated Edge in 33:10 (★★★★).

Glory By Honor XVIII Night #1 ★★
20-08-21, Philadelphia, Pennsylvania **ROH**
Silas Young defeated Rey Horus in 7:54 (★★); Demonic Flamita defeated Eli Isom, Dak Draper, Danhausen, Mike Bennett and PJ Black in a Six Man Mayhem Match in 11:47 (★★); Vita VonStarr and Max The Impaler defeated The Allure (Angelina Love and Mandy Leon) in 6:39 (★★); EC3 defeated Brian Johnson in 12:48 (★★); Mark Briscoe defeated Bateman in 6:19 (★★); Jonathan Gresham defeated Rhett Titus in a Pure Rules Match in 14:43 (★★★); VLNCE UNLTD (Brody King, Tony Deppen, Homicide and Chris Dickinson) vs. La Faccion Ingobernable (Dragon Lee, Kenny King, La Bestia del Ring and Rush) went to a no contest in 1:48 (★★); VLNCE UNLTD (Brody King, Tony Deppen, Homicide and Chris Dickinson) defeated La Faccion Ingobernable (Dragon Lee, Kenny King, La Bestia del Ring and Rush) in a Philadelphia Street Fight in 15:35 (★★★); Bandido defeated Flip Gordon in 17:18 (★★★).

Glory By Honor XVIII Night #2 ★★★
21-08-21, Philadelphia, Pennsylvania **ROH**
Dalton Castle defeated Danhausen in 8:08 (★★); LSG defeated The World Famous CB in a Pure Rules Match in 7:21 (★★); Miranda Alize and Rok-C defeated Chelsea Green and Willow in 7:45 (★★); Shane Taylor Promotions (Kaun, Moses and Shane Taylor) defeated Incoherence (Delirious, Frightmare and

Hallowicked) in 13:18 (★★); Mark Briscoe and Brian Johnson defeated Flip Gordon and Demonic Flamita in 11:23 (★★); The Foundation (Jay Lethal, Jonathan Gresham, Rhett Titus and Tracy Williams) defeated VLNCE UNLTD (Brody King, Tony Deppen, Homicide and Chris Dickinson) in 16:05 (★★★); La Faccion Ingobernable (Dragon Lee and Rush) defeated Bandido and Rey Horus in 13:02 (★★★); Vincent defeated Matt Taven in a Steel Cage Match in 19:37 (★★★).

SummerSlam '21 ★★★
21-08-21, Paradise, Nevada **WWE**

RK-Bro (Randy Orton and Riddle) defeated AJ Styles and Omos to win the WWE Raw Tag Team Title in 7:05 (★★); Alexa Bliss defeated Eva Marie in 3:50 (★); Damian Priest defeated Sheamus to win the WWE United States Title in 13:50 (★★★); The Usos (Jimmy Uso and Jey Uso) defeated Rey Mysterio and Dominik Mysterio in 10:50 (★★★); Becky Lynch defeated Bianca Belair to win the WWE SmackDown Women's Title in :27 (★); Drew McIntyre defeated Jinder Mahal in 4:40 (★★); Charlotte Flair defeated Nikki A.S.H. and Rhea Ripley in a Three Way Match to win the WWE Raw Women's Title in 13:05 (★★★); Edge defeated Seth Rollins in 21:15 (★★★★); Bobby Lashley defeated Goldberg in 7:10 (★★); Roman Reigns defeated John Cena in 23:00 (★★★★).

Takeover 36 ★★★
22-08-21, Orlando, Florida **NXT**

Cameron Grimes defeated LA Knight to win the Million Dollar Title in 16:31 (★★★); Raquel Gonzalez defeated Dakota Kai in 12:24 (★★★); Ilja Dragunov defeated Walter to win the NXT United Kingdom Title in 22:03 (★★★★★); Kyle O'Reilly defeated Adam Cole in a Three Stages Of Hell Match in 25:20 (★★★); Samoa Joe defeated Karrion Kross to win the NXT Title in 12:24 (★★).

EmPowerrr ★★
28-08-21, St. Louis, Missouri **NWA**

Diamante defeated Chik Tormenta and Kylie Rae in a Three Way Match in 8:14 (★★); The Hex (Allysin Kay and Marti Belle) defeated Hell On Heels (Renee Michelle and Sahara Seven) in 6:54 (★★); Red Velvet and KiLynn King defeated The Freebabes (Jazzy Yang and Miranda Gordy) in 6:44 (★★); Deonna Purrazzo defeated Melina Perez in 14:38 (★★); The Hex defeated Red Velvet and KiLynn King to win the vacant NWA Women's World Title in 9:41 (★★★); Kamille defeated Leyla Hirsch in 13:03 (★★★); Chelsea Green won a Gauntlet Match to win the NWA Women's Invitational Cip in 24:08 (★★).

73rd Anniversary Show ★★★
29-08-21, St. Louis, Missouri **NWA**

Tim Storm defeated Thom Latimer and Crimson in a Three Way No DQ Match in 9:10 (★★★); Mickie James defeated Kylie Rae in 5:35 (★★); Tyrus, The Masked Man and Jordan Clearwater defeated Da Pope and The End (Odinson and Parrow) in 12:52 (★★); Chris Adonis defeated James Storm in 14:03 (★★★); Judais won a Battle Royal in 20:08 (★★); Kamille defeated Chelsea Green in 12:33 (★★★); La Rebellion (Bestia 666 and Mecha Wolf) defeated Aron Stevens and JR Kratos to win the NWA World Tag Team Title in 14:04 (★★); Trevor Murdoch defeated Nick Aldis to win the NWA Worlds Heavyweight Title in 16:25 (★★★★).

All Out '21 ★★★★★
05-09-21, Hoffman Estates, Illinois **AEW**

Miro defeated Eddie Kingston in 13:25 (★★★★); Jon Moxley defeated Satoshi Kojima in 12:10 (★★★); Dr. Britt Baker D.M.D. defeated Kris Statlander in 11:25 (★★★); The Lucha Brothers (Penta El Zero Miedo and Rey Fenix) defeated The Young Bucks (Matt Jackson and Nick Jackson) in a Steel Cage Match to win the AEW World Tag Team Title in 22:05 (★★★★★); Ruby Soho won a Casino Battle Royal in 22:00 (★★★); Chris Jericho defeated MJF in 21:15 (★★★); CM Punk defeated Darby Allin in 16:40 (★★★★); Paul Wight defeated QT Marshall in 3:10 (★★); Kenny Omega defeated Christian Cage in 21:20 (★★★).

Death Before Dishonor XVIII ★★★
12-09-21, Philadelphia, Pennsylvania **ROH**

Dalton Castle defeated Eli Isom in 9:16 (★★); Taylor Rust defeated Jake Atlas in 6:55 (★★); VLNCE UNLTD (Homicide, Chris Dickinson and Tony Deppen) defeated John Walters, LSG and Lee Moriarty in 10:58 (★★★); The OGK (Matt Taven and

Mike Bennett) defeated The Briscoe Brothers (Jay Briscoe and Mark Briscoe) in 13:07 (★★★); Josh Woods defeated Jonathan Gresham in a Pure Rules Match to win the ROH Pure Title in 20:01 (★★★); Shane Taylor Promotions (Kaun, Moses and O'Shay Edwards) defeated La Faccion Ingobernable (Dragon Lee, Kenny King and La Bestia del Ring) in 11:27 (★★); Rok-C defeated Miranda Alize to win the vacant ROH Women's World Title in 18:13 (★★★); Bandido defeated Brody King, Demonic Flamita and EC3 in a Four Corner Survival Match in 17:09 (★★★).

Extreme Rules '21 ★★★
26-09-21, Columbus, Ohio **WWE**

The New Day (Big E, Kofi Kingston and Xavier Woods) defeated Bobby Lashley, AJ Styles and Omos in 18:15 (★★★); The Usos (Jimmy Uso and Jey Uso) defeated The Street Profits (Angelo Dawkins and Montez Ford) in 13:45 (★★★); Charlotte Flair defeated Alexa Bliss in 11:25 (★★★); Damian Priest defeated Jeff Hardy and Sheamus in a Three Way Match in 13:25 (★★★); Bianca Belair defeated Becky Lynch by DQ in 17:26 (★★★); Roman Reigns defeated Finn Balor in an Extreme Rules Match in 19:45 (★★★).

Crown Jewel '21 ★★★★
21-10-21, Riyadh, Saudi Arabia **WWE**

Edge defeated Seth Rollins in a Hell In A Cell Match in 27:40 (★★★★); Mansoor defeated Mustafa Ali in 10:00 (★★★); RK-Bro (Randy Orton and Riddle) defeated AJ Styles and Omos in 8:40 (★★); Zelina Vega defeated Doudrop to win the Queen's Crown Tournament in 5:51 (★★); Goldberg defeated Bobby Lashley in a No Holds Barred Falls Count Anywhere Match in 11:25 (★★★); Xavier Woods defeated Finn Balor to win the King Of The Ring Tournament in 9:40 (★★★); Big E defeated Drew McIntyre in 13:25 (★★★★); Becky Lynch defeated Bianca Belair and Sasha Banks in a Three Way Match in 19:25 (★★★); Roman Reigns defeated Brock Lesnar in 12:20 (★★★★).

Bound For Glory '21 ★★★
23-10-21, Las Vegas, Nevada **Impact**

The Iinspiration (Cassie Lee and Jessica McKay) defeated Decay (Havok and Rosemary) to win the Impact Knockouts Tag Team Title in 8:58 (★★); Trey Miguel defeated El Phantasmo and Steve Maclin in a Three Way Match to win the vacant Impact X Division Title in 13:21 (★★★); Heath and Rhino defeated Violent By Design (Deaner and Joe Doering) in 4:59 (★★); Moose won a Call Your Shot Gauntlet Match in 29:33 (★★); The Good Brothers (Luke Gallows and Karl Anderson) defeated FinJuice (David Finlay and Juice Robinson) and Chris Bey and Hikuleo in a Three Way Match in 9:55 (★★); Mickie James defeated Deonna Purrazzo to win the Impact Knockouts Title in 13:17 (★★★); Josh Alexander defeated Christian Cage to win the Impact World Title in 18:52 (★★★★); Moose defeated Josh Alexander to win the Impact World Title in :07 (★★).

Full Gear '21 ★★★★★
13-11-21, Minneapolis, Minnesota **AEW**

MJF defeated Darby Allin in 22:48 (★★★★★); The Lucha Brothers (Penta El Zero Miedo and Rey Fenix) defeated FTR (Cash Wheeler and Dax Hardwood) in 18:38 (★★★); Bryan Danielson defeated Miro in 20:00 (★★★★); Christian Cage and Jurassic Express (Jungle Boy and Luchasaurus) defeated Adam Cole and The Young Bucks (Matt Jackson and Nick Jackson) in a Falls Count Anywhere Match in 22:18 (★★★); Cody Rhodes and Pac defeated Malakai Black and Andrade El Idolo in 16:55 (★★★); Dr. Britt Baker D.M.D. defeated Tay Conti in 15:30 (★★); CM Punk defeated Eddie Kingston in 11:11 (★★★); The Inner Circle (Chris Jericho, Jake Hager, Sammy Guevara, Santana and Ortiz) defeated American Top Team (Dan Lambert, Andrei Arlovski, Junior Dos Santos, Ethan Page and Scorpio Sky) in a Street Fight in 20:01 (★★★); Hangman Page defeated Kenny Omega to win the AEW World Title in 25:06 (★★★★).

Honor For All '21 ★★
14-11-21, Baltimore, Maryland **ROH**

Taylor Rust defeated Tracy Williams in a Pure Rules Match in 11:47 (★★★); Holidead defeated Quinn McKay, Trish Adora and Vita VonStarr in a Four Corner Survival Match in 13:52 (★★); The Briscoe Brothers (Jay Briscoe and Mark Briscoe) defeated The Second Gear Crew (AJ Gray and Effy) in 8:33 (★★); Jonathan Gresham defeated Brody King in 10:51 (★★★); The OGK (Matt Taven and Mike Bennett) defeated La

Faccion Ingobernable (**Dragon Lee** and **Kenny King**) to win the ROH World Tag Team Title in 11:59 (★ ★); **Bandido** defeated **Demonic Flamita** in a No DQ Match in 13:33 (★ ★ ★).

Tribute To The Troops '21 ★ ★
14-11-21, Ontario, California **WWE**
Big E defeated **Dolph Ziggler** in 4:58 (★ ★); **Bianca Belair** defeated **Liv Morgan** in 3:53 (★ ★); **Roman Reigns** defeated **Shinsuke Nakamura** in 8:04 (★ ★ ★).

Survivor Series '21 ★ ★
21-11-21, Brooklyn, New York **WWE**
Becky Lynch defeated **Charlotte Flair** in 18:13 (★ ★ ★ ★); **Team Raw** (Austin Theory, Bobby Lashley, Finn Balor, Kevin Owens and Seth Rollins) defeated **Team SmackDown** (Drew McIntyre, Happy Corbin, Jeff Hardy, Xavier Woods and Sheamus) in an Elimination Match in 29:56 (★ ★ ★); **Omos** won a Battle Royal in 10:45 (★); **RK-Bro** (Randy Orton and Riddle) defeated **The Usos** (Jimmy Uso and Jey Uso) in 14:50 (★ ★ ★); **Team Raw** (Bianca Belair, Carmella, Liv Morgan, Queen Zelina and Rhea Ripley) defeated **Team SmackDown** (Natalya, Sasha Banks, Shayna Baszler, Shotzi and Toni Storm) in an Elimination Match in 23:45 (★ ★); **Roman Reigns** defeated **Big E** in 21:55 (★ ★ ★).

Hard Times 2 ★ ★
04-12-21, Atlanta, Georgia **NWA**
Austin Aries defeated **Rhett Titus** in 9:03 (★ ★); **The OGK** (Matt Taven and Mike Bennett) defeated **Aron Stevens** and **JR Kratos** in 10:57 (★ ★); **Colby Corino** defeated **Doug Williams** in 8:46 (★ ★); **Mickie James** defeated **Kiera Hogan** in 8:46 (★ ★); **Tyrus** defeated **Cyon** in a No DQ Match in 15:54 (★); **Chris Adonis** defeated **Judais** in 10:53 (★ ★); **La Rebelion** (Bestia 666 and Mecha Wolf) defeated **The End** (Odinson and Parrow) in 7:47 (★ ★); **Nick Aldis** defeated **Thom Latimer** in 11:16 (★ ★); **Kamille** defeated **Melina** in 12:42 (★); **Trevor Murdoch** defeated **Mike Knox** in 8:15 (★ ★).

WarGames V ★ ★ ★
05-12-21, Orlando, Florida **NXT 2.0**
Cora Jade, Io Shirai, Kay Lee Ray and **Raquel Gonzalez** defeated **Dakota Kai** and **Toxic Attraction** (Mandy Rose, Gigi Dolin) and **Jacy Jayne**) in a WarGames Match in 31:23 (★ ★); **Imperium** (Fabian Aichner and Marcel Barthel) defeated **Kyle O'Reilly** and **Von Wagner** in 14:54 (★ ★ ★ ★); **Cameron Grimes** defeated **Duke Hudson** in a Hair vs. Hair Match in 10:24 (★ ★); **Roderick Strong** defeated **Joe Gacy** in 8:27 (★ ★); **Bron Breakker, Carmelo Hayes, Grayson Waller** and **Tony D'Angelo** defeated **Johnny Gargano, LA Knight, Pete Dunne** and **Tommaso Ciampa** in a WarGames Match in 38:13 (★ ★ ★ ★).

Final Battle '21 ★ ★ ★
11-12-21, Baltimore, Maryland **ROH**
Dragon Lee defeated **Rey Horus** in 11:21 (★ ★ ★); **Rhett Titus** defeated **Dalton Castle, Joe Hendry** and **Silas Young** in a Four Way Match to win the ROH World Television Title in 8:30 (★ ★); **Josh Woods** defeated **Brian Johnson** in 12:59 (★ ★); **Shane Taylor** defeated **Kenny King** in a Fight Without Honor in 17:47 (★ ★ ★); **Rok-C** defeated **Willow** in 10:18 (★ ★); **VLNCE UNLTD** (Brody King, Homicide and Tony Deppen) and **Rocky Romero** defeated **EC3, Eli Isom, Taylor Rust** and **Tracy Williams** in 13:32 (★ ★ ★); **The Briscoe Brothers** (Mark Briscoe and Jay Briscoe) defeated **The OGK** (Matt Taven and Mike Bennett) to win the ROH World Tag Team Title in 15:56 (★ ★ ★ ★); **Jonathan Gresham** defeated **Jay Lethal** to win the vacant ROH World Title in 15:11 (★ ★ ★ ★).

Day 1 ★ ★ ★
01-01-22, Atlanta, Georgia **WWE**
The Usos (Jey Uso and Jimmy Uso) defeated **The New Day** (Kofi Kingston and Xavier Woods) in 18:05 (★ ★ ★); **Drew McIntyre** defeated **Madcap Moss** in 9:45 (★ ★); **RK-Bro** (Randy Orton and Riddle) defeated **The Street Profits** (Angelo Dawkins and Montez Ford) in 11:15 (★ ★); **Edge** defeated **The Miz** in 20:00 (★ ★ ★); **Becky Lynch** defeated **Liv Morgan** in 17:00 (★ ★); **Brock Lesnar** defeated **Big E, Seth Rollins, Kevin Owens** and **Bobby Lashley** in a Fatal Five-Way Match to win the WWE Title in 8:19 (★ ★ ★).

Battle Of The Belts I ★ ★
08-01-22, Charlotte, North Carolina **AEW**
Sammy Guevara defeated **Dustin Rhodes** in 16:15 (★ ★); **Ricky Starks** defeated **Matt Sydal** in 9:00 (★ ★); **Dr. Britt Baker D.M.D.** defeated **Riho** in 12:47 (★ ★).

Hard To Kill '22 ★ ★ ★ ★
08-01-22, Dallas, Texas **Impact**
Tasha Steelz defeated **Alisha Edwards, Chelsea Green, Jordynne Grace, Lady Frost** and **Rosemary** in an Ultimate X Match in 9:00 (★ ★ ★); **Trey Miguel** defeated **Steve Maclin** in 12:50 (★ ★ ★); **Jonathan Gresham** defeated **Chris Sabin** in 12:40 (★ ★ ★ ★); **Josh Alexander** defeated **Jonah** in 17:05 (★ ★ ★ ★); **Eddie Edwards, Rich Swann, Willie Mack, Heath** and **Rhyno** defeated **The Good Brothers** (Luke Gallows and Karl Anderson) and **Violent By Design** (Eric Young, Deaner and Joe Doering) in a Hardcore War in 23:25 (★ ★ ★); **Moose** defeated **Matt Cardona** and **W. Morrissey** in a Three Way Match in 16:00 (★ ★ ★); **Mickie James** defeated **Deonna Purrazzo** in a Texas Deathmatch in 19:40 (★ ★ ★).

Royal Rumble '22 ★ ★
29-01-22, St. Louis, Missouri **WWE**
Seth Rollins defeated **Roman Reigns** by DQ in 14:25 (★ ★ ★); **Ronda Rousey** won the 30-Woman Royal Rumble Match in 59:40 (★ ★); **Becky Lynch** defeated **Doudrop** in 13:00 (★ ★); **Bobby Lashley** defeated **Brock Lesnar** to win the WWE Title in 10:15 (★ ★); **Edge** and **Beth Phoenix** defeated **The Miz** and **Maryse** in 12:30 (★ ★); **Brock Lesnar** won the 30-Man Royal Rumble Match in 51:10 (★ ★).

Elimination Chamber '22 ★ ★
19-02-22, Jeddah, Saudi Arabia **WWE**
Roman Reigns defeated **Goldberg** in 6:00 (★ ★); **Bianca Belair** defeated **Alexa Bliss, Doudrop, Liv Morgan, Nikki A.S.H.** and **Rhea Ripley** in an Elimination Chamber Match in 15:45 (★ ★); **Naomi** and **Ronda Rousey** defeated **Charlotte Flair** and **Sonya Deville** in 9:14 (★ ★); **Drew McIntyre** defeated **Madcap Moss** in a Falls Count Anywhere Match in 9:00 (★ ★ ★); **Becky Lynch** defeated **Lita** in 12:10 (★ ★ ★); **Brock Lesnar** defeated **Bobby Lashley, AJ Styles, Austin Theory, Riddle** and **Seth Rollins** in an Elimination Chamber Match to win the WWE Title in 14:55 (★ ★).

Revolution '22 ★ ★ ★ ★
06-03-22, Orlando, Florida **AEW**
Eddie Kingston defeated **Chris Jericho** in 13:40 (★ ★ ★ ★); **Jurassic Express** (Jungle Boy and Luchasaurus) defeated **reDRagon** (Bobby Fish and Kyle O'Reilly) and **The Young Bucks** (Matt Jackson and Nick Jackson) in a Three Way Match in 18:55 (★ ★ ★ ★); **Wardlow** defeated **Christian Cage, Keith Lee, Orange Cassidy, Powerhouse Hobbs** and **Ricky Starks** in a Face Of The Revolution Ladder Match in 17:20 (★ ★ ★); **Jade Cargill** defeated **Tay Conti** in 6:40 (★ ★); **CM Punk** defeated **MJF** in a Dog Collar Match in 26:45 (★ ★ ★ ★ ★); **Dr. Britt Baker D.M.D.** defeated **Thunder Rosa** in 17:25 (★ ★); **Jon Moxley** defeated **Bryan Danielson** in 21:05 (★ ★ ★ ★); **Darby Allin, Sammy Guevara** and **Sting** defeated **The Andrade-Hardy Family Office** (Andrade El Idolo, Matt Hardy and Isiah Kassidy) in a Tornado Tag Team Match in 13:20 (★ ★ ★); **Hangman Page** defeated **Adam Cole** in 25:45 (★ ★ ★).

Crockett Cup '22 Night #1 ★ ★
19-03-22, Nashville, Tennessee **NWA**
Hawx Aerie (Luke Hawx and PJ Hawx) defeated **The End** (Odinson and Parrow) in 9:20 (★ ★); **The Cardonas** (Mike Knox and VSK) defeated **Da Pope** and **Mims** in 9:59 (★ ★); **The Dirty Sexy Boys** (Dirty Dango and JTG) defeated **Aron Stevens** and **The Blue Meanie** in 6:40 (★ ★); **Gold Rushhh** (Jordan Clearwater and Marshe Rockett) defeated **Strictly Business** (Chris Adonis and Thom Latimer) in 4:18 (★ ★); **The Commonwealth Connection** (Doug Williams and Harry Smith) defeated **The Ill Begotten** (Alex Taylor and Rush Freeman) in 6:38 (★ ★); **La Rebelion** (Bestia 666 and Mecha Wolf) defeated **The Bad News Boyz** (Brandon Tate and Brent Tate) in 8:59 (★ ★); **The Cardonas** (Mike Knox and VSK) defeated **The Fixers** (Jay Bradley and Wrecking Ball Legursky) in 7:03 (★ ★); **The Briscoe Brothers** (Jay Briscoe and Mark Briscoe) defeated **The Dirty Sexy Boys** (Dirty Dango and JTG) in 8:13 (★ ★); **La Rebelion** (Bestia 666 and Mecha Wolf) defeated **PJ Hawx** in a Handicap Match in 7:25 (★ ★); **The Commonwealth Connection** (Doug Williams and Harry Smith) defeated **Gold Rushhh** (Jordan Clearwater and Marshe Rockett) in 12:50 (★ ★).

Crockett Cup '22 Night #2 ★ ★ ★ ★
20-03-22, Nashville, Tennessee **NWA**
The Briscoe Brothers (Jay Briscoe and Mark Briscoe) defeated **The Cardonas** (Mike Knox and VSK) in 7:45 (★ ★); **The Commonwealth Connection** (Doug Williams and Harry Smith)

defeated **La Rebelion (Bestia 666** and **Mecha Wolf)** in 8:58 (★★★); **Anthony Mayweather** defeated **Jax Dane** in 10:11 (★★★); **Jax Dane** defeated **Anthony Mayweather** to win the NWA National Title in :31 (★); **The Hex (Allysin Kay** and **Marti Belle)** defeated **Pretty Empowered (Ella Envy** and **Kenzie Paige)** in 7:09 (★★); **Homicide** defeated **Austin Aries, Colby Corino** and **Darius Lockhart** in a Four Way Match to win the vacant NWA World Junior Heavyweight Title in 9:39 (★★★); **Kamille** defeated **Chelsea Green** and **Kylie Rae** in a Three Way Match in 12:02 (★★★); **Tyrus** defeated **Rodney Mack** in 8:14 (★); **The Briscoe Brothers (Jay Briscoe** and **Mark Briscoe)** defeated **The Commonwealth Connection (Doug Williams** and **Harry Smith)** to win the Crockett Cup in 13:55 (★★★); **Matt Cardona** defeated **Nick Aldis** by DQ in 21:11 (★★).

Multiverse Of Matches ★★★
01-04-22, Dallas, Texas **Impact**

Trey Miguel defeated **Chris Bey, Jordynne Grace, Rich Swann, Vincent** and **Willie Mack** in an Ultimate X Match in 7:27 (★★★); **Mickie James** and **Nick Aldis** defeated **Chelsea Green** and **Matt Cardona** in 7:04 (★); **Mike Bailey** defeated **Alex Shelley** in 15:03 (★★★★); **The Influence (Madison Rayne** and **Tenille Dashwood)** defeated **Tasha Steelz** and **Savannah Evans, Gisele Shaw** and **Lady Frost,** and **Decay (Havok** and **Rosemary)** in a Four Way Match in 9:02 (★★); **Tomohiro Ishii** defeated **Eddie Edwards** in 14:09 (★★★); **Josh Alexander** and **Jonah** defeated **Moose** and **PCO** in 12:47 (★★); **Deonna Purrazzo** defeated **Faby Apache** in 8:52 (★★); **Chris Sabin** defeated **Jay White** in 16:00 (★★★); **The Good Brothers (Luke Gallows** and **Karl Anderson)** defeated **The Briscoe Brothers (Jay Briscoe** and **Mark Briscoe)** in 9:46 (★★).

Supercard Of Honor XV ★★★
01-04-22, Garland, Texas **ROH**

Swerve Strickland defeated **Alex Zayne** in 11:40 (★★); **Brian Cage** defeated **Ninja Mack** in 2:50 (★★); **Jay Lethal** defeated **Lee Moriarty** in 14:50 (★★★); **Mercedes Martinez** defeated **Willow Nightingale** to win the interim ROH Women's World Title in 12:45 (★★); **FTR (Dax Harwood** and **Cash Wheeler)** defeated **The Briscoe Brothers (Jay Briscoe** and **Mark Briscoe)** to win the ROH World Tag Team Title in 27:25 (★★★★★★); **Minoru Suzuki** defeated **Rhett Titus** to win the ROH World Television Title in 6:00 (★★); **Wheeler Yuta** defeated **Josh Woods** in a Pure Wrestling Rules Match to win the ROH Pure Title in 12:55 (★★); **Jonathan Gresham** defeated **Bandido** in 24:55 (★★★★).

Stand & Deliver '22 ★★★
02-04-22, Dallas, Texas **NXT**

Cameron Grimes defeated **Carmelo Hayes, Santos Escobar, Solo Sikoa** and **Grayson Waller** in a Five Way Ladder Match to win the NXT North American Title in 21:01 (★★★★); **Tony D'Angelo** defeated **Tommaso Ciampa** in 13:11 (★★); **MSK (Nash Carter** and **Wes Lee)** defeated **Imperium (Fabian Aichner** and **Marcel Barthel)** and **The Creed Brothers (Brutus Creed** and **Julius Creed)** in a Three Way Match to win the NXT Tag Team Title in 11:22 (★★★); **Mandy Rose** defeated **Cora Jade, Kay Lee Ray** and **Io Shirai** in a Fatal Four-Way Match in 13:28 (★★★); **Gunther** defeated **LA Knight** in 10:24 (★★★); **Dolph Ziggler** defeated **Bron Breakker** in 16:13 (★★★).

WrestleMania XXXVIII Night #1 ★★★★★
02-04-22, Dallas, Texas **WWE**

The Usos (Jey Uso and **Jimmy Uso)** defeated **Shinsuke Nakamura** and **Rick Boogs** in 6:55 (★★); **Drew McIntyre** defeated **Happy Corbin** in 8:35 (★★); **The Miz** and **Logan Paul** defeated **The Mysterios (Rey Mysterio** and **Dominik Mysterio)** in 11:15 (★★★); **Bianca Belair** defeated **Becky Lynch** to win the WWE RAW Women's Title in 19:10 (★★★★); **Cody Rhodes** defeated **Seth Rollins** in 21:40 (★★★★); **Charlotte Flair** defeated **Ronda Rousey** in 18:30 (★★); **Steve Austin** defeated **Kevin Owens** in a No Holds Barred Match in 13:55 (★★★★).

WrestleMania XXXVIII Night #2 ★★★
03-04-22, Dallas, Texas **WWE**

RK-Bro (Randy Orton and **Riddle)** defeated **The Street Profits (Angelo Dawkins** and **Montez Ford)** and **Alpha Academy (Chad Gable** and **Otis)** in a Three Way Match in 11:30 (★★★); **Bobby Lashley** defeated **Omos** in 6:35 (★★); **Johnny Knoxville** defeated **Sami Zayn** in an Anything Goes Match in 14:25 (★★★); **Sasha Banks** and **Naomi** defeated **Carmella** and **Queen Zelina, Liv Morgan** and **Rhea Ripley,** and **Natalya** and **Shayna Baszler** in a Four Way Match to win the WWE Women's

Tag Team Title in 10:50 (★★); **Edge** defeated **AJ Styles** in 24:05 (★★★); **Sheamus** and **Ridge Holland** defeated **The New Day (Kofi Kingston** and **Xavier Woods)** in 1:40 (★); **Pat McAfee** defeated **Austin Theory** in 9:40 (★★); **Vince McMahon** defeated **Pat McAfee** in 3:45 (★); **Roman Reigns** defeated **Brock Lesnar** to win the WWE Title in 12:15 (★★★).

Battle Of The Belts II ★★
16-04-22, Garland, Texas **AEW**

Sammy Guevara defeated **Scorpio Sky** in 12:45 (★★); **Jonathan Gresham** defeated **Dalton Castle** in 10:35 (★★); **Thunder Rosa** defeated **Nyla Rose** in 14:10 (★★).

Rebellion '22 ★★★
23-04-22, Poughkeepsie, New York **Impact**

Steve Maclin defeated **Chris Sabin** and **Jay White** in a Three Way Match in 12:07 (★★★); **Taya Valkyrie** defeated **Deonna Purrazzo** to win the AAA Reina de Reinas Title in 9:03 (★★); **Ace Austin** defeated **Trey Miguel** and **Mike Bailey** in a Three Way Match to win the Impact X Division Title in 10:25 (★★★); **Tomohiro Ishii** defeated **Jonah** in 14:34 (★★★); **Violent By Design (Eric Young** and **Joe Doering)** won an Eight-Team Elimination Challenge Match in 33:02 (★★★); **Tasha Steelz** defeated **Rosemary** in 11:45 (★★); **Josh Alexander** defeated **Moose** to win the Impact World Title in 23:56 (★★★★).

WrestleMania Backlash '22 ★★★
08-05-22, Providence, Rhode Island **WWE**

Cody Rhodes defeated **Seth Rollins** in 20:45 (★★★★); **Omos** defeated **Bobby Lashley** in 8:50 (★★); **Edge** defeated **AJ Styles** in 16:25 (★★★); **Ronda Rousey** defeated **Charlotte Flair** in an "I Quit" Match to win the WWE SmackDown Women's Title in 16:35 (★★★); **Madcap Moss** defeated **Happy Corbin** in 8:40 (★★); **The Bloodline (Roman Reigns, Jey Uso** and **Jimmy Uso)** defeated **Drew McIntyre** and **RK-Bro (Randy Orton** and **Riddle)** in 22:20 (★★★★).

Double Or Nothing '22 ★★★
29-05-22, Paradise, Nevada **AEW**

Wardlow defeated **MJF** in 7:30 (★★); **The Hardys (Matt Hardy** and **Jeff Hardy)** defeated **The Young Bucks (Matt Jackson** and **Nick Jackson)** in 19:15 (★★★); **Jade Cargill** defeated **Anna Jay** in 7:25 (★); **The House Of Black (Malakai Black, Buddy Matthews** and **Brody King)** defeated **Death Triangle (Pac, Penta Oscuro** and **Rey Fenix)** in 15:35 (★★★★); **Adam Cole** defeated **Samoa Joe** to win the Men's Owen Hart Foundation Tournament in 12:30 (★★); **Dr. Britt Baker D.M.D.** defeated **Ruby Soho** to win the Women's Owen Hart Foundation Tournament in 13:20 (★★); **American Top Team (Ethan Page, Scorpio Sky** and **Paige VanZant)** defeated **Frankie Kazarian, Sammy Guevara** and **Tay Conti** in 12:30 (★★); **Kyle O'Reilly** defeated **Darby Allin** in 9:50 (★★★); **Thunder Rosa** defeated **Serena Deeb** in 16:55 (★★★); **The Jericho Appreciation Society (Chris Jericho, Daniel Garcia, Jake Hager, Angelo Parker** and **Matt Menard)** defeated **The Blackpool Combat Club (Bryan Danielson** and **Jon Moxley), Eddie Kingston, Santana** and **Ortiz** in an Anarchy In Arena Match in 22:45 (★★★★); **Jurassic Express (Jungle Boy** and **Luchasaurus)** defeated **Swerve In Our Glory (Keith Lee** and **Swerve Strickland)** and **Team Taz (Powerhouse Hobbs** and **Ricky Starks)** in a Three Way Match in 17:15 (★★★); **CM Punk** defeated **Hangman Page** to win the AEW World Title in 25:40 (★★★★).

In Your House '22 ★★
04-06-22, Orlando, Florida **NXT**

The D'Angelo Family (Tony D'Angelo, Channing Lorenzo and **Troy Donovan)** defeated **Legado del Fantasma (Santos Escobar, Cruz Del Toro** and **Joaquin Wilde)** in 12:45 (★★★); **Toxic Attraction (Gigi Dolin** and **Jacy Jayne)** defeated **Katana Chance** and **Kayden Carter** in 9:01 (★★); **Carmelo Hayes** defeated **Cameron Grimes** to win the NXT North American Title in 15:30 (★★★); **Mandy Rose** defeated **Wendy Choo** in 11:08 (★★); **The Creed Brothers (Brutus Creed** and **Julius Creed)** defeated **Pretty Deadly (Elton Prince** and **Kit Wilson)** to win the NXT Tag Team Title in 15:19 (★★★); **Bron Breakker** defeated **Joe Gacy** in 15:50 (★★).

Hell In A Cell '22 ★★★★
05-06-22, Rosemont, Illinois **WWE**

Bianca Belair defeated **Asuka** and **Becky Lynch** in a Three Way Match in 18:55 (★★★★); **Bobby Lashley** defeated **Omos** and **MVP** in a Handicap Match in 8:25 (★★); **Kevin Owens** defeated

Ezekiel in 9:20 (★★); The Judgment Day (Edge, Damian Priest and Rhea Ripley) defeated AJ Styles, Finn Balor and Liv Morgan in 16:00 (★★); Madcap Moss defeated Happy Corbin in a No Holds Barred Match in 12:05 (★★); Theory defeated Mustafa Ali in 10:25 (★★); Cody Rhodes defeated Seth Rollins in a Hell In A Cell Match in 24:20 (★★★★★).

Alwayz Ready '22 ★★★
11-06-22, Knoxville, Tennessee NWA

Trevor Murdoch defeated Aron Stevens in 4:38 (★★); Pretty Empowered (Ella Envy and Kenzie Paige) defeated The Hex (Allysin Kay and Marti Belle) to win the NWA World Women's Tag Team Title in 8:35 (★★); Homicide defeated PJ Hawx in 10:50 (★★); Homicide defeated Colby Corino in 9:06 (★★★); Natalia Markova defeated Taya Valkyrie in 8:43 (★★); Jax Dane defeated Chris Adonis in 10:19 (★★); Thom Latimer defeated Cyon in 12:30 (★★); Tyrus defeated Mims in 8:37 (★); The Commonwealth Connection (Doug Williams and Harry Smith) defeated La Rebelion (Bestia 666 and Mecha Wolf) to win the NWA World Tag Team Title in 13:54 (★★★); Kamille defeated KiLynn King in 17:25 (★★★); Trevor Murdoch defeated Nick Aldis, Thom Latimer and Sam Shaw in a Four Way Match to win the vacant NWA Worlds Heavyweight Title in 18:10 (★★★).

Slammiversary XX ★★★
19-06-22, Nashville, Tennessee Impact

Mike Bailey defeated Ace Austin, Alex Zayne, Andrew Everett, Kenny King and Trey Miguel in an Ultimate X Match to win the Impact X Divison Title in 9:50 (★★★); Rosemary and Taya Valkyrie defeated The Influence (Madison Rayne and Tenille Dashwood) to win the Impact Knockouts World Tag Team Title in 7:20 (★★); Sami Callihan defeated Moose in a Monster's Ball Match in 16:00 (★★★); The Good Brothers (Luke Gallows and Karl Anderson) defeated The Briscoe Brothers (Jay Briscoe and Mark Briscoe) to win the Impact World Tag Team Title in 10:00 (★★★); Impact Originals (Alex Shelley, Chris Sabin, Davey Richards, Frankie Kazarian and Magnus) defeated Honor No More (Eddie Edwards, Matt Taven, Mike Bennett, PCO and Vincent) in 18:45 (★★★); Jordynne Grace defeated Tasha Steelz, Chelsea Green, Deonna Purrazzo and Mia Yim in a Queen Of The Mountain Match to win the Impact Knockouts World Title in 18:15 (★★★); Josh Alexander defeated Eric Young in 18:50 (★★★★).

Forbidden Door ★★★★
26-06-22, Chicago, Illinois AEW/NJPW

Minoru Suzuki and Le Sex Gods (Chris Jericho and Sammy Guevara) defeated Eddie Kingston, Shota Umino and Wheeler Yuta in 18:58 (★★★★); FTR (Cash Wheeler and Dax Harwood) defeated United Empire (Great-O-Khan and Jeff Cobb) and Roppongi Vice (Rocky Romero and Trent Beretta) in a Three Way Match to win the IWGP Tag Team Title in 16:19 (★★★); Pac defeated Clark Connors, Miro and Malakai Black in a Four Way Match to win the inaugural AEW All-Atlantic Title in 15:10 (★★★); Dudes With Attitudes (Darby Allin, Sting and Shingo Takagi) defeated Bullet Club (El Phantasmo, Matt Jackson and Nick Jackson) in 13:01 (★★★★); Thunder Rosa defeated Toni Storm in 10:42 (★★); Will Ospreay defeated Orange Cassidy in 16:43 (★★★★); Claudio Castagnoli defeated Zack Sabre Jr. in 18:26 (★★★★); Jay White defeated Hangman Page, Kazuchika Okada and Adam Cole in a Four Way Match in 21:05 (★★★); Jon Moxley defeated Hiroshi Tanahashi to win the interim AEW World Title in 18:14 (★★★).

Money In The Bank '22 ★★
02-07-22, Paradise, Nevada WWE

Liv Morgan defeated Alexa Bliss, Asuka, Becky Lynch, Lacey Evans, Raquel Rodriguez and Shotzi in a Money In The Bank Ladder Match in 16:35 (★★); Bobby Lashley defeated Theory to win the WWE United States Title in 11:05 (★★); Bianca Belair defeated Carmella in 7:10 (★★); The Usos (Jey Uso and Jimmy Uso) defeated The Street Profits (Angelo Dawkins and Montez Ford) in 23:00 (★★★★); Ronda Rousey defeated Natalya in 12:30 (★★); Liv Morgan defeated Ronda Rousey to win the WWE SmackDown Women's Title in :35 (★★); Theory defeated Drew McIntyre, Madcap Moss, Omos, Riddle, Sami Zayn, Seth Rollins and Sheamus in a Money In The Bank Ladder Match in 25:25 (★★).

Death Before Dishonor XIX ★★★★
23-07-22, Lowell, Massachusetts ROH

Claudio Castagnoli defeated Jonathan Gresham to win the ROH World Title in 11:30 (★★★); Dalton Castle and The Boys (Brandon Tate and Brent Tate) defeated The Righteous (Vincent, Bateman and Dutch) to win the ROH World Six-Man Tag Team Title in 9:40 (★★); Wheeler Yuta defeated Daniel Garcia in a Pure Wrestling Rules Match in 15:55 (★★★★); Rush defeated Dragon Lee in 15:50 (★★★★); Mercedes Martinez defeated Serena Deeb in 17:20 (★★★); Samoa Joe defeated Jay Lethal in 12:20 (★★★); FTR (Cash Wheeler and Dax Harwood) defeated The Briscoe Brothers (Jay Briscoe and Mark Briscoe) 2-1 in a Best Two Out Of Three Falls Match in 43:25 (★★★★★).

SummerSlam '22 ★★★★
30-07-22, Nashville, Tennessee WWE

Bianca Belair defeated Becky Lynch in 15:10 (★★★★); Logan Paul defeated The Miz in 14:15 (★★★); Bobby Lashley defeated Theory in 4:45 (★★); The Mysterios (Rey Mysterio and Dominik Mysterio) defeated The Judgment Day (Finn Balor and Damian Priest) in 11:05 (★★); Pat McAfee defeated Happy Corbin in 10:40 (★★); The Usos (Jey Uso and Jimmy Uso) defeated The Street Profits (Angelo Dawkins and Montez Ford) in 13:25 (★★★); Liv Morgan defeated Ronda Rousey in 4:35 (★★); Roman Reigns defeated Brock Lesnar in a Last Man Standing Match in 23:00 (★★★★).

Ric Flair's Last Match ★★
31-07-22, Nashville, Tennessee JCP

The Motor City Machine Guns (Alex Shelley and Chris Sabin) defeated The Wolves (Davey Richards and Eddie Edwards) in 11:06 (★★★); Killer Kross defeated Davey Boy Smith Jr. in 5:22 (★★); Jonathan Gresham defeated Alan Angels, Konosuke Takeshita and Nick Wayne in a Four Way Match in 5:40 (★★); The Four Horsemen (Brian Pillman Jr. and Brock Anderson) defeated The Rock 'N' Roll Express (Ricky Morton and Kerry Morton) in 7:21 (★★); Rey Fenix defeated Bandido, Laredo Kid and Black Taurus in a Four Way Match in 11:45 (★★★★); Josh Alexander vs. Jacob Fatu ended in a no contest in 10:14 (★★★); The Briscoe Brothers (Jay Briscoe and Mark Briscoe) defeated The Von Erichs (Marshall Von Erich and Ross Von Erich) in 7:43 (★★); Jordynne Grace defeated Deonna Purrazzo and Rachael Ellering in a Three Way Match in 9:17 (★★); Ric Flair and Andrade El Idolo defeated Jay Lethal and Jeff Jarrett in 26:40 (★).

Battle Of The Belts III ★★★
06-08-22, Grand Rapids, Michigan AEW

Wardlow defeated Jay Lethal in 7:21 (★★); Thunder Rosa defeated Jamie Hayter in 11:31 (★★★); Claudio Castagnoli defeated Konosuke Takeshita in 19:59 (★★★★).

74th Anniversary Show Night #1 ★★
27-08-22, St. Louis, Missouri NWA

EC3 defeated Mims in 4:52 (★★); The Miserable Faithful (Judais, Sal The Pal and Gaagz The Gymp) defeated The Ill Begotten (Alex Taylor, Jeremiah Plunkett and Danny Dealz) in a Beelzebub's Bedlam Match in 9:41 (★★); Chris Adonis defeated Odinson by DQ in 7:26 (★★); Homicide defeated Kerry Morton in 12:38 (★★★); Rolando Freeman defeated Matt Cardona in 5:41 (★★); Max The Impaler won a Burke Invitational Gauntlet in 17:24 (★★); Cyon defeated Jax Dane in 7:26 (★★); Bully Ray defeated Mike Knox in a Tables Match in 8:38 (★★); La Rebelion (Bestia 666 and Mecha Wolf) defeated Hawx Aerie (Luke Hawx and PJ Hawx) to win the vacant NWA World Tag Team Title in 13:10 (★★); Kamille defeated Taya Valkyrie in 18:57 (★★★★).

74th Anniversary Show Night #2 ★★
28-08-22, St. Louis, Missouri NWA

Colby Corino defeated Caprice Coleman 2-1 in a Best Two Out Of Three Falls Match in 9:57 (★★); The Fixers (Jay Bradley and Wrecking Ball Legursky) won a Tag Team Battle Royal to win the vacant NWA World Tag Team Title in 14:07 (★★); Magic Jake Dumas defeated Mercurio in 7:15 (★★); Davey Richards defeated Thrillbilly Silas in 10:24 (★★); Cyon defeated Anthony Mayweather in 8:18 (★★); Pretty Empowered (Ella Envy and Kenzie Paige) defeated The Hex (Allysin Kay and Marti Belle) in a Kingshighway Street Fight in 10:02 (★★); Homicide defeated Ricky Morton in 6:12 (★★); Nick Aldis defeated Flip Gordon in 8:43 (★★); JR Kratos and Da Pope defeated Aron Stevens and

Rodney Mack in a Missouri Tornado Match in 9:40 (★★); Thom Latimer vs. EC3 ended in a no contest in 6:42 (★★); Kamille defeated Max The Impaler in 11:07 (★★); Trevor Murdoch defeated Tyrus in 13:44 (★).

Clash At The Castle ★★★★
03-09-22, Cardiff, Wales WWE
Damage CTRL (Bayley, Dakota Kai and Iyo Sky) defeated Bianca Belair, Alexa Bliss and Asuka in 18:44 (★★★); Gunther defeated Sheamus in 19:33 (★★★★★); Liv Morgan defeated Shayna Baszler in 11:02 (★★); Edge and Rey Mysterio defeated The Judgment Day (Finn Balor and Damian Priest) in 12:35 (★★); Seth Rollins defeated Matt Riddle in 17:22 (★★★★); Roman Reigns defeated Drew McIntyre in 30:47 (★★★★).

Worlds Collide '22 ★★★
04-09-22, Orlando, Florida NXT
Carmelo Hayes defeated Ricochet in 15:57 (★★★★); Pretty Deadly (Elton Prince and Kit Wilson) defeated The Creed Brothers (Brutus Creed and Julius Creed), Brooks Jensen and Josh Briggs, and Gallus (Mark Coffey and Wolfgang) in a Four Way Elimination Match to unify the NXT Tag Team Title and NXT UK Tag Team Title in 15:34 (★★); Mandy Rose defeated Meiko Satomura and Blair Davenport in a Three Way Match to unify the NXT Women's Title and NXT UK Women's Title in 13:17 (★★★); Katana Chance and Kayden Carter defeated Doudrop and Nikki A.S.H. in 10:19 (★★); Bron Breakker defeated Tyler Bate to unify the NXT Title and NXT United Kingdom Title in 17:11 (★★★★).

All Out '22 ★★★★
04-09-22, Hoffman Estates, Illinois AEW
MJF defeated Claudio Castagnoli, Wheeler Yuta, Penta El Zero M, Rey Fenix, Rush, Andrade El Idolo and Dante Martin in a Casino Ladder Match in 14:15 (★★); The Elite (Kenny Omega, Matt Jackson and Nick Jackson) defeated The Dark Order (Hangman Page, Alex Reynolds and John Silver) to win the inaugural AEW World Trios Title in 19:50 (★★★★); Jade Cargill defeated Athena in 4:20 (★★); Wardlow and FTR (Cash Wheeler and Dax Harwood) defeated Jay Lethal and The Motor City Machine Guns (Chris Sabin and Alex Shelley) in 16:30 (★★); Powerhouse Hobbs defeated Ricky Starks in 5:05 (★★); Swerve In Our Glory (Keith Lee and Swerve Strickland) defeated The Acclaimed (Anthony Bowens and Max Caster) in 22:30 (★★★★); Toni Storm defeated Dr. Britt Baker D.M.D., Jamie Hayter and Hikaru Shida in a Four Way Match to win the vacant interim AEW Women's World Title in 14:20 (★★); Christian Cage defeated Jungle Boy in :20 (★); Chris Jericho defeated Bryan Danielson in 23:40 (★★★); Darby Allin, Sting and Miro defeated The House Of Black (Malakai Black, Brody King and Buddy Matthews) in 12:10 (★★); CM Punk defeated Jon Moxley to win the AEW World Title in 19:55 (★★★★).

Bound For Glory '22 ★★★★
07-10-22, Albany, New York Impact
Frankie Kazarian defeated Mike Bailey to win the Impact X Division Title in 12:30 (★★★); Mickie James defeated Mia Yim in a Last Rodeo Match in 10:56 (★★★); The Death Dollz (Jessicka and Taya Valkyrie) defeated VXT (Chelsea Green and Deonna Purrazzo) to win the Impact Knockouts World Tag Team Title in 7:24 (★★); The Kingdom (Matt Taven and Mike Bennett) defeated The Motor City Machine Guns (Alex Shelley and Chris Sabin) in 16:35 (★★★); Bully Ray won a 20-Person Call Your Shot Gauntlet Match in 29:18 (★★); Jordynne Grace defeated Masha Slamovich in 16:00 (★★★★); Josh Alexander defeated Eddie Edwards in 28:02 (★★★★).

Battle Of The Belts IV ★★
07-10-22, Washington, D.C. AEW
Pac defeated Trent Beretta in 14:25 (★★★); Jade Cargill defeated Willow Nightingale in 7:30 (★★); FTR (Cash Wheeler and Dax Harwood) defeated Gates Of Agony (Toa Liona and Kaun) in 13:26 (★★).

Extreme Rules '22 ★★★
08-10-22, Philadelphia, Pennsylvania WWE
The Brawling Brutes (Sheamus, Butch and Ridge Holland) defeated Imperium (Gunther, Ludwig Kaiser and Giovanni Vinci) in a Good Old Fashioned Donnybrook Match in 17:50

(★★★); Ronda Rousey defeated Liv Morgan in an Extreme Rules Match to win the WWE SmackDown Women's Title in 12:05 (★★); Karrion Kross defeated Drew McIntyre in a Strap Match in 10:20 (★★); Bianca Belair defeated Bayley in a Ladder Match in 16:40 (★★★); Finn Balor defeated Edge in an "I Quit" Match in 29:55 (★★); Matt Riddle defeated Seth Rollins in a Fight Pit Match in 16:35 (★★★).

Halloween Havoc '22 ★★★
22-10-22, Orlando, Florida NXT
Wes Lee defeated Carmelo Hayes, Oro Mensa, Von Wagner and Nathan Frazer in a Ladder Match to win the vacant NXT North American Title in 22:25 (★★★); Apollo Crews defeated Grayson Waller in a Casket Match in 14:27 (★★); Roxanne Perez defeated Cora Jade in a Weapons Wild Match in 12:25 (★★); Julius Creed defeated Damon Kemp in an Ambulance Match in 14:09 (★★★); Mandy Rose defeated Alba Fyre in 7:07 (★★); Bron Breakker defeated Ilja Dragunov and JD McDonagh in a Three Way Match in 23:47 (★★★★).

Crown Jewel '22 ★★★
05-11-22, Riyadh, Saudi Arabia WWE
Brock Lesnar defeated Bobby Lashley in 6:00 (★★★); Damage CTRL (Dakota Kai and Iyo Sky) defeated Alexa Bliss and Asuka to win the WWE Women's Tag Team Title in 12:50 (★★★); Drew McIntyre defeated Karrion Kross in a Steel Cage Match in 13:00 (★★); The Judgment Day (Finn Balor, Damian Priest and Dominik Mysterio) defeated The O.C. (AJ Styles, Luke Gallows and Karl Anderson) in 14:00 (★★); Braun Strowman defeated Omos in 7:20 (★★); The Usos (Jey Uso and Jimmy Uso) defeated The Brawling Brutes (Ridge Holland and Butch) in 10:45 (★★★); Bianca Belair defeated Bayley in a Last Woman Standing Match in 20:20 (★★★); Roman Reigns defeated Logan Paul in 24:50 (★★★★).

Hard Times 3 ★★★
12-11-22, Chalmette, Louisiana NWA
Max The Impaler defeated Natalia Markova in a Voodoo Queen Casket Match in 8:14 (★★); Davey Richards defeated Colby Corino in 6:42 (★★); The Question Mark II defeated The Question Mark in a Mask vs. Mask Match in 6:00 (★★); Kerry Morton defeated Homicide to win the NWA World Junior Heavyweight Title in 10:02 (★★★); Thrillbilly Silas defeated Odinson in 4:43 (★★); The Fixers (Jay Bradley and Wrecking Ball Legursky) defeated The Spectaculars (Brady Pierce and Rush Freeman) in 9:15 (★★); Cyon defeated Dak Draper in 6:01 (★★); Pretty Empowered (Ella Envy and Kenzie Paige) defeated Madi Wrenkowski and Missa Kate in 8:12 (★★); EC3 defeated Thom Latimer by DQ in 8:31 (★★); La Rebelion (Bestia 666 and Mecha Wolf) defeated Hawx Aerie (Luke Hawx and PJ Hawx) in 10:48 (★★★); Kamille defeated Chelsea Green and Kilynn King in a Three Way Match in 8:59 (★★); Tyrus defeated Trevor Murdoch and Matt Cardona in a Three Way Match to win the NWA Worlds Heavyweight Title in 10:03 (★).

Full Gear '22 ★★★★
19-11-22, Newark, New Jersey AEW
Jungle Boy defeated Luchasaurus in a Steel Cage Match in 18:40 (★★★★); Death Triangle (Pac, Penta El Zero Miedo and Rey Fenix) defeated The Elite (Kenny Omega, Matt Jackson and Nick Jackson) in 18:40 (★★★★); Jade Cargill defeated Nyla Rose in 8:00 (★); Chris Jericho defeated Bryan Danielson, Claudio Castagnoli and Sammy Guevara in a Four Way Match in 21:30 (★★★★); Saraya defeated Dr. Britt Baker D.M.D. in 12:30 (★★); Samoa Joe defeated Wardlow and Powerhouse Hobbs in a Three Way Match to win the AEW TNT Title in 9:55 (★★); Sting and Darby Allin defeated Jeff Jarrett and Jay Lethal in a No DQ Match in 11:00 (★★★); Jamie Hayter defeated Toni Storm to win the interim AEW Women's Title in 15:00 (★★★); The Acclaimed (Anthony Bowens and Max Caster) defeated Swerve In Our Glory (Swerve Strickland and Keith Lee) in 19:40 (★★★); MJF defeated Jon Moxley to win the AEW World Title in 23:15 (★★★).

Survivor Series WarGames ★★★
26-11-22, Boston, Massachusetts WWE
Team Belair (Bianca Belair, Alexa Bliss, Asuka, Mia Yim and Becky Lynch) defeated Team Bayley (Bayley, Dakota Kai, Iyo Sky, Nikki Cross and Rhea Ripley) in a WarGames Match in 39:40 (★★); AJ Styles defeated Finn Balor in 18:25 (★★★); Ronda Rousey defeated Shotzi in 7:15 (★); Austin Theory defeated Seth Rollins and Bobby Lashley in a Three Way Match to win

the WWE United States Title in 14:50 (★ ★ ★); **The Bloodline (Roman Reigns, Sami Zayn, Solo Sikoa, Jey Uso** and **Jimmy Uso**) defeated **The Brawling Brutes (Sheamus, Butch** and **Ridge Holland), Drew McIntyre** and **Kevin Owens** in a WarGames Match in 38:30 (★ ★ ★).

Deadline ★ ★ ★
10-12-22, Orlando, Florida NXT

Roxanne Perez (2) defeated **Zoey Stark** (1), **Cora Jade** (1), **Indi Hartwell** (1) and **Kiana James** (0) in an Iron Survivor Challenge in 25:00 (★ ★ ★); **Isla Dawn** defeated **Alba Fyre** in 9:52 (★ ★); **The New Day (Kofi Kingston** and **Xavier Woods**) defeated **Pretty Deadly (Elton Prince** and **Kit Wilson**) to win the NXT Tag Team Title in 14:05 (★ ★ ★); **Grayson Waller** (3) defeated **Carmelo Hayes** (2), **Joe Gacy** (2), **Axiom** (2) and **JD McDonagh** (0) in an Iron Survivor Challenge in 25:00 (★ ★ ★); **Bron Breakker** defeated **Apollo Crews** in 14:34 (★ ★ ★).

Final Battle '22 ★ ★ ★
10-12-22, Arlington, Texas ROH

Blake Christian and **AR Fox** defeated **La Faccion Ingobernable (Rush** and **Dralistico**) in 10:35 (★ ★); **Athena** defeated **Mercedes Martinez** to win the ROH Women's World Title in 13:10 (★ ★); **Swerve In Our Glory (Keith Lee** and **Swerve Strickland**) defeated **Shane Taylor Promotions (Shane Taylor** and **JD Griffey**) in 13:50 (★ ★ ★); **The Embassy (Brian Cage, Kaun** and **Toa Liona**) defeated **Dalton Castle** and **The Boys (Brandon Tate** and **Brent Tate**) to win the ROH World Six-Man Tag Team Title in 10:05 (★ ★); **Wheeler Yuta** defeated **Daniel Garcia** in a Pure Rules Match to win the ROH Pure Title in 14:50 (★ ★ ★); **The Briscoe Brothers (Jay Briscoe** and **Mark Briscoe**) defeated **FTR (Cash Wheeler** and **Dax Harwood**) in a Double Dog Collar Match to win the ROH World Tag Team Title in 22:20 (★ ★ ★ ★ ★); **Samoa Joe** defeated **Juice Robinson** in 13:40 (★ ★); **Claudio Castagnoli** defeated **Chris Jericho** to win the ROH World Title in 17:15 (★ ★ ★).

Tribute To The Troops '22 ★ ★
17-12-22, Indianapolis, Indiana WWE

Braun Strowman defeated **LA Knight** in 2:12 (★ ★); **Ronda Rousey** and **Shayna Baszler** defeated **Emma** and **Tamina** in 7:34 (★ ★); **Drew McIntyre, Ricochet** and **Sheamus** defeated **Imperium (Gunther, Giovanni Vinci** and **Ludwig Kaiser**) in 16:34 (★ ★).

IN
MEMORIUM

DATE	KNOWN AS	AGE	CAUSE OF DEATH	REAL NAME
Jan 2	General Von Kessler	81	-	Galen Carpenter
Jan 4	Bill Fryman	84	-	William Harrison Fryman
Jan 7	Matilda The Hun	73	Lupus/Peripheral neuropathy	Deanna Booher
Jan 7	Osamu Inoue	38	Kidney failure	Osamu Inoue
Jan 8	Jake Slater	43	-	James William Sinyard
Jan 8	Stan Lavdas	86	-	Stamatios Savas Lavdas
Jan 9	The Samoan Predator	44	-	Shannon Hutchens
Jan 10	Big T	46	-	Tee Jay Lairson
Jan 11	Antonio Posa	84	-	Antonio Posa Gonzalez
Jan 11	Temuri Sakura	83	Heart failure	Temuri Sakura
Jan 11	Charles Bronson Mexicano	88	-	Ismael Ramirez Cruz
Jan 14	Tom Mix	-	-	-
Jan 18	Angel	58	COVID-19	Andrea Micheil
Jan 20	Vicki Askew	101	Natural causes	Victoria Hanner Askew
Jan 21	Bob Steele	70	Heart failure	Bruce Hemlow
Jan 24	Ken Raper	67	Heart failure	Ken Raper
Jan 25	Piraña	-	-	-
Jan 27	Roy Schiessl	85	-	Roy Schiessl
Jan 27	Adam Evans	35	Car accident	Adam Ellerman
Feb 8	David Williamson	70	-	David Williamson
Feb 8	Ricky Hunter	85	-	Charles B. Sprott
Feb 9	Candi Devine	63	Collapsed lung	Candace Maria Rummel
Feb 9	Super Muneco	59	COVID-19	Herbert Palafox
Feb 9	Arturo Rivera	67	COVID-19	Arturo Rivera
Feb 9	Aguila Dorada	87	-	Juan Alcazar
Feb 10	Shooter Storm	39	-	Shaun Balaban
Feb 10	Steel Fox	-	-	Octavio Gonzalez
Feb 11	Adam Turek	34	Illness	Adam Turek
Feb 11	La Garra	-	-	Rafael Miranda Farias
Feb 13	Sailor Jim Clark	93	-	James Edwin Clark
Feb 14	Mickie Jay	59	COVID-19	Mickie Jay Henson
Feb 16	Charrito de Oro	71	-	-
Feb 17	Gran Sebastian	61	-	Sebastian Plumajero
Feb 20	Crusher Bones	53	Liver failure	Scott Turner
Feb 20	Bubba Sutton	37	Car accident	Howard K. Alden
Feb 22	Donna Day	-	-	-
Feb 22	Boom Boom Comini	-	-	Aaron Comini
Feb 25	Big Doug	57	-	Doug Griffin
Feb 26	Terry Landell	59	-	Terry Bundren
Feb 28	Black Man	73	-	Alvaro Tibanez
Feb 28	Hysteria 2.0	37	-	Pablo Romero
Feb 28	Mr. Raff	-	-	-
Mar 1	Theo Koutsouliotas	79	-	Theodoros Koutsouliotas
Mar 7	Dan Mirade	42	Car accident	Daniel Michael Frongillo
Mar 8	Gulliver	67	-	Angel Mondragon
Mar 9	Joe D'Orazio	99	Natural causes	Giuseppe Scala
Mar 9	Caveman Broda	68	-	Ronald Cadman
Mar 9	Chucky	67	-	Angel Mondra Arias
Mar 11	JJ Maguire	68	-	John James Maguire
Mar 14	Razor Ramon	63	Heart attack	Scott Hall
Mar 14	Sol Yang	30	-	Leng Yang
Mar 17	Black Warrior Jr.	24	Heart attack	Ramces de Jesus Toral
Mar 18	Pepper Martin	85	Cancer	Howard Martin
Mar 18	Hatfield Hattie	83	-	Trucella Jane Marez
Mar 22	Energy Boy	-	Cancer	Ulises Gutierrez Martinez
Mar 24	Logan Legit	28	Car accident	Logan Roettger
Mar 27	Rocky King	64	Kidney failure	William Boulware Jr.
Mar 27	Sarapeno	72	-	Federico Lara Hernande
Mar 30	Mad Dog Johnson	64	-	Ken Johnson
Apr 4	Raziel	49	Heart attack	-
Apr 10	Jermaine Johnson	38	Heart failure	Jermaine Johnson
Apr 11	Bob Arnold	94	-	Robert W. Arnold
Apr 12	Sonny Caldinez	89	Ruptured aortic aneurysm	Sonny Caldinez
Apr 16	Tony "Banger" Walsh	72	Dementia	John Anthony Sheehan
Apr 16	Kid Krazy	37	-	Jarod Michael Hall
Apr 17	Unicorn	-	-	Jorge Maya
Apr 21	Adam Windsor	40	Heart failure	Adam Bryniarski
Apr 21	The Zebra Kid	73	-	Humberto Whijares
Apr 21	Big Mac Smack	-	-	Rob Roman
Apr 24	Anarchy Ash Aubrey	36	Heart attack	Jeff Greeno
Apr 24	Karl Lauer	83	-	Karl Konrad Lauer
Apr 25	Toro Bill Jr.	40	Heart attack	Roberto Rosete
Apr 26	Devoy Brunson	76	-	Devoy Harvey Brunson
May 2	Charlie Smith	92	Natural causes	Charlie Smith
May 4	Gengis Khan	61	-	Isaias Rodriguez
May 7	Bad Boy Buck	46	-	Buck Blevins
May 9	Doug Grant	90	-	Clair Douglas Grant
May 13	Apolo Chino	-	-	Anastacio Rodriguez
May 17	Juventud Rebelde	-	Shooting	Jerry Garcia
May 21	Nikolai Zouev	64	Heart disease	Nikolai Zouev
May 22	Torito Castillo	79	-	Mario Lopez Castillo

DATE	KNOWN AS	AGE	CAUSE OF DEATH	REAL NAME
May 23	Sebastian Night	-	-	Brian Recker
May 24	Brute Barreto	36	-	-
May 25	Tommy Seabolt	62	Stroke	Thomas Edward Seabolt
May 25	Big Pappa	45	-	John David Kroell
May 27	Aquiles	-	-	Joel Garcia Labatan
May 29	Tarzan Goto	58	Liver cancer	Seiji Goto
May 30	Black Master	-	-	Angel Pech
Jun 1	Melanie Pillman	56	-	Melanie Diane Pillman
Jun 6	Danger	-	-	Gabriel Mendoza
Jun 13	Bubbles	31	Car accident	Chelsey Cartwright
Jun 15	Luis Mariscal	73	-	Luis Mariscal
Jun 17	Dave Hebner	73	Illness	David Hebner
Jun 17	Jake McCoy	39	-	Jacob Manford Coffey
Jun 19	Tim White	68	-	Timothy Rhys White
Jun 24	Butcher Blackwell	58	-	Michael A. Sgro
Jun 24	Tackle	-	-	Fernando Rodriguez
Jun 26	John Riegler	66	-	John F. Riegler
Jun 27	Klondyke Jake	87	-	Barry Hawkins
Jun 29	Ray Lanier	82	-	Ernie Ray Lanier
Jul 6	Masashi Aoyagi	65	-	Masashi Aoyagi
Jul 6	Jim Quigley	48	Cancer	James F. Quigley IV
Jul 8	Tigre Hispano	84	-	Ventura Lahoz
Jul 15	Lourdes Grobet	81	-	Lourdes Grobet
Jul 16	Trajan Ender	38	-	Joshua Powell
Jul 18	Cyndi Heenan	74	-	Cynthia Jean Heenan
Jul 20	Matt Sinister	46	Heart attack	Matthew Obbema
Jul 23	Death Row 3260	63	-	Wendell Rozier
Jul 25	Wolfgang Saturski	81	-	Wolfgang Jakob-Saturski
Jul 26	Foob Dogg	-	-	Robert Tenorio
Jul 28	Gil Hayes	82	Heart attack	Gilbert Lee Hayes
Jul 29	Blackjack Brown	65	-	David Herman Brown
Jul 30	Mysterio	-	-	Mario Blancas
Aug 1	Invincible	52	-	Dave Maddison
Aug 4	Erick Snake	37	Illness	Erick Belmares
Aug 6	TNT	84	-	Jose Guadalupe Herrera
Aug 7	Eugene Palermo	57	-	Eugene Palermo
Aug 8	Mike Masters	68	Throat cancer	Michael Jones
Aug 9	Gene LeBell	89	Natural causes	Ivan Gene LeBell
Aug 10	Larry Katz	74	-	Larry Katz
Aug 14	Darling Pat Sherry	81	-	Mary Austin
Aug 14	Kalimaco	-	Suicide	-
Aug 15	Guerrero Espacial	43	-	Isidro Gonzalez
Aug 16	Vernon Love	-	-	Jim Wolverton
Aug 20	Bert Royal	91	-	Herbert Faulkner
Aug 21	Lepra MX	-	Kidnap and murder	Salvador Garcia Soto
Aug 22	Ray Wilson	94	-	Raymond Audley Wilson
Aug 24	Howard Brody	73	Infection	Howard Brody
Aug 26	Goro Tsurumi	73	Sepsis	Takao Tanaka
Aug 27	Maremoto	-	Kidnap and murder	Raul Salazar Santillan
Aug 28	Bill Ash	76	-	Bill Ash
Aug 29	Super Loco	52	-	Alejandro Alvaro Ortiz
Aug 29	Lasser	66	Stroke	Jorge Vega Oriel
Aug 31	Alan Denkenson	69	Illness	Alan Denkenson
Sep 1	Freddie Fargo	74	-	Alfred Raymond Bernard
Sep 10	Bubba Monroe	61	-	Quentin Bell
Sep 11	Elias Theodorou	34	Colon cancer	Elias Michael Theodorou
Sep 14	Ricky The Janitor	31	Organ failure	Ricky Dunlap
Sep 14	Vito Mussolini	55	-	Kenneth Michael Hreha
Sep 15	Soleil	44	Cancer	Roberto Hernandez
Sep 20	Mary Galaz	86	-	Mary Galaz
Sep 23	Starman	48	-	Othoniel Trejo
Sep 26	Fuerza K9	-	Illness	Mario Rodolfo Sandoval
Sep 27	Dan Masters	-	Car accident	Dan Henry
Oct 1	Antonio Inoki	79	Systemic transthyretin amyloisosis	Muhammad Inoki
Oct 5	Sara Lee	30	-	Sara Ann Weston
Oct 12	Katsuya Kitamura	36	-	Katsuya Kitamura
Oct 13	Hurricane Rivera	-	-	Jose Santiago
Oct 16	Humberto Garza Sr.	85	-	Don Humberto
Oct 19	Brian Muster	36	-	Brian Muster
Oct 20	Tristen Nash	26	Heart attack	Tristen Nash
Oct 25	Damien Van Horn	47	-	John Tighe
Oct 29	Ivannia Moreno Tolsa	38	-	Ivannia Moreno Tolsa
Oct 30	Chavo Lomeli	53	-	Ponciano Lomeli
Nov 1	Dexter P. Wyler	46	-	Gerric Dillon Walker
Nov 3	D'Lo Jordan	30	Illness	Jason Pearce
Nov 4	Cowboy Hank Dalton	41	-	Steven McGregor
Nov 5	Lord Conn MacIntosh	61	-	Randy Alan Woodward
Nov 8	Karl Von Steiger	80	Heart failure	Edward Lorne Corlett
Nov 11	El Caudillo	24	Illness	Roberto Garcia
Nov 14	Servio Tulio Rosada	-	Car accident	Servio Tulio Rosada
Nov 15	Lazzer Boy	40	-	Mario Alberto Contreras

DATE	KNOWN AS	AGE	CAUSE OF DEATH	REAL NAME
Nov 16	Bronco del Cibao	-	Shooting	Starlin Jaquez
Nov 18	Bobby Lane	69	Heart issues	Robert Pico Jr.
Nov 19	Bob Mulrenin	58	Esophageal cancer	Robert Mulrenin
Nov 20	Farmer Brooks	65	Illness	Clifford Lloyd Fraser
Nov 22	Todd Fulkerson	45	-	Todd Fulkerson
Nov 23	Ernie Moore	82	-	Ernest Moore
Nov 28	Tigre Colombiano	92	-	Bill Martinez Patino
Nov 28	Comando Ruso	58	-	Juan Torres Navarro
Dec 1	Len Davies	69		Len Davies
Dec 3	Babe The Farmer's Daughter	56	Cancer	Ursula Hayden
Dec 3	Leon Negro	75	Kidney failure	Rafael Leon Ochoa
Dec 5	Ultimo Samuray	37	-	Javier Perez
Dec 6	Mills Lane	85	-	Mills Lane
Dec 9	Mark Watson	61	-	Mark John Watson
Dec 9	Sexy Fly	30	Car accident	-
Dec 10	Damon Knight	43	-	Andrew N Smith
Dec 18	Karl Kramer	55	-	Carl Davis
Dec 22	Stephan Bonnar	45	Heart issues	Stephan Bonnar
Dec 23	Scrapyard Dog	54	-	Louis Mcnair
Dec 28	Doc Holliday	80	Cancer	Robert Holliday
Dec 29	Jaysin Strife	37	Illness	Nathan Blodgett
Dec 30	Johnny Powers	79	-	Dennis Waters
Dec 30	Don West	59	Cancer	Don West
Dec 31	Mike Pappas	81	Cancer	Manoli Savvenas

Printed in Great Britain
by Amazon

28053608R00331